"It is exactly what is needed in our time"

"It is always refreshing to be made aware of the unceasing efforts of concerned Christian authorities to make God's Word understood by today's generation of believers and skeptics. *The Evidence Bible* is specially designed to reinforce the faith of our times by offering hard evidence and scientific proof for the thinking mind. A welcome addition to the literature of apologetics."

Dr. D. James Kennedy
Coral Ridge Ministries

"*The Evidence Bible* is jam-packed with vignettes tucked right in the text that will help you in witnessing to your friends and in answering their objections to the gospel. If you're looking for a Bible with sneakers on that can run with you into life, *The Evidence Bible* is for you."

Dr. Woodrow Kroll, President
Back to the Bible

"In some countries, handing a pastor a study Bible like *The Evidence Bible* with all its solid teaching is like sending the pastor to seminary training. I look forward to distributing many of these Bibles to pastors all over the world."

Mike Weygandt, Director of International Ministries
The Voice of the Martyrs

"Clearly the Holy Spirit led you as you brought this wonderful document together. I could not be more impressed... It is like having a loving, mature Christian elder standing by your shoulder as you read the Scriptures. It is exactly what is needed in our time."

James D. Stambaugh, Director
Billy Graham Center Museum

"Ray Comfort's teaching is right on."

Joni Eareckson Tada
Joni & Friends

"I don't know of an evangelist today who has a better grasp of how to communicate Christ to the totally secular mind of our day than Ray Comfort. He is fearless and genuine. *The Evidence Bible* is filled with practical and theological insights to help anyone effectively communicate the gospel of Christ to their lost friends."

David E. Clippard, Associate Executive Director
Baptist General Convention of Oklahoma

"Any thinking person should demand evidence when it comes to the most important of all matters—eternity. If you are one of those, *The Evidence Bible* will bring your search to an end. It might even spur you on to talk about Christ with someone who's looking for evidence."

Ron DiCianni

"I love *The Evidence Bible*. It should be a great help in drawing others to Christ."

Dr. Kent Hovind, Director
Creation Science Evangelism

"Ray Comfort...cuts to the core of a man's spiritual dilemma. As we pray for revival and wonder what God's waiting for, we need to seriously consider this message. To ignore it puts us in spiritual peril."

Terry Meeuwsen, Co-host
The 700 Club

"*The Evidence Bible* is full of the wisdom of great Christian men, including Billy Graham, John MacArthur, and Oswald Chambers, to help answer all the 'why' questions, whether from the new believer, someone who's just beginning to seek the truth, or someone who has been in the faith for several years."

Ron Wheeler
Cartoonworks

The Evidence Bible

Presented to

_____

_____

by

_____

_____

Date

_____

The Way of the Master

The **Evidence Bible**

Irrefutable
evidence
for the
thinking mind

THE WAY OF THE MASTER
W D
L D
MARK 16:15

The Evidence Bible

Irrefutable evidence for the thinking mind

RAY COMFORT

Bridge-Logos
Alachua, Florida 32615

The Way of the Master Evidence Bible

Compiled by Ray Comfort and Kirk Cameron

Published by:

Bridge-Logos

Alachua, Florida 32615 USA
bridgelogos.com

Library of Congress Card Catalog Number: 2007928011

ISBN 978-0-88270-970-3 HARD COVER
ISBN 978-0-88270-905-5 SOFT COVER
ISBN 978-0-88270-906-2 BLACK LEATHER
ISBN 978-0-88270-955-0 BURGUNDY LEATHER

Information on Islam, Hinduism, Mormonism, and Buddhism is reprinted
with permission by the North American Mission Board (www.namb.net/evangelism/iev)
and may be reproduced in limited quantities for use by churches.
Permission to reprint this material does not constitute an endorsement of
Living Waters Publications or Bridge-Logos Publishers by the North
American Mission Board or the Southern Baptist Convention.

The text used in this Bible is a "Comfort-able KJV"—a sensitively revised
King James Version, in which archaic words have been simplified to make
God's Words more understandable.

Scriptural quotations designated *Amplified* are from *The Amplified Bible*,
©1965 by Zondervan Publishing House, Grand Rapids, Michigan. Used by
permission.

The Way of the Master is an evangelism training ministry and television program
produced and hosted by Kirk Cameron and Ray Comfort. Its sole purpose is to teach
Christians how to share their faith simply, effectively, and biblically . . . the way Jesus
did. For further information about this ministry see www.wayofthemaster.com.

G218.x.S.m902.352100

Contents

Foreword vii

Preface ix

How to Use this Bible xii

Acknowledgments xxvii

Books of the Old Testament

Genesis 1	Ecclesiastes 849
Exodus 89	Song of Solomon 859
Leviticus 153	Isaiah 865
Numbers 195	Jeremiah 931
Deuteronomy 253	Lamentations 1007
Joshua 301	Ezekiel 1015
Judges 335	Daniel 1081
Ruth 369	Hosea 1105
1 Samuel 375	Joel 1115
2 Samuel 417	Amos 1123
1 Kings 451	Obadiah 1133
2 Kings 493	Jonah 1135
1 Chronicles 533	Micah 1141
2 Chronicles 569	Nahum 1147
Ezra 615	Habakkuk 1151
Nehemiah 631	Zephaniah 1155
Esther 653	Haggai 1159
Job 665	Zechariah 1161
Psalms 707	Malachi 1173
Proverbs 811	

Books of the New Testament

Matthew	1181	1 Timothy	1569
Mark	1243	2 Timothy	1579
Luke	1279	Titus	1585
John	1337	Philemon	1589
Acts	1393	Hebrews	1591
Romans	1453	James	1613
1 Corinthians	1479	1 Peter	1623
2 Corinthians	1507	2 Peter	1633
Galatians	1523	1 John	1639
Ephesians	1533	2 John	1647
Philippians	1543	3 John	1651
Colossians	1549	Jude	1653
1 Thessalonians	1557	Revelation	1657
2 Thessalonians	1563		

Closing Words of Comfort 1683
The Wordless Gospel 1691
Bibliography 1695
Index 1697
Ray Comfort 1716
Timeline 1717

Foreword

AS ANY PROFESSIONAL ACTOR KNOWS, some roles initially feel out of character, difficult to grasp. In fact, some roles can seem impossible at first, that is, until a good director steps in to ease your fears and provide confident reassurance that you are the right person for this role. A good director might then remind you of the fundamental principles of acting, the tools you need to bring out your best as you step into any new and unfamiliar role.

As a Christian, you know that Jesus calls you to do some things that seem so far out of your character and even your ability that those roles may feel impossible. For many of us, sharing the gospel with non-believers is a challenge that can sometimes seem terrifying.

In the role of Christian witness, it helps to have a good friend come alongside and ease your fears with some reassuring reminders that God has personally chosen you for this very special role, to bring His light to those who are in darkness.

The Evidence Bible is a guiding friend, filled with helpful reminders of the basic principles of witnessing, including how Jesus shared His good news with sinners. Here you will find the tools you need to be the very best witness you can be. You'll find answers to the 100 most commonly asked questions about the Christian faith. You will also find fascinating quotes about God, the Bible and faith from presidents, scientists, and other famous people, including experienced evangelists. And you will find in-depth study notes and in-the-trenches, hands-on training for open-air preaching and one-to-one witnessing.

For learning how to share the gospel effectively and biblically in today's world, I have found Ray Comfort's *Evidence Bible* to be the absolute best.

Kirk Cameron, actor

Preface

I HAVE OFTEN SAID that if you want to see the evangelism section in your local Christian bookstore, take your magnifying glass with you. Someone once put my claim to the test. When he entered a Christian book store and asked for the "evangelism section," and the salesperson replied, "What's evangelism?"

Bill Bright, founder of the international ministry, Campus Crusade for Christ, in his book, *The Coming Revival,* reports that "only two percent of believers in America regularly share their faith in Christ with others" (p. 65). I believe one reason for this tragedy is that the Body of Christ hasn't been suitably equipped. What soldier is going to run into the heat of battle, facing modern warfare, but armed only with a feather duster?

However, a soldier who is thoroughly equipped with state-of-the-art weapons and a bulletproof vest will find that his very weapons give him courage. *The Evidence Bible* will equip the most timid of Christ's soldiers with powerful weapons to conquer disbelief, doubt, skepticism and fear.

As you read, you will learn how to trample underfoot grasshoppers that before may have seemed like daunting secular giants. No longer will themes such as evolution, atheism, modernism, skepticism, and secular intellectualism intimidate you.

Much of my commentary on evangelism is drawn from my experiences open-air preaching almost daily for twelve years at "Speaker's Corner" in the city of Christchurch in my native New Zealand. During those years, I collected information that again and again rebuffed hecklers who asked

Ray Comfort, foreground, responds to a heckler while open-air preaching in Venice Beach, California, 1998.

Ray Comfort open-air preaching in Speaker's Square at Christchurch, New Zealand, 1987.

me probing questions about my faith and who posed a range of objections to the gospel message I preached.

But the wisdom of this world stands on weak and shifting sand. And *The Evidence Bible* will show you that, as a Christian, you stand on intellectually solid and spiritually immovable rock. You will find in these pages quotes from many well-known secular people. The apostle Paul, when he preached to the Athenians on Mars Hill, likewise cited secular Greek poets (Acts 17:28). Obviously, Paul wasn't endorsing their sinful lifestyle, nor was he promoting their poetry. He was simply using their words, familiar to his listeners, as a springboard for the gospel. And you can learn to do the same thing.

While *The Evidence Bible* is a study Bible that can strengthen and encourage the faith of any believing Christian, it is also an evangelistic tool. And the primary purpose of this Bible is to bring the message of salvation to the yet unsaved.

In 1999, I had the incredible experience of floating in the Dead Sea. It is impossible to sink into its waters due to the high salt content and rich mineral deposits. The contemporary Body of Christ has become too much like the Dead Sea because there is insufficient outlet from the Church to the world. So the Body of Christ (though rich in many ways) is evangelistically dead because it has stopped giving out what it has received.

God forbid that *The Evidence Bible* should merely add more knowledge to the dead sea of contemporary Christianity. Make sure that you give out what you take in. Become familiar with the commentary and quotes included here. Take this Bible with you when you share your faith and don't hesitate to read portions to the unsaved. There is no higher calling than evangelism.

Many people don't realize how many great men and women of history believed and loved the Word of God. There are many who are ignorant of the Bible's wealth of scientific and medical knowledge. Perhaps one simple quote from a famous person of the past or present may be enough to spark a nonbeliever's interest in Holy Scripture. Perhaps God will use your words to bring the message of eternal life to those who sit in the shadow of death, unaware that eternal life is within their reach.

To help *The Evidence Bible* to be easily accessible, we have translated into contemporary English some archaic words from the King James Version, such as "concupiscence," "decketh," "eschew," "feigned," "hawn," "heretofore," "howbeit," "intreaty," "waxeth."

There may be concerns that in removing such archaic words from the King James Version we are somehow altering God's Word. But translating such words into contemporary English is not unlike translating the King James

Version into Chinese in order to publish the Bible in a Chinese-speaking country. Would I publish a Bible in the King James English for the Chinese? No, they don't speak that language. Will God's wrath come upon us because we translated the words of the Bible into Chinese so that the Bible could be easily read by the Chinese? I don't think so. Obviously, the Bible should be translated into the language spoken in each country, otherwise it won't make sense to readers there.

I'm sure Heaven rejoiced when the first English version of the Bible gave light to those whom the Roman Catholic church had kept in the dark by keeping the Word of God in Latin. I'm sure "in principio creavit Deus caelum et terram" makes more sense to you when you read it as "In the beginning God created the heavens and the earth."

Let's now go forward to this day and age. The King James English Bible was written for the English (another country) when they spoke another language (what we commonly call King James English). Satan didn't say "Yea, Hath God said?" (unless you think that Satan and Adam and Eve spoke English) The verse was originally written in Hebrew, but was translated into English by some kind folks so that the English in the 1700's could understand the Word of God.

We are doing exactly the same thing today. We are taking words that people don't understand and giving the contemporary equivalent. We would never think of dropping verses about the Blood of Christ, repentance, or the deity of Christ; nor would we change the meaning of any verse nor drop one jot or tittle from God's Word.

In closing, let me share one of the greatest encouragements of my personal life. It happened when actor Kirk Cameron called our ministry late in 2001. Even though he had been a Christian for many years, God had deeply touched his life through the book (which is now called), *The Way of the Master* and through a teaching I do called "Hell's Best Kept Secret." He was so excited about what he read and heard that we decided to combine ministries to get the teaching to the contemporary Church.

Some time later, Kirk preached "Hell's Best Kept Secret" on a major Christian TV network and the next day our website received over a million hits. We then produced a TV program called "The Way of the Master." This put principles of biblical evangelism into practice. We were delighted when it won a People's Choice Award 2004, 2005, 2006, and NRB's "Best Program" award 2005 and 2006. We then took the cream of the TV program and created "The Basic Training Course," an eight-week DVD course formatted for local churches and individuals to train them in biblical evangelism. Not long after that we started Way of The Master Radio (you can hear this daily on www.WayOfTheMasterRadio.com)

So if you like the principles expounded in the commentary of *The Evidence Bible* and you want more, tune into the radio program. You can also receive our free monthly email newsletter through www.WayOfTheMaster.com

May God bless you for picking up this Bible, and may He use you and this Bible to reach this dying world.

RAY COMFORT
SEPTEMBER 2006

How to Use this Bible

- **Meditate on evangelism verses:** Shaded, italic verses help give you the motivation to seek the lost.

  7 A thousand shall fall at your side, and ten thousand at your right hand; but it shall not come near you.

- **Memorize evangelistic verses:** Bold verses are passages for you to use in witnessing and preaching.

  10 The days of our years are threescore years and ten; and if by reason of strength they be fourscore years, yet is their strength labor and sorrow; for it is soon cut off, and we fly away.

- Look for **bold verse numbers,** indicating that the verse has a corresponding comment nearby.

  13 Those that be planted in the house of the LORD shall flourish in the courts of our God.

- Read **"Questions & Objections"** so you'll be ready to give a defense as you encounter these in witnessing.

- Follow **cross-references** to read more about a topic.

- Refer to the **index** to look up topics of interest.

- **Passages with bold verses and bold verse numbers** are for you to use in witnessing and preaching, and these verses have a corresponding comment nearby.

  12 So teach us to number our days, that we may apply our hearts unto wisdom.

Springboards for Preaching and Witnessing

Why do I Need a Savior? . . . . .Deuteronomy. 4:24

Hang in There . . . . .Job 6:11

The Bible and All It Contains . . . . .Psalms 119:162

The A-Frame Roof . . . . .Isaiah 28:16

The Key . . . . .Proverbs 14:12

Water or Money? . . . . .Matthew 16:26

Sting Operation . . . . .Luke 11:39

The Rush . . . . .Luke 16:17

Revolting Natives . . . . .John 15:13

Experiential Faith . . . . .John 17:3

The Sinking Ship . . . . .1 Corinthians 1:18

The Olympic High Diver . . . . .2 Corinthians 6:2

The Love of God . . . . .Ephesians 2:4,5

The Titanic . . . . .Hebrews 2:10

Solid Ice . . . . .Hebrews 8:6

The New Convert . . . . .Hebrews 11:29

The Will to Live . . . . .James 4:14

Principles of Growth for the New and Growing Christian

Prayer, Wait for a Minute . . . . .Matthew 6:9

Tithing-The Final Frontier . . . . .Mark 12:41-44

Evangelism, Our Most Sobering Task . . . . .Luke 10:2

Water Baptism-Sprinkle or Immerse? . . . . .Acts 2:38

Warfare-Praise the Lord and Pass the Ammunition . . . . .2 Corinthians 4:4

Thanksgiving, Do the Right Thing . . . . .Ephesians 5:20

Faith, Elevators Can Let You Down . . . . .Hebrews 6:18

Fellowship-Flutter by Butterfly . . . . .Hebrews 10:25

Feeding on the Word, Daily Nutrition . . . . .1 Peter 2:2

Points for Open-Air Preaching

Never Fear Hecklers .... Matthew 5:10-12

Make the Bullet Hit the Target .... Matthew 28:19-20

How to Draw a Crowd ....Acts 2:14

Crowd Etiquette ....Acts 3:4

Give Yourself a Lift ....Acts 17:22

Aim for Repentance Rather Than a Decision ....Acts 20:21

Raw Nerves ....Acts 21:30

Watch for "Red Herrings" or "Rabbit Trails" ....1 Corinthians 2:4

"Watch It, Blind Man!" ....2 Timothy 2:24-26

In-depth Comments

Evolution: True Science Fiction ....Genesis 2

Islam ....Genesis 21

The Ten Commandments ....Exodus 20:1-17

The World Dances Around Its Golden Calf of Mammon ....Exodus 32:1-6

Pascal's Wager ....Deuteronomy 30:19

Four Simple Laws ....Psalms 1

How to Confront Sinners ....Psalms 41:4

The Bible Stands Alone ....Psalms 119:105

What God's Word Says About Abortion ....Psalms 127:3

An Interesting Quiz ....Psalms 139:16

How to Use the Ten Commandments in Witnessing ....Psalms 51:6

Questions for Evolutionists ....Proverbs 3:19

Archaeology and History Attest to the Reliability of the Bible ..Matthew 4:4

The Sermon on the Mount ....Matthew 5:1

God's Love: The Biblical Presentation ....Matthew 10:22

Points to Ponder About the Flood and Noah's Ark ....Matthew 24:38,39

The Parable of the Fishless Fishermen ....Mark 1:17

How to Witness to Mormons ....Mark 11:25

Contradictions in the Bible: Why Are They There? ....Mark 15:26

The Witness . . . . .Mark 15:39

The Key to Reaching the Lost . . . . .Luke 11:52

The Hands of the Carpenter . . . . .Luke 23:53

The "Sinner's Prayer"- To Pray or Not To Pray? . . . . .John 1:13

The Significance of Moses' First Miracle . . . . .John 2:6-11

Is Repentance Necessary for Salvation? . . . . .John 3:16

Personal Witnessing, How Jesus Did It . . . . .John 4:7

The Deity of Jesus . . . . .John 10:36

How to Preach at a Funeral

for Someone You Suspect Died Unsaved . . . . .John 11:14

Is Suffering the Entrance to Heaven? . . . . .Acts 4:12

"Missing Link" Still Missing . . . . .Acts 14:15

How to Witness to Muslims . . . . .Acts 17:22

I Have a Problem . . . . .Acts 19

Memorize the Ten Commandments . . . . .Romans 15

Speaking the Truth in Love to Jehovah's Witnesses . . .1 Corinthians 13:2

Last Words of Famous People . . . . .1 Corinthians 15:55

The Gospel: Why not preach that Jesus gives happiness,

peace, and joy? . . . . .2 Corinthians 2:17

What is the Purpose of the Law? . . . . .Galatians 3:19

Ten Ways to Break the Stronghold of Pornography . . . . . . .Galatians 5:16

Freedom from Sabbath-keeping . . . . .Colossians 2:16

Two Prayers . . . . .1 Thessalonians 4

Hinduism . . . . .2 Thessalonians 3

The Great Commission . . . . .1 Timothy 1

Jehovah's Witnesses: Witnessing Tips . . . . .1 Timothy 3:16

Intelligence Tests . . . . .Philemon

Great Leaders Speak About the Bible . . . . .Philemon

Scientific Facts in the Bible . . . . .Hebrews 11:3

Optical Illusions . . . . .Hebrews 12

Mormonism . . . . .James 5

The Dead Sea Scrolls . . . . .1 Peter 1:25

Science Confirms the Bible . . . . .1 Peter 4

The Firefighters . . . . .1 John 4:8

Buddhism . . . . .2 John

Evangelistic Survey . . . . .3 John 1

Test Your I.Q. . . . . Jude

The Resurrection . . . . .Revelation 19

Q & O
Common Questions & Objections

God

"I will believe if God will appear to me" . . . . Exodus 33:18-23

"Who made God?" . . . . Psalms 90:2

"God said He would blot out all remembrance
of Amalek. The Bible itself disproves this statement by mentioning
Amalek to this day." . . . . Psalms 109:15

"Why does the Old Testament show a God of wrath
and the New Testament a God of mercy?" . . . . .Psalms 89:14

"The First Commandment says, 'You shall have no other gods
before Me.' That proves He isn't the only God!" . . . . .Psalms 115:4

"The Bible says 'God repented.' Doesn't that show
He is capable of sin?" . . . . .Psalms 135:14

"How can a perfect God be furious?" . . . . Nahum 2:13

"God is unfair in that Hitler and a dear old lady
(who never accepted Jesus) will both go to hell." . . . . .Matthew 11:24

"My God would never create hell." . . . . .Matthew 18:9

"I don't believe that God is knowable." . . . . John 17:3

"What should I say to someone who acknowledges his sins,
but says, 'I just hope God is forgiving'?" . . . . .Acts 26:28

"Why is there suffering?
That proves there is no 'loving' God." . . . . .Romans 5:12

"If God is perfect, why did He make
an imperfect creation?" . . . . .1 Corinthians 15:22

"God made me like this. Sin is His fault!" . . . . .1 Timothy 2:14

"If God is a God of love,
why hasn't He dealt with evil?" . . . . .1 Peter 3:12

"Why does God allow evil?" . . . . .2 Peter 3:9

"God told Joshua to kill every man, woman, and child, and He killed
masses of people in Revelation. If that's your 'God of love,'
I want nothing to do with Him!" . . . . .Revelation 8:11

Jesus Christ

"On the cross, Jesus cried, 'My God, My God, why have You forsaken Me?'
This proves He was a fake because God forsook Him." . . . . . . .Psalms 22:1
"Jesus wasn't sinless; He became angry
when He cleared the temple." . . . . .Mark 11:15
"Jesus taught hatred by saying that
a Christian should 'hate' his father and mother." . . . . .Luke 14:26
"Jesus didn't condemn the woman caught in the act of adultery,
but condemned those who judged her.
Therefore you shouldn't judge others." . . . . John 8:11
"It's intolerant to say that Jesus is the only way to God!" . . . . . . .John 14:6
"Is it possible that Jesus simply fainted on the cross,
and revived while He was in the tomb?" . . . . John 19:33-34
"Will people who have never heard about Jesus go to hell?" . . .Romans 2:12

The Bible

"Why does the Old Testament show a God of wrath
and the New Testament a God of mercy?" . . . . .Psalms 89:14
"God said He would blot out all remembrance of Amalek. But the Bible itself
disproves this statement by mentioning Amalek to this day." .Psalms 109:15
"The Bible has changed down through the ages." . . . . .Psalms 119:160
"The Bible calls the hare a cud-chewing animal.
As any veterinarian could tell you, this statement is false." . . . .Psalms 147:9
"The fact that there are so many versions proves
that the Bible has mistakes. Which one is right?" . . . . .Proverbs 30:5
"Christianity oppresses women by making them submit to their
husbands!" . . . . .Proverbs 31:10
"When the Bible says 'an eye for an eye,' it encourages us
to take the law in our own hands by avenging wrongdoing." Matthew 5:38

"There are contradictions in the resurrection accounts.

Did Christ appear first to the women or to His disciples?" . . .Matthew 28:9

"How many angels were at the tomb-one or two?" . . . . .Mark 16:6

If someone claims to have read the Bible

and says it's just a book of fairy tales . . . . .Luke 24:44,45

"Christians can't use 'circular reasoning' by trying

to prove the Bible by quoting from the Bible!" . . . . .Acts 17:2

"I've tried to read the Bible, but I can't understand it." . . .1 Corinthians 2:14

"Adam was a mythical figure who never really lived." . . .1 Corinthians 15:45

"Adam didn't die the day God said he would!" . . . . .Ephesians 4:18

"Isn't it blasphemous to call the Bible 'God's Word'

when it makes Him look so bad?" .1 Timothy 6:1

"Didn't men write the Bible?" . . . . .2 Peter 1:21

"The Bible teaches that the earth is flat." . . . . .Revelation 1:7

Sin

When the moral law is preached, should you also

use the ceremonial and civil law? . . . . Exodus 23

The Old Testament said that children were to be stoned to death

for being disobedient. Isn't that rather harsh? . . . . Deuteronomy 21:18

How to Confront Sinners . . . . .Psalms 41:4

"God couldn't forgive my sin." . . . . .Psalms 103:17

"What should I say if someone asks,

'Have you ever lusted?'" . . . . .Matthew 5:28

"You shouldn't talk about sin because Jesus didn't condemn anybody.

He was always loving and kind." .Matthew 23:13

"'Judge not lest you be judged.' You therefore have no right

to judge me when it comes to my sins!" . . . . .Luke 6:37

"What if someone says they've never lied, stolen, lusted, or

blasphemed? If they deny having any sin at all?" . . . . .Luke 18:21

"What should I say to someone who acknowledges his sins,

but says, I just hope God is forgiving?" . . . . .Acts 26:28

"Because Jesus died on the cross,

we are all forgiven of every sin." . . . . .2 Corinthians 5:14,15

"I know I'm a sinner, but I confess my sins to God daily.

I tell Him that I'm sorry and I won't sin again." . . . . .Ephesians 1:7

"God made me like this. Sin is His fault!" . . . . .1 Timothy 2:14

"Do you sin, as a Christian?" . . . . .1 Peter 4:1

Heaven & Hell

"Is it wrong to speak to the dead?" . . . . 1 Chronicles 10:13-14

"I don't mind going to hell. All my friends will be there." . . . .Psalms 55:15

"Could you be wrong in your claims about Judgment Day?" . . .Psalms 76:8

"My God would never create hell." . . . . .Matthew 18:9

"Hell isn't a place. This life is hell." . . . . .Mark 9:47

"Is 'hell-fire' preaching effective?" .Acts 24:25

"Will people who have never heard about Jesus go to hell?" . . .Romans 2:12

"Does someone go to hell for committing suicide?" . . . . .1 Corinthians 3:17

"You are using scare tactics by talking about hell

and Judgment Day." . . . . .Hebrews 10:31

"I hope I'm going to heaven when I die." . . . . .1 John 5:12,13

"Hell is just a metaphor for the grave." . . . . .Revelation 1:18

"How can people be happy in heaven, knowing

that their unsaved loved ones are suffering in hell?" . . . . . .Revelation 21:4

Excuses

"When you're dead, you're dead." . . . . .Psalms 49:15

"I'll wait until I am old, then I'll get right with God." . . . . .Luke 12:20

"I don't believe that God is knowable." . . . . .John 17:3

"If I submit to God, I'll just become a puppet!" . . . . .Acts 13:47

"There is no absolute truth." . . . . .1 Thessalonians 2:13

"God made me like this. Sin is His fault!" . . . . .1 Timothy 2:14

"I was once a born-again Christian.

Now I believe it's all rubbish!" . . . . .1 John 2:19

Faith

"If God gives me some 'sign,' then I will believe." . . . . .Matthew 12:39

"I will believe if God will appear to me." . . . . .John 1:18

"I made a commitment, but nothing happened." . . . . John 14:21

"Seeing is believing. If I can't see it, I don't believe it exists." . . . . John 20:25

"I find it difficult to have faith in God." . . . . 1 John 5:10

Evolution/Creation

"Doesn't the Big Bang theory disprove
the Genesis account of creation?" . . . . Psalms 19:1-4

"How does the young-earth theory explain
that we can see stars millions of light-years away?"

"How would the light have reached us?" . . . . Psalms 136:7-9

"Where do all the races come from?" . . . . Acts 17:26

"Evolution disproves the Bible!" . . . . 1 Corinthians 15:39

"Adam was a mythical figure who never really lived." . . 1 Corinthians 15:45

"The number of fossils in some areas is enormous.
How could earth have supported all those creatures
at the same time?" . . . . 2 Peter 3:3-6

"Where did Cain get his wife?" . . . . 1 John 3:12

Self-righteousness

"I have broken the Ten Commandments,
but I do good things for people." . . . . Proverbs 16:10

"I used to be a liar and a thief, but that was years ago.
Now I try to be a good person." . . . . Proverbs 20:9

"I need to get my life cleaned up first." . . . . Matthew 19:16

"I'm as good as any Christian!" . . . . Mark 10:18

"What if someone says they've never lied, stolen, lusted, or blasphemed?
If they deny having any sin at all?" . . . . Luke 18:21

"Do you think that Christians are better than non-Christians?" . Romans 3:9

"I believe I will go to heaven
because I live by the Golden Rule." . . . . Galatians 5:14

"I've made my peace with the 'Man upstairs.'" . . . . Colossians 1:20

"I'm doing fine. I don't need God." . . . . Hebrews 11:25

Hypocrisy

"Religion has caused more wars than anything else in history." . . .Luke 6:27

"The church is full of hypocrites." . . . . .2 Timothy 2:19

Pride

"Man is the master of his own destiny!" . . . . .Psalms 89:48

Guilt

"You are trying to make me feel guilty

by quoting the Ten Commandments." . . . . .John 8:9

"I don't feel guilty." . . . . .1 Timothy 4:2

Religion

"Why are there so many denominations?" . . . . .Psalms 1:6

"Why are there so many different religions?" . . . . .Romans 10:3

Salvation

"Is water baptism essential to salvation?" . . . . .Mark 1:4-5

"Jews don't need to be 'saved'; they're already God's chosen people.

Even the New Testament says 'so all Israel shall be saved.'" . . . . .Luke 3:7-9

"I have been born again many times." . . . . .John 3:3

"How can you know that you are saved?" . . . . .Galatians 4:6

The Ten Commandments

"What if someone says, 'I've broken every one

of the Ten Commandments'?" . . . . .Psalms 32:5

How to Use the Ten Commandments in Witnessing . . . . .Psalms 51:6

"You are trying to make me feel guilty

by quoting the Ten Commandments." . . . . .John 8:9

Personal Witnessing

"How do I reach my neighbors with the gospel?" . . . . .Proverbs 27:10

"How should I witness to someone who belongs to a denomination,

who I suspect isn't trusting the Savior?" . . . . .Matthew 8:14

"What should I say to someone who has lost a loved one
through cancer?" . . . . .Acts 9:37

"How should I witness to a Jew?" . . . . .Romans 3:1

"How do I witness to someone I know?" . . . . .Romans 14:12

"How should I witness to a homosexual?" . . . . .1 Timothy 1:8-10

"How should I witness to my coworkers?" . . . . .1 Peter 2:15

Women

"Christianity oppresses women by making them submit
to their husbands!" . . . . .Proverbs 31:10

"I know abortion isn't right, but if it is not legal,
we'll have all those poor girls slipping off to see
those butchers in dark alleys." . . . . Isaiah 57:5

Miscellaneous

"If the Jews are God's 'chosen people,'
why have they been so oppressed?" . . . . .Luke 21:24

"Mother Nature sure blew it ..." . . . . .Romans 8:22

"God made me to be a homosexual,
so He doesn't want me to change." . . . . Jude 7

The Function of God's Law

"People will never set their faces decidedly toward heaven and live like pilgrims,
until they really feel that they are in danger of hell." . . . . .Exodus 35:1

Do we remove words that might offend, such as "repentance" and
"hell" to make the message more acceptable,
or to make ourselves acceptable to a God-hating world? . . . . . . Numbers 2

"I was alive without the Law once: but when the commandment came,
sin revived" (Romans 7:9). . . . . .Numbers 7

Christians give their sons and their daughters to the world
by failing to train them up in God's good ways. . . . . . . .Deuteronomy 6:5-9

The trouble with people who are not seeking for a Savior and for salvation
is that they do not understand the nature of sin. . . . . . Deuteronomy 17:11

It is a great mistake to give a man who has not been convicted of sin

certain passages that were never meant for him. . . . . .Joshua 1:7

How the people were wounded with the words of the Law

that were read to them. . . . . .Nehemiah 8:9

Esther had the ten sons of Haman hanged. . . . . .Esther 9:13

If there is no hell, no ultimate justice,

then the answer to the question posed in this verse

must be "Yes. The Almighty does pervert justice." . . . . .Job 8:3

No one likes to admit that their heart is wicked. . . . . .Job 13:23

This is what God's Law does to the receptive sinner. . . . . .Job 40:4

This Law, then, should be arrayed in all its majesty

against selfishness and enmity of the sinner. . . . . .Psalms 5:5

God's Law is perfect. It is His tool to convert the soul. . . . .Psalms 19:7-11

It is amazing for a soul to discover that God gave a law to be observed,

but that its observance is not even taken into account

as a means of salvation. . . . . .Psalms 143:2

The absence of God's holy Law from modern preaching

is perhaps as responsible as any other factor for the evangelistic impotence

of our churches and missions. . . . . .Proverbs 6:23

People will never set their faces decidedly towards heaven

and live like pilgrims until they really feel

that they are in danger of hell... . . . . .Isaiah 4:4

When we judge ourselves against man's standards,

we come up reasonably clean. . . . . .Isaiah 42

A prophecy of a suffering Messiah . . . . .Isaiah 53

When preachers in pulpits have no respect for God's Law,

they preach a gospel devoid of reference to it. . . . . .Jeremiah 6:13-14

The great truth of this verse is hidden from any who do not understand

the spiritual nature of the moral Law. . . . . .Jeremiah 17:9

This is the new birth. . . . . .Jeremiah 31:33

There is a controversy between God and the world. . . . . .Hosea 4:1-3

"I was alive without the Law once:

but when the commandment came, sin revived" (Romans 7:9). . .Hosea 4:6

I do not believe that any man can preach the gospel

who does not preach the Law.   . . . . .Habakkuk 1:4

False prophets, whether during the time of Zephaniah,

or the Pharisees in Jesus' day, or the false prophets of our day,

all do "violence to the Law."   . . . . .Zephaniah 3:4

The covenant of the Law was given that we might fear God. . .Malachi 2:5-8

The reason for sorcery, adultery, false witness and other

transgressions of God's Law is a lack of the fear of God. . . . . . .Malachi 3:5

We are not to forget the Law

once we have accepted the Savior. . . . . .Malachi 4:4

Herein is the Law of God above all other laws,

that it is a spiritual law. . . . . .Matthew 5:22

The unsaved are in no condition today for the gospel

till the Law be applied to their hearts . . . . .Matthew 7:6

Sinners that think they need no physician

will not endure the healer's hand. . . . . .Matthew 9:12

Here is the master Evangelist showing us how to deal with a proud,

self-righteous person-a typical sinner. . . . . .Matthew 19:17-22

 Of this excellent use is the Law: it converts the soul, opens the eyes,

prepares the way of the Lord in the desert, rends the rocks,

levels the mountains, makes a people prepared for the Lord." . . . .Mark 1:3

Now, if you have your hearts broken up by the Law,

you will find the heart is more deceitful than the devil. . . . . . . .Mark 7:21

This man came running and fell to his knees before Jesus. . . . . .Mark 10:17

Ever more the Law must prepare the way for the gospel. . . . . . . .Luke 3:4

If I had my way, I would declare a moratorium on public preaching

of 'the plan of salvation' in America for one to two years. . . . . . .John 3:16

The wrath of the Law brought this woman

to the feet of the Savior. . . . . John 8:4,5

When we apply the tablets of the Law to the eyes of sinners,

it causes them to have reason to go to the cleansing pool

of the gospel. . . . . .John 9:7

Peter's audience was composed of "devout men" (v.2)

who were gathered at Pentecost

to celebrate the giving of God's Law on Mount Sinai. . . . . .Acts 2:37
The very first end of the Law is, namely, convicting men of sin;
awakening those who are still asleep on the brink of hell . . . . .Acts 12:7
Paul was preaching the essence of the First and Second Commandments
to show his hearers that they were idolaters. . . . . .Acts 17:29
Notice that Paul used both prophecy and the Law of Moses
in his evangelism. . . . . .Acts 28:23
The Law's part in transformation is to make a person aware of his sin
and of his need for divine forgiveness and redemption . . . . .Acts 28:23
Here Paul uses the Law to bring "the knowledge of sin." . . . . .Romans 2:21
Sin is like smog: it is not visible while you are in its midst. . . . Romans 3:20
The purpose of the Law is to stop the sinner's mouth
of justification . . . . .Romans 3:19
To slay the sinner is then the first use of the Law . . . . .Romans 7:11
God be thanked when the Law so works as to take off the sinner
all confidence in himself! . . . . .2 Corinthians 3:5,6
The Law's function is to bring death to the sinner in the same way
civil law brings capital punishment to a guilty murderer. . . . .Galatians 2:19
Lower the Law and you dim the light
by which man perceives his guilt . . . . .Galatians 3:24
Some may wonder whether using the Law in evangelism
produces legalism. . . . . .Colossians 2:21
As that which is straight discovers that which is crooked,
so there is no way of coming to that knowledge of sin,
which is necessary to repentance,
but by comparing our hearts and lives with the Law. . . . . .1 Timothy 1:8
When once God the Holy Spirit applies the Law to the conscience,
secret sins are dragged to light, little sins are magnified to their true size,
and things apparently harmless become exceedingly sinful. . .1 Timothy 4:2
While every true believer cries out, 'O what love have I unto thy Law!
All the day long is my study in it;' he sees daily, in that divine mirror,
more and more of his own sinfulness. . . . . .Hebrews 3:12
It is the ordinary method of the Spirit of God
to convict sinners by the Law. . . . . .Hebrews 4:12

You understand that the work of the Law
is the revealing of sin. . . . . .Hebrews 9:14
God, being a perfect God, had to give a perfect Law . . . . .James 1:25
It is of great importance that the sinner
should be made to feel his guilt . . . . James 2:10
The Law also shows us our great need: our need of cleansing,
cleansing with the water and the blood. . . . . .1 John 1:7
"This now is the Christian teaching and preaching,
which, God be praised, we know and possess." . . . . .Jude 3

Scientific Facts in the Bible

Psalm 8:8; 19:5,6; 25:14; 33:6; 95:4,5; 102:25,26; 104:2; 104:19; 135:7;
Luke 4:40; John 20:26; Acts 14:17; Heb. 11:3; 11:11

Acknowledgments

WITHOUT A DOUBT, it is the resurrection of the Savior that provides the ultimate evidence of the truth of Christianity. All the quality quotes and powerful arguments about creation, the folly of evolution, and other topics may not convince a man of the truth. However, an encounter with the resurrected Savior will.

Jesus is still stopping Sauls on the Road to Damascus. He still gives light to those who are in darkness. The indwelling Savior makes a man a new creature in Christ. He gives him a new heart with new desires, making him love the things he once hated, and hate the things he once loved. When a man is born again he needs no more convincing. Knowing Jesus is an infallible proof: "To whom also he showed himself alive after his passion by many infallible proofs, being seen of them forty days" (Acts 1:3).

I am also grateful to my lifelong friend Richard Gunther for his fine cartoons, and to Alex Ruiz, Joe Potter, Joel Hughs and Scott Harvey for their quality illustrations.

My gratitude also goes to my beloved wife, Sue; my sons, Daniel and Jacob; as well as to Rachel and Emeal Zwayne; Ron Meade; Sarah and Becky Comfort; Felicia Woodson; Pastor Garry Ansdell; and to my good friend Mark Spence. My very special thanks to Lynn Copeland of the Genesis Group for her patience, her love of the truth, her concern for the lost, and for her wonderful editorial work. She made a sow's ear into a silk purse.

I am also indebted to Guy Morrell, the owner of Bridge-Logos Publishers. There are not too many Christian men in positions of importance who remember the reason that the Church exists. When the idea of this publication was first conceived, he was told by a respected source to be careful because "evangelism Bibles don't sell." Guy's response was, "That's why we *must* do it." He has a deep passion to see this world reached for Jesus Christ. I count it an honor to work with him and his staff at Bridge-Logos.

The
Old
Testament

Who Can Tell Me?

"Who can tell me where I came from?"
The little boy would ask.
His question was a good one
Yet he faced a trying task.

Each man had different answers
As he was soon to learn.
This brought him great confusion
And it caused a deep concern.

He first went to his schoolmates
And they spoke with one another.
Then the smartest of the bunch said,
"You came from your mother."

Now this had satisfied him,
Yet only for a time.
For as he grew in years of age
His thoughts began to climb.

He then looked all around him
At all that he could see.
And his mind began to wonder
How it all had come to be.

He thought about the cosmos,
The infinitude of space;
And every star and planet
That exists in every place.

He thought about the rounded earth,
Spinning in rotation.
And all four seasons that occur
In yearly circulation.

He thought about the darkness
And he thought about the light.
He thought about the sun and moon
That help the day and night.

He thought of all the creatures
Of the land and sea and skies
Of all the different species
And their variance in size.

He thought of all the plants and trees
And all that each provides,
Each growing from a tiny seed
With roots the soil hides.

He then looked at humanity
With all the different faces.
Different tongues and characters
And all the different races.

He thought of mortal bodies
With features so profound;
All the senses: taste, and touch,
And smell, and sight, and sound.

He thought of reproduction
And the miracle of birth.
He thought of human life itself
And all that it is worth.

He then considered human will:
Weak and also strong.
He thought about the conscience
That discerns the right from wrong.

He thought about emotions
And feelings that arise.
He thought about the love and hate
And tears that flow from eyes.

He thought about the anger
And the joy that does abound.
He thought about the happiness
And sadness that is found.

And filled with curiosity,
This boy would daily strive.
In hopeful expectation
That his answer would arrive.

He spoke with scientific men
Who claimed his question solved.
They told him of a real big bang
And that all things evolved.

He then spoke with philosophers
And many did insist,
That there is no reality
And nothing does exist.

He spoke with many people
From various groups and sects.
And heard the vast opinions
Of various intellects.

Now baffled by confusion,
A very troubled youth;
Unable to discern
What is error, what is truth.

He almost gave up looking,
But he took a second look.
And very unexpectedly,
He found a special Book.

As he opened up the first page,
The mystery came undone.
His questions all were answered
In Genesis, chapter one.

With a nod of understanding,
He smiled, so elated.
For now he surely knew—
"In the Beginning, God created…"

Pastor Emeal Zwayne

Genesis

CHAPTER 1

IN the beginning God created the heaven and the earth.

2 And the earth was without form, and void; and darkness was upon the face of the deep. And the Spirit of God moved upon the face of the waters.

3 And God said, Let there be light: and there was light.

4 And God saw the light, that it was good: and God divided the light from the darkness.

5 And God called the light Day, and the darkness he called Night. And the evening and the morning were the first day.

6 And God said, Let there be a firmament in the midst of the waters, and let it divide the waters from the waters.

7 And God made the firmament, and divided the waters which were under the firmament from the waters which were above the firmament: and it was so.

8 And God called the firmament Heaven. And the evening and the morning were the second day.

9 And God said, Let the waters under the heaven be gathered together to one place, and let the dry land appear: and it was so.

10 And God called the dry land Earth; and the gathering together of the waters called he Seas: and God saw that it was good.

11 And God said, Let the earth bring forth grass, the herb yielding seed, and the fruit tree yielding fruit after his kind, whose seed is in itself, upon the earth: and it was so.

1:1 A simple way to study the Bible is to COMB the words: C: Context, O: Other related scriptures, M: Meaning of words, B: Background.

1:1 How old is creation? See Psalm 136:7-9 "Questions and Objections."

1:1 "Genesis is the seed-plot of the whole Bible. It is referred to or quoted 60 times in the New Testament, and divine authority is set like a seal on its historical facts. See Matthew 19:4-6, 24:37-39, Mark 7:4,10, 10:3-8, Luke 11:49-51, 17:26-29,32, John 1:51, 7:21-23, 8:44-56." Richard Gunther

1:3 The Gospel of John, Chapter One, tells us that the "Word" was in the beginning with God; that He made all things and that He became flesh in Jesus of Nazareth. Here we see the "Word" manifest in the voice of God. It was God's word, His voice that brought all things into existence. Through the incarnation of Jesus His "voice/word" became flesh and dwelt amongst us. That's why Jesus said strange things about His voice. He said, "Marvel not, but the hour is coming when all that are in their graves shall hear (My) voice." He said, "My words are spirit, they are life." It was His voice that brought Lazarus from the grave (see John 11:43). It is His voice that brings life. See Psalm 29:3-9. See John 1:3 comment.

1:9 For thoughts on the "Big Bang," see Psalm 19:1-4 "Questions and Objections."

12 And the earth brought forth grass, and herb yielding seed after his kind, and the tree yielding fruit, whose seed was in itself, after his kind: and God saw that it was good.

13 And the evening and the morning were the third day.

14 And God said, Let there be lights in the firmament of the heaven to divide the day from the night; and let them be for signs, and for seasons, and for days, and years:

15 And let them be for lights in the firmament of the heaven to give light upon the earth: and it was so.

16 And God made two great lights; the greater light to rule the day, and the lesser light to rule the night: he made the stars also.

17 And God set them in the firmament of the heaven to give light upon the earth,

18 And to rule over the day and over the night, and to divide the light from the darkness: and God saw that it was good.

19 And the evening and the morning were the fourth day.

20 And God said, Let the waters bring forth abundantly the moving creature that has life, and fowl that may fly above the earth in the open firmament of heaven.

21 And God created great whales, and every living creature that moves, which the waters brought forth abundantly, after their kind, and every winged fowl after his kind: and God saw that it was good.

22 And God blessed them, saying, Be fruitful, and multiply, and fill the waters in the seas, and let fowl multiply in the earth.

23 And the evening and the morning were the fifth day.

24 And God said, Let the earth bring forth the living creature after his kind, cattle, and creeping thing, and beast of the earth after his kind: and it was so.

25 And God made the beast of the earth after his kind, and cattle after their kind, and every thing that creeps upon the earth after his kind: and God saw that it was good.

26 And God said, Let us make man in our image, after our likeness: and let them have dominion over the fish of the sea, and over the fowl of the air, and over the cattle, and over all the earth, and over every creeping thing that creeps upon the earth.

27 So God created man in his own image, in the image of God created he him; male and female created he them.

28 And God blessed them, and God said to them, Be fruitful, and multiply, and replenish the earth, and subdue it: and have dominion over the fish of the sea, and over the fowl of the air, and over every living thing that moves upon the earth.

29 And God said, Behold, I have given you every herb bearing seed, which is upon the face of all the earth, and every tree, in the which is the fruit of a tree yielding seed; to you it shall be for meat.

30 And to every beast of the earth, and to every fowl of the air, and to every thing that creeps upon the earth, wherein there is life, I have given every green herb for meat: and it was so.

31 And God saw every thing that he had made, and, behold, it was very

---

1:24 For thoughts on microevolution, see Psalm 90:2 comments.

1:25 For the differences between men and animals, see Psalm 32:9 comment.

1:26 There is no contradiction between this verse and Genesis 2:7, as skeptics often maintain. Genesis 2:7 merely gives details of Genesis 1:26.

1:27 See "God made male and female," (Mark 10:6). Also "Questions for Evolutionists", page 6.

1:28 See Psalm 8:6 comment.

To suppose that the eye
could have been formed
by natural selection, seems,
I freely confess,
absurd in the highest degree.

Charles Darwin

---

good. And the evening and the morning were the sixth day.

CHAPTER 2

T HUS the heavens and the earth were finished, and all the host of them.

2 And on the seventh day God ended his work which he had made; and he rested on the seventh day from all his work which he had made.

3 And God blessed the seventh day, and sanctified it: because that in it he had rested from all his work which God created and made.

4 These are the generations of the heavens and of the earth when they were created, in the day that the LORD God made the earth and the heavens,

5 And every plant of the field before it was in the earth, and every herb of the field before it grew: for the LORD God had not caused it to rain upon the earth, and there was not a man to till the ground.

6 But there went up a mist from the earth, and watered the whole face of the ground.

7 And the LORD God formed man of the dust of the ground, and breathed into his nostrils the breath of life; and man became a living soul.

8 And the LORD God planted a garden eastward in Eden; and there he put the man whom he had formed.

9 And out of the ground made the LORD God to grow every tree that is pleasant to the sight, and good for food; the tree of life also in the midst of the garden, and the tree of knowledge of good and evil.

1:31 For Albert Einstein's appreciation of the Creator, see Psalm 33:8 comment.

2:1 "The heavens and the earth were finished." There is a fundamental law known to science that says that energy cannot be destroyed or created. In other words, the universe as we know it contains exactly the same amount of energy at all times. Richard Gunther (For interesting thoughts of scientists, see Proverbs 3:19 comment.)

2:7 Now that science is able to break material substances down to their basic constituents, it has been found that all matter consists of a limited number of elements, which are common to all living and non-living things. In other words, man is made of exactly the same things as soil. Richard Gunther

2:8 Evolution comes unglued. See comment at Psalm 104:24.

2:1 *The Scientist:*
"I want to know
how God created the world."
                        Albert Einstein

There are many who, in a vain attempt to show atheism to be "intellectual," have claimed that Albert Einstein was an atheist. However, the father of all scientists made a number of statements that clearly refute such a claim. He said, "In the view of such harmony in the cosmos which I, with my limited human mind, am able to recognize, there are yet people who say there is no God. But what makes me really angry is that they quote me for support of such views." (The Expanded Quotable Einstein, Princeton University Press, page 214). He also said, "We know nothing about God and the world at all. All our knowledge is but the knowledge of schoolchildren. Possibly we shall know a little more than we do now. But the real nature of things, that we shall never know, never." (The Expanded Quotable Einstein, Princeton University Press, page 207). He even revealed his insightful mind with, "I see a pattern, but my imagination cannot picture the maker of the pattern. I see a clock, but I cannot envision the clockmaker. The human mind is unable to conceive of the four dimensions, so how can it conceive of a God, before whom a thousand years and a thousand dimensions are as one." (The Expanded Quotable Einstein, Princeton University Press, page 208). He also said, "I want to know how God created this world. I am not interested in this or that phenomenon, in the spectrum of this or that element. I want to know His thoughts. The rest are details." (The Expanded Quotable Einstein, Princeton University Press, page 202).

Those who take the time to read the Bible can know how God created this world (see Genesis chapter 1), and they can read the thoughts of God throughout holy scripture. The problem is that the Bible is not merely a history book as some maintain. It is a moral book and for that reason sinful man refuses to open its pages. The Psalmist informs us, "The entrance of Your Word gives light" (Psalm 119:130) and the Bible further tells us that men love darkness rather than light, because their deeds are evil. They refuse to come to the light because it exposes their sinful deeds (see John 3:19-20).

In the light of these thoughts it is interesting to note that at the age of thirty-four a reasonably young Einstein unashamedly boasted, "I have firmly resolved to bite the dust, when my time comes, with the minimum of medical assistance, and up to then I will sin to my wicked heart's content." (The Expanded Quotable Einstein, Princeton University Press, page 61). However, time tends to make most thinking men somewhat philosophical. Two months before his death in 1955, he said, "To one bent on age, death will come as a release. I feel this quite strongly now that I have grown old myself and have come to regard death like an old debt, at long last to be discharged. Still, instinctively one does everything possible to postpone the final settlement. Such is the game that nature plays with us." (The Expanded Quotable Einstein, Princeton University Press, page 63). It seems that the great genius spoke biblical truth unawares. However, it isn't nature that seeks a "final settlement," it is the law of God. Like a criminal who has transgressed civil law, he (like the rest of humanity) was in debt to eternal justice because he had transgressed God's law. This great debt that he spoke of could not be satisfied with mere silver and gold. It is a debt that demands capital punishment. It calls for the death penalty for guilty transgressors…and eternal damnation in Hell. Its terrible decree demands, "The soul that sins shall die," but it is a demand that was fully satisfied by the One who cried from Calvary's cross, "It is finished!" It was paid in full by the precious Blood of Jesus.

From, God Doesn't Believe in Atheists, by Ray Comfort (Bridge-Logos Publishers)

Evolution:
True Science Fiction

LUCY
Nearly all experts agree Lucy was just a 3 foot tall chimpanzee.

HEIDELBERG MAN
Built from a jawbone that was conceded by many to be quite human.

NEBRASKA MAN
Scientifically built up from one tooth, later found to be the tooth of an extinct pig.

PILTDOWN MAN
The jawbone turned out to belong to a modern ape.

PEKING MAN
Supposedly 500,000 years old, but all evidence has disappeared.

NEANDERTHAL MAN
At the Int'l Congress of Zoology (1958) Dr. A.J.E. Cave said his examination showed that this famous skeleton found in France over 50 years ago is that of an old man who suffered from arthritis.

NEW GUINEA MAN
Dates way back to 1970. This species has been found in the region just north of Australia.

CRO-MAGNON MAN
One of the earliest and best established fossils is at least equal in physique and brain capacity to modern man... so what's the difference?

MODERN MAN
This genius thinks we came from a monkey.

"Professing themselves to be wise they became fools."
(Romans 1:22)

© Chick Publications, reprinted by permission.

1:27 *Questions for Evolutionists*

by Dr. Kent Hovind

The test of any theory is whether or not it provides answers to basic questions. Some well-meaning but misguided people think evolution is a reasonable theory to explain man's questions about the universe. Evolution is not a good theory—it is just a pagan religion masquerading as science.

1. Where did the space for the universe come from?

2. Where did matter come from?

3. Where did the laws of the universe come from (gravity, inertia, etc.)?

4. How did matter get so perfectly organized?

5. Where did the energy come from to do all the organizing?

6. When, where, why, and how did life come from dead matter?

7. When, where, why, and how did life learn to reproduce itself?

8. With what did the first cell capable of sexual reproduction reproduce?

9. Why would any plant or animal want to reproduce more of its kind since this would only make more mouths to feed and decrease the chances of survival? (Does the individual have a drive to survive, or the species? How do you explain this?)

10. How can mutations (recombining of the genetic code) create any new, improved varieties? (Recombining English letters will never produce Chinese books.)

11. Is it possible that similarities in design between different animals prove a common Creator instead of a common ancestor?

12. Natural selection only works with the genetic information available and tends only to keep a species stable. How would you explain the increasing complexity in the genetic code that must have occurred if evolution were true?

13. When, where, why, and how did:

    a) Single-celled plants become multi-celled? (Where are the two- and three-celled intermediates?)

    b) Single-celled animals evolve?

    c) Fish change to amphibians?

    d) Amphibians change to reptiles?

    e) Reptiles change to birds? (The lungs, bones, eyes, reproductive organs, heart, method of locomotion, body covering, etc., are all very different!) How did the intermediate forms live?

14. When, where, why, how, and from what did:

    a) Whales evolve?

    b) Sea horses evolve?

    c) Bats evolve?

    d) Eyes evolve?

    e) Ears evolve?

    f) Hair, skin, feathers, scales, nails, claws, etc., evolve?

15. Which evolved first (how, and how long, did it work without the others)?

    a) The digestive system, the food to be digested, the appetite, the ability to find and eat the food, the digestive juices, or the body's resistance to its own digestive juice (stomach, intestines, etc.)?

    b) The drive to reproduce or the ability to reproduce?

    c) The lungs, the mucus lining to protect them, the throat, or the perfect mixture of gases to be breathed into the lungs?

    d) DNA or RNA to carry the DNA message to cell parts?

    e) The termite or the flagella in its intestines that actually digest the cellulose?

    f) The plants or the insects that live on and pollinate the plants?

    g) The bones, ligaments, tendons, blood supply, or muscles to move the bones?

    h) The nervous system, repair system, or hormone system?

    i) The immune system or the need for it?

I could prove God statistically.
Take the human body alone.
The chance that all the functions of the individual
would just happen
is a statistical monstrosity.

GEORGE GALLUP
STATISTICIAN

1:27 *Fearfully and Wonderfully Made*

Do you realize that you sneeze at 120 miles per hour? Did you also know that every time you sneeze, you have been programmed to close your eyes? Where does your hair grow from? How can the thin layer of skin on your head send out a special hair? It has been formulated in your genes to send out a certain type of hair for the head, hair different from that which grows on the arm, or on the eyelids or the eyebrows. Imagine if you had eyebrows or eyelashes that grew to the length of the hair on your head. Think of the fine row of hair that makes up the eyelash or of the way the hairs face the same direction on the eyebrow.

Have you ever studied the ordinary garden snail and wondered how its shell is able to grow in proportion to its body? When it is a baby snail, it has a baby shell. As it doubles in size, it doesn't discard it. The hard shell also doubles in size. Do you credit the snail with having a mind brilliant enough to make its own shell?

How does a grubby little caterpillar get rid of all its legs while inside a cocoon, grow two fresh ones, then form itself into a beautiful butterfly? Perhaps you could mumble "evolution," and believe that it could happen if millions of years were involved. But all this happens in a few weeks.

Do you give a baby credit for having the ability to grow its own teeth? How did you grow both sets of yours? If you ever decide to get false teeth, will you have them made, or will you wait for "chance" to make a pair for you? Look at your fingernails. Where did they grow from? What makes up their substance? Look at how your hands are holding this publication. Notice how the fingers cradle it while the thumb holds the pages. One thumb comes from the right side, the other from the left. Both thumbs bend forward. If they bent the other way, you couldn't hold the book. Hands have been designed for the purpose of holding.

How is it that your lungs keep breathing irrespective of your will? You have been doing it without a second thought while you have been looking at your thumbs. In fact, becoming conscious of it can hinder the process. Lungs seem to work best without any conscious thought from the mind. How does your subconscious mind continually feed you with thoughts, even when you sleep? Listen to it talk to you and keep you company. It never stops. Try and stop it yourself. Put this book down and think of nothing for five minutes. Bet you can't. Your subconscious mind has been set in motion, and it has little to do with your will.

Think of the complexities of the human mind. It is feeding your understanding with knowledge right now by translating ink shapes on these pages, speaking them to your mind, and automatically filing them into your memory bank.

Right at this moment, your liver, kidneys, heart, pancreas, salivary glands, etc., are all working to keep your body going. You don't even have the power to switch them off and on. During your sleep tonight, your heart will pump seventy-five gallons of blood through your body each hour.

Continued on next page

Continued from previous page

Contrary to common belief, your lungs are more than just bags into which you breathe smoke. They are designed to filter oxygen out of the air you breathe. These organs contain 300,000,000,000 tiny blood vessels called capillaries. Your entire blood supply washes through your lungs once every minute. In your lifetime, the marrow in your bones will create approximately half a ton of red corpuscles.

You have focusing muscles in your eyes that move an estimated 100,000 times each day. That same eye has within it a retina that covers less than a square inch and contains 137,000,000 light-sensitive cells. Even a wide-eyed Charles Darwin said, "To suppose that the eye could have been formed by natural selection, seems, I freely confess, absurd in the highest degree."

Your brain contains 10,000,000,000 neurons, microscopic nerve cells. Your stomach, which produces four pints of gastric juice each day, has 35,000,000 glands lining it. Next time you eat a delicious meal, be thankful to God for the 8,000 taste buds that were put into your mouth. Imagine how boring eating would be without them.

George Gallup, the famous statistician, said, "I could prove God statistically; take the human body alone, the chance that all the functions of the individual would just happen, is a statistical monstrosity."

Was it an accident that your ears were designed to capture sound? The grooves, bumps and ridges are made to catch passing sound waves and channel them into the eardrum. Again, your hands were made to grip and feel. The tongue was made to taste food and to shape speech. The nose was made to smell. What if your ears faced backwards or your nose was upside down (what a nightmare in a rainstorm), or your mouth had two tongues? I am serious. If humanity just happened (with no purposeful design), why don't we see such creatures? In fact, we see the very opposite. From the teeth of a dog to the legs of a grasshopper, one can see practical design in everything that has been made.

Now, if the incredibly brilliant, creative "force" made all things, then it is not only infinitely more intelligent than man whom it made, but it is surely familiar with what it has made. Not only did it create every one of the 100,000 hairs on the average non-bald human head, but it is also familiar with each individual hair. If the force can make the eye, it is not blind itself (see Psalm 94:8,9).

Creation reflects the genius of the Creator's hand. Let's look at a common cow. Someone once said, "How is it that a brown cow eats green grass, which turns into white milk, then yellow butter, which is eaten by a man who grows red hair and has blue eyes?" Think of how grass-cuttings become milk, cheese, and butter...all from a little stirring and churning. Imagine if you were able to invent a machine that could turn your grass into milk. Yet the cow does just that. Tell me how she does it. If it is so simple, make your millions by inventing a machine that turns grass into milk. Call it a "Lawn-Mooer." The cow does it with little effort. Is she wiser than you?

Explain to me how a sparrow knows he is a sparrow and stays with other sparrows or how a baby knows how to look into the eyes of its mother when no one has taught it to do so. Tell me how strawberries can grow next to garlic, and yet both derive their own unique tastes from the same soil and water. How was a wasp made so that its wings flap at 100 times every second or the housefly at 190 per second or the mosquito at an amazing 500 times every second?

The most godless must be humbled by a sense of awe and wonder when standing beneath the mighty power of Niagara Falls or as he gazes into the Grand Canyon or stares into the infinity of space. How much more should we be humbled by the maker of these things?

1,2   *Contradictions in the Bible?*

Do Genesis chapters 1 and 2 conflict? When scoffers claim that the Bible is full of contradictions, they almost always cite Genesis 1 and 2 as examples.

1. Genesis 1:11 has the trees made on day three before man; Genesis 2:9 has the trees made on day six after man.

2. Genesis 1:20 has birds made out of the water on day five; Genesis 2:19 has birds made out of the ground (after man) on day six.

3. Genesis 1:24, 25 has the animals made on day 6 before man; Genesis 2:19 has the animals made on day six after man.

A careful reading of the two chapters will show the solution for each of the supposed contradictions.

Explanation of supposed contradiction 1:

A. Chapter 1 tells the entire story in the order it happened.

B. Genesis 2:4-6 gives a quick summary of the first five days of creation.

C. Genesis 2:7-25 is describing only the events that took place on day six in the Garden of Eden.

D. The trees described in Genesis 2:9 are only in the Garden of Eden; the rest of the world is already full of trees from day three. The purpose of this second creation of trees may have been to let Adam see that God did have power to create, that He was not just taking credit for the existing world. Notice that the second creation of trees was still on day six and was only those trees that are "pleasant to the sight and good for food."

Explanation of supposed contradiction 2:

The birds created out of the ground on day six are only one of each "kind" so that Adam can name them and select a wife. The rest of the world is full of birds from day five.

Explanation of supposed contradiction 3:

Genesis 2:19 is describing only the animals created in the Garden, after man. The purpose of this second batch of animals being created was so that Adam could name them (Genesis 2:19) and select a wife (Genesis 2:20). Since Adam could not find a suitable mate (God knew he wouldn't), He made Eve (Genesis 2:21-22).

There are no contradictions between these two chapters. Chapter 2 only describes in more detail the events in the Garden of Eden on day six. If ancient man had written the Bible (as some scoffers say), he would never have made it say that the light was made before the sun! Many ancient cultures worshiped the sun as the source of life. God is light. God made the light before He made the sun so we could see that He (not the sun) is the source of life.

Dr. Kent Hovind

THE FORMATION OF EVE

Genesis 2:23

10 And a river went out of Eden to water the garden; and from thence it was parted, and became into four heads.

11 The name of the first is Pison: that is it which compasses the whole land of Havilah, where there is gold;

12 And the gold of that land is good: there is bdellium and the onyx stone.

13 And the name of the second river is Gihon: the same is it that compasses the whole land of Ethiopia.

14 And the name of the third river is Hiddekel: that is it which goes toward the east of Assyria. And the fourth river is Euphrates.

15 And the LORD God took the man, and put him into the garden of Eden to dress it and to keep it.

16 And the LORD God commanded the man, saying, Of every tree of the garden you may freely eat:

17 But of the tree of the knowledge of good and evil, you shall not eat of it: for in the day that you eat thereof you shall surely die.

18 And the LORD God said, It is not good that the man should be alone; I will make him an help mate for him.

19 And out of the ground the LORD God formed every beast of the field, and every fowl of the air; and brought them to Adam to see what he would call them: and whatsoever Adam called every living creature, that was the name thereof.

20 And Adam gave names to all cattle, and to the fowl of the air, and to every beast of the field; but for Adam there was not found an help mate for him.

21 And the LORD God caused a deep sleep to fall upon Adam, and he slept: and he took one of his ribs, and closed up the flesh instead thereof;

22 And the rib, which the LORD God had taken from man, made he a woman, and brought her to the man.

23 And Adam said, This is now bone of my bones, and flesh of my flesh: she shall be called Woman, because she was taken out of Man.

24 Therefore shall a man leave his father and his mother, and shall cleave to his wife: and they shall be one flesh.

25 And they were both naked, the man and his wife, and were not ashamed.

CHAPTER 3

N OW the serpent was more subtle than any beast of the field which the LORD God had made. And he said to the woman, Yea, has God said, You shall not eat of every tree of the garden?

2:17 "When Adam sinned, God's warning that he would die began to come true. In Hebrew, the expression 'you shall die' means 'dying you shall die' - in other words, a process of dying was to begin. Science has found that death is a process that begins at conception. Within every cell, at the end of the DNA, are small pieces called telemeres. At each division of the cell a telemere is lost. Eventually all the telemeres are gone, and the cell dies. 'Dying you shall die' is literally fulfilled." Richard Gunther

Skeptics maintain that Adam didn't die that day. He certainly did. Death entered him: "As by one man sin entered the world, and death by sin..." Also, it must be remembered that the scriptures inform us that a day to the Lord is a thousand years to us (see 2 Peter 3:8). Adam died at the age of 930 years (Genesis 5:5).

2:25 "Slight variations in physical laws such as gravity or electromagnetism would make life impossible...The necessity to produce life lies at the center of the universe's whole machinery and design." John Wheeler, Princeton University professor of physics (Reader's Digest, Sept. 1986)

Even evolutionist Stephen Hawking acknowledges "the universe and the laws of physics seem to have been specifically designed for us. If any one of about 40 physical qualities had more than slightly different values, life as we know it could not exist: Either atoms would not be stable, or they wouldn't combine into molecules, or the stars wouldn't form the heavier elements, or the universe would collapse before life could develop, and so on..." (Austin American-Statesman, October 19, 1997)

2 And the woman said to the serpent, We may eat of the fruit of the trees of the garden:

3 But of the fruit of the tree which is in the midst of the garden, God has said, You shall not eat of it, neither shall you touch it, lest you die.

4 And the serpent said to the woman, You shall not surely die:

5 For God does know that in the day you eat thereof, then your eyes shall be opened, and you shall be as gods, knowing good and evil.

6 And when the woman saw that the tree was good for food, and that it was pleasant to the eyes, and a tree to be desired to make one wise, she took of the fruit thereof, and did eat, and gave also to her husband with her; and he did eat.

7 And the eyes of them both were opened, and they knew that they were naked; and they sewed fig leaves together, and made themselves aprons.

8 And they heard the voice of the LORD God walking in the garden in the cool of the day: and Adam and his wife hid themselves from the presence of the LORD God amongst the trees of the garden.

9 And the LORD God called to Adam, and said to him, Where are you?

10 And he said, I heard your voice in the garden, and I was afraid, because I was naked; and I hid myself.

11 And he said, Who told you that you were naked? Have you eaten of the tree,

"Ah! How foolish we are! How we repeat the folly of our first parent every day when we seek to hide sin from conscience, and then think it is hidden from God."

Charles Spurgeon

whereof I commanded you that you should not eat?

12 And the man said, The woman whom you gave to be with me, she gave me of the tree, and I did eat.

3:1 "He [Satan] will most thoroughly and carefully examine us, and if he shall find us to be, like Achilles, vulnerable nowhere else but in our heel, then he will shoot his arrows at our heel." Charles Spurgeon

3:7 "The fig leaves used by Adam and Eve are called aprons, which cover only a part of the body and are not sufficient for a complete covering. The fig leaf is soft like velvet, and, under the heat of the sun, shrinks to about a quarter the size. These leaves are a type of self-righteousness. After Adam and Eve made the aprons they still hid themselves from God because they knew they were still naked in His sight. No amount of self-righteousness, or religion, or church attendance, or donations to worthy causes, or religious acts...is sufficient to hide the sins of the heart from God's sight." From W.L. Wilson's *Diet of Types*

It is the light and heat of the law of God that withers self-righteousness and exposes the shame of our sin.

ADAM AND EVE DRIVEN OUT OF EDEN

Genesis 3:24

13 And the LORD God said to the woman, What is this that you have done? And the woman said, The serpent beguiled me, and I did eat.

14 And the LORD God said to the serpent, Because you have done this, you are cursed above all cattle, and above every beast of the field; upon your belly shall you go, and dust shall you eat all the days of your life:

15 And I will put enmity between you and the woman, and between your seed and her seed; it shall bruise your head, and you shall bruise his heel.

16 To the woman he said, I will greatly multiply your sorrow and your conception; in sorrow you shall bring forth children; and your desire shall be to your husband, and he shall rule over you.

17 And to Adam he said, Because you have hearkened to the voice of your wife, and have eaten of the tree, of which I commanded you, saying, You shall not eat of it: cursed is the ground for your sake; in sorrow shall you eat of it all the days of your life;

18 Thorns also and thistles shall it bring forth to you; and you shall eat the herb of the field;

19 *In the sweat of your face shall you eat bread, till you return to the ground; for out of it were you taken: for dust you are, and to dust shall you return.*

20 And Adam called his wife's name Eve; because she was the mother of all living.

21 To Adam also and to his wife did the LORD God make coats of skins, and clothed them.

22 And the LORD God said, Behold, the man is become as one of us, to know good and evil: and now, lest he put forth his hand, and take also of the tree of life, and eat, and live for ever:

23 Therefore the LORD God sent him forth from the garden of Eden, to till the ground from whence he was taken.

24 So he drove out the man; and he placed at the east of the garden of Eden Cherubims, and a flaming sword which

God whispers to us in our pleasures, speaks in our conscience, but shouts in our pain: it is His megaphone to rouse a deaf world.

**C. S. LEWIS
THE PROBLEM OF PAIN**

turned every way, to keep the way of the tree of life.

CHAPTER 4

AND Adam knew Eve his wife; and she conceived, and bare Cain, and said, I have gotten a man from the LORD.

2 And she again bare his brother Abel. And Abel was a keeper of sheep, but Cain was a tiller of the ground.

3 And in process of time it came to pass, that Cain brought of the fruit of the ground an offering to the LORD.

4 And Abel, he also brought of the firstlings of his flock and of the fat thereof. And the LORD had respect to Abel and to his offering:

5 But to Cain and to his offering he had not respect. And Cain was very wroth, and his countenance fell.

6 And the LORD said to Cain, Why are you wroth? and why is your countenance fallen?

7 If you do well, shall you not be accepted? and if you do not well, sin lies at the door. And to you shall be his desire, and you shall rule over him.

8 And Cain talked with Abel his brother: and it came to pass, when they were in the field, that Cain rose up against Abel his brother, and slew him.

9 And the LORD said to Cain, Where is Abel your brother? And he said, I know not: Am I my brother's keeper?

10 And he said, What have you done? the voice of your brother's blood cries to me from the ground.

11 And now are you cursed from the earth, which has opened her mouth to receive your brother's blood from your hand;

12 When you till the ground, it shall not henceforth yield to you her strength; a fugitive and a vagabond shall you be in the earth.

13 And Cain said to the LORD, My punishment is greater than I can bear.

14 Behold, you have driven me out this day from the face of the earth; and from your face shall I be hid; and I shall be a fugitive and a vagabond in the earth; and it shall come to pass, that every one that finds me shall slay me.

15 And the LORD said to him, Therefore whosoever slays Cain, vengeance shall be taken on him sevenfold. And the LORD set a mark upon Cain, lest any finding him should kill him.

16 And Cain went out from the presence of the LORD, and dwelt in the land of Nod, on the east of Eden.

17 And Cain knew his wife; and she conceived, and bare Enoch: and he built a city, and called the name of the city, after the name of his son, Enoch.

18 And to Enoch was born Irad: and Irad begat Mehujael: and Mehujael begat Methusael: and Methusael begat Lamech.

19 And Lamech took to him two wives: the name of the one was Adah, and the name of the other Zillah.

20 And Adah bare Jabal: he was the father of such as dwell in tents, and of such as have cattle.

21 And his brother's name was Jubal: he was the father of all such as handle the harp and organ.

22 And Zillah, she also bare Tubalcain, an instructer of every artificer in brass and iron: and the sister of Tubalcain was Naamah.

23 And Lamech said to his wives, Adah and Zillah, Hear my voice; you wives of Lamech, hearken to my speech: for I have slain a man to my wounding, and a young man to my hurt.

24 If Cain shall be avenged sevenfold, truly Lamech seventy and sevenfold.

25 And Adam knew his wife again; and she bare a son, and called his name Seth: For God, said she, has appointed me another seed instead of Abel, whom Cain slew.

26 And to Seth, to him also there was born a son; and he called his name Enos: then began men to call upon the name of the LORD.

CHAPTER 5

THIS is the book of the generations of Adam. In the day that God created

---

4:9 "The cool impudence of Cain is an indication of the state of heart which led up to his murdering his brother; and it was also a part of his having committed that terrible crime. He would not have proceeded to the cruel deed of bloodshed if he had not first cast off the fear of God and been ready to defy his Maker." Charles Spurgeon

4:17 Where did Cain get his wife? Many ask this question thinking they've found a "mistake" in the Bible-that there must have been other people besides Adam and Eve. Scripture tells us that Adam is "the first man" (1 Corinthians 15:45); that there were no other humans when he was created, because God said, "It is not good that the man should be alone" (Genesis 2:18); and that Eve is "the mother of all living" (Genesis 3:20). There are two thoughts: 1. Cain may have married a distant sister. Perhaps first-generation siblings married each other in order to populate the earth. At that time there was no law against incest. But as the population grew large enough, and as the risk of genetic problems increased because of sin's curse, God outlawed marriage between siblings. 2. Perhaps Cain got his wife from the same place Adam got Eve.

man, in the likeness of God made he him;

2 Male and female created he them; and blessed them, and called their name Adam, in the day when they were created.

3 And Adam lived an hundred and thirty years, and begat a son in his own likeness, and after his image; and called his name Seth:

4 And the days of Adam after he had begotten Seth were eight hundred years: and he begat sons and daughters:

5 And all the days that Adam lived were nine hundred and thirty years: and he died.

6 And Seth lived an hundred and five years, and begat Enos:

7 And Seth lived after he begat Enos eight hundred and seven years, and begat sons and daughters:

8 And all the days of Seth were nine hundred and twelve years: and he died.

9 And Enos lived ninety years, and begat Cainan:

10 And Enos lived after he begat Cainan eight hundred and fifteen years, and begat sons and daughters:

11 And all the days of Enos were nine hundred and five years: and he died.

12 And Cainan lived seventy years and begat Mahalaleel:

13 And Cainan lived after he begat Mahalaleel eight hundred and forty years, and begat sons and daughters:

14 And all the days of Cainan were nine hundred and ten years: and he died.

15 And Mahalaleel lived sixty and five years, and begat Jared:

16 And Mahalaleel lived after he begat Jared eight hundred and thirty years, and begat sons and daughters:

17 And all the days of Mahalaleel were eight hundred ninety and five years: and he died.

18 And Jared lived an hundred sixty and two years, and he begat Enoch:

19 And Jared lived after he begat Enoch eight hundred years, and begat sons and daughters:

20 And all the days of Jared were nine hundred sixty and two years: and he died.

21 And Enoch lived sixty and five years, and begat Methuselah:

22 And Enoch walked with God after he begat Methuselah three hundred years, and begat sons and daughters:

23 And all the days of Enoch were three hundred sixty and five years:

24 And Enoch walked with God: and he was not; for God took him.

25 And Methuselah lived an hundred eighty and seven years, and begat Lamech.

26 And Methuselah lived after he begat Lamech seven hundred eighty and two years, and begat sons and daughters:

27 And all the days of Methuselah were nine hundred sixty and nine years: and he died.

28 And Lamech lived an hundred eighty and two years, and begat a son:

29 And he called his name Noah, saying, This same shall comfort us concerning our work and toil of our hands, because of the ground which the LORD has cursed.

30 And Lamech lived after he begat Noah five hundred ninety and five years, and begat sons and daughters:

31 And all the days of Lamech were seven hundred seventy and seven years: and he died.

5:3 "Adam lived 930 years. Conditions then were at their optimum for health. In his day the climate was such that ultraviolet exposure was low (due to the water canopy) and the nutritional value of foods was extremely high.

There is talk today of extending life spans. Some of the means to do this are: to reduce ultraviolet exposure, because this tends to age the skin, to increase nutritional contents in foods." Richard Gunther.

32 And Noah was five hundred years old: and Noah begat Shem, Ham, and Japheth.

CHAPTER 6

AND it came to pass, when men began to multiply on the face of the earth, and daughters were born to them,

2 That the sons of God saw the daughters of men that they were fair; and they took them wives of all which they chose.

3 And the LORD said, My spirit shall not always strive with man, for that he also is flesh: yet his days shall be an hundred and twenty years.

4 There were giants in the earth in those days; and also after that, when the sons of God came in to the daughters of men, and they bare children to them, the same became mighty men which were of old, men of renown.

5 And God saw that the wickedness of man was great in the earth, and that every imagination of the thoughts of his heart was only evil continually.

6 And it repented the LORD that he had made man on the earth, and it grieved him at his heart.

7 And the LORD said, I will destroy man whom I have created from the face of the earth; both man, and beast, and the creeping thing, and the fowls of the air; for it repents me that I have made them.

8 But Noah found grace in the eyes of the LORD.

9 These are the generations of Noah: Noah was a just man and perfect in his generations, and Noah walked with God.

10 And Noah begat three sons, Shem, Ham, and Japheth.

11 The earth also was corrupt before God, and the earth was filled with violence.

12 And God looked upon the earth, and, behold, it was corrupt; for all flesh had corrupted his way upon the earth.

Never be afraid to try something new. Remember, amateurs built the ark; professionals built the Titanic.

UNKNOWN

13 And God said to Noah, The end of all flesh is come before me; for the earth is filled with violence through them; and, behold, I will destroy them with the earth.

14 Make you an ark of gopher wood; rooms shall you make in the ark, and shall pitch it within and without with pitch.

15 And this is the fashion which you shall make it of: The length of the ark shall be three hundred cubits, the breadth of it fifty cubits, and the height of it thirty cubits.

16 A window shall you make to the ark, and in a cubit shall you finish it above; and the door of the ark shall you set in the side thereof; with lower, second, and third stories shall you make it.

17 And, behold, I, even I, do bring a flood of waters upon the earth, to destroy all flesh, wherein is the breath of life, from under heaven; and every thing that is in the earth shall die.

18 But with you will I establish my covenant; and you shall come into the ark, you, and your sons, and your wife, and your sons' wives with you.

19 And of every living thing of all flesh, two of every sort shall you bring into the ark, to keep them alive with you; they shall be male and female.

20 Of fowls after their kind, and of cattle after their kind, of every creeping thing of the earth after his kind, two of every sort shall come to you, to keep them alive.

21 And take to you of all food that is eaten, and you shall gather it to you; and it shall be for food for you, and for them.

22 Thus did Noah; according to all that God commanded him, so did he.

6:17 For points to ponder about the flood see Matthew 24:38 comment.

CHAPTER 7

7:19-23

AND the LORD said to Noah, Come you and all your house into the ark; for you have I seen righteous before me in this generation.

2 Of every clean beast you shall take to you by sevens, the male and his female: and of beasts that are not clean by two, the male and his female.

3 Of fowls also of the air by sevens, the male and the female; to keep seed alive upon the face of all the earth.

4 For yet seven days, and I will cause it to rain upon the earth forty days and forty nights; and every living substance that I have made will I destroy from off the face of the earth.

5 And Noah did according to all that the LORD commanded him.

6 And Noah was six hundred years old when the flood of waters was upon the earth.

7 And Noah went in, and his sons, and his wife, and his sons' wives with him, into the ark, because of the waters of the flood.

8 Of clean beasts, and of beasts that are not clean, and of fowls, and of every thing that creeps upon the earth,

9 There went in two and two to Noah into the ark, the male and the female, as God had commanded Noah.

10 And it came to pass after seven days, that the waters of the flood were upon the earth.

11 In the six hundredth year of Noah's life, in the second month, the seventeenth day of the month, the same day were all the fountains of the great deep broken up, and the windows of heaven were opened.

12 And the rain was upon the earth forty days and forty nights.

13 In the selfsame day entered Noah, and Shem, and Ham, and Japheth, the sons of Noah, and Noah's wife, and the three wives of his sons with them, into the ark;

14 They, and every beast after his kind, and all the cattle after their kind, and

These verses make it clear that this was a world-wide flood.

every creeping thing that creeps upon the earth after his kind, and every fowl after his kind, every bird of every sort.

15 And they went in to Noah into the ark, two and two of all flesh, wherein is the breath of life.

16 And they that went in, went in male and female of all flesh, as God had commanded him: and the LORD shut him in.

17 And the flood was forty days upon the earth; and the waters increased, and bare up the ark, and it was lifted up above the earth.

18 And the waters prevailed, and were increased greatly upon the earth; and the ark went upon the face of the waters.

19 And the waters prevailed exceedingly upon the earth; and all the high hills, that were under the whole heaven, were covered.

20 Fifteen cubits upward did the waters prevail; and the mountains were covered.

21 And all flesh died that moved upon the earth, both of fowl, and of cattle, and of beast, and of every creeping thing that creeps upon the earth, and every man:

22 All in whose nostrils was the breath of life, of all that was in the dry land, died.

23 And every living substance was destroyed which was upon the face of the ground, both man, and cattle, and the creeping things, and the fowl of the heaven; and they were destroyed from the earth: and Noah only remained alive, and they that were with him in the ark.

24 And the waters prevailed upon the earth an hundred and fifty days.

CHAPTER 8

AND God remembered Noah, and every living thing, and all the cattle that was with him in the ark: and God made a wind to pass over the earth, and the waters asswaged;

2 The fountains also of the deep and the windows of heaven were stopped, and the rain from heaven was restrained;

3 And the waters returned from off the earth continually: and after the end of the hundred and fifty days the waters were abated.

4 And the ark rested in the seventh month, on the seventeenth day of the month, upon the mountains of Ararat.

5 And the waters decreased continually until the tenth month: in the tenth month, on the first day of the month, were the tops of the mountains seen.

6 And it came to pass at the end of forty days, that Noah opened the window of the ark which he had made:

7 And he sent forth a raven, which went forth to and fro, until the waters were dried up from off the earth.

8 Also he sent forth a dove from him, to see if the waters were abated from off the face of the ground;

9 But the dove found no rest for the sole of her foot, and she returned to him into the ark, for the waters were on the face of the whole earth: then he put forth his hand, and took her, and pulled her in to him into the ark.

10 And he stayed yet another seven days; and again he sent forth the dove out of the ark;

11 And the dove came in to him in the evening; and, lo, in her mouth was an olive leaf plucked off: so Noah knew that the waters were abated from off the earth.

12 And he stayed yet another seven days; and sent forth the dove; which returned not again to him any more.

13 And it came to pass in the six hundredth and first year, in the first month, the first day of the month, the waters were dried up from off the earth: and Noah removed the covering of the ark, and looked, and, behold, the face of the ground was dry.

14 And in the second month, on the seven and twentieth day of the month, was the earth dried.

15 And God spoke to Noah, saying,

16 Go forth of the ark, you, and your wife, and your sons, and your sons' wives with you.

17 Bring forth with you every living thing that is with you, of all flesh, both of fowl, and of cattle, and of every creeping thing that creeps upon the earth; that they may breed abundantly in the earth, and be fruitful, and multiply upon the earth.

18 And Noah went forth, and his sons, and his wife, and his sons' wives with him:

19 Every beast, every creeping thing, and every fowl, and whatsoever creeps upon the earth, after their kinds, went forth out of the ark.

20 And Noah built an altar to the LORD; and took of every clean beast, and of every clean fowl, and offered burnt offerings on the altar.

21 And the LORD smelled a sweet savor; and the LORD said in his heart, I will not again curse the ground any more for man's sake; for the imagination of man's heart is evil from his youth; neither will I again smite any more every thing living, as I have done.

22 While the earth remains, seedtime and harvest, and cold and heat, and summer and winter, and day and night shall not cease.

CHAPTER 9

AND God blessed Noah and his sons, and said to them, Be fruitful, and multiply, and replenish the earth.

2 And the fear of you and the dread of you shall be upon every beast of the

earth, and upon every fowl of the air, upon all that moves upon the earth, and upon all the fishes of the sea; into your hand are they delivered.

3 Every moving thing that lives shall be meat for you; even as the green herb have I given you all things.

4 But flesh with the life thereof, which is the blood thereof, shall you not eat.

5 And surely your blood of your lives will I require; at the hand of every beast will I require it, and at the hand of man; at the hand of every man's brother will I require the life of man.

6 Whoso sheds man's blood, by man shall his blood be shed: for in the image of God made he man.

7 And you, be fruitful, and multiply; bring forth abundantly in the earth, and multiply therein.

8 And God spoke to Noah, and to his sons with him, saying,

9 And I, behold, I establish my covenant with you, and with your seed after you;

10 And with every living creature that is with you, of the fowl, of the cattle, and of every beast of the earth with you; from all that go out of the ark, to every beast of the earth.

11 And I will establish my covenant with you, neither shall all flesh be cut off any more by the waters of a flood; neither shall there any more be a flood to destroy the earth.

12 And God said, This is the token of the covenant which I make between me and you and every living creature that is with you, for perpetual generations:

13 I do set my bow in the cloud, and it shall be for a token of a covenant between me and the earth.

14 And it shall come to pass, when I bring a cloud over the earth, that the bow shall be seen in the cloud:

15 And I will remember my covenant, which is between me and you and every living creature of all flesh; and the waters shall no more become a flood to destroy all flesh.

16 And the bow shall be in the cloud; and I will look upon it, that I may remember the everlasting covenant between God and every living creature of all flesh that is upon the earth.

17 And God said to Noah, This is the token of the covenant, which I have established between me and all flesh that is upon the earth.

18 And the sons of Noah, that went forth of the ark, were Shem, and Ham, and Japheth: and Ham is the father of Canaan.

19 These are the three sons of Noah: and of them was the whole earth overspread.

20 And Noah began to be an husbandman, and he planted a vineyard:

21 And he drank of the wine, and was drunken; and he was uncovered within his tent.

22 And Ham, the father of Canaan, saw the nakedness of his father, and told his two brethren without.

23 And Shem and Japheth took a garment, and laid it upon both their shoulders, and went backward, and covered the nakedness of their father; and their faces were backward, and they saw not their father's nakedness.

24 And Noah awoke from his wine, and knew what his younger son had done to him.

25 And he said, Cursed be Canaan; a servant of servants shall he be to his brethren.

26 And he said, Blessed be the LORD God of Shem; and Canaan shall be his servant.

27 God shall enlarge Japheth, and he shall dwell in the tents of Shem; and Canaan shall be his servant.

28 And Noah lived after the flood three hundred and fifty years.

29 And all the days of Noah were nine hundred and fifty years: and he died.

CHAPTER 10

NOW these are the generations of the sons of Noah, Shem, Ham, and

Japheth: and to them were sons born after the flood.

2 The sons of Japheth; Gomer, and Magog, and Madai, and Javan, and Tubal, and Meshech, and Tiras.

3 And the sons of Gomer; Ashkenaz, and Riphath, and Togarmah.

4 And the sons of Javan; Elishah, and Tarshish, Kittim, and Dodanim.

5 By these were the isles of the Gentiles divided in their lands; every one after his tongue, after their families, in their nations.

6 And the sons of Ham; Cush, and Mizraim, and Phut, and Canaan.

7 And the sons of Cush; Seba, and Havilah, and Sabtah, and Raamah, and Sabtechah: and the sons of Raamah; Sheba, and Dedan.

8 And Cush begat Nimrod: he began to be a mighty one in the earth.

9 He was a mighty hunter before the LORD: therefore it is said, Even as Nimrod the mighty hunter before the LORD.

10 And the beginning of his kingdom was Babel, and Erech, and Accad, and Calneh, in the land of Shinar.

11 Out of that land went forth Asshur, and built Nineveh, and the city Rehoboth, and Calah,

12 And Resen between Nineveh and Calah: the same is a great city.

13 And Mizraim begat Ludim, and Anamim, and Lehabim, and Naphtuhim,

14 And Pathrusim, and Casluhim, (out of whom came Philistim,) and Caphtorim.

15 And Canaan begat Sidon his first born, and Heth,

16 And the Jebusite, and the Amorite, and the Girgasite,

17 And the Hivite, and the Arkite, and the Sinite,

18 And the Arvadite, and the Zemarite, and the Hamathite: and afterward were the families of the Canaanites spread abroad.

19 And the border of the Canaanites was from Sidon, as you come to Gerar, to Gaza; as you go, to Sodom, and Gomorrah, and Admah, and Zeboim, even to Lasha.

20 These are the sons of Ham, after their families, after their tongues, in their countries, and in their nations.

21 To Shem also, the father of all the children of Eber, the brother of Japheth the elder, even to him were children born.

22 The children of Shem; Elam, and Asshur, and Arphaxad, and Lud, and Aram.

23 And the children of Aram; Uz, and Hul, and Gether, and Mash.

24 And Arphaxad begat Salah; and Salah begat Eber.

25 And to Eber were born two sons: the name of one was Peleg; for in his days was the earth divided; and his brother's name was Joktan.

26 And Joktan begat Almodad, and Sheleph, and Hazarmaveth, and Jerah,

27 And Hadoram, and Uzal, and Diklah,

28 And Obal, and Abimael, and Sheba,

29 And Ophir, and Havilah, and Jobab: all these were the sons of Joktan.

30 And their dwelling was from Mesha, as you go to Sephar a mount of the east.

31 These are the sons of Shem, after their families, after their tongues, in their lands, after their nations.

32 These are the families of the sons of Noah, after their generations, in their nations: and by these were the nations divided in the earth after the flood.

10:5 "God created all the distinct, separate languages. It was long held by science that all the languages in the world had common origins, but gradually this assumption has been abandoned. While some words have a common root, almost all distinct language groups are completely different from each other in many ways." Richard Gunther

CHAPTER 11

AND the whole earth was of one language, and of one speech.

2 And it came to pass, as they journeyed from the east, that they found a plain in the land of Shinar; and they dwelt there.

3 And they said one to another, Go to, let us make brick, and burn them thoroughly. And they had brick for stone, and slime had they for morter.

4 And they said, Go to, let us build us a city and a tower, whose top may reach to heaven; and let us make us a name, lest we be scattered abroad upon the face of the whole earth.

5 And the LORD came down to see the city and the tower, which the children of men built.

6 And the LORD said, Behold, the people are one, and they have all one language; and this they begin to do: and now nothing will be restrained from them, which they have imagined to do.

7 Go to, let us go down, and there confound their language, that they may not understand one another's speech.

8 So the LORD scattered them abroad from thence upon the face of all the earth: and they left off to build the city.

9 Therefore is the name of it called Babel; because the LORD did there confound the language of all the earth: and from thence did the LORD scatter them abroad upon the face of all the earth.

10 These are the generations of Shem: Shem was an hundred years old, and begat Arphaxad two years after the flood:

11 And Shem lived after he begat Arphaxad five hundred years, and begat sons and daughters.

12 And Arphaxad lived five and thirty years, and begat Salah:

13 And Arphaxad lived after he begat Salah four hundred and three years, and begat sons and daughters.

14 And Salah lived thirty years, and begat Eber:

15 And Salah lived after he begat Eber four hundred and three years, and begat sons and daughters.

16 And Eber lived four and thirty years, and begat Peleg:

17 And Eber lived after he begat Peleg four hundred and thirty years, and begat sons and daughters.

18 And Peleg lived thirty years, and begat Reu:

19 And Peleg lived after he begat Reu two hundred and nine years, and begat sons and daughters.

20 And Reu lived two and thirty years, and begat Serug:

21 And Reu lived after he begat Serug two hundred and seven years, and begat sons and daughters.

22 And Serug lived thirty years, and begat Nahor:

23 And Serug lived after he begat Nahor two hundred years, and begat sons and daughters.

24 And Nahor lived nine and twenty years, and begat Terah:

25 And Nahor lived after he begat Terah an hundred and nineteen years, and begat sons and daughters.

26 And Terah lived seventy years, and begat Abram, Nahor, and Haran.

27 Now these are the generations of Terah: Terah begat Abram, Nahor, and Haran; and Haran begat Lot.

28 And Haran died before his father Terah in the land of his nativity, in Ur of the Chaldees.

29 And Abram and Nahor took them wives: the name of Abram's wife was Sarai; and the name of Nahor's wife, Milcah, the daughter of Haran, the father of Milcah, and the father of Iscah.

30 But Sarai was barren; she had no child.

11:9 For witnessing to those who don't speak English, see the back of this Bible for the entire gospel in picture form.

THE CONFUSION OF TONGUES

Genesis 11:4.8

31 And Terah took Abram his son, and Lot the son of Haran his son's son, and Sarai his daughter in law, his son Abram's wife; and they went forth with them from Ur of the Chaldees, to go into the land of Canaan; and they came to Haran, and dwelt there.

32 And the days of Terah were two hundred and five years: and Terah died in Haran.

CHAPTER 12

N OW the LORD had said to Abram, Get you out of your country, and from your kindred, and from your father's house, to a land that I will show you:

2 And I will make of you a great nation, and I will bless you, and make your name great; and you shall be a blessing:

3 And I will bless them that bless you, and curse him that curseth you: and in you shall all families of the earth be blessed.

4 So Abram departed, as the LORD had spoken to him; and Lot went with him: and Abram was seventy and five years old when he departed out of Haran.

5 And Abram took Sarai his wife, and Lot his brother's son, and all their substance that they had gathered, and the souls that they had gotten in Haran; and they went forth to go into the land of Canaan; and into the land of Canaan they came.

6 And Abram passed through the land to the place of Sichem, to the plain of Moreh. And the Canaanite was then in the land.

7 And the LORD appeared to Abram, and said, To your seed will I give this land: and there built he an altar to the LORD, who appeared to him.

8 And he removed from thence to a mountain on the east of Bethel, and pitched his tent, having Bethel on the west, and Hai on the east: and there he built an altar to the LORD, and called upon the name of the LORD.

9 And Abram journeyed, going on still toward the south.

10 And there was a famine in the land: and Abram went down into Egypt to sojourn there; for the famine was grievous in the land.

11 And it came to pass, when he was come near to enter into Egypt, that he said to Sarai his wife, Behold now, I know that you are a fair woman to look upon:

12 Therefore it shall come to pass, when the Egyptians shall see you, that they shall say, This is his wife: and they will kill me, but they will save you alive.

13 Say, I pray you, you are my sister: that it may be well with me for your sake; and my soul shall live because of you.

14 And it came to pass, that, when Abram was come into Egypt, the Egyptians beheld the woman that she was very fair.

15 The princes also of Pharaoh saw her, and commended her before Pharaoh: and the woman was taken into Pharaoh's house.

16 And he entreated Abram well for her sake: and he had sheep, and oxen, and he asses, and menservants, and maidservants, and she asses, and camels.

17 And the LORD plagued Pharaoh and his house with great plagues because of Sarai Abram's wife.

18 And Pharaoh called Abram and said, What is this that you have done to me? why did you not tell me that she was your wife?

19 Why did you say, She is my sister? so I might have taken her to me to wife: now therefore behold your wife, take her, and go your way.

20 And Pharaoh commanded his men concerning him: and they sent him away, and his wife, and all that he had.

12:13 A lying generation. See Psalm 116:11 comment.

CHAPTER 13

AND Abram went up out of Egypt, he, and his wife, and all that he had, and Lot with him, into the south.

2 And Abram was very rich in cattle, in silver, and in gold.

3 And he went on his journeys from the south even to Bethel, to the place where his tent had been at the beginning, between Bethel and Hai;

4 To the place of the altar, which he had made there at the first: and there Abram called on the name of the LORD.

5 And Lot also, which went with Abram, had flocks, and herds, and tents.

6 And the land was not able to bear them, that they might dwell together: for their substance was great, so that they could not dwell together.

7 And there was a strife between the herdsmen of Abram's cattle and the herdsmen of Lot's cattle: and the Canaanite and the Perizzite dwelled then in the land.

8 And Abram said to Lot, Let there be no strife, I pray you, between me and you, and between my herdsmen and your herdsmen; for we be brethren.

9 Is not the whole land before you? separate yourself, I pray you, from me: if you will take the left hand, then I will go to the right; or if you depart to the right hand, then I will go to the left.

10 And Lot lifted up his eyes, and beheld all the plain of Jordan, that it was well watered every where, before the LORD destroyed Sodom and Gomorrah, even as the garden of the LORD, like the land of Egypt, as you come to Zoar.

11 Then Lot chose him all the plain of Jordan; and Lot journeyed east: and they separated themselves the one from the other.

12 Abram dwelled in the land of Canaan, and Lot dwelled in the cities of the plain, and pitched his tent toward Sodom.

13 But the men of Sodom were wicked and sinners before the LORD exceedingly.

14 And the LORD said to Abram, after that Lot was separated from him, Lift up now your eyes, and look from the place where you are northward, and southward, and eastward, and westward:

15 For all the land which you see, to you will I give it, and to your seed for ever.

16 And I will make your seed as the dust of the earth: so that if a man can number the dust of the earth, then shall your seed also be numbered.

17 Arise, walk through the land in the length of it and in the breadth of it; for I will give it to you.

18 Then Abram removed his tent, and came and dwelt in the plain of Mamre, which is in Hebron, and built there an altar to the LORD.

CHAPTER 14

AND it came to pass in the days of Amraphel king of Shinar, Arioch king of Ellasar, Chedorlaomer king of Elam, and Tidal king of nations;

2 That these made war with Bera king of Sodom, and with Birsha king of Gomorrah, Shinab king of Admah, and Shemeber king of Zeboiim, and the king of Bela, which is Zoar.

3 All these were joined together in the vale of Siddim, which is the salt sea.

4 Twelve years they served Chedorlaomer, and in the thirteenth year they rebelled.

5 And in the fourteenth year came Chedorlaomer, and the kings that were with him, and smote the Rephaims in Ashteroth Karnaim, and the Zuzims in Ham, and the Emins in Shaveh Kiriathaim,

6 And the Horites in their mount Seir, to Elparan, which is by the wilderness.

7 And they returned, and came to Enmishpat, which is Kadesh, and smote all the country of the Amalekites, and also the Amorites, that dwelt in Hazezontamar.

8 And there went out the king of Sodom, and the king of Gomorrah, and

the king of Admah, and the king of Zeboiim, and the king of Bela (the same is Zoar;) and they joined battle with them in the vale of Siddim;

9 With Chedorlaomer the king of Elam, and with Tidal king of nations, and Amraphel king of Shinar, and Arioch king of Ellasar; four kings with five.

10 And the vale of Siddim was full of slimepits; and the kings of Sodom and Gomorrah fled, and fell there; and they that remained fled to the mountain.

11 And they took all the goods of Sodom and Gomorrah, and all their victuals, and went their way.

12 And they took Lot, Abram's brother's son, who dwelt in Sodom, and his goods, and departed.

13 And there came one that had escaped, and told Abram the Hebrew; for he dwelt in the plain of Mamre the Amorite, brother of Eshcol, and brother of Aner: and these were confederate with Abram.

14 And when Abram heard that his brother was taken captive, he armed his trained servants, born in his own house, three hundred and eighteen, and pursued them to Dan.

15 And he divided himself against them, he and his servants, by night, and smote them, and pursued them to Hobah, which is on the left hand of Damascus.

16 And he brought back all the goods, and also brought again his brother Lot, and his goods, and the women also, and the people.

17 And the king of Sodom went out to meet him after his return from the slaughter of Chedorlaomer, and of the kings that were with him, at the valley of Shaveh, which is the king's dale.

18 And Melchizedek king of Salem brought forth bread and wine: and he was the priest of the most high God.

19 And he blessed him, and said, Blessed be Abram of the most high God, possessor of heaven and earth:

20 And blessed be the most high God, which has delivered your enemies into your hand. And he gave him tithes of all.

21 And the king of Sodom said to Abram, Give me the persons, and take the goods to yourself.

22 And Abram said to the king of Sodom, I have lifted up mine hand to the LORD, the most high God, the possessor of heaven and earth,

23 That I will not take from a thread even to a shoelatchet, and that I will not take anything that is yours, lest you should say, I have made Abram rich:

24 Save only that which the young men have eaten, and the portion of the men which went with me, Aner, Eshcol, and Mamre; let them take their portion.

CHAPTER 15

AFTER these things the word of the LORD came to Abram in a vision, saying, Fear not, Abram: I am your shield, and your exceeding great reward.

2 And Abram said, LORD God, what will you give me, seeing I go childless, and the steward of my house is this Eliezer of Damascus?

3 And Abram said, Behold, to me you have given no seed: and, lo, one born in my house is mine heir.

4 And, behold, the word of the LORD came to him, saying, This shall not be your heir; but he that shall come forth out of your own bowels shall be your heir.

5 And he brought him forth abroad, and said, Look now toward heaven, and tell the stars, if you be able to number them: and he said to him, So shall your seed be.

6 And he believed in the LORD; and he counted it to him for righteousness.

7 And he said to him, I am the LORD that brought you out of Ur of the Chaldees, to give you this land to inherit it.

8 And he said, LORD God, whereby shall I know that I shall inherit it?

9 And he said to him, Take me an heifer of three years old, and a she goat of three years old, and a ram of three years old, and a turtledove, and a young pigeon.

10 And he took to him all these, and divided them in the midst, and laid each piece one against another: but the birds divided he not.

11 And when the fowls came down upon the carcasses, Abram drove them away.

12 And when the sun was going down, a deep sleep fell upon Abram; and, lo, an horror of great darkness fell upon him.

13 And he said to Abram, Know of a surety that your seed shall be a stranger in a land that is not theirs, and shall serve them; and they shall afflict them four hundred years;

14 And also that nation, whom they shall serve, will I judge: and afterward shall they come out with great substance.

15 And you shall go to your fathers in peace; you shall be buried in a good old age.

16 But in the fourth generation they shall come hither again: for the iniquity of the Amorites is not yet full.

17 And it came to pass, that, when the sun went down, and it was dark, behold a smoking furnace, and a burning lamp that passed between those pieces.

18 In the same day the LORD made a covenant with Abram, saying, To your seed have I given this land, from the river of Egypt to the great river, the river Euphrates:

19 The Kenites, and the Kenizzites, and the Kadmonites,

20 And the Hittites, and the Perizzites, and the Rephaims,

21 And the Amorites, and the Canaanites, and the Girgashites, and the Jebusites.

CHAPTER 16

N OW Sarai Abram's wife bare him no children: and she had an hand-maid, an Egyptian, whose name was Hagar.

2 And Sarai said to Abram, Behold now, the LORD has restrained me from bearing: I pray you, go in to my maid; it may be that I may obtain children by her. And Abram hearkened to the voice of Sarai.

3 And Sarai Abram's wife took Hagar her maid the Egyptian, after Abram had dwelt ten years in the land of Canaan, and gave her to her husband Abram to be his wife.

4 And he went in to Hagar, and she conceived: and when she saw that she had conceived, her mistress was despised in her eyes.

5 And Sarai said to Abram, My wrong be upon you: I have given my maid into your bosom; and when she saw that she had conceived, I was despised in her eyes: the LORD judge between me and you.

6 But Abram said to Sarai, Behold, your maid is in your hand; do to her as it pleases you. And when Sarai dealt hardly with her, she fled from her face.

7 And the angel of the LORD found her by a fountain of water in the wilderness, by the fountain in the way to Shur.

8 And he said, Hagar, Sarai's maid, where have you come from? and where will you go? And she said, I flee from the face of my mistress Sarai.

9 And the angel of the LORD said to her, Return to your mistress, and submit yourself under her hands.

10 And the angel of the LORD said to her, I will multiply your seed exceedingly, that it shall not be numbered for multitude.

11 And the angel of the LORD said to her, Behold, you are with child and shall bear a son, and shall call his name Ishmael; because the LORD has heard your affliction.

12 And he will be a wild man; his hand will be against every man, and every man's hand against him; and he shall dwell in the presence of all his brethren.

13 And she called the name of the LORD that spoke to her, You are the God who sees me: for she said, Have I also here looked after him that sees me?

14 Therefore the well was called Beerlahairoi; behold, it is between Kadesh and Bered.

15 And Hagar bare Abram a son: and Abram called his son's name, which Hagar bare, Ishmael.

16 And Abram was fourscore and six years old, when Hagar bare Ishmael to Abram.

CHAPTER 17

AND when Abram was ninety years old and nine, the LORD appeared to Abram, and said to him, I am the Almighty God; walk before me, and be perfect.

2 And I will make my covenant between me and you, and will multiply you exceedingly.

3 And Abram fell on his face: and God talked with him, saying,

4 As for me, behold, my covenant is with you, and you shall be a father of many nations.

5 Neither shall your name any more be called Abram, but your name shall be Abraham; for a father of many nations have I made you.

6 And I will make you exceedingly fruitful, and I will make nations of you, and kings shall come out of you.

7 And I will establish my covenant between me and you and your seed after you in their generations for an everlasting covenant, to be a God to you, and to your seed after you.

8 And I will give to you, and to your seed after you, the land wherein you are a stranger, all the land of Canaan, for an everlasting possession; and I will be their God.

9 And God said to Abraham, You shall keep my covenant therefore, you, and your seed after you in their generations.

10 This is my covenant, which you shall keep, between me and you and your seed after you; Every man child among you shall be circumcised.

11 And you shall circumcise the flesh of your foreskin; and it shall be a token of the covenant between me and you.

12 And he that is eight days old shall be circumcised among you, every man child in your generations, he that is born in the house, or bought with money of any stranger, which is not of your seed.

13 He that is born in your house, and he that is bought with your money, must be circumcised: and my covenant shall be in your flesh for an everlasting covenant.

14 And the uncircumcised man child whose flesh of his foreskin is not circumcised, that soul shall be cut off from his people; he has broken my covenant.

15 And God said to Abraham, As for Sarai your wife, you shall not call her name Sarai, but Sarah shall her name be.

16 And I will bless her, and give you a son also of her: yea, I will bless her, and she shall be a mother of nations; kings of people shall be of her.

17 Then Abraham fell upon his face, and laughed, and said in his heart, Shall a child be born to him that is an hundred years old? and shall Sarah, that is ninety years old, bear?

18 And Abraham said to God, O that Ishmael might live before you!

19 And God said, Sarah your wife shall bear you a son indeed; and you shall call his name Isaac: and I will establish my covenant with him for an everlasting covenant, and with his seed after him.

20 And as for Ishmael, I have heard you: Behold, I have blessed him, and will make him fruitful, and will multiply him exceedingly; twelve princes shall he beget, and I will make him a great nation.

21 But my covenant will I establish with Isaac, which Sarah shall bear to you at this set time in the next year.

22 And he left off talking with him, and God went up from Abraham.

23 And Abraham took Ishmael his son, and all that were born in his house, and all that were bought with his money, every male among the men of Abraham's house; and circumcised the flesh of their foreskin in the selfsame day, as God had said to him.

24 And Abraham was ninety years old and nine, when he was circumcised in the flesh of his foreskin.

25 And Ishmael his son was thirteen years old, when he was circumcised in the flesh of his foreskin.

26 In the selfsame day was Abraham circumcised, and Ishmael his son.

27 And all the men of his house, born in the house, and bought with money of the stranger, were circumcised with him.

CHAPTER 18

A ND the LORD appeared to him in the plains of Mamre: and he sat in the tent door in the heat of the day;

2 And he lift up his eyes and looked, and, lo, three men stood by him: and when he saw them, he ran to meet them from the tent door, and bowed himself toward the ground,

3 And said, My LORD, if now I have found favor in your sight, pass not away, I pray you, from your servant:

4 Let a little water, I pray you, be fetched, and wash your feet, and rest yourselves under the tree:

5 And I will fetch a morsel of bread, and comfort you your hearts; after that you shall pass on: for therefore are you come to your servant. And they said, So do, as you have said.

6 And Abraham hastened into the tent to Sarah, and said, Make ready quickly three measures of fine meal, knead it, and make cakes upon the hearth.

7 And Abraham ran to the herd, and fetched a calf tender and good, and gave it to a young man; and he hasted to dress it.

8 And he took butter, and milk, and the calf which he had dressed, and set it before them; and he stood by them under the tree, and they did eat.

9 And they said to him, Where is Sarah your wife? And he said, Behold, in the tent.

10 And he said, I will certainly return to you according to the time of life; and, lo, Sarah your wife shall have a son. And Sarah heard it in the tent door, which was behind him.

11 Now Abraham and Sarah were old and well stricken in age; and it ceased to be with Sarah after the manner of women.

12 Therefore Sarah laughed within herself, saying, After I am waxed old shall I have pleasure, my lord being old also?

13 And the LORD said to Abraham, Why did Sarah laugh, saying, Shall I of a surety bear a child, which am old?

14 Is anything too hard for the LORD? At the time appointed I will return to you, according to the time of life, and Sarah shall have a son.

15 Then Sarah denied, saying, I laughed not; for she was afraid. And he said, Nay; but you did laugh.

16 And the men rose up from thence, and looked toward Sodom: and Abraham went with them to bring them on the way.

17 And the LORD said, Shall I hide from Abraham that thing which I do;

18 Seeing that Abraham shall surely become a great and mighty nation, and all the nations of the earth shall be blessed in him?

18:1 "Abraham saw Him and knew it was the Lord, yet Abraham also clearly saw that He had a physical body. He both had feet to wash (vs.4) and a mouth to eat (vs.8). This passage clearly shows us the second person of the Trinity, our Lord Jesus Christ. The scripture cannot be denied. It is written, he that has the Son has life, he that does not have the Son does not have life.

Jesus said ...for if you do not believe that I am He, you shall die in your sins." Jay Fowler

19 For I know him, that he will command his children and his household after him, and they shall keep the way of the LORD, to do justice and judgment; that the LORD may bring upon Abraham that which he has spoken of him.

20 And the LORD said, Because the cry of Sodom and Gomorrah is great, and because their sin is very grievous;

21 I will go down now, and see whether they have done altogether according to the cry of it, which is come to me; and if not, I will know.

22 And the men turned their faces from thence, and went toward Sodom: but Abraham stood yet before the LORD.

23 And Abraham drew near, and said, Will you also destroy the righteous with the wicked?

24 Peradventure there be fifty righteous within the city: will you also destroy and not spare the place for the fifty righteous that are therein?

25 That be far from you to do after this manner, to slay the righteous with the wicked: and that the righteous should be as the wicked, that be far from you: Shall not the Judge of all the earth do right?

26 And the LORD said, If I find in Sodom fifty righteous within the city, then I will spare all the place for their sakes.

27 And Abraham answered and said, Behold now, I have taken upon me to speak to the LORD, which am but dust and ashes:

28 Peradventure there shall lack five of the fifty righteous: will you destroy all the city for lack of five? And he said, If I find there forty and five, I will not destroy it.

29 And he spoke to him yet again, and said, Peradventure there shall be forty found there. And he said, I will not do it for forty's sake.

30 And he said to him, Oh let not the LORD be angry, and I will speak: Peradventure there shall thirty be found there. And he said, I will not do it, if I find thirty there.

31 And he said, Behold now, I have taken upon me to speak to the LORD: Peradventure there shall be twenty found there. And he said, I will not destroy it for twenty's sake.

32 And he said, Oh let not the LORD be angry, and I will speak yet but this once: Peradventure ten shall be found there. And he said, I will not destroy it for ten's sake.

33 And the LORD went his way, as soon as he had left communing with Abraham: and Abraham returned to his place.

CHAPTER 19

AND there came two angels to Sodom at even; and Lot sat in the gate of Sodom: and Lot seeing them rose up to meet them; and he bowed himself with his face toward the ground;

2 And he said, Behold now, my lords, turn in, I pray you, into your servant's house, and tarry all night, and wash your feet, and you shall rise up early, and go on your ways. And they said, No; but we will abide in the street all night.

3 And he pressed upon them greatly; and they turned in to him, and entered into his house; and he made them a feast, and did bake unleavened bread, and they did eat.

4 But before they lay down, the men of the city, even the men of Sodom, compassed the house round, both old and young, all the people from every quarter:

5 And they called to Lot, and said to him, Where are the men which came in to you this night? bring them out to us, that we may know them.

6 And Lot went out at the door to them, and shut the door after him,

7 And said, I pray you, brethren, do not so wickedly.

8 Behold now, I have two daughters which have not known man; let me, I pray you, bring them out to you, and do to them as is good in your eyes: only to these men do nothing; for therefore came they under the shadow of my roof.

9 And they said, Stand back. And they said again, This one fellow came in to sojourn, and he will needs be a judge: now will we deal worse with you, than with them. And they pressed sore upon the man, even Lot, and came near to break the door.

10 But the men put forth their hand, and pulled Lot into the house to them, and shut to the door.

11 And they smote the men that were at the door of the house with blindness, both small and great: so that they wearied themselves to find the door.

12 And the men said to Lot, Have you here any besides? son in law, and your sons, and your daughters, and whatsoever you have in the city, bring them out of this place:

13 For we will destroy this place, because the cry of them is waxen great before the face of the LORD; and the LORD has sent us to destroy it.

14 And Lot went out, and spoke to his sons in law, which married his daughters, and said, Up, get you out of this place; for the LORD will destroy this city. But he seemed as one that mocked to his sons in law.

15 And when the morning arose, then the angels hastened Lot, saying, Arise, take your wife, and your two daughters, which are here; lest you be consumed in the iniquity of the city.

16 And while he lingered, the men laid hold upon his hand, and upon the hand of his wife, and upon the hand of his two daughters; the LORD being merciful to him: and they brought him forth, and set him without the city.

17 And it came to pass, when they had brought them forth abroad, that he said, Escape for your life; look not behind you, neither stay you in all the plain; escape to the mountain, lest you be consumed.

18 And Lot said to them, Oh, not so, my LORD:

19 Behold now, your servant has found grace in your sight, and you have magnified your mercy, which you have showed to me in saving my life; and I cannot escape to the mountain, lest some evil take me, and I die:

20 Behold now, this city is near to flee unto, and it is a little one: Oh, let me escape thither, (is it not a little one?) and my soul shall live.

21 And he said to him, See, I have accepted you concerning this thing also, that I will not overthrow this city, for the which you have spoken.

22 Haste you, escape thither; for I cannot do anything till you be come thither. Therefore the name of the city was called Zoar.

23 The sun was risen upon the earth when Lot entered into Zoar.

24 Then the LORD rained upon Sodom and upon Gomorrah brimstone and fire from the LORD out of heaven;

25 And he overthrew those cities, and all the plain, and all the inhabitants of the cities, and that which grew upon the ground.

26 But his wife looked back from behind him, and she became a pillar of salt.

27 And Abraham gat up early in the morning to the place where he stood before the LORD:

28 And he looked toward Sodom and Gomorrah, and toward all the land of the plain, and beheld, and, lo, the smoke of the country went up as the smoke of a furnace.

29 And it came to pass, when God destroyed the cities of the plain, that God remembered Abraham, and sent Lot out of the midst of the overthrow, when he overthrew the cities in the which Lot dwelt.

30 And Lot went up out of Zoar, and dwelt in the mountain, and his two daughters with him; for he feared to dwell in Zoar: and he dwelt in a cave, he and his two daughters.

31 And the firstborn said to the younger, Our father is old, and there is

THE FLIGHT OF LOT

Genesis 19:24,26

God destroyed Sodom and Gomorrah and the three other cities. On the eastern edge of the Dead Sea are the remains of five cities, which, despite their location and the presence of fresh water, lie in ruins.

Richard Gunther

not a man in the earth to come in to us after the manner of all the earth:

32 Come, let us make our father drink wine, and we will lie with him, that we may preserve seed of our father.

33 And they made their father drink wine that night: and the firstborn went in, and lay with her father; and he perceived not when she lay down, nor when she arose.

34 And it came to pass on the morrow, that the firstborn said to the younger, Behold, I lay last night with my father: let us make him drink wine this night also; and go you in, and lie with him, that we may preserve seed of our father.

35 And they made their father drink wine that night also: and the younger arose, and lay with him; and he perceived not when she lay down, nor when she arose.

36 Thus were both the daughters of Lot with child by their father.

37 And the first born bare a son, and called his name Moab: the same is the father of the Moabites to this day.

38 And the younger, she also bare a son, and called his name Benammi: the same is the father of the children of Ammon to this day.

CHAPTER 20

A ND Abraham journeyed from thence toward the south country, and dwelled between Kadesh and Shur, and sojourned in Gerar.

2 And Abraham said of Sarah his wife, She is my sister: and Abimelech king of Gerar sent, and took Sarah.

3 But God came to Abimelech in a dream by night, and said to him, Behold, you are but a dead man, for the woman which you have taken; for she is a man's wife.

4 But Abimelech had not come near her: and he said, LORD, will you slay also a righteous nation?

5 Said he not to me, She is my sister? and she, even she herself said, He is my brother: in the integrity of my heart and innocency of my hands have I done this.

6 And God said to him in a dream, Yea, I know that you did this in the integrity of your heart; for I also withheld you from sinning against me: therefore suffered I you not to touch her.

7 Now therefore restore the man his wife; for he is a prophet, and he shall pray for you, and you shall live: and if you restore her not, know you that you shall surely die, you, and all that are yours.

8 Therefore Abimelech rose early in the morning, and called all his servants, and told all these things in their ears: and the men were sore afraid.

9 Then Abimelech called Abraham, and said to him, What have you done to us? and what have I offended you, that you have brought on me and on my kingdom a great sin? you have done deeds to me that ought not to be done.

10 And Abimelech said to Abraham, What did you see, that you have done this thing?

11 And Abraham said, Because I thought, Surely the fear of God is not in this place; and they will slay me for my wife's sake.

12 And yet indeed she is my sister; she is the daughter of my father, but not the daughter of my mother; and she became my wife.

13 And it came to pass, when God caused me to wander from my father's house, that I said to her, This is your kindness which you shall show to me; at every place whither we shall come, say of me, He is my brother.

14 And Abimelech took sheep, and oxen, and menservants, and women servants, and gave them to Abraham, and restored him Sarah his wife.

15 And Abimelech said, Behold, my land is before you: dwell where it pleases you.

16 And to Sarah he said, Behold, I have given your brother a thousand pieces of silver: behold, he is to you a covering of

the eyes, to all that are with you, and with all other: thus she was reproved.

17 So Abraham prayed to God: and God healed Abimelech, and his wife, and his maidservants; and they bare children.

18 For the LORD had fast closed up all the wombs of the house of Abimelech, because of Sarah, Abraham's wife.

CHAPTER 21

AND the LORD visited Sarah as he had said, and the LORD did to Sarah as he had spoken.

2 For Sarah conceived, and bare Abraham a son in his old age, at the set time of which God had spoken to him.

3 And Abraham called the name of his son that was born to him, whom Sarah bare to him, Isaac.

4 And Abraham circumcised his son Isaac being eight days old, as God had commanded him.

5 And Abraham was an hundred years old, when his son Isaac was born to him.

6 And Sarah said, God has made me to laugh, so that all that hear will laugh with me.

7 And she said, Who would have said to Abraham, that Sarah should have given children suck? for I have born him a son in his old age.

8 And the child grew, and was weaned: and Abraham made a great feast the same day that Isaac was weaned.

9 And Sarah saw the son of Hagar the Egyptian, which she had born to Abraham, mocking.

10 Therefore she said to Abraham, Cast out this bondwoman and her son: for the son of this bondwoman shall not be heir with my son, even with Isaac.

11 And the thing was very grievous in Abraham's sight because of his son.

12 And God said to Abraham, Let it not be grievous in your sight because of the lad, and because of your bondwoman; in all that Sarah has said to you, hearken to her voice; for in Isaac shall your seed be called.

13 And also of the son of the bond-woman will I make a nation, because he is your seed.

14 And Abraham rose up early in the morning, and took bread, and a bottle of water, and gave it to Hagar, putting it on her shoulder, and the child, and sent her away: and she departed, and wandered in the wilderness of Beersheba.

15 And the water was spent in the bottle, and she cast the child under one of the shrubs.

16 And she went, and sat her down over against him a good way off, as it were a bow shot: for she said, Let me not see the death of the child. And she sat over against him, and lift up her voice, and wept.

17 And God heard the voice of the lad; and the angel of God called to Hagar out of heaven, and said to her, What ails you, Hagar? fear not; for God has heard the voice of the lad where he is.

18 Arise, lift up the lad, and hold him in your hand; for I will make him a great nation.

19 And God opened her eyes, and she saw a well of water; and she went, and filled the bottle with water, and gave the lad drink.

20 And God was with the lad; and he grew, and dwelt in the wilderness, and became an archer.

21 And he dwelt in the wilderness of Paran: and his mother took him a wife out of the land of Egypt.

22 And it came to pass at that time, that Abimelech and Phichol the chief captain of his host spoke to Abraham, saying, God is with you in all that you do:

23 Now therefore swear to me here by God that you will not deal falsely with me, nor with my son, nor with my son's son: but according to the kindness that I have done to you, you shall do to me, and to the land wherein you have sojourned.

24 And Abraham said, I will swear.

25 And Abraham reproved Abimelech because of a well of water, which

HAGAR AND ISHMAEL IN THE WILDERNESS

Genesis 21:16-18

God heard Hagar's cry for help when her son, Ishmael, the son of Abraham, was near death in the desert. God opened Hagar's eyes so that she could see a well and give her son water. Ishmael means, "God hears."

IN-DEPTH COMMENT

21:18   *"Are Arabs the Descendents of Ishmael?"*

In responding to this frequently asked question, Dr. Robert A. Morey refers first to Genesis 12. When Abraham left Ur of the Chaldees, he went west to what is now called Israel. Abraham became a dweller in tents in that land.

It was in Israel that God made a covenant with Abraham for the land in which he was living at that time. It was in Israel that Abraham fathered Isaac, Ishmael and many other sons and daughters.

It was prophesied in the Torah that Ishmael and his family would "live to the East of all of his brothers (Gen. 16:12). The descendants of Ishmael were scattered in Northern Arabia from the wilderness of Shur to the ancient city of Havilah, a broad section of desert east of Egypt as one goes toward Assyria (Gen. 15:18).

Ishmael's twelve sons were named Nebaioth, Kedar, Adbeel, Mibsam, Mishma, Dumah, Massa, Hadad, Tema, Jetur, Naphish, and Kedemah (Gen. 25:13-15). They intermarried with the local population in North Arabia and produced several nomadic tribes known as the "Ishmaelites."

The Ishmaelites are mentioned as a distinct tribe in the Assyrian records. They later intermarried with and were absorbed by the Midianites and other local tribes. In Gen. 37:25-28; 39:1, the Ishmaelites are called the Midianites and in Judges 8:22-24 cf. 7:1f, the Midianites are called the Ishmaelites. The identification cannot be made any stronger.

But Arabia was already populated by the descendants of Cush and Shem long before Abraham or Ishmael were born (Gen. 10:7). Their cities and temples have been well documented by archeologists. The Arab people existed before, during and after Ishmael started roaming the wilderness in North Africa.

There is no historical or archeological evidence that Ishmael went south to Mecca and became the "Father" of the Arab race. Some modern Arab scholars admit that before Muhammad, Qahtan was said to be the "Father" of the Arab people, not Ishmael.

The Abrahamic Covenant was given only to Isaac and to his descendants. Ishmael and the other sons of Abraham were explicitly excluded by God from having any part of the covenant made with Abraham. (Gen. 18:18-21). Isaac was the only son of Abraham chosen by God to be the heir of the covenant.

According to Genesis 22:3, it was Isaac whom Abraham took to Mt. Moriah to be offered up as a sacrifice to God. But the Qua'ran, the scripture of Islam, states that Ishmael was the son Abraham offered as a sacrifice to God.

But while it is good to have a knowledge of what other religions believe, don't feel as though you have to soak your head in their doctrines. Rather, feed your mind on the truths of the Bible. Never argue with a Muslim. Instead, gently take him through the Ten Commandments. In doing so, you will circumvent the intellect (the place of argument) and speak directly to his conscience (the place of conviction). It is not your job to reveal the deity of Christ to him. That's the job of God (Matthew 16:17). Simply "shut" him up under the Law, then point to the only Door whereby he can be saved. (See also Matthew 19:17, John 4:7 and Acts 17:22 comments.)

Islam

OFFICIAL NAME: Islam

KEY FIGURE IN HISTORY: Muhammad (A.D. 570–632)

DATE OF ITS ESTABLISHMENT: A.D. 622

ADHERENTS: Worldwide: Estimated 800 million to 1 billion; 58 percent live in South and Southeast Asia; 28 percent in Africa; 9 percent in Near and Middle East; 5 percent other. U.S.: Estimated 6.5 to 8 million.

WHAT IS ISLAM?

Islam is the world's youngest major world religion. It claims to be the restoration of original monotheism and truth and thus supersedes both Judaism and Christianity. It stresses submission to *Allah*, the Arabic name for God, and conformity to the "five pillars" or disciplines of that religion as essential for salvation. From its inception, Islam was an aggressively missionary-oriented religion. Within one century of its formation, and often using military force, Islam had spread across the Middle East, most of North Africa, and as far east as India. While God is, in the understanding of most Muslims, unknowable personally, His will is believed to be perfectly revealed in the holy book, the *Qur'an*. The Qur'an is to be followed completely and its teaching forms a complete guide for life and society.

WHO WAS MUHAMMAD?

Muhammad is believed by Muslims to be the last and greatest prophet of God—"the seal of the prophets." It was through him that the Qur'an was dictated, thus according him the supreme place among the seers of God. A native of Mecca, Muhammad was forced to flee that city in A.D. 622 after preaching vigorously against the paganism of the city. Having secured his leadership in Medina, and with several military victories to his credit, Muhammad returned in triumph to Mecca in A.D. 630. There, he established Islam as the religion of all Arabia.

WHAT IS THE QUR'AN?

The Qur'an is the sacred book of Islam and the perfect word of God for the Muslim. It is claimed that the Qur'an was dictated in Arabic by the angel Gabriel to Muhammad and were God's precise words. As such, it had preexisted from eternity in heaven with God as the "Mother of the Book" and was in that form uncreated and co-eternal with God. Islam teaches that it contains the total and perfect revelation and will of God. The Qur'an is about four-fifths the length of the New Testament and is divided into 114 *surahs* or chapters. While Islam respects the Torah, the psalms of David, and the four Gospels, the Qur'an stands alone in its authority and absoluteness. It is believed to be most perfectly understood in Arabic and it is a religious obligation to seek to read and quote it in the original language.

WHAT ARE THE "FIVE PILLARS"?

They are the framework for the Muslims' life and discipline. Successful and satisfactory adherence to the pillars satisfies the will of Allah. They form the basis for the Muslim's hope for salvation along with faith and belief in Allah's existence, the authority of Muhammad as a prophet, and the finality and perfection of the Qur'an. The five pillars are:

The confession of Faith or *Shahada*: It is the declaration that there is no god but Allah and Muhammad is his prophet. Sincerity in the voicing of the confession is necessary for it to be valid. It must be held until death, and repudiation of the *Shahada* nullifies hope for salvation.

Prayer of *Salat*: Five times a day, preceded by ceremonial washing, the Muslim is required to pray facing Mecca. Specific formulas recited from the Qur'an (in Arabic), along with prostrations, are included. Prayer is, in this sense, an expression of submission to the will of Allah. While most of Islam has no hierarchical priesthood, prayers are led in mosques by respected lay leaders. The five times of prayer are before sunrise, noon, midafternoon, sunset, and prior to sleep.

Almsgiving or *Zakat*: The Qur'an teaches the giving of two-and-a-half percent of one's capital wealth to the poor and/or for the propagation of Islam. By doing so, the Muslim's remaining wealth is purified.

The Fast or *Sawm*: during the course of the lunar month of Ramadan, a fast is to be observed by every Muslim from sunrise to sunset. Nothing is to pass over the lips during this time, and they should refrain from sexual relations. After sunset, feasting and other celebrations often occur. The daylight hours are set aside for self-purification. The month is used to remember the giving of the Qur'an to Muhammad.

Pilgrimage or *Hajj*: All Muslims who are economically and physically able are required to journey to Mecca at least once in their lifetime. The required simple pilgrim's dress stresses the notion of equality before God. Another element of the Hajj is the mandatory walk of each pilgrim seven times around the *Kaabah*—the shrine of the black rock, the holiest site of Islam. Muhammad taught that the Kaabah was the original place of worship for Adam and later for Abraham. The Kaabah is thus venerated as the site of true religion, the absolute monotheism of Islam.

THE DOCTRINES OF ISLAM

God: He is numerically and absolutely one. Allah is beyond the understanding of man so that only his will may be revealed and known. He is confessed as the "merciful and compassionate one."

Sin: The most serious sin that can be ascribed to people is that of *shirk* or considering god as more than one. Original sin is viewed as a "lapse" by Adam. Humankind is considered weak and forgetful but not as fallen.

Angels: Islam affirms the reality of angels as messengers and agents of god. Evil spirits or *Jinn* also exist. Satan is a fallen angel. Angels perform important functions for Allah both now and at the end of time.

Final Judgment: The world will be judged at the end of time by Allah. The good deeds and obedience of all people to the five pillars and the Qur'an will serve as the basis of judgment.

Salvation: It is determined by faith, as defined by Islam, as well as by compiling good deeds primarily in conformity to the five pillars.

Marriage: Muslims uphold marriage as honorable and condemn adultery. While many Muslim marriages are monogamous, Islamic states allow as many as four wives. Men consider a woman as less than an equal, and while a man has the right to divorce his wife, the wife has no similar power (see Surah 2:228, 4:34).

Nonetheless, the female has a right to own and dispose of property. Modesty in dress is encouraged for both men and women.

War: The term *jihad* or "struggle" is often considered as both external and internal, both a physical and spiritual struggle. The enemies of Islam or "idolaters," states the Qur'an, may be slain "wherever you find them" (Surah:5). (See Surah 47:4). Paradise is promised for those who die fighting in the cause of Islam (see Surah 3:195, 2:224). Moderate Muslims emphasize the spiritual dimension of Jihad and not its political element.

ANSWERING MUSLIM OBJECTIONS TO CHRISTIANITY

Christians and Jews are acknowledged as "people of the book," although their failure to conform to the confession of Islam labels them as unbelievers. Following are several questions that Muslims have about Christianity.

Is the Trinity a belief in three gods?

Christians are monotheistic and believe that God is one. But both in His work in accomplishing salvation through the person of Jesus Christ and through biblical study it has become clear that His oneness in fact comprises three persons—Father, Son (Jesus Christ), and the third person of the Godhead, the Holy Spirit. Mary is not part of the Godhead. The notion of God, who is three-in-one, is part of both the mystery and greatness of God. God is in essence one while in persons three. This truth helps us understand God as truly personal and having the capacity to relate to other persons. As well, Christians confirm the holiness, sovereignty, and greatness of God.

How can Jesus be the Son of God?

Scripture affirms that Jesus was conceived supernaturally by the Holy Spirit and was born of the Virgin Mary. It does not in any way claim that Jesus was directly God the Father's biological and physical son. It rejects the notion of the Arabic word for son, *walad*, meaning physical son, for the-word *ibin*, which is the title of relationship. Jesus is the Son in a symbolic manner designating that He was God the Word who became man in order to save humankind from its sin. The virgin birth was supernatural as God the Holy Spirit conceived in Mary, without physical relations, Jesus the Messiah. In this manner even the Qur'an affirms the miraculous birth of Christ (see Surah 19:16–21). Jesus was in this sense "God's unique Son." During His earthly ministry He carried out the will of the Father. Notably the Qur'an affirms Jesus' supernatural birth, life of miracles, His compassion, and ascension to heaven (see Surah 19:16–21,29–31, 3:37–47, 5:110).

How could Jesus have died on the cross especially if He's God's son?

The testimony of history and the *Injil,* or the four Gospels, is that Jesus died on the cross. If it is understood that God is love, and that humankind is lost in sin, then is it not likely that God would have provided a sacrifice for sin? Jesus is God's sacrifice for all the sins of the world and is a bridge from a holy God to fallen and sinful humans.

This truth is revealed in the Injil, John 3:16. Even the Qur'an states in Surah 3:55 that "Allah said: O Isa [Jesus], I am going to terminate [to put to death] the period of your stay (on earth) and cause you to ascend unto Me." What other way could this concept have any meaning apart from Jesus' death for sin and His subsequent resurrection?

Muslims believe that God took Jesus from the cross and substituted Judas in His place, or at least someone who looked like Jesus. He was then taken to heaven where He is alive and from where one day He will return.

ANSWERING MUSLIMS' QUESTIONS TO CHRISTIANS ABOUT ISLAM
What do you think about the prophet Muhammad?

Muhammad was apparently a well-meaning man who sought to oppose paganism and evil in his day. While he succeeded in uniting the Arabian Peninsula and upheld several important virtues, we do not believe he received a fresh revelation from God. Jesus Christ fulfilled not only the final prophetic role from God, but He is the Savior of the world and God the Son. While Islam believes that some Bible passages refer to Muhammad (see Deut. 18:18–19; John 14:16; 15:26; 16:7), that is clearly not the meaning of the texts. Other passages may help in understanding and interpreting the previous texts (see Matthew 21:11; Luke 24:19; John 6;14; 7:40; Acts 1:8–16; 7:37).

What is your opinion of the Qur'an?

It is a greatly valued book for the Muslim. It is not received or believed to be a divine book by the Christian. The statements of the Qur'an are accepted only where they agree with the Bible.

What is your opinion about the five pillars?

Salvation is from God and comes only through the saving work of Jesus Christ. When we put our faith in Him, we may be saved (see John 3:16–21,31–36).

WITNESSING TO MUSLIMS

- Be courteous and loving.
- Reflect interest in their beliefs. Allow them time to articulate their views.
- Be acquainted with their basic beliefs.
- Be willing to examine passages of the Qur'an concerning their beliefs.
- Stick to the cardinal doctrines of the Christian faith but also take time to respond to all sincere questions.
- Point out the centrality of the person and work of Jesus Christ for salvation.
- Stress that because of Jesus, His cross, and resurrection, one may have the full assurance of salvation, both now and for eternity (see 1 John 5:13).
- Share the plan of salvation. Point out that salvation is a gift and not to be earned.
- Pray for the fullness of the Holy Spirit. Trust Him to provide wisdom and grace.
- Be willing to become a friend and a personal evangelist to Muslims.

Phil Roberts, Director of Interfaith Evangelism. Copyright 1996 North American Mission Board of the Southern Baptist Convention, Alpharetta, Georgia. All rights reserved. Reprinted with permission.

Abimelech's servants had violently taken away.

26 And Abimelech said, I did not know who did this thing; neither did you tell me, neither yet heard I of it, but today.

27 And Abraham took sheep and oxen, and gave them to Abimelech; and both of them made a covenant.

28 And Abraham set seven ewe lambs of the flock by themselves.

29 And Abimelech said to Abraham, What mean these seven ewe lambs which you have set by themselves?

30 And he said, For these seven ewe lambs shall you take of my hand, that they may be a witness to me, that I have dug this well.

31 Therefore he called that place Beersheba; because there they swore both of them.

32 Thus they made a covenant at Beersheba: then Abimelech rose up, and Phichol the chief captain of his host, and they returned into the land of the Philistines.

33 And Abraham planted a grove in Beersheba, and called there on the name of the LORD, the everlasting God.

34 And Abraham sojourned in the Philistines' land many days.

CHAPTER 22

A ND it came to pass after these things, that God did tempt Abraham, and said to him, Abraham: and he said, Behold, here I am.

2 And he said, Take now your son, your only son Isaac, whom you love, and get you into the land of Moriah; and offer him there for a burnt offering upon one of the mountains which I will tell you of.

3 And Abraham rose up early in the morning, and saddled his ass, and took two of his young men with him, and Isaac his son, and clave the wood for the burnt offering, and rose up, and went to the place of which God had told him.

4 Then on the third day Abraham lifted up his eyes, and saw the place afar off.

5 And Abraham said to his young men, Abide here with the ass; and I and the lad will go yonder and worship, and come again to you.

6 And Abraham took the wood of the burnt offering, and laid it upon Isaac his son; and he took the fire in his hand, and a knife; and they went both of them together.

7 And Isaac spoke to Abraham his father, and said, My father: and he said, Here am I, my son. And he said, Behold the fire and the wood: but where is the lamb for a burnt offering?

8 And Abraham said, My son, God will provide himself a lamb for a burnt offering: so they went both of them together.

9 And they came to the place which God had told him of; and Abraham built an altar there, and laid the wood in order, and bound Isaac his son, and laid him on the altar upon the wood.

10 And Abraham stretched forth his hand, and took the knife to slay his son.

11 And the angel of the LORD called to him out of heaven, and said, Abraham, Abraham: and he said, Here am I.

12 And he said, Lay not your hand upon the lad, neither do you any thing to him: for now I know that you fear God, seeing you have not withheld your son, your only son from me.

13 And Abraham lifted up his eyes, and looked, and behold behind him a ram

---

22:2 When skeptics attempt to slur the character of God by saying that He commanded human sacrifice, it may be good to point out that God did not tell Abraham to sacrifice his son. He told him to "offer" him (KJV). When Abraham tried to sacrifice Isaac, God stopped him (see verse 12).

22:8 This wasn't a reference to verse 13 because God didn't provide a lamb in this incident. It is an obvious reference to the Lamb of God, the Messiah. See John 1:36.

THE TRIAL OF ABRAHAM'S FAITH

Genesis 22:6-18

When God asked Abraham to offer his son Isaac as a sacrifice, Abraham believed that God would "provide Himself a lamb for the burnt offering" (v. 8). But seeing no lamb, Abraham raised a knife to slay his son (v. 10). Only when the angel stopped Abraham, saying, "Now I know you fear God; you have not withheld your son, your only son, from me," did Abraham see a ram caught in the thicket, and he sacrificed the ram instead of his son (v. 13). "And Abraham called the name of that place Jehovah-jireh . . . " (v. 14), which means, God provides.

God sacrificed His only son, Jesus, as the one, perfect and true sacrifice and atonement for sin. "For by one offering He has perfected for all time those who are sanctified" (Hebrews 10:14).

caught in a thicket by his horns: and Abraham went and took the ram, and offered him up for a burnt offering in the stead of his son.

14 And Abraham called the name of that place Jehovah Jireh: as it is said to this day, In the mount of the LORD it shall be seen.

15 And the angel of the LORD called to Abraham out of heaven the second time,

16 And said, By myself have I sworn, says the LORD, for because you have done this thing, and have not withheld your son, your only son:

17 That in blessing I will bless you, and in multiplying I will multiply your seed as the stars of the heaven, and as the sand which is upon the sea shore; and your seed shall possess the gate of his enemies;

18 And in your seed shall all the nations of the earth be blessed; because you have obeyed my voice.

19 So Abraham returned to his young men, and they rose up and went together to Beersheba; and Abraham dwelt at Beersheba.

20 And it came to pass after these things, that it was told Abraham, saying, Behold, Milcah, she has also born children to your brother Nahor;

21 Huz his firstborn, and Buz his brother, and Kemuel the father of Aram,

22 And Chesed, and Hazo, and Pildash, and Jidlaph, and Bethuel.

23 And Bethuel begat Rebekah: these eight Milcah did bear to Nahor, Abraham's brother.

24 And his concubine, whose name was Reumah, she bare also Tebah, and Gaham, and Thahash, and Maachah.

CHAPTER 23

AND Sarah was an hundred and seven and twenty years old: these were the years of the life of Sarah.

2 And Sarah died in Kirjatharba; the same is Hebron in the land of Canaan: and Abraham came to mourn for Sarah, and to weep for her.

3 And Abraham stood up from before his dead, and spoke to the sons of Heth, saying,

4 I am a stranger and a sojourner with you: give me a possession of a burying place with you, that I may bury my dead out of my sight.

5 And the children of Heth answered Abraham, saying to him,

6 Hear us, my lord: you are a mighty prince among us: in the choice of our sepulchers bury your dead; none of us shall withhold from you his sepulcher, but that you may bury your dead.

7 And Abraham stood up, and bowed himself to the people of the land, even to the children of Heth.

8 And he communed with them, saying, If it be your mind that I should bury my dead out of my sight; hear me, and entreat for me to Ephron the son of Zohar,

9 That he may give me the cave of Machpelah, which he has, which is in the end of his field; for as much money as it is worth he shall give it me for a possession of a burying place amongst you.

10 And Ephron dwelt among the children of Heth: and Ephron the Hittite answered Abraham in the audience of the children of Heth, even of all that went in at the gate of his city, saying,

11 Nay, my lord, hear me: the field give I you, and the cave that is therein, I give it you; in the presence of the sons of my people give I it you: bury your dead.

12 And Abraham bowed down himself before the people of the land.

13 And he spoke to Ephron in the audience of the people of the land, saying, But if you will give it, I pray you, hear me: I will give you money for the field; take it of me, and I will bury my dead there.

14 And Ephron answered Abraham, saying to him,

15 My lord, hearken to me: the land is worth four hundred shekels of silver;

what is that between me and you? bury therefore your dead.

16 And Abraham hearkened to Ephron; and Abraham weighed to Ephron the silver, which he had named in the audience of the sons of Heth, four hundred shekels of silver, current money with the merchant.

17 And the field of Ephron which was in Machpelah, which was before Mamre, the field, and the cave which was therein, and all the trees that were in the field, that were in all the borders round about, were made sure.

18 To Abraham for a possession in the presence of the children of Heth, before all that went in at the gate of his city.

19 And after this, Abraham buried Sarah his wife in the cave of the field of Machpelah before Mamre: the same is Hebron in the land of Canaan.

20 And the field, and the cave that is therein, were made sure to Abraham for a possession of a burying place by the sons of Heth.

CHAPTER 24

AND Abraham was old, and well stricken in age: and the LORD had blessed Abraham in all things.

2 And Abraham said to his eldest servant of his house, that ruled over all that he had, Put, I pray you, your hand under my thigh:

3 And I will make you swear by the LORD, the God of heaven, and the God of the earth, that you shall not take a wife to my son of the daughters of the Canaanites, among whom I dwell:

4 But you shall go to my country, and to my kindred, and take a wife to my son Isaac.

5 And the servant said to him, Peradventure the woman will not be willing to follow me to this land: must I bring your son again to the land from where you came?

6 And Abraham said to him, Beware you that you bring not my son thither again.

7 The LORD God of heaven, which took me from my father's house, and from the land of my kindred, and which spoke to me, and that swore to me, saying, To your seed will I give this land; he shall send his angel before you, and you shall take a wife to my son from thence.

8 And if the woman will not be willing to follow you, then you shall be clear from this my oath: only bring not my son thither again.

9 And the servant put his hand under the thigh of Abraham his master, and swore to him concerning that matter.

10 And the servant took ten camels of the camels of his master, and departed; for all the goods of his master were in his hand: and he arose, and went to Mesopotamia, to the city of Nahor.

11 And he made his camels to kneel down without the city by a well of water at the time of the evening, even the time that women go out to draw water.

12 And he said O LORD God of my master Abraham, I pray you, send me good speed this day, and show kindness to my master Abraham.

13 Behold, I stand here by the well of water; and the daughters of the men of the city come out to draw water:

14 And let it come to pass, that the damsel to whom I shall say, Let down your pitcher, I pray you, that I may drink; and she shall say, Drink, and I will give your camels drink also: let the same be she that you have appointed for your servant Isaac; and thereby shall I know that you have showed kindness to my master.

15 And it came to pass, before he had done speaking, that, behold, Rebekah came out, who was born to Bethuel, son of Milcah, the wife of Nahor, Abraham's brother, with her pitcher upon her shoulder.

16 And the damsel was very fair to look upon, a virgin, neither had any man known her: and she went down to the well, and filled her pitcher, and came up.

ELIEZER AND REBEKAH

Genesis 24:16

17 And the servant ran to meet her, and said, Let me, I pray you, drink a little water of your pitcher.

18 And she said, Drink, my lord: and she hasted, and let down her pitcher upon her hand, and gave him drink.

19 And when she had done giving him drink, she said, I will draw water for your camels also, until they have done drinking.

20 And she hasted, and emptied her pitcher into the trough, and ran again to the well to draw water, and drew for all his camels.

21 And the man wondering at her held his peace, to wit whether the LORD had made his journey prosperous or not.

22 And it came to pass, as the camels had done drinking, that the man took a golden earring of half a shekel weight, and two bracelets for her hands of ten shekels weight of gold;

23 And said, Whose daughter are thou? tell me, I pray you: is there room in your father's house for us to lodge in?

24 And she said to him, I am the daughter of Bethuel the son of Milcah, which she bare to Nahor.

25 She said moreover to him, We have both straw and provender enough, and room to lodge in.

26 And the man bowed down his head, and worshipped the LORD.

27 And he said, Blessed be the LORD God of my master Abraham, who has not left destitute my master of his mercy and his truth: I being in the way, the LORD led me to the house of my master's brethren.

28 And the damsel ran, and told them of her mother's house these things.

29 And Rebekah had a brother, and his name was Laban: and Laban ran out to the man, to the well.

30 And it came to pass, when he saw the earring and bracelets upon his sister's hands, and when he heard the words of Rebekah his sister, saying, Thus spoke the man to me; that he came to the man; and, behold, he stood by the camels at the well.

31 And he said, Come in, you blessed of the LORD; Why do you stand without? for I have prepared the house, and room for the camels.

32 And the man came into the house: and he ungirded his camels, and gave straw and provender for the camels, and water to wash his feet, and the men's feet that were with him.

33 And there was set meat before him to eat: but he said, I will not eat, until I have told mine errand. And he said, Speak on.

34 And he said, I am Abraham's servant.

35 And the LORD has blessed my master greatly; and he is become great: and he has given him flocks, and herds, and silver, and gold, and menservants, and maidservants, and camels, and asses.

36 And Sarah my master's wife bare a son to my master when she was old: and to him has he given all that he has.

37 And my master made me swear, saying, You shall not take a wife to my son of the daughters of the Canaanites, in whose land I dwell:

38 But you shall go to my father's house, and to my kindred, and take a wife to my son.

39 And I said to my master, Peradventure the woman will not follow me.

40 And he said to me, The LORD, before whom I walk, will send his angel with you, and prosper your way; and you shall take a wife for my son of my kindred, and of my father's house:

41 Then shall you be clear from this my oath, when you come to my kindred; and if they give not you one, you shall be clear from my oath.

42 And I came this day to the well, and said, O LORD God of my master Abraham, if now you do prosper my way which I go:

43 Behold, I stand by the well of water; and it shall come to pass, that when the

virgin cometh forth to draw water, and I say to her, Give me, I pray you, a little water of your pitcher to drink;

44 And she say to me, Both drink thou, and I will also draw for your camels: let the same be the woman whom the LORD has appointed out for my master's son.

45 And before I had done speaking in mine heart, behold, Rebekah came forth with her pitcher on her shoulder; and she went down to the well, and drew water: and I said to her, Let me drink, I pray you.

46 And she made haste, and let down her pitcher from her shoulder, and said, Drink, and I will give your camels drink also: so I drank, and she made the camels drink also.

47 And I asked her, and said, Whose daughter are thou? And she said, the daughter of Bethuel, Nahor's son, whom Milcah bare to him: and I put the earring upon her face, and the bracelets upon her hands.

48 And I bowed down my head, and worshipped the LORD, and blessed the LORD God of my master Abraham, which had led me in the right way to take my master's brother's daughter to his son.

49 And now if you will deal kindly and truly with my master, tell me: and if not, tell me; that I may turn to the right hand, or to the left.

50 Then Laban and Bethuel answered and said, The thing proceeds from the LORD: we cannot speak to you bad or good.

51 Behold, Rebekah is before you, take her, and go, and let her be your master's son's wife, as the LORD has spoken.

52 And it came to pass, that, when Abraham's servant heard their words, he worshipped the LORD, bowing himself to the earth.

53 And the servant brought forth jewels of silver, and jewels of gold, and raiment, and gave them to Rebekah: he gave also to her brother and to her mother precious things.

54 And they did eat and drink, he and the men that were with him, and tarried all night; and they rose up in the morning, and he said, Send me away to my master.

55 And her brother and her mother said, Let the damsel abide with us a few days, at the least ten; after that she shall go.

56 And he said to them, Hinder me not, seeing the LORD has prospered my way; send me away that I may go to my master.

57 And they said, We will call the damsel, and inquire at her mouth.

58 And they called Rebekah, and said to her, Will you go with this man? And she said, I will go.

59 And they sent away Rebekah their sister, and her nurse, and Abraham's servant, and his men.

60 And they blessed Rebekah, and said to her, You are our sister, be you the mother of thousands of millions, and let your seed possess the gate of those which hate them.

61 And Rebekah arose, and her damsels, and they rode upon the camels, and followed the man: and the servant took Rebekah, and went his way.

62 And Isaac came from the way of the well Lahairoi; for he dwelt in the south country.

63 And Isaac went out to meditate in the field at the eventide: and he lifted up his eyes, and saw, and, behold, the camels were coming.

64 And Rebekah lifted up her eyes, and when she saw Isaac, she lighted off the camel.

65 For she had said to the servant, What man is this that walks in the field to meet us? And the servant had said, It is my master: therefore she took a veil, and covered herself.

66 And the servant told Isaac all things that he had done.

67 And Isaac brought her into his mother Sarah's tent, and took Rebekah, and she became his wife; and he loved her: and Isaac was comforted after his mother's death.

CHAPTER 25

THEN again Abraham took a wife, and her name was Keturah.

2 And she bare him Zimran, and Jokshan, and Medan, and Midian, and Ishbak, and Shuah.

3 And Jokshan begat Sheba, and Dedan. And the sons of Dedan were Asshurim, and Letushim, and Leummim.

4 And the sons of Midian; Ephah, and Epher, and Hanoch, and Abidah, and Eldaah. All these were the children of Keturah.

5 And Abraham gave all that he had to Isaac.

6 But to the sons of the concubines, which Abraham had, Abraham gave gifts, and sent them away from Isaac his son, while he yet lived, eastward, to the east country.

7 And these are the days of the years of Abraham's life which he lived, an hundred threescore and fifteen years.

8 Then Abraham gave up the ghost, and died in a good old age, an old man, and full of years; and was gathered to his people.

9 And his sons Isaac and Ishmael buried him in the cave of Machpelah, in the field of Ephron the son of Zohar the Hittite, which is before Mamre;

10 The field which Abraham purchased of the sons of Heth: there was Abraham buried, and Sarah his wife.

11 And it came to pass after the death of Abraham, that God blessed his son Isaac; and Isaac dwelt by the well Lahairoi.

12 Now these are the generations of Ishmael, Abraham's son, whom Hagar the Egyptian, Sarah's handmaid, bare to Abraham:

13 And these are the names of the sons of Ishmael, by their names, according to their generations: the firstborn of Ishmael, Nebajoth; and Kedar, and Adbeel, and Mibsam,

14 And Mishma, and Dumah, and Massa,

15 Hadar, and Tema, Jetur, Naphish, and Kedemah:

16 These are the sons of Ishmael, and these are their names, by their towns, and by their castles; twelve princes according to their nations.

17 And these are the years of the life of Ishmael, an hundred and thirty and seven years: and he gave up the ghost and died; and was gathered to his people.

18 And they dwelt from Havilah to Shur, that is before Egypt, as you goest toward Assyria: and he died in the presence of all his brethren.

19 And these are the generations of Isaac, Abraham's son: Abraham begat Isaac:

20 And Isaac was forty years old when he took Rebekah to wife, the daughter of Bethuel the Syrian of Padanaram, the sister to Laban the Syrian.

21 And Isaac entreated the LORD for his wife, because she was barren: and the LORD was entreated of him, and Rebekah his wife conceived.

22 And the children struggled together within her; and she said, If it be so, why am I thus? And she went to inquire of the LORD.

23 And the LORD said to her, Two nations are in your womb, and two manner of people shall be separated from your bowels; and the one people shall be stronger than the other people; and the elder shall serve the younger.

24 And when her days to be delivered were fulfilled, behold, there were twins in her womb.

25 And the first came out red, all over like an hairy garment; and they called his name Esau.

26 And after that came his brother out, and his hand took hold on Esau's heel; and his name was called Jacob: and Isaac

was threescore years old when she bare them.

27 And the boys grew: and Esau was a cunning hunter, a man of the field; and Jacob was a plain man, dwelling in tents.

28 And Isaac loved Esau, because he did eat of his venison: but Rebekah loved Jacob.

29 And Jacob sod pottage: and Esau came from the field, and he was faint:

30 And Esau said to Jacob, Feed me, I pray you, with that same red pottage; for I am faint: therefore was his name called Edom.

31 And Jacob said, Sell me this day your birthright.

32 And Esau said, Behold, I am at the point to die: and what profit shall this birthright do to me?

33 And Jacob said, Swear to me this day; and he swore to him: and he sold his birthright to Jacob.

34 Then Jacob gave Esau bread and pottage of lentiles; and he did eat and drink, and rose up, and went his way: thus Esau despised his birthright.

CHAPTER 26

AND there was a famine in the land, beside the first famine that was in the days of Abraham. And Isaac went to Abimelech king of the Philistines to Gerar.

2 And the LORD appeared to him, and said, Go not down into Egypt; dwell in the land which I shall tell you of:

3 Sojourn in this land, and I will be with you, and will bless you; for to you, and to your seed, I will give all these countries, and I will perform the oath which I swore to Abraham your father;

4 And I will make your seed to multiply as the stars of heaven, and will give to your seed all these countries; and in your seed shall all the nations of the earth be blessed;

5 Because that Abraham obeyed my voice, and kept my charge, my commandments, my statutes, and my laws.

6 And Isaac dwelt in Gerar:

7 And the men of the place asked him of his wife; and he said, She is my sister: for he feared to say, She is my wife; lest, said he, the men of the place should kill me for Rebekah; because she was fair to look upon.

8 And it came to pass, when he had been there a long time, that Abimelech king of the Philistines looked out at a window, and saw, and, behold, Isaac was sporting with Rebekah his wife.

9 And Abimelech called Isaac, and said, Behold, of a surety she is your wife; and how could you say, She is my sister? And Isaac said to him, Because I said, Lest I die for her.

10 And Abimelech said, What is this you have done to us? one of the people might lightly have lain with your wife, and you should have brought guiltiness upon us.

11 And Abimelech charged all his people, saying, He that touches this man or his wife shall surely be put to death.

12 Then Isaac sewed in that land, and received in the same year an hundredfold: and the LORD blessed him.

13 And the man waxed great, and went forward, and grew until he became very great:

14 For he had possession of flocks, and possession of herds, and great store of servants: and the Philistines envied him.

15 For all the wells which his father's servants had dug in the days of Abraham his father, the Philistines had stopped them, and filled them with earth.

16 And Abimelech said to Isaac, Go from us; for you are much mightier than we.

17 And Isaac departed thence, and pitched his tent in the valley of Gerar, and dwelt there.

18 And Isaac dug again the wells of water, which they had dug in the days of Abraham his father; for the Philistines had stopped them after the death of Abraham: and he called their names after the names by which his father had called them.

19 And Isaac's servants dug in the valley, and found there a well of springing water.

20 And the herdsmen of Gerar did strive with Isaac's herdsmen, saying, The water is ours: and he called the name of the well Esek; because they strove with him.

21 And they dug another well, and strove for that also: and he called the name of it Sitnah.

22 And he removed from thence, and dug another well; and for that they strove not: and he called the name of it Rehoboth; and he said, For now the LORD has made room for us, and we shall be fruitful in the land.

23 And he went up from thence to Beersheba.

24 And the LORD appeared to him the same night, and said, I am the God of Abraham your father: fear not, for I am with you, and will bless you, and multiply your seed for my servant Abraham's sake.

25 And he built an altar there, and called upon the name of the LORD, and pitched his tent there: and there Isaac's servants dug a well.

26 Then Abimelech went to him from Gerar, and Ahuzzath one of his friends, and Phichol the chief captain of his army.

27 And Isaac said to them, Why do you come to me, seeing you hate me, and have sent me away from you?

28 And they said, We saw certainly that the LORD was with you: and we said, Let there be now an oath between us, even between us and you, and let us make a covenant with you;

29 That you will do us no hurt, as we have not touched you, and as we have done to you nothing but good, and have sent you away in peace: you are now the blessed of the LORD.

30 And he made them a feast, and they did eat and drink.

31 And they rose up early in the morning, and swore one to another: and Isaac sent them away, and they departed from him in peace.

32 And it came to pass the same day, that Isaac's servants came, and told him concerning the well which they had dug, and said to him, We have found water.

33 And he called it Shebah: therefore the name of the city is Beersheba to this day.

34 And Esau was forty years old when he took to wife Judith the daughter of Beeri the Hittite, and Bashemath the daughter of Elon the Hittite:

35 Which were a grief of mind to Isaac and to Rebekah.

CHAPTER 27

AND it came to pass, that when Isaac was old, and his eyes were dim, so that he could not see, he called Esau his eldest son, and said to him, My son: and he said to him, Behold, here am I.

2 And he said, Behold now, I am old, I know not the day of my death:

3 Now therefore take, I pray you, your weapons, your quiver and your bow, and go out to the field, and take me some venison;

4 And make me savory meat, such as I love, and bring it to me, that I may eat; that my soul may bless you before I die.

5 And Rebekah heard when Isaac spoke to Esau his son. And Esau went to the field to hunt for venison, and to bring it.

6 And Rebekah spoke to Jacob her son, saying, Behold, I heard your father speak to Esau your brother, saying,

7 Bring me venison, and make me savory meat, that I may eat, and bless you before the LORD before my death.

8 Now therefore, my son, obey my voice according to that which I command you.

9 Go now to the flock, and fetch me from thence two good kids of the goats; and I will make them savory meat for your father, such as he loves:

10 And you shall bring it to your father, that he may eat, and that he may bless you before his death.

ISAAC BLESSING JACOB

Genesis 27:1-29

11 And Jacob said to Rebekah his mother, Behold, Esau my brother is a hairy man, and I am a smooth man:

12 My father peradventure will feel me, and I shall seem to him as a deceiver; and I shall bring a curse upon me, and not a blessing.

13 And his mother said to him, Upon me be your curse, my son: only obey my voice, and go fetch me them.

14 And he went, and fetched, and brought them to his mother: and his mother made savory meat, such as his father loved.

15 And Rebekah took goodly raiment of her eldest son Esau, which were with her in the house, and put them upon Jacob her younger son:

16 And she put the skins of the kids of the goats upon his hands, and upon the smooth of his neck:

17 And she gave the savory meat and the bread, which she had prepared, into the hand of her son Jacob.

18 And he came to his father, and said, My father: and he said, Here am I; who are thou, my son?

19 And Jacob said to his father, I am Esau your first born; I have done according as you told me: arise, I pray you, sit and eat of my venison, that your soul may bless me.

20 And Isaac said to his son, How is it that you have found it so quickly, my son? And he said, Because the LORD your God brought it to me.

21 And Isaac said to Jacob, Come near, I pray you, that I may feel you, my son, whether you be my very son Esau or not.

22 And Jacob went near to Isaac his father; and he felt him, and said, The voice is Jacob's voice, but the hands are the hands of Esau.

23 And he discerned him not, because his hands were hairy, as his brother Esau's hands: so he blessed him.

24 And he said, are you my very son Esau? And he said, I am.

25 And he said, Bring it near to me, and I will eat of my son's venison, that my soul may bless you. And he brought it near to him, and he did eat: and he brought him wine and he drank.

26 And his father Isaac said to him, Come near now, and kiss me, my son.

27 And he came near, and kissed him: and he smelled the smell of his raiment, and blessed him, and said, See, the smell of my son is as the smell of a field which the LORD has blessed:

28 Therefore God give you of the dew of heaven, and the fatness of the earth, and plenty of corn and wine:

29 Let people serve you, and nations bow down to you: be lord over your brethren, and let your mother's sons bow down to you: cursed be every one that curses you, and blessed be he that blesses you.

30 And it came to pass, as soon as Isaac had made an end of blessing Jacob, and Jacob was yet scarce gone out from the presence of Isaac his father, that Esau his brother came in from his hunting.

31 And he also had made savory meat, and brought it to his father, and said to his father, Let my father arise, and eat of his son's venison, that your soul may bless me.

32 And Isaac his father said to him, Who are thou? And he said, I am your son, your firstborn Esau.

33 And Isaac trembled very exceedingly, and said, Who? where is he that has taken venison, and brought it me, and I have eaten of all before you came, and have blessed him? yea, and he shall be blessed.

34 And when Esau heard the words of his father, he cried with a great and exceeding bitter cry, and said to his father, Bless me, even me also, O my father.

35 And he said, Your brother came with subtlety, and has taken away your blessing.

36 And he said, Is not he rightly named Jacob? for he has supplanted me these two times: he took away my birthright; and, behold, now he has taken away my

blessing. And he said, Have you not reserved a blessing for me?

37 And Isaac answered and said to Esau, Behold, I have made him your lord, and all his brethren have I given to him for servants; and with corn and wine have I sustained him: and what shall I do now to you, my son?

38 And Esau said to his father, Have you but one blessing, my father? bless me, even me also, O my father. And Esau lifted up his voice, and wept.

39 And Isaac his father answered and said to him, Behold, your dwelling shall be the fatness of the earth, and of the dew of heaven from above;

40 And by your sword shall you live, and shall serve your brother; and it shall come to pass when you shall have the dominion, that you shall break his yoke from off your neck.

41 And Esau hated Jacob because of the blessing wherewith his father blessed him: and Esau said in his heart, The days of mourning for my father are at hand; then will I slay my brother Jacob.

42 And these words of Esau her elder son were told to Rebekah: and she sent and called Jacob her younger son, and said to him, Behold, your brother Esau, as touching you, doth comfort himself, purposing to kill you.

43 Now therefore, my son, obey my voice; arise, flee you to Laban my brother to Haran;

44 And tarry with him a few days, until your brother's fury turn away;

45 Until your brother's anger turn away from you, and he forget that which you have done to him: then I will send, and fetch you from thence: why should I be deprived also of you both in one day?

46 And Rebekah said to Isaac, I am weary of my life because of the daughters of Heth: if Jacob take a wife of the daughters of Heth, such as these which are of the daughters of the land, what good shall my life do me?

CHAPTER 28

AND Isaac called Jacob, and blessed him, and charged him, and said to him, You shall not take a wife of the daughters of Canaan.

2 Arise, go to Padanaram, to the house of Bethuel your mother's father; and take you a wife from thence of the daughers of Laban your mother's brother.

3 And God Almighty bless you, and make you fruitful, and multiply you, that you may be a multitude of people;

4 And give you the blessing of Abraham, to you, and to your seed with you; that you may inherit the land wherein you are a stranger, which God gave to Abraham.

5 And Isaac sent away Jacob: and he went to Padanaram to Laban, son of Bethuel the Syrian, the brother of Rebekah, Jacob's and Esau's mother.

6 When Esau saw that Isaac had blessed Jacob, and sent him away to Padanaram, to take him a wife from thence; and that as he blessed him he gave him a charge, saying, You shall not take a wife of the daughters of Canaan;

7 And that Jacob obeyed his father and his mother, and was gone to Padanaram;

8 And Esau seeing that the daughters of Canaan pleased not Isaac his father;

9 Then went Esau to Ishmael, and took to the wives which he had Mahalath the daughter of Ishmael Abraham's son, the sister of Nebajoth, to be his wife.

10 And Jacob went out from Beersheba, and went toward Haran.

11 And he lighted upon a certain place, and tarried there all night, because the sun was set; and he took of the stones of that place, and put them for his pillows, and lay down in that place to sleep.

12 And he dreamed, and behold a ladder set up on the earth, and the top of it reached to heaven: and behold the angels of God ascending and descending on it.

13 And, behold, the LORD stood above it, and said, I am the LORD God of Abraham your father, and the God of

JACOB'S DREAM

Genesis 28:11-22

Isaac: the land whereon you lie, to you will I give it, and to your seed;

14 And your seed shall be as the dust of the earth, and you shall spread abroad to the west, and to the east, and to the north, and to the south: and in you and in your seed shall all the families of the earth be blessed.

15 And, behold, I am with you, and will keep you in all places where you go, and will bring you again into this land; for I will not leave you, until I have done that which I have spoken to you of.

16 And Jacob awaked out of his sleep, and he said, Surely the LORD is in this place; and I knew it not.

17 And he was afraid, and said, How dreadful is this place! this is none other but the house of God, and this is the gate of heaven.

18 And Jacob rose up early in the morning, and took the stone that he had put for his pillows, and set it up for a pillar, and poured oil upon the top of it.

19 And he called the name of that place Bethel: but the name of that city was called Luz at the first.

20 And Jacob vowed a vow, saying, If God will be with me, and will keep me in this way that I go, and will give me bread to eat, and raiment to put on,

21 So that I come again to my father's house in peace; then shall the LORD be my God:

22 And this stone, which I have set for a pillar, shall be God's house: and of all that you shall give me I will surely give the tenth to you.

CHAPTER 29

THEN Jacob went on his journey, and came into the land of the people of the east.

2 And he looked, and behold a well in the field, and, lo, there were three flocks of sheep lying by it; for out of that well they watered the flocks: and a great stone was upon the well's mouth.

3 And thither were all the flocks gathered: and they rolled the stone from the well's mouth, and watered the sheep, and put the stone again upon the well's mouth in his place.

4 And Jacob said to them, My brethren, where are you from? And they said, Of Haran are we.

5 And he said to them, Do you know Laban the son of Nahor? And they said, We know him.

6 And he said to them, Is he well? And they said, He is well: and, behold, Rachel his daughter cometh with the sheep.

7 And he said, Lo, it is yet high day, neither is it time that the cattle should be gathered together: water the sheep, and go and feed them.

8 And they said, We cannot, until all the flocks be gathered together, and till they roll the stone from the well's mouth; then we water the sheep.

9 And while he yet spoke with them, Rachel came with her father's sheep; for she kept them.

10 And it came to pass, when Jacob saw Rachel the daughter of Laban his mother's brother, and the sheep of Laban his mother's brother, that Jacob went near, and rolled the stone from the well's mouth, and watered the flock of Laban his mother's brother.

11 And Jacob kissed Rachel, and lifted up his voice, and wept.

12 And Jacob told Rachel that he was her father's brother, and that he was Rebekah's son: and she ran and told her father.

13 And it came to pass, when Laban heard the tidings of Jacob his sister's son, that he ran to meet him, and embraced him, and kissed him, and brought him to his house. And he told Laban all these things.

14 And Laban said to him, Surely you are my bone and my flesh. And he abode with him the space of a month.

15 And Laban said to Jacob, Because you are my brother, should you therefore serve me for nothing? tell me, what shall your wages be?

16 And Laban had two daughters: the name of the elder was Leah, and the name of the younger was Rachel.

17 Leah was tender eyed; but Rachel was beautiful and well favored.

18 And Jacob loved Rachel; and said, I will serve you seven years for Rachel your younger daughter.

19 And Laban said, It is better that I give her to you, than that I should give her to another man: abide with me.

20 And Jacob served seven years for Rachel; and they seemed to him but a few days, for the love he had for her.

21 And Jacob said to Laban, Give me my wife, for my days are fulfilled, that I may go in to her.

22 And Laban gathered together all the men of the place, and made a feast.

23 And it came to pass in the evening, that he took Leah his daughter, and brought her to him; and he went in to her.

24 And Laban gave to his daughter Leah Zilpah his maid for an handmaid.

25 And it came to pass, that in the morning, behold, it was Leah: and he said to Laban, What is this you have done to me? did not I serve with you for Rachel? why then have you beguiled me?

26 And Laban said, It must not be so done in our country, to give the younger before the firstborn.

27 Fulfill her week, and we will give you this also for the service which you shall serve with me yet seven other years.

28 And Jacob did so, and fulfilled her week: and he gave him Rachel his daughter to wife also.

29 And Laban gave to Rachel his daughter Bilhah his handmaid to be her maid.

30 And he went in also to Rachel, and he loved also Rachel more than Leah, and served with him yet seven other years.

31 And when the LORD saw that Leah was hated, he opened her womb: but Rachel was barren.

32 And Leah conceived, and bare a son, and she called his name Reuben: for she said, Surely the LORD has looked upon my affliction; now therefore my husband will love me.

33 And she conceived again, and bare a son; and said, Because the LORD has heard I was hated, he has therefore given me this son also: and she called his name Simeon.

34 And she conceived again, and bare a son; and said, Now this time will my husband be joined to me, because I have born him three sons: therefore was his name called Levi.

35 And she conceived again, and bare a son: and she said, Now will I praise the LORD: therefore she called his name Judah; and left bearing.

CHAPTER 30

AND when Rachel saw that she bare Jacob no children, Rachel envied her sister; and said to Jacob, Give me children, or else I die.

2 And Jacob's anger was kindled against Rachel: and he said, Am I in God's stead, who has withheld from you the fruit of the womb?

3 And she said, Behold my maid Bilhah, go in to her; and she shall bear upon my knees, that I may also have children by her.

4 And she gave him Bilhah her handmaid to wife: and Jacob went in to her.

5 And Bilhah conceived, and bare Jacob a son.

6 And Rachel said, God has judged me, and has also heard my voice, and has given me a son: therefore called she his name Dan.

7 And Bilhah Rachel's maid conceived again, and bare Jacob a second son.

8 And Rachel said, With great wrestlings have I wrestled with my sister, and I have prevailed: and she called his name Naphtali.

9 When Leah saw that she had left bearing, she took Zilpah her maid, and gave her Jacob to wife.

10 And Zilpah Leah's maid bare Jacob a son.

11 And Leah said, A troop cometh: and she called his name Gad.

12 And Zilpah Leah's maid bare Jacob a second son.

13 And Leah said, Happy am I, for the daughters will call me blessed: and she called his name Asher.

14 And Reuben went in the days of wheat harvest, and found mandrakes in the field, and brought them to his mother Leah. Then Rachel said to Leah, Give me, I pray you, of your son's mandrakes.

15 And she said to her, Is it a small matter that you have taken my husband? and would you take away my son's mandrakes also? And Rachel said, Therefore he shall lie with you tonight for your son's mandrakes.

16 And Jacob came out of the field in the evening, and Leah went out to meet him, and said, You must come in to me; for surely I have hired you with my son's mandrakes. And he lay with her that night.

17 And God hearkened to Leah, and she conceived, and bare Jacob the fifth son.

18 And Leah said, God has given me my hire, because I have given my maiden to my husband: and she called his name Issachar.

19 And Leah conceived again, and bare Jacob the sixth son.

20 And Leah said, God has endued me with a good dowry; now will my husband dwell with me, because I have born him six sons: and she called his name Zebulun.

21 And afterwards she bare a daughter, and called her name Dinah.

22 And God remembered Rachel, and God hearkened to her, and opened her womb.

23 And she conceived, and bare a son; and said, God has taken away my reproach:

24 And she called his name Joseph; and said, The LORD shall add to me another son.

25 And it came to pass, when Rachel had born Joseph, that Jacob said to Laban, Send me away, that I may go to mine own place, and to my country.

26 Give me my wives and my children, for whom I have served you, and let me go: for you know my service which I have done you.

27 And Laban said to him, I pray you, if I have found favor in your eyes, tarry: for I have learned by experience that the LORD has blessed me for your sake.

28 And he said, Appoint me your wages, and I will give it.

29 And he said to him, You know how I have served you, and how your cattle was with me.

30 For it was little which you had before I came, and it is now increased to a multitude; and the LORD has blessed you since my coming: and now when shall I provide for mine own house also?

31 And he said, What shall I give you? And Jacob said, You shall not give me any thing: if you will do this thing for me, I will again feed and keep your flock.

32 I will pass through all your flock today, removing from thence all the speckled and spotted cattle, and all the brown cattle among the sheep, and the spotted and speckled among the goats: and of such shall be my hire.

33 So shall my righteousness answer for me in time to come, when it shall come for my hire before your face: every one that is not speckled and spotted among the goats, and brown among the sheep, that shall be counted stolen with me.

34 And Laban said, Behold, I would it might be according to your word.

35 And he removed that day the he goats that were ringstraked and spotted, and all the she goats that were speckled and spotted, and every one that had some white in it, and all the brown

among the sheep, and gave them into the hand of his sons.

36 And he set three days' journey between himself and Jacob: and Jacob fed the rest of Laban's flocks.

37 And Jacob took him rods of green poplar, and of the hazel and chesnut tree; and peeled white strakes in them, and made the white appear which was in the rods.

38 And he set the rods which he had peeled before the flocks in the gutters in the watering troughs when the flocks came to drink, that they should conceive when they came to drink.

39 And the flocks conceived before the rods, and brought forth cattle ringstraked, speckled, and spotted.

40 And Jacob did separate the lambs, and set the faces of the flocks toward the ringstraked, and all the brown in the flock of Laban; and he put his own flocks by themselves, and put them not to Laban's cattle.

41 And it came to pass, whensoever the stronger cattle did conceive, that Jacob laid the rods before the eyes of the cattle in the gutters, that they might conceive among the rods.

42 But when the cattle were feeble, he put them not in: so the feebler were Laban's, and the stronger Jacob's.

43 And the man increased exceedingly, and had much cattle, and maidservants, and menservants, and camels, and asses.

CHAPTER 31

A ND he heard the words of Laban's sons, saying, Jacob has taken away all that was our father's; and of that which was our father's has he gotten all this glory.

2 And Jacob beheld the countenance of Laban, and, behold, it was not toward him as before.

3 And the LORD said to Jacob, Return to the land of your fathers, and to your kindred; and I will be with you.

4 And Jacob sent and called Rachel and Leah to the field to his flock,

5 And said to them, I see your father's countenance, that it is not toward me as before; but the God of my father has been with me.

6 And you know that with all my power I have served your father.

7 And your father has deceived me, and changed my wages ten times; but God suffered him not to hurt me.

8 If he said thus, The speckled shall be your wages; then all the cattle bare speckled: and if he said thus, The ringstraked shall be your hire; then bare all the cattle ringstraked.

9 Thus God has taken away the cattle of your father, and given them to me.

10 And it came to pass at the time that the cattle conceived, that I lifted up mine eyes, and saw in a dream, and, behold, the rams which leaped upon the cattle were ringstraked, speckled, and grisled.

11 And the angel of God spoke to me in a dream, saying, Jacob: And I said, Here am I.

12 And he said, Lift up now your eyes, and see, all the rams which leap upon the cattle are ringstraked, speckled, and grisled: for I have seen all that Laban does to you.

13 I am the God of Bethel, where you anointed the pillar, and where you vowed a vow to me: now arise, get you out from this land, and return to the land of your kindred.

14 And Rachel and Leah answered and said to him, Is there yet any portion or inheritance for us in our father's house?

15 Are we not counted of him strangers? for he has sold us, and has quite devoured also our money.

16 For all the riches which God has taken from our father, that is ours, and our children's: now then, whatsoever God has said to you, do.

17 Then Jacob rose up, and set his sons and his wives upon camels;

18 And he carried away all his cattle, and all his goods which he had gotten, the cattle of his getting, which he had

gotten in Padanaram, for to go to Isaac his father in the land of Canaan.

19 And Laban went to shear his sheep: and Rachel had stolen the images that were her father's.

20 And Jacob stole away unawares to Laban the Syrian, in that he told him not that he fled.

21 So he fled with all that he had; and he rose up, and passed over the river, and set his face toward the mount Gilead.

22 And it was told Laban on the third day that Jacob was fled.

23 And he took his brethren with him, and pursued after him seven days' journey; and they overtook him in the mount Gilead.

24 And God came to Laban the Syrian in a dream by night, and said to him, Take heed that you speak not to Jacob either good or bad.

25 Then Laban overtook Jacob. Now Jacob had pitched his tent in the mount: and Laban with his brethren pitched in the mount of Gilead.

26 And Laban said to Jacob, What have you done, that you have stolen away unawares to me, and carried away my daughters, as captives taken with the sword?

27 Why did you flee away secretly, and steal away from me; and did not tell me, that I might have sent you away with mirth, and with songs, with tabret, and with harp?

28 And have not suffered me to kiss my sons and my daughters? you have now done foolishly in so doing.

29 It is in the power of my hand to do you hurt: but the God of your father spoke to me last night, saying, Take you heed that you speak not to Jacob either good or bad.

30 And now, though you would need to be gone, because you greatly longed after your father's house, yet why have you stolen my gods?

31 And Jacob answered and said to Laban, Because I was afraid: for I said, Peradventure you would take by force your daughters from me.

32 With whomsoever you find your gods, let him not live: before our brethren discern you what is yours with me, and take it to you. For Jacob knew not that Rachel had stolen them.

33 And Laban went into Jacob's tent, and into Leah's tent, and into the two maidservants' tents; but he found them not. Then went he out of Leah's tent, and entered into Rachel's tent.

34 Now Rachel had taken the images, and put them in the camel's furniture, and sat upon them. And Laban searched all the tent, but found them not.

35 And she said to her father, Let it not displease my lord that I cannot rise up before you; for the custom of women is upon me. And he searched but found not the images.

36 And Jacob was wroth, and chode with Laban: and Jacob answered and said to Laban, What is my trespass? what is my sin, that you have so hotly pursued after me?

37 Whereas you have searched all my stuff, what have you found of all your household stuff? set it here before my brethren and your brethren, that they may judge between us both.

38 This twenty years have I been with you; your ewes and your she goats have not cast their young, and the rams of your flock have I not eaten.

39 That which was torn of beasts I brought not to you; I bare the loss of it; of my hand did you require it, whether stolen by day, or stolen by night.

40 Thus I was; in the day the drought consumed me, and the frost by night; and my sleep departed from mine eyes.

41 Thus have I been twenty years in your house; I served you fourteen years for your two daughters, and six years for your cattle: and you have changed my wages ten times.

42 Except the God of my father, the God of Abraham, and the fear of Isaac, had been with me, surely you hadst sent

me away now empty. God has seen mine affliction and the labor of my hands, and rebuked you last night.

43 And Laban answered and said to Jacob, These daughters are my daughters, and these children are my children, and these cattle are my cattle, and all that you see is mine: and what can I do this day to these my daughters, or to their children which they have born?

44 Now therefore come thou, let us make a covenant, I and thou; and let it be for a witness between me and you.

45 And Jacob took a stone, and set it up for a pillar.

46 And Jacob said to his brethren, Gather stones; and they took stones, and made an heap: and they did eat there upon the heap.

47 And Laban called it Jegarsahadutha: but Jacob called it Galeed.

48 And Laban said, This heap is a witness between me and you this day. Therefore was the name of it called Galeed;

49 And Mizpah; for he said, The LORD watch between me and you, when we are absent one from another.

50 If you shall afflict my daughters, or if you shall take other wives beside my daughters, no man is with us; see, God is witness between me and you.

51 And Laban said to Jacob, Behold this heap, and behold this pillar, which I have cast between me and you:

52 This heap be witness, and this pillar be witness, that I will not pass over this heap to you, and that you shall not pass over this heap and this pillar to me, for harm.

53 The God of Abraham, and the God of Nahor, the God of their father, judge between us. And Jacob swore by the fear of his father Isaac.

54 Then Jacob offered sacrifice upon the mount, and called his brethren to eat bread: and they did eat bread, and tarried all night in the mount.

55 And early in the morning Laban rose up, and kissed his sons and his daughters, and blessed them: and Laban departed, and returned to his place.

CHAPTER 32

AND Jacob went on his way, and the angels of God met him.

2 And when Jacob saw them, he said, This is God's host: and he called the name of that place Mahanaim.

3 And Jacob sent messengers before him to Esau his brother to the land of Seir, the country of Edom.

4 And he commanded them, saying, Thus shall you speak to my lord Esau; Your servant Jacob says thus, I have sojourned with Laban, and stayed there until now:

5 And I have oxen, and asses, flocks, and menservants, and women servants: and I have sent to tell my lord, that I may find grace in your sight.

6 And the messengers returned to Jacob, saying, We came to your brother Esau, and also he cometh to meet you, and four hundred men with him.

7 Then Jacob was greatly afraid and distressed: and he divided the people that was with him, and the flocks, and herds, and the camels, into two bands;

8 And said, If Esau come to the one company, and smite it, then the other company which is left shall escape.

9 And Jacob said, O God of my father Abraham, and God of my father Isaac, the LORD which said to me, Return to your country, and to your kindred, and I will deal well with you:

10 I am not worthy of the least of all the mercies, and of all the truth, which you have showed to your servant; for with my staff I passed over this Jordan; and now I am become two bands.

11 Deliver me, I pray you, from the hand of my brother, from the hand of Esau: for I fear him, lest he will come and smite me, and the mother with the children.

12 And you said, I will surely do you good, and make your seed as the sand of

the sea, which cannot be numbered for multitude.

13 And he lodged there that same night; and took of that which came to his hand a present for Esau his brother;

14 Two hundred she goats, and twenty he goats, two hundred ewes, and twenty rams,

15 Thirty milch camels with their colts, forty kine, and ten bulls, twenty she asses, and ten foals.

16 And he delivered them into the hand of his servants, every drove by themselves; and said to his servants, Pass over before me, and put a space between drove and drove.

17 And he commanded the foremost, saying, When Esau my brother meets you, and ask you, saying, Whose are you? and where are you going? and whose are these before you?

18 Then you shall say, They be your servant Jacob's; it is a present sent to my lord Esau: and, behold, also he is behind us.

19 And so commanded he the second, and the third, and all that followed the droves, saying, On this manner shall you speak to Esau, when you find him.

20 And say moreover, Behold, your servant Jacob is behind us. For he said, I will appease him with the present that goes before me, and afterward I will see his face; peradventure he will accept of me.

21 So went the present over before him: and himself lodged that night in the company.

22 And he rose up that night, and took his two wives, and his two women servants, and his eleven sons, and passed over the ford Jabbok.

23 And he took them, and sent them over the brook, and sent over that he had.

24 And Jacob was left alone; and there wrestled a man with him until the breaking of the day.

25 And when he saw that he prevailed not against him, he touched the hollow of his thigh; and the hollow of Jacob's thigh was out of joint, as he wrestled with him.

26 And he said, Let me go, for the day breaks. And he said, I will not let you go, except you bless me.

27 And he said to him, What is your name? And he said, Jacob.

28 And he said, Your name shall be called no more Jacob, but Israel: for as a prince have you power with God and with men, and have prevailed.

29 And Jacob asked him, and said, Tell me, I pray you, your name. And he said, Why is it that you ask after my name? And he blessed him there.

30 And Jacob called the name of the place Peniel: for I have seen God face to face, and my life is preserved.

31 And as he passed over Peniel the sun rose upon him, and he halted upon his thigh.

32 Therefore the children of Israel eat not of the sinew which shrank, which is upon the hollow of the thigh, to this day: because he touched the hollow of Jacob's thigh in the sinew that shrank.

CHAPTER 33

AND Jacob lifted up his eyes, and looked, and, behold, Esau came, and with him four hundred men. And he divided the children to Leah, and to Rachel, and to the two handmaids.

2 And he put the handmaids and their children foremost, and Leah and her children after, and Rachel and Joseph hindermost.

3 And he passed over before them, and bowed himself to the ground seven times, until he came near to his brother.

4 And Esau ran to meet him, and embraced him, and fell on his neck, and kissed him: and they wept.

5 And he lifted up his eyes, and saw the women and the children; and said, Who are those with you? And he said, The children which God has graciously given your servant.

I t's been said that Jacob was as twisted as a cork screw, and it took an act of God to straighten him out.

Jacob, by an act of deceit, had robbed his older brother, Esau, of their father's blessing, a blessing that rightfully belonged to the oldest son.

It was Jacob's fear that his vengeful brother would kill him that drove Jacob to seek God's favor. Jacob was afraid he would reap the consequences of his wrong actions.

It is legitimate to come to the Savior in fear. We have greatly wronged the One who gave us life by violating His Law. His wrath abides upon us.

If we don't repent and trust in the Savior, we will reap the terrifying fruit of our actions–death and

JACOB WRESTLING WITH THE ANGEL

Genesis 32:24-29

everlasting Hell. What a fearful thing it is to fall into the hands of the living God! R.C. Sproul rightly said that Jesus doesn't save us to God, He saves us from God.

Those who have had a face-to-face encounter with God will, like Jacob, ever after walk with a limp. Whereas we once walked with a high look and proud heart, we now bow in quiet humility and walk in lowliness of mind. And like Jacob, who had a new name, Israel, as a result of his encounter, when we meet the Lord, we, too, become new creatures (2 Corinthians 5:17). We are born again, with a new heart and with new desires.

And just as Jacob wrestled alone with God, each of us must make our own peace with God. Nobody else can do it for us. Notice that Jacob said that he wouldn't let God go until He blessed him. God honors importunity. Whatever you do, seek God's blessing until you know that you have peace with Him. Call upon the Name of the Lord. Be as the blind man Bartimaeus, who in desperation called to Jesus, despite the censure of those around him (Mark 10:46). Don't give up until you have made your own calling and election sure.

The New Testament has many examples of importunity, including the woman who pushed through the crowds just to touch the hem of the garment of the Savior. It was her desperate need that drove her to the feet of Jesus, and God honored her importunity (Mark 5:25-34)..

After you have had your encounter with God, don't let it stop there. Be earnest always to keep His smile on your life. Revelation of the Cross will make sure you do that. Jacob asked God for His Name and then rejoiced that his life had been preserved.

Once you have seen the Cross and come to know Him who suffered for you, you will never forget the name of Jesus. You will rejoice with joy unspeakable and never forget the One whose blood preserved you for His everlasting Kingdom.

6 Then the handmaidens came near, they and their children, and they bowed themselves.

7 And Leah also with her children came near, and bowed themselves: and after came Joseph near and Rachel, and they bowed themselves.

8 And he said, What meanest you by all this drove which I met? And he said, These are to find grace in the sight of my lord.

9 And Esau said, I have enough, my brother; keep that you have to thyself.

10 And Jacob said, Nay, I pray you, if now I have found grace in your sight, then receive my present at my hand: for therefore I have seen your face, as though I had seen the face of God, and you were pleased with me.

11 Take, I pray you, my blessing that is brought to you; because God has dealt graciously with me, and because I have enough. And he urged him, and he took it.

12 And he said, Let us take our journey, and let us go, and I will go before you.

13 And he said to him, My lord knows that the children are tender, and the flocks and herds with young are with me: and if men should overdrive them one day, all the flock will die.

14 Let my lord, I pray you, pass over before his servant: and I will lead on softly, according as the cattle that goes before me and the children be able to endure, until I come to my lord to Seir.

15 And Esau said, Let me now leave with you some of the folk that are with me. And he said, What need is there? let me find grace in the sight of my lord.

16 So Esau returned that day on his way to Seir.

17 And Jacob journeyed to Succoth, and built him an house, and made booths for his cattle: therefore the name of the place is called Succoth.

18 And Jacob came to Shalem, a city of Shechem, which is in the land of Canaan, when he came from Padanaram; and pitched his tent before the city.

19 And he bought a parcel of a field, where he had spread his tent, at the hand of the children of Hamor, Shechem's father, for an hundred pieces of money.

20 And he erected there an altar, and called it El-Elohe-Israel.

CHAPTER 34

AND Dinah the daughter of Leah, which she bare to Jacob, went out to see the daughters of the land.

2 And when Shechem the son of Hamor the Hivite, prince of the country, saw her, he took her, and lay with her, and defiled her.

3 And his soul clave to Dinah the daughter of Jacob, and he loved the damsel, and spoke kindly to the damsel.

4 And Shechem spoke to his father Hamor, saying, Get me this damsel to wife.

5 And Jacob heard that he had defiled Dinah his daughter: now his sons were with his cattle in the field: and Jacob held his peace until they were come.

6 And Hamor the father of Shechem went out to Jacob to commune with him.

7 And the sons of Jacob came out of the field when they heard it: and the men were grieved, and they were very wroth, because he had wrought folly in Israel in lying with Jacob's daughter: which thing ought not to be done.

8 And Hamor communed with them, saying, The soul of my son Shechem longeth for your daughter: I pray you give her him to wife.

9 And make marriages with us, and give your daughters to us, and take our daughters to you.

10 And you shall dwell with us: and the land shall be before you; dwell and trade therein, and get possessions therein.

11 And Shechem said to her father and to her brethren, Let me find grace in

your eyes, and what you shall say to me I will give.

12 Ask me never so much dowry and gift, and I will give according as you shall say to me: but give me the damsel to wife.

13 And the sons of Jacob answered Shechem and Hamor his father deceitfully, and said, because he had defiled Dinah their sister:

14 And they said to them, We cannot do this thing, to give our sister to one that is uncircumcised; for that would be a reproach to us:

15 But in this will we consent to you: If you will be as we be, that every male of you be circumcised;

16 Then will we give our daughters to you, and we will take your daughters to us, and we will dwell with you, and we will become one people.

17 But if you will not hearken to us, to be circumcised; then will we take our daughter, and we will be gone.

18 And their words pleased Hamor, and Shechem Hamor's son.

19 And the young man deferred not to do the thing, because he had delight in Jacob's daughter: and he was more honorable than all the house of his father.

20 And Hamor and Shechem his son came to the gate of their city, and communed with the men of their city, saying,

21 These men are peaceable with us; therefore let them dwell in the land, and trade therein; for the land, behold, it is large enough for them; let us take their daughters to us for wives, and let us give them our daughters.

22 Only herein will the men consent to us for to dwell with us, to be one people, if every male among us be circumcised, as they are circumcised.

23 Shall not their cattle and their substance and every beast of theirs be ours? only let us consent to them, and they will dwell with us.

24 And to Hamor and to Shechem his son hearkened all that went out of the gate of his city; and every male was circumcised, all that went out of the gate of his city.

25 And it came to pass on the third day, when they were sore, that two of the sons of Jacob, Simeon and Levi, Dinah's brethren, took each man his sword, and came upon the city boldly, and slew all the males.

26 And they slew Hamor and Shechem his son with the edge of the sword, and took Dinah out of Shechem's house, and went out.

27 The sons of Jacob came upon the slain, and spoiled the city, because they had defiled their sister.

28 They took their sheep, and their oxen, and their asses, and that which was in the city, and that which was in the field,

29 And all their wealth, and all their little ones, and their wives took they captive, and spoiled even all that was in the house.

30 And Jacob said to Simeon and Levi, You have troubled me to make me to stink among the inhabitants of the land, among the Canaanites and the Perizzites: and I being few in number, they shall gather themselves together against me, and slay me; and I shall be destroyed, I and my house.

31 And they said, Should he deal with our sister as with an harlot?

CHAPTER 35

AND God said to Jacob, Arise, go up to Bethel, and dwell there: and make there an altar to God, that appeared to you when you fled from the face of Esau your brother.

2 Then Jacob said to his household, and to all that were with him, Put away the strange gods that are among you, and be clean, and change your garments:

3 And let us arise, and go up to Bethel; and I will make there an altar to God, who answered me in the day of my distress, and was with me in the way which I went.

4 And they gave to Jacob all the strange gods which were in their hand, and all their earrings which were in their ears; and Jacob hid them under the oak which was by Shechem.

5 And they journeyed: and the terror of God was upon the cities that were round about them, and they did not pursue after the sons of Jacob.

6 So Jacob came to Luz, which is in the land of Canaan, that is, Bethel, he and all the people that were with him.

7 And he built there an altar, and called the place Elbethel: because there God appeared to him, when he fled from the face of his brother.

8 But Deborah Rebekah's nurse died, and she was buried beneath Bethel under an oak: and the name of it was called Allonbachuth.

9 And God appeared to Jacob again, when he came out of Padanaram, and blessed him.

10 And God said to him, Your name is Jacob: your name shall not be called any more Jacob, but Israel shall be your name: and he called his name Israel.

11 And God said to him, I am God Almighty: be fruitful and multiply; a nation and a company of nations shall be of you, and kings shall come out of your loins;

12 And the land which I gave Abraham and Isaac, to you I will give it, and to your seed after you will I give the land.

13 And God went up from him in the place where he talked with him.

14 And Jacob set up a pillar in the place where he talked with him, even a pillar of stone: and he poured a drink offering thereon, and he poured oil thereon.

15 And Jacob called the name of the place where God spoke with him, Bethel.

16 And they journeyed from Bethel; and there was but a little way to come to Ephrath: and Rachel travailed, and she had hard labor.

17 And it came to pass, when she was in hard labor, that the midwife said to her, Fear not; you shall have this son also.

18 And it came to pass, as her soul was in departing, (for she died) that she called his name Benoni: but his father called him Benjamin.

19 And Rachel died, and was buried in the way to Ephrath, which is Bethlehem.

20 And Jacob set a pillar upon her grave: that is the pillar of Rachel's grave to this day.

21 And Israel journeyed, and spread his tent beyond the tower of Edar.

22 And it came to pass, when Israel dwelt in that land, that Reuben went and lay with Bilhah his father's concubine: and Israel heard it. Now the sons of Jacob were twelve:

23 The sons of Leah; Reuben, Jacob's firstborn, and Simeon, and Levi, and Judah, and Issachar, and Zebulun:

24 The sons of Rachel; Joseph, and Benjamin:

25 And the sons of Bilhah, Rachel's handmaid; Dan, and Naphtali:

26 And the sons of Zilpah, Leah's handmaid: Gad, and Asher: these are the sons of Jacob, which were born to him in Padanaram.

27 And Jacob came to Isaac his father to Mamre, to the city of Arbah, which is Hebron, where Abraham and Isaac sojourned.

28 And the days of Isaac were an hundred and fourscore years.

29 And Isaac gave up the ghost, and died, and was gathered to his people, being old and full of days: and his sons Esau and Jacob buried him.

CHAPTER 36

NOW these are the generations of Esau, who is Edom.

2 Esau took his wives of the daughters of Canaan; Adah the daughter of Elon the Hittite, and Aholibamah the daughter of Anah the daughter of Zibeon the Hivite;

3 And Bashemath Ishmael's daughter, sister of Nebajoth.

4 And Adah bare to Esau Eliphaz; and Bashemath bare Reuel;

5 And Aholibamah bare Jeush, and Jaalam, and Korah: these are the sons of Esau, which were born to him in the land of Canaan.

6 And Esau took his wives, and his sons, and his daughters, and all the persons of his house, and his cattle, and all his beasts, and all his substance, which he had got in the land of Canaan; and went into the country from the face of his brother Jacob.

7 For their riches were more than that they might dwell together; and the land wherein they were strangers could not bear them because of their cattle.

8 Thus dwelt Esau in mount Seir: Esau is Edom.

9 And these are the generations of Esau the father of the Edomites in mount Seir:

10 These are the names of Esau's sons; Eliphaz the son of Adah the wife of Esau, Reuel the son of Bashemath the wife of Esau.

11 And the sons of Eliphaz were Teman, Omar, Zepho, and Gatam, and Kenaz.

12 And Timna was concubine to Eliphaz Esau's son; and she bare to Eliphaz Amalek: these were the sons of Adah Esau's wife.

13 And these are the sons of Reuel; Nahath, and Zerah, Shammah, and Mizzah: these were the sons of Bashemath Esau's wife.

14 And these were the sons of Aholibamah, the daughter of Anah the daughter of Zibeon, Esau's wife: and she bare to Esau Jeush, and Jaalam, and Korah.

15 These were dukes of the sons of Esau: the sons of Eliphaz the firstborn son of Esau; duke Teman, duke Omar, duke Zepho, duke Kenaz,

16 Duke Korah, duke Gatam, and duke Amalek: these are the dukes that came of Eliphaz in the land of Edom; these were the sons of Adah.

17 And these are the sons of Reuel Esau's son; duke Nahath, duke Zerah, duke Shammah, duke Mizzah: these are the dukes that came of Reuel in the land of Edom; these are the sons of Bashemath Esau's wife.

18 And these are the sons of Aholibamah Esau's wife; duke Jeush, duke Jaalam, duke Korah: these were the dukes that came of Aholibamah the daughter of Anah, Esau's wife.

19 These are the sons of Esau, who is Edom, and these are their dukes.

20 These are the sons of Seir the Horite, who inhabited the land; Lotan, and Shobal, and Zibeon, and Anah,

21 And Dishon, and Ezer, and Dishan: these are the dukes of the Horites, the children of Seir in the land of Edom.

22 And the children of Lotan were Hori and Hemam; and Lotan's sister was Timna.

23 And the children of Shobal were these; Alvan, and Manahath, and Ebal, Shepho, and Onam.

24 And these are the children of Zibeon; both Ajah, and Anah: this was that Anah that found the mules in the wilderness, as he fed the asses of Zibeon his father.

25 And the children of Anah were these; Dishon, and Aholibamah the daughter of Anah.

26 And these are the children of Dishon; Hemdan, and Eshban, and Ithran, and Cheran.

27 The children of Ezer are these; Bilhan, and Zaavan, and Akan.

28 The children of Dishan are these; Uz, and Aran.

29 These are the dukes that came of the Horites; duke Lotan, duke Shobal, duke Zibeon, duke Anah,

30 Duke Dishon, duke Ezer, duke Dishan: these are the dukes that came of Hori, among their dukes in the land of Seir.

31 And these are the kings that reigned in the land of Edom, before there

reigned any king over the children of Israel.

32 And Bela the son of Beor reigned in Edom: and the name of his city was Dinhabah.

33 And Bela died, and Jobab the son of Zerah of Bozrah reigned in his stead.

34 And Jobab died, and Husham of the land of Temani reigned in his stead.

35 And Husham died, and Hadad the son of Bedad, who smote Midian in the field of Moab, reigned in his stead: and the name of his city was Avith.

36 And Hadad died, and Samlah of Masrekah reigned in his stead.

37 And Samlah died, and Saul of Rehoboth by the river reigned in his stead.

38 And Saul died, and Baalhanan the son of Achbor reigned in his stead.

39 And Baalhanan the son of Achbor died, and Hadar reigned in his stead: and the name of his city was Pau; and his wife's name was Mehetabel, the daughter of Matred, the daughter of Mezahab.

40 And these are the names of the dukes that came of Esau, according to their families, after their places, by their names; duke Timnah, duke Alvah, duke Jetheth,

41 Duke Aholibamah, duke Elah, duke Pinon,

42 Duke Kenaz, duke Teman, duke Mibzar,

43 Duke Magdiel, duke Iram: these be the dukes of Edom, according to their habitations in the land of their possession: he is Esau the father of the Edomites.

CHAPTER 37

AND Jacob dwelt in the land wherein his father was a stranger, in the land of Canaan.

2 These are the generations of Jacob. Joseph, being seventeen years old, was feeding the flock with his brethren; and the lad was with the sons of Bilhah, and with the sons of Zilpah, his father's wives: and Joseph brought to his father their evil report.

3 Now Israel loved Joseph more than all his children, because he was the son of his old age: and he made him a coat of many colors.

4 And when his brethren saw that their father loved him more than all his brethren, they hated him, and could not speak peaceably to him.

5 And Joseph dreamed a dream, and he told it his brethren: and they hated him yet the more.

6 And he said to them, Hear, I pray you, this dream which I have dreamed:

7 For, behold, we were binding sheaves in the field, and, lo, my sheaf arose, and also stood upright; and, behold, your sheaves stood round about, and made obeisance to my sheaf.

8 And his brethren said to him, Shall you indeed reign over us? or shall you indeed have dominion over us? And they hated him yet the more for his dreams, and for his words.

9 And he dreamed yet another dream, and told it his brethren, and said, Behold, I have dreamed a dream more; and, behold, the sun and the moon and the eleven stars made obeisance to me.

10 And he told it to his father, and to his brethren: and his father rebuked him, and said to him, What is this dream that you have dreamed? Shall I and your mother and your brethren indeed come to bow down ourselves to you to the earth?

11 And his brethren envied him; but his father observed the saying.

12 And his brethren went to feed their father's flock in Shechem.

13 And Israel said to Joseph, Do not your brethren feed the flock in Shechem? come, and I will send you to them. And he said to him, Here am I.

14 And he said to him, Go, I pray you, see whether it be well with your brethren, and well with the flocks; and bring me word again. So he sent him out

JOSEPH SOLD BY HIS BRETHREN

Genesis 37:1-28

T he history of Joseph, who saved his family and all of Egypt from death due
to starvation, foreshadows the Messiah to come, who has the power to save
us, whether Jew or Gentile, from eternal damnation.

Joseph was greatly favored by his father, Israel (v. 37:3). Israel sent Joseph into
the fields to find his brothers (v. 37:13-14). Joseph sought his brothers and found
them (v. 37:15-17). But when Joseph's brothers saw him coming, they conspired to
kill him (v. 37:18-20). And they stripped his coat off of him (v. 37:23) and eventually sold him into slavery for 20 pieces of silver (v. 37:28).

Jesus, too, was favored by His Heavenly Father (see Matthew 3:17 and Mark
1:11), who sent Jesus into the world in search of us, His brothers and sisters (see
Romans 8:17, Galatians 4:7 and Matthew 12:50 and 25:40).

But when Jesus "came unto his own . . . His own received him not (John 1:11)."
Those of the same blood line as Jesus (see Matthew 1:1-17) demanded that Jesus be
crucified (see John 19:6, 15). Jesus was eventually stripped and beaten (Matthew
27: 26, 28). And through an exchange of silver, Jesus was betrayed by his own disciple (Matthew 26:15 and 27:9).

of the vale of Hebron, and he came to Shechem.

15 And a certain man found him, and, behold, he was wandering in the field: and the man asked him, saying, What do you seek?

16 And he said, I seek my brethren: tell me, I pray you, where they feed their flocks.

17 And the man said, They are departed hence; for I heard them say, Let us go to Dothan. And Joseph went after his brethren, and found them in Dothan.

18 And when they saw him afar off, even before he came near to them, they conspired against him to slay him.

19 And they said one to another, Behold, this dreamer cometh.

20 Come now therefore, and let us slay him, and cast him into some pit, and we will say, Some evil beast has devoured him: and we shall see what will become of his dreams.

21 And Reuben heard it, and he delivered him out of their hands; and said, Let us not kill him.

22 And Reuben said to them, Shed no blood, but cast him into this pit that is in the wilderness, and lay no hand upon him; that he might rid him out of their hands, to deliver him to his father again.

23 And it came to pass, when Joseph was come to his brethren, that they stripped Joseph out of his coat, his coat of many colors that was on him;

24 And they took him, and cast him into a pit: and the pit was empty, there was no water in it.

25 And they sat down to eat bread: and they lifted up their eyes and looked, and, behold, a company of Ishmeelites came from Gilead with their camels bearing spicery and balm and myrrh, going to carry it down to Egypt.

26 And Judah said to his brethren, What profit is it if we slay our brother, and conceal his blood?

27 Come, and let us sell him to the Ishmeelites, and let not our hand be upon him; for he is our brother and our flesh. And his brethren were content.

28 Then there passed by Midianites merchantmen; and they drew and lifted up Joseph out of the pit, and sold Joseph to the Ishmeelites for twenty pieces of silver: and they brought Joseph into Egypt.

29 And Reuben returned to the pit; and, behold, Joseph was not in the pit; and he rent his clothes.

30 And he returned to his brethren, and said, The child is not; and I, where shall I go?

31 And they took Joseph's coat, and killed a kid of the goats, and dipped the coat in the blood;

32 And they sent the coat of many colors, and they brought it to their father; and said, This have we found: know now whether it be your son's coat or no.

33 And he knew it, and said, It is my son's coat; an evil beast has devoured him; Joseph is without doubt rent in pieces.

34 And Jacob rent his clothes, and put sackcloth upon his loins, and mourned for his son many days.

35 And all his sons and all his daughters rose up to comfort him; but he refused to be comforted; and he said, For I will go down into the grave to my son mourning. Thus his father wept for him.

36 And the Midianites sold him into Egypt to Potiphar, an officer of Pharaoh's, and captain of the guard.

CHAPTER 38

AND it came to pass at that time, that Judah went down from his brethren, and turned in to a certain Adullamite, whose name was Hirah.

2 And Judah saw there a daughter of a certain Canaanite, whose name was Shuah; and he took her, and went in to her.

3 And she conceived, and bare a son; and he called his name Er.

4 And she conceived again, and bare a son; and she called his name Onan.

5 And she yet again conceived, and bare a son; and called his name Shelah: and he was at Chezib, when she bare him.

6 And Judah took a wife for Er his firstborn, whose name was Tamar.

7 And Er, Judah's firstborn, was wicked in the sight of the LORD; and the LORD slew him.

8 And Judah said to Onan, Go in to your brother's wife, and marry her, and raise up seed to your brother.

9 And Onan knew that the seed should not be his; and it came to pass, when he went in to his brother's wife, that he spilled it on the ground, lest that he should give seed to his brother.

10 And the thing which he did displeased the LORD: therefore he slew him also.

11 Then said Judah to Tamar his daughter in law, Remain a widow at your father's house, till Shelah my son be grown: for he said, Lest peradventure he die also, as his brethren did. And Tamar went and dwelt in her father's house.

12 And in process of time the daughter of Shuah Judah's wife died; and Judah was comforted, and went up to his sheepshearers to Timnath, he and his friend Hirah the Adullamite.

13 And it was told Tamar, saying, Behold your father in law goes up to Timnath to shear his sheep.

14 And she put her widow's garments off from her, and covered her with a vail, and wrapped herself, and sat in an open place, which is by the way to Timnath; for she saw that Shelah was grown, and she was not given to him to wife.

15 When Judah saw her, he thought her to be an harlot; because she had covered her face.

16 And he turned to her by the way, and said, Go to, I pray you, let me come in to you; (for he knew not that she was his daughter in law.) And she said, What will you give me, that you may come in to me?

17 And he said, I will send you a kid from the flock. And she said, Will you give me a pledge, till you send it?

18 And he said, What pledge shall I give you? And she said, Your signet, and your bracelets, and your staff that is in your hand. And he gave it her, and came in to her, and she conceived by him.

19 And she arose, and went away, and laid by her veil from her, and put on the garments of her widowhood.

20 And Judah sent the kid by the hand of his friend the Adullamite, to receive his pledge from the woman's hand: but he found her not.

21 Then he asked the men of that place, saying, Where is the harlot, that was openly by the way side? And they said, There was no harlot in this place.

22 And he returned to Judah, and said, I cannot find her; and also the men of the place said, that there was no harlot in this place.

23 And Judah said, Let her take it to her, lest we be shamed: behold, I sent this kid, and you have not found her.

24 And it came to pass about three months after, that it was told Judah, saying, Tamar your daughter in law has played the harlot; and also, behold, she is with child by whoredom. And Judah said, Bring her forth, and let her be burnt.

25 When she was brought forth, she sent to her father in law, saying, By the man, whose these are, am I with child: and she said, Discern, I pray you, whose are these, the signet, and bracelets, and staff.

26 And Judah acknowledged them, and said, She has been more righteous than I; because that I gave her not to Shelah my son. And he knew her again no more.

27 And it came to pass in the time of her travail, that, behold, twins were in her womb.

28 And it came to pass, when she travailed, that the one put out his hand: and the midwife took and bound upon

his hand a scarlet thread, saying, This came out first.

29 And it came to pass, as he drew back his hand, that, behold, his brother came out: and she said, How have you broken forth? this breach be upon you: therefore his name was called Pharez.

30 And afterward came out his brother, that had the scarlet thread upon his hand: and his name was called Zarah.

CHAPTER 39

AND Joseph was brought down to Egypt; and Potiphar, an officer of Pharaoh, captain of the guard, an Egyptian, bought him of the hands of the Ishmeelites, which had brought him down thither.

2 And the LORD was with Joseph, and he was a prosperous man; and he was in the house of his master the Egyptian.

3 And his master saw that the LORD was with him, and that the LORD made all that he did to prosper in his hand.

4 And Joseph found grace in his sight, and he served him: and he made him overseer over his house, and all that he had he put into his hand.

5 And it came to pass from the time that he had made him overseer in his house, and over all that he had, that the LORD blessed the Egyptian's house for Joseph's sake; and the blessing of the LORD was upon all that he had in the house, and in the field.

6 And he left all that he had in Joseph's hand; and he knew not ought he had, save the bread which he did eat. And Joseph was a goodly person, and well favoured.

7 And it came to pass after these things, that his master's wife cast her eyes upon Joseph; and she said, Lie with me.

8 But he refused, and said to his master's wife, Behold, my master does not know what is with me in the house, and he has committed all that he has to my hand;

9 There is none greater in this house than I; neither has he kept back any

thing from me but you, because you are his wife: how then can I do this great wickedness, and sin against God?

10 And it came to pass, as she spoke to Joseph day by day, that he hearkened not to her, to lie by her, or to be with her.

11 And it came to pass about this time, that Joseph went into the house to do his business; and there was none of the men of the house there within.

12 And she caught him by his garment, saying, Lie with me: and he left his garment in her hand, and fled, and got him out.

13 And it came to pass, when she saw that he had left his garment in her hand, and was fled forth,

14 That she called to the men of her house, and spoke to them, saying, See, he has brought in an Hebrew to us to mock us; he came in to me to lie with me, and I cried with a loud voice:

15 And it came to pass, when he heard that I lifted up my voice and cried, that he left his garment with me, and fled, and got him out.

16 And she laid up his garment by her, until his lord came home.

17 And she spoke to him according to these words, saying, The Hebrew servant, which you have brought to us, came in to me to mock me:

18 And it came to pass, as I lifted up my voice and cried, that he left his garment with me, and fled out.

19 And it came to pass, when his master heard the words of his wife, which she spoke to him, saying, After this manner did your servant to me; that his wrath was kindled.

20 And Joseph's master took him, and put him into the prison, a place where the king's prisoners were bound: and he was there in the prison.

21 But the LORD was with Joseph, and showed him mercy, and gave him favor in the sight of the keeper of the prison.

22 And the keeper of the prison committed to Joseph's hand all the prisoners

that were in the prison; and whatsoever they did there, he was the doer of it.

23 The keeper of the prison looked not to any thing that was under his hand; because the LORD was with him, and that which he did, the LORD made it to prosper.

CHAPTER 40

AND it came to pass after these things, that the butler of the king of Egypt and his baker had offended their lord the king of Egypt.

2 And Pharaoh was wroth against two of his officers, against the chief of the butlers, and against the chief of the bakers.

3 And he put them in ward in the house of the captain of the guard, into the prison, the place where Joseph was bound.

4 And the captain of the guard charged Joseph with them, and he served them: and they continued a season in ward.

5 And they dreamed a dream both of them, each man his dream in one night, each man according to the interpretation of his dream, the butler and the baker of the king of Egypt, which were bound in the prison.

6 And Joseph came in to them in the morning, and looked upon them, and, behold, they were sad.

7 And he asked Pharaoh's officers that were with him in the ward of his lord's house, saying, Why do you look so sadly to day?

8 And they said to him, We have dreamed a dream, and there is no interpreter of it. And Joseph said to them, Do not interpretations belong to God? tell me them, I pray you.

9 And the chief butler told his dream to Joseph, and said to him, In my dream, behold, a vine was before me;

10 And in the vine were three branches: and it was as though it budded, and her blossoms shot forth; and the clusters thereof brought forth ripe grapes:

11 And Pharaoh's cup was in my hand: and I took the grapes, and pressed them into Pharaoh's cup, and I gave the cup into Pharaoh's hand.

12 And Joseph said to him, This is the interpretation of it: The three branches are three days:

13 Yet within three days shall Pharaoh lift up your head, and restore you to your place: and you shall deliver Pharaoh's cup into his hand, after the former manner when you were his butler.

14 But think on me when it shall be well with you, and show kindness, I pray you, to me, and make mention of me to Pharaoh, and bring me out of this house:

15 For indeed I was stolen away out of the land of the Hebrews: and here also have I done nothing that they should put me into the dungeon.

16 When the chief baker saw that the interpretation was good, he said to Joseph, I also was in my dream, and, behold, I had three white baskets on my head:

17 And in the uppermost basket there was of all manner of bakemeats for Pharaoh; and the birds did eat them out of the basket upon my head.

18 And Joseph answered and said, This is the interpretation thereof: The three baskets are three days:

19 Yet within three days shall Pharaoh lift up your head from off you, and shall hang you on a tree; and the birds shall eat your flesh from off you.

20 And it came to pass the third day, which was Pharaoh's birthday, that he made a feast to all his servants: and he lifted up the head of the chief butler and of the chief baker among his servants.

21 And he restored the chief butler to his butlership again; and he gave the cup into Pharaoh's hand:

22 But he hanged the chief baker: as Joseph had interpreted to them.

23 Yet did not the chief butler remember Joseph, but forgot him.

CHAPTER 41

AND it came to pass at the end of two full years, that Pharaoh dreamed: and, behold, he stood by the river.

2 And, behold, there came up out of the river seven well favored kine and fatfleshed; and they fed in a meadow.

3 And, behold, seven other kine came up after them out of the river, ill favored and leanfleshed; and stood by the other kine upon the brink of the river.

4 And the ill favored and leanfleshed kine did eat up the seven well favored and fat kine. So Pharaoh awoke.

5 And he slept and dreamed the second time: and, behold, seven ears of corn came up upon one stalk, rank and good.

6 And, behold, seven thin ears and blasted with the east wind sprung up after them.

7 And the seven thin ears devoured the seven rank and full ears. And Pharaoh awoke, and, behold, it was a dream.

8 And it came to pass in the morning that his spirit was troubled; and he sent and called for all the magicians of Egypt, and all the wise men thereof: and Pharaoh told them his dream; but there was none that could interpret them to Pharaoh.

9 Then spoke the chief butler to Pharaoh, saying, I do remember my faults this day:

10 Pharaoh was wroth with his servants, and put me in ward in the captain of the guard's house, both me and the chief baker:

11 And we dreamed a dream in one night, I and he; we dreamed each man according to the interpretation of his dream.

12 And there was there with us a young man, an Hebrew, servant to the captain of the guard; and we told him, and he interpreted to us our dreams; to each man according to his dream he did interpret.

13 And it came to pass, as he interpreted to us, so it was; me he restored to mine office, and him he hanged.

14 Then Pharaoh sent and called Joseph, and they brought him hastily out of the dungeon: and he shaved himself, and changed his raiment, and came in to Pharaoh.

15 And Pharaoh said to Joseph, I have dreamed a dream, and there is none that can interpret it: and I have heard say of you, that you can understand a dream to interpret it.

16 And Joseph answered Pharaoh, saying, It is not in me: God shall give Pharaoh an answer of peace.

17 And Pharaoh said to Joseph, In my dream, behold, I stood upon the bank of the river:

18 And, behold, there came up out of the river seven kine, fatfleshed and well favored; and they fed in a meadow:

19 And, behold, seven other kine came up after them, poor and very ill favored and leanfleshed, such as I never saw in all the land of Egypt for badness:

20 And the lean and the ill favored kine did eat up the first seven fat kine:

21 And when they had eaten them up, it could not be known that they had eaten them; but they were still ill favored, as at the beginning. So I awoke.

22 And I saw in my dream, and, behold, seven ears came up in one stalk, full and good:

23 And, behold, seven ears, withered, thin, and blasted with the east wind, sprung up after them:

24 And the thin ears devoured the seven good ears: and I told this to the magicians; but there was none that could declare it to me.

25 And Joseph said to Pharaoh, The dream of Pharaoh is one: God has showed Pharaoh what he is about to do.

26 The seven good kine are seven years; and the seven good ears are seven years: the dream is one.

27 And the seven thin and ill favored kine that came up after them are seven

JOSEPH INTERPRETING PHARAOH'S DREAM

Genesis 41:25

After a long imprisonment for a crime he did not commit, Joseph was called to serve Pharaoh. Pleased with Joseph's service, Pharaoh exalted Joseph to a high position of authority. When Joseph's brothers later came to him for help, Joseph forgave them their betrayal of him and saved their lives by providing the food they needed.

In these details, Joseph's history continues to foreshadow the Savior to come, who was crucified as a sacrifice for sins he did not commit, went to hell on account of those sins, and was then raised from death and exalted by God the Father to the highest position of authority.

Compare the account of Pharaoh's exalting Joseph in Genesis 41: 40-44 with descriptions of Jesus in Ephesians 1:19-22 and Matthew 28:18. And compare the risen Christ in John 17:2, " Even as You gave Him authority over all flesh, that to all whom You have given Him, He may give eternal life . . ." with Joseph's statement to his brothers in Genesis 45:7, "And God sent me before you . . . to save your lives by a great deliverance."

years; and the seven empty ears blasted with the east wind shall be seven years of famine.

28 This is the thing which I have spoken to Pharaoh: What God is about to do he shows to Pharaoh.

29 Behold, there come seven years of great plenty throughout all the land of Egypt:

30 And there shall arise after them seven years of famine; and all the plenty shall be forgotten in the land of Egypt; and the famine shall consume the land;

31 And the plenty shall not be known in the land by reason of that famine following; for it shall be very grievous.

32 And for that the dream was doubled to Pharaoh twice; it is because the thing is established by God, and God will shortly bring it to pass.

33 Now therefore let Pharaoh look out a man discreet and wise, and set him over the land of Egypt.

34 Let Pharaoh do this, and let him appoint officers over the land, and take up the fifth part of the land of Egypt in the seven plenteous years.

35 And let them gather all the food of those good years that come, and lay up corn under the hand of Pharaoh, and let them keep food in the cities.

36 And that food shall be for store to the land against the seven years of famine, which shall be in the land of Egypt; that the land perish not through the famine.

37 And the thing was good in the eyes of Pharaoh, and in the eyes of all his servants.

38 And Pharaoh said to his servants, Can we find such a one as this is, a man in whom the Spirit of God is?

39 And Pharaoh said to Joseph, Forasmuch as God has showed you all this, there is none so discreet and wise as you art:

40 You shall be over my house, and according to your word shall all my people be ruled: only in the throne will I be greater than thou.

41 And Pharaoh said to Joseph, See, I have set you over all the land of Egypt.

42 And Pharaoh took off his ring from his hand, and put it upon Joseph's hand, and arrayed him in vestures of fine linen, and put a gold chain about his neck;

43 And he made him to ride in the second chariot which he had; and they cried before him, Bow the knee: and he made him ruler over all the land of Egypt.

44 And Pharaoh said to Joseph, I am Pharaoh, and without you shall no man lift up his hand or foot in all the land of Egypt.

45 And Pharaoh called Joseph's name Zaphnathpaaneah; and he gave him to wife Asenath the daughter of Potipherah priest of On. And Joseph went out over all the land of Egypt.

46 And Joseph was thirty years old when he stood before Pharaoh king of Egypt. And Joseph went out from the presence of Pharaoh, and went throughout all the land of Egypt.

47 And in the seven plenteous years the earth brought forth by handfuls.

48 And he gathered up all the food of the seven years, which were in the land of Egypt, and laid up the food in the cities: the food of the field, which was round about every city, laid he up in the same.

49 And Joseph gathered corn as the sand of the sea, very much, until he left numbering; for it was without number.

50 And to Joseph were born two sons before the years of famine came, which Asenath the daughter of Potipherah priest of On bare to him.

51 And Joseph called the name of the firstborn Manasseh: For God, said he, has made me forget all my toil, and all my father's house.

52 And the name of the second called he Ephraim: For God has caused me to be fruitful in the land of my affliction.

53 And the seven years of plenteousness, that was in the land of Egypt, were ended.

54 And the seven years of dearth began to come, according as Joseph had said: and the dearth was in all lands; but in all the land of Egypt there was bread.

55 And when all the land of Egypt was famished, the people cried to Pharaoh for bread: and Pharaoh said to all the Egyptians, Go to Joseph; whatever he says to you, do.

56 And the famine was over all the face of the earth: and Joseph opened all the storehouses, and sold to the Egyptians; and the famine waxed sore in the land of Egypt.

57 And all countries came into Egypt to Joseph for to buy corn; because that the famine was so sore in all lands.

CHAPTER 42

NOW when Jacob saw that there was corn in Egypt, Jacob said to his sons, Why do you look one upon another?

2 And he said, Behold, I have heard that there is corn in Egypt: get down there, and buy for us from there; that we may live, and not die.

3 And Joseph's ten brethren went down to buy corn in Egypt.

4 But Benjamin, Joseph's brother, Jacob sent not with his brethren; for he said, Lest peradventure mischief befall him.

5 And the sons of Israel came to buy corn among those that came: for the famine was in the land of Canaan.

6 And Joseph was the governor over the land, and he it was that sold to all the people of the land: and Joseph's brethren came, and bowed down themselves before him with their faces to the earth.

7 And Joseph saw his brethren, and he knew them, but made himself strange to them, and spoke roughly to them; and he said to them, Where do you come from? And they said, From the land of Canaan to buy food.

8 And Joseph knew his brethren, but they knew not him.

9 And Joseph remembered the dreams which he dreamed of them, and said to them, You are spies; to see the nakedness of the land you are come.

10 And they said to him, No, my lord, but to buy food are your servants come.

11 We are all one man's sons; we are true men, your servants are no spies.

12 And he said to them, Nay, but to see the nakedness of the land you are come.

13 And they said, Your servants are twelve brethren, the sons of one man in the land of Canaan; and, behold, the youngest is this day with our father, and one is not.

14 And Joseph said to them, That is it that I spoke to you, saying, You are spies:

15 Hereby you shall be proved: By the life of Pharaoh you shall not go forth hence, except your youngest brother come here.

16 Send one of you, and let him fetch your brother, and you shall be kept in prison, that your words may be proved, whether there be any truth in you: or else by the life of Pharaoh surely you are spies.

17 And he put them all together into ward three days.

18 And Joseph said to them the third day, This do, and live; for I fear God:

19 If you be true men, let one of your brethren be bound in the house of your prison: go ye, carry corn for the famine of your houses:

20 But bring your youngest brother to me; so shall your words be verified, and you shall not die. And they did so.

21 And they said one to another, We are verily guilty concerning our brother, in that we saw the anguish of his soul, when he besought us, and we would not hear; therefore is this distress come upon us.

22 And Reuben answered them, saying, Spoke I not to you, saying, Do not sin against the child; and you would not hear? therefore, behold, also his blood is required.

23 And they knew not that Joseph understood them; for he spoke to them by an interpreter.

24 And he turned himself about from them, and wept; and returned to them again, and communed with them, and took from them Simeon, and bound him before their eyes.

25 Then Joseph commanded to fill their sacks with corn, and to restore every man's money into his sack, and to give them provision for the way: and thus did he to them.

26 And they laded their asses with the corn, and departed thence.

27 And as one of them opened his sack to give his ass provender in the inn, he espied his money; for, behold, it was in his sack's mouth.

28 And he said to his brethren, My money is restored; and, lo, it is even in my sack: and their heart failed them, and they were afraid, saying one to another, What is this that God has done to us?

29 And they came to Jacob their father to the land of Canaan, and told him all that befell to them; saying,

30 The man, who is the lord of the land, spoke roughly to us, and took us for spies of the country.

31 And we said to him, We are true men; we are no spies:

32 We be twelve brethren, sons of our father; one is not, and the youngest is this day with our father in the land of Canaan.

33 And the man, the lord of the country, said to us, Hereby shall I know that you are true men; leave one of your brethren here with me, and take food for the famine of your households, and be gone:

34 And bring your youngest brother to me: then shall I know that you are no spies, but that you are true men: so will I deliver you your brother, and you shall traffic in the land.

35 And it came to pass as they emptied their sacks, that, behold, every man's bundle of money was in his sack: and when both they and their father saw the bundles of money, they were afraid.

36 And Jacob their father said to them, Me have you bereaved of my children: Joseph is not, and Simeon is not, and you will take Benjamin away: all these things are against me.

37 And Reuben spoke to his father, saying, Slay my two sons, if I bring him not to you: deliver him into my hand, and I will bring him to you again.

38 And he said, My son shall not go down with you; for his brother is dead, and he is left alone: if mischief befall him by the way in the which you go, then shall you bring down my gray hairs with sorrow to the grave.

CHAPTER 43

AND the famine was sore in the land. 2 And it came to pass, when they had eaten up the corn which they had brought out of Egypt, their father said to them, Go again, buy us a little food.

3 And Judah spoke to him, saying, The man did solemnly protest to us, saying, You shall not see my face, except your brother be with you.

4 If you will send our brother with us, we will go down and buy you food:

5 But if you will not send him, we will not go down: for the man said to us, You shall not see my face, except your brother be with you.

6 And Israel said, Why did you deal so ill with me, as to tell the man whether you had yet a brother?

7 And they said, The man asked us straightly of our state, and of our kindred, saying, Is your father yet alive? have you another brother? and we told him according to the tenor of these words: could we certainly know that he would say, Bring your brother down?

8 And Judah said to Israel his father, Send the lad with me, and we will arise and go; that we may live, and not die, both we, and thou, and also our little ones.

9 I will be surety for him; of my hand shall you require him: if I bring him not to you, and set him before you, then let me bear the blame for ever:

10 For except we had lingered, surely now we had returned this second time.

11 And their father Israel said to them, If it must be so now, do this; take of the best fruits in the land in your vessels, and carry down the man a present, a little balm, and a little honey, spices, and myrrh, nuts, and almonds:

12 And take double money in your hand; and the money that was brought again in the mouth of your sacks, carry it again in your hand; peradventure it was an oversight:

13 Take also your brother, and arise, go again to the man:

14 And God Almighty give you mercy before the man, that he may send away your other brother, and Benjamin. If I be bereaved of my children, I am bereaved.

15 And the men took that present, and they took double money in their hand and Benjamin; and rose up, and went down to Egypt, and stood before Joseph.

16 And when Joseph saw Benjamin with them, he said to the ruler of his house, Bring these men home, and slay, and make ready; for these men shall dine with me at noon.

17 And the man did as Joseph bade; and the man brought the men into Joseph's house.

18 And the men were afraid, because they were brought into Joseph's house; and they said, Because of the money that was returned in our sacks at the first time are we brought in; that he may seek occasion against us, and fall upon us, and take us for bondmen, and our asses.

19 And they came near to the steward of Joseph's house, and they communed with him at the door of the house,

20 And said, O sir, we came indeed down at the first time to buy food:

21 And it came to pass, when we came to the inn, that we opened our sacks, and, behold, every man's money was in the mouth of his sack, our money in full weight: and we have brought it again in our hand.

22 And other money have we brought down in our hands to buy food: we cannot tell who put our money in our sacks.

23 And he said, Peace be to you, fear not: your God, and the God of your father, has given you treasure in your sacks: I had your money. And he brought Simeon out to them.

24 And the man brought the men into Joseph's house, and gave them water, and they washed their feet; and he gave their asses provender.

25 And they made ready the present against Joseph came at noon: for they heard that they should eat bread there.

26 And when Joseph came home, they brought him the present which was in their hand into the house, and bowed themselves to him to the earth.

27 And he asked them of their welfare, and said, Is your father well, the old man of whom you spoke? Is he yet alive?

28 And they answered, Your servant our father is in good health, he is yet alive. And they bowed down their heads, and made obeisance.

29 And he lifted up his eyes, and saw his brother Benjamin, his mother's son, and said, Is this your younger brother, of whom you spoke to me? And he said, God be gracious to you, my son.

30 And Joseph made haste; for his bowels did yearn upon his brother: and he sought where to weep; and he entered into his chamber, and wept there.

31 And he washed his face, and went out, and refrained himself, and said, Set on bread.

32 And they set on for him by himself, and for them by themselves, and for the Egyptians, which did eat with him, by themselves: because the Egyptians might not eat bread with the Hebrews; for that is an abomination to the Egyptians.

33 And they sat before him, the firstborn according to his birthright, and the

youngest according to his youth: and the men marveled one at another.

34 And he took and sent messes to them from before him: but Benjamin's mess was five times so much as any of theirs. And they drank, and were merry with him.

CHAPTER 44

A ND he commanded the steward of his house, saying, Fill the men's sacks with food, as much as they can carry, and put every man's money in his sack's mouth.

2 And put my cup, the silver cup, in the sack's mouth of the youngest, and his corn money. And he did according to the word that Joseph had spoken.

3 As soon as the morning was light, the men were sent away, they and their asses.

4 And when they were gone out of the city, and not yet far off, Joseph said to his steward, Up, follow after the men; and when you dost overtake them, say to them, Why have you rewarded evil for good?

5 Is not this it in which my lord drinks, and whereby indeed he divines? you have done evil in so doing.

6 And he overtook them, and he spoke to them these same words.

7 And they said to him, Why does my lord say these words? God forbid that your servants should do according to this thing:

8 Behold, the money, which we found in our sacks' mouths, we brought again to you out of the land of Canaan: how then should we steal out of your lord's house silver or gold?

9 With whomsoever of your servants it be found, both let him die, and we also will be my lord's bondmen.

10 And he said, Now also let it be according to your words: he with whom it is found shall be my servant; and you shall be blameless.

11 Then they speedily took down every man his sack to the ground, and opened every man his sack.

12 And he searched, and began at the eldest, and left at the youngest: and the cup was found in Benjamin's sack.

13 Then they rent their clothes, and laded every man his ass, and returned to the city.

14 And Judah and his brethren came to Joseph's house; for he was yet there: and they fell before him on the ground.

15 And Joseph said to them, What deed is this that you have done? Did you not know that such a man as I can certainly divine?

16 And Judah said, What shall we say to my lord? what shall we speak? or how shall we clear ourselves? God has found out the iniquity of your servants: behold, we are my lord's servants, both we, and he also with whom the cup is found.

17 And he said, God forbid that I should do so: but the man in whose hand the cup is found, he shall be my servant; and as for you, get you up in peace to your father.

18 Then Judah came near to him, and said, Oh my lord, let your servant, I pray you, speak a word in my lord's ears, and let not your anger burn against your servant: for you are even as Pharaoh.

19 My lord asked his servants, saying, Have you a father, or a brother?

20 And we said to my lord, We have a father, an old man, and a child of his old age, a little one; and his brother is dead, and he alone is left of his mother, and his father loves him.

21 And you said to your servants, Bring him down to me, that I may set mine eyes upon him.

22 And we said to my lord, The lad cannot leave his father: for if he should leave his father, his father would die.

23 And you said to your servants, Except your youngest brother come down with you, you shall see my face no more.

24 And it came to pass when we came up to your servant my father, we told him the words of my lord.

25 And our father said, Go again, and buy us a little food.

26 And we said, We cannot go down: if our youngest brother be with us, then will we go down: for we may not see the man's face, except our youngest brother be with us.

27 And your servant my father said to us, You know that my wife bare me two sons:

28 And the one went out from me, and I said, Surely he is torn in pieces; and I saw him not since:

29 And if you take this also from me, and mischief befall him, you shall bring down my gray hairs with sorrow to the grave.

30 Now therefore when I come to your servant my father, and the lad be not with us; seeing that his life is bound up in the lad's life;

31 It shall come to pass, when he sees that the lad is not with us, that he will die: and your servants shall bring down the gray hairs of your servant our father with sorrow to the grave.

32 For your servant became surety for the lad to my father, saying, If I bring him not to you, then I shall bear the blame to my father for ever.

33 Now therefore, I pray you, let your servant abide instead of the lad a bondman to my lord; and let the lad go up with his brethren.

34 For how shall I go up to my father, and the lad be not with me? lest peradventure I see the evil that shall come on my father.

CHAPTER 45

THEN Joseph could not refrain himself before all them that stood by him; and he cried, Cause every man to go out from me. And there stood no man with him, while Joseph made himself known to his brethren.

2 And he wept aloud: and the Egyptians and the house of Pharaoh heard.

3 And Joseph said to his brethren, I am Joseph; doth my father yet live? And his brethren could not answer him; for they were troubled at his presence.

4 And Joseph said to his brethren, Come near to me, I pray you. And they came near. And he said, I am Joseph your brother, whom you sold into Egypt.

5 Now therefore be not grieved, nor angry with yourselves, that you sold me hither: for God did send me before you to preserve life.

6 For these two years has the famine been in the land: and yet there are five years, in the which there shall neither be earing nor harvest.

7 And God sent me before you to preserve you a posterity in the earth, and to save your lives by a great deliverance.

8 So now it was not you that sent me hither, but God: and he has made me a father to Pharaoh, and lord of all his house, and a ruler throughout all the land of Egypt.

9 Haste ye, and go up to my father, and say to him, Thus says your son Joseph, God has made me lord of all Egypt: come down to me, tarry not:

10 And you shall dwell in the land of Goshen, and you shall be near to me, you, and your children, and your children's children, and your flocks, and your herds, and all that you have:

11 And there will I nourish you; for yet there are five years of famine; lest thou, and your household, and all that you hast, come to poverty.

12 And, behold, your eyes see, and the eyes of my brother Benjamin, that it is my mouth that speaks to you.

13 And you shall tell my father of all my glory in Egypt, and of all that you have seen; and you shall haste and bring down my father hither.

14 And he fell upon his brother Benjamin's neck, and wept; and Benjamin wept upon his neck.

JOSEPH MAKES HIMSELF KNOWN TO HIS BRETHREN

Genesis 45:1-6

Joseph forgives his brothers, the sons of Israel, and tells them that God used their act of betrayal as the means to bring him ahead of them to Egypt, so he could save their lives (v.5).

Jesus, during his trial before his crucifixion, told Pilate that his authority to sentence Him to death was due only to God's will. "You would have no authority over Me, unless it had been given you from above . . ." (John 19:11). Jesus, too, forgave those who crucified him (Luke 23:34).

15 Moreover he kissed all his brethren, and wept upon them: and after that his brethren talked with him.

16 And the fame thereof was heard in Pharaoh's house, saying, Joseph's brethren are come: and it pleased Pharaoh well, and his servants.

17 And Pharaoh said to Joseph, Say to your brethren, This do ye; lade your beasts, and go, get you to the land of Canaan;

18 And take your father and your households, and come to me: and I will give you the good of the land of Egypt, and you shall eat the fat of the land.

19 Now you are commanded, this do ye; take you wagons out of the land of Egypt for your little ones, and for your wives, and bring your father, and come.

20 Also regard not your stuff; for the good of all the land of Egypt is yours.

21 And the children of Israel did so: and Joseph gave them wagons, according to the commandment of Pharaoh, and gave them provision for the way.

22 To all of them he gave each man changes of raiment; but to Benjamin he gave three hundred pieces of silver, and five changes of raiment.

23 And to his father he sent after this manner; ten asses laden with the good things of Egypt, and ten she asses laden with corn and bread and meat for his father by the way.

24 So he sent his brethren away, and they departed: and he said to them, See that you fall not out by the way.

25 And they went up out of Egypt, and came into the land of Canaan to Jacob their father,

26 And told him, saying, Joseph is yet alive, and he is governor over all the land of Egypt. And Jacob's heart fainted, for he believed them not.

27 And they told him all the words of Joseph, which he had said to them: and when he saw the wagons which Joseph had sent to carry him, the spirit of Jacob their father revived:

28 And Israel said, It is enough; Joseph my son is yet alive: I will go and see him before I die.

CHAPTER 46

AND Israel took his journey with all that he had, and came to Beersheba, and offered sacrifices to the God of his father Isaac.

2 And God spoke to Israel in the visions of the night, and said, Jacob, Jacob. And he said, Here am I.

3 And he said, I am God, the God of your father: fear not to go down into Egypt; for I will there make of you a great nation:

4 I will go down with you into Egypt; and I will also surely bring you up again: and Joseph shall put his hand upon your eyes.

5 And Jacob rose up from Beersheba: and the sons of Israel carried Jacob their father, and their little ones, and their wives, in the wagons which Pharaoh had sent to carry him.

6 And they took their cattle, and their goods, which they had gotten in the land of Canaan, and came into Egypt, Jacob, and all his seed with him:

7 His sons, and his sons' sons with him, his daughters, and his sons' daughters, and all his seed brought he with him into Egypt.

8 And these are the names of the children of Israel, which came into Egypt, Jacob and his sons: Reuben, Jacob's first-born.

9 And the sons of Reuben; Hanoch, and Phallu, and Hezron, and Carmi.

10 And the sons of Simeon; Jemuel, and Jamin, and Ohad, and Jachin, and Zohar, and Shaul the son of a Canaanitish woman.

11 And the sons of Levi; Gershon, Kohath, and Merari.

12 And the sons of Judah; Er, and Onan, and Shelah, and Pharez, and Zarah: but Er and Onan died in the land of Canaan. And the sons of Pharez were Hezron and Hamul.

13 And the sons of Issachar; Tola, and Phuvah, and Job, and Shimron.

14 And the sons of Zebulun; Sered, and Elon, and Jahleel.

15 These be the sons of Leah, which she bare to Jacob in Padanaram, with his daughter Dinah: all the souls of his sons and his daughters were thirty and three.

16 And the sons of Gad; Ziphion, and Haggi, Shuni, and Ezbon, Eri, and Arodi, and Areli.

17 And the sons of Asher; Jimnah, and Ishuah, and Isui, and Beriah, and Serah their sister: and the sons of Beriah; Heber, and Malchiel.

18 These are the sons of Zilpah, whom Laban gave to Leah his daughter, and these she bare to Jacob, even sixteen souls.

19 The sons of Rachel Jacob's wife; Joseph, and Benjamin.

20 And to Joseph in the land of Egypt were born Manasseh and Ephraim, which Asenath the daughter of Potipherah priest of On bare to him.

21 And the sons of Benjamin were Belah, and Becher, and Ashbel, Gera, and Naaman, Ehi, and Rosh, Muppim, and Huppim, and Ard.

22 These are the sons of Rachel, which were born to Jacob: all the souls were fourteen.

23 And the sons of Dan; Hushim.

24 And the sons of Naphtali; Jahzeel, and Guni, and Jezer, and Shillem.

25 These are the sons of Bilhah, which Laban gave to Rachel his daughter, and she bare these to Jacob: all the souls were seven.

26 All the souls that came with Jacob into Egypt, which came out of his loins, besides Jacob's sons' wives, all the souls were threescore and six;

27 And the sons of Joseph, which were born him in Egypt, were two souls: all the souls of the house of Jacob, which came into Egypt, were threescore and ten.

28 And he sent Judah before him to Joseph, to direct his face to Goshen; and they came into the land of Goshen.

29 And Joseph made ready his chariot, and went up to meet Israel his father, to Goshen, and presented himself to him; and he fell on his neck, and wept on his neck a good while.

30 And Israel said to Joseph, Now let me die, since I have seen your face, because you are yet alive.

31 And Joseph said to his brethren, and to his father's house, I will go up, and show Pharaoh, and say to him, My brethren, and my father's house, which were in the land of Canaan, are come to me;

32 And the men are shepherds, for their trade has been to feed cattle; and they have brought their flocks, and their herds, and all that they have.

33 And it shall come to pass, when Pharaoh shall call you, and shall say, What is your occupation?

34 That you shall say, Your servants' trade has been about cattle from our youth even until now, both we, and also our fathers: that you may dwell in the land of Goshen; for every shepherd is an abomination to the Egyptians.

CHAPTER 47

THEN Joseph came and told Pharaoh, and said, My father and my brethren, and their flocks, and their herds, and all that they have, are come out of the land of Canaan; and, behold, they are in the land of Goshen.

2 And he took some of his brethren, even five men, and presented them to Pharaoh.

3 And Pharaoh said to his brethren, What is your occupation? And they said to Pharaoh, Your servants are shepherds, both we, and also our fathers.

4 They said to Pharaoh, For to sojourn in the land are we come; for your servants have no pasture for their flocks; for the famine is sore in the land of Canaan:

now therefore, we pray you, let your servants dwell in the land of Goshen.

5 And Pharaoh spoke to Joseph, saying, Your father and your brethren are come to you:

6 The land of Egypt is before you; in the best of the land make your father and brethren to dwell; in the land of Goshen let them dwell: and if you know any men of activity among them, then make them rulers over my cattle.

7 And Joseph brought in Jacob his father, and set him before Pharaoh: and Jacob blessed Pharaoh.

8 And Pharaoh said to Jacob, How old are thou?

9 And Jacob said to Pharaoh, The days of the years of my pilgrimage are an hundred and thirty years: few and evil have the days of the years of my life been, and have not attained to the days of the years of the life of my fathers in the days of their pilgrimage.

10 And Jacob blessed Pharaoh, and went out from before Pharaoh.

11 And Joseph placed his father and his brethren, and gave them a possession in the land of Egypt, in the best of the land, in the land of Rameses, as Pharaoh had commanded.

12 And Joseph nourished his father, and his brethren, and all his father's household, with bread, according to their families.

13 And there was no bread in all the land; for the famine was very sore, so that the land of Egypt and all the land of Canaan fainted by reason of the famine.

14 And Joseph gathered up all the money that was found in the land of Egypt, and in the land of Canaan, for the corn which they bought: and Joseph brought the money into Pharaoh's house.

15 And when money failed in the land of Egypt, and in the land of Canaan, all the Egyptians came to Joseph, and said, Give us bread: for why should we die in your presence? for the money fails.

16 And Joseph said, Give your cattle; and I will give you for your cattle, if money fail.

17 And they brought their cattle to Joseph: and Joseph gave them bread in exchange for horses, and for the flocks, and for the cattle of the herds, and for the asses: and he fed them with bread for all their cattle for that year.

18 When that year was ended, they came to him the second year, and said to him, We will not hide it from my lord, how that our money is spent; my lord also has our herds of cattle; there is not ought left in the sight of my lord, but our bodies, and our lands:

19 Why shall we die before your eyes, both we and our land? buy us and our land for bread, and we and our land will be servants to Pharaoh: and give us seed, that we may live, and not die, that the land be not desolate.

20 And Joseph bought all the land of Egypt for Pharaoh; for the Egyptians sold every man his field, because the famine prevailed over them: so the land became Pharaoh's.

21 And as for the people, he removed them to cities from one end of the borders of Egypt even to the other end thereof.

22 Only the land of the priests bought he not; for the priests had a portion assigned them of Pharaoh, and did eat their portion which Pharaoh gave them: therefore they sold not their lands.

23 Then Joseph said to the people, Behold, I have bought you this day and your land for Pharaoh: lo, here is seed for you, and you shall sow the land.

24 And it shall come to pass in the increase, that you shall give the fifth part to Pharaoh, and four parts shall be your own, for seed of the field, and for your food, and for them of your households, and for food for your little ones.

25 And they said, You have saved our lives: let us find grace in the sight of my lord, and we will be Pharaoh's servants.

26 And Joseph made it a law over the land of Egypt to this day, that Pharaoh should have the fifth part, except the land of the priests only, which became not Pharaoh's.

27 And Israel dwelt in the land of Egypt, in the country of Goshen; and they had possessions therein, and grew, and multiplied exceedingly.

28 And Jacob lived in the land of Egypt seventeen years: so the whole age of Jacob was an hundred forty and seven years.

29 And the time drew nigh that Israel must die: and he called his son Joseph, and said to him, If now I have found grace in your sight, put, I pray you, your hand under my thigh, and deal kindly and truly with me; bury me not, I pray you, in Egypt:

30 But I will lie with my fathers, and you shall carry me out of Egypt, and bury me in their buryingplace. And he said, I will do as you have said.

31 And he said, Swear to me. And he swore to him. And Israel bowed himself upon the bed's head.

CHAPTER 48

AND it came to pass after these things, that one told Joseph, Behold, your father is sick: and he took with him his two sons, Manasseh and Ephraim.

2 And one told Jacob, and said, Behold, your son Joseph cometh to you: and Israel strengthened himself, and sat upon the bed.

3 And Jacob said to Joseph, God Almighty appeared to me at Luz in the land of Canaan, and blessed me,

4 And said to me, Behold, I will make you fruitful, and multiply you, and I will make of you a multitude of people; and will give this land to your seed after you for an everlasting possession.

5 And now your two sons, Ephraim and Manasseh, which were born to you in the land of Egypt before I came to you into Egypt, are mine; as Reuben and Simeon, they shall be mine.

6 And your issue, which you beget after them, shall be yours, and shall be called after the name of their brethren in their inheritance.

7 And as for me, when I came from Padan, Rachel died by me in the land of Canaan in the way, when yet there was but a little way to come to Ephrath: and I buried her there in the way of Ephrath; the same is Bethlehem.

8 And Israel beheld Joseph's sons, and said, Who are these?

9 And Joseph said to his father, They are my sons, whom God has given me in this place. And he said, Bring them, I pray you, to me, and I will bless them.

10 Now the eyes of Israel were dim for age, so that he could not see. And he brought them near to him; and he kissed them, and embraced them.

11 And Israel said to Joseph, I had not thought to see your face: and, lo, God has showed me also your seed.

12 And Joseph brought them out from between his knees, and he bowed himself with his face to the earth.

13 And Joseph took them both, Ephraim in his right hand toward Israel's left hand, and Manasseh in his left hand toward Israel's right hand, and brought them near to him.

14 And Israel stretched out his right hand, and laid it upon Ephraim's head, who was the younger, and his left hand upon Manasseh's head, guiding his hands wittingly; for Manasseh was the firstborn.

15 And he blessed Joseph, and said, God, before whom my fathers Abraham and Isaac did walk, the God which fed me all my life long to this day,

16 The Angel which redeemed me from all evil, bless the lads; and let my name be named on them, and the name of my fathers Abraham and Isaac; and let them grow into a multitude in the midst of the earth.

17 And when Joseph saw that his father laid his right hand upon the head of Ephraim, it displeased him: and he held up his father's hand, to remove it from Ephraim's head to Manasseh's head.

18 And Joseph said to his father, Not so, my father: for this is the firstborn; put your right hand upon his head.

19 And his father refused, and said, I know it, my son, I know it: he also shall become a people, and he also shall be great: but truly his younger brother shall be greater than he, and his seed shall become a multitude of nations.

20 And he blessed them that day, saying, In you shall Israel bless, saying, God make you as Ephraim and as Manasseh: and he set Ephraim before Manasseh.

21 And Israel said to Joseph, Behold, I die: but God shall be with you, and bring you again to the land of your fathers.

22 Moreover I have given to you one portion above your brethren, which I took out of the hand of the Amorite with my sword and with my bow.

CHAPTER 49

AND Jacob called to his sons, and said, Gather yourselves together, that I may tell you that which shall befall you in the last days.

2 Gather yourselves together, and hear, you sons of Jacob; and hearken to Israel your father.

3 Reuben, you are my firstborn, my might, and the beginning of my strength, the excellency of dignity, and the excellency of power:

4 Unstable as water, you shall not excel; because you went up to your father's bed; then you defiled it: he went up to my couch.

5 Simeon and Levi are brethren; instruments of cruelty are in their habitations.

6 O my soul, come not you into their secret; to their assembly, mine honor, be not you united: for in their anger they slew a man, and in their selfwill they dug down a wall.

7 Cursed be their anger, for it was fierce; and their wrath, for it was cruel: I will divide them in Jacob, and scatter them in Israel.

8 Judah, you are he whom your brethren shall praise: your hand shall be in the neck of your enemies; your father's children shall bow down before you.

9 Judah is a lion's whelp: from the prey, my son, you are gone up: he stooped down, he crouched as a lion, and as an old lion; who shall rouse him up?

10 The scepter shall not depart from Judah, nor a lawgiver from between his feet, until Shiloh come; and to him shall the gathering of the people be.

11 Binding his foal to the vine, and his ass's colt to the choice vine; he washed his garments in wine, and his clothes in the blood of grapes:

12 His eyes shall be red with wine, and his teeth white with milk.

13 Zebulun shall dwell at the haven of the sea; and he shall be for an haven of ships; and his border shall be to Zidon.

14 Issachar is a strong ass crouching down between two burdens:

15 And he saw that rest was good, and the land that it was pleasant; and bowed his shoulder to bear, and became a servant to tribute.

16 Dan shall judge his people, as one of the tribes of Israel.

17 Dan shall be a serpent by the way, an adder in the path, that bites the horse heels, so that his rider shall fall backward.

18 I have waited for your salvation, O LORD.

49:10-12 It seems that Hollywood blew it with their blond and blue-eyed Jesus. In verse 12 we have what is possibly a physical description of Jesus of Nazareth.

19 Gad, a troop shall overcome him: but he shall overcome at the last.

20 Out of Asher his bread shall be fat, and he shall yield royal dainties.

21 Naphtali is a hind let loose: he gives goodly words.

22 Joseph is a fruitful bough, even a fruitful bough by a well; whose branches run over the wall:

23 The archers have sorely grieved him, and shot at him, and hated him:

24 But his bow abode in strength, and the arms of his hands were made strong by the hands of the mighty God of Jacob; (from thence is the shepherd, the stone of Israel:)

25 Even by the God of your father, who shall help you; and by the Almighty, who shall bless you with blessings of heaven above, blessings of the deep that lieth under, blessings of the breasts, and of the womb:

26 The blessings of your father have prevailed above the blessings of my progenitors to the utmost bound of the everlasting hills: they shall be on the head of Joseph, and on the crown of the head of him that was separate from his brethren.

27 Benjamin shall ravin as a wolf: in the morning he shall devour the prey, and at night he shall divide the spoil.

28 All these are the twelve tribes of Israel: and this is it that their father spoke to them, and blessed them; every one according to his blessing he blessed them.

29 And he charged them, and said to them, I am to be gathered to my people: bury me with my fathers in the cave that is in the field of Ephron the Hittite,

30 In the cave that is in the field of Machpelah, which is before Mamre, in the land of Canaan, which Abraham bought with the field of Ephron the Hittite for a possession of a burying-place.

31 There they buried Abraham and Sarah his wife; there they buried Isaac and Rebekah his wife; and there I buried Leah.

32 The purchase of the field and of the cave that is therein was from the children of Heth.

33 And when Jacob had made an end of commanding his sons, he gathered up his feet into the bed, and yielded up the ghost, and was gathered to his people.

CHAPTER 50

AND Joseph fell upon his father's face, and wept upon him, and kissed him.

2 And Joseph commanded his servants the physicians to embalm his father: and the physicians embalmed Israel.

3 And forty days were fulfilled for him; for so are fulfilled the days of those which are embalmed: and the Egyptians mourned for him threescore and ten days.

4 And when the days of his mourning were past, Joseph spoke to the house of Pharaoh, saying, If now I have found grace in your eyes, speak, I pray you, in the ears of Pharaoh, saying,

5 My father made me swear, saying, Lo, I die: in my grave which I have dug for me in the land of Canaan, there shall you bury me. Now therefore let me go up, I pray you, and bury my father, and I will come again.

6 And Pharaoh said, Go up, and bury your father, according as he made you swear.

7 And Joseph went up to bury his father: and with him went up all the servants of Pharaoh, the elders of his house, and all the elders of the land of Egypt,

8 And all the house of Joseph, and his brethren, and his father's house: only their little ones, and their flocks, and their herds, they left in the land of Goshen.

9 And there went up with him both chariots and horsemen: and it was a very great company.

10 And they came to the threshing floor of Atad, which is beyond Jordan, and

Exodus

CHAPTER 1

N OW these are the names of the children of Israel, which came into Egypt; every man and his household came with Jacob.

2 Reuben, Simeon, Levi, and Judah,

3 Issachar, Zebulun, and Benjamin,

4 Dan, and Naphtali, Gad, and Asher.

5 And all the souls that came out of the loins of Jacob were seventy souls: for Joseph was in Egypt already.

6 And Joseph died, and all his brethren, and all that generation.

7 And the children of Israel were fruitful, and increased abundantly, and multiplied, and waxed exceeding mighty; and the land was filled with them.

8 Now there arose up a new king over Egypt, which knew not Joseph.

9 And he said to his people, Behold, the people of the children of Israel are more and mightier than we:

10 Come on, let us deal wisely with them; lest they multiply, and it come to pass, that, when there falls out any war, they join also to our enemies, and fight against us, and so get them up out of the land.

11 Therefore they did set over them taskmasters to afflict them with their burdens. And they built for Pharaoh treasure cities, Pithom and Raamses.

12 But the more they afflicted them, the more they multiplied and grew. And they were grieved because of the children of Israel.

13 And the Egyptians made the children of Israel to serve with rigor:

14 And they made their lives bitter with hard bondage, in morter, and in brick, and in all manner of service in the field: all their service, wherein they made them serve, was with rigor.

15 And the king of Egypt spoke to the Hebrew midwives, of which the name of the one was Shiphrah, and the name of the other Puah:

16 And he said, When you do the office of a midwife to the Hebrew women, and see them upon the stools; if it be a son, then you shall kill him: but if it be a daughter, then she shall live.

17 But the midwives feared God, and did not as the king of Egypt commanded them, but saved the men children alive.

18 And the king of Egypt called for the midwives, and said to them, Why have you done this thing, and have saved the men children alive?

19 And the midwives said to Pharaoh, Because the Hebrew women are not as the Egyptian women; for they are lively, and are delivered ere the midwives come in to them.

20 Therefore God dealt well with the midwives: and the people multiplied, and waxed very mighty.

21 And it came to pass, because the midwives feared God, that he made them houses.

22 And Pharaoh charged all his people, saying, Every son that is born you shall

THE CHILD MOSES ON THE NILE

Exodus 2:3-4

cast into the river, and every daughter
you shall save alive.

CHAPTER 2

A ND there went a man of the house
of Levi, and took to wife a daughter
of Levi.

2 And the woman conceived, and bare a
son: and when she saw him that he was
a goodly child, she hid him three
months.

3 And when she could not longer hide
him, she took for him an ark of bulrushes, and daubed it with slime and with
pitch, and put the child therein; and she
laid it in the flags by the river's brink.

4 And his sister stood afar off, to wit
what would be done to him.

5 And the daughter of Pharaoh came
down to wash herself at the river; and

her maidens walked along by the river's
side; and when she saw the ark among
the flags, she sent her maid to fetch it.

6 And when she had opened it, she saw
the child: and, behold, the babe wept.
And she had compassion on him, and
said, This is one of the Hebrews' children.

7 Then said his sister to Pharaoh's
daughter, Shall I go and call to you a
nurse of the Hebrew women, that she
may nurse the child for you?

8 And Pharaoh's daughter said to her,
Go. And the maid went and called the
child's mother.

9 And Pharaoh's daughter said to her,
Take this child away, and nurse it for
me, and I will give you your wages. And
the women took the child, and nursed it.

10 And the child grew, and she brought him to Pharaoh's daughter, and he became her son. And she called his name Moses: and she said, Because I drew him out of the water.

11 And it came to pass in those days, when Moses was grown, that he went out to his brethren, and looked on their burdens: and he spied an Egyptian smiting an Hebrew, one of his brethren.

12 And he looked this way and that way, and when he saw that there was no man, he slew the Egyptian, and hid him in the sand.

13 And when he went out the second day, behold, two men of the Hebrews strove together: and he said to him that did the wrong, Why do you smite your fellow?

14 And he said, Who made you a prince and a judge over us? Do you intend to kill me, as you killed the Egyptian? And Moses feared, and said, Surely this thing is known.

15 Now when Pharaoh heard this thing, he sought to slay Moses. But Moses fled from the face of Pharaoh, and dwelt in the land of Midian: and he sat down by a well.

16 Now the priest of Midian had seven daughters: and they came and drew water, and filled the troughs to water their father's flock.

17 And the shepherds came and drove them away: but Moses stood up and helped them, and watered their flock.

18 And when they came to Reuel their father, he said, How is it that you are come so soon to day?

19 And they said, An Egyptian delivered us out of the hand of the shepherds, and also drew water enough for us, and watered the flock.

20 And he said to his daughters, And where is he? why is it that you have left the man? call him, that he may eat bread.

21 And Moses was content to dwell with the man: and he gave Moses Zipporah his daughter.

Earth's crammed with heaven,
and every common bush afire with God.
But only he who sees takes off his shoes.
The rest sit round and pluck blackberries.

E. B. Browning
1806-1861
BRITISH POET

22 And she bare him a son, and he called his name Gershom: for he said, I have been a stranger in a strange land.

23 And it came to pass in process of time, that the king of Egypt died: and the children of Israel sighed by reason of the bondage, and they cried, and their cry came up to God by reason of the bondage.

24 And God heard their groaning, and God remembered his covenant with Abraham, with Isaac, and with Jacob.

25 And God looked upon the children of Israel, and God had respect to them.

CHAPTER 3

NOW Moses kept the flock of Jethro his father in law, the priest of Midian: and he led the flock to the backside of the desert, and came to the mountain of God, even to Horeb.

2 And the angel of the LORD appeared to him in a flame of fire out of the midst of a bush: and he looked, and, behold,

the bush burned with fire, and the bush was not consumed.

3 And Moses said, I will now turn aside, and see this great sight, why the bush is not burnt.

4 And when the LORD saw that he turned aside to see, God called to him out of the midst of the bush, and said, Moses, Moses. And he said, Here am I.

5 And he said, Draw not nigh hither: put off your shoes from off your feet, for the place whereon you stand is holy ground.

6 Moreover he said, I am the God of your father, the God of Abraham, the God of Isaac, and the God of Jacob. And Moses hid his face; for he was afraid to look upon God.

7 And the LORD said, I have surely seen the affliction of my people which are in Egypt, and have heard their cry by reason of their taskmasters; for I know their sorrows;

8 And I am come down to deliver them out of the hand of the Egyptians, and to bring them up out of that land to a good land and a large, to a land flowing with milk and honey; to the place of the Canaanites, and the Hittites, and the Amorites, and the Perizzites, and the Hivites, and the Jebusites.

3.5 Moses was made to remove his sandals because the place on which he stood was holy ground.

In the gospel, God makes the believer holy. Now his feet are shod with the Gospel of peace (Ephesians 6:15) so that he can take the message of salvation to those who stand on unholy ground.

9 Now therefore, behold, the cry of the children of Israel is come to me: and I have also seen the oppression wherewith the Egyptians oppress them.

10 Come now therefore, and I will send you to Pharaoh, that you may bring forth my people the children of Israel out of Egypt.

11 And Moses said to God, Who am I, that I should go to Pharaoh, and that I should bring forth the children of Israel out of Egypt?

12 And he said, Certainly I will be with you; and this shall be a token to you, that I have sent you: When you have brought forth the people out of Egypt, you shall serve God upon this mountain.

13 And Moses said to God, Behold, when I come to the children of Israel, and shall say to them, The God of your fathers has sent me to you; and they shall say to me, What is his name? what shall I say to them?

14 And God said to Moses, I AM THAT I AM: and he said, Thus shall you say to the children of Israel, I AM has sent me to you.

15 And God said moreover to Moses, Thus shall you say to the children of Israel, the LORD God of your fathers, the God of Abraham, the God of Isaac, and the God of Jacob, has sent me to you: this is my name for ever, and this is my memorial to all generations.

16 Go, and gather the elders of Israel together, and say to them, The LORD God of your fathers, the God of Abraham, of Isaac, and of Jacob, appeared to me, saying, I have surely visited you, and seen that which is done to you in Egypt:

17 And I have said, I will bring you up out of the affliction of Egypt to the land of the Canaanites, and the Hittites, and the Amorites, and the Perizzites, and the Hivites, and the Jebusites, to a land flowing with milk and honey.

18 And they shall hearken to your voice: and you shall come, you and the elders of Israel, to the king of Egypt, and

you shall say to him, The LORD God of the Hebrews has met with us: and now let us go, we beseech you, three days' journey into the wilderness, that we may sacrifice to the LORD our God.

19 And I am sure that the king of Egypt will not let you go, no, not by a mighty hand.

20 And I will stretch out my hand, and smite Egypt with all my wonders which I will do in the midst thereof: and after that he will let you go.

21 And I will give this people favor in the sight of the Egyptians: and it shall come to pass, that, when you go, you shall not go empty.

22 But every woman shall borrow of her neighbor, and of her that sojourned in her house, jewels of silver, and jewels of gold, and raiment: and you shall put them upon your sons, and upon your daughters; and you shall spoil the Egyptians.

CHAPTER 4

AND Moses answered and said, But, behold, they will not believe me, nor hearken to my voice: for they will say, The LORD has not appeared to you.

2 And the LORD said to him, What is that in your hand? And he said, A rod.

3 And he said, Cast it on the ground. And he cast it on the ground, and it became a serpent; and Moses fled from before it.

4 And the LORD said to Moses, Put forth your hand, and take it by the tail. And he put forth his hand, and caught it, and it became a rod in his hand:

5 That they may believe that the LORD God of their fathers, the God of Abraham, the God of Isaac, and the God of Jacob, has appeared to you.

6 And the LORD said furthermore to him, Put now your hand into your bosom. And he put his hand into his bosom: and when he took it out, behold, his hand was leprous as snow.

7 And he said, Put your hand into your bosom again. And he put his hand into his bosom again; and plucked it out of his bosom, and, behold, it was turned again as his other flesh.

8 And it shall come to pass, if they will not believe you, neither hearken to the voice of the first sign, that they will believe the voice of the latter sign.

9 And it shall come to pass, if they will not believe also these two signs, neither hearken to your voice, that you shall take of the water of the river, and pour it upon the dry land: and the water which you take out of the river shall become blood upon the dry land.

10 And Moses said to the LORD, O my LORD, I am not eloquent, neither heretofore, nor since you have spoken to your servant: but I am slow of speech, and of a slow tongue.

11 And the LORD said to him, Who has made man's mouth? or who makes the dumb, or deaf, or the seeing, or the blind? have not I the LORD?

12 Now therefore go, and I will be with your mouth, and teach you what you shall say.

13 And he said, O my LORD, send, I pray you, by the hand of him whom you will send.

14 And the anger of the LORD was kindled against Moses, and he said, Is not Aaron the Levite your brother? I know

---

4:10 For how to battle the fear of man see Psalm 56:11 comment.

4:10-14 Moses said that he wasn't eloquent. In Syracuse, New York in June of 2001, doctors treated a man who had been shot multiple times as he sat in his car. They said that the man, who had driven himself to the hospital, survived the shooting because he weighed 400 pounds, and the bullets hadn't reached his vital organs. The moral is that what may seem a liability for one person can be an asset for others.

When it comes to being a spokesperson for God, your weakness can become your strength. It's your inability to speak that makes you rely on God's ability.

that he can speak well. And also, behold, he comes forth to meet you: and when he sees you, he will be glad in his heart.

15 And you shall speak to him, and put words in his mouth: and I will be with your mouth, and with his mouth, and will teach you what you shall do.

16 And he shall be your spokesman to the people: and he shall be, even he shall be to you instead of a mouth, and you shall be to him instead of God.

17 And you shall take this rod in your hand, wherewith you shall do signs.

18 And Moses went and returned to Jethro his father in law, and said to him, Let me go, I pray you, and return to my brethren which are in Egypt, and see whether they be yet alive. And Jethro said to Moses, Go in peace.

19 And the LORD said to Moses in Midian, Go, return into Egypt: for all the men are dead which sought your life.

20 And Moses took his wife and his sons, and set them upon an ass, and he returned to the land of Egypt: and Moses took the rod of God in his hand.

21 And the LORD said to Moses, When you go to return into Egypt, see that you do all those wonders before Pharaoh, which I have put in your hand: but I will harden his heart, that he shall not let the people go.

22 And you shall say to Pharaoh, Thus says the LORD, Israel is my son, even my firstborn:

23 And I say to you, Let my son go, that he may serve me: and if You refuse to let him go, behold, I will slay your son, even your firstborn.

24 And it came to pass by the way in the inn, that the LORD met him, and sought to kill him.

25 Then Zipporah took a sharp stone, and cut off the foreskin of her son, and cast it at his feet, and said, Surely a bloody husband are You to me.

26 So he let him go: then she said, A bloody husband You are, because of the circumcision.

27 And the LORD said to Aaron, Go into the wilderness to meet Moses. And he went, and met him in the mount of God, and kissed him.

28 And Moses told Aaron all the words of the LORD who had sent him, and all the signs which he had commanded him.

29 And Moses and Aaron went and gathered together all the elders of the children of Israel:

30 And Aaron spoke all the words which the LORD had spoken to Moses, and did the signs in the sight of the people.

31 And the people believed: and when they heard that the LORD had visited the children of Israel, and that he had looked upon their affliction, then they bowed their heads and worshipped.

CHAPTER 5

AND afterward Moses and Aaron went in, and told Pharaoh, Thus says the LORD God of Israel, Let my people go, that they may hold a feast to me in the wilderness.

2 And Pharaoh said, Who is the LORD, that I should obey his voice to let Israel go? I know not the LORD, neither will I let Israel go.

3 And they said, The God of the Hebrews has met with us: let us go, we pray you, three days' journey into the desert, and sacrifice to the LORD our God; lest he fall upon us with pestilence, or with the sword.

4 And the king of Egypt said to them, Why do you, Moses and Aaron, let the people from their works? get to your burdens.

5 And Pharaoh said, Behold, the people of the land now are many, and you make them rest from their burdens.

6 And Pharaoh commanded the same day the taskmasters of the people, and their officers, saying,

7 You shall no more give the people straw to make brick, as heretofore: let them go and gather straw for themselves.

8 And the tale of the bricks, which they did make heretofore, you shall lay upon them; you shall not diminish ought thereof: for they be idle; therefore they cry, saying, Let us go and sacrifice to our God.

9 Let there more work be laid upon the men, that they may labor therein; and let them not regard vain words.

10 And the taskmasters of the people went out, and their officers, and they spoke to the people, saying, Thus says Pharaoh, I will not give you straw.

11 Go, get straw where you can find it: yet not ought of your work shall be diminished.

12 So the people were scattered abroad throughout all the land of Egypt to gather stubble instead of straw.

13 And the taskmasters hasted them, saying, Fulfill your works, your daily tasks, as when there was straw.

14 And the officers of the children of Israel, which Pharaoh's taskmasters had set over them, were beaten, and demanded, Why have you not fulfilled your task in making brick both yesterday and to day, as heretofore?

15 Then the officers of the children of Israel came and cried to Pharaoh, saying, Why do you deal this way with your servants?

16 There is no straw given to your servants, and they say to us, Make brick: and, behold, your servants are beaten; but the fault is in your own people.

17 But he said, You are idle, you are idle: therefore you say, Let us go and do sacrifice to the LORD.

18 Go therefore now, and work; for there shall no straw be given you, yet shall you deliver the tale of bricks.

19 And the officers of the children of Israel did see that they were in evil case, after it was said, You shall not minish ought from your bricks of your daily task.

20 And they met Moses and Aaron, who stood in the way, as they came forth from Pharaoh:

21 And they said to them, The LORD look upon you, and judge; because you have made our savor to be abhorred in the eyes of Pharaoh, and in the eyes of his servants, to put a sword in their hand to slay us.

22 And Moses returned to the LORD, and said, LORD, why have You so evil entreated this people? why is it that You have sent me?

23 For since I came to Pharaoh to speak in your name, he has done evil to this people; neither have You delivered your people at all.

CHAPTER 6

THEN the LORD said to Moses, Now shall you see what I will do to Pharaoh: for with a strong hand shall he let them go, and with a strong hand shall he drive them out of his land.

2 And God spoke to Moses, and said to him, I am the LORD:

3 And I appeared to Abraham, to Isaac, and to Jacob, by the name of God Almighty, but by my name JEHOVAH was I not known to them.

4 And I have also established my covenant with them, to give them the land of Canaan, the land of their pilgrimage, wherein they were strangers.

5 And I have also heard the groaning of the children of Israel, whom the Egyptians keep in bondage; and I have remembered my covenant.

6 Therefore say to the children of Israel, I am the LORD, and I will bring you out from under the burdens of the Egyptians, and I will rid you out of their bondage, and I will redeem you with a stretched out arm, and with great judgments:

7 And I will take you to me for a people, and I will be to you a God: and you shall know that I am the LORD your God, which brings you out from under the burdens of the Egyptians.

8 And I will bring you in to the land, concerning the which I did swear to give it to Abraham, to Isaac, and to Jacob;

and I will give it you for an heritage: I am the LORD.

9 And Moses spoke so to the children of Israel: but they hearkened not to Moses for anguish of spirit, and for cruel bondage.

10 And the LORD spoke to Moses, saying,

11 Go in, speak to Pharaoh king of Egypt, that he let the children of Israel go out of his land.

12 And Moses spoke before the LORD, saying, Behold, the children of Israel have not hearkened to me; how then shall Pharaoh hear me, who am of uncircumcised lips?

13 And the LORD spoke to Moses and to Aaron, and gave them a charge to the children of Israel, and to Pharaoh king of Egypt, to bring the children of Israel out of the land of Egypt.

14 These be the heads of their fathers' houses: The sons of Reuben the firstborn of Israel; Hanoch, and Pallu, Hezron, and Carmi: these be the families of Reuben.

15 And the sons of Simeon; Jemuel, and Jamin, and Ohad, and Jachin, and Zohar, and Shaul the son of a Canaanitish woman: these are the families of Simeon.

16 And these are the names of the sons of Levi according to their generations; Gershon, and Kohath, and Merari: and the years of the life of Levi were an hundred thirty and seven years.

17 The sons of Gershon; Libni, and Shimi, according to their families.

18 And the sons of Kohath; Amram, and Izhar, and Hebron, and Uzziel: and the years of the life of Kohath were an hundred thirty and three years.

19 And the sons of Merari; Mahali and Mushi: these are the families of Levi according to their generations.

20 And Amram took him Jochebed his father's sister to wife; and she bare him Aaron and Moses: and the years of the life of Amram were an hundred and thirty and seven years.

21 And the sons of Izhar; Korah, and Nepheg, and Zichri.

22 And the sons of Uzziel; Mishael, and Elzaphan, and Zithri.

23 And Aaron took him Elisheba, daughter of Amminadab, sister of Naashon, to wife; and she bare him Nadab, and Abihu, Eleazar, and Ithamar.

24 And the sons of Korah; Assir, and Elkanah, and Abiasaph: these are the families of the Korhites.

25 And Eleazar Aaron's son took him one of the daughters of Putiel to wife; and she bare him Phinehas: these are the heads of the fathers of the Levites according to their families.

26 These are that Aaron and Moses, to whom the LORD said, Bring out the children of Israel from the land of Egypt according to their armies.

27 These are they which spoke to Pharaoh king of Egypt, to bring out the children of Israel from Egypt: these are that Moses and Aaron.

28 And it came to pass on the day when the LORD spoke to Moses in the land of Egypt,

29 That the LORD spoke to Moses, saying, I am the LORD: speak to Pharaoh king of Egypt all that I say to you.

30 And Moses said before the LORD, Behold, I am of uncircumcised lips, and how shall Pharaoh hearken to me?

CHAPTER 7

AND the LORD said to Moses, See, I have made you a god to Pharaoh: and Aaron your brother shall be your prophet.

2 You shall speak all that I command you: and Aaron your brother shall speak to Pharaoh, that he send the children of Israel out of his land.

3 And I will harden Pharaoh's heart, and multiply my signs and my wonders in the land of Egypt.

4 But Pharaoh shall not hearken to you, that I may lay my hand upon Egypt, and bring forth mine armies, and my people

MOSES AND AARON BEFORE PHAROAH

Exodus 7:10

the children of Israel, out of the land of Egypt by great judgments.

5 And the Egyptians shall know that I am the LORD, when I stretch forth mine hand upon Egypt, and bring out the children of Israel from among them.

6 And Moses and Aaron did as the LORD commanded them, so did they.

7 And Moses was fourscore years old, and Aaron fourscore and three years old, when they spoke to Pharaoh.

8 And the LORD spoke to Moses and to Aaron, saying,

9 When Pharaoh shall speak to you, saying, Show a miracle for you: then you shall say to Aaron, Take your rod, and cast it before Pharaoh, and it shall become a serpent.

10 And Moses and Aaron went in to Pharaoh, and they did so as the LORD had commanded: and Aaron cast down his rod before Pharaoh, and before his servants, and it became a serpent.

11 Then Pharaoh also called the wise men and the sorcerers: now the magicians of Egypt, they also did in like manner with their enchantments.

12 For they cast down every man his rod, and they became serpents: but Aaron's rod swallowed up their rods.

13 And he hardened Pharaoh's heart, that he hearkened not to them; as the LORD had said.

14 And the LORD said to Moses, Pharaoh's heart is hardened, he refuses to let the people go.

15 Get you to Pharaoh in the morning; lo, he goes out to the water; and you shall stand by the river's brink against he come; and the rod which was turned to a serpent shall you take in your hand.

16 And you shall say to him, The LORD God of the Hebrews has sent me to you, saying, Let my people go, that they may serve me in the wilderness: and, behold, hitherto you would not hear.

17 Thus says the LORD, In this you shall know that I am the LORD: behold, I will smite with the rod that is in mine hand upon the waters which are in the river, and they shall be turned to blood.

18 And the fish that is in the river shall die, and the river shall stink; and the Egyptians shall loath to drink of the water of the river.

19 And the LORD spoke to Moses, Say to Aaron, Take your rod, and stretch out your hand upon the waters of Egypt, upon their streams, upon their rivers, and upon their ponds, and upon all their pools of water, that they may become blood; and that there may be blood throughout all the land of Egypt, both in vessels of wood, and in vessels of stone.

20 And Moses and Aaron did so, as the LORD commanded; and he lifted up the rod, and smote the waters that were in the river, in the sight of Pharaoh, and in the sight of his servants; and all the waters that were in the river were turned to blood.

21 And the fish that was in the river died; and the river stank, and the Egyptians could not drink of the water of the river; and there was blood throughout all the land of Egypt.

22 And the magicians of Egypt did so with their enchantments: and Pharaoh's heart was hardened, neither did he hearken to them; as the LORD had said.

23 And Pharaoh turned and went into his house, neither did he set his heart to this also.

24 And all the Egyptians dug round about the river for water to drink; for they could not drink of the water of the river.

25 And seven days were fulfilled, after that the LORD had smitten the river.

CHAPTER 8

AND the LORD spoke to Moses, Go to Pharaoh, and say to him, Thus says the LORD, Let my people go, that they may serve me.

2 And if you refuse to let them go, behold, I will smite all your borders with frogs:

3 And the river shall bring forth frogs abundantly, which shall go up and come into your house, and into your bedchamber, and upon your bed, and into the house of your servants, and upon your people, and into your ovens, and into your kneading troughs:

4 And the frogs shall come up both on you, and upon your people, and upon all your servants.

5 And the LORD spoke to Moses, Say to Aaron, Stretch forth your hand with your rod over the streams, over the rivers, and over the ponds, and cause frogs to come up upon the land of Egypt.

6 And Aaron stretched out his hand over the waters of Egypt; and the frogs came up, and covered the land of Egypt.

7 And the magicians did so with their enchantments, and brought up frogs upon the land of Egypt.

8 Then Pharaoh called for Moses and Aaron, and said, Entreat the LORD, that he may take away the frogs from me, and from my people; and I will let the people go, that they may do sacrifice to the LORD.

9 And Moses said to Pharaoh, Glory over me: when shall I entreat for you, and for your servants, and for your people, to destroy the frogs from you and your houses, that they may remain in the river only?

10 And he said, Tomorrow. And he said, Be it according to your word: that you may know that there is none like the LORD our God.

11 And the frogs shall depart from you, and from your houses, and from your servants, and from your people; they shall remain in the river only.

12 And Moses and Aaron went out from Pharaoh: and Moses cried to the LORD because of the frogs which he had brought against Pharaoh.

13 And the LORD did according to the word of Moses; and the frogs died out of the houses, out of the villages, and out of the fields.

14 And they gathered them together upon heaps: and the land stank.

15 But when Pharaoh saw that there was respite, he hardened his heart, and hearkened not to them; as the LORD had said.

16 And the LORD said to Moses, Say to Aaron, Stretch out your rod, and smite the dust of the land, that it may become lice throughout all the land of Egypt.

17 And they did so; for Aaron stretched out his hand with his rod, and smote the dust of the earth, and it became lice in man, and in beast; all the dust of the land became lice throughout all the land of Egypt.

18 And the magicians did so with their enchantments to bring forth lice, but they could not: so there were lice upon man, and upon beast.

19 Then the magicians said to Pharaoh, This is the finger of God: and Pharaoh's heart was hardened, and he hearkened not to them; as the LORD had said.

20 And the LORD said to Moses, Rise up early in the morning, and stand before Pharaoh; lo, he comes forth to the water; and say to him, Thus says the LORD, Let my people go, that they may serve me.

21 Else, if you will not let my people go, behold, I will send swarms of flies upon you, and upon your servants, and upon your people, and into your houses: and the houses of the Egyptians shall be full of swarms of flies, and also the ground whereon they are.

22 And I will sever in that day the land of Goshen, in which my people dwell, that no swarms of flies shall be there; to the end you may know that I am the LORD in the midst of the earth.

23 And I will put a division between my people and your people: tomorrow shall this sign be.

24 And the LORD did so; and there came a grievous swarm of flies into the house of Pharaoh, and into his servants' houses, and into all the land of Egypt:

the land was corrupted by reason of the swarm of flies.

25 And Pharaoh called for Moses and for Aaron, and said, Go, sacrifice to your God in the land.

26 And Moses said, It is not meet so to do; for we shall sacrifice the abomination of the Egyptians to the LORD our God: lo, shall we sacrifice the abomination of the Egyptians before their eyes, and will they not stone us?

27 We will go three days' journey into the wilderness, and sacrifice to the LORD our God, as he shall command us.

28 And Pharaoh said, I will let you go, that you may sacrifice to the LORD your God in the wilderness; only you shall not go very far away: entreat for me.

29 And Moses said, Behold, I go out from you, and I will entreat the LORD that the swarms of flies may depart from Pharaoh, from his servants, and from his people, tomorrow: but let not Pharaoh deal deceitfully any more in not letting the people go to sacrifice to the LORD.

30 And Moses went out from Pharaoh, and entreated the LORD.

31 And the LORD did according to the word of Moses; and he removed the swarms of flies from Pharaoh, from his servants, and from his people; there remained not one.

32 And Pharaoh hardened his heart at this time also, neither would he let the people go.

CHAPTER 9

THEN the LORD said to Moses, Go in to Pharaoh, and tell him, Thus says the LORD God of the Hebrews, Let my people go, that they may serve me.

2 For if you refuse to let them go, and will hold them still,

3 Behold, the hand of the LORD is upon your cattle which is in the field, upon the horses, upon the asses, upon the camels, upon the oxen, and upon the sheep: there shall be a very grievous murrain.

4 And the LORD shall sever between the cattle of Israel and the cattle of Egypt: and there shall nothing die of all that is the children's of Israel.

5 And the LORD appointed a set time, saying, To morrow the LORD shall do this thing in the land.

6 And the LORD did that thing on the morrow, and all the cattle of Egypt died: but of the cattle of the children of Israel died not one.

7 And Pharaoh sent, and, behold, there was not one of the cattle of the Israelites dead. And the heart of Pharaoh was hardened, and he did not let the people go.

8 And the LORD said to Moses and to Aaron, Take to you handfuls of ashes of the furnace, and let Moses sprinkle it toward the heaven in the sight of Pharaoh.

9 And it shall become small dust in all the land of Egypt, and shall be a boil breaking forth with blains upon man, and upon beast, throughout all the land of Egypt.

10 And they took ashes of the furnace, and stood before Pharaoh; and Moses sprinkled it up toward heaven; and it became a boil breaking forth with blains upon man, and upon beast.

11 And the magicians could not stand before Moses because of the boils; for the boil was upon the magicians, and upon all the Egyptians.

12 And the LORD hardened the heart of Pharaoh, and he hearkened not to them; as the LORD had spoken to Moses.

13 And the LORD said to Moses, Rise up early in the morning, and stand before Pharaoh, and say to him, Thus says the LORD God of the Hebrews, Let my people go, that they may serve me.

14 For I will at this time send all my plagues upon your heart, and upon your servants, and upon your people; that you may know that there is none like me in all the earth.

15 For now I will stretch out my hand, that I may smite you and your people

with pestilence; and you shall be cut off from the earth.

16 And in very deed for this cause have I raised you up, for to show in you my power; and that my name may be declared throughout all the earth.

17 As yet you exalt yourself against my people, that you will not let them go?

18 Behold, tomorrow about this time I will cause it to rain a very grievous hail, such as has not been in Egypt since the foundation thereof even until now.

19 Send therefore now, and gather your cattle, and all that you have in the field; for upon every man and beast which shall be found in the field, and shall not be brought home, the hail shall come down upon them, and they shall die.

20 He that feared the word of the LORD among the servants of Pharaoh made his servants and his cattle flee into the houses:

21 And he that regarded not the word of the LORD left his servants and his cattle in the field.

22 And the LORD said to Moses, Stretch forth your hand toward heaven, that there may be hail in all the land of Egypt, upon man, and upon beast, and upon every herb of the field, throughout the land of Egypt.

23 And Moses stretched forth his rod toward heaven: and the LORD sent thunder and hail, and the fire ran along upon the ground; and the LORD rained hail upon the land of Egypt.

24 So there was hail, and fire mingled with the hail, very grievous, such as there was none like it in all the land of Egypt since it became a nation.

25 And the hail smote throughout all the land of Egypt all that was in the field, both man and beast; and the hail smote every herb of the field, and brake every tree of the field.

26 Only in the land of Goshen, where the children of Israel were, was there no hail.

27 And Pharaoh sent, and called for Moses and Aaron, and said to them, I have sinned this time: the LORD is righteous, and I and my people are wicked.

28 Entreat the LORD (for it is enough) that there be no more mighty thunderings and hail; and I will let you go, and you shall stay no longer.

29 And Moses said to him, As soon as I am gone out of the city, I will spread abroad my hands to the LORD; and the thunder shall cease, neither shall there be any more hail; that you may know how that the earth is the LORD's.

30 But as for you and your servants, I know that you will not yet fear the LORD God.

31 And the flax and the barley was smitten: for the barley was in the ear, and the flax was bolled.

32 But the wheat and the rie were not smitten: for they were not grown up.

33 And Moses went out of the city from Pharaoh, and spread abroad his hands to the LORD: and the thunders and hail ceased, and the rain was not poured upon the earth.

34 And when Pharaoh saw that the rain and the hail and the thunders were ceased, he sinned yet more, and hardened his heart, he and his servants.

35 And the heart of Pharaoh was hardened, neither would he let the children of Israel go; as the LORD had spoken by Moses.

CHAPTER 10

AND the LORD said to Moses, Go in to Pharaoh: for I have hardened his heart, and the heart of his servants, that I might show these my signs before him:

2 And that you may tell in the ears of your son, and of your son's son, what things I have wrought in Egypt, and my signs which I have done among them; that you may know how that I am the LORD.

3 And Moses and Aaron came in to Pharaoh, and said to him, Thus says the LORD God of the Hebrews, How long will you refuse to humble yourself before

me? let my people go, that they may serve me.

4 Else, if you refuse to let my people go, behold, tomorrow will I bring the locusts into your coast:

5 And they shall cover the face of the earth, that one cannot be able to see the earth: and they shall eat the residue of that which is escaped, which remains to you from the hail, and shall eat every tree which grows for you out of the field:

6 And they shall fill your houses, and the houses of all your servants, and the houses of all the Egyptians; which neither your fathers, nor your fathers' fathers have seen, since the day that they were upon the earth to this day. And he turned himself, and went out from Pharaoh.

7 And Pharaoh's servants said to him, How long shall this man be a snare to us? let the men go, that they may serve the LORD their God: do you not know yet that Egypt is destroyed?

8 And Moses and Aaron were brought again to Pharaoh: and he said to them, Go, serve the LORD your God: but who are they that shall go?

9 And Moses said, We will go with our young and with our old, with our sons and with our daughters, with our flocks and with our herds will we go; for we must hold a feast to the LORD.

10 And he said to them, Let the LORD be so with you, as I will let you go, and your little ones: look to it; for evil is before you.

11 Not so: go now you that are men, and serve the LORD; for that you did desire. And they were driven out from Pharaoh's presence.

12 And the LORD said to Moses, Stretch out your hand over the land of Egypt for the locusts, that they may come up upon the land of Egypt, and eat every herb of the land, even all that the hail has left.

13 And Moses stretched forth his rod over the land of Egypt, and the LORD brought an east wind upon the land all that day, and all that night; and when it was morning, the east wind brought the locusts.

14 And the locust went up over all the land of Egypt, and rested in all the coasts of Egypt: very grievous were they; before them there were no such locusts as they, neither after them shall be such.

15 For they covered the face of the whole earth, so that the land was darkened; and they did eat every herb of the land, and all the fruit of the trees which the hail had left: and there remained not any green thing in the trees, or in the herbs of the field, through all the land of Egypt.

16 Then Pharaoh called for Moses and Aaron in haste; and he said, I have sinned against the LORD your God, and against you.

17 Now therefore forgive, I pray you, my sin only this once, and entreat the LORD your God, that he may take away from me this death only.

18 And he went out from Pharaoh, and entreated the LORD.

19 And the LORD turned a mighty strong west wind, which took away the locusts, and cast them into the Red sea; there remained not one locust in all the coasts of Egypt.

20 But the LORD hardened Pharaoh's heart, so that he would not let the children of Israel go.

21 And the LORD said to Moses, Stretch out your hand toward heaven, that there may be darkness over the land of Egypt, even darkness which may be felt.

22 And Moses stretched forth his hand toward heaven; and there was a thick darkness in all the land of Egypt three days:

23 They saw not one another, neither rose any from his place for three days: but all the children of Israel had light in their dwellings.

24 And Pharaoh called to Moses, and said, Go, serve the LORD; only let your

flocks and your herds be stayed: let your little ones also go with you.

25 And Moses said, You must give us also sacrifices and burnt offerings, that we may sacrifice to the LORD our God.

26 Our cattle also shall go with us; there shall not an hoof be left behind; for thereof must we take to serve the LORD our God; and we know not with what we must serve the LORD, until we come thither.

27 But the LORD hardened Pharaoh's heart, and he would not let them go.

28 And Pharaoh said to him, Get you from me, take heed to yourself, see my face no more; for in that day you see my face you shall die.

29 And Moses said, You have spoken well, I will see your face again no more.

CHAPTER 11

AND the LORD said to Moses, Yet will I bring one plague more upon Pharaoh, and upon Egypt; afterwards he will let you go hence: when he shall let you go, he shall surely thrust you out hence altogether.

2 Speak now in the ears of the people, and let every man borrow of his neighbor, and every woman of her neighbor, jewels of silver and jewels of gold.

3 And the LORD gave the people favor in the sight of the Egyptians. Moreover the man Moses was very great in the land of Egypt, in the sight of Pharaoh's servants, and in the sight of the people.

4 And Moses said, Thus says the LORD, About midnight will I go out into the midst of Egypt:

5 And all the firstborn in the land of Egypt shall die, from the first born of Pharaoh that sits upon his throne, even to the firstborn of the maidservant that is behind the mill; and all the firstborn of beasts.

6 And there shall be a great cry throughout all the land of Egypt, such as there was none like it, nor shall be like it any more.

7 But against any of the children of Israel shall not a dog move his tongue, against man or beast: that you may know how that the LORD doth put a difference between the Egyptians and Israel.

8 And all these your servants shall come down to me, and bow down themselves to me, saying, Get out, and all the people that follow you: and after that I will go out. And he went out from Pharaoh in a great anger.

9 And the LORD said to Moses, Pharaoh shall not hearken to you; that my wonders may be multiplied in the land of Egypt.

10 And Moses and Aaron did all these wonders before Pharaoh: and the LORD hardened Pharaoh's heart, so that he would not let the children of Israel go out of his land.

CHAPTER 12

AND the LORD spoke to Moses and Aaron in the land of Egypt saying,

2 This month shall be to you the beginning of months: it shall be the first month of the year to you.

3 Speak to all the congregation of Israel, saying, In the tenth day of this month they shall take to them every man a lamb, according to the house of their fathers, a lamb for an house:

4 And if the household be too little for the lamb, let him and his neighbor next to his house take it according to the number of the souls; every man according to his eating shall make your count for the lamb.

5 Your lamb shall be without blemish, a male of the first year: you shall take it out from the sheep, or from the goats:

10:27 The same sunlight that melts wax hardens clay. The heart of the sinner determines his response to the Word of God.

11:5 See Psalm 139:16 comment for an interesting quiz.

6 And you shall keep it up until the fourteenth day of the same month: and the whole assembly of the congregation of Israel shall kill it in the evening.

7 And they shall take of the ·blood, and strike it on the two side posts and on the upper door post of the houses, wherein they shall eat it.

8 And they shall eat the flesh in that night, roast with fire, and unleavened bread; and with bitter herbs they shall eat it.

9 Eat not of it raw, nor sodden at all with water, but roast with fire; his head with his legs, and with the purtenance thereof.

10 And you shall let nothing of it remain until the morning; and that which remains of it until the morning you shall burn with fire.

11 And thus shall you eat it; with your loins girded, your shoes on your feet, and your staff in your hand; and you shall eat it in haste: it is the LORD's passover.

12 For I will pass through the land of Egypt this night, and will smite all the firstborn in the land of Egypt, both man and beast; and against all the gods of Egypt I will execute judgment: I am the LORD.

13 And the blood shall be to you for a token upon the houses where you are: and when I see the blood, I will pass over you, and the plague shall not be upon you to destroy you, when I smite the land of Egypt.

14 And this day shall be to you for a memorial; and you shall keep it a feast to the LORD throughout your generations; you shall keep it a feast by an ordinance for ever.

15 Seven days shall you eat unleavened bread; even the first day you shall put away leaven out of your houses: for whosoever eats leavened bread from the first day until the seventh day, that soul shall be cut off from Israel.

16 And in the first day there shall be an holy convocation, and in the seventh day there shall be an holy convocation to you; no manner of work shall be done in them, save that which every man must eat, that only may be done of you.

17 And you shall observe the feast of unleavened bread; for in this selfsame day have I brought your armies out of the land of Egypt: therefore shall you observe this day in your generations by an ordinance for ever.

18 In the first month, on the fourteenth day of the month at even, you shall eat unleavened bread, until the one and twentieth day of the month at even.

19 Seven days shall there be no leaven found in your houses: for whosoever eats that which is leavened, even that soul shall be cut off from the congregation of Israel, whether he be a stranger, or born in the land.

20 You shall eat nothing leavened; in all your habitations shall you eat unleavened bread.

21 Then Moses called for all the elders of Israel, and said to them, Draw out and take you a lamb according to your families, and kill the passover.

22 And you shall take a bunch of hyssop, and dip it in the blood that is in the bason, and strike the lintel and the two side posts with the blood that is in the bason; and none of you shall go out at the door of his house until the morning.

23 For the LORD will pass through to smite the Egyptians; and when he sees the blood upon the lintel, and on the two side posts, the LORD will pass over the door, and will not suffer the destroyer to come in to your houses to smite you.

24 And you shall observe this thing for an ordinance to you and to your sons for ever.

25 And it shall come to pass, when you be come to the land which the LORD will give you, according as he has promised, that you shall keep this service.

THE FIRSTBORN SLAIN

Exodus 12:1-29

The first Passover predicts salvation through the sacrificial blood of the Messiah. The sinner needs the Lamb of God (v. 3). The Lamb was to be killed by Israel (v. 6). The Savior's blood must be applied to the doorposts of the sinner's life (v. 7). He needs to eat the "bitter herbs" of contrition (v. 8). He must put on the whole armor of God (v. 11). He must have purity of doctrine (v. 15). He may then cease from his labors (v. 16).

26 And it shall come to pass, when your children shall say to you, What do you mean by this service?

27 That you shall say, It is the sacrifice of the LORD's passover, who passed over the houses of the children of Israel in Egypt, when he smote the Egyptians, and delivered our houses. And the people bowed the head and worshipped.

28 And the children of Israel went away, and did as the LORD had commanded Moses and Aaron, so did they.

29 And it came to pass, that at midnight the LORD smote all the firstborn in the land of Egypt, from the firstborn of Pharaoh that sat on his throne to the firstborn of the captive that was in the dungeon; and all the firstborn of cattle.

30 And Pharaoh rose up in the night, he, and all his servants, and all the Egyptians; and there was a great cry in Egypt; for there was not a house where there was not one dead.

31 And he called for Moses and Aaron by night, and said, Rise up, and get you forth from among my people, both you and the children of Israel; and go, serve the LORD, as you have said.

32 Also take your flocks and your herds, as you have said, and be gone; and bless me also.

33 And the Egyptians were urgent upon the people, that they might send them out of the land in haste; for they said, We be all dead men.

34 And the people took their dough before it was leavened, their kneading troughs being bound up in their clothes upon their shoulders.

35 And the children of Israel did according to the word of Moses; and they borrowed of the Egyptians jewels of silver, and jewels of gold, and raiment:

36 And the LORD gave the people favor in the sight of the Egyptians, so that they lent to them such things as they required. And they spoiled the Egyptians.

37 And the children of Israel journeyed from Rameses to Succoth, about six hundred thousand on foot that were men, beside children.

38 And a mixed multitude went up also with them; and flocks, and herds, even very much cattle.

39 And they baked unleavened cakes of the dough which they brought forth out of Egypt, for it was not leavened; because they were thrust out of Egypt, and could not tarry, neither had they prepared for themselves any victual.

40 Now the sojourning of the children of Israel, who dwelt in Egypt, was four hundred and thirty years.

41 And it came to pass at the end of the four hundred and thirty years, even the selfsame day it came to pass, that all the hosts of the LORD went out from the land of Egypt.

42 It is a night to be much observed to the LORD for bringing them out from the land of Egypt: this is that night of the LORD to be observed of all the children of Israel in their generations.

43 And the LORD said to Moses and Aaron, This is the ordinance of the passover: There shall no stranger eat thereof:

44 But every man's servant that is bought for money, when you have circumcised him, then shall he eat thereof.

45 A foreigner and an hired servant shall not eat thereof.

46 In one house shall it be eaten; you shall not carry forth ought of the flesh abroad out of the house; neither shall you break a bone thereof.

47 All the congregation of Israel shall keep it.

48 And when a stranger shall sojourn with you, and will keep the passover to

---

12:46 None of the Passover lamb's bones were to be broken. Just so, while others crucified with Jesus at Calvary had their legs broken by soldiers to hasten their death, Jesus' bones were not broken (see John 19:33, 36).

the LORD, let all his males be circumcised, and then let him come near and keep it; and he shall be as one that is born in the land: for no uncircumcised person shall eat thereof.

49 One law shall be to him that is homeborn, and to the stranger that sojourns among you.

50 Thus did all the children of Israel; as the LORD commanded Moses and Aaron, so did they.

51 And it came to pass the selfsame day, that the LORD did bring the children of Israel out of the land of Egypt by their armies.

CHAPTER 13

AND the LORD spoke to Moses, saying,

2 Sanctify to me all the firstborn, whatsoever opens the womb among the children of Israel, both of man and of beast: it is mine.

3 And Moses said to the people, Remember this day, in which you came out from Egypt, out of the house of bondage; for by strength of hand the LORD brought you out from this place: there shall no leavened bread be eaten.

4 This day you came out in the month Abib.

5 And it shall be when the LORD shall bring you into the land of the Canaanites, and the Hittites, and the Amorites, and the Hivites, and the Jebusites, which he swore to your fathers to give you, a land flowing with milk and honey, that you shall keep this service in this month.

6 Seven days you shall eat unleavened bread, and in the seventh day shall be a feast to the LORD.

7 Unleavened bread shall be eaten seven days; and there shall no leavened bread be seen with you, neither shall there be leaven seen with you in all your quarters.

8 And you shall show your son in that day, saying, This is done because of that which the LORD did to me when I came forth out of Egypt.

9 And it shall be for a sign to you upon your hand, and for a memorial between your eyes, that the LORD's law may be in your mouth: for with a strong hand has the LORD brought you out of Egypt.

10 You shall therefore keep this ordinance in his season from year to year.

11 And it shall be when the LORD shall bring you into the land of the Canaanites, as he swore to you and to your fathers, and shall give it you,

12 That you shall set apart to the LORD all that opens the matrix, and every firstling that comes of a beast which you have; the males shall be the LORD's.

13 And every firstling of an ass you shall redeem with a lamb; and if you will not redeem it, then you shall break his neck: and all the firstborn of man among your children shall you redeem.

14 And it shall be when your son asks you in time to come, saying, What is this? that you shall say to him, By strength of hand the LORD brought us out from Egypt, from the house of bondage:

15 And it came to pass, when Pharaoh would hardly let us go, that the LORD slew all the firstborn in the land of Egypt, both the firstborn of man, and the firstborn of beast: therefore I sacrifice to the LORD all that opens the matrix, being males; but all the firstborn of my children I redeem.

16 And it shall be for a token upon your hand, and for frontlets between your eyes: for by strength of hand the LORD brought us forth out of Egypt.

17 And it came to pass, when Pharaoh had let the people go, that God led them not through the way of the land of the Philistines, although that was near; for God said, Lest peradventure the people repent when they see war, and they return to Egypt:

18 But God led the people about, through the way of the wilderness of the

Red sea: and the children of Israel went up harnessed out of the land of Egypt.

19 And Moses took the bones of Joseph with him: for he had straightly sworn the children of Israel, saying, God will surely visit you; and you shall carry up my bones away hence with you.

20 And they took their journey from Succoth, and encamped in Etham, in the edge of the wilderness.

21 And the LORD went before them by day in a pillar of a cloud, to lead them the way; and by night in a pillar of fire, to give them light; to go by day and night:

22 He took not away the pillar of the cloud by day, nor the pillar of fire by night, from before the people.

THE FUNCTION OF THE LAW

14:16 The Law is the rod of God in the hand of Moses. It will open up the Red Sea and bring deliverance of those who have been "taken captive by the devil." It is a "schoolmaster to bring us to Christ" (Galatians 3:24).

CHAPTER 14

AND the LORD spoke to Moses, saying,

2 Speak to the children of Israel, that they turn and encamp before Pihahiroth, between Migdol and the sea, over against Baalzephon: before it shall you encamp by the sea.

3 For Pharaoh will say of the children of Israel, They are entangled in the land, the wilderness has shut them in.

4 And I will harden Pharaoh's heart, that he shall follow after them; and I will be honoured upon Pharaoh, and upon all his host; that the Egyptians may know that I am the LORD. And they did so.

5 And it was told the king of Egypt that the people fled: and the heart of Pharaoh and of his servants was turned against the people, and they said, Why have we done this, that we have let Israel go from serving us?

6 And he made ready his chariot, and took his people with him:

7 And he took six hundred chosen chariots, and all the chariots of Egypt, and captains over every one of them.

8 And the LORD hardened the heart of Pharaoh king of Egypt, and he pursued after the children of Israel: and the children of Israel went out with an high hand.

9 But the Egyptians pursued after them, all the horses and chariots of Pharaoh, and his horsemen, and his army, and overtook them encamping by the sea, beside Pihahiroth, before Baalzephon.

10 And when Pharaoh drew nigh, the children of Israel lifted up their eyes, and, behold, the Egyptians marched after them; and they were sore afraid: and the children of Israel cried out to the LORD.

11 And they said to Moses, Because there were no graves in Egypt, have you taken us away to die in the wilderness? why have you dealt thus with us, to carry us forth out of Egypt?

12 Is not this the word that we did tell you in Egypt, saying, Let us alone, that we may serve the Egyptians? For it had been better for us to serve the Egyptians, than that we should die in the wilderness.

13 And Moses said to the people, Fear not, stand still, and see the salvation of the LORD, which he will show to you to day: for the Egyptians whom you have seen to day, you shall see them again no more for ever.

14 The LORD shall fight for you, and you shall hold your peace.

15 And the LORD said to Moses, Why are you crying to me? speak to the children of Israel, that they go forward:

16 But lift up your rod, and stretch out your hand over the sea, and divide it: and the children of Israel shall go on dry ground through the midst of the sea.

17 And I, behold, I will harden the hearts of the Egyptians, and they shall follow them: and I will get me honour upon Pharaoh, and upon all his host, upon his chariots, and upon his horsemen.

18 And the Egyptians shall know that I am the LORD, when I have gotten me honour upon Pharaoh, upon his chariots, and upon his horsemen.

19 And the angel of God, which went before the camp of Israel, removed and went behind them; and the pillar of the cloud went from before their face, and stood behind them:

20 And it came between the camp of the Egyptians and the camp of Israel; and it was a cloud and darkness to them, but it gave light by night to these: so that the one came not near the other all the night.

21 And Moses stretched out his hand over the sea; and the LORD caused the sea to go back by a strong east wind all that night, and made the sea dry land, and the waters were divided.

22 And the children of Israel went into the midst of the sea upon the dry ground: and the waters were a wall to them on their right hand, and on their left.

23 And the Egyptians pursued, and went in after them to the midst of the sea, even all Pharaoh's horses, his chariots, and his horsemen.

24 And it came to pass, that in the morning watch the LORD looked to the host of the Egyptians through the pillar of fire and of the cloud, and troubled the host of the Egyptians,

25 And took off their chariot wheels, that they drive them heavily: so that the Egyptians said, Let us flee from the face

The Holy Spirit convicts us . . .
He shows us the Ten Commandments;
the Law is the schoolmaster
that leads us to Christ.
We look in the mirror
of the Ten Commandments,
and we see ourselves in that mirror.

Billy Graham
AMERICAN EVANGELIST
BORN 1918
IN NORTH CAROLINA

of Israel; for the LORD fights for them against the Egyptians.

26 And the LORD said to Moses, Stretch out your hand over the sea, that the waters may come again upon the Egyptians, upon their chariots, and upon their horsemen.

27 And Moses stretched forth his hand over the sea, and the sea returned to his strength when the morning appeared; and the Egyptians fled against it; and the LORD overthrew the Egyptians in the midst of the sea.

28 And the waters returned, and covered the chariots, and the horsemen, and all the host of Pharaoh that came into the sea after them; there remained not so much as one of them.

29 But the children of Israel walked upon dry land in the midst of the sea;

*In all my perplexities and distresses,
the Bible has never failed
to give me light and strength.*

Robert E. Lee
1807-1870
GENERAL OF THE CONFEDERACY
DURING THE AMERICAN CIVIL WAR

and the waters were a wall to them on their right hand, and on their left.

30 Thus the LORD saved Israel that day out of the hand of the Egyptians; and Israel saw the Egyptians dead upon the sea shore.

31 And Israel saw that great work which the LORD did upon the Egyptians: and the people feared the LORD, and believed the LORD, and his servant Moses.

CHAPTER 15

THEN sang Moses and the children of Israel this song to the LORD, and spoke, saying, I will sing to the LORD, for he has triumphed gloriously: the horse and his rider has he thrown into the sea.

2 The LORD is my strength and song, and he is become my salvation: he is my God, and I will prepare him an habita-tion; my father's God, and I will exalt him.

3 The LORD is a man of war: the LORD is his name.

4 Pharaoh's chariots and his host has he cast into the sea: his chosen captains also are drowned in the Red sea.

5 The depths have covered them: they sank into the bottom as a stone.

6 Your right hand, O LORD, is become glorious in power: your right hand, O LORD, has dashed in pieces the enemy.

7 And in the greatness of your excellency you have overthrown them that rose up against you: you sent forth your wrath, which consumed them as stubble.

8 And with the blast of your nostrils the waters were gathered together, the floods stood upright as an heap, and the depths were congealed in the heart of the sea.

9 The enemy said, I will pursue, I will overtake, I will divide the spoil; my lust shall be satisfied upon them; I will draw my sword, my hand shall destroy them.

10 You did blow with your wind, the sea covered them: they sank as lead in the mighty waters.

11 Who is like you, O LORD, among the gods? who is like you, glorious in holiness, fearful in praises, doing wonders?

12 You stretched out your right hand, the earth swallowed them.

13 You in your mercy have led forth the people which you have redeemed: you have guided them in your strength to your holy habitation.

14 The people shall hear, and be afraid: sorrow shall take hold on the inhabitants of Palestina.

15 Then the dukes of Edom shall be amazed; the mighty men of Moab, trembling shall take hold upon them; all the inhabitants of Canaan shall melt away.

16 Fear and dread shall fall upon them; by the greatness of your arm they shall be as still as a stone; till your people pass over, O LORD, till the people pass over, which you have purchased.

> So pure, so just, so uncompromising
> is the Law of God,
> that when it is really understood,
> it makes us quail,
> and brings us to our knees.

CHARLES SPURGEON

1834-1892

PRINCE OF PREACHERS

17 You shall bring them in, and plant them in the mountain of your inheritance, in the place, O LORD, which you have made for you to dwell in, in the Sanctuary, O LORD, which your hands have established.

18 The LORD shall reign for ever and ever.

19 For the horse of Pharaoh went in with his chariots and with his horsemen into the sea, and the LORD brought again the waters of the sea upon them; but the children of Israel went on dry land in the midst of the sea.

20 And Miriam the prophetess, the sister of Aaron, took a timbrel in her hand; and all the women went out after her with timbrels and with dances.

21 And Miriam answered them, Sing to the LORD, for he has triumphed gloriously; the horse and his rider has he thrown into the sea.

22 So Moses brought Israel from the Red sea, and they went out into the wilderness of Shur; and they went three days in the wilderness, and found no water.

23 And when they came to Marah, they could not drink of the waters of Marah, for they were bitter: therefore the name of it was called Marah.

24 And the people murmured against Moses, saying, What shall we drink?

25 And he cried to the LORD; and the LORD showed him a tree, which when he had cast into the waters, the waters were made sweet: there he made for them a statute and an ordinance, and there he proved them,

26 And said, If you will diligently hearken to the voice of the LORD your God, and will do that which is right in his sight, and will give ear to his commandments, and keep all his statutes, I will put none of these diseases upon you, which I have brought upon the Egyptians: for I am the LORD that heals you.

27 And they came to Elim, where were twelve wells of water, and threescore and ten palm trees: and they encamped there by the waters.

CHAPTER 16

AND they took their journey from Elim, and all the congregation of the children of Israel came to the wilderness of Sin, which is between Elim and Sinai, on the fifteenth day of the second month after their departing out of the land of Egypt.

2 And the whole congregation of the children of Israel murmured against Moses and Aaron in the wilderness:

3 And the children of Israel said to them, Would to God we had died by the hand of the LORD in the land of Egypt, when we sat by the flesh pots, and when we did eat bread to the full; for you have brought us forth into this wilderness, to kill this whole assembly with hunger.

4 Then said the LORD to Moses, Behold, I will rain bread from heaven for you; and the people shall go out and gather a certain rate every day, that I may prove them, whether they will walk in my law, or no.

5 And it shall come to pass, that on the sixth day they shall prepare that which they bring in; and it shall be twice as much as they gather daily.

6 And Moses and Aaron said to all the children of Israel, At even, then you shall

---

15:26 To learn about the healing power of Jesus' sacrifice, see Isaiah 53:5 and 1 Peter 2:24.

> The Law searches
> to the dividing asunder of joints
> and marrow,
> and it is a discerner of the thoughts
> and intents of the heart.
> Its excessive light strikes us
> like Saul of Tarsus,
> to the earth,
> and makes us cry for mercy.

CHARLES SPURGEON

1834-1892

PRINCE OF PREACHERS

know that the LORD has brought you out from the land of Egypt:

7 And in the morning, then you shall see the glory of the LORD; for that he hears your murmurings against the LORD: and what are we, that you murmur against us?

8 And Moses said, This shall be, when the LORD shall give you in the evening flesh to eat, and in the morning bread to the full; for that the LORD hears your murmurings which you murmur against him: and what are we? your murmurings are not against us, but against the LORD.

9 And Moses spoke to Aaron, Say to all the congregation of the children of Israel, Come near before the LORD: for he has heard your murmurings.

10 And it came to pass, as Aaron spoke to the whole congregation of the children of Israel, that they looked toward the wilderness, and, behold, the glory of the LORD appeared in the cloud.

11 And the LORD spoke to Moses, saying,

12 I have heard the murmurings of the children of Israel: speak to them, saying, At even you shall eat flesh, and in the morning you shall be filled with bread; and you shall know that I am the LORD your God.

13 And it came to pass, that at even the quails came up, and covered the camp: and in the morning the dew lay round about the host.

14 And when the dew that lay was gone up, behold, upon the face of the wilderness there lay a small round thing, as small as the hoar frost on the ground.

15 And when the children of Israel saw it, they said one to another, It is manna: for they did not know what it was. And Moses said to them, This is the bread which the LORD has given you to eat.

16 This is the thing which the LORD has commanded, Gather of it every man according to his eating, an omer for every man, according to the number of your persons; take you every man for them which are in his tents.

17 And the children of Israel did so, and gathered, some more, some less.

18 And when they did mete it with an omer, he that gathered much had nothing over, and he that gathered little had no lack; they gathered every man according to his eating.

19 And Moses said, Let no man leave of it till the morning.

20 Notwithstanding they hearkened not to Moses; but some of them left of it until the morning, and it bred worms, and stank: and Moses was wroth with them.

21 And they gathered it every morning, every man according to his eating: and when the sun waxed hot, it melted.

22 And it came to pass, that on the sixth day they gathered twice as much bread, two omers for one man: and all the rulers of the congregation came and told Moses.

23 And he said to them, This is that which the LORD has said, Tomorrow is the rest of the holy sabbath to the LORD: bake that which you will bake to day, and seethe that you will seethe; and that which remains over lay up for you to be kept until the morning.

16:12 For thoughts on vegetarianism see Psalm 66:15 comment.

24 And they laid it up till the morning, as Moses bade: and it did not stink, neither was there any worm therein.

25 And Moses said, Eat that to day; for to day is a sabbath to the LORD: to day you shall not find it in the field.

26 Six days you shall gather it; but on the seventh day, which is the sabbath, in it there shall be none.

27 And it came to pass, that there went out some of the people on the seventh day for to gather, and they found none.

28 And the LORD said to Moses, How long do you refuse to keep my commandments and my laws?

29 See, for that the LORD has given you the sabbath, therefore he gives you on the sixth day the bread of two days; abide every man in his place, let no man go out of his place on the seventh day.

30 So the people rested on the seventh day.

31 And the house of Israel called the name thereof Manna: and it was like coriander seed, white; and the taste of it was like wafers made with honey.

32 And Moses said, This is the thing which the LORD commands, Fill an omer of it to be kept for your generations; that they may see the bread wherewith I have fed you in the wilderness, when I brought you forth from the land of Egypt.

33 And Moses said to Aaron, Take a pot, and put an omer full of manna therein, and lay it up before the LORD, to be kept for your generations.

34 As the LORD commanded Moses, so Aaron laid it up before the Testimony, to be kept.

35 And the children of Israel did eat manna forty years, until they came to a land inhabited; they did eat manna, until they came to the borders of the land of Canaan.

36 Now an omer is the tenth part of an ephah.

CHAPTER 17

AND all the congregation of the children of Israel journeyed from the wilderness of Sin, after their journeys, according to the commandment of the LORD, and pitched in Rephidim: and there was no water for the people to drink.

2 Therefore the people did chide with Moses, and said, Give us water that we may drink. And Moses said to them, Why do you chide with me? why do you tempt the LORD?

3 And the people thirsted there for water; and the people murmured against Moses, and said, Why is this that you have brought us up out of Egypt, to kill us and our children and our cattle with thirst?

4 And Moses cried to the LORD, saying, What shall I do to this people? they be almost ready to stone me.

5 And the LORD said to Moses, Go on before the people, and take with you of the elders of Israel; and your rod, wherewith you smote the river, take in your hand, and go.

6 Behold, I will stand before you there upon the rock in Horeb; and you shall smite the rock, and there shall come water out of it, that the people may drink. And Moses did so in the sight of the elders of Israel.

7 And he called the name of the place Massah, and Meribah, because of the chiding of the children of Israel, and because they tempted the LORD, saying, Is the LORD among us, or not?

8 Then came Amalek, and fought with Israel in Rephidim.

9 And Moses said to Joshua, Choose us out men, and go out, fight with Amalek: to morrow I will stand on the top of the hill with the rod of God in mine hand.

10 So Joshua did as Moses had said to him, and fought with Amalek: and Moses, Aaron, and Hur went up to the top of the hill.

11 And it came to pass, when Moses held up his hand, that Israel prevailed:

MOSES STRIKING THE ROCK IN HOREB

Exodus 17:5-6

The rod of the law, punishment for sin, came down upon the rock (Christ) at the cross (see 1 Corinthians 10:4), and Jesus' life-saving blood issued forth with water (see John 19:34). Through this issue of blood and water, those who accept Jesus' sacrifice for their sins overcome the world (see 1 John 5:5-6). And those who believe on Him "shall never thirst" (John 6:35).

and when he let down his hand, Amalek prevailed.

12 But Moses hands were heavy; and they took a stone, and put it under him, and he sat thereon; and Aaron and Hur stayed up his hands, the one on the one side, and the other on the other side; and his hands were steady until the going down of the sun.

13 And Joshua discomfited Amalek and his people with the edge of the sword.

14 And the LORD said to Moses, Write this for a memorial in a book, and re-hearse it in the ears of Joshua: for I will utterly put out the remembrance of Amalek from under heaven.

15 And Moses built an altar, and called the name of it Jehovahnissi:

16 For he said, Because the LORD has sworn that the LORD will have war with Amalek from generation to generation.

CHAPTER 18

WHEN Jethro, the priest of Midian, Moses' father in law, heard of all that God had done for Moses, and for Israel his people, and that the LORD had brought Israel out of Egypt;

2 Then Jethro, Moses' father in law, took Zipporah, Moses' wife, after he had sent her back,

3 And her two sons; of which the name of the one was Gershom; for he said, I have been an alien in a strange land:

4 And the name of the other was Eliezer; for the God of my father, said he, was mine help, and delivered me from the sword of Pharaoh:

5 And Jethro, Moses' father in law, came with his sons and his wife to Moses into the wilderness, where he encamped at the mount of God:

6 And he said to Moses, I your father in law Jethro am come to you, and your wife, and her two sons with her.

7 And Moses went out to meet his fa-ther in law, and did obeisance, and kissed him; and they asked each other of their welfare; and they came into the tent.

8 And Moses told his father in law all that the LORD had done to Pharaoh and to the Egyptians for Israel's sake, and all the travail that had come upon them by the way, and how the LORD delivered them.

9 And Jethro rejoiced for all the good-ness which the LORD had done to Israel, whom he had delivered out of the hand of the Egyptians.

10 And Jethro said, Blessed be the LORD, who has delivered you out of the hand of the Egyptians, and out of the hand of Pharaoh, who has delivered the people from under the hand of the Egyptians.

11 Now I know that the LORD is greater than all gods: for in the thing wherein they dealt proudly he was above them.

12 And Jethro, Moses' father in law, took a burnt offering and sacrifices for God: and Aaron came, and all the elders of Israel, to eat bread with Moses' father in law before God.

13 And it came to pass on the morrow, that Moses sat to judge the people: and the people stood by Moses from the morning to the evening.

14 And when Moses' father in law saw all that he did to the people, he said, What is this thing that you do to the people? why do you sit alone, and all the people stand by you from morning to even?

15 And Moses said to his father in law, Because the people come to me to en-quire of God:

16 When they have a matter, they come to me; and I judge between one and an-other, and I do make them know the statutes of God, and his laws.

17 And Moses' father in law said to him, The thing that you do is not good.

18 You will surely wear away, both you, and this people that is with you: for this thing is too heavy for you; you are not able to perform it alone.

19 Hearken now to my voice, I will give you counsel, and God shall be with you:

Be you for the people to God-ward, that you may bring the causes to God:

20 And you shall teach them ordinances and laws, and shall show them the way wherein they must walk, and the work that they must do.

21 Moreover you shall provide out of all the people able men, such as fear God, men of truth, hating covetousness; and place such over them, to be rulers of thousands, and rulers of hundreds, rulers of fifties, and rulers of tens:

22 And let them judge the people at all seasons: and it shall be, that every great matter they shall bring to you, but every small matter they shall judge: so shall it be easier for yourself, and they shall bear the burden with you.

23 If you shall do this thing, and God command you so, then you shall be able to endure, and all this people shall also go to their place in peace.

24 So Moses hearkened to the voice of his father in law, and did all that he had said.

25 And Moses chose able men out of all Israel, and made them heads over the people, rulers of thousands, rulers of hundreds, rulers of fifties, and rulers of tens.

26 And they judged the people at all seasons: the hard causes they brought to Moses, but every small matter they judged themselves.

27 And Moses let his father in law depart; and he went his way into his own land.

CHAPTER 19

IN the third month, when the children of Israel were gone forth out of the land of Egypt, the same day came they into the wilderness of Sinai.

2 For they were departed from Rephidim, and were come to the desert of Sinai, and had pitched in the wilderness; and there Israel camped before the mount.

3 And Moses went up to God, and the LORD called to him out of the moun-tain, saying, Thus shall you say to the house of Jacob, and tell the children of Israel;

4 You have seen what I did to the Egyptians, and how I bare you on eagles' wings, and brought you to myself.

5 Now therefore, if you will obey my voice indeed, and keep my covenant, then you shall be a peculiar treasure to me above all people: for all the earth is mine:

6 And you shall be to me a kingdom of priests, and an holy nation. These are the words which you shall speak to the children of Israel.

7 And Moses came and called for the elders of the people, and laid before their faces all these words which the LORD commanded him.

8 And all the people answered together, and said, All that the LORD has spoken we will do. And Moses returned the words of the people to the LORD.

9 And the LORD said to Moses, Lo, I come to you in a thick cloud, that the people may hear when I speak with you, and believe you for ever. And Moses told the words of the people to the LORD.

10 And the LORD said to Moses, Go to the people, and sanctify them to day and tomorrow, and let them wash their clothes,

11 And be ready against the third day: for the third day the LORD will come down in the sight of all the people upon mount Sinai.

12 And you shall set bounds to the people round about, saying, Take heed to yourselves, that you go not up into the mount, or touch the border of it: whosoever touches the mount shall be surely put to death:

13 There shall not an hand touch it, but he shall surely be stoned, or shot through; whether it be beast or man, it shall not live: when the trumpet sounds long, they shall come up to the mount.

14 And Moses went down from the mount to the people, and sanctified the people; and they washed their clothes.

THE GIVING OF THE LAW UPON MOUNT SANAI

Exodus 19:16

15 And he said to the people, Be ready against the third day: come not at your wives.

16 And it came to pass on the third day in the morning, that there were thunders and lightnings, and a thick cloud upon the mount, and the voice of the trumpet exceeding loud; so that all the people that were in the camp trembled.

17 And Moses brought forth the people out of the camp to meet with God; and they stood at the nether part of the mount.

18 And mount Sinai was altogether on a smoke, because the LORD descended upon it in fire: and the smoke thereof ascended as the smoke of a furnace, and the whole mount quaked greatly.

19 And when the voice of the trumpet sounded long, and waxed louder and louder, Moses spoke, and God answered him by a voice.

20 And the LORD came down upon mount Sinai, on the top of the mount: and the LORD called Moses up to the top of the mount; and Moses went up.

21 And the LORD said to Moses, Go down, charge the people, lest they break through to the LORD to gaze, and many of them perish.

*Secure sinners must hear
the thundering of Mount Sinai
before we bring them to Mount Zion.*

*Every minister should be a Boanerges,
a son of thunder,
as well as Barnabas, a son of consolation.*

George Whitfield

1714-1770
FAMOUS OPEN-AIR PREACHER

22 And let the priests also, which come near to the LORD, sanctify themselves, lest the LORD break forth upon them.

23 And Moses said to the LORD, The people cannot come up to mount Sinai: for you charged us, saying, Set bounds about the mount, and sanctify it.

24 And the LORD said to him, Away, get down, and you shall come up, you, and Aaron with you: but let not the priests and the people break through to come up to the LORD, lest he break forth upon them.

25 So Moses went down to the people, and spoke to them.

CHAPTER 20

AND God spoke all these words, saying,

2 I am the LORD your God, which have brought you out of the land of Egypt, out of the house of bondage.

3 You shall have no other gods before me.

4 You shall not make for yourself any graven image, or any likeness of any thing that is in heaven above, or that is in the earth beneath, or that is in the water under the earth.

5 You shall not bow down yourself to them, nor serve them: for I the LORD your God am a jealous God, visiting the iniquity of the fathers upon the children to the third and fourth generation of them that hate me;

6 And showing mercy to thousands of them that love me, and keep my commandments.

7 You shall not take the name of the LORD your God in vain; for the LORD will not hold him guiltless that takes his name in vain.

8 Remember the sabbath day, to keep it holy.

9 Six days shall you labor, and do all your work:

10 But the seventh day is the sabbath of the LORD your God: in it you shall not do any work, you, nor your son, nor your daughter, your manservant, nor your maidservant, nor your cattle, nor your stranger that is within your gates:

11 For in six days the LORD made heaven and earth, the sea, and all that in them is, and rested the seventh day: therefore the LORD blessed the sabbath day, and hallowed it.

12 Honour your father and your mother: that your days may be long upon the land which the LORD your God gives you.

19:20 If the sinner will humble himself before God, God will draw near to the sinner (James 4:8-10).

13 You shall not kill.

14 You shall not commit adultery.

15 You shall not steal.

16 You shall not bear false witness against your neighbor.

17 You shall not covet your neighbor's house, you shall not covet your neighbor's wife, nor his manservant, nor his maidservant, nor his ox, nor his ass, nor any thing that is your neighbor's.

18 And all the people saw the thunderings, and the lightnings, and the noise of the trumpet, and the mountain smoking: and when the people saw it, they removed, and stood afar off.

19 And they said to Moses, Speak with us, and we will hear: but let not God speak with us, lest we die.

20 And Moses said to the people, Fear not: for God is come to prove you, and that his fear may be before your faces, that you sin not.

21 And the people stood afar off, and Moses drew near to the thick darkness where God was.

22 And the LORD said to Moses, Thus you shall say to the children of Israel, You have seen that I have talked with you from heaven.

The true function of the Law
is to accuse and to kill;

but the function of the gospel
is to make alive.

Martin Luther
1483-1546
GERMAN PRIEST
WHO FOUNDED
THE LUTHERAN CHURCH

23 You shall not make with me gods of silver, neither shall you make for yourselves gods of gold.

20:14 Don't rely solely on your conscience to save you from sin. Our love for sin can overwhelm the still, small voice of conscience.

A woman in her early 40s committed adultery and was so weighed down with a sense of guilt that she cried off and on for three months. In an effort to be free from guilt, she finally confessed her sin to her husband, who forgave her immediately. However, the woman still found no relief from her guilt, sinking deeper and deeper into depression. She would often sleep downstairs in their two-story home, wrapped in a blanket, weeping and praying.

One night, her loving husband crept down stairs and was relieved to see her wrapped in a blanket, soundly sleeping. In the morning, he went outside and picked a rose. He then wrote her a love note and left it on the table for her to find.

After some time, he went into the room and was horrified to find that she had committed suicide during the night.

We need more than our conscience to keep us from sin; we need a healthy fear of God. See Proverbs 2:1-5 comment.

For some repercussions of adultery see Psalm 107:17 comment.

20:18 "If the giving of the Law, while it was yet unbroken, was attended with such a display of awe-inspiring power, what will that day be when the Lord shall, with flaming fire, take vengeance on those who have willfully broken that Law?" Charles Spurgeon

*The only way we can know
whether we are sinning
is by knowing His moral Law.*

Jonathan Edwards

1703-1758

THIRD PRESIDENT OF PRINCETON

24 An altar of earth you shall make to me, and shall sacrifice thereon your burnt offerings, and your peace offerings, your sheep, and your oxen: in all places where I record my name I will come to you, and I will bless you.

25 And if you will make me an altar of stone, you shall not build it of hewn stone: for if you lift up your tool upon it, you have polluted it.

26 Neither shall you go up by steps to mine altar, that your nakedness be not discovered thereon.

CHAPTER 21

NOW these are the judgments which you shall set before them.

2 If you buy a Hebrew servant, six years he shall serve: and in the seventh he shall go out free for nothing.

3 If he came in by himself, he shall go out by himself: if he were married, then his wife shall go out with him.

4 If his master have given him a wife, and she have born him sons or daughters; the wife and her children shall be her master's, and he shall go out by himself.

5 And if the servant shall plainly say, I love my master, my wife, and my children; I will not go out free:

6 Then his master shall bring him to the judges; he shall also bring him to the door, or to the door post; and his master shall bore his ear through with an awl; and he shall serve him for ever.

7 And if a man sell his daughter to be a maidservant, she shall not go out as the menservants do.

8 If she please not her master, who has betrothed her to himself, then shall he let her be redeemed: to sell her to a strange nation he shall have no power, seeing he has dealt deceitfully with her.

9 And if he have betrothed her to his son, he shall deal with her after the manner of daughters.

10 If he take him another wife; her food, her raiment, and her duty of marriage, shall he not diminish.

11 And if he do not these three to her, then shall she go out free without money.

12 He that smites a man, so that he die, shall be surely put to death.

21:5-6 "The slavery which existed among the ancient Jews was a very different thing from that which has disgraced humanity in modern times. . . . [The slave then] was quite free to leave his master's house and go whither he pleased. But it seems that the servitude was so exceedingly light, and, indeed, was so much for the benefit of the person in it, that frequently he would not go free. They preferred to continue as they were, servants to their masters." Charles Spurgeon

21:5-6 The sinner, upon conversion, becomes a servant of Jesus Christ. He presents his body as a living sacrifice. His ear is forever open to the voice of the Savior (see John 10:9). He hears His voice.

Memorize
the Ten Commandments

Use these picture figures to memorize the Ten Commandments.
Then test your memory and grade yourself.
Put each picture in your mind, and it will remind you of each commandment.

1. You shall have no other gods before Me.
God should be number one.

2. You shall not make yourself any graven image.
Don't bow down to anything but God.

3. You shall not take the name of the Lord your God in vain.
Don't use your lips to dishonor God.

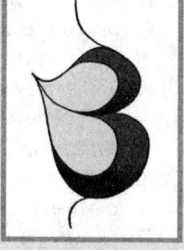

4. Remember the Sabbath Day to keep it holy.
Don't neglect the things of God.

5. Honor your father and your mother.

6. You shall not kill.

7. You shall not commit adultery.
Adultery leaves a heart broken.

8. You shall not steal.

9. You shall not lie.
(a "lying" nine)

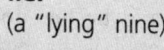

10. You shall not covet.
Don't want what others have.

13 And if a man lie not in wait, but God deliver him into his hand; then I will appoint you a place where he shall flee.

14 But if a man come presumptuously upon his neighbor, to slay him with guile; you shall take him from mine altar, that he may die.

15 And he that smites his father, or his mother, shall be surely put to death.

16 And he that steals a man, and sells him, or if he be found in his hand, he shall surely be put to death.

17 And he that curses his father, or his mother, shall surely be put to death.

18 And if men strive together, and one smite another with a stone, or with his fist, and he die not, but keeps his bed:

19 If he rise again, and walk abroad upon his staff, then shall he that smote him be quit: only he shall pay for the loss of his time, and shall cause him to be thoroughly healed.

20 And if a man smite his servant, or his maid, with a rod, and he die under his hand; he shall be surely punished.

21 Notwithstanding, if he continue a day or two, he shall not be punished: for he is his money.

22 If men strive, and hurt a woman with child, so that her fruit depart from her, and yet no mischief follow: he shall be surely punished, according as the woman's husband will lay upon him; and he shall pay as the judges determine.

23 And if any mischief follow, then you shall give life for life,

24 Eye for eye, tooth for tooth, hand for hand, foot for foot,

25 Burning for burning, wound for wound, stripe for stripe.

26 And if a man smite the eye of his servant, or the eye of his maid, that it perish; he shall let him go free for his eye's sake.

27 And if he smite out his manservant's tooth, or his maidservant's tooth; he shall let him go free for his tooth's sake.

The trouble with people. who are not seeking for a Savior, and for salvation, is that they do not understand the nature of sin. It is the peculiar function of the Law to bring such an understanding to a man's mind and conscience. That is why great evangelical preachers 300 years ago in the time of the Puritans, and 200 years ago in the time of Whitfield and others, always engaged in what they called a preliminary Law work.

Dr. Martin Lloyd-Jones

1899-1981
MINISTER, WESTMINSTER CHAPEL
LONDON

28 If an ox gore a man or a woman, that they die: then the ox shall be surely stoned, and his flesh shall not be eaten; but the owner of the ox shall be quit.

29 But if the ox were wont to push with his horn in time past, and it has been testified to his owner, and he has not kept him in, but that he has killed a man

or a woman; the ox shall be stoned, and his owner also shall be put to death.

30 If there be laid on him a sum of money, then he shall give for the ransom of his life whatsoever is laid upon him.

31 Whether he have gored a son, or have gored a daughter, according to this judgment shall it be done to him.

32 If the ox shall push a manservant or a maidservant; he shall give to their master thirty shekels of silver, and the ox shall be stoned.

33 And if a man shall open a pit, or if a man shall dig a pit, and not cover it, and an ox or an ass fall therein;

34 The owner of the pit shall make it good, and give money to the owner of them; and the dead beast shall be his.

35 And if one man's ox hurt another's, that he die; then they shall sell the live ox, and divide the money of it; and the dead ox also they shall divide.

36 Or if it be known that the ox has used to push in time past, and his owner has not kept him in; he shall surely pay ox for ox; and the dead shall be his own.

CHAPTER 22

IF a man shall steal an ox, or a sheep, and kill it, or sell it; he shall restore five oxen for an ox, and four sheep for a sheep.

2 If a thief be found breaking up, and be smitten that he die, there shall no blood be shed for him.

3 If the sun be risen upon him, there shall be blood shed for him; for he should make full restitution; if he have nothing, then he shall be sold for his theft.

4 If the theft be certainly found in his hand alive, whether it be ox, or ass, or sheep; he shall restore double.

5 If a man shall cause a field or vineyard to be eaten, and shall put in his beast, and shall feed in another man's field; of the best of his own field, and of the best of his own vineyard, shall he make restitution.

6 If fire break out, and catch in thorns, so that the stacks of corn, or the standing corn, or the field, be consumed therewith; he that kindled the fire shall surely make restitution.

7 If a man shall deliver to his neighbor money or stuff to keep, and it be stolen out of the man's house; if the thief be found, let him pay double.

8 If the thief be not found, then the master of the house shall be brought to the judges, to see whether he have put his hand to his neighbor's goods.

9 For all manner of trespass, whether it be for ox, for ass, for sheep, for raiment, or for any manner of lost thing which another challenges to be his, the cause of both parties shall come before the judges; and whom the judges shall condemn, he shall pay double to his neighbor.

10 If a man deliver to his neighbor an ass, or an ox, or a sheep, or any beast, to keep; and it die, or be hurt, or driven away, no man seeing it:

11 Then shall an oath of the LORD be between them both, that he has not put his hand to his neighbor's goods; and the owner of it shall accept thereof, and he shall not make it good.

12 And if it be stolen from him, he shall make restitution to the owner thereof.

13 If it be torn in pieces, then let him bring it for witness, and he shall not make good that which was torn.

14 And if a man borrow ought of his neighbor, and it be hurt, or die, the owner thereof being not with it, he shall surely make it good.

15 But if the owner thereof be with it, he shall not make it good: if it be an hired thing, it came for his hire.

16 And if a man entice a maid that is not betrothed, and lie with her, he shall surely endow her to be his wife.

17 If her father utterly refuse to give her to him, he shall pay money according to the dowry of virgins.

18 You shall not suffer a witch to live.

19 Whosoever lies with a beast shall surely be put to death.

20 He that sacrifices to any god, save to the LORD only, he shall be utterly destroyed.

21 You shall neither vex a stranger, nor oppress him: for you were strangers in the land of Egypt.

22 You shall not afflict any widow, or fatherless child.

23 If you afflict them in any wise, and they cry at all to me, I will surely hear their cry;

24 And my wrath shall wax hot, and I will kill you with the sword; and your wives shall be widows, and your children fatherless.

25 If you lend money to any of my people that is poor by you, you shall not be to him as an usurer, neither shall you lay upon him usury.

26 If you at all take your neighbor's raiment to pledge, you shall deliver it to him by that the sun goes down:

27 For that is his covering only, it is his raiment for his skin: wherein shall he sleep? and it shall come to pass, when he cries to me, that I will hear; for I am gracious.

28 You shall not revile the gods, nor curse the ruler of your people.

29 You shall not delay to offer the first of your ripe fruits, and of your liquors: the firstborn of your sons shall you give to me.

30 Likewise shall you do with your oxen, and with your sheep: seven days it shall be with his dam; on the eighth day you shall give it me.

31 And you shall be holy men to me: neither shall you eat any flesh that is torn of beasts in the field; you shall cast it to the dogs.

CHAPTER 23

YOU shall not raise a false report: put not your hand with the wicked to be an unrighteous witness.

2 You shall not follow a multitude to do evil; neither shall you speak in a cause to decline after many to wrest judgment:

3 Neither shall you countenance a poor man in his cause.

4 If you meet your enemy's ox or his ass going astray, you shall surely bring it back to him again.

5 If you see the ass of him that hates you lying under his burden, and would forbear to help him, you shall surely help with him.

6 You shall not wrest the judgment of your poor in his cause.

7 Keep far from a false matter; and the innocent and righteous do not slay: for I will not justify the wicked.

8 And you shall take no gift: for the gift blinds the wise, and perverts the words of the righteous.

9 Also you shall not oppress a stranger: for you know the heart of a stranger, seeing you were strangers in the land of Egypt.

10 And six years you shall sow your land, and shall gather in the fruits thereof:

11 But the seventh year you shall let it rest and lie still; that the poor of your people may eat: and what they leave the beasts of the field shall eat. In like manner you shall deal with your vineyard, and with your olive yard.

12 Six days you shall do your work, and on the seventh day you shall rest: that your ox and your ass may rest, and the son of your handmaid, and the stranger, may be refreshed.

13 And in all things that I have said to you be circumspect: and make no men-

---

22:31 "Before modern science identified bacteria, God made provision for humans by banning possibly diseased animals. As the blood carries most sickness, it was a wise precaution to avoid animals that had not been correctly drained of blood." Richard Gunther

23:4-5 Israel was commanded to love their enemies (see Matthew 5:44).

"When the moral Law is preached, should you also use the ceremonial and civil laws?"

Look to the example of how and which part of the Law is presented in scripture. Look at Paul in Romans (Romans 2:21-24), James (James 2:10-11), Jesus (Luke 18:18-20). Each used the moral Law to bring the knowledge of sin, specifically the Ten Commandments. That's what is written on the hearts of all men (see Romans 2:15).

tion of the name of other gods, neither let it be heard out of your mouth.

14 Three times you shall keep a feast to me in the year.

15 You shall keep the feast of unleavened bread: (you shall eat unleavened bread seven days, as I commanded you, in the time appointed of the month Abib; for in it you came out from Egypt: and none shall appear before me empty:)

16 And the feast of harvest, the first fruits of your labors, which you have sown in the field: and the feast of ingathering, which is in the end of the year, when you have gathered in your labors out of the field.

17 Three times in the year all your males shall appear before the LORD God.

18 You shall not offer the blood of my sacrifice with leavened bread; neither shall the fat of my sacrifice remain until the morning.

19 The first of the first fruits of your land you shall bring into the house of the LORD your God. You shall not seethe a kid in his mother's milk.

20 Behold, I send an Angel before you, to keep you in the way, and to bring you into the place which I have prepared.

21 Beware of him, and obey his voice, provoke him not; for he will not pardon your transgressions: for my name is in him.

22 But if you shall indeed obey his voice, and do all that I speak; then I will be an enemy to your enemies, and an adversary to your adversaries.

23 For mine Angel shall go before you, and bring you in to the Amorites, and the Hittites, and the Perizzites, and the Canaanites, the Hivites, and the Jebusites: and I will cut them off.

24 You shall not bow down to their gods, nor serve them, nor do after their works: but you shall utterly overthrow them, and quite break down their images.

25 And you shall serve the LORD your God, and he shall bless your bread, and your water; and I will take sickness away from the midst of you.

26 There shall nothing cast their young, nor be barren, in your land: the number of your days I will fulfill.

27 I will send my fear before you, and will destroy all the people to whom you shall come, and I will make all your enemies turn their backs to you.

28 And I will send hornets before you, which shall drive out the Hivite, the Canaanite, and the Hittite, from before you.

29 I will not drive them out from before you in one year; lest the land become desolate, and the beast of the field multiply against you.

30 By little and little I will drive them out from before you, until you be increased, and inherit the land.

31 And I will set your bounds from the Red sea even to the sea of the Philistines, and from the desert to the river: for I will deliver the inhabitants of the land into your hand; and you shall drive them out before you.

> First, then, before you can speak
> peace to your hearts,
> you must be made to see,
> made to feel, made to weep over,
> made to bewail,
> your actual transgressions
> against the Law of God.

GEORGE WHITFIELD
1714-1770
FAMOUS OPEN-AIR PREACHER

32 You shall make no covenant with them, nor with their gods.
33 They shall not dwell in your land, lest they make you sin against me: for if you serve their gods, it will surely be a snare to you.

CHAPTER 24

AND he said to Moses, Come up to the LORD, you, and Aaron, Nadab, and Abihu, and seventy of the elders of Israel; and worship afar off.
2 And Moses alone shall come near the LORD: but they shall not come nigh; neither shall the people go up with him.
3 And Moses came and told the people all the words of the LORD, and all the judgments: and all the people answered with one voice, and said, All the words which the LORD has said will we do.
4 And Moses wrote all the words of the LORD, and rose up early in the morning, and built an altar under the hill, and twelve pillars, according to the twelve tribes of Israel.
5 And he sent young men of the children of Israel, which offered burnt offerings, and sacrificed peace offerings of oxen to the LORD.
6 And Moses took half of the blood, and put it in basons; and half of the blood he sprinkled on the altar.
7 And he took the book of the covenant, and read in the audience of the people: and they said, All that the LORD has said will we do, and be obedient.

8 And Moses took the blood, and sprinkled it on the people, and said, Behold the blood of the covenant, which the LORD has made with you concerning all these words.
9 Then went up Moses, and Aaron, Nadab, and Abihu, and seventy of the elders of Israel:
10 And they saw the God of Israel: and there was under his feet as it were a paved work of a sapphire stone, and as it were the body of heaven in his clearness.
11 And upon the nobles of the children of Israel he laid not his hand: also they saw God, and did eat and drink.
12 And the LORD said to Moses, Come up to me into the mount, and be there: and I will give you tables of stone, and a law, and commandments which I have written; that you may teach them.
13 And Moses rose up, and his minister Joshua: and Moses went up into the mount of God.
14 And he said to the elders, Tarry here for us, until we come again to you: and, behold, Aaron and Hur are with you: if any man have any matters to do, let him come to them.
15 And Moses went up into the mount, and a cloud covered the mount.
16 And the glory of the LORD abode upon mount Sinai, and the cloud covered it six days: and the seventh day he called to Moses out of the midst of the cloud.
17 And the sight of the glory of the LORD was like devouring fire on the top of the mount in the eyes of the children of Israel.
18 And Moses went into the midst of the cloud, and gat him up into the mount: and Moses was in the mount forty days and forty nights.

CHAPTER 25

AND the LORD spoke to Moses, saying,
2 Speak to the children of Israel, that they bring me an offering: of every man

"We Christians too often substitute
prayer for playing the game.
Prayer is good;
but when used as a substitute
for obedience, it is nothing
but a blatant hypocrisy,
a despicable Pharisaism...
To your knees, man!
And to your Bible! Decide at once!
Don't hedge! Time flies!
Cease your insults to God.
Quit consulting flesh and blood.
Stop your lame, lying,
and cowardly excuses.
Enlist!"

C. T. STUDD
1860-1931
BRITISH MISSIONARY
WHO SERVED IN CHINA, INDIA
AND AFRICA

that gives it willingly with his heart you shall take my offering.

3 And this is the offering which you shall take of them; gold, and silver, and brass,

4 And blue, and purple, and scarlet, and fine linen, and goats' hair,

5 And rams' skins dyed red, and badgers' skins, and shittim wood,

6 Oil for the light, spices for anointing oil, and for sweet incense,

7 Onyx stones, and stones to be set in the ephod, and in the breastplate.

8 And let them make me a sanctuary; that I may dwell among them.

9 According to all that I show you, after the pattern of the tabernacle, and the pattern of all the instruments thereof, even so shall you make it.

10 And they shall make an ark of shittim wood: two cubits and a half shall be the length thereof, and a cubit and a half the breadth thereof, and a cubit and a half the height thereof.

11 And you shall overlay it with pure gold, within and without shall you overlay it, and shall make upon it a crown of gold round about.

12 And you shall cast four rings of gold for it, and put them in the four corners thereof; and two rings shall be in the one side of it, and two rings in the other side of it.

13 And you shall make staves of shittim wood, and overlay them with gold.

14 And you shall put the staves into the rings by the sides of the ark, that the ark may be borne with them.

15 The staves shall be in the rings of the ark: they shall not be taken from it.

16 And you shall put into the ark the testimony which I shall give you.

17 And you shall make a mercy seat of pure gold: two cubits and a half shall be the length thereof, and a cubit and a half the breadth thereof.

18 And you shall make two cherubims of gold, of beaten work shall you make them, in the two ends of the mercy seat.

19 And make one cherub on the one end, and the other cherub on the other end: even of the mercy seat shall you make the cherubims on the two ends thereof.

20 And the cherubims shall stretch forth their wings on high, covering the mercy seat with their wings, and their faces shall look one to another; toward the mercy seat shall the faces of the cherubims be.

21 And you shall put the mercy seat above upon the ark; and in the ark you shall put the testimony that I shall give you.

22 And there I will meet with you, and I will commune with you from above the mercy seat, from between the two cherubims which are upon the ark of the testimony, of all things which I will give you in commandment to the children of Israel.

23 You shall also make a table of shittim wood: two cubits shall be the length thereof, and a cubit the breadth thereof, and a cubit and a half the height thereof.

24 And you shall overlay it with pure gold, and make thereto a crown of gold round about.

25 And you shall make to it a border of an hand breadth round about, and you shall make a golden crown to the border thereof round about.

26 And you shall make for it four rings of gold, and put the rings in the four corners that are on the four feet thereof.

27 Over against the border shall the rings be for places of the staves to bear the table.

28 And you shall make the staves of shittim wood, and overlay them with gold, that the table may be borne with them.

29 And you shall make the dishes thereof, and spoons thereof, and covers thereof, and bowls thereof, to cover withal: of pure gold shall you make them.

30 And you shall set upon the table showbread before me always.

31 And you shall make a candlestick of pure gold: of beaten work shall the candlestick be made: his shaft, and his branches, his bowls, his knops, and his flowers, shall be of the same.

32 And six branches shall come out of the sides of it; three branches of the candlestick out of the one side, and three branches of the candlestick out of the other side:

33 Three bowls made like to almonds, with a knop and a flower in one branch; and three bowls made like almonds in the other branch, with a knop and a flower: so in the six branches that come out of the candlestick.

34 And in the candlesticks shall be four bowls made like to almonds, with their knops and their flowers.

35 And there shall be a knop under two branches of the same, and a knop under two branches of the same, and a knop under two branches of the same, according to the six branches that proceed out of the candlestick.

36 Their knops and their branches shall be of the same: all it shall be one beaten work of pure gold.

37 And you shall make the seven lamps thereof: and they shall light the lamps thereof, that they may give light over against it.

38 And the tongs thereof, and the snuffdishes thereof, shall be of pure gold.

39 Of a talent of pure gold shall he make it, with all these vessels.

40 And look that you make them after their pattern, which was showed you in the mount.

> No man knows the brightness of the gospel 'till he understands the blackness of those clouds which surround the Law of the Lord.
>
> **CHARLES SPURGEON**

CHAPTER 26

MOREOVER you shall make the tabernacle with ten curtains of fine twined linen, and blue, and purple, and scarlet: with cherubims of cunning work shall you make them.

2 The length of one curtain shall be eight and twenty cubits, and the breadth of one curtain four cubits: and every one of the curtains shall have one measure.

3 The five curtains shall be coupled together one to another; and other five curtains shall be coupled one to another.

4 And you shall make loops of blue upon the edge of the one curtain from the selvedge in the coupling; and likewise shall you make in the uttermost edge of another curtain, in the coupling of the second.

5 Fifty loops shall you make in the one curtain, and fifty loops shall you make in the edge of the curtain that is in the coupling of the second; that the loops may take hold one of another.

6 And you shall make fifty taches of gold, and couple the curtains together with the taches: and it shall be one tabernacle.

7 And you shall make curtains of goats' hair to be a covering upon the tabernacle: eleven curtains shall you make.

8 The length of one curtain shall be thirty cubits, and the breadth of one curtain four cubits: and the eleven curtains shall be all of one measure.

9 And you shall couple five curtains by themselves, and six curtains by themselves, and shall double the sixth curtain in the forefront of the tabernacle.

10 And you shall make fifty loops on the edge of the one curtain that is outmost in the coupling, and fifty loops in the edge of the curtain which couples the second.

11 And you shall make fifty taches of brass, and put the taches into the loops, and couple the tent together, that it may be one.

12 And the remnant that remains of the curtains of the tent, the half curtain that remains, shall hang over the backside of the tabernacle.

13 And a cubit on the one side, and a cubit on the other side of that which remains in the length of the curtains of the tent, it shall hang over the sides of the tabernacle on this side and on that side, to cover it.

14 And you shall make a covering for the tent of rams' skins dyed red, and a covering above of badgers' skins.

15 And you shall make boards for the tabernacle of shittim wood standing up.

16 Ten cubits shall be the length of a board, and a cubit and a half shall be the breadth of one board.

17 Two tenons shall there be in one board, set in order one against another: thus shall you make for all the boards of the tabernacle.

18 And you shall make the boards for the tabernacle, twenty boards on the south side southward.

19 And you shall make forty sockets of silver under the twenty boards; two sockets under one board for his two tenons, and two sockets under another board for his two tenons.

20 And for the second side of the tabernacle on the north side there shall be twenty boards:

21 And their forty sockets of silver; two sockets under one board, and two sockets under another board.

22 And for the sides of the tabernacle westward you shall make six boards.

23 And two boards shall you make for the corners of the tabernacle in the two sides.

24 And they shall be coupled together beneath, and they shall be coupled together above the head of it to one ring: thus shall it be for them both; they shall be for the two corners.

25 And they shall be eight boards, and their sockets of silver, sixteen sockets; two sockets under one board, and two sockets under another board.

26 And you shall make bars of shittim wood; five for the boards of the one side of the tabernacle,

27 And five bars for the boards of the other side of the tabernacle, and five bars for the boards of the side of the tabernacle, for the two sides westward.

28 And the middle bar in the midst of the boards shall reach from end to end.

29 And you shall overlay the boards with gold, and make their rings of gold for places for the bars: and you shall overlay the bars with gold.

30 And you shall rear up the tabernacle according to the fashion thereof which was shown you in the mount.

31 And you shall make a vail of blue, and purple, and scarlet, and fine twined linen of cunning work: with cherubims shall it be made:

32 And you shall hang it upon four pillars of shittim wood overlaid with gold: their hooks shall be of gold, upon the four sockets of silver.

33 And you shall hang up the vail under the taches, that you may bring in thither within the vail the ark of the testimony: and the vail shall divide to you between the holy place and the most holy.

34 And you shall put the mercy seat upon the ark of the testimony in the most holy place.

35 And you shall set the table without the vail, and the candlestick over against the table on the side of the tabernacle toward the south: and you shall put the table on the north side.

36 And you shall make an hanging for the door of the tent, of blue, and purple, and scarlet, and fine twined linen, wrought with needlework.

37 And you shall make for the hanging five pillars of shittim wood, and overlay them with gold, and their hooks shall be of gold: and you shall cast five sockets of brass for them.

CHAPTER 27

AND you shall make an altar of shittim wood, five cubits long, and five cubits broad; the altar shall be foursquare: and the height thereof shall be three cubits.

2 And you shall make the horns of it upon the four corners thereof: his horns shall be of the same: and you shall overlay it with brass.

3 And you shall make his pans to receive his ashes, and his shovels, and his basons, and his fleshhooks, and his firepans: all the vessels thereof you shall make of brass.

4 And you shall make for it a grate of network of brass; and upon the net shall you make four brasen rings in the four corners thereof.

5 And you shall put it under the compass of the altar beneath, that the net may be even to the midst of the altar.

6 And you shall make staves for the altar, staves of shittim wood, and overlay them with brass.

7 And the staves shall be put into the rings, and the staves shall be upon the two sides of the altar, to bear it.

8 Hollow with boards shall you make it: as it was shown you in the mount, so shall they make it.

9 And you shall make the court of the tabernacle: for the south side southward there shall be hangings for the court of fine twined linen of an hundred cubits long for one side:

10 And the twenty pillars thereof and their twenty sockets shall be of brass; the hooks of the pillars and their fillets shall be of silver.

11 And likewise for the north side in length there shall be hangings of an hundred cubits long, and his twenty pillars and their twenty sockets of brass; the hooks of the pillars and their fillets of silver.

12 And for the breadth of the court on the west side shall be hangings of fifty cubits: their pillars ten, and their sockets ten.

13 And the breadth of the court on the east side eastward shall be fifty cubits.

14 The hangings of one side of the gate shall be fifteen cubits: their pillars three, and their sockets three.

15 And on the other side shall be hangings fifteen cubits: their pillars three, and their sockets three.

16 And for the gate of the court shall be an hanging of twenty cubits, of blue, and purple, and scarlet, and fine twined linen, wrought with needlework: and their pillars shall be four, and their sockets four.

17 All the pillars round about the court shall be filleted with silver; their hooks shall be of silver, and their sockets of brass.

18 The length of the court shall be an hundred cubits, and the breadth fifty every where, and the height five cubits of fine twined linen, and their sockets of brass.

19 All the vessels of the tabernacle in all the service thereof, and all the pins thereof, and all the pins of the court, shall be of brass.

20 And you shall command the children of Israel, that they bring you pure oil olive beaten for the light, to cause the lamp to burn always.

21 In the tabernacle of the congregation without the vail, which is before the testimony, Aaron and his sons shall order it from evening to morning before the LORD: it shall be a statute for ever to their generations on the behalf of the children of Israel.

CHAPTER 28

AND take to yourself Aaron your brother, and his sons with him, from among the children of Israel, that he may minister to me in the priest's office, even Aaron, Nadab and Abihu, Eleazar and Ithamar, Aaron's sons.

2 And you shall make holy garments for Aaron your brother for glory and for beauty.

3 And you shall speak to all that are wise hearted, whom I have filled with the spirit of wisdom, that they may make Aaron's garments to consecrate him, that he may minister to me in the priest's office.

4 And these are the garments which they shall make; a breastplate, and an ephod, and a robe, and a broidered coat, a mitre, and a girdle: and they shall make holy garments for Aaron your brother, and his sons, that he may minister to me in the priest's office.

5 And they shall take gold, and blue, and purple, and scarlet, and fine linen.

6 And they shall make the ephod of gold, of blue, and of purple, of scarlet, and fine twined linen, with cunning work.

7 It shall have the two shoulderpieces thereof joined at the two edges thereof; and so it shall be joined together.

8 And the curious girdle of the ephod, which is upon it, shall be of the same, according to the work thereof; even of gold, of blue, and purple, and scarlet, and fine twined linen.

9 And you shall take two onyx stones, and grave on them the names of the children of Israel:

10 Six of their names on one stone, and the other six names of the rest on the other stone, according to their birth.

11 With the work of an engraver in stone, like the engravings of a signet, shall you engrave the two stones with the names of the children of Israel: you shall make them to be set in ouches of gold.

12 And you shall put the two stones upon the shoulders of the ephod for stones of memorial to the children of Israel: and Aaron shall bear their names before the LORD upon his two shoulders for a memorial.

13 And you shall make ouches of gold;

14 And two chains of pure gold at the ends; of wreathen work shall you make them, and fasten the wreathen chains to the ouches.

15 And you shall make the breastplate of judgment with cunning work; after the work of the ephod you shall make it; of gold, of blue, and of purple, and of scarlet, and of fine twined linen, shall you make it.

16 Foursquare it shall be being doubled; a span shall be the length thereof, and a span shall be the breadth thereof.

17 And you shall set in it settings of stones, even four rows of stones: the first row shall be a sardius, a topaz, and a carbuncle: this shall be the first row.

18 And the second row shall be an emerald, a sapphire, and a diamond.

19 And the third row a ligure, an agate, and an amethyst.

20 And the fourth row a beryl, and an onyx, and a jasper: they shall be set in gold in their inclosings.

21 And the stones shall be with the names of the children of Israel, twelve, according to their names, like the engravings of a signet; every one with his name shall they be according to the twelve tribes.

22 And you shall make upon the breastplate chains at the ends of wreathen work of pure gold.

23 And you shall make upon the breastplate two rings of gold, and shall put the two rings on the two ends of the breastplate.

24 And you shall put the two wreathen chains of gold in the two rings which are on the ends of the breastplate.

25 And the other two ends of the two wreathen chains you shall fasten in the two ouches, and put them on the shoulderpieces of the ephod before it.

26 And you shall make two rings of gold, and you shall put them upon the two ends of the breastplate in the border thereof, which is in the side of the ephod inward.

27 And two other rings of gold you shall make, and shall put them on the two sides of the ephod underneath, toward the forepart thereof, over against the other coupling thereof, above the curious girdle of the ephod.

28 And they shall bind the breastplate by the rings thereof to the rings of the ephod with a lace of blue, that it may be above the curious girdle of the ephod, and that the breastplate be not loosed from the ephod.

29 And Aaron shall bear the names of the children of Israel in the breastplate of judgment upon his heart, when he goes in to the holy place, for a memorial before the LORD continually.

30 And you shall put in the breastplate of judgment the Urim and the Thummim; and they shall be upon Aaron's heart, when he goes in before the LORD: and Aaron shall bear the judgment of the children of Israel upon his heart before the LORD continually.

31 And you shall make the robe of the ephod all of blue.

32 And there shall be an hole in the top of it, in the midst thereof: it shall have a binding of woven work round about the hole of it, as it were the hole of an habergeon, that it be not rent.

33 And beneath upon the hem of it you shall make pomegranates of blue, and of purple, and of scarlet, round about the hem thereof; and bells of gold between them round about:

34 A golden bell and a pomegranate, a golden bell and a pomegranate, upon the hem of the robe round about.

35 And it shall be upon Aaron to minister: and his sound shall be heard when he goes in to the holy place before the LORD, and when he comes out, that he die not.

36 And you shall make a plate of pure gold, and grave upon it, like the engravings of a signet, HOLINESS TO THE LORD.

37 And you shall put it on a blue lace, that it may be upon the mitre; upon the forefront of the mitre it shall be.

38 And it shall be upon Aaron's forehead, that Aaron may bear the iniquity of the holy things, which the children of Israel shall hallow in all their holy gifts; and it shall be always upon his forehead, that they may be accepted before the LORD.

39 And you shall embroider the coat of fine linen, and you shall make the mitre of fine linen, and you shall make the girdle of needlework.

40 And for Aaron's sons you shall make coats, and you shall make for them girdles, and bonnets shall you make for them, for glory and for beauty.

41 And you shall put them upon Aaron your brother, and his sons with him; and shall anoint them, and consecrate them, and sanctify them, that they may minister to me in the priest's office.

42 And you shall make them linen breeches to cover their nakedness; from the loins even to the thighs they shall reach:

43 And they shall be upon Aaron, and upon his sons, when they come in to the tabernacle of the congregation, or when they come near to the altar to minister in the holy place; that they bear not iniquity, and die: it shall be a statute for ever to him and his seed after him.

CHAPTER 29

AND this is the thing that you shall do to them to hallow them, to minister to me in the priest's office: Take one young bullock, and two rams without blemish,

2 And unleavened bread, and cakes unleavened tempered with oil, and wafers unleavened anointed with oil: of wheaten flour shall you make them.

3 And you shall put them into one basket, and bring them in the basket, with the bullock and the two rams.

4 And Aaron and his sons you shall bring to the door of the tabernacle of the congregation, and shall wash them with water.

5 And you shall take the garments, and put upon Aaron the coat, and the robe of the ephod, and the ephod, and the breastplate, and gird him with the curious girdle of the ephod:

6 And you shall put the mitre upon his head, and put the holy crown upon the mitre.

7 Then shall you take the anointing oil, and pour it upon his head, and anoint him.

8 And you shall bring his sons, and put coats upon them.

9 And you shall gird them with girdles, Aaron and his sons, and put the bonnets on them: and the priest's office shall be theirs for a perpetual statute: and you shall consecrate Aaron and his sons.

10 And you shall cause a bullock to be brought before the tabernacle of the congregation: and Aaron and his sons shall put their hands upon the head of the bullock.

11 And you shall kill the bullock before the LORD, by the door of the tabernacle of the congregation.

12 And you shall take of the blood of the bullock, and put it upon the horns of the altar with your finger, and pour all the blood beside the bottom of the altar.

13 And you shall take all the fat that covers the inwards, and the caul that is above the liver, and the two kidneys, and the fat that is upon them, and burn them upon the altar.

14 But the flesh of the bullock, and his skin, and his dung, shall you burn with fire without the camp: it is a sin offering.

15 You shall also take one ram; and Aaron and his sons shall put their hands upon the head of the ram.

16 And you shall slay the ram, and you shall take his blood, and sprinkle it round about upon the altar.

17 And you shall cut the ram in pieces, and wash the inwards of him, and his legs, and put them to his pieces, and to his head.

18 And you shall burn the whole ram upon the altar: it is a burnt offering to the LORD: it is a sweet savor, an offering made by fire to the LORD.

19 And you shall take the other ram; and Aaron and his sons shall put their hands upon the head of the ram.

20 Then shall you kill the ram, and take of his blood, and put it upon the tip of the right ear of Aaron, and upon the tip of the right ear of his sons, and upon the thumb of their right hand, and upon the great toe of their right foot, and sprinkle the blood upon the altar round about.

21 And you shall take of the blood that is upon the altar, and of the anointing oil, and sprinkle it upon Aaron, and upon his garments, and upon his sons, and upon the garments of his sons with him: and he shall be hallowed, and his garments, and his sons, and his sons' garments with him.

22 Also you shall take of the ram the fat and the rump, and the fat that covers the inwards, and the caul above the liver, and the two kidneys, and the fat that is upon them, and the right shoulder; for it is a ram of consecration:

23 And one loaf of bread, and one cake of oiled bread, and one wafer out of the basket of the unleavened bread that is before the LORD:

24 And you shall put all in the hands of Aaron, and in the hands of his sons; and

shall wave them for a wave offering before the LORD.

25 And you shall receive them of their hands, and burn them upon the altar for a burnt offering, for a sweet savor before the LORD: it is an offering made by fire to the LORD.

26 And you shall take the breast of the ram of Aaron's consecration, and wave it for a wave offering before the LORD: and it shall be your part.

27 And you shall sanctify the breast of the wave offering, and the shoulder of the heave offering, which is waved, and which is heaved up, of the ram of the consecration, even of that which is for Aaron, and of that which is for his sons:

28 And it shall be Aaron's and his sons' by a statute for ever from the children of Israel: for it is an heave offering: and it shall be an heave offering from the children of Israel of the sacrifice of their peace offerings, even their heave offering to the LORD.

29 And the holy garments of Aaron shall be his sons' after him, to be anointed therein, and to be consecrated in them.

30 And that son that is priest in his stead shall put them on seven days, when he comes into the tabernacle of the congregation to minister in the holy place.

31 And you shall take the ram of the consecration, and seethe his flesh in the holy place.

32 And Aaron and his sons shall eat the flesh of the ram, and the bread that is in the basket by the door of the tabernacle of the congregation.

33 And they shall eat those things wherewith the atonement was made, to consecrate and to sanctify them: but a stranger shall not eat thereof, because they are holy.

34 And if ought of the flesh of the consecrations, or of the bread, remain to the morning, then you shall burn the remainder with fire: it shall not be eaten, because it is holy.

35 And thus shall you do to Aaron, and to his sons, according to all things which I have commanded you: seven days shall you consecrate them.

36 And you shall offer every day a bullock for a sin offering for atonement: and you shall cleanse the altar, when you have made an atonement for it, and you shall anoint it, to sanctify it.

37 Seven days you shall make an atonement for the altar, and sanctify it; and it shall be an altar most holy: whatsoever touches the altar shall be holy.

38 Now this is that which you shall offer upon the altar; two lambs of the first year day by day continually.

39 The one lamb you shall offer in the morning; and the other lamb you shall offer at even:

40 And with the one lamb a tenth deal of flour mingled with the fourth part of an hin of beaten oil; and the fourth part of an hin of wine for a drink offering.

41 And the other lamb you shall offer at even, and shall do thereto according to the meat offering of the morning, and according to the drink offering thereof, for a sweet savor, an offering made by fire to the LORD.

42 This shall be a continual burnt offering throughout your generations at the door of the tabernacle of the congregation before the LORD: where I will meet you, to speak there to you.

43 And there I will meet with the children of Israel, and the tabernacle shall be sanctified by my glory.

44 And I will sanctify the tabernacle of the congregation, and the altar: I will sanctify also both Aaron and his sons, to minister to me in the priest's office.

45 And I will dwell among the children of Israel, and will be their God.

46 And they shall know that I am the LORD their God, that brought them forth out of the land of Egypt, that I may dwell among them: I am the LORD their God.

CHAPTER 30

AND you shall make an altar to burn incense upon: of shittim wood shall you make it.

2 A cubit shall be the length thereof, and a cubit the breadth thereof; foursquare shall it be: and two cubits shall be the height thereof: the horns thereof shall be of the same.

3 And you shall overlay it with pure gold, the top thereof, and the sides thereof round about, and the horns thereof; and you shall make to it a crown of gold round about.

4 And two golden rings shall you make to it under the crown of it, by the two corners thereof, upon the two sides of it shall you make it; and they shall be for places for the staves to bear it withal.

5 And you shall make the staves of shittim wood, and overlay them with gold.

6 And you shall put it before the vail that is by the ark of the testimony, before the mercy seat that is over the testimony, where I will meet with you.

7 And Aaron shall burn thereon sweet incense every morning: when he dresses the lamps, he shall burn incense upon it.

8 And when Aaron lights the lamps at even, he shall burn incense upon it, a perpetual incense before the LORD throughout your generations.

9 You shall offer no strange incense thereon, nor burnt sacrifice, nor meat offering; neither shall you pour drink offering thereon.

10 And Aaron shall make an atonement upon the horns of it once in a year with the blood of the sin offering of atonements: once in the year shall he make atonement upon it throughout your generations: it is most holy to the LORD.

11 And the LORD spoke to Moses, saying,

12 When you take the sum of the children of Israel after their number, then shall they give every man a ransom for his soul to the LORD, when you number them; that there be no plague among them, when you number them.

13 This they shall give, every one that passes among them that are numbered, half a shekel after the shekel of the sanctuary: (a shekel is twenty gerahs:) an half shekel shall be the offering of the LORD.

14 Every one that passes among them that are numbered, from twenty years old and above, shall give an offering to the LORD.

15 The rich shall not give more, and the poor shall not give less than half a shekel, when they give an offering to the LORD, to make an atonement for your souls.

16 And you shall take the atonement money of the children of Israel, and shall appoint it for the service of the tabernacle of the congregation; that it may be a memorial to the children of Israel before the LORD, to make an atonement for your souls.

17 And the LORD spoke to Moses, saying,

18 You shall also make a laver of brass, and his foot also of brass, to wash withal: and you shall put it between the tabernacle of the congregation and the altar, and you shall put water therein.

19 For Aaron and his sons shall wash their hands and their feet thereat:

20 When they go into the tabernacle of the congregation, they shall wash with water, that they die not; or when they come near to the altar to minister, to burn offering made by fire to the LORD:

21 So they shall wash their hands and their feet, that they die not: and it shall be a statute for ever to them, even to him and to his seed throughout their generations.

22 Moreover the LORD spoke to Moses, saying,

23 Take also to yourself principal spices, of pure myrrh five hundred shekels, and of sweet cinnamon half so much, even two hundred and fifty shekels, and of sweet calamus two hundred and fifty shekels,

24 And of cassia five hundred shekels, after the shekel of the sanctuary, and of oil olive an hin:

25 And you shall make it an oil of holy ointment, an ointment compound after the art of the apothecary: it shall be an holy anointing oil.

26 And you shall anoint the tabernacle of the congregation therewith, and the ark of the testimony,

27 And the table and all his vessels, and the candlestick and his vessels, and the altar of incense,

28 And the altar of burnt offering with all his vessels, and the laver and his foot.

29 And you shall sanctify them, that they may be most holy: whatsoever touches them shall be holy.

30 And you shall anoint Aaron and his sons, and consecrate them, that they may minister to me in the priest's office.

31 And you shall speak to the children of Israel, saying, This shall be an holy anointing oil to me throughout your generations.

32 Upon man's flesh shall it not be poured, neither shall you make any other like it, after the composition of it: it is holy, and it shall be holy to you.

33 Whosoever compounds any like it, or whosoever puts any of it upon a stranger, shall even be cut off from his people.

34 And the LORD said to Moses, Take to you sweet spices, stacte, and onycha, and galbanum; these sweet spices with pure frankincense: of each shall there be a like weight:

35 And you shall make it a perfume, a confection after the art of the apothecary, tempered together, pure and holy:

36 And you shall beat some of it very small, and put of it before the testimony in the tabernacle of the congregation, where I will meet with you: it shall be to you most holy.

37 And as for the perfume which you shall make, you shall not make to yourselves according to the composition thereof: it shall be to you holy for the LORD.

38 Whosoever shall make like to that, to smell thereto, shall even be cut off from his people.

CHAPTER 31

AND the LORD spoke to Moses, saying,

2 See, I have called by name Bezaleel the son of Uri, the son of Hur, of the tribe of Judah:

3 And I have filled him with the spirit of God, in wisdom, and in understanding, and in knowledge, and in all manner of workmanship,

4 To devise cunning works, to work in gold, and in silver, and in brass,

5 And in cutting of stones, to set them, and in carving of timber, to work in all manner of workmanship.

6 And I, behold, I have given with him Aholiab, the son of Ahisamach, of the tribe of Dan: and in the hearts of all that are wise hearted I have put wisdom, that they may make all that I have commanded you;

7 The tabernacle of the congregation, and the ark of the testimony, and the mercy seat that is thereupon, and all the furniture of the tabernacle,

8 And the table and his furniture, and the pure candlestick with all his furniture, and the altar of incense,

9 And the altar of burnt offering with all his furniture, and the laver and his foot,

10 And the cloths of service, and the holy garments for Aaron the priest, and the garments of his sons, to minister in the priest's office,

11 And the anointing oil, and sweet incense for the holy place: according to all that I have commanded you shall they do.

12 And the LORD spoke to Moses, saying,

13 Speak also to the children of Israel, saying, Verily my sabbaths you shall keep: for it is a sign between me and you throughout your generations; that you

THE WORLD DANCES AROUND ITS GOLDEN CALF OF MAMMON

32:1-6 "Whatever we make the most of is our God." Martin Luther

For those who worship idols, the idols' silence gives the worshiper an illusion of permission to sin, to rise up early and embrace the pleasures of sin.

may know that I am the LORD that doth sanctify you.

14 You shall keep the sabbath therefore; for it is holy to you: every one that defiles it shall surely be put to death: for whosoever does any work therein, that soul shall be cut off from among his people.

15 Six days may work be done; but in the seventh is the sabbath of rest, holy to the LORD: whosoever does any work in the sabbath day, he shall surely be put to death.

16 Therefore the children of Israel shall keep the sabbath, to observe the sabbath throughout their generations, for a perpetual covenant.

17 It is a sign between me and the children of Israel for ever: for in six days the LORD made heaven and earth, and on the seventh day he rested, and was refreshed.

18 And he gave to Moses, when he had made an end of communing with him upon mount Sinai, two tables of testimony, tables of stone, written with the finger of God.

CHAPTER 32

AND when the people saw that Moses delayed to come down out of the mount, the people gathered themselves together to Aaron, and said to him, Up, make us gods, which shall go before us; for as for this Moses, the man that brought us up out of the land of Egypt, we do not know what is become of him.

2 And Aaron said to them, Break off the golden earrings, which are in the ears of your wives, of your sons, and of your daughters, and bring them to me.

3 And all the people brake off the golden earrings which were in their ears, and brought them to Aaron.

4 And he received them at their hand, and fashioned it with a graving tool, after he had made it a molten calf: and they said, These be your gods, O Israel, which brought you up out of the land of Egypt.

5 And when Aaron saw it, he built an altar before it; and Aaron made proclamation, and said, To morrow is a feast to the LORD.

6 And they rose up early on the morrow, and offered burnt offerings, and brought peace offerings; and the people sat down to eat and to drink, and rose up to play.

7 And the LORD said to Moses, Go, get down; for your people, which you brought out of the land of Egypt, have corrupted themselves:

8 They have turned aside quickly out of the way which I commanded them: they have made them a molten calf, and have worshipped it, and have sacrificed thereunto, and said, These be your gods, O Israel, which have brought you up out of the land of Egypt.

9 And the LORD said to Moses, I have seen this people, and, behold, it is a stiffnecked people:

10 Now therefore let me alone, that my wrath may wax hot against them, and

---

31:14 For freedom from Sabbath-keeping see Colossians 2:16 comment.

31:15-16 The fact that there was capital punishment for Sabbath-breaking should send the sinner fleeing to the Savior.

that I may consume them: and I will make of you a great nation.

11 And Moses besought the LORD his God, and said, LORD, why doth your wrath wax hot against your people, which you have brought forth out of the land of Egypt with great power, and with a mighty hand?

12 Why should the Egyptians speak, and say, For mischief did he bring them out, to slay them in the mountains, and to consume them from the face of the earth? Turn from your fierce wrath, and repent of this evil against your people.

13 Remember Abraham, Isaac, and Israel, your servants, to whom you swore by your own self, and said to them, I will multiply your seed as the stars of heaven, and all this land that I have spoken of will I give to your seed, and they shall inherit it for ever.

14 And the LORD repented of the evil which he thought to do to his people.

15 And Moses turned, and went down from the mount, and the two tables of the testimony were in his hand: the tables were written on both their sides; on the one side and on the other were they written.

16 And the tables were the work of God, and the writing was the writing of God, graven upon the tables.

17 And when Joshua heard the noise of the people as they shouted, he said to Moses, There is a noise of war in the camp.

18 And he said, It is not the voice of them that shout for mastery, neither is it the voice of them that cry for being overcome: but the noise of them that sing do I hear.

19 And it came to pass, as soon as he came nigh to the camp, that he saw the calf, and the dancing: and Moses' anger waxed hot, and he cast the tables out of his hands, and brake them beneath the mount.

20 And he took the calf which they had made, and burnt it in the fire, and ground it to powder, and scattered it upon the water, and made the children of Israel drink of it.

21 And Moses said to Aaron, What did this people do to you, that you have brought so great a sin upon them?

22 And Aaron said, Let not the anger of my lord wax hot: you know the people, that they are set on mischief.

23 For they said to me, Make us gods, which shall go before us: for as for this Moses, the man that brought us up out of the land of Egypt, we know not what is become of him.

24 And I said to them, Whosoever has any gold, let them break it off. So they gave it me: then I cast it into the fire, and there came out this calf.

25 And when Moses saw that the people were naked; (for Aaron had made them naked to their shame among their enemies:)

26 Then Moses stood in the gate of the camp, and said, Who is on the LORD's side? let him come to me. And all the sons of Levi gathered themselves together to him.

27 And he said to them, Thus says the LORD God of Israel, Put every man his sword by his side, and go in and out from gate to gate throughout the camp, and slay every man his brother, and every man his companion, and every man his neighbor.

28 And the children of Levi did according to the word of Moses: and there fell of the people that day about three thousand men.

29 For Moses had said, Consecrate yourselves today to the LORD, even every man upon his son, and upon his brother; that he may bestow upon you a blessing this day.

30 And it came to pass on the morrow, that Moses said to the people, You have sinned a great sin: and now I will go up to the LORD; peradventure I shall make an atonement for your sin.

31 And Moses returned to the LORD, and said, Oh, this people have sinned a

MOSES COMING DOWN FROM MOUNT SINAI

The Ten Commandments

You shall have no other gods before Me.

You shall not make to yourself any graven image.

*You shall not take the name of the
Lord your God in vain.*

Remember the Sabbath day, to keep it holy.

Honor your father and your mother.

You shall not kill.

You shall not commit adultery.

You shall not steal.

*You shall not bear false witness
against your neighbor.*

You shall not covet.

Exodus 32:15

great sin, and have made them gods of gold.

32 Yet now, if you will forgive their sin; and if not, blot me, I pray you, out of your book which you have written.

33 And the LORD said to Moses, Whosoever has sinned against me, him will I blot out of my book.

34 Therefore now go, lead the people to the place of which I have spoken to you: behold, mine Angel shall go before you: nevertheless in the day when I visit I will visit their sin upon them.

35 And the LORD plagued the people, because they made the calf, which Aaron made.

CHAPTER 33

AND the LORD said to Moses, Depart, and go up hence, you and the people which you have brought up out of the land of Egypt, to the land which I swore to Abraham, to Isaac, and to Jacob, saying, To your seed will I give it:

2 And I will send an angel before you; and I will drive out the Canaanite, the Amorite, and the Hittite, and the Perizzite, the Hivite, and the Jebusite:

3 To a land flowing with milk and honey: for I will not go up in the midst of you; for you are a stiffnecked people: lest I consume you in the way.

4 And when the people heard these evil tidings, they mourned: and no man did put on him his ornaments.

5 For the LORD had said to Moses, Say to the children of Israel, You are a stiff-necked people: I will come up into the midst of you in a moment, and consume you: therefore now put off your ornaments from you, that I may know what to do to you.

6 And the children of Israel stripped themselves of their ornaments by the mount Horeb.

7 And Moses took the tabernacle, and pitched it without the camp, afar off from the camp, and called it the Tabernacle of the congregation. And it came to pass, that every one which sought the LORD went out to the tabernacle of the congregation, which was without the camp.

8 And it came to pass, when Moses went out to the tabernacle, that all the people rose up, and stood every man at his tent door, and looked after Moses, until he was gone into the tabernacle.

9 And it came to pass, as Moses entered into the tabernacle, the cloudy pillar descended, and stood at the door of the tabernacle, and the Lord talked with Moses.

10 And all the people saw the cloudy pillar stand at the tabernacle door: and all the people rose up and worshipped, every man in his tent door.

11 And the LORD spoke to Moses face to face, as a man speaks to his friend. And he turned again into the camp: but his servant Joshua, the son of Nun, a young man, departed not out of the tabernacle.

12 And Moses said to the LORD, See, you say to me, Bring up this people: and you have not let me know who you will send with me. Yet you have said, I know you by name, and you have also found grace in my sight.

13 Now therefore, I pray you, if I have found grace in your sight, show me now your way, that I may know you, that I may find grace in your sight: and consider that this nation is your people.

14 And he said, My presence shall go with you, and I will give you rest.

15 And he said to him, If your presence go not with me, carry us not up hence.

16 For wherein shall it be known here that I and your people have found grace in your sight? is it not in that you go with us? so shall we be separated, I and your people, from all the people that are upon the face of the earth.

17 And the LORD said to Moses, I will do this thing also that you have spoken: for you have found grace in my sight, and I know you by name.

QUESTIONS & OBJECTIONS

33:18-23 *"I will believe if God will appear to me."*

When a proud and ignorant sinner says, "I will believe if God will appear to me," he has no understanding of the nature of his Creator. If the mere "goodness" of God is manifest to any sinner, he would instantly die. His "goodness" would spill wrath upon evil man. We can understand that if an earthly judge is a good man, he would be outraged by a vicious murder and must do his best to make sure the wicked criminal is brought to justice. It is his goodness that makes him passionate for justice to be done.

It is the goodness of God that will make sure every murderer and rapist is brought to justice on Judgment Day. However, God is so good, so pure and holy, that He is utterly provoked to just retribution by any evil (anger, greed, envy, pride, lust, lying, jealousy, hatred, etc.). The only way man may live in the presence of a holy God is to be hidden in the rock of Jesus Christ (see 1 Corinthians 10:4). The pure in heart shall see God (see Matthew 5:8), and the only way we can become pure is through the righteousness of the Savior.

When God "appeared" to certain men in the Old Testament, He manifested himself in another form, such as a burning bush or the angel of the Lord. However, no man has seen the essence of God at any time (see John 1:18). When the Bible says that the Lord spoke to Moses "face to face" (Exodus 33:11), it is an example of anthropomorphism. When Moses simply gazed at where God had been, his own face so shone with the glory of God that Israel couldn't even look at him (see Exodus 34:29-35). The Christian has the light of the knowledge of the glory of God in the face of Jesus Christ (see 2 Corinthians 4:6).

---

18 And he said, I beseech you, show me your glory.

19 And he said, I will make all my goodness pass before you, and I will proclaim the name of the LORD before you; and will be gracious to whom I will be gracious, and will show mercy on whom I will show mercy.

20 And he said, You can not see my face: for there shall no man see me, and live.

21 And the LORD said, Behold, there is a place by me, and you shall stand upon a rock:

22 And it shall come to pass, while my glory passes by, that I will put you in a clift of the rock, and will cover you with my hand while I pass by:

23 And I will take away mine hand, and you shall see my back parts: but my face shall not be seen.

CHAPTER 34

AND the LORD said to Moses, Hew two tables of stone like to the first: and I will write upon these tables the words that were in the first tables, which you broke.

2 And be ready in the morning, and come up in the morning to mount Sinai, and present yourself there to me in the top of the mount.

3 And no man shall come up with you, neither let any man be seen throughout all the mount; neither let the flocks nor herds feed before that mount.

4 And he hewed two tables of stone like to the first; and Moses rose up early in the morning, and went up to mount Sinai, as the LORD had commanded him, and took in his hand the two tables of stone.

5 And the LORD descended in the cloud, and stood with him there, and proclaimed the name of the LORD.

6 And the LORD passed by before him, and proclaimed, The LORD, The LORD God, merciful and gracious, longsuffer-

We cannot come to Christ to be justified
until we have first been to Moses
to be condemned.
But once we have gone to Moses
and acknowledged our sin,
guilt and condemnation,
we must not stay there.

John Stott

1921-PRESENT
CHAPLAIN
TO THE QUEEN OF ENGLAND

ing, and abundant in goodness and truth,

7 Keeping mercy for thousands, forgiving iniquity and transgression and sin, and that will by no means clear the guilty; visiting the iniquity of the fathers upon the children, and upon the children's children, to the third and to the fourth generation.

8 And Moses made haste, and bowed his head toward the earth, and worshipped.

9 And he said, If now I have found grace in your sight, O LORD, let my LORD, I pray you, go among us; for it is a stiffnecked people; and pardon our iniquity and our sin, and take us for your inheritance.

10 And he said, Behold, I make a covenant: before all your people I will do marvels, such as have not been done in all the earth, nor in any nation: and all the people among which you are shall see the work of the LORD: for it is a terrible thing that I will do with you.

11 Observe you that which I command you this day: behold, I drive out before you the Amorite, and the Canaanite, and the Hittite, and the Perizzite, and the Hivite, and the Jebusite.

12 Take heed to yourself, lest you make a covenant with the inhabitants of the land where you go, lest it be for a snare in the midst of you:

13 But you shall destroy their altars, break their images, and cut down their groves:

14 For you shall worship no other god: for the LORD, whose name is Jealous, is a jealous God:

15 Lest you make a covenant with the inhabitants of the land, and they go a whoring after their gods, and do sacrifice to their gods, and one call you, and you eat of his sacrifice;

16 And you take of their daughters to your sons, and their daughters go a whoring after their gods, and make your sons go a whoring after their gods.

17 You shall make yourself no molten gods.

18 The feast of unleavened bread shall you keep. Seven days you shall eat unleavened bread, as I commanded you, in

---

34:6-9 Those who say that the God of the Old Testament is "vindictive" should also know that the Lord is merciful, gracious, slow to anger, longsuffering, full of goodness and truth. He will forgive iniquity (lawlessness), transgression (missing the mark of God's Law) and sin (missing the mark of the Law). If they refuse His mercy offered in the gospel, they will reap His judgment. He will by no means clear the guilty. Without His intervention through conversion, the sins of the fathers (immorality, drunkenness, wife beating, divorce, anger, racial prejudice, blasphemy, etc.) are often passed from father to son.

the time of the month Abib: for in the month Abib you came out from Egypt.

19 All that open the matrix is mine; and every firstling among your cattle, whether ox or sheep, that is male.

20 But the firstling of an ass you shall redeem with a lamb: and if you redeem him not, then shall you break his neck. All the firstborn of your sons you shall redeem. And none shall appear before me empty.

21 Six days you shall work, but on the seventh day you shall rest: in earing time and in harvest you shall rest.

22 And you shall observe the feast of weeks, of the firstfruits of wheat harvest, and the feast of ingathering at the year's end.

23 Thrice in the year shall all your menchildren appear before the LORD God, the God of Israel.

24 For I will cast out the nations before you, and enlarge your borders: neither shall any man desire your land, when you shall go up to appear before the LORD your God thrice in the year.

25 You shall not offer the blood of my sacrifice with leaven; neither shall the sacrifice of the feast of the passover be left to the morning.

26 The first of the firstfruits of your land you shall bring to the house of the LORD your God. You shall not seethe a kid in his mother's milk.

27 And the LORD said to Moses, Write these words: for after the tenor of these words I have made a covenant with you and with Israel.

28 And he was there with the LORD forty days and forty nights; he did neither eat bread, nor drink water. And he wrote upon the tables the words of the covenant, the ten commandments.

29 And it came to pass, when Moses came down from mount Sinai with the two tables of testimony in Moses' hand, when he came down from the mount, that Moses knew not that the skin of his face shone while he talked with him.

30 And when Aaron and all the children of Israel saw Moses, behold, the skin of his face shone; and they were afraid to come nigh him.

31 And Moses called to them; and Aaron and all the rulers of the congregation returned to him: and Moses talked with them.

32 And afterward all the children of Israel came nigh: and he gave them in commandment all that the LORD had spoken with him in mount Sinai.

33 And till Moses had done speaking with them, he put a vail on his face.

34 But when Moses went in before the LORD to speak with him, he took the vail off, until he came out. And he came out, and spoke to the children of Israel that which he was commanded.

35 And the children of Israel saw the face of Moses, that the skin of Moses' face shone: and Moses put the vail upon his face again, until he went in to speak with him.

CHAPTER 35

AND Moses gathered all the congregation of the children of Israel together, and said to them, These are the words which the LORD has commanded, that you should do them.

2 Six days shall work be done, but on the seventh day there shall be to you an holy day, a sabbath of rest to the LORD: whosoever does work therein shall be put to death.

3 You shall kindle no fire throughout your habitations upon the sabbath day.

4 And Moses spoke to all the congregation of the children of Israel, saying, This is the thing which the LORD commanded, saying,

5 Take from among you an offering to the LORD: whosoever is of a willing heart, let him bring it, an offering of the LORD; gold, and silver, and brass,

6 And blue, and purple, and scarlet, and fine linen, and goats' hair,

7 And rams' skins dyed red, and badgers' skins, and shittim wood,

THE FUNCTION OF THE LAW IN EVANGELISM

35:1 People will never set their faces decidedly toward heaven and live like pilgrims, until they really feel that they are in danger of hell . . .

Let us expound and beat out the Ten Commandments, and show the length, and breadth, and depth, and height of their requirements. This is the way of our Lord in the Sermon on the Mount. We cannot do better than follow His plan. We may depend on it, men will never come to Jesus, and stay with Jesus, and live for Jesus, unless they really know why they are to come, and what is their need. Those whom the Spirit draws to Jesus are those whom the Spirit has convinced of sin. Without thorough conviction of sin, men may seem to come to Jesus and follow Him for a season, but they will soon fall away and return to the world.

John C. Ryle
1816-1900
Evangelical Bishop of the Anglican Church

8 And oil for the light, and spices for anointing oil, and for the sweet incense,
9 And onyx stones, and stones to be set for the ephod, and for the breastplate.
10 And every wise hearted among you shall come, and make all that the LORD has commanded;
11 The tabernacle, his tent, and his covering, his taches, and his boards, his bars, his pillars, and his sockets,
12 The ark, and the staves thereof, with the mercy seat, and the vail of the covering,
13 The table, and his staves, and all his vessels, and the showbread,
14 The candlestick also for the light, and his furniture, and his lamps, with the oil for the light,
15 And the incense altar, and his staves, and the anointing oil, and the sweet incense, and the hanging for the door at the entering in of the tabernacle,
16 The altar of burnt offering, with his brasen grate, his staves, and all his vessels, the laver and his foot,

17 The hangings of the court, his pillars, and their sockets, and the hanging for the door of the court,
18 The pins of the tabernacle, and the pins of the court, and their cords,
19 The cloths of service, to do service in the holy place, the holy garments for Aaron the priest, and the garments of his sons, to minister in the priest's office.
20 And all the congregation of the children of Israel departed from the presence of Moses.
21 And they came, every one whose heart stirred him up, and every one whom his spirit made willing, and they brought the LORD's offering to the work of the tabernacle of the congregation, and for all his service, and for the holy garments.
22 And they came, both men and women, as many as were willing hearted, and brought bracelets, and earrings, and rings, and tablets, all jewels of gold: and every man that offered offered an offering of gold to the LORD.
23 And every man, with whom was found blue, and purple, and scarlet, and fine linen, and goats' hair, and red skins of rams, and badgers' skins, brought them.
24 Every one that did offer an offering of silver and brass brought the LORD's offering: and every man, with whom was found shittim wood for any work of the service, brought it.
25 And all the women that were wise hearted did spin with their hands, and brought that which they had spun, both of blue, and of purple, and of scarlet, and of fine linen.
26 And all the women whose heart stirred them up in wisdom spun goats' hair.
27 And the rulers brought onyx stones, and stones to be set, for the ephod, and for the breastplate;
28 And spice, and oil for the light, and for the anointing oil, and for the sweet incense.

29 The children of Israel brought a willing offering to the LORD, every man and woman, whose heart made them willing to bring for all manner of work, which the LORD had commanded to be made by the hand of Moses.

30 And Moses said to the children of Israel, See, the LORD has called by name Bezaleel the son of Uri, the son of Hur, of the tribe of Judah;

31 And he has filled him with the spirit of God, in wisdom, in understanding, and in knowledge, and in all manner of workmanship;

32 And to devise curious works, to work in gold, and in silver, and in brass,

33 And in the cutting of stones, to set them, and in carving of wood, to make any manner of cunning work.

34 And he has put in his heart that he may teach, both he, and Aholiab, the son of Ahisamach, of the tribe of Dan.

35 Them has he filled with wisdom of heart, to work all manner of work, of the engraver, and of the cunning workman, and of the embroiderer, in blue, and in purple, in scarlet, and in fine linen, and of the weaver, even of them that do any work, and of those that devise cunning work.

CHAPTER 36

THEN wrought Bezaleel and Aholiab, and every wise hearted man, in whom the LORD put wisdom and understanding to know how to work all manner of work for the service of the sanctuary, according to all that the LORD had commanded.

2 And Moses called Bezaleel and Aholiab, and every wise hearted man, in whose heart the LORD had put wisdom, even every one whose heart stirred him up to come to the work to do it:

3 And they received of Moses all the offering, which the children of Israel had brought for the work of the service of the sanctuary, to make it withal. And they brought yet to him free offerings every morning.

4 And all the wise men, that wrought all the work of the sanctuary, came every man from his work which they made;

5 And they spoke to Moses, saying, The people bring much more than enough for the service of the work, which the LORD commanded to make.

6 And Moses gave commandment, and they caused it to be proclaimed throughout the camp, saying, Let neither man nor woman make any more work for the offering of the sanctuary. So the people were restrained from bringing.

7 For the stuff they had was sufficient for all the work to make it, and too much.

8 And every wise hearted man among them that wrought the work of the tabernacle made ten curtains of fine twined linen, and blue, and purple, and scarlet: with cherubims of cunning work made he them.

9 The length of one curtain was twenty and eight cubits, and the breadth of one curtain four cubits: the curtains were all of one size.

10 And he coupled the five curtains one to another: and the other five curtains he coupled one to another.

11 And he made loops of blue on the edge of one curtain from the selvedge in the coupling: likewise he made in the uttermost side of another curtain, in the coupling of the second.

12 Fifty loops made he in one curtain, and fifty loops made he in the edge of the curtain which was in the coupling of the second: the loops held one curtain to another.

13 And he made fifty taches of gold, and coupled the curtains one to another with the taches: so it became one tabernacle.

14 And he made curtains of goats' hair for the tent over the tabernacle: eleven curtains he made them.

15 The length of one curtain was thirty cubits, and four cubits was the breadth of one curtain: the eleven curtains were of one size.

16 And he coupled five curtains by themselves, and six curtains by themselves.

17 And he made fifty loops upon the uttermost edge of the curtain in the coupling, and fifty loops made he upon the edge of the curtain which couples the second.

18 And he made fifty taches of brass to couple the tent together, that it might be one.

19 And he made a covering for the tent of rams' skins dyed red, and a covering of badgers' skins above that.

20 And he made boards for the tabernacle of shittim wood, standing up.

21 The length of a board was ten cubits, and the breadth of a board one cubit and a half.

22 One board had two tenons, equally distant one from another: thus did he make for all the boards of the tabernacle.

23 And he made boards for the tabernacle; twenty boards for the south side southward:

24 And forty sockets of silver he made under the twenty boards; two sockets under one board for his two tenons, and two sockets under another board for his two tenons.

25 And for the other side of the tabernacle, which is toward the north corner, he made twenty boards,

26 And their forty sockets of silver; two sockets under one board, and two sockets under another board.

27 And for the sides of the tabernacle westward he made six boards.

28 And two boards made he for the corners of the tabernacle in the two sides.

29 And they were coupled beneath, and coupled together at the head thereof, to one ring: thus he did to both of them in both the corners.

30 And there were eight boards; and their sockets were sixteen sockets of silver, under every board two sockets.

31 And he made bars of shittim wood; five for the boards of the one side of the tabernacle,

32 And five bars for the boards of the other side of the tabernacle, and five bars for the boards of the tabernacle for the sides westward.

33 And he made the middle bar to shoot through the boards from the one end to the other.

34 And he overlaid the boards with gold, and made their rings of gold to be places for the bars, and overlaid the bars with gold.

35 And he made a vail of blue, and purple, and scarlet, and fine twined linen: with cherubims made he it of cunning work.

36 And he made thereunto four pillars of shittim wood, and overlaid them with gold: their hooks were of gold; and he cast for them four sockets of silver.

37 And he made an hanging for the tabernacle door of blue, and purple, and scarlet, and fine twined linen, of needlework;

38 And the five pillars of it with their hooks: and he overlaid their chapiters and their fillets with gold: but their five sockets were of brass.

CHAPTER 37

AND Bezaleel made the ark of shittim wood: two cubits and a half was the length of it, and a cubit and a half the breadth of it, and a cubit and a half the height of it:

2 And he overlaid it with pure gold within and without, and made a crown of gold to it round about.

3 And he cast for it four rings of gold, to be set by the four corners of it; even two rings upon the one side of it, and two rings upon the other side of it.

4 And he made staves of shittim wood, and overlaid them with gold.

5 And he put the staves into the rings by the sides of the ark, to bear the ark.

6 And he made the mercy seat of pure gold: two cubits and a half was the

length thereof, and one cubit and a half the breadth thereof.

7 And he made two cherubims of gold, beaten out of one piece made he them, on the two ends of the mercy seat;

8 One cherub on the end on this side, and another cherub on the other end on that side: out of the mercy seat made he made the cherubims on the two ends thereof.

9 And the cherubims spread out their wings on high, and covered with their wings over the mercy seat, with their faces one to another; even to the mercy seatward were the faces of the cherubims.

10 And he made the table of shittim wood: two cubits was the length thereof, and a cubit the breadth thereof, and a cubit and a half the height thereof:

11 And he overlaid it with pure gold, and made thereunto a crown of gold round about.

12 Also he made thereunto a border of an handbreadth round about; and made a crown of gold for the border thereof round about.

13 And he cast for it four rings of gold, and put the rings upon the four corners that were in the four feet thereof.

14 Over against the border were the rings, the places for the staves to bear the table.

15 And he made the staves of shittim wood, and overlaid them with gold, to bear the table.

16 And he made the vessels which were upon the table, his dishes, and his spoons, and his bowls, and his covers to cover withal, of pure gold.

17 And he made the candlestick of pure gold: of beaten work made he the candlestick; his shaft, and his branch, his bowls, his knops, and his flowers, were of the same:

18 And six branches going out of the sides thereof; three branches of the candlestick out of the one side thereof, and three branches of the candlestick out of the other side thereof:

19 Three bowls made after the fashion of almonds in one branch, a knop and a flower; and three bowls made like almonds in another branch, a knop and a flower: so throughout the six branches going out of the candlestick.

20 And in the candlestick were four bowls made like almonds, his knops, and his flowers:

21 And a knop under two branches of the same, and a knop under two branches of the same, and a knop under two branches of the same, according to the six branches going out of it.

22 Their knops and their branches were of the same: all of it was one beaten work of pure gold.

23 And he made his seven lamps, and his snuffers, and his snuffdishes, of pure gold.

24 Of a talent of pure gold made he it, and all the vessels thereof.

25 And he made the incense altar of shittim wood: the length of it was a cubit, and the breadth of it a cubit; it was foursquare; and two cubits was the height of it; the horns thereof were of the same.

26 And he overlaid it with pure gold, both the top of it, and the sides thereof round about, and the horns of it: also he made to it a crown of gold round about.

27 And he made two rings of gold for it under the crown thereof, by the two corners of it, upon the two sides thereof, to be places for the staves to bear it withal.

28 And he made the staves of shittim wood, and overlaid them with gold.

29 And he made the holy anointing oil, and the pure incense of sweet spices, according to the work of the apothecary.

CHAPTER 38

A ND he made the altar of burnt offering of shittim wood: five cubits was the length thereof, and five cubits the breadth thereof; it was foursquare; and three cubits the height thereof.

2 And he made the horns thereof on the four corners of it; the horns thereof were

of the same: and he overlaid it with brass.

3 And he made all the vessels of the altar, the pots, and the shovels, and the basons, and the fleshhooks, and the firepans: all the vessels thereof made he of brass.

4 And he made for the altar a brasen grate of network under the compass thereof beneath to the midst of it.

5 And he cast four rings for the four ends of the grate of brass, to be places for the staves.

6 And he made the staves of shittim wood, and overlaid them with brass.

7 And he put the staves into the rings on the sides of the altar, to bear it withal; he made the altar hollow with boards.

8 And he made the laver of brass, and the foot of it of brass, of the looking-glasses of the women assembling, which assembled at the door of the tabernacle of the congregation.

9 And he made the court: on the south side southward the hangings of the court were of fine twined linen, an hundred cubits:

10 Their pillars were twenty, and their brasen sockets twenty; the hooks of the pillars and their fillets were of silver.

11 And for the north side the hangings were an hundred cubits, their pillars were twenty, and their sockets of brass twenty; the hooks of the pillars and their fillets of silver.

12 And for the west side were hangings of fifty cubits, their pillars ten, and their sockets ten; the hooks of the pillars and their fillets of silver.

13 And for the east side eastward fifty cubits.

14 The hangings of the one side of the gate were fifteen cubits; their pillars three, and their sockets three.

15 And for the other side of the court gate, on this hand and that hand, were hangings of fifteen cubits; their pillars three, and their sockets three.

16 All the hangings of the court round about were of fine twined linen.

17 And the sockets for the pillars were of brass; the hooks of the pillars and their fillets of silver; and the overlaying of their chapiters of silver; and all the pillars of the court were filleted with silver.

18 And the hanging for the gate of the court was needlework, of blue, and purple, and scarlet, and fine twined linen: and twenty cubits was the length, and the height in the breadth was five cubits, answerable to the hangings of the court.

19 And their pillars were four, and their sockets of brass four; their hooks of silver, and the overlaying of their chapiters and their fillets of silver.

20 And all the pins of the tabernacle, and of the court round about, were of brass.

21 This is the sum of the tabernacle, even of the tabernacle of testimony, as it was counted, according to the commandment of Moses, for the service of the Levites, by the hand of Ithamar, son to Aaron the priest.

22 And Bezaleel the son of Uri, the son of Hur, of the tribe of Judah, made all that the LORD commanded Moses.

23 And with him was Aholiab, son of Ahisamach, of the tribe of Dan, an engraver, and a cunning workman, and an embroiderer in blue, and in purple, and in scarlet, and fine linen.

24 All the gold that was occupied for the work in all the work of the holy place, even the gold of the offering, was twenty and nine talents, and seven hundred and thirty shekels, after the shekel of the sanctuary.

25 And the silver of them that were numbered of the congregation was an hundred talents, and a thousand seven hundred and threescore and fifteen shekels, after the shekel of the sanctuary:

26 A bekah for every man, that is, half a shekel, after the shekel of the sanctuary, for every one that went to be numbered, from twenty years old and upward, for six hundred thousand and three thousand and five hundred and fifty men.

27 And of the hundred talents of silver were cast the sockets of the sanctuary, and the sockets of the vail; an hundred sockets of the hundred talents, a talent for a socket.

28 And of the thousand seven hundred seventy and five shekels he made hooks for the pillars, and overlaid their chapiters, and filleted them.

29 And the brass of the offering was seventy talents, and two thousand and four hundred shekels.

30 And therewith he made the sockets to the door of the tabernacle of the congregation, and the brasen altar, and the brasen grate for it, and all the vessels of the altar,

31 And the sockets of the court round about, and the sockets of the court gate, and all the pins of the tabernacle, and all the pins of the court round about.

CHAPTER 39

A ND of the blue, and purple, and scarlet, they made cloths of service, to do service in the holy place, and made the holy garments for Aaron; as the LORD commanded Moses.

2 And he made the ephod of gold, blue, and purple, and scarlet, and fine twined linen.

3 And they did beat the gold into thin plates, and cut it into wires, to work it in the blue, and in the purple, and in the scarlet, and in the fine linen, with cunning work.

4 They made shoulderpieces for it, to couple it together: by the two edges was it coupled together.

5 And the curious girdle of his ephod, that was upon it, was of the same, according to the work thereof; of gold, blue, and purple, and scarlet, and fine twined linen; as the LORD commanded Moses.

6 And they wrought onyx stones inclosed in ouches of gold, graven, as signets are graven, with the names of the children of Israel.

7 And he put them on the shoulders of the ephod, that they should be stones for a memorial to the children of Israel; as the LORD commanded Moses.

8 And he made the breastplate of cunning work, like the work of the ephod; of gold, blue, and purple, and scarlet, and fine twined linen.

9 It was foursquare; they made the breastplate double: a span was the length thereof, and a span the breadth thereof, being doubled.

10 And they set in it four rows of stones: the first row was a sardius, a topaz, and a carbuncle: this was the first row.

11 And the second row, an emerald, a sapphire, and a diamond.

12 And the third row, a ligure, an agate, and an amethyst.

13 And the fourth row, a beryl, an onyx, and a jasper: they were inclosed in ouches of gold in their inclosings.

14 And the stones were according to the names of the children of Israel, twelve, according to their names, like the engravings of a signet, every one with his name, according to the twelve tribes.

15 And they made upon the breastplate chains at the ends, of wreathen work of pure gold.

16 And they made two ouches of gold, and two gold rings; and put the two rings in the two ends of the breastplate.

17 And they put the two wreathen chains of gold in the two rings on the ends of the breastplate.

18 And the two ends of the two wreathen chains they fastened in the two ouches, and put them on the shoulderpieces of the ephod, before it.

19 And they made two rings of gold, and put them on the two ends of the breastplate, upon the border of it, which was on the side of the ephod inward.

20 And they made two other golden rings, and put them on the two sides of the ephod underneath, toward the forepart of it, over against the other cou-

pling thereof, above the curious girdle of the ephod.

21 And they did bind the breastplate by his rings to the rings of the ephod with a lace of blue, that it might be above the curious girdle of the ephod, and that the breastplate might not be loosed from the ephod; as the LORD commanded Moses.

22 And he made the robe of the ephod of woven work, all of blue.

23 And there was an hole in the midst of the robe, as the hole of an habergeon, with a band round about the hole, that it should not rend.

24 And they made upon the hems of the robe pomegranates of blue, and purple, and scarlet, and twined linen.

25 And they made bells of pure gold, and put the bells between the pomegranates upon the hem of the robe, round about between the pomegranates;

26 A bell and a pomegranate, a bell and a pomegranate, round about the hem of the robe to minister in; as the LORD commanded Moses.

27 And they made coats of fine linen of woven work for Aaron, and for his sons,

28 And a mitre of fine linen, and goodly bonnets of fine linen, and linen breeches of fine twined linen,

29 And a girdle of fine twined linen, and blue, and purple, and scarlet, of needlework; as the LORD commanded Moses.

30 And they made the plate of the holy crown of pure gold, and wrote upon it a writing, like to the engravings of a signet, HOLINESS TO THE LORD.

31 And they tied to it a lace of blue, to fasten it on high upon the mitre; as the LORD commanded Moses.

32 Thus was all the work of the tabernacle of the tent of the congregation finished: and the children of Israel did according to all that the LORD commanded Moses, so did they.

33 And they brought the tabernacle to Moses, the tent, and all his furniture, his taches, his boards, his bars, and his pillars, and his sockets,

34 And the covering of rams' skins dyed red, and the covering of badgers' skins, and the vail of the covering,

35 The ark of the testimony, and the staves thereof, and the mercy seat,

36 The table, and all the vessels thereof, and the showbread,

37 The pure candlestick, with the lamps thereof, even with the lamps to be set in order, and all the vessels thereof, and the oil for light,

38 And the golden altar, and the anointing oil, and the sweet incense, and the hanging for the tabernacle door,

39 The brasen altar, and his grate of brass, his staves, and all his vessels, the laver and his foot,

40 The hangings of the court, his pillars, and his sockets, and the hanging for the court gate, his cords, and his pins, and all the vessels of the service of the tabernacle, for the tent of the congregation,

41 The cloths of service to do service in the holy place, and the holy garments for Aaron the priest, and his sons' garments, to minister in the priest's office.

42 According to all that the LORD commanded Moses, so the children of Israel made all the work.

43 And Moses did look upon all the work, and, behold, they had done it as the LORD had commanded, even so had they done it: and Moses blessed them.

CHAPTER 40

AND the LORD spoke to Moses, saying,

2 On the first day of the first month shall you set up the tabernacle of the tent of the congregation.

3 And you shall put therein the ark of the testimony, and cover the ark with the vail.

4 And you shall bring in the table, and set in order the things that are to be set in order upon it; and you shall bring in the candlestick, and light the lamps thereof.

5 And you shall set the altar of gold for the incense before the ark of the testimony, and put the hanging of the door to the tabernacle.

6 And you shall set the altar of the burnt offering before the door of the tabernacle of the tent of the congregation.

7 And you shall set the laver between the tent of the congregation and the altar, and shall put water therein.

8 And you shall set up the court round about, and hang up the hanging at the court gate.

9 And you shall take the anointing oil, and anoint the tabernacle, and all that is therein, and shall hallow it, and all the vessels thereof: and it shall be holy.

10 And you shall anoint the altar of the burnt offering, and all his vessels, and sanctify the altar: and it shall be an altar most holy.

11 And you shall anoint the laver and his foot, and sanctify it.

12 And you shall bring Aaron and his sons to the door of the tabernacle of the congregation, and wash them with water.

13 And you shall put upon Aaron the holy garments, and anoint him, and sanctify him; that he may minister to me in the priest's office.

14 And you shall bring his sons, and clothe them with coats:

15 And you shall anoint them, as you did anoint their father, that they may minister to me in the priest's office: for their anointing shall surely be an everlasting priesthood throughout their generations.

16 Thus did Moses: according to all that the LORD commanded him, so did he.

17 And it came to pass in the first month in the second year, on the first day of the month, that the tabernacle was reared up.

18 And Moses reared up the tabernacle, and fastened his sockets, and set up the boards thereof, and put in the bars thereof, and reared up his pillars.

19 And he spread abroad the tent over the tabernacle, and put the covering of the tent above upon it; as the LORD commanded Moses.

20 And he took and put the testimony into the ark, and set the staves on the ark, and put the mercy seat above upon the ark:

21 And he brought the ark into the tabernacle, and set up the vail of the covering, and covered the ark of the testimony; as the LORD commanded Moses.

22 And he put the table in the tent of the congregation, upon the side of the tabernacle northward, without the vail.

23 And he set the bread in order upon it before the LORD; as the LORD had commanded Moses.

24 And he put the candlestick in the tent of the congregation, over against the table, on the side of the tabernacle southward.

25 And he lighted the lamps before the LORD; as the LORD commanded Moses.

26 And he put the golden altar in the tent of the congregation before the vail:

27 And he burnt sweet incense thereon; as the LORD commanded Moses.

28 And he set up the hanging at the door of the tabernacle.

29 And he put the altar of burnt offering by the door of the tabernacle of the tent of the congregation, and offered upon it the burnt offering and the meat offering; as the LORD commanded Moses.

30 And he set the laver between the tent of the congregation and the altar, and put water there, to wash with.

31 And Moses and Aaron and his sons washed their hands and their feet thereat:

32 When they went into the tent of the congregation, and when they came near to the altar, they washed; as the LORD commanded Moses.

37 But if the cloud were not taken up, then they journeyed not till the day that it was taken up.

38 For the cloud of the LORD was upon the tabernacle by day, and fire was on it by night, in the sight of all the house of Israel, throughout all their journeys.

A zealous man feels that, like a lamp,
he is made to burn;
and if consumed in burning,
he has but done the work
for which God appointed him.
Such a one will always find a sphere
for his zeal.
If he cannot preach and work
and give money,
he will cry and sigh and pray.

John C. Ryle
1816-1900
EVANGELICAL BISHOP
OF THE ANGLICAN CHURCH

33 And he reared up the court round about the tabernacle and the altar, and set up the hanging of the court gate. So Moses finished the work.

34 Then a cloud covered the tent of the congregation, and the glory of the LORD filled the tabernacle.

35 And Moses was not able to enter into the tent of the congregation, because the cloud abode thereon, and the glory of the LORD filled the tabernacle.

36 And when the cloud was taken up from over the tabernacle, the children of Israel went onward in all their journeys:

Leviticus

CHAPTER 1

A ND the LORD called to Moses, and spoke to him out of the tabernacle of the congregation, saying,

2 Speak to the children of Israel, and say to them, If any man of you bring an offering to the LORD, you shall bring your offering of the cattle, even of the herd, and of the flock.

3 If his offering be a burnt sacrifice of the herd, let him offer a male without blemish: he shall offer it of his own voluntary will at the door of the tabernacle of the congregation before the LORD.

4 And he shall put his hand upon the head of the burnt offering; and it shall be accepted for him to make atonement for him.

5 And he shall kill the bullock before the LORD: and the priests, Aaron's sons, shall bring the blood, and sprinkle the blood round about upon the altar that is by the door of the tabernacle of the congregation.

6 And he shall flay the burnt offering, and cut it into his pieces.

7 And the sons of Aaron the priest shall put fire upon the altar, and lay the wood in order upon the fire:

8 And the priests, Aaron's sons, shall lay the parts, the head, and the fat, in order upon the wood that is on the fire which is upon the altar:

9 But his inwards and his legs shall he wash in water: and the priest shall burn all on the altar, to be a burnt sacrifice, an offering made by fire, of a sweet savor to the LORD.

10 And if his offering be of the flocks, namely, of the sheep, or of the goats, for a burnt sacrifice; he shall bring it a male without blemish.

11 And he shall kill it on the side of the altar northward before the LORD: and the priests, Aaron's sons, shall sprinkle his blood round about upon the altar.

12 And he shall cut it into his pieces, with his head and his fat: and the priest shall lay them in order on the wood that is on the fire which is upon the altar:

13 But he shall wash the inwards and the legs with water: and the priest shall bring it all, and burn it upon the altar: it is a burnt sacrifice, an offering made by fire, of a sweet savor to the LORD.

14 And if the burnt sacrifice for his offering to the LORD be of fowls, then he shall bring his offering of turtledoves, or of young pigeons.

15 And the priest shall bring it to the altar, and wring off his head, and burn it on the altar; and the blood thereof shall be wrung out at the side of the altar:

16 And he shall pluck away his crop with his feathers, and cast it beside the altar on the east part, by the place of the ashes:

17 And he shall cleave it with the wings thereof, but shall not divide it asunder: and the priest shall burn it upon the altar, upon the wood that is upon the fire: it is a burnt sacrifice, an offering

made by fire, of a sweet savor to the
LORD.

CHAPTER 2

AND when any will offer a meat offering to the LORD, his offering
shall be of fine flour; and he shall pour
oil upon it, and put frankincense thereon:

2 And he shall bring it to Aaron's sons
the priests: and he shall take thereout his
handful of the flour thereof, and of the
oil thereof, with all the frankincense
thereof; and the priest shall burn the
memorial of it upon the altar, to be an
offering made by fire, of a sweet savor to
the LORD:

3 And the remnant of the meat offering
shall be Aaron's and his sons': it is a
thing most holy of the offerings of the
LORD made by fire.

4 And if you bring an oblation of a meat
offering baken in the oven, it shall be
unleavened cakes of fine flour mingled
with oil, or unleavened wafers anointed
with oil.

5 And if your oblation be a meat offering baken in a pan, it shall be of fine
flour unleavened, mingled with oil.

6 You shall part it in pieces, and pour
oil thereon: it is a meat offering.

7 And if your oblation be a meat offering baken in the fryingpan, it shall be
made of fine flour with oil.

8 And you shall bring the meat offering
that is made of these things to the
LORD: and when it is presented to the
priest, he shall bring it to the altar.

9 And the priest shall take from the
meat offering a memorial thereof, and
shall burn it upon the altar: it is an offering made by fire, of a sweet savor to the
LORD.

10 And that which is left of the meat offering shall be Aaron's and his sons': it is
a thing most holy of the offerings of the
LORD made by fire.

11 No meat offering, which you shall
bring to the LORD, shall be made with
leaven: for you shall burn no leaven, nor

any honey, in any offering of the LORD
made by fire.

12 As for the oblation of the firstfruits,
you shall offer them to the LORD: but
they shall not be burnt on the altar for a
sweet savor.

13 And every oblation of your meat offering shall you season with salt; neither
shall you suffer the salt of the covenant
of your God to be lacking from your
meat offering: with all your offerings you
shall offer salt.

14 And if you offer a meat offering of
your firstfruits to the LORD, you shall
offer for the meat offering of your firstfruits green ears of corn dried by the fire,
even corn beaten out of full ears.

15 And you shall put oil upon it, and
lay frankincense thereon: it is a meat offering.

16 And the priest shall burn the memorial of it, part of the beaten corn thereof,
and part of the oil thereof, with all the
frankincense thereof: it is an offering
made by fire to the LORD.

CHAPTER 3

AND if his oblation be a sacrifice of
peace offering, if he offer it of the
herd; whether it be a male or female, he
shall offer it without blemish before the
LORD.

2 And he shall lay his hand upon the
head of his offering, and kill it at the
door of the tabernacle of the congregation: and Aaron's sons the priests shall
sprinkle the blood upon the altar round
about.

3 And he shall offer of the sacrifice of
the peace offering an offering made by
fire to the LORD; the fat that covers the
inwards, and all the fat that is upon the
inwards,

4 And the two kidneys, and the fat that
is on them, which is by the flanks, and
the caul above the liver, with the kidneys, it shall he take away.

5 And Aaron's sons shall burn it on the
altar upon the burnt sacrifice, which is
upon the wood that is on the fire: it is an

Are Christians bound by the law that Moses brought to the Jews?

The book of Leviticus is perhaps the least read and most misunderstood book in the entire Old Testament. From a New Covenant perspective, this God-breathed revelation, with all of its detailed dietary, sacrificial and sacerdotal Laws, is perceived to be wholly irrelevant by many evangelical Christians.

At the same time, however, it is considered by most Orthodox Jews and some professing Christians, in both this generation and generations past, to be an indispensable element in prescribing true godly conduct for God's chosen people.

But the question regarding the Levitical Law's relevance to Christians was perhaps the most hotly debated issue confronting the first century church. The issue was clearly settled at that time, during the first church counsel in Jerusalem. But some Christians today are still unclear as to whether they are obligated to observe the requirements of the Mosaic law as a whole, laws delineated in the pages of the Pentateuch, the first five books of the Old Testament.

God has not, however, left us without answer in this regard, but has in the pages of scripture outlined for us the express function of His Law and its relationship to the Christian.

The first Christians were Jews, and Jews predominated in the church in its developing stages. And these first century Messianic Jews did not initially forego their observance of God's Law, but rather continued in it, as was their custom from the days of their youth.

The question of the relevance of the Mosaic Law for Christians arose when God began adding Gentile believers to the body of Christ. In Acts chapter 10, God directed a God-fearing Gentile Centurion named Cornelius to summon the Apostle Peter. God subsequently revealed His will to the Apostle in a very disturbing vision. This vision eventually led to Peter proclaiming the gospel before Cornelius and all of his close friends and relatives. As a result, they converted to belief in Christ.

As the Lord began to raise up Paul the Apostle and use him mightily for His glory, this resulted in many more Gentile conversions. This great influx of Gentile believers into the early church brought much attention to the issue of the Mosaic Law's relevance for the Christian. In Acts 15:1, we learn, "And certain men came down from Judea and taught the brethren, unless you are circumcised according to the custom of Moses, you cannot be saved." And Acts 15:24 tells us that they were saying "you must be circumcised and keep the Law."

It was determined that Paul and Barnabas should go up to Jerusalem to meet with the apostles and elders in order to settle this dispute. And it was here that the historic decision was made regarding the Christian's relationship to the Law of Moses. Amidst much debate and discussion, the Apostle Peter asked regarding this matter: ". . .why do you test God by putting a yoke on the neck of the disciples which neither our fathers nor we were able to bear?"(Acts 15:10) It was then revealed by the Holy Spirit that the Gentile believers were not obligated to keep the Law of Moses, but they, as well as the Jews, are saved through the grace of the Lord Jesus.

It would seem at this point that the Law delivered by Moses to the Jews had no purposes whatsoever for the Christian, that it was altogether irrelevant. In Paul's Epistle to the Galatians he addressed this issue extensively as this church was also coming under the influence of "those of the circumcision," who were also known as the "Judaizers."

In the midst of his letter to the believers in Galatia, Paul proceeds to ask the following question: "What purpose then does the Law serve?" (Galatians 3:19) Paul then goes on to answer this question, and while doing so he makes the following statement: "...for if there had been a Law given which could have given life, truly righteousness would have been by the Law.

But the scripture has confined all under sin, that the promise by faith in Jesus Christ might be given to those who believe. But before faith came, we were kept under guard by the Law, kept for the faith which would afterward be revealed.

Continued next page . . .

Continued from previous page . . .

Therefore the Law was our tutor to bring us to Christ that we might be justified by faith. But after faith has come, we are no longer under a tutor" (Galatians 3:21-24).

According to Paul the Law was added because of "transgressions." This implies, as the NEB paraphrase suggests, that God's Law was used to "make wrongdoing a legal offence." In other words, it was intended to reveal to us our moral bankruptcy so that we might discover how sinful we really are.

After an individual has come to faith in Christ, the "tutor's" job in showing them their sinfulness and therefore leading them to the Savior is accomplished, and they are, at that point, no longer under the "schoolmaster." As Paul so aptly stated in Romans 3:20, "Therefore by the deeds of the Law no flesh shall be justified in His sight, for by the Law is the knowledge of sin." And again in Romans 7:7, "I would not have known sin except through the Law."

It is therefore indisputable that the Law of God is both relevant and pertinent. In its Levitical sense, God's Law continues to serve as that schoolmaster to those Jews who still adhere to it as the standard for their conduct. And in its general, moral sense, as found in the heart of the Law, the Ten Commandments, it continues to convict the consciences of men and women throughout the world as it reveals sinfulness and thus the true depth of need for the Savior.

The Apostle Paul said in 1 Timothy 1:9-10, "...we know that the Law is good if one uses it lawfully, knowing this: that the Law is not made for a righteous person, but for the lawless and insubordinate, for the ungodly and for sinners, for the unholy and profane, for murderers of fathers and murderers of mothers, for manslayers, for fornicators, for sodomites, for kidnappers, for liars, for perjurers, and if there is any other thing that is contrary to sound doctrine...".

It is, therefore, fitting for the wise and sensible servant of the Lord to lawfully wield the holy commandments of God while faithfully laboring in the field that is white for the harvest.

Pastor Emeal ("E.Z.") Zwayne
Vice President / General Manager
Living Waters Publications / The Way of the Master

offering made by fire, of a sweet savor to the LORD.

6 And if his offering for a sacrifice of peace offering to the LORD be of the flock; male or female, he shall offer it without blemish.

7 If he offer a lamb for his offering, then shall he offer it before the LORD.

8 And he shall lay his hand upon the head of his offering, and kill it before the tabernacle of the congregation: and Aaron's sons shall sprinkle the blood thereof round about upon the altar.

9 And he shall offer of the sacrifice of the peace offering an offering made by fire to the LORD; the fat thereof, and the whole rump, it shall he take off hard by the backbone; and the fat that covers the inwards, and all the fat that is upon the inwards,

10 And the two kidneys, and the fat that is upon them, which is by the flanks, and the caul above the liver, with the kidneys, it shall he take away.

11 And the priest shall burn it upon the altar: it is the food of the offering made by fire to the LORD.

12 And if his offering be a goat, then he shall offer it before the LORD.

13 And he shall lay his hand upon the head of it, and kill it before the tabernacle of the congregation: and the sons of Aaron shall sprinkle the blood thereof upon the altar round about.

14 And he shall offer thereof his offering, even an offering made by fire to the LORD; the fat that covers the inwards, and all the fat that is upon the inwards,

15 And the two kidneys, and the fat that is upon them, which is by the

flanks, and the caul above the liver, with the kidneys, it shall he take away.

16 And the priest shall burn them upon the altar: it is the food of the offering made by fire for a sweet savor: all the fat is the LORD's.

17 It shall be a perpetual statute for your generations throughout all your dwellings, that you eat neither fat nor blood.

CHAPTER 4

AND the LORD spoke to Moses, saying,

2 Speak to the children of Israel, saying, If a soul shall sin through ignorance against any of the commandments of the LORD concerning things which ought not to be done, and shall do against any of them:

3 If the priest that is anointed do sin according to the sin of the people; then let him bring for his sin, which he has sinned, a young bullock without blemish to the LORD for a sin offering.

4 And he shall bring the bullock to the door of the tabernacle of the congregation before the LORD; and shall lay his hand upon the bullock's head, and kill the bullock before the LORD.

5 And the priest that is anointed shall take of the bullock's blood, and bring it to the tabernacle of the congregation:

6 And the priest shall dip his finger in the blood, and sprinkle of the blood seven times before the LORD, before the vail of the sanctuary.

7 And the priest shall put some of the blood upon the horns of the altar of sweet incense before the LORD, which is in the tabernacle of the congregation; and shall pour all the blood of the bullock at the bottom of the altar of the burnt offering, which is at the door of the tabernacle of the congregation.

8 And he shall take off from it all the fat of the bullock for the sin offering; the fat that covers the inwards, and all the fat that is upon the inwards,

9 And the two kidneys, and the fat that is upon them, which is by the flanks, and the caul above the liver, with the kidneys, it shall he take away,

10 As it was taken off from the bullock of the sacrifice of peace offerings: and the priest shall burn them upon the altar of the burnt offering.

11 And the skin of the bullock, and all his flesh, with his head, and with his legs, and his inwards, and his dung,

12 Even the whole bullock shall he carry forth without the camp to a clean place, where the ashes are poured out, and burn him on the wood with fire: where the ashes are poured out shall he be burnt.

13 And if the whole congregation of Israel sin through ignorance, and the thing be hid from the eyes of the assembly, and they have done somewhat against any of the commandments of the LORD concerning things which should not be done, and are guilty;

14 When the sin, which they have sinned against it, is known, then the congregation shall offer a young bullock for the sin, and bring him before the tabernacle of the congregation.

15 And the elders of the congregation shall lay their hands upon the head of the bullock before the LORD: and the bullock shall be killed before the LORD.

It is the ordinary method of the Spirit of God to convict sinners by the law. It is this which, being set home on the conscience, generally breaketh the rocks in pieces.

It is more especially this part of the Word of God which is quick and powerful, full of life and energy and sharper than any two-edged sword.

JOHN WESLEY
1703—1791
BRITISH EVANGELIST
AND FOUNDER OF METHODISM

16 And the priest that is anointed shall bring of the bullock's blood to the tabernacle of the congregation:

17 And the priest shall dip his finger in some of the blood, and sprinkle it seven times before the LORD, even before the vail.

18 And he shall put some of the blood upon the horns of the altar which is before the LORD, that is in the tabernacle of the congregation, and shall pour out all the blood at the bottom of the altar of the burnt offering, which is at the door of the tabernacle of the congregation.

19 And he shall take all his fat from him, and burn it upon the altar.

20 And he shall do with the bullock as he did with the bullock for a sin offering, so shall he do with this: and the priest shall make an atonement for them, and it shall be forgiven them.

21 And he shall carry forth the bullock without the camp, and burn him as he burned the first bullock: it is a sin offering for the congregation.

22 When a ruler has sinned, and done somewhat through ignorance against any of the commandments of the LORD his God concerning things which should not be done, and is guilty;

23 Or if his sin, wherein he has sinned, come to his knowledge; he shall bring his offering, a kid of the goats, a male without blemish:

24 And he shall lay his hand upon the head of the goat, and kill it in the place where they kill the burnt offering before the LORD: it is a sin offering.

25 And the priest shall take of the blood of the sin offering with his finger, and put it upon the horns of the altar of burnt offering, and shall pour out his blood at the bottom of the altar of burnt offering.

26 And he shall burn all his fat upon the altar, as the fat of the sacrifice of peace offerings: and the priest shall make an atonement for him as concerning his sin, and it shall be forgiven him.

27 And if any one of the common people sin through ignorance, while he doeth somewhat against any of the commandments of the LORD concerning things which ought not to be done, and be guilty;

28 Or if his sin, which he has sinned, come to his knowledge: then he shall bring his offering, a kid of the goats, a female without blemish, for his sin which he has sinned.

29 And he shall lay his hand upon the head of the sin offering, and slay the sin offering in the place of the burnt offering.

30 And the priest shall take of the blood thereof with his finger, and put it upon the horns of the altar of burnt offering, and shall pour out all the blood thereof at the bottom of the altar.

31 And he shall take away all the fat thereof, as the fat is taken away from off the sacrifice of peace offerings; and the priest shall burn it upon the altar for a sweet savor to the LORD; and the priest shall make an atonement for him, and it shall be forgiven him.

32 And if he bring a lamb for a sin offering, he shall bring it a female without blemish.

33 And he shall lay his hand upon the head of the sin offering, and slay it for a sin offering in the place where they kill the burnt offering.

34 And the priest shall take of the blood of the sin offering with his finger, and put it upon the horns of the altar of burnt offering, and shall pour out all the blood thereof at the bottom of the altar:

35 And he shall take away all the fat thereof, as the fat of the lamb is taken away from the sacrifice of the peace offerings; and the priest shall burn them upon the altar, according to the offerings made by fire to the LORD: and the priest shall make an atonement for his sin that he has committed, and it shall be forgiven him.

CHAPTER 5

AND if a soul sin, and hear the voice of swearing, and is a witness, whether he has seen or known of it; if he do not utter it, then he shall bear his iniquity.

2 Or if a soul touch any unclean thing, whether it be a carcase of an unclean beast, or a carcase of unclean cattle, or the carcase of unclean creeping things, and if it be hidden from him; he also shall be unclean, and guilty.

3 Or if he touch the uncleanness of man, whatsoever uncleanness it be that a man shall be defiled with, and it be hid from him; when he knows of it, then he shall be guilty.

4 Or if a soul swear, pronouncing with his lips to do evil, or to do good, whatsoever it be that a man shall pronounce with an oath, and it be hid from him; when he knows of it, then he shall be guilty in one of these.

5 And it shall be, when he shall be guilty in one of these things, that he shall confess that he has sinned in that thing:

6 And he shall bring his trespass offering to the LORD for his sin which he has sinned, a female from the flock, a lamb or a kid of the goats, for a sin offering; and the priest shall make an atonement for him concerning his sin.

7 And if he be not able to bring a lamb, then he shall bring for his trespass, which he has committed, two turtledoves, or two young pigeons, to the LORD; one for a sin offering, and the other for a burnt offering.

8 And he shall bring them to the priest, who shall offer that which is for the sin offering first, and wring off his head from his neck, but shall not divide it asunder:

9 And he shall sprinkle of the blood of the sin offering upon the side of the altar; and the rest of the blood shall be wrung out at the bottom of the altar: it is a sin offering.

10 And he shall offer the second for a burnt offering, according to the manner: and the priest shall make an atonement for him for his sin which he has sinned, and it shall be forgiven him.

11 But if he be not able to bring two turtledoves, or two young pigeons, then he that sinned shall bring for his offering the tenth part of an ephah of fine flour for a sin offering; he shall put no oil upon it, neither shall he put any frankincense thereon: for it is a sin offering.

12 Then shall he bring it to the priest, and the priest shall take his handful of it, even a memorial thereof, and burn it on the altar, according to the offerings made by fire to the LORD: it is a sin offering.

13 And the priest shall make an atonement for him as touching his sin that he has sinned in one of these, and it shall be forgiven him: and the remnant shall be the priest's, as a meat offering.

14 And the LORD spoke to Moses, saying,

15 If a soul commit a trespass, and sin through ignorance, in the holy things of the LORD; then he shall bring for his trespass to the LORD a ram without blemish out of the flocks, with your estimation by shekels of silver, after the shekel of the sanctuary, for a trespass offering.

16 And he shall make amends for the harm that he has done in the holy thing, and shall add the fifth part thereto, and give it to the priest: and the priest shall make an atonement for him with the ram of the trespass offering, and it shall be forgiven him.

17 And if a soul sin, and commit any of these things which are forbidden to be done by the commandments of the LORD; though he know it not, yet is he guilty, and shall bear his iniquity.

18 And he shall bring a ram without blemish out of the flock, with your estimation, for a trespass offering, to the priest: and the priest shall make an atonement for him concerning his

ignorance wherein he erred and knew it not, and it shall be forgiven him.

19 It is a trespass offering: he has certainly trespassed against the LORD.

CHAPTER 6

AND the LORD spoke to Moses, saying,

2 If a soul sin, and commit a trespass against the LORD, and lie to his neighbor in that which was delivered him to keep, or in fellowship, or in a thing taken away by violence, or has deceived his neighbor;

3 Or have found that which was lost, and lies concerning it, and swears falsely; in any of all these that a man does, sinning therein:

4 Then it shall be, because he has sinned, and is guilty, that he shall restore that which he took violently away, or the thing which he has deceitfully gotten, or that which was delivered him to keep, or the lost thing which he found,

5 Or all that about which he has sworn falsely; he shall even restore it in the principal, and shall add the fifth part more thereto, and give it to him to whom it appertains, in the day of his trespass offering.

6 And he shall bring his trespass offering to the LORD, a ram without blemish out of the flock, with your estimation, for a trespass offering, to the priest:

7 And the priest shall make an atonement for him before the LORD: and it shall be forgiven him for any thing of all that he has done in trespassing therein.

8 And the LORD spoke to Moses, saying,

9 Command Aaron and his sons, saying, This is the law of the burnt offering: It is the burnt offering, because of the burning upon the altar all night to the morning, and the fire of the altar shall be burning in it.

10 And the priest shall put on his linen garment, and his linen breeches shall he put upon his flesh, and take up the ashes which the fire has consumed with the burnt offering on the altar, and he shall put them beside the altar.

11 And he shall put off his garments, and put on other garments, and carry forth the ashes without the camp to a clean place.

12 And the fire upon the altar shall be burning in it; it shall not be put out: and the priest shall burn wood on it every morning, and lay the burnt offering in order upon it; and he shall burn thereon the fat of the peace offerings.

13 The fire shall ever be burning upon the altar; it shall never go out.

14 And this is the law of the meat offering: the sons of Aaron shall offer it before the LORD, before the altar.

15 And he shall take of it his handful, of the flour of the meat offering, and of the oil thereof, and all the frankincense which is upon the meat offering, and shall burn it upon the altar for a sweet savor, even the memorial of it, to the LORD.

16 And the remainder thereof shall Aaron and his sons eat: with unleavened bread shall it be eaten in the holy place; in the court of the tabernacle of the congregation they shall eat it.

17 It shall not be baken with leaven. I have given it to them for their portion of my offerings made by fire; it is most holy, as is the sin offering, and as the trespass offering.

18 All the males among the children of Aaron shall eat of it. It shall be a statute for ever in your generations concerning the offerings of the LORD made by fire: every one that touches them shall be holy.

19 And the LORD spoke to Moses, saying,

20 This is the offering of Aaron and of his sons, which they shall offer to the LORD in the day when he is anointed; the tenth part of an ephah of fine flour for a meat offering perpetual, half of it in the morning, and half thereof at night.

21 In a pan it shall be made with oil; and when it is baken, you shall bring it

in: and the baken pieces of the meat offering shall you offer for a sweet savor to the LORD.

22 And the priest of his sons that is anointed in his stead shall offer it: it is a statute for ever to the LORD; it shall be wholly burnt.

23 For every meat offering for the priest shall be wholly burnt: it shall not be eaten.

24 And the LORD spoke to Moses, saying,

25 Speak to Aaron and to his sons, saying, This is the law of the sin offering: In the place where the burnt offering is killed shall the sin offering be killed before the LORD: it is most holy.

26 The priest that offers it for sin shall eat it: in the holy place shall it be eaten, in the court of the tabernacle of the congregation.

27 Whatsoever shall touch the flesh thereof shall be holy: and when there is sprinkled of the blood thereof upon any garment, you shall wash that whereon it was sprinkled in the holy place.

28 But the earthen vessel wherein it is sodden shall be broken: and if it be sodden in a brasen pot, it shall be both scoured, and rinsed in water.

29 All the males among the priests shall eat thereof: it is most holy.

30 And no sin offering, whereof any of the blood is brought into the tabernacle of the congregation to reconcile withal in the holy place, shall be eaten: it shall be burnt in the fire.

CHAPTER 7

LIKEWISE this is the law of the trespass offering: it is most holy.

2 In the place where they kill the burnt offering shall they kill the trespass offering: and the blood thereof shall he sprinkle round about upon the altar.

3 And he shall offer of it all the fat thereof; the rump, and the fat that covers the inwards,

4 And the two kidneys, and the fat that is on them, which is by the flanks, and the caul that is above the liver, with the kidneys, it shall he take away:

5 And the priest shall burn them upon the altar for an offering made by fire to the LORD: it is a trespass offering.

6 Every male among the priests shall eat thereof: it shall be eaten in the holy place: it is most holy.

7 As the sin offering is, so is the trespass offering: there is one law for them: the priest that makes atonement therewith shall have it.

8 And the priest that offers any man's burnt offering, even the priest shall have to himself the skin of the burnt offering which he has offered.

9 And all the meat offering that is baken in the oven, and all that is dressed in the fryingpan, and in the pan, shall be the priest's that offers it.

10 And every meat offering, mingled with oil, and dry, shall all the sons of Aaron have, one as much as another.

11 And this is the law of the sacrifice of peace offerings, which he shall offer to the LORD.

12 If he offer it for a thanksgiving, then he shall offer with the sacrifice of thanksgiving unleavened cakes mingled with oil, and unleavened wafers anointed with oil, and cakes mingled with oil, of fine flour, fried.

13 Besides the cakes, he shall offer for his offering leavened bread with the sacrifice of thanksgiving of his peace offerings.

14 And of it he shall offer one out of the whole oblation for an heave offering to the LORD, and it shall be the priest's that sprinkles the blood of the peace offerings.

15 And the flesh of the sacrifice of his peace offerings for thanksgiving shall be eaten the same day that it is offered; he shall not leave any of it until the morning.

16 But if the sacrifice of his offering be a vow, or a voluntary offering, it shall be eaten the same day that he offers his

sacrifice: and on the morrow also the remainder of it shall be eaten:

17 But the remainder of the flesh of the sacrifice on the third day shall be burnt with fire.

18 And if any of the flesh of the sacrifice of his peace offerings be eaten at all on the third day, it shall not be accepted, neither shall it be imputed to him that offers it: it shall be an abomination, and the soul that eats of it shall bear his iniquity.

19 And the flesh that touches any unclean thing shall not be eaten; it shall be burnt with fire: and as for the flesh, all that be clean shall eat thereof.

20 But the soul that eats of the flesh of the sacrifice of peace offerings, that pertain to the LORD, having his uncleanness upon him, even that soul shall be cut off from his people.

21 Moreover the soul that shall touch any unclean thing, as the uncleanness of man, or any unclean beast, or any abominable unclean thing, and eat of the flesh of the sacrifice of peace offerings, which pertain to the LORD, even that soul shall be cut off from his people.

22 And the LORD spoke to Moses, saying,

23 Speak to the children of Israel, saying, You shall eat no manner of fat, of ox, or of sheep, or of goat.

24 And the fat of the beast that dies of itself, and the fat of that which is torn with beasts, may be used in any other use: but you shall in no wise eat of it.

25 For whosoever eats the fat of the beast, of which men offer an offering made by fire to the LORD, even the soul that eats it shall be cut off from his people.

26 Moreover you shall eat no manner of blood, whether it be of fowl or of beast, in any of your dwellings.

27 Whatsoever soul it be that eats any manner of blood, even that soul shall be cut off from his people.

28 And the LORD spoke to Moses, saying,

29 Speak to the children of Israel, saying, He that offers the sacrifice of his peace offerings to the LORD shall bring his oblation to the LORD of the sacrifice of his peace offerings.

30 His own hands shall bring the offerings of the LORD made by fire, the fat with the breast, it shall he bring, that the breast may be waved for a wave offering before the LORD.

31 And the priest shall burn the fat upon the altar: but the breast shall be Aaron's and his sons'.

32 And the right shoulder shall you give to the priest for an heave offering of the sacrifices of your peace offerings.

33 He among the sons of Aaron, that offers the blood of the peace offerings, and the fat, shall have the right shoulder for his part.

34 For the wave breast and the heave shoulder have I taken of the children of Israel from off the sacrifices of their peace offerings, and have given them to Aaron the priest and to his sons by a statute for ever from among the children of Israel.

35 This is the portion of the anointing of Aaron, and of the anointing of his sons, out of the offerings of the LORD made by fire, in the day when he presented them to minister to the LORD in the priest's office;

36 Which the LORD commanded to be given them of the children of Israel, in the day that he anointed them, by a statute for ever throughout their generations.

37 This is the law of the burnt offering, of the meat offering, and of the sin offering, and of the trespass offering, and of the consecrations, and of the sacrifice of the peace offerings;

38 Which the LORD commanded Moses in mount Sinai, in the day that he commanded the children of Israel to offer their oblations to the LORD, in the wilderness of Sinai.

CHAPTER 8

A ND the LORD spoke to Moses, saying,

2 Take Aaron and his sons with him, and the garments, and the anointing oil, and a bullock for the sin offering, and two rams, and a basket of unleavened bread;

3 And gather all the congregation together to the door of the tabernacle of the congregation.

4 And Moses did as the LORD commanded him; and the assembly was gathered together to the door of the tabernacle of the congregation.

5 And Moses said to the congregation, This is the thing which the LORD commanded to be done.

6 And Moses brought Aaron and his sons, and washed them with water.

7 And he put upon him the coat, and girded him with the girdle, and clothed him with the robe, and put the ephod upon him, and he girded him with the curious girdle of the ephod, and bound it to him therewith.

8 And he put the breastplate upon him: also he put in the breastplate the Urim and the Thummim.

9 And he put the mitre upon his head; also upon the mitre, even upon his forefront, did he put the golden plate, the holy crown; as the LORD commanded Moses.

10 And Moses took the anointing oil, and anointed the tabernacle and all that was therein, and sanctified them.

11 And he sprinkled thereof upon the altar seven times, and anointed the altar and all his vessels, both the laver and his foot, to sanctify them.

12 And he poured of the anointing oil upon Aaron's head, and anointed him, to sanctify him.

13 And Moses brought Aaron's sons, and put coats upon them, and girded them with girdles, and put bonnets upon them; as the LORD commanded Moses.

14 And he brought the bullock for the sin offering: and Aaron and his sons laid their hands upon the head of the bullock for the sin offering.

15 And he slew it; and Moses took the blood, and put it upon the horns of the altar round about with his finger, and purified the altar, and poured the blood at the bottom of the altar, and sanctified it, to make reconciliation upon it.

16 And he took all the fat that was upon the inwards, and the caul above the liver, and the two kidneys, and their fat, and Moses burned it upon the altar.

17 But the bullock, and his hide, his flesh, and his dung, he burnt with fire without the camp; as the LORD commanded Moses.

18 And he brought the ram for the burnt offering: and Aaron and his sons laid their hands upon the head of the ram.

19 And he killed it; and Moses sprinkled the blood upon the altar round about.

20 And he cut the ram into pieces; and Moses burnt the head, and the pieces, and the fat.

21 And he washed the inwards and the legs in water; and Moses burnt the whole ram upon the altar: it was a burnt sacrifice for a sweet savor, and an offering made by fire to the LORD; as the LORD commanded Moses.

22 And he brought the other ram, the ram of consecration: and Aaron and his sons laid their hands upon the head of the ram.

23 And he slew it; and Moses took of the blood of it, and put it upon the tip of Aaron's right ear, and upon the thumb of his right hand, and upon the great toe of his right foot.

24 And he brought Aaron's sons, and Moses put of the blood upon the tip of their right ear, and upon the thumbs of their right hands, and upon the great toes of their right feet: and Moses sprinkled the blood upon the altar round about.

25 And he took the fat, and the rump, and all the fat that was upon the in-

wards, and the caul above the liver, and the two kidneys, and their fat, and the right shoulder:

26 And out of the basket of unleavened bread, that was before the LORD, he took one unleavened cake, and a cake of oiled bread, and one wafer, and put them on the fat, and upon the right shoulder:

27 And he put all upon Aaron's hands, and upon his sons' hands, and waved them for a wave offering before the LORD.

28 And Moses took them from off their hands, and burnt them on the altar upon the burnt offering: they were consecrations for a sweet savor: it is an offering made by fire to the LORD.

29 And Moses took the breast, and waved it for a wave offering before the LORD: for of the ram of consecration it was Moses' part; as the LORD commanded Moses.

30 And Moses took of the anointing oil, and of the blood which was upon the altar, and sprinkled it upon Aaron, and upon his garments, and upon his sons, and upon his sons' garments with him; and sanctified Aaron, and his garments, and his sons, and his sons' garments with him.

31 And Moses said to Aaron and to his sons, Boil the flesh at the door of the tabernacle of the congregation: and there eat it with the bread that is in the basket of consecrations, as I commanded, saying, Aaron and his sons shall eat it.

32 And that which remains of the flesh and of the bread shall you burn with fire.

33 And you shall not go out of the door of the tabernacle of the congregation in seven days, until the days of your consecration be at an end: for seven days shall he consecrate you.

34 As he has done this day, so the LORD has commanded to do, to make an atonement for you.

35 Therefore shall you abide at the door of the tabernacle of the congrega-

tion day and night seven days, and keep the charge of the LORD, that you die not: for so I am commanded.

36 So Aaron and his sons did all things which the LORD commanded by the hand of Moses.

CHAPTER 9

AND it came to pass on the eighth day, that Moses called Aaron and his sons, and the elders of Israel;

2 And he said to Aaron, Take a young calf for a sin offering, and a ram for a burnt offering, without blemish, and offer them before the LORD.

3 And to the children of Israel you shall speak, saying, Take a kid of the goats for a sin offering; and a calf and a lamb, both of the first year, without blemish, for a burnt offering;

4 Also a bullock and a ram for peace offerings, to sacrifice before the LORD; and a meat offering mingled with oil: for to day the LORD will appear to you.

5 And they brought that which Moses commanded before the tabernacle of the congregation: and all the congregation drew near and stood before the LORD.

6 And Moses said, This is the thing which the LORD commanded that you should do: and the glory of the LORD shall appear to you.

7 And Moses said to Aaron, Go to the altar, and offer your sin offering, and your burnt offering, and make an atonement for thyself, and for the people: and offer the offering of the people, and make an atonement for them; as the LORD commanded.

8 Aaron therefore went to the altar, and slew the calf of the sin offering, which was for himself.

9 And the sons of Aaron brought the blood to him: and he dipped his finger in the blood, and put it upon the horns of the altar, and poured out the blood at the bottom of the altar:

10 But the fat, and the kidneys, and the caul above the liver of the sin offering,

he burnt upon the altar; as the LORD commanded Moses.

11 And the flesh and the hide he burnt with fire without the camp.

12 And he slew the burnt offering; and Aaron's sons presented to him the blood, which he sprinkled round about upon the altar.

13 And they presented the burnt offering to him, with the pieces thereof, and the head: and he burnt them upon the altar.

14 And he did wash the inwards and the legs, and burnt them upon the burnt offering on the altar.

15 And he brought the people's offering, and took the goat, which was the sin offering for the people, and slew it, and offered it for sin, as the first.

16 And he brought the burnt offering, and offered it according to the manner.

17 And he brought the meat offering, and took an handful thereof, and burnt it upon the altar, beside the burnt sacrifice of the morning.

18 He slew also the bullock and the ram for a sacrifice of peace offerings, which was for the people: and Aaron's sons presented to him the blood, which he sprinkled upon the altar round about,

19 And the fat of the bullock and of the ram, the rump, and that which covers the inwards, and the kidneys, and the caul above the liver:

20 And they put the fat upon the breasts, and he burnt the fat upon the altar:

21 And the breasts and the right shoulder Aaron waved for a wave offering before the LORD; as Moses commanded.

22 And Aaron lifted up his hand toward the people, and blessed them, and came down from offering of the sin offering, and the burnt offering, and peace offerings.

23 And Moses and Aaron went into the tabernacle of the congregation, and came out, and blessed the people: and the glory of the LORD appeared to all the people.

24 And there came a fire out from before the LORD, and consumed upon the altar the burnt offering and the fat: which when all the people saw, they shouted, and fell on their faces.

CHAPTER 10

AND Nadab and Abihu, the sons of Aaron, took either of them his censer, and put fire therein, and put incense thereon, and offered strange fire before the LORD, which he commanded them not.

2 And there went out fire from the LORD, and devoured them, and they died before the LORD.

3 Then Moses said to Aaron, This is it that the LORD spoke, saying, I will be sanctified in them that come nigh me, and before all the people I will be glorified. And Aaron held his peace.

4 And Moses called Mishael and Elzaphan, the sons of Uzziel the uncle of Aaron, and said to them, Come near, carry your brethren from before the sanctuary out of the camp.

5 So they went near, and carried them in their coats out of the camp; as Moses had said.

6 And Moses said to Aaron, and to Eleazar and to Ithamar, his sons, Uncover not your heads, neither rend your clothes; lest you die, and lest wrath come upon all the people: but let your brethren, the whole house of Israel, bewail the burning which the LORD has kindled.

7 And you shall not go out from the door of the tabernacle of the congregation, lest you die: for the anointing oil of the LORD is upon you. And they did according to the word of Moses.

8 And the LORD spoke to Aaron, saying,

9 Do not drink wine nor strong drink, your, nor your sons with you, when you go into the tabernacle of the congregation, lest you die: it shall be a statute for ever throughout your generations:

10 And that you may put difference between holy and unholy, and between unclean and clean;

11 And that you may teach the children of Israel all the statutes which the LORD has spoken to them by the hand of Moses.

12 And Moses spoke to Aaron, and to Eleazar and to Ithamar, his sons that were left, Take the meat offering that remains of the offerings of the LORD made by fire, and eat it without leaven beside the altar: for it is most holy:

13 And you shall eat it in the holy place, because it is your due, and your sons' due, of the sacrifices of the LORD made by fire: for so I am commanded.

14 And the wave breast and heave shoulder shall you eat in a clean place; you, and your sons, and your daughters with you: for they are your due, and your sons' due, which are given out of the sacrifices of peace offerings of the children of Israel.

15 The heave shoulder and the wave breast shall they bring with the offerings made by fire of the fat, to wave it for a wave offering before the LORD; and it shall be yours, and your sons' with you, by a statute for ever; as the LORD has commanded.

16 And Moses diligently sought the goat of the sin offering, and, behold, it was burnt: and he was angry with Eleazar and Ithamar, the sons of Aaron which were left alive, saying,

17 Why have you not eaten the sin offering in the holy place, seeing it is most holy, and God has given it you to bear the iniquity of the congregation, to make atonement for them before the LORD?

18 Behold, the blood of it was not brought in within the holy place: you should indeed have eaten it in the holy place, as I commanded.

19 And Aaron said to Moses, Behold, this day have they offered their sin offering and their burnt offering before the LORD; and such things have befallen me: and if I had eaten the sin offering to day, should it have been accepted in the sight of the LORD?

20 And when Moses heard that, he was content.

CHAPTER 11

AND the LORD spoke to Moses and to Aaron, saying to them,

2 Speak to the children of Israel, saying, These are the beasts which you shall eat among all the beasts that are on the earth.

3 Whatsoever parts the hoof, and is clovenfooted, and chews the cud, among the beasts, that shall you eat.

4 Nevertheless these shall you not eat of them that chew the cud, or of them that divide the hoof: as the camel, because he chews the cud, but divides not the hoof; he is unclean to you.

5 And the coney, because he chews the cud, but divides not the hoof; he is unclean to you.

6 And the hare, because he chews the cud, but divides not the hoof; he is unclean to you.

7 And the swine, though he divide the hoof, and be clovenfooted, yet he chews not the cud; he is unclean to you.

8 Of their flesh shall you not eat, and their carcase shall you not touch; they are unclean to you.

9 These shall you eat of all that are in the waters: whatsoever has fins and scales in the waters, in the seas, and in the rivers, them shall you eat.

10 And all that have not fins and scales in the seas, and in the rivers, of all that move in the waters, and of any living thing which is in the waters, they shall be an abomination to you:

11 They shall be even an abomination to you; you shall not eat of their flesh, but you shall have their carcases in abomination.

12 Whatsoever has no fins nor scales in the waters, that shall be an abomination to you.

13 And these are they which you shall have in abomination among the fowls;

they shall not be eaten, they are an abomination: the eagle, and the ossifrage, and the ospray,

14 And the vulture, and the kite after his kind;

15 Every raven after his kind;

16 And the owl, and the night hawk, and the cuckow, and the hawk after his kind,

17 And the little owl, and the cormorant, and the great owl,

18 And the swan, and the pelican, and the gier eagle,

19 And the stork, the heron after her kind, and the lapwing, and the bat.

20 All fowls that creep, going upon all four, shall be an abomination to you.

21 Yet these may you eat of every flying creeping thing that goes upon all four, which have legs above their feet, to leap with upon the earth;

22 Even these of them you may eat; the locust after his kind, and the bald locust after his kind, and the beetle after his kind, and the grasshopper after his kind.

23 But all other flying creeping things, which have four feet, shall be an abomination to you.

24 And for these you shall be unclean: whosoever touches the carcase of them shall be unclean until the even.

25 And whosoever bears ought of the carcase of them shall wash his clothes, and be unclean until the even.

26 The carcases of every beast which divides the hoof, and is not clovenfooted, nor chews the cud, are unclean to you: every one that touches them shall be unclean.

27 And whatsoever goes upon his paws, among all manner of beasts that go on all four, those are unclean to you: whoso touches their carcase shall be unclean until the even.

28 And he that bears the carcase of them shall wash his clothes, and be unclean until the even: they are unclean to you.

29 These also shall be unclean to you among the creeping things that creep upon the earth; the weasel, and the mouse, and the tortoise after his kind,

30 And the ferret, and the chameleon, and the lizard, and the snail, and the mole.

31 These are unclean to you among all that creep: whosoever doth touch them, when they be dead, shall be unclean until the even.

32 And upon whatsoever any of them, when they are dead, doth fall, it shall be unclean; whether it be any vessel of wood, or raiment, or skin, or sack, whatsoever vessel it be, wherein any work is done, it must be put into water, and it shall be unclean until the even; so it shall be cleansed.

33 And every earthen vessel, whereinto any of them falls, whatsoever is in it shall be unclean; and you shall break it.

34 Of all meat which may be eaten, that on which such water cometh shall be unclean: and all drink that may be drunk in every such vessel shall be unclean.

35 And every thing whereupon any part of their carcase falls shall be unclean; whether it be oven, or ranges for pots, they shall be broken down: for they are unclean and shall be unclean to you.

36 Nevertheless a fountain or pit, wherein there is plenty of water, shall be clean: but that which touches their carcase shall be unclean.

37 And if any part of their carcase fall upon any sowing seed which is to be sown, it shall be clean.

38 But if any water be put upon the seed, and any part of their carcase fall thereon, it shall be unclean to you.

39 And if any beast, of which you may eat, die; he that touches the carcase thereof shall be unclean until the even.

40 And he that eats of the carcase of it shall wash his clothes, and be unclean until the even: he also that bears the carcase of it shall wash his clothes, and be unclean until the even.

41 And every creeping thing that creeps upon the earth shall be an abomination; it shall not be eaten.

42 Whatsoever goes upon the belly, and whatsoever goes upon all four, or whatsoever has more feet among all creeping things that creep upon the earth, them you shall not eat; for they are an abomination.

43 You shall not make yourselves abominable with any creeping thing that creeps, neither shall you make yourselves unclean with them, that you should be defiled thereby.

44 For I am the LORD your God: you shall therefore sanctify yourselves, and you shall be holy; for I am holy: neither shall you defile yourselves with any manner of creeping thing that creeps upon the earth.

45 For I am the LORD that brings you up out of the land of Egypt, to be your God: you shall therefore be holy, for I am holy.

46 This is the law of the beasts, and of the fowl, and of every living creature that moves in the waters, and of every creature that creeps upon the earth:

47 To make a difference between the unclean and the clean, and between the beast that may be eaten and the beast that may not be eaten.

CHAPTER 12

AND the LORD spoke to Moses, saying,

2 Speak to the children of Israel, saying, If a woman have conceived seed, and born a man child: then she shall be unclean seven days; according to the days of the separation for her infirmity shall she be unclean.

3 And in the eighth day the flesh of his foreskin shall be circumcised.

4 And she shall then continue in the blood of her purifying three and thirty days; she shall touch no hallowed thing,

nor come into the sanctuary, until the days of her purifying be fulfilled.

5 But if she bear a maid child, then she shall be unclean two weeks, as in her separation: and she shall continue in the blood of her purifying threescore and six days.

6 And when the days of her purifying are fulfilled, for a son, or for a daughter, she shall bring a lamb of the first year for a burnt offering, and a young pigeon, or a turtledove, for a sin offering, to the door of the tabernacle of the congregation, to the priest:

7 Who shall offer it before the LORD, and make an atonement for her; and she shall be cleansed from the issue of her blood. This is the law for her that has born a male or a female.

8 And if she be not able to bring a lamb, then she shall bring two turtles, or two young pigeons; the one for the burnt offering, and the other for a sin offering: and the priest shall make an atonement for her, and she shall be clean.

CHAPTER 13

AND the LORD spoke to Moses and Aaron, saying,

2 When a man shall have in the skin of his flesh a rising, a scab, or bright spot, and it be in the skin of his flesh like the plague of leprosy; then he shall be brought to Aaron the priest, or to one of his sons the priests:

3 And the priest shall look on the plague in the skin of the flesh: and when the hair in the plague is turned white, and the plague in sight be deeper than the skin of his flesh, it is a plague of leprosy: and the priest shall look on him, and pronounce him unclean.

4 If the bright spot be white in the skin of his flesh, and in sight be not deeper than the skin, and the hair thereof be not

---

13:5 For fascinating facts in the Bible see Psalm 38:11 comment.

turned white; then the priest shall shut up him that has the plague seven days:

5 And the priest shall look on him the seventh day: and, behold, if the plague in his sight be at a stay, and the plague spread not in the skin; then the priest shall shut him up seven days more:

6 And the priest shall look on him again the seventh day: and, behold, if the plague be somewhat dark, and the plague spread not in the skin, the priest shall pronounce him clean: it is but a scab: and he shall wash his clothes, and be clean.

7 But if the scab spread much abroad in the skin, after that he has been seen of the priest for his cleansing, he shall be seen of the priest again.

8 And if the priest see that, behold, the scab spreads in the skin, then the priest shall pronounce him unclean: it is a leprosy.

9 When the plague of leprosy is in a man, then he shall be brought to the priest;

10 And the priest shall see him: and, behold, if the rising be white in the skin, and it have turned the hair white, and there be quick raw flesh in the rising;

11 It is an old leprosy in the skin of his flesh, and the priest shall pronounce him unclean, and shall not shut him up: for he is unclean.

12 And if a leprosy break out abroad in the skin, and the leprosy cover all the skin of him that has the plague from his head even to his foot, wheresoever the priest looks;

13 Then the priest shall consider: and, behold, if the leprosy have covered all his flesh, he shall pronounce him clean that has the plague: it is all turned white: he is clean.

14 But when raw flesh appears in him, he shall be unclean.

15 And the priest shall see the raw flesh, and pronounce him to be unclean: for the raw flesh is unclean: it is a leprosy.

16 Or if the raw flesh turn again, and be changed to white, he shall come to the priest;

17 And the priest shall see him: and, behold, if the plague be turned into white; then the priest shall pronounce him clean that has the plague: he is clean.

18 The flesh also, in which, even in the skin thereof, was a boil, and is healed,

19 And in the place of the boil there be a white rising, or a bright spot, white, and somewhat reddish, and it be showed to the priest;

20 And if, when the priest sees it, behold, it be in sight lower than the skin, and the hair thereof be turned white; the priest shall pronounce him unclean: it is a plague of leprosy broken out of the boil.

21 But if the priest look on it, and, behold, there be no white hairs therein, and if it be not lower than the skin, but be somewhat dark; then the priest shall shut him up seven days:

22 And if it spread much abroad in the skin, then the priest shall pronounce him unclean: it is a plague.

23 But if the bright spot stay in his place, and spread not, it is a burning boil; and the priest shall pronounce him clean.

24 Or if there be any flesh, in the skin whereof there is a hot burning, and the quick flesh that burns have a white bright spot, somewhat reddish, or white;

25 Then the priest shall look upon it: and, behold, if the hair in the bright spot be turned white, and it be in sight deeper than the skin; it is a leprosy broken out of the burning: therefore the priest shall pronounce him unclean: it is the plague of leprosy.

26 But if the priest look on it, and, behold, there be no white hair in the bright spot, and it be no lower than the other skin, but be somewhat dark; then the priest shall shut him up seven days:

27 And the priest shall look upon him the seventh day: and if it be spread

much abroad in the skin, then the priest shall pronounce him unclean: it is the plague of leprosy.

28 And if the bright spot stay in his place, and spread not in the skin, but it be somewhat dark; it is a rising of the burning, and the priest shall pronounce him clean: for it is an inflammation of the burning.

29 If a man or woman have a plague upon the head or the beard;

30 Then the priest shall see the plague: and, behold, if it be in sight deeper than the skin; and there be in it a yellow thin hair; then the priest shall pronounce him unclean: it is a dry scall, even a leprosy upon the head or beard.

31 And if the priest look on the plague of the scall, and, behold, it be not in sight deeper than the skin, and that there is no black hair in it; then the priest shall shut up him that has the plague of the scall seven days:

32 And in the seventh day the priest shall look on the plague: and, behold, if the scall spread not, and there be in it no yellow hair, and the scall be not in sight deeper than the skin;

33 He shall be shaven, but the scall shall he not shave; and the priest shall shut up him that has the scall seven days more:

34 And in the seventh day the priest shall look on the scall: and, behold, if the scall be not spread in the skin, nor be in sight deeper than the skin; then the priest shall pronounce him clean: and he shall wash his clothes, and be clean.

35 But if the scall spread much in the skin after his cleansing;

36 Then the priest shall look on him: and, behold, if the scall be spread in the skin, the priest shall not seek for yellow hair; he is unclean.

37 But if the scall be in his sight at a stay, and that there is black hair grown up therein; the scall is healed, he is clean: and the priest shall pronounce him clean.

38 If a man also or a woman have in the skin of their flesh bright spots, even white bright spots;

39 Then the priest shall look: and, behold, if the bright spots in the skin of their flesh be darkish white; it is a freckled spot that grows in the skin; he is clean.

40 And the man whose hair is fallen off his head, he is bald; yet is he clean.

41 And he that has his hair fallen off from the part of his head toward his face, he is forehead bald: yet is he clean.

42 And if there be in the bald head, or bald forehead, a white reddish sore; it is a leprosy sprung up in his bald head, or his bald forehead.

43 Then the priest shall look upon it: and, behold, if the rising of the sore be white reddish in his bald head, or in his bald forehead, as the leprosy appears in the skin of the flesh;

44 He is a leprous man, he is unclean: the priest shall pronounce him utterly unclean; his plague is in his head.

45 And the leper in whom the plague is, his clothes shall be rent, and his head bare, and he shall put a covering upon his upper lip, and shall cry, Unclean, unclean.

46 All the days wherein the plague shall be in him he shall be defiled; he is unclean: he shall dwell alone; without the camp shall his habitation be.

47 The garment also that the plague of leprosy is in, whether it be a woollen garment, or a linen garment;

48 Whether it be in the warp, or woof; of linen, or of woollen; whether in a skin, or in any thing made of skin;

49 And if the plague be greenish or reddish in the garment, or in the skin, either in the warp, or in the woof, or in any thing of skin; it is a plague of leprosy, and shall be showed to the priest:

50 And the priest shall look upon the plague, and shut up it that has the plague seven days:

51 And he shall look on the plague on the seventh day: if the plague be spread

in the garment, either in the warp, or in the woof, or in a skin, or in any work that is made of skin; the plague is a fretting leprosy; it is unclean.

52 He shall therefore burn that garment, whether warp or woof, in woollen or in linen, or any thing of skin, wherein the plague is: for it is a fretting leprosy; it shall be burnt in the fire.

53 And if the priest shall look, and, behold, the plague be not spread in the garment, either in the warp, or in the woof, or in any thing of skin;

54 Then the priest shall command that they wash the thing wherein the plague is, and he shall shut it up seven days more:

55 And the priest shall look on the plague, after that it is washed: and, behold, if the plague have not changed his colour, and the plague be not spread; it is unclean; your shall burn it in the fire; it is fret inward, whether it be bare within or without.

56 And if the priest look, and, behold, the plague be somewhat dark after the washing of it; then he shall rend it out of the garment, or out of the skin, or out of the warp, or out of the woof:

57 And if it appear still in the garment, either in the warp, or in the woof, or in any thing of skin; it is a spreading plague: you shall burn that wherein the plague is with fire.

58 And the garment, either warp, or woof, or whatsoever thing of skin it be, which you shall wash, if the plague be departed from them, then it shall be washed the second time, and shall be clean.

59 This is the law of the plague of leprosy in a garment of woollen or linen, either in the warp, or woof, or any thing of skins, to pronounce it clean, or to pronounce it unclean.

CHAPTER 14

AND the LORD spoke to Moses, saying,

2 This shall be the law of the leper in the day of his cleansing: He shall be brought to the priest:

3 And the priest shall go forth out of the camp; and the priest shall look, and, behold, if the plague of leprosy be healed in the leper;

4 Then shall the priest command to take for him that is to be cleansed two birds alive and clean, and cedar wood, and scarlet, and hyssop:

5 And the priest shall command that one of the birds be killed in an earthen vessel over running water:

6 As for the living bird, he shall take it, and the cedar wood, and the scarlet, and the hyssop, and shall dip them and the living bird in the blood of the bird that was killed over the running water:

7 And he shall sprinkle upon him that is to be cleansed from the leprosy seven times, and shall pronounce him clean, and shall let the living bird loose into the open field.

8 And he that is to be cleansed shall wash his clothes, and shave off all his hair, and wash himself in water, that he may be clean: and after that he shall come into the camp, and shall tarry abroad out of his tent seven days.

9 But it shall be on the seventh day, that he shall shave all his hair off his head and his beard and his eyebrows, even all his hair he shall shave off: and he shall wash his clothes, also he shall wash his flesh in water, and he shall be clean.

10 And on the eighth day he shall take two he lambs without blemish, and one ewe lamb of the first year without blemish, and three tenth deals of fine flour for a meat offering, mingled with oil, and one log of oil.

11 And the priest that makes him clean shall present the man that is to be made clean, and those things, before the

LORD, at the door of the tabernacle of the congregation:

12 And the priest shall take one he lamb, and offer him for a trespass offering, and the log of oil, and wave them for a wave offering before the LORD:

13 And he shall slay the lamb in the place where he shall kill the sin offering and the burnt offering, in the holy place: for as the sin offering is the priest's, so is the trespass offering: it is most holy:

14 And the priest shall take some of the blood of the trespass offering, and the priest shall put it upon the tip of the right ear of him that is to be cleansed, and upon the thumb of his right hand, and upon the great toe of his right foot:

15 And the priest shall take some of the log of oil, and pour it into the palm of his own left hand:

16 And the priest shall dip his right finger in the oil that is in his left hand, and shall sprinkle of the oil with his finger seven times before the LORD:

17 And of the rest of the oil that is in his hand shall the priest put upon the tip of the right ear of him that is to be cleansed, and upon the thumb of his right hand, and upon the great toe of his right foot, upon the blood of the trespass offering:

18 And the remnant of the oil that is in the priest's hand he shall pour upon the head of him that is to be cleansed: and the priest shall make an atonement for him before the LORD.

19 And the priest shall offer the sin offering, and make an atonement for him that is to be cleansed from his uncleanness; and afterward he shall kill the burnt offering:

20 And the priest shall offer the burnt offering and the meat offering upon the altar: and the priest shall make an atonement for him, and he shall be clean.

21 And if he be poor, and cannot get so much; then he shall take one lamb for a trespass offering to be waved, to make an atonement for him, and one tenth deal of fine flour mingled with oil for a meat offering, and a log of oil;

22 And two turtledoves, or two young pigeons, such as he is able to get; and the one shall be a sin offering, and the other a burnt offering.

23 And he shall bring them on the eighth day for his cleansing to the priest, to the door of the tabernacle of the congregation, before the LORD.

24 And the priest shall take the lamb of the trespass offering, and the log of oil, and the priest shall wave them for a wave offering before the LORD:

25 And he shall kill the lamb of the trespass offering, and the priest shall take some of the blood of the trespass offering, and put it upon the tip of the right ear of him that is to be cleansed, and upon the thumb of his right hand, and upon the great toe of his right foot:

26 And the priest shall pour of the oil into the palm of his own left hand:

27 And the priest shall sprinkle with his right finger some of the oil that is in his left hand seven times before the LORD:

28 And the priest shall put of the oil that is in his hand upon the tip of the right ear of him that is to be cleansed, and upon the thumb of his right hand, and upon the great toe of his right foot, upon the place of the blood of the trespass offering:

29 And the rest of the oil that is in the priest's hand he shall put upon the head of him that is to be cleansed, to make an atonement for him before the LORD.

30 And he shall offer the one of the turtledoves, or of the young pigeons, such as he can get;

31 Even such as he is able to get, the one for a sin offering, and the other for a burnt offering, with the meat offering: and the priest shall make an atonement for him that is to be cleansed before the LORD.

32 This is the law of him in whom is the plague of leprosy, whose hand is not

able to get that which pertains to his cleansing.

33 And the LORD spoke to Moses and to Aaron, saying,

34 When you be come into the land of Canaan, which I give to you for a possession, and I put the plague of leprosy in a house of the land of your possession;

35 And he that owns the house shall come and tell the priest, saying, It seems to me there is as it were a plague in the house:

36 Then the priest shall command that they empty the house, before the priest go into it to see the plague, that all that is in the house be not made unclean: and afterward the priest shall go in to see the house:

37 And he shall look on the plague, and, behold, if the plague be in the walls of the house with hollow strakes, greenish or reddish, which in sight are lower than the wall;

38 Then the priest shall go out of the house to the door of the house, and shut up the house seven days:

39 And the priest shall come again the seventh day, and shall look: and, behold, if the plague be spread in the walls of the house;

40 Then the priest shall command that they take away the stones in which the plague is, and they shall cast them into an unclean place without the city:

41 And he shall cause the house to be scraped within round about, and they shall pour out the dust that they scrape off without the city into an unclean place:

42 And they shall take other stones, and put them in the place of those stones; and he shall take other morter, and shall plaister the house.

43 And if the plague come again, and break out in the house, after that he has taken away the stones, and after he has scraped the house, and after it is plaistered;

44 Then the priest shall come and look, and, behold, if the plague be spread in the house, it is a fretting leprosy in the house; it is unclean.

45 And he shall break down the house, the stones of it, and the timber thereof, and all the morter of the house; and he shall carry them forth out of the city into an unclean place.

46 Moreover he that goes into the house all the while that it is shut up shall be unclean until the even.

47 And he that lies in the house shall wash his clothes; and he that eats in the house shall wash his clothes.

48 And if the priest shall come in, and look upon it, and, behold, the plague has not spread in the house, after the house was plaistered: then the priest shall pronounce the house clean, because the plague is healed.

49 And he shall take to cleanse the house two birds, and cedar wood, and scarlet, and hyssop:

50 And he shall kill the one of the birds in an earthen vessel over running water:

51 And he shall take the cedar wood, and the hyssop, and the scarlet, and the living bird, and dip them in the blood of the slain bird, and in the running water, and sprinkle the house seven times:

52 And he shall cleanse the house with the blood of the bird, and with the running water, and with the living bird, and with the cedar wood, and with the hyssop, and with the scarlet:

53 But he shall let go the living bird out of the city into the open fields, and make an atonement for the house: and it shall be clean.

54 This is the law for all manner of plague of leprosy, and scall,

55 And for the leprosy of a garment, and of a house,

56 And for a rising, and for a scab, and for a bright spot:

57 To teach when it is unclean, and when it is clean: this is the law of leprosy.

CHAPTER 15

A ND the LORD spoke to Moses and to Aaron, saying,

2 Speak to the children of Israel, and say to them, When any man has a running issue out of his flesh, because of his issue he is unclean.

3 And this shall be his uncleanness in his issue: whether his flesh run with his issue, or his flesh be stopped from his issue, it is his uncleanness.

4 Every bed, whereon he lies that has the issue, is unclean: and every thing, whereon he sits, shall be unclean.

5 And whosoever touches his bed shall wash his clothes, and bathe himself in water, and be unclean until the even.

6 And he that sits on any thing whereon he sat that has the issue shall wash his clothes, and bathe himself in water, and be unclean until the even.

7 And he that touches the flesh of him that has the issue shall wash his clothes, and bathe himself in water, and be unclean until the even.

8 And if he that has the issue spit upon him that is clean; then he shall wash his clothes, and bathe himself in water, and be unclean until the even.

9 And what saddle soever he rides upon that has the issue shall be unclean.

10 And whosoever touches any thing that was under him shall be unclean until the even: and he that bears any of those things shall wash his clothes, and bathe himself in water, and be unclean until the even.

11 And whomsoever he touches that has the issue, and has not rinsed his hands in water, he shall wash his clothes, and bathe himself in water, and be unclean until the even.

12 And the vessel of earth, that he touches which has the issue, shall be broken: and every vessel of wood shall be rinsed in water.

13 And when he that has an issue is cleansed of his issue; then he shall number to himself seven days for his cleansing, and wash his clothes, and bathe his flesh in running water, and shall be clean.

14 And on the eighth day he shall take to him two turtledoves, or two young pigeons, and come before the LORD to the door of the tabernacle of the congregation, and give them to the priest:

15 And the priest shall offer them, the one for a sin offering, and the other for a burnt offering; and the priest shall make an atonement for him before the LORD for his issue.

16 And if any man's seed of copulation go out from him, then he shall wash all his flesh in water, and be unclean until the even.

17 And every garment, and every skin, whereon is the seed of copulation, shall be washed with water, and be unclean until the even.

18 The woman also with whom man shall lie with seed of copulation, they shall both bathe themselves in water, and be unclean until the even.

19 And if a woman have an issue, and her issue in her flesh be blood, she shall be put apart seven days: and whosoever touches her shall be unclean until the even.

20 And every thing that she lies upon in her separation shall be unclean: every thing also that she sits upon shall be unclean.

21 And whosoever touches her bed shall wash his clothes, and bathe himself in water, and be unclean until the even.

22 And whosoever touches any thing that she sat upon shall wash his clothes, and bathe himself in water, and be unclean until the even.

23 And if it be on her bed, or on any thing whereon she sits, when he touches it, he shall be unclean until the even.

24 And if any man lie with her at all, and her flowers be upon him, he shall be unclean seven days; and all the bed whereon he lies shall be unclean.

25 And if a woman have an issue of her blood many days out of the time of her separation, or if it run beyond the time

of her separation; all the days of the issue of her uncleanness shall be as the days of her separation: she shall be unclean.

26 Every bed whereon she lies all the days of her issue shall be to her as the bed of her separation: and whatsoever she sits upon shall be unclean, as the uncleanness of her separation.

27 And whosoever touches those things shall be unclean, and shall wash his clothes, and bathe himself in water, and be unclean until the even.

28 But if she be cleansed of her issue, then she shall number to herself seven days, and after that she shall be clean.

29 And on the eighth day she shall take to her two turtles, or two young pigeons, and bring them to the priest, to the door of the tabernacle of the congregation.

30 And the priest shall offer the one for a sin offering, and the other for a burnt offering; and the priest shall make an atonement for her before the LORD for the issue of her uncleanness.

31 Thus shall you separate the children of Israel from their uncleanness; that they die not in their uncleanness, when they defile my tabernacle that is among them.

32 This is the law of him that has an issue, and of him whose seed goes from him, and is defiled therewith;

33 And of her that is sick of her flowers, and of him that has an issue, of the man, and of the woman, and of him that lies with her that is unclean.

CHAPTER 16

AND the LORD spoke to Moses after the death of the two sons of Aaron, when they offered before the LORD, and died;

2 And the LORD said to Moses, Speak to Aaron your brother, that he come not at all times into the holy place within the vail before the mercy seat, which is upon the ark; that he die not: for I will appear in the cloud upon the mercy seat.

3 Thus shall Aaron come into the holy place: with a young bullock for a sin offering, and a ram for a burnt offering.

4 He shall put on the holy linen coat, and he shall have the linen breeches upon his flesh, and shall be girded with a linen girdle, and with the linen mitre shall he be attired: these are holy garments; therefore shall he wash his flesh in water, and so put them on.

5 And he shall take of the congregation of the children of Israel two kids of the goats for a sin offering, and one ram for a burnt offering.

6 And Aaron shall offer his bullock of the sin offering, which is for himself, and make an atonement for himself, and for his house.

7 And he shall take the two goats, and present them before the LORD at the door of the tabernacle of the congregation.

8 And Aaron shall cast lots upon the two goats; one lot for the LORD, and the other lot for the scapegoat.

9 And Aaron shall bring the goat upon which the LORD's lot fell, and offer him for a sin offering.

10 But the goat, on which the lot fell to be the scapegoat, shall be presented alive before the LORD, to make an atonement with him, and to let him go for a scapegoat into the wilderness.

11 And Aaron shall bring the bullock of the sin offering, which is for himself, and shall make an atonement for himself, and for his house, and shall kill the bullock of the sin offering which is for himself:

12 And he shall take a censer full of burning coals of fire from off the altar before the LORD, and his hands full of sweet incense beaten small, and bring it within the vail:

13 And he shall put the incense upon the fire before the LORD, that the cloud of the incense may cover the mercy seat that is upon the testimony, that he die not:

14 And he shall take of the blood of the bullock, and sprinkle it with his finger upon the mercy seat eastward; and before the mercy seat shall he sprinkle of the blood with his finger seven times.

15 Then shall he kill the goat of the sin offering, that is for the people, and bring his blood within the vail, and do with that blood as he did with the blood of the bullock, and sprinkle it upon the mercy seat, and before the mercy seat:

16 And he shall make an atonement for the holy place, because of the uncleanness of the children of Israel, and because of their transgressions in all their sins: and so shall he do for the tabernacle of the congregation, that remains among them in the midst of their uncleanness.

17 And there shall be no man in the tabernacle of the congregation when he goes in to make an atonement in the holy place, until he come out, and have made an atonement for himself, and for his household, and for all the congregation of Israel.

18 And he shall go out to the altar that is before the LORD, and make an atonement for it; and shall take of the blood of the bullock, and of the blood of the goat, and put it upon the horns of the altar round about.

19 And he shall sprinkle of the blood upon it with his finger seven times, and cleanse it, and hallow it from the uncleanness of the children of Israel.

20 And when he has made an end of reconciling the holy place, and the tabernacle of the congregation, and the altar, he shall bring the live goat:

21 And Aaron shall lay both his hands upon the head of the live goat, and confess over him all the iniquities of the children of Israel, and all their transgressions in all their sins, putting them upon the head of the goat, and shall send him away by the hand of a fit man into the wilderness:

22 And the goat shall bear upon him all their iniquities to a land not inhabited:

and he shall let go the goat in the wilderness.

23 And Aaron shall come into the tabernacle of the congregation, and shall put off the linen garments, which he put on when he went into the holy place, and shall leave them there:

24 And he shall wash his flesh with water in the holy place, and put on his garments, and come forth, and offer his burnt offering, and the burnt offering of the people, and make an atonement for himself, and for the people.

25 And the fat of the sin offering shall he burn upon the altar.

26 And he that let go the goat for the scapegoat shall wash his clothes, and bathe his flesh in water, and afterward come into the camp.

27 And the bullock for the sin offering, and the goat for the sin offering, whose blood was brought in to make atonement in the holy place, shall one carry forth without the camp; and they shall burn in the fire their skins, and their flesh, and their dung.

28 And he that burns them shall wash his clothes, and bathe his flesh in water, and afterward he shall come into the camp.

29 And this shall be a statute for ever to you: that in the seventh month, on the tenth day of the month, you shall afflict your souls, and do no work at all, whether it be one of your own country, or a stranger that sojourns among you:

30 For on that day shall the priest make an atonement for you, to cleanse you, that you may be clean from all your sins before the LORD.

31 It shall be a sabbath of rest to you, and you shall afflict your souls, by a statute for ever.

32 And the priest, whom he shall anoint, and whom he shall consecrate to minister in the priest's office in his father's stead, shall make the atonement, and shall put on the linen clothes, even the holy garments:

33 And he shall make an atonement for the holy sanctuary, and he shall make an atonement for the tabernacle of the congregation, and for the altar, and he shall make an atonement for the priests, and for all the people of the congregation.

34 And this shall be an everlasting statute to you, to make an atonement for the children of Israel for all their sins once a year. And he did as the LORD commanded Moses.

CHAPTER 17

A ND the LORD spoke to Moses, saying,

2 Speak to Aaron, and to his sons, and to all the children of Israel, and say to them; This is the thing which the LORD has commanded, saying,

3 What man soever there be of the house of Israel, that kills an ox, or lamb, or goat, in the camp, or that kills it out of the camp,

4 And brings it not to the door of the tabernacle of the congregation, to offer an offering to the LORD before the tabernacle of the LORD; blood shall be imputed to that man; he has shed blood; and that man shall be cut off from among his people:

5 To the end that the children of Israel may bring their sacrifices, which they offer in the open field, even that they may bring them to the LORD, to the door of the tabernacle of the congregation, to the priest, and offer them for peace offerings to the LORD.

6 And the priest shall sprinkle the blood upon the altar of the LORD at the door of the tabernacle of the congregation, and burn the fat for a sweet savor to the LORD.

7 And they shall no more offer their sacrifices to devils, after whom they have gone a whoring. This shall be a statute for ever to them throughout their generations.

8 And you shall say to them, Whatsoever man there be of the house of Israel, or of the strangers which sojourn among you, that offers a burnt offering or sacrifice,

9 And brings it not to the door of the tabernacle of the congregation, to offer it to the LORD; even that man shall be cut off from among his people.

10 And whatsoever man there be of the house of Israel, or of the strangers that sojourn among you, that eats any manner of blood; I will even set my face against that soul that eats blood, and will cut him off from among his people.

11 For the life of the flesh is in the blood: and I have given it to you upon the altar to make an atonement for your souls: for it is the blood that makes an atonement for the soul.

12 Therefore I said to the children of Israel, No soul of you shall eat blood, neither shall any stranger that sojourns among you eat blood.

13 And whatsoever man there be of the children of Israel, or of the strangers that sojourn among you, which hunts and catches any beast or fowl that may be eaten; he shall even pour out the blood thereof, and cover it with dust.

14 For it is the life of all flesh; the blood of it is for the life thereof: therefore I said to the children of Israel, You shall eat the blood of no manner of flesh: for the life of all flesh is the blood thereof: whosoever eats it shall be cut off.

15 And every soul that eats that which died of itself, or that which was torn with beasts, whether it be one of your own country, or a stranger, he shall both wash his clothes, and bathe himself in water, and be unclean until the even: then shall he be clean.

16 But if he wash them not, nor bathe his flesh; then he shall bear his iniquity.

Chapter 18: For thoughts on biblical sexuality, also see 1 Corinthians 7:2 comment.

Conscience is the internal perception of God's moral Law.

Oswald Chambers

1874-1917

AUTHOR

LED A BIBLE-TEACHING

MINISTRY IN THE U.S.,

THE UNITED KINGDOM AND JAPAN

CHAPTER 18

A ND the LORD spoke to Moses, saying,

2 Speak to the children of Israel, and say to them, I am the LORD your God.

3 After the doings of the land of Egypt, wherein you dwelt, shall you not do: and after the doings of the land of Canaan, where I bring you, shall you not do: neither shall you walk in their ordinances.

4 You shall do my judgments, and keep mine ordinances, to walk therein: I am the LORD your God.

5 You shall therefore keep my statutes, and my judgments: which if a man do, he shall live in them: I am the LORD.

6 None of you shall approach to any that is near of kin to him, to uncover their nakedness: I am the LORD.

7 The nakedness of your father, or the nakedness of your mother, you shall not uncover: she is your mother; you shall not uncover her nakedness.

8 The nakedness of your father's wife you shall not uncover: it is your father's nakedness.

9 The nakedness of your sister, the daughter of your father, or daughter of your mother, whether she be born at home, or born abroad, even their nakedness you shall not uncover.

10 The nakedness of your son's daughter, or of your daughter's daughter, even their nakedness you shall not uncover: for theirs is your own nakedness.

11 The nakedness of your father's wife's daughter, begotten of your father, she is your sister, you shall not uncover her nakedness.

12 You shall not uncover the nakedness of your father's sister: she is your father's near kinswoman.

13 You shall not uncover the nakedness of your mother's sister: for she is your mother's near kinswoman.

14 You shall not uncover the nakedness of your father's brother, you shall not approach to his wife: she is your aunt.

15 You shall not uncover the nakedness of your daughter in law: she is your son's wife; you shall not uncover her nakedness.

16 You shall not uncover the nakedness of your brother's wife: it is your brother's nakedness.

17 You shall not uncover the nakedness of a woman and her daughter, neither shall you take her son's daughter, or her daughter's daughter, to uncover her nakedness; for they are her near kinswomen: it is wickedness.

18 Neither shall you take a wife to her sister, to vex her, to uncover her nakedness, beside the other in her life time.

19 Also you shall not approach to a woman to uncover her nakedness, as long as she is put apart for her uncleanness.

QUESTIONS & OBJECTIONS

19:11 *"Aren't there some circumstances when violating God's Law is justified?"*

A man's wife is dying. She needs medicine that can only be gotten at one store, and it's currently closed. They're too far from any hospital, and the man doesn't have enough money to buy the medicine even if the store was open. So he breaks in that night, steals the medicine (and doesn't touch anything else) and saves his wife's life. Is this morally incorrect? Is this a sin?

The Bible says, "Men do not despise a thief, if he steals to satisfy his soul when he is hungry; But if he be found, he shall restore sevenfold; he shall give all the substance of his house" (Proverbs 6:30-31).

If a man steals to save the life of his wife, he "steals." He is therefore guilty of breaking both man's law and God's Law. However, any reasonable judge would take the motive for his transgression into account and be merciful. Obviously God will do the same on Judgment Day with those who have found themselves in such a predicament. God will do that which is right. However, if you dig a little into the motive of the person who is asking whether there are some circumstances where breaking the law is justifiable, you will more than likely find that neither he nor his loved ones are in a life-or-death predicament, but is merely creating imaginary scenarios to try and justify his love of sin.

20 Moreover you shall not lie carnally with your neighbour's wife, to defile thyself with her.

21 And you shall not let any of your seed pass through the fire to Molech, neither shall you profane the name of your God: I am the LORD.

22 You shall not lie with mankind, as with womankind: it is abomination.

23 Neither shall you lie with any beast to defile thyself therewith: neither shall any woman stand before a beast to lie down thereto: it is confusion.

24 Defile not yourselves in any of these things: for in all these the nations are defiled which I cast out before you:

25 And the land is defiled: therefore I do visit the iniquity thereof upon it, and the land itself vomits out her inhabitants.

26 You shall therefore keep my statutes and my judgments, and shall not commit any of these abominations; neither any of your own nation, nor any stranger that sojourns among you:

27 (For all these abominations have the men of the land done, which were before you, and the land is defiled;)

28 That the land spue not you out also, when you defile it, as it spued out the nations that were before you.

29 For whosoever shall commit any of these abominations, even the souls that commit them shall be cut off from among their people.

30 Therefore shall you keep mine ordinance, that you commit not any one of these abominable customs, which were committed before you, and that you defile not yourselves therein: I am the LORD your God.

CHAPTER 19

AND the LORD spoke to Moses, saying,

2 Speak to all the congregation of the children of Israel, and say to them, You shall be holy: for I the LORD your God am holy.

3 You shall fear every man his mother, and his father, and keep my sabbaths: I am the LORD your God.

4 Turn not to idols, nor make to yourselves molten gods: I am the LORD your God.

5 And if you offer a sacrifice of peace offerings to the LORD, you shall offer it at your own will.

6 It shall be eaten the same day you offer it, and on the morrow: and if ought remain until the third day, it shall be burnt in the fire.

7 And if it be eaten at all on the third day, it is abominable; it shall not be accepted.

8 Therefore every one that eats it shall bear his iniquity, because he has profaned the hallowed thing of the LORD: and that soul shall be cut off from among his people.

9 And when you reap the harvest of your land, you shall not wholly reap the corners of your field, neither shall you gather the gleanings of your harvest.

10 And you shall not glean your vineyard, neither shall you gather every grape of your vineyard; you shall leave them for the poor and stranger: I am the LORD your God.

11 You shall not steal, neither deal falsely, neither lie one to another.

12 And you shall not swear by my name falsely, neither shall you profane the name of your God: I am the LORD.

13 You shall not defraud your neighbour, neither rob him: the wages of him that is hired shall not abide with you all night until the morning.

14 You shall not curse the deaf, nor put a stumblingblock before the blind, but shall fear your God: I am the LORD.

15 You shall do no unrighteousness in judgment: you shall not respect the person of the poor, nor honor the person of the mighty: but in righteousness shall you judge your neighbour.

16 You shall not go up and down as a talebearer among your people: neither shall you stand against the blood of your neighbour; I am the LORD.

17 You shall not hate your brother in your heart: you shall in any wise rebuke your neighbour, and not suffer sin upon him.

> "Does it grieve you, my friends,
> that the name of God
> is being taken in vain and desecrated?
> Does it grieve you
> that we are living in a godless age?
> But we are living in such an age
> and the main reason we should be
> praying about revival
> is that we are anxious to see
> God's name vindicated
> and His glory manifested.
> We should be anxious to see
> something happening
> that will arrest the nations,
> all the peoples,
> and cause them to stop
> and to think again."

DR. MARTYN LLOYD-JONES

1899-1981

MINISTER, WESTMINSTER CHAPEL

LONDON

18 You shall not avenge, nor bear any grudge against the children of your people, but you shall love your neighbour as thyself: I am the LORD.

19 You shall keep my statutes. You shall not let your cattle gender with a diverse kind: you shall not sow your field with mingled seed: neither shall a garment mingled of linen and woollen come upon you.

20 And whosoever lies carnally with a woman, that is a bondmaid, betrothed to an husband, and not at all redeemed, nor freedom given her; she shall be scourged; they shall not be put to death, because she was not free.

21 And he shall bring his trespass offering to the LORD, to the door of the tabernacle of the congregation, even a ram for a trespass offering.

22 And the priest shall make an atonement for him with the ram of the trespass offering before the LORD for his sin which he has done: and the sin which he has done shall be forgiven him.

23 And when you shall come into the land, and shall have planted all manner of trees for food, then you shall count the fruit thereof as uncircumcised: three years shall it be as uncircumcised to you: it shall not be eaten of.

24 But in the fourth year all the fruit thereof shall be holy to praise the LORD withal.

25 And in the fifth year shall you eat of the fruit thereof, that it may yield to you the increase thereof: I am the LORD your God.

26 You shall not eat any thing with the blood: neither shall you use enchantment, nor observe times.

27 You shall not round the corners of your heads, neither shall you mar the corners of your beard.

28 You shall not make any cuttings in your flesh for the dead, nor print any marks upon you: I am the LORD.

29 Do not prostitute your daughter, to cause her to be a whore; lest the land fall to whoredom, and the land become full of wickedness.

30 You shall keep my sabbaths, and reverence my sanctuary: I am the LORD.

31 Regard not them that have familiar spirits, neither seek after wizards, to be defiled by them: I am the LORD your God.

32 You shall rise up before the hoary head, and honour the face of the old man, and fear your God: I am the LORD.

33 And if a stranger sojourn with you in your land, you shall not vex him.

34 But the stranger that dwells with you shall be to you as one born among you, and you shall love him as thyself; for you were strangers in the land of Egypt: I am the LORD your God.

35 You shall do no unrighteousness in judgment, in meteyard, in weight, or in measure.

36 Just balances, just weights, a just ephah, and a just hin, shall you have: I am the LORD your God, which brought you out of the land of Egypt.

37 Therefore shall you observe all my statutes, and all my judgments, and do them: I am the LORD.

CHAPTER 20

AND the LORD spoke to Moses, saying,

2 Again, you shall say to the children of Israel, Whosoever he be of the children of Israel, or of the strangers that sojourn in Israel, that gives any of his seed to Molech; he shall surely be put to death: the people of the land shall stone him with stones.

3 And I will set my face against that man, and will cut him off from among his people; because he has given of his seed to Molech, to defile my sanctuary, and to profane my holy name.

4 And if the people of the land do any ways hide their eyes from the man, when he gives of his seed to Molech, and kill him not:

5 Then I will set my face against that man, and against his family, and will cut him off, and all that go a whoring after him, to commit whoredom with Molech, from among their people.

6 And the soul that turns after such as have familiar spirits, and after wizards, to go a whoring after them, I will even set my face against that soul, and will cut him off from among his people.

7 Sanctify yourselves therefore, and be holy: for I am the LORD your God.

8 And you shall keep my statutes, and do them: I am the LORD which sanctify you.

9 For every one that curses his father or his mother shall be surely put to death: he has cursed his father or his mother; his blood shall be upon him.

10 And the man that commits adultery with another man's wife, even he that commits adultery with his neighbour's wife, the adulterer and the adulteress shall surely be put to death.

11 And the man that lies with his father's wife has uncovered his father's nakedness: both of them shall surely be

put to death; their blood shall be upon them.

12 And if a man lie with his daughter in law, both of them shall surely be put to death: they have wrought confusion; their blood shall be upon them.

13 If a man also lie with mankind, as he lies with a woman, both of them have committed an abomination: they shall surely be put to death; their blood shall be upon them.

14 And if a man take a wife and her mother, it is wickedness: they shall be burnt with fire, both he and they; that there be no wickedness among you.

15 And if a man lie with a beast, he shall surely be put to death: and you shall slay the beast.

16 And if a woman approach to any beast, and lie down thereto, you shall kill the woman, and the beast: they shall surely be put to death; their blood shall be upon them.

17 And if a man shall take his sister, his father's daughter, or his mother's daughter, and see her nakedness, and she see his nakedness; it is a wicked thing; and they shall be cut off in the sight of their people: he has uncovered his sister's nakedness; he shall bear his iniquity.

18 And if a man shall lie with a woman having her sickness, and shall uncover her nakedness; he has discovered her fountain, and she has uncovered the fountain of her blood: and both of them shall be cut off from among their people.

19 And you shall not uncover the nakedness of your mother's sister, nor of your father's sister: for he uncovers his near kin: they shall bear their iniquity.

20 And if a man shall lie with his uncle's wife, he has uncovered his uncle's nakedness: they shall bear their sin; they shall die childless.

21 And if a man shall take his brother's wife, it is an unclean thing: he has uncovered his brother's nakedness; they shall be childless.

22 You shall therefore keep all my statutes, and all my judgments, and do

them: that the land, where I bring you to dwell therein, spue you not out.

23 And you shall not walk in the manners of the nation, which I cast out before you: for they committed all these things, and therefore I abhorred them.

24 But I have said to you, You shall inherit their land, and I will give it to you to possess it, a land that flows with milk and honey: I am the LORD your God, which have separated you from other people.

25 You shall therefore put difference between clean beasts and unclean, and between unclean fowls and clean: and you shall not make your souls abominable by beast, or by fowl, or by any manner of living thing that creeps on the ground, which I have separated from you as unclean.

26 And you shall be holy to me: for I the LORD am holy, and have severed you from other people, that you should be mine.

27 A man also or woman that has a familiar spirit, or that is a wizard, shall surely be put to death: they shall stone them with stones: their blood shall be upon them.

CHAPTER 21

AND the LORD said to Moses, Speak to the priests the sons of Aaron, and say to them, There shall none be defiled for the dead among his people:

2 But for his kin, that is near to him, that is, for his mother, and for his father, and for his son, and for his daughter, and for his brother.

3 And for his sister a virgin, that is nigh to him, which has had no husband; for her may he be defiled.

4 But he shall not defile himself, being a chief man among his people, to profane himself.

5 They shall not make baldness upon their head, neither shall they shave off the corner of their beard, nor make any cuttings in their flesh.

6 They shall be holy to their God, and not profane the name of their God: for the offerings of the LORD made by fire, and the bread of their God, they do offer: therefore they shall be holy.

7 They shall not take a wife that is a whore, or profane; neither shall they take a woman put away from her husband: for he is holy to his God.

8 You shall sanctify him therefore; for he offers the bread of your God: he shall be holy to you: for I the LORD, which sanctify you, am holy.

9 And the daughter of any priest, if she profane herself by playing the whore, she profanes her father: she shall be burnt with fire.

10 And he that is the high priest among his brethren, upon whose head the anointing oil was poured, and that is consecrated to put on the garments, shall not uncover his head, nor rend his clothes;

11 Neither shall he go in to any dead body, nor defile himself for his father, or for his mother;

12 Neither shall he go out of the sanctuary, nor profane the sanctuary of his God; for the crown of the anointing oil of his God is upon him: I am the LORD.

13 And he shall take a wife in her virginity.

14 A widow, or a divorced woman, or profane, or an harlot, these shall he not take: but he shall take a virgin of his own people to wife.

15 Neither shall he profane his seed among his people: for I the LORD do sanctify him.

16 And the LORD spoke to Moses, saying,

17 Speak to Aaron, saying, Whosoever he be of your seed in their generations that has any blemish, let him not approach to offer the bread of his God.

18 For whatsoever man he be that has a blemish, he shall not approach: a blind man, or a lame, or he that has a flat nose, or any thing superfluous,

19 Or a man that is brokenfooted, or brokenhanded,

20 Or crookbackt, or a dwarf, or that has a blemish in his eye, or be scurvy, or scabbed, or has his stones broken;

21 No man that has a blemish of the seed of Aaron the priest shall come nigh to offer the offerings of the LORD made by fire: he has a blemish; he shall not come nigh to offer the bread of his God.

22 He shall eat the bread of his God, both of the most holy, and of the holy.

23 Only he shall not go in to the vail, nor come nigh to the altar, because he has a blemish; that he profane not my sanctuaries: for I the LORD do sanctify them.

24 And Moses told it to Aaron, and to his sons, and to all the children of Israel.

CHAPTER 22

AND the LORD spoke to Moses, saying,

2 Speak to Aaron and to his sons, that they separate themselves from the holy things of the children of Israel, and that they profane not my holy name in those things which they hallow to me: I am the LORD.

3 Say to them, Whosoever he be of all your seed among your generations, that goes to the holy things, which the children of Israel hallow to the LORD, having his uncleanness upon him, that soul shall be cut off from my presence: I am the LORD.

4 What man soever of the seed of Aaron is a leper, or has a running issue; he shall not eat of the holy things, until he be clean. And whoso touches any thing that is unclean by the dead, or a man whose seed goes from him;

5 Or whosoever touches any creeping thing, whereby he may be made unclean, or a man of whom he may take uncleanness, whatsoever uncleanness he has;

6 The soul which has touched any such shall be unclean until even, and shall not

eat of the holy things, unless he wash his flesh with water.

7 And when the sun is down, he shall be clean, and shall afterward eat of the holy things; because it is his food.

8 That which dies of itself, or is torn with beasts, he shall not eat to defile himself therewith; I am the LORD.

9 They shall therefore keep mine ordinance, lest they bear sin for it, and die therefore, if they profane it: I the LORD do sanctify them.

10 There shall no stranger eat of the holy thing: a sojourner of the priest, or an hired servant, shall not eat of the holy thing.

11 But if the priest buy any soul with his money, he shall eat of it, and he that is born in his house: they shall eat of his meat.

12 If the priest's daughter also be married to a stranger, she may not eat of an offering of the holy things.

13 But if the priest's daughter be a widow, or divorced, and have no child, and is returned to her father's house, as in her youth, she shall eat of her father's meat: but there shall be no stranger eat thereof.

14 And if a man eat of the holy thing unwittingly, then he shall put the fifth part thereof to it, and shall give it to the priest with the holy thing.

15 And they shall not profane the holy things of the children of Israel, which they offer to the LORD;

16 Or suffer them to bear the iniquity of trespass, when they eat their holy things: for I the LORD do sanctify them.

17 And the LORD spoke to Moses, saying,

18 Speak to Aaron, and to his sons, and to all the children of Israel, and say to them, Whatsoever he be of the house of Israel, or of the strangers in Israel, that will offer his oblation for all his vows, and for all his freewill offerings, which they will offer to the LORD for a burnt offering;

19 You shall offer at your own will a male without blemish, of the beeves, of the sheep, or of the goats.

20 But whatsoever has a blemish, that shall you not offer: for it shall not be acceptable for you.

21 And whosoever offers a sacrifice of peace offerings to the LORD to accomplish his vow, or a freewill offering in beeves or sheep, it shall be perfect to be accepted; there shall be no blemish therein.

22 Blind, or broken, or maimed, or having a wen, or scurvy, or scabbed, you shall not offer these to the LORD, nor make an offering by fire of them upon the altar to the LORD.

23 Either a bullock or a lamb that has any thing superfluous or lacking in his parts, that you may offer for a freewill offering; but for a vow it shall not be accepted.

24 You shall not offer to the LORD that which is bruised, or crushed, or broken, or cut; neither shall you make any offering thereof in your land.

25 Neither from a stranger's hand shall you offer the bread of your God of any of these; because their corruption is in them, and blemishes be in them: they shall not be accepted for you.

26 And the LORD spoke to Moses, saying,

27 When a bullock, or a sheep, or a goat, is brought forth, then it shall be seven days under the dam; and from the eighth day and thenceforth it shall be accepted for an offering made by fire to the LORD.

28 And whether it be cow, or ewe, you shall not kill it and her young both in one day.

29 And when you will offer a sacrifice of thanksgiving to the LORD, offer it at your own will.

30 On the same day it shall be eaten up; you shall leave none of it until the morrow: I am the LORD.

31 Therefore shall you keep my commandments, and do them: I am the LORD.

32 Neither shall you profane my holy name; but I will be hallowed among the children of Israel: I am the LORD which hallow you,

33 That brought you out of the land of Egypt, to be your God: I am the LORD.

CHAPTER 23

AND the LORD spoke to Moses, saying,

2 Speak to the children of Israel, and say to them, Concerning the feasts of the LORD, which you shall proclaim to be holy convocations, even these are my feasts.

3 Six days shall work be done: but the seventh day is the sabbath of rest, an holy convocation; you shall do no work therein: it is the sabbath of the LORD in all your dwellings.

4 These are the feasts of the LORD, even holy convocations, which you shall proclaim in their seasons.

5 In the fourteenth day of the first month at even is the LORD's passover.

6 And on the fifteenth day of the same month is the feast of unleavened bread to the LORD: seven days you must eat unleavened bread.

7 In the first day you shall have an holy convocation: you shall do no servile work therein.

8 But you shall offer an offering made by fire to the LORD seven days: in the seventh day is an holy convocation: you shall do no servile work therein.

9 And the LORD spoke to Moses, saying,

10 Speak to the children of Israel, and say to them, When you be come into the land which I give to you, and shall reap the harvest thereof, then you shall bring a sheaf of the firstfruits of your harvest to the priest:

11 And he shall wave the sheaf before the LORD, to be accepted for you: on the morrow after the sabbath the priest shall wave it.

12 And you shall offer that day when you wave the sheaf an he lamb without blemish of the first year for a burnt offering to the LORD.

13 And the meat offering thereof shall be two tenth deals of fine flour mingled with oil, an offering made by fire to the LORD for a sweet savor: and the drink offering thereof shall be of wine, the fourth part of an hin.

14 And you shall eat neither bread, nor parched corn, nor green ears, until the selfsame day that you have brought an offering to your God: it shall be a statute for ever throughout your generations in all your dwellings.

15 And you shall count to you from the morrow after the sabbath, from the day that you brought the sheaf of the wave offering; seven sabbaths shall be complete:

16 Even to the morrow after the seventh sabbath shall you number fifty days; and you shall offer a new meat offering to the LORD.

17 You shall bring out of your habitations two wave loaves of two tenth deals; they shall be of fine flour; they shall be baken with leaven; they are the firstfruits to the LORD.

18 And you shall offer with the bread seven lambs without blemish of the first year, and one young bullock, and two rams: they shall be for a burnt offering to the LORD, with their meat offering, and their drink offerings, even an offering made by fire, of sweet savor to the LORD.

19 Then you shall sacrifice one kid of the goats for a sin offering, and two lambs of the first year for a sacrifice of peace offerings.

20 And the priest shall wave them with the bread of the firstfruits for a wave offering before the LORD, with the two lambs: they shall be holy to the LORD for the priest.

21 And you shall proclaim on the self-same day, that it may be an holy convocation to you: you shall do no servile work therein: it shall be a statute for ever in all your dwellings throughout your generations.

22 And when you reap the harvest of your land, you shall not make clean riddance of the corners of your field when you reap, neither shall you gather any gleaning of your harvest: you shall leave them to the poor, and to the stranger: I am the LORD your God.

23 And the LORD spoke to Moses, saying,

24 Speak to the children of Israel, saying, In the seventh month, in the first day of the month, shall you have a sabbath, a memorial of blowing of trumpets, an holy convocation.

25 You shall do no servile work therein: but you shall offer an offering made by fire to the LORD.

26 And the LORD spoke to Moses, saying,

27 Also on the tenth day of this seventh month there shall be a day of atonement: it shall be an holy convocation to you; and you shall afflict your souls, and offer an offering made by fire to the LORD.

28 And you shall do no work in that same day: for it is a day of atonement, to make an atonement for you before the LORD your God.

29 For whatsoever soul it be that shall not be afflicted in that same day, he shall be cut off from among his people.

30 And whatsoever soul it be that doeth any work in that same day, the same soul will I destroy from among his people.

31 You shall do no manner of work: it shall be a statute for ever throughout your generations in all your dwellings.

32 It shall be to you a sabbath of rest, and you shall afflict your souls: in the ninth day of the month at even, from even to even, shall you celebrate your sabbath.

33 And the LORD spoke to Moses, saying,

34 Speak to the children of Israel, saying, The fifteenth day of this seventh month shall be the feast of tabernacles for seven days to the LORD.

35 On the first day shall be an holy convocation: you shall do no servile work therein.

36 Seven days you shall offer an offering made by fire to the LORD: on the eighth day shall be an holy convocation to you; and you shall offer an offering made by fire to the LORD: it is a solemn assembly; and you shall do no servile work therein.

37 These are the feasts of the LORD, which you shall proclaim to be holy convocations, to offer an offering made by fire to the LORD, a burnt offering, and a meat offering, a sacrifice, and drink offerings, every thing upon his day:

38 Beside the sabbaths of the LORD, and beside your gifts, and beside all your vows, and beside all your freewill offerings, which you give to the LORD.

39 Also in the fifteenth day of the seventh month, when you have gathered in the fruit of the land, you shall keep a feast to the LORD seven days: on the first day shall be a sabbath, and on the eighth day shall be a sabbath.

40 And you shall take you on the first day the boughs of goodly trees, branches of palm trees, and the boughs of thick trees, and willows of the brook; and you shall rejoice before the LORD your God seven days.

41 And you shall keep it a feast to the LORD seven days in the year. It shall be a statute for ever in your generations: you shall celebrate it in the seventh month.

42 You shall dwell in booths seven days; all that are Israelites born shall dwell in booths:

43 That your generations may know that I made the children of Israel to dwell in booths, when I brought them

out of the land of Egypt: I am the LORD your God.

44 And Moses declared to the children of Israel the feasts of the LORD.

CHAPTER 24

A ND the LORD spoke to Moses, saying,

2 Command the children of Israel, that they bring to you pure oil olive beaten for the light, to cause the lamps to burn continually.

3 Without the vail of the testimony, in the tabernacle of the congregation, shall Aaron order it from the evening to the morning before the LORD continually: it shall be a statute for ever in your generations.

4 He shall order the lamps upon the pure candlestick before the LORD continually.

5 And you shall take fine flour, and bake twelve cakes thereof: two tenth deals shall be in one cake.

6 And you shall set them in two rows, six on a row, upon the pure table before the LORD.

7 And you shall put pure frankincense upon each row, that it may be on the bread for a memorial, even an offering made by fire to the LORD.

8 Every sabbath he shall set it in order before the LORD continually, being taken from the children of Israel by an everlasting covenant.

9 And it shall be Aaron's and his sons'; and they shall eat it in the holy place: for it is most holy to him of the offerings of the LORD made by fire by a perpetual statute.

10 And the son of an Israelitish woman, whose father was an Egyptian, went out among the children of Israel: and this son of the Israelitish woman and a man of Israel strove together in the camp;

11 And the Israelitish woman's son blasphemed the name of the Lord, and cursed. And they brought him to Moses: (and his mother's name was Shelomith,

the daughter of Dibri, of the tribe of Dan:)

12 And they put him in ward, that the mind of the LORD might be showed them.

13 And the LORD spoke to Moses, saying,

14 Bring forth him that has cursed without the camp; and let all that heard him lay their hands upon his head, and let all the congregation stone him.

15 And you shall speak to the children of Israel, saying, Whosoever curses his God shall bear his sin.

16 And he that blasphemes the name of the LORD, he shall surely be put to death, and all the congregation shall certainly stone him: as well the stranger, as he that is born in the land, when he blasphemes the name of the Lord, shall be put to death.

17 And he that kills any man shall surely be put to death.

18 And he that kills a beast shall make it good; beast for beast.

19 And if a man cause a blemish in his neighbour; as he has done, so shall it be done to him;

20 Breach for breach, eye for eye, tooth for tooth: as he has caused a blemish in a man, so shall it be done to him again.

21 And he that kills a beast, he shall restore it: and he that kills a man, he shall be put to death.

22 You shall have one manner of law, as well for the stranger, as for one of your own country: for I am the LORD your God.

23 And Moses spoke to the children of Israel, that they should bring forth him that had cursed out of the camp, and stone him with stones. And the children of Israel did as the LORD commanded Moses.

> The proper effect of the Law
> is to lead us out of our tents
> and tabernacles,
> that is to say,
> from the quietness and security
> wherein we dwell,
> and from trusting in ourselves,
> and to bring us before
> the presence of God,
> to reveal His wrath to us
> and to set us before our sins.

MARTIN LUTHER

1483-1546

GERMAN PRIEST

WHOSE OBJECTIONS

TO ROMAN CATHOLICISM

SPARKED THE REFORMATION

CHAPTER 25

AND the LORD spoke to Moses in mount Sinai, saying,

2 Speak to the children of Israel, and say to them, When you come into the land which I give you, then shall the land keep a sabbath to the LORD.

3 Six years you shall sow your field, and six years you shall prune your vineyard, and gather in the fruit thereof;

4 But in the seventh year shall be a sabbath of rest to the land, a sabbath for the LORD: you shall neither sow your field, nor prune your vineyard.

5 That which grows of its own accord of your harvest you shall not reap, neither gather the grapes of your vine undressed: for it is a year of rest to the land.

6 And the sabbath of the land shall be meat for you; for you, and for your servant, and for your maid, and for your hired servant, and for your stranger that sojourns with you.

7 And for your cattle, and for the beast that are in your land, shall all the increase thereof be meat.

8 And you shall number seven sabbaths of years to yourself, seven times seven years; and the space of the seven sabbaths of years shall be to you forty and nine years.

9 Then shall you cause the trumpet of the jubile to sound on the tenth day of the seventh month, in the day of atonement shall you make the trumpet sound throughout all your land.

10 And you shall hallow the fiftieth year, and proclaim liberty throughout all the land to all the inhabitants thereof: it shall be a jubile to you; and you shall return every man to his possession, and you shall return every man to his family.

11 A jubile shall that fiftieth year be to you: you shall not sow, neither reap that which grows of itself in it, nor gather the grapes in it of your vine undressed.

12 For it is the jubile; it shall be holy to you: you shall eat the increase thereof out of the field.

13 In the year of this jubile you shall return every man to his possession.

14 And if you sell ought to your neighbour, or buy ought of your neighbour's hand, you shall not oppress one another:

15 According to the number of years after the jubile you shall buy of your neighbour, and according to the number of years of the fruits he shall sell to you:

16 According to the multitude of years you shall increase the price thereof, and according to the fewness of years you shall diminish the price of it: for according to the number of the years of the fruits doth he sell to you.

17 You shall not therefore oppress one another; but you shall fear your God: for I am the LORD your God.

18 Therefore you shall do my statutes, and keep my judgments, and do them; and you shall dwell in the land in safety.

19 And the land shall yield her fruit, and you shall eat your fill, and dwell therein in safety.

20 And if you shall say, What shall we eat the seventh year? behold, we shall not sow, nor gather in our increase:

21 Then I will command my blessing upon you in the sixth year, and it shall bring forth fruit for three years.

22 And you shall sow the eighth year, and eat yet of old fruit until the ninth year; until her fruits come in you shall eat of the old store.

23 The land shall not be sold for ever: for the land is mine, for you are strangers and sojourners with me.

24 And in all the land of your possession you shall grant a redemption for the land.

25 If your brother be waxen poor, and has sold away some of his possession, and if any of his kin come to redeem it, then shall he redeem that which his brother sold.

26 And if the man have none to redeem it, and himself be able to redeem it;

27 Then let him count the years of the sale thereof, and restore the overplus to the man to whom he sold it; that he may return to his possession.

28 But if he be not able to restore it to him, then that which is sold shall remain in the hand of him that has bought it until the year of jubile: and in the jubile it shall go out, and he shall return to his possession.

29 And if a man sell a dwelling house in a walled city, then he may redeem it within a whole year after it is sold; within a full year may he redeem it.

30 And if it be not redeemed within the space of a full year, then the house that is in the walled city shall be established for ever to him that bought it throughout his generations: it shall not go out in the jubile.

31 But the houses of the villages which have no wall round about them shall be counted as the fields of the country: they may be redeemed, and they shall go out in the jubile.

32 Notwithstanding the cities of the Levites, and the houses of the cities of their possession, may the Levites redeem at any time.

33 And if a man purchase of the Levites, then the house that was sold, and the city of his possession, shall go out in the year of jubile: for the houses of the cities of the Levites are their possession among the children of Israel.

34 But the field of the suburbs of their cities may not be sold; for it is their perpetual possession.

35 And if your brother be waxen poor, and fallen in decay with you; then you shall relieve him: yea, though he be a stranger, or a sojourner; that he may live with you.

36 Take no usury of him, or increase: but fear your God; that your brother may live with you.

37 You shall not give him your money upon usury, nor lend him your victuals for increase.

38 I am the LORD your God, which brought you forth out of the land of Egypt, to give you the land of Canaan, and to be your God.

39 And if your brother that dwells by you be waxen poor, and be sold to you; you shall not compel him to serve as a bondservant:

40 But as an hired servant, and as a sojourner, he shall be with you, and shall serve you to the year of jubile.

41 And then shall he depart from you, both he and his children with him, and shall return to his own family, and to the possession of his fathers shall he return.

42 For they are my servants, which I brought forth out of the land of Egypt: they shall not be sold as bondmen.

43 You shall not rule over him with rigour; but shall fear your God.

44 Both your bondmen, and your bondmaids, which you shall have, shall be of the heathen that are round about you; of them shall you buy bondmen and bondmaids.

45 Moreover of the children of the strangers that do sojourn among you, of them shall you buy, and of their families that are with you, which they begat in your land: and they shall be your possession.

46 And you shall take them as an inheritance for your children after you, to inherit them for a possession; they shall be

your bondmen for ever: but over your brethren the children of Israel, you shall not rule one over another with rigour.

47 And if a sojourner or stranger wax rich by you, and your brother that dwells by him wax poor, and sell himself to the stranger or sojourner by you, or to the stock of the stranger's family:

48 After that he is sold he may be redeemed again; one of his brethren may redeem him:

49 Either his uncle, or his uncle's son, may redeem him, or any that is nigh of kin to him of his family may redeem him; or if he be able, he may redeem himself.

50 And he shall reckon with him that bought him from the year that he was sold to him to the year of jubile: and the price of his sale shall be according to the number of years, according to the time of an hired servant shall it be with him.

51 If there be yet many years behind, according to them he shall give again the price of his redemption out of the money that he was bought for.

52 And if there remain but few years to the year of jubile, then he shall count with him, and according to his years shall he give him again the price of his redemption.

53 And as a yearly hired servant shall he be with him: and the other shall not rule with rigour over him in your sight.

54 And if he be not redeemed in these years, then he shall go out in the year of jubile, both he, and his children with him.

55 For to me the children of Israel are servants; they are my servants whom I brought forth out of the land of Egypt: I am the LORD your God.

CHAPTER 26

YOU shall make you no idols nor graven image, neither rear you up a standing image, neither shall you set up any image of stone in your land, to bow down to it: for I am the LORD your God.

2 You shall keep my sabbaths, and reverence my sanctuary: I am the LORD.

3 If you walk in my statutes, and keep my commandments, and do them;

4 Then I will give you rain in due season, and the land shall yield her increase, and the trees of the field shall yield their fruit.

5 And your threshing shall reach to the vintage, and the vintage shall reach to the sowing time: and you shall eat your bread to the full, and dwell in your land safely.

6 And I will give peace in the land, and you shall lie down, and none shall make you afraid: and I will rid evil beasts out of the land, neither shall the sword go through your land.

7 And you shall chase your enemies, and they shall fall before you by the sword.

8 And five of you shall chase an hundred, and an hundred of you shall put ten thousand to flight: and your enemies shall fall before you by the sword.

9 For I will have respect to you, and make you fruitful, and multiply you, and establish my covenant with you.

10 And you shall eat old store, and bring forth the old because of the new.

11 And I set my tabernacle among you: and my soul shall not abhor you.

12 And I will walk among you, and will be your God, and you shall be my people.

26:1-13 Look at these wonderful blessings that God promised to Israel if they would obey Him. The rain would come in due season. The land would yield its harvest. The trees would give their fruit. Their food would satisfy them. They would have peace in the land, and no wild beasts would devour them. Truly blessed is the nation whose God is the Lord (Psalm 144:15) .

Look, too, at the fearful curses that come with disobedience, which is so evident in our sinful nation, plagued with cancer and terrible diseases, violence, earthquakes, droughts, fires, tornadoes, killer bees, diseases in the soil, hurricanes and floods.

13 I am the LORD your God, which brought you forth out of the land of Egypt, that you should not be their bondmen;
and I have broken the bands of your yoke, and made you go upright.
14 But if you will not hearken to me, and will not do all these commandments;
15 And if you shall despise my statutes, or if your soul abhor my judgments, so that you will not do all my commandments, but that you break my covenant:
16 I also will do this to you; I will even appoint over you terror, consumption, and the burning ague, that shall consume the eyes, and cause sorrow of heart: and you shall sow your seed in vain, for your enemies shall eat it.
17 And I will set my face against you, and you shall be slain before your enemies: they that hate you shall reign over you; and you shall flee when none pursues you.
18 And if you will not yet for all this hearken to me, then I will punish you seven times more for your sins.
19 And I will break the pride of your power; and I will make your heaven as iron, and your earth as brass:
20 And your strength shall be spent in vain: for your land shall not yield her increase, neither shall the trees of the land yield their fruits.
21 And if you walk contrary to me, and will not hearken to me; I will bring seven times more plagues upon you according to your sins.
22 I will also send wild beasts among you, which shall rob you of your children, and destroy your cattle, and make you few in number; and your high ways shall be desolate.
23 And if you will not be reformed by me by these things, but will walk contrary to me;
24 Then will I also walk contrary to you, and will punish you yet seven times for your sins.

25 And I will bring a sword upon you, that shall avenge the quarrel of my covenant: and when you are gathered together within your cities, I will send the pestilence among you; and you shall be delivered into the hand of the enemy.
26 And when I have broken the staff of your bread, ten women shall bake your bread in one oven, and they shall deliver you your bread again by weight: and you shall eat, and not be satisfied.
27 And if you will not for all this hearken to me, but walk contrary to me;
28 Then I will walk contrary to you also in fury; and I, even I, will chastise you seven times for your sins.
29 And you shall eat the flesh of your sons, and the flesh of your daughters shall you eat.
30 And I will destroy your high places, and cut down your images, and cast your carcases upon the carcases of your idols, and my soul shall abhor you.
31 And I will make your cities waste, and bring your sanctuaries to desolation, and I will not smell the savor of your sweet odours.
32 And I will bring the land into desolation: and your enemies which dwell therein shall be astonished at it.
33 And I will scatter you among the heathen, and will draw out a sword after you: and your land shall be desolate, and your cities waste.
34 Then shall the land enjoy her sabbaths, as long as it lies desolate, and you be in your enemies' land; even then shall the land rest, and enjoy her sabbaths.
35 As long as it lies desolate it shall rest; because it did not rest in your sabbaths, when you dwelt upon it.
36 And upon them that are left alive of you I will send a faintness into their hearts in the lands of their enemies; and the sound of a shaken leaf shall chase them; and they shall flee, as fleeing from a sword; and they shall fall when none pursues.
37 And they shall fall one upon another, as it were before a sword, when none

pursues: and you shall have no power to stand before your enemies.

38 And you shall perish among the heathen, and the land of your enemies shall eat you up.

39 And they that are left of you shall pine away in their iniquity in your enemies' lands; and also in the iniquities of their fathers shall they pine away with them.

40 If they shall confess their iniquity, and the iniquity of their fathers, with their trespass which they trespassed against me, and that also they have walked contrary to me;

41 And that I also have walked contrary to them, and have brought them into the land of their enemies; if then their uncircumcised hearts be humbled, and they then accept of the punishment of their iniquity:

42 Then will I remember my covenant with Jacob, and also my covenant with Isaac, and also my covenant with Abraham will I remember; and I will remember the land.

43 The land also shall be left of them, and shall enjoy her sabbaths, while she lies desolate without them: and they shall accept of the punishment of their iniquity: because, even because they despised my judgments, and because their soul abhorred my statutes.

44 And yet for all that, when they be in the land of their enemies, I will not cast them away, neither will I abhor them, to destroy them utterly, and to break my covenant with them: for I am the LORD their God.

45 But I will for their sakes remember the covenant of their ancestors, whom I brought forth out of the land of Egypt in the sight of the heathen, that I might be their God: I am the LORD.

46 These are the statutes and judgments and laws, which the LORD made between him and the children of Israel in mount Sinai by the hand of Moses.

CHAPTER 27

AND the LORD spoke to Moses, saying,

2 Speak to the children of Israel, and say to them, When a man shall make a singular vow, the persons shall be for the LORD by your estimation.

3 And your estimation shall be of the male from twenty years old even to sixty years old, even your estimation shall be fifty shekels of silver, after the shekel of the sanctuary.

4 And if it be a female, then your estimation shall be thirty shekels.

5 And if it be from five years old even to twenty years old, then your estimation shall be of the male twenty shekels, and for the female ten shekels.

6 And if it be from a month old even to five years old, then your estimation shall be of the male five shekels of silver, and for the female your estimation shall be three shekels of silver.

7 And if it be from sixty years old and above; if it be a male, then your estimation shall be fifteen shekels, and for the female ten shekels.

8 But if he be poorer than your estimation, then he shall present himself before the priest, and the priest shall value him; according to his ability that vowed shall the priest value him.

9 And if it be a beast, whereof men bring an offering to the LORD, all that any man gives of such to the LORD shall be holy.

10 He shall not alter it, nor change it, a good for a bad, or a bad for a good: and if he shall at all change beast for beast, then it and the exchange thereof shall be holy.

11 And if it be any unclean beast, of which they do not offer a sacrifice to the LORD, then he shall present the beast before the priest:

12 And the priest shall value it, whether it be good or bad: as you value it, who are the priest, so shall it be.

13 But if he will at all redeem it, then he shall add a fifth part thereof to your estimation.

14 And when a man shall sanctify his house to be holy to the LORD, then the priest shall estimate it, whether it be good or bad: as the priest shall estimate it, so shall it stand.

15 And if he that sanctified it will redeem his house, then he shall add the fifth part of the money of your estimation to it, and it shall be his.

16 And if a man shall sanctify to the LORD some part of a field of his possession, then your estimation shall be according to the seed thereof: an homer of barley seed shall be valued at fifty shekels of silver.

17 If he sanctify his field from the year of jubile, according to your estimation it shall stand.

18 But if he sanctify his field after the jubile, then the priest shall reckon to him the money according to the years that remain, even to the year of the jubile, and it shall be abated from your estimation.

19 And if he that sanctified the field will in any wise redeem it, then he shall add the fifth part of the money of your estimation to it, and it shall be assured to him.

20 And if he will not redeem the field, or if he have sold the field to another man, it shall not be redeemed any more.

21 But the field, when it goes out in the jubile, shall be holy to the LORD, as a field devoted; the possession thereof shall be the priest's.

22 And if a man sanctify to the LORD a field which he has bought, which is not of the fields of his possession;

23 Then the priest shall reckon to him the worth of your estimation, even to the year of the jubile: and he shall give your estimation in that day, as a holy thing to the LORD.

24 In the year of the jubile the field shall return to him of whom it was bought, even to him to whom the possession of the land did belong.

25 And all your estimations shall be according to the shekel of the sanctuary: twenty gerahs shall be the shekel.

26 Only the firstling of the beasts, which should be the LORD's firstling, no man shall sanctify it; whether it be ox, or sheep: it is the LORD's.

27 And if it be of an unclean beast, then he shall redeem it according to your estimation, and shall add a fifth part of it thereto: or if it be not redeemed, then it shall be sold according to your estimation.

28 Notwithstanding no devoted thing, that a man shall devote to the LORD of all that he has, both of man and beast, and of the field of his possession, shall be sold or redeemed: every devoted thing is most holy to the LORD.

29 None devoted, which shall be devoted of men, shall be redeemed; but shall surely be put to death.

30 And all the tithe of the land, whether of the seed of the land, or of the fruit of the tree, is the LORD's: it is holy to the LORD.

31 And if a man will at all redeem ought of his tithes, he shall add thereto the fifth part thereof.

32 And concerning the tithe of the herd, or of the flock, even of whatsoever passes under the rod, the tenth shall be holy to the LORD.

33 He shall not search whether it be good or bad, neither shall he change it: and if he change it at all, then both it and the change thereof shall be holy; it shall not be redeemed.

34 These are the commandments, which the LORD commanded Moses for the children of Israel in mount Sinai.

Numbers

CHAPTER 1

A ND the LORD spoke to Moses in the wilderness of Sinai, in the tabernacle of the congregation, on the first day of the second month, in the second year after they were come out of the land of Egypt, saying,

2 Take the sum of all the congregation of the children of Israel, after their families, by the house of their fathers, with the number of their names, every male by their polls;

3 From twenty years old and upward, all that are able to go forth to war in Israel: you and Aaron shall number them by their armies.

4 And with you there shall be a man of every tribe; every one head of the house of his fathers.

5 And these are the names of the men that shall stand with you: of the tribe of Reuben; Elizur the son of Shedeur.

6 Of Simeon; Shelumiel the son of Zurishaddai.

7 Of Judah; Nahshon the son of Amminadab.

8 Of Issachar; Nethaneel the son of Zuar.

9 Of Zebulun; Eliab the son of Helon.

10 Of the children of Joseph: of Ephraim; Elishama the son of Ammihud: of Manasseh; Gamaliel the son of Pedahzur.

11 Of Benjamin; Abidan the son of Gideoni.

12 Of Dan; Ahiezer the son of Ammishaddai.

13 Of Asher; Pagiel the son of Ocran.

14 Of Gad; Eliasaph the son of Deuel.

15 Of Naphtali; Ahira the son of Enan.

16 These were the renowned of the congregation, princes of the tribes of their fathers, heads of thousands in Israel.

17 And Moses and Aaron took these men which are expressed by their names:

18 And they assembled all the congregation together on the first day of the second month, and they declared their pedigrees after their families, by the house of their fathers, according to the number of the names, from twenty years old and upward, by their polls.

19 As the LORD commanded Moses, so he numbered them in the wilderness of Sinai.

20 And the children of Reuben, Israel's eldest son, by their generations, after their families, by the house of their fathers, according to the number of the names, by their polls, every male from twenty years old and upward, all that were able to go forth to war;

21 Those that were numbered of them, even of the tribe of Reuben, were forty and six thousand and five hundred.

22 Of the children of Simeon, by their generations, after their families, by the house of their fathers, those that were numbered of them, according to the

number of the names, by their polls, every male from twenty years old and upward, all that were able to go forth to war;

23 Those that were numbered of them, even of the tribe of Simeon, were fifty and nine thousand and three hundred.

24 Of the children of Gad, by their generations, after their families, by the house of their fathers, according to the number of the names, from twenty years old and upward, all that were able to go forth to war;

25 Those that were numbered of them, even of the tribe of Gad, were forty and five thousand six hundred and fifty.

26 Of the children of Judah, by their generations, after their families, by the house of their fathers, according to the number of the names, from twenty years old and upward, all that were able to go forth to war;

27 Those that were numbered of them, even of the tribe of Judah, were threescore and fourteen thousand and six hundred.

28 Of the children of Issachar, by their generations, after their families, by the house of their fathers, according to the number of the names, from twenty years old and upward, all that were able to go forth to war;

29 Those that were numbered of them, even of the tribe of Issachar, were fifty and four thousand and four hundred.

30 Of the children of Zebulun, by their generations, after their families, by the house of their fathers, according to the number of the names, from twenty years old and upward, all that were able to go forth to war;

31 Those that were numbered of them, even of the tribe of Zebulun, were fifty and seven thousand and four hundred.

32 Of the children of Joseph, namely, of the children of Ephraim, by their generations, after their families, by the house of their fathers, according to the number of the names,

from twenty years old and upward, all that were able to go forth to war;

33 Those that were numbered of them, even of the tribe of Ephraim, were forty thousand and five hundred.

34 Of the children of Manasseh, by their generations, after their families, by the house of their fathers, according to the number of the names, from twenty years old and upward, all that were able to go forth to war;

35 Those that were numbered of them, even of the tribe of Manasseh, were thirty and two thousand and two hundred.

36 Of the children of Benjamin, by their generations, after their families, by the house of their fathers, according to the number of the names, from twenty years old and upward, all that were able to go forth to war;

37 Those that were numbered of them, even of the tribe of Benjamin, were thirty and five thousand and four hundred.

38 Of the children of Dan, by their generations, after their families, by the house of their fathers, according to the number of the names, from twenty years old and upward, all that were able to go forth to war;

39 Those that were numbered of them, even of the tribe of Dan, were threescore and two thousand and seven hundred.

40 Of the children of Asher, by their generations, after their families, by the house of their fathers, according to the number of the names, from twenty years old and upward, all that were able to go forth to war;

41 Those that were numbered of them, even of the tribe of Asher, were forty and one thousand and five hundred.

42 Of the children of Naphtali, throughout their generations, after their families, by the house of their fathers, according to the number of the names, from twenty years old and upward, all that were able to go forth to war;

43 Those that were numbered of them, even of the tribe of Naphtali, were fifty and three thousand and four hundred.

THE FUNCTION OF THE LAW IN EVANGELISM

Do we remove words that might offend, such as "repentance" and "hell" to make the message more acceptable, or to make ourselves acceptable to a God-hating world? God forbid that our concern should be for our own comfort, rather than for the eternal welfare of the world.

The 18th century British evangelist who founded Methodism, John Wesley, said of God's Law, "It drives us by force, rather than draws us by love. And yet love is the spring of all. It is the spirit of love which, by this painful means, tears away our confidence in the flesh, which leaves us no broken reed whereon to trust, and so constrains the sinner, stripped of all to cry out in the bitterness of his soul or groan in the depth of his heart, 'I give up every plea beside, Lord, I am damned; but thou hast died.'"

44 These are those that were numbered, which Moses and Aaron numbered, and the princes of Israel, being twelve men: each one was for the house of his fathers.

45 So were all those that were numbered of the children of Israel, by the house of their fathers, from twenty years old and upward, all that were able to go forth to war in Israel;

46 Even all they that were numbered were six hundred thousand and three thousand and five hundred and fifty.

47 But the Levites after the tribe of their fathers were not numbered among them.

48 For the LORD had spoken to Moses, saying,

49 Only you shall not number the tribe of Levi, neither take the sum of them among the children of Israel:

50 But you shall appoint the Levites over the tabernacle of testimony, and over all the vessels thereof, and over all things that belong to it: they shall bear the tabernacle, and all the vessels thereof; and they shall minister to it, and shall encamp round about the tabernacle.

51 And when the tabernacle sets forward, the Levites shall take it down: and when the tabernacle is to be pitched, the Levites shall set it up: and the stranger that cometh nigh shall be put to death.

52 And the children of Israel shall pitch their tents, every man by his own camp, and every man by his own standard, throughout their hosts.

53 But the Levites shall pitch round about the tabernacle of testimony, that there be no wrath upon the congregation of the children of Israel: and the Levites shall keep the charge of the tabernacle of testimony.

54 And the children of Israel did according to all that the LORD commanded Moses, so did they.

CHAPTER 2

AND the LORD spoke to Moses and to Aaron, saying,

2 Every man of the children of Israel shall pitch by his own standard, with the ensign of their father's house: far off about the tabernacle of the congregation shall they pitch.

3 And on the east side toward the rising of the sun shall they of the standard of the camp of Judah pitch throughout their armies: and Nahshon the son of Amminadab shall be captain of the children of Judah.

4 And his host, and those that were numbered of them, were threescore and fourteen thousand and six hundred.

5 And those that do pitch next to him shall be the tribe of Issachar: and Nethaneel the son of Zuar shall be captain of the children of Issachar.

6 And his host, and those that were numbered thereof, were fifty and four thousand and four hundred.

7 Then the tribe of Zebulun: and Eliab the son of Helon shall be captain of the children of Zebulun.

8 And his host, and those that were numbered thereof, were fifty and seven thousand and four hundred.

9 All that were numbered in the camp of Judah were an hundred thousand and fourscore thousand and six thousand and four hundred, throughout their armies. These shall first set forth.

10 On the south side shall be the standard of the camp of Reuben according to their armies: and the captain of the children of Reuben shall be Elizur the son of Shedeur.

11 And his host, and those that were numbered thereof, were forty and six thousand and five hundred.

12 And those which pitch by him shall be the tribe of Simeon: and the captain of the children of Simeon shall be Shelumiel the son of Zurishaddai.

13 And his host, and those that were numbered of them, were fifty and nine thousand and three hundred.

14 Then the tribe of Gad: and the captain of the sons of Gad shall be Eliasaph the son of Reuel.

15 And his host, and those that were numbered of them, were forty and five thousand and six hundred and fifty.

16 All that were numbered in the camp of Reuben were an hundred thousand and fifty and one thousand and four hundred and fifty, throughout their armies. And they shall set forth in the second rank.

17 Then the tabernacle of the congregation shall set forward with the camp of the Levites in the midst of the camp: as they encamp, so shall they set forward, every man in his place by their standards.

18 On the west side shall be the standard of the camp of Ephraim according to their armies: and the captain of the sons of Ephraim shall be Elishama the son of Ammihud.

19 And his host, and those that were numbered of them, were forty thousand and five hundred.

20 And by him shall be the tribe of Manasseh: and the captain of the children of Manasseh shall be Gamaliel the son of Pedahzur.

21 And his host, and those that were numbered of them, were thirty and two thousand and two hundred.

22 Then the tribe of Benjamin: and the captain of the sons of Benjamin shall be Abidan the son of Gideoni.

23 And his host, and those that were numbered of them, were thirty and five thousand and four hundred.

24 All that were numbered of the camp of Ephraim were an hundred thousand and eight thousand and an hundred, throughout their armies. And they shall go forward in the third rank.

25 The standard of the camp of Dan shall be on the north side by their armies: and the captain of the children of Dan shall be Ahiezer the son of Ammishaddai.

26 And his host, and those that were numbered of them, were threescore and two thousand and seven hundred.

27 And those that encamp by him shall be the tribe of Asher:
and the captain of the children of Asher shall be Pagiel the son of Ocran.

28 And his host, and those that were numbered of them, were forty and one thousand and five hundred.

29 Then the tribe of Naphtali: and the captain of the children of Naphtali shall be Ahira the son of Enan.

30 And his host, and those that were numbered of them, were fifty and three thousand and four hundred.

31 All they that were numbered in the camp of Dan were an hundred thousand and fifty and seven thousand and six hundred. They shall go hindmost with their standards.

32 These are those which were numbered of the children of Israel by the house of their fathers: all those that were numbered of the camps throughout their hosts were six hundred thousand and

three thousand and five hundred and
fifty.

33 But the Levites were not numbered
among the children of Israel; as the
LORD commanded Moses.

34 And the children of Israel did according to all that the LORD commanded Moses: so they pitched by their standards, and so they set forward, every one
after their families, according to the
house of their fathers.

CHAPTER 3

THESE also are the generations of
Aaron and Moses in the day that the
LORD spoke with Moses in mount Sinai.
2 And these are the names of the sons
of Aaron; Nadab the firstborn, and
Abihu, Eleazar, and Ithamar.

3 These are the names of the sons of
Aaron, the priests which were anointed,
whom he consecrated to minister in the
priest's office.

4 And Nadab and Abihu died before the
LORD, when they offered strange fire
before the LORD, in the wilderness of
Sinai, and they had no children: and
Eleazar and Ithamar ministered in the
priest's office in the sight of Aaron their
father.

5 And the LORD spoke to Moses, saying,

6 Bring the tribe of Levi near, and present them before Aaron the priest, that
they may minister to him.

7 And they shall keep his charge, and
the charge of the whole congregation before the tabernacle of the congregation,
to do the service of the tabernacle.

8 And they shall keep all the instruments of the tabernacle of the congregation, and the charge of the children of
Israel, to do the service of the tabernacle.

9 And you shall give the Levites to
Aaron and to his sons: they are wholly
given to him out of the children of Israel.

10 And you shall appoint Aaron and his
sons, and they shall wait on their priest's
office: and the stranger that cometh nigh
shall be put to death.

11 And the LORD spoke to Moses, saying,

12 And I, behold, I have taken the
Levites from among the children of Israel
instead of all the firstborn that opens the
matrix among the children of Israel:
therefore the Levites shall be mine;

13 Because all the firstborn are mine;
for on the day that I smote all the firstborn in the land of Egypt I hallowed to
me all the firstborn in Israel, both man
and beast: mine shall they be: I am the
LORD.

14 And the LORD spoke to Moses in
the wilderness of Sinai, saying,

15 Number the children of Levi after
the house of their fathers, by their families: every male from a month old and
upward shall you number them.

16 And Moses numbered them according to the word of the LORD, as he was
commanded.

17 And these were the sons of Levi by
their names; Gershon, and Kohath, and
Merari.

18 And these are the names of the sons
of Gershon by their families; Libni, and
Shimei.

19 And the sons of Kohath by their
families; Amram, and Izehar, Hebron,
and Uzziel.

20 And the sons of Merari by their families; Mahli, and Mushi. These are the
families of the Levites according to the
house of their fathers.

21 Of Gershon was the family of the
Libnites, and the family of the Shimites:
these are the families of the Gershonites.

22 Those that were numbered of them,
according to the number of all the males,
from a month old and upward, even
those that were numbered of them were
seven thousand and five hundred.

23 The families of the Gershonites shall
pitch behind the tabernacle westward.

24 And the chief of the house of the father of the Gershonites shall be Eliasaph
the son of Lael.

25 And the charge of the sons of
Gershon in the tabernacle of the congre-

gation shall be the tabernacle, and the tent, the covering thereof, and the hanging for the door of the tabernacle of the congregation,

26 And the hangings of the court, and the curtain for the door of the court, which is by the tabernacle, and by the altar round about, and the cords of it for all the service thereof.

27 And of Kohath was the family of the Amramites, and the family of the Izeharites, and the family of the Hebronites, and the family of the Uzzielites: these are the families of the Kohathites.

28 In the number of all the males, from a month old and upward, were eight thousand and six hundred, keeping the charge of the sanctuary.

29 The families of the sons of Kohath shall pitch on the side of the tabernacle southward.

30 And the chief of the house of the father of the families of the Kohathites shall be Elizaphan the son of Uzziel.

31 And their charge shall be the ark, and the table, and the candlestick, and the altars, and the vessels of the sanctuary wherewith they minister, and the hanging, and all the service thereof.

32 And Eleazar the son of Aaron the priest shall be chief over the chief of the Levites, and have the oversight of them that keep the charge of the sanctuary.

33 Of Merari was the family of the Mahlites, and the family of the Mushites: these are the families of Merari.

34 And those that were numbered of them, according to the number of all the males, from a month old and upward, were six thousand and two hundred.

35 And the chief of the house of the father of the families of Merari was Zuriel the son of Abihail: these shall pitch on the side of the tabernacle northward.

36 And under the custody and charge of the sons of Merari shall be the boards of the tabernacle, and the bars thereof, and the pillars thereof, and the sockets

thereof, and all the vessels thereof, and all that serves thereto,

37 And the pillars of the court round about, and their sockets, and their pins, and their cords.

38 But those that encamp before the tabernacle toward the east, even before the tabernacle of the congregation eastward, shall be Moses, and Aaron and his sons, keeping the charge of the sanctuary for the charge of the children of Israel; and the stranger that cometh nigh shall be put to death.

39 All that were numbered of the Levites, which Moses and Aaron numbered at the commandment of the LORD, throughout their families, all the males from a month old and upward, were twenty and two thousand.

40 And the LORD said to Moses, Number all the firstborn of the males of the children of Israel from a month old and upward, and take the number of their names.

41 And you shall take the Levites for me (I am the LORD) instead of all the firstborn among the children of Israel; and the cattle of the Levites instead of all the firstlings among the cattle of the children of Israel.

42 And Moses numbered, as the LORD commanded him, all the firstborn among the children of Israel.

43 And all the firstborn males by the number of names, from a month old and upward, of those that were numbered of them, were twenty and two thousand two hundred and threescore and thirteen.

44 And the LORD spoke to Moses, saying,

45 Take the Levites instead of all the firstborn among the children of Israel, and the cattle of the Levites instead of their cattle; and the Levites shall be mine: I am the LORD.

46 And for those that are to be redeemed of the two hundred and threescore and thirteen of the firstborn of the

children of Israel, which are more than the Levites;

47 You shall even take five shekels apiece by the poll, after the shekel of the sanctuary shall you take them: (the shekel is twenty gerahs:)

48 And you shall give the money, wherewith the odd number of them is to be redeemed, to Aaron and to his sons.

49 And Moses took the redemption money of them that were over and above them that were redeemed by the Levites:

50 Of the firstborn of the children of Israel took he the money; a thousand three hundred and threescore and five shekels, after the shekel of the sanctuary:

51 And Moses gave the money of them that were redeemed to Aaron and to his sons, according to the word of the LORD, as the LORD commanded Moses.

CHAPTER 4

A ND the LORD spoke to Moses and to Aaron, saying,

2 Take the sum of the sons of Kohath from among the sons of Levi, after their families, by the house of their fathers,

3 From thirty years old and upward even until fifty years old, all that enter into the host, to do the work in the tabernacle of the congregation.

4 This shall be the service of the sons of Kohath in the tabernacle of the congregation, about the most holy things:

5 And when the camp sets forward, Aaron shall come, and his sons, and they shall take down the covering vail, and cover the ark of testimony with it:

6 And shall put thereon the covering of badgers' skins, and shall spread over it a cloth wholly of blue, and shall put in the staves thereof.

7 And upon the table of shewbread they shall spread a cloth of blue, and put thereon the dishes, and the spoons, and the bowls, and covers to cover withal: and the continual bread shall be thereon:

8 And they shall spread upon them a cloth of scarlet, and cover the same with a covering of badgers' skins, and shall put in the staves thereof.

9 And they shall take a cloth of blue, and cover the candlestick of the light, and his lamps, and his tongs, and his snuffdishes, and all the oil vessels thereof, wherewith they minister to it:

10 And they shall put it and all the vessels thereof within a covering of badgers' skins, and shall put it upon a bar.

11 And upon the golden altar they shall spread a cloth of blue, and cover it with a covering of badgers' skins, and shall put to the staves thereof:

12 And they shall take all the instruments of ministry, wherewith they minister in the sanctuary, and put them in a cloth of blue, and cover them with a covering of badgers' skins, and shall put them on a bar:

13 And they shall take away the ashes from the altar, and spread a purple cloth thereon:

14 And they shall put upon it all the vessels thereof, wherewith they minister about it, even the censers, the flesh-hooks, and the shovels, and the basons, all the vessels of the altar; and they shall spread upon it a covering of badgers' skins, and put to the staves of it.

15 And when Aaron and his sons have made an end of covering the sanctuary, and all the vessels of the sanctuary, as the camp is to set forward; after that, the sons of Kohath shall come to bear it: but they shall not touch any holy thing, lest they die. These things are the burden of the sons of Kohath in the tabernacle of the congregation.

16 And to the office of Eleazar the son of Aaron the priest pertains the oil for the light, and the sweet incense, and the daily meat offering, and the anointing oil, and the oversight of all the tabernacle, and of all that therein is, in the sanctuary, and in the vessels thereof.

17 And the LORD spoke to Moses and to Aaron saying,

18 Cut not off the tribe of the families of the Kohathites from among the Levites:

19 But thus do to them, that they may live, and not die, when they approach to the most holy things: Aaron and his sons shall go in, and appoint them every one to his service and to his burden:

20 But they shall not go in to see when the holy things are covered, lest they die.

21 And the LORD spoke to Moses, saying,

22 Take also the sum of the sons of Gershon, throughout the houses of their fathers, by their families;

23 From thirty years old and upward until fifty years old shall you number them; all that enter in to perform the service, to do the work in the tabernacle of the congregation.

24 This is the service of the families of the Gershonites, to serve, and for burdens:

25 And they shall bear the curtains of the tabernacle, and the tabernacle of the congregation, his covering, and the covering of the badgers' skins that is above upon it, and the hanging for the door of the tabernacle of the congregation,

26 And the hangings of the court, and the hanging for the door of the gate of the court, which is by the tabernacle and by the altar round about, and their cords, and all the instruments of their service, and all that is made for them: so shall they serve.

27 At the appointment of Aaron and his sons shall be all the service of the sons of the Gershonites, in all their burdens, and in all their service: and you shall appoint to them in charge all their burdens.

28 This is the service of the families of the sons of Gershon in the tabernacle of the congregation: and their charge shall be under the hand of Ithamar the son of Aaron the priest.

29 As for the sons of Merari, you shall number them after their families, by the house of their fathers;

30 From thirty years old and upward even to fifty years old shall you number them, every one that enters into the service, to do the work of the tabernacle of the congregation.

31 And this is the charge of their burden, according to all their service in the tabernacle of the congregation; the boards of the tabernacle, and the bars thereof, and the pillars thereof, and sockets thereof,

32 And the pillars of the court round about, and their sockets, and their pins, and their cords, with all their instruments, and with all their service: and by name you shall reckon the instruments of the charge of their burden.

33 This is the service of the families of the sons of Merari, according to all their service, in the tabernacle of the congregation, under the hand of Ithamar the son of Aaron the priest.

34 And Moses and Aaron and the chief of the congregation numbered the sons of the Kohathites after their families, and after the house of their fathers,

35 From thirty years old and upward even to fifty years old, every one that enters into the service, for the work in the tabernacle of the congregation:

36 And those that were numbered of them by their families were two thousand seven hundred and fifty.

37 These were they that were numbered of the families of the Kohathites, all that might do service in the tabernacle of the congregation, which Moses and Aaron did number according to the commandment of the LORD by the hand of Moses.

38 And those that were numbered of the sons of Gershon, throughout their families, and by the house of their fathers,

39 From thirty years old and upward even to fifty years old, every one that enters into the service, for the work in the tabernacle of the congregation,

40 Even those that were numbered of them, throughout their families, by the

house of their fathers, were two thousand and six hundred and thirty.

41 These are they that were numbered of the families of the sons of Gershon, of all that might do service in the tabernacle of the congregation, whom Moses and Aaron did number according to the commandment of the LORD.

42 And those that were numbered of the families of the sons of Merari, throughout their families, by the house of their fathers,

43 From thirty years old and upward even to fifty years old, every one that enters into the service, for the work in the tabernacle of the congregation,

44 Even those that were numbered of them after their families, were three thousand and two hundred.

45 These be those that were numbered of the families of the sons of Merari, whom Moses and Aaron numbered according to the word of the LORD by the hand of Moses.

46 All those that were numbered of the Levites, whom Moses and Aaron and the chief of Israel numbered, after their families, and after the house of their fathers,

47 From thirty years old and upward even to fifty years old, every one that came to do the service of the ministry, and the service of the burden in the tabernacle of the congregation.

48 Even those that were numbered of them, were eight thousand and five hundred and fourscore,

49 According to the commandment of the LORD they were numbered by the hand of Moses, every one according to his service, and according to his burden: thus were they numbered of him, as the LORD commanded Moses.

CHAPTER 5

AND the LORD spoke to Moses, saying,

2 Command the children of Israel, that they put out of the camp every leper, and every one that has an issue, and whosoever is defiled by the dead:

3 Both male and female shall you put out, without the camp shall you put them; that they defile not their camps, in the midst whereof I dwell.

4 And the children of Israel did so, and put them out without the camp: as the LORD spoke to Moses, so did the children of Israel.

5 And the LORD spoke to Moses, saying,

6 Speak to the children of Israel, When a man or woman shall commit any sin that men commit, to do a trespass against the LORD, and that person be guilty;

7 Then they shall confess their sin which they have done: and he shall recompense his trespass with the principal thereof, and add to it the fifth part thereof, and give it to him against whom he has trespassed.

8 But if the man have no kinsman to recompense the trespass to, let the trespass be recompensed to the LORD, even to the priest; beside the ram of the atonement, whereby an atonement shall be made for him.

9 And every offering of all the holy things of the children of Israel, which they bring to the priest, shall be his.

10 And every man's hallowed things shall be his: whatsoever any man gives the priest, it shall be his.

11 And the LORD spoke to Moses, saying,

12 Speak to the children of Israel, and say to them, If any man's wife go aside, and commit a trespass against him,

13 And a man lie with her carnally, and it be hid from the eyes of her husband, and be kept close, and she be defiled, and there be no witness against her, neither she be taken with the manner;

14 And the spirit of jealousy come upon him, and he be jealous of his wife, and she be defiled: or if the spirit of jealousy come upon him, and he be jealous of his wife, and she be not defiled:

15 Then shall the man bring his wife to the priest, and he shall bring her offering

for her, the tenth part of an ephah of
barley meal; he shall pour no oil upon it,
nor put frankincense thereon; for it is an
offering of jealousy, an offering of
memorial, bringing iniquity to remembrance.

16 And the priest shall bring her near,
and set her before the LORD:

17 And the priest shall take holy water
in an earthen vessel; and of the dust that
is in the floor of the tabernacle the priest
shall take, and put it into the water:

18 And the priest shall set the woman
before the LORD, and uncover the
woman's head, and put the offering of
memorial in her hands, which is the jealousy offering: and the priest shall have
in his hand the bitter water that causes
the curse:

19 And the priest shall charge her by an
oath, and say to the woman, If no man
have lain with you, and if you have not
gone aside to uncleanness with another
instead of your husband, be free from
this bitter water that causes the curse:

20 But if you have gone aside to another instead of your husband, and if you
be defiled, and some man have lain with
you beside your husband:

21 Then the priest shall charge the
woman with an oath of cursing, and the
priest shall say to the woman, The LORD
make you a curse and an oath among
your people, when the LORD doth make
your thigh to rot, and your belly to
swell;

22 And this water that causes the curse
shall go into your bowels, to make your
belly to swell, and your thigh to rot: And
the woman shall say, Amen, amen.

23 And the priest shall write these curses in a book, and he shall blot them out
with the bitter water:

24 And he shall cause the woman to
drink the bitter water that causes the
curse: and the water that causes the
curse shall enter into her, and become
bitter.

25 Then the priest shall take the jealousy offering out of the woman's hand,
and shall wave the offering before the
LORD, and offer it upon the altar:

26 And the priest shall take an handful
of the offering, even the memorial thereof, and burn it upon the altar, and afterward shall cause the woman to drink the
water.

27 And when he has made her to drink
the water, then it shall come to pass,
that, if she be defiled, and have done
trespass against her husband, that the
water that causes the curse shall enter
into her, and become bitter, and her
belly shall swell, and her thigh shall rot:
and the woman shall be a curse among
her people.

28 And if the woman be not defiled,
but be clean; then she shall be free, and
shall conceive seed.

29 This is the law of jealousies, when a
wife goes aside to another instead of her
husband, and is defiled;

30 Or when the spirit of jealousy
cometh upon him, and he be jealous
over his wife, and shall set the woman
before the LORD, and the priest shall execute upon her all this law.

31 Then shall the man be guiltless from
iniquity, and this woman shall bear her
iniquity.

CHAPTER 6

A ND the LORD spoke to Moses, saying,

2 Speak to the children of Israel, and
say to them, When either man or woman
shall separate themselves to vow a vow
of a Nazarite, to separate themselves to
the LORD:

3 He shall separate himself from wine
and strong drink, and shall drink no
vinegar of wine, or vinegar of strong
drink, neither shall he drink any liquor
of grapes, nor eat moist grapes, or dried.

4 All the days of his separation shall he
eat nothing that is made of the vine tree,
from the kernels even to the husk.

5 All the days of the vow of his separation there shall no razor come upon his
head: until the days be fulfilled, in the

which he separates himself to the LORD, he shall be holy, and shall let the locks of the hair of his head grow.

6 All the days that he separates himself to the LORD he shall come at no dead body.

7 He shall not make himself unclean for his father, or for his mother, for his brother, or for his sister, when they die: because the consecration of his God is upon his head.

8 All the days of his separation he is holy to the LORD.

9 And if any man die very suddenly by him, and he has defiled the head of his consecration; then he shall shave his head in the day of his cleansing, on the seventh day shall he shave it.

10 And on the eighth day he shall bring two turtles, or two young pigeons, to the priest, to the door of the tabernacle of the congregation:

11 And the priest shall offer the one for a sin offering, and the other for a burnt offering, and make an atonement for him, for that he sinned by the dead, and shall hallow his head that same day.

12 And he shall consecrate to the LORD the days of his separation, and shall bring a lamb of the first year for a trespass offering: but the days that were before shall be lost, because his separation was defiled.

13 And this is the law of the Nazarite, when the days of his separation are fulfilled: he shall be brought to the door of the tabernacle of the congregation:

14 And he shall offer his offering to the LORD, one he lamb of the first year without blemish for a burnt offering, and one ewe lamb of the first year without blemish for a sin offering, and one ram without blemish for peace offerings,

15 And a basket of unleavened bread, cakes of fine flour mingled with oil, and wafers of unleavened bread anointed with oil, and their meat offering, and their drink offerings.

16 And the priest shall bring them before the LORD, and shall offer his sin offering, and his burnt offering:

17 And he shall offer the ram for a sacrifice of peace offerings to the LORD, with the basket of unleavened bread: the priest shall offer also his meat offering, and his drink offering.

18 And the Nazarite shall shave the head of his separation at the door of the tabernacle of the congregation, and shall take the hair of the head of his separation, and put it in the fire which is under the sacrifice of the peace offerings.

19 And the priest shall take the sodden shoulder of the ram, and one unleavened cake out of the basket, and one unleavened wafer, and shall put them upon the hands of the Nazarite, after the hair of his separation is shaven:

20 And the priest shall wave them for a wave offering before the LORD: this is holy for the priest, with the wave breast and heave shoulder: and after that the Nazarite may drink wine.

21 This is the law of the Nazarite who has vowed, and of his offering to the LORD for his separation, beside that that his hand shall get: according to the vow which he vowed, so he must do after the law of his separation.

22 And the LORD spoke to Moses, saying,

23 Speak to Aaron and to his sons, saying, On this wise you shall bless the children of Israel, saying to them,

24 The LORD bless you, and keep you:

25 The LORD make his face shine upon you, and be gracious to you:

26 The LORD lift up his countenance upon you, and give you peace.

27 And they shall put my name upon the children of Israel, and I will bless them.

CHAPTER 7

AND it came to pass on the day that Moses had fully set up the tabernacle, and had anointed it, and sanctified it, and all the instruments thereof, both the altar and all the vessels thereof, and had anointed them, and sanctified them;

2 That the princes of Israel, heads of the house of their fathers, who were the princes of the tribes, and were over them that were numbered, offered:

3 And they brought their offering before the LORD, six covered wagons, and twelve oxen; a wagon for two of the princes, and for each one an ox: and they brought them before the tabernacle.

4 And the LORD spoke to Moses, saying,

5 Take it of them, that they may be to do the service of the tabernacle of the congregation; and you shall give them to the Levites, to every man according to his service.

6 And Moses took the wagons and the oxen, and gave them to the Levites.

7 Two wagons and four oxen he gave to the sons of Gershon, according to their service:

8 And four wagons and eight oxen he gave to the sons of Merari, according to their service, under the hand of Ithamar the son of Aaron the priest.

9 But to the sons of Kohath he gave none: because the service of the sanctuary belonging to them was that they should bear upon their shoulders.

10 And the princes offered for dedicating of the altar in the day that it was anointed, even the princes offered their offering before the altar.

11 And the LORD said to Moses, They shall offer their offering, each prince on his day, for the dedicating of the altar.

12 And he that offered his offering the first day was Nahshon the son of Amminadab, of the tribe of Judah:

13 And his offering was one silver charger, the weight thereof was an hundred and thirty shekels, one silver bowl of seventy shekels, after the shekel of the sanctuary; both of them were full of fine flour mingled with oil for a meat offering:

14 One spoon of ten shekels of gold, full of incense:

15 One young bullock, one ram, one lamb of the first year, for a burnt offering:

16 One kid of the goats for a sin offering:

17 And for a sacrifice of peace offerings, two oxen, five rams, five he goats, five lambs of the first year: this was the offering of Nahshon the son of Amminadab.

18 On the second day Nethaneel the son of Zuar, prince of Issachar, did offer:

19 He offered for his offering one silver charger, the weight whereof was an hundred and thirty shekels, one silver bowl of seventy shekels, after the shekel of the sanctuary; both of them full of fine flour mingled with oil for a meat offering:

20 One spoon of gold of ten shekels, full of incense:

21 One young bullock, one ram, one lamb of the first year, for a burnt offering:

22 One kid of the goats for a sin offering:

23 And for a sacrifice of peace offerings, two oxen, five rams, five he goats, five lambs of the first year: this was the offering of Nethaneel the son of Zuar.

24 On the third day Eliab the son of Helon, prince of the children of Zebulun, did offer:

25 His offering was one silver charger, the weight whereof was an hundred and thirty shekels, one silver bowl of seventy shekels, after the shekel of the sanctuary; both of them full of fine flour mingled with oil for a meat offering:

26 One golden spoon of ten shekels, full of incense:

27 One young bullock, one ram, one lamb of the first year, for a burnt offering:

28 One kid of the goats for a sin offering:

29 And for a sacrifice of peace offerings, two oxen, five rams, five he goats, five lambs of the first year: this was the offering of Eliab the son of Helon.

THE FUNCTION OF THE LAW IN EVANGELISM

 Martin Luther, the German priest who in the 16th century broke with the Roman Catholic Church and founded the Lutheran Church, said, "I was alive without the Law once: but when the commandment came, sin revived' (Romans 7:9).
"So it is with the work-righteous and the proud unbelievers. Because they do not know the Law of God, which is directed against them, it is impossible for them to know their sin. Therefore also, they are not amenable to instruction. If they would know the Law, they would also know their sin; and sin to which they are now dead would become alive in them."

30 On the fourth day Elizur the son of Shedeur, prince of the children of Reuben, did offer:

31 His offering was one silver charger of the weight of an hundred and thirty shekels, one silver bowl of seventy shekels, after the shekel of the sanctuary; both of them full of fine flour mingled with oil for a meat offering:

32 One golden spoon of ten shekels, full of incense:

33 One young bullock, one ram, one lamb of the first year, for a burnt offering:

34 One kid of the goats for a sin offering:

35 And for a sacrifice of peace offerings, two oxen, five rams, five he goats, five lambs of the first year: this was the offering of Elizur the son of Shedeur.

36 On the fifth day Shelumiel the son of Zurishaddai, prince of the children of Simeon, did offer:

37 His offering was one silver charger, the weight whereof was an hundred and thirty shekels, one silver bowl of seventy shekels, after the shekel of the sanctuary; both of them full of fine flour mingled with oil for a meat offering:

38 One golden spoon of ten shekels, full of incense:

39 One young bullock, one ram, one lamb of the first year, for a burnt offering:

40 One kid of the goats for a sin offering:

41 And for a sacrifice of peace offerings, two oxen, five rams, five he goats, five lambs of the first year: this was the offer-

ing of Shelumiel the son of Zurishaddai.

42 On the sixth day Eliasaph the son of Deuel, prince of the children of Gad, offered:

43 His offering was one silver charger of the weight of an hundred and thirty shekels, a silver bowl of seventy shekels, after the shekel of the sanctuary; both of them full of fine flour mingled with oil for a meat offering:

44 One golden spoon of ten shekels, full of incense:

45 One young bullock, one ram, one lamb of the first year, for a burnt offering:

46 One kid of the goats for a sin offering:

47 And for a sacrifice of peace offerings, two oxen, five rams, five he goats, five lambs of the first year: this was the offering of Eliasaph the son of Deuel.

48 On the seventh day Elishama the son of Ammihud, prince of the children of Ephraim, offered:

49 His offering was one silver charger, the weight whereof was an hundred and thirty shekels, one silver bowl of seventy shekels, after the shekel of the sanctuary; both of them full of fine flour mingled with oil for a meat offering:

50 One golden spoon of ten shekels, full of incense:

51 One young bullock, one ram, one lamb of the first year, for a burnt offering:

52 One kid of the goats for a sin offering:

53 And for a sacrifice of peace offerings, two oxen, five rams, five he goats, five

lambs of the first year: this was the offering of Elishama the son of Ammihud.

54 On the eighth day offered Gamaliel the son of Pedahzur, prince of the children of Manasseh:

55 His offering was one silver charger of the weight of an hundred and thirty shekels, one silver bowl of seventy shekels, after the shekel of the sanctuary; both of them full of fine flour mingled with oil for a meat offering:

56 One golden spoon of ten shekels, full of incense:

57 One young bullock, one ram, one lamb of the first year, for a burnt offering:

58 One kid of the goats for a sin offering:

59 And for a sacrifice of peace offerings, two oxen, five rams, five he goats, five lambs of the first year: this was the offering of Gamaliel the son of Pedahzur.

60 On the ninth day Abidan the son of Gideoni, prince of the children of Benjamin, offered:

61 His offering was one silver charger, the weight whereof was an hundred and thirty shekels, one silver bowl of seventy shekels, after the shekel of the sanctuary; both of them full of fine flour mingled with oil for a meat offering:

62 One golden spoon of ten shekels, full of incense:

63 One young bullock, one ram, one lamb of the first year, for a burnt offering:

64 One kid of the goats for a sin offering:

65 And for a sacrifice of peace offerings, two oxen, five rams, five he goats, five lambs of the first year: this was the offering of Abidan the son of Gideoni.

66 On the tenth day Ahiezer the son of Ammishaddai, prince of the children of Dan, offered:

67 His offering was one silver charger, the weight whereof was an hundred and thirty shekels, one silver bowl of seventy shekels, after the shekel of the sanctuary;

both of them full of fine flour mingled with oil for a meat offering:

68 One golden spoon of ten shekels, full of incense:

69 One young bullock, one ram, one lamb of the first year, for a burnt offering:

70 One kid of the goats for a sin offering:

71 And for a sacrifice of peace offerings, two oxen, five rams, five he goats, five lambs of the first year: this was the offering of Ahiezer the son of Ammishaddai.

72 On the eleventh day Pagiel the son of Ocran, prince of the children of Asher, offered:

73 His offering was one silver charger, the weight whereof was an hundred and thirty shekels, one silver bowl of seventy shekels, after the shekel of the sanctuary; both of them full of fine flour mingled with oil for a meat offering:

74 One golden spoon of ten shekels, full of incense:

75 One young bullock, one ram, one lamb of the first year, for a burnt offering:

76 One kid of the goats for a sin offering:

77 And for a sacrifice of peace offerings, two oxen, five rams, five he goats, five lambs of the first year: this was the offering of Pagiel the son of Ocran.

78 On the twelfth day Ahira the son of Enan, prince of the children of Naphtali, offered:

79 His offering was one silver charger, the weight whereof was an hundred and thirty shekels, one silver bowl of seventy shekels, after the shekel of the sanctuary; both of them full of fine flour mingled with oil for a meat offering:

80 One golden spoon of ten shekels, full of incense:

81 One young bullock, one ram, one lamb of the first year, for a burnt offering:

82 One kid of the goats for a sin offering:

83 And for a sacrifice of peace offerings, two oxen, five rams, five he goats, five lambs of the first year: this was the offering of Ahira the son of Enan.

84 This was the dedication of the altar, in the day when it was anointed, by the princes of Israel: twelve chargers of silver, twelve silver bowls, twelve spoons of gold:

85 Each charger of silver weighing an hundred and thirty shekels, each bowl seventy: all the silver vessels weighed two thousand and four hundred shekels, after the shekel of the sanctuary:

86 The golden spoons were twelve, full of incense, weighing ten shekels apiece, after the shekel of the sanctuary: all the gold of the spoons was an hundred and twenty shekels.

87 All the oxen for the burnt offering were twelve bullocks, the rams twelve, the lambs of the first year twelve, with their meat offering: and the kids of the goats for sin offering twelve.

88 And all the oxen for the sacrifice of the peace offerings were twenty and four bullocks, the rams sixty, the he goats sixty, the lambs of the first year sixty. This was the dedication of the altar, after that it was anointed.

89 And when Moses was gone into the tabernacle of the congregation to speak with him, then he heard the voice of one speaking to him from off the mercy seat that was upon the ark of testimony, from between the two cherubims: and he spoke to him.

CHAPTER 8

AND the LORD spoke to Moses, saying,

2 Speak to Aaron and say to him, When you light the lamps, the seven lamps shall give light over against the candlestick.

3 And Aaron did so; he lighted the lamps thereof over against the candlestick, as the LORD commanded Moses.

4 And this work of the candlestick was of beaten gold, to the shaft thereof, to the flowers thereof, was beaten work: according to the pattern which the LORD had showed Moses, so he made the candlestick.

5 And the LORD spoke to Moses, saying,

6 Take the Levites from among the children of Israel, and cleanse them.

7 And thus shall you do to them, to cleanse them: Sprinkle water of purifying upon them, and let them shave all their flesh, and let them wash their clothes, and so make themselves clean.

8 Then let them take a young bullock with his meat offering, even fine flour mingled with oil, and another young bullock shall you take for a sin offering.

9 And you shall bring the Levites before the tabernacle of the congregation: and you shall gather the whole assembly of the children of Israel together:

10 And you shall bring the Levites before the LORD: and the children of Israel shall put their hands upon the Levites:

11 And Aaron shall offer the Levites before the LORD for an offering of the children of Israel, that they may execute the service of the LORD.

12 And the Levites shall lay their hands upon the heads of the bullocks: and you shall offer the one for a sin offering, and the other for a burnt offering, to the LORD, to make an atonement for the Levites.

13 And you shall set the Levites before Aaron, and before his sons, and offer them for an offering to the LORD.

14 Thus shall you separate the Levites from among the children of Israel: and the Levites shall be mine.

15 And after that shall the Levites go in to do the service of the tabernacle of the congregation: and you shall cleanse them, and offer them for an offering.

16 For they are wholly given to me from among the children of Israel; instead of such as open every womb, even instead of the firstborn of all the children of Israel, have I taken them to me.

17 For all the firstborn of the children of Israel are mine, both man and beast: on the day that I smote every firstborn in the land of Egypt I sanctified them for myself.

18 And I have taken the Levites for all the firstborn of the children of Israel.

19 And I have given the Levites as a gift to Aaron and to his sons from among the children of Israel, to do the service of the children of Israel in the tabernacle of the congregation, and to make an atonement for the children of Israel: that there be no plague among the children of Israel, when the children of Israel come nigh to the sanctuary.

20 And Moses, and Aaron, and all the congregation of the children of Israel, did to the Levites according to all that the LORD commanded Moses concerning the Levites, so did the children of Israel to them.

21 And the Levites were purified, and they washed their clothes; and Aaron offered them as an offering before the LORD; and Aaron made an atonement for them to cleanse them.

22 And after that went the Levites in to do their service in the tabernacle of the congregation before Aaron, and before his sons: as the LORD had commanded Moses concerning the Levites, so did they to them.

23 And the LORD spoke to Moses, saying,

24 This is it that belongs to the Levites: from twenty and five years old and upward they shall go in to wait upon the service of the tabernacle of the congregation:

25 And from the age of fifty years they shall cease waiting upon the service thereof, and shall serve no more:

26 But shall minister with their brethren in the tabernacle of the congregation, to keep the charge, and shall do no service. Thus shall you do to the Levites touching their charge.

CHAPTER 9

AND the LORD spoke to Moses in the wilderness of Sinai, in the first month of the second year after they were come out of the land of Egypt, saying,

2 Let the children of Israel also keep the passover at his appointed season.

3 In the fourteenth day of this month, at even, you shall keep it in his appointed season: according to all the rites of it, and according to all the ceremonies thereof, shall you keep it.

4 And Moses spoke to the children of Israel, that they should keep the passover.

5 And they kept the passover on the fourteenth day of the first month at even in the wilderness of Sinai: according to all that the LORD commanded Moses, so did the children of Israel.

6 And there were certain men, who were defiled by the dead body of a man, that they could not keep the passover on that day: and they came before Moses and before Aaron on that day:

7 And those men said to him, We are defiled by the dead body of a man: why are we kept back, that we may not offer an offering of the LORD in his appointed season among the children of Israel?

8 And Moses said to them, Stand still, and I will hear what the LORD will command concerning you.

9 And the LORD spoke to Moses, saying,

10 Speak to the children of Israel, saying, If any man of you or of your posterity shall be unclean by reason of a dead body, or be in a journey afar off, yet he shall keep the passover to the LORD.

11 The fourteenth day of the second month at even they shall keep it, and eat it with unleavened bread and bitter herbs.

12 They shall leave none of it to the morning, nor break any bone of it: according to all the ordinances of the passover they shall keep it.

13 But the man that is clean, and is not in a journey, and forbears to keep the

> The Law cuts into the core of the evil;
>
> it reveals the seat of the malady
>
> and informs us
>
> that the leprosy lies deep within.

CHARLES SPURGEON

1834-1892

PRINCE OF PREACHERS

passover, even the same soul shall be cut off from among his people: because he brought not the offering of the LORD in his appointed season, that man shall bear his sin.

14 And if a stranger shall sojourn among you, and will keep the passover to the LORD; according to the ordinance of the passover, and according to the manner thereof, so shall he do: you shall have one ordinance, both for the stranger, and for him that was born in the land.

15 And on the day that the tabernacle was reared up the cloud covered the tabernacle, namely, the tent of the testimony: and at even there was upon the tabernacle as it were the appearance of fire, until the morning.

16 So it was alway: the cloud covered it by day, and the appearance of fire by night.

17 And when the cloud was taken up from the tabernacle, then after that the children of Israel journeyed: and in the place where the cloud abode, there the children of Israel pitched their tents.

18 At the commandment of the LORD the children of Israel journeyed, and at the commandment of the LORD they pitched: as long as the cloud abode upon the tabernacle they rested in their tents.

19 And when the cloud tarried long upon the tabernacle many days, then the children of Israel kept the charge of the LORD, and journeyed not.

20 And so it was, when the cloud was a few days upon the tabernacle; according to the commandment of the LORD they abode in their tents, and according to

the commandment of the LORD they journeyed.

21 And so it was, when the cloud abode from even to the morning, and that the cloud was taken up in the morning, then they journeyed: whether it was by day or by night that the cloud was taken up, they journeyed.

22 Or whether it were two days, or a month, or a year, that the cloud tarried upon the tabernacle, remaining thereon, the children of Israel abode in their tents, and journeyed not: but when it was taken up, they journeyed.

23 At the commandment of the LORD they rested in the tents, and at the commandment of the LORD they journeyed: they kept the charge of the LORD, at the commandment of the LORD by the hand of Moses.

CHAPTER 10

AND the LORD spoke to Moses, saying,

2 Make you two trumpets of silver; of a whole piece shall you make them: that you may use them for the calling of the assembly, and for the journeying of the camps.

3 And when they shall blow with them, all the assembly shall assemble themselves to you at the door of the tabernacle of the congregation.

4 And if they blow but with one trumpet, then the princes, which are heads of the thousands of Israel, shall gather themselves to you.

5 When you blow an alarm, then the camps that lie on the east parts shall go forward.

6 When you blow an alarm the second time, then the camps that lie on the south side shall take their journey: they shall blow an alarm for their journeys.

7 But when the congregation is to be gathered together, you shall blow, but you shall not sound an alarm.

8 And the sons of Aaron, the priests, shall blow with the trumpets; and they

shall be to you for an ordinance for ever throughout your generations.

9 And if you go to war in your land against the enemy that oppresses you, then you shall blow an alarm with the trumpets; and you shall be remembered before the LORD your God, and you shall be saved from your enemies.

10 Also in the day of your gladness, and in your solemn days, and in the beginnings of your months, you shall blow with the trumpets over your burnt offerings, and over the sacrifices of your peace offerings; that they may be to you for a memorial before your God: I am the LORD your God.

11 And it came to pass on the twentieth day of the second month, in the second year, that the cloud was taken up from off the tabernacle of the testimony.

12 And the children of Israel took their journeys out of the wilderness of Sinai; and the cloud rested in the wilderness of Paran.

13 And they first took their journey according to the commandment of the LORD by the hand of Moses.

14 In the first place went the standard of the camp of the children of Judah according to their armies: and over his host was Nahshon the son of Amminadab.

15 And over the host of the tribe of the children of Issachar was Nethaneel the son of Zuar.

16 And over the host of the tribe of the children of Zebulun was Eliab the son of Helon.

17 And the tabernacle was taken down; and the sons of Gershon and the sons of Merari set forward, bearing the tabernacle.

18 And the standard of the camp of Reuben set forward according to their armies: and over his host was Elizur the son of Shedeur.

19 And over the host of the tribe of the children of Simeon was Shelumiel the son of Zurishaddai.

20 And over the host of the tribe of the children of Gad was Eliasaph the son of Deuel.

21 And the Kohathites set forward, bearing the sanctuary: and the other did set up the tabernacle against they came.

22 And the standard of the camp of the children of Ephraim set forward according to their armies: and over his host was Elishama the son of Ammihud.

23 And over the host of the tribe of the children of Manasseh was Gamaliel the son of Pedahzur.

24 And over the host of the tribe of the children of Benjamin was Abidan the son of Gideoni.

25 And the standard of the camp of the children of Dan set forward, which was the rereward of all the camps throughout their hosts: and over his host was Ahiezer the son of Ammishaddai.

26 And over the host of the tribe of the children of Asher was Pagiel the son of Ocran.

27 And over the host of the tribe of the children of Naphtali was Ahira the son of Enan.

28 Thus were the journeys of the children of Israel according to their armies, when they set forward.

29 And Moses said to Hobab, the son of Raguel the Midianite, Moses' father in law, We are journeying to the place of which the LORD said, I will give it you: come with us, and we will do you good: for the LORD has spoken good concerning Israel.

30 And he said to him, I will not go; but I will depart to mine own land, and to my kindred.

31 And he said, Leave us not, I pray you; forasmuch as you know how we are to encamp in the wilderness, and you may be to us instead of eyes.

32 And it shall be, if you go with us, yea, it shall be, that what goodness the LORD shall do to us, the same will we do to you.

33 And they departed from the mount of the LORD three days' journey: and the

ark of the covenant of the LORD went before them in the three days' journey, to search out a resting place for them.

34 And the cloud of the LORD was upon them by day, when they went out of the camp.

35 And it came to pass, when the ark set forward, that Moses said, Rise up, LORD, and let your enemies be scattered; and let them that hate you flee before you.

36 And when it rested, he said, Return, O LORD, to the many thousands of Israel.

CHAPTER 11

AND when the people complained, it displeased the LORD: and the LORD heard it; and his anger was kindled; and the fire of the LORD burnt among them, and consumed them that were in the uttermost parts of the camp.

2 And the people cried to Moses; and when Moses prayed to the LORD, the fire was quenched.

3 And he called the name of the place Taberah: because the fire of the LORD burnt among them.

4 And the mixt multitude that was among them fell a lusting: and the children of Israel also wept again, and said, Who shall give us flesh to eat?

5 We remember the fish, which we did eat in Egypt freely; the cucumbers, and the melons, and the leeks, and the onions, and the garlick:

6 But now our soul is dried away: there is nothing at all, beside this manna, before our eyes.

7 And the manna was as coriander seed, and the colour thereof as the colour of bdellium.

8 And the people went about, and gathered it, and ground it in mills, or beat it in a mortar, and baked it in pans, and made cakes of it: and the taste of it was as the taste of fresh oil.

9 And when the dew fell upon the camp in the night, the manna fell upon it.

10 Then Moses heard the people weep throughout their families, every man in the door of his tent: and the anger of the LORD was kindled greatly; Moses also was displeased.

11 And Moses said to the LORD, Why have you afflicted your servant? and why have I not found favour in your sight, that you lay the burden of all this people upon me?

12 Have I conceived all this people? have I begotten them, that you should say to me, Carry them in your bosom, as a nursing father bears the sucking child, to the land which you swore to their fathers?

13 Whence should I have flesh to give to all this people? for they weep to me, saying, Give us flesh, that we may eat.

14 I am not able to bear all this people alone, because it is too heavy for me.

15 And if you deal thus with me, kill me, I pray you, out of hand, if I have found favour in your sight; and let me not see my wretchedness.

16 And the LORD said to Moses, Gather to me seventy men of the elders of Israel, whom you know to be the elders of the people, and officers over them; and bring them to the tabernacle of the congregation, that they may stand there with you.

17 And I will come down and talk with you there: and I will take of the spirit which is upon you, and will put it upon them; and they shall bear the burden of the people with you, that you bear it not yourself alone.

18 And say to the people, Sanctify yourselves against to morrow, and you shall eat flesh: for you have wept in the ears of the LORD, saying, Who shall give us flesh to eat? for it was well with us in Egypt: therefore the LORD will give you flesh, and you shall eat.

19 You shall not eat one day, nor two days, nor five days, neither ten days, nor twenty days;

20 But even a whole month, until it come out at your nostrils, and it be

loathsome to you: because that you have despised the LORD which is among you, and have wept before him, saying, Why came we forth out of Egypt?

21 And Moses said, The people, among whom I am, are six hundred thousand footmen; and you have said, I will give them flesh, that they may eat a whole month.

22 Shall the flocks and the herds be slain for them, to suffice them? or shall all the fish of the sea be gathered together for them, to suffice them?

23 And the LORD said to Moses, Is the LORD's hand waxed short? you shall see now whether my word shall come to pass to you or not.

24 And Moses went out, and told the people the words of the LORD, and gathered the seventy men of the elders of the people, and set them round about the tabernacle.

25 And the LORD came down in a cloud, and spoke to him, and took of the spirit that was upon him, and gave it to the seventy elders: and it came to pass, that, when the spirit rested upon them, they prophesied, and did not cease.

26 But there remained two of the men in the camp, the name of the one was Eldad, and the name of the other Medad: and the spirit rested upon them; and they were of them that were written, but went not out to the tabernacle: and they prophesied in the camp.

27 And there ran a young man, and told Moses, and said, Eldad and Medad do prophesy in the camp.

28 And Joshua the son of Nun, the servant of Moses, one of his young men, answered and said, My lord Moses, forbid them.

29 And Moses said to him, are you jealous for my sake? would God that all the LORD's people were prophets, and that the LORD would put his spirit upon them!

30 And Moses gat him into the camp, he and the elders of Israel.

31 And there went forth a wind from the LORD, and brought quails from the sea, and let them fall by the camp, as it were a day's journey on this side, and as it were a day's journey on the other side, round about the camp, and as it were two cubits high upon the face of the earth.

32 And the people stood up all that day, and all that night, and all the next day, and they gathered the quails: he that gathered least gathered ten homers: and they spread them all abroad for themselves round about the camp.

33 And while the flesh was yet between their teeth, ere it was chewed, the wrath of the LORD was kindled against the people, and the LORD smote the people with a very great plague.

34 And he called the name of that place Kibrothhattaavah: because there they buried the people that lusted.

35 And the people journeyed from Kibrothhattaavah to Hazeroth; and abode at Hazeroth.

CHAPTER 12

AND Miriam and Aaron spoke against Moses because of the Ethiopian woman whom he had married: for he had married an Ethiopian woman.

2 And they said, Has the LORD indeed spoken only by Moses? has he not spoken also by us? And the LORD heard it.

3 (Now the man Moses was very meek, above all the men which were upon the face of the earth.)

4 And the LORD spoke suddenly to Moses, and to Aaron, and to Miriam, Come out you three to the tabernacle of the congregation. And they three came out.

5 And the LORD came down in the pillar of the cloud, and stood in the door of the tabernacle, and called Aaron and Miriam: and they both came forth.

6 And he said, Hear now my words: If there be a prophet among you, I the LORD will make myself known to him

in a vision, and will speak to him in a dream.

7 My servant Moses is not so, who is faithful in all mine house.

8 With him will I speak mouth to mouth, even apparently, and not in dark speeches; and the similitude of the LORD shall he behold: why then were you not afraid to speak against my servant Moses?

9 And the anger of the LORD was kindled against them; and he departed.

10 And the cloud departed from off the tabernacle; and, behold, Miriam became leprous, white as snow: and Aaron looked upon Miriam, and, behold, she was leprous.

11 And Aaron said to Moses, Alas, my lord, I beseech you, lay not the sin upon us, wherein we have done foolishly, and wherein we have sinned.

12 Let her not be as one dead, of whom the flesh is half consumed when he cometh out of his mother's womb.

13 And Moses cried to the LORD, saying, Heal her now, O God, I beseech you.

14 And the LORD said to Moses, If her father had but spit in her face, should she not be ashamed seven days? let her be shut out from the camp seven days, and after that let her be received in again.

15 And Miriam was shut out from the camp seven days: and the people journeyed not till Miriam was brought in again.

16 And afterward the people removed from Hazeroth, and pitched in the wilderness of Paran.

CHAPTER 13

AND the LORD spoke to Moses, saying,

2 Send men, that they may search the land of Canaan, which I give to the children of Israel: of every tribe of their fathers shall you send a man, every one a ruler among them.

3 And Moses by the commandment of the LORD sent them from the wilderness of Paran: all those men were heads of the children of Israel.

4 And these were their names: of the tribe of Reuben, Shammua the son of Zaccur.

5 Of the tribe of Simeon, Shaphat the son of Hori.

6 Of the tribe of Judah, Caleb the son of Jephunneh.

7 Of the tribe of Issachar, Igal the son of Joseph.

8 Of the tribe of Ephraim, Oshea the son of Nun.

9 Of the tribe of Benjamin, Palti the son of Raphu.

10 Of the tribe of Zebulun, Gaddiel the son of Sodi.

11 Of the tribe of Joseph, namely, of the tribe of Manasseh, Gaddi the son of Susi.

12 Of the tribe of Dan, Ammiel the son of Gemalli.

13 Of the tribe of Asher, Sethur the son of Michael.

14 Of the tribe of Naphtali, Nahbi the son of Vophsi.

15 Of the tribe of Gad, Geuel the son of Machi.

16 These are the names of the men which Moses sent to spy out the land. And Moses called Oshea the son of Nun Jehoshua.

17 And Moses sent them to spy out the land of Canaan, and said to them, Get you up this way southward, and go up into the mountain:

18 And see the land, what it is, and the people that dwelleth therein, whether they be strong or weak, few or many;

19 And what the land is that they dwell in, whether it be good or bad; and what cities they be that they dwell in, whether in tents, or in strong holds;

20 And what the land is, whether it be fat or lean, whether there be wood therein, or not. And be of good courage, and bring of the fruit of the land. Now the time was the time of the firstripe grapes.

RETURN OF THE SPIES FROM THE LAND OF PROMISE

Numbers 13:26-27

21 So they went up, and searched the land from the wilderness of Zin to Rehob, as men come to Hamath.

22 And they ascended by the south, and came to Hebron; where Ahiman, Sheshai, and Talmai, the children of Anak, were. (Now Hebron was built seven years before Zoan in Egypt.)

23 And they came to the brook of Eshcol, and cut down from thence a branch with one cluster of grapes, and they bare it between two upon a staff; and they brought of the pomegranates, and of the figs.

24 The place was called the brook Eshcol, because of the cluster of grapes which the children of Israel cut down from thence.

25 And they returned from searching of the land after forty days.

26 And they went and came to Moses, and to Aaron, and to all the congregation of the children of Israel, to the wilderness of Paran, to Kadesh; and brought back word to them, and to all the congregation, and showed them the fruit of the land.

27 And they told him, and said, We came to the land whither you sent us,

and surely it flows with milk and honey; and this is the fruit of it.

28 Nevertheless the people be strong that dwell in the land, and the cities are walled, and very great: and moreover we saw the children of Anak there.

29 The Amalekites dwell in the land of the south: and the Hittites, and the Jebusites, and the Amorites, dwell in the mountains: and the Canaanites dwell by the sea, and by the coast of Jordan.

30 And Caleb stilled the people before Moses, and said, Let us go up at once, and possess it; for we are well able to overcome it.

31 But the men that went up with him said, We be not able to go up against the people; for they are stronger than we.

32 And they brought up an evil report of the land which they had searched to the children of Israel, saying, The land, through which we have gone to search it, is a land that eats up the inhabitants thereof; and all the people that we saw in it are men of a great stature.

33 And there we saw the giants, the sons of Anak, which come of the giants: and we were in our own sight as grasshoppers, and so we were in their sight.

CHAPTER 14

AND all the congregation lifted up their voice, and cried; and the people wept that night.

2 And all the children of Israel murmured against Moses and against Aaron: and the whole congregation said to them, Would God that we had died in the land of Egypt! or would God we had died in this wilderness!

3 And why has the LORD brought us to this land, to fall by the sword, that our wives and our children should be a prey? were it not better for us to return into Egypt?

4 And they said one to another, Let us make a captain, and let us return into Egypt.

5 Then Moses and Aaron fell on their faces before all the assembly of the congregation of the children of Israel.

6 And Joshua the son of Nun, and Caleb the son of Jephunneh, which were of them that searched the land, rent their clothes:

7 And they spoke to all the company of the children of Israel, saying, The land, which we passed through to search it, is an exceeding good land.

8 If the LORD delight in us, then he will bring us into this land, and give it us; a land which flows with milk and honey.

9 Only rebel not against the LORD, neither fear the people of the land; for they are bread for us: their defence is departed from them, and the LORD is with us: fear them not.

10 But all the congregation bade stone them with stones. And the glory of the LORD appeared in the tabernacle of the congregation before all the children of Israel.

11 And the LORD said to Moses, How long will this people provoke me? and how long will it be ere they believe me, for all the signs which I have showed among them?

12 I will smite them with the pestilence, and disinherit them, and will make of you a greater nation and mightier than they.

13 And Moses said to the LORD, Then the Egyptians shall hear it, (for you brought up this people in your might from among them;)

14 And they will tell it to the inhabitants of this land: for they have heard that you LORD are among this people, that you LORD are seen face to face, and that your cloud stands over them, and that you go before them, by day time in a pillar of a cloud, and in a pillar of fire by night.

15 Now if you shall kill all this people as one man, then the nations which have heard the fame of you will speak, saying,

16 Because the LORD was not able to

bring this people into the land which he swore to them, therefore he has slain them in the wilderness.

17 And now, I beseech you, let the power of my LORD be great, according as you have spoken, saying,

18 The LORD is longsuffering, and of great mercy, forgiving iniquity and transgression, and by no means clearing the guilty, visiting the iniquity of the fathers upon the children to the third and fourth generation.

19 Pardon, I beseech you, the iniquity of this people according to the greatness of your mercy, and as you have forgiven this people, from Egypt even until now.

20 And the LORD said, I have pardoned according to your word:

21 But as truly as I live, all the earth shall be filled with the glory of the LORD.

22 Because all those men which have seen my glory, and my miracles, which I did in Egypt and in the wilderness, and have tempted me now these ten times, and have not hearkened to my voice;

23 Surely they shall not see the land which I swore to their fathers, neither shall any of them that provoked me see it:

24 But my servant Caleb, because he had another spirit with him, and has followed me fully, him will I bring into the land whereinto he went; and his seed shall possess it.

25 (Now the Amalekites and the Canaanites dwelt in the valley.) Tomorrow turn you, and get you into the wilderness by the way of the Red sea.

26 And the LORD spoke to Moses and to Aaron, saying,

27 How long shall I bear with this evil congregation, which murmur against me? I have heard the murmurings of the children of Israel, which they murmur against me.

28 Say to them, As truly as I live, says the LORD, as you have spoken in mine ears, so will I do to you:

29 Your carcases shall fall in this wilderness; and all that were numbered of you, according to your whole number, from twenty years old and upward which have murmured against me.

30 Doubtless you shall not come into the land, concerning which I swore to make you dwell therein, save Caleb the son of Jephunneh, and Joshua the son of Nun.

31 But your little ones, which you said should be a prey, them will I bring in, and they shall know the land which you have despised.

32 But as for you, your carcases, they shall fall in this wilderness.

33 And your children shall wander in the wilderness forty years, and bear your whoredoms, until your carcases be wasted in the wilderness.

34 After the number of the days in which you searched the land, even forty days, each day for a year, shall you bear your iniquities, even forty years, and you shall know my breach of promise.

35 I the LORD have said, I will surely do it to all this evil congregation, that are gathered together against me: in this wilderness they shall be consumed, and there they shall die.

36 And the men, which Moses sent to search the land, who returned, and made all the congregation to murmur against him, by bringing up a slander upon the land,

37 Even those men that did bring up the evil report upon the land, died by the plague before the LORD.

38 But Joshua the son of Nun, and Caleb the son of Jephunneh, which were of the men that went to search the land, lived still.

39 And Moses told these sayings to all the children of Israel: and the people mourned greatly.

40 And they rose up early in the morning, and gat them up into the top of the mountain, saying, Lo, we be here, and will go up to the place which the LORD has promised: for we have sinned.

41 And Moses said, Why now do you transgress the commandment of the LORD? but it shall not prosper.

42 Go not up, for the LORD is not among you; that you be not smitten before your enemies.

43 For the Amalekites and the Canaanites are there before you, and you shall fall by the sword: because you are turned away from the LORD, therefore the LORD will not be with you.

44 But they presumed to go up to the hill top: nevertheless the ark of the covenant of the LORD, and Moses, departed not out of the camp.

45 Then the Amalekites came down, and the Canaanites which dwelt in that hill, and smote them, and discomfited them, even to Hormah.

CHAPTER 15

AND the LORD spoke to Moses, saying,

2 Speak to the children of Israel, and say to them, When you be come into the land of your habitations, which I give to you,

3 And will make an offering by fire to the LORD, a burnt offering, or a sacrifice in performing a vow, or in a freewill offering, or in your solemn feasts, to make a sweet savour to the LORD, of the herd or of the flock:

4 Then shall he that offers his offering to the LORD bring a meat offering of a tenth deal of flour mingled with the fourth part of an hin of oil.

5 And the fourth part of an hin of wine for a drink offering shall you prepare with the burnt offering or sacrifice, for one lamb.

6 Or for a ram, you shall prepare for a meat offering two tenth deals of flour mingled with the third part of an hin of oil.

7 And for a drink offering you shall offer the third part of an hin of wine, for a sweet savour to the LORD.

8 And when you prepare a bullock for a burnt offering, or for a sacrifice in per-

forming a vow, or peace offerings to the LORD:

9 Then shall he bring with a bullock a meat offering of three tenth deals of flour mingled with half an hin of oil.

10 And you shall bring for a drink offering half an hin of wine, for an offering made by fire, of a sweet savour to the LORD.

11 Thus shall it be done for one bullock, or for one ram, or for a lamb, or a kid.

12 According to the number that you shall prepare, so shall you do to every one according to their number.

13 All that are born of the country shall do these things after this manner, in offering an offering made by fire, of a sweet savour to the LORD.

14 And if a stranger sojourn with you, or whosoever be among you in your generations, and will offer an offering made by fire, of a sweet savour to the LORD; as you do, so he shall do.

15 One ordinance shall be both for you of the congregation, and also for the stranger that sojourns with you, an ordinance for ever in your generations: as you are, so shall the stranger be before the LORD.

16 One law and one manner shall be for you, and for the stranger that sojourns with you.

17 And the LORD spoke to Moses, saying,

18 Speak to the children of Israel, and say to them, When you come into the land whither I bring you,

19 Then it shall be, that, when you eat of the bread of the land, you shall offer up an heave offering to the LORD.

20 You shall offer up a cake of the first of your dough for an heave offering: as you do the heave offering of the threshingfloor, so shall you heave it.

21 Of the first of your dough you shall give to the LORD an heave offering in your generations.

22 And if you have erred, and not observed all these commandments, which the LORD has spoken to Moses,

23 Even all that the LORD has commanded you by the hand of Moses, from the day that the LORD commanded Moses, and henceforward among your generations;

24 Then it shall be, if ought be committed by ignorance without the knowledge of the congregation, that all the congregation shall offer one young bullock for a burnt offering, for a sweet savour to the LORD, with his meat offering, and his drink offering, according to the manner, and one kid of the goats for a sin offering.

25 And the priest shall make an atonement for all the congregation of the children of Israel, and it shall be forgiven them; for it is ignorance: and they shall bring their offering, a sacrifice made by fire to the LORD, and their sin offering before the LORD, for their ignorance:

26 And it shall be forgiven all the congregation of the children of Israel, and the stranger that sojourns among them; seeing all the people were in ignorance.

27 And if any soul sin through ignorance, then he shall bring a she goat of the first year for a sin offering.

28 And the priest shall make an atonement for the soul that sins ignorantly, when he sins by ignorance before the LORD, to make an atonement for him; and it shall be forgiven him.

29 You shall have one law for him that sins through ignorance, both for him that is born among the children of Israel, and for the stranger that sojourns among them.

30 But the soul that doeth ought presumptuously, whether he be born in the land, or a stranger, the same reproaches the LORD; and that soul shall be cut off from among his people.

31 Because he has despised the word of the LORD, and has broken his commandment, that soul shall utterly be cut off; his iniquity shall be upon him.

32 And while the children of Israel were in the wilderness, they found a man that gathered sticks upon the sabbath day.

33 And they that found him gathering sticks brought him to Moses and Aaron, and to all the congregation.

34 And they put him in ward, because it was not declared what should be done to him.

35 And the LORD said to Moses, The man shall be surely put to death: all the congregation shall stone him with stones without the camp.

36 And all the congregation brought him without the camp, and stoned him with stones, and he died; as the LORD commanded Moses.

37 And the LORD spoke to Moses, saying,

38 Speak to the children of Israel, and bid them that they make them fringes in the borders of their garments throughout their generations, and that they put upon the fringe of the borders a ribband of blue:

39 And it shall be to you for a fringe, that you may look upon it, and remember all the commandments of the LORD, and do them; and that you seek not after your own heart and your own eyes, after which you use to go a whoring:

40 That you may remember, and do all my commandments, and be holy to your God.

41 I am the LORD your God, which brought you out of the land of Egypt, to be your God: I am the LORD your God.

15:32–36 These verses show how God's Law is without mercy. Those who object to the harshness of this Law should realize that it is this same Law that will judge them on Judgment Day. Such thoughts should make us flee evil and cleave to the Savior.

CHAPTER 16

NOW Korah, the son of Izhar, the son of Kohath, the son of Levi, and Dathan and Abiram, the sons of Eliab, and On, the son of Peleth, sons of Reuben, took men:

2 And they rose up before Moses, with certain of the children of Israel, two hundred and fifty princes of the assembly, famous in the congregation, men of renown:

3 And they gathered themselves together against Moses and against Aaron, and said to them, You take too much upon you, seeing all the congregation are holy, every one of them, and the LORD is among them: why then lift up yourselves above the congregation of the LORD?

4 And when Moses heard it, he fell upon his face:

5 And he spoke to Korah and to all his company, saying, Even tomorrow the LORD will show who are his, and who is holy; and will cause him to come near to him: even him whom he has chosen will he cause to come near to him.

6 This do; Take you censers, Korah, and all his company;

7 And put fire therein, and put incense in them before the LORD tomorrow: and it shall be that the man whom the LORD doth choose, he shall be holy: you take too much upon you, you sons of Levi.

8 And Moses said to Korah, Hear, I pray you, you sons of Levi:

9 Seems it but a small thing to you, that the God of Israel has separated you from the congregation of Israel, to bring you near to himself to do the service of the tabernacle of the LORD, and to stand before the congregation to minister to them?

10 And he has brought you near to him, and all your brethren the sons of Levi with you: and seek you the priesthood also?

11 For which cause both you and all your company are gathered together against the LORD: and what is Aaron, that you murmur against him?

12 And Moses sent to call Dathan and Abiram, the sons of Eliab: which said, We will not come up:

13 Is it a small thing that you have brought us up out of a land that flows with milk and honey, to kill us in the wilderness, except you make yourself altogether a prince over us?

14 Moreover you have not brought us into a land that flows with milk and honey, or given us inheritance of fields and vineyards: will you put out the eyes of these men? we will not come up.

15 And Moses was very wroth, and said to the LORD, Respect not you their offering: I have not taken one ass from them, neither have I hurt one of them.

16 And Moses said to Korah, Be you and all your company before the LORD, you, and they, and Aaron, tomorrow:

17 And take every man his censer, and put incense in them, and bring before the LORD every man his censer, two hundred and fifty censers; you also, and Aaron, each of you his censer.

18 And they took every man his censer, and put fire in them, and laid incense thereon, and stood in the door of the tabernacle of the congregation with Moses and Aaron.

19 And Korah gathered all the congregation against them to the door of the tabernacle of the congregation: and the glory of the LORD appeared to all the congregation.

20 And the LORD spoke to Moses and to Aaron, saying,

21 Separate yourselves from among this congregation, that I may consume them in a moment.

22 And they fell upon their faces, and said, O God, the God of the spirits of all flesh, shall one man sin, and will you be wroth with all the congregation?

23 And the LORD spoke to Moses, saying,

24 Speak to the congregation, saying, Get you up from about the tabernacle of Korah, Dathan, and Abiram.

25 And Moses rose up and went to Dathan and Abiram; and the elders of Israel followed him.

26 And he spoke to the congregation, saying, Depart, I pray you, from the tents of these wicked men, and touch nothing of their's, lest you be consumed in all their sins.

27 So they gat up from the tabernacle of Korah, Dathan, and Abiram, on every side: and Dathan and Abiram came out, and stood in the door of their tents, and their wives, and their sons, and their little children.

28 And Moses said, Hereby you shall know that the LORD has sent me to do all these works; for I have not done them of mine own mind.

29 If these men die the common death of all men, or if they be visited after the visitation of all men; then the LORD has not sent me.

30 But if the LORD make a new thing, and the earth open her mouth, and swallow them up, with all that appertain to them, and they go down quick into the pit; then you shall understand that these men have provoked the LORD.

31 And it came to pass, as he had made an end of speaking all these words, that the ground clave asunder that was under them:

32 And the earth opened her mouth, and swallowed them up, and their houses, and all the men that appertained to Korah, and all their goods.

33 They, and all that appertained to them, went down alive into the pit, and the earth closed upon them: and they perished from among the congregation.

34 And all Israel that were round about them fled at the cry of them: for they said, Lest the earth swallow us up also.

35 And there came out a fire from the LORD, and consumed the two hundred and fifty men that offered incense.

36 And the LORD spoke to Moses, saying,

37 Speak to Eleazar the son of Aaron the priest, that he take up the censers out of the burning, and scatter the fire yonder; for they are hallowed.

38 The censers of these sinners against their own souls, let them make them broad plates for a covering of the altar: for they offered them before the LORD, therefore they are hallowed: and they shall be a sign to the children of Israel.

39 And Eleazar the priest took the brasen censers, wherewith they that were burnt had offered; and they were made broad plates for a covering of the altar:

40 To be a memorial to the children of Israel, that no stranger, which is not of the seed of Aaron, come near to offer incense before the LORD; that he be not as Korah, and as his company: as the LORD said to him by the hand of Moses.

41 But on the morrow all the congregation of the children of Israel murmured against Moses and against Aaron, saying, You have killed the people of the LORD.

42 And it came to pass, when the congregation was gathered against Moses and against Aaron, that they looked toward the tabernacle of the congregation: and, behold, the cloud covered it, and the glory of the LORD appeared.

43 And Moses and Aaron came before the tabernacle of the congregation.

44 And the LORD spoke to Moses, saying,

45 Get you up from among this congregation, that I may consume them as in a moment. And they fell upon their faces.

46 And Moses said to Aaron, Take a censer, and put fire therein from off the altar, and put on incense, and go quickly to the congregation, and make an atonement for them: for there is wrath gone out from the LORD; the plague is begun.

47 And Aaron took as Moses commanded, and ran into the midst of the congregation; and, behold, the plague was begun among the people: and he put on incense, and made an atonement for the people.

48 And he stood between the dead and the living; and the plague was stayed.

49 Now they that died in the plague were fourteen thousand and seven hundred, beside them that died about the matter of Korah.

50 And Aaron returned to Moses to the door of the tabernacle of the congregation: and the plague was stayed.

CHAPTER 17

AND the LORD spoke to Moses, saying,

2 Speak to the children of Israel, and take of every one of them a rod according to the house of their fathers, of all their princes according to the house of their fathers twelve rods: write every man's name upon his rod.

3 And you shall write Aaron's name upon the rod of Levi: for one rod shall be for the head of the house of their fathers.

4 And you shall lay them up in the tabernacle of the congregation before the testimony, where I will meet with you.

5 And it shall come to pass, that the man's rod, whom I shall choose, shall blossom: and I will make to cease from me the murmurings of the children of Israel, whereby they murmur against you.

6 And Moses spoke to the children of Israel, and every one of their princes gave him a rod apiece, for each prince one, according to their fathers' houses, even twelve rods: and the rod of Aaron was among their rods.

7 And Moses laid up the rods before the LORD in the tabernacle of witness.

8 And it came to pass, that on the morrow Moses went into the tabernacle of witness; and, behold, the rod of Aaron for the house of Levi was budded, and brought forth buds, and bloomed blossoms, and yielded almonds.

9 And Moses brought out all the rods from before the LORD to all the children of Israel: and they looked, and took every man his rod.

10 And the LORD said to Moses, Bring Aaron's rod again before the testimony, to be kept for a token against the rebels; and you shall quite take away their murmurings from me, that they die not.

11 And Moses did so: as the LORD commanded him, so did he.

12 And the children of Israel spoke to Moses, saying, Behold, we die, we perish, we all perish.

13 Whosoever comes any where near to the tabernacle of the LORD shall die: shall we be consumed with dying?

CHAPTER 18

AND the LORD said to Aaron, You and your sons and your father's house with you shall bear the iniquity of the sanctuary: and you and your sons with you shall bear the iniquity of your priesthood.

2 And your brethren also of the tribe of Levi, the tribe of your father, bring with you, that they may be joined to you, and minister to you: but you and your sons with you shall minister before the tabernacle of witness.

3 And they shall keep your charge, and the charge of all the tabernacle: only they shall not come nigh the vessels of the sanctuary and the altar, that neither they, nor you also, die.

4 And they shall be joined to you, and keep the charge of the tabernacle of the congregation, for all the service of the tabernacle: and a stranger shall not come nigh to you.

5 And you shall keep the charge of the sanctuary, and the charge of the altar: that there be no wrath any more upon the children of Israel.

6 And I, behold, I have taken your brethren the Levites from among the children of Israel: to you they are given as a gift for the LORD, to do the service of the tabernacle of the congregation.

7 Therefore you and your sons with you shall keep your priest's office for everything of the altar, and within the vail; and you shall serve: I have given your priest's office to you as a service of gift:

and the stranger that cometh nigh shall be put to death.

8 And the LORD spoke to Aaron, Behold, I also have given you the charge of mine heave offerings of all the hallowed things of the children of Israel; to you have I given them by reason of the anointing, and to your sons, by an ordinance for ever.

9 This shall be yours of the most holy things, reserved from the fire: every oblation of theirs, every meat offering of theirs, and every sin offering of theirs, and every trespass offering of theirs which they shall render to me, shall be most holy for you and for your sons.

10 In the most holy place shall you eat it; every male shall eat it: it shall be holy to you.

11 And this is yours; the heave offering of their gift, with all the wave offerings of the children of Israel: I have given them to you, and to your sons and to your daughters with you, by a statute for ever: every one that is clean in your house shall eat of it.

12 All the best of the oil, and all the best of the wine, and of the wheat, the firstfruits of them which they shall offer to the LORD, them have I given you.

13 And whatsoever is first ripe in the land, which they shall bring to the LORD, shall be yours; every one that is clean in your house shall eat of it.

14 Every thing devoted in Israel shall be yours.

15 Every thing that opens the matrix in all flesh, which they bring to the LORD, whether it be of men or beasts, shall be yours: nevertheless the firstborn of man shall you surely redeem, and the firstling of unclean beasts shall you redeem.

16 And those that are to be redeemed from a month old shall you redeem, according to your estimation, for the money of five shekels, after the shekel of the sanctuary, which is twenty gerahs.

17 But the firstling of a cow, or the firstling of a sheep, or the firstling of a goat, you shall not redeem; they are

holy: you shall sprinkle their blood upon the altar, and shall burn their fat for an offering made by fire, for a sweet savour to the LORD.

18 And the flesh of them shall be yours, as the wave breast and as the right shoulder are yours.

19 All the heave offerings of the holy things, which the children of Israel offer to the LORD, have I given you, and your sons and your daughters with you, by a statute for ever: it is a covenant of salt for ever before the LORD to you and to your seed with you.

20 And the LORD spoke to Aaron, You shall have no inheritance in their land, neither shall you have any part among them: I am your part and your inheritance among the children of Israel.

21 And, behold, I have given the children of Levi all the tenth in Israel for an inheritance, for their service which they serve, even the service of the tabernacle of the congregation.

22 Neither must the children of Israel henceforth come nigh the tabernacle of the congregation, lest they bear sin, and die.

23 But the Levites shall do the service of the tabernacle of the congregation, and they shall bear their iniquity: it shall be a statute for ever throughout your generations, that among the children of Israel they have no inheritance.

24 But the tithes of the children of Israel, which they offer as an heave offering to the LORD, I have given to the Levites to inherit: therefore I have said to them, Among the children of Israel they shall have no inheritance.

25 And the LORD spoke to Moses, saying,

26 Thus speak to the Levites, and say to them, When you take of the children of Israel the tithes which I have given you from them for your inheritance, then you shall offer up an heave offering of it for the LORD, even a tenth part of the tithe.

27 And this your heave offering shall be reckoned to you, as though it were the corn of the threshingfloor, and as the fullness of the winepress.

28 Thus you also shall offer an heave offering to the LORD of all your tithes, which you receive of the children of Israel; and you shall give thereof the LORD's heave offering to Aaron the priest.

29 Out of all your gifts you shall offer every heave offering of the LORD, of all the best thereof, even the hallowed part thereof out of it.

30 Therefore you shall say to them, When you have heaved the best thereof from it, then it shall be counted to the Levites as the increase of the threshingfloor, and as the increase of the winepress.

31 And you shall eat it in every place, you and your households: for it is your reward for your service in the tabernacle of the congregation.

32 And you shall bear no sin by reason of it, when you have heaved from it the best of it: neither shall you pollute the holy things of the children of Israel, lest you die.

CHAPTER 19

AND the LORD spoke to Moses and to Aaron, saying,

2 This is the ordinance of the law which the LORD has commanded, saying, Speak to the children of Israel, that they bring you a red heifer without spot, wherein is no blemish, and upon which never came yoke:

3 And you shall give her to Eleazar the priest, that he may bring her forth without the camp, and one shall slay her before his face:

4 And Eleazar the priest shall take of her blood with his finger, and sprinkle of her blood directly before the tabernacle of the congregation seven times:

5 And one shall burn the heifer in his sight; her skin, and her flesh, and her blood, with her dung, shall he burn:

6 And the priest shall take cedar wood, and hyssop, and scarlet, and cast it into the midst of the burning of the heifer.

7 Then the priest shall wash his clothes, and he shall bathe his flesh in water, and afterward he shall come into the camp, and the priest shall be unclean until the even.

8 And he that burns her shall wash his clothes in water, and bathe his flesh in water, and shall be unclean until the even.

9 And a man that is clean shall gather up the ashes of the heifer, and lay them up without the camp in a clean place, and it shall be kept for the congregation of the children of Israel for a water of separation: it is a purification for sin.

10 And he that gathers the ashes of the heifer shall wash his clothes, and be unclean until the even: and it shall be to the children of Israel, and to the stranger that sojourns among them, for a statute for ever.

11 He that touches the dead body of any man shall be unclean seven days.

12 He shall purify himself with it on the third day, and on the seventh day he shall be clean: but if he purify not himself the third day, then the seventh day he shall not be clean.

13 Whosoever touches the dead body of any man that is dead, and purifies not himself, defiles the tabernacle of the LORD; and that soul shall be cut off from Israel: because the water of separation was not sprinkled upon him, he shall be unclean; his uncleanness is yet upon him.

14 This is the law, when a man dies in a tent: all that come into the tent, and all that is in the tent, shall be unclean seven days.

15 And every open vessel, which has no covering bound upon it, is unclean.

16 And whosoever touches one that is slain with a sword in the open fields, or a dead body, or a bone of a man, or a grave, shall be unclean seven days.

17 And for an unclean person they shall take of the ashes of the burnt heifer of purification for sin, and running water shall be put thereto in a vessel:

18 And a clean person shall take hyssop, and dip it in the water, and sprinkle it upon the tent, and upon all the vessels, and upon the persons that were there, and upon him that touched a bone, or one slain, or one dead, or a grave:

19 And the clean person shall sprinkle upon the unclean on the third day, and on the seventh day: and on the seventh day he shall purify himself, and wash his clothes, and bathe himself in water, and shall be clean at even.

20 But the man that shall be unclean, and shall not purify himself, that soul shall be cut off from among the congregation, because he has defiled the sanctuary of the LORD: the water of separation has not been sprinkled upon him; he is unclean.

21 And it shall be a perpetual statute to them, that he that sprinkles the water of separation shall wash his clothes; and he that touches the water of separation shall be unclean until even.

22 And whatsoever the unclean person touches shall be unclean; and the soul that touches it shall be unclean until even.

CHAPTER 20

THEN came the children of Israel, even the whole congregation, into the desert of Zin in the first month: and the people abode in Kadesh; and Miriam died there, and was buried there.

2 And there was no water for the congregation: and they gathered themselves together against Moses and against Aaron.

3 And the people chode with Moses, and spoke, saying, Would God that we had died when our brethren died before the LORD!

4 And why have you brought up the congregation of the LORD into this wilderness, that we and our cattle should die there?

5 And why have you made us to come up out of Egypt, to bring us in to this evil place? it is no place of seed, or of figs, or of vines, or of pomegranates; neither is there any water to drink.

6 And Moses and Aaron went from the presence of the assembly to the door of the tabernacle of the congregation, and they fell upon their faces: and the glory of the LORD appeared to them.

7 And the LORD spoke to Moses, saying,

8 Take the rod, and gather the assembly together, you, and Aaron your brother, and speak to the rock before their eyes; and it shall give forth his water, and you shall bring forth to them water out of the rock: so you shall give the congregation and their beasts drink.

9 And Moses took the rod from before the LORD, as he commanded him.

10 And Moses and Aaron gathered the congregation together before the rock, and he said to them, Hear now, you rebels; must we fetch you water out of this rock?

11 And Moses lifted up his hand, and with his rod he smote the rock twice: and the water came out abundantly, and the congregation drank, and their beasts also.

12 And the LORD spoke to Moses and Aaron, Because you believed me not, to sanctify me in the eyes of the children of Israel, therefore you shall not bring this congregation into the land which I have given them.

13 This is the water of Meribah; because the children of Israel strove with the LORD, and he was sanctified in them.

14 And Moses sent messengers from Kadesh to the king of Edom, Thus says your brother Israel, You know all the travail that has befallen us:

15 How our fathers went down into Egypt, and we have dwelt in Egypt

a long time; and the Egyptians vexed us, and our fathers:

16 And when we cried to the LORD, he heard our voice, and sent an angel, and has brought us forth out of Egypt: and, behold, we are in Kadesh, a city in the uttermost of your border:

17 Let us pass, I pray you, through your country: we will not pass through the fields, or through the vineyards, neither will we drink of the water of the wells: we will go by the king's high way, we will not turn to the right hand nor to the left, until we have passed your borders.

18 And Edom said to him, You shall not pass by me, lest I come out against you with the sword.

19 And the children of Israel said to him, We will go by the high way: and if I and my cattle drink of your water, then I will pay for it: I will only, without doing anything else, go through on my feet.

20 And he said, You shall not go through. And Edom came out against him with much people, and with a strong hand.

21 Thus Edom refused to give Israel passage through his border: therefore Israel turned away from him.

22 And the children of Israel, even the whole congregation, journeyed from Kadesh, and came to mount Hor.

23 And the LORD spoke to Moses and Aaron in mount Hor, by the coast of the land of Edom, saying,

24 Aaron shall be gathered to his people: for he shall not enter into the land which I have given to the children of Israel, because you rebelled against my word at the water of Meribah.

25 Take Aaron and Eleazar his son, and bring them up to mount Hor:

26 And strip Aaron of his garments, and put them upon Eleazar his son: and Aaron shall be gathered to his people, and shall die there.

27 And Moses did as the LORD commanded: and they went up into mount Hor in the sight of all the congregation.

28 And Moses stripped Aaron of his garments, and put them upon Eleazar his son; and Aaron died there in the top of the mount: and Moses and Eleazar came down from the mount.

29 And when all the congregation saw that Aaron was dead, they mourned for Aaron thirty days, even all the house of Israel.

CHAPTER 21

AND when king Arad the Canaanite, which dwelt in the south, heard tell that Israel came by the way of the spies; then he fought against Israel, and took some of them prisoners.

2 And Israel vowed a vow to the LORD, and said, If you will indeed deliver this people into my hand, then I will utterly destroy their cities.

3 And the LORD hearkened to the voice of Israel, and delivered up the Canaanites; and they utterly destroyed them and their cities: and he called the name of the place Hormah.

4 And they journeyed from mount Hor by the way of the Red sea, to compass the land of Edom: and the soul of the people was much discouraged because of the way.

5 And the people spoke against God, and against Moses, Why have you brought us up out of Egypt to die in the wilderness? for there is no bread, neither is there any water; and our soul loathes this light bread.

6 And the LORD sent fiery serpents among the people, and they bit the people; and much people of Israel died.

7 Therefore the people came to Moses, and said, We have sinned, for we have spoken against the LORD, and against you; pray to the LORD, that he take away the serpents from us. And Moses prayed for the people.

8 And the LORD said to Moses, Make you a fiery serpent, and set it upon a pole: and it shall come to pass, that every one that is bitten, when he looks upon it, shall live.

9 And Moses made a serpent of brass, and put it upon a pole, and it came to pass, that if a serpent had bitten any man, when he beheld the serpent of brass, he lived.

10 And the children of Israel set forward, and pitched in Oboth.

11 And they journeyed from Oboth, and pitched at Ijeabarim, in the wilderness which is before Moab, toward the sunrising.

12 From thence they removed, and pitched in the valley of Zared.

13 From thence they removed, and pitched on the other side of Arnon, which is in the wilderness that cometh out of the coasts of the Amorites: for Arnon is the border of Moab, between Moab and the Amorites.

14 Therefore it is said in the book of the wars of the LORD, What he did in the Red sea, and in the brooks of Arnon,

15 And at the stream of the brooks that goes down to the dwelling of Ar, and lies upon the border of Moab.

16 And from thence they went to Beer: that is the well whereof the LORD spoke to Moses, Gather the people together, and I will give them water.

17 Then Israel sang this song, Spring up, O well; sing you to it:

18 The princes digged the well, the nobles of the people digged it, by the direction of the lawgiver, with their staves. And from the wilderness they went to Mattanah:

19 And from Mattanah to Nahaliel: and from Nahaliel to Bamoth:

20 And from Bamoth in the valley, that is in the country of Moab, to the top of Pisgah, which looks toward Jeshimon.

21 And Israel sent messengers to Sihon king of the Amorites, saying,

22 Let me pass through your land: we will not turn into the fields, or into the vineyards; we will not drink of the waters of the well: but we will go along by the king's high way, until we be past your borders.

23 And Sihon would not suffer Israel to pass through his border: but Sihon gathered all his people together, and went out against Israel into the wilderness: and he came to Jahaz, and fought against Israel.

24 And Israel smote him with the edge of the sword, and possessed his land from Arnon to Jabbok, even to the children of Ammon: for the border of the children of Ammon was strong.

25 And Israel took all these cities: and Israel dwelt in all the cities of the Amorites, in Heshbon, and in all the villages thereof.

26 For Heshbon was the city of Sihon the king of the Amorites, who had fought against the former king of Moab, and taken all his land out of his hand, even to Arnon.

27 Therefore they that speak in proverbs say, Come into Heshbon, let the city of Sihon be built and prepared:

28 For there is a fire gone out of Heshbon, a flame from the city of Sihon: it has consumed Ar of Moab, and the lords of the high places of Arnon.

29 Woe to you, Moab! you are undone, O people of Chemosh: he has given his sons that escaped, and his daughters, into captivity to Sihon king of the Amorites.

30 We have shot at them; Heshbon is perished even to Dibon, and we have laid them waste even to Nophah, which reaches to Medeba.

31 Thus Israel dwelt in the land of the Amorites.

32 And Moses sent to spy out Jaazer, and they took the villages thereof, and drove out the Amorites that were there.

33 And they turned and went up by the way of Bashan: and Og the king of Bashan went out against them, he, and all his people, to the battle at Edrei.

34 And the LORD said to Moses, Fear him not: for I have delivered him into your hand, and all his people, and his land; and you shall do to him as you did

THE BRAZEN SERPENT

Numbers 21:4-9

When the Israelites doubted God, God sent serpents among them. The deadly bite of the serpents caused the Israelites to admit that they had sinned. God also sent a cure for the serpent bite; He told Moses to make a bronze serpent and place it on a pole. When the people looked up at the bronze serpent, they were saved from death. Later, Jesus specifically cited this passage in reference to salvation from sin (see John 3:14).

The Ten Commandments are like ten biting serpents that carry with them the deadly venom of God's Law. This Law convicts us of our sinful nature and drives us to look up to the One who is lifted up on a cross, the Messiah, who saves us from what would otherwise be our certain death due to our judgment under God's Law.

to Sihon king of the Amorites, which dwelt at Heshbon.

35 So they smote him, and his sons, and all his people, until there was none left him alive: and they possessed his land.

CHAPTER 22

AND the children of Israel set forward, and pitched in the plains of Moab on this side Jordan by Jericho.

2 And Balak the son of Zippor saw all that Israel had done to the Amorites.

3 And Moab was sore afraid of the people, because they were many: and Moab was distressed because of the children of Israel.

4 And Moab said to the elders of Midian, Now shall this company lick up all that are round about us, as the ox licks up the grass of the field. And Balak the son of Zippor was king of the Moabites at that time.

5 He sent messengers therefore to Balaam the son of Beor to Pethor, which is by the river of the land of the children of his people, to call him, saying, Behold, there is a people come out from Egypt: behold, they cover the face of the earth, and they abide over against me:

6 Come now therefore, I pray you, curse me this people; for they are too mighty for me: peradventure I shall prevail, that we may smite them, and that I may drive them out of the land: for I wot that he whom you blesses is blessed, and he whom you curses is cursed.

7 And the elders of Moab and the elders of Midian departed with the rewards of divination in their hand; and they came to Balaam, and spoke to him the words of Balak.

8 And he said to them, Lodge here this night, and I will bring you word again, as the LORD shall speak to me: and the princes of Moab abode with Balaam.

9 And God came to Balaam, and said, What men are these with you?

10 And Balaam said to God, Balak the son of Zippor, king of Moab, has sent to me, saying,

11 Behold, there is a people come out of Egypt, which covers the face of the earth: come now, curse me them; peradventure I shall be able to overcome them, and drive them out.

12 And God said to Balaam, You shall not go with them; you shall not curse the people: for they are blessed.

13 And Balaam rose up in the morning, and said to the princes of Balak, Get you into your land: for the LORD refuses to give me leave to go with you.

14 And the princes of Moab rose up, and they went to Balak, and said, Balaam refuses to come with us.

15 And Balak sent yet again princes, more, and more honourable than they.

16 And they came to Balaam, and said to him, Thus says Balak the son of Zippor, Let nothing, I pray you, hinder you from coming to me:

17 For I will promote you to very great honour, and I will do whatsoever you say to me: come therefore, I pray you, curse me this people.

18 And Balaam answered and said to the servants of Balak, If Balak would give me his house full of silver and gold, I cannot go beyond the word of the LORD my God, to do less or more.

19 Now therefore, I pray you, tarry also here this night, that I may know what the LORD will say to me more.

20 And God came to Balaam at night, and said to him, If the men come to call you, rise up, and go with them; but yet the word which I shall say to you, that shall you do.

21 And Balaam rose up in the morning, and saddled his ass, and went with the princes of Moab.

22 And God's anger was kindled because he went: and the angel of the LORD stood in the way for an adversary against him. Now he was riding upon his ass, and his two servants were with him.

23 And the ass saw the angel of the LORD standing in the way, and his sword drawn in his hand: and the ass turned aside out of the way, and went into the field: and Balaam smote the ass, to turn her into the way.

24 But the angel of the LORD stood in a path of the vineyards, a wall being on this side, and a wall on that side.

25 And when the ass saw the angel of the LORD, she thrust herself to the wall, and crushed Balaam's foot against the wall: and he smote her again.

26 And the angel of the LORD went further, and stood in a narrow place, where was no way to turn either to the right hand or to the left.

27 And when the ass saw the angel of the LORD, she fell down under Balaam: and Balaam's anger was kindled, and he smote the ass with a staff.

28 And the LORD opened the mouth of the ass, and she said to Balaam, What have I done to you, that you have smitten me these three times?

29 And Balaam said to the ass, Because you have mocked me: I would there were a sword in mine hand, for now would I kill you.

30 And the ass said to Balaam, Am not I your ass, upon which you have ridden ever since I was yours to this day? was I ever wont to do so to you? And he said, Nay.

31 Then the LORD opened the eyes of Balaam, and he saw the angel of the LORD standing in the way, and his sword drawn in his hand: and he bowed down his head, and fell flat on his face.

32 And the angel of the LORD said to him, Why have you smitten your ass these three times? behold, I went out to withstand you, because your way is perverse before me:

33 And the ass saw me, and turned from me these three times: unless she had turned from me, surely now also I had slain you, and saved her alive.

34 And Balaam said to the angel of the LORD, I have sinned; for I knew not that

Faith sees the invisible,
believes the unbelievable,
and receives the impossible.

Corrie Ten Boom

1892 - 1983
OPERATED GIRLS CLUBS
IN HER NATIVE HOLLAND
AND WAS IMPRISONED IN WWII
BECAUSE SHE SHELTERED JEWS
FROM NAZI PERSECUTION

you stood in the way against me: now therefore, if it displease you, I will get me back again.

35 And the angel of the LORD said to Balaam, Go with the men: but only the word that I shall speak to you, that you shall speak. So Balaam went with the princes of Balak.

36 And when Balak heard that Balaam was come, he went out to meet him to a city of Moab, which is in the border of Arnon, which is in the utmost coast.

37 And Balak said to Balaam, Did I not earnestly send to you to call you? why came you not to me? am I not able indeed to promote you to honour?

38 And Balaam said to Balak, Lo, I am come to you: have I now any power at all to say any thing? the word that God puts in my mouth, that shall I speak.

Numbers 22:23

39 And Balaam went with Balak, and they came to Kirjathhuzoth.

40 And Balak offered oxen and sheep, and sent to Balaam, and to the princes that were with him.

41 And it came to pass on the morrow, that Balak took Balaam, and brought him up into the high places of Baal, that thence he might see the utmost part of the people.

CHAPTER 23

AND Balaam said to Balak, Build me here seven altars, and prepare me here seven oxen and seven rams.

2 And Balak did as Balaam had spoken; and Balak and Balaam offered on every altar a bullock and a ram.

3 And Balaam said to Balak, Stand by your burnt offering, and I will go: peradventure the LORD will come to meet me: and whatsoever he shows me I will tell you. And he went to an high place.

4 And God met Balaam: and he said to him, I have prepared seven altars, and I have offered upon every altar a bullock and a ram.

5 And the LORD put a word in Balaam's mouth, and said, Return to Balak, and thus you shall speak.

6 And he returned to him, and, lo, he stood by his burnt sacrifice, he, and all the princes of Moab.

7 And he took up his parable, and said, Balak the king of Moab has brought me from Aram, out of the mountains of the east, saying, Come, curse me Jacob, and come, defy Israel.

8 How shall I curse, whom God has not cursed? or how shall I defy, whom the LORD has not defied?

9 For from the top of the rocks I see him, and from the hills I behold him: lo, the people shall dwell alone, and shall not be reckoned among the nations.

10 Who can count the dust of Jacob, and the number of the fourth part of Israel?
Let me die the death of the righteous, and let my last end be like his!

11 And Balak said to Balaam, What have you done to me? I took you to curse mine enemies, and, behold, you have blessed them altogether.

12 And he answered and said, Must I not take heed to speak that which the LORD has put in my mouth?

13 And Balak said to him, Come, I pray you, with me to another place, from whence you may see them: you shall see but the utmost part of them, and shall not see them all: and curse me them from thence.

14 And he brought him into the field of Zophim, to the top of Pisgah, and built seven altars, and offered a bullock and a ram on every altar.

15 And he said to Balak, Stand here by your burnt offering, while I meet the LORD yonder.

16 And the LORD met Balaam, and put a word in his mouth, and said, Go again to Balak, and say thus.

17 And when he came to him, behold, he stood by his burnt offering, and the princes of Moab with him. And Balak said to him, What has the LORD spoken?

18 And he took up his parable, and said, Rise up, Balak, and hear; hearken to me, you son of Zippor:

19 God is not a man, that he should lie; neither the son of man, that he should repent: has he said, and shall he not do it? or has he spoken, and shall he not make it good?

20 Behold, I have received commandment to bless: and he has blessed; and I cannot reverse it.

21 He has not beheld iniquity in Jacob, neither has he seen perverseness in Israel: the LORD his God is with him, and the shout of a king is among them.

22 God brought them out of Egypt; he has as it were the strength of an unicorn.

23 Surely there is no enchantment against Jacob, neither is there any divination against Israel: according to this time it shall be said of Jacob and of Israel, What has God wrought!

24 Behold, the people shall rise up as a great lion, and lift up himself as a young lion: he shall not lie down until he eat of the prey, and drink the blood of the slain.

25 And Balak said to Balaam, Neither curse them at all, nor bless them at all.

26 But Balaam answered and said to Balak, Told not I you, saying, All that the LORD speaks, that I must do?

27 And Balak said to Balaam, Come, I pray you, I will bring you to another place; peradventure it will please God that you may curse me them from thence.

28 And Balak brought Balaam to the top of Peor, that looks toward Jeshimon.

29 And Balaam said to Balak, Build me here seven altars, and prepare me here seven bullocks and seven rams.

30 And Balak did as Balaam had said, and offered a bullock and a ram on every altar.

CHAPTER 24

AND when Balaam saw that it pleased the LORD to bless Israel, he went not, as at other times, to seek for enchantments, but he set his face toward the wilderness.

2 And Balaam lifted up his eyes, and he saw Israel abiding in his tents according to their tribes; and the spirit of God came upon him.

3 And he took up his parable, and said, Balaam the son of Beor has said, and the man whose eyes are open has said:

4 He has said, which heard the words of God, which saw the vision of the Almighty, falling into a trance, but having his eyes open:

5 How goodly are your tents, O Jacob, and your tabernacles, O Israel!

6 As the valleys are they spread forth, as gardens by the river's side, as the trees of lign aloes which the LORD has planted, and as cedar trees beside the waters.

7 He shall pour the water out of his buckets, and his seed shall be in many waters, and his king shall be higher than Agag, and his kingdom shall be exalted.

8 God brought him forth out of Egypt; he has as it were the strength of a unicorn: he shall eat up the nations his enemies, and shall break their bones, and pierce them through with his arrows.

9 He couched, he lay down as a lion, and as a great lion: who shall stir him up? Blessed is he that blesses you, and cursed is he that curses you.

10 And Balak's anger was kindled against Balaam, and he smote his hands together: and Balak said to Balaam, I called you to curse mine enemies, and, behold, you have altogether blessed them these three times.

11 Therefore now flee to your place: I thought to promote you to great honour; but, lo, the LORD has kept you back from honour.

12 And Balaam said to Balak, Spoke I not also to your messengers which you sent to me, saying,

13 If Balak would give me his house full of silver and gold, I cannot go beyond the commandment of the LORD, to do either good or bad of mine own mind; but what the LORD says, that will I speak?

14 And now, behold, I go to my people: come therefore, and I will advertise you what this people shall do to your people in the latter days.

15 And he took up his parable, and said, Balaam the son of Beor has said, and the man whose eyes are open has said:

16 He has said, which heard the words of God, and knew the knowledge of the most High, which saw the vision of the Almighty, falling into a trance, but having his eyes open:

17 I shall see him, but not now: I shall behold him, but not nigh: there shall come a Star out of Jacob, and a Sceptre shall rise out of Israel, and shall smite the corners of Moab, and destroy all the children of Sheth.

18 And Edom shall be a possession, Seir also shall be a possession for his enemies; and Israel shall do valiantly.

19 Out of Jacob shall come he that shall have dominion, and shall destroy him that remains of the city.

20 And when he looked on Amalek, he took up his parable, and said, Amalek was the first of the nations; but his latter end shall be that he perish for ever.

21 And he looked on the Kenites, and took up his parable, and said, Strong is

24:16-17

" In science we have been reading only the notes to a poem; in Christianity we find the poem itself.

C. S. LEWIS

your dwellingplace, and you put your
nest in a rock.

22 Nevertheless the Kenite shall be
wasted, until Asshur shall carry you
away captive.

23 And he took up his parable, and
said, Alas, who shall live when God does
this!

24 And ships shall come from the coast
of Chittim, and shall afflict Asshur, and
shall afflict Eber, and he also shall perish
for ever.

25 And Balaam rose up, and went and
returned to his place: and Balak also
went his way.

CHAPTER 25

A ND Israel abode in Shittim, and the
people began to commit whoredom
with the daughters of Moab.

2 And they called the people to the sacrifices of their gods: and the people did
eat, and bowed down to their gods.

3 And Israel joined himself to Baalpeor:
and the anger of the LORD was kindled
against Israel.

4 And the LORD said to Moses, Take all
the heads of the people, and hang them
up before the LORD against the sun, that
the fierce anger of the LORD may be
turned away from Israel.

5 And Moses said to the judges of
Israel, Slay every one his men that were
joined to Baalpeor.

6 And, behold, one of the children of
Israel came and brought to his brethren
a Midianitish woman in the sight of
Moses, and in the sight of all the congregation of the children of Israel, who were
weeping before the door of the tabernacle of the congregation.

7 And when Phinehas, the son of
Eleazar, the son of Aaron the priest, saw
it, he rose up from among the congregation, and took a javelin in his hand;

8 And he went after the man of Israel
into the tent, and thrust both of them
through, the man of Israel, and the
woman through her belly. So the plague
was stayed from the children of Israel.

9 And those that died in the plague
were twenty and four thousand.

10 And the LORD spoke to Moses, saying,

11 Phinehas, the son of Eleazar, the son
of Aaron the priest, has turned my wrath
away from the children of Israel, while
he was zealous for my sake among them,
that I consumed not the children of
Israel in my jealousy.

12 Therefore say, Behold, I give to him
my covenant of peace:

13 And he shall have it, and his seed
after him, even the covenant of an everlasting priesthood; because he was zealous for his God, and made an atonement
for the children of Israel.

14 Now the name of the Israelite that
was slain, even that was slain with the
Midianitish woman, was Zimri, the son
of Salu, a prince of a chief house among
the Simeonites.

15 And the name of the Midianitish
woman that was slain was Cozbi, the
daughter of Zur; he was head over a people, and of a chief house in Midian.

16 And the LORD spoke to Moses, saying,

17 Vex the Midianites, and smite them:

18 For they vex you with their wiles,
wherewith they have beguiled you in the
matter of Peor, and in the matter of
Cozbi, the daughter of a prince of
Midian, their sister, which was slain in
the day of the plague for Peor's sake.

CHAPTER 26

A ND it came to pass after the plague,
that the LORD spoke to Moses and
to Eleazar the son of Aaron the priest,
saying,

2 Take the sum of all the congregation
of the children of Israel, from twenty
years old and upward, throughout their
fathers' house, all that are able to go to
war in Israel.

3 And Moses and Eleazar the priest
spoke with them in the plains of Moab
by Jordan near Jericho, saying,

4 Take the sum of the people, from twenty years old and upward; as the LORD commanded Moses and the children of Israel, which went forth out of the land of Egypt.

5 Reuben, the eldest son of Israel: the children of Reuben; Hanoch, of whom cometh the family of the Hanochites: of Pallu, the family of the Palluites:

6 Of Hezron, the family of the Hezronites: of Carmi, the family of the Carmites.

7 These are the families of the Reubenites: and they that were numbered of them were forty and three thousand and seven hundred and thirty.

8 And the sons of Pallu; Eliab.

9 And the sons of Eliab; Nemuel, and Dathan, and Abiram. This is that Dathan and Abiram, which were famous in the congregation, who strove against Moses and against Aaron in the company of Korah,

when they strove against the LORD:

10 And the earth opened her mouth, and swallowed them up together with Korah, when that company died, what time the fire devoured two hundred and fifty men: and they became a sign.

11 Notwithstanding the children of Korah died not.

12 The sons of Simeon after their families: of Nemuel, the family of the Nemuelites: of Jamin, the family of the Jaminites: of Jachin, the family of the Jachinites:

13 Of Zerah, the family of the Zarhites: of Shaul, the family of the Shaulites.

14 These are the families of the Simeonites, twenty and two thousand and two hundred.

15 The children of Gad after their families: of Zephon, the family of the Zephonites: of Haggi, the family of the Haggites: of Shuni, the family of the Shunites:

16 Of Ozni, the family of the Oznites: of Eri, the family of the Erites:

17 Of Arod, the family of the Arodites: of Areli, the family of the Arelites.

18 These are the families of the children of Gad according to those that were numbered of them, forty thousand and five hundred.

19 The sons of Judah were Er and Onan: and Er and Onan died in the land of Canaan.

20 And the sons of Judah after their families were; of Shelah, the family of the Shelanites: of Pharez, the family of the Pharzites: of Zerah, the family of the Zarhites.

21 And the sons of Pharez were; of Hezron, the family of the Hezronites: of Hamul, the family of the Hamulites.

22 These are the families of Judah according to those that were numbered of them, threescore and sixteen thousand and five hundred.

23 Of the sons of Issachar after their families: of Tola, the family of the Tolaites: of Pua, the family of the Punites:

24 Of Jashub, the family of the Jashubites: of Shimron, the family of the Shimronites.

25 These are the families of Issachar according to those that were numbered of them, threescore and four thousand and three hundred.

26 Of the sons of Zebulun after their families: of Sered, the family of the Sardites: of Elon, the family of the Elonites: of Jahleel, the family of the Jahleelites.

27 These are the families of the Zebulunites according to those that were numbered of them, threescore thousand and five hundred.

28 The sons of Joseph after their families were Manasseh and Ephraim.

29 Of the sons of Manasseh: of Machir, the family of the Machirites: and Machir begat Gilead: of Gilead come the family of the Gileadites.

30 These are the sons of Gilead: of Jeezer, the family of the Jeezerites: of Helek, the family of the Helekites:

31 And of Asriel, the family of the Asrielites: and of Shechem, the family of the Shechemites:

32 And of Shemida, the family of the Shemidaites: and of Hepher, the family of the Hepherites.

33 And Zelophehad the son of Hepher had no sons, but daughters: and the names of the daughters of Zelophehad were Mahlah, and Noah, Hoglah, Milcah, and Tirzah.

34 These are the families of Manasseh, and those that were numbered of them, fifty and two thousand and seven hundred.

35 These are the sons of Ephraim after their families: of Shuthelah, the family of the Shuthalhites: of Becher, the family of the Bachrites: of Tahan, the family of the Tahanites.

36 And these are the sons of Shuthelah: of Eran, the family of the Eranites.

37 These are the families of the sons of Ephraim according to those that were numbered of them, thirty and two thousand and five hundred. These are the sons of Joseph after their families.

38 The sons of Benjamin after their families: of Bela, the family of the Belaites: of Ashbel, the family of the Ashbelites: of Ahiram, the family of the Ahiramites:

39 Of Shupham, the family of the Shuphamites: of Hupham, the family of the Huphamites.

40 And the sons of Bela were Ard and Naaman: of Ard, the family of the Ardites: and of Naaman, the family of the Naamites.

41 These are the sons of Benjamin after their families: and they that were numbered of them were forty and five thousand and six hundred.

42 These are the sons of Dan after their families: of Shuham, the family of the Shuhamites. These are the families of Dan after their families.

43 All the families of the Shuhamites, according to those that were numbered

of them, were threescore and four thousand and four hundred.

44 Of the children of Asher after their families: of Jimna, the family of the Jimnites: of Jesui, the family of the Jesuites: of Beriah, the family of the Beriites.

45 Of the sons of Beriah: of Heber, the family of the Heberites: of Malchiel, the family of the Malchielites.

46 And the name of the daughter of Asher was Sarah.

47 These are the families of the sons of Asher according to those that were numbered of them; who were fifty and three thousand and four hundred.

48 Of the sons of Naphtali after their families: of Jahzeel, the family of the Jahzeelites: of Guni, the family of the Gunites:

49 Of Jezer, the family of the Jezerites: of Shillem, the family of the Shillemites.

50 These are the families of Naphtali according to their families: and they that were numbered of them were forty and five thousand and four hundred.

51 These were the numbered of the children of Israel, six hundred thousand and a thousand seven hundred and thirty.

52 And the LORD spoke to Moses, saying,

53 To these the land shall be divided for an inheritance according to the number of names.

54 To many you shall give the more inheritance, and to few you shall give the less inheritance: to every one shall his inheritance be given according to those that were numbered of him.

55 Notwithstanding the land shall be divided by lot: according to the names of the tribes of their fathers they shall inherit.

56 According to the lot shall the possession thereof be divided between many and few.

57 And these are they that were numbered of the Levites after their families: of Gershon, the family of the

Gershonites: of Kohath, the family of the Kohathites: of Merari, the family of the Merarites.

58 These are the families of the Levites: the family of the Libnites, the family of the Hebronites, the family of the Mahlites, the family of the Mushites, the family of the Korathites. And Kohath begat Amram.

59 And the name of Amram's wife was Jochebed, the daughter of Levi, whom her mother bare to Levi in Egypt: and she bare to Amram Aaron and Moses, and Miriam their sister.

60 And to Aaron was born Nadab, and Abihu, Eleazar, and Ithamar.

61 And Nadab and Abihu died, when they offered strange fire before the LORD.

62 And those that were numbered of them were twenty and three thousand, all males from a month old and upward: for they were not numbered among the children of Israel, because there was no inheritance given them among the children of Israel.

63 These are they that were numbered by Moses and Eleazar the priest, who numbered the children of Israel in the plains of Moab by Jordan near Jericho.

64 But among these there was not a man of them whom Moses and Aaron the priest numbered, when they numbered the children of Israel in the wilderness of Sinai.

65 For the LORD had said of them, They shall surely die in the wilderness. And there was not left a man of them, save Caleb the son of Jephunneh, and Joshua the son of Nun.

CHAPTER 27

THEN came the daughters of Zelophehad, the son of Hepher, the son of Gilead, the son of Machir, the son of Manasseh, of the families of Manasseh the son of Joseph: and these are the names of his daughters; Mahlah, Noah, and Hoglah, and Milcah, and Tirzah.

2 And they stood before Moses, and before Eleazar the priest, and before the princes and all the congregation, by the door of the tabernacle of the congregation, saying,

3 Our father died in the wilderness, and he was not in the company of them that gathered themselves together against the LORD in the company of Korah; but died in his own sin, and had no sons.

4 Why should the name of our father be done away from among his family, because he has no son? Give to us therefore a possession among the brethren of our father.

5 And Moses brought their cause before the LORD.

6 And the LORD spoke to Moses, saying,

7 The daughters of Zelophehad speak right: you shall surely give them a possession of an inheritance among their father's brethren; and you shall cause the inheritance of their father to pass to them.

8 And you shall speak to the children of Israel, saying, If a man die, and have no son, then you shall cause his inheritance to pass to his daughter.

9 And if he has no daughter, then you shall give his inheritance to his brethren.

10 And if he has no brethren, then you shall give his inheritance to his father's brethren.

11 And if his father has no brethren, then you shall give his inheritance to his kinsman that is next to him of his family, and he shall possess it: and it shall be to the children of Israel a statute of judgment, as the LORD commanded Moses.

12 And the LORD said to Moses, Get up into this mount Abarim, and see the land which I have given to the children of Israel.

13 And when you have seen it, you also shall be gathered to your people, as Aaron your brother was gathered.

14 For you rebelled against my commandment in the desert of Zin, in the strife of the congregation, to sanctify me

at the water before their eyes: that is the water of Meribah in Kadesh in the wilderness of Zin.

15 And Moses spoke to the LORD, saying,

16 Let the LORD, the God of the spirits of all flesh, set a man over the congregation,

17 Which may go out before them, and which may go in before them, and which may lead them out, and which may bring them in; that the congregation of the LORD be not as sheep which have no shepherd.

18 And the LORD said to Moses, Take Joshua the son of Nun, a man in whom is the spirit, and lay your hand upon him;

19 And set him before Eleazar the priest, and before all the congregation; and give him a charge in their sight.

20 And you shall put some of your honour upon him, that all the congregation of the children of Israel may be obedient.

21 And he shall stand before Eleazar the priest, who shall ask counsel for him after the judgment of Urim before the LORD: at his word shall they go out, and at his word they shall come in, both he, and all the children of Israel with him, even all the congregation.

22 And Moses did as the LORD commanded him: and he took Joshua, and set him before Eleazar the priest, and before all the congregation:

23 And he laid his hands upon him, and gave him a charge, as the LORD commanded by the hand of Moses.

CHAPTER 28

A ND the LORD spoke to Moses, saying,

2 Command the children of Israel, and say to them, My offering, and my bread for my sacrifices made by fire, for a sweet savour to me, shall you observe to offer to me in their due season.

3 And you shall say to them, This is the offering made by fire which you shall offer to the LORD; two lambs of the first year without spot day by day, for a continual burnt offering.

4 The one lamb shall you offer in the morning, and the other lamb shall you offer at even;

5 And a tenth part of an ephah of flour for a meat offering, mingled with the fourth part of an hin of beaten oil.

6 It is a continual burnt offering, which was ordained in Mount Sinai for a sweet savour, a sacrifice made by fire to the LORD.

7 And the drink offering thereof shall be the fourth part of a hin for the one lamb: in the holy place shall you cause the strong wine to be poured to the LORD for a drink offering.

8 And the other lamb shall you offer at even: as the meat offering of the morning, and as the drink offering thereof, you shall offer it, a sacrifice made by fire, of a sweet savour to the LORD.

9 And on the sabbath day two lambs of the first year without spot, and two tenth deals of flour for a meat offering, mingled with oil, and the drink offering thereof:

10 This is the burnt offering of every sabbath, beside the continual burnt offering, and his drink offering.

11 And in the beginnings of your months you shall offer a burnt offering to the LORD; two young bullocks, and one ram, seven lambs of the first year without spot;

12 And three tenth deals of flour for a meat offering, mingled with oil, for one bullock; and two tenth deals of flour for a meat offering, mingled with oil, for one ram;

13 And a several tenth deal of flour mingled with oil for a meat offering to one lamb; for a burnt offering of a sweet savour, a sacrifice made by fire to the LORD.

14 And their drink offerings shall be half a hin of wine to a bullock, and the third part of an hin to a ram, and a fourth part of a hin to a lamb: this is the

burnt offering of every month throughout the months of the year.

15 And one kid of the goats for a sin offering to the LORD shall be offered, beside the continual burnt offering, and his
drink offering.

16 And in the fourteenth day of the first
month is the Passover of the LORD.

17 And in the fifteenth day of this
month is the feast: seven days shall unleavened bread be eaten.

18 In the first day shall be a holy convocation; you shall do no manner of
servile work therein:

19 But you shall offer a sacrifice made
by fire for a burnt offering to the LORD;
two young bullocks, and one ram, and
seven lambs of the first year: they shall
be to you without blemish:

20 And their meat offering shall be of
flour mingled with oil: three tenth deals
shall you offer for a bullock, and two
tenth deals for a ram;

21 A several tenth deal shall you offer
for every lamb, throughout the seven
lambs:

22 And one goat for a sin offering, to
make an atonement for you.

23 You shall offer these beside the
burnt offering in the morning, which is
for a continual burnt offering.

24 After this manner you shall offer
daily, throughout the seven days, the
meat of the sacrifice made by fire, of a
sweet savour to the LORD: it shall be offered beside the continual burnt offering,
and his drink offering.

25 And on the seventh day you shall
have an holy convocation; you shall do
no servile work.

26 Also in the day of the firstfruits,
when you bring a new meat offering to
the LORD, after your weeks be out, you
shall have an holy convocation; you shall
do no servile work:

27 But you shall offer the burnt offering
for a sweet savour to the LORD; two
young bullocks, one ram, seven lambs of
the first year;

28 And their meat offering of flour mingled with oil, three tenth deals to one
bullock, two tenth deals to one ram,

29 A several tenth deal to one lamb,
throughout the seven lambs;

30 And one kid of the goats, to make
an atonement for you.

31 You shall offer them beside the continual burnt offering, and his meat offering, (they shall be to you without blemish) and their drink offerings.

CHAPTER 29

AND in the seventh month, on the
first day of the month, you shall
have an holy convocation; you shall do
no servile work: it is a day of blowing
the trumpets to you.

2 And you shall offer a burnt offering
for a sweet savour to the LORD; one
young bullock, one ram, and seven
lambs of the first year without blemish:

3 And their meat offering shall be of
flour mingled with oil, three tenth deals
for a bullock, and two tenth deals for a
ram,

4 And one tenth deal for one lamb,
throughout the seven lambs:

5 And one kid of the goats for a sin offering, to make an atonement for you:

6 Beside the burnt offering of the
month, and his meat offering, and the
daily burnt offering, and his meat offering, and their drink offerings, according
to their manner, for a sweet savour, a
sacrifice made by fire to the LORD.

7 And you shall have on the tenth day
of this seventh month an holy convocation; and you shall afflict your souls: you
shall not do any work therein:

8 But you shall offer a burnt offering to
the LORD for a sweet savour; one young
bullock, one ram, and seven lambs of
the first year; they shall be to you without blemish:

9 And their meat offering shall be of
flour mingled with oil, three tenth deals
to a bullock, and two tenth deals to one
ram,

10 A several tenth deal for one lamb, throughout the seven lambs:

11 One kid of the goats for a sin offering; beside the sin offering of atonement, and the continual burnt offering, and the meat offering of it, and their drink offerings.

12 And on the fifteenth day of the seventh month you shall have an holy convocation; you shall do no servile work, and you shall keep a feast to the LORD seven days:

13 And you shall offer a burnt offering, a sacrifice made by fire, of a sweet savour to the LORD; thirteen young bullocks, two rams, and fourteen lambs of the first year; they shall be without blemish:

14 And their meat offering shall be of flour mingled with oil, three tenth deals to every bullock of the thirteen bullocks, two tenth deals to each ram of the two rams,

15 And a several tenth deal to each lamb of the fourteen lambs:

16 And one kid of the goats for a sin offering; beside the continual burnt offering, his meat offering, and his drink offering.

17 And on the second day you shall offer twelve young bullocks, two rams, fourteen lambs of the first year without spot:

18 And their meat offering and their drink offerings for the bullocks, for the rams, and for the lambs, shall be according to their number, after the manner:

19 And one kid of the goats for a sin offering; beside the continual burnt offering, and the meat offering thereof, and their drink offerings.

20 And on the third day eleven bullocks, two rams, fourteen lambs of the first year without blemish;

21 And their meat offering and their drink offerings for the bullocks, for the rams, and for the lambs, shall be according to their number, after the manner:

22 And one goat for a sin offering; beside the continual burnt offering, and his meat offering, and his drink offering.

23 And on the fourth day ten bullocks, two rams, and fourteen lambs of the first year without blemish:

24 Their meat offering and their drink offerings for the bullocks, for the rams, and for the lambs, shall be according to their number, after the manner:

25 And one kid of the goats for a sin offering; beside the continual burnt offering, his meat offering, and his drink offering.

26 And on the fifth day nine bullocks, two rams, and fourteen lambs of the first year without spot:

27 And their meat offering and their drink offerings for the bullocks, for the rams, and for the lambs, shall be according to their number, after the manner:

28 And one goat for a sin offering; beside the continual burnt offering, and his meat offering, and his drink offering.

29 And on the sixth day eight bullocks, two rams, and fourteen lambs of the first year without blemish:

30 And their meat offering and their drink offerings for the bullocks, for the rams, and for the lambs, shall be according to their number, after the manner:

31 And one goat for a sin offering; beside the continual burnt offering, his meat offering, and his drink offering.

32 And on the seventh day seven bullocks, two rams, and fourteen lambs of the first year without blemish:

33 And their meat offering and their drink offerings for the bullocks, for the rams, and for the lambs, shall be according to their number, after the manner:

34 And one goat for a sin offering; beside the continual burnt offering, his meat offering, and his drink offering.

35 On the eighth day you shall have a solemn assembly: you shall do no servile work therein:

36 But you shall offer a burnt offering, a sacrifice made by fire, of a sweet savour to the LORD: one bullock, one

ram, seven lambs of the first year without blemish:

37 Their meat offering and their drink offerings for the bullock, for the ram, and for the lambs, shall be according to their number, after the manner:

38 And one goat for a sin offering; beside the continual burnt offering, and his meat offering, and his drink offering.

39 These things you shall do to the LORD in your set feasts, beside your vows, and your freewill offerings, for your burnt offerings, and for your meat offerings, and for your drink offerings, and for your peace offerings.

40 And Moses told the children of Israel according to all that the LORD commanded Moses.

CHAPTER 30

AND Moses spoke to the heads of the tribes concerning the children of Israel, saying, This is the thing which the LORD has commanded.

2 If a man vow a vow to the LORD, or swear an oath to bind his soul with a bond; he shall not break his word, he shall do according to all that proceeds out of his mouth.

3 If a woman also vow a vow to the LORD, and bind herself by a bond, being in her father's house in her youth;

4 And her father hears her vow, and her bond wherewith she has bound her soul, and her father shall hold his peace at her; then all her vows shall stand, and every bond wherewith she has bound her soul shall stand.

5 But if her father disallow her in the day that he hears; not any of her vows, or of her bonds wherewith she has bound her soul, shall stand: and the LORD shall forgive her, because her father disallowed her.

6 And if she had at all an husband, when she vowed, or uttered ought out of her lips, wherewith she bound her soul;

7 And her husband heard it, and held his peace at her in the day that he heard it: then her vows shall stand, and her

bonds wherewith she bound her soul shall stand.

8 But if her husband disallowed her on the day that he heard it; then he shall make her vow which she vowed, and that which she uttered with her lips, wherewith she bound her soul, of none effect: and the LORD shall forgive her.

9 But every vow of a widow, and of her that is divorced, wherewith they have bound their souls, shall stand against her.

10 And if she vowed in her husband's house, or bound her soul by a bond with an oath;

11 And her husband heard it, and held his peace at her, and disallowed her not: then all her vows shall stand, and every bond wherewith she bound her soul shall stand.

12 But if her husband has utterly made them void on the day he heard them; then whatsoever proceeded out of her lips concerning her vows, or concerning the bond of her soul, shall not stand: her husband has made them void; and the LORD shall forgive her.

13 Every vow, and every binding oath to afflict the soul, her husband may establish it, or her husband may make it void.

14 But if her husband altogether hold his peace at her from day to day; then he establishes all her vows, or all her bonds, which are upon her: he confirms them, because he held his peace at her in the day that he heard them.

15 But if he shall any ways make them void after that he has heard them; then he shall bear her iniquity.

16 These are the statutes, which the LORD commanded Moses, between a man and his wife, between the father and his daughter, being yet in her youth in her father's house.

CHAPTER 31

AND the LORD spoke to Moses, saying,

2 Avenge the children of Israel of the Midianites: afterward shall you be gathered to your people.

3 And Moses spoke to the people, saying, Arm some of yourselves to the war, and let them go against the Midianites, and avenge the LORD of Midian.

4 Of every tribe a thousand, throughout all the tribes of Israel, shall you send to the war.

5 So there were delivered out of the thousands of Israel, a thousand of every tribe, twelve thousand armed for war.

6 And Moses sent them to the war, a thousand of every tribe, them and Phinehas the son of Eleazar the priest, to the war, with the holy instruments, and the trumpets to blow in his hand.

7 And they warred against the Midianites, as the LORD commanded Moses; and they slew all the males.

8 And they slew the kings of Midian, beside the rest of them that were slain; namely, Evi, and Rekem, and Zur, and Hur, and Reba, five kings of Midian: Balaam also the son of Beor they slew with the sword.

9 And the children of Israel took all the women of Midian captives, and their little ones, and took the spoil of all their cattle, and all their flocks, and all their goods.

10 And they burnt all their cities wherein they dwelt, and all their goodly castles, with fire.

11 And they took all the spoil, and all the prey, both of men and of beasts.

12 And they brought the captives, and the prey, and the spoil, to Moses, and Eleazar the priest, and to the congregation of the children of Israel, to the camp at the plains of Moab, which are by Jordan near Jericho.

13 And Moses, and Eleazar the priest, and all the princes of the congregation, went forth to meet them without the camp.

14 And Moses was wroth with the officers of the host, with the captains over thousands, and captains over hundreds, which came from the battle.

15 And Moses said to them, Have you saved all the women alive?

16 Behold, these caused the children of Israel, through the counsel of Balaam, to commit trespass against the LORD in the matter of Peor, and there was a plague among the congregation of the LORD.

17 Now therefore kill every male among the little ones, and kill every woman that has known man by lying with him.

18 But all the women children, that have not known a man by lying with him, keep alive for yourselves.

19 And do you abide without the camp seven days: whosoever has killed any person, and whosoever has touched any slain, purify both yourselves and your captives on the third day, and on the seventh day.

20 And purify all your raiment, and all that is made of skins, and all work of goats' hair, and all things made of wood.

21 And Eleazar the priest said to the men of war which went to the battle, This is the ordinance of the law which the LORD commanded Moses;

22 Only the gold, and the silver, the brass, the iron, the tin, and the lead,

23 Every thing that may abide the fire, you shall make it go through the fire, and it shall be clean: nevertheless it shall be purified with the water of separation: and all that abides not the fire you shall make go through the water.

24 And you shall wash your clothes on the seventh day, and you shall be clean, and afterward you shall come into the camp.

25 And the LORD spoke to Moses, saying,

26 Take the sum of the prey that was taken, both of man and of beast, you, and Eleazar the priest, and the chief fathers of the congregation:

27 And divide the prey into two parts; between them that took the war upon them, who went out to battle, and between all the congregation:

28 And levy a tribute to the Lord of the men of war which went out to battle: one soul of five hundred, both of the persons, and of the beeves, and of the asses, and of the sheep:

29 Take it of their half, and give it to Eleazar the priest, for an heave offering of the LORD.

30 And of the children of Israel's half, you shall take one portion of fifty, of the persons, of the beeves, of the asses, and of the flocks, of all manner of beasts, and give them to the Levites, which keep the charge of the tabernacle of the LORD.

31 And Moses and Eleazar the priest did as the LORD commanded Moses.

32 And the booty, being the rest of the prey which the men of war had caught, was six hundred thousand and seventy thousand and five thousand sheep,

33 And threescore and twelve thousand beeves,

34 And threescore and one thousand asses,

35 And thirty and two thousand persons in all, of women that had not known man by lying with him.

36 And the half, which was the portion of them that went out to war, was in number three hundred thousand and seven and thirty thousand and five hundred sheep:

37 And the LORD's tribute of the sheep was six hundred and threescore and fifteen.

38 And the beeves were thirty and six thousand; of which the LORD's tribute was threescore and twelve.

39 And the asses were thirty thousand and five hundred; of which the LORD's tribute was threescore and one.

40 And the persons were sixteen thousand; of which the LORD's tribute was thirty and two persons.

41 And Moses gave the tribute, which was the LORD's heave offering, to Eleazar the priest, as the LORD commanded Moses.

42 And of the children of Israel's half, which Moses divided from the men that warred,

43 (Now the half that pertained to the congregation was three hundred thousand and thirty thousand and seven thousand and five hundred sheep,

44 And thirty and six thousand beeves,

45 And thirty thousand asses and five hundred,

46 And sixteen thousand persons;)

47 Even of the children of Israel's half, Moses took one portion of fifty, both of man and of beast, and gave them to the Levites, which kept the charge of the tabernacle of the LORD; as the LORD commanded Moses.

48 And the officers which were over thousands of the host, the captains of thousands, and captains of hundreds, came near to Moses:

49 And they said to Moses, Your servants have taken the sum of the men of war which are under our charge, and there lacks not one man of us.

50 We have therefore brought an oblation for the LORD, what every man has gotten, of jewels of gold, chains, and bracelets, rings, earrings, and tablets, to make an atonement for our souls before the LORD.

51 And Moses and Eleazar the priest took the gold of them, even all wrought jewels.

52 And all the gold of the offering that they offered up to the LORD, of the captains of thousands, and of the captains of hundreds, was sixteen thousand seven hundred and fifty shekels.

53 (For the men of war had taken spoil, every man for himself.)

54 And Moses and Eleazar the priest took the gold of the captains of thousands and of hundreds, and brought it into the tabernacle of the congregation, for a memorial for the children of Israel before the LORD.

CHAPTER 32

NOW the children of Reuben and the children of Gad had a very great multitude of cattle: and when they saw the land of Jazer, and the land of Gilead, that, behold, the place was a place for cattle;

2 The children of Gad and the children of Reuben came and spoke to Moses, and to Eleazar the priest, and to the princes of the congregation, saying,

3 Ataroth, and Dibon, and Jazer, and Nimrah, and Heshbon, and Elealeh, and Shebam, and Nebo, and Beon,

4 Even the country which the LORD smote before the congregation of Israel, is a land for cattle, and your servants have cattle:

5 Therefore, said they, if we have found grace in your sight, let this land be given to your servants for a possession, and bring us not over Jordan.

6 And Moses said to the children of Gad and to the children of Reuben, Shall your brethren go to war, and shall you sit here?

7 And why do you discourage the heart of the children of Israel from going over into the land which the LORD has given them?

8 Thus did your fathers, when I sent them from Kadeshbarnea to see the land.

9 For when they went up to the valley of Eshcol, and saw the land, they discouraged the heart of the children of Israel, that they should not go into the land which the LORD had given them.

10 And the LORD's anger was kindled the same time, and he swore, saying,

11 Surely none of the men that came up out of Egypt, from twenty years old and upward, shall see the land which I swore to Abraham, to Isaac, and to Jacob; because they have not wholly followed me:

12 Save Caleb the son of Jephunneh the Kenezite, and Joshua the son of Nun: for they have wholly followed the LORD.

13 And the LORD's anger was kindled against Israel, and he made them wander in the wilderness forty years, until all the generation, that had done evil in the sight of the LORD, was consumed.

14 And, behold, you are risen up in your fathers' stead, an increase of sinful men, to augment yet the fierce anger of the LORD toward Israel.

15 For if you turn away from after him, he will yet again leave them in the wilderness; and you shall destroy all this people.

16 And they came near to him, and said, We will build sheepfolds here for our cattle, and cities for our little ones:

17 But we ourselves will go ready armed before the children of Israel, until we have brought them to their place: and our little ones shall dwell in the fenced cities because of the inhabitants of the land.

18 We will not return to our houses, until the children of Israel have inherited every man his inheritance.

19 For we will not inherit with them on yonder side Jordan, or forward; because our inheritance is fallen to us on this side Jordan eastward.

20 And Moses said to them, If you will do this thing, if you will go armed before the LORD to war,

21 And will go all of you armed over Jordan before the LORD, until he has driven out his enemies from before him,

22 And the land be subdued before the LORD: then afterward you shall return, and be guiltless before the LORD, and before Israel; and this land shall be your possession before the LORD.

23 But if you will not do so, behold, you have sinned against the LORD: and be sure your sin will find you out.

24 Build you cities for your little ones, and folds for your sheep; and do that which has proceeded out of your mouth.

25 And the children of Gad and the children of Reuben spoke to Moses, saying, Your servants will do as my lord commands.

26 Our little ones, our wives, our flocks, and all our cattle, shall be there in the cities of Gilead:

27 But your servants will pass over, every man armed for war, before the LORD to battle, as my lord says.

28 So concerning them Moses commanded Eleazar the priest, and Joshua the son of Nun, and the chief fathers of the tribes of the children of Israel:

29 And Moses said to them, If the children of Gad and the children of Reuben will pass with you over Jordan, every man armed to battle, before the LORD, and the land shall be subdued before you; then you shall give them the land of Gilead for a possession:

30 But if they will not pass over with you armed, they shall have possessions among you in the land of Canaan.

31 And the children of Gad and the children of Reuben answered, saying, As the LORD has said to your servants, so will we do.

32 We will pass over armed before the LORD into the land of Canaan, that the possession of our inheritance on this side Jordan may be ours.

33 And Moses gave to them, even to the children of Gad, and to the children of Reuben, and to half the tribe of Manasseh the son of Joseph, the kingdom of Sihon king of the Amorites, and the kingdom of Og king of Bashan, the land, with the cities thereof in the coasts, even the cities of the country round about.

34 And the children of Gad built Dibon, and Ataroth, and Aroer,

35 And Atroth, Shophan, and Jaazer, and Jogbehah,

36 And Bethnimrah, and Bethharan, fenced cities: and folds for sheep.

37 And the children of Reuben built Heshbon, and Elealeh, and Kirjathaim,

38 And Nebo, and Baalmeon, (their names being changed,) and Shibmah: and gave other names to the cities which they builded.

39 And the children of Machir the son of Manasseh went to Gilead, and took it, and dispossessed the Amorite which was in it.

40 And Moses gave Gilead to Machir the son of Manasseh; and he dwelt therein.

41 And Jair the son of Manasseh went and took the small towns thereof, and called them Havothjair.

42 And Nobah went and took Kenath, and the villages thereof, and called it Nobah, after his own name.

CHAPTER 33

THESE are the journeys of the children of Israel, which went forth out of the land of Egypt with their armies under the hand of Moses and Aaron.

2 And Moses wrote their goings out according to their journeys by the commandment of the LORD: and these are their journeys according to their goings out.

3 And they departed from Rameses in the first month, on the fifteenth day of the first month; on the morrow after the passover the children of Israel went out with an high hand in the sight of all the Egyptians.

4 For the Egyptians buried all their firstborn, which the LORD had smitten among them: upon their gods also the LORD executed judgments.

5 And the children of Israel removed from Rameses, and pitched in Succoth.

6 And they departed from Succoth, and pitched in Etham, which is in the edge of the wilderness.

7 And they removed from Etham, and turned again to Pihahiroth, which is before Baalzephon: and they pitched before Migdol.

8 And they departed from before Pihahiroth, and passed through the midst of the sea into the wilderness, and went three days' journey in the wilderness of Etham, and pitched in Marah.

9 And they removed from Marah, and came to Elim: and in Elim were twelve

One single soul saved

shall outlive and outweigh

all the kingdoms of the world.

John C. Ryle

1816-1900

EVANGELICAL BISHOP
OF THE ANGLICAN CHURCH

fountains of water, and threescore and ten palm trees; and they pitched there.

10 And they removed from Elim, and encamped by the Red sea.

11 And they removed from the Red sea, and encamped in the wilderness of Sin.

12 And they took their journey out of the wilderness of Sin, and encamped in Dophkah.

13 And they departed from Dophkah, and encamped in Alush.

14 And they removed from Alush, and encamped at Rephidim, where was no water for the people to drink.

15 And they departed from Rephidim, and pitched in the wilderness of Sinai.

16 And they removed from the desert of Sinai, and pitched at Kibrothhattaavah.

17 And they departed from Kibrothhattaavah, and encamped at Hazeroth.

18 And they departed from Hazeroth, and pitched in Rithmah.

19 And they departed from Rithmah, and pitched at Rimmonparez.

20 And they departed from Rimmonparez, and pitched in Libnah.

21 And they removed from Libnah, and pitched at Rissah.

22 And they journeyed from Rissah, and pitched in Kehelathah.

23 And they went from Kehelathah, and pitched in mount Shapher.

24 And they removed from mount Shapher, and encamped in Haradah.

25 And they removed from Haradah, and pitched in Makheloth.

26 And they removed from Makheloth, and encamped at Tahath.

27 And they departed from Tahath, and pitched at Tarah.

28 And they removed from Tarah, and pitched in Mithcah.

29 And they went from Mithcah, and pitched in Hashmonah.

30 And they departed from Hashmonah, and encamped at Moseroth.

31 And they departed from Moseroth, and pitched in Benejaakan.

32 And they removed from Benejaakan, and encamped at Horhagidgad.

33 And they went from Horhagidgad, and pitched in Jotbathah.

34 And they removed from Jotbathah, and encamped at Ebronah.

35 And they departed from Ebronah, and encamped at Eziongaber.

36 And they removed from Eziongaber, and pitched in the wilderness of Zin, which is Kadesh.

37 And they removed from Kadesh, and pitched in mount Hor, in the edge of the land of Edom.

38 And Aaron the priest went up into mount Hor at the commandment of the LORD, and died there, in the fortieth year after the children of Israel were come out of the land of Egypt, in the first day of the fifth month.

39 And Aaron was an hundred and twenty and three years old when he died in mount Hor.

40 And king Arad the Canaanite, which dwelt in the south in the land of Canaan, heard of the coming of the children of Israel.

41 And they departed from mount Hor, and pitched in Zalmonah.

42 And they departed from Zalmonah, and pitched in Punon.

43 And they departed from Punon, and pitched in Oboth.

44 And they departed from Oboth, and pitched in Ijeabarim, in the border of Moab.

45 And they departed from Iim, and pitched in Dibongad.

46 And they removed from Dibongad, and encamped in Almondiblathaim.

47 And they removed from Almondiblathaim, and pitched in the mountains of Abarim, before Nebo.

48 And they departed from the mountains of Abarim, and pitched in the plains of Moab by Jordan near Jericho.

49 And they pitched by Jordan, from Bethjesimoth even to Abelshittim in the plains of Moab.

50 And the LORD spoke to Moses in the plains of Moab by Jordan near Jericho, saying,

51 Speak to the children of Israel, and say to them, When you are passed over Jordan into the land of Canaan;

52 Then you shall drive out all the inhabitants of the land from before you, and destroy all their pictures, and destroy all their molten images, and quite pluck down all their high places:

53 And you shall dispossess the inhabitants of the land, and dwell therein: for I have given you the land to possess it.

54 And you shall divide the land by lot for an inheritance among your families: and to the more you shall give the more inheritance, and to the fewer you shall give the less inheritance: every man's inheritance shall be in the place where his lot falls; according to the tribes of your fathers you shall inherit.

55 But if you will not drive out the inhabitants of the land from before you; then it shall come to pass, that those which you let remain of them shall be pricks in your eyes, and thorns in your sides, and shall vex you in the land wherein you dwell.

56 Moreover it shall come to pass, that I shall do to you, as I thought to do to them.

CHAPTER 34

AND the LORD spoke to Moses, saying,

2 Command the children of Israel, and say to them, When you come into the land of Canaan; (this is the land that shall fall to you for an inheritance, even the land of Canaan with the coasts thereof:)

3 Then your south quarter shall be from the wilderness of Zin along by the coast of Edom, and your south border shall be the outmost coast of the salt sea eastward:

4 And your border shall turn from the south to the ascent of Akrabbim, and pass on to Zin: and the going forth thereof shall be from the south to Kadeshbarnea, and shall go on to Hazaraddar, and pass on to Azmon:

5 And the border shall fetch a compass from Azmon to the river of Egypt, and the goings out of it shall be at the sea.

6 And as for the western border, you shall even have the great sea for a border: this shall be your west border.

7 And this shall be your north border: from the great sea you shall point out for you mount Hor:

8 From mount Hor you shall point out your border to the entrance of Hamath; and the goings forth of the border shall be to Zedad:

9 And the border shall go on to Ziphron, and the goings out of it shall be at Hazarenan: this shall be your north border.

10 And you shall point out your east border from Hazarenan to Shepham:

11 And the coast shall go down from Shepham to Riblah, on the east side of Ain; and the border shall descend, and shall reach to the side of the sea of Chinnereth eastward:

12 And the border shall go down to Jordan, and the goings out of it shall be at the salt sea: this shall be your land with the coasts thereof round about.

13 And Moses commanded the children of Israel, saying, This is the land which you shall inherit by lot, which the LORD commanded to give to the nine tribes, and to the half tribe:

14 For the tribe of the children of Reuben according to the house of their fathers, and the tribe of the children of Gad according to the house of their fathers, have received their inheritance; and half the tribe of Manasseh have received their inheritance:

15 The two tribes and the half tribe have received their inheritance on this side Jordan near Jericho eastward, toward the sunrising.

16 And the LORD spoke to Moses, saying,

17 These are the names of the men which shall divide the land to you: Eleazar the priest, and Joshua the son of Nun.

18 And you shall take one prince of every tribe, to divide the land by inheritance.

19 And the names of the men are these: Of the tribe of Judah, Caleb the son of Jephunneh.

20 And of the tribe of the children of Simeon, Shemuel the son of Ammihud.

21 Of the tribe of Benjamin, Elidad the son of Chislon.

22 And the prince of the tribe of the children of Dan, Bukki the son of Jogli.

23 The prince of the children of Joseph, for the tribe of the children of Manasseh, Hanniel the son of Ephod.

24 And the prince of the tribe of the children of Ephraim, Kemuel the son of Shiphtan.

25 And the prince of the tribe of the children of Zebulun, Elizaphan the son of Parnach.

26 And the prince of the tribe of the children of Issachar, Paltiel the son of Azzan.

27 And the prince of the tribe of the children of Asher, Ahihud the son of Shelomi.

28 And the prince of the tribe of the children of Naphtali, Pedahel the son of Ammihud.

29 These are they whom the LORD commanded to divide the inheritance to the children of Israel in the land of Canaan.

CHAPTER 35

AND the LORD spoke to Moses in the plains of Moab by Jordan near Jericho, saying,

2 Command the children of Israel, that they give to the Levites of the inheritance of their possession cities to dwell in; and you shall give also to the Levites suburbs for the cities round about them.

3 And the cities shall they have to dwell in; and the suburbs of them shall be for their cattle, and for their goods, and for all their beasts.

4 And the suburbs of the cities, which you shall give to the Levites, shall reach from the wall of the city and outward a thousand cubits round about.

5 And you shall measure from without the city on the east side two thousand cubits, and on the south side two thousand cubits, and on the west side two thousand cubits, and on the north side two thousand cubits; and the city shall be in the midst: this shall be to them the suburbs of the cities.

6 And among the cities which you shall give to the Levites there shall be six cities for refuge, which you shall appoint for the manslayer, that he may flee thither:

and to them you shall add forty and two cities.

7 So all the cities which you shall give to the Levites shall be forty and eight cities: them shall you give with their suburbs.

8 And the cities which you shall give shall be of the possession of the children of Israel: from them that have many you shall give many; but from them that have few you shall give few: every one shall give of his cities to the Levites according to his inheritance which he inherits.

9 And the LORD spoke to Moses, saying,

10 Speak to the children of Israel, and say to them, When you be come over Jordan into the land of Canaan;

11 Then you shall appoint you cities to be cities of refuge for you; that the slayer may flee thither, which kills any person at unawares.

12 And they shall be to you cities for refuge from the avenger; that the manslayer die not, until he stand before the congregation in judgment.

13 And of these cities which you shall give six cities shall you have for refuge.

14 You shall give three cities on this side Jordan, and three cities shall you give in the land of Canaan, which shall be cities of refuge.

15 These six cities shall be a refuge, both for the children of Israel, and for the stranger, and for the sojourner among them: that every one that kills any person unawares may flee thither.

16 And if he smite him with an instrument of iron, so that he die, he is a murderer: the murderer shall surely be put to death.

17 And if he smite him with throwing a stone, wherewith he may die, and he die, he is a murderer: the murderer shall surely be put to death.

18 Or if he smite him with an hand weapon of wood, wherewith he may die, and he die, he is a murderer: the murderer shall surely be put to death.

19 The revenger of blood himself shall slay the murderer: when he meets him, he shall slay him.

20 But if he thrust him of hatred, or hurl at him by laying of wait, that he die;

21 Or in enmity smite him with his hand, that he die: he that smote him shall surely be put to death; for he is a murderer: the revenger of blood shall slay the murderer, when he meets him.

22 But if he thrust him suddenly without enmity, or have cast upon him any thing without laying of wait,

23 Or with any stone, wherewith a man may die, seeing him not, and cast it upon him, that he die, and was not his enemy, neither sought his harm:

24 Then the congregation shall judge between the slayer and the revenger of blood according to these judgments:

25 And the congregation shall deliver the slayer out of the hand of the revenger of blood, and the congregation shall restore him to the city of his refuge, whither he was fled: and he shall abide in it to the death of the high priest, which was anointed with the holy oil.

26 But if the slayer shall at any time come without the border of the city of his refuge, whither he was fled;

27 And the revenger of blood find him without the borders of the city of his refuge, and the revenger of blood kill the slayer; he shall not be guilty of blood:

28 Because he should have remained in the city of his refuge until the death of the high priest: but after the death of the high priest the slayer shall return into the land of his possession.

29 So these things shall be for a statute of judgment to you throughout your generations in all your dwellings.

30 Whoso kills any person, the murderer shall be put to death by the mouth of witnesses: but one witness shall not testify against any person to cause him to die.

31 Moreover you shall take no satisfaction for the life of a murderer, which is

guilty of death: but he shall be surely put to death.

32 And you shall take no satisfaction for him that is fled to the city of his refuge, that he should come again to dwell in the land, until the death of the priest.

33 So you shall not pollute the land wherein you are: for blood it defiles the land: and the land cannot be cleansed of the blood that is shed therein, but by the blood of him that shed it.

34 Defile not therefore the land which you shall inhabit, wherein I dwell: for I the LORD dwell among the children of Israel.

CHAPTER 36

AND the chief fathers of the families of the children of Gilead, the son of Machir, the son of Manasseh, of the families of the sons of Joseph, came near, and spoke before Moses, and before the princes, the chief fathers of the children of Israel:

2 And they said, The LORD commanded my lord to give the land for an inheritance by lot to the children of Israel: and my lord was commanded by the LORD to give the inheritance of Zelophehad our brother to his daughters.

3 And if they be married to any of the sons of the other tribes of the children of Israel, then shall their inheritance be taken from the inheritance of our fathers, and shall be put to the inheritance of the tribe whereunto they are received: so shall it be taken from the lot of our inheritance.

4 And when the jubile of the children of Israel shall be, then shall their inheritance be put to the inheritance of the tribe whereunto they are received: so shall their inheritance be taken away from the inheritance of the tribe of our fathers.

5 And Moses commanded the children of Israel according to the word of the LORD, saying, The tribe of the sons of Joseph has said well.

6 This is the thing which the LORD doth command concerning the daughters of Zelophehad, saying, Let them marry to whom they think best; only to the family of the tribe of their father shall they marry.

7 So shall not the inheritance of the children of Israel remove from tribe to tribe: for every one of the children of Israel shall keep himself to the inheritance of the tribe of his fathers.

8 And every daughter, that possesses an inheritance in any tribe of the children of Israel, shall be wife to one of the family of the tribe of her father, that the children of Israel may enjoy every man the inheritance of his fathers.

9 Neither shall the inheritance remove from one tribe to another tribe; but every one of the tribes of the children of Israel shall keep himself to his own inheritance.

10 Even as the LORD commanded Moses, so did the daughters of Zelophehad:

11 For Mahlah, Tirzah, and Hoglah, and Milcah, and Noah, the daughters of Zelophehad, were married to their father's brothers' sons:

12 And they were married into the families of the sons of Manasseh the son of Joseph, and their inheritance remained in the tribe of the family of their father.

13 These are the commandments and the judgments, which the LORD commanded by the hand of Moses to the children of Israel in the plains of Moab by Jordan near Jericho.

Deuteronomy

CHAPTER 1

THESE be the words which Moses spoke to all Israel on this side Jordan in the wilderness, in the plain over against the Red sea, between Paran, and Tophel, and Laban, and Hazeroth, and Dizahab.

2 (There are eleven days' journey from Horeb by the way of mount Seir to Kadeshbarnea.)

3 And it came to pass in the fortieth year, in the eleventh month, on the first day of the month, that Moses spoke to the children of Israel, according to all that the LORD had given him in commandment to them;

4 After he had slain Sihon the king of the Amorites, which dwelt in Heshbon, and Og the king of Bashan, which dwelt at Astaroth in Edrei:

5 On this side Jordan, in the land of Moab, began Moses to declare this law, saying,

6 The LORD our God spoke to us in Horeb, saying, You have dwelt long enough in this mount:

7 Turn, and take your journey, and go to the mount of the Amorites, and to all the places nigh thereunto, in the plain, in the hills, and in the vale, and in the south, and by the sea side, to the land of the Canaanites, and to Lebanon, to the great river, the river Euphrates.

8 Behold, I have set the land before you: go in and possess the land which the LORD swore to your fathers, Abraham, Isaac, and Jacob, to give to them and to their seed after them.

9 And I spoke to you at that time, saying, I am not able to bear you myself alone:

10 The LORD your God has multiplied you, and, behold, you are this day as the stars of heaven for multitude.

11 (The LORD God of your fathers make you a thousand times so many more as you are, and bless you, as he has promised you!)

12 How can I myself alone bear your cumbrance, and your burden, and your strife?

13 Take you wise men, and understanding, and known among your tribes, and I will make them rulers over you.

14 And you answered me, and said, The thing which you have spoken is good for us to do.

15 So I took the chief of your tribes, wise men, and known, and made them heads over you, captains over thousands, and captains over hundreds, and captains over fifties, and captains over tens, and officers among your tribes.

16 And I charged your judges at that time, saying, Hear the causes between your brethren, and judge righteously between every man and his brother, and the stranger that is with him.

17 You shall not respect persons in judgment; but you shall hear the small as well as the great; you shall not be afraid of the face of man; for the judg-

ment is God's: and the cause that is too hard for you, bring it to me, and I will hear it.

18 And I commanded you at that time all the things which you should do.

19 And when we departed from Horeb, we went through all that great and terrible wilderness, which you saw by the way of the mountain of the Amorites, as the LORD our God commanded us; and we came to Kadeshbarnea.

20 And I said to you, You are come to the mountain of the Amorites, which the LORD our God gives to us.

21 Behold, the LORD your God has set the land before you: go up and possess it, as the LORD God of your fathers has said to you; fear not, neither be discouraged.

22 And you came near to me every one of you, and said, We will send men before us, and they shall search us out the land, and bring us word again by what way we must go up, and into what cities we shall come.

23 And the saying pleased me well: and I took twelve men of you, one of a tribe:

24 And they turned and went up into the mountain, and came to the valley of Eshcol, and searched it out.

25 And they took of the fruit of the land in their hands, and brought it down to us, and brought us word again, and said, It is a good land which the LORD our God doth give us.

26 Notwithstanding you would not go up, but rebelled against the commandment of the LORD your God:

27 And you murmured in your tents, and said, Because the LORD hated us, he has brought us forth out of the land of Egypt, to deliver us into the hand of the Amorites, to destroy us.

28 Whither shall we go up? our brethren have discouraged our heart, saying, The people are greater and taller than we; the cities are great and walled up to heaven; and moreover we have seen the sons of the Anakims there.

29 Then I said to you, Dread not, neither be afraid of them.

30 The LORD your God which goes before you, he shall fight for you, according to all that he did for you in Egypt before your eyes;

31 And in the wilderness, where you have seen how that the LORD your God bare you, as a man doth bear his son, in all the way that you went, until you came into this place.

32 Yet in this thing you did not believe the LORD your God,

33 Who went in the way before you, to search you out a place to pitch your tents in, in fire by night, to show you by what way you should go, and in a cloud by day.

34 And the LORD heard the voice of your words, and was wroth, and swore, saying,

35 Surely there shall not one of these men of this evil generation see that good land, which I swore to give to your fathers.

36 Save Caleb the son of Jephunneh; he shall see it, and to him will I give the land that he has trodden upon, and to his children, because he has wholly followed the LORD.

37 Also the LORD was angry with me for your sakes, saying, You also shall not go in thither.

38 But Joshua the son of Nun, which stands before you, he shall go in thither: encourage him: for he shall cause Israel to inherit it.

39 Moreover your little ones, which you said should be a prey, and your children, which in that day had no knowledge between good and evil, they shall go in thither, and to them will I give it, and they shall possess it.

40 But as for you, turn you, and take your journey into the wilderness by the way of the Red Sea.

41 Then you answered and said to me, We have sinned against the LORD, we will go up and fight, according to all that the LORD our God commanded us. And

when you had girded on every man his weapons of war, you were ready to go up into the hill.

42 And the LORD said to me, Say to them. Go not up, neither fight; for I am not among you; lest you be smitten before your enemies.

43 So I spoke to you; and you would not hear, but rebelled against the commandment of the LORD, and went presumptuously up into the hill.

44 And the Amorites, which dwelt in that mountain, came out against you, and chased you, as bees do, and destroyed you in Seir, even to Hormah.

45 And you returned and wept before the LORD; but the LORD would not hearken to your voice, nor give ear to you.

46 So you abode in Kadesh many days, according to the days that you abode there.

CHAPTER 2

THEN we turned, and took our journey into the wilderness by the way of the Red sea, as the LORD spoke to me: and we compassed mount Seir many days.

2 And the LORD spoke to me, saying,

3 You have compassed this mountain long enough: turn you northward.

4 And command you the people, saying, You are to pass through the coast of your brethren the children of Esau, which dwell in Seir; and they shall be afraid of you: take you good heed to yourselves therefore:

5 Meddle not with them; for I will not give you of their land, no, not so much as a foot breadth; because I have given mount Seir to Esau for a possession.

6 You shall buy meat of them for money, that you may eat; and you shall also buy water of them for money, that you may drink.

7 For the LORD your God has blessed you in all the works of your hand: he knows your walking through this great wilderness: these forty years the LORD your God has been with you; you have lacked nothing.

8 And when we passed by from our brethren the children of Esau, which dwelt in Seir, through the way of the plain from Elath, and from Eziongaber, we turned and passed by the way of the wilderness of Moab.

9 And the LORD said to me, Distress not the Moabites, neither contend with them in battle: for I will not give you of their land for a possession; because I have given Ar to the children of Lot for a possession.

10 The Emims dwelt therein in times past, a people great, and many, and tall, as the Anakims;

11 Which also were accounted giants, as the Anakims; but the Moabites called them Emims.

12 The Horims also dwelt in Seir beforetime; but the children of Esau succeeded them, when they had destroyed them from before them, and dwelt in their stead; as Israel did to the land of his possession, which the LORD gave to them.

13 Now rise up, said I, and get you over the brook Zered. And we went over the brook Zered.

14 And the space in which we came from Kadeshbarnea, until we were come over the brook Zered, was thirty and eight years; until all the generation of the men of war were wasted out from among the host, as the LORD swore to them.

15 For indeed the hand of the LORD was against them, to destroy them from among the host, until they were consumed.

16 So it came to pass, when all the men of war were consumed and dead from among the people,

17 That the LORD spoke to me, saying,

18 You are to pass over through Ar, the coast of Moab, this day:

19 And when you come nigh over against the children of Ammon, distress them not, nor meddle with them: for I will not give you of the land of the chil-

dren of Ammon any possession; because I have given it to the children of Lot for a possession.

20 (That also was accounted a land of giants: giants dwelt therein in old time; and the Ammonites call them Zamzummims;

21 A people great, and many, and tall, as the Anakims; but the LORD destroyed them before them; and they succeeded them, and dwelt in their stead:

22 As he did to the children of Esau, which dwelt in Seir, when he destroyed the Horims from before them; and they succeeded them, and dwelt in their stead even to this day:

23 And the Avims which dwelt in Hazerim, even to Azzah, the Caphtorims, which came forth out of Caphtor, destroyed them, and dwelt in their stead.)

24 Rise up, take your journey, and pass over the river Arnon: behold, I have given into your hand Sihon the Amorite, king of Heshbon, and his land: begin to possess it, and contend with him in battle.

25 This day will I begin to put the dread of you and the fear of you upon the nations that are under the whole heaven, who shall hear report of you, and shall tremble, and be in anguish because of you.

26 And I sent messengers out of the wilderness of Kedemoth to Sihon king of Heshbon with words of peace, saying,

27 Let me pass through your land: I will go along by the high way, I will neither turn to the right hand nor to the left.

28 You shall sell me meat for money, that I may eat; and give me water for money, that I may drink: only I will pass through on my feet;

29 (As the children of Esau which dwell in Seir, and the Moabites which dwell in Ar, did to me;) until I shall pass over Jordan into the land which the LORD our God gives us.

30 But Sihon king of Heshbon would not let us pass by him: for the LORD your God hardened his spirit, and made his heart obstinate, that he might deliver him into your hand, as appears this day.

31 And the LORD said to me, Behold, I have begun to give Sihon and his land before you: begin to possess, that you may inherit his land.

32 Then Sihon came out against us, he and all his people, to fight at Jahaz.

33 And the LORD our God delivered him before us; and we smote him, and his sons, and all his people.

34 And we took all his cities at that time, and utterly destroyed the men, and the women, and the little ones, of every city, we left none to remain:

35 Only the cattle we took for a prey to ourselves, and the spoil of the cities which we took.

36 From Aroer, which is by the brink of the river of Arnon, and from the city that is by the river, even to Gilead, there was not one city too strong for us: the LORD our God delivered all to us:

37 Only to the land of the children of Ammon you came not, nor to any place of the river Jabbok, nor to the cities in the mountains, nor to whatsoever the LORD our God forbad us.

CHAPTER 3

THEN we turned, and went up the way to Bashan: and Og the king of Bashan came out against us, he and all his people, to battle at Edrei.

2 And the LORD said to me, Fear him not: for I will deliver him, and all his people, and his land, into your hand; and you shall do to him as you did to Sihon king of the Amorites, which dwelt at Heshbon.

3 So the LORD our God delivered into our hands Og also, the king of Bashan, and all his people: and we smote him until none was left to him remaining.

4 And we took all his cities at that time, there was not a city which we took not from them, threescore cities, all the

region of Argob, the kingdom of Og in Bashan.

5 All these cities were fenced with high walls, gates, and bars; beside unwalled towns a great many.

6 And we utterly destroyed them, as we did to Sihon king of Heshbon, utterly destroying the men, women, and children, of every city.

7 But all the cattle, and the spoil of the cities, we took for a prey to ourselves.

8 And we took at that time out of the hand of the two kings of the Amorites the land that was on this side Jordan, from the river of Arnon to mount Hermon;

9 (Which Hermon the Sidonians call Sirion; and the Amorites call it Shenir;)

10 All the cities of the plain, and all Gilead, and all Bashan, to Salchah and Edrei, cities of the kingdom of Og in Bashan.

11 For only Og king of Bashan remained of the remnant of giants; behold his bedstead was a bedstead of iron; is it not in Rabbath of the children of Ammon? nine cubits was the length thereof, and four cubits the breadth of it, after the cubit of a man.

12 And this land, which we possessed at that time, from Aroer, which is by the river Arnon, and half mount Gilead, and the cities thereof, gave I to the Reubenites and to the Gadites.

13 And the rest of Gilead, and all Bashan, being the kingdom of Og, gave I to the half tribe of Manasseh; all the region of Argob, with all Bashan, which was called the land of giants.

14 Jair the son of Manasseh took all the country of Argob to the coasts of Geshuri and Maachathi; and called them after his own name, Bashanhavothjair, to this day.

15 And I gave Gilead to Machir.

16 And to the Reubenites and to the Gadites I gave from Gilead even to the river Arnon half the valley, and the border even to the river Jabbok, which is the border of the children of Ammon;

17 The plain also, and Jordan, and the coast thereof, from Chinnereth even to the sea of the plain, even the salt sea, under Ashdothpisgah eastward.

18 And I commanded you at that time, saying, The LORD your God has given you this land to possess it: you shall pass over armed before your brethren the children of Israel, all that are meet for the war.

19 But your wives, and your little ones, and your cattle, (for I know that you have much cattle,) shall abide in your cities which I have given you;

20 Until the LORD have given rest to your brethren, as well as to you, and until they also possess the land which the LORD your God has given them beyond Jordan: and then shall you return every man to his possession, which I have given you.

21 And I commanded Joshua at that time, saying, Your eyes have seen all that the LORD your God has done to these two kings: so shall the LORD do to all the kingdoms whither you pass.

22 You shall not fear them: for the LORD your God he shall fight for you.

23 And I besought the LORD at that time, saying,

24 O Lord GOD, you have begun to show your servant your greatness, and your mighty hand: for what God is there in heaven or in earth, that can do according to your works, and according to your might?

25 I pray you, let me go over, and see the good land that is beyond Jordan, that goodly mountain, and Lebanon.

26 But the LORD was wroth with me for your sakes, and would not hear me: and the LORD said to me, Let it suffice you; speak no more to me of this matter.

27 Get up into the top of Pisgah, and lift up your eyes westward, and northward, and southward, and eastward, and behold it with your eyes: for you shall not go over this Jordan.

28 But charge Joshua, and encourage him, and strengthen him: for he shall go

over before this people, and he shall cause them to inherit the land which you shall see.

29 So we abode in the valley over against Bethpeor.

CHAPTER 4

NOW therefore hearken, O Israel, to the statutes and to the judgments, which I teach you, for to do them, that you may live, and go in and possess the land which the LORD God of your fathers gives you.

2 You shall not add to the word which I command you, neither shall you diminish ought from it, that you may keep the commandments of the LORD your God which I command you.

3 Your eyes have seen what the LORD did because of Baalpeor: for all the men that followed Baalpeor, the LORD your God has destroyed them from among you.

4 But you that did cleave to the LORD your God are alive every one of you this day.

5 Behold, I have taught you statutes and judgments, even as the LORD my God commanded me, that you should do so in the land whither you go to possess it.

6 Keep therefore and do them; for this is your wisdom and your understanding in the sight of the nations, which shall hear all these statutes, and say, Surely this great nation is a wise and understanding people.

7 For what nation is there so great, who has God so nigh to them, as the LORD our God is in all things that we call upon him for?

8 And what nation is there so great, that has statutes and judgments so righteous as all this law, which I set before you this day?

9 Only take heed to yourself, and keep your soul diligently, lest you forget the things which your eyes have seen, and lest they depart from your heart all the days of your life: but teach them your sons, and your sons' sons;

4:10

Any parent who doesn't make time for family devotions should not be mystified when their children turn from the things of God in teenage years.

Parents whose love for their children is deep enough to include concern for their children's eternal welfare will build a solid spiritual foundation for their children during the children's years of impression (See Psalm 78:4-5).

10 Specially the day that you stood before the LORD your God in Horeb, when the LORD said to me, Gather me the people together, and I will make them hear my words, that they may learn to fear me all the days that they shall live upon the earth, and that they may teach their children.

11 And you came near and stood under the mountain; and the mountain burned with fire to the midst of heaven, with darkness, clouds, and thick darkness.

12 And the LORD spoke to you out of the midst of the fire: you heard the voice of the words, but saw no similitude; only you heard a voice.

13 And he declared to you his covenant, which he commanded you to perform, even ten commandments; and he wrote them upon two tables of stone.

14 And the LORD commanded me at that time to teach you statutes and judgments, that you might do them in the land whither you go over to possess it.

15 Take you therefore good heed to yourselves; for you saw no manner of similitude on the day that the LORD

SPRINGBOARDS FOR PREACHING AND WITNESSING

4:24   *Why do I need a savior?*

If you were to place a dried-out leaf into the presence of fire, you would notice that the fire would not hesitate to consume the leaf in a matter of seconds. The fire must consume the leaf because of its very nature. Even if the fire didn't want to dispose of the leaf, it wouldn't matter; it still must consume it because their natures are diametrically opposed one to the other.

As in Deuteronomy 4:24, Hebrews 12:29 also describes God as a consuming fire. By His very nature, God must consume anything and everything that opposes His nature. We must put on the Lord Jesus Christ, or we will be consumed by the ever-pure burning holiness of the King of Kings.

---

spoke to you in Horeb out of the midst of the fire:

16 Lest you corrupt yourselves, and make you a graven image, the similitude of any figure, the likeness of male or female,

17 The likeness of any beast that is on the earth, the likeness of any winged fowl that flies in the air,

18 The likeness of any thing that creeps on the ground, the likeness of any fish that is in the waters beneath the earth:

19 And lest you lift up your eyes to heaven, and when you see the sun, and the moon, and the stars, even all the host of heaven, should be driven to worship them, and serve them, which the LORD your God has divided to all nations under the whole heaven.

20 But the LORD has taken you, and brought you forth out of the iron furnace, even out of Egypt, to be to him a people of inheritance, as you are this day.

21 Furthermore the LORD was angry with me for your sakes, and swore that I should not go over Jordan, and that I should not go in to that good land, which the LORD your God gives you for an inheritance:

22 But I must die in this land, I must not go over Jordan: but you shall go over, and possess that good land.

23 Take heed to yourselves, lest you forget the covenant of the LORD your God, which he made with you, and make you a graven image, or the likeness of any thing, which the LORD your God has forbidden you.

24 For the LORD your God is a consuming fire, even a jealous God.

25 When you shall beget children, and children's children, and you shall have remained long in the land, and shall corrupt yourselves, and make a graven image, or the likeness of any thing, and shall do evil in the sight of the LORD your God, to provoke him to anger:

26 I call heaven and earth to witness against you this day, that you shall soon utterly perish from off the land whereunto you go over Jordan to possess it; you shall not prolong your days upon it, but shall utterly be destroyed.

27 And the LORD shall scatter you among the nations, and you shall be left few in number among the heathen, whither the LORD shall lead you.

28 And there you shall serve gods, the work of men's hands, wood and stone, which neither see, nor hear, nor eat, nor smell.

29 But if from thence you shall seek the LORD your God, you shall find him, if you seek him with all your heart and with all your soul.

30 When you are in tribulation, and all these things are come upon you, even in the latter days, if you turn to the LORD your God, and shall be obedient to his voice;

31 (For the LORD your God is a merciful God;) he will not forsake you, neither destroy you, nor forget the covenant of your fathers which he swore to them.

32 For ask now of the days that are past, which were before you, since the day that God created man upon the earth, and ask from the one side of heaven to the other, whether there has been any such thing as this great thing is, or has been heard like it?

33 Did ever people hear the voice of God speaking out of the midst of the fire, as you have heard, and live?

34 Or has God assayed to go and take him a nation from the midst of another nation, by temptations, by signs, and by wonders, and by war, and by a mighty hand, and by a stretched out arm, and by great terrors, according to all that the LORD your God did for you in Egypt before your eyes?

35 To you it was shown, that you might know that the LORD he is God; there is none else beside him.

36 Out of heaven he made you to hear his voice, that he might instruct you: and upon earth he showed you his great fire; and you heard his words out of the midst of the fire.

37 And because he loved your fathers, therefore he chose their seed after them, and brought you out in his sight with his mighty power out of Egypt;

38 To drive out nations from before you greater and mightier than you are, to bring you in, to give you their land for an inheritance, as it is this day.

39 Know therefore this day, and consider it in your heart, that the LORD he is God in heaven above, and upon the earth beneath: there is none else.

40 You shall keep therefore his statutes, and his commandments, which I command you this day, that it may go well with you, and with your children after you, and that you may prolong your days upon the earth, which the LORD your God gives you, for ever.

41 Then Moses severed three cities on this side Jordan toward the sunrising;

42 That the slayer might flee thither, which should kill his neighbour unawares, and hated him not in times past; and that fleeing to one of these cities he might live:

43 Namely, Bezer in the wilderness, in the plain country, of the Reubenites; and Ramoth in Gilead, of the Gadites; and Golan in Bashan, of the Manassites.

44 And this is the law which Moses set before the children of Israel:

45 These are the testimonies, and the statutes, and the judgments, which Moses spoke to the children of Israel, after they came forth out of Egypt.

46 On this side Jordan, in the valley over against Bethpeor, in the land of Sihon king of the Amorites, who dwelt at Heshbon, whom Moses and the children of Israel smote, after they were come forth out of Egypt:

47 And they possessed his land, and the land of Og king of Bashan, two kings of the Amorites, which were on this side Jordan toward the sunrising;

48 From Aroer, which is by the bank of the river Arnon, even to mount Sion, which is Hermon,

49 And all the plain on this side Jordan eastward, even to the sea of the plain, under the springs of Pisgah.

CHAPTER 5

AND Moses called all Israel, and said to them, Hear, O Israel, the statutes and judgments which I speak in your ears this day, that you may learn them, and keep, and do them.

2 The LORD our God made a covenant with us in Horeb.

3 The LORD made not this covenant with our fathers, but with us, even us, who are all of us here alive this day.

4 The LORD talked with you face to face in the mount out of the midst of the fire,

5 (I stood between the LORD and you at that time, to show you the word of the LORD: for you were afraid by reason of the fire, and went not up into the mount;) saying,

6 I am the LORD your God, which brought you out of the land of Egypt, from the house of bondage.

7 You shall have none other gods before me.

8 You shall not make for yourself any graven image, or any likeness of any thing that is in heaven above, or that is in the earth beneath, or that is in the waters beneath the earth:

9 You shall not bow down yourself to them, nor serve them: for I the LORD your God am a jealous God, visiting the iniquity of the fathers upon the children to the third and fourth generation of them that hate me,

10 And showing mercy to thousands of them that love me and keep my commandments.

11 You shall not take the name of the LORD your God in vain: for the LORD will not hold him guiltless that takes his name in vain.

12 Keep the sabbath day to sanctify it, as the LORD your God has commanded you.

13 Six days you shall labour, and do all your work:

14 But the seventh day is the sabbath of the LORD your God: in it you shall not do any work, you, nor your son, nor your daughter, nor your manservant, nor your maidservant, nor your ox, nor your ass, nor any of your cattle, nor your stranger that is within your gates; that your manservant and your maidservant may rest as well as you.

15 And remember that you were a servant in the land of Egypt, and that the LORD your God brought you out thence through a mighty hand and by a stretched out arm: therefore the LORD your God commanded you to keep the sabbath day.

16 Honour your father and your mother, as the LORD your God has commanded you; that your days may be prolonged, and that it may go well with you, in the land which the LORD your God gives you.

17 You shall not kill.

18 Neither shall you commit adultery.

19 Neither shall you steal.

20 Neither shall you bear false witness against your neighbour.

21 Neither shall you desire your neighbour's wife, neither shall you covet your neighbour's house, his field, or his manservant, or his maidservant, his ox, or his ass, or any thing that is your neighbour's.

22 These words the LORD spoke to all your assembly in the mount out of the midst of the fire, of the cloud, and of the thick darkness, with a great voice: and he added no more. And he wrote them in two tables of stone, and delivered them to me.

23 And it came to pass, when you heard the voice out of the midst of the darkness, (for the mountain did burn with fire,) that you came near to me, even all the heads of your tribes, and your elders;

24 And you said, Behold, the LORD our God has showed us his glory and his greatness, and we have heard his voice out of the midst of the fire: we have seen this day that God doth talk with man, and he lives.

25 Now therefore why should we die? for this great fire will consume us: if we hear the voice of the LORD our God any more, then we shall die.

26 For who is there of all flesh, that has heard the voice of the living God speaking out of the midst of the fire, as we have, and lived?

27 You go near, and hear all that the LORD our God shall say: and speak to us all that the LORD our God shall speak to you; and we will hear it, and do it.

THE FUNCTION OF THE LAW

6:5-9 Christians give their sons and their daughters to the world by failing to train them up in God's good ways. (See Proverbs 22:6)

Every Christian home should have established within it a family altar made of the solid rocks of resolution, an alter whose foundation should be memorization and understanding of God's law. The Bible tells us that the Ten Commandments should be diligently spoken of when we walk with our children, talk with them, lie down with them and when we rise up with them. Yet the average Christian parent doesn't even know all ten of these commandments, much less teach them to their children.

The purpose of God's law is to teach the holiness of God, so that they will see our need for the Savior (see Galatians 3:24).

No wonder the enemy hates God's law.

28 And the LORD heard the voice of your words, when you spoke to me; and the LORD said to me, I have heard the voice of the words of this people, which they have spoken to you: they have well said all that they have spoken.

29 O that there were such an heart in them, that they would fear me, and keep all my commandments always, that it might be well with them, and with their children for ever!

30 Go say to them, Get you into your tents again.

31 But as for you, stand here by me, and I will speak to you all the commandments, and the statutes, and the judgments, which you shall teach them, that they may do them in the land which I give them to possess it.

32 You shall observe to do therefore as the LORD your God has commanded you: you shall not turn aside to the right hand or to the left.

33 You shall walk in all the ways which the LORD your God has commanded you, that you may live, and that it may be well with you, and that you may prolong your days in the land which you shall possess.

CHAPTER 6

N OW these are the commandments, the statutes, and the judgments, which the LORD your God commanded to teach you, that you might do them in the land whither you go to possess it:

2 That you might fear the LORD your God, to keep all his statutes and his commandments, which I command you, you, and your son, and your son's son, all the days of your life; and that your days may be prolonged.

3 Hear therefore, O Israel, and observe to do it; that it may be well with you, and that you may increase mightily, as the LORD God of your fathers has promised you, in the land that flows with milk and honey.

4 Hear, O Israel: The LORD our God is one LORD:

5 And you shall love the LORD your God with all your heart, and with all your soul, and with all your might.

6 And these words, which I command you this day, shall be in your heart:

7 And you shall teach them diligently to your children, and shall talk of them when you sit in your house, and when you walk by the way, and when you lie down, and when you rise up.

8 And you shall bind them for a sign upon your hand, and they shall be as frontlets between your eyes.

9 And you shall write them upon the posts of your house, and on your gates.

10 And it shall be, when the LORD your God shall have brought you into the land which he swore to your fathers,

to Abraham, to Isaac, and to Jacob, to give you great and goodly cities, which you built not,

11 And houses full of all good things, which you filled not, and wells dug, which you dug not, vineyards and olive trees, which you planted not; when you shall have eaten and be full;

12 Then beware lest you forget the LORD, which brought you forth out of the land of Egypt, from the house of bondage.

13 You shall fear the LORD your God, and serve him, and shall swear by his name.

14 You shall not go after other gods, of the gods of the people which are round about you;

15 (For the LORD your God is a jealous God among you) lest the anger of the LORD your God be kindled against you, and destroy you from off the face of the earth.

16 You shall not tempt the LORD your God, as you tempted him in Massah.

17 You shall diligently keep the commandments of the LORD your God, and his testimonies, and his statutes, which he has commanded you.

18 And you shall do that which is right and good in the sight of the LORD: that it may be well with you, and that you may go in and possess the good land which the LORD swore to your fathers.

19 To cast out all your enemies from before you, as the LORD has spoken.

20 And when your son asks you in time to come, saying, What do the testimonies mean, and the statutes, and the judgments, which the LORD our God has commanded you?

21 Then you shall say to your son, We were Pharaoh's bondmen in Egypt; and the LORD brought us out of Egypt with a mighty hand:

22 And the LORD showed signs and wonders, great and sore, upon Egypt, upon Pharaoh, and upon all his household, before our eyes:

23 And he brought us out from thence, that he might bring us in, to give us the land which he swore to our fathers.

24 And the LORD commanded us to do all these statutes, to fear the LORD our God, for our good always, that he might preserve us alive, as it is at this day.

25 And it shall be our righteousness, if we observe to do all these commandments before the LORD our God, as he has commanded us.

CHAPTER 7

WHEN the LORD your God shall bring you into the land whither you go to possess it, and has cast out many nations before you, the Hittites, and the Girgashites, and the Amorites, and the Canaanites, and the Perizzites, and the Hivites, and the Jebusites, seven nations greater and mightier than you;

2 And when the LORD your God shall deliver them before you; you shall smite them, and utterly destroy them; you shall make no covenant with them, nor show mercy to them:

3 Neither shall you make marriages with them; your daughter you shall not give to his son, nor his daughter shall you take to your son.

4 For they will turn away your son from following me, that they may serve other gods: so will the anger of the LORD be kindled against you, and destroy you suddenly.

5 But thus shall you deal with them; you shall destroy their altars, and break down their images, and cut down their groves, and burn their graven images with fire.

6 For you are an holy people to the LORD your God: the LORD your God has chosen you to be a special people to himself, above all people that are upon the face of the earth.

7 The LORD did not set his love upon you, nor choose you, because you were more in number than any people; for you were the fewest of all people:

8 But because the LORD loved you, and because he would keep the oath which he had sworn to your fathers, has the LORD brought you out with a mighty hand, and redeemed you out of the house of bondmen, from the hand of Pharaoh king of Egypt.

9 Know therefore that the LORD your God, he is God, the faithful God, which keeps covenant and mercy with them that love him and keep his commandments to a thousand generations;

10 And repays them that hate him to their face, to destroy them: he will not be slack to him that hates him, he will repay him to his face.

11 You shall therefore keep the commandments, and the statutes, and the judgments, which I command you this day, to do them.

12 Therefore it shall come to pass, if you hearken to these judgments, and keep, and do them, that the LORD your God shall keep to you the covenant and the mercy which he swore to your fathers:

13 And he will love you, and bless you, and multiply you: he will also bless the fruit of your womb, and the fruit of your land, your corn, and your wine, and your oil, the increase of your kine, and the flocks of your sheep, in the land which he swore to your fathers to give you.

14 You shall be blessed above all people: there shall not be male or female barren among you, or among your cattle.

15 And the LORD will take away from you all sickness, and will put none of the evil diseases of Egypt, which you know, upon you; but will lay them upon all them that hate you.

16 And you shall consume all the people which the LORD your God shall deliver you; your eye shall have no pity upon them: neither shall you serve their gods; for that will be a snare to you.

17 If you shall say in your heart, These nations are more than I; how can I dispossess them?

18 You shall not be afraid of them: but shall well remember what the LORD your God did to Pharaoh, and to all Egypt;

19 The great temptations which your eyes saw, and the signs, and the wonders, and the mighty hand, and the stretched out arm, whereby the LORD your God brought you out: so shall the LORD your God do to all the people of whom you are afraid.

20 Moreover the LORD your God will send the hornet among them, until they that are left, and hide themselves from you, be destroyed.

21 You shall not be affrighted at them: for the LORD your God is among you, a mighty God and terrible.

22 And the LORD your God will put out those nations before you by little and little: you may not consume them at once, lest the beasts of the field increase upon you.

23 But the LORD your God shall deliver them to you, and shall destroy them with a mighty destruction, until they be destroyed.

24 And he shall deliver their kings into your hand, and you shall destroy their name from under heaven: there shall no man be able to stand before you, until you have destroyed them.

25 The graven images of their gods shall you burn with fire: you shall not desire the silver or gold that is on them, nor take it to you, lest you be snared therin: for it is an abomination to the LORD your God.

26 Neither shall you bring an abomination into your house, lest you be a cursed thing like it: but you shall utterly detest it, and you shall utterly abhor it; for it is a cursed thing.

CHAPTER 8

ALL the commandments which I command you this day shall you observe to do, that you may live, and multiply, and go in and possess the land which the LORD swore to your fathers.

2 And you shall remember all the way which the LORD your God led you these forty years in the wilderness, to humble you, and to prove you, to know what was in your heart, whether you would keep his commandments, or no.

3 And he humbled you, and suffered you to hunger, and fed you with manna, which you knew not, neither did your fathers know; that he might make you know that man doth not live by bread only, but by every word that proceeds out of the mouth of the LORD doth man live.

4 Your raiment waxed not old upon you, neither did your foot swell, these forty years.

5 You shall also consider in your heart, that, as a man chastens his son, so the LORD your God chastens you.

6 Therefore you shall keep the commandments of the LORD your God, to walk in his ways, and to fear him.

7 For the LORD your God brings you into a good land, a land of brooks of water, of fountains and depths that spring out of valleys and hills;

8 A land of wheat, and barley, and vines, and fig trees, and pomegranates; a land of oil olive, and honey;

9 A land wherein you shall eat bread without scarceness, you shall not lack any thing in it; a land whose stones are iron, and out of whose hills you may dig brass.

10 When you have eaten and are full, then you shall bless the LORD your God for the good land which he has given you.

11 Beware that you forget not the LORD your God, in not keeping his commandments, and his judgments, and his statutes, which I command you this day:

12 Lest when you have eaten and are full, and have built goodly houses, and dwelt therein;

13 And when your herds and your flocks multiply, and your silver and your gold is multiplied, and all that you have is multiplied;

14 Then your heart be lifted up, and you forget the LORD your God, which brought you forth out of the land of Egypt, from the house of bondage;

15 Who led you through that great and terrible wilderness, wherein were fiery serpents, and scorpions, and drought, where there was no water; who brought you forth water out of the rock of flint;

16 Who fed you in the wilderness with manna, which your fathers knew not, that he might humble you, and that he might prove you, to do you good at your latter end;

17 And you say in your heart, My power and the might of mine hand has gotten me this wealth.

18 But you shall remember the LORD your God: for it is he that gives you power to get wealth, that he may establish his covenant which he swore to your fathers, as it is this day.

19 And it shall be, if you do at all forget the LORD your God, and walk after other gods, and serve them, and worship them, I testify against you this day that you shall surely perish.

20 As the nations which the LORD destroys before your face, so shall you perish; because you would not be obedient to the voice of the LORD your God.

CHAPTER 9

HEAR, O Israel: You are to pass over Jordan this day, to go in to possess nations greater and mightier than yourself, cities great and fenced up to heaven,

2 A people great and tall, the children of the Anakims, whom you know, and of whom you have heard say, Who can stand before the children of Anak!

3 Understand therefore this day, that the LORD your God is he which goes over before you; as a consuming fire he shall destroy them, and he shall bring them down before your face: so shall you drive them out, and destroy them quickly, as the LORD has said to you.

4 Speak not in your heart, after that the LORD your God has cast them out from before you, saying, For my righteousness the LORD has brought me in to possess this land: but for the wickedness of these nations the LORD doth drive them out from before you.

5 Not for your righteousness, or for the uprightness of your heart, dost you go to possess their land: but for the wickedness of these nations the LORD your God doth drive them out from before you, and that he may perform the word which the LORD swore to your fathers, Abraham, Isaac, and Jacob.

6 Understand therefore, that the LORD your God gives you not this good land to possess it for your righteousness; for you are a stiffnecked people.

7 Remember, and forget not, how you provoked the LORD your God to wrath in the wilderness: from the day that you did depart out of the land of Egypt, until you came to this place, you have been rebellious against the LORD.

8 Also in Horeb you provoked the LORD to wrath, so that the LORD was angry with you to have destroyed you.

9 When I was gone up into the mount to receive the tables of stone, even the tables of the covenant which the LORD made with you, then I abode in the mount forty days and forty nights, I neither did eat bread nor drink water:

10 And the LORD delivered to me two tables of stone written with the finger of God; and on them was written according to all the words, which the LORD spoke with you in the mount out of the midst of the fire in the day of the assembly.

11 And it came to pass at the end of forty days and forty nights, that the LORD gave me the two tables of stone, even the tables of the covenant.

12 And the LORD said to me, Arise, get down quickly from hence; for your people which you have brought forth out of Egypt have corrupted themselves; they are quickly turned aside out of the way which I commanded them; they have made them a molten image.

13 Furthermore the LORD spoke to me, saying, I have seen this people, and, behold, it is a stiffnecked people:

14 Let me alone, that I may destroy them, and blot out their name from under heaven: and I will make of you a nation mightier and greater than they.

15 So I turned and came down from the mount, and the mount burned with fire: and the two tables of the covenant were in my two hands.

16 And I looked, and, behold, you had sinned against the LORD your God, and had made you a molten calf: you had turned aside quickly out of the way which the LORD had commanded you.

17 And I took the two tables, and cast them out of my two hands, and brake them before your eyes.

18 And I fell down before the LORD, as at the first, forty days and forty nights: I did neither eat bread, nor drink water, because of all your sins which you sinned, in doing wickedly in the sight of the LORD, to provoke him to anger.

19 For I was afraid of the anger and hot displeasure, wherewith the LORD was wroth against you to destroy you. But the LORD hearkened to me at that time also.

20 And the LORD was very angry with Aaron to have destroyed him: and I prayed for Aaron also the same time.

21 And I took your sin, the calf which you had made, and burnt it with fire, and stamped it, and ground it very small, even until it was as small as dust: and I cast the dust thereof into the brook that descended out of the mount.

22 And at Taberah, and at Massah, and at Kibrothhattaavah, you provoked the LORD to wrath.

23 Likewise when the LORD sent you from Kadeshbarnea, saying, Go up and possess the land which I have given you; then you rebelled against the commandment of the LORD your God, and you

believed him not, nor hearkened to his voice.

24 You have been rebellious against the LORD from the day that I knew you.

25 Thus I fell down before the LORD forty days and forty nights, as I fell down at the first; because the LORD had said he would destroy you.

26 I prayed therefore to the LORD, and said, O Lord GOD, destroy not your people and your inheritance, which you have redeemed through your greatness, which you have brought forth out of Egypt with a mighty hand.

27 Remember your servants, Abraham, Isaac, and Jacob; look not to the stubbornness of this people, nor to their wickedness, nor to their sin:

28 Lest the land whence you brought us out say, Because the LORD was not able to bring them into the land which he promised them, and because he hated them, he has brought them out to slay them in the wilderness.

29 Yet they are your people and your inheritance, which you brought out by your mighty power and by your stretched out arm.

CHAPTER 10

A T that time the LORD said to me, Hew for yourself two tables of stone like to the first, and come up to me into the mount, and make for yourself an ark of wood.

2 And I will write on the tables the words that were in the first tables which you broke, and you shall put them in the ark.

3 And I made an ark of shittim wood, and hewed two tables of stone like to the first, and went up into the mount, having the two tables in mine hand.

4 And he wrote on the tables, according to the first writing, the ten commandments, which the LORD spoke to you in the mount out of the midst of the fire in the day of the assembly: and the LORD gave them to me.

5 And I turned myself and came down from the mount, and put the tables in the ark which I had made; and there they be, as the LORD commanded me.

6 And the children of Israel took their journey from Beeroth of the children of Jaakan to Mosera: there Aaron died, and there he was buried; and Eleazar his son ministered in the priest's office in his stead.

7 From thence they journeyed to Gudgodah; and from Gudgodah to Jotbath, a land of rivers of waters.

8 At that time the LORD separated the tribe of Levi, to bear the ark of the covenant of the LORD, to stand before the LORD to minister to him, and to bless in his name, to this day.

9 Therefore Levi has no part nor inheritance with his brethren; the LORD is his inheritance, according as the LORD your God promised him.

10 And I stayed in the mount, according to the first time, forty days and forty nights; and the LORD hearkened to me at that time also, and the LORD would not destroy you.

11 And the LORD said to me, Arise, take your journey before the people, that they may go in and possess the land, which I swore to their fathers to give to them.

12 And now, Israel, what doth the LORD your God require of you, but to fear the LORD your God, to walk in all his ways, and to love him, and to serve the LORD your God with all your heart and with all your soul,

13 To keep the commandments of the LORD, and his statutes, which I command you this day for your good?

14 Behold, the heaven and the heaven of heavens is the LORD's your God, the earth also, with all that therein is.

15 Only the LORD had a delight in your fathers to love them, and he chose their seed after them, even you above all people, as it is this day.

16 Circumcise therefore the foreskin of your heart, and be no more stiffnecked.

17 For the LORD your God is God of gods, and Lord of lords, a great God, a mighty, and a terrible, which regards not persons, nor takes reward:

18 He doth execute the judgment of the fatherless and widow, and loves the stranger, in giving him food and raiment.

19 Love therefore the stranger: for you were strangers in the land of Egypt.

20 You shall fear the LORD your God; him shall you serve, and to him shall you cleave, and swear by his name.

21 He is your praise, and he is your God, that has done for you these great and terrible things, which your eyes have seen.

22 Your fathers went down into Egypt with threescore and ten persons; and now the LORD your God has made you as the stars of heaven for multitude.

CHAPTER 11

THEREFORE you shall love the LORD your God, and keep his charge, and his statutes, and his judgments, and his commandments, alway.

2 And know you this day: for I speak not with your children which have not known, and which have not seen the chastisement of the LORD your God, his greatness, his mighty hand, and his stretched out arm,

3 And his miracles, and his acts, which he did in the midst of Egypt to Pharaoh the king of Egypt, and to all his land;

4 And what he did to the army of Egypt, to their horses, and to their chariots; how he made the water of the Red sea to overflow them as they pursued after you, and how the LORD has destroyed them to this day;

5 And what he did to you in the wilderness, until you came into this place;

6 And what he did to Dathan and Abiram, the sons of Eliab, the son of Reuben: how the earth opened her mouth, and swallowed them up, and their households, and their tents, and all the substance that was in their possession, in the midst of all Israel:

7 But your eyes have seen all the great acts of the LORD which he did.

8 Therefore shall you keep all the commandments which I command you this day, that you may be strong, and go in and possess the land, whither you go to possess it;

9 And that you may prolong your days in the land, which the LORD swore to your fathers to give to them and to their seed, a land that flows with milk and honey.

10 For the land, whither you go in to possess it, is not as the land of Egypt, from whence you came out, where you sowed your seed, and watered it with your foot, as a garden of herbs:

11 But the land, whither you go to possess it, is a land of hills and valleys, and drinks water of the rain of heaven:

12 A land which the LORD your God cares for: the eyes of the LORD your God are always upon it, from the beginning of the year even to the end of the year.

13 And it shall come to pass, if you shall hearken diligently to my commandments which I command you this day, to love the LORD your God, and to serve him with all your heart and with all your soul,

14 That I will give you the rain of your land in his due season, the first rain and the latter rain, that you may gather in your corn, and your wine, and your oil.

15 And I will send grass in your fields for your cattle, that you may eat and be full.

16 Take heed to yourselves, that your heart be not deceived, and you turn aside, and serve other gods, and worship them;

17 And then the LORD's wrath be kindled against you, and he shut up the heaven, that there be no rain, and that the land yield not her fruit; and lest you perish quickly from off the good land which the LORD gives you.

18 Therefore shall you lay up these my words in your heart and in your soul, and bind them for a sign upon your hand, that they may be as frontlets between your eyes.

19 And you shall teach them your children, speaking of them when you sit in your house, and when you walk by the way, when you lie down, and when you rise up.

20 And you shall write them upon the door posts of your house, and upon your gates:

21 That your days may be multiplied, and the days of your children, in the land which the LORD swore to your fathers to give them, as the days of heaven upon the earth.

22 For if you shall diligently keep all these commandments which I command you, to do them, to love the LORD your God, to walk in all his ways, and to cleave to him;

23 Then will the LORD drive out all these nations from before you, and you shall possess greater nations and mightier than yourselves.

24 Every place whereon the soles of your feet shall tread shall be yours: from the wilderness and Lebanon, from the river, the river Euphrates, even to the uttermost sea shall your coast be.

25 There shall no man be able to stand before you: for the LORD your God shall lay the fear of you and the dread of you upon all the land that you shall tread upon, as he has said to you.

26 Behold, I set before you this day a blessing and a curse;

27 A blessing, if you obey the commandments of the LORD your God, which I command you this day:

28 And a curse, if you will not obey the commandments of the LORD your God, but turn aside out of the way which I command you this day, to go after other gods, which you have not known.

29 And it shall come to pass, when the LORD your God has brought you in to the land whither you go to possess it, that you shall put the blessing upon mount Gerizim, and the curse upon mount Ebal.

30 Are they not on the other side Jordan, by the way where the sun goes down, in the land of the Canaanites, which dwell in the champaign over against Gilgal, beside the plains of Moreh?

31 For you shall pass over Jordan to go in to possess the land which the LORD your God gives you, and you shall possess it, and dwell therein.

32 And you shall observe to do all the statutes and judgments which I set before you this day.

CHAPTER 12

THESE are the statutes and judgments, which you shall observe to do in the land, which the LORD God of your fathers gives you to possess it, all the days that you live upon the earth.

2 You shall utterly destroy all the places, wherein the nations which you shall possess served their gods, upon the high mountains, and upon the hills, and under every green tree:

3 And you shall overthrow their altars, and break their pillars, and burn their groves with fire; and you shall hew down the graven images of their gods, and destroy the names of them out of that place.

4 You shall not do so to the LORD your God.

5 But to the place which the LORD your God shall choose out of all your tribes to put his name there, even to his habitation shall you seek, and thither you shall come:

6 And thither you shall bring your burnt offerings, and your sacrifices, and your tithes, and heave offerings of your hand, and your vows, and your freewill offerings, and the firstlings of your herds and of your flocks:

7 And there you shall eat before the LORD your God, and you shall rejoice in all that you put your hand to, you and

your households, wherein the LORD your God has blessed you.

8 You shall not do after all the things that we do here this day, every man whatsoever is right in his own eyes.

9 For you are not as yet come to the rest and to the inheritance, which the LORD your God gives you.

10 But when you go over Jordan, and dwell in the land which the LORD your God gives you to inherit, and when he gives you rest from all your enemies round about, so that you dwell in safety;

11 Then there shall be a place which the LORD your God shall choose to cause his name to dwell there; thither shall you bring all that I command you; your burnt offerings, and your sacrifices, your tithes, and the heave offering of your hand, and all your choice vows which you vow to the LORD:

12 And you shall rejoice before the LORD your God, you, and your sons, and your daughters, and your menservants, and your maidservants, and the Levite that is within your gates; forasmuch as he has no part nor inheritance with you.

13 Take heed to yourself that you offer not your burnt offerings in every place that you see:

14 But in the place which the LORD shall choose in one of your tribes, there you shall offer your burnt offerings, and there you shall do all that I command you.

15 Notwithstanding you may kill and eat flesh in all your gates, whatsoever your soul lusts after, according to the blessing of the LORD your God which he has given you: the unclean and the clean may eat thereof, as of the roebuck, and as of the hart.

16 Only you shall not eat the blood; you shall pour it upon the earth as water.

17 You may not eat within your gates the tithe of your corn, or of your wine, or of your oil, or the firstlings of your herds or of your flock, nor any of your

vows which you vow, nor your freewill offerings, or heave offering of your hand:

18 But you must eat them before the LORD your God in the place which the LORD your God shall choose, you, and your son, and your daughter, and your manservant, and your maidservant, and the Levite that is within your gates: and you shall rejoice before the LORD your God in all that you put your hands to.

19 Take heed to yourself that you forsake not the Levite as long as you live upon the earth.

20 When the LORD your God shall enlarge your border, as he has promised you, and you shall say, I will eat flesh, because your soul longs to eat flesh; you may eat flesh, whatsoever your soul lusts after.

21 If the place which the LORD your God has chosen to put his name there be too far from you, then you shall kill of your herd and of your flock, which the LORD has given you, as I have commanded you, and you shall eat in your gates whatsoever your soul lusts after.

22 Even as the roebuck and the hart is eaten, so you shall eat them: the unclean and the clean shall eat of them alike.

23 Only be sure that you eat not the blood: for the blood is the life; and you may not eat the life with the flesh.

24 You shall not eat it; you shall pour it upon the earth as water.

25 You shall not eat it; that it may go well with you, and with your children after you, when you shall do that which is right in the sight of the LORD.

26 Only your holy things which you have, and your vows, you shall take, and go to the place which the LORD shall choose:

27 And you shall offer your burnt offerings, the flesh and the blood, upon the altar of the LORD your God: and the blood of your sacrifices shall be poured out upon the altar of the LORD your God, and you shall eat the flesh.

28 Observe and hear all these words which I command you, that it may go

well with you, and with your children after you for ever, when you do that which is good and right in the sight of the LORD your God.

29 When the LORD your God shall cut off the nations from before you, whither you go to possess them, and you succeed them, and dwell in their land;

30 Take heed to yourself that you be not snared by following them, after that they be destroyed from before you; and that you enquire not after their gods, saying, How did these nations serve their gods? even so will I do likewise.

31 You shall not do so to the LORD your God: for every abomination to the LORD, which he hates, have they done to their gods; for even their sons and their daughters they have burnt in the fire to their gods.

32 What thing soever I command you, observe to do it: you shall not add thereto, nor diminish from it.

CHAPTER 13

IF there arise among you a prophet, or a dreamer of dreams, and gives you a sign or a wonder,

2 And the sign or the wonder come to pass, whereof he spoke to you, saying, Let us go after other gods, which you have not known, and let us serve them;

3 You shall not hearken to the words of that prophet, or that dreamer of dreams: for the LORD your God proves you, to know whether you love the LORD your God with all your heart and with all your soul.

4 You shall walk after the LORD your God, and fear him, and keep his commandments, and obey his voice, and you shall serve him, and cleave to him.

5 And that prophet, or that dreamer of dreams, shall be put to death; because he has spoken to turn you away from the LORD your God, which brought you out of the land of Egypt, and redeemed you out of the house of bondage, to thrust you out of the way which the LORD your God commanded you to walk in.

*It shall greatly help thee
to understand scripture
if thou mark not only what is spoken
or written,
but of whom, and to whom,
and with what words,
at what time, where, to what intent,
and with what circumstances,
considering what goeth before
and what followeth.*

John Wycliffe

1330-1384
OXFORD PROFESSOR
WHO ADVOCATED THE BIBLE
AS SUPREME AUTHORITY
AND IS CREDITED WITH THE FIRST
COMPLETE TRANSLATION
OF THE BIBLE
INTO MIDDLE ENGLISH

So shall you put the evil away from the midst of you.

6 If your brother, the son of your mother, or your son, or your daughter, or the wife of your bosom, or your friend, which is as your own soul, entice you secretly, saying, Let us go and serve other gods, which you have not known, you, nor your fathers;

7 Namely, of the gods of the people which are round about you, nigh to you,

or far off from you, from the one end of the earth even to the other end of the earth;

8 You shall not consent to him, nor hearken to him; neither shall your eye pity him, neither shall you spare, neither shall you conceal him:

9 But you shall surely kill him; your hand shall be first upon him to put him to death, and afterwards the hand of all the people.

10 And you shall stone him with stones, that he die; because he has sought to thrust you away from the LORD your God, which brought you out of the land of Egypt, from the house of bondage.

11 And all Israel shall hear, and fear, and shall do no more any such wickedness as this is among you.

12 If you shall hear say in one of your cities, which the LORD your God has given you to dwell there, saying,

13 Certain men, the children of Belial, are gone out from among you, and have withdrawn the inhabitants of their city, saying, Let us go and serve other gods, which you have not known;

14 Then shall you inquire, and make search, and ask diligently; and, behold, if it be truth, and the thing certain, that such abomination is wrought among you;

15 You shall surely smite the inhabitants of that city with the edge of the sword, destroying it utterly, and all that is therein, and the cattle thereof, with the edge of the sword.

16 And you shall gather all the spoil of it into the midst of the street thereof, and shall burn with fire the city, and all the spoil thereof every whit, for the LORD your God: and it shall be an heap for ever; it shall not be built again.

17 And there shall cleave nought of the cursed thing to your hand: that the LORD may turn from the fierceness of his anger, and show you mercy, and have compassion upon you, and multiply you, as he has sworn to your fathers;

18 When you shall hearken to the voice of the LORD your God, to keep all his commandments which I command you this day, to do that which is right in the eyes of the LORD your God.

CHAPTER 14

YOU are the children of the LORD your God: you shall not cut yourselves, nor make any baldness between your eyes for the dead.

2 For you are an holy people to the LORD your God, and the LORD has chosen you to be a peculiar people to himself, above all the nations that are upon the earth.

3 You shall not eat any abominable thing.

4 These are the beasts which you shall eat: the ox, the sheep, and the goat,

5 The hart, and the roebuck, and the fallow deer, and the wild goat, and the pygarg, and the wild ox, and the chamois.

6 And every beast that parts the hoof, and cleaves the cleft into two claws, and chews the cud among the beasts, that you shall eat.

7 Nevertheless these you shall not eat of them that chew the cud, or of them that divide the cloven hoof; as the camel, and the hare, and the coney: for they chew the cud, but divide not the hoof; therefore they are unclean to you.

8 And the swine, because it divides the hoof, yet chews not the cud, it is unclean to you: you shall not eat of their flesh, nor touch their dead carcase.

9 These you shall eat of all that are in the waters: all that have fins and scales shall you eat:

10 And whatsoever has not fins and scales you may not eat; it is unclean to you.

11 Of all clean birds you shall eat.

12 But these are they of which you shall not eat: the eagle, and the ossifrage, and the ospray,

13 And the glede, and the kite, and the vulture after his kind,

14 And every raven after his kind,
15 And the owl, and the night hawk, and the cuckow, and the hawk after his kind,
16 The little owl, and the great owl, and the swan,
17 And the pelican, and the gier eagle, and the cormorant,
18 And the stork, and the heron after her kind, and the lapwing, and the bat.
19 And every creeping thing that flies is unclean to you: they shall not be eaten.
20 But of all clean fowls you may eat.
21 You shall not eat of anything that dies of itself: you shall give it to the stranger that is in your gates, that he may eat it; or you may sell it to an alien: for you are an holy people to the LORD your God. You shall not seethe a kid in his mother's milk.
22 You shall truly tithe all the increase of your seed, that the field brings forth year by year.
23 And you shall eat before the LORD your God, in the place which he shall choose to place his name there, the tithe of your corn, of your wine, and of your oil, and the firstlings of your herds and of your flocks; that you may learn to fear the LORD your God always.
24 And if the way be too long for you, so that you are not able to carry it; or if the place be too far from you, which the LORD your God shall choose to set his name there, when the LORD your God has blessed you:
25 Then shall you turn it into money, and bind up the money in your hand, and shall go to the place which the LORD your God shall choose:
26 And you shall bestow that money for whatsoever your soul lusts after, for oxen, or for sheep, or for wine, or for strong drink, or for whatsoever your soul desires: and you shall eat there before the LORD your God, and you shall rejoice, you, and your household,
27 And the Levite that is within your gates; you shall not forsake him; for he has no part nor inheritance with you.

28 At the end of three years you shall bring forth all the tithe of your increase the same year, and shall lay it up within your gates:
29 And the Levite, (because he has no part nor inheritance with you,) and the stranger, and the fatherless, and the widow, which are within your gates, shall come, and shall eat and be satisfied; that the LORD your God may bless you in all the work of your hand which you do.

CHAPTER 15

AT the end of every seven years you shall make a release.
2 And this is the manner of the release: Every creditor that lends ought to his neighbour shall release it; he shall not exact it of his neighbour, or of his brother; because it is called the LORD's release.
3 Of a foreigner you may exact it again: but that which is yours with your brother your hand shall release;
4 Save when there shall be no poor among you; for the LORD shall greatly bless you in the land which the LORD your God gives you for an inheritance to possess it:
5 Only if you carefully hearken to the voice of the LORD your God, to observe to do all these commandments which I command you this day.
6 For the LORD your God blesses you, as he promised you: and you shall lend to many nations, but you shall not borrow; and you shall reign over many nations, but they shall not reign over you.
7 If there be among you a poor man of one of your brethren within any of your gates in your land which the LORD your God gives you, you shall not harden your heart, nor shut your hand from your poor brother:
8 But you shall open your hand wide to him, and shall surely lend him sufficient for his need, in that which he wants.
9 Beware that there be not a thought in your wicked heart, saying, The seventh

year, the year of release, is at hand; and your eye be evil against your poor brother, and you give him nought; and he cry to the LORD against you, and it be sin to you.

10 You shall surely give him, and your heart shall not be grieved when you give to him: because that for this thing the LORD your God shall bless you in all your works, and in all that you put your hand to.

11 For the poor shall never cease out of the land: therefore I command you, saying, You shall open your hand wide to your brother, to your poor, and to your needy, in your land.

12 And if your brother, an Hebrew man, or an Hebrew woman, be sold to you, and serve you six years; then in the seventh year you shall let him go free from you.

13 And when you send him out free from you, you shall not let him go away empty:

14 You shall furnish him liberally out of your flock, and out of your floor, and out of your winepress: of that wherewith the LORD your God has blessed you, you shall give to him.

15 And you shall remember that you were a bondman in the land of Egypt, and the LORD your God redeemed you: therefore I command you this thing to day.

16 And it shall be, if he say to you, I will not go away from you; because he loves you and your house, because he is well with you;

17 Then you shall take an aul, and thrust it through his ear to the door, and he shall be your servant for ever. And also to your maidservant you shall do likewise.

18 It shall not seem hard to you, when you send him away free from you; for he has been worth a double hired servant to you, in serving you six years: and the LORD your God shall bless you in all that you do.

19 All the firstling males that come of your herd and of your flock you shall sanctify to the LORD your God: you shall do no work with the firstling of your bullock, nor shear the firstling of your sheep.

20 You shall eat it before the LORD your God year by year in the place which the LORD shall choose, you and your household.

21 And if there be any blemish therein, as if it be lame, or blind, or have any ill blemish, you shall not sacrifice it to the LORD your God.

22 You shall eat it within your gates: the unclean and the clean person shall eat it alike, as the roebuck, and as the hart.

23 Only you shall not eat the blood thereof; you shall pour it upon the ground as water.

CHAPTER 16

OBSERVE the month of Abib, and keep the passover to the LORD your God: for in the month of Abib the LORD your God brought you forth out of Egypt by night.

2 You shall therefore sacrifice the passover to the LORD your God, of the flock and the herd, in the place which the LORD shall choose to place his name there.

3 You shall eat no leavened bread with it; seven days shall you eat unleavened bread therewith, even the bread of affliction; for you came forth out of the land of Egypt in haste: that you may remember the day when you came forth out of the land of Egypt all the days of your life.

4 And there shall be no leavened bread seen with you in all your coast seven days; neither shall there any thing of the flesh, which you sacrificed the first day at even, remain all night until the morning.

5 You may not sacrifice the passover within any of your gates, which the LORD your God gives you:

6 But at the place which the LORD your God shall choose to place his name in, there you shall sacrifice the passover at even, at the going down of the sun, at the season that you came forth out of Egypt.

7 And you shall roast and eat it in the place which the LORD your God shall choose: and you shall turn in the morning, and go to your tents.

8 Six days you shall eat unleavened bread: and on the seventh day shall be a solemn assembly to the LORD your God: you shall do no work therein.

9 Seven weeks shall you number to you: begin to number the seven weeks from such time as you begin to put the sickle to the corn.

10 And you shall keep the feast of weeks to the LORD your God with a tribute of a freewill offering of your hand, which you shall give to the LORD your God, according as the LORD your God has blessed you:

11 And you shall rejoice before the LORD your God, you, and your son, and your daughter, and your manservant, and your maidservant, and the Levite that is within your gates, and the stranger, and the fatherless, and the widow, that are among you, in the place which the LORD your God has chosen to place his name there.

12 And you shall remember that you were a bondman in Egypt: and you shall observe and do these statutes.

13 You shall observe the feast of tabernacles seven days, after that you have gathered in your corn and your wine:

14 And you shall rejoice in your feast, you, and your son, and your daughter, and your manservant, and your maidservant, and the Levite, the stranger, and the fatherless, and the widow, that are within your gates.

15 Seven days shall you keep a solemn feast to the LORD your God in the place which the LORD shall choose: because the LORD your God shall bless you in all your increase, and in all the works of your hands, therefore you shall surely rejoice.

16 Three times in a year shall all your males appear before the LORD your God in the place which he shall choose; in the feast of unleavened bread, and in the feast of weeks, and in the feast of tabernacles: and they shall not appear before the LORD empty:

17 Every man shall give as he is able, according to the blessing of the LORD your God which he has given you.

18 Judges and officers shall you make you in all your gates, which the LORD your God gives you, throughout your tribes: and they shall judge the people with just judgment.

19 You shall not wrest judgment; you shall not respect persons, neither take a gift: for a gift doth blind the eyes of the wise, and pervert the words of the righteous.

20 That which is altogether just shall you follow, that you may live, and inherit the land which the LORD your God gives you.

21 You shall not plant for yourself a grove of any trees near to the altar of the LORD your God, which you shall make for yourself.

22 Neither shall you set up any image; which the LORD your God hates.

CHAPTER 17

YOU shall not sacrifice to the LORD your God any bullock, or sheep, wherein is blemish, or any evilfavouredness: for that is an abomination to the LORD your God.

2 If there be found among you, within any of your gates which the LORD your God gives you, man or woman, that has wrought wickedness in the sight of the LORD your God, in transgressing his covenant,

3 And has gone and served other gods, and worshipped them, either the sun, or moon, or any of the host of heaven, which I have not commanded;

THE FUNCTION OF THE LAW IN EVANGELISM

17:11 The trouble with people who are not seeking the Savior and His salvation is that they do not understand the nature of sin. It is the peculiar function of the Law to bring such an understanding to a man's mind and conscience. That is why great evangelical preachers 300 years ago, in the time of the Puritans, and 200 years ago, in the time of Whitfield and others, always engaged in what they called a preliminary 'Law work.'

Dr. Martyn Lloyd-Jones

4 And it be told you, and you have heard of it, and inquired diligently, and, behold, it be true, and the thing certain, that such abomination is wrought in Israel:

5 Then shall you bring forth that man or that woman, which have committed that wicked thing, to your gates, even that man or that woman, and shall stone them with stones, till they die.

6 At the mouth of two witnesses, or three witnesses, shall he that is worthy of death be put to death; but at the mouth of one witness he shall not be put to death.

7 The hands of the witnesses shall be first upon him to put him to death, and afterward the hands of all the people. So you shall put the evil away from among you.

8 If there arise a matter too hard for you in judgment, between blood and blood, between plea and plea, and between stroke and stroke, being matters of controversy within your gates: then shall you arise, and get up into the place which the LORD your God shall choose;

9 And you shall come to the priests the Levites, and to the judge that shall be in those days, and inquire; and they shall show you the sentence of judgment:

10 And you shall do according to the sentence, which they of that place which the LORD shall choose shall show you; and you shall observe to do according to all that they inform you:

11 According to the sentence of the law which they shall teach you, and according to the judgment which they shall tell you, you shall do: you shall not decline from the sentence which they shall show you, to the right hand, nor to the left.

12 And the man that will do presumptuously, and will not hearken to the priest that stands to minister there before the LORD your God, or to the judge, even that man shall die: and you shall put away the evil from Israel.

13 And all the people shall hear, and fear, and do no more presumptuously.

14 When you are come to the land which the LORD your God gives you, and shall possess it, and shall dwell therein, and shall say, I will set a king over me, like as all the nations that are about me;

15 You shall in any wise set him king over you, whom the LORD your God shall choose: one from among your brethren shall you set king over you: you may not set a stranger over you, which is not your brother.

16 But he shall not multiply horses to himself, nor cause the people to return to Egypt, to the end that he should multiply horses: forasmuch as the LORD has said to you, You shall henceforth return no more that way.

17 Neither shall he multiply wives to himself, that his heart turn not away: neither shall he greatly multiply to himself silver and gold.

18 And it shall be, when he sits upon the throne of his kingdom, that he shall write him a copy of this law in a book out of that which is before the priests the Levites:

19 And it shall be with him, and he shall read therein all the days of his life: that he may learn to fear the LORD his

Some men's passion is for gold.
Some men's passion is for art.
Some men's passion is for fame.
My passion is for souls.

William Booth

1829-1912
FOUNDED THE SALVATION ARMY
TO MINISTER TO THE POOR
OF VICTORIAN LONDON

God, to keep all the words of this law and these statutes, to do them:

20 That his heart be not lifted up above his brethren, and that he turn not aside from the commandment, to the right hand, or to the left: to the end that he may prolong his days in his kingdom, he, and his children, in the midst of Israel.

CHAPTER 18

THE priests the Levites, and all the tribe of Levi, shall have no part nor inheritance with Israel: they shall eat the offerings of the LORD made by fire, and his inheritance.

2 Therefore shall they have no inheritance among their brethren: the LORD is their inheritance, as he has said to them.

3 And this shall be the priest's due from the people, from them that offer a sacrifice, whether it be ox or sheep; and they shall give to the priest the shoulder, and the two cheeks, and the maw.

4 The firstfruit also of your corn, of your wine, and of your oil, and the first of the fleece of your sheep, shall you give him.

5 For the LORD your God has chosen him out of all your tribes, to stand to minister in the name of the LORD, him and his sons for ever.

6 And if a Levite come from any of your gates out of all Israel, where he sojourned, and come with all the desire of his mind to the place which the LORD shall choose;

7 Then he shall minister in the name of the LORD his God, as all his brethren the Levites do, which stand there before the LORD.

8 They shall have like portions to eat, beside that which cometh of the sale of his patrimony.

9 When you are come into the land which the LORD your God gives you, you shall not learn to do after the abominations of those nations.

10 There shall not be found among you any one that makes his son or his daughter to pass through the fire, or that uses divination, or an observer of times, or an enchanter, or a witch.

11 Or a charmer, or a consulter with familiar spirits, or a wizard, or a necromancer.

12 For all that do these things are an abomination to the LORD: and because of these abominations the LORD your God doth drive them out from before you.

13 You shall be perfect with the LORD your God.

14 For these nations, which you shall possess, hearkened to observers of times, and to diviners: but as for you, the LORD your God has not suffered you so to do.

15 The LORD your God will raise up to you a Prophet from the midst of you, of

your brethren, like to me; to him you shall hearken;

16 According to all that you desired of the LORD your God in Horeb in the day of the assembly, saying, Let me not hear again the voice of the LORD my God, neither let me see this great fire any more, that I die not.

17 And the LORD said to me, They have well spoken that which they have spoken.

18 I will raise them up a Prophet from among their brethren, like to you, and will put my words in his mouth; and he shall speak to them all that I shall command him.

19 And it shall come to pass, that whosoever will not hearken to my words which he shall speak in my name, I will require it of him.

20 But the prophet, which shall presume to speak a word in my name, which I have not commanded him to speak, or that shall speak in the name of other gods, even that prophet shall die.

21 And if you say in your heart, How shall we know the word which the LORD has not spoken?

22 When a prophet speaks in the name of the LORD, if the thing follow not, nor come to pass, that is the thing which the LORD has not spoken, but the prophet has spoken it presumptuously: you shall not be afraid of him.

CHAPTER 19

WHEN the LORD your God has cut off the nations, whose land the LORD your God gives you, and you succeed them, and dwell in their cities, and in their houses;

2 You shall separate three cities for you in the midst of your land, which the LORD your God gives you to possess it.

3 You shall prepare you a way, and divide the coasts of your land, which the LORD your God gives you to inherit, into three parts, that every slayer may flee thither.

4 And this is the case of the slayer, which shall flee thither, that he may live: Whoso kills his neighbour ignorantly, whom he hated not in time past;

5 As when a man goes into the wood with his neighbour to hew wood, and his hand fetches a stroke with the axe to cut down the tree, and the head slips from the helve, and lights upon his neighbour, that he die; he shall flee to one of those cities, and live:

6 Lest the avenger of the blood pursue the slayer, while his heart is hot, and overtake him, because the way is long, and slay him; whereas he was not worthy of death, inasmuch as he hated him not in time past.

7 Therefore I command you, saying, You shall separate three cities for you.

8 And if the LORD your God enlarge your coast, as he has sworn to your fathers, and give you all the land which he promised to give to your fathers;

9 If you shall keep all these commandments to do them, which I command you this day, to love the LORD your God, and to walk ever in his ways; then shall you add three cities more for you, beside these three:

10 That innocent blood be not shed in your land, which the LORD your God gives you for an inheritance, and so blood be upon you.

11 But if any man hate his neighbour, and lie in wait for him, and rise up against him, and smite him mortally that he die, and flees into one of these cities:

12 Then the elders of his city shall send and fetch him thence, and deliver him into the hand of the avenger of blood, that he may die.

13 Your eye shall not pity him, but you shall put away the guilt of innocent blood from Israel, that it may go well with you.

14 You shall not remove your neighbour's landmark, which they of old time have set in your inheritance, which you shall inherit in the land that the LORD your God gives you to possess it.

15 One witness shall not rise up against a man for any iniquity, or for any sin, in any sin that he sins: at the mouth of two witnesses, or at the mouth of three witnesses, shall the matter be established.

16 If a false witness rise up against any man to testify against him that which is wrong;

17 Then both the men, between whom the controversy is, shall stand before the LORD, before the priests and the judges, which shall be in those days;

18 And the judges shall make diligent inquisition: and, behold, if the witness be a false witness, and has testified falsely against his brother;

19 Then shall you do to him, as he had thought to have done to his brother: so shall you put the evil away from among you.

20 And those which remain shall hear, and fear, and shall henceforth commit no more any such evil among you.

21 And your eye shall not pity; but life shall go for life, eye for eye, tooth for tooth, hand for hand, foot for foot.

CHAPTER 20

WHEN you go out to battle against your enemies, and see horses, and chariots, and a people more than you, be not afraid of them: for the LORD your God is with you, which brought you up out of the land of Egypt.

2 And it shall be, when you are come nigh to the battle, that the priest shall approach and speak to the people,

3 And shall say to them, Hear, O Israel, you approach this day to battle against your enemies: let not your hearts faint, fear not, and do not tremble, neither be terrified because of them;

4 For the LORD your God is he that goes with you, to fight for you against your enemies, to save you.

5 And the officers shall speak to the people, saying, What man is there that has built a new house, and has not dedicated it? let him go and return to his house, lest he die in the battle, and another man dedicate it.

6 And what man is he that has planted a vineyard, and has not yet eaten of it? let him also go and return to his house, lest he die in the battle, and another man eat of it.

7 And what man is there that has betrothed a wife, and has not taken her? let him go and return to his house, lest he die in the battle, and another man take her.

8 And the officers shall speak further to the people, and they shall say, What man is there that is fearful and fainthearted? let him go and return to his house, lest his brethren's heart faint as well as his heart.

9 And it shall be, when the officers have made an end of speaking to the people that they shall make captains of the armies to lead the people.

10 When you come nigh to a city to fight against it, then proclaim peace to it.

11 And it shall be, if it make you answer of peace, and open to you, then it shall be, that all the people that is found therein shall be tributaries to you, and they shall serve you.

12 And if it will make no peace with you, but will make war against you, then you shall besiege it:

13 And when the LORD your God has delivered it into your hands, you shall smite every male thereof with the edge of the sword:

14 But the women, and the little ones, and the cattle, and all that is in the city, even all the spoil thereof, shall you take to yourself; and you shall eat the spoil of your enemies, which the LORD your God has given you.

15 Thus shall you do to all the cities which are very far off from you, which are not of the cities of these nations.

16 But of the cities of these people, which the LORD your God doth give you for an inheritance, you shall save alive nothing that breathes:

17 But you shall utterly destroy them; namely, the Hittites, and the Amorites, the Canaanites, and the Perizzites, the Hivites, and the Jebusites; as the LORD your God has commanded you:

18 That they teach you not to do after all their abominations, which they have done to their gods; so should you sin against the LORD your God.

19 When you shall besiege a city a long time, in making war against it to take it, you shall not destroy the trees thereof by forcing an axe against them: for you may eat of them, and you shall not cut them down (for the tree of the field is man's life) to employ them in the siege:

20 Only the trees which you know that they be not trees for meat, you shall destroy and cut them down; and you shall build bulwarks against the city that makes war with you, until it be subdued.

CHAPTER 21

IF one be found slain in the land which the LORD your God gives you to possess it, lying in the field, and it be not known who has slain him:

2 Then your elders and your judges shall come forth, and they shall measure to the cities which are round about him that is slain:

3 And it shall be, that the city which is next to the slain man, even the elders of that city shall take an heifer, which has not been wrought with, and which has not drawn in the yoke;

4 And the elders of that city shall bring down the heifer to a rough valley, which is neither eared nor sown, and shall strike off the heifer's neck there in the valley:

5 And the priests the sons of Levi shall come near; for them the LORD your God has chosen to minister to him, and to bless in the name of the LORD; and by their word shall every controversy and every stroke be tried:

6 And all the elders of that city, that are next to the slain man, shall wash their hands over the heifer that is beheaded in the valley:

7 And they shall answer and say, Our hands have not shed this blood, neither have our eyes seen it.

8 Be merciful, O LORD, to your people Israel, whom you have redeemed, and lay not innocent blood to your people of Israel's charge. And the blood shall be forgiven them.

9 So shall you put away the guilt of innocent blood from among you, when you shall do that which is right in the sight of the LORD.

10 When you go forth to war against your enemies, and the LORD your God has delivered them into your hands, and you have taken them captive,

11 And see among the captives a beautiful woman, and have a desire to her, that you would have her to your wife;

12 Then you shall bring her home to your house, and she shall shave her head, and pare her nails;

13 And she shall put the raiment of her captivity from off her, and shall remain in your house, and bewail her father and her mother a full month: and after that you shall go in to her, and be her husband, and she shall be your wife.

14 And it shall be, if you have no delight in her, then you shall let her go whither she will; but you shall not sell her at all for money, you shall not make merchandise of her, because you have humbled her.

15 If a man have two wives, one beloved, and another hated, and they have born him children, both the beloved and the hated; and if the firstborn son be hers that was hated:

16 Then it shall be, when he makes his sons to inherit that which he has, that he may not make the son of the beloved firstborn before the son of the hated, which is indeed the firstborn:

17 But he shall acknowledge the son of the hated for the firstborn, by giving him a double portion of all that he has:

for he is the beginning of his strength; the right of the firstborn is his.

18 If a man have a stubborn and rebellious son, which will not obey the voice of his father, or the voice of his mother, and that, when they have chastened him, will not hearken to them:

19 Then shall his father and his mother lay hold on him, and bring him out to the elders of his city, and to the gate of his place;

20 And they shall say to the elders of his city, This our son is stubborn and rebellious, he will not obey our voice; he is a glutton, and a drunkard.

21 And all the men of his city shall stone him with stones, that he die: so shall you put evil away from among you; and all Israel shall hear, and fear.

22 And if a man have committed a sin worthy of death, and he be to be put to death, and you hang him on a tree:

23 His body shall not remain all night upon the tree, but you shall in any wise bury him that day; (for he that is hanged is accursed of God;) that your land be not defiled, which the LORD your God gives you for an inheritance.

CHAPTER 22

YOU shall not see your brother's ox or his sheep go astray, and hide yourself from them: you shall in any case bring them again to your brother.

2 And if your brother be not nigh to you, or if you know him not, then you shall bring it to your own house, and it shall be with you until your brother seek after it, and you shall restore it to him again.

3 In like manner shall you do with his ass; and so shall you do with his raiment; and with all lost thing of your brother's, which he has lost, and you have found, shall you do likewise: you may not hide yourself.

4 You shall not see your brother's ass or his ox fall down by the way, and hide yourself from them: you shall surely help him to lift them up again.

5 The woman shall not wear that which pertains to a man, neither shall a man put on a woman's garment: for all that do so are abomination to the LORD your God.

6 If a bird's nest chance to be before you in the way in any tree, or on the ground, whether they be young ones, or eggs, and the dam sitting upon the young, or upon the eggs, you shall not take the dam with the young:

7 But you shall in any wise let the dam go, and take the young to you; that it may be well with you, and that you may prolong your days.

8 When you build a new house, then you shall make a battlement for your roof, that you bring not blood upon your house, if any man fall from thence.

9 You shall not sow your vineyard with divers seeds: lest the fruit of your seed which you have sown, and the fruit of your vineyard, be defiled.

10 You shall not plow with an ox and an ass together.

11 You shall not wear a garment of divers sorts, as of woollen and linen together.

12 You shall make fringes upon the four quarters of your vesture, wherewith you cover yourself.

13 If any man take a wife, and go in to her, and hate her,

14 And give occasions of speech against her, and bring up an evil name upon her, and say, I took this woman, and when I came to her, I found her not a maid:

15 Then shall the father of the damsel, and her mother, take and bring forth the tokens of the damsel's virginity to the elders of the city in the gate:

16 And the damsel's father shall say to the elders, I gave my daughter to this man to wife, and he hates her;

17 And, lo, he has given occasions of speech against her, saying, I found not your daughter a maid; and yet these are the tokens of my daughter's virginity. And they shall spread the cloth before the elders of the city.

18 And the elders of that city shall take that man and chastise him;

19 And they shall amerce him in an hundred shekels of silver, and give them to the father of the damsel, because he has brought up an evil name upon a virgin of Israel: and she shall be his wife; he may not put her away all his days.

20 But if this thing be true, and the tokens of virginity be not found for the damsel:

21 Then they shall bring out the damsel to the door of her father's house, and the men of her city shall stone her with stones that she die: because she has wrought folly in Israel, to play the whore in her father's house: so shall you put evil away from among you.

22 If a man be found lying with a woman married to an husband, then they shall both of them die, both the man that lay with the woman, and the woman: so shall you put away evil from Israel.

23 If a damsel that is a virgin be betrothed to an husband, and a man find her in the city, and lie with her;

24 Then you shall bring them both out to the gate of that city, and you shall stone them with stones that they die; the damsel, because she cried not, being in the city; and the man, because he has humbled his neighbour's wife: so you shall put away evil from among you.

25 But if a man find a betrothed damsel in the field, and the man force her, and lie with her: then the man only that lay with her shall die.

26 But to the damsel you shall do nothing; there is in the damsel no sin worthy of death: for as when a man rises against his neighbour, and slays him, even so is this matter:

27 For he found her in the field, and the betrothed damsel cried, and there was none to save her.

28 If a man find a damsel that is a virgin, which is not betrothed, and lay hold on her, and lie with her, and they be found;

29 Then the man that lay with her shall give to the damsel's father fifty shekels of silver, and she shall be his wife; because he has humbled her, he may not put her away all his days.

30 A man shall not take his father's wife, nor discover his father's skirt.

CHAPTER 23

H E that is wounded in the stones, or has his privy member cut off, shall not enter into the congregation of the LORD.

2 A bastard shall not enter into the congregation of the LORD; even to his tenth generation shall he not enter into the congregation of the LORD.

3 An Ammonite or Moabite shall not enter into the congregation of the LORD; even to their tenth generation shall they not enter into the congregation of the LORD for ever:

4 Because they met you not with bread and with water in the way, when you came forth out of Egypt; and because they hired against you Balaam the son of Beor of Pethor of Mesopotamia, to curse you.

5 Nevertheless the LORD your God would not hearken to Balaam; but the LORD your God turned the curse into a blessing to you, because the LORD your God loved you.

6 You shall not seek their peace nor their prosperity all your days for ever.

7 You shall not abhor an Edomite; for he is your brother: you shall not abhor an Egyptian; because you were a stranger in his land.

8 The children that are begotten of them shall enter into the congregation of the LORD in their third generation.

9 When the host goes forth against your enemies, then keep you from every wicked thing.

10 If there be among you any man, that is not clean by reason of uncleanness that chances him by night, then shall he go abroad out of the camp, he shall not come within the camp:

11 But it shall be, when evening cometh on, he shall wash himself with water: and when the sun is down, he shall come into the camp again.

12 You shall have a place also without the camp, whither you shall go forth abroad:

13 And you shall have a paddle upon your weapon; and it shall be, when you will ease yourself abroad, you shall dig therewith, and shall turn back and cover that which cometh from you:

14 For the LORD your God walks in the midst of your camp, to deliver you, and to give up your enemies before you; therefore shall your camp be holy: that he see no unclean thing in you, and turn away from you.

15 You shall not deliver to his master the servant which is escaped from his master to you:

16 He shall dwell with you, even among you, in that place which he shall choose in one of your gates, where it likes him best: you shall not oppress him.

17 There shall be no whore of the daughters of Israel, nor a sodomite of the sons of Israel.

18 You shall not bring the hire of a whore, or the price of a dog, into the house of the LORD your God for any vow: for even both these are abomination to the LORD your God.

19 You shall not lend upon usury to your brother; usury of money, usury of victuals, usury of any thing that is lent upon usury:

20 To a stranger you may lend upon usury; but to your brother you shall not lend upon usury: that the LORD your God may bless you in all that you set your hand to in the land whither you go to possess it.

21 When you shall vow a vow to the LORD your God, you shall not slack to pay it: for the LORD your God will surely require it of you; and it would be sin in you.

22 But if you shall forbear to vow, it shall be no sin in you.

23 That which is gone out of your lips

23:5 For the biblical presentation of God's love, see comment at Matthew 10:22.

you shall keep and perform; even a freewill offering, according as you have vowed to the LORD your God, which you have promised with your mouth.

24 When you come into your neighbour's vineyard, then you may eat grapes your fill at your own pleasure; but you shall not put any in your vessel.

25 When you come into the standing corn of your neighbour, then you may pluck the ears with your hand; but you shall not move a sickle to your neighbour's standing corn.

CHAPTER 24

WHEN a man has taken a wife, and married her, and it come to pass that she find no favour in his eyes, because he has found some uncleanness in her: then let him write her a bill of divorcement, and give it in her hand, and send her out of his house.

2 And when she is departed out of his house, she may go and be another man's wife.

3 And if the latter husband hate her, and write her a bill of divorcement, and gives it in her hand, and sends her out of his house; or if the latter husband die, which took her to be his wife;

4 Her former husband, which sent her away, may not take her again to be his wife, after that she is defiled; for that is abomination before the LORD: and you shall not cause the land to sin, which the LORD your God gives you for an inheritance.

5 When a man has taken a new wife, he shall not go out to war, neither shall he be charged with any business: but he shall be free at home one year, and shall cheer up his wife which he has taken.

6 No man shall take the nether or the upper millstone to pledge: for he takes a man's life to pledge.

7 If a man be found stealing any of his brethren of the children of Israel, and makes merchandise of him, or sells him; then that thief shall die; and you shall put evil away from among you.

8 Take heed in the plague of leprosy, that you observe diligently, and do according to all that the priests the Levites shall teach you: as I commanded them, so you shall observe to do.

9 Remember what the LORD your God did to Miriam by the way, after that you were come forth out of Egypt.

10 When you dost lend your brother any thing, you shall not go into his house to fetch his pledge.

11 You shall stand abroad, and the man to whom you dost lend shall bring out the pledge abroad to you.

12 And if the man be poor, you shall not sleep with his pledge:

13 In any case you shall deliver him the pledge again when the sun goes down, that he may sleep in his own raiment, and bless you: and it shall be righteousness to you before the LORD your God.

14 You shall not oppress an hired servant that is poor and needy, whether he be of your brethren, or of your strangers that are in your land within your gates:

15 At his day you shall give him his hire, neither shall the sun go down upon it; for he is poor, and sets his heart upon it: lest he cry against you to the LORD, and it be sin to you.

16 The fathers shall not be put to death for the children, neither shall the children be put to death for the fathers: every man shall be put to death for his own sin.

17 You shall not pervert the judgment of the stranger, nor of the fatherless; nor take a widow's raiment to pledge:

18 But you shall remember that you were a bondman in Egypt, and the LORD your God redeemed you thence: therefore I command you to do this thing.

19 When you cut down your harvest in your field, and have forgot a sheaf in the field, you shall not go again to fetch it: it shall be for the stranger, for the fatherless, and for the widow: that the LORD your God may bless you in all the work of your hands.

20 When you beat your olive tree, you shall not go over the boughs again: it shall be for the stranger, for the fatherless, and for the widow.

21 When you gather the grapes of your vineyard, you shall not glean it afterward: it shall be for the stranger, for the fatherless, and for the widow.

22 And you shall remember that you were a bondman in the land of Egypt: therefore I command you to do this thing.

CHAPTER 25

IF there be a controversy between men, and they come to judgment, that the judges may judge them; then they shall justify the righteous, and condemn the wicked.

2 And it shall be, if the wicked man be worthy to be beaten, that the judge shall cause him to lie down, and to be beaten before his face, according to his fault, by a certain number.

3 Forty stripes he may give him, and not exceed: lest, if he should exceed, and beat him above these with many stripes, then your brother should seem vile to you.

4 You shall not muzzle the ox when he treads out the corn.

5 If brethren dwell together, and one of them die, and have no child, the wife of the dead shall not marry without to a stranger: her husband's brother shall go in to her, and take her to him to wife, and perform the duty of an husband's brother to her.

6 And it shall be, that the firstborn which she bears shall succeed in the name of his brother which is dead, that his name be not put out of Israel.

7 And if the man like not to take his brother's wife, then let his brother's wife go up to the gate to the elders, and say, My husband's brother refuses to raise up to his brother a name in Israel, he will not perform the duty of my husband's brother.

8 Then the elders of his city shall call him, and speak to him: and if he stand to it, and say, I like not to take her;

9 Then shall his brother's wife come to him in the presence of the elders, and loose his shoe from off his foot, and spit in his face, and shall answer and say, So shall it be done to that man that will not build up his brother's house.

10 And his name shall be called in Israel, The house of him that has his shoe loosed.

11 When men strive together one with another, and the wife of the one draws near for to deliver her husband out of the hand of him that smites him, and puts forth her hand, and takes him by the secrets:

12 Then you shall cut off her hand, your eye shall not pity her.

13 You shall not have in your bag divers weights, a great and a small.

14 You shall not have in your house divers measures, a great and a small.

15 But you shall have a perfect and just weight, a perfect and just measure shall you have: that your days may be lengthened in the land which the LORD your God gives you.

16 For all that do such things, and all that do unrighteously, are an abomination to the LORD your God.

17 Remember what Amalek did to you by the way, when you were come forth out of Egypt;

18 How he met you by the way, and smote the hindmost of you, even all that were feeble behind you, when you was faint and weary; and he feared not God.

19 Therefore it shall be, when the LORD your God has given you rest from all your enemies round about, in the land which the LORD your God gives you for an inheritance to possess it, that you shall blot out the remembrance of Amalek from under heaven; you shall not forget it.

CHAPTER 26

AND it shall be, when you are come in to the land which the LORD your God gives you for an inheritance, and possesses it, and dwells therein;

2 That you shall take of the first of all the fruit of the earth, which you shall bring of your land that the LORD your God gives you, and shall put it in a basket, and shall go to the place which the LORD your God shall choose to place his name there.

3 And you shall go to the priest that shall be in those days, and say to him, I profess this day to the LORD your God, that I am come to the country which the LORD swore to our fathers for to give us.

4 And the priest shall take the basket out of your hand, and set it down before the altar of the LORD your God.

5 And you shall speak and say before the LORD your God, A Syrian ready to perish was my father, and he went down into Egypt, and sojourned there with a few, and became there a nation, great, mighty, and populous:

6 And the Egyptians evil entreated us, and afflicted us, and laid upon us hard bondage:

7 And when we cried to the LORD God of our fathers, the LORD heard our voice, and looked on our affliction, and our labour, and our oppression:

8 And the LORD brought us forth out of Egypt with a mighty hand, and with an outstretched arm, and with great terribleness, and with signs, and with wonders:

9 And he has brought us into this place, and has given us this land, even a land that flows with milk and honey.

10 And now, behold, I have brought the firstfruits of the land, which you, O LORD, have given me. And you shall set it before the LORD your God, and worship before the LORD your God:

11 And you shall rejoice in every good thing which the LORD your God has given to you, and to your house, you, and the Levite, and the stranger that is among you.

12 When you have made an end of tithing all the tithes of your increase the third year, which is the year of tithing, and have given it to the Levite, the stranger, the fatherless, and the widow, that they may eat within your gates, and be filled;

13 Then you shall say before the LORD your God, I have brought away the hallowed things out of mine house, and also have given them to the Levite, and to the stranger, to the fatherless, and to the widow, according to all your commandments which you have commanded me: I have not transgressed your commandments, neither have I forgotten them.

14 I have not eaten thereof in my mourning, neither have I taken away ought thereof for any unclean use, nor given ought thereof for the dead: but I have hearkened to the voice of the LORD my God, and have done according to all that you have commanded me.

15 Look down from your holy habitation, from heaven, and bless your people Israel, and the land which you have given us, as you swore to our fathers, a land that flows with milk and honey.

16 This day the LORD your God has commanded you to do these statutes and judgments: you shall therefore keep and do them with all your heart, and with all your soul.

17 You have avouched the LORD this day to be your God, and to walk in his ways, and to keep his statutes, and his commandments, and his judgments, and to hearken to his voice:

18 And the LORD has avouched you this day to be his peculiar people, as he has promised you, and that you should keep all his commandments;

19 And to make you high above all nations which he has made, in praise, and in name, and in honour; and that you may be an holy people to the LORD your God, as he has spoken.

CHAPTER 27

AND Moses with the elders of Israel commanded the people, saying, Keep all the commandments which I command you this day.

2 And it shall be on the day when you shall pass over Jordan to the land which the LORD your God gives you, that you shall set up for yourselves great stones, and plaister them with plaister:

3 And you shall write upon them all the words of this law, when you are passed over, that you may go in to the land which the LORD your God gives you, a land that flows with milk and honey; as the LORD God of your fathers has promised you.

4 Therefore it shall be when you be gone over Jordan, that you shall set up these stones, which I command you this day, in mount Ebal, and you shall plaister them with plaister.

5 And there shall you build an altar to the LORD your God, an altar of stones: you shall not lift up any iron tool upon them.

6 You shall build the altar of the LORD your God of whole stones: and you shall offer burnt offerings thereon to the LORD your God:

7 And you shall offer peace offerings, and shall eat there, and rejoice before the LORD your God.

8 And you shall write upon the stones all the words of this law very plainly.

9 And Moses and the priests the Levites spoke to all Israel, saying, Take heed, and hearken, O Israel; this day you are become the people of the LORD your God.

10 You shall therefore obey the voice of the LORD your God, and do his commandments and his statutes, which I command you this day.

11 And Moses charged the people the same day, saying,

12 These shall stand upon mount Gerizim to bless the people, when you are come over Jordan; Simeon, and Levi, and Judah, and Issachar, and Joseph, and Benjamin:

13 And these shall stand upon mount Ebal to curse; Reuben, Gad, and Asher, and Zebulun, Dan, and Naphtali.

14 And the Levites shall speak, and say to all the men of Israel with a loud voice,

15 Cursed be the man that makes any graven or molten image, an abomination to the LORD, the work of the hands of the craftsman, and puts it in a secret place. And all the people shall answer and say, Amen.

16 Cursed be he that sets light by his father or his mother. And all the people shall say, Amen.

17 Cursed be he that removes his neighbour's landmark. And all the people shall say, Amen.

18 Cursed be he that makes the blind to wander out of the way. And all the people shall say, Amen.

19 Cursed be he that perverts the judgment of the stranger, fatherless, and widow. And all the people shall say, Amen.

20 Cursed be he that lies with his father's wife; because he uncovers his father's skirt. And all the people shall say, Amen.

21 Cursed be he that lies with any manner of beast. And all the people shall say, Amen.

22 Cursed be he that lies with his sister, the daughter of his father, or the daughter of his mother. And all the people shall say, Amen.

23 Cursed be he that lies with his mother in law. And all the people shall say, Amen.

24 Cursed be he that smites his neighbour secretly. And all the people shall say, Amen.

25 Cursed be he that takes reward to slay an innocent person. And all the people shall say, Amen.

26 Cursed be he that confirms not all the words of this law to do them. And all the people shall say, Amen.

CHAPTER 28

AND it shall come to pass, if you shall hearken diligently to the voice of the LORD your God, to observe and to do all his commandments which I command you this day, that the LORD your God will set you on high above all nations of the earth:

2 And all these blessings shall come on you, and overtake you, if you shall hearken to the voice of the LORD your God.

3 Blessed shall you be in the city, and blessed shall you be in the field.

4 Blessed shall be the fruit of your body, and the fruit of your ground, and the fruit of your cattle, the increase of your kine, and the flocks of your sheep.

5 Blessed shall be your basket and your store.

6 Blessed shall you be when you come in, and blessed shall you be when you go out.

7 The LORD shall cause your enemies that rise up against you to be smitten before your face: they shall come out against you one way, and flee before you seven ways.

8 The LORD shall command the blessing upon you in your storehouses, and in all that you set your hand to; and he shall bless you in the land which the LORD your God gives you.

9 The LORD shall establish you an holy people to himself, as he has sworn to you, if you shall keep the commandments of the LORD your God, and walk in his ways.

10 And all people of the earth shall see that you are called by the name of the LORD; and they shall be afraid of you.

11 And the LORD shall make you plenteous in goods, in the fruit of your body, and in the fruit of your cattle, and in the fruit of your ground, in the land which the LORD swore to your fathers to give you.

12 The LORD shall open to you his good treasure, the heaven to give the rain to your land in his season, and to bless all the work of your hand: and you shall lend to many nations, and you shall not borrow.

13 And the LORD shall make you the head, and not the tail; and you shall be above only, and you shall not be beneath; if that you hearken to the commandments of the LORD your God, which I command you this day, to observe and to do them:

14 And you shall not go aside from any of the words which I command you this day, to the right hand, or to the left, to go after other gods to serve them.

15 But it shall come to pass, if you will not hearken to the voice of the LORD your God, to observe to do all his commandments and his statutes which I command you this day; that all these curses shall come upon you, and overtake you:

16 Cursed shall you be in the city, and cursed shall you be in the field.

17 Cursed shall be your basket and your store.

28:15-68 Compare these curses to what has come upon the United States. More than 200,000 people were murdered in the last decade. We are plagued with diseases both on our crops and upon our children. We have terrible droughts; in August 2000, three hundred fires were started by lightning strikes in just one week. Many live in adultery. Many fall into bankruptcy and suffer repossession of their property. Theft is rampant. We have masses of missing children through both kidnapping and runaways. We are seeing the untimely dropping of fruit from our trees.

The U.S. has also suffered an attack that came "from the end of the earth, as swift as the eagle flies" and from a nation "whose tongue you shall not understand . . .".

These sufferings have come to us because we have not been thankful to God, but instead have forsaken His law. If we heeded the Ten Commandments, they would show us our sinful state and drive us to the cleansing blood of the Savior. Hearts and minds that are responsive to God, and not political change, is the key to healing for our land.

18 Cursed shall be the fruit of your body, and the fruit of your land, the increase of your kine, and the flocks of your sheep.

19 Cursed shall you be when you come in, and cursed shall you be when you go out.

20 The LORD shall send upon you cursing, vexation, and rebuke, in all that you set your hand to for to do, until you be destroyed, and until you perish quickly; because of the wickedness of your doings, whereby you have forsaken me.

21 The LORD shall make the pestilence cleave to you, until he have consumed you from off the land, whither you go to possess it.

22 The LORD shall smite you with a consumption, and with a fever, and with an inflammation, and with an extreme burning, and with the sword, and with blasting, and with mildew; and they shall pursue you until you perish.

23 And your heaven that is over your head shall be brass, and the earth that is under you shall be iron.

24 The LORD shall make the rain of your land powder and dust: from heaven shall it come down upon you, until you be destroyed.

25 The LORD shall cause you to be smitten before your enemies: you shall go out one way against them, and flee seven ways before them: and shall be removed into all the kingdoms of the earth.

26 And your carcase shall be meat to all fowls of the air, and to the beasts of the earth, and no man shall fray them away.

27 The LORD will smite you with the botch of Egypt, and with the emerods, and with the scab, and with the itch, whereof you canst not be healed.

28 The LORD shall smite you with madness, and blindness, and astonishment of heart:

29 And you shall grope at noonday, as the blind gropes in darkness, and you shall not prosper in your ways: and you shall be only oppressed and spoiled evermore, and no man shall save you.

30 You shall betroth a wife, and another man shall lie with her: you shall build an house, and you shall not dwell therein: you shall plant a vineyard, and shall not gather the grapes thereof.

31 Your ox shall be slain before your eyes, and you shall not eat thereof: your ass shall be violently taken away from before your face, and shall not be restored to you: your sheep shall be given to your enemies, and you shall have none to rescue them.

32 Your sons and your daughters shall be given to another people, and your eyes shall look, and fail with longing for them all the day long; and there shall be no might in your hand.

33 The fruit of your land, and all your labours, shall a nation which you know not eat up; and you shall be only oppressed and crushed alway:

34 So that you shall be mad for the sight of your eyes which you shall see.

35 The LORD shall smite you in the knees, and in the legs, with a sore botch that cannot be healed, from the sole of your foot to the top of your head.

36 The LORD shall bring you, and your king which you shall set over you, to a nation which neither you nor your fathers have known; and there shall you serve other gods, wood and stone.

37 And you shall become an astonishment, a proverb, and a byword, among all nations whither the LORD shall lead you.

38 You shall carry much seed out into the field, and shall gather but little in; for the locust shall consume it.

39 You shall plant vineyards, and dress them, but shall neither drink of the wine, nor gather the grapes; for the worms shall eat them.

40 You shall have olive trees throughout all your coasts, but you shall not anoint yourself with the oil; for your olive shall cast his fruit.

41 You shall beget sons and daughters, but you shall not enjoy them; for they shall go into captivity.

42 All your trees and fruit of your land shall the locust consume.

43 The stranger that is within you shall get up above you very high; and you shall come down very low.

44 He shall lend to you, and you shall not lend to him: he shall be the head, and you shall be the tail.

45 Moreover all these curses shall come upon you, and shall pursue you, and overtake you, till you be destroyed; because you hearkened not to the voice of the LORD your God, to keep his commandments and his statutes which he commanded you:

46 And they shall be upon you for a sign and for a wonder, and upon your seed for ever.

47 Because you served not the LORD your God with joyfulness, and with gladness of heart, for the abundance of all things;

48 Therefore shall you serve your enemies which the LORD shall send against you, in hunger, and in thirst, and in nakedness, and in want of all things: and he shall put a yoke of iron upon your neck, until he have destroyed you.

49 The LORD shall bring a nation against you from far, from the end of the earth, as swift as the eagle flies; a nation whose tongue you shall not understand;

50 A nation of fierce countenance, which shall not regard the person of the old, nor show favour to the young:

51 And he shall eat the fruit of your cattle, and the fruit of your land, until you be destroyed: which also shall not leave you either corn, wine, or oil, or the increase of your kine, or flocks of your sheep, until he has destroyed you.

52 And he shall besiege you in all your gates, until your high and fenced walls come down, wherein you trusted, throughout all your land: and he shall besiege you in all your gates throughout all your land, which the LORD your God has given you.

53 And you shall eat the fruit of your own body, the flesh of your sons and of your daughters, which the LORD your God has given you, in the siege, and in the straitness, wherewith your enemies shall distress you:

54 So that the man that is tender among you, and very delicate, his eye shall be evil toward his brother, and toward the wife of his bosom, and toward the remnant of his children which he shall leave:

55 So that he will not give to any of them of the flesh of his children whom he shall eat: because he has nothing left him in the siege, and in the straitness, wherewith your enemies shall distress you in all your gates.

56 The tender and delicate woman among you, which would not adventure to set the sole of her foot upon the ground for delicateness and tenderness, her eye shall be evil toward the husband of her bosom, and toward her son, and toward her daughter,

57 And toward her young one that comes out from between her feet, and toward her children which she shall bear: for she shall eat them for want of all things secretly in the siege and straitness, wherewith your enemy shall distress you in your gates.

58 If you will not observe to do all the words of this law that are written in this book, that you may fear this glorious and fearful name, THE LORD YOUR GOD;

59 Then the LORD will make your plagues wonderful, and the plagues of your seed, even great plagues, and of long continuance, and sore sicknesses, and of long continuance.

60 Moreover he will bring upon you all the diseases of Egypt, which you were afraid of; and they shall cleave to you.

61 Also every sickness, and every plague, which is not written in the book of this law, them will the LORD bring upon you, until you be destroyed.

62 And you shall be left few in number, whereas you were as the stars of heaven for multitude; because you would not obey the voice of the LORD your God.

63 And it shall come to pass, that as the LORD rejoiced over you to do you good, and to multiply you; so the LORD will rejoice over you to destroy you, and to bring you to nought; and you shall be plucked from off the land whither you go to possess it.

64 And the LORD shall scatter you among all people, from the one end of the earth even to the other; and there you shall serve other gods, which neither you nor your fathers have known, even wood and stone.

65 And among these nations shall you find no ease, neither shall the sole of your foot have rest: but the LORD shall give you there a trembling heart, and failing of eyes, and sorrow of mind:

66 And your life shall hang in doubt before you; and you shall fear day and night, and shall have none assurance of your life:

67 In the morning you shall say, Would God it were even! and at even you shall say, Would God it were morning! for the fear of your heart wherewith you shall fear, and for the sight of your eyes which you shall see.

68 And the LORD shall bring you into Egypt again with ships, by the way whereof I spoke to you, You shall see it no more again: and there you shall be sold to your enemies for bondmen and bondwomen, and no man shall buy you.

CHAPTER 29

THESE are the words of the covenant, which the LORD commanded Moses to make with the children of Israel in the land of Moab, beside the covenant which he made with them in Horeb.

2 And Moses called to all Israel, and said to them, You have seen all that the LORD did before your eyes in the land of Egypt to Pharaoh, and to all his servants, and to all his land;

3 The great temptations which your eyes have seen, the signs, and those great miracles:

4 Yet the LORD has not given you an heart to perceive, and eyes to see, and ears to hear, to this day.

5 And I have led you forty years in the wilderness: your clothes are not waxen old upon you, and your shoe is not waxen old upon your foot.

6 You have not eaten bread, neither have you drunk wine or strong drink: that you might know that I am the LORD your God.

7 And when you came to this place, Sihon the king of Heshbon, and Og the king of Bashan, came out against us to battle, and we smote them:

8 And we took their land, and gave it for an inheritance to the Reubenites, and to the Gadites, and to the half tribe of Manasseh.

9 Keep therefore the words of this covenant, and do them, that you may prosper in all that you do.

10 You stand this day all of you before the LORD your God; your captains of your tribes, your elders, and your officers, with all the men of Israel,

11 Your little ones, your wives, and your stranger that is in your camp, from the hewer of your wood to the drawer of your water:

12 That you should enter into covenant with the LORD your God, and into his oath, which the LORD your God makes with you this day:

13 That he may establish you to day for a people to himself, and that he may be to you a God, as he has said to you, and as he has sworn to your fathers, to Abraham, to Isaac, and to Jacob.

14 Neither with you only do I make this covenant and this oath;

15 But with him that stands here with us this day before the LORD our God, and also with him that is not here with us this day:

16 (For you know how we have dwelt in the land of Egypt; and how we came through the nations which you passed by;

17 And you have seen their abominations, and their idols, wood and stone, silver and gold, which were among them:)

18 Lest there should be among you man, or woman, or family, or tribe, whose heart turns away this day from the LORD our God, to go and serve the gods of these nations; lest there should be among you a root that bears gall and wormwood;

19 And it come to pass, when he hears the words of this curse, that he bless himself in his heart, saying, I shall have peace, though I walk in the imagination of mine heart, to add drunkenness to thirst:

20 The LORD will not spare him, but then the anger of the LORD and his jealousy shall smoke against that man, and all the curses that are written in this book shall lie upon him, and the LORD shall blot out his name from under heaven.

21 And the LORD shall separate him to evil out of all the tribes of Israel, according to all the curses of the covenant that are written in this book of the law:

22 So that the generation to come of your children that shall rise up after you, and the stranger that shall come from a far land, shall say, when they see the plagues of that land, and the sicknesses which the LORD has laid upon it;

23 And that the whole land thereof is brimstone, and salt, and burning, that it is not sown, nor bears, nor any grass grows therein, like the overthrow of Sodom, and Gomorrah, Admah, and Zeboim, which the LORD overthrew in his anger, and in his wrath:

24 Even all nations shall say, Why has the LORD done thus to this land? what means the heat of this great anger?

25 Then men shall say, Because they have forsaken the covenant of the LORD God of their fathers, which he made with them when he brought them forth out of the land of Egypt:

26 For they went and served other gods, and worshipped them, gods whom they knew not, and whom he had not given to them:

27 And the anger of the LORD was kindled against this land, to bring upon it all the curses that are written in this book:

28 And the LORD rooted them out of their land in anger, and in wrath, and in great indignation, and cast them into another land, as it is this day.

29 The secret things belong to the LORD our God: but those things which are revealed belong to us and to our children for ever, that we may do all the words of this law.

CHAPTER 30

A ND it shall come to pass, when all these things are come upon you, the blessing and the curse, which I have set before you, and you shall call them to mind among all the nations, whither the LORD your God has driven you,

2 And shall return to the LORD your God, and shall obey his voice according to all that I command you this day, you and your children, with all your heart, and with all your soul;

3 That then the LORD your God will turn your captivity, and have compassion upon you, and will return and gather you from all the nations, whither the LORD your God has scattered you.

4 If any of yours be driven out to the outmost parts of heaven, from thence will the LORD your God gather you, and from thence will he fetch you:

5 And the LORD your God will bring you into the land which your fathers possessed, and you shall possess it; and he will do you good, and multiply you above your fathers.

30:19

Pascal's Wager

Blaise Pascal was a seventeenth-century genius, a mathematician and a physicist, renowned for his faith and for his understanding of probability theory. He invented the world's first working computer, vacuum cleaner and public transportation system.

Here is his famous wager:

"Who then will condemn Christians for being unable to give rational grounds for their belief...They declare that it is folly, *stultitiam*, in expounding it to the world, and then you complain that they do not prove it...

"Let us examine this point, and let us say: 'Either God is or He is not.' But to which view shall we be inclined? Reason cannot decide this question. Infinite chaos separates us. At the far end of this infinite distance a coin is being spun which will come down heads or tails. How will you wager? Reason cannot make you choose either, reason cannot prove either wrong.

"Do not then condemn as wrong those who have made a choice, for you know nothing about it. 'No, but I will condemn them not for having made this particular choice, for, although the one who calls heads and the other one are equally at fault, that fact is that they are both at fault: the right thing is not to wager at all.'

. . .your gain is so certain
and your risk so negligible,
that in the end you will realize
that you have wagered
on something certain and infinite
for which you have paid nothing.

Blaise Pascal

1623 -1662

FRENCH MATHEMATICIAN
AND PHYSICIST

"Yes, but you must wager. There is no choice, you are already committed. Which will you choose then? Let us see: since a choice must be made, let us see which offers you the least interest.

"You have two things to lose: the true and the good; and two things to stake: your reason and your will, your knowledge and your happiness; and your nature has two things to avoid: error and wretchedness. Since you must necessarily choose, your reason is no more affronted by choosing one rather than the other. That is one point cleared up.

"But your happiness? Let us weigh up the gain and the loss involved in calling heads that God exists. Let us assess the two cases: if you win you win everything, if you lose you lose nothing. Do not hesitate then; wager that He does exist. That is wonderful. Yes, I must wager, but perhaps I am wagering too much. Let us see: since there is an equal chance of gain and loss, if you stood to win only two lives for one you could still wager, but supposing you stood to win three?

"I tell you that you will gain even in this life, and that at every step you take along this road you will see that your gain is so certain and your risk so negligible that in the end you will realize that you have wagered on something certain and infinite for which you have paid nothing."

from *Christianity for Modern Pagans*

6 And the LORD your God will circumcise your heart, and the heart of your seed, to love the LORD your God with all your heart, and with all your soul, that you may live.

7 And the LORD your God will put all these curses upon your enemies, and on them that hate you, which persecuted you.

8 And you shall return and obey the voice of the LORD, and do all his commandments which I command you this day.

9 And the LORD your God will make you plenteous in every work of your hand, in the fruit of your body, and in the fruit of your cattle, and in the fruit of your land, for good: for the LORD will again rejoice over you for good, as he rejoiced over your fathers:

10 If you shall hearken to the voice of the LORD your God, to keep his commandments and his statutes which are written in this book of the law, and if you turn to the LORD your God with all your heart, and with all your soul.

11 For this commandment which I command you this day, it is not hidden from you, neither is it far off.

12 It is not in heaven, that you should say, Who shall go up for us to heaven, and bring it to us, that we may hear it, and do it?

13 Neither is it beyond the sea, that you should say, Who shall go over the sea for us, and bring it to us, that we may hear it, and do it?

14 But the word is very nigh to you, in your mouth, and in your heart, that you may do it.

15 See, I have set before you this day life and good, and death and evil;

16 In that I command you this day to love the LORD your God, to walk in his ways, and to keep his commandments and his statutes and his judgments, that you may live and multiply: and the LORD your God shall bless you in the land whither you go to possess it.

17 But if your heart turn away, so that you will not hear, but shall be drawn away, and worship other gods, and serve them;

18 I denounce to you this day, that you shall surely perish, and that you shall not prolong your days upon the land, whither you pass over Jordan to go to possess it.

19 I call heaven and earth to record this day against you, that I have set before you life and death, blessing and cursing: therefore choose life, that both you and your seed may live:

20 That you may love the LORD your God, and that you may obey his voice, and that you may cleave to him: for he is your life, and the length of your days: that you may dwell in the land which the LORD swore to your fathers, to Abraham, to Isaac, and to Jacob, to give them.

CHAPTER 31

AND Moses went and spoke these words to all Israel.

2 And he said to them, I am an hundred and twenty years old this day; I can no more go out and come in: also the LORD has said to me, You shall not go over this Jordan.

3 The LORD your God, he will go over before you, and he will destroy these nations from before you, and you shall possess them: and Joshua, he shall go over before you, as the LORD has said.

4 And the LORD shall do to them as he did to Sihon and to Og, kings of the Amorites, and to the land of them, whom he destroyed.

5 And the LORD shall give them up before your face, that you may do to them according to all the commandments which I have commanded you.

6 Be strong and of a good courage, fear not, nor be afraid of them: for the LORD your God, he it is that doth go with you; he will not fail you, nor forsake you.

7 And Moses called to Joshua, and said to him in the sight of all Israel, Be strong

and of a good courage: for you must go with this people to the land which the LORD has sworn to their fathers to give them; and you shall cause them to inherit it.

8 And the LORD, he it is that doth go before you; he will be with you, he will not fail you, neither forsake you: fear not, neither be dismayed.

9 And Moses wrote this law, and delivered it to the priests the sons of Levi, which bare the ark of the covenant of the LORD, and to all the elders of Israel.

10 And Moses commanded them, saying, At the end of every seven years, in the solemnity of the year of release, in the feast of tabernacles,

11 When all Israel is come to appear before the LORD your God in the place which he shall choose, you shall read this law before all Israel in their hearing.

12 Gather the people together, men and women, and children, and your stranger that is within your gates, that they may hear, and that they may learn, and fear the LORD your God, and observe to do all the words of this law:

13 And that their children, which have not known any thing, may hear, and learn to fear the LORD your God, as long as you live in the land whither you go over Jordan to possess it.

14 And the LORD said to Moses, Behold, your days approach that you must die: call Joshua, and present yourselves in the tabernacle of the congregation, that I may give him a charge. And Moses and Joshua went, and presented themselves in the tabernacle of the congregation.

15 And the LORD appeared in the tabernacle in a pillar of a cloud: and the pillar of the cloud stood over the door of the tabernacle.

16 And the LORD said to Moses, Behold, you shall sleep with your fathers; and this people will rise up, and go a whoring after the gods of the strangers of the land, whither they go to be among them, and will forsake me, and break my covenant which I have made with them.

17 Then my anger shall be kindled against them in that day, and I will forsake them, and I will hide my face from them, and they shall be devoured, and many evils and troubles shall befall them; so that they will say in that day, Are not these evils come upon us, because our God is not among us?

18 And I will surely hide my face in that day for all the evils which they shall have wrought, in that they are turned to other gods.

19 Now therefore write you this song for you, and teach it the children of Israel: put it in their mouths, that this song may be a witness for me against the children of Israel.

20 For when I shall have brought them into the land which I swore to their fathers, that flows with milk and honey; and they shall have eaten and filled themselves, and waxen fat; then will they turn to other gods, and serve them, and provoke me, and break my covenant.

21 And it shall come to pass, when many evils and troubles are befallen them, that this song shall testify against them as a witness; for it shall not be forgotten out of the mouths of their seed: for I know their imagination which they go about, even now, before I have brought them into the land which I swore.

22 Moses therefore wrote this song the same day, and taught it the children of Israel.

23 And he gave Joshua the son of Nun a charge, and said, Be strong and of a good courage: for you shall bring the children of Israel into the land which I swore to them: and I will be with you.

24 And it came to pass, when Moses had made an end of writing the words of this law in a book, until they were finished,

25 That Moses commanded the Levites, which bare the ark of the covenant of the LORD, saying,

26 Take this book of the law, and put it in the side of the ark of the covenant of the LORD your God, that it may be there for a witness against you.

27 For I know your rebellion, and your stiff neck: behold, while I am yet alive with you this day, you have been rebellious against the LORD; and how much more after my death?

28 Gather to me all the elders of your tribes, and your officers, that I may speak these words in their ears, and call heaven and earth to record against them.

29 For I know that after my death you will utterly corrupt yourselves, and turn aside from the way which I have commanded you; and evil will befall you in the latter days; because you will do evil in the sight of the LORD, to provoke him to anger through the work of your hands.

30 And Moses spoke in the ears of all the congregation of Israel the words of this song, until they were ended.

CHAPTER 32

GIVE ear, O you heavens, and I will speak; and hear, O earth, the words of my mouth.

2 My doctrine shall drop as the rain, my speech shall distil as the dew, as the small rain upon the tender herb, and as the showers upon the grass:

3 Because I will publish the name of the LORD: ascribe greatness to our God.

4 He is the Rock, his work is perfect: for all his ways are judgment: a God of truth and without iniquity, just and right is he.

5 They have corrupted themselves, their spot is not the spot of his children: they are a perverse and crooked generation.

6 Do you thus requite the LORD, O foolish people and unwise? is not he your father that has bought you? has he not made you, and established you?

7 Remember the days of old, consider the years of many generations: ask your father, and he will show you; your elders, and they will tell you.

8 When the Most High divided to the nations their inheritance, when he separated the sons of Adam, he set the bounds of the people according to the number of the children of Israel.

9 For the LORD's portion is his people; Jacob is the lot of his inheritance.

10 He found him in a desert land, and in the waste howling wilderness; he led him about, he instructed him, he kept him as the apple of his eye.

11 As an eagle stirs up her nest, flutters over her young, spreads abroad her wings, takes them, bears them on her wings:

12 So the LORD alone did lead him, and there was no strange god with him.

13 He made him ride on the high places of the earth, that he might eat the increase of the fields; and he made him to suck honey out of the rock, and oil out of the flinty rock;

14 Butter of kine, and milk of sheep, with fat of lambs, and rams of the breed of Bashan, and goats, with the fat of kidneys of wheat; and you did drink the pure blood of the grape.

15 But Jeshurun waxed fat, and kicked: you are waxen fat, you are grown thick, you are covered with fatness; then he forsook God which made him, and lightly esteemed the Rock of his salvation.

16 They provoked him to jealousy with strange gods, with abominations provoked they him to anger.

17 They sacrificed to devils, not to God; to gods whom they knew not, to new gods that came newly up, whom your fathers feared not.

18 Of the Rock that begat you you are unmindful, and have forgotten God that formed you.

19 And when the LORD saw it, he abhorred them, because of the provoking of his sons, and of his daughters.

20 And he said, I will hide my face from them, I will see what their end shall be: for they are a very froward generation, children in whom is no faith.

21 They have moved me to jealousy with that which is not God; they have provoked me to anger with their vanities: and I will move them to jealousy with those which are not a people; I will provoke them to anger with a foolish nation.

22 For a fire is kindled in mine anger, and shall burn to the lowest hell, and shall consume the earth with her increase, and set on fire the foundations of the mountains.

23 I will heap mischiefs upon them; I will spend mine arrows upon them.

24 They shall be burnt with hunger, and devoured with burning heat, and with bitter destruction: I will also send the teeth of beasts upon them, with the poison of serpents of the dust.

25 The sword without, and terror within, shall destroy both the young man and the virgin, the suckling also with the man of gray hairs.

26 I said, I would scatter them into corners, I would make the remembrance of them to cease from among men:

27 Were it not that I feared the wrath of the enemy, lest their adversaries should behave themselves strangely, and lest they should say, Our hand is high, and the LORD has not done all this.

28 For they are a nation void of counsel, neither is there any understanding in them.

29 O that they were wise, that they understood this, that they would consider their latter end!

30 How should one chase a thousand, and two put ten thousand to flight, except their Rock had sold them, and the LORD had shut them up?

31 For their rock is not as our Rock, even our enemies themselves being judges.

32 For their vine is of the vine of Sodom, and of the fields of Gomorrah: their grapes are grapes of gall, their clusters are bitter:

33 Their wine is the poison of dragons, and the cruel venom of asps.

34 Is not this laid up in store with me, and sealed up among my treasures?

35 To me belongs vengeance and recompence; their foot shall slide in due time: for the day of their calamity is at hand, and the things that shall come upon them make haste.

36 For the LORD shall judge his people, and repent himself for his servants, when he sees that their power is gone, and there is none shut up, or left.

37 And he shall say, Where are their gods, their rock in whom they trusted,

38 Which did eat the fat of their sacrifices, and drank the wine of their drink offerings? let them rise up and help you, and be your protection.

39 See now that I, even I, am he, and there is no god with me: I kill, and I make alive; I wound, and I heal: neither is there any that can deliver out of my hand.

40 For I lift up my hand to heaven, and say, I live for ever.

41 If I whet my glittering sword, and mine hand take hold on judgment; I will render vengeance to mine enemies, and will reward them that hate me.

42 I will make mine arrows drunk with blood, and my sword shall devour flesh; and that with the blood of the slain and of the captives, from the beginning of revenges upon the enemy.

43 Rejoice, O you nations, with his people: for he will avenge the blood of his servants, and will render vengeance to his adversaries, and will be merciful to his land, and to his people.

44 And Moses came and spoke all the words of this song in the ears of the people, he, and Hoshea the son of Nun.

45 And Moses made an end of speaking all these words to all Israel:

46 And he said to them, Set your hearts to all the words which I testify among you this day, which you shall command

your children to observe to do, all the words of this law.

47 For it is not a vain thing for you; because it is your life: and through this thing you shall prolong your days in the land, whither you go over Jordan to possess it.

48 And the LORD spoke to Moses that selfsame day, saying,

49 Get up into this mountain Abarim, to mount Nebo, which is in the land of Moab, that is over against Jericho; and behold the land of Canaan, which I give to the children of Israel for a possession:

50 And die in the mount whither you go up, and be gathered to your people; as Aaron your brother died in mount Hor, and was gathered to his people:

51 Because you trespassed against me among the children of Israel at the waters of MeribahKadesh, in the wilderness of Zin; because you sanctified me not in the midst of the children of Israel.

52 Yet you shall see the land before you; but you shall not go thither to the land which I give the children of Israel.

CHAPTER 33

AND this is the blessing, wherewith Moses the man of God blessed the children of Israel before his death.

2 And he said, The LORD came from Sinai, and rose up from Seir to them; he shined forth from mount Paran, and he came with ten thousands of saints: from his right hand went a fiery law for them.

3 Yea, he loved the people; all his saints are in your hand: and they sat down at your feet; every one shall receive of your words.

4 Moses commanded us a law, even the inheritance of the congregation of Jacob.

5 And he was king in Jeshurun, when the heads of the people and the tribes of Israel were gathered together.

6 Let Reuben live, and not die; and let not his men be few.

7 And this is the blessing of Judah: and he said, Hear, LORD, the voice of Judah, and bring him to his people: let his hands be sufficient for him; and be you an help to him from his enemies.

8 And of Levi he said, Let your Thummim and your Urim be with your holy one, whom you did prove at Massah, and with whom you did strive at the waters of Meribah;

9 Who said to his father and to his mother, I have not seen him; neither did he acknowledge his brethren, nor knew his own children: for they have observed your word, and kept your covenant.

10 They shall teach Jacob your judgments, and Israel your law: they shall put incense before you, and whole burnt sacrifice upon your altar.

11 Bless, LORD, his substance, and accept the work of his hands; smite through the loins of them that rise against him, and of them that hate him, that they rise not again.

12 And of Benjamin he said, The beloved of the LORD shall dwell in safety by him; and the Lord shall cover him all the day long, and he shall dwell between his shoulders.

13 And of Joseph he said, Blessed of the LORD be his land, for the precious things of heaven, for the dew, and for the deep that couches beneath,

14 And for the precious fruits brought forth by the sun, and for the precious things put forth by the moon,

15 And for the chief things of the ancient mountains, and for the precious things of the lasting hills,

16 And for the precious things of the earth and fullness thereof, and for the good will of him that dwelt in the bush: let the blessing come upon the head of Joseph, and upon the top of the head of him that was separated from his brethren.

17 His glory is like the firstling of his bullock, and his horns are like the horns of unicorns: with them he shall push the people together to the ends of the earth: and they are the ten thousands of

Ephraim, and they are the thousands of Manasseh.

18 And of Zebulun he said, Rejoice, Zebulun, in your going out; and, Issachar, in your tents.

19 They shall call the people to the mountain; there they shall offer sacrifices of righteousness: for they shall suck of the abundance of the seas, and of treasures hid in the sand.

20 And of Gad he said, Blessed be he that enlarges Gad: he dwells as a lion, and tears the arm with the crown of the head.

21 And he provided the first part for himself, because there, in a portion of the lawgiver, was he seated; and he came with the heads of the people, he executed the justice of the LORD, and his judgments with Israel.

22 And of Dan he said, Dan is a lion's whelp: he shall leap from Bashan.

23 And of Naphtali he said, O Naphtali, satisfied with favour, and full with the blessing of the LORD: possess you the west and the south.

24 And of Asher he said, Let Asher be blessed with children; let him be acceptable to his brethren, and let him dip his foot in oil.

25 Your shoes shall be iron and brass; and as your days, so shall your strength be.

26 There is none like to the God of Jeshurun, who rides upon the heaven in your help, and in his excellency on the sky.

27 The eternal God is your refuge, and underneath are the everlasting arms: and he shall thrust out the enemy from before you; and shall say, Destroy them.

28 Israel then shall dwell in safety alone: the fountain of Jacob shall be upon a land of corn and wine; also his heavens shall drop down dew.

29 Happy are you, O Israel: who is like to you, O people saved by the LORD, the shield of your help, and who is the sword of your excellency! and your enemies shall be found liars to you; and you shall tread upon their high places.

CHAPTER 34

AND Moses went up from the plains of Moab to the mountain of Nebo, to the top of Pisgah, that is over against Jericho. And the LORD showed him all the land of Gilead, to Dan,

2 And all Naphtali, and the land of Ephraim, and Manasseh, and all the land of Judah, to the utmost sea,

3 And the south, and the plain of the valley of Jericho, the city of palm trees, to Zoar.

4 And the LORD said to him, This is the land which I swore to Abraham, to Isaac, and to Jacob, saying, I will give it to your seed: I have caused you to see it with your eyes, but you shall not go over thither.

5 So Moses the servant of the LORD died there in the land of Moab, according to the word of the LORD.

6 And he buried him in a valley in the land of Moab, over against Bethpeor: but no man knows of his sepulchre to this day.

7 And Moses was an hundred and twenty years old when he died: his eye was not dim, nor his natural force abated.

8 And the children of Israel wept for Moses in the plains of Moab thirty days: so the days of weeping and mourning for Moses were ended.

9 And Joshua the son of Nun was full of the spirit of wisdom; for Moses had laid his hands upon him: and the children of Israel hearkened to him, and did as the LORD commanded Moses.

10 And there arose not a prophet since in Israel like to Moses, whom the LORD knew face to face,

11 In all the signs and the wonders, which the LORD sent him to do in the land of Egypt to Pharaoh, and to all his servants, and to all his land,

12 And in all that mighty hand, and in all the great terror which Moses showed in the sight of all Israel.

Joshua

CHAPTER 1

NOW after the death of Moses the servant of the LORD it came to pass, that the LORD spoke to Joshua the son of Nun, Moses' minister, saying,

2 Moses my servant is dead; now therefore arise, go over this Jordan, you, and all this people, to the land which I do give to them, even to the children of Israel.

3 Every place that the sole of your foot shall tread upon, that have I given to you, as I said to Moses.

4 From the wilderness and this Lebanon even to the great river, the river Euphrates, all the land of the Hittites, and to the great sea toward the going down of the sun, shall be your coast.

5 There shall not any man be able to stand before you all the days of your life: as I was with Moses, so I will be with you: I will not fail you, nor forsake you.

6 Be strong and of a good courage: for to this people shall you divide for an inheritance the land, which I swore to their fathers to give them.

7 Only be strong and very courageous, that you may observe to do according to all the law, which Moses my servant commanded you: turn not from it to the right hand or to the left, that you may prosper withersoever you go.

8 This book of the law shall not depart out of your mouth; but you shall meditate therein day and night, that you may observe to do according to all that is written therein: for then you shall make your way prosperous, and then you shall have good success.

9 Have not I commanded you? Be strong and of a good courage; be not afraid, neither be dismayed: for the LORD your God is with you wherever you go.

10 Then Joshua commanded the officers of the people, saying,

11 Pass through the host, and command the people, saying, Prepare you victuals; for within three days you shall pass over this Jordan, to go in to possess the land, which the LORD your God gives you to possess it.

12 And to the Reubenites, and to the Gadites, and to half the tribe of Manasseh, spoke Joshua, saying,

13 Remember the word which Moses the servant of the LORD commanded you, saying, The LORD your God has given you rest, and has given you this land.

14 Your wives, your little ones, and your cattle, shall remain in the land which Moses gave you on this side of the Jordan; but you shall pass before your

---

1:6-9 The key to biblical prosperity and evangelistic "good success" is obedience.

THE FUNCTION OF THE LAW IN EVANGELISM

1:7 It is a great mistake to give a man who has not been convicted of sin certain passages that were never meant for him. The Law is what he needs . . .Do not offer the consolation of the gospel until he sees and knows he is guilty before God. We must give enough of the Law to take away all self-righteousness. I pity the man who preaches only one side of the truth, always the Gospel and never the Law.

D. L. Moody

brethren armed, all the mighty men of valour, and help them;

15 Until the LORD have given your brethren rest, as he has given you, and they also have possessed the land which the LORD your God gives them: then you shall return to the land of your possession, and enjoy it, which Moses the LORD's servant gave you on this side Jordan toward the sunrising.

16 And they answered Joshua, saying, All that you command us we will do, and wherever you send us, we will go.

17 According as we hearkened to Moses in all things, so will we hearken to you: only the LORD your God be with you, as he was with Moses.

18 Whosoever he be that does rebel against your commandment, and will not hearken to your words in all that you command him, he shall be put to death: only be strong and of a good courage.

CHAPTER 2

AND Joshua the son of Nun sent out of Shittim two men to spy secretly, saying, Go view the land, even Jericho. And they went, and came into an harlot's house, named Rahab, and lodged there.

2 And it was told the king of Jericho, saying, Behold, there came men in hither to night of the children of Israel to search out the country.

3 And the king of Jericho sent to Rahab, saying, Bring forth the men that are come to you, which are entered into your house: for they be come to search out all the country.

4 And the woman took the two men, and hid them, and said thus, There came men to me, but I knew not whence they were:

5 And it came to pass about the time of shutting of the gate, when it was dark, that the men went out: where the men went I wot not: pursue after them quickly; for you shall overtake them.

6 But she had brought them up to the roof of the house, and hid them with the stalks of flax, which she had laid in order upon the roof.

7 And the men pursued after them the way to Jordan to the fords: and as soon as they which pursued after them were gone out, they shut the gate.

8 And before they were laid down, she came up to them upon the roof;

9 And she said to the men, I know that the LORD has given you the land, and that your terror is fallen upon us, and that all the inhabitants of the land faint because of you.

10 For we have heard how the LORD dried up the water of the Red sea for you, when you came out of Egypt; and what you did to the two kings of the Amorites, that were on the other side Jordan, Sihon and Og, whom you utterly destroyed.

11 And as soon as we had heard these things, our hearts did melt, neither did there remain any more courage in any man, because of you: for the LORD your God, he is God in heaven above, and in earth beneath.

12 Now therefore, I pray you, swear to me by the LORD, since I have showed you kindness, that you will also show kindness to my father's house, and give me a true token:

13 And that you will save alive my father, and my mother, and my brethren, and my sisters, and all that they have, and deliver our lives from death.

14 And the men answered her, Our life for yours, if you utter not this our business. And it shall be, when the LORD has given us the land, that we will deal kindly and truly with you.

15 Then she let them down by a cord through the window: for her house was upon the town wall, and she dwelt upon the wall.

16 And she said to them, Get you to the mountain, lest the pursuers meet you; and hide yourselves there three days, until the pursuers be returned: and afterward may you go your way.

17 And the men said to her, We will be blameless of this your oath which you have made us swear.

18 Behold, when we come into the land, you shall bind this line of scarlet thread in the window which you did let us down by: and you shall bring your father, and your mother, and your brethren, and all your father's household, home to you.

19 And it shall be, that whosoever shall go out of the doors of your house into the street, his blood shall be upon his head, and we will be guiltless: and whosoever shall be with you in the house, his blood shall be on our head, if any hand be upon him.

20 And if you utter this our business, then we will be quit of your oath which you have made us to swear.

21 And she said, According to your words, so be it. And she sent them away, and they departed: and she bound the scarlet line in the window.

22 And they went, and came to the mountain, and abode there three days, until the pursuers were returned: and the pursuers sought them throughout all the way, but found them not.

23 So the two men returned, and descended from the mountain, and passed over, and came to Joshua the son of Nun, and told him all things that befell them:

24 And they said to Joshua, Truly the LORD has delivered into our hands all the land; for even all the inhabitants of the country do faint because of us.

CHAPTER 3

AND Joshua rose early in the morning; and they removed from Shittim, and came to Jordan, he and all the children of Israel, and lodged there before they passed over.

2 And it came to pass after three days, that the officers went through the host;

3 And they commanded the people, saying, When you see the ark of the covenant of the LORD your God, and the priests the Levites bearing it, then you shall remove from your place, and go after it.

4 Yet there shall be a space between you and it, about two thousand cubits by measure: come not near to it, that you may know the way by which you must go: for you have not passed this way heretofore.

5 And Joshua said to the people, Sanctify yourselves: for tomorrow the LORD will do wonders among you.

6 And Joshua spoke to the priests, saying, Take up the ark of the covenant, and pass over before the people. And they took up the ark of the covenant, and went before the people.

7 And the LORD said to Joshua, This day will I begin to magnify you in the sight of all Israel, that they may know that, as I was with Moses, so I will be with you.

8 And you shall command the priests that bear the ark of the covenant, saying, When you are come to the brink of the water of Jordan, you shall stand still in Jordan.

9 And Joshua said to the children of Israel, Come hither, and hear the words of the LORD your God.

10 And Joshua said, Hereby you shall know that the living God is among you,

and that he will without fail drive out from before you the Canaanites, and the Hittites, and the Hivites, and the Perizzites, and the Girgashites, and the Amorites, and the Jebusites.

11 Behold, the ark of the covenant of the LORD of all the earth passes over before you into Jordan.

12 Now therefore take you twelve men out of the tribes of Israel, out of every tribe a man.

13 And it shall come to pass, as soon as the soles of the feet of the priests that bear the ark of the LORD, the LORD of all the earth, shall rest in the waters of Jordan, that the waters of Jordan shall be cut off from the waters that come down from above; and they shall stand upon an heap.

14 And it came to pass, when the people removed from their tents, to pass over Jordan, and the priests bearing the ark of the covenant before the people;

15 And as they that bare the ark were come to Jordan, and the feet of the priests that bare the ark were dipped in the brim of the water, (for Jordan overflows all his banks all the time of harvest,)

16 That the waters which came down from above stood and rose up upon an heap very far from the city Adam, that is beside Zaretan: and those that came down toward the sea of the plain, even the salt sea, failed, and were cut off: and the people passed over right against Jericho.

17 And the priests that bare the ark of the covenant of the LORD stood firm on dry ground in the midst of Jordan, and all the Israelites passed over on dry ground, until all the people were passed clean over Jordan.

CHAPTER 4

AND it came to pass, when all the people were clean passed over Jordan, that the LORD spoke to Joshua, saying,

2 Take you twelve men out of the people, out of every tribe a man,

3 And command them, saying, Take you hence out of the midst of Jordan, out of the place where the priests' feet stood firm, twelve stones, and you shall carry them over with you, and leave them in the lodging place, where you shall lodge this night.

4 Then Joshua called the twelve men, whom he had prepared of the children of Israel, out of every tribe a man:

5 And Joshua said to them, Pass over before the ark of the LORD your God into the midst of Jordan, and take you up every man of you a stone upon his shoulder, according to the number of the tribes of the children of Israel:

6 That this may be a sign among you, that when your children ask their fathers in time to come, saying, What do these stones mean to you?

7 Then you shall answer them, That the waters of Jordan were cut off before the ark of the covenant of the LORD; when it passed over Jordan, the waters of Jordan were cut off: and these stones shall be for a memorial to the children of Israel for ever.

8 And the children of Israel did so as Joshua commanded, and took up twelve stones out of the midst of Jordan, as the LORD spoke to Joshua, according to the number of the tribes of the children of Israel, and carried them over with them

4:1-7

Just as the twelve stones were placed as immovable witnesses, the Church, too, was established with twelve witnesses (see Acts 1:21-26).

THE CHILDREN OF ISRAEL CROSSING JORDAN

Joshua 3:14-17

to the place where they lodged, and laid them down there.

9 And Joshua set up twelve stones in the midst of Jordan, in the place where the feet of the priests which bare the ark of the covenant stood: and they are there to this day.

10 For the priests which bare the ark stood in the midst of Jordan, until everything was finished that the LORD commanded Joshua to speak to the people, according to all that Moses commanded Joshua: and the people hasted and passed over.

11 And it came to pass, when all the people were clean passed over, that the ark of the LORD passed over, and the priests, in the presence of the people.

12 And the children of Reuben, and the children of Gad, and half the tribe of Manasseh, passed over armed before the children of Israel, as Moses spoke to them:

13 About forty thousand prepared for war passed over before the LORD to battle, to the plains of Jericho.

14 On that day the LORD magnified Joshua in the sight of all Israel; and they feared him, as they feared Moses, all the days of his life.

15 And the LORD spoke to Joshua, saying,

16 Command the priests that bear the ark of the testimony, that they come up out of Jordan.

17 Joshua therefore commanded the priests, saying, Come up out of Jordan.

18 And it came to pass, when the priests that bare the ark of the covenant of the LORD were come up out of the midst of Jordan, and the soles of the priests' feet were lifted up to the dry land, that the waters of Jordan returned to their place, and flowed over all his banks, as they did before.

19 And the people came up out of Jordan on the tenth day of the first month, and encamped in Gilgal, in the east border of Jericho.

20 And those twelve stones, which they took out of Jordan, did Joshua pitch in Gilgal.

21 And he spoke to the children of Israel, saying, When your children shall ask their fathers in time to come, saying, What mean these stones?

22 Then you shall let your children know, saying, Israel came over this Jordan on dry land.

23 For the LORD your God dried up the waters of Jordan from before you, until you were passed over, as the LORD your God did to the Red sea, which he dried up from before us, until we were gone over:

24 That all the people of the earth might know the hand of the LORD, that it is mighty: that you might fear the LORD your God for ever.

CHAPTER 5

AND it came to pass, when all the kings of the Amorites, which were on the side of Jordan westward, and all the kings of the Canaanites, which were by the sea, heard that the LORD had dried up the waters of Jordan from before the children of Israel, until we were passed over, that their heart melted, neither was there spirit in them any more, because of the children of Israel.

2 At that time the LORD said to Joshua, Make for yourself sharp knives, and circumcise again the children of Israel the second time.

3 And Joshua made him sharp knives, and circumcised the children of Israel at the hill of the foreskins.

4 And this is the cause why Joshua did circumcise: All the people that came out of Egypt, that were males, even all the men of war, died in the wilderness by the way, after they came out of Egypt.

5 Now all the people that came out were circumcised: but all the people that were born in the wilderness by the way as they came forth out of Egypt, them they had not circumcised.

6 For the children of Israel walked forty years in the wilderness, till all the people that were men of war, which came out of Egypt, were consumed, because they obeyed not the voice of the LORD: to whom the LORD swore that he would not show them the land, which the LORD swore to their fathers that he would give us, a land that flows with milk and honey.

7 And their children, whom he raised up in their stead, them Joshua circumcised: for they were uncircumcised, because they had not circumcised them by the way.

8 And it came to pass, when they had done circumcising all the people, that they abode in their places in the camp, till they were whole.

9 And the LORD said to Joshua, This day have I rolled away the reproach of Egypt from off you. Therefore the name of the place is called Gilgal to this day.

10 And the children of Israel encamped in Gilgal, and kept the passover on the fourteenth day of the month at even in the plains of Jericho.

11 And they did eat of the old corn of the land on the morrow after the passover, unleavened cakes, and parched corn in the selfsame day.

12 And the manna ceased on the morrow after they had eaten of the old corn of the land; neither had the children of Israel manna any more; but they did eat of the fruit of the land of Canaan that year.

13 And it came to pass, when Joshua was by Jericho, that he lifted up his eyes and looked, and, behold, there stood a man over against him with his sword drawn in his hand: and Joshua went to him, and said to him, Are you for us, or for our adversaries?

14 And he said, Nay; but as captain of the host of the LORD am I now come. And Joshua fell on his face to the earth, and did worship, and said to him, What says my Lord to his servant?

15 And the captain of the LORD's host said to Joshua, Loose your shoe from off your foot; for the place whereon you stand is holy. And Joshua did so.

THE WALLS OF JERICHO FALLING DOWN

Joshua 6:1-20

In this incident, when Joshua seizes the City of Jericho, notice the emphasis on the presence of the Ark of the Lord, which contained God's law. The Ark is mentioned 10 times in this chapter before the city walls fall down. If we want to see the downfall of the enemy, the presentation of the Ten Commandments must precede the victorious shout of the gospel.

CHAPTER 6

NOW Jericho was straitly shut up because of the children of Israel: none went out, and none came in.

2 And the LORD said to Joshua, See, I have given into your hand Jericho, and the king thereof, and the mighty men of valour.

3 And you shall compass the city, all you men of war, and go round about the city once. Thus shall you do six days.

4 And seven priests shall bear before the ark seven trumpets of rams' horns: and the seventh day you shall compass the city seven times, and the priests shall blow with the trumpets.

5 And it shall come to pass, that when they make a long blast with the ram's horn, and when you hear the sound of the trumpet, all the people shall shout with a great shout; and the wall of the city shall fall down flat, and the people shall ascend up every man straight before him.

6 And Joshua the son of Nun called the priests, and said to them, Take up the ark of the covenant, and let seven priests bear seven trumpets of rams' horns before the ark of the LORD.

7 And he said to the people, Pass on, and compass the city, and let him that is armed pass on before the ark of the LORD.

8 And it came to pass, when Joshua had spoken to the people, that the seven priests bearing the seven trumpets of rams' horns passed on before the LORD, and blew with the trumpets: and the ark of the covenant of the LORD followed them.

9 And the armed men went before the priests that blew with the trumpets, and the rearward came after the ark, the priests going on, and blowing with the trumpets.

10 And Joshua had commanded the people, saying, You shall not shout, nor make any noise with your voice, neither shall any word proceed out of your mouth, until the day I bid you shout; then shall you shout.

11 So the ark of the LORD compassed the city, going about it once: and they came into the camp, and lodged in the camp.

12 And Joshua rose early in the morning, and the priests took up the ark of the LORD.

13 And seven priests bearing seven trumpets of rams' horns before the ark of the LORD went on continually, and blew with the trumpets: and the armed men went before them; but the rearward came after the ark of the LORD, the priests going on, and blowing with the trumpets.

14 And the second day they compassed the city once, and returned into the camp: so they did six days.

15 And it came to pass on the seventh day, that they rose early about the dawning of the day, and compassed the city after the same manner seven times: only on that day they compassed the city seven times.

16 And it came to pass at the seventh time, when the priests blew with the trumpets, Joshua said to the people, Shout; for the LORD has given you the city.

17 And the city shall be accursed, even it, and all that are therein, to the LORD: only Rahab the harlot shall live, she and all that are with her in the house, because she hid the messengers that we sent.

18 And you, in any wise keep yourselves from the accursed thing, lest you make yourselves accursed, when you take of the accursed thing, and make the camp of Israel a curse, and trouble it.

19 But all the silver, and gold, and vessels of brass and iron, are consecrated to the LORD: they shall come into the treasury of the LORD.

20 So the people shouted when the priests blew with the trumpets: and it came to pass, when the people heard the sound of the trumpet, and the people shouted with a great shout, that the wall fell down flat, so that the people went up into the city, every man straight before him, and they took the city.

21 And they utterly destroyed all that was in the city, both man and woman, young and old, and ox, and sheep, and ass, with the edge of the sword.

22 But Joshua had said to the two men that had spied out the country, Go into the harlot's house, and bring out thence the woman, and all that she has, as you swore to her.

23 And the young men that were spies went in, and brought out Rahab, and her father, and her mother, and her brethren, and all that she had; and they brought out all her kindred, and left them without the camp of Israel.

24 And they burnt the city with fire, and all that was therein: only the silver, and the gold, and the vessels of brass and of iron, they put into the treasury of the house of the LORD.

25 And Joshua saved Rahab the harlot alive, and her father's household, and all that she had; and she dwells in Israel even to this day; because she hid the messengers, which Joshua sent to spy out Jericho.

26 And Joshua adjured them at that time, saying, Cursed be the man before the LORD, that rises up and builds this city Jericho: he shall lay the foundation thereof in his firstborn, and in his youngest son shall he set up the gates of it.

27 So the LORD was with Joshua; and his fame was noised throughout all the country.

CHAPTER 7

BUT the children of Israel committed a trespass in the accursed thing: for Achan, the son of Carmi, the son of Zabdi, the son of Zerah, of the tribe of Judah, took of the accursed thing: and the anger of the LORD was kindled against the children of Israel.

2 And Joshua sent men from Jericho to Ai, which is beside Bethaven, on the east of Bethel, and spoke to them, saying, Go up and view the country. And the men went up and viewed Ai.

3 And they returned to Joshua, and said to him, Let not all the people go up; but let about two or three thousand men go up and smite Ai; and make not all the people to labour thither; for they are but few.

4 So there went up thither of the people about three thousand men: and they fled before the men of Ai.

5 And the men of Ai smote of them about thirty and six men: for they chased them from before the gate even to Shebarim, and smote them in the going

down: therefore the hearts of the people melted, and became as water.

6 And Joshua rent his clothes, and fell to the earth upon his face before the ark of the LORD until the eventide, he and the elders of Israel, and put dust upon their heads.

7 And Joshua said, Alas, O LORD God, why have you at all brought this people over Jordan, to deliver us into the hand of the Amorites, to destroy us? would to God we had been content, and dwelt on the other side Jordan!

8 O LORD, what shall I say, when Israel turns their backs before their enemies!

9 For the Canaanites and all the inhabitants of the land shall hear of it, and shall environ us round, and cut off our name from the earth: and what will you do to your great name?

10 And the LORD said to Joshua, Get up; why do you lie thus upon your face?

11 Israel has sinned, and they have also transgressed my covenant which I commanded them: for they have even taken of the accursed thing, and have also stolen, and dissembled also, and they have put it even among their own stuff.

12 Therefore the children of Israel could not stand before their enemies, but turned their backs before their enemies, because they were accursed: neither will I be with you any more, except you destroy the accursed from among you.

13 Up, sanctify the people, and say, Sanctify yourselves against tomorrow: for thus says the LORD God of Israel, There is an accursed thing in the midst of you, O Israel: you can not stand before your enemies, until you take away the accursed thing from among you.

14 In the morning therefore you shall be brought according to your tribes: and it shall be, that the tribe which the LORD takes shall come according to the families thereof; and the family which the LORD shall take shall come by households; and the household which

the LORD shall take shall come man by man.

15 And it shall be, that he that is taken with the accursed thing shall be burnt with fire, he and all that he has: because he has transgressed the covenant of the LORD, and because he has wrought folly in Israel.

16 So Joshua rose up early in the morning, and brought Israel by their tribes; and the tribe of Judah was taken:

17 And he brought the family of Judah; and he took the family of the Zarhites: and he brought the family of the Zarhites man by man; and Zabdi was taken:

18 And he brought his household man by man; and Achan, the son of Carmi, the son of Zabdi, the son of Zerah, of the tribe of Judah, was taken.

19 And Joshua said to Achan, My son, give, I pray you, glory to the LORD God of Israel, and make confession to him; and tell me now what you have done; hide it not from me.

20 And Achan answered Joshua, and said, Indeed I have sinned against the LORD God of Israel, and thus and thus have I done:

21 When I saw among the spoils a goodly Babylonish garment, and two hundred shekels of silver, and a wedge of gold of fifty shekels weight, then I coveted them, and took them; and, behold, they are hid in the earth in the midst of my tent, and the silver under it.

22 So Joshua sent messengers, and they ran to the tent; and, behold, it was hid in his tent, and the silver under it.

23 And they took them out of the midst of the tent, and brought them to Joshua, and to all the children of Israel, and laid them out before the LORD.

24 And Joshua, and all Israel with him, took Achan the son of Zerah, and the silver, and the garment, and the wedge of gold, and his sons, and his daughters, and his oxen, and his asses, and his sheep, and his tent, and all that he had: and they brought them to the valley of Achor.

25 And Joshua said, Why have you troubled us? the LORD shall trouble you this day. And all Israel stoned him with stones, and burned them with fire, after they had stoned them with stones.

26 And they raised over him a great heap of stones to this day. So the LORD turned from the fierceness of his anger. Therefore the name of that place was called, The valley of Achor, to this day.

CHAPTER 8

AND the LORD said to Joshua, Fear not, neither be dismayed: take all the people of war with you, and arise, go up to Ai: see, I have given into your hand the king of Ai, and his people, and his city, and his land:

2 And you shall do to Ai and her king as you did to Jericho and her king: only the spoil thereof, and the cattle thereof, shall you take for a prey to yourselves: lay an ambush for the city behind it.

3 So Joshua arose, and all the people of war, to go up against Ai: and Joshua chose out thirty thousand mighty men of valour, and sent them away by night.

4 And he commanded them, saying, Behold, you shall lie in wait against the city, even behind the city: go not very far from the city, but all of you be ready:

5 And I, and all the people that are with me, will approach to the city: and it shall come to pass, when they come out against us, as at the first, that we will flee before them,

6 (For they will come out after us) till we have drawn them from the city; for they will say, They flee before us, as at the first: therefore we will flee before them.

7 Then you shall rise up from the ambush, and seize upon the city: for the LORD your God will deliver it into your hand.

8 And it shall be, when you have taken the city, that you shall set the city on fire: according to the commandment

of the LORD shall you do. See, I have commanded you.

9 Joshua therefore sent them forth: and they went to lie in ambush, and abode between Bethel and Ai, on the west side of Ai: but Joshua lodged that night among the people.

10 And Joshua rose up early in the morning, and numbered the people, and went up, he and the elders of Israel, before the people to Ai.

11 And all the people, even the people of war that were with him, went up, and drew nigh, and came before the city, and pitched on the north side of Ai: now there was a valley between them and Ai.

12 And he took about five thousand men, and set them to lie in ambush between Bethel and Ai, on the west side of the city.

13 And when they had set the people, even all the host that was on the north of the city, and their liers in wait on the west of the city, Joshua went that night into the midst of the valley.

14 And it came to pass, when the king of Ai saw it, that they hasted and rose up early, and the men of the city went out against Israel to battle, he and all his people, at a time appointed, before the plain; but he knew not that there were liers in ambush against him behind the city.

15 And Joshua and all Israel made as if they were beaten before them, and fled by the way of the wilderness.

16 And all the people that were in Ai were called together to pursue after them: and they pursued after Joshua, and were drawn away from the city.

17 And there was not a man left in Ai or Bethel, that went not out after Israel: and they left the city open, and pursued after Israel.

18 And the LORD said to Joshua, Stretch out the spear that is in your hand toward Ai; for I will give it into your hand. And Joshua stretched out the spear that he had in his hand toward the city.

19 And the ambush arose quickly out of their place, and they ran as soon as he had stretched out his hand: and they entered into the city, and took it, and hasted and set the city on fire.

20 And when the men of Ai looked behind them, they saw, and, behold, the smoke of the city ascended up to heaven, and they had no power to flee this way or that way: and the people that fled to the wilderness turned back upon the pursuers.

21 And when Joshua and all Israel saw that the ambush had taken the city, and that the smoke of the city ascended, then they turned again, and slew the men of Ai.

22 And the other issued out of the city against them; so they were in the midst of Israel, some on this side, and some on that side: and they smote them, so that they let none of them remain or escape.

23 And the king of Ai they took alive, and brought him to Joshua.

24 And it came to pass, when Israel had made an end of slaying all the inhabitants of Ai in the field, in the wilderness wherein they chased them, and when they were all fallen on the edge of the sword, until they were consumed, that all the Israelites returned to Ai, and smote it with the edge of the sword.

25 And so it was, that all that fell that day, both of men and women, were twelve thousand, even all the men of Ai.

26 For Joshua drew not his hand back, wherewith he stretched out the spear, until he had utterly destroyed all the inhabitants of Ai.

27 Only the cattle and the spoil of that city Israel took for a prey to themselves, according to the word of the LORD which he commanded Joshua.

28 And Joshua burnt Ai, and made it an heap for ever, even a desolation to this day.

29 And the king of Ai he hanged on a tree until eventide: and as soon as the sun was down, Joshua commanded that they should take his carcase down from

the tree, and cast it at the entering of the gate of the city, and raise thereon a great heap of stones, that remains to this day.

30 Then Joshua built an altar to the LORD God of Israel in mount Ebal,

31 As Moses the servant of the LORD commanded the children of Israel, as it is written in the book of the law of Moses, an altar of whole stones, over which no man has lift up any iron: and they offered thereon burnt offerings to the LORD, and sacrificed peace offerings.

32 And he wrote there upon the stones a copy of the law of Moses, which he wrote in the presence of the children of Israel.

33 And all Israel, and their elders, and officers, and their judges, stood on this side the ark and on that side before the priests the Levites, which bare the ark of the covenant of the LORD, as well the stranger, as he that was born among them; half of them over against mount Gerizim, and half of them over against mount Ebal; as Moses the servant of the LORD had commanded before, that they should bless the people of Israel.

34 And afterward he read all the words of the law, the blessings and cursings, according to all that is written in the book of the law.

35 There was not a word of all that Moses commanded, which Joshua read not before all the congregation of Israel, with the women, and the little ones, and the strangers that were conversant among them.

CHAPTER 9

AND it came to pass, when all the kings which were on this side Jordan, in the hills, and in the valleys, and in all the coasts of the great sea over against Lebanon, the Hittite, and the Amorite, the Canaanite, the Perizzite, the Hivite, and the Jebusite, heard thereof;

2 That they gathered themselves together, to fight with Joshua and with Israel, with one accord.

3 And when the inhabitants of Gibeon heard what Joshua had done to Jericho and to Ai,

4 They did work wilily, and went and made as if they had been ambassadors, and took old sacks upon their asses, and wine bottles, old, and rent, and bound up;

5 And old shoes and clouted upon their feet, and old garments upon them; and all the bread of their provision was dry and mouldy.

6 And they went to Joshua to the camp at Gilgal, and said to him, and to the men of Israel, We be come from a far country: now therefore make a league with us.

7 And the men of Israel said to the Hivites, Peradventure you dwell among us; and how shall we make a league with you?

8 And they said to Joshua, We are your servants. And Joshua said to them, Who are you? And where do you come from?

9 And they said to him, From a very far country your servants are come because of the name of the LORD your God: for we have heard the fame of him, and all that he did in Egypt,

10 And all that he did to the two kings of the Amorites, that were beyond Jordan, to Sihon king of Heshbon, and to Og king of Bashan, which was at Ashtaroth.

11 Therefore our elders and all the inhabitants of our country spoke to us, saying, Take victuals with you for the journey, and go to meet them, and say to them, We are your servants: therefore now make a league with us.

12 This our bread we took hot for our provision out of our houses on the day we came forth to go to you; but now, behold, it is dry, and it is mouldy:

13 And these bottles of wine, which we filled, were new; and, behold, they be rent: and these our garments and our shoes are become old by reason of the very long journey.

14 And the men took of their victuals, and asked not counsel at the mouth of the LORD.

15 And Joshua made peace with them, and made a league with them, to let them live: and the princes of the congregation swore to them.

16 And it came to pass at the end of three days after they had made a league with them, that they heard that they were their neighbours, and that they dwelt among them.

17 And the children of Israel journeyed, and came to their cities on the third day. Now their cities were Gibeon, and Chephirah, and Beeroth, and Kirjathjearim.

18 And the children of Israel smote them not, because the princes of the congregation had sworn to them by the LORD God of Israel. And all the congregation murmured against the princes.

19 But all the princes said to all the congregation, We have sworn to them by the LORD God of Israel: now therefore we may not touch them.

20 This we will do to them; we will even let them live, lest wrath be upon us, because of the oath which we swore to them.

21 And the princes said to them, Let them live; but let them be hewers of wood and drawers of water to all the congregation; as the princes had promised them.

22 And Joshua called for them, and he spoke to them, saying, Why have you beguiled us, saying, We are very far from you; when you dwell among us?

23 Now therefore you are cursed, and there shall none of you be freed from being bondmen, and hewers of wood and drawers of water for the house of my God.

24 And they answered Joshua, and said, Because it was certainly told your servants, how that the LORD your God commanded his servant Moses to give you all the land, and to destroy all the inhabitants of the land from before you,

therefore we were sore afraid of our lives because of you, and have done this thing.

25 And now, behold, we are in your hand: as it seems good and right to you to do to us, do.

26 And so did he to them, and delivered them out of the hand of the children of Israel, that they slew them not.

27 And Joshua made them that day hewers of wood and drawers of water for the congregation, and for the altar of the LORD, even to this day, in the place which he should choose.

CHAPTER 10

NOW it came to pass, when Adonizedec king of Jerusalem had heard how Joshua had taken Ai, and had utterly destroyed it; as he had done to Jericho and her king, so he had done to Ai and her king; and how the inhabitants of Gibeon had made peace with Israel, and were among them;

2 That they feared greatly, because Gibeon was a great city, as one of the royal cities, and because it was greater than Ai, and all the men thereof were mighty.

3 Therefore Adonizedec king of Jerusalem, sent to Hoham king of Hebron, and to Piram king of Jarmuth, and to Japhia king of Lachish, and to Debir king of Eglon, saying,

4 Come up to me, and help me, that we may smite Gibeon: for it has made peace with Joshua and with the children of Israel.

5 Therefore the five kings of the Amorites, the king of Jerusalem, the king of Hebron, the king of Jarmuth, the king of Lachish, the king of Eglon, gathered themselves together, and went up, they and all their hosts, and encamped before Gibeon, and made war against it.

6 And the men of Gibeon sent to Joshua to the camp to Gilgal, saying, Slack not your hand from your servants; come up to us quickly, and save us, and help us: for all the kings of the Amorites that

JOSHUA COMMANDING THE SUN TO STAND STILL

Joshua 10:12

dwell in the mountains are gathered together against us.

7 So Joshua ascended from Gilgal, he, and all the people of war with him, and all the mighty men of valour.

8 And the LORD said to Joshua, Fear them not: for I have delivered them into your hand; there shall not a man of them stand before you.

9 Joshua therefore came to them suddenly, and went up from Gilgal all night.

10 And the LORD discomfited them before Israel, and slew them with a great slaughter at Gibeon, and chased them along the way that goes up to Bethhoron, and smote them to Azekah, and to Makkedah.

11 And it came to pass, as they fled from before Israel, and were in the going down to Bethhoron, that the LORD cast down great stones from heaven upon them to Azekah, and they died: they were more which died with hailstones than they whom the children of Israel slew with the sword.

12 Then spoke Joshua to the LORD in the day when the LORD delivered up the Amorites before the children of Israel, and he said in the sight of Israel, Sun, stand still upon Gibeon; and you, Moon, in the valley of Ajalon.

13 And the sun stood still, and the moon stayed, until the people had avenged themselves upon their enemies. Is not this written in the book of Jasher? So the sun stood still in the midst of heaven, and hasted not to go down about a whole day.

14 And there was no day like that before it or after it, that the LORD hear-

kened to the voice of a man: for the LORD fought for Israel.

15 And Joshua returned, and all Israel with him, to the camp to Gilgal.

16 But these five kings fled, and hid themselves in a cave at Makkedah.

17 And it was told Joshua, saying, The five kings are found hid in a cave at Makkedah.

18 And Joshua said, Roll great stones upon the mouth of the cave, and set men by it for to keep them:

19 And stay you not, but pursue after your enemies, and smite the hindmost of them; suffer them not to enter into their cities: for the LORD your God has delivered them into your hand.

20 And it came to pass, when Joshua and the children of Israel had made an end of slaying them with a very great slaughter, till they were consumed, that the rest which remained of them entered into fenced cities.

21 And all the people returned to the camp to Joshua at Makkedah in peace: none moved his tongue against any of the children of Israel.

22 Then said Joshua, Open the mouth of the cave, and bring out those five kings to me out of the cave.

23 And they did so, and brought forth those five kings to him out of the cave, the king of Jerusalem, the king of Hebron, the king of Jarmuth, the king of Lachish, and the king of Eglon.

24 And it came to pass, when they brought out those kings to Joshua, that Joshua called for all the men of Israel, and said to the captains of the men of war which went with him, Come near, put your feet upon the necks of these kings. And they came near, and put their feet upon the necks of them.

25 And Joshua said to them, Fear not, nor be dismayed, be strong and of good courage: for thus shall the LORD do to all your enemies against whom you fight.

26 And afterward Joshua smote them, and slew them, and hanged them on five trees: and they were hanging upon the trees until the evening.

27 And it came to pass at the time of the going down of the sun, that Joshua commanded, and they took them down off the trees, and cast them into the cave wherein they had been hid, and laid great stones in the cave's mouth, which remain until this very day.

28 And that day Joshua took Makkedah, and smote it with the edge of the sword, and the king thereof he utterly destroyed, them, and all the souls that were therein; he let none remain: and he did to the king of Makkedah as he did to the king of Jericho.

29 Then Joshua passed from Makkedah, and all Israel with him, to Libnah, and fought against Libnah:

30 And the LORD delivered it also, and the king thereof, into the hand of Israel; and he smote it with the edge of the sword, and all the souls that were therein; he let none remain in it; but did to the king thereof as he did to the king of Jericho.

31 And Joshua passed from Libnah, and all Israel with him, to Lachish, and encamped against it, and fought against it:

32 And the LORD delivered Lachish into the hand of Israel, which took it on the second day, and smote it with the edge of the sword, and all the souls that were therein, according to all that he had done to Libnah.

33 Then Horam king of Gezer came up to help Lachish; and Joshua smote him and his people, until he had left him none remaining.

34 And from Lachish Joshua passed to Eglon, and all Israel with him; and they encamped against it, and fought against it:

35 And they took it on that day, and smote it with the edge of the sword, and all the souls that were therein he utterly destroyed that day, according to all that he had done to Lachish.

> While women weep, as they do now,
>   I'll fight;
> while children go hungry
>   as they do now,
>   I'll fight;
> while men go to prison,
>   in and out, in and out,
>   as they do now,
>   I'll fight;
> while there is a drunkard left,
> while there is a poor lost girl
>   upon the streets,
> while there remains one dark soul
>   without the light of God,
>   I'll fight;
> I'll fight to the very end!

WILLIAM BOOTH
1829-1912
FOUNDED THE SALVATION ARMY
TO MINISTER TO THE POOR
OF VICTORIAN LONDON

36 And Joshua went up from Eglon, and all Israel with him, to Hebron; and they fought against it:

37 And they took it, and smote it with the edge of the sword, and the king thereof, and all the cities thereof, and all the souls that were therein; he left none remaining, according to all that he had done to Eglon; but destroyed it utterly, and all the souls that were therein.

38 And Joshua returned, and all Israel with him, to Debir; and fought against it:

39 And he took it, and the king thereof, and all the cities thereof; and they smote them with the edge of the sword, and utterly destroyed all the souls that were therein; he left none remaining: as he had done to Hebron, so he did to Debir, and to the king thereof; as he had done also to Libnah, and to her king.

40 So Joshua smote all the country of the hills, and of the south, and of the vale, and of the springs, and all their kings: he left none remaining, but utterly destroyed all that breathed, as the LORD God of Israel commanded.

41 And Joshua smote them from Kadeshbarnea even to Gaza, and all the country of Goshen, even to Gibeon.

42 And all these kings and their land did Joshua take at one time, because the LORD God of Israel fought for Israel.

43 And Joshua returned, and all Israel with him, to the camp to Gilgal.

CHAPTER 11

AND it came to pass, when Jabin king of Hazor had heard those things, that he sent to Jobab king of Madon, and to the king of Shimron, and to the king of Achshaph,

2 And to the kings that were on the north of the mountains, and of the plains south of Chinneroth, and in the valley, and in the borders of Dor on the west,

3 And to the Canaanite on the east and on the west, and to the Amorite, and the Hittite, and the Perizzite, and the Jebusite in the mountains, and to the Hivite under Hermon in the land of Mizpeh.

4 And they went out, they and all their hosts with them, much people, even as the sand that is upon the sea shore in multitude, with horses and chariots very many.

5 And when all these kings were met together, they came and pitched together at the waters of Merom, to fight against Israel.

6 And the LORD said to Joshua, Be not afraid because of them: for tomorrow about this time will I deliver them up all slain before Israel: you shall hough their horses, and burn their chariots with fire.

7 So Joshua came, and all the people of war with him, against them by the waters of Merom suddenly; and they fell upon them.

8 And the LORD delivered them into the hand of Israel, who smote them, and chased them to great Zidon, and to Misrephothmaim, and to the valley of

Mizpeh eastward; and they smote them, until they left them none remaining.

9 And Joshua did to them as the LORD bade him: he houghed their horses, and burnt their chariots with fire.

10 And Joshua at that time turned back, and took Hazor, and smote the king thereof with the sword: for Hazor beforetime was the head of all those kingdoms.

11 And they smote all the souls that were therein with the edge of the sword, utterly destroying them: there was not any left to breathe: and he burnt Hazor with fire.

12 And all the cities of those kings, and all the kings of them, did Joshua take, and smote them with the edge of the sword, and he utterly destroyed them, as Moses the servant of the LORD commanded.

13 But as for the cities that stood still in their strength, Israel burned none of them, save Hazor only; that did Joshua burn.

14 And all the spoil of these cities, and the cattle, the children of Israel took for a prey to themselves; but every man they smote with the edge of the sword, until they had destroyed them, neither left they any to breathe.

15 As the LORD commanded Moses his servant, so did Moses command Joshua, and so did Joshua; he left nothing undone of all that the LORD commanded Moses.

16 So Joshua took all that land, the hills, and all the south country, and all the land of Goshen, and the valley, and the plain, and the mountain of Israel, and the valley of the same;

17 Even from the mount Halak, that goes up to Seir, even to Baalgad in the valley of Lebanon under mount Hermon: and all their kings he took, and smote them, and slew them.

18 Joshua made war a long time with all those kings.

19 There was not a city that made peace with the children of Israel, save the Hivites the inhabitants of Gibeon: all other they took in battle.

20 For it was of the LORD to harden their hearts, that they should come against Israel in battle, that he might destroy them utterly, and that they might have no favour, but that he might destroy them, as the LORD commanded Moses.

21 And at that time came Joshua, and cut off the Anakims from the mountains, from Hebron, from Debir, from Anab, and from all the mountains of Judah, and from all the mountains of Israel: Joshua destroyed them utterly with their cities.

22 There was none of the Anakims left in the land of the children of Israel: only in Gaza, in Gath, and in Ashdod, there remained.

23 So Joshua took the whole land, according to all that the LORD said to Moses; and Joshua gave it for an inheritance to Israel according to their divisions by their tribes. And the land rested from war.

CHAPTER 12

NOW these are the kings of the land, which the children of Israel smote, and possessed their land on the other side Jordan toward the rising of the sun, from the river Arnon to mount Hermon, and all the plain on the east:

2 Sihon king of the Amorites, who dwelt in Heshbon, and ruled from Aroer, which is upon the bank of the river Arnon, and from the middle of the river, and from half Gilead, even to the river Jabbok, which is the border of the children of Ammon;

3 And from the plain to the sea of Chinneroth on the east, and to the sea of the plain, even the salt sea on the east, the way to Bethjeshimoth; and from the south, under Ashdothpisgah:

4 And the coast of Og king of Bashan, which was of the remnant of the giants, that dwelt at Ashtaroth and at Edrei,

5 And reigned in mount Hermon, and in Salcah, and in all Bashan, to the border of the Geshurites and the Maachathites, and half Gilead, the border of Sihon king of Heshbon.

6 Them did Moses the servant of the LORD and the children of Israel smite: and Moses the servant of the LORD gave it for a possession to the Reubenites, and the Gadites, and the half tribe of Manasseh.

7 And these are the kings of the country which Joshua and the children of Israel smote on this side Jordan on the west, from Baalgad in the valley of Lebanon even to the mount Halak, that goes up to Seir; which Joshua gave to the tribes of Israel for a possession according to their divisions;

8 In the mountains, and in the valleys, and in the plains, and in the springs, and in the wilderness, and in the south country; the Hittites, the Amorites, and the Canaanites, the Perizzites, the Hivites, and the Jebusites:

9 The king of Jericho, one; the king of Ai, which is beside Bethel, one;

10 The king of Jerusalem, one; the king of Hebron, one;

11 The king of Jarmuth, one; the king of Lachish, one;

12 The king of Eglon, one; the king of Gezer, one;

13 The king of Debir, one; the king of Geder, one;

14 The king of Hormah, one; the king of Arad, one;

15 The king of Libnah, one; the king of Adullam, one;

16 The king of Makkedah, one; the king of Bethel, one;

17 The king of Tappuah, one; the king of Hepher, one;

18 The king of Aphek, one; the king of Lasharon, one;

19 The king of Madon, one; the king of Hazor, one;

20 The king of Shimronmeron, one; the king of Achshaph, one;

21 The king of Taanach, one; the king of Megiddo, one;

22 The king of Kedesh, one; the king of Jokneam of Carmel, one;

23 The king of Dor in the coast of Dor, one; the king of the nations of Gilgal, one;

24 The king of Tirzah, one: all the kings thirty and one.

CHAPTER 13

NOW Joshua was old and stricken in years; and the LORD said to him, You are old and stricken in years, and there remains yet very much land to be possessed.

2 This is the land that yet remains: all the borders of the Philistines, and all Geshuri,

3 From Sihor, which is before Egypt, even to the borders of Ekron northward, which is counted to the Canaanite: five lords of the Philistines; the Gazathites, and the Ashdothites, the Eshkalonites, the Gittites, and the Ekronites; also the Avites:

4 From the south, all the land of the Canaanites, and Mearah that is beside the Sidonians to Aphek, to the borders of the Amorites:

5 And the land of the Giblites, and all Lebanon, toward the sunrising, from Baalgad under mount Hermon to the entering into Hamath.

6 All the inhabitants of the hill country from Lebanon to Misrephothmaim, and all the Sidonians, them will I drive out from before the children of Israel: only divide it by lot to the Israelites for an inheritance, as I have commanded you.

7 Now therefore divide this land for an inheritance to the nine tribes, and the half tribe of Manasseh,

8 With whom the Reubenites and the Gadites have received their inheritance, which Moses gave them, beyond Jordan eastward, even as Moses the servant of the LORD gave them;

9 From Aroer, that is upon the bank of the river Arnon, and the city that is in

the midst of the river, and all the plain of Medeba to Dibon;

10 And all the cities of Sihon king of the Amorites, which reigned in Heshbon, to the border of the children of Ammon;

11 And Gilead, and the border of the Geshurites and Maachathites, and all mount Hermon, and all Bashan to Salcah;

12 All the kingdom of Og in Bashan, which reigned in Ashtaroth and in Edrei, who remained of the remnant of the giants: for these did Moses smite, and cast them out.

13 Nevertheless the children of Israel expelled not the Geshurites, nor the Maachathites: but the Geshurites and the Maachathites dwell among the Israelites until this day.

14 Only to the tribes of Levi he gave none inheritance; the sacrifices of the LORD God of Israel made by fire are their inheritance, as he said to them.

15 And Moses gave to the tribe of the children of Reuben inheritance according to their families.

16 And their coast was from Aroer, that is on the bank of the river Arnon, and the city that is in the midst of the river, and all the plain by Medeba;

17 Heshbon, and all her cities that are in the plain; Dibon, and Bamothbaal, and Bethbaalmeon,

18 And Jahaza, and Kedemoth, and Mephaath,

19 And Kirjathaim, and Sibmah, and Zarethshahar in the mount of the valley,

20 And Bethpeor, and Ashdothpisgah, and Bethjeshimoth,

21 And all the cities of the plain, and all the kingdom of Sihon king of the Amorites, which reigned in Heshbon, whom Moses smote with the princes of Midian, Evi, and Rekem, and Zur, and Hur, and Reba, which were dukes of Sihon, dwelling in the country.

22 Balaam also the son of Beor, the soothsayer, did the children of Israel slay with the sword among them that were slain by them.

23 And the border of the children of Reuben was Jordan, and the border thereof. This was the inheritance of the children of Reuben after their families, the cities and the villages thereof.

24 And Moses gave inheritance to the tribe of Gad, even to the children of Gad according to their families.

25 And their coast was Jazer, and all the cities of Gilead, and half the land of the children of Ammon, to Aroer that is before Rabbah;

26 And from Heshbon to Ramathmizpeh, and Betonim; and from Mahanaim to the border of Debir;

27 And in the valley, Betharam, and Bethnimrah, and Succoth, and Zaphon, the rest of the kingdom of Sihon king of Heshbon, Jordan and his border, even to the edge of the sea of Chinnereth on the other side Jordan eastward.

28 This is the inheritance of the children of Gad after their families, the cities, and their villages.

29 And Moses gave inheritance to the half tribe of Manasseh: and this was the possession of the half tribe of the children of Manasseh by their families.

30 And their coast was from Mahanaim, all Bashan, all the kingdom of Og king of Bashan, and all the towns of Jair, which are in Bashan, threescore cities:

31 And half Gilead, and Ashtaroth, and Edrei, cities of the kingdom of Og in Bashan, were pertaining to the children of Machir the son of Manasseh, even to the one half of the children of Machir by their families.

32 These are the countries which Moses did distribute for inheritance in the plains of Moab, on the other side Jordan, by Jericho, eastward.

33 But to the tribe of Levi Moses gave not any inheritance: the LORD God of Israel was their inheritance, as he said to them.

CHAPTER 14

AND these are the countries which the children of Israel inherited in the land of Canaan, which Eleazar the priest, and Joshua the son of Nun, and the heads of the fathers of the tribes of the children of Israel, distributed for inheritance to them.

2 By lot was their inheritance, as the LORD commanded by the hand of Moses, for the nine tribes, and for the half tribe.

3 For Moses had given the inheritance of two tribes and an half tribe on the other side Jordan: but to the Levites he gave none inheritance among them.

4 For the children of Joseph were two tribes, Manasseh and Ephraim: therefore they gave no part to the Levites in the land, save cities to dwell in, with their suburbs for their cattle and for their substance.

5 As the LORD commanded Moses, so the children of Israel did, and they divided the land.

6 Then the children of Judah came to Joshua in Gilgal: and Caleb the son of Jephunneh the Kenezite said to him, You know the thing that the LORD said to Moses the man of God concerning me and you in Kadeshbarnea.

7 Forty years old was I when Moses the servant of the LORD sent me from Kadeshbarnea to espy out the land; and I brought him word again as it was in mine heart.

8 Nevertheless my brethren that went up with me made the heart of the people melt: but I wholly followed the LORD my God.

9 And Moses swore on that day, saying, Surely the land whereon your feet have trodden shall be your inheritance, and your children's for ever, because you have wholly followed the LORD my God.

10 And now, behold, the LORD has kept me alive, as he said, these forty and five years, even since the LORD spoke this word to Moses, while the children of Israel wandered in the wilderness: and now, lo, I am this day fourscore and five years old.

11 As yet I am as strong this day as I was in the day that Moses sent me: as my strength was then, even so is my strength now, for war, both to go out, and to come in.

12 Now therefore give me this mountain, whereof the LORD spoke in that day; for you heard in that day how the Anakims were there, and that the cities were great and fenced: if so be the LORD will be with me, then I shall be able to drive them out, as the LORD said.

13 And Joshua blessed him, and gave to Caleb the son of Jephunneh Hebron for an inheritance.

14 Hebron therefore became the inheritance of Caleb the son of Jephunneh the Kenezite to this day, because that he wholly followed the LORD God of Israel.

15 And the name of Hebron before was Kirjatharba; which Arba was a great man among the Anakims. And the land had rest from war.

CHAPTER 15

THIS then was the lot of the tribe of the children of Judah by their families; even to the border of Edom the wilderness of Zin southward was the uttermost part of the south coast.

2 And their south border was from the shore of the salt sea, from the bay that looks southward:

3 And it went out to the south side to Maalehacrabbim, and passed along to Zin, and ascended up on the south side to Kadeshbarnea, and passed along to Hezron, and went up to Adar, and fetched a compass to Karkaa:

4 From thence it passed toward Azmon, and went out to the river of Egypt; and the goings out of that coast were at the sea: this shall be your south coast.

5 And the east border was the salt sea, even to the end of Jordan. And their border in the north quarter was from the

bay of the sea at the uttermost part of Jordan:

6 And the border went up to Bethhogla, and passed along by the north of Betharabah; and the border went up to the stone of Bohan the son of Reuben:

7 And the border went up toward Debir from the valley of Achor, and so northward, looking toward Gilgal, that is before the going up to Adummim, which is on the south side of the river: and the border passed toward the waters of Enshemesh, and the goings out thereof were at Enrogel:

8 And the border went up by the valley of the son of Hinnom to the south side of the Jebusite; the same is Jerusalem: and the border went up to the top of the mountain that lies before the valley of Hinnom westward, which is at the end of the valley of the giants northward:

9 And the border was drawn from the top of the hill to the fountain of the water of Nephtoah, and went out to the cities of mount Ephron; and the border was drawn to Baalah, which is Kirjathjearim:

10 And the border compassed from Baalah westward to mount Seir, and passed along to the side of mount Jearim, which is Chesalon, on the north side, and went down to Bethshemesh, and passed on to Timnah:

11 And the border went out to the side of Ekron northward: and the border was drawn to Shicron, and passed along to mount Baalah, and went out to Jabneel; and the goings out of the border were at the sea.

12 And the west border was to the great sea, and the coast thereof. This is the coast of the children of Judah round about according to their families.

13 And to Caleb the son of Jephunneh he gave a part among the children of Judah, according to the commandment of the LORD to Joshua, even the city of Arba the father of Anak, which city is Hebron.

14 And Caleb drove thence the three sons of Anak, Sheshai, and Ahiman, and Talmai, the children of Anak.

15 And he went up thence to the inhabitants of Debir: and the name of Debir before was Kirjathsepher.

16 And Caleb said, He that smites Kirjathsepher, and takes it, to him will I give Achsah my daughter to wife.

17 And Othniel the son of Kenaz, the brother of Caleb, took it: and he gave him Achsah his daughter to wife.

18 And it came to pass, as she came to him, that she moved him to ask of her father a field: and she lighted off her ass; and Caleb said to her, What would you?

19 Who answered, Give me a blessing; for you have given me a south land; give me also springs of water. And he gave her the upper springs, and the nether springs.

20 This is the inheritance of the tribe of the children of Judah according to their families.

21 And the uttermost cities of the tribe of the children of Judah toward the coast of Edom southward were Kabzeel, and Eder, and Jagur,

22 And Kinah, and Dimonah, and Adadah,

23 And Kedesh, and Hazor, and Ithnan,

24 Ziph, and Telem, and Bealoth,

25 And Hazor, Hadattah, and Kerioth, and Hezron, which is Hazor,

26 Amam, and Shema, and Moladah,

27 And Hazargaddah, and Heshmon, and Bethpalet,

28 And Hazarshual, and Beersheba, and Bizjothjah,

29 Baalah, and Iim, and Azem,

30 And Eltolad, and Chesil, and Hormah,

31 And Ziklag, and Madmannah, and Sansannah,

32 And Lebaoth, and Shilhim, and Ain, and Rimmon: all the cities are twenty and nine, with their villages:

33 And in the valley, Eshtaol, and Zoreah, and Ashnah,

34 And Zanoah, and Engannim, Tappuah, and Enam,

35 Jarmuth, and Adullam, Socoh, and Azekah,

36 And Sharaim, and Adithaim, and Gederah, and Gederothaim; fourteen cities with their villages:

37 Zenan, and Hadashah, and Migdalgad,

38 And Dilean, and Mizpeh, and Joktheel,

39 Lachish, and Bozkath, and Eglon,

40 And Cabbon, and Lahmam, and Kithlish,

41 And Gederoth, Bethdagon, and Naamah, and Makkedah; sixteen cities with their villages:

42 Libnah, and Ether, and Ashan,

43 And Jiphtah, and Ashnah, and Nezib,

44 And Keilah, and Achzib, and Mareshah; nine cities with their villages:

45 Ekron, with her towns and her villages:

46 From Ekron even to the sea, all that lay near Ashdod, with their villages:

47 Ashdod with her towns and her villages, Gaza with her towns and her villages, to the river of Egypt, and the great sea, and the border thereof:

48 And in the mountains, Shamir, and Jattir, and Socoh,

49 And Dannah, and Kirjathsannah, which is Debir,

50 And Anab, and Eshtemoh, and Anim,

51 And Goshen, and Holon, and Giloh; eleven cities with their villages:

52 Arab, and Dumah, and Eshean,

53 And Janum, and Bethtappuah, and Aphekah,

54 And Humtah, and Kirjatharba, which is Hebron, and Zior; nine cities with their villages:

55 Maon, Carmel, and Ziph, and Juttah,

56 And Jezreel, and Jokdeam, and Zanoah,

57 Cain, Gibeah, and Timnah; ten cities with their villages:

58 Halhul, Bethzur, and Gedor,

59 And Maarath, and Bethanoth, and Eltekon; six cities with their villages:

60 Kirjathbaal, which is Kirjathjearim, and Rabbah; two cities with their villages:

61 In the wilderness, Betharabah, Middin, and Secacah,

62 And Nibshan, and the city of Salt, and Engedi; six cities with their villages.

63 As for the Jebusites the inhabitants of Jerusalem, the children of Judah could not drive them out; but the Jebusites dwell with the children of Judah at Jerusalem to this day.

CHAPTER 16

A ND the lot of the children of Joseph fell from Jordan by Jericho, to the water of Jericho on the east, to the wilderness that goeth up from Jericho throughout mount Bethel,

2 And goeth out from Bethel to Luz, and passes along to the borders of Archi to Ataroth,

3 And goeth down westward to the coast of Japhleti, to the coast of Bethhoron the nether, and to Gezer; and the goings out thereof are at the sea.

4 So the children of Joseph, Manasseh and Ephraim, took their inheritance.

5 And the border of the children of Ephraim according to their families was thus: even the border of their inheritance on the east side was Atarothaddar, to Bethhoron the upper;

6 And the border went out toward the sea to Michmethah on the north side; and the border went about eastward to Taanathshiloh, and passed by it on the east to Janohah;

7 And it went down from Janohah to Ataroth, and to Naarath, and came to Jericho, and went out at Jordan.

8 The border went out from Tappuah westward to the river Kanah; and the goings out thereof were at the sea. This is the inheritance of the tribe of the children of Ephraim by their families.

9 And the separate cities for the children of Ephraim were among the inheritance of the children of Manasseh, all the cities with their villages.

10 And they drove not out the Canaanites that dwelt in Gezer: but the Canaanites dwell among the Ephraimites to this day, and serve under tribute.

CHAPTER 17

THERE was also a lot for the tribe of Manasseh; for he was the firstborn of Joseph; to wit, for Machir the firstborn of Manasseh, the father of Gilead: because he was a man of war, therefore he had Gilead and Bashan.

2 There was also a lot for the rest of the children of Manasseh by their families; for the children of Abiezer, and for the children of Helek, and for the children of Asriel, and for the children of Shechem, and for the children of Hepher, and for the children of Shemida: these were the male children of Manasseh the son of Joseph by their families.

3 But Zelophehad, the son of Hepher, the son of Gilead, the son of Machir, the son of Manasseh, had no sons, but daughters: and these are the names of his daughters, Mahlah, and Noah, Hoglah, Milcah, and Tirzah.

4 And they came near before Eleazar the priest, and before Joshua the son of Nun, and before the princes, saying, The LORD commanded Moses to give us an inheritance among our brethren. Therefore according to the commandment of the LORD he gave them an inheritance among the brethren of their father.

5 And there fell ten portions to Manasseh, beside the land of Gilead and Bashan, which were on the other side Jordan;

6 Because the daughters of Manasseh had an inheritance among his sons: and the rest of Manasseh's sons had the land of Gilead.

7 And the coast of Manasseh was from Asher to Michmethah, that lies before Shechem; and the border went along on the right hand to the inhabitants of Entappuah.

8 Now Manasseh had the land of Tappuah: but Tappuah on the border of Manasseh belonged to the children of Ephraim;

9 And the coast descended to the river Kanah, southward of the river: these cities of Ephraim are among the cities of Manasseh: the coast of Manasseh also was on the north side of the river, and the outgoings of it were at the sea:

10 Southward it was Ephraim's, and northward it was Manasseh's, and the sea is his border; and they met together in Asher on the north, and in Issachar on the east.

11 And Manasseh had in Issachar and in Asher Bethshean and her towns, and Ibleam and her towns, and the inhabitants of Dor and her towns, and the inhabitants of Endor and her towns, and the inhabitants of Taanach and her towns, and the inhabitants of Megiddo and her towns, even three countries.

12 Yet the children of Manasseh could not drive out the inhabitants of those cities; but the Canaanites would dwell in that land.

13 Yet it came to pass, when the children of Israel were waxen strong, that they put the Canaanites to tribute, but did not utterly drive them out.

14 And the children of Joseph spake to Joshua, saying, Why have you given me but one lot and one portion to inherit, seeing I am a great people, forasmuch as the LORD has blessed me hitherto?

15 And Joshua answered them, If you are a great people, then get up to the wood country, and cut down for yourself there in the land of the Perizzites and of the giants, if mount Ephraim be too narrow for you.

16 And the children of Joseph said, The hill is not enough for us: and all the Canaanites that dwell in the land of the

valley have chariots of iron, both they who are of Bethshean and her towns, and they who are of the valley of Jezreel.

17 And Joshua spoke to the house of Joseph, even to Ephraim and to Manasseh, saying, You are a great people, and have great power: you shall not have one lot only:

18 But the mountain shall be yours; for it is a wood, and you shall cut it down: and the outgoings of it shall be yours: for you shall drive out the Canaanites, though they have iron chariots, and though they be strong.

CHAPTER 18

AND the whole congregation of the children of Israel assembled together at Shiloh, and set up the tabernacle of the congregation there. And the land was subdued before them.

2 And there remained among the children of Israel seven tribes, which had not yet received their inheritance.

3 And Joshua said to the children of Israel, How long are you slack to go to possess the land, which the LORD God of your fathers has given you?

4 Give out from among you three men for each tribe: and I will send them, and they shall rise, and go through the land, and describe it according to the inheritance of them; and they shall come again to me.

5 And they shall divide it into seven parts: Judah shall abide in their coast on the south, and the house of Joseph shall abide in their coasts on the north.

6 You shall therefore describe the land into seven parts, and bring the description hither to me, that I may cast lots for you here before the LORD our God.

7 But the Levites have no part among you; for the priesthood of the LORD is their inheritance: and Gad, and Reuben, and half the tribe of Manasseh, have received their inheritance beyond Jordan on the east, which Moses the servant of the LORD gave them.

8 And the men arose, and went away: and Joshua charged them that went to describe the land, saying, Go and walk through the land, and describe it, and come again to me, that I may here cast lots for you before the LORD in Shiloh.

9 And the men went and passed through the land, and described it by cities into seven parts in a book, and came again to Joshua to the host at Shiloh.

10 And Joshua cast lots for them in Shiloh before the LORD: and there Joshua divided the land to the children of Israel according to their divisions.

11 And the lot of the tribe of the children of Benjamin came up according to their families: and the coast of their lot came forth between the children of Judah and the children of Joseph.

12 And their border on the north side was from Jordan; and the border went up to the side of Jericho on the north side, and went up through the mountains westward; and the goings out thereof were at the wilderness of Bethaven.

13 And the border went over from thence toward Luz, to the side of Luz, which is Bethel, southward; and the border descended to Atarothadar, near the hill that lies on the south side of the nether Bethhoron.

14 And the border was drawn thence, and compassed the corner of the sea southward, from the hill that lies before Bethhoron southward; and the goings out thereof were at Kirjathbaal, which is Kirjathjearim, a city of the children of Judah: this was the west quarter.

15 And the south quarter was from the end of Kirjathjearim, and the border went out on the west, and went out to the well of waters of Nephtoah:

16 And the border came down to the end of the mountain that lies before the valley of the son of Hinnom, and which is in the valley of the giants on the north, and descended to the valley of Hinnom,

to the side of Jebusi on the south, and descended to Enrogel,

17 And was drawn from the north, and went forth to Enshemesh, and went forth toward Geliloth, which is over against the going up of Adummim, and descended to the stone of Bohan the son of Reuben,

18 And passed along toward the side over against Arabah northward, and went down to Arabah:

19 And the border passed along to the side of Bethhoglah northward: and the outgoings of the border were at the north bay of the salt sea at the south end of Jordan: this was the south coast.

20 And Jordan was the border of it on the east side. This was the inheritance of the children of Benjamin, by the coasts thereof round about, according to their families.

21 Now the cities of the tribe of the children of Benjamin according to their families were Jericho, and Bethhoglah, and the valley of Keziz,

22 And Betharabah, and Zemaraim, and Bethel,

23 And Avim, and Pharah, and Ophrah,

24 And Chepharhaammonai, and Ophni, and Gaba; twelve cities with their villages:

25 Gibeon, and Ramah, and Beeroth,

26 And Mizpeh, and Chephirah, and Mozah,

27 And Rekem, and Irpeel, and Taralah,

28 And Zelah, Eleph, and Jebusi, which is Jerusalem, Gibeath, and Kirjath; fourteen cities with their villages. This is the inheritance of the children of Benjamin according to their families.

CHAPTER 19

AND the second lot came forth to Simeon, even for the tribe of the children of Simeon according to their families: and their inheritance was within the inheritance of the children of Judah.

2 And they had in their inheritance Beersheba, and Sheba, and Moladah,

3 And Hazarshual, and Balah, and Azem,

4 And Eltolad, and Bethul, and Hormah,

5 And Ziklag, and Bethmarcaboth, and Hazarsusah,

6 And Bethlebaoth, and Sharuhen; thirteen cities and their villages:

7 Ain, Remmon, and Ether, and Ashan; four cities and their villages:

8 And all the villages that were round about these cities to Baalathbeer, Ramath of the south. This is the inheritance of the tribe of the children of Simeon according to their families.

9 Out of the portion of the children of Judah was the inheritance of the children of Simeon: for the part of the children of Judah was too much for them: therefore the children of Simeon had their inheritance within the inheritance of them.

10 And the third lot came up for the children of Zebulun according to their families: and the border of their inheritance was to Sarid:

11 And their border went up toward the sea, and Maralah, and reached to Dabbasheth, and reached to the river that is before Jokneam;

12 And turned from Sarid eastward toward the sunrising to the border of Chislothtabor, and then goeth out to Daberath, and goeth up to Japhia,

13 And from thence passes on along on the east to Gittahhepher, to Ittahkazin, and goeth out to Remmonmethoar to Neah;

14 And the border compasses it on the north side to Hannathon: and the outgoings thereof are in the valley of Jiphthahel:

15 And Kattath, and Nahallal, and Shimron, and Idalah, and Bethlehem: twelve cities with their villages.

16 This is the inheritance of the children of Zebulun according to their families, these cities with their villages.

17 And the fourth lot came out to Issachar, for the children of Issachar according to their families.

18 And their border was toward Jezreel, and Chesulloth, and Shunem,

19 And Haphraim, and Shihon, and Anaharath,

20 And Rabbith, and Kishion, and Abez,

21 And Remeth, and Engannim, and Enhaddah, and Bethpazzez;

22 And the coast reaches to Tabor, and Shahazimah, and Bethshemesh; and the outgoings of their border were at Jordan: sixteen cities with their villages.

23 This is the inheritance of the tribe of the children of Issachar according to their families, the cities and their villages.

24 And the fifth lot came out for the tribe of the children of Asher according to their families.

25 And their border was Helkath, and Hali, and Beten, and Achshaph,

26 And Alammelech, and Amad, and Misheal; and reacheth to Carmel westward, and to Shihorlibnath;

27 And turns toward the sunrising to Bethdagon, and reaches to Zebulun, and to the valley of Jiphthahel toward the north side of Bethemek, and Neiel, and goeth out to Cabul on the left hand,

28 And Hebron, and Rehob, and Hammon, and Kanah, even to great Zidon;

29 And then the coast turns to Ramah, and to the strong city Tyre; and the coast turns to Hosah; and the outgoings thereof are at the sea from the coast to Achzib:

30 Ummah also, and Aphek, and Rehob: twenty and two cities with their villages.

31 This is the inheritance of the tribe of the children of Asher according to their families, these cities with their villages.

32 The sixth lot came out to the children of Naphtali, even for the children of Naphtali according to their families.

33 And their coast was from Heleph, from Allon to Zaanannim, and Adami, Nekeb, and Jabneel, to Lakum; and the outgoings thereof were at Jordan:

34 And then the coast turns westward to Aznothtabor, and goeth out from thence to Hukkok, and reaches to Zebulun on the south side, and reaches to Asher on the west side, and to Judah upon Jordan toward the sunrising.

35 And the fenced cities are Ziddim, Zer, and Hammath, Rakkath, and Chinnereth,

36 And Adamah, and Ramah, and Hazor,

37 And Kedesh, and Edrei, and Enhazor,

38 And Iron, and Migdalel, Horem, and Bethanath, and Bethshemesh; nineteen cities with their villages.

39 This is the inheritance of the tribe of the children of Naphtali according to their families, the cities and their villages.

40 And the seventh lot came out for the tribe of the children of Dan according to their families.

41 And the coast of their inheritance was Zorah, and Eshtaol, and Irshemesh,

42 And Shaalabbin, and Ajalon, and Jethlah,

43 And Elon, and Thimnathah, and Ekron,

44 And Eltekeh, and Gibbethon, and Baalath,

45 And Jehud, and Beneberak, and Gathrimmon,

46 And Mejarkon, and Rakkon, with the border before Japho.

47 And the coast of the children of Dan went out too little for them: therefore the children of Dan went up to fight against Leshem, and took it, and smote it with the edge of the sword, and possessed it, and dwelt therein, and called Leshem, Dan, after the name of Dan their father.

48 This is the inheritance of the tribe of the children of Dan according to their families, these cities with their villages.

49 When they had made an end of dividing the land for inheritance by their

coasts, the children of Israel gave an inheritance to Joshua the son of Nun among them:

50 According to the word of the LORD they gave him the city which he asked, even Timnathserah in mount Ephraim: and he built the city, and dwelt therein.

51 These are the inheritances, which Eleazar the priest, and Joshua the son of Nun, and the heads of the fathers of the tribes of the children of Israel, divided for an inheritance by lot in Shiloh before the LORD, at the door of the tabernacle of the congregation. So they made an end of dividing the country.

CHAPTER 20

THE LORD also spoke to Joshua, saying,

2 Speak to the children of Israel, saying, Appoint out for you cities of refuge, whereof I spoke to you by the hand of Moses:

3 That the slayer that kills any person unawares and unwittingly may flee thither: and they shall be your refuge from the avenger of blood.

4 And when he that does flee to one of those cities shall stand at the entering of the gate of the city, and shall declare his cause in the ears of the elders of that city, they shall take him into the city to them, and give him a place, that he may dwell among them.

5 And if the avenger of blood pursue after him, then they shall not deliver the slayer up into his hand; because he smote his neighbour unwittingly, and hated him not beforetime.

6 And he shall dwell in that city, until he stand before the congregation for judgment, and until the death of the high priest that shall be in those days: then shall the slayer return, and come to his own city, and to his own house, to the city from whence he fled.

7 And they appointed Kedesh in Galilee in mount Naphtali, and Shechem in mount Ephraim, and Kirjatharba, which is Hebron, in the mountain of Judah.

8 And on the other side Jordan by Jericho eastward, they assigned Bezer in the wilderness upon the plain out of the tribe of Reuben, and Ramoth in Gilead out of the tribe of Gad, and Golan in Bashan out of the tribe of Manasseh.

9 These were the cities appointed for all the children of Israel, and for the stranger that sojourns among them, that whosoever kills any person at unawares might flee thither, and not die by the hand of the avenger of blood, until he stood before the congregation.

CHAPTER 21

THEN came near the heads of the fathers of the Levites to Eleazar the priest, and to Joshua the son of Nun, and to the heads of the fathers of the tribes of the children of Israel;

2 And they spoke to them at Shiloh in the land of Canaan, saying, The LORD commanded by the hand of Moses to give us cities to dwell in, with the suburbs thereof for our cattle.

3 And the children of Israel gave to the Levites out of their inheritance, at the commandment of the LORD, these cities and their suburbs.

4 And the lot came out for the families of the Kohathites: and the children of Aaron the priest, which were of the Levites, had by lot out of the tribe of Judah, and out of the tribe of Simeon, and out of the tribe of Benjamin, thirteen cities.

5 And the rest of the children of Kohath had by lot out of the families of the tribe of Ephraim, and out of the tribe of Dan, and out of the half tribe of Manasseh, ten cities.

6 And the children of Gershon had by lot out of the families of the tribe of Issachar, and out of the tribe of Asher, and out of the tribe of Naphtali, and out of the half tribe of Manasseh in Bashan, thirteen cities.

7 The children of Merari by their families had out of the tribe of Reuben,

and out of the tribe of Gad, and out of the tribe of Zebulun, twelve cities.

8 And the children of Israel gave by lot to the Levites these cities with their suburbs, as the LORD commanded by the hand of Moses.

9 And they gave out of the tribe of the children of Judah, and out of the tribe of the children of Simeon, these cities which are here mentioned by name.

10 Which the children of Aaron, being of the families of the Kohathites, who were of the children of Levi, had: for theirs was the first lot.

11 And they gave them the city of Arba the father of Anak, which city is Hebron, in the hill country of Judah, with the suburbs thereof round about it.

12 But the fields of the city, and the villages thereof, gave they to Caleb the son of Jephunneh for his possession.

13 Thus they gave to the children of Aaron the priest Hebron with her suburbs, to be a city of refuge for the slayer; and Libnah with her suburbs,

14 And Jattir with her suburbs, and Eshtemoa with her suburbs,

15 And Holon with her suburbs, and Debir with her suburbs,

16 And Ain with her suburbs, and Juttah with her suburbs, and Bethshemesh with her suburbs; nine cities out of those two tribes.

17 And out of the tribe of Benjamin, Gibeon with her suburbs, Geba with her suburbs,

18 Anathoth with her suburbs, and Almon with her suburbs; four cities.

19 All the cities of the children of Aaron, the priests, were thirteen cities with their suburbs.

20 And the families of the children of Kohath, the Levites which remained of the children of Kohath, even they had the cities of their lot out of the tribe of Ephraim.

21 For they gave them Shechem with her suburbs in mount Ephraim, to be a city of refuge for the slayer; and Gezer with her suburbs,

22 And Kibzaim with her suburbs, and Bethhoron with her suburbs; four cities.

23 And out of the tribe of Dan, Eltekeh with her suburbs, Gibbethon with her suburbs,

24 Aijalon with her suburbs, Gathrimmon with her suburbs; four cities.

25 And out of the half tribe of Manasseh, Tanach with her suburbs, and Gathrimmon with her suburbs; two cities.

26 All the cities were ten with their suburbs for the families of the children of Kohath that remained.

27 And to the children of Gershon, of the families of the Levites, out of the other half tribe of Manasseh they gave Golan in Bashan with her suburbs, to be a city of refuge for the slayer; and Beeshterah with her suburbs; two cities.

28 And out of the tribe of Issachar, Kishon with her suburbs, Dabareh with her suburbs,

29 Jarmuth with her suburbs, Engannim with her suburbs; four cities.

30 And out of the tribe of Asher, Mishal with her suburbs, Abdon with her suburbs,

31 Helkath with her suburbs, and Rehob with her suburbs; four cities.

32 And out of the tribe of Naphtali, Kedesh in Galilee with her suburbs, to be a city of refuge for the slayer; and Hammothdor with her suburbs, and Kartan with her suburbs; three cities.

33 All the cities of the Gershonites according to their families were thirteen cities with their suburbs.

34 And to the families of the children of Merari, the rest of the Levites, out of the tribe of Zebulun, Jokneam with her suburbs, and Kartah with her suburbs,

35 Dimnah with her suburbs, Nahalal with her suburbs; four cities.

36 And out of the tribe of Reuben, Bezer with her suburbs, and Jahazah with her suburbs,

37 Kedemoth with her suburbs, and Mephaath with her suburbs; four cities.

38 And out of the tribe of Gad, Ramoth in Gilead with her suburbs, to be a city of refuge for the slayer; and Mahanaim with her suburbs,

39 Heshbon with her suburbs, Jazer with her suburbs; four cities in all.

40 So all the cities for the children of Merari by their families, which were remaining of the families of the Levites, were by their lot twelve cities.

41 All the cities of the Levites within the possession of the children of Israel were forty and eight cities with their suburbs.

42 These cities were every one with their suburbs round about them: thus were all these cities.

43 And the LORD gave to Israel all the land which he swore to give to their fathers; and they possessed it, and dwelt therein.

44 And the LORD gave them rest round about, according to all that he swore to their fathers: and there stood not a man of all their enemies before them; the LORD delivered all their enemies into their hand.

45 There failed not ought of any good thing which the LORD had spoken to the house of Israel; all came to pass.

CHAPTER 22

THEN Joshua called the Reubenites, and the Gadites, and the half tribe of Manasseh,

2 And said to them, You have kept all that Moses the servant of the LORD commanded you, and have obeyed my voice in all that I commanded you:

3 You have not left your brethren these many days to this day, but have kept the charge of the commandment of the LORD your God.

4 And now the LORD your God has given rest to your brethren, as he promised them: therefore now return, and get to your tents, and to the land of your possession, which Moses the servant of the LORD gave you on the other side Jordan.

5 But take diligent heed to do the commandment and the law, which Moses the servant of the LORD charged you, to love the LORD your God, and to walk in all his ways, and to keep his commandments, and to cleave to him, and to serve him with all your heart and with all your soul.

6 So Joshua blessed them, and sent them away: and they went to their tents.

7 Now to the one half of the tribe of Manasseh Moses had given possession in Bashan: but to the other half thereof gave Joshua among their brethren on this side Jordan westward. And when Joshua sent them away also to their tents, then he blessed them,

8 And he spoke to them, saying, Return with much riches to your tents, and with very much cattle, with silver, and with gold, and with brass, and with iron, and with very much raiment: divide the spoil of your enemies with your brethren.

9 And the children of Reuben and the children of Gad and the half tribe of Manasseh returned, and departed from the children of Israel out of Shiloh, which is in the land of Canaan, to go to the country of Gilead, to the land of their possession, whereof they were possessed, according to the word of the LORD by the hand of Moses.

10 And when they came to the borders of Jordan, that are in the land of Canaan, the children of Reuben and the children of Gad and the half tribe of Manasseh built there an altar by Jordan, a great altar to see to.

11 And the children of Israel heard say, Behold, the children of Reuben and the children of Gad and the half tribe of Manasseh have built an altar over against the land of Canaan, in the borders of Jordan, at the passage of the children of Israel.

12 And when the children of Israel heard of it, the whole congregation of the children of Israel gathered themselves together at Shiloh, to go up to war against them.

13 And the children of Israel sent to the children of Reuben, and to the children of Gad, and to the half tribe of Manasseh, into the land of Gilead, Phinehas the son of Eleazar the priest,

14 And with him ten princes, of each chief house a prince throughout all the tribes of Israel; and each one was an head of the house of their fathers among the thousands of Israel.

15 And they came to the children of Reuben, and to the children of Gad, and to the half tribe of Manasseh, to the land of Gilead, and they spoke with them, saying,

16 Thus says the whole congregation of the LORD, What trespass is this that you have committed against the God of Israel, to turn away this day from following the LORD, in that you have built for yourselves an altar, that you might rebel this day against the LORD?

17 Is the iniquity of Peor too little for us, from which we are not cleansed until this day, although there was a plague in the congregation of the LORD,

18 But that you must turn away this day from following the LORD? and it will be, seeing you rebel to day against the LORD, that tomorrow he will be wroth with the whole congregation of Israel.

19 Notwithstanding, if the land of your possession be unclean, then pass over to the land of the possession of the LORD, wherein the LORD's tabernacle dwells, and take possession among us: but rebel not against the LORD, nor rebel against us, in building you an altar beside the altar of the LORD our God.

20 Did not Achan the son of Zerah commit a trespass in the accursed thing, and wrath fell on all the congregation of Israel? and that man perished not alone in his iniquity.

21 Then the children of Reuben and the children of Gad and the half tribe of Manasseh answered, and said to the heads of the thousands of Israel,

22 The LORD God of gods, the LORD God of gods, he knows, and Israel he shall know; if it be in rebellion, or if in transgression against the LORD, (save us not this day,)

23 That we have built us an altar to turn from following the LORD, or if to offer thereon burnt offering or meat offering, or if to offer peace offerings thereon, let the LORD himself require it;

24 And if we have not rather done it for fear of this thing, saying, In time to come your children might speak to our children, saying, What have you to do with the LORD God of Israel?

25 For the LORD has made Jordan a border between us and you, you children of Reuben and children of Gad; you have no part in the LORD: so shall your children make our children cease from fearing the LORD.

26 Therefore we said, Let us now prepare to build us an altar, not for burnt offering, nor for sacrifice:

27 But that it may be a witness between us, and you, and our generations after us, that we might do the service of the LORD before him with our burnt offerings, and with our sacrifices, and with our peace offerings; that your children may not say to our children in time to come, You have no part in the LORD.

28 Therefore said we, that it shall be, when they should so say to us or to our generations in time to come, that we may say again, Behold the pattern of the altar of the LORD, which our fathers made, not for burnt offerings, nor for sacrifices; but it is a witness between us and you.

29 God forbid that we should rebel against the LORD, and turn this day from following the LORD, to build an altar for burnt offerings, for meat offerings, or for sacrifices, beside the altar of the LORD our God that is before his tabernacle.

30 And when Phinehas the priest, and the princes of the congregation and heads of the thousands of Israel which were with him, heard the words that the

children of Reuben and the children of Gad and the children of Manasseh spoke, it pleased them.

31 And Phinehas the son of Eleazar the priest said to the children of Reuben, and to the children of Gad, and to the children of Manasseh, This day we perceive that the LORD is among us, because you have not committed this trespass against the LORD: now you have delivered the children of Israel out of the hand of the LORD.

32 And Phinehas the son of Eleazar the priest, and the princes, returned from the children of Reuben, and from the children of Gad, out of the land of Gilead, to the land of Canaan, to the children of Israel, and brought them word again.

33 And the thing pleased the children of Israel; and the children of Israel blessed God, and did not intend to go up against them in battle, to destroy the land wherein the children of Reuben and Gad dwelt.

34 And the children of Reuben and the children of Gad called the altar Ed: for it shall be a witness between us that the LORD is God.

CHAPTER 23

AND it came to pass a long time after that the LORD had given rest to Israel from all their enemies round about, that Joshua waxed old and stricken in age.

2 And Joshua called for all Israel, and for their elders, and for their heads, and for their judges, and for their officers, and said to them, I am old and stricken in age:

3 And you have seen all that the LORD your God has done to all these nations because of you; for the LORD your God is he that has fought for you.

4 Behold, I have divided to you by lot these nations that remain, to be an inheritance for your tribes, from Jordan, with all the nations that I have cut off, even to the great sea westward.

5 And the LORD your God, he shall expel them from before you, and drive them from out of your sight; and you shall possess their land, as the LORD your God has promised to you.

6 Be you therefore very courageous to keep and to do all that is written in the book of the law of Moses, that you turn not aside therefrom to the right hand or to the left;

7 That you come not among these nations, these that remain among you; neither make mention of the name of their gods, nor cause to swear by them, neither serve them, nor bow yourselves to them:

8 But cleave to the LORD your God, as you have done to this day.

9 For the LORD has driven out from before you great nations and strong: but as for you, no man has been able to stand before you to this day.

10 One man of you shall chase a thousand: for the LORD your God, he it is that fights for you, as he has promised you.

11 Take good heed therefore to yourselves, that you love the LORD your God.

12 Else if you do in any wise go back, and cleave to the remnant of these nations, even these that remain among you, and shall make marriages with them, and go in to them, and they to you:

13 Know for a certainty that the LORD your God will no more drive out any of these nations from before you; but they shall be snares and traps to you, and scourges in your sides, and thorns in your eyes, until you perish from off this good land which the LORD your God has given you.

14 And, behold, this day I am going the way of all the earth: and you know in all your hearts and in all your souls, that not one thing has failed of all the good things which the LORD your God spoke concerning you; all are come to pass

to you, and not one thing has failed thereof.

15 Therefore it shall come to pass, that as all good things are come upon you, which the LORD your God promised you; so shall the LORD bring upon you all evil things, until he have destroyed you from off this good land which the LORD your God has given you.

16 When you have transgressed the covenant of the LORD your God, which he commanded you, and have gone and served other gods, and bowed yourselves to them; then shall the anger of the LORD be kindled against you, and you shall perish quickly from off the good land which he has given to you.

CHAPTER 24

AND Joshua gathered all the tribes of Israel to Shechem, and called for the elders of Israel, and for their heads, and for their judges, and for their officers; and they presented themselves before God.

2 And Joshua said to all the people, Thus says the LORD God of Israel, Your fathers dwelt on the other side of the flood in old time, even Terah, the father of Abraham, and the father of Nachor: and they served other gods.

3 And I took your father Abraham from the other side of the flood, and led him throughout all the land of Canaan, and multiplied his seed, and gave him Isaac.

4 And I gave to Isaac Jacob and Esau: and I gave to Esau mount Seir, to possess it; but Jacob and his children went down into Egypt.

5 I sent Moses also and Aaron, and I plagued Egypt, according to that which I did among them: and afterward I brought you out.

6 And I brought your fathers out of Egypt: and you came to the sea; and the Egyptians pursued after your fathers with chariots and horsemen to the Red sea.

7 And when they cried to the LORD, he put darkness between you and the Egyptians, and brought the sea upon them, and covered them; and your eyes have seen what I have done in Egypt: and you dwelt in the wilderness a long season.

8 And I brought you into the land of the Amorites, which dwelt on the other side Jordan; and they fought with you: and I gave them into your hand, that you might possess their land; and I destroyed them from before you.

9 Then Balak the son of Zippor, king of Moab, arose and warred against Israel, and sent and called Balaam the son of Beor to curse you:

10 But I would not hearken to Balaam; therefore he blessed you still: so I delivered you out of his hand.

11 And you went over Jordan, and came to Jericho: and the men of Jericho fought against you, the Amorites, and the Perizzites, and the Canaanites, and the Hittites, and the Girgashites, the Hivites, and the Jebusites; and I delivered them into your hand.

12 And I sent the hornet before you, which drove them out from before you, even the two kings of the Amorites; but not with your sword, nor with your bow.

13 And I have given you a land for which you did not labour, and cities which you built not, and you dwell in them; of the vineyards and oliveyards which you planted not do you eat.

14 Now therefore fear the LORD, and serve him in sincerity and in truth: and put away the gods which your fathers served on the other side of the flood, and in Egypt; and serve the LORD.

15 And if it seem evil to you to serve the LORD, choose this day whom you will serve; whether the gods which your fathers served that were on the other side of the flood, or the gods of the Amorites, in whose land you dwell: but as for me and my house, we will serve the LORD.

16 And the people answered and said, God forbid that we should forsake the LORD, to serve other gods;

17 For the LORD our God, he it is that brought us up and our fathers out of the land of Egypt, from the house of bondage, and which did those great signs in our sight, and preserved us in all the way wherein we went, and among all the people through whom we passed:

18 And the LORD drove out from before us all the people, even the Amorites which dwelt in the land: therefore will we also serve the LORD; for he is our God.

19 And Joshua said to the people, You cannot serve the LORD: for he is an holy God; he is a jealous God; he will not forgive your transgressions nor your sins.

20 If you forsake the LORD, and serve strange gods, then he will turn and do you hurt, and consume you, after that he has done you good.

21 And the people said to Joshua, Nay; but we will serve the LORD.

22 And Joshua said to the people, You are witnesses against yourselves that you have chosen you the LORD, to serve him. And they said, We are witnesses.

23 Now therefore put away, said he, the strange gods which are among you, and incline your heart to the LORD God of Israel.

24 And the people said to Joshua, The LORD our God will we serve, and his voice will we obey.

25 So Joshua made a covenant with the people that day, and set them a statute and an ordinance in Shechem.

26 And Joshua wrote these words in the book of the law of God, and took a great stone, and set it up there under an oak, that was by the sanctuary of the LORD.

27 And Joshua said to all the people, Behold, this stone shall be a witness to us; for it has heard all the words of the LORD which he spoke to us: it shall be therefore a witness to you, lest you deny your God.

28 So Joshua let the people depart, every man to his inheritance.

29 And it came to pass after these things, that Joshua the son of Nun, the servant of the LORD, died, being an hundred and ten years old.

30 And they buried him in the border of his inheritance in Timnathserah, which is in mount Ephraim, on the north side of the hill of Gaash.

31 And Israel served the LORD all the days of Joshua, and all the days of the elders that overlived Joshua, and which had known all the works of the LORD, that he had done for Israel.

32 And the bones of Joseph, which the children of Israel brought up out of Egypt, buried they in Shechem, in a parcel of ground which Jacob bought of the sons of Hamor the father of Shechem for an hundred pieces of silver: and it became the inheritance of the children of Joseph.

33 And Eleazar the son of Aaron died; and they buried him in a hill that pertained to Phinehas his son, which was given him in mount Ephraim.

Judges

CHAPTER 1

NOW after the death of Joshua it came to pass, that the children of Israel asked the LORD, saying, Who shall go up for us against the Canaanites first, to fight against them?

2 And the LORD said, Judah shall go up: behold, I have delivered the land into his hand.

3 And Judah said to Simeon his brother, Come up with me into my lot, that we may fight against the Canaanites; and I likewise will go with you into your lot. So Simeon went with him.

4 And Judah went up; and the LORD delivered the Canaanites and the Perizzites into their hand: and they slew of them in Bezek ten thousand men.

5 And they found Adonibezek in Bezek: and they fought against him, and they slew the Canaanites and the Perizzites.

6 But Adonibezek fled; and they pursued after him, and caught him, and cut off his thumbs and his great toes.

7 And Adonibezek said, Threescore and ten kings, having their thumbs and their great toes cut off, gathered their meat under my table: as I have done, so God has requited me. And they brought him to Jerusalem, and there he died.

8 Now the children of Judah had fought against Jerusalem, and had taken it, and smitten it with the edge of the sword, and set the city on fire.

9 And afterward the children of Judah went down to fight against the Canaanites, that dwelt in the mountain, and in the south, and in the valley.

10 And Judah went against the Canaanites that dwelt in Hebron: (now the name of Hebron before was Kirjatharba:) and they slew Sheshai, and Ahiman, and Talmai.

11 And from thence he went against the inhabitants of Debir: and the name of Debir before was Kirjathsepher:

12 And Caleb said, He that smiteth Kirjathsepher, and takes it, to him will I give Achsah my daughter to wife.

13 And Othniel the son of Kenaz, Caleb's younger brother, took it: and he gave him Achsah his daughter to wife.

14 And it came to pass, when she came to him, that she moved him to ask of her father a field: and she lighted from off her ass; and Caleb said to her, What do you want?

15 And she said to him, Give me a blessing: for you have given me a south land; give me also springs of water. And Caleb gave her the upper springs and the nether springs.

16 And the children of the Kenite, Moses' father in law, went up out of the city of palm trees with the children of Judah into the wilderness of Judah, which lies in the south of Arad; and they went and dwelt among the people.

17 And Judah went with Simeon his brother, and they slew the Canaanites that inhabited Zephath, and utterly

destroyed it. And the name of the city was called Hormah.

18 Also Judah took Gaza with the coast thereof, and Askelon with the coast thereof, and Ekron with the coast thereof.

19 And the LORD was with Judah; and he drove out the inhabitants of the mountain; but could not drive out the inhabitants of the valley, because they had chariots of iron.

20 And they gave Hebron to Caleb, as Moses said: and he expelled thence the three sons of Anak.

21 And the children of Benjamin did not drive out the Jebusites that inhabited Jerusalem; but the Jebusites dwell with the children of Benjamin in Jerusalem to this day.

22 And the house of Joseph, they also went up against Bethel: and the LORD was with them.

23 And the house of Joseph sent to descry Bethel. (Now the name of the city before was Luz.)

24 And the spies saw a man come forth out of the city, and they said to him, Show us, we pray you, the entrance into the city, and we will show you mercy.

25 And when he showed them the entrance into the city, they smote the city with the edge of the sword; but they let go the man and all his family.

26 And the man went into the land of the Hittites, and built a city, and called the name thereof Luz: which is the name thereof to this day.

27 Neither did Manasseh drive out the inhabitants of Bethshean and her towns, nor Taanach and her towns, nor the inhabitants of Dor and her towns, nor the inhabitants of Ibleam and her towns, nor the inhabitants of Megiddo and her towns: but the Canaanites would dwell in that land.

28 And it came to pass, when Israel was strong, that they put the Canaanites to tribute, and did not utterly drive them out.

29 Neither did Ephraim drive out the Canaanites that dwelt in Gezer; but the Canaanites dwelt in Gezer among them.

30 Neither did Zebulun drive out the inhabitants of Kitron, nor the inhabitants of Nahalol; but the Canaanites dwelt among them, and became tributaries.

31 Neither did Asher drive out the inhabitants of Accho, nor the inhabitants of Zidon, nor of Ahlab, nor of Achzib, nor of Helbah, nor of Aphik, nor of Rehob:

32 But the Asherites dwelt among the Canaanites, the inhabitants of the land: for they did not drive them out.

33 Neither did Naphtali drive out the inhabitants of Bethshemesh, nor the inhabitants of Bethanath; but he dwelt among the Canaanites, the inhabitants of the land: nevertheless the inhabitants of Bethshemesh and of Bethanath became tributaries to them.

34 And the Amorites forced the children of Dan into the mountain: for they would not suffer them to come down to the valley:

35 But the Amorites would dwell in mount Heres in Aijalon, and in Shaalbim: yet the hand of the house of Joseph prevailed, so that they became tributaries.

36 And the coast of the Amorites was from the going up to Akrabbim, from the rock, and upward.

CHAPTER 2

A ND an angel of the LORD came up from Gilgal to Bochim, and said, I made you to go up out of Egypt, and have brought you to the land which I swore to your fathers; and I said, I will never break my covenant with you.

2 And you shall make no league with the inhabitants of this land; you shall throw down their altars: but you have not obeyed my voice: why have you done this?

3 Therefore I also said, I will not drive them out from before you; but they shall

be as thorns in your sides, and their gods shall be a snare to you.

4 And it came to pass, when the angel of the LORD spoke these words to all the children of Israel, that the people lifted up their voice, and wept.

5 And they called the name of that place Bochim: and they sacrificed there to the LORD.

6 And when Joshua had let the people go, the children of Israel went every man to his inheritance to possess the land.

7 And the people served the LORD all the days of Joshua, and all the days of the elders that outlived Joshua, who had seen all the great works of the LORD, that he did for Israel.

8 And Joshua the son of Nun, the servant of the LORD, died, being an hundred and ten years old.

9 And they buried him in the border of his inheritance in Timnathheres, in the mount of Ephraim, on the north side of the hill Gaash.

10 And also all that generation were gathered to their fathers: and there arose another generation after them, which knew not the LORD, nor yet the works which he had done for Israel.

11 And the children of Israel did evil in the sight of the LORD, and served Baalim:

12 And they forsook the LORD God of their fathers, which brought them out of the land of Egypt, and followed other gods, of the gods of the people that were round about them, and bowed themselves to them, and provoked the LORD to anger.

13 And they forsook the LORD, and served Baal and Ashtaroth.

14 And the anger of the LORD was hot against Israel, and he delivered them into the hands of spoilers that spoiled them, and he sold them into the hands of their enemies round about, so that they could not any longer stand before their enemies.

15 Wherever they went out, the hand of the LORD was against them for evil, as the LORD had said, and as the LORD had sworn to them: and they were greatly distressed.

16 Nevertheless the LORD raised up judges, which delivered them out of the hand of those that spoiled them.

17 And yet they would not hearken to their judges, but they went a whoring after other gods, and bowed themselves to them: they turned quickly out of the way which their fathers walked in, obeying the commandments of the LORD; but they did not so.

18 And when the LORD raised them up judges, then the LORD was with the judge, and delivered them out of the hand of their enemies all the days of the judge: for it repented the LORD because of their groanings by reason of them that oppressed them and vexed them.

19 And it came to pass, when the judge was dead, that they returned, and corrupted themselves more than their fathers, in following other gods to serve them, and to bow down to them; they ceased not from their own doings, nor from their stubborn way.

20 And the anger of the LORD was hot against Israel; and he said, Because that this people has transgressed my covenant which I commanded their fathers, and have not hearkened to my voice;

21 I also will not henceforth drive out any from before them of the nations which Joshua left when he died:

22 That through them I may prove Israel, whether they will keep the way of the LORD to walk therein, as their fathers did keep it, or not.

23 Therefore the LORD left those nations, without driving them out hastily; neither delivered he them into the hand of Joshua.

CHAPTER 3

NOW these are the nations which the LORD left, to prove Israel by them, even as many of Israel as had not known all the wars of Canaan;

2 Only that the generations of the children of Israel might know, to teach them war, at the least such as before knew nothing thereof;

3 Namely, five lords of the Philistines, and all the Canaanites, and the Sidonians, and the Hivites that dwelt in mount Lebanon, from mount Baalhermon to the entering in of Hamath.

4 And they were to prove Israel by them, to know whether they would hearken to the commandments of the LORD, which he commanded their fathers by the hand of Moses.

5 And the children of Israel dwelt among the Canaanites, Hittites, and Amorites, and Perizzites, and Hivites, and Jebusites:

6 And they took their daughters to be their wives, and gave their daughters to their sons, and served their gods.

7 And the children of Israel did evil in the sight of the LORD, and forgot the LORD their God, and served Baalim and the groves.

8 Therefore the anger of the LORD was hot against Israel, and he sold them into the hand of Chushanrishathaim king of Mesopotamia: and the children of Israel served Chushanrishathaim eight years.

9 And when the children of Israel cried to the LORD, the LORD raised up a deliverer to the children of Israel, who delivered them, even Othniel the son of Kenaz, Caleb's younger brother.

10 And the Spirit of the LORD came upon him, and he judged Israel, and went out to war: and the LORD delivered Chushanrishathaim king of Mesopotamia into his hand; and his hand prevailed against Chushanrishathaim.

11 And the land had rest forty years. And Othniel the son of Kenaz died.

12 And the children of Israel did evil again in the sight of the LORD: and the LORD strengthened Eglon the king of Moab against Israel, because they had done evil in the sight of the LORD.

13 And he gathered to him the children of Ammon and Amalek, and went and smote Israel, and possessed the city of palm trees.

14 So the children of Israel served Eglon the king of Moab eighteen years.

15 But when the children of Israel cried to the LORD, the LORD raised them up a deliverer, Ehud the son of Gera, a Benjamite, a man lefthanded: and by him the children of Israel sent a present to Eglon the king of Moab.

16 But Ehud made him a dagger which had two edges, of a cubit length; and he did gird it under his raiment upon his right thigh.

17 And he brought the present to Eglon king of Moab: and Eglon was a very fat man.

18 And when he had made an end to offer the present, he sent away the people that bare the present.

19 But he himself turned again from the quarries that were by Gilgal, and said, I have a secret errand to you, O king: who said, Keep silence. And all that stood by him went out from him.

20 And Ehud came to him; and he was sitting in a summer parlour, which he had for himself alone. And Ehud said, I have a message from God to you. And he arose out of his seat.

21 And Ehud put forth his left hand, and took the dagger from his right thigh, and thrust it into his belly:

22 And the haft also went in after the blade; and the fat closed upon the blade, so that he could not draw the dagger out of his belly; and the dirt came out.

23 Then Ehud went forth through the porch, and shut the doors of the parlour upon him, and locked them.

24 When he was gone out, his servants came; and when they saw that, behold, the doors of the parlour were locked, they said, Surely he covers his feet in his summer chamber.

25 And they tarried till they were ashamed: and, behold, he opened not the doors of the parlour; therefore they

took a key, and opened them: and, behold, their lord was fallen down dead on the earth.

26 And Ehud escaped while they tarried, and passed beyond the quarries, and escaped to Seirath.

27 And it came to pass, when he was come, that he blew a trumpet in the mountain of Ephraim, and the children of Israel went down with him from the mount, and he before them.

28 And he said to them, Follow after me: for the LORD has delivered your enemies the Moabites into your hand. And they went down after him, and took the fords of Jordan toward Moab, and suffered not a man to pass over.

29 And they slew of Moab at that time about ten thousand men, all lusty, and all men of valour; and there escaped not a man.

30 So Moab was subdued that day under the hand of Israel. And the land had rest fourscore years.

31 And after him was Shamgar the son of Anath, which slew of the Philistines six hundred men with an ox goad: and he also delivered Israel.

CHAPTER 4

AND the children of Israel again did evil in the sight of the LORD, when Ehud was dead.

2 And the LORD sold them into the hand of Jabin king of Canaan, that reigned in Hazor; the captain of whose host was Sisera, which dwelt in Harosheth of the Gentiles.

3 And the children of Israel cried to the LORD: for he had nine hundred chariots of iron; and twenty years he mightily oppressed the children of Israel.

4 And Deborah, a prophetess, the wife of Lapidoth, she judged Israel at that time.

5 And she dwelt under the palm tree of Deborah between Ramah and Bethel in mount Ephraim: and the children of Israel came up to her for judgment.

6 And she sent and called Barak the son of Abinoam out of Kedeshnaphtali, and said to him, Has not the LORD God of Israel commanded, saying, Go and draw toward mount Tabor, and take with you ten thousand men of the children of Naphtali and of the children of Zebulun?

7 And I will draw to you to the river Kishon Sisera, the captain of Jabin's army, with his chariots and his multitude; and I will deliver him into your hand.

8 And Barak said to her, If you will go with me, then I will go: but if you will not go with me, then I will not go.

9 And she said, I will surely go with you: notwithstanding the journey that you take shall not be for your honour; for the LORD shall sell Sisera into the hand of a woman. And Deborah arose, and went with Barak to Kedesh.

10 And Barak called Zebulun and Naphtali to Kedesh; and he went up with ten thousand men at his feet: and Deborah went up with him.

11 Now Heber the Kenite, which was of the children of Hobab the father in law of Moses, had severed himself from the Kenites, and pitched his tent to the plain of Zaanaim, which is by Kedesh.

12 And they showed Sisera that Barak the son of Abinoam was gone up to mount Tabor.

13 And Sisera gathered together all his chariots, even nine hundred chariots of iron, and all the people that were with him, from Harosheth of the Gentiles to the river of Kishon.

14 And Deborah said to Barak, Up; for this is the day in which the LORD has delivered Sisera into your hand: is not the LORD gone out before you? So Barak went down from mount Tabor, and ten thousand men after him.

15 And the LORD discomfited Sisera, and all his chariots, and all his host, with the edge of the sword before Barak; so that Sisera lighted down off his chariot, and fled away on his feet.

16 But Barak pursued after the chariots, and after the host, to Harosheth of the Gentiles: and all the host of Sisera fell upon the edge of the sword; and there was not a man left.

17 Howbeit Sisera fled away on his feet to the tent of Jael the wife of Heber the Kenite: for there was peace between Jabin the king of Hazor and the house of Heber the Kenite.

18 And Jael went out to meet Sisera, and said to him, Turn in, my lord, turn in to me; fear not. And when he had turned in to her into the tent, she covered him with a mantle.

19 And he said to her, Give me, I pray you, a little water to drink; for I am thirsty. And she opened a bottle of milk, and gave him drink, and covered him.

20 Again he said to her, Stand in the door of the tent, and it shall be, when any man does come and enquire of you, and say, Is there any man here? that you shall say, No.

21 Then Jael Heber's wife took a nail of the tent, and took an hammer in her hand, and went softly to him, and smote the nail into his temples, and fastened it into the ground: for he was fast asleep and weary. So he died.

22 And, behold, as Barak pursued Sisera, Jael came out to meet him, and said to him, Come, and I will show you the man whom you seek. And when he came into her tent, behold, Sisera lay dead, and the nail was in his temples.

23 So God subdued on that day Jabin the king of Canaan before the children of Israel.

24 And the hand of the children of Israel prospered, and prevailed against Jabin the king of Canaan, until they had destroyed Jabin king of Canaan.

CHAPTER 5

THEN sang Deborah and Barak the son of Abinoam on that day, saying,

2 Praise you the LORD for the avenging of Israel, when the people willingly offered themselves.

3 Hear, O you kings; give ear, O you princes; I, even I, will sing to the LORD; I will sing praise to the LORD God of Israel.

4 LORD, when you went out of Seir, when you marched out of the field of Edom, the earth trembled, and the heavens dropped, the clouds also dropped water.

5 The mountains melted from before the LORD, even that Sinai from before the LORD God of Israel.

6 In the days of Shamgar the son of Anath, in the days of Jael, the highways were unoccupied, and the travellers walked through byways.

7 The inhabitants of the villages ceased, they ceased in Israel, until that I Deborah arose, that I arose a mother in Israel.

8 They chose new gods; then was war in the gates: was there a shield or spear seen among forty thousand in Israel?

9 My heart is toward the governors of Israel, that offered themselves willingly among the people. Bless you the LORD.

10 Speak, you that ride on white asses, you that sit in judgment, and walk by the way.

11 They that are delivered from the noise of archers in the places of drawing water, there shall they rehearse the righteous acts of the LORD, even the righteous acts toward the inhabitants of his villages in Israel: then shall the people of the LORD go down to the gates.

12 Awake, awake, Deborah: awake, awake, utter a song: arise, Barak, and lead your captivity captive, you son of Abinoam.

13 Then he made him that remains have dominion over the nobles among the people: the LORD made me have dominion over the mighty.

14 Out of Ephraim was there a root of them against Amalek; after you, Benjamin, among your people; out of Machir came down governors, and out of Zebulun they that handle the pen of the writer.

15 And the princes of Issachar were with Deborah; even Issachar, and also Barak: he was sent on foot into the valley. For the divisions of Reuben there were great thoughts of heart.

16 Why do you sit among the sheepfolds, to hear the bleatings of the flocks? For the divisions of Reuben there were great searchings of heart.

17 Gilead abode beyond Jordan: and why did Dan remain in ships? Asher continued on the sea shore, and abode in his breaches.

18 Zebulun and Naphtali were a people that jeoparded their lives to the death in the high places of the field.

19 The kings came and fought, then fought the kings of Canaan in Taanach by the waters of Megiddo; they took no gain of money.

20 They fought from heaven; the stars in their courses fought against Sisera.

21 The river of Kishon swept them away, that ancient river, the river Kishon. O my soul, you have trodden down strength.

22 Then were the horsehoofs broken by the means of the pransings, the pransings of their mighty ones.

23 Curse you Meroz, said the angel of the LORD, curse you bitterly the inhabitants thereof; because they came not to the help of the LORD, to the help of the LORD against the mighty.

24 Blessed above women shall Jael the wife of Heber the Kenite be, blessed shall she be above women in the tent.

25 He asked water, and she gave him milk; she brought forth butter in a lordly dish.

26 She put her hand to the nail, and her right hand to the workmen's hammer; and with the hammer she smote Sisera, she smote off his head, when she had pierced and stricken through his temples.

27 At her feet he bowed, he fell, he lay down: at her feet he bowed, he fell: where he bowed, there he fell down dead.

28 The mother of Sisera looked out at a window, and cried through the lattice, Why is his chariot so long in coming? why tarry the wheels of his chariots?

29 Her wise ladies answered her, yea, she returned answer to herself,

30 Have they not sped? have they not divided the prey; to every man a damsel or two; to Sisera a prey of divers colours, a prey of divers colours of needlework, of divers colours of needlework on both sides, meet for the necks of them that take the spoil?

31 So let all your enemies perish, O LORD: but let them that love him be as the sun when he goeth forth in his might. And the land had rest forty years.

CHAPTER 6

AND the children of Israel did evil in the sight of the LORD: and the LORD delivered them into the hand of Midian seven years.

2 And the hand of Midian prevailed against Israel: and because of the Midianites the children of Israel made them the dens which are in the mountains, and caves, and strong holds.

3 And so it was, when Israel had sown, that the Midianites came up, and the Amalekites, and the children of the east, even they came up against them;

4 And they encamped against them, and destroyed the increase of the earth, till you come to Gaza, and left no sustenance for Israel, neither sheep, nor ox, nor ass.

5 For they came up with their cattle and their tents, and they came as grasshoppers for multitude; for both they and their camels were without number: and they entered into the land to destroy it.

6 And Israel was greatly impoverished because of the Midianites; and the children of Israel cried to the LORD.

7 And it came to pass, when the children of Israel cried to the LORD because of the Midianites,

8 That the LORD sent a prophet to the children of Israel, which said to them, Thus says the LORD God of Israel, I brought you up from Egypt, and brought you forth out of the house of bondage;

9 And I delivered you out of the hand of the Egyptians, and out of the hand of all that oppressed you, and drove them out from before you, and gave you their land;

10 And I said to you, I am the LORD your God; fear not the gods of the Amorites, in whose land you dwell: but you have not obeyed my voice.

11 And there came an angel of the LORD, and sat under an oak which was in Ophrah, that pertained to Joash the Abiezrite: and his son Gideon threshed wheat by the winepress, to hide it from the Midianites.

12 And the angel of the LORD appeared to him, and said to him, The LORD is with you, you mighty man of valour.

13 And Gideon said to him, Oh my Lord, if the LORD be with us, why then is all this befallen us? and where be all his miracles which our fathers told us of, saying, Did not the LORD bring us up from Egypt? but now the LORD has forsaken us, and delivered us into the hands of the Midianites.

14 And the LORD looked upon him, and said, Go in this your might, and you shall save Israel from the hand of the Midianites: have not I sent you?

15 And he said to him, Oh my Lord, wherewith shall I save Israel? behold, my family is poor in Manasseh, and I am the least in my father's house.

> How shall I feel at the judgment,
> if multitudes of missed opportunities
> pass before me in full review,
> and all my excuses
> prove to be disguises
> of my cowardice and pride?
> **W. E. SANGSTER**
> BRITISH PASTOR
> OF THE WESLEYAN CHURCH

16 And the LORD said to him, Surely I will be with you, and you shall smite the Midianites as one man.

17 And he said to him, If now I have found grace in your sight, then show me a sign that you talk with me.

18 Depart not hence, I pray you, until I come to you, and bring forth my present, and set it before you. And he said, I will tarry until you come again.

19 And Gideon went in, and made ready a kid, and unleavened cakes of an ephah of flour: the flesh he put in a basket, and he put the broth in a pot, and brought it out to him under the oak, and presented it.

20 And the angel of God said to him, Take the flesh and the unleavened cakes, and lay them upon this rock, and pour out the broth. And he did so.

21 Then the angel of the LORD put forth the end of the staff that was in his hand, and touched the flesh and the unleavened cakes; and there rose up fire out of the rock, and consumed the flesh and the unleavened cakes. Then the angel of the LORD departed out of his sight.

22 And when Gideon perceived that he was an angel of the LORD, Gideon said, Alas, O LORD God! for because I have seen an angel of the LORD face to face.

23 And the LORD said to him, Peace be to you; fear not: you shall not die.

24 Then Gideon built an altar there to the LORD, and called it Jehovahshalom: to this day it is yet in Ophrah of the Abiezrites.

25 And it came to pass the same night, that the LORD said to him, Take your fa-

---

6:12 As a Christian, you may feel inadequate for the task of reaching out to the lost, but you too are a mighty man or woman of valor because the Lord is with you. See Romans 8:31.

ther's young bullock, even the second bullock of seven years old, and throw down the altar of Baal that your father has, and cut down the grove that is by it:

26 And build an altar to the LORD your God upon the top of this rock, in the ordered place, and take the second bullock, and offer a burnt sacrifice with the wood of the grove which you shall cut down.

27 Then Gideon took ten men of his servants, and did as the LORD had said to him: and so it was, because he feared his father's household, and the men of the city, that he could not do it by day, that he did it by night.

28 And when the men of the city arose early in the morning, behold, the altar of Baal was cast down, and the grove was cut down that was by it, and the second bullock was offered upon the altar that was built.

29 And they said one to another, Who has done this thing? And when they enquired and asked, they said, Gideon the son of Joash has done this thing.

30 Then the men of the city said to Joash, Bring out your son, that he may die: because he has cast down the altar of Baal, and because he has cut down the grove that was by it.

31 And Joash said to all that stood against him, Will you plead for Baal? will you save him? he that will plead for him, let him be put to death whilst it is yet morning: if he be a god, let him plead for himself, because one has cast down his altar.

32 Therefore on that day he called him Jerubbaal, saying, Let Baal plead against him, because he has thrown down his altar.

33 Then all the Midianites and the Amalekites and the children of the east were gathered together, and went over, and pitched in the valley of Jezreel.

34 But the Spirit of the LORD came upon Gideon, and he blew a trumpet; and Abiezer was gathered after him.

35 And he sent messengers throughout all Manasseh; who also was gathered after him: and he sent messengers to Asher, and to Zebulun, and to Naphtali; and they came up to meet them.

36 And Gideon said to God, If you will save Israel by mine hand, as you have said,

37 Behold, I will put a fleece of wool in the floor; and if the dew be on the fleece only, and it be dry upon all the earth beside, then shall I know that you will save Israel by mine hand, as you have said.

38 And it was so: for he rose up early on the morrow, and thrust the fleece together, and wringed the dew out of the fleece, a bowl full of water.

39 And Gideon said to God, Let not your anger be hot against me, and I will speak but this once: let me prove, I pray you, but this once with the fleece;

> "The only saving faith is that which casts itself on God for life or death."
>
> **MARTIN LUTHER**
> 1483-1546
> GERMAN PRIEST
> FOUNDED LUTHERAN CHURCH

6:27 There is no denying that when God asks us to reach out to the unsaved that we battle with fear. Gideon also had a battle with fear. However, he didn't let it paralyze him. Notice that what he couldn't do during the day, he did at night. One great key was that he took "ten men of his servants and did what the Lord had said." Do the same. Take the Ten Commandments and use them (as Jesus did--see Mark 10:17-22) as servants to do what God has said (see Mark 16:15). If you can't open-air preach, then witness one-to-one. If you can't do that, then give out tracts. If you can't do that, then discretely leave a tract somewhere. Whatever you do, don't let fear paralyze you into doing nothing. If you can't evangelize in the sight of men, then evangelize when no one is looking.

GIDEON CHOOSING HIS SOLDIERS

Judges 7:3-7

Don't be surprised if, in a church of 22,000, you can only find 300 who are prepared to reach out to the lost. Sadly, most Christians are afraid to share their faith with non-believers and would rather stay home than evangelize. Such reluctance among church-going Christians is a tragedy, but it will leave you with an army (small though it may be) of soldiers who keep their eyes peeled for opportunities to present the Gospel message to the unsaved.

These soldiers know that the fear they battle isn't from God. They are aware that "we wrestle not against flesh and blood, but against principalities, against powers, against the rulers of the darkness of this world, against spiritual wickedness in high places" (see Ephesians 6:11-20), and they are the ones who God will use for His purposes.

let it now be dry only upon the fleece, and upon all the ground let there be dew.

40 And God did so that night: for it was dry upon the fleece only, and there was dew on all the ground.

CHAPTER 7

THEN Jerubbaal, who is Gideon, and all the people that were with him, rose up early, and pitched beside the well of Harod: so that the host of the Midianites were on the north side of them, by the hill of Moreh, in the valley.

2 And the LORD said to Gideon, The people that are with you are too many for me to give the Midianites into their hands, lest Israel vaunt themselves against me, saying, Mine own hand has saved me.

3 Now therefore go to, proclaim in the ears of the people, saying, Whosoever is fearful and afraid, let him return and depart early from mount Gilead. And there returned of the people twenty and two thousand; and there remained ten thousand.

4 And the LORD said to Gideon, The people are yet too many; bring them down to the water, and I will try them for you there: and it shall be, that of whom I say to you, This shall go with you, the same shall go with you; and of whomsoever I say to you, This shall not go with you, the same shall not go.

5 So he brought down the people to the water: and the LORD said to Gideon, Every one that laps of the water with his tongue, as a dog laps, him shall you set by himself; likewise every one that bows down upon his knees to drink.

6 And the number of them that lapped, putting their hand to their mouth, were three hundred men: but all the rest of the people bowed down upon their knees to drink water.

7 And the LORD said to Gideon, By the three hundred men that lapped will I save you, and deliver the Midianites into your hand: and let all the other people go every man to his place.

8 So the people took victuals in their hand, and their trumpets: and he sent all the rest of Israel every man to his tent, and retained those three hundred men: and the host of Midian was beneath him in the valley.

9 And it came to pass the same night, that the LORD said to him, Arise, get down to the host; for I have delivered it into your hand.

10 But if you fear to go down, go with Phurah your servant down to the host:

11 And you shall hear what they say; and afterward shall your hands be strengthened to go down to the host. Then went he down with Phurah his servant to the outside of the armed men that were in the host.

> Bear up the hands that hang down,
> by faith and prayer;
> support the tottering knees.
> Have you any days
> of fasting and prayer?
> Storm the throne of grace
> and persevere therein,
> and mercy will come down.
>
> **JOHN WESLEY**
> 1703 - 1791
> BRITISH EVANGELIST
> FOUNDER OF METHODIST CHURCH

12 And the Midianites and the Amalekites and all the children of the east lay along in the valley like grasshoppers for multitude; and their camels were without number, as the sand by the sea side for multitude.

13 And when Gideon was come, behold, there was a man that told a dream to his fellow, and said, Behold, I dreamed a dream, and, lo, a cake of barley bread tumbled into the host of Midian, and came to a tent, and smote it that it fell, and overturned it, that the tent lay along.

14 And his fellow answered and said, This is nothing else save the sword of Gideon the son of Joash, a man of Israel: for into his hand has God delivered Midian, and all the host.

15 And it was so, when Gideon heard the telling of the dream, and the interpretation thereof, that he worshipped, and returned into the host of Israel, and said, Arise; for the LORD has delivered into your hand the host of Midian.

16 And he divided the three hundred men into three companies, and he put a trumpet in every man's hand, with empty pitchers, and lamps within the pitchers.

17 And he said to them, Look on me, and do likewise: and, behold, when I come to the outside of the camp, it shall be that, as I do, so shall you do.

18 When I blow with a trumpet, I and all that are with me, then blow you the trumpets also on every side of all the camp, and say, The sword of the LORD, and of Gideon.

19 So Gideon, and the hundred men that were with him, came to the outside of the camp in the beginning of the middle watch; and they had but newly set

the watch: and they blew the trumpets, and brake the pitchers that were in their hands.

20 And the three companies blew the trumpets, and brake the pitchers, and held the lamps in their left hands, and the trumpets in their right hands to blow withal: and they cried, The sword of the LORD, and of Gideon.

21 And they stood every man in his place round about the camp; and all the host ran, and cried, and fled.

22 And the three hundred blew the trumpets, and the LORD set every man's sword against his fellow, even throughout all the host: and the host fled to Bethshittah in Zererath, and to the border of Abelmeholah, to Tabbath.

23 And the men of Israel gathered themselves together out of Naphtali, and out of Asher, and out of all Manasseh, and pursued after the Midianites.

24 And Gideon sent messengers throughout all mount Ephraim, saying, come down against the Midianites, and take before them the waters to Bethbarah and Jordan. Then all the men of Ephraim gathered themselves together, and took the waters to Bethbarah and Jordan.

25 And they took two princes of the Midianites, Oreb and Zeeb; and they slew Oreb upon the rock Oreb, and Zeeb they slew at the winepress of Zeeb, and pursued Midian, and brought the heads of Oreb and Zeeb to Gideon on the other side Jordan.

CHAPTER 8

A ND the men of Ephraim said to him, Why have you served us thus, that you called us not, when you went to fight with the Midianites? And they did chide with him sharply.

2 And he said to them, What have I done now in comparison of you? Is not the gleaning of the grapes of Ephraim better than the vintage of Abiezer?

3 God has delivered into your hands the princes of Midian, Oreb and Zeeb: and what was I able to do in comparison of you? Then their anger was abated toward him, when he had said that.

4 And Gideon came to Jordan, and passed over, he, and the three hundred men that were with him, faint, yet pursuing them.

5 And he said to the men of Succoth, Give, I pray you, loaves of bread to the people that follow me; for they be faint, and I am pursuing after Zebah and Zalmunna, kings of Midian.

6 And the princes of Succoth said, Are the hands of Zebah and Zalmunna now in your hand, that we should give bread to your army?

7 And Gideon said, Therefore when the LORD has delivered Zebah and Zalmunna into mine hand, then I will tear your flesh with the thorns of the wilderness and with briers.

8 And he went up thence to Penuel, and spoke to them likewise: and the men of Penuel answered him as the men of Succoth had answered him.

9 And he spoke also to the men of Penuel, saying, When I come again in peace, I will break down this tower.

10 Now Zebah and Zalmunna were in Karkor, and their hosts with them, about fifteen thousand men, all that were left of all the hosts of the children of the east: for there fell an hundred and twenty thousand men that drew sword.

11 And Gideon went up by the way of them that dwelt in tents on the east of Nobah and Jogbehah, and smote the host; for the host was secure.

12 And when Zebah and Zalmunna fled, he pursued after them, and took the two kings of Midian, Zebah and Zalmunna, and discomfited all the host.

7:15-19 God wants broken vessels who will then let their light shine before men. He wants soldiers of Christ who will take up the two-edged sword of the Word of God in their hand and boldly lift up their voice as a trumpet and show this people their transgression (see Isaiah 58:1).

13 And Gideon the son of Joash returned from battle before the sun was up,

14 And caught a young man of the men of Succoth, and enquired of him: and he described to him the princes of Succoth, and the elders thereof, even threescore and seventeen men.

15 And he came to the men of Succoth, and said, Behold Zebah and Zalmunna, with whom you did upbraid me, saying, Are the hands of Zebah and Zalmunna now in your hand, that we should give bread to your men that are weary?

16 And he took the elders of the city, and thorns of the wilderness and briers, and with them he taught the men of Succoth.

17 And he beat down the tower of Penuel, and slew the men of the city.

18 Then said he to Zebah and Zalmunna, What manner of men were they whom you slew at Tabor? And they answered, As you are, so were they; each one resembled the children of a king.

19 And he said, They were my brethren, even the sons of my mother: as the LORD lives, if you had saved them alive, I would not slay you.

20 And he said to Jether his firstborn, Up, and slay them. But the youth drew not his sword: for he feared, because he was yet a youth.

21 Then Zebah and Zalmunna said, Rise you, and fall upon us: for as the man is, so is his strength. And Gideon arose, and slew Zebah and Zalmunna, and took away the ornaments that were on their camels' necks.

22 Then the men of Israel said to Gideon, Rule over us, both you, and your son, and your son's son also: for you have delivered us from the hand of Midian.

23 And Gideon said to them, I will not rule over you, neither shall my son rule over you: the LORD shall rule over you.

24 And Gideon said to them, I would desire a request of you, that you would give me every man the earrings of his prey. (For they had golden earrings, because they were Ishmaelites.)

25 And they answered, We will willingly give them. And they spread a garment, and did cast therein every man the earrings of his prey.

26 And the weight of the golden earrings that he requested was a thousand and seven hundred shekels of gold; beside ornaments, and collars, and purple raiment that was on the kings of Midian, and beside the chains that were about their camels' necks.

27 And Gideon made an ephod thereof, and put it in his city, even in Ophrah: and all Israel went there a whoring after it: which thing became a snare to Gideon, and to his house.

28 Thus was Midian subdued before the children of Israel, so that they lifted up their heads no more. And the country was in quietness forty years in the days of Gideon.

29 And Jerubbaal the son of Joash went and dwelt in his own house.

30 And Gideon had threescore and ten sons of his body begotten: for he had many wives.

31 And his concubine that was in Shechem, she also bare him a son, whose name he called Abimelech.

32 And Gideon the son of Joash died in a good old age, and was buried in the sepulchre of Joash his father, in Ophrah of the Abiezrites.

33 And it came to pass, as soon as Gideon was dead, that the children of Israel turned again, and went a whoring after Baalim, and made Baalberith their god.

34 And the children of Israel remembered not the LORD their God, who had delivered them out of the hands of all their enemies on every side:

35 Neither showed they kindness to the house of Jerubbaal, namely, Gideon, according to all the goodness which he had showed to Israel.

CHAPTER 9

AND Abimelech the son of Jerubbaal went to Shechem to his mother's brethren, and communed with them, and with all the family of the house of his mother's father, saying,

2 Speak, I pray you, in the ears of all the men of Shechem, Whether is better for you, either that all the sons of Jerubbaal, which are threescore and ten persons, reign over you, or that one reign over you? remember also that I am your bone and your flesh.

3 And his mother's brethren spoke of him in the ears of all the men of Shechem all these words: and their hearts inclined to follow Abimelech; for they said, He is our brother.

4 And they gave him threescore and ten pieces of silver out of the house of Baalberith, wherewith Abimelech hired vain and light persons, which followed him.

5 And he went to his father's house at Ophrah, and slew his brethren the sons of Jerubbaal, being threescore and ten persons, upon one stone: notwithstanding yet Jotham the youngest son of Jerubbaal was left; for he hid himself.

6 And all the men of Shechem gathered together, and all the house of Millo, and went, and made Abimelech king, by the plain of the pillar that was in Shechem.

7 And when they told it to Jotham, he went and stood in the top of mount Gerizim, and lifted up his voice, and cried, and said to them, Hearken to me, you men of Shechem, that God may hearken to you.

8 The trees went forth on a time to anoint a king over them; and they said to the olive tree, Reign over us.

9 But the olive tree said to them, Should I leave my fatness, wherewith by me they honour God and man, and go to be promoted over the trees?

10 And the trees said to the fig tree, You come, and reign over us.

11 But the fig tree said to them, Should I forsake my sweetness, and my good fruit, and go to be promoted over the trees?

12 Then said the trees to the vine, You come, and reign over us.

13 And the vine said to them, Should I leave my wine, which cheereth God and man, and go to be promoted over the trees?

14 Then said all the trees to the bramble, You come, and reign over us.

15 And the bramble said to the trees, If in truth you anoint me king over you, then come and put your trust in my shadow: and if not, let fire come out of the bramble, and devour the cedars of Lebanon.

16 Now therefore, if you have done truly and sincerely, in that you have made Abimelech king, and if you have dealt well with Jerubbaal and his house, and have done to him according to the deserving of his hands;

17 (For my father fought for you, and adventured his life far, and delivered you out of the hand of Midian:

18 And you are risen up against my father's house this day, and have slain his sons, threescore and ten persons, upon one stone, and have made Abimelech, the son of his maidservant, king over the men of Shechem, because he is your brother;)

19 If you then have dealt truly and sincerely with Jerubbaal and with his house this day, then rejoice in Abimelech, and let him also rejoice in you:

20 But if not, let fire come out from Abimelech, and devour the men of Shechem, and the house of Millo; and let fire come out from the men of Shechem, and from the house of Millo, and devour Abimelech.

21 And Jotham ran away, and fled, and went to Beer, and dwelt there, for fear of Abimelech his brother.

22 When Abimelech had reigned three years over Israel,

23 Then God sent an evil spirit between Abimelech and the men of Shechem; and

the men of Shechem dealt treacherously with Abimelech:

24 That the cruelty done to the threescore and ten sons of Jerubbaal might come, and their blood be laid upon Abimelech their brother, which slew them; and upon the men of Shechem, which aided him in the killing of his brethren.

25 And the men of Shechem set liers in wait for him in the top of the mountains, and they robbed all that came along that way by them: and it was told Abimelech.

26 And Gaal the son of Ebed came with his brethren, and went over to Shechem: and the men of Shechem put their confidence in him.

27 And they went out into the fields, and gathered their vineyards, and trode the grapes, and made merry, and went into the house of their god, and did eat and drink, and cursed Abimelech.

28 And Gaal the son of Ebed said, Who is Abimelech, and who is Shechem, that we should serve him? is not he the son of Jerubbaal? and Zebul his officer? serve the men of Hamor the father of Shechem: for why should we serve him?

29 And would to God this people were under my hand! then would I remove Abimelech. And he said to Abimelech, Increase your army, and come out.

30 And when Zebul the ruler of the city heard the words of Gaal the son of Ebed, his anger was kindled.

31 And he sent messengers to Abimelech privily, saying, Behold, Gaal the son of Ebed and his brethren be come to Shechem; and, behold, they fortify the city against you.

32 Now therefore up by night, you and the people that is with you, and lie in wait in the field:

33 And it shall be, that in the morning, as soon as the sun is up, you shall rise early, and set upon the city: and, behold, when he and the people that is with him come out against you, then may you do to them as you shall find occasion.

34 And Abimelech rose up, and all the people that were with him, by night, and they laid wait against Shechem in four companies.

35 And Gaal the son of Ebed went out, and stood in the entering of the gate of the city: and Abimelech rose up, and the people that were with him, from lying in wait.

36 And when Gaal saw the people, he said to Zebul, Behold, there come people down from the top of the mountains. And Zebul said to him, You see the shadow of the mountains as if they were men.

37 And Gaal spoke again, and said, See there come people down by the middle of the land, and another company come along by the plain of Meonenim.

38 Then said Zebul to him, Where is now your mouth, wherewith you said, Who is Abimelech, that we should serve him? is not this the people that you have despised? go out, I pray now, and fight with them.

39 And Gaal went out before the men of Shechem, and fought with Abimelech.

40 And Abimelech chased him, and he fled before him, and many were overthrown and wounded, even to the entering of the gate.

41 And Abimelech dwelt at Arumah: and Zebul thrust out Gaal and his brethren, that they should not dwell in Shechem.

42 And it came to pass on the morrow, that the people went out into the field; and they told Abimelech.

43 And he took the people, and divided them into three companies, and laid wait in the field, and looked, and, behold, the people were come forth out of the city; and he rose up against them, and smote them.

44 And Abimelech, and the company that was with him, rushed forward, and stood in the entering of the gate of the city: and the two other companies ran upon all the people that were in the fields, and slew them.

45 And Abimelech fought against the city all that day; and he took the city, and slew the people that was therein, and beat down the city, and sowed it with salt.

46 And when all the men of the tower of Shechem heard that, they entered into an hold of the house of the god Berith.

47 And it was told Abimelech, that all the men of the tower of Shechem were gathered together.

48 And Abimelech gat him up to mount Zalmon, he and all the people that were with him; and Abimelech took an axe in his hand, and cut down a bough from the trees, and took it, and laid it on his shoulder, and said to the people that were with him, What you have seen me do, make haste, and do as I have done.

49 And all the people likewise cut down every man his bough, and followed Abimelech, and put them to the hold, and set the hold on fire upon them; so that all the men of the tower of Shechem died also, about a thousand men and women.

50 Then went Abimelech to Thebez, and encamped against Thebez, and took it.

51 But there was a strong tower within the city, and there fled all the men and women, and all they of the city, and shut it to them, and gat them up to the top of the tower.

52 And Abimelech came to the tower, and fought against it, and went hard to the door of the tower to burn it with fire.

53 And a certain woman cast a piece of a millstone upon Abimelech's head, and all to brake his skull.

54 Then he called hastily to the young man his armourbearer, and said to him, Draw your sword, and slay me, that men say not of me, A women slew him. And his young man thrust him through, and he died.

55 And when the men of Israel saw that Abimelech was dead, they departed every man to his place.

56 Thus God rendered the wickedness of Abimelech, which he did to his father, in slaying his seventy brethren:

57 And all the evil of the men of Shechem did God render upon their heads: and upon them came the curse of Jotham the son of Jerubbaal.

CHAPTER 10

AND after Abimelech there arose to defend Israel Tola the son of Puah, the son of Dodo, a man of Issachar; and he dwelt in Shamir in mount Ephraim.

2 And he judged Israel twenty and three years, and died, and was buried in Shamir.

3 And after him arose Jair, a Gileadite, and judged Israel twenty and two years.

4 And he had thirty sons that rode on thirty ass colts, and they had thirty cities, which are called Havothjair to this day, which are in the land of Gilead.

5 And Jair died, and was buried in Camon.

6 And the children of Israel did evil again in the sight of the LORD, and served Baalim, and Ashtaroth, and the gods of Syria, and the gods of Zidon, and the gods of Moab, and the gods of the children of Ammon, and the gods of the Philistines, and forsook the LORD, and served not him.

7 And the anger of the LORD was hot against Israel, and he sold them into the hands of the Philistines, and into the hands of the children of Ammon.

8 And that year they vexed and oppressed the children of Israel: eighteen years, all the children of Israel that were on the other side Jordan in the land of the Amorites, which is in Gilead.

9 Moreover the children of Ammon passed over Jordan to fight also against Judah, and against Benjamin, and against the house of Ephraim; so that Israel was sore distressed.

10 And the children of Israel cried to the LORD, saying, We have sinned against you, both because we have forsaken our God, and also served Baalim.

11 And the LORD said to the children of Israel, Did not I deliver you from the Egyptians, and from the Amorites, from the children of Ammon, and from the Philistines?

12 The Zidonians also, and the Amalekites, and the Maonites, did oppress you; and you cried to me, and I delivered you out of their hand.

13 Yet you have forsaken me, and served other gods: therefore I will deliver you no more.

14 Go and cry to the gods which you have chosen; let them deliver you in the time of your tribulation.

15 And the children of Israel said to the LORD, We have sinned: do to us whatsoever seems good to you; deliver us only, we pray you, this day.

16 And they put away the strange gods from among them, and served the LORD: and his soul was grieved for the misery of Israel.

17 Then the children of Ammon were gathered together, and encamped in Gilead. And the children of Israel assembled themselves together, and encamped in Mizpeh.

18 And the people and princes of Gilead said one to another, What man is he that will begin to fight against the children of Ammon? he shall be head over all the inhabitants of Gilead.

CHAPTER 11

NOW Jephthah the Gileadite was a mighty man of valour, and he was the son of an harlot: and Gilead begat Jephthah.

2 And Gilead's wife bare him sons; and his wife's sons grew up, and they thrust out Jephthah, and said to him, You shall not inherit in our father's house; for you are the son of a strange woman.

3 Then Jephthah fled from his brethren, and dwelt in the land of Tob: and there were gathered vain men to Jephthah, and went out with him.

4 And it came to pass in process of time, that the children of Ammon made war against Israel.

5 And it was so, that when the children of Ammon made war against Israel, the elders of Gilead went to fetch Jephthah out of the land of Tob:

6 And they said to Jephthah, Come, and be our captain, that we may fight with the children of Ammon.

7 And Jephthah said to the elders of Gilead, Did not you hate me, and expel me out of my father's house? and why are you come to me now when you are in distress?

8 And the elders of Gilead said to Jephthah, Therefore we turn again to you now, that you may go with us, and fight against the children of Ammon, and be our head over all the inhabitants of Gilead.

9 And Jephthah said to the elders of Gilead, If you bring me home again to fight against the children of Ammon, and the LORD deliver them before me, shall I be your head?

10 And the elders of Gilead said to Jephthah, The LORD be witness between us, if we do not so according to your words.

11 Then Jephthah went with the elders of Gilead, and the people made him head and captain over them: and Jephthah uttered all his words before the LORD in Mizpeh.

12 And Jephthah sent messengers to the king of the children of Ammon, saying, What have you to do with me, that you are come against me to fight in my land?

13 And the king of the children of Ammon answered to the messengers of Jephthah, Because Israel took away my land, when they came up out of Egypt, from Arnon even to Jabbok, and to Jordan: now therefore restore those lands again peaceably.

14 And Jephthah sent messengers again to the king of the children of Ammon:

15 And said to him, Thus says Jephthah, Israel took not away the land of Moab, nor the land of the children of Ammon:

16 But when Israel came up from Egypt, and walked through the wilderness to the Red sea, and came to Kadesh;

17 Then Israel sent messengers to the king of Edom, saying, Let me, I pray you, pass through your land: but the king of Edom would not hearken thereto. And in like manner they sent to the king of Moab: but he would not consent: and Israel abode in Kadesh.

18 Then they went along through the wilderness, and compassed the land of Edom, and the land of Moab, and came by the east side of the land of Moab, and pitched on the other side of Arnon, but came not within the border of Moab: for Arnon was the border of Moab.

19 And Israel sent messengers to Sihon king of the Amorites, the king of Heshbon; and Israel said to him, Let us pass, we pray you, through your land into my place.

20 But Sihon trusted not Israel to pass through his coast: but Sihon gathered all his people together, and pitched in Jahaz, and fought against Israel.

21 And the LORD God of Israel delivered Sihon and all his people into the hand of Israel, and they smote them: so Israel possessed all the land of the Amorites, the inhabitants of that country.

22 And they possessed all the coasts of the Amorites, from Arnon even to Jabbok, and from the wilderness even to Jordan.

23 So now the LORD God of Israel has dispossessed the Amorites from before his people Israel, and should you possess it?

24 Will not you possess that which Chemosh your god gives you to possess? So whomsoever the LORD our God shall drive out from before us, them will we possess.

25 And now are you any thing better than Balak the son of Zippor, king of Moab? did he ever strive against Israel, or did he ever fight against them,

26 While Israel dwelt in Heshbon and her towns, and in Aroer and her towns, and in all the cities that be along by the coasts of Arnon, three hundred years? why therefore did you not recover them within that time?

27 Therefore I have not sinned against you, but you do me wrong to war against me: the LORD the Judge be judge this day between the children of Israel and the children of Ammon.

28 Howbeit the king of the children of Ammon hearkened not to the words of Jephthah which he sent him.

29 Then the Spirit of the LORD came upon Jephthah, and he passed over Gilead, and Manasseh, and passed over Mizpeh of Gilead, and from Mizpeh of Gilead he passed over to the children of Ammon.

30 And Jephthah vowed a vow to the LORD, and said, If you shall without fail deliver the children of Ammon into mine hands,

31 Then it shall be, that whatsoever cometh forth of the doors of my house to meet me, when I return in peace from the children of Ammon, shall surely be the LORD's, and I will offer it up for a burnt offering.

32 So Jephthah passed over to the children of Ammon to fight against them; and the LORD delivered them into his hands.

33 And he smote them from Aroer, even till you come to Minnith, even twenty cities, and to the plain of the vineyards, with a very great slaughter. Thus the children of Ammon were subdued before the children of Israel.

34 And Jephthah came to Mizpeh to his house, and, behold, his daughter came out to meet him with timbrels and with dances: and she was his only child; beside her he had neither son nor daughter.

35 And it came to pass, when he saw her, that he rent his clothes, and said, Alas, my daughter! you have brought me very low, and you are one of them that trouble me: for I have opened my mouth to the LORD, and I cannot go back.

36 And she said to him, My father, if you have opened your mouth to the LORD, do to me according to that which has proceeded out of your mouth; forasmuch as the LORD has taken vengeance for you of your enemies, even of the children of Ammon.

37 And she said to her father, Let this thing be done for me: let me alone two months, that I may go up and down upon the mountains, and bewail my virginity, I and my fellows.

38 And he said, Go. And he sent her away for two months: and she went with her companions, and bewailed her virginity upon the mountains.

39 And it came to pass at the end of two months, that she returned to her father, who did with her according to his vow which he had vowed: and she knew no man. And it was a custom in Israel,

40 That the daughters of Israel went yearly to lament the daughter of Jephthah the Gileadite four days in a year.

CHAPTER 12

AND the men of Ephraim gathered themselves together, and went northward, and said to Jephthah, Why did you pass over to fight against the children of Ammon, and did not call us to go with you? we will burn your house upon you with fire.

2 And Jephthah said to them, I and my people were at great strife with the children of Ammon; and when I called you, you delivered me not out of their hands.

3 And when I saw that you delivered me not, I put my life in my hands, and passed over against the children of Ammon, and the LORD delivered them into my hand: why then are you come up to me this day, to fight against me?

4 Then Jephthah gathered together all the men of Gilead, and fought with Ephraim: and the men of Gilead smote Ephraim, because they said, You Gileadites are fugitives of Ephraim among the Ephraimites, and among the Manassites.

5 And the Gileadites took the passages of Jordan before the Ephraimites: and it was so, that when those Ephraimites which were escaped said, Let me go over; that the men of Gilead said to him, Are you an Ephraimite? If he said, Nay;

6 Then said they to him, Say now Shibboleth: and he said Sibboleth: for he could not frame to pronounce it right. Then they took him, and slew him at the passages of Jordan: and there fell at that time of the Ephraimites forty and two thousand.

7 And Jephthah judged Israel six years. Then died Jephthah the Gileadite, and was buried in one of the cities of Gilead.

8 And after him Ibzan of Bethlehem judged Israel.

9 And he had thirty sons, and thirty daughters, whom he sent abroad, and took in thirty daughters from abroad for his sons. And he judged Israel seven years.

10 Then died Ibzan, and was buried at Bethlehem.

11 And after him Elon, a Zebulonite, judged Israel; and he judged Israel ten years.

12 And Elon the Zebulonite died, and was buried in Aijalon in the country of Zebulun.

13 And after him Abdon the son of Hillel, a Pirathonite, judged Israel.

14 And he had forty sons and thirty nephews, that rode on threescore and ten ass colts: and he judged Israel eight years.

15 And Abdon the son of Hillel the Pirathonite died, and was buried in Pirathon in the land of Ephraim, in the mount of the Amalekites.

CHAPTER 13

AND the children of Israel did evil again in the sight of the LORD; and the LORD delivered them into the hand of the Philistines forty years.

2 And there was a certain man of Zorah, of the family of the Danites, whose name was Manoah; and his wife was barren, and bare not.

3 And the angel of the LORD appeared to the woman, and said to her, Behold now, you are barren, and bear not: but you shall conceive, and bear a son.

4 Now therefore beware, I pray you, and drink not wine nor strong drink, and eat not any unclean thing:

5 For, lo, you shall conceive, and bear a son; and no razor shall come on his head: for the child shall be a Nazarite to God from the womb: and he shall begin to deliver Israel out of the hand of the Philistines.

6 Then the woman came and told her husband, saying, A man of God came to me, and his countenance was like the countenance of an angel of God, very terrible: but I asked him not whence he was, neither told he me his name:

7 But he said to me, Behold, you shall conceive, and bear a son; and now drink no wine nor strong drink, neither eat any unclean thing: for the child shall be a Nazarite to God from the womb to the day of his death.

8 Then Manoah intreated the LORD, and said, O my Lord, let the man of God which you didst send come again to us, and teach us what we shall do to the child that shall be born.

9 And God hearkened to the voice of Manoah; and the angel of God came again to the woman as she sat in the field: but Manoah her husband was not with her.

10 And the woman made haste, and ran, and showed her husband, and said to him, Behold, the man has appeared to me, that came to me the other day.

11 And Manoah arose, and went after his wife, and came to the man, and said to him, Are you the man that spoke to the woman? And he said, I am.

12 And Manoah said, Now let your words come to pass. How shall we order the child, and how shall we do to him?

13 And the angel of the LORD said to Manoah, Of all that I said to the woman let her beware.

14 She may not eat of any thing that cometh of the vine, neither let her drink wine or strong drink, nor eat any unclean thing: all that I commanded her let her observe.

15 And Manoah said to the angel of the LORD, I pray you, let us detain you, until we shall have made ready a kid for you.

16 And the angel of the LORD said to Manoah, Though you detain me, I will not eat of your bread: and if you will offer a burnt offering, you must offer it to the LORD. For Manoah knew not that he was an angel of the LORD.

17 And Manoah said to the angel of the LORD, What is your name, that when your sayings come to pass we may do you honour?

18 And the angel of the LORD said to him, Why do you ask my name, seeing it is secret?

19 So Manoah took a kid with a meat offering, and offered it upon a rock to the LORD: and the angel did wonderously; and Manoah and his wife looked on.

20 For it came to pass, when the flame went up toward heaven from off the altar, that the angel of the LORD ascended in the flame of the altar. And Manoah and his wife looked on it, and fell on their faces to the ground.

21 But the angel of the LORD did no more appear to Manoah and to his wife. Then Manoah knew that he was an angel of the LORD.

22 And Manoah said to his wife, We shall surely die, because we have seen God.

23 But his wife said to him, If the LORD were pleased to kill us, he would

not have received a burnt offering and a meat offering at our hands, neither would he have showed us all these things, nor would as at this time have told us such things as these.

24 And the woman bare a son, and called his name Samson: and the child grew, and the LORD blessed him.

25 And the Spirit of the LORD began to move him at times in the camp of Dan between Zorah and Eshtaol.

CHAPTER 14

AND Samson went down to Timnath, and saw a woman in Timnath of the daughters of the Philistines.

2 And he came up, and told his father and his mother, and said, I have seen a woman in Timnath of the daughters of the Philistines: now therefore get her for me to wife.

3 Then his father and his mother said to him, Is there never a woman among the daughters of your brethren, or among all my people, that you go to take a wife of the uncircumcised Philistines? And Samson said to his father, Get her for me; for she pleases me well.

4 But his father and his mother knew not that it was of the LORD, that he sought an occasion against the Philistines: for at that time the Philistines had dominion over Israel.

5 Then went Samson down, and his father and his mother, to Timnath, and came to the vineyards of Timnath: and, behold, a young lion roared against him.

6 And the Spirit of the LORD came mightily upon him, and he rent him as he would have rent a kid, and he had nothing in his hand: but he told not his father or his mother what he had done.

7 And he went down, and talked with the woman; and she pleased Samson well.

8 And after a time he returned to take her, and he turned aside to see the carcase of the lion: and, behold, there was a swarm of bees and honey in the carcase of the lion.

9 And he took thereof in his hands, and went on eating, and came to his father and mother, and he gave them, and they did eat: but he told not them that he had taken the honey out of the carcase of the lion.

10 So his father went down to the woman: and Samson made there a feast; for so used the young men to do.

11 And it came to pass, when they saw him, that they brought thirty companions to be with him.

12 And Samson said to them, I will now put forth a riddle to you: if you can certainly declare it me within the seven days of the feast, and find it out, then I will give you thirty sheets and thirty change of garments:

13 But if you cannot declare it me, then shall you give me thirty sheets and thirty change of garments. And they said to him, Put forth your riddle, that we may hear it.

14 And he said to them, Out of the eater came forth meat, and out of the strong came forth sweetness. And they could not in three days expound the riddle.

15 And it came to pass on the seventh day, that they said to Samson's wife, Entice your husband, that he may declare to us the riddle, lest we burn you and your father's house with fire: have you called us to take that we have? is it not so?

16 And Samson's wife wept before him, and said, You dost but hate me, and love me not: you have put forth a riddle to the children of my people, and have not told it me. And he said to her, Behold, I have not told it my father nor my mother, and shall I tell it to you?

17 And she wept before him the seven days, while their feast lasted: and it came to pass on the seventh day, that he told her, because she lay sore upon him: and she told the riddle to the children of her people.

18 And the men of the city said to him on the seventh day before the sun went

down, What is sweeter than honey? And what is stronger than a lion? and he said to them, If you had not plowed with my heifer, you had not found out my riddle.
19 And the Spirit of the LORD came upon him, and he went down to Ashkelon, and slew thirty men of them, and took their spoil, and gave change of garments to them which expounded the riddle. And his anger was kindled, and he went up to his father's house.
20 But Samson's wife was given to his companion, whom he had used as his friend.

CHAPTER 15

BUT it came to pass within a while after, in the time of wheat harvest, that Samson visited his wife with a kid; and he said, I will go in to my wife into the chamber. But her father would not suffer him to go in.
2 And her father said, I verily thought that you had utterly hated her; therefore I gave her to your companion: is not her younger sister fairer than she? take her, I pray you, instead of her.
3 And Samson said concerning them, Now shall I be more blameless than the Philistines, though I do them a displeasure.
4 And Samson went and caught three hundred foxes, and took firebrands, and turned tail to tail, and put a firebrand in the midst between two tails.
5 And when he had set the brands on fire, he let them go into the standing corn of the Philistines, and burnt up both the shocks, and also the standing corn, with the vineyards and olives.
6 Then the Philistines said, Who has done this? And they answered, Samson, the son in law of the Timnite, because he had taken his wife, and given her to his companion. And the Philistines came up, and burnt her and her father with fire.
7 And Samson said to them, Though you have done this, yet will I be avenged of you, and after that I will cease.

8 And he smote them hip and thigh with a great slaughter: and he went down and dwelt in the top of the rock Etam.
9 Then the Philistines went up, and pitched in Judah, and spread themselves in Lehi.
10 And the men of Judah said, Why are you come up against us? And they answered, To bind Samson are we come up, to do to him as he has done to us.
11 Then three thousand men of Judah went to the top of the rock Etam, and said to Samson, Know you not that the Philistines are rulers over us? what is this that you have done to us? And he said to them, As they did to me, so have I done to them.
12 And they said to him, We are come down to bind you, that we may deliver you into the hand of the Philistines. And Samson said to them, Swear to me, that you will not fall upon me yourselves.
13 And they spoke to him, saying, No; but we will bind you fast, and deliver you into their hand: but surely we will not kill you. And they bound him with two new cords, and brought him up from the rock.
14 And when he came to Lehi, the Philistines shouted against him: and the Spirit of the LORD came mightily upon him, and the cords that were upon his arms became as flax that was burnt with fire, and his bands loosed from off his hands.
15 And he found a new jawbone of an ass, and put forth his hand, and took it, and slew a thousand men therewith.
16 And Samson said, With the jawbone of an ass, heaps upon heaps, with the jaw of an ass have I slain a thousand men.
17 And it came to pass, when he had made an end of speaking, that he cast away the jawbone out of his hand, and called that place Ramathlehi.
18 And he was sore athirst, and called on the LORD, and said, You have given this great deliverance into the hand of

SAMSON AND DELILAH

Judges 16:4-20

your servant: and now shall I die for thirst, and fall into the hand of the uncircumcised?

19 But God clave an hollow place that was in the jaw, and there came water thereout; and when he had drunk, his spirit came again, and he revived: therefore he called the name thereof Enhakkore, which is in Lehi to this day.

20 And he judged Israel in the days of the Philistines twenty years.

CHAPTER 16

THEN went Samson to Gaza, and saw there an harlot, and went in to her.

2 And it was told the Gazites, saying, Samson is come here. And they compassed him in, and laid wait for him all night in the gate of the city, and were quiet all the night, saying, In the morning, when it is day, we shall kill him.

3 And Samson lay till midnight, and arose at midnight, and took the doors of the gate of the city, and the two posts,

and went away with them, bar and all, and put them upon his shoulders, and carried them up to the top of an hill that is before Hebron.

4 And it came to pass afterward, that he loved a woman in the valley of Sorek, whose name was Delilah.

5 And the lords of the Philistines came up to her, and said to her, Entice him, and see wherein his great strength lieth, and by what means we may prevail against him, that we may bind him to afflict him; and we will give you every one of us eleven hundred pieces of silver.

6 And Delilah said to Samson, Tell me, I pray you, wherein your great strength lies, and wherewith you might be bound to afflict you.

7 And Samson said to her, If they bind me with seven green withs that were never dried, then shall I be weak, and be as another man.

8 Then the lords of the Philistines brought up to her seven green withs which had not been dried, and she bound him with them.

9 Now there were men lying in wait, abiding with her in the chamber. And she said to him, The Philistines be upon you, Samson. And he brake the withs, as a thread of tow is broken when it touches the fire. So his strength was not known.

10 And Delilah said to Samson, Behold, you have mocked me, and told me lies: now tell me, I pray you, wherewith you might be bound.

11 And he said to her, If they bind me fast with new ropes that never were occupied, then shall I be weak, and be as another man.

12 Delilah therefore took new ropes, and bound him therewith, and said to him, The Philistines be upon you, Samson. And there were liers in wait abiding in the chamber. And he brake them from off his arms like a thread.

13 And Delilah said to Samson, Until now you have mocked me, and told me lies: tell me wherewith you might be bound. And he said to her, If you weave the seven locks of my head with the web.

14 And she fastened it with the pin, and said to him, The Philistines be upon you, Samson. And he awaked out of his sleep, and went away with the pin of the beam, and with the web.

15 And she said to him, How canst you say, I love you, when your heart is not with me? you have mocked me these three times, and have not told me wherein your great strength lieth.

16 And it came to pass, when she pressed him daily with her words, and urged him, so that his soul was vexed to death;

17 That he told her all his heart, and said to her, There has not come a razor upon mine head; for I have been a Nazarite to God from my mother's womb: if I be shaven, then my strength will go from me, and I shall become weak, and be like any other man.

18 And when Delilah saw that he had told her all his heart, she sent and called for the lords of the Philistines, saying, Come up this once, for he has showed me all his heart. Then the lords of the Philistines came up to her, and brought money in their hand.

19 And she made him sleep upon her knees; and she called for a man, and she caused him to shave off the seven locks of his head; and she began to afflict him, and his strength went from him.

20 And she said, The Philistines be upon you, Samson. And he awoke out of his sleep, and said, I will go out as at other times before, and shake myself. And he knew not that the LORD was departed from him.

21 But the Philistines took him, and put out his eyes, and brought him down to Gaza, and bound him with fetters of brass; and he did grind in the prison house.

22 Howbeit the hair of his head began to grow again after he was shaven.

DEATH OF SAMSON

Judges 16:25-30

The enemy has blinded the Church as to the use of God's law in evangelism. Be the lad who takes the hands of the blinded Church and places them on the pillars of God's Law. Then we will see a revival of the power of the Church.

23 Then the lords of the Philistines gathered them together for to offer a great sacrifice to Dagon their god, and to rejoice: for they said, Our god has delivered Samson our enemy into our hand.

24 And when the people saw him, they praised their god: for they said, Our god has delivered into our hands our enemy, and the destroyer of our country, which slew many of us.

25 And it came to pass, when their hearts were merry, that they said, Call for Samson, that he may make us sport. And they called for Samson out of the

prison house; and he made them sport: and they set him between the pillars.

26 And Samson said to the lad that held him by the hand, Suffer me that I may feel the pillars whereupon the house stands, that I may lean upon them.

27 Now the house was full of men and women; and all the lords of the Philistines were there; and there were upon the roof about three thousand men and women, that beheld while Samson made sport.

28 And Samson called to the LORD, and said, O Lord God, remember me, I pray you, and strengthen me, I pray you, only this once, O God, that I may be at once avenged of the Philistines for my two eyes.

29 And Samson took hold of the two middle pillars upon which the house stood, and on which it was borne up, of the one with his right hand, and of the other with his left.

30 And Samson said, Let me die with the Philistines. And he bowed himself with all his might; and the house fell upon the lords, and upon all the people that were therein. So the dead which he slew at his death were more than they which he slew in his life.

31 Then his brethren and all the house of his father came down, and took him, and brought him up, and buried him between Zorah and Eshtaol in the burying-place of Manoah his father. And he judged Israel twenty years.

CHAPTER 17

AND there was a man of mount Ephraim, whose name was Micah.

2 And he said to his mother, The eleven hundred shekels of silver that were taken from you, about which you cursed, and spoke of also in mine ears, behold, the silver is with me; I took it. And his mother said, Blessed be you of the LORD, my son.

3 And when he had restored the eleven hundred shekels of silver to his mother, his mother said, I had wholly dedicated the silver to the LORD from my hand for my son, to make a graven image and a molten image: now therefore I will restore it to you.

4 Yet he restored the money to his mother; and his mother took two hundred shekels of silver, and gave them to the founder, who made thereof a graven image and a molten image: and they were in the house of Micah.

5 And the man Micah had an house of gods, and made an ephod, and teraphim, and consecrated one of his sons, who became his priest.

6 In those days there was no king in Israel, but every man did that which was right in his own eyes.

7 And there was a young man out of Bethlehemjudah of the family of Judah, who was a Levite, and he sojourned there.

8 And the man departed out of the city from Bethlehemjudah to sojourn where he could find a place: and he came to mount Ephraim to the house of Micah, as he journeyed.

9 And Micah said to him, Where do you come from? And he said to him, I am a Levite of Bethlehemjudah, and I go to sojourn where I may find a place.

10 And Micah said to him, Dwell with me, and be to me a father and a priest, and I will give you ten shekels of silver by the year, and a suit of apparel, and your victuals. So the Levite went in.

11 And the Levite was content to dwell with the man; and the young man was to him as one of his sons.

12 And Micah consecrated the Levite; and the young man became his priest, and was in the house of Micah.

13 Then said Micah, Now know I that the LORD will do me good, seeing I have a Levite to my priest.

CHAPTER 18

IN those days there was no king in Israel: and in those days the tribe of the Danites sought them an inheritance to dwell in; for to that day all their inheritance had not fallen to them among the tribes of Israel.

2 And the children of Dan sent of their family five men from their coasts, men of valour, from Zorah, and from Eshtaol, to spy out the land, and to search it; and they said to them, Go, search the land: who when they came to mount Ephraim, to the house of Micah, they lodged there.

3 When they were by the house of Micah, they knew the voice of the young man the Levite: and they turned in there, and said to him, Who brought you here? and what are you doing in this place? and what have you here?

4 And he said to them, Thus and thus deals Micah with me, and has hired me, and I am his priest.

5 And they said to him, Ask counsel, we pray you, of God, that we may know whether our way which we go shall be prosperous.

6 And the priest said to them, Go in peace: before the LORD is your way wherein you go.

7 Then the five men departed, and came to Laish, and saw the people that were therein, how they dwelt careless, after the manner of the Zidonians, quiet and secure; and there was no magistrate in the land, that might put them to shame in any thing; and they were far from the Zidonians, and had no business with any man.

8 And they came to their brethren to Zorah and Eshtaol: and their brethren said to them, What do you report?

9 And they said, Arise, that we may go up against them: for we have seen the land, and, behold, it is very good: and are you still? be not slothful to go, and to enter to possess the land.

10 When you go, you shall come to a people secure, and to a large land: for God has given it into your hands; a place where there is no want of any thing that is in the earth.

11 And there went from thence of the family of the Danites, out of Zorah and out of Eshtaol, six hundred men appointed with weapons of war.

12 And they went up, and pitched in Kirjathjearim, in Judah: therefore they called that place Mahanehdan to this day: behold, it is behind Kirjathjearim.

13 And they passed thence to mount Ephraim, and came to the house of Micah.

14 Then answered the five men that went to spy out the country of Laish, and said to their brethren, Do you know that there is in these houses an ephod, and teraphim, and a graven image, and a molten image? now therefore consider what you have to do.

15 And they turned aside there, and came to the house of the young man the Levite, even to the house of Micah, and saluted him.

16 And the six hundred men appointed with their weapons of war, which were of the children of Dan, stood by the entering of the gate.

17 And the five men that went to spy out the land went up, and came in there, and took the graven image, and the ephod, and the teraphim, and the molten image: and the priest stood in the entering of the gate with the six hundred men that were appointed with weapons of war.

18 And these went into Micah's house, and fetched the carved image, the ephod, and the teraphim, and the molten image. Then said the priest to them, What are you doing?

19 And they said to him, Hold your peace, lay your hand upon your mouth, and go with us, and be to us a father and a priest: is it better for you to be a priest to the house of one man, or that you be a priest to a tribe and a family in Israel?

20 And the priest's heart was glad, and he took the ephod, and the teraphim, and the graven image, and went in the midst of the people.

21 So they turned and departed, and put the little ones and the cattle and the carriage before them.

22 And when they were a good way from the house of Micah, the men that were in the houses near to Micah's house were gathered together, and overtook the children of Dan.

23 And they cried to the children of Dan. And they turned their faces, and said to Micah, What ails you, that you come with such a company?

24 And he said, You have taken away my gods which I made, and the priest, and you are gone away: and what have I more? and what is this that you say to me, What ails you?

25 And the children of Dan said to him, Let not your voice be heard among us, lest angry fellows run upon you, and you lose your life, with the lives of your household.

26 And the children of Dan went their way: and when Micah saw that they were too strong for him, he turned and went back to his house.

27 And they took the things which Micah had made, and the priest which he had, and came to Laish, to a people that were at quiet and secure: and they smote them with the edge of the sword, and burnt the city with fire.

28 And there was no deliverer, because it was far from Zidon, and they had no business with any man; and it was in the valley that lieth by Bethrehob. And they built a city, and dwelt therein.

29 And they called the name of the city Dan, after the name of Dan their father, who was born to Israel: howbeit the name of the city was Laish at the first.

30 And the children of Dan set up the graven image: and Jonathan, the son of Gershom, the son of Manasseh, he and his sons were priests to the tribe of Dan until the day of the captivity of the land.

31 And they set them up Micah's graven image, which he made, all the time that the house of God was in Shiloh.

CHAPTER 19

AND it came to pass in those days, when there was no king in Israel, that there was a certain Levite sojourning on the side of mount Ephraim, who took to him a concubine out of Bethlehemjudah.

2 And his concubine played the whore against him, and went away from him to her father's house to Bethlehemjudah, and was there four whole months.

3 And her husband arose, and went after her, to speak friendly to her, and to bring her again, having his servant with him, and a couple of asses: and she brought him into her father's house: and when the father of the damsel saw him, he rejoiced to meet him.

4 And his father in law, the damsel's father, retained him; and he abode with him three days: so they did eat and drink, and lodged there.

5 And it came to pass on the fourth day, when they arose early in the morning, that he rose up to depart: and the damsel's father said to his son in law, Comfort your heart with a morsel of bread, and afterward go your way.

6 And they sat down, and did eat and drink both of them together: for the damsel's father had said to the man, Be content, I pray you, and tarry all night, and let your heart be merry.

7 And when the man rose up to depart, his father in law urged him: therefore he lodged there again.

8 And he arose early in the morning on the fifth day to depart; and the damsel's father said, Comfort your heart, I pray you. And they tarried until afternoon, and they did eat both of them.

9 And when the man rose up to depart, he, and his concubine, and his servant, his father in law, the damsel's father, said to him, Behold, now the day draws toward evening, I pray you tarry all night: behold, the day grows to an end, lodge here, that your heart may be merry; and to morrow get you early on your way, that you may go home.

10 But the man would not tarry that night, but he rose up and departed, and came over against Jebus, which is Jerusalem; and there were with him two asses saddled, his concubine also was with him.

11 And when they were by Jebus, the day was far spent; and the servant said to his master, Come, I pray you, and let us turn in into this city of the Jebusites, and lodge in it.

12 And his master said to him, We will not turn aside there into the city of a stranger, that is not of the children of Israel; we will pass over to Gibeah.

13 And he said to his servant, Come, and let us draw near to one of these places to lodge all night, in Gibeah, or in Ramah.

14 And they passed on and went their way; and the sun went down upon them when they were by Gibeah, which belongs to Benjamin.

15 And they turned aside there, to go in and to lodge in Gibeah: and when he went in, he sat him down in a street of the city: for there was no man that took them into his house to lodging.

16 And, behold, there came an old man from his work out of the field at even, which was also of mount Ephraim; and he sojourned in Gibeah: but the men of the place were Benjamites.

17 And when he had lifted up his eyes, he saw a wayfaring man in the street of the city: and the old man said, Where are you going? and where do you come from?

18 And he said to him, We are passing from Bethlehemjudah toward the side of mount Ephraim; from thence am I: and I went to Bethlehemjudah, but I am now going to the house of the LORD; and there is no man that receives me to house.

19 Yet there is both straw and provender for our asses; and there is bread and wine also for me, and for your handmaid, and for the young man which is with your servants: there is no want of any thing.

20 And the old man said, Peace be with you; howsoever let all your wants lie upon me; only lodge not in the street.

21 So he brought him into his house, and gave provender to the asses: and they washed their feet, and did eat and drink.

22 Now as they were making their hearts merry, behold, the men of the city, certain sons of Belial, beset the house round about, and beat at the door, and spoke to the master of the house, the old man, saying, Bring forth the man that came into your house, that we may know him.

23 And the man, the master of the house, went out to them, and said to them, Nay, my brethren, nay, I pray you, do not so wickedly; seeing that this man is come into mine house, do not this folly.

24 Behold, here is my daughter a maiden, and his concubine; them I will bring out now, and humble you them, and do with them what seems good to you: but to this man do not so vile a thing.

25 But the men would not hearken to him: so the man took his concubine, and brought her forth to them; and they knew her, and abused her all the night until the morning: and when the day began to spring, they let her go.

26 Then came the woman in the dawning of the day, and fell down at the door of the man's house where her lord was, till it was light.

27 And her lord rose up in the morning, and opened the doors of the house, and went out to go his way: and, behold, the woman his concubine was fallen down at the door of the house, and her hands were upon the threshold.

28 And he said to her, Up, and let us be going. But none answered. Then the man took her up upon an ass, and the man rose up, and gat him to his place.

29 And when he was come into his house, he took a knife, and laid hold on

his concubine, and divided her, together with her bones, into twelve pieces, and sent her into all the coasts of Israel.

30 And it was so, that all that saw it said, There was no such deed done nor seen from the day that the children of Israel came up out of the land of Egypt to this day: consider of it, take advice, and speak your minds.

CHAPTER 20

THEN all the children of Israel went out, and the congregation was gathered together as one man, from Dan even to Beersheba, with the land of Gilead, to the LORD in Mizpeh.

2 And the chief of all the people, even of all the tribes of Israel, presented themselves in the assembly of the people of God, four hundred thousand footmen that drew sword.

3 (Now the children of Benjamin heard that the children of Israel were gone up to Mizpeh.) Then said the children of Israel, Tell us, how was this wickedness?

4 And the Levite, the husband of the woman that was slain, answered and said, I came into Gibeah that belongs to Benjamin, I and my concubine, to lodge.

5 And the men of Gibeah rose against me, and beset the house round about upon me by night, and thought to have slain me: and my concubine have they forced, that she is dead.

6 And I took my concubine, and cut her in pieces, and sent her throughout all the country of the inheritance of Israel: for they have committed lewdness and folly in Israel.

7 Behold, you are all children of Israel; give here your advice and counsel.

8 And all the people arose as one man, saying, We will not any of us go to his tent, neither will we any of us turn into his house.

9 But now this shall be the thing which we will do to Gibeah; we will go up by lot against it;

10 And we will take ten men of an hundred throughout all the tribes of Israel, and an hundred of a thousand, and a thousand out of ten thousand, to fetch victual for the people, that they may do, when they come to Gibeah of Benjamin, according to all the folly that they have wrought in Israel.

11 So all the men of Israel were gathered against the city, knit together as one man.

12 And the tribes of Israel sent men through all the tribe of Benjamin, saying, What wickedness is this that is done among you?

13 Now therefore deliver us the men, the children of Belial, which are in Gibeah, that we may put them to death, and put away evil from Israel. But the children of Benjamin would not hearken to the voice of their brethren the children of Israel.

14 But the children of Benjamin gathered themselves together out of the cities to Gibeah, to go out to battle against the children of Israel.

15 And the children of Benjamin were numbered at that time out of the cities twenty and six thousand men that drew sword, beside the inhabitants of Gibeah, which were numbered seven hundred chosen men.

16 Among all this people there were seven hundred chosen men lefthanded; every one could sling stones at an hair breadth, and not miss.

17 And the men of Israel, beside Benjamin, were numbered four hundred thousand men that drew sword: all these were men of war.

18 And the children of Israel arose, and went up to the house of God, and asked counsel of God, and said, Which of us shall go up first to the battle against the children of Benjamin? And the LORD said, Judah shall go up first.

19 And the children of Israel rose up in the morning, and encamped against Gibeah.

20 And the men of Israel went out to battle against Benjamin; and the men of

Israel put themselves in array to fight against them at Gibeah.

21 And the children of Benjamin came forth out of Gibeah, and destroyed down to the ground of the Israelites that day twenty and two thousand men.

22 And the people the men of Israel encouraged themselves, and set their battle again in array in the place where they put themselves in array the first day.

23 (And the children of Israel went up and wept before the LORD until even, and asked counsel of the LORD, saying, Shall I go up again to battle against the children of Benjamin my brother? And the LORD said, Go up against him.)

24 And the children of Israel came near against the children of Benjamin the second day.

25 And Benjamin went forth against them out of Gibeah the second day, and destroyed down to the ground of the children of Israel again eighteen thousand men; all these drew the sword.

26 Then all the children of Israel, and all the people, went up, and came to the house of God, and wept, and sat there before the LORD, and fasted that day until even, and offered burnt offerings and peace offerings before the LORD.

27 And the children of Israel enquired of the LORD, (for the ark of the covenant of God was there in those days,

28 And Phinehas, the son of Eleazar, the son of Aaron, stood before it in those days,) saying, Shall I yet again go out to battle against the children of Benjamin my brother, or shall I cease? And the LORD said, Go up; for tomorrow I will deliver them into your hand.

29 And Israel set liers in wait round about Gibeah.

30 And the children of Israel went up against the children of Benjamin on the third day, and put themselves in array against Gibeah, as at other times.

31 And the children of Benjamin went out against the people, and were drawn away from the city; and they began to smite of the people, and kill, as at other times, in the highways, of which one goeth up to the house of God, and the other to Gibeah in the field, about thirty men of Israel.

32 And the children of Benjamin said, They are smitten down before us, as at the first. But the children of Israel said, Let us flee, and draw them from the city to the highways.

33 And all the men of Israel rose up out of their place, and put themselves in array at Baaltamar: and the liers in wait of Israel came forth out of their places, even out of the meadows of Gibeah.

34 And there came against Gibeah ten thousand chosen men out of all Israel, and the battle was sore: but they knew not that evil was near them.

35 And the LORD smote Benjamin before Israel: and the children of Israel destroyed of the Benjamites that day twenty and five thousand and an hundred men: all these drew the sword.

36 So the children of Benjamin saw that they were smitten: for the men of Israel gave place to the Benjamites, because they trusted to the liers in wait which they had set beside Gibeah.

37 And the liers in wait hasted, and rushed upon Gibeah; and the liers in wait drew themselves along, and smote all the city with the edge of the sword.

38 Now there was an appointed sign between the men of Israel and the liers in wait, that they should make a great flame with smoke rise up out of the city.

39 And when the men of Israel retired in the battle, Benjamin began to smite and kill of the men of Israel about thirty persons: for they said, Surely they are smitten down before us, as in the first battle.

40 But when the flame began to arise up out of the city with a pillar of smoke, the Benjamites looked behind them, and, behold, the flame of the city ascended up to heaven.

41 And when the men of Israel turned again, the men of Benjamin were

amazed: for they saw that evil was come upon them.

42 Therefore they turned their backs before the men of Israel to the way of the wilderness; but the battle overtook them; and them which came out of the cities they destroyed in the midst of them.

43 Thus they inclosed the Benjamites round about, and chased them, and trode them down with ease over against Gibeah toward the sunrising.

44 And there fell of Benjamin eighteen thousand men; all these were men of valour.

45 And they turned and fled toward the wilderness to the rock of Rimmon: and they gleaned of them in the highways five thousand men; and pursued hard after them to Gidom, and slew two thousand men of them.

46 So that all which fell that day of Benjamin were twenty and five thousand men that drew the sword; all these were men of valour.

47 But six hundred men turned and fled to the wilderness to the rock Rimmon, and abode in the rock Rimmon four months.

48 And the men of Israel turned again upon the children of Benjamin, and smote them with the edge of the sword, as well the men of every city, as the beast, and all that came to hand: also they set on fire all the cities that they came to.

CHAPTER 21

NOW the men of Israel had sworn in Mizpeh, saying, There shall not any of us give his daughter to Benjamin to wife.

2 And the people came to the house of God, and abode there till even before God, and lifted up their voices, and wept sore;

3 And said, O LORD God of Israel, why is this come to pass in Israel, that there should be to day one tribe lacking in Israel?

4 And it came to pass on the morrow, that the people rose early, and built there an altar, and offered burnt offerings and peace offerings.

5 And the children of Israel said, Who is there among all the tribes of Israel that came not up with the congregation to the LORD? For they had made a great oath concerning him that came not up to the LORD to Mizpeh, saying, He shall surely be put to death.

6 And the children of Israel repented them for Benjamin their brother, and said, There is one tribe cut off from Israel this day.

7 How shall we do for wives for them that remain, seeing we have sworn by the LORD that we will not give them of our daughters to wives?

8 And they said, What one is there of the tribes of Israel that came not up to Mizpeh to the LORD? And, behold, there came none to the camp from Jabeshgilead to the assembly.

9 For the people were numbered, and, behold, there were none of the inhabitants of Jabeshgilead there.

10 And the congregation sent there twelve thousand of the most valiant men, and commanded them, saying, Go and smite the inhabitants of Jabeshgilead with the edge of the sword, with the women and the children.

11 And this is the thing that you shall do, You shall utterly destroy every male, and every woman that has lain by man.

12 And they found among the inhabitants of Jabeshgilead four hundred young virgins, that had known no man by lying with any male: and they brought them to the camp to Shiloh, which is in the land of Canaan.

13 And the whole congregation sent some to speak to the children of Benjamin that were in the rock Rimmon, and to call peaceably to them.

14 And Benjamin came again at that time; and they gave them wives which they had saved alive of the women of

Ruth

CHAPTER 1

NOW it came to pass in the days when the judges ruled, that there was a famine in the land. And a certain man of Bethlehemjudah went to sojourn in the country of Moab, he, and his wife, and his two sons.

2 And the name of the man was Elimelech, and the name of his wife Naomi, and the name of his two sons Mahlon and Chilion, Ephrathites of Bethlehemjudah. And they came into the country of Moab, and continued there.

3 And Elimelech Naomi's husband died; and she was left, and her two sons.

4 And they took them wives of the women of Moab; the name of the one was Orpah, and the name of the other Ruth: and they dwelled there about ten years.

5 And Mahlon and Chilion died also both of them; and the woman was left of her two sons and her husband.

6 Then she arose with her daughters in law, that she might return from the country of Moab: for she had heard in the country of Moab how that the LORD had visited his people in giving them bread.

7 Therefore she went forth out of the place where she was, and her two daughters in law with her; and they went on the way to return to the land of Judah.

8 And Naomi said to her two daughters in law, Go, return each to her mother's house: the LORD deal kindly with you, as you have dealt with the dead, and with me.

9 The LORD grant you that you may find rest, each of you in the house of her husband. Then she kissed them; and they lifted up their voice, and wept.

10 And they said to her, Surely we will return with you to your people.

11 And Naomi said, Turn again, my daughters: why will you go with me? are there yet any more sons in my womb, that they may be your husbands?

12 Turn again, my daughters, go your way; for I am too old to have an husband. If I should say, I have hope, if I should have an husband also tonight, and should also bear sons;

13 Would you tarry for them till they were grown? would you stay for them from having husbands? nay, my daughters; for it grieves me much for your sakes that the hand of the LORD is gone out against me.

14 And they lifted up their voice, and wept again: and Orpah kissed her mother in law; but Ruth clave to her.

15 And she said, Behold, your sister in law is gone back to her people, and to her gods: return you after your sister in law.

16 And Ruth said, Intreat me not to leave you, or to return from following after you: for where you go, I will go; and where you lodge, I will lodge:

NAOMI AND HER DAUGHTERS IN LAW

Ruth 1:15

your people shall be my people, and your God my God:

17 Where you die, will I die, and there will I be buried: the LORD do so to me, and more also, if ought but death part you and me.

18 When she saw that she was stedfastly minded to go with her, then she left speaking to her.

19 So they two went until they came to Bethlehem. And it came to pass, when they were come to Bethlehem, that all the city was moved about them, and they said, Is this Naomi?

20 And she said to them, Call me not Naomi, call me Mara: for the Almighty has dealt very bitterly with me.

21 I went out full and the LORD has brought me home again empty: why then do you call me Naomi, seeing the LORD has testified against me, and the Almighty has afflicted me?

22 So Naomi returned, and Ruth the Moabitess, her daughter in law, with her, which returned out of the country of Moab: and they came to Bethlehem in the beginning of barley harvest.

BOAZ AND RUTH

Ruth 2:12-16

CHAPTER 2

AND Naomi had a kinsman of her husband's, a mighty man of wealth, of the family of Elimelech; and his name was Boaz.

2 And Ruth the Moabitess said to Naomi, Let me now go to the field, and glean ears of corn after him in whose sight I shall find grace. And she said to her, Go, my daughter.

3 And she went, and came, and gleaned in the field after the reapers: and her hap was to light on a part of the field belonging to Boaz, who was of the kindred of Elimelech.

4 And, behold, Boaz came from Bethlehem, and said to the reapers, The LORD be with you. And they answered him, The LORD bless you.

5 Then said Boaz to his servant that was set over the reapers, Whose damsel is this?

6 And the servant that was set over the reapers answered and said, It is the Moabitish damsel that came back with Naomi out of the country of Moab:

7 And she said, I pray you, let me glean and gather after the reapers among the sheaves: so she came, and has continued even from the morning until now, that she tarried a little in the house.

8 Then said Boaz to Ruth, Hear you not, my daughter? Go not to glean in another field, neither go from hence, but abide here fast by my maidens:

9 Let your eyes be on the field that they do reap, and go after them: have I not charged the young men that they shall not touch you? and when you are athirst, go to the vessels, and drink of that which the young men have drawn.

10 Then she fell on her face, and bowed herself to the ground, and said to him, Why have I found grace in your eyes, that you should take knowledge of me, seeing I am a stranger?

11 And Boaz answered and said to her, It has fully been showed me, all that you have done to your mother in law since the death of your husband: and how you have left your father and your mother, and the land of your nativity, and are come to a people which you knew not heretofore.

12 **The LORD recompense your work, and a full reward be given you of the LORD God of Israel, under whose wings you are come to trust.**

13 Then she said, Let me find favour in your sight, my lord; for that you have comforted me, and for that you have spoken friendly to your handmaid, though I be not like one of your handmaidens.

14 And Boaz said to her, at mealtime come here, and eat of the bread, and dip your morsel in the vinegar. And she sat beside the reapers: and he reached her parched corn, and she did eat, and was sufficed, and left.

15 And when she was risen up to glean, Boaz commanded his young men, saying, Let her glean even among the sheaves, and reproach her not:

16 And let fall also some of the handfuls on purpose for her, and leave them, that she may glean them, and rebuke her not.

17 So she gleaned in the field until even, and beat out that she had gleaned: and it was about an ephah of barley.

18 And she took it up, and went into the city: and her mother in law saw what she had gleaned: and she brought forth, and gave to her that she had reserved after she was sufficed.

19 And her mother in law said to her, Where have you gleaned today? and where did you work? blessed be he that did take knowledge of you. And she showed her mother in law with whom she had wrought, and said, The man's name with whom I wrought today is Boaz.

20 And Naomi said to her daughter in law, Blessed be he of the LORD, who has not left off his kindness to the living and to the dead. And Naomi said to her, The man is near of kin to us, one of our next kinsmen.

21 And Ruth the Moabitess said, He said to me also, You shall keep fast by my young men, until they have ended all my harvest.

22 And Naomi said to Ruth her daughter in law, It is good, my daughter, that you go out with his maidens, that they meet you not in any other field.

23 So she kept fast by the maidens of Boaz to glean to the end of barley harvest and of wheat harvest; and dwelt with her mother in law.

CHAPTER 3

THEN Naomi her mother in law said to her, My daughter, shall I not seek rest for you, that it may be well with you?

2 And now is not Boaz of our kindred, with whose maidens you were? Behold, he winnows barley tonight in the threshing floor.

3 Wash yourself therefore, and anoint you, and put your raiment upon you, and get down to the floor: but make not

yourself known to the man, until he shall have done eating and drinking.

4 And it shall be, when he lieth down, that you shall mark the place where he shall lie, and you shall go in, and uncover his feet, and lay down; and he will tell you what you shall do.

5 And she said to her, All that you say to me I will do.

6 And she went down to the floor, and did according to all that her mother in law bade her.

7 And when Boaz had eaten and drunk, and his heart was merry, he went to lie down at the end of the heap of corn: and she came softly, and uncovered his feet, and laid her down.

8 And it came to pass at midnight, that the man was afraid, and turned himself: and, behold, a woman lay at his feet.

9 And he said, Who are you? And she answered, I am Ruth your handmaid: spread therefore your skirt over your handmaid; for you are a near kinsman.

10 And he said, Blessed are you of the LORD, my daughter: for you have showed more kindness in the latter end than at the beginning, inasmuch as you followed not young men, whether poor or rich.

11 And now, my daughter, fear not; I will do to you all that you require: for all the city of my people know that you are a virtuous woman.

12 And now it is true that I am your near kinsman: howbeit there is a kinsman nearer than I.

13 Tarry this night, and it shall be in the morning, that if he will perform to you the part of a kinsman, well; let him do the kinsman's part: but if he will not do the part of a kinsman to you, then will I do the part of a kinsman to you, as the LORD lives: lie down until the morning.

14 And she lay at his feet until the morning: and she rose up before one could know another. And he said, Let it not be known that a woman came into the floor.

15 Also he said, Bring the vail that you have upon you, and hold it. And when she held it, he measured six measures of barley, and laid it on her: and she went into the city.

16 And when she came to her mother in law, she said, Who are you, my daughter? And she told her all that the man had done to her.

17 And she said, These six measures of barley gave he me; for he said to me, Go not empty to your mother in law.

18 Then said she, Sit still, my daughter, until you know how the matter will fall: for the man will not be in rest, until he have finished the thing this day.

CHAPTER 4

THEN went Boaz up to the gate, and sat him down there: and, behold, the kinsman of whom Boaz spoke came by; to whom he said, Ho, such a one! turn aside, sit down here. And he turned aside, and sat down.

2 And he took ten men of the elders of the city, and said, Sit down here. And they sat down.

3 And he said to the kinsman, Naomi, that is come again out of the country of Moab, sells a parcel of land, which was our brother Elimelech's:

4 And I thought to advertise you, saying, Buy it before the inhabitants, and before the elders of my people. If you will redeem it, redeem it: but if you will not redeem it, then tell me, that I may know: for there is none to redeem it beside you; and I am after you. And he said, I will redeem it.

5 Then said Boaz, What day you buy the field of the hand of Naomi, you must buy it also of Ruth the Moabitess, the wife of the dead, to raise up the name of the dead upon his inheritance.

6 And the kinsman said, I cannot redeem it for myself, lest I mar mine own inheritance: you redeem my right to yourself; for I cannot redeem it.

7 Now this was the manner in former time in Israel concerning redeeming and

*I have found that there are three stages
in every great work of God:
first it is impossible, then it is difficult,
then it is done.*

James H. Taylor
1832-1905
PIONEER MISSIONARY

concerning changing, for to confirm all things; a man plucked off his shoe, and gave it to his neighbour: and this was a testimony in Israel.

8 Therefore the kinsman said to Boaz, Buy it for yourself. So he drew off his shoe.

9 And Boaz said to the elders, and to all the people, You are witnesses this day, that I have bought all that was Elimelech's, and all that was Chilion's and Mahlon's, of the hand of Naomi.

10 Moreover Ruth the Moabitess, the wife of Mahlon, have I purchased to be my wife, to raise up the name of the dead upon his inheritance, that the name of the dead be not cut off from among his brethren, and from the gate of his place: you are witnesses this day.

11 And all the people that were in the gate, and the elders, said, We are witnesses. The LORD make the woman that is come into your house like Rachel and like Leah, which two did build the house of Israel: and you do worthily in Ephratah, and be famous in Bethlehem:

12 And let your house be like the house of Pharez, whom Tamar bare to Judah, of the seed which the LORD shall give you of this young woman.

13 So Boaz took Ruth, and she was his wife: and when he went in to her, the LORD gave her conception, and she bare a son.

14 And the women said to Naomi, Blessed be the LORD, which has not left you this day without a kinsman, that his name may be famous in Israel.

15 And he shall be to you a restorer of your life, and a nourisher of your old age: for your daughter in law, which loves you, which is better to you than seven sons, has born him.

16 And Naomi took the child, and laid it in her bosom, and became nurse to it.

17 And the women her neighbours gave it a name, saying, There is a son born to Naomi; and they called his name Obed: he is the father of Jesse, the father of David.

18 Now these are the generations of Pharez: Pharez begat Hezron,

19 And Hezron begat Ram, and Ram begat Amminadab,

20 And Amminadab begat Nahshon, and Nahshon begat Salmon,

21 And Salmon begat Boaz, and Boaz begat Obed,

22 And Obed begat Jesse, and Jesse begat David.

1 Samuel

CHAPTER 1

NOW there was a certain man of Ramathaimzophim, of mount Ephraim, and his name was Elkanah, the son of Jeroham, the son of Elihu, the son of Tohu, the son of Zuph, an Ephrathite:
2 And he had two wives; the name of the one was Hannah, and the name of the other Peninnah: and Peninnah had children, but Hannah had no children.
3 And this man went up out of his city yearly to worship and to sacrifice to the LORD of hosts in Shiloh. And the two sons of Eli, Hophni and Phinehas, the priests of the LORD, were there.
4 And when the time was that Elkanah offered, he gave to Peninnah his wife, and to all her sons and her daughters, portions:
5 But to Hannah he gave a worthy portion; for he loved Hannah: but the LORD had shut up her womb.
6 And her adversary also provoked her sore, for to make her fret, because the LORD had shut up her womb.
7 And as he did so year by year, when she went up to the house of the LORD, so she provoked her; therefore she wept, and did not eat.
8 Then said Elkanah her husband to her, Hannah, why do you weep? and why do you not eat? and why is your heart grieved? am not I better to you than ten sons?
9 So Hannah rose up after they had eaten in Shiloh, and after they had drunk. Now Eli the priest sat upon a seat by a post of the temple of the LORD.
10 And she was in bitterness of soul, and prayed to the LORD, and wept sore.
11 And she vowed a vow, and said, O LORD of hosts, if you will indeed look on the affliction of your handmaid, and remember me, and not forget your handmaid, but will give to your handmaid a man child, then I will give him to the LORD all the days of his life, and there shall no razor come upon his head.
12 And it came to pass, as she continued praying before the LORD, that Eli marked her mouth.
13 Now Hannah, she spoke in her heart; only her lips moved, but her voice was not heard: therefore Eli thought she had been drunken.
14 And Eli said to her, How long will you be drunken? put away your wine from you.
15 And Hannah answered and said, No, my lord, I am a woman of a sorrowful spirit: I have drunk neither wine nor strong drink, but have poured out my soul before the LORD.
16 Count not your handmaid for a daughter of Belial: for out of the abundance of my complaint and grief have I spoken hitherto.
17 Then Eli answered and said, Go in peace: and the God of Israel grant your petition that you have asked of him.
18 And she said, Let your handmaid find grace in your sight. So the woman

went her way, and did eat, and her countenance was no more sad.

19 And they rose up in the morning early, and worshipped before the LORD, and returned, and came to their house to Ramah: and Elkanah knew Hannah his wife; and the LORD remembered her.

20 Therefore it came to pass, when the time was come about after Hannah had conceived, that she bare a son, and called his name Samuel, saying, Because I have asked him of the LORD.

21 And the man Elkanah, and all his house, went up to offer to the LORD the yearly sacrifice, and his vow.

22 But Hannah went not up; for she said to her husband, I will not go up until the child be weaned, and then I will bring him, that he may appear before the LORD, and there abide for ever.

23 And Elkanah her husband said to her, Do what seems good to you; tarry until you have weaned him; only the LORD establish his word. So the woman abode, and gave her son suck until she weaned him.

24 And when she had weaned him, she took him up with her, with three bullocks, and one ephah of flour, and a bottle of wine, and brought him to the house of the LORD in Shiloh: and the child was young.

25 And they slew a bullock, and brought the child to Eli.

26 And she said, Oh my lord, as your soul lives, my lord, I am the woman that stood by you here, praying to the LORD.

27 For this child I prayed; and the LORD has given me my petition which I asked of him:

28 Therefore also I have lent him to the LORD; as long as he lives he shall be lent to the LORD. And he worshipped the LORD there.

CHAPTER 2

AND Hannah prayed, and said, My heart rejoices in the LORD, mine horn is exalted in the LORD: my mouth is enlarged over mine enemies; because I rejoice in your salvation.

2 There is none holy as the LORD: for there is none beside you: neither is there any rock like our God.

3 Talk no more so exceeding proudly; let not arrogancy come out of your mouth: for the LORD is a God of knowledge, and by him actions are weighed.

4 The bows of the mighty men are broken, and they that stumbled are girded with strength.

5 They that were full have hired out themselves for bread; and they that were hungry ceased: so that the barren has born seven; and she that has many children is waxed feeble.

6 The LORD kills, and makes alive: he brings down to the grave, and brings up.

7 The LORD makes poor, and makes rich: he brings low, and lifts up.

8 He raises up the poor out of the dust, and lifts up the beggar from the dunghill, to set them among princes, and to make them inherit the throne of glory: for the pillars of the earth are the LORD's, and he has set the world upon them.

9 He will keep the feet of his saints, and the wicked shall be silent in darkness; for by strength shall no man prevail.

10 The adversaries of the LORD shall be broken to pieces; out of heaven shall he thunder upon them: the LORD shall judge the ends of the earth; and he shall give strength to his king, and exalt the horn of his anointed.

11 And Elkanah went to Ramah to his house. And the child did minister to the LORD before Eli the priest.

12 Now the sons of Eli were sons of Belial; they knew not the LORD.

13 And the priest's custom with the people was, that, when any man offered sacrifice, the priest's servant came,

while the flesh was in seething, with a fleshhook of three teeth in his hand;

14 And he struck it into the pan, or kettle, or caldron, or pot; all that the fleshhook brought up the priest took for himself. So they did in Shiloh to all the Israelites that came there.

15 Also before they burnt the fat, the priest's servant came, and said to the man that sacrificed, Give flesh to roast for the priest; for he will not have sodden flesh of you, but raw.

16 And if any man said to him, Let them not fail to burn the fat presently, and then take as much as your soul desires; then he would answer him, Nay; but you shall give it me now: and if not, I will take it by force.

17 Therefore the sin of the young men was very great before the LORD: for men abhorred the offering of the LORD.

18 But Samuel ministered before the LORD, being a child, girded with a linen ephod.

19 Moreover his mother made him a little coat, and brought it to him from year to year, when she came up with her husband to offer the yearly sacrifice.

20 And Eli blessed Elkanah and his wife, and said, The LORD give you seed of this woman for the loan which is lent to the LORD. And they went to their own home.

21 And the LORD visited Hannah, so that she conceived, and bare three sons and two daughters. And the child Samuel grew before the LORD.

22 Now Eli was very old, and heard all that his sons did to all Israel; and how they lay with the women that assembled at the door of the tabernacle of the congregation.

23 And he said to them, Why do you do such things? for I hear of your evil dealings by all this people.

24 Nay, my sons; for it is no good report that I hear: you make the LORD's people to transgress.

25 If one man sin against another, the judge shall judge him: but if a man sin against the LORD, who shall intreat for him? Notwithstanding they hearkened not to the voice of their father, because the LORD would slay them.

26 And the child Samuel grew on, and was in favour both with the LORD, and also with men.

27 And there came a man of God to Eli, and said to him, Thus says the LORD, Did I plainly appear to the house of your father, when they were in Egypt in Pharaoh's house?

28 And did I choose him out of all the tribes of Israel to be my priest, to offer upon mine altar, to burn incense, to wear an ephod before me? and did I give to the house of your father all the offerings made by fire of the children of Israel?

29 Why do you kick at my sacrifice and at mine offering, which I have commanded in my habitation; and honourest your sons above me, to make yourselves fat with the chiefest of all the offerings of Israel my people?

30 Therefore the LORD God of Israel says, I said indeed that your house, and the house of your father, should walk before me for ever: but now the LORD says, Be it far from me; for them that honour me I will honour, and they that despise me shall be lightly esteemed.

31 Behold, the days come, that I will cut off your arm, and the arm of your father's house, that there shall not be an old man in your house.

32 And you shall see an enemy in my habitation, in all the wealth which God shall give Israel: and there shall not be an old man in your house for ever.

33 And the man of yours, whom I shall not cut off from mine altar, shall be to consume your eyes, and to grieve your heart: and all the increase of your house shall die in the flower of their age.

34 And this shall be a sign to you, that shall come upon your two sons, on Hophni and Phinehas; in one day they shall die both of them.

35 And I will raise me up a faithful priest, that shall do according to that which is in mine heart and in my mind: and I will build him a sure house; and he shall walk before mine anointed for ever.

36 And it shall come to pass, that every one that is left in your house shall come and crouch to him for a piece of silver and a morsel of bread, and shall say, Put me, I pray you, into one of the priests' offices, that I may eat a piece of bread.

CHAPTER 3

A ND the child Samuel ministered to the LORD before Eli. And the word of the LORD was precious in those days; there was no open vision.

2 And it came to pass at that time, when Eli was laid down in his place, and his eyes began to wax dim, that he could not see;

3 And ere the lamp of God went out in the temple of the LORD, where the ark of God was, and Samuel was laid down to sleep;

4 That the LORD called Samuel: and he answered, Here am I.

5 And he ran to Eli, and said, Here am I; for you called me. And he said, I called not; lie down again. And he went and lay down.

6 And the LORD called yet again, Samuel. And Samuel arose and went to Eli, and said, Here am I; for you did call me. And he answered, I called not, my son; lie down again.

7 Now Samuel did not yet know the LORD, neither was the word of the LORD yet revealed to him.

8 And the LORD called Samuel again the third time. And he arose and went to Eli, and said, Here am I; for you did call me. And Eli perceived that the LORD had called the child.

9 Therefore Eli said to Samuel, Go, lie down: and it shall be, if he call you, that you shall say, Speak, LORD; for your servant hears. So Samuel went and lay down in his place.

10 And the LORD came, and stood, and called as at other times, Samuel, Samuel. Then Samuel answered, Speak; for your servant hears.

11 And the LORD said to Samuel, Behold, I will do a thing in Israel, at which both the ears of every one that hears it shall tingle.

12 In that day I will perform against Eli all things which I have spoken concerning his house: when I begin, I will also make an end.

13 For I have told him that I will judge his house for ever for the iniquity which he knows; because his sons made themselves vile, and he restrained them not.

14 And therefore I have sworn to the house of Eli, that the iniquity of Eli's house shall not be purged with sacrifice nor offering for ever.

15 And Samuel lay until the morning, and opened the doors of the house of the LORD. And Samuel feared to show Eli the vision.

16 Then Eli called Samuel, and said, Samuel, my son. And he answered, Here am I.

17 And he said, What is the thing that the LORD has said to you? I pray you hide it not from me: God do so to you, and more also, if you hide any thing from me of all the things that he said to you.

18 And Samuel told him every whit, and hid nothing from him. And he said, It is the LORD: let him do what seems him good.

19 And Samuel grew, and the LORD was with him, and did let none of his words fall to the ground.

20 And all Israel from Dan even to Beersheba knew that Samuel was established to be a prophet of the LORD.

21 And the LORD appeared again in Shiloh: for the LORD revealed himself to Samuel in Shiloh by the word of the LORD.

CHAPTER 4

AND the word of Samuel came to all Israel. Now Israel went out against the Philistines to battle, and pitched beside Ebenezer: and the Philistines pitched in Aphek.

2 And the Philistines put themselves in array against Israel: and when they joined battle, Israel was smitten before the Philistines: and they slew of the army in the field about four thousand men.

3 And when the people were come into the camp, the elders of Israel said, Why has the LORD smitten us to day before the Philistines? Let us fetch the ark of the covenant of the LORD out of Shiloh to us, that, when it cometh among us, it may save us out of the hand of our enemies.

4 So the people sent to Shiloh, that they might bring from thence the ark of the covenant of the LORD of hosts, which dwells between the cherubims: and the two sons of Eli, Hophni and Phinehas, were there with the ark of the covenant of God.

5 And when the ark of the covenant of the LORD came into the camp, all Israel shouted with a great shout, so that the earth rang again.

6 And when the Philistines heard the noise of the shout, they said, What does the noise of this great shout in the camp of the Hebrews mean? And they understood that the ark of the LORD was come into the camp.

7 And the Philistines were afraid, for they said, God is come into the camp. And they said, Woe to us! for there has not been such a thing heretofore.

8 Woe to us! who shall deliver us out of the hand of these mighty Gods? these are the Gods that smote the Egyptians with all the plagues in the wilderness.

9 Be strong and quit yourselves like men, O you Philistines, that you be not servants to the Hebrews, as they have been to you: quit yourselves like men, and fight.

10 And the Philistines fought, and Israel was smitten, and they fled every man into his tent: and there was a very great slaughter; for there fell of Israel thirty thousand footmen.

11 And the ark of God was taken; and the two sons of Eli, Hophni and Phinehas, were slain.

12 And there ran a man of Benjamin out of the army, and came to Shiloh the same day with his clothes rent, and with earth upon his head.

13 And when he came, lo, Eli sat upon a seat by the wayside watching: for his heart trembled for the ark of God. And when the man came into the city, and told it, all the city cried out.

14 And when Eli heard the noise of the crying, he said, What does the noise of this tumult mean? And the man came in hastily, and told Eli.

15 Now Eli was ninety and eight years old; and his eyes were dim, that he could not see.

16 And the man said to Eli, I am he that came out of the army, and I fled to day out of the army. And he said, What is there done, my son?

17 And the messenger answered and said, Israel is fled before the Philistines, and there has been also a great slaughter among the people, and your two sons also, Hophni and Phinehas, are dead, and the ark of God is taken.

18 And it came to pass, when he made mention of the ark of God, that he fell from off the seat backward by the side of the gate, and his neck brake, and he died: for he was an old man, and heavy. And he had judged Israel forty years.

19 And his daughter in law, Phinehas' wife, was with child, near to be delivered: and when she heard the tidings that the ark of God was taken, and that her father in law and her husband were dead, she bowed herself and travailed; for her pains came upon her.

20 And about the time of her death the women that stood by her said to her, Fear not; for you have born a son. But

she answered not, neither did she regard it.

21 And she named the child Ichabod, saying, The glory is departed from Israel: because the ark of God was taken, and because of her father in law and her husband.

22 And she said, The glory is departed from Israel: for the ark of God is taken.

CHAPTER 5

AND the Philistines took the ark of God, and brought it from Ebenezer to Ashdod.

2 When the Philistines took the ark of God, they brought it into the house of Dagon, and set it by Dagon.

3 And when they of Ashdod arose early on the morrow, behold, Dagon was fallen upon his face to the earth before the ark of the LORD. And they took Dagon, and set him in his place again.

4 And when they arose early on the morrow morning, behold, Dagon was fallen upon his face to the ground before the ark of the LORD; and the head of Dagon and both the palms of his hands were cut off upon the threshold; only the stump of Dagon was left to him.

5 Therefore neither the priests of Dagon, nor any that come into Dagon's house, tread on the threshold of Dagon in Ashdod to this day.

6 But the hand of the LORD was heavy upon them of Ashdod, and he destroyed them, and smote them with emerods, even Ashdod and the coasts thereof.

7 And when the men of Ashdod saw that it was so, they said, The ark of the God of Israel shall not abide with us: for his hand is sore upon us, and upon Dagon our god.

8 They sent therefore and gathered all the lords of the Philistines to them, and said, What shall we do with the ark of the God of Israel? And they answered, Let the ark of the God of Israel be carried about to Gath. And they carried the ark of the God of Israel about there.

9 And it was so, that, after they had carried it about, the hand of the LORD was against the city with a very great destruction: and he smote the men of the city, both small and great, and they had emerods in their secret parts.

10 Therefore they sent the ark of God to Ekron. And it came to pass, as the ark of God came to Ekron, that the Ekronites cried out, saying, They have brought about the ark of the God of Israel to us, to slay us and our people.

11 So they sent and gathered together all the lords of the Philistines, and said, Send away the ark of the God of Israel, and let it go again to his own place, that it slay us not, and our people: for there was a deadly destruction throughout all the city; the hand of God was very heavy there.

12 And the men that died not were smitten with the emerods: and the cry of the city went up to heaven.

CHAPTER 6

AND the ark of the LORD was in the country of the Philistines seven months.

2 And the Philistines called for the priests and the diviners, saying, What shall we do to the ark of the LORD? tell us wherewith we shall send it to his place.

3 And they said, If you send away the ark of the God of Israel, send it not empty; but in any wise return him a trespass offering: then you shall be healed, and it shall be known to you why his hand is not removed from you.

4 Then said they, What shall be the trespass offering which we shall return to him? They answered, Five golden emerods, and five golden mice, according to the number of the lords of the Philistines: for one plague was on you all, and on your lords.

5 Therefore you shall make images of your emerods, and images of your mice that mar the land; and you shall give glory to the God of Israel: peradventure

RETURN OF THE ARK TO BETH-SHEMESH

1 Samuel 6:13

he will lighten his hand from off you, and from off your gods, and from off your land.

6 Why then do you harden your hearts, as the Egyptians and Pharaoh hardened their hearts? when he had wrought wonderfully among them, did they not let the people go, and they departed?

7 Now therefore make a new cart, and take two milch kine, on which there has come no yoke, and tie the kine to the cart, and bring their calves home from them:

8 And take the ark of the LORD, and lay it upon the cart; and put the jewels of gold, which you return him for a trespass offering, in a coffer by the side thereof; and send it away, that it may go.

9 And see, if it goeth up by the way of his own coast to Bethshemesh, then he has done us this great evil: but if not, then we shall know that it is not his hand that smote us: it was a chance that happened to us.

10 And the men did so; and took two milch kine, and tied them to the cart, and shut up their calves at home:

11 And they laid the ark of the LORD upon the cart, and the coffer with the mice of gold and the images of their emerods.

12 And the kine took the straight way to the way of Bethshemesh, and went along the highway, lowing as they went, and turned not aside to the right hand or to the left; and the lords of the Philistines went after them to the border of Bethshemesh.

13 And they of Bethshemesh were reaping their wheat harvest in the valley: and they lifted up their eyes, and saw the ark, and rejoiced to see it.

14 And the cart came into the field of Joshua, a Bethshemite, and stood there, where there was a great stone: and they clave the wood of the cart, and offered the kine a burnt offering to the LORD.

15 And the Levites took down the ark of the LORD, and the coffer that was with it, wherein the jewels of gold were, and put them on the great stone: and the men of Bethshemesh offered burnt offerings and sacrificed sacrifices the same day to the LORD.

16 And when the five lords of the Philistines had seen it, they returned to Ekron the same day.

17 And these are the golden emerods which the Philistines returned for a trespass offering to the LORD; for Ashdod one, for Gaza one, for Askelon one, for Gath one, for Ekron one;

18 And the golden mice, according to the number of all the cities of the Philistines belonging to the five lords, both of fenced cities, and of country villages, even to the great stone of Abel, whereon they set down the ark of the LORD: which stone remains to this day in the field of Joshua, the Bethshemite.

19 And he smote the men of Bethshemesh, because they had looked into the ark of the LORD, even he smote of the people fifty thousand and threescore and ten men: and the people lamented, because the LORD had smitten many of the people with a great slaughter.

20 And the men of Bethshemesh said, Who is able to stand before this holy LORD God? and to whom shall he go up from us?

21 And they sent messengers to the inhabitants of Kirjathjearim, saying, The Philistines have brought again the ark of the LORD; come down, and fetch it up to you.

CHAPTER 7

AND the men of Kirjathjearim came, and fetched up the ark of the LORD, and brought it into the house of Abinadab in the hill, and sanctified Eleazar his son to keep the ark of the LORD.

2 And it came to pass, while the ark abode in Kirjathjearim, that the time was long; for it was twenty years: and all the house of Israel lamented after the LORD.

3 And Samuel spoke to all the house of Israel, saying, If you do return to the LORD with all your hearts, then put away the strange gods and Ashtaroth from among you, and prepare your hearts to the LORD, and serve him only: and he will deliver you out of the hand of the Philistines.

4 Then the children of Israel did put away Baalim and Ashtaroth, and served the LORD only.

5 And Samuel said, Gather all Israel to Mizpeh, and I will pray for you to the LORD.

6 And they gathered together to Mizpeh, and drew water, and poured it out before the LORD, and fasted on that day, and said there, We have sinned against the LORD. And Samuel judged the children of Israel in Mizpeh.

7 And when the Philistines heard that the children of Israel were gathered together to Mizpeh, the lords of the Philistines went up against Israel. And when the children of Israel heard it, they were afraid of the Philistines.

8 And the children of Israel said to Samuel, Cease not to cry to the LORD our God for us, that he will save us out of the hand of the Philistines.

9 And Samuel took a sucking lamb, and offered it for a burnt offering wholly to the LORD: and Samuel cried to the LORD for Israel; and the LORD heard him.

10 And as Samuel was offering up the burnt offering, the Philistines drew near to battle against Israel: but the LORD thundered with a great thunder on that day upon the Philistines, and discomfited them; and they were smitten before Israel.

11 And the men of Israel went out of Mizpeh, and pursued the Philistines, and smote them, until they came under Bethcar.

12 Then Samuel took a stone, and set it between Mizpeh and Shen, and called

the name of it Ebenezer, saying, Thus far has the LORD helped us.

13 So the Philistines were subdued, and they came no more into the coast of Israel: and the hand of the LORD was against the Philistines all the days of Samuel.

14 And the cities which the Philistines had taken from Israel were restored to Israel, from Ekron even to Gath; and the coasts thereof did Israel deliver out of the hands of the Philistines. And there was peace between Israel and the Amorites.

15 And Samuel judged Israel all the days of his life.

16 And he went from year to year in circuit to Bethel, and Gilgal, and Mizpeh, and judged Israel in all those places.

17 And his return was to Ramah; for there was his house; and there he judged Israel; and there he built an altar to the LORD.

CHAPTER 8

AND it came to pass, when Samuel was old, that he made his sons judges over Israel.

2 Now the name of his firstborn was Joel; and the name of his second, Abiah: they were judges in Beersheba.

3 And his sons walked not in his ways, but turned aside after lucre, and took bribes, and perverted judgment.

4 Then all the elders of Israel gathered themselves together, and came to Samuel to Ramah,

5 And said to him, Behold, you are old, and your sons walk not in your ways: now make us a king to judge us like all the nations.

6 But the thing displeased Samuel, when they said, Give us a king to judge us. And Samuel prayed to the LORD.

7 And the LORD said to Samuel, Hearken to the voice of the people in all that they say to you: for they have not rejected you, but they have rejected me, that I should not reign over them.

8 According to all the works which they have done since the day that I brought them up out of Egypt even to this day, wherewith they have forsaken me, and served other gods, so do they also to you.

9 Now therefore hearken to their voice: howbeit yet protest solemnly to them, and show them the manner of the king that shall reign over them.

10 And Samuel told all the words of the LORD to the people that asked of him a king.

11 And he said, This will be the manner of the king that shall reign over you: He will take your sons, and appoint them for himself, for his chariots, and to be his horsemen; and some shall run before his chariots.

12 And he will appoint him captains over thousands, and captains over fifties; and will set them to ear his ground, and to reap his harvest, and to make his instruments of war, and instruments of his chariots.

13 And he will take your daughters to be confectionaries, and to be cooks, and to be bakers.

14 And he will take your fields, and your vineyards, and your oliveyards, even the best of them, and give them to his servants.

15 And he will take the tenth of your seed, and of your vineyards, and give to his officers, and to his servants.

16 And he will take your menservants, and your maidservants, and your goodliest young men, and your asses, and put them to his work.

17 He will take the tenth of your sheep: and you shall be his servants.

18 And you shall cry out in that day because of your king which you shall have chosen you; and the LORD will not hear you in that day.

19 Nevertheless the people refused to obey the voice of Samuel; and they said, Nay; but we will have a king over us;

20 That we also may be like all the nations; and that our king may judge us,

and go out before us, and fight our battles.

21 And Samuel heard all the words of the people, and he rehearsed them in the ears of the LORD.

22 And the LORD said to Samuel, Hearken to their voice, and make them a king. And Samuel said to the men of Israel, Go every man to his city.

CHAPTER 9

NOW there was a man of Benjamin, whose name was Kish, the son of Abiel, the son of Zeror, the son of Bechorath, the son of Aphiah, a Benjamite, a mighty man of power.

2 And he had a son, whose name was Saul, a choice young man, and a goodly: and there was not among the children of Israel a goodlier person than he: from his shoulders and upward he was higher than any of the people.

3 And the asses of Kish Saul's father were lost. And Kish said to Saul his son, Take now one of the servants with you, and arise, go seek the asses.

4 And he passed through mount Ephraim, and passed through the land of Shalisha, but they found them not: then they passed through the land of Shalim, and there they were not: and he passed through the land of the Benjamites, but they found them not.

5 And when they were come to the land of Zuph, Saul said to his servant that was with him, Come, and let us return; lest my father leave caring for the asses, and take thought for us.

6 And he said to him, Behold now, there is in this city a man of God, and he is an honourable man; all that he says cometh surely to pass: now let us go there; peradventure he can show us our way that we should go.

7 Then said Saul to his servant, But, behold, if we go, what shall we bring the man? for the bread is spent in our vessels, and there is not a present to bring to the man of God: what have we?

8 And the servant answered Saul again, and said, Behold, I have here at hand the fourth part of a shekel of silver: that will I give to the man of God, to tell us our way.

9 (Beforetime in Israel, when a man went to inquire of God, thus he spoke, Come, and let us go to the seer: for he that is now called a Prophet was beforetime called a Seer.)

10 Then said Saul to his servant, Well said; come, let us go. So they went to the city where the man of God was.

11 And as they went up the hill to the city, they found young maidens going out to draw water, and said to them, Is the seer here?

12 And they answered them, and said, He is; behold, he is before you: make haste now, for he came to day to the city; for there is a sacrifice of the people to day in the high place:

13 As soon as you come into the city, you shall straightway find him, before he go up to the high place to eat: for the people will not eat until he come, because he does bless the sacrifice; and afterwards they eat that be bidden. Now therefore get you up; for about this time you shall find him.

14 And they went up into the city: and when they were come into the city, behold, Samuel came out against them, for to go up to the high place.

15 Now the LORD had told Samuel in his ear a day before Saul came, saying,

16 Tomorrow about this time I will send you a man out of the land of Benjamin, and you shall anoint him to be captain over my people Israel, that he may save my people out of the hand of the Philistines: for I have looked upon my people, because their cry is come to me.

17 And when Samuel saw Saul, the LORD said to him, Behold the man whom I spoke to you of! this same shall reign over my people.

18 Then Saul drew near to Samuel in the gate, and said, Tell me, I pray you, where the seer's house is.

SAMUEL BLESSING SAUL

1 Samuel 9:17

19 And Samuel answered Saul, and said, I am the seer: go up before me to the high place; for you shall eat with me to day, and tomorrow I will let you go, and will tell you all that is in your heart.

20 And as for your asses that were lost three days ago, set not your mind on them; for they are found. And on whom is all the desire of Israel? Is it not on you, and on all your father's house?

21 And Saul answered and said, Am not I a Benjamite, of the smallest of the tribes of Israel? and my family the least of all the families of the tribe of Benjamin? Why then do you speak like this to me?

22 And Samuel took Saul and his servant, and brought them into the parlour, and made them sit in the chiefest place among them that were bidden, which were about thirty persons.

23 And Samuel said to the cook, Bring the portion which I gave you, of which I said to you, Set it by you.

24 And the cook took up the shoulder, and that which was upon it, and set it before Saul. And Samuel said, Behold that which is left! set it before you, and eat: for to this time has it been kept for you since I said, I have invited the people. So Saul did eat with Samuel that day.

25 And when they were come down from the high place into the city, Samuel communed with Saul upon the top of the house.

26 And they arose early: and it came to pass about the spring of the day, that Samuel called Saul to the top of the house, saying, Up, that I may send you away. And Saul arose, and they went out both of them, he and Samuel, abroad.

27 And as they were going down to the end of the city, Samuel said to Saul, Bid the servant pass on before us, (and he passed on), but you stand still a while, that I may show you the word of God.

CHAPTER 10

THEN Samuel took a vial of oil, and poured it upon his head, and kissed him, and said, Is it not because the LORD has anointed you to be captain over his inheritance?

2 When you are departed from me to day, then you shall find two men by Rachel's sepulchre in the border of Benjamin at Zelzah; and they will say to you, The asses which you went to seek are found: and, lo, your father has left the care of the asses, and sorrows for you, saying, What shall I do for my son?

3 Then shall you go on forward from thence, and you shall come to the plain of Tabor, and there shall meet you three men going up to God to Bethel, one carrying three kids, and another carrying three loaves of bread, and another carrying a bottle of wine:

4 And they will salute you, and give you two loaves of bread; which you shall receive of their hands.

5 After that you shall come to the hill of God, where is the garrison of the Philistines: and it shall come to pass, when you are come there to the city, that you shall meet a company of prophets coming down from the high place with a psaltery, and a tabret, and a pipe, and a harp, before them; and they shall prophesy:

6 And the Spirit of the LORD will come upon you, and you shall prophesy with them, and shalt be turned into another man.

7 And let it be, when these signs are come to you, that you do as occasion serve you; for God is with you.

8 And you shall go down before me to Gilgal; and, behold, I will come down to you, to offer burnt offerings, and to sacrifice sacrifices of peace offerings: seven days shall you tarry, till I come to you, and show you what you shall do.

9 And it was so, that when he had turned his back to go from Samuel, God gave him another heart: and all those signs came to pass that day.

10 And when they came there to the hill, behold, a company of prophets met him; and the Spirit of God came upon him, and he prophesied among them.

11 And it came to pass, when all that knew him beforetime saw that, behold, he prophesied among the prophets, then the people said one to another, What is this that is come to the son of Kish? Is Saul also among the prophets?

12 And one of the same place answered and said, But who is their father?

Therefore it became a proverb, Is Saul also among the prophets?

13 And when he had made an end of prophesying, he came to the high place.

14 And Saul's uncle said to him and to his servant, Where did you go? And he said, To seek the asses: and when we saw that they were no where, we came to Samuel.

15 And Saul's uncle said, Tell me, I pray you, what Samuel said to you.

16 And Saul said to his uncle, He told us plainly that the asses were found. But of the matter of the kingdom, whereof Samuel spoke, he told him not.

17 And Samuel called the people together to the LORD to Mizpeh;

18 And said to the children of Israel, Thus says the LORD God of Israel, I brought up Israel out of Egypt, and delivered you out of the hand of the Egyptians, and out of the hand of all kingdoms, and of them that oppressed you:

19 And you have this day rejected your God, who himself saved you out of all your adversities and your tribulations; and you have said to him, Nay, but set a king over us. Now therefore present yourselves before the LORD by your tribes, and by your thousands.

20 And when Samuel had caused all the tribes of Israel to come near, the tribe of Benjamin was taken.

21 When he had caused the tribe of Benjamin to come near by their families, the family of Matri was taken, and Saul the son of Kish was taken: and when they sought him, he could not be found.

22 Therefore they inquired of the LORD further, if the man should yet come there. And the LORD answered, Behold he has hid himself among the stuff.

23 And they ran and fetched him thence: and when he stood among the people, he was higher than any of the people from his shoulders and upward.

24 And Samuel said to all the people, Do you see him whom the LORD has chosen, that there is none like him among all the people? And all the people shouted, and said, God save the king.

25 Then Samuel told the people the manner of the kingdom, and wrote it in a book, and laid it up before the LORD. And Samuel sent all the people away, every man to his house.

26 And Saul also went home to Gibeah; and there went with him a band of men, whose hearts God had touched.

27 But the children of Belial said, How shall this man save us? And they despised him, and brought no presents. But he held his peace.

CHAPTER 11

THEN Nahash the Ammonite came up, and encamped against Jabeshgilead: and all the men of Jabesh said to Nahash, Make a covenant with us, and we will serve you.

2 And Nahash the Ammonite answered them, On this condition will I make a covenant with you, that I may thrust out all your right eyes, and lay it for a reproach upon all Israel.

3 And the elders of Jabesh said to him, Give us seven days' respite, that we may send messengers to all the coasts of Israel: and then, if there be no man to save us, we will come out to you.

4 Then came the messengers to Gibeah of Saul, and told the tidings in the ears of the people: and all the people lifted up their voices, and wept.

5 And, behold, Saul came after the herd out of the field; and Saul said, What ails the people that they weep? And they told him the tidings of the men of Jabesh.

6 And the Spirit of God came upon Saul when he heard those tidings, and his anger was kindled greatly.

7 And he took a yoke of oxen, and hewed them in pieces, and sent them throughout all the coasts of Israel by the hands of messengers, saying, Whosoever cometh not forth after Saul and after Samuel, so shall it be done to his oxen. And the fear of the LORD fell on the

people, and they came out with one consent.

8 And when he numbered them in Bezek, the children of Israel were three hundred thousand, and the men of Judah thirty thousand.

9 And they said to the messengers that came, Thus shall you say to the men of Jabeshgilead, Tomorrow, by that time the sun be hot, you shall have help. And the messengers came and showed it to the men of Jabesh; and they were glad.

10 Therefore the men of Jabesh said, To morrow we will come out to you, and you shall do with us all that seems good to you.

11 And it was so on the morrow, that Saul put the people in three companies; and they came into the midst of the host in the morning watch, and slew the Ammonites until the heat of the day: and it came to pass, that they which remained were scattered, so that two of them were not left together.

12 And the people said to Samuel, Who is he that said, Shall Saul reign over us? bring the men, that we may put them to death.

13 And Saul said, There shall not a man be put to death this day: for to day the LORD has wrought salvation in Israel.

14 Then said Samuel to the people, Come, and let us go to Gilgal, and renew the kingdom there.

15 And all the people went to Gilgal; and there they made Saul king before the LORD in Gilgal; and there they sacrificed sacrifices of peace offerings before the LORD; and there Saul and all the men of Israel rejoiced greatly.

CHAPTER 12

AND Samuel said to all Israel, Behold, I have hearkened to your voice in all that you said to me, and have made a king over you.

2 And now, behold, the king walks before you: and I am old and grayheaded; and, behold, my sons are with you:

and I have walked before you from my childhood to this day.

3 Behold, here I am: witness against me before the LORD, and before his anointed: whose ox have I taken? or whose ass have I taken? or whom have I defrauded? whom have I oppressed? or of whose hand have I received any bribe to blind mine eyes therewith? and I will restore it you.

4 And they said, You have not defrauded us, nor oppressed us, neither have you taken ought of any man's hand.

5 And he said to them, The LORD is witness against you, and his anointed is witness this day, that you have not found ought in my hand. And they answered, He is witness.

6 And Samuel said to the people, It is the LORD that advanced Moses and Aaron, and that brought your fathers up out of the land of Egypt.

7 Now therefore stand still, that I may reason with you before the LORD of all the righteous acts of the LORD, which he did to you and to your fathers.

8 When Jacob was come into Egypt, and your fathers cried to the LORD, then the LORD sent Moses and Aaron, which brought forth your fathers out of Egypt, and made them dwell in this place.

9 And when they forgot the LORD their God, he sold them into the hand of Sisera, captain of the host of Hazor, and into the hand of the Philistines, and into the hand of the king of Moab, and they fought against them.

10 And they cried to the LORD, and said, We have sinned, because we have forsaken the LORD, and have served Baalim and Ashtaroth: but now deliver us out of the hand of our enemies, and we will serve you.

11 And the LORD sent Jerubbaal, and Bedan, and Jephthah, and Samuel, and delivered you out of the hand of your enemies on every side, and you dwelled safe.

12 And when you saw that Nahash the king of the children of Ammon came

against you, you said to me, Nay; but a king shall reign over us: when the LORD your God was your king.

13 Now therefore behold the king whom you have chosen, and whom you have desired! and, behold, the LORD has set a king over you.

14 If you will fear the LORD, and serve him, and obey his voice, and not rebel against the commandment of the LORD, then shall both you and also the king that reigns over you continue following the LORD your God:

15 But if you will not obey the voice of the LORD, but rebel against the commandment of the LORD, then shall the hand of the LORD be against you, as it was against your fathers.

16 Now therefore stand and see this great thing, which the LORD will do before your eyes.

17 Is it not wheat harvest to day? I will call to the LORD, and he shall send thunder and rain; that you may perceive and see that your wickedness is great, which you have done in the sight of the LORD, in asking you a king.

18 So Samuel called to the LORD; and the LORD sent thunder and rain that day: and all the people greatly feared the LORD and Samuel.

19 And all the people said to Samuel, Pray for your servants to the LORD your God, that we die not: for we have added to all our sins this evil, to ask us a king.

20 And Samuel said to the people, Fear not: you have done all this wickedness: yet turn not aside from following the LORD, but serve the LORD with all your heart;

21 And do not turn aside: for then should you go after vain things, which cannot profit nor deliver; for they are vain.

> "The ultimate proof of the sinner is that he doesn't know his own sin. Our job is to make him see it."
>
> **MARTIN LUTHER**
> 1483-1546
> GERMAN PRIEST
> FOUNDED THE LUTHERAN CHURCH

22 For the LORD will not forsake his people for his great name's sake: because it has pleased the LORD to make you his people.

23 Moreover as for me, God forbid that I should sin against the LORD in ceasing to pray for you: but I will teach you the good and the right way:

24 Only fear the LORD, and serve him in truth with all your heart: for consider how great things he has done for you.

25 But if you shall still do wickedly, you shall be consumed, both you and your king.

CHAPTER 13

SAUL reigned one year; and when he had reigned two years over Israel,

2 Saul chose him three thousand men of Israel; whereof two thousand were with Saul in Michmash and in mount Bethel, and a thousand were with Jonathan in Gibeah of Benjamin: and the rest of the people he sent every man to his tent.

3 And Jonathan smote the garrison of the Philistines that was in Geba, and the Philistines heard of it. And Saul blew the trumpet throughout all the land, saying, Let the Hebrews hear.

4 And all Israel heard say that Saul had smitten a garrison of the Philistines, and that Israel also was had in abomination with the Philistines. And the people were called together after Saul to Gilgal.

5 And the Philistines gathered themselves together to fight with Israel, thirty thousand chariots, and six thousand horsemen, and people as the sand which is on the sea shore in multitude: and they came up, and pitched in Michmash, eastward from Bethaven.

6 When the men of Israel saw that they were in a strait, (for the people were distressed,) then the people did hide them-

selves in caves, and in thickets, and in rocks, and in high places, and in pits.

7 And some of the Hebrews went over Jordan to the land of Gad and Gilead. As for Saul, he was yet in Gilgal, and all the people followed him trembling.

8 And he tarried seven days, according to the set time that Samuel had appointed: but Samuel came not to Gilgal; and the people were scattered from him.

9 And Saul said, Bring here a burnt offering to me, and peace offerings. And he offered the burnt offering.

10 And it came to pass, that as soon as he had made an end of offering the burnt offering, behold, Samuel came; and Saul went out to meet him, that he might salute him.

11 And Samuel said, What have you done? And Saul said, Because I saw that the people were scattered from me, and that you camest not within the days appointed, and that the Philistines gathered themselves together at Michmash;

12 Therefore said I, The Philistines will come down now upon me to Gilgal, and I have not made supplication to the LORD: I forced myself therefore, and offered a burnt offering.

13 And Samuel said to Saul, You have done foolishly: you have not kept the commandment of the LORD your God, which he commanded you: for now would the LORD have established your kingdom upon Israel for ever.

14 But now your kingdom shall not continue: the LORD has sought him a man after his own heart, and the LORD has commanded him to be captain over his people, because you have not kept that which the LORD commanded you.

15 And Samuel arose, and gat him up from Gilgal to Gibeah of Benjamin. And Saul numbered the people that were present with him, about six hundred men.

16 And Saul, and Jonathan his son, and the people that were present with them, abode in Gibeah of Benjamin: but the Philistines encamped in Michmash.

17 And the spoilers came out of the camp of the Philistines in three companies: one company turned to the way that leads to Ophrah, to the land of Shual:

18 And another company turned the way to Bethhoron: and another company turned to the way of the border that looks to the valley of Zeboim toward the wilderness.

19 Now there was no smith found throughout all the land of Israel: for the Philistines said, Lest the Hebrews make them swords or spears:

20 But all the Israelites went down to the Philistines, to sharpen every man his share, and his coulter, and his axe, and his mattock.

21 Yet they had a file for the mattocks, and for the coulters, and for the forks, and for the axes, and to sharpen the goads.

22 So it came to pass in the day of battle, that there was neither sword nor spear found in the hand of any of the people that were with Saul and Jonathan: but with Saul and with Jonathan his son was there found.

23 And the garrison of the Philistines went out to the passage of Michmash.

CHAPTER 14

N OW it came to pass upon a day, that Jonathan the son of Saul said to the young man that bare his armour, Come, and let us go over to the Philistines' garrison, that is on the other side. But he told not his father.

2 And Saul tarried in the uttermost part of Gibeah under a pomegranate tree which is in Migron: and the people that were with him were about six hundred men;

3 And Ahiah, the son of Ahitub, Ichabod's brother, the son of Phinehas, the son of Eli, the LORD's priest in Shiloh, wearing an ephod. And the people knew not that Jonathan was gone.

4 And between the passages, by which Jonathan sought to go over to the

Philistines' garrison, there was a sharp rock on the one side, and a sharp rock on the other side: and the name of the one was Bozez, and the name of the other Seneh.

5 The forefront of the one was situate northward over against Michmash, and the other southward over against Gibeah.

6 And Jonathan said to the young man that bare his armour, Come, and let us go over to the garrison of these uncircumcised: it may be that the LORD will work for us: for there is no restraint to the LORD to save by many or by few.

7 And his armourbearer said to him, Do all that is in your heart: turn yourself; behold, I am with you according to your heart.

8 Then said Jonathan, Behold, we will pass over to these men, and we will discover ourselves to them.

9 If they say thus to us, Tarry until we come to you; then we will stand still in our place, and will not go up to them.

10 But if they say thus, Come up to us; then we will go up: for the LORD has delivered them into our hand: and this shall be a sign to us.

11 And both of them discovered themselves to the garrison of the Philistines: and the Philistines said, Behold, the Hebrews come forth out of the holes where they had hid themselves.

12 And the men of the garrison answered Jonathan and his armourbearer, and said, Come up to us, and we will show you a thing. And Jonathan said to his armourbearer, Come up after me: for the LORD has delivered them into the hand of Israel.

13 And Jonathan climbed up upon his hands and upon his feet, and his armourbearer after him: and they fell before Jonathan; and his armourbearer slew after him.

14 And that first slaughter, which Jonathan and his armourbearer made, was about twenty men, within as it were an half acre of land, which a yoke of oxen might plow.

15 And there was trembling in the host, in the field, and among all the people: the garrison, and the spoilers, they also trembled, and the earth quaked: so it was a very great trembling.

16 And the watchmen of Saul in Gibeah of Benjamin looked; and, behold, the multitude melted away, and they went on beating down one another.

17 Then said Saul to the people that were with him, Number now, and see who is gone from us. And when they had numbered, behold, Jonathan and his armourbearer were not there.

18 And Saul said to Ahiah, Bring here the ark of God. For the ark of God was at that time with the children of Israel.

19 And it came to pass, while Saul talked to the priest, that the noise that was in the host of the Philistines went on and increased: and Saul said to the priest, Withdraw your hand.

20 And Saul and all the people that were with him assembled themselves, and they came to the battle: and, behold, every man's sword was against his fellow, and there was a very great discomfiture.

21 Moreover the Hebrews that were with the Philistines before that time, which went up with them into the camp from the country round about, even they also turned to be with the Israelites that were with Saul and Jonathan.

22 Likewise all the men of Israel which had hid themselves in mount Ephraim, when they heard that the Philistines fled, even they also followed hard after them in the battle.

23 So the LORD saved Israel that day: and the battle passed over to Bethaven.

24 And the men of Israel were distressed that day: for Saul had adjured the people, saying, Cursed be the man that eats any food until evening, that I may be avenged on mine enemies. So none of the people tasted any food.

25 And all they of the land came to a wood; and there was honey upon the ground.

26 And when the people were come into the wood, behold, the honey dropped; but no man put his hand to his mouth: for the people feared the oath.

27 But Jonathan heard not when his father charged the people with the oath: therefore he put forth the end of the rod that was in his hand, and dipped it in an honeycomb, and put his hand to his mouth; and his eyes were enlightened.

28 Then answered one of the people, and said, Your father straitly charged the people with an oath, saying, Cursed be the man that eats any food this day. And the people were faint.

29 Then said Jonathan, My father has troubled the land: see, I pray you, how mine eyes have been enlightened, because I tasted a little of this honey.

30 How much more, if haply the people had eaten freely to day of the spoil of their enemies which they found? for had there not been now a much greater slaughter among the Philistines?

31 And they smote the Philistines that day from Michmash to Aijalon: and the people were very faint.

32 And the people flew upon the spoil, and took sheep, and oxen, and calves, and slew them on the ground: and the people did eat them with the blood.

33 Then they told Saul, saying, Behold, the people sin against the LORD, in that they eat with the blood. And he said, You have transgressed: roll a great stone to me this day.

34 And Saul said, Disperse yourselves among the people, and say to them, Bring me here every man his ox, and every man his sheep, and slay them here, and eat; and sin not against the LORD in eating with the blood. And all the people brought every man his ox with him that night, and slew them there.

35 And Saul built an altar to the LORD: the same was the first altar that he built to the LORD.

36 And Saul said, Let us go down after the Philistines by night, and spoil them until the morning light, and let us not leave a man of them. And they said, Do whatsoever seems good to you. Then said the priest, Let us draw near here to God.

37 And Saul asked counsel of God, Shall I go down after the Philistines? will you deliver them into the hand of Israel? But he answered him not that day.

38 And Saul said, Draw near here, all the chief of the people: and know and see wherein this sin has been this day.

39 For, as the LORD lives, which saves Israel, though it be in Jonathan my son, he shall surely die. But there was not a man among all the people that answered him.

40 Then said he to all Israel, You be on one side, and I and Jonathan my son will be on the other side. And the people said to Saul, Do what seems good to you.

41 Therefore Saul said to the LORD God of Israel, Give a perfect lot. And Saul and Jonathan were taken: but the people escaped.

42 And Saul said, Cast lots between me and Jonathan my son. And Jonathan was taken.

43 Then Saul said to Jonathan, Tell me what you have done. And Jonathan told him, and said, I did but taste a little honey with the end of the rod that was in mine hand, and, lo, I must die.

44 And Saul answered, God do so and more also: for you shall surely die, Jonathan.

45 And the people said to Saul, Shall Jonathan die, who has wrought this great salvation in Israel? God forbid: as the

---

14:27 God's Law is the rod that dips into the honeycomb of the gospel. This Law enlightens the eyes. "The commandment of the Lord is pure, enlightening the eyes" (Psalm 19:8).

LORD lives, there shall not one hair of his head fall to the ground; for he has wrought with God this day. So the people rescued Jonathan, that he died not.

46 Then Saul went up from following the Philistines: and the Philistines went to their own place.

47 So Saul took the kingdom over Israel, and fought against all his enemies on every side, against Moab, and against the children of Ammon, and against Edom, and against the kings of Zobah, and against the Philistines: and wherever he turned himself, he vexed them.

48 And he gathered an host, and smote the Amalekites, and delivered Israel out of the hands of them that spoiled them.

49 Now the sons of Saul were Jonathan, and Ishui, and Melchishua: and the names of his two daughters were these; the name of the firstborn Merab, and the name of the younger Michal:

50 And the name of Saul's wife was Ahinoam, the daughter of Ahimaaz: and the name of the captain of his host was Abner, the son of Ner, Saul's uncle.

51 And Kish was the father of Saul; and Ner the father of Abner was the son of Abiel.

52 And there was sore war against the Philistines all the days of Saul: and when Saul saw any strong man, or any valiant man, he took him to him.

CHAPTER 15

SAMUEL also said to Saul, The LORD sent me to anoint you to be king over his people, over Israel: now therefore hearken to the voice of the words of the LORD.

2 Thus says the LORD of hosts, I remember that which Amalek did to Israel, how he laid wait for him in the way, when he came up from Egypt.

3 Now go and smite Amalek, and utterly destroy all that they have, and spare them not; but slay both man and woman, infant and suckling, ox and sheep, camel and ass.

4 And Saul gathered the people together, and numbered them in Telaim, two hundred thousand footmen, and ten thousand men of Judah.

5 And Saul came to a city of Amalek, and laid wait in the valley.

6 And Saul said to the Kenites, Go, depart, get you down from among the Amalekites, lest I destroy you with them: for you showed kindness to all the children of Israel, when they came up out of Egypt. So the Kenites departed from among the Amalekites.

7 And Saul smote the Amalekites from Havilah until you come to Shur, that is over against Egypt.

8 And he took Agag the king of the Amalekites alive, and utterly destroyed all the people with the edge of the sword.

9 But Saul and the people spared Agag, and the best of the sheep, and of the oxen, and of the fatlings, and the lambs, and all that was good, and would not utterly destroy them: but every thing that was vile and refuse, that they destroyed utterly.

10 Then came the word of the LORD to Samuel, saying,

11 It repented me that I have set up Saul to be king: for he is turned back from following me, and has not performed my commandments. And it grieved Samuel; and he cried to the LORD all night.

12 And when Samuel rose early to meet Saul in the morning, it was told Samuel, saying, Saul came to Carmel, and, behold, he set him up a place, and is gone about, and passed on, and gone down to Gilgal.

13 And Samuel came to Saul: and Saul said to him, Blessed are you of the LORD: I have performed the commandment of the LORD.

14 And Samuel said, What then is this bleating of the sheep in mine ears, and the lowing of the oxen which I hear?

15 And Saul said, They have brought them from the Amalekites: for the peo-

ple spared the best of the sheep and of the oxen, to sacrifice to the LORD your God; and the rest we have utterly destroyed.

16 Then Samuel said to Saul, Stay, and I will tell you what the LORD has said to me this night. And he said to him, Say on.

17 And Samuel said, When you were little in your own sight, were you not made the head of the tribes of Israel, and the LORD anointed you king over Israel?

18 And the LORD sent you on a journey, and said, Go and utterly destroy the sinners the Amalekites, and fight against them until they be consumed.

19 Why then did you not obey the voice of the LORD, but did fly upon the spoil, and did evil in the sight of the LORD?

20 And Saul said to Samuel, Yea, I have obeyed the voice of the LORD, and have gone the way which the LORD sent me, and have brought Agag the king of Amalek, and have utterly destroyed the Amalekites.

21 But the people took of the spoil, sheep and oxen, the chief of the things which should have been utterly destroyed, to sacrifice to the LORD your God in Gilgal.

22 And Samuel said, Has the LORD as great delight in burnt offerings and sacrifices, as in obeying the voice of the LORD? Behold, to obey is better than sacrifice, and to hearken than the fat of rams.

23 For rebellion is as the sin of witchcraft, and stubbornness is as iniquity and idolatry. Because you have rejected the word of the LORD, he has also rejected you from being king.

24 And Saul said to Samuel, I have sinned: for I have transgressed the commandment of the LORD, and your words: because I feared the people, and obeyed their voice.

25 Now therefore, I pray you, pardon my sin, and turn again with me, that I may worship the LORD.

26 And Samuel said to Saul, I will not return with you: for you have rejected the word of the LORD, and the LORD has rejected you from being king over Israel.

27 And as Samuel turned about to go away, he laid hold upon the skirt of his mantle, and it rent.

28 And Samuel said to him, The LORD has rent the kingdom of Israel from you this day, and has given it to a neighbour of your, that is better than you.

29 And also the Strength of Israel will not lie nor repent: for he is not a man, that he should repent.

30 Then he said, I have sinned: yet honour me now, I pray you, before the elders of my people, and before Israel, and turn again with me, that I may worship the LORD your God.

31 So Samuel turned again after Saul; and Saul worshipped the LORD.

32 Then said Samuel, Bring here to me Agag the king of the Amalekites. And Agag came to him delicately. And Agag said, Surely the bitterness of death is past.

33 And Samuel said, As the sword has made women childless, so shall your mother be childless among women. And Samuel hewed Agag in pieces before the LORD in Gilgal.

34 Then Samuel went to Ramah; and Saul went up to his house to Gibeah of Saul.

35 And Samuel came no more to see Saul until the day of his death: nevertheless Samuel mourned for Saul: and the LORD repented that he had made Saul king over Israel.

CHAPTER 16

AND the LORD said to Samuel, How long will you mourn for Saul, seeing I have rejected him from reigning over Israel? fill your horn with oil, and go, I will send you to Jesse the Bethlehemite: for I have provided me a king among his sons.

2 And Samuel said, How can I go? if Saul hear it, he will kill me. And the LORD said, Take an heifer with you, and say, I am come to sacrifice to the LORD.

3 And call Jesse to the sacrifice, and I will show you what you shall do: and you shall anoint to me him whom I name to you.

4 And Samuel did that which the LORD spoke, and came to Bethlehem. And the elders of the town trembled at his coming, and said, Do you come peaceably?

5 And he said, Peaceably: I am come to sacrifice to the LORD: sanctify yourselves, and come with me to the sacrifice. And he sanctified Jesse and his sons, and called them to the sacrifice.

6 And it came to pass, when they were come, that he looked on Eliab, and said, Surely the LORD's anointed is before him.

7 But the LORD said to Samuel, Look not on his countenance, or on the height of his stature; because I have refused him: for the LORD sees not as man sees; for man looks on the outward appearance, but the LORD looks on the heart.

8 Then Jesse called Abinadab, and made him pass before Samuel. And he said, Neither has the LORD chosen this.

9 Then Jesse made Shammah to pass by. And he said, Neither has the LORD chosen this.

10 Again, Jesse made seven of his sons to pass before Samuel. And Samuel said to Jesse, The LORD has not chosen these.

11 And Samuel said to Jesse, Are here all your children? And he said, There remains yet the youngest, and, behold, he keeps the sheep. And Samuel said to Jesse, Send and fetch him: for we will not sit down till he come here.

12 And he sent, and brought him in. Now he was ruddy, and withal of a beautiful countenance, and goodly to look to. And the LORD said, Arise, anoint him: for this is he.

13 Then Samuel took the horn of oil, and anointed him in the midst of his brethren: and the Spirit of the LORD came upon David from that day forward. So Samuel rose up, and went to Ramah.

14 But the Spirit of the LORD departed from Saul, and an evil spirit from the LORD troubled him.

15 And Saul's servants said to him, Behold now, an evil spirit from God troubles you.

16 Let our lord now command your servants, which are before you, to seek out a man, who is a cunning player on an harp: and it shall come to pass, when the evil spirit from God is upon you, that he shall play with his hand, and you shall be well.

17 And Saul said to his servants, Provide me now a man that can play well, and bring him to me.

18 Then answered one of the servants, and said, Behold, I have seen a son of Jesse the Bethlehemite, that is cunning in playing, and a mighty valiant man, and a man of war, and prudent in matters, and a comely person, and the LORD is with him.

19 Therefore Saul sent messengers to Jesse, and said, Send me David your son, which is with the sheep.

20 And Jesse took an ass laden with bread, and a bottle of wine, and a kid, and sent them by David his son to Saul.

21 And David came to Saul, and stood before him: and he loved him greatly; and he became his armourbearer.

22 And Saul sent to Jesse, saying, Let David, I pray you, stand before me; for he has found favour in my sight.

23 And it came to pass, when the evil spirit from God was upon Saul, that David took an harp, and played with his hand: so Saul was refreshed, and was

---

16:7 True repentance requires the understanding of how God looks at our hearts, our thought-life. He requires truth in the "inward parts" (Psalm 51:6).

well, and the evil spirit departed from him.

CHAPTER 17

NOW the Philistines gathered together their armies to battle, and were gathered together at Shochoh, which belongs to Judah, and pitched between Shochoh and Azekah, in Ephesdammim.

2 And Saul and the men of Israel were gathered together, and pitched by the valley of Elah, and set the battle in array against the Philistines.

3 And the Philistines stood on a mountain on the one side, and Israel stood on a mountain on the other side: and there was a valley between them.

4 And there went out a champion out of the camp of the Philistines, named Goliath, of Gath, whose height was six cubits and a span.

5 And he had an helmet of brass upon his head, and he was armed with a coat of mail; and the weight of the coat was five thousand shekels of brass.

6 And he had greaves of brass upon his legs, and a target of brass between his shoulders.

7 And the staff of his spear was like a weaver's beam; and his spear's head weighed six hundred shekels of iron: and one bearing a shield went before him.

8 And he stood and cried to the armies of Israel, and said to them, Why are you come out to set your battle in array? am not I a Philistine, and you servants to Saul? choose you a man for you, and let him come down to me.

9 If he be able to fight with me, and to kill me, then will we be your servants: but if I prevail against him, and kill him, then shall you be our servants, and serve us.

10 And the Philistine said, I defy the armies of Israel this day; give me a man, that we may fight together.

11 When Saul and all Israel heard those words of the Philistine, they were dismayed, and greatly afraid.

12 Now David was the son of that Ephrathite of Bethlehemjudah, whose name was Jesse; and he had eight sons: and the man went among men for an old man in the days of Saul.

13 And the three eldest sons of Jesse went and followed Saul to the battle: and the names of his three sons that went to the battle were Eliab the firstborn, and next to him Abinadab, and the third Shammah.

14 And David was the youngest: and the three eldest followed Saul.

15 But David went and returned from Saul to feed his father's sheep at Bethlehem.

16 And the Philistine drew near morning and evening, and presented himself forty days.

17 And Jesse said to David his son, Take now for your brethren an ephah of this parched corn, and these ten loaves, and run to the camp of your brethren;

18 And carry these ten cheeses to the captain of their thousand, and look how your brethren fare, and take their pledge.

19 Now Saul, and they, and all the men of Israel, were in the valley of Elah, fighting with the Philistines.

20 And David rose up early in the morning, and left the sheep with a keeper, and took, and went, as Jesse had commanded him; and he came to the trench, as the host was going forth to the fight, and shouted for the battle.

21 For Israel and the Philistines had put the battle in array, army against army.

22 And David left his carriage in the hand of the keeper of the carriage, and ran into the army, and came and saluted his brethren.

23 And as he talked with them, behold, there came up the champion, the Philistine of Gath, Goliath by name, out of the armies of the Philistines, and

spoke according to the same words: and David heard them.

24 And all the men of Israel, when they saw the man, fled from him, and were sore afraid.

25 And the men of Israel said, Have you seen this man that is come up? surely to defy Israel is he come up: and it shall be, that the man who kills him, the king will enrich him with great riches, and will give him his daughter, and make his father's house free in Israel.

26 And David spoke to the men that stood by him, saying, What shall be done to the man that kills this Philistine, and takes away the reproach from Israel? for who is this uncircumcised Philistine, that he should defy the armies of the living God?

27 And the people answered him after this manner, saying, So shall it be done to the man that kills him.

28 And Eliab his eldest brother heard when he spoke to the men; and Eliab's anger was kindled against David, and he said, Why did you come down here? and with whom have you left those few sheep in the wilderness? I know your pride, and the naughtiness of your heart; for you are come down that you might see the battle.

29 And David said, What have I now done? Is there not a cause?

30 And he turned from him toward another, and spoke after the same manner: and the people answered him again after the former manner.

31 And when the words were heard which David spoke, they rehearsed them before Saul: and he sent for him.

32 And David said to Saul, Let no man's heart fail because of him; your servant will go and fight with this Philistine.

33 And Saul said to David, You are not able to go against this Philistine to fight

with him: for you are but a youth, and he a man of war from his youth.

34 And David said to Saul, Your servant kept his father's sheep, and there came a lion, and a bear, and took a lamb out of the flock:

35 And I went out after him, and smote him, and delivered it out of his mouth: and when he arose against me, I caught him by his beard, and smote him, and slew him.

36 Your servant slew both the lion and the bear: and this uncircumcised Philistine shall be as one of them, seeing he has defied the armies of the living God.

37 David said moreover, The LORD that delivered me out of the paw of the lion, and out of the paw of the bear, he will deliver me out of the hand of this Philistine. And Saul said to David, Go, and the LORD be with you.

38 And Saul armed David with his armour, and he put an helmet of brass upon his head; also he armed him with a coat of mail.

39 And David girded his sword upon his armour, and he assayed to go; for he had not proved it. And David said to Saul, I cannot go with these; for I have not proved them. And David put them off him.

40 And he took his staff in his hand, and chose him five smooth stones out of the brook, and put them in a shepherd's bag which he had, even in a scrip; and his sling was in his hand: and he drew near to the Philistine.

41 And the Philistine came on and drew near to David; and the man that bare the shield went before him.

42 And when the Philistine looked about, and saw David, he disdained him: for he was but a youth, and ruddy, and of a fair countenance.

17:40 Jesus took the staff of the Law in His hand (Isaiah 42:1-4) and chose for Himself the five-fold ministry of the Church (see Ephesians 4:11) to bring about the downfall of the enemy.

43 And the Philistine said to David, Am I a dog, that you come to me with staves? And the Philistine cursed David by his gods.

44 And the Philistine said to David, Come to me, and I will give your flesh to the fowls of the air, and to the beasts of the field.

45 Then said David to the Philistine, You come to me with a sword, and with a spear, and with a shield: but I come to you in the name of the LORD of hosts, the God of the armies of Israel, whom you have defied.

46 This day will the LORD deliver you into mine hand; and I will smite you, and take your head from you; and I will give the carcases of the host of the Philistines this day to the fowls of the air, and to the wild beasts of the earth; that all the earth may know that there is a God in Israel.

47 And all this assembly shall know that the LORD saves not with sword and spear: for the battle is the LORD's, and he will give you into our hands.

48 And it came to pass, when the Philistine arose, and came, and drew nigh to meet David, that David hastened, and ran toward the army to meet the Philistine.

49 And David put his hand in his bag, and took thence a stone, and slang it, and smote the Philistine in his forehead, that the stone sunk into his forehead; and he fell upon his face to the earth.

50 So David prevailed over the Philistine with a sling and with a stone, and smote the Philistine, and slew him; but there was no sword in the hand of David.

51 Therefore David ran, and stood upon the Philistine, and took his sword, and drew it out of the sheath thereof, and slew him, and cut off his head therewith. And when the Philistines saw their champion was dead, they fled.

52 And the men of Israel and of Judah arose, and shouted, and pursued the Philistines, until you come to the valley, and to the gates of Ekron. And the wounded of the Philistines fell down by the way to Shaaraim, even to Gath, and to Ekron.

53 And the children of Israel returned from chasing after the Philistines, and they spoiled their tents.

54 And David took the head of the Philistine, and brought it to Jerusalem; but he put his armour in his tent.

55 And when Saul saw David go forth against the Philistine, he said to Abner, the captain of the host, Abner, whose son is this youth? And Abner said, As your soul lives, O king, I cannot tell.

56 And the king said, Inquire whose son the stripling is.

57 And as David returned from the slaughter of the Philistine, Abner took him, and brought him before Saul with the head of the Philistine in his hand.

58 And Saul said to him, Whose son are you, young man? And David answered, I am the son of your servant Jesse the Bethlehemite.

CHAPTER 18

AND it came to pass, when he had made an end of speaking to Saul, that the soul of Jonathan was knit with the soul of David, and Jonathan loved him as his own soul.

2 And Saul took him that day, and would let him go no more home to his father's house.

17:48 We must run towards the task that God has set before us.

17:50 God's Law is the sling that gives the stone of the gospel its thrust to conquer the enemy. Without God's Law, the gospel doesn't penetrate the mind of the sinner. Why should he repent and believe and accept the Savior if he has no understanding of the true nature of sin? That understanding is something only the Law can give (Romans 7:7).

SAUL ATTEMPTS TO TAKE THE LIFE OF DAVID

1 Samuel 18:11

3 Then Jonathan and David made a covenant, because he loved him as his own soul.

4 And Jonathan stripped himself of the robe that was upon him, and gave it to David, and his garments, even to his sword, and to his bow, and to his girdle.

5 And David went out wherever Saul sent him, and behaved himself wisely: and Saul set him over the men of war, and he was accepted in the sight of all the people, and also in the sight of Saul's servants.

6 And it came to pass as they came, when David was returned from the slaughter of the Philistine, that the women came out of all cities of Israel, singing and dancing, to meet king Saul,

with tabrets, with joy, and with instruments of music.

7 And the women answered one another as they played, and said, Saul has slain his thousands, and David his ten thousands.

8 And Saul was very wroth, and the saying displeased him; and he said, They have ascribed to David ten thousands, and to me they have ascribed but thousands: and what can he have more but the kingdom?

9 And Saul eyed David from that day and forward.

10 And it came to pass on the morrow, that the evil spirit from God came upon Saul, and he prophesied in the midst of the house: and David played with his

hand, as at other times: and there was a javelin in Saul's hand.

11 And Saul cast the javelin; for he said, I will smite David even to the wall with it. And David avoided out of his presence twice.

12 And Saul was afraid of David, because the LORD was with him, and was departed from Saul.

13 Therefore Saul removed him from him, and made him his captain over a thousand; and he went out and came in before the people.

14 And David behaved himself wisely in all his ways; and the LORD was with him.

15 Therefore when Saul saw that he behaved himself very wisely, he was afraid of him.

16 But all Israel and Judah loved David, because he went out and came in before them.

17 And Saul said to David, Behold my elder daughter Merab, her will I give you to wife: only be valiant for me, and fight the LORD's battles. For Saul said, Let not mine hand be upon him, but let the hand of the Philistines be upon him.

18 And David said to Saul, Who am I? and what is my life, or my father's family in Israel, that I should be son in law to the king?

19 But it came to pass at the time when Merab Saul's daughter should have been given to David, that she was given to Adriel the Meholathite to wife.

20 And Michal Saul's daughter loved David: and they told Saul, and the thing pleased him.

21 And Saul said, I will give him her, that she may be a snare to him, and that the hand of the Philistines may be against him. Therefore Saul said to David, You shall this day be my son in law in the one of the twain.

22 And Saul commanded his servants, saying, Commune with David secretly, and say, Behold, the king has delight in you, and all his servants love you: now therefore be the king's son in law.

23 And Saul's servants spoke those words in the ears of David. And David said, Does it seem to you a light thing to be a king's son in law, seeing that I am a poor man, and lightly esteemed?

24 And the servants of Saul told him, saying, On this manner spoke David.

25 And Saul said, Thus shall you say to David, The king desires not any dowry, but an hundred foreskins of the Philistines, to be avenged of the king's enemies. But Saul thought to make David fall by the hand of the Philistines.

26 And when his servants told David these words, it pleased David well to be the king's son in law: and the days were not expired.

27 Therefore David arose and went, he and his men, and slew of the Philistines two hundred men; and David brought their foreskins, and they gave them in full tale to the king, that he might be the king's son in law. And Saul gave him Michal his daughter to wife.

28 And Saul saw and knew that the LORD was with David, and that Michal Saul's daughter loved him.

29 And Saul was yet the more afraid of David; and Saul became David's enemy continually.

30 Then the princes of the Philistines went forth: and it came to pass, after they went forth, that David behaved himself more wisely than all the servants of Saul; so that his name was much set by.

CHAPTER 19

AND Saul spoke to Jonathan his son, and to all his servants, that they should kill David.

2 But Jonathan Saul's son delighted much in David: and Jonathan told David, saying, Saul my father seeks to kill you: now therefore, I pray you, take heed to yourself until the morning, and abide in a secret place, and hide yourself:

3 And I will go out and stand beside my father in the field where you are, and I

will commune with my father of you; and what I see, that I will tell you.

4 And Jonathan spoke good of David to Saul his father, and said to him, Let not the king sin against his servant, against David; because he has not sinned against you, and because his works have been very good towards you:

5 For he did put his life in his hand, and slew the Philistine, and the LORD wrought a great salvation for all Israel: you saw it, and did rejoice: why then will you sin against innocent blood, to slay David without a cause?

6 And Saul hearkened to the voice of Jonathan: and Saul swore, As the LORD lives, he shall not be slain.

7 And Jonathan called David, and Jonathan showed him all those things. And Jonathan brought David to Saul, and he was in his presence, as in times past.

8 And there was war again: and David went out, and fought with the Philistines, and slew them with a great slaughter; and they fled from him.

9 And the evil spirit from the LORD was upon Saul, as he sat in his house with his javelin in his hand: and David played with his hand.

10 And Saul sought to smite David even to the wall with the javelin: but he slipped away out of Saul's presence, and he smote the javelin into the wall: and David fled, and escaped that night.

11 Saul also sent messengers to David's house, to watch him, and to slay him in the morning: and Michal David's wife told him, saying, If you save not your life tonight, tomorrow you shall be slain.

12 So Michal let David down through a window: and he went, and fled, and escaped.

13 And Michal took an image, and laid it in the bed, and put a pillow of goats' hair for his bolster, and covered it with a cloth.

14 And when Saul sent messengers to take David, she said, He is sick.

15 And Saul sent the messengers again to see David, saying, Bring him up to me in the bed, that I may slay him.

16 And when the messengers were come in, behold, there was an image in the bed, with a pillow of goats' hair for his bolster.

17 And Saul said to Michal, Why have you deceived me so, and sent away mine enemy, that he is escaped? And Michal answered Saul, He said to me, Let me go; why should I kill you?

18 So David fled, and escaped, and came to Samuel to Ramah, and told him all that Saul had done to him. And he and Samuel went and dwelt in Naioth.

19 And it was told Saul, saying, Behold, David is at Naioth in Ramah.

20 And Saul sent messengers to take David: and when they saw the company of the prophets prophesying, and Samuel standing as appointed over them, the Spirit of God was upon the messengers of Saul, and they also prophesied.

21 And when it was told Saul, he sent other messengers, and they prophesied likewise. And Saul sent messengers again the third time, and they prophesied also.

22 Then went he also to Ramah, and came to a great well that is in Sechu: and he asked and said, Where are Samuel and David? And one said, Behold, they be at Naioth in Ramah.

23 And he went there to Naioth in Ramah: and the Spirit of God was upon him also, and he went on, and prophesied, until he came to Naioth in Ramah.

24 And he stripped off his clothes also, and prophesied before Samuel in like manner, and lay down naked all that day and all that night. Therefore they say, Is Saul also among the prophets?

CHAPTER 20

AND David fled from Naioth in Ramah, and came and said before Jonathan, What have I done? what is mine iniquity? and what is my sin before your father, that he seeks my life?

2 And he said to him, God forbid; you shall not die: behold, my father will do nothing either great or small, but that he will show it me: and why should my father hide this thing from me? it is not so.

3 And David swore moreover, and said, Your father certainly knows that I have found grace in your eyes; and he says, Let not Jonathan know this, lest he be grieved: but truly as the LORD lives, and as your soul lives, there is but a step between me and death.

4 Then said Jonathan to David, Whatsoever your soul desires, I will even do it for you.

5 And David said to Jonathan, Behold, to morrow is the new moon, and I should not fail to sit with the king at meat: but let me go, that I may hide myself in the field to the third day at even.

6 If your father at all miss me, then say, David earnestly asked leave of me that he might run to Bethlehem his city: for there is a yearly sacrifice there for all the family.

7 If he say thus, It is well; your servant shall have peace: but if he be very wroth, then be sure that evil is determined by him.

8 Therefore you shall deal kindly with your servant; for you have brought your servant into a covenant of the LORD with you: notwithstanding, if there be in me iniquity, slay me yourself; for why should you bring me to your father?

9 And Jonathan said, Far be it from you: for if I knew certainly that evil were determined by my father to come upon you, then would not I tell it you?

10 Then said David to Jonathan, Who shall tell me? or what if your father answer you roughly?

11 And Jonathan said to David, Come, and let us go out into the field. And they went out both of them into the field.

12 And Jonathan said to David, O LORD God of Israel, when I have sounded my father about tomorrow any time, or the third day, and, behold, if there be good toward David, and I then send not to you, and show it you;

13 The LORD do so and much more to Jonathan: but if it please my father to do you evil, then I will show it you, and send you away, that you may go in peace: and the LORD be with you, as he has been with my father.

14 And you shall not only while yet I live show me the kindness of the LORD, that I die not:

15 But also you shall not cut off your kindness from my house for ever: no, not when the LORD has cut off the enemies of David every one from the face of the earth.

16 So Jonathan made a covenant with the house of David, saying, Let the LORD even require it at the hand of David's enemies.

17 And Jonathan caused David to swear again, because he loved him: for he loved him as he loved his own soul.

18 Then Jonathan said to David, To morrow is the new moon: and you shall be missed, because your seat will be empty.

19 And when you have stayed three days, then you shall go down quickly, and come to the place where you did hide yourself when the business was in hand, and shall remain by the stone Ezel.

20 And I will shoot three arrows on the side thereof, as though I shot at a mark.

21 And, behold, I will send a lad, saying, Go, find out the arrows. If I expressly say to the lad, Behold, the arrows are on this side of you, take them; then come: for there is peace to you, and no hurt; as the LORD lives.

22 But if I say thus to the young man, Behold, the arrows are beyond you; go your way: for the LORD has sent you away.

23 And as touching the matter which you and I have spoken of, behold, the LORD be between you and me for ever.

24 So David hid himself in the field: and when the new moon was come, the king sat him down to eat meat.

25 And the king sat upon his seat, as at other times, even upon a seat by the wall: and Jonathan arose, and Abner sat by Saul's side, and David's place was empty.

26 Nevertheless Saul spoke not any thing that day: for he thought, Something has befallen him, he is not clean; surely he is not clean.

27 And it came to pass on the morrow, which was the second day of the month, that David's place was empty: and Saul said to Jonathan his son, Why cometh not the son of Jesse to meat, neither yesterday, nor to day?

28 And Jonathan answered Saul, David earnestly asked leave of me to go to Bethlehem:

29 And he said, Let me go, I pray you; for our family has a sacrifice in the city; and my brother, he has commanded me to be there: and now, if I have found favour in your eyes, let me get away, I pray you, and see my brethren. Therefore he cometh not to the king's table.

30 Then Saul's anger was kindled against Jonathan, and he said to him, You son of the perverse rebellious woman, do not I know that you have chosen the son of Jesse to your own confusion, and to the confusion of your mother's nakedness?

31 For as long as the son of Jesse lives upon the ground, you shall not be established, nor your kingdom. Therefore now send and fetch him to me, for he shall surely die.

32 And Jonathan answered Saul his father, and said to him, Why shall he be slain? what has he done?

33 And Saul cast a javelin at him to smite him: whereby Jonathan knew that it was determined of his father to slay David.

34 So Jonathan arose from the table in fierce anger, and did eat no meat the second day of the month: for he was grieved for David, because his father had done him shame.

35 And it came to pass in the morning, that Jonathan went out into the field at the time appointed with David, and a little lad with him.

36 And he said to his lad, Run, find out now the arrows which I shoot. And as the lad ran, he shot an arrow beyond him.

37 And when the lad was come to the place of the arrow which Jonathan had shot, Jonathan cried after the lad, and said, Is not the arrow beyond you?

38 And Jonathan cried after the lad, Make speed, haste, stay not. And Jonathan's lad gathered up the arrows, and came to his master.

39 But the lad knew not any thing: only Jonathan and David knew the matter.

40 And Jonathan gave his artillery to his lad, and said to him, Go, carry them to the city.

41 And as soon as the lad was gone, David arose out of a place toward the south, and fell on his face to the ground, and bowed himself three times: and they kissed one another, and wept one with another, until David exceeded.

42 And Jonathan said to David, Go in peace, forasmuch as we have sworn both of us in the name of the LORD, saying, The LORD be between me and you, and between my seed and your seed for ever. And he arose and departed: and Jonathan went into the city.

CHAPTER 21

THEN came David to Nob to Ahimelech the priest: and Ahimelech was afraid at the meeting of David, and said to him, Why are you alone, and no man with you?

2 And David said to Ahimelech the priest, The king has commanded me a business, and has said to me, Let no man know any thing of the business whereabout I send you, and what I have

commanded you: and I have appointed my servants to such and such a place.

3 Now therefore what is under your hand? give me five loaves of bread in mine hand, or what there is present.

4 And the priest answered David, and said, There is no common bread under mine hand, but there is hallowed bread; if the young men have kept themselves at least from women.

5 And David answered the priest, and said to him, Of a truth women have been kept from us about these three days, since I came out, and the vessels of the young men are holy, and the bread is in a manner common, yea, though it were sanctified this day in the vessel.

6 So the priest gave him hallowed bread: for there was no bread there but the shewbread, that was taken from before the LORD, to put hot bread in the day when it was taken away.

7 Now a certain man of the servants of Saul was there that day, detained before the LORD; and his name was Doeg, an Edomite, the chiefest of the herdmen that belonged to Saul.

8 And David said to Ahimelech, And is there not here under your hand spear or sword? for I have neither brought my sword nor my weapons with me, because the king's business required haste.

9 And the priest said, The sword of Goliath the Philistine, whom you slew in the valley of Elah, behold, it is here wrapped in a cloth behind the ephod: if you will take that, take it: for there is no other save that here. And David said, There is none like that; give it me.

10 And David arose and fled that day for fear of Saul, and went to Achish the king of Gath.

11 And the servants of Achish said to him, Is not this David the king of the land? did they not sing one to another of him in dances, saying, Saul has slain his thousands, and David his ten thousands?

12 And David laid up these words in his heart, and was sore afraid of Achish the king of Gath.

13 And he changed his behaviour before them, and feigned himself mad in their hands, and scrabbled on the doors of the gate, and let his spittle fall down upon his beard.

14 Then said Achish to his servants, Lo, you see the man is mad: why then have you brought him to me?

15 Have I need of mad men, that you have brought this fellow to play the mad man in my presence? shall this fellow come into my house?

CHAPTER 22

DAVID therefore departed thence, and escaped to the cave Adullam: and when his brethren and all his father's house heard it, they went down there to him.

2 And every one that was in distress, and every one that was in debt, and every one that was discontented, gathered themselves to him; and he became a captain over them: and there were with him about four hundred men.

3 And David went thence to Mizpeh of Moab: and he said to the king of Moab, Let my father and my mother, I pray you, come forth, and be with you, till I know what God will do for me.

4 And he brought them before the king of Moab: and they dwelt with him all the while that David was in the hold.

5 And the prophet Gad said to David, Abide not in the hold; depart, and get into the land of Judah. Then David departed, and came into the forest of Hareth.

6 When Saul heard that David was discovered, and the men that were with him, (now Saul abode in Gibeah under a tree in Ramah, having his spear in his hand, and all his servants were standing about him;)

7 Then Saul said to his servants that stood about him, Hear now, you Benjamites; will the son of Jesse give every one of you fields and vineyards, and make you all captains of thousands, and captains of hundreds;

8 That all of you have conspired against me, and there is none that shows me that my son has made a league with the son of Jesse, and there is none of you that is sorry for me, or shows to me that my son has stirred up my servant against me, to lie in wait, as at this day?

9 Then answered Doeg the Edomite, which was set over the servants of Saul, and said, I saw the son of Jesse coming to Nob, to Ahimelech the son of Ahitub.

10 And he enquired of the LORD for him, and gave him victuals, and gave him the sword of Goliath the Philistine.

11 Then the king sent to call Ahimelech the priest, the son of Ahitub, and all his father's house, the priests that were in Nob: and they came all of them to the king.

12 And Saul said, Hear now, son of Ahitub. And he answered, Here I am, my lord.

13 And Saul said to him, Why have you conspired against me, you and the son of Jesse, in that you have given him bread, and a sword, and have inquired of God for him, that he should rise against me, to lie in wait, as at this day?

14 Then Ahimelech answered the king, and said, And who is so faithful among all your servants as David, which is the king's son in law, and goeth at your bidding, and is honourable in your house?

15 Did I then begin to inquire of God for him? be it far from me: let not the king impute any thing to his servant, nor to all the house of my father: for your servant knew nothing of all this, less or more.

16 And the king said, You shall surely die, Ahimelech, you, and all your father's house.

17 And the king said to the footmen that stood about him, Turn, and slay the priests of the LORD: because their hand also is with David, and because they knew when he fled, and did not show it to me. But the servants of the king would not put forth their hand to fall upon the priests of the LORD.

18 And the king said to Doeg, You turn, and fall upon the priests. And Doeg the Edomite turned, and he fell upon the priests, and slew on that day fourscore and five persons that did wear a linen ephod.

19 And Nob, the city of the priests, smote he with the edge of the sword, both men and women, children and sucklings, and oxen, and asses, and sheep, with the edge of the sword.

20 And one of the sons of Ahimelech the son of Ahitub, named Abiathar, escaped, and fled after David.

21 And Abiathar showed David that Saul had slain the LORD's priests.

22 And David said to Abiathar, I knew it that day, when Doeg the Edomite was there, that he would surely tell Saul: I have occasioned the death of all the persons of your father's house.

23 Abide with me, fear not: for he that seeks my life seeks your life: but with me you shall be in safeguard.

CHAPTER 23

THEN they told David, saying, Behold, the Philistines fight against Keilah, and they rob the threshingfloors.

2 Therefore David enquired of the LORD, saying, Shall I go and smite these Philistines? And the LORD said to David, Go, and smite the Philistines, and save Keilah.

3 And David's men said to him, Behold, we be afraid here in Judah: how much more then if we come to Keilah against the armies of the Philistines?

4 Then David enquired of the LORD yet again. And the LORD answered him and said, Arise, go down to Keilah; for I will deliver the Philistines into your hand.

5 So David and his men went to Keilah, and fought with the Philistines, and brought away their cattle, and smote them with a great slaughter. So David saved the inhabitants of Keilah.

6 And it came to pass, when Abiathar the son of Ahimelech fled to David to

Keilah, that he came down with an ephod in his hand.

7 And it was told Saul that David was come to Keilah. And Saul said, God has delivered him into mine hand; for he is shut in, by entering into a town that has gates and bars.

8 And Saul called all the people together to war, to go down to Keilah, to besiege David and his men.

9 And David knew that Saul secretly practised mischief against him; and he said to Abiathar the priest, Bring here the ephod.

10 Then said David, O LORD God of Israel, your servant has certainly heard that Saul seeks to come to Keilah, to destroy the city for my sake.

11 Will the men of Keilah deliver me up into his hand? will Saul come down, as your servant has heard? O LORD God of Israel, I beseech you, tell your servant. And the LORD said, He will come down.

12 Then said David, Will the men of Keilah deliver me and my men into the hand of Saul? And the LORD said, They will deliver you up.

13 Then David and his men, which were about six hundred, arose and departed out of Keilah, and went wherever they could go. And it was told Saul that David was escaped from Keilah; and he forbare to go forth.

14 And David abode in the wilderness in strong holds, and remained in a mountain in the wilderness of Ziph. And Saul sought him every day, but God delivered him not into his hand.

15 And David saw that Saul was come out to seek his life: and David was in the wilderness of Ziph in a wood.

16 And Jonathan Saul's son arose, and went to David into the wood, and strengthened his hand in God.

17 And he said to him, Fear not: for the hand of Saul my father shall not find you; and you shall be king over Israel, and I shall be next to you; and that also Saul my father knows.

18 And they two made a covenant before the LORD: and David abode in the wood, and Jonathan went to his house.

19 Then came up the Ziphites to Saul to Gibeah, saying, Does not David hide himself with us in strong holds in the wood, in the hill of Hachilah, which is on the south of Jeshimon?

20 Now therefore, O king, come down according to all the desire of your soul to come down; and our part shall be to deliver him into the king's hand.

21 And Saul said, Blessed are you of the LORD; for you have compassion on me.

22 Go, I pray you, prepare yet, and know and see his place where his haunt is, and who has seen him there: for it is told me that he deals very subtilly.

23 See therefore, and take knowledge of all the lurking places where he hides himself, and come again to me with the certainty, and I will go with you: and it shall come to pass, if he be in the land, that I will search him out throughout all the thousands of Judah.

24 And they arose, and went to Ziph before Saul: but David and his men were in the wilderness of Maon, in the plain on the south of Jeshimon.

25 Saul also and his men went to seek him. And they told David; therefore he came down into a rock, and abode in the wilderness of Maon. And when Saul heard that, he pursued after David in the wilderness of Maon.

26 And Saul went on this side of the mountain, and David and his men on that side of the mountain: and David made haste to get away for fear of Saul; for Saul and his men compassed David and his men round about to take them.

27 But there came a messenger to Saul, saying, Hasten, and come; for the Philistines have invaded the land.

28 Therefore Saul returned from pursuing after David, and went against the Philistines: therefore they called that place Selahammahlekoth.

29 And David went up from thence, and dwelt in strong holds at Engedi.

CHAPTER 24

AND it came to pass, when Saul was returned from following the Philistines, that it was told him, saying, Behold, David is in the wilderness of Engedi.

2 Then Saul took three thousand chosen men out of all Israel, and went to seek David and his men upon the rocks of the wild goats.

3 And he came to the sheepcotes by the way, where was a cave; and Saul went in to cover his feet: and David and his men remained in the sides of the cave.

4 And the men of David said to him, Behold the day of which the LORD said to you, Behold, I will deliver your enemy into your hand, that you may do to him as it shall seem good to you. Then David arose, and cut off the skirt of Saul's robe privily.

5 And it came to pass afterward, that David's heart smote him, because he had cut off Saul's skirt.

6 And he said to his men, The LORD forbid that I should do this thing to my master, the LORD's anointed, to stretch forth mine hand against him, seeing he is the anointed of the LORD.

7 So David stayed his servants with these words, and suffered them not to rise against Saul. But Saul rose up out of the cave, and went on his way.

8 David also arose afterward, and went out of the cave, and cried after Saul, saying, My lord the king. And when Saul looked behind him, David stooped with his face to the earth, and bowed himself.

DAVID SHOWING SAUL THAT HE HAD SPARED HIS LIFE

1 Samuel 24:11

9 And David said to Saul, Why do you listen to men's words, saying, Behold, David seeks your hurt?

10 Behold, this day your eyes have seen how that the LORD had delivered you to day into mine hand in the cave: and some bade me kill you: but mine eye spared you; and I said, I will not put forth mine hand against my lord; for he is the LORD's anointed.

11 Moreover, my father, see, yea, see the skirt of your robe in my hand: for in that I cut off the skirt of your robe, and killed you not, know and see that there is neither evil nor transgression in mine hand, and I have not sinned against you; yet you hunt my soul to take it.

12 The LORD judge between me and you, and the LORD avenge me of you: but mine hand shall not be upon you.

13 As says the proverb of the ancients, Wickedness proceeds from the wicked: but mine hand shall not be upon you.

14 After whom is the king of Israel come out? after whom do you pursue? after a dead dog, after a flea.

15 The LORD therefore be judge, and judge between me and you, and see, and plead my cause, and deliver me out of your hand.

16 And it came to pass, when David had made an end of speaking these words to Saul, that Saul said, Is this your voice, my son David? And Saul lifted up his voice, and wept.

17 And he said to David, You are more righteous than I: for you have rewarded me good, whereas I have rewarded you evil.

18 And you have showed this day how that you have dealt well with me: forasmuch as when the LORD had delivered me into your hand, you killed me not.

19 For if a man find his enemy, will he let him go well away? therefore the LORD reward you good for that you have done to me this day.

20 And now, behold, I know well that you shall surely be king, and that the kingdom of Israel shall be established in your hand.

21 Swear now therefore to me by the LORD, that you will not cut off my seed after me, and that you will not destroy my name out of my father's house.

22 And David swore to Saul. And Saul went home; but David and his men gat them up to the hold.

CHAPTER 25

AND Samuel died; and all the Israelites were gathered together, and lamented him, and buried him in his house at Ramah. And David arose, and went down to the wilderness of Paran.

2 And there was a man in Maon, whose possessions were in Carmel; and the man was very great, and he had three thousand sheep, and a thousand goats: and he was shearing his sheep in Carmel.

3 Now the name of the man was Nabal; and the name of his wife Abigail: and she was a woman of good understanding, and of a beautiful countenance: but the man was churlish and evil in his doings; and he was of the house of Caleb.

4 And David heard in the wilderness that Nabal did shear his sheep.

5 And David sent out ten young men, and David said to the young men, Get you up to Carmel, and go to Nabal, and greet him in my name:

6 And thus shall you say to him that lives in prosperity, Peace be both to you, and peace be to your house, and peace be to all that you have .

7 And now I have heard that you have shearers: now your shepherds which were with us, we hurt them not, neither was there ought missing to them, all the while they were in Carmel.

8 Ask your young men, and they will show you. Therefore let the young men find favour in your eyes: for we come in a good day: give, I pray you, whatsoever cometh to your hand to your servants, and to your son David.

9 And when David's young men came, they spoke to Nabal according to all those words in the name of David, and ceased.

10 And Nabal answered David's servants, and said, Who is David? and who is the son of Jesse? there be many servants now a days that break away every man from his master.

11 Shall I then take my bread, and my water, and my flesh that I have killed for my shearers, and give it to men, whom I know not whence they be?

12 So David's young men turned their way, and went again, and came and told him all those sayings.

13 And David said to his men, Gird on every man his sword. And they girded on every man his sword; and David also girded on his sword: and there went up after David about four hundred men; and two hundred abode by the stuff.

14 But one of the young men told Abigail, Nabal's wife, saying, Behold, David sent messengers out of the wilderness to salute our master; and he railed on them.

15 But the men were very good to us, and we were not hurt, neither missed we any thing, as long as we were conversant with them, when we were in the fields:

16 They were a wall to us both by night and day, all the while we were with them keeping the sheep.

17 Now therefore know and consider what you will do; for evil is determined against our master, and against all his household: for he is such a son of Belial, that a man cannot speak to him.

18 Then Abigail made haste, and took two hundred loaves, and two bottles of wine, and five sheep ready dressed, and five measures of parched corn, and an hundred clusters of raisins, and two hundred cakes of figs, and laid them on asses.

19 And she said to her servants, Go on before me; behold, I come after you. But she told not her husband Nabal.

20 And it was so, as she rode on the ass, that she came down by the covert on the hill, and, behold, David and his men came down against her; and she met them.

21 Now David had said, Surely in vain have I kept all that this fellow has in the wilderness, so that nothing was missed of all that pertained to him: and he has requited me evil for good.

22 So and more also do God to the enemies of David, if I leave of all that pertain to him by the morning light any that urinates against the wall.

23 And when Abigail saw David, she hasted, and lighted off the ass, and fell before David on her face, and bowed herself to the ground,

24 And fell at his feet, and said, Upon me, my lord, upon me let this iniquity be: and let your handmaid, I pray you, speak in your audience, and hear the words of your handmaid.

25 Let not my lord, I pray you, regard this man of Belial, even Nabal: for as his name is, so is he; Nabal is his name, and folly is with him: but I your handmaid saw not the young men of my lord, whom you did send.

26 Now therefore, my lord, as the LORD lives, and as your soul lives, seeing the LORD has withholden you from coming to shed blood, and from avenging yourself with your own hand, now let your enemies, and they that seek evil to my lord, be as Nabal.

27 And now this blessing which your handmaid has brought to my lord, let it even be given to the young men that follow my lord.

28 I pray you, forgive the trespass of your handmaid: for the LORD will certainly make my lord a sure house; because my lord fights the battles of the LORD, and evil has not been found in you all your days.

29 Yet a man is risen to pursue you, and to seek your soul: but the soul of my lord shall be bound in the bundle of life with the LORD your God; and the souls

of your enemies, them shall he sling out, as out of the middle of a sling.

30 And it shall come to pass, when the LORD shall have done to my lord according to all the good that he has spoken concerning you, and shall have appointed you ruler over Israel;

31 That this shall be no grief to you, nor offence of heart to my lord, either that you have shed blood causeless, or that my lord has avenged himself: but when the LORD shall have dealt well with my lord, then remember your handmaid.

32 And David said to Abigail, Blessed be the LORD God of Israel, which sent you this day to meet me:

33 And blessed be your advice, and blessed are you, which have kept me this day from coming to shed blood, and from avenging myself with mine own hand.

34 For in very deed, as the LORD God of Israel lives, which has kept me back from hurting you, except you had hasted and come to meet me, surely there had not been left to Nabal by the morning light any that urinates against the wall.

35 So David received of her hand that which she had brought him, and said to her, Go up in peace to your house; see, I have hearkened to your voice, and have accepted your person.

36 And Abigail came to Nabal; and, behold, he held a feast in his house, like the feast of a king; and Nabal's heart was merry within him, for he was very drunken: therefore she told him nothing, less or more, until the morning light.

37 But it came to pass in the morning, when the wine was gone out of Nabal, and his wife had told him these things, that his heart died within him, and he became as a stone.

38 And it came to pass about ten days after, that the LORD smote Nabal, that he died.

39 And when David heard that Nabal was dead, he said, Blessed be the LORD, that has pleaded the cause of my reproach from the hand of Nabal, and has kept his servant from evil: for the LORD has returned the wickedness of Nabal upon his own head. And David sent and communed with Abigail, to take her to him to wife.

40 And when the servants of David were come to Abigail to Carmel, they spoke to her, saying, David sent us to you, to take you to him to wife.

41 And she arose, and bowed herself on her face to the earth, and said, Behold, let your handmaid be a servant to wash the feet of the servants of my lord.

42 And Abigail hasted, and arose and rode upon an ass, with five damsels of hers that went after her; and she went after the messengers of David, and became his wife.

43 David also took Ahinoam of Jezreel; and they were also both of them his wives.

44 But Saul had given Michal his daughter, David's wife, to Phalti the son of Laish, which was of Gallim.

CHAPTER 26

AND the Ziphites came to Saul to Gibeah, saying, Does not David hide himself in the hill of Hachilah, which is before Jeshimon?

2 Then Saul arose, and went down to the wilderness of Ziph, having three thousand chosen men of Israel with him, to seek David in the wilderness of Ziph.

3 And Saul pitched in the hill of Hachilah, which is before Jeshimon, by the way. But David abode in the wilderness, and he saw that Saul came after him into the wilderness.

4 David therefore sent out spies, and understood that Saul was come in very deed.

5 And David arose, and came to the place where Saul had pitched: and David beheld the place where Saul lay, and Abner the son of Ner, the captain of his host: and Saul lay in the trench, and the people pitched round about him.

6 Then answered David and said to Ahimelech the Hittite, and to Abishai the son of Zeruiah, brother to Joab, saying, Who will go down with me to Saul to the camp? And Abishai said, I will go down with you.

7 So David and Abishai came to the people by night: and, behold, Saul lay sleeping within the trench, and his spear stuck in the ground at his bolster: but Abner and the people lay round about him.

8 Then said Abishai to David, God has delivered your enemy into your hand this day: now therefore let me smite him, I pray you, with the spear even to the earth at once, and I will not smite him the second time.

9 And David said to Abishai, Destroy him not: for who can stretch forth his hand against the LORD's anointed, and be guiltless?

10 David said furthermore, As the LORD lives, the LORD shall smite him; or his day shall come to die; or he shall descend into battle, and perish.

11 The LORD forbid that I should stretch forth mine hand against the LORD's anointed: but, I pray you, take now the spear that is at his bolster, and the cruse of water, and let us go.

12 So David took the spear and the cruse of water from Saul's bolster; and they gat them away, and no man saw it, nor knew it, neither awaked: for they were all asleep; because a deep sleep from the LORD was fallen upon them.

13 Then David went over to the other side, and stood on the top of an hill afar off; a great space being between them:

14 And David cried to the people, and to Abner the son of Ner, saying, Do you not answer, Abner? Then Abner answered and said, Who are you that cries to the king?

15 And David said to Abner, Are not you a valiant man? and who is like to you in Israel? why then have you not kept your lord the king? for there came one of the people in to destroy the king your lord.

16 This thing is not good that you have done. As the LORD lives, you are worthy to die, because you have not kept your master, the LORD's anointed. And now see where the king's spear is, and the cruse of water that was at his bolster.

17 And Saul knew David's voice, and said, Is this your voice, my son David? And David said, It is my voice, my lord, O king.

18 And he said, Why does my lord thus pursue after his servant? for what have I done? or what evil is in mine hand?

19 Now therefore, I pray you, let my lord the king hear the words of his servant. If the LORD have stirred you up against me, let him accept an offering: but if they be the children of men, cursed be they before the LORD; for they have driven me out this day from abiding in the inheritance of the LORD, saying, Go, serve other gods.

20 Now therefore, let not my blood fall to the earth before the face of the LORD: for the king of Israel is come out to seek a flea, as when one does hunt a partridge in the mountains.

21 Then said Saul, I have sinned: return, my son David: for I will no more do you harm, because my soul was precious in your eyes this day: behold, I have played the fool, and have erred exceedingly.

22 And David answered and said, Behold the king's spear! and let one of the young men come over and fetch it.

23 The LORD render to every man his righteousness and his faithfulness; for the LORD delivered you into my hand to day, but I would not stretch forth mine hand against the LORD's anointed.

24 And, behold, as your life was much set by this day in mine eyes, so let my life be much set by in the eyes of the LORD, and let him deliver me out of all tribulation.

25 Then Saul said to David, Blessed are you, my son David: you shall both do

great things, and also shall still prevail. So David went on his way, and Saul returned to his place.

CHAPTER 27

AND David said in his heart, I shall now perish one day by the hand of Saul: there is nothing better for me than that I should speedily escape into the land of the Philistines; and Saul shall despair of me, to seek me any more in any coast of Israel: so shall I escape out of his hand.

2 And David arose, and he passed over with the six hundred men that were with him to Achish, the son of Maoch, king of Gath.

3 And David dwelt with Achish at Gath, he and his men, every man with his household, even David with his two wives, Ahinoam the Jezreelitess, and Abigail the Carmelitess, Nabal's wife.

4 And it was told Saul that David was fled to Gath: and he sought no more again for him.

5 And David said to Achish, If I have now found grace in your eyes, let them give me a place in some town in the country, that I may dwell there: for why should your servant dwell in the royal city with you?

6 Then Achish gave him Ziklag that day: therefore Ziklag pertains to the kings of Judah to this day.

7 And the time that David dwelt in the country of the Philistines was a full year and four months.

8 And David and his men went up, and invaded the Geshurites, and the Gezrites, and the Amalekites: for those nations were of old the inhabitants of the land, as you go to Shur, even to the land of Egypt.

9 And David smote the land, and left neither man nor woman alive, and took away the sheep, and the oxen, and the asses, and the camels, and the apparel, and returned, and came to Achish.

10 And Achish said, Where have you made a road to day? And David said,

Against the south of Judah, and against the south of the Jerahmeelites, and against the south of the Kenites.

11 And David saved neither man nor woman alive, to bring tidings to Gath, saying, Lest they should tell on us, saying, So did David, and so will be his manner all the while he dwells in the country of the Philistines.

12 And Achish believed David, saying, He has made his people Israel utterly to abhor him; therefore he shall be my servant for ever.

CHAPTER 28

AND it came to pass in those days, that the Philistines gathered their armies together for warfare, to fight with Israel. And Achish said to David, Know you assuredly, that you shall go out with me to battle, you and your men.

2 And David said to Achish, Surely you shall know what your servant can do. And Achish said to David, Therefore will I make you keeper of mine head for ever.

3 Now Samuel was dead, and all Israel had lamented him, and buried him in Ramah, even in his own city. And Saul had put away those that had familiar spirits, and the wizards, out of the land.

4 And the Philistines gathered themselves together, and came and pitched in Shunem: and Saul gathered all Israel together, and they pitched in Gilboa.

5 And when Saul saw the host of the Philistines, he was afraid, and his heart greatly trembled.

6 And when Saul inquired of the LORD, the LORD answered him not, neither by dreams, nor by Urim, nor by prophets.

7 Then said Saul to his servants, Seek me a woman that has a familiar spirit, that I may go to her, and inquire of her. And his servants said to him, Behold, there is a woman that has a familiar spirit at Endor.

8 And Saul disguised himself, and put on other raiment, and he went, and two

men with him, and they came to the woman by night: and he said, I pray you, divine to me by the familiar spirit, and bring me him up, whom I shall name to you.

9 And the woman said to him, Behold, you know what Saul has done, how he has cut off those that have familiar spirits, and the wizards, out of the land: why then do you lay a snare for my life, to cause me to die?

10 And Saul swore to her by the LORD, saying, As the LORD lives, there shall no punishment happen to you for this thing.

11 Then said the woman, Whom shall I bring up to you? And he said, Bring me up Samuel.

12 And when the woman saw Samuel, she cried with a loud voice: and the woman spoke to Saul, saying, Why have you deceived me? for you are Saul.

13 And the king said to her, Be not afraid: for what did you see? And the woman said to Saul, I saw gods ascending out of the earth.

14 And he said to her, What form is he of? And she said, An old man cometh up; and he is covered with a mantle. And Saul perceived that it was Samuel, and he stooped with his face to the ground, and bowed himself.

15 And Samuel said to Saul, Why have you disquieted me, to bring me up? And Saul answered, I am sore distressed; for the Philistines make war against me, and God is departed from me, and answers me no more, neither by prophets, nor by dreams: therefore I have called you, that you may make known to me what I shall do.

16 Then said Samuel, Why then do you ask of me, seeing the LORD is departed from you, and is become your enemy?

17 And the LORD has done to him, as he spoke by me: for the LORD has rent the kingdom out of your hand, and given it to your neighbour, even to David:

18 Because you obeyed not the voice of the LORD, nor executed his fierce wrath upon Amalek, therefore has the LORD done this thing to you this day.

19 Moreover the LORD will also deliver Israel with you into the hand of the Philistines: and to morrow shall you and your sons be with me: the LORD also shall deliver the host of Israel into the hand of the Philistines.

20 Then Saul fell straightway all along on the earth, and was sore afraid, because of the words of Samuel: and there was no strength in him; for he had eaten no bread all the day, nor all the night.

21 And the woman came to Saul, and saw that he was sore troubled, and said to him, Behold, your handmaid has obeyed your voice, and I have put my life in my hand, and have hearkened to your words which you spoke to me.

22 Now therefore, I pray you, hearken also to the voice of your handmaid, and let me set a morsel of bread before you; and eat, that you may have strength, when you go on your way.

23 But he refused, and said, I will not eat. But his servants, together with the woman, compelled him; and he hearkened to their voice. So he arose from the earth, and sat upon the bed.

24 And the woman had a fat calf in the house; and she hasted, and killed it, and took flour, and kneaded it, and did bake unleavened bread thereof:

25 And she brought it before Saul, and before his servants; and they did eat. Then they rose up, and went away that night.

CHAPTER 29

NOW the Philistines gathered together all their armies to Aphek: and the Israelites pitched by a fountain which is in Jezreel.

2 And the lords of the Philistines passed on by hundreds, and by thousands: but David and his men passed on in the rearward with Achish.

3 Then said the princes of the Philistines, What do these Hebrews here? And Achish said to the princes of the Philistines, Is not this David, the servant of Saul the king of Israel, which has been with me these days, or these years, and I have found no fault in him since he fell to me to this day?

4 And the princes of the Philistines were wroth with him; and the princes of the Philistines said to him, Make this fellow return, that he may go again to his place which you have appointed him, and let him not go down with us to battle, lest in the battle he be an adversary to us: for wherewith should he reconcile himself to his master? should it not be with the heads of these men?

5 Is not this David, of whom they sang one to another in dances, saying, Saul slew his thousands, and David his ten thousands?

6 Then Achish called David, and said to him, Surely, as the LORD lives, you have been upright, and your going out and your coming in with me in the host is good in my sight: for I have not found evil in you since the day of your coming to me to this day: nevertheless the lords favour you not.

7 Therefore now return, and go in peace, that you displease not the lords of the Philistines.

8 And David said to Achish, But what have I done? and what have you found in your servant so long as I have been with you to this day, that I may not go fight against the enemies of my lord the king?

9 And Achish answered and said to David, I know that you are good in my sight, as an angel of God: notwithstanding the princes of the Philistines have said, He shall not go up with us to the battle.

10 Therefore now rise up early in the morning with your master's servants that are come with you: and as soon as you are up early in the morning, and have light, depart.

11 So David and his men rose up early to depart in the morning, to return into the land of the Philistines. And the Philistines went up to Jezreel.

CHAPTER 30

AND it came to pass, when David and his men were come to Ziklag on the third day, that the Amalekites had invaded the south, and Ziklag, and smitten Ziklag, and burned it with fire;

2 And had taken the women captives, that were therein: they slew not any, either great or small, but carried them away, and went on their way.

3 So David and his men came to the city, and, behold, it was burned with fire; and their wives, and their sons, and their daughters, were taken captives.

4 Then David and the people that were with him lifted up their voice and wept, until they had no more power to weep.

5 And David's two wives were taken captives, Ahinoam the Jezreelitess, and Abigail the wife of Nabal the Carmelite.

6 And David was greatly distressed; for the people spoke of stoning him, because the soul of all the people was grieved, every man for his sons and for his daughters: but David encouraged himself in the LORD his God.

7 And David said to Abiathar the priest, Ahimelech's son, I pray you, bring me here the ephod. And Abiathar brought there the ephod to David.

8 And David inquired at the LORD, saying, Shall I pursue after this troop? shall I overtake them? And he answered him, Pursue: for you shall surely overtake them, and without fail recover all.

9 So David went, he and the six hundred men that were with him, and came to the brook Besor, where those that were left behind stayed.

10 But David pursued, he and four hundred men: for two hundred abode behind, which were so faint that they could not go over the brook Besor.

11 And they found an Egyptian in the field, and brought him to David, and

gave him bread, and he did eat; and they made him drink water;

12 And they gave him a piece of a cake of figs, and two clusters of raisins: and when he had eaten, his spirit came again to him: for he had eaten no bread, nor drunk any water, three days and three nights.

13 And David said to him, To whom do you belong? and where are you from? And he said, I am a young man of Egypt, servant to an Amalekite; and my master left me, because three days ago I fell sick.

14 We made an invasion upon the south of the Cherethites, and upon the coast which belongs to Judah, and upon the south of Caleb; and we burned Ziklag with fire.

15 And David said to him, Can you bring me down to this company? And he said, Swear to me by God, that you will neither kill me, nor deliver me into the hands of my master, and I will bring you down to this company.

16 And when he had brought him down, behold, they were spread abroad upon all the earth, eating and drinking, and dancing, because of all the great spoil that they had taken out of the land of the Philistines, and out of the land of Judah.

17 And David smote them from the twilight even to the evening of the next day: and there escaped not a man of them, save four hundred young men, which rode upon camels, and fled.

18 And David recovered all that the Amalekites had carried away: and David rescued his two wives.

19 And there was nothing lacking to them, neither small nor great, neither sons nor daughters, neither spoil, nor any thing that they had taken to them: David recovered all.

20 And David took all the flocks and the herds, which they drove before those other cattle, and said, This is David's spoil.

21 And David came to the two hundred men, which were so faint that they could not follow David, whom they had made also to abide at the brook Besor: and they went forth to meet David, and to meet the people that were with him: and when David came near to the people, he saluted them.

22 Then answered all the wicked men and men of Belial, of those that went with David, and said, Because they went not with us, we will not give them ought of the spoil that we have recovered, save to every man his wife and his children, that they may lead them away, and depart.

23 Then said David, You shall not do so, my brethren, with that which the LORD has given us, who has preserved us, and delivered the company that came against us into our hand.

24 For who will hearken to you in this matter? but as his part is that goeth down to the battle, so shall his part be that tarries by the stuff: they shall part alike.

25 And it was so from that day forward, that he made it a statute and an ordinance for Israel to this day.

26 And when David came to Ziklag, he sent of the spoil to the elders of Judah, even to his friends, saying, Behold a present for you of the spoil of the enemies of the LORD;

27 To them which were in Bethel, and to them which were in south Ramoth, and to them which were in Jattir,

28 And to them which were in Aroer, and to them which were in Siphmoth, and to them which were in Eshtemoa,

29 And to them which were in Rachal, and to them which were in the cities of the Jerahmeelites, and to them which were in the cities of the Kenites,

30 And to them which were in Hormah, and to them which were in Chorashan, and to them which were in Athach,

31 And to them which were in Hebron, and to all the places where David himself and his men were wont to haunt.

CHAPTER 31

N OW the Philistines fought against Israel: and the men of Israel fled from before the Philistines, and fell down slain in mount Gilboa.

2 And the Philistines followed hard upon Saul and upon his sons; and the Philistines slew Jonathan, and Abinadab, and Melchishua, Saul's sons.

3 And the battle went sore against Saul, and the archers hit him; and he was sore wounded of the archers.

4 Then said Saul to his armourbearer, Draw your sword, and thrust me through therewith; lest these uncircumcised come and thrust me through, and abuse me. But his armourbearer would not; for he was sore afraid. Therefore Saul took a sword, and fell upon it.

5 And when his armourbearer saw that Saul was dead, he fell likewise upon his sword, and died with him.

6 So Saul died, and his three sons, and his armourbearer, and all his men, that same day together.

7 And when the men of Israel that were on the other side of the valley, and they that were on the other side Jordan, saw that the men of Israel fled, and that Saul and his sons were dead, they forsook the cities, and fled; and the Philistines came and dwelt in them.

8 And it came to pass on the morrow, when the Philistines came to strip the slain, that they found Saul and his three sons fallen in mount Gilboa.

9 And they cut off his head, and stripped off his armour, and sent into the land of the Philistines round about, to publish it in the house of their idols, and among the people.

10 And they put his armour in the house of Ashtaroth: and they fastened his body to the wall of Bethshan.

11 And when the inhabitants of Jabeshgilead heard of that which the Philistines had done to Saul;

12 All the valiant men arose, and went all night, and took the body of Saul and the bodies of his sons from the wall of Bethshan, and came to Jabesh, and burnt them there.

13 And they took their bones, and buried them under a tree at Jabesh, and fasted seven days.

DEATH OF SAUL

1 Samuel 31:4-5

2 Samuel

CHAPTER 1

N OW it came to pass after the death of Saul, when David was returned from the slaughter of the Amalekites, and David had abode two days in Ziklag;

2 It came even to pass on the third day, that, behold, a man came out of the camp from Saul with his clothes rent, and earth upon his head: and so it was, when he came to David, that he fell to the earth, and did obeisance.

3 And David said to him, Where do you come from? And he said to him, Out of the camp of Israel am I escaped.

4 And David said to him, How went the matter? I pray you, tell me. And he answered, That the people are fled from the battle, and many of the people also are fallen and dead; and Saul and Jonathan his son are dead also.

5 And David said to the young man that told him, How know you that Saul and Jonathan his son be dead?

6 And the young man that told him said, As I happened by chance upon mount Gilboa, behold, Saul leaned upon his spear; and, lo, the chariots and horsemen followed hard after him.

7 And when he looked behind him, he saw me, and called to me. And I answered, Here am I.

8 And he said to me, Who are you? And I answered him, I am an Amalekite.

9 He said to me again, Stand, I pray you, upon me, and slay me:

for anguish is come upon me, because my life is yet whole in me.

10 So I stood upon him, and slew him, because I was sure that he could not live after that he was fallen: and I took the crown that was upon his head, and the bracelet that was on his arm, and have brought them here to my lord.

11 Then David took hold on his clothes, and rent them; and likewise all the men that were with him:

12 And they mourned, and wept, and fasted until even, for Saul, and for Jonathan his son, and for the people of the LORD, and for the house of Israel; because they were fallen by the sword.

13 And David said to the young man that told him, Where are you from? And he answered, I am the son of a stranger, an Amalekite.

14 And David said to him, How were you not afraid to stretch forth your hand to destroy the LORD's anointed?

15 And David called one of the young men, and said, Go near, and fall upon him. And he smote him that he died.

16 And David said to him, Your blood be upon your head; for your mouth has testified against you, saying, I have slain the LORD's anointed.

17 And David lamented with this lamentation over Saul and over Jonathan his son:

18 (Also he bade them teach the children of Judah the use of the bow: behold, it is written in the book of Jasher.)

19 The beauty of Israel is slain upon your high places: how are the mighty fallen!

20 Tell it not in Gath, publish it not in the streets of Askelon; lest the daughters of the Philistines rejoice, lest the daughters of the uncircumcised triumph.

21 You mountains of Gilboa, let there be no dew, neither let there be rain, upon you, nor fields of offerings: for there the shield of the mighty is vilely cast away, the shield of Saul, as though he had not been anointed with oil.

22 From the blood of the slain, from the fat of the mighty, the bow of Jonathan turned not back, and the sword of Saul returned not empty.

23 Saul and Jonathan were lovely and pleasant in their lives, and in their death they were not divided: they were swifter than eagles, they were stronger than lions.

24 You daughters of Israel, weep over Saul, who clothed you in scarlet, with other delights, who put on ornaments of gold upon your apparel.

25 How are the mighty fallen in the midst of the battle! O Jonathan, you were slain in your high places.

26 I am distressed for you, my brother Jonathan: very pleasant have you been to me: your love to me was wonderful, passing the love of women.

27 How are the mighty fallen, and the weapons of war perished!

CHAPTER 2

AND it came to pass after this, that David inquired of the LORD, saying, Shall I go up into any of the cities of Judah? And the LORD said to him, Go up. And David said, Where shall I go up? And he said, To Hebron.

2 So David went up there, and his two wives also, Ahinoam the Jezreelitess, and Abigail Nabal's wife the Carmelite.

3 And his men that were with him did David bring up, every man with his household: and they dwelt in the cities of Hebron.

4 And the men of Judah came, and there they anointed David king over the house of Judah. And they told David, saying, That the men of Jabeshgilead were they that buried Saul.

5 And David sent messengers to the men of Jabeshgilead, and said to them, Blessed be you of the LORD, that you have showed this kindness to your lord, even to Saul, and have buried him.

6 And now the LORD show kindness and truth to you: and I also will requite you this kindness, because you have done this thing.

7 Therefore now let your hands be strengthened, and be valiant: for your master Saul is dead, and also the house of Judah have anointed me king over them.

8 But Abner the son of Ner, captain of Saul's host, took Ishbosheth the son of Saul, and brought him over to Mahanaim;

9 And made him king over Gilead, and over the Ashurites, and over Jezreel, and over Ephraim, and over Benjamin, and over all Israel.

10 Ishbosheth Saul's son was forty years old when he began to reign over Israel, and reigned two years. But the house of Judah followed David.

11 And the time that David was king in Hebron over the house of Judah was seven years and six months.

12 And Abner the son of Ner, and the servants of Ishbosheth the son of Saul, went out from Mahanaim to Gibeon.

13 And Joab the son of Zeruiah, and the servants of David, went out, and met together by the pool of Gibeon: and they sat down, the one on the one side of the pool, and the other on the other side of the pool.

14 And Abner said to Joab, Let the young men now arise, and play before us. And Joab said, Let them arise.

15 Then there arose and went over by number twelve of Benjamin, which pertained to Ishbosheth the son of Saul, and twelve of the servants of David.

16 And they caught every one his fellow by the head, and thrust his sword in his fellow's side; so they fell down together: therefore that place was called Helkathhazzurim, which is in Gibeon.

17 And there was a very sore battle that day; and Abner was beaten, and the men of Israel, before the servants of David.

18 And there were three sons of Zeruiah there, Joab, and Abishai, and Asahel: and Asahel was as light of foot as a wild roe.

19 And Asahel pursued after Abner; and in going he turned not to the right hand nor to the left from following Abner.

20 Then Abner looked behind him, and said, Are you Asahel? And he answered, I am.

21 And Abner said to him, Turn aside to your right hand or to your left, and lay hold on one of the young men, and take his armour for yourself. But Asahel would not turn aside from following of him.

22 And Abner said again to Asahel, Turn aside from following me: why should I smite you to the ground? how then should I hold up my face to Joab your brother?

23 Howbeit he refused to turn aside: therefore Abner with the hinder end of the spear smote him under the fifth rib, that the spear came out behind him; and he fell down there, and died in the same place: and it came to pass, that as many as came to the place where Asahel fell down and died stood still.

24 Joab also and Abishai pursued after Abner: and the sun went down when they were come to the hill of Ammah, that lies before Giah by the way of the wilderness of Gibeon.

25 And the children of Benjamin gathered themselves together after Abner, and became one troop, and stood on the top of an hill.

26 Then Abner called to Joab, and said, Shall the sword devour for ever? know you not that it will be bitterness in the latter end? how long shall it be then, ere you bid the people return from following their brethren?

27 And Joab said, As God lives, unless you had spoken, surely then in the morning the people had gone up every one from following his brother.

28 So Joab blew a trumpet, and all the people stood still, and pursued after Israel no more, neither fought they any more.

29 And Abner and his men walked all that night through the plain, and passed over Jordan, and went through all Bithron, and they came to Mahanaim.

30 And Joab returned from following Abner: and when he had gathered all the people together, there lacked of David's servants nineteen men and Asahel.

31 But the servants of David had smitten of Benjamin, and of Abner's men, so that three hundred and threescore men died.

32 And they took up Asahel, and buried him in the sepulchre of his father, which was in Bethlehem. And Joab and his men went all night, and they came to Hebron at break of day.

CHAPTER 3

NOW there was long war between the house of Saul and the house of David: but David waxed stronger and stronger, and the house of Saul waxed weaker and weaker.

2 And to David were sons born in Hebron: and his firstborn was Amnon, of Ahinoam the Jezreelitess;

3 And his second, Chileab, of Abigail the wife of Nabal the Carmelite; and the third, Absalom the son of Maacah the daughter of Talmai king of Geshur;

4 And the fourth, Adonijah the son of Haggith; and the fifth, Shephatiah the son of Abital;

5 And the sixth, Ithream, by Eglah David's wife. These were born to David in Hebron.

6 And it came to pass, while there was war between the house of Saul and the

house of David, that Abner made himself strong for the house of Saul.

7 And Saul had a concubine, whose name was Rizpah, the daughter of Aiah: and Ishbosheth said to Abner, Why have you gone in to my father's concubine?

8 Then was Abner very wroth for the words of Ishbosheth, and said, Am I a dog's head, which against Judah do show kindness this day to the house of Saul your father, to his brethren, and to his friends, and have not delivered you into the hand of David, that you charge me to day with a fault concerning this woman?

9 So do God to Abner, and more also, except, as the LORD has sworn to David, even so I do to him;

10 To translate the kingdom from the house of Saul, and to set up the throne of David over Israel and over Judah, from Dan even to Beersheba.

11 And he could not answer Abner a word again, because he feared him.

12 And Abner sent messengers to David on his behalf, saying, Whose is the land? saying also, Make your league with me, and, behold, my hand shall be with you, to bring about all Israel to you.

13 And he said, Well; I will make a league with you: but one thing I require of you, that is, You shall not see my face, except you first bring Michal Saul's daughter, when you come to see my face.

14 And David sent messengers to Ishbosheth Saul's son, saying, Deliver me my wife Michal, which I espoused to me for an hundred foreskins of the Philistines.

15 And Ishbosheth sent, and took her from her husband, even from Phaltiel the son of Laish.

16 And her husband went with her along weeping behind her to Bahurim. Then said Abner to him, Go, return. And he returned.

17 And Abner had communication with the elders of Israel, saying,

You sought for David in times past to be king over you:

18 Now then do it: for the LORD has spoken of David, saying, By the hand of my servant David I will save my people Israel out of the hand of the Philistines, and out of the hand of all their enemies.

19 And Abner also spoke in the ears of Benjamin: and Abner went also to speak in the ears of David in Hebron all that seemed good to Israel, and that seemed good to the whole house of Benjamin.

20 So Abner came to David to Hebron, and twenty men with him. And David made Abner and the men that were with him a feast.

21 And Abner said to David, I will arise and go, and will gather all Israel to my lord the king, that they may make a league with you, and that you may reign over all that your heart desires. And David sent Abner away; and he went in peace.

22 And, behold, the servants of David and Joab came from pursuing a troop, and brought in a great spoil with them: but Abner was not with David in Hebron; for he had sent him away, and he was gone in peace.

23 When Joab and all the host that was with him were come, they told Joab, saying, Abner the son of Ner came to the king, and he has sent him away, and he is gone in peace.

24 Then Joab came to the king, and said, What have you done? behold, Abner came to you; why is it that you have sent him away, and he is quite gone?

25 You know Abner the son of Ner, that he came to deceive you, and to know your going out and your coming in, and to know all that you do.

26 And when Joab was come out from David, he sent messengers after Abner, which brought him again from the well of Sirah: but David knew it not.

27 And when Abner was returned to Hebron, Joab took him aside in the gate to speak with him quietly, and smote

him there under the fifth rib, that he died, for the blood of Asahel his brother.

28 And afterward when David heard it, he said, I and my kingdom are guiltless before the LORD for ever from the blood of Abner the son of Ner:

29 Let it rest on the head of Joab, and on all his father's house; and let there not fail from the house of Joab one that has an issue, or that is a leper, or that leans on a staff, or that falls on the sword, or that lacks bread.

30 So Joab, and Abishai his brother slew Abner, because he had slain their brother Asahel at Gibeon in the battle.

31 And David said to Joab, and to all the people that were with him, Rend your clothes, and gird you with sackcloth, and mourn before Abner. And king David himself followed the bier.

32 And they buried Abner in Hebron: and the king lifted up his voice, and wept at the grave of Abner; and all the people wept.

33 And the king lamented over Abner, and said, Died Abner as a fool dies?

34 Your hands were not bound, nor your feet put into fetters: as a man falls before wicked men, so you fell. And all the people wept again over him.

35 And when all the people came to cause David to eat meat while it was yet day, David swore, saying, So do God to me, and more also, if I taste bread, or ought else, till the sun be down.

36 And all the people took notice of it, and it pleased them: as whatsoever the king did pleased all the people.

37 For all the people and all Israel understood that day that it was not of the king to slay Abner the son of Ner.

38 And the king said to his servants, Know you not that there is a prince and a great man fallen this day in Israel?

39 And I am this day weak, though anointed king; and these men the sons of Zeruiah be too hard for me: the LORD shall reward the doer of evil according to his wickedness.

CHAPTER 4

AND when Saul's son heard that Abner was dead in Hebron, his hands were feeble, and all the Israelites were troubled.

2 And Saul's son had two men that were captains of bands: the name of the one was Baanah, and the name of the other Rechab, the sons of Rimmon a Beerothite, of the children of Benjamin: (for Beeroth also was reckoned to Benjamin.

3 And the Beerothites fled to Gittaim, and were sojourners there until this day.)

4 And Jonathan, Saul's son, had a son that was lame of his feet. He was five years old when the tidings came of Saul and Jonathan out of Jezreel, and his nurse took him up, and fled: and it came to pass, as she made haste to flee, that he fell, and became lame. And his name was Mephibosheth.

5 And the sons of Rimmon the Beerothite, Rechab and Baanah, went, and came about the heat of the day to the house of Ishbosheth, who lay on a bed at noon.

6 And they came there into the midst of the house, as though they would have fetched wheat; and they smote him under the fifth rib: and Rechab and Baanah his brother escaped.

7 For when they came into the house, he lay on his bed in his bedchamber, and they smote him, and slew him, and beheaded him, and took his head, and gat them away through the plain all night.

8 And they brought the head of Ishbosheth to David to Hebron, and said to the king, Behold the head of Ishbosheth the son of Saul your enemy, which sought your life; and the LORD has avenged my lord the king this day of Saul, and of his seed.

9 And David answered Rechab and Baanah his brother, the sons of Rimmon the Beerothite, and said to them,

As the LORD lives, who has redeemed my soul out of all adversity,

10 When one told me, saying, Behold, Saul is dead, thinking to have brought good tidings, I took hold of him, and slew him in Ziklag, who thought that I would have given him a reward for his tidings:

11 How much more, when wicked men have slain a righteous person in his own house upon his bed? shall I not therefore now require his blood of your hand, and take you away from the earth?

12 And David commanded his young men, and they slew them, and cut off their hands and their feet, and hanged them up over the pool in Hebron. But they took the head of Ishbosheth, and buried it in the sepulchre of Abner in Hebron.

CHAPTER 5

THEN came all the tribes of Israel to David to Hebron, and spoke, saying, Behold, we are your bone and your flesh.

2 Also in time past, when Saul was king over us, you were he that led out and brought in Israel: and the LORD said to you, You shall feed my people Israel, and you shall be a captain over Israel.

3 So all the elders of Israel came to the king to Hebron; and king David made a league with them in Hebron before the LORD: and they anointed David king over Israel.

4 David was thirty years old when he began to reign, and he reigned forty years.

5 In Hebron he reigned over Judah seven years and six months: and in Jerusalem he reigned thirty and three years over all Israel and Judah.

6 And the king and his men went to Jerusalem to the Jebusites, the inhabitants of the land: which spoke to David, saying, Except you take away the blind and the lame, you shall not come in here: thinking, David cannot come in here.

7 Nevertheless David took the strong hold of Zion: the same is the city of David.

8 And David said on that day, Whosoever gets up to the gutter, and smites the Jebusites, and the lame and the blind that are hated of David's soul, he shall be chief and captain. Therefore they said, The blind and the lame shall not come into the house.

9 So David dwelt in the fort, and called it the city of David. And David built round about from Millo and inward.

10 And David went on, and grew great, and the LORD God of hosts was with him.

11 And Hiram king of Tyre sent messengers to David, and cedar trees, and carpenters, and masons: and they built David an house.

12 And David perceived that the LORD had established him king over Israel, and that he had exalted his kingdom for his people Israel's sake.

13 And David took him more concubines and wives out of Jerusalem, after he was come from Hebron: and there were yet sons and daughters born to David.

14 And these be the names of those that were born to him in Jerusalem; Shammuah, and Shobab, and Nathan, and Solomon,

15 Ibhar also, and Elishua, and Nepheg, and Japhia,

16 And Elishama, and Eliada, and Eliphalet.

17 But when the Philistines heard that they had anointed David king over Israel, all the Philistines came up to seek David; and David heard of it, and went down to the hold.

18 The Philistines also came and spread themselves in the valley of Rephaim.

19 And David inquired of the LORD, saying, Shall I go up to the Philistines? will you deliver them into mine hand? And the LORD said to David, Go up: for I will doubtless deliver the Philistines into your hand.

20 And David came to Baalperazim, and David smote them there, and said, The LORD has broken forth upon mine enemies before me, as the breach of waters. Therefore he called the name of that place Baalperazim.

21 And there they left their images, and David and his men burned them.

22 And the Philistines came up yet again, and spread themselves in the valley of Rephaim.

23 And when David enquired of the LORD, he said, You shall not go up; but fetch a compass behind them, and come upon them over against the mulberry trees.

24 And let it be, when you hear the sound of a going in the tops of the mulberry trees, that then you shall bestir yourself: for then shall the LORD go out before you, to smite the host of the Philistines.

25 And David did so, as the LORD had commanded him; and smote the Philistines from Geba until you come to Gazer.

CHAPTER 6

AGAIN, David gathered together all the chosen men of Israel, thirty thousand.

2 And David arose, and went with all the people that were with him from Baale of Judah, to bring up from thence the ark of God, whose name is called by the name of the LORD of hosts that dwells between the cherubims.

3 And they set the ark of God upon a new cart, and brought it out of the house of Abinadab that was in Gibeah: and Uzzah and Ahio, the sons of Abinadab, drove the new cart.

4 And they brought it out of the house of Abinadab which was at Gibeah, accompanying the ark of God: and Ahio went before the ark.

5 And David and all the house of Israel played before the LORD on all manner of instruments made of fir wood, even on harps, and on psalteries, and on timbrels, and on cornets, and on cymbals.

6 And when they came to Nachon's threshingfloor, Uzzah put forth his hand to the ark of God, and took hold of it; for the oxen shook it.

7 And the anger of the LORD was kindled against Uzzah; and God smote him there for his error; and there he died by the ark of God.

8 And David was displeased, because the LORD had made a breach upon Uzzah: and he called the name of the place Perezuzzah to this day.

9 And David was afraid of the LORD that day, and said, How shall the ark of the LORD come to me?

10 So David would not remove the ark of the LORD to him into the city of David: but David carried it aside into the house of Obededom the Gittite.

11 And the ark of the LORD continued in the house of Obededom the Gittite three months: and the LORD blessed Obededom, and all his household.

12 And it was told king David, saying, The LORD has blessed the house of Obededom, and all that pertained to him, because of the ark of God. So David went and brought up the ark of God from the house of Obededom into the city of David with gladness.

13 And it was so, that when they that bare the ark of the LORD had gone six paces, he sacrificed oxen and fatlings.

14 And David danced before the LORD with all his might; and David was girded with a linen ephod.

15 So David and all the house of Israel brought up the ark of the LORD with shouting, and with the sound of the trumpet.

16 And as the ark of the LORD came into the city of David, Michal Saul's daughter looked through a window, and saw king David leaping and dancing before the LORD; and she despised him in her heart.

17 And they brought in the ark of the LORD, and set it in his place, in the

midst of the tabernacle that David had pitched for it: and David offered burnt offerings and peace offerings before the LORD.

18 And as soon as David had made an end of offering burnt offerings and peace offerings, he blessed the people in the name of the LORD of hosts.

19 And he dealt among all the people, even among the whole multitude of Israel, as well to the women as men, to every one a cake of bread, and a good piece of flesh, and a flagon of wine. So all the people departed every one to his house.

20 Then David returned to bless his household. And Michal the daughter of Saul came out to meet David, and said, How glorious was the king of Israel to day, who uncovered himself to day in the eyes of the handmaids of his servants, as one of the vain fellows shamelessly uncovers himself!

21 And David said to Michal, It was before the LORD, which chose me before your father, and before all his house, to appoint me ruler over the people of the LORD, over Israel: therefore will I play before the LORD.

22 And I will yet be more vile than thus, and will be base in mine own sight: and of the maidservants which you have spoken of, of them shall I be had in honour.

23 Therefore Michal the daughter of Saul had no child to the day of her death.

CHAPTER 7

AND it came to pass, when the king sat in his house, and the LORD had given him rest round about from all his enemies;

2 That the king said to Nathan the prophet, See now, I dwell in an house of cedar, but the ark of God dwells within curtains.

3 And Nathan said to the king, Go, do all that is in your heart; for the LORD is with you.

4 And it came to pass that night, that the word of the LORD came to Nathan, saying,

5 Go and tell my servant David, Thus says the LORD, Shall you build me an house for me to dwell in?

6 Whereas I have not dwelt in any house since the time that I brought up the children of Israel out of Egypt, even to this day, but have walked in a tent and in a tabernacle.

7 In all the places wherein I have walked with all the children of Israel spoke I a word with any of the tribes of Israel, whom I commanded to feed my people Israel, saying, Why have you not built me a house of cedar?

8 Now therefore so shall you say to my servant David, Thus says the LORD of hosts, I took you from the sheepcote, from following the sheep, to be ruler over my people, over Israel:

9 And I was with you wherever you went, and have cut off all your enemies out of your sight, and have made you a great name, like to the name of the great men that are in the earth.

10 Moreover I will appoint a place for my people Israel, and will plant them, that they may dwell in a place of their own, and move no more; neither shall the children of wickedness afflict them any more, as beforetime,

11 And as since the time that I commanded judges to be over my people Israel, and have caused you to rest from all your enemies. Also the LORD tells you that he will make you an house.

12 And when your days be fulfilled, and you shall sleep with your fathers, I will set up your seed after you, which shall proceed out of your bowels, and I will establish his kingdom.

13 He shall build an house for my name, and I will stablish the throne of his kingdom for ever.

14 I will be his father, and he shall be my son. If he commit iniquity, I will chasten him with the rod of men, and with the stripes of the children of men:

15 But my mercy shall not depart away from him, as I took it from Saul, whom I put away before you.

16 And your house and your kingdom shall be established for ever before you: your throne shall be established for ever.

17 According to all these words, and according to all this vision, so did Nathan speak to David.

18 Then went king David in, and sat before the LORD, and he said, Who am I, O Lord GOD? and what is my house, that you have brought me hitherto?

19 And this was yet a small thing in your sight, O Lord GOD; but you have spoken also of your servant's house for a great while to come. And is this the manner of man, O Lord GOD?

20 And what can David say more to you? for you, Lord GOD, knows your servant.

21 For your word's sake, and according to your own heart, have you done all these great things, to make your servant know them.

22 Therefore you are great, O LORD God: for there is none like you, neither is there any God beside you, according to all that we have heard with our ears.

23 And what one nation in the earth is like your people, even like Israel, whom God went to redeem for a people to himself, and to make him a name, and to do for you great things and terrible, for your land, before your people, which you redeemed to you from Egypt, from the nations and their gods?

24 For you have confirmed to yourself your people Israel to be a people to you for ever: and you, LORD, are become their God.

25 And now, O LORD God, the word that you have spoken concerning your servant, and concerning his house, establish it for ever, and do as you have said.

26 And let your name be magnified for ever, saying, The LORD of hosts is the God over Israel: and let the house of your servant David be established before you.

27 For you, O LORD of hosts, God of Israel, have revealed to your servant, saying, I will build you an house: therefore has your servant found in his heart to pray this prayer to you.

28 And now, O Lord GOD, you are that God, and your words be true, and you have promised this goodness to your servant:

29 Therefore now let it please you to bless the house of your servant, that it may continue for ever before you: for you, O Lord GOD, have spoken it: and with your blessing let the house of your servant be blessed for ever.

CHAPTER 8

AND after this it came to pass that David smote the Philistines, and subdued them: and David took Methegammah out of the hand of the Philistines.

2 And he smote Moab, and measured them with a line, casting them down to the ground; even with two lines measured he to put to death, and with one full line to keep alive. And so the Moabites became David's servants, and brought gifts.

3 David smote also Hadadezer, the son of Rehob, king of Zobah, as he went to recover his border at the river Euphrates.

4 And David took from him a thousand chariots, and seven hundred horsemen, and twenty thousand footmen: and David houghed all the chariot horses, but reserved of them for an hundred chariots.

5 And when the Syrians of Damascus came to succour Hadadezer king of Zobah, David slew of the Syrians two and twenty thousand men.

6 Then David put garrisons in Syria of Damascus: and the Syrians became servants to David, and brought gifts. And the LORD preserved David wherever he went.

7 And David took the shields of gold that were on the servants of Hadadezer, and brought them to Jerusalem.

8 And from Betah, and from Berothai, cities of Hadadezer, king David took exceeding much brass.

9 When Toi king of Hamath heard that David had smitten all the host of Hadadezer,

10 Then Toi sent Joram his son to king David, to salute him, and to bless him, because he had fought against Hadadezer, and smitten him: for Hadadezer had wars with Toi. And Joram brought with him vessels of silver, and vessels of gold, and vessels of brass:

11 Which also king David did dedicate to the LORD, with the silver and gold that he had dedicated of all nations which he subdued;

12 Of Syria, and of Moab, and of the children of Ammon, and of the Philistines, and of Amalek, and of the spoil of Hadadezer, son of Rehob, king of Zobah.

13 And David gat him a name when he returned from smiting of the Syrians in the valley of salt, being eighteen thousand men.

14 And he put garrisons in Edom; throughout all Edom put he garrisons, and all they of Edom became David's servants. And the LORD preserved David wherever he went.

15 And David reigned over all Israel; and David executed judgment and justice to all his people.

16 And Joab the son of Zeruiah was over the host; and Jehoshaphat the son of Ahilud was recorder;

17 And Zadok the son of Ahitub, and Ahimelech the son of Abiathar, were the priests; and Seraiah was the scribe;

18 And Benaiah the son of Jehoiada was over both the Cherethites and the Pelethites; and David's sons were chief rulers.

CHAPTER 9

AND David said, Is there yet any that is left of the house of Saul, that I may show him kindness for Jonathan's sake?

2 And there was of the house of Saul a servant whose name was Ziba. And when they had called him to David, the king said to him, Are you Ziba? And he said, Your servant is he.

3 And the king said, Is there not yet any of the house of Saul, that I may show the kindness of God to him? And Ziba said to the king, Jonathan has yet a son, which is lame on his feet.

4 And the king said to him, Where is he? And Ziba said to the king, Behold, he is in the house of Machir, the son of Ammiel, in Lodebar.

5 Then king David sent, and fetched him out of the house of Machir, the son of Ammiel, from Lodebar.

6 Now when Mephibosheth, the son of Jonathan, the son of Saul, was come to David, he fell on his face, and did reverence. And David said, Mephibosheth. And he answered, Behold your servant!

7 And David said to him, Fear not: for I will surely show you kindness for Jonathan your father's sake, and will restore you all the land of Saul your father; and you shall eat bread at my table continually.

8 And he bowed himself, and said, What is your servant, that you should look upon such a dead dog as I am?

9 Then the king called to Ziba, Saul's servant, and said to him, I have given to your master's son all that pertained to Saul and to all his house.

10 You therefore, and your sons, and your servants, shall till the land for him, and you shall bring in the fruits, that your master's son may have food to eat: but Mephibosheth your master's son shall eat bread always at my table. Now Ziba had fifteen sons and twenty servants.

11 Then said Ziba to the king, According to all that my lord the king

has commanded his servant, so shall your servant do. As for Mephibosheth, said the king, he shall eat at my table, as one of the king's sons.

12 And Mephibosheth had a young son, whose name was Micha. And all that dwelt in the house of Ziba were servants to Mephibosheth.

13 So Mephibosheth dwelt in Jerusalem: for he did eat continually at the king's table; and was lame on both his feet.

CHAPTER 10

AND it came to pass after this, that the king of the children of Ammon died, and Hanun his son reigned in his stead.

2 Then said David, I will show kindness to Hanun the son of Nahash, as his father showed kindness to me. And David sent to comfort him by the hand of his servants for his father. And David's servants came into the land of the children of Ammon.

3 And the princes of the children of Ammon said to Hanun their lord, Do you think that David does honour your father, that he has sent comforters to you? has not David rather sent his servants to you, to search the city, and to spy it out, and to overthrow it?

4 Therefore Hanun took David's servants, and shaved off the one half of their beards, and cut off their garments in the middle, even to their buttocks, and sent them away.

5 When they told it to David, he sent to meet them, because the men were greatly ashamed: and the king said, Tarry at Jericho until your beards be grown, and then return.

6 And when the children of Ammon saw that they stank before David, the children of Ammon sent and hired the Syrians of Bethrehob and the Syrians of Zoba, twenty thousand footmen, and of king Maacah a thousand men, and of Ishtob twelve thousand men.

7 And when David heard of it, he sent Joab, and all the host of the mighty men.

8 And the children of Ammon came out, and put the battle in array at the entering in of the gate: and the Syrians of Zoba, and of Rehob, and Ishtob, and Maacah, were by themselves in the field.

9 When Joab saw that the front of the battle was against him before and behind, he chose of all the choice men of Israel, and put them in array against the Syrians:

10 And the rest of the people he delivered into the hand of Abishai his brother, that he might put them in array against the children of Ammon.

11 And he said, If the Syrians be too strong for me, then you shall help me: but if the children of Ammon be too strong for you, then I will come and help you.

12 Be of good courage, and let us play the men for our people, and for the cities of our God: and the LORD do that which seems good to him.

13 And Joab drew nigh, and the people that were with him, to the battle against the Syrians: and they fled before him.

14 And when the children of Ammon saw that the Syrians were fled, then fled they also before Abishai, and entered into the city. So Joab returned from the children of Ammon, and came to Jerusalem.

15 And when the Syrians saw that they were smitten before Israel, they gathered themselves together.

16 And Hadarezer sent, and brought out the Syrians that were beyond the river: and they came to Helam; and Shobach the captain of the host of Hadarezer went before them.

17 And when it was told David, he gathered all Israel together, and passed over Jordan, and came to Helam. And the Syrians set themselves in array against David, and fought with him.

18 And the Syrians fled before Israel; and David slew the men of seven hundred chariots of the Syrians, and forty

thousand horsemen, and smote Shobach the captain of their host, who died there. 19 And when all the kings that were servants to Hadarezer saw that they were smitten before Israel, they made peace with Israel, and served them. So the Syrians feared to help the children of Ammon any more.

CHAPTER 11

AND it came to pass, after the year was expired, at the time when kings go forth to battle, that David sent Joab, and his servants with him, and all Israel; and they destroyed the children of Ammon, and besieged Rabbah. But David tarried still at Jerusalem.

2 And it came to pass in an eveningtide, that David arose from off his bed, and walked upon the roof of the king's house: and from the roof he saw a woman washing herself; and the woman was very beautiful to look upon.

3 And David sent and inquired after the woman. And one said, Is not this Bathsheba, the daughter of Eliam, the wife of Uriah the Hittite?

4 And David sent messengers, and took her; and she came in to him, and he lay with her; for she was purified from her uncleanness: and she returned to her house.

5 And the woman conceived, and sent and told David, and said, I am with child.

6 And David sent to Joab, saying, Send me Uriah the Hittite. And Joab sent Uriah to David.

7 And when Uriah was come to him, David demanded of him how Joab did, and how the people did, and how the war prospered.

8 And David said to Uriah, Go down to your house, and wash your feet. And Uriah departed out of the king's house, and there followed him a mess of meat from the king.

9 But Uriah slept at the door of the king's house with all the servants of his lord, and went not down to his house.

10 And when they had told David, saying, Uriah went not down to his house, David said to Uriah, Did you not come from your journey? Why then did you not go down to your house?

11 And Uriah said to David, The ark, and Israel, and Judah, abide in tents; and my lord Joab, and the servants of my lord, are encamped in the open fields; shall I then go into mine house, to eat and to drink, and to lie with my wife? as you live, and as your soul lives, I will not do this thing.

12 And David said to Uriah, Tarry here to day also, and to morrow I will let you depart. So Uriah abode in Jerusalem that day, and the morrow.

13 And when David had called him, he did eat and drink before him; and he made him drunk: and at even he went out to lie on his bed with the servants of his lord, but went not down to his house.

14 And it came to pass in the morning, that David wrote a letter to Joab, and sent it by the hand of Uriah.

15 And he wrote in the letter, saying, Set Uriah in the forefront of the hottest battle, and retire from him, that he may be smitten, and die.

16 And it came to pass, when Joab observed the city, that he assigned Uriah to a place where he knew that valiant men were.

17 And the men of the city went out, and fought with Joab: and there fell some of the people of the servants of David; and Uriah the Hittite died also.

18 Then Joab sent and told David all the things concerning the war;

19 And charged the messenger, saying, When you have made an end of telling the matters of the war to the king,

20 And if so be that the king's wrath arise, and he say to you, Why approached you so near to the city when you did fight? Did you not know that they would shoot from the wall?

21 Who smote Abimelech the son of Jerubbesheth? did not a woman cast a

piece of a millstone upon him from the wall, that he died in Thebez? why did you go near the wall? then say you, Your servant Uriah the Hittite is dead also.

22 So the messenger went, and came and showed David all that Joab had sent him for.

23 And the messenger said to David, Surely the men prevailed against us, and came out to us into the field, and we were upon them even to the entering of the gate.

24 And the shooters shot from off the wall upon your servants; and some of the king's servants be dead, and your servant Uriah the Hittite is dead also.

25 Then David said to the messenger, Thus shall you say to Joab, Let not this thing displease you, for the sword devours one as well as another: make your battle more strong against the city, and overthrow it: and encourage you him.

26 And when the wife of Uriah heard that Uriah her husband was dead, she mourned for her husband.

27 And when the mourning was past, David sent and fetched her to his house, and she became his wife, and bare him a son. But the thing that David had done displeased the LORD.

CHAPTER 12

AND the LORD sent Nathan to David. And he came to him, and said to him, There were two men in one city; the one rich, and the other poor.

2 The rich man had exceeding many flocks and herds:

3 But the poor man had nothing, save one little ewe lamb, which he had bought and nourished up: and it grew up together with him, and with his children; it did eat of his own meat, and drank of his own cup, and lay in his bosom, and was to him as a daughter.

4 And there came a traveller to the rich man, and he spared to take of his own flock and of his own herd, to dress for the wayfaring man that was come to him; but took the poor man's lamb, and dressed it for the man that was come to him.

5 And David's anger was greatly kindled against the man; and he said to Nathan, As the LORD lives, the man that has done this thing shall surely die:

6 And he shall restore the lamb fourfold, because he did this thing, and because he had no pity.

7 And Nathan said to David, You are the man. Thus says the LORD God of Israel, I anointed you king over Israel, and I delivered you out of the hand of Saul;

8 And I gave you your master's house, and your master's wives into your bosom, and gave you the house of Israel and of Judah; and if that had been too little, I would moreover have given to you such and such things.

9 Why have you despised the commandment of the LORD, to do evil in his sight? you have killed Uriah the Hittite with the sword, and have taken his wife to be your wife, and have slain him with the sword of the children of Ammon.

10 Now therefore the sword shall never depart from your house; because you have despised me, and have taken the wife of Uriah the Hittite to be your wife.

11 Thus says the LORD, Behold, I will raise up evil against you out of your own house, and I will take your wives before your eyes, and give them to your neighbour, and he shall lie with your wives in the sight of this sun.

12 For you did it secretly: but I will do this thing before all Israel, and before the sun.

13 And David said to Nathan, I have sinned against the LORD. And Nathan said to David, The LORD also has put away your sin; you shall not die.

12:1-14 See Psalm 41:4 comment: "How to Confront Sinners."

14 Howbeit, because by this deed you have given great occasion to the enemies of the LORD to blaspheme, the child also that is born to you shall surely die.

15 And Nathan departed to his house. And the LORD struck the child that Uriah's wife bare to David, and it was very sick.

16 David therefore besought God for the child; and David fasted, and went in, and lay all night upon the earth.

17 And the elders of his house arose, and went to him, to raise him up from the earth: but he would not, neither did he eat bread with them.

18 And it came to pass on the seventh day, that the child died. And the servants of David feared to tell him that the child was dead: for they said, Behold, while the child was yet alive, we spoke to him, and he would not hearken to our voice: how will he then vex himself, if we tell him that the child is dead?

19 But when David saw that his servants whispered, David perceived that the child was dead: therefore David said to his servants, Is the child dead? And they said, He is dead.

20 Then David arose from the earth, and washed, and anointed himself, and changed his apparel, and came into the house of the LORD, and worshipped: then he came to his own house; and when he required, they set bread before him, and he did eat.

21 Then said his servants to him, What thing is this that you have done? you did fast and weep for the child, while it was alive; but when the child was dead, you did rise and eat bread.

22 And he said, While the child was yet alive, I fasted and wept: for I said, Who can tell whether GOD will be gracious to me, that the child may live?

23 But now he is dead, why should I fast? can I bring him back again? I shall go to him, but he shall not return to me.

24 And David comforted Bathsheba his wife, and went in to her, and lay with her: and she bare a son, and he called his name Solomon: and the LORD loved him.

25 And he sent by the hand of Nathan the prophet; and he called his name Jedidiah, because of the LORD.

26 And Joab fought against Rabbah of the children of Ammon, and took the royal city.

27 And Joab sent messengers to David, and said, I have fought against Rabbah, and have taken the city of waters.

28 Now therefore gather the rest of the people together, and encamp against the city, and take it: lest I take the city, and it be called after my name.

29 And David gathered all the people together, and went to Rabbah, and fought against it, and took it.

30 And he took their king's crown from off his head, the weight whereof was a talent of gold with the precious stones: and it was set on David's head. And he brought forth the spoil of the city in great abundance.

31 And he brought forth the people that were therein, and put them under saws, and under harrows of iron, and under axes of iron, and made them pass through the brick-kiln: and thus did he to all the cities of the children of Ammon. So David and all the people returned to Jerusalem.

CHAPTER 13

AND it came to pass after this, that Absalom the son of David had a fair sister, whose name was Tamar; and Amnon the son of David loved her.

2 And Amnon was so vexed, that he fell sick for his sister Tamar; for she was a virgin; and Amnon thought it hard for him to do anything to her.

3 But Amnon had a friend, whose name was Jonadab, the son of Shimeah David's brother: and Jonadab was a very subtil man.

4 And he said to him, Why are you, being the king's son, lean from day to day? will you not tell me?

And Amnon said to him, I love Tamar, my brother Absalom's sister.

5 And Jonadab said to him, Lay down on your bed, and make yourself sick: and when your father cometh to see you, say to him, I pray you, let my sister Tamar come, and give me meat, and dress the meat in my sight, that I may see it, and eat it at her hand.

6 So Amnon lay down, and made himself sick: and when the king was come to see him, Amnon said to the king, I pray you, let Tamar my sister come, and make me a couple of cakes in my sight, that I may eat at her hand.

7 Then David sent home to Tamar, saying, Go now to your brother Amnon's house, and dress him meat.

8 So Tamar went to her brother Amnon's house; and he was laid down. And she took flour, and kneaded it, and made cakes in his sight, and did bake the cakes.

9 And she took a pan, and poured them out before him; but he refused to eat. And Amnon said, Have out all men from me. And they went out every man from him.

10 And Amnon said to Tamar, Bring the meat into the chamber, that I may eat of your hand. And Tamar took the cakes which she had made, and brought them into the chamber to Amnon her brother.

11 And when she had brought them to him to eat, he took hold of her, and said to her, Come lie with me, my sister.

12 And she answered him, Nay, my brother, do not force me; for no such thing ought to be done in Israel: do not do this folly.

13 And I, where shall I cause my shame to go? and as for you, you shall be as one of the fools in Israel. Now therefore, I pray you, speak to the king; for he will not withhold me from you.

14 Howbeit he would not hearken to her voice: but, being stronger than she, forced her, and lay with her.

15 Then Amnon hated her exceedingly; so that the hatred wherewith he hated her was greater than the love wherewith he had loved her. And Amnon said to her, Arise, be gone.

16 And she said to him, There is no cause: this evil in sending me away is greater than the other that you did to me. But he would not hearken to her.

17 Then he called his servant that ministered to him, and said, Put now this woman out from me, and bolt the door after her.

18 And she had a garment of divers colours upon her: for with such robes were the king's daughters that were virgins apparelled. Then his servant brought her out, and bolted the door after her.

19 And Tamar put ashes on her head, and rent her garment of divers colours that was on her, and laid her hand on her head, and went on crying.

20 And Absalom her brother said to her, Has Amnon your brother been with you? but hold now your peace, my sister: he is your brother; regard not this thing. So Tamar remained desolate in her brother Absalom's house.

21 But when king David heard of all these things, he was very wroth.

22 And Absalom spoke to his brother Amnon neither good nor bad: for Absalom hated Amnon, because he had forced his sister Tamar.

23 And it came to pass after two full years, that Absalom had sheepshearers in Baalhazor, which is beside Ephraim: and Absalom invited all the king's sons.

24 And Absalom came to the king, and said, Behold now, your servant has sheepshearers; let the king, I beseech you, and his servants go with your servant.

25 And the king said to Absalom, Nay, my son, let us not all now go, lest we be chargeable to you. And he pressed him: howbeit he would not go, but blessed him.

26 Then said Absalom, If not, I pray you, let my brother Amnon go with us. And the king said to him, Why should he go with you?

27 But Absalom pressed him, that he let Amnon and all the king's sons go with him.

28 Now Absalom had commanded his servants, saying, Mark now when Amnon's heart is merry with wine, and when I say to you, Smite Amnon; then kill him, fear not: have not I commanded you? be courageous, and be valiant.

29 And the servants of Absalom did to Amnon as Absalom had commanded. Then all the king's sons arose, and every man gat him up upon his mule, and fled.

30 And it came to pass, while they were in the way, that tidings came to David, saying, Absalom has slain all the king's sons, and there is not one of them left.

31 Then the king arose, and tare his garments, and lay on the earth; and all his servants stood by with their clothes rent.

32 And Jonadab, the son of Shimeah David's brother, answered and said, Let not my lord suppose that they have slain all the young men the king's sons; for Amnon only is dead: for by the appointment of Absalom this has been determined from the day that he forced his sister Tamar.

33 Now therefore let not my lord the king take the thing to his heart, to think that all the king's sons are dead: for Amnon only is dead.

34 But Absalom fled. And the young man that kept the watch lifted up his eyes, and looked, and, behold, there came much people by the way of the hill side behind him.

35 And Jonadab said to the king, Behold, the king's sons come: as your servant said, so it is.

36 And it came to pass, as soon as he had made an end of speaking, that, behold, the king's sons came, and lifted up their voice and wept: and the king also and all his servants wept very sore.

37 But Absalom fled, and went to Talmai, the son of Ammihud, king of Geshur. And David mourned for his son every day.

38 So Absalom fled, and went to Geshur, and was there three years.

39 And the soul of king David longed to go forth to Absalom: for he was comforted concerning Amnon, seeing he was dead.

CHAPTER 14

NOW Joab the son of Zeruiah perceived that the king's heart was toward Absalom.

2 And Joab sent to Tekoah, and fetched thence a wise woman, and said to her, I pray you, feign yourself to be a mourner, and put on now mourning apparel, and anoint not yourself with oil, but be as a woman that had a long time mourned for the dead:

3 And come to the king, and speak on this manner to him. So Joab put the words in her mouth.

4 And when the woman of Tekoah spoke to the king, she fell on her face to the ground, and did obeisance, and said, Help, O king.

5 And the king said to her, What ails you? And she answered, I am indeed a widow woman, and mine husband is dead.

6 And your handmaid had two sons, and they two strove together in the field, and there was none to part them, but the one smote the other, and slew him.

7 And, behold, the whole family is risen against your handmaid, and they said, Deliver him that smote his brother, that we may kill him, for the life of his brother whom he slew; and we will destroy the heir also: and so they shall quench my coal which is left, and shall not leave to my husband neither name nor remainder upon the earth.

8 And the king said to the woman, Go to your house, and I will give charge concerning you.

> I reckon him a Christian indeed
> who is not ashamed of the gospel
> or a shame to it.
> **MATTHEW HENRY**
> 1662-1714
> BRITISH PASTOR
> NOTED
> FOR HIS COMMENTARY
> ON THE BIBLE

9 And the woman of Tekoah said to the king, My lord, O king, the iniquity be on me, and on my father's house: and the king and his throne be guiltless.

10 And the king said, Whoever says ought to you, bring him to me, and he shall not touch you any more.

11 Then said she, I pray you, let the king remember the LORD your God, that you would not suffer the revengers of blood to destroy any more, lest they destroy my son. And he said, As the LORD lives, there shall not one hair of your son fall to the earth.

12 Then the woman said, Let your handmaid, I pray you, speak one word to my lord the king. And he said, Say on.

13 And the woman said, Why then have you thought such a thing against the people of God? for the king does speak this thing as one which is faulty, in that the king does not fetch home again his banished.

14 For we must needs die, and are as water spilt on the ground, which cannot be gathered up again; neither does God respect any person: yet does he devise means, that his banished be not expelled from him.

15 Now therefore that I am come to speak of this thing to my lord the king, it is because the people have made me afraid: and your handmaid said, I will now speak to the king; it may be that the king will perform the request of his handmaid.

16 For the king will hear, to deliver his handmaid out of the hand of the man that would destroy me and my son together out of the inheritance of God.

17 Then your handmaid said, The word of my lord the king shall now be comfortable: for as an angel of God, so is my lord the king to discern good and bad: therefore the LORD your God will be with you.

18 Then the king answered and said to the woman, Hide not from me, I pray you, the thing that I shall ask you. And the woman said, Let my lord the king now speak.

19 And the king said, Is not the hand of Joab with you in all this? And the woman answered and said, As your soul lives, my lord the king, none can turn to the right hand or to the left from ought that my lord the king has spoken: for your servant Joab, he bade me, and he put all these words in the mouth of your handmaid:

20 To fetch about this form of speech has your servant Joab done this thing: and my lord is wise, according to the wisdom of an angel of God, to know all things that are in the earth.

21 And the king said to Joab, Behold now, I have done this thing: go therefore, bring the young man Absalom again.

22 And Joab fell to the ground on his face, and bowed himself, and thanked the king: and Joab said, Today your servant knows that I have found grace in your sight, my lord, O king, in that the king has fulfilled the request of his servant.

23 So Joab arose and went to Geshur, and brought Absalom to Jerusalem.

24 And the king said, Let him turn to his own house, and let him not see my face. So Absalom returned to his own house, and saw not the king's face.

25 But in all Israel there was none to be so much praised as Absalom for his beauty: from the sole of his foot even to the crown of his head there was no blemish in him.

26 And when he polled his head, (for it was at every year's end that he polled it:

because the hair was heavy on him, therefore he polled it:) he weighed the hair of his head at two hundred shekels after the king's weight.

27 And to Absalom there were born three sons, and one daughter, whose name was Tamar: she was a woman of a fair countenance.

28 So Absalom dwelt two full years in Jerusalem, and saw not the king's face.

29 Therefore Absalom sent for Joab, to have sent him to the king; but he would not come to him: and when he sent again the second time, he would not come.

30 Therefore he said to his servants, See, Joab's field is near mine, and he has barley there; go and set it on fire. And Absalom's servants set the field on fire.

31 Then Joab arose, and came to Absalom to his house, and said to him, Why have your servants set my field on fire?

32 And Absalom answered Joab, Behold, I sent to you, saying, Come here, that I may send you to the king, to say, Why am I come from Geshur? it had been good for me to have been there still: now therefore let me see the king's face; and if there be any iniquity in me, let him kill me.

33 So Joab came to the king, and told him: and when he had called for Absalom, he came to the king, and bowed himself on his face to the ground before the king: and the king kissed Absalom.

CHAPTER 15

AND it came to pass after this, that Absalom prepared him chariots and horses, and fifty men to run before him.

2 And Absalom rose up early, and stood beside the way of the gate: and it was so, that when any man that had a controversy came to the king for judgment, then Absalom called to him, and said, Of what city are you? And he said, Your servant is of one of the tribes of Israel.

3 And Absalom said to him, See, your matters are good and right; but there is no man deputed of the king to hear you.

4 Absalom said moreover, Oh that I were made judge in the land, that every man which has any suit or cause might come to me, and I would do him justice!

5 And it was so, that when any man came nigh to him to do him obeisance, he put forth his hand, and took him, and kissed him.

6 And on this manner did Absalom to all Israel that came to the king for judgment: so Absalom stole the hearts of the men of Israel.

7 And it came to pass after forty years, that Absalom said to the king, I pray you, let me go and pay my vow, which I have vowed to the LORD, in Hebron.

8 For your servant vowed a vow while I abode at Geshur in Syria, saying, If the LORD shall bring me again indeed to Jerusalem, then I will serve the LORD.

9 And the king said to him, Go in peace. So he arose, and went to Hebron.

10 But Absalom sent spies throughout all the tribes of Israel, saying, As soon as you hear the sound of the trumpet, then you shall say, Absalom reigns in Hebron.

11 And with Absalom went two hundred men out of Jerusalem, that were called; and they went in their simplicity, and they knew not any thing.

12 And Absalom sent for Ahithophel the Gilonite, David's counselor, from his city, even from Giloh, while he offered sacrifices. And the conspiracy was strong; for the people increased continually with Absalom.

13 And there came a messenger to David, saying, The hearts of the men of Israel are after Absalom.

14 And David said to all his servants that were with him at Jerusalem, Arise, and let us flee; for we shall not else escape from Absalom: make speed to depart, lest he overtake us suddenly, and bring evil upon us, and smite the city with the edge of the sword.

15 And the king's servants said to the king, Behold, your servants are ready to do whatsoever my lord the king shall appoint.

16 And the king went forth, and all his household after him. And the king left ten women, which were concubines, to keep the house.

17 And the king went forth, and all the people after him, and tarried in a place that was far off.

18 And all his servants passed on beside him; and all the Cherethites, and all the Pelethites, and all the Gittites, six hundred men which came after him from Gath, passed on before the king.

19 Then said the king to Ittai the Gittite, Why are you also going with us? return to your place, and abide with the king: for you are a stranger, and also an exile.

20 Whereas you came but yesterday, should I this day make you go up and down with us? seeing I go where I may, return, and take back your brethren: mercy and truth be with you.

21 And Ittai answered the king, and said, As the LORD lives, and as my lord the king lives, surely in what place my lord the king shall be, whether in death or life, even there also will your servant be.

22 And David said to Ittai, Go and pass over. And Ittai the Gittite passed over, and all his men, and all the little ones that were with him.

23 And all the country wept with a loud voice, and all the people passed over: the king also himself passed over the brook Kidron, and all the people passed over, toward the way of the wilderness.

24 And lo Zadok also, and all the Levites were with him, bearing the ark of the covenant of God: and they set down the ark of God; and Abiathar went up, until all the people had done passing out of the city.

25 And the king said to Zadok, Carry back the ark of God into the city: if I shall find favour in the eyes of the LORD, he will bring me again, and show me both it, and his habitation:

26 But if he thus say, I have no delight in you; behold, here am I, let him do to me as seems good to him.

27 The king said also to Zadok the priest, Are not you a seer? return into the city in peace, and your two sons with you, Ahimaaz your son, and Jonathan the son of Abiathar.

28 See, I will tarry in the plain of the wilderness, until there come word from you to certify me.

29 Zadok therefore and Abiathar carried the ark of God again to Jerusalem: and they tarried there.

30 And David went up by the ascent of mount Olivet, and wept as he went up, and had his head covered, and he went barefoot: and all the people that was with him covered every man his head, and they went up, weeping as they went up.

31 And one told David, saying, Ahithophel is among the conspirators with Absalom. And David said, O LORD, I pray you, turn the counsel of Ahithophel into foolishness.

32 And it came to pass, that when David was come to the top of the mount, where he worshipped God, behold, Hushai the Archite came to meet him with his coat rent, and earth upon his head:

33 To whom David said, If you pass on with me, then you shall be a burden to me:

34 But if you return to the city, and say to Absalom, I will be your servant, O king; as I have been your father's servant hitherto, so will I now also be your servant: then may you for me defeat the counsel of Ahithophel.

35 And have you not there with you Zadok and Abiathar the priests? therefore it shall be, that what thing soever you shall hear out of the king's house, you shall tell it to Zadok and Abiathar the priests.

36 Behold, they have there with them their two sons, Ahimaaz Zadok's son, and Jonathan Abiathar's son; and by them you shall send to me every thing that you can hear.

37 So Hushai David's friend came into the city, and Absalom came into Jerusalem.

CHAPTER 16

AND when David was a little past the top of the hill, behold, Ziba the servant of Mephibosheth met him, with a couple of asses saddled, and upon them two hundred loaves of bread, and an hundred bunches of raisins, and an hundred of summer fruits, and a bottle of wine.

2 And the king said to Ziba, What do you mean by these? And Ziba said, The asses be for the king's household to ride on; and the bread and summer fruit for the young men to eat; and the wine, that such as be faint in the wilderness may drink.

3 And the king said, And where is your master's son? And Ziba said to the king, Behold, he abides at Jerusalem: for he said, To day shall the house of Israel restore me the kingdom of my father.

4 Then said the king to Ziba, Behold, you are all that pertained to Mephibosheth. And Ziba said, I humbly beseech you that I may find grace in your sight, my lord, O king.

5 And when king David came to Bahurim, behold, thence came out a man of the family of the house of Saul, whose name was Shimei, the son of Gera: he came forth, and cursed still as he came.

6 And he cast stones at David, and at all the servants of king David: and all the people and all the mighty men were on his right hand and on his left.

7 And thus said Shimei when he cursed, Come out, come out, you bloody man, and you man of Belial:

8 The LORD has returned upon you all the blood of the house of Saul, in whose stead you have reigned; and the LORD has delivered the kingdom into the hand of Absalom your son: and, behold, you are taken in your mischief, because you are a bloody man.

9 Then said Abishai the son of Zeruiah to the king, Why should this dead dog curse my lord the king? let me go over, I pray you, and take off his head.

10 And the king said, What have I to do with you, you sons of Zeruiah? so let him curse, because the LORD has said to him, Curse David. Who shall then say, Why have you done so?

11 And David said to Abishai, and to all his servants, Behold, my son, which came forth of my bowels, seeks my life: how much more now may this Benjamite do it? let him alone, and let him curse; for the LORD has bidden him.

12 It may be that the LORD will look on mine affliction, and that the LORD will requite me good for his cursing this day.

13 And as David and his men went by the way, Shimei went along on the hill's side over against him, and cursed as he went, and threw stones at him, and cast dust.

14 And the king, and all the people that were with him, came weary, and refreshed themselves there.

15 And Absalom, and all the people the men of Israel, came to Jerusalem, and Ahithophel with him.

16 And it came to pass, when Hushai the Archite, David's friend, was come to Absalom, that Hushai said to Absalom, God save the king, God save the king.

17 And Absalom said to Hushai, Is this your kindness to your friend? why did you not go with your friend?

18 And Hushai said to Absalom, Nay; but whom the LORD, and this people, and all the men of Israel, choose, his will I be, and with him will I abide.

19 And again, whom should I serve? should I not serve in the presence of his

son? as I have served in your father's presence, so will I be in your presence.

20 Then said Absalom to Ahithophel, Give counsel among you what we shall do.

21 And Ahithophel said to Absalom, Go in to your father's concubines, which he has left to keep the house; and all Israel shall hear that you are abhorred of your father: then shall the hands of all that are with you be strong.

22 So they spread Absalom a tent upon the top of the house; and Absalom went in to his father's concubines in the sight of all Israel.

23 And the counsel of Ahithophel, which he counseled in those days, was as if a man had inquired at the oracle of God: so was all the counsel of Ahithophel both with David and with Absalom.

CHAPTER 17

MOREOVER Ahithophel said to Absalom, Let me now choose out twelve thousand men, and I will arise and pursue after David this night:

2 And I will come upon him while he is weary and weak handed, and will make him afraid: and all the people that are with him shall flee; and I will smite the king only:

3 And I will bring back all the people to you: the man whom you seek is as if all returned: so all the people shall be in peace.

4 And the saying pleased Absalom well, and all the elders of Israel.

5 Then said Absalom, Call now Hushai the Archite also, and let us hear likewise what he says.

6 And when Hushai was come to Absalom, Absalom spoke to him, saying, Ahithophel has spoken after this manner: shall we do after his saying? if not; you speak.

7 And Hushai said to Absalom, The counsel that Ahithophel has given is not good at this time.

8 For, said Hushai, you know your father and his men, that they be mighty men, and they be chafed in their minds, as a bear robbed of her whelps in the field: and your father is a man of war, and will not lodge with the people.

9 Behold, he is hid now in some pit, or in some other place: and it will come to pass, when some of them be overthrown at the first, that whosoever hears it will say, There is a slaughter among the people that follow Absalom.

10 And he also that is valiant, whose heart is as the heart of a lion, shall utterly melt: for all Israel knows that your father is a mighty man, and they which be with him are valiant men.

11 Therefore I counsel that all Israel be generally gathered to you, from Dan even to Beersheba, as the sand that is by the sea for multitude; and that you go to battle in your own person.

12 So shall we come upon him in some place where he shall be found, and we will light upon him as the dew falls on the ground: and of him and of all the men that are with him there shall not be left so much as one.

13 Moreover, if he be gotten into a city, then shall all Israel bring ropes to that city, and we will draw it into the river, until there be not one small stone found there.

14 And Absalom and all the men of Israel said, The counsel of Hushai the Archite is better than the counsel of Ahithophel. For the LORD had appointed to defeat the good counsel of Ahithophel, to the intent that the LORD might bring evil upon Absalom.

15 Then said Hushai to Zadok and to Abiathar the priests, Thus and thus did Ahithophel counsel Absalom and the elders of Israel; and thus and thus have I counseled.

16 Now therefore send quickly, and tell David, saying, Lodge not this night in the plains of the wilderness, but speedily pass over; lest the king be swallowed up, and all the people that are with him.

17 Now Jonathan and Ahimaaz stayed by Enrogel; for they might not be seen to come into the city: and a wench went and told them; and they went and told king David.

18 Nevertheless a lad saw them, and told Absalom: but they went both of them away quickly, and came to a man's house in Bahurim, which had a well in his court; where they went down.

19 And the woman took and spread a covering over the well's mouth, and spread ground corn thereon; and the thing was not known.

20 And when Absalom's servants came to the woman to the house, they said, Where is Ahimaaz and Jonathan? And the woman said to them, They be gone over the brook of water. And when they had sought and could not find them, they returned to Jerusalem.

21 And it came to pass, after they were departed, that they came up out of the well, and went and told king David, and said to David, Arise, and pass quickly over the water: for thus has Ahithophel counselled against you.

22 Then David arose, and all the people that were with him, and they passed over Jordan: by the morning light there lacked not one of them that was not gone over Jordan.

23 And when Ahithophel saw that his counsel was not followed, he saddled his ass, and arose, and gat him home to his house, to his city, and put his household in order, and hanged himself, and died, and was buried in the sepulchre of his father.

24 Then David came to Mahanaim. And Absalom passed over Jordan, he and all the men of Israel with him.

25 And Absalom made Amasa captain of the host instead of Joab: which Amasa was a man's son, whose name was Ithra an Israelite, that went in to Abigail the daughter of Nahash, sister to Zeruiah Joab's mother.

26 So Israel and Absalom pitched in the land of Gilead.

27 And it came to pass, when David was come to Mahanaim, that Shobi the son of Nahash of Rabbah of the children of Ammon, and Machir the son of Ammiel of Lodebar, and Barzillai the Gileadite of Rogelim,

28 Brought beds, and basons, and earthen vessels, and wheat, and barley, and flour, and parched corn, and beans, and lentiles, and parched pulse,

29 And honey, and butter, and sheep, and cheese of kine, for David, and for the people that were with him, to eat: for they said, The people is hungry, and weary, and thirsty, in the wilderness.

CHAPTER 18

AND David numbered the people that were with him, and set captains of thousands, and captains of hundreds over them.

2 And David sent forth a third part of the people under the hand of Joab, and a third part under the hand of Abishai the son of Zeruiah, Joab's brother, and a third part under the hand of Ittai the Gittite. And the king said to the people, I will surely go forth with you myself also.

3 But the people answered, You shall not go forth: for if we flee away, they will not care for us; neither if half of us die, will they care for us: but now you are worth ten thousand of us: therefore now it is better that you succour us out of the city.

4 And the king said to them, What seems best to you I will do. And the king stood by the gate side, and all the people came out by hundreds and by thousands.

5 And the king commanded Joab and Abishai and Ittai, saying, Deal gently for my sake with the young man, even with Absalom. And all the people heard when the king gave all the captains charge concerning Absalom.

6 So the people went out into the field against Israel: and the battle was in the wood of Ephraim;

7 Where the people of Israel were slain before the servants of David, and there was there a great slaughter that day of twenty thousand men.

8 For the battle was there scattered over the face of all the country: and the wood devoured more people that day than the sword devoured.

9 And Absalom met the servants of David. And Absalom rode upon a mule, and the mule went under the thick boughs of a great oak, and his head caught hold of the oak, and he was taken up between the heaven and the earth; and the mule that was under him went away.

10 And a certain man saw it, and told Joab, and said, Behold, I saw Absalom hanged in an oak.

11 And Joab said to the man that told him, And, behold, you saw him, and why did you not smite him there to the ground? and I would have given you ten shekels of silver, and a girdle.

12 And the man said to Joab, Though I should receive a thousand shekels of silver in mine hand, yet would I not put forth mine hand against the king's son: for in our hearing the king charged you and Abishai and Ittai, saying, Beware that none touch the young man Absalom.

13 Otherwise I should have wrought falsehood against mine own life: for there is no matter hid from the king, and you yourself would have set yourself against me.

14 Then said Joab, I may not tarry thus with you. And he took three darts in his hand, and thrust them through the heart of Absalom, while he was yet alive in the midst of the oak.

15 And ten young men that bare Joab's armour compassed about and smote Absalom, and slew him.

16 And Joab blew the trumpet, and the people returned from pursuing after Israel: for Joab held back the people.

17 And they took Absalom, and cast him into a great pit in the wood, and laid a very great heap of stones upon him: and all Israel fled every one to his tent.

18 Now Absalom in his lifetime had taken and reared up for himself a pillar, which is in the king's dale: for he said, I have no son to keep my name in remembrance: and he called the pillar after his own name: and it is called to this day, Absalom's place.

19 Then said Ahimaaz the son of Zadok, Let me now run, and bear the king tidings, how that the LORD has avenged him of his enemies.

20 And Joab said to him, You shall not bear tidings this day, but you shall bear tidings another day: but this day you shall bear no tidings, because the king's son is dead.

21 Then said Joab to Cushi, Go tell the king what you have seen. And Cushi bowed himself to Joab, and ran.

22 Then said Ahimaaz the son of Zadok yet again to Joab, But howsoever, let me, I pray you, also run after Cushi. And Joab said, Why will you run, my son, seeing that you have no tidings ready?

23 But howsoever, said he, let me run. And he said to him, Run. Then Ahimaaz ran by the way of the plain, and overran Cushi.

24 And David sat between the two gates: and the watchman went up to the roof over the gate to the wall, and lifted up his eyes, and looked, and behold a man running alone.

25 And the watchman cried, and told the king. And the king said, If he be alone, there is tidings in his mouth. And he came apace, and drew near.

26 And the watchman saw another man running: and the watchman called to the porter, and said, Behold another man running alone. And the king said, He also brings tidings.

27 And the watchman said, I think the running of the foremost is like the running of Ahimaaz the son of Zadok. And the king said, He is a good man, and cometh with good tidings.

DAVID MOURNING THE DEATH OF ABSALOM

2 Samuel 18:33

28 And Ahimaaz called, and said to the king, All is well. And he fell down to the earth upon his face before the king, and said, Blessed be the LORD your God, which has delivered up the men that lifted up their hand against my lord the king.
29 And the king said, Is the young man Absalom safe? And Ahimaaz answered, When Joab sent the king's servant, and me your servant, I saw a great tumult, but I knew not what it was.
30 And the king said to him, Turn aside, and stand here. And he turned aside, and stood still.

31 And, behold, Cushi came; and Cushi said, Tidings, my lord the king: for the LORD has avenged you this day of all them that rose up against you.
32 And the king said to Cushi, Is the young man Absalom safe? And Cushi answered, The enemies of my lord the king, and all that rise against you to do you hurt, be as that young man is.
33 And the king was much moved, and went up to the chamber over the gate, and wept: and as he went, thus he said, O my son Absalom, my son, my son Absalom! would God I had died for you, O Absalom, my son, my son!

CHAPTER 19

AND it was told Joab, Behold, the king weeps and mourns for Absalom.

2 And the victory that day was turned into mourning to all the people: for the people heard say that day how the king was grieved for his son.

3 And the people gat them by stealth that day into the city, as people being ashamed steal away when they flee in battle.

4 But the king covered his face, and the king cried with a loud voice, O my son Absalom, O Absalom, my son, my son!

5 And Joab came into the house to the king, and said, You have shamed this day the faces of all your servants, which this day have saved your life, and the lives of your sons and of your daughters, and the lives of your wives, and the lives of your concubines;

6 In that you love your enemies, and hate your friends. For you have declared this day, that you regard neither princes nor servants: for this day I perceive, that if Absalom had lived, and all we had died this day, then it had pleased you well.

7 Now therefore arise, go forth, and speak comfortably to your servants: for I swear by the LORD, if you go not forth, there will not tarry one with you this night: and that will be worse to you than all the evil that befell you from your youth until now.

8 Then the king arose, and sat in the gate. And they told to all the people, saying, Behold, the king does sit in the gate. And all the people came before the king: for Israel had fled every man to his tent.

9 And all the people were at strife throughout all the tribes of Israel, saying, The king saved us out of the hand of our enemies, and he delivered us out of the hand of the Philistines; and now he is fled out of the land for Absalom.

10 And Absalom, whom we anointed over us, is dead in battle.

Now therefore why do you speak not a word of bringing the king back?

11 And king David sent to Zadok and to Abiathar the priests, saying, Speak to the elders of Judah, saying, Why are you the last to bring the king back to his house? seeing the speech of all Israel is come to the king, even to his house.

12 You are my brethren, you are my bones and my flesh: why then are you the last to bring back the king?

13 And say to Amasa, Are you not of my bone, and of my flesh? God do so to me, and more also, if you are not captain of the host before me continually in the room of Joab.'

14 And he bowed the heart of all the men of Judah, even as the heart of one man; so that they sent this word to the king, Return, and all your servants.

15 So the king returned, and came to Jordan. And Judah came to Gilgal, to go to meet the king, to conduct the king over Jordan.

16 And Shimei the son of Gera, a Benjamite, which was of Bahurim, hasted and came down with the men of Judah to meet king David.

17 And there were a thousand men of Benjamin with him, and Ziba the servant of the house of Saul, and his fifteen sons and his twenty servants with him; and they went over Jordan before the king.

18 And there went over a ferry boat to carry over the king's household, and to do what he thought good. And Shimei the son of Gera fell down before the king, as he was come over Jordan;

19 And said to the king, Let not my lord impute iniquity to me, neither do you remember that which your servant did perversely the day that my lord the king went out of Jerusalem, that the king should take it to his heart.

20 For your servant does know that I have sinned: therefore, behold, I am come the first this day of all the house of Joseph to go down to meet my lord the king.

21 But Abishai the son of Zeruiah answered and said, Shall not Shimei be put to death for this, because he cursed the LORD's anointed?

22 And David said, What have I to do with you, you sons of Zeruiah, that you should this day be adversaries to me? shall there any man be put to death this day in Israel? for do not I know that I am this day king over Israel?

23 Therefore the king said to Shimei, You shall not die. And the king swore to him.

24 And Mephibosheth the son of Saul came down to meet the king, and had neither dressed his feet, nor trimmed his beard, nor washed his clothes, from the day the king departed until the day he came again in peace.

25 And it came to pass, when he was come to Jerusalem to meet the king, that the king said to him, Why did you not go with me, Mephibosheth?

26 And he answered, My lord, O king, my servant deceived me: for your servant said, I will saddle me an ass, that I may ride thereon, and go to the king; because your servant is lame.

27 And he has slandered your servant to my lord the king; but my lord the king is as an angel of God: do therefore what is good in your eyes.

28 For all of my father's house were but dead men before my lord the king: yet did you set your servant among them that did eat at your own table. What right therefore have I yet to cry any more to the king?

29 And the king said to him, Why do you speak any more of your matters? I have said, You and Ziba divide the land.

30 And Mephibosheth said to the king, Yea, let him take all, forasmuch as my lord the king is come again in peace to his own house.

31 And Barzillai the Gileadite came down from Rogelim, and went over Jordan with the king, to conduct him over Jordan.

32 Now Barzillai was a very aged man, even fourscore years old: and he had provided the king of sustenance while he lay at Mahanaim; for he was a very great man.

33 And the king said to Barzillai, Come over with me, and I will feed you with me in Jerusalem.

34 And Barzillai said to the king, How long have I to live, that I should go up with the king to Jerusalem?

35 I am this day fourscore years old: and can I discern between good and evil? can your servant taste what I eat or what I drink? can I hear any more the voice of singing men and singing women? why then should your servant be yet a burden to my lord the king?

36 Your servant will go a little way over Jordan with the king: and why should the king recompense it me with such a reward?

37 Let your servant, I pray you, turn back again, that I may die in mine own city, and be buried by the grave of my father and of my mother. But behold your servant Chimham; let him go over with my lord the king; and do to him what shall seem good to you.

38 And the king answered, Chimham shall go over with me, and I will do to him that which shall seem good to you: and whatsoever you shall require of me, that will I do for you.

39 And all the people went over Jordan. And when the king was come over, the king kissed Barzillai, and blessed him; and he returned to his own place.

40 Then the king went on to Gilgal, and Chimham went on with him: and all the people of Judah conducted the king, and also half the people of Israel.

41 And, behold, all the men of Israel came to the king, and said to the king, Why have our brethren the men of Judah stolen you away, and have brought the king, and his household, and all David's men with him, over Jordan?

42 And all the men of Judah answered the men of Israel, Because the king is near of kin to us: why then are you angry for this matter? have we eaten at all of the king's cost? or has he given us any gift?

43 And the men of Israel answered the men of Judah, and said, We have ten parts in the king, and we have also more right in David than you: why then did you despise us, that our advice should not be first had in bringing back our king? And the words of the men of Judah were fiercer than the words of the men of Israel.

CHAPTER 20

AND there happened to be there a man of Belial, whose name was Sheba, the son of Bichri, a Benjamite: and he blew a trumpet, and said, We have no part in David, neither have we inheritance in the son of Jesse: every man to his tents, O Israel.

2 So every man of Israel went up from after David, and followed Sheba the son of Bichri: but the men of Judah clave to their king, from Jordan even to Jerusalem.

3 And David came to his house at Jerusalem; and the king took the ten women his concubines, whom he had left to keep the house, and put them in ward, and fed them, but went not in to them. So they were shut up to the day of their death, living in widowhood.

4 Then said the king to Amasa, Assemble me the men of Judah within three days, and be present here yourself.

5 So Amasa went to assemble the men of Judah: but he tarried longer than the set time which he had appointed him.

6 And David said to Abishai, Now shall Sheba the son of Bichri do us more harm than did Absalom: take your lord's servants, and pursue after him, lest he get him fenced cities, and escape us.

7 And there went out after him Joab's men, and the Cherethites, and the Pelethites, and all the mighty men: and they went out of Jerusalem, to pursue after Sheba the son of Bichri.

8 When they were at the great stone which is in Gibeon, Amasa went before them. And Joab's garment that he had put on was girded to him, and upon it a girdle with a sword fastened upon his loins in the sheath thereof; and as he went forth it fell out.

9 And Joab said to Amasa, Are you in health, my brother? And Joab took Amasa by the beard with the right hand to kiss him.

10 But Amasa took no heed to the sword that was in Joab's hand: so he smote him therewith in the fifth rib, and shed out his bowels to the ground, and struck him not again; and he died. So Joab and Abishai his brother pursued after Sheba the son of Bichri.

11 And one of Joab's men stood by him, and said, He that favours Joab, and he that is for David, let him go after Joab.

12 And Amasa wallowed in blood in the midst of the highway. And when the man saw that all the people stood still, he removed Amasa out of the highway into the field, and cast a cloth upon him, when he saw that every one that came by him stood still.

13 When he was removed out of the highway, all the people went on after Joab, to pursue after Sheba the son of Bichri.

14 And he went through all the tribes of Israel to Abel, and to Bethmaachah, and all the Berites: and they were gathered together, and went also after him.

15 And they came and besieged him in Abel of Bethmaachah, and they cast up a bank against the city, and it stood in the trench: and all the people that were with Joab battered the wall, to throw it down.

16 Then cried a wise woman out of the city, Hear, hear; say, I pray you, to Joab, Come near here, that I may speak with you.

17 And when he was come near to her, the woman said, Are you Joab? And he

answered, I am he. Then she said to him, Hear the words of your handmaid. And he answered, I do hear.

18 Then she spoke, saying, They were wont to speak in old time, saying, They shall surely ask counsel at Abel: and so they ended the matter.

19 I am one of them that are peaceable and faithful in Israel: you seek to destroy a city and a mother in Israel: why will you swallow up the inheritance of the LORD?

20 And Joab answered and said, Far be it, far be it from me, that I should swallow up or destroy.

21 The matter is not so: but a man of mount Ephraim, Sheba the son of Bichri by name, has lifted up his hand against the king, even against David: deliver him only, and I will depart from the city. And the woman said to Joab, Behold, his head shall be thrown to you over the wall.

22 Then the woman went to all the people in her wisdom. And they cut off the head of Sheba the son of Bichri, and cast it out to Joab. And he blew a trumpet, and they retired from the city, every man to his tent. And Joab returned to Jerusalem to the king.

23 Now Joab was over all the host of Israel: and Benaiah the son of Jehoiada was over the Cherethites and over the Pelethites:

24 And Adoram was over the tribute: and Jehoshaphat the son of Ahilud was recorder:

25 And Sheva was scribe: and Zadok and Abiathar were the priests:

26 And Ira also the Jairite was a chief ruler about David.

CHAPTER 21

THEN there was a famine in the days of David three years, year after year; and David enquired of the LORD. And the LORD answered, It is for Saul, and for his bloody house, because he slew the Gibeonites.

2 And the king called the Gibeonites, and said to them; (now the Gibeonites were not of the children of Israel, but of the remnant of the Amorites; and the children of Israel had sworn to them: and Saul sought to slay them in his zeal to the children of Israel and Judah.)

3 Therefore David said to the Gibeonites, What shall I do for you? and wherewith shall I make the atonement, that you may bless the inheritance of the LORD?

4 And the Gibeonites said to him, We will have no silver nor gold of Saul, nor of his house; neither for us shall you kill any man in Israel. And he said, What you shall say, that will I do for you.

5 And they answered the king, The man that consumed us, and that devised against us that we should be destroyed from remaining in any of the coasts of Israel,

6 Let seven men of his sons be delivered to us, and we will hang them up to the LORD in Gibeah of Saul, whom the LORD did choose. And the king said, I will give them.

7 But the king spared Mephibosheth, the son of Jonathan the son of Saul, because of the LORD's oath that was between them, between David and Jonathan the son of Saul.

8 But the king took the two sons of Rizpah the daughter of Aiah, whom she bare to Saul, Armoni and Mephibosheth; and the five sons of Michal the daughter of Saul, whom she brought up for Adriel the son of Barzillai the Meholathite:

9 And he delivered them into the hands of the Gibeonites, and they hanged them in the hill before the LORD: and they fell all seven together, and were put to death in the days of harvest, in the first days, in the beginning of barley harvest.

10 And Rizpah the daughter of Aiah took sackcloth, and spread it for her upon the rock, from the beginning of harvest until water dropped upon them out of heaven, and suffered neither the

LORD, at the blast of the breath of his nostrils.

17 He sent from above, he took me; he drew me out of many waters;

18 He delivered me from my strong enemy, and from them that hated me: for they were too strong for me.

19 They prevented me in the day of my calamity: but the LORD was my stay.

20 He brought me forth also into a large place: he delivered me, because he delighted in me.

21 The LORD rewarded me according to my righteousness: according to the cleanness of my hands has he recompensed me.

22 For I have kept the ways of the LORD, and have not wickedly departed from my God.

23 For all his judgments were before me: and as for his statutes, I did not depart from them.

24 I was also upright before him, and have kept myself from mine iniquity.

25 Therefore the LORD has recompensed me according to my righteousness; according to my cleanness in his eye sight.

26 With the merciful you will show yourself merciful, and with the upright man you will show yourself upright.

27 With the pure you will show yourself pure; and with the froward you will show yourself unsavoury.

28 And the afflicted people you will save: but your eyes are upon the haughty, that you may bring them down.

29 For you are my lamp, O LORD: and the LORD will lighten my darkness.

30 For by you I have run through a troop: by my God have I leaped over a wall.

31 As for God, his way is perfect; the word of the LORD is tried: he is a buckler to all them that trust in him.

32 For who is God, save the LORD? and who is a rock, save our God?

33 God is my strength and power: and he makes my way perfect.

34 He makes my feet like hinds' feet: and sets me upon my high places.

35 He teaches my hands to war; so that a bow of steel is broken by mine arms.

36 You have also given me the shield of your salvation: and your gentleness has made me great.

37 You have enlarged my steps under me; so that my feet did not slip.

38 I have pursued mine enemies, and destroyed them; and turned not again until I had consumed them.

39 And I have consumed them, and wounded them, that they could not arise: yea, they are fallen under my feet.

40 For you have girded me with strength to battle: them that rose up against me have you subdued under me.

41 You have also given me the necks of mine enemies, that I might destroy them that hate me.

42 They looked, but there was none to save; even to the LORD, but he answered them not.

43 Then did I beat them as small as the dust of the earth, I did stamp them as the mire of the street, and did spread them abroad.

44 You also have delivered me from the strivings of my people, you have kept me to be head of the heathen: a people which I knew not shall serve me.

45 Strangers shall submit themselves to me: as soon as they hear, they shall be obedient to me.

46 Strangers shall fade away, and they shall be afraid out of their close places.

47 The LORD lives; and blessed be my rock; and exalted be the God of the rock of my salvation.

48 It is God that avenges me, and that brings down the people under me.

49 And that brings me forth from mine enemies: you also have lifted me up on high above them that rose up against me: you have delivered me from the violent man.

50 Therefore I will give thanks to you, O LORD, among the heathen, and I will sing praises to your name.

51 He is the tower of salvation for his king: and shows mercy to his anointed, to David, and to his seed for evermore.

CHAPTER 23

NOW these be the last words of David. David the son of Jesse said, and the man who was raised up on high, the anointed of the God of Jacob, and the sweet psalmist of Israel, said,

2 The Spirit of the LORD spoke by me, and his word was in my tongue.

3 The God of Israel said, the Rock of Israel spoke to me, He that rules over men must be just, ruling in the fear of God.

4 And he shall be as the light of the morning, when the sun rises, even a morning without clouds; as the tender grass springing out of the earth by clear shining after rain.

5 Although my house be not so with God; yet he has made with me an everlasting covenant, ordered in all things, and sure: for this is all my salvation, and all my desire, although he make it not to grow.

6 But the sons of Belial shall be all of them as thorns thrust away, because they cannot be taken with hands:

7 But the man that shall touch them must be fenced with iron and the staff of a spear; and they shall be utterly burned with fire in the same place.

8 These be the names of the mighty men whom David had: The Tachmonite that sat in the seat, chief among the captains; the same was Adino the Eznite: he lift up his spear against eight hundred, whom he slew at one time.

9 And after him was Eleazar the son of Dodo the Ahohite, one of the three mighty men with David, when they defied the Philistines that were there gathered together to battle, and the men of Israel were gone away:

10 He arose, and smote the Philistines until his hand was weary, and his hand clave to the sword: and the LORD brought about a great victory that day;

and the people returned after him only to spoil.

11 And after him was Shammah the son of Agee the Hararite. And the Philistines were gathered together into a troop, where was a piece of ground full of lentiles: and the people fled from the Philistines.

12 But he stood in the midst of the ground, and defended it, and slew the Philistines: and the LORD brought about a great victory.

13 And three of the thirty chief went down, and came to David in the harvest time to the cave of Adullam: and the troop of the Philistines pitched in the valley of Rephaim.

14 And David was then in an hold, and the garrison of the Philistines was then in Bethlehem.

15 And David longed, and said, Oh that one would give me drink of the water of the well of Bethlehem, which is by the gate!

16 And the three mighty men brake through the host of the Philistines, and drew water out of the well of Bethlehem, that was by the gate, and took it, and brought it to David: nevertheless he would not drink thereof, but poured it out to the LORD.

17 And he said, Be it far from me, O LORD, that I should do this: is not this the blood of the men that went in jeopardy of their lives? therefore he would not drink it. These things did these three mighty men.

18 And Abishai, the brother of Joab, the son of Zeruiah, was chief among three. And he lifted up his spear against three hundred, and slew them, and had the name among three.

19 Was he not most honourable of three? therefore he was their captain: howbeit he attained not to the first three.

20 And Benaiah the son of Jehoiada, the son of a valiant man, of Kabzeel, who had done many acts, he slew two lionlike men of Moab: he went down also

and slew a lion in the midst of a pit in time of snow:

21 And he slew an Egyptian, a goodly man: and the Egyptian had a spear in his hand; but he went down to him with a staff, and plucked the spear out of the Egyptian's hand, and slew him with his own spear.

22 These things did Benaiah the son of Jehoiada, and had the name among three mighty men.

23 He was more honourable than the thirty, but he attained not to the first three. And David set him over his guard.

24 Asahel the brother of Joab was one of the thirty; Elhanan the son of Dodo of Bethlehem,

25 Shammah the Harodite, Elika the Harodite,

26 Helez the Paltite, Ira the son of Ikkesh the Tekoite,

27 Abiezer the Anethothite, Mebunnai the Hushathite,

28 Zalmon the Ahohite, Maharai the Netophathite,

29 Heleb the son of Baanah, a Netophathite, Ittai the son of Ribai out of Gibeah of the children of Benjamin,

30 Benaiah the Pirathonite, Hiddai of the brooks of Gaash,

31 Abialbon the Arbathite, Azmaveth the Barhumite,

32 Eliahba the Shaalbonite, of the sons of Jashen, Jonathan,

33 Shammah the Hararite, Ahiam the son of Sharar the Hararite,

34 Eliphelet the son of Ahasbai, the son of the Maachathite, Eliam the son of Ahithophel the Gilonite,

35 Hezrai the Carmelite, Paarai the Arbite,

36 Igal the son of Nathan of Zobah, Bani the Gadite,

37 Zelek the Ammonite, Nahari the Beerothite, armourbearer to Joab the son of Zeruiah,

38 Ira an Ithrite, Gareb an Ithrite,

39 Uriah the Hittite: thirty and seven in all.

CHAPTER 24

AND again the anger of the LORD was kindled against Israel, and he moved David against them to say, Go, number Israel and Judah.

2 For the king said to Joab the captain of the host, which was with him, Go now through all the tribes of Israel, from Dan even to Beersheba, and number you the people, that I may know the number of the people.

3 And Joab said to the king, Now the LORD your God add to the people, how many soever they be, an hundredfold, and that the eyes of my lord the king may see it: but why does my lord the king delight in this thing?

4 Notwithstanding the king's word prevailed against Joab, and against the captains of the host. And Joab and the captains of the host went out from the presence of the king, to number the people of Israel.

5 And they passed over Jordan, and pitched in Aroer, on the right side of the city that lies in the midst of the river of Gad, and toward Jazer:

6 Then they came to Gilead, and to the land of Tahtimhodshi; and they came to Danjaan, and about to Zidon,

7 And came to the strong hold of Tyre, and to all the cities of the Hivites, and of the Canaanites: and they went out to the south of Judah, even to Beersheba.

8 So when they had gone through all the land, they came to Jerusalem at the end of nine months and twenty days.

9 And Joab gave up the sum of the number of the people to the king: and there were in Israel eight hundred thousand valiant men that drew the sword; and the men of Judah were five hundred thousand men.

10 And David's heart smote him after that he had numbered the people. And David said to the LORD, I have sinned greatly in that I have done: and now, I beseech you, O LORD, take away the iniquity of your servant; for I have done very foolishly.

11 For when David was up in the morning, the word of the LORD came to the prophet Gad, David's seer, saying,

12 Go and say to David, Thus says the LORD, I offer you three things; choose one of them for yourself, that I may do it to you.

13 So Gad came to David, and told him, and said to him, Shall seven years of famine come to you in your land? or will you flee three months before your enemies, while they pursue you? or that there be three days' pestilence in your land? now advise, and see what answer I shall return to him that sent me.

14 And David said to Gad, I am in a great strait: let us fall now into the hand of the LORD; for his mercies are great: and let me not fall into the hand of man.

15 So the LORD sent a pestilence upon Israel from the morning even to the time appointed: and there died of the people from Dan even to Beersheba seventy thousand men.

16 And when the angel stretched out his hand upon Jerusalem to destroy it, the LORD repented him of the evil, and said to the angel that destroyed the people, It is enough: stay now your hand. And the angel of the LORD was by the threshing place of Araunah the Jebusite.

17 And David spoke to the LORD when he saw the angel that smote the people, and said, Lo, I have sinned, and I have done wickedly: but these sheep, what have they done? let your hand, I pray you, be against me, and against my father's house.

18 And Gad came that day to David, and said to him, Go up, rear an altar to the LORD in the threshingfloor of Araunah the Jebusite.

19 And David, according to the saying of Gad, went up as the LORD commanded.

20 And Araunah looked, and saw the king and his servants coming on toward him: and Araunah went out, and bowed himself before the king on his face upon the ground.

21 And Araunah said, Why is my lord the king come to his servant? And David said, To buy the threshingfloor from you, to build an altar to the LORD, that the plague may be stayed from the people.

22 And Araunah said to David, Let my lord the king take and offer up what seems good to him: behold, here be oxen for burnt sacrifice, and threshing instruments and other instruments of the oxen for wood.

23 All these things did Araunah, as a king, give to the king. And Araunah said to the king, The LORD your God accept you.

24 And the king said to Araunah, Nay; but I will surely buy it of you at a price: neither will I offer burnt offerings to the LORD my God of that which does cost me nothing. So David bought the threshingfloor and the oxen for fifty shekels of silver.

25 And David built there an altar to the LORD, and offered burnt offerings and peace offerings. So the LORD was intreated for the land, and the plague was stayed from Israel.

1 Kings

CHAPTER 1

NOW king David was old and stricken in years; and they covered him with clothes, but he gat no heat.

2 Therefore his servants said to him, Let there be sought for my lord the king a young virgin: and let her stand before the king, and let her cherish him, and let her lie in your bosom, that my lord the king may get heat.

3 So they sought for a fair damsel throughout all the coasts of Israel, and found Abishag a Shunammite, and brought her to the king.

4 And the damsel was very fair, and cherished the king, and ministered to him: but the king knew her not.

5 Then Adonijah the son of Haggith exalted himself, saying, I will be king: and he prepared him chariots and horsemen, and fifty men to run before him.

6 And his father had not displeased him at any time in saying, Why have you done so? and he also was a very goodly man; and his mother bare him after Absalom.

7 And he conferred with Joab the son of Zeruiah, and with Abiathar the priest: and they following Adonijah helped him.

8 But Zadok the priest, and Benaiah the son of Jehoiada, and Nathan the prophet, and Shimei, and Rei, and the mighty men which belonged to David, were not with Adonijah.

9 And Adonijah slew sheep and oxen and fat cattle by the stone of Zoheleth, which is by Enrogel, and called all his brethren the king's sons, and all the men of Judah the king's servants:

10 But Nathan the prophet, and Benaiah, and the mighty men, and Solomon his brother, he called not.

11 Therefore Nathan spoke to Bathsheba the mother of Solomon, saying, Have you not heard that Adonijah the son of Haggith does reign, and David our lord knows it not?

12 Now therefore come, let me, I pray you, give you counsel, that you may save your own life, and the life of your son Solomon.

13 Go and get in to king David, and say to him, Did not you, my lord, O king, swear to your handmaid, saying, Assuredly Solomon your son shall reign after me, and he shall sit upon my throne? why then does Adonijah reign?

14 Behold, while you yet talk there with the king, I also will come in after you, and confirm your words.

15 And Bathsheba went in to the king into the chamber: and the king was very old; and Abishag the Shunammite ministered to the king.

16 And Bathsheba bowed, and did obeisance to the king. And the king said, What would you?

17 And she said to him, My lord, you swore by the LORD your God to your handmaid, saying, Assuredly Solomon

your son shall reign after me, and he shall sit upon my throne.

18 And now, behold, Adonijah reigns; and now, my lord the king, you know it not:

19 And he has slain oxen and fat cattle and sheep in abundance, and has called all the sons of the king, and Abiathar the priest, and Joab the captain of the host: but Solomon your servant has he not called.

20 And you, my lord, O king, the eyes of all Israel are upon you, that you should tell them who shall sit on the throne of my lord the king after him.

21 Otherwise it shall come to pass, when my lord the king shall sleep with his fathers, that I and my son Solomon shall be counted offenders.

22 And, lo, while she yet talked with the king, Nathan the prophet also came in.

23 And they told the king, saying, Behold Nathan the prophet. And when he was come in before the king, he bowed himself before the king with his face to the ground.

24 And Nathan said, My lord, O king, have you said, Adonijah shall reign after me, and he shall sit upon my throne?

25 For he is gone down this day, and has slain oxen and fat cattle and sheep in abundance, and has called all the king's sons, and the captains of the host, and Abiathar the priest; and, behold, they eat and drink before him, and say, God save king Adonijah.

26 But me, even me your servant, and Zadok the priest, and Benaiah the son of Jehoiada, and your servant Solomon, has he not called.

27 Is this thing done by my lord the king, and you have not showed it to your servant, who should sit on the throne of my lord the king after him?

28 Then king David answered and said, Call me Bathsheba. And she came into the king's presence, and stood before the king.

29 And the king swore, and said, As the LORD lives, that has redeemed my soul out of all distress,

30 Even as I swore to you by the LORD God of Israel, saying, Assuredly Solomon your son shall reign after me, and he shall sit upon my throne in my stead; even so will I certainly do this day.

31 Then Bathsheba bowed with her face to the earth, and did reverence to the king, and said, Let my lord king David live for ever.

32 And king David said, Call me Zadok the priest, and Nathan the prophet, and Benaiah the son of Jehoiada. And they came before the king.

33 The king also said to them, Take with you the servants of your lord, and cause Solomon my son to ride upon mine own mule, and bring him down to Gihon:

34 And let Zadok the priest and Nathan the prophet anoint him there king over Israel: and blow you with the trumpet, and say, God save king Solomon.

35 Then you shall come up after him, that he may come and sit upon my throne; for he shall be king in my stead: and I have appointed him to be ruler over Israel and over Judah.

36 And Benaiah the son of Jehoiada answered the king, and said, Amen: the LORD God of my lord the king say so too.

37 As the LORD has been with my lord the king, even so be he with Solomon, and make his throne greater than the throne of my lord king David.

38 So Zadok the priest, and Nathan the prophet, and Benaiah the son of Jehoiada, and the Cherethites, and the Pelethites, went down, and caused Solomon to ride upon king David's mule, and brought him to Gihon.

39 And Zadok the priest took an horn of oil out of the tabernacle, and anointed Solomon. And they blew the trumpet; and all the people said, God save king Solomon.

40 And all the people came up after him, and the people piped with pipes, and rejoiced with great joy, so that the earth rent with the sound of them.

41 And Adonijah and all the guests that were with him heard it as they had made an end of eating. And when Joab heard the sound of the trumpet, he said, Why is this noise of the city being in an uproar?

42 And while he yet spoke, behold, Jonathan the son of Abiathar the priest came; and Adonijah said to him, Come in; for you are a valiant man, and bring good tidings.

43 And Jonathan answered and said to Adonijah, Verily our lord king David has made Solomon king.

44 And the king has sent with him Zadok the priest, and Nathan the prophet, and Benaiah the son of Jehoiada, and the Cherethites, and the Pelethites, and they have caused him to ride upon the king's mule:

45 And Zadok the priest and Nathan the prophet have anointed him king in Gihon: and they are come up from thence rejoicing, so that the city rang again. This is the noise that you have heard.

46 And also Solomon sits on the throne of the kingdom.

47 And moreover the king's servants came to bless our lord king David, saying, God make the name of Solomon better than your name, and make his throne greater than your throne. And the king bowed himself upon the bed.

48 And also thus said the king, Blessed be the LORD God of Israel, which has given one to sit on my throne this day, mine eyes even seeing it.

49 And all the guests that were with Adonijah were afraid, and rose up, and went every man his way.

50 And Adonijah feared because of Solomon, and arose, and went, and caught hold on the horns of the altar.

51 And it was told Solomon, saying, Behold, Adonijah fears king Solomon:

for, lo, he has caught hold on the horns of the altar, saying, Let king Solomon swear to me today that he will not slay his servant with the sword.

52 And Solomon said, If he will show himself a worthy man, there shall not an hair of him fall to the earth: but if wickedness shall be found in him, he shall die.

53 So king Solomon sent, and they brought him down from the altar. And he came and bowed himself to king Solomon: and Solomon said to him, Go to your house.

CHAPTER 2

NOW the days of David drew nigh that he should die; and he charged Solomon his son, saying,

2 I go the way of all the earth: be strong therefore, and show yourself a man;

3 And keep the charge of the LORD your God, to walk in his ways, to keep his statutes, and his commandments, and his judgments, and his testimonies, as it is written in the law of Moses, that you may prosper in all that you do, and wherever you turn yourself:

4 That the LORD may continue his word which he spoke concerning me, saying, If your children take heed to their way, to walk before me in truth with all their heart and with all their soul, there shall not fail you (said he) a man on the throne of Israel.

5 Moreover you know also what Joab the son of Zeruiah did to me, and what he did to the two captains of the hosts of Israel, to Abner the son of Ner, and to Amasa the son of Jether, whom he slew, and shed the blood of war in peace, and put the blood of war upon his girdle that was about his loins, and in his shoes that were on his feet.

6 Do therefore according to your wisdom, and let not his hoar head go down to the grave in peace.

7 But show kindness to the sons of Barzillai the Gileadite, and let them be of those that eat at your table: for so they

came to me when I fled because of Absalom your brother.

8 And, behold, you have with you Shimei the son of Gera, a Benjamite of Bahurim, which cursed me with a grievous curse in the day when I went to Mahanaim: but he came down to meet me at Jordan, and I swore to him by the LORD, saying, I will not put you to death with the sword.

9 Now therefore hold him not guiltless: for you are a wise man, and know what you ought to do to him; but his hoar head bring down to the grave with blood.

10 So David slept with his fathers, and was buried in the city of David.

11 And the days that David reigned over Israel were forty years: seven years reigned he in Hebron, and thirty and three years reigned he in Jerusalem.

12 Then sat Solomon upon the throne of David his father; and his kingdom was established greatly.

13 And Adonijah the son of Haggith came to Bathsheba the mother of Solomon. And she said, Do you come peaceably? And he said, Peaceably.

14 He said moreover, I have somewhat to say to you. And she said, Say on.

15 And he said, You know that the kingdom was mine, and that all Israel set their faces on me, that I should reign: howbeit the kingdom is turned about, and is become my brother's: for it was his from the LORD.

16 And now I ask one petition of you, deny me not. And she said to him, Say on.

17 And he said, Speak, I pray you, to Solomon the king, (for he will not say you nay,) that he give me Abishag the Shunammite to wife.

18 And Bathsheba said, Well; I will speak for you to the king.

19 Bathsheba therefore went to king Solomon, to speak to him for Adonijah. And the king rose up to meet her, and bowed himself to her, and sat down on his throne, and caused a seat to be set for the king's mother; and she sat on his right hand.

20 Then she said, I desire one small petition of you; I pray you, do not refuse me. And the king said to her, Ask on, my mother: for I will not say you nay.

21 And she said, Let Abishag the Shunammite be given to Adonijah your brother to wife.

22 And king Solomon answered and said to his mother, And why do you ask Abishag the Shunammite for Adonijah? ask for him the kingdom also; for he is mine elder brother; even for him, and for Abiathar the priest, and for Joab the son of Zeruiah.

23 Then king Solomon swore by the LORD, saying, God do so to me, and more also, if Adonijah have not spoken this word against his own life.

24 Now therefore, as the LORD lives, which has established me, and set me on the throne of David my father, and who has made me an house, as he promised, Adonijah shall be put to death this day.

25 And king Solomon sent by the hand of Benaiah the son of Jehoiada; and he fell upon him that he died.

26 And to Abiathar the priest said the king, Get to Anathoth, to your own fields; for you are worthy of death: but I will not at this time put you to death, because you bare the ark of the LORD God before David my father, and because you have been afflicted in all wherein my father was afflicted.

27 So Solomon thrust out Abiathar from being priest to the LORD; that he might fulfill the word of the LORD, which he spoke concerning the house of Eli in Shiloh.

28 Then tidings came to Joab: for Joab had turned after Adonijah, though he turned not after Absalom. And Joab fled to the tabernacle of the LORD, and caught hold on the horns of the altar.

29 And it was told king Solomon that Joab was fled to the tabernacle of the LORD; and, behold, he is by the altar. Then Solomon sent Benaiah the son of

Jehoiada, saying, Go, fall upon him.

30 And Benaiah came to the tabernacle of the LORD, and said to him, Thus says the king, Come forth. And he said, Nay; but I will die here. And Benaiah brought the king word again, saying, Thus said Joab, and thus he answered me.

31 And the king said to him, Do as he has said, and fall upon him, and bury him; that you may take away the innocent blood, which Joab shed, from me, and from the house of my father.

32 And the LORD shall return his blood upon his own head, who fell upon two men more righteous and better than he, and slew them with the sword, my father David not knowing thereof, to wit, Abner the son of Ner, captain of the host of Israel, and Amasa the son of Jether, captain of the host of Judah.

33 Their blood shall therefore return upon the head of Joab, and upon the head of his seed for ever: but upon David, and upon his seed, and upon his house, and upon his throne, shall there be peace for ever from the LORD.

34 So Benaiah the son of Jehoiada went up, and fell upon him, and slew him: and he was buried in his own house in the wilderness.

35 And the king put Benaiah the son of Jehoiada in his room over the host: and Zadok the priest did the king put in the room of Abiathar.

36 And the king sent and called for Shimei, and said to him, Build yourself a house in Jerusalem, and dwell there, and go not forth thence any where.

37 For it shall be, that on the day you go out, and pass over the brook Kidron, you shall know for certain that you shall surely die: your blood shall be upon your own head.

38 And Shimei said to the king, The saying is good: as my lord the king has said, so will your servant do. And Shimei dwelt in Jerusalem many days.

39 And it came to pass at the end of three years, that two of the servants of Shimei ran away to Achish son of Maachah king of Gath. And they told Shimei, saying, Behold, your servants are in Gath.

40 And Shimei arose, and saddled his ass, and went to Gath to Achish to seek his servants: and Shimei went, and brought his servants from Gath.

41 And it was told Solomon that Shimei had gone from Jerusalem to Gath, and was come again.

42 And the king sent and called for Shimei, and said to him, Did I not make you to swear by the LORD, and protested to you, saying, Know for a certain, on the day you go out, and walk abroad any where, that you shall surely die? and you said to me, The word that I have heard is good.

43 Why then have you not kept the oath of the LORD, and the commandment that I have charged you with?

44 The king said moreover to Shimei, You know all the wickedness which your heart is privy to, that you did to David my father: therefore the LORD shall return your wickedness upon your own head;

45 And king Solomon shall be blessed, and the throne of David shall be established before the LORD for ever.

46 So the king commanded Benaiah the son of Jehoiada; which went out, and fell upon him, that he died. And the kingdom was established in the hand of Solomon.

CHAPTER 3

AND Solomon made affinity with Pharaoh king of Egypt, and took Pharaoh's daughter, and brought her into the city of David, until he had made an end of building his own house, and the house of the LORD, and the wall of Jerusalem round about.

2 Only the people sacrificed in high places, because there was no house built to the name of the LORD, until those days.

3 And Solomon loved the LORD, walking in the statutes of David his father:

only he sacrificed and burnt incense in high places.

4 And the king went to Gibeon to sacrifice there; for that was the great high place: a thousand burnt offerings did Solomon offer upon that altar.

5 In Gibeon the LORD appeared to Solomon in a dream by night: and God said, Ask what I shall give you.

6 And Solomon said, You have showed to your servant David my father great mercy, according as he walked before you in truth, and in righteousness, and in uprightness of heart with you; and you have kept for him this great kindness, that you have given him a son to sit on his throne, as it is this day.

7 And now, O LORD my God, you have made your servant king instead of David my father: and I am but a little child: I know not how to go out or come in.

8 And your servant is in the midst of your people which you have chosen, a great people, that cannot be numbered nor counted for multitude.

9 Give therefore your servant an understanding heart to judge your people, that I may discern between good and bad: for who is able to judge this great people of yours?

10 And the speech pleased the LORD, that Solomon had asked this thing.

11 And God said to him, Because you have asked this thing, and have not asked for yourself long life; neither have asked riches for yourself, nor have asked the life of your enemies; but have asked for yourself understanding to discern judgment;

12 Behold, I have done according to your words: lo, I have given you a wise and an understanding heart; so that there was none like you before you, neither after you shall any arise like to you.

13 And I have also given you that which you have not asked, both riches, and honour: so that there shall not be any among the kings like to you all your days.

14 And if you will walk in my ways, to keep my statutes and my commandments, as your father David did walk, then I will lengthen your days.

15 And Solomon awoke; and, behold, it was a dream. And he came to Jerusalem, and stood before the ark of the covenant of the LORD, and offered up burnt offerings, and offered peace offerings, and made a feast to all his servants.

16 Then came there two women, that were harlots, to the king, and stood before him.

17 And the one woman said, O my lord, I and this woman dwell in one house; and I was delivered of a child with her in the house.

18 And it came to pass the third day after that I was delivered, that this woman was delivered also: and we were together; there was no stranger with us in the house, save we two in the house.

19 And this woman's child died in the night; because she overlaid it.

20 And she arose at midnight, and took my son from beside me, while your handmaid slept, and laid it in her bosom, and laid her dead child in my bosom.

21 And when I rose in the morning to give my child suck, behold, it was dead: but when I had considered it in the morning, behold, it was not my son, which I did bear.

22 And the other woman said, Nay; but the living is my son, and the dead is your son. And this said, No; but the dead is your son, and the living is my son. Thus they spoke before the king.

23 Then said the king, The one says, This is my son that lives, and your son is the dead: and the other says, Nay; but your son is the dead, and my son is the living.

3:5 See John 14:14 comment.

JUDGMENT OF SOLOMON

1 Kings 3:27

24 And the king said, Bring me a sword. And they brought a sword before the king.

25 And the king said, Divide the living child in two, and give half to the one, and half to the other.

26 Then spoke the woman whose the living child was to the king, for her bowels yearned upon her son, and she said, O my lord, give her the living child, and in no wise slay it. But the other said, Let it be neither mine nor yours, but divide it.

27 Then the king answered and said, Give her the living child, and in no wise slay it: she is the mother thereof.

28 And all Israel heard of the judgment which the king had judged; and they feared the king: for they saw that the wisdom of God was in him, to do judgment.

CHAPTER 4

SO king Solomon was king over all Israel.

2 And these were the princes which he had; Azariah the son of Zadok the priest,

3 Elihoreph and Ahiah, the sons of Shisha, scribes; Jehoshaphat the son of Ahilud, the recorder.

4 And Benaiah the son of Jehoiada was over the host: and Zadok and Abiathar were the priests:

5 And Azariah the son of Nathan was over the officers: and Zabud the son of Nathan was principal officer, and the king's friend:

6 And Ahishar was over the household: and Adoniram the son of Abda was over the tribute.

7 And Solomon had twelve officers over all Israel, which provided victuals for the king and his household: each man his month in a year made provision.

8 And these are their names: The son of Hur, in mount Ephraim:

9 The son of Dekar, in Makaz, and in Shaalbim, and Bethshemesh, and Elonbethhanan:

10 The son of Hesed, in Aruboth; to him pertained Sochoh, and all the land of Hepher:

11 The son of Abinadab, in all the region of Dor; which had Taphath the daughter of Solomon to wife:

12 Baana the son of Ahilud; to him pertained Taanach and Megiddo, and all Bethshean, which is by Zartanah beneath Jezreel, from Bethshean to Abelmeholah, even to the place that is beyond Jokneam:

13 The son of Geber, in Ramothgilead; to him pertained the towns of Jair the son of Manasseh, which are in Gilead; to him also pertained the region of Argob, which is in Bashan, threescore great cities with walls and brasen bars:

14 Ahinadab the son of Iddo had Mahanaim:

15 Ahimaaz was in Naphtali; he also took Basmath the daughter of Solomon to wife:

16 Baanah the son of Hushai was in Asher and in Aloth:

17 Jehoshaphat the son of Paruah, in Issachar:

18 Shimei the son of Elah, in Benjamin:

19 Geber the son of Uri was in the country of Gilead, in the country of Sihon king of the Amorites, and of Og king of Bashan; and he was the only officer which was in the land.

20 Judah and Israel were many, as the sand which is by the sea in multitude, eating and drinking, and making merry.

21 And Solomon reigned over all kingdoms from the river to the land of the Philistines, and to the border of Egypt: they brought presents, and served Solomon all the days of his life.

22 And Solomon's provision for one day was thirty measures of fine flour, and threescore measures of meal,

23 Ten fat oxen, and twenty oxen out of the pastures, and an hundred sheep, beside harts, and roebucks, and fallowdeer, and fatted fowl.

24 For he had dominion over all the region on this side the river, from Tiphsah even to Azzah, over all the kings on this side the river: and he had peace on all sides round about him.

25 And Judah and Israel dwelt safely, every man under his vine and under his fig tree, from Dan even to Beersheba, all the days of Solomon.

26 And Solomon had forty thousand stalls of horses for his chariots, and twelve thousand horsemen.

27 And those officers provided victual for king Solomon, and for all that came to king Solomon's table, every man in his month: they lacked nothing.

28 Barley also and straw for the horses and dromedaries brought they to the place where the officers were, every man according to his charge.

29 And God gave Solomon wisdom and understanding exceeding much, and largeness of heart, even as the sand that is on the sea shore.

CUTTING DOWN CEDARS FOR THE CONSTRUCTION OF THE TEMPLE

1 Kings 5:5-6

30 And Solomon's wisdom excelled the wisdom of all the children of the east country, and all the wisdom of Egypt.

31 For he was wiser than all men; than Ethan the Ezrahite, and Heman, and Chalcol, and Darda, the sons of Mahol: and his fame was in all nations round about.

32 And he spoke three thousand proverbs: and his songs were a thousand and five.

33 And he spoke of trees, from the cedar tree that is in Lebanon even to the hyssop that springs out of the wall: he spoke also of beasts, and of fowl, and of creeping things, and of fishes.

34 And there came of all people to hear the wisdom of Solomon, from all kings of the earth, which had heard of his wisdom.

CHAPTER 5

AND Hiram king of Tyre sent his servants to Solomon; for he had heard that they had anointed him king in the room of his father: for Hiram was ever a lover of David.

2 And Solomon sent to Hiram, saying,

3 You know how that David my father could not build an house to the name of the LORD his God for the wars which were about him on every side, until the LORD put them under the soles of his feet.

4 But now the LORD my God has given me rest on every side, so that there is neither adversary nor evil occurrent.

5 And, behold, I purpose to build an house to the name of the LORD my God, as the LORD spoke to David my father, saying, Your son, whom I will set upon

your throne in your room, he shall build an house to my name.

6 Now therefore command that they hew me cedar trees out of Lebanon; and my servants shall be with your servants: and to you will I give hire for your servants according to all that you shall appoint: for you know that there is not among us any that can skill to hew timber like to the Sidonians.

7 And it came to pass, when Hiram heard the words of Solomon, that he rejoiced greatly, and said, Blessed be the LORD this day, which has given to David a wise son over this great people.

8 And Hiram sent to Solomon, saying, I have considered the things which you sent to me for: and I will do all your desire concerning timber of cedar, and concerning timber of fir.

9 My servants shall bring them down from Lebanon to the sea: and I will convey them by sea in floats to the place that you shall appoint me, and will cause them to be discharged there, and you shall receive them: and you shall accomplish my desire, in giving food for my household.

10 So Hiram gave Solomon cedar trees and fir trees according to all his desire.

11 And Solomon gave Hiram twenty thousand measures of wheat for food to his household, and twenty measures of pure oil: thus gave Solomon to Hiram year by year.

12 And the LORD gave Solomon wisdom, as he promised him: and there was peace between Hiram and Solomon; and they two made a league together.

13 And king Solomon raised a levy out of all Israel; and the levy was thirty thousand men.

14 And he sent them to Lebanon, ten thousand a month by courses: a month they were in Lebanon, and two months at home: and Adoniram was over the levy.

15 And Solomon had threescore and ten thousand that bare burdens, and fourscore thousand hewers in the mountains;

16 Beside the chief of Solomon's officers which were over the work, three thousand and three hundred, which ruled over the people that labored in the work.

17 And the king commanded, and they brought great stones, costly stones, and hewed stones, to lay the foundation of the house.

18 And Solomon's builders and Hiram's builders did hew them, and the stonesquarers: so they prepared timber and stones to build the house.

CHAPTER 6

AND it came to pass in the four hundred and eightieth year after the children of Israel were come out of the land of Egypt, in the fourth year of Solomon's reign over Israel, in the month Zif, which is the second month, that he began to build the house of the LORD.

2 And the house which king Solomon built for the LORD, the length thereof was threescore cubits, and the breadth thereof twenty cubits, and the height thereof thirty cubits.

3 And the porch before the temple of the house, twenty cubits was the length thereof, according to the breadth of the house; and ten cubits was the breadth thereof before the house.

4 And for the house he made windows of narrow lights.

5 And against the wall of the house he built chambers round about, against the walls of the house round about, both of the temple and of the oracle: and he made chambers round about:

6 The nethermost chamber was five cubits broad, and the middle was six cubits broad, and the third was seven cubits broad: for without in the wall of the house he made narrowed rests round about, that the beams should not be fastened in the walls of the house.

7 And the house, when it was in building, was built of stone made ready before it was brought there: so that there was neither hammer nor axe nor any tool of iron heard in the house, while it was in building.

8 The door for the middle chamber was in the right side of the house: and they went up with winding stairs into the middle chamber, and out of the middle into the third.

9 So he built the house, and finished it; and covered the house with beams and boards of cedar.

10 And then he built chambers against all the house, five cubits high: and they rested on the house with timber of cedar.

11 And the word of the LORD came to Solomon, saying,

12 Concerning this house which you are in building, if you will walk in my statutes, and execute my judgments, and keep all my commandments to walk in them; then will I perform my word with you, which I spoke to David your father:

13 And I will dwell among the children of Israel, and will not forsake my people Israel.

14 So Solomon built the house, and finished it.

15 And he built the walls of the house within with boards of cedar, both the floor of the house, and the walls of the ceiling: and he covered them on the inside with wood, and covered the floor of the house with planks of fir.

16 And he built twenty cubits on the sides of the house, both the floor and the walls with boards of cedar: he even built them for it within, even for the oracle, even for the most holy place.

17 And the house, that is, the temple before it, was forty cubits long.

18 And the cedar of the house within was carved with knops and open flowers: all was cedar; there was no stone seen.

19 And the oracle he prepared in the house within, to set there the ark of the covenant of the LORD.

20 And the oracle in the forepart was twenty cubits in length, and twenty cubits in breadth, and twenty cubits in the height thereof: and he overlaid it with pure gold; and so covered the altar which was of cedar.

21 So Solomon overlaid the house within with pure gold: and he made a partition by the chains of gold before the oracle; and he overlaid it with gold.

22 And the whole house he overlaid with gold, until he had finished all the house: also the whole altar that was by the oracle he overlaid with gold.

23 And within the oracle he made two cherubims of olive tree, each ten cubits high.

24 And five cubits was the one wing of the cherub, and five cubits the other wing of the cherub: from the uttermost part of the one wing to the uttermost part of the other were ten cubits.

25 And the other cherub was ten cubits: both the cherubims were of one measure and one size.

26 The height of the one cherub was ten cubits, and so was it of the other cherub.

27 And he set the cherubims within the inner house: and they stretched forth the wings of the cherubims, so that the wing of the one touched the one wall, and the wing of the other cherub touched the other wall; and their wings touched one another in the midst of the house.

28 And he overlaid the cherubims with gold.

29 And he carved all the walls of the house round about with carved figures of cherubims and palm trees and open flowers, within and without.

30 And the floors of the house he overlaid with gold, within and without.

31 And for the entering of the oracle he made doors of olive tree: the lintel and side posts were a fifth part of the wall.

32 The two doors also were of olive tree; and he carved upon them carvings of cherubims and palm trees and open flowers, and overlaid them with gold, and spread gold upon the cherubims, and upon the palm trees.

33 So also made he for the door of the temple posts of olive tree, a fourth part of the wall.

34 And the two doors were of fir tree: the two leaves of the one door were folding, and the two leaves of the other door were folding.

35 And he carved thereon cherubims and palm trees and open flowers: and covered them with gold fitted upon the carved work.

36 And he built the inner court with three rows of hewed stone, and a row of cedar beams.

37 In the fourth year was the foundation of the house of the LORD laid, in the month Zif:

38 And in the eleventh year, in the month Bul, which is the eighth month, was the house finished throughout all the parts thereof, and according to all the fashion of it. So was he seven years in building it.

CHAPTER 7

BUT Solomon was building his own house thirteen years, and he finished all his house.

2 He built also the house of the forest of Lebanon; the length thereof was an hundred cubits, and the breadth thereof fifty cubits, and the height thereof thirty cubits, upon four rows of cedar pillars, with cedar beams upon the pillars.

3 And it was covered with cedar above upon the beams, that lay on forty five pillars, fifteen in a row.

4 And there were windows in three rows, and light was against light in three ranks.

5 And all the doors and posts were square, with the windows: and light was against light in three ranks.

6 And he made a porch of pillars; the length thereof was fifty cubits, and the breadth thereof thirty cubits: and the porch was before them: and the other pillars and the thick beam were before them.

7 Then he made a porch for the throne where he might judge, even the porch of judgment: and it was covered with cedar from one side of the floor to the other.

8 And his house where he dwelt had another court within the porch, which was of the like work. Solomon made also an house for Pharaoh's daughter, whom he had taken to wife, like to this porch.

9 All these were of costly stones, according to the measures of hewed stones, sawed with saws, within and without, even from the foundation to the coping, and so on the outside toward the great court.

10 And the foundation was of costly stones, even great stones, stones of ten cubits, and stones of eight cubits.

11 And above were costly stones, after the measures of hewed stones, and cedars.

12 And the great court round about was with three rows of hewed stones, and a row of cedar beams, both for the inner court of the house of the LORD, and for the porch of the house.

13 And king Solomon sent and fetched Hiram out of Tyre.

14 He was a widow's son of the tribe of Naphtali, and his father was a man of Tyre, a worker in brass: and he was filled with wisdom, and understanding, and cunning to work all works in brass. And he came to king Solomon, and did all his work.

15 For he cast two pillars of brass, of eighteen cubits high apiece: and a line of twelve cubits did compass either of them about.

16 And he made two chapiters of molten brass, to set upon the tops of the pillars: the height of the one chapiter was five cubits, and the height of the other chapiter was five cubits:

17 And nets of checker work, and wreaths of chain work, for the chapiters which were upon the top of the pillars; seven for the one chapiter, and seven for the other chapiter.

18 And he made the pillars, and two rows round about upon the one network, to cover the chapiters that were upon the top, with pomegranates: and so did he for the other chapiter.

19 And the chapiters that were upon the top of the pillars were of lily work in the porch, four cubits.

20 And the chapiters upon the two pillars had pomegranates also above, over against the belly which was by the network: and the pomegranates were two hundred in rows round about upon the other chapiter.

21 And he set up the pillars in the porch of the temple: and he set up the right pillar, and called the name thereof Jachin: and he set up the left pillar, and called the name thereof Boaz.

22 And upon the top of the pillars was lily work: so was the work of the pillars finished.

23 And he made a molten sea, ten cubits from the one brim to the other: it was round all about, and his height was five cubits: and a line of thirty cubits did compass it round about.

24 And under the brim of it round about there were knops compassing it, ten in a cubit, compassing the sea round about: the knops were cast in two rows, when it was cast.

25 It stood upon twelve oxen, three looking toward the north, and three looking toward the west, and three looking toward the south, and three looking toward the east: and the sea was set above upon them, and all their hinder parts were inward.

26 And it was an hand breadth thick, and the brim thereof was shaped like the brim of a cup, with flowers of lilies: it contained two thousand baths.

27 And he made ten bases of brass; four cubits was the length of one base, and four cubits the breadth thereof, and three cubits the height of it.

28 And the work of the bases was on this manner: they had borders, and the borders were between the ledges:

29 And on the borders that were between the ledges were lions, oxen, and cherubims: and upon the ledges there was a base above: and beneath the lions and oxen were certain additions made of thin work.

30 And every base had four brasen wheels, and plates of brass: and the four corners thereof had undersetters: under the laver were undersetters molten, at the side of every addition.

31 And the mouth of it within the chapiter and above was a cubit: but the mouth thereof was round after the work of the base, a cubit and an half: and also upon the mouth of it were gravings with their borders, foursquare, not round.

32 And under the borders were four wheels; and the axletrees of the wheels were joined to the base: and the height of a wheel was a cubit and half a cubit.

33 And the work of the wheels was like the work of a chariot wheel: their axletrees, and their naves, and their felloes, and their spokes, were all molten.

34 And there were four undersetters to the four corners of one base: and the undersetters were of the very base itself.

35 And in the top of the base was there a round compass of half a cubit high: and on the top of the base the ledges thereof and the borders thereof were of the same.

36 For on the plates of the ledges thereof, and on the borders thereof, he graved cherubims, lions, and palm trees, according to the proportion of every one, and additions round about.

37 After this manner he made the ten bases: all of them had one casting, one measure, and one size.

38 Then made he ten lavers of brass: one laver contained forty baths: and every laver was four cubits: and upon every one of the ten bases one laver.

39 And he put five bases on the right side of the house, and five on the left side of the house: and he set the sea on the right side of the house eastward over against the south.

40 And Hiram made the lavers, and the shovels, and the basons. So Hiram made an end of doing all the work that he made king Solomon for the house of the LORD:

41 The two pillars, and the two bowls of the chapiters that were on the top of the two pillars; and the two networks, to cover the two bowls of the chapiters which were upon the top of the pillars;

42 And four hundred pomegranates for the two networks, even two rows of pomegranates for one network, to cover the two bowls of the chapiters that were upon the pillars;

43 And the ten bases, and ten lavers on the bases;

44 And one sea, and twelve oxen under the sea;

45 And the pots, and the shovels, and the basons: and all these vessels, which Hiram made to king Solomon for the house of the LORD, were of bright brass.

46 In the plain of Jordan did the king cast them, in the clay ground between Succoth and Zarthan.

47 And Solomon left all the vessels unweighed, because they were exceeding many: neither was the weight of the brass found out.

48 And Solomon made all the vessels that pertained to the house of the LORD: the altar of gold, and the table of gold, whereupon the shewbread was,

49 And the candlesticks of pure gold, five on the right side, and five on the left, before the oracle, with the flowers, and the lamps, and the tongs of gold,

50 And the bowls, and the snuffers, and the basons, and the spoons, and the censers of pure gold; and the hinges of gold, both for the doors of the inner house, the most holy place, and for the doors of the house, to wit, of the temple.

51 So was ended all the work that king Solomon made for the house of the LORD. And Solomon brought in the things which David his father had dedicated; even the silver, and the gold, and the vessels, did he put among the treasures of the house of the LORD.

CHAPTER 8

THEN Solomon assembled the elders of Israel, and all the heads of the tribes, the chief of the fathers of the children of Israel, to king Solomon in Jerusalem, that they might bring up the ark of the covenant of the LORD out of the city of David, which is Zion.

2 And all the men of Israel assembled themselves to king Solomon at the feast in the month Ethanim, which is the seventh month.

3 And all the elders of Israel came, and the priests took up the ark.

4 And they brought up the ark of the LORD, and the tabernacle of the congregation, and all the holy vessels that were in the tabernacle, even those did the priests and the Levites bring up.

5 And king Solomon, and all the congregation of Israel, that were assembled to him, were with him before the ark, sacrificing sheep and oxen, that could not be told nor numbered for multitude.

6 And the priests brought in the ark of the covenant of the LORD to his place, into the oracle of the house, to the most holy place, even under the wings of the cherubims.

7 For the cherubims spread forth their two wings over the place of the ark, and the cherubims covered the ark and the staves thereof above.

8 And they drew out the staves, that the ends of the staves were seen out in the holy place before the oracle, and they were not seen without: and there they are to this day.

9 There was nothing in the ark save the two tables of stone, which Moses put there at Horeb, when the LORD made a covenant with the children of Israel,

when they came out of the land of Egypt.

10 And it came to pass, when the priests were come out of the holy place, that the cloud filled the house of the LORD,

11 So that the priests could not stand to minister because of the cloud: for the glory of the LORD had filled the house of the LORD.

12 Then spoke Solomon, The LORD said that he would dwell in the thick darkness.

13 I have surely built you an house to dwell in, a settled place for you to abide in for ever.

14 And the king turned his face about, and blessed all the congregation of Israel: (and all the congregation of Israel stood;)

15 And he said, Blessed be the LORD God of Israel, which spoke with his mouth to David my father, and has with his hand fulfilled it, saying,

16 Since the day that I brought forth my people Israel out of Egypt, I chose no city out of all the tribes of Israel to build an house, that my name might be therein; but I chose David to be over my people Israel.

17 And it was in the heart of David my father to build an house for the name of the LORD God of Israel.

18 And the LORD said to David my father, Whereas it was in your heart to build an house to my name, you did well that it was in your heart.

19 Nevertheless you shall not build the house; but your son that shall come forth out of your loins, he shall build the house to my name.

20 And the LORD has performed his word that he spoke, and I am risen up in the room of David my father, and sit on the throne of Israel, as the LORD promised, and have built an house for the name of the LORD God of Israel.

21 And I have set there a place for the ark, wherein is the covenant of the LORD, which he made with our fathers,

when he brought them out of the land of Egypt.

22 And Solomon stood before the altar of the LORD in the presence of all the congregation of Israel, and spread forth his hands toward heaven:

23 And he said, LORD God of Israel, there is no God like you, in heaven above, or on earth beneath, who keeps covenant and mercy with your servants that walk before you with all their heart:

24 Who have kept with your servant David my father that you promised him: you spoke also with your mouth, and have fulfilled it with your hand, as it is this day.

25 Therefore now, LORD God of Israel, keep with your servant David my father that you promised him, saying, There shall not fail you a man in my sight to sit on the throne of Israel; so that your children take heed to their way, that they walk before me as you have walked before me.

26 And now, O God of Israel, let your word, I pray you, be verified, which you spoke to your servant David my father.

27 But will God indeed dwell on the earth? behold, the heaven and heaven of heavens cannot contain you; how much less this house that I have built?

28 Yet have you respect to the prayer of your servant, and to his supplication, O LORD my God, to hearken to the cry and to the prayer, which your servant prays before you to day:

29 That your eyes may be open toward this house night and day, even toward the place of which you have said, My name shall be there: that you may hearken to the prayer which your servant shall make toward this place.

30 And hearken to the supplication of your servant, and of your people Israel, when they shall pray toward this place: and hear you in heaven your dwelling place: and when you hear, forgive.

31 If any man trespass against his neighbour, and an oath be laid upon

him to cause him to swear, and the oath come before your altar in this house:

32 Then hear you in heaven, and do, and judge your servants, condemning the wicked, to bring his way upon his head; and justifying the righteous, to give him according to his righteousness.

33 When your people Israel be smitten down before the enemy, because they have sinned against you, and shall turn again to you, and confess your name, and pray, and make supplication to you in this house:

34 Then hear you in heaven, and forgive the sin of your people Israel, and bring them again to the land which you gave to their fathers.

35 When heaven is shut up, and there is no rain, because they have sinned against you; if they pray toward this place, and confess your name, and turn from their sin, when you afflict them:

36 Then hear you in heaven, and forgive the sin of your servants, and of your people Israel, that you teach them the good way wherein they should walk, and give rain upon your land, which you have given to your people for an inheritance.

37 If there be in the land famine, if there be pestilence, blasting, mildew, locust, or if there be caterpiller; if their enemy besiege them in the land of their cities; whatsoever plague, whatsoever sickness there be;

38 What prayer and supplication soever be made by any man, or by all your people Israel, which shall know every man the plague of his own heart, and spread forth his hands toward this house:

39 Then hear you in heaven your dwelling place, and forgive, and do, and give to every man according to his ways, whose heart you know; (for you, even you only, know the hearts of all the children of men;)

40 That they may fear you all the days that they live in the land which you gave to our fathers.

41 Moreover concerning a stranger, that is not of your people Israel, but cometh out of a far country for your name's sake;

42 (For they shall hear of your great name, and of your strong hand, and of your stretched out arm;) when he shall come and pray toward this house;

43 Hear you in heaven your dwelling place, and do according to all that the stranger calls to you for: that all people of the earth may know your name, to fear you, as do your people Israel; and that they may know that this house, which I have built, is called by your name.

44 If your people go out to battle against their enemy, wherever you shall send them, and shall pray to the LORD toward the city which you have chosen, and toward the house that I have built for your name:

45 Then hear you in heaven their prayer and their supplication, and maintain their cause.

46 If they sin against you, (for there is no man that sins not,) and you be angry with them, and deliver them to the enemy, so that they carry them away captives to the land of the enemy, far or near;

47 Yet if they shall bethink themselves in the land where they were carried captives, and repent, and make supplication to you in the land of them that carried them captives, saying, We have sinned, and have done perversely, we have committed wickedness;

48 And so return to you with all their heart, and with all their soul, in the land of their enemies, which led them away captive, and pray to you toward their land, which you gave to their fathers, the city which you have chosen, and the house which I have built for your name:

49 Then hear you their prayer and their supplication in heaven your dwelling place, and maintain their cause,

50 And forgive your people that have sinned against you, and all their transgressions wherein they have transgressed

against you, and give them compassion before them who carried them captive, that they may have compassion on them:

51 For they are your people, and your inheritance, which you brought forth out of Egypt, from the midst of the furnace of iron:

52 That your eyes may be open to the supplication of your servant, and to the supplication of your people Israel, to hearken to them in all that they call for to you.

53 For you did separate them from among all the people of the earth, to be your inheritance, as you spoke by the hand of Moses your servant, when you brought our fathers out of Egypt, O LORD God.

54 And it was so, that when Solomon had made an end of praying all this prayer and supplication to the LORD, he arose from before the altar of the LORD, from kneeling on his knees with his hands spread up to heaven.

55 And he stood, and blessed all the congregation of Israel with a loud voice, saying,

56 Blessed be the LORD, that has given rest to his people Israel, according to all that he promised: there has not failed one word of all his good promise, which he promised by the hand of Moses his servant.

57 The LORD our God be with us, as he was with our fathers: let him not leave us, nor forsake us:

58 That he may incline our hearts to him, to walk in all his ways, and to keep his commandments, and his statutes, and his judgments, which he commanded our fathers.

59 And let these my words, wherewith I have made supplication before the LORD, be nigh to the LORD our God day and night, that he maintain the cause of his servant, and the cause of his people Israel at all times, as the matter shall require:

60 That all the people of the earth may know that the LORD is God, and that there is none else.

61 Let your heart therefore be perfect with the LORD our God, to walk in his statutes, and to keep his commandments, as at this day.

62 And the king, and all Israel with him, offered sacrifice before the LORD.

63 And Solomon offered a sacrifice of peace offerings, which he offered to the LORD, two and twenty thousand oxen, and an hundred and twenty thousand sheep. So the king and all the children of Israel dedicated the house of the LORD.

64 The same day did the king hallow the middle of the court that was before the house of the LORD: for there he offered burnt offerings, and meat offerings, and the fat of the peace offerings: because the brasen altar that was before the LORD was too little to receive the burnt offerings, and meat offerings, and the fat of the peace offerings.

65 And at that time Solomon held a feast, and all Israel with him, a great congregation, from the entering in of Hamath to the river of Egypt, before the LORD our God, seven days and seven days, even fourteen days.

66 On the eighth day he sent the people away: and they blessed the king, and went to their tents joyful and glad of heart for all the goodness that the LORD had done for David his servant, and for Israel his people.

CHAPTER 9

AND it came to pass, when Solomon had finished the building of the house of the LORD, and the king's house, and all Solomon's desire which he was pleased to do,

2 That the LORD appeared to Solomon the second time, as he had appeared to him at Gibeon.

3 And the LORD said to him, I have heard your prayer and your supplication, that you have made before me: I have hallowed this house, which you

have built, to put my name there for ever; and mine eyes and mine heart shall be there perpetually.

4 And if you will walk before me, as David your father walked, in integrity of heart, and in uprightness, to do according to all that I have commanded you, and will keep my statutes and my judgments:

5 Then I will establish the throne of your kingdom upon Israel for ever, as I promised to David your father, saying, There shall not fail you a man upon the throne of Israel.

6 But if you shall at all turn from following me, you or your children, and will not keep my commandments and my statutes which I have set before you, but go and serve other gods, and worship them:

7 Then will I cut off Israel out of the land which I have given them; and this house, which I have hallowed for my name, will I cast out of my sight; and Israel shall be a proverb and a byword among all people:

8 And at this house, which is high, every one that passes by it shall be astonished, and shall hiss; and they shall say, Why has the LORD done thus to this land, and to this house?

9 And they shall answer, Because they forsook the LORD their God, who brought forth their fathers out of the land of Egypt, and have taken hold upon other gods, and have worshipped them, and served them: therefore has the LORD brought upon them all this evil.

10 And it came to pass at the end of twenty years, when Solomon had built the two houses, the house of the LORD, and the king's house,

11 (Now Hiram the king of Tyre had furnished Solomon with cedar trees and fir trees, and with gold, according to all his desire,) that then king Solomon gave Hiram twenty cities in the land of Galilee.

12 And Hiram came out from Tyre to see the cities which Solomon had given him; and they pleased him not.

13 And he said, What cities are these which you have given me, my brother? And he called them the land of Cabul to this day.

14 And Hiram sent to the king sixscore talents of gold.

15 And this is the reason of the levy which king Solomon raised; for to build the house of the LORD, and his own house, and Millo, and the wall of Jerusalem, and Hazor, and Megiddo, and Gezer.

16 For Pharaoh king of Egypt had gone up, and taken Gezer, and burnt it with fire, and slain the Canaanites that dwelt in the city, and given it for a present to his daughter, Solomon's wife.

17 And Solomon built Gezer, and Bethhoron the nether,

18 And Baalath, and Tadmor in the wilderness, in the land,

19 And all the cities of store that Solomon had, and cities for his chariots, and cities for his horsemen, and that which Solomon desired to build in Jerusalem, and in Lebanon, and in all the land of his dominion.

20 And all the people that were left of the Amorites, Hittites, Perizzites, Hivites, and Jebusites, which were not of the children of Israel,

21 Their children that were left after them in the land, whom the children of Israel also were not able utterly to destroy, upon those did Solomon levy a tribute of bondservice to this day.

22 But of the children of Israel did Solomon make no bondmen: but they were men of war, and his servants, and his princes, and his captains, and rulers of his chariots, and his horsemen.

23 These were the chief of the officers that were over Solomon's work, five hundred and fifty, which bare rule over the people that wrought in the work.

24 But Pharaoh's daughter came up out of the city of David to her house which

Solomon had built for her: then did he build Millo.

25 And three times in a year did Solomon offer burnt offerings and peace offerings upon the altar which he built to the LORD, and he burnt incense upon the altar that was before the LORD. So he finished the house.

26 And king Solomon made a navy of ships in Eziongeber, which is beside Eloth, on the shore of the Red sea, in the land of Edom.

27 And Hiram sent in the navy his servants, shipmen that had knowledge of the sea, with the servants of Solomon.

28 And they came to Ophir, and fetched from thence gold, four hundred and twenty talents, and brought it to king Solomon.

CHAPTER 10

AND when the queen of Sheba heard of the fame of Solomon concerning the name of the LORD, she came to prove him with hard questions.

2 And she came to Jerusalem with a very great train, with camels that bare spices, and very much gold, and precious stones: and when she was come to Solomon, she communed with him of all that was in her heart.

3 And Solomon told her all her questions: there was not any thing hid from the king, which he told her not.

4 And when the queen of Sheba had seen all Solomon's wisdom, and the house that he had built,

5 And the meat of his table, and the sitting of his servants, and the attendance of his ministers, and their apparel, and his cupbearers, and his ascent by which he went up to the house of the LORD; there was no more spirit in her.

6 And she said to the king, It was a true report that I heard in mine own land of your acts and of your wisdom.

7 Howbeit I believed not the words, until I came, and mine eyes had seen it: and, behold, the half was not told me:

your wisdom and prosperity exceeds the fame which I heard.

8 Happy are your men, happy are these your servants, which stand continually before you, and that hear your wisdom.

9 Blessed be the LORD your God, which delighted in you, to set you on the throne of Israel: because the LORD loved Israel for ever, therefore made he you king, to do judgment and justice.

10 And she gave the king an hundred and twenty talents of gold, and of spices very great store, and precious stones: there came no more such abundance of spices as these which the queen of Sheba gave to king Solomon.

11 And the navy also of Hiram, that brought gold from Ophir, brought in from Ophir great plenty of almug trees, and precious stones.

12 And the king made of the almug trees pillars for the house of the LORD, and for the king's house, harps also and psalteries for singers: there came no such almug trees, nor were seen to this day.

13 And king Solomon gave to the queen of Sheba all her desire, whatsoever she asked, beside that which Solomon gave her of his royal bounty. So she turned and went to her own country, she and her servants.

14 Now the weight of gold that came to Solomon in one year was six hundred threescore and six talents of gold,

15 Beside that he had of the merchantmen, and of the traffick of the spice merchants, and of all the kings of Arabia, and of the governors of the country.

16 And king Solomon made two hundred targets of beaten gold: six hundred shekels of gold went to one target.

17 And he made three hundred shields of beaten gold; three pound of gold went to one shield: and the king put them in the house of the forest of Lebanon.

18 Moreover the king made a great throne of ivory, and overlaid it with the best gold.

19 The throne had six steps, and the top of the throne was round behind: and

there were stays on either side on the place of the seat, and two lions stood beside the stays.

20 And twelve lions stood there on the one side and on the other upon the six steps: there was not the like made in any kingdom.

21 And all king Solomon's drinking vessels were of gold, and all the vessels of the house of the forest of Lebanon were of pure gold; none were of silver: it was nothing accounted of in the days of Solomon.

22 For the king had at sea a navy of Tharshish with the navy of Hiram: once in three years came the navy of Tharshish, bringing gold, and silver, ivory, and apes, and peacocks.

23 So king Solomon exceeded all the kings of the earth for riches and for wisdom.

24 And all the earth sought to Solomon, to hear his wisdom, which God had put in his heart.

25 And they brought every man his present, vessels of silver, and vessels of gold, and garments, and armour, and spices, horses, and mules, a rate year by year.

26 And Solomon gathered together chariots and horsemen: and he had a thousand and four hundred chariots, and twelve thousand horsemen, whom he bestowed in the cities for chariots, and with the king at Jerusalem.

27 And the king made silver to be in Jerusalem as stones, and cedars made he to be as the sycamore trees that are in the vale, for abundance.

28 And Solomon had horses brought out of Egypt, and linen yarn: the king's merchants received the linen yarn at a price.

29 And a chariot came up and went out of Egypt for six hundred shekels of silver, and an horse for an hundred and fifty: and so for all the kings of the Hittites, and for the kings of Syria, did they bring them out by their means.

CHAPTER 11

BUT king Solomon loved many strange women, together with the daughter of Pharaoh, women of the Moabites, Ammonites, Edomites, Zidonians, and Hittites:

2 Of the nations concerning which the LORD said to the children of Israel, You shall not go in to them, neither shall they come in to you: for surely they will turn away your heart after their gods: Solomon clave to these in love.

3 And he had seven hundred wives, princesses, and three hundred concubines: and his wives turned away his heart.

4 For it came to pass, when Solomon was old, that his wives turned away his heart after other gods: and his heart was not perfect with the LORD his God, as was the heart of David his father.

5 For Solomon went after Ashtoreth the goddess of the Zidonians, and after Milcom the abomination of the Ammonites.

6 And Solomon did evil in the sight of the LORD, and went not fully after the LORD, as did David his father.

7 Then did Solomon build an high place for Chemosh, the abomination of Moab, in the hill that is before Jerusalem, and for Molech, the abomination of the children of Ammon.

8 And likewise did he for all his strange wives, which burnt incense and sacrificed to their gods.

9 And the LORD was angry with Solomon, because his heart was turned from the LORD God of Israel, which had appeared to him twice,

10 And had commanded him concerning this thing, that he should not go after other gods: but he kept not that which the LORD commanded.

11 Therefore the LORD said to Solomon, Forasmuch as this is done of you, and you have not kept my covenant and my statutes, which I have commanded you, I will surely rend the king-

dom from you, and will give it to your servant.

12 Notwithstanding in your days I will not do it for David your father's sake: but I will rend it out of the hand of your son.

13 Howbeit I will not rend away all the kingdom; but will give one tribe to your son for David my servant's sake, and for Jerusalem's sake which I have chosen.

14 And the LORD stirred up an adversary to Solomon, Hadad the Edomite: he was of the king's seed in Edom.

15 For it came to pass, when David was in Edom, and Joab the captain of the host was gone up to bury the slain, after he had smitten every male in Edom;

16 (For six months did Joab remain there with all Israel, until he had cut off every male in Edom:)

17 That Hadad fled, he and certain Edomites of his father's servants with him, to go into Egypt; Hadad being yet a little child.

18 And they arose out of Midian, and came to Paran: and they took men with them out of Paran, and they came to Egypt, to Pharaoh king of Egypt; which gave him an house, and appointed him victuals, and gave him land.

19 And Hadad found great favour in the sight of Pharaoh, so that he gave him to wife the sister of his own wife, the sister of Tahpenes the queen.

20 And the sister of Tahpenes bare him Genubath his son, whom Tahpenes weaned in Pharaoh's house: and Genubath was in Pharaoh's household among the sons of Pharaoh.

21 And when Hadad heard in Egypt that David slept with his fathers, and that Joab the captain of the host was dead, Hadad said to Pharaoh, Let me depart, that I may go to mine own country.

22 Then Pharaoh said to him, But what have you lacked with me, that, behold, you seek to go to your own country? And he answered, Nothing: howbeit let me go in any wise.

23 And God stirred him up another adversary, Rezon the son of Eliadah, which fled from his lord Hadadezer king of Zobah:

24 And he gathered men to him, and became captain over a band, when David slew them of Zobah: and they went to Damascus, and dwelt therein, and reigned in Damascus.

25 And he was an adversary to Israel all the days of Solomon, beside the mischief that Hadad did: and he abhorred Israel, and reigned over Syria.

26 And Jeroboam the son of Nebat, an Ephrathite of Zereda, Solomon's servant, whose mother's name was Zeruah, a widow woman, even he lifted up his hand against the king.

27 And this was the cause that he lifted up his hand against the king: Solomon built Millo, and repaired the breaches of the city of David his father.

28 And the man Jeroboam was a mighty man of valour: and Solomon seeing the young man that he was industrious, he made him ruler over all the charge of the house of Joseph.

29 And it came to pass at that time when Jeroboam went out of Jerusalem, that the prophet Ahijah the Shilonite found him in the way; and he had clad himself with a new garment; and they two were alone in the field:

30 And Ahijah caught the new garment that was on him, and rent it in twelve pieces:

31 And he said to Jeroboam, Take you ten pieces: for thus says the LORD, the God of Israel, Behold, I will rend the kingdom out of the hand of Solomon, and will give ten tribes to you:

32 (But he shall have one tribe for my servant David's sake, and for Jerusalem's sake, the city which I have chosen out of all the tribes of Israel:)

33 Because that they have forsaken me, and have worshipped Ashtoreth the goddess of the Zidonians, Chemosh the god of the Moabites, and Milcom the god of the children of Ammon, and have not

walked in my ways, to do that which is right in mine eyes, and to keep my statutes and my judgments, as did David his father.

34 Howbeit I will not take the whole kingdom out of his hand: but I will make him prince all the days of his life for David my servant's sake, whom I chose, because he kept my commandments and my statutes:

35 But I will take the kingdom out of his son's hand, and will give it to you, even ten tribes.

36 And to his son will I give one tribe, that David my servant may have a light alway before me in Jerusalem, the city which I have chosen me to put my name there.

37 And I will take you, and you shall reign according to all that your soul desires, and shall be king over Israel.

38 And it shall be, if you will hearken to all that I command you, and will walk in my ways, and do that is right in my sight, to keep my statutes and my commandments, as David my servant did; that I will be with you, and build you a sure house, as I built for David, and will give Israel to you.

39 And I will for this afflict the seed of David, but not for ever.

40 Solomon sought therefore to kill Jeroboam. And Jeroboam arose, and fled into Egypt, to Shishak king of Egypt, and was in Egypt until the death of Solomon.

41 And the rest of the acts of Solomon, and all that he did, and his wisdom, are they not written in the book of the acts of Solomon?

42 And the time that Solomon reigned in Jerusalem over all Israel was forty years.

43 And Solomon slept with his fathers, and was buried in the city of David his father: and Rehoboam his son reigned in his stead.

CHAPTER 12

AND Rehoboam went to Shechem: for all Israel were come to Shechem to make him king.

2 And it came to pass, when Jeroboam the son of Nebat, who was yet in Egypt, heard of it, (for he was fled from the presence of king Solomon, and Jeroboam dwelt in Egypt;)

3 That they sent and called him. And Jeroboam and all the congregation of Israel came, and spoke to Rehoboam, saying,

4 Your father made our yoke grievous: now therefore make the grievous service of your father, and his heavy yoke which he put upon us, lighter, and we will serve you.

5 And he said to them, Depart yet for three days, then come again to me. And the people departed.

6 And king Rehoboam consulted with the old men, that stood before Solomon his father while he yet lived, and said, How do you advise that I may answer this people?

7 And they spoke to him, saying, If you will be a servant to this people this day, and will serve them, and answer them, and speak good words to them, then they will be your servants for ever.

8 But he forsook the counsel of the old men, which they had given him, and consulted with the young men that were grown up with him, and which stood before him:

9 And he said to them, What counsel do you give that we may answer this people, who have spoken to me, saying, Make the yoke which your father did put upon us lighter?

10 And the young men that were grown up with him spoke to him, saying, Thus shall you speak to this people that spoke to you, saying, Your father made our yoke heavy, but you make it lighter to us; thus shall you say to them, My little finger shall be thicker than my father's loins.

11 And now whereas my father did lade you with a heavy yoke, I will add to your yoke: my father has chastised you with whips, but I will chastise you with scorpions.

12 So Jeroboam and all the people came to Rehoboam the third day, as the king had appointed, saying, Come to me again the third day.

13 And the king answered the people roughly, and forsook the old men's counsel that they gave him;

14 And spoke to them after the counsel of the young men, saying, My father made your yoke heavy, and I will add to your yoke: my father also chastised you with whips, but I will chastise you with scorpions.

15 Therefore the king hearkened not to the people; for the cause was from the LORD, that he might perform his saying, which the LORD spoke by Ahijah the Shilonite to Jeroboam the son of Nebat.

16 So when all Israel saw that the king hearkened not to them, the people answered the king, saying, What portion have we in David? neither have we inheritance in the son of Jesse: to your tents, O Israel: now see to your own house, David. So Israel departed to their tents.

17 But as for the children of Israel which dwelt in the cities of Judah, Rehoboam reigned over them.

18 Then king Rehoboam sent Adoram, who was over the tribute; and all Israel stoned him with stones, that he died. Therefore king Rehoboam made speed to get him up to his chariot, to flee to Jerusalem.

19 So Israel rebelled against the house of David to this day.

20 And it came to pass, when all Israel heard that Jeroboam was come again, that they sent and called him to the congregation, and made him king over all Israel: there was none that followed the house of David, but the tribe of Judah only.

21 And when Rehoboam was come to Jerusalem, he assembled all the house of Judah, with the tribe of Benjamin, an hundred and fourscore thousand chosen men, which were warriors, to fight against the house of Israel, to bring the kingdom again to Rehoboam the son of Solomon.

22 But the word of God came to Shemaiah the man of God, saying,

23 Speak to Rehoboam, the son of Solomon, king of Judah, and to all the house of Judah and Benjamin, and to the remnant of the people, saying,

24 Thus says the LORD, You shall not go up, nor fight against your brethren the children of Israel: return every man to his house; for this thing is from me. They hearkened therefore to the word of the LORD, and returned to depart, according to the word of the LORD.

25 Then Jeroboam built Shechem in mount Ephraim, and dwelt therein; and went out from thence, and built Penuel.

26 And Jeroboam said in his heart, Now shall the kingdom return to the house of David:

27 If this people go up to do sacrifice in the house of the LORD at Jerusalem, then shall the heart of this people turn again to their lord, even to Rehoboam king of Judah, and they shall kill me, and go again to Rehoboam king of Judah.

28 Whereupon the king took counsel, and made two calves of gold, and said to them, It is too much for you to go up to Jerusalem: behold your gods, O Israel, which brought you up out of the land of Egypt.

29 And he set the one in Bethel, and the other put he in Dan.

30 And this thing became a sin: for the people went to worship before the one, even to Dan.

31 And he made an house of high places, and made priests of the lowest of the people, which were not of the sons of Levi.

32 And Jeroboam ordained a feast in the eighth month, on the fifteenth day of the month, like to the feast that is in Judah, and he offered upon the altar. So did he in Bethel, sacrificing to the calves that he had made: and he placed in Bethel the priests of the high places which he had made.

33 So he offered upon the altar which he had made in Bethel the fifteenth day of the eighth month, even in the month which he had devised of his own heart; and ordained a feast to the children of Israel: and he offered upon the altar, and burnt incense.

CHAPTER 13

AND, behold, there came a man of God out of Judah by the word of the LORD to Bethel: and Jeroboam stood by the altar to burn incense.

2 And he cried against the altar in the word of the LORD, and said, O altar, altar, thus says the LORD; Behold, a child shall be born to the house of David, Josiah by name; and upon you shall he offer the priests of the high places that burn incense upon you, and men's bones shall be burnt upon you.

3 And he gave a sign the same day, saying, This is the sign which the LORD has spoken; Behold, the altar shall be rent, and the ashes that are upon it shall be poured out.

4 And it came to pass, when king Jeroboam heard the saying of the man of God, which had cried against the altar in Bethel, that he put forth his hand from the altar, saying, Lay hold on him. And his hand, which he put forth against him, dried up, so that he could not pull it in again to him.

5 The altar also was rent, and the ashes poured out from the altar, according to the sign which the man of God had given by the word of the LORD.

6 And the king answered and said to the man of God, Intreat now the face of the LORD your God, and pray for me, that my hand may be restored me again. And the man of God besought the LORD, and the king's hand was restored him again, and became as it was before.

7 And the king said to the man of God, Come home with me, and refresh yourself, and I will give you a reward.

8 And the man of God said to the king, If you will give me half your house, I will not go in with you, neither will I eat bread nor drink water in this place:

9 For so was it charged me by the word of the LORD, saying, Eat no bread, nor drink water, nor turn again by the same way that you came.

10 So he went another way, and returned not by the way that he came to Bethel.

11 Now there dwelt an old prophet in Bethel; and his sons came and told him all the works that the man of God had done that day in Bethel: the words which he had spoken to the king, them they told also to their father.

12 And their father said to them, What way went he? For his sons had seen what way the man of God went, which came from Judah.

13 And he said to his sons, Saddle me the ass. So they saddled him the ass: and he rode thereon,

14 And went after the man of God, and found him sitting under an oak: and he said to him, Are you the man of God that came from Judah? And he said, I am.

15 Then he said to him, Come home with me, and eat bread.

16 And he said, I may not return with you, nor go in with you: neither will I eat bread nor drink water with you in this place:

17 For it was said to me by the word of the LORD, You shall eat no bread nor drink water there, nor turn again to go by the way that you came.

18 He said to him, I am a prophet also as you are; and an angel spoke to me by the word of the LORD, saying, Bring him back with you into your house, that he

may eat bread and drink water. But he lied to him.

19 So he went back with him, and did eat bread in his house, and drank water.

20 And it came to pass, as they sat at the table, that the word of the LORD came to the prophet that brought him back:

21 And he cried to the man of God that came from Judah, saying, Thus says the LORD, Forasmuch as you have disobeyed the mouth of the LORD, and have not kept the commandment which the LORD your God commanded you,

22 But came back, and have eaten bread and drunk water in the place, of the which the Lord did say to you, Eat no bread, and drink no water; your carcase shall not come to the sepulchre of your fathers.

23 And it came to pass, after he had eaten bread, and after he had drunk, that he saddled for him the ass, to wit, for the prophet whom he had brought back.

24 And when he was gone, a lion met him by the way, and slew him: and his carcase was cast in the way, and the ass stood by it, the lion also stood by the carcase.

25 And, behold, men passed by, and saw the carcase cast in the way, and the lion standing by the carcase: and they came and told it in the city where the old prophet dwelt.

26 And when the prophet that brought him back from the way heard thereof, he said, It is the man of God, who was disobedient to the word of the LORD: therefore the LORD has delivered him to the lion, which has torn him, and slain him, according to the word of the LORD, which he spoke to him.

27 And he spoke to his sons, saying, Saddle me the ass. And they saddled him.

28 And he went and found his carcase cast in the way, and the ass and the lion standing by the carcase: the lion had not eaten the carcase, nor torn the ass.

29 And the prophet took up the carcase of the man of God, and laid it upon the ass, and brought it back: and the old prophet came to the city, to mourn and to bury him.

30 And he laid his carcase in his own grave; and they mourned over him, saying, Alas, my brother!

31 And it came to pass, after he had buried him, that he spoke to his sons, saying, When I am dead, then bury me in the sepulchre wherein the man of God is buried; lay my bones beside his bones:

32 For the saying which he cried by the word of the LORD against the altar in Bethel, and against all the houses of the high places which are in the cities of Samaria, shall surely come to pass.

33 After this thing Jeroboam returned not from his evil way, but made again of the lowest of the people priests of the high places: whosoever would, he consecrated him, and he became one of the priests of the high places.

34 And this thing became sin to the house of Jeroboam, even to cut it off, and to destroy it from off the face of the earth.

CHAPTER 14

AT that time Abijah the son of Jeroboam fell sick.

2 And Jeroboam said to his wife, Arise, I pray you, and disguise yourself, that you be not known to be the wife of Jeroboam; and get to Shiloh: behold, there is Ahijah the prophet, which told me that I should be king over this people.

3 And take with you ten loaves, and cracknels, and a cruse of honey, and go to him: he shall tell you what shall become of the child.

4 And Jeroboam's wife did so, and arose, and went to Shiloh, and came to the house of Ahijah. But Ahijah could not see; for his eyes were set by reason of his age.

5 And the LORD said to Ahijah, Behold, the wife of Jeroboam cometh to ask a

thing of you for her son; for he is sick: thus and thus shall you say to her: for it shall be, when she cometh in, that she shall feign herself to be another woman.

6 And it was so, when Ahijah heard the sound of her feet, as she came in at the door, that he said, Come in, wife of Jeroboam; why do you pretend to be another? for I am sent to you with heavy tidings.

7 Go, tell Jeroboam, Thus says the LORD God of Israel, Forasmuch as I exalted you from among the people, and made you prince over my people Israel,

8 And rent the kingdom away from the house of David, and gave it to you: and yet you have not been as my servant David, who kept my commandments, and who followed me with all his heart, to do that only which was right in mine eyes;

9 But have done evil above all that were before you: for you have gone and made for yourself other gods, and molten images, to provoke me to anger, and have cast me behind your back:

10 Therefore, behold, I will bring evil upon the house of Jeroboam, and will cut off from Jeroboam him that urinates against the wall, and him that is shut up and left in Israel, and will take away the remnant of the house of Jeroboam, as a man takes away dung, till it be all gone.

11 Him that dies of Jeroboam in the city shall the dogs eat; and him that dies in the field shall the fowls of the air eat: for the LORD has spoken it.

12 Arise therefore, get to your own house: and when your feet enter into the city, the child shall die.

13 And all Israel shall mourn for him, and bury him: for he only of Jeroboam shall come to the grave, because in him there is found some good thing toward the LORD God of Israel in the house of Jeroboam.

14 Moreover the LORD shall raise him up a king over Israel, who shall cut off the house of Jeroboam that day: but what? even now.

15 For the LORD shall smite Israel, as a reed is shaken in the water, and he shall root up Israel out of this good land, which he gave to their fathers, and shall scatter them beyond the river, because they have made their groves, provoking the LORD to anger.

16 And he shall give Israel up because of the sins of Jeroboam, who did sin, and who made Israel to sin.

17 And Jeroboam's wife arose, and departed, and came to Tirzah: and when she came to the threshold of the door, the child died;

18 And they buried him; and all Israel mourned for him, according to the word of the LORD, which he spoke by the hand of his servant Ahijah the prophet.

19 And the rest of the acts of Jeroboam, how he warred, and how he reigned, behold, they are written in the book of the chronicles of the kings of Israel.

20 And the days which Jeroboam reigned were two and twenty years: and he slept with his fathers, and Nadab his son reigned in his stead.

21 And Rehoboam the son of Solomon reigned in Judah. Rehoboam was forty and one years old when he began to reign, and he reigned seventeen years in Jerusalem, the city which the LORD did choose out of all the tribes of Israel, to put his name there. And his mother's name was Naamah an Ammonitess.

22 And Judah did evil in the sight of the LORD, and they provoked him to jealousy with their sins which they had committed, above all that their fathers had done.

23 For they also built them high places, and images, and groves, on every high hill, and under every green tree.

24 And there were also sodomites in the land: and they did according to all the abominations of the nations which the LORD cast out before the children of Israel.

25 And it came to pass in the fifth year of king Rehoboam, that Shishak king of Egypt came up against Jerusalem:

26 And he took away the treasures of the house of the LORD, and the treasures of the king's house; he even took away all: and he took away all the shields of gold which Solomon had made.

27 And king Rehoboam made in their stead brasen shields, and committed them to the hands of the chief of the guard, which kept the door of the king's house.

28 And it was so, when the king went into the house of the LORD, that the guard bare them, and brought them back into the guard chamber.

29 Now the rest of the acts of Rehoboam, and all that he did, are they not written in the book of the chronicles of the kings of Judah?

30 And there was war between Rehoboam and Jeroboam all their days.

31 And Rehoboam slept with his fathers, and was buried with his fathers in the city of David. And his mother's name was Naamah an Ammonitess. And Abijam his son reigned in his stead.

CHAPTER 15

N OW in the eighteenth year of king Jeroboam the son of Nebat reigned Abijam over Judah.

2 Three years reigned he in Jerusalem. and his mother's name was Maachah, the daughter of Abishalom.

3 And he walked in all the sins of his father, which he had done before him: and his heart was not perfect with the LORD his God, as the heart of David his father.

4 Nevertheless for David's sake did the LORD his God give him a lamp in Jerusalem, to set up his son after him, and to establish Jerusalem:

5 Because David did that which was right in the eyes of the LORD, and turned not aside from any thing that he commanded him all the days of his life, save only in the matter of Uriah the Hittite.

6 And there was war between Rehoboam and Jeroboam all the days of his life.

7 Now the rest of the acts of Abijam, and all that he did, are they not written in the book of the chronicles of the kings of Judah? And there was war between Abijam and Jeroboam.

8 And Abijam slept with his fathers; and they buried him in the city of David: and Asa his son reigned in his stead.

9 And in the twentieth year of Jeroboam king of Israel reigned Asa over Judah.

10 And forty and one years reigned he in Jerusalem. And his mother's name was Maachah, the daughter of Abishalom.

11 And Asa did that which was right in the eyes of the LORD, as did David his father.

12 And he took away the sodomites out of the land, and removed all the idols that his fathers had made.

13 And also Maachah his mother, even her he removed from being queen, because she had made an idol in a grove; and Asa destroyed her idol, and burnt it by the brook Kidron.

14 But the high places were not removed: nevertheless Asa's heart was perfect with the LORD all his days.

15 And he brought in the things which his father had dedicated, and the things which himself had dedicated, into the house of the LORD, silver, and gold, and vessels.

16 And there was war between Asa and Baasha king of Israel all their days.

17 And Baasha king of Israel went up against Judah, and built Ramah, that he might not suffer any to go out or come in to Asa king of Judah.

18 Then Asa took all the silver and the gold that were left in the treasures of the house of the LORD, and the treasures of the king's house, and delivered them into the hand of his servants: and king Asa sent them to Benhadad, the son of Tabrimon, the son of Hezion, king of Syria, that dwelt at Damascus, saying,

19 There is a league between me and you, and between my father and your father: behold, I have sent to you a present of silver and gold; come and break your league with Baasha king of Israel, that he may depart from me.

20 So Benhadad hearkened to king Asa, and sent the captains of the hosts which he had against the cities of Israel, and smote Ijon, and Dan, and Abelbethmaachah, and all Cinneroth, with all the land of Naphtali.

21 And it came to pass, when Baasha heard thereof, that he left off building of Ramah, and dwelt in Tirzah.

22 Then king Asa made a proclamation throughout all Judah; none was exempted: and they took away the stones of Ramah, and the timber thereof, wherewith Baasha had builded; and king Asa built with them Geba of Benjamin, and Mizpah.

23 The rest of all the acts of Asa, and all his might, and all that he did, and the cities which he built, are they not written in the book of the chronicles of the kings of Judah? Nevertheless in the time of his old age he was diseased in his feet.

24 And Asa slept with his fathers, and was buried with his fathers in the city of David his father: and Jehoshaphat his son reigned in his stead.

25 And Nadab the son of Jeroboam began to reign over Israel in the second year of Asa king of Judah, and reigned over Israel two years.

26 And he did evil in the sight of the LORD, and walked in the way of his father, and in his sin wherewith he made Israel to sin.

27 And Baasha the son of Ahijah, of the house of Issachar, conspired against him; and Baasha smote him at Gibbethon, which belonged to the Philistines; for Nadab and all Israel laid siege to Gibbethon.

28 Even in the third year of Asa king of Judah did Baasha slay him, and reigned in his stead.

29 And it came to pass, when he reigned, that he smote all the house of Jeroboam; he left not to Jeroboam any that breathed, until he had destroyed him, according to the saying of the LORD, which he spoke by his servant Ahijah the Shilonite:

30 Because of the sins of Jeroboam which he sinned, and which he made Israel sin, by his provocation wherewith he provoked the LORD God of Israel to anger.

31 Now the rest of the acts of Nadab, and all that he did, are they not written in the book of the chronicles of the kings of Israel?

32 And there was war between Asa and Baasha king of Israel all their days.

33 In the third year of Asa king of Judah began Baasha the son of Ahijah to reign over all Israel in Tirzah, twenty and four years.

34 And he did evil in the sight of the LORD, and walked in the way of Jeroboam, and in his sin wherewith he made Israel to sin.

CHAPTER 16

THEN the word of the LORD came to Jehu the son of Hanani against Baasha, saying,

2 Forasmuch as I exalted you out of the dust, and made you prince over my people Israel; and you have walked in the way of Jeroboam, and have made my people Israel to sin, to provoke me to anger with their sins;

3 Behold, I will take away the posterity of Baasha, and the posterity of his house; and will make your house like the house of Jeroboam the son of Nebat.

4 Him that dies of Baasha in the city shall the dogs eat; and him that dies of his in the fields shall the fowls of the air eat.

5 Now the rest of the acts of Baasha, and what he did, and his might, are they not written in the book of the chronicles of the kings of Israel?

6 So Baasha slept with his fathers, and was buried in Tirzah: and Elah his son reigned in his stead.

7 And also by the hand of the prophet Jehu the son of Hanani came the word of the LORD against Baasha, and against his house, even for all the evil that he did in the sight of the LORD, in provoking him to anger with the work of his hands, in being like the house of Jeroboam; and because he killed him.

8 In the twenty and sixth year of Asa king of Judah began Elah the son of Baasha to reign over Israel in Tirzah, two years.

9 And his servant Zimri, captain of half his chariots, conspired against him, as he was in Tirzah, drinking himself drunk in the house of Arza steward of his house in Tirzah.

10 And Zimri went in and smote him, and killed him, in the twenty and seventh year of Asa king of Judah, and reigned in his stead.

11 And it came to pass, when he began to reign, as soon as he sat on his throne, that he slew all the house of Baasha: he left him not one that urinates against a wall, neither of his kinsfolks, nor of his friends.

12 Thus did Zimri destroy all the house of Baasha, according to the word of the LORD, which he spoke against Baasha by Jehu the prophet.

13 For all the sins of Baasha, and the sins of Elah his son, by which they sinned, and by which they made Israel to sin, in provoking the LORD God of Israel to anger with their vanities.

14 Now the rest of the acts of Elah, and all that he did, are they not written in the book of the chronicles of the kings of Israel?

15 In the twenty and seventh year of Asa king of Judah did Zimri reign seven days in Tirzah. And the people were encamped against Gibbethon, which belonged to the Philistines.

16 And the people that were encamped heard say, Zimri has conspired, and has also slain the king: therefore all Israel made Omri, the captain of the host, king over Israel that day in the camp.

17 And Omri went up from Gibbethon, and all Israel with him, and they besieged Tirzah.

18 And it came to pass, when Zimri saw that the city was taken, that he went into the palace of the king's house, and burnt the king's house over him with fire, and died.

19 For his sins which he sinned in doing evil in the sight of the LORD, in walking in the way of Jeroboam, and in his sin which he did, to make Israel to sin.

20 Now the rest of the acts of Zimri, and his treason that he committed, are they not written in the book of the chronicles of the kings of Israel?

21 Then were the people of Israel divided into two parts: half of the people followed Tibni the son of Ginath, to make him king; and half followed Omri.

22 But the people that followed Omri prevailed against the people that followed Tibni the son of Ginath: so Tibni died, and Omri reigned.

23 In the thirty and first year of Asa king of Judah began Omri to reign over Israel, twelve years: six years reigned he in Tirzah.

24 And he bought the hill Samaria of Shemer for two talents of silver, and built on the hill, and called the name of the city which he built, after the name of Shemer, owner of the hill, Samaria.

25 But Omri did evil in the eyes of the LORD, and did worse than all that were before him.

26 For he walked in all the way of Jeroboam the son of Nebat, and in his sin wherewith he made Israel to sin, to provoke the LORD God of Israel to anger with their vanities.

27 Now the rest of the acts of Omri which he did, and his might that he showed, are they not written in the book of the chronicles of the kings of Israel?

28 So Omri slept with his fathers, and was buried in Samaria: and Ahab his son reigned in his stead.

29 And in the thirty and eighth year of Asa king of Judah began Ahab the son of Omri to reign over Israel: and Ahab the son of Omri reigned over Israel in Samaria twenty and two years.

30 And Ahab the son of Omri did evil in the sight of the LORD above all that were before him.

31 And it came to pass, as if it had been a light thing for him to walk in the sins of Jeroboam the son of Nebat, that he took to wife Jezebel the daughter of Ethbaal king of the Zidonians, and went and served Baal, and worshipped him.

32 And he reared up an altar for Baal in the house of Baal, which he had built in Samaria.

33 And Ahab made a grove; and Ahab did more to provoke the LORD God of Israel to anger than all the kings of Israel that were before him.

34 In his days did Hiel the Bethelite build Jericho: he laid the foundation thereof in Abiram his firstborn, and set up the gates thereof in his youngest son Segub, according to the word of the LORD, which he spoke by Joshua the son of Nun.

CHAPTER 17

AND Elijah the Tishbite, who was of the inhabitants of Gilead, said to Ahab, As the LORD God of Israel lives, before whom I stand, there shall not be dew nor rain these years, but according to my word.

2 And the word of the LORD came to him, saying,

3 Get away from here, and turn eastward, and hide yourself by the brook Cherith, that is before Jordan.

4 And it shall be, that you shall drink of the brook; and I have commanded the ravens to feed you there.

5 So he went and did according to the word of the LORD: for he went

and dwelt by the brook Cherith, that is before Jordan.

6 And the ravens brought him bread and flesh in the morning, and bread and flesh in the evening; and he drank of the brook.

7 And it came to pass after a while, that the brook dried up, because there had been no rain in the land.

8 And the word of the LORD came to him, saying,

9 Arise, get to Zarephath, which belongs to Zidon, and dwell there: behold, I have commanded a widow woman there to sustain you.

10 So he arose and went to Zarephath. And when he came to the gate of the city, behold, the widow woman was there gathering of sticks: and he called to her, and said, Fetch me, I pray you, a little water in a vessel, that I may drink.

11 And as she was going to fetch it, he called to her, and said, Bring me, I pray you, a morsel of bread in your hand.

12 And she said, As the LORD your God liveth, I have not a cake, but an handful of meal in a barrel, and a little oil in a cruse: and, behold, I am gathering two sticks, that I may go in and dress it for me and my son, that we may eat it, and die.

13 And Elijah said to her, Fear not; go and do as you have said: but make me thereof a little cake first, and bring it to me, and after make for you and for your son.

14 For thus says the LORD God of Israel, The barrel of meal shall not waste, neither shall the cruse of oil fail, until the day that the LORD sends rain upon the earth.

15 And she went and did according to the saying of Elijah: and she, and he, and her house, did eat many days.

16 And the barrel of meal wasted not, neither did the cruse of oil fail, according to the word of the LORD, which he spoke by Elijah.

17 And it came to pass after these things, that the son of the woman, the

ELIJAH RAISETH THE SON OF THE WIDOW OF ZAREPHATH

1 Kings 17:23

mistress of the house, fell sick; and his sickness was so sore, that there was no breath left in him.

18 And she said to Elijah, What have I to do with you, O you man of God? are you come to me to call my sin to remembrance, and to slay my son?

19 And he said to her, Give me your son. And he took him out of her bosom, and carried him up into a loft, where he abode, and laid him upon his own bed.

20 And he cried to the LORD, and said, O LORD my God, have you also brought evil upon the widow with whom I sojourn, by slaying her son?

21 And he stretched himself upon the child three times, and cried to the LORD, and said, O LORD my God, I pray you, let this child's soul come into him again.

22 And the LORD heard the voice of Elijah; and the soul of the child came into him again, and he revived.

23 And Elijah took the child, and brought him down out of the chamber into the house, and delivered him to his mother: and Elijah said, See, your son lives.

24 And the woman said to Elijah, Now by this I know that you are a man of God, and that the word of the LORD in your mouth is truth.

CHAPTER 18

AND it came to pass after many days, that the word of the LORD came to Elijah in the third year, saying, Go, show yourself to Ahab; and I will send rain upon the earth.

2 And Elijah went to show himself to Ahab. And there was a sore famine in Samaria.

3 And Ahab called Obadiah, which was the governor of his house. (Now Obadiah feared the LORD greatly:

4 For it was so, when Jezebel cut off the prophets of the LORD, that Obadiah took an hundred prophets, and hid them by fifty in a cave, and fed them with bread and water.)   ·

5 And Ahab said to Obadiah, Go into the land, to all fountains of water, and to all brooks: peradventure we may find grass to save the horses and mules alive, that we lose not all the beasts.

6 So they divided the land between them to pass throughout it: Ahab went one way by himself, and Obadiah went another way by himself.

7 And as Obadiah was in the way, behold, Elijah met him: and he knew him, and fell on his face, and said, Are you that my lord Elijah?

8 And he answered him, I am: go, tell your lord, Behold, Elijah is here.

9 And he said, What have I sinned, that you would deliver your servant into the hand of Ahab, to slay me?

10 As the LORD your God lives, there is no nation or kingdom, where my lord has not sent to seek you: and when they said, He is not there; he took an oath of the kingdom and nation, that they found you not.

11 And now you say, Go, tell your lord, Behold, Elijah is here.

12 And it shall come to pass, as soon as I am gone from you, that the Spirit of the LORD shall carry you where I know not; and so when I come and tell Ahab, and he cannot find you, he shall slay me: but I your servant fear the LORD from my youth.

13 Was it not told my lord what I did when Jezebel slew the prophets of the LORD, how I hid an hundred men of the LORD's prophets by fifty in a cave, and fed them with bread and water?

14 And now you say, Go, tell your lord, Behold, Elijah is here: and he shall slay me.

15 And Elijah said, As the LORD of hosts liveth, before whom I stand, I will surely show myself to him to day.

16 So Obadiah went to meet Ahab, and told him: and Ahab went to meet Elijah.

17 And it came to pass, when Ahab saw Elijah, that Ahab said to him, Are you he that troubles Israel?

18 And he answered, I have not troubled Israel; but you, and your father's house, in that you have forsaken the commandments of the LORD, and you have followed Baalim.

19 Now therefore send, and gather to me all Israel to mount Carmel, and the prophets of Baal four hundred and fifty, and the prophets of the groves four hundred, which eat at Jezebel's table.

20 So Ahab sent to all the children of Israel, and gathered the prophets together to mount Carmel.

21 And Elijah came to all the people, and said, How long will you halt between two opinions? if the LORD be God, follow him: but if Baal, then follow him. And the people answered him not a word.

22 Then said Elijah to the people, I, even I only, remain a prophet of the LORD; but Baal's prophets are four hundred and fifty men.

23 Let them therefore give us two bullocks; and let them choose one bullock for themselves, and cut it in pieces, and lay it on wood, and put no fire under: and I will dress the other bullock, and lay it on wood, and put no fire under:

24 And you call on the name of your gods, and I will call on the name of the LORD: and the God that answers by fire,

18:17 Those who stand for righteousness will be considered a "troubler" in the world's eyes. The Apostle Paul was called a "pestilent fellow," a "mover of sedition" and the "ringleader" of a "sect" (see Acts 24:5 comment).

let him be God. And all the people answered and said, It is well spoken.

25 And Elijah said to the prophets of Baal, Choose you one bullock for yourselves, and dress it first; for you are many; and call on the name of your gods, but put no fire under.

26 And they took the bullock which was given them, and they dressed it, and called on the name of Baal from morning even until noon, saying, O Baal, hear us. But there was no voice, nor any that answered. And they leaped upon the altar which was made.

27 And it came to pass at noon, that Elijah mocked them, and said, Cry aloud: for he is a god; either he is talking, or he is pursuing, or he is in a journey, or peradventure he sleeps, and must be awaked.

28 And they cried aloud, and cut themselves after their manner with knives and lancets, till the blood gushed out upon them.

29 And it came to pass, when midday was past, and they prophesied until the time of the offering of the evening sacrifice, that there was neither voice, nor any to answer, nor any that regarded.

30 And Elijah said to all the people, Come near to me. And all the people came near to him. And he repaired the altar of the LORD that was broken down.

31 And Elijah took twelve stones, according to the number of the tribes of the sons of Jacob, to whom the word of the LORD came, saying, Israel shall be your name:

32 And with the stones he built an altar in the name of the LORD: and he made a trench about the altar, as great as would contain two measures of seed.

33 And he put the wood in order, and cut the bullock in pieces, and laid him on the wood, and said, Fill four barrels with water, and pour it on the burnt sacrifice, and on the wood.

34 And he said, Do it the second time. And they did it the second time. And he said, Do it the third time. And they did it the third time.

35 And the water ran round about the altar; and he filled the trench also with water.

36 And it came to pass at the time of the offering of the evening sacrifice, that Elijah the prophet came near, and said, LORD God of Abraham, Isaac, and of Israel, let it be known this day that you are God in Israel, and that I am your servant, and that I have done all these things at your word.

37 Hear me, O LORD, hear me, that this people may know that you are the LORD God, and that you have turned their heart back again.

38 Then the fire of the LORD fell, and consumed the burnt sacrifice, and the wood, and the stones, and the dust, and licked up the water that was in the trench.

39 And when all the people saw it, they fell on their faces: and they said, The LORD, he is the God; the LORD, he is the God.

40 And Elijah said to them, Take the prophets of Baal; let not one of them escape. And they took them: and Elijah brought them down to the brook Kishon, and slew them there.

41 And Elijah said to Ahab, Get up, eat and drink; for there is a sound of abundance of rain.

42 So Ahab went up to eat and to drink. And Elijah went up to the top of Carmel; and he cast himself down upon the earth, and put his face between his knees,

43 And said to his servant, Go up now, look toward the sea. And he went up, and looked, and said, There is nothing. And he said, Go again seven times.

44 And it came to pass at the seventh time, that he said, Behold, there arises a little cloud out of the sea, like a man's hand. And he said, Go up, say to Ahab, Prepare your chariot, and get down that the rain stop you not.

ELIJAH NOURISHED BY AN ANGEL

1 Kings 19:5

45 And it came to pass in the mean while, that the heaven was black with clouds and wind, and there was a great rain. And Ahab rode, and went to Jezreel.

46 And the hand of the LORD was on Elijah; and he girded up his loins, and ran before Ahab to the entrance of Jezreel.

CHAPTER 19

AND Ahab told Jezebel all that Elijah had done, and withal how he had slain all the prophets with the sword.

2 Then Jezebel sent a messenger to Elijah, saying, So let the gods do to me, and more also, if I make not your life as the life of one of them by to morrow about this time.

3 And when he saw that, he arose, and went for his life, and came to Beersheba, which belongs to Judah, and left his servant there.

4 But he himself went a day's journey into the wilderness, and came and sat down under a juniper tree: and he requested for himself that he might die; and said, It is enough; now, O LORD, take away my life; for I am not better than my fathers.

5 And as he lay and slept under a juniper tree, behold, then an angel

19:10 See Acts 18:10 comment.

touched him, and said to him, Arise and eat.

6 And he looked, and, behold, there was a cake baked on the coals, and a cruse of water at his head. And he did eat and drink, and laid him down again.

7 And the angel of the LORD came again the second time, and touched him, and said, Arise and eat; because the journey is too great for you.

8 And he arose, and did eat and drink, and went in the strength of that meat forty days and forty nights to Horeb the mount of God.

9 And he came there to a cave, and lodged there; and, behold, the word of the LORD came to him, and he said to him, What are you doing here, Elijah?

10 And he said, I have been very jealous for the LORD God of hosts: for the children of Israel have forsaken your covenant, thrown down your altars, and slain your prophets with the sword; and I, even I only, am left; and they seek my life, to take it away.

11 And he said, Go forth, and stand upon the mount before the LORD. And, behold, the LORD passed by, and a great and strong wind rent the mountains, and brake in pieces the rocks before the LORD; but the LORD was not in the wind: and after the wind an earthquake; but the LORD was not in the earthquake:

12 And after the earthquake a fire; but the LORD was not in the fire: and after the fire a still small voice.

13 And it was so, when Elijah heard it, that he wrapped his face in his mantle, and went out, and stood in the entering in of the cave. And, behold, there came a voice to him, and said, What are you doing here, Elijah?

14 And he said, I have been very jealous for the LORD God of hosts: because the children of Israel have forsaken your covenant, thrown down your altars, and slain your prophets with the sword; and I, even I only, am left; and they seek my life, to take it away.

15 And the LORD said to him, Go, return on your way to the wilderness of Damascus: and when you come, anoint Hazael to be king over Syria:

16 And Jehu the son of Nimshi shall you anoint to be king over Israel: and Elisha the son of Shaphat of Abelmeholah shall you anoint to be prophet in your room.

17 And it shall come to pass, that him that escapes the sword of Hazael shall Jehu slay: and him that escapes from the sword of Jehu shall Elisha slay.

18 Yet I have left me seven thousand in Israel, all the knees which have not bowed to Baal, and every mouth which has not kissed him.

19 So he departed thence, and found Elisha the son of Shaphat, who was plowing with twelve yoke of oxen before him, and he with the twelfth: and Elijah passed by him, and cast his mantle upon him.

20 And he left the oxen, and ran after Elijah, and said, Let me, I pray you, kiss my father and my mother, and then I will follow you. And he said to him, Go back again: for what have I done to you?

21 And he returned back from him, and took a yoke of oxen, and slew them, and boiled their flesh with the instruments of the oxen, and gave to the people, and they did eat. Then he arose, and went after Elijah, and ministered to him.

CHAPTER 20

AND Benhadad the king of Syria gathered all his host together: and there were thirty and two kings with him, and horses, and chariots; and he went up and besieged Samaria, and warred against it.

2 And he sent messengers to Ahab king of Israel into the city, and said to him, Thus says Benhadad,

3 Your silver and your gold is mine; your wives also and your children, even the goodliest, are mine.

4 And the king of Israel answered and said, My lord, O king, according to your saying, I am yours, and all that I have.

5 And the messengers came again, and said, Thus speaks Benhadad, saying, Although I have sent to you, saying, You shall deliver me your silver, and your gold, and your wives, and your children;

6 Yet I will send my servants to you to morrow about this time, and they shall search your house, and the houses of your servants; and it shall be, that whatsoever is pleasant in your eyes, they shall put it in their hand, and take it away.

7 Then the king of Israel called all the elders of the land, and said, Mark, I pray you, and see how this man seeks mischief: for he sent to me for my wives, and for my children, and for my silver, and for my gold; and I denied him not.

8 And all the elders and all the people said to him, Hearken not to him, nor consent.

9 Therefore he said to the messengers of Benhadad, Tell my lord the king, All that you did send for to your servant at the first I will do: but this thing I may not do. And the messengers departed, and brought him word again.

10 And Benhadad sent to him, and said, The gods do so to me, and more also, if the dust of Samaria shall suffice for handfuls for all the people that follow me.

11 And the king of Israel answered and said, Tell him, Let not him that girds on his harness boast himself as he that puts it off.

12 And it came to pass, when Benhadad heard this message, as he was drinking, he and the kings in the pavilions, that he said to his servants, Set yourselves in array. And they set themselves in array against the city.

13 And, behold, there came a prophet to Ahab king of Israel, saying, Thus says the LORD, Have you seen all this great multitude? behold, I will deliver it into your hand this day; and you shall know that I am the LORD.

14 And Ahab said, By whom? And he said, Thus says the LORD, Even by the young men of the princes of the provinces. Then he said, Who shall order the battle? And he answered, You.

15 Then he numbered the young men of the princes of the provinces, and they were two hundred and thirty two: and after them he numbered all the people, even all the children of Israel, being seven thousand.

16 And they went out at noon. But Benhadad was drinking himself drunk in the pavilions, he and the kings, the thirty and two kings that helped him.

17 And the young men of the princes of the provinces went out first; and Benhadad sent out, and they told him, saying, There are men come out of Samaria.

18 And he said, Whether they be come out for peace, take them alive; or whether they be come out for war, take them alive.

19 So these young men of the princes of the provinces came out of the city, and the army which followed them.

20 And they slew every one his man: and the Syrians fled; and Israel pursued them: and Benhadad the king of Syria escaped on an horse with the horsemen.

21 And the king of Israel went out, and smote the horses and chariots, and slew the Syrians with a great slaughter.

22 And the prophet came to the king of Israel, and said to him, Go, strengthen yourself, and mark, and see what you should do: for at the return of the year the king of Syria will come up against you.

23 And the servants of the king of Syria said to him, Their gods are gods of the hills; therefore they were stronger than we; but let us fight against them in the plain, and surely we shall be stronger than they.

24 And do this thing, Take the kings away, every man out of his place, and put captains in their rooms:

25 And you number an army, like the army that you have lost, horse for horse, and chariot for chariot: and we will fight against them in the plain, and surely we shall be stronger than they. And he hearkened to their voice, and did so.

26 And it came to pass at the return of the year, that Benhadad numbered the Syrians, and went up to Aphek, to fight against Israel.

27 And the children of Israel were numbered, and were all present, and went against them: and the children of Israel pitched before them like two little flocks of kids; but the Syrians filled the country.

28 And there came a man of God, and spoke to the king of Israel, and said, Thus says the LORD, Because the Syrians have said, The LORD is God of the hills, but he is not God of the valleys, therefore will I deliver all this great multitude into your hand, and you shall know that I am the LORD.

29 And they pitched one over against the other seven days. And so it was, that in the seventh day the battle was joined: and the children of Israel slew of the Syrians an hundred thousand footmen in one day.

30 But the rest fled to Aphek, into the city; and there a wall fell upon twenty and seven thousand of the men that were left. And Benhadad fled, and came into the city, into an inner chamber.

31 And his servants said to him, Behold now, we have heard that the kings of the house of Israel are merciful kings: let us, I pray you, put sackcloth on our loins, and ropes upon our heads, and go out to the king of Israel: peradventure he will save your life.

32 So they girded sackcloth on their loins, and put ropes on their heads, and came to the king of Israel, and said, Your servant Benhadad says, I pray you, let me live. And he said, Is he yet alive? he is my brother.

33 Now the men did diligently observe whether any thing would come from him, and did hastily catch it: and they said, Your brother Benhadad. Then he said, Go, bring him. Then Benhadad came forth to him; and he caused him to come up into the chariot.

34 And Ben-hadad said to him, The cities, which my father took from your father, I will restore; and you shall make streets for you in Damascus, as my father made in Samaria. Then said Ahab, I will send you away with this covenant. So he made a covenant with him, and sent him away.

35 And a certain man of the sons of the prophets said to his neighbour in the word of the LORD, Smite me, I pray you. And the man refused to smite him.

36 Then said he to him, Because you have not obeyed the voice of the LORD, behold, as soon as you are departed from me, a lion shall slay you. And as soon as he was departed from him, a lion found him, and slew him.

37 Then he found another man, and said, Smite me, I pray you. And the man smote him, so that in smiting he wounded him.

38 So the prophet departed, and waited for the king by the way, and disguised himself with ashes upon his face.

39 And as the king passed by, he cried to the king: and he said, Your servant went out into the midst of the battle; and, behold, a man turned aside, and brought a man to me, and said, Keep this man: if by any means he be missing, then shall your life be for his life, or else you shall pay a talent of silver.

40 And as your servant was busy here and there, he was gone. And the king of Israel said to him, So shall your judgment be; yourself have decided it.

41 And he hasted, and took the ashes away from his face; and the king of Israel discerned him that he was of the prophets.

42 And he said to him, Thus says the LORD, Because you have let go out of your hand a man whom I appointed to utter destruction, therefore your life

shall go for his life, and your people for his people.

43 And the king of Israel went to his house heavy and displeased, and came to Samaria.

CHAPTER 21

AND it came to pass after these things, that Naboth the Jezreelite had a vineyard, which was in Jezreel, hard by the palace of Ahab king of Samaria.

2 And Ahab spoke to Naboth, saying, Give me your vineyard, that I may have it for a garden of herbs, because it is near to my house: and I will give you for it a better vineyard than it; or, if it seem

good to you, I will give you the worth of it in money.

3 And Naboth said to Ahab, The LORD forbid it me, that I should give the inheritance of my fathers to you.

4 And Ahab came into his house heavy and displeased because of the word which Naboth the Jezreelite had spoken to him: for he had said, I will not give you the inheritance of my fathers. And he laid him down upon his bed, and turned away his face, and would eat no bread.

5 But Jezebel his wife came to him, and said to him, Why is your spirit so sad, that you eat no bread?

6 And he said to her, Because I spoke to Naboth the Jezreelite, and said to him, Give me your vineyard for money; or else, if it please you, I will give you another vineyard for it: and he answered, I will not give you my vineyard.

7 And Jezebel his wife said to him, Do you now govern the kingdom of Israel? arise, and eat bread, and let your heart be merry: I will give you the vineyard of Naboth the Jezreelite.

8 So she wrote letters in Ahab's name, and sealed them with his seal, and sent the letters to the elders and to the nobles that were in his city, dwelling with Naboth.

9 And she wrote in the letters, saying, Proclaim a fast, and set Naboth on high among the people:

10 And set two men, sons of Belial, before him, to bear witness against him, saying, You did blaspheme God and the king. And then carry him out, and stone him, that he may die.

11 And the men of his city, even the elders and the nobles who were the inhabitants in his city, did as Jezebel had sent to them, and as it was written in the letters which she had sent to them.

12 They proclaimed a fast, and set Naboth on high among the people.

13 And there came in two men, children of Belial, and sat before him: and the men of Belial witnessed against him, even against Naboth, in the presence of the people, saying, Naboth did blaspheme God and the king. Then they carried him forth out of the city, and stoned him with stones, that he died.

14 Then they sent to Jezebel, saying, Naboth is stoned, and is dead.

15 And it came to pass, when Jezebel heard that Naboth was stoned, and was dead, that Jezebel said to Ahab, Arise, take possession of the vineyard of Naboth the Jezreelite, which he refused to give you for money: for Naboth is not alive, but dead.

16 And it came to pass, when Ahab heard that Naboth was dead, that Ahab rose up to go down to the vineyard of Naboth the Jezreelite, to take possession of it.

17 And the word of the LORD came to Elijah the Tishbite, saying,

18 Arise, go down to meet Ahab king of Israel, which is in Samaria: behold, he is in the vineyard of Naboth, where he is gone down to possess it.

19 And you shall speak to him, saying, Thus says the LORD, Have you killed, and also taken possession? And you shall speak to him, saying, Thus says the LORD, In the place where dogs licked the blood of Naboth shall dogs lick your blood, even yours.

20 And Ahab said to Elijah, Have you found me, O mine enemy? And he answered, I have found you: because you have sold yourself to work evil in the sight of the LORD.

21 Behold, I will bring evil upon you, and will take away your posterity, and will cut off from Ahab him that urinates against the wall, and him that is shut up and left in Israel,

22 And will make your house like the house of Jeroboam the son of Nebat, and like the house of Baasha the son of Ahijah, for the provocation wherewith you have provoked me to anger, and made Israel to sin.

23 And of Jezebel also spoke the LORD, saying, The dogs shall eat Jezebel by the wall of Jezreel.

24 Him that dies of Ahab in the city the dogs shall eat; and him that dies in the field shall the fowls of the air eat.

25 But there was none like to Ahab, which did sell himself to work wickedness in the sight of the LORD, whom Jezebel his wife stirred up.

26 And he did very abominably in following idols, according to all things as did the Amorites, whom the LORD cast out before the children of Israel.

27 And it came to pass, when Ahab heard those words, that he rent his clothes, and put sackcloth upon his flesh, and fasted, and lay in sackcloth, and went softly.

28 And the word of the LORD came to Elijah the Tishbite, saying,

29 Do you see how Ahab humbles himself before me? because he humbles himself before me, I will not bring the evil in his days: but in his son's days will I bring the evil upon his house.

CHAPTER 22

AND they continued three years without war between Syria and Israel.

2 And it came to pass in the third year, that Jehoshaphat the king of Judah came down to the king of Israel.

3 And the king of Israel said to his servants, Know you that Ramoth in Gilead is ours, and we be still, and take it not out of the hand of the king of Syria?

4 And he said to Jehoshaphat, Will you go with me to battle to Ramothgilead? And Jehoshaphat said to the king of Israel, I am as you are, my people as your people, my horses as your horses.

5 And Jehoshaphat said to the king of Israel, Inquire, I pray you, at the word of the LORD to day.

6 Then the king of Israel gathered the prophets together, about four hundred men, and said to them, Shall I go against Ramothgilead to battle, or shall I forbear? And they said, Go up; for the LORD shall deliver it into the hand of the king.

7 And Jehoshaphat said, Is there not here a prophet of the LORD besides, that we might inquire of him?

8 And the king of Israel said to Jehoshaphat, There is yet one man, Micaiah the son of Imlah, by whom we may inquire of the LORD: but I hate him; for he does not prophesy good concerning me, but evil. And Jehoshaphat said, Let not the king say so.

9 Then the king of Israel called an officer, and said, Hasten here Micaiah the son of Imlah.

10 And the king of Israel and Jehoshaphat the king of Judah sat each on his throne, having put on their robes, in a void place in the entrance of the gate of Samaria; and all the prophets prophesied before them.

11 And Zedekiah the son of Chenaanah made him horns of iron: and he said, Thus says the LORD, With these shall you push the Syrians, until you have consumed them.

12 And all the prophets prophesied so, saying, Go up to Ramothgilead, and prosper: for the LORD shall deliver it into the king's hand.

13 And the messenger that was gone to call Micaiah spoke to him, saying, Behold now, the words of the prophets

declare good to the king with one
mouth: let your word, I pray you, be like
the word of one of them, and speak that
which is good.

14 And Micaiah said, As the LORD
liveth, what the LORD says to me, that
will I speak.

15 So he came to the king. And the
king said to him, Micaiah, shall we go
against Ramothgilead to battle, or shall
we forbear? And he answered him, Go,
and prosper: for the LORD shall deliver
it into the hand of the king.

16 And the king said to him, How
many times shall I adjure you that you
tell me nothing but that which is true in
the name of the LORD?

17 And he said, I saw all Israel scattered
upon the hills, as sheep that have not a
shepherd: and the LORD said, These
have no master: let them return every
man to his house in peace.

18 And the king of Israel said to
Jehoshaphat, Did I not tell you that he
would prophesy no good concerning
me, but evil?

19 And he said, Hear you therefore the
word of the LORD: I saw the LORD sitting on his throne, and all the host of
heaven standing by him on his right
hand and on his left.

20 And the LORD said, Who shall persuade Ahab, that he may go up and fall
at Ramothgilead? And one said on this
manner, and another said on that manner.

21 And there came forth a spirit, and
stood before the LORD, and said, I will
persuade him.

22 And the LORD said to him,
Wherewith? And he said, I will go forth,
and I will be a lying spirit in the mouth
of all his prophets. And he said, You
shall persude him, and prevail also: go
forth, and do so.

23 Now therefore, behold, the LORD
has put a lying spirit in the mouth of all
these your prophets, and the LORD has
spoken evil concerning you.

24 But Zedekiah the son of Chenaanah
went near, and smote Micaiah on the
cheek, and said, Which way went the
Spirit of the LORD from me to speak to
you?

25 And Micaiah said, Behold, you shall
see in that day, when you shall go into
an inner chamber to hide yourself.

26 And the king of Israel said, Take
Micaiah, and carry him back to Amon
the governor of the city, and to Joash the
king's son;

27 And say, Thus says the king, Put this
fellow in the prison, and feed him with
bread of affliction and with water of affliction, until I come in peace.

28 And Micaiah said, If you return at all
in peace, the LORD has not spoken by
me. And he said, Hearken, O people,
every one of you.

29 So the king of Israel and
Jehoshaphat the king of Judah went up
to Ramothgilead.

30 And the king of Israel said to
Jehoshaphat, I will disguise myself, and
enter into the battle; but you put on
your robes. And the king of Israel disguised himself, and went into the battle.

31 But the king of Syria commanded
his thirty and two captains that had rule
over his chariots, saying, Fight neither
with small nor great, save only with the
king of Israel.

32 And it came to pass, when the captains of the chariots saw Jehoshaphat,
that they said, Surely it is the king of
Israel. And they turned aside to fight
against him: and Jehoshaphat cried out.

33 And it came to pass, when the captains of the chariots perceived that it was
not the king of Israel, that they turned
back from pursuing him.

34 And a certain man drew a bow at a
venture, and smote the king of Israel between the joints of the harness: therefore
he said to the driver of his chariot, Turn
your hand, and carry me out of the host;
for I am wounded.

35 And the battle increased that day:
and the king was stayed up in his chariot

against the Syrians, and died at even: and the blood ran out of the wound into the midst of the chariot.

36 And there went a proclamation throughout the host about the going down of the sun, saying, Every man to his city, and every man to his own country.

37 So the king died, and was brought to Samaria; and they buried the king in Samaria.

38 And one washed the chariot in the pool of Samaria; and the dogs licked up his blood; and they washed his armour; according to the word of the LORD which he spoke.

39 Now the rest of the acts of Ahab, and all that he did, and the ivory house which he made, and all the cities that he built, are they not written in the book of the chronicles of the kings of Israel?

40 So Ahab slept with his fathers; and Ahaziah his son reigned in his stead.

41 And Jehoshaphat the son of Asa began to reign over Judah in the fourth year of Ahab king of Israel.

42 Jehoshaphat was thirty and five years old when he began to reign; and he reigned twenty and five years in Jerusalem. And his mother's name was Azubah the daughter of Shilhi.

43 And he walked in all the ways of Asa his father; he turned not aside from it, doing that which was right in the eyes of the LORD: nevertheless the high places were not taken away; for the people offered and burnt incense yet in the high places.

44 And Jehoshaphat made peace with the king of Israel.

45 Now the rest of the acts of Jehoshaphat, and his might that he showed, and how he warred, are they not written in the book of the chronicles of the kings of Judah?

46 And the remnant of the sodomites, which remained in the days of his father Asa, he took out of the land.

47 There was then no king in Edom: a deputy was king.

48 Jehoshaphat made ships of Tharshish to go to Ophir for gold: but they went not; for the ships were broken at Eziongeber.

49 Then said Ahaziah the son of Ahab to Jehoshaphat, Let my servants go with your servants in the ships. But Jehoshaphat would not.

50 And Jehoshaphat slept with his fathers, and was buried with his fathers in the city of David his father: and Jehoram his son reigned in his stead.

51 Ahaziah the son of Ahab began to reign over Israel in Samaria the seventeenth year of Jehoshaphat king of Judah, and reigned two years over Israel.

52 And he did evil in the sight of the LORD, and walked in the way of his father, and in the way of his mother, and in the way of Jeroboam the son of Nebat, who made Israel to sin:

53 For he served Baal, and worshipped him, and provoked to anger the LORD God of Israel, according to all that his father had done.

2 Kings

CHAPTER 1

THEN Moab rebelled against Israel after the death of Ahab.

2 And Ahaziah fell down through a lattice in his upper chamber that was in Samaria, and was sick: and he sent messengers, and said to them, Go, inquire of Baalzebub the god of Ekron whether I shall recover of this disease.

3 But the angel of the LORD said to Elijah the Tishbite, Arise, go up to meet the messengers of the king of Samaria, and say to them, Is it not because there is not a God in Israel, that you go to inquire of Baalzebub the god of Ekron?

4 Now therefore thus says the LORD, You shall not come down from that bed on which you are gone up, but shall surely die. And Elijah departed.

5 And when the messengers turned back to him, he said to them, Why are you now turned back?

6 And they said to him, There came a man up to meet us, and said to us, Go, turn again to the king that sent you, and say to him, Thus says the LORD, Is it not because there is not a God in Israel, that you send to inquire of Baalzebub the god of Ekron? therefore you shall not come down from that bed on which you are gone up, but shall surely die.

7 And he said to them, What manner of man was he which came up to meet you, and told you these words?

8 And they answered him, He was an hairy man, and girt with a girdle of leather about his loins. And he said, It is Elijah the Tishbite.

9 Then the king sent to him a captain of fifty with his fifty. And he went up to him: and, behold, he sat on the top of an hill. And he spoke to him, You man of God, the king has said, Come down.

10 And Elijah answered and said to the captain of fifty, If I be a man of God, then let fire come down from heaven, and consume you and your fifty. And there came down fire from heaven, and consumed him and his fifty.

11 Again also he sent to him another captain of fifty with his fifty. And he answered and said to him, O man of God, thus has the king said, Come down quickly.

12 And Elijah answered and said to them, If I be a man of God, let fire come down from heaven, and consume you and your fifty. And the fire of God came down from heaven, and consumed him and his fifty.

13 And he sent again a captain of the third fifty with his fifty. And the third captain of fifty went up, and came and fell on his knees before Elijah, and besought him, and said to him, O man of God, I pray you, let my life, and the life of these fifty your servants, be precious in your sight.

14 Behold, there came fire down from heaven, and burnt up the two captains of the former fifties with their fifties:

ELIJAH TAKEN UP TO HEAVEN IN A CHARIOT OF FIRE

2 Kings 2:11-12

therefore let my life now be precious in your sight.

15 And the angel of the LORD said to Elijah, Go down with him: be not afraid of him. And he arose, and went down with him to the king.

16 And he said to him, Thus says the LORD, Forasmuch as you have sent messengers to inquire of Baalzebub the god of Ekron, is it not because there is no God in Israel to inquire of his word? therefore you shall not come down off that bed on which you are gone up, but shall surely die.

17 So he died according to the word of the LORD which Elijah had spoken. And Jehoram reigned in his stead in the second year of Jehoram the son of Jehoshaphat king of Judah; because he had no son.

18 Now the rest of the acts of Ahaziah which he did, are they not written in the book of the chronicles of the kings of Israel?

CHAPTER 2

AND it came to pass, when the LORD would take up Elijah into heaven by a whirlwind, that Elijah went with Elisha from Gilgal.

2 And Elijah said to Elisha, Tarry here, I pray you; for the LORD has sent me to Bethel. And Elisha said to him, As the LORD lives, and as your soul lives, I will not leave you. So they went down to Bethel.

3 And the sons of the prophets that were at Bethel came forth to Elisha, and said to him, Do you know that the LORD will take away your master from your head to day? And he said, Yea, I know it; hold your peace.

4 And Elijah said to him, Elisha, tarry here, I pray you; for the LORD has sent me to Jericho. And he said, As the LORD lives, and as your soul lives, I will not leave you. So they came to Jericho.

5 And the sons of the prophets that were at Jericho came to Elisha, and said to him, Do you know that the LORD will

take away your master from your head to day? And he answered, Yea, I know it; hold your peace.

6 And Elijah said to him, Tarry, I pray you, here; for the LORD has sent me to Jordan. And he said, As the LORD lives, and as your soul lives, I will not leave you. And they two went on.

7 And fifty men of the sons of the prophets went, and stood to view afar off: and they two stood by Jordan.

8 And Elijah took his mantle, and wrapped it together, and smote the waters, and they were divided here and there, so that they two went over on dry ground.

9 And it came to pass, when they were gone over, that Elijah said to Elisha, Ask what I shall do for you, before I be taken away from you. And Elisha said, I pray you, let a double portion of your spirit be upon me.

10 And he said, You hast asked a hard thing: nevertheless, if you see me when I am taken from you, it shall be so to you; but if not, it shall not be so.

11 And it came to pass, as they still went on, and talked, that, behold, there appeared a chariot of fire, and horses of fire, and parted them both asunder; and Elijah went up by a whirlwind into heaven.

12 And Elisha saw it, and he cried, My father, my father, the chariot of Israel, and the horsemen thereof. And he saw him no more: and he took hold of his own clothes, and rent them in two pieces.

13 He took up also the mantle of Elijah that fell from him, and went back, and stood by the bank of Jordan;

14 And he took the mantle of Elijah that fell from him, and smote the waters, and said, Where is the LORD God of Elijah? and when he also had smitten the waters, they parted here and there: and Elisha went over.

15 And when the sons of the prophets which were to view at Jericho saw him, they said, The spirit of Elijah does rest

on Elisha. And they came to meet him, and bowed themselves to the ground before him.

16 And they said to him, Behold now, there be with your servants fifty strong men; let them go, we pray you, and seek your master: lest peradventure the Spirit of the LORD has taken him up, and cast him upon some mountain, or into some valley. And he said, You shall not send.

17 And when they urged him till he was ashamed, he said, Send. They sent therefore fifty men; and they sought three days, but found him not.

18 And when they came again to him, (for he tarried at Jericho,) he said to them, Did I not say to you, Go not?

19 And the men of the city said to Elisha, Behold, I pray you, the situation of this city is pleasant, as my lord sees: but the water is naught, and the ground barren.

20 And he said, Bring me a new cruse, and put salt therein. And they brought it to him.

21 And he went forth to the spring of the waters, and cast the salt in there, and said, Thus says the LORD, I have healed these waters; there shall not be from thence any more death or barren land.

22 So the waters were healed to this day, according to the saying of Elisha which he spoke.

23 And he went up from thence to Bethel: and as he was going up by the way, there came forth little children out of the city, and mocked him, and said to him, Go up, you bald head; go up, you bald head.

24 And he turned back, and looked on them, and cursed them in the name of the LORD. And there came forth two she bears out of the wood, and tare forty and two children of them.

25 And he went from thence to mount Carmel, and from thence he returned to Samaria.

CHAPTER 3

NOW Jehoram the son of Ahab began to reign over Israel in Samaria the eighteenth year of Jehoshaphat king of Judah, and reigned twelve years.

2 And he did evil in the sight of the LORD; but not like his father, and like his mother: for he put away the image of Baal that his father had made.

3 Nevertheless he cleaved to the sins of Jeroboam the son of Nebat, which made Israel to sin; he departed not therefrom.

4 And Mesha king of Moab was a sheepmaster, and rendered to the king of Israel an hundred thousand lambs, and an hundred thousand rams, with the wool.

5 But it came to pass, when Ahab was dead, that the king of Moab rebelled against the king of Israel.

6 And king Jehoram went out of Samaria the same time, and numbered all Israel.

7 And he went and sent to Jehoshaphat the king of Judah, saying, The king of Moab has rebelled against me: will you go with me against Moab to battle? And he said, I will go up: I am as you are, my people as your people, and my horses as your horses.

8 And he said, Which way shall we go up? And he answered, The way through the wilderness of Edom.

9 So the king of Israel went, and the king of Judah, and the king of Edom: and they fetched a compass of seven days' journey: and there was no water for the host, and for the cattle that followed them.

10 And the king of Israel said, Alas! that the LORD has called these three kings together, to deliver them into the hand of Moab!

11 But Jehoshaphat said, Is there not here a prophet of the LORD, that we may inquire of the LORD by him? And one of the king of Israel's servants answered and said, Here is Elisha the son

of Shaphat, which poured water on the hands of Elijah.

12 And Jehoshaphat said, The word of the LORD is with him. So the king of Israel and Jehoshaphat and the king of Edom went down to him.

13 And Elisha said to the king of Israel, What have I to do with you? get you to the prophets of your father, and to the prophets of your mother. And the king of Israel said to him, Nay: for the LORD has called these three kings together, to deliver them into the hand of Moab.

14 And Elisha said, As the LORD of hosts lives, before whom I stand, surely, were it not that I regard the presence of Jehoshaphat the king of Judah, I would not look toward you, nor see you.

15 But now bring me a minstrel. And it came to pass, when the minstrel played, that the hand of the LORD came upon him.

16 And he said, Thus says the LORD, Make this valley full of ditches.

17 For thus says the LORD, You shall not see wind, neither shall you see rain; yet that valley shall be filled with water, that you may drink, both you, and your cattle, and your beasts.

18 And this is but a light thing in the sight of the LORD: he will deliver the Moabites also into your hand.

19 And you shall smite every fenced city, and every choice city, and shall fell every good tree, and stop all wells of water, and mar every good piece of land with stones.

20 And it came to pass in the morning, when the meat offering was offered, that, behold, there came water by the way of Edom, and the country was filled with water.

21 And when all the Moabites heard that the kings were come up to fight against them, they gathered all that were able to put on armour, and upward, and stood in the border.

22 And they rose up early in the morning, and the sun shone upon the water,

and the Moabites saw the water on the other side as red as blood:

23 And they said, This is blood: the kings are surely slain, and they have smitten one another: now therefore, Moab, to the spoil.

24 And when they came to the camp of Israel, the Israelites rose up and smote the Moabites, so that they fled before them: but they went forward smiting the Moabites, even in their country.

25 And they beat down the cities, and on every good piece of land cast every man his stone, and filled it; and they stopped all the wells of water, and felled all the good trees: only in Kirharaseth left they the stones thereof; howbeit the slingers went about it, and smote it.

26 And when the king of Moab saw that the battle was too sore for him, he took with him seven hundred men that drew swords, to break through even to the king of Edom: but they could not.

27 Then he took his eldest son that should have reigned in his stead, and offered him for a burnt offering upon the wall. And there was great indignation against Israel: and they departed from him, and returned to their own land.

CHAPTER 4

NOW there cried a certain woman of the wives of the sons of the prophets to Elisha, saying, Your servant my husband is dead; and you know that your servant did fear the LORD: and the creditor is come to take to him my two sons to be bondmen.

2 And Elisha said to her, What shall I do for you? tell me, what have you in the house? And she said, Your handmaid has not any thing in the house, save a pot of oil.

3 Then he said, Go, borrow vessels abroad of all your neighbours, even empty vessels; borrow not a few.

4 And when you are come in, you shall shut the door upon you and upon your sons, and shall pour out into all those

vessels, and you shall set aside that which is full.

5 So she went from him, and shut the door upon her and upon her sons, who brought the vessels to her; and she poured out.

6 And it came to pass, when the vessels were full, that she said to her son, Bring me yet a vessel. And he said to her, There is not a vessel more. And the oil stayed.

7 Then she came and told the man of God. And he said, Go, sell the oil, and pay your debt, and you and your children live on the rest.

8 And it fell on a day, that Elisha passed to Shunem, where was a great woman; and she constrained him to eat bread. And so it was, that as oft as he passed by, he turned in there to eat bread.

9 And she said to her husband, Behold now, I perceive that this is an holy man of God, which passes by us continually.

10 Let us make a little chamber, I pray you, on the wall; and let us set for him there a bed, and a table, and a stool, and a candlestick: and it shall be, when he cometh to us, that he shall turn in there.

11 And it fell on a day, that he came there, and he turned into the chamber, and lay there.

12 And he said to Gehazi his servant, Call this Shunammite. And when he had called her, she stood before him.

13 And he said to him, Say now to her, Behold, you have been careful for us with all this care; what is to be done for you? would you be spoken for to the king, or to the captain of the host? And she answered, I dwell among mine own people.

14 And he said, What then is to be done for her? And Gehazi answered, Verily she has no child, and her husband is old.

15 And he said, Call her. And when he had called her, she stood in the door.

16 And he said, About this season, according to the time of life, you shall embrace a son. And she said, Nay, my lord,

you man of God, do not lie to your handmaid.

17 And the woman conceived, and bare a son at that season that Elisha had said to her, according to the time of life.

18 And when the child was grown, it fell on a day, that he went out to his father to the reapers.

19 And he said to his father, My head, my head. And he said to a lad, Carry him to his mother.

20 And when he had taken him, and brought him to his mother, he sat on her knees till noon, and then died.

21 And she went up, and laid him on the bed of the man of God, and shut the door upon him, and went out.

22 And she called to her husband, and said, Send me, I pray you, one of the young men, and one of the asses, that I may run to the man of God, and come again.

23 And he said, Why will you go to him to day? it is neither new moon, nor sabbath. And she said, It shall be well.

24 Then she saddled an ass, and said to her servant, Drive, and go forward; slack not your riding for me, except I bid you.

25 So she went and came to the man of God to mount Carmel. And it came to pass, when the man of God saw her afar off, that he said to Gehazi his servant, Behold, yonder is that Shunammite:

26 Run now, I pray you, to meet her, and say to her, Is it well with you? is it well with your husband? is it well with the child? And she answered, It is well:

27 And when she came to the man of God to the hill, she caught him by the feet: but Gehazi came near to thrust her away. And the man of God said, Let her alone; for her soul is vexed within her: and the LORD has hid it from me, and has not told me.

28 Then she said, Did I desire a son of my lord? did I not say, Do not deceive me?

29 Then he said to Gehazi, Gird up your loins, and take my staff in your hand, and go your way: if you meet any

man, salute him not; and if any salute you, answer him not again: and lay my staff upon the face of the child.

30 And the mother of the child said, As the LORD lives, and as your soul lives, I will not leave you. And he arose, and followed her.

31 And Gehazi passed on before them, and laid the staff upon the face of the child; but there was neither voice, nor hearing. Therefore he went again to meet him, and told him, saying, The child is not awaked.

32 And when Elisha was come into the house, behold, the child was dead, and laid upon his bed.

33 He went in therefore, and shut the door upon them twain, and prayed to the LORD.

34 And he went up, and lay upon the child, and put his mouth upon his mouth, and his eyes upon his eyes, and his hands upon his hands: and stretched himself upon the child; and the flesh of the child waxed warm.

35 Then he returned, and walked in the house to and fro; and went up, and stretched himself upon him: and the child sneezed seven times, and the child opened his eyes.

36 And he called Gehazi, and said, Call this Shunammite. So he called her. And when she was come in to him, he said, Take up your son.

37 Then she went in, and fell at his feet, and bowed herself to the ground, and took up her son, and went out.

38 And Elisha came again to Gilgal: and there was a dearth in the land; and the sons of the prophets were sitting before him: and he said to his servant, Set on the great pot, and seethe pottage for the sons of the prophets.

39 And one went out into the field to gather herbs, and found a wild vine, and gathered thereof wild gourds his lap full, and came and shred them into the pot of pottage: for they knew them not.

40 So they poured out for the men to eat. And it came to pass, as they were eating of the pottage, that they cried out, and said, O you man of God, there is death in the pot. And they could not eat thereof.

41 But he said, Then bring meal. And he cast it into the pot; and he said, Pour out for the people, that they may eat. And there was no harm in the pot.

42 And there came a man from Baalshalisha, and brought the man of God bread of the firstfruits, twenty loaves of barley, and full ears of corn in the husk thereof. And he said, Give to the people, that they may eat.

43 And his servitor said, What, should I set this before an hundred men? He said again, Give the people, that they may eat: for thus says the LORD, They shall eat, and shall leave thereof.

44 So he set it before them, and they did eat, and left thereof, according to the word of the LORD.

CHAPTER 5

NOW Naaman, captain of the host of the king of Syria, was a great man with his master, and honourable, because by him the LORD had given deliverance to Syria: he was also a mighty man in valour, but he was a leper.

2 And the Syrians had gone out by companies, and had brought away captive out of the land of Israel a little maid; and she waited on Naaman's wife.

3 And she said to her mistress, Would God my lord were with the prophet that is in Samaria! for he would recover him of his leprosy.

4:44 Compare this incident with Jesus' feeding of the 5000 men plus women and children. In both instances, there was enough bread for all to eat and some left over (see Matthew 14:17-20). We have eaten from the Bread of Life, and now we must take that Bread to a starving world.

4 And one went in, and told his lord, saying, Thus and thus said the maid that is of the land of Israel.

5 And the king of Syria said, Go to, go, and I will send a letter to the king of Israel. And he departed, and took with him ten talents of silver, and six thousand pieces of gold, and ten changes of raiment.

6 And he brought the letter to the king of Israel, saying, Now when this letter is come to you, behold, I have therewith sent Naaman my servant to you, that you may recover him of his leprosy.

7 And it came to pass, when the king of Israel had read the letter, that he rent his clothes, and said, Am I God, to kill and to make alive, that this man does send to me to recover a man of his leprosy? therefore consider, I pray you, and see how he seeks a quarrel against me.

8 And it was so, when Elisha the man of God had heard that the king of Israel had rent his clothes, that he sent to the king, saying, Why have you rent your clothes? let him come now to me, and he shall know that there is a prophet in Israel.

9 So Naaman came with his horses and with his chariot, and stood at the door of the house of Elisha.

10 And Elisha sent a messenger to him, saying, Go and wash in Jordan seven times, and your flesh shall come again to you, and you shall be clean.

11 But Naaman was wroth, and went away, and said, Behold, I thought, He will surely come out to me, and stand, and call on the name of the LORD his God, and strike his hand over the place, and recover the leper.

12 Are not Abana and Pharpar, rivers of Damascus, better than all the waters of Israel? may I not wash in them, and be clean? So he turned and went away in a rage.

13 And his servants came near, and spoke to him, and said, My father, if the prophet had bid you do some great thing, would you not have done it? how much rather then, when he says to you, Wash, and be clean?

14 Then went he down, and dipped himself seven times in Jordan, according to the saying of the man of God: and his flesh came again like to the flesh of a little child, and he was clean.

15 And he returned to the man of God, he and all his company, and came, and stood before him: and he said, Behold, now I know that there is no God in all the earth, but in Israel: now therefore, I pray you, take a blessing of your servant.

16 But he said, As the LORD lives, before whom I stand, I will receive none. And he urged him to take it; but he refused.

17 And Naaman said, Shall there not then, I pray you, be given to your servant two mules' burden of earth? for your servant will henceforth offer neither burnt offering nor sacrifice to other gods, but to the LORD.

18 In this thing the LORD pardon your servant, that when my master goeth into the house of Rimmon to worship there, and he leans on my hand, and I bow myself in the house of Rimmon: when I bow down myself in the house of Rimmon, the LORD pardon your servant in this thing.

19 And he said to him, Go in peace. So he departed from him a little way.

20 But Gehazi, the servant of Elisha the man of God, said, Behold, my master has spared Naaman this Syrian, in not receiving at his hands that which he brought: but, as the LORD lives, I will run after him, and take somewhat of him.

21 So Gehazi followed after Naaman. And when Naaman saw him running after him, he lighted down from the chariot to meet him, and said, Is all well?

22 And he said, All is well. My master has sent me, saying, Behold, even now there be come to me from mount Ephraim two young men of the sons of the prophets: give them, I pray you,

a talent of silver, and two changes of garments.

23 And Naaman said, Be content, take two talents. And he urged him, and bound two talents of silver in two bags, with two changes of garments, and laid them upon two of his servants; and they bare them before him.

24 And when he came to the tower, he took them from their hand, and bestowed them in the house: and he let the men go, and they departed.

25 But he went in, and stood before his master. And Elisha said to him, Where do you come from, Gehazi? And he said, Your servant went no where.

26 And he said to him, Went not mine heart with you, when the man turned again from his chariot to meet you? Is it a time to receive money, and to receive garments, and oliveyards, and vineyards, and sheep, and oxen, and menservants, and maidservants?

27 The leprosy therefore of Naaman shall cleave to you, and to your seed for ever. And he went out from his presence a leper as white as snow.

CHAPTER 6

AND the sons of the prophets said to Elisha, Behold now, the place where we dwell with you is too strait for us.

2 Let us go, we pray you, to Jordan, and take thence every man a beam, and let us make us a place there, where we may dwell. And he answered, Go.

3 And one said, Be content, I pray you, and go with your servants. And he answered, I will go.

4 So he went with them. And when they came to Jordan, they cut down wood.

5 But as one was felling a beam, the axe head fell into the water: and he cried, and said, Alas, master! for it was borrowed.

6 And the man of God said, Where fell it? And he showed him the place. And he cut down a stick, and cast it in there; and the iron did swim.

7 Therefore said he, Take it up to you. And he put out his hand, and took it.

8 Then the king of Syria warred against Israel, and took counsel with his servants, saying, In such and such a place shall be my camp.

9 And the man of God sent to the king of Israel, saying, Beware that you pass not such a place; for there the Syrians are come down.

10 And the king of Israel sent to the place which the man of God told him and warned him of, and saved himself there, not once nor twice.

11 Therefore the heart of the king of Syria was sore troubled for this thing; and he called his servants, and said to them, Will you not show me which of us is for the king of Israel?

12 And one of his servants said, None, my lord, O king: but Elisha, the prophet that is in Israel, tells the king of Israel the words that you speak in your bedchamber.

13 And he said, Go and spy where he is, that I may send and fetch him. And it was told him, saying, Behold, he is in Dothan.

14 Therefore sent he there horses, and chariots, and a great host: and they came by night, and compassed the city about.

15 And when the servant of the man of God was risen early, and gone forth, behold, an host compassed the city both with horses and chariots. And his servant said to him, Alas, my master! how shall we do?

16 And he answered, Fear not: for they that be with us are more than they that be with them.

17 And Elisha prayed, and said, LORD, I pray you, open his eyes, that he may see. And the LORD opened the eyes of the young man; and he saw: and, behold, the mountain was full of horses and chariots of fire round about Elisha.

18 And when they came down to him, Elisha prayed to the LORD, and said, Smite this people, I pray you, with blindness. And he smote them with

blindness according to the word of Elisha.

19 And Elisha said to them, This is not the way, neither is this the city: follow me, and I will bring you to the man whom you seek. But he led them to Samaria.

20 And it came to pass, when they were come into Samaria, that Elisha said, LORD, open the eyes of these men, that they may see. And the LORD opened their eyes, and they saw; and, behold, they were in the midst of Samaria.

21 And the king of Israel said to Elisha, when he saw them, My father, shall I smite them? shall I smite them?

22 And he answered, You shall not smite them: would you smite those whom you have taken captive with your sword and with your bow? set bread and water before them, that they may eat and drink, and go to their master.

23 And he prepared great provision for them: and when they had eaten and drunk, he sent them away, and they went to their master. So the bands of Syria came no more into the land of Israel.

24 And it came to pass after this, that Benhadad king of Syria gathered all his host, and went up, and besieged Samaria.

25 And there was a great famine in Samaria: and, behold, they besieged it, until an ass's head was sold for fourscore pieces of silver, and the fourth part of a cab of dove's dung for five pieces of silver.

26 And as the king of Israel was passing by upon the wall, there cried a woman to him, saying, Help, my lord, O king.

27 And he said, If the LORD do not help you, whence shall I help you? out of the barnfloor, or out of the winepress?

28 And the king said to her, What ails you? And she answered, This woman said to me, Give your son, that we may eat him to day, and we will eat my son tomorrow.

29 So we boiled my son, and did eat him: and I said to her on the next day, Give your son, that we may eat him: and she has hid her son.

30 And it came to pass, when the king heard the words of the woman, that he rent his clothes; and he passed by upon the wall, and the people looked, and, behold, he had sackcloth within upon his flesh.

31 Then he said, God do so and more also to me, if the head of Elisha the son of Shaphat shall stand on him this day.

32 But Elisha sat in his house, and the elders sat with him; and the king sent a man from before him: but ere the messenger came to him, he said to the elders, Do you see how this son of a murderer has sent to take away mine head? look, when the messenger cometh, shut the door, and hold him fast at the door: is not the sound of his master's feet behind him?

33 And while he yet talked with them, behold, the messenger came down to him: and he said, Behold, this evil is of the LORD; what should I wait for the LORD any longer?

CHAPTER 7

THEN Elisha said, Hear the word of the LORD; Thus says the LORD, To morrow about this time shall a measure of fine flour be sold for a shekel, and two measures of barley for a shekel, in the gate of Samaria.

2 Then a lord on whose hand the king leaned answered the man of God, and said, Behold, if the LORD would make windows in heaven, might this thing be? And he said, Behold, you shall see it with your eyes, but shall not eat thereof.

3 And there were four leprous men at the entering in of the gate: and they said one to another, Why sit we here until we die?

4 If we say, We will enter into the city, then the famine is in the city, and we shall die there: and if we sit still here, we die also. Now therefore come, and let us

fall to the host of the Syrians: if they save us alive, we shall live; and if they kill us, we shall but die.

5 And they rose up in the twilight, to go to the camp of the Syrians: and when they were come to the uttermost part of the camp of Syria, behold, there was no man there.

6 For the LORD had made the host of the Syrians to hear a noise of chariots, and a noise of horses, even the noise of a great host: and they said one to another, Lo, the king of Israel has hired against us the kings of the Hittites, and the kings of the Egyptians, to come upon us.

7 Therefore they arose and fled in the twilight, and left their tents, and their horses, and their asses, even the camp as it was, and fled for their life.

8 And when these lepers came to the uttermost part of the camp, they went into one tent, and did eat and drink, and carried thence silver, and gold, and raiment, and went and hid it; and came again, and entered into another tent, and carried thence also, and went and hid it.

9 Then they said one to another, We do not well: this day is a day of good tidings, and we hold our peace: if we tarry till the morning light, some mischief will come upon us: now therefore come, that we may go and tell the king's household.

10 So they came and called to the porter of the city: and they told them, saying, We came to the camp of the Syrians, and, behold, there was no man there, neither voice of man, but horses tied, and asses tied, and the tents as they were.

11 And he called the porters; and they told it to the king's house within.

12 And the king arose in the night, and said to his servants, I will now show you what the Syrians have done to us. They know that we be hungry; therefore are they gone out of the camp to hide themselves in the field, saying, When they come out of the city, we shall catch them alive, and get into the city.

13 And one of his servants answered and said, Let some take, I pray you, five of the horses that remain, which are left in the city, (behold, they are as all the multitude of Israel that are left in it: behold, I say, they are even as all the multitude of the Israelites that are consumed:) and let us send and see.

14 They took therefore two chariot horses; and the king sent after the host of the Syrians, saying, Go and see.

15 And they went after them to Jordan: and, lo, all the way was full of garments and vessels, which the Syrians had cast away in their haste. And the messengers returned, and told the king.

16 And the people went out, and spoiled the tents of the Syrians. So a measure of fine flour was sold for a shekel, and two measures of barley for a shekel, according to the word of the LORD.

17 And the king appointed the lord on whose hand he leaned to have the charge of the gate: and the people trode upon him in the gate, and he died, as the man of God had said, who spoke when the king came down to him.

18 And it came to pass as the man of God had spoken to the king, saying, Two measures of barley for a shekel, and a measure of fine flour for a shekel, shall be to morrow about this time in the gate of Samaria:

19 And that lord answered the man of God, and said, Now, behold, if the LORD should make windows in heaven,

---

7:9 How could these lepers keep this good news to themselves? Their conscience spoke to them of their moral obligations. How much more should we feel an obligation to take the Good News of everlasting life to a dying world? We have been cleansed from the leprosy of sin and have found the Bread of Life. We, therefore, must take it to the world. Like Paul, we are in "debt" to those who haven't heard the gospel (See Romans 1:14-17).

might such a thing be? And he said, Behold, you shall see it with your eyes, but shall not eat thereof.

20 And so it fell out to him: for the people trode upon him in the gate, and he died.

CHAPTER 8

THEN Elisha spoke to the woman, whose son he had restored to life, saying, Arise and go, you and your household, and sojourn wherever you can sojourn: for the LORD has called for a famine; and it shall also come upon the land seven years.

2 And the woman arose, and did after the saying of the man of God: and she went with her household, and sojourned in the land of the Philistines seven years.

3 And it came to pass at the seven years' end, that the woman returned out of the land of the Philistines: and she went forth to cry to the king for her house and for her land.

4 And the king talked with Gehazi the servant of the man of God, saying, Tell me, I pray you, all the great things that Elisha has done.

5 And it came to pass, as he was telling the king how he had restored a dead body to life, that, behold, the woman, whose son he had restored to life, cried to the king for her house and for her land. And Gehazi said, My lord, O king, this is the woman, and this is her son, whom Elisha restored to life.

6 And when the king asked the woman, she told him. So the king appointed to her a certain officer, saying, Restore all that was hers, and all the fruits of the field since the day that she left the land, even until now.

7 And Elisha came to Damascus; and Benhadad the king of Syria was sick; and it was told him, saying, The man of God is come here.

8 And the king said to Hazael, Take a present in your hand, and go, meet the man of God, and inquire of the LORD by him, saying, Shall I recover of this disease?

9 So Hazael went to meet him, and took a present with him, even of every good thing of Damascus, forty camels' burden, and came and stood before him, and said, Your son Benhadad king of Syria has sent me to you, saying, Shall I recover of this disease?

10 And Elisha said to him, Go, say to him, You may certainly recover: howbeit the LORD has showed me that he shall surely die.

11 And he settled his countenance stedfastly, until he was ashamed: and the man of God wept.

12 And Hazael said, Why is my lord weeping? And he answered, Because I know the evil that you will do to the children of Israel: their strong holds will you set on fire, and their young men will you slay with the sword, and will dash their children, and rip up their women with child.

13 And Hazael said, But what, is your servant a dog, that he should do this great thing? And Elisha answered, The LORD has showed me that you shall be king over Syria.

14 So he departed from Elisha, and came to his master; who said to him, What said Elisha to you? And he answered, He told me that you should surely recover.

15 And it came to pass on the morrow, that he took a thick cloth, and dipped it in water, and spread it on his face, so that he died: and Hazael reigned in his stead.

16 And in the fifth year of Joram the son of Ahab king of Israel, Jehoshaphat being then king of Judah, Jehoram the son of Jehoshaphat king of Judah began to reign.

17 Thirty and two years old was he when he began to reign; and he reigned eight years in Jerusalem.

18 And he walked in the way of the kings of Israel, as did the house of Ahab:

for the daughter of Ahab was his wife: and he did evil in the sight of the LORD.

19 Yet the LORD would not destroy Judah for David his servant's sake, as he promised him to give him alway a light, and to his children.

20 In his days Edom revolted from under the hand of Judah, and made a king over themselves.

21 So Joram went over to Zair, and all the chariots with him: and he rose by night, and smote the Edomites which compassed him about, and the captains of the chariots: and the people fled into their tents.

22 Yet Edom revolted from under the hand of Judah to this day. Then Libnah revolted at the same time.

23 And the rest of the acts of Joram, and all that he did, are they not written in the book of the chronicles of the kings of Judah?

24 And Joram slept with his fathers, and was buried with his fathers in the city of David: and Ahaziah his son reigned in his stead.

25 In the twelfth year of Joram the son of Ahab king of Israel did Ahaziah the son of Jehoram king of Judah begin to reign.

26 Two and twenty years old was Ahaziah when he began to reign; and he reigned one year in Jerusalem. And his mother's name was Athaliah, the daughter of Omri king of Israel.

27 And he walked in the way of the house of Ahab, and did evil in the sight of the LORD, as did the house of Ahab: for he was the son in law of the house of Ahab.

28 And he went with Joram the son of Ahab to the war against Hazael king of Syria in Ramothgilead; and the Syrians wounded Joram.

29 And king Joram went back to be healed in Jezreel of the wounds which the Syrians had given him at Ramah, when he fought against Hazael king of Syria. And Ahaziah the son of Jehoram king of Judah went down to see Joram the son of Ahab in Jezreel, because he was sick.

CHAPTER 9

AND Elisha the prophet called one of the children of the prophets, and said to him, Gird up your loins, and take this box of oil in your hand, and go to Ramothgilead:

2 And when you come there, look out there Jehu the son of Jehoshaphat the son of Nimshi, and go in, and make him arise up from among his brethren, and carry him to an inner chamber;

3 Then take the box of oil, and pour it on his head, and say, Thus says the LORD, I have anointed you king over Israel. Then open the door, and flee, and tarry not.

4 So the young man, even the young man the prophet, went to Ramothgilead.

5 And when he came, behold, the captains of the host were sitting; and he said, I have an errand to you, O captain. And Jehu said, To which of all us? And he said, To you, O captain.

6 And he arose, and went into the house; and he poured the oil on his head, and said to him, Thus says the LORD God of Israel, I have anointed you king over the people of the LORD, even over Israel.

7 And you shall smite the house of Ahab your master, that I may avenge the blood of my servants the prophets, and the blood of all the servants of the LORD, at the hand of Jezebel.

8 For the whole house of Ahab shall perish: and I will cut off from Ahab him that pisses against the wall, and him that is shut up and left in Israel:

9 And I will make the house of Ahab like the house of Jeroboam the son of Nebat, and like the house of Baasha the son of Ahijah:

10 And the dogs shall eat Jezebel in the portion of Jezreel, and there shall be none to bury her. And he opened the door, and fled.

11 Then Jehu came forth to the servants of his lord: and one said to him, Is all well? why came this mad fellow to you? And he said to them, You know the man, and his communication.

12 And they said, It is false; tell us now. And he said, Thus and thus spoke he to me, saying, Thus says the LORD, I have anointed you king over Israel.

13 Then they hasted, and took every man his garment, and put it under him on the top of the stairs, and blew with trumpets, saying, Jehu is king.

14 So Jehu the son of Jehoshaphat the son of Nimshi conspired against Joram. (Now Joram had kept Ramothgilead, he and all Israel, because of Hazael king of Syria.

15 But king Joram was returned to be healed in Jezreel of the wounds which the Syrians had given him, when he fought with Hazael king of Syria.) And Jehu said, If it be your minds, then let none go forth nor escape out of the city to go to tell it in Jezreel.

16 So Jehu rode in a chariot, and went to Jezreel; for Joram lay there. And Ahaziah king of Judah was come down to see Joram.

17 And there stood a watchman on the tower in Jezreel, and he spied the company of Jehu as he came, and said, I see a company. And Joram said, Take an horseman, and send to meet them, and let him say, Is it peace?

18 So there went one on horseback to meet him, and said, Thus says the king, Is it peace? And Jehu said, What have you to do with peace? turn behind me. And the watchman told, saying, The messenger came to them, but he cometh not again.

19 Then he sent out a second on horseback, which came to them, and said, Thus says the king, Is it peace? And Jehu answered, What have you to do with peace? turn behind me.

20 And the watchman told, saying, He came even to them, and cometh not again: and the driving is like the driving of Jehu the son of Nimshi; for he drives furiously.

21 And Joram said, Make ready. And his chariot was made ready. And Joram king of Israel and Ahaziah king of Judah went out, each in his chariot, and they went out against Jehu, and met him in the portion of Naboth the Jezreelite.

22 And it came to pass, when Joram saw Jehu, that he said, Is it peace, Jehu? And he answered, What peace, so long as the whoredoms of your mother Jezebel and her witchcrafts are so many?

23 And Joram turned his hands, and fled, and said to Ahaziah, There is treachery, O Ahaziah.

24 And Jehu drew a bow with his full strength, and smote Jehoram between his arms, and the arrow went out at his heart, and he sunk down in his chariot.

25 Then said Jehu to Bidkar his captain, Take up, and cast him in the portion of the field of Naboth the Jezreelite: for remember how that, when I and you rode together after Ahab his father, the LORD laid this burden upon him;

26 Surely I have seen yesterday the blood of Naboth, and the blood of his sons, says the LORD; and I will repay you in this plat, says the LORD. Now therefore take and cast him into the plat of ground, according to the word of the LORD.

27 But when Ahaziah the king of Judah saw this, he fled by the way of the garden house. And Jehu followed after him, and said, Smite him also in the chariot. And they did so at the going up to Gur, which is by Ibleam. And he fled to Megiddo, and died there.

28 And his servants carried him in a chariot to Jerusalem, and buried him in his sepulchre with his fathers in the city of David.

29 And in the eleventh year of Joram the son of Ahab began Ahaziah to reign over Judah.

30 And when Jehu was come to Jezreel, Jezebel heard of it; and she painted her

THE DEATH OF JEZEBEL

2 Kings 9:33

face, and tired her head, and looked out at a window.

31 And as Jehu entered in at the gate, she said, Had Zimri peace, who slew his master?

32 And he lifted up his face to the window, and said, Who is on my side? who?

And there looked out to him two or three eunuchs.

33 And he said, Throw her down. So they threw her down: and some of her blood was sprinkled on the wall, and on the horses: and he trode her under foot.

34 And when he was come in, he did eat and drink, and said, Go, see now this

cursed woman, and bury her: for she is a king's daughter.

35 And they went to bury her: but they found no more of her than the skull, and the feet, and the palms of her hands.

36 Therefore they came again, and told him. And he said, This is the word of the LORD, which he spoke by his servant Elijah the Tishbite, saying, In the portion of Jezreel shall dogs eat the flesh of Jezebel:

37 And the carcase of Jezebel shall be as dung upon the face of the field in the portion of Jezreel; so that they shall not say, This is Jezebel.

CHAPTER 10

AND Ahab had seventy sons in Samaria. And Jehu wrote letters, and sent to Samaria, to the rulers of Jezreel, to the elders, and to them that brought up Ahab's children, saying,

2 Now as soon as this letter cometh to you, seeing your master's sons are with you, and there are with you chariots and horses, a fenced city also, and armour;

3 Look even out the best and most upright of your master's sons, and set him on his father's throne, and fight for your master's house.

4 But they were exceedingly afraid, and said, Behold, two kings stood not before him: how then shall we stand?

5 And he that was over the house, and he that was over the city, the elders also, and the bringers up of the children, sent to Jehu, saying, We are your servants, and will do all that you shall bid us; we will not make any king: do that which is good in your eyes.

6 Then he wrote a letter the second time to them, saying, If you are mine, and if you will hearken to my voice, take the heads of the men your master's sons, and come to me to Jezreel by to morrow this time. Now the king's sons, being seventy persons, were with the great men of the city, which brought them up.

7 And it came to pass, when the letter came to them, that they took the king's sons, and slew seventy persons, and put their heads in baskets, and sent him them to Jezreel.

8 And there came a messenger, and told him, saying, They have brought the heads of the king's sons. And he said, Lay them in two heaps at the entering in of the gate until the morning.

9 And it came to pass in the morning, that he went out, and stood, and said to all the people, You are righteous: behold, I conspired against my master, and slew him: but who slew all these?

10 Know now that there shall fall to the earth nothing of the word of the LORD, which the LORD spoke concerning the house of Ahab: for the LORD has done that which he spoke by his servant Elijah.

11 So Jehu slew all that remained of the house of Ahab in Jezreel, and all his great men, and his kinsfolks, and his priests, until he left him none remaining.

12 And he arose and departed, and came to Samaria. And as he was at the shearing house in the way,

13 Jehu met with the brethren of Ahaziah king of Judah, and said, Who are you? And they answered, We are the brethren of Ahaziah; and we go down to salute the children of the king and the children of the queen.

14 And he said, Take them alive. And they took them alive, and slew them at the pit of the shearing house, even two and forty men; neither left he any of them.

15 And when he was departed thence, he lighted on Jehonadab the son of Rechab coming to meet him: and he saluted him, and said to him, Is your heart right, as my heart is with your heart? And Jehonadab answered, It is. If it be, give me your hand. And he gave him his hand; and he took him up to him into the chariot.

16 And he said, Come with me, and see my zeal for the LORD. So they made him ride in his chariot.

17 And when he came to Samaria, he slew all that remained to Ahab in Samaria, till he had destroyed him, according to the saying of the LORD, which he spoke to Elijah.

18 And Jehu gathered all the people together, and said to them, Ahab served Baal a little; but Jehu shall serve him much.

19 Now therefore call to me all the prophets of Baal, all his servants, and all his priests; let none be wanting: for I have a great sacrifice to do to Baal; whosoever shall be wanting, he shall not live. But Jehu did it in subtilty, to the intent that he might destroy the worshippers of Baal.

20 And Jehu said, Proclaim a solemn assembly for Baal. And they proclaimed it.

21 And Jehu sent through all Israel: and all the worshippers of Baal came, so that there was not a man left that came not. And they came into the house of Baal; and the house of Baal was full from one end to another.

22 And he said to him that was over the vestry, Bring forth vestments for all the worshippers of Baal. And he brought them forth vestments.

23 And Jehu went, and Jehonadab the son of Rechab, into the house of Baal, and said to the worshippers of Baal, Search, and look that there be here with you none of the servants of the LORD, but the worshippers of Baal only.

24 And when they went in to offer sacrifices and burnt offerings, Jehu appointed fourscore men without, and said, If any of the men whom I have brought into your hands escape, he that lets him go, his life shall be for the life of him.

25 And it came to pass, as soon as he had made an end of offering the burnt offering, that Jehu said to the guard and to the captains, Go in, and slay them; let none come forth. And they smote them with the edge of the sword; and the guard and the captains cast them out, and went to the city of the house of Baal.

26 And they brought forth the images out of the house of Baal, and burned them.

27 And they brake down the image of Baal, and brake down the house of Baal, and made it a draught house to this day.

28 Thus Jehu destroyed Baal out of Israel.

29 Howbeit from the sins of Jeroboam the son of Nebat, who made Israel to sin, Jehu departed not from after them, to wit, the golden calves that were in Bethel, and that were in Dan.

30 And the LORD said to Jehu, Because you have done well in executing that which is right in mine eyes, and have done to the house of Ahab according to all that was in mine heart, your children of the fourth generation shall sit on the throne of Israel.

31 But Jehu took no heed to walk in the law of the LORD God of Israel with all his heart: for he departed not from the sins of Jeroboam, which made Israel to sin.

32 In those days the LORD began to cut Israel short: and Hazael smote them in all the coasts of Israel;

33 From Jordan eastward, all the land of Gilead, the Gadites, and the Reubenites, and the Manassites, from Aroer, which is by the river Arnon, even Gilead and Bashan.

34 Now the rest of the acts of Jehu, and all that he did, and all his might, are they not written in the book of the chronicles of the kings of Israel?

35 And Jehu slept with his fathers: and they buried him in Samaria. And Jehoahaz his son reigned in his stead.

36 And the time that Jehu reigned over Israel in Samaria was twenty and eight years.

CHAPTER 11

AND when Athaliah the mother of Ahaziah saw that her son was dead, she arose and destroyed all the seed royal.

2 But Jehosheba, the daughter of king Joram, sister of Ahaziah, took Joash the son of Ahaziah, and stole him from among the king's sons which were slain; and they hid him, even him and his nurse, in the bedchamber from Athaliah, so that he was not slain.

3 And he was with her hid in the house of the LORD six years. And Athaliah did reign over the land.

4 And the seventh year Jehoiada sent and fetched the rulers over hundreds, with the captains and the guard, and brought them to him into the house of the LORD, and made a covenant with them, and took an oath of them in the house of the LORD, and showed them the king's son.

5 And he commanded them, saying, This is the thing that you shall do; A third part of you that enter in on the sabbath shall even be keepers of the watch of the king's house;

6 And a third part shall be at the gate of Sur; and a third part at the gate behind the guard: so shall you keep the watch of the house, that it be not broken down.

7 And two parts of all you that go forth on the sabbath, even they shall keep the watch of the house of the LORD about the king.

8 And you shall compass the king round about, every man with his weapons in his hand: and he that cometh within the ranges, let him be slain: and you are to be with the king as he goeth out and as he cometh in.

9 And the captains over the hundreds did according to all things that Jehoiada the priest commanded: and they took every man his men that were to come in on the sabbath, with them that should go out on the sabbath, and came to Jehoiada the priest.

10 And to the captains over hundreds did the priest give king David's spears and shields, that were in the temple of the LORD.

11 And the guard stood, every man with his weapons in his hand, round about the king, from the right corner of the temple to the left corner of the temple, along by the altar and the temple.

12 And he brought forth the king's son, and put the crown upon him, and gave him the testimony; and they made him king, and anointed him; and they clapped their hands, and said, God save the king.

13 And when Athaliah heard the noise of the guard and of the people, she came to the people into the temple of the LORD.

14 And when she looked, behold, the king stood by a pillar, as the manner was, and the princes and the trumpeters by the king, and all the people of the land rejoiced, and blew with trumpets: and Athaliah rent her clothes, and cried, Treason, Treason.

15 But Jehoiada the priest commanded the captains of the hundreds, the officers of the host, and said to them, Have her forth without the ranges: and him that follows her kill with the sword. For the priest had said, Let her not be slain in the house of the LORD.

16 And they laid hands on her; and she went by the way by the which the horses came into the king's house: and there was she slain.

17 And Jehoiada made a covenant between the LORD and the king and the people, that they should be the LORD's people; between the king also and the people.

18 And all the people of the land went into the house of Baal, and brake it down; his altars and his images brake they in pieces thoroughly, and slew Mattan the priest of Baal before the altars. And the priest appointed officers over the house of the LORD.

19 And he took the rulers over hundreds, and the captains, and the guard, and all the people of the land; and they brought down the king from the house of the LORD, and came by the way of the gate of the guard to the king's house. And he sat on the throne of the kings.

20 And all the people of the land rejoiced, and the city was in quiet: and they slew Athaliah with the sword beside the king's house.

21 Seven years old was Jehoash when he began to reign.

CHAPTER 12

IN the seventh year of Jehu Jehoash began to reign; and forty years reigned he in Jerusalem. And his mother's name was Zibiah of Beersheba.

2 And Jehoash did that which was right in the sight of the LORD all his days wherein Jehoiada the priest instructed him.

3 But the high places were not taken away: the people still sacrificed and burnt incense in the high places.

4 And Jehoash said to the priests, All the money of the dedicated things that is brought into the house of the LORD, even the money of every one that passes the account, the money that every man is set at, and all the money that cometh into any man's heart to bring into the house of the LORD,

5 Let the priests take it to them, every man of his acquaintance: and let them repair the breaches of the house, wherever any breach shall be found.

6 But it was so, that in the three and twentieth year of king Jehoash the priests had not repaired the breaches of the house.

7 Then king Jehoash called for Jehoiada the priest, and the other priests, and said to them, Why do you not repair the breaches of the house? now therefore receive no more money of your acquaintance, but deliver it for the breaches of the house.

8 And the priests consented to receive no more money of the people, neither to repair the breaches of the house.

9 But Jehoiada the priest took a chest, and bored a hole in the lid of it, and set it beside the altar, on the right side as one cometh into the house of the LORD: and the priests that kept the door put therein all the money that was brought into the house of the LORD.

10 And it was so, when they saw that there was much money in the chest, that the king's scribe and the high priest came up, and they put up in bags, and told the money that was found in the house of the LORD.

11 And they gave the money, being told, into the hands of them that did the work, that had the oversight of the house of the LORD: and they laid it out to the carpenters and builders, that worked upon the house of the LORD,

12 And to masons, and hewers of stone, and to buy timber and hewed stone to repair the breaches of the house of the LORD, and for all that was laid out for the house to repair it.

13 Howbeit there were not made for the house of the LORD bowls of silver, snuffers, basons, trumpets, any vessels of gold, or vessels of silver, of the money that was brought into the house of the LORD:

14 But they gave that to the workmen, and repaired therewith the house of the LORD.

15 Moreover they reckoned not with the men, into whose hand they delivered the money to be bestowed on workmen: for they dealt faithfully.

16 The trespass money and sin money was not brought into the house of the LORD: it was the priests'.

17 Then Hazael king of Syria went up, and fought against Gath, and took it: and Hazael set his face to go up to Jerusalem.

18 And Jehoash king of Judah took all the hallowed things that Jehoshaphat, and Jehoram, and Ahaziah, his fathers,

kings of Judah, had dedicated, and his own hallowed things, and all the gold that was found in the treasures of the house of the LORD, and in the king's house, and sent it to Hazael king of Syria: and he went away from Jerusalem.

19 And the rest of the acts of Joash, and all that he did, are they not written in the book of the chronicles of the kings of Judah?

20 And his servants arose, and made a conspiracy, and slew Joash in the house of Millo, which goeth down to Silla.

21 For Jozachar the son of Shimeath, and Jehozabad the son of Shomer, his servants, smote him, and he died; and they buried him with his fathers in the city of David: and Amaziah his son reigned in his stead.

CHAPTER 13

IN the three and twentieth year of Joash the son of Ahaziah king of Judah Jehoahaz the son of Jehu began to reign over Israel in Samaria, and reigned seventeen years.

2 And he did that which was evil in the sight of the LORD, and followed the sins of Jeroboam the son of Nebat, which made Israel to sin; he departed not therefrom.

3 And the anger of the LORD was kindled against Israel, and he delivered them into the hand of Hazael king of Syria, and into the hand of Benhadad the son of Hazael, all their days.

4 And Jehoahaz besought the LORD, and the LORD hearkened to him: for he saw the oppression of Israel, because the king of Syria oppressed them.

5 (And the LORD gave Israel a saviour, so that they went out from under the hand of the Syrians: and the children of Israel dwelt in their tents, as beforetime.

6 Nevertheless they departed not from the sins of the house of Jeroboam, who made Israel sin, but walked therein: and there remained the grove also in Samaria.)

7 Neither did he leave of the people to Jehoahaz but fifty horsemen, and ten chariots, and ten thousand footmen; for the king of Syria had destroyed them, and had made them like the dust by threshing.

8 Now the rest of the acts of Jehoahaz, and all that he did, and his might, are they not written in the book of the chronicles of the kings of Israel?

9 And Jehoahaz slept with his fathers; and they buried him in Samaria: and Joash his son reigned in his stead.

10 In the thirty and seventh year of Joash king of Judah began Jehoash the son of Jehoahaz to reign over Israel in Samaria, and reigned sixteen years.

11 And he did that which was evil in the sight of the LORD; he departed not from all the sins of Jeroboam the son of Nebat, who made Israel sin: but he walked therein.

12 And the rest of the acts of Joash, and all that he did, and his might wherewith he fought against Amaziah king of Judah, are they not written in the book of the chronicles of the kings of Israel?

13 And Joash slept with his fathers; and Jeroboam sat upon his throne: and Joash was buried in Samaria with the kings of Israel.

14 Now Elisha was fallen sick of his sickness whereof he died. And Joash the king of Israel came down to him, and wept over his face, and said, O my father, my father, the chariot of Israel, and the horsemen thereof.

15 And Elisha said to him, Take bow and arrows. And he took to him bow and arrows.

16 And he said to the king of Israel, Put your hand upon the bow. And he put his hand upon it: and Elisha put his hands upon the king's hands.

17 And he said, Open the window eastward. And he opened it. Then Elisha said, Shoot. And he shot. And he said, The arrow of the LORD's deliverance, and the arrow of deliverance from Syria:

> Satan, the god of all dissension,
> stirreth up daily new sects,
> and last of all,
> which of all other
> I should never have foreseen
> or once suspected,
> he hath raised up a sect
> as such as teach . . .
> that men should not be terrified
> by the Law,
> but gently exhorted by the preaching
> of the grace of Christ.

MARTIN LUTHER

1483-1546

GERMAN PRIEST

FOUNDER

OF THE LUTHERAN CHURCH

for you shall smite the Syrians in Aphek, till you have consumed them.

18 And he said, Take the arrows. And he took them. And he said to the king of Israel, Smite upon the ground. And he smote thrice, and stayed.

19 And the man of God was wroth with him, and said, You should have smitten five or six times; then had you smitten Syria till you had consumed it: whereas now you shall smite Syria but thrice.

20 And Elisha died, and they buried him. And the bands of the Moabites invaded the land at the coming in of the year.

21 And it came to pass, as they were burying a man, that, behold, they spied a band of men; and they cast the man into the sepulchre of Elisha: and when the man was let down, and touched the bones of Elisha, he revived, and stood up on his feet.

22 But Hazael king of Syria oppressed Israel all the days of Jehoahaz.

23 And the LORD was gracious to them, and had compassion on them, and had respect to them, because of his covenant with Abraham, Isaac, and Jacob, and would not destroy them, neither cast he them from his presence as yet.

24 So Hazael king of Syria died; and Benhadad his son reigned in his stead.

25 And Jehoash the son of Jehoahaz took again out of the hand of Benhadad the son of Hazael the cities, which he had taken out of the hand of Jehoahaz his father by war. Three times did Joash beat him, and recovered the cities of Israel.

CHAPTER 14

IN the second year of Joash son of Jehoahaz king of Israel reigned Amaziah the son of Joash king of Judah.

2 He was twenty and five years old when he began to reign, and reigned twenty and nine years in Jerusalem. And his mother's name was Jehoaddan of Jerusalem.

3 And he did that which was right in the sight of the LORD, yet not like David his father: he did according to all things as Joash his father did.

4 Howbeit the high places were not taken away: as yet the people did sacrifice and burnt incense on the high places.

5 And it came to pass, as soon as the kingdom was confirmed in his hand, that he slew his servants which had slain the king his father.

6 But the children of the murderers he slew not: according to that which is written in the book of the law of Moses, wherein the LORD commanded, saying, The fathers shall not be put to death for the children, nor the children be put to death for the fathers; but every man shall be put to death for his own sin.

7 He slew of Edom in the valley of salt ten thousand, and took Selah by war, and called the name of it Joktheel to this day.

8 Then Amaziah sent messengers to Jehoash, the son of Jehoahaz son of Jehu, king of Israel, saying, Come, let us look one another in the face.

9 And Jehoash the king of Israel sent to Amaziah king of Judah, saying, The thistle that was in Lebanon sent to the cedar

that was in Lebanon, saying, Give your daughter to my son to wife: and there passed by a wild beast that was in Lebanon, and trode down the thistle.

10 You have indeed smitten Edom, and your heart has lifted you up: glory of this, and tarry at home: for why should you meddle to your hurt, that you should fall, even you, and Judah with you?

11 But Amaziah would not hear. Therefore Jehoash king of Israel went up; and he and Amaziah king of Judah looked one another in the face at Bethshemesh, which belongs to Judah.

12 And Judah was put to the worse before Israel; and they fled every man to their tents.

13 And Jehoash king of Israel took Amaziah king of Judah, the son of Jehoash the son of Ahaziah, at Bethshemesh, and came to Jerusalem, and brake down the wall of Jerusalem from the gate of Ephraim to the corner gate, four hundred cubits.

14 And he took all the gold and silver, and all the vessels that were found in the house of the LORD, and in the treasures of the king's house, and hostages, and returned to Samaria.

15 Now the rest of the acts of Jehoash which he did, and his might, and how he fought with Amaziah king of Judah, are they not written in the book of the chronicles of the kings of Israel?

16 And Jehoash slept with his fathers, and was buried in Samaria with the kings of Israel; and Jeroboam his son reigned in his stead.

17 And Amaziah the son of Joash king of Judah lived after the death of Jehoash son of Jehoahaz king of Israel fifteen years.

18 And the rest of the acts of Amaziah, are they not written in the book of the chronicles of the kings of Judah?

19 Now they made a conspiracy against him in Jerusalem: and he fled to Lachish; but they sent after him to Lachish, and slew him there.

20 And they brought him on horses: and he was buried at Jerusalem with his fathers in the city of David.

21 And all the people of Judah took Azariah, which was sixteen years old, and made him king instead of his father Amaziah.

22 He built Elath, and restored it to Judah, after that the king slept with his fathers.

23 In the fifteenth year of Amaziah the son of Joash king of Judah Jeroboam the son of Joash king of Israel began to reign in Samaria, and reigned forty and one years.

24 And he did that which was evil in the sight of the LORD: he departed not from all the sins of Jeroboam the son of Nebat, who made Israel to sin.

25 He restored the coast of Israel from the entering of Hamath to the sea of the plain, according to the word of the LORD God of Israel, which he spoke by the hand of his servant Jonah, the son of Amittai, the prophet, which was of Gathhepher.

26 For the LORD saw the affliction of Israel, that it was very bitter: for there was not any shut up, nor any left, nor any helper for Israel.

27 And the LORD said not that he would blot out the name of Israel from under heaven: but he saved them by the hand of Jeroboam the son of Joash.

28 Now the rest of the acts of Jeroboam, and all that he did, and his might, how he warred, and how he recovered Damascus, and Hamath, which belonged to Judah, for Israel, are they not written in the book of the chronicles of the kings of Israel?

29 And Jeroboam slept with his fathers, even with the kings of Israel; and Zachariah his son reigned in his stead.

CHAPTER 15

IN the twenty and seventh year of Jeroboam king of Israel began Azariah son of Amaziah king of Judah to reign.

2 Sixteen years old was he when he began to reign, and he reigned two and fifty years in Jerusalem. And his mother's name was Jecholiah of Jerusalem.

3 And he did that which was right in the sight of the LORD, according to all that his father Amaziah had done;

4 Save that the high places were not removed: the people sacrificed and burnt incense still on the high places.

5 And the LORD smote the king, so that he was a leper to the day of his death, and dwelt in a several house. And Jotham the king's son was over the house, judging the people of the land.

6 And the rest of the acts of Azariah, and all that he did, are they not written in the book of the chronicles of the kings of Judah?

7 So Azariah slept with his fathers; and they buried him with his fathers in the city of David: and Jotham his son reigned in his stead.

8 In the thirty and eighth year of Azariah king of Judah did Zachariah the son of Jeroboam reign over Israel in Samaria six months.

9 And he did that which was evil in the sight of the LORD, as his fathers had done: he departed not from the sins of Jeroboam the son of Nebat, who made Israel to sin.

10 And Shallum the son of Jabesh conspired against him, and smote him before the people, and slew him, and reigned in his stead.

11 And the rest of the acts of Zachariah, behold, they are written in the book of the chronicles of the kings of Israel.

12 This was the word of the LORD which he spoke to Jehu, saying, Your sons shall sit on the throne of Israel to the fourth generation. And so it came to pass.

13 Shallum the son of Jabesh began to reign in the nine and thirtieth year of Uzziah king of Judah; and he reigned a full month in Samaria.

14 For Menahem the son of Gadi went up from Tirzah, and came to Samaria, and smote Shallum the son of Jabesh in Samaria, and slew him, and reigned in his stead.

15 And the rest of the acts of Shallum, and his conspiracy which he made, behold, they are written in the book of the chronicles of the kings of Israel.

16 Then Menahem smote Tiphsah, and all that were therein, and the coasts thereof from Tirzah: because they opened not to him, therefore he smote it; and all the women therein that were with child he ripped up.

17 In the nine and thirtieth year of Azariah king of Judah began Menahem the son of Gadi to reign over Israel, and reigned ten years in Samaria.

18 And he did that which was evil in the sight of the LORD: he departed not all his days from the sins of Jeroboam the son of Nebat, who made Israel to sin.

19 And Pul the king of Assyria came against the land: and Menahem gave Pul a thousand talents of silver, that his hand might be with him to confirm the kingdom in his hand.

20 And Menahem exacted the money of Israel, even of all the mighty men of wealth, of each man fifty shekels of silver, to give to the king of Assyria. So the king of Assyria turned back, and stayed not there in the land.

21 And the rest of the acts of Menahem, and all that he did, are they not written in the book of the chronicles of the kings of Israel?

22 And Menahem slept with his fathers; and Pekahiah his son reigned in his stead.

23 In the fiftieth year of Azariah king of Judah Pekahiah the son of Menahem began to reign over Israel in Samaria, and reigned two years.

24 And he did that which was evil in the sight of the LORD: he departed not

from the sins of Jeroboam the son of Nebat, who made Israel to sin.

25 But Pekah the son of Remaliah, a captain of his, conspired against him, and smote him in Samaria, in the palace of the king's house, with Argob and Arieh, and with him fifty men of the Gileadites: and he killed him, and reigned in his room.

26 And the rest of the acts of Pekahiah, and all that he did, behold, they are written in the book of the chronicles of the kings of Israel.

27 In the two and fiftieth year of Azariah king of Judah Pekah the son of Remaliah began to reign over Israel in Samaria, and reigned twenty years.

28 And he did that which was evil in the sight of the LORD: he departed not from the sins of Jeroboam the son of Nebat, who made Israel to sin.

29 In the days of Pekah king of Israel came Tiglathpileser king of Assyria, and took Ijon, and Abelbethmaachah, and Janoah, and Kedesh, and Hazor, and Gilead, and Galilee, all the land of Naphtali, and carried them captive to Assyria.

30 And Hoshea the son of Elah made a conspiracy against Pekah the son of Remaliah, and smote him, and slew him, and reigned in his stead, in the twentieth year of Jotham the son of Uzziah.

31 And the rest of the acts of Pekah, and all that he did, behold, they are written in the book of the chronicles of the kings of Israel.

32 In the second year of Pekah the son of Remaliah king of Israel began Jotham the son of Uzziah king of Judah to reign.

33 Five and twenty years old was he when he began to reign, and he reigned sixteen years in Jerusalem. And his mother's name was Jerusha, the daughter of Zadok.

34 And he did that which was right in the sight of the LORD: he did according to all that his father Uzziah had done.

35 Howbeit the high places were not removed: the people sacrificed and burned incense still in the high places. He built the higher gate of the house of the LORD.

36 Now the rest of the acts of Jotham, and all that he did, are they not written in the book of the chronicles of the kings of Judah?

37 In those days the LORD began to send against Judah Rezin the king of Syria, and Pekah the son of Remaliah.

38 And Jotham slept with his fathers, and was buried with his fathers in the city of David his father: and Ahaz his son reigned in his stead.

CHAPTER 16

IN the seventeenth year of Pekah the son of Remaliah Ahaz the son of Jotham king of Judah began to reign.

2 Twenty years old was Ahaz when he began to reign, and reigned sixteen years in Jerusalem, and did not that which was right in the sight of the LORD his God, like David his father.

3 But he walked in the way of the kings of Israel, yea, and made his son to pass through the fire, according to the abominations of the heathen, whom the LORD cast out from before the children of Israel.

4 And he sacrificed and burnt incense in the high places, and on the hills, and under every green tree.

5 Then Rezin king of Syria and Pekah son of Remaliah king of Israel came up to Jerusalem to war: and they besieged Ahaz, but could not overcome him.

6 At that time Rezin king of Syria recovered Elath to Syria, and drove the Jews from Elath: and the Syrians came to Elath, and dwelt there to this day.

7 So Ahaz sent messengers to Tiglathpileser king of Assyria, saying, I am your servant and your son: come up, and save me out of the hand of the king of Syria, and out of the hand of the king of Israel, which rise up against me.

8 And Ahaz took the silver and gold that was found in the house of the LORD, and in the treasures of the king's

house, and sent it for a present to the king of Assyria.

9 And the king of Assyria hearkened to him: for the king of Assyria went up against Damascus, and took it, and carried the people of it captive to Kir, and slew Rezin.

10 And king Ahaz went to Damascus to meet Tiglathpileser king of Assyria, and saw an altar that was at Damascus: and king Ahaz sent to Urijah the priest the fashion of the altar, and the pattern of it, according to all the workmanship thereof.

11 And Urijah the priest built an altar according to all that king Ahaz had sent from Damascus: so Urijah the priest made it against king Ahaz came from Damascus.

12 And when the king was come from Damascus, the king saw the altar: and the king approached to the altar, and offered thereon.

13 And he burnt his burnt offering and his meat offering, and poured his drink offering, and sprinkled the blood of his peace offerings, upon the altar.

14 And he brought also the brasen altar, which was before the LORD, from the forefront of the house, from between the altar and the house of the LORD, and put it on the north side of the altar.

15 And king Ahaz commanded Urijah the priest, saying, Upon the great altar burn the morning burnt offering, and the evening meat offering, and the king's burnt sacrifice, and his meat offering, with the burnt offering of all the people of the land, and their meat offering, and their drink offerings; and sprinkle upon it all the blood of the burnt offering, and all the blood of the sacrifice: and the brasen altar shall be for me to enquire by.

16 Thus did Urijah the priest, according to all that king Ahaz commanded.

17 And king Ahaz cut off the borders of the bases, and removed the laver from off them; and took down the sea from off the brasen oxen that were under it, and put it upon the pavement of stones.

18 And the covert for the sabbath that they had built in the house, and the king's entry without, turned he from the house of the LORD for the king of Assyria.

19 Now the rest of the acts of Ahaz which he did, are they not written in the book of the chronicles of the kings of Judah?

20 And Ahaz slept with his fathers, and was buried with his fathers in the city of David: and Hezekiah his son reigned in his stead.

CHAPTER 17

IN the twelfth year of Ahaz king of Judah began Hoshea the son of Elah to reign in Samaria over Israel nine years.

2 And he did that which was evil in the sight of the LORD, but not as the kings of Israel that were before him.

3 Against him came up Shalmaneser king of Assyria; and Hoshea became his servant, and gave him presents.

4 And the king of Assyria found conspiracy in Hoshea: for he had sent messengers to So king of Egypt, and brought no present to the king of Assyria, as he had done year by year: therefore the king of Assyria shut him up, and bound him in prison.

5 Then the king of Assyria came up throughout all the land, and went up to Samaria, and besieged it three years.

6 In the ninth year of Hoshea the king of Assyria took Samaria, and carried Israel away into Assyria, and placed them in Halah and in Habor by the river of Gozan, and in the cities of the Medes.

7 For so it was, that the children of Israel had sinned against the LORD their God, which had brought them up out of the land of Egypt, from under the hand of Pharaoh king of Egypt, and had feared other gods,

8 And walked in the statutes of the heathen, whom the LORD cast out from be-

fore the children of Israel, and of the kings of Israel, which they had made.

9 And the children of Israel did secretly those things that were not right against the LORD their God, and they built them high places in all their cities, from the tower of the watchmen to the fenced city.

10 And they set them up images and groves in every high hill, and under every green tree:

11 And there they burnt incense in all the high places, as did the heathen whom the LORD carried away before them; and did wicked things to provoke the LORD to anger:

12 For they served idols, whereof the LORD had said to them, You shall not do this thing.

13 Yet the LORD testified against Israel, and against Judah, by all the prophets, and by all the seers, saying, Turn from your evil ways, and keep my commandments and my statutes, according to all the law which I commanded your fathers, and which I sent to you by my servants the prophets.

14 Notwithstanding they would not hear, but hardened their necks, like to the neck of their fathers, that did not believe in the LORD their God.

15 And they rejected his statutes, and his covenant that he made with their fathers, and his testimonies which he testified against them; and they followed vanity, and became vain, and went after the heathen that were round about them, concerning whom the LORD had charged them, that they should not do like them.

16 And they left all the commandments of the LORD their God, and made them molten images, even two calves, and made a grove, and worshipped all the host of heaven, and served Baal.

17 And they caused their sons and their daughters to pass through the fire, and used divination and enchantments, and sold themselves to do evil in the sight of the LORD, to provoke him to anger.

18 Therefore the LORD was very angry with Israel, and removed them out of his sight: there was none left but the tribe of Judah only.

19 Also Judah kept not the commandments of the LORD their God, but walked in the statutes of Israel which they made.

20 And the LORD rejected all the seed of Israel, and afflicted them, and delivered them into the hand of spoilers, until he had cast them out of his sight.

21 For he rent Israel from the house of David; and they made Jeroboam the son of Nebat king: and Jeroboam drove Israel from following the LORD, and made them sin a great sin.

22 For the children of Israel walked in all the sins of Jeroboam which he did; they departed not from them;

23 Until the LORD removed Israel out of his sight, as he had said by all his servants the prophets. So was Israel carried away out of their own land to Assyria to this day.

24 And the king of Assyria brought men from Babylon, and from Cuthah, and from Ava, and from Hamath, and from Sepharvaim, and placed them in the cities of Samaria instead of the children of Israel: and they possessed Samaria, and dwelt in the cities thereof.

25 And so it was at the beginning of their dwelling there, that they feared not the LORD: therefore the LORD sent lions among them, which slew some of them.

26 Therefore they spoke to the king of Assyria, saying, The nations which you have removed, and placed in the cities of Samaria, know not the manner of the God of the land: therefore he has sent lions among them, and, behold, they slay them, because they know not the manner of the God of the land.

27 Then the king of Assyria commanded, saying, Carry there one of the priests whom you brought from thence; and let them go and dwell there, and let him

teach them the manner of the God of the land.

28 Then one of the priests whom they had carried away from Samaria came and dwelt in Bethel, and taught them how they should fear the LORD.

29 Howbeit every nation made gods of their own, and put them in the houses of the high places which the Samaritans had made, every nation in their cities wherein they dwelt.

30 And the men of Babylon made Succothbenoth, and the men of Cuth made Nergal, and the men of Hamath made Ashima,

31 And the Avites made Nibhaz and Tartak, and the Sepharvites burnt their children in fire to Adrammelech and Anammelech, the gods of Sepharvaim.

32 So they feared the LORD, and made to themselves of the lowest of them priests of the high places, which sacrificed for them in the houses of the high places.

33 They feared the LORD, and served their own gods, after the manner of the nations whom they carried away from thence.

34 To this day they do after the former manners: they fear not the LORD, neither do they after their statutes, or after their ordinances, or after the law and commandment which the LORD commanded the children of Jacob, whom he named Israel;

35 With whom the LORD had made a covenant, and charged them, saying, You shall not fear other gods, nor bow yourselves to them, nor serve them, nor sacrifice to them:

36 But the LORD, who brought you up out of the land of Egypt with great power and a stretched out arm, him shall you fear, and him shall you worship, and to him shall you do sacrifice.

37 And the statutes, and the ordinances, and the law, and the commandment, which he wrote for you, you shall observe to do for evermore; and you shall not fear other gods.

38 And the covenant that I have made with you you shall not forget; neither shall you fear other gods.

39 But the LORD your God you shall fear; and he shall deliver you out of the hand of all your enemies.

40 Howbeit they did not hearken, but they did after their former manner.

41 So these nations feared the LORD, and served their graven images, both their children, and their children's children: as did their fathers, so do they to this day.

CHAPTER 18

N OW it came to pass in the third year of Hoshea son of Elah king of Israel, that Hezekiah the son of Ahaz king of Judah began to reign.

2 Twenty and five years old was he when he began to reign; and he reigned twenty and nine years in Jerusalem. His mother's name also was Abi, the daughter of Zachariah.

3 And he did that which was right in the sight of the LORD, according to all that David his father did.

4 He removed the high places, and brake the images, and cut down the groves, and brake in pieces the brasen serpent that Moses had made: for to those days the children of Israel did burn incense to it: and he called it Nehushtan.

5 He trusted in the LORD God of Israel; so that after him was none like him among all the kings of Judah, nor any that were before him.

6 For he clave to the LORD, and departed not from following him, but kept his commandments, which the LORD commanded Moses.

7 And the LORD was with him; and he prospered wherever he went forth: and he rebelled against the king of Assyria, and served him not.

8 He smote the Philistines, even to Gaza, and the borders thereof, from the tower of the watchmen to the fenced city.

9 And it came to pass in the fourth year of king Hezekiah, which was the seventh year of Hoshea son of Elah king of Israel, that Shalmaneser king of Assyria came up against Samaria, and besieged it.

10 And at the end of three years they took it: even in the sixth year of Hezekiah, that is in the ninth year of Hoshea king of Israel, Samaria was taken.

11 And the king of Assyria did carry away Israel to Assyria, and put them in Halah and in Habor by the river of Gozan, and in the cities of the Medes:

12 Because they obeyed not the voice of the LORD their God, but transgressed his covenant, and all that Moses the servant of the LORD commanded, and would not hear them, nor do them.

13 Now in the fourteenth year of king Hezekiah did Sennacherib king of Assyria come up against all the fenced cities of Judah, and took them.

14 And Hezekiah king of Judah sent to the king of Assyria to Lachish, saying, I have offended; return from me: that which you put on me will I bear. And the king of Assyria appointed to Hezekiah king of Judah three hundred talents of silver and thirty talents of gold.

15 And Hezekiah gave him all the silver that was found in the house of the LORD, and in the treasures of the king's house.

16 At that time did Hezekiah cut off the gold from the doors of the temple of the LORD, and from the pillars which Hezekiah king of Judah had overlaid, and gave it to the king of Assyria.

17 And the king of Assyria sent Tartan and Rabsaris and Rabshakeh from Lachish to king Hezekiah with a great host against Jerusalem. And they went up and came to Jerusalem. And when they were come up, they came and stood by the conduit of the upper pool, which is in the highway of the fuller's field.

18 And when they had called to the king, there came out to them Eliakim the son of Hilkiah, which was over the household, and Shebna the scribe, and Joah the son of Asaph the recorder.

19 And Rabshakeh said to them, Speak now to Hezekiah, Thus says the great king, the king of Assyria, What confidence is this wherein you trust?

20 You say, (but they are but vain words,) I have counsel and strength for the war. Now on whom do you trust, that you rebel against me?

21 Now, behold, you trust upon the staff of this bruised reed, even upon Egypt, on which if a man lean, it will go into his hand, and pierce it: so is Pharaoh king of Egypt to all that trust on him.

22 But if you say to me, We trust in the LORD our God: is not that he, whose high places and whose altars Hezekiah has taken away, and has said to Judah and Jerusalem, You shall worship before this altar in Jerusalem?

23 Now therefore, I pray you, give pledges to my lord the king of Assyria, and I will deliver you two thousand horses, if you are able on your part to set riders upon them.

24 How then will you turn away the face of one captain of the least of my master's servants, and put your trust on Egypt for chariots and for horsemen?

25 Am I now come up without the LORD against this place to destroy it? The LORD said to me, Go up against this land, and destroy it.

26 Then said Eliakim the son of Hilkiah, and Shebna, and Joah, to Rabshakeh, Speak, I pray you, to your servants in the Syrian language; for we understand it: and talk not with us in the Jews' language in the ears of the people that are on the wall.

27 But Rabshakeh said to them, Has my master sent me to your master, and to you, to speak these words? has he not sent me to the men which sit on the wall, that they may eat their own dung, and drink their own piss with you?

28 Then Rabshakeh stood and cried with a loud voice in the Jews' language,

and spoke, saying, Hear the word of the great king, the king of Assyria:

29 Thus says the king, Let not Hezekiah deceive you: for he shall not be able to deliver you out of his hand:

30 Neither let Hezekiah make you trust in the LORD, saying, The LORD will surely deliver us, and this city shall not be delivered into the hand of the king of Assyria.

31 Hearken not to Hezekiah: for thus says the king of Assyria, Make an agreement with me by a present, and come out to me, and then every man eat of his own vine, and every one of his fig tree, and every one of you drink the waters of his cistern:

32 Until I come and take you away to a land like your own land, a land of corn and wine, a land of bread and vineyards, a land of oil olive and of honey, that you may live, and not die: and hearken not to Hezekiah, when he persuades you, saying, The LORD will deliver us.

33 Has any of the gods of the nations delivered at all his land out of the hand of the king of Assyria?

34 Where are the gods of Hamath, and of Arpad? where are the gods of Sepharvaim, Hena, and Ivah? have they delivered Samaria out of mine hand?

35 Who are they among all the gods of the countries, that have delivered their country out of mine hand, that the LORD should deliver Jerusalem out of mine hand?

36 But the people held their peace, and answered him not a word: for the king's commandment was, saying, Answer him not.

37 Then came Eliakim the son of Hilkiah, which was over the household, and Shebna the scribe, and Joah the son of Asaph the recorder, to Hezekiah with their clothes rent, and told him the words of Rabshakeh.

CHAPTER 19

AND it came to pass, when king Hezekiah heard it, that he rent his clothes, and covered himself with sackcloth, and went into the house of the LORD.

2 And he sent Eliakim, which was over the household, and Shebna the scribe, and the elders of the priests, covered with sackcloth, to Isaiah the prophet the son of Amoz.

3 And they said to him, Thus says Hezekiah, This day is a day of trouble, and of rebuke, and blasphemy; for the children are come to the birth, and there is not strength to bring forth.

4 It may be the LORD your God will hear all the words of Rabshakeh, whom the king of Assyria his master has sent to reproach the living God; and will reprove the words which the LORD your God has heard: therefore lift up your prayer for the remnant that are left.

5 So the servants of king Hezekiah came to Isaiah.

6 And Isaiah said to them, Thus shall you say to your master, Thus says the LORD, Be not afraid of the words which you have heard, with which the servants of the king of Assyria have blasphemed me.

7 Behold, I will send a blast upon him, and he shall hear a rumour, and shall return to his own land; and I will cause him to fall by the sword in his own land.

8 So Rabshakeh returned, and found the king of Assyria warring against Libnah: for he had heard that he was departed from Lachish.

9 And when he heard say of Tirhakah king of Ethiopia, Behold, he is come out to fight against you: he sent messengers again to Hezekiah, saying,

10 Thus shall you speak to Hezekiah king of Judah, saying, Let not your God in whom you trust deceive you, saying, Jerusalem shall not be delivered into the hand of the king of Assyria.

11 Behold, you have heard what the kings of Assyria have done to all lands,

by destroying them utterly: and shall you be delivered?

12 Have the gods of the nations delivered them which my fathers have destroyed; as Gozan, and Haran, and Rezeph, and the children of Eden which were in Thelasar?

13 Where is the king of Hamath, and the king of Arpad, and the king of the city of Sepharvaim, of Hena, and Ivah?

14 And Hezekiah received the letter of the hand of the messengers, and read it: and Hezekiah went up into the house of the LORD, and spread it before the LORD.

15 And Hezekiah prayed before the LORD, and said, O LORD God of Israel, which dwells between the cherubims, you are the God, even you alone, of all the kingdoms of the earth; you have made heaven and earth.

16 LORD, bow down your ear, and hear: open, LORD, your eyes, and see: and hear the words of Sennacherib, which has sent him to reproach the living God.

17 Of a truth, LORD, the kings of Assyria have destroyed the nations and their lands,

18 And have cast their gods into the fire: for they were no gods, but the work of men's hands, wood and stone: therefore they have destroyed them.

19 Now therefore, O LORD our God, I beseech you, save you us out of his hand, that all the kingdoms of the earth may know that you are the LORD God, even you only.

20 Then Isaiah the son of Amoz sent to Hezekiah, saying, Thus says the LORD God of Israel, That which you have prayed to me against Sennacherib king of Assyria I have heard.

21 This is the word that the LORD has spoken concerning him; The virgin the daughter of Zion has despised you, and laughed you to scorn; the daughter of Jerusalem has shaken her head at you.

22 Whom have you reproached and blasphemed? and against whom have you exalted your voice, and lifted up your eyes on high? even against the Holy One of Israel.

23 By your messengers you have reproached the LORD, and have said, With the multitude of my chariots I am come up to the height of the mountains, to the sides of Lebanon, and will cut down the tall cedar trees thereof, and the choice fir trees thereof: and I will enter into the lodgings of his borders, and into the forest of his Carmel.

24 I have dug and drunk strange waters, and with the sole of my feet have I dried up all the rivers of besieged places.

25 Have you not heard long ago how I have done it, and of ancient times that I have formed it? now have I brought it to pass, that you should be to lay waste fenced cities into ruinous heaps.

26 Therefore their inhabitants were of small power, they were dismayed and confounded; they were as the grass of the field, and as the green herb, as the grass on the house tops, and as corn blasted before it be grown up.

27 But I know your abode, and your going out, and your coming in, and your rage against me.

28 Because your rage against me and your tumult is come up into mine ears, therefore I will put my hook in your nose, and my bridle in your lips, and I will turn you back by the way by which you came.

29 And this shall be a sign to you, You shall eat this year such things as grow of themselves, and in the second year that which springs of the same; and in the third year sow and reap, and plant vineyards, and eat the fruits thereof.

30 And the remnant that is escaped of the house of Judah shall yet again take root downward, and bear fruit upward.

31 For out of Jerusalem shall go forth a remnant, and they that escape out of mount Zion: the zeal of the LORD of hosts shall do this.

32 Therefore thus says the LORD concerning the king of Assyria, He shall not

come into this city, nor shoot an arrow there, nor come before it with shield, nor cast a bank against it.

33 By the way that he came, by the same shall he return, and shall not come into this city, says the LORD.

34 For I will defend this city, to save it, for mine own sake, and for my servant David's sake.

35 And it came to pass that night, that the angel of the LORD went out, and smote in the camp of the Assyrians an hundred fourscore and five thousand: and when they arose early in the morning, behold, they were all dead corpses.

36 So Sennacherib king of Assyria departed, and went and returned, and dwelt at Nineveh.

37 And it came to pass, as he was worshipping in the house of Nisroch his god, that Adrammelech and Sharezer his sons smote him with the sword: and they escaped into the land of Armenia. And Esarhaddon his son reigned in his stead.

CHAPTER 20

IN those days was Hezekiah sick to death. And the prophet Isaiah the son of Amoz came to him, and said to him, Thus says the LORD, Set your house in order; for you shall die, and not live.

2 Then he turned his face to the wall, and prayed to the LORD, saying,

3 I beseech you, O LORD, remember now how I have walked before you in truth and with a perfect heart, and have done that which is good in your sight. And Hezekiah wept sore.

4 And it came to pass, afore Isaiah was gone out into the middle court, that the word of the LORD came to him, saying,

5 Turn again, and tell Hezekiah the captain of my people, Thus says the LORD, the God of David your father, I have heard your prayer, I have seen your tears: behold, I will heal you: on the third day you shall go up to the house of the LORD.

6 And I will add to your days fifteen years; and I will deliver you and this city out of the hand of the king of Assyria; and I will defend this city for mine own sake, and for my servant David's sake.

7 And Isaiah said, Take a lump of figs. And they took and laid it on the boil, and he recovered.

8 And Hezekiah said to Isaiah, What shall be the sign that the LORD will heal me, and that I shall go up into the house of the LORD the third day?

9 And Isaiah said, This sign shall you have of the LORD, that the LORD will do the thing that he has spoken: shall the shadow go forward ten degrees, or go back ten degrees?

10 And Hezekiah answered, It is a light thing for the shadow to go down ten degrees: nay, but let the shadow return backward ten degrees.

11 And Isaiah the prophet cried to the LORD: and he brought the shadow ten degrees backward, by which it had gone down in the dial of Ahaz.

12 At that time Berodachbaladan, the son of Baladan, king of Babylon, sent letters and a present to Hezekiah: for he had heard that Hezekiah had been sick.

13 And Hezekiah hearkened to them, and showed them all the house of his precious things, the silver, and the gold, and the spices, and the precious ointment, and all the house of his armour, and all that was found in his treasures: there was nothing in his house, nor in all

---

20:1 God's Law makes a sinner see that he is about to perish. It causes him to turn away from the world's distractions, put his face to the wall and seek the Savior for deliverance. It is a "schoolmaster" to bring him to Christ (see Galatians 3:24).

20:7 "Today orthodox medicine is beginning to concede that some natural' remedies, such as poultices, really do work just as effectively as 'modern' medicines." Richard Gunther

his dominion, that Hezekiah showed them not.

14 Then came Isaiah the prophet to king Hezekiah, and said to him, What said these men? and from where did they come to you? And Hezekiah said, They are come from a far country, even from Babylon.

15 And he said, What have they seen in your house? And Hezekiah answered, All the things that are in mine house have they seen: there is nothing among my treasures that I have not showed them.

16 And Isaiah said to Hezekiah, Hear the word of the LORD.

17 Behold, the days come, that all that is in your house, and that which your fathers have laid up in store to this day, shall be carried into Babylon: nothing shall be left, says the LORD.

18 And of your sons that shall issue from you, which you shall beget, shall they take away; and they shall be eunuchs in the palace of the king of Babylon.

19 Then said Hezekiah to Isaiah, Good is the word of the LORD which you have spoken. And he said, Is it not good, if peace and truth be in my days?

20 And the rest of the acts of Hezekiah, and all his might, and how he made a pool, and a conduit, and brought water into the city, are they not written in the book of the chronicles of the kings of Judah?

21 And Hezekiah slept with his fathers: and Manasseh his son reigned in his stead.

CHAPTER 21

MANASSEH was twelve years old when he began to reign, and reigned fifty and five years in Jerusalem. And his mother's name was Hephzibah.

2 And he did that which was evil in the sight of the LORD, after the abominations of the heathen, whom the LORD cast out before the children of Israel.

3 For he built up again the high places which Hezekiah his father had destroyed; and he reared up altars for Baal, and made a grove, as did Ahab king of Israel; and worshipped all the host of heaven, and served them.

4 And he built altars in the house of the LORD, of which the LORD said, In Jerusalem will I put my name.

5 And he built altars for all the host of heaven in the two courts of the house of the LORD.

6 And he made his son pass through the fire, and observed times, and used enchantments, and dealt with familiar spirits and wizards: he did much wickedness in the sight of the LORD, to provoke him to anger.

7 And he set a graven image of the grove that he had made in the house, of which the LORD said to David, and to Solomon his son, In this house, and in Jerusalem, which I have chosen out of all tribes of Israel, will I put my name for ever:

8 Neither will I make the feet of Israel move any more out of the land which I gave their fathers; only if they will observe to do according to all that I have commanded them, and according to all the law that my servant Moses commanded them.

9 But they hearkened not: and Manasseh seduced them to do more evil than did the nations whom the LORD destroyed before the children of Israel.

10 And the LORD spoke by his servants the prophets, saying,

11 Because Manasseh king of Judah has done these abominations, and has done wickedly above all that the Amorites did, which were before him, and has made Judah also to sin with his idols:

12 Therefore thus says the LORD God of Israel, Behold, I am bringing such evil upon Jerusalem and Judah, that whosoever hears of it, both his ears shall tingle.

13 And I will stretch over Jerusalem the line of Samaria, and the plummet of the house of Ahab: and I will wipe Jerusalem as a man wipes a dish, wiping it, and turning it upside down.

14 And I will forsake the remnant of mine inheritance, and deliver them into the hand of their enemies; and they shall become a prey and a spoil to all their enemies;

15 Because they have done that which was evil in my sight, and have provoked me to anger, since the day their fathers came forth out of Egypt, even to this day.

16 Moreover Manasseh shed innocent blood very much, till he had filled Jerusalem from one end to another; beside his sin wherewith he made Judah to sin, in doing that which was evil in the sight of the LORD.

17 Now the rest of the acts of Manasseh, and all that he did, and his sin that he sinned, are they not written in the book of the chronicles of the kings of Judah?

18 And Manasseh slept with his fathers, and was buried in the garden of his own house, in the garden of Uzza: and Amon his son reigned in his stead.

19 Amon was twenty and two years old when he began to reign, and he reigned two years in Jerusalem. And his mother's name was Meshullemeth, the daughter of Haruz of Jotbah.

20 And he did that which was evil in the sight of the LORD, as his father Manasseh did.

21 And he walked in all the way that his father walked in, and served the idols that his father served, and worshipped them:

22 And he forsook the LORD God of his fathers, and walked not in the way of the LORD.

23 And the servants of Amon conspired against him, and slew the king in his own house.

24 And the people of the land slew all them that had conspired against king Amon; and the people of the land made Josiah his son king in his stead.

25 Now the rest of the acts of Amon which he did, are they not written in the book of the chronicles of the kings of Judah?

26 And he was buried in his sepulchre in the garden of Uzza: and Josiah his son reigned in his stead.

CHAPTER 22

JOSIAH was eight years old when he began to reign, and he reigned thirty and one years in Jerusalem. And his mother's name was Jedidah, the daughter of Adaiah of Boscath.

2 And he did that which was right in the sight of the LORD, and walked in all the way of David his father, and turned not aside to the right hand or to the left.

3 And it came to pass in the eighteenth year of king Josiah, that the king sent Shaphan the son of Azaliah, the son of Meshullam, the scribe, to the house of the LORD, saying,

4 Go up to Hilkiah the high priest, that he may sum the silver which is brought into the house of the LORD, which the keepers of the door have gathered of the people:

5 And let them deliver it into the hand of the doers of the work, that have the oversight of the house of the LORD: and let them give it to the doers of the work which is in the house of the LORD, to repair the breaches of the house,

6 To carpenters, and builders, and masons, and to buy timber and hewn stone to repair the house.

7 Howbeit there was no reckoning made with them of the money that was delivered into their hand, because they dealt faithfully.

8 And Hilkiah the high priest said to Shaphan the scribe, I have found the book of the law in the house of the LORD. And Hilkiah gave the book to Shaphan, and he read it.

9 And Shaphan the scribe came to the king, and brought the king word again, and said, Your servants have gathered the money that was found in the house, and have delivered it into the hand of

them that do the work, that have the oversight of the house of the LORD.

10 And Shaphan the scribe showed the king, saying, Hilkiah the priest has delivered me a book. And Shaphan read it before the king.

11 And it came to pass, when the king had heard the words of the book of the law, that he rent his clothes.

12 And the king commanded Hilkiah the priest, and Ahikam the son of Shaphan, and Achbor the son of Michaiah, and Shaphan the scribe, and Asahiah a servant of the king's, saying,

13 Go, enquire of the LORD for me, and for the people, and for all Judah, concerning the words of this book that is found: for great is the wrath of the LORD that is kindled against us, because our fathers have not hearkened to the words of this book, to do according to all that which is written concerning us.

14 So Hilkiah the priest, and Ahikam, and Achbor, and Shaphan, and Asahiah, went to Huldah the prophetess, the wife of Shallum the son of Tikvah, the son of Harhas, keeper of the wardrobe; (now she dwelt in Jerusalem in the college;) and they communed with her.

15 And she said to them, Thus says the LORD God of Israel, Tell the man that sent you to me,

16 Thus says the LORD, Behold, I will bring evil upon this place, and upon the inhabitants thereof, even all the words of the book which the king of Judah has read:

17 Because they have forsaken me, and have burned incense to other gods, that they might provoke me to anger with all the works of their hands; therefore my wrath shall be kindled against this place, and shall not be quenched.

18 But to the king of Judah which sent you to inquire of the LORD, thus shall you say to him, Thus says the LORD God of Israel, As touching the words which you have heard;

19 Because your heart was tender, and you have humbled yourself before the LORD, when you heard what I spoke against this place, and against the inhabitants thereof, that they should become a desolation and a curse, and have rent your clothes, and wept before me; I also have heard you, says the LORD.

20 Behold therefore, I will gather you to your fathers, and you shall be gathered into your grave in peace; and your eyes shall not see all the evil which I will bring upon this place. And they brought the king word again.

CHAPTER 23

AND the king sent, and they gathered to him all the elders of Judah and of Jerusalem.

2 And the king went up into the house of the LORD, and all the men of Judah and all the inhabitants of Jerusalem with him, and the priests, and the prophets, and all the people, both small and great: and he read in their ears all the words of the book of the covenant which was found in the house of the LORD.

3 And the king stood by a pillar, and made a covenant before the LORD, to walk after the LORD, and to keep his commandments and his testimonies and his statutes with all their heart and all their soul, to perform the words of this covenant that were written in this book. And all the people stood to the covenant.

4 And the king commanded Hilkiah the high priest, and the priests of the second order, and the keepers of the door, to bring forth out of the temple of the LORD all the vessels that were made for Baal, and for the grove, and for all the host of heaven: and he burned them without Jerusalem in the fields of Kidron, and carried the ashes of them to Bethel.

5 And he put down the idolatrous priests, whom the kings of Judah had ordained to burn incense in the high places in the cities of Judah, and in the places round about Jerusalem; them also that burned incense to Baal, to the sun,

and to the moon, and to the planets, and to all the host of heaven.

6 And he brought out the grove from the house of the LORD, without Jerusalem, to the brook Kidron, and burned it at the brook Kidron, and stamped it small to powder, and cast the powder thereof upon the graves of the children of the people.

7 And he brake down the houses of the sodomites, that were by the house of the LORD, where the women wove hangings for the grove.

8 And he brought all the priests out of the cities of Judah, and defiled the high places where the priests had burned incense, from Geba to Beersheba, and brake down the high places of the gates that were in the entering in of the gate of Joshua the governor of the city, which were on a man's left hand at the gate of the city.

9 Nevertheless the priests of the high places came not up to the altar of the LORD in Jerusalem, but they did eat of the unleavened bread among their brethren.

10 And he defiled Topheth, which is in the valley of the children of Hinnom, that no man might make his son or his daughter to pass through the fire to Molech.

11 And he took away the horses that the kings of Judah had given to the sun, at the entering in of the house of the LORD, by the chamber of Nathanmelech the chamberlain, which was in the suburbs, and burned the chariots of the sun with fire.

12 And the altars that were on the top of the upper chamber of Ahaz, which the kings of Judah had made, and the altars which Manasseh had made in the two courts of the house of the LORD, did the king beat down, and brake them down from thence, and cast the dust of them into the brook Kidron.

13 And the high places that were before Jerusalem, which were on the right hand of the mount of corruption, which Solomon the king of Israel had built for Ashtoreth the abomination of the Zidonians, and for Chemosh the abomination of the Moabites, and for Milcom the abomination of the children of Ammon, did the king defile.

14 And he brake in pieces the images, and cut down the groves, and filled their places with the bones of men.

15 Moreover the altar that was at Bethel, and the high place which Jeroboam the son of Nebat, who made Israel to sin, had made, both that altar and the high place he brake down, and burned the high place, and stamped it small to powder, and burned the grove.

16 And as Josiah turned himself, he spied the sepulchres that were there in the mount, and sent, and took the bones out of the sepulchres, and burned them upon the altar, and polluted it, according to the word of the LORD which the man of God proclaimed, who proclaimed these words.

17 Then he said, What title is that that I see? And the men of the city told him, It is the sepulchre of the man of God, which came from Judah, and proclaimed these things that you have done against the altar of Bethel.

18 And he said, Let him alone; let no man move his bones. So they let his bones alone, with the bones of the prophet that came out of Samaria.

19 And all the houses also of the high places that were in the cities of Samaria, which the kings of Israel had made to provoke the Lord to anger, Josiah took away, and did to them according to all the acts that he had done in Bethel.

20 And he slew all the priests of the high places that were there upon the altars, and burned men's bones upon them, and returned to Jerusalem.

21 And the king commanded all the people, saying, Keep the passover to the LORD your God, as it is written in the book of this covenant.

22 Surely there was not holden such a passover from the days of the judges that

judged Israel, nor in all the days of the kings of Israel, nor of the kings of Judah;
23 But in the eighteenth year of king Josiah, wherein this passover was holden to the LORD in Jerusalem.
24 Moreover the workers with familiar spirits, and the wizards, and the images, and the idols, and all the abominations that were spied in the land of Judah and in Jerusalem, did Josiah put away, that he might perform the words of the law which were written in the book that Hilkiah the priest found in the house of the LORD.
25 And like to him was there no king before him, that turned to the LORD with all his heart, and with all his soul, and with all his might, according to all the law of Moses; neither after him arose there any like him.
26 Notwithstanding the LORD turned not from the fierceness of his great wrath, wherewith his anger was kindled against Judah, because of all the provocations that Manasseh had provoked him withal.
27 And the LORD said, I will remove Judah also out of my sight, as I have removed Israel, and will cast off this city Jerusalem which I have chosen, and the house of which I said, My name shall be there.
28 Now the rest of the acts of Josiah, and all that he did, are they not written in the book of the chronicles of the kings of Judah?
29 In his days Pharaohnechoh king of Egypt went up against the king of Assyria to the river Euphrates: and king Josiah went against him; and he slew him at Megiddo, when he had seen him.
30 And his servants carried him in a chariot dead from Megiddo, and brought him to Jerusalem, and buried him in his own sepulchre. And the people of the land took Jehoahaz the son of Josiah, and anointed him, and made him king in his father's stead.
31 Jehoahaz was twenty and three years old when he began to reign; and he reigned three months in Jerusalem. And his mother's name was Hamutal, the daughter of Jeremiah of Libnah.
32 And he did that which was evil in the sight of the LORD, according to all that his fathers had done.
33 And Pharaohnechoh put him in bands at Riblah in the land of Hamath, that he might not reign in Jerusalem; and put the land to a tribute of an hundred talents of silver, and a talent of gold.
34 And Pharaohnechoh made Eliakim the son of Josiah king in the room of Josiah his father, and turned his name to Jehoiakim, and took Jehoahaz away: and he came to Egypt, and died there.
35 And Jehoiakim gave the silver and the gold to Pharaoh; but he taxed the land to give the money according to the commandment of Pharaoh: he exacted the silver and the gold of the people of the land, of every one according to his taxation, to give it to Pharaohnechoh.
36 Jehoiakim was twenty and five years old when he began to reign; and he reigned eleven years in Jerusalem. And his mother's name was Zebudah, the daughter of Pedaiah of Rumah.
37 And he did that which was evil in the sight of the LORD, according to all that his fathers had done.

CHAPTER 24

IN his days Nebuchadnezzar king of Babylon came up, and Jehoiakim became his servant three years: then he turned and rebelled against him.
2 And the LORD sent against him bands of the Chaldees, and bands of the Syrians, and bands of the Moabites, and bands of the children of Ammon, and sent them against Judah to destroy it, according to the word of the LORD, which he spoke by his servants the prophets.
3 Surely at the commandment of the LORD came this upon Judah, to remove them out of his sight, for the sins of Manasseh, according to all that he did;

*I would rather win souls
than be the greatest king
or emperor on earth;
I would rather win souls
than be the greatest general
that ever commanded an army...
my one ambition in life
is to win as many as possible.
Oh, it is the only thing worth doing;
to save souls;
and, men and women,
we can all do it.*

R. A. Torrey

1856 - 1928

AUTHOR, PASTOR AND
DEAN OF THE BIBLE INSTITUTE
OF LOS ANGELES

4 And also for the innocent blood that he shed: for he filled Jerusalem with innocent blood; which the LORD would not pardon.

5 Now the rest of the acts of Jehoiakim, and all that he did, are they not written in the book of the chronicles of the kings of Judah?

6 So Jehoiakim slept with his fathers: and Jehoiachin his son reigned in his stead.

7 And the king of Egypt came not again any more out of his land: for the king of Babylon had taken from the river of Egypt to the river Euphrates all that pertained to the king of Egypt.

8 Jehoiachin was eighteen years old when he began to reign, and he reigned in Jerusalem three months. And his mother's name was Nehushta, the daughter of Elnathan of Jerusalem.

9 And he did that which was evil in the sight of the LORD, according to all that his father had done.

10 At that time the servants of Nebuchadnezzar king of Babylon came up against Jerusalem, and the city was besieged.

11 And Nebuchadnezzar king of Babylon came against the city, and his servants did besiege it.

12 And Jehoiachin the king of Judah went out to the king of Babylon, he, and his mother, and his servants, and his princes, and his officers: and the king of Babylon took him in the eighth year of his reign.

13 And he carried out thence all the treasures of the house of the LORD, and the treasures of the king's house, and cut in pieces all the vessels of gold which Solomon king of Israel had made in the temple of the LORD, as the LORD had said.

14 And he carried away all Jerusalem, and all the princes, and all the mighty men of valour, even ten thousand captives, and all the craftsmen and smiths: none remained, save the poorest sort of the people of the land.

15 And he carried away Jehoiachin to Babylon, and the king's mother, and the king's wives, and his officers, and the mighty of the land, those carried he into captivity from Jerusalem to Babylon.

16 And all the men of might, even seven thousand, and craftsmen and smiths a thousand, all that were strong and apt for war, even them the king of Babylon brought captive to Babylon.

17 And the king of Babylon made Mattaniah his father's brother king in his

SLAUGHTER OF THE SONS OF ZEDEKIAH BEFORE THEIR FATHER

2 Kings 25:7

stead, and changed his name to Zedekiah.

18 Zedekiah was twenty and one years old when he began to reign, and he reigned eleven years in Jerusalem. And his mother's name was Hamutal, the daughter of Jeremiah of Libnah.

19 And he did that which was evil in the sight of the LORD, according to all that Jehoiakim had done.

20 For through the anger of the LORD it came to pass in Jerusalem and Judah, until he had cast them out from his presence, that Zedekiah rebelled against the king of Babylon.

CHAPTER 25

AND it came to pass in the ninth year of his reign, in the tenth month, in the tenth day of the month, that Nebuchadnezzar king of Babylon came, he, and all his host, against Jerusalem, and pitched against it; and they built forts against it round about.

2 And the city was besieged to the eleventh year of king Zedekiah.

3 And on the ninth day of the fourth month the famine prevailed in the city, and there was no bread for the people of the land.

4 And the city was broken up, and all the men of war fled by night by the way of the gate between two walls, which is by the king's garden: (now the Chaldees

were against the city round about) and the king went the way toward the plain.

5 And the army of the Chaldees pursued after the king, and overtook him in the plains of Jericho: and all his army were scattered from him.

6 So they took the king, and brought him up to the king of Babylon to Riblah; and they gave judgment upon him.

7 And they slew the sons of Zedekiah before his eyes, and put out the eyes of Zedekiah, and bound him with fetters of brass, and carried him to Babylon.

8 And in the fifth month, on the seventh day of the month, which is the nineteenth year of king Nebuchadnezzar king of Babylon, came Nebuzaradan, captain of the guard, a servant of the king of Babylon, to Jerusalem:

9 And he burnt the house of the LORD, and the king's house, and all the houses of Jerusalem, and every great man's house burnt he with fire.

10 And all the army of the Chaldees, that were with the captain of the guard, brake down the walls of Jerusalem round about.

11 Now the rest of the people that were left in the city, and the fugitives that fell away to the king of Babylon, with the remnant of the multitude, did Nebuzaradan the captain of the guard carry away.

12 But the captain of the guard left of the door of the poor of the land to be vinedressers and husbandmen.

13 And the pillars of brass that were in the house of the LORD, and the bases, and the brasen sea that was in the house of the LORD, did the Chaldees break in pieces, and carried the brass of them to Babylon.

14 And the pots, and the shovels, and the snuffers, and the spoons, and all the vessels of brass wherewith they ministered, took they away.

15 And the firepans, and the bowls, and such things as were of gold, in gold, and of silver, in silver, the captain of the guard took away.

16 The two pillars, one sea, and the bases which Solomon had made for the house of the LORD; the brass of all these vessels was without weight.

17 The height of the one pillar was eighteen cubits, and the chapiter upon it was brass: and the height of the chapiter three cubits; and the wreathen work, and pomegranates upon the chapiter round about, all of brass: and like to these had the second pillar with wreathen work.

18 And the captain of the guard took Seraiah the chief priest, and Zephaniah the second priest, and the three keepers of the door:

19 And out of the city he took an officer that was set over the men of war, and five men of them that were in the king's presence, which were found in the city, and the principal scribe of the host, which mustered the people of the land, and threescore men of the people of the land that were found in the city:

20 And Nebuzaradan captain of the guard took these, and brought them to the king of Babylon to Riblah:

21 And the king of Babylon smote them, and slew them at Riblah in the land of Hamath. So Judah was carried away out of their land.

22 And as for the people that remained in the land of Judah, whom Nebuchadnezzar king of Babylon had left, even over them he made Gedaliah the son of Ahikam, the son of Shaphan, ruler.

23 And when all the captains of the armies, they and their men, heard that the king of Babylon had made Gedaliah governor, there came to Gedaliah to Mizpah, even Ishmael the son of Nethaniah, and Johanan the son of Careah, and Seraiah the son of Tanhumeth the Netophathite, and Jaazaniah the son of a Maachathite, they and their men.

24 And Gedaliah sware to them, and to their men, and said to them, Fear not to be the servants of the Chaldees: dwell in

the land, and serve the king of Babylon;
and it shall be well with you.

25 But it came to pass in the seventh
month, that Ishmael the son of
Nethaniah, the son of Elishama, of the
seed royal, came, and ten men with him,
and smote Gedaliah, that he died, and
the Jews and the Chaldees that were
with him at Mizpah.

26 And all the people, both small and
great, and the captains of the armies,
arose, and came to Egypt: for they were
afraid of the Chaldees.

27 And it came to pass in the seven and
thirtieth year of the captivity of
Jehoiachin king of Judah, in the twelfth
month, on the seven and twentieth day
of the month, that Evilmerodach king of
Babylon in the year that he began to
reign did lift up the head of Jehoiachin
king of Judah out of prison;

28 And he spoke kindly to him, and set
his throne above the throne of the kings
that were with him in Babylon;

29 And changed his prison garments:
and he did eat bread continually before
him all the days of his life.

30 And his allowance was a continual
allowance given him of the king, a daily
rate for every day, all the days of his life.

1 Chronicles

CHAPTER 1

ADAM, Sheth, Enosh, (2) Kenan, Mahalaleel, Jered,

3 Henoch, Methuselah, Lamech,

4 Noah, Shem, Ham, and Japheth.

5 The sons of Japheth; Gomer, and Magog, and Madai, and Javan, and Tubal, and Meshech, and Tiras.

6 And the sons of Gomer; Ashchenaz, and Riphath, and Togarmah.

7 And the sons of Javan; Elishah, and Tarshish, Kittim, and Dodanim.

8 The sons of Ham; Cush, and Mizraim, Put, and Canaan.

9 And the sons of Cush; Seba, and Havilah, and Sabta, and Raamah, and Sabtecha. And the sons of Raamah; Sheba, and Dedan.

10 And Cush begat Nimrod: he began to be mighty upon the earth.

11 And Mizraim begat Ludim, and Anamim, and Lehabim, and Naphtuhim,

12 And Pathrusim, and Casluhim, (of whom came the Philistines,) and Caphthorim.

13 And Canaan begat Zidon his first-born, and Heth,

14 The Jebusite also, and the Amorite, and the Girgashite,

15 And the Hivite, and the Arkite, and the Sinite,

16 And the Arvadite, and the Zemarite, and the Hamathite.

17 The sons of Shem; Elam, and Asshur, and Arphaxad, and Lud, and Aram, and Uz, and Hul, and Gether, and Meshech.

18 And Arphaxad begat Shelah, and Shelah begat Eber.

19 And to Eber were born two sons: the name of the one was Peleg; because in his days the earth was divided: and his brother's name was Joktan.

20 And Joktan begat Almodad, and Sheleph, and Hazarmaveth, and Jerah,

21 Hadoram also, and Uzal, and Diklah,

22 And Ebal, and Abimael, and Sheba,

23 And Ophir, and Havilah, and Jobab. All these were the sons of Joktan.

24 Shem, Arphaxad, Shelah,

25 Eber, Peleg, Reu,

26 Serug, Nahor, Terah,

27 Abram; the same is Abraham.

28 The sons of Abraham; Isaac, and Ishmael.

29 These are their generations: The firstborn of Ishmael, Nebaioth; then Kedar, and Adbeel, and Mibsam,

30 Mishma, and Dumah, Massa, Hadad, and Tema,

31 Jetur, Naphish, and Kedemah. These are the sons of Ishmael.

32 Now the sons of Keturah, Abraham's concubine: she bare Zimran, and Jokshan, and Medan, and Midian, and Ishbak, and Shuah. And the sons of Jokshan; Sheba, and Dedan.

33 And the sons of Midian; Ephah, and Epher, and Henoch, and Abida, and Eldaah. All these are the sons of Keturah.

34 And Abraham begat Isaac. The sons of Isaac; Esau and Israel.

35 The sons of Esau; Eliphaz, Reuel, and Jeush, and Jaalam, and Korah.

36 The sons of Eliphaz; Teman, and Omar, Zephi, and Gatam, Kenaz, and Timna, and Amalek.

37 The sons of Reuel; Nahath, Zerah, Shammah, and Mizzah.

38 And the sons of Seir; Lotan, and Shobal, and Zibeon, and Anah, and Dishon, and Ezar, and Dishan.

39 And the sons of Lotan; Hori, and Homam: and Timna was Lotan's sister.

40 The sons of Shobal; Alian, and Manahath, and Ebal, Shephi, and Onam. and the sons of Zibeon; Aiah, and Anah.

41 The sons of Anah; Dishon. And the sons of Dishon; Amram, and Eshban, and Ithran, and Cheran.

42 The sons of Ezer; Bilhan, and Zavan, and Jakan. The sons of Dishan; Uz, and Aran.

43 Now these are the kings that reigned in the land of Edom before any king reigned over the children of Israel; Bela the son of Beor: and the name of his city was Dinhabah.

44 And when Bela was dead, Jobab the son of Zerah of Bozrah reigned in his stead.

45 And when Jobab was dead, Husham of the land of the Temanites reigned in his stead.

46 And when Husham was dead, Hadad the son of Bedad, which smote Midian in the field of Moab, reigned in his stead: and the name of his city was Avith.

47 And when Hadad was dead, Samlah of Masrekah reigned in his stead.

48 And when Samlah was dead, Shaul of Rehoboth by the river reigned in his stead.

49 And when Shaul was dead, Baalhanan the son of Achbor reigned in his stead.

50 And when Baalhanan was dead, Hadad reigned in his stead: and the name of his city was Pai; and his wife's name was Mehetabel, the daughter of Matred, the daughter of Mezahab.

51 Hadad died also. And the dukes of Edom were; duke Timnah, duke Aliah, duke Jetheth,

52 Duke Aholibamah, duke Elah, duke Pinon,

53 Duke Kenaz, duke Teman, duke Mibzar,

54 Duke Magdiel, duke Iram. These are the dukes of Edom.

CHAPTER 2

THESE are the sons of Israel; Reuben, Simeon, Levi, and Judah, Issachar, and Zebulun,

2 Dan, Joseph, and Benjamin, Naphtali, Gad, and Asher.

3 The sons of Judah; Er, and Onan, and Shelah: which three were born to him of the daughter of Shua the Canaanitess. And Er, the firstborn of Judah, was evil in the sight of the LORD; and he slew him.

4 And Tamar his daughter in law bore him Pharez and Zerah. All the sons of Judah were five.

5 The sons of Pharez; Hezron, and Hamul.

6 And the sons of Zerah; Zimri, and Ethan, and Heman, and Calcol, and Dara: five of them in all.

7 And the sons of Carmi; Achar, the troubler of Israel, who transgressed in the thing accursed.

8 And the sons of Ethan; Azariah.

9 The sons also of Hezron, that were born to him; Jerahmeel, and Ram, and Chelubai.

10 And Ram begat Amminadab; and Amminadab begat Nahshon, prince of the children of Judah;

11 And Nahshon begat Salma, and Salma begat Boaz,

12 And Boaz begat Obed, and Obed begat Jesse,

13 And Jesse begat his firstborn Eliab, and Abinadab the second, and Shimma the third,

14 Nethaneel the fourth, Raddai the fifth,

15 Ozem the sixth, David the seventh:

16 Whose sisters were Zeruiah, and Abigail. And the sons of Zeruiah; Abishai, and Joab, and Asahel, three.

17 And Abigail bare Amasa: and the father of Amasa was Jether the Ishmeelite.

18 And Caleb the son of Hezron begat children of Azubah his wife, and of Jerioth: her sons are these; Jesher, and Shobab, and Ardon.

19 And when Azubah was dead, Caleb took to him Ephrath, which bare him Hur.

20 And Hur begat Uri, and Uri begat Bezaleel.

21 And afterward Hezron went in to the daughter of Machir the father of Gilead, whom he married when he was threescore years old; and she bare him Segub.

22 And Segub begat Jair, who had three and twenty cities in the land of Gilead.

23 And he took Geshur, and Aram, with the towns of Jair, from them, with Kenath, and the towns thereof, even threescore cities. All these belonged to the sons of Machir the father of Gilead.

24 And after that Hezron was dead in Calebephratah, then Abiah Hezron's wife bare him Ashur the father of Tekoa.

25 And the sons of Jerahmeel the firstborn of Hezron were, Ram the firstborn, and Bunah, and Oren, and Ozem, and Ahijah.

26 Jerahmeel had also another wife, whose name was Atarah; she was the mother of Onam.

27 And the sons of Ram the firstborn of Jerahmeel were, Maaz, and Jamin, and Eker.

28 And the sons of Onam were, Shammai, and Jada. And the sons of Shammai; Nadab and Abishur.

29 And the name of the wife of Abishur was Abihail, and she bare him Ahban, and Molid.

30 And the sons of Nadab; Seled, and Appaim: but Seled died without children.

31 And the sons of Appaim; Ishi. And the sons of Ishi; Sheshan. And the children of Sheshan; Ahlai.

32 And the sons of Jada the brother of Shammai; Jether, and Jonathan: and Jether died without children.

33 And the sons of Jonathan; Peleth, and Zaza. These were the sons of Jerahmeel.

34 Now Sheshan had no sons, but daughters. And Sheshan had a servant, an Egyptian, whose name was Jarha.

35 And Sheshan gave his daughter to Jarha his servant to wife; and she bare him Attai.

36 And Attai begat Nathan, and Nathan begat Zabad,

37 And Zabad begat Ephlal, and Ephlal begat Obed,

38 And Obed begat Jehu, and Jehu begat Azariah,

39 And Azariah begat Helez, and Helez begat Eleasah,

40 And Eleasah begat Sisamai, and Sisamai begat Shallum,

41 And Shallum begat Jekamiah, and Jekamiah begat Elishama.

42 Now the sons of Caleb the brother of Jerahmeel were, Mesha his firstborn, which was the father of Ziph; and the sons of Mareshah the father of Hebron.

43 And the sons of Hebron; Korah, and Tappuah, and Rekem, and Shema.

44 And Shema begat Raham, the father of Jorkoam: and Rekem begat Shammai.

45 And the son of Shammai was Maon: and Maon was the father of Bethzur.

46 And Ephah, Caleb's concubine, bare Haran, and Moza, and Gazez: and Haran begat Gazez.

47 And the sons of Jahdai; Regem, and Jotham, and Gesham, and Pelet, and Ephah, and Shaaph.

48 Maachah, Caleb's concubine, bare Sheber, and Tirhanah.

49 She bare also Shaaph the father of Madmannah, Sheva the father of

Machbenah, and the father of Gibea: and the daughter of Caleb was Achsa.

50 These were the sons of Caleb the son of Hur, the firstborn of Ephratah; Shobal the father of Kirjathjearim.

51 Salma the father of Bethlehem, Hareph the father of Bethgader.

52 And Shobal the father of Kirjathjearim had sons; Haroeh, and half of the Manahethites.

53 And the families of Kirjathjearim; the Ithrites, and the Puhites, and the Shumathites, and the Mishraites; of them came the Zareathites, and the Eshtaulites,

54 The sons of Salma; Bethlehem, and the Netophathites, Ataroth, the house of Joab, and half of the Manahethites, the Zorites.

55 And the families of the scribes which dwelt at Jabez; the Tirathites, the Shimeathites, and Suchathites. These are the Kenites that came of Hemath, the father of the house of Rechab.

CHAPTER 3

N OW these were the sons of David, which were born to him in Hebron; the firstborn Amnon, of Ahinoam the Jezreelitess; the second Daniel, of Abigail the Carmelitess:

2 The third, Absalom the son of Maachah the daughter of Talmai king of Geshur: the fourth, Adonijah the son of Haggith:

3 The fifth, Shephatiah of Abital: the sixth, Ithream by Eglah his wife.

4 These six were born to him in Hebron; and there he reigned seven years and six months: and in Jerusalem he reigned thirty and three years.

5 And these were born to him in Jerusalem; Shimea, and Shobab, and Nathan, and Solomon, four, of Bathshua the daughter of Ammiel:

6 Ibhar also, and Elishama, and Eliphelet,

7 And Nogah, and Nepheg, and Japhia,

8 And Elishama, and Eliada, and Eliphelet, nine.

9 These were all the sons of David, beside the sons of the concubines, and Tamar their sister.

10 And Solomon's son was Rehoboam, Abia his son, Asa his son, Jehoshaphat his son,

11 Joram his son, Ahaziah his son, Joash his son,

12 Amaziah his son, Azariah his son, Jotham his son,

13 Ahaz his son, Hezekiah his son, Manasseh his son,

14 Amon his son, Josiah his son.

15 And the sons of Josiah were, the firstborn Johanan, the second Jehoiakim, the third Zedekiah, the fourth Shallum.

16 And the sons of Jehoiakim: Jeconiah his son, Zedekiah his son.

17 And the sons of Jeconiah; Assir, Salathiel his son,

18 Malchiram also, and Pedaiah, and Shenazar, Jecamiah, Hoshama, and Nedabiah.

19 And the sons of Pedaiah were, Zerubbabel, and Shimei: and the sons of Zerubbabel; Meshullam, and Hananiah, and Shelomith their sister:

20 And Hashubah, and Ohel, and Berechiah, and Hasadiah, Jushabhesed, five.

21 And the sons of Hananiah; Pelatiah, and Jesaiah: the sons of Rephaiah, the sons of Arnan, the sons of Obadiah, the sons of Shechaniah.

22 And the sons of Shechaniah; Shemaiah: and the sons of Shemaiah; Hattush, and Igeal, and Bariah, and Neariah, and Shaphat, six.

23 And the sons of Neariah; Elioenai, and Hezekiah, and Azrikam, three.

24 And the sons of Elioenai were, Hodaiah, and Eliashib, and Pelaiah, and Akkub, and Johanan, and Dalaiah, and Anani, seven.

CHAPTER 4

T HE sons of Judah; Pharez, Hezron, and Carmi, and Hur, and Shobal.

2 And Reaiah the son of Shobal begat Jahath; and Jahath begat Ahumai, and

Lahad. These are the families of the Zorathites.

3 And these were of the father of Etam; Jezreel, and Ishma, and Idbash: and the name of their sister was Hazelelponi:

4 And Penuel the father of Gedor, and Ezer the father of Hushah. These are the sons of Hur, the firstborn of Ephratah, the father of Bethlehem.

5 And Ashur the father of Tekoa had two wives, Helah and Naarah.

6 And Naarah bare him Ahuzam, and Hepher, and Temeni, and Haahashtari. These were the sons of Naarah.

7 And the sons of Helah were, Zereth, and Jezoar, and Ethnan.

8 And Coz begat Anub, and Zobebah, and the families of Aharhel the son of Harum.

9 And Jabez was more honourable than his brethren: and his mother called his name Jabez, saying, Because I bare him with sorrow.

10 And Jabez called on the God of Israel, saying, Oh that you would bless me indeed, and enlarge my coast, and that your hand might be with me, and that you would keep me from evil, that it may not grieve me! And God granted him that which he requested.

11 And Chelub the brother of Shuah begat Mehir, which was the father of Eshton.

12 And Eshton begat Bethrapha, and Paseah, and Tehinnah the father of Irnahash. These are the men of Rechah.

13 And the sons of Kenaz; Othniel, and Seraiah: and the sons of Othniel; Hathath.

14 And Meonothai begat Ophrah: and Seraiah begat Joab, the father of the valley of Charashim; for they were craftsmen.

15 And the sons of Caleb the son of Jephunneh; Iru, Elah, and Naam: and the sons of Elah, even Kenaz.

16 And the sons of Jehaleleel; Ziph, and Ziphah, Tiria, and Asareel.

17 And the sons of Ezra were, Jether, and Mered, and Epher, and Jalon: and she bare Miriam, and Shammai, and Ishbah the father of Eshtemoa.

18 And his wife Jehudijah bare Jered the father of Gedor, and Heber the father of Socho, and Jekuthiel the father of Zanoah. And these are the sons of Bithiah the daughter of Pharaoh, which Mered took.

19 And the sons of his wife Hodiah the sister of Naham, the father of Keilah the Garmite, and Eshtemoa the Maachathite.

20 And the sons of Shimon were, Amnon, and Rinnah, Benhanan, and Tilon. And the sons of Ishi were, Zoheth, and Benzoheth.

21 The sons of Shelah the son of Judah were, Er the father of Lecah, and Laadah the father of Mareshah, and the families of the house of them that worked fine linen, of the house of Ashbea,

22 And Jokim, and the men of Chozeba, and Joash, and Saraph, who had the dominion in Moab, and Jashubilehem. And these are ancient things.

23 These were the potters, and those that dwelt among plants and hedges: there they dwelt with the king for his work.

24 The sons of Simeon were, Nemuel, and Jamin, Jarib, Zerah, and Shaul:

25 Shallum his son, Mibsam his son, Mishma his son.

26 And the sons of Mishma; Hamuel his son, Zacchur his son, Shimei his son.

27 And Shimei had sixteen sons and six daughters: but his brethren had not many children, neither did all their family multiply, like to the children of Judah.

28 And they dwelt at Beersheba, and Moladah, and Hazarshual,

29 And at Bilhah, and at Ezem, and at Tolad,

30 And at Bethuel, and at Hormah, and at Ziklag,

31 And at Bethmarcaboth, and Hazarsusim, and at Bethbirei, and at Shaaraim. These were their cities to the reign of David.

32 And their villages were, Etam, and Ain, Rimmon, and Tochen, and Ashan, five cities:

33 And all their villages that were round about the same cities, to Baal. These were their habitations, and their genealogy.

34 And Meshobab, and Jamlech, and Joshah, the son of Amaziah,

35 And Joel, and Jehu the son of Josibiah, the son of Seraiah, the son of Asiel,

36 And Elioenai, and Jaakobah, and Jeshohaiah, and Asaiah, and Adiel, and Jesimiel, and Benaiah,

37 And Ziza the son of Shiphi, the son of Allon, the son of Jedaiah, the son of Shimri, the son of Shemaiah;

38 These mentioned by their names were princes in their families: and the house of their fathers increased greatly.

39 And they went to the entrance of Gedor, even to the east side of the valley, to seek pasture for their flocks.

40 And they found fat pasture and good, and the land was wide, and quiet, and peaceable; for they of Ham had dwelt there of old.

41 And these written by name came in the days of Hezekiah king of Judah, and smote their tents, and the habitations that were found there, and destroyed them utterly to this day, and dwelt in their rooms: because there was pasture there for their flocks.

42 And some of them, even of the sons of Simeon, five hundred men, went to mount Seir, having for their captains Pelatiah, and Neariah, and Rephaiah, and Uzziel, the sons of Ishi.

43 And they smote the rest of the Amalekites that were escaped, and dwelt there to this day.

CHAPTER 5

NOW the sons of Reuben the first-born of Israel, (for he was the firstborn; but forasmuch as he defiled his father's bed, his birthright was given to the sons of Joseph the son of Israel: and the genealogy is not to be reckoned after the birthright.

2 For Judah prevailed above his brethren, and of him came the chief ruler; but the birthright was Joseph's:)

3 The sons, I say, of Reuben the first-born of Israel were, Hanoch, and Pallu, Hezron, and Carmi.

4 The sons of Joel; Shemaiah his son, Gog his son, Shimei his son,

5 Micah his son, Reaia his son, Baal his son,

6 Beerah his son, whom Tilgathpilneser king of Assyria carried away captive: he was prince of the Reubenites.

7 And his brethren by their families, when the genealogy of their generations was reckoned, were the chief, Jeiel, and Zechariah,

8 And Bela the son of Azaz, the son of Shema, the son of Joel, who dwelt in Aroer, even to Nebo and Baalmeon:

9 And eastward he inhabited to the entering in of the wilderness from the river Euphrates: because their cattle were multiplied in the land of Gilead.

10 And in the days of Saul they made war with the Hagarites, who fell by their hand: and they dwelt in their tents throughout all the east land of Gilead.

11 And the children of Gad dwelt over against them, in the land of Bashan to Salcah:

12 Joel the chief, and Shapham the next, and Jaanai, and Shaphat in Bashan.

13 And their brethren of the house of their fathers were, Michael, and Meshullam, and Sheba, and Jorai, and Jachan, and Zia, and Heber, seven.

14 These are the children of Abihail the son of Huri, the son of Jaroah, the son of Gilead, the son of Michael, the son of Jeshishai, the son of Jahdo, the son of Buz;

15 Ahi the son of Abdiel, the son of Guni, chief of the house of their fathers.

16 And they dwelt in Gilead in Bashan, and in her towns, and in all the suburbs of Sharon, upon their borders.

17 All these were reckoned by genealogies in the days of Jotham king of Judah, and in the days of Jeroboam king of Israel.

18 The sons of Reuben, and the Gadites, and half the tribe of Manasseh, of valiant men, men able to bear buckler and sword, and to shoot with bow, and skilful in war, were four and forty thousand seven hundred and threescore, that went out to the war.

19 And they made war with the Hagarites, with Jetur, and Nephish, and Nodab.

20 And they were helped against them, and the Hagarites were delivered into their hand, and all that were with them: for they cried to God in the battle, and he was intreated of them; because they put their trust in him.

21 And they took away their cattle; of their camels fifty thousand, and of sheep two hundred and fifty thousand, and of asses two thousand, and of men an hundred thousand.

22 For there fell down many slain, because the war was of God. And they dwelt in their steads until the captivity.

23 And the children of the half tribe of Manasseh dwelt in the land: they increased from Bashan to Baalhermon and Senir, and to mount Hermon.

24 And these were the heads of the house of their fathers, even Epher, and Ishi, and Eliel, and Azriel, and Jeremiah, and Hodaviah, and Jahdiel, mighty men of valour, famous men, and heads of the house of their fathers.

25 And they transgressed against the God of their fathers, and went a whoring after the gods of the people of the land, whom God destroyed before them.

26 And the God of Israel stirred up the spirit of Pul king of Assyria, and the spirit of Tilgathpilneser king of Assyria, and he carried them away, even the Reubenites, and the Gadites, and the half tribe of Manasseh, and brought them to Halah, and Habor, and Hara, and to the river Gozan, to this day.

CHAPTER 6

THE sons of Levi; Gershon, Kohath, and Merari.

2 And the sons of Kohath; Amram, Izhar, and Hebron, and Uzziel.

3 And the children of Amram; Aaron, and Moses, and Miriam. The sons also of Aaron; Nadab, and Abihu, Eleazar, and Ithamar.

4 Eleazar begat Phinehas, Phinehas begat Abishua,

5 And Abishua begat Bukki, and Bukki begat Uzzi,

6 And Uzzi begat Zerahiah, and Zerahiah begat Meraioth,

7 Meraioth begat Amariah, and Amariah begat Ahitub,

8 And Ahitub begat Zadok, and Zadok begat Ahimaaz,

9 And Ahimaaz begat Azariah, and Azariah begat Johanan,

10 And Johanan begat Azariah, (he it is that executed the priest's office in the temple that Solomon built in Jerusalem:)

11 And Azariah begat Amariah, and Amariah begat Ahitub,

12 And Ahitub begat Zadok, and Zadok begat Shallum,

13 And Shallum begat Hilkiah, and Hilkiah begat Azariah,

14 And Azariah begat Seraiah, and Seraiah begat Jehozadak,

15 And Jehozadak went into captivity, when the LORD carried away Judah and Jerusalem by the hand of Nebuchadnezzar.

5:18-20 A "valiant" soldier of Christ is one who is able to bear the shield of faith and carry the sword of the Word of God. He is also able to "shoot with bow." The bow of God's Law gives the arrow of the Gospel its power. This is what makes him "skillful in war." His power exists because he doesn't trust in himself; he cries out to God in battle. His strength is in the Lord. For witnessing to those who don't speak English, see the back of this publication for the entire gospel in picture form.

16 The sons of Levi; Gershom, Kohath, and Merari.

17 And these be the names of the sons of Gershom; Libni, and Shimei.

18 And the sons of Kohath were, Amram, and Izhar, and Hebron, and Uzziel.

19 The sons of Merari; Mahli, and Mushi. And these are the families of the Levites according to their fathers.

20 Of Gershom; Libni his son, Jahath his son, Zimmah his son,

21 Joah his son, Iddo his son, Zerah his son, Jeaterai his son.

22 The sons of Kohath; Amminadab his son, Korah his son, Assir his son,

23 Elkanah his son, and Ebiasaph his son, and Assir his son,

24 Tahath his son, Uriel his son, Uzziah his son, and Shaul his son.

25 And the sons of Elkanah; Amasai, and Ahimoth.

26 As for Elkanah: the sons of Elkanah; Zophai his son, and Nahath his son,

27 Eliab his son, Jeroham his son, Elkanah his son.

28 And the sons of Samuel; the first-born Vashni, and Abiah.

29 The sons of Merari; Mahli, Libni his son, Shimei his son, Uzza his son,

30 Shimea his son, Haggiah his son, Asaiah his son.

31 And these are they whom David set over the service of song in the house of the LORD, after that the ark had rest.

32 And they ministered before the dwelling place of the tabernacle of the congregation with singing, until Solomon had built the house of the LORD in Jerusalem: and then they waited on their office according to their order.

33 And these are they that waited with their children. Of the sons of the Kohathites: Heman a singer, the son of Joel, the son of Shemuel,

34 The son of Elkanah, the son of Jeroham, the son of Eliel, the son of Toah,

35 The son of Zuph, the son of Elkanah, the son of Mahath, the son of Amasai,

36 The son of Elkanah, the son of Joel, the son of Azariah, the son of Zephaniah,

37 The son of Tahath, the son of Assir, the son of Ebiasaph, the son of Korah,

38 The son of Izhar, the son of Kohath, the son of Levi, the son of Israel.

39 And his brother Asaph, who stood on his right hand, even Asaph the son of Berachiah, the son of Shimea,

40 The son of Michael, the son of Baaseiah, the son of Malchiah,

41 The son of Ethni, the son of Zerah, the son of Adaiah,

42 The son of Ethan, the son of Zimmah, the son of Shimei,

43 The son of Jahath, the son of Gershom, the son of Levi.

44 And their brethren the sons of Merari stood on the left hand: Ethan the son of Kishi, the son of Abdi, the son of Malluch,

45 The son of Hashabiah, the son of Amaziah, the son of Hilkiah,

46 The son of Amzi, the son of Bani, the son of Shamer,

47 The son of Mahli, the son of Mushi, the son of Merari, the son of Levi.

48 Their brethren also the Levites were appointed to all manner of service of the tabernacle of the house of God.

49 But Aaron and his sons offered upon the altar of the burnt offering, and on the altar of incense, and were appointed for all the work of the place most holy, and to make an atonement for Israel, according to all that Moses the servant of God had commanded.

50 And these are the sons of Aaron; Eleazar his son, Phinehas his son, Abishua his son,

51 Bukki his son, Uzzi his son, Zerahiah his son,

52 Meraioth his son, Amariah his son, Ahitub his son,

53 Zadok his son, Ahimaaz his son.

54 Now these are their dwelling places throughout their castles in their coasts,

of the sons of Aaron, of the families of the Kohathites: for theirs was the lot.

55 And they gave them Hebron in the land of Judah, and the suburbs thereof round about it.

56 But the fields of the city, and the villages thereof, they gave to Caleb the son of Jephunneh.

57 And to the sons of Aaron they gave the cities of Judah, namely, Hebron, the city of refuge, and Libnah with her suburbs, and Jattir, and Eshtemoa, with their suburbs,

58 And Hilen with her suburbs, Debir with her suburbs,

59 And Ashan with her suburbs, and Bethshemesh with her suburbs:

60 And out of the tribe of Benjamin; Geba with her suburbs, and Alemeth with her suburbs, and Anathoth with her suburbs. All their cities throughout their families were thirteen cities.

61 And to the sons of Kohath, which were left of the family of that tribe, were cities given out of the half tribe, namely, out of the half tribe of Manasseh, by lot, ten cities.

62 And to the sons of Gershom throughout their families out of the tribe of Issachar, and out of the tribe of Asher, and out of the tribe of Naphtali, and out of the tribe of Manasseh in Bashan, thirteen cities.

63 To the sons of Merari were given by lot, throughout their families, out of the tribe of Reuben, and out of the tribe of Gad, and out of the tribe of Zebulun, twelve cities.

64 And the children of Israel gave to the Levites these cities with their suburbs.

65 And they gave by lot out of the tribe of the children of Judah, and out of the tribe of the children of Simeon, and out of the tribe of the children of Benjamin, these cities, which are called by their names.

66 And the residue of the families of the sons of Kohath had cities of their coasts out of the tribe of Ephraim.

67 And they gave to them, of the cities of refuge, Shechem in mount Ephraim with her suburbs; they gave also Gezer with her suburbs,

68 And Jokmeam with her suburbs, and Bethhoron with her suburbs,

69 And Aijalon with her suburbs, and Gathrimmon with her suburbs:

70 And out of the half tribe of Manasseh; Aner with her suburbs, and Bileam with her suburbs, for the family of the remnant of the sons of Kohath.

71 To the sons of Gershom were given out of the family of the half tribe of Manasseh, Golan in Bashan with her suburbs, and Ashtaroth with her suburbs:

72 And out of the tribe of Issachar; Kedesh with her suburbs, Daberath with her suburbs,

73 And Ramoth with her suburbs, and Anem with her suburbs:

74 And out of the tribe of Asher; Mashal with her suburbs, and Abdon with her suburbs,

75 And Hukok with her suburbs, and Rehob with her suburbs:

76 And out of the tribe of Naphtali; Kedesh in Galilee with her suburbs, and Hammon with her suburbs, and Kirjathaim with her suburbs.

77 To the rest of the children of Merari were given out of the tribe of Zebulun, Rimmon with her suburbs, Tabor with her suburbs:

78 And on the other side Jordan by Jericho, on the east side of Jordan, were given them out of the tribe of Reuben, Bezer in the wilderness with her suburbs, and Jahzah with her suburbs,

79 Kedemoth also with her suburbs, and Mephaath with her suburbs:

80 And out of the tribe of Gad; Ramoth in Gilead with her suburbs, and Mahanaim with her suburbs,

81 And Heshbon with her suburbs, and Jazer with her suburbs.

CHAPTER 7

NOW the sons of Issachar were, Tola, and Puah, Jashub, and Shimrom, four.

2 And the sons of Tola; Uzzi, and Rephaiah, and Jeriel, and Jahmai, and Jibsam, and Shemuel, heads of their father's house, to wit, of Tola: they were valiant men of might in their generations; whose number was in the days of David two and twenty thousand and six hundred.

3 And the sons of Uzzi; Izrahiah: and the sons of Izrahiah; Michael, and Obadiah, and Joel, Ishiah, five: all of them chief men.

4 And with them, by their generations, after the house of their fathers, were bands of soldiers for war, six and thirty thousand men: for they had many wives and sons.

5 And their brethren among all the families of Issachar were valiant men of might, reckoned in all by their genealogies fourscore and seven thousand.

6 The sons of Benjamin; Bela, and Becher, and Jediael, three.

7 And the sons of Bela; Ezbon, and Uzzi, and Uzziel, and Jerimoth, and Iri, five; heads of the house of their fathers, mighty men of valour; and were reckoned by their genealogies twenty and two thousand and thirty and four.

8 And the sons of Becher; Zemira, and Joash, and Eliezer, and Elioenai, and Omri, and Jerimoth, and Abiah, and Anathoth, and Alameth. All these are the sons of Becher.

9 And the number of them, after their genealogy by their generations, heads of the house of their fathers, mighty men of valour, was twenty thousand and two hundred.

10 The sons also of Jediael; Bilhan: and the sons of Bilhan; Jeush, and Benjamin, and Ehud, and Chenaanah, and Zethan, and Tharshish, and Ahishahar.

11 All these the sons of Jediael, by the heads of their fathers, mighty men of valour, were seventeen thousand and two hundred soldiers, fit to go out for war and battle.

12 Shuppim also, and Huppim, the children of Ir, and Hushim, the sons of Aher.

13 The sons of Naphtali; Jahziel, and Guni, and Jezer, and Shallum, the sons of Bilhah.

14 The sons of Manasseh; Ashriel, whom she bare: (but his concubine the Aramitess bare Machir the father of Gilead:

15 And Machir took to wife the sister of Huppim and Shuppim, whose sister's name was Maachah;) and the name of the second was Zelophehad: and Zelophehad had daughters.

16 And Maachah the wife of Machir bare a son, and she called his name Peresh; and the name of his brother was Sheresh; and his sons were Ulam and Rakem.

17 And the sons of Ulam; Bedan. These were the sons of Gilead, the son of Machir, the son of Manasseh.

18 And his sister Hammoleketh bare Ishod, and Abiezer, and Mahalah.

19 And the sons of Shemidah were, Ahian, and Shechem, and Likhi, and Aniam.

20 And the sons of Ephraim; Shuthelah, and Bered his son, and Tahath his son, and Eladah his son, and Tahath his son,

21 And Zabad his son, and Shuthelah his son, and Ezer, and Elead, whom the men of Gath that were born in that land slew, because they came down to take away their cattle.

22 And Ephraim their father mourned many days, and his brethren came to comfort him.

23 And when he went in to his wife, she conceived, and bare a son, and he called his name Beriah, because it went evil with his house.

24 (And his daughter was Sherah, who built Bethhoron the nether, and the upper, and Uzzensherah.)

25 And Rephah was his son, also Resheph, and Telah his son, and Tahan his son.

26 Laadan his son, Ammihud his son, Elishama his son.

27 Non his son, Jehoshuah his son.

28 And their possessions and habitations were, Bethel and the towns thereof, and eastward Naaran, and westward Gezer, with the towns thereof; Shechem also and the towns thereof, to Gaza and the towns thereof:

29 And by the borders of the children of Manasseh, Bethshean and her towns, Taanach and her towns, Megiddo and her towns, Dor and her towns. In these dwelt the children of Joseph the son of Israel.

30 The sons of Asher; Imnah, and Isuah, and Ishuai, and Beriah, and Serah their sister.

31 And the sons of Beriah; Heber, and Malchiel, who is the father of Birzavith.

32 And Heber begat Japhlet, and Shomer, and Hotham, and Shua their sister.

33 And the sons of Japhlet; Pasach, and Bimhal, and Ashvath. These are the children of Japhlet.

34 And the sons of Shamer; Ahi, and Rohgah, Jehubbah, and Aram.

35 And the sons of his brother Helem; Zophah, and Imna, and Shelesh, and Amal.

36 The sons of Zophah; Suah, and Harnepher, and Shual, and Beri, and Imrah,

37 Bezer, and Hod, and Shamma, and Shilshah, and Ithran, and Beera.

38 And the sons of Jether; Jephunneh, and Pispah, and Ara.

39 And the sons of Ulla; Arah, and Haniel, and Rezia.

40 All these were the children of Asher, heads of their father's house, choice and mighty men of valour, chief of the princes. And the number throughout the genealogy of them that were apt to the war and to battle was twenty and six thousand men.

CHAPTER 8

NOW Benjamin begat Bela his first-born, Ashbel the second, and Aharah the third,

2 Nohah the fourth, and Rapha the fifth.

3 And the sons of Bela were, Addar, and Gera, and Abihud,

4 And Abishua, and Naaman, and Ahoah,

5 And Gera, and Shephuphan, and Huram.

6 And these are the sons of Ehud: these are the heads of the fathers of the inhabitants of Geba, and they removed them to Manahath:

7 And Naaman, and Ahiah, and Gera, he removed them, and begat Uzza, and Ahihud.

8 And Shaharaim begat children in the country of Moab, after he had sent them away; Hushim and Baara were his wives.

9 And he begat of Hodesh his wife, Jobab, and Zibia, and Mesha, and Malcham,

10 And Jeuz, and Shachia, and Mirma. These were his sons, heads of the fathers.

11 And of Hushim he begat Abitub, and Elpaal.

12 The sons of Elpaal; Eber, and Misham, and Shamed, who built Ono, and Lod, with the towns thereof:

13 Beriah also, and Shema, who were heads of the fathers of the inhabitants of Aijalon, who drove away the inhabitants of Gath:

14 And Ahio, Shashak, and Jeremoth,

15 And Zebadiah, and Arad, and Ader,

16 And Michael, and Ispah, and Joha, the sons of Beriah;

17 And Zebadiah, and Meshullam, and Hezeki, and Heber,

18 Ishmerai also, and Jezliah, and Jobab, the sons of Elpaal;

19 And Jakim, and Zichri, and Zabdi,

20 And Elienai, and Zilthai, and Eliel,

21 And Adaiah, and Beraiah, and Shimrath, the sons of Shimhi;

22 And Ishpan, and Heber, and Eliel,
23 And Abdon, and Zichri, and Hanan,
24 And Hananiah, and Elam, and Antothijah,
25 And Iphedeiah, and Penuel, the sons of Shashak;
26 And Shamsherai, and Shehariah, and Athaliah,
27 And Jaresiah, and Eliah, and Zichri, the sons of Jeroham.
28 These were heads of the fathers, by their generations, chief men. These dwelt in Jerusalem.
29 And at Gibeon dwelt the father of Gibeon; whose wife's name was Maachah:
30 And his firstborn son Abdon, and Zur, and Kish, and Baal, and Nadab,
31 And Gedor, and Ahio, and Zacher.
32 And Mikloth begat Shimeah. And these also dwelt with their brethren in Jerusalem, over against them.
33 And Ner begat Kish, and Kish begat Saul, and Saul begat Jonathan, and Malchishua, and Abinadab, and Eshbaal.
34 And the son of Jonathan was Meribbaal; and Meribbaal begat Micah.
35 And the sons of Micah were, Pithon, and Melech, and Tarea, and Ahaz.
36 And Ahaz begat Jehoadah; and Jehoadah begat Alemeth, and Azmaveth, and Zimri; and Zimri begat Moza,
37 And Moza begat Binea: Rapha was his son, Eleasah his son, Azel his son:
38 And Azel had six sons, whose names are these, Azrikam, Bocheru, and Ishmael, and Sheariah, and Obadiah, and Hanan. All these were the sons of Azel.
39 And the sons of Eshek his brother were, Ulam his firstborn, Jehush the second, and Eliphelet the third.
40 And the sons of Ulam were mighty men of valour, archers, and had many sons, and sons' sons, an hundred and fifty. All these are of the sons of Benjamin.

CHAPTER 9

SO all Israel were reckoned by genealogies; and, behold, they were written in the book of the kings of Israel and Judah, who were carried away to Babylon for their transgression.
2 Now the first inhabitants that dwelt in their possessions in their cities were, the Israelites, the priests, Levites, and the Nethinims.
3 And in Jerusalem dwelt of the children of Judah, and of the children of Benjamin, and of the children of Ephraim, and Manasseh;
4 Uthai the son of Ammihud, the son of Omri, the son of Imri, the son of Bani, of the children of Pharez the son of Judah.
5 And of the Shilonites; Asaiah the firstborn, and his sons.
6 And of the sons of Zerah; Jeuel, and their brethren, six hundred and ninety.
7 And of the sons of Benjamin; Sallu the son of Meshullam, the son of Hodaviah, the son of Hasenuah,
8 And Ibneiah the son of Jeroham, and Elah the son of Uzzi, the son of Michri, and Meshullam the son of Shephathiah, the son of Reuel, the son of Ibnijah;
9 And their brethren, according to their generations, nine hundred and fifty and six. All these men were chief of the fathers in the house of their fathers.
10 And of the priests; Jedaiah, and Jehoiarib, and Jachin,
11 And Azariah the son of Hilkiah, the son of Meshullam, the son of Zadok, the son of Meraioth, the son of Ahitub, the ruler of the house of God;
12 And Adaiah the son of Jeroham, the son of Pashur, the son of Malchijah, and Maasiai the son of Adiel, the son of Jahzerah, the son of Meshullam, the son of Meshillemith, the son of Immer;
13 And their brethren, heads of the house of their fathers, a thousand and seven hundred and threescore; very able men for the work of the service of the house of God.

14 And of the Levites; Shemaiah the son of Hasshub, the son of Azrikam, the son of Hashabiah, of the sons of Merari;

15 And Bakbakkar, Heresh, and Galal, and Mattaniah the son of Micah, the son of Zichri, the son of Asaph;

16 And Obadiah the son of Shemaiah, the son of Galal, the son of Jeduthun, and Berechiah the son of Asa, the son of Elkanah, that dwelt in the villages of the Netophathites.

17 And the porters were, Shallum, and Akkub, and Talmon, and Ahiman, and their brethren: Shallum was the chief;

18 Who hitherto waited in the king's gate eastward: they were porters in the companies of the children of Levi.

19 And Shallum the son of Kore, the son of Ebiasaph, the son of Korah, and his brethren, of the house of his father, the Korahites, were over the work of the service, keepers of the gates of the tabernacle: and their fathers, being over the host of the LORD, were keepers of the entry.

20 And Phinehas the son of Eleazar was the ruler over them in time past, and the LORD was with him.

21 And Zechariah the son of Meshelemiah was porter of the door of the tabernacle of the congregation.

22 All these which were chosen to be porters in the gates were two hundred and twelve. These were reckoned by their genealogy in their villages, whom David and Samuel the seer did ordain in their set office.

23 So they and their children had the oversight of the gates of the house of the LORD, namely, the house of the tabernacle, by wards.

24 In four quarters were the porters, toward the east, west, north, and south.

25 And their brethren, which were in their villages, were to come after seven days from time to time with them.

26 For these Levites, the four chief porters, were in their set office, and were over the chambers and treasuries of the house of God.

27 And they lodged round about the house of God, because the charge was upon them, and the opening thereof every morning pertained to them.

28 And certain of them had the charge of the ministering vessels, that they should bring them in and out by tale.

29 Some of them also were appointed to oversee the vessels, and all the instruments of the sanctuary, and the fine flour, and the wine, and the oil, and the frankincense, and the spices.

30 And some of the sons of the priests made the ointment of the spices.

31 And Mattithiah, one of the Levites, who was the firstborn of Shallum the Korahite, had the set office over the things that were made in the pans.

32 And other of their brethren, of the sons of the Kohathites, were over the shewbread, to prepare it every sabbath.

33 And these are the singers, chief of the fathers of the Levites, who remaining in the chambers were free: for they were employed in that work day and night.

34 These chief fathers of the Levites were chief throughout their generations; these dwelt at Jerusalem.

35 And in Gibeon dwelt the father of Gibeon, Jehiel, whose wife's name was Maachah:

36 And his firstborn son Abdon, then Zur, and Kish, and Baal, and Ner, and Nadab.

37 And Gedor, and Ahio, and Zechariah, and Mikloth.

38 And Mikloth begat Shimeam. And they also dwelt with their brethren at Jerusalem, over against their brethren.

39 And Ner begat Kish; and Kish begat Saul; and Saul begat Jonathan, and Malchishua, and Abinadab, and Eshbaal.

40 And the son of Jonathan was Meribbaal: and Meribbaal begat Micah.

41 And the sons of Micah were, Pithon, and Melech, and Tahrea, and Ahaz.

42 And Ahaz begat Jarah; and Jarah begat Alemeth, and Azmaveth, and Zimri; and Zimri begat Moza;

QUESTIONS & OBJECTIONS

10:13-14 *Is it wrong to "speak to the dead"?*

Those who do so are dabbling with the demonic realm, something the Bible refers to as a "familiar spirit." *Unger's Bible Dictionary* tells us "[A] familiar spirit is a divining demon present in the physical body of the conjurer. . . . The term "familiar" is used to describe the foreboding demon because it was regarded by the English translators as a secret (famulus), belonging to the family (familiaris), who was on intimate terms with and might be readily summoned by the one possessing it." Those who seek the supernatural should seek God through prayer and through His Word. God killed King Saul because he sought guidance through a familiar spirit, rather than through the Lord.

43 And Moza begat Binea; and Rephaiah his son, Eleasah his son, Azel his son.

44 And Azel had six sons, whose names are these, Azrikam, Bocheru, and Ishmael, and Sheariah, and Obadiah, and Hanan: these were the sons of Azel.

CHAPTER 10

NOW the Philistines fought against Israel; and the men of Israel fled from before the Philistines, and fell down slain in mount Gilboa.

2 And the Philistines followed hard after Saul, and after his sons; and the Philistines slew Jonathan, and Abinadab, and Malchishua, the sons of Saul.

3 And the battle went sore against Saul, and the archers hit him, and he was wounded of the archers.

4 Then said Saul to his armourbearer, Draw your sword, and thrust me through therewith; lest these uncircumcised come and abuse me. But his armourbearer would not; for he was sore afraid. So Saul took a sword, and fell upon it.

5 And when his armourbearer saw that Saul was dead, he fell likewise on the sword, and died.

6 So Saul died, and his three sons, and all his house died together.

7 And when all the men of Israel that were in the valley saw that they fled, and that Saul and his sons were dead, then they forsook their cities, and fled: and the Philistines came and dwelt in them.

8 And it came to pass on the morrow, when the Philistines came to strip the slain, that they found Saul and his sons fallen in mount Gilboa.

9 And when they had stripped him, they took his head, and his armour, and sent into the land of the Philistines round about, to carry tidings to their idols, and to the people.

10 And they put his armour in the house of their gods, and fastened his head in the temple of Dagon.

11 And when all Jabeshgilead heard all that the Philistines had done to Saul,

12 They arose, all the valiant men, and took away the body of Saul, and the bodies of his sons, and brought them to Jabesh, and buried their bones under the oak in Jabesh, and fasted seven days.

13 So Saul died for his transgression which he committed against the LORD, even against the word of the LORD, which he kept not, and also for asking counsel of one that had a familiar spirit, to inquire of it;

14 And inquired not of the LORD: therefore he slew him, and turned the kingdom to David the son of Jesse.

CHAPTER 11

THEN all Israel gathered themselves to David to Hebron, saying, Behold, we are your bone and your flesh.

2 And moreover in time past, even when Saul was king, you was he that led out and brought in Israel: and the LORD your God said to you, You shall feed my

people Israel, and you shall be ruler over my people Israel.

3 Therefore came all the elders of Israel to the king to Hebron; and David made a covenant with them in Hebron before the LORD; and they anointed David king over Israel, according to the word of the LORD by Samuel.

4 And David and all Israel went to Jerusalem, which is Jebus; where the Jebusites were, the inhabitants of the land.

5 And the inhabitants of Jebus said to David, You shall not come here. Nevertheless David took the castle of Zion, which is the city of David.

6 And David said, Whosoever smiteth the Jebusites first shall be chief and captain. So Joab the son of Zeruiah went first up, and was chief.

7 And David dwelt in the castle; therefore they called it the city of David.

8 And he built the city round about, even from Millo round about: and Joab repaired the rest of the city.

9 So David waxed greater and greater: for the LORD of hosts was with him.

10 These also are the chief of the mighty men whom David had, who strengthened themselves with him in his kingdom, and with all Israel, to make him king, according to the word of the LORD concerning Israel.

11 And this is the number of the mighty men whom David had; Jashobeam, an Hachmonite, the chief of the captains: he lifted up his spear against three hundred slain by him at one time.

12 And after him was Eleazar the son of Dodo, the Ahohite, who was one of the three mighties.

13 He was with David at Pasdammim, and there the Philistines were gathered together to battle, where was a parcel of ground full of barley; and the people fled from before the Philistines.

14 And they set themselves in the midst of that parcel, and delivered it, and slew the Philistines; and the LORD saved them by a great deliverance.

15 Now three of the thirty captains went down to the rock to David, into the cave of Adullam; and the host of the Philistines encamped in the valley of Rephaim.

16 And David was then in the hold, and the Philistines' garrison was then at Bethlehem.

17 And David longed, and said, Oh that one would give me drink of the water of the well of Bethlehem, that is at the gate!

18 And the three brake through the host of the Philistines, and drew water out of the well of Bethlehem, that was by the gate, and took it, and brought it to David: but David would not drink of it, but poured it out to the LORD.

19 And said, My God forbid it me, that I should do this thing: shall I drink the blood of these men that have put their lives in jeopardy? for with the jeopardy of their lives they brought it. Therefore he would not drink it. These things did these three mightiest.

20 And Abishai the brother of Joab, he was chief of the three: for lifting up his spear against three hundred, he slew them, and had a name among the three.

21 Of the three, he was more honourable than the two; for he was their captain: howbeit he attained not to the first three.

22 Benaiah the son of Jehoiada, the son of a valiant man of Kabzeel, who had done many acts; he slew two lionlike men of Moab: also he went down and slew a lion in a pit in a snowy day.

23 And he slew an Egyptian, a man of great stature, five cubits high; and in the Egyptian's hand was a spear like a weaver's beam; and he went down to him with a staff, and plucked the spear out of the Egyptian's hand, and slew him with his own spear.

24 These things did Benaiah the son of Jehoiada, and had the name among the three mighties.

25 Behold, he was honourable among the thirty, but attained not to the first three: and David set him over his guard.

26 Also the valiant men of the armies were, Asahel the brother of Joab, Elhanan the son of Dodo of Bethlehem,

27 Shammoth the Harorite, Helez the Pelonite,

28 Ira the son of Ikkesh the Tekoite, Abiezer the Antothite,

29 Sibbecai the Hushathite, Ilai the Ahohite,

30 Maharai the Netophathite, Heled the son of Baanah the Netophathite,

31 Ithai the son of Ribai of Gibeah, that pertained to the children of Benjamin, Benaiah the Pirathonite,

32 Hurai of the brooks of Gaash, Abiel the Arbathite,

33 Azmaveth the Baharumite, Eliahba the Shaalbonite,

34 The sons of Hashem the Gizonite, Jonathan the son of Shage the Hararite,

35 Ahiam the son of Sacar the Hararite, Eliphal the son of Ur,

36 Hepher the Mecherathite, Ahijah the Pelonite,

37 Hezro the Carmelite, Naarai the son of Ezbai,

38 Joel the brother of Nathan, Mibhar the son of Haggeri,

39 Zelek the Ammonite, Naharai the Berothite, the armourbearer of Joab the son of Zeruiah,

40 Ira the Ithrite, Gareb the Ithrite,

41 Uriah the Hittite, Zabad the son of Ahlai,

42 Adina the son of Shiza the Reubenite, a captain of the Reubenites, and thirty with him,

43 Hanan the son of Maachah, and Joshaphat the Mithnite,

44 Uzzia the Ashterathite, Shama and Jehiel the sons of Hothan the Aroerite,

45 Jediael the son of Shimri, and Joha his brother, the Tizite,

46 Eliel the Mahavite, and Jeribai, and Joshaviah, the sons of Elnaam, and Ithmah the Moabite,

47 Eliel, and Obed, and Jasiel the Mesobaite.

CHAPTER 12

NOW these are they that came to David to Ziklag, while he yet kept himself close because of Saul the son of Kish: and they were among the mighty men, helpers of the war.

2 They were armed with bows, and could use both the right hand and the left in hurling stones and shooting arrows out of a bow, even of Saul's brethren of Benjamin.

3 The chief was Ahiezer, then Joash, the sons of Shemaah the Gibeathite; and Jeziel, and Pelet, the sons of Azmaveth; and Berachah, and Jehu the Antothite,

4 And Ismaiah the Gibeonite, a mighty man among the thirty, and over the thirty; and Jeremiah, and Jahaziel, and Johanan, and Josabad the Gederathite,

5 Eluzai, and Jerimoth, and Bealiah, and Shemariah, and Shephatiah the Haruphite,

6 Elkanah, and Jesiah, and Azareel, and Joezer, and Jashobeam, the Korhites,

7 And Joelah, and Zebadiah, the sons of Jeroham of Gedor.

8 And of the Gadites there separated themselves to David into the hold to the wilderness men of might, and men of war fit for the battle, that could handle shield and buckler, whose faces were like the faces of lions, and were as swift as the roes upon the mountains;

9 Ezer the first, Obadiah the second, Eliab the third,

10 Mishmannah the fourth, Jeremiah the fifth,

11 Attai the sixth, Eliel the seventh,

12 Johanan the eighth, Elzabad the ninth,

13 Jeremiah the tenth, Machbanai the eleventh.

14 These were of the sons of Gad, captains of the host: one of the least was over an hundred, and the greatest over a thousand.

15 These are they that went over Jordan in the first month, when it had over-flown all his banks; and they put to flight all them of the valleys, both toward the east, and toward the west.

16 And there came of the children of Benjamin and Judah to the hold to David.

17 And David went out to meet them, and answered and said to them, If you have come peaceably to me to help me, mine heart shall be knit to you: but if to betray me to mine enemies, seeing there is no wrong in mine hands, the God of our fathers look thereon, and rebuke it.

18 Then the spirit came upon Amasai, who was chief of the captains, and he said, We are yours, David, and on your side, you son of Jesse: peace, peace be to you, and peace be to your helpers; for your God helps you. Then David received them, and made them captains of the band.

19 And there fell some of Manasseh to David, when he came with the Philistines against Saul to battle: but they helped them not: for the lords of the Philistines upon advisement sent him away, saying, He will fall to his master Saul to the jeopardy of our heads.

20 As he went to Ziklag, there fell to him of Manasseh, Adnah, and Jozabad, and Jediael, and Michael, and Jozabad, and Elihu, and Zilthai, captains of the thousands that were of Manasseh.

21 And they helped David against the band of the rovers: for they were all mighty men of valour, and were captains in the host.

22 For at that time day by day there came to David to help him, until it was a great host, like the host of God.

23 And these are the numbers of the bands that were ready armed to the war, and came to David to Hebron, to turn the kingdom of Saul to him, according to the word of the LORD.

24 The children of Judah that bare shield and spear were six thousand and eight hundred, ready armed to the war.

25 Of the children of Simeon, mighty men of valour for the war, seven thousand and one hundred.

26 Of the children of Levi four thousand and six hundred.

27 And Jehoiada was the leader of the Aaronites, and with him were three thousand and seven hundred;

28 And Zadok, a young man mighty of valour, and of his father's house twenty and two captains.

29 And of the children of Benjamin, the kindred of Saul, three thousand: for hitherto the greatest part of them had kept the ward of the house of Saul.

30 And of the children of Ephraim twenty thousand and eight hundred, mighty men of valour, famous throughout the house of their fathers.

31 And of the half tribe of Manasseh eighteen thousand, which were expressed by name, to come and make David king.

32 And of the children of Issachar, which were men that had understanding of the times, to know what Israel ought to do; the heads of them were two hundred; and all their brethren were at their commandment.

33 Of Zebulun, such as went forth to battle, expert in war, with all instruments of war, fifty thousand, which could keep rank: they were not of double heart.

34 And of Naphtali a thousand captains, and with them with shield and spear thirty and seven thousand.

35 And of the Danites expert in war twenty and eight thousand and six hundred.

36 And of Asher, such as went forth to battle, expert in war, forty thousand.

37 And on the other side of Jordan, of the Reubenites, and the Gadites, and of the half tribe of Manasseh, with all manner of instruments of war for the battle, an hundred and twenty thousand.

38 All these men of war, that could keep rank, came with a perfect heart to Hebron, to make David king over all

Israel: and all the rest also of Israel were of one heart to make David king.

39 And there they were with David three days, eating and drinking: for their brethren had prepared for them.

40 Moreover they that were nigh them, even to Issachar and Zebulun and Naphtali, brought bread on asses, and on camels, and on mules, and on oxen, and meat, meal, cakes of figs, and bunches of raisins, and wine, and oil, and oxen, and sheep abundantly: for there was joy in Israel.

CHAPTER 13

AND David consulted with the captains of thousands and hundreds, and with every leader.

2 And David said to all the congregation of Israel, If it seem good to you, and that it be of the LORD our God, let us send abroad to our brethren every where, that are left in all the land of Israel, and with them also to the priests and Levites which are in their cities and suburbs, that they may gather themselves to us:

3 And let us bring again the ark of our God to us: for we inquired not at it in the days of Saul.

4 And all the congregation said that they would do so: for the thing was right in the eyes of all the people.

5 So David gathered all Israel together, from Shihor of Egypt even to the entering of Hemath, to bring the ark of God from Kirjathjearim.

6 And David went up, and all Israel, to Baalah, that is, to Kirjathjearim, which belonged to Judah, to bring up thence the ark of God the LORD, that dwells between the cherubims, whose name is called on it.

7 And they carried the ark of God in a new cart out of the house of Abinadab: and Uzza and Ahio drove the cart.

8 And David and all Israel played before God with all their might, and with singing, and with harps, and with psalteries, and with timbrels, and with cymbals, and with trumpets.

9 And when they came to the threshingfloor of Chidon, Uzza put forth his hand to hold the ark; for the oxen stumbled.

10 And the anger of the LORD was kindled against Uzza, and he smote him, because he put his hand to the ark: and there he died before God.

11 And David was displeased, because the LORD had made a breach upon Uzza: therefore that place is called Perezuzza to this day.

12 And David was afraid of God that day, saying, How shall I bring the ark of God home to me?

13 So David brought not the ark home to himself to the city of David, but carried it aside into the house of Obededom the Gittite.

14 And the ark of God remained with the family of Obededom in his house three months. And the LORD blessed the house of Obededom, and all that he had.

CHAPTER 14

NOW Hiram king of Tyre sent messengers to David, and timber of cedars, with masons and carpenters, to build him an house.

2 And David perceived that the LORD had confirmed him king over Israel, for his kingdom was lifted up on high, because of his people Israel.

3 And David took more wives at Jerusalem: and David begat more sons and daughters.

4 Now these are the names of his children which he had in Jerusalem; Shammua, and Shobab, Nathan, and Solomon,

---

13:10 It has been rightly said that Uzza considered his hand to be cleaner than the dirt.

5 And Ibhar, and Elishua, and Elpalet,

6 And Nogah, and Nepheg, and Japhia,

7 And Elishama, and Beeliada, and Eliphalet.

8 And when the Philistines heard that David was anointed king over all Israel, all the Philistines went up to seek David. And David heard of it, and went out against them.

9 And the Philistines came and spread themselves in the valley of Rephaim.

10 And David enquired of God, saying, Shall I go up against the Philistines? And will you deliver them into mine hand? And the LORD said to him, Go up; for I will deliver them into your hand.

11 So they came up to Baalperazim; and David smote them there. Then David said, God has broken in upon mine enemies by mine hand like the breaking forth of waters: therefore they called the name of that place Baalperazim.

12 And when they had left their gods there, David gave a commandment, and they were burned with fire.

13 And the Philistines yet again spread themselves abroad in the valley.

14 Therefore David inquired again of God; and God said to him, Go not up after them; turn away from them, and come upon them over against the mulberry trees.

15 And it shall be, when you shall hear a sound of going in the tops of the mulberry trees, that then you shall go out to battle: for God is gone forth before you to smite the host of the Philistines.

16 David therefore did as God commanded him: and they smote the host of the Philistines from Gibeon even to Gazer.

17 And the fame of David went out into all lands; and the LORD brought the fear of him upon all nations.

CHAPTER 15

AND David made him houses in the city of David, and prepared a place for the ark of God, and pitched for it a tent.

2 Then David said, None ought to carry the ark of God but the Levites: for them has the LORD chosen to carry the ark of God, and to minister to him for ever.

3 And David gathered all Israel together to Jerusalem, to bring up the ark of the LORD to his place, which he had prepared for it.

4 And David assembled the children of Aaron, and the Levites:

5 Of the sons of Kohath; Uriel the chief, and his brethren an hundred and twenty:

6 Of the sons of Merari; Asaiah the chief, and his brethren two hundred and twenty:

7 Of the sons of Gershom; Joel the chief and his brethren an hundred and thirty:

8 Of the sons of Elizaphan; Shemaiah the chief, and his brethren two hundred:

9 Of the sons of Hebron; Eliel the chief, and his brethren fourscore:

10 Of the sons of Uzziel; Amminadab the chief, and his brethren an hundred and twelve.

11 And David called for Zadok and Abiathar the priests, and for the Levites, for Uriel, Asaiah, and Joel, Shemaiah, and Eliel, and Amminadab,

12 And said to them, You are the chief of the fathers of the Levites: sanctify yourselves, both you and your brethren, that you may bring up the ark of the LORD God of Israel to the place that I have prepared for it.

13 For because you did it not at the first, the LORD our God made a breach upon us, for that we sought him not after the due order.

14 So the priests and the Levites sanctified themselves to bring up the ark of the LORD God of Israel.

15 And the children of the Levites bare the ark of God upon their shoulders with the staves thereon, as Moses com-

manded according to the word of the LORD.

16 And David spoke to the chief of the Levites to appoint their brethren to be the singers with instruments of music, psalteries and harps and cymbals, sounding, by lifting up the voice with joy.

17 So the Levites appointed Heman the son of Joel; and of his brethren, Asaph the son of Berechiah; and of the sons of Merari their brethren, Ethan the son of Kushaiah;

18 And with them their brethren of the second degree, Zechariah, Ben, and Jaaziel, and Shemiramoth, and Jehiel, and Unni, Eliab, and Benaiah, and Maaseiah, and Mattithiah, and Elipheleh, and Mikneiah, and Obededom, and Jeiel, the porters.

19 So the singers, Heman, Asaph, and Ethan, were appointed to sound with cymbals of brass;

20 And Zechariah, and Aziel, and Shemiramoth, and Jehiel, and Unni, and Eliab, and Maaseiah, and Benaiah, with psalteries on Alamoth;

21 And Mattithiah, and Elipheleh, and Mikneiah, and Obededom, and Jeiel, and Azaziah, with harps on the Sheminith to excel.

22 And Chenaniah, chief of the Levites, was for song: he instructed about the song, because he was skilful.

23 And Berechiah and Elkanah were doorkeepers for the ark.

24 And Shebaniah, and Jehoshaphat, and Nethaneel, and Amasai, and Zechariah, and Benaiah, and Eliezer, the priests, did blow with the trumpets before the ark of God: and Obededom and Jehiah were doorkeepers for the ark.

25 So David, and the elders of Israel, and the captains over thousands, went to bring up the ark of the covenant of the LORD out of the house of Obededom with joy.

26 And it came to pass, when God helped the Levites that bare the ark of the covenant of the LORD, that they offered seven bullocks and seven rams.

27 And David was clothed with a robe of fine linen, and all the Levites that bare the ark, and the singers, and Chenaniah the master of the song with the singers: David also had upon him an ephod of linen.

28 Thus all Israel brought up the ark of the covenant of the LORD with shouting, and with sound of the cornet, and with trumpets, and with cymbals, making a noise with psalteries and harps.

29 And it came to pass, as the ark of the covenant of the LORD came to the city of David, that Michal, the daughter of Saul looking out at a window saw king David dancing and playing: and she despised him in her heart.

CHAPTER 16

SO they brought the ark of God, and set it in the midst of the tent that David had pitched for it: and they offered burnt sacrifices and peace offerings before God.

2 And when David had made an end of offering the burnt offerings and the peace offerings, he blessed the people in the name of the LORD.

3 And he dealt to every one of Israel, both man and woman, to every one a loaf of bread, and a good piece of flesh, and a flagon of wine.

4 And he appointed certain of the Levites to minister before the ark of the LORD, and to record, and to thank and praise the LORD God of Israel:

5 Asaph the chief, and next to him Zechariah, Jeiel, and Shemiramoth, and Jehiel, and Mattithiah, and Eliab, and Benaiah, and Obededom: and Jeiel with psalteries and with harps; but Asaph made a sound with cymbals;

6 Benaiah also and Jahaziel the priests with trumpets continually before the ark of the covenant of God.

7 Then on that day David delivered first this psalm to thank the LORD into the hand of Asaph and his brethren.

8 Give thanks to the LORD, call upon his name, make known his deeds among the people.

9 Sing to him, sing psalms to him, talk of all his wondrous works.

10 Glory in his holy name: let the heart of them rejoice that seek the LORD.

11 Seek the LORD and his strength, seek his face continually.

12 Remember his marvelous works that he has done, his wonders, and the judgments of his mouth;

13 O you seed of Israel his servant, you children of Jacob, his chosen ones.

14 He is the LORD our God; his judgments are in all the earth.

15 Be mindful always of his covenant; the word which he commanded to a thousand generations;

16 Even of the covenant which he made with Abraham, and of his oath to Isaac;

17 And has confirmed the same to Jacob for a law, and to Israel for an everlasting covenant,

18 Saying, To you will I give the land of Canaan, the lot of your inheritance;

19 When you were but few, even a few, and strangers in it.

20 And when they went from nation to nation, and from one kingdom to another people;

21 He suffered no man to do them wrong: yea, he reproved kings for their sakes,

22 Saying, Touch not mine anointed, and do my prophets no harm.

23 Sing to the LORD, all the earth; show forth from day to day his salvation.

24 Declare his glory among the heathen; his marvelous works among all nations.

25 For great is the LORD, and greatly to be praised: he also is to be feared above all gods.

26 For all the gods of the people are idols: but the LORD made the heavens.

27 Glory and honour are in his presence; strength and gladness are in his place.

> If I had my way,
> I would declare a moratorium
> on public preaching
> of 'the plan of salvation' in America
> for one to two years.
> Then I would call on everyone
> who has use of the airwaves
> and the pulpits
> to preach the holiness of God,
> the righteousness of God
> and the Law of God
> until sinners would cry out,
> 'What must we do to be saved?'
> Then I would take them off
> in a corner
> and whisper the gospel to them.
>
> **PARIS REIDHEAD**
> 20TH CENTURY AMERICAN
> BIBLE TEACHER AND AUTHOR

28 Give to the LORD, you kindreds of the people, give to the LORD glory and strength.

29 Give to the LORD the glory due to his name: bring an offering, and come before him: worship the LORD in the beauty of holiness.

30 Fear before him, all the earth: the world also shall be stable, that it be not moved.

31 Let the heavens be glad, and let the earth rejoice: and let men say among the nations, The LORD reigns.

32 Let the sea roar, and the fullness thereof: let the fields rejoice, and all that is therein.

33 Then shall the trees of the wood sing out at the presence of the LORD, because he cometh to judge the earth.

34 O give thanks to the LORD; for he is good; for his mercy endures for ever.

35 And say, Save us, O God of our salvation, and gather us together, and deliver us from the heathen, that we may give thanks to your holy name, and glory in your praise.

36 Blessed be the LORD God of Israel for ever and ever. And all the people said, Amen, and praised the LORD.

37 So he left there before the ark of the covenant of the LORD Asaph and his brethren, to minister before the ark continually, as every day's work required:

38 And Obededom with their brethren, threescore and eight; Obededom also the son of Jeduthun and Hosah to be porters:

39 And Zadok the priest, and his brethren the priests, before the tabernacle of the LORD in the high place that was at Gibeon,

40 To offer burnt offerings to the LORD upon the altar of the burnt offering continually morning and evening, and to do according to all that is written in the law of the LORD, which he commanded Israel;

41 And with them Heman and Jeduthun, and the rest that were chosen, who were expressed by name, to give thanks to the LORD, because his mercy endures for ever;

42 And with them Heman and Jeduthun with trumpets and cymbals for those that should make a sound, and with musical instruments of God. And the sons of Jeduthun were porters.

43 And all the people departed every man to his house: and David returned to bless his house.

CHAPTER 17

NOW it came to pass, as David sat in his house, that David said to Nathan the prophet, Lo, I dwell in an house of cedars, but the ark of the covenant of the LORD remains under curtains.

2 Then Nathan said to David, Do all that is in your heart; for God is with you.

3 And it came to pass the same night, that the word of God came to Nathan, saying,

4 Go and tell David my servant, Thus says the LORD, You shall not build me an house to dwell in:

5 For I have not dwelt in an house since the day that I brought up Israel to this day; but have gone from tent to tent, and from one tabernacle to another.

6 Wherever I have walked with all Israel, spoke I a word to any of the judges of Israel, whom I commanded to feed my people, saying, Why have you not built me an house of cedars?

7 Now therefore thus shall you say to my servant David, Thus says the LORD of hosts, I took you from the sheepcote, even from following the sheep, that you should be ruler over my people Israel:

8 And I have been with you wherever you have walked, and have cut off all your enemies from before you, and have made you a name like the name of the great men that are in the earth.

9 Also I will ordain a place for my people Israel, and will plant them, and they shall dwell in their place, and shall be moved no more; neither shall the children of wickedness waste them any more, as at the beginning,

10 And since the time that I commanded judges to be over my people Israel. Moreover I will subdue all your enemies. Furthermore I tell you that the LORD will build you an house.

11 And it shall come to pass, when your days be expired that you must go to be with your fathers, that I will raise up your seed after you, which shall be of your sons; and I will establish his kingdom.

12 He shall build me an house, and I will stablish his throne for ever.

13 I will be his father, and he shall be my son: and I will not take my mercy away from him, as I took it from him that was before you:

14 But I will settle him in mine house and in my kingdom for ever: and his throne shall be established for evermore.

15 According to all these words, and according to all this vision, so did Nathan speak to David.

16 And David the king came and sat before the LORD, and said, Who am I, O LORD God, and what is mine house, that you have brought me hitherto?

A person fully confident
that he is able to do God's work
is often the one that fails
to submit to God.
It is the humble servant,
fully dependent upon God,
who succeeds.
CHARLES F. STANLEY
CONTEMPORARY PASTOR
FIRST BAPTIST CHURCH
ATLANTA

17 And yet this was a small thing in your eyes, O God; for you have also spoken of your servant's house for a great while to come, and have regarded me according to the estate of a man of high degree, O LORD God.

18 What can David speak more to you for the honour of your servant? for you know your servant.

19 O LORD, for your servant's sake, and according to your own heart, have you done all this greatness, in making known all these great things.

20 O LORD, there is none like you, neither is there any God beside you, according to all that we have heard with our ears.

21 And what one nation in the earth is like your people Israel, whom God went to redeem to be his own people, to make you a name of greatness and terribleness, by driving out nations from before your people whom you have redeemed out of Egypt?

22 For your people Israel did you make your own people for ever; and you, LORD, became their God.

23 Therefore now, LORD, let the thing that you have spoken concerning your servant and concerning his house be established for ever, and do as you have said.

24 Let it even be established, that your name may be magnified for ever, saying, The LORD of hosts is the God of Israel, even a God to Israel: and let the house of David your servant be established before you.

25 For you, O my God, have told your servant that you will build him an house: therefore your servant has found in his heart to pray before you.

26 And now, LORD, you are God, and have promised this goodness to your servant:

27 Now therefore let it please you to bless the house of your servant, that it may be before you for ever: for you bless, O LORD, and it shall be blessed for ever.

CHAPTER 18

NOW after this it came to pass, that David smote the Philistines, and subdued them, and took Gath and her towns out of the hand of the Philistines.

2 And he smote Moab; and the Moabites became David's servants, and brought gifts.

3 And David smote Hadarezer king of Zobah to Hamath, as he went to stablish his dominion by the river Euphrates.

4 And David took from him a thousand chariots, and seven thousand horsemen, and twenty thousand footmen: David also hamstrung all the chariot horses, but reserved of them an hundred chariots.

5 And when the Syrians of Damascus came to help Hadarezer king of Zobah, David slew of the Syrians two and twenty thousand men.

6 Then David put garrisons in Syria-damascus; and the Syrians became David's servants, and brought gifts. Thus the LORD preserved David wherever he went.

7 And David took the shields of gold that were on the servants of Hadarezer, and brought them to Jerusalem.

8 Likewise from Tibhath, and from Chun, cities of Hadarezer, brought David very much brass, wherewith Solomon made the brasen sea, and the pillars, and the vessels of brass.

9 Now when Tou king of Hamath heard how David had smitten all the host of Hadarezer king of Zobah;

10 He sent Hadoram his son to king David, to inquire of his welfare, and to congratulate him, because he had fought against Hadarezer, and smitten him; (for Hadarezer had war with Tou;) and with him all manner of vessels of gold and silver and brass.

11 Them also king David dedicated to the LORD, with the silver and the gold that he brought from all these nations; from Edom, and from Moab, and from the children of Ammon, and from the Philistines, and from Amalek.

12 Moreover Abishai the son of Zeruiah slew of the Edomites in the valley of salt eighteen thousand.

13 And he put garrisons in Edom; and all the Edomites became David's servants. Thus the LORD preserved David wherever he went.

14 So David reigned over all Israel, and executed judgment and justice among all his people.

15 And Joab the son of Zeruiah was over the host; and Jehoshaphat the son of Ahilud, recorder.

16 And Zadok the son of Ahitub, and Abimelech the son of Abiathar, were the priests; and Shavsha was scribe;

17 And Benaiah the son of Jehoiada was over the Cherethites and the Pelethites; and the sons of David were chief about the king.

CHAPTER 19

NOW it came to pass after this, that Nahash the king of the children of Ammon died, and his son reigned in his stead.

2 And David said, I will show kindness to Hanun the son of Nahash, because his father showed kindness to me. And David sent messengers to comfort him concerning his father. So the servants of David came into the land of the children of Ammon to Hanun, to comfort him.

3 But the princes of the children of Ammon said to Hanun, Do you think that David does honour your father, that he has sent comforters to you? are not his servants come to you for to search, and to overthrow, and to spy out the land?

4 Therefore Hanun took David's servants, and shaved them, and cut off their garments in the midst hard by their buttocks, and sent them away.

5 Then there went certain, and told David how the men were served. And he sent to meet them: for the men were greatly ashamed. And the king said, Tarry at Jericho until your beards be grown, and then return.

6 And when the children of Ammon saw that they had made themselves odious to David, Hanun and the children of Ammon sent a thousand talents of silver to hire them chariots and horsemen out of Mesopotamia, and out of Syriamaachah, and out of Zobah.

7 So they hired thirty and two thousand chariots, and the king of Maachah and his people; who came and pitched before Medeba. And the children of Ammon gathered themselves together from their cities, and came to battle.

8 And when David heard of it, he sent Joab, and all the host of the mighty men.

9 And the children of Ammon came out, and put the battle in array before the gate of the city: and the kings that were come were by themselves in the field.

10 Now when Joab saw that the battle was set against him before and behind, he chose out of all the choice of Israel, and put them in array against the Syrians.

11 And the rest of the people he delivered to the hand of Abishai his brother, and they set themselves in array against the children of Ammon.

12 And he said, If the Syrians be too strong for me, then you shall help me: but if the children of Ammon be too strong for you, then I will help you.

13 Be of good courage, and let us behave ourselves valiantly for our people, and for the cities of our God: and let the LORD do that which is good in his sight.
14 So Joab and the people that were with him drew nigh before the Syrians to the battle; and they fled before him.
15 And when the children of Ammon saw that the Syrians were fled, they likewise fled before Abishai his brother, and entered into the city. Then Joab came to Jerusalem.
16 And when the Syrians saw that they were put to the worse before Israel, they sent messengers, and drew forth the Syrians that were beyond the river: and Shophach the captain of the host of Hadarezer went before them.
17 And it was told David; and he gathered all Israel, and passed over Jordan, and came upon them, and set the battle in array against them. So when David had put the battle in array against the Syrians, they fought with him.
18 But the Syrians fled before Israel; and David slew of the Syrians seven thousand men which fought in chariots, and forty thousand footmen, and killed Shophach the captain of the host.
19 And when the servants of Hadarezer saw that they were put to the worse before Israel, they made peace with David, and became his servants: neither would the Syrians help the children of Ammon any more.

CHAPTER 20

AND it came to pass, that after the year was expired, at the time that kings go out to battle, Joab led forth the power of the army, and wasted the country of the children of Ammon, and came and besieged Rabbah. But David tarried at Jerusalem. And Joab smote Rabbah, and destroyed it.
2 And David took the crown of their king from off his head, and found it to weigh a talent of gold, and there were precious stones in it; and it was set upon David's head: and he brought also exceeding much spoil out of the city.
3 And he brought out the people that were in it, and cut them with saws, and with harrows of iron, and with axes. Even so dealt David with all the cities of the children of Ammon. And David and all the people returned to Jerusalem.
4 And it came to pass after this, that there arose war at Gezer with the Philistines; at which time Sibbechai the Hushathite slew Sippai, that was of the children of the giant: and they were subdued.
5 And there was war again with the Philistines; and Elhanan the son of Jair slew Lahmi the brother of Goliath the Gittite, whose spear staff was like a weaver's beam.
6 And yet again there was war at Gath, where was a man of great stature, whose fingers and toes were four and twenty, six on each hand, and six on each foot and he also was the son of the giant.
7 But when he defied Israel, Jonathan the son of Shimea David's brother slew him.
8 These were born to the giant in Gath; and they fell by the hand of David, and by the hand of his servants.

CHAPTER 21

AND Satan stood up against Israel, and provoked David to number Israel.
2 And David said to Joab and to the rulers of the people, Go, number Israel from Beersheba even to Dan; and bring the number of them to me, that I may know it.
3 And Joab answered, The LORD make his people an hundred times so many more as they be: but, my lord the king, are they not all my lord's servants? why then does my lord require this thing? why will he be a cause of trespass to Israel?
4 Nevertheless the king's word prevailed against Joab. Therefore Joab

departed, and went throughout all Israel, and came to Jerusalem.

5 And Joab gave the sum of the number of the people to David. And all they of Israel were a thousand thousand and an hundred thousand men that drew sword: and Judah was four hundred threescore and ten thousand men that drew sword.

6 But Levi and Benjamin counted he not among them: for the king's word was abominable to Joab.

7 And God was displeased with this thing; therefore he smote Israel.

8 And David said to God, I have sinned greatly, because I have done this thing: but now, I beseech you, do away the iniquity of your servant; for I have done very foolishly.

9 And the LORD spoke to Gad, David's seer, saying,

10 Go and tell David, saying, Thus says the LORD, I offer you three things: choose one of them for yourself, that I may do it to you.

11 So Gad came to David, and said to him, Thus says the LORD, Choose for yourself,

12 Either three years' famine; or three months to be destroyed before your foes, while that the sword of your enemies overtakes you; or else three days the sword of the LORD, even the pestilence, in the land, and the angel of the LORD destroying throughout all the coasts of Israel. Now therefore advise yourself what word I shall bring again to him that sent me.

13 And David said to Gad, I am in a great strait: let me fall now into the hand of the LORD; for very great are his mercies: but let me not fall into the hand of man.

14 So the LORD sent pestilence upon Israel: and there fell of Israel seventy thousand men.

15 And God sent an angel to Jerusalem to destroy it: and as he was destroying, the LORD beheld, and he repented him of the evil, and said to the angel that destroyed, It is enough, stay now your hand. And the angel of the LORD stood by the threshingfloor of Ornan the Jebusite.

16 And David lifted up his eyes, and saw the angel of the LORD stand between the earth and the heaven, having a drawn sword in his hand stretched out over Jerusalem. Then David and the elders of Israel, who were clothed in sackcloth, fell upon their faces.

17 And David said to God, Is it not I that commanded the people to be numbered? even I it is that have sinned and done evil indeed; but as for these sheep, what have they done? let your hand, I pray you, O LORD my God, be on me, and on my father's house; but not on your people, that they should be plagued.

18 Then the angel of the LORD commanded Gad to say to David, that David should go up, and set up an altar to the LORD in the threshingfloor of Ornan the Jebusite.

19 And David went up at the saying of Gad, which he spoke in the name of the LORD.

20 And Ornan turned back, and saw the angel; and his four sons with him hid themselves. Now Ornan was threshing wheat.

21 And as David came to Ornan, Ornan looked and saw David, and went out of the threshingfloor, and bowed himself to David with his face to the ground.

22 Then David said to Ornan, Grant me the place of this threshingfloor, that I may build an altar therein to the LORD: you shall grant it me for the full price: that the plague may be stayed from the people.

23 And Ornan said to David, Take it to you, and let my lord the king do that which is good in his eyes: lo, I give you the oxen also for burnt offerings, and the threshing instruments for wood, and the wheat for the meat offering; I give it all.

24 And king David said to Ornan, Nay; but I will verily buy it for the full price:

for I will not take that which is yours for the LORD, nor offer burnt offerings without cost.

25 So David gave to Ornan for the place six hundred shekels of gold by weight.

26 And David built there an altar to the LORD, and offered burnt offerings and peace offerings, and called upon the LORD; and he answered him from heaven by fire upon the altar of burnt offering.

27 And the LORD commanded the angel; and he put up his sword again into the sheath thereof.

28 At that time when David saw that the LORD had answered him in the threshingfloor of Ornan the Jebusite, then he sacrificed there.

29 For the tabernacle of the LORD, which Moses made in the wilderness, and the altar of the burnt offering, were at that season in the high place at Gibeon.

30 But David could not go before it to enquire of God: for he was afraid because of the sword of the angel of the LORD.

CHAPTER 22

THEN David said, This is the house of the LORD God, and this is the altar of the burnt offering for Israel.

2 And David commanded to gather together the strangers that were in the land of Israel; and he set masons to hew out stones to build the house of God.

3 And David prepared iron in abundance for the nails for the doors of the gates, and for the joinings; and brass in abundance without weight;

4 Also cedar trees in abundance: for the Zidonians and they of Tyre brought much cedar wood to David.

5 And David said, Solomon my son is young and tender, and the house that is to be built for the LORD must be exceeding magnifical, of fame and of glory throughout all countries: I will therefore now make preparation for it. So David prepared abundantly before his death.

6 Then he called for Solomon his son, and charged him to build an house for the LORD God of Israel.

7 And David said to Solomon, My son, as for me, it was in my mind to build an house to the name of the LORD my God:

8 But the word of the LORD came to me, saying, You have shed blood abundantly, and have made great wars: you shall not build an house to my name, because you have shed much blood upon the earth in my sight.

9 Behold, a son shall be born to you, who shall be a man of rest; and I will give him rest from all his enemies round about: for his name shall be Solomon, and I will give peace and quietness to Israel in his days.

10 He shall build an house for my name; and he shall be my son, and I will be his father; and I will establish the throne of his kingdom over Israel for ever.

11 Now, my son, the LORD be with you; and prosper you, and build the house of the LORD your God, as he has said of you.

12 Only the LORD give you wisdom and understanding, and give you charge concerning Israel, that you may keep the law of the LORD your God.

13 Then shall you prosper, if you take heed to fulfil the statutes and judgments which the LORD charged Moses with concerning Israel: be strong, and of good courage; dread not, nor be dismayed.

14 Now, behold, in my trouble I have prepared for the house of the LORD an hundred thousand talents of gold, and a thousand thousand talents of silver; and of brass and iron without weight; for it is in abundance: timber also and stone have I prepared; and you may add thereto.

15 Moreover there are workmen with you in abundance, hewers and workers of stone and timber, and all manner of cunning men for every manner of work.

16 Of the gold, the silver, and the brass, and the iron, there is no number.

Arise therefore, and be doing, and the LORD be with you.

17 David also commanded all the princes of Israel to help Solomon his son, saying,

18 Is not the LORD your God with you? and has he not given you rest on every side? for he has given the inhabitants of the land into mine hand; and the land is subdued before the LORD, and before his people.

19 Now set your heart and your soul to seek the LORD your God; arise therefore, and build the sanctuary of the LORD God, to bring the ark of the covenant of the LORD, and the holy vessels of God, into the house that is to be built to the name of the LORD.

CHAPTER 23

SO when David was old and full of days, he made Solomon his son king over Israel.

2 And he gathered together all the princes of Israel, with the priests and the Levites.

3 Now the Levites were numbered from the age of thirty years and upward: and their number by their polls, man by man, was thirty and eight thousand.

4 Of which, twenty and four thousand were to set forward the work of the house of the LORD; and six thousand were officers and judges:

5 Moreover four thousand were porters; and four thousand praised the LORD with the instruments which I made, said David, to praise therewith.

6 And David divided them into courses among the sons of Levi, namely, Gershon, Kohath, and Merari.

7 Of the Gershonites were, Laadan, and Shimei.

8 The sons of Laadan; the chief was Jehiel, and Zetham, and Joel, three.

9 The sons of Shimei; Shelomith, and Haziel, and Haran, three. These were the chief of the fathers of Laadan.

10 And the sons of Shimei were, Jahath, Zina, and Jeush, and Beriah. These four were the sons of Shimei.

11 And Jahath was the chief, and Zizah the second: but Jeush and Beriah had not many sons; therefore they were in one reckoning, according to their father's house.

12 The sons of Kohath; Amram, Izhar, Hebron, and Uzziel, four.

13 The sons of Amram; Aaron and Moses: and Aaron was separated, that he should sanctify the most holy things, he and his sons for ever, to burn incense before the LORD, to minister to him, and to bless in his name for ever.

14 Now concerning Moses the man of God, his sons were named of the tribe of Levi.

15 The sons of Moses were, Gershom, and Eliezer.

16 Of the sons of Gershom, Shebuel was the chief.

17 And the sons of Eliezer were, Rehabiah the chief. And Eliezer had none other sons; but the sons of Rehabiah were very many.

18 Of the sons of Izhar; Shelomith the chief.

19 Of the sons of Hebron; Jeriah the first, Amariah the second, Jahaziel the third, and Jekameam the fourth.

20 Of the sons of Uzziel; Micah the first and Jesiah the second.

21 The sons of Merari; Mahli, and Mushi. The sons of Mahli; Eleazar, and Kish.

22 And Eleazar died, and had no sons, but daughters: and their brethren the sons of Kish took them.

23 The sons of Mushi; Mahli, and Eder, and Jeremoth, three.

24 These were the sons of Levi after the house of their fathers; even the chief of the fathers, as they were counted by number of names by their polls, that did the work for the service of the house of the LORD, from the age of twenty years and upward.

25 For David said, The LORD God of Israel has given rest to his people, that they may dwell in Jerusalem for ever:

26 And also to the Levites; they shall no more carry the tabernacle, nor any vessels of it for the service thereof.

27 For by the last words of David the Levites were numbered from twenty years old and above:

28 Because their office was to wait on the sons of Aaron for the service of the house of the LORD, in the courts, and in the chambers, and in the purifying of all holy things, and the work of the service of the house of God;

29 Both for the shewbread, and for the fine flour for meat offering, and for the unleavened cakes, and for that which is baked in the pan, and for that which is fried, and for all manner of measure and size;

30 And to stand every morning to thank and praise the LORD, and likewise at even:

31 And to offer all burnt sacrifices to the LORD in the sabbaths, in the new moons, and on the set feasts, by number, according to the order commanded to them, continually before the LORD:

32 And that they should keep the charge of the tabernacle of the congregation, and the charge of the holy place, and the charge of the sons of Aaron their brethren, in the service of the house of the LORD.

CHAPTER 24

NOW these are the divisions of the sons of Aaron. The sons of Aaron; Nadab, and Abihu, Eleazar, and Ithamar.

2 But Nadab and Abihu died before their father, and had no children: therefore Eleazar and Ithamar executed the priest's office.

3 And David distributed them, both Zadok of the sons of Eleazar, and Ahimelech of the sons of Ithamar, according to their offices in their service.

4 And there were more chief men found of the sons of Eleazar than of the sons of Ithamar, and thus were they divided. Among the sons of Eleazar there were sixteen chief men of the house of their fathers, and eight among the sons of Ithamar according to the house of their fathers.

5 Thus were they divided by lot, one sort with another; for the governors of the sanctuary, and governors of the house of God, were of the sons of Eleazar, and of the sons of Ithamar.

6 And Shemaiah the son of Nethaneel the scribe, one of the Levites, wrote them before the king, and the princes, and Zadok the priest, and Ahimelech the son of Abiathar, and before the chief of the fathers of the priests and Levites: one principal household being taken for Eleazar, and one taken for Ithamar.

7 Now the first lot came forth to Jehoiarib, the second to Jedaiah,

8 The third to Harim, the fourth to Seorim,

9 The fifth to Malchijah, the sixth to Mijamin,

10 The seventh to Hakkoz, the eighth to Abijah,

11 The ninth to Jeshuah, the tenth to Shecaniah,

12 The eleventh to Eliashib, the twelfth to Jakim,

13 The thirteenth to Huppah, the fourteenth to Jeshebeab,

14 The fifteenth to Bilgah, the sixteenth to Immer,

15 The seventeenth to Hezir, the eighteenth to Aphses,

16 The nineteenth to Pethahiah, the twentieth to Jehezekel,

17 The one and twentieth to Jachin, the two and twentieth to Gamul,

18 The three and twentieth to Delaiah, the four and twentieth to Maaziah.

19 These were the orderings of them in their service to come into the house of the LORD, according to their manner, under Aaron their father, as the LORD God of Israel had commanded him.

20 And the rest of the sons of Levi were these: Of the sons of Amram; Shubael: of the sons of Shubael; Jehdeiah.

21 Concerning Rehabiah: of the sons of Rehabiah, the first was Isshiah.

22 Of the Izharites; Shelomoth: of the sons of Shelomoth; Jahath.

23 And the sons of Hebron; Jeriah the first, Amariah the second, Jahaziel the third, Jekameam the fourth.

24 Of the sons of Uzziel; Michah: of the sons of Michah; Shamir.

25 The brother of Michah was Isshiah: of the sons of Isshiah; Zechariah.

26 The sons of Merari were Mahli and Mushi: the sons of Jaaziah; Beno.

27 The sons of Merari by Jaaziah; Beno, and Shoham, and Zaccur, and Ibri.

28 Of Mahli came Eleazar, who had no sons.

29 Concerning Kish: the son of Kish was Jerahmeel.

30 The sons also of Mushi; Mahli, and Eder, and Jerimoth. These were the sons of the Levites after the house of their fathers.

31 These likewise cast lots over against their brethren the sons of Aaron in the presence of David the king, and Zadok, and Ahimelech, and the chief of the fathers of the priests and Levites, even the principal fathers over against their younger brethren.

CHAPTER 25

M OREOVER David and the captains of the host separated to the service of the sons of Asaph, and of Heman, and of Jeduthun, who should prophesy with harps, with psalteries, and with cymbals: and the number of the workmen according to their service was:

2 Of the sons of Asaph; Zaccur, and Joseph, and Nethaniah, and Asarelah, the sons of Asaph under the hands of Asaph, which prophesied according to the order of the king.

3 Of Jeduthun: the sons of Jeduthun; Gedaliah, and Zeri, and Jeshaiah, Hashabiah, and Mattithiah, six, under the hands of their father Jeduthun, who prophesied with a harp, to give thanks and to praise the LORD.

4 Of Heman: the sons of Heman: Bukkiah, Mattaniah, Uzziel, Shebuel, and Jerimoth, Hananiah, Hanani, Eliathah, Giddalti, and Romamtiezer, Joshbekashah, Mallothi, Hothir, and Mahazioth:

5 All these were the sons of Heman the king's seer in the words of God, to lift up the horn. And God gave to Heman fourteen sons and three daughters.

6 All these were under the hands of their father for song in the house of the LORD, with cymbals, psalteries, and harps, for the service of the house of God, according to the king's order to Asaph, Jeduthun, and Heman.

7 So the number of them, with their brethren that were instructed in the songs of the LORD, even all that were cunning, was two hundred fourscore and eight.

8 And they cast lots, ward against ward, as well the small as the great, the teacher as the scholar.

9 Now the first lot came forth for Asaph to Joseph: the second to Gedaliah, who with his brethren and sons were twelve:

10 The third to Zaccur, he, his sons, and his brethren, were twelve:

11 The fourth to Izri, he, his sons, and his brethren, were twelve:

12 The fifth to Nethaniah, he, his sons, and his brethren, were twelve:

13 The sixth to Bukkiah, he, his sons, and his brethren, were twelve:

14 The seventh to Jesharelah; he, his sons, and his brethren, were twelve:

15 The eighth to Jeshaiah, he, his sons, and his brethren, were twelve:

16 The ninth to Mattaniah, he, his sons, and his brethren, were twelve:

17 The tenth to Shimei, he, his sons, and his brethren, were twelve:

18 The eleventh to Azareel, he, his sons, and his brethren, were twelve:

19 The twelfth to Hashabiah, he, his sons, and his brethren, were twelve:

20 The thirteenth to Shubael, he, his sons, and his brethren, were twelve:

21 The fourteenth to Mattithiah, he, his sons, and his brethren, were twelve:

22 The fifteenth to Jeremoth, he, his sons, and his brethren, were twelve:

23 The sixteenth to Hananiah, he, his sons, and his brethren, were twelve:

24 The seventeenth to Joshbekashah, he, his sons, and his brethren, were twelve:

25 The eighteenth to Hanani, he, his sons, and his brethren, were twelve:

26 The nineteenth to Mallothi, he, his sons, and his brethren, were twelve:

27 The twentieth to Eliathah, he, his sons, and his brethren, were twelve:

28 The one and twentieth to Hothir, he, his sons, and his brethren, were twelve:

29 The two and twentieth to Giddalti, he, his sons, and his brethren, were twelve:

30 The three and twentieth to Mahazioth, he, his sons, and his brethren, were twelve:

31 The four and twentieth to Romamtiezer, he, his sons, and his brethren, were twelve.

CHAPTER 26

CONCERNING the divisions of the porters: Of the Korhites was Meshelemiah the son of Kore, of the sons of Asaph.

2 And the sons of Meshelemiah were, Zechariah the firstborn, Jediael the second, Zebadiah the third, Jathniel the fourth,

3 Elam the fifth, Jehohanan the sixth, Elioenai the seventh.

4 Moreover the sons of Obededom were, Shemaiah the firstborn, Jehozabad the second, Joah the third, and Sacar the fourth, and Nethaneel the fifth.

5 Ammiel the sixth, Issachar the seventh, Peulthai the eighth: for God blessed him.

6 Also to Shemaiah his son were sons born, that ruled throughout the house of their father: for they were mighty men of valour.

7 The sons of Shemaiah; Othni, and Rephael, and Obed, Elzabad, whose brethren were strong men, Elihu, and Semachiah.

8 All these of the sons of Obededom: they and their sons and their brethren, able men for strength for the service, were threescore and two of Obededom.

9 And Meshelemiah had sons and brethren, strong men, eighteen.

10 Also Hosah, of the children of Merari, had sons; Simri the chief, (for though he was not the firstborn, yet his father made him the chief;)

11 Hilkiah the second, Tebaliah the third, Zechariah the fourth: all the sons and brethren of Hosah were thirteen.

12 Among these were the divisions of the porters, even among the chief men, having wards one against another, to minister in the house of the LORD.

13 And they cast lots, as well the small as the great, according to the house of their fathers, for every gate.

14 And the lot eastward fell to Shelemiah. Then for Zechariah his son, a wise counselor, they cast lots; and his lot came out northward.

15 To Obededom southward; and to his sons the house of Asuppim.

16 To Shuppim and Hosah the lot came forth westward, with the gate Shallecheth, by the causeway of the going up, ward against ward.

17 Eastward were six Levites, northward four a day, southward four a day, and toward Asuppim two and two.

18 At Parbar westward, four at the causeway, and two at Parbar.

19 These are the divisions of the porters among the sons of Kore, and among the sons of Merari.

20 And of the Levites, Ahijah was over the treasures of the house of God, and over the treasures of the dedicated things.

21 As concerning the sons of Laadan; the sons of the Gershonite Laadan, chief

fathers, even of Laadan the Gershonite, were Jehieli.

22 The sons of Jehieli; Zetham, and Joel his brother, which were over the treasures of the house of the LORD.

23 Of the Amramites, and the Izharites, the Hebronites, and the Uzzielites:

24 And Shebuel the son of Gershom, the son of Moses, was ruler of the treasures.

25 And his brethren by Eliezer; Rehabiah his son, and Jeshaiah his son, and Joram his son, and Zichri his son, and Shelomith his son.

26 Which Shelomith and his brethren were over all the treasures of the dedicated things, which David the king, and the chief fathers, the captains over thousands and hundreds, and the captains of the host, had dedicated.

27 Out of the spoils won in battles did they dedicate to maintain the house of the LORD.

28 And all that Samuel the seer, and Saul the son of Kish, and Abner the son of Ner, and Joab the son of Zeruiah, had dedicated; and whosoever had dedicated any thing, it was under the hand of Shelomith, and of his brethren.

29 Of the Izharites, Chenaniah and his sons were for the outward business over Israel, for officers and judges.

30 And of the Hebronites, Hashabiah and his brethren, men of valour, a thousand and seven hundred, were officers among them of Israel on this side Jordan westward in all the business of the LORD, and in the service of the king.

31 Among the Hebronites was Jerijah the chief, even among the Hebronites, according to the generations of his fathers. In the fortieth year of the reign of David they were sought for, and there were found among them mighty men of valour at Jazer of Gilead.

32 And his brethren, men of valour, were two thousand and seven hundred chief fathers, whom king David made rulers over the Reubenites, the Gadites, and the half tribe of Manasseh, for every

matter pertaining to God, and affairs of the king.

CHAPTER 27

NOW the children of Israel after their number, to wit, the chief fathers and captains of thousands and hundreds, and their officers that served the king in any matter of the courses, which came in and went out month by month throughout all the months of the year, of every course were twenty and four thousand.

2 Over the first course for the first month was Jashobeam the son of Zabdiel: and in his course were twenty and four thousand.

3 Of the children of Perez was the chief of all the captains of the host for the first month.

4 And over the course of the second month was Dodai an Ahohite, and of his course was Mikloth also the ruler: in his course likewise were twenty and four thousand.

5 The third captain of the host for the third month was Benaiah the son of Jehoiada, a chief priest: and in his course were twenty and four thousand.

6 This is that Benaiah, who was mighty among the thirty, and above the thirty: and in his course was Ammizabad his son.

7 The fourth captain for the fourth month was Asahel the brother of Joab, and Zebadiah his son after him: and in his course were twenty and four thousand.

8 The fifth captain for the fifth month was Shamhuth the Izrahite: and in his course were twenty and four thousand.

9 The sixth captain for the sixth month was Ira the son of Ikkesh the Tekoite: and in his course were twenty and four thousand.

10 The seventh captain for the seventh month was Helez the Pelonite, of the children of Ephraim: and in his course were twenty and four thousand.

11 The eighth captain for the eighth month was Sibbecai the Hushathite, of the Zarhites: and in his course were twenty and four thousand.

12 The ninth captain for the ninth month was Abiezer the Anetothite, of the Benjamites: and in his course were twenty and four thousand.

13 The tenth captain for the tenth month was Maharai the Netophathite, of the Zarhites: and in his course were twenty and four thousand.

14 The eleventh captain for the eleventh month was Benaiah the Pirathonite, of the children of Ephraim: and in his course were twenty and four thousand.

15 The twelfth captain for the twelfth month was Heldai the Netophathite, of Othniel: and in his course were twenty and four thousand.

16 Furthermore over the tribes of Israel: the ruler of the Reubenites was Eliezer the son of Zichri: of the Simeonites, Shephatiah the son of Maachah:

17 Of the Levites, Hashabiah the son of Kemuel: of the Aaronites, Zadok:

18 Of Judah, Elihu, one of the brethren of David: of Issachar, Omri the son of Michael:

19 Of Zebulun, Ishmaiah the son of Obadiah: of Naphtali, Jerimoth the son of Azriel:

20 Of the children of Ephraim, Hoshea the son of Azaziah: of the half tribe of Manasseh, Joel the son of Pedaiah:

21 Of the half tribe of Manasseh in Gilead, Iddo the son of Zechariah: of Benjamin, Jaasiel the son of Abner:

22 Of Dan, Azareel the son of Jeroham. These were the princes of the tribes of Israel.

23 But David took not the number of them from twenty years old and under: because the LORD had said he would increase Israel like to the stars of the heavens.

24 Joab the son of Zeruiah began to number, but he finished not, because there fell wrath for it against Israel; neither was the number put in the account of the chronicles of king David.

25 And over the king's treasures was Azmaveth the son of Adiel: and over the storehouses in the fields, in the cities, and in the villages, and in the castles, was Jehonathan the son of Uzziah:

26 And over them that did the work of the field for tillage of the ground was Ezri the son of Chelub:

27 And over the vineyards was Shimei the Ramathite: over the increase of the vineyards for the wine cellars was Zabdi the Shiphmite:

28 And over the olive trees and the sycomore trees that were in the low plains was Baalhanan the Gederite: and over the cellars of oil was Joash:

29 And over the herds that fed in Sharon was Shitrai the Sharonite: and over the herds that were in the valleys was Shaphat the son of Adlai:

30 Over the camels also was Obil the Ishmaelite: and over the asses was Jehdeiah the Meronothite:

31 And over the flocks was Jaziz the Hagerite. All these were the rulers of the substance which was king David's.

32 Also Jonathan David's uncle was a counsellor, a wise man, and a scribe: and Jehiel the son of Hachmoni was with the king's sons:

33 And Ahithophel was the king's counsellor: and Hushai the Archite was the king's companion:

34 And after Ahithophel was Jehoiada the son of Benaiah, and Abiathar: and the general of the king's army was Joab.

CHAPTER 28

AND David assembled all the princes of Israel, the princes of the tribes, and the captains of the companies that ministered to the king by course, and the captains over the thousands, and captains over the hundreds, and the stewards over all the substance and possession of the king, and of his sons, with the officers, and with the mighty men, and with all the valiant men, to Jerusalem.

2 Then David the king stood up upon his feet, and said, Hear me, my brethren, and my people: As for me, I had in mine heart to build an house of rest for the ark of the covenant of the LORD, and for the footstool of our God, and had made ready for the building:

3 But God said to me, You shall not build an house for my name, because you have been a man of war, and have shed blood.

4 Howbeit the LORD God of Israel chose me before all the house of my father to be king over Israel for ever: for he has chosen Judah to be the ruler; and of the house of Judah, the house of my father; and among the sons of my father he liked me to make me king over all Israel:

5 And of all my sons, (for the LORD has given me many sons,) he has chosen Solomon my son to sit upon the throne of the kingdom of the LORD over Israel.

6 And he said to me, Solomon your son, he shall build my house and my courts: for I have chosen him to be my son, and I will be his father.

7 Moreover I will establish his kingdom for ever, if he be constant to do my commandments and my judgments, as at this day.

8 Now therefore in the sight of all Israel the congregation of the LORD, and in the audience of our God, keep and seek for all the commandments of the LORD your God: that you may possess this good land, and leave it for an inheritance for your children after you for ever.

9 And you, Solomon my son, know the God of your father, and serve him with a perfect heart and with a willing mind: for the LORD searches all hearts, and understands all the imaginations of the thoughts: if you seek him, he will be found of you; but if you forsake him, he will cast you off for ever.

10 Take heed now; for the LORD has chosen you to build an house for the sanctuary: be strong, and do it.

11 Then David gave to Solomon his son the pattern of the porch, and of the houses thereof, and of the treasuries thereof, and of the upper chambers thereof, and of the inner parlours thereof, and of the place of the mercy seat,

12 And the pattern of all that he had by the spirit, of the courts of the house of the LORD, and of all the chambers round about, of the treasuries of the house of God, and of the treasuries of the dedicated things:

13 Also for the courses of the priests and the Levites, and for all the work of the service of the house of the LORD, and for all the vessels of service in the house of the LORD.

14 He gave of gold by weight for things of gold, for all instruments of all manner of service; silver also for all instruments of silver by weight, for all instruments of every kind of service:

15 Even the weight for the candlesticks of gold, and for their lamps of gold, by weight for every candlestick, and for the lamps thereof: and for the candlesticks of silver by weight, both for the candlestick, and also for the lamps thereof, according to the use of every candlestick.

16 And by weight he gave gold for the tables of shewbread, for every table; and likewise silver for the tables of silver:

17 Also pure gold for the fleshhooks, and the bowls, and the cups: and for the golden basons he gave gold by weight for every bason; and likewise silver by weight for every bason of silver:

18 And for the altar of incense refined gold by weight; and gold for the pattern of the chariot of the cherubims, that spread out their wings, and covered the ark of the covenant of the LORD.

19 All this, said David, the LORD made me understand in writing by his hand upon me, even all the works of this pattern.

20 And David said to Solomon his son, Be strong and of good courage, and do it: fear not, nor be dismayed: for the LORD God, even my God, will be with you; he will not fail you, nor forsake you, until you have finished all the work for the service of the house of the LORD. 21 And, behold, the courses of the priests and the Levites, even they shall be with you for all the service of the house of God: and there shall be with you for all manner of workmanship every willing skilful man, for any manner of service: also the princes and all the people will be wholly at your commandment.

CHAPTER 29

FURTHERMORE David the king said to all the congregation, Solomon my son, whom alone God has chosen, is yet young and tender, and the work is great: for the palace is not for man, but for the LORD God.
2 Now I have prepared with all my might for the house of my God the gold for things to be made of gold, and the silver for things of silver, and the brass for things of brass, the iron for things of iron, and wood for things of wood; onyx stones, and stones to be set, glistering stones, and of divers colours, and all manner of precious stones, and marble stones in abundance.
3 Moreover, because I have set my affection to the house of my God, I have of mine own proper good, of gold and silver, which I have given to the house of my God, over and above all that I have prepared for the holy house.
4 Even three thousand talents of gold, of the gold of Ophir, and seven thousand talents of refined silver, to overlay the walls of the houses withal:
5 The gold for things of gold, and the silver for things of silver, and for all manner of work to be made by the hands of artificers. And who then is willing to consecrate his service this day to the LORD?

6 Then the chief of the fathers and princes of the tribes of Israel and the captains of thousands and of hundreds, with the rulers of the king's work, offered willingly,
7 And gave for the service of the house of God of gold five thousand talents and ten thousand drams, and of silver ten thousand talents, and of brass eighteen thousand talents, and one hundred thousand talents of iron.
8 And they with whom precious stones were found gave them to the treasure of the house of the LORD, by the hand of Jehiel the Gershonite.
9 Then the people rejoiced, for that they offered willingly, because with perfect heart they offered willingly to the LORD: and David the king also rejoiced with great joy.
10 Therefore David blessed the LORD before all the congregation: and David said, Blessed are you, LORD God of Israel our father, for ever and ever.
11 Yours, O LORD is the greatness, and the power, and the glory, and the victory, and the majesty: for all that is in the heaven and in the earth is yours; yours is the kingdom, O LORD, and you are exalted as head above all.
12 Both riches and honour come of you, and you reign over all; and in your hand is power and might; and in your hand it is to make great, and to give strength to all.
13 Now therefore, our God, we thank you, and praise your glorious name.
14 But who am I, and what is my people, that we should be able to offer so willingly after this sort? for all things come of you, and of your own have we given you.
15 For we are strangers before you, and sojourners, as were all our fathers: our days on the earth are as a shadow, and there is none abiding.
16 O LORD our God, all this store that we have prepared to build you an house for your holy name comes of your hand, and is all your own.

17 I know also, my God, that you try the heart, and have pleasure in uprightness. As for me, in the uprightness of mine heart I have willingly offered all these things: and now have I seen with joy your people, which are present here, to offer willingly to you.

18 O LORD God of Abraham, Isaac, and of Israel, our fathers, keep this for ever in the imagination of the thoughts of the heart of your people, and prepare their heart to you:

19 And give to Solomon my son a perfect heart, to keep your commandments, your testimonies, and your statutes, and to do all these things, and to build the palace, for the which I have made provision.

20 And David said to all the congregation, Now bless the LORD your God. And all the congregation blessed the LORD God of their fathers, and bowed down their heads, and worshipped the LORD, and the king.

21 And they sacrificed sacrifices to the LORD, and offered burnt offerings to the LORD, on the morrow after that day, even a thousand bullocks, a thousand rams, and a thousand lambs, with their drink offerings, and sacrifices in abundance for all Israel:

22 And did eat and drink before the LORD on that day with great gladness. And they made Solomon the son of David king the second time, and anointed him to the LORD to be the chief governor, and Zadok to be priest.

23 Then Solomon sat on the throne of the LORD as king instead of David his father, and prospered; and all Israel obeyed him.

24 And all the princes, and the mighty men, and all the sons likewise of king David, submitted themselves to Solomon the king.

25 And the LORD magnified Solomon exceedingly in the sight of all Israel, and bestowed upon him such royal majesty as had not been on any king before him in Israel.

26 Thus David the son of Jesse reigned over all Israel.

27 And the time that he reigned over Israel was forty years; seven years reigned he in Hebron, and thirty and three years reigned he in Jerusalem.

28 And he died in a good old age, full of days, riches, and honour: and Solomon his son reigned in his stead.

29 Now the acts of David the king, first and last, behold, they are written in the book of Samuel the seer, and in the book of Nathan the prophet, and in the book of Gad the seer,

30 With all his reign and his might, and the times that went over him, and over Israel, and over all the kingdoms of the countries.

29:19 Did Jesus really say to be perfect? See Matthew 5:48 comment.

2 Chronicles

CHAPTER 1

AND Solomon the son of David was strengthened in his kingdom, and the LORD his God was with him, and magnified him exceedingly.

2 Then Solomon spoke to all Israel, to the captains of thousands and of hundreds, and to the judges, and to every governor in all Israel, the chief of the fathers.

3 So Solomon, and all the congregation with him, went to the high place that was at Gibeon; for there was the tabernacle of the congregation of God, which Moses the servant of the LORD had made in the wilderness.

4 But the ark of God had David brought up from Kirjathjearim to the place which David had prepared for it: for he had pitched a tent for it at Jerusalem.

5 Moreover the brasen altar, that Bezaleel the son of Uri, the son of Hur, had made, he put before the tabernacle of the LORD: and Solomon and the congregation sought to it.

6 And Solomon went up there to the brasen altar before the LORD, which was at the tabernacle of the congregation, and offered a thousand burnt offerings upon it.

7 In that night did God appear to Solomon, and said to him, Ask what I shall give you.

8 And Solomon said to God, You have showed great mercy to David my father, and have made me to reign in his stead.

9 Now, O LORD God, let your promise to David my father be established: for you have made me king over a people like the dust of the earth in multitude.

10 Give me now wisdom and knowledge, that I may go out and come in before this people: for who can judge this your people, that is so great?

11 And God said to Solomon, Because this was in your heart, and you have not asked riches, wealth, or honour, nor the life of enemies, neither yet have asked long life; but have asked wisdom and knowledge for yourself, that you may judge my people, over whom I have made you king:

12 Wisdom and knowledge is granted to you; and I will give you riches, and wealth, and honour, such as none of the kings have had that have been before you, neither shall there any after you have the like.

13 Then Solomon came from his journey to the high place that was at Gibeon to Jerusalem, from before the tabernacle of the congregation, and reigned over Israel.

14 And Solomon gathered chariots and horsemen: and he had a thousand and four hundred chariots, and twelve thou-

---

1:6-7 Notice that God didn't rebuke Solomon for killing a thousand animals. See 2 Chron. 7:5.

SOLOMON

2 Chronicles 1:10

If we have wisdom we will think right, do right and speak right. God was overjoyed that Solomon asked Him for wisdom. We have the same opportunity as Solomon to ask for something that pleases God. The Bible implores us, "If any of you lack wisdom, let him ask of God, that gives to all men liberally, and upbraids not; and it shall be given him" (James 1:5).

sand horsemen, which he placed in the chariot cities, and with the king at Jerusalem.

15 And the king made silver and gold at Jerusalem as plenteous as stones, and cedar trees made he as the sycamore trees that are in the vale for abundance.

16 And Solomon had horses brought out of Egypt, and linen yarn: the king's merchants received the linen yarn at a price.

17 And they fetched up, and brought forth out of Egypt a chariot for six hundred shekels of silver, and an horse for an hundred and fifty: and so brought they out horses for all the kings of the Hittites, and for the kings of Syria, by their means.

CHAPTER 2

AND Solomon determined to build an house for the name of the LORD, and an house for his kingdom.

2 And Solomon told out threescore and ten thousand men to bear burdens, and fourscore thousand to hew in the mountain, and three thousand and six hundred to oversee them.

3 And Solomon sent to Huram the king of Tyre, saying, As you did deal with David my father, and did send him cedars to build him an house to dwell therein, even so deal with me.

4 Behold, I build an house to the name of the LORD my God, to dedicate it to him, and to burn before him sweet incense, and for the continual shewbread, and for the burnt offerings morning and evening, on the sabbaths, and on the new moons, and on the solemn feasts of the LORD our God. This is an ordinance for ever to Israel.

5 And the house which I build is great: for great is our God above all gods.

6 But who is able to build him an house, seeing the heaven and heaven of heavens cannot contain him? who am I then, that I should build him an house, save only to burn sacrifice before him?

7 Send me now therefore a man cunning to work in gold, and in silver, and in brass, and in iron, and in purple, and crimson, and blue, and that can skill to grave with the cunning men that are with me in Judah and in Jerusalem, whom David my father did provide.

8 Send me also cedar trees, fir trees, and algum trees, out of Lebanon: for I know that your servants can skill to cut timber in Lebanon; and, behold, my servants shall be with your servants,

9 Even to prepare me timber in abundance: for the house which I am about to build shall be wonderful great.

10 And, behold, I will give to your servants, the hewers that cut timber, twenty thousand measures of beaten wheat, and twenty thousand measures of barley, and twenty thousand baths of wine, and twenty thousand baths of oil.

11 Then Huram the king of Tyre answered in writing, which he sent to Solomon, Because the LORD has loved his people, he has made you king over them.

12 Huram said moreover, Blessed be the LORD God of Israel, that made heaven and earth, who has given to David the king a wise son, endued with prudence and understanding, that might build an house for the LORD, and an house for his kingdom.

13 And now I have sent a cunning man, endued with understanding, of Huram my father's,

14 The son of a woman of the daughters of Dan, and his father was a man of Tyre, skilful to work in gold, and in silver, in brass, in iron, in stone, and in timber, in purple, in blue, and in fine linen, and in crimson; also to grave any manner of graving, and to find out every device which shall be put to him, with your cunning men, and with the cunning men of my lord David your father.

15 Now therefore the wheat, and the barley, the oil, and the wine, which my lord has spoken of, let him send to his servants:

16 And we will cut wood out of Lebanon, as much as you shall need: and we will bring it to you in floats by sea to Joppa; and you shall carry it up to Jerusalem.

17 And Solomon numbered all the strangers that were in the land of Israel, after the numbering wherewith David his father had numbered them; and they were found an hundred and fifty thousand and three thousand and six hundred.

18 And he set threescore and ten thousand of them to be bearers of burdens, and fourscore thousand to be hewers in the mountain, and three thousand and six hundred overseers to set the people a work.

CHAPTER 3

THEN Solomon began to build the house of the LORD at Jerusalem in mount Moriah, where the Lord appeared to David his father, in the place that David had prepared in the threshingfloor of Ornan the Jebusite.

2 And he began to build in the second day of the second month, in the fourth year of his reign.

3 Now these are the things wherein Solomon was instructed for the building of the house of God. The length by cubits after the first measure was threescore cubits, and the breadth twenty cubits.

4 And the porch that was in the front of the house, the length of it was according to the breadth of the house, twenty cubits, and the height was an hundred and twenty: and he overlaid it within with pure gold.

5 And the greater house he cieled with fir tree, which he overlaid with fine gold, and set thereon palm trees and chains.

6 And he garnished the house with precious stones for beauty: and the gold was gold of Parvaim.

7 He overlaid also the house, the beams, the posts, and the walls thereof, and the doors thereof, with gold; and graved cherubims on the walls.

8 And he made the most holy house, the length whereof was according to the breadth of the house, twenty cubits, and the breadth thereof twenty cubits: and he overlaid it with fine gold, amounting to six hundred talents.

9 And the weight of the nails was fifty shekels of gold. And he overlaid the upper chambers with gold.

10 And in the most holy house he made two cherubims of image work, and overlaid them with gold.

11 And the wings of the cherubims were twenty cubits long: one wing of the one cherub was five cubits, reaching to the wall of the house: and the other wing was likewise five cubits, reaching to the wing of the other cherub.

12 And one wing of the other cherub was five cubits, reaching to the wall of the house: and the other wing was five cubits also, joining to the wing of the other cherub.

13 The wings of these cherubims spread themselves forth twenty cubits: and they stood on their feet, and their faces were inward.

14 And he made the vail of blue, and purple, and crimson, and fine linen, and wove cherubims thereon.

15 Also he made before the house two pillars of thirty and five cubits high, and the chapiter that was on the top of each of them was five cubits.

16 And he made chains, as in the oracle, and put them on the heads of the pillars; and made an hundred pomegranates, and put them on the chains.

17 And he reared up the pillars before the temple, one on the right hand, and the other on the left; and called the name of that on the right hand Jachin, and the name of that on the left Boaz.

CHAPTER 4

MOREOVER he made an altar of brass, twenty cubits the length thereof, and twenty cubits the breadth thereof, and ten cubits the height thereof.

2 Also he made a molten sea of ten cubits from brim to brim, round in compass, and five cubits the height thereof; and a line of thirty cubits did compass it round about.

3 And under it was the similitude of oxen, which did compass it round about: ten in a cubit, compassing the sea round about. Two rows of oxen were cast, when it was cast.

4 It stood upon twelve oxen, three looking toward the north, and three looking toward the west, and three looking toward the south, and three looking toward the east: and the sea was set above upon them, and all their hinder parts were inward.

5 And the thickness of it was an handbreadth, and the brim of it like the work of the brim of a cup, with flowers of lilies; and it received and held three thousand baths.

6 He made also ten lavers, and put five on the right hand, and five on the left, to wash in them: such things as they offered for the burnt offering they washed in them; but the sea was for the priests to wash in.

7 And he made ten candlesticks of gold according to their form, and set them in the temple, five on the right hand, and five on the left.

8 He made also ten tables, and placed them in the temple, five on the right side, and five on the left. And he made an hundred basons of gold.

9 Furthermore he made the court of the priests, and the great court, and doors for the court, and overlaid the doors of them with brass.

10 And he set the sea on the right side of the east end, over against the south.

11 And Huram made the pots, and the shovels, and the basons. And Huram finished the work that he was to make for king Solomon for the house of God;

12 To wit, the two pillars, and the pommels, and the chapiters which were on the top of the two pillars, and the two wreaths to cover the two pommels of the chapiters which were on the top of the pillars;

13 And four hundred pomegranates on the two wreaths; two rows of pomegranates on each wreath, to cover the two pommels of the chapiters which were upon the pillars.

14 He made also bases, and lavers made he upon the bases;

15 One sea, and twelve oxen under it.

16 The pots also, and the shovels, and the fleshhooks, and all their instruments, did Huram his father make to king Solomon for the house of the LORD of bright brass.

17 In the plain of Jordan did the king cast them, in the clay ground between Succoth and Zeredathah.

18 Thus Solomon made all these vessels in great abundance: for the weight of the brass could not be found out.

19 And Solomon made all the vessels that were for the house of God, the golden altar also, and the tables whereon the shewbread was set;

20 Moreover the candlesticks with their lamps, that they should burn after the manner before the oracle, of pure gold;

21 And the flowers, and the lamps, and the tongs, made he of gold, and that perfect gold;

22 And the snuffers, and the basons, and the spoons, and the censers, of pure gold: and the entry of the house, the inner doors thereof for the most holy place, and the doors of the house of the temple, were of gold.

CHAPTER 5

THUS all the work that Solomon made for the house of the LORD was finished: and Solomon brought in all the things that David his father had dedicated; and the silver, and the gold, and all the instruments, put he among the treasures of the house of God.

2 Then Solomon assembled the elders of Israel, and all the heads of the tribes, the chief of the fathers of the children of Israel, to Jerusalem, to bring up the ark of the covenant of the LORD out of the city of David, which is Zion.

3 Therefore all the men of Israel assembled themselves to the king in the feast which was in the seventh month.

4 And all the elders of Israel came; and the Levites took up the ark.

5 And they brought up the ark, and the tabernacle of the congregation, and all the holy vessels that were in the tabernacle, these did the priests and the Levites bring up.

6 Also king Solomon, and all the congregation of Israel that were assembled to him before the ark, sacrificed sheep and oxen, which could not be told nor numbered for multitude.

7 And the priests brought in the ark of the covenant of the LORD to his place, to the oracle of the house, into the most holy place, even under the wings of the cherubims:

8 For the cherubims spread forth their wings over the place of the ark, and the cherubims covered the ark and the staves thereof above.

9 And they drew out the staves of the ark, that the ends of the staves were seen from the ark before the oracle; but they were not seen without. And there it is to this day.

10 There was nothing in the ark save the two tables which Moses put therein at Horeb, when the LORD made a covenant with the children of Israel, when they came out of Egypt.

11 And it came to pass, when the priests were come out of the holy place: (for all the priests that were present were sanctified, and did not then wait by course:

12 Also the Levites which were the singers, all of them of Asaph, of Heman, of Jeduthun, with their sons and their brethren, being arrayed in white linen, having cymbals and psalteries and harps, stood at the east end of the altar, and with them an hundred and twenty priests sounding with trumpets:)

13 It came even to pass, as the trumpeters and singers were as one, to make one sound to be heard in praising and thanking the LORD; and when they lifted up their voice with the trumpets and cymbals and instruments of music, and praised the LORD, saying, For he is good; for his mercy endures for ever: that then the house was filled with a cloud, even the house of the LORD;

14 So that the priests could not stand to minister by reason of the cloud: for the glory of the LORD had filled the house of God.

CHAPTER 6

THEN said Solomon, The LORD has said that he would dwell in the thick darkness.

2 But I have built an house of habitation for you, and a place for your dwelling for ever.

3 And the king turned his face, and blessed the whole congregation of Israel: and all the congregation of Israel stood.

4 And he said, Blessed be the LORD God of Israel, who has with his hands fulfilled that which he spoke with his mouth to my father David, saying,

5 Since the day that I brought forth my people out of the land of Egypt I chose no city among all the tribes of Israel to build an house in, that my name might be there; neither chose I any man to be a ruler over my people Israel:

6 But I have chosen Jerusalem, that my name might be there; and have chosen David to be over my people Israel.

7 Now it was in the heart of David my father to build an house for the name of the LORD God of Israel.

8 But the LORD said to David my father, Forasmuch as it was in your heart to build an house for my name, you did well in that it was in your heart:

9 Notwithstanding you shall not build the house; but your son which shall come forth out of your loins, he shall build the house for my name.

10 The LORD therefore has performed his word that he has spoken: for I am risen up in the room of David my father, and am set on the throne of Israel, as the LORD promised, and have built the house for the name of the LORD God of Israel.

11 And in it have I put the ark, wherein is the covenant of the LORD, that he made with the children of Israel.

12 And he stood before the altar of the LORD in the presence of all the congregation of Israel, and spread forth his hands:

13 For Solomon had made a brasen scaffold of five cubits long, and five cubits broad, and three cubits high, and had set it in the midst of the court: and upon it he stood, and kneeled down upon his knees before all the congregation of Israel, and spread forth his hands toward heaven.

14 And said, O LORD God of Israel, there is no God like you in the heaven, nor in the earth; which keep covenant, and show mercy to your servants, that walk before you with all their hearts:

15 You which have kept with your servant David my father that which you have promised him; and spoke with your mouth, and have fulfilled it with your hand, as it is this day.

16 Now therefore, O LORD God of Israel, keep with your servant David my father that which you have promised him, saying, There shall not fail you a man in my sight to sit upon the throne of Israel; yet so that your children take heed to their way to walk in my law, as you have walked before me.

17 Now then, O LORD God of Israel, let your word be verified, which you have spoken to your servant David.

18 But will God in very deed dwell with men on the earth? behold, heaven and the heaven of heavens cannot contain you; how much less this house which I have built!

19 Have respect therefore to the prayer of your servant, and to his supplication, O LORD my God, to hearken to the cry and the prayer which your servant prays before you:

20 That your eyes may be open upon this house day and night, upon the place whereof you have said that you would put your name there; to hearken to the prayer which your servant prays toward this place.

21 Hearken therefore to the supplications of your servant, and of your people Israel, which they shall make toward this place: hear from your dwelling place, even from heaven; and when you hear, forgive.

22 If a man sin against his neighbour, and an oath be laid upon him to make him swear, and the oath come before your altar in this house;

23 Then hear you from heaven, and do, and judge your servants, by requiting the wicked, by recompensing his way upon his own head; and by justifying the righteous, by giving him according to his righteousness.

24 And if your people Israel be put to the worse before the enemy, because they have sinned against you; and shall return and confess your name, and pray and make supplication before you in this house;

25 Then hear from the heavens, and forgive the sin of your people Israel, and bring them again to the land which you gave to them and to their fathers.

26 When the heaven is shut up, and there is no rain, because they have sinned against you; yet if they pray toward this place, and confess your name, and turn from their sin, when you dost afflict them;

27 Then hear from heaven, and forgive the sin of your servants, and of your people Israel, when you have taught them the good way, wherein they should walk; and send rain upon your land,

which you have given to your people for an inheritance.

28 If there be dearth in the land, if there be pestilence, if there be blasting, or mildew, locusts, or caterpillers; if their enemies besiege them in the cities of their land; whatsoever sore or whatsoever sickness there be:

29 Then what prayer or what supplication soever shall be made of any man, or of all your people Israel, when every one shall know his own sore and his own grief, and shall spread forth his hands in this house:

30 Then hear from heaven your dwelling place, and forgive, and render to every man according to all his ways, whose heart you know; (for you only know the hearts of the children of men:)

31 That they may fear you, to walk in your ways, so long as they live in the land which you gave to our fathers.

32 Moreover concerning the stranger, which is not of your people Israel, but is come from a far country for your great name's sake, and your mighty hand, and your stretched out arm; if they come and pray in this house;

33 Then hear from the heavens, even from your dwelling place, and do according to all that the stranger calls to you for; that all people of the earth may know your name, and fear you, as does your people Israel, and may know that this house which I have built is called by your name.

34 If your people go out to war against their enemies by the way that you shall send them, and they pray to you toward this city which you have chosen, and the house which I have built for your name;

35 Then hear from the heavens their prayer and their supplication, and maintain their cause.

36 If they sin against you, (for there is no man which sinneth not,) and you are angry with them, and deliver them over before their enemies, and they carry them away captives to a land far off or near;

37 Yet if they bethink themselves in the land where they are carried captive, and turn and pray to you in the land of their captivity, saying, We have sinned, we have done amiss, and have dealt wickedly;

38 If they return to you with all their heart and with all their soul in the land of their captivity, where they have carried them captives, and pray toward their land, which you gave to their fathers, and toward the city which you have chosen, and toward the house which I have built for your name:

39 Then hear from the heavens, even from your dwelling place, their prayer and their supplications, and maintain their cause, and forgive your people which have sinned against you.

40 Now, my God, let, I beseech you, your eyes be open, and let your ears be attent to the prayer that is made in this place.

41 Now therefore arise, O LORD God, into your resting place, you, and the ark of your strength: let your priests, O LORD God, be clothed with salvation, and let your saints rejoice in goodness.

42 O LORD God, turn not away the face of your anointed: remember the mercies of David your servant.

CHAPTER 7

NOW when Solomon had made an end of praying, the fire came down from heaven, and consumed the burnt offering and the sacrifices; and the glory of the LORD filled the house.

2 And the priests could not enter into the house of the LORD, because the glory of the LORD had filled the LORD's house.

3 And when all the children of Israel saw how the fire came down, and the glory of the LORD upon the house, they bowed themselves with their faces to the ground upon the pavement, and worshipped, and praised the LORD, saying, For he is good; for his mercy endures for ever.

4 Then the king and all the people offered sacrifices before the LORD.

5 And king Solomon offered a sacrifice of twenty and two thousand oxen, and an hundred and twenty thousand sheep: so the king and all the people dedicated the house of God.

6 And the priests waited on their offices: the Levites also with instruments of music of the LORD, which David the king had made to praise the LORD, because his mercy endures for ever, when David praised by their ministry; and the priests sounded trumpets before them, and all Israel stood.

7 Moreover Solomon hallowed the middle of the court that was before the house of the LORD: for there he offered burnt offerings, and the fat of the peace offerings, because the brasen altar which Solomon had made was not able to receive the burnt offerings, and the meat offerings, and the fat.

8 Also at the same time Solomon kept the feast seven days, and all Israel with him, a very great congregation, from the entering in of Hamath to the river of Egypt.

9 And in the eighth day they made a solemn assembly: for they kept the dedication of the altar seven days, and the feast seven days.

10 And on the three and twentieth day of the seventh month he sent the people away into their tents, glad and merry in heart for the goodness that the LORD had showed to David, and to Solomon, and to Israel his people.

11 Thus Solomon finished the house of the LORD, and the king's house: and all that came into Solomon's heart to make in the house of the LORD, and in his own house, he prosperously effected.

12 And the LORD appeared to Solomon by night, and said to him, I have heard your prayer, and have chosen this place to myself for an house of sacrifice.

13 If I shut up heaven that there be no rain, or if I command the locusts to devour the land, or if I send pestilence among my people;

14 If my people, which are called by my name, shall humble themselves, and pray, and seek my face, and turn from their wicked ways; then will I hear from heaven, and will forgive their sin, and will heal their land.

15 Now mine eyes shall be open, and mine ears attent to the prayer that is made in this place.

16 For now have I chosen and sanctified this house, that my name may be there for ever: and mine eyes and mine heart shall be there perpetually.

17 And as for you, if you will walk before me, as David your father walked, and do according to all that I have commanded you, and shall observe my statutes and my judgments;

18 Then will I stablish the throne of your kingdom, according as I have covenanted with David your father, saying, There shall not fail you a man to be ruler in Israel.

19 But if you turn away, and forsake my statutes and my commandments, which I have set before you, and shall go and serve other gods, and worship them;

20 Then will I pluck them up by the roots out of my land which I have given them; and this house, which I have sanctified for my name, will I cast out of my

---

7:5 Animal-rights advocates who insist that "meat is murder" are misguided. God didn't chide the king for his sacrificial worship. The slaying of 22,000 bulls and 120,000 sheep as part of a religious rite would today be an animal-rights nightmare.

7:14 This verse is often applied to God's people. The Church is made up of true believers who live in holiness. They have already turned from their wicked ways. If they haven't, they are playing the hypocrite. Rather, the promise is to Israel, and its principle may be applied to any nation that calls upon the name of the Lord.

sight, and will make it to be a proverb and a byword among all nations.

21 And this house, which is high, shall be an astonishment to every one that passes by it; so that he shall say, Why has the LORD done thus to this land, and to this house?

22 And it shall be answered, Because they forsook the LORD God of their fathers, which brought them forth out of the land of Egypt, and laid hold on other gods, and worshipped them, and served them: therefore has he brought all this evil upon them.

CHAPTER 8

AND it came to pass at the end of twenty years, wherein Solomon had built the house of the LORD, and his own house,

2 That the cities which Huram had restored to Solomon, Solomon built them, and caused the children of Israel to dwell there.

3 And Solomon went to Hamathzobah, and prevailed against it.

4 And he built Tadmor in the wilderness, and all the store cities, which he built in Hamath.

5 Also he built Bethhoron the upper, and Bethhoron the nether, fenced cities, with walls, gates, and bars;

6 And Baalath, and all the store cities that Solomon had, and all the chariot cities, and the cities of the horsemen, and all that Solomon desired to build in Jerusalem, and in Lebanon, and throughout all the land of his dominion.

7 As for all the people that were left of the Hittites, and the Amorites, and the Perizzites, and the Hivites, and the Jebusites, which were not of Israel,

8 But of their children, who were left after them in the land, whom the children of Israel consumed not, them did Solomon make to pay tribute until this day.

9 But of the children of Israel did Solomon make no servants for his work; but they were men of war, and chief of his captains, and captains of his chariots and horsemen.

10 And these were the chief of king Solomon's officers, even two hundred and fifty, that bare rule over the people.

11 And Solomon brought up the daughter of Pharaoh out of the city of David to the house that he had built for her: for he said, My wife shall not dwell in the house of David king of Israel, because the places are holy, whereunto the ark of the LORD has come.

12 Then Solomon offered burnt offerings to the LORD on the altar of the LORD, which he had built before the porch,

13 Even after a certain rate every day, offering according to the commandment of Moses, on the sabbaths, and on the new moons, and on the solemn feasts, three times in the year, even in the feast of unleavened bread, and in the feast of weeks, and in the feast of tabernacles.

14 And he appointed, according to the order of David his father, the courses of the priests to their service, and the Levites to their charges, to praise and minister before the priests, as the duty of every day required: the porters also by their courses at every gate: for so had David the man of God commanded.

15 And they departed not from the commandment of the king to the priests and Levites concerning any matter, or concerning the treasures.

16 Now all the work of Solomon was prepared to the day of the foundation of the house of the LORD, and until it was finished. So the house of the LORD was perfected.

17 Then went Solomon to Eziongeber, and to Eloth, at the sea side in the land of Edom.

18 And Huram sent him by the hands of his servants ships, and servants that had knowledge of the sea; and they went with the servants of Solomon to Ophir, and took thence four hundred and fifty talents of gold, and brought them to king Solomon.

SOLOMON RECEIVING THE QUEEN OF SHEBA

2 Chronicles 9:1

CHAPTER 9

AND when the queen of Sheba heard of the fame of Solomon, she came to prove Solomon with hard questions at Jerusalem, with a very great company, and camels that bare spices, and gold in abundance, and precious stones: and when she was come to Solomon, she communed with him of all that was in her heart.

2 And Solomon told her all her questions: and there was nothing hid from Solomon which he told her not.

3 And when the queen of Sheba had seen the wisdom of Solomon, and the house that he had built,

4 And the meat of his table, and the sitting of his servants, and the attendance of his ministers, and their apparel; his cupbearers also, and their apparel; and his ascent by which he went up into the house of the LORD; there was no more spirit in her.

5 And she said to the king, It was a true report which I heard in mine own land of your acts, and of your wisdom:

6 Howbeit I believed not their words, until I came, and mine eyes had seen it: and, behold, the one half of the greatness of your wisdom was not told me: for you exceed the fame that I heard.

7 Happy are your men, and happy are these your servants, which stand continually before you, and hear your wisdom.

8 Blessed be the LORD your God, which delighted in you to set you on his throne, to be king for the LORD your God: because your God loved Israel, to establish them for ever, therefore he made you king over them, to do judgment and justice.

9 And she gave the king an hundred and twenty talents of gold, and of spices great abundance, and precious stones: neither was there any such spice as the queen of Sheba gave king Solomon.

10 And the servants also of Huram, and the servants of Solomon, which brought gold from Ophir, brought algum trees and precious stones.

11 And the king made of the algum trees terraces to the house of the LORD, and to the king's palace, and harps and psalteries for singers: and there were none such seen before in the land of Judah.

12 And king Solomon gave to the queen of Sheba all her desire, whatsoever she asked, beside that which she had brought to the king. So she turned, and went away to her own land, she and her servants.

13 Now the weight of gold that came to Solomon in one year was six hundred and threescore and six talents of gold;

14 Beside that which chapmen and merchants brought. And all the kings of Arabia and governors of the country brought gold and silver to Solomon.

15 And king Solomon made two hundred targets of beaten gold: six hundred shekels of beaten gold went to one target.

16 And three hundred shields made he of beaten gold: three hundred shekels of gold went to one shield. And the king put them in the house of the forest of Lebanon.

17 Moreover the king made a great throne of ivory, and overlaid it with pure gold.

18 And there were six steps to the throne, with a footstool of gold, which were fastened to the throne, and stays on each side of the sitting place, and two lions standing by the stays:

19 And twelve lions stood there on the one side and on the other upon the six steps. There was not the like made in any kingdom.

20 And all the drinking vessels of king Solomon were of gold, and all the vessels of the house of the forest of Lebanon were of pure gold: none were of silver; it was not any thing accounted of in the days of Solomon.

21 For the king's ships went to Tarshish with the servants of Huram: every three years once came the ships of Tarshish bringing gold, and silver, ivory, and apes, and peacocks.

22 And king Solomon passed all the kings of the earth in riches and wisdom.

9:5-8 We have One who is (infinitely) greater than Solomon. We once didn't believe, but now we can say with the Queen of Sheba that we have come to know Him personally. How the heart thrills to see the wisdom of God in Christ through the holy scripture. Even the Pharisees marveled at Him. Those who know Him more than marvel; they worship Him.

23 And all the kings of the earth sought the presence of Solomon, to hear his wisdom, that God had put in his heart.

24 And they brought every man his present, vessels of silver, and vessels of gold, and raiment, harness, and spices, horses, and mules, a rate year by year.

25 And Solomon had four thousand stalls for horses and chariots, and twelve thousand horsemen; whom he bestowed in the chariot cities, and with the king at Jerusalem.

26 And he reigned over all the kings from the river even to the land of the Philistines, and to the border of Egypt.

27 And the king made silver in Jerusalem as stones, and cedar trees made he as the sycamore trees that are in the low plains in abundance.

28 And they brought to Solomon horses out of Egypt, and out of all lands.

29 Now the rest of the acts of Solomon, first and last, are they not written in the book of Nathan the prophet, and in the prophecy of Ahijah the Shilonite, and in the visions of Iddo the seer against Jeroboam the son of Nebat?

30 And Solomon reigned in Jerusalem over all Israel forty years.

31 And Solomon slept with his fathers, and he was buried in the city of David his father: and Rehoboam his son reigned in his stead.

CHAPTER 10

AND Rehoboam went to Shechem: for to Shechem were all Israel come to make him king.

2 And it came to pass, when Jeroboam the son of Nebat, who was in Egypt, where he fled from the presence of Solomon the king, heard it, that Jeroboam returned out of Egypt.

3 And they sent and called him. So Jeroboam and all Israel came and spoke to Rehoboam, saying,

4 Your father made our yoke grievous: now therefore ease somewhat the grievous servitude of your father, and his heavy yoke that he put upon us, and we will serve you.

5 And he said to them, Come again to me after three days. And the people departed.

6 And king Rehoboam took counsel with the old men that had stood before Solomon his father while he yet lived, saying, What counsel do you give me to return answer to this people?

7 And they spoke to him, saying, If you are kind to this people, and please them, and speak good words to them, they will be your servants for ever.

8 But he forsook the counsel which the old men gave him, and took counsel with the young men that were brought up with him, that stood before him.

9 And he said to them, What advice do you give that we may return answer to this people, which have spoken to me, saying, Ease somewhat the yoke that your father did put upon us?

10 And the young men that were brought up with him spoke to him, saying, Thus shall you answer the people that spoke to you, saying, Your father made our yoke heavy, but you make it somewhat lighter for us; thus shall you say to them, My little finger shall be thicker than my father's loins.

11 For whereas my father put a heavy yoke upon you, I will put more to your yoke: my father chastised you with whips, but I will chastise you with scorpions.

12 So Jeroboam and all the people came to Rehoboam on the third day,

---

10:8 God forbid that we should ignore godly advice gained by experience in life. A wise man said that parents should never worry if teenagers don't seem to listen to their advice because, in time, those teenagers will become parents and then will give the same advice to their kids.

as the king bade, saying, Come again to me on the third day.

13 And the king answered them roughly; and king Rehoboam forsook the counsel of the old men,

14 And answered them after the advice of the young men, saying, My father made your yoke heavy, but I will add thereto: my father chastised you with whips, but I will chastise you with scorpions.

15 So the king hearkened not to the people: for the cause was of God, that the LORD might perform his word, which he spoke by the hand of Ahijah the Shilonite to Jeroboam the son of Nebat.

16 And when all Israel saw that the king would not hearken to them, the people answered the king, saying, What portion have we in David? and we have none inheritance in the son of Jesse: every man to your tents, O Israel: and now, David, see to your own house. So all Israel went to their tents.

17 But as for the children of Israel that dwelt in the cities of Judah, Rehoboam reigned over them.

18 Then king Rehoboam sent Hadoram that was over the tribute; and the children of Israel stoned him with stones, that he died. But king Rehoboam made speed to get him up to his chariot, to flee to Jerusalem.

19 And Israel rebelled against the house of David to this day.

CHAPTER 11

AND when Rehoboam was come to Jerusalem, he gathered of the house of Judah and Benjamin an hundred and fourscore thousand chosen men, which were warriors, to fight against Israel, that he might bring the kingdom again to Rehoboam.

2 But the word of the LORD came to Shemaiah the man of God, saying,

3 Speak to Rehoboam the son of Solomon, king of Judah, and to all Israel in Judah and Benjamin, saying,

4 Thus says the LORD, You shall not go up, nor fight against your brethren: return every man to his house: for this thing is done of me. And they obeyed the words of the LORD, and returned from going against Jeroboam.

5 And Rehoboam dwelt in Jerusalem, and built cities for defence in Judah.

6 He built even Bethlehem, and Etam, and Tekoa,

7 And Bethzur, and Shoco, and Adullam,

8 And Gath, and Mareshah, and Ziph,

9 And Adoraim, and Lachish, and Azekah,

10 And Zorah, and Aijalon, and Hebron, which are in Judah and in Benjamin fenced cities.

11 And he fortified the strong holds, and put captains in them, and store of victual, and of oil and wine.

12 And in every several city he put shields and spears, and made them exceeding strong, having Judah and Benjamin on his side.

13 And the priests and the Levites that were in all Israel resorted to him out of all their coasts.

14 For the Levites left their suburbs and their possession, and came to Judah and Jerusalem: for Jeroboam and his sons had cast them off from executing the priest's office to the LORD:

15 And he ordained him priests for the high places, and for the devils, and for the calves which he had made.

16 And after them out of all the tribes of Israel such as set their hearts to seek the LORD God of Israel came to Jerusalem, to sacrifice to the LORD God of their fathers.

17 So they strengthened the kingdom of Judah, and made Rehoboam the son of Solomon strong, three years: for three years they walked in the way of David and Solomon.

18 And Rehoboam took him Mahalath the daughter of Jerimoth the son of David to wife, and Abihail the daughter of Eliab the son of Jesse;

19 Which bare him children; Jeush, and Shamariah, and Zaham.

20 And after her he took Maachah the daughter of Absalom; which bare him Abijah, and Attai, and Ziza, and Shelomith.

21 And Rehoboam loved Maachah the daughter of Absalom above all his wives and his concubines: (for he took eighteen wives, and threescore concubines; and begat twenty and eight sons, and threescore daughters.)

22 And Rehoboam made Abijah the son of Maachah the chief, to be ruler among his brethren: for he thought to make him king.

23 And he dealt wisely, and dispersed of all his children throughout all the countries of Judah and Benjamin, to every fenced city: and he gave them victual in abundance. And he desired many wives.

CHAPTER 12

AND it came to pass, when Rehoboam had established the kingdom, and had strengthened himself, he forsook the law of the LORD, and all Israel with him.

2 And it came to pass, that in the fifth year of king Rehoboam Shishak king of Egypt came up against Jerusalem, because they had transgressed against the LORD,

3 With twelve hundred chariots, and threescore thousand horsemen: and the people were without number that came with him out of Egypt; the Lubims, the Sukkiims, and the Ethiopians.

4 And he took the fenced cities which pertained to Judah, and came to Jerusalem.

5 Then came Shemaiah the prophet to Rehoboam, and to the princes of Judah, that were gathered together to Jerusalem because of Shishak, and said to them, Thus says the LORD, You have forsaken me, and therefore have I also left you in the hand of Shishak.

6 Whereupon the princes of Israel and the king humbled themselves; and they said, The LORD is righteous.

7 And when the LORD saw that they humbled themselves, the word of the LORD came to Shemaiah, saying, They have humbled themselves; therefore I will not destroy them, but I will grant them some deliverance; and my wrath shall not be poured out upon Jerusalem by the hand of Shishak.

8 Nevertheless they shall be his servants; that they may know my service, and the service of the kingdoms of the countries.

9 So Shishak king of Egypt came up against Jerusalem, and took away the treasures of the house of the LORD, and the treasures of the king's house; he took all: he carried away also the shields of gold which Solomon had made.

10 Instead of which king Rehoboam made shields of brass, and committed them to the hands of the chief of the guard, that kept the entrance of the king's house.

11 And when the king entered into the house of the LORD, the guard came and fetched them, and brought them again into the guard chamber.

12 And when he humbled himself, the wrath of the LORD turned from him, that he would not destroy him altogether: and also in Judah things went well.

13 So king Rehoboam strengthened himself in Jerusalem, and reigned: for Rehoboam was one and forty years old when he began to reign, and he reigned seventeen years in Jerusalem, the city which the LORD had chosen out of all the tribes of Israel, to put his name there. And his mother's name was Naamah an Ammonitess.

14 And he did evil, because he prepared not his heart to seek the LORD.

12:6 Repentance follows naturally from the humble acknowledgment that God is righteous. See Psalm 51:4.

15 Now the acts of Rehoboam, first and last, are they not written in the book of Shemaiah the prophet, and of Iddo the seer concerning genealogies? And there were wars between Rehoboam and Jeroboam continually.

16 And Rehoboam slept with his fathers, and was buried in the city of David: and Abijah his son reigned in his stead.

CHAPTER 13

NOW in the eighteenth year of king Jeroboam began Abijah to reign over Judah.

2 He reigned three years in Jerusalem. His mother's name also was Michaiah the daughter of Uriel of Gibeah. And there was war between Abijah and Jeroboam.

3 And Abijah set the battle in array with an army of valiant men of war, even four hundred thousand chosen men: Jeroboam also set the battle in array against him with eight hundred thousand chosen men, being mighty men of valour.

4 And Abijah stood up upon mount Zemaraim, which is in mount Ephraim, and said, Hear me, Jeroboam, and all Israel;

5 Do you not know that the LORD God of Israel gave the kingdom over Israel to David for ever, even to him and to his sons by a covenant of salt?

6 Yet Jeroboam the son of Nebat, the servant of Solomon the son of David, is risen up, and has rebelled against his lord.

7 And there are gathered to him vain men, the children of Belial, and have strengthened themselves against Rehoboam the son of Solomon, when Rehoboam was young and tenderhearted, and could not withstand them.

8 And now you think to withstand the kingdom of the LORD in the hand of the sons of David; and you are a great multitude, and there are with your golden calves, which Jeroboam made you for gods.

9 Have you not cast out the priests of the LORD, the sons of Aaron, and the Levites, and have made you priests after the manner of the nations of other lands? so that whosoever cometh to consecrate himself with a young bullock and seven rams, the same may be a priest of them that are no gods.

10 But as for us, the LORD is our God, and we have not forsaken him; and the priests, which minister to the LORD, are the sons of Aaron, and the Levites wait upon their business:

11 And they burn to the LORD every morning and every evening burnt sacrifices and sweet incense: the shewbread also set they in order upon the pure table; and the candlestick of gold with the lamps thereof, to burn every evening: for we keep the charge of the LORD our God; but you have forsaken him.

12 And, behold, God himself is with us for our captain, and his priests with sounding trumpets to cry alarm against you. O children of Israel, do not fight against the LORD God of your fathers; for you shall not prosper.

13 But Jeroboam caused an ambushment to come about behind them: so they were before Judah, and the ambushment was behind them.

14 And when Judah looked back, behold, the battle was before and behind: and they cried to the LORD, and the priests sounded with the trumpets.

15 Then the men of Judah gave a shout: and as the men of Judah shouted, it came to pass, that God smote Jeroboam and all Israel before Abijah and Judah.

16 And the children of Israel fled before Judah: and God delivered them into their hand.

17 And Abijah and his people slew them with a great slaughter: so there fell down slain of Israel five hundred thousand chosen men.

18 Thus the children of Israel were brought under at that time, and the children of Judah prevailed, because they relied upon the LORD God of their fathers.

19 And Abijah pursued after Jeroboam, and took cities from him, Bethel with the towns thereof, and Jeshanah with the towns thereof, and Ephraim with the towns thereof.

20 Neither did Jeroboam recover strength again in the days of Abijah: and the LORD struck him, and he died.

21 But Abijah waxed mighty, and married fourteen wives, and begat twenty and two sons, and sixteen daughters.

22 And the rest of the acts of Abijah, and his ways, and his sayings, are written in the story of the prophet Iddo.

CHAPTER 14

SO Abijah slept with his fathers, and they buried him in the city of David: and Asa his son reigned in his stead. In his days the land was quiet ten years.

2 And Asa did that which was good and right in the eyes of the LORD his God:

3 For he took away the altars of the strange gods, and the high places, and brake down the images, and cut down the groves:

4 And commanded Judah to seek the LORD God of their fathers, and to do the law and the commandment.

5 Also he took away out of all the cities of Judah the high places and the images: and the kingdom was quiet before him.

6 And he built fenced cities in Judah: for the land had rest, and he had no war in those years; because the LORD had given him rest.

7 Therefore he said to Judah, Let us build these cities, and make about them walls, and towers, gates, and bars, while the land is yet before us; because we have sought the LORD our God, we have sought him, and he has given us rest on every side. So they built and prospered.

8 And Asa had an army of men that bare targets and spears, out of Judah three hundred thousand; and out of Benjamin, that bare shields and drew bows, two hundred and fourscore thousand: all these were mighty men of valour.

9 And there came out against them Zerah the Ethiopian with an host of a thousand thousand, and three hundred chariots; and came to Mareshah.

10 Then Asa went out against him, and they set the battle in array in the valley of Zephathah at Mareshah.

11 And Asa cried to the LORD his God, and said, LORD, it is nothing with you to help, whether with many, or with them that have no power: help us, O LORD our God; for we rest on you, and in your name we go against this multitude. O LORD, you are our God; let no man prevail against you.

12 So the LORD smote the Ethiopians before Asa, and before Judah; and the Ethiopians fled.

13 And Asa and the people that were with him pursued them to Gerar: and the Ethiopians were overthrown, that they could not recover themselves; for they were destroyed before the LORD, and before his host; and they carried away very much spoil.

14 And they smote all the cities round about Gerar; for the fear of the LORD came upon them: and they spoiled all the cities; for there was exceeding much spoil in them.

15 They smote also the tents of cattle, and carried away sheep and camels in abundance, and returned to Jerusalem.

CHAPTER 15

AND the Spirit of God came upon Azariah the son of Oded:

2 And he went out to meet Asa, and said to him, Hear me, Asa, and all Judah and Benjamin; The LORD is with you, while you are with him; and if you seek him, he will be found of you; but if you forsake him, he will forsake you.

3 Now for a long season Israel has been without the true God, and without a teaching priest, and without law.

4 But when they in their trouble did turn to the LORD God of Israel, and sought him, he was found of them.

5 And in those times there was no peace to him that went out, nor to him that came in, but great vexations were upon all the inhabitants of the countries.

6 And nation was destroyed of nation, and city of city: for God did vex them with all adversity.

7 Be strong therefore, and let not your hands be weak: for your work shall be rewarded.

8 And when Asa heard these words, and the prophecy of Oded the prophet, he took courage, and put away the abominable idols out of all the land of Judah and Benjamin, and out of the cities which he had taken from mount Ephraim, and renewed the altar of the LORD, that was before the porch of the LORD.

9 And he gathered all Judah and Benjamin, and the strangers with them out of Ephraim and Manasseh, and out of Simeon: for they fell to him out of Israel in abundance, when they saw that the LORD his God was with him.

10 So they gathered themselves together at Jerusalem in the third month, in the fifteenth year of the reign of Asa.

11 And they offered to the LORD the same time, of the spoil which they had brought, seven hundred oxen and seven thousand sheep.

12 And they entered into a covenant to seek the LORD God of their fathers with all their heart and with all their soul;

13 That whosoever would not seek the LORD God of Israel should be put to death, whether small or great, whether man or woman.

14 And they swore to the LORD with a loud voice, and with shouting, and with trumpets, and with cornets.

15 And all Judah rejoiced at the oath: for they had sworn with all their heart, and sought him with their whole desire; and he was found of them: and the LORD gave them rest round about.

16 And also concerning Maachah the mother of Asa the king, he removed her from being queen, because she had made an idol in a grove: and Asa cut down her idol, and stamped it, and burnt it at the brook Kidron.

17 But the high places were not taken away out of Israel: nevertheless the heart of Asa was perfect all his days.

18 And he brought into the house of God the things that his father had dedicated, and that he himself had dedicated, silver, and gold, and vessels.

19 And there was no more war to the five and thirtieth year of the reign of Asa.

CHAPTER 16

IN the six and thirtieth year of the reign of Asa Baasha king of Israel came up against Judah, and built Ramah, to the intent that he might let none go out or come in to Asa king of Judah.

2 Then Asa brought out silver and gold out of the treasures of the house of the LORD and of the king's house, and sent to Benhadad king of Syria, that dwelt at Damascus, saying,

3 There is a league between me and you, as there was between my father and your father: behold, I have sent you silver and gold; go, break your league with Baasha king of Israel, that he may depart from me.

4 And Benhadad hearkened to king Asa, and sent the captains of his armies against the cities of Israel; and they smote Ijon, and Dan, and Abelmaim, and all the store cities of Naphtali.

5 And it came to pass, when Baasha heard it, that he left off building of Ramah, and let his work cease.

15:4 Sadly, tribulation doesn't always turn sinners towards Heaven. Some harden their heart and become bitter at God.

6 Then Asa the king took all Judah; and they carried away the stones of Ramah, and the timber thereof, wherewith Baasha was building; and he built therewith Geba and Mizpah.

7 And at that time Hanani the seer came to Asa king of Judah, and said to him, Because you have relied on the king of Syria, and not relied on the LORD your God, therefore is the host of the king of Syria escaped out of your hand.

8 Were not the Ethiopians and the Lubims a huge host, with very many chariots and horsemen? yet, because you did rely on the LORD, he delivered them into your hand.

9 For the eyes of the LORD run to and fro throughout the whole earth, to show himself strong in the behalf of them whose heart is perfect toward him. Herein you have done foolishly: therefore from henceforth you shall have wars.

10 Then Asa was wroth with the seer, and put him in a prison house; for he was in a rage with him because of this thing. And Asa oppressed some of the people the same time.

11 And, behold, the acts of Asa, first and last, lo, they are written in the book of the kings of Judah and Israel.

12 And Asa in the thirty and ninth year of his reign was diseased in his feet, until his disease was exceeding great: yet in his disease he sought not to the LORD, but to the physicians.

13 And Asa slept with his fathers, and died in the one and fortieth year of his reign.

14 And they buried him in his own sepulchres, which he had made for himself in the city of David, and laid him in the bed which was filled with sweet odours and divers kinds of spices prepared by the apothecaries' art: and they made a very great burning for him.

CHAPTER 17

AND Jehoshaphat his son reigned in his stead, and strengthened himself against Israel.

2 And he placed forces in all the fenced cities of Judah, and set garrisons in the land of Judah, and in the cities of Ephraim, which Asa his father had taken.

3 And the LORD was with Jehoshaphat, because he walked in the first ways of his father David, and did not seek the baals;

4 But sought to the Lord God of his father, and walked in his commandments, and not after the doings of Israel.

5 Therefore the LORD stablished the kingdom in his hand; and all Judah brought to Jehoshaphat presents; and he had riches and honour in abundance.

6 And his heart was lifted up in the ways of the LORD: moreover he took away the high places and groves out of Judah.

7 Also in the third year of his reign he sent to his princes, even to Benhail, and to Obadiah, and to Zechariah, and to Nethaneel, and to Michaiah, to teach in the cities of Judah.

8 And with them he sent Levites, even Shemaiah, and Nethaniah, and Zebadiah, and Asahel, and Shemiramoth, and Jehonathan, and Adonijah, and Tobijah, and Tobadonijah, Levites; and with them Elishama and Jehoram, priests.

9 And they taught in Judah, and had the book of the law of the LORD with them, and went about throughout all the cities of Judah, and taught the people.

10 And the fear of the LORD fell upon all the kingdoms of the lands that were round about Judah, so that they made no war against Jehoshaphat.

11 Also some of the Philistines brought Jehoshaphat presents, and tribute silver;

16:9 The word "perfect" doesn't mean sinless perfection for no one is without sin. It means to be blameless and to have a completely willing heart before God. It means to have a "Here I am, send me!" attitude.

and the Arabians brought him flocks, seven thousand and seven hundred rams, and seven thousand and seven hundred he goats.

12 And Jehoshaphat waxed great exceedingly; and he built in Judah castles, and cities of store.

13 And he had much business in the cities of Judah: and the men of war, mighty men of valour, were in Jerusalem.

14 And these are the numbers of them according to the house of their fathers: Of Judah, the captains of thousands; Adnah the chief, and with him mighty men of valour three hundred thousand.

15 And next to him was Jehohanan the captain, and with him two hundred and fourscore thousand.

16 And next him was Amasiah the son of Zichri, who willingly offered himself to the LORD; and with him two hundred thousand mighty men of valour.

17 And of Benjamin; Eliada a mighty man of valour, and with him armed men with bow and shield two hundred thousand.

18 And next him was Jehozabad, and with him an hundred and fourscore thousand ready prepared for the war.

19 These waited on the king, beside those whom the king put in the fenced cities throughout all Judah.

CHAPTER 18

NOW Jehoshaphat had riches and honour in abundance, and joined affinity with Ahab.

2 And after certain years he went down to Ahab to Samaria. And Ahab killed sheep and oxen for him in abundance, and for the people that he had with him, and persuaded him to go up with him to Ramothgilead.

3 And Ahab king of Israel said to Jehoshaphat king of Judah, Will you go with me to Ramothgilead? And he answered him, I am as you are, and my people as your people; and we will be with you in the war.

4 And Jehoshaphat said to the king of Israel, inquire, I pray you, at the word of the LORD to day.

5 Therefore the king of Israel gathered together of prophets four hundred men, and said to them, Shall we go to Ramothgilead to battle, or shall I forbear? And they said, Go up; for God will deliver it into the king's hand.

6 But Jehoshaphat said, Is there not here a prophet of the LORD besides, that we might enquire of him?

7 And the king of Israel said to Jehoshaphat, There is yet one man, by whom we may inquire of the LORD: but I hate him; for he never prophesied good to me, but always evil: the same is Micaiah the son of Imla. And Jehoshaphat said, Let not the king say so.

8 And the king of Israel called for one of his officers, and said, Fetch quickly Micaiah the son of Imla.

9 And the king of Israel and Jehoshaphat king of Judah sat either of them on his throne, clothed in their robes, and they sat in a void place at the entering in of the gate of Samaria; and all the prophets prophesied before them.

10 And Zedekiah the son of Chenaanah had made him horns of iron, and said, Thus says the LORD, With these you shall push Syria until they be consumed.

11 And all the prophets prophesied so, saying, Go up to Ramothgilead, and prosper: for the LORD shall deliver it into the hand of the king.

12 And the messenger that went to call Micaiah spoke to him, saying, Behold, the words of the prophets declare good to the king with one assent; let your word therefore, I pray you, be like one of their's, and speak good.

18:7 Perhaps if Ahab had lived a more virtuous life, the prophet may have had something good to tell him.

13 And Micaiah said, As the LORD liveth, even what my God says, that will I speak.

14 And when he was come to the king, the king said to him, Micaiah, shall we go to Ramothgilead to battle, or shall I forbear? And he said, Go up, and prosper, and they shall be delivered into your hand.

15 And the king said to him, How many times shall I adjure you that you say nothing but the truth to me in the name of the LORD?

16 Then he said, I did see all Israel scattered upon the mountains, as sheep that have no shepherd: and the LORD said, These have no master; let them return therefore every man to his house in peace.

17 And the king of Israel said to Jehoshaphat, Did I not tell you that he would not prophesy good to me, but evil?

18 Again he said, Therefore hear the word of the LORD; I saw the LORD sitting upon his throne, and all the host of heaven standing on his right hand and on his left.

19 And the LORD said, Who shall entice Ahab king of Israel, that he may go up and fall at Ramothgilead? And one spoke saying after this manner, and another saying after that manner.

20 Then there came out a spirit, and stood before the LORD, and said, I will entice him. And the LORD said to him, Wherewith?

21 And he said, I will go out, and be a lying spirit in the mouth of all his prophets. And the Lord said, You shall entice him, and you shall also prevail: go out, and do even so.

22 Now therefore, behold, the LORD has put a lying spirit in the mouth of these your prophets, and the LORD has spoken evil against you.

23 Then Zedekiah the son of Chenaanah came near, and smote Micaiah upon the cheek, and said, Which way went the Spirit of the LORD from me to speak to you?

24 And Micaiah said, Behold, you shall see on that day when you shall go into an inner chamber to hide yourself.

25 Then the king of Israel said, Take Micaiah, and carry him back to Amon the governor of the city, and to Joash the king's son;

26 And say, Thus says the king, Put this fellow in the prison, and feed him with bread of affliction and with water of affliction, until I return in peace.

27 And Micaiah said, If you certainly return in peace, then has not the LORD spoken by me. And he said, Hearken, all you people.

28 So the king of Israel and Jehoshaphat the king of Judah went up to Ramothgilead.

29 And the king of Israel said to Jehoshaphat, I will disguise myself, and I will go to the battle; but put on your robes. So the king of Israel disguised himself; and they went to the battle.

30 Now the king of Syria had commanded the captains of the chariots that were with him, saying, Fight with no one small or great, save only with the king of Israel.

31 And it came to pass, when the captains of the chariots saw Jehoshaphat, that they said, It is the king of Israel. Therefore they compassed about him to fight: but Jehoshaphat cried out, and the LORD helped him; and God moved them to depart from him.

32 For it came to pass, that, when the captains of the chariots perceived that it

---

18:16 See Matthew 9:36.

18:22 Those who run to this verse to try and accuse God of sin are throwing mud at the heavens; the mud will fall on those who throw it. God is without sin. All of His judgments are righteous and true altogether.

was not the king of Israel, they turned back again from pursuing him.

33 And a certain man drew a bow at a venture, and smote the king of Israel between the joints of the harness: therefore he said to his chariot man, Turn your hand, that you may carry me out of the host; for I am wounded.

34 And the battle increased that day: howbeit the king of Israel stayed himself up in his chariot against the Syrians until the even: and about the time of the sun going down he died.

CHAPTER 19

AND Jehoshaphat the king of Judah returned to his house in peace to Jerusalem.

2 And Jehu the son of Hanani the seer went out to meet him, and said to king Jehoshaphat, Should you help the ungodly, and love them that hate the LORD? therefore is wrath upon you from before the LORD.

3 Nevertheless there are good things found in you, in that you have taken away the groves out of the land, and have prepared your heart to seek God.

4 And Jehoshaphat dwelt at Jerusalem: and he went out again through the people from Beersheba to mount Ephraim, and brought them back to the LORD God of their fathers.

5 And he set judges in the land throughout all the fenced cities of Judah, city by city,

6 And said to the judges, Take heed what you do: for you judge not for man, but for the LORD, who is with you in the judgment.

7 Therefore now let the fear of the LORD be upon you; take heed and do it: for there is no iniquity with the LORD our God, nor respect of persons, nor taking of gifts.

8 Moreover in Jerusalem did Jehoshaphat set of the Levites, and of the priests, and of the chief of the fathers of Israel, for the judgment of the LORD, and for controversies, when they returned to Jerusalem.

9 And he charged them, saying, Thus shall you do in the fear of the LORD, faithfully, and with a perfect heart.

10 And what cause soever shall come to you of your brethren that dwell in your cities, between blood and blood, between law and commandment, statutes and judgments, you shall even warn them that they trespass not against the LORD, and so wrath come upon you, and upon your brethren: this do, and you shall not trespass.

11 And, behold, Amariah the chief priest is over you in all matters of the LORD; and Zebadiah the son of Ishmael, the ruler of the house of Judah, for all the king's matters: also the Levites shall be officers before you. Deal courageously, and the LORD shall be with the good.

CHAPTER 20

IT came to pass after this also, that the children of Moab, and the children of Ammon, and with them other beside the Ammonites, came against Jehoshaphat to battle.

2 Then there came some that told Jehoshaphat, saying, There cometh a great multitude against you from beyond the sea on this side Syria; and, behold, they be in Hazazontamar, which is Engedi.

3 And Jehoshaphat feared, and set himself to seek the LORD, and proclaimed a fast throughout all Judah.

4 And Judah gathered themselves together, to ask help of the LORD: even out of all the cities of Judah they came to seek the LORD.

19:7 The judge we must face on Judgment Day is perfect, holy, and righteous. He is without iniquity. He will not be bribed. Our money, status, fame, etc., will have no relevance. All that will matter is the question of whether we have accepted the righteousness of Jesus Christ. Are we sheltered in Him?

5 And Jehoshaphat stood in the congregation of Judah and Jerusalem, in the house of the LORD, before the new court,

6 And said, O LORD God of our fathers, are not you God in heaven? and do you not rule over all the kingdoms of the heathen? and in your hand is there not power and might, so that none is able to withstand you?

7 Are not you our God, who did drive out the inhabitants of this land before your people Israel, and gave it to the seed of Abraham your friend for ever?

8 And they dwelt therein, and have built you a sanctuary therein for your name, saying,

9 If, when evil cometh upon us, as the sword, judgment, or pestilence, or famine, we stand before this house, and in your presence, (for your name is in this house,) and cry to you in our affliction, then you will hear and help.

10 And now, behold, the children of Ammon and Moab and mount Seir, whom you would not let Israel invade, when they came out of the land of Egypt, but they turned from them, and destroyed them not;

11 Behold, I say, how they reward us, to come to cast us out of your possession, which you have given us to inherit.

12 O our God, will you not judge them? for we have no might against this great company that cometh against us; neither know we what to do: but our eyes are upon you.

13 And all Judah stood before the LORD, with their little ones, their wives, and their children.

14 Then upon Jahaziel the son of Zechariah, the son of Benaiah, the son of Jeiel, the son of Mattaniah, a Levite of the sons of Asaph, came the Spirit of the LORD in the midst of the congregation;

15 And he said, Hearken, all you of Judah, and you inhabitants of Jerusalem, and you king Jehoshaphat, Thus says the LORD to you, Be not afraid nor dismayed by reason of this great multitude; for the battle is not yours, but God's.

16 Tomorrow go down against them: behold, they come up by the cliff of Ziz; and you shall find them at the end of the brook, before the wilderness of Jeruel.

17 You shall not need to fight in this battle: set yourselves, stand still, and see the salvation of the LORD with you, O Judah and Jerusalem: fear not, nor be dismayed; tomorrow go out against them: for the LORD will be with you.

18 And Jehoshaphat bowed his head with his face to the ground: and all Judah and the inhabitants of Jerusalem fell before the LORD, worshipping the LORD.

19 And the Levites, of the children of the Kohathites, and of the children of the Korhites, stood up to praise the LORD God of Israel with a loud voice on high.

20 And they rose early in the morning, and went forth into the wilderness of Tekoa: and as they went forth, Jehoshaphat stood and said, Hear me, O Judah, and you inhabitants of Jerusalem; Believe in the LORD your God, so shall you be established; believe his prophets, so shall you prosper.

21 And when he had consulted with the people, he appointed singers to the LORD, and that should praise the beauty of holiness, as they went out before the army, and to say, Praise the LORD; for his mercy endures for ever.

22 And when they began to sing and to praise, the LORD set ambushments against the children of Ammon, Moab, and mount Seir, which were come against Judah; and they were smitten.

23 For the children of Ammon and Moab stood up against the inhabitants of mount Seir, utterly to slay and destroy them: and when they had made an end of the inhabitants of Seir, every one helped to destroy another.

24 And when Judah came toward the watch tower in the wilderness, they

looked to the multitude, and, behold, they were dead bodies fallen to the earth, and none escaped.

25 And when Jehoshaphat and his people came to take away the spoil of them, they found among them in abundance both riches with the dead bodies, and precious jewels, which they stripped off for themselves, more than they could carry away: and they were three days in gathering of the spoil, it was so much.

26 And on the fourth day they assembled themselves in the valley of Berachah; for there they blessed the LORD: therefore the name of the same place was called, The valley of Berachah, to this day.

27 Then they returned, every man of Judah and Jerusalem, and Jehoshaphat in the forefront of them, to go again to Jerusalem with joy; for the LORD had made them to rejoice over their enemies.

28 And they came to Jerusalem with psalteries and harps and trumpets to the house of the LORD.

29 And the fear of God was on all the kingdoms of those countries, when they had heard that the LORD fought against the enemies of Israel.

30 So the realm of Jehoshaphat was quiet: for his God gave him rest round about.

31 And Jehoshaphat reigned over Judah: he was thirty and five years old when he began to reign, and he reigned twenty and five years in Jerusalem. And his mother's name was Azubah the daughter of Shilhi.

32 And he walked in the way of Asa his father, and departed not from it, doing that which was right in the sight of the LORD.

33 Howbeit the high places were not taken away: for as yet the people had not prepared their hearts to the God of their fathers.

34 Now the rest of the acts of Jehoshaphat, first and last, behold, they are written in the book of Jehu the son of Hanani, who is mentioned in the book of the kings of Israel.

35 And after this did Jehoshaphat king of Judah join himself with Ahaziah king of Israel, who did very wickedly:

36 And he joined himself with him to make ships to go to Tarshish: and they made the ships in Eziongaber.

37 Then Eliezer the son of Dodavah of Mareshah prophesied against Jehoshaphat, saying, Because you have joined yourself with Ahaziah, the LORD has broken your works. And the ships were broken, that they were not able to go to Tarshish.

CHAPTER 21

NOW Jehoshaphat slept with his fathers, and was buried with his fathers in the city of David. And Jehoram his son reigned in his stead.

2 And he had brethren the sons of Jehoshaphat, Azariah, and Jehiel, and Zechariah, and Azariah, and Michael, and Shephatiah: all these were the sons of Jehoshaphat king of Israel.

3 And their father gave them great gifts of silver, and of gold, and of precious things, with fenced cities in Judah: but the kingdom gave he to Jehoram; because he was the firstborn.

4 Now when Jehoram was risen up to the kingdom of his father, he strengthened himself, and slew all his brethren with the sword, and divers also of the princes of Israel.

5 Jehoram was thirty and two years old when he began to reign, and he reigned eight years in Jerusalem.

6 And he walked in the way of the kings of Israel, like as did the house of Ahab: for he had the daughter of Ahab to wife: and he did that which was evil in the eyes of the LORD.

7 Howbeit the LORD would not destroy the house of David, because of the covenant that he had made with David, and as he promised to give a light to him and to his sons for ever.

8 In his days the Edomites revolted from under the dominion of Judah, and made themselves a king.

9 Then Jehoram went forth with his princes, and all his chariots with him: and he rose up by night, and smote the Edomites which compassed him in, and the captains of the chariots.

10 So the Edomites revolted from under the hand of Judah to this day. The same time also did Libnah revolt from under his hand; because he had forsaken the LORD God of his fathers.

11 Moreover he made high places in the mountains of Judah and caused the inhabitants of Jerusalem to commit fornication, and compelled Judah thereto.

12 And there came a writing to him from Elijah the prophet, saying, Thus says the LORD God of David your father, Because you have not walked in the ways of Jehoshaphat your father, nor in the ways of Asa king of Judah,

13 But have walked in the way of the kings of Israel, and have made Judah and the inhabitants of Jerusalem to go a whoring, like to the whoredoms of the house of Ahab, and also have slain your brethren of your father's house, which were better than yourself:

14 Behold, with a great plague will the LORD smite your people, and your children, and your wives, and all your goods:

15 And you shall have great sickness by disease of your bowels, until your bowels fall out by reason of the sickness day by day.

16 Moreover the LORD stirred up against Jehoram the spirit of the Philistines, and of the Arabians, that were near the Ethiopians:

17 And they came up into Judah, and brake into it, and carried away all the substance that was found in the king's house, and his sons also, and his wives; so that there was never a son left him, save Jehoahaz, the youngest of his sons.

18 And after all this the LORD smote him in his bowels with an incurable disease.

19 And it came to pass, that in process of time, after the end of two years, his bowels fell out by reason of his sickness: so he died of sore diseases. And his people made no burning for him, like the burning of his fathers.

20 Thirty and two years old was he when he began to reign, and he reigned in Jerusalem eight years, and departed without being desired. Howbeit they buried him in the city of David, but not in the sepulchres of the kings.

CHAPTER 22

AND the inhabitants of Jerusalem made Ahaziah his youngest son king in his stead: for the band of men that came with the Arabians to the camp had slain all the eldest. So Ahaziah the son of Jehoram king of Judah reigned.

2 Forty and two years old was Ahaziah when he began to reign, and he reigned one year in Jerusalem. His mother's name also was Athaliah the daughter of Omri.

3 He also walked in the ways of the house of Ahab: for his mother was his counselor to do wickedly.

4 Therefore he did evil in the sight of the LORD like the house of Ahab: for they were his counselors after the death of his father to his destruction.

5 He walked also after their counsel, and went with Jehoram the son of Ahab king of Israel to war against Hazael king of Syria at Ramothgilead: and the Syrians smote Joram.

6 And he returned to be healed in Jezreel because of the wounds which were given him at Ramah, when he fought with Hazael king of Syria. And Azariah the son of Jehoram king of Judah went down to see Jehoram the son of Ahab at Jezreel, because he was sick.

7 And the destruction of Ahaziah was of God by coming to Joram: for when he was come, he went out with Jehoram against Jehu the son of Nimshi, whom

the LORD had anointed to cut off the house of Ahab.

8 And it came to pass, that, when Jehu was executing judgment upon the house of Ahab, and found the princes of Judah, and the sons of the brethren of Ahaziah, that ministered to Ahaziah, he slew them.

9 And he sought Ahaziah: and they caught him, (for he was hid in Samaria,) and brought him to Jehu: and when they had slain him, they buried him: Because, said they, he is the son of Jehoshaphat, who sought the LORD with all his heart. So the house of Ahaziah had no power to keep still the kingdom.

10 But when Athaliah the mother of Ahaziah saw that her son was dead, she arose and destroyed all the seed royal of the house of Judah.

11 But Jehoshabeath, the daughter of the king, took Joash the son of Ahaziah, and stole him from among the king's sons that were slain, and put him and his nurse in a bedchamber. So Jehoshabeath, the daughter of king Jehoram, the wife of Jehoiada the priest, (for she was the sister of Ahaziah,) hid him from Athaliah, so that she slew him not.

12 And he was with them hid in the house of God six years: and Athaliah reigned over the land.

CHAPTER 23

AND in the seventh year Jehoiada strengthened himself, and took the captains of hundreds, Azariah the son of Jeroham, and Ishmael the son of Jehohanan, and Azariah the son of Obed, and Maaseiah the son of Adaiah, and Elishaphat the son of Zichri, into covenant with him.

2 And they went about in Judah, and gathered the Levites out of all the cities of Judah, and the chief of the fathers of Israel, and they came to Jerusalem.

3 And all the congregation made a covenant with the king in the house of God. And he said to them, Behold, the king's son shall reign, as the LORD has said of the sons of David.

4 This is the thing that you shall do; A third part of you entering on the sabbath, of the priests and of the Levites, shall be porters of the doors;

5 And a third part shall be at the king's house; and a third part at the gate of the foundation: and all the people shall be in the courts of the house of the LORD.

6 But let none come into the house of the LORD, save the priests, and they that minister of the Levites; they shall go in, for they are holy: but all the people shall keep the watch of the LORD.

7 And the Levites shall compass the king round about, every man with his weapons in his hand; and whosoever else cometh into the house, he shall be put to death: but you are to be with the king when he comes in, and when he goes out.

8 So the Levites and all Judah did according to all things that Jehoiada the priest had commanded, and took every man his men that were to come in on the sabbath, with them that were to go out on the sabbath: for Jehoiada the priest dismissed not the courses.

9 Moreover Jehoiada the priest delivered to the captains of hundreds spears, and bucklers, and shields, that had been king David's, which were in the house of God.

10 And he set all the people, every man having his weapon in his hand, from the right side of the temple to the left side of the temple, along by the altar and the temple, by the king round about.

11 Then they brought out the king's son, and put upon him the crown, and gave him the testimony, and made him king. And Jehoiada and his sons anointed him, and said, God save the king.

12 Now when Athaliah heard the noise of the people running and praising the king, she came to the people into the house of the LORD:

13 And she looked, and, behold, the king stood at his pillar at the entering in,

and the princes and the trumpets by the king: and all the people of the land rejoiced, and sounded with trumpets, also the singers with instruments of music, and such as taught to sing praise. Then Athaliah rent her clothes, and said, Treason, Treason.

14 Then Jehoiada the priest brought out the captains of hundreds that were set over the host, and said to them, Have her forth of the ranges: and whoso follows her, let him be slain with the sword. For the priest said, Slay her not in the house of the LORD.

15 So they laid hands on her; and when she was come to the entering of the horse gate by the king's house, they slew her there.

16 And Jehoiada made a covenant between him, and between all the people, and between the king, that they should be the LORD's people.

17 Then all the people went to the house of Baal, and brake it down, and brake his altars and his images in pieces, and slew Mattan the priest of Baal before the altars.

18 Also Jehoiada appointed the offices of the house of the LORD by the hand of the priests the Levites, whom David had distributed in the house of the LORD, to offer the burnt offerings of the LORD, as it is written in the law of Moses, with rejoicing and with singing, as it was ordained by David.

19 And he set the porters at the gates of the house of the LORD, that none which was unclean in any thing should enter in.

20 And he took the captains of hundreds, and the nobles, and the governors of the people, and all the people of the land, and brought down the king from the house of the LORD: and they came through the high gate into the king's house, and set the king upon the throne of the kingdom.

21 And all the people of the land rejoiced: and the city was quiet, after that they had slain Athaliah with the sword.

CHAPTER 24

JOASH was seven years old when he began to reign, and he reigned forty years in Jerusalem. His mother's name also was Zibiah of Beersheba.

2 And Joash did that which was right in the sight of the LORD all the days of Jehoiada the priest.

3 And Jehoiada took for him two wives; and he begat sons and daughters.

4 And it came to pass after this, that Joash was minded to repair the house of the LORD.

5 And he gathered together the priests and the Levites, and said to them, Go out to the cities of Judah, and gather of all Israel money to repair the house of your God from year to year, and see that you hasten the matter. Howbeit the Levites hastened it not.

6 And the king called for Jehoiada the chief, and said to him, Why have you not required of the Levites to bring in out of Judah and out of Jerusalem the collection, according to the commandment of Moses the servant of the LORD, and of the congregation of Israel, for the tabernacle of witness?

7 For the sons of Athaliah, that wicked woman, had broken up the house of God; and also all the dedicated things of the house of the LORD did they bestow upon Baalim.

8 And at the king's commandment they made a chest, and set it without at the gate of the house of the LORD.

9 And they made a proclamation through Judah and Jerusalem, to bring in to the LORD the collection that Moses the servant of God laid upon Israel in the wilderness.

10 And all the princes and all the people rejoiced, and brought in, and cast into the chest, until they had made an end.

11 Now it came to pass, that at what time the chest was brought to the king's office by the hand of the Levites, and when they saw that there was much money, the king's scribe and the high

priest's officer came and emptied the chest, and took it, and carried it to his place again. Thus they did day by day, and gathered money in abundance.

12 And the king and Jehoiada gave it to such as did the work of the service of the house of the LORD, and hired masons and carpenters to repair the house of the LORD, and also such as worked iron and brass to mend the house of the LORD.

13 So the workmen laboured, and the work was perfected by them, and they set the house of God in his state, and strengthened it.

14 And when they had finished it, they brought the rest of the money before the king and Jehoiada, whereof were made vessels for the house of the LORD, even vessels to minister, and to offer withal, and spoons, and vessels of gold and silver. And they offered burnt offerings in the house of the LORD continually all the days of Jehoiada.

15 But Jehoiada waxed old, and was full of days when he died; an hundred and thirty years old was he when he died.

16 And they buried him in the city of David among the kings, because he had done good in Israel, both toward God, and toward his house.

17 Now after the death of Jehoiada came the princes of Judah, and made obeisance to the king. Then the king hearkened to them.

18 And they left the house of the LORD God of their fathers, and served groves and idols: and wrath came upon Judah and Jerusalem for this their trespass.

19 Yet he sent prophets to them, to bring them again to the LORD; and they testified against them: but they would not give ear.

20 And the Spirit of God came upon Zechariah the son of Jehoiada the priest, which stood above the people, and said to them, Thus says God, Why do you transgress the commandments of the LORD, that you cannot prosper? because you have forsaken the LORD, he has also forsaken you.

21 And they conspired against him, and stoned him with stones at the commandment of the king in the court of the house of the LORD.

22 Thus Joash the king remembered not the kindness which Jehoiada his father had done to him, but slew his son. And when he died, he said, The LORD look upon it, and require it.

23 And it came to pass at the end of the year, that the host of Syria came up against him: and they came to Judah and Jerusalem, and destroyed all the princes of the people from among the people, and sent all the spoil of them to the king of Damascus.

24 For the army of the Syrians came with a small company of men, and the LORD delivered a very great host into their hand, because they had forsaken the LORD God of their fathers. So they executed judgment against Joash.

25 And when they were departed from him, (for they left him in great diseases,) his own servants conspired against him for the blood of the sons of Jehoiada the priest, and slew him on his bed, and he died: and they buried him in the city of David, but they buried him not in the sepulchres of the kings.

26 And these are they that conspired against him; Zabad the son of Shimeath an Ammonitess, and Jehozabad the son of Shimrith a Moabitess.

27 Now concerning his sons, and the greatness of the burdens laid upon him, and the repairing of the house of God, behold, they are written in the story of the book of the kings. And Amaziah his son reigned in his stead.

CHAPTER 25

AMAZIAH was twenty and five years old when he began to reign, and he reigned twenty and nine years in Jerusalem. And his mother's name was Jehoaddan of Jerusalem.

2 And he did that which was right in the sight of the LORD, but not with a perfect heart.

3 Now it came to pass, when the kingdom was established to him, that he slew his servants that had killed the king his father.

4 But he slew not their children, but did as it is written in the law in the book of Moses, where the LORD commanded, saying, The fathers shall not die for the children, neither shall the children die for the fathers, but every man shall die for his own sin.

5 Moreover Amaziah gathered Judah together, and made them captains over thousands, and captains over hundreds, according to the houses of their fathers, throughout all Judah and Benjamin: and he numbered them from twenty years old and above, and found them three hundred thousand choice men, able to go forth to war, that could handle spear and shield.

6 He hired also an hundred thousand mighty men of valour out of Israel for an hundred talents of silver.

7 But there came a man of God to him, saying, O king, let not the army of Israel go with you; for the LORD is not with Israel, to wit, with all the children of Ephraim.

8 But if you will go, do it; be strong for the battle: God shall make you fall before the enemy: for God has power to help, and to cast down.

9 And Amaziah said to the man of God, But what shall we do for the hundred talents which I have given to the army of Israel? And the man of God answered, The LORD is able to give you much more than this.

10 Then Amaziah separated them, to wit, the army that was come to him out of Ephraim, to go home again: therefore their anger was greatly kindled against Judah, and they returned home in great anger.

11 And Amaziah strengthened himself, and led forth his people, and went to the valley of salt, and smote of the children of Seir ten thousand.

12 And other ten thousand left alive did the children of Judah carry away captive, and brought them to the top of the rock, and cast them down from the top of the rock, that they all were broken in pieces.

13 But the soldiers of the army which Amaziah sent back, that they should not go with him to battle, fell upon the cities of Judah, from Samaria even to Bethhoron, and smote three thousand of them, and took much spoil.

14 Now it came to pass, after that Amaziah was come from the slaughter of the Edomites, that he brought the gods of the children of Seir, and set them up to be his gods, and bowed down himself before them, and burned incense to them.

15 Therefore the anger of the LORD was kindled against Amaziah, and he sent to him a prophet, which said to him, Why have you sought after the gods of the people, which could not deliver their own people out of your hand?

16 And it came to pass, as he talked with him, that the king said to him, Are you made of the king's counsel? forbear; why should you be smitten? Then the prophet forbare, and said, I know that God has determined to destroy you, because you have done this, and have not hearkened to my counsel.

17 Then Amaziah king of Judah took advice, and sent to Joash, the son of Jehoahaz, the son of Jehu, king of Israel, saying, Come, let us see one another in the face.

18 And Joash king of Israel sent to Amaziah king of Judah, saying, The thistle that was in Lebanon sent to the cedar that was in Lebanon, saying, Give your daughter to my son to wife: and there passed by a wild beast that was in Lebanon, and trode down the thistle.

19 You say, Lo, you have smitten the Edomites; and your heart lifts you up to boast: abide now at home; why should you meddle to your hurt, that you

should fall, even you, and Judah with you?

20 But Amaziah would not hear; for it came of God, that he might deliver them into the hand of their enemies, because they sought after the gods of Edom.

21 So Joash the king of Israel went up; and they saw one another in the face, both he and Amaziah king of Judah, at Bethshemesh, which belongeth to Judah.

22 And Judah was put to the worse before Israel, and they fled every man to his tent.

23 And Joash the king of Israel took Amaziah king of Judah, the son of Joash, the son of Jehoahaz, at Bethshemesh, and brought him to Jerusalem, and brake down the wall of Jerusalem from the gate of Ephraim to the corner gate, four hundred cubits.

24 And he took all the gold and the silver, and all the vessels that were found in the house of God with Obededom, and the treasures of the king's house, the hostages also, and returned to Samaria.

25 And Amaziah the son of Joash king of Judah lived after the death of Joash son of Jehoahaz king of Israel fifteen years.

26 Now the rest of the acts of Amaziah, first and last, behold, are they not written in the book of the kings of Judah and Israel?

27 Now after the time that Amaziah did turn away from following the LORD they made a conspiracy against him in Jerusalem; and he fled to Lachish: but they sent to Lachish after him, and slew him there.

28 And they brought him upon horses, and buried him with his fathers in the city of Judah.

CHAPTER 26

THEN all the people of Judah took Uzziah, who was sixteen years old, and made him king in the room of his father Amaziah.

2 He built Eloth, and restored it to Judah, after that the king slept with his fathers.

3 Sixteen years old was Uzziah when he began to reign, and he reigned fifty and two years in Jerusalem. His mother's name also was Jecoliah of Jerusalem.

4 And he did that which was right in the sight of the LORD, according to all that his father Amaziah did.

5 And he sought God in the days of Zechariah, who had understanding in the visions of God: and as long as he sought the LORD, God made him to prosper.

6 And he went forth and warred against the Philistines, and brake down the wall of Gath, and the wall of Jabneh, and the wall of Ashdod, and built cities about Ashdod, and among the Philistines.

7 And God helped him against the Philistines, and against the Arabians that dwelt in Gurbaal, and the Mehunims.

8 And the Ammonites gave gifts to Uzziah: and his name spread abroad even to the entering in of Egypt; for he strengthened himself exceedingly.

9 Moreover Uzziah built towers in Jerusalem at the corner gate, and at the valley gate, and at the turning of the wall, and fortified them.

10 Also he built towers in the desert, and dug many wells: for he had much cattle, both in the low country, and in the plains: husbandmen also, and vine dressers in the mountains, and in Carmel: for he loved husbandry.

11 Moreover Uzziah had an host of fighting men, that went out to war by bands, according to the number of their account by the hand of Jeiel the scribe and Maaseiah the ruler, under the hand of Hananiah, one of the king's captains.

12 The whole number of the chief of the fathers of the mighty men of valour were two thousand and six hundred.

13 And under their hand was an army, three hundred thousand and seven thousand and five hundred, that made war

with mighty power, to help the king against the enemy.

14 And Uzziah prepared for them throughout all the host shields, and spears, and helmets, and habergeons, and bows, and slings to cast stones.

15 And he made in Jerusalem engines, invented by cunning men, to be on the towers and upon the bulwarks, to shoot arrows and great stones withal. And his name spread far abroad; for he was marvellously helped, till he was strong.

16 But when he was strong, his heart was lifted up to his destruction: for he transgressed against the LORD his God, and went into the temple of the LORD to burn incense upon the altar of incense.

17 And Azariah the priest went in after him, and with him fourscore priests of the LORD, that were valiant men:

18 And they withstood Uzziah the king, and said to him, It appertains not to you, Uzziah, to burn incense to the LORD, but to the priests the sons of Aaron, that are consecrated to burn incense: go out of the sanctuary; for you have trespassed; neither shall it be for your honour from the LORD God.

19 Then Uzziah was wroth, and had a censer in his hand to burn incense: and while he was wroth with the priests, the leprosy even rose up in his forehead before the priests in the house of the LORD, from beside the incense altar.

20 And Azariah the chief priest, and all the priests, looked upon him, and, behold, he was leprous in his forehead, and they thrust him out from thence; yea, himself hasted also to go out, because the LORD had smitten him.

21 And Uzziah the king was a leper to the day of his death, and dwelt in a several house, being a leper; for he was cut off from the house of the LORD: and Jotham his son was over the king's house, judging the people of the land.

22 Now the rest of the acts of Uzziah, first and last, did Isaiah the prophet, the son of Amoz, write.

23 So Uzziah slept with his fathers, and they buried him with his fathers in the field of the burial which belonged to the kings; for they said, He is a leper: and Jotham his son reigned in his stead.

CHAPTER 27

JOTHAM was twenty and five years old when he began to reign, and he reigned sixteen years in Jerusalem. His mother's name also was Jerushah, the daughter of Zadok.

2 And he did that which was right in the sight of the LORD, according to all that his father Uzziah did: howbeit he entered not into the temple of the LORD. And the people did yet corruptly.

3 He built the high gate of the house of the LORD, and on the wall of Ophel he built much.

4 Moreover he built cities in the mountains of Judah, and in the forests he built castles and towers.

5 He fought also with the king of the Ammonites, and prevailed against them. And the children of Ammon gave him the same year an hundred talents of silver, and ten thousand measures of wheat, and ten thousand of barley. So much did the children of Ammon pay to him, both the second year, and the third.

6 So Jotham became mighty, because he prepared his ways before the LORD his God.

7 Now the rest of the acts of Jotham, and all his wars, and his ways, lo, they are written in the book of the kings of Israel and Judah.

8 He was five and twenty years old when he began to reign, and reigned sixteen years in Jerusalem.

9 And Jotham slept with his fathers, and they buried him in the city of David: and Ahaz his son reigned in his stead.

CHAPTER 28

AHAZ was twenty years old when he began to reign, and he reigned sixteen years in Jerusalem: but he did not that which was right in the sight of the LORD, like David his father:

2 For he walked in the ways of the kings of Israel, and made also molten images for Baalim.

3 Moreover he burnt incense in the valley of the son of Hinnom, and burnt his children in the fire, after the abominations of the heathen whom the LORD had cast out before the children of Israel.

4 He sacrificed also and burnt incense in the high places, and on the hills, and under every green tree.

5 Therefore the LORD his God delivered him into the hand of the king of Syria; and they smote him, and carried away a great multitude of them captives, and brought them to Damascus. And he was also delivered into the hand of the king of Israel, who smote him with a great slaughter.

6 For Pekah the son of Remaliah slew in Judah an hundred and twenty thousand in one day, which were all valiant men; because they had forsaken the LORD God of their fathers.

7 And Zichri, a mighty man of Ephraim, slew Maaseiah the king's son, and Azrikam the governor of the house, and Elkanah that was next to the king.

8 And the children of Israel carried away captive of their brethren two hundred thousand, women, sons, and daughters, and took also away much spoil from them, and brought the spoil to Samaria.

9 But a prophet of the LORD was there, whose name was Oded: and he went out before the host that came to Samaria, and said to them, Behold, because the LORD God of your fathers was wroth with Judah, he has delivered them into your hand, and you have slain them in a rage that reaches up to heaven.

10 And now you purpose to keep under the children of Judah and Jerusalem for bondmen and bondwomen to you: but are there not with you, even with you, sins against the LORD your God?

11 Now hear me therefore, and deliver the captives again, which you have taken captive of your brethren: for the fierce wrath of the LORD is upon you.

12 Then certain of the heads of the children of Ephraim, Azariah the son of Johanan, Berechiah the son of Meshillemoth, and Jehizkiah the son of Shallum, and Amasa the son of Hadlai, stood up against them that came from the war,

13 And said to them, You shall not bring in the captives here: for whereas we have offended against the LORD already, you intend to add more to our sins and to our trespass: for our trespass is great, and there is fierce wrath against Israel.

14 So the armed men left the captives and the spoil before the princes and all the congregation.

15 And the men which were expressed by name rose up, and took the captives, and with the spoil clothed all that were naked among them, and arrayed them, and shod them, and gave them to eat and to drink, and anointed them, and carried all the feeble of them upon asses, and brought them to Jericho, the city of palm trees, to their brethren: then they returned to Samaria.

16 At that time did king Ahaz send to the kings of Assyria to help him.

17 For again the Edomites had come and smitten Judah, and carried away captives.

18 The Philistines also had invaded the cities of the low country, and of the south of Judah, and had taken Bethshemesh, and Ajalon, and Gederoth, and Shocho with the villages thereof, and Timnah with the villages thereof, Gimzo also and the villages thereof: and they dwelt there.

19 For the LORD brought Judah low because of Ahaz king of Israel; for he

made Judah naked, and transgressed sore against the LORD.

20 And Tilgathpilneser king of Assyria came to him, and distressed him, but strengthened him not.

21 For Ahaz took away a portion out of the house of the LORD, and out of the house of the king, and of the princes, and gave it to the king of Assyria: but he helped him not.

22 And in the time of his distress did he trespass yet more against the LORD: this is that king Ahaz.

23 For he sacrificed to the gods of Damascus, which smote him: and he said, Because the gods of the kings of Syria help them, therefore will I sacrifice to them, that they may help me. But they were the ruin of him, and of all Israel.

24 And Ahaz gathered together the vessels of the house of God, and cut in pieces the vessels of the house of God, and shut up the doors of the house of the LORD, and he made him altars in every corner of Jerusalem.

25 And in every several city of Judah he made high places to burn incense to other gods, and provoked to anger the LORD God of his fathers.

26 Now the rest of his acts and of all his ways, first and last, behold, they are written in the book of the kings of Judah and Israel.

27 And Ahaz slept with his fathers, and they buried him in the city, even in Jerusalem: but they brought him not into the sepulchres of the kings of Israel: and Hezekiah his son reigned in his stead.

CHAPTER 29

HEZEKIAH began to reign when he was five and twenty years old, and he reigned nine and twenty years in Jerusalem. And his mother's name was Abijah, the daughter of Zechariah.

2 And he did that which was right in the sight of the LORD, according to all that David his father had done.

3 He in the first year of his reign, in the first month, opened the doors of the house of the LORD, and repaired them.

4 And he brought in the priests and the Levites, and gathered them together into the east street,

5 And said to them, Hear me, you Levites, sanctify now yourselves, and sanctify the house of the LORD God of your fathers, and carry forth the filthiness out of the holy place.

6 For our fathers have trespassed, and done that which was evil in the eyes of the LORD our God, and have forsaken him, and have turned away their faces from the habitation of the LORD, and turned their backs.

7 Also they have shut up the doors of the porch, and put out the lamps, and have not burned incense nor offered burnt offerings in the holy place to the God of Israel.

8 Therefore the wrath of the LORD was upon Judah and Jerusalem, and he has delivered them to trouble, to astonishment, and to hissing, as you see with your eyes.

9 For, lo, our fathers have fallen by the sword, and our sons and our daughters and our wives are in captivity for this.

10 Now it is in mine heart to make a covenant with the LORD God of Israel, that his fierce wrath may turn away from us.

11 My sons, be not now negligent: for the LORD has chosen you to stand before him, to serve him, and that you should minister to him, and burn incense.

12 Then the Levites arose, Mahath the son of Amasai, and Joel the son of Azariah, of the sons of the Kohathites: and of the sons of Merari, Kish the son of Abdi, and Azariah the son of Jehalelel: and of the Gershonites; Joah the son of Zimmah, and Eden the son of Joah:

13 And of the sons of Elizaphan; Shimri, and Jeiel: and of the sons of Asaph; Zechariah, and Mattaniah:

14 And of the sons of Heman; Jehiel, and Shimei: and of the sons of Jeduthun; Shemaiah, and Uzziel.

15 And they gathered their brethren, and sanctified themselves, and came, according to the commandment of the king, by the words of the LORD, to cleanse the house of the LORD.

16 And the priests went into the inner part of the house of the LORD, to cleanse it, and brought out all the uncleanness that they found in the temple of the LORD into the court of the house of the LORD. And the Levites took it, to carry it out abroad into the brook Kidron.

17 Now they began on the first day of the first month to sanctify, and on the eighth day of the month came they to the porch of the LORD: so they sanctified the house of the LORD in eight days; and in the sixteenth day of the first month they made an end.

18 Then they went in to Hezekiah the king, and said, We have cleansed all the house of the LORD, and the altar of burnt offering, with all the vessels thereof, and the shewbread table, with all the vessels thereof.

19 Moreover all the vessels, which king Ahaz in his reign did cast away in his transgression, have we prepared and sanctified, and, behold, they are before the altar of the LORD.

20 Then Hezekiah the king rose early, and gathered the rulers of the city, and went up to the house of the LORD.

21 And they brought seven bullocks, and seven rams, and seven lambs, and seven he goats, for a sin offering for the kingdom, and for the sanctuary, and for Judah. And he commanded the priests the sons of Aaron to offer them on the altar of the LORD.

22 So they killed the bullocks, and the priests received the blood, and sprinkled it on the altar: likewise, when they had killed the rams, they sprinkled the blood upon the altar: they killed also the lambs, and they sprinkled the blood upon the altar.

23 And they brought forth the he goats for the sin offering before the king and the congregation; and they laid their hands upon them:

24 And the priests killed them, and they made reconciliation with their blood upon the altar, to make an atonement for all Israel: for the king commanded that the burnt offering and the sin offering should be made for all Israel.

25 And he set the Levites in the house of the LORD with cymbals, with psalteries, and with harps, according to the commandment of David, and of Gad the king's seer, and Nathan the prophet: for so was the commandment of the LORD by his prophets.

26 And the Levites stood with the instruments of David, and the priests with the trumpets.

27 And Hezekiah commanded to offer the burnt offering upon the altar. And when the burnt offering began, the song of the LORD began also with the trumpets, and with the instruments ordained by David king of Israel.

28 And all the congregation worshipped, and the singers sang, and the trumpeters sounded: and all this continued until the burnt offering was finished.

29 And when they had made an end of offering, the king and all that were present with him bowed themselves, and worshipped.

30 Moreover Hezekiah the king and the princes commanded the Levites to sing praise to the LORD with the words of David, and of Asaph the seer. And they sang praises with gladness, and they bowed their heads and worshipped.

31 Then Hezekiah answered and said, Now you have consecrated yourselves to the LORD, come near and bring sacrifices and thank offerings into the house of the LORD. And the congregation brought in sacrifices and thank offerings; and as many as were of a free heart burnt offerings.

> God will sometimes bend
> the ceremonial laws
> because of circumstances.
> However, His moral Law,
> He will not compromise.
> He is the same
> yesterday, today, and forever.
> God will judge humanity
> with His law, written in stone
> and written upon every man's heart
> **JAY FOWLER**
> AMERICAN BIBLE SCHOLAR
> BORN 1977

32 And the number of the burnt offerings, which the congregation brought, was threescore and ten bullocks, an hundred rams, and two hundred lambs: all these were for a burnt offering to the LORD.

33 And the consecrated things were six hundred oxen and three thousand sheep.

34 But the priests were too few, so that they could not flay all the burnt offerings: therefore their brethren the Levites did help them, till the work was ended, and until the other priests had sanctified themselves: for the Levites were more upright in heart to sanctify themselves than the priests.

35 And also the burnt offerings were in abundance, with the fat of the peace offerings, and the drink offerings for every burnt offering. So the service of the house of the LORD was set in order.

36 And Hezekiah rejoiced, and all the people, that God had prepared the people: for the thing was done suddenly.

CHAPTER 30

AND Hezekiah sent to all Israel and Judah, and wrote letters also to Ephraim and Manasseh, that they should come to the house of the LORD at Jerusalem, to keep the passover to the LORD God of Israel.

2 For the king had taken counsel, and his princes, and all the congregation in Jerusalem, to keep the passover in the second month.

3 For they could not keep it at that time, because the priests had not sanctified themselves sufficiently, neither had the people gathered themselves together to Jerusalem.

4 And the thing pleased the king and all the congregation.

5 So they established a decree to make proclamation throughout all Israel, from Beersheba even to Dan, that they should come to keep the passover to the LORD God of Israel at Jerusalem: for they had not done it of a long time in such sort as it was written.

6 So the posts went with the letters from the king and his princes throughout all Israel and Judah, and according to the commandment of the king, saying, You children of Israel, turn again to the LORD God of Abraham, Isaac, and Israel, and he will return to the remnant of you, that are escaped out of the hand of the kings of Assyria.

7 And do not be like your fathers, and like your brethren, which trespassed against the LORD God of their fathers, who therefore gave them up to desolation, as you see.

8 Now do not be stiffnecked, as your fathers were, but yield yourselves to the LORD, and enter into his sanctuary, which he has sanctified for ever: and serve the LORD your God, that the fierceness of his wrath may turn away from you.

9 For if you turn again to the LORD, your brethren and your children shall find compassion before them that lead them captive, so that they shall come again into this land: for the LORD your God is gracious and merciful, and will not turn away his face from you, if you return to him.

10 So the posts passed from city to city through the country of Ephraim and Manasseh even to Zebulun: but they laughed them to scorn, and mocked them.

11 Nevertheless divers of Asher and Manasseh and of Zebulun humbled themselves, and came to Jerusalem.

12 Also in Judah the hand of God was to give them one heart to do the commandment of the king and of the princes, by the word of the LORD.

13 And there assembled at Jerusalem much people to keep the feast of unleavened bread in the second month, a very great congregation.

14 And they arose and took away the altars that were in Jerusalem, and all the altars for incense took they away, and cast them into the brook Kidron.

15 Then they killed the passover on the fourteenth day of the second month: and the priests and the Levites were ashamed, and sanctified themselves, and brought in the burnt offerings into the house of the LORD.

16 And they stood in their place after their manner, according to the law of Moses the man of God: the priests sprinkled the blood, which they received of the hand of the Levites.

17 For there were many in the congregation that were not sanctified: therefore the Levites had the charge of the killing of the passovers for every one that was not clean, to sanctify them to the LORD.

18 For a multitude of the people, even many of Ephraim, and Manasseh, Issachar, and Zebulun, had not cleansed themselves, yet did they eat the passover otherwise than it was written. But Hezekiah prayed for them, saying, The good LORD pardon every one

19 That prepares his heart to seek God, the LORD God of his fathers, though he be not cleansed according to the purification of the sanctuary.

20 And the LORD hearkened to Hezekiah, and healed the people.

21 And the children of Israel that were present at Jerusalem kept the feast of unleavened bread seven days with great gladness: and the Levites and the priests praised the LORD day by day, singing with loud instruments to the LORD.

22 And Hezekiah spoke comfortably to all the Levites that taught the good knowledge of the LORD: and they did eat throughout the feast seven days, offering peace offerings, and making confession to the LORD God of their fathers.

23 And the whole assembly took counsel to keep other seven days: and they kept other seven days with gladness.

24 For Hezekiah king of Judah did give to the congregation a thousand bullocks and seven thousand sheep; and the princes gave to the congregation a thousand bullocks and ten thousand sheep: and a great number of priests sanctified themselves.

25 And all the congregation of Judah, with the priests and the Levites, and all the congregation that came out of Israel, and the strangers that came out of the land of Israel, and that dwelt in Judah, rejoiced.

26 So there was great joy in Jerusalem: for since the time of Solomon the son of David king of Israel there was not the like in Jerusalem.

27 Then the priests the Levites arose and blessed the people: and their voice was heard, and their prayer came up to his holy dwelling place, even to heaven.

CHAPTER 31

NOW when all this was finished, all Israel that were present went out to the cities of Judah, and brake the images in pieces, and cut down the groves, and threw down the high places and the altars out of all Judah and Benjamin, in Ephraim also and Manasseh, until they had utterly destroyed them all. Then all the children of Israel returned, every man to his possession, into their own cities.

2 And Hezekiah appointed the courses of the priests and the Levites after their courses, every man according to his service, the priests and Levites for burnt offerings and for peace offerings, to minister, and to give thanks, and to praise in the gates of the tents of the LORD.

3 He appointed also the king's portion of his substance for the burnt offerings, to wit, for the morning and evening burnt offerings, and the burnt offerings for the sabbaths, and for the new moons, and for the set feasts, as it is written in the law of the LORD.

4 Moreover he commanded the people that dwelt in Jerusalem to give the portion of the priests and the Levites, that they might be encouraged in the law of the LORD.

5 And as soon as the commandment came abroad, the children of Israel brought in abundance the firstfruits of corn, wine, and oil, and honey, and of all the increase of the field; and the tithe of all things brought they in abundantly.

6 And concerning the children of Israel and Judah, that dwelt in the cities of Judah, they also brought in the tithe of oxen and sheep, and the tithe of holy things which were consecrated to the LORD their God, and laid them by heaps.

7 In the third month they began to lay the foundation of the heaps, and finished them in the seventh month.

8 And when Hezekiah and the princes came and saw the heaps, they blessed the LORD, and his people Israel.

9 Then Hezekiah questioned with the priests and the Levites concerning the heaps.

10 And Azariah the chief priest of the house of Zadok answered him, and said, Since the people began to bring the offerings into the house of the LORD, we have had enough to eat, and have left plenty: for the LORD has blessed his people; and that which is left is this great store.

11 Then Hezekiah commanded to prepare chambers in the house of the LORD; and they prepared them,

12 And brought in the offerings and the tithes and the dedicated things faithfully: over which Cononiah the Levite was ruler, and Shimei his brother was the next.

13 And Jehiel, and Azaziah, and Nahath, and Asahel, and Jerimoth, and Jozabad, and Eliel, and Ismachiah, and Mahath, and Benaiah, were overseers under the hand of Cononiah and Shimei his brother, at the commandment of Hezekiah the king, and Azariah the ruler of the house of God.

14 And Kore the son of Imnah the Levite, the porter toward the east, was over the freewill offerings of God, to distribute the oblations of the LORD, and the most holy things.

15 And next him were Eden, and Miniamin, and Jeshua, and Shemaiah, Amariah, and Shecaniah, in the cities of the priests, in their set office, to give to their brethren by courses, as well to the great as to the small:

16 Beside their genealogy of males, from three years old and upward, even to every one that enters into the house of the LORD, his daily portion for their service in their charges according to their courses;

17 Both to the genealogy of the priests by the house of their fathers, and the Levites from twenty years old and upward, in their charges by their courses;

18 And to the genealogy of all their little ones, their wives, and their sons, and their daughters, through all the congregation: for in their set office they sanctified themselves in holiness:

19 Also of the sons of Aaron the priests, which were in the fields of the suburbs of their cities, in every several city, the men that were expressed by name, to give portions to all the males among the priests, and to all that were reckoned by genealogies among the Levites.

20 And thus did Hezekiah throughout all Judah, and worked that which was good and right and truth before the LORD his God.

21 And in every work that he began in the service of the house of God, and in the law, and in the commandments, to seek his God, he did it with all his heart, and prospered.

CHAPTER 32

1 After these things, and the establishment thereof, Sennacherib king of Assyria came, and entered into Judah, and encamped against the fenced cities, and thought to win them for himself.

2 And when Hezekiah saw that Sennacherib was come, and that he was purposed to fight against Jerusalem,

3 He took counsel with his princes and his mighty men to stop the waters of the fountains which were without the city: and they did help him.

4 So there was gathered much people together, who stopped all the fountains, and the brook that ran through the midst of the land, saying, Why should the kings of Assyria come, and find much water?

5 Also he strengthened himself, and built up all the wall that was broken, and raised it up to the towers, and another wall without, and repaired Millo in the city of David, and made darts and shields in abundance.

6 And he set captains of war over the people, and gathered them together to him in the street of the gate of the city, and spoke comfortably to them, saying,

7 Be strong and courageous, be not afraid nor dismayed for the king of Assyria, nor for all the multitude that is with him: for there be more with us than with him:

8 With him is an arm of flesh; but with us is the LORD our God to help us, and to fight our battles. And the people rested themselves upon the words of Hezekiah king of Judah.

9 After this did Sennacherib king of Assyria send his servants to Jerusalem, (but he himself laid siege against Lachish, and all his power with him,) to Hezekiah king of Judah, and to all Judah that were at Jerusalem, saying,

10 Thus says Sennacherib king of Assyria, Whereon do you trust, that you abide in the siege in Jerusalem?

11 Does not Hezekiah persuade you to give over yourselves to die by famine and by thirst, saying, The LORD our God shall deliver us out of the hand of the king of Assyria?

12 Has not the same Hezekiah taken away his high places and his altars, and commanded Judah and Jerusalem, saying, You shall worship before one altar, and burn incense upon it?

13 Do you not know what I and my fathers have done to all the people of other lands? were the gods of the nations of those lands any ways able to deliver their lands out of mine hand?

14 Who was there among all the gods of those nations that my fathers utterly destroyed, that could deliver his people out of mine hand, that your God should be able to deliver you out of mine hand?

15 Now therefore let not Hezekiah deceive you, nor persuade you on this manner, neither yet believe him: for no god of any nation or kingdom was able to deliver his people out of mine hand, and out of the hand of my fathers: how much less shall your God deliver you out of mine hand?

16 And his servants spoke yet more against the LORD God, and against his servant Hezekiah.

17 He wrote also letters to rail on the LORD God of Israel, and to speak against him, saying, As the gods of the nations of other lands have not delivered their people out of mine hand, so shall not the God of Hezekiah deliver his people out of mine hand.

18 Then they cried with a loud voice in the Jews' speech to the people of Jerusalem that were on the wall, to affright them, and to trouble them; that they might take the city.

19 And they spoke against the God of Jerusalem, as against the gods of the people of the earth, which were the work of the hands of man.

20 And for this cause Hezekiah the king, and the prophet Isaiah the son of Amoz, prayed and cried to heaven.

21 And the LORD sent an angel, which cut off all the mighty men of valour, and

the leaders and captains in the camp of the king of Assyria. So he returned with shame of face to his own land. And when he was come into the house of his god, they that came forth of his own bowels slew him there with the sword.

22 Thus the LORD saved Hezekiah and the inhabitants of Jerusalem from the hand of Sennacherib the king of Assyria, and from the hand of all other, and guided them on every side.

23 And many brought gifts to the LORD to Jerusalem, and presents to Hezekiah king of Judah: so that he was magnified in the sight of all nations from thenceforth.

24 In those days Hezekiah was sick to the death, and prayed to the LORD: and he spoke to him, and he gave him a sign.

25 But Hezekiah rendered not again according to the benefit done to him; for his heart was lifted up: therefore there was wrath upon him, and upon Judah and Jerusalem.

26 Notwithstanding Hezekiah humbled himself for the pride of his heart, both he and the inhabitants of Jerusalem, so that the wrath of the LORD came not upon them in the days of Hezekiah.

27 And Hezekiah had exceeding much riches and honour: and he made himself treasuries for silver, and for gold, and for precious stones, and for spices, and for shields, and for all manner of pleasant jewels;

28 Storehouses also for the increase of corn, and wine, and oil; and stalls for all manner of beasts, and cotes for flocks.

29 Moreover he provided him cities, and possessions of flocks and herds in abundance: for God had given him substance very much.

30 This same Hezekiah also stopped the upper watercourse of Gihon, and brought it straight down to the west side of the city of David. And Hezekiah prospered in all his works.

31 Howbeit in the business of the ambassadors of the princes of Babylon, who sent to him to inquire of the wonder that was done in the land, God left him, to try him, that he might know all that was in his heart.

32 Now the rest of the acts of Hezekiah, and his goodness, behold, they are written in the vision of Isaiah the prophet, the son of Amoz, and in the book of the kings of Judah and Israel.

33 And Hezekiah slept with his fathers, and they buried him in the chiefest of the sepulchres of the sons of David: and all Judah and the inhabitants of Jerusalem did him honour at his death. And Manasseh his son reigned in his stead.

CHAPTER 33

MANASSEH was twelve years old when he began to reign, and he reigned fifty and five years in Jerusalem:

2 But did that which was evil in the sight of the LORD, like to the abominations of the heathen, whom the LORD had cast out before the children of Israel.

3 For he built again the high places which Hezekiah his father had broken down, and he reared up altars for Baalim, and made groves, and worshipped all the host of heaven, and served them.

4 Also he built altars in the house of the LORD, whereof the LORD had said, In Jerusalem shall my name be for ever.

5 And he built altars for all the host of heaven in the two courts of the house of the LORD.

6 And he caused his children to pass through the fire in the valley of the son of Hinnom: also he observed times, and used enchantments, and used witchcraft, and dealt with a familiar spirit, and with wizards: he worked much evil in the sight of the LORD, to provoke him to anger.

7 And he set a carved image, the idol which he had made, in the house of God, of which God had said to David and to Solomon his son, In this house, and in Jerusalem, which I have chosen

before all the tribes of Israel, will I put my name for ever:

8 Neither will I any more remove the foot of Israel from out of the land which I have appointed for your fathers; so that they will take heed to do all that I have commanded them, according to the whole law and the statutes and the ordinances by the hand of Moses.

9 So Manasseh made Judah and the inhabitants of Jerusalem to err, and to do worse than the heathen, whom the LORD had destroyed before the children of Israel.

10 And the LORD spoke to Manasseh, and to his people: but they would not hearken.

11 Therefore the LORD brought upon them the captains of the host of the king of Assyria, which took Manasseh among the thorns, and bound him with fetters, and carried him to Babylon.

12 And when he was in affliction, he besought the LORD his God, and humbled himself greatly before the God of his fathers,

13 And prayed to him: and he was intreated of him, and heard his supplication, and brought him again to Jerusalem into his kingdom. Then Manasseh knew that the LORD he was God.

14 Now after this he built a wall without the city of David, on the west side of Gihon, in the valley, even to the entering in at the fish gate, and compassed about Ophel, and raised it up a very great height, and put captains of war in all the fenced cities of Judah.

15 And he took away the strange gods, and the idol out of the house of the LORD, and all the altars that he had built in the mount of the house of the LORD, and in Jerusalem, and cast them out of the city.

16 And he repaired the altar of the LORD, and sacrificed thereon peace offerings and thank offerings, and commanded Judah to serve the LORD God of Israel.

17 Nevertheless the people did sacrifice still in the high places, yet to the LORD their God only.

18 Now the rest of the acts of Manasseh, and his prayer to his God, and the words of the seers that spoke to him in the name of the LORD God of Israel, behold, they are written in the book of the kings of Israel.

19 His prayer also, and how God was intreated of him, and all his sins, and his trespass, and the places wherein he built high places, and set up groves and graven images, before he was humbled: behold, they are written among the sayings of the seers.

20 So Manasseh slept with his fathers, and they buried him in his own house: and Amon his son reigned in his stead.

21 Amon was two and twenty years old when he began to reign, and reigned two years in Jerusalem.

22 But he did that which was evil in the sight of the LORD, as did Manasseh his father: for Amon sacrificed to all the carved images which Manasseh his father had made, and served them;

23 And humbled not himself before the LORD, as Manasseh his father had humbled himself; but Amon trespassed more and more.

24 And his servants conspired against him, and slew him in his own house.

25 But the people of the land slew all them that had conspired against king Amon; and the people of the land made Josiah his son king in his stead.

CHAPTER 34

JOSIAH was eight years old when he began to reign, and he reigned in Jerusalem one and thirty years.

2 And he did that which was right in the sight of the LORD, and walked in the ways of David his father, and declined neither to the right hand, nor to the left.

3 For in the eighth year of his reign, while he was yet young, he began to seek after the God of David his father: and in the twelfth year he began to

purge Judah and Jerusalem from the high places, and the groves, and the carved images, and the molten images.

4 And they brake down the altars of Baalim in his presence; and the images, that were on high above them, he cut down; and the groves, and the carved images, and the molten images, he brake in pieces, and made dust of them, and strowed it upon the graves of them that had sacrificed to them.

5 And he burnt the bones of the priests upon their altars, and cleansed Judah and Jerusalem.

6 And so did he in the cities of Manasseh, and Ephraim, and Simeon, even to Naphtali, with their mattocks round about.

7 And when he had broken down the altars and the groves, and had beaten the graven images into powder, and cut down all the idols throughout all the land of Israel, he returned to Jerusalem.

8 Now in the eighteenth year of his reign, when he had purged the land, and the house, he sent Shaphan the son of Azaliah, and Maaseiah the governor of the city, and Joah the son of Joahaz the recorder, to repair the house of the LORD his God.

9 And when they came to Hilkiah the high priest, they delivered the money that was brought into the house of God, which the Levites that kept the doors had gathered of the hand of Manasseh and Ephraim, and of all the remnant of Israel, and of all Judah and Benjamin; and they returned to Jerusalem.

10 And they put it in the hand of the workmen that had the oversight of the house of the LORD, and they gave it to the workmen that worked in the house of the LORD, to repair and amend the house:

11 Even to the artificers and builders gave they it, to buy hewn stone, and timber for couplings, and to floor the houses which the kings of Judah had destroyed.

12 And the men did the work faithfully: and the overseers of them were Jahath and Obadiah, the Levites, of the sons of Merari; and Zechariah and Meshullam, of the sons of the Kohathites, to set it forward; and other of the Levites, all that could skill of instruments of music.

13 Also they were over the bearers of burdens, and were overseers of all that worked the work in any manner of service: and of the Levites there were scribes, and officers, and porters.

14 And when they brought out the money that was brought into the house of the LORD, Hilkiah the priest found a book of the law of the LORD given by Moses.

15 And Hilkiah answered and said to Shaphan the scribe, I have found the book of the law in the house of the LORD. And Hilkiah delivered the book to Shaphan.

16 And Shaphan carried the book to the king, and brought the king word back again, saying, All that was committed to your servants, they do it.

17 And they have gathered together the money that was found in the house of the LORD, and have delivered it into the hand of the overseers, and to the hand of the workmen.

18 Then Shaphan the scribe told the king, saying, Hilkiah the priest has given me a book. And Shaphan read it before the king.

19 And it came to pass, when the king had heard the words of the law, that he rent his clothes.

20 And the king commanded Hilkiah, and Ahikam the son of Shaphan, and Abdon the son of Micah, and Shaphan the scribe, and Asaiah a servant of the king's, saying,

21 Go, inquire of the LORD for me, and for them that are left in Israel and in Judah, concerning the words of the book that is found: for great is the wrath of the LORD that is poured out upon us, because our fathers have not kept the word

of the LORD, to do after all that is written in this book.

22 And Hilkiah, and they that the king had appointed, went to Huldah the prophetess, the wife of Shallum the son of Tikvath, the son of Hasrah, keeper of the wardrobe; (now she dwelt in Jerusalem in the college:) and they spoke to her to that effect.

23 And she answered them, Thus says the LORD God of Israel, Tell the man that sent you to me,

24 Thus says the LORD, Behold, I will bring evil upon this place, and upon the inhabitants thereof, even all the curses that are written in the book which they have read before the king of Judah:

25 Because they have forsaken me, and have burned incense to other gods, that they might provoke me to anger with all the works of their hands; therefore my wrath shall be poured out upon this place, and shall not be quenched.

26 And as for the king of Judah, who sent you to inquire of the LORD, so shall you say to him, Thus says the LORD God of Israel concerning the words which you have heard;

27 Because your heart was tender, and you did humble yourself before God, when you heard his words against this place, and against the inhabitants thereof, and humbled yourself before me, and did rend your clothes, and weep before me; I have even heard you also, says the LORD.

28 Behold, I will gather you to your fathers, and you shall be gathered to your grave in peace, neither shall your eyes see all the evil that I will bring upon this place, and upon the inhabitants of the same. So they brought the king word again.

29 Then the king sent and gathered together all the elders of Judah and Jerusalem.

30 And the king went up into the house of the LORD, and all the men of Judah, and the inhabitants of Jerusalem, and the priests, and the Levites, and all the people, great and small: and he read in their ears all the words of the book of the covenant that was found in the house of the LORD.

31 And the king stood in his place, and made a covenant before the LORD, to walk after the LORD, and to keep his commandments, and his testimonies, and his statutes, with all his heart, and with all his soul, to perform the words of the covenant which are written in this book.

32 And he caused all that were present in Jerusalem and Benjamin to stand to it. And the inhabitants of Jerusalem did according to the covenant of God, the God of their fathers.

33 And Josiah took away all the abominations out of all the countries that pertained to the children of Israel, and made all that were present in Israel to serve, even to serve the LORD their God. And all his days they departed not from following the LORD, the God of their fathers.

CHAPTER 35

MOREOVER Josiah kept a passover to the LORD in Jerusalem: and they killed the passover on the fourteenth day of the first month.

2 And he set the priests in their charges, and encouraged them to the service of the house of the LORD,

3 And said to the Levites that taught all Israel, which were holy to the LORD, Put the holy ark in the house which Solomon the son of David king of Israel did build; it shall not be a burden upon your shoulders: serve now the LORD your God, and his people Israel,

4 And prepare yourselves by the houses of your fathers, after your courses, according to the writing of David king of Israel, and according to the writing of Solomon his son.

5 And stand in the holy place according to the divisions of the families of the fathers of your brethren the people, and

after the division of the families of the Levites.

6 So kill the passover, and sanctify yourselves, and prepare your brethren, that they may do according to the word of the LORD by the hand of Moses.

7 And Josiah gave to the people, of the flock, lambs and kids, all for the passover offerings, for all that were present, to the number of thirty thousand, and three thousand bullocks: these were of the king's substance.

8 And his princes gave willingly to the people, to the priests, and to the Levites: Hilkiah and Zechariah and Jehiel, rulers of the house of God, gave to the priests for the passover offerings two thousand and six hundred small cattle and three hundred oxen.

9 Conaniah also, and Shemaiah and Nethaneel, his brethren, and Hashabiah and Jeiel and Jozabad, chief of the Levites, gave to the Levites for passover offerings five thousand small cattle, and five hundred oxen.

10 So the service was prepared, and the priests stood in their place, and the Levites in their courses, according to the king's commandment.

11 And they killed the passover, and the priests sprinkled the blood from their hands, and the Levites flayed them.

12 And they removed the burnt offerings, that they might give according to the divisions of the families of the people, to offer to the LORD, as it is written in the book of Moses. And so did they with the oxen.

13 And they roasted the passover with fire according to the ordinance: but the other holy offerings sod they in pots, and in caldrons, and in pans, and divided them speedily among all the people.

14 And afterward they made ready for themselves, and for the priests: because the priests the sons of Aaron were busied in offering of burnt offerings and the fat until night; therefore the Levites prepared for themselves, and for the priests the sons of Aaron.

15 And the singers the sons of Asaph were in their place, according to the commandment of David, and Asaph, and Heman, and Jeduthun the king's seer; and the porters waited at every gate; they might not depart from their service; for their brethren the Levites prepared for them.

16 So all the service of the LORD was prepared the same day, to keep the passover, and to offer burnt offerings upon the altar of the LORD, according to the commandment of king Josiah.

17 And the children of Israel that were present kept the passover at that time, and the feast of unleavened bread seven days.

18 And there was no passover like to that kept in Israel from the days of Samuel the prophet; neither did all the kings of Israel keep such a passover as Josiah kept, and the priests, and the Levites, and all Judah and Israel that were present, and the inhabitants of Jerusalem.

19 In the eighteenth year of the reign of Josiah was this passover kept.

20 After all this, when Josiah had prepared the temple, Necho king of Egypt came up to fight against Charchemish by Euphrates: and Josiah went out against him.

21 But he sent ambassadors to him, saying, What have I to do with you, you king of Judah? I come not against you this day, but against the house wherewith I have war: for God commanded me to make haste: forbear you from meddling with God, who is with me, that he may not destroy you.

22 Nevertheless Josiah would not turn his face from him, but disguised himself, that he might fight with him, and hearkened not to the words of Necho from the mouth of God, and came to fight in the valley of Megiddo.

23 And the archers shot at king Josiah; and the king said to his servants, Have me away; for I am sore wounded.

> Perhaps if there were more
> of that intense distress for souls
> that leads to tears,
> we should more frequently see
> the results we desire.
> Sometimes it may be
> that while we are complaining
> of the hardness of the hearts
> of those we are seeking to benefit,
> the hardness of our own hearts
> and our feeble apprehension
> of the solemn reality of eternal things
> may be the true cause
> of our want of success.
> **JAMES H. TAYLOR**
> 1832-1905
> PIONEER MISSIONARY

24 His servants therefore took him out of that chariot, and put him in the second chariot that he had; and they brought him to Jerusalem, and he died, and was buried in one of the sepulchres of his fathers. And all Judah and Jerusalem mourned for Josiah.

25 And Jeremiah lamented for Josiah: and all the singing men and the singing women spoke of Josiah in their lamentations to this day, and made them an ordinance in Israel: and, behold, they are written in the lamentations.

26 Now the rest of the acts of Josiah, and his goodness, according to that which was written in the law of the LORD,

27 And his deeds, first and last, behold, they are written in the book of the kings of Israel and Judah.

CHAPTER 36

THEN the people of the land took Jehoahaz the son of Josiah, and made him king in his father's stead in Jerusalem.

2 Jehoahaz was twenty and three years old when he began to reign, and he reigned three months in Jerusalem.

3 And the king of Egypt put him down at Jerusalem, and condemned the land in an hundred talents of silver and a talent of gold.

4 And the king of Egypt made Eliakim his brother king over Judah and Jerusalem, and turned his name to Jehoiakim. And Necho took Jehoahaz his brother, and carried him to Egypt.

5 Jehoiakim was twenty and five years old when he began to reign, and he reigned eleven years in Jerusalem: and he did that which was evil in the sight of the LORD his God.

6 Against him came up Nebuchadnezzar king of Babylon, and bound him in fetters, to carry him to Babylon.

7 Nebuchadnezzar also carried of the vessels of the house of the LORD to Babylon, and put them in his temple at Babylon.

8 Now the rest of the acts of Jehoiakim, and his abominations which he did, and that which was found in him, behold, they are written in the book of the kings of Israel and Judah: and Jehoiachin his son reigned in his stead.

9 Jehoiachin was eight years old when he began to reign, and he reigned three months and ten days in Jerusalem: and he did that which was evil in the sight of the LORD.

10 And when the year was expired, king Nebuchadnezzar sent, and brought him to Babylon, with the goodly vessels of the house of the LORD, and made Zedekiah his brother king over Judah and Jerusalem.

11 Zedekiah was one and twenty years old when he began to reign, and reigned eleven years in Jerusalem.

12 And he did that which was evil in the sight of the LORD his God, and humbled not himself before Jeremiah the prophet speaking from the mouth of the LORD.

13 And he also rebelled against king Nebuchadnezzar, who had made him swear by God: but he stiffened his neck, and hardened his heart from turning to the LORD God of Israel.

14 Moreover all the chief of the priests, and the people, transgressed very much after all the abominations of the heathen; and polluted the house of the LORD which he had hallowed in Jerusalem.

15 And the LORD God of their fathers sent to them by his messengers, rising up betimes, and sending; because he had compassion on his people, and on his dwelling place:

16 But they mocked the messengers of God, and despised his words, and misused his prophets, until the wrath of the LORD arose against his people, till there was no remedy.

17 Therefore he brought upon them the king of the Chaldees, who slew their young men with the sword in the house of their sanctuary, and had no compassion upon young man or maiden, old man, or him that stooped for age: he gave them all into his hand.

18 And all the vessels of the house of God, great and small, and the treasures of the house of the LORD, and the treasures of the king, and of his princes; all these he brought to Babylon.

19 And they burnt the house of God, and brake down the wall of Jerusalem, and burnt all the palaces thereof with fire, and destroyed all the goodly vessels thereof.

20 And them that had escaped from the sword carried he away to Babylon; where they were servants to him and his sons until the reign of the kingdom of Persia:

21 To fulfill the word of the LORD by the mouth of Jeremiah, until the land had enjoyed her sabbaths: for as long as she lay desolate she kept sabbath, to fulfill threescore and ten years.

22 Now in the first year of Cyrus king of Persia, that the word of the LORD spoken by the mouth of Jeremiah might be accomplished, the LORD stirred up the spirit of Cyrus king of Persia, that he made a proclamation throughout all his kingdom, and put it also in writing, saying,

23 Thus says Cyrus king of Persia, All the kingdoms of the earth has the LORD God of heaven given me; and he has charged me to build him an house in Jerusalem, which is in Judah. Who is there among you of all his people? The LORD his God be with him, and let him go up.

Ezra

CHAPTER 1

NOW in the first year of Cyrus king of Persia, that the word of the LORD by the mouth of Jeremiah might be fulfilled, the LORD stirred up the spirit of Cyrus king of Persia, that he made a proclamation throughout all his kingdom, and put it also in writing, saying,

2 Thus says Cyrus king of Persia, The LORD God of heaven has given me all the kingdoms of the earth; and he has charged me to build him an house at Jerusalem, which is in Judah.

3 Who is there among you of all his people? his God be with him, and let him go up to Jerusalem, which is in

CYRUS RESTORING THE VESSELS OF THE TEMPLE

Ezra 1:7

615

Judah, and build the house of the LORD God of Israel, (he is the God,) which is in Jerusalem.

4 And whosoever remains in any place where he sojourns, let the men of his place help him with silver, and with gold, and with goods, and with beasts, beside the freewill offering for the house of God that is in Jerusalem.

5 Then rose up the chief of the fathers of Judah and Benjamin, and the priests, and the Levites, with all them whose spirit God had raised, to go up to build the house of the LORD which is in Jerusalem.

6 And all they that were about them strengthened their hands with vessels of silver, with gold, with goods, and with beasts, and with precious things, beside all that was willingly offered.

7 Also Cyrus the king brought forth the vessels of the house of the LORD, which Nebuchadnezzar had brought forth out of Jerusalem, and had put them in the house of his gods;

8 Even those did Cyrus king of Persia bring forth by the hand of Mithredath the treasurer, and numbered them to Sheshbazzar, the prince of Judah.

9 And this is the number of them: thirty chargers of gold, a thousand chargers of silver, nine and twenty knives,

10 Thirty basons of gold, silver basons of a second sort four hundred and ten, and other vessels a thousand.

11 All the vessels of gold and of silver were five thousand and four hundred. All these did Sheshbazzar bring up with them of the captivity that were brought up from Babylon to Jerusalem.

CHAPTER 2

NOW these are the children of the province that went up out of the captivity, of those which had been carried away, whom Nebuchadnezzar the king of Babylon had carried away to Babylon, and came again to Jerusalem and Judah, every one to his city;

2 Which came with Zerubbabel: Jeshua, Nehemiah, Seraiah, Reelaiah, Mordecai, Bilshan, Mizpar, Bigvai, Rehum, Baanah. The number of the men of the people of Israel:

3 The children of Parosh, two thousand an hundred seventy and two.

4 The children of Shephatiah, three hundred seventy and two.

5 The children of Arah, seven hundred seventy and five.

6 The children of Pahathmoab, of the children of Jeshua and Joab, two thousand eight hundred and twelve.

7 The children of Elam, a thousand two hundred fifty and four.

8 The children of Zattu, nine hundred forty and five.

9 The children of Zaccai, seven hundred and threescore.

10 The children of Bani, six hundred forty and two.

11 The children of Bebai, six hundred twenty and three.

12 The children of Azgad, a thousand two hundred twenty and two.

13 The children of Adonikam, six hundred sixty and six.

14 The children of Bigvai, two thousand fifty and six.

15 The children of Adin, four hundred fifty and four.

16 The children of Ater of Hezekiah, ninety and eight.

17 The children of Bezai, three hundred twenty and three.

18 The children of Jorah, an hundred and twelve.

19 The children of Hashum, two hundred twenty and three.

20 The children of Gibbar, ninety and five.

21 The children of Bethlehem, an hundred twenty and three.

22 The men of Netophah, fifty and six.

23 The men of Anathoth, an hundred twenty and eight.

24 The children of Azmaveth, forty and two.

25 The children of Kirjatharim, Chephirah, and Beeroth, seven hundred and forty and three.

26 The children of Ramah and Gaba, six hundred twenty and one.

27 The men of Michmas, an hundred twenty and two.

28 The men of Bethel and Ai, two hundred twenty and three.

29 The children of Nebo, fifty and two.

30 The children of Magbish, an hundred fifty and six.

31 The children of the other Elam, a thousand two hundred fifty and four.

32 The children of Harim, three hundred and twenty.

33 The children of Lod, Hadid, and Ono, seven hundred twenty and five.

34 The children of Jericho, three hundred forty and five.

35 The children of Senaah, three thousand and six hundred and thirty.

36 The priests: the children of Jedaiah, of the house of Jeshua, nine hundred seventy and three.

37 The children of Immer, a thousand fifty and two.

38 The children of Pashur, a thousand two hundred forty and seven.

39 The children of Harim, a thousand and seventeen.

40 The Levites: the children of Jeshua and Kadmiel, of the children of Hodaviah, seventy and four.

41 The singers: the children of Asaph, an hundred twenty and eight.

42 The children of the porters: the children of Shallum, the children of Ater, the children of Talmon, the children of Akkub, the children of Hatita, the children of Shobai, in all an hundred thirty and nine.

43 The Nethinims: the children of Ziha, the children of Hasupha, the children of Tabbaoth,

44 The children of Keros, the children of Siaha, the children of Padon,

45 The children of Lebanah, the children of Hagabah, the children of Akkub,

46 The children of Hagab, the children of Shalmai, the children of Hanan,

47 The children of Giddel, the children of Gahar, the children of Reaiah,

48 The children of Rezin, the children of Nekoda, the children of Gazzam,

49 The children of Uzza, the children of Paseah, the children of Besai,

50 The children of Asnah, the children of Mehunim, the children of Nephusim,

51 The children of Bakbuk, the children of Hakupha, the children of Harhur,

52 The children of Bazluth, the children of Mehida, the children of Harsha,

53 The children of Barkos, the children of Sisera, the children of Thamah,

54 The children of Neziah, the children of Hatipha.

55 The children of Solomon's servants: the children of Sotai, the children of Sophereth, the children of Peruda,

56 The children of Jaalah, the children of Darkon, the children of Giddel,

57 The children of Shephatiah, the children of Hattil, the children of Pochereth of Zebaim, the children of Ami.

58 All the Nethinims, and the children of Solomon's servants, were three hundred ninety and two.

59 And these were they which went up from Telmelah, Telharsa, Cherub, Addan, and Immer: but they could not show their father's house, and their seed, whether they were of Israel:

60 The children of Delaiah, the children of Tobiah, the children of Nekoda, six hundred fifty and two.

61 And of the children of the priests: the children of Habaiah, the children of Koz, the children of Barzillai; which took a wife of the daughters of Barzillai the Gileadite, and was called after their name:

62 These sought their register among those that were reckoned by genealogy, but they were not found: therefore were they, as polluted, put from the priesthood.

63 And the Tirshatha said to them, that they should not eat of the most holy things, till there stood up a priest with Urim and with Thummim.

64 The whole congregation together was forty and two thousand three hundred and threescore,

65 Beside their servants and their maids, of whom there were seven thousand three hundred thirty and seven: and there were among them two hundred singing men and singing women.

66 Their horses were seven hundred thirty and six; their mules, two hundred forty and five;

67 Their camels, four hundred thirty and five; their asses, six thousand seven hundred and twenty.

68 And some of the chief of the fathers, when they came to the house of the LORD which is at Jerusalem, offered freely for the house of God to set it up in his place:

69 They gave after their ability to the treasure of the work threescore and one thousand drams of gold, and five thousand pound of silver, and one hundred priests' garments.

70 So the priests, and the Levites, and some of the people, and the singers, and the porters, and the Nethinims, dwelt in their cities, and all Israel in their cities.

CHAPTER 3

AND when the seventh month was come, and the children of Israel were in the cities, the people gathered themselves together as one man to Jerusalem.

2 Then stood up Jeshua the son of Jozadak, and his brethren the priests, and Zerubbabel the son of Shealtiel, and his brethren, and built the altar of the God of Israel, to offer burnt offerings thereon, as it is written in the law of Moses the man of God.

3 And they set the altar upon his bases; for fear was upon them because of the people of those countries: and they offered burnt offerings thereon to the LORD, even burnt offerings morning and evening.

4 They kept also the feast of tabernacles, as it is written, and offered the daily burnt offerings by number, according to the custom, as the duty of every day required;

5 And afterward offered the continual burnt offering, both of the new moons, and of all the set feasts of the LORD that were consecrated, and of every one that willingly offered a freewill offering to the LORD.

6 From the first day of the seventh month began they to offer burnt offerings to the LORD. But the foundation of the temple of the LORD was not yet laid.

7 They gave money also to the masons, and to the carpenters; and meat, and drink, and oil, to them of Zidon, and to them of Tyre, to bring cedar trees from Lebanon to the sea of Joppa, according to the grant that they had of Cyrus king of Persia.

8 Now in the second year of their coming to the house of God at Jerusalem, in the second month, began Zerubbabel the son of Shealtiel, and Jeshua the son of Jozadak, and the remnant of their brethren the priests and the Levites, and all they that were come out of the captivity to Jerusalem; and appointed the Levites, from twenty years old and upward, to set forward the work of the house of the LORD.

9 Then stood Jeshua with his sons and his brethren, Kadmiel and his sons, the sons of Judah, together, to set forward the workmen in the house of God: the sons of Henadad, with their sons and their brethren the Levites.

2:62 It is a tragic day when unsaved men and women find their way into places of leadership within the Church.

10 And when the builders laid the foundation of the temple of the LORD, they set the priests in their apparel with trumpets, and the Levites the sons of Asaph with cymbals, to praise the LORD, after the ordinance of David king of Israel.

11 And they sang together by course in praising and giving thanks to the LORD; because he is good, for his mercy endures for ever toward Israel. And all the people shouted with a great shout, when they praised the LORD, because the foundation of the house of the LORD was laid.

12 But many of the priests and Levites and chief of the fathers, who were ancient men, that had seen the first house, when the foundation of this house was laid before their eyes, wept with a loud voice; and many shouted aloud for joy:

13 So that the people could not discern the noise of the shout of joy from the noise of the weeping of the people: for the people shouted with a loud shout, and the noise was heard afar off.

CHAPTER 4

NOW when the adversaries of Judah and Benjamin heard that the children of the captivity built the temple to the LORD God of Israel;

2 Then they came to Zerubbabel, and to the chief of the fathers, and said to them, Let us build with you: for we seek your God, as you do; and we do sacrifice to him since the days of Esarhaddon king of Assur, which brought us up here.

3 But Zerubbabel, and Jeshua, and the rest of the chief of the fathers of Israel, said to them, You have nothing to do with us to build an house to our God;

but we ourselves together will build to the LORD God of Israel, as king Cyrus the king of Persia has commanded us.

4 Then the people of the land weakened the hands of the people of Judah, and troubled them in building,

5 And hired counsellors against them, to frustrate their purpose, all the days of Cyrus king of Persia, even until the reign of Darius king of Persia.

6 And in the reign of Ahasuerus, in the beginning of his reign, wrote they to him an accusation against the inhabitants of Judah and Jerusalem.

7 And in the days of Artaxerxes wrote Bishlam, Mithredath, Tabeel, and the rest of their companions, to Artaxerxes king of Persia; and the writing of the letter was written in the Syrian tongue, and interpreted in the Syrian tongue.

8 Rehum the chancellor and Shimshai the scribe wrote a letter against Jerusalem to Artaxerxes the king in this sort:

9 Then wrote Rehum the chancellor, and Shimshai the scribe, and the rest of their companions; the Dinaites, the Apharsathchites, the Tarpelites, the Apharsites, the Archevites, the Babylonians, the Susanchites, the Dehavites, and the Elamites,

10 And the rest of the nations whom the great and noble Asnapper brought over, and set in the cities of Samaria, and the rest that are on this side the river, and at such a time.

11 This is the copy of the letter that they sent to him, even to Artaxerxes the king; Your servants the men on this side the river, and at such a time.

12 Be it known to the king, that the Jews which came up from you to us are

---

3:11 We have the same reasons they had to rejoice and give thanks to God: God is good, and He showers us, too, with blessings, and not treating us according to our sins. See Psalm 136:1 and Romans 1:20-21.

Chapter 4 The believer has become the Temple of God. The adversary wants to weaken our hands and frustrate our purposes. That's why we must pray that God strengthens our hands and encourages our evangelistic objectives.

come to Jerusalem, building the rebellious and the bad city, and have set up the walls thereof, and joined the foundations.

13 Be it known now to the king, that, if this city be built, and the walls set up again, then will they not pay toll, tribute, and custom, and so you shall endamage the revenue of the kings.

14 Now because we have maintenance from the king's palace, and it was not meet for us to see the king's dishonour, therefore have we sent and certified the king;

15 That search may be made in the book of the records of your fathers: so shall you find in the book of the records, and know that this city is a rebellious city, and hurtful to kings and provinces, and that they have moved sedition within the same of old time: for which cause was this city destroyed.

16 We certify the king that, if this city be built again, and the walls thereof set up, by this means you shall have no portion on this side the river.

17 Then sent the king an answer to Rehum the chancellor, and to Shimshai the scribe, and to the rest of their companions that dwell in Samaria, and to the rest beyond the river, Peace, and at such a time.

18 The letter which you sent to us has been plainly read before me.

19 And I commanded, and search has been made, and it is found that this city of old time has made insurrection against kings, and that rebellion and sedition have been made therein.

20 There have been mighty kings also over Jerusalem, which have ruled over all countries beyond the river; and toll, tribute, and custom, was paid to them.

21 Give now commandment to cause these men to cease, and that this city be not built, until another commandment shall be given from me.

22 Take heed now that you fail not to do this: why should damage grow to the hurt of the kings?

23 Now when the copy of king Artaxerxes' letter was read before Rehum, and Shimshai the scribe, and their companions, they went up in haste to Jerusalem to the Jews, and made them to cease by force and power.

24 Then ceased the work of the house of God which is at Jerusalem. So it ceased to the second year of the reign of Darius king of Persia.

CHAPTER 5

THEN the prophets, Haggai the prophet, and Zechariah the son of Iddo, prophesied to the Jews that were in Judah and Jerusalem in the name of the God of Israel, even to them.

2 Then rose up Zerubbabel the son of Shealtiel, and Jeshua the son of Jozadak, and began to build the house of God which is at Jerusalem: and with them were the prophets of God helping them.

3 At the same time came to them Tatnai, governor on this side the river, and Shetharboznai and their companions, and said thus to them, Who has commanded you to build this house, and to make up this wall?

4 Then said we to them after this manner, What are the names of the men that make this building?

5 But the eye of their God was upon the elders of the Jews, that they could not cause them to cease, till the matter came to Darius: and then they returned answer by letter concerning this matter.

6 The copy of the letter that Tatnai, governor on this side the river, and Shetharboznai and his companions the Apharsachites, which were on this side the river, sent to Darius the king:

7 They sent a letter to him, wherein was written thus; To Darius the king, all peace.

8 Be it known to the king, that we went into the province of Judea, to the house of the great God, which is built with great stones, and timber is laid in the walls, and this work goeth fast on, and prospers in their hands.

9 Then asked we those elders, and said to them thus, Who commanded you to build this house, and to make up these walls?

10 We asked their names also, to certify you, that we might write the names of the men that were the chief of them.

11 And thus they returned us answer, saying, We are the servants of the God of heaven and earth, and build the house that was built these many years ago, which a great king of Israel built and set up.

12 But after that our fathers had provoked the God of heaven to wrath, he gave them into the hand of Nebuchadnezzar the king of Babylon, the Chaldean, who destroyed this house, and carried the people away into Babylon.

13 But in the first year of Cyrus the king of Babylon the same king Cyrus made a decree to build this house of God.

14 And the vessels also of gold and silver of the house of God, which Nebuchadnezzar took out of the temple that was in Jerusalem, and brought them into the temple of Babylon, those did Cyrus the king take out of the temple of Babylon, and they were delivered to one, whose name was Sheshbazzar, whom he had made governor;

15 And said to him, Take these vessels, go, carry them into the temple that is in Jerusalem, and let the house of God be built in his place.

16 Then came the same Sheshbazzar, and laid the foundation of the house of God which is in Jerusalem: and since that time even until now has it been in building, and yet it is not finished.

17 Now therefore, if it seem good to the king, let there be search made in the king's treasure house, which is there at Babylon, whether it be so, that a decree was made of Cyrus the king to build this house of God at Jerusalem, and let the king send his pleasure to us concerning this matter.

CHAPTER 6

THEN Darius the king made a decree, and search was made in the house of the rolls, where the treasures were laid up in Babylon.

2 And there was found at Achmetha, in the palace that is in the province of the Medes, a roll, and therein was a record thus written:

3 In the first year of Cyrus the king the same Cyrus the king made a decree concerning the house of God at Jerusalem, Let the house be built, the place where they offered sacrifices, and let the foundations thereof be strongly laid; the height thereof threescore cubits, and the breadth thereof threescore cubits;

4 With three rows of great stones, and a row of new timber: and let the expenses be given out of the king's house:

5 And also let the golden and silver vessels of the house of God, which Nebuchadnezzar took forth out of the temple which is at Jerusalem, and brought to Babylon, be restored, and brought again to the temple which is at Jerusalem, every one to his place, and place them in the house of God.

6 Now therefore, Tatnai, governor beyond the river, Shetharboznai, and your companions the Apharsachites, which are beyond the river, keep yourselves far from there:

7 Let the work of this house of God alone; let the governor of the Jews and the elders of the Jews build this house of God in his place.

8 Moreover I make a decree what you shall do to the elders of these Jews for the building of this house of God: that of the king's goods, even of the tribute beyond the river, forthwith expenses be

---

5:12 Sin is a lightning rod for eternal justice.

given to these men, that they be not hindered.

9 And that which they have need of, both young bullocks, and rams, and lambs, for the burnt offerings of the God of heaven, wheat, salt, wine, and oil, according to the appointment of the priests which are at Jerusalem, let it be given them day by day without fail:

10 That they may offer sacrifices of sweet savours to the God of heaven, and pray for the life of the king, and of his sons.

11 Also I have made a decree, that whosoever shall alter this word, let timber be pulled down from his house, and being set up, let him be hanged thereon; and let his house be made a dunghill for this.

12 And the God that has caused his name to dwell there destroy all kings and people, that shall put to their hand to alter and to destroy this house of God which is at Jerusalem. I Darius have made a decree; let it be done with speed.

13 Then Tatnai, governor on this side the river, Shetharboznai, and their companions, according to that which Darius the king had sent, so they did speedily.

14 And the elders of the Jews built, and they prospered through the prophesying of Haggai the prophet and Zechariah the son of Iddo. And they built, and finished it, according to the commandment of the God of Israel, and according to the commandment of Cyrus, and Darius, and Artaxerxes king of Persia.

15 And this house was finished on the third day of the month Adar, which was in the sixth year of the reign of Darius the king.

16 And the children of Israel, the priests, and the Levites, and the rest of the children of the captivity, kept the dedication of this house of God with joy.

17 And offered at the dedication of this house of God an hundred bullocks, two hundred rams, four hundred lambs; and for a sin offering for all Israel, twelve he

goats, according to the number of the tribes of Israel.

18 And they set the priests in their divisions, and the Levites in their courses, for the service of God, which is at Jerusalem; as it is written in the book of Moses.

19 And the children of the captivity kept the passover upon the fourteenth day of the first month.

20 For the priests and the Levites were purified together, all of them were pure, and killed the passover for all the children of the captivity, and for their brethren the priests, and for themselves.

21 And the children of Israel, which were come again out of captivity, and all such as had separated themselves to them from the filthiness of the heathen of the land, to seek the LORD God of Israel, did eat,

22 And kept the feast of unleavened bread seven days with joy: for the LORD had made them joyful, and turned the heart of the king of Assyria to them, to strengthen their hands in the work of the house of God, the God of Israel.

CHAPTER 7

NOW after these things, in the reign of Artaxerxes king of Persia, Ezra the son of Seraiah, the son of Azariah, the son of Hilkiah,

2 The son of Shallum, the son of Zadok, the son of Ahitub,

3 The son of Amariah, the son of Azariah, the son of Meraioth,

4 The son of Zerahiah, the son of Uzzi, the son of Bukki,

5 The son of Abishua, the son of Phinehas, the son of Eleazar, the son of Aaron the chief priest:

6 This Ezra went up from Babylon; and he was a ready scribe in the law of Moses, which the LORD God of Israel had given: and the king granted him all his request, according to the hand of the LORD his God upon him.

7 And there went up some of the children of Israel, and of the priests, and the

Levites, and the singers, and the porters, and the Nethinims, to Jerusalem, in the seventh year of Artaxerxes the king.

8 And he came to Jerusalem in the fifth month, which was in the seventh year of the king.

9 For upon the first day of the first month began he to go up from Babylon, and on the first day of the fifth month came he to Jerusalem, according to the good hand of his God upon him.

10 For Ezra had prepared his heart to seek the law of the LORD, and to do it, and to teach in Israel statutes and judgments.

11 Now this is the copy of the letter that the king Artaxerxes gave to Ezra the priest, the scribe, even a scribe of the words of the commandments of the LORD, and of his statutes to Israel.

12 Artaxerxes, king of kings, to Ezra the priest, a scribe of the law of the God of heaven, perfect peace, and at such a time.

13 I make a decree, that all they of the people of Israel, and of his priests and Levites, in my realm, which are minded of their own freewill to go up to Jerusalem, go with you.

14 Forasmuch as you are sent of the king, and of his seven counsellors, to enquire concerning Judah and Jerusalem, according to the law of your God which is in your hand;

15 And to carry the silver and gold, which the king and his counselors have freely offered to the God of Israel, whose habitation is in Jerusalem,

16 And all the silver and gold that you can find in all the province of Babylon,

ARTAXERXES GRANTING LIBERTY TO THE JEWS

Ezra 7:13

The only way we can know whether we are sinning is by knowing His moral law.

Jonathan Edwards

1703-1758

THIRD PRESIDENT OF PRINCETON

with the freewill offering of the people, and of the priests, offering willingly for the house of their God which is in Jerusalem:

17 That you may buy speedily with this money bullocks, rams, lambs, with their meat offerings and their drink offerings, and offer them upon the altar of the house of your God which is in Jerusalem.

18 And whatsoever shall seem good to you, and to your brethren, to do with the rest of the silver and the gold, that do after the will of your God.

19 The vessels also that are given you for the service of the house of your God, those deliver before the God of Jerusalem.

20 And whatsoever more shall be needful for the house of your God, which you shall have occasion to bestow, bestow it out of the king's treasure house.

21 And I, even I Artaxerxes the king, do make a decree to all the treasurers which are beyond the river, that whatsoever Ezra the priest, the scribe of the law of the God of heaven, shall require of you, it be done speedily,

22 To an hundred talents of silver, and to an hundred measures of wheat, and to an hundred baths of wine, and to an hundred baths of oil, and salt without prescribing how much.

23 Whatsoever is commanded by the God of heaven, let it be diligently done for the house of the God of heaven: for why should there be wrath against the realm of the king and his sons?

24 Also we certify you, that touching any of the priests and Levites, singers, porters, Nethinims, or ministers of this house of God, it shall not be lawful to impose toll, tribute, or custom, upon them.

25 And you, Ezra, after the wisdom of your God, that is in your hand, set magistrates and judges, which may judge all the people that are beyond the river, all such as know the laws of your God; and teach them that know them not.

26 And whosoever will not do the law of your God, and the law of the king, let judgment be executed speedily upon him, whether it be to death, or to banishment, or to confiscation of goods, or to imprisonment.

27 Blessed be the LORD God of our fathers, which has put such a thing as this in the king's heart, to beautify the house of the LORD which is in Jerusalem:

28 And has extended mercy to me before the king, and his counselors, and before all the king's mighty princes. And I was strengthened as the hand of the LORD my God was upon me, and I gathered together out of Israel chief men to go up with me.

CHAPTER 8

THESE are now the chief of their fathers, and this is the genealogy of them that went up with me from Babylon, in the reign of Artaxerxes the king.

2 Of the sons of Phinehas; Gershom: of the sons of Ithamar; Daniel: of the sons of David; Hattush.

3 Of the sons of Shechaniah, of the sons of Pharosh; Zechariah: and with him were reckoned by genealogy of the males an hundred and fifty.

4 Of the sons of Pahathmoab; Elihoenai the son of Zerahiah, and with him two hundred males.

5 Of the sons of Shechaniah; the son of Jahaziel, and with him three hundred males.

6 Of the sons also of Adin; Ebed the son of Jonathan, and with him fifty males.

7 And of the sons of Elam; Jeshaiah the son of Athaliah, and with him seventy males.

8 And of the sons of Shephatiah; Zebadiah the son of Michael, and with him fourscore males.

9 Of the sons of Joab; Obadiah the son of Jehiel, and with him two hundred and eighteen males.

10 And of the sons of Shelomith; the son of Josiphiah, and with him an hundred and threescore males.

11 And of the sons of Bebai; Zechariah the son of Bebai, and with him twenty and eight males.

12 And of the sons of Azgad; Johanan the son of Hakkatan, and with him an hundred and ten males.

13 And of the last sons of Adonikam, whose names are these, Eliphelet, Jeiel, and Shemaiah, and with them threescore males.

14 Of the sons also of Bigvai; Uthai, and Zabbud, and with them seventy males.

15 And I gathered them together to the river that runs to Ahava; and there abode we in tents three days: and I viewed the people, and the priests, and found there none of the sons of Levi.

16 Then sent I for Eliezer, for Ariel, for Shemaiah, and for Elnathan, and for Jarib, and for Elnathan, and for Nathan, and for Zechariah, and for Meshullam, chief men; also for Joiarib, and for Elnathan, men of understanding.

17 And I sent them with commandment to Iddo the chief at the place Casiphia, and I told them what they should say to Iddo, and to his brethren the Nethinims, at the place Casiphia, that they should bring to us ministers for the house of our God.

18 And by the good hand of our God upon us they brought us a man of understanding, of the sons of Mahli, the son of Levi, the son of Israel; and Sherebiah, with his sons and his brethren, eighteen;

19 And Hashabiah, and with him Jeshaiah of the sons of Merari, his brethren and their sons, twenty;

20 Also of the Nethinims, whom David and the princes had appointed for the service of the Levites, two hundred and twenty Nethinims: all of them were expressed by name.

21 Then I proclaimed a fast there, at the river of Ahava, that we might afflict ourselves before our God, to seek of him a right way for us, and for our little ones, and for all our substance.

22 For I was ashamed to require of the king a band of soldiers and horsemen to help us against the enemy in the way: because we had spoken to the king, saying, The hand of our God is upon all them for good that seek him; but his

> God's grace
> cannot be faithfully preached
> to unbelievers
> until the Law is preached,
> and man's corrupt nature is exposed.
> It is impossible
> for a person to fully realize
> his need for God's grace
> until he sees how terribly he has failed
> the standards of God's law.

JOHN MACARTHUR, JR.

PASTOR

GRACE COMMUNITY CHURCH

SUN VALLEY

power and his wrath is against all them that forsake him.

23 So we fasted and besought our God for this: and he was intreated of us.

24 Then I separated twelve of the chief of the priests, Sherebiah, Hashabiah, and ten of their brethren with them,

25 And weighed to them the silver, and the gold, and the vessels, even the offering of the house of our God, which the king, and his counsellors, and his lords, and all Israel there present, had offered:

26 I even weighed to their hand six hundred and fifty talents of silver, and silver vessels an hundred talents, and of gold an hundred talents;

27 Also twenty basons of gold, of a thousand drams; and two vessels of fine copper, precious as gold.

28 And I said to them, You are holy to the LORD; the vessels are holy also; and the silver and the gold are a freewill offering to the LORD God of your fathers.

29 Watch, and keep them, until you weigh them before the chief of the priests and the Levites, and chief of the fathers of Israel, at Jerusalem, in the chambers of the house of the LORD.

30 So took the priests and the Levites the weight of the silver, and the gold, and the vessels, to bring them to Jerusalem to the house of our God.

31 Then we departed from the river of Ahava on the twelfth day of the first month, to go to Jerusalem: and the hand of our God was upon us, and he delivered us from the hand of the enemy, and of such as lay in wait by the way.

32 And we came to Jerusalem, and abode there three days.

33 Now on the fourth day was the silver and the gold and the vessels weighed in the house of our God by the hand of Meremoth the son of Uriah the priest; and with him was Eleazar the son of Phinehas; and with them was Jozabad the son of Jeshua, and Noadiah the son of Binnui, Levites;

34 By number and by weight of every one: and all the weight was written at that time.

35 Also the children of those that had been carried away, which were come out of the captivity, offered burnt offerings to the God of Israel, twelve bullocks for all Israel, ninety and six rams, seventy and seven lambs, twelve he goats for a sin offering: all this was a burnt offering to the LORD.

36 And they delivered the king's commissions to the king's lieutenants, and to the governors on this side the river: and they furthered the people, and the house of God.

CHAPTER 9

NOW when these things were done, the princes came to me, saying, The people of Israel, and the priests, and the Levites, have not separated themselves from the people of the lands, doing according to their abominations, even of the Canaanites, the Hittites, the Perizzites, the Jebusites, the Ammonites, the Moabites, the Egyptians, and the Amorites.

2 For they have taken of their daughters for themselves, and for their sons: so that the holy seed have mingled themselves with the people of those lands: yea, the hand of the princes and rulers has been chief in this trespass.

3 And when I heard this thing, I rent my garment and my mantle, and

EZRA IN PRAYER

Ezra 9:1-6

E zra was burdened and ashamed to face his Creator because of the compromise of God's people. Compromise in the Christian takes away his confidence before God.

plucked off the hair of my head and of my beard, and sat down astonied.
4 Then were assembled to me every one that trembled at the words of the God of Israel, because of the transgression of those that had been carried away; and I sat astonied until the evening sacrifice.
5 And at the evening sacrifice I arose up from my heaviness; and having rent my garment and my mantle, I fell upon my knees, and spread out my hands to the LORD my God,
6 And said, O my God, I am ashamed and blush to lift up my face to you, my God: for our iniquities are increased over our head, and our trespass is grown up to the heavens.

7 Since the days of our fathers have we been in a great trespass to this day; and for our iniquities have we, our kings, and our priests, been delivered into the hand of the kings of the lands, to the sword, to captivity, and to a spoil, and to confusion of face, as it is this day.
8 And now for a little space grace has been showed from the LORD our God, to leave us a remnant to escape, and to give us a nail in his holy place, that our God may lighten our eyes, and give us a little reviving in our bondage.
9 For we were bondmen; yet our God has not forsaken us in our bondage, but has extended mercy to us in the sight of the kings of Persia, to give us a reviving,

to set up the house of our God, and to repair the desolations thereof, and to give us a wall in Judah and in Jerusalem.

10 And now, O our God, what shall we say after this? for we have forsaken your commandments,

11 Which you have commanded by your servants the prophets, saying, The land, to which you go to possess it, is an unclean land with the filthiness of the people of the lands, with their abominations, which have filled it from one end to another with their uncleanness.

12 Now therefore give not your daughters to their sons, neither take their daughters to your sons, nor seek their peace or their wealth for ever: that you may be strong, and eat the good of the land, and leave it for an inheritance to your children for ever.

13 And after all that is come upon us for our evil deeds, and for our great trespass, seeing that you our God have punished us less than our iniquities deserve, and have given us such deliverance as this;

14 Should we again break your commandments, and join in affinity with the people of these abominations? would not you be angry with us till you had consumed us, so that there should be no remnant nor escaping?

15 O LORD God of Israel, you are righteous: for we remain yet escaped, as it is this day: behold, we are before you in our trespasses: for we cannot stand before you because of this.

CHAPTER 10

NOW when Ezra had prayed, and when he had confessed, weeping and casting himself down before the house of God, there assembled to him out of Israel a very great congregation of men and women and children: for the people wept very sore.

2 And Shechaniah the son of Jehiel, one of the sons of Elam, answered and said to Ezra, We have trespassed against our God, and have taken strange wives of the people of the land: yet now there is hope in Israel concerning this thing.

3 Now therefore let us make a covenant with our God to put away all the wives, and such as are born of them, according to the counsel of my lord, and of those that tremble at the commandment of our God; and let it be done according to the law.

4 Arise; for this matter belongs to you: we also will be with you: be of good courage, and do it.

5 Then arose Ezra, and made the chief priests, the Levites, and all Israel, to swear that they should do according to this word. And they swore.

6 Then Ezra rose up from before the house of God, and went into the chamber of Johanan the son of Eliashib: and when he came there, he did eat no bread, nor drink water: for he mourned because of the transgression of them that had been carried away.

7 And they made proclamation throughout Judah and Jerusalem to all the children of the captivity, that they should gather themselves together to Jerusalem;

8 And that whosoever would not come within three days, according to the counsel of the princes and the elders, all his substance should be forfeited, and himself separated from the congregation of those that had been carried away.

9 Then all the men of Judah and Benjamin gathered themselves together to Jerusalem within three days. It was the ninth month, on the twentieth day of the month; and all the people sat in the street of the house of God, trembling because of this matter, and for the great rain.

10 And Ezra the priest stood up, and said to them, You have transgressed, and have taken strange wives, to increase the trespass of Israel.

11 Now therefore make confession to the LORD God of your fathers, and do his pleasure: and separate yourselves

from the people of the land, and from the strange wives.

12 Then all the congregation answered and said with a loud voice, As you have said, so must we do.

13 But the people are many, and it is a time of much rain, and we are not able to stand without, neither is this a work of one day or two: for we are many that have transgressed in this thing.

14 Let now our rulers of all the congregation stand, and let all them which have taken strange wives in our cities come at appointed times, and with them the elders of every city, and the judges thereof, until the fierce wrath of our God for this matter be turned from us.

15 Only Jonathan the son of Asahel and Jahaziah the son of Tikvah were employed about this matter: and Meshullam and Shabbethai the Levite helped them.

16 And the children of the captivity did so. And Ezra the priest, with certain chief of the fathers, after the house of their fathers, and all of them by their names, were separated, and sat down in the first day of the tenth month to examine the matter.

17 And they made an end with all the men that had taken strange wives by the first day of the first month.

18 And among the sons of the priests there were found that had taken strange wives: namely, of the sons of Jeshua the son of Jozadak, and his brethren; Maaseiah, and Eliezer, and Jarib, and Gedaliah.

19 And they gave their hands that they would put away their wives; and being guilty, they offered a ram of the flock for their trespass.

20 And of the sons of Immer; Hanani, and Zebadiah.

21 And of the sons of Harim; Maaseiah, and Elijah, and Shemaiah, and Jehiel, and Uzziah.

22 And of the sons of Pashur; Elioenai, Maaseiah, Ishmael, Nethaneel, Jozabad, and Elasah.

23 Also of the Levites; Jozabad, and Shimei, and Kelaiah, (the same is Kelita,) Pethahiah, Judah, and Eliezer.

24 Of the singers also; Eliashib: and of the porters; Shallum, and Telem, and Uri.

25 Moreover of Israel: of the sons of Parosh; Ramiah, and Jeziah, and Malchiah, and Miamin, and Eleazar, and Malchijah, and Benaiah.

26 And of the sons of Elam; Mattaniah, Zechariah, and Jehiel, and Abdi, and Jeremoth, and Eliah.

27 And of the sons of Zattu; Elioenai, Eliashib, Mattaniah, and Jeremoth, and Zabad, and Aziza.

28 Of the sons also of Bebai; Jehohanan, Hananiah, Zabbai, and Athlai.

29 And of the sons of Bani; Meshullam, Malluch, and Adaiah, Jashub, and Sheal, and Ramoth.

30 And of the sons of Pahathmoab; Adna, and Chelal, Benaiah, Maaseiah, Mattaniah, Bezaleel, and Binnui, and Manasseh.

31 And of the sons of Harim; Eliezer, Ishijah, Malchiah, Shemaiah, Shimeon,

32 Benjamin, Malluch, and Shemariah.

33 Of the sons of Hashum; Mattenai, Mattathah, Zabad, Eliphelet, Jeremai, Manasseh, and Shimei.

34 Of the sons of Bani; Maadai, Amram, and Uel,

35 Benaiah, Bedeiah, Chelluh,

36 Vaniah, Meremoth, Eliashib,

37 Mattaniah, Mattenai, and Jaasau,

38 And Bani, and Binnui, Shimei,

39 And Shelemiah, and Nathan, and Adaiah,

40 Machnadebai, Shashai, Sharai,

41 Azareel, and Shelemiah, Shemariah,

42 Shallum, Amariah, and Joseph.

43 Of the sons of Nebo; Jeiel, Mattithiah, Zabad, Zebina, Jadau, and Joel, Benaiah.

44 All these had taken strange wives: and some of them had wives by whom they had children.

Nehemiah

CHAPTER 1

THE words of Nehemiah the son of Hachaliah. And it came to pass in the month Chisleu, in the twentieth year, as I was in Shushan the palace,

2 That Hanani, one of my brethren, came, he and certain men of Judah; and I asked them concerning the Jews that had escaped, which were left of the captivity, and concerning Jerusalem.

3 And they said to me, The remnant that are left of the captivity there in the province are in great affliction and reproach: the wall of Jerusalem also is broken down, and the gates thereof are burned with fire.

4 And it came to pass, when I heard these words, that I sat down and wept, and mourned certain days, and fasted, and prayed before the God of heaven,

5 And said, I beseech you, O LORD God of heaven, the great and terrible God, that keeps covenant and mercy for them that love him and observe his commandments:

6 Let your ear now be attentive, and your eyes open, that you may hear the prayer of your servant, which I pray before you now, day and night, for the children of Israel your servants, and confess the sins of the children of Israel, which we have sinned against you: both I and my father's house have sinned.

7 We have dealt very corruptly against you, and have not kept the commandments, nor the statutes, nor the judgments, which you commanded your servant Moses.

8 Remember, I beseech you, the word that you commanded your servant Moses, saying, If you transgress, I will scatter you abroad among the nations:

9 But if you turn to me, and keep my commandments, and do them; though there were of you cast out to the uttermost part of the heaven, yet will I gather them from thence, and will bring them to the place that I have chosen to set my name there.

10 Now these are your servants and your people, whom you have redeemed by your great power, and by your strong hand.

11 O LORD, I beseech you, let now your ear be attentive to the prayer of your servant, and to the prayer of your servants, who desire to fear your name: and prosper, I pray you, your servant

---

1: 4 In this book, Nehemiah seeks God in prayer eleven times.

1:11 The key to being heard by God is to be a servant who delights in the fear of the Lord. Jesus was heard in that He feared; "Who in the days of his flesh, when he had offered up prayers and supplications with strong crying and ears unto Him that was able to save Him from death, and was heard in that He feared" (Hebrews 5:7).

this day, and grant him mercy in the sight of this man. For I was the king's cupbearer.

CHAPTER 2

AND it came to pass in the month Nisan, in the twentieth year of Artaxerxes the king, that wine was before him: and I took up the wine, and gave it to the king. Now I had not been beforetime sad in his presence.

2 Therefore the king said to me, Why is your countenance sad, seeing you are not sick? this is nothing else but sorrow of heart. Then I was very sore afraid,

3 And said to the king, Let the king live forever: why should not my countenance be sad, when the city, the place of my fathers' sepulchres, lieth waste, and the gates thereof are consumed with fire?

4 Then the king said to me, For what do you make request? So I prayed to the God of heaven.

5 And I said to the king, If it please the king, and if your servant have found favour in your sight, that you would send me to Judah, to the city of my fathers' sepulchres, that I may build it.

6 And the king said to me, (the queen also sitting by him,) For how long shall your journey be? and when will you return? So it pleased the king to send me; and I set him a time.

7 Moreover I said to the king, If it please the king, let letters be given me to the governors beyond the river, that they may convey me over till I come into Judah;

8 And a letter to Asaph the keeper of the king's forest, that he may give me timber to make beams for the gates of the palace which appertained to the house, and for the wall of the city, and for the house that I shall enter into.

And the king granted me, according to the good hand of my God upon me.

9 Then I came to the governors beyond the river, and gave them the king's letters. Now the king had sent captains of the army and horsemen with me.

10 When Sanballat the Horonite, and Tobiah the servant, the Ammonite, heard of it, it grieved them exceedingly that there was come a man to seek the welfare of the children of Israel.

11 So I came to Jerusalem, and was there three days.

12 And I arose in the night, I and some few men with me; neither told I any man what my God had put in my heart to do at Jerusalem: neither was there any beast with me, save the beast that I rode upon.

13 And I went out by night by the gate of the valley, even before the dragon well, and to the dung port, and viewed the walls of Jerusalem, which were broken down, and the gates thereof were consumed with fire.

14 Then I went on to the gate of the fountain, and to the king's pool: but there was no place for the beast that was under me to pass.

15 Then went I up in the night by the brook, and viewed the wall, and turned back, and entered by the gate of the valley, and so returned.

16 And the rulers knew not where I went, or what I did; neither had I as yet told it to the Jews, nor to the priests, nor to the nobles, nor to the rulers, nor to the rest that did the work.

17 Then said I to them, You see the distress that we are in, how Jerusalem lieth waste, and the gates thereof are burned with fire: come, and let us build up the wall of Jerusalem, that we be no more a reproach.

18 Then I told them of the hand of my God which was good upon me; as also

---

2:8-9 We have not only been given authority from the King to build the Kingdom of God; we are also co-laborers with the Captain of our salvation and the hosts of Heaven (see Hebrews 1:13-14).

2:12 Check out the mind of God; see the comment at 1 Corinthians 2:16.

NEHEMIAH SECRETLY VIEWED THE RUINS OF THE WALLS OF JERUSALEM

Nehemiah 2:17

the king's words that he had spoken to me. And they said, Let us rise up and build. So they strengthened their hands for this good work.

19 But when Sanballat the Horonite, and Tobiah the servant, the Ammonite, and Geshem the Arabian, heard it, they laughed us to scorn, and despised us,

and said, What is this thing that you do? will you rebel against the king?

20 Then answered I them, and said to them, The God of heaven, he will prosper us; therefore we his servants will arise and build: but you have no portion, nor right, nor memorial, in Jerusalem.

CHAPTER 3

THEN Eliashib the high priest rose up with his brethren the priests, and they built the sheep gate; they sanctified it, and set up the doors of it; even to the tower of Meah they sanctified it, to the tower of Hananeel.

2 And next to him built the men of Jericho. And next to them built Zaccur the son of Imri.

3 But the fish gate did the sons of Hassenaah build, who also laid the beams thereof, and set up the doors thereof, the locks thereof, and the bars thereof.

4 And next to them repaired Meremoth the son of Urijah, the son of Koz. And next to them repaired Meshullam the son of Berechiah, the son of Meshezabeel. And next to them repaired Zadok the son of Baana.

5 And next to them the Tekoites repaired; but their nobles put not their necks to the work of their LORD.

6 Moreover the old gate repaired Jehoiada the son of Paseah, and Meshullam the son of Besodeiah; they laid the beams thereof, and set up the doors thereof, and the locks thereof, and the bars thereof.

7 And next to them repaired Melatiah the Gibeonite, and Jadon the Meronothite, the men of Gibeon, and of Mizpah, to the throne of the governor on this side the river.

8 Next to him repaired Uzziel the son of Harhaiah, of the goldsmiths. Next to him also repaired Hananiah the son of one of the apothecaries, and they fortified Jerusalem to the broad wall.

9 And next to them repaired Rephaiah the son of Hur, the ruler of the half part of Jerusalem.

10 And next to them repaired Jedaiah the son of Harumaph, even over against his house. And next to him repaired Hattush the son of Hashabniah.

11 Malchijah the son of Harim, and Hashub the son of Pahathmoab, repaired the other piece, and the tower of the furnaces.

12 And next to him repaired Shallum the son of Halohesh, the ruler of the half part of Jerusalem, he and his daughters.

13 The valley gate repaired Hanun, and the inhabitants of Zanoah; they built it, and set up the doors thereof, the locks thereof, and the bars thereof, and a thousand cubits on the wall to the dung gate.

14 But the dung gate repaired Malchiah the son of Rechab, the ruler of part of Bethhaccerem; he built it, and set up the doors thereof, the locks thereof, and the bars thereof.

15 But the gate of the fountain repaired Shallun the son of Colhozeh, the ruler of part of Mizpah; he built it, and covered it, and set up the doors thereof, the locks thereof, and the bars thereof, and the wall of the pool of Siloah by the king's garden, and to the stairs that go down from the city of David.

16 After him repaired Nehemiah the son of Azbuk, the ruler of the half part of Bethzur, to the place over against the sepulchres of David, and to the pool

---

3:1-3 To build up the walls of the Church we must build the sheep gate and sanctify it. We have a mandate from the King. It is believed that the Tower of Hananeel connected the sheep gate and the fish gate. The people of God should be connected by prayer to the task of evangelism. We should first of all be fishers of men. Notice that the fish gate had locks and bars (verse 3). It is easy to forget that the Church exists to seek the lost. Once we have become fishers of men we should lock ourselves into that task, and then bar any distraction.

that was made, and to the house of the mighty.

17 After him repaired the Levites, Rehum the son of Bani. Next to him repaired Hashabiah, the ruler of the half part of Keilah, in his part.

18 After him repaired their brethren, Bavai the son of Henadad, the ruler of the half part of Keilah.

19 And next to him repaired Ezer the son of Jeshua, the ruler of Mizpah, another piece over against the going up to the armoury at the turning of the wall.

20 After him Baruch the son of Zabbai earnestly repaired the other piece, from the turning of the wall to the door of the house of Eliashib the high priest.

21 After him repaired Meremoth the son of Urijah the son of Koz another piece, from the door of the house of Eliashib even to the end of the house of Eliashib.

22 And after him repaired the priests, the men of the plain.

23 After him repaired Benjamin and Hashub over against their house. After him repaired Azariah the son of Maaseiah the son of Ananiah by his house.

24 After him repaired Binnui the son of Henadad another piece, from the house of Azariah to the turning of the wall, even to the corner.

25 Palal the son of Uzai, over against the turning of the wall, and the tower which lieth out from the king's high house, that was by the court of the prison. After him Pedaiah the son of Parosh.

26 Moreover the Nethinims dwelt in Ophel, to the place over against the water gate toward the east, and the tower that lieth out.

27 After them the Tekoites repaired another piece, over against the great tower that lieth out, even to the wall of Ophel.

28 From above the horse gate repaired the priests, every one over against his house.

29 After them repaired Zadok the son of Immer over against his house. After him repaired also Shemaiah the son of Shechaniah, the keeper of the east gate.

30 After him repaired Hananiah the son of Shelemiah, and Hanun the sixth son of Zalaph, another piece. After him repaired Meshullam the son of Berechiah over against his chamber.

31 After him repaired Malchiah the goldsmith's son to the place of the Nethinims, and of the merchants, over against the gate Miphkad, and to the going up of the corner.

32 And between the going up of the corner to the sheep gate repaired the goldsmiths and the merchants.

CHAPTER 4

BUT it came to pass, that when Sanballat heard that we built the wall, he was wroth, and took great indignation, and mocked the Jews.

2 And he spoke before his brethren and the army of Samaria, and said, What do these feeble Jews? will they fortify themselves? will they sacrifice? will they make an end in a day? will they revive the stones out of the heaps of the rubbish which are burned?

3 Now Tobiah the Ammonite was by him, and he said, Even that which they build, if a fox go up, he shall even break down their stone wall.

4 Hear, O our God; for we are despised: and turn their reproach upon their own head, and give them for a prey in the land of captivity:

4:1-6 In the world's incongruent attitude toward the Church, Christians are, on the one hand, considered by non-Christians to be a feeble folk engaged in a futile work. At the same time, however, these same non-Christians are often greatly threatened by the Church and will work hard to hamper its work even though they say that the work of the Church is futile. But those of us who labor for the King give ourselves to prayer and have a mind to work.

5 And cover not their iniquity, and let not their sin be blotted out from before you: for they have provoked you to anger before the builders.

6 So built we the wall; and all the wall was joined together to the half thereof: for the people had a mind to work.

7 But it came to pass, that when Sanballat, and Tobiah, and the Arabians, and the Ammonites, and the Ashdodites, heard that the walls of Jerusalem were made up, and that the breaches began to be stopped, then they were very wroth,

8 And conspired all of them together to come and to fight against Jerusalem, and to hinder it.

9 Nevertheless we made our prayer to our God, and set a watch against them day and night, because of them.

10 And Judah said, The strength of the bearers of burdens is decayed, and there is much rubbish; so that we are not able to build the wall.

11 And our adversaries said, They shall not know, neither see, till we come in the midst among them, and slay them, and cause the work to cease.

12 And it came to pass, that when the Jews which dwelt by them came, they said to us ten times, From all places where you shall return to us they will be upon you.

13 Therefore set I in the lower places behind the wall, and on the higher places, I even set the people after their families with their swords, their spears, and their bows.

14 And I looked, and rose up, and said to the nobles, and to the rulers, and to the rest of the people, Be not afraid of them: remember the LORD, which is great and terrible, and fight for your brethren, your sons, and your daughters, your wives, and your houses.

15 And it came to pass, when our enemies heard that it was known to us, and God had brought their counsel to nothing, that we returned all of us to the wall, every one to his work.

16 And it came to pass from that time forth, that the half of my servants worked in the work, and the other half of them held both the spears, the shields, and the bows, and the habergeons; and the rulers were behind all the house of Judah.

17 They which built on the wall, and they that bare burdens, with those that laded, every one with one of his hands worked in the work, and with the other hand held a weapon.

18 For the builders, every one had his sword girded by his side, and so built. And he that sounded the trumpet was by me.

19 And I said to the nobles, and to the rulers, and to the rest of the people, The work is great and large, and we are separated upon the wall, one far from another.

4:8-9 When the world conspires to hinder the work of evangelism, we watch and pray (see Matthew 26:41).

4:13 See Ephesians 6:12-20.

4:17-20 As we work to build the Lord's kingdom on earth, we may sometimes be separated as Christians far from one another. Even so, however, each of us must not only keep our spiritual weapons ready at our sides; we must also keep listening for the sound of the trumpet of God and the voice of the archangel (see 1 Thessalonians 4:16).

It is then that "the Lord Jesus shall be revealed from heaven with his mighty angels, in flaming fire taking vengeance on them that know not God and that obey not the gospel of our Lord Jesus Christ: Who shall be punished with everlasting destruction from the presence of the Lord, and from the glory of his power" (2 Thessalonians 1: 7-9).

Our unified efforts will keep our mind working while it is yet day. For the night is coming when no man shall work (see John 9:4).

20 In what place, therefore, you hear the sound of the trumpet, resort there to us: our God shall fight for us.

21 So we laboured in the work: and half of them held the spears from the rising of the morning till the stars appeared.

22 Likewise at the same time said I to the people, Let every one with his servant lodge within Jerusalem, that in the night they may be a guard to us, and labour on the day.

23 So neither I, nor my brethren, nor my servants, nor the men of the guard which followed me, none of us put off our clothes, saving that every one put them off for washing.

CHAPTER 5

AND there was a great cry of the people and of their wives against their brethren the Jews.

2 For there were that said, We, our sons, and our daughters, are many: therefore we take up corn for them, that we may eat, and live.

3 Some also there were that said, We have mortgaged our lands, vineyards, and houses, that we might buy corn, because of the dearth.

4 There were also that said, We have borrowed money for the king's tribute, and that upon our lands and vineyards.

5 Yet now our flesh is as the flesh of our brethren, our children as their children: and, lo, we bring into bondage our sons and our daughters to be servants, and some of our daughters are brought to bondage already: neither is it in our power to redeem them; for other men have our lands and vineyards.

6 And I was very angry when I heard their cry and these words.

7 Then I consulted with myself, and I rebuked the nobles, and the rulers, and said to them, You exact usury, every one of his brother. And I set a great assembly against them.

8 And I said to them, We after our ability have redeemed our brethren the Jews, which were sold to the heathen; and will you even sell your brethren? or shall they be sold to us? Then held they their peace, and found nothing to answer.

9 Also I said, It is not good that you do: should you not to walk in the fear of our God because of the reproach of the heathen our enemies?

10 I likewise, and my brethren, and my servants, might exact of them money and corn: I pray you, let us leave off this usury.

11 Restore, I pray you, to them, even this day, their lands, their vineyards, their oliveyards, and their houses, also the hundredth part of the money, and of the corn, the wine, and the oil, that you exact of them.

12 Then said they, We will restore them, and will require nothing of them; so will we do as you say. Then I called the priests, and took an oath of them, that they should do according to this promise.

13 Also I shook my lap, and said, So God shake out every man from his house, and from his labour, that performs not this promise, even thus be he shaken out, and emptied. And all the congregation said, Amen, and praised the LORD. And the people did according to this promise.

14 Moreover from the time that I was appointed to be their governor in the land of Judah, from the twentieth year even to the two and thirtieth year of Artaxerxes the king, that is, twelve years, I and my brethren have not eaten the bread of the governor.

5:16 Every leader should condescend to do the work of evangelism. The Apostle Paul had the highest calling and yet pleaded for prayer that he would open his mouth and speak the mystery of the Gospel " ... as I ought to speak " (Ephesians 6:20).

15 But the former governors that had been before me were chargeable to the people, and had taken of them bread and wine, beside forty shekels of silver; yea, even their servants bare rule over the people: but so did not I, because of the fear of God.

16 Yea, also I continued in the work of this wall, neither bought we any land: and all my servants were gathered there to the work.

17 Moreover there were at my table an hundred and fifty of the Jews and rulers, beside those that came to us from among the heathen that are about us.

18 Now that which was prepared for me daily was one ox and six choice sheep; also fowls were prepared for me, and once in ten days store of all sorts of wine: yet for all this required not I the bread of the governor, because the bondage was heavy upon this people.

19 Think upon me, my God, for good, according to all that I have done for this people.

CHAPTER 6

NOW it came to pass when Sanballat, and Tobiah, and Geshem the Arabian, and the rest of our enemies, heard that I had built the wall, and that there was no breach left therein; (though at that time I had not set up the doors upon the gates;)

2 That Sanballat and Geshem sent to me, saying, Come, let us meet together in some one of the villages in the plain of Ono. But they thought to do me mischief.

3 And I sent messengers to them, saying, I am doing a great work, so that I cannot come down: why should the work cease, whilst I leave it, and come down to you?

4 Yet they sent to me four times after this sort; and I answered them after the same manner.

5 Then sent Sanballat his servant to me in like manner the fifth time with an open letter in his hand;

6 Wherein was written, It is reported among the heathen, and Gashmu says it, that you and the Jews think to rebel: for which cause you built the wall, that you may be their king, according to these words.

7 And you have also appointed prophets to preach of you at Jerusalem, saying, There is a king in Judah: and now shall it be reported to the king according to these words. Come now therefore, and let us take counsel together.

8 Then I sent to him, saying, There are no such things done as you say, but you feign them out of your own heart.

9 For they all made us afraid, saying, Their hands shall be weakened from the work, that it be not done. Now therefore, O God, strengthen my hands.

10 Afterward I came to the house of Shemaiah the son of Delaiah the son of Mehetabeel, who was shut up; and he said, Let us meet together in the house of God, within the temple, and let us shut the doors of the temple: for they will come to slay you; yea, in the night will they come to slay you.

11 And I said, Should such a man as I flee? and who is there, that, being as I am, would go into the temple to save his life? I will not go in.

12 And, lo, I perceived that God had not sent him; but that he pronounced this prophecy against me: for Tobiah and Sanballat had hired him.

13 Therefore was he hired, that I should be afraid, and do so, and sin, and

---

6:3 The enemy's aim is to have the Church cease from the work of evangelism. But we know that we are doing the greatest of all works that man can be involved in on earth. We will not cease. We cannot cease (see 1 Corinthians 15:58).

6:9 If the enemy cannot use apathy to cause us to cease from our labors on behalf of the gospel, he will use intimidation (see verse 14). Fear is his poison, but faith is the antidote.

that they might have matter for an evil report, that they might reproach me.

14 My God, think upon Tobiah and Sanballat according to these their works, and on the prophetess Noadiah, and the rest of the prophets, that would have put me in fear.

15 So the wall was finished in the twenty and fifth day of the month Elul, in fifty and two days.

16 And it came to pass, that when all our enemies heard thereof, and all the heathen that were about us saw these things, they were much cast down in their own eyes: for they perceived that this work was done of our God.

17 Moreover in those days the nobles of Judah sent many letters to Tobiah, and the letters of Tobiah came to them.

18 For there were many in Judah sworn to him, because he was the son in law of Shechaniah the son of Arah; and his son Johanan had taken the daughter of Meshullam the son of Berechiah.

19 Also they reported his good deeds before me, and uttered my words to him. And Tobiah sent letters to put me in fear.

CHAPTER 7

N OW it came to pass, when the wall was built, and I had set up the doors, and the porters and the singers and the Levites were appointed,

2 That I gave my brother Hanani, and Hananiah the ruler of the palace, charge over Jerusalem: for he was a faithful man, and feared God above many.

3 And I said to them, Let not the gates of Jerusalem be opened until the sun be hot; and while they stand by, let them shut the doors, and bar them: and appoint watches of the inhabitants of Jerusalem, every one in his watch, and every one to be over against his house.

4 Now the city was large and great: but the people were few therein, and the houses were not built.

5 And my God put into mine heart to gather together the nobles, and the rulers, and the people, that they might be reckoned by genealogy. And I found a register of the genealogy of them which came up at the first, and found written therein,

6 These are the children of the province, that went up out of the captivity, of those that had been carried away, whom Nebuchadnezzar the king of Babylon had carried away, and came again to Jerusalem and to Judah, every one to his city;

7 Who came with Zerubbabel, Jeshua, Nehemiah, Azariah, Raamiah, Nahamani, Mordecai, Bilshan, Mispereth, Bigvai, Nehum, Baanah. The number, I say, of the men of the people of Israel was this;

8 The children of Parosh, two thousand an hundred seventy and two.

9 The children of Shephatiah, three hundred seventy and two.

10 The children of Arah, six hundred fifty and two.

11 The children of Pahathmoab, of the children of Jeshua and Joab, two thousand and eight hundred and eighteen.

12 The children of Elam, a thousand two hundred fifty and four.

13 The children of Zattu, eight hundred forty and five.

14 The children of Zaccai, seven hundred and threescore.

15 The children of Binnui, six hundred forty and eight.

16 The children of Bebai, six hundred twenty and eight.

17 The children of Azgad, two thousand three hundred twenty and two.

18 The children of Adonikam, six hundred threescore and seven.

7: 2 The Church needs men and women who are faithful to and fearful of nothing but God.

19 The children of Bigvai, two thousand threescore and seven.

20 The children of Adin, six hundred fifty and five.

21 The children of Ater of Hezekiah, ninety and eight.

22 The children of Hashum, three hundred twenty and eight.

23 The children of Bezai, three hundred twenty and four.

24 The children of Hariph, an hundred and twelve.

25 The children of Gibeon, ninety and five.

26 The men of Bethlehem and Netophah, an hundred fourscore and eight.

27 The men of Anathoth, an hundred twenty and eight.

28 The men of Bethazmaveth, forty and two.

29 The men of Kirjathjearim, Chephirah, and Beeroth, seven hundred forty and three.

30 The men of Ramah and Gaba, six hundred twenty and one.

31 The men of Michmas, an hundred and twenty and two.

32 The men of Bethel and Ai, an hundred twenty and three.

33 The men of the other Nebo, fifty and two.

34 The children of the other Elam, a thousand two hundred fifty and four.

35 The children of Harim, three hundred and twenty.

36 The children of Jericho, three hundred forty and five.

37 The children of Lod, Hadid, and Ono, seven hundred twenty and one.

38 The children of Senaah, three thousand nine hundred and thirty.

39 The priests: the children of Jedaiah, of the house of Jeshua, nine hundred seventy and three.

40 The children of Immer, a thousand fifty and two.

41 The children of Pashur, a thousand two hundred forty and seven.

42 The children of Harim, a thousand and seventeen.

43 The Levites: the children of Jeshua, of Kadmiel, and of the children of Hodevah, seventy and four.

44 The singers: the children of Asaph, an hundred forty and eight.

45 The porters: the children of Shallum, the children of Ater, the children of Talmon, the children of Akkub, the children of Hatita, the children of Shobai, an hundred thirty and eight.

46 The Nethinims: the children of Ziha, the children of Hashupha, the children of Tabbaoth,

47 The children of Keros, the children of Sia, the children of Padon,

48 The children of Lebana, the children of Hagaba, the children of Shalmai,

49 The children of Hanan, the children of Giddel, the children of Gahar,

50 The children of Reaiah, the children of Rezin, the children of Nekoda,

51 The children of Gazzam, the children of Uzza, the children of Phaseah,

52 The children of Besai, the children of Meunim, the children of Nephishesim,

53 The children of Bakbuk, the children of Hakupha, the children of Harhur,

54 The children of Bazlith, the children of Mehida, the children of Harsha,

55 The children of Barkos, the children of Sisera, the children of Tamah,

56 The children of Neziah, the children of Hatipha.

57 The children of Solomon's servants: the children of Sotai, the children of Sophereth, the children of Perida,

58 The children of Jaala, the children of Darkon, the children of Giddel,

59 The children of Shephatiah, the children of Hattil, the children of Pochereth of Zebaim, the children of Amon.

60 All the Nethinims, and the children of Solomon's servants, were three hundred ninety and two.

61 And these were they which went up also from Telmelah, Telharesha, Cherub,

Addon, and Immer: but they could not shew their father's house, nor their seed, whether they were of Israel.

62 The children of Delaiah, the children of Tobiah, the children of Nekoda, six hundred forty and two.

63 And of the priests: the children of Habaiah, the children of Koz, the children of Barzillai, which took one of the daughters of Barzillai the Gileadite to wife, and was called after their name.

64 These sought their register among those that were reckoned by genealogy, but it was not found: therefore were they, as polluted, put from the priesthood.

65 And the Tirshatha said to them, that they should not eat of the most holy things, till there stood up a priest with Urim and Thummim.

66 The whole congregation together was forty and two thousand three hundred and threescore,

67 Beside their manservants and their maidservants, of whom there were seven thousand three hundred thirty and seven: and they had two hundred forty and five singing men and singing women.

68 Their horses, seven hundred thirty and six: their mules, two hundred forty and five:

69 Their camels, four hundred thirty and five: six thousand seven hundred and twenty asses.

70 And some of the chief of the fathers gave to the work. The Tirshatha gave to the treasure a thousand drams of gold, fifty basons, five hundred and thirty priests' garments.

71 And some of the chief of the fathers gave to the treasure of the work twenty thousand drams of gold, and two thousand and two hundred pound of silver.

72 And that which the rest of the people gave was twenty thousand drams of gold, and two thousand pound of silver, and threescore and seven priests' garments.

73 So the priests, and the Levites, and the porters, and the singers, and some of the people, and the Nethinims, and all Israel, dwelt in their cities; and when the seventh month came, the children of Israel were in their cities.

CHAPTER 8

AND all the people gathered themselves together as one man into the street that was before the water gate; and they spoke to Ezra the scribe to bring the book of the law of Moses, which the LORD had commanded to Israel.

2 And Ezra the priest brought the law before the congregation both of men and women, and all that could hear with understanding, upon the first day of the seventh month.

3 And he read therein before the street that was before the water gate from the morning until midday, before the men and the women, and those that could understand; and the ears of all the people were attentive to the book of the law.

4 And Ezra the scribe stood upon a pulpit of wood, which they had made for the purpose; and beside him stood Mattithiah, and Shema, and Anaiah, and Urijah, and Hilkiah, and Maaseiah, on his right hand; and on his left hand, Pedaiah, and Mishael, and Malchiah, and Hashum, and Hashbadana, Zechariah, and Meshullam.

5 And Ezra opened the book in the sight of all the people; (for he was above all the people;) and when he opened it, all the people stood up:

6 And Ezra blessed the LORD, the great God. And all the people answered, Amen, Amen, with lifting up their hands: and they bowed their heads, and worshipped the LORD with their faces to the ground.

7 Also Jeshua, and Bani, and Sherebiah, Jamin, Akkub, Shabbethai, Hodijah, Maaseiah, Kelita, Azariah, Jozabad, Hanan, Pelaiah, and the Levites, caused the people to understand the law: and the people stood in their place.

EZRA READING THE LAW IN THE HEARING OF THE PEOPLE

Nehemiah 8:2-9

We must bring God's Law to the people. They will not come to it. Men love darkness rather than light. Neither will they come to the light lest their deeds be exposed (see John 3:19-21).

It is the light of this Law that exposes sin (see Romans 7:7). The Law faces the Watergate; it causes those who hear with understanding to thirst for the righteousness that can only be found in Jesus Christ.

Notice in these verses that they caused the people to understand the Law by presenting it distinctly, giving it sense and causing them to understand its meaning. We do the same by opening up the spirituality of the Ten Commandments. We tell our hearers that God sees their thoughts, and He requires truth in the inward parts. We make clear that God considers lust to be adultery and hatred to be murder, etc. We explain that God's holy, perfect, just and good Law is the measure against which they will be judged. Those who hear and understand will find a place of contrition before God (verse 9) and at that point will be receptive to the gospel of grace.

THE FUNCTION OF THE LAW IN EVANGELISM

8:9 How the people were wounded with the words of the Law that were read to them. The Law works death and speaks terror; shows men their sins and their misery and danger because of sin, and it thunders a curse against every one that continues not in every part of his duty.

Therefore, when they heard it they all wept. It was a good sign that their hearts were tender, like Josiah's when he heard the words of the Law. They wept to think how they had offended God and exposed themselves, by their many violations of the Law; when some wept, all wept, for they all saw themselves guilty before God.

Matthew Henry

8 So they read in the book in the law of God distinctly, and gave the sense, and caused them to understand the reading.

9 And Nehemiah, which is the Tirshatha, and Ezra the priest the scribe, and the Levites that taught the people, said to all the people, This day is holy to the LORD your God; mourn not, nor weep. For all the people wept, when they heard the words of the law.

10 Then he said to them, Go your way, eat the fat, and drink the sweet, and send portions to them for whom nothing is prepared: for this day is holy to our LORD: neither be sorry; for the joy of the LORD is your strength.

11 So the Levites stilled all the people, saying, Hold your peace, for the day is holy; neither be grieved.

12 And all the people went their way to eat, and to drink, and to send portions, and to make great mirth, because they had understood the words that were declared to them.

13 And on the second day were gathered together the chief of the fathers of all the people, the priests, and the Levites, to Ezra the scribe, even to understand the words of the law.

14 And they found written in the law which the LORD had commanded by Moses, that the children of Israel should dwell in booths in the feast of the seventh month:

15 And that they should publish and proclaim in all their cities, and in Jerusalem, saying, Go forth to the mount, and fetch olive branches, and pine branches, and myrtle branches, and palm branches, and branches of thick trees, to make booths, as it is written.

16 So the people went forth, and brought them, and made themselves booths, every one upon the roof of his house, and in their courts, and in the courts of the house of God, and in the street of the water gate, and in the street of the gate of Ephraim.

17 And all the congregation of them that were come again out of the captivity made booths, and sat under the booths: for since the days of Jeshua the son of Nun to that day had not the children of Israel done so. And there was very great gladness.

18 Also day by day, from the first day to the last day, he read in the book of the law of God. And they kept the feast seven days; and on the eighth day was a solemn assembly, according to the manner.

CHAPTER 9

NOW in the twenty and fourth day of this month the children of Israel were assembled with fasting, and with sackclothes, and earth upon them.

2 And the seed of Israel separated themselves from all strangers, and stood and confessed their sins, and the iniquities of their fathers.

3 And they stood up in their place, and read in the book of the law of the LORD their God one fourth part of the day; and

another fourth part they confessed, and worshipped the LORD their God.

4 Then stood up upon the stairs, of the Levites, Jeshua, and Bani, Kadmiel, Shebaniah, Bunni, Sherebiah, Bani, and Chenani, and cried with a loud voice to the LORD their God.

5 Then the Levites, Jeshua, and Kadmiel, Bani, Hashabniah, Sherebiah, Hodijah, Shebaniah, and Pethahiah, said, Stand up and bless the LORD your God for ever and ever: and blessed be your glorious name, which is exalted above all blessing and praise.

6 You, even you, are LORD alone; you have made heaven, the heaven of heavens, with all their host, the earth, and all things that are therein, the seas, and all that is therein, and you preserve them all; and the host of heaven worships you.

7 You are the LORD the God, who did choose Abram, and brought him forth out of Ur of the Chaldees, and gave him the name of Abraham;

8 And found his heart faithful before you, and made a covenant with him to give the land of the Canaanites, the Hittites, the Amorites, and the Perizzites, and the Jebusites, and the Girgashites, to give it, I say, to his seed, and have performed your words; for you are righteous:

9 And did see the affliction of our fathers in Egypt, and heard their cry by the Red sea;

10 And showed signs and wonders upon Pharaoh, and on all his servants, and on all the people of his land: for you knew that they dealt proudly against them. So did you get for yourself a name, as it is this day.

11 And you did divide the sea before them, so that they went through the midst of the sea on the dry land; and their persecutors you threw into the deeps, as a stone into the mighty waters.

12 Moreover you led them in the day by a cloudy pillar; and in the night by a pillar of fire, to give them light in the way wherein they should go.

13 You came down also upon mount Sinai, and spoke with them from heaven, and gave them right judgments, and true laws, good statutes and commandments:

14 And made known to them your holy sabbath, and commanded them precepts, statutes, and laws, by the hand of Moses your servant:

15 And gave them bread from heaven for their hunger, and brought forth water for them out of the rock for their thirst, and promised them that they should go in to possess the land which you had sworn to give them.

16 But they and our fathers dealt proudly, and hardened their necks, and hearkened not to your commandments,

17 And refused to obey, neither were mindful of your wonders that you did among them; but hardened their necks, and in their rebellion appointed a captain to return to their bondage: but you are a God ready to pardon, gracious and merciful, slow to anger, and of great kindness, and forsook them not.

18 Yea, when they had made them a molten calf, and said, This is your God that brought you up out of Egypt, and had worked great provocations;

19 Yet you in your manifold mercies forsook them not in the wilderness: the pillar of the cloud departed not from

---

9:6 God made the heavens with "all" their hosts. He made the earth and "all" that are in it. He made the seas and "all" that are in them. There is no room for theories that anything evolved of its own accord.

9:15 Jesus is the bread from Heaven (see John 6:33-35). He is also the rock from which flows the water of life (see 1 Corinthians 10:4).

9:17 God hasn't changed. He is still patiently waiting, not willing that any perish, but that all come to repentance.

them by day, to lead them in the way;
neither the pillar of fire by night, to
show them light, and the way wherein
they should go.

20 You gave also your good spirit to instruct them, and withheld not your
manna from their mouth, and gave them
water for their thirst.

21 Yea, forty years did you sustain
them in the wilderness, so that they
lacked nothing; their clothes waxed not
old, and their feet swelled not.

22 Moreover you gave them kingdoms
and nations, and did divide them into
corners: so they possessed the land of
Sihon, and the land of the king of
Heshbon, and the land of Og king of
Bashan.

23 Their children also multiplied you as
the stars of heaven, and brought them
into the land, concerning which you had
promised to their fathers, that they
should go in to possess it.

24 So the children went in and possessed the land, and you subdued before
them the inhabitants of the land, the
Canaanites, and gave them into their
hands, with their kings, and the people
of the land, that they might do with
them as they would.

25 And they took strong cities, and a fat
land, and possessed houses full of all
goods, wells dug, vineyards, and oliveyards, and fruit trees in abundance: so
they did eat, and were filled, and became
fat, and delighted themselves in your
great goodness.

26 Nevertheless they were disobedient,
and rebelled against you, and cast your
law behind their backs, and slew your
prophets which testified against them to
turn them to you, and they worked great
provocations.

27 Therefore you delivered them into
the hand of their enemies, who vexed
them: and in the time of their trouble,
when they cried to you, you heard them
from heaven; and according to your
manifold mercies you gave them saviours, who saved them out of the hand
of their enemies.

28 But after they had rest, they did evil
again before you: therefore you left them
in the land of their enemies, so that they
had the dominion over them: yet when
they returned, and cried to you, you
heard them from heaven; and many
times did you deliver them according to
your mercies;

29 And testified against them, that you
might bring them again to your law: yet
they dealt proudly, and hearkened not to
your commandments, but sinned against
your judgments, (which if a man do, he
shall live in them;) and withdrew the
shoulder, and hardened their neck, and
would not hear.

30 Yet many years did you forbear
them, and testified against them by your
spirit in your prophets: yet would they
not give ear: therefore you gave them
into the hand of the people of the lands.

31 Nevertheless for your great mercies'
sake you did not utterly consume them,
nor forsake them; for you are a gracious
and merciful God.

32 Now therefore, our God, the great,
the mighty, and the terrible God, who
keeps covenant and mercy, let not all the
trouble seem little before you, that has
come upon us, on our kings, on our
princes, and on our priests, and on our
prophets, and on our fathers, and on all
your people, since the time of the kings
of Assyria to this day.

9:26 The disobedient and rebellious hate God's Law. They think that their moral dilemma will be
solved and they can sin with guilt-free abandonment if they expel the Ten Commandments and
those who preach God's Law. However, God wrote His Law in stone with His own finger, and He
engraved its work on the tables of their heart (see Romans 2:15). They will still have to face Him
and His Law on the Day of Wrath.

33 Howbeit you are just in all that is brought upon us; for you have done right, but we have done wickedly:

34 Neither have our kings, our princes, our priests, nor our fathers, kept your law, nor hearkened to your commandments and your testimonies, wherewith you did testify against them.

35 For they have not served you in their kingdom, and in your great goodness that you gave them, and in the large and fat land which you gave before them, neither turned they from their wicked works.

36 Behold, we are servants this day, and for the land that you gave to our fathers to eat the fruit thereof and the good thereof, behold, we are servants in it:

37 And it yielded much increase to the kings whom you have set over us because of our sins: also they have dominion over our bodies, and over our cattle, at their pleasure, and we are in great distress.

38 And because of all this we make a sure covenant, and write it; and our princes, Levites, and priests, seal to it.

CHAPTER 10

NOW those that sealed were, Nehemiah, the Tirshatha, the son of Hachaliah, and Zidkijah,

2 Seraiah, Azariah, Jeremiah,

3 Pashur, Amariah, Malchijah,

4 Hattush, Shebaniah, Malluch,

5 Harim, Meremoth, Obadiah,

6 Daniel, Ginnethon, Baruch,

7 Meshullam, Abijah, Mijamin,

8 Maaziah, Bilgai, Shemaiah: these were the priests.

9 And the Levites: both Jeshua the son of Azaniah, Binnui of the sons of Henadad, Kadmiel;

10 And their brethren, Shebaniah, Hodijah, Kelita, Pelaiah, Hanan,

11 Micha, Rehob, Hashabiah,

12 Zaccur, Sherebiah, Shebaniah,

13 Hodijah, Bani, Beninu.

14 The chief of the people; Parosh, Pahathmoab, Elam, Zatthu, Bani,

15 Bunni, Azgad, Bebai,

16 Adonijah, Bigvai, Adin,

17 Ater, Hizkijah, Azzur,

18 Hodijah, Hashum, Bezai,

19 Hariph, Anathoth, Nebai,

20 Magpiash, Meshullam, Hezir,

21 Meshezabeel, Zadok, Jaddua,

22 Pelatiah, Hanan, Anaiah,

23 Hoshea, Hananiah, Hashub,

24 Hallohesh, Pileha, Shobek,

25 Rehum, Hashabnah, Maaseiah,

26 And Ahijah, Hanan, Anan,

27 Malluch, Harim, Baanah.

28 And the rest of the people, the priests, the Levites, the porters, the singers, the Nethinims, and all they that had separated themselves from the people of the lands to the law of God, their wives, their sons, and their daughters, every one having knowledge, and having understanding;

29 They clave to their brethren, their nobles, and entered into a curse, and into an oath, to walk in God's law, which was given by Moses the servant of God, and to observe and do all the commandments of the LORD our Lord, and his judgments and his statutes;

30 And that we would not give our daughters to the people of the land, not take their daughters for our sons:

31 And if the people of the land bring ware or any victuals on the sabbath day to sell, that we would not buy it of them on the sabbath, or on the holy day: and that we would leave the seventh year, and the exaction of every debt.

32 Also we made ordinances for us, to charge ourselves yearly with the third part of a shekel for the service of the house of our God;

33 For the shewbread, and for the continual meat offering, and for the continu-

---

10:29 For the spiritual nature of God's Law, see comment at Matthew 15:19.

al burnt offering, of the sabbaths, of the new moons, for the set feasts, and for the holy things, and for the sin offerings to make an atonement for Israel, and for all the work of the house of our God.

34 And we cast the lots among the priests, the Levites, and the people, for the wood offering, to bring it into the house of our God, after the houses of our fathers, at times appointed year by year, to burn upon the altar of the LORD our God, as it is written in the law:

35 And to bring the firstfruits of our ground, and the firstfruits of all fruit of all trees, year by year, to the house of the LORD:

36 Also the firstborn of our sons, and of our cattle, as it is written in the law, and the firstlings of our herds and of our flocks, to bring to the house of our God, to the priests that minister in the house of our God:

37 And that we should bring the firstfruits of our dough, and our offerings, and the fruit of all manner of trees, of wine and of oil, to the priests, to the chambers of the house of our God; and the tithes of our ground to the Levites, that the same Levites might have the tithes in all the cities of our tillage.

38 And the priest the son of Aaron shall be with the Levites, when the Levites take tithes: and the Levites shall bring up the tithe of the tithes to the house of our God, to the chambers, into the treasure house.

39 For the children of Israel and the children of Levi shall bring the offering of the corn, of the new wine, and the oil, to the chambers, where are the vessels of the sanctuary, and the priests that minister, and the porters, and the singers: and we will not forsake the house of our God.

CHAPTER 11

AND the rulers of the people dwelt at Jerusalem: the rest of the people also cast lots, to bring one of ten to dwell in Jerusalem the holy city, and nine parts to dwell in other cities.

2 And the people blessed all the men, that willingly offered themselves to dwell at Jerusalem.

3 Now these are the chief of the province that dwelt in Jerusalem: but in the cities of Judah dwelt every one in his possession in their cities, to wit, Israel, the priests, and the Levites, and the Nethinims, and the children of Solomon's servants.

4 And at Jerusalem dwelt certain of the children of Judah, and of the children of Benjamin. Of the children of Judah; Athaiah the son of Uzziah, the son of Zechariah, the son of Amariah, the son of Shephatiah, the son of Mahalaleel, of the children of Perez;

5 And Maaseiah the son of Baruch, the son of Colhozeh, the son of Hazaiah, the son of Adaiah, the son of Joiarib, the son of Zechariah, the son of Shiloni.

6 All the sons of Perez that dwelt at Jerusalem were four hundred threescore and eight valiant men.

7 And these are the sons of Benjamin; Sallu the son of Meshullam, the son of Joed, the son of Pedaiah, the son of Kolaiah, the son of Maaseiah, the son of Ithiel, the son of Jesaiah.

8 And after him Gabbai, Sallai, nine hundred twenty and eight.

9 And Joel the son of Zichri was their overseer: and Judah the son of Senuah was second over the city.

10 Of the priests: Jedaiah the son of Joiarib, Jachin.

11 Seraiah the son of Hilkiah, the son of Meshullam, the son of Zadok, the son of Meraioth, the son of Ahitub, was the ruler of the house of God.

12 And their brethren that did the work of the house were eight hundred twenty and two: and Adaiah the son of Jeroham, the son of Pelaliah, the son of Amzi, the

son of Zechariah, the son of Pashur, the son of Malchiah.

13 And his brethren, chief of the fathers, two hundred forty and two: and Amashai the son of Azareel, the son of Ahasai, the son of Meshillemoth, the son of Immer,

14 And their brethren, mighty men of valour, an hundred twenty and eight: and their overseer was Zabdiel, the son of one of the great men.

15 Also of the Levites: Shemaiah the son of Hashub, the son of Azrikam, the son of Hashabiah, the son of Bunni;

16 And Shabbethai and Jozabad, of the chief of the Levites, had the oversight of the outward business of the house of God.

17 And Mattaniah the son of Micha, the son of Zabdi, the son of Asaph, was the principal to begin the thanksgiving in prayer: and Bakbukiah the second among his brethren, and Abda the son of Shammua, the son of Galal, the son of Jeduthun.

18 All the Levites in the holy city were two hundred fourscore and four.

19 Moreover the porters, Akkub, Talmon, and their brethren that kept the gates, were an hundred seventy and two.

20 And the residue of Israel, of the priests, and the Levites, were in all the cities of Judah, every one in his inheritance.

21 But the Nethinims dwelt in Ophel: and Ziha and Gispa were over the Nethinims.

22 The overseer also of the Levites at Jerusalem was Uzzi the son of Bani, the son of Hashabiah, the son of Mattaniah, the son of Micha. Of the sons of Asaph, the singers were over the business of the house of God.

23 For it was the king's commandment concerning them, that a certain portion should be for the singers, due for every day.

24 And Pethahiah the son of Meshezabeel, of the children of Zerah the son of Judah, was at the king's hand in all matters concerning the people.

25 And for the villages, with their fields, some of the children of Judah dwelt at Kirjatharba, and in the villages thereof, and at Dibon, and in the villages thereof, and at Jekabzeel, and in the villages thereof,

26 And at Jeshua, and at Moladah, and at Bethphelet,

27 And at Hazarshual, and at Beersheba, and in the villages thereof,

28 And at Ziklag, and at Mekonah, and in the villages thereof,

29 And at Enrimmon, and at Zareah, and at Jarmuth,

30 Zanoah, Adullam, and in their villages, at Lachish, and the fields thereof, at Azekah, and in the villages thereof. And they dwelt from Beersheba to the valley of Hinnom.

31 The children also of Benjamin from Geba dwelt at Michmash, and Aija, and Bethel, and in their villages.

32 And at Anathoth, Nob, Ananiah,

33 Hazor, Ramah, Gittaim,

34 Hadid, Zeboim, Neballat,

35 Lod, and Ono, the valley of craftsmen.

36 And of the Levites were divisions in Judah, and in Benjamin.

CHAPTER 12

NOW these are the priests and the Levites that went up with Zerubbabel the son of Shealtiel, and Jeshua: Seraiah, Jeremiah, Ezra,

2 Amariah, Malluch, Hattush,

3 Shechaniah, Rehum, Meremoth,

4 Iddo, Ginnetho, Abijah,

5 Miamin, Maadiah, Bilgah,

6 Shemaiah, and Joiarib, Jedaiah,

7 Sallu, Amok, Hilkiah, Jedaiah. These were the chief of the priests and of their brethren in the days of Jeshua.

8 Moreover the Levites: Jeshua, Binnui, Kadmiel, Sherebiah, Judah, and Mattaniah, which was over the thanksgiving, he and his brethren.

9 Also Bakbukiah and Unni, their brethren, were over against them in the watches.

10 And Jeshua begat Joiakim, Joiakim also begat Eliashib, and Eliashib begat Joiada,

11 And Joiada begat Jonathan, and Jonathan begat Jaddua.

12 And in the days of Joiakim were priests, the chief of the fathers: of Seraiah, Meraiah; of Jeremiah, Hananiah;

13 Of Ezra, Meshullam; of Amariah, Jehohanan;

14 Of Melicu, Jonathan; of Shebaniah, Joseph;

15 Of Harim, Adna; of Meraioth, Helkai;

16 Of Iddo, Zechariah; of Ginnethon, Meshullam;

17 Of Abijah, Zichri; of Miniamin, of Moadiah, Piltai:

18 Of Bilgah, Shammua; of Shemaiah, Jehonathan;

19 And of Joiarib, Mattenai; of Jedaiah, Uzzi;

20 Of Sallai, Kallai; of Amok, Eber;

21 Of Hilkiah, Hashabiah; of Jedaiah, Nethaneel.

22 The Levites in the days of Eliashib, Joiada, and Johanan, and Jaddua, were recorded chief of the fathers: also the priests, to the reign of Darius the Persian.

23 The sons of Levi, the chief of the fathers, were written in the book of the chronicles, even until the days of Johanan the son of Eliashib.

24 And the chief of the Levites: Hashabiah, Sherebiah, and Jeshua the son of Kadmiel, with their brethren over against them, to praise and to give thanks, according to the commandment of David the man of God, ward over against ward.

25 Mattaniah, and Bakbukiah, Obadiah, Meshullam, Talmon, Akkub, were porters keeping the ward at the thresholds of the gates.

26 These were in the days of Joiakim the son of Jeshua, the son of Jozadak, and in the days of Nehemiah the governor, and of Ezra the priest, the scribe.

27 And at the dedication of the wall of Jerusalem they sought the Levites out of all their places, to bring them to Jerusalem, to keep the dedication with gladness, both with thanksgivings, and with singing, with cymbals, psalteries, and with harps.

28 And the sons of the singers gathered themselves together, both out of the plain country round about Jerusalem, and from the villages of Netophathi;

29 Also from the house of Gilgal, and out of the fields of Geba and Azmaveth: for the singers had built them villages round about Jerusalem.

30 And the priests and the Levites purified themselves, and purified the people, and the gates, and the wall.

31 Then I brought up the princes of Judah upon the wall, and appointed two great companies of them that gave thanks, whereof one went on the right hand upon the wall toward the dung gate:

32 And after them went Hoshaiah, and half of the princes of Judah,

33 And Azariah, Ezra, and Meshullam,

34 Judah, and Benjamin, and Shemaiah, and Jeremiah,

35 And certain of the priests' sons with trumpets; namely, Zechariah the son of Jonathan, the son of Shemaiah, the son of Mattaniah, the son of Michaiah, the son of Zaccur, the son of Asaph:

36 And his brethren, Shemaiah, and Azarael, Milalai, Gilalai, Maai, Nethaneel, and Judah, Hanani, with the musical instruments of David the man of God, and Ezra the scribe before them.

37 And at the fountain gate, which was over against them, they went up by the stairs of the city of David, at the going up of the wall, above the house of David, even to the water gate eastward.

38 And the other company of them that gave thanks went over against them, and I after them, and the half of the people

upon the wall, from beyond the tower of the furnaces even to the broad wall;

39 And from above the gate of Ephraim, and above the old gate, and above the fish gate, and the tower of Hananeel, and the tower of Meah, even to the sheep gate: and they stood still in the prison gate.

40 So stood the two companies of them that gave thanks in the house of God, and I, and the half of the rulers with me:

41 And the priests; Eliakim, Maaseiah, Miniamin, Michaiah, Elioenai, Zechariah, and Hananiah, with trumpets;

42 And Maaseiah, and Shemaiah, and Eleazar, and Uzzi, and Jehohanan, and Malchijah, and Elam, and Ezer. And the singers sang loud, with Jezrahiah their overseer.

43 Also that day they offered great sacrifices, and rejoiced: for God had made them rejoice with great joy: the wives also and the children rejoiced: so that the joy of Jerusalem was heard even afar off.

44 And at that time were some appointed over the chambers for the treasures, for the offerings, for the firstfruits, and for the tithes, to gather into them out of the fields of the cities the portions of the law for the priests and Levites: for Judah rejoiced for the priests and for the Levites that waited.

45 And both the singers and the porters kept the ward of their God, and the ward of the purification, according to the commandment of David, and of Solomon his son.

46 For in the days of David and Asaph of old there were chief of the singers, and songs of praise and thanksgiving to God.

47 And all Israel in the days of Zerubbabel, and in the days of Nehemiah, gave the portions of the singers and the porters, every day his portion: and they sanctified holy things to the Levites; and the Levites sanctified them to the children of Aaron.

CHAPTER 13

ON that day they read in the book of Moses in the audience of the people; and therein was found written, that the Ammonite and the Moabite should not come into the congregation of God forever;

2 Because they met not the children of Israel with bread and with water, but hired Balaam against them, that he should curse them: howbeit our God turned the curse into a blessing.

3 Now it came to pass, when they had heard the law, that they separated from Israel all the mixed multitude.

4 And before this, Eliashib the priest, having the oversight of the chamber of the house of our God, was allied to Tobiah:

5 And he had prepared for him a great chamber, where aforetime they laid the meat offerings, the frankincense, and the vessels, and the tithes of the corn, the new wine, and the oil, which was commanded to be given to the Levites, and the singers, and the porters; and the offerings of the priests.

6 But in all this time was not I at Jerusalem: for in the two and thirtieth year of Artaxerxes king of Babylon came I to the king, and after certain days obtained I leave of the king:

7 And I came to Jerusalem, and understood of the evil that Eliashib did for Tobiah, in preparing him a chamber in the courts of the house of God.

8 And it grieved me sore: therefore I cast forth all the household stuff to Tobiah out of the chamber.

Chapter 13 The Church needs to thunder God's Law from its pulpits. It will not only awaken the sinner in the pew, but it will separate those who are tares among the wheat. God's Law will arouse the false convert to his true condition before a holy God.

9 Then I commanded, and they cleansed the chambers: and there brought I again the vessels of the house of God, with the meat offering and the frankincense.

10 And I perceived that the portions of the Levites had not been given them: for the Levites and the singers, that did the work, were fled every one to his field.

11 Then contended I with the rulers, and said, Why is the house of God forsaken? And I gathered them together, and set them in their place.

12 Then brought all Judah the tithe of the corn and the new wine and the oil to the treasuries.

13 And I made treasurers over the treasuries, Shelemiah the priest, and Zadok the scribe, and of the Levites, Pedaiah: and next to them was Hanan the son of Zaccur, the son of Mattaniah: for they were counted faithful, and their office was to distribute to their brethren.

14 Remember me, O my God, concerning this, and wipe not out my good deeds that I have done for the house of my God, and for the offices thereof.

15 In those days saw I in Judah some treading wine presses on the sabbath, and bringing in sheaves, and lading asses; as also wine, grapes, and figs, and all manner of burdens, which they brought into Jerusalem on the sabbath day: and I testified against them in the day wherein they sold victuals.

16 There dwelt men of Tyre also therein, which brought fish, and all manner of ware, and sold on the sabbath to the children of Judah, and in Jerusalem.

17 Then I contended with the nobles of Judah, and said to them, What evil thing is this that you do, and profane the sabbath day?

18 Did not your fathers thus, and did not our God bring all this evil upon us, and upon this city? yet you bring more wrath upon Israel by profaning the sabbath.

19 And it came to pass, that when the gates of Jerusalem began to be dark before the sabbath, I commanded that the gates should be shut, and charged that they should not be opened till after the sabbath: and some of my servants set I at the gates, that there should no burden be brought in on the sabbath day.

20 So the merchants and sellers of all kind of ware lodged without Jerusalem once or twice.

21 Then I testified against them, and said to them, Why do you lodge about the wall? if you do so again, I will lay hands on you. From that time forth came they no more on the sabbath.

22 And I commanded the Levites that they should cleanse themselves, and that they should come and keep the gates, to sanctify the sabbath day. Remember me, O my God, concerning this also, and spare me according to the greatness of your mercy.

23 In those days also saw I Jews that had married wives of Ashdod, of Ammon, and of Moab:

24 And their children spoke half in the speech of Ashdod, and could not speak in the Jews' language, but according to the language of each people.

25 And I contended with them, and cursed them, and smote certain of them, and plucked off their hair, and made them swear by God, saying, You shall not give your daughters to their sons, nor take their daughters to your sons, or for yourselves.

26 Did not Solomon king of Israel sin by these things? yet among many nations was there no king like him, who was beloved of his God, and God made him king over all Israel: nevertheless even him did outlandish women cause to sin.

27 Shall we then hearken to you to do all this great evil, to transgress against our God in marrying strange wives?

28 And one of the sons of Joiada, the son of Eliashib the high priest, was son in law to Sanballat the Horonite: therefore I chased him from me.

29 Remember them, O my God, because they have defiled the priesthood,

and the covenant of the priesthood, and of the Levites.

30 Thus cleansed I them from all strangers, and appointed the wards of the priests and the Levites, every one in his business;

31 And for the wood offering, at times appointed, and for the firstfruits. Remember me, O my God, for good.

Esther

CHAPTER 1

NOW it came to pass in the days of Ahasuerus, (this is Ahasuerus which reigned, from India even to Ethiopia, over an hundred and seven and twenty provinces:)

2 That in those days, when the king Ahasuerus sat on the throne of his kingdom, which was in Shushan the palace,

3 In the third year of his reign, he made a feast to all his princes and his servants; the power of Persia and Media, the nobles and princes of the provinces, being before him:

4 When he showed the riches of his glorious kingdom and the honour of his excellent majesty many days, even an hundred and fourscore days.

5 And when these days were expired, the king made a feast to all the people that were present in Shushan the palace, both to great and small, seven days, in the court of the garden of the king's palace;

6 Where were white, green, and blue, hangings, fastened with cords of fine linen and purple to silver rings and pillars of marble: the beds were of gold and silver, upon a pavement of red, and blue, and white, and black, marble.

7 And they gave them drink in vessels of gold, (the vessels being diverse one from another,) and royal wine in abundance, according to the state of the king.

8 And the drinking was according to the law; none did compel: for so the king had appointed to all the officers of his house, that they should do according to every man's pleasure.

9 Also Vashti the queen made a feast for the women in the royal house which belonged to king Ahasuerus.

10 On the seventh day, when the heart of the king was merry with wine, he commanded Mehuman, Biztha, Harbona, Bigtha, and Abagtha, Zethar, and Carcas, the seven chamberlains that served in the presence of Ahasuerus the king,

11 To bring Vashti the queen before the king with the crown royal, to show the people and the princes her beauty: for she was fair to look on.

12 But the queen Vashti refused to come at the king's commandment by his chamberlains: therefore was the king very wroth, and his anger burned in him.

13 Then the king said to the wise men, which knew the times, (for so was the king's manner toward all that knew law and judgment:

14 And the next to him was Carshena, Shethar, Admatha, Tarshish, Meres, Marsena, and Memucan, the seven princes of Persia and Media, which saw the king's face, and which sat the first in the kingdom;)

15 What shall we do to the queen Vashti according to law, because she has not performed the commandment of the king Ahasuerus by the chamberlains?

16 And Memucan answered before the king and the princes, Vashti the queen has not done wrong to the king only, but also to all the princes, and to all the people that are in all the provinces of the king Ahasuerus.

17 For this deed of the queen shall come abroad to all women, so that they shall despise their husbands in their eyes, when it shall be reported, The king Ahasuerus commanded Vashti the queen to be brought in before him, but she came not.

18 Likewise shall the ladies of Persia and Media say this day to all the king's princes, which have heard of the deed of the queen. Thus shall there arise too much contempt and wrath.

19 If it please the king, let there go a royal commandment from him, and let it be written among the laws of the Persians and the Medes, that it be not altered, That Vashti come no more before king Ahasuerus; and let the king give her royal estate to another that is better than she.

20 And when the king's decree which he shall make shall be published throughout all his empire, (for it is great,) all the wives shall give to their husbands honour, both to great and small.

21 And the saying pleased the king and the princes; and the king did according to the word of Memucan:

22 For he sent letters into all the king's provinces, into every province according to the writing thereof, and to every people after their language, that every man should bear rule in his own house, and that it should be published according to the language of every people.

CHAPTER 2

AFTER these things, when the wrath of king Ahasuerus was appeased, he remembered Vashti, and what she had done, and what was decreed against her.

2 Then said the king's servants that ministered to him, Let there be fair young virgins sought for the king:

3 And let the king appoint officers in all the provinces of his kingdom, that they may gather together all the fair young virgins to Shushan the palace, to the house of the women, to the custody of Hege the king's chamberlain, keeper of the women; and let their things for purification be given them:

4 And let the maiden which pleases the king be queen instead of Vashti. And the thing pleased the king; and he did so.

5 Now in Shushan the palace there was a certain Jew, whose name was Mordecai, the son of Jair, the son of Shimei, the son of Kish, a Benjamite;

6 Who had been carried away from Jerusalem with the captivity which had been carried away with Jeconiah king of Judah, whom Nebuchadnezzar the king of Babylon had carried away.

7 And he brought up Hadassah, that is, Esther, his uncle's daughter: for she had neither father nor mother, and the maid was fair and beautiful; whom Mordecai, when her father and mother were dead, took for his own daughter.

8 So it came to pass, when the king's commandment and his decree was heard, and when many maidens were gathered together to Shushan the palace, to the custody of Hegai, that Esther was brought also to the king's house, to the custody of Hegai, keeper of the women.

9 And the maiden pleased him, and she obtained kindness of him; and he speedily gave her her things for purification, with such things as belonged to her, and seven maidens, which were meet to be given her, out of the king's house: and he preferred her and her maids to the best place of the house of the women.

10 Esther had not showed her people nor her kindred: for Mordecai had charged her that she should not show it.

11 And Mordecai walked every day before the court of the women's house, to

know how Esther did, and what should become of her.

12 Now when every maid's turn was come to go in to king Ahasuerus, after that she had been twelve months, according to the manner of the women, (for so were the days of their purifications accomplished, to wit, six months with oil of myrrh, and six months with sweet odours, and with other things for the purifying of the women;)

13 Then thus came every maiden to the king; whatsoever she desired was given her to go with her out of the house of the women to the king's house.

14 In the evening she went, and on the morrow she returned into the second house of the women, to the custody of Shaashgaz, the king's chamberlain, which kept the concubines: she came in to the king no more, except the king delighted in her, and that she were called by name.

15 Now when the turn of Esther, the daughter of Abihail the uncle of Mordecai, who had taken her for his daughter, was come to go in to the king, she required nothing but what Hegai the king's chamberlain, the keeper of the women, appointed. And Esther obtained favour in the sight of all them that looked upon her.

16 So Esther was taken to king Ahasuerus into his house royal in the tenth month, which is the month Tebeth, in the seventh year of his reign.

17 And the king loved Esther above all the women, and she obtained grace and favour in his sight more than all the virgins; so that he set the royal crown upon her head, and made her queen instead of Vashti.

18 Then the king made a great feast to all his princes and his servants, even Esther's feast; and he made a release to the provinces, and gave gifts, according to the state of the king.

19 And when the virgins were gathered together the second time, then Mordecai sat in the king's gate.

20 Esther had not yet showed her kindred nor her people; as Mordecai had charged her: for Esther did the commandment of Mordecai, like as when she was brought up with him.

21 In those days, while Mordecai sat in the king's gate, two of the king's chamberlains, Bigthan and Teresh, of those which kept the door, were wroth, and sought to lay hands on the king Ahasuerus.

22 And the thing was known to Mordecai, who told it to Esther the queen; and Esther certified the king thereof in Mordecai's name.

23 And when inquisition was made of the matter, it was found out; therefore they were both hanged on a tree: and it was written in the book of the chronicles before the king.

CHAPTER 3

AFTER these things did king Ahasuerus promote Haman the son of Hammedatha the Agagite, and advanced him, and set his seat above all the princes that were with him.

2 And all the king's servants, that were in the king's gate, bowed, and reverenced Haman: for the king had so commanded concerning him. But Mordecai bowed not, nor did him reverence.

3 Then the king's servants, which were in the king's gate, said to Mordecai, Why do you transgress the king's commandment?

4 Now it came to pass, when they spoke daily to him, and he hearkened not to them, that they told Haman, to see whether Mordecai's matters would stand: for he had told them that he was a Jew.

5 And when Haman saw that Mordecai bowed not, nor did him reverence, then was Haman full of wrath.

6 And he thought scorn to lay hands on Mordecai alone; for they had showed him the people of Mordecai: therefore Haman sought to destroy all the Jews that were throughout the whole king-

dom of Ahasuerus, even the people of Mordecai.

7 In the first month, that is, the month Nisan, in the twelfth year of king Ahasuerus, they cast Pur, that is, the lot, before Haman from day to day, and from month to month, to the twelfth month, that is, the month Adar.

8 And Haman said to king Ahasuerus, There is a certain people scattered abroad and dispersed among the people in all the provinces of your kingdom; and their laws are diverse from all people; neither keep they the king's laws: therefore it is not for the king's profit to suffer them.

9 If it please the king, let it be written that they may be destroyed: and I will pay ten thousand talents of silver to the hands of those that have the charge of the business, to bring it into the king's treasuries.

10 And the king took his ring from his hand, and gave it to Haman the son of Hammedatha the Agagite, the Jews' enemy.

11 And the king said to Haman, The silver is given to you, the people also, to do with them as it seems good to you.

12 Then were the king's scribes called on the thirteenth day of the first month, and there was written according to all that Haman had commanded to the king's lieutenants, and to the governors that were over every province, and to the rulers of every people of every province according to the writing thereof, and to every people after their language; in the name of king Ahasuerus was it written, and sealed with the king's ring.

13 And the letters were sent by posts into all the king's provinces, to destroy, to kill, and to cause to perish, all Jews, both young and old, little children and women, in one day, even upon the thirteenth day of the twelfth month, which

is the month Adar, and to take the spoil of them for a prey.

14 The copy of the writing for a commandment to be given in every province was published to all people, that they should be ready against that day.

15 The posts went out, being hastened by the king's commandment, and the decree was given in Shushan the palace. And the king and Haman sat down to drink; but the city Shushan was perplexed.

CHAPTER 4

WHEN Mordecai perceived all that was done, Mordecai rent his clothes, and put on sackcloth with ashes, and went out into the midst of the city, and cried with a loud and a bitter cry;

2 And came even before the king's gate: for none might enter into the king's gate clothed with sackcloth.

3 And in every province, wherever the king's commandment and his decree came, there was great mourning among the Jews, and fasting, and weeping, and wailing; and many lay in sackcloth and ashes.

4 So Esther's maids and her chamberlains came and told it her. Then was the queen exceedingly grieved; and she sent raiment to clothe Mordecai, and to take away his sackcloth from him: but he received it not.

5 Then called Esther for Hatach, one of the king's chamberlains, whom he had appointed to attend upon her, and gave him a commandment to Mordecai, to know what it was, and why it was.

6 So Hatach went forth to Mordecai to the street of the city, which was before the king's gate.

7 And Mordecai told him of all that had happened to him, and of the sum of the money that Haman had promised to pay

---

3:12-13 The rulers of this world have a mandate to kill, steal and destroy (see Ephesians 6:12 and John 10:10). Satan roams about as a roaring lion seeking whom he may devour (see 1 Peter 5:8). Unrepentant sin gives the enemy permission to destroy.

to the king's treasuries for the Jews, to destroy them.

8 Also he gave him the copy of the writing of the decree that was given at Shushan to destroy them, to show it to Esther, and to declare it to her, and to charge her that she should go in to the king, to make supplication to him, and to make request before him for her people.

9 And Hatach came and told Esther the words of Mordecai.

10 Again Esther spoke to Hatach, and gave him commandment to Mordecai;

11 All the king's servants, and the people of the king's provinces, do know, that whosoever, whether man or women, shall come to the king into the inner court, who is not called, there is one law of his to put him to death, except such to whom the king shall hold out the golden sceptre, that he may live: but I have not been called to come in to the king these thirty days.

12 And they told to Mordecai Esther's words.

13 Then Mordecai commanded to answer Esther, Think not with yourself that you shall escape in the king's house, more than all the Jews.

14 For if you altogether hold your peace at this time, then shall there enlargement and deliverance arise to the Jews from another place; but you and your father's house shall be destroyed: and who knows whether you are come to the kingdom for such a time as this?

15 Then Esther bade them return Mordecai this answer,

16 Go, gather together all the Jews that are present in Shushan, and fast for me, and neither eat nor drink three days, night or day: I also and my maidens will fast likewise; and so will I go in to the king, which is not according to the law: and if I perish, I perish.

17 So Mordecai went his way, and did according to all that Esther had commanded him.

CHAPTER 5

NOW it came to pass on the third day, that Esther put on her royal apparel, and stood in the inner court of the king's house, over against the king's house: and the king sat upon his royal throne in the royal house, over against the gate of the house.

2 And it was so, when the king saw Esther the queen standing in the court, that she obtained favour in his sight: and the king held out to Esther the golden sceptre that was in his hand. So Esther drew near, and touched the top of the sceptre.

3 Then said the king to her, What will you, queen Esther? and what is your request? it shall be even given you to the half of the kingdom.

4 And Esther answered, If it seem good to the king, let the king and Haman come this day to the banquet that I have prepared for him.

5 Then the king said, Cause Haman to make haste, that he may do as Esther has said. So the king and Haman came to the banquet that Esther had prepared.

6 And the king said to Esther at the banquet of wine, What is your petition?

4:14-16 We have come into the Kingdom for such a time as this. God gave us life and saved us at the end of this age for a reason. We must abandon ourselves to the cause of evangelism—with Esther's courageous attitude: "If I perish, I perish." Heroic warriors had had this attitude to obtain a piece of land in Israel, Korea or Vietnam, and the land has been given back in peace negotiations some years later. But the cause for which we give our lives is eternal.

5:2 God extends favor towards us as we stand before Him clothed in the righteousness of Christ. We can boldly draw near the Throne of Grace, having obtained redemption in Christ. It is now the Father's good pleasure to give us the Kingdom (Luke 12:32).

TRIUMPH OF MORDECAI

Esther 6:10

and it shall be granted you: and what is your request? even to the half of the kingdom it shall be performed.

7 Then answered Esther, and said, My petition and my request is;

8 If I have found favour in the sight of the king, and if it please the king to grant my petition, and to perform my request, let the king and Haman come to the banquet that I shall prepare for them, and I will do to morrow as the king has said.

9 Then went Haman forth that day joyful and with a glad heart: but when

Haman saw Mordecai in the king's gate, that he stood not up, nor moved for him, he was full of indignation against Mordecai.

10 Nevertheless Haman refrained himself: and when he came home, he sent and called for his friends, and Zeresh his wife.

11 And Haman told them of the glory of his riches, and the multitude of his children, and all the things wherein the king had promoted him, and how he had advanced him above the princes and servants of the king.

12 Haman said moreover, Yea, Esther the queen did let no man come in with the king to the banquet that she had prepared but myself; and tomorrow am I invited to her also with the king.

13 Yet all this avails me nothing, so long as I see Mordecai the Jew sitting at the king's gate.

14 Then said Zeresh his wife and all his friends to him, Let a gallows be made of fifty cubits high, and tomorrow speak to the king that Mordecai may be hanged thereon: then go in merrily with the king to the banquet. And the thing pleased Haman; and he caused the gallows to be made.

CHAPTER 6

ON that night could not the king sleep, and he commanded to bring the book of records of the chronicles; and they were read before the king.

2 And it was found written, that Mordecai had told of Bigthana and Teresh, two of the king's chamberlains, the keepers of the door, who sought to lay hand on the king Ahasuerus.

3 And the king said, What honour and dignity has been done to Mordecai for this? Then said the king's servants that ministered to him, There is nothing done for him.

4 And the king said, Who is in the court? Now Haman was come into the outward court of the king's house, to speak to the king to hang Mordecai on the gallows that he had prepared for him.

5 And the king's servants said to him, Behold, Haman stands in the court. And the king said, Let him come in.

6 So Haman came in. And the king said to him, What shall be done to the man whom the king delights to honour? Now Haman thought in his heart, To whom would the king delight to do honour more than to myself?

7 And Haman answered the king, For the man whom the king delights to honour,

8 Let the royal apparel be brought which the king uses to wear, and the horse that the king rides upon, and the crown royal which is set upon his head:

9 And let this apparel and horse be delivered to the hand of one of the king's most noble princes, that they may array the man withal whom the king delights to honour, and bring him on horseback through the street of the city, and proclaim before him, Thus shall it be done to the man whom the king delights to honour.

10 Then the king said to Haman, Make haste, and take the apparel and the horse, as you have said, and do even so to Mordecai the Jew, that sits at the king's gate: let nothing fail of all that you have spoken.

11 Then took Haman the apparel and the horse, and arrayed Mordecai, and brought him on horseback through the street of the city, and proclaimed before him, Thus shall it be done to the man whom the king delights to honour.

12 And Mordecai came again to the king's gate. But Haman hasted to his house mourning, and having his head covered.

13 And Haman told Zeresh his wife and all his friends every thing that had befallen him. Then said his wise men and Zeresh his wife to him, If Mordecai be of the seed of the Jews, before whom you have begun to fall, you shall not prevail

ESTHER ACCUSING HAMAN

Esther 7:4-6

against him, but shall surely fall before him.

14 And while they were yet talking with him, came the king's chamberlains, and hasted to bring Haman to the banquet that Esther had prepared.

CHAPTER 7

SO the king and Haman came to banquet with Esther the queen.

2 And the king said again to Esther on the second day at the banquet of wine, What is your petition, queen Esther? and it shall be granted you: and what is your

7:9-10

The proud who erect gallows with the intention of destroying God's witnesses, the loyal servants of the King, have strung just enough rope to hang themselves. See Romans 2:3.

request? and it shall be performed, even to the half of the kingdom.

3 Then Esther the queen answered and said, If I have found favour in your sight, O king, and if it please the king, let my life be given me at my petition, and my people at my request:

4 For we are sold, I and my people, to be destroyed, to be slain, and to perish. But if we had been sold for bondmen and bondwomen, I had held my tongue, although the enemy could not countervail the king's damage.

5 Then the king Ahasuerus answered and said to Esther the queen, Who is he, and where is he, that durst presume in his heart to do so?

6 And Esther said, The adversary and enemy is this wicked Haman. Then Haman was afraid before the king and the queen.

7 And the king arising from the banquet of wine in his wrath went into the palace garden: and Haman stood up to make request for his life to Esther the queen; for he saw that there was evil determined against him by the king.

8 Then the king returned out of the palace garden into the place of the banquet of wine; and Haman was fallen upon the bed whereon Esther was. Then said the king, Will he force the queen also before me in the house? As the word

went out of king's mouth, they covered Haman's face.

9 And Harbonah, one of the chamberlains, said before the king, Behold also, the gallows fifty cubits high, which Haman had made for Mordecai, who spoken good for the king, stands in the house of Haman. Then the king said, Hang him thereon.

10 So they hanged Haman on the gallows that he had prepared for Mordecai. Then was the king's wrath pacified.

CHAPTER 8

ON that day did the king Ahasuerus give the house of Haman the Jews' enemy to Esther the queen. And Mordecai came before the king; for Esther had told what he was to her.

2 And the king took off his ring, which he had taken from Haman, and gave it to Mordecai. And Esther set Mordecai over the house of Haman.

3 And Esther spoke yet again before the king, and fell down at his feet, and besought him with tears to put away the mischief of Haman the Agagite, and his device that he had devised against the Jews.

4 Then the king held out the golden sceptre toward Esther. So Esther arose, and stood before the king,

5 And said, If it please the king, and if I have favour in his sight, and the thing seem right before the king, and I be pleasing in his eyes, let it be written to reverse the letters devised by Haman the son of Hammedatha the Agagite, which he wrote to destroy the Jews which are in all the king's provinces:

6 For how can I endure to see the evil that shall come to my people? or how can I endure to see the destruction of my kindred?

7 Then the king Ahasuerus said to Esther the queen and to Mordecai the Jew, Behold, I have given Esther the house of Haman, and him they have hanged upon the gallows, because he laid his hand upon the Jews.

8 You write also for the Jews, as it likes you, in the king's name, and seal it with the king's ring: for the writing which is written in the king's name, and sealed with the king's ring, may no man reverse.

9 Then were the king's scribes called at that time in the third month, that is, the month Sivan, on the three and twentieth day thereof; and it was written according to all that Mordecai commanded to the Jews, and to the lieutenants, and the deputies and rulers of the provinces which are from India to Ethiopia, an hundred twenty and seven provinces, to every province according to the writing thereof, and to every people after their language, and to the Jews according to their writing, and according to their language.

10 And he wrote in the king Ahasuerus' name, and sealed it with the king's ring, and sent letters by posts on horseback, and riders on mules, camels, and young dromedaries:

11 Wherein the king granted the Jews which were in every city to gather themselves together, and to stand for their life, to destroy, to slay and to cause to perish, all the power of the people and province that would assault them, both little ones and women, and to take the spoil of them for a prey,

12 Upon one day in all the provinces of king Ahasuerus, namely, upon the thirteenth day of the twelfth month, which is the month Adar.

13 The copy of the writing for a commandment to be given in every province was published to all people, and that the Jews should be ready against that day to avenge themselves on their enemies.

14 So the posts that rode upon mules and camels went out, being hastened and pressed on by the king's commandment. And the decree was given at Shushan the palace.

15 And Mordecai went out from the presence of the king in royal apparel of blue and white, and with a great crown of gold, and with a garment of fine linen and purple: and the city of Shushan rejoiced and was glad.

16 The Jews had light, and gladness, and joy, and honour.

17 And in every province, and in every city, wherever the king's commandment and his decree came, the Jews had joy and gladness, a feast and a good day. And many of the people of the land became Jews; for the fear of the Jews fell upon them.

CHAPTER 9

NOW in the twelfth month, that is, the month Adar, on the thirteenth day of the same, when the king's commandment and his decree drew near to be put in execution, in the day that the enemies of the Jews hoped to have power over them, (though it was turned to the contrary, that the Jews had rule over them that hated them;)

2 The Jews gathered themselves together in their cities throughout all the provinces of the king Ahasuerus, to lay hand on such as sought their hurt: and no man could withstand them; for the fear of them fell upon all people.

3 And all the rulers of the provinces, and the lieutenants, and the deputies, and officers of the king, helped the Jews; because the fear of Mordecai fell upon them.

4 For Mordecai was great in the king's house, and his fame went out throughout all the provinces: for this man Mordecai waxed greater and greater.

5 Thus the Jews smote all their enemies with the stroke of the sword, and slaughter, and destruction, and did what they would to those that hated them.

6 And in Shushan the palace the Jews slew and destroyed five hundred men.

7 And Parshandatha, and Dalphon, and Aspatha,

8 And Poratha, and Adalia, and Aridatha,

9 And Parmashta, and Arisai, and Aridai, and Vajezatha,

The Function of the Law

9:13 **Esther had the ten sons of Haman hanged.** This is a picture of "repentance towards God," when we rid ourselves of the enemy by putting to death the works of the flesh, the result of the nature that came to us from the devil (see John 8:44, Ephesians 2:2).

The works of the flesh are traced back to transgression of the Ten Commandments (see 1 John 3:4). The ten sons of Haman (the ten sins of humanity) are rebellion against God, idolatry, blasphemy, Sabbath breaking, parental dishonor, murder, adultery, theft, lying and covetousness.

10 The ten sons of Haman the son of Hammedatha, the enemy of the Jews, slew they; but on the spoil laid they not their hand.

11 On that day the number of those that were slain in Shushan the palace was brought before the king.

12 And the king said to Esther the queen, The Jews have slain and destroyed five hundred men in Shushan the palace, and the ten sons of Haman; what have they done in the rest of the king's provinces? now what is your petition? and it shall be granted you: or what is your request further? and it shall be done.

13 Then said Esther, If it please the king, let it be granted to the Jews which are in Shushan to do tomorrow also according to this day's decree, and let Haman's ten sons be hanged upon the gallows.

14 And the king commanded it so to be done: and the decree was given at Shushan; and they hanged Haman's ten sons.

15 For the Jews that were in Shushan gathered themselves together on the fourteenth day also of the month Adar, and slew three hundred men at Shushan; but on the prey they laid not their hand.

16 But the other Jews that were in the king's provinces gathered themselves together, and stood for their lives, and had rest from their enemies, and slew of their foes seventy and five thousand, but they laid not their hands on the prey,

17 On the thirteenth day of the month Adar; and on the fourteenth day of the same rested they, and made it a day of feasting and gladness.

18 But the Jews that were at Shushan assembled together on the thirteenth day thereof, and on the fourteenth thereof; and on the fifteenth day of the same they rested, and made it a day of feasting and gladness.

19 Therefore the Jews of the villages, that dwelt in the unwalled towns, made the fourteenth day of the month Adar a day of gladness and feasting, and a good day, and of sending portions one to another.

20 And Mordecai wrote these things, and sent letters to all the Jews that were in all the provinces of the king Ahasuerus, both nigh and far,

21 To stablish this among them, that they should keep the fourteenth day of the month Adar, and the fifteenth day of the same, yearly,

22 As the days wherein the Jews rested from their enemies, and the month which was turned to them from sorrow to joy, and from mourning into a good day: that they should make them days of feasting and joy, and of sending portions one to another, and gifts to the poor.

23 And the Jews undertook to do as they had begun, and as Mordecai had written to them;

24 Because Haman the son of Hammedatha, the Agagite, the enemy of all the Jews, had devised against the Jews to destroy them, and had cast Pur, that is, the lot, to consume them, and to destroy them;

25 But when Esther came before the king, he commanded by letters that his wicked device, which he devised against the Jews, should return upon his own head, and that he and his sons should be hanged on the gallows.

26 Therefore they called these days Purim after the name of Pur. Therefore for all the words of this letter, and of that which they had seen concerning this matter, and which had come to them,

27 The Jews ordained, and took upon them, and upon their seed, and upon all such as joined themselves to them, so as it should not fail, that they would keep these two days according to their writing, and according to their appointed time every year;

28 And that these days should be remembered and kept throughout every generation, every family, every province, and every city; and that these days of Purim should not fail from among the Jews, nor the memorial of them perish from their seed.

29 Then Esther the queen, the daughter of Abihail, and Mordecai the Jew, wrote with all authority, to confirm this second letter of Purim.

30 And he sent the letters to all the Jews, to the hundred twenty and seven provinces of the kingdom of Ahasuerus, with words of peace and truth,

31 To confirm these days of Purim in their times appointed, according as Mordecai the Jew and Esther the queen had enjoined them, and as they had decreed for themselves and for their seed, the matters of the fastings and their cry.

32 And the decree of Esther confirmed these matters of Purim; and it was written in the book.

CHAPTER 10

A ND the king Ahasuerus laid a tribute upon the land, and upon the isles of the sea.

2 And all the acts of his power and of his might, and the declaration of the greatness of Mordecai, whereunto the king advanced him, are they not written in the book of the chronicles of the kings of Media and Persia?

3 For Mordecai the Jew was next to king Ahasuerus, and great among the Jews, and accepted of the multitude of his brethren, seeking the wealth of his people, and speaking peace to all his seed.

Job

CHAPTER 1

THERE was a man in the land of Uz, whose name was Job; and that man was perfect and upright, and one that feared God, and eschewed evil.

2 And there were born to him seven sons and three daughters.

3 His substance also was seven thousand sheep, and three thousand camels, and five hundred yoke of oxen, and five hundred she asses, and a very great household; so that this man was the greatest of all the men of the east.

4 And his sons went and feasted in their houses, every one his day; and sent and called for their three sisters to eat and to drink with them.

5 And it was so, when the days of their feasting were gone about, that Job sent and sanctified them, and rose up early in the morning, and offered burnt offerings according to the number of them all: for Job said, It may be that my sons have sinned, and cursed God in their hearts. Thus did Job continually.

6 Now there was a day when the sons of God came to present themselves before the LORD, and Satan came also among them.

7 And the LORD said to Satan, From where do you come? Then Satan answered the LORD, and said, From going to and fro in the earth, and from walking up and down in it.

8 And the LORD said to Satan, Have you considered my servant Job, that there is none like him in the earth, a perfect and an upright man, one that fears God, and eschews evil?

9 Then Satan answered the LORD, and said, Does Job fear God for nothing?

10 Have you not made an hedge about him, and about his house, and about all that he has on every side? you have blessed the work of his hands, and his substance is increased in the land.

11 But put forth your hand now, and touch all that he has, and he will curse you to your face.

12 And the LORD said to Satan, Behold, all that he has is in your power; only upon himself put not forth your hand. So Satan went forth from the presence of the LORD.

13 And there was a day when his sons and his daughters were eating and drinking wine in their eldest brother's house:

14 And there came a messenger to Job, and said, The oxen were plowing, and the asses feeding beside them:

15 And the Sabeans fell upon them, and took them away; yea, they have slain the servants with the edge of the sword; and I only am escaped alone to tell you.

16 While he was yet speaking, there came also another, and said, The fire of God is fallen from heaven, and has burned up the sheep, and the servants, and consumed them; and I only am escaped alone to tell you.

JOB HEARING OF HIS RUIN

Job 1:21

17 While he was yet speaking, there came also another, and said, The Chaldeans made out three bands, and fell upon the camels, and have carried them away, yea, and slain the servants with the edge of the sword; and I only am escaped alone to tell you.

18 While he was yet speaking, there came also another, and said, Your sons and your daughters were eating and drinking wine in their eldest brother's house:

19 And, behold, there came a great wind from the wilderness, and smote the four corners of the house, and it fell upon the young men, and they are dead; and I only am escaped alone to tell you.

20 Then Job arose, and rent his mantle, and shaved his head, and fell down upon the ground, and worshipped,

21 And said, Naked came I out of my mother's womb, and naked shall I return there: the LORD gave, and the LORD

has taken away; blessed be the name of the LORD.

22 In all this Job sinned not, nor charged God foolishly.

CHAPTER 2

AGAIN there was a day when the sons of God came to present themselves before the LORD, and Satan came also among them to present himself before the LORD.

2 And the LORD said to Satan, From where do you come? And Satan answered the LORD, and said, From going to and fro in the earth, and from walking up and down in it.

3 And the LORD said to Satan, Have you considered my servant Job, that there is none like him in the earth, a perfect and an upright man, one that fears God, and eschews evil? and still he holds fast his integrity, although you moved me against him, to destroy him without cause.

4 And Satan answered the LORD, and said, Skin for skin, yea, all that a man has will he give for his life.

5 But put forth your hand now, and touch his bone and his flesh, and he will curse you to your face.

6 And the LORD said to Satan, Behold, he is in your hand; but save his life.

7 So went Satan forth from the presence of the LORD, and smote Job with sore boils from the sole of his foot to his crown.

8 And he took him a potsherd to scrape himself withal; and he sat down among the ashes.

9 Then said his wife to him, Do you still retain your integrity? curse God, and die.

10 But he said to her, You speak as one of the foolish women speaks. What? shall we receive good at the hand of God, and shall we not receive evil? In all this did not Job sin with his lips.

11 Now when Job's three friends heard of all this evil that was come upon him, they came every one from his own place; Eliphaz the Temanite, and Bildad the Shuhite, and Zophar the Naamathite: for they had made an appointment together to come to mourn with him and to comfort him.

12 And when they lifted up their eyes afar off, and knew him not, they lifted up their voice, and wept; and they rent every one his mantle, and sprinkled dust upon their heads toward heaven.

13 So they sat down with him upon the ground seven days and seven nights, and none spoke a word to him: for they saw that his grief was very great.

CHAPTER 3

AFTER this opened Job his mouth, and cursed his day.

2 And Job spoke, and said,

3 Let the day perish wherein I was born, and the night in which it was said, There is a man child conceived.

4 Let that day be darkness; let not God regard it from above, neither let the light shine upon it.

5 Let darkness and the shadow of death stain it; let a cloud dwell upon it; let the blackness of the day terrify it.

6 As for that night, let darkness seize upon it; let it not be joined to the days of the year, let it not come into the number of the months.

7 Lo, let that night be solitary, let no joyful voice come therein.

8 Let them curse it that curse the day, who are ready to raise up their mourning.

9 Let the stars of the twilight thereof be dark; let it look for light, but have none; neither let it see the dawning of the day:

10 Because it shut not up the doors of my mother's womb, nor hid sorrow from my eyes.

11 Why died I not from the womb? why did I not give up the ghost when I came out of the belly?

12 Why did the knees prevent me? or why the breasts that I should suck?

13 For now should I have lain still and been quiet, I should have slept: then had I been at rest,

14 With kings and counselors of the earth, which build desolate places for themselves;

15 Or with princes that had gold, who filled their houses with silver:

16 Or as an hidden untimely birth I had not been; as infants which never saw light.

17 There the wicked cease from troubling; and there the weary be at rest.

18 There the prisoners rest together; they hear not the voice of the oppressor.

19 The small and great are there; and the servant is free from his master.

20 Why is light given to him that is in misery, and life to the bitter in soul;

21 Which long for death, but it does not come; and dig for it more than for hid treasures;

22 Which rejoice exceedingly, and are glad, when they can find the grave?

23 Why is light given to a man whose way is hid, and whom God has hedged in?

24 For my sighing comes before I eat, and my groanings are poured out like the waters.

25 For the thing which I greatly feared is come upon me, and that which I was afraid of is come to me.

26 I was not in safety, neither had I rest, neither was I quiet; yet trouble came.

CHAPTER 4

THEN Eliphaz the Temanite answered and said,

2 If we attempt to commune with you, will you be grieved? but who can withhold himself from speaking?

3 Behold, you have instructed many, and you have strengthened the weak hands.

4 Your words have upholden him that was falling, and you have strengthened the feeble knees.

5 But now it is come upon you, and you faint; it touches you, and you are troubled.

6 Is not this your fear, your confidence, your hope, and the uprightness of your ways?

7 Remember, I pray you, who ever perished, being innocent? or where were the righteous cut off?

8 Even as I have seen, they that plow iniquity, and sow wickedness, reap the same.

9 By the blast of God they perish, and by the breath of his nostrils are they consumed.

10 The roaring of the lion, and the voice of the fierce lion, and the teeth of the young lions, are broken.

11 The old lion perishes for lack of prey, and the stout lion's whelps are scattered abroad.

12 Now a thing was secretly brought to me, and my ear received a little thereof.

13 In thoughts from the visions of the night, when deep sleep falls on men,

14 Fear came upon me, and trembling, which made all my bones to shake.

15 Then a spirit passed before my face; the hair of my flesh stood up:

16 It stood still, but I could not discern the form thereof: an image was before my eyes, there was silence, and I heard a voice, saying,

17 Shall mortal man be more just than God? shall a man be more pure than his maker?

18 Behold, he put no trust in his servants; and his angels he charged with folly:

19 How much less in them that dwell

4:20 Before my conversion I had thoughts that I was compelled to keep to myself. I would think, "It makes no sense that the whole of humanity are heading for death, and instead of seeking a cure to the aging process, they are searching for intelligent life in space or for a cure to the common cold. No one seems concerned about our big problem. No one even talks about death." But now that I have found that God has provided a cure to man's greatest disease, salvation through Jesus Christ, I cannot and will not stop talking about it.

in houses of clay, whose foundation is in the dust, which are crushed before the moth?

20 They are destroyed from morning to evening: they perish for ever without any regarding it.

21 Does not their excellency which is in them go away? they die, even without wisdom.

CHAPTER 5

CALL now, if there be any that will answer you; and to which of the saints will you turn?

2 For wrath kills the foolish man, and envy slays the silly one.

3 I have seen the foolish taking root: but suddenly I cursed his habitation.

4 His children are far from safety, and they are crushed in the gate, neither is there any to deliver them.

5 Whose harvest the hungry eats up, and takes it even out of the thorns, and the robber swallows up their substance.

6 Although affliction does not come forth of the dust, neither does trouble spring out of the ground;

7 Yet man is born to trouble, as the sparks fly upward.

8 I would seek God, and to God would I commit my cause:

9 Which does great things and unsearchable; marvelous things without number:

10 Who gives rain upon the earth, and sends waters upon the fields:

11 To set up on high those that be low; that those which mourn may be exalted to safety.

12 He disappoints the devices of the crafty, so that their hands cannot perform their enterprise.

13 He takes the wise in their own craftiness: and the counsel of the froward is carried headlong.

14 They meet with darkness in the day time, and grope in the noonday as in the night.

15 But he saves the poor from the sword, from their mouth, and from the hand of the mighty.

16 So the poor has hope, and iniquity stops her mouth.

17 Behold, happy is the man whom God corrects: therefore do not despise the chastening of the Almighty:

18 For he makes sore, and binds up: he wounds, and his hands make whole.

19 He shall deliver you in six troubles: yea, in seven there shall no evil touch you.

20 In famine he shall redeem you from death: and in war from the power of the sword.

21 You shall be hid from the scourge of the tongue: neither shall you be afraid of destruction when it comes.

22 At destruction and famine you shall laugh: neither shall you be afraid of the beasts of the earth.

23 For you shall be in league with the stones of the field: and the beasts of the field shall be at peace with you.

24 And you shall know that your tabernacle shall be in peace; and you shall visit your habitation, and shall not sin.

25 You shall know also that your seed shall be great, and your offspring as the grass of the earth.

26 You shall come to your grave in a full age, like as a shock of corn comes in in his season.

27 Lo this, we have searched it, so it is; hear it, and know it for your good.

5:11-14 See 1 Corinthians 3:19.

5:18 God's Law makes us sore, so that the Gospel can heal us. It wounds so that the hand of grace can make us whole.

Hang in There

6:11

There was once a daring escape from a Nazi war prison. The inmates had dug a tunnel, which sadly had surfaced twenty feet short of the cover of a wooded area. So they waited until a moonless night and sent one man into the woods to watch for the time when the guard would turn his back. His job was to pull on a piece of string which ran from the woods, down into the tunnel. This would let the next prisoner know it was safe for him to emerge. One by one, the men felt the tug of the string and surfaced, running into the safety of the dark woods. Unfortunately the guard heard a sound and walked across to the area where the hole was located. He didn't see the opening but stood by it for some time, looking suspiciously around the locality. Time seemed to stand still for the next prisoner who was waiting underground for the tug on the string.

Suddenly, he lost his patience. He could stand it no longer. He moved forward, then up and out of the hole in the dark. It was the last thing he did. The guard swung around and fired on him with his machine gun, filling him full of lead.

We can learn from that man's fatal mistake. His error was threefold. He lacked patience, faith, and obedience. If only he had trusted the one on the other end. If only he had obeyed instructions given to him, he would have found his freedom. Instead, he lost his very life.

The Bible tells us that we inherit the promises of God through "faith and patience." There are times when a Christian asks God for something, and there is a delay. But he doesn't lose patience. He hangs in there. The One holding onto the string can see things he can't, and He knows what is best for him. The Bible says "Trust in the Lord with all your heart; and lean not unto your own understanding" (Proverbs 3:5).

CHAPTER 6

BUT Job answered and said,
2 Oh that my grief were throughly weighed, and my calamity laid in the balances together!

3 For now it would be heavier than the sand of the sea: therefore my words are swallowed up.

4 For the arrows of the Almighty are within me, the poison whereof drinks up my spirit: the terrors of God do set themselves in array against me.

5 Does the wild ass bray when he has grass? or low the ox over his fodder?

6 Can that which is unsavoury be eaten without salt? or is there any taste in the white of an egg?

7 The things that my soul refused to touch are as my sorrowful meat.

8 Oh that I might have my request; and that God would grant me the thing that I long for!

9 Even that it would please God to destroy me; that he would let loose his hand, and cut me off!

10 Then should I yet have comfort; yea, I would harden myself in sorrow: let him not spare; for I have not concealed the words of the Holy One.

11 What is my strength, that I should hope? and what is my end, that I should prolong my life?

12 Is my strength the strength of stones? or is my flesh of brass?

13 Is not my help in me? and is wisdom driven quite from me?

14 To him that is afflicted pity should be showed from his friend; but he forsakes the fear of the Almighty.

15 My brethren have dealt deceitfully as a brook, and as the stream of brooks they pass away;

16 Which are blackish by reason of the ice, and wherein the snow is hid:

17 What time they wax warm, they vanish: when it is hot, they are consumed out of their place.

18 The paths of their way are turned aside; they go to nothing, and perish.

19 The troops of Tema looked, the companies of Sheba waited for them.

20 They were confounded because they had hoped; they came there, and were ashamed.

21 For now you are nothing; you see my casting down, and are afraid.

22 Did I say, Bring to me? or, Give a reward for me of your substance?

23 Or, Deliver me from the enemy's hand? or, Redeem me from the hand of the mighty?

24 Teach me, and I will hold my tongue: and cause me to understand wherein I have erred.

25 How forcible are right words! but what does your arguing reprove?

26 Do you imagine to reprove words, and the speeches of one that is desperate, which are as wind?

27 Yea, you overwhelm the fatherless, and you dig a pit for your friend.

28 Now therefore be content, look upon me; for it is evident to you if I lie.

29 Return, I pray you, let it not be iniquity; yea, return again, my righteousness is in it.

30 Is there iniquity in my tongue? cannot my taste discern perverse things?

CHAPTER 7

IS there not an appointed time to man upon earth? are not his days also like the days of an hireling?

2 As a servant earnestly desires the shadow, and as an hireling looks for the reward of his work:

3 So am I made to possess months of vanity, and wearisome nights are appointed to me.

4 When I lie down, I say, When shall I arise, and the night be gone? and I am full of tossings to and fro to the dawning of the day.

5 My flesh is clothed with worms and clods of dust; my skin is broken, and become loathsome.

6 My days are swifter than a weaver's shuttle, and are spent without hope.

7 O remember that my life is wind: my eye shall no more see good.

8 The eye of him that has seen me shall see me no more: your eyes are upon me, and I am not.

9 As the cloud is consumed and vanishes away: so he that goes down to the grave shall come up no more.

10 He shall return no more to his house, neither shall his place know him any more.

11 Therefore I will not refrain my mouth; I will speak in the anguish of my spirit; I will complain in the bitterness of my soul.

12 Am I a sea, or a whale, that you set a watch over me?

13 When I say, My bed shall comfort me, my couch shall ease my complaints;

14 Then you scare me with dreams, and terrify me through visions:

15 So that my soul chooses strangling, and death rather than my life.

16 I loathe it; I would not live alway: let me alone; for my days are vanity.

17 What is man, that you should magnify him? and that you should set your heart upon him?

18 And that you should visit him every morning, and try him every moment?

19 How long will you not depart from me, nor let me alone till I swallow down my spittle?

20 I have sinned; what shall I do to you, O you preserver of men? why have you set me as a mark against you, so that I am a burden to myself?

21 And why do you not pardon my transgression, and take away my iniqui-

---

7:6 How frightening life is for the unsaved. They live in futility, and are held captive to the fear of death (see Hebrews 2:14-15). It is therefore legitimate to confront the ungodly with these things, to awaken them to their plight before death seizes them. The only way to effectively do this is to then say why they live in futility; why they are swiftly being drawn towards death, transgression of the Law of God.

THE FUNCTION OF THE LAW

8:3 **If there is no hell, no ultimate justice,** then the answer to the question posed in this verse must be "Yes. The Almighty does pervert justice."

In July, 2001, a Washington DC police chief boasted that his state was not too far behind the 51% national success rate in solving homicides in the United States. During the 1990's the average annual murder rate was around 22,000 per year. That means approximately half of those homicides were never solved, which means that more than 100,000 murderers were never brought to justice from 1990 - 2000. Think of it. During those ten years over 100,000 people were stabbed, shot, had their throats cut, were strangled, or poisoned, and the murderer went away free. If God isn't going the punish them for such terrible crimes, then He is unjust.

However, the opposite is the case. God will bring to justice every secret thing, whether it is good or evil. He will be so thorough, so sweeping in His justice that he will consider hatred to be murder and will judge humanity right down to their thoughts and intents of the heart.

In 2001, a man in the U.S. was given twelve years in jail for conspiring to kill his wife. She was going to take all he had through a bitter divorce, and he decided that murdering her would solve his problem. The reason he was given twelve years was because his hateful thoughts were made manifest to a hit man, who recorded them on video. True hatred conspires to murder (within the mind) and as God has access to human thought, He also considers the person guilty, even though they haven't physically carried out the crime.

ty? for now shall I sleep in the dust; and you shall seek me in the morning, but I shall not be.

CHAPTER 8

THEN answered Bildad the Shuhite, and said,

2 How long will you speak these things? and how long shall the words of your mouth be like a strong wind?

3 Does God pervert judgment? or does the Almighty pervert justice?

4 If your children have sinned against him, and he have cast them away for their transgression;

5 If you would seek God betimes, and make your supplication to the Almighty;

6 If you were pure and upright; surely now he would awake for you, and make the habitation of your righteousness prosperous.

7 Though your beginning was small, yet your latter end should greatly increase.

8 For enquire, I pray you, of the former age, and prepare yourself to the search of their fathers:

9 (For we are but of yesterday, and know nothing, because our days upon earth are a shadow:)

10 Shall they not teach you, and tell you, and utter words out of their heart?

11 Can the rush grow up without mire? can the flag grow without water?

12 Whilst it is yet in his greenness, and not cut down, it withers before any other herb.

13 So are the paths of all that forget God; and the hypocrite's hope shall perish:

14 Whose hope shall be cut off, and whose trust shall be a spider's web.

15 He shall lean upon his house, but it shall not stand: he shall hold it fast, but it shall not endure.

16 He is green before the sun, and his branch shoots forth in his garden.

17 His roots are wrapped about the heap, and sees the place of stones.

18 If he destroy him from his place, then it shall deny him, saying, I have not seen you.

19 Behold, this is the joy of his way, and out of the earth shall others grow.

20 Behold, God will not cast away a perfect man, neither will he help the evil doers:

21 Till he fill your mouth with laughing, and your lips with rejoicing.

22 They that hate you shall be clothed with shame; and the dwelling place of the wicked shall come to nothing.

CHAPTER 9

THEN Job answered and said, (2) I know it is so of a truth: but how should man be just with God?

3 If he will contend with him, he cannot answer him one of a thousand.

4 He is wise in heart, and mighty in strength: who has hardened himself against him, and has prospered?

5 Which removes the mountains, and they know not: which overturns them in his anger.

6 Which shakes the earth out of her place, and the pillars thereof tremble.

7 Which commands the sun, and it rises not; and seals up the stars.

8 Which alone spreads out the heavens, and treads upon the waves of the sea.

9 Which makes Arcturus, Orion, and Pleiades, and the chambers of the south.

10 Which doeth great things past finding out; yea, and wonders without number.

11 Lo, he goes by me, and I see him not: he passes on also, but I perceive him not.

12 Behold, he takes away, who can hinder him? who will say to him, What are you doing?

13 If God will not withdraw his anger, the proud helpers do stoop under him.

14 How much less shall I answer him, and choose out my words to reason with him?

15 Whom, though I were righteous, yet would I not answer, but I would make supplication to my judge.

16 If I had called, and he had answered me; yet would I not believe that he had hearkened to my voice.

17 For he breaks me with a tempest, and multiplies my wounds without cause.

18 He will not suffer me to take my breath, but fills me with bitterness.

19 If I speak of strength, lo, he is strong: and if of judgment, who shall set me a time to plead?

20 If I justify myself, my own mouth shall condemn me: if I say, I am perfect, it shall also prove me perverse.

21 Though I were perfect, yet would I not know my soul: I would despise my life.

22 This is one thing, therefore I said it, He destroys the perfect and the wicked.

23 If the scourge slay suddenly, he will laugh at the trial of the innocent.

24 The earth is given into the hand of the wicked: he covers the faces of the judges thereof; if not, where, and who is he?

25 Now my days are swifter than a post: they flee away, they see no good.

26 They are passed away as the swift ships: as the eagle that hastens to the prey.

27 If I say, I will forget my complaint, I will leave off my heaviness, and comfort myself:

28 I am afraid of all my sorrows, I know that you will not hold me innocent.

29 If I be wicked, why then labour I in vain?

30 If I wash myself with snow water, and make my hands never so clean;

31 Yet shall you plunge me in the ditch, and my own clothes shall abhor me.

9:2 The answer to such a profound question is that a man can be made righteous by grace, through faith. See Ephesians 2:8-9.

9:10-12 The immortal, invisible Creator does what He wants when He wants. See Romans 11:33.

32 For he is not a man, as I am, that I should answer him, and we should come together in judgment.

33 Neither is there any mediator between us, that might lay his hand upon us both.

34 Let him take his rod away from me, and let not his fear terrify me:

35 Then would I speak, and not fear him; but it is not so with me.

CHAPTER 10

MY soul is weary of my life; I will leave my complaint upon myself; I will speak in the bitterness of my soul.

2 I will say to God, Do not condemn me; show me why you contend with me.

3 Is it good to you that you should oppress, that you should despise the work of your hands, and shine upon the counsel of the wicked?

4 Have you eyes of flesh? or do you see as man sees?

5 Are your days as the days of man? are your years as man's days,

6 That you enquire after my iniquity, and search after my sin?

7 You know that I am not wicked; and there is none that can deliver out of your hand.

8 Your hands have made me and fashioned me together round about; yet you would destroy me.

9 Remember, I beseech you, that you have made me as the clay; and will you bring me into dust again?

10 Have you not poured me out as milk, and curdled me like cheese?

11 You have clothed me with skin and flesh, and have fenced me with bones and sinews.

12 You have granted me life and favour, and your visitation has preserved my spirit.

13 And these things have you hid in your heart: I know that this is with you.

14 If I sin, then you mark me, and you will not acquit me from my iniquity.

15 If I be wicked, woe to me; and if I be righteous, yet will I not lift up my head. I am full of confusion; therefore see my affliction;

16 For it increases. You hunt me as a fierce lion: and again you show yourself marvelous upon me.

17 You renew your witnesses against me, and increase your indignation upon me; changes and war are against me.

18 Why then have you brought me forth out of the womb? Oh that I had given up the ghost, and no eye had seen me!

19 I should have been as though I had not been; I should have been carried from the womb to the grave.

20 Are not my days few? cease then, and let me alone, that I may take comfort a little,

21 Before I go where I shall not return, even to the land of darkness and the shadow of death;

22 A land of darkness, as darkness itself; and of the shadow of death, without any order, and where the light is as darkness.

CHAPTER 11

THEN answered Zophar the Naamathite, and said,

2 Should not the multitude of words be answered? and should a man full of talk be justified?

3 Should your lies make men hold their peace? and when you mock, shall no man make you ashamed?

4 For you have said, My doctrine is pure, and I am clean in your eyes.

10:4 Little did Job realize that one day this would happen, God would become flesh and dwell among us. See 1 Timothy 3:16.

10:7,15 No one likes to admit that his heart is wicked. This is because we are ignorant of God's righteousness until the Law is applied to the conscience. See verse 15. Then see Job 13:23.

5 But oh that God would speak, and open his lips against you;

6 And that he would show you the secrets of wisdom, that they are double to that which is! Know therefore that God exacts of you less than your iniquity deserves.

7 Can you by searching find out God? can you find out the Almighty to perfection?

8 It is as high as heaven; what can you do? deeper than hell; what can you know?

9 The measure thereof is longer than the earth, and broader than the sea.

10 If he cut off, and shut up, or gather together, then who can hinder him?

11 For he knows vain men: he sees wickedness also; will he not then consider it?

12 For vain men would be wise, though man be born like a wild ass's colt.

13 If you prepare your heart, and stretch out your hands toward him;

14 If iniquity be in your hand, put it far away, and let not wickedness dwell in your tabernacles.

15 For then shall you lift up your face without spot; yea, you shall be stedfast, and shall not fear:

16 Because you shall forget your misery, and remember it as waters that pass away:

17 And your age shall be clearer than the noonday: you shall shine forth, you shall be as the morning.

18 And you shall be secure, because there is hope; yea, you shall dig about you, and you shall take your rest in safety.

19 Also you shall lie down, and none shall make you afraid; yea, many shall make suit to you.

20 But the eyes of the wicked shall fail, and they shall not escape, and their hope shall be as the giving up of the ghost.

CHAPTER 12

AND Job answered and said, (2) No doubt but you are the people, and wisdom shall die with you.

3 But I have understanding as well as you; I am not inferior to you: yea, who does not know such things as these?

4 I am as one mocked of his neighbour, who calls upon God, and he answers him: the just upright man is laughed to scorn.

5 He that is ready to slip with his feet is as a lamp despised in the thought of him that is at ease.

6 The tabernacles of robbers prosper, and they that provoke God are secure; into whose hand God brings abundantly.

7 But ask now the beasts, and they shall teach you; and the fowls of the air, and they shall tell you:

8 Or speak to the earth, and it shall teach you: and the fishes of the sea shall declare to you.

9 Who does not know in all these that the hand of the LORD has done this?

10 In whose hand is the soul of every living thing, and the breath of all mankind.

11 Does not the ear try words? and the mouth taste his meat?

12 With the ancient is wisdom; and in length of days understanding.

13 With him is wisdom and strength, he has counsel and understanding.

14 Behold, he breaks down, and it cannot be built again: he shuts up a man, and there can be no opening.

15 Behold, he withholds the waters, and they dry up: also he sends them out, and they overturn the earth.

12:6 The ungodly see that they live as well if not better than those who refrain from sin (see Matthew 5:45). Instead of being humbled by God's goodness, they see Heaven's silence as Heaven's approval.

16 With him is strength and wisdom: the deceived and the deceiver are his.

17 He leads counselors away spoiled, and makes the judges fools.

18 He looses the bond of kings, and girds their loins with a girdle.

19 He leads princes away spoiled, and overthrows the mighty.

20 He removes away the speech of the trusty, and takes away the understanding of the aged.

21 He pours contempt upon princes, and weakens the strength of the mighty.

22 He discovers deep things out of darkness, and brings out to light the shadow of death.

23 He increases the nations, and destroys them: he enlarges the nations, and straitens them again.

24 He takes away the heart of the chief of the people of the earth, and causes them to wander in a wilderness where there is no way.

25 They grope in the dark without light, and he makes them to stagger like a drunken man.

CHAPTER 13

LO, my eye has seen all this, my ear has heard and understood it.

2 What you know, the same do I know also: I am not inferior to you.

3 Surely I would speak to the Almighty, and I desire to reason with God.

4 But you are forgers of lies, you are all physicians of no value.

5 O that you would altogether hold your peace! and it should be your wisdom.

6 Hear now my reasoning, and hearken to the pleadings of my lips.

7 Will you speak wickedly for God? and talk deceitfully for him?

THE FUNCTION OF THE LAW

13:23 No one likes to admit that their heart is wicked. We are all ignorant of God's righteousness until His Law is applied to the conscience.

8 Will you accept his person? will you contend for God?

9 Is it good that he should search you out? or as one man mocks another, do you so mock him?

10 He will surely reprove you, if you do secretly accept persons.

11 Shall not his excellency make you afraid? and his dread fall upon you?

12 Your remembrances are like to ashes, your bodies to bodies of clay.

13 Hold your peace, let me alone, that I may speak, and let come on me what will.

14 Why do I take my flesh in my teeth, and put my life in my hand?

15 Though he slay me, yet will I trust in him: but I will maintain my own ways before him.

16 He also shall be my salvation: for an hypocrite shall not come before him.

17 Hear diligently my speech, and my declaration with your ears.

18 Behold now, I have ordered my cause; I know that I shall be justified.

19 Who is he that will plead with me? for now, if I hold my tongue, I shall give up the ghost.

20 Only do not two things to me: then will I not hide myself from you.

21 Withdraw your hand far from me: and let not your dread make me afraid.

22 Then call, and I will answer: or let me speak, and answer me.

12:22 This is what Jesus did. See Luke 1:79.

13:15 In these words, Job reveals his great faith. Despite his misery and pain, Job did trust God's judgments. May God help each of us to have such faith in Him, no matter what He allows to come our way.

JOB HEARING OF HIS RUIN

Job 14:1

23 How many are my iniquities and sins? make me to know my transgression and my sin.

24 Why do you hide your face, and hold me for your enemy?

25 Will you break a leaf driven to and fro? and will you pursue the dry stubble?

26 For you write bitter things against me, and make me to possess the iniquities of my youth.

27 You put my feet also in the stocks, and look narrowly to all my paths; you set a print upon the heels of my feet.

28 And he, as a rotten thing, consumes, as a garment that is moth eaten.

CHAPTER 14

MAN that is born of a woman is of few days and full of trouble.

2 He comes forth like a flower, and is cut down: he flees also as a shadow, and continues not.

3 And do you open your eyes upon such an one, and bring me into judgment with you?

4 Who can bring a clean thing out of an unclean? not one.

5 Seeing his days are determined, the number of his months are with you, you have appointed his bounds that he cannot pass;

6 Turn from him, that he may rest, till he shall accomplish, as an hireling, his day.

7 For there is hope of a tree, if it be cut down, that it will sprout again, and that the tender branch thereof will not cease.

8 Though the root thereof wax old in the earth, and the stock thereof die in the ground;

9 Yet through the scent of water it will bud, and bring forth boughs like a plant.

10 But man dies, and wastes away: yea, man gives up the ghost, and where is he?

11 As the waters fail from the sea, and the flood decays and dries up:

12 So man lies down, and does not rise: till the heavens be no more, they shall not awake, nor be raised out of their sleep.

13 O that you would hide me in the grave, that you would keep me secret, until your wrath be past, that you would appoint me a set time, and remember me!

14 If a man die, shall he live again? all the days of my appointed time will I wait, till my change come.

15 You shall call, and I will answer you: you will have a desire to the work of your hands.

16 For now you number my steps: do you not watch over my sin?

17 My transgression is sealed up in a bag, and you sew up my iniquity.

18 And surely the mountains falling comes to nothing, and the rock is removed out of his place.

19 The waters wear the stones: you wash away the things which grow out of the dust of the earth; and you destroy the hope of man.

20 You prevail for ever against him, and he passes: you change his countenance, and send him away.

21 His sons come to honour, and he knows it not; and they are brought low, but he does not perceive it of them.

22 But his flesh upon him shall have pain, and his soul within him shall mourn.

CHAPTER 15

THEN answered Eliphaz the Temanite, and said,

2 Should a wise man utter vain knowledge, and fill his belly with the east wind?

3 Should he reason with unprofitable talk? or with speeches wherewith he can do no good?

4 Yea, you cast off fear, and restrain prayer before God.

5 For your mouth utters your iniquity, and you choose the tongue of the crafty.

6 Your own mouth condemns you, and not I: yea, your own lips testify against you.

7 Are you the first man that was born? or were you made before the hills?

8 Have you heard the secret of God? and do you restrain wisdom to yourself?

9 What do you know, that we do not know? what do you understand, which is not in us?

10 With us are both the grayheaded and very aged men, much elder than your father.

14:1 See Isaiah 40:6.

14:4 In Christ, God doesn't make a clean thing out of an unclean thing. Instead He makes us new creatures. See 2 Corinthians 5:17.

14:14 Every man and woman who dies will stand before God in judgment. It has been well-said, "Death is not the termination of existence; but the entrance into an eternal and unchanging state."

11 Are the consolations of God small with you? is there any secret thing with you?

12 Why does your heart carry you away? and what do your eyes wink at,

13 That you turn your spirit against God, and let such words go out of your mouth?

14 What is man, that he should be clean? and he which is born of a woman, that he should be righteous?

15 Behold, he puts no trust in his saints; yea, the heavens are not clean in his sight.

16 How much more abominable and filthy is man, which drinks iniquity like water?

17 I will show you, hear me; and that which I have seen I will declare;

18 Which wise men have told from their fathers, and have not hid it:

19 To whom alone the earth was given, and no stranger passed among them.

20 The wicked man travails with pain all his days, and the number of years is hidden to the oppressor.

21 A dreadful sound is in his ears: in prosperity the destroyer shall come upon him.

22 He believeth not that he shall return out of darkness, and he is waited for of the sword.

23 He wanders abroad for bread, saying, Where is it? he knows that the day of darkness is ready at his hand.

24 Trouble and anguish shall make him afraid; they shall prevail against him, as a king ready to the battle.

25 For he stretches out his hand against God, and strengthens himself against the Almighty.

26 He runs upon him, even on his neck, upon the thick bosses of his bucklers:

27 Because he covers his face with his fatness, and makes collops of fat on his flanks.

28 And he dwells in desolate cities, and in houses which no man inhabits, which are ready to become heaps.

29 He shall not be rich, neither shall his substance continue, neither shall he prolong the perfection thereof upon the earth.

30 He shall not depart out of darkness; the flame shall dry up his branches, and by the breath of his mouth shall he go away.

31 Let not him that is deceived trust in vanity: for vanity shall be his reward.

32 It shall be accomplished before his time, and his branch shall not be green.

33 He shall shake off his unripe grape as the vine, and shall cast off his flower as the olive.

34 For the congregation of hypocrites shall be desolate, and fire shall consume the tabernacles of bribery.

35 They conceive mischief, and bring forth vanity, and their belly prepares deceit.

CHAPTER 16

THEN Job answered and said,

2 I have heard many such things: miserable comforters are you all.

3 Shall vain words have an end? or what emboldens you that you answer?

4 I also could speak as you do: if your soul were in my soul's stead, I could heap up words against you, and shake my head at you.

5 But I would strengthen you with my mouth, and the moving of my lips should relieve your grief.

6 Though I speak, my grief is not relieved: and though I forbear, what am I eased?

15:15-16 One doesn't have to look too far to see the truth of this; just visit a secular video store or a magazine rack and see what the unsaved thirst for (refer to Psalms 14:3).

7 But now he has made me weary: you have made desolate all my company.

8 And you have filled me with wrinkles, which is a witness against me: and my leanness rising up in me bears witness to my face.

9 He tears me in his wrath, who hates me: he gnashes upon me with his teeth; my enemy sharpens his eyes upon me.

10 They have gaped upon me with their mouth; they have smitten me upon the cheek reproachfully; they have gathered themselves together against me.

11 God has delivered me to the ungodly, and turned me over into the hands of the wicked.

12 I was at ease, but he has broken me asunder: he has also taken me by my neck, and shaken me to pieces, and set me up for his mark.

13 His archers compass me round about, he cleaves my reins asunder, and does not spare; he pours out my gall upon the ground.

14 He breaks me with breach upon breach, he runs upon me like a giant.

15 I have sewed sackcloth upon my skin, and defiled my horn in the dust.

16 My face is foul with weeping, and on my eyelids is the shadow of death;

17 .Not for any injustice in my hands: also my prayer is pure.

18 O earth, do not cover my blood, and let my cry have no place.

19 Also now, behold, my witness is in heaven, and my record is on high.

20 My friends scorn me: but my eye pours out tears to God.

21 O that one might plead for a man with God, as a man pleads for his neighbour!

22 When a few years are come, then I shall go the way where I shall not return.

CHAPTER 17

MY breath is corrupt, my days are extinct, the graves are ready for me.

2 Are there not mockers with me? and does not my eye continue in their provocation?

3 Lay down now, put me in a surety with you; who is he that will strike hands with me?

4 For you have hid their heart from understanding: therefore shall you not exalt them.

5 He that speaks flattery to his friends, even the eyes of his children shall fail.

6 He has made me also a byword of the people; and aforetime I was as a tabret.

7 My eye also is dim by reason of sorrow, and all my members are as a shadow.

8 Upright men shall be astonished at this, and the innocent shall stir up himself against the hypocrite.

9 The righteous also shall hold on his way, and he that has clean hands shall be stronger and stronger.

10 But as for you all, do you return, and come now: for I cannot find one wise man among you.

11 My days are past, my purposes are broken off, even the thoughts of my heart.

12 They change the night into day: the light is short because of darkness.

13 If I wait, the grave is my house: I have made my bed in the darkness.

14 I have said to corruption, You are my father: to the worm, You are my mother, and my sister.

15 And where is now my hope? as for my hope, who shall see it?

16 They shall go down to the bars of the pit, when our rest together is in the dust.

16:10-11 This is a Messianic prophesy (see Psalm 22:13).

16:21 We have an advocate, one to plead for us in the presence of God, Jesus Christ the righteous (see 1 John 2:1-2).

CHAPTER 18

THEN answered Bildad the Shuhite, and said,

2 How long will it be till you make an end of words? mark, and afterwards we will speak.

3 Why are we counted as beasts, and reputed vile in your sight?

4 He tears himself in his anger: shall the earth be forsaken for you? and shall the rock be removed out of his place?

5 Yea, the light of the wicked shall be put out, and the spark of his fire shall not shine.

6 The light shall be dark in his tabernacle, and his candle shall be put out with him.

7 The steps of his strength shall be straitened, and his own counsel shall cast him down.

8 For he is cast into a net by his own feet, and he walks upon a snare.

9 The gin shall take him by the heel, and the robber shall prevail against him.

10 The snare is laid for him in the ground, and a trap for him in the way.

11 Terrors shall make him afraid on every side, and shall drive him to his feet.

12 His strength shall be hungerbitten, and destruction shall be ready at his side.

13 It shall devour the strength of his skin: even the firstborn of death shall devour his strength.

14 His confidence shall be rooted out of his tabernacle, and it shall bring him to the king of terrors.

15 It shall dwell in his tabernacle, because it is none of his: brimstone shall be scattered upon his habitation.

16 His roots shall be dried up beneath, and above shall his branch be cut off.

17 His remembrance shall perish from the earth, and he shall have no name in the street.

18 He shall be driven from light into darkness, and chased out of the world.

19 He shall neither have son nor nephew among his people, nor any remaining in his dwellings.

20 They that come after him shall be astonished at his day, as they that went before were affrighted.

21 Surely such are the dwellings of the wicked, and this is the place of him that knows not God.

CHAPTER 19

THEN Job answered and said, (2) How long will you vex my soul, and break me in pieces with words?

3 These ten times have you reproached me: you are not ashamed that you make yourselves strange to me.

4 And be it indeed that I have erred, my error remains with myself.

5 If indeed you will magnify yourselves against me, and plead against me my reproach:

6 Know now that God has overthrown me, and has compassed me with his net.

7 Behold, I cry out of wrong, but I am not heard: I cry aloud, but there is no judgment.

8 He has fenced up my way that I cannot pass, and he has set darkness in my paths.

9 He has stripped me of my glory, and taken the crown from my head.

10 He has destroyed me on every side, and I am gone: and my hope has he removed like a tree.

11 He has also kindled his wrath against me, and he counts me to him as one of his enemies.

12 His troops come together, and raise up their way against me, and encamp round about my tabernacle.

13 He has put my brethren far from me, and my acquaintance are verily estranged from me.

14 My kinsfolk have failed, and my familiar friends have forgotten me.

15 They that dwell in my house, and my maids, count me for a stranger: I am an alien in their sight.

16 I called my servant, and he gave me no answer; I intreated him with my mouth.

17 My breath is strange to my wife, though I intreated for the children's sake of my own body.

18 Yea, young children despised me; I arose, and they spoke against me.

19 All my inward friends abhorred me: and they whom I loved are turned against me.

20 My bone cleaves to my skin and to my flesh, and I am escaped with the skin of my teeth.

21 Have pity upon me, have pity upon me, O you my friends; for the hand of God has touched me.

22 Why do you persecute me as God, and are not satisfied with my flesh?

23 Oh that my words were now written! oh that they were printed in a book!

24 That they were graven with an iron pen and lead in the rock for ever!

25 For I know that my redeemer lives, and that he shall stand at the latter day upon the earth:

26 And though after my skin worms destroy this body, yet in my flesh shall I see God:

27 Whom I shall see for myself, and my eyes shall behold, and not another; though my reins be consumed within me.

28 But you should say, Why persecute we him, seeing the root of the matter is found in me?

29 Be afraid of the sword: for wrath brings the punishments of the sword, that you may know there is a judgment.

CHAPTER 20

THEN answered Zophar the Naamathite, and said,

2 Therefore do my thoughts cause me to answer, and for this I make haste.

3 I have heard the check of my reproach, and the spirit of my understanding causes me to answer.

4 Do you not know this of old, since man was placed upon earth,

5 That the triumphing of the wicked is short, and the joy of the hypocrite but for a moment?

6 Though his excellency mount up to the heavens, and his head reach to the clouds;

7 Yet he shall perish for ever like his own dung: they which have seen him shall say, Where is he?

8 He shall fly away as a dream, and shall not be found: yea, he shall be chased away as a vision of the night.

9 The eye also which saw him shall see him no more; neither shall his place any more behold him.

10 His children shall seek to please the poor, and his hands shall restore their goods.

11 His bones are full of the sin of his youth, which shall lie down with him in the dust.

12 Though wickedness be sweet in his mouth, though he hide it under his tongue;

19:25 In this verse, we see that this man, who existed thousands of years before the coming of the Messiah, had faith that God would deliver him from death. Jesus said that Abraham rejoiced to see his day. Job looked ahead, along with Isaac, Jacob, Joseph, Moses, Joshua, Rahab and others, who "through faith "subdued kingdoms...not accepting deliverance, that they might obtain a better resurrection" (see Hebrews 11:35). Their salvation would come by grace through their faith in the coming Messiah.

20:5 The world often complains about the hypocrites they think are "in the Church." Yet hypocrites are not in the "Church" (which is made up of true believers). Hypocrites merely dwell as goats among the Lord's sheep, bad fish among the good, tares among wheat until the day God separates them. This scripture confirms that sin can bring joy (see Jeremiah 12:1 & Hebrews 11:24-25, also Job 27:8-9).

13 Though he spare it, and forsake it not; but keep it still within his mouth:

14 Yet his meat in his bowels is turned, it is the gall of asps within him.

15 He has swallowed down riches, and he shall vomit them up again: God shall cast them out of his belly.

16 He shall suck the poison of asps: the viper's tongue shall slay him.

17 He shall not see the rivers, the floods, the brooks of honey and butter.

18 That which he laboured for shall he restore, and shall not swallow it down: according to his substance shall the restitution be, and he shall not rejoice therein.

19 Because he has oppressed and has forsaken the poor; because he has violently taken away an house which he did not build;

20 Surely he shall not feel quietness in his belly, he shall not save of that which he desired.

21 There shall none of his meat be left; therefore shall no man look for his goods.

22 In the fullness of his sufficiency he shall be in straits: every hand of the wicked shall come upon him.

23 When he is about to fill his belly, God shall cast the fury of his wrath upon him, and shall rain it upon him while he is eating.

24 He shall flee from the iron weapon, and the bow of steel shall strike him through.

25 It is drawn, and comes out of the body; yea, the glittering sword comes out of his gall: terrors are upon him.

26 All darkness shall be hid in his secret places: a fire not blown shall consume him; it shall go ill with him that is left in his tabernacle.

27 The heaven shall reveal his iniquity; and the earth shall rise up against him.

28 The increase of his house shall depart, and his goods shall flow away in the day of his wrath.

29 This is the portion of a wicked man from God, and the heritage appointed to him by God.

CHAPTER 21

B UT Job answered and said, (2) Hear diligently my speech, and let this be your consolations.

3 Suffer me that I may speak; and after that I have spoken, mock on.

4 As for me, is my complaint to man? and if it were so, why should not my spirit be troubled?

5 Mark me, and be astonished, and lay your hand upon your mouth.

6 Even when I remember I am afraid, and trembling takes hold on my flesh.

7 Why do the wicked live, become old, yea, are mighty in power?

8 Their seed is established in their sight with them, and their offspring before their eyes.

9 Their houses are safe from fear, neither is the rod of God upon them.

10 Their bull genders, and fails not; their cow calves, and castes not her calf.

11 They send forth their little ones like a flock, and their children dance.

12 They take the timbrel and harp, and rejoice at the sound of the organ.

13 They spend their days in wealth, and in a moment go down to the grave.

14 Therefore they say to God, Depart from us; for we desire not the knowledge of your ways.

15 What is the Almighty, that we should serve him? and what profit should we have, if we pray to him?

16 Lo, their good is not in their hand: the counsel of the wicked is far from me.

17 How oft is the candle of the wicked put out! and how oft comes their destruction upon them! God distributes sorrows in his anger.

18 They are as stubble before the wind, and as chaff that the storm carries away.

19 God lays up his iniquity for his children: he rewards him, and he shall know it.

20 His eyes shall see his destruction, and he shall drink of the wrath of the Almighty.

21 For what pleasure has he in his house after him, when the number of his months is cut off in the midst?

22 Shall any teach God knowledge? seeing he judges those that are high.

23 One dies in his full strength, being wholly at ease and quiet.

24 His breasts are full of milk, and his bones are moistened with marrow.

25 And another dies in the bitterness of his soul, and never eats with pleasure.

26 They shall lie down alike in the dust, and the worms shall cover them.

27 Behold, I know your thoughts, and the devices which you wrongfully imagine against me.

28 For you say, Where is the house of the prince? and where are the dwelling places of the wicked?

29 Have you not asked them that go by the way? and do you not know their tokens,

30 That the wicked is reserved to the day of destruction? they shall be brought forth to the day of wrath.

31 Who shall declare his way to his face? and who shall repay him what he has done?

32 Yet shall he be brought to the grave, and shall remain in the tomb.

33 The clods of the valley shall be sweet to him, and every man shall draw after him, as there are innumerable before him.

34 How then can you comfort me in vain, seeing in your answers there remains falsehood?

CHAPTER 22

THEN Eliphaz the Temanite answered and said,

2 Can a man be profitable to God, as he that is wise may be profitable to himself?

3 Is it any pleasure to the Almighty, that you are righteous? or is it gain to him, that you make your ways perfect?

4 Will he reprove you for fear of you? will he enter with you into judgment?

5 Is not your wickedness great? and your iniquities infinite?

6 For you have taken a pledge from your brother for nothing, and stripped the naked of their clothing.

7 You have not given water to the weary to drink, and you have withholden bread from the hungry.

8 But as for the mighty man, he had the earth; and the honourable man dwelt in it.

9 You have sent widows away empty, and the arms of the fatherless have been broken.

10 Therefore snares are round about you, and sudden fear troubles you;

11 Or darkness, that you can not see; and abundance of waters cover you.

12 Is not God in the height of heaven? and behold the height of the stars, how high they are!

13 And you say, How does God know? can he judge through the dark cloud?

14 Thick clouds are a covering to him, that he sees not; and he walks in the circuit of heaven.

15 Have you marked the old way which wicked men have trodden?

16 Which were cut down out of time, whose foundation was overflown with a flood:

17 Which said to God, Depart from us: and what can the Almighty do for them?

18 Yet he filled their houses with good things: but the counsel of the wicked is far from me.

19 The righteous see it, and are glad: and the innocent laugh them to scorn.

20 Whereas our substance is not cut down, but the remnant of them the fire consumes.

22:21-22 We are born not acquainted with God; neither are we at peace with Him. It is the Law that acquaints us with God's character and brings us to the foot of the cross. See Galatians 3:24.

21 Acquaint now yourself with him, and be at peace: thereby good shall come to you.

22 Receive, I pray you, the law from his mouth, and lay up his words in your heart.

23 If you return to the Almighty, you shall be built up, you shall put away iniquity far from your tabernacles.

24 Then shall you lay up gold as dust, and the gold of Ophir as the stones of the brooks.

25 Yea, the Almighty shall be your defence, and you shall have plenty of silver.

26 For then shall you have your delight in the Almighty, and shall lift up your face to God.

27 You shall make your prayer to him, and he shall hear you, and you shall pay your vows.

28 You shall also decree a thing, and it shall be established to you: and the light shall shine upon your ways.

29 When men are cast down, then you shall say, There is lifting up; and he shall save the humble person.

30 He shall deliver the island of the innocent: and it is delivered by the pureness of your hands.

CHAPTER 23

THEN Job answered and said, (2) Even to day is my complaint bitter: my stroke is heavier than my groaning.

3 Oh that I knew where I might find him! that I might come even to his seat!

4 I would order my cause before him, and fill my mouth with arguments.

5 I would know the words which he would answer me, and understand what he would say to me.

6 Will he plead against me with his great power? No; but he would put strength in me.

7 There the righteous might dispute with him; so should I be delivered for ever from my judge.

8 Behold, I go forward, but he is not there; and backward, but I cannot perceive him:

9 On the left hand, where he does work, but I cannot behold him: he hides himself on the right hand, that I cannot see him:

10 But he knows the way that I take: when he has tried me, I shall come forth as gold.

11 My foot has held his steps, his way have I kept, and not declined.

12 Neither have I gone back from the commandment of his lips; I have esteemed the words of his mouth more than my necessary food.

13 But he is in one mind, and who can turn him? and what his soul desires, even that he doeth.

14 For he performs the thing that is appointed for me: and many such things are with him.

15 Therefore am I troubled at his presence: when I consider, I am afraid of him.

16 For God makes my heart soft, and the Almighty troubles me:

17 Because I was not cut off before the darkness, neither has he covered the darkness from my face.

22:26 What a blessing to be able to lift up our face to God! All our sins are washed away through the blood of the cross. We no longer need to hide our face in shame.

23:2 See Romans 10:8-9

23:12 Do you read the Bible every day without fail? Do you esteem the words of His mouth more than your necessary food? Which comes first, your Bible or your belly? If you put God's Word first in your life and fulfill the requirements of Psalm One, then you can also reap the Psalm's promised blessings.

CHAPTER 24

WHY, seeing times are not hidden from the Almighty, do they that know him not see his days?

2 Some remove the landmarks; they violently take away flocks, and feed thereof.

3 They drive away the ass of the fatherless, they take the widow's ox for a pledge.

4 They turn the needy out of the way: the poor of the earth hide themselves together.

5 Behold, as wild asses in the desert, go they forth to their work; rising betimes for a prey: the wilderness yields food for them and for their children.

6 They reap every one his corn in the field: and they gather the vintage of the wicked.

7 They cause the naked to lodge without clothing, that they have no covering in the cold.

8 They are wet with the showers of the mountains, and embrace the rock for want of a shelter.

9 They pluck the fatherless from the breast, and take a pledge of the poor.

10 They cause him to go naked without clothing, and they take away the sheaf from the hungry;

11 Which make oil within their walls, and tread their winepresses, and suffer thirst.

12 Men groan from out of the city, and the soul of the wounded cry out: yet God does not lay folly to them.

13 They are of those that rebel against the light; they know not the ways thereof, nor abide in the paths thereof.

14 The murderer rising with the light kills the poor and needy, and in the night is as a thief.

15 The eye also of the adulterer waits for the twilight, saying, No eye shall see me: and disguises his face.

16 In the dark they dig through houses, which they had marked for themselves in the daytime: they know not the light.

17 For the morning is to them even as the shadow of death: if one know them, they are in the terrors of the shadow of death.

18 He is swift as the waters; their portion is cursed in the earth: he beholds not the way of the vineyards.

19 Drought and heat consume the snow waters: so does the grave those which have sinned.

20 The womb shall forget him; the worm shall feed sweetly on him; he shall be no more remembered; and wickedness shall be broken as a tree.

21 He evil entreats the barren that bears not: and doeth not good to the widow.

22 He draws also the mighty with his power: he rises up, and no man is sure of life.

23 Though it be given him to be in safety, whereon he rests; yet his eyes are upon their ways.

24 They are exalted for a little while, but are gone and brought low; they are taken out of the way as all other, and cut off as the tops of the ears of corn.

25 And if it be not so now, who will make me a liar, and make my speech nothing worth?

CHAPTER 25

THEN answered Bildad the Shuhite, and said,

2 Dominion and fear are with him, he makes peace in his high places.

3 Is there any number of his armies? and upon whom does not his light arise?

24:15 Some primitive tribes paint their faces so that their gods cannot recognize them when they kill. We may smile at such absurdity, but western man is no different. He thinks that God, who made his eyes, cannot see his sin. But it is the sinner, and not God, who is blind. See Psalm 94:7-11.

25:4 See John 3:3.

4 How then can man be justified with God? or how can he be clean that is born of a woman?

5 Behold even to the moon, and it shines not; yea, the stars are not pure in his sight.

6 How much less man, that is a worm? and the son of man, which is a worm?

CHAPTER 26

B UT Job answered and said, (2) How have you helped him that is without power? how have you saved the arm that has no strength?

3 How have you counseled him that has no wisdom? and how have you plentifully declared the thing as it is?

4 To whom have you uttered words? and whose spirit came from you?

5 Dead things are formed from under the waters, and the inhabitants thereof.

6 Hell is naked before him, and destruction has no covering.

7 He stretches out the north over the empty place, and hangs the earth upon nothing.

8 He binds up the waters in his thick clouds; and the cloud is not rent under them.

9 He holds back the face of his throne, and spreads his cloud upon it.

10 He has compassed the waters with bounds, until the day and night come to an end.

11 The pillars of heaven tremble and are astonished at his reproof.

12 He divides the sea with his power, and by his understanding he smiteth through the proud.

13 By his spirit he has garnished the heavens; his hand has formed the crooked serpent.

14 Lo, these are parts of his ways: but how little a portion is heard of him? but the thunder of his power who can understand?

CHAPTER 27

M OREOVER Job continued his parable, and said,

2 As God lives, who has taken away my judgment; and the Almighty, who has vexed my soul;

3 All the while my breath is in me, and the spirit of God is in my nostrils;

4 My lips shall not speak wickedness, nor my tongue utter deceit.

5 God forbid that I should justify you: till I die I will not remove my integrity from me.

6 My righteousness I hold fast, and will not let it go: my heart shall not reproach me so long as I live.

7 Let my enemy be as the wicked, and he that rises up against me as the unrighteous.

8 For what is the hope of the hypocrite, though he has gained, when God takes away his soul?

9 Will God hear his cry when trouble comes upon him?

10 Will he delight himself in the Almighty? will he always call upon God?

11 I will teach you by the hand of God: that which is with the Almighty will I not conceal.

12 Behold, all of you have seen it; why then are you thus altogether vain?

26:7 See *Scientific Facts in the Bible*, Hebrews 11:3

26:8 "The average thunderstorm contains about 100,000 tons of water. Imagine, 100,000 tons of water floating about in the sky! All that water just sits there, without crashing down, or 'rending' the cloud." Richard Gunther

26:14 In the city of Christchurch, New Zealand, (population 350,000) the first part of this verse is carved into stone across the top of the doorway of the city's museum. How few gaze at the marvels of God's creation and see the unspeakable genius of His incredible creative hand. They admire the painting and ignore the painter (see Romans 1:25).

13 This is the portion of a wicked man with God, and the heritage of oppressors, which they shall receive of the Almighty.

14 If his children be multiplied, it is for the sword: and his offspring shall not be satisfied with bread.

15 Those that remain of him shall be buried in death: and his widows shall not weep.

16 Though he heap up silver as the dust, and prepare raiment as the clay;

17 He may prepare it, but the just shall put it on, and the innocent shall divide the silver.

18 He builds his house as a moth, and as a booth that the keeper makes.

19 The rich man shall lie down, but he shall not be gathered: he opens his eyes, and he is not.

20 Terrors take hold on him as waters, a tempest steals him away in the night.

21 The east wind carries him away, and he departs: and as a storm hurls him out of his place.

22 For God shall cast upon him, and not spare: he would fain flee out of his hand.

23 Men shall clap their hands at him, and shall hiss him out of his place.

CHAPTER 28

SURELY there is a vein for the silver, and a place for gold where they fine it.

2 Iron is taken out of the earth, and brass is molten out of the stone.

3 He sets an end to darkness, and searches out all perfection: the stones of darkness, and the shadow of death.

4 The flood breaks out from the inhabitant; even the waters forgotten of the foot: they are dried up, they are gone away from men.

5 As for the earth, out of it comes bread: and under it is turned up as it were fire.

6 The stones of it are the place of sapphires: and it has dust of gold.

7 There is a path which no fowl knows, and which the vulture's eye has not seen:

8 The lion's whelps have not trodden it, nor the fierce lion passed by it.

9 He puts forth his hand upon the rock; he overturns the mountains by the roots.

10 He cuts out rivers among the rocks; and his eye sees every precious thing.

11 He binds the floods from overflowing; and the thing that is hid he brings forth to light.

12 But where shall wisdom be found? and where is the place of understanding?

13 Man does not know the price thereof; neither is it found in the land of the living.

14 The depth says, It is not in me: and the sea says, It is not with me.

15 It cannot be gotten for gold, neither shall silver be weighed for the price thereof.

16 It cannot be valued with the gold of Ophir, with the precious onyx, or the sapphire.

17 The gold and the crystal cannot equal it: and the exchange of it shall not be for jewels of fine gold.

18 No mention shall be made of coral, or of pearls: for the price of wisdom is above rubies.

19 The topaz of Ethiopia shall not equal it, neither shall it be valued with pure gold.

20 From where then does wisdom come? and where is the place of understanding?

21 Seeing it is hid from the eyes of all living, and kept close from the fowls of the air.

28:5 All food (including meat) traces itself back to the soil.

28:7-8 No one knows the "path" of God. Jesus likened His way to the wind (see John 3:8). It is amazing to think that God is omnipresent and yet can have an immediate presence. He can manifest Himself through the Angel of the Lord, come as a rushing mighty wind, speak out of a whirlwind, or in a burning bush.

22 Destruction and death say, We have heard the fame thereof with our ears.

23 God understands the way thereof, and he knows the place thereof.

24 For he looks to the ends of the earth, and sees under the whole heaven;

25 To make the weight for the winds; and he weighs the waters by measure.

26 When he made a decree for the rain, and a way for the lightning of the thunder:

27 Then did he see it, and declare it; he prepared it, yea, and searched it out.

28 And to man he said, Behold, the fear of the LORD, that is wisdom; and to depart from evil is understanding.

CHAPTER 29

MOREOVER Job continued his parable, and said,

2 Oh that I were as in months past, as in the days when God preserved me;

3 When his candle shined upon my head, and when by his light I walked through darkness;

4 As I was in the days of my youth, when the secret of God was upon my tabernacle;

5 When the Almighty was yet with me, when my children were about me;

6 When I washed my steps with butter, and the rock poured me out rivers of oil;

7 When I went out to the gate through the city, when I prepared my seat in the street!

8 The young men saw me, and hid themselves: and the aged arose, and stood up.

9 The princes refrained talking, and laid their hand on their mouth.

10 The nobles held their peace, and their tongue cleaved to the roof of their mouth.

11 When the ear heard me, then it blessed me; and when the eye saw me, it gave witness to me:

12 Because I delivered the poor that cried, and the fatherless, and him that had none to help him.

13 The blessing of him that was ready to perish came upon me: and I caused the widow's heart to sing for joy.

14 I put on righteousness, and it clothed me: my judgment was as a robe and a diadem.

15 I was eyes to the blind, and feet was I to the lame.

16 I was a father to the poor: and the cause which I knew not I searched out.

17 And I brake the jaws of the wicked, and plucked the spoil out of his teeth.

18 Then I said, I shall die in my nest, and I shall multiply my days as the sand.

19 My root was spread out by the waters, and the dew lay all night upon my branch.

20 My glory was fresh in me, and my bow was renewed in my hand.

21 To me men gave ear, and waited, and kept silence at my counsel.

22 After my words they spoke not again; and my speech dropped upon them.

23 And they waited for me as for the rain; and they opened their mouth wide as for the latter rain.

24 If I laughed on them, they believed it not; and the light of my countenance they cast not down.

25 I chose out their way, and sat chief, and dwelt as a king in the army, as one that comforts the mourners.

28:25 "Long before it was scientifically recognized that the air had weight, the Bible said that it did. It also tells us that the water has weight - but the fact that so much water covers the Earth, means that the effects of the sun and moon's gravity are balanced perfectly. The energy is dissipated in the water - the weight of the water is precisely measured." Richard Gunther

CHAPTER 30

BUT now they that are younger than I have me in derision, whose fathers I would have disdained to have set with the dogs of my flock.

2 Yea, whereto might the strength of their hands profit me, in whom old age was perished?

3 For want and famine they were solitary; fleeing into the wilderness in former time desolate and waste.

4 Who cut up mallows by the bushes, and juniper roots for their meat.

5 They were driven forth from among men, (they cried after them as after a thief;)

6 To dwell in the cliffs of the valleys, in caves of the earth, and in the rocks.

7 Among the bushes they brayed; under the nettles they were gathered together.

8 They were children of fools, yea, children of base men: they were viler than the earth.

9 And now am I their song, yea, I am their byword.

10 They abhor me, they flee far from me, and spare not to spit in my face.

11 Because he has loosed my cord, and afflicted me, they have also let loose the bridle before me.

12 Upon my right hand rise the youth; they push away my feet, and they raise up against me the ways of their destruction.

13 They mar my path, they set forward my calamity, they have no helper.

14 They came upon me as a wide breaking in of waters: in the desolation they rolled themselves upon me.

15 Terrors are turned upon me: they pursue my soul as the wind: and my welfare passes away as a cloud.

16 And now my soul is poured out upon me; the days of affliction have taken hold upon me.

17 My bones are pierced in me in the night season: and my sinews take no rest.

18 By the great force of my disease is my garment changed: it binds me about as the collar of my coat.

19 He has cast me into the mire, and I am become like dust and ashes.

20 I cry to you, and you do not hear me: I stand up, and you regard me not.

21 You have become cruel to me: with your strong hand you oppose yourself against me.

22 You lift me up to the wind; you cause me to ride upon it, and dissolve my substance.

23 For I know that you will bring me to death, and to the house appointed for all living.

24 Howbeit he will not stretch out his hand to the grave, though they cry in his destruction.

25 Did not I weep for him that was in trouble? was not my soul grieved for the poor?

26 When I looked for good, then evil came to me: and when I waited for light, there came darkness.

27 My bowels boiled, and rested not: the days of affliction prevented me.

28 I went mourning without the sun: I stood up, and I cried in the congregation.

29 I am a brother to dragons, and a companion to owls.

30 My skin is black upon me, and my bones are burned with heat.

31 My harp also is turned to mourning, and my organ into the voice of them that weep.

CHAPTER 31

I made a covenant with my eyes; why then should I think upon a maid?

2 For what portion of God is there from above? and what inheritance of the Almighty from on high?

3 Is not destruction to the wicked? and a strange punishment to the workers of iniquity?

4 Does not he see my ways, and count all my steps?

5 If I have walked with vanity, or if my foot has hastened to deceit;

6 Let me be weighed in an even balance that God may know my integrity.

7 If my step has turned out of the way, and my heart walked after my eyes, and if any blot has cleaved to my hands;

8 Then let me sow, and let another eat; yea, let my offspring be rooted out.

9 If my heart have been deceived by a woman, or if I have laid wait at my neighbour's door;

10 Then let my wife grind to another, and let others bow down upon her.

11 For this is an heinous crime; yea, it is an iniquity to be punished by the judges.

12 For it is a fire that consumes to destruction, and would root out all my increase.

13 If I did despise the cause of my manservant or of my maidservant, when they contended with me;

14 What then shall I do when God rises up? and when he visits, what shall I answer him?

15 Did not he that made me in the womb make him? and did not one fashion us in the womb?

16 If I have withheld the poor from their desire, or have caused the eyes of the widow to fail;

17 Or have eaten my morsel myself alone, and the fatherless has not eaten thereof;

18 (For from my youth he was brought up with me, as with a father, and I have guided her from my mother's womb;)

19 If I have seen any perish for want of clothing, or any poor without covering;

20 If his loins have not blessed me, and if he were not warmed with the fleece of my sheep;

21 If I have lifted up my hand against the fatherless, when I saw my help in the gate:

22 Then let my arm fall from my shoulder blade, and my arm be broken from the bone.

23 For destruction from God was a terror to me, and by reason of his highness I could not endure.

24 If I have made gold my hope, or have said to the fine gold, You are my confidence;

25 If I rejoice because my wealth was great, and because my hand had gotten much;

26 If I beheld the sun when it shined, or the moon walking in brightness;

27 And my heart has been secretly enticed, or my mouth has kissed my hand:

28 This also were an iniquity to be punished by the judge: for I should have denied the God that is above.

29 If I rejoice at the destruction of him that hated me, or lifted up myself when evil found him:

30 Neither have I suffered my mouth to sin by wishing a curse to his soul.

31 If the men of my tabernacle said not, Oh that we had of his flesh! we cannot be satisfied.

32 The stranger did not lodge in the street: but I opened my doors to the traveller.

33 If I covered my transgressions as Adam, by hiding my iniquity in my bosom:

34 Did I fear a great multitude, or did the contempt of families terrify me, that I kept silence, and went not out of the door?

35 Oh that one would hear me! behold, my desire is, that the Almighty would answer me, and that my adversary had written a book.

36 Surely I would take it upon my shoulder, and bind it as a crown to me.

37 I would declare to him the number of my steps; as a prince would I go near to him.

31:1 Jesus took this a little further. See Matthew 5:27-29. See also Galatians 5:16 and Philippians 4:8.

38 If my land cry against me, or that the furrows likewise thereof complain;

39 If I have eaten the fruits thereof without money, or have caused the owners thereof to lose their life:

40 Let thistles grow instead of wheat, and cockle instead of barley. The words of Job are ended.

CHAPTER 32

SO these three men ceased to answer Job, because he was righteous in his own eyes.

2 Then was kindled the wrath of Elihu the son of Barachel the Buzite, of the kindred of Ram: against Job was his wrath kindled, because he justified himself rather than God.

3 Also against his three friends was his wrath kindled, because they had found no answer, and yet had condemned Job.

4 Now Elihu had waited till Job had spoken, because they were elder than he.

5 When Elihu saw that there was no answer in the mouth of these three men, then his wrath was kindled.

6 And Elihu the son of Barachel the Buzite answered and said, I am young, and you are very old; therefore I was afraid, and dared not show you my opinion.

7 I said, Days should speak, and multitude of years should teach wisdom.

> Job's friends chose the right time to visit him, but took not the right course of improving their visit; had they spent the time in praying for him which they did in hot disputes with him, they would have profited him, and pleased God more.
>
> **WILLIAM GURNALL**
> **17TH CENTURY PURITAN**

8 But there is a spirit in man: and the inspiration of the Almighty gives them understanding.

9 Great men are not always wise: neither do the aged understand judgment.

10 Therefore I said, Hearken to me; I also will show my opinion.

11 Behold, I waited for your words; I gave ear to your reasons, while you searched out what to say.

12 Yea, I attended to you, and, behold, there was none of you that convinced Job, or that answered his words:

13 Lest you should say, We have found out wisdom: God thrusts him down, not man.

14 Now he has not directed his words against me: neither will I answer him with your speeches.

15 They were amazed, they answered no more: they left off speaking.

32:2 Eluhu was angry because Job tried to justify himself rather than justify God. This is so often what sinners do when they are confronted with the Law of God. Instead of blaming themselves for sin, they blame God — "He made me like this!"

But when Jesus spoke, we are told that the opposite took place: "And all the people that heard him, and the publicans justified God, being baptized with the baptism of John" (Luke 7:29, italics added).

When a natural tragedy happens, the world calls it "an act of God." Instead of saying that we live in a fallen creation and suffering and tragedies happen as a direct result of our sin, they blame God. The godly would never do that. We would rather justify a holy God than sinful man.

It is normal to have Elihu's experience. He was not only indignant, but he felt as though he was about to burst because of the lies that were being fed to Job. We should react the same with the lies that are being fed to this sick and suffering world. Each of us should feel as though we are about to burst with the new wine of the Holy Spirit (the Spirit of Truth), constraining us to preach that which we know to be true (see verse 19).

16 When I had waited, (for they spoke not, but stood still, and answered no more;)

17 I said, I will answer also my part, I also will show my opinion.

18 For I am full of matter, the spirit within me constrains me

19 Behold, my belly is as wine which has no vent; it is ready to burst like new bottles.

20 I will speak, that I may be refreshed: I will open my lips and answer.

21 Let me not, I pray you, accept any man's person, neither let me give flattering titles to man.

22 For I know not to give flattering titles; in so doing my maker would soon take me away.

CHAPTER 33

THEREFORE, Job, I pray you, hear my speeches, and hearken to all my words.

2 Behold, now I have opened my mouth, my tongue has spoken in my mouth.

3 My words shall be of the uprightness of my heart: and my lips shall utter knowledge clearly.

4 The spirit of God has made me, and the breath of the Almighty has given me life.

5 If you can answer me, set your words in order before me, stand up.

6 Behold, I am according to your wish in God's stead: I also am formed out of the clay.

7 Behold, my terror shall not make you afraid, neither shall my hand be heavy upon you.

8 Surely you have spoken in my hearing, and I have heard the voice of your words, saying,

9 I am clean without transgression, I am innocent; neither is there iniquity in me.

10 Behold, he finds occasions against me, he counts me for his enemy,

11 He puts my feet in the stocks, he marks all my paths.

12 Behold, in this you are not just: I will answer you, that God is greater than man.

13 Why do you strive against him? for he gives not account of any of his matters.

14 For God speaks once, yea twice, yet man does not perceive it.

15 In a dream, in a vision of the night, when deep sleep falls upon men, in slumberings upon the bed;

16 Then he opens the ears of men, and seals their instruction,

17 That he may withdraw man from his purpose, and hide pride from man.

18 He keeps back his soul from the pit, and his life from perishing by the sword.

19 He is chastened also with pain upon his bed, and the multitude of his bones with strong pain:

20 So that his life abhors bread, and his soul dainty meat.

21 His flesh is consumed away, that it cannot be seen; and his bones that were not seen stick out.

22 Yea, his soul draws near to the grave, and his life to the destroyers.

23 If there be a messenger with him, an interpreter, one among a thousand, to show to man his uprightness:

24 Then he is gracious to him, and says, Deliver him from going down to the pit: I have found a ransom.

25 His flesh shall be fresher than a child's: he shall return to the days of his youth:

26 He shall pray to God, and he will be favourable to him: and he shall see his face with joy: for he will render to man his righteousness.

27 He looks upon men, and if any say, I have sinned, and perverted that which was right, and it profited me not;

28 He will deliver his soul from going into the pit, and his life shall see the light.

29 Lo, God works all these things oftentimes with man,

30 To bring back his soul from the pit, to be enlightened with the light of the living.

31 Mark well, O Job, hearken to me: hold your peace, and I will speak.

32 If you have anything to say, answer me: speak, for I desire to justify you.

33 If not, hearken to me: hold your peace, and I shall teach you wisdom.

CHAPTER 34

FURTHERMORE Elihu answered and said,

2 Hear my words, O you wise men; and give ear to me, you that have knowledge.

3 For the ear tries words, as the mouth tastes meat.

4 Let us choose to us judgment: let us know among ourselves what is good.

5 For Job has said, I am righteous: and God has taken away my judgment.

6 Should I lie against my right? my wound is incurable without transgression.

7 What man is like Job, who drinks up scorning like water?

8 Which goes in company with the workers of iniquity, and walks with wicked men.

9 For he has said, It profits a man nothing that he should delight himself with God.

10 Therefore hearken to me you men of understanding: far be it from God, that he should do wickedness; and from the Almighty, that he should commit iniquity.

11 For the work of a man shall he render to him, and cause every man to find according to his ways.

12 Yea, surely God will not do wickedly, neither will the Almighty pervert judgment.

13 Who has given him a charge over the earth? or who has disposed the whole world?

> In the moral conflict
> now raging around us,
> whoever is on God's side
> is on the winning side
> and cannot lose;
> whoever is on the other side
> is on the losing side and cannot win.
> Here there is no chance, no gamble.
> There is freedom to choose
> which side we shall be on,
> but no freedom
> to negotiate the results
> of the choice once it is made.
>
> **AIDEN WILSON TOZER**
> 1897 - 1963
> 20TH CENTURY PREACHER

14 If he set his heart upon man, if he gather to himself his spirit and his breath;

15 All flesh shall perish together, and man shall turn again to dust.

16 If now you have understanding, hear this: hearken to the voice of my words.

17 Shall even he that hates right govern? and will you condemn him that is most just?

18 Is it fit to say to a king, You are wicked? and to princes, You are ungodly?

19 How much less to him that accepts not the persons of princes, nor regards the rich more than the poor? for they all are the work of his hands.

20 In a moment shall they die, and the people shall be troubled at midnight, and pass away: and the mighty shall be taken away without hand.

21 For his eyes are upon the ways of man, and he sees all his goings.

22 There is no darkness, nor shadow of death, where the workers of iniquity may hide themselves.

23 For he will not lay upon man more than right; that he should enter into judgment with God.

34:21 Even the grave will not hide sinful man from the justice of Almighty God.

24 He shall break in pieces mighty men without number, and set others in their stead.

25 Therefore he knows their works, and he overturns them in the night, so that they are destroyed.

26 He strikes them as wicked men in the open sight of others;

27 Because they turned back from him, and would not consider any of his ways:

28 So that they cause the cry of the poor to come to him, and he hears the cry of the afflicted.

29 When he gives quietness, who then can make trouble? and when he hides his face, who then can behold him? whether it be done against a nation, or against a man only:

30 That the hypocrite reign not, lest the people be ensnared.

31 Surely it is meet to be said to God, I have borne chastisement, I will not offend any more:

32 Teach me what I do not see: if I have done iniquity, I will do no more.

33 Should it be according to your mind? he will recompense it, whether you refuse, or whether you choose; and not I: therefore speak what you know.

34 Let men of understanding tell me, and let a wise man hearken to me.

35 Job has spoken without knowledge, and his words were without wisdom.

36 My desire is that Job may be tried to the end because of his answers for wicked men.

37 For he adds rebellion to his sin, he claps his hands among us, and multiplies his words against God.

CHAPTER 35

ELIHU spoke moreover, and said, (2) Do you think this is right, that you said, My righteousness is more than God's?

3 For you said, What advantage will it be to you? and, What profit shall I have, if I be cleansed from my sin?

4 I will answer you, and your companions with you.

5 Look to the heavens, and see; and behold the clouds which are higher than you.

6 If you sin, what do you accomplish against him? or if your transgressions be multiplied, what are you doing to him?

7 If you are righteous, what do you give him? or what does he receive of your hand?

8 Your wickedness may hurt a man such as you; and your righteousness may profit the son of man.

9 By reason of the multitude of oppressions they make the oppressed to cry: they cry out by reason of the arm of the mighty.

10 But none says, Where is God my maker, who gives songs in the night;

11 Who teaches us more than the beasts of the earth, and makes us wiser than the fowls of heaven?

12 There they cry, but none gives answer, because of the pride of evil men.

13 Surely God will not hear vanity, neither will the Almighty regard it.

14 Although you say you shall not see him, yet judgment is before him; therefore trust in him.

15 But now, because it is not so, he has visited in his anger; yet he knows it not in great extremity:

16 Therefore does Job open his mouth in vain; he multiplies words without knowledge.

35:10-12 God has created man with more understanding than animals and birds have, and yet blinding pride stops so many from giving God thanks for His wonderful blessings. Pride is such a wicked thing. It destroys families. A proud husband or wife will not humble him or herself and apologize. They would rather destroy their marriage, leave their family in ruin and keep their cursed pride. The Bible says, "Everyone who is proud of heart is an abomination to the Lord" (Proverbs 16:5.) God resists the proud and gives grace to the humble.

CHAPTER 36

ELIHU also proceeded, and said,
(2) Suffer me a little, and I will show
you that I have yet to speak on God's behalf.

3 I will fetch my knowledge from afar,
and will ascribe righteousness to my
Maker.

4 For truly my words shall not be false:
he that is perfect in knowledge is with
you.

5 Behold, God is mighty, and despises
not any: he is mighty in strength and
wisdom.

6 He preserves not the life of the
wicked: but gives right to the poor.

7 He does not withdraw his eyes from
the righteous: but with kings are they on
the throne; yea, he does establish them
for ever, and they are exalted.

8 And if they be bound in fetters, and
be holden in cords of affliction;

9 Then he shows them their work, and
their transgressions that they have exceeded.

10 He opens also their ear to discipline,
and commands that they return from iniquity.

11 If they obey and serve him, they
shall spend their days in prosperity, and
their years in pleasures.

12 But if they obey not, they shall perish by the sword, and they shall die
without knowledge.

13 But the hypocrites in heart heap up
wrath: they cry not when he binds them.

14 They die in youth, and their life is
among the unclean.

15 He delivers the poor in his affliction,
and opens their ears in oppression.

16 Even so would he have removed you
out of the strait into a broad place,
where there is no straitness; and that
which should be set on your table
should be full of fatness.

17 But you have fulfilled the judgment
of the wicked: judgment and justice take
hold on you.

18 Because there is wrath, beware lest
he take you away with his stroke: then a
great ransom cannot deliver you.

19 Will he esteem your riches? no, not
gold, nor all the forces of strength.

20 Desire not the night, when people
are cut off in their place.

21 Take heed, regard not iniquity: for
this have you chosen rather than affliction.

22 Behold, God exalts by his power:
who teaches like him?

23 Who has enjoined him his way? or
who can say, You have done iniquity?

24 Remember that you magnify his
work, which men behold.

25 Every man may see it; man may behold it afar off.

26 Behold, God is great, and we know
him not, neither can the number of his
years be searched out.

27 For he makes small the drops of
water: they pour down rain according to
the vapour thereof:

28 Which the clouds do drop and distil
upon man abundantly.

29 Also can any understand the spread-
ings of the clouds, or the noise of his
tabernacle?

30 Behold, he spreads his light upon it,
and covers the bottom of the sea.

31 For by them he judges the people;
he gives meat in abundance.

32 With clouds he covers the light; and
commands it not to shine by the cloud
that comes between.

33 The noise thereof shows concerning
it, the cattle also concerning the vapour.

CHAPTER 37

AT this also my heart trembles, and is
moved out of his place.

2 Hear attentively the noise of his voice,
and the sound that goes out of his
mouth.

3 He directs it under the whole heaven,
and his lightning to the ends of the
earth.

4 After it a voice roars: he thunders
with the voice of his excellency; and he

will not stay them when his voice is heard.

5 God thunders marvelously with his voice; great things doeth he, which we cannot comprehend.

6 For he says to the snow, Be on the earth; likewise to the small rain, and to the great rain of his strength.

7 He seals up the hand of every man; that all men may know his work.

8 Then the beasts go into dens, and remain in their places.

9 Out of the south comes the whirlwind: and cold out of the north.

10 By the breath of God frost is given: and the breadth of the waters is straitened.

11 Also by watering he wearies the thick cloud: he scatters his bright cloud:

12 And it is turned round about by his counsels: that they may do whatsoever he commands them upon the face of the world in the earth.

13 He causes it to come, whether for correction, or for his land, or for mercy.

14 Hearken to this, O Job: stand still, and consider the wondrous works of God.

15 Do you know when God disposed them, and caused the light of his cloud to shine?

16 Do you know the balancings of the clouds, the wondrous works of him which is perfect in knowledge?

17 How your garments are warm, when he quiets the earth by the south wind?

18 Have you with him spread out the sky, which is strong, and as a molten looking glass?

19 Teach us what we shall say to him; for we cannot order our speech by reason of darkness.

20 Shall it be told him that I speak? if a man speak, surely he shall be swallowed up.

21 And now men see not the bright light which is in the clouds: but the wind passes, and cleanses them.

22 Fair weather comes out of the north: with God is terrible majesty.

23 Touching the Almighty, we cannot find him out: he is excellent in power, and in judgment, and in plenty of justice: he will not afflict.

24 Men do therefore fear him: he does not respect any that are wise of heart.

CHAPTER 38

THEN the LORD answered Job out of the whirlwind, and said,

2 Who is this that darkens counsel by words without knowledge?

3 Gird up now your loins like a man;

38:1-2

It took 38 chapters before God spoke to Job. His words, spoken out of a whirlwind, are meaningful for contemporary evangelism.

There is no question as to the sincerity of the many who preach the gospel but fail to precede it with God's moral Law. Such preachers ignore the fact that the Law brings the knowledge of sin (Romans 3:20), and thus the counsel of the gospel remains darkened words without knowledge to lost sinners.

The preaching of the cross will be foolishness to the world as long as we fail to walk in the footsteps of Jesus and open up the Divine Law (see Mark 10:17-21, Luke 10:25-37, and Luke 18:18-22) before we preach the gospel.

for I will demand of you, and you shall answer me.

4 Where were you when I laid the foundations of the earth? declare, if you have understanding.

5 Who has laid the measures thereof, if

38:11

Have you ever watched surfers drop down the face of a mountainous Hawaiian wave, then wondered why, a few moments later, that great wall of water swishes its way up the beach and amounts to nothing?

Gigantic, proud waves can smash through giant steel walls and push them aside as if they were soggy cardboard. Yet, in a moment, those waves humbly fade into nothingness because God has decreed, "Thus far, and no further."

you know? or who has stretched the line upon it?

6 Whereupon are the foundations thereof fastened? or who laid the corner stone thereof;

7 When the morning stars sang together, and all the sons of God shouted for joy?

8 Or who shut up the sea with doors, when it brake forth, as if it had issued out of the womb?

9 When I made the cloud the garment thereof, and thick darkness a swaddling-band for it,

10 And brake up for it my decreed place, and set bars and doors,

11 And said, This far shall you come, but no further: and here shall your proud waves be stayed?

12 Have you commanded the morning since your days; and caused the dayspring to know his place;

13 That it might take hold of the ends of the earth, that the wicked might be shaken out of it?

14 It is turned as clay to the seal; and they stand as a garment.

15 And from the wicked their light is withholden, and the high arm shall be broken.

16 Have you entered into the springs of the sea? or have you walked in the search of the depth?

17 Have the gates of death been opened to you? or have you seen the doors of the shadow of death?

18 Have you perceived the breadth of the earth? declare if you know it all.

19 Where is the way where light dwells? and as for darkness, where is the place thereof,

20 That you should take it to the bound thereof, and that you should know the paths to the house thereof?

38:17

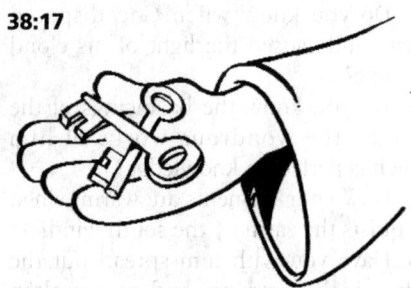

Jesus holds the keys to this gate. (See Revelation 1:18)

37:14 Every man and woman should stop from the business of life and consider the wondrous works of God. They should study the clouds, the birds, the trees, the flowers, the stars, the animals, the vast array of fruits, the marvels of the human body, and look at all this in the light of God's creative hand. There comes a time when audible praise doesn't express the incredible greatness of our God. We instead bow our heads and remain still in worshipful adoration of this Creator who gave us life and redeemed us by His blood.

38:16 "Modern deep sea diving cameras have discovered amazing hot-water vents on the floor of the oceans. These thermal vents release huge amounts of mineral rich super-heated water-springs in the darkness." Richard Gunther

21 Do you know it, because you were then born? or because the number of your days is great?

22 Have you entered into the treasures of the snow? or have you seen the treasures of the hail,

23 Which I have reserved against the time of trouble, against the day of battle and war?

24 By what way is the light parted, which scatters the east wind upon the earth?

25 Who has divided a watercourse for the overflowing of waters, or a way for the lightning of thunder;

26 To cause it to rain on the earth, where no man is; on the wilderness, wherein there is no man;

27 To satisfy the desolate and waste ground; and to cause the bud of the tender herb to spring forth?

28 Has the rain a father? or who has begotten the drops of dew?

29 Out of whose womb came the ice? and the hoary frost of heaven, who has gendered it?

30 The waters are hid as with a stone, and the face of the deep is frozen.

31 Can you bind the sweet influences of Pleiades, or loose the bands of Orion?

32 Can you bring forth Mazzaroth in his season? or can you guide Arcturus with his sons?

33 Do you know the ordinances of heaven? can you set the dominion thereof in the earth?

34 Can you lift up your voice to the clouds, that abundance of waters may cover you?

35 Can you send lightnings, that they may go and say to you, Here we are?

36 Who has put wisdom in the inward parts? or who has given understanding to the heart?

37 Who can number the clouds in wisdom? or who can stay the bottles of heaven,

38 When the dust grows into hardness, and the clods cleave fast together?

39 Will you hunt the prey for the lion? or fill the appetite of the young lions,

40 When they couch in their dens, and abide in the covert to lie in wait?

41 Who provides for the raven his food? when his young ones cry to God, they wander for lack of meat.

CHAPTER 39

DO you know the time when the wild goats of the rock bring forth? or can you mark when the hinds do calve?

2 Can you number the months that they fulfil? or do you know the time when they bring forth?

3 They bow themselves, they bring forth their young ones, they cast out their sorrows.

38:22 See *Scientific Facts in the Bible*, Hebrews 11:3.

38:24 "Sir Isaac Newton studied light and discovered that white light is made of seven colors, which can be 'parted' from the white, and then recombined to make white again." Richard Gunther

38:31 "Here reference is made to some very distant constellations, thought by most people to be too far away to have any effect on our planet. However, modern science has confirmed that Pleiades is a remarkable point in the solar system, like the center of a gigantic wheel. But even more remarkable is the fact that now scientists agree on the all-pervasive power of gravity. Anything with mass affects, even in unimaginably tiny ways, everything else in the universe. Gravity has an effect through all things and over all distances. The "bands" of Orion cannot be loosed, because gravity is a force that no human can shake off or defeat." Richard Gunther

38:35 See *Scientific Facts in the Bible*, Hebrews 11:3.

38:36 When we think we have caught a glimpse of the genius of God, He outdoes our estimation of His greatness. We haven't begun to see what God can do. (See 1 Corinthians 2:9)

4 Their young ones are in good liking, they grow up with corn; they go forth, and return not to them.

5 Who has sent out the wild ass free? or who has loosed the bands of the wild ass?

6 Whose house I have made the wilderness, and the barren land his dwellings.

7 He scorns the multitude of the city, neither does he regard the crying of the driver.

8 The range of the mountains is his pasture, and he searches after every green thing.

9 Will the unicorn be willing to serve you, or abide by your crib?

10 Can you bind the unicorn with his band in the furrow? or will he harrow the valleys after you?

11 Will you trust him, because his strength is great? or will you leave your labour to him?

12 Will you believe him, that he will bring home your seed, and gather it into your barn?

13 Did you give the goodly wings to the peacocks? or wings and feathers to the ostrich?

14 Which leaves her eggs in the earth, and warms them in dust,

15 And forgets that the foot may crush them, or that the wild beast may break them.

16 She is hardened against her young ones, as though they were not her's: her labour is in vain without fear;

17 Because God has deprived her of wisdom, neither has he imparted to her understanding.

18 What time she lifts up herself on high, she scorns the horse and his rider.

19 Have you given the horse strength? have you clothed his neck with thunder?

20 Can you make him afraid as a grasshopper? the glory of his nostrils is terrible.

21 He paws in the valley, and rejoices in his strength: he goes on to meet the armed men.

22 He mocks at fear, and is not affrighted; neither does he turn back from the sword.

23 The quiver rattles against him, the glittering spear and the shield.

24 He swallows the ground with fierceness and rage: neither believeth he that it is the sound of the trumpet.

25 He says among the trumpets, Ha, ha; and he smells the battle afar off, the thunder of the captains, and the shouting.

26 Does the hawk fly by your wisdom, and stretch her wings toward the south?

27 Does the eagle mount up at your command, and make her nest on high?

28 She dwells and abides on the rock, upon the crag of the rock, and the strong place.

29 From thence she seeks the prey, and her eyes behold afar off.

30 Her young ones also suck up blood: and where the slain are, there is she.

39:10-11 This is what God did through the cross of Jesus Christ. His wrath fell upon the Messiah so that proud sinners could live.

39:15-24 See *Scientific Facts in the Bible*, Hebrews 11:3.

39:19-25 We take the horse for granted. Look at how it has been made for man to ride. See its back is curved for his form. Look at its magnificent neck and its glorious mane. A bit and bridle makes him useful to man. Look at his courage as he runs into battle, stirred by the sound of the trumpet. What a picture of how the Christian should be! We have been made for God's habitation. Our reins should instruct us because they are in the hands of our Master. May God bridle our energy and direct us to run courageously into the heat of battle for the souls of humanity.

39:26-30 One marvels at the incredible intricacies of the human eye, but man's eye is but a Brownie box camera compared to the high-tech eye of the eagle. When we think we have caught a glimpse of the genius of God, He outdoes our estimation of His greatness. Yet, in this creation we haven't begun to see what God can do. See 1 Corinthians 2:9.

THE FUNCTION OF THE LAW

40:4 **This is what God's Law does to the receptive sinner.** He sees his own desperately wicked heart revealed under the brilliant light of the Ten Commandments. And he suddenly sees sin as being "exceedingly sinful" (see Romans 7:13).

He has a straight-edge so that he can understand how crooked he is. It halts the mouth of justification. That's what God's Law does, it "stops every mouth and leaves the whole world guilty before God" (Romans 3:19). See Job 42:5-6

CHAPTER 40

MOREOVER the LORD answered Job, and said,

2 Shall he that contends with the Almighty instruct him? he that reproves God, let him answer it.

3 Then Job answered the LORD, and said,

4 Behold, I am vile; what shall I answer you? I will lay my hand upon my mouth.

5 Once have I spoken; but I will not answer: yea, twice; but I will proceed no further.

6 Then answered the LORD to Job out of the whirlwind, and said,

7 Gird up your loins now like a man: I will demand of you, and you declare to me.

8 Will you also disannul my judgment? will you condemn me, that you may be righteous?

9 Have you an arm like God? or can you thunder with a voice like him?

10 Deck yourself now with majesty and excellency; and array yourself with glory and beauty.

11 Cast abroad the rage of your wrath: and behold every one that is proud, and abase him.

12 Look on every one that is proud, and bring him low; and tread down the wicked in their place.

13 Hide them in the dust together; and bind their faces in secret.

14 Then will I also confess to you that your own right hand can save you.

15 Behold now behemoth, which I made with you; he eats grass as an ox.

16 Lo now, his strength is in his loins, and his force is in the navel of his belly.

17 He moves his tail like a cedar: the sinews of his stones are wrapped together.

18 His bones are as strong pieces of brass; his bones are like bars of iron.

19 He is the chief of the ways of God: he that made him can make his sword to approach to him.

20 Surely the mountains bring him forth food, where all the beasts of the field play.

21 He lieth under the shady trees, in the covert of the reed, and fens.

22 The shady trees cover him with their shadow; the willows of the brook compass him about.

23 Behold, he drinks up a river, and hastens not: he trusts that he can draw up Jordan into his mouth.

24 He takes it with his eyes: his nose pierces through snares.

CHAPTER 41

CAN you draw out leviathan with an hook? or his tongue with a cord which you let down?

2 Can you put an hook into his nose? or bore his jaw through with a thorn?

3 Will he make many supplications to you? will he speak soft words to you?

4 Will he make a covenant with you? will you take him for a servant for ever?

5 Will you play with him as with a bird? or will you bind him for your maidens?

6 Shall the companions make a banquet of him? shall they part him among the merchants?

7 Can you fill his skin with barbed irons? or his head with fish spears?

8 Lay your hand upon him, remember the battle, do no more.

9 Behold, the hope of him is in vain: shall not one be cast down even at the sight of him?

10 None is so fierce that dare stir him up: who then is able to stand before me?

11 Who has prevented me, that I should repay him? whatsoever is under the whole heaven is mine.

12 I will not conceal his parts, nor his power, nor his comely proportion.

13 Who can discover the face of his garment? or who can come to him with his double bridle?

14 Who can open the doors of his face? his teeth are terrible round about.

15 His scales are his pride, shut up together as with a close seal.

16 One is so near to another, that no air can come between them.

17 They are joined one to another, they stick together, that they cannot be sundered.

18 By his sneezings a light does shine, and his eyes are like the eyelids of the morning.

19 Out of his mouth go burning lamps, and sparks of fire leap out.

20 Smoke goes out of his nostrils, as out of a seething pot or caldron.

21 His breath kindles coals, and a flame goes out of his mouth.

22 In his neck remains strength, and sorrow is turned into joy before him.

23 The flakes of his flesh are joined together: they are firm in themselves; they cannot be moved.

24 His heart is as firm as a stone; yea, as hard as a piece of the nether millstone.

25 When he raises up himself, the mighty are afraid: by reason of breakings they purify themselves.

26 The sword of him that lays at him cannot hold: the spear, the dart, nor the habergeon.

27 He esteems iron as straw, and brass as rotten wood.

28 The arrow cannot make him flee: slingstones are turned with him into stubble.

29 Darts are counted as stubble: he laughs at the shaking of a spear.

30 Sharp stones are under him: he spreads sharp pointed things upon the mire.

31 He makes the deep to boil like a pot: he makes the sea like a pot of ointment.

32 He makes a path to shine after him; one would think the deep to be hoary.

33 Upon earth there is not his like, who is made without fear.

34 He beholds all high things: he is a king over all the children of pride.

CHAPTER 42

THEN Job answered the LORD, and said,

2 I know that you can do every thing, and that no thought can be withholden from you.

3 Who is he that hides counsel without knowledge? therefore have I uttered that I understood not; things too wonderful for me, which I knew not.

4 Hear, I beseech you, and I will speak: I will demand of you, and you declare to me.

5 I have heard of you by the hearing of the ear: but now my eye sees you.

6 Therefore I abhor myself, and repent in dust and ashes.

7 And it was so, that after the LORD had spoken these words to Job, the LORD said to Eliphaz the Temanite, My wrath is kindled against you, and against your two friends: for you have not spoken of me the thing that is right, as my servant Job has.

8 Therefore take to you now seven bullocks and seven rams, and go to my servant Job, and offer up for yourselves a burnt offering; and my servant Job shall pray for you: for him will I accept: lest I deal with you after your folly, in that you have not spoken of me the thing which is right, like my servant Job.

9 So Eliphaz the Temanite and Bildad the Shuhite and Zophar the Naamathite went, and did according as the LORD commanded them: the LORD also accepted Job.

10 And the LORD turned the captivity of Job, when he prayed for his friends: also the LORD gave Job twice as much as he had before.

11 Then all his brethren, and all his sisters, and all they that had been of his acquaintance before, came to him and did eat bread with him in his house: and they bemoaned him, and comforted him over all the evil that the LORD had brought upon him: every man also gave him a piece of money, and every one an earring of gold.

12 So the LORD blessed the latter end of Job more than his beginning: for he had fourteen thousand sheep, and six thousand camels, and a thousand yoke of oxen, and a thousand she asses.

13 He had also seven sons and three daughters.

14 And he called the name of the first, Jemima; and the name of the second, Kezia; and the name of the third, Kerenhappuch.

15 And in all the land were no women found so fair as the daughters of Job: and their father gave them inheritance among their brethren.

16 After this lived Job an hundred and forty years, and saw his sons, and his sons' sons, even four generations.

17 So Job died, being old and full of days.

Going through a real tough time?
See "Closing Words of Comfort"
in the back of this Bible.

Psalms
and
Proverbs

Four Simple Laws

. . . .

God is holy and just:

"For God shall bring every work into judgment,
with every secret thing,
whether it be good or whether it be evil" *(Ecclesiastes 12:14).*

The wages of sin is death:

"Sin is the transgression of the Law" *(1 John 3:4).*

God is rich in mercy:

"But God, who is rich in mercy,
for his great love wherewith He loved us…" *(Ephesians 2:4).*

Eternal life is in Jesus Christ:

"For God so loved the world,
that he gave his only begotten Son,
that whosoever believes in Him
should not perish, but have everlasting life" *(John 3:16).*

"[God] now commands all men every where to repent:
because he has appointed a day, in which he will judge
the world in righteousness" *(Acts 17:30).*

A Model Prayer of Repentance

God, please forgive me for sinning against You.
I understand that, according to Your Law, I deserve to go to hell.
However, You are not willing that I perish.
Thank You that Jesus suffered and died for me
and rose again on the third day.
I now repent and yield myself to Him to be my Lord and Savior.
I will read Your Word daily and obey what I read.
In Jesus' Name I pray.
Amen.

Psalms

PSALM 1

BLESSED is the man that walks not in the counsel of the ungodly, nor stands in the way of sinners, nor sits in the seat of the scornful.

2 But his delight is in the law of the LORD; and in his law does he meditate day and night.

3 And he shall be like a tree planted by the rivers of water, that brings forth his fruit in his season; his leaf also shall not wither; and whatsoever he does shall prosper.

4 The ungodly are not so: but are like the chaff which the wind drives away.

5 Therefore the ungodly shall not stand in the judgment, nor sinners in the congregation of the righteous.

6 For the LORD knows the way of the righteous: but the way of the ungodly shall perish.

PSALM 2

WHY do the heathen rage, and the people imagine a vain thing?

2 The kings of the earth set themselves, and the rulers take counsel together, against the LORD, and against his anointed, saying,

3 Let us break their bands asunder, and cast away their cords from us.

4 He that sits in the heavens shall laugh: the LORD shall have them in derision.

5 Then shall he speak unto them in his wrath, and vex them in his sore displeasure.

6 Yet have I set my king upon my holy hill of Zion.

7 I will declare the decree: the LORD has said unto me, You are my Son; this day have I begotten you.

8 Ask of me, and I shall give you the heathen for your inheritance, and the uttermost parts of the earth for your possession.

9 You shall break them with a rod of iron; you shall dash them in pieces like a potter's vessel.

10 **Be wise now therefore, O you kings: be instructed, you judges of the earth.**

11 **Serve the LORD with fear, and rejoice with trembling.**

1:1–3 Here is the biblical formula for success. The key to fruitfulness as a Christian is to meditate on God's Word every day, without fail. Have you ever gone one day when you have been too busy or have forgotten to read the Bible? Have you ever gone one day when you have been too busy or have forgotten to feed your stomach? Which comes first—your Bible or your belly? Be like Job, who "esteemed the words of His mouth more than [his] necessary food" (Job 23:12). Then whatever we do "shall prosper" (v. 3), including our evangelistic endeavors.

1:5 If the fate of the ungodly is our continual meditation, concern for their salvation will be our continual motivation.

QUESTIONS & OBJECTIONS

Q 1:6 "Why are there so many denominations?"

In the early 1500s, a German monk named Martin Luther was so conscious of his sins that he spent up to six hours in the confessional. Through study of the Scriptures he found that salvation didn't come through anything he did, but simply through trusting in the finished work of the cross of Jesus Christ. He listed the contradictions between what the Scriptures said and what his church taught, and nailed his "95 Theses" to the church door in Wittenberg, Germany.

Martin Luther became the first to "protest" against the Roman church, and thus he became the father of the Protestant church. Since that split, there have been many disagreements about how much water one should baptize with, how to sing what and why, who should govern who, etc., causing thousands of splinter groups. Many of these groups are convinced that they alone are right. These have become known as Protestant "denominations." Despite the confusion, these churches subscribe to certain foundational beliefs such as the deity, death, burial, and resurrection of Jesus Christ. The Bible says, "The foundation of God stands sure, having this seal, The Lord knows them that are his" (2 Timothy 2:19).

Thomas Jefferson once wrote of a preacher, *Richard Mote*, who "exclaimed aloud to his congregation that he did not believe there was a Quaker, Presbyterian, Methodist, or Baptist in heaven, having paused to give his hearers time to stare and to wonder. He added that, in heaven, God knew no distinctions."

---

12 Kiss the Son, lest he be angry, and you perish from the way, when his wrath is kindled but a little. Blessed are all they that put their trust in him.

PSALM 3

LORD, how are they increased that trouble me! many are they that rise up against me.

2 Many there be which say of my soul, There is no help for him in God. Selah.

3 But you, O LORD, are a shield for me; my glory, and the lifter up of my head.

4 I cried unto the LORD with my voice, and he heard me out of his holy hill. Selah.

5 I laid me down and slept; I awaked; for the LORD sustained me.

6 I will not be afraid of ten thousands of people, that have set themselves against me round about.

7 Arise, O LORD; save me, O my God: for you have smitten all my enemies upon the cheek bone; you have broken the teeth of the ungodly.

8 Salvation belongs unto the LORD: your blessing is upon your people. Selah.

2:12 The warning of God's wrath. In 1969, twenty-four people decided to ignore warnings that Hurricane Camille was heading for Mississippi. They instead made up their minds that they were going to ride it out. Twenty-three of them died in the hurricane.

The cross is a warning of the fierce hurricane of God's wrath, which no one will "ride out" on Judgment Day. The only way to flee the coming wrath is to "kiss the Son"—to yield to the Lordship of the Savior, Jesus Christ. Those who put their trust in Him are blessed with forgiveness and eternal life.

3:8 Salvation belongs to the Lord. Scripture tells us that there are none who seek after God, and that no man can come to the Son unless the Father draws him (John 6:44). We have as much to do with our salvation as Lazarus had to do with his own raising from the dead. It is the Lord who quickens the believer. He makes us come alive, then we respond to His voice.

PSALM 4

HEAR me when I call, O God of my righteousness: you have enlarged me when I was in distress; have mercy upon me, and hear my prayer.

2 O you sons of men, how long will you turn my glory into shame? how long will you love vanity, and seek after leasing? Selah.

3 But know that the LORD has set apart him that is godly for himself: the LORD will hear when I call unto him.

4 Stand in awe, and sin not: commune with your own heart upon your bed, and be still. Selah.

5 Offer the sacrifices of righteousness, and put your trust in the LORD.

6 There be many that say, Who will show us any good? LORD, lift up the light of your countenance upon us.

7 You have put gladness in my heart, more than in the time that their corn and their wine increased.

8 I will both lay me down in peace, and sleep: for you, LORD, only make me dwell in safety.

PSALM 5

GIVE ear to my words, O LORD, consider my meditation.

2 Hearken unto the voice of my cry, my King, and my God: for unto you will I pray.

3 My voice shall you hear in the morning, O LORD; in the morning will I direct my prayer unto you, and will look up.

4 For you are not a God that has pleasure in wickedness: neither shall evil dwell with you.

5 The foolish shall not stand in your sight: you hate all workers of iniquity.

THE FUNCTION OF THE LAW

5:5 This Law, then, should be arrayed in all its majesty against selfishness and enmity of the sinner. All men know that they have sinned, but all are not convicted of the guilt and ill dessert of sin. But without this they cannot understand or appreciate the Gospel method of salvation. Away with this milk-and-water preaching of a love of Christ that has no holiness or moral discrimination in it. Away with preaching a love of God that is not angry with sinners every day.

Charles Finney

6 You shall destroy them that speak leasing: the LORD will abhor the bloody and deceitful man.

7 But as for me, I will come into your house in the multitude of your mercy: and in your fear will I worship toward your holy temple.

8 Lead me, O LORD, in your righteousness because of my enemies; make your way straight before my face.

9 For there is no faithfulness in their mouth; their inward part is very wickedness; their throat is an open sepulcher; they flatter with their tongue.

10 Destroy them, O God; let them fall by their own counsels; cast them out in the multitude of their transgressions; for they have rebelled against you.

11 But let all those that put their trust in you rejoice: let them ever shout for joy, because you defend them: let them also that love your name be joyful in you.

12 For you, LORD, will bless the righteous; with favor will you compass him as with a shield.

5:5 Does God hate sinners? How can God hate sinners when John 3:16 says that He loves them? *Norman Geisler* and *Thomas Howe* write, "There is no contradiction in these statements. The difficulty arises when we wrongly assume that God hates in the same way men hate. Hatred in human beings is generally thought of in terms of strong emotional distaste or dislike for someone or something. However, in God, hate is a judicial act on the part of the righteous judge who separates the sinner from Himself" *(When Critics Ask)*. See Psalm 7:11–13 comment.

5:9 Sinful man speaks from the abundance of his depraved heart. See Jeremiah 17:9; Mark 7:21–23; Romans 3:10–18.

PSALM 6

O LORD, rebuke me not in your anger, neither chasten me in your hot displeasure.

2 Have mercy upon me, O LORD; for I am weak: O LORD, heal me; for my bones are vexed.

3 My soul is also sore vexed: but you, O LORD, how long?

4 Return, O LORD, deliver my soul: oh save me for your mercies' sake.

5 For in death there is no remembrance of you: in the grave who shall give you thanks?

6 I am weary with my groaning; all the night make I my bed to swim; I water my couch with my tears.

7 My eye is consumed because of grief; it waxes old because of all my enemies.

8 Depart from me, all you workers of iniquity; for the LORD has heard the voice of my weeping.

9 The LORD has heard my supplication; the LORD will receive my prayer.

10 Let all my enemies be ashamed and sore vexed: let them return and be ashamed suddenly.

PSALM 7

O LORD my God, in you do I put my trust: save me from all them that persecute me, and deliver me:

2 Lest he tear my soul like a lion, rending it in pieces, while there is none to deliver.

3 O LORD my God, If I have done this; if there be iniquity in my hands;

4 If I have rewarded evil unto him that was at peace with me; (yes, I have delivered him that without cause is my enemy:)

5 Let the enemy persecute my soul, and take it; yes, let him tread down my life upon the earth, and lay my honor in the dust. Selah.

6 Arise, O LORD, in your anger, lift up yourself because of the rage of my enemies: and awake for me to the judgment that you have commanded.

7 So shall the congregation of the people compass you about: for their sakes therefore return on high.

8 The LORD shall judge the people: judge me, O LORD, according to my righteousness, and according to my integrity that is in me.

9 Oh let the wickedness of the wicked come to an end; but establish the just: for the righteous God tries the hearts and reins.

10 My defense is of God, which saves the upright in heart.

11 God judges the righteous, and God is angry with the wicked every day.

12 If he turn not, he will whet his sword; he has bent his bow, and made it ready.

13 He has also prepared for him the instruments of death; he ordains his arrows against the persecutors.

14 Behold, he travails with iniquity, and has conceived mischief, and brought forth falsehood.

15 He made a pit, and digged it, and is fallen into the ditch which he made.

16 His mischief shall return upon his own head, and his violent dealing shall come down upon his own pate.

17 I will praise the LORD according to his righteousness: and will sing praise to the name of the LORD most high.

PSALM 8

O LORD, our Lord, how excellent is your name in all the earth! who have set your glory above the heavens.

2 Out of the mouth of babes and sucklings have you ordained strength because

---

7:11–13 This is the message we must bring to a sinful world. God is angry with the wicked every day. His wrath abides on them (John 3:36). Every time they sin, they are storing up for themselves wrath that will be revealed on the Day of Judgment (Romans 2:5). Unless they are convinced that there is wrath to come, they will not flee to the One who can deliver them from the wrath to come (1 Thessalonians 1:10). See 1 Timothy 1:8–10 comment.

of your enemies, that you might still the enemy and the avenger.

3 When I consider your heavens, the work of your fingers, the moon and the stars, which you have ordained;

4 What is man, that you are mindful of him? and the son of man, that you visit him?

5 For you have made him a little lower than the angels, and have crowned him with glory and honor.

6 You made him to have dominion over the works of your hands; you have put all things under his feet:

7 All sheep and oxen, yes, and the beasts of the field;

8 The fowl of the air, and the fish of the sea, and whatsoever passes through the paths of the seas.

9 O LORD our Lord, how excellent is your name in all the earth!

PSALM 9

I WILL praise you, O LORD, with my whole heart; I will show forth all your marvelous works.

2 I will be glad and rejoice in you: I will sing praise to your name, O you most High.

3 When my enemies are turned back, they shall fall and perish at your presence.

4 For you have maintained my right and my cause; you sat in the throne judging right.

5 You have rebuked the heathen, you have destroyed the wicked, you have put out their name for ever and ever.

6 O you enemy, destructions are come to a perpetual end: and you have destroyed cities; their memorial is perished with them.

7 But the LORD shall endure forever: he has prepared his throne for judgment.

8 And he shall judge the world in righteousness, he shall minister judgment to the people in uprightness.

8:5 "See what wickedness there is in the nature of man. How much are we beholden to the restraining grace of God! For, were it not for this, man, who was made but a little lower than angels, would make himself a great deal lower than the devils." *Matthew Henry*

8:6 Man's dominion. Man is not just an animal on the evolutionary food chain. God has given him dominion (authority) over all the animals (Genesis 1:28). He is intellectually superior to them and has *priority* over them—every animal is "under his feet" and may be brought into submission by him (James 3:7). Birds (parrots) can be taught to speak. With a crack of a whip lions will do what he says. Even killer whales obey his voice.

Man's dominion is obvious. Cows yield milk for his cereal, cheese for his hamburger, butter for his bread, yogurt to keep him healthy, and ice cream to delight his taste buds on hot days. The same cow gives him meat to keep him strong and leather to keep him warm. Sheep and goats also yield many of these same products. The chicken makes eggs for his breakfast and provides finger-licking meat for his dinner. The sea overflows with an incredible variety of fish for him to catch and eat. Dogs protect his property and herd his sheep. Elephants lift great weights for him. Camels carry him across deserts. The horse is perfectly designed to be ridden by him. See also Matthew 6:26 comment.

8:8 *Scientific Facts in the Bible.* The Bible says, "...and the fish of the sea, and whatsoever passes through the paths of the seas" (Psalm 8:8). What does the Bible mean by "paths of the seas"? Man discovered the existence of ocean currents in the 1850s, but the Bible declared the science of oceanography 2,800 years ago. *Matthew Maury* (1806–1873) is considered the father of oceanography. He noticed the expression "paths of the sea" in Psalm 8:8. "If God said there are paths in the sea," Maury said, "I am going to find them." Maury took God at His word and went looking for these paths. We are indebted to his discovery of the warm and cold continental currents. His book on oceanography remains a basic text on the subject and is still used in universities. Maury used the Bible as a guide to a scientific discovery; if only more would use the Bible as a guide in their personal lives.

9 The LORD also will be a refuge for the oppressed, a refuge in times of trouble.

10 And they that know your name will put their trust in you: for you, LORD, have not forsaken them that seek you.

11 Sing praises to the LORD, which dwells in Zion: declare among the people his doings.

12 When he makes inquisition for blood, he remembers them: he forgets not the cry of the humble.

13 Have mercy upon me, O LORD; consider my trouble which I suffer of them that hate me, you that lift me up from the gates of death:

14 That I may show forth all your praise in the gates of the daughter of Zion: I will rejoice in your salvation.

15 The heathen are sunk down in the pit that they made: in the net which they hid is their own foot taken.

16 The LORD is known by the judgment which he executes: the wicked is snared in the work of his own hands. Higgaion. Selah.

17 The wicked shall be turned into hell, and all the nations that forget God.

18 For the needy shall not always be forgotten: the expectation of the poor shall not perish for ever.

19 Arise, O LORD; let not man prevail: let the heathen be judged in your sight.

20 Put them in fear, O LORD: that the nations may know themselves to be but men. Selah.

PSALM 10

WHY stand afar off, O LORD? why hide yourself in times of trouble?

2 The wicked in his pride does persecute the poor: let them be taken in the devices that they have imagined.

3 For the wicked boasts of his heart's desire, and blesses the covetous, whom the LORD abhors.

4 The wicked, through the pride of his countenance, will not seek after God: God is not in all his thoughts.

5 His ways are always grievous; your judgments are far above out of his sight: as for all his enemies, he puffs at them.

6 He has said in his heart, I shall not be moved: for I shall never be in adversity.

7 His mouth is full of cursing and deceit and fraud: under his tongue is mischief and vanity.

8 He sits in the lurking places of the villages: in the secret places does he murder the innocent: his eyes are privily set against the poor.

9 He lies in wait secretly as a lion in his den: he lies in wait to catch the poor: he does catch the poor, when he draws him into his net.

10 He crouches, and humbles himself, that the poor may fall by his strong ones.

11 He has said in his heart, God has forgotten: he hides his face; he will never see it.

12 Arise, O LORD; O God, lift up your hand: forget not the humble.

9:8 See Acts 17:31.

9:17 How wrong it is for us to forget the One who gave us life. When nations, like individuals, forget God, they therefore die in their sins and reap His great wrath. See 1 John 1:9 comment.

10:3–6,11,13 The thoughts of sinners. Scripture gives us insight into the thoughts of the unsaved: 1) His pride keeps him from seeking God. Any admittance of guilt is a blow to the pride of the human heart. 2) Because he's self-centered and self-sufficient, he feels no need to even consider God. 3) He thinks that he's in control of his life and that adversity will never come to him. 4) His willful ignorance leaves him without understanding of God's righteous judgments. 5) He believes that either God is blinded to his sinful lifestyle, or He has no sense of justice and will therefore not require any account for his lawlessness.

10:4 The reason that the proud don't seek after God is that they don't want to—they *will* not seek after God because they don't want to leave their sins. It's not that they cannot find Him, but that they *will* not.

13 Wherefore does the wicked contemn God? he has said in his heart, You will not require it.

14 You have seen it; for you behold mischief and spite, to requite it with your hand: the poor commits himself unto you; you are the helper of the fatherless.

15 Break the arm of the wicked and the evil man: seek out his wickedness till you find none.

16 The LORD is King for ever and ever: the heathen are perished out of his land.

17 LORD, you have heard the desire of the humble: you will prepare their heart, you will cause your ear to hear:

18 To judge the fatherless and the oppressed, that the man of the earth may no more oppress.

> All men who are eminently useful are made to feel their weakness in a supreme degree.
>
> **CHARLES SPURGEON**

PSALM 11

IN the LORD put I my trust: how say to my soul, Flee as a bird to your mountain?

2 For, lo, the wicked bend their bow, they make ready their arrow upon the string, that they may privily shoot at the upright in heart.

3 If the foundations be destroyed, what can the righteous do?

4 The LORD is in his holy temple, the LORD's throne is in heaven: his eyes behold, his eyelids try, the children of men.

5 The LORD tries the righteous: but the wicked and him that loves violence his soul hates.

6 Upon the wicked he shall rain snares, fire and brimstone, and an horrible tempest: this shall be the portion of their cup.

7 For the righteous LORD loves righteousness; his countenance does behold the upright.

PSALM 12

HELP, LORD; for the godly man ceases; for the faithful fail from among the children of men.

2 They speak vanity every one with his neighbor: with flattering lips and with a double heart do they speak.

3 The LORD shall cut off all flattering lips, and the tongue that speaks proud things:

4 Who have said, With our tongue will we prevail; our lips are our own: who is lord over us?

5 For the oppression of the poor, for the sighing of the needy, now will I arise, says the LORD; I will set him in safety from him that puffs at him.

6 The words of the LORD are pure words: as silver tried in a furnace of earth, purified seven times.

7 You shall keep them, O LORD, you shall preserve them from this generation for ever.

8 The wicked walk on every side, when the vilest men are exalted.

PSALM 13

HOW long will you forget me, O LORD? for ever? how long will you hide your face from me?

2 How long shall I take counsel in my soul, having sorrow in my heart daily? how long shall my enemy be exalted over me?

3 Consider and hear me, O LORD my God: lighten my eyes, lest I sleep the sleep of death;

4 Lest my enemy say, I have prevailed against him; and those that trouble me rejoice when I am moved.

5 But I have trusted in your mercy; my heart shall rejoice in your salvation.

12:6-7 Men may list what they consider to be mistakes in the Bible. However, all Scripture is given by inspiration of God (2 Timothy 3:16); every word of the Lord is pure. Therefore any seeming "mistakes" are there because God has put them there, and they are therefore not mistakes. In time, we will find that the "mistakes" are actually ours. See Mark 15:26 comment.

6 I will sing unto the LORD, because he has dealt bountifully with me.

PSALM 14

THE fool has said in his heart, There is no God. They are corrupt, they have done abominable works, there is none that does good.

2 The LORD looked down from heaven upon the children of men, to see if there were any that did understand, and seek God.

3 They are all gone aside, they are all together become filthy: there is none that does good, no, not one.

4 Have all the workers of iniquity no knowledge? who eat up my people as they eat bread, and call not upon the LORD.

5 There were they in great fear: for God is in the generation of the righteous.

6 You have shamed the counsel of the poor, because the LORD is his refuge.

7 Oh that the salvation of Israel were come out of Zion! when the LORD brings back the captivity of his people, Jacob shall rejoice, and Israel shall be glad.

PSALM 15

LORD, who shall abide in your tabernacle? who shall dwell in your holy hill?

2 He that walks uprightly, and works righteousness, and speaks the truth in his heart.

3 He that backbites not with his tongue, nor does evil to his neighbor, nor takes up a reproach against his neighbor.

4 In whose eyes a vile person is contemned; but he honors them that fear the LORD. He that swears to his own hurt, and changes not.

5 He that puts not out his money to usury, nor takes reward against the innocent. He that does these things shall never be moved.

PSALM 16

PRESERVE me, O God: for in you do I put my trust.

2 O my soul, you have said unto the LORD, You are my Lord: my goodness extends not to you;

3 But to the saints that are in the earth, and to the excellent, in whom is all my delight.

4 Their sorrows shall be multiplied that hasten after another god: their drink offerings of blood will I not offer, nor take up their names into my lips.

5 The LORD is the portion of my inheritance and of my cup: you maintain my lot.

6 The lines are fallen unto me in pleasant places; yes, I have a goodly heritage.

7 I will bless the LORD, who has given me counsel: my reins also instruct me in the night seasons.

8 I have set the LORD always before me: because he is at my right hand, I shall not be moved.

14:1 There is no such thing as an "atheist." He is a "fool." See Psalm 53:1 comment.

14:1–3 Who is "good"? As far as the world is concerned, there are many people who do good. However, here is God's view of humanity: 1) All people are corrupt and do abominable things. 2) No one understands or seeks God. 3) All have turned away from God. 4) They have together become filthy. 5) There is no one who does good, not even one.

The world may consider it a good deed when a celebrity gives millions to charity. God, however, sees the motive for the act, which may be guilt for a past adulterous lifestyle. As long as the world is ignorant of God's Law (which Romans 7:12 says is "good"), it will have no idea of what "good" is.

15:1–5 This is the standard by which the Christian should live. We must walk in righteousness, speak the truth, keep our heart free from sin, keep our word, and be free from any corruption and covetousness. Those who fear God and want to be effective in their witness will gladly conform.

16:7 It is most profitable to arise from bed, pray, then allow your reins to instruct you in the night season. If you have allowed God to break your spirit, He is the one who has hold of the reins, and He will guide you in the way you should go. See Psalm 119:62.

9 Therefore my heart is glad, and my glory rejoices: my flesh also shall rest in hope.

10 For you will not leave my soul in hell; neither will you suffer your Holy One to see corruption.

11 You will show me the path of life: in your presence is fullness of joy; at your right hand there are pleasures for evermore.

· · · · · ·

*To learn the damage of gossip,
see Proverbs 11:13 comment.*

· · · · · ·

PSALM 17

HEAR the right, O LORD, attend unto my cry, give ear unto my prayer, that goes not out of feigned lips.

2 Let my sentence come forth from your presence; let your eyes behold the things that are equal.

3 You have proved my heart; you have visited me in the night; you have tried me, and shall find nothing; I am purposed that my mouth shall not transgress.

4 Concerning the works of men, by the word of your lips I have kept me from the paths of the destroyer.

5 Hold up my goings in your paths, that my footsteps slip not.

6 I have called upon you, for you will hear me, O God: incline your ear unto me, and hear my speech.

7 Show your marvelous lovingkindness, O you that save by your right hand them which put their trust in you from those that rise up against them.

8 Keep me as the apple of the eye, hide me under the shadow of your wings,

9 From the wicked that oppress me, from my deadly enemies, who compass me about.

10 They are enclosed in their own fat: with their mouth they speak proudly.

11 They have now compassed us in our steps: they have set their eyes bowing down to the earth;

12 Like as a lion that is greedy of his prey, and as it were a young lion lurking in secret places.

13 Arise, O LORD, disappoint him, cast him down: deliver my soul from the wicked, which is your sword:

14 From men which are your hand, O LORD, from men of the world, which have their portion in this life, and whose belly you fill with your hid treasure: they are full of children, and leave the rest of their substance to their babes.

15 As for me, I will behold your face in righteousness: I shall be satisfied, when I awake, with your likeness.

PSALM 18

I WILL love you, O LORD, my strength.

2 The LORD is my rock, and my fortress, and my deliverer; my God, my strength, in whom I will trust; my buckler, and the horn of my salvation, and my high tower.

3 I will call upon the LORD, who is worthy to be praised: so shall I be saved from my enemies.

4 The sorrows of death compassed me, and the floods of ungodly men made me afraid.

5 The sorrows of hell compassed me about: the snares of death prevented me.

6 In my distress I called upon the LORD, and cried unto my God: he heard my voice out of his temple, and my cry came before him, even into his ears.

7 Then the earth shook and trembled; the foundations also of the hills moved and were shaken, because he was wroth.

8 There went up a smoke out of his nostrils, and fire out of his mouth devoured: coals were kindled by it.

9 He bowed the heavens also, and came down: and darkness was under his feet.

16:10 **Messianic prophecy:** This was fulfilled in Acts 2:31.

10 And he rode upon a cherub, and did fly: yes, he did fly upon the wings of the wind.

11 He made darkness his secret place; his pavilion round about him were dark waters and thick clouds of the skies.

12 At the brightness that was before him his thick clouds passed, hail stones and coals of fire.

13 The LORD also thundered in the heavens, and the Highest gave his voice; hail stones and coals of fire.

14 Yes, he sent out his arrows, and scattered them; and he shot out lightnings, and discomfited them.

15 Then the channels of waters were seen, and the foundations of the world were discovered at your rebuke, O LORD, at the blast of the breath of your nostrils.

16 He sent from above, he took me, he drew me out of many waters.

17 He delivered me from my strong enemy, and from them which hated me: for they were too strong for me.

18 They prevented me in the day of my calamity: but the LORD was my stay.

19 He brought me forth also into a large place; he delivered me, because he delighted in me.

20 The LORD rewarded me according to my righteousness; according to the cleanness of my hands has he recompensed me.

21 For I have kept the ways of the LORD, and have not wickedly departed from my God.

22 For all his judgments were before me, and I did not put away his statutes from me.

23 I was also upright before him, and I kept myself from my iniquity.

24 Therefore has the LORD recompensed me according to my righteousness, according to the cleanness of my hands in his eyesight.

25 With the merciful you will show yourself merciful; with an upright man you will show yourself upright;

26 With the pure you will show yourself pure; and with the froward you will show yourself froward.

27 For you will save the afflicted people; but will bring down high looks.

28 For you will light my candle: the LORD my God will enlighten my darkness.

29 For by you I have run through a troop; and by my God have I leaped over a wall.

30 As for God, his way is perfect: the word of the LORD is tried: he is a buckler to all those that trust in him.

31 For who is God save the LORD? or who is a rock save our God?

32 It is God that girds me with strength, and makes my way perfect.

33 He makes my feet like hinds' feet, and sets me upon my high places.

34 He teaches my hands to war, so that a bow of steel is broken by my arms.

35 You have also given me the shield of your salvation: and your right hand has held me up, and your gentleness has made me great.

36 You have enlarged my steps under me, that my feet did not slip.

37 I have pursued my enemies, and overtaken them: neither did I turn again till they were consumed.

38 I have wounded them that they were not able to rise: they are fallen under my feet.

39 For you have girded me with strength unto the battle: you have subdued under me those that rose up against me.

18:30 A perfect God gave a perfect Law that demands that we live up to its perfection. He makes us perfect in Christ (Colossians 1:28). See verse 32.

18:39 We must run to the battle for the souls of men. Our aim is not to kill, but to make alive. Men have rushed into battle merely to obtain dirt. Many have given their lives to get back a hill in Vietnam, Korea, or Israel—a hill that may be returned to the enemy through peace negotiations twenty years later. Their costly efforts proved to be futile. Our labor, however, is not in vain (1 Corinthians 15:58).

"Doesn't the Big Bang theory disprove the Genesis account of creation?"

19:1–4

Try to think of any explosion that has produced order. Does a terrorist bomb create harmony? Big bangs cause chaos. How could a Big Bang produce a rose, apple trees, fish, sunsets, the seasons, hummingbirds, polar bears—thousands of birds and animals, each with its own eyes, nose, and mouth? A *child* can see that there is "grand design" in creation.

Try this interesting experiment: Empty your garage of every piece of metal, wood, paint, rubber and plastic. *Make sure there is nothing there.* Nothing. Then wait for ten years and see if a Mercedes evolves. Try it. If it doesn't appear, leave it for 20 years. If that doesn't work, try it for 100 years. Then try leaving it for 10,000 years.

Here's what will produce the necessary blind faith to make the evolutionary process believable: leave it for 250 million years.

"New scientific revelations about supernovas, black holes, quarks, and the big bang even suggest to some scientists that there is a 'grand design' in the universe." (*U.S. News & World Report*, March 31, 1997)

"The universe suddenly exploded into being...The big bang bears an uncanny resemblance to the Genesis command." (Jim Holt, science writer, *Wall Street Journal*)

---

40 You have also given me the necks of my enemies; that I might destroy them that hate me.
41 They cried, but there was none to save them: even unto the LORD, but he answered them not.
42 Then did I beat them small as the dust before the wind: I did cast them out as the dirt in the streets.
43 You have delivered me from the strivings of the people; and you have made me the head of the heathen: a people whom I have not known shall serve me.
44 As soon as they hear of me, they shall obey me: the strangers shall submit themselves unto me.
45 The strangers shall fade away, and be afraid out of their close places.
46 The LORD lives and blessed be my rock; and let the God of my salvation be exalted.
47 It is God that avenges me, and subdues the people under me.

48 He delivers me from my enemies: yes, you lift me up above those that rise up against me: you have delivered me from the violent man.
49 Therefore will I give thanks unto you, O LORD, among the heathen, and sing praises unto your name.
50 Great deliverance gives he to his king; and shows mercy to his anointed, to David, and to his seed for evermore.

PSALM 19

THE heavens declare the glory of God; and the firmament shows his handiwork.
2 Day unto day utters speech, and night unto night shows knowledge.
3 There is no speech nor language, where their voice is not heard.
4 Their line is gone out through all the earth, and their words to the end of the world. In them has he set a tabernacle for the sun,

---

19:1–4 Creation reveals the genius of God's creative hand. Men are without excuse when it comes to believing in God's existence. See Psalm 33:8 comment and Romans 1:20.

5 Which is as a bridegroom coming out of his chamber, and rejoices as a strong man to run a race.

6 His going forth is from the end of the heaven, and his circuit unto the ends of it: and there is nothing hid from the heat thereof.

7 The law of the LORD is perfect, converting the soul: the testimony of the LORD is sure, making wise the simple.

8 The statutes of the LORD are right, rejoicing the heart: the commandment of the LORD is pure, enlightening the eyes.

9 The fear of the LORD is clean, enduring for ever: the judgments of the LORD are true and righteous altogether.

10 More to be desired are they than gold, yes, than much fine gold: sweeter also than honey and the honeycomb.

11 Moreover by them is your servant warned: and in keeping of them there is great reward.

12 Who can understand his errors? cleanse me from secret faults.

13 Keep back your servant also from presumptuous sins; let them not have dominion over me: then shall I be upright, and I shall be innocent from the great transgression.

14 Let the words of my mouth, and the meditation of my heart, be acceptable in your sight, O LORD, my strength, and my redeemer.

THE FUNCTION OF THE LAW

19:7–11 "God's Law is perfect. It is His tool to convert the soul. When a sinner is confronted with God's holy Law, his conscience affirms its truth. The Law gives understanding to the unregenerate mind. It reveals God's absolutes and therefore produces the fear of God, leading to repentance. It is of great worth. It is sweet to the converted soul. Its function is to warn sinners of the wrath to come and lead them to shelter in the Savior.

"The law of the Lord...is of use to convert the soul, to bring us back to ourselves, to our God, to our duty; for it shows us our sinfulness and misery in our departures from God and the indispensable necessity of our return to Him.

"Those who would know sin must get the knowledge of the Law in its strictness, extent, and spiritual nature."

Matthew Henry

PSALM 20

THE LORD hear you in the day of trouble; the name of the God of Jacob defend you;

2 Send you help from the sanctuary, and strengthen you out of Zion;

3 Remember all your offerings, and accept your burnt sacrifice; Selah.

4 Grant you according to your own heart, and fulfill all your counsel.

19:5-6 God's Law is like the sun. On Judgment Day it will arise with its burning heat and shine the brilliant light of eternal justice on the dark corners of the human heart. Nothing will be hidden from its consuming heat.

19:5-6 *Scientific Facts in the Bible.* In speaking of the sun, the psalmist says that "his going forth is from the end of the heaven, and his circuit unto the ends of it: and there is nothing hid from the heat thereof." For many years critics scoffed at these verses, claiming that they taught the old false doctrine of geocentricity (i.e., the sun revolves around the earth). Scientists thought the sun was stationary. Then it was discovered in recent years that the sun is in fact moving through space at approximately 600,000 miles per hour. It is traveling through the heavens and has a "circuit" just as the Bible says. Its circuit is so large that it would take approximately 200 million years to complete one orbit.

19:7-11 God's Law does the following: 1) converts the soul; 2) makes wise the simple; 3) makes the heart rejoice; 4) enlightens the eyes; 5) produces the fear of the Lord; 6) reveals God's true and righteous judgments; 7) is more to be desired than gold; 8) is sweeter than honey; 9) warns us of God's wrath; 10) provides a great reward.

22:1

"On the cross, Jesus cried, 'My God, my God, why have You forsaken Me?' This proves He was a fake; God forsook Him."

Jesus' words recorded in Matthew 27:46 and Mark 15:34 were the fulfillment of David's prophecy in Psalm 22:1. Verse 3 of this psalm then gives us insight into why God forsook Jesus on the cross: "But You are holy..." A holy Creator cannot have fellowship with sin. When Jesus was on the cross, the sin of the entire world was laid upon Him (Isaiah 53:6; 2 Corinthians 5:21), but Scripture says God is "of purer eyes than to behold evil, and cannot look on iniquity" (Habakkuk 1:13).

5 We will rejoice in your salvation, and in the name of our God we will set up our banners: the LORD fulfill all your petitions.

6 Now know I that the LORD saves his anointed; he will hear him from his holy heaven with the saving strength of his right hand.

7 Some trust in chariots, and some in horses: but we will remember the name of the LORD our God.

8 They are brought down and fallen: but we are risen, and stand upright.

9 Save, LORD: let the king hear us when we call.

PSALM 21

THE king shall joy in your strength, O LORD; and in your salvation how greatly shall he rejoice!

2 You have given him his heart's desire, and have not withheld the request of his lips. Selah.

3 For you prevent him with the blessings of goodness: you set a crown of pure gold on his head.

4 He asked life of you, and you gave it him, even length of days for ever and ever.

5 His glory is great in your salvation: honor and majesty have you laid upon him.

6 For you have made him most blessed for ever: you have made him exceeding glad with your countenance.

7 For the king trusts in the LORD, and through the mercy of the most High he shall not be moved.

8 Your hand shall find out all your enemies: your right hand shall find out those that hate you.

9 You shall make them as a fiery oven in the time of your anger: the LORD shall swallow them up in his wrath, and the fire shall devour them.

10 Their fruit shall you destroy from the earth, and their seed from among the children of men.

11 For they intended evil against you: they imagined a mischievous device, which they are not able to perform.

12 Therefore shall you make them turn their back, when you shall make ready your arrows upon your strings against the face of them.

13 Be exalted, LORD, in your own strength: so will we sing and praise your power.

PSALM 22

MY God, my God, why have you forsaken me? why are you so far from helping me, and from the words of my roaring?

21:9 "There's probably no concept in theology more repugnant to modern America than the idea of divine wrath." R. C. Sproul

2 O my God, I cry in the day time, but you hear not; and in the night season, and am not silent.

3 But you are holy, O you that inhabit the praises of Israel.

4 Our fathers trusted in you: they trusted, and you did deliver them.

5 They cried unto you, and were delivered: they trusted in you, and were not confounded.

6 But I am a worm, and no man; a reproach of men, and despised of the people.

7 All they that see me laugh me to scorn: they shoot out the lip, they shake the head, saying,

8 He trusted on the LORD that he would deliver him: let him deliver him, seeing he delighted in him.

9 But you are he that took me out of the womb: you did make me hope when I was upon my mother's breasts.

10 I was cast upon you from the womb: you are my God from my mother's belly.

11 Be not far from me; for trouble is near; for there is none to help.

12 Many bulls have compassed me: strong bulls of Bashan have beset me round.

13 They gaped upon me with their mouths, as a ravening and a roaring lion.

14 I am poured out like water, and all my bones are out of joint: my heart is like wax; it is melted in the midst of my bowels.

15 My strength is dried up like a potsherd; and my tongue cleaves to my jaws; and you have brought me into the dust of death.

22:6–8   Christ's suffering on the cross. "Man, at the best, is a worm; but he [Jesus] became a worm, and no man. If he had not made himself a worm, he could not have been trampled upon as he was. The word signifies such a worm as was used in dyeing scarlet or purple, whence some make it an allusion to his bloody sufferings. See what abuses were put upon him. He was ridiculed as a foolish man, and one that not only deceived others, but himself too. Those that saw him hanging on the cross laughed him to scorn. So far were they from pitying him, or concerning themselves for him, that they added to his afflictions, with all the gestures and expressions of insolence upbraiding him with his fall. They make mouths at him, make merry over him and make a jest of his sufferings: They shoot out the lip; they shake their head, saying, 'This was he that said he trusted God would deliver him; now let him deliver him.'

"David was sometimes taunted for his confidence in God; but in the sufferings of Christ this was literally and exactly fulfilled. Those very gestures were used by those that reviled him (Matt. 27:39); they wagged their heads, nay, and so far did their malice make them forget themselves that they used the very words (v. 43), 'He trusted in God; let him deliver him.' Our Lord Jesus, having undertaken to satisfy for the dishonor we had done to God by our sins, did it by submitting to the lowest possible instance of ignominy and disgrace."

Matthew Henry, *Commentary on the Whole Bible, New Modern Edition*

22:12–18   Messianic prophecy: This was clearly fulfilled in the crucifixion of Jesus of Nazareth. See John 19:28,37; Luke 23:35; and Matthew 27:35. Here is a graphic description of the Messiah on the cross:

- He was aware of their scorn (vv. 6-7).
- He could hear the mocking words (v. 8).
- He was praying (vv. 9–13).
- The strain of crucifixion pulled His bones out of joint (v. 14).
- Loss of blood made His heart feel as though it were melting (v. 14).
- His strength completely left Him (v. 15).
- Thirst caused His tongue to adhere to His mouth (v. 15).
- They pierced His hands and feet (v. 16).
- He could see them gambling for His clothes (v. 18).

16 For dogs have compassed me: the assembly of the wicked have enclosed me: they pierced my hands and my feet.

17 I may tell all my bones: they look and stare upon me.

18 They part my garments among them, and cast lots upon my vesture.

19 But be not far from me, O LORD: O my strength, haste to help me.

20 Deliver my soul from the sword; my darling from the power of the dog.

21 Save me from the lion's mouth: for you have heard me from the horns of the unicorns.

22 I will declare your name unto my brethren: in the midst of the congregation will I praise you.

23 You that fear the LORD, praise him; all you the seed of Jacob, glorify him; and fear him, all you the seed of Israel.

24 For he has not despised nor abhorred the affliction of the afflicted; neither has he hid his face from him; but when he cried unto him, he heard.

25 My praise shall be of you in the great congregation: I will pay my vows before them that fear him.

26 The meek shall eat and be satisfied: they shall praise the LORD that seek him: your heart shall live for ever.

Those who will not be governed by God will be ruled by tyrants.

William Penn

1644 - 1718

BRITISH QUAKER

FOUNDER OF PENNSYLVANIA

22:14 When commenting on this verse, *Charles Spurgeon* said: "The placing of the cross in its socket had shaken Him with great violence, had strained all the ligaments, pained every nerve, and more or less dislocated all His bones. Burdened with His own weight, the august sufferer felt the strain increasing every moment of those six long hours. His sense of faintness and general weakness were overpowering; while to His own consciousness He became nothing but a mass of misery and swooning sickness…To us, sensations such as our Lord endured would have been insupportable, and kind unconsciousness would have come to our rescue; but in His case, He was wounded and *felt* the sword; He drained the cup and *tasted* every drop."

22:16 Messianic prophecy: This was fulfilled in Luke 24:39.

22:18 *Matthew Henry* wrote, "The shame of nakedness was the immediate consequence of sin (Genesis 3:7), and therefore our Lord Jesus was stripped of His clothes, when He was crucified, that the shame of our nakedness might not appear." (See Revelation 3:17, 18; 16:15.)

22:18 Messianic prophecy: This was fulfilled in Mark 15:24.

22:28 "Men, in a word, must necessarily be controlled, either by a power within them, or by a power without them; either by the word of God, or by the strong arm of man; either by the Bible, or by the bayonet." Robert Winthrop

"We staked the whole future of American civilization, not upon the power of government, far from it. We have staked the future of all our political institutions upon the capacity of mankind for self government; upon the capacity of each and all of us to govern ourselves, to control ourselves according to the Commandments of God." James Madison

27 All the ends of the world shall remember and turn unto the LORD: and all the kindreds of the nations shall worship before you.

28 For the kingdom is the LORD's: and he is the governor among the nations.

29 All they that be fat upon earth shall eat and worship: all they that go down to the dust shall bow before him: and none can keep alive his own soul.

30 A seed shall serve him; it shall be accounted to the Lord for a generation.

31 They shall come, and shall declare his righteousness unto a people that shall be born, that he has done this.

PSALM 23

THE LORD is my shepherd; I shall not want.

2 He makes me to lie down in green pastures: he leads me beside the still waters.

3 He restores my soul: he leads me in the paths of righteousness for his name's sake.

4 Yes, though I walk through the valley of the shadow of death, I will fear no evil: for thou art with me; thy rod and thy staff they comfort me.

5 You prepare a table before me in the presence of my enemies: you anoint my head with oil; my cup runs over.

6 Surely goodness and mercy shall follow me all the days of my life: and I will dwell in the house of the LORD for ever.

PSALM 24

THE earth is the LORD's, and the fullness thereof; the world, and they that dwell therein.

2 For he has founded it upon the seas, and established it upon the floods.

3 Who shall ascend into the hill of the LORD? or who shall stand in his holy place?

4 He that has clean hands, and a pure heart; who has not lifted up his soul unto vanity, nor sworn deceitfully.

5 He shall receive the blessing from the LORD, and righteousness from the God of his salvation.

6 This is the generation of them that seek him, that seek your face, O Jacob. Selah.

7 Lift up your heads, O you gates; and be lift up, you everlasting doors; and the King of glory shall come in.

8 Who is this King of glory? The LORD strong and mighty, the LORD mighty in battle.

9 Lift up your heads, O you gates; even lift them up, you everlasting doors; and the King of glory shall come in.

10 Who is this King of glory? The LORD of hosts, he is the King of glory. Selah.

PSALM 25

UNTO you, O LORD, do I lift up my soul.

2 O my God, I trust in you: let me not be ashamed, let not my enemies triumph over me.

3 Yes, let none that wait on you be ashamed: let them be ashamed which transgress without cause.

4 Show me your ways, O LORD; teach me your paths.

5 Lead me in your truth, and teach me: for you are the God of my salvation; on you do I wait all the day.

23:1 See John 10:11 comment.

23:4 This life is the valley of the shadow of death. The Scriptures describe all of humanity as sitting in darkness and the shadow of death, because they rebelled against the words of God (Psalm 107:10,11). The birth of the Savior gives "light to those who sit in darkness and the shadow of death" (Luke 1:79). The light of the gospel not only banishes the shadow of death, but the believer fears no evil because God is now for him, rather than against him.

24:1 No one truly "owns" anything. We are merely temporary custodians of that which God has entrusted to us. The entire earth and all who dwell in it belong to the Lord.

6 Remember, O LORD, your tender mercies and your lovingkindnesses; for they have been ever of old.

7 Remember not the sins of my youth, nor my transgressions: according to your mercy remember me for your goodness' sake, O LORD.

8 Good and upright is the LORD: therefore will he teach sinners in the way.

9 The meek will he guide in judgment: and the meek will he teach his way.

10 All the paths of the LORD are mercy and truth unto such as keep his covenant and his testimonies.

11 For your name's sake, O LORD, pardon my iniquity; for it is great.

12 What man is he that fears the LORD? him shall he teach in the way that he shall choose.

13 His soul shall dwell at ease; and his seed shall inherit the earth.

25:12–14 Look at what wonderful fruit comes from the fear of the Lord: God Himself will teach us. We will dwell in prosperity. Our descendants will be blessed, and we will be partakers of His incredible covenant.

25:14 Samuel Morse, famous for his invention of the telegraph, gave God the glory for his inventions. It's fitting that the first message he ever sent over the wire was taken from Scripture: "What hath God wrought!" (Numbers 23:23).

Morse, who graduated from Yale in 1810, wrote these words four years before he died: "The nearer I approach the end of my pilgrimage, the clearer is the evidence of the divine origin of the Bible. The grandeur and sublimity of God's remedy for fallen man are more appreciated and the future is illuminated with hope and joy."

25:14 **Scientists Who Believe.** "Most of the great scientists of the past who founded and developed the key disciplines of science were creationists. Note the following sampling:

Physics: Newton, Faraday, Maxwell, Kelvin
Chemistry: Boyle, Dalton, Pascal, Ramsay
Biology: Ray, Linnaeus, Mendel, Pasteur
Geology: Steno, Woodward, Brewster, Agassiz
Astronomy: Kepler, Galileo, Herschel, Maunder

"These men, as well as scores of others who could be mentioned, were creationists, not evolutionists, and their names are practically synonymous with the rise of modern science. To them, the scientific enterprise was a high calling, one dedicated to "thinking God's thoughts after Him." Henry M. Morris and Gary E. Parker, *What is Creation Science?*

"Science is the glimpse of God's purpose in nature. The very existence of the amazing world of the atom and radiation points to a purposeful creation, to the idea that there is a God and an intelligent purpose back of everything…An orderly universe testifies to the greatest statement ever uttered: 'In the beginning, God…'" Arthur H. Compton, winner of Nobel Prize in Physics

"The chief aim of all investigation of the external world should be to discover the rational order and harmony which has been imposed on it by God." Johann Kepler

"With regard to the origin of life, science…positively affirms creative power." Lord Kelvin

"All material things seem to have been composed of the hard and solid particles above mentioned, variously associated in the first creation by the counsel of an intelligent Agent. For it became Him who created them to set them in order. And if He did so, it's unphilosophical to seek for any other origin of the world, or to pretend that it might arise out of a chaos by the mere laws of nature." Sir Isaac Newton

"An increasing number of scientists, most particularly a growing number of evolutionists…argue that Darwinian evolutionary theory is no genuine scientific theory at all…Many of the critics have the highest intellectual credentials." Michael Ruse, "Darwin's Theory: An Exercise in Science," *New Scientist*

See also Psalm 33:8 comment.

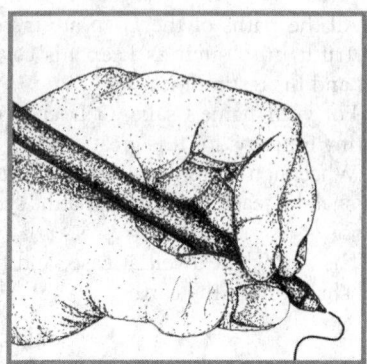

Who wrote the Bible—God or men?
See 2 Peter 2:21 comment.

14 The secret of the LORD is with them that fear him; and he will show them his covenant.

15 My eyes are ever toward the LORD; for he shall pluck my feet out of the net.

16 Turn you unto me, and have mercy upon me; for I am desolate and afflicted.

17 The troubles of my heart are enlarged: O bring me out of my distresses.

18 Look upon my affliction and my pain; and forgive all my sins.

19 Consider my enemies; for they are many; and they hate me with cruel hatred.

20 O keep my soul, and deliver me: let me not be ashamed; for I put my trust in you.

21 Let integrity and uprightness preserve me; for I wait on you.

22 Redeem Israel, O God, out of all his troubles.

PSALM 26

JUDGE me, O LORD; for I have walked in my integrity: I have trusted also in the LORD; therefore I shall not slide.

2 Examine me, O LORD, and prove me; try my reins and my heart.

3 For your lovingkindness is before my eyes: and I have walked in your truth.

4 I have not sat with vain persons, neither will I go in with dissemblers.

5 I have hated the congregation of evil doers; and will not sit with the wicked.

6 I will wash my hands in innocency: so will I compass your altar, O LORD:

7 That I may publish with the voice of thanksgiving, and tell of all your wondrous works.

8 LORD, I have loved the habitation of your house, and the place where your honor dwells.

9 Gather not my soul with sinners, nor my life with bloody men:

10 In whose hands is mischief, and their right hand is full of bribes.

11 But as for me, I will walk in my integrity: redeem me, and be merciful unto me.

12 My foot stands in an even place: in the congregations will I bless the LORD.

PSALM 27

THE LORD is my light and my salvation; whom shall I fear? the LORD is the strength of my life; of whom shall I be afraid?

2 When the wicked, even my enemies and my foes, came upon me to eat up my flesh, they stumbled and fell.

3 Though an host should encamp against me, my heart shall not fear: though war should rise against me, in this will I be confident.

4 One thing have I desired of the LORD, that will I seek after; that I may dwell in the house of the LORD all the days of my life, to behold the beauty of the LORD, and to inquire in his temple.

5 For in the time of trouble he shall hide me in his pavilion: in the secret of his tabernacle shall he hide me; he shall set me up upon a rock.

6 And now shall my head be lifted up above my enemies round about me: therefore will I offer in his tabernacle sacrifices of joy; I will sing, yes, I will sing praises unto the LORD.

7 Hear, O LORD, when I cry with my voice: have mercy also upon me, and answer me.

8 When you said, Seek my face; my heart said unto you, Your face, LORD, will I seek.

9 Hide not your face far from me; put not your servant away in anger: you have been my help; leave me not, neither forsake me, O God of my salvation.

10 When my father and my mother forsake me, then the LORD will take me up.

11 Teach me your way, O LORD, and lead me in a plain path, because of my enemies.

12 Deliver me not over unto the will of my enemies: for false witnesses are risen up against me, and such as breathe out cruelty.

13 I had fainted, unless I had believed to see the goodness of the LORD in the land of the living.

14 Wait on the LORD: be of good courage, and he shall strengthen your heart: wait, I say, on the LORD.

PSALM 28

UNTO you will I cry, O LORD my rock; be not silent to me: lest, if you be silent to me, I become like them that go down into the pit.

2 Hear the voice of my supplications, when I cry unto you, when I lift up my hands toward your holy oracle.

3 Draw me not away with the wicked, and with the workers of iniquity, which speak peace to their neighbors, but mischief is in their hearts.

4 Give them according to their deeds, and according to the wickedness of their endeavors: give them after the work of their hands; render to them their desert.

5 Because they regard not the works of the LORD, nor the operation of his hands, he shall destroy them, and not build them up.

6 Blessed be the LORD, because he has heard the voice of my supplications.

7 The LORD is my strength and my shield; my heart trusted in him, and I am helped: therefore my heart greatly rejoices; and with my song will I praise him.

8 The LORD is their strength, and he is the saving strength of his anointed.

9 Save your people, and bless your inheritance: feed them also, and lift them up for ever.

PSALM 29

GIVE unto the LORD, O you mighty, give unto the LORD glory and strength.

2 Give unto the LORD the glory due unto his name; worship the LORD in the beauty of holiness.

3 The voice of the LORD is upon the waters: the God of glory thunders: the LORD is upon many waters.

4 The voice of the LORD is powerful; the voice of the LORD is full of majesty.

5 The voice of the LORD breaks the cedars; yes, the LORD breaks the cedars of Lebanon.

6 He makes them also to skip like a calf; Lebanon and Sirion like a young unicorn.

7 The voice of the LORD divides the flames of fire.

8 The voice of the LORD shakes the wilderness; the LORD shakes the wilderness of Kadesh.

9 The voice of the LORD makes the hinds to calve, and discovers the forests: and in his temple does every one speak of his glory.

27:12 Messianic prophecy: This was fulfilled in Matthew 26:60.

28:4-5 It is a fearful thing for sinners to be given exactly what they deserve.

29:3–9 The Voice of the Lord. It was His Word that brought creation into existence (see Genesis 1:3; John 1:1–3). God's voice then became flesh in the person of Jesus of Nazareth (John 1:14; 1 John 1:1–3). That's why Jesus said strange things about His voice: "Marvel not at this: for the hour is coming, in which all that are in the graves shall hear [My] voice" (John 5:28). He said, "The words that I speak to you, they are spirit, and they are life" (John 6:63). It was the voice of the Savior that brought Lazarus back to life (John 11:43), and it is His voice that will bring the dead out of their graves at the resurrection (John 5:28-29). His voice brings life.

This is just one example of a wonderfully unique aspect of the Bible. One can study a multitude of subjects in its different books, and find incredible continuity, despite the fact that the books were written thousands of years apart.

10 The LORD sits upon the flood; yes, the LORD sits King for ever.

11 The LORD will give strength unto his people; the LORD will bless his people with peace.

PSALM 30

I WILL extol you, O LORD; for you have lifted me up, and have not made my foes to rejoice over me.

2 O LORD my God, I cried unto you, and you have healed me.

3 O LORD, you have brought up my soul from the grave: you have kept me alive, that I should not go down to the pit.

4 Sing unto the LORD, O you saints of his, and give thanks at the remembrance of his holiness.

5 For his anger endures but a moment; in his favor is life: weeping may endure for a night, but joy comes in the morning.

6 And in my prosperity I said, I shall never be moved.

7 LORD, by your favor you have made my mountain to stand strong: you did hide your face, and I was troubled.

8 I cried to you, O LORD; and unto the LORD I made supplication.

9 What profit is there in my blood, when I go down to the pit? Shall the dust praise you? shall it declare your truth?

10 Hear, O LORD, and have mercy upon me: LORD, be my helper.

11 You have turned for me my mourning into dancing: you have put off my sackcloth, and girded me with gladness;

12 To the end that my glory may sing praise to you, and not be silent. O LORD my God, I will give thanks unto you for ever.

PSALM 31

I N you, O LORD, do I put my trust; let me never be ashamed: deliver me in your righteousness.

2 Bow down your ear to me; deliver me speedily: be my strong rock, for an house of defense to save me.

3 For you are my rock and my fortress; therefore for your name's sake lead me, and guide me.

4 Pull me out of the net that they have laid privily for me: for you are my strength.

5 Into your hand I commit my spirit: you have redeemed me, O LORD God of truth.

6 I have hated them that regard lying vanities: but I trust in the LORD.

7 I will be glad and rejoice in your mercy: for you have considered my trouble; you have known my soul in adversities;

8 And have not shut me up into the hand of the enemy: you have set my feet in a large room.

9 Have mercy upon me, O LORD, for I am in trouble: my eye is consumed with grief, yes, my soul and my belly.

10 For my life is spent with grief, and my years with sighing: my strength fails because of my iniquity, and my bones are consumed.

11 I was a reproach among all my enemies, but especially among my neighbors, and a fear to my acquaintance: they that did see me without fled from me.

12 I am forgotten as a dead man out of mind: I am like a broken vessel.

13 For I have heard the slander of many: fear was on every side: while they took counsel together against me, they devised to take away my life.

14 But I trusted in you, O LORD: I said, You are my God.

15 My times are in your hand: deliver me from the hand of my enemies, and from them that persecute me.

16 Make your face to shine upon your servant: save me for your mercies' sake.

17 Let me not be ashamed, O LORD; for I have called upon you: let the wicked be ashamed, and let them be silent in the grave.

18 Let the lying lips be put to silence; which speak grievous things proudly and contemptuously against the righteous.

19 *Oh how great is your goodness, which you have laid up for them that fear you; which you have wrought for*

Q 32:5 *What if someone says, "I've broken every one of the Ten Commandments."*

Do not take this statement to mean that the person has seen the gravity of his sinful state before God. He may say something like, "I'm a really *bad* person!" It is often used as a way of shrugging off conviction. Say to him, "Well let's take the time to go through them one by one and see if you have." As he is confronted with the righteous standard of God's Moral Law, pray that the Holy Spirit brings conviction of sin.

them that trust in you before the sons of men!
20 You shall hide them in the secret of your presence from the pride of man: you shall keep them secretly in a pavilion from the strife of tongues.
21 Blessed be the LORD: for he has showed me his marvelous kindness in a strong city.
22 For I said in my haste, I am cut off from before your eyes: nevertheless you heard the voice of my supplications when I cried unto you.
23 O love the LORD, all you his saints: for the LORD preserve the faithful, and plentifully reward the proud doer.
24 Be of good courage, and he shall strengthen your heart, all you that hope in the LORD.

PSALM 32

BLESSED is he whose transgression is forgiven, whose sin is covered.
2 Blessed is the man unto whom the LORD imputes not iniquity, and in whose spirit there is no guile.
3 When I kept silence, my bones waxed old through my roaring all the day long.

4 For day and night your hand was heavy upon me: my moisture is turned into the drought of summer. Selah.
5 I acknowledge my sin unto you, and my iniquity have I not hid. I said, I will confess my transgressions unto the LORD; and you forgave the iniquity of my sin. Selah.
6 For this shall every one that is godly pray unto you in a time when you may be found: surely in the floods of great waters they shall not come near unto him.
7 You are my hiding place; you shall preserve me from trouble; you shall compass me about with songs of deliverance. Selah.
8 I will instruct you and teach you in the way which you shall go: I will guide you with my eye.
9 Be not as the horse, or as the mule, which have no understanding: whose mouth must be held in with bit and bridle, lest they come near unto you.
10 Many sorrows shall be to the wicked: but he that trusts in the LORD, mercy shall compass him about.

31:19 Here is an amazing promise to those who are not ashamed to bear the reproach of the Gospel.

32:1-2 *Transgression* is violation of the Law. *Sin* is falling short of the Law's standard. *Iniquity* is lawlessness.

32:5 Contrition does not save us. Its outworking can be seen in these verses: we acknowledge our sin to God rather than justifying ourselves. No longer do we try to hide anything from God, but we confess our transgressions to Him.

11 Be glad in the LORD, and rejoice, you righteous: and shout for joy, all you that are upright in heart.

PSALM 33

REJOICE in the LORD, O you right-eous: for praise is comely for the up-right.

32:9 Differences Between Men and Animals. The Bible tells us that animals are created "without understanding." Human beings are different from animals. We are made in God's "image." As human beings, we are aware of our "being." God is "I AM," and we know that "we are." We have understanding that we exist.

Among other unique characteristics, we have an innate ability to appreciate God's creation. What animal gazes with awe at a sunset, or at the magnificence of the Grand Canyon? What animal obtains joy from the sounds of music or takes the time to form itself into an orchestra to create music? What animal among the beasts sets up court systems and apportions justice to its fellow creatures? We are moral beings.

While birds and other creatures have instincts to create (nests, etc.), we have the ability to uncover the hidden laws of electricity. We can utilize the law of aerodynamics to transport ourselves around the globe. We also have the God-given ability to appreciate the *value* of creation. We unearth the hidden treasures of gold, silver, diamonds, and oil and make use of them for our own benefit. Only humans have the unique ability to appreciate God for this incredible creation and to respond to His love.

33:6 *Scientific Facts in the Bible.* The Scriptures say, "Thus the heavens and the earth were finished, and all the host of them" (Genesis 2:1). The original Hebrew uses the past definite tense for the verb "finished," indicating an action completed in the past, never again to occur. The creation was "finished"—once and for all. That is exactly what the First Law of Thermodynamics says. This law (often referred to as the Law of the Conservation of Energy and/or Mass) states that neither matter nor energy can be either created or destroyed. It was because of this Law that Sir Fred Hoyle's "Steady-State" (or "Continuous Creation") Theory was discarded. Hoyle stated that at points in the universe called "irtrons," matter (or energy) was constantly being created. But, the First Law states just the opposite. Indeed, there is no "creation" ongoing today. It is "finished" exactly as the Bible states.

33:8 Awe for the Creator. "Science can only be created by those who are thoroughly imbued with the aspiration toward truth and understanding. This source of feeling, however, springs from the sphere of religion. To this there also belongs the faith in the possibility that the regulations valid for the world of existence are rational, that is, comprehensible to reason. I cannot conceive of a genuine scientist without that profound faith." *Albert Einstein*

Sir John Frederick Herschel, an English astronomer who discovered over 500 stars, stated: "All human discoveries seem to be made only for the purpose of confirming more and more strongly the truths that come from on high and are contained in the Sacred Writings." His father, *Sir William Herschel*, also a renowned astronomer, insisted, "The undevout astronomer must be mad." See also Psalm 25:14 comment.

"In antiquity and in what is called the Dark Ages, men did not know what they now know about humanity and the cosmos. They did not know the lock but they possessed the key, which is God. Now many have excellent descriptions of the lock, but they have lost the key. The proper solution is union between religion and science. We should be owners of the lock *and* the key. The fact is that as science advances, it discovers what was said thousands of years ago in the Bible." Richard Wurmbrand, *Proofs of God's Existence*

"Calvin said that the Bible—God's special revelation—was spectacles that we must put on if we are to correctly read the book of nature—God's revelation in creation. Unfortunately, between the beginning of science and our day, many scientists have discarded these glasses, and many distortions have followed." D. James Kennedy and Jerry Newcombe, *What if Jesus Had Never Been Born?*

2 Praise the LORD with harp: sing unto him with the psaltery and an instrument of ten strings.

3 Sing unto him a new song; play skillfully with a loud noise.

4 For the word of the LORD is right; and all his works are done in truth.

5 He loves righteousness and judgment: the earth is full of the goodness of the LORD.

6 By the word of the LORD were the heavens made; and all the host of them by the breath of his mouth.

7 He gathers the waters of the sea together as an heap: he lays up the depth in storehouses.

8 Let all the earth fear the LORD: let all the inhabitants of the world stand in awe of him.

9 For he spoke, and it was done; he commanded, and it stood fast.

10 The LORD brings the counsel of the heathen to nought: he makes the devices of the people of none effect.

11 The counsel of the LORD stands for ever, the thoughts of his heart to all generations.

12 Blessed is the nation whose God is the LORD; and the people whom he has chosen for his own inheritance.

13 **The LORD looks from heaven; he beholds all the sons of men.**

14 **From the place of his habitation he looks upon all the inhabitants of the earth.**

15 **He fashions their hearts alike; he considers all their works.**

16 There is no king saved by the multitude of an host: a mighty man is not delivered by much strength.

17 An horse is a vain thing for safety: neither shall he deliver any by his great strength.

18 Behold, the eye of the LORD is upon them that fear him, upon them that hope in his mercy;

19 To deliver their soul from death, and to keep them alive in famine.

20 Our soul waits for the LORD: he is our help and our shield.

21 For our heart shall rejoice in him, because we have trusted in his holy name.

22 Let your mercy, O LORD, be upon us, according as we hope in you.

PSALM 34

I WILL bless the LORD at all times: his praise shall continually be in my mouth.

2 My soul shall make her boast in the LORD: the humble shall hear thereof, and be glad.

3 O magnify the LORD with me, and let us exalt his name together.

33:12 The Source of a Nation's Blessings. In Leviticus 26:1–13, God promises Israel many wonderful blessings if they would simply obey Him: The rain would come in due season; the land would yield its harvest and the trees would yield their fruit; their food would satisfy them; they would have peace and safety in the land (no violence), and they would prevail over their enemies. Truly, blessed is the nation whose God is the Lord.

"Suppose a nation in some distant region should take the Bible for their only law book, and every member should regulate his conduct by the precepts there exhibited! Every member would be obliged in conscience, to temperance, frugality, and industry; to justice, kindness, and charity towards his fellow men; and to piety, love, and reverence toward Almighty God...What a Utopia, what a Paradise would this region be." John Adams

"If we abide by the principles taught in the Bible, our country will go on prospering and to prosper; but if we and our posterity neglect its instructions and authority, no man can tell how sudden a catastrophe may overwhelm us and bury all our glory in profound obscurity." Daniel Webster

34:2 The proud are not glad to hear a soul boast in the Lord. Try telling a proud unsaved person about an obvious answer to prayer, and watch him try to explain it away as coincidence. It is a humble heart that can hear a boast about God.

4 I sought the LORD, and he heard me, and delivered me from all my fears.

5 They looked unto him, and were lightened: and their faces were not ashamed.

6 This poor man cried, and the LORD heard him, and saved him out of all his troubles.

7 The angel of the LORD encamps round about them that fear him, and delivers them.

8 O taste and see that the LORD is good: blessed is the man that trusts in him.

9 O fear the LORD, you his saints: for there is no want to them that fear him.

10 The young lions do lack, and suffer hunger: but they that seek the LORD shall not want any good thing.

11 Come, you children, hearken unto me: I will teach you the fear of the LORD.

12 What man is he that desires life, and loves many days, that he may see good?

13 Keep your tongue from evil, and your lips from speaking guile.

14 Depart from evil, and do good; seek peace, and pursue it.

15 The eyes of the LORD are upon the righteous, and his ears are open unto their cry.

16 The face of the LORD is against them that do evil, to cut off the remembrance of them from the earth.

17 The righteous cry, and the LORD hears, and delivers them out of all their troubles.

18 The LORD is near unto them that are of a broken heart; and saves such as be of a contrite spirit.

19 Many are the afflictions of the righteous: but the LORD delivers him out of them all.

20 He keeps all his bones: not one of them is broken.

21 Evil shall slay the wicked: and they that hate the righteous shall be desolate.

22 The LORD redeems the soul of his servants: and none of them that trust in him shall be desolate.

PSALM 35

PLEAD my cause, O LORD, with them that strive with me: fight against them that fight against me.

2 Take hold of shield and buckler, and stand up for my help.

3 Draw out also the spear, and stop the way against them that persecute me: say unto my soul, I am your salvation.

4 Let them be confounded and put to shame that seek after my soul: let them be turned back and brought to confusion that devise my hurt.

5 Let them be as chaff before the wind: and let the angel of the LORD chase them.

6 Let their way be dark and slippery: and let the angel of the LORD persecute them.

7 For without cause have they hid for me their net in a pit, which without cause they have digged for my soul.

8 Let destruction come upon him at unawares; and let his net that he has hid catch himself: into that very destruction let him fall.

9 And my soul shall be joyful in the LORD: it shall rejoice in his salvation.

10 All my bones shall say, LORD, who is like unto you, who delivers the poor from him that is too strong for him, yes, the poor and the needy from him that spoils him?

11 False witnesses did rise up; they laid to my charge things that I knew not.

12 They rewarded me evil for good to the spoiling of my soul.

13 But as for me, when they were sick, my clothing was sackcloth: I humbled my

---

34:8 See John 17:3 comment, "Experiential Faith."

34:8-9 The goodness of God cannot be separated from the fear of the Lord. Those who maintain that it is "the goodness of God" that leads to repentance, and therefore we need only speak of His goodness, need to study the context of Romans 2:3–11.

34:20 Messianic prophecy: This was fulfilled in John 19:33.

> I remember two things:
> I am a great sinner
> and I have a great Savior;
> and I don't suppose an old slave trader
> needs to remember
> much more than that.
>
> **JOHN NEWTON**
> 1725-1807
> AUTHOR OF "AMAZING GRACE"

soul with fasting; and my prayer returned into my own bosom.

14 I behaved myself as though he had been my friend or brother: I bowed down heavily, as one that mourns for his mother.

15 But in my adversity they rejoiced, and gathered themselves together: yes, the abjects gathered themselves together against me, and I knew it not; they did tear me, and ceased not:

16 With hypocritical mockers in feasts, they gnashed upon me with their teeth.

17 Lord, how long will you look on? rescue my soul from their destructions, my darling from the lions.

18 I will give you thanks in the great congregation: I will praise you among much people.

19 Let not them that are my enemies wrongfully rejoice over me: neither let them wink with the eye that hate me without a cause.

20 For they speak not peace: but they devise deceitful matters against them that are quiet in the land.

21 Yes, they opened their mouth wide against me, and said, Aha, aha, our eye has seen it.

22 This you have seen, O LORD: keep not silence: O Lord, be not far from me.

23 Stir up yourself, and awake to my judgment, even unto my cause, my God and my Lord.

24 Judge me, O LORD my God, according to your righteousness; and let them not rejoice over me.

25 Let them not say in their hearts, Ah, so would we have it: let them not say, We have swallowed him up.

26 Let them be ashamed and brought to confusion together that rejoice at my hurt: let them be clothed with shame and dishonor that magnify themselves against me.

27 Let them shout for joy, and be glad, that favor my righteous cause: yes, let them say continually, Let the LORD be magnified, which has pleasure in the prosperity of his servant.

28 And my tongue shall speak of your righteousness and of your praise all the day long.

PSALM 36

THE transgression of the wicked says within my heart, that there is no fear of God before his eyes.

2 For he flatters himself in his own eyes, until his iniquity be found to be hateful.

3 The words of his mouth are iniquity and deceit: he has left off to be wise, and to do good.

4 He devises mischief upon his bed; he sets himself in a way that is not good; he abhors not evil.

5 Your mercy, O LORD, is in the heavens; and your faithfulness reaches unto the clouds.

6 Your righteousness is like the great mountains; your judgments are a great deep: O LORD, you preserve man and beast.

7 How excellent is your lovingkindness, O God! therefore the children of men put their trust under the shadow of your wings.

35:13 It is wise to make fasting a way of life. Missing a meal on a regular basis will help you to keep your appetite in check. It will also put a joyful thanksgiving in your heart every time you sit down to a meal.

36:2 "The greatest fault is to be conscious of none." Thomas Carlyle

8 They shall be abundantly satisfied with the fatness of your house; and you shall make them drink of the river of your pleasures.

9 For with you is the fountain of life: in your light shall we see light.

10 O continue your lovingkindness unto them that know you; and your righteousness to the upright in heart.

11 Let not the foot of pride come against me, and let not the hand of the wicked remove me.

12 There are the workers of iniquity fallen: they are cast down, and shall not be able to rise.

PSALM 37

FRET not yourself because of evildoers, neither be envious against the workers of iniquity.

2 For they shall soon be cut down like the grass, and wither as the green herb.

3 Trust in the LORD, and do good; so shall you dwell in the land, and verily you shall be fed.

4 Delight yourself also in the LORD: and he shall give you the desires of your heart.

5 Commit your way unto the LORD; trust also in him; and he shall bring it to pass.

6 And he shall bring forth your righteousness as the light, and your judgment as the noonday.

7 Rest in the LORD, and wait patiently for him: fret not yourself because of him who prospers in his way, because of the man who brings wicked devices to pass.

8 Cease from anger, and forsake wrath: fret not yourself in any wise to do evil.

9 For evildoers shall be cut off: but those that wait upon the LORD, they shall inherit the earth.

10 For yet a little while, and the wicked shall not be: yes, you shall diligently consider his place, and it shall not be.

11 But the meek shall inherit the earth; and shall delight themselves in the abundance of peace.

12 The wicked plots against the just, and gnashes upon him with his teeth.

13 The LORD shall laugh at him: for he sees that his day is coming.

14 The wicked have drawn out the sword, and have bent their bow, to cast down the poor and needy, and to slay such as be of upright conversation.

15 Their sword shall enter into their own heart, and their bows shall be broken.

16 A little that a righteous man has is better than the riches of many wicked.

17 For the arms of the wicked shall be broken: but the LORD upholds the righteous.

18 The LORD knows the days of the upright: and their inheritance shall be for ever.

19 They shall not be ashamed in the evil time: and in the days of famine they shall be satisfied.

20 But the wicked shall perish, and the enemies of the LORD shall be as the fat of lambs: they shall consume; into smoke shall they consume away.

21 The wicked borrows, and pays not again: but the righteous shows mercy, and gives.

37:4 Desires of the Heart. What are our desires? What do we want most in life? Do we desire above all things to have a better paying job, a bigger house, thicker carpet, a superior car, and more money? Are we controlled by the lust of the flesh, the lust of the eyes, and the pride of life? Or have we been transformed from the way of this world by "the renewing of [our] mind" (Romans 12:2), that we may prove what is that good, and acceptable, and perfect will of God? Are our desires now in line with God's desires? Are we above all things "not willing that any should perish, but that all should come to repentance" (2 Peter 3:9)? If we delight ourselves in the Lord, the desires of our heart will match His—and those are the desires He will grant.

37:9 Does the reference to the wicked being "cut off" mean that they are annihilated? "If it did, then the Messiah would have been annihilated when He died, since the same word (*karath*) is used of the death of the Messiah (in Daniel 9:26)." Norman Geisler and Thomas Howe, *When Critics Ask*

22 For such as be blessed of him shall inherit the earth; and they that be cursed of him shall be cut off.

23 The steps of a good man are ordered by the LORD: and he delights in his way.

24 Though he fall, he shall not be utterly cast down: for the LORD upholds him with his hand.

25 I have been young, and now am old; yet have I not seen the righteous forsaken, nor his seed begging bread.

26 He is ever merciful, and lends; and his seed is blessed.

27 Depart from evil, and do good; and dwell for evermore.

28 For the LORD loves judgment, and forsakes not his saints; they are preserved for ever: but the seed of the wicked shall be cut off.

29 The righteous shall inherit the land, and dwell therein for ever.

30 *The mouth of the righteous speaks wisdom, and his tongue talks of judgment.*

31 *The law of his God is in his heart; none of his steps shall slide.*

32 The wicked watches the righteous, and seeks to slay him.

33 The LORD will not leave him in his hand, nor condemn him when he is judged.

34 Wait on the LORD, and keep his way, and he shall exalt you to inherit the land: when the wicked are cut off, you shall see it.

35 I have seen the wicked in great power, and spreading himself like a green bay tree.

36 Yet he passed away, and, lo, he was not: yes, I sought him, but he could not be found.

37 Mark the perfect man, and behold the upright: for the end of that man is peace.

38 But the transgressors shall be destroyed together: the end of the wicked shall be cut off.

39 But the salvation of the righteous is of the LORD: he is their strength in the time of trouble.

40 And the LORD shall help them, and deliver them: he shall deliver them from the wicked, and save them, because they trust in him.

PSALM 38

O LORD, rebuke me not in your wrath: neither chasten me in your hot displeasure.

2 For your arrows stick fast in me, and your hand presses me sore.

3 There is no soundness in my flesh because of your anger; neither is there any rest in my bones because of my sin.

4 For my iniquities are gone over my head: as an heavy burden they are too heavy for me.

5 My wounds stink and are corrupt because of my foolishness.

6 I am troubled; I am bowed down greatly; I go mourning all the day long.

7 For my loins are filled with a loathsome disease: and there is no soundness in my flesh.

8 I am feeble and sore broken: I have roared by reason of the disquietness of my heart.

9 Lord, all my desire is before you; and my groaning is not hid from you.

10 My heart pants, my strength fails me: as for the light of my eyes, it also is gone from me.

11 My lovers and my friends stand aloof from my sore; and my kinsmen stand afar off.

12 They also that seek after my life lay snares for me: and they that seek my hurt

37:30-31 When we share the gospel, we speak the wisdom of God in Christ and of the justice of a holy God, revealed in a perfect Law.

38:11 The Bible's Fascinating Facts. If, down through the ages, scriptural principles had been applied during epidemics such as the Black Plague, millions of lives would have been saved. Long before man understood the principles of quarantine, the Bible spoke of the importance of isolating those who had a contagious disease and of disinfecting their houses. See Leviticus 13 and 14.

speak mischievous things, and imagine deceits all the day long.

13 But I, as a deaf man, heard not; and I was as a dumb man that opens not his mouth.

14 Thus I was as a man that hears not, and in whose mouth are no reproofs.

15 For in you, O LORD, do I hope: you will hear, O Lord my God.

16 For I said, Hear me, lest otherwise they should rejoice over me: when my foot slips, they magnify themselves against me.

17 For I am ready to halt, and my sorrow is continually before me.

18 For I will declare my iniquity; I will be sorry for my sin.

19 But my enemies are lively, and they are strong: and they that hate me wrongfully are multiplied.

20 They also that render evil for good are my adversaries; because I follow the thing that good is.

21 Forsake me not, O LORD: O my God, be not far from me.

22 Make haste to help me, O Lord my salvation.

PSALM 39

I SAID, I will take heed to my ways, that I sin not with my tongue: I will keep my mouth with a bridle, while the wicked is before me.

2 I was dumb with silence, I held my peace, even from good; and my sorrow was stirred.

3 *My heart was hot within me, while I was musing the fire burned: then spoke I with my tongue,*

4 *LORD, make me to know my end, and the measure of my days, what it is: that I may know how frail I am.*

5 Behold, you have made my days as an handbreadth; and my age is as nothing before you: verily every man at his best state is altogether vanity. Selah.

6 Surely every man walks in a vain show: surely they are disquieted in vain: he heaps up riches, and knows not who shall gather them.

7 And now, Lord, what wait I for? my hope is in you.

8 Deliver me from all my transgressions: make me not the reproach of the foolish.

9 I was dumb, I opened not my mouth; because you did it.

10 Remove your stroke away from me: I am consumed by the blow of your hand.

11 When you with rebukes do correct man for iniquity, you make his beauty to consume away like a moth: surely every man is vanity. Selah.

12 Hear my prayer, O LORD, and give ear unto my cry; hold not your peace at my tears: for I am a stranger with you, and a sojourner, as all my fathers were.

13 O spare me, that I may recover strength, before I go hence, and be no more.

PSALM 40

I WAITED *patiently for the* LORD; *and he inclined unto me, and heard my cry.*

2 *He brought me up also out of an horrible pit, out of the miry clay, and set my feet upon a rock, and established my goings.*

3 *And he has put a new song in my mouth, even praise unto our God: many shall see it, and fear, and shall trust in the* LORD.

4 Blessed is that man that makes the LORD his trust, and respects not the proud, nor such as turn aside to lies.

5 Many, O LORD my God, are your wonderful works which you have done, and your thoughts which are to us-ward: they cannot be reckoned up in order unto you: if I would declare and speak of them, they are more than can be numbered.

6 Sacrifice and offering you did not desire; my ears have you opened: burnt offering and sin offering have you not required.

7 Then said I, Lo, I come: in the volume of the book it is written of me,

8 *I delight to do your will, O my God: yes, your law is within my heart.*

9 *I have preached righteousness in the great congregation: lo, I have not refrained my lips, O LORD, you know.*

10 I have not hid your righteousness within my heart; I have declared your faithfulness and your salvation: I have not concealed your lovingkindness and your truth from the great congregation.

11 Withhold not your tender mercies from me, O LORD: let your lovingkindness and your truth continually preserve me.

12 For innumerable evils have compassed me about: my iniquities have taken hold upon me, so that I am not able to look up; they are more than the hairs of my head: therefore my heart fails me.

13 Be pleased, O LORD, to deliver me: O LORD, make haste to help me.

14 Let them be ashamed and confounded together that seek after my soul to destroy it; let them be driven backward and put to shame that wish me evil.

15 Let them be desolate for a reward of their shame that say unto me, Aha, aha.

16 Let all those that seek you rejoice and be glad in you: let such as love your salvation say continually, The LORD be magnified.

17 But I am poor and needy; yet the Lord thinks upon me: you are my help and my deliverer; make no tarrying, O my God.

PSALM 41

B LESSED is he that considers the poor: the LORD will deliver him in time of trouble.

2 The LORD will preserve him, and keep him alive; and he shall be blessed upon the earth: and you will not deliver him unto the will of his enemies.

3 The LORD will strengthen him upon the bed of languishing: you will make all his bed in his sickness.

4 I said, LORD, be merciful unto me: heal my soul; for I have sinned against you.

5 My enemies speak evil of me, When shall he die, and his name perish?

6 And if he come to see me, he speaks vanity: his heart gathers iniquity to itself; when he goes abroad, he tells it.

7 All that hate me whisper together against me: against me do they devise my hurt.

8 An evil disease, say they, cleaves fast unto him: and now that he lies he shall rise up no more.

9 Yes, my own familiar friend, in whom I trusted, which did eat of my bread, has lifted up his heel against me.

10 But you, O LORD, be merciful unto me, and raise me up, that I may requite them.

11 By this I know that you favor me, because my enemy does not triumph over me.

12 And as for me, you uphold me in my integrity, and set me before your face for ever.

13 Blessed be the LORD God of Israel from everlasting, and to everlasting. Amen, and Amen.

· · · · · ·

Read how Charles Spurgeon used the Law. See Galatians 3:19 comment.

· · · · · ·

40:7–9 This is a direct reference to the Messiah (see Hebrews 10:7). Jesus preached righteousness because God's Law was within His heart. When God's Law is written in our hearts, we will delight to do His will and will proclaim the good news of righteousness. We do this by preaching "the righteousness which is of the Law" (Romans 10:5). This will show men that they have sinned, and therefore need a Savior. See Romans 3:19-20.

40:17 King David had great wealth and had his every need met, so he is speaking here in a spiritual sense. Describing himself as "poor and needy" shows he recognized his moral poverty and desperate need for God. See Luke 4:18 comment.

41:9 Messianic Prophecy: This was fulfilled in Mark 14:10.

41:4 *How to Confront Sinners*

When David sinned with Bathsheba, he broke *all* of the Ten Commandments. He coveted his neighbor's wife, lived a lie, stole her, committed adultery, murdered her husband, dishonored his parents, and thus broke the remaining four Commandments by dishonoring God. Therefore, the Lord sent Nathan the prophet to reprove him (2 Samuel 12:1–14).

There is great significance in the order in which the reproof came. Nathan gave David (the shepherd of Israel) a parable about something that David could understand—sheep. He began with the natural realm, rather than immediately exposing the king's sin. He told a story about a rich man who, instead of taking a sheep from his own flock, killed a poor man's pet lamb to feed a stranger.

David was indignant, and sat up on his high throne of self-righteousness. He revealed his knowledge of the Law by declaring that the guilty party must restore fourfold and must die for his crime. Nathan then exposed the king's sin of taking another man's "lamb," saying, "You are the man...Why have you despised the commandment of the Lord, to do evil in his sight?" When David cried, "I have sinned against the Lord," the prophet *then* gave him grace and said, "The Lord also has put away your sin; you shall not die."

Imagine if Nathan, fearful of rejection, changed things around a little, and instead told David, "God loves you and has a wonderful plan for your life. However, there is something that is keeping you from enjoying this wonderful plan; it is called 'sin.'"

Imagine if he had glossed over the *personal nature* of David's sin, with a general reference to *all* men having sinned and fallen short of the glory of God. David's reaction may have been, "What *sin* are you talking about?" rather than to admit his terrible transgression. Think of it —why should he cry, "I have sinned against the Lord" at the sound of *that* message? Instead, he may have, in a sincere desire to experience this "wonderful plan," admitted that he, like all men, had sinned and fallen short of the glory of God.

If David had not been made to *tremble* under the wrath of the Law, the prophet would have removed the very means of producing godly sorrow, which was so necessary for David's repentance. It is "godly sorrow" that produces repentance (2 Corinthians 7:10). It was the weight of David's guilt that caused him to cry out, "I have sinned against the Lord." The Law caused him to labor and become heavy laden; it made him hunger and thirst for righteousness. It enlightened him as to the *serious* nature of sin as far as God was concerned.

PSALM 42

AS the hart pants after the water brooks, so pants my soul after you, O God.

2 My soul thirsts for God, for the living God: when shall I come and appear before God?

3 My tears have been my meat day and night, while they continually say unto me, Where is your God?

4 When I remember these things, I pour out my soul in me: for I had gone with the multitude, I went with them to the house of God, with the voice of joy and praise, with a multitude that kept holyday.

5 Why are you cast down, O my soul? and why are you disquieted in me? hope in God: for I shall yet praise him for the help of his countenance.

6 O my God, my soul is cast down within me: therefore will I remember you from the land of Jordan, and of the Hermonites, from the hill Mizar.

7 Deep calls unto deep at the noise of your waterspouts: all your waves and your billows are gone over me.

8 Yet the LORD will command his lovingkindness in the day time, and in the night his song shall be with me, and my prayer unto the God of my life.

9 I will say unto God my rock, Why have you forgotten me? why go I mourning because of the oppression of the enemy?

10 As with a sword in my bones, my enemies reproach me; while they say daily unto me, Where is your God?

11 Why are you cast down, O my soul? and why are you disquieted within me? hope in God: for I shall yet praise him, who is the health of my countenance, and my God.

PSALM 43

JUDGE me, O God, and plead my cause against an ungodly nation: O deliver me from the deceitful and unjust man.

2 For you are the God of my strength: why do you cast me off? why go I mourning because of the oppression of the enemy?

3 O send out your light and your truth: let them lead me; let them bring me unto your holy hill, and to your tabernacles.

4 Then will I go unto the altar of God, unto God my exceeding joy: yes, upon the harp will I praise you, O God my God.

5 Why are you cast down, O my soul? and why are you disquieted within me? hope in God: for I shall yet praise him, who is the health of my countenance, and my God.

PSALM 44

WE have heard with our ears, O God, our fathers have told us, what work you did in their days, in the times of old.

2 How you did drive out the heathen with your hand, and plant them; how you did afflict the people, and cast them out.

3 For they got not the land in possession by their own sword, neither did their own arm save them: but your right hand, and your arm, and the light of your countenance, because you had a favor unto them.

4 You are my King, O God: command deliverances for Jacob.

5 Through you will we push down our enemies: through your name will we tread them under that rise up against us.

6 For I will not trust in my bow, neither shall my sword save me.

7 But you have saved us from our enemies, and have put them to shame that hated us.

8 In God we boast all the day long, and praise your name for ever. Selah.

9 But you have cast off, and put us to shame; and go not forth with our armies.

10 You make us to turn back from the enemy: and they which hate us spoil for themselves.

11 You have given us like sheep appointed for meat; and have scattered us among the heathen.

12 You sell your people for nought, and do not increase your wealth by their price.

13 You make us a reproach to our neighbors, a scorn and a derision to them that are round about us.

14 You make us a byword among the heathen, a shaking of the head among the people.

15 My confusion is continually before me, and the shame of my face has covered me,

16 For the voice of him that reproaches and blasphemes; by reason of the enemy and avenger.

17 All this is come upon us; yet have we not forgotten you, neither have we dealt falsely in your covenant.

18 Our heart is not turned back, neither have our steps declined from your way;

19 Though you have sore broken us in the place of dragons, and covered us with the shadow of death.

20 If we have forgotten the name of our God, or stretched out our hands to a strange god;

44:21 It is so easy to say, "God sees the heart." Think for a moment how incredible God must be to be able to search the thoughts of even one person. He sees the motives, the desires, and the deepest secrets. Sometimes our thoughts are so numerous that even we have trouble tracking them. Yet God sees the thoughts of every living person on this earth. This can either be a great comfort or a great terror, depending on whether or not our sins are forgiven.

21 Shall not God search this out? for he knows the secrets of the heart.

22 Yes, for your sake are we killed all the day long; we are counted as sheep for the slaughter.

23 Awake, why do you sleep, O Lord? arise, cast us not off for ever.

24 Why do you hide your face, and forget our affliction and our oppression?

25 For our soul is bowed down to the dust: our belly cleaves unto the earth.

26 Arise for our help, and redeem us for your mercies' sake.

PSALM 45

MY heart is inditing a good matter: I speak of the things which I have made touching the king: my tongue is the pen of a ready writer.

2 You are fairer than the children of men: grace is poured into your lips: therefore God has blessed you for ever.

3 Gird your sword upon your thigh, O most mighty, with your glory and your majesty.

4 And in your majesty ride prosperously because of truth and meekness and righteousness; and your right hand shall teach you terrible things.

5 Your arrows are sharp in the heart of the king's enemies; whereby the people fall under you.

6 Your throne, O God, is for ever and ever: the sceptre of your kingdom is a right sceptre.

7 You love righteousness, and hate wickedness: therefore God, your God, has anointed you with the oil of gladness above your fellows.

8 All your garments smell of myrrh, and aloes, and cassia, out of the ivory palaces, whereby they have made you glad.

9 Kings' daughters were among your honorable women: upon your right hand did stand the queen in gold of Ophir.

10 Hearken, O daughter, and consider, and incline your ear; forget also your own people, and your father's house;

> A man can no more possess a private religion than he can possess a private sun and moon.
>
> **G. K. CHESTERTON**

11 So shall the king greatly desire your beauty: for he is your Lord; and worship him.

12 And the daughter of Tyre shall be there with a gift; even the rich among the people shall entreat your favor.

13 The king's daughter is all glorious within: her clothing is of wrought gold.

14 She shall be brought unto the king in raiment of needlework: the virgins her companions that follow her shall be brought unto you.

15 With gladness and rejoicing shall they be brought: they shall enter into the king's palace.

16 Instead of your fathers shall be your children, whom you may make princes in all the earth.

17 I will make your name to be remembered in all generations: therefore shall the people praise you for ever and ever.

PSALM 46

GOD is our refuge and strength, a very present help in trouble.

2 Therefore will not we fear, though the earth be removed, and though the mountains be carried into the midst of the sea;

3 Though the waters thereof roar and be troubled, though the mountains shake with the swelling thereof. Selah.

4 There is a river, the streams whereof shall make glad the city of God, the holy place of the tabernacles of the most High.

5 God is in the midst of her; she shall not be moved: God shall help her, and that right early.

6 The heathen raged, the kingdoms were moved: he uttered his voice, the earth melted.

7 The LORD of hosts is with us; the God of Jacob is our refuge. Selah.

8 Come, behold the works of the LORD, what desolations he has made in the earth.

9 He makes wars to cease unto the end of the earth; he breaks the bow, and cuts the spear in sunder; he burns the chariot in the fire.

10 Be still, and know that I am God: I will be exalted among the heathen, I will be exalted in the earth.

11 The LORD of hosts is with us; the God of Jacob is our refuge. Selah.

PSALM 47

O CLAP your hands, all you people; shout unto God with the voice of triumph.

2 For the LORD most high is terrible; he is a great King over all the earth.

3 He shall subdue the people under us, and the nations under our feet.

4 He shall choose our inheritance for us, the excellency of Jacob whom he loved. Selah.

5 God is gone up with a shout, the LORD with the sound of a trumpet.

6 Sing praises to God, sing praises: sing praises unto our King, sing praises.

7 For God is the King of all the earth: sing praises with understanding.

8 God reigns over the heathen: God sits upon the throne of his holiness.

9 The princes of the people are gathered together, even the people of the God of Abraham: for the shields of the earth belong unto God: he is greatly exalted.

PSALM 48

G REAT is the LORD, and greatly to be praised in the city of our God, in the mountain of his holiness.

2 Beautiful for situation, the joy of the whole earth, is mount Zion, on the sides of the north, the city of the great King.

3 God is known in her palaces for a refuge.

4 For, lo, the kings were assembled, they passed by together.

5 They saw it, and so they marveled; they were troubled, and hasted away.

6 Fear took hold upon them there, and pain, as of a woman in travail.

7 You break the ships of Tarshish with an east wind.

8 As we have heard, so have we seen in the city of the LORD of hosts, in the city of our God: God will establish it for ever. Selah.

9 We have thought of your lovingkindness, O God, in the midst of your temple.

10 According to your name, O God, so is your praise unto the ends of the earth: your right hand is full of righteousness.

11 Let mount Zion rejoice, let the daughters of Judah be glad, because of your judgments.

12 Walk about Zion, and go round about her: tell the towers thereof.

13 Mark well her bulwarks, consider her palaces; that you may tell it to the generation following.

14 For this God is our God for ever and ever: he will be our guide even unto death.

PSALM 49

H EAR this, all you people; give ear, all you inhabitants of the world:

2 Both low and high, rich and poor, together.

49:7   Grief for the Lost. Many of us have felt sorrow and grief over loved ones who don't know the salvation of God. If there was something we could do to save them, we would gladly do it. But often there is nothing we can do but pray—none of us can by any means redeem his brother or give God a ransom for him. We can however, trust God in the fact that One has already become a curse for Israel and for our loved ones. One has already provided the necessary redemption—He has paid the ransom for them. We inherit the promises of God through faith and patience, and therefore rest in the knowledge that God will answer our prayers for our loved ones.

But our zeal for the salvation of sinners shouldn't be limited to our loved ones. Salvation in the heart of the Christian should cause him to love his neighbor as he loves himself.

49:7-8 The blood of Jesus Christ was the precious cost of our redemption, something that humanity could not provide. See 1 Peter 1:18,19.

49:15 *"When you're dead, you're dead."*

What if you are wrong? What if God, Jesus, the prophets, the Jews, and Christians are right and you are wrong? If there is no afterlife, no Judgment Day, no heaven, and no hell, then God is unjust and each of the above is guilty of being a false witness. It means that Almighty God couldn't care less about the fact that a man rapes a woman, then cuts her throat and is never brought to justice. If you are right, and there is no ultimate justice, you won't even have the joy of saying, "I told you so." However, if you are wrong, you will lose your soul and end up eternally damned. You are playing Russian roulette with a fully loaded gun. See Hebrews 9:27 comment.

3 My mouth shall speak of wisdom; and the meditation of my heart shall be of understanding.

4 I will incline my ear to a parable: I will open my dark saying upon the harp.

5 Wherefore should I fear in the days of evil, when the iniquity of my heels shall compass me about?

6 *They that trust in their wealth, and boast themselves in the multitude of their riches;*

7 *None of them can by any means redeem his brother, nor give to God a ransom for him:*

8 *(For the redemption of their soul is precious, and it ceases for ever:)*

9 *That he should still live for ever, and not see corruption.*

10 *For he sees that wise men die, likewise the fool and the brutish person perish, and leave their wealth to others.*

11 *Their inward thought is, that their houses shall continue for ever, and their dwelling places to all generations; they call their lands after their own names.*

12 *Nevertheless man being in honor abides not: he is like the beasts that perish.*

13 *This their way is their folly: yet their posterity approve their sayings. Selah.*

14 *Like sheep they are laid in the grave; death shall feed on them; and the upright shall have dominion over them in the morning; and their beauty shall consume in the grave from their dwelling.*

15 But God will redeem my soul from the power of the grave: for he shall receive me. Selah.

16 Be not afraid when one is made rich, when the glory of his house is increased;

17 For when he dies he shall carry nothing away: his glory shall not descend after him.

18 Though while he lived he blessed his soul: and men will praise you, when you do well to yourself.

19 He shall go to the generation of his fathers; they shall never see light.

20 Man that is in honor, and understands not, is like the beasts that perish.

PSALM 50

THE mighty God, even the LORD, has spoken, and called the earth from the rising of the sun unto the going down thereof.

2 Out of Zion, the perfection of beauty, God has shined.

3 Our God shall come, and shall not keep silence: a fire shall devour before him, and it shall be very tempestuous round about him.

49:17 "When we die we leave behind all that we have, and take with us all that we are."
Chapel of the Air

4 He shall call to the heavens from above, and to the earth, that he may judge his people.

5 Gather my saints together unto me; those that have made a covenant with me by sacrifice.

6 And the heavens shall declare his righteousness: for God is judge himself. Selah.

7 Hear, O my people, and I will speak; O Israel, and I will testify against you: I am God, even your God.

8 I will not reprove you for your sacrifices or your burnt offerings, to have been continually before me.

9 I will take no bullock out of your house, nor he goats out of your folds.

10 For every beast of the forest is mine, and the cattle upon a thousand hills.

11 I know all the fowls of the mountains: and the wild beasts of the field are mine.

12 If I were hungry, I would not tell you: for the world is mine, and the fullness thereof.

13 Will I eat the flesh of bulls, or drink the blood of goats?

14 Offer unto God thanksgiving; and pay your vows unto the most High:

15 **And call upon me in the day of trouble: I will deliver you, and you shall glorify me.**

16 But unto the wicked God says, What have you to do to declare my statutes, or that you should take my covenant in your mouth?

17 Seeing you hate instruction, and cast my words behind you.

18 When you saw a thief, then you consented with him, and have been partaker with adulterers.

19 You give your mouth to evil, and your tongue frames deceit.

20 You sit and speak against your brother; you slander your own mother's son.

21 These things have you done, and I kept silence; you thought that I was altogether such an one as yourself: but I will reprove you, and set them in order before your eyes.

22 **Now consider this, you that forget God, lest I tear you in pieces, and there be none to deliver.**

23 **Whoso offers praise glorifies me: and to him that orders his conversation aright will I show the salvation of God.**

PSALM 51

HAVE mercy upon me, O God, according to your lovingkindness: according unto the multitude of your tender mercies blot out my transgressions.

2 **Wash me thoroughly from my iniquity, and cleanse me from my sin.**

3 **For I acknowledge my transgressions: and my sin is ever before me.**

4 **Against you, you only, have I sinned, and done this evil in your sight: that you might be justified when you speak, and be clear when you judge.**

5 **Behold, I was shaped in iniquity; and in sin did my mother conceive me.**

50:16 Verses 16–23 contain a fearful word for a godless world that delights in entertainment glorifying theft, violence, adultery, and hatred. They assume that heaven's silence is heaven's sanction. God threatens fearful wrath, then offers salvation to those who will listen. This is the biblical order of gospel proclamation—Law before grace.

51:1–4 When a sinner is ready for salvation, he exhibits personal responsibility for his sins. In these four verses David uses the words *me*, *my*, and *I* ten times in reference to his sins. See also Luke 15:21 comment.

51:6 Civil law can, under some circumstances, search your house, your car and even your person. But under no circumstances can civil law search your heart. Civil law cannot detect human thoughts or desires. God's Law, however, searches the inward parts. Like ten hungry bloodhounds, it chases the scent of injustice. It will pursue the guilty criminal until he is brought to justice. There is only one way for the ten ravenous hounds to leave the trail: sinners must cross over a "river." There is a river of blood that flows from Calvary's cross. Only the blood of Jesus Christ satisfies the Law's insatiable appetite for righteousness. See Hebrews 9:22.

51:6 How to Use the Ten Commandments in Witnessing

This should be done in a spirit of love and gentleness:

"Do you think you have kept the Ten Commandments? Have you ever told a lie (including 'white lies,' half-truths, exaggerations, etc.)? If you have, then you are a 'liar,' and you cannot enter the kingdom of God. Have you ever stolen (the value is irrelevant)? Then you are a thief. Jesus said that if you look with lust, you have committed adultery in your heart. If you hate someone, then you have committed murder in your heart. God requires truth 'in the inward parts'—He sees even the thought-life.

"Have you loved God above all else? Has He always been first in your affections? Have you made a 'god' to suit yourself (having your own beliefs about God)? That is called idolatry, and the Bible warns that no idolater will enter the kingdom of God. Have you ever used God's holy name to curse, or been greedy? Have you kept the Sabbath holy? Have you always implicitly honored your parents? Have you broken any of the Ten Commandments?

"Knowing that God has seen your thought-life and every deed done in darkness, will you be innocent or guilty on Judgment Day? You know you will be guilty. So, will you end up in heaven or hell?"

The Law brings individuals to a point of seeing that they have sinned against God— that His wrath abides on them. It causes them to see that their own "goodness" can't save them. It stops their mouth of justification (Romans 3:19), and prepares the heart for the good news of the gospel:

"The only thing you can do to be saved from His wrath is to repent and put your faith in the Savior, Jesus Christ. When He died on the cross, He took the punishment for our sins. He, once and for all, stepped into the Courtroom and completely paid the fine for us. Then He rose from the dead, defeating death. If you want to be saved from God's wrath, confess and forsake your sins, put your faith in Jesus for your eternal salvation, and you will pass from death into life. Then read the Bible daily and obey what you read (see John 14:21). God will never let you down."

6 Behold, you desire truth in the inward parts: and in the hidden part you shall make me to know wisdom.

7 Purge me with hyssop, and I shall be clean: wash me, and I shall be whiter than snow.

8 Make me to hear joy and gladness; that the bones which you have broken may rejoice.

9 Hide your face from my sins, and blot out all my iniquities.

10 Create in me a clean heart, O God; and renew a right spirit within me.

11 Cast me not away from your presence; and take not your holy spirit from me.

12 Restore unto me the joy of your salvation; and uphold me with your free spirit.

13 Then will I teach transgressors your ways; and sinners shall be converted unto you.

51:7 "Direct my thoughts, words, and work. Wash away my sins in the immaculate Blood of the Lamb, and purge my heart by Thy Holy Spirit...Daily frame me more and more into the likeness of Thy Son Jesus Christ." George Washington, in his prayer book

51:10 Those who confess and forsake their sins are given a clean heart in Christ, and the fruit of genuine salvation is a concern for the lost. See verse 13.

51:13–17 "Transgressors" are those who have transgressed the Moral Law. It is the "schoolmaster" (Galatians 3:24) that teaches them that they are sinners in the eyes of God (Romans 3:19-20). It is the Law that sings aloud of God's righteousness, breaks the human spirit, and gives the sinner reason to be contrite over sins in which he previously delighted. See Romans 7:13,24-25.

14 Deliver me from bloodguiltiness, O God, you God of my salvation: and my tongue shall sing aloud of your righteousness.

15 O Lord, open my lips; and my mouth shall show forth your praise.

16 For you desire not sacrifice; else would I give it: you delight not in burnt offering.

17 **The sacrifices of God are a broken spirit: a broken and a contrite heart, O God, you will not despise.**

18 Do good in your good pleasure unto Zion: build the walls of Jerusalem.

19 Then shall you be pleased with the sacrifices of righteousness, with burnt offering and whole burnt offering: then shall they offer bullocks upon your altar.

PSALM 52

WHY boast yourself in mischief, O mighty man? the goodness of God endures continually.

2 The tongue devises mischiefs; like a sharp razor, working deceitfully.

3 You love evil more than good; and lying rather than to speak righteousness. Selah.

4 You love all devouring words, O you deceitful tongue.

5 God shall likewise destroy you for ever, he shall take you away, and pluck you out of your dwelling place, and root you out of the land of the living. Selah.

6 The righteous also shall see, and fear, and shall laugh at him:

7 Lo, this is the man that made not God his strength; but trusted in the abundance of his riches, and strengthened himself in his wickedness.

8 But I am like a green olive tree in the house of God: I trust in the mercy of God for ever and ever.

9 I will praise you for ever, because you have done it: and I will wait on your name; for it is good before your saints.

PSALM 53

THE fool has said in his heart, There is no God. Corrupt are they, and have done abominable iniquity: there is none that does good.

2 God looked down from heaven upon the children of men, to see if there were any that did understand, that did seek God.

3 Every one of them is gone back: they are altogether become filthy; there is none that does good, no, not one.

52:7 The New Testament reminds us of this truth: We cannot love God *and* mammon (Luke 16:13).

53:1 Atheism. It is much more reasonable to believe that this publication had no printer than to believe that there is no God. Who in his right mind would ever believe that no one compiled its pages, no one produced the graphic art, and no one printed it. The publication happened by chance...from nothing. There was no paper, no ink, no cardboard, and no glue. The paper just came into being (from nothing), then trimmed itself into perfectly straight edges. All the words fell into place, forming coherent sentences, and then the graphic art appeared. The pages fell into numerical order, and finally the book bound itself.

The fact that there was a printer is axiomatic (self-evident), so it would be intellectually insulting to even begin to argue for the case of the printer's existence. For the same reason, the Bible does not enter into the case for God's existence. It simply begins by stating, "In the beginning God..." (Genesis 1:1). See Psalm 90:2 comment.

"It takes no brains to be an atheist. Any stupid person can deny the existence of a supernatural power because man's physical senses cannot detect it. But there cannot be ignored the influence of conscience, the respect we feel for the Moral Law, the mystery of first life...or the marvelous order in which the universe moves about us on this earth. All these evidence the handiwork of the beneficent Deity...That Deity is the God of the Bible and Jesus Christ, His Son." Dwight Eisenhower

53:1–3 There are many "good" people from man's viewpoint. However, here is *God's* point of view. These verses leave no room for the self-righteous.

4 Have the workers of iniquity no knowledge? who eat up my people as they eat bread: they have not called upon God.

5 There were they in great fear, where no fear was: for God has scattered the bones of him that encamps against you: you have put them to shame, because God has despised them.

6 Oh that the salvation of Israel were come out of Zion! When God brings back the captivity of his people, Jacob shall rejoice, and Israel shall be glad.

PSALM 54

SAVE me, O God, by your name, and judge me by your strength.

2 Hear my prayer, O God; give ear to the words of my mouth.

3 For strangers are risen up against me, and oppressors seek after my soul: they have not set God before them. Selah.

4 Behold, God is my helper: the Lord is with them that uphold my soul.

5 He shall reward evil unto my enemies: cut them off in your truth.

6 I will freely sacrifice unto you: I will praise your name, O LORD; for it is good.

7 For he has delivered me out of all trouble: and my eye has seen his desire upon my enemies.

PSALM 55

GIVE ear to my prayer, O God; and hide not yourself from my supplication.

2 Attend unto me, and hear me: I mourn in my complaint, and make a noise;

3 Because of the voice of the enemy, because of the oppression of the wicked: for they cast iniquity upon me, and in wrath they hate me.

4 My heart is sore pained within me: and the terrors of death are fallen upon me.

5 Fearfulness and trembling are come upon me, and horror has overwhelmed me.

6 And I said, Oh that I had wings like a dove! for then would I fly away, and be at rest.

> Holy practice
> is the most decisive evidence
> of the reality of our repentance.
>
> **JONATHAN EDWARDS**
> 1703-1758
> THEOLOGIAN AND
> THIRD PRESIDENT OF PRINCETON

7 Lo, then would I wander far off, and remain in the wilderness. Selah.

8 I would hasten my escape from the windy storm and tempest.

9 Destroy, O Lord, and divide their tongues: for I have seen violence and strife in the city.

10 Day and night they go about it upon the walls thereof: mischief also and sorrow are in the midst of it.

11 Wickedness is in the midst thereof: deceit and guile depart not from her streets.

12 For it was not an enemy that reproached me; then I could have borne it: neither was it he that hated me that did magnify himself against me; then I would have hid myself from him:

13 But it was you, a man my equal, my guide, and my acquaintance.

14 We took sweet counsel together, and walked unto the house of God in company.

15 Let death seize upon them, and let them go down quick into hell: for wickedness is in their dwellings, and among them.

16 As for me, I will call upon God; and the LORD shall save me.

17 Evening, and morning, and at noon, will I pray, and cry aloud: and he shall hear my voice.

18 He has delivered my soul in peace from the battle that was against me: for there were many with me.

19 God shall hear, and afflict them, even he that abides of old. Selah. Because they have no changes, therefore they fear not God.

20 He has put forth his hands against such as be at peace with him: he has broken his covenant.

55:15   *"I don't mind going to hell. All my friends will be there."*

Obviously, those who flippantly say such things don't believe in the biblical concept of hell. Their understanding of the nature of God is erroneous. The slow-witted criminal thinks that the electric chair is a place to put up his feet for a while and relax.

It may be wise therefore to speak with him for a few moments about the *reasonableness* of a place called hell. Reason with him by saying, "If a judge turns a blind eye to the unlawful dealings of the Mafia, if he sees their murderous acts and deliberately turns the other way, is he a good or bad judge? He's obviously corrupt, and should be brought to justice himself. If he is a good judge, he will do everything within his power to bring those murderers to justice. He should make sure that they are justly punished.

"If Almighty God sees a man rape and strangle to death your sister or mother, do you think He should look the other way, or bring that murderer to justice? If He looks the other way, He's corrupt and should be brought to justice Himself. It makes sense then, that if God is good, He will do everything in His power to ensure justice is done. The Bible tells us that He *will* punish murderers, and the place of punishment—the prison God will send them to—is a place called hell.

"God should punish murderers and rapists. However, God is so good, He will also punish thieves, liars, adulterers, fornicators, and blasphemers. He will even punish those who *desired* to murder and rape but never took the opportunity. He warns that if we hate someone, we commit murder in our hearts. If we lust, we commit adultery in the heart, etc."

Then take the time to tell him of the *reality* of hell. Sinners like to picture hell as a fun, hedonistic, pleasure-filled place where they can engage in all the sensual sins that are forbidden here. But Jesus said that it is a place of torment, where the worm never dies and the fire is never quenched (Mark 9:43-44). We tend to forget what pain is like when we don't have it. Can you begin to imagine how terrible it would be to be in agony, with no hope of relief?

Many human beings go insane if they are merely isolated for a long time from other people. Imagine how terrible it would be if God simply withdrew all the things we hold so dear—friendship, love, color, light, peace, joy, laughter, and security. Hell isn't just a place with an absence of God's blessings, it is punishment for sin. It is literal torment, forever. That's why the Bible warns that it is a fearful thing to fall into the hands of the living God.

God has given His Law to convince men of their sins, and unless a sinner is convinced that he has sinned against God, he won't see that hell is his eternal destiny. He may consider it a fit place for others, but not for himself. That's why we mustn't hesitate to open up the Law and show that each individual is personally responsible for sin, and that God's wrath abides on him because of it.

Ask him to consider why you would say such a thing to him if it wasn't true. Tell him to examine your motives. You are so concerned for his eternal welfare that you are prepared to risk offending him.

Then ask him if he would sell an eye for a million dollars. Would he sell *both* for ten million? No one in his right mind would. Our eyes are precious to us. How much more then is our eternal soul worth? (For a biblical description of hell, see Revelation 1:18 comment.)

21 The words of his mouth were smoother than butter, but war was in his heart: his words were softer than oil, yet were they drawn swords.

22 Cast your burden upon the LORD, and he shall sustain you: he shall never suffer the righteous to be moved.

55:22 What an incredible promise—we have an anchor for the soul. See Matthew 6:25–34 for some of the ways the Lord sustains us.

23 But you, O God, shall bring them down into the pit of destruction: bloody and deceitful men shall not live out half their days; but I will trust in you.

PSALM 56

BE merciful unto me, O God: for man would swallow me up; he fighting daily oppresses me.

2 My enemies would daily swallow me up: for they be many that fight against me, O you most High.

3 *What time I am afraid, I will trust in you.*

4 *In God I will praise his word, in God I have put my trust; I will not fear what flesh can do unto me.*

5 Every day they wrest my words: all their thoughts are against me for evil.

6 They gather themselves together, they hide themselves, they mark my steps, when they wait for my soul.

7 Shall they escape by iniquity? in your anger cast down the people, O God.

8 You tell my wanderings: put my tears into your bottle: are they not in your book?

9 When I cry unto you, then shall my enemies turn back: this I know; for God is for me.

10 In God will I praise his word: in the LORD will I praise his word.

11 In God have I put my trust: I will not be afraid what man can do unto me.

12 Your vows are upon me, O God: I will render praises unto you.

13 For you have delivered my soul from death: will not you deliver my feet from falling, that I may walk before God in the light of the living?

PSALM 57

BE merciful unto me, O God, be merciful unto me: for my soul trusts in you: yes, in the shadow of your wings will I make my refuge, until these calamities be overpast.

2 I will cry unto God most high; unto God that performs all things for me.

3 He shall send from heaven, and save me from the reproach of him that would swallow me up. Selah. God shall send forth his mercy and his truth.

4 My soul is among lions: and I lie even among them that are set on fire, even the sons of men, whose teeth are spears and arrows, and their tongue a sharp sword.

5 Be exalted, O God, above the heavens; let your glory be above all the earth.

6 They have prepared a net for my steps; my soul is bowed down: they have digged a pit before me, into the midst whereof they are fallen themselves. Selah.

7 My heart is fixed, O God, my heart is fixed: I will sing and give praise.

8 Awake up, my glory; awake, psaltery and harp: I myself will awake early.

9 I will praise you, O Lord, among the people: I will sing unto you among the nations.

10 For your mercy is great unto the heavens, and your truth unto the clouds.

11 Be exalted, O God, above the heavens: let your glory be above all the earth.

PSALM 58

DO you indeed speak righteousness, O congregation? do you judge uprightly, O you sons of men?

56:11 The fear of man is the devil's paralyzing poison. Faith in God is the antidote. When the enemy feeds you the lie that you cannot share your faith, answer him with, "I can do all things through Christ which strengthens me" (Philippians 4:13). Then put works with your faith—follow your convictions. Don't be concerned if you don't *feel* compassion for the lost. If a firefighter rescues someone from a burning building, he may have saved the person because he was motivated by compassion or because it was the job he had committed himself to do. His motive is of little concern to the person who has been pulled from the flames.

56:11 "Stop caring about what people think; begin to think about caring for people." Emeal Zwayne

2 Yes, in heart you work wickedness; you weigh the violence of your hands in the earth.

3 The wicked are estranged from the womb: they go astray as soon as they be born, speaking lies.

4 Their poison is like the poison of a serpent: they are like the deaf adder that stops her ear;

5 Which will not hearken to the voice of charmers, charming never so wisely.

6 Break their teeth, O God, in their mouth: break out the great teeth of the young lions, O LORD.

7 Let them melt away as waters which run continually: when he bends his bow to shoot his arrows, let them be as cut in pieces.

8 As a snail which melts, let every one of them pass away: like the untimely birth of a woman, that they may not see the sun.

9 Before your pots can feel the thorns, he shall take them away as with a whirlwind, both living, and in his wrath.

10 The righteous shall rejoice when he sees the vengeance: he shall wash his feet in the blood of the wicked.

11 So that a man shall say, Verily there is a reward for the righteous: verily he is a God that judges in the earth.

PSALM 59

DELIVER me from my enemies, O my God: defend me from them that rise up against me.

2 Deliver me from the workers of iniquity, and save me from bloody men.

3 For, lo, they lie in wait for my soul: the mighty are gathered against me; not for my transgression, nor for my sin, O LORD.

To learn the beliefs of Hindus and how to witness to them, see comment in 2 Thessalonians, Chapter 3

4 They run and prepare themselves without my fault: awake to help me, and behold.

5 You therefore, O LORD God of hosts, the God of Israel, awake to visit all the heathen: be not merciful to any wicked transgressors. Selah.

6 They return at evening: they make a noise like a dog, and go round about the city.

7 Behold, they belch out with their mouth: swords are in their lips: for who, say they, does hear?

8 But you, O LORD, shall laugh at them; you shall have all the heathen in derision.

9 Because of his strength will I wait upon you: for God is my defense.

10 The God of my mercy shall prevent me: God shall let me see my desire upon my enemies.

11 Slay them not, lest my people forget: scatter them by your power; and bring them down, O Lord our shield.

12 For the sin of their mouth and the words of their lips let them even be taken in their pride: and for cursing and lying which they speak.

58:6 Some have wondered how David could possibly be "a man after [God's] own heart" (Acts 13:22) when he exhibited such a vindictive attitude. However, he was merely pouring out his anger in prayer. Let it be a lesson to those of us who would like to seek vengeance—take it to God in prayer. Those who learn that secret prayer is the place to leave grievances will find that like David, they can then show mercy to those who have wronged them (see 1 Samuel 26:1–12).

> The root of joy is gratefulness...
> It is not joy that makes us grateful;
> it is gratitude that makes us joyful.
>
> **DAVID STEINDL-RAST**

13 Consume them in wrath, consume them, that they may not be: and let them know that God rules in Jacob unto the ends of the earth. Selah.

14 And at evening let them return; and let them make a noise like a dog, and go round about the city.

15 Let them wander up and down for meat, and grudge if they be not satisfied.

16 But I will sing of your power; yes, I will sing aloud of your mercy in the morning: for you have been my defense and refuge in the day of my trouble.

17 Unto you, O my strength, will I sing: for God is my defense, and the God of my mercy.

PSALM 60

O GOD, you have cast us off, you have scattered us, you have been displeased; O turn yourself to us again.

2 You have made the earth to tremble; you have broken it: heal the breaches thereof; for it shakes.

3 You have showed your people hard things: you have made us to drink the wine of astonishment.

4 You have given a banner to them that fear you, that it may be displayed because of the truth. Selah.

5 That your beloved may be delivered; save with your right hand, and hear me.

6 God has spoken in his holiness; I will rejoice, I will divide Shechem, and mete out the valley of Succoth.

7 Gilead is mine, and Manasseh is mine; Ephraim also is the strength of my head; Judah is my lawgiver;

8 Moab is my washpot; over Edom will I cast out my shoe: Philistia, triumph because of me.

9 Who will bring me into the strong city? who will lead me into Edom?

10 Will not you, O God, which had cast us off? and you, O God, which did not go out with our armies?

11 Give us help from trouble: for vain is the help of man.

12 Through God we shall do valiantly: for he it is that shall tread down our enemies.

PSALM 61

H EAR my cry, O God; attend unto my prayer.

2 From the end of the earth will I cry unto you, when my heart is overwhelmed: lead me to the rock that is higher than I.

3 For you have been a shelter for me, and a strong tower from the enemy.

4 I will abide in your tabernacle for ever: I will trust in the covert of your wings. Selah.

5 For you, O God, have heard my vows: you have given me the heritage of those that fear your name.

6 You will prolong the king's life: and his years as many generations.

7 He shall abide before God for ever: O prepare mercy and truth, which may preserve him.

8 So will I sing praise unto your name for ever, that I may daily perform my vows.

PSALM 62

T RULY my soul waits upon God: from him comes my salvation.

2 He only is my rock and my salvation; he is my defense; I shall not be greatly moved.

3 How long will you imagine mischief against a man? you shall be slain all of you: as a bowing wall shall you be, and as a tottering fence.

4 They only consult to cast him down from his excellency: they delight in lies: they bless with their mouth, but they curse inwardly. Selah.

5 My soul, wait only upon God; for my expectation is from him.

6 He only is my rock and my salvation: he is my defense; I shall not be moved.

7 In God is my salvation and my glory: the rock of my strength, and my refuge, is in God.

8 **Trust in him at all times; you people, pour out your heart before him: God is a refuge for us. Selah.**

9 Surely men of low degree are vanity, and men of high degree are a lie: to be laid in the balance, they are altogether lighter than vanity.

10 Trust not in oppression, and become not vain in robbery: if riches increase, set not your heart upon them.

11 God has spoken once; twice have I heard this; that power belongs unto God.

12 Also unto you, O Lord, belongs mercy: for you render to every man according to his work.

PSALM 63

O GOD, you are my God; early will I seek you: my soul thirsts for you, my flesh longs for you in a dry and thirsty land, where no water is;

2 To see your power and your glory, so as I have seen you in the sanctuary.

3 Because your lovingkindness is better than life, my lips shall praise you.

4 Thus will I bless you while I live: I will lift up my hands in your name.

5 My soul shall be satisfied as with marrow and fatness; and my mouth shall praise you with joyful lips:

6 When I remember you upon my bed, and meditate on you in the night watches.

7 Because you have been my help, therefore in the shadow of your wings will I rejoice.

8 My soul follows hard after you: your right hand upholds me.

9 But those that seek my soul, to destroy it, shall go into the lower parts of the earth.

10 They shall fall by the sword: they shall be a portion for foxes.

11 But the king shall rejoice in God; every one that swears by him shall glory: but the mouth of them that speak lies shall be stopped.

Worshipping God and the Lamb in the temple: God, for his benefaction in creating all things, and the Lamb, for his benefaction in redeeming us with His blood.

Isaac Newton

1642-1747

BRITISH PHYSICIST

AND MATHEMATICIAN

PSALM 64

H EAR my voice, O God, in my prayer: preserve my life from fear of the enemy.

2 Hide me from the secret counsel of the wicked; from the insurrection of the workers of iniquity:

3 Who whet their tongue like a sword, and bend their bows to shoot their arrows, even bitter words:

4 That they may shoot in secret at the perfect: suddenly do they shoot at him, and fear not.

5 They encourage themselves in an evil matter: they commune of laying snares privily; they say, Who shall see them?

6 They search out iniquities; they accomplish a diligent search: both the inward thought of every one of them, and the heart, is deep.

7 But God shall shoot at them with an arrow; suddenly shall they be wounded.

8 So they shall make their own tongue to fall upon themselves: all that see them shall flee away.

9 And all men shall fear, and shall declare the work of God; for they shall wisely consider of his doing.

10 The righteous shall be glad in the LORD, and shall trust in him; and all the upright in heart shall glory.

PSALM 65

P RAISE waits for you, O God, in Sion: and unto you shall the vow be performed.

2 O you that hears prayer, unto you shall all flesh come.

3 Iniquities prevail against me: as for our transgressions, you shall purge them away.

4 Blessed is the man whom you choose, and cause to approach unto you, that he may dwell in your courts: we shall be satisfied with the goodness of your house, even of your holy temple.

5 By terrible things in righteousness will you answer us, O God of our salvation; who are the confidence of all the ends of the earth, and of them that are afar off upon the sea:

6 Which by his strength set fast the mountains; being girded with power:

7 Which still the noise of the seas, the noise of their waves, and the tumult of the people.

8 They also that dwell in the uttermost parts are afraid at your tokens: you make the outgoings of the morning and evening to rejoice.

9 You visit the earth, and water it: you greatly enrich it with the river of God, which is full of water: you prepare them corn, when you have so provided for it.

10 You water the ridges thereof abundantly: you set the furrows thereof: you make it soft with showers: you bless the springing thereof.

11 You crown the year with your goodness; and your paths drop fatness.

12 They drop upon the pastures of the wilderness: and the little hills rejoice on every side.

13 The pastures are clothed with flocks; the valleys also are covered over with corn; they shout for joy, they also sing.

PSALM 66

M AKE a joyful noise unto God, all you lands:

2 Sing forth the honor of his name: make his praise glorious.

3 Say unto God, How terrible are you in your works! through the greatness of your power shall your enemies submit themselves unto you.

4 All the earth shall worship you, and shall sing unto you; they shall sing to your name. Selah.

5 Come and see the works of God: he is terrible in his doing toward the children of men.

6 He turned the sea into dry land: they went through the flood on foot: there did we rejoice in him.

7 He rules by his power for ever; his eyes behold the nations: let not the rebellious exalt themselves. Selah.

8 O bless our God, you people, and make the voice of his praise to be heard:

9 Which hold our soul in life, and suffers not our feet to be moved.

10 For you, O God, have proved us: you have tried us, as silver is tried.

11 You brought us into the net; you laid affliction upon our loins.

12 You have caused men to ride over our heads; we went through fire and through

---

66:10–12 We often blame tribulation on the enemy when God uses this very instrument to fulfill His will for our lives. God takes us through the fire, not to burn us, but to purify us. He takes us through the water, not to drown us, but to wash us. Understanding that the Lord chastens those He loves enables us to endure trials. The psalmist wrote, "It is good for me that I have been afflicted; that I might learn your statutes" (119:71). See also Hebrews 12:10–13.

water: but you brought us out into a wealthy place.

13 I will go into your house with burnt offerings: I will pay you my vows,

14 Which my lips have uttered, and my mouth has spoken, when I was in trouble.

15 I will offer unto you burnt sacrifices of fatlings, with the incense of rams; I will offer bullocks with goats. Selah.

16 Come and hear, all you that fear God, and I will declare what he has done for my soul.

17 I cried unto him with my mouth, and he was extolled with my tongue.

18 If I regard iniquity in my heart, the Lord will not hear me:

19 But verily God has heard me; he has attended to the voice of my prayer.

20 Blessed be God, which has not turned away my prayer, nor his mercy from me.

PSALM 67

GOD be merciful unto us, and bless us; and cause his face to shine upon us; Selah.

2 That your way may be known upon earth, your saving health among all nations.

3 Let the people praise you, O God; let all the people praise you.

4 O let the nations be glad and sing for joy: for you shall judge the people righteously, and govern the nations upon earth. Selah.

5 Let the people praise you, O God; let all the people praise you.

6 Then shall the earth yield her increase; and God, even our own God, shall bless us.

7 God shall bless us; and all the ends of the earth shall fear him.

· · · · · ·

Read a challenging letter from an atheist. See Romans 9:2-3 comment.

· · · · · ·

PSALM 68

LET God arise, let his enemies be scattered: let them also that hate him flee before him.

2 As smoke is driven away, so drive them away: as wax melts before the fire, so let the wicked perish at the presence of God.

3 But let the righteous be glad; let them rejoice before God: yes, let them exceedingly rejoice.

4 Sing unto God, sing praises to his name: extol him that rides upon the heavens by his name JAH, and rejoice before him.

5 A father of the fatherless, and a judge of the widows, is God in his holy habitation.

6 God sets the solitary in families: he brings out those which are bound with chains: but the rebellious dwell in a dry land.

66:15 Animal rights advocates who insist that "meat is murder" are misguided. God was the first to kill an animal (Genesis 3:21). In Exodus 12:5–8 God told Israel to kill and eat lambs. King Solomon sacrificed 22,000 oxen and 120,000 sheep when he dedicated the temple to God (1 Kings 8:63). When three angels appeared to Abraham, he killed a "tender and good" calf for them to eat (Genesis 18:7-8). In Genesis 27:7 we are told that Jacob ate venison (deer meat), which was his favorite food. Jesus ate the Passover lamb (Mark 14:12,18). In the parable of the prodigal son, the father rejoiced at his son's return by "killing the fatted calf" (which was eaten). See 1 Timothy 4:3,4 comment.

67:4 "It is the duty of all nations to acknowledge the Providence of Almighty God, to obey His will, to be grateful for His benefits, and humbly to implore His protection and favor." George Washington

"The foundations of our society and our government rest so much on the teachings of the Bible that it would be difficult to support them if faith in these teachings would cease to be practically universal in our country." Calvin Coolidge

> Beloved, we must win souls;
> we cannot live and see men damned.
>
> **CHARLES SPURGEON**

7 O God, when you went forth before your people, when you did march through the wilderness; Selah:

8 The earth shook, the heavens also dropped at the presence of God: even Sinai itself was moved at the presence of God, the God of Israel.

9 You, O God, did send a plentiful rain, whereby you did confirm your inheritance, when it was weary.

10 Your congregation has dwelt therein: you, O God, have prepared of your goodness for the poor.

11 The Lord gave the word: great was the company of those that published it.

12 Kings of armies did flee apace: and she that tarried at home divided the spoil.

13 Though you have lien among the pots, yet shall you be as the wings of a dove covered with silver, and her feathers with yellow gold.

14 When the Almighty scattered kings in it, it was white as snow in Salmon.

15 The hill of God is as the hill of Bashan; an high hill as the hill of Bashan.

16 Why do you leap, you high hills? this is the hill which God desires to dwell in; yes, the LORD will dwell in it for ever.

17 The chariots of God are twenty thousand, even thousands of angels: the Lord is among them, as in Sinai, in the holy place.

18 You have ascended on high, you have led captivity captive: you have received gifts for men; yes, for the rebellious also, that the LORD God might dwell among them.

19 Blessed be the Lord, who daily loads us with benefits, even the God of our salvation. Selah.

20 He that is our God is the God of salvation; and unto GOD the Lord belong the issues from death.

21 But God shall wound the head of his enemies, and the hairy scalp of such an one as goes on still in his trespasses.

22 The Lord said, I will bring again from Bashan, I will bring my people again from the depths of the sea:

23 That your foot may be dipped in the blood of your enemies, and the tongue of your dogs in the same.

24 They have seen your goings, O God; even the goings of my God, my King, in the sanctuary.

25 The singers went before, the players on instruments followed after; among them were the damsels playing with timbrels.

26 Bless God in the congregations, even the Lord, from the fountain of Israel.

27 There is little Benjamin with their ruler, the princes of Judah and their council, the princes of Zebulun, and the princes of Naphtali.

28 Your God has commanded your strength: strengthen, O God, that which you have wrought for us.

29 Because of your temple at Jerusalem shall kings bring presents unto you.

30 Rebuke the company of spearmen, the multitude of the bulls, with the calves of the people, till every one submit himself with pieces of silver: scatter the people that delight in war.

31 Princes shall come out of Egypt; Ethiopia shall soon stretch out her hands unto God.

32 Sing unto God, you kingdoms of the earth; O sing praises unto the Lord; Selah:

33 To him that rides upon the heavens of heavens, which were of old; lo, he does send out his voice, and that a mighty voice.

34 Ascribe strength unto God: his excellency is over Israel, and his strength is in the clouds.

35 O God, you are terrible out of your holy places: the God of Israel is he that gives strength and power unto his people. Blessed be God.

PSALM 69

SAVE me, O God; for the waters are come in unto my soul.

2 I sink in deep mire, where there is no standing: I am come into deep waters, where the floods overflow me.

3 I am weary of my crying: my throat is dried: my eyes fail while I wait for my God.

4 They that hate me without a cause are more than the hairs of my head: they that would destroy me, being my enemies wrongfully, are mighty: then I restored that which I took not away.

5 O God, you know my foolishness; and my sins are not hid from you.

6 Let not them that wait on you, O Lord GOD of hosts, be ashamed for my sake: let not those that seek you be confounded for my sake, O God of Israel.

7 Because for your sake I have borne reproach; shame has covered my face.

8 I am become a stranger unto my brethren, and an alien unto my mother's children.

9 For the zeal of your house has eaten me up; and the reproaches of them that reproached you are fallen upon me.

10 When I wept, and chastened my soul with fasting, that was to my reproach.

11 I made sackcloth also my garment; and I became a proverb to them.

12 They that sit in the gate speak against me; and I was the song of the drunkards.

13 But as for me, my prayer is unto you, O LORD, in an acceptable time: O God, in the multitude of your mercy hear me, in the truth of your salvation.

14 Deliver me out of the mire, and let me not sink: let me be delivered from them that hate me, and out of the deep waters.

15 Let not the waterflood overflow me, neither let the deep swallow me up, and let not the pit shut her mouth upon me.

16 Hear me, O LORD; for your lovingkindness is good: turn unto me according to the multitude of your tender mercies.

17 And hide not your face from your servant; for I am in trouble: hear me speedily.

18 Draw near unto my soul, and redeem it: deliver me because of my enemies.

19 You have known my reproach, and my shame, and my dishonor: my adversaries are all before you.

20 Reproach has broken my heart; and I am full of heaviness: and I looked for some to take pity, but there was none; and for comforters, but I found none.

21 They gave me also gall for my meat; and in my thirst they gave me vinegar to drink.

22 Let their table become a snare before them: and that which should have been for their welfare, let it become a trap.

23 Let their eyes be darkened, that they see not; and make their loins continually to shake.

24 Pour out your indignation upon them, and let your wrathful anger take hold of them.

25 Let their habitation be desolate; and let none dwell in their tents.

26 For they persecute him whom you have smitten; and they talk to the grief of those whom you have wounded.

27 Add iniquity unto their iniquity: and let them not come into your righteousness.

28 Let them be blotted out of the book of the living, and not be written with the righteous.

29 But I am poor and sorrowful: let your salvation, O God, set me up on high.

30 I will praise the name of God with a song, and will magnify him with thanksgiving.

31 This also shall please the LORD better than an ox or bullock that has horns and hoofs.

32 The humble shall see this, and be glad: and your heart shall live that seek God.

69:9 This is a direct reference to the Messiah. See John 2:17.

69:21 Messianic prophecy: This was fulfilled in John 19:29.

33 For the LORD hears the poor, and despises not his prisoners.

34 Let the heaven and earth praise him, the seas, and every thing that moves therein.

35 For God will save Zion, and will build the cities of Judah: that they may dwell there, and have it in possession.

36 The seed also of his servants shall inherit it: and they that love his name shall dwell therein.

PSALM 70

MAKE haste, O God, to deliver me; make haste to help me, O LORD.

2 Let them be ashamed and confounded that seek after my soul: let them be turned backward, and put to confusion, that desire my hurt.

3 Let them be turned back for a reward of their shame that say, Aha, aha.

4 Let all those that seek you rejoice and be glad in you: and let such as love your salvation say continually, Let God be magnified.

5 But I am poor and needy: make haste unto me, O God: you are my help and my deliverer; O LORD, make no tarrying.

PSALM 71

IN you, O LORD, do I put my trust: let me never be put to confusion.

2 Deliver me in your righteousness, and cause me to escape: incline your ear unto me, and save me.

3 Be my strong habitation, whereunto I may continually resort: you have given commandment to save me; for you are my rock and my fortress.

4 Deliver me, O my God, out of the hand of the wicked, out of the hand of the unrighteous and cruel man.

5 For you are my hope, O Lord GOD: you are my trust from my youth.

6 By you have I been held up from the womb: you are he that took me out of my mother's bowels: my praise shall be continually of you.

7 I am as a wonder unto many; but you are my strong refuge.

8 Let my mouth be filled with your praise and with your honor all the day.

9 Cast me not off in the time of old age; forsake me not when my strength fails.

10 For my enemies speak against me; and they that lay wait for my soul take counsel together,

11 Saying, God has forsaken him: persecute and take him; for there is none to deliver him.

12 O God, be not far from me: O my God, make haste for my help.

13 Let them be confounded and consumed that are adversaries to my soul; let them be covered with reproach and dishonor that seek my hurt.

14 But I will hope continually, and will yet praise you more and more.

15 My mouth shall show forth your righteousness and your salvation all the day; for I know not the numbers thereof.

16 I will go in the strength of the Lord GOD: I will make mention of your righteousness, even of yours only.

17 O God, you have taught me from my youth: and hitherto have I declared your wondrous works.

18 Now also when I am old and greyheaded, O God, forsake me not; until I have showed your strength unto this generation, and your power to every one that is to come.

19 Your righteousness also, O God, is very high, who have done great things: O God, who is like unto you!

20 You, who have showed me great and sore troubles, shall quicken me again, and shall bring me up again from the depths of the earth.

70:3 An accusing world is quick to point out the slightest weakness in the Christian. If we become impatient, they say, "Aha...you're supposed to be a Christian." They are unaware that they will be judged by the same measure by which they judge. See Romans 2:1-3.

*No educated man
can afford to be ignorant of the Bible.*

Theodore Roosevelt

1858-1919

26TH PRESIDENT

OF THE UNITED STATES

21 You shall increase my greatness, and comfort me on every side.

22 I will also praise you with the psaltery, even your truth, O my God: unto you will I sing with the harp, O you Holy One of Israel.

23 My lips shall greatly rejoice when I sing unto you; and my soul, which you have redeemed.

24 My tongue also shall talk of your righteousness all the day long: for they are confounded, for they are brought unto shame, that seek my hurt.

PSALM 72

GIVE the king your judgments, O God, and your righteousness unto the king's son.

2 He shall judge your people with righteousness, and your poor with judgment.

3 The mountains shall bring peace to the people, and the little hills, by righteousness.

4 He shall judge the poor of the people, he shall save the children of the needy, and shall break in pieces the oppressor.

5 They shall fear you as long as the sun and moon endure, throughout all generations.

6 He shall come down like rain upon the mown grass: as showers that water the earth.

7 In his days shall the righteous flourish; and abundance of peace so long as the moon endures.

8 He shall have dominion also from sea to sea, and from the river unto the ends of the earth.

9 They that dwell in the wilderness shall bow before him; and his enemies shall lick the dust.

10 The kings of Tarshish and of the isles shall bring presents: the kings of Sheba and Seba shall offer gifts.

11 Yes, all kings shall fall down before him: all nations shall serve him.

12 For he shall deliver the needy when he cries; the poor also, and him that has no helper.

13 He shall spare the poor and needy, and shall save the souls of the needy.

14 He shall redeem their soul from deceit and violence: and precious shall their blood be in his sight.

15 And he shall live, and to him shall be given of the gold of Sheba: prayer also shall be made for him continually; and daily shall he be praised.

16 There shall be an handful of corn in the earth upon the top of the mountains; the fruit thereof shall shake like Lebanon: and they of the city shall flourish like grass of the earth.

17 His name shall endure for ever: his name shall be continued as long as the sun: and men shall be blessed in him: all nations shall call him blessed.

18 Blessed be the LORD God, the God of Israel, who only does wondrous things.

19 And blessed be his glorious name for ever: and let the whole earth be filled with his glory; Amen, and Amen.

20　The prayers of David the son of Jesse are ended.

PSALM 73

TRULY God is good to Israel, even to such as are of a clean heart.

2　But as for me, my feet were almost gone; my steps had well near slipped.

3　For I was envious at the foolish, when I saw the prosperity of the wicked.

4　For there are no bands in their death: but their strength is firm.

5　They are not in trouble as other men; neither are they plagued like other men.

6　Therefore pride compasses them about as a chain; violence covers them as a garment.

7　Their eyes stand out with fatness: they have more than heart could wish.

8　They are corrupt, and speak wickedly concerning oppression: they speak loftily.

9　They set their mouth against the heavens, and their tongue walks through the earth.

10　Therefore his people return hither: and waters of a full cup are wrung out to them.

11　And they say, How does God know? and is there knowledge in the most High?

12　Behold, these are the ungodly, who prosper in the world; they increase in riches.

13　Verily I have cleansed my heart in vain, and washed my hands in innocency.

14　For all the day long have I been plagued, and chastened every morning.

15　If I say, I will speak thus; behold, I should offend against the generation of your children.

16　When I thought to know this, it was too painful for me;

17　Until I went into the sanctuary of God; then understood I their end.

18　Surely you did set them in slippery places: you cast them down into destruction.

19　How are they brought into desolation, as in a moment! they are utterly consumed with terrors.

20　As a dream when one awakes; so, O Lord, when you awake, you shall despise their image.

21　Thus my heart was grieved, and I was pricked in my reins.

22　So foolish was I, and ignorant: I was as a beast before you.

23　Nevertheless I am continually with you: you have held me by my right hand.

24　You shall guide me with your counsel, and afterward receive me to glory.

25　Whom have I in heaven but you? and there is none upon earth that I desire beside you.

26　My flesh and my heart fails: but God is the strength of my heart, and my portion for ever.

27　For, lo, they that are far from you shall perish: you have destroyed all them that go a whoring from you.

28　But it is good for me to draw near to God: I have put my trust in the Lord GOD, that I may declare all your works.

PSALM 74

O GOD, why have you cast us off for ever? why does your anger smoke against the sheep of your pasture?

2　Remember your congregation, which you have purchased of old; the rod of your inheritance, which you have redeemed; this mount Zion, wherein you have dwelt.

3　Lift up your feet unto the perpetual desolations; even all that the enemy has done wickedly in the sanctuary.

4　Your enemies roar in the midst of your congregations; they set up their ensigns for signs.

5　A man was famous according as he had lifted up axes upon the thick trees.

6　But now they break down the carved work thereof at once with axes and hammers.

7　They have cast fire into your sanctuary, they have defiled by casting down the dwelling place of your name to the ground.

8　They said in their hearts, Let us destroy them together: they have burned up all the synagogues of God in the land.

> There is no doctrine
> which I would more willingly remove
> from Christianity
> than the doctrine of hell,
> if it lay in my power.
> But it has the full support of scripture
> and, especially,
> of our Lord's own words;
> it has always been held
> by the Christian Church,
> and it has the support of reason.

C. S. LEWIS

1898-1963

BRITISH SCHOLAR

9 We see not our signs: there is no more any prophet: neither is there among us any that knows how long.

10 O God, how long shall the adversary reproach? shall the enemy blaspheme your name for ever?

11 Why do you withdraw your hand, even your right hand? pluck it out of your bosom.

12 For God is my King of old, working salvation in the midst of the earth.

13 You did divide the sea by your strength: you brake the heads of the dragons in the waters.

14 You brake the heads of leviathan in pieces, and gave him to be meat to the people inhabiting the wilderness.

15 You did cleave the fountain and the flood: you dried up mighty rivers.

16 The day is yours, the night also is yours: you have prepared the light and the sun.

17 You have set all the borders of the earth: you have made summer and winter.

18 Remember this, that the enemy has reproached, O LORD, and that the foolish people have blasphemed your name.

19 O deliver not the soul of your turtledove unto the multitude of the wicked:

forget not the congregation of your poor for ever.

20 Have respect unto the covenant: for the dark places of the earth are full of the habitations of cruelty.

21 O let not the oppressed return ashamed: let the poor and needy praise your name.

22 Arise, O God, plead your own cause: remember how the foolish man reproaches you daily.

23 Forget not the voice of your enemies: the tumult of those that rise up against you increases continually.

PSALM 75

UNTO you, O God, do we give thanks, unto you do we give thanks: for that your name is near your wondrous works declare.

2 When I shall receive the congregation I will judge uprightly.

3 The earth and all the inhabitants thereof are dissolved: I bear up the pillars of it. Selah.

4 I said unto the fools, Deal not foolishly: and to the wicked, Lift not up the horn:

5 Lift not up your horn on high: speak not with a stiff neck.

6 For promotion comes neither from the east, nor from the west, nor from the south.

7 But God is the judge: he puts down one, and sets up another.

8 For in the hand of the LORD there is a cup, and the wine is red; it is full of mixture; and he pours out of the same: but the dregs thereof, all the wicked of the earth shall wring them out, and drink them.

9 But I will declare for ever; I will sing praises to the God of Jacob.

10 All the horns of the wicked also will I cut off; but the horns of the righteous shall be exalted.

75:1 "It is a terrible thing, I found, to be grateful and have no one to thank, to be awed and have no one to worship." Philip Yancey, *What's So Amazing About Grace?*

PSALM 76

IN Judah is God known: his name is great in Israel.

2 In Salem also is his tabernacle, and his dwelling place in Zion.

3 There brake he the arrows of the bow, the shield, and the sword, and the battle. Selah.

4 You are more glorious and excellent than the mountains of prey.

5 The stouthearted are spoiled, they have slept their sleep: and none of the men of might have found their hands.

6 At your rebuke, O God of Jacob, both the chariot and horse are cast into a dead sleep.

7 You, even you, are to be feared: and who may stand in your sight when once you are angry?

8 You did cause judgment to be heard from heaven; the earth feared, and was still,

9 When God arose to judgment, to save all the meek of the earth. Selah.

10 Surely the wrath of man shall praise you: the remainder of wrath shall you restrain.

11 Vow, and pay unto the LORD your God: let all that be round about him bring presents unto him that ought to be feared.

12 He shall cut off the spirit of princes: he is terrible to the kings of the earth.

PSALM 77

I CRIED unto God with my voice, even unto God with my voice; and he gave ear unto me.

2 In the day of my trouble I sought the Lord: my sore ran in the night, and ceased not: my soul refused to be comforted.

3 I remembered God, and was troubled: I complained, and my spirit was overwhelmed. Selah.

4 You hold my eyes waking: I am so troubled that I cannot speak.

5 I have considered the days of old, the years of ancient times.

6 I call to remembrance my song in the night: I commune with my own heart: and my spirit made diligent search.

7 Will the Lord cast off for ever? and will he be favorable no more?

8 Is his mercy clean gone for ever? does his promise fail for evermore?

9 Has God forgotten to be gracious? has he in anger shut up his tender mercies? Selah.

10 And I said, This is my infirmity: but I will remember the years of the right hand of the most High.

11 I will remember the works of the LORD: surely I will remember your wonders of old.

12 I will meditate also of all your work, and talk of your doings.

13 Your way, O God, is in the sanctuary: who is so great a God as our God?

14 You are the God that does wonders: you have declared your strength among the people.

15 You have with your arm redeemed your people, the sons of Jacob and Joseph. Selah.

16 The waters saw you, O God, the waters saw you; they were afraid: the depths also were troubled.

17 The clouds poured out water: the skies sent out a sound: your arrows also went abroad.

18 The voice of your thunder was in the heaven: the lightnings lightened the world: the earth trembled and shook.

19 Your way is in the sea, and your path in the great waters, and your footsteps are not known.

20 You led your people like a flock by the hand of Moses and Aaron.

PSALM 78

GIVE ear, O my people, to my law: incline your ears to the words of my mouth.

2 I will open my mouth in a parable: I will utter dark sayings of old:

3 Which we have heard and known, and our fathers have told us.

4 We will not hide them from their children, showing to the generation to come the praises of the LORD, and his strength, and his wonderful works that he has done.

QUESTIONS & OBJECTIONS

Q 76:8 *"Could you be wrong in your claims about Judgment Day and the existence of hell?"*

The existence of hell and the surety of the judgment are not the claims of fallible man. The Bible is the source of the claim, and it is utterly infallible.

When someone becomes a Christian, he is admitting that he was in the wrong, and that God is justified in His declarations that we have sinned against Him. However, let's surmise for a moment that there is no Judgment Day and no hell. That would mean that the Bible is a huge hoax, in which more than forty authors collaborated (over a period of 3,000 years) to produce a document revealing God's character as "just." They portrayed Him as a just judge, who warned that He would eventually punish murderers, rapists, liars, thieves, adulterers, etc. Each of those writers (who professed to be godly) therefore bore false witness, transgressing the very commandments they claimed to be true. It would mean that Jesus Christ was a liar, and that all the claims He made about the reality of judgment were therefore false. It would also mean that He gave His life in vain, as did multitudes of martyrs who have given their lives for the cause of Christ. Add to that the thought that if there is no ultimate justice, it means that the Creator of all things is unjust—that He sees murder and rape and couldn't care less, making Him worse than a corrupt human judge who refuses to bring criminals to justice.

Here's the good news, though, if there is no hell: You won't know a thing after you die. It will be the end. No heaven, no hell. Just nothing. You won't even realize that it's good news. Here's the bad news if the Bible is right and that there is eternal justice: You will find yourself standing before the judgment throne of a holy God, who has seen every sin you have ever committed. Think of it. A holy and perfect Creator has seen your thought-life and every secret sin you have ever committed. You have a multitude of sins, and God must by nature carry out justice. Ask Him to remind you of the sins of your youth. Ask Him to bring to remembrance your secret sexual sins, the lies, the gossip, and other idle words. You may have forgotten your past sins, but God hasn't. Hell will be your just desert (exactly what you deserve), and you will have no one to blame but yourself. This is the claim of the Bible. If you don't believe it, it is still true. It will still happen.

Yet, there is good news—incredibly good news. We deserve judgment, but God offers us mercy through the cross. He paid our fine so that we could leave the courtroom. He destroyed the power of the grave for all who obey Him. Simply obey the gospel, and live. By doing that you will find out for yourself that the gospel is indeed the "gospel truth." Jesus said that if you obey Him, you will know the truth, and the truth will make you free (see John 8:31,32). Get on your knees today, confess and forsake your sins. Tell God you are truly sorry, then trust the Savior as you would trust yourself to a parachute. Then you will find yourself in a terrible dilemma. You will know for certain that hell is a reality. When you get up the courage to warn people you care about, they will smile passively, and say, "Could you be wrong in your claims about Judgment Day and the existence of hell?"

---

5 For he established a testimony in Jacob, and appointed a law in Israel, which he commanded our fathers, that they should make them known to their children:

6 That the generation to come might know them, even the children which should be born; who should arise and declare them to their children:

78:2 Messianic Prophecy: Jesus fulfilled this in Matthew 13:34-35.

7 That they might set their hope in God, and not forget the works of God, but keep his commandments:

8 And might not be as their fathers, a stubborn and rebellious generation; a generation that set not their heart aright, and whose spirit was not steadfast with God.

9 The children of Ephraim, being armed, and carrying bows, turned back in the day of battle.

10 They kept not the covenant of God, and refused to walk in his law;

11 And forgot his works, and his wonders that he had showed them.

12 Marvelous things did he in the sight of their fathers, in the land of Egypt, in the field of Zoan.

13 He divided the sea, and caused them to pass through; and he made the waters to stand as an heap.

14 In the daytime also he led them with a cloud, and all the night with a light of fire.

15 He clave the rocks in the wilderness, and gave them drink as out of the great depths.

16 He brought streams also out of the rock, and caused waters to run down like rivers.

17 And they sinned yet more against him by provoking the most High in the wilderness.

> The beginning of anxiety
> is the end of faith,
> and the beginning of true faith
> is the end of anxiety.
>
> **GEORGE MUELLER**
>
> 1805-1898
>
> ENGLISH EVANGELIST
>
> AND PHILANTHROPIST

18 And they tempted God in their heart by asking meat for their lust.

19 Yes, they spoke against God; they said, Can God furnish a table in the wilderness?

20 Behold, he smote the rock, that the waters gushed out, and the streams overflowed; can he give bread also? can he provide flesh for his people?

21 Therefore the LORD heard this, and was wroth: so a fire was kindled against Jacob, and anger also came up against Israel;

22 Because they believed not in God, and trusted not in his salvation:

23 Though he had commanded the clouds from above, and opened the doors of heaven,

24 And had rained down manna upon them to eat, and had given them of the corn of heaven.

25 Man did eat angels' food: he sent them meat to the full.

26 He caused an east wind to blow in the heaven: and by his power he brought in the south wind.

27 He rained flesh also upon them as dust, and feathered fowls like as the sand of the sea:

28 And he let it fall in the midst of their camp, round about their habitations.

29 So they did eat, and were well filled: for he gave them their own desire;

78:5-6 If you want to bring children to the Savior, teach them the Ten Commandments in light of New Testament revelation (lust is adultery, hatred is murder, etc.). Immediately after giving God's Moral Law (the Ten Commandments) to Israel, Moses said to teach them diligently. In Deuteronomy 6:6–9, he explains how to do that: speak of the Commandments when you sit with your children at home, as you go for walks together, at their bedtime, and when they get up (nighttime and morning devotions). Bind the Commandments on your hands, in front of your eyes, and at the entry of your house—in other words, do not forget them. Can you name the Ten Commandments? Can your children name them? See Exodus 20:1–17 and Deuteronomy 11:18–21.

To help your kids memorize the Ten Commandments, see comment in Exodus, Chapter 21.

30 They were not estranged from their lust. But while their meat was yet in their mouths,

31 The wrath of God came upon them, and slew the fattest of them, and smote down the chosen men of Israel.

32 For all this they sinned still, and believed not for his wondrous works.

33 Therefore their days did he consume in vanity, and their years in trouble.

34 When he slew them, then they sought him: and they returned and enquired early after God.

35 And they remembered that God was their rock, and the high God their redeemer.

36 Nevertheless they did flatter him with their mouth, and they lied unto him with their tongues.

37 For their heart was not right with him, neither were they steadfast in his covenant.

38 But he, being full of compassion, forgave their iniquity, and destroyed them not: yes, many a time turned he his anger away, and did not stir up all his wrath.

39 For he remembered that they were but flesh; a wind that passes away, and comes not again.

40 How oft did they provoke him in the wilderness, and grieve him in the desert!

41 Yes, they turned back and tempted God, and limited the Holy One of Israel.

42 They remembered not his hand, nor the day when he delivered them from the enemy.

43 How he had wrought his signs in Egypt, and his wonders in the field of Zoan.

44 And had turned their rivers into blood; and their floods, that they could not drink.

45 He sent divers sorts of flies among them, which devoured them; and frogs, which destroyed them.

46 He gave also their increase unto the caterpillar, and their labor unto the locust.

47 He destroyed their vines with hail, and their sycamore trees with frost.

48 He gave up their cattle also to the hail, and their flocks to hot thunderbolts.

49 He cast upon them the fierceness of his anger, wrath, and indignation, and trouble, by sending evil angels among them.

50 He made a way to his anger; he spared not their soul from death, but gave their life over to the pestilence;

51 And smote all the firstborn in Egypt; the chief of their strength in the tabernacles of Ham:

52 But made his own people to go forth like sheep, and guided them in the wilderness like a flock.

53 And he led them on safely, so that they feared not: but the sea overwhelmed their enemies.

54 And he brought them to the border of his sanctuary, even to this mountain, which his right hand had purchased.

55 He cast out the heathen also before them, and divided them an inheritance by line, and made the tribes of Israel to dwell in their tents.

56 Yet they tempted and provoked the most high God, and kept not his testimonies:

57 But turned back, and dealt unfaithfully like their fathers: they were turned aside like a deceitful bow.

58 For they provoked him to anger with their high places, and moved him to jealousy with their graven images.

59 When God heard this, he was wroth, and greatly abhorred Israel:

60 So that he forsook the tabernacle of Shiloh, the tent which he placed among men;

61 And delivered his strength into captivity, and his glory into the enemy's hand.

62 He gave his people over also unto the sword; and was wroth with his inheritance.

63 The fire consumed their young men; and their maidens were not given to marriage.

64 Their priests fell by the sword; and their widows made no lamentation.

65 Then the LORD awaked as one out of sleep, and like a mighty man that shouts by reason of wine.

66 And he smote his enemies in the hinder parts: he put them to a perpetual reproach.

67 Moreover he refused the tabernacle of Joseph, and chose not the tribe of Ephraim:

68 But chose the tribe of Judah, the mount Zion which he loved.

69 And he built his sanctuary like high palaces, like the earth which he has established for ever.

70 He chose David also his servant, and took him from the sheepfolds:

71 From following the ewes great with young he brought him to feed Jacob his people, and Israel his inheritance.

72 So he fed them according to the integrity of his heart; and guided them by the skillfulness of his hands.

PSALM 79

O GOD, the heathen are come into your inheritance; your holy temple have they defiled; they have laid Jerusalem on heaps.

2 The dead bodies of your servants have they given to be meat unto the fowls of the heaven, the flesh of your saints unto the beasts of the earth.

3 Their blood have they shed like water round about Jerusalem; and there was none to bury them.

4 We are become a reproach to our neighbors, a scorn and derision to them that are round about us.

5 How long, LORD? will you be angry for ever? shall your jealousy burn like fire?

6 Pour out your wrath upon the heathen that have not known you, and upon the kingdoms that have not called upon your name.

7 For they have devoured Jacob, and laid waste his dwelling place.

8 O remember not against us former iniquities: let your tender mercies speedily prevent us: for we are brought very low.

9 Help us, O God of our salvation, for the glory of your name: and deliver us, and purge away our sins, for your name's sake.

10 Wherefore should the heathen say, Where is their God? let him be known among the heathen in our sight by the revenging of the blood of your servants which is shed.

11 Let the sighing of the prisoner come before you; according to the greatness of your power preserve those that are appointed to die;

12 And render unto our neighbors sevenfold into their bosom their reproach, wherewith they have reproached you, O Lord.

13 So we your people and sheep of your pasture will give you thanks for ever: we will show forth your praise to all generations.

PSALM 80

G IVE ear, O Shepherd of Israel, you that lead Joseph like a flock; you that dwell between the cherubims, shine forth.

2 Before Ephraim and Benjamin and Manasseh stir up your strength, and come and save us.

3 Turn us again, O God, and cause your face to shine; and we shall be saved.

4 O LORD God of hosts, how long will you be angry against the prayer of your people?

5 You feed them with the bread of tears; and give them tears to drink in great measure.

6 You make us a strife unto our neighbors: and our enemies laugh among themselves.

7 Turn us again, O God of hosts, and cause your face to shine; and we shall be saved.

8 You have brought a vine out of Egypt: you have cast out the heathen, and planted it.

9 You prepared room before it, and did cause it to take deep root, and it filled the land.

10 The hills were covered with the shadow of it, and the boughs thereof were like the goodly cedars.

11 She sent out her boughs unto the sea, and her branches unto the river.

12 Why have you then broken down her hedges, so that all they which pass by the way do pluck her?

13 The boar out of the wood does waste it, and the wild beast of the field does devour it.

14 Return, we beseech you, O God of hosts: look down from heaven, and behold, and visit this vine;

15 And the vineyard which your right hand has planted, and the branch that you made strong for yourself.

16 It is burned with fire, it is cut down: they perish at the rebuke of your countenance.

17 Let your hand be upon the man of your right hand, upon the son of man whom you made strong for yourself.

18 So will not we go back from you: quicken us, and we will call upon your name.

19 Turn us again, O LORD God of hosts, cause your face to shine; and we shall be saved.

PSALM 81

SING aloud unto God our strength: make a joyful noise unto the God of Jacob.

2 Take a psalm, and bring hither the timbrel, the pleasant harp with the psaltery.

3 Blow up the trumpet in the new moon, in the time appointed, on our solemn feast day.

4 For this was a statute for Israel, and a law of the God of Jacob.

5 This he ordained in Joseph for a testimony, when he went out through the land of Egypt: where I heard a language that I understood not.

6 I removed his shoulder from the burden: his hands were delivered from the pots.

7 You called in trouble, and I delivered you; I answered you in the secret place of thunder: I proved you at the waters of Meribah. Selah.

8 Hear, O my people, and I will testify unto you: O Israel, if you will hearken unto me;

9 There shall no strange god be in you; neither shall you worship any strange god.

10 I am the LORD your God, which brought you out of the land of Egypt: open your mouth wide, and I will fill it.

11 But my people would not hearken to my voice; and Israel would none of me.

12 So I gave them up unto their own hearts' lust: and they walked in their own counsels.

13 Oh that my people had hearkened unto me, and Israel had walked in my ways!

14 I should soon have subdued their enemies, and turned my hand against their adversaries.

15 The haters of the LORD should have submitted themselves unto him: but their time should have endured for ever.

16 He should have fed them also with the finest of the wheat: and with honey out of the rock should I have satisfied you.

PSALM 82

GOD stands in the congregation of the mighty; he judges among the gods.

2 How long will you judge unjustly, and accept the persons of the wicked? Selah.

3 Defend the poor and fatherless: do justice to the afflicted and needy.

4 Deliver the poor and needy: rid them out of the hand of the wicked.

5 They know not, neither will they understand; they walk on in darkness: all the foundations of the earth are out of course.

6 I have said, You are gods; and all of you are children of the most High.

7 But you shall die like men, and fall like one of the princes.

8 Arise, O God, judge the earth: for you shall inherit all nations.

PSALM 83

KEEP not silence, O God: hold not your peace, and be not still, O God.

2 For, lo, your enemies make a tumult: and they that hate you have lifted up the head.

3 They have taken crafty counsel against your people, and consulted against your hidden ones.

4 They have said, Come, and let us cut them off from being a nation; that the name of Israel may be no more in remembrance.

5 For they have consulted together with one consent: they are confederate against you:

6 The tabernacles of Edom, and the Ishmaelites; of Moab, and the Hagarenes;

7 Gebal, and Ammon, and Amalek; the Philistines with the inhabitants of Tyre;

8 Assur also is joined with them: they have helped the children of Lot. Selah.

9 Do unto them as unto the Midianites; as to Sisera, as to Jabin, at the brook of Kison:

10 Which perished at Endor: they became as dung for the earth.

11 Make their nobles like Oreb, and like Zeeb: yes, all their princes as Zebah, and as Zalmunna:

12 Who said, Let us take to ourselves the houses of God in possession.

13 O my God, make them like a wheel; as the stubble before the wind.

14 As the fire burns a wood, and as the flame sets the mountains on fire;

15 So persecute them with your tempest, and make them afraid with your storm.

16 Fill their faces with shame; that they may seek your name, O LORD.

17 Let them be confounded and troubled for ever; yes, let them be put to shame, and perish:

18 That men may know that you, whose name alone is JEHOVAH, are the most high over all the earth.

PSALM 84

HOW amiable are your tabernacles, O LORD of hosts!

2 My soul longs, yes, even faints for the courts of the LORD: my heart and my flesh cries out for the living God.

3 Yes, the sparrow has found an house, and the swallow a nest for herself, where she may lay her young, even your altars, O LORD of hosts, my King, and my God.

4 Blessed are they that dwell in your house: they will be still praising you. Selah.

5 Blessed is the man whose strength is in you; in whose heart are the ways of them.

6 Who passing through the valley of Baca make it a well; the rain also fills the pools.

7 They go from strength to strength, every one of them in Zion appears before God.

8 O LORD God of hosts, hear my prayer: give ear, O God of Jacob. Selah.

9 Behold, O God our shield, and look upon the face of your anointed.

10 For a day in your courts is better than a thousand. I had rather be a doorkeeper in the house of my God, than to dwell in the tents of wickedness.

11 For the LORD God is a sun and shield: the LORD will give grace and glory: no good thing will he withhold from them that walk uprightly.

12 O LORD of hosts, blessed is the man that trusts in you.

PSALM 85

LORD, you have been favorable unto your land: you have brought back the captivity of Jacob.

2 You have forgiven the iniquity of your people, you have covered all their sin. Selah.

3 You have taken away all your wrath: you have turned yourself from the fierceness of your anger.

82:7 "Every man must do two things alone: he must do his own believing, and he must do his own dying." Martin Luther

4 Turn us, O God of our salvation, and cause your anger toward us to cease.

5 Will you be angry with us for ever? will you draw out your anger to all generations?

6 Will you not revive us again: that your people may rejoice in you?

7 Show us your mercy, O Lord, and grant us your salvation.

8 I will hear what God the Lord will speak: for he will speak peace unto his people, and to his saints: but let them not turn again to folly.

9 Surely his salvation is near them that fear him; that glory may dwell in our land.

10 Mercy and truth are met together; righteousness and peace have kissed each other.

11 Truth shall spring out of the earth; and righteousness shall look down from heaven.

12 Yes, the Lord shall give that which is good; and our land shall yield her increase.

13 Righteousness shall go before him; and shall set us in the way of his steps.

PSALM 86

Bow down your ear, O Lord, hear me: for I am poor and needy.

2 Preserve my soul; for I am holy: O you my God, save your servant that trusts in you.

3 Be merciful unto me, O Lord: for I cry unto you daily.

4 Rejoice the soul of your servant: for unto you, O Lord, do I lift up my soul.

5 For you, Lord, are good, and ready to forgive; and plenteous in mercy unto all them that call upon you.

6 Give ear, O Lord, unto my prayer; and attend to the voice of my supplications.

7 In the day of my trouble I will call upon you: for you will answer me.

8 Among the gods there is none like unto you, O Lord; neither are there any works like unto your works.

9 All nations whom you have made shall come and worship before you, O Lord; and shall glorify your name.

10 For you are great, and do wondrous things: you are God alone.

11 Teach me your way, O Lord; I will walk in your truth: unite my heart to fear your name.

12 I will praise you, O Lord my God, with all my heart: and I will glorify your name for evermore.

13 For great is your mercy toward me: and you have delivered my soul from the lowest hell.

14 O God, the proud are risen against me, and the assemblies of violent men have sought after my soul; and have not set you before them.

15 But you, O Lord, are a God full of compassion, and gracious, long suffering, and plenteous in mercy and truth.

16 O turn unto me, and have mercy upon me; give your strength unto your servant, and save the son of your handmaid.

17 Show me a token for good; that they which hate me may see it, and be ashamed: because you, Lord, have helped me, and comforted me.

PSALM 87

His foundation is in the holy mountains.

2 The Lord loves the gates of Zion more than all the dwellings of Jacob.

3 Glorious things are spoken of you, O city of God. Selah.

4 I will make mention of Rahab and Babylon to them that know me: behold Philistia, and Tyre, with Ethiopia; this man was born there.

5 And of Zion it shall be said, This and that man was born in her: and the highest himself shall establish her.

6 The Lord shall count, when he writes up the people, that this man was born there. Selah.

85:10 The cross of Calvary is where righteousness and peace kissed each other.

7 As well the singers as the players on instruments shall be there: all my springs are in you.

PSALM 88

O LORD God of my salvation, I have cried day and night before you:

2 Let my prayer come before you: incline your ear unto my cry;

3 For my soul is full of troubles: and my life draws near unto the grave.

4 I am counted with them that go down into the pit: I am as a man that has no strength:

5 Free among the dead, like the slain that lie in the grave, whom you remember no more: and they are cut off from your hand.

6 You have laid me in the lowest pit, in darkness, in the deeps.

7 Your wrath lies hard upon me, and you have afflicted me with all your waves. Selah.

8 You have put away my acquaintance far from me; you have made me an abomination unto them: I am shut up, and I cannot come forth.

9 My eye mourns by reason of affliction: LORD, I have called daily upon you, I have stretched out my hands unto you.

10 Will you show wonders to the dead? shall the dead arise and praise you? Selah.

11 Shall your lovingkindness be declared in the grave? or your faithfulness in destruction?

12 Shall your wonders be known in the dark? and your righteousness in the land of forgetfulness?

13 But unto you have I cried, O LORD; and in the morning shall my prayer prevent you.

14 LORD, why cast off my soul? why hide your face from me?

15 I am afflicted and ready to die from my youth up: while I suffer your terrors I am distracted.

16 Your fierce wrath goes over me; your terrors have cut me off.

17 They came round about me daily like water; they compassed me about together.

18 Lover and friend have you put far from me, and my acquaintance into darkness.

PSALM 89

I WILL sing of the mercies of the LORD for ever: with my mouth will I make known your faithfulness to all generations.

2 For I have said, Mercy shall be built up for ever: your faithfulness shall you establish in the very heavens.

3 I have made a covenant with my chosen, I have sworn unto David my servant,

4 Your seed will I establish for ever, and build up your throne to all generations. Selah.

5 And the heavens shall praise your wonders, O LORD: your faithfulness also in the congregation of the saints.

6 For who in the heaven can be compared unto the LORD? who among the sons of the mighty can be likened unto the LORD?

7 God is greatly to be feared in the assembly of the saints, and to be had in reverence of all them that are about him.

8 O LORD God of hosts, who is a strong LORD like unto you? or to your faithfulness round about you?

9 You rule the raging of the sea: when the waves thereof arise, you stillest them.

10 You have broken Rahab in pieces, as one that is slain; you have scattered your enemies with your strong arm.

11 The heavens are yours, the earth also is yours: as for the world and the fullness thereof, you have founded them.

12 The north and the south you have created them: Tabor and Hermon shall rejoice in your name.

13 You have a mighty arm: strong is your hand, and high is your right hand.

14 Justice and judgment are the habitation of your throne: mercy and truth shall go before your face.

89:6 Nothing on this earth or in heaven compares to God. Even the regenerate mind can't begin to comprehend His infinite greatness.

QUESTIONS & OBJECTIONS

89:14 **"Why does the Old Testament show a God of wrath and the New Testament a God of mercy?"**

The God of the New Testament is the same as the God of the Old Testament. The Bible says that He *never* changes. He is just as merciful in the Old Testament as He is in the New Testament. Read Nehemiah 9 for a summary of how God mercifully forgave Israel, again and again, after they repeatedly sinned and turned their back on Him. The Psalms of David often speak of God's mercy, poured out on sinners.

He is also just as wrath-filled in the New Testament as He is in the Old. He killed a husband and wife in the Book of Acts, simply because they told one lie. Jesus warned that He was to be feared because He has the power to cast the body and soul into hell. The apostle Paul said that he persuaded men to come to the Savior because he knew the "terror of the Lord." Read the dreadful judgments of the New Testament's Book of Revelation. That will put the "fear of God" in you, which incidentally is "the beginning of wisdom."

Perhaps the most fearful display of His wrath is seen in the cross of Jesus Christ. His fury so came upon the Messiah that it seems God enshrouded the face of Jesus in darkness so that creation couldn't gaze upon His unspeakable agony. Whether we like it or not, our God is a consuming fire of holiness (Hebrews 12:29). He isn't going to change, so we had better...before the Day of Judgment. If we repent, God, in His mercy, will forgive us and grant us eternal life in heaven with Him.

15 Blessed is the people that know the joyful sound: they shall walk, O LORD, in the light of your countenance.

16 In your name shall they rejoice all the day: and in your righteousness shall they be exalted.

17 For you are the glory of their strength: and in your favor our horn shall be exalted.

18 For the LORD is our defense; and the Holy One of Israel is our king.

19 Then you spoke in vision to your holy one, and said, I have laid help upon one that is mighty; I have exalted one chosen out of the people.

20 I have found David my servant; with my holy oil have I anointed him:

21 With whom my hand shall be established: my arm also shall strengthen him.

22 The enemy shall not exact upon him; nor the son of wickedness afflict him.

23 And I will beat down his foes before his face, and plague them that hate him.

24 But my faithfulness and my mercy shall be with him: and in my name shall his horn be exalted.

25 I will set his hand also in the sea, and his right hand in the rivers.

26 He shall cry unto me, You are my father, my God, and the rock of my salvation.

27 Also I will make him my firstborn, higher than the kings of the earth.

28 My mercy will I keep for him for evermore, and my covenant shall stand fast with him.

29 His seed also will I make to endure for ever, and his throne as the days of heaven.

30 If his children forsake my law, and walk not in my judgments;

31 If they break my statutes, and keep not my commandments;

32 Then will I visit their transgression with the rod, and their iniquity with stripes.

33 Nevertheless my lovingkindness will I not utterly take from him, nor suffer my faithfulness to fail.

34 My covenant will I not break, nor alter the thing that is gone out of my lips.

89:48 *"Man is the master of his own destiny!"*

If man is in total control of his future, then he should at least be in control of his own body. Instead, he is subject to involuntary yawning, sneezing, breathing, swallowing, sleeping, salivating, dreaming, blinking, and thinking. He can't even control hair and nail growth. He automatically does these things, irrespective of his will. God has set his body in motion and there is little he can do about it. He also has minimal control over his daily bodily functions. His kidneys, bladder, intestines, heart, liver, lungs, etc., work independently of his will. It is ludicrous to say that man controls his future when he has trouble predicting the stock market, political outcomes, earthquakes, and even the weather, let alone having control over these things.

35 Once have I sworn by my holiness that I will not lie unto David.
36 His seed shall endure for ever, and his throne as the sun before me.
37 It shall be established for ever as the moon, and as a faithful witness in heaven. Selah.
38 But you have cast off and abhorred, you have been wroth with your anointed.
39 You have made void the covenant of your servant: you have profaned his crown by casting it to the ground.
40 You have broken down all his hedges; you have brought his strong holds to ruin.
41 All that pass by the way spoil him: he is a reproach to his neighbors.
42 You have set up the right hand of his adversaries; you have made all his enemies to rejoice.
43 You have also turned the edge of his sword, and have not made him to stand in the battle.
44 You have made his glory to cease, and cast his throne down to the ground.
45 The days of his youth have you shortened: you have covered him with shame. Selah.
46 How long, LORD? will you hide yourself for ever? shall your wrath burn like fire?
47 Remember how short my time is: wherefore have you made all men in vain?

48 **What man is he that lives, and shall not see death? shall he deliver his soul from the hand of the grave? Selah.**
49 Lord, where are your former lovingkindnesses, which you swore unto David in your truth?
50 Remember, Lord, the reproach of your servants; how I do bear in my bosom the reproach of all the mighty people;
51 Wherewith your enemies have reproached, O LORD; wherewith they have reproached the footsteps of your anointed.
52 Blessed be the LORD for evermore. Amen, and Amen.

PSALM 90

LORD, you have been our dwelling place in all generations.
2 Before the mountains were brought forth, or ever you had formed the earth and the world, even from everlasting to everlasting, you are God.
3 You turn man to destruction; and say, Return, you children of men.
4 For a thousand years in your sight are but as yesterday when it is past, and as a watch in the night.
5 You carry them away as with a flood; they are as a sleep: in the morning they are like grass which grows up.
6 In the morning it flourishes, and grows up; in the evening it is cut down, and withers.

89:48 See James 4:14 comment, "The Will to Live."

QUESTIONS & OBJECTIONS

90:2   *"Who made God?"*

To one who examines the evidence, there can be no doubt that
God exists. *Every* building has a builder. Everything made has
a maker. The fact of the existence of the Creator is axiomatic (self-evident). That's why the Bible says, "The fool has said in his
heart, 'There is no God'" (Psalm 14:1). The professing atheist denies the common
sense given to him by God, and defends his belief by thinking that the question "Who made
God?" can't be answered. This, he thinks, gives him license to deny the existence of God.

The question of who made God can be answered by simply looking at space and asking,
"Does space have an end?" Obviously, it doesn't. If there is a brick wall with "The End" written
on it, the question arises, "What is behind the brick wall?" Strain the mind though it may, we
have to believe (have faith) that space has no beginning and no end. The same applies to
God. He has no beginning and no end. He is eternal.

The Bible also informs us that time is a dimension that God created, into which man was
subjected. It even tells us that one day time will no longer exist. That will be called "eternity."
God Himself dwells outside of the dimension He created (2 Timothy 1:9, Titus 1:2). He dwells in
eternity and is not subject to time. God spoke history before it came into being. He can move
through time as a man flips through a history book. Because we live in the dimension of time,
logic and reason demand that everything *must* have a beginning and an end. We can understand the concept of God's eternal nature the same way we understand the concept of space
having no beginning and end—by faith. We simply *have* to believe they are so, even though
such thoughts put a strain on our distinctly insufficient cerebrum.

---

7 For we are consumed by your anger,
and by your wrath are we troubled.

8 You have set our iniquities before you,
our secret sins in the light of your countenance.

9 For all our days are passed away in your
wrath: we spend our years as a tale that is
told.

**10 The days of our years are three-
score years and ten; and if by reason of**
**strength they be fourscore years, yet is
their strength labor and sorrow; for it is
soon cut off, and we fly away.**

11 Who knows the power of your anger? even according to your fear, so is
your wrath.

**12 So teach us to number our days,
that we may apply our hearts unto wisdom.**

90:2 Microevolution vs. Macroevolution. While we *do* see what's called "microevolution"—variations within species (different types of dogs, for instance)—we *don't* see any evidence of
"macroevolution"—one species evolving into another species. Microevolution is observable, while
macroevolution takes a tremendous leap of faith. If Christians had as much faith in God as atheists
have in the theory of evolution, we would see revival. Like little children, atheists believe without a
shred of evidence. *Ken Ham* writes, "Adaptation and natural selection are biological facts; amoeba-
to-man evolution is not. Natural selection can only work on the genetic information present in a
population of organisms—it cannot create new information. For example, since no known reptiles
have genes for feathers, no amount of selection will produce a feathered reptile. Mutations in
genes can only modify or eliminate existing structures, not create new ones" (*The Answers Book*).

Evolutionists claim that the appendix has no purpose—that it's left over from evolution. The
truth is that the appendix is part of the human immune system. They also say that we have a tailbone (another leftover), proving that man is the product of evolution. The "tailbone" actually supports muscles that are necessary for daily bodily functions.

The average person dies at 70 years old.

IF YOU ARE:	YOU HAVE:
20 years old	2,600 weekends left
30 years old	2,080 weekends left
40 years old	1,560 weekends left
50 years old	1,040 weekends left
60 years old	520 weekends left

According to the U.S Census Bureau, 150,000 people die every 24 hours.

13 Return, O LORD, how long? and let it repent you concerning your servants.

14 O satisfy us early with your mercy; that we may rejoice and be glad all our days.

15 Make us glad according to the days wherein you have afflicted us, and the years wherein we have seen evil.

16 Let your work appear unto your servants, and your glory unto their children.

17 And let the beauty of the LORD our God be upon us: and establish the work of our hands upon us; yes, the work of our hands establish it.

PSALM 91

HE that dwells in the secret place of the most High shall abide under the shadow of the Almighty.

2 I will say of the LORD, He is my refuge and my fortress: my God; in him will I trust.

3 Surely he shall deliver you from the snare of the fowler, and from the noisome pestilence.

4 He shall cover you with his feathers, and under his wings shall you trust: his truth shall be your shield and buckler.

5 You shall not be afraid for the terror by night; nor for the arrow that flies by day;

6 Nor for the pestilence that walks in darkness; nor for the destruction that wastes at noonday.

7 *A thousand shall fall at your side, and ten thousand at your right hand; but it shall not come near you.*

8 Only with your eyes shall you behold and see the reward of the wicked.

9 Because you have made the LORD, which is my refuge, even the most High, your habitation;

10 There shall no evil befall you, neither shall any plague come near your dwelling.

11 For he shall give his angels charge over you, to keep you in all your ways.

12 They shall bear you up in their hands, lest you dash your foot against a stone.

13 You shall tread upon the lion and adder: the young lion and the dragon shall you trample under feet.

14 Because he has set his love upon me, therefore will I deliver him: I will set him on high, because he has known my name.

15 He shall call upon me, and I will answer him: I will be with him in trouble; I will deliver him, and honor him.

16 With long life will I satisfy him, and show him my salvation.

90:4 Time is God's creation. He Himself is not subject to the dimension of time. See 2 Peter 3:8 comment.

90:7-8 The ungodly must be made to understand that every secret sin as well as sins of the heart are seen by God. He will bring every work to judgment, including every hidden thing, whether it is good or evil.

"When we merely say that we are bad, the 'wrath' of God seems a barbarous doctrine; as soon as we perceive our bad-ness, it appears inevitable, a mere corollary from God's goodness." *C. S. Lewis*

90:12 "Your days at the most cannot be very long, so use them to the best of your ability for the glory of God and the benefit of your generation. " *General William Booth*

91:1 This Psalm is good medicine for those of us who sometimes feel sick with fear at the thought of evangelism. How can we not draw courage from such incredible promises?

PSALM 92

IT is a good thing to give thanks unto the LORD, and to sing praises unto your name, O Most High:

2 To show forth your lovingkindness in the morning, and your faithfulness every night,

3 Upon an instrument of ten strings, and upon the psaltery; upon the harp with a solemn sound.

4 For you, LORD, have made me glad through your work: I will triumph in the works of your hands.

5 *O LORD, how great are your works! and your thoughts are very deep.*

6 *A brutish man knows not; neither does a fool understand this.*

7 When the wicked spring as the grass, and when all the workers of iniquity do flourish; it is that they shall be destroyed for ever:

8 But you, LORD, are most high for evermore.

9 For, lo, your enemies, O LORD, for, lo, your enemies shall perish; all the workers of iniquity shall be scattered.

10 But my horn shall you exalt like the horn of an unicorn: I shall be anointed with fresh oil.

11 My eye also shall see my desire on my enemies, and my ears shall hear my desire of the wicked that rise up against me.

12 The righteous shall flourish like the palm tree: he shall grow like a cedar in Lebanon.

13 Those that be planted in the house of the LORD shall flourish in the courts of our God.

14 They shall still bring forth fruit in old age; they shall be fat and flourishing;

15 To show that the LORD is upright: he is my rock, and there is no unrighteousness in him.

PSALM 93

THE LORD reigns, he is clothed with majesty; the LORD is clothed with strength, wherewith he has girded himself: the world also is established, that it cannot be moved.

2 Your throne is established of old: you are from everlasting.

3 The floods have lifted up, O LORD, the floods have lifted up their voice; the floods lift up their waves.

4 The LORD on high is mightier than the noise of many waters, yes, than the mighty waves of the sea.

5 Your testimonies are very sure: holiness becomes your house, O LORD, for ever.

PSALM 94

O LORD God, to whom vengeance belongs; O God, to whom vengeance belongs, show yourself.

2 Lift up yourself, you judge of the earth: render a reward to the proud.

92:5-6 The unregenerate mind is able to see God's creation and not begin to comprehend how great God is. His understanding is darkened. He is alienated from the life of God through the ignorance that is in him (Ephesians 4:18). This ignorance is a willful blindness brought about by a hardened heart. See John 3:19-20 comment.

92:13 "Most people think churches are like cafeterias; they pick and choose what they like! They feel the freedom to stay as long as there are no problems. But this does not agree at all with what the Bible teaches. You are not the one who chooses where you go to church. God does! The Bible does not say, 'God has set the members, each one of them, in the body *just as they please.*' Rather it says, 'But now God has set the members, each one of them, in the body *just as He pleased*' (1 Corinthians 12:18).

"Remember that, if you're in the place where God wants you, the devil will try to offend you to get you out. He wants to uproot men and women from the place where God plants them. If he can get you out, he has been successful. If you will not budge, even in the midst of great conflict, you will spoil his plans." John Bevere, *The Bait of Satan*

3 LORD, how long shall the wicked, how long shall the wicked triumph?

4 How long shall they utter and speak hard things? and all the workers of iniquity boast themselves?

5 They break in pieces your people, O LORD, and afflict your heritage.

6 They slay the widow and the stranger, and murder the fatherless.

7 Yet they say, The LORD shall not see, neither shall the God of Jacob regard it.

8 Understand, you brutish among the people: and you fools, when will you be wise?

9 He that planted the ear, shall he not hear? he that formed the eye, shall he not see?

10 He that chastises the heathen, shall not he correct? he that teaches man knowledge, shall not he know?

11 The LORD knows the thoughts of man, that they are vanity.

12 Blessed is the man whom you chasten, O LORD, and teach him out of your law;

13 That you may give him rest from the days of adversity, until the pit be digged for the wicked.

14 For the LORD will not cast off his people, neither will he forsake his inheritance.

15 But judgment shall return unto righteousness: and all the upright in heart shall follow it.

16 *Who will rise up for me against the evildoers? or who will stand up for me against the workers of iniquity?*

17 *Unless the LORD had been my help, my soul had almost dwelt in silence.*

18 When I said, My foot slips; your mercy, O LORD, held me up.

19 In the multitude of my thoughts within me your comforts delight my soul.

20 Shall the throne of iniquity have fellowship with you, which frames mischief by a law?

21 They gather themselves together against the soul of the righteous, and condemn the innocent blood.

22 But the LORD is my defense; and my God is the rock of my refuge.

23 And he shall bring upon them their own iniquity, and shall cut them off in their own wickedness; yes, the LORD our God shall cut them off.

PSALM 95

O COME, let us sing unto the LORD: let us make a joyful noise to the rock of our salvation.

2 Let us come before his presence with thanksgiving, and make a joyful noise unto him with psalms.

3 For the LORD is a great God, and a great King above all gods.

4 In his hand are the deep places of the earth: the strength of the hills is his also.

5 The sea is his, and he made it: and his hands formed the dry land.

6 O come, let us worship and bow down: let us kneel before the LORD our maker.

94:1 "God is not disillusioned with us. He never had any illusions to begin with." Luis Palau

94:7-10 This is the great error of the ungodly. They don't consider the fact that if God can create an ear, He can therefore hear everything they say. If He can create an eye, He therefore can see everything they do.

94:12 Blessed is the man who is instructed out of God's Law. When God uses His Law to bring "the knowledge of sin," it acts as a "schoolmaster" (Galatians 3:24) to bring a sinner to the Savior.

95:4-5 *Scientific Facts in the Bible.* Only in recent years has man discovered that there are mountains on the ocean floor. This was revealed in the Bible thousands of years ago. While deep in the ocean, Jonah cried, "I went down to the bottoms of the mountains..." (Jonah 2:6). The reason the Bible and true science harmonize is that they have the same author.

95:6 "I can safely say, on the authority of all that is revealed in the Word of God, that any man or woman on this earth who is bored and turned off by worship is not ready for heaven." A. W. Tozer

7 For he is our God; and we are the people of his pasture, and the sheep of his hand. To day if you will hear his voice,

8 Harden not your heart, as in the provocation, and as in the day of temptation in the wilderness:

9 When your fathers tempted me, proved me, and saw my work.

10 Forty years long was I grieved with this generation, and said, It is a people that do err in their heart, and they have not known my ways:

11 Unto whom I swore in my wrath that they should not enter into my rest.

PSALM 96

O SING unto the LORD a new song: sing unto the LORD, all the earth.

2 Sing unto the LORD, bless his name; show forth his salvation from day to day.

3 Declare his glory among the heathen, his wonders among all people.

4 For the LORD is great, and greatly to be praised: he is to be feared above all gods.

5 For all the gods of the nations are idols: but the LORD made the heavens.

6 Honor and majesty are before him: strength and beauty are in his sanctuary.

7 Give unto the LORD, O you kindreds of the people, give unto the LORD glory and strength.

8 Give unto the LORD the glory due unto his name: bring an offering, and come into his courts.

9 O worship the LORD in the beauty of holiness: fear before him, all the earth.

10 Say among the heathen that the LORD reigns: the world also shall be established

that it shall not be moved: he shall judge the people righteously.

11 *Let the heavens rejoice, and let the earth be glad; let the sea roar, and the fullness thereof.*

12 *Let the field be joyful, and all that is therein: then shall all the trees of the wood rejoice*

13 *Before the LORD: for he comes, for he comes to judge the earth: he shall judge the world with righteousness, and the people with his truth.*

PSALM 97

T HE LORD reigns; let the earth rejoice; let the multitude of isles be glad thereof.

2 Clouds and darkness are round about him: righteousness and judgment are the habitation of his throne.

3 A fire goes before him, and burns up his enemies round about.

4 His lightnings enlightened the world: the earth saw, and trembled.

5 The hills melted like wax at the presence of the LORD, at the presence of the Lord of the whole earth.

6 The heavens declare his righteousness, and all the people see his glory.

7 Confounded be all they that serve graven images, that boast themselves of idols: worship him, all you gods.

8 Zion heard, and was glad; and the daughters of Judah rejoiced because of your judgments, O LORD.

9 For you, LORD, are high above all the earth: you are exalted far above all gods.

10 You that love the LORD, hate evil: he preserves the souls of his saints; he delivers them out of the hand of the wicked.

96:11–13 When a murderer is brought to justice, good people rejoice. Justice is sweet to the upright in heart. We are informed that the whole of creation rejoices because God is going to judge the world with righteousness and truth. This is what Paul preached in Acts 17:30-31, and it is what we must preach if we want the world to be saved.

97:2 Righteousness and justice are the very essence of God's character.

97:3–6 This is perhaps a reference to the giving of the Law on Mount Sinai (Exodus 19).

97:10 Do we truly hate evil, or do we secretly embrace lust and take pleasure in violent entertainment?

11 Light is sown for the righteous, and gladness for the upright in heart.
12 Rejoice in the LORD, you righteous; and give thanks at the remembrance of his holiness.

. . . . . .

Is "hell-fire" preaching effective?
See Acts 24:25.

. . . . .

PSALM 98

O SING unto the LORD a new song; for he has done marvelous things: his right hand, and his holy arm, has gotten him the victory.
2 The LORD has made known his salvation: his righteousness has he openly showed in the sight of the heathen.
3 He has remembered his mercy and his truth toward the house of Israel: all the ends of the earth have seen the salvation of our God.
4 Make a joyful noise unto the LORD, all the earth: make a loud noise, and rejoice, and sing praise.
5 Sing unto the LORD with the harp; with the harp, and the voice of a psalm.
6 With trumpets and sound of cornet make a joyful noise before the LORD, the King.
7 *Let the sea roar, and the fullness thereof; the world, and they that dwell therein.*
8 *Let the floods clap their hands: let the hills be joyful together*
9 *Before the LORD; for he comes to judge the earth: with righteousness shall he judge the world, and the people with equity.*

PSALM 99

T HE LORD reigns; let the people tremble: he sits between the cherubims; let the earth be moved.
2 The LORD is great in Zion; and he is high above all the people.
3 Let them praise your great and terrible name; for it is holy.
4 The king's strength also loves judgment; you do establish equity, you execute judgment and righteousness in Jacob.
5 Exalt the LORD our God, and worship at his footstool; for he is holy.
6 Moses and Aaron among his priests, and Samuel among them that call upon his name; they called upon the LORD, and he answered them.
7 He spoke unto them in the cloudy pillar: they kept his testimonies, and the ordinance that he gave them.
8 You answered them, O LORD our God: you were a God that forgave them, though you took vengeance of their inventions.
9 Exalt the LORD our God, and worship at his holy hill; for the LORD our God is holy.

PSALM 100

M AKE a joyful noise unto the LORD, all you lands.
2 Serve the LORD with gladness: come before his presence with singing.
3 Know that the LORD he is God: it is he that has made us, and not we ourselves; we are his people, and the sheep of his pasture.
4 Enter into his gates with thanksgiving, and into his courts with praise: be thankful unto him, and bless his name.
5 For the LORD is good; his mercy is everlasting; and his truth endures to all generations.

98:7–9 The whole of creation rejoices at the thought of God coming to judge the earth. Justice is a joy to the upright. See Psalm 96:11–13 comment.

PSALM 101

I WILL sing of mercy and judgment:
unto you, O LORD, will I sing.
2 I will behave myself wisely in a perfect way. O when will you come unto me?
I will walk within my house with a perfect heart.
3 I will set no wicked thing before my
eyes: I hate the work of them that turn
aside; it shall not cleave to me.
4 A froward heart shall depart from me:
I will not know a wicked person.
5 Whoso privily slanders his neighbor,
him will I cut off: him that has an high
look and a proud heart will not I suffer.
6 My eyes shall be upon the faithful of
the land, that they may dwell with me: he
that walks in a perfect way, he shall serve
me.
7 He that works deceit shall not dwell
within my house: he that tells lies shall
not tarry in my sight.
8 I will early destroy all the wicked of
the land; that I may cut off all wicked
doers from the city of the LORD.

PSALM 102

H EAR my prayer, O LORD, and let my
cry come unto you.
2 Hide not your face from me in the day
when I am in trouble; incline your ear unto me: in the day when I call answer me
speedily.
3 For my days are consumed like smoke,
and my bones are burned as an hearth.
4 My heart is smitten, and withered like
grass; so that I forget to eat my bread.
5 By reason of the voice of my groaning
my bones cleave to my skin.
6 I am like a pelican of the wilderness: I
am like an owl of the desert.
7 I watch, and am as a sparrow alone upon the house top.
8 My enemies reproach me all the day;
and they that are mad against me are
sworn against me.

9 For I have eaten ashes like bread, and
mingled my drink with weeping.
10 Because of your indignation and your
wrath: for you have lifted me up, and cast
me down.
11 My days are like a shadow that declines; and I am withered like grass.
12 But you, O LORD, shall endure for
ever; and your remembrance unto all generations.
13 You shall arise, and have mercy upon Zion: for the time to favor her, yes, the
set time, is come.
14 For your servants take pleasure in
her stones, and favor the dust thereof.
15 So the heathen shall fear the name of
the LORD, and all the kings of the earth
your glory.
16 When the LORD shall build up Zion,
he shall appear in his glory.
17 He will regard the prayer of the destitute, and not despise their prayer.
18 This shall be written for the generation to come: and the people which shall
be created shall praise the LORD.
19 For he has looked down from the
height of his sanctuary; from heaven did
the LORD behold the earth;
20 To hear the groaning of the prisoner;
to loose those that are appointed to death;
21 To declare the name of the LORD in
Zion, and his praise in Jerusalem;
22 When the people are gathered together, and the kingdoms, to serve the
LORD.
23 He weakened my strength in the way;
he shortened my days.
24 I said, O my God, take me not away
in the midst of my days: your years are
throughout all generations.
25 Of old have you laid the foundation
of the earth: and the heavens are the work
of your hands.
26 They shall perish, but you shall endure: yes, all of them shall wax old like a
garment; as a vesture shall you change
them, and they shall be changed:

101:1 Mercy and judgment met at the cross of Calvary. See Galatians 6:14.

QUESTIONS & OBJECTIONS

103:17 *"God couldn't forgive my sin."*

Those who think they are too sinful for God to accept them don't understand how merciful God is. The Bible says that He is "rich in mercy" (Ephesians 2:4). The Scriptures also tell us that "the mercy of the LORD is from everlasting to everlasting upon them that fear him" (Psalm 103:17). God was merciful to King David and forgave him when he committed adultery and murder. He forgave Moses when he committed murder. He also forgave Saul of Tarsus for murdering Christians (Acts 22:4). God promises to save "all" who call upon the name of Jesus (Romans 10:13). Those who think this promise isn't worth the paper it's written on are calling God a liar (see 1 John 5:10). Jesus shed His precious blood to pay for their sins. Wasn't it good enough for them? It was good enough for God. God *commands* them to repent. To offer any excuse is to remain in rebellion to His command—no matter how "noble" it may seem to say that they are too sinful.

---

27 But you are the same, and your years shall have no end.

28 The children of your servants shall continue, and their seed shall be established before you.

PSALM 103

B LESS the LORD, O my soul: and all that is within me, bless his holy name.
2 Bless the LORD, O my soul, and forget not all his benefits:
3 Who forgives all your iniquities; who heals all your diseases;
4 Who redeems your life from destruction; who crowns you with lovingkindness and tender mercies;
5 Who satisfies your mouth with good things; so that your youth is renewed like the eagle's.

6 The LORD executes righteousness and judgment for all that are oppressed.
7 He made known his ways unto Moses, his acts unto the children of Israel.
8 The LORD is merciful and gracious, slow to anger, and plenteous in mercy.
9 He will not always chide: neither will he keep his anger for ever.
10 He has not dealt with us after our sins; nor rewarded us according to our iniquities.
11 **For as the heaven is high above the earth, so great is his mercy toward them that fear him.**
12 **As far as the east is from the west, so far has he removed our transgressions from us.**
13 **Like as a father pities his children, so the LORD pities them that fear him.**

102:25-26 *Scientific Facts in the Bible.* Three different places in the Bible (Isaiah 51:6; Psalm 102:25-26; Hebrews 1:11) indicate that the earth is wearing out. This is what the Second Law of Thermodynamics (the Law of Increasing Entropy) states: that in all physical processes, every ordered system over time tends to become more disordered. Everything is running down and wearing out as energy is becoming less and less available for use. That means the universe will eventually "wear out" to the extent that (theoretically speaking) there will be a "heat death" and therefore no more energy available for use. This wasn't discovered by man until fairly recently, but the Bible states it in clear, succinct terms.

102:27 See Hebrews 13:8 comment.

103:10 How true it is that God hasn't dealt with us according to our iniquities (vv. 10–18). He hasn't treated us as He treated Ananias and Sapphira (Acts 5:1–10). He has held back His just wrath and instead lavished us with mercy.

14 **For he knows our frame; he remembers that we are dust.**

15 **As for man, his days are as grass: as a flower of the field, so he flourishes.**

16 **For the wind passes over it, and it is gone; and the place thereof shall know it no more.**

17 **But the mercy of the Lord is from everlasting to everlasting upon them that fear him, and his righteousness unto children's children;**

18 To such as keep his covenant, and to those that remember his commandments to do them.

19 The Lord has prepared his throne in the heavens; and his kingdom rules over all.

20 Bless the Lord, you his angels, that excel in strength, that do his commandments, hearkening unto the voice of his word.

21 Bless the Lord, all his hosts; you ministers of his, that do his pleasure.

22 Bless the Lord, all his works in all places of his dominion: bless the Lord, O my soul.

PSALM 104

B LESS the Lord, O my soul. O Lord my God, you are very great; you are clothed with honor and majesty.

2 Who covers yourself with light as with a garment: who stretches out the heavens like a curtain:

3 Who lays the beams of his chambers in the waters: who makes the clouds his chariot: who walks upon the wings of the wind:

4 Who makes his angels spirits; his ministers a flaming fire:

5 Who laid the foundations of the earth, that it should not be removed for ever.

6 You covered it with the deep as with a garment: the waters stood above the mountains.

7 At your rebuke they fled; at the voice of your thunder they hasted away.

8 They go up by the mountains; they go down by the valleys unto the place which you have founded for them.

9 You have set a bound that they may not pass over; that they turn not again to cover the earth.

10 He sends the springs into the valleys, which run among the hills.

11 They give drink to every beast of the field: the wild asses quench their thirst.

12 By them shall the fowls of the heaven have their habitation, which sing among the branches.

13 He waters the hills from his chambers: the earth is satisfied with the fruit of your works.

14 He causes the grass to grow for the cattle, and herb for the service of man: that he may bring forth food out of the earth;

15 And wine that makes glad the heart of man, and oil to make his face to shine, and bread which strengthens man's heart.

16 The trees of the Lord are full of sap; the cedars of Lebanon, which he has planted;

104:2 *Scientific Facts in the Bible.* It is interesting to note that scientists are beginning to understand that the universe is expanding or stretching out. At least seven times in Scripture we are told that God *stretches* out the heavens like a curtain (Isaiah 40:22). See also Hebrews 11:3 comment.

104:19 *Scientific Facts in the Bible.* God created the "lights" in the heavens "for signs, and for seasons, and for days and years" (Genesis 1:14). Through the marvels of astronomy we now understand that a year is the time required for the earth to travel once around the sun. The seasons are caused by the changing position of the earth in relation to the sun—"astronomers can tell exactly from the earth's motion around the sun when one season ends and the next one begins" (*Worldbook Multimedia Encyclopedia*). We also now understand that a "month [is] the time of one revolution of the moon around the earth with respect to the sun" (*Encyclopedia Britannica*). How could Moses (the accepted author of Genesis) have known 3,500 years ago that the "lights" of the sun and moon were the actual determining factors of the year's length, unless his words were inspired by God? (See also Psalm 136:7–9.)

17 Where the birds make their nests: as for the stork, the fir trees are her house.

18 The high hills are a refuge for the wild goats; and the rocks for the conies.

19 He appointed the moon for seasons: the sun knows his going down.

20 You make darkness, and it is night: wherein all the beasts of the forest do creep forth.

21 The young lions roar after their prey, and seek their meat from God.

22 The sun arises, they gather themselves together, and lay them down in their dens.

23 Man goes forth unto his work and to his labor until the evening.

24 O LORD, how manifold are your works! in wisdom have you made them all: the earth is full of your riches.

25 So is this great and wide sea, wherein are things creeping innumerable, both small and great beasts.

26 There go the ships: there is that leviathan, whom you have made to play therein.

27 These wait all upon you; that you may give them their meat in due season.

28 That you give them they gather: you open your hand, they are filled with good.

29 You hide your face, they are troubled: you take away their breath, they die, and return to their dust.

30 You send forth your spirit, they are created: and you renew the face of the earth.

31 The glory of the LORD shall endure for ever: the LORD shall rejoice in his works.

32 He looks on the earth, and it trembles: he touches the hills, and they smoke.

104:24 The Peppered Moth: Evolution Comes Unglued. "Almost all textbooks on evolution include the peppered moth as *the* classic example of evolution by natural selection. There are two types of peppered moths, a light-colored speckled variety and a dark variety. Most peppered moths in England were the light variety, which were camouflaged as they rested on tree trunks. The black variety stood out against the light bark and were easily seen and eaten by birds. But as the industrial revolution created pollution that covered tree trunks with soot, the dark variety was camouflaged better, so birds ate more of the light moths.

"The peppered moth story has been trumpeted since the 1950s as proof positive that evolution by natural selection is true. In 1978, one famous geneticist called the peppered moth 'the clearest case in which a conspicuous evolutionary process has actually been observed.'

"However, this 'clearest case' of purported Darwinian evolution by natural selection is not true! The nocturnal peppered moth does not rest on the trunks of trees during the day. In fact, despite over 40 years of intense field study, only two peppered moths have ever been seen naturally resting on tree trunks!

"So where did all the evolution textbook pictures of peppered moths on different colored tree trunks come from? They were all staged. The moths were glued, pinned, or placed onto tree trunks and their pictures taken. The scientists who used these pictures in their books to prove evolution *all* conveniently forgot to tell their readers this fact. If the *best* example of evolution is not true, how about all their *other* supposed examples? It makes you wonder, doesn't it?" Mark Varney

Evolutionary Humor. It's humorous that evolutionists cite the peppered moth as their best example, enabling them to "watch evolution in action." Watch closely: Before the moth's environment changed, some of the moths were mostly white, some were mostly black. After their environment changed, some were mostly white, some were mostly black. No new color or variety came into being, yet we have supposedly just witnessed evolution.

Evolutionist John Reader *(Missing Links)* explains this biased interpretation: "Ever since Darwin's work..., preconceptions have led evidence by the nose." Harvard professor and evolutionist Steven Jay Gould admits this scientific bias, "Facts do not 'speak for themselves'; they are read in light of theory."

Even Charles Darwin concedes, "Alas, how frequent, how almost universal it is in an author to persuade himself of the truth of his own dogmas." Keep this in mind when scientists proclaim the theory of evolution as "fact."

33 I will sing unto the LORD as long as I live: I will sing praise to my God while I have my being.

34 My meditation of him shall be sweet: I will be glad in the LORD.

35 Let the sinners be consumed out of the earth, and let the wicked be no more. Bless the LORD, O my soul. Praise the LORD.

PSALM 105

O GIVE thanks unto the LORD; call upon his name: make known his deeds among the people.

2 Sing unto him, sing psalms unto him: talk of all his wondrous works.

3 Glory in his holy name: let the heart of them rejoice that seek the LORD.

4 Seek the LORD, and his strength: seek his face evermore.

5 Remember his marvelous works that he has done; his wonders, and the judgments of his mouth;

6 O you seed of Abraham his servant, you children of Jacob his chosen.

7 He is the LORD our God: his judgments are in all the earth.

8 He has remembered his covenant for ever, the word which he commanded to a thousand generations.

9 Which covenant he made with Abraham, and his oath unto Isaac;

10 And confirmed the same unto Jacob for a law, and to Israel for an everlasting covenant:

11 Saying, Unto you will I give the land of Canaan, the lot of your inheritance:

12 When they were but a few men in number; yes, very few, and strangers in it.

13 When they went from one nation to another, from one kingdom to another people;

14 He suffered no man to do them wrong: yes, he reproved kings for their sakes;

15 Saying, Touch not my anointed, and do my prophets no harm.

16 Moreover he called for a famine upon the land: he brake the whole staff of bread.

17 He sent a man before them, even Joseph, who was sold for a servant:

18 Whose feet they hurt with fetters: he was laid in iron:

19 Until the time that his word came: the word of the LORD tried him.

20 The king sent and loosed him; even the ruler of the people, and let him go free.

21 He made him lord of his house, and ruler of all his substance:

22 To bind his princes at his pleasure; and teach his senators wisdom.

> A little science estranges men from God, but much science leads them back to Him.
>
> **LOUIS PASTEUR**
> 1822-1895
> FRENCH CHEMIST AND
> BACTERIOLOGIST

23 Israel also came into Egypt; and Jacob sojourned in the land of Ham.

24 And he increased his people greatly; and made them stronger than their enemies.

25 He turned their heart to hate his people, to deal subtly with his servants.

26 He sent Moses his servant; and Aaron whom he had chosen.

27 They showed his signs among them, and wonders in the land of Ham.

28 He sent darkness, and made it dark; and they rebelled not against his word.

29 He turned their waters into blood, and slew their fish.

105:17–19 If God is going to use you to reach the lost, be ready to be "tested." Your own family may turn against you. You may find yourself "laid in iron"—in a hardship in which there seems to be no escape. Don't get discouraged, and don't become passive in your evangelism. See 1 Peter 1:7 and "Closing Words of Comfort" in the appendix.

30 Their land brought forth frogs in abundance, in the chambers of their kings.

31 He spoke, and there came divers sorts of flies, and lice in all their coasts.

32 He gave them hail for rain, and flaming fire in their land.

33 He smote their vines also and their fig trees; and brake the trees of their coasts.

34 He spoke, and the locusts came, and caterpillars, and that without number,

35 And did eat up all the herbs in their land, and devoured the fruit of their ground.

36 He smote also all the firstborn in their land, the chief of all their strength.

37 He brought them forth also with silver and gold: and there was not one feeble person among their tribes.

38 Egypt was glad when they departed: for the fear of them fell upon them.

39 He spread a cloud for a covering; and fire to give light in the night.

40 The people asked, and he brought quails, and satisfied them with the bread of heaven.

41 He opened the rock, and the waters gushed out; they ran in the dry places like a river.

42 For he remembered his holy promise, and Abraham his servant.

43 And he brought forth his people with joy, and his chosen with gladness:

44 And gave them the lands of the heathen: and they inherited the labor of the people;

45 That they might observe his statutes, and keep his laws. Praise the LORD.

PSALM 106

P RAISE the LORD. O give thanks unto the LORD; for he is good: for his mercy endures for ever.

2 Who can utter the mighty acts of the LORD? who can show forth all his praise?

3 Blessed are they that keep judgment, and he that does righteousness at all times.

4 Remember me, O LORD, with the favor that you bear unto your people: O visit me with your salvation;

5 That I may see the good of your chosen, that I may rejoice in the gladness of your nation, that I may glory with your inheritance.

6 We have sinned with our fathers, we have committed iniquity, we have done wickedly.

7 Our fathers understood not your wonders in Egypt; they remembered not the multitude of your mercies; but provoked him at the sea, even at the Red sea.

8 Nevertheless he saved them for his name's sake, that he might make his mighty power to be known.

9 He rebuked the Red sea also, and it was dried up: so he led them through the depths, as through the wilderness.

10 And he saved them from the hand of him that hated them, and redeemed them from the hand of the enemy.

11 And the waters covered their enemies: there was not one of them left.

12 Then believed they his words; they sang his praise.

13 They soon forgot his works; they waited not for his counsel:

14 But lusted exceedingly in the wilderness, and tempted God in the desert.

15 And he gave them their request; but sent leanness into their soul.

16 They envied Moses also in the camp, and Aaron the saint of the LORD.

17 The earth opened and swallowed up Dathan and covered the company of Abiram.

18 And a fire was kindled in their company; the flame burned up the wicked.

19 They made a calf in Horeb, and worshipped the molten image.

20 Thus they changed their glory into the similitude of an ox that eats grass.

21 They forgot God their savior, which had done great things in Egypt;

22 Wondrous works in the land of Ham, and terrible things by the Red sea.

23 Therefore he said that he would destroy them, had not Moses his chosen stood before him in the breach, to turn away his wrath, lest he should destroy them.

24 Yes, they despised the pleasant land, they believed not his word:

25 But murmured in their tents, and hearkened not unto the voice of the LORD.

26 Therefore he lifted up his hand against them, to overthrow them in the wilderness:

27 To overthrow their seed also among the nations, and to scatter them in the lands.

28 They joined themselves also unto Baalpeor, and ate the sacrifices of the dead.

29 Thus they provoked him to anger with their inventions: and the plague brake in upon them.

30 Then stood up Phinehas, and executed judgment: and so the plague was stayed.

31 And that was counted unto him for righteousness unto all generations for evermore.

32 They angered him also at the waters of strife, so that it went ill with Moses for their sakes:

33 Because they provoked his spirit, so that he spoke unadvisedly with his lips.

34 They did not destroy the nations, concerning whom the LORD commanded them:

35 But were mingled among the heathen, and learned their works.

36 And they served their idols: which were a snare unto them.

37 Yes, they sacrificed their sons and their daughters unto devils,

38 And shed innocent blood, even the blood of their sons and of their daughters, whom they sacrificed unto the idols of Canaan: and the land was polluted with blood.

39 Thus were they defiled with their own works, and went a whoring with their own inventions.

40 Therefore was the wrath of the LORD kindled against his people, insomuch that he abhorred his own inheritance.

41 And he gave them into the hand of the heathen; and they that hated them ruled over them.

42 Their enemies also oppressed them, and they were brought into subjection under their hand.

43 Many times did he deliver them; but they provoked him with their counsel, and were brought low for their iniquity.

44 Nevertheless he regarded their affliction, when he heard their cry:

45 And he remembered for them his covenant, and repented according to the multitude of his mercies.

46 He made them also to be pitied of all those that carried them captives.

47 Save us, O LORD our God, and gather us from among the heathen, to give thanks unto your holy name, and to triumph in your praise.

48 Blessed be the LORD God of Israel from everlasting to everlasting: and let all the people say, Amen. Praise the LORD.

106:35–39 Abortion, a Result of Idolatry. How can people believe in God and yet believe in the killing of children through abortion? Simply because they "serve idols." Idolatry is perhaps the greatest of all sins because it opens the door to unrestrained evil—"My god gives me the right to choose!" etc. It gives sinners license not only to tolerate sin, but to sanction it, fanned by demonic influence. Those who create a god in their own image feel at liberty to go "a whoring with their own inventions."

The following is typical of how easy it is to create your own god:

Over the years, Ed and Joanne Liverani have found many reasons to summon God. But now, at middle age, they've boiled it down to one essential: "Not to get clobbered by life."

So sometime in the past ten years the Liveranis began to build their own church, salvaging bits of their old religion that they liked and chucking the rest. The first to go were an angry, vengeful God and hell—"That's just something they say to scare you," Ed said. They kept Jesus, "because Jesus is big on love." *The Washington Post* (January 9, 2000)

PSALM 107

O GIVE thanks unto the LORD, for he is good: for his mercy endures for ever.

2 Let the redeemed of the LORD say so, whom he has redeemed from the hand of the enemy;

3 And gathered them out of the lands, from the east, and from the west, from the north, and from the south.

4 They wandered in the wilderness in a solitary way; they found no city to dwell in.

5 Hungry and thirsty, their soul fainted in them.

6 Then they cried unto the LORD in their trouble, and he delivered them out of their distresses.

7 And he led them forth by the right way, that they might go to a city of habitation.

8 Oh that men would praise the LORD for his goodness, and for his wonderful works to the children of men!

9 **For he satisfies the longing soul, and fills the hungry soul with goodness.**

10 **Such as sit in darkness and in the shadow of death, being bound in affliction and iron;**

11 **Because they rebelled against the words of God, and contemned the counsel of the most High:**

12 **Therefore he brought down their heart with labor; they fell down, and there was none to help.**

13 **Then they cried unto the LORD in their trouble, and he saved them out of their distresses.**

14 **He brought them out of darkness and the shadow of death, and brake their bands in sunder.**

15 **Oh that men would praise the LORD for his goodness, and for his wonderful works to the children of men!**

16 **For he has broken the gates of brass, and cut the bars of iron in sunder.**

17 **Fools because of their transgression, and because of their iniquities, are afflicted.**

18 **Their soul abhors all manner of meat; and they draw near unto the gates of death.**

19 **Then they cry unto the LORD in their trouble, and he saves them out of their distresses.**

20 He sent his word, and healed them, and delivered them from their destructions.

21 Oh that men would praise the LORD for his goodness, and for his wonderful works to the children of men!

22 And let them sacrifice the sacrifices of thanksgiving, and declare his works with rejoicing.

23 They that go down to the sea in ships, that do business in great waters;

24 These see the works of the LORD, and his wonders in the deep.

25 For he commands, and raises the stormy wind, which lifts up the waves thereof.

107:2 How can the redeemed not "say so"? We have been redeemed from the cold hand of death. See verse 14.

107:17 Self-inflicted Misery. So much of the world's misery is self-inflicted: AIDS, alcoholism, obesity, guilt, drug addiction, nicotine addiction and its related diseases, etc. Look at the repercussions of adultery, revealed in this unsigned letter: "Eleven years ago, I walked out on a 12-year marriage. My wife was a good person, but for a long time she was under a lot of stress. Instead of helping her, I began an affair with her best friend. It was a disaster. This is what I gave up: 1) seeing my daughter grow up; 2) the respect of many long-time friends; 3) the enjoyment of living as a family; 4) a wife who was loyal, was appreciative and tried to make me happy. This is what I got: 1) two stepchildren who treated me like dirt; 2) a wife who didn't know how to make anything for dinner but reservations; 3) a wife whose only interest in me was how much money she could get; 4) a wife who made disparaging remarks about my family and ruined all my existing friendships; 5) finally, the best thing I got was a bitter, expensive divorce."

26 They mount up to the heaven, they go down again to the depths: their soul is melted because of trouble.

27 They reel to and fro, and stagger like a drunken man, and are at their wit's end.

28 Then they cry unto the LORD in their trouble, and he brings them out of their distresses.

29 He makes the storm a calm, so that the waves thereof are still.

30 Then are they glad because they be quiet; so he brings unto their desired haven.

31 Oh that men would praise the LORD for his goodness, and for his wonderful works to the children of men!

32 Let them exalt him also in the congregation of the people, and praise him in the assembly of the elders.

33 He turns rivers into a wilderness, and the watersprings into dry ground;

34 A fruitful land into barrenness, for the wickedness of them that dwell therein.

35 He turns the wilderness into a standing water, and dry ground into watersprings.

36 And there he makes the hungry to dwell, that they may prepare a city for habitation;

37 And sow the fields, and plant vineyards, which may yield fruits of increase.

38 He blesses them also, so that they are multiplied greatly; and suffers not their cattle to decrease.

39 Again, they are minished and brought low through oppression, affliction, and sorrow.

40 He pours contempt upon princes, and causes them to wander in the wilderness, where there is no way.

41 Yet sets he the poor on high from affliction, and makes him families like a flock.

42 The righteous shall see it, and rejoice: and all iniquity shall stop her mouth.

43 Whoso is wise, and will observe these things, even they shall understand the lovingkindness of the LORD.

PSALM 108

O GOD, my heart is fixed; I will sing and give praise, even with my glory.

2 Awake, psaltery and harp: I myself will awake early.

3 I will praise you, O LORD, among the people: and I will sing praises unto you among the nations.

4 For your mercy is great above the heavens: and your truth reaches unto the clouds.

5 Be exalted, O God, above the heavens: and your glory above all the earth;

6 That your beloved may be delivered: save with your right hand, and answer me.

7 God has spoken in his holiness; I will rejoice, I will divide Shechem, and mete out the valley of Succoth.

8 Gilead is mine; Manasseh is mine; Ephraim also is the strength of my head; Judah is my lawgiver;

9 Moab is my washpot; over Edom will I cast out my shoe; over Philistia will I triumph.

10 Who will bring me into the strong city? who will lead me into Edom?

11 Will not you, O God, who have cast us off? and will not you, O God, go forth with our hosts?

12 Give us help from trouble: for vain is the help of man.

13 Through God we shall do valiantly: for he it is that shall tread down our enemies.

PSALM 109

H OLD not your peace, O God of my praise;

2 For the mouth of the wicked and the mouth of the deceitful are opened against me: they have spoken against me with a lying tongue.

109:1–4 When the world turns against you because of your faith, and you find yourself in the valley of discouragement, climb up onto the high place of prayer.

109:15 *"God said He would blot out all remembrance of Amalek. The Bible itself disproves this statement by mentioning Amalek to this day."*

In Exodus 17:14, God told Moses to "write this for a memorial in a book…" Moses did that and God preserved the Book for 5,000 years, so skeptics would know that God keeps every promise He makes. The phrase, "I will utterly put out the remembrance of Amalek from under heaven," means that he will blot them out as a nation from the earth. There are no descendants of the Amalekites on the earth. They don't exist.

3 They compassed me about also with words of hatred; and fought against me without a cause.

4 For my love they are my adversaries: but I give myself unto prayer.

5 And they have rewarded me evil for good, and hatred for my love.

6 Set a wicked man over him: and let Satan stand at his right hand.

7 When he shall be judged, let him be condemned: and let his prayer become sin.

8 Let his days be few; and let another take his office.

9 Let his children be fatherless, and his wife a widow.

10 Let his children be continually vagabonds, and beg: let them seek their bread also out of their desolate places.

11 Let the extortioner catch all that he has; and let the strangers spoil his labor.

12 Let there be none to extend mercy unto him: neither let there be any to favor his fatherless children.

13 Let his posterity be cut off; and in the generation following let their name be blotted out.

14 Let the iniquity of his fathers be remembered with the LORD; and let not the sin of his mother be blotted out.

15 Let them be before the LORD continually, that he may cut off the memory of them from the earth.

16 Because that he remembered not to show mercy, but persecuted the poor and needy man, that he might even slay the broken in heart.

17 As he loved cursing, so let it come unto him: as he delighted not in blessing, so let it be far from him.

18 As he clothed himself with cursing like as with his garment, so let it come into his bowels like water, and like oil into his bones.

19 Let it be unto him as the garment which covers him, and for a girdle wherewith he is girded continually.

20 Let this be the reward of my adversaries from the LORD, and of them that speak evil against my soul.

21 But do for me, O GOD the Lord, for your name's sake: because your mercy is good, deliver me.

22 For I am poor and needy, and my heart is wounded within me.

23 I am gone like the shadow when it declines: I am tossed up and down as the locust.

24 My knees are weak through fasting; and my flesh fails of fatness.

25 I became also a reproach unto them: when they looked upon me they shook their heads.

26 Help me, O LORD my God: O save me according to your mercy:

109:8 This is a direct reference to Judas Iscariot. See Acts 1:20.

27 That they may know that this is your hand; that you, LORD, have done it.

28 Let them curse, but you bless: when they arise, let them be ashamed; but let your servant rejoice.

29 Let my adversaries be clothed with shame, and let them cover themselves with their own confusion, as with a mantle.

30 I will greatly praise the LORD with my mouth; yes, I will praise him among the multitude.

31 For he shall stand at the right hand of the poor, to save him from those that condemn his soul.

PSALM 110

THE LORD said unto my Lord, Sit at my right hand, until I make your enemies your footstool.

2 The LORD shall send the rod of your strength out of Zion: rule in the midst of your enemies.

3 Your people shall be willing in the day of your power, in the beauties of holiness from the womb of the morning: you have the dew of your youth.

4 The LORD has sworn, and will not repent, You are a priest for ever after the order of Melchizedek.

5 The Lord at your right hand shall strike through kings in the day of his wrath.

6 He shall judge among the heathen, he shall fill the places with the dead bodies; he shall wound the heads over many countries.

7 He shall drink of the brook in the way: therefore shall he lift up the head.

PSALM 111

PRAISE the LORD. I will praise the LORD with my whole heart, in the assembly of the upright, and in the congregation.

2 The works of the LORD are great, sought out of all them that have pleasure therein.

3 His work is honorable and glorious: and his righteousness endures for ever.

4 He has made his wonderful works to be remembered: the LORD is gracious and full of compassion.

5 He has given meat unto them that fear him: he will ever be mindful of his covenant.

6 He has showed his people the power of his works, that he may give them the heritage of the heathen.

7 The works of his hands are verity and judgment; all his commandments are sure.

8 They stand fast for ever and ever, and are done in truth and uprightness.

9 He sent redemption unto his people: he has commanded his covenant for ever: holy and reverend is his name.

10 The fear of the LORD is the beginning of wisdom: a good understanding have all they that do his commandments: his praise endures for ever.

. . . . . .

For how to use the Law in evangelism, see Matthew 19:17–22 comment.

. . . . . .

PSALM 112

PRAISE the LORD. Blessed is the man that fears the LORD, that delights greatly in his commandments.

2 His seed shall be mighty upon earth: the generation of the upright shall be blessed.

3 Wealth and riches shall be in his house: and his righteousness endures for ever.

4 Unto the upright there arises light in the darkness: he is gracious, and full of compassion, and righteous.

5 A good man shows favor, and lends: he will guide his affairs with discretion.

---

110 These verses speak of the coming Messiah. Hebrews 5:5-6 tells us that Jesus is our High Priest "after the order of Melchisedec" (v. 4), and John 5:22 says that God has committed all judgment to Jesus (v. 6). See also Hebrews 4:14; 7:22–26; Acts 10:42.

112:1 The apostle Paul is one who delighted in the Law of God. See Romans 7:22.

6 Surely he shall not be moved for ever: the righteous shall be in everlasting remembrance.

7 He shall not be afraid of evil tidings: his heart is fixed, trusting in the LORD.

8 His heart is established, he shall not be afraid, until he see his desire upon his enemies.

9 He has dispersed, he has given to the poor; his righteousness endures for ever; his horn shall be exalted with honor.

10 The wicked shall see it, and be grieved; he shall gnash with his teeth, and melt away: the desire of the wicked shall perish.

PSALM 113

P RAISE the LORD. Praise, O you servants of the LORD, praise the name of the LORD.

2 Blessed be the name of the LORD from this time forth and for evermore.

3 From the rising of the sun unto the going down of the same the LORD's name is to be praised.

4 The LORD is high above all nations, and his glory above the heavens.

5 Who is like unto the LORD our God, who dwells on high,

6 Who humbles himself to behold the things that are in heaven, and in the earth!

7 He raises up the poor out of the dust, and lifts the needy out of the dunghill;

8 That he may set him with princes, even with the princes of his people.

9 He makes the barren woman to keep house, and to be a joyful mother of children. Praise the LORD.

PSALM 114

W HEN Israel went out of Egypt, the house of Jacob from a people of strange language;

2 Judah was his sanctuary, and Israel his dominion.

3 The sea saw it, and fled: Jordan was driven back.

4 The mountains skipped like rams, and the little hills like lambs.

5 What ailed you, O you sea, that you fled? you Jordan, that you were driven back?

6 You mountains, that skipped like rams; and you little hills, like lambs?

7 Tremble, you earth, at the presence of the Lord, at the presence of the God of Jacob;

8 Who turned the rock into a standing water, the flint into a fountain of waters.

PSALM 115

N OT unto us, O LORD, not unto us, but unto your name give glory, for your mercy, and for your truth's sake.

2 Wherefore should the heathen say, Where is now their God?

3 But our God is in the heavens: he has done whatsoever he has pleased.

4 Their idols are silver and gold, the work of men's hands.

5 They have mouths, but they speak not: eyes have they, but they see not:

6 They have ears, but they hear not: noses have they, but they smell not:

7 They have hands, but they handle not: feet have they, but they walk not: neither speak they through their throat.

8 They that make them are like unto them; so is every one that trusts in them.

9 O Israel, trust in the LORD: he is their help and their shield.

10 O house of Aaron, trust in the LORD: he is their help and their shield.

11 You that fear the LORD, trust in the LORD: he is their help and their shield.

12 The LORD has been mindful of us: he will bless us; he will bless the house of Israel; he will bless the house of Aaron.

13 He will bless them that fear the LORD, both small and great.

113:3 As the Declaration of Independence was being signed, Samuel Adams stated, "We have this day restored the Sovereign to Whom all men ought to be obedient. He reigns in heaven and from the rising to the setting of the sun, let His kingdom come."

115:4-9 *"The First Commandment says, 'You shall have no other gods before Me.' That proves He isn't the only God!"*

That's true. Man has always made false gods. An old adage says, "God created man in His own image, and man has been returning the favor ever since." Hindus have millions of gods. Sometimes gods are made of wood or stone, other times man makes up a god in his mind. Whatever the case, making a god to suit yourself is called "idolatry," and is a transgression of both the First and Second of the Ten Commandments.

---

14 The LORD shall increase you more and more, you and your children.

15 You are blessed of the LORD which made heaven and earth.

16 The heaven, even the heavens, are the LORD's: but the earth has he given to the children of men.

17 The dead praise not the LORD, neither any that go down into silence.

18 But we will bless the LORD from this time forth and for evermore. Praise the LORD.

PSALM 116

I LOVE the LORD, because he has heard my voice and my supplications.

2 Because he has inclined his ear unto me, therefore will I call upon him as long as I live.

3 The sorrows of death compassed me, and the pains of hell gat hold upon me: I found trouble and sorrow.

4 Then called I upon the name of the LORD; O LORD, I beseech you, deliver my soul.

5 Gracious is the LORD, and righteous; yes, our God is merciful.

6 The LORD preserves the simple: I was brought low, and he helped me.

7 Return unto your rest, O my soul; for the LORD has dealt bountifully with you.

8 For you have delivered my soul from death, my eyes from tears, and my feet from falling.

9 I will walk before the LORD in the land of the living.

10 I believed, therefore have I spoken: I was greatly afflicted:

11 I said in my haste, All men are liars.

12 What shall I render unto the LORD for all his benefits toward me?

13 I will take the cup of salvation, and call upon the name of the LORD.

14 I will pay my vows unto the LORD now in the presence of all his people.

15 Precious in the sight of the LORD is the death of his saints.

16 O LORD, truly I am your servant; I am your servant, and the son of your handmaid: you have loosed my bonds.

17 I will offer to you the sacrifice of thanksgiving, and will call upon the name of the LORD.

18 I will pay my vows unto the LORD now in the presence of all his people.

19 In the courts of the LORD's house, in the midst of you, O Jerusalem. Praise the LORD.

116:11 "...20,000 middle and high-schoolers were surveyed by the Josephson Institute of Ethics —a nonprofit organization in Marina del Rey, Calif., devoted to character education. Ninety-two percent of the teenagers admitted having lied to their parents in the previous year, and 73 percent characterized themselves as 'serial liars,' meaning they told lies weekly. Despite these admissions, 91 percent of all respondents said they were 'satisfied with my own ethics and character.'" *Reader's Digest*, November 1999

PSALM 117

O PRAISE the LORD, all you nations: praise him, all you people.

2 For his merciful kindness is great toward us: and the truth of the LORD endures for ever. Praise the LORD.

PSALM 118

O GIVE thanks unto the LORD; for he is good: because his mercy endures for ever.

2 Let Israel now say, that his mercy endures for ever.

3 Let the house of Aaron now say, that his mercy endures for ever.

4 Let them now that fear the LORD say, that his mercy endures for ever.

5 I called upon the LORD in distress: the LORD answered me, and set me in a large place.

6 *The LORD is on my side; I will not fear: what can man do unto me?*

7 *The LORD takes my part with them that help me: therefore shall I see my desire upon them that hate me.*

8 *It is better to trust in the LORD than to put confidence in man.*

9 *It is better to trust in the LORD than to put confidence in princes.*

10 All nations compassed me about: but in the name of the LORD will I destroy them.

11 They compassed me about; yes, they compassed me about: but in the name of the LORD I will destroy them.

12 They compassed me about like bees: they are quenched as the fire of thorns:

for in the name of the LORD I will destroy them.

13 You have thrust sore at me that I might fall: but the LORD helped me.

14 The LORD is my strength and song, and is become my salvation.

15 The voice of rejoicing and salvation is in the tabernacles of the righteous: the right hand of the LORD does valiantly.

16 The right hand of the LORD is exalted: the right hand of the LORD does valiantly.

17 I shall not die, but live, and declare the works of the LORD.

18 The LORD has chastened me sore: but he has not given me over unto death.

19 Open to me the gates of righteousness: I will go into them, and I will praise the LORD:

20 This gate of the LORD, into which the righteous shall enter.

21 I will praise you: for you have heard me, and are become my salvation.

22 The stone which the builders refused is become the head stone of the corner.

23 This is the LORD's doing; it is marvelous in our eyes.

24 This is the day which the LORD has made; we will rejoice and be glad in it.

25 Save now, I beseech you, O LORD: O LORD, I beseech you, send now prosperity.

26 Blessed be he that comes in the name of the LORD: we have blessed you out of the house of the LORD.

27 God is the LORD, which has showed us light: bind the sacrifice with cords, even unto the horns of the altar.

118:6 Remember that courage isn't the absence of fear, but the conquering of it. If we really care for the lost, each of us must learn to push aside fear and replace it with faith in God. You do your part, and God will do His.

118:8 The middle of the Bible. Psalm 118 is the middle chapter of the entire Bible. Psalm 117 is the shortest chapter in the Bible. Psalm 119 is the longest chapter in the Bible. The Scriptures have 594 chapters before Psalm 118, and 594 chapters after Psalm 118. If you add up all the chapters except 118, you get a total of 1188 chapters. Psalm 118:8 is the middle verse of the entire Bible. It goes without saying that the central verse has an important message: "It is better to trust in the Lord than to put confidence in man."

118:22 This is a direct reference to the Messiah. See 1 Peter 2:7-8.

118:27 We must "bind" our bodies as living sacrifices on the altar of service for God (see Romans 12:1).

28 You are my God, and I will praise you: you are my God, I will exalt you.

29 O give thanks unto the LORD; for he is good: for his mercy endures for ever.

PSALM 119

B LESSED are the undefiled in the way, who walk in the law of the LORD.

2 Blessed are they that keep his testimonies, and that seek him with the whole heart.

3 They also do no iniquity: they walk in his ways.

4 You have commanded us to keep your precepts diligently.

5 O that my ways were directed to keep your statutes!

6 Then shall I not be ashamed, when I have respect unto all your commandments.

7 I will praise you with uprightness of heart, when I shall have learned your righteous judgments.

8 I will keep your statutes: O forsake me not utterly.

9 Wherewithal shall a young man cleanse his way? by taking heed thereto according to your word.

10 With my whole heart have I sought you: O let me not wander from your commandments.

11 Your word have I hid in my heart, that I might not sin against you.

12 Blessed are you, O LORD: teach me your statutes.

13 With my lips have I declared all the judgments of your mouth.

14 I have rejoiced in the way of your testimonies, as much as in all riches.

> If you pick up a dog
> and make him prosperous,
> he will not bite you.
> This is the principal difference
> between a dog and a man.

MARK TWAIN

1835-1910

AMERICAN WRITER AND HUMORIST

15 I will meditate in your precepts, and have respect unto your ways.

16 I will delight myself in your statutes: I will not forget your word.

17 Deal bountifully with your servant, that I may live, and keep your word.

18 Open my eyes, that I may behold wondrous things out of your law.

19 I am a stranger in the earth: hide not your commandments from me.

20 My soul breaks for the longing that it has unto your judgments at all times.

21 You have rebuked the proud that are cursed, which do err from your commandments.

22 Remove from me reproach and contempt; for I have kept your testimonies.

23 Princes also did sit and speak against me: but your servant did meditate in your statutes.

24 Your testimonies also are my delight and my counselors.

25 My soul cleaves unto the dust: quicken me according to your word.

26 I have declared my ways, and you heard me: teach me your statutes.

119:2 This wonderful Psalm gives us insight into the rewards of meditating on God's Word. It reveals the great key to living a life of victory as a Christian. That key is to seek and serve Him with a "whole heart."

119:14 "I believe the Bible is the best gift God has given to man. All the good Savior gave to the world was communicated through this Book." Abraham Lincoln

119:16 "God's Word is our primary weapon in evangelism. It is not designed to destroy life, but to give it. It is not to be used to harm but like a surgeon's scalpel, to save. Just as a builder knows his tools and an artist knows his brushes and pens, we need to know the Bible." Greg Laurie

119:18 "Ignorance of the nature and design of the Law is at the bottom of most religious mistakes." John Newton

119:105 *The Bible Stands Alone*

In 1889 a schoolteacher told a ten-year-old boy, "You will never amount to very much." That boy was Albert Einstein. In 1954 a music manager told a young singer, "You ought to go back to driving a truck." That singer was Elvis Presley. In 1962 a record company told a group of singers, "We don't like your sound. Groups with guitars are definitely on their way out." They said that to the Beatles. Man is prone to make mistakes. Those who reject the Bible should take the time to look at the evidence before they come to a verdict.

1. It is unique in its continuity. If just 10 people today were picked who were from the same place, born around the same time, spoke the same language, and made about the same amount of money, and were asked to write on just one controversial subject, they would have trouble agreeing with each other. But the Bible stands alone. It was written over a period of 1,600 years by more than 40 writers from all walks of life. Some were fishermen; some were politicians. Others were generals or kings, shepherds or historians. They were from three different continents, and wrote in three different languages. They wrote on hundreds of controversial subjects yet they wrote with agreement and harmony. They wrote in dungeons, in temples, on beaches, and on hillsides, during peacetime and during war. Yet their words sound like they came from the same source. So even though 10 people today couldn't write on one controversial subject and agree, God picked 40 different people to write the Bible—and it stands the test of time.

2. It is unique in its circulation. The invention of the printing press in 1450 made it possible to print books in large quantities. The first book printed was the Bible. Since then, the Bible has been read by more people and printed more times than any other book in history. By 1930, over one billion Bibles had been distributed by Bible societies around the world. By 1977, Bible societies alone were printing over 200 million Bibles each year, and this number doesn't include the many other Bible publishers. No one who is interested in knowing the truth can ignore such an important book.

3. It is unique in its translation. The Bible has been translated into over 1,400 languages. No other book even comes close.

4. It is unique in its survival. In ancient times, books were copied by hand onto manuscripts which were made from parchment and would decay over time. Ancient books are available today only because someone made copies of the originals to preserve them. For example, the original writings of Julius Caesar are no longer around. We know what he wrote only by the copies we have. Only 10 copies still exist, and they were made 1,000 years after he died. Only 600 copies of Homer's *The Iliad* exist, made 1,300 years after the originals were written. No other book has as many copies of the ancient manuscripts as the Bible. In fact, there are over 24,000 copies of New Testament manuscripts, some written within 35 years of the writer's death.

5. It is unique in withstanding attack. No other book has been so attacked throughout history as the Bible. In A.D. 300 the Roman emperor Diocletian ordered every Bible burned because he thought that by destroying the Scriptures he could destroy Christianity. Anyone caught with a Bible would be executed. But just 25 years later, the Roman emperor Constantine ordered that 50 perfect copies of the Bible be made at government expense. The French philosopher Voltaire, a skeptic who destroyed the faith of many people, boasted that within 100 years of his death, the Bible would disappear from the face of the earth. Voltaire died in 1728, but the Bible lives on. The irony of history is that 50 years after his death, the Geneva Bible Society moved into his former house and used his printing presses to print thousands of Bibles.

The Bible has also survived criticism. No book has been more attacked for its accuracy. And yet archeologists are proving every year that the Bible's detailed descriptions of historic events are correct. See Matthew 4:4 and 1 Peter 1:25 comments.

Compiled by Justin and Jordan Drake

*Hold fast to the Bible as the sheet anchor
of your liberties;
write its precepts in your hearts,
and practice them in your lives.*

Ulysses S. Grant

1822-1885
18TH PRESIDENT OF THE UNITED STATES
COMMANDER OF UNION FORCES
DURING THE CIVIL WAR

27 Make me to understand the way of your precepts: so shall I talk of your wondrous works.

28 My soul melts for heaviness: strengthen me according unto your word.

29 Remove from me the way of lying: and grant me your law graciously.

30 I have chosen the way of truth: your judgments have I laid before me.

31 I have stuck unto your testimonies: O LORD, put me not to shame.

32 I will run the way of your commandments, when you shall enlarge my heart.

33 Teach me, O LORD, the way of your statutes; and I shall keep it unto the end.

34 Give me understanding, and I shall keep your law; yes, I shall observe it with my whole heart.

35 Make me to go in the path of your commandments; for therein do I delight.

36 Incline my heart unto your testimonies, and not to covetousness.

37 Turn away my eyes from beholding vanity; and quicken me in your way.

38 Establish your word unto your servant, who is devoted to your fear.

39 Turn away my reproach which I fear: for your judgments are good.

40 Behold, I have longed after your precepts: quicken me in your righteousness.

41 Let your mercies come also unto me, O LORD, even your salvation, according to your word.

42 So shall I have wherewith to answer him that reproaches me: for I trust in your word.

43 And take not the word of truth utterly out of my mouth; for I have hoped in your judgments.

44 So shall I keep your law continually for ever and ever.

45 And I will walk at liberty: for I seek your precepts.

46 I will speak of your testimonies also before kings, and will not be ashamed.

47 And I will delight myself in your commandments, which I have loved.

48 My hands also will I lift up unto your commandments, which I have loved; and I will meditate in your statutes.

49 Remember the word unto your servant, upon which you have caused me to hope.

50 This is my comfort in my affliction: for your word has quickened me.

51 The proud have had me greatly in derision: yet have I not declined from your law.

52 I remembered your judgments of old, O LORD; and have comforted myself.

53 Horror has taken hold upon me because of the wicked that forsake your law.

54 Your statutes have been my songs in the house of my pilgrimage.

55 I have remembered your name, O LORD, in the night, and have kept your law.

56 This I had, because I kept your precepts.

57 You are my portion, O LORD: I have said that I would keep your words.

58 I entreated your favor with my whole heart: be merciful unto me according to your word.

59 I thought on my ways, and turned my feet unto your testimonies.

60 I made haste, and delayed not to keep your commandments.

61 The bands of the wicked have robbed me: but I have not forgotten your law.

62 At midnight I will rise to give thanks unto you because of your righteous judgments.

63 I am a companion of all them that fear you, and of them that keep your precepts.

64 The earth, O LORD, is full of your mercy: teach me your statutes.

65 You have dealt well with your servant, O LORD, according unto your word.

66 Teach me good judgment and knowledge: for I have believed your commandments.

67 Before I was afflicted I went astray: but now have I kept your word.

68 You are good, and do good; teach me your statutes.

69 The proud have forged a lie against me: but I will keep your precepts with my whole heart.

70 Their heart is as fat as grease; but I delight in your law.

71 It is good for me that I have been afflicted; that I might learn your statutes.

72 The law of your mouth is better unto me than thousands of gold and silver.

73 Your hands have made me and fashioned me: give me understanding, that I may learn your commandments.

74 They that fear you will be glad when they see me; because I have hoped in your word.

75 I know, O LORD, that your judgments are right, and that you in faithfulness have afflicted me.

76 Let, I pray you, your merciful kindness be for my comfort, according to your word unto your servant.

77 Let your tender mercies come unto me, that I may live: for your law is my delight.

78 Let the proud be ashamed; for they dealt perversely with me without a cause: but I will meditate in your precepts.

79 Let those that fear you turn unto me, and those that have known your testimonies.

80 Let my heart be sound in your statutes; that I be not ashamed.

81 My soul faints for your salvation: but I hope in your word.

82 My eyes fail for your word, saying, When will you comfort me?

83 For I am become like a bottle in the smoke; yet do I not forget your statutes.

84 How many are the days of your servant? when will you execute judgment on them that persecute me?

85 The proud have digged pits for me, which are not after your law.

86 All your commandments are faithful: they persecute me wrongfully; help me.

87 They had almost consumed me upon earth; but I forsook not your precepts.

88 Quicken me after your lovingkindness; so shall I keep the testimony of your mouth.

89 For ever, O LORD, your word is settled in heaven.

90 Your faithfulness is unto all generations: you have established the earth, and it abides.

91 They continue this day according to your ordinances: for all are your servants.

92 Unless your law had been my delights, I should then have perished in my affliction.

93 I will never forget your precepts: for with them you have quickened me.

94 I am yours, save me: for I have sought your precepts.

119:72 "A thorough knowledge of the Bible is worth more than a college education." Theodore Roosevelt

95 The wicked have waited for me to destroy me: but I will consider your testimonies.

96 I have seen an end of all perfection: but your commandment is exceeding broad.

97 O how I love your law! it is my meditation all the day.

98 You through your commandments have made me wiser than my enemies: for they are ever with me.

99 I have more understanding than all my teachers: for your testimonies are my meditation.

100 I understand more than the ancients, because I keep your precepts.

101 I have refrained my feet from every evil way, that I might keep your word.

102 I have not departed from your judgments: for you have taught me.

103 How sweet are your words unto my taste! yes, sweeter than honey to my mouth!

104 Through your precepts I get understanding: therefore I hate every false way.

105 Your word is a lamp unto my feet, and a light unto my path.

106 I have sworn, and I will perform it, that I will keep your righteous judgments.

107 I am afflicted very much: quicken me, O Lord, according unto your word.

108 Accept, I beseech you, the freewill offerings of my mouth, O Lord, and teach me your judgments.

109 My soul is continually in my hand: yet do I not forget your law.

110 The wicked have laid a snare for me: yet I erred not from your precepts.

111 Your testimonies have I taken as an heritage for ever: for they are the rejoicing of my heart.

112 I have inclined my heart to perform your statutes always, even unto the end.

113 I hate vain thoughts: but your law do I love.

114 You are my hiding place and my shield: I hope in your word.

115 Depart from me, you evildoers: for I will keep the commandments of my God.

116 Uphold me according unto your word, that I may live: and let me not be ashamed of my hope.

117 Hold me up, and I shall be safe: and I will have respect unto your statutes continually.

118 You have trodden down all them that err from your statutes: for their deceit is falsehood.

119 You put away all the wicked of the earth like dross: therefore I love your testimonies.

120 My flesh trembles for fear of you; and I am afraid of your judgments.

121 I have done judgment and justice: leave me not to my oppressors.

122 Be surety for your servant for good: let not the proud oppress me.

123 My eyes fail for your salvation, and for the word of your righteousness.

124 Deal with your servant according unto your mercy, and teach me your statutes.

125 I am your servant; give me understanding, that I may know your testimonies.

126 *It is time for you, Lord, to work: for they have made void your law.*

127 *Therefore I love your commandments above gold; yes, above fine gold.*

128 Therefore I esteem all your precepts concerning all things to be right; and I hate every false way.

129 Your testimonies are wonderful: therefore does my soul keep them.

119:104 "But for this Book [the Bible], we could not know right from wrong...Take all you can of this Book upon reason, and the balance on faith, and you will live and die a happier man." Abraham Lincoln

119:128 This verse covers all of God's judgments over sinners—harsh though they may seem to our darkened minds.

QUESTIONS & OBJECTIONS

119:160 *"The Bible has changed down through the ages."*

No, it hasn't. God has preserved His Word. In the spring of 1947, the Dead Sea Scrolls were discovered. These manuscripts were copies of large portions of the Old Testament, a thousand years older than any other existing copies. Study of the scrolls has revealed that the Bible hasn't changed in content down through the ages as many skeptics had surmised. (See 1 Peter 1:25 comment.)

Anyone can now obtain access to computer programs that give the original Hebrew and Greek words, and the only "changes" have been made for clarity. For example, the old English translation of 2 Corinthians 12:8 is "For this thing I besought the Lord thrice...," while a contemporary translation is "Concerning this thing I pleaded with the Lord three times..."

---

130 The entrance of your words gives light; it gives understanding unto the simple.

131 I opened my mouth, and panted: for I longed for your commandments.

132 Look upon me, and be merciful unto me, as you used to do unto those that love your name.

133 Order my steps in your word: and let not any iniquity have dominion over me.

134 Deliver me from the oppression of man: so will I keep your precepts.

135 Make your face to shine upon your servant; and teach me your statutes.

136 Rivers of waters run down my eyes, because they keep not your law.

137 Righteous are you, O LORD, and upright are your judgments.

138 Your testimonies that you have commanded are righteous and very faithful.

139 My zeal has consumed me, because my enemies have forgotten your words.

140 Your word is very pure: therefore your servant loves it.

141 I am small and despised: yet do not I forget your precepts.

142 Your righteousness is an everlasting righteousness, and your law is the truth.

143 Trouble and anguish have taken hold on me: yet your commandments are my delights.

144 The righteousness of your testimonies is everlasting: give me understanding, and I shall live.

145 I cried with my whole heart; hear me, O LORD: I will keep your statutes.

146 I cried unto you; save me, and I shall keep your testimonies.

147 I prevented the dawning of the morning, and cried: I hoped in your word.

148 My eyes prevent the night watches, that I might meditate in your word.

149 Hear my voice according unto your lovingkindness: O LORD, quicken me according to your judgment.

150 They draw near that follow after mischief: they are far from your law.

151 You are near, O LORD; and all your commandments are truth.

119:133   Sin may beset the Christian, but those whose steps are in God's Word prevent sin from having dominion over them. See Romans 6:12–18. See also Galatians 5:16 comment.

119:136   "And you, too, who are moral enough in your conversation, and regular in your attendance on the outward forms of religion, you who never weep over sinners, you who never pray for them, you who never speak to them, you who leave all that to your minister, and think you have nothing to do with it, the voice of your brother's blood crieth from the ground to heaven." Charles Spurgeon

The Bible and All It Contains

119:162

A young man once received a letter from a lawyer stating that his grandmother had left him an inheritance. To his astonishment, it was $50,000 plus "my Bible and all it contains."

The youth was delighted to receive the money. However, he knew what the Bible contained, and because he wasn't into religion he didn't bother to open it. Instead, he put it on a high shelf.

He gambled the $50,000, and over the next fifty years he lived as a pauper, scraping for every meal. Finally he became so destitute, he had to move in with his relatives.

When he cleaned out his room, he reached up to get the dusty old Bible from the shelf. As he took it down, his trembling hands dropped it onto the floor, flinging it open to reveal a $100 bill between every page.

The man had lived as a pauper, simply because of his prejudice. He thought he knew what the Bible "contained."

152 Concerning your testimonies, I have known of old that you have founded them for ever.

153 Consider my affliction, and deliver me: for I do not forget your law.

154 Plead my cause, and deliver me: quicken me according to your word.

155 Salvation is far from the wicked: for they seek not your statutes.

156 Great are your tender mercies, O LORD: quicken me according to your judgments.

157 Many are my persecutors and my enemies; yet do I not decline from your testimonies.

158 I beheld the transgressors, and was grieved; because they kept not your word.

159 Consider how I love your precepts: quicken me, O LORD, according to your lovingkindness.

160 Your word is true from the beginning: and every one of your righteous judgments endures for ever.

161 Princes have persecuted me without a cause: but my heart stands in awe of your word.

162 I rejoice at your word, as one that finds great spoil.

163 I hate and abhor lying: but your law do I love.

164 Seven times a day do I praise you because of your righteous judgments.

165 *Great peace have they which love your law: and nothing shall offend them.*

166 LORD, I have hoped for your salvation, and done your commandments.

167 My soul has kept your testimonies; and I love them exceedingly.

168 I have kept your precepts and your testimonies: for all my ways are before you.

169 Let my cry come near before you, O LORD: give me understanding according to your word.

170 Let my supplication come before you: deliver me according to your word.

171 My lips shall utter praise, when you have taught me your statutes.

172 My tongue shall speak of your word: for all your commandments are righteousness.

173 Let your hand help me; for I have chosen your precepts.

174 I have longed for your salvation, O LORD; and your law is my delight.

175 Let my soul live, and it shall praise you; and let your judgments help me.

176 I have gone astray like a lost sheep; seek your servant; for I do not forget your commandments.

PSALM 120

IN my distress I cried unto the LORD, and he heard me.

2 Deliver my soul, O LORD, from lying lips, and from a deceitful tongue.

3 What shall be given unto you? or what shall be done unto you, you false tongue?

4 Sharp arrows of the mighty, with coals of juniper.

5 Woe is me, that I sojourn in Mesech, that I dwell in the tents of Kedar!

6 My soul has long dwelt with him that hates peace.

7 I am for peace: but when I speak, they are for war.

> What health is to the heart,
>
> holiness is to the soul.
>
> **JOHN FLAVEL**
>
> 1630-1691
>
> ENGLISH PURITAN

PSALM 121

I WILL lift up my eyes unto the hills, from whence comes my help.

2 My help comes from the LORD, who made heaven and earth.

3 He will not suffer your foot to be moved: he that keeps you will not slumber.

4 Behold, he that keeps Israel shall neither slumber nor sleep.

5 The LORD is your keeper: the LORD is your shade upon your right hand.

6 The sun shall not smite you by day, nor the moon by night.

7 The LORD shall preserve you from all evil: he shall preserve your soul.

8 The LORD shall preserve your going out and your coming in from this time forth, and even for evermore.

PSALM 122

I WAS glad when they said unto me, Let us go into the house of the LORD.

2 Our feet shall stand within your gates, O Jerusalem.

3 Jerusalem is built as a city that is compact together:

4 Whither the tribes go up, the tribes of the LORD, unto the testimony of Israel, to give thanks unto the name of the LORD.

5 For there are set thrones of judgment, the thrones of the house of David.

6 Pray for the peace of Jerusalem: they shall prosper that love you.

7 Peace be within your walls, and prosperity within your palaces.

8 For my brethren and companions' sakes, I will now say, Peace be within you.

9 Because of the house of the LORD our God I will seek your good.

PSALM 123

U NTO you lift I up my eyes, O you that dwells in the heavens.

2 Behold, as the eyes of servants look unto the hand of their masters, and as the eyes of a maiden unto the hand of her mistress; so our eyes wait upon the Lord our God, until that he have mercy upon us.

3 Have mercy upon us, O LORD, have mercy upon us: for we are exceedingly filled with contempt.

4 Our soul is exceedingly filled with the scorning of those that are at ease, and with the contempt of the proud.

PSALM 124

I F it had not been the LORD who was on our side, now may Israel say;

2 If it had not been the LORD who was on our side, when men rose up against us:

3 Then they had swallowed us up quick, when their wrath was kindled against us:

4 Then the waters had overwhelmed us, the stream had gone over our soul:

5 Then the proud waters had gone over our soul.

6 Blessed be the LORD, who has not given us as a prey to their teeth.

7 Our soul is escaped as a bird out of the snare of the fowlers: the snare is broken, and we are escaped.

125:1 If we are "moved" by adversity, it is because we lack trust in the Lord. The amount of joy we retain in tribulation reveals the depth of our trust in God. The apostle Paul said, "I am exceeding joyful in all our tribulation" (2 Corinthians 7:4).

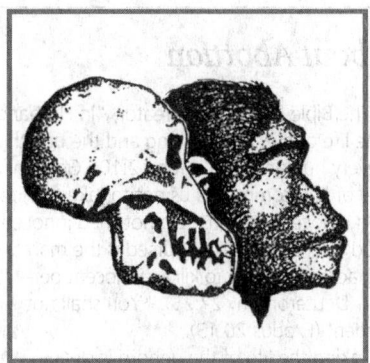

To see how the theory of evolution clashes with the facts, see Acts 14:15 comment.

2 Then was our mouth filled with laughter, and our tongue with singing: then said they among the heathen, The LORD has done great things for them.

3 The LORD has done great things for us; whereof we are glad.

4 Turn again our captivity, O LORD, as the streams in the south.

5 *They that sow in tears shall reap in joy.*

6 *He that goes forth and weeping, bearing precious seed, shall doubtless come again with rejoicing, bringing his sheaves with him.*

PSALM 127

EXCEPT the LORD build the house, they labor in vain that build it: except the LORD keep the city, the watchman wakes but in vain.

2 It is vain for you to rise up early, to sit up late, to eat the bread of sorrows: for so he gives his beloved sleep.

3 Lo, children are an heritage of the LORD: and the fruit of the womb is his reward.

4 As arrows are in the hand of a mighty man; so are children of the youth.

5 Happy is the man that has his quiver full of them: they shall not be ashamed, but they shall speak with the enemies in the gate.

8 Our help is in the name of the LORD, who made heaven and earth.

PSALM 125

THEY that trust in the LORD shall be as mount Zion, which cannot be removed, but abides for ever.

2 As the mountains are round about Jerusalem, so the LORD is round about his people from henceforth even for ever.

3 For the rod of the wicked shall not rest upon the lot of the righteous; lest the righteous put forth their hands unto iniquity.

4 Do good, O LORD, unto those that be good, and to them that are upright in their hearts.

5 As for such as turn aside unto their crooked ways, the LORD shall lead them forth with the workers of iniquity: but peace shall be upon Israel.

PSALM 126

WHEN the LORD turned again the captivity of Zion, we were like them that dream.

PSALM 128

BLESSED is every one that fears the LORD; that walks in his ways.

2 For you shall eat the labor of your hands: happy shall you be, and it shall be well with you.

3 Your wife shall be as a fruitful vine by the sides of your house: your children like olive plants round about your table.

4 Behold, that thus shall the man be blessed that fears the LORD.

126:6 Sowing in tears. "But from whence shall I fetch my argument? With what shall I win them? Oh, that I could tell! I would write to them in tears, I would weep out every argument, I would empty my veins for ink, I would petition them on my knees. Oh how thankful I would be if they would be prevailed with to repent and turn!" Joseph Alleine

"Jesus Christ wept over Jerusalem, and you will have to weep over sinners if they are to be saved through you." Charles Spurgeon

127:3   *What God's Word Says About Abortion*

By Lynn Copeland

God speaks very clearly in the Bible on the value of unborn children.

God's Word says that He personally made each one of us, and has a plan for each life: "Before I formed you in the womb I knew you, before you were born I set you apart" (Jeremiah 1:5). "Even before I was born, God had chosen me to be His" (Galatians 1:15). "For You created my inmost being; You knit me together in my mother's womb...Your eyes saw my unformed body. All the days ordained for me were written in Your book before one of them came to be" (Psalm 139:13, 16). "Your hands shaped me and made me ... Did You not clothe me with skin and flesh and knit me together with bones and sinews? You gave me life" (Job 10:8–12). "This is what the Lord says—He who made you, who formed you in the womb" (Isaiah 44:2). "Did not He who made me in the womb make them? Did not the same One form us both within our mothers?" (Job 31:15).

Because man is made in God's own image (Genesis 1:27), each life is of great value to God: "Children are a gift from God" (Psalm 127:3). He even calls our children His own: "You took *your* sons and daughters whom you bore to Me and sacrificed them...You slaughtered *My* children" (Ezekiel 16:20-21).

The Bible says of our Creator, "In His hand is the life of every living thing and the breath of every human being" (Job 12:10). God, the giver of life, commands us not to take the life of an innocent person: "Do not shed innocent blood" (Jeremiah 7:6); "Cursed is the man who accepts a bribe to kill an innocent person" (Deuteronomy 27:25). "You shall not murder" (Exodus 20:13).

Taking the life of the unborn is clearly murder—"He didn't *kill* me in the womb, with my mother as my grave" (Jeremiah 20:17)—and God vowed to punish those who "ripped open the women with child" (Amos 1:13). The unborn child was granted equal protection in the law; if he lost his life, the one who caused his death must lose his own life: "If men who are fighting hit a pregnant woman and she gives birth prematurely but there is no serious injury, the offender must be fined...
But if there is serious injury, you are to take life for life" (Exodus 21:22,23).

Life is a gift created by God, and is not to be taken away by abortion. God is "pro-choice," but He tells us clearly the only acceptable choice to make:

"I have set before you life and death, blessings and curses. Now choose life, so that you and your children may live" (Deuteronomy 30:19).

---

5 The LORD shall bless you out of Zion: and you shall see the good of Jerusalem all the days of your life.

6 Yes, you shall see your children's children, and peace upon Israel.

PSALM 129

MANY a time have they afflicted me from my youth, may Israel now say:

2 Many a time have they afflicted me from my youth: yet they have not prevailed against me.

3 The plowers plowed upon my back: they made long their furrows.

4 The LORD is righteous: he has cut asunder the cords of the wicked.

5 Let them all be confounded and turned back that hate Zion.

6 Let them be as the grass upon the housetops, which withers before it grows up:

7 Wherewith the mower fills not his hand; nor he that binds sheaves his bosom.

8 Neither do they which go by say, The blessing of the LORD be upon you: we bless you in the name of the LORD.

PSALM 130

OUT of the depths have I cried unto you, O LORD.

2 Lord, hear my voice: let your ears be attentive to the voice of my supplications.

> There is no point
> on which men make greater mistakes
> than on the relation
> which exists between the Law
> and the gospel.

CHARLES SPURGEON

1834-1892

FOREMOST PREACHER

OF THE 19TH CENTURY

3 If you, LORD, should mark iniquities, O Lord, who shall stand?

4 But there is forgiveness with you, that you may be feared.

5 I wait for the LORD, my soul does wait, and in his word do I hope.

6 My soul waits for the Lord more than they that watch for the morning: I say, more than they that watch for the morning.

7 Let Israel hope in the LORD: for with the LORD there is mercy, and with him is plenteous redemption.

8 And he shall redeem Israel from all his iniquities.

PSALM 131

LORD, my heart is not haughty, nor my eyes lofty: neither do I exercise myself in great matters, or in things too high for me.

2 Surely I have behaved and quieted myself, as a child that is weaned of his mother: my soul is even as a weaned child.

3 Let Israel hope in the LORD from henceforth and for ever.

PSALM 132

LORD, remember David, and all his afflictions:

2 How he swore unto the LORD, and vowed unto the mighty God of Jacob;

3 Surely I will not come into the tabernacle of my house, nor go up into my bed;

4 I will not give sleep to my eyes, or slumber to my eyelids,

5 Until I find out a place for the LORD, an habitation for the mighty God of Jacob.

6 Lo, we heard of it at Ephratah: we found it in the fields of the wood.

7 We will go into his tabernacles: we will worship at his footstool.

8 Arise, O LORD, into your rest; you, and the ark of your strength.

9 Let your priests be clothed with righteousness; and let your saints shout for joy.

10 For your servant David's sake turn not away the face of your anointed.

11 The LORD has sworn in truth unto David; he will not turn from it; Of the fruit of your body will I set upon your throne.

12 If your children will keep my covenant and my testimony that I shall teach them, their children shall also sit upon your throne for evermore.

13 For the LORD has chosen Zion; he has desired it for his habitation.

14 This is my rest for ever: here will I dwell; for I have desired it.

15 I will abundantly bless her provision: I will satisfy her poor with bread.

16 I will also clothe her priests with salvation: and her saints shall shout aloud for joy.

17 There will I make the horn of David to bud: I have ordained a lamp for my anointed.

18 His enemies will I clothe with shame: but upon himself shall his crown flourish.

130:1–4 Here is true contrition—a humble cry to God for mercy. Those who obtain the mercy of the cross and see the cost of redemption live their lives in the fear of the Lord, knowing that they were not redeemed with silver and gold, but with the precious blood of Christ. See 1 Peter 1:17-19.

131:1 Beware of "intellectual Christianity." It is easy to become puffed up with a theology that forgets "the simplicity that is in Christ" (2 Corinthians 11:3). The measure of the quality of our Christian theology will be evidenced by the depth of our concern for the lost.

QUESTIONS & OBJECTIONS

135:14   ***"The Bible says 'God repented.'***
Doesn't that show He is capable of sin?"

"Repent" means "to have a change of mind." When the Bible tells sinners to repent, it means to change their direction, to turn from their sins. God's "repenting" is when He turns away from His fierce anger toward sinners. He warns men of the consequences of their disobedience. If they repent (turn from their sins), He will "repent" by not pouring out His promised wrath on them. For instance, Jonah 3:8-9 says, "Let them turn every one from his evil way...Who can tell if God will turn and repent, and turn away from his fierce anger, that we perish not?" (See also Jeremiah 18:8.)

PSALM 133

BEHOLD, how good and how pleasant it is for brethren to dwell together in unity!

2 It is like the precious ointment upon the head, that ran down upon the beard, even Aaron's beard: that went down to the skirts of his garments;

3 As the dew of Hermon, and as the dew that descended upon the mountains of Zion: for there the LORD commanded the blessing, even life for evermore.

PSALM 134

BEHOLD, bless the LORD, all you servants of the LORD, which by night stand in the house of the LORD.

2 Lift up your hands in the sanctuary, and bless the LORD.

3 The LORD that made heaven and earth bless you out of Zion.

PSALM 135

PRAISE the LORD. Praise the name of the LORD; praise him, O you servants of the LORD.

2 You that stand in the house of the LORD, in the courts of the house of our God.

3 Praise the LORD; for the LORD is good: sing praises unto his name; for it is pleasant.

4 For the LORD has chosen Jacob unto himself, and Israel for his peculiar treasure.

5 For I know that the LORD is great, and that our Lord is above all gods.

6 Whatsoever the LORD pleased, that did he in heaven, and in earth, in the seas, and all deep places.

7 He causes the vapors to ascend from the ends of the earth; he makes lightnings for the rain; he brings the wind out of his treasuries.

8 Who smote the firstborn of Egypt, both of man and beast.

135:7 *Scientific Facts in the Bible.* The Scriptures inform us, "All the rivers run into the sea; yet the sea is not full; unto the place from whence the rivers come, there they return again" (Ecclesiastes 1:7). This statement alone may not seem profound. But, when considered with other biblical passages, it becomes all the more remarkable. For example, the Mississippi River dumps approximately 6 million gallons of water per second into the Gulf of Mexico. Where does all that water go? And that's just one of thousands of rivers.

The answer lies in the hydrologic cycle, so well brought out in the Bible. Ecclesiastes 11:3 states that "if the clouds be full of rain, they empty themselves upon the earth." Amos 9:6 tells us, "He...calls for the waters of the sea, and pours them out upon the face of the earth." The idea of a complete water cycle was not fully understood until the seventeenth century. However, more than 2,000 years prior to the discoveries of Pierre Perrault, Edme Mariotte, Edmund Halley, and others, the Scriptures clearly spoke of a water cycle.

QUESTIONS & OBJECTIONS

Q 136:7–9 *"How does the young-earth theory explain that we can see stars millions of light-years away? How would the light have reached us?"*

Since God made the sun, moon, and stars "to give light upon the earth" (Genesis 1:14–18), those lights would be immediately visible on earth. They fulfilled their purpose on the day God spoke them into being, because He "saw that it was good." No doubt God also made Adam as a fully-grown man—perhaps with the appearance of being 30 years old, even though he was only minutes old. Likewise, herbs and trees were already mature and fruit-bearing, to provide a ready supply of food. That would be the case with all of His creation.

9 Who sent tokens and wonders into the midst of you, O Egypt, upon Pharaoh, and upon all his servants.

10 Who smote great nations, and slew mighty kings;

11 Sihon king of the Amorites, and Og king of Bashan, and all the kingdoms of Canaan:

12 And gave their land for an heritage, an heritage unto Israel his people.

13 Your name, O LORD, endures for ever; and your memorial, O LORD, throughout all generations.

14 For the LORD will judge his people, and he will repent himself concerning his servants.

15 The idols of the heathen are silver and gold, the work of men's hands.

16 They have mouths, but they speak not; eyes have they, but they see not;

17 They have ears, but they hear not; neither is there any breath in their mouths.

18 They that make them are like unto them: so is every one that trusts in them.

19 Bless the LORD, O house of Israel: bless the LORD, O house of Aaron:

20 Bless the LORD, O house of Levi: you that fear the LORD, bless the LORD.

21 Blessed be the LORD out of Zion, which dwells at Jerusalem. Praise the LORD.

PSALM 136

O GIVE thanks unto the LORD; for he is good: for his mercy endures for ever.

2 O give thanks unto the God of gods: for his mercy endures for ever.

3 O give thanks to the Lord of lords: for his mercy endures for ever.

4 To him who alone does great wonders: for his mercy endures for ever.

5 To him that by wisdom made the heavens: for his mercy endures for ever.

6 To him that stretched out the earth above the waters: for his mercy endures for ever.

7 To him that made great lights: for his mercy endures for ever:

136:4–6 Worshiping a Faithful Creator. We should pray, "Open my eyes that I might continually see the genius of Your mind displayed in creation." If we could walk in such a spirit of illumination, we would walk around awestruck! We would continually worship God. We would be filled with such faith, we would see no problem too great for our God. As the revelation of His greatness astounds us, we would say, "Ah, Lord God! Behold You have made the heavens and the earth by Your great power and outstretched arm. There is nothing too hard for You!" (Jeremiah 32:17).

Such knowledge of His power and ability would cause us to have faith that produces joy, even at the edge of the Red Sea, even in the lion's *mouth*. We can look at the world with all its problems, sins, and pains, and know that with one small breath of Almighty God's Spirit, our nation can be saved. If the mere tip of the finger of God is for us, nothing can be against us.

> Is sin so luscious
> that you will burn in hell forever for it?

CHARLES SPURGEON

8 The sun to rule by day: for his mercy endures for ever:

9 The moon and stars to rule by night: for his mercy endures for ever.

10 To him that smote Egypt in their firstborn: for his mercy endures for ever:

11 And brought out Israel from among them: for his mercy endures for ever:

12 With a strong hand, and with a stretched out arm: for his mercy endures for ever.

13 To him which divided the Red sea into parts: for his mercy endures for ever:

14 And made Israel to pass through the midst of it: for his mercy endures for ever:

15 But overthrew Pharaoh and his host in the Red sea: for his mercy endures for ever.

16 To him which led his people through the wilderness: for his mercy endures for ever.

17 To him which smote great kings: for his mercy endures for ever:

18 And slew famous kings: for his mercy endures for ever:

19 Sihon king of the Amorites: for his mercy endures for ever:

20 And Og the king of Bashan: for his mercy endures for ever:

21 And gave their land for an heritage: for his mercy endures for ever:

22 Even an heritage unto Israel his servant: for his mercy endures for ever.

23 Who remembered us in our low estate: for his mercy endures for ever:

24 And has redeemed us from our enemies: for his mercy endures for ever.

25 Who gives food to all flesh: for his mercy endures for ever.

26 O give thanks unto the God of heaven: for his mercy endures for ever.

PSALM 137

BY the rivers of Babylon, there we sat down, yes, we wept, when we remembered Zion.

2 We hanged our harps upon the willows in the midst thereof.

3 For there they that carried us away captive required of us a song; and they that wasted us required of us mirth, saying, Sing us one of the songs of Zion.

4 How shall we sing the LORD's song in a strange land?

5 If I forget you, O Jerusalem, let my right hand forget her cunning.

6 If I do not remember you, let my tongue cleave to the roof of my mouth; if I prefer not Jerusalem above my chief joy.

7 Remember, O LORD, the children of Edom in the day of Jerusalem; who said, Rase it, rase it, even to the foundation thereof.

8 O daughter of Babylon, who are to be destroyed; happy shall he be, that rewards you as you have served us.

9 Happy shall he be, that takes and dashes your little ones against the stones.

PSALM 138

I WILL praise you with my whole heart: before the gods will I sing praise unto you.

2 I will worship toward your holy temple, and praise your name for your lovingkindness and for your truth: for you have magnified your word above all your name.

3 In the day when I cried you answered me, and strengthened me with strength in my soul.

4 All the kings of the earth shall praise you, O LORD, when they hear the words of your mouth.

5 Yes, they shall sing in the ways of the LORD: for great is the glory of the LORD.

6 Though the LORD be high, yet has he respect unto the lowly: but the proud he knows afar off.

7 Though I walk in the midst of trouble, you will revive me: you shall stretch forth your hand against the wrath of my

enemies, and your right hand shall save me.

8 The LORD will perfect that which concerns me: your mercy, O LORD, endures for ever: forsake not the works of your own hands.

PSALM 139

O LORD, you have searched me, and known me.

2 You know my down sitting and my uprising, you understand my thought afar off.

3 You compass my path and my lying down, and are acquainted with all my ways.

4 For there is not a word in my tongue, but, lo, O LORD, you know it altogether.

5 You have beset me behind and before, and laid your hand upon me.

6 **Such knowledge is too wonderful for me; it is high, I cannot attain unto it.**

7 **Whither shall I go from your spirit? or whither shall I flee from your presence?**

8 **If I ascend up into heaven, you are there: if I make my bed in hell, behold, you are there.**

9 **If I take the wings of the morning, and dwell in the uttermost parts of the sea;**

10 **Even there shall your hand lead me, and your right hand shall hold me.**

11 **If I say, Surely the darkness shall cover me; even the night shall be light about me.**

12 **Yes, the darkness hides not from you; but the night shines as the day: the darkness and the light are both alike to you.**

139:2 God's Presence. The ungodly are unaware of the immediate presence of a holy Creator. They think that God somehow becomes present when we bow our head in prayer or walk reverently into a lofty cathedral. In truth, our Creator is ever-present. He knows when we sit down and when we stand up (vv. 2–12). He searches our heart and sees our innermost thoughts. He knows every detail of our lives, including every whispered word.

The knowledge that a holy God sees every thought and deed is disconcerting to the guilty, but wonderfully comforting to the forgiven and saved soul (see v. 17). It is with this understanding that we should regularly cry with the psalmist, "Search me, O God, and know my heart: try me, and know my thoughts: and see if there be any wicked way in me, and lead me in the way of everlasting" (vv. 23-24).

139:14 We Are Wonderfully Made. In his book, *Darwin's Black Box*, biochemistry professor Michael J. Behe, acknowledges an extremely "powerful challenge to Darwinian evolution"— something he refers to as "irreducible complexity." He gives a simple example: the humble mousetrap. The mousetrap has five major components that make it functional. If any one of these components is missing, it will not function. It becomes worthless as a mousetrap.

Charles Darwin admitted, "If it could be demonstrated that any complex organ existed which could not possibly have been formed by numerous, successive, slight modifications, my theory would absolutely break down" *(The Origin of Species)*.

If we just take the human eye, one small part of an incredibly complex creation, we will see this same principle of irreducible complexity. The eye cannot be reduced to anything less than what it is. It has thousands of co-equal functions to make it work. If we take away just one of those functions, the rest of the eye is worthless as an eye. How then did the eye evolve when all functions had to be present at once to give it any worth at all? We are indeed fearfully and wonderfully made.

"To suppose that the eye, with all its inimitable contrivances for adjusting the focus to different distances, for admitting different amounts of light, and for the correction of spherical and chromatic aberration, could have been formed by natural selection, seems, I freely confess, absurd in the highest degree." Charles Darwin, *The Origin of Species*

(No wonder—the focusing muscles in the eye move an estimated 100,000 times each day. The retina contains 137 million light-sensitive cells.)

139:16   *An Interesting Quiz...*

How would you respond in these situations?

1. A preacher and his wife are very, very poor. They already have 14 kids. Now she finds out she's pregnant with the 15th. They're living in tremendous poverty. Considering their poverty and the excessive world population, would you consider recommending she get an abortion?

2. The father is sick with sniffles, the mother has TB. Of their four children, the first is blind, the second has died, the third is deaf, the fourth has TB. She finds she's pregnant again. Given this extreme situation, would you consider recommending abortion?

3. A white man raped a 13-year-old black girl and she's now pregnant. If you were her parents, would you consider recommending abortion?

4. A teenage girl is pregnant. She's not married. Her fiancé is not the father of the baby, and her fiancé is upset. Would you recommend abortion?

In the first case, you would have killed John Wesley, one of the great evangelists in the 19th century.

In the second case, you would have killed Beethoven.

In the third case, you would have killed Ethel Waters, the great black gospel singer.

If you said yes to the fourth case, you would have declared the murder of Jesus Christ!

God is the author of life, and He has given every single individual supreme value. Each life—whether inside or outside the womb—should therefore be valued by us. God knows the plans He has for each individual and has written in His book all the days ordained for us before one of them came to be.

When we presume to know better than God who should be given life, we are putting ourselves in the place of God and are guilty of idolatry.

See also Psalm 127:3 comment.

---

13 For you have possessed my reins: you have covered me in my mother's womb.

14 I will praise you; for I am fearfully and wonderfully made: marvelous are your works; and that my soul knows right well.

15 My substance was not hid from you, when I was made in secret, and curiously wrought in the lowest parts of the earth.

16 Your eyes did see my substance, yet being imperfect; and in your book all my members were written, which in continuance were fashioned, when as yet there was none of them.

17 How precious also are your thoughts unto me, O God! how great is the sum of them!

18 If I should count them, they are more in number than the sand: when I awake, I am still with you.

19 Surely you will slay the wicked, O God: depart from me therefore, you bloody men.

20 For they speak against you wickedly, and your enemies take your name in vain.

21 Do not I hate them, O LORD, that hate you? and am not I grieved with those that rise up against you?

22 I hate them with perfect hatred: I count them my enemies.

23 Search me, O God, and know my heart: try me, and know my thoughts:

24 And see if there be any wicked way in me, and lead me in the way everlasting.

PSALM 140

DELIVER me, O LORD, from the evil man: preserve me from the violent man;

2 Which imagine mischiefs in their heart; continually are they gathered together for war.

3 They have sharpened their tongues like a serpent; adders' poison is under their lips. Selah.

4 Keep me, O Lord, from the hands of the wicked; preserve me from the violent man; who have purposed to overthrow my goings.

5 The proud have hid a snare for me, and cords; they have spread a net by the wayside; they have set gins for me. Selah.

6 I said unto the Lord, You are my God: hear the voice of my supplications, O Lord.

7 O God the Lord, the strength of my salvation, you have covered my head in the day of battle.

8 Grant not, O Lord, the desires of the wicked: further not his wicked device; lest they exalt themselves. Selah.

9 As for the head of those that compass me about, let the mischief of their own lips cover them.

10 Let burning coals fall upon them: let them be cast into the fire; into deep pits, that they rise not up again.

11 Let not an evil speaker be established in the earth: evil shall hunt the violent man to overthrow him.

12 I know that the Lord will maintain the cause of the afflicted, and the right of the poor.

13 Surely the righteous shall give thanks unto your name: the upright shall dwell in your presence.

I have always said, and always will say, that the studious perusal of the Sacred Volume will make better citizens, better fathers, and better husbands.

Thomas Jefferson

1743-1826
THIRD PRESIDENT OF THE U.S.
AUTHOR OF THE U.S. DECLARATION
OF INDEPENDENCE

PSALM 141

Lord, I cry unto you: make haste unto me; give ear unto my voice, when I cry unto you.

2 Let my prayer be set forth before you as incense; and the lifting up of my hands as the evening sacrifice.

3 Set a watch, O Lord, before my mouth; keep the door of my lips.

4 Incline not my heart to any evil thing, to practice wicked works with men that work iniquity: and let me not eat of their dainties.

5 Let the righteous smite me; it shall be a kindness: and let him reprove me; it shall be an excellent oil, which shall not break my head: for yet my prayer also shall be in their calamities.

6 When their judges are overthrown in stony places, they shall hear my words; for they are sweet.

7 Our bones are scattered at the grave's mouth, as when one cuts and cleaves wood upon the earth.

8 But my eyes are unto you, O God the Lord: in you is my trust; leave not my soul destitute.

140:2-3 "The heart is like a viper, hissing and spitting poison at God." Jonathan Edwards

141:5 This is a test of our humility. Are we prepared to submit ourselves to godly counsel?

THE FUNCTION OF THE LAW

143:2 It is amazing for a soul to discover that God gave a law to be observed, but that its observance is not even taken into account as a means of salvation. Then why was the law given? What good are moral standards? They were not given because God had the illusion that we could conform our lives to them. God knows that we are a degenerate race and that there is nothing good in our carnal nature.

"The law serves another purpose: to show us our sins. Man is confronted with a moral law that is just and good. His mind, while acknowledging that here is the truth, confesses at the same time that he does not live according to this law. And no matter how hard he tries, he realizes he does not reach the ideal. This is how he discovers he is a lost sinner.

"This is the great purpose of the law. It teaches us what sin is and it shows us how wrong we are, just as a mirror reveals to us how filthy we are and what needs cleansing. But just as a mirror does not and cannot wash us but only reveals our condition, so the law cannot correct us but only shows us what great sinners we are.

"The purpose of the law is to make you know your sin so that you will begin to pray with the psalmist, 'Do not enter into judgment with Your servant, for in Your sight no one living is righteous' (Psalm 143:2)."

Richard Wurmbrand

9 Keep me from the snares which they have laid for me, and the gins of the workers of iniquity.

10 Let the wicked fall into their own nets, while I withal escape.

PSALM 142

I CRIED unto the LORD with my voice; with my voice unto the LORD did I make my supplication.

2 I poured out my complaint before him; I showed before him my trouble.

3 When my spirit was overwhelmed within me, then you knew my path. In the way wherein I walked have they privily laid a snare for me.

4 I looked on my right hand, and beheld, but there was no man that would know me: refuge failed me; no man cared for my soul.

5 I cried unto you, O LORD: I said, You are my refuge and my portion in the land of the living.

6 Attend unto my cry; for I am brought very low: deliver me from my persecutors; for they are stronger than I.

7 Bring my soul out of prison, that I may praise your name: the righteous shall compass me about; for you shall deal bountifully with me.

PSALM 143

H EAR my prayer, O LORD, give ear to my supplications: in your faithfulness answer me, and in your righteousness.

2 And enter not into judgment with your servant: for in your sight shall no man living be justified.

3 For the enemy has persecuted my soul; he has smitten my life down to the ground; he has made me to dwell in darkness, as those that have been long dead.

4 Therefore is my spirit overwhelmed within me; my heart within me is desolate.

5 I remember the days of old; I meditate on all your works; I muse on the work of your hands.

6 I stretch forth my hands unto you: my soul thirsts after you, as a thirsty land. Selah.

7 Hear me speedily, O LORD: my spirit fails: hide not your face from me, lest I be

---

143:2 How fearful it would be stand in judgment and be judged by the standard of God's Law. See Galatians 2:16 for what God did so that we could live.

like unto them that go down into the pit.
8 Cause me to hear your lovingkindness in the morning; for in you do I trust: cause me to know the way wherein I should walk; for I lift up my soul unto you.
9 Deliver me, O LORD, from my enemies: I flee unto you to hide me.
10 Teach me to do your will; for you are my God: your spirit is good; lead me into the land of uprightness.
11 Quicken me, O LORD, for your name's sake: for your righteousness' sake bring my soul out of trouble.
12 And of your mercy cut off my enemies, and destroy all them that afflict my soul: for I am your servant.

PSALM 144

BLESSED be the LORD my strength which teaches my hands to war, and my fingers to fight:
2 My goodness, and my fortress; my high tower, and my deliverer; my shield, and he in whom I trust; who subdues my people under me.
3 *LORD, what is man, that you take knowledge of him! or the son of man, that you make account of him!*
4 *Man is like to vanity: his days are as a shadow that passes away.*
5 Bow your heavens, O LORD, and come down: touch the mountains, and they shall smoke.
6 Cast forth lightning, and scatter them: shoot out your arrows, and destroy them.
7 Send your hand from above; rid me, and deliver me out of great waters, from the hand of strange children;
8 Whose mouth speaks vanity, and their right hand is a right hand of falsehood.
9 I will sing a new song unto you, O God: upon a psaltery and an instrument of ten strings will I sing praises unto you.
10 It is he that gives salvation unto kings: who delivers David his servant from the hurtful sword.

11 Rid me, and deliver me from the hand of strange children, whose mouth speaks vanity, and their right hand is a right hand of falsehood:
12 That our sons may be as plants grown up in their youth; that our daughters may be as corner stones, polished after the similitude of a palace:
13 That our garners may be full, affording all manner of store: that our sheep may bring forth thousands and ten thousands in our streets:
14 That our oxen may be strong to labor; that there be no breaking in, nor going out; that there be no complaining in our streets.

> I believe the holier a man becomes,
> the more he mourns
> over the unholiness
> which remains in him.
> **CHARLES SPURGEON**

15 Happy is that people, that is in such a case: yes, happy is that people, whose God is the LORD.

PSALM 145

I WILL extol you, my God, O king; and I will bless your name for ever and ever.
2 Every day will I bless you; and I will praise your name for ever and ever.
3 Great is the LORD, and greatly to be praised; and his greatness is unsearchable.
4 One generation shall praise your works to another, and shall declare your mighty acts.
5 I will speak of the glorious honor of your majesty, and of your wondrous works.
6 And men shall speak of the might of your terrible acts: and I will declare your greatness.

145:8 This is why we have the cross of Calvary. Nothing in man's character drew out God's love for us. It came simply because the Lord is gracious and full of compassion.

> The church is like manure.
> Pile it up,
> and it stinks up the neighborhood.
> Spread it out,
> and it enriches the world.

LUIS PALAU
ARGENTINIAN EVANGELIST
BORN 1934 IN BUENOS AIRES

7 They shall abundantly utter the memory of your great goodness, and shall sing of your righteousness.

8 The LORD is gracious, and full of compassion; slow to anger, and of great mercy.

9 The LORD is good to all: and his tender mercies are over all his works.

10 All your works shall praise you, O LORD; and your saints shall bless you.

11 They shall speak of the glory of your kingdom, and talk of your power;

12 To make known to the sons of men his mighty acts, and the glorious majesty of his kingdom.

13 Your kingdom is an everlasting kingdom, and your dominion endures throughout all generations.

14 The LORD upholds all that fall, and raises up all those that be bowed down.

15 The eyes of all wait upon you; and you give them their meat in due season.

16 You open your hand, and satisfy the desire of every living thing.

17 The LORD is righteous in all his ways, and holy in all his works.

18 The LORD is near unto all them that call upon him, to all that call upon him in truth.

19 He will fulfill the desire of them that fear him: he also will hear their cry, and will save them.

20 The LORD preserves all them that love him: but all the wicked will he destroy.

21 My mouth shall speak the praise of the LORD: and let all flesh bless his holy name for ever and ever.

PSALM 146

PRAISE the LORD. Praise the LORD, O my soul.

2 While I live will I praise the LORD: I will sing praises unto my God while I have any being.

3 Put not your trust in princes, nor in the son of man, in whom there is no help.

4 His breath goes forth, he returns to his earth; in that very day his thoughts perish.

5 Happy is he that has the God of Jacob for his help, whose hope is in the LORD his God:

6 Which made heaven, and earth, the sea, and all that therein is: which keeps truth for ever:

7 Which executes judgment for the oppressed: which gives food to the hungry. The LORD looses the prisoners:

145:17-18 Notice the word "all" in these verses.

146:6 Evolution's Circular Reasoning. "At least six different radiometric dating methods are available. The assumed age of the sample will dictate which dating method is used because each will give a different result.

"For example: when dinosaur bones containing carbon are found, they are *not* carbon dated because the result would be only a few thousand years. Because this would not match the assumed age based on the geologic column, scientists use another method of dating to give an age closer to the desired result. All radiometric results that do not match the preassigned ages of the geologic column are discarded." Dr. Kent Hovind

"Contrary to what most scientists write, the fossil record does not support the Darwinian theory of evolution because it is this theory (there are several) which we use to interpret the fossil record. By doing so we are guilty of circular reasoning if we then say the fossil record supports this theory." Ronald R. West, Ph.D.

146:7–9 Here is the Ministry of the Savior. Jesus fed the hungry, loosed the prisoners of sin and suffering, opened the eyes of the blind, and raised up those who were bowed down.

8 The LORD opens the eyes of the blind: the LORD raises them that are bowed down: the LORD loves the righteous:

9 The LORD preserves the strangers; he relieves the fatherless and widow: but the way of the wicked he turns upside down.

10 The LORD shall reign for ever, even your God, O Zion, unto all generations. Praise the LORD.

PSALM 147

P RAISE the LORD: for it is good to sing praises unto our God; for it is pleasant; and praise is comely.

2 The LORD does build up Jerusalem: he gathers together the outcasts of Israel.

3 He heals the broken in heart, and binds up their wounds.

4 He tells the number of the stars; he calls them all by their names.

5 Great is our Lord, and of great power: his understanding is infinite.

6 The LORD lifts up the meek: he casts the wicked down to the ground.

7 Sing unto the LORD with thanksgiving; sing praise upon the harp unto our God:

8 Who covers the heaven with clouds, who prepares rain for the earth, who makes grass to grow upon the mountains.

9 He gives to the beast his food, and to the young ravens which cry.

10 **He delights not in the strength of the horse: he takes not pleasure in the legs of a man.**

11 **The LORD takes pleasure in them that fear him, in those that hope in his mercy.**

12 Praise the LORD, O Jerusalem; praise your God, O Zion.

13 For he has strengthened the bars of your gates; he has blessed your children within you.

14 He makes peace in your borders, and fills you with the finest of the wheat.

15 He sends forth his commandment upon earth: his word runs very swiftly.

16 He gives snow like wool: he scatters the hoarfrost like ashes.

17 He casts forth his ice like morsels: who can stand before his cold?

147:4 In Jeremiah 33:22, the Bible states that "the host of heaven cannot be numbered, neither the sand of the sea measured." When this was written, 2,500 years ago, no one knew how vast the stars were since only about 1,100 were visible. Now we know that there are billions of stars, and that they cannot be numbered.

18 He sends out his word, and melts them: he causes his wind to blow, and the waters flow.
19 He showed his word unto Jacob, his statutes and his judgments unto Israel.
20 He has not dealt so with any nation: and as for his judgments, they have not known them. Praise the LORD.

PSALM 148

P RAISE the LORD. Praise the LORD from the heavens: praise him in the heights.
2 Praise him, all his angels: praise him, all his hosts.
3 Praise him, sun and moon: praise him, all stars of light.
4 Praise him, heavens of heavens, and waters that be above the heavens.
5 Let them praise the name of the LORD: for he commanded, and they were created.
6 He has also established them for ever and ever: he has made a decree which shall not pass.
7 Praise the LORD from the earth, dragons, and all deeps:
8 Fire, and hail; snow, and vapors; stormy wind fulfilling his word:
9 Mountains, and all hills; fruitful trees, and all cedars:
10 Beasts, and all cattle; creeping things, and flying fowl:
11 Kings of the earth, and all people; princes, and all judges of the earth:
12 Both young men, and maidens; old men, and children:
13 Let them praise the name of the LORD: for his name alone is excellent; his glory is above the earth and heaven.
14 He also exalts the horn of his people, the praise of all his saints; even of the children of Israel, a people near unto him. Praise the LORD.

PSALM 149

P RAISE the LORD. Sing unto the LORD a new song, and his praise in the congregation of saints.
2 Let Israel rejoice in him that made him: let the children of Zion be joyful in their King.

Any man who declares children
to be born perfect
was never a father.
Your child without evil?
You without eyes, you mean!
CHARLES SPURGEON

3 Let them praise his name in the dance: let them sing praises unto him with the timbrel and harp.
4 For the LORD takes pleasure in his people: he will beautify the meek with salvation.
5 Let the saints be joyful in glory: let them sing aloud upon their beds.
6 Let the high praises of God be in their mouth, and a two-edged sword in their hand;
7 To execute vengeance upon the heathen, and punishments upon the people;
8 To bind their kings with chains, and their nobles with fetters of iron;
9 To execute upon them the judgment written: this honor have all his saints. Praise the LORD.

PSALM 150

P RAISE the LORD. Praise God in his sanctuary: praise him in the firmament of his power.
2 Praise him for his mighty acts: praise him according to his excellent greatness.
3 Praise him with the sound of the trumpet: praise him with the psaltery and harp.
4 Praise him with the timbrel and dance: praise him with stringed instruments and organs.
5 Praise him upon the loud cymbals: praise him upon the high sounding cymbals.
6 Let every thing that has breath praise the LORD. Praise the LORD.

. . . . . .

*For the biblical way
to present God's love,
see Matthew 10:22 comment.*

Proverbs

CHAPTER 1

THE proverbs of Solomon the son of David, king of Israel;

2 To know wisdom and instruction; to perceive the words of understanding;

3 To receive the instruction of wisdom, justice, and judgment, and equity;

4 To give subtlety to the simple, to the young man knowledge and discretion.

5 A wise man will hear, and will increase learning; and a man of understanding shall attain unto wise counsels:

6 To understand a proverb, and the interpretation; the words of the wise, and their dark sayings.

7 The fear of the LORD is the beginning of knowledge: but fools despise wisdom and instruction.

8 My son, hear the instruction of your father, and forsake not the law of your mother:

9 For they shall be an ornament of grace unto your head, and chains about your neck.

10 My son, if sinners entice you, consent not.

11 If they say, Come with us, let us lay wait for blood, let us lurk privily for the innocent without cause:

12 Let us swallow them up alive as the grave; and whole, as those that go down into the pit:

13 We shall find all precious substance, we shall fill our houses with spoil:

14 Cast in your lot among us; let us all have one purse:

15 My son, walk not in the way with them; refrain your foot from their path:

16 For their feet run to evil, and make haste to shed blood.

17 Surely in vain the net is spread in the sight of any bird.

18 And they lay wait for their own blood; they lurk privily for their own lives.

19 So are the ways of every one that is greedy of gain; which takes away the life of the owners thereof.

20 Wisdom cries without; she utters her voice in the streets:

21 She cries in the chief place of concourse, in the openings of the gates: in the city she utters her words, saying,

---

1:2 It is wise to read a proverb for each day of the month. They were written that we might have wisdom, instruction, and understanding.

1:22-23 One just has to observe the gospel being preached in the open air to know the truth of these words. When presented with the knowledge of how to be saved from death and hell, the world delights in scorn. Yet despite their contempt, our Creator offers salvation to a God-hating humanity. He will make His words known to all who turn to His reproof.

22 How long, you simple ones, will you love simplicity? and the scorners delight in their scorning, and fools hate knowledge?

23 Turn you at my reproof: behold, I will pour out my spirit unto you, I will make known my words unto you.

24 Because I have called, and you refused; I have stretched out my hand, and no man regarded;

25 But you have set at nought all my counsel, and would none of my reproof:

26 I also will laugh at your calamity; I will mock when your fear comes;

27 When your fear comes as desolation, and your destruction comes as a whirlwind; when distress and anguish comes upon you.

28 Then shall they call upon me, but I will not answer; they shall seek me early, but they shall not find me:

29 For that they hated knowledge, and did not choose the fear of the LORD:

30 They would none of my counsel: they despised all my reproof.

31 Therefore shall they eat of the fruit of their own way, and be filled with their own devices.

32 For the turning away of the simple shall slay them, and the prosperity of fools shall destroy them.

33 But whoso hearkens unto me shall dwell safely, and shall be quiet from fear of evil.

CHAPTER 2

M Y son, if you will receive my words, and hide my commandments with you;

2 So that you incline your ear unto wisdom, and apply your heart to understanding;

3 Yes, if you cry after knowledge, and lift up your voice for understanding;

4 If you seek her as silver, and search for her as for hidden treasures;

5 Then shall you understand the fear of the LORD, and find the knowledge of God.

6 For the LORD gives wisdom: out of his mouth comes knowledge and understanding.

7 He lays up sound wisdom for the righteous: he is a buckler to them that walk uprightly.

8 He keeps the paths of judgment, and preserves the way of his saints.

9 Then shall you understand righteousness, and judgment, and equity; yes, every good path.

10 When wisdom enters into your heart, and knowledge is pleasant unto your soul;

11 Discretion shall preserve you, understanding shall keep you:

12 To deliver you from the way of the evil man, from the man that speaks froward things;

13 Who leave the paths of uprightness, to walk in the ways of darkness;

14 Who rejoice to do evil, and delight in the frowardness of the wicked;

15 Whose ways are crooked, and they froward in their paths:

16 To deliver you from the strange woman, even from the stranger which flatters with her words;

17 Who forsakes the guide of her youth, and forgets the covenant of her God.

18 For her house inclines unto death, and her paths unto the dead.

19 None that go unto her return again, neither take they hold of the paths of life.

20 That you may walk in the way of good men, and keep the paths of the righteous.

2:1–5 The Fear of the Lord. This is how to obtain the fear of the Lord, the most necessary virtue: 1) receive the Word of God; 2) hide His commandments within you; 3) incline your ear to wisdom; 4) apply your heart to understanding; 5) cry out for knowledge and discernment; 6) seek it as you would for silver or hidden treasures.

2:12 Wisdom, knowledge, discretion, and understanding will keep you from perversity and sexual sin. They give the blind light as to the end result of sin (see verse 18).

21 For the upright shall dwell in the land, and the perfect shall remain in it.

22 But the wicked shall be cut off from the earth, and the transgressors shall be rooted out of it.

CHAPTER 3

M Y son, forget not my law; but let your heart keep my commandments:

2 For length of days, and long life, and peace, shall they add to you.

3 Let not mercy and truth forsake you: bind them about your neck; write them upon the table of your heart:

4 So shall you find favor and good understanding in the sight of God and man.

5 Trust in the Lord with all your heart; and lean not unto your own understanding.

6 In all your ways acknowledge him, and he shall direct your paths.

7 Be not wise in your own eyes: fear the Lord, and depart from evil.

8 It shall be health to your navel, and marrow to your bones.

9 Honor the LORD with your substance, and with the firstfruits of all your increase:

10 So shall your barns be filled with plenty, and your presses shall burst out with new wine.

11 My son, despise not the chastening of the LORD; neither be weary of his correction:

12 For whom the LORD loves he corrects; even as a father the son in whom he delights.

13 Happy is the man that finds wisdom, and the man that gets understanding.

14 For the merchandise of it is better than the merchandise of silver, and the gain thereof than fine gold.

15 She is more precious than rubies: and all the things you canst desire are not to be compared unto her.

16 Length of days is in her right hand; and in her left hand riches and honor.

17 Her ways are ways of pleasantness, and all her paths are peace.

18 She is a tree of life to them that lay hold upon her: and happy is every one that retains her.

19 The LORD by wisdom has founded the earth; by understanding has he established the heavens.

20 By his knowledge the depths are broken up, and the clouds drop down the dew.

21 My son, let not them depart from your eyes: keep sound wisdom and discretion:

22 So shall they be life unto your soul, and grace to your neck.

3:1–3 The Law leads to mercy and truth. See John 1:17 and Galatians 3:24.

3:5 The world says the opposite—doubt the Word of God and have faith in yourself.

3:6 "It was the Lord who put it into my mind...I could feel His hand upon me...There is no question the inspiration was from the Holy Spirit because He comforted me with rays of marvelous illumination from the Holy Scriptures...No one should fear to undertake any task in the name of our Savior if it is just and if the intention is purely for His holy service. The gospel must still be preached to so many lands in such a short time. This is what convinces me." Christopher Columbus (from his diary, in reference to his discovery of "the New World").

3:19 "Slight variations in physical laws such as gravity or electromagnetism would make life impossible...The necessity to produce life lies at the center of the universe's whole machinery and design." John Wheeler, Princeton University professor of physics (Reader's Digest, Sept. 1986)

Even evolutionist Stephen Hawking, considered the best-known scientist since Albert Einstein, acknowledges "the universe and the laws of physics seem to have been specifically designed for us. If any one of about 40 physical qualities had more than slightly different values, life as we know it could not exist: Either atoms would not be stable, or they wouldn't combine into molecules, or the stars wouldn't form the heavier elements, or the universe would collapse before life could develop, ... " (Austin American-Statesman, Oct 19th 1997).

23 Then shall you walk in your way safely, and your foot shall not stumble.

24 When you lie down, you shall not be afraid: yes, you shall lie down, and your sleep shall be sweet.

25 Be not afraid of sudden fear, neither of the desolation of the wicked, when it comes.

26 For the LORD shall be your confidence, and shall keep your foot from being taken.

27 Withhold not good from them to whom it is due, when it is in the power of your hand to do it.

28 Say not unto your neighbor, Go, and come again, and tomorrow I will give; when you have it by you.

29 Devise not evil against your neighbor, seeing he dwells securely by you.

30 Strive not with a man without cause, if he has done you no harm.

31 Envy not the oppressor, and choose none of his ways.

32 For the froward is abomination to the LORD: but his secret is with the righteous.

33 The curse of the LORD is in the house of the wicked: but he blesses the habitation of the just.

34 Surely he scorns the scorners: but he gives grace unto the lowly.

35 The wise shall inherit glory: but shame shall be the promotion of fools.

CHAPTER 4

HEAR, you children, the instruction of a father, and attend to know understanding.

2 For I give you good doctrine, forsake not my law.

3 For I was my father's son, tender and only beloved in the sight of my mother.

4 He taught me also, and said unto me, Let your heart retain my words: keep my commandments, and live.

5 Get wisdom, get understanding: forget it not; neither decline from the words of my mouth.

6 Forsake her not, and she shall preserve you: love her, and she shall keep you.

7 Wisdom is the principal thing; therefore get wisdom: and with all your getting get understanding.

3:27-28 We must never lose sight of love for our neighbor. A good deed can be a stronger evangelistic witness than a thousand words. See Proverbs 27:10 comment.

3:34 It has been said that the Italian dictator Mussolini, in his youth, stood on a high pinnacle and cried, "God, if you are there, strike me dead!" When God did not bow to his dictates, Mussolini concluded that there is no God. God did, however, answer his prayer some time later.

4:1–5 Training our children. We are responsible to God to train our children in the way they should go (Proverbs 22:6), and must constantly be on guard against humanism, atheism, relativism, evolution, and any other teaching that opposes the Christian worldview. See also Ephesians 6:4 comment.

"I think that the most important factor moving us toward a secular society has been the educational factor. Our schools may not teach Johnny how to read properly, but the fact that Johnny is in school until he is sixteen tends toward the elimination of religious superstition. The average American child now acquires a high school education, and this militates against Adam and Eve and all other myths of alleged history." P. Blanchard, "Three Cheers for Our Secular State," The Humanist

"Education is thus a most powerful ally of humanism. What can a theistic Sunday school's meeting for an hour once a week and teaching only a fraction of the children, do to stem the tide of the five-day program of humanistic teaching?" Humanism: A New Religion, 1930

"Fundamental parents have no right to indoctrinate their children in their beliefs. We are preparing their children for the year 2000 and life in a global one-world society, and those children will not fit in." Senator Paul Hoagland, 1984

8 Exalt her, and she shall promote you: she shall bring you to honor, when you do embrace her.

9 She shall give to your head an ornament of grace: a crown of glory shall she deliver to you.

10 Hear, O my son, and receive my sayings; and the years of your life shall be many.

11 I have taught you in the way of wisdom; I have led you in right paths.

12 When you go, your steps shall not be straitened; and when you run, you shall not stumble.

13 Take fast hold of instruction; let her not go: keep her; for she is your life.

14 Enter not into the path of the wicked, and go not in the way of evil men.

15 Avoid it, pass not by it, turn from it, and pass away.

16 For they sleep not, except they have done mischief; and their sleep is taken away, unless they cause some to fall.

17 For they eat the bread of wickedness, and drink the wine of violence.

18 But the path of the just is as the shining light, that shines more and more unto the perfect day.

19 The way of the wicked is as darkness: they know not at what they stumble.

20 My son, attend to my words; incline your ear unto my sayings.

21 Let them not depart from your eyes; keep them in the midst of your heart.

22 For they are life unto those that find them, and health to all their flesh.

23 Keep your heart with all diligence; for out of it are the issues of life.

24 Put away from you a froward mouth, and perverse lips put far from you.

25 Let your eyes look right on, and let your eyelids look straight before you.

26 Ponder the path of your feet, and let all your ways be established.

27 Turn not to the right hand nor to the left: remove your foot from evil.

CHAPTER 5

MY son, attend unto my wisdom, and bow your ear to my understanding:

2 That you may regard discretion, and that your lips may keep knowledge.

3 For the lips of a strange woman drop as an honeycomb, and her mouth is smoother than oil:

4 But her end is bitter as wormwood, sharp as a two-edged sword.

5 Her feet go down to death; her steps take hold on hell.

6 Lest you should ponder the path of life, her ways are moveable, that you can not know them.

7 Hear me now therefore, O you children, and depart not from the words of my mouth.

8 Remove your way far from her, and come not near the door of her house:

9 Lest you give your honor unto others, and your years unto the cruel:

10 Lest strangers be filled with your wealth; and your labors be in the house of a stranger;

11 And you mourn at the last, when your flesh and your body are consumed,

12 And say, How have I hated instruction, and my heart despised reproof;

13 And have not obeyed the voice of my teachers, nor inclined my ear to them that instructed me!

14 I was almost in all evil in the midst of the congregation and assembly.

15 Drink waters out of your own cistern, and running waters out of your own well.

16 Let your fountains be dispersed abroad, and rivers of waters in the streets.

17 Let them be only your own, and not strangers' with you.

18 Let your fountain be blessed: and rejoice with the wife of your youth.

19 Let her be as the loving hind and pleasant roe; let her breasts satisfy you at all times; and be ravished always with her

---

4:7 How do we get this "principal thing" that preserves and promotes? Primarily through prayer and Proverbs. Seek God and feed on this wealth of wisdom daily.

love.

20 And why will you, my son, be ravished with a strange woman, and embrace the bosom of a stranger?

21 For the ways of man are before the eyes of the Lord, and he ponders all his goings.

22 His own iniquities shall take the wicked himself, and he shall be held with the cords of his sins.

23 He shall die without instruction; and in the greatness of his folly he shall go astray.

CHAPTER 6

M Y son, if you be surety for your friend, if you have stricken your hand with a stranger,

2 You are snared with the words of your mouth, you are taken with the words of your mouth.

3 Do this now, my son, and deliver yourself, when you are come into the hand of your friend; go, humble yourself, and make sure your friend.

4 Give not sleep to your eyes, nor slumber to your eyelids.

5 Deliver yourself as a roe from the hand of the hunter, and as a bird from the hand of the fowler.

6 Go to the ant, you sluggard; consider her ways, and be wise:

7 Which having no guide, overseer, or ruler,

8 Provides her meat in the summer, and gathers her food in the harvest.

9 How long will you sleep, O sluggard? when will you arise out of your sleep?

THE FUNCTION OF THE LAW

 6:23 "The absence of God's holy Law from modern preaching is perhaps as responsible as any other factor for the evangelistic impotence of our churches and missions. Only by the light of the Law can the vermin of sin in the heart be exposed. Satan has effectively used a very clever device to silence the Law, which is needed as an instrument to bring perishing men to Christ.

"It is imperative that preachers of today learn how to declare the spiritual Law of God; for, until we learn how to wound consciences, we shall have no wounds to bind with gospel bandages."
Walter Chantry
Today's Gospel: Authentic or Synthetic?

"The Law is the God-given light to illuminate the dark soul of man."
Mark A. Spence

"Unless we see our shortcomings in the light of the Law and holiness of God, we do not see them as sin at all."
J. I. Packer

---

10 Yet a little sleep, a little slumber, a little folding of the hands to sleep:

11 So shall your poverty come as one that travels, and your want as an armed man.

12 A naughty person, a wicked man, walks with a froward mouth.

13 He winks with his eyes, he speaks with his feet, he teaches with his fingers;

5:19 Biblical Sexuality. It comes as a shock to the world that God's Word speaks so openly about sex. It is a gift of God given for both procreation and pleasure, within the bounds of marriage. Those who refuse to keep sexual intimacy within the bounds of the marriage bed will suffer the consequences of their actions (vv. 20–23). It is interesting to note that a man and a woman can have sexual relations thousands of times within their marriage with no fear of AIDS or any sexually transmitted diseases. See verse 11.

6:6–8 The ant is an example of the Christian who knows the will of God—to seek and save that which is lost. He understands that God isn't willing that any should perish, so he sets about the task of reaching the lost with the gospel. The ant doesn't need anyone telling him what to do. He just does it. See 1 Corinthians 15:58.

14 Frowardness is in his heart, he devises mischief continually; he sows discord.

15 Therefore shall his calamity come suddenly; suddenly shall he be broken without remedy.

16 These six things does the LORD hate: yes, seven are an abomination unto him:

17 A proud look, a lying tongue, and hands that shed innocent blood,

18 An heart that devises wicked imaginations, feet that be swift in running to mischief,

19 A false witness that speaks lies, and he that sows discord among brethren.

20 My son, keep your father's commandment, and forsake not the law of your mother:

21 Bind them continually upon your heart, and tie them about your neck.

22 When you go, it shall lead you; when you sleep, it shall keep you; and when you awake, it shall talk with you.

23 For the commandment is a lamp; and the law is light; and reproofs of instruction are the way of life:

24 To keep you from the evil woman, from the flattery of the tongue of a strange woman.

25 Lust not after her beauty in your heart; neither let her take you with her eyelids.

26 For by means of a whorish woman a man is brought to a piece of bread: and the adulteress will hunt for the precious life.

27 Can a man take fire in his bosom, and his clothes not be burned?

28 Can one go upon hot coals, and his feet not be burned?

29 So he that goes in to his neighbor's wife; whosoever touches her shall not be innocent.

30 Men do not despise a thief, if he steal to satisfy his soul when he is hungry;

I do not believe that any man can preach the gospel who does not preach the Law.

Charles Spurgeon
1834–1892
FOREMOST PREACHER OF THE 19TH CENTURY

31 But if he be found, he shall restore sevenfold; he shall give all the substance of his house.

32 But whoso commits adultery with a woman lacks understanding: he that does it destroys his own soul.

33 A wound and dishonor shall he get; and his reproach shall not be wiped away.

34 For jealousy is the rage of a man: therefore he will not spare in the day of vengeance.

35 He will not regard any ransom; neither will he rest content, though you give many gifts.

6:23–30 Never fall into the trap of thinking that God's Law has no relevance for the Christian. Not only is it a schoolmaster to bring him to Christ (Galatians 3:24), but it leaves him with knowledge that will guide him for the rest of his life. We shouldn't disregard instruction of the schoolmaster after we graduate. The Ten Commandments will keep the Christian from fornication (v. 24), lust (v. 25), adultery (v. 29), and theft (v. 30).

CHAPTER 7

MY son, keep my words, and lay up my commandments with you.

2 Keep my commandments, and live; and my law as the apple of your eye.

3 Bind them upon your fingers, write them upon the table of your heart.

4 Say unto wisdom, You are my sister; and call understanding your kinswoman:

5 That they may keep you from the strange woman, from the stranger which flatters with her words.

6 For at the window of my house I looked through my casement,

7 And beheld among the simple ones, I discerned among the youths, a young man void of understanding,

8 Passing through the street near her corner; and he went the way to her house,

9 In the twilight, in the evening, in the black and dark night:

10 And, behold, there met him a woman with the attire of an harlot, and subtle of heart.

11 (She is loud and stubborn; her feet abide not in her house:

12 Now is she without, now in the streets, and lies in wait at every corner.)

13 So she caught him, and kissed him, and with an impudent face said unto him,

14 I have peace offerings with me; this day have I paid my vows.

15 Therefore came I forth to meet you, diligently to seek your face, and I have found you.

16 I have decked my bed with coverings of tapestry, with carved works, with fine linen of Egypt.

17 I have perfumed my bed with myrrh, aloes, and cinnamon.

18 Come, let us take our fill of love until the morning: let us solace ourselves with loves.

19 For the goodman is not at home, he is gone a long journey:

20 He has taken a bag of money with him, and will come home at the day appointed.

21 With her much fair speech she caused him to yield, with the flattering of her lips she forced him.

22 He goes after her straightway, as an ox goes to the slaughter, or as a fool to the correction of the stocks;

23 Till a dart strike through his liver; as a bird hastens to the snare, and knows not that it is for his life.

24 Hearken unto me now therefore, O you children, and attend to the words of my mouth.

25 Let not your heart decline to her ways, go not astray in her paths.

26 For she has cast down many wounded: yes, many strong men have been slain by her.

27 Her house is the way to hell, going down to the chambers of death.

CHAPTER 8

DOES not wisdom cry? and understanding put forth her voice?

2 She stands in the top of high places, by the way in the places of the paths.

3 She cries at the gates, at the entry of the city, at the coming in at the doors.

4 Unto you, O men, I call; and my voice is to the sons of man.

5 O you simple, understand wisdom: and, you fools, be you of an understanding heart.

6 Hear; for I will speak of excellent things; and the opening of my lips shall be right things.

7 For my mouth shall speak truth; and wickedness is an abomination to my lips.

8 All the words of my mouth are in righteousness; there is nothing froward or perverse in them.

9 They are all plain to him that understands, and right to them that find knowledge.

10 Receive my instruction, and not silver; and knowledge rather than choice gold.

11 For wisdom is better than rubies; and all the things that may be desired are not to be compared to it.

12 I wisdom dwell with prudence, and find out knowledge of witty inventions.

13 The fear of the LORD is to hate evil: pride, and arrogance, and the evil way, and the froward mouth, do I hate.

14 Counsel is mine, and sound wisdom: I am understanding; I have strength.

15 By me kings reign, and princes decree justice.

16 By me princes rule, and nobles, even all the judges of the earth.

17 I love them that love me; and those that seek me early shall find me.

18 Riches and honor are with me; yes, durable riches and righteousness.

19 My fruit is better than gold, yes, than fine gold; and my revenue than choice silver.

20 I lead in the way of righteousness, in the midst of the paths of judgment:

21 That I may cause those that love me to inherit substance; and I will fill their treasures.

22 The LORD possessed me in the beginning of his way, before his works of old.

23 I was set up from everlasting, from the beginning, or ever the earth was.

24 When there were no depths, I was brought forth; when there were no fountains abounding with water.

25 Before the mountains were settled, before the hills was I brought forth:

26 While as yet he had not made the earth, nor the fields, nor the highest part of the dust of the world.

27 When he prepared the heavens, I was there: when he set a compass upon the face of the depth:

28 When he established the clouds above: when he strengthened the fountains of the deep:

29 When he gave to the sea his decree, that the waters should not pass his commandment: when he appointed the foundations of the earth:

30 Then I was by him, as one brought up with him: and I was daily his delight, rejoicing always before him;

31 Rejoicing in the habitable part of his earth; and my delights were with the sons of men.

32 Now therefore hearken unto me, O you children: for blessed are they that keep my ways.

33 Hear instruction, and be wise, and refuse it not.

34 Blessed is the man that hears me, watching daily at my gates, waiting at the posts of my doors.

35 For whoso finds me finds life, and shall obtain favor of the LORD.

36 But he that sins against me wrongs his own soul: all they that hate me love death.

> **If you will not have death unto sin, you shall have sin unto death. There is no alternative. If you do not die to sin, you shall die for sin. If you do not slay sin, sin will slay you.**
>
> **CHARLES SPURGEON**

8:22 Jehovah's Witnesses. When Jehovah's Witnesses maintain that Jesus was "made" of the seed of David (that Jesus was a god "created" by Jehovah to die for our sins), they may point to Proverbs 8:22–35 for justification. However, the Bible is speaking here of "wisdom" (v. 12).

They also may refer to John 14:28 in which Jesus said, "I go to the Father: for my Father is greater than I," but they fail to show why Jesus said the Father was greater: "But we see Jesus, who was made a little lower than the angels for the suffering of death,...that he by the grace of God should taste death for every man" (Hebrews 2:9, emphasis added).

In Romans 1:3, the word used to refer to the incarnation ("made") is ginomai, which means "assembled." A body was prepared for God to manifest Himself in the flesh—"And without controversy great is the mystery of godliness: God was manifest in the flesh, justified in the Spirit, seen of angels, preached to the Gentiles, believed on in the world, received up into glory" (1 Timothy 3:16).

CHAPTER 9

WISDOM has built her house, she has hewn out her seven pillars:

2 She has killed her beasts; she has mingled her wine; she has also furnished her table.

3 She has sent forth her maidens: she cries upon the highest places of the city,

4 Whoso is simple, let him turn in hither: as for him that wants understanding, she says to him,

5 Come, eat of my bread, and drink of the wine which I have mingled.

6 Forsake the foolish, and live; and go in the way of understanding.

7 He that reproves a scorner gets to himself shame: and he that rebukes a wicked man gets himself a blot.

8 Reprove not a scorner, lest he hate you: rebuke a wise man, and he will love you.

9 Give instruction to a wise man, and he will be yet wiser: teach a just man, and he will increase in learning.

10 **The fear of the Lord is the beginning of wisdom: and the knowledge of the holy is understanding.**

11 For by me your days shall be multiplied, and the years of your life shall be increased.

12 If you be wise, you shall be wise for yourself: but if you scorn, you alone shall bear it.

13 A foolish woman is clamorous: she is simple, and knows nothing.

14 For she sits at the door of her house, on a seat in the high places of the city,

15 To call passengers who go right on their ways:

16 Whoso is simple, let him turn in hither: and as for him that wants understanding, she says to him,

17 Stolen waters are sweet, and bread eaten in secret is pleasant.

18 But he knows not that the dead are there; and that her guests are in the depths of hell.

· · · · · ·

Will a sinner go to hell because
he doesn't trust in Jesus?
See John 16:9 comment.

· · · · · ·

CHAPTER 10

THE proverbs of Solomon. A wise son makes a glad father: but a foolish son is the heaviness of his mother.

2 **Treasures of wickedness profit nothing: but righteousness delivers from death.**

3 The LORD will not suffer the soul of the righteous to famish: but he casts away the substance of the wicked.

4 He becomes poor that deals with a slack hand: but the hand of the diligent makes rich.

5 He that gathers in summer is a wise son: but he that sleeps in harvest is a son that causes shame.

6 Blessings are upon the head of the just: but violence covers the mouth of the wicked.

7 The memory of the just is blessed: but the name of the wicked shall rot.

8 The wise in heart will receive commandments: but a prating fool shall fall.

9 He that walks uprightly walks surely: but he that perverts his ways shall be known.

10 He that winks with the eye causes sorrow: but a prating fool shall fall.

9:17 Our sinful hearts are so perverse that sin promises excitement. Despite the claim of modern evangelism that we can't find happiness until we come to Jesus, sin is indeed enticing and pleasurable, and can make a man or woman happy. See Jeremiah 12:1 and Hebrews 11:25.

10:2 All the money in the world will not turn the head of the Judge of the Universe. Money may buy a pardon from a civil court, but only righteousness will deliver the guilty from the wrath of Eternal Justice. See Proverbs 11:4.

11 The mouth of a righteous man is a well of life: but violence covers the mouth of the wicked.

12 Hatred stirs up strifes: but love covers all sins.

13 In the lips of him that has understanding wisdom is found: but a rod is for the back of him that is void of understanding.

14 Wise men lay up knowledge: but the mouth of the foolish is near destruction.

15 The rich man's wealth is his strong city: the destruction of the poor is their poverty.

16 The labor of the righteous tends to life: the fruit of the wicked to sin.

17 He is in the way of life that keeps instruction: but he that refuses reproof errs.

18 He that hides hatred with lying lips, and he that utters a slander, is a fool.

19 In the multitude of words there wants not sin: but he that refrains his lips is wise.

20 The tongue of the just is as choice silver: the heart of the wicked is little worth.

21 The lips of the righteous feed many: but fools die for want of wisdom.

22 The blessing of the LORD, it makes rich, and he adds no sorrow with it.

23 It is as sport to a fool to do mischief: but a man of understanding has wisdom.

24 The fear of the wicked, it shall come upon him: but the desire of the righteous shall be granted.

25 As the whirlwind passes, so is the wicked no more: but the righteous is an everlasting foundation.

26 As vinegar to the teeth, and as smoke to the eyes, so is the sluggard to them that send him.

27 The fear of the LORD prolongs days: but the years of the wicked shall be shortened.

28 The hope of the righteous shall be gladness: but the expectation of the wicked shall perish.

29 The way of the LORD is strength to the upright: but destruction shall be to the workers of iniquity.

30 The righteous shall never be removed: but the wicked shall not inhabit the earth.

31 The mouth of the just brings forth wisdom: but the froward tongue shall be cut out.

32 The lips of the righteous know what is acceptable: but the mouth of the wicked speaks frowardness.

CHAPTER 11

A FALSE balance is abomination to the LORD: but a just weight is his delight.

2 When pride comes, then comes shame: but with the lowly is wisdom.

3 The integrity of the upright shall guide them: but the perverseness of transgressors shall destroy them.

4 Riches profit not in the day of wrath: but righteousness delivers from death.

5 The righteousness of the perfect shall direct his way: but the wicked shall fall by his own wickedness.

10:7 Perhaps this is why not too many people name their children Adolf, Judas, or Jezebel.

10:32 Knowing What's Acceptable. There is no record of David seeking God for His will before he confronted Goliath. How could this be? The Scriptures say, "In all your ways acknowledge him, and he shall direct your paths" (Proverbs 3:6). Shouldn't David have acknowledged the Lord in some way? No doubt, he did pray as he faced his enemy, but there is no proof that David asked God whether he should attack the giant Philistine. The reason for this is clear. The Bible tells us, "The lips of the righteous know what is acceptable." There are certain things that we know are not acceptable. If you saw an elderly woman fall to the ground, would you ask God whether or not you should help her up? Some things should be obvious to the godly. David took one look at the situation and saw that such a thing was completely unacceptable—that this "uncircumcised Philistine" was defying the armies of the Living God.

David could draw that conclusion because he had a relationship with God. His senses were "exercised to discern both good and evil" (Hebrews 5:14). He knew the Lord, and those who "know their God shall be strong, and do exploits" (Daniel 11:32).

6 The righteousness of the upright shall deliver them: but transgressors shall be taken in their own naughtiness.

7 When a wicked man dies, his expectation shall perish: and the hope of unjust men perishes.

8 The righteous is delivered out of trouble, and the wicked comes in his stead.

9 An hypocrite with his mouth destroys his neighbor: but through knowledge shall the just be delivered.

10 When it goes well with the righteous, the city rejoices: and when the wicked perish, there is shouting.

11 By the blessing of the upright the city is exalted: but it is overthrown by the mouth of the wicked.

12 He that is void of wisdom despises his neighbor: but a man of understanding holds his peace.

13 A talebearer reveals secrets: but he that is of a faithful spirit conceals the matter.

14 Where no counsel is, the people fall: but in the multitude of counselors there is safety.

15 He that is surety for a stranger shall smart for it: and he that hates suretiship is sure.

16 A gracious woman retains honor: and strong men retain riches.

17 The merciful man does good to his own soul: but he that is cruel troubles his own flesh.

18 The wicked works a deceitful work: but to him that sows righteousness shall be a sure reward.

19 As righteousness tends to life: so he that pursues evil pursues it to his own death.

20 They that are of a froward heart are abomination to the LORD: but such as are upright in their way are his delight.

21 Though hand join in hand, the wicked shall not be unpunished: but the seed of the righteous shall be delivered.

22 As a jewel of gold in a swine's snout, so is a fair woman who is without discretion.

23 The desire of the righteous is only good: but the expectation of the wicked is wrath.

24 There is that scatters, and yet increases; and there is that withholds more than is meet, but it tends to poverty.

25 The liberal soul shall be made fat: and he that waters shall be watered also himself.

26 He that withholds corn, the people shall curse him: but blessing shall be upon the head of him that sells it.

27 He that diligently seeks good procures favor: but he that seeks mischief, it shall come unto him.

28 He that trusts in his riches shall fall: but the righteous shall flourish as a branch.

11:5–7 Notice the surety of these verses. They shall come to pass.

11:9 If we wouldn't say it in prayer, we shouldn't say it at all.

11:13 The damage of gossip. A woman once spread some hot gossip about a local pastor. What he had supposedly done became common knowledge around town. Then she found that what she had heard wasn't true. She gallantly went to the pastor and asked for his forgiveness. The pastor forgave her, but then told her to take a pillow full of tiny feathers to a corner of the town, and in high winds, shake the feathers out. Then he told her to try to pick up every feather. He explained that the damage had already been done. She had destroyed his good reputation, and trying to repair the damage was like trying to pick up feathers in high winds.

The Bible says that there is life and death in the power of the tongue (Proverbs 18:21). Pray with the psalmist, "Set a watch, O Lord, before my mouth; keep the door of my lips" (Psalm 141:3). Remember the old saying, "He that gossips to you will gossip about you."

11:21 Though the entire world joins hands in a unity of spirit and says that there is no hell, it is still a reality. There will be a Judgment Day and justice will be done.

29 He that troubles his own house shall inherit the wind: and the fool shall be servant to the wise of heart.

30 *The fruit of the righteous is a tree of life; and he that wins souls is wise.*

31 Behold, the righteous shall be recompensed in the earth: much more the wicked and the sinner.

CHAPTER 12

WHOSO loves instruction loves knowledge: but he that hates reproof is brutish.

2 A good man obtains favor of the LORD: but a man of wicked devices will he condemn.

3 A man shall not be established by wickedness: but the root of the righteous shall not be moved.

4 A virtuous woman is a crown to her husband: but she that makes ashamed is as rottenness in his bones.

5 The thoughts of the righteous are right: but the counsels of the wicked are deceit.

6 The words of the wicked are to lie in wait for blood: but the mouth of the upright shall deliver them.

7 The wicked are overthrown, and are not: but the house of the righteous shall stand.

8 A man shall be commended according to his wisdom: but he that is of a perverse heart shall be despised.

9 He that is despised, and has a servant, is better than he that honors himself, and lacks bread.

10 A righteous man regards the life of his beast: but the tender mercies of the wicked are cruel.

11 He that tills his land shall be satisfied with bread: but he that follows vain persons is void of understanding.

12 The wicked desires the net of evil men: but the root of the righteous yields fruit.

13 The wicked is snared by the transgression of his lips: but the just shall come out of trouble.

14 A man shall be satisfied with good by the fruit of his mouth: and the recompense of a man's hands shall be rendered unto him.

15 **The way of a fool is right in his own eyes: but he that hearkens unto counsel is wise.**

16 A fool's wrath is presently known: but a prudent man covers shame.

17 He that speaks truth shows forth righteousness: but a false witness deceit.

18 There is that speaks like the piercings of a sword: but the tongue of the wise is health.

11:24 The wallet is the final frontier. There is nothing wrong with riches. However, those who have wealth must not trust in money (v. 28) and must be willing to share their prosperity with others. See 1 Timothy 6:17–19.

11:30 "Even if I were utterly selfish and had no care for anything but my own happiness, I would choose, if God allowed, to be a soul winner, for never did I know perfect, overflowing, unutterable happiness of the purest and most ennobling order 'till I first heard of one who had sought and found a Savior through my means." Charles Spurgeon

11:30 Lifestyle evangelism. Here's how to cultivate true lifestyle evangelism: 1) Pray that God uses you to reach the lost. 2) Ask for wisdom to use the time you have effectively for evangelism. Treat every day as though it were your last opportunity to share Christ. One day you will be right. 3) Study how to answer every man who asks you a reason for the hope that is in you (1 Peter 3:15; see Proverbs 16:23). 4) Find a "fishing hole" and go there regularly. Don't wait for sinners to approach you; go to them (Mark 16:15). 5) Use any anxiety as a catalyst to drive you to prayer and trust in God. Don't let the fear of man paralyze you (Philippians 1:28). You will realize the spiritual nature of fear after you conquer it. Confront it with the Word of God—"I can do all things through Christ who strengthens me" (Philippians 4:13). 6) Encourage others (by example and exhortation) into the task of evangelism.

19 The lip of truth shall be established for ever: but a lying tongue is but for a moment.

20 Deceit is in the heart of them that imagine evil: but to the counselors of peace is joy.

21 There shall no evil happen to the just: but the wicked shall be filled with mischief.

22 Lying lips are abomination to the Lord: but they that deal truly are his delight.

23 A prudent man conceals knowledge: but the heart of fools proclaims foolishness.

24 The hand of the diligent shall bear rule: but the slothful shall be under tribute.

25 Heaviness in the heart of man makes it stoop: but a good word makes it glad.

26 The righteous is more excellent than his neighbor: but the way of the wicked seduces them.

27 The slothful man roasts not that which he took in hunting: but the substance of a diligent man is precious.

28 In the way of righteousness is life: and in the pathway thereof there is no death.

CHAPTER 13

A WISE son hears his father's instruction: but a scorner hears not rebuke.

2 A man shall eat good by the fruit of his mouth: but the soul of the transgressors shall eat violence.

3 He that keeps his mouth keeps his life: but he that opens wide his lips shall have destruction.

4 The soul of the sluggard desires, and has nothing: but the soul of the diligent shall be made fat.

5 A righteous man hates lying: but a wicked man is loathsome, and comes to shame.

6 Righteousness keeps him that is upright in the way: but wickedness overthrows the sinner.

7 There is that makes himself rich, yet has nothing: there is that makes himself poor, yet has great riches.

8 The ransom of a man's life are his riches: but the poor hears not rebuke.

9 The light of the righteous rejoices: but the lamp of the wicked shall be put out.

10 Only by pride comes contention: but with the well advised is wisdom.

11 Wealth gotten by vanity shall be diminished: but he that gathers by labor shall increase.

12 Hope deferred makes the heart sick: but when the desire comes, it is a tree of life.

13 Whoso despises the word shall be destroyed: but he that fears the commandment shall be rewarded.

14 The law of the wise is a fountain of life, to depart from the snares of death.

15 Good understanding gives favor: but the way of transgressors is hard.

16 Every prudent man deals with knowledge: but a fool lays open his folly.

17 A wicked messenger falls into mischief: but a faithful ambassador is health.

18 Poverty and shame shall be to him that refuses instruction: but he that regards reproof shall be honored.

12:15 This verse sums up the philosophy of a world that professes to be wise yet ignores the counsel of God's Word.

12:17 We are to follow the example of Jesus, who "preached righteousness in the great congregation" (see Psalm 40:6–10).

12:22 The ungodly try to justify themselves by saying that a "fib" or "white lie" never hurts anybody. Sin offends a holy God who demands retribution. See Proverbs 13:5.

12:25 Are you worried and depressed about the future? Then read and believe the "good word" of God's Word. Nothing banishes fear like faith. Trusting in God's promises is like switching on a bright light in a dark room of gloom.

19 The desire accomplished is sweet to the soul: but it is abomination to fools to depart from evil.

20 He that walks with wise men shall be wise: but a companion of fools shall be destroyed.

21 Evil pursues sinners: but to the righteous good shall be repaid.

22 A good man leaves an inheritance to his children's children: and the wealth of the sinner is laid up for the just.

23 Much food is in the tillage of the poor: but there is that is destroyed for want of judgment.

24 He that spares his rod hates his son: but he that loves him chastens him betimes.

25 The righteous eats to the satisfying of his soul: but the belly of the wicked shall want.

CHAPTER 14

E VERY wise woman builds her house: but the foolish plucks it down with her hands.

2 He that walks in his uprightness fears the LORD: but he that is perverse in his ways despises him.

3 In the mouth of the foolish is a rod of pride: but the lips of the wise shall preserve them.

4 Where no oxen are, the crib is clean: but much increase is by the strength of the ox.

5 A faithful witness will not lie: but a false witness will utter lies.

6 A scorner seeks wisdom, and finds it not: but knowledge is easy unto him that understands.

7 Go from the presence of a foolish man, when you perceive not in him the lips of knowledge.

8 The wisdom of the prudent is to understand his way: but the folly of fools is deceit.

9 Fools make a mock at sin: but among the righteous there is favor.

10 The heart knows his own bitterness; and a stranger does not intermeddle with his joy.

11 The house of the wicked shall be overthrown: but the tabernacle of the upright shall flourish.

12 There is a way which seems right unto a man, but the end thereof are the ways of death.

13 Even in laughter the heart is sorrowful; and the end of that mirth is heaviness.

14 The backslider in heart shall be filled with his own ways: and a good man shall be satisfied from himself.

15 The simple believes every word: but the prudent man looks well to his going.

16 A wise man fears, and departs from evil: but the fool rages, and is confident.

17 He that is soon angry deals foolishly: and a man of wicked devices is hated.

18 The simple inherit folly: but the prudent are crowned with knowledge.

19 The evil bow before the good; and the wicked at the gates of the righteous.

20 The poor is hated even of his own neighbor: but the rich has many friends.

21 He that despises his neighbor sins: but he that has mercy on the poor, happy is he.

22 Do they not err that devise evil? but mercy and truth shall be to them that devise good.

13:13 The Word will judge and condemn the guilty on the Last Day. Those who fear when they realize that they have sinned against God by transgressing His Law will be rewarded in the Gospel. See Galatians 3:24.

13:19 Sinners love darkness; it is their security. See Proverbs 14:9; John 3:19,20.

14:5 See verse 25.

14:14 False converts have no concern for God's will to reach the lost. Those who manage to find themselves in a pulpit will build their own kingdom rather than God's. See also Acts 20:30.

SPRINGBOARDS FOR PREACHING AND WITNESSING

The Key

14:12 Back in the Old West, a number of men were upstairs in a boarding house amusing themselves with a game of cards when there was a cry from the street below of "Fire! Fire!" The men looked at one another in disbelief. One of the windows grew orange with the flames. "Wait!" said the dealer. "Let's just finish this hand; we've got plenty of time—I have a key to the back door." The men nodded in approval, then quickly picked up the dealt cards.

Precious minutes passed. One of the men became nervous as the flames licked through the now broken window. With darting eyes and a sweat-filled brow, he asked for the key. "Coward!" muttered the dealer as he tossed across the key. Each of them then rushed to the door and waited with bated breath as the key was placed into the lock. "It won't turn!" was the cry. "Let me have it!" said the dealer. As he tried in vain to turn the key, he whispered in horror, "It's the wrong key!"

---

23 In all labor there is profit: but the talk of the lips tends only to penury.

24 The crown of the wise is their riches: but the foolishness of fools is folly.

25 A true witness delivers souls: but a deceitful witness speaks lies.

26 In the fear of the LORD is strong confidence: and his children shall have a place of refuge.

27 The fear of the LORD is a fountain of life, to depart from the snares of death.

28 In the multitude of people is the king's honor: but in the want of people is the destruction of the prince.

29 He that is slow to wrath is of great understanding: but he that is hasty of spirit exalts folly.

30 A sound heart is the life of the flesh: but envy the rottenness of the bones.

31 He that oppresses the poor reproaches his Maker: but he that honors him has mercy on the poor.

32 The wicked is driven away in his wickedness: but the righteous has hope in his death.

33 Wisdom rests in the heart of him that has understanding: but that which is in the midst of fools is made known.

34 Righteousness exalts a nation: but sin is a reproach to any people.

35 The king's favor is toward a wise servant: but his wrath is against him that causes shame.

CHAPTER 15

A SOFT answer turns away wrath: but grievous words stir up anger.

2 The tongue of the wise uses knowledge aright: but the mouth of fools pours out foolishness.

3 The eyes of the LORD are in every place, beholding the evil and the good.

4 A wholesome tongue is a tree of life: but perverseness therein is a breach in the spirit.

14:25 A "witness" is not called upon to give an eloquent speech, but to merely testify to what he has seen and heard.

14:27 Here is a fountain from which most men refuse to drink. Their prejudicial minds think that its waters are bitter, when in truth they are incredibly sweet. The fear of the Lord helps men shake off that beast called "sin"—which is sucking from them their very life's blood.

14:34 "The moral principles and precepts contained in the Scriptures ought to form the basis of all our civil constitutions and laws. All the miseries and evils which men suffer from—vice, crime, ambition, injustice, oppression, slavery, and war—proceed from their despising or neglecting the precepts contained in the Bible." Noah Webster

5 A fool despises his father's instruction: but he that regards reproof is prudent.

6 In the house of the righteous is much treasure: but in the revenues of the wicked is trouble.

7 The lips of the wise disperse knowledge: but the heart of the foolish does not so.

8 **The sacrifice of the wicked is an abomination to the Lord: but the prayer of the upright is his delight.**

9 **The way of the wicked is an abomination unto the Lord: but he loves him that follows after righteousness.**

10 Correction is grievous unto him that forsakes the way: and he that hates reproof shall die.

11 Hell and destruction are before the LORD: how much more then the hearts of the children of men?

12 A scorner loves not one that reproves him: neither will he go unto the wise.

13 A merry heart makes a cheerful countenance: but by sorrow of the heart the spirit is broken.

14 The heart of him that has understanding seeks knowledge: but the mouth of fools feeds on foolishness.

15 All the days of the afflicted are evil: but he that is of a merry heart has a continual feast.

16 Better is little with the fear of the LORD than great treasure and trouble therewith.

17 Better is a dinner of herbs where love is, than a stalled ox and hatred therewith.

18 A wrathful man stirs up strife: but he that is slow to anger appeases strife.

19 The way of the slothful man is as an hedge of thorns: but the way of the righteous is made plain.

20 A wise son makes a glad father: but a foolish man despises his mother.

21 Folly is joy to him that is destitute of wisdom: but a man of understanding walks uprightly.

22 Without counsel purposes are disappointed: but in the multitude of counselors they are established.

23 A man has joy by the answer of his mouth: and a word spoken in due season, how good is it!

24 The way of life is above to the wise, that he may depart from hell beneath.

25 The Lord will destroy the house of the proud: but he will establish the border of the widow.

15:1 Speak softly. This verse needs to be written on the hearts of all who preach the gospel, whether they share their faith with sinners one-on-one or preach open-air. If sinners become angry when you witness to them, speak softly. If you think you are about to be hit, ask the person his name to help diffuse the situation. Don't be afraid to gently change the subject, and don't wait to be a martyr. Jesus said to flee from a city that persecutes you (Matthew 10:23). Paul left one city in a basket (2 Corinthians 11:33). For other verses on the spirit in which we should share our faith, see Proverbs 16:32.

15:7 God's Law gives knowledge (see Romans 3:20,21). Those who are wise will tell sinners of its righteous requirements.

15:8 When sinners think they are righteous because they give money, attend church, or live what they consider to be a virtuous life, it is an "abomination to the Lord." Even their thoughts are an abomination to Him (v. 26). This is because they stand guilty before Him. Their good works are provoked by a guilty conscience. Like a despicable criminal trying to pervert justice by offering the judge a bribe, they think their good deeds will outweigh their sins (see Hebrews 9:14).

"Good works, as they are called, in sinners are nothing but splendid sins." Augustine

15:15 Laughter is the enemy of legalism. Liberty and joy go hand in hand.

15:21 Use your time to further the gospel (see Ephesians 5:15,16). So much of today's entertainment is folly. If shallow entertainment gives us joy, it reveals our shallow understanding of the precious nature of time.

26 The thoughts of the wicked are an abomination to the Lord: but the words of the pure are pleasant words.

27 He that is greedy of gain troubles his own house; but he that hates gifts shall live.

28 *The heart of the righteous studies to answer: but the mouth of the wicked pours out evil things.*

29 The Lord is far from the wicked: but he hears the prayer of the righteous.

30 The light of the eyes rejoices the heart: and a good report makes the bones fat.

31 The ear that hears the reproof of life abides among the wise.

32 He that refuses instruction despises his own soul: but he that hears reproof gets understanding.

33 The fear of the Lord is the instruction of wisdom; and before honor is humility.

CHAPTER 16

The *preparations of the heart in man, and the answer of the tongue, is from the Lord.*

2 All the ways of a man are clean in his own eyes; but the Lord weighs the spirits.

3 *Commit your works unto the Lord, and your thoughts shall be established.*

4 The Lord has made all things for himself: yes, even the wicked for the day of evil.

5 Every one that is proud in heart is an abomination to the Lord: though hand join in hand, he shall not be unpunished.

6 *By mercy and truth iniquity is purged: and by the fear of the Lord men depart from evil.*

7 *When a man's ways please the Lord, he makes even his enemies to be at peace with him.*

8 Better is a little with righteousness than great revenues without right.

9 A man's heart devises his way: but the LORD directs his steps.

10 A divine sentence is in the lips of the king: his mouth transgresses not in judgment.

11 A just weight and balance are the LORD's: all the weights of the bag are his work.

12 It is an abomination to kings to commit wickedness: for the throne is established by righteousness.

13 Righteous lips are the delight of kings; and they love him that speaks right.

14 The wrath of a king is as messengers of death: but a wise man will pacify it.

15 In the light of the king's countenance is life; and his favour is as a cloud of the latter rain.

16 How much better is it to get wisdom than gold! and to get understanding rather to be chosen than silver!

15:23 What a joy it is to direct a lost sinner to the Savior. The gospel is always in season. See 2 Timothy 4:2.

16:2 This is never so evident as when you ask a guilty sinner if he thinks he is a good person (see Proverbs 21:2; Luke 16:15). When the Law is used properly, it strips a man of self-righteousness (See Luke 18:18–23).

16:5 God resists those who are proud. Grace is only for the humble. Biblical evangelism is "Law to the proud; grace to the humble." With the Law, we break the hard heart. With the gospel, we heal the broken heart.

16:6 Men will not let go of their beloved sins unless the fear of the Lord grips their sin-loving hearts. Sinners are like a child whose eyes sparkle with delight as he holds a stick of lighted dynamite. He will not let go of it unless he is convinced that he is in terrible danger. The Law of God coupled with future punishment is the convincing agent that God has chosen to awaken the sinner. He must be told that God (who has the power to cast his soul into hell) will judge the world (on Judgment Day) in righteousness (by the perfect and righteous standard of His Law).

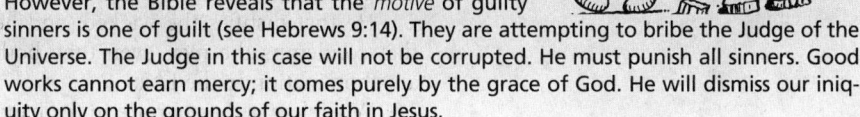

16:10 *"I have broken the Ten Commandments, but I do good things for people."*

Many people do similar things. They may steal from their employer or cheat on their taxes, then give to a charity or spend Thanksgiving helping at a soup kitchen. They think they are balancing the scales: they have done bad, and now they are doing good. However, the Bible reveals that the *motive* of guilty sinners is one of guilt (see Hebrews 9:14). They are attempting to bribe the Judge of the Universe. The Judge in this case will not be corrupted. He must punish all sinners. Good works cannot earn mercy; it comes purely by the grace of God. He will dismiss our iniquity only on the grounds of our faith in Jesus.

17 The highway of the upright is to depart from evil: he that keeps his way preserves his soul.

18 Pride goes before destruction, and an haughty spirit before a fall.

19 Better it is to be of an humble spirit with the lowly, than to divide the spoil with the proud.

20 He that handles a matter wisely shall find good: and whoso trusts in the LORD, happy is he.

21 The wise in heart shall be called prudent: and the sweetness of the lips increases learning.

22 Understanding is a wellspring of life unto him that has it: but the instruction of fools is folly.

23 *The heart of the wise teaches his mouth, and adds learning to his lips.*

24 Pleasant words are as an honeycomb, sweet to the soul, and health to the bones.

25 There is a way that seems right unto a man, but the end thereof are the ways of death.

26 He that labors labors for himself; for his mouth craves it of him.

27 An ungodly man digs up evil: and in his lips there is as a burning fire.

28 A froward man sows strife: and a whisperer separates chief friends.

29 A violent man entices his neighbor, and leads him into the way that is not good.

30 He shuts his eyes to devise froward things: moving his lips he brings evil to pass.

31 The hoary head is a crown of glory, if it be found in the way of righteousness.

32 *He that is slow to anger is better than the mighty; and he that rules his spirit than he that takes a city.*

33 The lot is cast into the lap; but the whole disposing thereof is of the LORD.

CHAPTER 17

BETTER is a dry morsel, and quietness therewith, than an house full of sacrifices with strife.

2 A wise servant shall have rule over a son that causes shame, and shall have part of the inheritance among the brethren.

16:25 See Proverbs 12:15. The way of self-righteousness seems right to men. (See Proverbs 15:8 comment.)

16:32 This is the spirit in which we should share our faith. See Luke 6:28.

"He who masters his passions is a king even while in chains. He who is ruled by his passions is a slave even while sitting on a throne." Richard Wurmbrand

*Do I not destroy my enemies
when I make them my friends?*

Abraham Lincoln

1809–1865

16TH PRESIDENT OF THE U.S.

ABOLISHED SLAVERY

3 The fining pot is for silver, and the furnace for gold: but the LORD tries the hearts.

4 A wicked doer gives heed to false lips; and a liar gives ear to a naughty tongue.

5 Whoso mocks the poor reproaches his Maker: and he that is glad at calamities shall not be unpunished.

6 Children's children are the crown of old men; and the glory of children are their fathers.

7 Excellent speech becomes not a fool: much less do lying lips a prince.

8 A gift is as a precious stone in the eyes of him that has it: whithersoever it turns, it prospers.

9 He that covers a transgression seeks love; but he that repeats a matter separates very friends.

10 A reproof enters more into a wise man than an hundred stripes into a fool.

11 An evil man seeks only rebellion: therefore a cruel messenger shall be sent against him.

12 Let a bear robbed of her whelps meet a man, rather than a fool in his folly.

13 Whoso rewards evil for good, evil shall not depart from his house.

14 The beginning of strife is as when one lets out water: therefore leave off contention, before it be meddled with.

15 He that justifies the wicked, and he that condemns the just, even they both are abomination to the LORD.

16 Wherefore is there a price in the hand of a fool to get wisdom, seeing he has no heart to it?

17 A friend loves at all times, and a brother is born for adversity.

18 A man void of understanding strikes hands, and becomes surety in the presence of his friend.

19 He loves transgression that loves strife: and he that exalts his gate seeks destruction.

20 He that has a froward heart finds no good: and he that has a perverse tongue falls into mischief.

21 He that begets a fool does it to his sorrow: and the father of a fool has no joy.

22 A merry heart does good like a medicine: but a broken spirit dries the bones.

23 A wicked man takes a gift out of the bosom to pervert the ways of judgment.

24 Wisdom is before him that has understanding; but the eyes of a fool are in the ends of the earth.

25 A foolish son is a grief to his father, and bitterness to her that bare him.

26 Also to punish the just is not good, nor to strike princes for equity.

27 He that has knowledge spares his words: and a man of understanding is of an excellent spirit.

28 Even a fool, when he holds his peace, is counted wise: and he that shuts his lips is esteemed a man of understanding.

17:11 A rebellious heart is an open door to the demonic realm. This was the case with King Saul.

17:14 See Matthew 12:36 comment.

CHAPTER 18

THROUGH desire a man, having separated himself, seeks and intermeddles with all wisdom.

2 A fool has no delight in understanding, but that his heart may discover itself.

3 When the wicked comes, then comes also contempt, and with ignominy reproach.

4 The words of a man's mouth are as deep waters, and the wellspring of wisdom as a flowing brook.

5 It is not good to accept the person of the wicked, to overthrow the righteous in judgment.

6 A fool's lips enter into contention, and his mouth calls for strokes.

7 A fool's mouth is his destruction, and his lips are the snare of his soul.

8 The words of a talebearer are as wounds, and they go down into the innermost parts of the belly.

9 He also that is slothful in his work is brother to him that is a great waster.

10 The name of the LORD is a strong tower: the righteous runs into it, and is safe.

11 The rich man's wealth is his strong city, and as an high wall in his own conceit.

12 **Before destruction the heart of man is haughty, and before honor is humility.**

13 *He that answers a matter before he hears it, it is folly and shame unto him.*

14 The spirit of a man will sustain his infirmity; but a wounded spirit who can bear?

15 The heart of the prudent gets knowledge; and the ear of the wise seeks knowledge.

16 A man's gift makes room for him, and brings him before great men.

17 He that is first in his own cause seems just; but his neighbor comes and searches him.

18 The lot causes contentions to cease, and parts between the mighty.

19 A brother offended is harder to be won than a strong city: and their contentions are like the bars of a castle.

20 A man's belly shall be satisfied with the fruit of his mouth; and with the increase of his lips shall he be filled.

21 Death and life are in the power of the tongue: and they that love it shall eat the fruit thereof.

22 Whoso finds a wife finds a good thing, and obtains favor of the LORD.

23 The poor uses entreaties; but the rich answers roughly.

24 A man that has friends must show himself friendly: and there is a friend that sticks closer than a brother.

17:22 Let the joy of the Lord be your strength. See Proverbs 15:15 comment.

17:24 True riches are laid before us in the Word of God. Those who ignore these "exceedingly great and precious promises" (2 Peter 1:4) will never be content.

18:1 Never isolate yourself from other Christians. Those who are not in regular fellowship with other believers make themselves an easier target for the enemy. Satan is as a roaring lion, seeking to devour us (1 Peter 5:8). The first thing a lion does in stalking its prey is to isolate individual members from the herd. See Hebrews 10:25.

18:13 Be patient when sinners ramble. It is a discredit to our Christian witness to interrupt someone who is trying to tell us something, even though we have heard the empty argument many times before. Love will listen.

18:16 If you are wanting God to use you, He will open the doors in His time.

18:19 Make it a rule of life not to argue over petty doctrinal or prophetic interpretations. Strive to keep the unity of the Spirit. See Philippians 1:27.

CHAPTER 19

BETTER is the poor that walks in his integrity, than he that is perverse in his lips, and is a fool.

2 Also, that the soul be without knowledge, it is not good; and he that hastens with his feet sins.

3 The foolishness of man perverts his way: and his heart frets against the LORD.

4 Wealth makes many friends; but the poor is separated from his neighbor.

5 A false witness shall not be unpunished, and he that speaks lies shall not escape.

6 Many will entreat the favor of the prince: and every man is a friend to him that gives gifts.

7 All the brethren of the poor do hate him: how much more do his friends go far from him? he pursues them with words, yet they are wanting to him.

8 He that gets wisdom loves his own soul: he that keeps understanding shall find good.

9 **A false witness shall not be unpunished, and he that speaks lies shall perish.**

10 Delight is not seemly for a fool; much less for a servant to have rule over princes.

11 *The discretion of a man defers his anger; and it is his glory to pass over a transgression.*

12 The king's wrath is as the roaring of a lion; but his favor is as dew upon the grass.

13 A foolish son is the calamity of his father: and the contentions of a wife are a continual dropping.

14 House and riches are the inheritance of fathers: and a prudent wife is from the LORD.

15 Slothfulness casts into a deep sleep; and an idle soul shall suffer hunger.

16 He that keeps the commandment keeps his own soul; but he that despises his ways shall die.

17 He that has pity upon the poor lends unto the LORD; and that which he has given will he pay him again.

18 Chasten your son while there is hope, and let not your soul spare for his crying.

19 A man of great wrath shall suffer punishment: for if you deliver him, yet you must do it again.

20 Hear counsel, and receive instruction, that you may be wise in your latter end.

21 There are many devices in a man's heart; nevertheless the counsel of the LORD, that shall stand.

22 The desire of a man is his kindness: and a poor man is better than a liar.

23 The fear of the LORD tends to life: and he that has it shall abide satisfied; he shall not be visited with evil.

24 A slothful man hides his hand in his bosom, and will not so much as bring it to his mouth again.

25 Smite a scorner, and the simple will beware: and reprove one that has understanding, and he will understand knowledge.

26 He that wastes his father, and chases away his mother, is a son that causes shame, and brings reproach.

27 Cease, my son, to hear the instruction that causes to err from the words of knowledge.

28 An ungodly witness scorns judgment: and the mouth of the wicked devours iniquity.

29 Judgments are prepared for scorners, and stripes for the back of fools.

CHAPTER 20

WINE is a mocker, strong drink is raging: and whosoever is deceived thereby is not wise.

19:3 See Romans 8:7.

19:5 Those who transgress the Ninth Commandment have a fearful fate. See Revelation 21:8.

19:17 "We make a living by what we get, but we make a life by what we give." Winston Churchill

2 The fear of a king is as the roaring of a lion: whoso provokes him to anger sins against his own soul.

3 It is an honor for a man to cease from strife: but every fool will be meddling.

4 The sluggard will not plow by reason of the cold; therefore shall he beg in harvest, and have nothing.

5 Counsel in the heart of man is like deep water; but a man of understanding will draw it out.

6 Most men will proclaim every one his own goodness: but a faithful man who can find?

7 The just man walks in his integrity: his children are blessed after him.

8 A king that sits in the throne of judgment scatters away all evil with his eyes.

9 Who can say, I have made my heart clean, I am pure from my sin?

10 Divers weights, and divers measures, both of them are alike abomination to the LORD.

11 Even a child is known by his doings, whether his work be pure, and whether it be right.

12 The hearing ear, and the seeing eye, the LORD has made even both of them.

13 Love not sleep, lest you come to poverty; open your eyes, and you shall be satisfied with bread.

14 It is naught, it is naught, says the buyer: but when he is gone his way, then he boasts.

15 There is gold, and a multitude of rubies: but the lips of knowledge are a precious jewel.

16 Take his garment that is surety for a stranger: and take a pledge of him for a strange woman.

17 Bread of deceit is sweet to a man; but afterwards his mouth shall be filled with gravel.

18 Every purpose is established by counsel: and with good advice make war.

19 He that goes about as a talebearer reveals secrets: therefore meddle not with him that flatters with his lips.

20:1 Alcohol is a poison. When someone is in-toxic-ated, he is "poisoned." The body protests with confused thinking, slurred speech, and impaired vision, memory, and judgment. The victim vomits. The next day his head throbs with pain, yet he still drinks the poison. Hundreds of thousands of innocent people have been maimed on the roads by drunk drivers, yet the world cannot bring itself to say, "Don't drink." It can only say, "Don't drink and drive." This is because alcohol is the only enemy man has succeeded in loving. It destroys his liver, heart, and kidneys. It gives him high blood pressure and causes blood vessels to burst in his skin. It leads him to beat his wife and abuse his kids. It will eventually destroy his ability to enjoy the intimacies of the marriage bed. Yet he still drinks.

He thinks alcohol is a "stimulant." In truth, it is a suppressant that reduces his inhibitions. It dulls the naggings of his conscience so that he can commit sexual and other sins that he couldn't indulge in while sober. A man who gives himself to the demon of alcohol becomes a slave to its addictive properties. It mocks him. It steals his dignity. It takes control of his will. Whoever is deceived by it (and there are millions) is not wise. See Proverbs 23:29–35.

20:3 It takes no skill to "argue" with sinners. We are called to reason—to plead with love and gentleness.

20:6 If you ask a man if he thinks he is a good person, he usually will say that he is. That's why we need to use the Law (which the Bible says is "good") to give him understanding about what "good" is (Romans 7:12). See Proverbs 21:2.

20:9 No man can do this. Only God can cleanse man's heart of sin and make him pure. See 1 John 1:9.

20:11 Those who deny the reality of the sinful nature haven't had children. See Proverbs 29:15 comment.

20:12 See Psalm 94:7–11.

20:9

"I used to be a liar and a thief, but that was years ago. Now I try to be a good person."

Time doesn't forgive sin. If a man commits murder on Monday, but on Tuesday he is kind to others, he is still a murderer. If a man lies and steals, unless he comes to the Savior, his sins remain with him until he stands before God in judgment.

20 Whoso curses his father or his mother, his lamp shall be put out in obscure darkness.

21 An inheritance may be gotten hastily at the beginning; but the end thereof shall not be blessed.

22 Say not, I will recompense evil; but wait on the LORD, and he shall save you.

23 Divers weights are an abomination unto the LORD; and a false balance is not good.

24 Man's goings are of the LORD; how can a man then understand his own way?

25 It is a snare to the man who devours that which is holy, and after vows to make enquiry.

26 A wise king scatters the wicked, and brings the wheel over them.

27 The spirit of man is the candle of the LORD, searching all the inward parts of the belly.

28 Mercy and truth preserve the king: and his throne is upheld by mercy.

29 The glory of young men is their strength: and the beauty of old men is the grey head.

30 The blueness of a wound cleanses away evil: so do stripes the inward parts of the belly.

CHAPTER 21

THE king's heart is in the hand of the LORD, as the rivers of water: he turns it whithersoever he will.

2 **Every way of a man is right in his own eyes: but the Lord ponders the hearts.**

3 To do justice and judgment is more acceptable to the LORD than sacrifice.

4 An high look, and a proud heart, and the plowing of the wicked, is sin.

21:1 This is our great confidence when preaching to sinners. God has control of the hearts of men and women.

21:2 Right in his own eyes. Consider the way dogs cross the road. A dog will wander onto a freeway oblivious to the danger. His tail wags as he steps between cars without a second thought. Cars swerve. Tires squeal. The noise is deafening as vehicles smash into each other. The sleepy dog stops wagging his tail for a moment and looks at the pile of smoldering, broken cars on the freeway. His expression betrays his thoughts. His bone-burying brain doesn't realize for one moment that he is responsible for the disaster.

When man wanders onto the freeway of sin, his tail wags with delight. He thinks that this is what he was made for. His thoughts of any repercussions for his actions are shallow. His mind wanders into lust, then predictably he wanders onto the path of adultery. Suddenly a disaster sits before him. His marriage is shattered, his name is slurred, his children are twisted and scarred. But like the dumb dog, he doesn't realize for one moment that he is solely responsible for his sin.

This is why the perfect Law of God needs to be arrayed before his darkened eyes—to show him that his way is not right in the eyes of a perfect God.

5 The thoughts of the diligent tend only to plenteousness; but of every one that is hasty only to want.

6 The getting of treasures by a lying tongue is a vanity tossed to and fro of them that seek death.

7 The robbery of the wicked shall destroy them; because they refuse to do judgment.

8 The way of man is froward and strange: but as for the pure, his work is right.

9 It is better to dwell in a corner of the housetop, than with a brawling woman in a wide house.

10 The soul of the wicked desires evil: his neighbor finds no favor in his eyes.

11 When the scorner is punished, the simple is made wise: and when the wise is instructed, he receives knowledge.

12 The righteous man wisely considers the house of the wicked: but God overthrows the wicked for their wickedness.

13 Whoso stops his ears at the cry of the poor, he also shall cry himself, but shall not be heard.

14 A gift in secret pacifies anger: and a reward in the bosom strong wrath.

15 It is joy to the just to do judgment: but destruction shall be to the workers of iniquity.

16 The man that wanders out of the way of understanding shall remain in the congregation of the dead.

17 He that loves pleasure shall be a poor man: he that loves wine and oil shall not be rich.

18 The wicked shall be a ransom for the righteous, and the transgressor for the upright.

19 It is better to dwell in the wilderness, than with a contentious and an angry woman.

20 There is treasure to be desired and oil in the dwelling of the wise; but a foolish man spends it up.

21 He that follows after righteousness and mercy finds life, righteousness, and honor.

22 A wise man scales the city of the mighty, and casts down the strength of the confidence thereof.

23 Whoso keeps his mouth and his tongue keeps his soul from troubles.

24 Proud and haughty scorner is his name, who deals in proud wrath.

25 The desire of the slothful kills him; for his hands refuse to labor.

26 He covets greedily all the day long: but the righteous gives and spares not.

27 The sacrifice of the wicked is abomination: how much more, when he brings it with a wicked mind?

28 A false witness shall perish: but the man that hears speaks constantly.

29 A wicked man hardens his face: but as for the upright, he directs his way.

30 There is no wisdom nor understanding nor counsel against the LORD.

31 The horse is prepared against the day of battle: but safety is of the LORD.

CHAPTER 22

A GOOD name is rather to be chosen than great riches, and loving favor rather than silver and gold.

2 The rich and poor meet together: the LORD is the maker of them all.

21:6 It has been rightly said that taking the easy path is what makes men and rivers crooked.

21:10 Sinful men have no trouble seeing other people's sins. **21:23** Be slow to speak your personal opinions, and save yourself a great deal of trouble.

21:24 The proud, arrogant, and angry scorner gravitates to open-air preaching. These will be prevalent in the last days (2 Peter 3:3). The Scriptures reveal that the reason for their contention is that they are given to lust.

21:27 Mankind can never atone for his own sins and buy immortality by giving to charitable causes. Eternal life is a gift of God. See Romans 6:23; Ephesians 2:8,9.

3 A prudent man foresees the evil, and hides himself: but the simple pass on, and are punished.

4 By humility and the fear of the LORD are riches, and honor, and life.

5 Thorns and snares are in the way of the froward: he that does keep his soul shall be far from them.

6 Train up a child in the way he should go: and when he is old, he will not depart from it.

7 The rich rules over the poor, and the borrower is servant to the lender.

8 He that sows iniquity shall reap vanity: and the rod of his anger shall fail.

9 He that has a bountiful eye shall be blessed; for he gives of his bread to the poor.

10 Cast out the scorner, and contention shall go out; yes, strife and reproach shall cease.

11 He that loves pureness of heart, for the grace of his lips the king shall be his friend.

12 The eyes of the LORD preserve knowledge, and he overthrows the words of the transgressor.

13 The slothful man says, There is a lion without, I shall be slain in the streets.

14 The mouth of strange women is a deep pit: he that is abhorred of the LORD shall fall therein.

15 Foolishness is bound in the heart of a child; but the rod of correction shall drive it far from him.

16 He that oppresses the poor to increase his riches, and he that gives to the rich, shall surely come to want.

17 Bow down your ear, and hear the words of the wise, and apply your heart unto my knowledge.

18 For it is a pleasant thing if you keep them within you; they shall withal be fitted in your lips.

19 That your trust may be in the LORD, I have made known to you this day, even to you.

20 Have not I written to you excellent things in counsels and knowledge,

21 That I might make you know the certainty of the words of truth; that you might answer the words of truth to them that send unto you?

22 Rob not the poor, because he is poor: neither oppress the afflicted in the gate:

23 For the LORD will plead their cause, and spoil the soul of those that spoiled them.

24 Make no friendship with an angry man; and with a furious man you shall not go:

25 Lest you learn his ways, and get a snare to your soul.

26 Be not one of them that strike hands, or of them that are sureties for debts.

27 If you have nothing to pay, why should he take away your bed from under you?

28 Remove not the ancient landmark, which your fathers have set.

29 See a man diligent in his business? he shall stand before kings; he shall not stand before mean men.

22:1 We must guard our name, character, and reputation for the sake of the gospel. If men think evil of us, let it be only for the cause of righteousness.

22:4 Those who refuse to humble themselves will eventually lose their possessions, their dignity, and their very life. However, those who walk in humility of heart and obey God store up an eternal treasure in heaven. They will preserve their life and be honored by God Himself. See John 12:25.

22:6 Training our children. "Let the children...be carefully instructed in the principles and obligations of the Christian religion. This is the most essential part of education. The great enemy of the salvation of man, in my opinion, never invented a more effectual means of extirpating [removing] Christianity from the world than by persuading mankind that it was improper to read the Bible at schools." Benjamin Rush (See also Proverbs 4:1–5 and Ephesians 6:4 comments.)

CHAPTER 23

WHEN you sit to eat with a ruler, consider diligently what is before you:

2 And put a knife to your throat, if you be a man given to appetite.

3 Be not desirous of his dainties: for they are deceitful meat.

4 Labor not to be rich: cease from your own wisdom.

5 Will you set your eyes upon that which is not? for riches certainly make themselves wings; they fly away as an eagle toward heaven.

6 Eat not the bread of him that has an evil eye, neither desire his dainty meats:

7 For as he thinks in his heart, so is he: Eat and drink, says he to you; but his heart is not with you.

8 The morsel which you have eaten shall you vomit up, and lose your sweet words.

9 Speak not in the ears of a fool: for he will despise the wisdom of your words.

10 Remove not the old landmark; and enter not into the fields of the fatherless:

11 For their redeemer is mighty; he shall plead their cause with you.

12 Apply your heart unto instruction, and your ears to the words of knowledge.

13 Withhold not correction from the child: for if you beat him with the rod, he shall not die.

14 You shall beat him with the rod, and shall deliver his soul from hell.

15 My son, if your heart be wise, my heart shall rejoice, even mine.

16 Yes, my reins shall rejoice, when your lips speak right things.

17 Let not your heart envy sinners: but be in the fear of the LORD all the day long.

18 For surely there is an end; and your expectation shall not be cut off.

19 Hear, my son, and be wise, and guide your heart in the way.

20 Be not among winebibbers; among riotous eaters of flesh:

21 For the drunkard and the glutton shall come to poverty: and drowsiness shall clothe a man with rags.

22 Hearken unto your father that begat you, and despise not your mother when she is old.

23 Buy the truth, and sell it not; also wisdom, and instruction, and understanding.

24 The father of the righteous shall greatly rejoice: and he that begets a wise child shall have joy of him.

25 Your father and your mother shall be glad, and she that bare you shall rejoice.

26 My son, give me your heart, and let your eyes observe my ways.

27 For a whore is a deep ditch; and a strange woman is a narrow pit.

28 She also lies in wait as for a prey, and increases the transgressors among men.

29 Who has woe? who has sorrow? who has contentions? who has babbling? who has wounds without cause? who has redness of eyes?

30 They that tarry long at the wine; they that go to seek mixed wine.

31 Look not upon the wine when it is red, when it gives his color in the cup, when it moves itself aright.

32 At the last it bites like a serpent, and stings like an adder.

23:12 There is no greater way to do this than to read and meditate on God's Word every day. Say to yourself, "No Bible, no breakfast. No read, no feed." Put your Bible before your belly. See Psalm 1, and mediate on the promises for those who do this.

23:17 See Psalm 73.

23:23 It is sad that so many Christian ministries demand money from their audience, often with the promise that God will bless them if they give. God knows the motives of the preacher, but the unsaved don't, and are therefore easily deceived by the practice. We should be careful never to give the impression that our motivation is the love of money.

23:24-25 This is the fruit of obedience to the Fifth Commandment.

33 Your eyes shall behold strange women, and your heart shall utter perverse
things.

34 Yes, you shall be as he that lies down
in the midst of the sea, or as he that lies
upon the top of a mast.

35 They have stricken me, shall you say,
and I was not sick; they have beaten me,
and I felt it not: when shall I awake? I will
seek it yet again.

CHAPTER 24

B E not envious against evil men, neither desire to be with them.

2 For their heart studies destruction,
and their lips talk of mischief.

3 Through wisdom is an house built;
and by understanding it is established:

4 And by knowledge shall the chambers
be filled with all precious and pleasant
riches.

5 A wise man is strong; yes, a man of
knowledge increases strength.

6 For by wise counsel you shall make
your war: and in multitude of counselors
there is safety.

7 Wisdom is too high for a fool: he opens
not his mouth in the gate.

8 He that devises to do evil shall be called
a mischievous person.

9 The thought of foolishness is sin: and
the scorner is an abomination to men.

10 If you faint in the day of adversity,
your strength is small.

11 If you forbear to deliver them that are
drawn unto death, and those that are ready
to be slain;

12 If you say, Behold, we knew it not;
does not he that ponders the heart consider it? and he that keeps your soul, does
not he know it? and shall not he render to

> Nothing can damn a man
> but his own righteousness;
> nothing can save him
> but the righteousness of Christ.
>
> **CHARLES SPURGEON**

every man according to his works?

13 My son, eat honey, because it is good;
and the honeycomb, which is sweet to
your taste:

14 So shall the knowledge of wisdom
be unto your soul: when you have found
it, then there shall be a reward, and your
expectation shall not be cut off.

15 Lay not wait, O wicked man, against
the dwelling of the righteous; spoil not
his resting place:

16 For a just man falls seven times, and
rises up again: but the wicked shall fall
into mischief.

17 Rejoice not when your enemy falls,
and let not your heart be glad when he
stumbles:

18 Lest the LORD see it, and it displease
him, and he turn away his wrath from
him.

19 Fret not thyself because of evil men,
neither be envious at the wicked:

20 For there shall be no reward to the
evil man; the candle of the wicked shall
be put out.

21 My son, fear the LORD and the king:
and meddle not with them that are given
to change:

22 For their calamity shall rise suddenly; and who knows the ruin of them both?

23 These things also belong to the wise.
It is not good to have respect of persons
in judgment.

23:29–35 See Proverbs 20:1 comment.

24:3-4 Jesus Christ and His teachings are the only sure foundation. See Colossians 1:9; Matthew 7:24.

24:9 Never be discouraged when a man mocks you when you are preaching the gospel. Your love, gentleness, and reasonableness will be seen to contrast his foolishness.

24:11-12 Surely these verses were written for those slothful servants who shun the task of evange-lism. See Matthew 25:14–30.

24 *He that says unto the wicked, You are righteous; him shall the people curse, nations shall abhor him:*

25 *But to them that rebuke him shall be delight, and a good blessing shall come upon them.*

26 *Every man shall kiss his lips that gives a right answer.*

27 Prepare your work without, and make it fit for thyself in the field; and afterwards build your house.

28 Be not a witness against your neighbor without cause; and deceive not with your lips.

29 Say not, I will do so to him as he has done to me: I will render to the man according to his work.

30 I went by the field of the slothful, and by the vineyard of the man void of understanding;

31 And, lo, it was all grown over with thorns, and nettles had covered the face thereof, and the stone wall thereof was broken down.

32 Then I saw, and considered it well: I looked upon it, and received instruction.

33 Yet a little sleep, a little slumber, a little folding of the hands to sleep:

34 So shall your poverty come as one that travels; and your want as an armed man.

CHAPTER 25

THESE are also proverbs of Solomon, which the men of Hezekiah king of Judah copied out.

2 It is the glory of God to conceal a thing: but the honor of kings is to search out a matter.

3 The heaven for height, and the earth for depth, and the heart of kings is unsearchable.

4 Take away the dross from the silver, and there shall come forth a vessel for the finer.

5 Take away the wicked from before the king, and his throne shall be established in righteousness.

6 Put not forth yourself in the presence of the king, and stand not in the place of great men:

7 For better it is that it be said unto you, Come up hither; than that you should be put lower in the presence of the prince whom your eyes have seen.

8 Go not forth hastily to strive, lest you know not what to do in the end thereof, when your neighbor has put you to shame.

9 Debate your cause with your neighbor himself; and discover not a secret to another:

10 Lest he that hears it put you to shame, and your infamy turn not away.

11 A word fitly spoken is like apples of gold in pictures of silver.

12 As an earring of gold, and an ornament of fine gold, so is a wise reprover upon an obedient ear.

13 As the cold of snow in the time of harvest, so is a faithful messenger to them that send him: for he refreshes the soul of his masters.

14 Whoso boasts himself of a false gift is like clouds and wind without rain.

15 By long forbearing is a prince persuaded, and a soft tongue breaks the bone.

16 Have you found honey? eat so much as is sufficient for you, lest you be filled therewith, and vomit it.

17 Withdraw your foot from your neighbor's house; lest he be weary of you, and so hate you.

18 A man that bears false witness against his neighbor is a maul, and a sword, and a sharp arrow.

19 *Confidence in an unfaithful man in time of trouble is like a broken tooth, and a foot out of joint.*

20 As he that takes away a garment in cold weather, and as vinegar upon nitre, so is he that sings songs to an heavy heart.

24:25 **We are to "preach the word;** be instant in season, [and] out of season," and to "reprove, rebuke, exhort with all longsuffering and doctrine" (2 Timothy 4:2). Do this, and you will have the promise of the blessing of God.

21 If your enemy be hungry, give him bread to eat; and if he be thirsty, give him water to drink:

22 For you shall heap coals of fire upon his head, and the LORD shall reward you.

23 The north wind drives away rain: so does an angry countenance a backbiting tongue.

24 It is better to dwell in the corner of the housetop, than with a brawling woman and in a wide house.

25 As cold waters to a thirsty soul, so is good news from a far country.

26 A righteous man falling down before the wicked is as a troubled fountain, and a corrupt spring.

27 It is not good to eat much honey: so for men to search their own glory is not glory.

28 He that has no rule over his own spirit is like a city that is broken down, and without walls.

CHAPTER 26

AS snow in summer, and as rain in harvest, so honor is not seemly for a fool.

2 As the bird by wandering, as the swallow by flying, so the curse causeless shall not come.

3 A whip for the horse, a bridle for the ass, and a rod for the fool's back.

4 Answer not a fool according to his folly, lest you also be like unto him.

5 Answer a fool according to his folly, lest he be wise in his own conceit.

6 He that sends a message by the hand of a fool cuts off the feet, and drinks damage.

7 The legs of the lame are not equal: so is a parable in the mouth of fools.

8 As he that binds a stone in a sling, so is he that gives honor to a fool.

9 As a thorn goes up into the hand of a drunkard, so is a parable in the mouths of fools.

10 The great God that formed all things both rewards the fool, and rewards transgressors.

11 As a dog returns to his vomit, so a fool returns to his folly.

12 See a man wise in his own conceit? there is more hope of a fool than of him.

13 The slothful man says, There is a lion in the way; a lion is in the streets.

14 As the door turns upon his hinges, so does the slothful upon his bed.

15 The slothful hides his hand in his bosom; it grieves him to bring it again to his mouth.

16 The sluggard is wiser in his own conceit than seven men that can render a reason.

17 He that passes by, and meddles with strife belonging not to him, is like one that takes a dog by the ears.

18 As a mad man who casts firebrands, arrows, and death,

25:19 A broken tooth or a foot out of joint cause the most pain when they are put under pressure. How do we react when we are put under pressure to share our faith?

25:28 We allow the enemy entrance when we give the flesh free reign, having no self-control over our spirit.

26:10 The word "great" cannot describe how great God is. Worship takes over where words fail. Our God formed all things. They didn't evolve after a big bang.

26:12 New Age Blasphemy. The inevitable result of man's darkened understanding is that he will think that he is God. His pride takes over his brain.

"We no longer feel ourselves to be guests in someone else's home and therefore obliged to make our behavior conform with a set of preexisting cosmic rules. It is our creation now. We make the rules. We establish the parameters of reality. We create the world, and because we do, we no longer feel beholden to outside forces. We no longer have to justify our behavior, for we are now the architects of the universe. We are responsible to nothing outside ourselves, for we are the kingdom, the power, and the glory forever and ever." Jeremy Rifkin, Algeny

19 So is the man that deceives his neighbor, and says, Am not I in sport?

20 Where no wood is, there the fire goes out: so where there is no talebearer, the strife ceases.

21 As coals are to burning coals, and wood to fire; so is a contentious man to kindle strife.

22 The words of a talebearer are as wounds, and they go down into the innermost parts of the belly.

23 Burning lips and a wicked heart are like a potsherd covered with silver dross.

24 He that hates dissembles with his lips, and lays up deceit within him;

25 When he speaks fair, believe him not: for there are seven abominations in his heart.

26 Whose hatred is covered by deceit, his wickedness shall be showed before the whole congregation.

27 Whoso digs a pit shall fall therein: and he that rolls a stone, it will return upon him.

28 A lying tongue hates those that are afflicted by it; and a flattering mouth works ruin.

CHAPTER 27

Boast not yourself of tomorrow; for you know not what a day may bring forth.

2   *Let another man praise you, and not your own mouth; a stranger, and not your own lips.*

3 A stone is heavy, and the sand weighty; but a fool's wrath is heavier than them both.

4 Wrath is cruel, and anger is outrageous; but who is able to stand before envy?

5   *Open rebuke is better than secret love.*

6 Faithful are the wounds of a friend; but the kisses of an enemy are deceitful.

7 The full soul loathes an honeycomb; but to the hungry soul every bitter thing is sweet.

8 As a bird that wanders from her nest, so is a man that wanders from his place.

9 Ointment and perfume rejoice the heart: so does the sweetness of a man's friend by hearty counsel.

10 Your own friend, and your father's friend, forsake not; neither go into your brother's house in the day of your calamity: for better is a neighbor that is near than a brother far off.

11 My son, be wise, and make my heart glad, that I may answer him that reproaches me.

12 A prudent man foresees the evil, and hides himself; but the simple pass on, and are punished.

13 Take his garment that is surety for a stranger, and take a pledge of him for a strange woman.

14 He that blesses his friend with a loud voice, rising early in the morning, it shall be counted a curse to him.

15 A continual dropping in a very rainy day and a contentious woman are alike.

16 Whosoever hides her hides the wind, and the ointment of his right hand, which bewrays itself.

17 Iron sharpens iron; so a man sharpens the countenance of his friend.

18 Whoso keeps the fig tree shall eat the fruit thereof: so he that waits on his master shall be honored.

19 As in water face answers to face, so the heart of man to man.

20 Hell and destruction are never full; so the eyes of man are never satisfied.

21 As the fining pot for silver, and the furnace for gold; so is a man to his praise.

26:17 This is wonderful guidance for the sincere Christian on what not to do. He who meddles will get hurt. The only thing we can be sure of is the breath going into our lungs at this moment. **27:1** We can't be sure of the next breath. That comes only by the permission of God. See James 4:13–16 and Luke 12:20 comment.

27:5 We openly rebuke those in the world for their sin because we love them and are concerned for their eternal welfare.

27:10 *"How do I reach my neighbors with the gospel?"*

Neighbors are like family. We don't want to offend them unnecessarily, because we have to live with them. We need to be rich in good works toward all men, but especially our neighbors. The Bible reveals that this is a legitimate means of evangelism. Jesus said, "Let your light so shine before men, that they may see your good works, and glorify your Father who is in heaven" (Matthew 5:16). It is God's will that "with well doing you may put to silence the ignorance of foolish men" (1 Peter 2:15). Sinners may disagree with what you believe, but seeing your good works makes them think, "I don't believe what he believes, but he sure does. He certainly is sincere in his faith."

A friendly wave, a gift for no reason, fresh-baked goods, etc., can pave the way for evangelism. Offer to mow your neighbors' lawn or help do some painting. Volunteer to pick up their mail and newspapers while they're on vacation. Compliment them on their landscaping and ask for gardening tips. Invite them over for a barbecue or dessert. Pray for an opportunity to share the gospel, and be prepared for it when it comes.

22 Though you should bray a fool in a mortar among wheat with a pestle, yet will not his foolishness depart from him.
23 Be diligent to know the state of your flocks, and look well to your herds.
24 For riches are not for ever: and does the crown endure to every generation?
25 The hay appears, and the tender grass shows itself, and herbs of the mountains are gathered.
26 The lambs are for your clothing, and the goats are the price of the field.
27 And you shall have goats' milk enough for your food, for the food of your household, and for the maintenance for your maidens.

CHAPTER 28

THE wicked flee when no man pursues: but the righteous are bold as a lion.
2 For the transgression of a land many are the princes thereof: but by a man of understanding and knowledge the state thereof shall be prolonged.
3 A poor man that oppresses the poor is like a sweeping rain which leaves no food.
4 *They that forsake the law praise the wicked: but such as keep the law contend with them.*
5 Evil men understand not judgment: but they that seek the LORD understand all things.
6 Better is the poor that walks in his uprightness, than he that is perverse in his ways, though he be rich.

27:20 **Men can never satisfy lust.** It is an unquenchable inferno. The more it is given fuel, the more it continues to burn. Desire will make him crave sexual pleasure, money, fame, and power. He will continue to "want" until the Lord becomes his shepherd. See Psalm 23:1.

27:25 **Marijuana advocates often point to Genesis** 1:11 ("Let the earth bring forth grass") and other verses (Genesis 1:29; 3:18) to justify the smoking of what they refer to as "grass." They claim that God declared marijuana "good." However, He also made sand (which is good), but if we eat it by the spoonful we shouldn't complain if we get sick. Those who inhale the burning fumes of a weed shouldn't complain when it mentally impairs them. It is called "dope" for a reason.

7 Whoso keeps the law is a wise son: but he that is a companion of riotous men shames his father.

8 He that by usury and unjust gain increases his substance, he shall gather it for him that will pity the poor.

9 He that turns away his ear from hearing the law, even his prayer shall be abomination.

10 Whoso causes the righteous to go astray in an evil way, he shall fall himself into his own pit: but the upright shall have good things in possession.

11 The rich man is wise in his own conceit; but the poor that has understanding searches him out.

12 When righteous men do rejoice, there is great glory: but when the wicked rise, a man is hidden.

13 He that covers his sins shall not prosper: but whoso confesses and forsakes them shall have mercy.

14 Happy is the man that fears always: but he that hardens his heart shall fall into mischief.

15 As a roaring lion, and a ranging bear; so is a wicked ruler over the poor people.

16 The prince that wants understanding is also a great oppressor: but he that hates covetousness shall prolong his days.

17 A man that does violence to the blood of any person shall flee to the pit; let no man stay him.

28:4 When the Church forsakes the proclamation of God's Law, iniquity floods the land. Daniel Webster stated: "If truth is not diffused, error will be. If God and His Word are not known and received, the devil and his works will gain the ascendancy. If the evangelical volume does not reach every hamlet, the pages of a corrupt and licentious literature will.

"If the power of the Gospel is not felt throughout the length and breadth of this land, anarchy and misrule, degradation and misery, corruption and darkness will reign without mitigation or end."

28:5 God's justice stands forever against the sinner in utter severity. The vague and tenuous hope that God is too kind to punish the ungodly has become a deadly opiate for the consciences of millions. It hushes their fears and allows them to practice all pleasant forms of iniquity while death draws every day nearer and the command to repent goes unregarded. As responsible moral beings, we dare not so trifle with our eternal future. A. W. Tozer, *The Knowledge of the Holy*

28:9 If a professing Christian thinks that he can willfully serve sin by transgressing the Moral Law and still have peace with God, he is deceived.

28:13 Sin cannot be covered from the eyes of a holy Creator. Biblical conversion not only comes from confessing sin to God, but also from forsaking sin. Those who do that and trust the Savior partake in the mercy of God.

Confessing our sins. "Whereas, it is the duty of nations as well as of men to own their dependence upon the overruling power of God, to confess their sins and transgressions in humble sorrow yet with assured hope that genuine repentance will lead to mercy and pardon, and to recognize the sublime truth, announced in the Holy Scriptures and proven by all history: that those nations only are blessed whose God is the Lord...

"We have been the recipients of the choicest bounties of Heaven. We have been preserved these many years in peace and prosperity. We have grown in numbers, wealth and power as no other nation has ever grown. But we have forgotten God. We have forgotten the gracious Hand which preserved us in peace, and multiplied and enriched and strengthened us; and we have vainly imagined, in the deceitfulness of our hearts, that all these blessings were produced by some superior wisdom and virtue of our own.

"Intoxicated with unbroken success, we have become too self-sufficient to feel the necessity of redeeming and preserving grace, too proud to pray to the God that made us!

"It behooves us then to humble ourselves before the offended Power, to confess our national sins and to pray for clemency and forgiveness." Abraham Lincoln, 1863, in declaring a day of national fasting, prayer, and humiliation

18 Whoso walks uprightly shall be saved: but he that is perverse in his ways shall fall at once.

19 He that tills his land shall have plenty of bread: but he that follows after vain persons shall have poverty enough.

20 A faithful man shall abound with blessings: but he that makes haste to be rich shall not be innocent.

21 To have respect of persons is not good: for for a piece of bread that man will transgress.

22 He that hastens to be rich has an evil eye, and considers not that poverty shall come upon him.

23 *He that rebukes a man afterwards shall find more favor than he that flatters with the tongue.*

24 Whoso robs his father or his mother, and says, It is no transgression; the same is the companion of a destroyer.

25 He that is of a proud heart stirs up strife: but he that puts his trust in the LORD shall be made fat.

26 **He that trusts in his own heart is a fool: but whoso walks wisely, he shall be delivered.**

27 He that gives unto the poor shall not lack: but he that hides his eyes shall have many a curse.

28 When the wicked rise, men hide themselves: but when they perish, the righteous increase.

CHAPTER 29

HE, that being often reproved hardens his neck, shall suddenly be destroyed, and that without remedy.

2 When the righteous are in authority, the people rejoice: but when the wicked bears rule, the people mourn.

3 Whoso loves wisdom rejoices his father: but he that keeps company with harlots spends his substance.

4 The king by judgment establishes the land: but he that receives gifts overthrows it.

5 A man that flatters his neighbor spreads a net for his feet.

6 In the transgression of an evil man there is a snare: but the righteous does sing and rejoice.

7 The righteous considers the cause of the poor: but the wicked regards not to know it.

8 Scornful men bring a city into a snare: but wise men turn away wrath.

9 If a wise man contends with a foolish man, whether he rage or laugh, there is no rest.

10 The bloodthirsty hate the upright: but the just seek his soul.

28:26 Never give in to the temptation to trust your feelings over God's promises. **See Proverbs 3:5-6.**

29:1 It is a fearful thought that God would lose patience with those who harden their hearts against Him. Jesus spoke of a man to whom God said, "This night your soul shall be required of you" (Luke 12:20). It is prudent to warn sinners that God may lose patience with them and let death seize them, as He did with Ananias and Sapphira (Acts 5:1–10).

29:2 Righteous authority. When believers fulfill their responsibility to elect righteous leaders, the entire country benefits.

"In selecting men for office, let principle be your guide. Regard not the particular sect or denomination of the candidate—look to his character...It is alleged by men of loose principles, or defective views of the subject, that religion and morality are not necessary or important qualifications for political stations. But the Scriptures teach a different doctrine. They direct that rulers should be men who rule in the fear of God, able men, such as fear God, men of truth, hating covetousness...

"When a citizen gives his vote to a man of known immorality, he abuses his civic responsibility; he sacrifices not only his own interest, but that of his neighbor; he betrays the interest of his country." Noah Webster

11 A fool utters all his mind: but a wise man keeps it in till afterwards.

12 If a ruler hearken to lies, all his servants are wicked.

13 The poor and the deceitful man meet together: the Lord lightens both their eyes.

14 The king that faithfully judges the poor, his throne shall be established for ever.

15 The rod and reproof give wisdom: but a child left to himself brings his mother to shame.

16 When the wicked are multiplied, transgression increases: but the righteous shall see their fall.

17 Correct your son, and he shall give you rest; yes, he shall give delight unto your soul.

18 Where there is no vision, the people perish: but he that keeps the law, happy is he.

19 A servant will not be corrected by words: for though he understand he will not answer.

20 See a man that is hasty in his words? there is more hope of a fool than of him.

21 He that delicately brings up his servant from a child shall have him become his son at the length.

22 An angry man stirs up strife, and a furious man abounds in transgression.

23 A man's pride shall bring him low: but honor shall uphold the humble in spirit.

24 Whoso is partner with a thief hates his own soul: he hears cursing, and bewrays it not.

25 The fear of man brings a snare: but whoso puts his trust in the LORD shall be safe.

26 Many seek the ruler's favor; but every man's judgment comes from the Lord.

27 An unjust man is an abomination to the just: and he that is upright in the way is abomination to the wicked.

CHAPTER 30

THE words of Agur the son of Jakeh, even the prophecy: the man spoke unto Ithiel, even unto Ithiel and Ucal,

2 Surely I am more brutish than any man, and have not the understanding of a man.

3 I neither learned wisdom, nor have the knowledge of the holy.

4 Who has ascended up into heaven, or descended? who has gathered the wind in his fists? who has bound the waters in a garment? who has established all the ends of the earth? what is his name, and what is his son's name, if you can tell?

5 **Every word of God is pure: he is a shield unto them that put their trust in him.**

6 Add not unto his words, lest he reprove you, and you be found a liar.

7 Two things have I required of you; deny me them not before I die:

8 Remove far from me vanity and lies: give me neither poverty nor riches; feed me with food convenient for me:

29:9 It has been well said that a wise man will learn more from a fool's question than a fool will learn from a wise man's answer.

29:15 A child doesn't learn to do evil; he naturally knows how to be selfish and lie. However, he must be taught to share and be truthful. See Proverbs 20:11.

29:25 See Psalm 56:11 comment

29:27 This is why the world hates the Christian. See John 15:18,19.

30:1-2 This is the foundational key to learning. See 1 Corinthians 1:21; 3:18.

30:4 His name is "I AM," and His Son's name is Jesus Christ. See Psalm 2:12.

30:5 All Scripture is given by inspiration of God (2 Timothy 3:16), and is His complete revelation to mankind. Many religions accept the words of Scripture, but consider them to be only part of the truth. Those who have added anything to God's Holy Word are in great error.

30:5

"The fact that there are so many versions proves that the Bible has mistakes. Which one is right?"

True, there are many different versions of the Bible. There are versions in Chinese for the Chinese. There are versions in Russian for the Russian people. There are actually thousands of versions of the Bible—some are in modern languages, some in foreign languages, and some are in old English. Few, in the printing age, can claim that they don't have access to the Scriptures in their own language. However, each translation is based on the original biblical texts. See Psalm 119:105 comment.

9 Lest I be full, and deny you, and say, Who is the Lord? or lest I be poor, and steal, and take the name of my God in vain.

10 Accuse not a servant unto his master, lest he curse you, and you be found guilty.

11 There is a generation that curses their father, and does not bless their mother.

12 There is a generation that are pure in their own eyes, and yet is not washed from their filthiness.

13 There is a generation, O how lofty are their eyes! and their eyelids are lifted up.

14 There is a generation, whose teeth are as swords, and their jaw teeth as knives, to devour the poor from off the earth, and the needy from among men.

15 The horseleach has two daughters, crying, Give, give. There are three things that are never satisfied, yes, four things say not, It is enough:

16 The grave; and the barren womb; the earth that is not filled with water; and the fire that says not, It is enough.

17 The eye that mocks at his father, and despises to obey his mother, the ravens of the valley shall pick it out, and the young eagles shall eat it.

18 There be three things which are too wonderful for me, yes, four which I know not:

19 The way of an eagle in the air; the way of a serpent upon a rock; the way of a ship in the midst of the sea; and the way of a man with a maid.

20 Such is the way of an adulterous woman; she eats and wipes her mouth, and says, I have done no wickedness.

21 For three things the earth is disquieted, and for four which it cannot bear:

22 For a servant when he reigns; and a fool when he is filled with meat;

23 For an odious woman when she is married; and an handmaid that is heir to her mistress.

24 There be four things which are little upon the earth, but they are exceeding wise:

25 The ants are a people not strong, yet they prepare their meat in the summer;

26 The conies are but a feeble folk, yet make they their houses in the rocks;

27 The locusts have no king, yet go they forth all of them by bands;

30:11-12 What better description do we have of this lawless generation? By transgressing the Fifth Commandment, it reaps the fearful consequences of disobedience and fails to receive the promise given in Ephesians 6:1–3. Because they have been left without the light of the Moral Law, they consider themselves pure and have therefore become a law to themselves.

30:15-16 Perhaps one more can be added to this list of those who never say "It is enough"—the money-hungry television preacher. See 2 Peter 2:1–3.

28 The spider takes hold with her hands, and is in kings' palaces.

29 There be three things which go well, yes, four are comely in going:

30 A lion which is strongest among beasts, and turns not away for any;

31 A greyhound; an he goat also; and a king, against whom there is no rising up.

32 If you have done foolishly in lifting up yourself, or if you have thought evil, lay your hand upon your mouth.

33 Surely the churning of milk brings forth butter, and the wringing of the nose brings forth blood: so the forcing of wrath brings forth strife.

CHAPTER 31

THE words of king Lemuel, the prophecy that his mother taught him.

2 What, my son? and what, the son of my womb? and what, the son of my vows?

3 Give not your strength unto women, nor your ways to that which destroys kings.

4 It is not for kings, O Lemuel, it is not for kings to drink wine; nor for princes strong drink:

5 Lest they drink, and forget the law, and pervert the judgment of any of the afflicted.

6 Give strong drink unto him that is ready to perish, and wine unto those that be of heavy hearts.

7 Let him drink, and forget his poverty, and remember his misery no more.

8 Open your mouth for the dumb in the cause of all such as are appointed to destruction.

9 Open your mouth, judge righteously, and plead the cause of the poor and needy.

10 Who can find a virtuous woman? for her price is far above rubies.

11 The heart of her husband does safely trust in her, so that he shall have no need of spoil.

12 She will do him good and not evil all the days of her life.

13 She seeks wool, and flax, and works willingly with her hands.

14 She is like the merchants' ships; she brings her food from afar.

15 She rises also while it is yet night, and gives meat to her household, and a portion to her maidens.

16 She considers a field, and buys it: with the fruit of her hands she plants a vineyard.

17 She girds her loins with strength, and strengthens her arms.

18 She perceives that her merchandise is good: her candle goes not out by night.

19 She lays her hands to the spindle, and her hands hold the distaff.

20 She stretches out her hand to the poor; yes, she reaches forth her hands to the needy.

21 She is not afraid of the snow for her household: for all her household are clothed with scarlet.

22 She makes herself coverings of tapestry; her clothing is silk and purple.

23 Her husband is known in the gates, when he sits among the elders of the land.

24 She makes fine linen, and sells it; and delivers girdles unto the merchant.

25 Strength and honor are her clothing; and she shall rejoice in time to come.

26 She opens her mouth with wisdom; and in her tongue is the law of kindness.

27 She looks well to the ways of her household, and eats not the bread of idleness.

30:20 Some people seem to have no conscience. In truth, they have a seared conscience (see 1 Timothy 4:2)—one that has become so hardened that it has lost its ability to function. A correct use of the Law will resurrect it. When you speak directly to the conscience of a hardened sinner by saying, "You know that it's wrong to steal, to lie, to commit adultery, etc.," the conscience affirms the truth of the Commandment. See Romans 2:15.

30:25–28 Here are four virtues needed to be an effective witness: initiative (1 Corinthians 15:58); wisdom (Matthew 7:24); unity (Philippians 1:27); and persistence (Acts 4:18–20).

QUESTIONS & OBJECTIONS

31:10   *"Christianity oppresses women by making them submit to their husbands!"*

The Bible does say, "Wives, submit yourselves to your own husbands, as to the Lord," but it also instructs, "Husbands, love your wives, even as Christ also loved the church, and gave Himself for it" (Ephesians 5:22,25). A man who understands that Jesus Christ sacrificed His life's blood for the Church will likewise love his wife sacrificially and passionately. He will honor her, respect her, protect, love, and cherish her as much as he does his own body, as he is instructed to do (Ephesians 5:28). He will never say or do anything to harm or demean her. It is in this atmosphere of love and security that a godly wife willingly submits herself to the protective arms of her husband. She does this not because he is better than she is, but simply because this is God's order for His creation.

A godless world rejects the God-given formula to make marriage work. It thinks it knows best, and suffers the heartbreaking consequences of destroyed marriages and ruined lives. The Christian ideal of marriage is not one of an authoritarian and chauvinistic male holding his cringing wife in submission like an obedient dog. It's the very opposite. While most of the great religions treat women as inferior to men, the Bible gives them a place of dignity, honor, and unspeakable worth, expressed so evidently in Proverbs 31.

28 Her children arise up, and call her blessed; her husband also, and he praises her.

29 Many daughters have done virtuously, but you excel them all.

30 Favor is deceitful, and beauty is vain: but a woman that fears the LORD, she shall be praised.

31 Give her of the fruit of her hands; and let her own works praise her in the gates.

FACTS ABOUT THE BIBLE

Number of books in the Bible: 66
Chapters: 1,189; Verses: 31,101
Words: 783,137; Letters: 3,566,480
Longest word (and name):
Mahershalalhashbaz (Isaiah 8:1)
Longest verse: Esther 8:9 (78 words)
Shortest verse: John 11:35 (2 words: "Jesus wept")
Middle books: Micah and Nahum
Middle chapter: Psalm 118
Middle verse: Psalm 118:8
Shortest book (number of words): 3 John
Shortest chapter (number of words): Psalm 117
Longest book: Psalms (150 chapters)
Longest chapter: Psalm 119 (176 verses)
Number of times the word "God" appears: 3,358
Number of times the word "Lord" appears: 7,736
Number of different authors: Approximately 40
Number of languages the Bible has been translated into: More than 1,200
Number of new Bibles distributed (sold or given away) in the U.S every day: About 168,000

Ecclesiastes

CHAPTER 1

THE words of the Preacher, the son of David, king in Jerusalem.

2 Vanity of vanities, says the Preacher, vanity of vanities; all is vanity.

3 What profit has a man of all his labour which he takes under the sun?

4 One generation passes away, and another generation comes: but the earth abides for ever.

5 The sun also arises, and the sun goes down, and hastens to his place where he arose.

6 The wind goes toward the south, and turns about to the north; it whirls about continually, and the wind returns again according to his circuits.

7 All the rivers run into the sea; yet the sea is not full; unto the place from where the rivers come, there they return again.

8 All things are full of labour; man cannot utter it: the eye is not satisfied with seeing, nor the ear filled with hearing.

9 The thing that has been, it is that which shall be; and that which is done is that which shall be done: and there is no new thing under the sun.

10 Is there any thing whereof it may be said, See, this is new? it has been already of old time, which was before us.

11 There is no remembrance of former things; neither shall there be any remembrance of things that are to come with those that shall come after.

12 I the Preacher was king over Israel in Jerusalem.

13 And I gave my heart to seek and search out by wisdom concerning all things that are done under heaven: this sore travail has God given to the sons of man to be exercised therewith.

14 I have seen all the works that are done under the sun; and, behold, all is vanity and vexation of spirit.

15 That which is crooked cannot be made straight: and that which is wanting cannot be numbered.

16 I communed with my own heart, saying, Lo, I am come to great estate, and have gotten more wisdom than all they that have been before me in Jerusalem: yea, my heart had great experience of wisdom and knowledge.

17 And I gave my heart to know wisdom, and to know madness and folly: I perceived that this also is vexation of spirit.

18 For in much wisdom is much grief: and he that increases knowledge increases sorrow.

1:6 "Modern science has confirmed that the air around the planet turns in huge circles, clockwise in one hemisphere and counterclockwise in the other." Richard Gunther

CHAPTER 2

I said in my heart, Go to now, I will prove you with mirth, therefore enjoy pleasure: and, behold, this also is vanity.

2 I said of laughter, It is mad: and of mirth, What doeth it?

3 I sought in my heart to give myself unto wine, yet acquainting my heart with wisdom; and to lay hold on folly, till I might see what was that good for the sons of men, which they should do under the heaven all the days of their life.

4 I made my great works; I built myself houses; I planted myself vineyards:

5 I made myself gardens and orchards, and I planted trees in them of all kind of fruits:

6 I made myself pools of water, to water therewith the wood that brings forth trees:

7 I got myself servants and maidens, and had servants born in my house; also I had great possessions of great and small cattle above all that were in Jerusalem before me:

8 I also gathered for myself silver and gold, and the peculiar treasure of kings and of the provinces: I got for myself men singers and women singers, and the delights of the sons of men, as musical instruments, and that of all sorts.

9 So I was great, and increased more than all that were before me in Jerusalem: also my wisdom remained with me.

10 And whatsoever my eyes desired I kept not from them, I withheld not my heart from any joy; for my heart rejoiced in all my labour: and this was my portion of all my labour.

11 Then I looked on all the works that my hands had done, and on the labour that I had laboured to do: and, behold, all was vanity and vexation of spirit, and there was no profit under the sun.

12 And I turned myself to behold wisdom, and madness, and folly: for what can the man do that comes after the king? even that which has been already done.

13 Then I saw that wisdom excels folly, as far as light excels darkness.

14 The wise man's eyes are in his head; but the fool walks in darkness: and I myself perceived also that one event happens to them all.

15 Then said I in my heart, As it happens to the fool, so it happens even to me; and why was I then more wise? Then I said in my heart, that this also is vanity.

16 For there is no remembrance of the wise more than of the fool for ever; seeing that which now is in the days to come shall all be forgotten. And how does a wise man die? as the fool.

17 Therefore I hated life; because the work that is done under the sun is grievous unto me: for all is vanity and vexation of spirit.

18 Yea, I hated all my labour which I had taken under the sun: because I should leave it unto the man that shall be after me.

19 And who knows whether he shall be a wise man or a fool? yet shall he have rule over all my labour wherein I have laboured, and wherein I have showed myself wise under the sun. This is also vanity.

20 Therefore I went about to cause my heart to despair of all the labour which I took under the sun.

21 For there is a man whose labour is in wisdom, and in knowledge, and in equity; yet to a man that has not laboured therein shall he leave it for his portion. This also is vanity and a great evil.

22 For what has man of all his labour, and of the vexation of his heart, wherein he has laboured under the sun?

23 For all his days are sorrows, and his travail grief; yea, his heart takes no rest in the night. This is also vanity.

24 There is nothing better for a man, than that he should eat and drink, and that he should make his soul enjoy good

in his labour. This also I saw, that it was from the hand of God.

25 For who can eat, or who else can hasten hereunto, more than I?

26 For God gives to a man that is good in his sight wisdom, and knowledge, and joy: but to the sinner he gives travail, to gather and to heap up, that he may give to him that is good before God. This also is vanity and vexation of spirit.

CHAPTER 3

TO every thing there is a season, and a time to every purpose under the heaven:

2 A time to be born, and a time to die; a time to plant, and a time to pluck up that which is planted;

3 A time to kill, and a time to heal; a time to break down, and a time to build up;

4 A time to weep, and a time to laugh; a time to mourn, and a time to dance;

5 A time to cast away stones, and a time to gather stones together; a time to embrace, and a time to refrain from embracing;

6 A time to get, and a time to lose; a time to keep, and a time to cast away;

7 A time to rend, and a time to sew; a time to keep silence, and a time to speak;

8 A time to love, and a time to hate; a time of war, and a time of peace.

9 What profit has he that works in that wherein he labours?

10 I have seen the travail, which God has given to the sons of men to be exercised in it.

11 He has made every thing beautiful in his time: also he has set the world in their heart, so that no man can find out the work that God makes from the beginning to the end.

12 I know that there is no good in them, but for a man to rejoice, and to do good in his life.

13 And also that every man should eat and drink, and enjoy the good of all his labour, it is the gift of God.

> Today comes but once
> and comes never to return.
> We hope it will come again tomorrow;
> but it does not.
> It is gone forever,
> with its inexhaustible possibilities,
> privileges and responsibilities.
>
> *RECORD OF CHRISTIAN WORK*
> OCTOBER 1908

14 I know that, whatsoever God doeth, it shall be for ever: nothing can be put to it, nor any thing taken from it: and God doeth it, that men should fear before him.

15 That which has been is now; and that which is to be has already been; and God requires that which is past.

16 And moreover I saw under the sun the place of judgment, that wickedness was there; and the place of righteousness, that iniquity was there.

17 I said in my heart, God shall judge the righteous and the wicked: for there is a time there for every purpose and for every work.

18 I said in my heart concerning the estate of the sons of men, that God might manifest them, and that they might see that they themselves are beasts.

19 For that which befalls the sons of men befalls beasts; even one thing befalls them: as the one dies, so dies the other; yea, they have all one breath; so that a man has no preeminence above a beast: for all is vanity.

20 All go unto one place; all are of the dust, and all turn to dust again.

21 Who knows the spirit of man that goes upward, and the spirit of the beast that goes downward to the earth?

22 Therefore I perceive that there is nothing better, than that a man should rejoice in his own works; for that is his portion: for who shall bring him to see what shall be after him?

CHAPTER 4

S O I returned, and considered all the oppressions that are done under the sun: and behold the tears of such as were oppressed, and they had no comforter; and on the side of their oppressors there was power; but they had no comforter.

2 Therefore I praised the dead which are already dead more than the living which are yet alive.

3 Yea, better is he than both they, which has not yet been, who has not seen the evil work that is done under the sun.

4 Again, I considered all travail, and every right work, that for this a man is envied of his neighbour. This is also vanity and vexation of spirit.

5 The fool folds his hands together, and eats his own flesh.

6 Better is an handful with quietness, than both the hands full with travail and vexation of spirit.

7 Then I returned, and I saw vanity under the sun.

8 There is one alone, and there is not a second; yea, he has neither child nor brother: yet is there no end of all his labour; neither is his eye satisfied with riches; neither does he say, For whom do I labour, and bereave my soul of good? This is also vanity, yea, it is a sore travail.

9 Two are better than one; because they have a good reward for their labour.

10 For if they fall, the one will lift up his fellow: but woe to him that is alone when he falls; for he has not another to help him up.

11 Again, if two lie together, then they have heat: but how can one be warm alone?

12 And if one prevail against him, two shall withstand him; and a threefold cord is not quickly broken.

13 Better is a poor and a wise child than an old and foolish king, who will no more be admonished.

14 For out of prison he comes to reign; whereas also he that is born in his kingdom becomes poor.

15 I considered all the living which walk under the sun, with the second child that shall stand up in his stead.

16 There is no end of all the people, even of all that have been before them: they also that come after shall not rejoice in him. Surely this also is vanity and vexation of spirit.

CHAPTER 5

K EEP your foot when you go to the house of God, and be more ready to hear, than to give the sacrifice of fools: for they consider not that they do evil.

2 Do not be rash with your mouth, and let not your heart be hasty to utter any thing before God: for God is in heaven, and you upon earth: therefore let your words be few.

3 For a dream comes through the multitude of business; and a fool's voice is known by multitude of words.

4 When you vow a vow unto God, defer not to pay it; for he has no pleasure in fools: pay that which you have vowed.

5 Better is it that you should not vow, than that you should vow and not pay.

6 Do not let your mouth to cause your flesh to sin; neither say before the angel, that it was an error: why should God be angry at your voice, and destroy the work of your hands?

7 For in the multitude of dreams and many words there are also divers vanities: but fear God.

8 If you see the oppression of the poor, and violent perverting of judgment and justice in a province, marvel not at the matter: for he that is higher than the highest regards; and there be higher than they.

9 Moreover the profit of the earth is for all: the king himself is served by the field.

10 He that loves silver shall not be satisfied with silver; nor he that loves abundance with increase: this is also vanity.

11 When goods increase, they are increased that eat them: and what good is there to the owners thereof, saving the beholding of them with their eyes?

12 The sleep of a labouring man is sweet, whether he eat little or much: but the abundance of the rich will not suffer him to sleep.

13 There is a sore evil which I have seen under the sun, namely, riches kept for the owners thereof to their hurt.

14 But those riches perish by evil travail: and he begets a son, and there is nothing in his hand.

15 As he came forth of his mother's womb, naked shall he return to go as he came, and shall take nothing of his labour, which he may carry away in his hand.

16 And this also is a sore evil, that in all points as he came, so shall he go: and what profit has he that has laboured for the wind?

17 All his days also he eats in darkness, and he has much sorrow and wrath with his sickness.

18 Behold that which I have seen: it is good and comely for one to eat and to drink, and to enjoy the good of all his labour that he takes under the sun all the days of his life, which God gives him: for it is his portion.

19 Every man also to whom God has given riches and wealth, and has given him power to eat thereof, and to take his portion, and to rejoice in his labour; this is the gift of God.

20 For he shall not much remember the days of his life; because God answers him in the joy of his heart.

CHAPTER 6

THERE is an evil which I have seen under the sun, and it is common among men:

2 A man to whom God has given riches, wealth, and honour, so that he wants nothing for his soul of all that he desires, yet God gives him not power to eat thereof, but a stranger eats it: this is vanity, and it is an evil disease.

3 If a man beget an hundred children, and live many years, so that the days of his years be many, and his soul be not filled with good, and also that he have no burial; I say, that an untimely birth is better than he.

4 For he comes in with vanity, and departs in darkness, and his name shall be covered with darkness.

5 Moreover he has not seen the sun, nor known any thing: this has more rest than the other.

6 Yea, though he live a thousand years twice told, yet has he seen no good: do not all go to one place?

7 All the labour of man is for his mouth, and yet the appetite is not filled.

8 For what has the wise more than the fool? what has the poor, that knows to walk before the living?

9 Better is the sight of the eyes than the wandering of the desire: this is also vanity and vexation of spirit.

10 That which has been is named already, and it is known that it is man: neither may he contend with him that is mightier than he.

11 Seeing there be many things that increase vanity, what is man the better?

12 For who knows what is good for man in this life, all the days of his vain life which he spends as a shadow? for who can tell a man what shall be after him under the sun?

CHAPTER 7

A good name is better than precious ointment; and the day of death than the day of one's birth.

2 It is better to go to the house of mourning, than to go to the house of feasting: for that is the end of all men; and the living will lay it to his heart.

3 Sorrow is better than laughter: for by the sadness of the countenance the heart is made better.

4 The heart of the wise is in the house of mourning; but the heart of fools is in the house of mirth.

5 It is better to hear the rebuke of the wise, than for a man to hear the song of fools.

6 For as the crackling of thorns under a pot, so is the laughter of the fool: this also is vanity.

7 Surely oppression makes a wise man mad; and a gift destroys the heart.

8 Better is the end of a thing than the beginning thereof: and the patient in spirit is better than the proud in spirit.

9 Be not hasty in your spirit to be angry: for anger rests in the bosom of fools.

10 Do not say, What is the cause that the former days were better than these? for you do not enquire wisely concerning this.

11 Wisdom is good with an inheritance: and by it there is profit to them that see the sun.

12 For wisdom is a defence, and money is a defence: but the excellency of knowledge is, that wisdom gives life to them that have it.

13 Consider the work of God: for who can make that straight, which he has made crooked?

14 In the day of prosperity be joyful, but in the day of adversity consider: God also has set the one over against the other, to the end that man should find nothing after him.

15 All things have I seen in the days of my vanity: there is a just man that perishes in his righteousness, and there is a wicked man that prolongs his life in his wickedness.

16 Be not righteous over much; neither make yourself over wise: why should you destroy yourself?

17 Be not over much wicked, neither be foolish: why should you die before your time?

18 It is good that you should take hold of this; yea, also from this do not withdraw your hand: for he that fears God shall come forth of them all.

19 Wisdom strengthens the wise more than ten mighty men which are in the city.

20 For there is not a just man upon earth, that does good, and does not sin.

21 Also take no heed unto all words that are spoken; lest you hear your servant curse you:

22 For oftentimes also your own heart knows that you yourself likewise have cursed others.

23 All this have I proved by wisdom: I said, I will be wise; but it was far from me.

24 That which is far off, and exceeding deep, who can find it out?

25 I applied my heart to know, and to search, and to seek out wisdom, and the reason of things, and to know the wickedness of folly, even of foolishness and madness:

26 And I find more bitter than death the woman, whose heart is snares and nets, and her hands as bands: whoso pleases God shall escape from her; but the sinner shall be taken by her.

27 Behold, this have I found, says the preacher, counting one by one, to find out the account:

28 Which yet my soul seeks, but I find not: one man among a thousand have I found; but a woman among all those have I not found.

29 Lo, this only have I found, that God has made man upright; but they have sought out many inventions.

CHAPTER 8

WHO is as the wise man? and who knows the interpretation of a thing? a man's wisdom makes his face to shine, and the boldness of his face shall be changed.

2 I counsel you to keep the king's commandment, and that in regard of the oath of God.

3 Be not hasty to go out of his sight: stand not in an evil thing; for he doeth whatsoever pleases him.

4 Where the word of a king is, there is power: and who may say unto him, What are you doing?

5 Whoso keeps the commandment shall feel no evil thing: and a wise man's heart discerns both time and judgment.

6 Because to every purpose there is time and judgment, therefore the misery of man is great upon him.

7 For he does not know that which shall be: for who can tell him when it shall be?

8 There is no man that has power over the spirit to retain the spirit; neither has he power in the day of death: and there is no discharge in that war; neither shall wickedness deliver those that are given to it.

9 All this have I seen, and applied my heart unto every work that is done under the sun: there is a time wherein one man rules over another to his own hurt.

10 And so I saw the wicked buried, who had come and gone from the place of the holy, and they were forgotten in the city where they had so done: this is also vanity.

11 Because sentence against an evil work is not executed speedily, therefore the heart of the sons of men is fully set in them to do evil.

12 Though a sinner do evil an hundred times, and his days be prolonged, yet surely I know that it shall be well with them that fear God, which fear before him:

13 But it shall not be well with the wicked, neither shall he prolong his days, which are as a shadow; because he does not fear before God.

14 There is a vanity which is done upon the earth; that there be just men, unto whom it happens according to the work of the wicked; again, there be wicked men, to whom it happens according to the work of the righteous: I said that this also is vanity.

15 Then I commended mirth, because a man has no better thing under the sun, than to eat, and to drink, and to be merry: for that shall abide with him of his labour the days of his life, which God gives him under the sun.

16 When I applied my heart to know wisdom, and to see the business that is done upon the earth: (for also there is that neither day nor night sees sleep with his eyes:)

17 Then I beheld all the work of God, that a man cannot find out the work that is done under the sun: because though a man labour to seek it out, yet he shall not find it; yea farther; though a wise man think to know it, yet shall he not be able to find it.

CHAPTER 9

FOR all this I considered in my heart even to declare all this, that the righteous, and the wise, and their works, are in the hand of God: no man knows either love or hatred by all that is before them.

2 All things come alike to all: there is one event to the righteous, and to the wicked; to the good and to the clean, and to the unclean; to him that sacrifices, and to him that does not sacrifice: as is the good, so is the sinner; and he that swears, as he that fears an oath.

3 This is an evil among all things that are done under the sun, that there is one event unto all: yea, also the heart of the sons of men is full of evil, and madness is in their heart while they live, and after that they go to the dead.

4 For to him that is joined to all the living there is hope: for a living dog is better than a dead lion.

5 For the living know that they shall die: but the dead know not any thing, neither have they any more a reward; for the memory of them is forgotten.

6 Also their love, and their hatred, and their envy, is now perished; neither have they any more a portion for ever in any thing that is done under the sun.

7 Go your way, eat your bread with joy, and drink your wine with a merry heart; for God now accepts your works.

8 Let your garments be always white; and let your head lack no ointment.

9 Live joyfully with the wife whom you love all the days of the life of your vanity, which he has given you under the sun, all the days of your vanity: for that is your portion in this life, and in your labour which you take under the sun.

10 Whatsoever your hand finds to do, do it with your might; for there is no work, nor device, nor knowledge, nor wisdom, in the grave, where you go.

11 I returned, and saw under the sun, that the race is not to the swift, nor the battle to the strong, neither yet bread to the wise, nor yet riches to men of understanding, nor yet favour to men of skill; but time and chance happen to them all.

12 For man also does not know his time: as the fishes that are taken in an evil net, and as the birds that are caught in the snare; so are the sons of men snared in an evil time, when it falls suddenly upon them.

13 This wisdom have I seen also under the sun, and it seemed great unto me:

14 There was a little city, and few men within it; and there came a great king against it, and besieged it, and built great bulwarks against it:

15 Now there was found in it a poor wise man, and he by his wisdom delivered the city; yet no man remembered that same poor man.

16 Then said I, Wisdom is better than strength: nevertheless the poor man's wisdom is despised, and his words are not heard.

17 The words of wise men are heard in quiet more than the cry of him that rules among fools.

18 Wisdom is better than weapons of war: but one sinner destroys much good.

CHAPTER 10

DEAD flies cause the ointment of the apothecary to send forth a stinking savour: so does a little folly him that is in reputation for wisdom and honour.

2 A wise man's heart is at his right hand; but a fool's heart at his left.

3 Yea also, when he that is a fool walks by the way, his wisdom fails him, and he says to every one that he is a fool.

4 If the spirit of the ruler rise up against you, do not leave your place; for yielding pacifies great offences.

5 There is an evil which I have seen under the sun, as an error which proceeds from the ruler:

6 Folly is set in great dignity, and the rich sit in low place.

7 I have seen servants upon horses, and princes walking as servants upon the earth.

8 He that digs a pit shall fall into it; and whoso breaks a hedge, a serpent shall bite him.

9 Whoso removes stones shall be hurt therewith; and he that cleaves wood shall be endangered thereby.

10 If the iron be blunt, and he do not whet the edge, then must he put to more strength: but wisdom is profitable to direct.

11 Surely the serpent will bite without enchantment; and a babbler is no better.

12 The words of a wise man's mouth are gracious; but the lips of a fool will swallow up himself.

13 The beginning of the words of his mouth is foolishness: and the end of his talk is mischievous madness.

14 A fool also is full of words: a man cannot tell what shall be; and what shall be after him, who can tell him?

15 The labour of the foolish wearies every one of them, because he knows not how to go to the city.

16 Woe to you, O land, when your king is a child, and your princes eat in the morning!

17 Blessed are you, O land, when your king is the son of nobles, and your

princes eat in due season, for strength, and not for drunkenness!

18 By much slothfulness the building decays; and through idleness of the hands the house drops through.

19 A feast is made for laughter, and wine makes merry: but money answers all things.

20 Do not curse the king, no not in your thought; and do not curse the rich in your bedchamber: for a bird of the air shall carry the voice, and that which has wings shall tell the matter.

CHAPTER 11

CAST your bread upon the waters: for you shall find it after many days.

2 Give a portion to seven, and also to eight; for you do not know what evil shall be upon the earth.

3 If the clouds be full of rain, they empty themselves upon the earth: and if the tree fall toward the south, or toward the north, in the place where the tree falls, there it shall be.

4 He that observes the wind shall not sow; and he that regards the clouds shall not reap.

5 As you do not know what is the way of the spirit, nor how the bones do grow in the womb of her that is with child: even so you know not the works of God who makes all.

6 In the morning sow your seed, and in the evening do not withhold your hand: for you do not know which shall prosper, either this or that, or whether they both shall be alike good.

7 Truly the light is sweet, and a pleasant thing it is for the eyes to behold the sun:

8 But if a man live many years, and rejoice in them all; yet let him remember the days of darkness; for they shall be many. All that comes is vanity.

9 Rejoice, O young man, in your youth; and let your heart cheer you in the days of your youth, and walk in the ways of your heart, and in the sight of your eyes:

but know, that for all these things God will bring you into judgment.

10 Therefore remove sorrow from your heart, and put away evil from your flesh: for childhood and youth are vanity.

CHAPTER 12

REMEMBER now your Creator in the days of your youth, while the evil days come not, nor the years draw nigh, when you shall say, I have no pleasure in them;

2 While the sun, or the light, or the moon, or the stars, be not darkened, nor the clouds return after the rain:

3 In the day when the keepers of the house shall tremble, and the strong men shall bow themselves, and the grinders cease because they are few, and those that look out of the windows be darkened,

4 And the doors shall be shut in the streets, when the sound of the grinding is low, and he shall rise up at the voice of the bird, and all the daughters of music shall be brought low;

5 Also when they shall be afraid of that which is high, and fears shall be in the way, and the almond tree shall flourish, and the grasshopper shall be a burden, and desire shall fail: because man goes to his long home, and the mourners go about the streets:

6 Or ever the silver cord be loosed, or the golden bowl be broken, or the pitcher be broken at the fountain, or the wheel broken at the cistern.

7 Then shall the dust return to the earth as it was: and the spirit shall return unto God who gave it.

8 Vanity of vanities, says the preacher; all is vanity.

9 And moreover, because the preacher was wise, he still taught the people knowledge; yea, he gave good heed, and sought out, and set in order many proverbs.

10 The preacher sought to find out acceptable words: and that which was

written was upright, even words of truth.

11 The words of the wise are as goads, and as nails fastened by the masters of assemblies, which are given from one shepherd.

12 And further, by these, my son, be admonished: of making many books there is no end; and much study is a weariness of the flesh.

13 Let us hear the conclusion of the whole matter: Fear God, and keep his commandments: for this is the whole duty of man.

14 For God shall bring every work into judgment, with every secret thing, whether it be good, or whether it be evil.

12:13-14 There is nothing as important in life as this great truth. It will bring us to the cross of Jesus and drive us to seek to present every man perfect in Jesus Christ before that great and terrible Day of the Lord.

Song of Solomon

CHAPTER 1

THE song of songs, which is Solomon's.

2 Let him kiss me with the kisses of his mouth: for your love is better than wine.

3 Because of the savour of your good ointments your name is as ointment poured forth, therefore do the virgins love you.

4 Draw me, we will run after you: the king has brought me into his chambers: we will be glad and rejoice in you, we will remember your love more than wine: the upright love you.

5 I am black, but comely, O you daughters of Jerusalem, as the tents of Kedar, as the curtains of Solomon.

6 Look not upon me, because I am black, because the sun has looked upon me: my mother's children were angry with me; they made me the keeper of the vineyards; but my own vineyard have I not kept.

7 Tell me, O you whom my soul loves, where you feed, where you make your flock to rest at noon: for why should I be as one that turns aside by the flocks of your companions?

8 If you do not know, O fairest among women, go your way forth by the footsteps of the flock, and feed your kids beside the shepherds' tents.

9 I have compared you, O my love, to a company of horses in Pharaoh's chariots.

10 Your cheeks are comely with rows of jewels, your neck with chains of gold.

11 We will make you borders of gold with studs of silver.

12 While the king sits at his table, my spikenard sends forth the smell thereof.

13 A bundle of myrrh is my well-beloved to me; he shall lie all night betwixt my breasts.

14 My beloved is to me as a cluster of camphire in the vineyards of Engedi.

15 Behold, you are fair, my love; behold, you are fair; you have doves' eyes.

16 Behold, you are fair, my beloved, yea, pleasant: also our bed is green.

17 The beams of our house are cedar, and our rafters of fir.

CHAPTER 2

I am the rose of Sharon, and the lily of the valleys.

2 As the lily among thorns, so is my love among the daughters.

3 As the apple tree among the trees of the wood, so is my beloved among the sons. I sat down under his shadow with great delight, and his fruit was sweet to my taste.

4 He brought me to the banqueting house, and his banner over me was love.

5 Stay me with flagons, comfort me with apples: for I am sick of love.

6 His left hand is under my head, and his right hand does embrace me.

7 I charge you, O you daughters of Jerusalem, by the roes, and by the hinds of the field, that you stir not up, nor awake my love, till he please.

8 The voice of my beloved! behold, he comes leaping upon the mountains, skipping upon the hills.

9 My beloved is like a roe or a young hart: behold, he stands behind our wall, he looks forth at the windows, showing himself through the lattice.

10 My beloved spoke, and said to me, Rise up, my love, my fair one, and come away.

11 For, lo, the winter is past, the rain is over and gone;

12 The flowers appear on the earth; the time of the singing of birds is come, and the voice of the turtle is heard in our land;

13 The fig tree puts forth her green figs, and the vines with the tender grape give a good smell. Arise, my love, my fair one, and come away.

14 O my dove, that is in the clefts of the rock, in the secret places of the stairs, let me see your countenance, let me hear your voice; for sweet is your voice, and your countenance is comely.

15 Take us the foxes, the little foxes, that spoil the vines: for our vines have tender grapes.

16 My beloved is mine, and I am his: he feeds among the lilies.

17 Until the day break, and the shadows flee away, turn, my beloved, and be like a roe or a young hart upon the mountains of Bether.

CHAPTER 3

BY night on my bed I sought him whom my soul loves: I sought him, but I found him not.

2 I will rise now, and go about the city in the streets, and in the broad ways I will seek him whom my soul loves: I sought him, but I did not find him.

3 The watchmen that go about the city found me: to whom I said, Have you seen him whom my soul loves?

4 It was but a little that I passed from them, but I found him whom my soul loves: I held him, and would not let him go, until I had brought him into my mother's house, and into the chamber of her that conceived me.

5 I charge you, O you daughters of Jerusalem, by the roes, and by the hinds of the field, that you do not stir up nor awaken my love, till he please.

6 Who is this that comes out of the wilderness like pillars of smoke, perfumed with myrrh and frankincense, with all powders of the merchant?

7 Behold his bed, which is Solomon's; threescore valiant men are about it, of the valiant of Israel.

8 They all hold swords, being expert in war: every man has his sword upon his thigh because of fear in the night.

9 King Solomon made himself a chariot of the wood of Lebanon.

10 He made the pillars thereof of silver, the bottom thereof of gold, the covering of it of purple, the midst thereof being paved with love, for the daughters of Jerusalem.

11 Go forth, O you daughters of Zion, and behold king Solomon with the crown wherewith his mother crowned him in the day of his espousals, and in the day of the gladness of his heart.

CHAPTER 4

BEHOLD, you are fair, my love; behold, you are fair; you have doves' eyes within your locks: your hair is as a flock of goats, that appear from mount Gilead.

2 Your teeth are like a flock of sheep that are even shorn, which came up from the washing; whereof every one

---

2:16 We belong to the Savior. He is our Lord, and we love Him. The next time you speak with a Jehovah's Witness or a Mormon, ask him if he loves Jesus, is He his "beloved?" Salvation depends upon this (see 1 Corinthians 16:22).

bear twins, and none is barren among them.

3 Your lips are like a thread of scarlet, and your speech is comely: your temples are like a piece of a pomegranate within your locks.

4 Your neck is like the tower of David built for an armoury, whereon there hang a thousand bucklers, all shields of mighty men.

5 Your two breasts are like two young roes that are twins, which feed among the lilies.

6 Until the day break, and the shadows flee away, I will get me to the mountain of myrrh, and to the hill of frankincense.

7 You are all fair, my love; there is no spot in you.

8 Come with me from Lebanon, my spouse, with me from Lebanon: look from the top of Amana, from the top of Shenir and Hermon, from the lions' dens, from the mountains of the leopards.

9 You have ravished my heart, my sister, my spouse; you have ravished my heart with one of your eyes, with one chain of your neck.

10 How fair is your love, my sister, my spouse! how much better is your love than wine! and the smell of your ointments than all spices!

11 Your lips, O my spouse, drop as the honeycomb: honey and milk are under your tongue; and the smell of your garments is like the smell of Lebanon.

12 A garden inclosed is my sister, my spouse; a spring shut up, a fountain sealed.

13 Your plants are an orchard of pomegranates, with pleasant fruits; camphire, with spikenard,

14 Spikenard and saffron; calamus and cinnamon, with all trees of frankincense; myrrh and aloes, with all the chief spices:

15 A fountain of gardens, a well of living waters, and streams from Lebanon.

16 Awake, O north wind; and come, you south; blow upon my garden, that the spices thereof may flow out. Let my beloved come into his garden, and eat his pleasant fruits.

CHAPTER 5

I am come into my garden, my sister, my spouse: I have gathered my myrrh with my spice; I have eaten my honeycomb with my honey; I have drunk my wine with my milk: eat, O friends; drink, yea, drink abundantly, O beloved.

2 I sleep, but my heart wakes: it is the voice of my beloved that knocks, saying, Open to me, my sister, my love, my dove, my undefiled: for my head is filled with dew, and my locks with the drops of the night.

3 I have put off my coat; how shall I put it on? I have washed my feet; how shall I defile them?

4 My beloved put in his hand by the hole of the door, and my bowels were moved for him.

5 I rose up to open to my beloved; and my hands dropped with myrrh, and my fingers with sweet smelling myrrh, upon the handles of the lock.

6 I opened to my beloved; but my beloved had withdrawn himself, and was gone: my soul failed when he spoke: I sought him, but I could not find him; I called him, but he gave me no answer.

7 The watchmen that went about the city found me, they smote me, they wounded me; the keepers of the walls took away my veil from me.

8 I charge you, O daughters of Jerusalem, if you find my beloved, that you tell him, that I am sick of love.

9 What is your beloved more than another beloved, O fairest among women? what is your beloved more than another beloved, that you so charge us?

10 My beloved is white and ruddy, the chiefest among ten thousand.

11 His head is as the most fine gold, his locks are bushy, and black as a raven.

12 His eyes are as the eyes of doves by the rivers of waters, washed with milk, and fitly set.

13 His cheeks are as a bed of spices, as sweet flowers: his lips like lilies, dropping sweet smelling myrrh.

14 His hands are as gold rings set with the beryl: his belly is as bright ivory overlaid with sapphires.

15 His legs are as pillars of marble, set upon sockets of fine gold: his countenance is as Lebanon, excellent as the cedars.

16 His mouth is most sweet: yea, he is altogether lovely. This is my beloved, and this is my friend, O daughters of Jerusalem.

CHAPTER 6

WHERE is your beloved gone, O fairest among women? where is your beloved turned aside? that we may seek him with you.

2 My beloved is gone down into his garden, to the beds of spices, to feed in the gardens, and to gather lilies.

3 I am my beloved's, and my beloved is mine: he feeds among the lilies.

4 You are beautiful, O my love, as Tirzah, comely as Jerusalem, terrible as an army with banners.

5 Turn your eyes away from me, for they have overcome me: your hair is as a flock of goats that appear from Gilead.

6 Your teeth are as a flock of sheep which go up from the washing, whereof every one bears twins, and there is not one barren among them.

7 As a piece of a pomegranate are your temples within your locks.

8 There are threescore queens, and fourscore concubines, and virgins without number.

9 My dove, my undefiled is but one; she is the only one of her mother, she is the choice one of her that bare her. The daughters saw her, and blessed her; yea, the queens and the concubines, and they praised her.

10 Who is she that looks forth as the morning, fair as the moon, clear as the sun, and terrible as an army with banners?

11 I went down into the garden of nuts to see the fruits of the valley, and to see whether the vine flourished and the pomegranates budded.

12 Or ever I was aware, my soul made me like the chariots of Amminadib.

13 Return, return, O Shulamite; return, return, that we may look upon you. What will you see in the Shulamite? As it were the company of two armies.

CHAPTER 7

HOW beautiful are your feet with shoes, O prince's daughter! the joints of your thighs are like jewels, the work of the hands of a cunning workman.

2 Your navel is like a round goblet, which lacks no liquor: your belly is like an heap of wheat set about with lilies.

3 Your two breasts are like two young roes that are twins.

4 Your neck is as a tower of ivory; your eyes like the fishpools in Heshbon, by the gate of Bathrabbim: your nose is as the tower of Lebanon which looks toward Damascus.

5 Your head upon you is like Carmel, and the hair of your head like purple; the king is held in the galleries.

6 How fair and how pleasant are you, O love, for delights!

7 This your stature is like to a palm tree, and your breasts to clusters of grapes.

8 I said, I will go up to the palm tree, I will take hold of the boughs thereof: now also your breasts shall be as clusters of the vine, and the smell of your nose like apples;

9 And the roof of your mouth like the best wine for my beloved, that goeth

---

7:10 The Christian is a chaste virgin, waiting to be presented to Jesus Christ. See 2 Corinthians 11:2. See also Psalm 45:11.

down sweetly, causing the lips of those that are asleep to speak.

10 I am my beloved's, and his desire is toward me.

11 Come, my beloved, let us go forth into the field; let us lodge in the villages.

12 Let us get up early to the vineyards; let us see if the vine flourish, whether the tender grape appear, and the pomegranates bud forth: there will I give you my loves.

13 The mandrakes give a smell, and at our gates are all manner of pleasant fruits, new and old, which I have laid up for you, O my beloved.

CHAPTER 8

O that you were as my brother, that sucked the breasts of my mother! when I should find you without, I would kiss you; yea, I should not be despised.

2 I would lead you, and bring you into my mother's house, who would instruct me: I would cause you to drink of spiced wine of the juice of my pomegranate.

3 His left hand should be under my head, and his right hand should embrace me.

4 I charge you, O daughters of Jerusalem, that you do not stir up nor awaken my love, until he please.

5 Who is this that comes up from the wilderness, leaning upon her beloved? I raised you up under the apple tree: there your mother brought you forth: there she brought you forth that bore you.

6 Set me as a seal upon your heart, as a seal upon your arm: for love is strong as death; jealousy is cruel as the grave: the coals thereof are coals of fire, which has a most vehement flame.

7 Many waters cannot quench love, neither can the floods drown it: if a man would give all the substance of his house for love, it would utterly be contemned.

8 We have a little sister, and she has no breasts: what shall we do for our sister in the day when she shall be spoken for?

9 If she be a wall, we will build upon her a palace of silver: and if she be a door, we will inclose her with boards of cedar.

10 I am a wall, and my breasts like towers: then was I in his eyes as one that found favour.

11 Solomon had a vineyard at Baalhamon; he let out the vineyard to keepers; every one for the fruit thereof was to bring a thousand pieces of silver.

12 My vineyard, which is mine, is before me: you, O Solomon, must have a thousand, and those that keep the fruit thereof two hundred.

13 You that dwell in the gardens, the companions hearken to your voice: cause me to hear it.

14 Make haste, my beloved, and be like to a roe or to a young hart upon the mountains of spices.

Isaiah

CHAPTER 1

THE vision of Isaiah the son of Amoz, which he saw concerning Judah and Jerusalem in the days of Uzziah, Jotham, Ahaz, and Hezekiah, kings of Judah.

2 Hear, O heavens, and give ear, O earth: for the LORD has spoken, I have nourished and brought up children, and they have rebelled against me.

3 The ox knows his owner, and the ass his master's crib: but Israel does not know, my people does not consider.

4 Ah sinful nation, a people laden with iniquity, a seed of evildoers, children that are corrupters: they have forsaken the LORD, they have provoked the Holy One of Israel to anger, they are gone away backward.

5 Why should you be stricken any more? you will revolt more and more: the whole head is sick, and the whole heart faint.

6 From the sole of the foot even to the head there is no soundness in it; but wounds, and bruises, and putrifying sores: they have not been closed, neither bound up, neither mollified with ointment.

7 Your country is desolate, your cities are burned with fire: your land, strangers devour it in your presence, and it is desolate, as overthrown by strangers.

8 And the daughter of Zion is left as a cottage in a vineyard, as a lodge in a garden of cucumbers, as a besieged city.

9 Except the LORD of hosts had left to us a very small remnant, we should have been as Sodom, and we should have been like Gomorrah.

10 Hear the word of the LORD, you rulers of Sodom; give ear to the law of our God, you people of Gomorrah.

11 To what purpose is the multitude of your sacrifices to me? says the LORD: I am full of the burnt offerings of rams, and the fat of fed beasts; and I delight not in the blood of bullocks, or of lambs, or of he goats.

12 When you come to appear before me, who has required this at your hand, to tread my courts?

13 Bring no more vain oblations; incense is an abomination to me; the new moons and sabbaths, the calling of assemblies, I cannot away with; it is iniquity, even the solemn meeting.

14 Your new moons and your appointed feasts my soul hates: they are a trouble to me; I am weary to bear them.

15 And when you spread forth your hands, I will hide my eyes from you: yea, when you make many prayers, I will not hear: your hands are full of blood.

16 Wash you, make you clean; put away the evil of your doings from before my eyes; cease to do evil;

17 Learn to do well; seek judgment, relieve the oppressed, judge the fatherless, plead for the widow.

18 Come now, and let us reason together, says the LORD: though your sins be

as scarlet, they shall be as white as snow; though they be red like crimson, they shall be as wool.

19 If you are willing and obedient, you shall eat the good of the land:

20 But if you refuse and rebel, you shall be devoured with the sword: for the mouth of the LORD has spoken it.

21 How is the faithful city become an harlot! it was full of judgment; righteousness lodged in it; but now murderers.

22 Your silver is become dross, your wine mixed with water:

23 Your princes are rebellious, and companions of thieves: every one loves gifts, and follows after rewards: they judge not the fatherless, neither does the cause of the widow come to them.

24 Therefore says the LORD, the LORD of hosts, the mighty One of Israel, Ah, I will ease me of my adversaries, and avenge me of my enemies:

25 And I will turn my hand upon you, and purely purge away your dross, and take away all your tin:

26 And I will restore your judges as at the first, and your counselors as at the beginning: afterward you shall be called, The city of righteousness, the faithful city.

27 Zion shall be redeemed with judgment, and her converts with righteousness.

28 And the destruction of the transgressors and of the sinners shall be together, and they that forsake the LORD shall be consumed.

29 For they shall be ashamed of the oaks which you have desired, and you shall be confounded for the gardens that you have chosen.

30 For you shall be as an oak whose leaf fades, and as a garden that has no water.

31 And the strong shall be as tow, and the maker of it as a spark, and they shall both burn together, and none shall quench them.

CHAPTER 2

THE word that Isaiah the son of Amoz saw concerning Judah and Jerusalem.

2 And it shall come to pass in the last days, that the mountain of the LORD's house shall be established in the top of the mountains, and shall be exalted above the hills; and all nations shall flow to it.

3 And many people shall go and say, Come, and let us go up to the mountain of the LORD, to the house of the God of Jacob; and he will teach us of his ways, and we will walk in his paths: for out of Zion shall go forth the law, and the word of the LORD from Jerusalem.

4 And he shall judge among the nations, and shall rebuke many people: and they shall beat their swords into plowshares, and their spears into pruninghooks: nation shall not lift up sword against nation, neither shall they learn war any more.

5 O house of Jacob, come, and let us walk in the light of the LORD.

6 Therefore you have forsaken your people the house of Jacob, because they be replenished from the east, and are soothsayers like the Philistines, and they please themselves in the children of strangers.

7 Their land also is full of silver and gold, neither is there any end of their treasures; their land is also full of horses, neither is there any end of their chariots:

8 Their land also is full of idols; they worship the work of their own hands, that which their own fingers have made:

9 And the mean man bows down, and the great man humbles himself: therefore forgive them not.

10 Enter into the rock, and hide in the dust, for fear of the LORD, and for the glory of his majesty.

11 The lofty looks of man shall be humbled, and the haughtiness of men shall be bowed down, and the LORD alone shall be exalted in that day.

12 For the day of the LORD of hosts shall be upon every one that is proud and lofty, and upon every one that is lifted up; and he shall be brought low:

13 And upon all the cedars of Lebanon, that are high and lifted up, and upon all the oaks of Bashan,

14 And upon all the high mountains, and upon all the hills that are lifted up,

15 And upon every high tower, and upon every fenced wall,

16 And upon all the ships of Tarshish, and upon all pleasant pictures.

17 And the loftiness of man shall be bowed down, and the haughtiness of men shall be made low: and the LORD alone shall be exalted in that day.

18 And the idols he shall utterly abolish.

19 And they shall go into the holes of the rocks, and into the caves of the earth, for fear of the LORD, and for the glory of his majesty, when he arises to shake terribly the earth.

20 In that day a man shall cast his idols of silver, and his idols of gold, which they made each one for himself to worship, to the moles and to the bats;

21 To go into the clefts of the rocks, and into the tops of the ragged rocks, for fear of the LORD, and for the glory of his majesty, when he arises to shake terribly the earth.

22 Sever yourselves from such a man, whose breath is in his nostrils: for wherein is he to be accounted of?

CHAPTER 3

FOR, behold, the Lord, the LORD of hosts, takes away from Jerusalem and from Judah the stay and the staff, the whole stay of bread, and the whole stay of water.

2 The mighty man, and the man of war, the judge, and the prophet, and the prudent, and the ancient,

3 The captain of fifty, and the honourable man, and the counselor, and the cunning artificer, and the eloquent orator.

4 And I will give children to be their princes, and babes shall rule over them.

5 And the people shall be oppressed, every one by another, and every one by his neighbour: the child shall behave himself proudly against the ancient, and the base against the honourable.

6 When a man shall take hold of his brother of the house of his father, saying, You have clothing, You be our ruler, and let this ruin be under your hand:

7 In that day shall he swear, saying, I will not be an healer; for in my house is neither bread nor clothing: make me not a ruler of the people.

8 For Jerusalem is ruined, and Judah is fallen: because their tongue and their doings are against the LORD, to provoke the eyes of his glory.

9 The show of their countenance does witness against them; and they declare their sin as Sodom, they hide it not. Woe to their soul! for they have rewarded evil to themselves.

10 Say to the righteous, that it shall be well with him: for they shall eat the fruit of their doings.

11 Woe to the wicked! it shall be ill with him: for the reward of his hands shall be given him.

12 As for my people, children are their oppressors, and women rule over them. O my people, they which lead you cause you to err, and destroy the way of your paths.

13 The LORD stands up to plead, and stands to judge the people.

14 The LORD will enter into judgment with the ancients of his people, and the princes thereof: for you have eaten up the vineyard; the spoil of the poor is in your houses.

3:9 Homosexuals are proud of their lifestyle, parading it to the world, despite God's judgment against homosexuality and despite the agony of AIDS, which afflicts many homosexual men.

The Function of the Law in Evangelism

4:4 People will never set their faces decidedly towards heaven and live like pilgrims until they really feel that they are in danger of hell . . . Let us expound and beat out the Ten Commandments and show the length, and breadth and depth and height of their requirements. This is the way of our Lord in the Sermon on the Mount. We cannot do better than follow His plan.

We may depend on it, men will never come to Jesus, and stay with Jesus, and live for Jesus, unless they really know why they are to come and what is their need. Those whom the Spirit draws to Jesus are those whom the Spirit has convinced of sin. Without thorough conviction of sin, men may seem to come to Jesus and follow Him for a season, but they will soon fall away and return to the world.

Faithfulness and Holiness : The Witness of J.C. Ryle.

15 What do you mean that you beat my people to pieces, and grind the faces of the poor? says the Lord GOD of hosts.

16 Moreover the LORD says, Because the daughters of Zion are haughty, and walk with stretched forth necks and wanton eyes, walking and mincing as they go, and making a tinkling with their feet:

17 Therefore the LORD will smite with a scab the crown of the head of the daughters of Zion, and the LORD will discover their secret parts.

18 In that day the Lord will take away the bravery of their tinkling ornaments about their feet, and their cauls, and their round tires like the moon,

19 The chains, and the bracelets, and the mufflers,

20 The bonnets, and the ornaments of the legs, and the headbands, and the tablets, and the earrings,

21 The rings, and nose jewels,

22 The changeable suits of apparel, and the mantles, and the wimples, and the crisping pins,

23 The glasses, and the fine linen, and the hoods, and the vails.

24 And it shall come to pass, that instead of sweet smell there shall be stink; and instead of a girdle a rent; and instead of well set hair baldness; and instead of a stomacher a girding of sackcloth; and burning instead of beauty.

25 Your men shall fall by the sword, and your mighty in the war.

26 And her gates shall lament and mourn; and she being desolate shall sit upon the ground.

CHAPTER 4

AND in that day seven women shall take hold of one man, saying, We will eat our own bread, and wear our own apparel: only let us be called by your name, to take away our reproach.

2 In that day shall the branch of the LORD be beautiful and glorious, and the fruit of the earth shall be excellent and comely for them that are escaped of Israel.

3 And it shall come to pass, that he that is left in Zion, and he that remains in Jerusalem, shall be called holy, even every one that is written among the living in Jerusalem:

4 When the Lord shall have washed away the filth of the daughters of Zion, and shall have purged the blood of Jerusalem from the midst thereof by the spirit of judgment, and by the spirit of burning.

5 And the LORD will create upon every dwelling place of mount Zion, and upon her assemblies, a cloud and smoke by day, and the shining of a flaming fire by night: for upon all the glory shall be a defence.

6 And there shall be a tabernacle for a shadow in the day time from the heat, and for a place of refuge, and for a covert from storm and from rain.

CHAPTER 5

NOW will I sing to my wellbeloved a song of my beloved touching his vineyard. My wellbeloved has a vineyard in a very fruitful hill:

2 And he fenced it, and gathered out the stones thereof, and planted it with the choicest vine, and built a tower in the midst of it, and also made a winepress therein: and he looked that it should bring forth grapes, and it brought forth wild grapes.

3 And now, O inhabitants of Jerusalem, and men of Judah, judge, I pray you, betwixt me and my vineyard.

4 What could have been done more to my vineyard, that I have not done in it? why, when I looked that it should bring forth grapes, brought it forth wild grapes?

5 And now go to; I will tell you what I will do to my vineyard: I will take away the hedge thereof, and it shall be eaten up; and break down the wall thereof, and it shall be trodden down:

6 And I will lay it waste: it shall not be pruned, nor dug; but there shall come up briers and thorns: I will also command the clouds that they rain no rain upon it.

7 For the vineyard of the LORD of hosts is the house of Israel, and the men of Judah his pleasant plant: and he looked for judgment, but behold oppression; for righteousness, but behold a cry.

8 Woe to them that join house to house, that lay field to field, till there be no place, that they may be placed alone in the midst of the earth!

9 In my ears said the LORD of hosts, Of a truth many houses shall be desolate, even great and fair, without inhabitant.

10 Yea, ten acres of vineyard shall yield one bath, and the seed of an homer shall yield an ephah.

11 Woe to them that rise up early in the morning, that they may follow strong drink; that continue until night, till wine inflame them!

12 And the harp, and the viol, the tabret, and pipe, and wine, are in their feasts: but they regard not the work of the LORD, neither consider the operation of his hands.

13 Therefore my people are gone into captivity, because they have no knowledge: and their honourable men are famished, and their multitude dried up with thirst.

14 Therefore hell has enlarged herself, and opened her mouth without measure: and their glory, and their multitude, and their pomp, and he that rejoices, shall descend into it.

15 And the mean man shall be brought down, and the mighty man shall be humbled, and the eyes of the lofty shall be humbled:

16 But the LORD of hosts shall be exalted in judgment, and God that is holy shall be sanctified in righteousness.

17 Then shall the lambs feed after their manner, and the waste places of the fat ones shall strangers eat.

18 Woe to them that draw iniquity with cords of vanity, and sin as it were with a cart rope:

19 That say, Let him make speed, and hasten his work, that we may see it: and let the counsel of the Holy One of Israel draw nigh and come, that we may know it!

20 **Woe to them that call evil good, and good evil; that put darkness for light, and light for darkness; that put bitter for sweet, and sweet for bitter!**

21 **Woe to them that are wise in their own eyes, and prudent in their own sight!**

22 Woe to them that are mighty to drink wine, and men of strength to mingle strong drink:

23 Which justify the wicked for reward, and take away the righteousness of the righteous from him!

24 Therefore as the fire devours the stubble, and the flame consumes the chaff, so their root shall be as rottenness, and their blossom shall go up as dust: because they have cast away the law of the LORD of hosts, and despised the word of the Holy One of Israel.

25 Therefore is the anger of the LORD kindled against his people, and he has stretched forth his hand against them, and has smitten them: and the hills did tremble, and their carcases were torn in the midst of the streets. For all this his anger is not turned away, but his hand is stretched out still.

26 And he will lift up an ensign to the nations from far, and will hiss to them from the end of the earth: and, behold, they shall come with speed swiftly:

27 None shall be weary nor stumble among them; none shall slumber nor sleep; neither shall the girdle of their loins be loosed, nor the latchet of their shoes be broken:

28 Whose arrows are sharp, and all their bows bent, their horses' hoofs shall be counted like flint, and their wheels like a whirlwind:

29 Their roaring shall be like a lion, they shall roar like young lions: yea, they shall roar, and lay hold of the prey, and shall carry it away safe, and none shall deliver it.

30 And in that day they shall roar against them like the roaring of the sea: and if one look to the land, behold darkness and sorrow, and the light is darkened in the heavens thereof.

CHAPTER 6

IN the year that king Uzziah died I saw also the LORD sitting upon a throne, high and lifted up, and his train filled the temple.

2 Above it stood the seraphims: each one had six wings; with twain he cov-ered his face, and with twain he covered his feet, and with twain he did fly.

3 And one cried to another, and said, Holy, holy, holy, is the LORD of hosts: the whole earth is full of his glory.

4 And the posts of the door moved at the voice of him that cried, and the house was filled with smoke.

5 Then said I, Woe is me! for I am un-done; because I am a man of unclean lips, and I dwell in the midst of a people of unclean lips: for my eyes have seen the King, the LORD of hosts.

6 Then flew one of the seraphims to me, having a live coal in his hand, which he had taken with the tongs from off the altar:

7 And he laid it upon my mouth, and said, Lo, this has touched your lips; and your iniquity is taken away, and your sin purged.

8 Also I heard the voice of the Lord, saying, Whom shall I send, and who will go for us? Then said I, Here am I; send me.

9 And he said, Go, and tell this people, Hear indeed, but understand not; and see indeed, but perceive not.

10 Make the heart of this people fat, and make their ears heavy, and shut their eyes; lest they see with their eyes, and hear with their ears, and understand with their heart, and convert, and be healed.

11 Then said I, Lord, how long? And he answered, Until the cities be wasted without inhabitant, and the houses with-out man, and the land be utterly deso-late,

12 And the LORD have removed men far away, and there be a great forsaking in the midst of the land.

13 But yet in it shall be a tenth, and it shall return, and shall be eaten: as a teil tree, and as an oak, whose substance is in them, when they cast their leaves: so

---

6:1-9 Those who see God's holiness will cry out for cleansing. They are the ones who willingly obey the command to take the gospel to the world. God did a similar thing to Jeremiah (see Jeremiah 1:7-10).

ISAIAH

Isaiah 6:8

the holy seed shall be the substance thereof.

CHAPTER 7

AND it came to pass in the days of Ahaz the son of Jotham, the son of Uzziah, king of Judah, that Rezin the king of Syria, and Pekah the son of Remaliah, king of Israel, went up toward Jerusalem to war against it, but could not prevail against it.

2 And it was told the house of David, saying, Syria is confederate with Ephraim. And his heart was moved, and the heart of his people, as the trees of the wood are moved with the wind.

3 Then said the LORD to Isaiah, Go forth now to meet Ahaz, you, and Shearjashub your son, at the end of the conduit of the upper pool in the highway of the fuller's field;

4 And say to him, Take heed, and be quiet; fear not, neither be fainthearted for the two tails of these smoking firebrands, for the fierce anger of Rezin with Syria, and of the son of Remaliah.

5 Because Syria, Ephraim, and the son of Remaliah, have taken evil counsel against you, saying,

6 Let us go up against Judah, and vex it, and let us make a breach therein for us, and set a king in the midst of it, even the son of Tabeal:

7 Thus says the Lord GOD, It shall not stand, neither shall it come to pass.

8 For the head of Syria is Damascus, and the head of Damascus is Rezin; and within threescore and five years shall Ephraim be broken, that it be not a people.

9 And the head of Ephraim is Samaria, and the head of Samaria is Remaliah's son. If you will not believe, surely you shall not be established.

10 Moreover the LORD spoke again to Ahaz, saying,

11 Ask a sign for yourself from the LORD your God; ask it either in the depth, or in the height above.

12 But Ahaz said, I will not ask, neither will I tempt the LORD.

13 And he said, Hear now, O house of David; Is it a small thing for you to weary men, but will you weary my God also?

14 Therefore the Lord himself shall give you a sign; Behold, a virgin shall conceive, and bear a son, and shall call his name Immanuel.

15 Butter and honey shall he eat, that he may know to refuse the evil, and choose the good.

16 For before the child shall know to refuse the evil, and choose the good, the land that you abhor shall be forsaken of both her kings.

17 The LORD shall bring upon you, and upon your people, and upon your father's house, days that have not come, from the day that Ephraim departed from Judah; even the king of Assyria.

18 And it shall come to pass in that day, that the LORD shall hiss for the fly that is in the uttermost part of the rivers of Egypt, and for the bee that is in the land of Assyria.

19 And they shall come, and shall rest all of them in the desolate valleys, and in the holes of the rocks, and upon all thorns, and upon all bushes.

20 In the same day shall the Lord shave with a razor that is hired, namely, by them beyond the river, by the king of Assyria, the head, and the hair of the feet: and it shall also consume the beard.

21 And it shall come to pass in that day, that a man shall nourish a young cow, and two sheep;

22 And it shall come to pass, for the abundance of milk that they shall give he shall eat butter: for butter and honey shall every one eat that is left in the land.

23 And it shall come to pass in that day, that every place shall be, where there were a thousand vines at a thousand silverlings, it shall even be for briers and thorns.

24 With arrows and with bows shall men come there; because all the land shall become briers and thorns.

25 And on all hills that shall be dug with the mattock, there shall not come there the fear of briers and thorns: but it shall be for the sending forth of oxen, and for the treading of lesser cattle.

CHAPTER 8

MOREOVER the LORD said to me, Take a great roll, and write in it with a man's pen concerning Mahershalalhashbaz.

2 And I took to me faithful witnesses to record, Uriah the priest, and Zechariah the son of Jeberechiah.

7:14 If the word "virgin" merely means a "young maiden," as some argue, it would not be a "sign" from God.

3 And I went to the prophetess; and she conceived, and bare a son. Then said the LORD to me, Call his name Mahershalalhashbaz.

4 For before the child shall have knowledge to cry, My father, and my mother, the riches of Damascus and the spoil of Samaria shall be taken away before the king of Assyria.

5 The LORD spoke also to me again, saying,

6 Forasmuch as this people refuses the waters of Shiloah that go softly, and rejoice in Rezin and Remaliah's son;

7 Now therefore, behold, the Lord brings up upon them the waters of the river, strong and many, even the king of Assyria, and all his glory: and he shall come up over all his channels, and go over all his banks:

8 And he shall pass through Judah; he shall overflow and go over, he shall reach even to the neck; and the stretching out of his wings shall fill the breadth of your land, O Immanuel.

9 Associate yourselves, O you people, and you shall be broken in pieces; and give ear, all you of far countries: gird yourselves, and you shall be broken in pieces; gird yourselves, and you shall be broken in pieces.

10 Take counsel together, and it shall come to nothing; speak the word, and it shall not stand: for God is with us.

11 For the LORD spoke thus to me with a strong hand, and instructed me that I should not walk in the way of this people, saying,

12 Say not, A confederacy, to all them to whom this people shall say, A confederacy; neither fear what they fear, nor be afraid.

13 Sanctify the LORD of hosts himself; and let him be your fear, and let him be your dread.

14 And he shall be for a sanctuary; but for a stone of stumbling and for a rock of offence to both the houses of Israel, for a gin and for a snare to the inhabitants of Jerusalem.

15 And many among them shall stumble, and fall, and be broken, and be snared, and be taken.

16 Bind up the testimony, seal the law among my disciples.

17 And I will wait upon the LORD, that hides his face from the house of Jacob, and I will look for him.

18 Behold, I and the children whom the LORD has given me are for signs and for wonders in Israel from the LORD of hosts, which dwells in mount Zion.

19 And when they shall say to you, Seek them that have familiar spirits, and to wizards that peep, and that mutter: should not a people seek to their God? for the living to the dead?

20 To the law and to the testimony: if they speak not according to this word, it is because there is no light in them.

21 And they shall pass through it, hardly bestead and hungry: and it shall come to pass, that when they shall be hungry, they shall fret themselves, and curse their king and their God, and look upward.

22 And they shall look to the earth; and behold trouble and darkness, dimness of anguish; and they shall be driven to darkness.

CHAPTER 9

NEVERTHELESS the dimness shall not be such as was in her vexation, when at the first he lightly afflicted the land of Zebulun and the land of Naphtali, and afterward did more grievously afflict her by the way of the sea, beyond Jordan, in Galilee of the nations.

2 The people that walked in darkness have seen a great light: they that dwell in the land of the shadow of death, upon them has the light shined.

3 You have multiplied the nation, and not increased the joy: they joy before you according to the joy in harvest, and as men rejoice when they divide the spoil.

4 For you have broken the yoke of his burden, and the staff of his shoulder, the

rod of his oppressor, as in the day of Midian.

5 For every battle of the warrior is with confused noise, and garments rolled in blood; but this shall be with burning and fuel of fire.

6 For unto us a child is born, unto us a son is given: and the government shall be upon his shoulder: and his name shall be called Wonderful, Counselor, The mighty God, The everlasting Father, The Prince of Peace.

7 Of the increase of his government and peace there shall be no end, upon the throne of David, and upon his kingdom, to order it, and to establish it with judgment and with justice from henceforth even for ever. The zeal of the LORD of hosts will perform this.

8 The Lord sent a word into Jacob, and it has lighted upon Israel.

9 And all the people shall know, even Ephraim and the inhabitant of Samaria, that say in the pride and stoutness of heart,

10 The bricks are fallen down, but we will build with hewn stones: the sycomores are cut down, but we will change them into cedars.

11 Therefore the LORD shall set up the adversaries of Rezin against him, and join his enemies together;

12 The Syrians before, and the Philistines behind; and they shall devour Israel with open mouth. For all this his anger is not turned away, but his hand is stretched out still.

13 For the people do not turn to him that smites them, neither do they seek the LORD of hosts.

14 Therefore the LORD will cut off from Israel head and tail, branch and rush, in one day.

15 The ancient and honourable, he is the head; and the prophet that teaches lies, he is the tail.

16 For the leaders of this people cause them to err; and they that are led of them are destroyed.

17 Therefore the LORD shall have no joy in their young men, neither shall have mercy on their fatherless and widows: for every one is an hypocrite and an evildoer, and every mouth speaks folly. For all this his anger is not turned away, but his hand is stretched out still.

18 For wickedness burns as the fire: it shall devour the briers and thorns, and shall kindle in the thickets of the forest, and they shall mount up like the lifting up of smoke.

19 Through the wrath of the LORD of hosts is the land darkened, and the people shall be as the fuel of the fire: no man shall spare his brother.

20 And he shall snatch on the right hand, and be hungry; and he shall eat on the left hand, and they shall not be satisfied: they shall eat every man the flesh of his own arm:

21 Manasseh, Ephraim; and Ephraim, Manasseh: and they together shall be against Judah. For all this his anger is not turned away, but his hand is stretched out still.

CHAPTER 10

WOE to them that decree unrighteous decrees, and that write grievousness which they have prescribed;

2 To turn aside the needy from judgment, and to take away the right from the poor of my people, that widows may be their prey, and that they may rob the fatherless!

3 And what will you do in the day of visitation, and in the desolation which shall come from far? to whom will you flee for help? and where will you leave your glory?

4 Without me they shall bow down under the prisoners, and they shall fall

---

9:6-7 This is a direct reference to the Messiah.

under the slain. For all this his anger is not turned away, but his hand is stretched out still.

5 O Assyrian, the rod of my anger, and the staff in their hand is my indignation.

6 I will send him against an hypocritical nation, and against the people of my wrath will I give him a charge, to take the spoil, and to take the prey, and to tread them down like the mire of the streets.

7 Howbeit he does not mean so, neither does his heart think so; but it is in his heart to destroy and cut off nations not a few.

8 For he says, Are not my princes altogether kings?

9 Is not Calno as Carchemish? is not Hamath as Arpad? is not Samaria as Damascus?

10 As my hand has found the kingdoms of the idols, and whose graven images did excel them of Jerusalem and of Samaria;

11 Shall I not, as I have done to Samaria and her idols, so do to Jerusalem and her idols?

12 Therefore it shall come to pass, that when the Lord has performed his whole work upon mount Zion and on Jerusalem, I will punish the fruit of the stout heart of the king of Assyria, and the glory of his high looks.

13 For he says, By the strength of my hand I have done it, and by my wisdom; for I am prudent: and I have removed the bounds of the people, and have robbed their treasures, and I have put down the inhabitants like a valiant man:

14 And my hand has found as a nest the riches of the people: and as one gathered eggs that are left, have I gathered all the earth; and there was none that moved the wing, or opened the mouth, or peeped.

15 Shall the axe boast itself against him that hews therewith? or shall the saw magnify itself against him that shakes it? as if the rod should shake itself against them that lift it up, or as if the staff should lift up itself, as if it were no wood.

16 Therefore shall the Lord, the Lord of hosts, send among his fat ones leanness; and under his glory he shall kindle a burning like the burning of a fire.

17 And the light of Israel shall be for a fire, and his Holy One for a flame: and it shall burn and devour his thorns and his briers in one day;

18 And shall consume the glory of his forest, and of his fruitful field, both soul and body: and they shall be as when a standard-bearer faints.

19 And the rest of the trees of his forest shall be few, that a child may write them.

20 And it shall come to pass in that day, that the remnant of Israel, and such as are escaped of the house of Jacob, shall no more again stay upon him that smote them; but shall stay upon the LORD, the Holy One of Israel, in truth.

21 The remnant shall return, even the remnant of Jacob, to the mighty God.

22 For though your people Israel be as the sand of the sea, yet a remnant of them shall return: the consumption decreed shall overflow with righteousness.

23 For the Lord GOD of hosts shall make a consumption, even determined, in the midst of all the land.

24 Therefore thus says the Lord GOD of hosts, O my people that dwell in Zion, be not afraid of the Assyrian: he shall smite you with a rod, and shall lift up his staff against you, after the manner of Egypt.

25 For yet a very little while, and the indignation shall cease, and my anger in their destruction.

26 And the LORD of hosts shall stir up a scourge for him according to the slaughter of Midian at the rock of Oreb: and as his rod was upon the sea, so shall he lift it up after the manner of Egypt.

27 And it shall come to pass in that day, that his burden shall be taken away from off your shoulder, and his yoke

from off your neck, and the yoke shall be destroyed because of the anointing.

28 He is come to Aiath, he is passed to Migron; at Michmash he has laid up his carriages:

29 They are gone over the passage: they have taken up their lodging at Geba; Ramah is afraid; Gibeah of Saul is fled.

30 Lift up your voice, O daughter of Gallim: cause it to be heard to Laish, O poor Anathoth.

31 Madmenah is removed; the inhabitants of Gebim gather themselves to flee.

32 As yet shall he remain at Nob that day: he shall shake his hand against the mount of the daughter of Zion, the hill of Jerusalem.

33 Behold, the Lord, the LORD of hosts, shall lop the bough with terror: and the high ones of stature shall be hewn down, and the haughty shall be humbled.

34 And he shall cut down the thickets of the forest with iron, and Lebanon shall fall by a mighty one.

CHAPTER 11

AND there shall come forth a rod out of the stem of Jesse, and a Branch shall grow out of his roots:

2 And the spirit of the LORD shall rest upon him, the spirit of wisdom and understanding, the spirit of counsel and might, the spirit of knowledge and of the fear of the LORD;

3 And shall make him of quick understanding in the fear of the LORD: and he shall not judge after the sight of his eyes, neither reprove after the hearing of his ears:

4 But with righteousness shall he judge the poor, and reprove with equity for the meek of the earth: and he shall smite the earth: with the rod of his mouth, and with the breath of his lips shall he slay the wicked.

5 And righteousness shall be the girdle of his loins, and faithfulness the girdle of his reins.

6 The wolf also shall dwell with the lamb, and the leopard shall lie down with the kid; and the calf and the young lion and the fatling together; and a little child shall lead them.

7 And the cow and the bear shall feed; their young ones shall lie down together: and the lion shall eat straw like the ox.

8 And the sucking child shall play on the hole of the asp, and the weaned child shall put his hand on the cockatrice' den.

9 They shall not hurt nor destroy in all my holy mountain: for the earth shall be full of the knowledge of the LORD, as the waters cover the sea.

10 And in that day there shall be a root of Jesse, which shall stand for an ensign of the people; to it shall the Gentiles seek: and his rest shall be glorious.

11 And it shall come to pass in that day, that the Lord shall set his hand again the second time to recover the remnant of his people, which shall be left, from Assyria, and from Egypt, and from Pathros, and from Cush, and from Elam, and from Shinar, and from Hamath, and from the islands of the sea.

12 And he shall set up an ensign for the nations, and shall assemble the outcasts of Israel, and gather together the dispersed of Judah from the four corners of the earth.

13 The envy also of Ephraim shall depart, and the adversaries of Judah shall be cut off: Ephraim shall not envy Judah, and Judah shall not vex Ephraim.

14 But they shall fly upon the shoulders of the Philistines toward the west; they shall spoil them of the east together: they shall lay their hand upon Edom and Moab; and the children of Ammon shall obey them.

15 And the LORD shall utterly destroy the tongue of the Egyptian sea; and with his mighty wind shall he shake his hand over the river, and shall smite it in the seven streams, and make men go over dryshod.

16 And there shall be an highway for the remnant of his people, which shall be left, from Assyria; like as it was to Israel in the day that he came up out of the land of Egypt.

CHAPTER 12

AND in that day you shall say, O LORD, I will praise you: though you were angry with me, your anger is turned away, and you comforted me.

2 Behold, God is my salvation; I will trust, and not be afraid: for the LORD JEHOVAH is my strength and my song; he also is become my salvation.

3 Therefore with joy shall you draw water out of the wells of salvation.

4 And in that day shall you say, Praise the LORD, call upon his name, declare his doings among the people, make mention that his name is exalted.

5 Sing to the LORD; for he has done excellent things: this is known in all the earth.

6 Cry out and shout, you inhabitant of Zion: for great is the Holy One of Israel in the midst of you.

CHAPTER 13

THE burden of Babylon, which Isaiah the son of Amoz did see.

2 Lift up a banner upon the high mountain, exalt the voice to them, shake the hand, that they may go into the gates of the nobles.

3 I have commanded my sanctified ones, I have also called my mighty ones for my anger, even them that rejoice in my highness.

4 The noise of a multitude in the mountains, like as of a great people; a tumultuous noise of the kingdoms of nations gathered together: the LORD of hosts musters the host of the battle.

5 They come from a far country, from the end of heaven, even the LORD, and the weapons of his indignation, to destroy the whole land.

6 Howl; for the day of the LORD is at hand; it shall come as a destruction from the Almighty.

7 Therefore shall all hands be faint, and every man's heart shall melt:

8 And they shall be afraid: pangs and sorrows shall take hold of them; they shall be in pain as a woman that travails: they shall be amazed one at another; their faces shall be as flames.

9 Behold, the day of the LORD comes, cruel both with wrath and fierce anger, to lay the land desolate: and he shall destroy the sinners thereof out of it.

10 For the stars of heaven and the constellations thereof shall not give their light: the sun shall be darkened in his going forth, and the moon shall not cause her light to shine.

11 And I will punish the world for their evil, and the wicked for their iniquity; and I will cause the arrogancy of the proud to cease, and will lay low the haughtiness of the terrible.

12 I will make a man more precious than fine gold; even a man than the golden wedge of Ophir.

13 Therefore I will shake the heavens, and the earth shall remove out of her place, in the wrath of the LORD of hosts, and in the day of his fierce anger.

14 And it shall be as the chased roe, and as a sheep that no man takes up: they shall every man turn to his own people, and flee every one into his own land.

15 Every one that is found shall be thrust through; and every one that is joined to them shall fall by the sword.

16 Their children also shall be dashed to pieces before their eyes; their houses shall be spoiled, and their wives ravished.

17 Behold, I will stir up the Medes against them, which shall not regard silver; and as for gold, they shall not delight in it.

13:11 God's promise to bring justice to an evil world still remains steadfast.

18 Their bows also shall dash the young men to pieces; and they shall have no pity on the fruit of the womb; their eye shall not spare children.

19 And Babylon, the glory of kingdoms, the beauty of the Chaldees' excellency, shall be as when God overthrew Sodom and Gomorrah.

20 It shall never be inhabited, neither shall it be dwelt in from generation to generation: neither shall the Arabian pitch tent there; neither shall the shepherds make their fold there.

21 But wild beasts of the desert shall lie there; and their houses shall be full of doleful creatures; and owls shall dwell there, and satyrs shall dance there.

22 And the wild beasts of the islands shall cry in their desolate houses, and dragons in their pleasant palaces: and her time is near to come, and her days shall not be prolonged.

CHAPTER 14

FOR the LORD will have mercy on Jacob, and will yet choose Israel, and set them in their own land: and the strangers shall be joined with them, and they shall cleave to the house of Jacob.

2 And the people shall take them, and bring them to their place: and the house of Israel shall possess them in the land of the LORD for servants and handmaids: and they shall take them captives, whose captives they were; and they shall rule over their oppressors.

3 And it shall come to pass in the day that the LORD shall give you rest from your sorrow, and from your fear, and from the hard bondage wherein you were made to serve,

4 That you shall take up this proverb against the king of Babylon, and say, How has the oppressor ceased! the golden city ceased!

5 The LORD has broken the staff of the wicked, and the sceptre of the rulers.

6 He who smote the people in wrath with a continual stroke, he that ruled the nations in anger, is persecuted, and none hinders.

7 The whole earth is at rest, and is quiet: they break forth into singing.

8 Yea, the fir trees rejoice at you, and the cedars of Lebanon, saying, Since you are laid down, no woodsman is come up against us.

9 Hell from beneath is moved for you to meet you at your coming: it stirs up the dead for you, even all the chief ones of the earth; it has raised up from their thrones all the kings of the nations.

10 All they shall speak and say to you, Are you also become weak as we? are you become like us?

11 Your pomp is brought down to the grave, and the noise of your viols: the worm is spread under you, and the worms cover you.

12 How are you fallen from heaven, O Lucifer, son of the morning! how are you cut down to the ground, which did weaken the nations!

13 For you have said in your heart, I will ascend into heaven, I will exalt my throne above the stars of God: I will sit also upon the mount of the congregation, in the sides of the north:

14 I will ascend above the heights of the clouds; I will be like the most High.

15 Yet you shall be brought down to hell, to the sides of the pit.

16 They that see you shall narrowly look upon you, and consider you, saying, Is this the man that made the earth to tremble, that did shake kingdoms;

17 That made the world as a wilderness, and destroyed the cities thereof; that opened not the house of his prisoners?

18 All the kings of the nations, even all of them, lie in glory, every one in his own house.

19 But you are cast out of your grave like an abominable branch, and as the

---

14:19 How long was Jesus in the tomb? For an answer, see comment at Matthew 12:40.

raiment of those that are slain, thrust through with a sword, that go down to the stones of the pit; as a carcase trodden under feet.

20 You shall not be joined with them in burial, because you have destroyed your land, and slain your people: the seed of evildoers shall never be renowned.

21 Prepare slaughter for his children for the iniquity of their fathers; that they do not rise, nor possess the land, nor fill the face of the world with cities.

22 For I will rise up against them, says the LORD of hosts, and cut off from Babylon the name, and remnant, and son, and nephew, says the LORD.

23 I will also make it a possession for the bittern, and pools of water: and I will sweep it with the besom of destruction, says the LORD of hosts.

24 The LORD of hosts has sworn, saying, Surely as I have thought, so shall it come to pass; and as I have purposed, so shall it stand:

25 That I will break the Assyrian in my land, and upon my mountains tread him under foot: then shall his yoke depart from off them, and his burden depart from off their shoulders.

26 This is the purpose that is purposed upon the whole earth: and this is the hand that is stretched out upon all the nations.

27 For the LORD of hosts has purposed, and who shall disannul it? and his hand is stretched out, and who shall turn it back?

28 In the year that king Ahaz died was this burden.

29 Do not rejoice, whole Palestina, because the rod of him that smote you is broken: for out of the serpent's root shall come forth a cockatrice, and his fruit shall be a fiery flying serpent.

30 And the firstborn of the poor shall feed, and the needy shall lie down in safety: and I will kill your root with famine, and he shall slay your remnant.

31 Howl, O gate; cry, O city; you, whole Palestina, are dissolved: for there shall come from the north a smoke, and none shall be alone in his appointed times.

32 What shall one then answer the messengers of the nation? That the LORD has founded Zion, and the poor of his people shall trust in it.

CHAPTER 15

THE burden of Moab. Because in the night Ar of Moab is laid waste, and brought to silence; because in the night Kir of Moab is laid waste, and brought to silence;

2 He is gone up to Bajith, and to Dibon, the high places, to weep: Moab shall howl over Nebo, and over Medeba: on all their heads shall be baldness, and every beard cut off.

3 In their streets they shall gird themselves with sackcloth: on the tops of their houses, and in their streets, every one shall howl, weeping abundantly.

4 And Heshbon shall cry, and Elealeh: their voice shall be heard even to Jahaz: therefore the armed soldiers of Moab shall cry out; his life shall be grievous to him.

5 My heart shall cry out for Moab; his fugitives shall flee to Zoar, an heifer of three years old: for by the mounting up of Luhith with weeping shall they go it up; for in the way of Horonaim they shall raise up a cry of destruction.

6 For the waters of Nimrim shall be desolate: for the hay is withered away, the grass fails, there is no green thing.

7 Therefore the abundance they have gotten, and that which they have laid up, shall they carry away to the brook of the willows.

8 For the cry is gone round about the borders of Moab; the howling thereof to Eglaim, and the howling thereof to Beerelim.

9 For the waters of Dimon shall be full of blood: for I will bring more upon Dimon, lions upon him that escapes of Moab, and upon the remnant of the land.

CHAPTER 16

SEND the lamb to the ruler of the land from Sela to the wilderness, to the mount of the daughter of Zion.

2 For it shall be, that, as a wandering bird cast out of the nest, so the daughters of Moab shall be at the fords of Arnon.

3 Take counsel, execute judgment; make your shadow as the night in the midst of the noonday; hide the outcasts; do not bewray him that wanders.

4 Let my outcasts dwell with you, Moab; be a covert to them from the face of the spoiler: for the extortioner is at an end, the spoiler ceases, the oppressors are consumed out of the land.

5 And in mercy shall the throne be established: and he shall sit upon it in truth in the tabernacle of David, judging, and seeking judgment, and hasting righteousness.

6 We have heard of the pride of Moab; he is very proud: even of his haughtiness, and his pride, and his wrath: but his lies shall not be so.

7 Therefore shall Moab howl for Moab, every one shall howl: for the foundations of Kirhareseth shall you mourn; surely they are stricken.

8 For the fields of Heshbon languish, and the vine of Sibmah: the lords of the heathen have broken down the principal plants thereof, they are come even to Jazer, they wandered through the wilderness: her branches are stretched out, they are gone over the sea.

9 Therefore I will bewail with the weeping of Jazer the vine of Sibmah: I will water you with my tears, O Heshbon, and Elealeh: for the shouting for your summer fruits and for your harvest is fallen.

10 And gladness is taken away, and joy out of the plentiful field; and in the vineyards there shall be no singing, neither shall there be shouting: the treaders shall tread out no wine in their presses; I have made their vintage shouting to cease.

11 Therefore my bowels shall sound like an harp for Moab, and my inward parts for Kirharesh.

12 And it shall come to pass, when it is seen that Moab is weary on the high place, that he shall come to his sanctuary to pray; but he shall not prevail.

13 This is the word that the LORD has spoken concerning Moab since that time.

14 But now the LORD has spoken, saying, Within three years, as the years of an hireling, and the glory of Moab shall be contemned, with all that great multitude; and the remnant shall be very small and feeble.

CHAPTER 17

THE burden of Damascus. Behold, Damascus is taken away from being a city, and it shall be a ruinous heap.

2 The cities of Aroer are forsaken: they shall be for flocks, which shall lie down, and none shall make them afraid.

3 The fortress also shall cease from Ephraim, and the kingdom from Damascus, and the remnant of Syria: they shall be as the glory of the children of Israel, says the LORD of hosts.

4 And in that day it shall come to pass, that the glory of Jacob shall be made thin, and the fatness of his flesh shall wax lean.

5 And it shall be as when the harvestman gathers the corn, and reaps the ears with his arm; and it shall be as he that gathers ears in the valley of Rephaim.

6 Yet gleaning grapes shall be left in it, as the shaking of an olive tree, two or three berries in the top of the uppermost bough, four or five in the outmost fruitful branches thereof, says the LORD God of Israel.

7 At that day shall a man look to his Maker, and his eyes shall have respect to the Holy One of Israel.

8 And he shall not look to the altars, the work of his hands, neither shall respect that which his fingers have made, either the groves, or the images.

9 In that day shall his strong cities be as a forsaken bough, and an uppermost branch, which they left because of the children of Israel: and there shall be desolation.

10 Because you have forgotten the God of your salvation, and have not been mindful of the rock of your strength, therefore shall you plant pleasant plants, and shall set it with strange slips:

11 In the day shall you make your plant to grow, and in the morning shall you make your seed to flourish: but the harvest shall be a heap in the day of grief and of desperate sorrow.

12 Woe to the multitude of many people, which make a noise like the noise of the seas; and to the rushing of nations, that make a rushing like the rushing of mighty waters!

13 The nations shall rush like the rushing of many waters: but God shall rebuke them, and they shall flee far off, and shall be chased as the chaff of the mountains before the wind, and like a rolling thing before the whirlwind.

14 And behold at eveningtide trouble; and before the morning he is not. This is the portion of them that spoil us, and the lot of them that rob us.

CHAPTER 18

WOE to the land shadowing with wings, which is beyond the rivers of Ethiopia:

2 That sends ambassadors by the sea, even in vessels of bulrushes upon the waters, saying, Go, you swift messengers, to a nation scattered and peeled, to a people terrible from their beginning hitherto; a nation meted out and trodden down, whose land the rivers have spoiled!

3 All you inhabitants of the world, and dwellers on the earth, you see it, when he lifts up an ensign on the mountains; and when he blows a trumpet, you hear it.

4 For so the LORD said to me, I will take my rest, and I will consider in my dwelling place like a clear heat upon herbs, and like a cloud of dew in the heat of harvest.

5 For afore the harvest, when the bud is perfect, and the sour grape is ripening in the flower, he shall both cut off the sprigs with pruning hooks, and take away and cut down the branches.

6 They shall be left together to the fowls of the mountains, and to the beasts of the earth: and the fowls shall summer upon them, and all the beasts of the earth shall winter upon them.

7 In that time shall the present be brought to the LORD of hosts of a people scattered and peeled, and from a people terrible from their beginning hitherto; a nation meted out and trodden under foot, whose land the rivers have spoiled, to the place of the name of the LORD of hosts, the mount Zion.

CHAPTER 19

THE burden of Egypt. Behold, the LORD rides upon a swift cloud, and shall come into Egypt: and the idols of Egypt shall be moved at his presence, and the heart of Egypt shall melt in the midst of it.

2 And I will set the Egyptians against the Egyptians: and they shall fight every one against his brother, and every one against his neighbour; city against city, and kingdom against kingdom.

3 And the spirit of Egypt shall fail in the midst thereof; and I will destroy the counsel thereof: and they shall seek to the idols, and to the charmers, and to them that have familiar spirits, and to the wizards.

4 And the Egyptians will I give over into the hand of a cruel lord; and a fierce king shall rule over them, says the Lord, the LORD of hosts.

5 And the waters shall fail from the sea, and the river shall be wasted and dried up.

6 And they shall turn the rivers far away; and the brooks of defence shall be

emptied and dried up: the reeds and flags shall wither.

7 The paper reeds by the brooks, by the mouth of the brooks, and every thing sown by the brooks, shall wither, be driven away, and be no more.

8 The fishers also shall mourn, and all they that cast angle into the brooks shall lament, and they that spread nets upon the waters shall languish.

9 Moreover they that work in fine flax, and they that weave networks, shall be confounded.

10 And they shall be broken in the purposes thereof, all that make sluices and ponds for fish.

11 Surely the princes of Zoan are fools, the counsel of the wise counselors of Pharaoh is become brutish: how do you say to Pharaoh, I am the son of the wise, the son of ancient kings?

12 Where are they? where are your wise men? and let them tell you now, and let them know what the LORD of hosts has purposed upon Egypt.

13 The princes of Zoan are become fools, the princes of Noph are deceived; they have also seduced Egypt, even they that are the stay of the tribes thereof.

14 The LORD has mingled a perverse spirit in the midst thereof: and they have caused Egypt to err in every work thereof, as a drunken man staggers in his vomit.

15 Neither shall there be any work for Egypt, which the head or tail, branch or rush, may do.

16 In that day shall Egypt be like women: and it shall be afraid and fear because of the shaking of the hand of the LORD of hosts, which he shakes over it.

17 And the land of Judah shall be a terror to Egypt, every one that makes mention thereof shall be afraid in himself, because of the counsel of the LORD of hosts, which he has determined against it.

18 In that day shall five cities in the land of Egypt speak the language of Canaan, and swear to the LORD of hosts; one shall be called, The city of destruction.

19 In that day shall there be an altar to the LORD in the midst of the land of Egypt, and a pillar at the border thereof to the LORD.

20 And it shall be for a sign and for a witness to the LORD of hosts in the land of Egypt: for they shall cry to the LORD because of the oppressors, and he shall send them a saviour, and a great one, and he shall deliver them.

21 And the LORD shall be known to Egypt, and the Egyptians shall know the LORD in that day, and shall do sacrifice and oblation; yea, they shall vow a vow to the LORD, and perform it.

22 And the LORD shall smite Egypt: he shall smite and heal it: and they shall return even to the LORD, and he shall be intreated of them, and shall heal them.

23 In that day shall there be a highway out of Egypt to Assyria, and the Assyrian shall come into Egypt, and the Egyptian into Assyria, and the Egyptians shall serve with the Assyrians.

24 In that day shall Israel be the third with Egypt and with Assyria, even a blessing in the midst of the land:

25 Whom the LORD of hosts shall bless, saying, Blessed be Egypt my people, and Assyria the work of my hands, and Israel my inheritance.

CHAPTER 20

IN the year that Tartan came to Ashdod, (when Sargon the king of Assyria sent him,) and fought against Ashdod, and took it;

2 At the same time spoke the LORD by Isaiah the son of Amoz, saying, Go and loose the sackcloth from off your loins, and put off your shoe from your foot. And he did so, walking naked and barefoot.

19:20 Was Jesus God in human form? See Matthew 8:2 comment.

3 And the LORD said, Like as my servant Isaiah has walked naked and barefoot three years for a sign and wonder upon Egypt and upon Ethiopia;
4 So shall the king of Assyria lead away the Egyptians prisoners, and the Ethiopians captives, young and old, naked and barefoot, even with their buttocks uncovered, to the shame of Egypt.
5 And they shall be afraid and ashamed of Ethiopia their expectation, and of Egypt their glory.
6 And the inhabitant of this isle shall say in that day, Behold, such is our expectation, where we flee for help to be delivered from the king of Assyria: and how shall we escape?

CHAPTER 21

THE burden of the desert of the sea. As whirlwinds in the south pass through; so it comes from the desert, from a terrible land.
2 A grievous vision is declared to me; the treacherous dealer deals treacherously, and the spoiler spoils. Go up, O Elam: besiege, O Media; all the sighing thereof have I made to cease.
3 Therefore are my loins filled with pain: pangs have taken hold upon me, as the pangs of a woman that travails: I was bowed down at the hearing of it; I was dismayed at the seeing of it.
4 My heart panted, fearfulness affrighted me: the night of my pleasure has he turned into fear to me.
5 Prepare the table, watch in the watchtower, eat, drink: arise, you princes, and anoint the shield.
6 For thus has the LORD said to me, Go, set a watchman, let him declare what he sees.
7 And he saw a chariot with a couple of horsemen, a chariot of asses, and a chariot of camels; and he hearkened diligently with much heed:
8 And he cried, A lion: My lord, I stand continually upon the watchtower in the daytime, and I am set in my ward whole nights:

9 And, behold, here comes a chariot of men, with a couple of horsemen. And he answered and said, Babylon is fallen, is fallen; and all the graven images of her gods he has broken to the ground.
10 O my threshing, and the corn of my floor: that which I have heard of the LORD of hosts, the God of Israel, have I declared to you.
11 The burden of Dumah. He calls to me out of Seir, Watchman, what of the night? Watchman, what of the night?
12 The watchman said, The morning comes, and also the night: if you will enquire, enquire: return, come.
13 The burden upon Arabia. In the forest in Arabia shall you lodge, O you travelling companies of Dedanim.
14 The inhabitants of the land of Tema brought water to him that was thirsty, they prevented with their bread him that fled.
15 For they fled from the swords, from the drawn sword, and from the bent bow, and from the grievousness of war.
16 For thus has the LORD said to me, Within a year, according to the years of an hireling, and all the glory of Kedar shall fail:
17 And the residue of the number of archers, the mighty men of the children of Kedar, shall be diminished: for the LORD God of Israel has spoken it.

CHAPTER 22

THE burden of the valley of vision. What ails you now, that you are wholly gone up to the housetops?
2 You that are full of stirs, a tumultuous city, joyous city: your slain men are not slain with the sword, nor dead in battle.
3 All your rulers are fled together, they are bound by the archers: all that are found in you are bound together, which have fled from far.
4 Therefore said I, Look away from me; I will weep bitterly, labour not to comfort me, because of the spoiling of the daughter of my people.

5 For it is a day of trouble, and of treading down, and of perplexity by the Lord GOD of hosts in the valley of vision, breaking down the walls, and of crying to the mountains.

6 And Elam bare the quiver with chariots of men and horsemen, and Kir uncovered the shield.

7 And it shall come to pass, that your choicest valleys shall be full of chariots, and the horsemen shall set themselves in array at the gate.

8 And he discovered the covering of Judah, and you did look in that day to the armour of the house of the forest.

9 You have seen also the breaches of the city of David, that they are many: and you gathered together the waters of the lower pool.

10 And you have numbered the houses of Jerusalem, and the houses have you broken down to fortify the wall.

11 You made also a ditch between the two walls for the water of the old pool: but you have not looked to the maker thereof, neither had respect to him that fashioned it long ago.

12 And in that day did the Lord GOD of hosts call to weeping, and to mourning, and to baldness, and to girding with sackcloth:

13 And behold joy and gladness, slaying oxen, and killing sheep, eating flesh, and drinking wine: let us eat and drink; for tomorrow we shall die.

14 And it was revealed in my ears by the LORD of hosts, Surely this iniquity shall not be purged from you till you die, says the Lord GOD of hosts.

15 Thus says the Lord GOD of hosts, Go, get to this treasurer, even to Shebna, which is over the house, and say,

16 What have you here? and whom have you here, that you have hewed out a sepulchre here, as he that hews him out a sepulchre on high, and that carves a habitation for himself in a rock?

17 Behold, the LORD will carry you away with a mighty captivity, and will surely cover you.

18 He will surely violently turn and toss you like a ball into a large country: there shall you die, and there the chariots of your glory shall be the shame of your lord's house.

19 And I will drive you from your station, and from your state shall he pull you down.

20 And it shall come to pass in that day, that I will call my servant Eliakim the son of Hilkiah:

21 And I will clothe him with your robe, and strengthen him with your girdle, and I will commit your government into his hand: and he shall be a father to the inhabitants of Jerusalem, and to the house of Judah.

22 And the key of the house of David will I lay upon his shoulder; so he shall open, and none shall shut; and he shall shut, and none shall open.

23 And I will fasten him as a nail in a sure place; and he shall be for a glorious throne to his father's house.

24 And they shall hang upon him all the glory of his father's house, the offspring and the issue, all vessels of small quantity, from the vessels of cups, even to all the vessels of flagons.

25 In that day, says the LORD of hosts, shall the nail that is fastened in the sure place be removed, and be cut down, and fall; and the burden that was upon it shall be cut off: for the LORD has spoken it.

CHAPTER 23

THE burden of Tyre. Howl, you ships of Tarshish; for it is laid waste, so that there is no house, no entering in: from the land of Chittim it is revealed to them.

2 Be still, you inhabitants of the isle; you whom the merchants of Zidon, that pass over the sea, have replenished.

3 And by great waters the seed of Sihor, the harvest of the river, is her revenue; and she is a mart of nations.

4 Be ashamed, O Zidon: for the sea has spoken, even the strength of the sea, say-

ing, I travail not, nor bring forth children, neither do I nourish up young men, nor bring up virgins.

5 As at the report concerning Egypt, so shall they be sorely pained at the report of Tyre.

6 Pass over to Tarshish; howl, you inhabitants of the isle.

7 Is this your joyous city, whose antiquity is of ancient days? her own feet shall carry her afar off to sojourn.

8 Who has taken this counsel against Tyre, the crowning city, whose merchants are princes, whose traffickers are the honourable of the earth?

9 The LORD of hosts has purposed it, to stain the pride of all glory, and to bring into contempt all the honourable of the earth.

10 Pass through your land as a river, O daughter of Tarshish: there is no more strength.

11 He stretched out his hand over the sea, he shook the kingdoms: the LORD has given a commandment against the merchant city, to destroy the strong holds thereof.

12 And he said, You shall no more rejoice, O you oppressed virgin, daughter of Zidon: arise, pass over to Chittim; there also you will have no rest.

13 Behold the land of the Chaldeans; this people was not, till the Assyrian founded it for them that dwell in the wilderness: they set up the towers thereof, they raised up the palaces thereof; and he brought it to ruin.

14 Howl, you ships of Tarshish: for your strength is laid waste.

15 And it shall come to pass in that day, that Tyre shall be forgotten seventy years, according to the days of one king: after the end of seventy years shall Tyre sing as an harlot.

16 Take a harp, go about the city, you harlot that has been forgotten; make sweet melody, sing many songs, that you may be remembered.

17 And it shall come to pass after the end of seventy years, that the LORD will visit Tyre, and she shall turn to her hire, and shall commit fornication with all the kingdoms of the world upon the face of the earth.

18 And her merchandise and her hire shall be holiness to the LORD: it shall not be treasured nor laid up; for her merchandise shall be for them that dwell before the LORD, to eat sufficiently, and for durable clothing.

CHAPTER 24

B EHOLD, the LORD makes the earth empty, and makes it waste, and turns it upside down, and scatters abroad the inhabitants thereof.

2 And it shall be, as with the people, so with the priest; as with the servant, so with his master; as with the maid, so with her mistress; as with the buyer, so with the seller; as with the lender, so with the borrower; as with the taker of usury, so with the giver of usury to him.

3 The land shall be utterly emptied, and utterly spoiled: for the LORD has spoken this word.

4 The earth mourns and fades away, the world languishes and fades away, the haughty people of the earth do languish.

5 The earth also is defiled under the inhabitants thereof; because they have transgressed the laws, changed the ordinance, broken the everlasting covenant.

6 Therefore has the curse devoured the earth, and they that dwell therein are desolate: therefore the inhabitants of the earth are burned, and few men left.

7 The new wine mourns, the vine languishes, all the merryhearted do sigh.

8 The mirth of tabrets ceases, the noise of them that rejoice ends, the joy of the harp ceases.

9 They shall not drink wine with a song; strong drink shall be bitter to them that drink it.

10 The city of confusion is broken down: every house is shut up, that no man may come in.

11 There is a crying for wine in the streets; all joy is darkened, the mirth of the land is gone.

12 In the city is left desolation, and the gate is smitten with destruction.

13 When thus it shall be in the midst of the land among the people, there shall be as the shaking of an olive tree, and as the gleaning grapes when the vintage is done.

14 They shall lift up their voice, they shall sing for the majesty of the LORD, they shall cry aloud from the sea.

15 Therefore glorify the LORD in the fires, even the name of the LORD God of Israel in the isles of the sea.

16 From the uttermost part of the earth have we heard songs, even glory to the righteous. But I said, My leanness, my leanness, woe to me! the treacherous dealers have dealt treacherously; yea, the treacherous dealers have dealt very treacherously.

17 Fear, and the pit, and the snare, are upon you, O inhabitant of the earth.

18 And it shall come to pass, that he who flees from the noise of the fear shall fall into the pit; and he that comes up out of the midst of the pit shall be taken in the snare: for the windows from on high are open, and the foundations of the earth do shake.

19 The earth is utterly broken down, the earth is clean dissolved, the earth is moved exceedingly.

20 The earth shall reel to and fro like a drunkard, and shall be removed like a cottage; and the transgression thereof shall be heavy upon it; and it shall fall, and not rise again.

21 And it shall come to pass in that day, that the LORD shall punish the host of the high ones that are on high, and the kings of the earth upon the earth.

22 And they shall be gathered together, as prisoners are gathered in the pit, and shall be shut up in the prison, and after many days shall they be visited.

23 Then the moon shall be confounded, and the sun ashamed, when the LORD of hosts shall reign in mount Zion, and in Jerusalem, and before his ancients gloriously.

CHAPTER 25

O LORD, you are my God; I will exalt you, I will praise your name; for you have done wonderful things; your counsels of old are faithfulness and truth.

2 For you have made of a city an heap; of a defenced city a ruin: a palace of strangers to be no city; it shall never be built.

3 Therefore shall the strong people glorify you, the city of the terrible nations shall fear you.

4 For you have been a strength to the poor, a strength to the needy in his distress, a refuge from the storm, a shadow from the heat, when the blast of the terrible ones is as a storm against the wall.

5 You shall bring down the noise of strangers, as the heat in a dry place; even the heat with the shadow of a cloud: the branch of the terrible ones shall be brought low.

6 And in this mountain shall the LORD of hosts make for all people a feast of fat things, a feast of wines on the lees, of fat things full of marrow, of wines on the lees well refined.

7 And he will destroy in this mountain the face of the covering cast over all people, and the vail that is spread over all nations.

8 **He will swallow up death in victory; and the Lord GOD will wipe away tears from off all faces; and the rebuke of his people shall he take away from off all the earth: for the LORD has spoken it.**

9 **And it shall be said in that day, Lo, this is our God; we have waited for him,**

25:8-9 God spoke to death, and it could not hold Him. (Also see: Isaiah 9:1-2 and Matthew 4:16) How we long for this day; and how the world will regret beyond words its rejection of the gospel.

and he will save us: this is the LORD; we have waited for him, we will be glad and rejoice in his salvation.

10 For in this mountain shall the hand of the LORD rest, and Moab shall be trodden down under him, even as straw is trodden down for the dunghill.

11 And he shall spread forth his hands in the midst of them, as he that swims spreads forth his hands to swim: and he shall bring down their pride together with the spoils of their hands.

12 And the fortress of the high fort of your walls shall he bring down, lay low, and bring to the ground, even to the dust.

CHAPTER 26

IN that day shall this song be sung in the land of Judah; We have a strong city; salvation will God appoint for walls and bulwarks.

2 Open the gates, that the righteous nation which keeps the truth may enter in.

3 You will keep him in perfect peace, whose mind is stayed on you: because he trusts in you.

4 Trust in the LORD for ever: for in the LORD JEHOVAH is everlasting strength:

5 For he brings down them that dwell on high; the lofty city, he lays it low; he lays it low, even to the ground; he brings it even to the dust.

6 The foot shall tread it down, even the feet of the poor, and the steps of the needy.

7 The way of the just is uprightness: you, most upright, dost weigh the path of the just.

8 Yea, in the way of your judgments, O LORD, have we waited for you; the desire of our soul is to your name, and to the remembrance of you.

9 With my soul have I desired you in the night; yea, with my spirit within me will I seek you early: for when your judgments are in the earth, the inhabitants of the world will learn righteousness.

10 Let favour be shown to the wicked, yet will he not learn righteousness: in the land of uprightness will he deal unjustly, and will not behold the majesty of the LORD.

11 LORD, when your hand is lifted up, they will not see: but they shall see, and be ashamed for their envy at the people; yea, the fire of your enemies shall devour them.

12 LORD, you will ordain peace for us: for you also have done all our works in us.

13 O LORD our God, other lords beside you have had dominion over us: but by you only will we make mention of your name.

14 They are dead, they shall not live; they are deceased, they shall not rise: therefore have you visited and destroyed them, and made all their memory to perish.

15 You have increased the nation, O LORD, you have increased the nation: you are glorified: you had removed it far to all the ends of the earth.

16 LORD, in trouble have they visited you, they poured out a prayer when your chastening was upon them.

17 Like as a woman with child, that draws near the time of her delivery, is in pain, and cries out in her pangs; so have we been in your sight, O LORD.

18 We have been with child, we have been in pain, we have as it were brought forth wind; we have not accomplished any deliverance in the earth; neither have the inhabitants of the world fallen.

19 Your dead men shall live, together with my dead body shall they arise. Awake and sing, you that dwell in dust: for your dew is as the dew of herbs, and the earth shall cast out the dead.

20 Come, my people, enter into your chambers, and shut your doors about you: hide yourself as it were for a little moment, until the indignation is overpast.

21 For, behold, the LORD comes out of his place to punish the inhabitants of the

earth for their iniquity: the earth also shall disclose her blood, and shall no more cover her slain.

CHAPTER 27

IN that day the LORD with his sore and great and strong sword shall punish leviathan the piercing serpent, even leviathan that crooked serpent; and he shall slay the dragon that is in the sea.

> "The effect of not believing in God is to believe in anything."
>
> **GILBERT K. CHESTERTON**
>
> **1874 - 1936**
>
> **ENGLISH AUTHOR**

2 In that day sing to her, A vineyard of red wine.
3 I the LORD do keep it; I will water it every moment: lest any hurt it, I will keep it night and day.
4 Fury is not in me: who would set the briers and thorns against me in battle? I would go through them, I would burn them together.
5 Or let him take hold of my strength, that he may make peace with me; and he shall make peace with me.
6 He shall cause them that come of Jacob to take root: Israel shall blossom and bud, and fill the face of the world with fruit.
7 Has he smitten him, as he smote those that smote him? or is he slain according to the slaughter of them that are slain by him?
8 In measure, when it shoots forth, you will debate with it: he stays his rough wind in the day of the east wind.
9 By this therefore shall the iniquity of Jacob be purged; and this is all the fruit to take away his sin; when he makes all the stones of the altar as chalkstones that are beaten in sunder, the groves and images shall not stand up.
10 Yet the defenced city shall be desolate, and the habitation forsaken, and left like a wilderness: there shall the calf feed, and there shall he lie down, and consume the branches thereof.
11 When the boughs thereof are withered, they shall be broken off: the women come, and set them on fire: for it is a people of no understanding: therefore he that made them will not have mercy on them, and he that formed them will show them no favour.
12 And it shall come to pass in that day, that the LORD shall beat off from the channel of the river to the stream of Egypt, and you shall be gathered one by one, O you children of Israel.
13 And it shall come to pass in that day, that the great trumpet shall be blown, and they shall come which were ready to perish in the land of Assyria, and the outcasts in the land of Egypt, and shall worship the LORD in the holy mount at Jerusalem.

CHAPTER 28

WOE to the crown of pride, to the drunkards of Ephraim, whose glorious beauty is a fading flower, which are on the head of the fat valleys of them that are overcome with wine!
2 Behold, the Lord has a mighty and strong one, which as a tempest of hail and a destroying storm, as a flood of mighty waters overflowing, shall cast down to the earth with the hand.
3 The crown of pride, the drunkards of Ephraim, shall be trodden under feet:
4 And the glorious beauty, which is on the head of the fat valley, shall be a fading flower, and as the hasty fruit before the summer; which when he that looks upon it sees, while it is yet in his hand he eats it up.
5 In that day shall the LORD of hosts be for a crown of glory, and for a diadem of beauty, to the residue of his people,
6 And for a spirit of judgment to him that sits in judgment, and for strength to them that turn the battle to the gate.
7 But they also have erred through wine, and through strong drink are out of the way; the priest and the prophet

SPRINGBOARDS FOR PREACHING AND WITNESSING

The A-Frame Roof

28:16

A TV news reporter once said, "Tonight we will look at the buying and selling of the world's most priceless commodity-information." He was right; information is the world's most priceless commodity. If you have information as to where oil deposits are, or you have information about the location of gold or diamonds in the earth, you can be a billionaire overnight. Information can even save your life. If you are in a building that is on fire, and you know the location of the fire escapes, you can find your way out. If you are without that information, you will probably die. Your actions will be governed by information, what you know and what you don't know.

This principle is demonstrated by the story of a man who wanted to paint his steep, A-frame roof. As his ladder was too short to reach the top, he threw a strong rope over the roof, went around the other side and carefully secured the rope to the back of his car. Then he went around the back of the house, climbed up onto his roof, tied the rope firmly around his waist and began painting. His wife, not knowing what he had done, came out of the house, car keys in hand, got into the car and drove off. He was pulled over the top of the roof and was seriously injured.

Perhaps you see nothing wrong with believing the theory of evolution or some other theory about our origins. But remember, your information will govern your actions. If you believe a drink contains poison, you won't drink it. If you believe it is okay, you will drink it. If you believe evolution is true, and from that premise believe that the Bible is false, you won't then repent. Why should you? Like the man who secured himself to the car, you will find you are only as secure as that to which you have secured yourself. If your faith is placed in evolution and not in God's promises, you will find that what you have tied yourself to will be your eternal downfall. You will perish because you refused information that would have saved you.

---

have erred through strong drink, they are swallowed up of wine, they are out of the way through strong drink; they err in vision, they stumble in judgment.

8 For all tables are full of vomit and filthiness, so that there is no place clean.

9 Whom shall he teach knowledge? and whom shall he make to understand doctrine? them that are weaned from the milk, and drawn from the breasts.

10 For precept must be upon precept, precept upon precept; line upon line, line upon line; here a little, and there a little:

11 For with stammering lips and another tongue will he speak to this people.

12 To whom he said, This is the rest wherewith you may cause the weary to rest; and this is the refreshing: yet they would not hear.

13 But the word of the LORD was to them precept upon precept, precept upon precept; line upon line, line upon line; here a little, and there a little; that they might go, and fall backward, and be broken, and snared, and taken.

14 Therefore hear the word of the LORD, you scornful men, that rule this people which is in Jerusalem.

15 Because you have said, We have made a covenant with death, and with hell are we at agreement; when the overflowing scourge shall pass through, it shall not come to us: for we have made lies our refuge, and under falsehood have we hid ourselves:

16 Therefore thus says the Lord GOD, Behold, I lay in Zion for a foundation a stone, a tried stone, a precious corner stone, a sure foundation: he that believeth shall not make haste.

17 Judgment also will I lay to the line, and righteousness to the plummet: and the hail shall sweep away the refuge of lies, and the waters shall overflow the hiding place.

18 And your covenant with death shall be disannulled, and your agreement with hell shall not stand; when the overflowing scourge shall pass through, then you shall be trodden down by it.

19 From the time that it goeth forth it shall take you: for morning by morning shall it pass over, by day and by night: and it shall be a vexation only to understand the report.

20 For the bed is shorter than that a man can stretch himself on it: and the covering narrower than that he can wrap himself in it.

21 For the LORD shall rise up as in mount Perazim, he shall be wroth as in the valley of Gibeon, that he may do his work, his strange work; and bring to pass his act, his strange act.

22 Now therefore do not be mockers, lest your bands be made strong: for I have heard from the Lord GOD of hosts a consumption, even determined upon the whole earth.

23 Give ear, and hear my voice; hearken, and hear my speech.

24 Does the plowman plow all day to sow? does he open and break the clods of his ground?

25 When he has made plain the face thereof, does he not cast abroad the fitches, and scatter the cummin, and cast in the principal wheat and the appointed barley and the rie in their place?

26 For his God does instruct him to discretion, and does teach him.

27 For the fitches are not threshed with a threshing instrument, neither is a cart wheel turned about upon the cummin; but the fitches are beaten out with a staff, and the cummin with a rod.

28 Bread corn is bruised; because he will not ever be threshing it, nor break it with the wheel of his cart, nor bruise it with his horsemen.

29 This also comes forth from the LORD of hosts, which is wonderful in counsel, and excellent in working.

CHAPTER 29

WOE to Ariel, to Ariel, the city where David dwelt! add year to year; let them kill sacrifices.

2 Yet I will distress Ariel, and there shall be heaviness and sorrow: and it shall be to me as Ariel.

3 And I will camp against you round about, and will lay siege against you with a mount, and I will raise forts against you.

4 And you shall be brought down, and shall speak out of the ground, and your speech shall be low out of the dust, and your voice shall be, as of one that has a familiar spirit, out of the ground, and your speech shall whisper out of the dust.

5 Moreover the multitude of your strangers shall be like small dust, and the multitude of the terrible ones shall be as chaff that passes away: yea, it shall be at an instant suddenly.

6 You shall be visited of the LORD of hosts with thunder, and with earthquake, and great noise, with storm and tempest, and the flame of devouring fire.

7 And the multitude of all the nations that fight against Ariel, even all that fight against her and her munition, and that distress her, shall be as a dream of a night vision.

8 It shall even be as when an hungry man dreams, and, behold, he eats; but he awakes, and his soul is empty: or as when a thirsty man dreams, and, behold, he drinks; but he awakes, and, behold, he is faint, and his soul has appetite: so shall the multitude of all the nations be, that fight against mount Zion.

9 Stay yourselves, and wonder; cry out, and cry: they are drunken, but not with wine; they stagger, but not with strong drink.

10 For the LORD has poured out upon you the spirit of deep sleep, and has closed your eyes: the prophets and your rulers, the seers has he covered.

11 And the vision of all is become to you as the words of a book that is sealed,

which men deliver to one that is learned, saying, Read this, I pray you: and he says, I cannot; for it is sealed:

12 And the book is delivered to him that is not learned, saying, Read this, I pray you: and he says, I am not learned.

13 Therefore the Lord said, Forasmuch as this people draw near me with their mouth, and with their lips do honour me, but have removed their heart far from me, and their fear toward me is taught by the precept of men:

14 Therefore, behold, I will proceed to do a marvelous work among this people, even a marvelous work and a wonder: for the wisdom of their wise men shall perish, and the understanding of their prudent men shall be hid.

15 Woe to them that seek deep to hide their counsel from the LORD, and their works are in the dark, and they say, Who sees us? and who knows us?

16 Surely your turning of things upside down shall be esteemed as the potter's clay: for shall the work say of him that made it, He made me not? or shall the thing framed say of him that framed it, He had no understanding?

17 Is it not yet a very little while, and Lebanon shall be turned into a fruitful field, and the fruitful field shall be esteemed as a forest?

18 And in that day shall the deaf hear the words of the book, and the eyes of the blind shall see out of obscurity, and out of darkness.

19 The meek also shall increase their joy in the LORD, and the poor among men shall rejoice in the Holy One of Israel.

20 For the terrible one is brought to nothing, and the scorner is consumed, and all that watch for iniquity are cut off:

21 That make a man an offender for a word, and lay a snare for him that reproves in the gate, and turn aside the just for a thing of nought.

22 Therefore thus says the LORD, who redeemed Abraham, concerning the house of Jacob, Jacob shall not now be

> "From beginning to ending, there is not a word or syllable or revelation in the Word of God that has contradicted, or ever will contradict, any true, substantiated scientific fact."
>
> **WALLIE AMOS CRISWELL**
> **1909-2002**
> **PASTOR**
> **FIRST BAPTIST CHURCH, DALLAS**

ashamed, neither shall his face now wax pale.

23 But when he sees his children, the work of my hands, in the midst of him, they shall sanctify my name, and sanctify the Holy One of Jacob, and shall fear the God of Israel.

24 They also that erred in spirit shall come to understanding, and they that murmured shall learn doctrine.

CHAPTER 30

WOE to the rebellious children, says the LORD, that take counsel, but not of me; and that cover with a covering, but not of my spirit, that they may add sin to sin:

2 That walk to go down into Egypt, and have not asked at my mouth; to strengthen themselves in the strength of Pharaoh, and to trust in the shadow of Egypt!

3 Therefore shall the strength of Pharaoh be your shame, and the trust in the shadow of Egypt your confusion.

4 For his princes were at Zoan, and his ambassadors came to Hanes.

5 They were all ashamed of a people that could not profit them, nor be an help nor profit, but a shame, and also a reproach.

6 The burden of the beasts of the south: into the land of trouble and anguish, from which come the young and old lion, the viper and fiery flying serpent, they will carry their riches upon the shoulders of young asses, and their trea-

sures upon the bunches of camels, to a people that shall not profit them.

7 For the Egyptians shall help in vain, and to no purpose: therefore have I cried concerning this, Their strength is to sit still.

8 Now go, write it before them in a table, and note it in a book, that it may be for the time to come for ever and ever:

9 That this is a rebellious people, lying children, children that will not hear the law of the LORD:

10 Which say to the seers, See not; and to the prophets, Prophesy not to us right things, speak to us smooth things, prophesy deceits:

11 Get you out of the way, turn aside out of the path, cause the Holy One of Israel to cease from before us.

12 Therefore thus says the Holy One of Israel, Because you despise this word, and trust in oppression and perverseness, and stay thereon:

13 Therefore this iniquity shall be to you as a breach ready to fall, swelling out in a high wall, whose breaking comes suddenly at an instant.

14 And he shall break it as the breaking of the potters' vessel that is broken in pieces; he shall not spare: so that there shall not be found in the bursting of it a sherd to take fire from the hearth, or to take water withal out of the pit.

15 For thus says the Lord GOD, the Holy One of Israel; In returning and rest shall you be saved; in quietness and in confidence shall be your strength: and you would not.

16 But you said, No; for we will flee upon horses; therefore shall you flee: and, We will ride upon the swift; therefore shall they that pursue you be swift.

17 One thousand shall flee at the rebuke of one; at the rebuke of five shall you flee: till you are left as a beacon upon the top of a mountain, and as an ensign on an hill.

18 And therefore will the LORD wait, that he may be gracious to you, and therefore will he be exalted, that he may have mercy upon you: for the LORD is a God of judgment: blessed are all they that wait for him.

19 For the people shall dwell in Zion at Jerusalem: you shall weep no more: he will be very gracious to you at the voice of your cry; when he shall hear it, he will answer you.

20 And though the Lord give you the bread of adversity, and the water of affliction, yet your teachers shall not be removed into a corner any more, but your eyes shall see your teachers:

21 And your ears shall hear a word behind you, saying, This is the way, walk in it, when you turn to the right hand, and when you turn to the left.

22 You shall defile also the covering of your graven images of silver, and the ornament of your molten images of gold: you shall cast them away as a menstruous cloth; you shall say to it, Get thee hence.

23 Then shall he give the rain of your seed, that you shall sow the ground withal; and bread of the increase of the earth, and it shall be fat and plenteous: in that day shall your cattle feed in large pastures.

24 The oxen likewise and the young asses that ear the ground shall eat clean provender, which has been winnowed with the shovel and with the fan.

25 And there shall be upon every high mountain, and upon every high hill, rivers and streams of waters in the day of the great slaughter, when the towers fall.

26 Moreover the light of the moon shall be as the light of the sun, and the light of the sun shall be sevenfold, as the light of seven days, in the day that the LORD binds up the breach of his people, and heals the stroke of their wound.

27 Behold, the name of the LORD comes from far, burning with his anger, and the burden thereof is heavy: his lips are full of indignation, and his tongue as a devouring fire:

28 And his breath, as an overflowing stream, shall reach to the midst of the neck, to sift the nations with the sieve of vanity: and there shall be a bridle in the jaws of the people, causing them to err.

29 You shall have a song, as in the night when a holy solemnity is kept; and gladness of heart, as when one goeth with a pipe to come into the mountain of the LORD, to the mighty One of Israel.

30 And the LORD shall cause his glorious voice to be heard, and shall show the lighting down of his arm, with the indignation of his anger, and with the flame of a devouring fire, with scattering, and tempest, and hailstones.

31 For through the voice of the LORD shall the Assyrian be beaten down, which smote with a rod.

32 And in every place where the grounded staff shall pass, which the LORD shall lay upon him, it shall be with tabrets and harps: and in battles of shaking will he fight with it.

33 For Tophet is ordained of old; yea, for the king it is prepared; he has made it deep and large: the pile thereof is fire and much wood; the breath of the LORD, like a stream of brimstone, does kindle it.

CHAPTER 31

WOE to them that go down to Egypt for help; and stay on horses, and trust in chariots, because they are many; and in horsemen, because they are very strong; but they look not to the Holy One of Israel, neither seek the LORD!

2 Yet he also is wise, and will bring evil, and will not call back his words: but will arise against the house of the evildoers, and against the help of them that work iniquity.

3 Now the Egyptians are men, and not God; and their horses flesh, and not spirit. When the LORD shall stretch out his hand, both he that helps shall fall, and he that is helped shall fall down, and they all shall fail together.

4 For thus has the LORD spoken to me, Like as the lion and the young lion roaring on his prey, when a multitude of shepherds is called forth against him, he will not be afraid of their voice, nor abase himself for the noise of them: so shall the LORD of hosts come down to fight for mount Zion, and for the hill thereof.

5 As birds flying, so will the LORD of hosts defend Jerusalem; defending also he will deliver it; and passing over he will preserve it.

6 Turn to him from whom the children of Israel have deeply revolted.

7 For in that day every man shall cast away his idols of silver, and his idols of gold, which your own hands have made to you for a sin.

8 Then shall the Assyrian fall with the sword, not of a mighty man; and the sword, not of a mean man, shall devour him: but he shall flee from the sword, and his young men shall be discomfited.

9 And he shall pass over to his strong hold for fear, and his princes shall be afraid of the ensign, says the LORD, whose fire is in Zion, and his furnace in Jerusalem.

CHAPTER 32

BEHOLD, a king shall reign in righteousness, and princes shall rule in judgment.

2 And a man shall be as an hiding place from the wind, and a covert from the tempest; as rivers of water in a dry place, as the shadow of a great rock in a weary land.

3 And the eyes of them that see shall not be dim, and the ears of them that hear shall hearken.

4 The heart also of the rash shall understand knowledge, and the tongue of the stammerers shall be ready to speak plainly.

5 The vile person shall be no more called liberal, nor the churl said to be bountiful.

6 For the vile person will speak villany, and his heart will work iniquity, to practise hypocrisy, and to utter error against the LORD, to make empty the soul of the hungry, and he will cause the drink of the thirsty to fail.

7 The instruments also of the churl are evil: he devises wicked devices to destroy the poor with lying words, even when the needy speaks right.

8 But the liberal devises liberal things; and by liberal things shall he stand.

9 Rise up, you women that are at ease; hear my voice, you careless daughters; give ear to my speech.

10 Many days and years shall you be troubled, you careless women: for the vintage shall fail, the gathering shall not come.

11 Tremble, you women that are at ease; be troubled, you careless ones: strip you, and make you bare, and gird sackcloth upon your loins.

12 They shall lament for the teats, for the pleasant fields, for the fruitful vine.

13 Upon the land of my people shall come up thorns and briers; yea, upon all the houses of joy in the joyous city:

14 Because the palaces shall be forsaken; the multitude of the city shall be left; the forts and towers shall be for dens for ever, a joy of wild asses, a pasture of flocks;

15 Until the spirit be poured upon us from on high, and the wilderness be a fruitful field, and the fruitful field be counted for a forest.

16 Then judgment shall dwell in the wilderness, and righteousness remain in the fruitful field.

17 And the work of righteousness shall be peace; and the effect of righteousness quietness and assurance for ever.

18 And my people shall dwell in a peaceable habitation, and in sure dwellings, and in quiet resting places;

19 When it shall hail, coming down on the forest; and the city shall be low in a low place.

20 Blessed are you that sow beside all waters, that send forth there the feet of the ox and the ass.

CHAPTER 33

WOE to you that spoils, and you were not spoiled; and deal treacherously, and they dealt not treacherously with you! when you shall cease to spoil, you shall be spoiled; and when you shall make an end to deal treacherously, they shall deal treacherously with you.

2 O LORD, be gracious to us; we have waited for you: be their arm every morning, our salvation also in the time of trouble.

3 At the noise of the tumult the people fled; at the lifting up of yourself the nations were scattered.

4 And your spoil shall be gathered like the gathering of the caterpiller: as the running to and fro of locusts shall he run upon them.

5 The LORD is exalted; for he dwells on high: he has filled Zion with judgment and righteousness.

6 And wisdom and knowledge shall be the stability of your times, and strength of salvation: the fear of the LORD is his treasure.

7 Behold, their valiant ones shall cry without: the ambassadors of peace shall weep bitterly.

8 The highways lie waste, the wayfaring man ceases: he has broken the covenant, he has despised the cities, he regards no man.

9 The earth mourns and languishes: Lebanon is ashamed and hewn down: Sharon is like a wilderness; and Bashan and Carmel shake off their fruits.

10 Now will I rise, says the LORD; now will I be exalted; now will I lift up myself.

11 You shall conceive chaff, you shall bring forth stubble: your breath, as fire, shall devour you.

12 And the people shall be as the burnings of lime: as thorns cut up shall they be burned in the fire.

13 Hear, you that are far off, what I have done; and, you that are near, acknowledge my might.

14 The sinners in Zion are afraid; fearfulness has surprised the hypocrites. Who among us shall dwell with the devouring fire? who among us shall dwell with everlasting burnings?

15 He that walks righteously, and speaks uprightly; he that despises the gain of oppressions, that shakes his hands from holding of bribes, that stops his ears from hearing of blood, and shuts his eyes from seeing evil;

16 He shall dwell on high: his place of defence shall be the munitions of rocks: bread shall be given him; his waters shall be sure.

17 Your eyes shall see the king in his beauty: they shall behold the land that is very far off.

18 Your heart shall meditate terror. Where is the scribe? where is the receiver? where is he that counted the towers?

19 You shall not see a fierce people, a people of a deeper speech than you can perceive; of a stammering tongue, that you can not understand.

20 Look upon Zion, the city of our solemnities: your eyes shall see Jerusalem a quiet habitation, a tabernacle that shall not be taken down; not one of the stakes thereof shall ever be removed, neither shall any of the cords thereof be broken.

21 But there the glorious LORD will be to us a place of broad rivers and streams; wherein shall go no galley with oars, neither shall gallant ship pass thereby.

22 For the LORD is our judge, the LORD is our lawgiver, the LORD is our king; he will save us.

23 Your tacklings are loosed; they could not well strengthen their mast, they could not spread the sail: then is the prey of a great spoil divided; the lame take the prey.

24 And the inhabitant shall not say, I am sick: the people that dwell therein shall be forgiven their iniquity.

CHAPTER 34

COME near, you nations, to hear; and hearken, you people: let the earth hear, and all that is therein; the world, and all things that come forth of it.

2 For the indignation of the LORD is upon all nations, and his fury upon all their armies: he has utterly destroyed them, he has delivered them to the slaughter.

3 Their slain also shall be cast out, and their stink shall come up out of their carcases, and the mountains shall be melted with their blood.

4 And all the host of heaven shall be dissolved, and the heavens shall be rolled together as a scroll: and all their host shall fall down, as the leaf falls off from the vine, and as a falling fig from the fig tree.

5 For my sword shall be bathed in heaven: behold, it shall come down upon Idumea, and upon the people of my curse, to judgment.

6 The sword of the LORD is filled with blood, it is made fat with fatness, and with the blood of lambs and goats, with the fat of the kidneys of rams: for the LORD has a sacrifice in Bozrah, and a great slaughter in the land of Idumea.

7 And the unicorns shall come down with them, and the bullocks with the bulls; and their land shall be soaked with blood, and their dust made fat with fatness.

8 For it is the day of the LORD's vengeance, and the year of recompences for the controversy of Zion.

9 And the streams thereof shall be turned into pitch, and the dust thereof into brimstone, and the land thereof shall become burning pitch.

10 It shall not be quenched night nor day; the smoke thereof shall go up for ever: from generation to generation it

shall lie waste; none shall pass through it for ever and ever.

11 But the cormorant and the bittern shall possess it; the owl also and the raven shall dwell in it: and he shall stretch out upon it the line of confusion, and the stones of emptiness.

12 They shall call the nobles thereof to the kingdom, but none shall be there, and all her princes shall be nothing.

13 And thorns shall come up in her palaces, nettles and brambles in the fortresses thereof: and it shall be an habitation of dragons, and a court for owls.

14 The wild beasts of the desert shall also meet with the wild beasts of the island, and the satyr shall cry to his fellow; the screech owl also shall rest there, and find for herself a place of rest.

15 There shall the great owl make her nest, and lay, and hatch, and gather under her shadow: there shall the vultures also be gathered, every one with her mate.

16 Seek out of the book of the LORD, and read: no one of these shall fail, none shall want her mate: for my mouth it has commanded, and his spirit it has gathered them.

17 And he has cast the lot for them, and his hand has divided it to them by line: they shall possess it for ever, from generation to generation shall they dwell therein.

CHAPTER 35

THE wilderness and the solitary place shall be glad for them; and the desert shall rejoice, and blossom as the rose.

2 It shall blossom abundantly, and rejoice even with joy and singing: the glory of Lebanon shall be given to it, the excellency of Carmel and Sharon, they shall see the glory of the LORD, and the excellency of our God.

3 *Strengthen the weak hands, and confirm the feeble knees.*

4 *Say to them that are of a fearful heart, Be strong, fear not: behold, your God will come with vengeance, even God with a recompence; he will come and save you.*

5 *Then the eyes of the blind shall be opened, and the ears of the deaf shall be unstopped.*

6 *Then shall the lame man leap as an hart, and the tongue of the dumb sing: for in the wilderness shall waters break out, and streams in the desert.*

7 *And the parched ground shall become a pool, and the thirsty land springs of water: in the habitation of dragons, where each lay, shall be grass with reeds and rushes.*

8 *And an highway shall be there, and a way, and it shall be called The way of holiness; the unclean shall not pass over it; but it shall be for those: the wayfaring men, though fools, shall not err therein.*

9 *No lion shall be there, nor any ravenous beast shall go up thereon, it shall not be found there; but the redeemed shall walk there:*

10 *And the ransomed of the LORD shall return, and come to Zion with songs and everlasting joy upon their heads: they shall obtain joy and gladness, and sorrow and sighing shall flee away.*

CHAPTER 36

NOW it came to pass in the fourteenth year of king Hezekiah, that Sennacherib king of Assyria came up against all the defenced cities of Judah, and took them.

2 And the king of Assyria sent Rabshakeh from Lachish to Jerusalem to king Hezekiah with a great army. And he stood by the conduit of the upper pool in the highway of the fuller's field.

3 Then came forth to him Eliakim, Hilkiah's son, which was over the house, and Shebna the scribe, and Joah, Asaph's son, the recorder.

4 And Rabshakeh said to them, Say now to Hezekiah, Thus says the great

king, the king of Assyria, What confidence is this wherein you trust?

5 I say, you say, (but they are but vain words) I have counsel and strength for war: now on whom do you trust, that you rebel against me?

6 Lo, you trust in the staff of this broken reed, on Egypt; whereon if a man lean, it will go into his hand, and pierce it: so is Pharaoh king of Egypt to all that trust in him.

7 But if you say to me, We trust in the LORD our God: is it not he, whose high places and whose altars Hezekiah has taken away, and said to Judah and to Jerusalem, You shall worship before this altar?

8 Now therefore give pledges, I pray you, to my master the king of Assyria, and I will give you two thousand horses, if you are able on your part to set riders upon them.

9 How then will you turn away the face of one captain of the least of my master's servants, and put your trust on Egypt for chariots and for horsemen?

10 And am I now come up without the LORD against this land to destroy it? the LORD said to me, Go up against this land, and destroy it.

11 Then said Eliakim and Shebna and Joah to Rabshakeh, Speak, I pray you, to your servants in the Syrian language; for we understand it: and speak not to us in the Jews' language, in the ears of the people that are on the wall.

12 But Rabshakeh said, Has my master sent me to your master and to you to speak these words? has he not sent me to the men that sit upon the wall, that they may eat their own dung, and drink their own piss with you?

13 Then Rabshakeh stood, and cried with a loud voice in the Jews' language, and said, Hear the words of the great king, the king of Assyria.

14 Thus says the king, Let not Hezekiah deceive you: for he shall not be able to deliver you.

15 Neither let Hezekiah make you trust in the LORD, saying, The LORD will surely deliver us: this city shall not be delivered into the hand of the king of Assyria.

16 Hearken not to Hezekiah: for thus says the king of Assyria, Make an agreement with me by a present, and come out to me: and every one of you eat from his own vine, and every one from his own fig tree, and every one of you drink the waters of his own cistern;

17 Until I come and take you away to a land like your own land, a land of corn and wine, a land of bread and vineyards.

18 Beware lest Hezekiah persuade you, saying, the LORD will deliver us. Has any of the gods of the nations delivered his land out of the hand of the king of Assyria?

19 Where are the gods of Hamath and Arphad? where are the gods of Sepharvaim? and have they delivered Samaria out of my hand?

20 Who are they among all the gods of these lands, that have delivered their land out of my hand, that the LORD should deliver Jerusalem out of my hand?

21 But they held their peace, and answered him not a word: for the king's commandment was, saying, Answer him not.

22 Then came Eliakim, the son of Hilkiah, that was over the household, and Shebna the scribe, and Joah, the son of Asaph, the recorder, to Hezekiah with their clothes rent, and told him the words of Rabshakeh.

CHAPTER 37

AND it came to pass, when king Hezekiah heard it, that he rent his clothes, and covered himself with sackcloth, and went into the house of the LORD.

2 And he sent Eliakim, who was over the household, and Shebna the scribe, and the elders of the priests covered

with sackcloth, to Isaiah the prophet the son of Amoz.

3 And they said to him, Thus says Hezekiah, This day is a day of trouble, and of rebuke, and of blasphemy: for the children are come to the birth, and there is not strength to bring forth.

4 It may be the LORD your God will hear the words of Rabshakeh, whom the king of Assyria his master has sent to reproach the living God, and will reprove the words which the LORD your God has heard: therefore lift up your prayer for the remnant that is left.

5 So the servants of king Hezekiah came to Isaiah.

6 And Isaiah said to them, Thus shall you say to your master, Thus says the LORD, Be not afraid of the words that you have heard, wherewith the servants of the king of Assyria have blasphemed me.

7 Behold, I will send a blast upon him, and he shall hear a rumour, and return to his own land; and I will cause him to fall by the sword in his own land.

8 So Rabshakeh returned, and found the king of Assyria warring against Libnah: for he had heard that he was departed from Lachish.

9 And he heard say concerning Tirhakah king of Ethiopia, He is come forth to make war with you. And when he heard it, he sent messengers to Hezekiah, saying,

10 Thus shall you speak to Hezekiah king of Judah, saying, Do not let your God, in whom you trust, deceive you, saying, Jerusalem shall not be given into the hand of the king of Assyria.

11 Behold, you have heard what the kings of Assyria have done to all lands by destroying them utterly; and shall you be delivered?

12 Have the gods of the nations delivered them which my fathers have destroyed, as Gozan, and Haran, and Rezeph, and the children of Eden which were in Telassar?

13 Where is the king of Hamath, and the king of Arphad, and the king of the city of Sepharvaim, Hena, and Ivah?

14 And Hezekiah received the letter from the hand of the messengers, and read it: and Hezekiah went up to the house of the LORD, and spread it before the LORD.

15 And Hezekiah prayed to the LORD, saying,

16 O LORD of hosts, God of Israel, that dwell between the cherubims, you are the God, even you alone, of all the kingdoms of the earth: you have made heaven and earth.

17 Incline your ear, O LORD, and hear; open your eyes, O LORD, and see: and hear all the words of Sennacherib, which has sent to reproach the living God.

18 Of a truth, LORD, the kings of Assyria have laid waste all the nations, and their countries,

19 And have cast their gods into the fire: for they were no gods, but the work of men's hands, wood and stone: therefore they have destroyed them.

20 Now therefore, O LORD our God, save us from his hand, that all the kingdoms of the earth may know that you are the LORD, even you only.

21 Then Isaiah the son of Amoz sent to Hezekiah, saying, Thus says the LORD God of Israel, Whereas you have prayed to me against Sennacherib king of Assyria:

22 This is the word which the LORD has spoken concerning him; The virgin, the daughter of Zion, has despised you, and laughed you to scorn; the daughter of Jerusalem has shaken her head at you.

23 Whom have you reproached and blasphemed? and against whom have you exalted your voice, and lifted up your eyes on high? even against the Holy One of Israel.

24 By your servants have you reproached the Lord, and have said, By the multitude of my chariots am I come up to the height of the mountains, to the sides of Lebanon; and I will cut down

the tall cedars thereof, and the choice fir trees thereof: and I will enter into the height of his border, and the forest of his Carmel.

25 I have dug, and drunk water; and with the sole of my feet have I dried up all the rivers of the besieged places.

26 Have you not heard long ago, how I have done it; and of ancient times, that I have formed it? now have I brought it to pass, that you should be to lay waste defenced cities into ruinous heaps.

27 Therefore their inhabitants were of small power, they were dismayed and confounded: they were as the grass of the field, and as the green herb, as the grass on the housetops, and as corn blasted before it be grown up.

28 But I know your abode, and your going out, and your coming in, and your rage against me.

29 Because your rage against me, and your tumult, is come up into my ears, therefore will I put my hook in your nose, and my bridle in your lips, and I will turn you back by the way by which you came.

30 And this shall be a sign to you, You shall eat this year such as grows of itself; and the second year that which springs of the same: and in the third year sow, and reap, and plant vineyards, and eat the fruit thereof.

31 And the remnant that is escaped of the house of Judah shall again take root downward, and bear fruit upward:

32 For out of Jerusalem shall go forth a remnant, and they that escape out of mount Zion: the zeal of the LORD of hosts shall do this.

33 Therefore thus says the LORD concerning the king of Assyria, He shall not come into this city, nor shoot an arrow there, nor come before it with shields, nor cast a bank against it.

34 By the way that he came, by the same shall he return, and shall not come into this city, says the LORD.

35 For I will defend this city to save it for my own sake, and for my servant David's sake.

36 Then the angel of the LORD went forth, and smote in the camp of the Assyrians a hundred and fourscore and five thousand: and when they arose early in the morning, behold, they were all dead corpses.

37 So Sennacherib king of Assyria departed, and went and returned, and dwelt at Nineveh.

38 And it came to pass, as he was worshipping in the house of Nisroch his god, that Adrammelech and Sharezer his sons smote him with the sword; and they escaped into the land of Armenia: and Esarhaddon his son reigned in his stead.

CHAPTER 38

IN those days was Hezekiah sick to death. And Isaiah the prophet the son of Amoz came to him, and said to him, Thus says the LORD, Set your house in order: for you shall die, and not live.

2 Then Hezekiah turned his face toward the wall, and prayed to the LORD,

3 And said, Remember now, O LORD, I beseech you, how I have walked before you in truth and with a perfect heart, and have done that which is good in your sight. And Hezekiah wept sore.

4 Then the word of the LORD came to Isaiah, saying,

5 Go, and say to Hezekiah, Thus says the LORD, the God of David your father, I have heard your prayer, I have seen your tears: behold, I will add to your days fifteen years.

6 And I will deliver you and this city out of the hand of the king of Assyria: and I will defend this city.

7 And this shall be a sign to you from the LORD, that the LORD will do this thing that he has spoken;

8 Behold, I will bring again the shadow of the degrees, which is gone down in the sun dial of Ahaz, ten degrees backward. So the sun returned ten

degrees, by which degrees it was gone down.

9 The writing of Hezekiah king of Judah, when he had been sick, and was recovered of his sickness:

10 I said in the cutting off of my days, I shall go to the gates of the grave: I am deprived of the residue of my years.

11 I said, I shall not see the LORD, even the LORD, in the land of the living: I shall behold man no more with the inhabitants of the world.

12 My age is departed, and is removed from me as a shepherd's tent: I have cut off like a weaver my life: he will cut me off with pining sickness: from day even to night will you make an end of me.

13 I reckoned till morning, that, as a lion, so will he break all my bones: from day even to night will you make an end of me.

14 Like a crane or a swallow, so did I chatter: I did mourn as a dove: my eyes fail with looking upward: O LORD, I am oppressed; undertake for me.

15 What shall I say? he has both spoken to me, and himself has done it: I shall go softly all my years in the bitterness of my soul.

16 O LORD, by these things men live, and in all these things is the life of my spirit: so will you recover me, and make me to live.

17 Behold, for peace I had great bitterness: but you have in love to my soul delivered it from the pit of corruption: for you have cast all my sins behind your back.

18 For the grave cannot praise you, death can not celebrate you: they that go down into the pit cannot hope for your truth.

19 The living, the living, he shall praise you, as I do this day: the father to the children shall make known your truth.

20 The LORD was ready to save me: therefore we will sing my songs to the stringed instruments all the days of our life in the house of the LORD.

21 For Isaiah had said, Let them take a lump of figs, and lay it for a plaister upon the boil, and he shall recover.

22 Hezekiah also had said, What is the sign that I shall go up to the house of the LORD?

CHAPTER 39

AT that time Merodachbaladan, the son of Baladan, king of Babylon, sent letters and a present to Hezekiah: for he had heard that he had been sick, and was recovered.

2 And Hezekiah was glad of them, and showed them the house of his precious things, the silver, and the gold, and the spices, and the precious ointment, and all the house of his armour, and all that was found in his treasures: there was nothing in his house, nor in all his dominion, that Hezekiah did not show them.

3 Then came Isaiah the prophet to king Hezekiah, and said to him, What said these men? and from where did they come to you? And Hezekiah said, They are come from a far country to me, even from Babylon.

4 Then said he, What have they seen in your house? And Hezekiah answered, All that is in my house have they seen: there is nothing among my treasures that I have not showed them.

5 Then said Isaiah to Hezekiah, Hear the word of the LORD of hosts:

6 Behold, the days come, that all that is in your house, and that which your fathers have laid up in store until this day, shall be carried to Babylon: nothing shall be left, says the LORD.

7 And of your sons that shall issue from you, which you shall beget, shall they take away; and they shall be eunuchs in the palace of the king of Babylon.

8 Then said Hezekiah to Isaiah, Good is the word of the LORD which you have spoken. He said moreover, For there shall be peace and truth in my days.

CHAPTER 40

COMFORT, yes, comfort my people, says your God.

2 You speak comfortably to Jerusalem, and cry to her, that her warfare is accomplished, that her iniquity is pardoned: for she has received of the LORD's hand double for all her sins.

3 The voice of him that cries in the wilderness, Prepare the way of the LORD, make straight in the desert a highway for our God.

4 Every valley shall be exalted, and every mountain and hill shall be made low: and the crooked shall be made straight, and the rough places plain:

5 And the glory of the LORD shall be revealed, and all flesh shall see it together: for the mouth of the LORD has spoken it.

6 The voice said, Cry. And he said, What shall I cry? All flesh is grass, and all the goodliness thereof is as the flower of the field:

7 The grass withers, the flower fades: because the spirit of the LORD blows upon it: surely the people are grass.

8 The grass withers, the flower fades: but the word of our God shall stand for ever.

9 O Zion, that brings good tidings, get up into the high mountain; O Jerusalem, that brings good tidings, lift up your voice with strength; lift it up, be not afraid; say to the cities of Judah, Behold your God!

10 Behold, the Lord GOD will come with strong hand, and his arm shall rule for him: behold, his reward is with him, and his work before him.

11 He shall feed his flock like a shepherd: he shall gather the lambs with his arm, and carry them in his bosom, and shall gently lead those that are with young.

12 Who has measured the waters in the hollow of his hand, and meted out heaven with the span, and comprehended the dust of the earth in a measure, and weighed the mountains in scales, and the hills in a balance?

13 Who has directed the Spirit of the LORD, or being his counselor has taught him?

14 With whom took he counsel, and who instructed him, and taught him in the path of judgment, and taught him knowledge, and showed to him the way of understanding?

15 Behold, the nations are as a drop of a bucket, and are counted as the small dust of the balance: behold, he takes up the isles as a very little thing.

16 And Lebanon is not sufficient to burn, nor the beasts thereof sufficient for a burnt offering.

17 All nations before him are as nothing; and they are counted to him less than nothing, and vanity.

18 To whom then will you liken God? or what likeness will you compare to him?

19 The workman melts a graven image, and the goldsmith spreads it over with gold, and casts silver chains.

20 He that is so impoverished that he has no oblation chooses a tree that will not rot; he seeks for himself a cunning workman to prepare a graven image, that shall not be moved.

21 Have you not known? have you not heard? has it not been told you from the beginning? have you not understood from the foundations of the earth?

22 It is he that sits upon the circle of the earth, and the inhabitants thereof are as grasshoppers; that stretches out the heavens as a curtain, and spreads them out as a tent to dwell in:

40:6-8 The Christian message to this world is that all its pleasures are but for a season. This life is a vapor; it is vanity. There is only One who is eternal, the Word of God, and He will grant eternal life to all who trust in Him.

41:10

When we are fearful to preach or to witness, we must stand firmly upon this wonderful promise; we must not fear. God is with us; He will strengthen, help and uphold us.

23 That brings the princes to nothing; he makes the judges of the earth as vanity.

24 Yea, they shall not be planted; yea, they shall not be sown: yea, their stock shall not take root in the earth: and he shall also blow upon them, and they shall wither, and the whirlwind shall take them away as stubble.

25 To whom then will you liken me, or shall I be equal? says the Holy One.

26 Lift up your eyes on high, and behold who has created these things, that brings out their host by number: he calls them all by names by the greatness of his might, for that he is strong in power; not one fails.

27 Why do you say, O Jacob, and speak, O Israel, My way is hid from the LORD, and my judgment is passed over from my God?

28 Have you not known? have you not heard, that the everlasting God, the LORD, the Creator of the ends of the earth, neither faints nor is weary? there is no searching of his understanding.

29 He gives power to the faint; and to them that have no might he increases strength.

30 Even the youths shall faint and be weary, and the young men shall utterly fall:

31 But they that wait upon the LORD shall renew their strength; they shall mount up with wings as eagles; they shall run, and not be weary; and they shall walk, and not faint.

CHAPTER 41

KEEP silence before me, O islands; and let the people renew their strength: let them come near; then let them speak: let us come near together to judgment.

2 Who raised up the righteous man from the east, called him to his foot, gave the nations before him, and made him rule over kings? he gave them as the dust to his sword, and as driven stubble to his bow.

3 He pursued them, and passed safely; even by the way that he had not gone with his feet.

4 Who has performed and done it, calling the generations from the beginning? I the LORD, the first, and with the last; I am he.

5 The isles saw it, and feared; the ends of the earth were afraid, drew near, and came.

6 They helped every one his neighbour; and every one said to his brother, Be of good courage.

7 So the carpenter encouraged the goldsmith, and he that smoothes with the hammer him that smote the anvil, saying, It is ready for the sodering: and he fastened it with nails, that it should not be moved.

8 But you, Israel, are my servant, Jacob whom I have chosen, the seed of Abraham my friend.

9 You whom I have taken from the ends of the earth, and called you from the chief men thereof, and said to you, You are my servant; I have chosen you, and not cast you away.

10 *Fear not; for I am with you: be not dismayed; for I am your God: I will* *strengthen you; yea, I will help you; yea, I will uphold you with the right hand of my righteousness.*

11 Behold, all they that were incensed against you shall be ashamed and confounded: they shall be as nothing; and they that strive with you shall perish.

12 You shall seek them, and shall not find them, even them that contended with you: they that war against you shall be as nothing, and as a thing of nought.

13 *For I the LORD your God will hold your right hand, saying to you, Fear not; I will help you.*

14 Fear not, you worm Jacob, and you men of Israel; I will help you, says the LORD, and your redeemer, the Holy One of Israel.

15 Behold, I will make you a new sharp threshing instrument having teeth: you shall thresh the mountains, and beat them small, and shall make the hills as chaff.

16 You shall fan them, and the wind shall carry them away, and the whirlwind shall scatter them: and you shall rejoice in the LORD, and shall glory in the Holy One of Israel.

17 When the poor and needy seek water, and there is none, and their tongue fails for thirst, I the LORD will hear them, I the God of Israel will not forsake them.

18 I will open rivers in high places, and fountains in the midst of the valleys: I will make the wilderness a pool of water, and the dry land springs of water.

19 I will plant in the wilderness the cedar, the shittah tree, and the myrtle, and the oil tree; I will set in the desert the fir tree, and the pine, and the box tree together:

20 That they may see, and know, and consider, and understand together, that the hand of the LORD has done this, and the Holy One of Israel has created it.

21 Produce your cause, says the LORD; bring forth your strong reasons, says the King of Jacob.

22 Let them bring them forth, and show us what shall happen: let them show the former things, what they be, that we may consider them, and know the latter end of them; or declare us things for to come.

23 Show the things that are to come hereafter, that we may know that you are gods: yea, do good, or do evil, that we may be dismayed, and behold it together.

24 Behold, you are of nothing, and your work of nought: an abomination is he that chooses you.

25 I have raised up one from the north, and he shall come: from the rising of the sun shall he call upon my name: and he shall come upon princes as upon morter, and as the potter treads clay.

26 Who has declared from the beginning, that we may know? and beforetime, that we may say, He is righteous? yea, there is none that shows, yea, there is none that declares, yea, there is none that hears your words.

27 The first shall say to Zion, Behold, behold them: and I will give to Jerusalem one that brings good tidings.

28 For I beheld, and there was no man; even among them, and there was no counsellor, that, when I asked of them, could answer a word.

29 Behold, they are all vanity; their works are nothing: their molten images are wind and confusion.

CHAPTER 42

BEHOLD my servant, whom I uphold; my elect, in whom my soul delights; I have put my spirit upon him: he shall bring forth judgment to the Gentiles.

2 He shall not cry, nor lift up, nor cause his voice to be heard in the street.

42:1-4 Jesus was never *dis*couraged (He never lost His courage); He did not fail (see Romans 8:31-39).

THE FUNCTION OF THE LAW

When we judge ourselves against man's standards, many of us come up reasonably clean. Adolf Hitler's life, for instance, makes most of us look almost pure.

However, when we use the Law of God as our measure, we see that we are not as clean as we like to think. We need to apply the spiritual nature of God's Law to the conscience of the sinner so he can see that his own righteousnesses is as filthy rags in the sight of a holy God.

3 A bruised reed shall he not break, and the smoking flax shall he not quench: he shall bring forth judgment to truth.

4 He shall not fail nor be discouraged, till he have set judgment in the earth: and the isles shall wait for his law.

5 Thus says God the LORD, he that created the heavens, and stretched them out; he that spread forth the earth, and that which comes out of it; he that gives breath to the people upon it, and spirit to them that walk therein:

6 I the LORD have called you in righteousness, and will hold your hand, and will keep you, and give you for a covenant of the people, for a light of the Gentiles;

7 To open the blind eyes, to bring out the prisoners from the prison, and them that sit in darkness out of the prison house.

8 I am the LORD: that is my name: and my glory will I not give to another, neither my praise to graven images.

9 Behold, the former things are come to pass, and new things do I declare: before they spring forth I tell you of them.

10 Sing to the LORD a new song, and his praise from the end of the earth, you that go down to the sea, and all that is therein; the isles, and the inhabitants thereof.

11 Let the wilderness and the cities thereof lift up their voice, the villages that Kedar does inhabit: let the inhabitants of the rock sing, let them shout from the top of the mountains.

12 Let them give glory to the LORD, and declare his praise in the islands.

13 The LORD shall go forth as a mighty man, he shall stir up jealousy like a man of war: he shall cry, yea, roar; he shall prevail against his enemies.

14 I have long time holden my peace; I have been still, and refrained myself: now will I cry like a travailing woman; I will destroy and devour at once.

15 I will make waste mountains and hills, and dry up all their herbs; and I will make the rivers islands, and I will dry up the pools.

16 And I will bring the blind by a way that they knew not; I will lead them in paths that they have not known: I will make darkness light before them, and crooked things straight. These things will I do to them, and not forsake them.

17 They shall be turned back, they shall be greatly ashamed, that trust in graven images, that say to the molten images, You are our gods.

18 Hear, you deaf; and look, you blind, that you may see.

19 Who is blind, but my servant? or deaf, as my messenger that I sent? who is blind as he that is perfect, and blind as the LORD's servant?

20 Seeing many things, but you do not observe; opening the ears, but he does not hear.

21 The LORD is well pleased for his righteousness' sake; he will magnify the law, and make it honourable.

22 But this is a people robbed and spoiled; they are all of them snared in holes, and they are hid in prison houses: they are for a prey, and none delivers; for a spoil, and none says, Restore.

42:21 Jesus magnified the Law and made it honorable in His Sermon on the Mount (see Matthew 5-7).

23 Who among you will give ear to this? who will hearken and hear for the time to come?

24 Who gave Jacob for a spoil, and Israel to the robbers? did not the LORD, he against whom we have sinned? for they would not walk in his ways, neither were they obedient to his law.

25 Therefore he has poured upon him the fury of his anger, and the strength of battle: and it has set him on fire round about, yet he knew not; and it burned him, yet he laid it not to heart.

CHAPTER 43

BUT now thus says the LORD that created you, O Jacob, and he that formed you, O Israel, Fear not: for I have redeemed you, I have called you by your name; you are mine.

2 When you pass through the waters, I will be with you; and through the rivers, they shall not overflow you: when you walk through the fire, you shall not be burned; neither shall the flame kindle upon you.

3 For I am the LORD your God, the Holy One of Israel, your Saviour: I gave Egypt for your ransom, Ethiopia and Seba for you.

4 Since you were precious in my sight, you have been honourable, and I have loved you: therefore will I give men for you, and people for your life.

5 Fear not: for I am with you: I will bring your seed from the east, and gather you from the west;

6 I will say to the north, Give up; and to the south, Keep not back: bring my sons from far, and my daughters from the ends of the earth;

7 Even every one that is called by my name: for I have created him for my glory, I have formed him; yea, I have made him.

8 Bring forth the blind people that have eyes, and the deaf that have ears.

9 Let all the nations be gathered together, and let the people be assembled: who among them can declare this, and show us former things? let them bring forth their witnesses, that they may be justified: or let them hear, and say, It is truth.

10 You are my witnesses, says the LORD, and my servant whom I have chosen: that you may know and believe me, and understand that I am he: before me there was no God formed, neither shall there be after me.

11 I, even I, am the LORD; and beside me there is no saviour.

12 I have declared, and have saved, and I have showed, when there was no strange god among you: therefore you are my witnesses, says the LORD, that I am God.

13 Yea, before the day was I am he; and there is none that can deliver out of my hand: I will work, and who shall let it?

14 Thus says the LORD, your redeemer, the Holy One of Israel; For your sake I have sent to Babylon, and have brought down all their nobles, and the Chaldeans, whose cry is in the ships.

15 I am the LORD, your Holy One, the creator of Israel, your King.

16 Thus says the LORD, which makes a way in the sea, and a path in the mighty waters;

17 Which brings forth the chariot and horse, the army and the power; they shall lie down together, they shall not rise: they are extinct, they are quenched as tow.

18 Do not remember the former things, neither consider the things of old.

19 Behold, I will do a new thing; now it shall spring forth; shall you not know it? I will even make a way in the wilderness, and rivers in the desert.

20 The beast of the field shall honour me, the dragons and the owls: because I give waters in the wilderness, and rivers

---

43:25 This was done once and for all through the Cross of Calvary (see Isaiah 44:22).

in the desert, to give drink to my people, my chosen.

21 This people have I formed for myself; they shall show forth my praise.

22 But you have not called upon me, O Jacob; but you have been weary of me, O Israel.

23 You have not brought me the small cattle of your burnt offerings; neither have you honoured me with your sacrifices. I have not caused you to serve with an offering, nor wearied you with incense.

24 You have bought me no sweet cane with money, neither have you filled me with the fat of your sacrifices: but you have made me to serve with your sins, you have wearied me with your iniquities.

25 I, even I, am he that blots out your transgressions for my own sake, and will not remember your sins.

26 Put me in remembrance: let us plead together: you declare, that you may be justified.

27 Your first father has sinned, and your teachers have transgressed against me.

28 Therefore I have profaned the princes of the sanctuary, and have given Jacob to the curse, and Israel to reproaches.

CHAPTER 44

YET now hear, O Jacob my servant; and Israel, whom I have chosen:

2 Thus says the LORD that made you, and formed you from the womb, which will help you; Fear not, O Jacob, my servant; and you, Jesurun, whom I have chosen.

3 For I will pour water upon him that is thirsty, and floods upon the dry ground: I will pour my spirit upon your seed, and my blessing upon your offspring:

4 And they shall spring up as among the grass, as willows by the water courses.

5 One shall say, I am the LORD's; and another shall call himself by the name of Jacob; and another shall subscribe with his hand to the LORD, and surname himself by the name of Israel.

6 Thus says the LORD the King of Israel, and his redeemer the LORD of hosts; I am the first, and I am the last; and beside me there is no God.

7 And who, as I, shall call, and shall declare it, and set it in order for me, since I appointed the ancient people? and the things that are coming, and shall come, let them show to them.

8 Fear not, neither be afraid: have not I told you from that time, and have declared it? you are even my witnesses. Is there a God beside me? yea, there is no God; I know not any.

9 They that make a graven image are all of them vanity; and their delectable things shall not profit; and they are their own witnesses; they see not, nor know; that they may be ashamed.

10 Who has formed a god, or molten a graven image that is profitable for nothing?

11 Behold, all his fellows shall be ashamed: and the workmen, they are of men: let them all be gathered together, let them stand up; yet they shall fear, and they shall be ashamed together.

12 The smith with the tongs both works in the coals, and fashions it with hammers, and works it with the strength of his arms: yea, he is hungry, and his strength fails: he drinks no water, and is faint.

13 The carpenter stretches out his rule; he marks it out with a line; he fits it with planes, and he marks it out with the compass, and makes it after the figure of a man, according to the beauty of a man; that it may remain in the house.

14 He hews him down cedars, and takes the cypress and the oak, which he strengthens for himself among the trees of the forest: he plants an ash, and the rain does nourish it.

15 Then shall it be for a man to burn: for he will take thereof, and warm himself; yea, he kindles it, and bakes bread;

> First, then, before you can speak
> peace to your hearts,
> you must be made to see,
> made to feel,
> made to weep over,
> made to bewail,
> your actual transgressions
> against the Law of God.

GEORGE WHITEFIELD
1714-1770
PREACHED IN ENGLAND,
SCOTLAND, WALES, GIBRALTAR,
BERMUDA
AND THE AMERICAN COLONIES

yea, he makes a god, and worships it; he makes it a graven image, and falls down thereto.

16 He burns part thereof in the fire; with part thereof he eats flesh; he roasts roast, and is satisfied: yea, he warms himself, and says, Aha, I am warm, I have seen the fire:

17 And the residue thereof he makes a god, even his graven image: he falls down to it, and worships it, and prays to it, and says, Deliver me; for you are my god.

18 They have not known nor understood: for he has shut their eyes, that they cannot see; and their hearts, that they cannot understand.

19 And none considers in his heart, neither is there knowledge nor understanding to say, I have burned part of it in the fire; yea, also I have baked bread upon the coals thereof; I have roasted flesh, and eaten it: and shall I make the residue thereof an abomination? shall I fall down to the stock of a tree?

20 He feeds on ashes: a deceived heart has turned him aside, that he cannot deliver his soul, nor say, Is there not a lie in my right hand?

21 Remember these, O Jacob and Israel; for you are my servant: I have formed you; you are my servant: O Israel, you shall not be forgotten of me.

22 I have blotted out, as a thick cloud, your transgressions, and, as a cloud, your sins: return to me; for I have redeemed you.

23 Sing, O you heavens; for the LORD has done it: shout, you lower parts of the earth: break forth into singing, you mountains, O forest, and every tree therein: for the LORD has redeemed Jacob, and glorified himself in Israel.

24 Thus says the LORD, your redeemer, and he that formed you from the womb, I am the LORD that makes all things; that stretches forth the heavens alone; that spreads abroad the earth by myself;

25 That frustrates the tokens of the liars, and makes diviners mad; that turns wise men backward, and makes their knowledge foolish;

26 That confirms the word of his servant, and performs the counsel of his messengers; that says to Jerusalem, You shall be inhabited; and to the cities of Judah, You shall be built, and I will raise up the decayed places thereof:

27 That says to the deep, Be dry, and I will dry up your rivers:

28 That says of Cyrus, He is my shepherd, and shall perform all my pleasure: even saying to Jerusalem, You shall be built; and to the temple, Your foundation shall be laid.

CHAPTER 45

THUS says the LORD to his anointed, to Cyrus, whose right hand I have holden, to subdue nations before him; and I will loose the loins of kings, to open before him the two leaved gates; and the gates shall not be shut;

2 I will go before you, and make the crooked places straight: I will break in pieces the gates of brass, and cut in sunder the bars of iron:

3 And I will give you the treasures of darkness, and hidden riches of secret places, that you may know that I, the LORD, which call you by your name, am the God of Israel.

4 For Jacob my servant's sake, and Israel my elect, I have even called you by your name: I have surnamed you, though you have not known me.

5 I am the LORD, and there is none else, there is no God beside me: I girded you, though you have not known me:

6 That they may know from the rising of the sun, and from the west, that there is none beside me. I am the LORD, and there is none else.

7 I form the light, and create darkness: I make peace, and create evil: I the LORD do all these things.

8 Drop down, you heavens, from above, and let the skies pour down righteousness: let the earth open, and let them bring forth salvation, and let righteousness spring up together; I the LORD have created it.

9 Woe to him that strives with his Maker! Let the potsherd strive with the potsherds of the earth. Shall the clay say to him that fashioned it, What are you making? or your work, He has no hands?

10 Woe to him that says to his father, What are you begetting? or to the woman, What have you brought forth?

11 Thus says the LORD, the Holy One of Israel, and his Maker, Ask me of things to come concerning my sons, and concerning the work of my hands you command me.

12 I have made the earth, and created man upon it: I, even my hands, have stretched out the heavens, and all their host have I commanded.

13 I have raised him up in righteousness, and I will direct all his ways: he shall build my city, and he shall let go my captives, not for price nor reward, says the LORD of hosts.

14 Thus says the LORD, The labour of Egypt, and merchandise of Ethiopia and of the Sabeans, men of stature, shall come over to you, and they shall be yours: they shall come after you; in chains they shall come over, and they shall fall down to you, they shall make supplication to you, saying, Surely God is in you; and there is none else, there is no God.

15 Verily you are a God that hides yourself, O God of Israel, the Saviour.

16 They shall be ashamed, and also confounded, all of them: they shall go to confusion together that are makers of idols.

17 But Israel shall be saved in the LORD with an everlasting salvation: you shall not be ashamed nor confounded world without end.

18 For thus says the LORD that created the heavens; God himself that formed the earth and made it; he has established it, he created it not in vain, he formed it to be inhabited: I am the LORD; and there is none else.

19 I have not spoken in secret, in a dark place of the earth: I did not say to the seed of Jacob, Seek me in vain: I the LORD speak righteousness, I declare things that are right.

20 Assemble yourselves and come; draw near together, you that are escaped of the nations: they have no knowledge that set up the wood of their graven image, and pray to a god that cannot save.

21 Tell, and bring them near; yea, let them take counsel together: who has declared this from ancient time? who has told it from that time? have not I the LORD? and there is no God else beside me; a just God and a Saviour; there is none beside me.

22 Look to me, and be saved, all the ends of the earth: for I am God, and there is none else.

23 I have sworn by myself, the word is gone out of my mouth in righteousness, and shall not return, That to me every knee shall bow, every tongue shall swear.

45:22 The call of the gospel is universal.

24 Surely, shall one say, in the LORD have I righteousness and strength: even to him shall men come; and all that are incensed against him shall be ashamed.

25 In the LORD shall all the seed of Israel be justified, and shall glory.

CHAPTER 46

B EL bows down, Nebo stoops, their idols were upon the beasts, and upon the cattle: your carriages were heavy loaden; they are a burden to the weary beast.

2 They stoop, they bow down together; they could not deliver the burden, but themselves are gone into captivity.

3 Hearken to me, O house of Jacob, and all the remnant of the house of Israel, which are borne by me from the belly, which are carried from the womb:

4 And even to your old age I am he; and even to hoar hairs will I carry you: I have made, and I will bear; even I will carry, and will deliver you.

5 To whom will you liken me, and make me equal, and compare me, that we may be like?

6 They lavish gold out of the bag, and weigh silver in the balance, and hire a goldsmith; and he makes it a god: they fall down, yea, they worship.

7 They bear him upon the shoulder, they carry him, and set him in his place, and he stands; from his place shall he not remove: yea, one shall cry to him, yet can he not answer, nor save him out of his trouble.

8 **Remember this, and show yourselves men: bring it again to mind, O you transgressors.**

9 **Remember the former things of old: for I am God, and there is none else; I am God, and there is none like me,**

10 **Declaring the end from the beginning, and from ancient times the things that are not yet done, saying, My counsel shall stand, and I will do all my pleasure:**

11 Calling a ravenous bird from the east, the man that executes my counsel from a far country: yea, I have spoken it, I will also bring it to pass; I have purposed it, I will also do it.

12 Hearken to me, you stouthearted, that are far from righteousness:

13 I bring near my righteousness; it shall not be far off, and my salvation shall not tarry: and I will place salvation in Zion for Israel my glory.

CHAPTER 47

C OME down, and sit in the dust, O virgin daughter of Babylon, sit on the ground: there is no throne, O daughter of the Chaldeans: for you shall no more be called tender and delicate.

2 Take the millstones, and grind meal: uncover your locks, make bare the leg, uncover the thigh, pass over the rivers.

3 Your nakedness shall be uncovered, yea, your shame shall be seen: I will take vengeance, and I will not meet you as a man.

4 As for our redeemer, the LORD of hosts is his name, the Holy One of Israel.

5 Sit silently, and go into darkness, O daughter of the Chaldeans: for you shall no more be called, The lady of kingdoms.

6 I was wroth with my people, I have polluted my inheritance, and given them into your hand: you did show them no mercy; upon the elderly you laid your yoke very heavily.

7 And you said, I shall be a lady for ever: so that you did not lay these things to your heart, neither did remember the latter end of it.

8 Therefore hear now this, you that are given to pleasures, that dwell carelessly, that say in your heart, I am, and none else beside me; I shall not sit as a widow, neither shall I know the loss of children:

9 But these two things shall come to you in a moment in one day, the loss of children, and widowhood: they shall come upon you in their perfection for the multitude of your sorceries, and for the great abundance of your enchantments.

10 For you have trusted in your wickedness: you have said, None sees me. Your wisdom and your knowledge, it has perverted you; and you have said in your heart, I am, and none else beside me.

11 Therefore shall evil come upon you; you shall not know from where it rises: and mischief shall fall upon you; you shall not be able to put it off: and desolation shall come upon you suddenly, which you shall not know.

12 Stand now with your enchantments, and with the multitude of your sorceries, wherein you have laboured from your youth; if so be you shall be able to profit, if so be you may prevail.

13 You are wearied in the multitude of your counsels. Let now the astrologers, the stargazers, the monthly prognosticators, stand up, and save you from these things that shall come upon you.

14 Behold, they shall be as stubble; the fire shall burn them; they shall not deliver themselves from the power of the flame: there shall not be a coal to warm at, nor fire to sit before it.

15 Thus shall they be to you with whom you have laboured, even your merchants, from your youth: they shall wander every one to his quarter; none shall save you.

CHAPTER 48

HEAR this, O house of Jacob, which are called by the name of Israel, and are come forth out of the waters of Judah, which swear by the name of the LORD, and make mention of the God of Israel, but not in truth, nor in righteousness.

2 For they call themselves of the holy city, and stay themselves upon the God of Israel; The LORD of hosts is his name.

3 I have declared the former things from the beginning; and they went forth out of my mouth, and I showed them; I did them suddenly, and they came to pass.

4 Because I knew that you are obstinate, and your neck is an iron sinew, and your brow brass;

5 I have even from the beginning declared it to you; before it came to pass I showed it to you: lest you should say, My idol has done them, and my graven image, and my molten image, has commanded them.

6 You have heard, see all this; and will you not declare it? I have showed you new things from this time, even hidden things, and you did not know them.

7 They are created now, and not from the beginning; even before the day when you heard them not; lest you should say, Behold, I knew them.

8 Yea, you did not hear; yea, you did not know; yea, from that time that your ear was not opened: for I knew that you would deal very treacherously, and were called a transgressor from the womb.

9 For my name's sake will I defer my anger, and for my praise will I refrain for you, so that I do not cut you off.

10 Behold, I have refined you, but not with silver; I have chosen you in the furnace of affliction.

11 For my own sake, even for my own sake, will I do it: for how should my name be polluted? and I will not give my glory to another.

12 Hearken to me, O Jacob and Israel, my called; I am he; I am the first, I also am the last.

13 My hand also has laid the foundation of the earth, and my right hand has spanned the heavens: when I call to them, they stand up together.

14 All you, assemble yourselves, and hear; which among them has declared these things? The LORD has loved him: he will do his pleasure on Babylon, and his arm shall be on the Chaldeans.

15 I, even I, have spoken; yea, I have called him: I have brought him, and he shall make his way prosperous.

16 Come near to me, hear this; I have not spoken in secret from the beginning; from the time that it was, there am I: and

now the Lord GOD, and his Spirit, has sent me.

17 Thus says the LORD, your Redeemer, the Holy One of Israel; I am the LORD your God which teaches you to profit, which leads you by the way that you should go.

18 O that you had hearkened to my commandments! then had your peace been as a river, and your righteousness as the waves of the sea:

19 Your seed also had been as the sand, and the offspring of your bowels like the gravel thereof; his name should not have been cut off nor destroyed from before me.

20 Go forth of Babylon, flee from the Chaldeans, with a voice of singing Declare, tell this, utter it even to the end of the earth; say, The LORD has redeemed his servant Jacob.

21 And they thirsted not when he led them through the deserts: he caused the waters to flow out of the rock for them: he clave the rock also, and the waters gushed out.

22 There is no peace, says the LORD, to the wicked.

CHAPTER 49

LISTEN, O isles, to me; and hearken, you people, from far; The LORD has called me from the womb; from the bowels of my mother has he made mention of my name.

2 And he has made my mouth like a sharp sword; in the shadow of his hand has he hid me, and made me a polished shaft; in his quiver has he hid me;

3 And said to me, You are my servant, O Israel, in whom I will be glorified.

4 Then I said, I have laboured in vain, I have spent my strength for nought, and in vain: yet surely my judgment is with the LORD, and my work with my God.

5 And now, says the LORD that formed me from the womb to be his servant, to bring Jacob again to him, Though Israel be not gathered, yet shall I be glorious in the eyes of the LORD, and my God shall be my strength.

6 And he said, It is a light thing that you should be my servant to raise up the tribes of Jacob, and to restore the preserved of Israel: I will also give you for a light to the Gentiles, that you may be my salvation to the end of the earth.

7 Thus says the LORD, the Redeemer of Israel, and his Holy One, to him whom man despises, to him whom the nation abhors, to a servant of rulers, Kings shall see and arise, princes also shall worship, because of the LORD that is faithful, and the Holy One of Israel, and he shall choose you.

8 Thus says the LORD, In an acceptable time have I heard you, and in a day of salvation have I helped you: and I will preserve you, and give you for a covenant of the people, to establish the earth, to cause to inherit the desolate heritages;

9 That you may say to the prisoners, Go forth; to them that are in darkness, Show yourselves. They shall feed in the ways, and their pastures shall be in all high places.

10 They shall not hunger nor thirst; neither shall the heat nor sun smite them: for he that has mercy on them shall lead them, even by the springs of water shall he guide them.

11 And I will make all my mountains a way, and my highways shall be exalted.

12 Behold, these shall come from far: and, lo, these from the north and from the west; and these from the land of Sinim.

13 Sing, O heavens; and be joyful, O earth; and break forth into singing, O mountains: for the LORD has comforted his people, and will have mercy upon his afflicted.

14 But Zion said, The LORD has forsaken me, and my Lord has forgotten me.

15 Can a woman forget her sucking child, that she should not have compassion on the son of her womb? yea, they may forget, yet will I not forget you.

16 Behold, I have graven you upon the palms of my hands; your walls are continually before me.

17 Your children shall make haste; your destroyers and they that made you waste shall go forth of you.

18 Lift up your eyes round about, and behold: all these gather themselves together, and come to you. As I live, says the LORD, you shall surely clothe yourselves with them all, as with an ornament, and bind them on you, as a bride does.

19 For your waste and your desolate places, and the land of your destruction, shall even now be too narrow by reason of the inhabitants, and they that swallowed you up shall be far away.

20 The children which you shall have, after you have lost the other, shall say again in your ears, The place is too strait for me: give place to me that I may dwell.

21 Then shall you say in your heart, Who has begotten me these, seeing I have lost my children, and am desolate, a captive, and removing to and fro? and who has brought up these? Behold, I was left alone; these, where had they been?

22 Thus says the Lord GOD, Behold, I will lift up my hand to the Gentiles, and set up my standard to the people: and they shall bring your sons in their arms, and your daughters shall be carried upon their shoulders.

23 And kings shall be your nursing fathers, and their queens your nursing mothers: they shall bow down to you with their face toward the earth, and lick up the dust of your feet; and you shall know that I am the LORD: for they shall not be ashamed that wait for me.

24 Shall the prey be taken from the mighty, or the lawful captive delivered?

25 But thus says the LORD, Even the captives of the mighty shall be taken away, and the prey of the terrible shall be delivered: for I will contend with him that contends with you, and I will save your children.

26 And I will feed them that oppress you with their own flesh; and they shall be drunken with their own blood, as with sweet wine: and all flesh shall know that I the LORD am your Saviour and your Redeemer, the mighty One of Jacob.

CHAPTER 50

THUS says the LORD, Where is the bill of your mother's divorcement, whom I have put away? or which of my creditors is it to whom I have sold you? Behold, for your iniquities have you sold yourselves, and for your transgressions is your mother put away.

2 Why, when I came, was there no man? when I called, was there none to answer? Is my hand shortened at all, that it cannot redeem? or have I no power to deliver? behold, at my rebuke I dry up the sea, I make the rivers a wilderness: their fish stink, because there is no water, and die for thirst.

3 I clothe the heavens with blackness, and I make sackcloth their covering.

4 *The Lord GOD has given me the tongue of the learned, that I should know how to speak a word in season to him that is weary: he wakens morning by morning, he wakens my ear to hear as the learned.*

5 The Lord GOD has opened my ear, and I was not rebellious, neither turned away back.

6 I gave my back to the smiters, and my cheeks to them that plucked off the hair: I hid not my face from shame and spitting.

7 For the Lord GOD will help me; therefore shall I not be confounded: therefore have I set my face like a flint, and I know that I shall not be ashamed.

50:6 The fulfillment of this prophecy is recorded in Matthew 27:26, 30.

8 He is near that justifies me; who will contend with me? let us stand together: who is my adversary? let him come near to me.

9 Behold, the Lord GOD will help me; who is he that shall condemn me? lo, they all shall wax old as a garment; the moth shall eat them up.

10 Who is among you that fears the LORD, that obeys the voice of his servant, that walks in darkness, and has no light? let him trust in the name of the LORD, and stay upon his God.

11 Behold, all you that kindle a fire, that compass yourselves about with sparks: walk in the light of your fire, and in the sparks that you have kindled. This shall you have of my hand; you shall lie down in sorrow.

CHAPTER 51

HEARKEN to me, you that follow after righteousness, you that seek the LORD: look to the rock from which you are hewn, and to the hole of the pit from which you were dug.

2 Look to Abraham your father, and to Sarah that bare you: for I called him alone, and blessed him, and increased him.

3 For the LORD shall comfort Zion: he will comfort all her waste places; and he will make her wilderness like Eden, and her desert like the garden of the LORD; joy and gladness shall be found therein, thanksgiving, and the voice of melody.

4 Hearken to me, my people; and give ear to me, O my nation: for a law shall proceed from me, and I will make my judgment to rest for a light of the people.

5 My righteousness is near; my salvation is gone forth, and my arms shall judge the people; the isles shall wait

upon me, and on my arm shall they trust.

6 Lift up your eyes to the heavens, and look upon the earth beneath: for the heavens shall vanish away like smoke, and the earth shall wax old like a garment, and they that dwell therein shall die in like manner: but my salvation shall be for ever, and my righteousness shall not be abolished.

7 Hearken to me, you that know righteousness, the people in whose heart is my law; do not fear the reproach of men, neither be afraid of their revilings.

8 For the moth shall eat them up like a garment, and the worm shall eat them like wool: but my righteousness shall be for ever, and my salvation from generation to generation.

9 Awake, awake, put on strength, O arm of the LORD; awake, as in the ancient days, in the generations of old. Are you not it that has cut Rahab, and wounded the dragon?

10 Are you not it which has dried the sea, the waters of the great deep; that has made the depths of the sea a way for the ransomed to pass over?

11 Therefore the redeemed of the LORD shall return, and come with singing to Zion; and everlasting joy shall be upon their head: they shall obtain gladness and joy; and sorrow and mourning shall flee away.

12 I, even I, am he that comforts you: who are you, that you should be afraid of a man that shall die, and of the son of man which shall be made as grass;

13 And forget the LORD your maker, that has stretched forth the heavens, and laid the foundations of the earth; and have feared continually every day because of the fury of the oppressor, as if

---

51:7 The Christian must stand for righteousness, not only because of the fearful consequences of sin, but also because we have had God's Law written on our heart (see Hebrews 10:16). Righteousness makes no sense to a sin-loving world. To them, we are the ultimate party-poopers, so we shouldn't be surprised when men reproach and revile us.

he were ready to destroy? and where is the fury of the oppressor?

14 The captive exile hastens that he may be loosed, and that he should not die in the pit, nor that his bread should fail.

15 But I am the LORD your God, that divided the sea, whose waves roared: The LORD of hosts is his name.

16 And I have put my words in your mouth, and I have covered you in the shadow of my hand, that I may plant the heavens, and lay the foundations of the earth, and say to Zion, You are my people.

17 Awake, awake, stand up, O Jerusalem, which have drunk at the hand of the LORD the cup of his fury; you have drunken the dregs of the cup of trembling, and wrung them out.

18 There is none to guide her among all the sons whom she has brought forth; neither is there any that takes her by the hand of all the sons that she has brought up.

19 These two things are come to you; who shall be sorry for you? desolation, and destruction, and the famine, and the sword: by whom shall I comfort you?

20 Your sons have fainted, they lie at the head of all the streets, as a wild bull in a net: they are full of the fury of the LORD, the rebuke of your God.

21 Therefore hear now this, you afflicted, and drunken, but not with wine:

52:7

"How can they hear without someone preaching to them?" (Romans 10:14-15) God sees as beautiful the lowly feet of those who preach His glorious gospel.

22 Thus says your Lord the LORD, and your God that pleads the cause of his people, Behold, I have taken out of your hand the cup of trembling, even the dregs of the cup of my fury; you shall no more drink it again:

23 But I will put it into the hand of them that afflict you; which have said to your soul, Bow down, that we may go over: and you have laid your body as the ground, and as the street, to them that went over.

CHAPTER 52

AWAKE, awake; put on your strength, O Zion; put on your beautiful garments, O Jerusalem, the holy city: for henceforth there shall no more come into you the uncircumcised and the unclean.

2 Shake yourself from the dust; arise, and sit down, O Jerusalem: loose yourself from the bands of your neck, O captive daughter of Zion.

3 For thus says the LORD, You have sold yourselves for nought; and you shall be redeemed without money.

4 For thus says the Lord GOD, My people went down aforetime into Egypt to sojourn there; and the Assyrian oppressed them without cause.

5 Now therefore, what have I here, says the LORD, that my people is taken away for nought? they that rule over them make them to howl, says the LORD; and my name continually every day is blasphemed.

6 Therefore my people shall know my name: therefore they shall know in that day that I am he that does speak: behold, it is I.

7 *How beautiful upon the mountains are the feet of him that brings good tidings, that publishes peace; that brings good tidings of good, that publishes salvation; that says to Zion, Your God reigns!*

8 Your watchmen shall lift up the voice; with the voice together shall they sing:

for they shall see eye to eye, when the LORD shall bring again Zion.

9 Break forth into joy, sing together, you waste places of Jerusalem: for the LORD has comforted his people, he has redeemed Jerusalem.

10 The LORD has made bare his holy arm in the eyes of all the nations; and all the ends of the earth shall see the salvation of our God.

11 Depart, depart, go out from there, touch no unclean thing; go out of the midst of her; be clean, you that bear the vessels of the LORD.

12 For you shall not go out with haste, nor go by flight: for the LORD will go before you; and the God of Israel will be your rearward.

13 Behold, my servant shall deal prudently, he shall be exalted and extolled, and be very high.

14 As many were astonished at you; his visage was so marred more than any man, and his form more than the sons of men:

15 So shall he sprinkle many nations; the kings shall shut their mouths at him: for that which had not been told them shall they see; and that which they had not heard shall they consider.

CHAPTER 53

WHO has believed our report? and to whom is the arm of the LORD revealed?

2 For he shall grow up before him as a tender plant, and as a root out of a dry ground: he has no form nor comeliness; and when we shall see him, there is no beauty that we should desire him.

52:3

A penny held close to the eye can blot out all of creation, and a dollar held too close to the heart can make a man forget his eternal destiny (See also Judges 16:18).

3 He is despised and rejected of men; a man of sorrows, and acquainted with grief: and we hid as it were our faces from him; he was despised, and we esteemed him not.

4 Surely he has borne our griefs, and carried our sorrows: yet we did esteem him stricken, smitten of God, and afflicted.

5 But he was wounded for our transgressions, he was bruised for our iniquities: the chastisement of our peace was upon him; and with his stripes we are healed.

6 All we like sheep have gone astray; we have turned every one to his own way; and the LORD has laid on him the iniquity of us all.

7 He was oppressed, and he was afflicted, yet he opened not his mouth: he is brought as a lamb to the slaughter, and as a sheep before her shearers is dumb, so he opened not his mouth.

52:14 Paintings of a "suffering Savior" on the Cross can never do justice to the agony He endured for us.

53:1 One would think that a terminally ill world would gladly embrace the cure of the gospel, but few, so few, believe our report (see John 12:38-40).

53:3 The ungodly still despise and reject the name of Jesus Christ. It is used worldwide as a cuss word to express disgust. Adolf Hitler's name wasn't despised enough to use in such a way.

53:7 Pilate marveled at the silence of God's Lamb (see Matthew 27:12-14).

THE FUNCTION OF THE LAW

53 After reading Chapter 53 of Isaiah, one might wonder how any Jew who professes to believe God's Word could not see this entire chapter as a prophecy of a "suffering" Messiah, especially the detailed description found in verses 3 through 12.

The obstacle to a Jew's belief in Jesus as Savior could be because the professing Jew has not been "shut up under the Law." As long as anyone believes he can provide for his own atonement, he won't understand his need for the Savior and won't, therefore, search the scriptures.

The evangelist must confront both Gentile and Jew with the spiritual nature of God's Law (see Jeremiah 9:25). Open up the commandments as Jesus did.

Don't take for granted that the Jew knows God's Law as he should. Many Jews today are steeped in tradition, but make void the Law as did the Jews in the day of Christ.

8 He was taken from prison and from judgment: and who shall declare his generation? for he was cut off out of the land of the living: for the transgression of my people was he stricken.

9 And he made his grave with the wicked, and with the rich in his death; because he had done no violence, neither was any deceit in his mouth.

10 Yet it pleased the LORD to bruise him; he has put him to grief: when you shall make his soul an offering for sin, he shall see his seed, he shall prolong his days, and the pleasure of the LORD shall prosper in his hand.

11 He shall see of the travail of his soul, and shall be satisfied: by his knowledge shall my righteous servant justify many; for he shall bear their iniquities.

12 Therefore will I divide him a portion with the great, and he shall divide the spoil with the strong; because he has poured out his soul to death: and he was numbered with the transgressors; and he bare the sin of many, and made intercession for the transgressors.

CHAPTER 54

SING, O barren, you that did not bear; break forth into singing, and cry aloud, you that did not travail with child: for more are the children of the desolate than the children of the married wife, says the LORD.

2 Enlarge the place of your tent, and let them stretch forth the curtains of your habitations: spare not, lengthen your cords, and strengthen your stakes;

3 For you shall break forth on the right hand and on the left; and your seed shall inherit the Gentiles, and make the desolate cities to be inhabited.

4 Fear not; for you shall not be ashamed: neither be confounded; for you shall not be put to shame: for you shall forget the shame of your youth, and shall not remember the reproach of your widowhood any more.

5 For your Maker is your husband; the LORD of hosts is his name; and your Redeemer the Holy One of Israel; The God of the whole earth shall he be called.

6 For the LORD has called you as a woman forsaken and grieved in spirit, and a wife of youth, when you were refused, says your God.

7 For a small moment have I forsaken you; but with great mercies will I gather you.

8 In a little wrath I hid my face from you for a moment; but with everlasting

53:9 See Matthew 27:57-60. Also see 1 Peter 2:22.

53:10 See 2 Corinthians 5:21.

53:11 See 1 John 2:1, Isaiah 42:1 and Romans 5:15-18.

53:12 See Psalm 2:8, Colossians 2:15, Isaiah 50:6, Romans 3:25, Matthew 27:38, Mark 15:28, Luke 22:37 and 2 Corinthians 5:21.

kindness will I have mercy on you, says the LORD your Redeemer.

9 For this is as the waters of Noah to me: for as I have sworn that the waters of Noah should no more go over the earth; so have I sworn that I would not be wroth with you, nor rebuke you.

10 For the mountains shall depart, and the hills be removed; but my kindness shall not depart from you, neither shall the covenant of my peace be removed, says the LORD that has mercy on you.

11 O you afflicted, tossed with tempest, and not comforted, behold, I will lay your stones with fair colours, and lay your foundations with sapphires.

12 And I will make your windows of agates, and your gates of carbuncles, and all your borders of pleasant stones.

13 And all your children shall be taught of the LORD; and great shall be the peace of your children.

14 In righteousness shall you be established: you shall be far from oppression; for you shall not fear: and from terror; for it shall not come near you.

15 Behold, they shall surely gather together, but not by me: whosoever shall gather together against you shall fall for your sake.

16 Behold, I have created the smith that blows the coals in the fire, and that brings forth an instrument for his work; and I have created the waster to destroy.

17 No weapon that is formed against you shall prosper; and every tongue that shall rise against you in judgment you shall condemn. This is the heritage of the servants of the LORD, and their righteousness is of me, says the LORD.

CHAPTER 55

H O, every one that thirsts, come to the waters, and he that has no money; come, buy, and eat; yea, come, buy wine and milk without money and without price.

> Each of us has been created
> in the likeness of God
> and after His image,
> 'Let Us make man (male and female)
> in Our image,
> according to Our likeness.'
> We are three in one—
> spirit, soul, and body.
> Like God, we are immortal.
> The most important thing about us
> is our immortality—
> our everlasting soul.
> Paul said that he was called to preach
> the immortality
> that Jesus brought to light
> (see 2 Timothy 1:10-11).
> Each of us, no matter the color,
> shape, size, intellect or gender,
> are human beings (being human).
> But our real label is not who we are,
> what we do, or what we know, etc.
> What really matters
> is that we are immortal.

GARRY T. ANSDELL
BORN 1946 IN CANADA
SENIOR PASTOR, HOSANNA CHAPEL
BELLFLOWER, CALIFORNIA.

2 Why do you spend money for that which is not bread? and your labour for that which does not satisfy? hearken diligently to me, and eat that which is good, and let your soul delight itself in fatness.

3 Incline your ear, and come to me: hear, and your soul shall live; and I will make an everlasting covenant with you, even the sure mercies of David.

4 Behold, I have given him for a witness to the people, a leader and commander to the people.

5 Behold, you shall call a nation that you do not know, and nations that do not know you shall run to you because of the LORD your God, and for the Holy One of Israel; for he has glorified you.

54:17 Our confidence before God is only because we stand in the Savior's righteousness.

55:1-3

Here is God's universal offer to humanity; "incline your ear and come to Me, and your soul shall live." God has mercy on the soul upon conversion (see Romans 8:1). Those who "thirst" for righteousness are most likely to listen for God's voice (see John 7:37).

6 Seek the LORD while he may be found, call upon him while he is near:
7 Let the wicked forsake his way, and the unrighteous man his thoughts: and let him return to the LORD, and he will have mercy upon him; and to our God, for he will abundantly pardon.
8 For my thoughts are not your thoughts, neither are your ways my ways, says the LORD.
9 For as the heavens are higher than the earth, so are my ways higher than your ways, and my thoughts than your thoughts.
10 For as the rain comes down, and the snow from heaven, and do not return

there, but waters the earth, and makes it bring forth and bud, that it may give seed to the sower, and bread to the eater:
11 So shall my word be that goeth forth out of my mouth: it shall not return to me void, but it shall accomplish that which I please, and it shall prosper in the thing whereto I sent it.
12 For you shall go out with joy, and be led forth with peace: the mountains and the hills shall break forth before you into singing, and all the trees of the field shall clap their hands.
13 Instead of the thorn shall come up the fir tree, and instead of the brier shall come up the myrtle tree: and it shall be to the LORD for a name, for an everlasting sign that shall not be cut off.

CHAPTER 56

THUS says the LORD, Keep judgment, and do justice: for my salvation is near to come, and my righteousness to be revealed.
2 Blessed is the man that doeth this, and the son of man that lays hold on it; that keeps the sabbath from polluting it, and keeps his hand from doing any evil.
3 Neither let the son of the stranger, that has joined himself to the LORD, speak, saying, The LORD has utterly separated me from his people: neither let the eunuch say, Behold, I am a dry tree.
4 For thus says the LORD to the eunuchs that keep my sabbaths, and choose the things that please me, and take hold of my covenant;
5 Even to them will I give in my house and within my walls a place and a name better than of sons and of daughters:

55:6 This verse suggests that the patience of God is exhaustible. For those who refuse to accept the Gospel, the time may come when the Lord will refuse to "be found" (see Proverbs 1:24-31). Unbelievers should be made aware that they may not get the deathbed conversion they may be planning on.

55:7 True repentance means to forsake the thoughts, as well as the deeds.

55:11 This verse is the reason for our confidence when we preach an uncompromising gospel message, even if we see no visible results (see also 1 Corinthians 15:58).

QUESTIONS & OBJECTIONS

Q **57:5** *"I know abortion isn't right, but if it is not legal, we'll have all those poor girls slipping off to see those butchers in dark alleys. At least this way they get counseling."*

You're right. Think of all those poor murderers who are condemned to slip around and kill in secret. We ought to legalize murder too! Then they can kill in a nice clean safe environment. They'll be protected from getting splashed with blood that might contain diseases, and we can offer counseling so they don't have any post murder trauma from the choices they've made. (See also Exodus 23:7)

I will give them an everlasting name, that shall not be cut off.

6 Also the sons of the stranger, that join themselves to the LORD, to serve him, and to love the name of the LORD, to be his servants, every one that keeps the sabbath from polluting it, and takes hold of my covenant;

7 Even them will I bring to my holy mountain, and make them joyful in my house of prayer: their burnt offerings and their sacrifices shall be accepted upon my altar; for my house shall be called an house of prayer for all people.

8 The Lord GOD, which gathers the outcasts of Israel says, Yet will I gather others to him, beside those that are gathered to him.

9 All you beasts of the field, come to devour, yea, all you beasts in the forest.

10 His watchmen are blind: they are all ignorant, they are all dumb dogs, they cannot bark; sleeping, lying down, loving to slumber.

11 Yea, they are greedy dogs which can never have enough, and they are shepherds that cannot understand: they all look to their own way, every one for his gain, from his quarter.

12 Come, say they, I will fetch wine, and we will fill ourselves with strong drink; and tomorrow shall be as this day, and much more abundant.

CHAPTER 57

THE righteous perish, and no man lays it to heart: and merciful men are taken away, none considering that the righteous is taken away from the evil to come.

2 He shall enter into peace: they shall rest in their beds, each one walking in his uprightness.

3 But draw near here, you sons of the sorceress, the seed of the adulterer and the whore.

4 Against whom do you sport yourselves? against whom do you make a wide mouth, and draw out the tongue? are you not children of transgression, a seed of falsehood.

57:4

The symbol of rebellion among occultist heavy-metal fans is a wide mouth and a sticking-out tongue. They are children of transgression, a seed of falsehood.

5 Enflaming yourselves with idols under every green tree, slaying the children in the valleys under the clifts of the rocks?

6 Among the smooth stones of the stream is your portion; they, they are your lot: even to them have you poured a drink offering, you have offered a meat offering. Should I receive comfort in these?

7 Upon a lofty and high mountain have you set your bed: even there you went up to offer sacrifice.

8 Behind the doors also and the posts have you set up your remembrance: for you have discovered yourself to another than me, and are gone up; you have enlarged your bed, and made you a covenant with them; you loved their bed where you saw it.

9 And you went to the king with ointment, and did increase your perfumes, and did send your messengers far off, and did debase yourself even to hell.

10 You are wearied in the greatness of your way; yet you did not say, There is no hope: you have found the life of your hand; therefore you were not grieved.

11 And of whom have you been afraid or feared, that you have lied, and have not remembered me, nor laid it to your heart? have not I held my peace even of old, and you do not fear me?

12 I will declare your righteousness, and your works; for they shall not profit you.

13 When you cry, let your companies deliver you; but the wind shall carry them all away; vanity shall take them: but he that puts his trust in me shall possess the land, and shall inherit my holy mountain;

14 And shall say, Cast up, cast up, prepare the way, take up the stumblingblock out of the way of my people.

15 For thus says the high and lofty One that inhabits eternity, whose name is Holy; I dwell in the high and holy place, with him also that is of a contrite and humble spirit, to revive the spirit of the humble, and to revive the heart of the contrite ones.

16 For I will not contend for ever, neither will I be always wroth: for the spirit should fail before me, and the souls which I have made.

17 For the iniquity of his covetousness was I wroth, and smote him: I hid me, and was wroth, and he went on frowardly in the way of his heart.

18 I have seen his ways, and will heal him: I will lead him also, and restore comforts to him and to his mourners.

19 I create the fruit of the lips; Peace, peace to him that is far off, and to him that is near, says the LORD; and I will heal him.

20 But the wicked are like the troubled sea, when it cannot rest, whose waters cast up mire and dirt.

21 There is no peace, says my God, to the wicked.

CHAPTER 58

CRY aloud, spare not, lift up your voice like a trumpet, and show my people their transgression, and the house of Jacob their sins.

58:1

If you obey this verse, the world will reprove you. They will tell you to instead speak about God's love. They will accuse you of being self-righteous. They will say "Judge not lest you be judged," and will even tell you that Jesus didn't talk about sin (see Matthew 23:13, Luke 6:37 and John 8:11 comments).

57:15 The essence of repentance is a humble and contrite heart (see Psalm 34:18 & Psalm 51:17).

2 Yet they seek me daily, and delight to know my ways, as a nation that did righteousness, and forsook not the ordinance of their God: they ask of me the ordinances of justice; they take delight in approaching to God.

3 Why have we fasted, say they, and you have not seen? why have we afflicted our soul, and you take no knowledge? Behold, in the day of your fast you find pleasure, and exact all your labours.

4 Behold, you fast for strife and debate, and to smite with the fist of wickedness: you shall not fast as you do this day, to make your voice to be heard on high.

5 Is it such a fast that I have chosen? a day for a man to afflict his soul? is it to bow down his head as a bulrush, and to spread sackcloth and ashes under him? will you call this a fast, and an acceptable day to the LORD?

6 Is not this the fast that I have chosen? to loose the bands of wickedness, to undo the heavy burdens, and to let the oppressed go free, and that you break every yoke?

7 Is it not to deal your bread to the hungry, and that you bring the poor that are cast out to your house? when you see the naked, that you cover him; and not hide yourself from your own flesh?

8 Then shall your light break forth as the morning, and your health shall spring forth speedily: and your righteousness shall go before you; the glory of the LORD shall be your rearward.

9 Then shall you call, and the LORD shall answer; you shall cry, and he shall say, Here I am. If you take away from the midst of you the yoke, the putting forth of the finger, and speaking vanity;

10 And if you draw out your soul to the hungry, and satisfy the afflicted soul; then shall your light rise in obscurity, and your darkness be as the noon day:

11 And the LORD shall guide you continually, and satisfy your soul in drought, and make fat your bones: and you shall be like a watered garden, and like a spring of water, whose waters fail not.

12 And they that shall be of you shall build the old waste places: you shall raise up the foundations of many generations; and you shall be called, The repairer of the breach, The restorer of paths to dwell in.

13 If you turn away your foot from the sabbath, from doing your pleasure on my holy day; and call the sabbath a delight, the holy of the LORD, honourable; and shall honour him, not doing your own ways, nor finding your own pleasure, nor speaking your own words:

14 Then shall you delight yourself in the LORD; and I will cause you to ride upon the high places of the earth, and feed you with the heritage of Jacob your father: for the mouth of the LORD has spoken it.

CHAPTER 59

BEHOLD, the LORD's hand is not shortened, that it cannot save; neither his ear heavy, that it cannot hear:

2 But your iniquities have separated between you and your God, and your sins have hid his face from you, that he will not hear.

3 For your hands are defiled with blood, and your fingers with iniquity; your lips have spoken lies, your tongue has muttered perverseness.

4 None calls for justice, nor any pleads for truth: they trust in vanity, and speak lies; they conceive mischief, and bring forth iniquity.

5 They hatch cockatrice' eggs, and weave the spider's web: he that eats of

---

59:1-2 Sometimes when sinners say that they pray and don't think that God even hears them, they may be right. If I am aware of sin in my heart, the Bible says that the Lord will not hear me (see Psalm 66:18).

their eggs dies, and that which is crushed breaks out into a viper.

6 Their webs shall not become garments, neither shall they cover themselves with their works: their works are works of iniquity, and the act of violence is in their hands.

7 Their feet run to evil, and they make haste to shed innocent blood: their thoughts are thoughts of iniquity; wasting and destruction are in their paths.

8 The way of peace they know not; and there is no judgment in their goings: they have made them crooked paths: whosoever goeth therein shall not know peace.

9 Therefore is judgment far from us, neither does justice overtake us: we wait for light, but behold obscurity; for brightness, but we walk in darkness.

10 We grope for the wall like the blind, and we grope as if we had no eyes: we stumble at noon day as in the night; we are in desolate places as dead men.

11 We roar all like bears, and mourn sore like doves: we look for judgment, but there is none; for salvation, but it is far off from us.

12 For our transgressions are multiplied before you, and our sins testify against us: for our transgressions are with us; and as for our iniquities, we know them;

13 In transgressing and lying against the LORD, and departing away from our God, speaking oppression and revolt, conceiving and uttering from the heart words of falsehood.

14 And judgment is turned away backward, and justice stands afar off: for truth is fallen in the street, and equity cannot enter.

15 Yea, truth fails; and he that departs from evil makes himself a prey: and the LORD saw it, and it displeased him that there was no judgment.

16 And he saw that there was no man, and wondered that there was no intercessor: therefore his arm brought salvation to him; and his righteousness, it sustained him.

17 For he put on righteousness as a breastplate, and an helmet of salvation upon his head; and he put on the garments of vengeance for clothing, and was clad with zeal as a cloak.

18 According to their deeds, accordingly he will repay, fury to his adversaries, recompence to his enemies; to the islands he will repay recompence.

19 So shall they fear the name of the LORD from the west, and his glory from the rising of the sun. When the enemy shall come in like a flood, the Spirit of the LORD shall lift up a standard against him.

20 And the Redeemer shall come to Zion, and to them that turn from transgression in Jacob, says the LORD.

21 As for me, this is my covenant with them, says the LORD; My spirit that is upon you, and my words which I have put in your mouth, shall not depart out of your mouth, nor out of the mouth of your seed, nor out of the mouth of your seed's seed, says the LORD, from henceforth and for ever.

CHAPTER 60

ARISE, shine; for your light is come, and the glory of the LORD is risen upon you.

2 For, behold, the darkness shall cover the earth, and gross darkness the people: but the LORD shall arise upon you, and his glory shall be seen upon you.

3 And the Gentiles shall come to your light, and kings to the brightness of your rising.

4 Lift up your eyes round about, and see: all they gather themselves together, they come to you: your sons shall come

---

59:7 See Psalm 127:3 comment.

59:13 For thoughts on atheism see Psalm 53:1 comment.

from far, and your daughters shall be nursed at your side.

5 Then you shall see, and flow together, and your heart shall fear, and be enlarged; because the abundance of the sea shall be converted to you, the forces of the Gentiles shall come to you.

6 The multitude of camels shall cover you, the dromedaries of Midian and Ephah; all they from Sheba shall come: they shall bring gold and incense; and they shall show forth the praises of the LORD.

7 All the flocks of Kedar shall be gathered together to you, the rams of Nebaioth shall minister to you: they shall come up with acceptance on my altar, and I will glorify the house of my glory.

8 Who are these that fly as a cloud, and as the doves to their windows?

9 Surely the isles shall wait for me, and the ships of Tarshish first, to bring your sons from far, their silver and their gold with them, to the name of the LORD your God, and to the Holy One of Israel, because he has glorified you.

10 And the sons of strangers shall build up your walls, and their kings shall minister to you: for in my wrath I smote you, but in my favour have I had mercy on you.

11 Therefore your gates shall be open continually; they shall not be shut day nor night; that men may bring to you the forces of the Gentiles, and that their kings may be brought.

12 For the nation and kingdom that will not serve you shall perish; yea, those nations shall be utterly wasted.

13 The glory of Lebanon shall come to you, the fir tree, the pine tree, and the box together, to beautify the place of my sanctuary; and I will make the place of my feet glorious.

14 The sons also of them that afflicted you shall come bending to you; and all they that despised you shall bow themselves down at the soles of your feet; and they shall call you; The city of the LORD, The Zion of the Holy One of Israel.

15 Whereas you has been forsaken and hated, so that no man went through you, I will make you an eternal excellency, a joy of many generations.

16 You shall also suck the milk of the Gentiles, and shall suck the breast of kings: and you shall know that I the LORD am your Saviour and your Redeemer, the mighty One of Jacob.

17 For brass I will bring gold, and for iron I will bring silver, and for wood brass, and for stones iron: I will also make your officers peace, and your exactors righteousness.

18 Violence shall no more be heard in your land, wasting nor destruction within your borders; but you shall call your walls Salvation, and your gates Praise.

19 The sun shall no more be your light by day; neither for brightness shall the moon give light to you: but the LORD shall be to you an everlasting light, and your God your glory.

20 Your sun shall no longer go down; neither shall your moon withdraw itself: for the LORD shall be your everlasting light, and the days of your mourning shall be ended.

21 Your people also shall be all righteous: they shall inherit the land for ever, the branch of my planting, the work of my hands, that I may be glorified.

22 A little one shall become a thousand, and a small one a strong nation: I the LORD will hasten it in his time.

CHAPTER 61

THE Spirit of the Lord GOD is upon me; because the LORD has anointed me to preach good tidings to the meek; he has sent me to bind up the brokenhearted, to proclaim liberty to the cap-

---

61:1 See Luke 4:18 comment, "Who is the gospel for?"

tives, and the opening of the prison to them that are bound;

2 To proclaim the acceptable year of the LORD, and the day of vengeance of our God; to comfort all that mourn;

3 To appoint to them that mourn in Zion, to give to them beauty for ashes, the oil of joy for mourning, the garment of praise for the spirit of heaviness; that they might be called trees of righteousness, the planting of the LORD, that he might be glorified.

4 And they shall build the old wastes, they shall raise up the former desolations, and they shall repair the waste cities, the desolations of many generations.

5 And strangers shall stand and feed your flocks, and the sons of the alien shall be your plowmen and your vinedressers.

6 But you shall be named the Priests of the LORD: men shall call you the Ministers of our God: you shall eat the riches of the Gentiles, and in their glory shall you boast yourselves.

7 For your shame you shall have double; and for confusion they shall rejoice in their portion: therefore in their land they shall possess the double: everlasting joy shall be to them.

8 For I the LORD love judgment, I hate robbery for burnt offering; and I will direct their work in truth, and I will make an everlasting covenant with them.

9 And their seed shall be known among the Gentiles, and their offspring among the people: all that see them shall acknowledge them, that they are the seed which the LORD has blessed.

10 I will greatly rejoice in the LORD, my soul shall be joyful in my God; for he has clothed me with the garments of salvation, he has covered me with the robe of righteousness, as a bridegroom decks himself with ornaments, and as a bride adorns herself with her jewels.

11 For as the earth brings forth her bud, and as the garden causes the things that are sown in it to spring forth; so the Lord GOD will cause righteousness and praise to spring forth before all the nations.

CHAPTER 62

FOR Zion's sake will I not hold my peace, and for Jerusalem's sake I will not rest, until the righteousness thereof go forth as brightness, and the salvation thereof as a lamp that burns.

2 And the Gentiles shall see your righteousness, and all kings your glory: and you shall be called by a new name, which the mouth of the LORD shall name.

3 You shall also be a crown of glory in the hand of the LORD, and a royal diadem in the hand of your God.

4 You shall no more be termed Forsaken; neither shall your land any more be termed Desolate: but you shall be called Hephzibah, and your land Beulah: for the LORD delights in you, and your land shall be married.

5 For as a young man marries a virgin, so shall your sons marry you: and as the bridegroom rejoices over the bride, so shall your God rejoice over you.

6 I have set watchmen upon your walls, O Jerusalem, which shall never hold their peace day nor night: you that make mention of the LORD, keep not silence,

7 And give him no rest, till he establish, and till he make Jerusalem a praise in the earth.

8 The LORD has sworn by his right hand, and by the arm of his strength, Surely I will no more give your corn to

---

61:3 Here is the order of conversion; a sinner should "mourn" for his sinful state. He should have the spirit of heaviness (be laboring and heavy laden over his sinful heart--see Matthew 11:28-30). It is these converts that become trees of righteousness because they are the planting of the Lord; they are born of God (see John 1:13).

be meat for your enemies; and the sons of the stranger shall not drink your wine, for the which you have laboured:

9 But they that have gathered it shall eat it, and praise the LORD; and they that have brought it together shall drink it in the courts of my holiness.

10 Go through, go through the gates; prepare the way of the people; cast up, cast up the highway; gather out the stones; lift up a standard for the people.

11 Behold, the LORD has proclaimed to the end of the world, Say to the daughter of Zion, Behold, your salvation comes; behold, his reward is with him, and his work before him.

12 And they shall call them, The holy people, The redeemed of the LORD: and you shall be called, Sought out, A city not forsaken.

CHAPTER 63

WHO is this that comes from Edom, with dyed garments from Bozrah? this that is glorious in his apparel, travelling in the greatness of his strength? I that speak in righteousness, mighty to save.

2 Why are you red in your apparel, and your garments like him that treads in the winefat?

3 I have trodden the winepress alone; and of the people there was none with me: for I will tread them in my anger, and trample them in my fury; and their blood shall be sprinkled upon my garments, and I will stain all my raiment.

4 For the day of vengeance is in my heart, and the year of my redeemed is come.

5 And I looked, and there was none to help; and I wondered that there was none to uphold: therefore my own arm brought salvation to me; and my fury, it upheld me.

6 And I will tread down the people in my anger, and make them drunk in my

> Oh, to realize that souls,
> precious, never dying souls,
> are perishing all around us,
> going out into the blackness
> of darkness and despair,
> eternally lost,
> and yet to feel no anguish,
> shed no tears, know no travail!
> How little we know
> of the compassion of Jesus!
> **OSWALD J. SMITH**
> EVANGELICAL PREACHER,
> MISSIONARY
> AND HYMN COMPOSER
> BORN 1890 IN TORONTO

fury, and I will bring down their strength to the earth.

7 I will mention the lovingkindnesses of the LORD, and the praises of the LORD, according to all that the LORD has bestowed on us, and the great goodness toward the house of Israel, which he has bestowed on them according to his mercies, and according to the multitude of his lovingkindnesses.

8 For he said, Surely they are my people, children that will not lie: so he was their Saviour.

9 In all their affliction he was afflicted, and the angel of his presence saved them: in his love and in his pity he redeemed them; and he bare them, and carried them all the days of old.

10 But they rebelled, and vexed his holy Spirit: therefore he was turned to be their enemy, and he fought against them.

11 Then he remembered the days of old, Moses, and his people, saying, Where is he that brought them up out of the sea with the shepherd of his flock? where is he that put his holy Spirit within him?

12 That led them by the right hand of Moses with his glorious arm, dividing

62:10 We obey this verse when we preach the whole counsel of God.

the water before them, to make himself an everlasting name?

13 That led them through the deep, as an horse in the wilderness, that they should not stumble?

14 As a beast goeth down into the valley, the Spirit of the LORD caused him to rest: so did you lead your people, to make yourself a glorious name.

15 Look down from heaven, and behold from the habitation of your holiness and of your glory: where is your zeal and your strength, the sounding of your bowels and of your mercies toward me? are they restrained?

16 Doubtless you are our father, though Abraham be ignorant of us, and Israel acknowledge us not: you, O LORD, are our father, our redeemer; your name is from everlasting.

17 O LORD, why have you made us to err from your ways, and hardened our heart from your fear? Return for your servants' sake, the tribes of your inheritance.

18 The people of your holiness have possessed it but a little while: our adversaries have trodden down your sanctuary.

19 We are yours: you never ruled over them; they were not called by your name.

CHAPTER 64

*O*H that you wouldest rend the heavens, that you wouldest come down, that the mountains might flow down at your presence,

2 As when the melting fire burns, the fire causes the waters to boil, to make your name known to your adversaries, that the nations may tremble at your presence!

3 When you did terrible things which we looked not for, you came down, the mountains flowed down at your presence.

4 For since the beginning of the world men have not heard, nor perceived by the ear, neither has the eye seen, O God, beside you, what he has prepared for him that waits for him.

5 You meet him that rejoices and works righteousness, those that remember you in your ways: behold, you are wroth; for we have sinned: in those is continuance, and we shall be saved.

6 But we are all as an unclean thing, and all our righteousnesses are as filthy rags; and we all do fade as a leaf; and our iniquities, like the wind, have taken us away.

7 And there is none that calls upon your name, that stirs up himself to take hold of you: for you have hid your face from us, and have consumed us, because of our iniquities.

8 But now, O LORD, you are our father; we are the clay, and you our potter; and we all are the work of your hand.

9 Be not wroth very sore, O LORD, neither remember iniquity for ever: behold, see, we beseech you, we are all your people.

10 Your holy cities are a wilderness, Zion is a wilderness, Jerusalem a desolation.

11 Our holy and our beautiful house, where our fathers praised you, is burned up with fire: and all our pleasant things are laid waste.

12 Will you refrain yourself for these things, O LORD? will you hold your peace, and afflict us very sore?

64:1 The prophet's cry was for the world to give God His due honor. This is our prayer also.

64:6 See Luke 16:15.

CHAPTER 65

I AM sought of them that asked not for me; I am found of them that sought me not: I said, Behold me, behold me, to a nation that was not called by my name.

2 I have spread out my hands all the day to a rebellious people, which walks in a way that was not good, after their own thoughts;

3 A people that provokes me to anger continually to my face; that sacrifices in gardens, and burns incense upon altars of brick;

4 Which remain among the graves, and lodge in the monuments, which eat swine's flesh, and broth of abominable things is in their vessels;

5 Which say, Stand by yourself, do not come near me; for I am holier than you. These are a smoke in my nose, a fire that burns all the day.

6 Behold, it is written before me: I will not keep silence, but will recompense, even recompense into their bosom,

7 Your iniquities, and the iniquities of your fathers together, says the LORD, which have burned incense upon the mountains, and blasphemed me upon the hills: therefore will I measure their former work into their bosom.

8 Thus says the LORD, As the new wine is found in the cluster, and one says, Destroy it not; for a blessing is in it: so will I do for my servants' sakes, that I may not destroy them all.

9 And I will bring forth a seed out of Jacob, and out of Judah an inheritor of my mountains: and my elect shall inherit it, and my servants shall dwell there.

10 And Sharon shall be a fold of flocks, and the valley of Achor a place for the herds to lie down in, for my people that have sought me.

11 But you are they that forsake the LORD, that forget my holy mountain, that prepare a table for that troop, and that furnish the drink offering to that number.

12 Therefore will I number you to the sword, and you shall all bow down to the slaughter: because when I called, you did not answer; when I spoke, you did not hear; but did evil before my eyes, and did choose that wherein I delighted not.

13 Therefore thus says the Lord GOD, Behold, my servants shall eat, but you shall be hungry: behold, my servants shall drink, but you shall be thirsty: behold, my servants shall rejoice, but you shall be ashamed:

14 Behold, my servants shall sing for joy of heart, but you shall cry for sorrow of heart, and shall howl for vexation of spirit.

15 And you shall leave your name for a curse to my chosen: for the Lord GOD shall slay you, and call his servants by another name:

16 That he who blesses himself in the earth shall bless himself in the God of truth; and he that swears in the earth shall swear by the God of truth; because the former troubles are forgotten, and because they are hid from my eyes.

17 For, behold, I create new heavens and a new earth: and the former shall not be remembered, nor come into mind.

18 But be glad and rejoice for ever in that which I create: for, behold, I create Jerusalem a rejoicing, and her people a joy.

19 And I will rejoice in Jerusalem, and joy in my people: and the voice of weeping shall be no more heard in her, nor the voice of crying.

20 There shall be no more thence an infant of days, nor an old man that has not filled his days: for the child shall die an hundred years old; but the sinner being an hundred years old shall be accursed.

65:15 See Acts 11:26.

21 And they shall build houses, and inhabit them; and they shall plant vineyards, and eat the fruit of them.

22 They shall not build, and another inhabit; they shall not plant, and another eat: for as the days of a tree are the days of my people, and my elect shall long enjoy the work of their hands.

23 They shall not labour in vain, nor bring forth for trouble; for they are the seed of the blessed of the LORD, and their offspring with them.

24 And it shall come to pass, that before they call, I will answer; and while they are yet speaking, I will hear.

25 The wolf and the lamb shall feed together, and the lion shall eat straw like the bullock: and dust shall be the serpent's meat. They shall not hurt nor destroy in all my holy mountain, says the LORD.

CHAPTER 66

THUS says the LORD, The heaven is my throne, and the earth is my footstool: where is the house that you build to me? and where is the place of my rest?

2 For all those things has my hand made, and all those things have been, says the LORD: but to this man will I look, even to him that is poor and of a contrite spirit, and trembles at my word.

3 He that kills an ox is as if he slew a man; he that sacrifices a lamb, as if he cut off a dog's neck; he that offers an oblation, as if he offered swine's blood; he that burns incense, as if he blessed an idol. Yea, they have chosen their own ways, and their soul delights in their abominations.

4 I also will choose their delusions, and will bring their fears upon them; because when I called, none did answer; when I spoke, they did not hear: but they did evil before my eyes, and chose that in which I delighted not.

5 Hear the word of the LORD, you that tremble at his word; Your brethren that hated you, that cast you out for my name's sake, said, Let the LORD be glorified: but he shall appear to your joy, and they shall be ashamed.

6 A voice of noise from the city, a voice from the temple, a voice of the LORD that renders recompence to his enemies.

7 Before she travailed, she brought forth; before her pain came, she was delivered of a man child.

8 Who has heard such a thing? who has seen such things? Shall the earth be made to bring forth in one day? or shall a nation be born at once? for as soon as Zion travailed, she brought forth her children.

9 Shall I bring to the birth, and not cause to bring forth? says the LORD: shall I cause to bring forth, and shut the womb? says your God.

10 Rejoice with Jerusalem, and be glad with her, all you that love her: rejoice for joy with her, all you that mourn for her:

11 That you may suck, and be satisfied with the breasts of her consolations; that you may milk out, and be delighted with the abundance of her glory.

12 For thus says the LORD, Behold, I will extend peace to her like a river, and the glory of the Gentiles like a flowing stream: then shall you suck, you shall be borne upon her sides, and be dandled upon her knees.

13 As one whom his mother comforts, so will I comfort you; and you shall be comforted in Jerusalem.

14 And when you see this, your heart shall rejoice, and your bones shall flourish like an herb: and the hand of the LORD shall be known toward his

---

65:25 This is often misquoted as "The lion will lie down with the lamb."

66:2 See Isaiah 61:3 comment.

66:15 See 2 Thessalonians 1:8..

servants, and his indignation toward his enemies.

15 For, behold, the LORD will come with fire, and with his chariots like a whirlwind, to render his anger with fury, and his rebuke with flames of fire.

16 For by fire and by his sword will the LORD plead with all flesh: and the slain of the LORD shall be many.

17 They that sanctify themselves, and purify themselves in the gardens behind one tree in the midst, eating swine's flesh, and the abomination, and the mouse, shall be consumed together, says the LORD.

18 For I know their works and their thoughts: it shall come, that I will gather all nations and tongues; and they shall come, and see my glory.

19 And I will set a sign among them, and I will send those that escape of them to the nations, to Tarshish, Pul, and Lud, that draw the bow, to Tubal, and Javan, to the isles afar off, that have not heard my fame, neither have seen my glory;and they shall declare my glory among the Gentiles.

20 And they shall bring all your brethren for an offering to the LORD out of all nations upon horses, and in chariots, and in litters, and upon mules, and upon swift beasts, to my holy mountain Jerusalem, says the LORD, as the children of Israel bring an offering in a clean vessel into the house of the LORD.

21 And I will also take of them for priests and for Levites, says the LORD.

22 For as the new heavens and the new earth, which I will make, shall remain before me, says the LORD, so shall your seed and your name remain.

23 And it shall come to pass, that from one new moon to another, and from one sabbath to another, shall all flesh come to worship before me, says the LORD.

24 And they shall go forth, and look upon the carcases of the men that have transgressed against me: for their worm shall not die, neither shall their fire be quenched; and they shall be an abhorring to all flesh.

66:24 See Mark 9:44-48

Jeremiah

CHAPTER 1

THE words of Jeremiah the son of Hilkiah, of the priests that were in Anathoth in the land of Benjamin:

2 To whom the word of the LORD came in the days of Josiah the son of Amon king of Judah, in the thirteenth year of his reign.

3 It came also in the days of Jehoiakim the son of Josiah king of Judah, to the end of the eleventh year of Zedekiah the son of Josiah king of Judah, to the carrying away of Jerusalem captive in the fifth month.

4 Then the word of the LORD came to me, saying,

5 Before I formed you in the belly I knew you; and before you came forth out of the womb I sanctified you, and I ordained you a prophet to the nations.

6 Then said I, Ah, Lord GOD! behold, I cannot speak: for I am a child.

7 But the LORD said to me, Say not, I am a child: for you shall go to all that I shall send you, and whatsoever I command you you shall speak.

8 Do not be afraid of their faces: for I am with you to deliver you, says the LORD.

9 Then the LORD put forth his hand, and touched my mouth. And the LORD said to me, Behold, I have put my words in your mouth.

10 See, I have this day set you over the nations and over the kingdoms, to root out, and to pull down, and to destroy, and to throw down, to build, and to plant.

11 Moreover the word of the LORD came to me, saying, Jeremiah, what do you see? And I said, I see a rod of an almond tree.

12 Then said the LORD to me, You have well seen: for I will hasten my word to perform it.

13 And the word of the LORD came to me the second time, saying, What do you see? And I said, I see a seething pot; and the face thereof is toward the north.

1:2 Since Jesus' incarnation, death and resurrection, we don't need special revelation to know the Word of the Lord. His Word has been manifest to us through His Son (see Hebrews 1:1-2).

1:5 We, too, have been formed (created by God), known (known of God), sanctified (by the blood of the Savior) and ordained (given the Great Commission (see Mark 16:15; see also Galatians 1:15).

1:6-7 Matthew Henry said, "'Thou hast God's precept, and let not thy being young hinder thee from obeying it. 'Go to all to whom I shall send thee and speak whatsoever I command thee.' Note, though a sense of our own weakness and insufficiency should make us go humbly about our work, yet it should not make us draw back from it when God calls us to it. God was angry with Moses even for his modest excuses" (Exodus 4:14).

> **I am tired of hearing the words, "I can't."**
> Jeremiah said, "I am a child;" but the Lord didn't pat him on the back and say,
> "Jeremiah, that is very good; I like that in you. Your humility is beautiful."
> Oh no! God didn't want any such mock humility. He reproved and rebuked it.
> I do not like the humility that is too humble to do as it is bid.
> When my children are too humble to do as they are bid,
> I pretty soon find a way to make them.
> I say, "Go and do it!"
> The Lord wants us to "Go and do it."

CATHERINE BOOTH

1829-1890

CO-FOUNDER WITH HER HUSBAND, WILLIAM, OF THE SALVATION ARMY

14 Then the LORD said to me, Out of the north an evil shall break forth upon all the inhabitants of the land.

15 For, lo, I will call all the families of the kingdoms of the north, says the LORD; and they shall come, and they shall set every one his throne at the entering of the gates of Jerusalem, and against all the walls thereof round about, and against all the cities of Judah.

16 And I will utter my judgments against them touching all their wickedness, who have forsaken me, and have burned incense to other gods, and worshipped the works of their own hands.

17 You therefore gird up your loins, and arise, and speak to them all that I command you: be not dismayed at their faces, lest I confound you before them.

18 For, behold, I have made you this day a defenced city, and an iron pillar, and brasen walls against the whole land, against the kings of Judah, against the princes thereof, against the priests thereof, and against the people of the land.

19 And they shall fight against you; but they shall not prevail against you; for I am with you, says the LORD, to deliver you.

CHAPTER 2

MOREOVER the word of the LORD came to me, saying,

2 Go and cry in the ears of Jerusalem, saying, Thus says the LORD; I remember you, the kindness of your youth, the love of your espousals, when you went after me in the wilderness, in a land that was not sown.

3 Israel was holiness to the LORD, and the firstfruits of his increase: all that devour him shall offend; evil shall come upon them, says the LORD.

4 Hear the word of the LORD, O house of Jacob, and all the families of the house of Israel:

5 Thus says the LORD, What iniquity have your fathers found in me, that they are gone far from me, and have walked after vanity, and are become vain?

6 Neither said they, Where is the LORD that brought us up out of the land of Egypt, that led us through the wilderness, through a land of deserts and of

1:17 God gives a similar commission to the Christian. We are to prepare ourselves, then arise with the gospel. It is not an option; it is God's command.

1:18 May God make us a fortified city, stubborn for the truth.

1:19 We need nothing else if God is with us (see Romans 8:31).

2:1 God forbid that we should ever preach without a "cry." We are warning men and women that they will be damned for eternity. Passion should be our fuel.

2:5 Men may point a sinful finger of accusation at a holy God; but what injustice can be found in God? His ways are perfect (see Micah 6:3).

Jeremiah 1:9-10

Notice the order. Jeremiah is to root out, pull down, destroy, throw down, then build and plant. Before we can build the Kingdom of God by planting the seed of God's Word, we must prepare the ground. It is the function of the moral Law in the hand of the Holy Spirit to root out sin, pull down strongholds and destroy the sinner's self-righteousness so that he understands his need to throw himself on the mercy of God.

pits, through a land of drought, and of the shadow of death, through a land that no man passed through, and where no man dwelt?

7 And I brought you into a plentiful country, to eat the fruit thereof and the goodness thereof; but when you entered, you defiled my land, and made my heritage an abomination.

8 The priests said not, Where is the LORD? and they that handle the law knew me not: the pastors also transgressed against me, and the prophets prophesied by Baal, and walked after things that do not profit.

9 Therefore I will yet plead with you, says the LORD, and with your children's children will I plead.

10 For pass over the isles of Chittim, and see; and send to Kedar, and consider diligently, and see if there be such a thing.

11 Has a nation changed their gods, which are yet no gods? but my people have changed their glory for that which does not profit.

12 Be astonished, O you heavens, at this, and be horribly afraid, be very desolate, says the LORD.

13 For my people have committed two evils; they have forsaken me the fountain of living waters, and hewed them out cisterns, broken cisterns, that can hold no water.

14 Is Israel a servant? is he a homeborn slave? why is he spoiled?

15 The young lions roared upon him, and yelled, and they made his land waste: his cities are burned without inhabitant.

16 Also the children of Noph and Tahapanes have broken the crown of your head.

17 Have you not procured this to yourself, in that you have forsaken the LORD your God, when he led you by the way?

18 And now what have you to do in the way of Egypt, to drink the waters of Sihor? or what have you to do in the way of Assyria, to drink the waters of the river?

19 Your own wickedness shall correct you, and your backslidings shall reprove you: know therefore and see that it is an evil thing and bitter, that you have forsaken the LORD your God, and that my fear is not in you, says the Lord GOD of hosts.

20 For of old time I have broken your yoke, and burst your bands; and you said, I will not transgress; when upon every high hill and under every green tree you wander, playing the harlot.

21 Yet I had planted you a noble vine, wholly a right seed: how then are you turned into the degenerate plant of a strange vine to me?

22 For though you wash yourself with nitre, and use much soap, yet your iniquity is marked before me, says the Lord GOD.

23 How can you say, I am not polluted, I have not gone after Baalim? see your way in the valley, know what you have done: you are a swift dromedary traversing her ways;

24 A wild ass used to the wilderness, that snuffeth up the wind at her pleasure; in her occasion who can turn her away? all they that seek her will not

---

2:1–5 The Fear of the Lord. This is how to obtain the fear of the Lord, the most necessary virtue: 1) receive the Word of God; 2) hide His commandments within you; 3) incline your ear to wisdom; 4) apply your heart to understanding; 5) cry out for knowledge and discernment; 6) seek it as you would for silver or hidden treasures.

2:12 Wisdom, knowledge, discretion, and understanding will keep you from perversity and sexual sin. They give the blind light as to the end result of sin: see verse 18.

2:19 This is the law of sowing and reaping.

2:22 The Law of God "marks" iniquity.

weary themselves; in her month they shall find her.

25 Withhold your foot from being unshod, and your throat from thirst: but you said, There is no hope: no; for I have loved strangers, and after them will I go.

26 As the thief is ashamed when he is found, so is the house of Israel ashamed; they, their kings, their princes, and their priests, and their prophets.

27 Saying to a stock, You are my father; and to a stone, You have brought me forth: for they have turned their back to me, and not their face: but in the time of their trouble they will say, Arise, and save us.

28 But where are your gods that you have made for yourselves? let them arise, if they can save you in the time of your trouble: for according to the number of your cities are your gods, O Judah.

29 Why will you plead with me? you all have transgressed against me, says the LORD.

30 In vain have I smitten your children; they received no correction: your own sword has devoured your prophets, like a destroying lion.

31 O generation, see the word of the LORD. Have I been a wilderness to Israel? a land of darkness? why do my people say, We are lords; we will come no more to you?

32 Can a maid forget her ornaments, or a bride her attire? yet my people have forgotten me days without number.

33 Why do you trim your way to seek love? therefore have you also taught the wicked ones your ways.

34 Also in your skirts is found the blood of the souls of the poor innocents: I have not found it by secret search, but upon all these.

35 Yet you say, Because I am innocent, surely his anger shall turn from me. Behold, I will plead with you, because you say, I have not sinned.

36 Why do you gad about so much to change your way? you also shall be ashamed of Egypt, as you were ashamed of Assyria.

37 Yea, you shall go forth from him, and your hands upon your head: for the LORD has rejected your confidences, and you shall not prosper in them.

CHAPTER 3

THEY say, If a man put away his wife, and she go from him, and become another man's, shall he return to her again? shall not that land be greatly polluted? but you have played the harlot with many lovers; yet return again to me, says the LORD.

2 Lift up your eyes to the high places, and see where you have not been lien with. In the ways have you sat for them, as the Arabian in the wilderness; and you have polluted the land with your whoredoms and with your wickedness.

3 Therefore the showers have been withholden, and there has been no latter rain; and you had a whore's forehead, you refused to be ashamed.

4 Will you not from this time cry to me, My father, you are the guide of my youth?

5 Will he reserve his anger for ever? will he keep it to the end? Behold, you have spoken and done evil things as you could.

6 The LORD said also to me in the days of Josiah the king, Have you seen that which backsliding Israel has done? she is gone up upon every high mountain and under every green tree, and there has played the harlot.

2:29 The ungodly don't understand that their sin is against God (see Psalm 51). They say that certain sinful actions are morally acceptable "as long as they don't hurt anybody." But all sin offends God. The true convert understands that he has sinned against God (see also Jeremiah 3:13).

2:34-35 How aptly these verses apply to abortion. Blood drips from the hands of those who have murdered innocent children, and yet they plead "not guilty."

7 And I said after she had done all these things, Turn to me. But she returned not. And her treacherous sister Judah saw it.

8 And I saw, when for all the causes whereby backsliding Israel committed adultery I had put her away, and given her a bill of divorce; yet her treacherous sister Judah feared not, but went and played the harlot also.

9 And it came to pass through the lightness of her whoredom, that she defiled the land, and committed adultery with stones and with stocks.

10 And yet for all this her treacherous sister Judah has not turned to me with her whole heart, but feignedly, says the LORD.

11 And the LORD said to me, The backsliding Israel has justified herself more than treacherous Judah.

12 Go and proclaim these words toward the north, and say, Return, you backsliding Israel, says the LORD; and I will not cause my anger to fall upon you: for I am merciful, says the LORD, and I will not keep anger for ever.

13 Only acknowledge your iniquity, that you have transgressed against the LORD your God, and have scattered your ways to the strangers under every green tree, and you have not obeyed my voice, says the LORD.

14 Turn, O backsliding children, says the LORD; for I am married to you: and I will take you one of a city, and two of a family, and I will bring you to Zion:

15 And I will give you pastors according to my heart, which shall feed you with knowledge and understanding.

16 And it shall come to pass, when you are multiplied and increased in the land, in those days, says the LORD, they shall say no more, The ark of the covenant of the LORD: neither shall it come to mind: neither shall they remember it; neither shall they visit it; neither shall that be done any more.

17 At that time they shall call Jerusalem the throne of the LORD; and all the nations shall be gathered to it, to the name of the LORD, to Jerusalem: neither shall they walk any more after the imagination of their evil heart.

18 In those days the house of Judah shall walk with the house of Israel, and they shall come together out of the land of the north to the land that I have given for an inheritance to your fathers.

19 But I said, How shall I put you among the children, and give you a pleasant land, a goodly heritage of the hosts of nations? and I said, You shall call me, My father; and shall not turn away from me.

20 Surely as a wife treacherously departs from her husband, so have you dealt treacherously with me, O house of Israel, says the LORD.

21 A voice was heard upon the high places, weeping and supplications of the children of Israel: for they have perverted their way, and they have forgotten the LORD their God.

22 Return, you backsliding children, and I will heal your backslidings. Behold, we come to you; for you are the LORD our God.

23 Truly in vain is salvation hoped for from the hills, and from the multitude of

---

3:8 Some try to justify "backsliding" by pointing to the use of the word, "backsliders" in the Old Testament. However, that word is used in reference to the nation of Israel. We cannot justify any believer's falling away from following Jesus in the light of Luke 9:62, where Jesus said that if we as much as look back, we are not fit for the kingdom. The true convert says with Peter, "Where would we go; you have the words of eternal life." (John 6:68). It is the false convert who is like a dog that returns to his vomit and the pig who goes back to the mire. A genuine convert would rather die than despise the Spirit of grace and trample the blood of Christ under his feet.

3:21 See Psalm 50:22-23.

mountains: truly in the LORD our God is the salvation of Israel.

24 For shame has devoured the labour of our fathers from our youth; their flocks and their herds, their sons and their daughters.

25 We lie down in our shame, and our confusion covers us: for we have sinned against the LORD our God, we and our fathers, from our youth even to this day, and have not obeyed the voice of the LORD our God.

CHAPTER 4

I F you will return, O Israel, says the LORD, return to me: and if you will put away your abominations out of my sight, then shall you not remove.

2 And you shall swear, The LORD lives, in truth, in judgment, and in righteousness; and the nations shall bless themselves in him, and in him shall they glory.

3 For thus says the LORD to the men of Judah and Jerusalem, Break up your fallow ground, and do not sow among thorns.

4 Circumcise yourselves to the LORD, and take away the foreskins of your heart, you men of Judah and inhabitants of Jerusalem: lest my fury come forth like fire, and burn that none can quench it, because of the evil of your doings.

5 Declare in Judah, and publish in Jerusalem; and say, Blow the trumpet in the land: cry, gather together, and say, Assemble yourselves, and let us go into the defenced cities.

6 Set up the standard toward Zion: retire, stay not: for I will bring evil from the north, and a great destruction.

7 The lion is come up from his thicket, and the destroyer of the Gentiles is on his way; he is gone forth from his place to make your land desolate; and your cities shall be laid waste, without an inhabitant.

8 For this gird you with sackcloth, lament and howl: for the fierce anger of the LORD is not turned back from us.

9 And it shall come to pass at that day, says the LORD, that the heart of the king shall perish, and the heart of the princes; and the priests shall be astonished, and the prophets shall wonder.

3:23 We can easily forget that "salvation is in the Lord." He is our salvation; it's not what we know or who we are, but who we know: "And this is life eternal, that they might know you the only true God, and Jesus Christ, whom you have sent" (John 17:3). "He that has the Son has life" (1 John 5:12).

3:25 Holy scripture consistently reveals that God holds us responsible for the sins of our youth, not the sins of our childhood.

4:2 So often the world gravitates to the vision of a God who is "all loving." The inference is that God is so loving that He would never judge a soul and damn that soul to hell. It is more biblical to say that God is love, but He is also the essence of truth, justice and righteousness. Therefore, God is bound by His own character to do that which is true, just, and right.

4:3 We need to break the fallow ground of a hard heart that has no concern for the eternal welfare of the lost. We also need to make sure we prepare the ground with the Law of God before we sow the seed of the gospel into the hearts of men and women.

4:4 God's fury against sin is held back by His long suffering. It is only His mercy that holds back the lightning of His wrath. Our God is a consuming fire (see Hebrews 12:25-29).

4:10 Jeremiah was in error to think that God could sin. Matthew Henry said, "Now, was it God that deceived them? No, He had often given them warning of judgments in general and of this in particular; but their own prophets deceive them and cry peace to those to whom the God of heaven does not speak peace. It is a pitiable thing, and that which every good man greatly laments, to see people flattered into their own ruin and promising themselves peace when war is at the door; and this we should complain of to God, who alone can prevent such a fatal delusion."

10 Then said I, Ah, Lord GOD! surely you have greatly deceived this people and Jerusalem, saying, You shall have peace; whereas the sword reaches to the soul.

11 At that time shall it be said to this people and to Jerusalem, A dry wind of the high places in the wilderness toward the daughter of my people, not to fan, nor to cleanse,

12 Even a full wind from those places shall come to me: now also will I give sentence against them.

13 Behold, he shall come up as clouds, and his chariots shall be as a whirlwind: his horses are swifter than eagles. Woe to us! for we are spoiled.

14 O Jerusalem, wash your heart from wickedness, that you may be saved. How long shall your vain thoughts lodge within you?

15 For a voice declares from Dan, and publishes affliction from mount Ephraim.

16 Make mention to the nations; behold, publish against Jerusalem, that watchers come from a far country, and give out their voice against the cities of Judah.

17 As keepers of a field, are they against her round about; because she has been rebellious against me, says the LORD.

18 Your way and your doings have procured these things to you; this is your wickedness, because it is bitter, because it reaches to your heart.

19 My bowels, my bowels! I am pained at my very heart; my heart makes a noise in me; I cannot hold my peace, because you have heard, O my soul, the sound of the trumpet, the alarm of war.

20 Destruction upon destruction is cried; for the whole land is spoiled: suddenly are my tents spoiled, and my curtains in a moment.

21 How long shall I see the standard, and hear the sound of the trumpet?

22 For my people are foolish, they have not known me; they are silly children, and they have none understanding: they are wise to do evil, but to do good they have no knowledge.

23 I beheld the earth, and, lo, it was without form, and void; and the heavens, and they had no light.

24 I beheld the mountains, and, lo, they trembled, and all the hills moved lightly.

25 I beheld, and, lo, there was no man, and all the birds of the heavens were fled.

26 I beheld, and, lo, the fruitful place was a wilderness, and all the cities thereof were broken down at the presence of the LORD, and by his fierce anger.

27 For thus has the LORD said, The whole land shall be desolate; yet will I not make a full end.

28 For this shall the earth mourn, and the heavens above be black; because I have spoken it, I have purposed it, and will not repent, neither will I turn back from it.

29 The whole city shall flee for the noise of the horsemen and bowmen; they shall go into thickets, and climb up upon the rocks: every city shall be forsaken, and not a man dwell therein.

30 And when you are spoiled, what will you do? Though you clothe yourself with crimson, though you deck yourself with ornaments of gold, though you rent

---

4:19 This is the heart-cry of the Christian. This is the prayer of those who catch a glimpse of sinful man and the holiness of God. In horror, they groan in prayer and plead in their preaching. They cannot hold their peace because they know that God's wrath abides on sinners, that they are enemies of God, who, without the Savior, will know the judgment of eternal fire.

4:22 Here is a summation of godless humanity, which believes itself wise, but is foolish. The unsaved lack the understanding and the knowledge that is provided by the Law of God (see Jeremiah 9:23; also see also Hosea 4:6).

your face with painting, in vain shall you make yourself fair; your lovers will despise you, they will seek your life.

31 For I have heard a voice as of a woman in travail, and the anguish as of her that brings forth her first child, the voice of the daughter of Zion, that bewails herself, that spreads her hands, saying, Woe is me now! for my soul is wearied because of murderers.

CHAPTER 5

RUN to and fro through the streets of Jerusalem, and see now, and know, and seek in the broad places thereof, if you can find a man, if there be any that executes judgment, that seeks the truth; and I will pardon it.

2 And though they say, The LORD lives; surely they swear falsely.

3 O LORD, are not your eyes upon the truth? you have stricken them, but they have not grieved; you have consumed them, but they have refused to receive correction: they have made their faces harder than a rock; they have refused to return.

4 Therefore I said, Surely these are poor; they are foolish: for they do not know the way of the LORD, nor the judgment of their God.

5 I will go to the great men, and will speak to them; for they have known the way of the LORD, and the judgment of their God: but these have altogether broken the yoke, and burst the bonds.

6 Therefore a lion out of the forest shall slay them, and a wolf of the evenings shall spoil them, a leopard shall watch over their cities: every one that goeth out thence shall be torn in pieces: because

their transgressions are many, and their backslidings are increased.

7 How shall I pardon you for this? your children have forsaken me, and sworn by them that are no gods: when I had fed them to the full, they then committed adultery, and assembled themselves by troops in the harlots' houses.

8 They were as fed horses in the morning: every one neighed after his neighbour's wife.

9 Shall I not visit for these things? says the LORD: and shall not my soul be avenged on such a nation as this?

10 Go up on her walls, and destroy; but do not make a full end: take away her battlements; for they are not the LORD's.

11 For the house of Israel and the house of Judah have dealt very treacherously against me, says the LORD.

12 They have belied the LORD, and said, It is not he; neither shall evil come upon us; neither shall we see sword nor famine:

13 And the prophets shall become wind, and the word is not in them: thus shall it be done to them.

14 Therefore thus says the LORD God of hosts, Because you speak this word, behold, I will make my words in your mouth fire, and this people wood, and it shall devour them.

15 Lo, I will bring a nation upon you from far, O house of Israel, says the LORD: it is a mighty nation, it is an ancient nation, a nation whose language you do not know, neither understand what they say.

16 Their quiver is as an open sepulchre, they are all mighty men.

5:1-5 God testifies that there was not one person in Jerusalem who seeks truth and justice, and Jeremiah agrees with the testimony of the Lord. Even though God chastened them, they refused correction. It is always a mystery when tragedy comes to sinful men, that instead of being broken in humility before God, they become bitter, angry, and harden their hearts further against God.

5:3 See Abraham Lincoln's call to national repentance in the comment at Proverbs 28:13.

5:7 America is so much like the Israel described in this verse. God has fed her to the full and blessed her as no other nation, and, yet, instead of living in humble thanksgiving to God, the land is full of idolatry, adultery and covetousness.

17 And they shall eat up your harvest, and your bread, which your sons and your daughters should eat: they shall eat up your flocks and your herds: they shall eat up your vines and your fig trees: they shall impoverish your fenced cities, wherein you trusted, with the sword.

18 Nevertheless in those days, says the LORD, I will not make a full end with you.

19 And it shall come to pass, when you shall say, Why does the LORD our God do all these things to us? then shall you answer them, Like as you have forsaken me, and served strange gods in your land, so shall you serve strangers in a land that is not your's.

20 Declare this in the house of Jacob, and publish it in Judah, saying,

21 Hear now this, O foolish people, and without understanding; which have eyes, and see not; which have ears, and hear not:

22 Do you not fear me? says the LORD: will you not tremble at my presence, which have placed the sand for the bound of the sea by a perpetual decree, that it cannot pass it: and though the waves thereof toss themselves, yet can they not prevail; though they roar, yet can they not pass over it?

23 But this people has a revolting and a rebellious heart; they are revolted and gone.

24 Neither say they in their heart, Let us now fear the LORD our God, that gives rain, both the former and the latter, in his season: he reserves to us the appointed weeks of the harvest.

25 Your iniquities have turned away these things, and your sins have withholden good things from you.

26 For among my people are found wicked men: they lay wait, as he that sets snares; they set a trap, they catch men.

27 As a cage is full of birds, so are their houses full of deceit: therefore they are become great, and grown rich.

28 They are grown fat, they shine: yea, they overpass the deeds of the wicked: they judge not the cause, the cause of the fatherless, yet they prosper; and the right of the needy do they not judge.

29 Shall I not visit for these things? says the LORD: shall not my soul be avenged on such a nation as this?

30 A wonderful and horrible thing is committed in the land;

31 The prophets prophesy falsely, and the priests bear rule by their means; and my people love to have it so: and what will you do in the end thereof?

CHAPTER 6

O you children of Benjamin, gather yourselves to flee out of the midst of Jerusalem, and blow the trumpet in Tekoa, and set up a sign of fire in Bethhaccerem: for evil appears out of the north, and great destruction.

2 I have likened the daughter of Zion to a comely and delicate woman.

3 The shepherds with their flocks shall come to her; they shall pitch their tents against her round about; they shall feed every one in his place.

4 Prepare war against her; arise, and let us go up at noon. Woe to us! for the day goeth away, for the shadows of the evening are stretched out.

5 Arise, and let us go by night, and let us destroy her palaces.

6 For thus has the LORD of hosts said, Hew down trees, and cast a mount against Jerusalem: this is the city to be visited; she is wholly oppression in the midst of her.

7 As a fountain casts out her waters, so she casts out her wickedness: violence and spoil is heard in her; before me continually is grief and wounds.

8 Be instructed, O Jerusalem, lest my soul depart from you; lest I make you desolate, a land not inhabited.

9 Thus says the LORD of hosts, They shall throughly glean the remnant of Israel as a vine: turn back your hand as a grapegatherer into the baskets.

THE FUNCTION OF THE LAW

6:13-14   **When preachers in pulpits have no respect for God's Law,** they preach a gospel devoid of reference to it. But God save us from a message that heals the hurt slightly, saying, "Peace, peace, when there is no peace" (Jeremiah 8:11-12). The preaching of our day too often leaves out the necessity of the Law and the reality of Judgment Day and in this way reaps a harvest of professed conversions. These folks refrain from the vices that once decimated their lives. Therefore, they find a measure of healing. No longer is their marriage in jeopardy; there has been an instigation of biblical principles.

Friendship and vocation flourish because there is a new understanding of the importance of being trustworthy, loving and showing respect for others. However, if there is no understanding of the nature of sin and the need for biblical repentance, these "converts" are still hellbound. If they haven't been born of God, it doesn't matter how much they have been slightly healed or from which pulpit they have been assured that they have peace with God (see John 3:16 comment).

10 To whom shall I speak, and give warning, that they may hear? behold, their ear is uncircumcised, and they cannot hearken: behold, the word of the LORD is to them a reproach; they have no delight in it.

11 Therefore I am full of the fury of the LORD; I am weary with holding in: I will pour it out upon the children abroad, and upon the assembly of young men together: for even the husband with the wife shall be taken, the aged with him that is full of days.

12 And their houses shall be turned to others, with their fields and wives together: for I will stretch out my hand upon the inhabitants of the land, says the LORD.

13 For from the least of them even to the greatest of them every one is given to covetousness; and from the prophet even to the priest every one deals falsely.

14 They have healed also the hurt of the daughter of my people slightly, saying, Peace, peace; when there is no peace.

15 Were they ashamed when they had committed abomination? nay, they were not at all ashamed, neither could they blush: therefore they shall fall among them that fall: at the time that I visit them they shall be cast down, says the LORD.

16 Thus says the LORD, Stand in the ways, and see, and ask for the old paths, where is the good way, and walk therein, and you shall find rest for your souls. But they said, We will not walk therein.

17 Also I set watchmen over you, saying, Hearken to the sound of the trumpet. But they said, We will not hearken.

18 Therefore hear, you nations, and know, O congregation, what is among them.

19 Hear, O earth: behold, I will bring evil upon this people, even the fruit of their thoughts, because they have not hearkened to my words, nor to my law, but rejected it.

20 For what purpose to me comes incense from Sheba, and the sweet cane from a far country? your burnt offerings are not acceptable, nor your sacrifices sweet to me.

21 Therefore thus says the LORD, Behold, I will lay stumblingblocks before this people, and the fathers and the sons together shall fall upon them; the neighbour and his friend shall perish.

22 Thus says the LORD, Behold, a people comes from the north country, and a great nation shall be raised from the sides of the earth.

23 They shall lay hold on bow and spear; they are cruel, and have no mercy; their voice roars like the sea; and they

ride upon horses, set in array as men for war against you, O daughter of Zion.

24 We have heard the fame thereof: our hands grow feeble: anguish has taken hold of us, and pain, as of a woman in travail.

25 Go not forth into the field, nor walk by the way; for the sword of the enemy and fear is on every side.

26 O daughter of my people, gird yourself with sackcloth, and wallow yourself in ashes: make mourning, as for an only son, most bitter lamentation: for the spoiler shall suddenly come upon us.

27 I have set you for a tower and a fortress among my people, that you may know and try their way.

28 They are all grievous revolters, walking with slanders: they are brass and iron; they are all corrupters.

29 The bellows are burned, the lead is consumed of the fire; the founder melts in vain: for the wicked are not plucked away.

30 Reprobate silver shall men call them, because the LORD has rejected them.

CHAPTER 7

THE word that came to Jeremiah from the LORD, saying,

2 Stand in the gate of the LORD's house, and proclaim there this word, and say, Hear the word of the LORD, all you of Judah, that enter in at these gates to worship the LORD.

3 Thus says the LORD of hosts, the God of Israel, Amend your ways and your doings, and I will cause you to dwell in this place.

4 Do not trust in lying words, saying, The temple of the LORD, The temple of the LORD, The temple of the LORD, are these.

5 For if you throughly amend your ways and your doings; if you throughly

execute judgment between a man and his neighbour;

6 If you do not oppress the stranger, the fatherless, and the widow, and do not shed innocent blood in this place, neither walk after other gods to your hurt:

7 Then will I cause you to dwell in this place, in the land that I gave to your fathers, for ever and ever.

8 Behold, you trust in lying words, that cannot profit.

9 Will you steal, murder, and commit adultery, and swear falsely, and burn incense to Baal, and walk after other gods whom you do not know;

10 And come and stand before me in this house, which is called by my name, and say, We are delivered to do all these abominations?

11 Is this house, which is called by my name, become a den of robbers in your eyes? Behold, even I have seen it, says the LORD.

12 But go now to my place which was in Shiloh, where I set my name at the first, and see what I did to it for the wickedness of my people Israel.

13 And now, because you have done all these works, says the LORD, and I spoke to you, rising up early and speaking, but you did not hear; and I called you, but you did not answer;

14 Therefore will I do to this house, which is called by my name, wherein you trust, and to the place which I gave to you and to your fathers, as I have done to Shiloh.

15 And I will cast you out of my sight, as I have cast out all your brethren, even the whole seed of Ephraim.

16 Therefore do not pray for this people, neither lift up cry nor prayer for them, neither make intercession to me: for I will not hear you.

7:8-10 This message is to those who have transgressed the moral Law of the Ten Commandments. They stole (eighth), murdered (sixth), committed adultery (seventh), swore falsely (ninth), and walked after other gods (first and second).

17 Do you not see what they do in the cities of Judah and in the streets of Jerusalem?

18 The children gather wood, and the fathers kindle the fire, and the women knead their dough, to make cakes to the queen of heaven, and to pour out drink offerings to other gods, that they may provoke me to anger.

19 Do they provoke me to anger? says the LORD: do they not provoke themselves to the confusion of their own faces?

20 Therefore thus says the Lord GOD; Behold, my anger and my fury shall be poured out upon this place, upon man, and upon beast, and upon the trees of the field, and upon the fruit of the ground; and it shall burn, and shall not be quenched.

21 Thus says the LORD of hosts, the God of Israel; Put your burnt offerings to your sacrifices, and eat flesh.

22 For I did not speak to your fathers, nor command them in the day that I brought them out of the land of Egypt, concerning burnt offerings or sacrifices:

23 But this thing I commanded them, saying, Obey my voice, and I will be your God, and you shall be my people: and walk in all the ways that I have commanded you, that it may be well with you.

24 But they did not hearken, nor incline their ear, but walked in the counsels and in the imagination of their evil heart, and went backward, and not forward.

25 Since the day that your fathers came forth out of the land of Egypt to this day I have even sent to you all my servants the prophets, daily rising up early and sending them:

26 Yet they did not hearken to me, nor inclined their ear, but hardened their neck: they did worse than their fathers.

27 Therefore you shall speak all these words to them; but they will not hearken to you: you shall also call to them; but they will not answer you.

28 But you shall say to them, This is a nation that does not obey the voice of the LORD their God, nor receives correction: truth is perished, and is cut off from their mouth.

29 Cut off your hair, O Jerusalem, and cast it away, and take up a lamentation on high places; for the LORD has rejected and forsaken the generation of his wrath.

30 For the children of Judah have done evil in my sight, says the LORD: they have set their abominations in the house which is called by my name, to pollute it.

31 And they have built the high places of Tophet, which is in the valley of the son of Hinnom, to burn their sons and their daughters in the fire; which I commanded them not, neither came it into my heart.

32 Therefore, behold, the days come, says the LORD, that it shall no more be called Tophet, nor the valley of the son of Hinnom, but the valley of slaughter: for they shall bury in Tophet, till there be no place.

33 And the carcases of this people shall be meat for the fowls of the heaven, and for the beasts of the earth; and none shall fray them away.

34 Then will I cause to cease from the cities of Judah, and from the streets of Jerusalem, the voice of mirth, and the voice of gladness, the voice of the bridegroom, and the voice of the bride: for the land shall be desolate.

CHAPTER 8

AT that time, says the LORD, they shall bring out the bones of the kings of Judah, and the bones of his princes, and the bones of the priests, and the bones of the prophets, and the bones of the inhabitants of Jerusalem, out of their graves:

2 And they shall spread them before the sun, and the moon, and all the host of heaven, whom they have loved, and whom they have served, and after whom

they have walked, and whom they have sought, and whom they have worshipped: they shall not be gathered, nor be buried; they shall be for dung upon the face of the earth.

3 And death shall be chosen rather than life by all the residue of them that remain of this evil family, which remain in all the places where I have driven them, says the LORD of hosts.

4 Moreover you shall say to them, Thus says the LORD; Shall they fall, and not arise? shall he turn away, and not return?

5 Why then is this people of Jerusalem slidden back by a perpetual backsliding? they hold fast deceit, they refuse to return.

6 I hearkened and heard, but they do not speak aright: no man repented him of his wickedness, saying, What have I done? every one turned to his course, as the horse rushes into the battle.

7 Yea, the stork in the heaven knows her appointed times; and the turtle and the crane and the swallow observe the time of their coming; but my people know not the judgment of the LORD.

8 How do you say, We are wise, and the law of the LORD is with us? Lo, certainly in vain made he it; the pen of the scribes is in vain.

9 The wise men are ashamed, they are dismayed and taken: lo, they have rejected the word of the LORD; and what wisdom is in them?

10 Therefore will I give their wives to others, and their fields to them that shall inherit them: for every one from the least even to the greatest is given to covetousness, from the prophet even to the priest every one deals falsely.

11 For they have healed the hurt of the daughter of my people slightly, saying, Peace, peace; when there is no peace.

12 Were they ashamed when they had committed abomination? nay, they were

8:1-12

Do we delight in the Word of God? Do we rejoice in God's Word as one who finds great spoil? (See Psalms 119:162).

The key is to consume the Word of God, to mediate upon the Word, digest it and let it become part of us.The Bible is a supernatural book. It can give us supernatural energy to do the will of God (see also Nehemiah 8:1-12). Too many fail to read the Bible every day. They find time to feed their stomach each day, but refuse to make time to read God's Word. Don't let your belly take precedenc e over reading the Bible. Forget your food rather than forget the Word of God. (See Exodus 34:28).

not at all ashamed, neither could they blush: therefore shall they fall among them that fall: in the time of their visitation they shall be cast down, says the LORD.

13 I will surely consume them, says the LORD: there shall be no grapes on the vine, nor figs on the fig tree, and the leaf shall fade; and the things that I have given them shall pass away from them.

14 Why do we sit still? assemble yourselves, and let us enter into the defenced cities, and let us be silent there: for the LORD our God has put us to silence, and given us water of gall to drink, because we have sinned against the LORD.

15 We looked for peace, but no good came; and for a time of health, and behold trouble!

16 The snorting of his horses was heard from Dan: the whole land trembled at the sound of the neighing of his strong

---

8:6 We also live in an age where people refuse personal responsibility; they rush at sin like a horse rushes into battle and then say, "What have I done?"

ones; for they are come, and have devoured the land, and all that is in it; the city, and those that dwell therein.

17 For, behold, I will send serpents, cockatrices, among you, which will not be charmed, and they shall bite you, says the LORD.

18 When I would comfort myself against sorrow, my heart is faint in me.

19 Behold the voice of the cry of the daughter of my people because of them that dwell in a far country: Is not the LORD in Zion? is not her king in her? Why have they provoked me to anger with their graven images, and with strange vanities?

20 The harvest is past, the summer is ended, and we are not saved.

21 For the hurt of the daughter of my people am I hurt; I am black; astonishment has taken hold on me.

22 Is there no balm in Gilead; is there no physician there? why then is not the health of the daughter of my people recovered?

CHAPTER 9

OH that my head were waters, and my eyes a fountain of tears, that I might weep day and night for the slain of the daughter of my people!

2 Oh that I had in the wilderness a lodging place of wayfaring men; that I might leave my people, and go from them! for they be all adulterers, an assembly of treacherous men.

3 And they bend their tongues like their bow for lies: but they are not valiant for the truth upon the earth; for they proceed from evil to evil, and they know not me, says the LORD.

4 Take heed every one of his neighbour, and do not trust any brother: for every brother will utterly supplant, and every neighbour will walk with slanders.

5 And they will deceive every one his neighbour, and will not speak the truth: they have taught their tongue to speak lies, and weary themselves to commit iniquity.

6 Your habitation is in the midst of deceit; through deceit they refuse to know me, says the LORD.

7 Therefore thus says the LORD of hosts, Behold, I will melt them, and try them; for how shall I do for the daughter of my people?

8 Their tongue is as an arrow shot out; it speaks deceit: one speaks peaceably to his neighbour with his mouth, but in heart he lies in wait.

9 Shall I not visit them for these things? says the LORD: shall not my soul be avenged on such a nation as this?

10 For the mountains will I take up a weeping and wailing, and for the habitations of the wilderness a lamentation, because they are burned up, so that none can pass through them; neither can men hear the voice of the cattle; both the fowl of the heavens and the beast are fled; they are gone.

11 And I will make Jerusalem heaps, and a den of dragons; and I will make the cities of Judah desolate, without an inhabitant.

12 Who is the wise man, that may understand this? and who is he to whom the mouth of the LORD has spoken, that he may declare it, for what the land perishes and is burned up like a wilderness, that none passes through?

13 And the LORD says, Because they have forsaken my law which I set before them, and have not obeyed my voice, neither walked therein;

14 But have walked after the imagination of their own heart, and after Baalim, which their fathers taught them:

9:1-2 We weep for the pain of sinners and want to run away from them because of their wickedness. However, we are not called to become monastic monks, but to be in the midst of a crooked and perverse nation, among whom we shine as lights in the world, holding forth the Word of life.

15 Therefore thus says the LORD of hosts, the God of Israel; Behold, I will feed them, even this people, with wormwood, and give them water of gall to drink.

16 I will scatter them also among the heathen, whom neither they nor their fathers have known: and I will send a sword after them, till I have consumed them.

17 Thus says the LORD of hosts, Consider, and call for the mourning women, that they may come; and send for cunning women, that they may come:

18 And let them make haste, and take up a wailing for us, that our eyes may run down with tears, and our eyelids gush out with waters.

19 For a voice of wailing is heard out of Zion, How are we spoiled! we are greatly confounded, because we have forsaken the land, because our dwellings have cast us out.

20 Yet hear the word of the LORD, O women, and let your ear receive the word of his mouth, and teach your daughters wailing, and every one her neighbour lamentation.

21 For death is come up into our windows, and is entered into our palaces, to cut off the children from without, and the young men from the streets.

22 Speak, Thus says the LORD, Even the carcases of men shall fall as dung upon the open field, and as the handful after the harvestman, and none shall gather them.

23 Thus says the LORD, Let not the wise man glory in his wisdom, neither let the mighty man glory in his might, let not the rich man glory in his riches:

24 But let him that glories glory in this, that he understands and knows me, that I am the LORD which exercise lovingkindness, judgment, and righteousness, in the earth: for in these things I delight, says the LORD.

25 Behold, the days come, says the LORD, that I will punish all them which are circumcised with the uncircumcised;

26 Egypt, and Judah, and Edom, and the children of Ammon, and Moab, and all that are in the utmost corners, that dwell in the wilderness: for all these nations are uncircumcised, and all the house of Israel are uncircumcised in the heart.

CHAPTER 10

HEAR the word which the LORD speaks to you, O house of Israel:

2 Thus says the LORD, Learn not the way of the heathen, and be not dismayed at the signs of heaven; for the heathen are dismayed at them.

3 For the customs of the people are vain: for one cuts a tree out of the forest, the work of the hands of the workman, with the axe.

4 They deck it with silver and with gold; they fasten it with nails and with hammers, that it move not.

5 They are upright as the palm tree, but speak not: they must needs be borne, because they cannot go. Be not afraid of

---

9:23-24 Though a man has the wisdom of Solomon, the strength of Samson, the riches of Abraham, he has nothing to glory in compared to the lowliest Christian who knows the Lord (see John 17:3). It is in this knowledge that we find eternal life. It was in the cross that God demonstrated His loving kindness, His judgment, and His righteousness. It is there that we find peace with God. This is why Paul gloried in the cross (see Galatians 6:14; also see the comment for Isaiah 6:5).

Misguided man is more interested in living in harmony with nature than he is in living in harmony with his God. He thinks that mother nature has given him life, and he will, therefore, tie himself to a tree rather than let a logging company cut it down. The Christian, however, knows that it is God who gave him life in this world and in the next. May we tie ourselves to the old wooden cross rather than let the world hide it away.

them; for they cannot do evil, neither also is it in them to do good.

6 Forasmuch as there is none like you, O LORD; you are great, and your name is great in might.

7 Who would not fear you, O King of nations? for to you does it appertain: forasmuch as among all the wise men of the nations, and in all their kingdoms, there is none like you.

8 But they are altogether brutish and foolish: the stock is a doctrine of vanities.

9 Silver spread into plates is brought from Tarshish, and gold from Uphaz, the work of the workman, and of the hands of the founder: blue and purple is their clothing: they are all the work of cunning men.

10 But the LORD is the true God, he is the living God, and an everlasting king: at his wrath the earth shall tremble, and the nations shall not be able to abide his indignation.

11 Thus shall you say to them, The gods that have not made the heavens and the earth, even they shall perish from the earth, and from under these heavens.

12 He has made the earth by his power, he has established the world by his wisdom, and has stretched out the heavens by his discretion.

13 When he utters his voice, there is a multitude of waters in the heavens, and he causes the vapours to ascend from the ends of the earth; he makes lightnings with rain, and brings forth the wind out of his treasures.

14 Every man is brutish in his knowledge: every founder is confounded by the graven image: for his molten image is falsehood, and there is no breath in them.

15 They are vanity, and the work of errors: in the time of their visitation they shall perish.

16 The portion of Jacob is not like them: for he is the former of all things;

and Israel is the rod of his inheritance: The LORD of hosts is his name.

17 Gather up your wares out of the land, O inhabitant of the fortress.

18 For thus says the LORD, Behold, I will sling out the inhabitants of the land at this once, and will distress them, that they may find it so.

19 Woe is me for my hurt! my wound is grievous; but I said, Truly this is a grief, and I must bear it.

20 My tabernacle is spoiled, and all my cords are broken: my children are gone forth of me, and they are not: there is none to stretch forth my tent any more, and to set up my curtains.

21 For the pastors are become brutish, and have not sought the LORD: therefore they shall not prosper, and all their flocks shall be scattered.

22 Behold, the noise of the bruit is come, and a great commotion out of the north country, to make the cities of Judah desolate, and a den of dragons.

23 O LORD, I know that the way of man is not in himself: it is not in man that walks to direct his steps.

24 O LORD, correct me, but with judgment; not in your anger, lest you bring me to nothing.

25 Pour out your fury upon the heathen who do not know you, and upon the families that do not call on your name: for they have eaten up Jacob, and devoured him, and consumed him, and have made his habitation desolate.

CHAPTER 11

THE word that came to Jeremiah from the LORD saying,

2 Hear the words of this covenant, and speak to the men of Judah, and to the inhabitants of Jerusalem;

3 And say to them, Thus says the LORD God of Israel; Cursed be the man that does not obey the words of this covenant,

4 Which I commanded your fathers in the day that I brought them forth out of the land of Egypt, from the iron furnace,

saying, Obey my voice, and do them, according to all which I command you: so shall you be my people, and I will be your God:

5 That I may perform the oath which I have sworn to your fathers, to give them a land flowing with milk and honey, as it is this day. Then answered I, and said, So be it, O LORD.

6 Then the LORD said to me, Proclaim all these words in the cities of Judah, and in the streets of Jerusalem, saying, Hear the words of this covenant, and do them.

7 For I earnestly protested to your fathers in the day that I brought them up out of the land of Egypt, even to this day, rising early and protesting, saying, Obey my voice.

8 Yet they obeyed not, nor inclined their ear, but walked every one in the imagination of their evil heart: therefore I will bring upon them all the words of this covenant, which I commanded them to do: but they did them not.

9 And the LORD said to me, A conspiracy is found among the men of Judah, and among the inhabitants of Jerusalem.

10 They are turned back to the iniquities of their forefathers, which refused to hear my words; and they went after other gods to serve them: the house of Israel and the house of Judah have broken my covenant which I made with their fathers.

11 Therefore thus says the LORD, Behold, I will bring evil upon them, which they shall not be able to escape; and though they shall cry to me, I will not hearken to them.

12 Then shall the cities of Judah and inhabitants of Jerusalem go, and cry to the gods to whom they offer incense: but they shall not save them at all in the time of their trouble.

13 For according to the number of your cities were your gods, O Judah; and according to the number of the streets of Jerusalem have you set up altars to that shameful thing, even altars to burn incense to Baal.

14 Therefore do not pray for this people, neither lift up a cry or prayer for them: for I will not hear them in the time that they cry to me for their trouble.

15 What has my beloved to do in my house, seeing she has done lewd deeds with many, and the holy flesh is passed from you? when you do evil, then you rejoice.

16 The LORD called your name, A green olive tree, fair, and of goodly fruit: with the noise of a great tumult he has kindled fire upon it, and the branches of it are broken.

17 For the LORD of hosts, that planted you, has pronounced evil against you, for the evil of the house of Israel and of the house of Judah, which they have done against themselves to provoke me to anger in offering incense to Baal.

18 And the LORD has given me knowledge of it, and I know it: then you showed me their doings.

19 But I was like a lamb or an ox that is brought to the slaughter; and I knew not that they had devised devices against me, saying, Let us destroy the tree with the fruit thereof, and let us cut him off from the land of the living, that his name may be no more remembered.

20 But, O LORD of hosts, that judges righteously, that tries the reins and the heart, let me see your vengeance on them: for to you have I revealed my cause.

21 Therefore thus says the LORD of the men of Anathoth, that seek your life, saying, Prophesy not in the name of the LORD, that you die not by our hand:

22 Therefore thus says the LORD of hosts, Behold, I will punish them: the young men shall die by the sword; their sons and their daughters shall die by famine:

23 And there shall be no remnant of them: for I will bring evil upon the men

of Anathoth, even the year of their visitation.

CHAPTER 12

RIGHTEOUS are you, O LORD, when I plead with you: yet let me talk with you of your judgments: Why does the way of the wicked prosper? why are all they happy that deal very treacherously?

2 You have planted them, yea, they have taken root: they grow, yea, they bring forth fruit: you are near in their mouth, and far from their reins.

3 But you, O LORD, know me: you have seen me, and tried my heart toward you: pull them out like sheep for the slaughter, and prepare them for the day of slaughter.

4 How long shall the land mourn, and the herbs of every field wither, for the wickedness of them that dwell therein? the beasts are consumed, and the birds; because they said, He shall not see our last end.

5 If you have run with the footmen, and they have wearied you, then how can you contend with horses? and if in the land of peace, wherein you trust, they wearied you, then how will you do in the swelling of Jordan?

6 For even your brethren, and the house of your father, even they have dealt treacherously with you; yea, they have called a multitude after you: believe them not, though they speak fair words to you.

7 I have forsaken my house, I have left my heritage; I have given the dearly beloved of my soul into the hand of her enemies.

8 My heritage is to me as a lion in the forest; it cries out against me: therefore have I hated it.

9 My heritage is to me as a speckled bird, the birds round about are against her; come, assemble all the beasts of the field, come to devour.

10 Many pastors have destroyed my vineyard, they have trodden my portion under foot, they have made my pleasant portion a desolate wilderness.

11 They have made it desolate, and being desolate it mourns to me; the whole land is made desolate, because no man lays it to heart.

12 The spoilers are come upon all high places through the wilderness: for the sword of the LORD shall devour from the one end of the land even to the other end of the land: no flesh shall have peace.

13 They have sown wheat, but shall reap thorns: they have put themselves to pain, but shall not profit: and they shall be ashamed of your revenues because of the fierce anger of the LORD.

14 Thus says the LORD against all my evil neighbours, that touch the inheritance which I have caused my people Israel to inherit; Behold, I will pluck them out of their land, and pluck out the house of Judah from among them.

15 And it shall come to pass, after that I have plucked them out I will return, and have compassion on them, and will bring them again, every man to his heritage, and every man to his land.

16 And it shall come to pass, if they will diligently learn the ways of my people, to swear by my name, The LORD lives; as they taught my people to swear by Baal; then shall they be built in the midst of my people.

17 But if they will not obey, I will utterly pluck up and destroy that nation, says the LORD.

12:1 The modern gospel tells us that the world can't find happiness without Jesus (see 2 Corinthians 2:17 comment).

CHAPTER 13

THUS says the LORD to me, Go and get you a linen girdle, and put it upon your loins, and put it not in water.

2 So I got a girdle according to the word of the LORD, and put it on my loins.

3 And the word of the LORD came to me the second time, saying,

4 Take the girdle that you have got, which is upon your loins, and arise, go to Euphrates, and hide it there in a hole of the rock.

5 So I went, and hid it by Euphrates, as the LORD commanded me.

6 And it came to pass after many days, that the LORD said to me, Arise, go to Euphrates, and take the girdle from thence, which I commanded you to hide there.

7 Then I went to Euphrates, and dug, and took the girdle from the place where I had hid it: and, behold, the girdle was marred, it was profitable for nothing.

8 Then the word of the LORD came to me, saying,

9 Thus says the LORD, After this manner will I mar the pride of Judah, and the great pride of Jerusalem.

10 This evil people, which refuse to hear my words, which walk in the imagination of their heart, and walk after other gods, to serve them, and to worship them, shall even be as this girdle, which is good for nothing.

11 For as the girdle cleaves to the loins of a man, so have I caused to cleave to me the whole house of Israel and the whole house of Judah, says the LORD; that they might be to me for a people, and for a name, and for a praise, and for a glory: but they would not hear.

12 Therefore you shall speak to them this word; Thus says the LORD God of Israel, Every bottle shall be filled with wine: and they shall say to you, Do we not certainly know that every bottle shall be filled with wine?

13 Then shall you say to them, Thus says the LORD, Behold, I will fill all the inhabitants of this land, even the kings that sit upon David's throne, and the priests, and the prophets, and all the inhabitants of Jerusalem, with drunkenness.

14 And I will dash them one against another, even the fathers and the sons together, says the LORD: I will not pity, nor spare, nor have mercy, but destroy them.

15 Hear, and give ear; do not be proud: for the LORD has spoken.

16 Give glory to the LORD your God, before he cause darkness, and before your feet stumble upon the dark mountains, and, while you look for light, he turn it into the shadow of death, and make it gross darkness.

17 But if you will not hear it, my soul shall weep in secret places for your pride; and my eye shall weep sore, and run down with tears, because the LORD's flock is carried away captive.

18 Say to the king and to the queen, Humble yourselves, sit down: for your principalities shall come down, even the crown of your glory.

19 The cities of the south shall be shut up, and none shall open them: Judah shall be carried away captive all of it, it shall be wholly carried away captive.

20 Lift up your eyes, and behold them that come from the north: where is the flock that was given to you, your beautiful flock?

21 What will you say when he shall punish you? for you have taught them to be captains, and as chief over you: shall not sorrows take you, as a woman in travail?

22 And if you say in your heart, Why have these things come upon me? For the greatness of your iniquity are your skirts discovered, and your heels made bare.

23 Can the Ethiopian change his skin, or the leopard his spots? then may you also do good, that are accustomed to do evil.

24 Therefore will I scatter them as the stubble that passes away by the wind of the wilderness.

25 This is your lot, the portion of your measures from me, says the LORD; because you have forgotten me, and trusted in falsehood.

26 Therefore will I discover your skirts upon your face, that your shame may appear.

27 I have seen your adulteries, and your neighings, the lewdness of your whoredom, and your abominations on the hills in the fields. Woe to you, O Jerusalem! will you not be made clean? when shall it once be?

CHAPTER 14

THE word of the LORD that came to Jeremiah concerning the dearth.

2 Judah mourns, and the gates thereof languish; they are black to the ground; and the cry of Jerusalem is gone up.

3 And their nobles have sent their little ones to the waters: they came to the pits, and found no water; they returned with their vessels empty; they were ashamed and confounded, and covered their heads.

4 Because the ground is chapped, for there was no rain in the earth, the plowmen were ashamed, they covered their heads.

5 Yea, the hind also calved in the field, and forsook it, because there was no grass.

6 And the wild asses did stand in the high places, they snuffed up the wind like dragons; their eyes did fail, because there was no grass.

7 O LORD, though our iniquities testify against us, do it for your name's sake: for our backslidings are many; we have sinned against you.

8 O the hope of Israel, the saviour thereof in time of trouble, why should you be as a stranger in the land, and as a wayfaring man that turns aside to tarry for a night?

9 Why should you be as a man astonished, as a mighty man that cannot save? yet you, O LORD, are in the midst of us, and we are called by your name; leave us not.

10 Thus says the LORD to this people, Thus have they loved to wander, they have not refrained their feet, therefore the LORD does not accept them; he will now remember their iniquity, and visit their sins.

11 Then said the LORD to me, Pray not for this people for their good.

12 When they fast, I will not hear their cry; and when they offer burnt offering and an oblation, I will not accept them: but I will consume them by the sword, and by the famine, and by the pestilence.

13 Then said I, Ah, Lord GOD! behold, the prophets say to them, You shall not see the sword, neither shall you have famine; but I will give you assured peace in this place.

14 Then the LORD said to me, The prophets prophesy lies in my name: I have not sent them, neither have I commanded them, neither spoken to them: they prophesy to you a false vision and divination, and a thing of nought, and the deceit of their heart.

15 Therefore thus says the LORD concerning the prophets that prophesy in my name, and I sent them not, yet they say, Sword and famine shall not be in this land; By sword and famine shall those prophets be consumed.

16 And the people to whom they prophesy shall be cast out in the streets of Jerusalem because of the famine and the sword; and they shall have none to bury them, them, their wives, nor their sons, nor their daughters: for I will pour their wickedness upon them.

17 Therefore you shall say this word to them; Let my eyes run down with tears night and day, and let them not cease: for the virgin daughter of my people is broken with a great breach, with a very grievous blow.

18 If I go forth into the field, then behold the slain with the sword! and if I enter into the city, then behold them that are sick with famine! yea, both the prophet and the priest go about into a land that they know not.

19 Have you utterly rejected Judah? has your soul lothed Zion? why have you smitten us, and there is no healing for us? we looked for peace, and there is no good; and for the time of healing, and behold trouble!

20 We acknowledge, O LORD, our wickedness, and the iniquity of our fathers: for we have sinned against you.

21 Do not abhor us, for your name's sake, do not disgrace the throne of your glory: remember, do not break your covenant with us.

22 Are there any among the vanities of the Gentiles that can cause rain? or can the heavens give showers? are you not he, O LORD our God? therefore we will wait upon you: for you have made all these things.

CHAPTER 15

THEN said the LORD to me, Though Moses and Samuel stood before me, yet my mind could not be toward this people: cast them out of my sight, and let them go forth.

2 And it shall come to pass, if they say to you, Where shall we go forth? then you shall tell them, Thus says the LORD; Such as are for death, to death; and such as are for the sword, to the sword; and such as are for the famine, to the famine; and such as are for the captivity, to the captivity.

3 And I will appoint over them four kinds, says the LORD: the sword to slay, and the dogs to tear, and the fowls of the heaven, and the beasts of the earth, to devour and destroy.

4 And I will cause them to be removed into all kingdoms of the earth, because of Manasseh the son of Hezekiah king of Judah, for that which he did in Jerusalem.

5 For who shall have pity upon you, O Jerusalem? or who shall bemoan you? or who shall go aside to ask how you do?

6 You have forsaken me, says the LORD, you are gone backward: therefore will I stretch out my hand against you, and destroy you; I am weary with repenting.

7 And I will fan them with a fan in the gates of the land; I will bereave them of children, I will destroy my people since they return not from their ways.

8 Their widows are increased to me above the sand of the seas: I have brought upon them against the mother of the young men a spoiler at noonday: I have caused him to fall upon it suddenly, and terrors upon the city.

9 She that has borne seven languishes: she has given up the ghost; her sun is gone down while it was yet day: she has been ashamed and confounded: and the residue of them will I deliver to the sword before their enemies, says the LORD.

10 Woe is me, my mother, that you have borne me a man of strife and a man of contention to the whole earth! I have neither lent on usury, nor men have lent to me on usury; yet every one of them does curse me.

11 The LORD said, Verily it shall be well with your remnant; verily I will cause the enemy to entreat you well in the time of evil and in the time of affliction.

12 Shall iron break the northern iron and the steel?

13 Your substance and your treasures will I give to the spoil without price, and that for all your sins, even in all your borders.

14 And I will make you to pass with your enemies into a land which you do not know: for a fire is kindled in my anger, which shall burn upon you.

15 O LORD, you know: remember me, and visit me, and revenge me of my persecutors; take me not away in your

longsuffering: know that for your sake I have suffered rebuke.

16 Your words were found, and I did eat them; and your word was to me the joy and rejoicing of my heart: for I am called by your name, O LORD God of hosts.

17 I sat not in the assembly of the mockers, nor rejoiced; I sat alone because of your hand: for you have filled me with indignation.

18 Why is my pain perpetual, and my wound incurable, which refuses to be healed? will you be altogether to me as a liar, and as waters that fail?

19 Therefore thus says the LORD, If you return, then will I bring you again, and you shall stand before me: and if you take forth the precious from the vile, you shall be as my mouth: let them return to you; but you do not return to them.

20 And I will make you to this people a fenced brasen wall: and they shall fight against you, but they shall not prevail against you: for I am with you to save you and to deliver you, says the LORD.

21 And I will deliver you out of the hand of the wicked, and I will redeem you out of the hand of the terrible.

CHAPTER 16

THE word of the LORD came also to me, saying,

2 You shall not take a wife, neither shall you have sons or daughters in this place.

3 For thus says the LORD concerning the sons and concerning the daughters that are born in this place, and concerning their mothers that bare them, and concerning their fathers that begat them in this land;

4 They shall die of grievous deaths; they shall not be lamented; neither shall they be buried; but they shall be as dung upon the face of the earth: and they shall be consumed by the sword, and by famine; and their carcases shall be meat for the fowls of heaven, and for the beasts of the earth.

5 For thus says the LORD, Enter not into the house of mourning, neither go to lament nor bemoan them: for I have taken away my peace from this people, says the LORD, even lovingkindness and mercies.

6 Both the great and the small shall die in this land: they shall not be buried, neither shall men lament for them, nor cut themselves, nor make themselves bald for them:

7 Neither shall men tear themselves for them in mourning, to comfort them for the dead; neither shall men give them the cup of consolation to drink for their father or for their mother.

8 You shall not also go into the house of feasting, to sit with them to eat and to drink.

9 For thus says the LORD of hosts, the God of Israel; Behold, I will cause to cease out of this place in your eyes, and in your days, the voice of mirth, and the voice of gladness, the voice of the bridegroom, and the voice of the bride.

10 And it shall come to pass, when you shall show this people all these words, and they shall say to you, Why has the LORD pronounced all this great evil against us? or what is our iniquity? or what is our sin that we have committed against the LORD our God?

11 Then shall you say to them, Because your fathers have forsaken me, says the LORD, and have walked after other gods, and have served them, and have worshipped them, and have forsaken me, and have not kept my law;

12 And you have done worse than your fathers; for, behold, you walk every one after the imagination of his evil heart, that they may not hearken to me:

13 Therefore will I cast you out of this land into a land that you know not, nei-

16:10-12 God has principles with which He deals with nations.

ther you nor your fathers; and there shall you serve other gods day and night; where I will not show you favour.

14 Therefore, behold, the days come, says the LORD, that it shall no more be said, The LORD lives, that brought up the children of Israel out of the land of Egypt;

15 But, The LORD lives, that brought up the children of Israel from the land of the north, and from all the lands where he had driven them: and I will bring them again into their land that I gave to their fathers.

16 Behold, I will send for many fishers, says the LORD, and they shall fish them; and after will I send for many hunters, and they shall hunt them from every mountain, and from every hill, and out of the holes of the rocks.

17 For my eyes are upon all their ways: they are not hid from my face, neither is their iniquity hid from my eyes.

18 And first I will recompense their iniquity and their sin double; because they have defiled my land, they have filled my inheritance with the carcases of their detestable and abominable things.

19 O LORD, my strength, and my fortress, and my refuge in the day of affliction, the Gentiles shall come to you from the ends of the earth, and shall say, Surely our fathers have inherited lies, vanity, and things wherein there is no profit.

20 Shall a man make gods for himself, and they are no gods?

21 Therefore, behold, I will this once cause them to know, I will cause them to know my hand and my might; and they shall know that my name is The LORD.

CHAPTER 17

THE sin of Judah is written with a pen of iron, and with the point of a diamond: it is graven upon the table of their heart, and upon the horns of your altars;

2 Whilst their children remember their altars and their groves by the green trees upon the high hills.

3 O my mountain in the field, I will give your substance and all your treasures to the spoil, and your high places for sin, throughout all your borders.

4 And you, even yourself, shall discontinue from your heritage that I gave you; and I will cause you to serve your enemies in the land which you do not know: for you have kindled a fire in my anger, which shall burn for ever.

5 Thus says the LORD; Cursed be the man that trusts in man, and makes flesh his arm, and whose heart departs from the LORD.

6 For he shall be like the heath in the desert, and shall not see when good comes; but shall inhabit the parched places in the wilderness, in a salt land and not inhabited.

7 Blessed is the man that trusts in the LORD, and whose hope the LORD is.

8 For he shall be as a tree planted by the waters, and that spreads out her roots by the river, and shall not see when heat comes, but her leaf shall be green; and shall not be careful in the year of drought, neither shall cease from yielding fruit.

9 The heart is deceitful above all things, and desperately wicked: who can know it?

10 I the LORD search the heart, I try the reins, even to give every man according to his ways, and according to the fruit of his doings.

11 As the partridge sits on eggs, and does not hatch them; so he that gets riches, and not by right, shall leave them

17:7-8 Compare Psalm 1.

THE FUNCTION OF THE LAW

 17:9 The great truth of this verse is hidden from any who do not understand the spiritual nature of the moral Law.

Many years ago we had in our home a stubborn spider that kept building a web against our house. No matter how many times we swept it away, the spider and its web would reappear the next morning. One day I enlisted the help of one of my sons, as well as a small stick and a can of insect spray. I then had my son gently tap the stick on the web while I made the sound of a fly in distress. The hungry spider came out of his hiding place, and that's when I killed him with the insect spray.

There is a stubborn web of sin that continually plagues mankind. It is the web of violence, corruption, rape, greed, wars, theft, etc. We try and sweep it away through political means. Yet these crimes remain, and few seem to identify the root cause of the problem. That remains in hiding.

We must use the stick of God's Law to gently tap on the human heart. Suddenly, the cause of sin appears. And that's when sin can be put to death with the power of the gospel. It is God's Law that reveals the human heart as desperately wicked, and it is the gospel that delivers us from the power of sin. In Christ we are born again (John 3:3) and become new creatures.

in the midst of his days, and at his end shall be a fool.

12 A glorious high throne from the beginning is the place of our sanctuary.

13 O LORD, the hope of Israel, all that forsake you shall be ashamed, and they that depart from me shall be written in the earth, because they have forsaken the LORD, the fountain of living waters.

14 Heal me, O LORD, and I shall be healed; save me, and I shall be saved: for you are my praise.

15 Behold, they say to me, Where is the word of the LORD? let it come now.

16 As for me, I have not hastened from being a pastor to follow you: neither have I desired the woeful day; you know: that which came out of my lips was right before you.

17 Do not be a terror to me: you are my hope in the day of evil.

18 Let them be confounded that persecute me, but let not me be confounded: let them be dismayed, but let not me be dismayed: bring upon them the day of evil, and destroy them with double destruction.

19 Thus said the LORD to me; Go and stand in the gate of the children of the people, whereby the kings of Judah

come in, and by the which they go out, and in all the gates of Jerusalem;

20 And say to them, Hear the word of the LORD, you kings of Judah, and all Judah, and all the inhabitants of Jerusalem, that enter in by these gates:

21 Thus says the LORD; Take heed to yourselves, and bear no burden on the sabbath day, nor bring it in by the gates of Jerusalem;

22 Neither carry forth a burden out of your houses on the sabbath day, neither do any work, but hallow the sabbath day, as I commanded your fathers.

23 But they obeyed not, neither inclined their ear, but made their neck stiff, that they might not hear, nor receive instruction.

24 And it shall come to pass, if you diligently hearken to me, says the LORD, to bring in no burden through the gates of this city on the sabbath day, but hallow the sabbath day, to do no work therein;

25 Then shall there enter into the gates of this city kings and princes sitting upon the throne of David, riding in chariots and on horses, they, and their princes, the men of Judah, and the inhabitants of Jerusalem: and this city shall remain for ever.

26 And they shall come from the cities of Judah, and from the places about Jerusalem, and from the land of Benjamin, and from the plain, and from the mountains, and from the south, bringing burnt offerings, and sacrifices, and meat offerings, and incense, and bringing sacrifices of praise, to the house of the LORD.

27 But if you will not hearken to me to hallow the sabbath day, and not to bear a burden, even entering in at the gates of Jerusalem on the sabbath day; then will I kindle a fire in the gates thereof, and it shall devour the palaces of Jerusalem, and it shall not be quenched.

CHAPTER 18

THE word which came to Jeremiah from the LORD, saying,

2 Arise, and go down to the potter's house, and there I will cause you to hear my words.

3 Then I went down to the potter's house, and, behold, he wrought a work on the wheels.

4 And the vessel that he made of clay was marred in the hand of the potter: so he made it again another vessel, as seemed good to the potter to make it.

5 Then the word of the LORD came to me, saying,

6 O house of Israel, cannot I do with you as this potter? says the LORD. Behold, as the clay is in the potter's hand, so are you in my hand, O house of Israel.

7 At what instant I shall speak concerning a nation, and concerning a kingdom, to pluck up, and to pull down, and to destroy it;

8 If that nation, against whom I have pronounced, turn from their evil, I will repent of the evil that I thought to do to them.

9 And at what instant I shall speak concerning a nation, and concerning a kingdom, to build and to plant it;

10 If it do evil in my sight, that it obey not my voice, then I will repent of the good, wherewith I said I would benefit them.

11 Now therefore go to, speak to the men of Judah, and to the inhabitants of Jerusalem, saying, Thus says the LORD; Behold, I frame evil against you, and devise a device against you: return now every one from his evil way, and make your ways and your doings good.

12 And they said, There is no hope: but we will walk after our own devices, and we will every one do the imagination of his evil heart.

13 Therefore thus says the LORD; Ask now among the heathen, who has heard such things: the virgin of Israel has done a very horrible thing.

14 Will a man leave the snow of Lebanon which comes from the rock of the field? or shall the cold flowing waters that come from another place be forsaken?

15 Because my people have forgotten me, they have burned incense to vanity, and they have caused them to stumble in their ways from the ancient paths, to walk in paths, in a way not cast up;

16 To make their land desolate, and a perpetual hissing; every one that passes thereby shall be astonished, and wag his head.

17 I will scatter them as with an east wind before the enemy; I will show them the back, and not the face, in the day of their calamity.

18 Then said they, Come and let us devise devices against Jeremiah; for the law shall not perish from the priest, nor counsel from the wise, nor the word from the prophet. Come, and let us smite him with the tongue, and let us not give heed to any of his words.

19 Give heed to me, O LORD, and hearken to the voice of them that contend with me.

20 Shall evil be recompensed for good? for they have dug a pit for my soul. Remember that I stood before you to speak good for them, and to turn away your wrath from them.

21 Therefore deliver up their children to the famine, and pour out their blood by the force of the sword; and let their wives be bereaved of their children, and be widows; and let their men be put to death; let their young men be slain by the sword in battle.

22 Let a cry be heard from their houses, when you shall bring a troop suddenly upon them: for they have dug a pit to take me, and hid snares for my feet.

23 Yet, LORD, you know all their counsel against me to slay me: forgive not their iniquity, neither blot out their sin from your sight, but let them be overthrown before you; deal thus with them in the time of your anger.

CHAPTER 19

THUS says the LORD, Go and get a potter's earthen bottle, and take of the ancients of the people, and of the ancients of the priests;

2 And go forth to the valley of the son of Hinnom, which is by the entry of the east gate, and proclaim there the words that I shall tell you,

3 And say, Hear the word of the LORD, O kings of Judah, and inhabitants of Jerusalem; Thus says the LORD of hosts, the God of Israel; Behold, I will bring evil upon this place, that whoever hears of it, his ears shall tingle.

4 Because they have forsaken me, and have estranged this place, and have burned incense in it to other gods, whom neither they nor their fathers have known, nor the kings of Judah, and have filled this place with the blood of innocents;

5 They have built also the high places of Baal, to burn their sons with fire for burnt offerings to Baal, which I did not command, nor speak it, neither did it come into my mind:

6 Therefore, behold, the days come, says the LORD, that this place shall no more be called Tophet, nor The valley of the son of Hinnom, but The valley of slaughter.

7 And I will make void the counsel of Judah and Jerusalem in this place; and I will cause them to fall by the sword before their enemies, and by the hands of them that seek their lives: and their carcases will I give to be meat for the fowls of the heaven, and for the beasts of the earth.

8 And I will make this city desolate, and an hissing; every one that passes thereby shall be astonished and hiss because of all the plagues thereof.

9 And I will cause them to eat the flesh of their sons and the flesh of their daughters, and they shall eat every one the flesh of his friend in the siege and straitness, wherewith their enemies, and they that seek their lives, shall straiten them.

10 Then shall you break the bottle in the sight of the men that go with you,

11 And shall say to them, Thus says the LORD of hosts; Even so will I break this people and this city, as one breaks a potter's vessel, that cannot be made whole again: and they shall bury them in Tophet, till there be no place to bury.

12 Thus will I do to this place, says the LORD, and to the inhabitants thereof, and even make this city as Tophet:

13 And the houses of Jerusalem, and the houses of the kings of Judah, shall be defiled as the place of Tophet, because of all the houses upon whose roofs they have burned incense to all the host of heaven, and have poured out drink offerings to other gods.

14 Then came Jeremiah from Tophet, where the LORD had sent him to prophesy; and he stood in the court of the LORD's house; and said to all the people,

15 Thus says the LORD of hosts, the God of Israel; Behold, I will bring upon

---

19:8-9 God warned in Deuteronomy 28:53 that this would happen to Israel if they refused to walk in obedience.

this city and upon all her towns all the evil that I have pronounced against it, because they have hardened their necks, that they might not hear my words.

CHAPTER 20

NOW Pashur the son of Immer the priest, who was also chief governor in the house of the LORD, heard that Jeremiah prophesied these things.

2 Then Pashur smote Jeremiah the prophet, and put him in the stocks that were in the high gate of Benjamin, which was by the house of the LORD.

3 And it came to pass on the morrow, that Pashur brought forth Jeremiah out of the stocks. Then Jeremiah said to him, The LORD has not called your name Pashur, but Magormissabib.

4 For thus says the LORD, Behold, I will make you a terror to yourself, and to all your friends: and they shall fall by the sword of their enemies, and your eyes shall behold it: and I will give all Judah into the hand of the king of Babylon, and he shall carry them captive into Babylon, and shall slay them with the sword.

5 Moreover I will deliver all the strength of this city, and all the labours thereof, and all the precious things thereof, and all the treasures of the kings of Judah will I give into the hand of their enemies, which shall spoil them, and take them, and carry them to Babylon.

6 And you, Pashur, and all that dwell in your house shall go into captivity: and you shall come to Babylon, and there you shall die, and shall be buried there, you, and all your friends, to whom you have prophesied lies.

7 O LORD, you have deceived me, and I was deceived; you are stronger than I, and have prevailed: I am in derision daily, every one mocks me.

> Lord, grant that the fire of my heart
> may melt the lead in my feet.
> **UNKNOWN**

20:9

Persecution almost persuaded Jeremiah not to speak in God's name, but God's Word burned so within Jeremiah that he could not keep it to himself (see Psalm 39:3).

How much more then should we be forthright in presenting the good news of eternal life through our Savior Jesus! (See John 17:14 comment.)

8 For since I spoke, I cried out, I cried violence and spoil; because the word of the LORD was made a reproach to me, and a derision, daily.

9 Then I said, I will not make mention of him, nor speak any more in his name. But his word was in my heart as a burning fire shut up in my bones, and I was weary with forbearing, and I could not stay.

10 For I heard the defaming of many, fear on every side. Report, say they, and we will report it. All my familiars watched for my halting, saying, Peradventure he will be enticed, and we shall prevail against him, and we shall take our revenge on him.

11 But the LORD is with me as a mighty terrible one: therefore my persecutors shall stumble, and they shall not prevail: they shall be greatly ashamed; for they shall not prosper: their everlasting confusion shall never be forgotten.

12 But, O LORD of hosts, that tries the righteous, and sees the reins and the heart, let me see your vengeance on them: for to you have I opened my cause.

13 Sing to the LORD, praise you the LORD: for he has delivered the soul of the poor from the hand of evildoers.

14 Cursed be the day wherein I was born: let not the day wherein my mother bare me be blessed.

15 Cursed be the man who brought tidings to my father, saying, A man child is born to you; making him very glad.

16 And let that man be as the cities which the LORD overthrew, and repented not: and let him hear the cry in the morning, and the shouting at noontide;

17 Because he slew me not from the womb; or that my mother might have been my grave, and her womb to be always great with me.

18 Therefore I came forth out of the womb to see labour and sorrow, that my days should be consumed with shame?

CHAPTER 21

THE word which came to Jeremiah from the LORD, when king Zedekiah sent to him Pashur the son of Melchiah, and Zephaniah the son of Maaseiah the priest, saying,

2 Enquire, I pray you, of the LORD for us; for Nebuchadrezzar king of Babylon makes war against us; if so be that the LORD will deal with us according to all his wondrous works, that he may go up from us.

3 Then Jeremiah said to them, Thus shall you say to Zedekiah:

4 Thus says the LORD God of Israel; Behold, I will turn back the weapons of war that are in your hands, wherewith you fight against the king of Babylon, and against the Chaldeans, which besiege you without the walls, and I will assemble them into the midst of this city.

5 And I myself will fight against you with an outstretched hand and with a strong arm, even in anger, and in fury, and in great wrath.

6 And I will smite the inhabitants of this city, both man and beast: they shall die of a great pestilence.

7 And afterward, says the LORD, I will deliver Zedekiah king of Judah, and his servants, and the people, and such as are left in this city from the pestilence, from the sword, and from the famine, into the hand of Nebuchadrezzar king of Babylon, and into the hand of their enemies, and into the hand of those that seek their life: and he shall smite them with the edge of the sword; he shall not spare them, neither have pity, nor have mercy.

8 And to this people you shall say, Thus says the LORD; Behold, I set before you the way of life, and the way of death.

9 He that abides in this city shall die by the sword, and by the famine, and by the pestilence: but he that goeth out, and falls to the Chaldeans that besiege you, he shall live, and his life shall be to him for a prey.

10 For I have set my face against this city for evil, and not for good, says the LORD: it shall be given into the hand of the king of Babylon, and he shall burn it with fire.

11 And touching the house of the king of Judah, say, Hear the word of the LORD;

12 O house of David, thus says the LORD; Execute judgment in the morning, and deliver him that is spoiled out of the hand of the oppressor, lest my fury go out like fire, and burn that none can quench it, because of the evil of your doings.

13 Behold, I am against you, O inhabitant of the valley, and rock of the plain, says the LORD; which say, Who shall

---

21:5 This is perhaps the most dreadful verse in the Bible. If God be for us, who can be against us? And if God be against us, who can be for us?

21:8 See Deuteronomy 30:15-19.

come down against us? or who shall enter into our habitations?

14 But I will punish you according to the fruit of your doings, says the LORD: and I will kindle a fire in the forest thereof, and it shall devour all things round about it.

CHAPTER 22

THUS says the LORD; Go down to the house of the king of Judah, and speak there this word,

2 And say, Hear the word of the LORD, O king of Judah, that sits upon the throne of David, you, and your servants, and your people that enter in by these gates:

3 Thus says the LORD; Execute judgment and righteousness, and deliver the spoiled out of the hand of the oppressor: and do no wrong, do no violence to the stranger, the fatherless, nor the widow, neither shed innocent blood in this place.

4 For if you do this thing indeed, then shall there enter in by the gates of this house kings sitting upon the throne of David, riding in chariots and on horses, he, and his servants, and his people.

5 But if you will not hear these words, I swear by myself, says the LORD, that this house shall become a desolation.

6 For thus says the LORD to the king's house of Judah; You are Gilead to me, and the head of Lebanon: yet surely I will make you a wilderness, and cities which are not inhabited.

7 And I will prepare destroyers against you, every one with his weapons: and they shall cut down your choice cedars, and cast them into the fire.

8 And many nations shall pass by this city, and they shall say every man to his neighbour, Why has the LORD done thus to this great city?

9 Then they shall answer, Because they have forsaken the covenant of the LORD their God, and worshipped other gods, and served them.

10 Weep not for the dead, neither bemoan him: but weep sore for him that goes away: for he shall return no more, nor see his native country.

11 For thus says the LORD touching Shallum the son of Josiah king of Judah, which reigned instead of Josiah his father, which went forth out of this place; He shall not return there any more:

12 But he shall die in the place where they have led him captive, and shall see this land no more.

13 Woe to him that builds his house by unrighteousness, and his chambers by wrong; that uses his neighbour's service without wages, and gives him nothing for his work;

14 That says, I will build me a wide house and large chambers, and cuts him out windows; and it is cieled with cedar, and painted with vermilion.

15 Shall you reign, because you enclose yourself in cedar? did not your father eat and drink, and do judgment and justice, and then it was well with him?

16 He judged the cause of the poor and needy; then it was well with him: was not this to know me? says the LORD.

17 But your eyes and your heart are not but for your covetousness, and for to shed innocent blood, and for oppression, and for violence, to do it.

18 Therefore thus says the LORD concerning Jehoiakim the son of Josiah king of Judah; They shall not lament for him, saying, Ah my brother! or, Ah sister!they shall not lament for him, saying, Ah lord! or, Ah his glory!

19 He shall be buried with the burial of an ass, drawn and cast forth beyond the gates of Jerusalem.

20 Go up to Lebanon, and cry; and lift up your voice in Bashan, and cry from the passages: for all your lovers are destroyed.

21 I spoke to you in your prosperity; but you said, I will not hear. This has been your manner from your youth, that you did not obey my voice.

22 The wind shall eat up all your pastors, and your lovers shall go into captivity: surely then shall you be ashamed and confounded for all your wickedness.

23 O inhabitant of Lebanon, that makes your nest in the cedars, how gracious shall you be when pangs come upon you, the pain as of a woman in travail!

24 As I live, says the LORD, though Coniah the son of Jehoiakim king of Judah were the signet upon my right hand, yet would I pluck you off;

25 And I will give you into the hand of them that seek your life, and into the hand of them whose face you fear, even into the hand of Nebuchadrezzar king of Babylon, and into the hand of the Chaldeans.

26 And I will cast you out, and your mother that bare you, into another country, where you were not born; and there shall you die.

27 But to the land which they desire to return, there they shall not return.

28 Is this man Coniah a despised broken idol? is he a vessel wherein is no pleasure? why are they cast out, he and his seed, and are cast into a land which they know not?

29 O earth, earth, earth, hear the word of the LORD.

30 Thus says the LORD, Write this man childless, a man that shall not prosper in his days: for no man of his seed shall prosper, sitting upon the throne of David, and ruling any more in Judah.

CHAPTER 23

WOE be to the pastors that destroy and scatter the sheep of my pasture! says the LORD.

2 Therefore thus says the LORD God of Israel against the pastors that feed my people; You have scattered my flock, and driven them away, and have not visited them: behold, I will visit upon you the evil of your doings, says the LORD.

3 And I will gather the remnant of my flock out of all countries where I have driven them, and will bring them again to their folds; and they shall be fruitful and increase.

4 And I will set up shepherds over them which shall feed them: and they shall fear no more, nor be dismayed, neither shall they be lacking, says the LORD.

5 Behold, the days come, says the LORD, that I will raise to David a righteous Branch, and a King shall reign and prosper, and shall execute judgment and justice in the earth.

6 In his days Judah shall be saved, and Israel shall dwell safely: and this is his name whereby he shall be called, THE LORD OUR RIGHTEOUSNESS.

7 Therefore, behold, the days come, says the LORD, that they shall no more say, The LORD lives, which brought up the children of Israel out of the land of Egypt;

8 But, The LORD lives, which brought up and which led the seed of the house of Israel out of the north country, and from all countries where I had driven them; and they shall dwell in their own land.

9 My heart within me is broken because of the prophets; all my bones shake; I am like a drunken man, and like a man whom wine has overcome, because of the LORD, and because of the words of his holiness.

10 For the land is full of adulterers; for because of swearing the land mourns; the pleasant places of the wilderness are dried up, and their course is evil, and their force is not right.

11 For both prophet and priest are profane; yea, in my house have I found their wickedness, says the LORD.

12 Therefore their way shall be to them as slippery ways in the darkness: they shall be driven on, and fall therein:

23:5-8 This is a Messianic prophecy. This will come to pass.

for I will bring evil upon them, even the year of their visitation, says the LORD.

13 And I have seen folly in the prophets of Samaria; they prophesied in Baal, and caused my people Israel to err.

14 I have seen also in the prophets of Jerusalem an horrible thing: they commit adultery, and walk in lies: they strengthen also the hands of evildoers, that none does return from his wickedness; they are all of them to me as Sodom, and the inhabitants thereof as Gomorrah.

15 Therefore thus says the LORD of hosts concerning the prophets; Behold, I will feed them with wormwood, and make them drink the water of gall: for from the prophets of Jerusalem is profaneness gone forth into all the land.

16 Thus says the LORD of hosts, do not hearken to the words of the prophets that prophesy to you: they make you vain: they speak a vision of their own heart, and not out of the mouth of the LORD.

17 They say still to them that despise me, The LORD has said, You shall have peace; and they say to every one that walks after the imagination of his own heart, No evil shall come upon you.

18 For who has stood in the counsel of the LORD, and has perceived and heard his word? who has marked his word, and heard it?

19 Behold, a whirlwind of the LORD is gone forth in fury, even a grievous whirlwind: it shall fall grievously upon the head of the wicked.

20 The anger of the LORD shall not return, until he has executed, and till he has performed the thoughts of his heart: in the latter days you shall consider it perfectly.

21 I have not sent these prophets, yet they ran: I have not spoken to them, yet they prophesied.

22 *But if they had stood in my counsel, and had caused my people to hear my words, then they should have turned them from their evil way, and from the evil of their doings.*

23 Am I a God at hand, says the LORD, and not a God afar off?

24 Can any hide himself in secret places that I shall not see him? says the LORD. Do not I fill heaven and earth? says the LORD.

25 I have heard what the prophets said, that prophesy lies in my name, saying, I have dreamed, I have dreamed.

26 How long shall this be in the heart of the prophets that prophesy lies? yea, they are prophets of the deceit of their own heart;

27 Which think to cause my people to forget my name by their dreams which they tell every man to his neighbour, as their fathers have forgotten my name for Baal.

28 *The prophet that has a dream, let him tell a dream; and he that has my word, let him speak my word faithfully. What is the chaff to the wheat? says the LORD.*

29 *Is not my word like as a fire? says the LORD; and like a hammer that breaks the rock in pieces?*

23:17 This is the message that is preached too often in churches today, a promise of roses without thorns (see 2 Corinthians 2:17 comment).

23:18 Feel free to underline your Bible.

23:24 This is a rhetorical question (see Psalm 139:7).

23:28-29 All who mount a pulpit or soapbox to preach must keep these words foremost in their thoughts. All God requires is faithfulness to the task He has set before us. When the gospel is preached in truth, heat and light will naturally accompany the message. The Word of God is a stone upon which the prideful sinner is broken in the day of grace. If not, it will fall heavily upon him and "grind him to powder" on the day of God's wrath (see Matthew 21:44).

30 Therefore, behold, I am against the prophets, says the LORD, that steal my words every one from his neighbour.

31 Behold, I am against the prophets, says the LORD, that use their tongues, and say, He says.

32 Behold, I am against them that prophesy false dreams, says the LORD, and do tell them, and cause my people to err by their lies, and by their lightness; yet I sent them not, nor commanded them: therefore they shall not profit this people at all, says the LORD.

33 And when this people, or the prophet, or a priest, shall ask you, saying, What is the burden of the LORD? you shall then say to them, What burden? I will even forsake you, says the LORD.

34 And as for the prophet, and the priest, and the people, that shall say, The burden of the LORD, I will even punish that man and his house.

35 Thus shall you say every one to his neighbour, and every one to his brother, What has the LORD answered? and, What has the LORD spoken?

36 And the burden of the LORD shall you mention no more: for every man's word shall be his burden; for you have perverted the words of the living God, of the LORD of hosts our God.

37 Thus shall you say to the prophet, What has the LORD answered you? and, What has the LORD spoken?

38 But since you say, The burden of the LORD; therefore thus says the LORD; Because you say this word, The burden of the LORD, and I have sent to you, saying, You shall not say, The burden of the LORD;

39 Therefore, behold, I, even I, will utterly forget you, and I will forsake you, and the city that I gave you and your fathers, and cast you out of my presence:

40 And I will bring an everlasting reproach upon you, and a perpetual shame, which shall not be forgotten.

CHAPTER 24

THE LORD showed me, and, behold, two baskets of figs were set before the temple of the LORD, after that Nebuchadrezzar king of Babylon had carried away captive Jeconiah the son of Jehoiakim king of Judah, and the princes of Judah, with the carpenters and smiths, from Jerusalem, and had brought them to Babylon.

2 One basket had very good figs, even like the figs that are first ripe: and the other basket had very naughty figs, which could not be eaten, they were so bad.

3 Then said the LORD to me, What do you see, Jeremiah? And I said, Figs; the good figs, very good; and the evil, very evil, that cannot be eaten, they are so evil.

4 Again the word of the LORD came to me, saying,

5 Thus says the LORD, the God of Israel; Like these good figs, so will I acknowledge them that are carried away captive of Judah, whom I have sent out of this place into the land of the Chaldeans for their good.

6 For I will set my eyes upon them for good, and I will bring them again to this land: and I will build them, and not pull them down; and I will plant them, and not pluck them up.

7 And I will give them an heart to know me, that I am the LORD: and they shall be my people, and I will be their God: for they shall return to me with their whole heart.

8 And as the evil figs, which cannot be eaten, they are so evil; surely thus says the LORD, So will I give Zedekiah the king of Judah, and his princes, and the residue of Jerusalem, that remain in this land, and them that dwell in the land of Egypt:

9 And I will deliver them to be removed into all the kingdoms of the earth for their hurt, to be a reproach and a proverb, a taunt and a curse, in all places where I shall drive them.

10 And I will send the sword, the famine, and the pestilence, among them, till they be consumed from off the land that I gave to them and to their fathers.

CHAPTER 25

THE word that came to Jeremiah concerning all the people of Judah in the fourth year of Jehoiakim the son of Josiah king of Judah, that was the first year of Nebuchadrezzar king of Babylon;

2 The which Jeremiah the prophet spoke to all the people of Judah, and to all the inhabitants of Jerusalem, saying,

3 From the thirteenth year of Josiah the son of Amon king of Judah, even to this day, that is the three and twentieth year, the word of the LORD has come to me, and I have spoken to you, rising early and speaking; but you have not hearkened.

4 And the LORD has sent to you all his servants the prophets, rising early and sending them; but you have not hearkened, nor inclined your ear to hear.

5 They said, Turn now every one from his evil way, and from the evil of your doings, and dwell in the land that the LORD has given to you and to your fathers for ever and ever:

6 And go not after other gods to serve them, and to worship them, and provoke me not to anger with the works of your hands; and I will do you no hurt.

7 Yet you have not hearkened to me, says the LORD; that you might provoke me to anger with the works of your hands to your own hurt.

8 Therefore thus says the LORD of hosts; Because you have not heard my words,

9 Behold, I will send and take all the families of the north, says the LORD, and Nebuchadrezzar the king of Babylon, my servant, and will bring them against this land, and against the inhabitants thereof, and against all these nations round about, and will utterly destroy them, and make them an astonishment, and an hissing, and perpetual desolations.

10 Moreover I will take from them the voice of mirth, and the voice of gladness, the voice of the bridegroom, and the voice of the bride, the sound of the millstones, and the light of the candle.

11 And this whole land shall be a desolation, and an astonishment; and these nations shall serve the king of Babylon seventy years.

12 And it shall come to pass, when seventy years are accomplished, that I will punish the king of Babylon, and that nation, says the LORD, for their iniquity, and the land of the Chaldeans, and will make it perpetual desolations.

13 And I will bring upon that land all my words which I have pronounced against it, even all that is written in this book, which Jeremiah has prophesied against all the nations.

14 For many nations and great kings shall serve themselves of them also: and I will recompense them according to their deeds, and according to the works of their own hands.

15 For thus says the LORD God of Israel to me; Take the wine cup of this fury at my hand, and cause all the nations, to whom I send you, to drink it.

16 And they shall drink, and be moved, and be mad, because of the sword that I will send among them.

17 Then took I the cup at the LORD's hand, and made all the nations to drink, to whom the LORD had sent me:

18 To wit, Jerusalem, and the cities of Judah, and the kings thereof, and the princes thereof, to make them a desolation, an astonishment, an hissing, and a curse; as it is this day;

19 Pharaoh king of Egypt, and his servants, and his princes, and all his people;

25:29-33 God's judgments are not confined to the nation of Israel.

20 And all the mingled people, and all the kings of the land of Uz, and all the kings of the land of the Philistines, and Ashkelon, and Azzah, and Ekron, and the remnant of Ashdod,

21 Edom, and Moab, and the children of Ammon,

22 And all the kings of Tyrus, and all the kings of Zidon, and the kings of the isles which are beyond the sea,

23 Dedan, and Tema, and Buz, and all that are in the utmost corners,

24 And all the kings of Arabia, and all the kings of the mingled people that dwell in the desert,

25 And all the kings of Zimri, and all the kings of Elam, and all the kings of the Medes,

26 And all the kings of the north, far and near, one with another, and all the kingdoms of the world, which are upon the face of the earth: and the king of Sheshach shall drink after them.

27 Therefore you shall say to them, Thus says the LORD of hosts, the God of Israel; Drink, and be drunken, and spue, and fall, and rise no more, because of the sword which I will send among you.

28 And it shall be, if they refuse to take the cup at your hand to drink, then shall you say to them, Thus says the LORD of hosts; You shall certainly drink.

29 For, lo, I begin to bring evil on the city which is called by my name, and should you be utterly unpunished? You shall not be unpunished: for I will call for a sword upon all the inhabitants of the earth, says the LORD of hosts.

30 *Therefore prophesy against them all these words, and say to them, The LORD shall roar from on high, and utter his voice from his holy habitation; he shall mightily roar upon his habitation; he shall give a shout, as they that tread the grapes, against all the inhabitants of the earth.*

31 A noise shall come even to the ends of the earth; for the LORD has a controversy with the nations, he will plead with all flesh; he will give them that are wicked to the sword, says the LORD.

32 Thus says the LORD of hosts, Behold, evil shall go forth from nation to nation, and a great whirlwind shall be raised up from the coasts of the earth.

33 And the slain of the LORD shall be at that day from one end of the earth even to the other end of the earth: they shall not be lamented, neither gathered, nor buried; they shall be dung upon the ground.

34 Howl, you shepherds, and cry; and wallow yourselves in the ashes, you principal of the flock: for the days of your slaughter and of your dispersions are accomplished; and you shall fall like a pleasant vessel.

35 And the shepherds shall have no way to flee, nor the principal of the flock to escape.

36 A voice of the cry of the shepherds, and an howling of the principal of the flock, shall be heard: for the LORD has spoiled their pasture.

37 And the peaceable habitations are cut down because of the fierce anger of the LORD.

38 He has forsaken his covert, as the lion: for their land is desolate because of the fierceness of the oppressor, and because of his fierce anger.

CHAPTER 26

IN the beginning of the reign of Jehoiakim the son of Josiah king of Judah came this word from the LORD, saying,

2 *Thus says the LORD; Stand in the court of the LORD's house, and speak*

26:2 In our presentation of the gospel, many of us are guilty of diminishing the significance of Biblical words, such as "repentance," "hell," "judgment day," and "sin." Perhaps we downplay the significance of these words because we fear persecution and are trying to make ourselves more acceptable to the unsaved (see Acts 20:27).

to all the cities of Judah, which come to worship in the LORD's house, all the words that I command you to speak to them; diminish not a word:

3 If so be they will hearken, and turn every man from his evil way, that I may repent me of the evil, which I purpose to do to them because of the evil of their doings.

4 And you shall say to them, Thus says the LORD; If you will not hearken to me, to walk in my law, which I have set before you,

5 To hearken to the words of my servants the prophets, whom I sent to you, both rising up early, and sending them, but you have not hearkened;

6 Then will I make this house like Shiloh, and will make this city a curse to all the nations of the earth.

7 So the priests and the prophets and all the people heard Jeremiah speaking these words in the house of the LORD.

8 Now it came to pass, when Jeremiah had made an end of speaking all that the LORD had commanded him to speak to all the people, that the priests and the prophets and all the people took him, saying, You shall surely die.

9 Why have you prophesied in the name of the LORD, saying, This house shall be like Shiloh, and this city shall be desolate without an inhabitant? And all the people were gathered against Jeremiah in the house of the LORD.

10 When the princes of Judah heard these things, then they came up from the king's house to the house of the LORD, and sat down in the entry of the new gate of the LORD's house.

11 Then spoke the priests and the prophets to the princes and to all the people, saying, This man is worthy to die; for he has prophesied against this city, as you have heard with your ears.

12 Then Jeremiah spoke to all the princes and to all the people, saying, The LORD sent me to prophesy against this house and against this city all the words that you have heard.

13 Therefore now amend your ways and your doings, and obey the voice of the LORD your God; and the LORD will repent him of the evil that he has pronounced against you.

14 As for me, behold, I am in your hand: do with me as seems good and meet to you.

15 But know for certain, that if you put me to death, you shall surely bring innocent blood upon yourselves, and upon this city, and upon the inhabitants thereof: for of a truth the LORD has sent me to you to speak all these words in your ears.

16 Then said the princes and all the people to the priests and to the prophets; This man is not worthy to die: for he has spoken to us in the name of the LORD our God.

17 Then rose up certain of the elders of the land, and spoke to all the assembly of the people, saying,

18 Micah the Morasthite prophesied in the days of Hezekiah king of Judah, and spoke to all the people of Judah, saying, Thus says the LORD of hosts; Zion shall be plowed like a field, and Jerusalem shall become heaps, and the mountain of the house as the high places of a forest.

19 Did Hezekiah king of Judah and all Judah put him at all to death? did he not fear the LORD, and besought the LORD, and the LORD repented him of the evil which he had pronounced against them?

26:8 One result of Jeremiah's obedience to his commission (see verse 2) was a death threat. Although Jeremiah was not killed (see verses 16 and 24), other prophets had been killed (see verse 20-23). In either case, we should not diminish one word from the whole counsel of God. Later, God allowed Stephen and James to die for their faith in the Savior and yet delivered Peter from prison (see Acts 12:5; also see Acts 7:55 and the comments accompanying Revelation Chapter 12).

Thus might we procure great evil against our souls.

20 And there was also a man that prophesied in the name of the LORD, Urijah the son of Shemaiah of Kirjathjearim, who prophesied against this city and against this land according to all the words of Jeremiah.

21 And when Jehoiakim the king, with all his mighty men, and all the princes, heard his words, the king sought to put him to death: but when Urijah heard it, he was afraid, and fled, and went into Egypt;

22 And Jehoiakim the king sent men into Egypt, namely, Elnathan the son of Achbor, and certain men with him into Egypt.

23 And they fetched forth Urijah out of Egypt, and brought him to Jehoiakim the king; who slew him with the sword, and cast his dead body into the graves of the common people.

24 Nevertheless the hand of Ahikam the son of Shaphan was with Jeremiah, that they should not give him into the hand of the people to put him to death.

CHAPTER 27

IN the beginning of the reign of Jehoiakim the son of Josiah king of Judah came this word to Jeremiah from the LORD, saying,

2 Thus says the LORD to me; Make for yourselves bonds and yokes, and put them upon your neck,

3 And send them to the king of Edom, and to the king of Moab, and to the king of the Ammonites, and to the king of Tyrus, and to the king of Zidon, by the hand of the messengers which come to Jerusalem to Zedekiah king of Judah;

4 And command them to say to their masters, Thus says the LORD of hosts, the God of Israel; Thus shall you say to your masters;

5 I have made the earth, the man and the beast that are upon the ground, by my great power and by my outstretched arm, and have given it to whom it seemed meet to me.

6 And now have I given all these lands into the hand of Nebuchadnezzar the king of Babylon, my servant; and the beasts of the field have I given him also to serve him.

7 And all nations shall serve him, and his son, and his son's son, until the very time of his land come: and then many nations and great kings shall serve themselves of him.

8 And it shall come to pass, that the nation and kingdom which will not serve the same Nebuchadnezzar the king of Babylon, and that will not put their neck under the yoke of the king of Babylon, that nation will I punish, says the LORD, with the sword, and with the famine, and with the pestilence, until I have consumed them by his hand.

9 Therefore do not hearken to your prophets, nor to your diviners, nor to your dreamers, nor to your enchanters, nor to your sorcerers, which speak to you, saying, You shall not serve the king of Babylon:

10 For they prophesy a lie to you, to remove you far from your land; and that I should drive you out, and you should perish.

11 But the nations that bring their neck under the yoke of the king of Babylon, and serve him, those will I let remain still in their own land, says the LORD; and they shall till it, and dwell therein.

12 I spoke also to Zedekiah king of Judah according to all these words, saying, Bring your necks under the yoke of the king of Babylon, and serve him and his people, and live.

13 Why will you die, you and your people, by the sword, by the famine, and by the pestilence, as the LORD has spoken against the nation that will not serve the king of Babylon?

14 Therefore do not hearken to the words of the prophets that speak to you, saying, You shall not serve the king of Babylon: for they prophesy a lie to you.

15 For I have not sent them, says the LORD, yet they prophesy a lie in my name; that I might drive you out, and that you might perish, you, and the prophets that prophesy to you.

16 Also I spoke to the priests and to all this people, saying, Thus says the LORD; Do not hearken to the words of your prophets that prophesy to you, saying, Behold, the vessels of the LORD's house shall now shortly be brought again from Babylon: for they prophesy a lie to you.

17 Do not hearken to them; serve the king of Babylon, and live: why should this city be laid waste?

18 But if they be prophets, and if the word of the LORD be with them, let them now make intercession to the LORD of hosts, that the vessels which are left in the house of the LORD, and in the house of the king of Judah, and at Jerusalem, go not to Babylon.

19 For thus says the LORD of hosts concerning the pillars, and concerning the sea, and concerning the bases, and concerning the residue of the vessels that remain in this city,

20 Which Nebuchadnezzar king of Babylon took not, when he carried away captive Jeconiah the son of Jehoiakim king of Judah from Jerusalem to Babylon, and all the nobles of Judah and Jerusalem;

21 Yea, thus says the LORD of hosts, the God of Israel, concerning the vessels that remain in the house of the LORD, and in the house of the king of Judah and of Jerusalem;

22 They shall be carried to Babylon, and there shall they be until the day that I visit them, says the LORD; then will I bring them up, and restore them to this place.

CHAPTER 28

AND it came to pass the same year, in the beginning of the reign of Zedekiah king of Judah, in the fourth year, and in the fifth month, that Hananiah the son of Azur the prophet, which was of Gibeon, spoke to me in the house of the LORD, in the presence of the priests and of all the people, saying,

2 Thus speaks the LORD of hosts, the God of Israel, saying, I have broken the yoke of the king of Babylon.

3 Within two full years will I bring again into this place all the vessels of the LORD's house, that Nebuchadnezzar king of Babylon took away from this place, and carried them to Babylon:

4 And I will bring again to this place Jeconiah the son of Jehoiakim king of Judah, with all the captives of Judah, that went into Babylon, says the LORD: for I will break the yoke of the king of Babylon.

5 Then the prophet Jeremiah said to the prophet Hananiah in the presence of the priests, and in the presence of all the people that stood in the house of the LORD,

6 Even the prophet Jeremiah said, Amen: the LORD do so: the LORD perform your words which you have prophesied, to bring again the vessels of the LORD's house, and all that is carried away captive, from Babylon into this place.

7 Nevertheless hear now this word that I speak in your ears, and in the ears of all the people;

8 The prophets that have been before me and before you of old prophesied both against many countries, and against great kingdoms, of war, and of evil, and of pestilence.

9 The prophet which prophesies of peace, when the word of the prophet shall come to pass, then shall the prophet be known, that the LORD has truly sent him.

10 Then Hananiah the prophet took the yoke from off the prophet Jeremiah's neck, and brake it.

11 And Hananiah spoke in the presence of all the people, saying, Thus says the LORD; Even so will I break the yoke of Nebuchadnezzar king of Babylon from the neck of all nations within the space

of two full years. And the prophet Jeremiah went his way.

12 Then the word of the LORD came to Jeremiah the prophet, after that Hananiah the prophet had broken the yoke from off the neck of the prophet Jeremiah, saying,

13 Go and tell Hananiah, saying, Thus says the LORD; You have broken the yokes of wood; but you shall make for them yokes of iron.

14 For thus says the LORD of hosts, the God of Israel; I have put a yoke of iron upon the neck of all these nations, that they may serve Nebuchadnezzar king of Babylon; and they shall serve him: and I have given him the beasts of the field also.

15 Then said the prophet Jeremiah to Hananiah the prophet, Hear now, Hananiah; The LORD has not sent you; but you make this people to trust in a lie.

16 Therefore thus says the LORD; Behold, I will cast you from off the face of the earth: this year you shall die, because you have taught rebellion against the LORD.

17 So Hananiah the prophet died the same year in the seventh month.

CHAPTER 29

N OW these are the words of the letter that Jeremiah the prophet sent from Jerusalem to the residue of the elders which were carried away captives, and to the priests, and to the prophets, and to all the people whom Nebuchadnezzar had carried away captive from Jerusalem to Babylon;

2 (After that Jeconiah the king, and the queen, and the eunuchs, the princes of Judah and Jerusalem, and the carpenters, and the smiths, were departed from Jerusalem;)

3 By the hand of Elasah the son of Shaphan, and Gemariah the son of Hilkiah, (whom Zedekiah king of Judah sent to Babylon to Nebuchadnezzar king of Babylon) saying,

4 Thus says the LORD of hosts, the God of Israel, to all that are carried away captives, whom I have caused to be carried away from Jerusalem to Babylon;

5 Build houses, and dwell in them; and plant gardens, and eat the fruit of them;

6 Take wives, and beget sons and daughters; and take wives for your sons, and give your daughters to husbands, that they may bear sons and daughters; that you may be increased there, and not diminished.

7 And seek the peace of the city where I have caused you to be carried away captives, and pray to the LORD for it: for in the peace thereof shall you have peace.

8 For thus says the LORD of hosts, the God of Israel; Let not your prophets and your diviners, that be in the midst of you, deceive you, neither hearken to your dreams which you cause to be dreamed.

9 For they prophesy falsely to you in my name: I have not sent them, says the LORD.

10 For thus says the LORD, That after seventy years be accomplished at Babylon I will visit you, and perform my good word toward you, in causing you to return to this place.

11 For I know the thoughts that I think toward you, says the LORD, thoughts of peace, and not of evil, to give you an expected end.

12 Then shall you call upon me, and you shall go and pray to me, and I will hearken to you.

13 And you shall seek me, and find me, when you shall search for me with all your heart.

14 And I will be found of you, says the LORD: and I will turn away your captivity, and I will gather you from all the nations, and from all the places where I have driven you, says the LORD; and I will bring you again into the place from which I caused you to be carried away captive.

15 Because you have said, The LORD has raised us up prophets in Babylon;

16 Know that thus says the LORD of the king that sits upon the throne of David, and of all the people that dwells in this city, and of your brethren that are not gone forth with you into captivity;

17 Thus says the LORD of hosts; Behold, I will send upon them the sword, the famine, and the pestilence, and will make them like vile figs, that cannot be eaten, they are so evil.

18 And I will persecute them with the sword, with the famine, and with the pestilence, and will deliver them to be removed to all the kingdoms of the earth, to be a curse, and an astonishment, and an hissing, and a reproach, among all the nations where I have driven them:

19 Because they have not hearkened to my words, says the LORD, which I sent to them by my servants the prophets, rising up early and sending them; but you would not hear, says the LORD.

20 Therefore hear the word of the LORD, all you of the captivity, whom I have sent from Jerusalem to Babylon:

21 Thus says the LORD of hosts, the God of Israel, of Ahab the son of Kolaiah, and of Zedekiah the son of Maaseiah, which prophesy a lie to you in my name; Behold, I will deliver them into the hand of Nebuchadrezzar king of Babylon; and he shall slay them before your eyes;

22 And of them shall be taken up a curse by all the captivity of Judah which are in Babylon, saying, The LORD make you like Zedekiah and like Ahab, whom the king of Babylon roasted in the fire;

23 Because they have committed villany in Israel, and have committed adultery with their neighbours' wives, and have spoken lying words in my name, which I have not commanded them; even I know, and am a witness, says the LORD.

24 Thus shall you also speak to Shemaiah the Nehelamite, saying,

25 Thus speaks the LORD of hosts, the God of Israel, saying, Because you have sent letters in your name to all the people that are at Jerusalem, and to Zephaniah the son of Maaseiah the priest, and to all the priests, saying,

26 The LORD has made you priest in the stead of Jehoiada the priest, that you should be officers in the house of the LORD, for every man that is mad, and makes himself a prophet, that you should put him in prison, and in the stocks.

27 Now therefore why have you not reproved Jeremiah of Anathoth, which makes himself a prophet to you?

28 For therefore he sent to us in Babylon, saying, This captivity is long: build houses, and dwell in them; and plant gardens, and eat the fruit of them.

29 And Zephaniah the priest read this letter in the ears of Jeremiah the prophet.

30 Then came the word of the LORD to Jeremiah, saying,

31 Send to all them of the captivity, saying, Thus says the LORD concerning Shemaiah the Nehelamite; Because that Shemaiah has prophesied to you, and I sent him not, and he caused you to trust in a lie:

32 Therefore thus says the LORD; Behold, I will punish Shemaiah the Nehelamite, and his seed: he shall not have a man to dwell among this people; neither shall he behold the good that I will do for my people, says the LORD; because he has taught rebellion against the LORD.

CHAPTER 30

THE word that came to Jeremiah from the LORD, saying,

2 Thus speaks the LORD God of Israel, saying, Write for yourself all the words that I have spoken to you in a book.

29:13 This conditional invitation differs considerably from the arrogant view often expressed by the unsaved sinner: "I will become a Christian when God shows Himself to me!"

3 For, lo, the days come, says the LORD, that I will bring again the captivity of my people Israel and Judah, says the LORD: and I will cause them to return to the land that I gave to their fathers, and they shall possess it.

4 And these are the words that the LORD spoke concerning Israel and concerning Judah.

5 For thus says the LORD; We have heard a voice of trembling, of fear, and not of peace.

6 Ask now, and see whether a man does travail with child? why do I see every man with his hands on his loins, as a woman in travail, and all faces are turned into paleness?

7 Alas! for that day is great, so that none is like it: it is even the time of Jacob's trouble, but he shall be saved out of it.

8 For it shall come to pass in that day, says the LORD of hosts, that I will break his yoke from off your neck, and will burst your bonds, and strangers shall no more serve themselves of him:

9 But they shall serve the LORD their God, and David their king, whom I will raise up to them.

10 Therefore fear not, O my servant Jacob, says the LORD; neither be dismayed, O Israel: for, lo, I will save you from afar, and your seed from the land of their captivity; and Jacob shall return, and shall be in rest, and be quiet, and none shall make him afraid.

11 For I am with you, says the LORD, to save you: though I make a full end of all nations where I have scattered you, yet I will not make a full end of you: but I will correct you in measure, and will not leave you altogether unpunished.

12 For thus says the LORD, Your bruise is incurable, and your wound is grievous.

13 There is none to plead your cause, that you may be bound up: you have no healing medicines.

14 All your lovers have forgotten you; they do not seek you; for I have wounded you with the wound of an enemy, with the chastisement of a cruel one, for the multitude of your iniquity; because your sins were increased.

15 Why do you cry for your affliction? your sorrow is incurable for the multitude of your iniquity: because your sins were increased, I have done these things to you.

16 Therefore all they that devour you shall be devoured; and all your adversaries, every one of them, shall go into captivity; and they that spoil you shall be a spoil, and all that prey upon you will I give for a prey.

17 For I will restore health to you, and I will heal you of your wounds, says the LORD; because they called you an Outcast, saying, This is Zion, whom no man seeks after.

18 Thus says the LORD; Behold, I will bring again the captivity of Jacob's tents, and have mercy on his dwellingplaces; and the city shall be built upon her own heap, and the palace shall remain after the manner thereof.

19 And out of them shall proceed thanksgiving and the voice of them that make merry: and I will multiply them, and they shall not be few; I will also glorify them, and they shall not be small.

20 Their children also shall be as aforetime, and their congregation shall be established before me, and I will punish all that oppress them.

21 And their nobles shall be of themselves, and their governor shall proceed from the midst of them; and I will cause him to draw near, and he shall approach to me: for who is this that engaged his heart to approach me? says the LORD.

22 And you shall be my people, and I will be your God.

23 Behold, the whirlwind of the LORD goeth forth with fury, a continuing whirlwind: it shall fall with pain upon the head of the wicked.

24 The fierce anger of the LORD shall not return, until he has done it, and until he have performed the intents of

his heart: in the latter days you shall consider it.

CHAPTER 31

AT the same time, says the LORD, will I be the God of all the families of Israel, and they shall be my people.

2 Thus says the LORD, The people which were left of the sword found grace in the wilderness; even Israel, when I went to cause him to rest.

3 The LORD has appeared of old to me, saying, Yea, I have loved you with an everlasting love: therefore with lovingkindness have I drawn you.

4 Again I will build you, and you shall be built, O virgin of Israel: you shall again be adorned with your tabrets, and shall go forth in the dances of them that make merry.

5 You shall yet plant vines upon the mountains of Samaria: the planters shall plant, and shall eat them as common things.

6 For there shall be a day, that the watchmen upon the mount Ephraim shall cry, Arise, and let us go up to Zion to the LORD our God.

7 *For thus says the LORD; Sing with gladness for Jacob, and shout among the chief of the nations: publish, give praise, and say, O LORD, save your people, the remnant of Israel.*

8 Behold, I will bring them from the north country, and gather them from the coasts of the earth, and with them the blind and the lame, the woman with child and her that travails with child together: a great company shall return there.

9 They shall come with weeping, and with supplications will I lead them: I will cause them to walk by the rivers of wa-

ters in a straight way, wherein they shall not stumble: for I am a father to Israel, and Ephraim is my firstborn.

10 Hear the word of the LORD, O you nations, and declare it in the isles afar off, and say, He that scattered Israel will gather him, and keep him, as a shepherd does his flock.

11 For the LORD has redeemed Jacob, and ransomed him from the hand of him that was stronger than he.

12 Therefore they shall come and sing in the height of Zion, and shall flow together to the goodness of the LORD, for wheat, and for wine, and for oil, and for the young of the flock and of the herd: and their soul shall be as a watered garden; and they shall not sorrow any more at all.

13 Then shall the virgin rejoice in the dance, both young men and old together: for I will turn their mourning into joy, and will comfort them, and make them rejoice from their sorrow.

14 And I will satiate the soul of the priests with fatness, and my people shall be satisfied with my goodness, says the LORD.

15 Thus says the LORD; A voice was heard in Ramah, lamentation, and bitter weeping; Rachel weeping for her children refused to be comforted for her children, because they were not.

16 Thus says the LORD; Refrain your voice from weeping, and your eyes from tears: for your work shall be rewarded, says the LORD; and they shall come again from the land of the enemy.

17 And there is hope in your end, says the LORD, that your children shall come again to their own border.

18 I have surely heard Ephraim bemoaning himself thus; You have chas-

---

30:24 We have the privilege of looking back at the dealings of God with His people (through the Bible and through history) and "consider it."

31:3 It was His love that drew us to our Savior. No man can come to the Son, unless the Father draws him (see John 6:44).

31:8-10 We have seen this happen in our generation.

tised me, and I was chastised, as a bullock unaccustomed to the yoke: you turn me, and I shall be turned; for you are the LORD my God.

19 Surely after that I was turned, I repented; and after that I was instructed, I smote upon my thigh: I was ashamed, yea, even confounded, because I did bear the reproach of my youth.

20 Is Ephraim my dear son? is he a pleasant child? for since I spoke against him, I do earnestly remember him still: therefore my bowels are troubled for him; I will surely have mercy upon him, says the LORD.

21 Set up waymarks, make high heaps: set your heart toward the highway, even the way which you went: turn again, O virgin of Israel, turn again to these your cities.

22 How long will you go about, O you backsliding daughter? for the LORD has created a new thing in the earth, A woman shall compass a man.

23 Thus says the LORD of hosts, the God of Israel; As yet they shall use this speech in the land of Judah and in the cities thereof, when I shall bring again their captivity; The LORD bless you, O habitation of justice, and mountain of holiness.

24 And there shall dwell in Judah itself, and in all the cities thereof together, husbandmen, and they that go forth with flocks.

25 For I have satiated the weary soul, and I have replenished every sorrowful soul.

26 Upon this I awaked, and beheld; and my sleep was sweet to me.

27 Behold, the days come, says the LORD, that I will sow the house of Israel and the house of Judah with the seed of man, and with the seed of beast.

28 And it shall come to pass, that like as I have watched over them, to pluck up, and to break down, and to throw down, and to destroy, and to afflict; so will I watch over them, to build, and to plant, says the LORD.

29 In those days they shall say no more, The fathers have eaten a sour grape, and the children's teeth are set on edge.

30 But every one shall die for his own iniquity: every man that eats the sour grape, his teeth shall be set on edge.

31 Behold, the days come, says the LORD, that I will make a new covenant with the house of Israel, and with the house of Judah:

32 Not according to the covenant that I made with their fathers in the day that I took them by the hand to bring them out of the land of Egypt; which my covenant they brake, although I was an husband to them, says the LORD:

33 But this shall be the covenant that I will make with the house of Israel; After those days, says the LORD, I will put my law in their inward parts, and write it in their hearts; and will be their God, and they shall be my people.

34 And they shall teach no more every man his neighbour, and every man his brother, saying, Know the LORD: for they shall all know me, from the least of them to the greatest of them, says the LORD: for I will forgive their iniquity, and I will remember their sin no more.

35 Thus says the LORD, which gives the sun for a light by day, and the ordinances of the moon and of the stars for a light by night, which divides the sea when the waves thereof roar; The LORD of hosts is his name:

36 If those ordinances depart from before me, says the LORD, then the seed of Israel also shall cease from being a nation before me for ever.

THE FUNCTION OF THE LAW

31:33 **This is the new birth.** It happens when God writes His Law on our hearts so that we desire to obey His Commandments and walk in His statutes. This is why the true convert delights to seek and save that which is lost. Evangelism is both an expression of love for God and love for one's neighbor. That is the essence of the Law of God.

37 Thus says the LORD; If heaven above can be measured, and the foundations of the earth searched out beneath, I will also cast off all the seed of Israel for all that they have done, says the LORD.

38 Behold, the days come, says the LORD, that the city shall be built to the LORD from the tower of Hananeel to the gate of the corner.

39 And the measuring line shall yet go forth over against it upon the hill Gareb, and shall compass about to Goath.

40 And the whole valley of the dead bodies, and of the ashes, and all the fields to the brook of Kidron, to the corner of the horse gate toward the east, shall be holy to the LORD; it shall not be plucked up, nor thrown down any more for ever.

CHAPTER 32

THE word that came to Jeremiah from the LORD in the tenth year of Zedekiah king of Judah, which was the eighteenth year of Nebuchadrezzar.

2 For then the king of Babylon's army besieged Jerusalem: and Jeremiah the prophet was shut up in the court of the prison, which was in the king of Judah's house.

3 For Zedekiah king of Judah had shut him up, saying, Why do you prophesy, and say, Thus says the LORD, Behold, I will give this city into the hand of the king of Babylon, and he shall take it;

4 And Zedekiah king of Judah shall not escape out of the hand of the Chaldeans, but shall surely be delivered into the hand of the king of Babylon, and shall speak with him mouth to mouth, and his eyes shall behold his eyes;

5 And he shall lead Zedekiah to Babylon, and there shall he be until I visit him, says the LORD: though you fight with the Chaldeans, you shall not prosper.

6 And Jeremiah said, The word of the LORD came to me, saying,

7 Behold, Hanameel the son of Shallum your uncle shall come to you saying, Buy my field that is in Anathoth: for the right of redemption is yours to buy it.

8 So Hanameel my uncle's son came to me in the court of the prison according to the word of the LORD, and said to me, Buy my field, I pray you, that is in Anathoth, which is in the country of Benjamin: for the right of inheritance is yours, and the redemption is yours; buy it for yourself. Then I knew that this was the word of the LORD.

9 And I bought the field of Hanameel my uncle's son, that was in Anathoth, and weighed him the money, even seventeen shekels of silver.

10 And I subscribed the evidence, and sealed it, and took witnesses, and weighed him the money in the balances.

11 So I took the evidence of the purchase, both that which was sealed according to the law and custom, and that which was open:

12 And I gave the evidence of the purchase to Baruch the son of Neriah, the son of Maaseiah, in the sight of Hanameel my uncle's son, and in the presence of the witnesses that subscribed the book of the purchase, before all the Jews that sat in the court of the prison.

13 And I charged Baruch before them, saying,

14 Thus says the LORD of hosts, the God of Israel; Take these evidences, this evidence of the purchase, both which is sealed, and this evidence which is open; and put them in an earthen vessel, that they may continue many days.

15 For thus says the LORD of hosts, the God of Israel; Houses and fields and

---

31:34 The biblical challenge to a sinner is "Do you know the Lord?" (See John 17:3)

32:4-5 See Mark 15:26 comment.

32:6-8 Jeremiah's comment, "Then I knew that this was the word of the Lord," reveals that the prophet walked by faith.

vineyards shall be possessed again in this land.

16 Now when I had delivered the evidence of the purchase to Baruch the son of Neriah, I prayed to the LORD, saying,

17 Ah Lord GOD! behold, you have made the heaven and the earth by your great power and stretched out arm, and there is nothing too hard for you:

18 You show lovingkindness to thousands, and recompense the iniquity of the fathers into the bosom of their children after them: the Great, the Mighty God, the LORD of hosts, is his name,

19 Great in counsel, and mighty in work: for your eyes are open upon all the ways of the sons of men: to give every one according to his ways, and according to the fruit of his doings:

20 Which have set signs and wonders in the land of Egypt, even to this day, and in Israel, and among other men; and have made you a name, as at this day;

21 And have brought forth your people Israel out of the land of Egypt with signs, and with wonders, and with a strong hand, and with a stretched out arm, and with great terror;

22 And have given them this land, which you did swear to their fathers to give them, a land flowing with milk and honey;

23 And they came in, and possessed it; but they have not obeyed your voice, neither walked in your law; they have done nothing of all that you commanded them to do: therefore you have caused all this evil to come upon them:

24 Behold the mounts, they are come to the city to take it; and the city is given into the hand of the Chaldeans, that fight against it, because of the sword, and of the famine, and of the pestilence:

and what you have spoken is come to pass; and, behold, you see it.

25 And you have said to me, O Lord GOD, Buy the field for money, and take witnesses; for the city is given into the hand of the Chaldeans.

26 Then came the word of the LORD to Jeremiah, saying,

27 Behold, I am the LORD, the God of all flesh: is there any thing too hard for me?

28 Therefore thus says the LORD; Behold, I will give this city into the hand of the Chaldeans, and into the hand of Nebuchadrezzar king of Babylon, and he shall take it:

29 And the Chaldeans, that fight against this city, shall come and set fire on this city, and burn it with the houses, upon whose roofs they have offered incense to Baal, and poured out drink offerings to other gods, to provoke me to anger.

30 For the children of Israel and the children of Judah have only done evil before me from their youth: for the children of Israel have only provoked me to anger with the work of their hands, says the LORD.

31 For this city has been to me as a provocation of my anger and of my fury from the day that they built it even to this day; that I should remove it from before my face,

32 Because of all the evil of the children of Israel and of the children of Judah, which they have done to provoke me to anger, they, their kings, their princes, their priests, and their prophets, and the men of Judah, and the inhabitants of Jerusalem.

33 And they have turned to me the back, and not the face: though I taught

---

32:14 The field is the world from which the Church has been purchased by the blood of the Savior. We are earthen vessels that have been sealed with the Holy Spirit of promise.

32:17 "Ah, Lord God" is an expression of overwhelming awe—that God could create such a creation as surrounds us. Words cannot express our wonder. When one has such a revelation, it leads to the great truth that nothing is too hard for God (see also Luke 1:37).

them, rising up early and teaching them, yet they have not hearkened to receive instruction.

34 But they set their abominations in the house, which is called by my name, to defile it.

35 And they built the high places of Baal, which are in the valley of the son of Hinnom, to cause their sons and their daughters to pass through the fire to Molech; which I commanded them not, neither came it into my mind, that they should do this abomination, to cause Judah to sin.

36 And now therefore thus says the LORD, the God of Israel, concerning this city, whereof you say, It shall be delivered into the hand of the king of Babylon by the sword, and by the famine, and by the pestilence;

37 Behold, I will gather them out of all countries, where I have driven them in my anger, and in my fury, and in great wrath; and I will bring them again to this place, and I will cause them to dwell safely:

38 And they shall be my people, and I will be their God:

39 **And I will give them one heart, and one way, that they may fear me for ever, for the good of them, and of their children after them:**

40 **And I will make an everlasting covenant with them, that I will not turn away from them, to do them good; but I will put my fear in their hearts, that they shall not depart from me.**

41 Yea, I will rejoice over them to do them good, and I will plant them in this land assuredly with my whole heart and with my whole soul.

42 For thus says the LORD; Like as I have brought all this great evil upon this people, so will I bring upon them all the good that I have promised them.

43 And fields shall be bought in this land, whereof you say, It is desolate without man or beast; it is given into the hand of the Chaldeans.

44 Men shall buy fields for money, and subscribe evidences, and seal them, and take witnesses in the land of Benjamin, and in the places about Jerusalem, and in the cities of Judah, and in the cities of the mountains, and in the cities of the valley, and in the cities of the south: for I will cause their captivity to return, says the LORD.

CHAPTER 33

MOREOVER the word of the LORD came to Jeremiah the second time, while he was yet shut up in the court of the prison, saying,

2 Thus says the LORD the maker thereof, the LORD that formed it, to establish it; the LORD is his name;

3 **Call to me, and I will answer you, and show you great and mighty things, which you do not know.**

4 For thus says the LORD, the God of Israel, concerning the houses of this city, and concerning the houses of the kings of Judah, which are thrown down by the mounts, and by the sword;

5 They come to fight with the Chaldeans, but it is to fill them with the dead bodies of men, whom I have slain in my anger and in my fury, and for all whose wickedness I have hid my face from this city.

32:37 History attests to the truth of this prophecy.

32:40 This is true conversion; "I will put My fear in their hearts, that they shall not depart from Me." The reason modern evangelism loses so many of its converts is because they fail to preach the Law of God, which produces the fear of the Lord in the heart of the sinner.

32:44 Jesus purchased the fields, the world and its inhabitants; He signed for them in His blood, sealed them with the Holy Spirit and made them His witnesses.

33:3 This is an open challenge to call upon the Lord for great and mighty things.

6 Behold, I will bring it health and cure, and I will cure them, and will reveal to them the abundance of peace and truth.

7 And I will cause the captivity of Judah and the captivity of Israel to return, and will build them, as at the first.

8 And I will cleanse them from all their iniquity, whereby they have sinned against me; and I will pardon all their iniquities, whereby they have sinned, and whereby they have transgressed against me.

9 And it shall be to me a name of joy, a praise and an honour before all the nations of the earth, which shall hear all the good that I do to them: and they shall fear and tremble for all the goodness and for all the prosperity that I procure to it.

10 Thus says the LORD; Again there shall be heard in this place, which you say shall be desolate without man and without beast, even in the cities of Judah, and in the streets of Jerusalem, that are desolate, without man, and without inhabitant, and without beast,

11 The voice of joy, and the voice of gladness, the voice of the bridegroom, and the voice of the bride, the voice of them that shall say, Praise the LORD of hosts: for the LORD is good; for his mercy endures for ever: and of them that shall bring the sacrifice of praise into the house of the LORD. For I will cause to return the captivity of the land, as at the first, says the LORD.

12 Thus says the LORD of hosts; Again in this place, which is desolate without man and without beast, and in all the cities thereof, shall be an habitation of shepherds causing their flocks to lie down.

13 In the cities of the mountains, in the cities of the vale, and in the cities of the south, and in the land of Benjamin, and in the places about Jerusalem, and in the cities of Judah, shall the flocks pass again under the hands of him that tells them, says the LORD.

14 Behold, the days come, says the LORD, that I will perform that good thing which I have promised to the house of Israel and to the house of Judah.

15 In those days, and at that time, will I cause the Branch of righteousness to grow up to David; and he shall execute judgment and righteousness in the land.

16 In those days shall Judah be saved, and Jerusalem shall dwell safely: and this is the name wherewith she shall be called, The LORD our righteousness.

17 For thus says the LORD; David shall never want a man to sit upon the throne of the house of Israel;

18 Neither shall the priests the Levites want a man before me to offer burnt offerings, and to kindle meat offerings, and to do sacrifice continually.

19 And the word of the LORD came to Jeremiah, saying,

20 Thus says the LORD; If you can break my covenant of the day, and my covenant of the night, and that there should not be day and night in their season;

21 Then may also my covenant be broken with David my servant, that he should not have a son to reign upon his throne; and with the Levites the priests, my ministers.

22 As the host of heaven cannot be numbered, neither the sand of the sea measured: so will I multiply the seed of David my servant, and the Levites that minister to me.

23 Moreover the word of the LORD came to Jeremiah, saying,

24 Have you not considered what these people have spoken, saying, The two families which the LORD has chosen, he has even cast them off? thus they have despised my people, that they should be no more a nation before them.

33:8 When we sin, we transgress the moral Law and sin against God.

25 Thus says the LORD; If my covenant be not with day and night, and if I have not appointed the ordinances of heaven and earth;

26 Then will I cast away the seed of Jacob and David my servant, so that I will not take any of his seed to be rulers over the seed of Abraham, Isaac, and Jacob: for I will cause their captivity to return, and have mercy on them.

CHAPTER 34

THE word which came to Jeremiah from the LORD, when Nebuchadnezzar king of Babylon, and all his army, and all the kingdoms of the earth of his dominion, and all the people, fought against Jerusalem, and against all the cities thereof, saying,

2 Thus says the LORD, the God of Israel; Go and speak to Zedekiah king of Judah, and tell him, Thus says the LORD; Behold, I will give this city into the hand of the king of Babylon, and he shall burn it with fire:

3 And you shall not escape out of his hand, but shall surely be taken, and delivered into his hand; and your eyes shall behold the eyes of the king of Babylon, and he shall speak with you mouth to mouth, and you shall go to Babylon.

4 Yet hear the word of the LORD, O Zedekiah king of Judah; Thus says the LORD of you, You shall not die by the sword:

5 But you shall die in peace: and with the burnings of your fathers, the former kings which were before you, so shall they burn odours for you; and they will lament you, saying, Ah lord! for I have pronounced the word, says the LORD.

6 Then Jeremiah the prophet spoke all these words to Zedekiah king of Judah in Jerusalem,

7 When the king of Babylon's army fought against Jerusalem, and against all the cities of Judah that were left, against Lachish, and against Azekah: for these defenced cities remained of the cities of Judah.

8 This is the word that came to Jeremiah from the LORD, after that the king Zedekiah had made a covenant with all the people which were at Jerusalem, to proclaim liberty to them;

9 That every man should let his manservant, and every man his maidservant, being an Hebrew or an Hebrewess, go free; that none should serve himself of them, to wit, of a Jew his brother.

10 Now when all the princes, and all the people, which had entered into the covenant, heard that every one should let his manservant, and every one his maidservant, go free, that none should serve themselves of them any more, then they obeyed, and let them go.

11 But afterward they turned, and caused the servants and the handmaids, whom they had let go free, to return, and brought them into subjection for servants and for handmaids.

12 Therefore the word of the LORD came to Jeremiah from the LORD, saying,

13 Thus says the LORD, the God of Israel; I made a covenant with your fathers in the day that I brought them forth out of the land of Egypt, out of the house of bondmen, saying,

14 At the end of seven years let go every man his brother an Hebrew, which has been sold to you; and when he has served you six years, you shall let him go free from you: but your fathers did not hearken to me, neither inclined their ear.

15 And you were now turned, and had done right in my sight, in proclaiming liberty every man to his neighbour; and you had made a covenant before me in the house which is called by my name:

33:22 See Hebrews 11:3, *Scientific Facts in the Bible*.
34:3 See Mark 15:26 comment.

16 But you turned and polluted my name, and caused every man his servant, and every man his handmaid, whom he had set at liberty at their pleasure, to return, and brought them into subjection, to be to you for servants and for handmaids.

17 Therefore thus says the LORD; You have not hearkened to me, in proclaiming liberty, every one to his brother, and every man to his neighbour: behold, I proclaim a liberty for you, says the LORD, to the sword, to the pestilence, and to the famine; and I will make you to be removed into all the kingdoms of the earth.

18 And I will give the men that have transgressed my covenant, which have not performed the words of the covenant which they had made before me, when they cut the calf in twain, and passed between the parts thereof,

19 The princes of Judah, and the princes of Jerusalem, the eunuchs, and the priests, and all the people of the land, which passed between the parts of the calf;

20 I will even give them into the hand of their enemies, and into the hand of them that seek their life: and their dead bodies shall be for meat to the fowls of the heaven, and to the beasts of the earth.

21 And Zedekiah king of Judah and his princes will I give into the hand of their enemies, and into the hand of them that seek their life, and into the hand of the king of Babylon's army, which are gone up from you.

22 Behold, I will command, says the LORD, and cause them to return to this city; and they shall fight against it, and take it, and burn it with fire: and I will make the cities of Judah a desolation without an inhabitant.

CHAPTER 35

THE word which came to Jeremiah from the LORD in the days of Jehoiakim the son of Josiah king of Judah, saying,

2 Go to the house of the Rechabites, and speak to them, and bring them into the house of the LORD, into one of the chambers, and give them wine to drink.

3 Then I took Jaazaniah the son of Jeremiah, the son of Habaziniah, and his brethren, and all his sons, and the whole house of the Rechabites;

4 And I brought them into the house of the LORD, into the chamber of the sons of Hanan, the son of Igdaliah, a man of God, which was by the chamber of the princes, which was above the chamber of Maaseiah the son of Shallum, the keeper of the door:

5 And I set before the sons of the house of the Rechabites pots full of wine, and cups, and I said to them, Drink wine.

6 But they said, We will drink no wine: for Jonadab the son of Rechab our father commanded us, saying, You shall drink no wine, neither you, nor your sons for ever:

7 Neither shall you build house, nor sow seed, nor plant vineyard, nor have any: but all your days you shall dwell in tents; that you may live many days in the land where you are strangers.

8 Thus have we obeyed the voice of Jonadab the son of Rechab our father in all that he has charged us, to drink no wine all our days, we, our wives, our sons, nor our daughters;

9 Nor to build houses for us to dwell in: neither have we vineyard, nor field, nor seed:

10 But we have dwelt in tents, and have obeyed, and done according to all that Jonadab our father commanded us.

11 But it came to pass, when Nebuchadrezzar king of Babylon came up into the land, that we said, Come, and let us go to Jerusalem for fear of the army of the Chaldeans, and for fear

of the army of the Syrians: so we dwell at Jerusalem.

12 Then came the word of the LORD to Jeremiah, saying,

13 Thus says the LORD of hosts, the God of Israel; Go and tell the men of Judah and the inhabitants of Jerusalem, Will you not receive instruction to hearken to my words? says the LORD.

14 The words of Jonadab the son of Rechab, that he commanded his sons not to drink wine, are performed; for to this day they drink none, but obey their father's commandment: notwithstanding I have spoken to you, rising early and speaking; but you did not hearken to me.

15 I have sent also to you all my servants the prophets, rising up early and sending them, saying, Return now every man from his evil way, and amend your doings, and go not after other gods to serve them, and you shall dwell in the land which I have given to you and to your fathers: but you have not inclined your ear, nor hearkened to me.

16 Because the sons of Jonadab the son of Rechab have performed the commandment of their father, which he commanded them; but this people has not hearkened to me:

17 Therefore thus says the LORD God of hosts, the God of Israel; Behold, I will bring upon Judah and upon all the inhabitants of Jerusalem all the evil that I have pronounced against them: because I have spoken to them, but they have not heard; and I have called to them, but they have not answered.

18 And Jeremiah said to the house of the Rechabites, Thus says the LORD of hosts, the God of Israel; Because you have obeyed the commandment of Jonadab your father, and kept all his precepts, and done according to all that he has commanded you:

19 Therefore thus says the LORD of hosts, the God of Israel; Jonadab the son of Rechab shall not want a man to stand before me for ever.

CHAPTER 36

AND it came to pass in the fourth year of Jehoiakim the son of Josiah king of Judah, that this word came to Jeremiah from the LORD, saying,

2 Take a roll of a book, and write therein all the words that I have spoken to you against Israel, and against Judah, and against all the nations, from the day I spoke to you, from the days of Josiah, even to this day.

3 It may be that the house of Judah will hear all the evil which I purpose to do to them; that they may return every man from his evil way; that I may forgive their iniquity and their sin.

4 Then Jeremiah called Baruch the son of Neriah: and Baruch wrote from the mouth of Jeremiah all the words of the LORD, which he had spoken to him, upon a roll of a book.

5 And Jeremiah commanded Baruch, saying, I am shut up; I cannot go into the house of the LORD:

6 You go, therefore, and read in the roll, which you have written from my mouth, the words of the LORD in the ears of the people in the LORD's house upon the fasting day: and also you shall read them in the ears of all Judah that come out of their cities.

7 It may be they will present their supplication before the LORD, and will return every one from his evil way: for great is the anger and the fury that the LORD has pronounced against this people.

8 And Baruch the son of Neriah did according to all that Jeremiah the prophet commanded him, reading in the book

---

36:1-3 Sinners must hear all the adversity that the law threatens so that they may turn from their evil ways, and God may forgive their iniquity and their sin through the gospel.

BARUCH WRITING JEREMIAH'S PROPHECIES

Jeremiah 36:4

the words of the LORD in the LORD's house.

9 And it came to pass in the fifth year of Jehoiakim the son of Josiah king of Judah, in the ninth month, that they proclaimed a fast before the LORD to all the people in Jerusalem, and to all the people that came from the cities of Judah to Jerusalem.

10 Then read Baruch in the book the words of Jeremiah in the house of the LORD, in the chamber of Gemariah the son of Shaphan the scribe, in the higher court, at the entry of the new gate of the LORD's house, in the ears of all the people.

11 When Michaiah the son of Gemariah, the son of Shaphan, had heard out of the book all the words of the LORD,

12 Then he went down into the king's house, into the scribe's chamber: and, lo, all the princes sat there, even Elishama the scribe, and Delaiah the son of Shemaiah, and Elnathan the son of Achbor, and Gemariah the son of Shaphan, and Zedekiah the son of Hananiah, and all the princes.

13 Then Michaiah declared to them all the words that he had heard, when Baruch read the book in the ears of the people.

14 Therefore all the princes sent Jehudi the son of Nethaniah, the son of Shelemiah, the son of Cushi, to Baruch, saying, Take in your hand the roll wherein you have read in the ears of the people, and come. So Baruch the son of Neriah took the roll in his hand, and came to them.

15 And they said to him, Sit down now, and read it in our ears. So Baruch read it in their ears.

16 Now it came to pass, when they had heard all the words, they were afraid both one and other, and said to Baruch, We will surely tell the king of all these words.

17 And they asked Baruch, saying, Tell us now, How did you write all these words at his mouth?

18 Then Baruch answered them, He pronounced all these words to me with his mouth, and I wrote them with ink in the book.

19 Then said the princes to Baruch, Go, hide, you and Jeremiah; and let no man know where you are.

20 And they went in to the king into the court, but they laid up the roll in the chamber of Elishama the scribe, and told all the words in the ears of the king.

21 So the king sent Jehudi to fetch the roll: and he took it out of Elishama the scribe's chamber. And Jehudi read it in the ears of the king, and in the ears of all the princes which stood beside the king.

22 Now the king sat in the winterhouse in the ninth month: and there was a fire on the hearth burning before him.

23 And it came to pass, that when Jehudi had read three or four leaves, he cut it with the penknife, and cast it into the fire that was on the hearth, until all the roll was consumed in the fire that was on the hearth.

24 Yet they were not afraid, nor rent their garments, neither the king, nor any of his servants that heard all these words.

25 Nevertheless Elnathan and Delaiah and Gemariah had made intercession to the king that he would not burn the roll: but he would not hear them.

26 But the king commanded Jerahmeel the son of Hammelech, and Seraiah the son of Azriel, and Shelemiah the son of Abdeel, to take Baruch the scribe and Jeremiah the prophet: but the LORD hid them.

27 Then the word of the LORD came to Jeremiah, after that the king had burned the roll, and the words which Baruch wrote at the mouth of Jeremiah, saying,

28 Take again another roll, and write in it all the former words that were in the first roll, which Jehoiakim the king of Judah has burned.

29 And you shall say to Jehoiakim king of Judah, Thus says the LORD; You have burned this roll, saying, Why have you written therein, saying, The king of Babylon shall certainly come and destroy this land, and shall cause to cease from thence man and beast?

30 Therefore thus says the LORD of Jehoiakim king of Judah; He shall have none to sit upon the throne of David: and his dead body shall be cast out in the day to the heat, and in the night to the frost.

31 And I will punish him and his seed and his servants for their iniquity; and I will bring upon them, and upon the inhabitants of Jerusalem, and upon the men of Judah, all the evil that I have pronounced against them; but they did not hearken.

32 Then took Jeremiah another roll, and gave it to Baruch the scribe, the son of Neriah; who wrote therein from the mouth of Jeremiah all the words of the book which Jehoiakim king of Judah had burned in the fire: and there were added besides to them many like words.

CHAPTER 37

AND king Zedekiah the son of Josiah reigned instead of Coniah the son of Jehoiakim, whom Nebuchadrezzar king of Babylon made king in the land of Judah.

2 But neither he, nor his servants, nor the people of the land, did hearken to the words of the LORD, which he spoke by the prophet Jeremiah.

3 And Zedekiah the king sent Jehucal the son of Shelemiah and Zephaniah the son of Maaseiah the priest to the prophet Jeremiah, saying, Pray now to the LORD our God for us.

4 Now Jeremiah came in and went out among the people: for they had not put him into prison.

5 Then Pharaoh's army was come forth out of Egypt: and when the Chaldeans that besieged Jerusalem heard tidings of them, they departed from Jerusalem.

6 Then came the word of the LORD to the prophet Jeremiah saying,

7 Thus says the LORD, the God of Israel; Thus shall you say to the king of Judah, that sent you to me to enquire of me; Behold, Pharaoh's army, which is come forth to help you, shall return to Egypt into their own land.

8 And the Chaldeans shall come again, and fight against this city, and take it, and burn it with fire.

9 Thus says the LORD; Deceive not yourselves, saying, The Chaldeans shall surely depart from us: for they shall not depart.

10 For though you had smitten the whole army of the Chaldeans that fight against you, and there remained but wounded men among them, yet should they rise up every man in his tent, and burn this city with fire.

11 And it came to pass, that when the army of the Chaldeans was broken up from Jerusalem for fear of Pharaoh's army,

12 Then Jeremiah went forth out of Jerusalem to go into the land of Benjamin, to separate himself thence in the midst of the people.

13 And when he was in the gate of Benjamin, a captain of the ward was there, whose name was Irijah, the son of Shelemiah, the son of Hananiah; and he took Jeremiah the prophet, saying, You fall away to the Chaldeans.

14 Then said Jeremiah, It is false; I fall not away to the Chaldeans. But he did not hearken to him: so Irijah took Jeremiah, and brought him to the princes.

15 Therefore the princes were wroth with Jeremiah, and smote him, and put him in prison in the house of Jonathan the scribe: for they had made that the prison.

16 When Jeremiah was entered into the dungeon, and into the cabins, and Jeremiah had remained there many days;

17 Then Zedekiah the king sent, and took him out: and the king asked him

secretly in his house, and said, Is there any word from the LORD? And Jeremiah said, There is: for, said he, you shall be delivered into the hand of the king of Babylon.

18 Moreover Jeremiah said to king Zedekiah, What have I offended against you, or against your servants, or against this people, that you have put me in prison?

19 Where are now your prophets which prophesied to you, saying, The king of Babylon shall not come against you, nor against this land?

20 Therefore hear now, I pray you, O my lord the king: let my supplication, I pray you, be accepted before you; that you do not cause me to return to the house of Jonathan the scribe, lest I die there.

21 Then Zedekiah the king commanded that they should commit Jeremiah into the court of the prison, and that they should give him daily a piece of bread out of the bakers' street, until all the bread in the city were spent. Thus Jeremiah remained in the court of the prison.

CHAPTER 38

THEN Shephatiah the son of Mattan, and Gedaliah the son of Pashur, and Jucal the son of Shelemiah, and Pashur the son of Malchiah, heard the words that Jeremiah had spoken to all the people, saying,

2 Thus says the LORD, He that remains in this city shall die by the sword, by the famine, and by the pestilence: but he that goeth forth to the Chaldeans shall live; for he shall have his life for a prey, and shall live.

3 Thus says the LORD, This city shall surely be given into the hand of the king of Babylon's army, which shall take it.

4 Therefore the princes said to the king, We beseech you, let this man be put to death: for thus he weakens the hands of the men of war that remain in this city, and the hands of all the people, in speaking such words to them: for this man does not seek the welfare of this people, but the hurt.

5 Then Zedekiah the king said, Behold, he is in your hand: for the king is not he that can do any thing against you.

6 Then took they Jeremiah, and cast him into the dungeon of Malchiah the son of Hammelech, that was in the court of the prison: and they let down Jeremiah with cords. And in the dungeon there was no water, but mire: so Jeremiah sunk in the mire.

7 Now when Ebedmelech the Ethiopian, one of the eunuchs which was in the king's house, heard that they had put Jeremiah in the dungeon; the king then sitting in the gate of Benjamin;

8 Ebedmelech went forth out of the king's house, and spoke to the king saying,

9 My lord the king, these men have done evil in all that they have done to Jeremiah the prophet, whom they have cast into the dungeon; and he is like to die for hunger in the place where he is: for there is no more bread in the city.

10 Then the king commanded Ebedmelech the Ethiopian, saying, Take from hence thirty men with you, and take up Jeremiah the prophet out of the dungeon, before he die.

11 So Ebedmelech took the men with him, and went into the house of the king under the treasury, and took thence old cast clouts and old rotten rags, and let them down by cords into the dungeon to Jeremiah.

12 And Ebedmelech the Ethiopian said to Jeremiah, Put now these old cast clouts and rotten rags under your arm-

---

38:4 They beseeched the king for the death of the prophet. The world is passionate about stopping the mouth of the evangelistic Christian. In their error, they are convinced that Christians want the ruin, not the good of humanity.

holes under the cords. And Jeremiah did so.

13 So they drew up Jeremiah with cords, and took him up out of the dungeon: and Jeremiah remained in the court of the prison.

14 Then Zedekiah the king sent, and took Jeremiah the prophet to him into the third entry that is in the house of the LORD: and the king said to Jeremiah, I will ask you a thing; hide nothing from me.

15 Then Jeremiah said to Zedekiah, If I declare it to you, will you not surely put me to death? and if I give you counsel, will you not hearken to me?

16 So Zedekiah the king swore secretly to Jeremiah, saying, As the LORD lives, that made us this soul, I will not put you to death, neither will I give you into the hand of these men that seek your life.

17 Then said Jeremiah to Zedekiah, Thus says the LORD, the God of hosts, the God of Israel; If you will assuredly go forth to the king of Babylon's princes, then your soul shall live, and this city shall not be burned with fire; and you shall live, and your house:

18 But if you will not go forth to the king of Babylon's princes, then shall this city be given into the hand of the Chaldeans, and they shall burn it with fire, and you shall not escape out of their hand.

19 And Zedekiah the king said to Jeremiah, I am afraid of the Jews that are fallen to the Chaldeans, lest they deliver me into their hand, and they mock me.

20 But Jeremiah said, They shall not deliver you. Obey, I beseech you, the voice of the LORD, which I speak to you: so it shall be well with you, and your soul shall live.

21 But if you refuse to go forth, this is the word that the LORD has shown me:

22 And, behold, all the women that are left in the king of Judah's house shall be brought forth to the king of Babylon's princes, and those women shall say, Your friends have set upon you, and have prevailed against you: your feet are sunk in the mire, and they are turned away back.

23 So they shall bring out all your wives and your children to the Chaldeans: and you shall not escape out of their hand, but shall be taken by the hand of the king of Babylon: and you shall cause this city to be burned with fire.

24 Then said Zedekiah to Jeremiah, Let no man know of these words, and you shall not die.

25 But if the princes hear that I have talked with you, and they come to you, and say to you, Declare to us now what you have said to the king, hide it not from us, and we will not put you to death; also what the king said to you:

26 Then you shall say to them, I presented my supplication before the king, that he would not cause me to return to Jonathan's house, to die there.

27 Then came all the princes to Jeremiah, and asked him: and he told them according to all these words that the king had commanded. So they left off speaking with him; for the matter was not perceived.

28 So Jeremiah abode in the court of the prison until the day that Jerusalem was taken: and he was there when Jerusalem was taken.

CHAPTER 39

IN the ninth year of Zedekiah king of Judah, in the tenth month, came Nebuchadrezzar king of Babylon and all his army against Jerusalem, and they besieged it.

2 And in the eleventh year of Zedekiah, in the fourth month, the ninth day of the month, the city was broken up.

3 And all the princes of the king of Babylon came in, and sat in the middle gate, even Nergalsharezer, Samgarnebo, Sarsechim, Rabsaris, Nergalsharezer, Rabmag, with all the residue of the princes of the king of Babylon.

4 And it came to pass, that when Zedekiah the king of Judah saw them, and all the men of war, then they fled, and went forth out of the city by night, by the way of the king's garden, by the gate betwixt the two walls: and he went out the way of the plain.

5 But the Chaldeans' army pursued after them, and overtook Zedekiah in the plains of Jericho: and when they had taken him, they brought him up to Nebuchadnezzar king of Babylon to Riblah in the land of Hamath, where he gave judgment upon him.

6 Then the king of Babylon slew the sons of Zedekiah in Riblah before his eyes: also the king of Babylon slew all the nobles of Judah.

7 Moreover he put out Zedekiah's eyes, and bound him with chains, to carry him to Babylon.

8 And the Chaldeans burned the king's house, and the houses of the people, with fire, and brake down the walls of Jerusalem.

9 Then Nebuzaradan the captain of the guard carried away captive into Babylon the remnant of the people that remained in the city, and those that fell away, that fell to him, with the rest of the people that remained.

10 But Nebuzaradan the captain of the guard left of the poor of the people, which had nothing, in the land of Judah, and gave them vineyards and fields at the same time.

11 Now Nebuchadrezzar king of Babylon gave charge concerning Jeremiah to Nebuzaradan the captain of the guard, saying,

12 Take him, and look well to him, and do him no harm; but do to him even as he shall say to you.

13 So Nebuzaradan the captain of the guard sent, and Nebushasban, Rabsaris, and Nergalsharezer, Rabmag, and all the king of Babylon's princes;

14 Even they sent, and took Jeremiah out of the court of the prison, and committed him to Gedaliah the son of Ahikam the son of Shaphan, that he should carry him home: so he dwelt among the people.

15 Now the word of the LORD came to Jeremiah, while he was shut up in the court of the prison, saying,

16 Go and speak to Ebedmelech the Ethiopian, saying, Thus says the LORD of hosts, the God of Israel; Behold, I will bring my words upon this city for evil, and not for good; and they shall be accomplished in that day before you.

17 But I will deliver you in that day, says the LORD: and you shall not be given into the hand of the men of whom you are afraid.

18 For I will surely deliver you, and you shall not fall by the sword, but your life shall be for a prey to you: because you have put your trust in me, says the LORD.

CHAPTER 40

THE word that came to Jeremiah from the LORD, after that Nebuzaradan the captain of the guard had let him go from Ramah, when he had taken him being bound in chains among all that were carried away captive of Jerusalem and Judah, which were carried away captive to Babylon.

2 And the captain of the guard took Jeremiah, and said to him, The LORD your God has pronounced this evil upon this place.

3 Now the LORD has brought it, and done according as he has said: because you have sinned against the LORD, and have not obeyed his voice, therefore this thing is come upon you.

4 And now, behold, I loose you this day from the chains which were upon your hand. If it seem good to you to come with me into Babylon, come; and I will

---

39:6 See Mark 15:26 "comment."

look well to you: but if it seem ill to you to come with me into Babylon, forbear: behold, all the land is before you: where it seems good and convenient for you to go, go there.

5 Now while he was not yet gone back, he said, Go back also to Gedaliah the son of Ahikam the son of Shaphan, whom the king of Babylon has made governor over the cities of Judah, and dwell with him among the people: or go wherever it seems convenient to you to go. So the captain of the guard gave him victuals and a reward, and let him go.

6 Then went Jeremiah to Gedaliah the son of Ahikam to Mizpah; and dwelt with him among the people that were left in the land.

7 Now when all the captains of the forces which were in the fields, even they and their men, heard that the king of Babylon had made Gedaliah the son of Ahikam governor in the land, and had committed to him men, and women, and children, and of the poor of the land, of them that were not carried away captive to Babylon;

8 Then they came to Gedaliah to Mizpah, even Ishmael the son of Nethaniah, and Johanan and Jonathan the sons of Kareah, and Seraiah the son of Tanhumeth, and the sons of Ephai the Netophathite, and Jezaniah the son of a Maachathite, they and their men.

9 And Gedaliah the son of Ahikam the son of Shaphan swore to them and to their men, saying, Fear not to serve the Chaldeans: dwell in the land, and serve the king of Babylon, and it shall be well with you.

10 As for me, behold, I will dwell at Mizpah, to serve the Chaldeans, which will come to us: but you, gather wine, and summer fruits, and oil, and put them in your vessels, and dwell in your cities that you have taken.

11 Likewise when all the Jews that were in Moab, and among the Ammonites, and in Edom, and that were in all the countries, heard that the king of Babylon

had left a remnant of Judah, and that he had set over them Gedaliah the son of Ahikam the son of Shaphan;

12 Even all the Jews returned out of all places where they were driven, and came to the land of Judah, to Gedaliah, to Mizpah, and gathered wine and summer fruits very much.

13 Moreover Johanan the son of Kareah, and all the captains of the forces that were in the fields, came to Gedaliah to Mizpah,

14 And said to him, Dost you certainly know that Baalis the king of the Ammonites has sent Ishmael the son of Nethaniah to slay you? But Gedaliah the son of Ahikam believed them not.

15 Then Johanan the son of Kareah spoke to Gedaliah in Mizpah secretly saying, Let me go, I pray you, and I will slay Ishmael the son of Nethaniah, and no man shall know it: why should he slay you, that all the Jews which are gathered to you should be scattered, and the remnant in Judah perish?

16 But Gedaliah the son of Ahikam said to Johanan the son of Kareah, You shall not do this thing: for you speak falsely of Ishmael.

CHAPTER 41

NOW it came to pass in the seventh month, that Ishmael the son of Nethaniah the son of Elishama, of the seed royal, and the princes of the king, even ten men with him, came to Gedaliah the son of Ahikam to Mizpah; and there they did eat bread together in Mizpah.

2 Then arose Ishmael the son of Nethaniah, and the ten men that were with him, and smote Gedaliah the son of Ahikam the son of Shaphan with the sword, and slew him, whom the king of Babylon had made governor over the land.

3 Ishmael also slew all the Jews that were with him, even with Gedaliah, at Mizpah, and the Chaldeans that were found there, and the men of war.

4 And it came to pass the second day after he had slain Gedaliah, and no man knew it,

5 That there came certain from Shechem, from Shiloh, and from Samaria, even fourscore men, having their beards shaven, and their clothes rent, and having cut themselves, with offerings and incense in their hand, to bring them to the house of the LORD.

6 And Ishmael the son of Nethaniah went forth from Mizpah to meet them, weeping all along as he went: and it came to pass, as he met them, he said to them, Come to Gedaliah the son of Ahikam.

7 And it was so, when they came into the midst of the city, that Ishmael the son of Nethaniah slew them, and cast them into the midst of the pit, he, and the men that were with him.

8 But ten men were found among them that said to Ishmael, Slay us not: for we have treasures in the field, of wheat, and of barley, and of oil, and of honey. So he forbare, and slew them not among their brethren.

9 Now the pit wherein Ishmael had cast all the dead bodies of the men, whom he had slain because of Gedaliah, was it which Asa the king had made for fear of Baasha king of Israel: and Ishmael the son of Nethaniah filled it with them that were slain.

10 Then Ishmael carried away captive all the residue of the people that were in Mizpah, even the king's daughters, and all the people that remained in Mizpah, whom Nebuzaradan the captain of the guard had committed to Gedaliah the son of Ahikam: and Ishmael the son of Nethaniah carried them away captive, and departed to go over to the Ammonites.

11 But when Johanan the son of Kareah, and all the captains of the forces that were with him, heard of all the evil that Ishmael the son of Nethaniah had done,

12 Then they took all the men, and went to fight with Ishmael the son of Nethaniah, and found him by the great waters that are in Gibeon.

13 Now it came to pass, that when all the people which were with Ishmael saw Johanan the son of Kareah, and all the captains of the forces that were with him, then they were glad.

14 So all the people that Ishmael had carried away captive from Mizpah cast about and returned, and went to Johanan the son of Kareah.

15 But Ishmael the son of Nethaniah escaped from Johanan with eight men, and went to the Ammonites.

16 Then took Johanan the son of Kareah, and all the captains of the forces that were with him, all the remnant of the people whom he had recovered from Ishmael the son of Nethaniah, from Mizpah, after that he had slain Gedaliah the son of Ahikam, even mighty men of war, and the women, and the children, and the eunuchs, whom he had brought again from Gibeon:

17 And they departed, and dwelt in the habitation of Chimham, which is by Bethlehem, to go to enter into Egypt,

18 Because of the Chaldeans: for they were afraid of them, because Ishmael the son of Nethaniah had slain Gedaliah the son of Ahikam, whom the king of Babylon made governor in the land.

CHAPTER 42

THEN all the captains of the forces, and Johanan the son of Kareah, and Jezaniah the son of Hoshaiah, and all the people from the least even to the greatest, came near,

2 And said to Jeremiah the prophet, Let, we beseech you, our supplication be accepted before you, and pray for us to the LORD your God, even for all this remnant; (for we are left but a few of many, as your eyes do behold us:)

3 That the LORD your God may show us the way wherein we may walk, and the thing that we may do.

4 Then Jeremiah the prophet said to them, I have heard you; behold, I will pray to the LORD your God according to your words; and it shall come to pass, that whatsoever thing the LORD shall answer you, I will declare it to you; I will keep nothing back from you.

5 Then they said to Jeremiah, The LORD be a true and faithful witness between us, if we do not even according to all things for the which the LORD your God shall send you to us.

6 Whether it be good, or whether it be evil, we will obey the voice of the LORD our God, to whom we send you; that it may be well with us, when we obey the voice of the LORD our God.

7 And it came to pass after ten days, that the word of the LORD came to Jeremiah.

8 Then called he Johanan the son of Kareah, and all the captains of the forces which were with him, and all the people from the least even to the greatest,

9 And said to them, Thus says the LORD, the God of Israel, to whom you sent me to present your supplication before him;

10 If you will still abide in this land, then will I build you, and not pull you down, and I will plant you, and not pluck you up: for I repent of the evil that I have done to you.

11 Be not afraid of the king of Babylon, of whom you are afraid; be not afraid of him, says the LORD: for I am with you to save you, and to deliver you from his hand.

12 And I will show mercies to you, that he may have mercy upon you, and cause you to return to your own land.

13 But if you say, We will not dwell in this land, neither obey the voice of the LORD your God,

14 Saying, No; but we will go into the land of Egypt, where we shall see no war, nor hear the sound of the trumpet, nor have hunger of bread; and there will we dwell:

15 And now therefore hear the word of the LORD, you remnant of Judah; Thus says the LORD of hosts, the God of Israel; If you wholly set your faces to enter into Egypt, and go to sojourn there;

16 Then it shall come to pass, that the sword, which you feared, shall overtake you there in the land of Egypt, and the famine, whereof you were afraid, shall follow close after you there in Egypt; and there you shall die.

17 So shall it be with all the men that set their faces to go into Egypt to sojourn there; they shall die by the sword, by the famine, and by the pestilence: and none of them shall remain or escape from the evil that I will bring upon them.

18 For thus says the LORD of hosts, the God of Israel; As my anger and my fury has been poured forth upon the inhabitants of Jerusalem; so shall my fury be poured forth upon you, when you shall enter into Egypt: and you shall be an execration, and an astonishment, and a curse, and a reproach; and you shall see this place no more.

19 The LORD has said concerning you, O you remnant of Judah; Do not go into Egypt: know certainly that I have admonished you this day.

20 For you dissembled in your hearts, when you sent me to the LORD your God, saying, Pray for us to the LORD our God; and according to all that the LORD our God shall say, so declare to us, and we will do it.

21 And now I have this day declared it to you; but you have not obeyed the voice of the LORD your God, nor any thing for the which he has sent me to you.

22 Now therefore know certainly that you shall die by the sword, by the famine, and by the pestilence, in the place where you desire to go and to sojourn.

CHAPTER 43

AND it came to pass, that when Jeremiah had made an end of speaking to all the people all the words of the LORD their God, for which the LORD their God had sent him to them, even all these words,

2 Then spoke Azariah the son of Hoshaiah, and Johanan the son of Kareah, and all the proud men, saying to Jeremiah, You speak falsely: the LORD our God has not sent you to say, Go not into Egypt to sojourn there:

3 But Baruch the son of Neriah sets you on against us, for to deliver us into the hand of the Chaldeans, that they might put us to death, and carry us away captives into Babylon.

4 So Johanan the son of Kareah, and all the captains of the forces, and all the people, obeyed not the voice of the LORD, to dwell in the land of Judah.

5 But Johanan the son of Kareah, and all the captains of the forces, took all the remnant of Judah, that were returned from all nations, where they had been driven, to dwell in the land of Judah;

6 Even men, and women, and children, and the king's daughters, and every person that Nebuzaradan the captain of the guard had left with Gedaliah the son of Ahikam the son of Shaphan, and Jeremiah the prophet, and Baruch the son of Neriah.

7 So they came into the land of Egypt: for they obeyed not the voice of the LORD: thus came they even to Tahpanhes.

8 Then came the word of the LORD to Jeremiah in Tahpanhes, saying,

9 Take great stones in your hand, and hide them in the clay in the brickkiln, which is at the entry of Pharaoh's house in Tahpanhes, in the sight of the men of Judah;

10 And say to them, Thus says the LORD of hosts, the God of Israel; Behold, I will send and take Nebuchadrezzar the king of Babylon, my servant, and will set his throne upon these stones that I have hid; and he shall spread his royal pavilion over them.

11 And when he comes, he shall smite the land of Egypt, and deliver such as are for death to death; and such as are for captivity to captivity; and such as are for the sword to the sword.

12 And I will kindle a fire in the houses of the gods of Egypt; and he shall burn them, and carry them away captives: and he shall array himself with the land of Egypt, as a shepherd puts on his garment; and he shall go forth from thence in peace.

13 He shall break also the images of Bethshemesh, that is in the land of Egypt; and the houses of the gods of the Egyptians shall he burn with fire.

CHAPTER 44

THE word that came to Jeremiah concerning all the Jews which dwell in the land of Egypt, which dwell at Migdol, and at Tahpanhes, and at Noph, and in the country of Pathros, saying,

2 Thus says the LORD of hosts, the God of Israel; You have seen all the evil that I have brought upon Jerusalem, and upon all the cities of Judah; and, behold, this day they are a desolation, and no man dwells therein,

3 Because of their wickedness which they have committed to provoke me to anger, in that they went to burn incense, and to serve other gods, whom they knew not, neither they, you, nor your fathers.

4 Howbeit I sent to you all my servants the prophets, rising early and sending them, saying, Oh, do not this abominable thing that I hate.

5 But they did not hearken, nor incline their ear to turn from their wickedness, to burn no incense to other gods.

6 Therefore my fury and my anger was poured forth, and was kindled in the cities of Judah and in the streets of Jerusalem; and they are wasted and desolate, as at this day.

7 Therefore now thus says the LORD, the God of hosts, the God of Israel; Why do you commit this great evil against your souls, to cut off from you man and woman, child and suckling, out of Judah, to leave you none to remain;

8 In that you provoke me to wrath with the works of your hands, burning incense to other gods in the land of Egypt, where you have gone to dwell, that you might cut yourselves off, and that you might be a curse and a reproach among all the nations of the earth?

9 Have you forgotten the wickedness of your fathers, and the wickedness of the kings of Judah, and the wickedness of their wives, and your own wickedness, and the wickedness of your wives, which they have committed in the land of Judah, and in the streets of Jerusalem?

10 They are not humbled even to this day, neither have they feared, nor walked in my law, nor in my statutes, that I set before you and before your fathers.

11 Therefore thus says the LORD of hosts, the God of Israel; Behold, I will set my face against you for evil, and to cut off all Judah.

12 And I will take the remnant of Judah, that have set their faces to go into the land of Egypt to sojourn there, and they shall all be consumed, and fall in the land of Egypt; they shall even be consumed by the sword and by the famine: they shall die, from the least even to the greatest, by the sword and by the famine: and they shall be an execration, and an astonishment, and a curse, and a reproach.

13 For I will punish them that dwell in the land of Egypt, as I have punished Jerusalem, by the sword, by the famine, and by the pestilence:

14 So that none of the remnant of Judah, which are gone into the land of Egypt to sojourn there, shall escape or remain, that they should return into the land of Judah, to the which they have a desire to return to dwell there: for none shall return but such as shall escape.

15 Then all the men which knew that their wives had burned incense to other gods, and all the women that stood by, a great multitude, even all the people that dwelt in the land of Egypt, in Pathros, answered Jeremiah, saying,

16 As for the word that you have spoken to us in the name of the LORD, we will not hearken to you.

17 But we will certainly do whatsoever thing goeth forth out of our own mouth, to burn incense to the queen of heaven, and to pour out drink offerings to her, as we have done, we, and our fathers, our kings, and our princes, in the cities of Judah, and in the streets of Jerusalem: for then had we plenty of victuals, and were well, and saw no evil.

18 But since we left off to burn incense to the queen of heaven, and to pour out drink offerings to her, we have wanted all things, and have been consumed by the sword and by the famine.

19 And when we burned incense to the queen of heaven, and poured out drink offerings to her, did we make her cakes to worship her, and pour out drink offerings to her, without our men?

20 Then Jeremiah said to all the people, to the men, and to the women, and to all the people which had given him that answer, saying,

21 The incense that you burned in the cities of Judah, and in the streets of Jerusalem, you, and your fathers, your kings, and your princes, and the people of the land, did not the LORD remember them, and came it not into his mind?

22 So that the LORD could no longer bear, because of the evil of your doings, and because of the abominations which you have committed; therefore is your land a desolation, and an astonishment, and a curse, without an inhabitant, as at this day.

23 Because you have burned incense, and because you have sinned against the

LORD, and have not obeyed the voice of the LORD, nor walked in his law, nor in his statutes, nor in his testimonies; therefore this evil is happened to you, as at this day.

24 Moreover Jeremiah said to all the people, and to all the women, Hear the word of the LORD, all Judah that are in the land of Egypt:

25 Thus says the LORD of hosts, the God of Israel, saying; You and your wives have both spoken with your mouths, and fulfilled with your hand, saying, We will surely perform our vows that we have vowed, to burn incense to the queen of heaven, and to pour out drink offerings to her: you will surely accomplish your vows, and surely perform your vows.

26 Therefore hear the word of the LORD, all Judah that dwell in the land of Egypt; Behold, I have sworn by my great name, says the LORD, that my name shall no more be named in the mouth of any man of Judah in all the land of Egypt, saying, The Lord GOD lives.

27 Behold, I will watch over them for evil, and not for good: and all the men of Judah that are in the land of Egypt shall be consumed by the sword and by the famine, until there be an end of them.

28 Yet a small number that escape the sword shall return out of the land of Egypt into the land of Judah, and all the remnant of Judah, that are gone into the land of Egypt to sojourn there, shall know whose words shall stand, mine, or their's.

29 And this shall be a sign to you, says the LORD, that I will punish you in this place, that you may know that my words shall surely stand against you for evil:

30 Thus says the LORD; Behold, I will give Pharaohhophra king of Egypt into the hand of his enemies, and into the hand of them that seek his life; as I gave Zedekiah king of Judah into the hand of Nebuchadrezzar king of Babylon, his enemy, and that sought his life.

CHAPTER 45

THE word that Jeremiah the prophet spoke to Baruch the son of Neriah, when he had written these words in a book at the mouth of Jeremiah, in the fourth year of Jehoiakim the son of Josiah king of Judah, saying,

2 Thus says the LORD, the God of Israel, to you, O Baruch:

3 You did say, Woe is me now! for the LORD has added grief to my sorrow; I fainted in my sighing, and I find no rest.

4 Thus shall you say to him, The LORD says thus; Behold, that which I have built will I break down, and that which I have planted I will pluck up, even this whole land.

5 And do you seek great things for yourself? seek them not: for, behold, I will bring evil upon all flesh, says the LORD: but your life will I give to you for a prey in all places where you go.

CHAPTER 46

THE word of the LORD which came to Jeremiah the prophet against the Gentiles;

2 Against Egypt, against the army of Pharaohnecho king of Egypt, which was by the river Euphrates in Carchemish, which Nebuchadrezzar king of Babylon smote in the fourth year of Jehoiakim the son of Josiah king of Judah.

3 Order the buckler and shield, and draw near to battle.

4 Harness the horses; and get up, you horsemen, and stand forth with your helmets; furbish the spears, and put on the brigandines.

5 Why have I seen them dismayed and turned away back? and their mighty ones are beaten down, and are fled apace, and look not back: for fear was round about, says the LORD.

6 Let not the swift flee away, nor the mighty man escape; they shall stumble, and fall toward the north by the river Euphrates.

7 Who is this that comes up as a flood, whose waters are moved as the rivers?

8 Egypt rises up like a flood, and his waters are moved like the rivers; and he says, I will go up, and will cover the earth; I will destroy the city and the inhabitants thereof.

9 Come up, you horses; and rage, you chariots; and let the mighty men come forth; the Ethiopians and the Libyans, that handle the shield; and the Lydians, that handle and bend the bow.

10 For this is the day of the Lord GOD of hosts, a day of vengeance, that he may avenge him of his adversaries: and the sword shall devour, and it shall be satiate and made drunk with their blood: for the Lord GOD of hosts has a sacrifice in the north country by the river Euphrates.

11 Go up into Gilead, and take balm, O virgin, the daughter of Egypt: in vain shall you use many medicines; for you shall not be cured.

12 The nations have heard of your shame, and your cry has filled the land: for the mighty man has stumbled against the mighty, and they are fallen both together.

13 The word that the LORD spoke to Jeremiah the prophet, how Nebuchadrezzar king of Babylon should come and smite the land of Egypt.

14 Declare in Egypt, and publish in Migdol, and publish in Noph and in Tahpanhes: say, Stand fast, and prepare yourselves; for the sword shall devour round about you.

15 Why are your valiant men swept away? they stood not, because the LORD did drive them.

16 He made many to fall, yea, one fell upon another: and they said, Arise, and let us go again to our own people, and to the land of our nativity, from the oppressing sword.

17 They did cry there, Pharaoh king of Egypt is but a noise; he has passed the time appointed.

18 As I live, says the King, whose name is the LORD of hosts, Surely as Tabor is among the mountains, and as Carmel by the sea, so shall he come.

19 O you daughter dwelling in Egypt, furnish yourself to go into captivity: for Noph shall be waste and desolate without an inhabitant.

20 Egypt is like a very fair heifer, but destruction comes; it comes out of the north.

21 Also her hired men are in the midst of her like fatted bullocks; for they also are turned back, and are fled away together: they did not stand, because the day of their calamity was come upon them, and the time of their visitation.

22 The voice thereof shall go like a serpent; for they shall march with an army, and come against her with axes, as hewers of wood.

23 They shall cut down her forest, says the LORD, though it cannot be searched; because they are more than the grasshoppers, and are innumerable.

24 The daughter of Egypt shall be confounded; she shall be delivered into the hand of the people of the north.

25 The LORD of hosts, the God of Israel, says; Behold, I will punish the multitude of No, and Pharaoh, and Egypt, with their gods, and their kings; even Pharaoh, and all them that trust in him:

26 And I will deliver them into the hand of those that seek their lives, and into the hand of Nebuchadrezzar king of Babylon, and into the hand of his servants: and afterward it shall be inhabited, as in the days of old, says the LORD.

27 But do not fear, O my servant Jacob, and do not be dismayed, O Israel: for, behold, I will save you from afar off, and your seed from the land of their captivity; and Jacob shall return, and be in rest and at ease, and none shall make him afraid.

28 Fear not, O Jacob my servant, says the LORD: for I am with you; for I will make a full end of all the nations where I have driven you: but I will not make a full end of you, but correct you in mea-

sure; yet will I not leave you wholly unpunished.

CHAPTER 47

THE word of the LORD that came to Jeremiah the prophet against the Philistines, before that Pharaoh smote Gaza.

2 Thus says the LORD; Behold, waters rise up out of the north, and shall be an overflowing flood, and shall overflow the land, and all that is therein; the city, and them that dwell therein: then the men shall cry, and all the inhabitants of the land shall howl.

3 At the noise of the stamping of the hoofs of his strong horses, at the rushing of his chariots, and at the rumbling of his wheels, the fathers shall not look back to their children for feebleness of hands;

4 Because of the day that comes to spoil all the Philistines, and to cut off from Tyrus and Zidon every helper that remains: for the LORD will spoil the Philistines, the remnant of the country of Caphtor.

5 Baldness is come upon Gaza; Ashkelon is cut off with the remnant of their valley: how long will you cut yourself?

6 O you sword of the LORD, how long will it be until you are quiet? put up yourself into your scabbard, rest, and be still.

7 How can it be quiet, seeing the LORD has given it a charge against Ashkelon, and against the sea shore? there has he appointed it.

CHAPTER 48

AGAINST Moab thus says the LORD of hosts, the God of Israel; Woe to Nebo! for it is spoiled: Kiriathaim is confounded and taken: Misgab is confounded and dismayed.

2 There shall be no more praise of Moab: in Heshbon they have devised evil against it; come, and let us cut it off from being a nation. Also you shall be cut down, O Madmen; the sword shall pursue you.

3 A voice of crying shall be from Horonaim, spoiling and great destruction.

4 Moab is destroyed; her little ones have caused a cry to be heard.

5 For in the going up of Luhith continual weeping shall go up; for in the going down of Horonaim the enemies have heard a cry of destruction.

6 Flee, save your lives, and be like the heath in the wilderness.

7 For because you have trusted in your works and in your treasures, you shall also be taken: and Chemosh shall go forth into captivity with his priests and his princes together.

8 And the spoiler shall come upon every city, and no city shall escape: the valley also shall perish, and the plain shall be destroyed, as the LORD has spoken.

9 Give wings to Moab, that it may flee and get away: for the cities thereof shall be desolate, without any to dwell therein.

10 Cursed is he that does the work of the LORD deceitfully, and cursed is he that keeps back his sword from blood.

11 Moab has been at ease from his youth, and he has settled on his lees, and has not been emptied from vessel to vessel, neither has he gone into captivity: therefore his taste remained in him, and his scent is not changed.

12 Therefore, behold, the days come, says the LORD, that I will send to him wanderers, that shall cause him to wander, and shall empty his vessels, and break their bottles.

13 And Moab shall be ashamed of Chemosh, as the house of Israel was ashamed of Bethel their confidence.

14 How can you say, We are mighty and strong men for the war?

15 Moab is spoiled, and gone up out of her cities, and his chosen young men are gone down to the slaughter, says the King, whose name is the LORD of hosts.

16 The calamity of Moab is near to come, and his affliction comes quickly.

17 All you that are about him, bemoan him; and all you that know his name, say, How is the strong staff broken, and the beautiful rod!

18 You daughter that dost inhabit Dibon, come down from your glory, and sit in thirst; for the spoiler of Moab shall come upon you, and he shall destroy your strong holds.

19 O inhabitant of Aroer, stand by the way, and espy; ask him that flees, and her that escapes, and say, What is done?

20 Moab is confounded; for it is broken down: howl and cry; tell it in Arnon, that Moab is spoiled,

21 And judgment is come upon the plain country; upon Holon, and upon Jahazah, and upon Mephaath,

22 And upon Dibon, and upon Nebo, and upon Bethdiblathaim,

23 And upon Kiriathaim, and upon Bethgamul, and upon Bethmeon,

24 And upon Kerioth, and upon Bozrah, and upon all the cities of the land of Moab, far or near.

25 The horn of Moab is cut off, and his arm is broken, says the LORD.

26 Make him drunk: for he magnified himself against the LORD: Moab also shall wallow in his vomit, and he also shall be in derision.

27 For was not Israel a derision to you? was he found among thieves? for since you spoke of him, you skipped for joy.

28 O you that dwell in Moab, leave the cities, and dwell in the rock, and be like the dove that makes her nest in the sides of the hole's mouth.

29 We have heard the pride of Moab, (he is exceeding proud) his loftiness, and his arrogancy, and his pride, and the haughtiness of his heart.

30 I know his wrath, says the LORD; but it shall not be so; his lies shall not so effect it.

31 Therefore will I howl for Moab, and I will cry out for all Moab; my heart shall mourn for the men of Kirheres.

32 O vine of Sibmah, I will weep for you with the weeping of Jazer: your plants are gone over the sea, they reach even to the sea of Jazer: the spoiler is fallen upon your summer fruits and upon your vintage.

33 And joy and gladness is taken from the plentiful field, and from the land of Moab, and I have caused wine to fail from the winepresses: none shall tread with shouting; their shouting shall be no shouting.

34 From the cry of Heshbon even to Elealeh, and even to Jahaz, have they uttered their voice, from Zoar even to Horonaim, as an heifer of three years old: for the waters also of Nimrim shall be desolate.

35 Moreover I will cause to cease in Moab, says the LORD, him that offers in the high places, and him that burns incense to his gods.

36 Therefore my heart shall sound for Moab like pipes, and my heart shall sound like pipes for the men of Kirheres: because the riches that he has gotten are perished.

37 For every head shall be bald, and every beard clipped: upon all the hands shall be cuttings, and upon the loins sackcloth.

38 There shall be lamentation generally upon all the housetops of Moab, and in the streets thereof: for I have broken Moab like a vessel wherein is no pleasure, says the LORD.

39 They shall howl, saying, How is it broken down! how has Moab turned the back with shame! so shall Moab be a derision and a dismaying to all them about him.

40 For thus says the LORD; Behold, he shall fly as an eagle, and shall spread his wings over Moab.

41 Kerioth is taken, and the strong holds are surprised, and the mighty men's hearts in Moab at that day shall be as the heart of a woman in her pangs.

42 And Moab shall be destroyed from being a people, because he has magnified himself against the LORD.

43 Fear, and the pit, and the snare, shall be upon you, O inhabitant of Moab, says the LORD.

44 He that flees from the fear shall fall into the pit; and he that gets up out of the pit shall be taken in the snare: for I will bring upon it, even upon Moab, the year of their visitation, says the LORD.

45 They that fled stood under the shadow of Heshbon because of the force: but a fire shall come forth out of Heshbon, and a flame from the midst of Sihon, and shall devour the corner of Moab, and the crown of the head of the tumultuous ones.

46 Woe to you, O Moab! the people of Chemosh perishes: for your sons are taken captives, and your daughters captives.

47 Yet will I bring again the captivity of Moab in the latter days, says the LORD. Thus far is the judgment of Moab.

CHAPTER 49

CONCERNING the Ammonites, thus says the LORD; Has Israel no sons? has he no heir? why then does their king inherit Gad, and his people dwell in his cities?

2 Therefore, behold, the days come, says the LORD, that I will cause an alarm of war to be heard in Rabbah of the Ammonites; and it shall be a desolate heap, and her daughters shall be burned with fire: then shall Israel be heir to them that were his heirs, says the LORD.

3 Howl, O Heshbon, for Ai is spoiled: cry, you daughters of Rabbah, gird you with sackcloth; lament, and run to and fro by the hedges; for their king shall go into captivity, and his priests and his princes together.

4 Why do you glory in the valleys, your flowing valley, O backsliding daughter? that trusted in her treasures, saying, Who shall come to me?

5 Behold, I will bring a fear upon you, says the Lord GOD of hosts, from all those that are about you; and you shall be driven out every man right forth; and none shall gather up him that wanders.

6 And afterward I will bring again the captivity of the children of Ammon, says the LORD.

7 Concerning Edom, thus says the LORD of hosts; Is wisdom no more in Teman? is counsel perished from the prudent? is their wisdom vanished?

8 Flee, turn back, dwell deep, O inhabitants of Dedan; for I will bring the calamity of Esau upon him, the time that I will visit him.

9 If grapegatherers come to you, would they not leave some gleaning grapes? if thieves by night, they will destroy till they have enough.

10 But I have made Esau bare, I have uncovered his secret places, and he shall not be able to hide himself: his seed is spoiled, and his brethren, and his neighbours, and he is not.

11 Leave your fatherless children, I will preserve them alive; and let your widows trust in me.

12 For thus says the LORD; Behold, they whose judgment was not to drink of the cup have assuredly drunken; and are you he that shall altogether go unpunished? you shall not go unpunished, but you shall surely drink of it.

13 For I have sworn by myself, says the LORD, that Bozrah shall become a desolation, a reproach, a waste, and a curse; and all the cities thereof shall be perpetual wastes.

14 I have heard a rumour from the LORD, and an ambassador is sent to the heathen, saying, Gather together, and come against her, and rise up to the battle.

15 For, lo, I will make you small among the heathen, and despised among men.

16 Your terribleness has deceived you, and the pride of your heart, O you that dwell in the clefts of the rock, that hold the height of the hill: though you should

make your nest as high as the eagle, I will bring you down from thence, says the LORD.

17 Also Edom shall be a desolation: every one that goeth by it shall be astonished, and shall hiss at all the plagues thereof.

18 As in the overthrow of Sodom and Gomorrah and the neighbour cities thereof, says the LORD, no man shall abide there, neither shall a son of man dwell in it.

19 Behold, he shall come up like a lion from the swelling of Jordan against the habitation of the strong: but I will suddenly make him run away from her: and who is a chosen man, that I may appoint over her? for who is like me? and who will appoint me the time? and who is that shepherd that will stand before me?

20 Therefore hear the counsel of the LORD, that he has taken against Edom; and his purposes, that he has purposed against the inhabitants of Teman: Surely the least of the flock shall draw them out: surely he shall make their habitations desolate with them.

21 The earth is moved at the noise of their fall, at the cry the noise thereof was heard in the Red sea.

22 Behold, he shall come up and fly as the eagle, and spread his wings over Bozrah: and at that day shall the heart of the mighty men of Edom be as the heart of a woman in her pangs.

23 Concerning Damascus. Hamath is confounded, and Arpad: for they have heard evil tidings: they are fainthearted; there is sorrow on the sea; it cannot be quiet.

24 Damascus is grown feeble, and turns herself to flee, and fear has seized on her: anguish and sorrows have taken her, as a woman in travail.

25 How is the city of praise not left, the city of my joy!

26 Therefore her young men shall fall in her streets, and all the men of war shall be cut off in that day, says the LORD of hosts.

27 And I will kindle a fire in the wall of Damascus, and it shall consume the palaces of Benhadad.

28 Concerning Kedar, and concerning the kingdoms of Hazor, which Nebuchadrezzar king of Babylon shall smite, thus says the LORD; Arise, go up to Kedar, and spoil the men of the east.

29 Their tents and their flocks shall they take away: they shall take to themselves their curtains, and all their vessels, and their camels; and they shall cry to them, Fear is on every side.

30 Flee, get far off, dwell deep, O inhabitants of Hazor, says the LORD; for Nebuchadrezzar king of Babylon has taken counsel against you, and has conceived a purpose against you.

31 Arise, go up to the wealthy nation, that dwells without care, says the LORD, which have neither gates nor bars, which dwell alone.

32 And their camels shall be a booty, and the multitude of their cattle a spoil: and I will scatter into all winds them that are in the utmost corners; and I will bring their calamity from all sides thereof, says the LORD.

33 And Hazor shall be a dwelling for dragons, and a desolation for ever: there shall no man abide there, nor any son of man dwell in it.

34 The word of the LORD that came to Jeremiah the prophet against Elam in the beginning of the reign of Zedekiah king of Judah, saying,

35 Thus says the LORD of hosts; Behold, I will break the bow of Elam, the chief of their might.

36 And upon Elam will I bring the four winds from the four quarters of heaven, and will scatter them toward all those winds; and there shall be no nation where the outcasts of Elam shall not come.

37 For I will cause Elam to be dismayed before their enemies, and before them that seek their life: and I will bring evil upon them, even my fierce anger,

says the LORD; and I will send the sword after them, till I have consumed them:

38 And I will set my throne in Elam, and will destroy from thence the king and the princes, says the LORD.

39 But it shall come to pass in the latter days, that I will bring again the captivity of Elam, says the LORD.

CHAPTER 50

THE word that the LORD spoke against Babylon and against the land of the Chaldeans by Jeremiah the prophet.

2 Declare among the nations, and publish, and set up a standard; publish, and conceal not: say, Babylon is taken, Bel is confounded, Merodach is broken in pieces; her idols are confounded, her images are broken in pieces.

3 For out of the north there comes up a nation against her, which shall make her land desolate, and none shall dwell therein: they shall remove, they shall depart, both man and beast.

4 In those days, and in that time, says the LORD, the children of Israel shall come, they and the children of Judah together, going and weeping: they shall go, and seek the LORD their God.

5 They shall ask the way to Zion with their faces towards it, saying, Come, and let us join ourselves to the LORD in a perpetual covenant that shall not be forgotten.

6 My people have been lost sheep: their shepherds have caused them to go astray, they have turned them away on the mountains: they have gone from mountain to hill, they have forgotten their restingplace.

7 All that found them have devoured them: and their adversaries said, We offend not, because they have sinned against the LORD, the habitation of justice, even the LORD, the hope of their fathers.

8 Remove out of the midst of Babylon, and go forth out of the land of the Chaldeans, and be as the he goats before the flocks.

9 For, lo, I will raise and cause to come up against Babylon an assembly of great nations from the north country: and they shall set themselves in array against her; from thence she shall be taken: their arrows shall be as of a mighty expert man; none shall return in vain.

10 And Chaldea shall be a spoil: all that spoil her shall be satisfied, says the LORD.

11 Because you were glad, because you rejoiced, O you destroyers of my heritage, because you are grown fat as the heifer at grass, and bellow as bulls;

12 Your mother shall be sore confounded; she that bare you shall be ashamed: behold, the hindermost of the nations shall be a wilderness, a dry land, and a desert.

13 Because of the wrath of the LORD it shall not be inhabited, but it shall be wholly desolate: every one that goeth by Babylon shall be astonished, and hiss at all her plagues.

14 Put yourselves in array against Babylon round about: all you that bend the bow, shoot at her, spare no arrows: for she has sinned against the LORD.

15 Shout against her round about: she has given her hand: her foundations are fallen, her walls are thrown down: for it is the vengeance of the LORD: take vengeance upon her; as she has done, do to her.

16 Cut off the sower from Babylon, and him that handles the sickle in the time of harvest: for fear of the oppressing sword they shall turn every one to his people, and they shall flee every one to his own land.

50:7 God is the very habitation of eternal justice.

17 Israel is a scattered sheep; the lions have driven him away: first the king of Assyria has devoured him; and last this Nebuchadrezzar king of Babylon has broken his bones.

18 Therefore thus says the LORD of hosts, the God of Israel; Behold, I will punish the king of Babylon and his land, as I have punished the king of Assyria.

19 And I will bring Israel again to his habitation, and he shall feed on Carmel and Bashan, and his soul shall be satisfied upon mount Ephraim and Gilead.

20 In those days, and in that time, says the LORD, the iniquity of Israel shall be sought for, and there shall be none; and the sins of Judah, and they shall not be found: for I will pardon them whom I reserve.

21 Go up against the land of Merathaim, even against it, and against the inhabitants of Pekod: waste and utterly destroy after them, says the LORD, and do according to all that I have commanded you.

22 A sound of battle is in the land, and of great destruction.

23 How is the hammer of the whole earth cut asunder and broken! how is Babylon become a desolation among the nations!

24 I have laid a snare for you, and you are also taken, O Babylon, and you were not aware: you are found, and also caught, because you have striven against the LORD.

25 The LORD has opened his armoury, and has brought forth the weapons of his indignation: for this is the work of the Lord GOD of hosts in the land of the Chaldeans.

26 Come against her from the utmost border, open her storehouses: cast her up as heaps, and destroy her utterly: let nothing of her be left.

27 Slay all her bullocks; let them go down to the slaughter: woe to them! for their day is come, the time of their visitation.

28 The voice of them that flee and escape out of the land of Babylon, to declare in Zion the vengeance of the LORD our God, the vengeance of his temple.

29 Call together the archers against Babylon: all you that bend the bow, camp against it round about; let none thereof escape: recompense her according to her work; according to all that she has done, do to her: for she has been proud against the LORD, against the Holy One of Israel.

30 Therefore shall her young men fall in the streets, and all her men of war shall be cut off in that day, says the LORD.

31 Behold, I am against you, O you most proud, says the Lord GOD of hosts: for your day is come, the time that I will visit you.

32 And the most proud shall stumble and fall, and none shall raise him up: and I will kindle a fire in his cities, and it shall devour all round about him.

33 Thus says the LORD of hosts; The children of Israel and the children of Judah were oppressed together: and all that took them captives held them fast; they refused to let them go.

34 Their Redeemer is strong; the LORD of hosts is his name: he shall throughly plead their cause, that he may give rest to the land, and disquiet the inhabitants of Babylon.

35 A sword is upon the Chaldeans, says the LORD, and upon the inhabitants of Babylon, and upon her princes, and upon her wise men.

36 A sword is upon the liars; and they shall dote: a sword is upon her mighty men; and they shall be dismayed.

37 A sword is upon their horses, and upon their chariots, and upon all the mingled people that are in the midst of her; and they shall become as women: a sword is upon her treasures; and they shall be robbed.

38 A drought is upon her waters; and they shall be dried up: for it is the land

of graven images, and they are mad upon their idols.

39 Therefore the wild beasts of the desert with the wild beasts of the islands shall dwell there, and the owls shall dwell therein: and it shall be no more inhabited for ever; neither shall it be dwelt in from generation to generation.

40 As God overthrew Sodom and Gomorrah and the neighbour cities thereof, says the LORD; so shall no man abide there, neither shall any son of man dwell therein.

41 Behold, a people shall come from the north, and a great nation, and many kings shall be raised up from the coasts of the earth.

42 They shall hold the bow and the lance: they are cruel, and will not show mercy: their voice shall roar like the sea, and they shall ride upon horses, every one put in array, like a man to the battle, against you, O daughter of Babylon.

43 The king of Babylon has heard the report of them, and his hands grow feeble: anguish took hold of him, and pangs as of a woman in travail.

44 Behold, he shall come up like a lion from the swelling of Jordan to the habitation of the strong: but I will make them suddenly run away from her: and who is a chosen man, that I may appoint over her? for who is like me? and who will appoint me the time? and who is that shepherd that will stand before me?

45 Therefore hear the counsel of the LORD, that he has taken against Babylon; and his purposes, that he has purposed against the land of the Chaldeans: Surely the least of the flock shall draw them out: surely he shall make their habitation desolate with them.

46 At the noise of the taking of Babylon the earth is moved, and the cry is heard among the nations.

CHAPTER 51

THUS says the LORD; Behold, I will raise up against Babylon, and against them that dwell in the midst of them that rise up against me, a destroying wind;

2 And will send to Babylon fanners, that shall fan her, and shall empty her land: for in the day of trouble they shall be against her round about.

3 Against him that bends let the archer bend his bow, and against him that lifts himself up in his brigandine: and do not spare her young men; utterly destroy all her host.

4 Thus the slain shall fall in the land of the Chaldeans, and they that are thrust through in her streets.

5 For Israel has not been forsaken, nor Judah of his God, of the LORD of hosts; though their land was filled with sin against the Holy One of Israel.

6 Flee out of the midst of Babylon, and deliver every man his soul: be not cut off in her iniquity; for this is the time of the LORD's vengeance; he will render to her a recompence.

7 Babylon has been a golden cup in the LORD's hand, that made all the earth drunken: the nations have drunken of her wine; therefore the nations are mad.

8 Babylon is suddenly fallen and destroyed: howl for her; take balm for her pain, if so be she may be healed.

9 We would have healed Babylon, but she is not healed: forsake her, and let us go every one into his own country: for her judgment reaches to heaven, and is lifted up even to the skies.

10 The LORD has brought forth our righteousness: come, and let us declare in Zion the work of the LORD our God.

11 Make bright the arrows; gather the shields: the LORD has raised up the spirit of the kings of the Medes: for his device is against Babylon, to destroy it; because it is the vengeance of the LORD, the vengeance of his temple.

12 Set up the standard upon the walls of Babylon, make the watch strong, set

up the watchmen, prepare the ambushes: for the LORD has both devised and done that which he spoke against the inhabitants of Babylon.

13 O you that dwell upon many waters, abundant in treasures, your end is come, and the measure of your covetousness.

14 The LORD of hosts has sworn by himself, saying, Surely I will fill you with men, as with caterpillers; and they shall lift up a shout against you.

15 He has made the earth by his power, he has established the world by his wisdom, and has stretched out the heaven by his understanding.

16 When he utters his voice, there is a multitude of waters in the heavens; and he causes the vapours to ascend from the ends of the earth: he makes lightnings with rain, and brings forth the wind out of his treasures.

17 Every man is brutish by his knowledge; every founder is confounded by the graven image: for his molten image is falsehood, and there is no breath in them.

18 They are vanity, the work of errors: in the time of their visitation they shall perish.

19 The portion of Jacob is not like them; for he is the former of all things: and Israel is the rod of his inheritance: the LORD of hosts is his name.

20 You are my battle axe and weapons of war: for with you will I break in pieces the nations, and with you will I destroy kingdoms;

21 And with you will I break in pieces the horse and his rider; and with you will I break in pieces the chariot and his rider;

22 With you also will I break in pieces man and woman; and with you will I break in pieces old and young; and with you will I break in pieces the young man and the maid;

23 I will also break in pieces with you the shepherd and his flock; and with you will I break in pieces the husbandman and his yoke of oxen; and with you will I break in pieces captains and rulers.

24 And I will render to Babylon and to all the inhabitants of Chaldea all their evil that they have done in Zion in your sight, says the LORD.

25 Behold, I am against you, O destroying mountain, says the LORD, which destroys all the earth: and I will stretch out my hand upon you, and roll you down from the rocks, and will make you a burnt mountain.

26 And they shall not take from you a stone for a corner, nor a stone for foundations; but you shall be desolate for ever, says the LORD.

27 Set up a standard in the land, blow the trumpet among the nations, prepare the nations against her, call together against her the kingdoms of Ararat, Minni, and Ashchenaz; appoint a captain against her; cause the horses to come up as the rough caterpillers.

28 Prepare against her the nations with the kings of the Medes, the captains thereof, and all the rulers thereof, and all the land of his dominion.

29 And the land shall tremble and sorrow: for every purpose of the LORD shall be performed against Babylon, to make the land of Babylon a desolation without an inhabitant.

30 The mighty men of Babylon have ceased to fight, they have remained in their holds: their might has failed; they became as women: they have burned her dwellingplaces; her bars are broken.

31 One post shall run to meet another, and one messenger to meet another, to show the king of Babylon that his city is taken at one end,

32 And that the passages are stopped, and the reeds they have burned with fire, and the men of war are affrighted.

33 For thus says the LORD of hosts, the God of Israel; The daughter of Babylon is like a threshingfloor, it is time to thresh her: yet a little while, and the time of her harvest shall come.

34 Nebuchadrezzar the king of Babylon has devoured me, he has crushed me, he

has made me an empty vessel, he has swallowed me up like a dragon, he has filled his belly with my delicates, he has cast me out.

35 The violence done to me and to my flesh be upon Babylon, shall the inhabitant of Zion say; and my blood upon the inhabitants of Chaldea, shall Jerusalem say.

36 Therefore thus says the LORD; Behold, I will plead your cause, and take vengeance for you; and I will dry up her sea, and make her springs dry.

37 And Babylon shall become heaps, a dwellingplace for dragons, an astonishment, and an hissing, without an inhabitant.

38 They shall roar together like lions: they shall yell as lions' whelps.

39 In their heat I will make their feasts, and I will make them drunken, that they may rejoice, and sleep a perpetual sleep, and not wake, says the LORD.

40 I will bring them down like lambs to the slaughter, like rams with he goats.

41 How is Sheshach taken! and how is the praise of the whole earth surprised! how is Babylon become an astonishment among the nations!

42 The sea is come up upon Babylon: she is covered with the multitude of the waves thereof.

43 Her cities are a desolation, a dry land, and a wilderness, a land wherein no man dwells, neither does any son of man pass thereby.

44 And I will punish Bel in Babylon, and I will bring forth out of his mouth that which he has swallowed up: and the nations shall not flow together any more to him: yea, the wall of Babylon shall fall.

45 My people, go out of the midst of her, and let every man deliver his soul from the fierce anger of the LORD.

46 And lest your heart faint, and you fear for the rumour that shall be heard in the land; a rumour shall both come one year, and after that in another year shall come a rumour, and violence in the land, ruler against ruler.

47 Therefore, behold, the days come, that I will do judgment upon the graven images of Babylon: and her whole land shall be confounded, and all her slain shall fall in the midst of her.

48 Then the heaven and the earth, and all that is therein, shall sing for Babylon: for the spoilers shall come to her from the north, says the LORD.

49 As Babylon has caused the slain of Israel to fall, so at Babylon shall fall the slain of all the earth.

50 You that have escaped the sword, go away, stand not still: remember the LORD afar off, and let Jerusalem come into your mind.

51 We are confounded, because we have heard reproach: shame has covered our faces: for strangers are come into the sanctuaries of the LORD's house.

52 Therefore, behold, the days come, says the LORD, that I will do judgment upon her graven images: and through all her land the wounded shall groan.

53 Though Babylon should mount up to heaven, and though she should fortify the height of her strength, yet from me shall spoilers come to her, says the LORD.

54 A sound of a cry comes from Babylon, and great destruction from the land of the Chaldeans:

55 Because the LORD has spoiled Babylon, and destroyed out of her the great voice; when her waves do roar like great waters, a noise of their voice is uttered:

56 Because the spoiler is come upon her, even upon Babylon, and her mighty men are taken, every one of their bows is broken: for the LORD God of recompences shall surely requite.

57 And I will make drunk her princes, and her wise men, her captains, and her rulers, and her mighty men: and they shall sleep a perpetual sleep, and not wake, says the King, whose name is the LORD of hosts.

58 Thus says the LORD of hosts; The broad walls of Babylon shall be utterly broken, and her high gates shall be burned with fire; and the people shall labour in vain, and the folk in the fire, and they shall be weary.

59 The word which Jeremiah the prophet commanded Seraiah the son of Neriah, the son of Maaseiah, when he went with Zedekiah the king of Judah into Babylon in the fourth year of his reign. And this Seraiah was a quiet prince.

60 So Jeremiah wrote in a book all the evil that should come upon Babylon, even all these words that are written against Babylon.

61 And Jeremiah said to Seraiah, When you come to Babylon, and shall see, and shall read all these words;

62 Then shall you say, O LORD, you have spoken against this place, to cut it off, that none shall remain in it, neither man nor beast, but that it shall be desolate for ever.

63 And it shall be, when you have made an end of reading this book, that you shall bind a stone to it, and cast it into the midst of Euphrates:

64 And you shall say, Thus shall Babylon sink, and shall not rise from the evil that I will bring upon her: and they shall be weary. Thus far are the words of Jeremiah.

CHAPTER 52

ZEDEKIAH was one and twenty years old when he began to reign, and he reigned eleven years in Jerusalem. And his mother's name was Hamutal the daughter of Jeremiah of Libnah.

2 And he did that which was evil in the eyes of the LORD, according to all that Jehoiakim had done.

3 For through the anger of the LORD it came to pass in Jerusalem and Judah, till he had cast them out from his presence, that Zedekiah rebelled against the king of Babylon.

4 And it came to pass in the ninth year of his reign, in the tenth month, in the tenth day of the month, that Nebuchadrezzar king of Babylon came, he and all his army, against Jerusalem, and pitched against it, and built forts against it round about.

5 So the city was besieged to the eleventh year of king Zedekiah.

6 And in the fourth month, in the ninth day of the month, the famine was sore in the city, so that there was no bread for the people of the land.

7 Then the city was broken up, and all the men of war fled, and went forth out of the city by night by the way of the gate between the two walls, which was by the king's garden; (now the Chaldeans were by the city round about:) and they went by the way of the plain.

8 But the army of the Chaldeans pursued after the king, and overtook Zedekiah in the plains of Jericho; and all his army was scattered from him.

9 Then they took the king, and carried him up to the king of Babylon to Riblah in the land of Hamath; where he gave judgment upon him.

10 And the king of Babylon slew the sons of Zedekiah before his eyes: he slew also all the princes of Judah in Riblah.

11 Then he put out the eyes of Zedekiah; and the king of Babylon bound him in chains, and carried him to Babylon, and put him in prison till the day of his death.

12 Now in the fifth month, in the tenth day of the month, which was the nineteenth year of Nebuchadrezzar king of Babylon, came Nebuzaradan, captain of the guard, which served the king of Babylon, into Jerusalem,

13 And burned the house of the LORD,

52:10-11 See Mark 15:26 "comment."

and the king's house; and all the houses of Jerusalem, and all the houses of the great men, burned he with fire:

14 And all the army of the Chaldeans, that were with the captain of the guard, brake down all the walls of Jerusalem round about.

15 Then Nebuzaradan the captain of the guard carried away captive certain of the poor of the people, and the residue of the people that remained in the city, and those that fell away, that fell to the king of Babylon, and the rest of the multitude.

16 But Nebuzaradan the captain of the guard left certain of the poor of the land for vinedressers and for husbandmen.

17 Also the pillars of brass that were in the house of the LORD, and the bases, and the brasen sea that was in the house of the LORD, the Chaldeans brake, and carried all the brass of them to Babylon.

18 The caldrons also, and the shovels, and the snuffers, and the bowls, and the spoons, and all the vessels of brass wherewith they ministered, took they away.

19 And the basons, and the firepans, and the bowls, and the caldrons, and the candlesticks, and the spoons, and the cups; that which was of gold in gold, and that which was of silver in silver, took the captain of the guard away.

20 The two pillars, one sea, and twelve brasen bulls that were under the bases, which king Solomon had made in the house of the LORD: the brass of all these vessels was without weight.

21 And concerning the pillars, the height of one pillar was eighteen cubits; and a fillet of twelve cubits did compass it; and the thickness thereof was four fingers: it was hollow.

22 And a chapiter of brass was upon it; and the height of one chapiter was five cubits, with network and pomegranates upon the chapiters round about, all of brass. The second pillar also and the pomegranates were like these.

23 And there were ninety and six pomegranates on a side; and all the pomegranates upon the network were an hundred round about.

24 And the captain of the guard took Seraiah the chief priest, and Zephaniah the second priest, and the three keepers of the door:

25 He took also out of the city an eunuch, which had the charge of the men of war; and seven men of them that were near the king's person, which were found in the city; and the principal scribe of the host, who mustered the people of the land; and threescore men of the people of the land, that were found in the midst of the city.

26 So Nebuzaradan the captain of the guard took them, and brought them to the king of Babylon to Riblah.

27 And the king of Babylon smote them, and put them to death in Riblah in the land of Hamath. Thus Judah was carried away captive out of his own land.

28 This is the people whom Nebuchadrezzar carried away captive: in the seventh year three thousand Jews and three and twenty:

29 In the eighteenth year of Nebuchadrezzar he carried away captive from Jerusalem eight hundred thirty and two persons:

30 In the three and twentieth year of Nebuchadrezzar Nebuzaradan the captain of the guard carried away captive of the Jews seven hundred forty and five persons: all the persons were four thousand and six hundred.

31 And it came to pass in the seven and thirtieth year of the captivity of Jehoiachin king of Judah, in the twelfth month, in the five and twentieth day of the month, that Evilmerodach king of Babylon in the first year of his reign lifted up the head of Jehoiachin king of Judah, and brought him forth out of prison.

32 And spoke kindly to him, and set his throne above the throne of the kings that were with him in Babylon,

33 And changed his prison garments:
and he did continually eat bread before
him all the days of his life.

34 And for his diet, there was a continual diet given him of the king of
Babylon, every day a portion until the
day of his death, all the days of his life.

Lamentations 1:1

The Christian should live in the spirit of lamentation. The Bible says that Jesus was a man of sorrows, acquainted with grief (see Isaiah 53:3). Those who acquaint themselves with the sufferings of this life and the sufferings of the next for those who die in their sins will lament in horror and then preach with passion.

Lamentations

CHAPTER 1

HOW does the city sit solitary, that was full of people! how is she become as a widow! she that was great among the nations, and princess among the provinces, how is she become tributary!

2 She weeps sore in the night, and her tears are on her cheeks: among all her lovers she has none to comfort her: all her friends have dealt treacherously with her, they are become her enemies.

3 Judah is gone into captivity because of affliction, and because of great servitude: she dwells among the heathen, she finds no rest: all her persecutors overtook her between the straits.

4 The ways of Zion do mourn, because none come to the solemn feasts: all her gates are desolate: her priests sigh, her virgins are afflicted, and she is in bitterness.

5 Her adversaries are the chief, her enemies prosper; for the LORD has afflicted her for the multitude of her transgressions: her children are gone into captivity before the enemy.

6 And from the daughter of Zion all her beauty is departed: her princes are become like harts that find no pasture, and they are gone without strength before the pursuer.

7 Jerusalem remembered in the days of her affliction and of her miseries all her pleasant things that she had in the days of old, when her people fell into the hand of the enemy, and none did help her: the adversaries saw her, and did mock at her sabbaths.

8 Jerusalem has grievously sinned; therefore she is removed: all that honoured her despise her, because they have seen her nakedness: yea, she sighs, and turns backward.

9 Her filthiness is in her skirts; she remembers not her last end; therefore she came down wonderfully: she had no comforter. O LORD, behold my affliction: for the enemy has magnified himself.

10 The adversary has spread out his hand upon all her pleasant things: for she has seen that the heathen entered into her sanctuary, whom you did command that they should not enter into your congregation.

11 All her people sigh, they seek bread; they have given their pleasant things for meat to relieve the soul: see, O LORD, and consider; for I am become vile.

12 Is it nothing to you, all you that pass by? behold, and see if there is any sorrow like my sorrow, which is done to me, wherewith the LORD has afflicted me in the day of his fierce anger.

13 From above has he sent fire into my bones, and it prevails against them: he has spread a net for my feet, he has turned me back: he has made me desolate and faint all the day.

14 The yoke of my transgressions is bound by his hand: they are wreathed,

and come up upon my neck: he has made my strength to fall, the LORD has delivered me into their hands, from whom I am not able to rise up.

15 The LORD has trodden under foot all my mighty men in the midst of me: he has called an assembly against me to crush my young men: the LORD has trodden the virgin, the daughter of Judah, as in a winepress.

16 For these things I weep; my eye, my eye runs down with water, because the comforter that should relieve my soul is far from me: my children are desolate, because the enemy prevailed.

17 Zion spreads forth her hands, and there is none to comfort her: the LORD has commanded concerning Jacob, that his adversaries should be round about him: Jerusalem is as a menstruous woman among them.

18 The LORD is righteous; for I have rebelled against his commandment: hear, I pray you, all people, and behold my sorrow: my virgins and my young men are gone into captivity.

19 I called for my lovers, but they deceived me: my priests and my elders gave up the ghost in the city, while they sought their meat to relieve their souls.

20 Behold, O LORD; for I am in distress: my bowels are troubled; my heart is turned within me; for I have grievously rebelled: abroad the sword bereaves, at home there is as death.

21 They have heard that I sigh: there is none to comfort me: all my enemies have heard of my trouble; they are glad that you have done it: you will bring the day that you have called, and they shall be like me.

22 Let all their wickedness come before you; and do to them, as you have done to me for all my transgressions: for my sighs are many, and my heart is faint.

CHAPTER 2

HOW has the LORD covered the daughter of Zion with a cloud in his anger, and cast down from heaven to the earth the beauty of Israel, and remembered not his footstool in the day of his anger!

2 The LORD has swallowed up all the habitations of Jacob, and has not pitied: he has thrown down in his wrath the strong holds of the daughter of Judah; he has brought them down to the ground: he has polluted the kingdom and the princes thereof.

3 He has cut off in his fierce anger all the horn of Israel: he has drawn back his right hand from before the enemy, and he burned against Jacob like a flaming fire, which devours round about.

4 He has bent his bow like an enemy: he stood with his right hand as an adversary, and slew all that were pleasant to the eye in the tabernacle of the daughter of Zion: he poured out his fury like fire.

5 The LORD was as an enemy: he has swallowed up Israel, he has swallowed up all her palaces: he has destroyed his strong holds, and has increased in the daughter of Judah mourning and lamentation.

6 And he has violently taken away his tabernacle, as if it were of a garden: he has destroyed his places of the assembly: the LORD has caused the solemn feasts and sabbaths to be forgotten in Zion, and has despised in the indignation of his anger the king and the priest.

7 The LORD has cast off his altar, he has abhorred his sanctuary, he has given up into the hand of the enemy the walls of her palaces; they have made a noise in the house of the LORD, as in the day of a solemn feast.

8 The LORD has purposed to destroy the wall of the daughter of Zion: he has stretched out a line, he has not with-

---

1:12 This verse is often seen as Messianic. How can anyone "pass by" Jesus on the cross, knowing that it is for them He suffers, aware that the Father allowed Jesus to be bruised so that we could live?

drawn his hand from destroying: therefore he made the rampart and the wall to lament; they languished together.

9 Her gates are sunk into the ground; he has destroyed and broken her bars: her king and her princes are among the Gentiles: the law is no more; her prophets also find no vision from the LORD.

10 The elders of the daughter of Zion sit upon the ground, and keep silence: they have cast up dust upon their heads; they have girded themselves with sackcloth: the virgins of Jerusalem hang down their heads to the ground.

11 My eyes do fail with tears, my bowels are troubled, my liver is poured upon the earth, for the destruction of the daughter of my people; because the children and the sucklings swoon in the streets of the city.

12 They say to their mothers, Where is corn and wine? when they swooned as the wounded in the streets of the city, when their soul was poured out into their mothers' bosom.

13 What thing shall I take to witness for you? what thing shall I liken to you, O daughter of Jerusalem? what shall I equal to you, that I may comfort you, O virgin daughter of Zion? for your breach is great like the sea: who can heal you?

14 Your prophets have seen vain and foolish things for you: and they have not discovered your iniquity, to turn away your captivity; but have seen for you false burdens and causes of banishment.

15 All that pass by clap their hands at you; they hiss and wag their head at the daughter of Jerusalem, saying, Is this the city that men call The perfection of beauty, The joy of the whole earth?

16 All your enemies have opened their mouth against you: they hiss and gnash the teeth: they say, We have swallowed her up: certainly this is the day that we looked for; we have found, we have seen it.

17 The LORD has done that which he had devised; he has fulfilled his word

that he had commanded in the days of old: he has thrown down, and has not pitied: and he has caused your enemy to rejoice over you, he has set up the horn of your adversaries.

18 Their heart cried to the LORD, O wall of the daughter of Zion, let tears run down like a river day and night: give yourself no rest; do not let the apple of your eye cease.

19 Arise, cry out in the night: in the beginning of the watches pour out your heart like water before the face of the LORD: lift up your hands toward him for the life of your young children, that faint for hunger in the top of every street.

20 Behold, O LORD, and consider to whom you have done this. Shall the women eat their fruit, and children of a span long? shall the priest and the prophet be slain in the sanctuary of the Lord?

21 The young and the old lie on the ground in the streets: my virgins and my young men are fallen by the sword; you have slain them in the day of your anger; you have killed, and not pitied.

22 You have called as in a solemn day my terrors round about, so that in the day of the LORD's anger none escaped nor remained: those that I have swaddled and brought up has my enemy consumed.

CHAPTER 3

I AM the man that has seen affliction by the rod of his wrath.

2 He has led me, and brought me into darkness, but not into light.

3 Surely against me is he turned; he turns his hand against me all the day.

4 My flesh and my skin has he made old; he has broken my bones.

5 He has built against me, and compassed me with gall and travail.

6 He has set me in dark places, as they that be dead of old.

7 He has hedged me about, that I cannot get out: he has made my chain heavy.

8 Also when I cry and shout, he shuts out my prayer.

9 He has inclosed my ways with hewn stone, he has made my paths crooked.

10 He was to me as a bear lying in wait, and as a lion in secret places.

11 He has turned aside my ways, and pulled me in pieces: he has made me desolate.

12 He has bent his bow, and set me as a mark for the arrow.

13 He has caused the arrows of his quiver to enter into my reins.

14 I was a derision to all my people; and their song all the day.

15 He has filled me with bitterness, he has made me drunken with wormwood.

16 He has also broken my teeth with gravel stones, he has covered me with ashes.

17 And you have removed my soul far off from peace: I forgot prosperity.

18 And I said, My strength and my hope is perished from the LORD:

19 Remembering my affliction and my misery, the wormwood and the gall.

3:22-36

In these verses, Jeremiah, in the midst of the desert of despair and God's judgment, remembers the wonderful oasis of God's mercy. God's compassion is still there, "new every morning." Great is His faithfulness.

Here, three things are named as being "good:" God is good to those who wait upon Him; it is good to hope and quietly wait for the salvation of the Lord, and it is good for a man to bear the yoke of his youth.

20 My soul has them still in remembrance, and is humbled in me.

21 This I recall to my mind, therefore have I hope.

22 It is of the LORD's mercies that we are not consumed, because his compassions fail not.

23 They are new every morning: great is your faithfulness.

24 The LORD is my portion, says my soul; therefore will I hope in him.

25 The LORD is good to them that wait for him, to the soul that seeks him.

26 It is good that a man should both hope and quietly wait for the salvation of the LORD.

27 It is good for a man that he bear the yoke of his youth.

28 He sits alone and keeps silence, because he has borne it upon him.

29 He puts his mouth in the dust; if so be there may be hope.

30 He gives his cheek to him that smites him: he is filled full with reproach.

31 For the LORD will not cast off for ever:

32 But though he cause grief, yet will he have compassion according to the multitude of his mercies.

33 For he does not afflict willingly nor grieve the children of men.

34 To crush under his feet all the prisoners of the earth.

35 To turn aside the right of a man before the face of the most High,

36 To subvert a man in his cause, the LORD does not approve.

37 Who is he that says, and it comes to pass, when the Lord does not command it?

38 Out of the mouth of the most High proceed not evil and good?

39 Why does a living man complain, a man for the punishment of his sins?

40 Let us search and try our ways, and turn again to the LORD.

41 Let us lift up our heart with our hands to God in the heavens.

42 We have transgressed and have rebelled: you have not pardoned.

43 You have covered with anger, and persecuted us: you have slain, you have not pitied.

44 You have covered yourself with a cloud, that our prayer should not pass through.

45 You have made us as the offscouring and refuse in the midst of the people.

46 All our enemies have opened their mouths against us.

47 Fear and a snare is come upon us, desolation and destruction.

48 My eye runs down with rivers of water for the destruction of the daughter of my people.

49 My eye trickles down, and does not cease, without any intermission.

50 Till the LORD look down, and behold from heaven.

51 My eye affects my heart because of all the daughters of my city.

52 My enemies chased me sore, like a bird, without cause.

53 They have cut off my life in the dungeon, and cast a stone upon me.

54 Waters flowed over my head; then I said, I am cut off.

55 I called upon your name, O LORD, out of the low dungeon.

56 You have heard my voice: do not hide your ear at my breathing, at my cry.

57 You drew near in the day that I called upon you: you said, Fear not.

58 O LORD, you have pleaded the causes of my soul; you have redeemed my life.

59 O LORD, you have seen my wrong: judge my cause.

60 You have seen all their vengeance and all their imaginations against me.

61 You have heard their reproach, O LORD, and all their imaginations against me;

62 The lips of those that rose up against me, and their device against me all the day.

63 Behold their sitting down, and their rising up; I am their music.

64 Render to them a recompence, O LORD, according to the work of their hands.

65 Give them sorrow of heart, your curse to them.

66 Persecute and destroy them in anger from under the heavens of the LORD.

CHAPTER 4

HOW is the gold become dim! how is the most fine gold changed! the stones of the sanctuary are poured out in the top of every street.

2 The precious sons of Zion, comparable to fine gold, how are they esteemed as earthen pitchers, the work of the hands of the potter!

3 Even the sea monsters draw out the breast, they give suck to their young ones: the daughter of my people is become cruel, like the ostriches in the wilderness.

4 The tongue of the sucking child cleaves to the roof of his mouth for thirst: the young children ask bread, and no man breaks it for them.

5 They that did feed delicately are desolate in the streets: they that were brought up in scarlet embrace dunghills.

6 For the punishment of the iniquity of the daughter of my people is greater than the punishment of the sin of Sodom, that was overthrown as in a moment, and no hands stayed on her.

7 Her Nazarites were purer than snow, they were whiter than milk, they were more ruddy in body than rubies, their polishing was of sapphire:

8 Their visage is blacker than a coal; they are not known in the streets: their

---

3:48 Do we ever shed a tear for the destruction of humanity? Do our eyes run down with water? Do we even care for their eternal salvation? Then our evangelistic lifestyle should be evident. (Also see Paul's lament in his letter to the Romans, 9:1-3.)

skin cleaves to their bones; it is withered, it is become like a stick.

9 They that be slain with the sword are better than they that be slain with hunger: for these pine away, stricken through for want of the fruits of the field.

10 The hands of the pitiful women have sodden their own children: they were their meat in the destruction of the daughter of my people.

11 The LORD has accomplished his fury; he has poured out his fierce anger, and has kindled a fire in Zion, and it has devoured the foundations thereof.

12 The kings of the earth, and all the inhabitants of the world, would not have believed that the adversary and the enemy should have entered into the gates of Jerusalem.

13 For the sins of her prophets, and the iniquities of her priests, that have shed the blood of the just in the midst of her,

14 They have wandered as blind men in the streets, they have polluted themselves with blood, so that men could not touch their garments.

15 They cried to them, Depart; it is unclean; depart, depart, touch not: when they fled away and wandered, they said among the heathen, They shall no more sojourn there.

16 The anger of the LORD has divided them; he will no more regard them: they did not respect the persons of the priests, they did not favour the elders.

17 As for us, our eyes as yet failed for our vain help: in our watching we have watched for a nation that could not save us.

18 They hunt our steps, that we cannot go in our streets: our end is near, our days are fulfilled; for our end is come.

19 Our persecutors are swifter than the eagles of the heaven: they pursued us upon the mountains, they laid wait for us in the wilderness.

20 The breath of our nostrils, the anointed of the LORD, was taken in their pits, of whom we said, Under his shadow we shall live among the heathen.

21 Rejoice and be glad, O daughter of Edom, that dwell in the land of Uz; the cup also shall pass through to you: you shall be drunken, and shall make yourself naked.

22 The punishment of your iniquity is accomplished, O daughter of Zion; he will no more carry you away into captivity: he will visit your iniquity, O daughter of Edom; he will discover your sins.

CHAPTER 5

REMEMBER, O LORD, what is come upon us: consider, and behold our reproach.

2 Our inheritance is turned to strangers, our houses to aliens.

3 We are orphans and fatherless, our mothers are as widows.

4 We have drunken our water for money; our wood is sold to us.

5 Our necks are under persecution: we labour, and have no rest.

6 We have given the hand to the Egyptians, and to the Assyrians, to be satisfied with bread.

7 Our fathers have sinned, and are not; and we have borne their iniquities.

8 Servants have ruled over us: there is none that delivers us out of their hand.

9 We gat our bread with the peril of our lives because of the sword of the wilderness.

10 Our skin was black like an oven because of the terrible famine.

11 They ravished the women in Zion, and the maids in the cities of Judah.

12 Princes are hanged up by their hand: the faces of elders were not honoured.

13 They took the young men to grind, and the children fell under the wood.

14 The elders have ceased from the gate, the young men from their music.

15 The joy of our heart is ceased; our dance is turned into mourning.

16 The crown is fallen from our head: woe to us, that we have sinned!

17 For this our heart is faint; for these things our eyes are dim.

18 Because of the mountain of Zion, which is desolate, the foxes walk upon it.

19 You, O LORD, remain for ever; your throne from generation to generation.

20 Why do you forget us for ever, and forsake us so long time?

21 Turn us to you, O LORD, and we shall be turned; renew our days as of old.

22 But you have utterly rejected us; you are very wroth against us.

Ezekiel 1:1

Ezekiel

CHAPTER 1

N OW it came to pass in the thirtieth year, in the fourth month, in the fifth day of the month, as I was among the captives by the river of Chebar, that the heavens were opened, and I saw visions of God.

2 In the fifth day of the month, which was the fifth year of king Jehoiachin's captivity,

3 The word of the LORD came expressly to Ezekiel the priest, the son of Buzi, in the land of the Chaldeans by the river Chebar; and the hand of the LORD was there upon him.

4 And I looked, and, behold, a whirlwind came out of the north, a great cloud, and a fire infolding itself, and a brightness was about it, and out of the midst thereof as the colour of amber, out of the midst of the fire.

5 Also out of the midst thereof came the likeness of four living creatures. And this was their appearance; they had the likeness of a man.

6 And every one had four faces, and every one had four wings.

7 And their feet were straight feet; and the sole of their feet was like the sole of a calf's foot: and they sparkled like the colour of burnished brass.

8 And they had the hands of a man under their wings on their four sides; and they four had their faces and their wings.

9 Their wings were joined one to another; they turned not when they went; they went every one straight forward.

10 As for the likeness of their faces, they four had the face of a man, and the face of a lion, on the right side: and they four had the face of an ox on the left side; they four also had the face of an eagle.

11 Thus were their faces: and their wings were stretched upward; two wings of every one were joined one to another, and two covered their bodies.

12 And they went every one straight forward: where the spirit was to go, they went; and they turned not when they went.

13 As for the likeness of the living creatures, their appearance was like burning coals of fire, and like the appearance of lamps: it went up and down among the living creatures; and the fire was bright, and out of the fire went forth lightning.

14 And the living creatures ran and returned as the appearance of a flash of lightning.

15 Now as I beheld the living creatures, behold one wheel upon the earth by the living creatures, with his four faces.

16 The appearance of the wheels and their work was like the colour of a beryl: and they four had one likeness: and their appearance and their work was as it were a wheel in the middle of a wheel.

17 When they went, they went upon their four sides: and they turned not when they went.

18 As for their rings, they were so high that they were dreadful; and their rings were full of eyes round about them four.

19 And when the living creatures went, the wheels went by them: and when the living creatures were lifted up from the earth, the wheels were lifted up.

20 Wherever the spirit was to go, they went, there was their spirit to go; and the wheels were lifted up over against them: for the spirit of the living creature was in the wheels.

21 When those went, these went; and when those stood, these stood; and when those were lifted up from the earth, the wheels were lifted up over against them: for the spirit of the living creature was in the wheels.

22 And the likeness of the firmament upon the heads of the living creature was as the colour of the terrible crystal, stretched forth over their heads above.

23 And under the firmament were their wings straight, the one toward the other: every one had two, which covered on this side, and every one had two, which covered on that side, their bodies.

24 And when they went, I heard the noise of their wings, like the noise of great waters, as the voice of the Almighty, the voice of speech, as the noise of an host: when they stood, they let down their wings.

25 And there was a voice from the firmament that was over their heads, when they stood, and had let down their wings.

26 And above the firmament that was over their heads was the likeness of a throne, as the appearance of a sapphire stone: and upon the likeness of the throne was the likeness as the appearance of a man above upon it.

27 And I saw as the colour of amber, as the appearance of fire round about within it, from the appearance of his loins even upward, and from the appearance of his loins even downward, I saw as it were the appearance of fire, and it had brightness round about.

28 As the appearance of the bow that is in the cloud in the day of rain, so was the appearance of the brightness round about. This was the appearance of the likeness of the glory of the LORD. And when I saw it, I fell upon my face, and I heard a voice of one that spoke.

CHAPTER 2

AND he said to me, Son of man, stand upon your feet, and I will speak to you.

2 And the spirit entered into me when he spoke to me, and set me upon my feet, that I heard him that spoke to me.

3 And he said to me, Son of man, I send you to the children of Israel, to a rebellious nation that has rebelled against me: they and their fathers have transgressed against me, even to this very day.

4 For they are impudent children and stiffhearted. I do send you to them; and you shall say to them, Thus says the Lord GOD.

5 And they, whether they will hear, or whether they will forbear, (for they are a rebellious house,) yet shall know that there has been a prophet among them.

6 And you, son of man, be not afraid of them, neither be afraid of their words, though briers and thorns be with you, and you dost dwell among scorpions: be not afraid of their words, nor be dismayed at their looks, though they be a rebellious house.

7 And you shall speak my words to them, whether they will hear, or whether they will forbear: for they are most rebellious.

8 But you, son of man, hear what I say to you; Do not be rebellious like that rebellious house: open your mouth, and eat what I give you.

9 And when I looked, behold, an hand was sent to me; and, lo, a roll of a book was therein;

10 And he spread it before me; and it was written within and without: and there was written therein lamentations, and mourning, and woe.

CHAPTER 3

MOREOVER he said to me, Son of man, eat what you find; eat this roll, and go speak to the house of Israel.
2 So I opened my mouth, and he caused me to eat that roll.
3 And he said to me, Son of man, cause your belly to eat, and fill your bowels with this roll that I give you. Then did I eat it; and it was in my mouth as honey for sweetness.
4 And he said to me, Son of man, go, get to the house of Israel, and speak with my words to them.
5 For you are not sent to a people of a strange speech and of an hard language, but to the house of Israel;
6 Not to many people of a strange speech and of an hard language, whose words you can not understand. Surely, had I sent you to them, they would have hearkened to you.
7 But the house of Israel will not hearken to you; for they will not hearken to me: for all the house of Israel are impudent and hardhearted.
8 Behold, I have made your face strong against their faces, and your forehead strong against their foreheads.
9 As an adamant harder than flint have I made your forehead: fear them not, neither be dismayed at their looks, though they be a rebellious house.
10 Moreover he said to me, Son of man, all my words that I shall speak to you receive in your heart, and hear with your ears.

11 And go, get to them of the captivity, to the children of your people, and speak to them, and tell them, Thus says the Lord GOD; whether they will hear, or whether they will forbear.
12 Then the spirit took me up, and I heard behind me a voice of a great rushing, saying, Blessed be the glory of the LORD from his place.
13 I heard also the noise of the wings of the living creatures that touched one another, and the noise of the wheels over against them, and a noise of a great rushing.
14 So the spirit lifted me up, and took me away, and I went in bitterness, in the heat of my spirit; but the hand of the LORD was strong upon me.
15 Then I came to them of the captivity at Telabib, that dwelt by the river of Chebar, and I sat where they sat, and remained there astonished among them seven days.
16 And it came to pass at the end of seven days, that the word of the LORD came to me, saying,
17 Son of man, I have made you a watchman for the house of Israel: therefore hear the word at my mouth, and give them warning from me.
18 When I say to the wicked, You shall surely die; and you did not give him warning, nor speak to warn the wicked from his wicked way, to save his life; the same wicked man shall die in his iniquity; but his blood will I require at your hand.
19 Yet if you warn the wicked, and he turn not from his wickedness, nor from his wicked way, he shall die in his iniquity; but you have delivered your soul.

3:8 May God make us stubborn for His kingdom, so that we never back down in the face of a godless world. We need faces and foreheads like flints. When you strike a flint, you get sparks. Such sparks are what Peter experienced, too, when he tried to deter Jesus from following the will of the Father (see Matthew 16:22-23).

3:18 In this verse and in Ezekiel 33:6, God made it plain to the prophet that he was responsible for warning the wicked of impending judgment.

20 Again, When a righteous man turns from his righteousness, and commits iniquity, and I lay a stumbling-block before him, he shall die: because you have not given him warning, he shall die in his sin, and his righteousness which he has done shall not be remembered; but his blood will I require at your hand.

21 Nevertheless if you warn the righteous man, that the righteous sin not, and he does not sin, he shall surely live, because he is warned; also you have delivered your soul.

22 And the hand of the LORD was there upon me; and he said to me, Arise, go forth into the plain, and I will there talk with you.

23 Then I arose, and went forth into the plain: and, behold, the glory of the LORD stood there, as the glory which I saw by the river of Chebar: and I fell on my face.

24 Then the spirit entered into me, and set me upon my feet, and spoke with me, and said to me, Go, shut yourself within your house.

25 But you, O son of man, behold, they shall put bands upon you, and shall bind you with them, and you shall not go out among them:

26 And I will make your tongue cleave to the roof of your mouth, that you shall be dumb, and shall not be to them a reprover: for they are a rebellious house.

27 But when I speak with you, I will open your mouth, and you shall say to them, Thus says the Lord GOD; He that hears, let him hear; and he that forbears, let him forbear: for they are a rebellious house.

CHAPTER 4

YOU also, son of man, take a tile, and lay it before you, and portray upon it the city, even Jerusalem:

2 And lay siege against it, and build a fort against it, and cast a mount against it; set the camp also against it, and set battering rams against it round about.

3 Moreover take for yourself an iron pan, and set it for a wall of iron between you and the city: and set your face against it, and it shall be besieged, and you shall lay siege against it. This shall be a sign to the house of Israel.

4 Lie also upon your left side, and lay the iniquity of the house of Israel upon it: according to the number of the days that you shall lie upon it you shall bear their iniquity.

5 For I have laid upon you the years of their iniquity, according to the number of the days, three hundred and ninety days: so shall you bear the iniquity of the house of Israel.

6 And when you have accomplished them, lie again on your right side, and you shall bear the iniquity of the house of Judah forty days: I have appointed you each day for a year.

7 Therefore you shall set your face toward the siege of Jerusalem, and your arm shall be uncovered, and you shall prophesy against it.

8 And, behold, I will lay bands upon you, and you shall not turn from one side to another, till you have ended the days of your siege.

9 Also take for yourself wheat, and barley, and beans, and lentiles, and millet, and fitches, and put them in one vessel, and make bread thereof for yourself, according to the number of the days that you shall lie upon your side, three hundred and ninety days shall you eat thereof.

10 And your meat which you shall eat shall be by weight, twenty shekels a day: from time to time shall you eat it.

11 You shall drink also water by measure, the sixth part of an hin: from time to time shall you drink.

12 And you shall eat it as barley cakes, and you shall bake it with dung that comes out of man, in their sight.

13 And the LORD said, Even thus shall the children of Israel eat their defiled bread among the Gentiles, where I will drive them.

14 Then said I, Ah Lord GOD! behold, my soul has not been polluted: for from my youth up even till now have I not eaten of that which dies of itself, or is torn in pieces; neither came there abominable flesh into my mouth.

15 Then he said to me, Lo, I have given you cow's dung for man's dung, and you shall prepare your bread therewith.

16 Moreover he said to me, Son of man, behold, I will break the staff of bread in Jerusalem: and they shall eat bread by weight, and with care; and they shall drink water by measure, and with astonishment:

17 That they may want bread and water, and be dismayed one with another, and consume away for their iniquity.

CHAPTER 5

AND you, son of man, take a sharp knife, take a barber's razor, and cause it to pass upon your head and upon your beard: then take balances to weigh, and divide the hair.

2 You shall burn with fire a third part in the midst of the city, when the days of the siege are fulfilled: and you shall take a third part, and smite about it with a knife: and a third part you shall scatter in the wind; and I will draw out a sword after them.

3 You shall also take thereof a few in number, and bind them in your skirts.

4 Then take of them again, and cast them into the midst of the fire, and burn them in the fire; for thereof shall a fire come forth into all the house of Israel.

5 Thus says the Lord GOD; This is Jerusalem: I have set it in the midst of the nations and countries that are round about her.

6 And she has changed my judgments into wickedness more than the nations, and my statutes more than the countries that are round about her: for they have refused my judgments and my statutes, they have not walked in them.

7 Therefore thus says the Lord GOD; Because you multiplied more than the nations that are round about you, and have not walked in my statutes, neither have kept my judgments, neither have done according to the judgments of the nations that are round about you;

8 Therefore thus says the Lord GOD; Behold, I, even I, am against you, and will execute judgments in the midst of you in the sight of the nations.

9 And I will do in you that which I have not done, and whereunto I will not do any more the like, because of all your abominations.

10 Therefore the fathers shall eat the sons in the midst of you, and the sons shall eat their fathers; and I will execute judgments in you, and the whole remnant of you will I scatter into all the winds.

11 Therefore, as I live, says the Lord GOD; Surely, because you have defiled my sanctuary with all your detestable things, and with all your abominations, therefore will I also diminish you; neither shall my eye spare, neither will I have any pity.

12 A third part of you shall die with the pestilence, and with famine shall they be consumed in the midst of you: and a third part shall fall by the sword round about you; and I will scatter a third part into all the winds, and I will draw out a sword after them.

13 Thus shall my anger be accomplished, and I will cause my fury to rest upon them, and I will be comforted: and they shall know that I the LORD have spoken it in my zeal, when I have accomplished my fury in them.

14 Moreover I will make you waste, and a reproach among the nations that are round about you, in the sight of all that pass by.

15 So it shall be a reproach and a taunt, an instruction and an astonishment to the nations that are round about you, when I shall execute judgments in you in anger and in fury and in furious rebukes. I the LORD have spoken it.

16 When I shall send upon them the evil arrows of famine, which shall be for their destruction, and which I will send to destroy you: and I will increase the famine upon you, and will break your staff of bread:

17 So will I send upon you famine and evil beasts, and they shall bereave you: and pestilence and blood shall pass through you; and I will bring the sword upon you. I the LORD have spoken it.

CHAPTER 6

AND the word of the LORD came to me, saying,

2 Son of man, set your face toward the mountains of Israel, and prophesy against them,

3 And say, You mountains of Israel, hear the word of the Lord GOD; Thus says the Lord GOD to the mountains, and to the hills, to the rivers, and to the valleys; Behold, I, even I, will bring a sword upon you, and I will destroy your high places.

4 And your altars shall be desolate, and your images shall be broken: and I will cast down your slain men before your idols.

5 And I will lay the dead carcases of the children of Israel before their idols; and I will scatter your bones round about your altars.

6 In all your dwelling places the cities shall be laid waste, and the high places shall be desolate; that your altars may be laid waste and made desolate, and your idols may be broken and cease, and your images may be cut down, and your works may be abolished.

7 And the slain shall fall in the midst of you, and you shall know that I am the LORD.

8 Yet will I leave a remnant, that you may have some that shall escape the sword among the nations, when you shall be scattered through the countries.

9 And they that escape of you shall remember me among the nations where they shall be carried captives, because I am broken with their whorish heart, which has departed from me, and with their eyes, which go a whoring after their idols: and they shall lothe themselves for the evils which they have committed in all their abominations.

10 And they shall know that I am the LORD, and that I have not said in vain that I would do this evil to them.

11 Thus says the Lord GOD; Smite with your hand, and stamp with your foot, and say, Alas for all the evil abominations of the house of Israel! for they shall fall by the sword, by the famine, and by the pestilence.

12 He that is far off shall die of the pestilence; and he that is near shall fall by the sword; and he that remains and is besieged shall die by the famine: thus will I accomplish my fury upon them.

13 Then shall you know that I am the LORD, when their slain men shall be among their idols round about their altars, upon every high hill, in all the tops of the mountains, and under every green tree, and under every thick oak, the place where they did offer sweet savour to all their idols.

14 So will I stretch out my hand upon them, and make the land desolate, yea, more desolate than the wilderness toward Diblath, in all their habitations: and they shall know that I am the LORD.

CHAPTER 7

MOREOVER the word of the LORD came to me, saying,

2 Also, you son of man, thus says the Lord GOD to the land of Israel; An end, the end is come upon the four corners of the land.

3 Now is the end come upon you, and I will send my anger upon you, and will judge you according to your ways, and will recompense upon you all your abominations.

4 And my eye shall not spare you, neither will I have pity: but I will recompense your ways upon you, and your

abominations shall be in the midst of you: and you shall know that I am the LORD.

5 Thus says the Lord GOD; An evil, an only evil, behold, is come.

6 An end is come, the end is come: it watches for you; behold, it is come.

7 The morning is come to you, O you that dwell in the land: the time is come, the day of trouble is near, and not the sounding again of the mountains.

8 Now will I shortly pour out my fury upon you, and accomplish my anger upon you: and I will judge you according to your ways, and will recompense you for all your abominations.

9 And my eye shall not spare, neither will I have pity: I will recompense you according to your ways and your abominations that are in the midst of you; and you shall know that I am the LORD that smites.

10 Behold the day, behold, it is come: the morning is gone forth; the rod has blossomed, pride has budded.

11 Violence is risen up into a rod of wickedness: none of them shall remain, nor of their multitude, nor of any of their's: neither shall there be wailing for them.

12 The time is come, the day draws near: let not the buyer rejoice, nor the seller mourn: for wrath is upon all the multitude thereof.

> Why does the Church stay indoors?
> They have a theology
> that has dwindled into a philosophy,
> in which there is no thrill of faith,
> no terror of doom
> and no concern for souls.
> Unbelief has put out
> the fires of passion,
> and worldliness garlands the altar
> of sacrifice
> with the tawdry glitter of unreality.

SAMUEL CHADWICK

1860-1932

ENGLISH PREACHER

13 For the seller shall not return to that which is sold, although they were yet alive: for the vision is touching the whole multitude thereof, which shall not return; neither shall any strengthen himself in the iniquity of his life.

14 They have blown the trumpet, even to make all ready; but none goeth to the battle: for my wrath is upon all the multitude thereof.

15 The sword is without, and the pestilence and the famine within: he that is in the field shall die with the sword; and he that is in the city, famine and pestilence shall devour him.

16 But they that escape of them shall escape, and shall be on the mountains like doves of the valleys, all of them mourning, every one for his iniquity.

17 All hands shall be feeble, and all knees shall be weak as water.

18 They shall also gird themselves with sackcloth, and horror shall cover them; and shame shall be upon all faces, and baldness upon all their heads.

19 They shall cast their silver in the streets, and their gold shall be removed: their silver and their gold shall not be able to deliver them in the day of the wrath of the LORD: they shall not satisfy their souls, neither fill their bowels: because it is the stumblingblock of their iniquity.

7:19 The love of money will always be an overwhelming temptation until a man deals with the stumbling block of his iniquity (see 1 Timothy 6:9-10). Once sin is forgiven and he is given a new heart with new desires, the saved can see through the folly of chasing riches. It has been well said, "Man seeks both wealth and wisdom. Having found one, he seldom seeks the other." The love of money may turn the head of a judge and cause him to pervert justice. But all the gold and silver in the world will not turn the head of the judge of the universe on the day of wrath.

20 As for the beauty of his ornament, he set it in majesty: but they made the images of their abominations and of their detestable things therein: therefore have I set it far from them.

21 And I will give it into the hands of the strangers for a prey, and to the wicked of the earth for a spoil; and they shall pollute it.

22 My face will I turn also from them, and they shall pollute my secret place: for the robbers shall enter into it, and defile it.

23 Make a chain: for the land is full of bloody crimes, and the city is full of violence.

24 Therefore I will bring the worst of the heathen, and they shall possess their houses: I will also make the pomp of the strong to cease; and their holy places shall be defiled.

25 Destruction comes; and they shall seek peace, and there shall be none.

26 Mischief shall come upon mischief, and rumour shall be upon rumour; then shall they seek a vision of the prophet; but the law shall perish from the priest, and counsel from the elders.

27 The king shall mourn, and the prince shall be clothed with desolation, and the hands of the people of the land shall be troubled: I will do to them after their way, and according to their deserts will I judge them; and they shall know that I am the LORD.

CHAPTER 8

AND it came to pass in the sixth year, in the sixth month, in the fifth day of the month, as I sat in my house, and the elders of Judah sat before me, that the hand of the Lord GOD fell there upon me.

2 Then I beheld, and lo a likeness as the appearance of fire: from the appearance of his loins even downward, fire; and from his loins even upward, as the appearance of brightness, as the colour of amber.

3 And he put forth the form of an hand, and took me by a lock of my head; and the spirit lifted me up between the earth and the heaven, and brought me in the visions of God to Jerusalem, to the door of the inner gate that looks toward the north; where was the seat of the image of jealousy, which provokes to jealousy.

4 And, behold, the glory of the God of Israel was there, according to the vision that I saw in the plain.

5 Then said he to me, Son of man, lift up your eyes now the way toward the north. So I lifted up my eyes the way toward the north, and behold northward at the gate of the altar this image of jealousy in the entry.

6 He said furthermore to me, Son of man, do you see what they do? even the great abominations that the house of Israel commits here, that I should go far off from my sanctuary? but turn yet again, and you shall see greater abominations.

7 And he brought me to the door of the court; and when I looked, behold a hole in the wall.

8 Then said he to me, Son of man, dig now in the wall: and when I had dug in the wall, behold a door.

9 And he said to me, Go in, and behold the wicked abominations that they do here.

10 So I went in and saw; and behold every form of creeping things, and abominable beasts, and all the idols of the house of Israel, portrayed upon the wall round about.

11 And there stood before them seventy men of the elders of the house of Israel, and in the midst of them stood Jaazaniah the son of Shaphan, with every man his censer in his hand; and a thick cloud of incense went up.

12 Then said he to me, Son of man, have you seen what the elders of the house of Israel do in the dark, every man in the chambers of his imagery? for they say, the LORD does not see us; the LORD has forsaken the earth.

13 He said also to me, Turn yet again, and you shall see greater abominations that they do.

14 Then he brought me to the door of the gate of the LORD's house which was toward the north; and, behold, there sat women weeping for Tammuz.

15 Then said he to me, Have you seen this, O son of man? turn yet again, and you shall see greater abominations than these.

16 And he brought me into the inner court of the LORD's house, and, behold, at the door of the temple of the LORD, between the porch and the altar, were about five and twenty men, with their backs toward the temple of the LORD, and their faces toward the east; and they worshipped the sun toward the east.

17 Then he said to me, Have you seen this, O son of man? Is it a light thing to the house of Judah that they commit the abominations which they commit here? for they have filled the land with violence, and have returned to provoke me to anger: and, lo, they put the branch to their nose.

18 Therefore will I also deal in fury: my eye shall not spare, neither will I have pity: and though they cry in my ears with a loud voice, yet will I not hear them.

CHAPTER 9

H E cried also in my ears with a loud voice, saying, Cause them that have charge over the city to draw near, even every man with his destroying weapon in his hand.

2 And, behold, six men came from the way of the higher gate, which lieth toward the north, and every man a slaughter weapon in his hand; and one man among them was clothed with linen, with a writer's inkhorn by his side: and they went in, and stood beside the brasen altar.

3 And the glory of the God of Israel was gone up from the cherub, whereupon he was, to the threshold of the house. And he called to the man clothed with linen, which had the writer's inkhorn by his side;

4 And the LORD said to him, Go through the midst of the city, through the midst of Jerusalem, and set a mark upon the foreheads of the men that sigh and that cry for all the abominations that be done in the midst thereof.

5 And to the others he said in my hearing, Go after him through the city, and smite: do not let your eye spare, neither have pity:

6 Slay utterly old and young, both maids, and little children, and women: but come not near any man upon whom is the mark; and begin at my sanctuary. Then they began at the ancient men which were before the house.

7 And he said to them, Defile the house, and fill the courts with the slain: go forth. And they went forth, and slew in the city.

8 And it came to pass, while they were slaying them, and I was left, that I fell upon my face, and cried, and said, Ah Lord GOD! will you destroy all the residue of Israel in your pouring out of your fury upon Jerusalem?

9 Then said he to me, The iniquity of the house of Israel and Judah is exceeding great, and the land is full of blood,

---

8:12 The error of the unsaved is that they think that God doesn't see the secret sins of the heart (see Romans 1:21).

8:15 There isn't a word that enters our mind nor comes off our tongue that God isn't intimately acquainted with. All the ways of men are known to God (see Psalm 139:3, Jeremiah 16:17 and 32:19).

9:4 How can a pastor reach his city with the message of salvation? See 1 Corinthians 4:16 comment.

and the city full of perverseness: for they say, The LORD has forsaken the earth, and the LORD does not see.

10 And as for me also, my eye shall not spare, neither will I have pity, but I will recompense their way upon their head.

11 And, behold, the man clothed with linen, which had the inkhorn by his side, reported the matter, saying, I have done as you have commanded me.

CHAPTER 10

THEN I looked, and, and, behold, in the firmament that was above the head of the cherubims there appeared over them as it were a sapphire stone, as the appearance of the likeness of a throne.

2 And he spoke to the man clothed with linen, and said, Go in between the wheels, even under the cherub, and fill your hand with coals of fire from between the cherubims, and scatter them over the city. And he went in in my sight.

3 Now the cherubims stood on the right side of the house, when the man went in; and the cloud filled the inner court.

4 Then the glory of the LORD went up from the cherub, and stood over the threshold of the house; and the house was filled with the cloud, and the court was full of the brightness of the LORD's glory.

5 And the sound of the cherubims' wings was heard even to the outer court, as the voice of the Almighty God when he speaks.

6 And it came to pass, that when he had commanded the man clothed with linen, saying, Take fire from between the wheels, from between the cherubims; then he went in, and stood beside the wheels.

7 And one cherub stretched forth his hand from between the cherubims to the fire that was between the cherubims, and took thereof, and put it into the hands of him that was clothed with linen: who took it, and went out.

8 And there appeared in the cherubims the form of a man's hand under their wings.

9 And when I looked, behold the four wheels by the cherubims, one wheel by one cherub, and another wheel by another cherub: and the appearance of the wheels was as the colour of a beryl stone.

10 And as for their appearances, they four had one likeness, as if a wheel had been in the midst of a wheel.

11 When they went, they went upon their four sides; they turned not as they went, but to the place where the head looked they followed it; they turned not as they went.

12 And their whole body, and their backs, and their hands, and their wings, and the wheels, were full of eyes round about, even the wheels that they four had.

13 As for the wheels, it was cried to them in my hearing, O wheel.

14 And every one had four faces: the first face was the face of a cherub, and the second face was the face of a man, and the third the face of a lion, and the fourth the face of an eagle.

15 And the cherubims were lifted up. This is the living creature that I saw by the river of Chebar.

16 And when the cherubims went, the wheels went by them: and when the cherubims lifted up their wings to mount up from the earth, the same wheels also turned not from beside them.

17 When they stood, these stood; and when they were lifted up, these lifted up themselves also: for the spirit of the living creature was in them.

18 Then the glory of the LORD departed from off the threshold of the house, and stood over the cherubims.

19 And the cherubims lifted up their wings, and mounted up from the earth in my sight: when they went out, the wheels also were beside them, and every one stood at the door of the east gate of

the LORD's house; and the glory of the God of Israel was over them above.

20 This is the living creature that I saw under the God of Israel by the river of Chebar; and I knew that they were the cherubims.

21 Every one had four faces apiece, and every one four wings; and the likeness of the hands of a man was under their wings.

22 And the likeness of their faces was the same faces which I saw by the river of Chebar, their appearances and themselves: they went every one straight forward.

CHAPTER 11

MOREOVER the spirit lifted me up, and brought me to the east gate of the LORD's house, which looks eastward: and behold at the door of the gate five and twenty men; among whom I saw Jaazaniah the son of Azur, and Pelatiah the son of Benaiah, princes of the people.

2 Then said he to me, Son of man, these are the men that devise mischief, and give wicked counsel in this city:

3 Which say, It is not near; let us build houses: this city is the caldron, and we be the flesh.

4 Therefore prophesy against them, prophesy, O son of man.

5 And the Spirit of the LORD fell upon me, and said to me, Speak; Thus says the LORD; Thus have you said, O house of Israel: for I know the things that come into your mind, every one of them.

6 You have multiplied your slain in this city, and you have filled the streets thereof with the slain.

7 Therefore thus says the Lord GOD; Your slain whom you have laid in the midst of it, they are the flesh, and this city is the caldron: but I will bring you forth out of the midst of it.

8 You have feared the sword; and I will bring a sword upon you, says the Lord GOD.

9 And I will bring you out of the midst thereof, and deliver you into the hands of strangers, and will execute judgments among you.

10 You shall fall by the sword; I will judge you in the border of Israel; and you shall know that I am the LORD.

11 This city shall not be your caldron, neither shall you be the flesh in the midst thereof; but I will judge you in the border of Israel:

12 And you shall know that I am the LORD: for you have not walked in my statutes, neither executed my judgments, but have done after the manners of the heathen that are round about you.

13 And it came to pass, when I prophesied, that Pelatiah the son of Benaiah died. Then fell I down upon my face, and cried with a loud voice, and said, Ah Lord GOD! will you make a full end of the remnant of Israel?

14 Again the word of the LORD came to me, saying,

15 Son of man, your brethren, even your brethren, the men of your kindred, and all the house of Israel wholly, are they to whom the inhabitants of Jerusalem have said, Get far from the LORD: to us is this land given in possession.

16 Therefore say, Thus says the Lord GOD; Although I have cast them far off among the heathen, and although I have scattered them among the countries, yet will I be to them as a little sanctuary in the countries where they shall come.

17 Therefore say, Thus says the Lord GOD; I will even gather you from the people, and assemble you out of the countries where you have been scattered, and I will give you the land of Israel.

11:17 The history of the Jews is a testimony of this promise of God. He has scattered them throughout the whole earth then gathered them back into the land of Israel.

18 And they shall come there, and they shall take away all the detestable things thereof and all the abominations thereof from thence.

19 And I will give them one heart, and I will put a new spirit within you; and I will take the stony heart out of their flesh, and will give them an heart of flesh:

20 That they may walk in my statutes, and keep my ordinances, and do them: and they shall be my people, and I will be their God.

21 But as for them whose heart walks after the heart of their detestable things and their abominations, I will recompense their way upon their own heads, says the Lord GOD.

22 Then did the cherubims lift up their wings, and the wheels beside them; and the glory of the God of Israel was over them above.

23 And the glory of the LORD went up from the midst of the city, and stood upon the mountain which is on the east side of the city.

24 Afterwards the spirit took me up, and brought me in a vision by the Spirit of God into Chaldea, to them of the captivity. So the vision that I had seen went up from me.

25 Then I spoke to them of the captivity all the things that the LORD had showed me.

CHAPTER 12

THE word of the LORD also came to me, saying,

2 Son of man, you dwell in the midst of a rebellious house, which have eyes to see, and see not; they have ears to hear, and hear not: for they are a rebellious house.

3 Therefore, you son of man, prepare stuff for removing, and remove by day in their sight; and you shall remove from your place to another place in their sight: it may be they will consider, though they be a rebellious house.

12:2

This verse sums up contemporary, secular America, where eyes and ears are firmly shut against God's Truth.

4 Then shall you bring forth your stuff by day in their sight, as stuff for removing: and you shall go forth at even in their sight, as they that go forth into captivity.

5 Dig through the wall in their sight, and carry out thereby.

6 In their sight shall you bear it upon your shoulders, and carry it forth in the twilight: you shall cover your face, that you see not the ground: for I have set you for a sign to the house of Israel.

7 And I did so as I was commanded: I brought forth my stuff by day, as stuff for captivity, and in the even I dug through the wall with my hand; I brought it forth in the twilight, and I bare it upon my shoulder in their sight.

8 And in the morning the word of the LORD came to me, saying,

9 Son of man, has not the house of Israel, the rebellious house, said to you, What are you doing?

10 Say to them, Thus says the Lord GOD; This burden concerns the prince in Jerusalem, and all the house of Israel that are among them.

11 Say, I am your sign: like as I have done, so shall it be done to them: they shall remove and go into captivity.

12 And the prince that is among them shall bear upon his shoulder in the twilight, and shall go forth: they shall dig through the wall to carry out thereby:

he shall cover his face, that he see not the ground with his eyes.

13 My net also will I spread upon him, and he shall be taken in my snare: and I will bring him to Babylon to the land of the Chaldeans; yet shall he not see it, though he shall die there.

14 And I will scatter toward every wind all that are about him to help him, and all his bands; and I will draw out the sword after them.

15 And they shall know that I am the LORD, when I shall scatter them among the nations, and disperse them in the countries.

16 But I will leave a few men of them from the sword, from the famine, and from the pestilence; that they may declare all their abominations among the heathen where they go; and they shall know that I am the LORD.

17 Moreover the word of the LORD came to me, saying,

18 Son of man, eat your bread with quaking, and drink your water with trembling and with carefulness;

19 And say to the people of the land, Thus says the Lord GOD of the inhabitants of Jerusalem, and of the land of Israel; They shall eat their bread with carefulness, and drink their water with astonishment, that her land may be desolate from all that is therein, because of the violence of all them that dwell therein.

20 And the cities that are inhabited shall be laid waste, and the land shall be desolate; and you shall know that I am the LORD.

21 And the word of the LORD came to me, saying,

22 Son of man, what is that proverb that you have in the land of Israel, saying, The days are prolonged, and every vision fails?

23 Tell them therefore, Thus says the Lord GOD; I will make this proverb to cease, and they shall no more use it as a proverb in Israel; but say to them,

The days are at hand, and the effect of every vision.

24 For there shall be no more any vain vision nor flattering divination within the house of Israel.

25 For I am the LORD: I will speak, and the word that I shall speak shall come to pass; it shall be no more prolonged: for in your days, O rebellious house, will I say the word, and will perform it, says the Lord GOD.

26 Again the word of the LORD came to me, saying,

27 Son of man, behold, they of the house of Israel say, The vision that he sees is for many days to come, and he prophesies of the times that are far off.

28 Therefore say to them, Thus says the Lord GOD; There shall none of my words be prolonged any more, but the word which I have spoken shall be done, says the Lord GOD.

CHAPTER 13

AND the word of the LORD came to me, saying,

2 Son of man, prophesy against the prophets of Israel that prophesy, and say to them that prophesy out of their own hearts, Hear the word of the LORD;

3 Thus says the Lord GOD; Woe to the foolish prophets, that follow their own spirit, and have seen nothing!

4 O Israel, your prophets are like the foxes in the deserts.

5 You have not gone up into the gaps, neither made up the hedge for the house of Israel to stand in the battle in the day of the LORD.

6 They have seen vanity and lying divination, saying, The LORD says: and the LORD has not sent them: and they have made others to hope that they would confirm the word.

7 Have you not seen a vain vision, and have you not spoken a lying divination, whereas you say, The LORD says it; albeit I have not spoken?

8 Therefore thus says the Lord GOD; Because you have spoken vanity,

and seen lies, therefore, behold, I am against you, says the Lord GOD.

9 And my hand shall be upon the prophets that see vanity, and that divine lies: they shall not be in the assembly of my people, neither shall they be written in the writing of the house of Israel, neither shall they enter into the land of Israel; and you shall know that I am the Lord GOD.

10 Because, even because they have seduced my people, saying, Peace; and there was no peace; and one built up a wall, and, lo, others daubed it with untempered morter:

11 Say to them which daub it with untempered morter, that it shall fall: there shall be an overflowing shower; and you, O great hailstones, shall fall; and a stormy wind shall rend it.

12 Lo, when the wall is fallen, shall it not be said to you, Where is the daubing wherewith you have daubed it?

13 Therefore thus says the Lord GOD; I will even rend it with a stormy wind in my fury; and there shall be an overflowing shower in my anger, and great hailstones in my fury to consume it.

14 So will I break down the wall that you have daubed with untempered morter, and bring it down to the ground, so that the foundation thereof shall be discovered, and it shall fall, and you shall be consumed in the midst thereof: and you shall know that I am the LORD.

15 Thus will I accomplish my wrath upon the wall, and upon them that have daubed it with untempered morter, and will say to you, The wall is no more, neither they that daubed it;

16 To wit, the prophets of Israel which prophesy concerning Jerusalem, and which see visions of peace for her, and there is no peace, says the Lord GOD.

17 Likewise, you son of man, set your face against the daughters of your people, which prophesy out of their own heart; and prophesy against them,

18 And say, Thus says the Lord GOD; Woe to the women that sew pillows to all armholes, and make kerchiefs upon the head of every stature to hunt souls! Will you hunt the souls of my people, and will you save the souls alive that come to you?

19 And will you pollute me among my people for handfuls of barley and for pieces of bread, to slay the souls that should not die, and to save the souls alive that should not live, by your lying to my people that hear your lies?

20 Therefore thus says the Lord GOD; Behold, I am against your pillows, wherewith you there hunt the souls to make them fly, and I will tear them from your arms, and will let the souls go, even the souls that you hunt to make them fly.

21 Your kerchiefs also will I tear, and deliver my people out of your hand, and they shall be no more in your hand to be hunted; and you shall know that I am the LORD.

22 Because with lies you have made the heart of the righteous sad, whom I have not made sad; and strengthened the hands of the wicked, that he should not return from his wicked way, by promising him life:

23 Therefore you shall see no more vanity, nor divine divinations: for I will deliver my people out of your hand: and you shall know that I am the LORD.

13:10 and15-16 Although these passages speak of prophets who have visions of peace for Jerusalem when there was no peace, these verses should make us tremble. The modern message of evangelism is too quick to say that a sinner has peace with God merely because he has recited a sinner's prayer. If there is no God-given repentance, there is no peace. The sinner is still under the wrath of God.

CHAPTER 14

THEN came certain of the elders of Israel to me, and sat before me.

2 And the word of the LORD came to me, saying,

3 Son of man, these men have set up their idols in their heart, and put the stumblingblock of their iniquity before their face: should I be inquired of at all by them?

4 Therefore speak to them, and say to them, Thus says the Lord GOD; Every man of the house of Israel that sets up his idols in his heart, and puts the stumblingblock of his iniquity before his face, and comes to the prophet; I the LORD will answer him that comes according to the multitude of his idols;

5 That I may take the house of Israel in their own heart, because they are all estranged from me through their idols.

6 Therefore say to the house of Israel, Thus says the Lord GOD; Repent, and turn yourselves from your idols; and turn away your faces from all your abominations.

7 For every one of the house of Israel, or of the stranger that sojourns in Israel, which separates himself from me, and sets up his idols in his heart, and puts the stumblingblock of his iniquity before his face, and comes to a prophet to inquire of him concerning me; I the LORD will answer him by myself:

8 And I will set my face against that man, and will make him a sign and a proverb, and I will cut him off from the midst of my people; and you shall know that I am the LORD.

9 And if the prophet be deceived when he has spoken a thing, I the LORD have deceived that prophet, and I will stretch out my hand upon him, and will destroy him from the midst of my people Israel.

10 And they shall bear the punishment of their iniquity: the punishment of the prophet shall be even as the punishment of him that seeks him;

11 That the house of Israel may go no more astray from me, neither be polluted any more with all their transgressions; but that they may be my people, and I may be their God, says the Lord GOD.

12 The word of the LORD came again to me, saying,

13 Son of man, when the land sins against me by trespassing grievously, then will I stretch out my hand upon it, and will break the staff of the bread thereof, and will send famine upon it, and will cut off man and beast from it:

14 Though these three men, Noah, Daniel, and Job, were in it, they should deliver but their own souls by their righteousness, says the Lord GOD.

15 If I cause noisome beasts to pass through the land, and they spoil it, so that it be desolate, that no man may pass through because of the beasts:

16 Though these three men were in it, as I live, says the Lord GOD, they shall deliver neither sons nor daughters; they only shall be delivered, but the land shall be desolate.

17 Or if I bring a sword upon that land, and say, Sword, go through the land; so that I cut off man and beast from it:

18 Though these three men were in it, as I live, says the Lord GOD, they shall deliver neither sons nor daughters, but they only shall be delivered themselves.

19 Or if I send a pestilence into that land, and pour out my fury upon it in blood, to cut off from it man and beast:

20 Though Noah, Daniel, and Job were in it, as I live, says the Lord GOD, they shall deliver neither son nor daughter; they shall but deliver their own souls by their righteousness.

21 For thus says the Lord GOD; How much more when I send my four sore judgments upon Jerusalem, the sword, and the famine, and the noisome beast, and the pestilence, to cut off from it man and beast?

22 Yet, behold, therein shall be left a remnant that shall be brought forth, both sons and daughters: behold, they shall come forth to you, and you shall see their way and their doings: and you

shall be comforted concerning the evil that I have brought upon Jerusalem, even concerning all that I have brought upon it.

23 And they shall comfort you, when you see their ways and their doings: and you shall know that I have not done without cause all that I have done in it, says the Lord GOD.

CHAPTER 15

AND the word of the LORD came to me, saying,

2 Son of man, what is the vine tree more than any tree, or than a branch which is among the trees of the forest?

3 Shall wood be taken thereof to do any work? or will men take a pin of it to hang any vessel thereon?

4 Behold, it is cast into the fire for fuel; the fire devours both the ends of it, and the midst of it is burned. Is it meet for any work?

5 Behold, when it was whole, it was meet for no work: how much less shall it be meet yet for any work, when the fire has devoured it, and it is burned?

6 Therefore thus says the Lord GOD; As the vine tree among the trees of the forest, which I have given to the fire for fuel, so will I give the inhabitants of Jerusalem.

7 And I will set my face against them; they shall go out from one fire, and another fire shall devour them; and you shall know that I am the LORD, when I set my face against them.

8 And I will make the land desolate, because they have committed a trespass, says the Lord GOD.

CHAPTER 16

AGAIN the word of the LORD came to me, saying,

2 Son of man, cause Jerusalem to know her abominations,

3 And say, Thus says the Lord GOD to Jerusalem; Your birth and your nativity is of the land of Canaan; your father was an Amorite, and your mother an Hittite.

4 And as for your nativity, in the day you were born your navel was not cut, neither were you washed in water to cleanse you; you were not salted at all, nor swaddled at all.

5 None eye pitied you, to do any of these to you, to have compassion upon you; but you were cast out in the open field, to the lothing of your person, in the day that you were born.

6 And when I passed by you, and saw you polluted in your own blood, I said to you when you were in your blood, Live; yea, I said to you when you were in your blood, Live.

7 I have caused you to multiply as the bud of the field, and you have increased and grew great, and you are come to excellent ornaments: your breasts are fashioned, and your hair is grown, whereas you were naked and bare.

8 Now when I passed by you, and looked upon you, behold, your time was the time of love; and I spread my skirt over you, and covered your nakedness: yea, I swore to you, and entered into a covenant with you, says the Lord GOD, and you became mine.

9 Then I washed you with water; yea, I throughly washed away your blood from you, and I anointed you with oil.

10 I clothed you also with broidered work, and shod you with badgers' skin, and I girded you about with fine linen, and I covered you with silk.

11 I decked you also with ornaments, and I put bracelets upon your hands, and a chain on your neck.

12 And I put a jewel on your forehead, and earrings in your ears, and a beautiful crown upon your head.

13 Thus were you decked with gold and silver; and your raiment was of fine

---

16:9 Does water baptism save us? See Acts 10:47 comment.

linen, and silk, and broidered work; you did eat fine flour, and honey, and oil: and you were exceeding beautiful, and you did prosper into a kingdom.

14 And your renown went forth among the heathen for your beauty: for it was perfect through my comeliness, which I had put upon you, says the Lord GOD.

15 But you did trust in your own beauty, and played the harlot because of your renown, and poured out your fornications on every one that passed by; his it was.

16 And of your garments you did take, and decked your high places with divers colours, and played the harlot thereupon: the like things shall not come, neither shall it be so.

17 You have also taken your fair jewels of my gold and of my silver, which I had given you, and made to yourself images of men, and did commit whoredom with them,

18 And took your broidered garments, and covered them: and you have set my oil and my incense before them.

19 My meat also which I gave you, fine flour, and oil, and honey, wherewith I fed you, you have even set it before them for a sweet savour: and thus it was, says the Lord GOD.

20 Moreover you have taken your sons and your daughters, whom you have borne to me, and these have you sacrificed to them to be devoured. Is this of your whoredoms a small matter,

21 That you have slain my children, and delivered them to cause them to pass through the fire for them?

22 And in all your abominations and your whoredoms you have not remembered the days of your youth, when you were naked and bare, and were polluted in your blood.

23 And it came to pass after all your wickedness, (woe, woe to you! says the LORD GOD;)

24 That you have also built for yourself an eminent place, and have made you a high place in every street.

25 You have built your high place at every head of the way, and have made your beauty to be abhorred, and have opened your feet to every one that passed by, and multiplied your whoredoms.

26 You have also committed fornication with the Egyptians your neighbours, great of flesh; and have increased your whoredoms, to provoke me to anger.

27 Behold, therefore I have stretched out my hand over you, and have diminished your ordinary food, and delivered you to the will of them that hate you, the daughters of the Philistines, which are ashamed of your lewd way.

28 You have played the whore also with the Assyrians, because you were unsatiable; yea, you have played the harlot with them, and yet could not be satisfied.

29 You have moreover multiplied your fornication in the land of Canaan to Chaldea; and yet you were not satisfied therewith.

30 How weak is your heart, says the LORD GOD, seeing you do all these things, the work of an imperious whorish woman;

31 In that you build your eminent place in the head of every way, and make your high place in every street; and have not been as an harlot, in that you scorn hire;

32 But as a wife that commits adultery, which takes strangers instead of her husband!

33 They give gifts to all whores: but you give your gifts to all your lovers, and hire them, that they may come to you on every side for your whoredom.

34 And the contrary is in you from other women in your whoredoms, whereas none follows you to commit whoredoms: and in that you give a reward, and no reward is given to you, therefore you are contrary.

35 Therefore, O harlot, hear the word of the LORD:

36 Thus says the Lord GOD; Because your filthiness was poured out, and your

nakedness discovered through your whoredoms with your lovers, and with all the idols of your abominations, and by the blood of your children, which you did give to them;

37 Behold, therefore I will gather all your lovers, with whom you have taken pleasure, and all them that you have loved, with all them that you have hated; I will even gather them round about against you, and will discover your nakedness to them, that they may see all your nakedness.

38 And I will judge you, as women that break wedlock and shed blood are judged; and I will give you blood in fury and jealousy.

39 And I will also give you into their hand, and they shall throw down your eminent place, and shall break down your high places: they shall strip you also of your clothes, and shall take your fair jewels, and leave you naked and bare.

40 They shall also bring up a company against you, and they shall stone you with stones, and thrust you through with their swords.

41 And they shall burn your houses with fire, and execute judgments upon you in the sight of many women: and I will cause you to cease from playing the harlot, and you also shall give no hire any more.

42 So will I make my fury toward you to rest, and my jealousy shall depart from you, and I will be quiet, and will be no more angry.

43 Because you have not remembered the days of your youth, but have fretted me in all these things; behold, therefore I also will recompense your way upon your head, says the Lord GOD: and you shall not commit this lewdness above all your abominations.

44 Behold, every one that uses proverbs shall use this proverb against you, saying, As is the mother, so is her daughter.

45 You are your mother's daughter, that lothes her husband and her children; and you are the sister of your sisters, which lothed their husbands and their children: your mother was an Hittite, and your father an Amorite.

46 And your elder sister is Samaria, she and her daughters that dwell at your left hand: and your younger sister, that dwells at your right hand, is Sodom and her daughters.

47 Yet have you not walked after their ways, nor done after their abominations: but, as if that were a very little thing, you were corrupted more than they in all your ways.

48 As I live, says the Lord GOD, Sodom your sister has not done, she nor her daughters, as you have done, you and your daughters.

49 Behold, this was the iniquity of your sister Sodom, pride, fullness of bread, and abundance of idleness was in her and in her daughters, neither did she strengthen the hand of the poor and needy.

50 And they were haughty, and committed abomination before me: therefore I took them away as I saw good.

51 Neither has Samaria committed half of your sins; but you have multiplied your abominations more than they, and have justified your sisters in all your abominations which you have done.

52 You also, which have judged your sisters, bear your own shame for your sins that you have committed more abominable than they: they are more righteous than you: yea, be confounded also, and bear your shame, in that you have justified your sisters.

53 When I shall bring again their captivity, the captivity of Sodom and her daughters, and the captivity of Samaria and her daughters, then will I bring again the captivity of your captives in the midst of them:

54 That you may bear your own shame, and may be confounded in all that you have done, in that you are a comfort to them.

55 When your sisters, Sodom and her daughters, shall return to their former estate, and Samaria and her daughters shall return to their former estate, then you and your daughters shall return to your former estate.

56 For your sister Sodom was not mentioned by your mouth in the day of your pride,

57 Before your wickedness was discovered, as at the time of your reproach of the daughters of Syria, and all that are round about her, the daughters of the Philistines, which despise you round about.

58 You have borne your lewdness and your abominations, says the LORD.

59 For thus says the Lord GOD; I will even deal with you as you have done, which have despised the oath in breaking the covenant.

60 Nevertheless I will remember my covenant with you in the days of your youth, and I will establish with you an everlasting covenant.

61 Then you shall remember your ways, and be ashamed, when you shall receive your sisters, your elder and your younger: and I will give them to you for daughters, but not by your covenant.

62 And I will establish my covenant with you; and you shall know that I am the LORD:

63 That you may remember, and be confounded, and never open your mouth any more because of your shame, when I am pacified toward you for all that you have done, says the Lord GOD.

CHAPTER 17

AND the word of the LORD came to me, saying,

2 Son of man, put forth a riddle, and speak a parable to the house of Israel;

3 And say, Thus says the Lord GOD; A great eagle with great wings, long-winged, full of feathers, which had divers colours, came to Lebanon, and took the highest branch of the cedar:

4 He cropped off the top of his young twigs, and carried it into a land of traffick; he set it in a city of merchants.

5 He took also of the seed of the land, and planted it in a fruitful field; he placed it by great waters, and set it as a willow tree.

6 And it grew, and became a spreading vine of low stature, whose branches turned toward him, and the roots thereof were under him: so it became a vine, and brought forth branches, and shot forth sprigs.

7 There was also another great eagle with great wings and many feathers: and, behold, this vine did bend her roots toward him, and shot forth her branches toward him, that he might water it by the furrows of her plantation.

8 It was planted in a good soil by great waters, that it might bring forth branches, and that it might bear fruit, that it might be a goodly vine.

9 Say, Thus says the Lord GOD; Shall it prosper? shall he not pull up the roots thereof, and cut off the fruit thereof, that it wither? it shall wither in all the leaves of her spring, even without great power or many people to pluck it up by the roots thereof.

10 Yea, behold, being planted, shall it prosper? shall it not utterly wither, when the east wind touches it? it shall wither in the furrows where it grew.

11 Moreover the word of the LORD came to me, saying,

12 Say now to the rebellious house, Do you not know what these things mean? tell them, Behold, the king of Babylon is come to Jerusalem, and has taken the king thereof, and the princes thereof, and led them with him to Babylon;

13 And has taken of the king's seed, and made a covenant with him, and has taken an oath of him: he has also taken the mighty of the land:

14 That the kingdom might be base, that it might not lift itself up, but that by keeping of his covenant it might stand.

15 But he rebelled against him in sending his ambassadors into Egypt, that they might give him horses and much people. Shall he prosper? shall he escape that doeth such things? or shall he break the covenant, and be delivered?

16 As I live, says the Lord GOD, surely in the place where the king dwells that made him king, whose oath he despised, and whose covenant he brake, even with him in the midst of Babylon he shall die.

17 Neither shall Pharaoh with his mighty army and great company make for him in the war, by casting up mounts, and building forts, to cut off many persons:

18 Seeing he despised the oath by breaking the covenant, when, lo, he had given his hand, and has done all these things, he shall not escape.

19 Therefore thus says the Lord GOD; As I live, surely my oath that he has despised, and my covenant that he has broken, even it will I recompense upon his own head.

20 And I will spread my net upon him, and he shall be taken in my snare, and I will bring him to Babylon, and will plead with him there for his trespass that he has trespassed against me.

21 And all his fugitives with all his bands shall fall by the sword, and they that remain shall be scattered toward all winds: and you shall know that I the LORD have spoken it.

22 Thus says the Lord GOD; I will also take of the highest branch of the high cedar, and will set it; I will crop off from the top of his young twigs a tender one, and will plant it upon an high mountain and eminent:

23 In the mountain of the height of Israel will I plant it: and it shall bring forth boughs, and bear fruit, and be a goodly cedar: and under it shall dwell all fowl of every wing; in the shadow of the branches thereof shall they dwell.

24 And all the trees of the field shall know that I the LORD have brought down the high tree, have exalted the low tree, have dried up the green tree, and have made the dry tree to flourish: I the LORD have spoken and have done it.

CHAPTER 18

THE word of the LORD came to me again, saying,

2 What do you mean, that you use this proverb concerning the land of Israel, saying, The fathers have eaten sour grapes, and the children's teeth are set on edge?

3 As I live, says the Lord GOD, you shall not have occasion any more to use this proverb in Israel.

4 Behold, all souls are mine; as the soul of the father, so also the soul of the son is mine: the soul that sins, it shall die.

5 But if a man be just, and do that which is lawful and right,

6 And has not eaten upon the mountains, neither has lifted up his eyes to the idols of the house of Israel, neither has defiled his neighbour's wife, neither has come near to a menstruous woman,

7 And has not oppressed any, but has restored to the debtor his pledge, has spoiled none by violence, has given his bread to the hungry, and has covered the naked with a garment;

8 He that has not given forth upon usury, neither has taken any increase, that has withdrawn his hand from iniquity, has executed true judgment between man and man,

9 Has walked in my statutes, and has kept my judgments, to deal truly; he is just, he shall surely live, says the Lord GOD.

18:4, 20 Violating God's moral Law is deadly to our souls. We are saved only through Jesus' sacrifice, including His descent into hell on our behalf, the only atonement for the sins of the whole world. (See Romans 6:23).

10 If he beget a son that is a robber, a shedder of blood, and that doeth the like to any one of these things,

11 And that doeth not any of those duties, but even has eaten upon the mountains, and defiled his neighbour's wife,

12 Has oppressed the poor and needy, has spoiled by violence, has not restored the pledge, and has lifted up his eyes to the idols, has committed abomination,

13 Has given forth upon usury, and has taken increase: shall he then live? he shall not live: he has done all these abominations; he shall surely die; his blood shall be upon him.

14 Now, lo, if he beget a son, that sees all his father's sins which he has done, and considers, and does not such like,

15 That has not eaten upon the mountains, neither has lifted up his eyes to the idols of the house of Israel, has not defiled his neighbour's wife,

16 Neither has oppressed any, has not withholden the pledge, neither has spoiled by violence, but has given his bread to the hungry, and has covered the naked with a garment,

17 That has taken off his hand from the poor, that has not received usury nor increase, has executed my judgments, has walked in my statutes; he shall not die for the iniquity of his father, he shall surely live.

18 As for his father, because he cruelly oppressed, spoiled his brother by violence, and did that which is not good among his people, lo, even he shall die in his iniquity.

19 Yet you say, Why? does not the son bear the iniquity of the father? When the son has done that which is lawful and right, and has kept all my statutes, and has done them, he shall surely live.

20 The soul that sins, it shall die. The son shall not bear the iniquity of the father, neither shall the father bear the in-iquity of the son: the righteousness of the righteous shall be upon him, and the wickedness of the wicked shall be upon him.

21 But if the wicked will turn from all his sins that he has committed, and keep all my statutes, and do that which is lawful and right, he shall surely live, he shall not die.

22 All his transgressions that he has committed, they shall not be mentioned to him: in his righteousness that he has done he shall live.

23 Have I any pleasure at all that the wicked should die? says the Lord GOD: and not that he should return from his ways, and live?

24 But when the righteous turns away from his righteousness, and commits iniquity, and doeth according to all the abominations that the wicked man doeth, shall he live? All his righteousness that he has done shall not be mentioned: in his trespass that he has trespassed, and in his sin that he has sinned, in them shall he die.

25 Yet you say, The way of the LORD is not equal. Hear now, O house of Israel; Is not my way equal? are not your ways unequal?

26 When a righteous man turns away from his righteousness, and commits iniquity, and dies in them; for his iniquity that he has done shall he die.

27 Again, when the wicked man turns away from his wickedness that he has committed, and doeth that which is lawful and right, he shall save his soul alive.

28 Because he considers, and turns away from all his transgressions that he has committed, he shall surely live, he shall not die.

29 Yet the house of Israel says, The way of the LORD is not equal. O house of Israel, are not my ways equal? are not your ways unequal?

18:25 None of God's judgments are unjust. Rather, our understanding is darkened (see Ephesians 4:18).

30 Therefore I will judge you, O house of Israel, every one according to his ways, says the Lord GOD. Repent, and turn yourselves from all your transgressions; so iniquity shall not be your ruin.

31 Cast away from you all your transgressions, whereby you have transgressed; and make you a new heart and a new spirit: for why will you die, O house of Israel?

32 For I have no pleasure in the death of him that dies, says the Lord GOD: therefore turn yourselves, and live.

CHAPTER 19

MOREOVER take up a lamentation for the princes of Israel,

2 And say, What is your mother? A lioness: she lay down among lions, she nourished her whelps among young lions.

3 And she brought up one of her whelps: it became a young lion, and it learned to catch the prey; it devoured men.

4 The nations also heard of him; he was taken in their pit, and they brought him with chains to the land of Egypt.

5 Now when she saw that she had waited, and her hope was lost, then she took another of her whelps, and made him a young lion.

6 And he went up and down among the lions, he became a young lion, and learned to catch the prey, and devoured men.

7 And he knew their desolate palaces, and he laid waste their cities; and the land was desolate, and the fulness thereof, by the noise of his roaring.

8 Then the nations set against him on every side from the provinces, and spread their net over him: he was taken in their pit.

9 And they put him in ward in chains, and brought him to the king of Babylon: they brought him into holds, that his voice should no more be heard upon the mountains of Israel.

10 Your mother is like a vine in your blood, planted by the waters: she was fruitful and full of branches by reason of many waters.

11 And she had strong rods for the sceptres of them that bare rule, and her stature was exalted among the thick branches, and she appeared in her height with the multitude of her branches.

12 But she was plucked up in fury, she was cast down to the ground, and the east wind dried up her fruit: her strong rods were broken and withered; the fire consumed them.

13 And now she is planted in the wilderness, in a dry and thirsty ground.

14 And fire is gone out of a rod of her branches, which has devoured her fruit, so that she has no strong rod to be a sceptre to rule. This is a lamentation, and shall be for a lamentation.

CHAPTER 20

AND it came to pass in the seventh year, in the fifth month, the tenth day of the month, that certain of the elders of Israel came to inquire of the LORD, and sat before me.

2 Then came the word of the LORD to me, saying,

3 Son of man, speak to the elders of Israel, and say to them, Thus says the Lord GOD; Are you come to inquire of me? As I live, says the Lord GOD, I will not be inquired of by you.

4 Will you judge them, son of man, will you judge them? cause them to know the abominations of their fathers:

5 And say to them, Thus says the Lord GOD; In the day when I chose Israel, and lifted up my hand to the seed of the house of Jacob, and made myself known

---

18:31 This should be the cry within the heart of every Christian. We should be horror-struck by sinners' disregard for their eternal salvation.

to them in the land of Egypt, when I lifted up my hand to them, saying, I am the LORD your God;

6 In the day that I lifted up my hand to them, to bring them forth of the land of Egypt into a land that I had espied for them, flowing with milk and honey, which is the glory of all lands:

7 Then I said to them, Every man cast away the abominations of his eyes, and do not defile yourselves with the idols of Egypt: I am the LORD your God.

8 But they rebelled against me, and would not hearken to me: they did not every man cast away the abominations of their eyes, neither did they forsake the idols of Egypt: then I said, I will pour out my fury upon them, to accomplish my anger against them in the midst of the land of Egypt.

9 But I acted for my name's sake, that it should not be polluted before the heathen, among whom they were, in whose sight I made myself known to them, in bringing them forth out of the land of Egypt.

10 Therefore I caused them to go forth out of the land of Egypt, and brought them into the wilderness.

11 And I gave them my statutes, and showed them my judgments, which if a man do, he shall even live in them.

12 Moreover also I gave them my sabbaths, to be a sign between me and them, that they might know that I am the LORD that sanctify them.

13 But the house of Israel rebelled against me in the wilderness: they walked not in my statutes, and they despised my judgments, which if a man do, he shall even live in them; and my sabbaths they greatly polluted: then I said, I would pour out my fury upon them in the wilderness, to consume them.

14 But I acted for my name's sake, that it should not be polluted before the heathen, in whose sight I brought them out.

15 Yet also I lifted up my hand to them in the wilderness, that I would not bring them into the land which I had given them, flowing with milk and honey, which is the glory of all lands;

16 Because they despised my judgments, and walked not in my statutes, but polluted my sabbaths: for their heart went after their idols.

17 Nevertheless my eye spared them from destroying them, neither did I make an end of them in the wilderness.

18 But I said to their children in the wilderness, Do not walk in the statutes of your fathers, neither observe their judgments, nor defile yourselves with their idols:

19 I am the LORD your God; walk in my statutes, and keep my judgments, and do them;

20 And hallow my sabbaths; and they shall be a sign between me and you, that you may know that I am the LORD your God.

21 Notwithstanding the children rebelled against me: they did not walk in my statutes, neither kept my judgments to do them, which if a man do, he shall even live in them; they polluted my sabbaths: then I said, I would pour out my fury upon them, to accomplish my anger against them in the wilderness.

22 Nevertheless I withdrew my hand, and acted for my name's sake, that it should not be polluted in the sight of the heathen, in whose sight I brought them forth.

23 I lifted up my hand to them also in the wilderness, that I would scatter them among the heathen, and disperse them through the countries;

24 Because they had not executed my judgments, but had despised my

---

20: 8 The essence of sin is a rebellious heart. It is not that they cannot seek God, but that they "will" not. See Psalm 10:4.

statutes, and had polluted my sabbaths, and their eyes were after their fathers' idols.

25 Therefore I gave them also statutes that were not good, and judgments whereby they should not live;

26 And I polluted them in their own gifts, in that they caused to pass through the fire all that opens the womb, that I might make them desolate, to the end that they might know that I am the LORD.

27 Therefore, son of man, speak to the house of Israel, and say to them, Thus says the Lord GOD; Yet in this your fathers have blasphemed me, in that they have committed a trespass against me.

28 For when I had brought them into the land, for the which I lifted up my hand to give it to them, then they saw every high hill, and all the thick trees, and they offered there their sacrifices, and there they presented the provocation of their offering: there also they made their sweet savour, and poured out there their drink offerings.

29 Then I said to them, What is the high place whereunto you go? And the name whereof is called Bamah to this day.

30 Therefore say to the house of Israel, Thus says the Lord GOD; Are you polluted after the manner of your fathers? and committing whoredom after their abominations?

31 For when you offer your gifts, when you make your sons to pass through the fire, you pollute yourselves with all your idols, even to this day: and shall I be enquired of by you, O house of Israel? As I live, says the Lord GOD, I will not be inquired of by you.

32 And that which comes into your mind shall not be at all, that you say, We will be as the heathen, as the families of the countries, to serve wood and stone.

33 As I live, says the Lord GOD, surely with a mighty hand, and with a stretched out arm, and with fury poured out, will I rule over you:

34 And I will bring you out from the people, and will gather you out of the countries wherein you are scattered, with a mighty hand, and with a stretched out arm, and with fury poured out.

35 And I will bring you into the wilderness of the people, and there will I plead with you face to face.

36 Like as I pleaded with your fathers in the wilderness of the land of Egypt, so will I plead with you, says the Lord GOD.

37 And I will cause you to pass under the rod, and I will bring you into the bond of the covenant:

38 And I will purge out from among you the rebels, and them that transgress against me: I will bring them forth out of the country where they sojourn, and they shall not enter into the land of Israel: and you shall know that I am the LORD.

39 As for you, O house of Israel, thus says the Lord GOD; Go, serve every one of you his idols, and hereafter also, if you will not hearken to me: but pollute my holy name no more with your gifts, and with your idols.

40 For in my holy mountain, in the mountain of the height of Israel, says the Lord GOD, there shall all the house of Israel, all of them in the land, serve me: there will I accept them, and there will I require your offerings, and the firstfruits of your oblations, with all your holy things.

41 I will accept you with your sweet savour, when I bring you out from the people, and gather you out of the countries wherein you have been scattered; and I will be sanctified in you before the heathen.

42 And you shall know that I am the LORD, when I shall bring you into the land of Israel, into the country for the which I lifted up my hand to give it to your fathers.

43 And there shall you remember your ways, and all your doings, wherein you

have been defiled; and you shall lothe yourselves in your own sight for all your evils that you have committed.

44 And you shall know that I am the LORD when I have dealt with you for my name's sake, not according to your wicked ways, nor according to your corrupt doings, O you house of Israel, says the Lord GOD.

45 Moreover the word of the LORD came to me, saying,

46 Son of man, set your face toward the south, and drop your word toward the south, and prophesy against the forest of the south field;

47 And say to the forest of the south, Hear the word of the LORD; Thus says the Lord GOD; Behold, I will kindle a fire in you, and it shall devour every green tree in you, and every dry tree: the flaming flame shall not be quenched, and all faces from the south to the north shall be burned therein.

48 And all flesh shall see that I the LORD have kindled it: it shall not be quenched.

49 Then said I, Ah Lord GOD! they say of me, Does he not speak parables?

CHAPTER 21

AND the word of the LORD came to me, saying,

2 Son of man, set your face toward Jerusalem, and drop your word toward the holy places, and prophesy against the land of Israel,

3 And say to the land of Israel, Thus says the LORD; Behold, I am against you, and will draw forth my sword out of his sheath, and will cut off from you the righteous and the wicked.

4 Seeing then that I will cut off from you the righteous and the wicked, therefore shall my sword go forth out of his sheath against all flesh from the south to the north:

5 That all flesh may know that I the LORD have drawn forth my sword out of his sheath: it shall not return any more.

6 Sigh therefore, you son of man, with the breaking of your loins; and with bitterness sigh before their eyes.

7 And it shall be, when they say to you, Why are you sighing? that you shall answer, For the tidings; because it comes: and every heart shall melt, and all hands shall be feeble, and every spirit shall faint, and all knees shall be weak as water: behold, it comes, and shall be brought to pass, says the Lord GOD.

8 Again the word of the LORD came to me, saying,

9 Son of man, prophesy, and say, Thus says the LORD; Say, A sword, a sword is sharpened, and also furbished:

10 It is sharpened to make a sore slaughter; it is furbished that it may glitter: should we then make mirth? it contemneth the rod of my son, as every tree.

11 And he has given it to be furbished, that it may be handled: this sword is sharpened, and it is furbished, to give it into the hand of the slayer.

12 Cry and howl, son of man: for it shall be upon my people, it shall be upon all the princes of Israel: terrors by reason of the sword shall be upon my people: smite therefore upon your thigh.

13 Because it is a trial, and what if the sword contemn even the rod? it shall be no more, says the Lord GOD.

14 You therefore, son of man, prophesy, and smite your hands together. and let the sword be doubled the third time, the sword of the slain: it is the sword of the great men that are slain, which enters into their privy chambers.

15 I have set the point of the sword against all their gates, that their heart may faint, and their ruins be multiplied: ah! it is made bright, it is wrapped up for the slaughter.

16 You go one way or other, either on the right hand, or on the left, wherever your face is set.

17 I will also smite my hands together, and I will cause my fury to rest: I the LORD have said it.

18 The word of the LORD came to me again, saying,

19 Also, you son of man, appoint for yourself two ways, that the sword of the king of Babylon may come: both twain shall come forth out of one land: and choose you a place, choose it at the head of the way to the city.

20 Appoint a way, that the sword may come to Rabbath of the Ammonites, and to Judah in Jerusalem the defenced.

21 For the king of Babylon stood at the parting of the way, at the head of the two ways, to use divination: he made his arrows bright, he consulted with images, he looked in the liver.

22 At his right hand was the divination for Jerusalem, to appoint captains, to open the mouth in the slaughter, to lift up the voice with shouting, to appoint battering rams against the gates, to cast a mount, and to build a fort.

23 And it shall be to them as a false divination in their sight, to them that have sworn oaths: but he will call to remembrance the iniquity, that they may be taken.

24 Therefore thus says the Lord GOD; Because you have made your iniquity to be remembered, in that your transgressions are discovered, so that in all your doings your sins do appear; because, I say, that you are come to remembrance, you shall be taken with the hand.

25 And you, profane wicked prince of Israel, whose day is come, when iniquity shall have an end,

26 Thus says the Lord GOD; Remove the diadem, and take off the crown: this shall not be the same: exalt him that is low, and abase him that is high.

27 I will overturn, overturn, overturn, it: and it shall be no more, until he come whose right it is; and I will give it him.

28 And you, son of man, prophesy and say, Thus says the Lord GOD concerning the Ammonites, and concerning their reproach; even say, The sword, the sword is drawn: for the slaughter it is furbished, to consume because of the glittering:

29 Whiles they see vanity for you, whiles they divine a lie to you, to bring you upon the necks of them that are slain, of the wicked, whose day is come, when their iniquity shall have an end.

30 Shall I cause it to return into his sheath? I will judge you in the place where you were created, in the land of your nativity.

31 And I will pour out my indignation upon you, I will blow against you in the fire of my wrath, and deliver you into the hand of brutish men, and skilful to destroy.

32 You shall be for fuel to the fire; your blood shall be in the midst of the land; you shall be no more remembered: for I the LORD have spoken it.

CHAPTER 22

MOREOVER the word of the LORD came to me, saying,

2 Now, you son of man, will you judge, will you judge the bloody city? yea, you shall show her all her abominations.

3 Then say, Thus says the Lord GOD, The city sheds blood in the midst of it, that her time may come, and makes idols against herself to defile herself.

4 You are become guilty in your blood that you have shed; and have defiled yourself in your idols which you have made; and you have caused your days to draw near, and are come even to your years: therefore I have made you a reproach to the heathen, and a mocking to all countries.

5 Those that are near, and those that are far from you, shall mock you, which are infamous and much vexed.

6 Behold, the princes of Israel, every one were in you to their power to shed blood.

7 In you have they set light by father and mother: in the midst of you have they dealt by oppression with the stranger: in you have they vexed the fatherless and the widow.

8 You have despised my holy things, and have profaned my sabbaths.

9 In you are men that carry tales to shed blood: and in you they eat upon the mountains: in the midst of you they commit lewdness.

10 In you have they discovered their fathers' nakedness: in you have they humbled her that was set apart for pollution.

11 And one has committed abomination with his neighbour's wife; and another has lewdly defiled his daughter in law; and another in you has humbled his sister, his father's daughter.

12 In you have they taken gifts to shed blood; you have taken usury and increase, and you have greedily gained of your neighbours by extortion, and have forgotten me, says the Lord GOD.

13 Behold, therefore I have smitten my hand at your dishonest gain which you have made, and at your blood which has been in the midst of you.

14 Can your heart endure, or can your hands be strong, in the days that I shall deal with you? I the LORD have spoken it, and will do it.

15 And I will scatter you among the heathen, and disperse you in the countries, and will consume your filthiness out of you.

16 And you shall take your inheritance in yourself in the sight of the heathen, and you shall know that I am the LORD.

17 And the word of the LORD came to me, saying,

18 Son of man, the house of Israel is to me become dross: all they are brass, and tin, and iron, and lead, in the midst of the furnace; they are even the dross of silver.

19 Therefore thus says the Lord GOD; Because you are all become dross, behold, therefore I will gather you into the midst of Jerusalem.

20 As they gather silver, and brass, and iron, and lead, and tin, into the midst of the furnace, to blow the fire upon it, to melt it; so will I gather you in my anger and in my fury, and I will leave you there, and melt you.

21 Yea, I will gather you, and blow upon you in the fire of my wrath, and you shall be melted in the midst therof.

22 As silver is melted in the midst of the furnace, so shall you be melted in the midst thereof; and you shall know that I the LORD have poured out my fury upon you.

23 And the word of the LORD came to me, saying,

24 Son of man, say to her, You are the land that is not cleansed, nor rained upon in the day of indignation.

25 There is a conspiracy of her prophets in the midst thereof, like a roaring lion ravening the prey; they have devoured souls; they have taken the treasure and precious things; they have made her many widows in the midst thereof.

26 Her priests have violated my law, and have profaned my holy things: they have put no difference between the holy and profane, neither have they shown difference between the unclean and the clean, and have hid their eyes from my sabbaths, and I am profaned among them.

27 Her princes in the midst thereof are like wolves ravening the prey, to shed blood, and to destroy souls, to get dishonest gain.

28 And her prophets have daubed them with untempered morter, seeing vanity, and divining lies to them, saying, Thus says the Lord GOD, when the LORD has not spoken.

29 The people of the land have used oppression, and exercised robbery, and

---

22:26 When a nation violates God's Law, they no longer make any distinction between good and evil. Abortion, pornography, homosexuality, adultery, lying and stealing become an accepted part of its culture.

have vexed the poor and needy: yea, they have oppressed the stranger wrongfully.

30 And I sought for a man among them, that should make up the hedge, and stand in the gap before me for the land, that I should not destroy it: but I found none.

31 Therefore have I poured out my indignation upon them; I have consumed them with the fire of my wrath: their own way have I recompensed upon their heads, says the Lord GOD.

CHAPTER 23

THE word of the LORD came again to me, saying,

2 Son of man, there were two women, the daughters of one mother:

3 And they committed whoredoms in Egypt; they committed whoredoms in their youth: there were their breasts pressed, and there they bruised the teats of their virginity.

4 And the names of them were Aholah the elder, and Aholibah her sister: and they were mine, and they bare sons and daughters. Thus were their names; Samaria is Aholah, and Jerusalem Aholibah.

5 And Aholah played the harlot when she was mine; and she doted on her lovers, on the Assyrians her neighbours,

6 Which were clothed with blue, captains and rulers, all of them desirable young men, horsemen riding upon horses.

7 Thus she committed her whoredoms with them, with all them that were the chosen men of Assyria, and with all on whom she doted: with all their idols she defiled herself.

8 Neither left she her whoredoms brought from Egypt: for in her youth they lay with her, and they bruised the breasts of her virginity, and poured their whoredom upon her.

9 Therefore I have delivered her into the hand of her lovers, into the hand of the Assyrians, upon whom she doted.

10 These discovered her nakedness: they took her sons and her daughters, and slew her with the sword: and she became famous among women; for they had executed judgment upon her.

11 And when her sister Aholibah saw this, she was more corrupt in her inordinate love than she, and in her whoredoms more than her sister in her whoredoms.

12 She doted upon the Assyrians her neighbours, captains and rulers clothed most gorgeously, horsemen riding upon horses, all of them desirable young men.

13 Then I saw that she was defiled, that they took both one way,

14 And that she increased her whoredoms: for when she saw men portrayed upon the wall, the images of the Chaldeans portrayed with vermilion,

15 Girded with girdles upon their loins, exceeding in dyed attire upon their heads, all of them princes to look to, after the manner of the Babylonians of Chaldea, the land of their nativity:

16 And as soon as she saw them with her eyes, she doted upon them, and sent messengers to them into Chaldea.

17 And the Babylonians came to her into the bed of love, and they defiled her with their whoredom, and she was polluted with them, and her mind was alienated from them.

18 So she discovered her whoredoms, and discovered her nakedness: then my mind was alienated from her, like as my mind was alienated from her sister.

19 Yet she multiplied her whoredoms, in calling to remembrance the days of her youth, wherein she had played the harlot in the land of Egypt.

22:30 This is why there is hope for America. There are many faithful Christians who stand in the righteousness of Christ and therefore can "stand in the gap" for this nation. Pray as though everything depended on God and plead with men as though everything depended on your words.

20 For she doted upon their para-
mours, whose flesh is as the flesh of
asses, and whose issue is like the issue of
horses.

21 Thus you called to remembrance the
lewdness of your youth, in bruising your
teats by the Egyptians for the paps of
your youth.

22 Therefore, O Aholibah, thus says the
Lord GOD; Behold, I will raise up your
lovers against you, from whom your
mind is alienated, and I will bring them
against you on every side;

23 The Babylonians, and all the
Chaldeans, Pekod, and Shoa, and Koa,
and all the Assyrians with them: all of
them desirable young men, captains and
rulers, great lords and renowned, all of
them riding upon horses.

24 And they shall come against you
with chariots, wagons, and wheels, and
with an assembly of people, which shall
set against you buckler and shield and
helmet round about: and I will set judgment before them, and they shall judge
you according to their judgments.

25 And I will set my jealousy against
you, and they shall deal furiously with
you: they shall take away your nose and
your ears; and your remnant shall fall by
the sword: they shall take your sons and
your daughters; and your residue shall
be devoured by the fire.

26 They shall also strip you out of your
clothes, and take away your fair jewels.

27 Thus will I make your lewdness to
cease from you, and your whoredom
brought from the land of Egypt: so that
you shall not lift up your eyes to them,
nor remember Egypt any more.

28 For thus says the Lord GOD;
Behold, I will deliver you into the hand
of them whom you hate, into the hand
of them from whom your mind is alienated:

29 And they shall deal with you hate-
fully, and shall take away all your
labour, and shall leave you naked and
bare: and the nakedness of your

whoredoms shall be discovered, both
your lewdness and your whoredoms.

30 I will do these things to you, because you have gone a whoring after the
heathen, and because you are polluted
with their idols.

31 You have walked in the way of your
sister; therefore will I give her cup into
your hand.

32 Thus says the Lord GOD; You shall
drink of your sister's cup deep and large:
you shall be laughed to scorn and had in
derision; it contains much.

33 You shall be filled with drunkenness
and sorrow, with the cup of astonishment and desolation, with the cup of
your sister Samaria.

34 You shall even drink it and suck it
out, and you shall break the sherds
thereof, and pluck off your own breasts:
for I have spoken it, says the Lord GOD.

35 Therefore thus says the Lord GOD;
Because you have forgotten me, and cast
me behind your back, therefore you also
bear your lewdness and your whoredoms.

36 The LORD said moreover to me;
Son of man, will you judge Aholah and
Aholibah? yea, declare to them their
abominations;

37 That they have committed adultery,
and blood is in their hands, and with
their idols have they committed adultery, and have also caused their sons,
whom they bare to me, to pass for them
through the fire, to devour them.

38 Moreover this they have done to me:
they have defiled my sanctuary in the
same day, and have profaned my sabbaths.

39 For when they had slain their children to their idols, then they came the
same day into my sanctuary to profane
it; and, lo, thus have they done in the
midst of my house.

40 And furthermore, that you have sent
for men to come from far, to whom a
messenger was sent; and, lo, they came:
for whom you did wash yourself,

painted your eyes, and decked yourself with ornaments,

41 And sat upon a stately bed, and a table prepared before it, whereupon you have set my incense and my oil.

42 And a voice of a multitude being at ease was with her: and with the men of the common sort were brought Sabeans from the wilderness, which put bracelets upon their hands, and beautiful crowns upon their heads.

43 Then I said to her that was old in adulteries, Will they now commit whoredoms with her, and she with them?

44 Yet they went in to her, as they go in to a woman that plays the harlot: so they went in to Aholah and Aholibah, the lewd women.

45 And the righteous men, they shall judge them after the manner of adulteresses, and after the manner of women that shed blood; because they are adulteresses, and blood is in their hands.

46 For thus says the Lord GOD; I will bring up a company upon them, and will give them to be removed and spoiled.

47 And the company shall stone them with stones, and dispatch them with their swords; they shall slay their sons and their daughters, and burn up their houses with fire.

48 Thus will I cause lewdness to cease out of the land, that all women may be taught not to do after your lewdness.

49 And they shall recompense your lewdness upon you, and you shall bear the sins of your idols: and you shall know that I am the Lord GOD.

CHAPTER 24

AGAIN in the ninth year, in the tenth month, in the tenth day of the month, the word of the LORD came to me, saying,

2 Son of man, write the name of the day, even of this same day: the king of Babylon set himself against Jerusalem this same day.

3 And utter a parable to the rebellious house, and say to them, Thus says the Lord GOD; Set on a pot, set it on, and also pour water into it:

4 Gather the pieces thereof into it, even every good piece, the thigh, and the shoulder; fill it with the choice bones.

5 Take the choice of the flock, and burn also the bones under it, and make it boil well, and let them seethe the bones of it therein.

6 Therefore thus says the Lord GOD; Woe to the bloody city, to the pot whose scum is therein, and whose scum is not gone out of it! bring it out piece by piece; let no lot fall upon it.

7 For her blood is in the midst of her; she set it upon the top of a rock; she poured it not upon the ground, to cover it with dust;

8 That it might cause fury to come up to take vengeance; I have set her blood upon the top of a rock, that it should not be covered.

9 Therefore thus says the Lord GOD; Woe to the bloody city! I will even make the pile for fire great.

10 Heap on wood, kindle the fire, consume the flesh, and spice it well, and let the bones be burned.

11 Then set it empty upon the coals thereof, that the brass of it may be hot, and may burn, and that the filthiness of it may be molten in it, that the scum of it may be consumed.

12 She has wearied herself with lies, and her great scum went not forth out of her: her scum shall be in the fire.

13 In your filthiness is lewdness: because I have purged you, and you were not purged, you shall not be purged from your filthiness any more, till I have caused my fury to rest upon you.

14 I the LORD have spoken it: it shall come to pass, and I will do it; I will not go back, neither will I spare, neither will I repent; according to your ways, and according to your doings, shall they judge you, says the Lord GOD.

15 Also the word of the LORD came to me, saying,

16 Son of man, behold, I take away from you the desire of your eyes with a stroke: yet neither shall you mourn nor weep, neither shall your tears run down.

17 Forbear to cry, make no mourning for the dead, bind the tire of your head upon you, and put on your shoes upon your feet, and do not cover your lips, and do not eat the bread of men.

18 So I spoke to the people in the morning: and at even my wife died; and I did in the morning as I was commanded.

19 And the people said to me, Will you not tell us what these things are to us, that you do so?

20 Then I answered them, The word of the LORD came to me, saying,

21 Speak to the house of Israel, Thus says the Lord GOD; Behold, I will profane my sanctuary, the excellency of your strength, the desire of your eyes, and that which your soul pities; and your sons and your daughters whom you have left shall fall by the sword.

22 And you shall do as I have done: you shall not cover your lips, nor eat the bread of men.

23 And your tires shall be upon your heads, and your shoes upon your feet: you shall not mourn nor weep; but you shall pine away for your iniquities, and mourn one toward another.

24 Thus Ezekiel is to you a sign: according to all that he has done shall you do: and when this comes, you shall know that I am the Lord GOD.

25 Also, you son of man, shall it not be in the day when I take from them their strength, the joy of their glory, the desire of their eyes, and that whereupon they set their minds, their sons and their daughters,

26 That he that escapes in that day shall come to you, to cause you to hear it with your ears?

27 In that day shall your mouth be opened to him which is escaped, and you shall speak, and be no more dumb: and you shall be a sign to them; and they shall know that I am the LORD.

CHAPTER 25

THE word of the LORD came again to me, saying,

2 Son of man, set your face against the Ammonites, and prophesy against them;

3 And say to the Ammonites, Hear the word of the Lord GOD; Thus says the Lord GOD; Because you said, Aha, against my sanctuary, when it was profaned; and against the land of Israel, when it was desolate; and against the house of Judah, when they went into captivity;

4 Behold, therefore I will deliver you to the men of the east for a possession, and they shall set their palaces in you, and make their dwellings in you: they shall eat your fruit, and they shall drink your milk.

5 And I will make Rabbah a stable for camels, and the Ammonites a couching place for flocks: and you shall know that I am the LORD.

6 For thus says the Lord GOD; Because you have clapped your hands, and stamped with the feet, and rejoiced in heart with all your despite against the land of Israel;

7 Behold, therefore I will stretch out my hand upon you, and will deliver you for a spoil to the heathen; and I will cut you off from the people, and I will cause you to perish out of the countries: I will destroy you; and you shall know that I am the LORD.

8 Thus says the Lord GOD; Because that Moab and Seir do say, Behold, the house of Judah is like all the heathen;

9 Therefore, behold, I will open the side of Moab from the cities, from his cities which are on his frontiers, the glory of the country, Bethjeshimoth, Baalmeon, and Kiriathaim,

10 To the men of the east with the Ammonites, and will give them in

possession, that the Ammonites may not be remembered among the nations.

11 And I will execute judgments upon Moab; and they shall know that I am the LORD.

12 Thus says the Lord GOD; Because that Edom has dealt against the house of Judah by taking vengeance, and has greatly offended, and revenged himself upon them;

13 Therefore thus says the Lord GOD; I will also stretch out my hand upon Edom, and will cut off man and beast from it; and I will make it desolate from Teman; and they of Dedan shall fall by the sword.

14 And I will lay my vengeance upon Edom by the hand of my people Israel: and they shall do in Edom according to my anger and according to my fury; and they shall know my vengeance, says the Lord GOD.

15 Thus says the Lord GOD; Because the Philistines have dealt by revenge, and have taken vengeance with a despiteful heart, to destroy it for the old hatred;

16 Therefore thus says the Lord GOD; Behold, I will stretch out my hand upon the Philistines, and I will cut off the Cherethims, and destroy the remnant of the sea coast.

17 And I will execute great vengeance upon them with furious rebukes; and they shall know that I am the LORD, when I shall lay my vengeance upon them.

CHAPTER 26

AND it came to pass in the eleventh year, in the first day of the month, that the word of the LORD came to me, saying,

2 Son of man, because that Tyrus has said against Jerusalem, Aha, she is broken that was the gates of the people: she is turned to me: I shall be replenished, now she is laid waste:

3 Therefore thus says the Lord GOD; Behold, I am against you, O Tyrus, and will cause many nations to come up against you, as the sea causes his waves to come up.

4 And they shall destroy the walls of Tyrus, and break down her towers: I will also scrape her dust from her, and make her like the top of a rock.

5 It shall be a place for the spreading of nets in the midst of the sea: for I have spoken it, says the Lord GOD: and it shall become a spoil to the nations.

6 And her daughters which are in the field shall be slain by the sword; and they shall know that I am the LORD.

7 For thus says the Lord GOD; Behold, I will bring upon Tyrus Nebuchadrezzar king of Babylon, a king of kings, from the north, with horses, and with chariots, and with horsemen, and companies, and much people.

8 He shall slay with the sword your daughters in the field: and he shall make a fort against you, and cast a mount against you, and lift up the buckler against you.

9 And he shall set engines of war against your walls, and with his axes he shall break down your towers.

10 By reason of the abundance of his horses their dust shall cover you: your walls shall shake at the noise of the horsemen, and of the wheels, and of the chariots, when he shall enter into your gates, as men enter into a city wherein is made a breach.

11 With the hoofs of his horses shall he tread down all your streets: he shall slay your people by the sword, and your strong garrisons shall go down to the ground.

12 And they shall make a spoil of your riches, and make a prey of your merchandise: and they shall break down your walls, and destroy your pleasant houses: and they shall lay your stones and your timber and your dust in the midst of the water.

13 And I will cause the noise of your songs to cease; and the sound of your harps shall be no more heard.

14 And I will make you like the top of a rock: you shall be a place to spread nets upon; you shall be built no more: for I the LORD have spoken it, says the Lord GOD.

15 Thus says the Lord GOD to Tyrus; Shall not the isles shake at the sound of your fall, when the wounded cry, when the slaughter is made in the midst of you?

16 Then all the princes of the sea shall come down from their thrones, and lay away their robes, and put off their broidered garments: they shall clothe themselves with trembling; they shall sit upon the ground, and shall tremble at every moment, and be astonished at you.

17 And they shall take up a lamentation for you, and say to you, How are you destroyed, that were inhabited of seafaring men, the renowned city, which was strong in the sea, she and her inhabitants, which cause their terror to be on all that haunt it!

18 Now shall the isles tremble in the day of your fall; yea, the isles that are in the sea shall be troubled at your departure.

19 For thus says the Lord GOD; When I shall make you a desolate city, like the cities that are not inhabited; when I shall bring up the deep upon you, and great waters shall cover you;

20 When I shall bring you down with them that descend into the pit, with the people of old time, and shall set you in the low parts of the earth, in places desolate of old, with them that go down to the pit, that you be not inhabited; and I shall set glory in the land of the living;

21 I will make you a terror, and you shall be no more: though you are sought for, yet you shall never be found again, says the Lord GOD.

CHAPTER 27

THE word of the LORD came again to me, saying,

2 Now, you son of man, take up a lamentation for Tyrus;

3 And say to Tyrus, O you that are situate at the entry of the sea, which are a merchant of the people for many isles, Thus says the Lord GOD; O Tyrus, you have said, I am of perfect beauty.

4 Your borders are in the midst of the seas, your builders have perfected your beauty.

5 They have made all your ship boards of fir trees of Senir: they have taken cedars from Lebanon to make masts for you.

6 Of the oaks of Bashan have they made your oars; the company of the Ashurites have made your benches of ivory, brought out of the isles of Chittim.

7 Fine linen with broidered work from Egypt was that which you spread forth to be your sail; blue and purple from the isles of Elishah was that which covered you.

8 The inhabitants of Zidon and Arvad were your mariners: your wise men, O Tyrus, that were in you, were your pilots.

9 The elders of Gebal and the wise men thereof were in you your calkers: all the ships of the sea with their mariners were in you to occupy your merchandise.

10 They of Persia and of Lud and of Phut were in your army, your men of war: they hanged the shield and helmet in you; they set forth your splendor.

11 The men of Arvad with your army were upon your walls round about, and the Gammadims were in your towers: they hanged their shields upon your walls round about; they have made your beauty perfect.

12 Tarshish was your merchant by reason of the multitude of all kind of riches; with silver, iron, tin, and lead, they traded in your fairs.

13 Javan, Tubal, and Meshech, they were your merchants: they traded the persons of men and vessels of brass in your market.

14 They of the house of Togarmah traded in your fairs with horses and horsemen and mules.

15 The men of Dedan were your merchants; many isles were the merchandise of your hand: they brought you for a present horns of ivory and ebony.

16 Syria was your merchant by reason of the multitude of the wares of your making: they occupied in your fairs with emeralds, purple, and broidered work, and fine linen, and coral, and agate.

17 Judah, and the land of Israel, they were your merchants: they traded in your market wheat of Minnith, and Pannag, and honey, and oil, and balm.

18 Damascus was your merchant in the multitude of the wares of your making, for the multitude of all riches; in the wine of Helbon, and white wool.

19 Dan also and Javan going to and fro occupied in your fairs: bright iron, cassia, and calamus, were in your market.

20 Dedan was your merchant in precious clothes for chariots.

21 Arabia, and all the princes of Kedar, they occupied with you in lambs, and rams, and goats: in these were they your merchants.

22 The merchants of Sheba and Raamah, they were your merchants: they occupied in your fairs with chief of all spices, and with all precious stones, and gold.

23 Haran, and Canneh, and Eden, the merchants of Sheba, Asshur, and Chilmad, were your merchants.

24 These were your merchants in all sorts of things, in blue clothes, and broidered work, and in chests of rich apparel, bound with cords, and made of cedar, among your merchandise.

25 The ships of Tarshish did sing of you in your market: and you were replenished, and made very glorious in the midst of the seas.

26 Your rowers have brought you into great waters: the east wind has broken you in the midst of the seas.

27 Your riches, and your fairs, your merchandise, your mariners, and your pilots, your calkers, and the occupiers of your merchandise, and all your men of war, that are in you, and in all your company which is in the midst of you, shall fall into the midst of the seas in the day of your ruin.

28 The suburbs shall shake at the sound of the cry of your pilots.

29 And all that handle the oar, the mariners, and all the pilots of the sea, shall come down from their ships, they shall stand upon the land;

30 And shall cause their voice to be heard against you, and shall cry bitterly, and shall cast up dust upon their heads, they shall wallow themselves in the ashes:

31 And they shall make themselves utterly bald for you, and gird them with sackcloth, and they shall weep for you with bitterness of heart and bitter wailing.

32 And in their wailing they shall take up a lamentation for you, and lament over you, saying, What city is like Tyrus, like the destroyed in the midst of the sea?

33 When your wares went forth out of the seas, you filled many people; you did enrich the kings of the earth with the multitude of your riches and of your merchandise.

34 In the time when you shall be broken by the seas in the depths of the waters your merchandise and all your company in the midst of you shall fall.

35 All the inhabitants of the isles shall be astonished at you, and their kings shall be sore afraid, they shall be troubled in their countenance.

36 The merchants among the people shall hiss at you; you shall be a terror, and never shall be any more.

CHAPTER 28

THE word of the LORD came again to me, saying,

2 Son of man, say to the prince of Tyrus, Thus says the Lord GOD; Because your heart is lifted up, and you have said, I am a God, I sit in the seat of God, in the midst of the seas; yet you are a

man, and not God, though you set your heart as the heart of God:

3 Behold, you are wiser than Daniel; there is no secret that they can hide from you:

4 With your wisdom and with your understanding you have gained riches for yourself, and have gathered gold and silver into your treasures:

5 By your great wisdom and by your traffick have you increased your riches, and your heart is lifted up because of your riches:

6 Therefore thus says the Lord GOD; Because you have set your heart as the heart of God;

7 Behold, therefore I will bring strangers upon you, the terrible of the nations: and they shall draw their swords against the beauty of your wisdom, and they shall defile your brightness.

8 They shall bring you down to the pit, and you shall die the deaths of them that are slain in the midst of the seas.

9 Will you yet say before him that slays you, I am God? but you shall be a man, and no God, in the hand of him that slays you.

10 You shall die the deaths of the uncircumcised by the hand of strangers: for I have spoken it, says the Lord GOD.

11 Moreover the word of the LORD came to me, saying,

12 Son of man, take up a lamentation upon the king of Tyrus, and say to him, Thus says the Lord GOD; You seal up the sum, full of wisdom, and perfect in beauty.

13 You have been in Eden the garden of God; every precious stone was your covering, the sardius, topaz, and the diamond, the beryl, the onyx, and the jasper, the sapphire, the emerald, and the carbuncle, and gold: the workmanship of your tabrets and of your pipes was prepared in you in the day that you were created.

14 You are the anointed cherub that covers; and I have set you so: you were upon the holy mountain of God; you have walked up and down in the midst of the stones of fire.

15 You were perfect in your ways from the day that you were created, till iniquity was found in you.

16 By the multitude of your merchandise they have filled the midst of you with violence, and you have sinned: therefore I will cast you as profane out of the mountain of God: and I will destroy you, O covering cherub, from the midst of the stones of fire.

17 Your heart was lifted up because of your beauty, you have corrupted your wisdom by reason of your brightness: I will cast you to the ground, I will lay you before kings, that they may behold you.

18 You have defiled your sanctuaries by the multitude of your iniquities, by the iniquity of your traffick; therefore will I bring forth a fire from the midst of you, it shall devour you, and I will bring you to ashes upon the earth in the sight of all them that behold you.

19 All they that know you among the people shall be astonished at you: you shall be a terror, and never shall you be any more.

20 Again the word of the LORD came to me, saying,

21 Son of man, set your face against Zidon, and prophesy against it,

22 And say, Thus says the Lord GOD; Behold, I am against you, O Zidon; and I will be glorified in the midst of you: and they shall know that I am the LORD, when I shall have executed judgments in her, and shall be sanctified in her.

23 For I will send into her pestilence, and blood into her streets; and the wounded shall be judged in the midst of her by the sword upon her on every side; and they shall know that I am the LORD.

24 And there shall be no more a pricking brier to the house of Israel, nor any grieving thorn of all that are round about

them, that despised them; and they shall know that I am the Lord GOD.

25 Thus says the Lord GOD; When I shall have gathered the house of Israel from the people among whom they are scattered, and shall be sanctified in them in the sight of the heathen, then shall they dwell in their land that I have given to my servant Jacob.

26 And they shall dwell safely therein, and shall build houses, and plant vineyards; yea, they shall dwell with confidence, when I have executed judgments upon all those that despise them round about them; and they shall know that I am the LORD their God.

CHAPTER 29

IN the tenth year, in the tenth month, in the twelfth day of the month, the word of the LORD came to me, saying,

2 Son of man, set your face against Pharaoh king of Egypt, and prophesy against him, and against all Egypt:

3 Speak, and say, Thus says the Lord GOD; Behold, I am against you, Pharaoh king of Egypt, the great dragon that lieth in the midst of his rivers, which has said, My river is my own, and I have made it for myself.

4 But I will put hooks in your jaws, and I will cause the fish of your rivers to stick to your scales, and I will bring you up out of the midst of your rivers, and all the fish of your rivers shall stick to your scales.

5 And I will leave you thrown into the wilderness, you and all the fish of your rivers: you shall fall upon the open fields; you shall not be brought together, nor gathered: I have given you for meat to the beasts of the field and to the fowls of the heaven.

6 And all the inhabitants of Egypt shall know that I am the LORD, because they have been a staff of reed to the house of Israel.

7 When they took hold of you by your hand, you did break, and rend all their shoulder: and when they leaned upon you, you broke, and made all their loins to be at a stand.

8 Therefore thus says the Lord GOD; Behold, I will bring a sword upon you, and cut off man and beast out of you.

9 And the land of Egypt shall be desolate and waste; and they shall know that I am the LORD: because he has said, The river is mine, and I have made it.

10 Behold, therefore I am against you, and against your rivers, and I will make the land of Egypt utterly waste and desolate, from the tower of Syene even to the border of Ethiopia.

11 No foot of man shall pass through it, nor foot of beast shall pass through it, neither shall it be inhabited forty years.

12 And I will make the land of Egypt desolate in the midst of the countries that are desolate, and her cities among the cities that are laid waste shall be desolate forty years: and I will scatter the Egyptians among the nations, and will disperse them through the countries.

13 Yet thus says the Lord GOD; At the end of forty years will I gather the Egyptians from the people where they were scattered:

14 And I will bring again the captivity of Egypt, and will cause them to return into the land of Pathros, into the land of their habitation; and they shall be there a base kingdom.

15 It shall be the basest of the kingdoms; neither shall it exalt itself any more above the nations: for I will diminish them, that they shall no more rule over the nations.

16 And it shall be no more the confidence of the house of Israel, which brings their iniquity to remembrance, when they shall look after them: but they shall know that I am the Lord GOD.

17 And it came to pass in the seven and twentieth year, in the first month, in the first day of the month, the word of the LORD came to me, saying,

18 Son of man, Nebuchadrezzar king of Babylon caused his army to serve a great

> In the Irish Revival of 1859, people became so weak
> that they could not get back to their homes.
> Men and women would fall by the wayside
> and would be found hours later pleading with God to save their souls.
> They felt that they were slipping into hell and that nothing else in life mattered
> but to get right with God...
> To them eternity meant everything. Nothing else was of any consequence.
> They felt that if God did not have mercy on them and save them,
> they were doomed for all time to come.

OSWALD J. SMITH
BORN 1890 IN CANADA
EVANGELICAL PREACHER, MISSIONARY AND HYMN COMPOSER

service against Tyrus: every head was made bald, and every shoulder was peeled: yet had he no wages, nor his army, for Tyrus, for the service that he had served against it:

19 Therefore thus says the Lord GOD; Behold, I will give the land of Egypt to Nebuchadrezzar king of Babylon; and he shall take her multitude, and take her spoil, and take her prey; and it shall be the wages for his army.

20 I have given him the land of Egypt for his labour wherewith he served against it, because they worked for me, says the Lord GOD.

21 In that day will I cause the horn of the house of Israel to bud forth, and I will give you the opening of the mouth in the midst of them; and they shall know that I am the LORD.

CHAPTER 30

THE word of the LORD came again to me, saying,

2 Son of man, prophesy and say, Thus says the Lord GOD; Howl, Woe worth the day!

3 For the day is near, even the day of the LORD is near, a cloudy day; it shall be the time of the heathen.

4 And the sword shall come upon Egypt, and great pain shall be in Ethiopia, when the slain shall fall in Egypt, and they shall take away her multitude, and her foundations shall be broken down.

5 Ethiopia, and Libya, and Lydia, and all the mingled people, and Chub, and the men of the land that is in league, shall fall with them by the sword.

6 Thus says the LORD; They also that uphold Egypt shall fall; and the pride of her power shall come down: from the tower of Syene shall they fall in it by the sword, says the Lord GOD.

7 And they shall be desolate in the midst of the countries that are desolate, and her cities shall be in the midst of the cities that are wasted.

8 And they shall know that I am the LORD, when I have set a fire in Egypt, and when all her helpers shall be destroyed.

9 In that day shall messengers go forth from me in ships to make the careless Ethiopians afraid, and great pain shall come upon them, as in the day of Egypt: for, lo, it comes.

10 Thus says the Lord GOD; I will also make the multitude of Egypt to cease by the hand of Nebuchadrezzar king of Babylon.

11 He and his people with him, the terrible of the nations, shall be brought to destroy the land: and they shall draw their swords against Egypt, and fill the land with the slain.

12 And I will make the rivers dry, and sell the land into the hand of the wicked: and I will make the land waste, and all that is therein, by the hand of strangers: I the LORD have spoken it.

13 Thus says the Lord GOD; I will also destroy the idols, and I will cause their images to cease out of Noph; and there shall be no more a prince of the land of Egypt: and I will put a fear in the land of Egypt.

14 And I will make Pathros desolate, and will set fire in Zoan, and will execute judgments in No.

15 And I will pour my fury upon Sin, the strength of Egypt; and I will cut off the multitude of No.

16 And I will set fire in Egypt: Sin shall have great pain, and No shall be rent asunder, and Noph shall have distresses daily.

17 The young men of Aven and of Pibeseth shall fall by the sword: and these cities shall go into captivity.

18 At Tehaphnehes also the day shall be darkened, when I shall break there the yokes of Egypt: and the pomp of her strength shall cease in her: as for her, a cloud shall cover her, and her daughters shall go into captivity.

19 Thus will I execute judgments in Egypt: and they shall know that I am the LORD.

20 And it came to pass in the eleventh year, in the first month, in the seventh day of the month, that the word of the LORD came to me, saying,

21 Son of man, I have broken the arm of Pharaoh king of Egypt; and, lo, it shall not be bound up to be healed, to put a roller to bind it, to make it strong to hold the sword.

22 Therefore thus says the Lord GOD; Behold, I am against Pharaoh king of Egypt, and will break his arms, the strong, and that which was broken; and I will cause the sword to fall out of his hand.

23 And I will scatter the Egyptians among the nations, and will disperse them through the countries.

24 And I will strengthen the arms of the king of Babylon, and put my sword in his hand: but I will break Pharaoh's arms, and he shall groan before him with the groanings of a deadly wounded man.

25 But I will strengthen the arms of the king of Babylon, and the arms of Pharaoh shall fall down; and they shall know that I am the LORD, when I shall put my sword into the hand of the king of Babylon, and he shall stretch it out upon the land of Egypt.

26 And I will scatter the Egyptians among the nations, and disperse them among the countries; and they shall know that I am the LORD.

CHAPTER 31

AND it came to pass in the eleventh year, in the third month, in the first day of the month, that the word of the LORD came to me, saying,

2 Son of man, speak to Pharaoh king of Egypt, and to his multitude; Whom are you like in your greatness?

3 Behold, the Assyrian was a cedar in Lebanon with fair branches, and with a shadowing shroud, and of an high stature; and his top was among the thick boughs.

4 The waters made him great, the deep set him up on high with her rivers running round about his plants, and sent her little rivers to all the trees of the field.

5 Therefore his height was exalted above all the trees of the field, and his boughs were multiplied, and his branches became long because of the multitude of waters, when he shot forth.

6 All the fowls of heaven made their nests in his boughs, and under his branches did all the beasts of the field bring forth their young, and under his shadow dwelt all great nations.

7 Thus was he fair in his greatness, in the length of his branches: for his root was by great waters.

8 The cedars in the garden of God could not hide him: the fir trees were not like his boughs, and the chestnut trees were not like his branches; nor any tree in the garden of God was like him in his beauty.

9 I have made him fair by the multitude of his branches: so that all the trees of Eden, that were in the garden of God, envied him.

10 Therefore thus says the Lord GOD; Because you have lifted up yourself in height, and he has shot up his top among the thick boughs, and his heart is lifted up in his height;

11 I have therefore delivered him into the hand of the mighty one of the heathen; he shall surely deal with him: I have driven him out for his wickedness.

12 And strangers, the terrible of the nations, have cut him off, and have left him: upon the mountains and in all the valleys his branches are fallen, and his boughs are broken by all the rivers of the land; and all the people of the earth are gone down from his shadow, and have left him.

13 Upon his ruin shall all the fowls of the heaven remain, and all the beasts of the field shall be upon his branches:

14 To the end that none of all the trees by the waters exalt themselves for their height, neither shoot up their top among the thick boughs, neither their trees stand up in their height, all that drink water: for they are all delivered to death, to the nether parts of the earth, in the midst of the children of men, with them that go down to the pit.

15 Thus says the Lord GOD; In the day when he went down to the grave I caused a mourning: I covered the deep for him, and I restrained the floods thereof, and the great waters were stayed: and I caused Lebanon to mourn for him, and all the trees of the field fainted for him.

16 I made the nations to shake at the sound of his fall, when I cast him down to hell with them that descend into the pit: and all the trees of Eden, the choice and best of Lebanon, all that drink water, shall be comforted in the nether parts of the earth.

17 They also went down into hell with him to them that be slain with the sword; and they that were his arm, that dwelt under his shadow in the midst of the heathen.

18 To whom are you thus like in glory and in greatness among the trees of Eden? yet shall you be brought down with the trees of Eden to the nether parts of the earth: you shall lie in the midst of the uncircumcised with them that be slain by the sword. This is Pharaoh and all his multitude, says the Lord GOD.

CHAPTER 32

AND it came to pass in the twelfth year, in the twelfth month, in the first day of the month, that the word of the LORD came to me, saying,

2 Son of man, take up a lamentation for Pharaoh king of Egypt, and say to him, You are like a young lion of the nations, and you are as a whale in the seas: and you came forth with your rivers, and troubled the waters with your feet, and fouled their rivers.

3 Thus says the Lord GOD; I will therefore spread out my net over you with a company of many people; and they shall bring you up in my net.

4 Then will I leave you upon the land, I will cast you forth upon the open field, and will cause all the fowls of the heaven to remain upon you, and I will fill the beasts of the whole earth with you.

5 And I will lay your flesh upon the mountains, and fill the valleys with your height.

6 I will also water with your blood the land wherein you swim, even to the mountains; and the rivers shall be full of you.

7 And when I shall put you out, I will cover the heaven, and make the stars thereof dark; I will cover the sun with a cloud, and the moon shall not give her light.

8 All the bright lights of heaven will I make dark over you, and set darkness upon your land, says the Lord GOD.

9 I will also vex the hearts of many people, when I shall bring your destruction among the nations, into the countries which you have not known.

10 Yea, I will make many people amazed at you, and their kings shall be horribly afraid for you, when I shall brandish my sword before them; and they shall tremble at every moment, every man for his own life, in the day of your fall.

11 For thus says the Lord GOD; The sword of the king of Babylon shall come upon you.

12 By the swords of the mighty will I cause your multitude to fall, the terrible of the nations, all of them: and they shall spoil the pomp of Egypt, and all the multitude thereof shall be destroyed.

13 I will destroy also all the beasts thereof from beside the great waters; neither shall the foot of man trouble them any more, nor the hoofs of beasts trouble them.

14 Then will I make their waters deep, and cause their rivers to run like oil, says the Lord GOD.

15 When I shall make the land of Egypt desolate, and the country shall be destitute of that whereof it was full, when I shall smite all them that dwell therein, then shall they know that I am the LORD.

16 This is the lamentation wherewith they shall lament her: the daughters of the nations shall lament her: they shall lament for her, even for Egypt, and for all her multitude, says the Lord GOD.

17 It came to pass also in the twelfth year, in the fifteenth day of the month, that the word of the LORD came to me, saying,

18 Son of man, wail for the multitude of Egypt, and cast them down, even her, and the daughters of the famous nations, to the nether parts of the earth, with them that go down into the pit.

19 Whom dost you pass in beauty? go down, and be laid with the uncircumcised.

20 They shall fall in the midst of them that are slain by the sword: she is delivered to the sword: draw her and all her multitudes.

21 The strong among the mighty shall speak to him out of the midst of hell with them that help him: they are gone down, they lie uncircumcised, slain by the sword.

22 Asshur is there and all her company: his graves are about him: all of them slain, fallen by the sword:

23 Whose graves are set in the sides of the pit, and her company is round about her grave: all of them slain, fallen by the sword, which caused terror in the land of the living.

24 There is Elam and all her multitude round about her grave, all of them slain, fallen by the sword, which are gone down uncircumcised into the nether parts of the earth, which caused their terror in the land of the living; yet have they borne their shame with them that go down to the pit.

25 They have set her a bed in the midst of the slain with all her multitude: her graves are round about him: all of them uncircumcised, slain by the sword: though their terror was caused in the land of the living, yet have they borne their shame with them that go down to the pit: he is put in the midst of them that be slain.

26 There is Meshech, Tubal, and all her multitude: her graves are round about him: all of them uncircumcised, slain by the sword, though they caused their terror in the land of the living.

27 And they shall not lie with the mighty that are fallen of the uncircumcised, which are gone down to hell with their weapons of war: and they have laid their swords under their heads, but their iniquities shall be upon their bones, though they were the terror of the mighty in the land of the living.

28 Yea, you shall be broken in the midst of the uncircumcised, and shall lie with them that are slain with the sword.

29 There is Edom, her kings, and all her princes, which with their might are laid by them that were slain by the sword: they shall lie with the uncircumcised, and with them that go down to the pit.

30 There be the princes of the north, all of them, and all the Zidonians, which are gone down with the slain; with their terror they are ashamed of their might; and they lie uncircumcised with them that be slain by the sword, and bear their shame with them that go down to the pit.

31 Pharaoh shall see them, and shall be comforted over all his multitude, even Pharaoh and all his army slain by the sword, says the Lord GOD.

32 For I have caused my terror in the land of the living: and he shall be laid in the midst of the uncircumcised with them that are slain with the sword, even Pharaoh and all his multitude, says the Lord GOD.

CHAPTER 33

AGAIN the word of the LORD came to me, saying,

2 Son of man, speak to the children of your people, and say to them, When I bring the sword upon a land, if the people of the land take a man of their coasts, and set him for their watchman:

3 If when he sees the sword come upon the land, he blow the trumpet, and warn the people;

4 Then whosoever hears the sound of the trumpet, and does not take warning; if the sword come, and take him away, his blood shall be upon his own head.

5 He heard the sound of the trumpet, and took not warning; his blood shall be upon him. But he that takes warning shall deliver his soul.

6 But if the watchman see the sword come, and blow not the trumpet, and the people be not warned; if the sword come, and take any person from among them, he is taken away in his iniquity; but his blood will I require at the watchman's hand.

7 *So you, O son of man, I have set you a watchman to the house of Israel; therefore you shall hear the word at my mouth, and warn them from me.*

8 *When I say to the wicked, O wicked man, you shall surely die; if you do not speak to warn the wicked from his way, that wicked man shall die in his iniquity; but his blood will I require at your hand.*

9 *Nevertheless, if you warn the wicked of his way to turn from it; if he do not turn from his way, he shall die in his iniquity; but you have delivered your soul.*

10 Therefore, O you son of man, speak to the house of Israel; Thus you speak, saying, If our transgressions and our sins be upon us, and we pine away in them, how should we then live?

11 Say to them, As I live, says the Lord GOD, I have no pleasure in the death of the wicked; but that the wicked turn from his way and live: you turn, turn from your evil ways; for why will you die, O house of Israel?

12 Therefore, you son of man, say to the children of your people, The righteousness of the righteous shall not deliver him in the day of his transgression: as for the wickedness of the wicked, he shall not fall thereby in the day that he turns from his wickedness; neither shall the righteous be able to live for his righteousness in the day that he sins.

33:3-9 These verses should make every one of us tremble, when we realize how many professed Christians within the Church don't bother to warn a soul of the coming judgment of God. It would seem that Paul had these verses in mind when he spoke of his responsibility to God and man (see Acts 20:26-27). To bring sobriety to the minds of your hearers (whether you are speaking to a crowd or just one person), you may like to say, "If you refuse to repent, and you die in your sins, if your eyes and mine meet on the Day of Judgment, I am free from your blood because I haven't held back from telling you the truth."

13 When I shall say to the righteous, that he shall surely live; if he trust to his own righteousness, and commit iniquity, all his righteousnesses shall not be remembered; but for his iniquity that he has committed, he shall die for it.

14 Again, when I say to the wicked, You shall surely die; if he turn from his sin, and do that which is lawful and right;

15 If the wicked restore the pledge, give again that he had robbed, walk in the statutes of life, without committing iniquity; he shall surely live, he shall not die.

16 None of his sins that he has committed shall be mentioned to him: he has done that which is lawful and right; he shall surely live.

17 Yet the children of your people say, The way of the Lord is not equal: but as for them, their way is not equal.

18 When the righteous turns from his righteousness, and commits iniquity, he shall even die thereby.

19 But if the wicked turn from his wickedness, and do that which is lawful and right, he shall live thereby.

20 Yet you say, The way of the Lord is not equal. O you house of Israel, I will judge you every one after his ways.

21 And it came to pass in the twelfth year of our captivity, in the tenth month, in the fifth day of the month, that one that had escaped out of Jerusalem came to me, saying, The city is smitten.

22 Now the hand of the LORD was upon me in the evening, afore he that was escaped came; and had opened my mouth, until he came to me in the morning; and my mouth was opened, and I was no more dumb.

23 Then the word of the LORD came to me, saying,

24 Son of man, they that inhabit those wastes of the land of Israel speak, saying, Abraham was one, and he inherited the land: but we are many; the land is given us for inheritance.

25 Therefore say to them, Thus says the Lord GOD; You eat with the blood, and lift up your eyes toward your idols, and shed blood: and shall you possess the land?

26 You stand upon your sword, you work abomination, and you defile every one his neighbour's wife: and shall you possess the land?

27 Say thus to them, Thus says the Lord GOD; As I live, surely they that are in the wastes shall fall by the sword, and him that is in the open field will I give to the beasts to be devoured, and they that be in the forts and in the caves shall die of the pestilence.

28 For I will lay the land most desolate, and the pomp of her strength shall cease; and the mountains of Israel shall be desolate, that none shall pass through.

29 Then shall they know that I am the LORD, when I have laid the land most desolate because of all their abominations which they have committed.

30 Also, you son of man, the children of your people still are talking against you by the walls and in the doors of the houses, and speak one to another, every one to his brother, saying, Come, I pray you, and hear what is the word that comes forth from the LORD.

31 And they come to you as the people come, and they sit before you as my people, and they hear your words, but they will not do them: for with their mouth they show much love, but their heart goeth after their covetousness.

33:11 God takes no pleasure in the death of the wicked. He is not willing that any perish, but that all come to repentance (see 2 Peter 3:9). This is why it is biblical to tell sinners that God doesn't want them to go to hell. It isn't His will. He doesn't send anyone to hell in the same way a righteous judge doesn't delight to send anyone to prison. The criminal's crimes send him to prison. The judge merely executes justice. In the case of our salvation, God prefers mercy over judgment, but if we refuse His mercy, Jesus' sacrifice for us, we will get exactly what we deserve.

32 And, lo, you are to them as a very lovely song of one that has a pleasant voice, and can play well on an instrument: for they hear your words, but they do them not.

33 And when this comes to pass, (lo, it will come,) then shall they know that a prophet has been among them.

CHAPTER 34

AND the word of the LORD came to me, saying,

2 Son of man, prophesy against the shepherds of Israel, prophesy, and say to them, Thus says the Lord GOD to the shepherds; Woe be to the shepherds of Israel that do feed themselves! should not the shepherds feed the flocks?

3 You eat the fat, and you clothe you with the wool, you kill them that are fed: but you do not feed the flock.

4 The diseased have you not strengthened, neither have you healed that which was sick, neither have you bound up that which was broken, neither have you brought again that which was driven away, neither have you sought that which was lost; but with force and with cruelty have you ruled them.

5 And they were scattered, because there is no shepherd: and they became meat to all the beasts of the field, when they were scattered.

6 My sheep wandered through all the mountains, and upon every high hill: yea, my flock was scattered upon all the face of the earth, and none did search or seek after them.

7 Therefore, you shepherds, hear the word of the LORD;

8 As I live, says the Lord GOD, surely because my flock became a prey, and my flock became meat to every beast of the field, because there was no shepherd, neither did my shepherds search for my flock, but the shepherds fed themselves, and fed not my flock;

9 Therefore, O you shepherds, hear the word of the LORD;

10 Thus says the Lord GOD; Behold, I am against the shepherds; and I will require my flock at their hand, and cause them to cease from feeding the flock; neither shall the shepherds feed themselves any more; for I will deliver my flock from their mouth, that they may not be meat for them.

11 For thus says the Lord GOD; Behold, I, even I, will both search my sheep, and seek them out.

12 As a shepherd seeks out his flock in the day that he is among his sheep that are scattered; so will I seek out my sheep, and will deliver them out of all places where they have been scattered in the cloudy and dark day.

13 And I will bring them out from the people, and gather them from the countries, and will bring them to their own land, and feed them upon the mountains of Israel by the rivers, and in all the inhabited places of the country.

14 I will feed them in a good pasture, and upon the high mountains of Israel shall their fold be: there shall they lie in a good fold, and in a fat pasture shall they feed upon the mountains of Israel.

15 I will feed my flock, and I will cause them to lie down, says the Lord GOD.

16 I will seek that which was lost, and bring again that which was driven away, and will bind up that which was broken, and will strengthen that which was sick: but I will destroy the fat and the strong; I will feed them with judgment.

33:32 God forbid that any preacher should become an entertainer to his hearers.

34:13 This was a promise that God reiterated many times (see Deuteronomy 30:3, Isaiah 11:11, Jeremiah 16:15, 23:3, Zephaniah 3:20, Zachariah 10:10 and Ezekiel 34:13) The promise commenced to find fulfillment in 1949, when the Jews took hold of the land of Palestine and began to return from throughout the earth. The Jews regained Jerusalem in 1967, fulfilling the prophecy of Jesus (see Luke 21:24).

17 And as for you, O my flock, thus says the Lord GOD; Behold, I judge between cattle and cattle, between the rams and the he goats.

18 Does it seem a small thing to you to have eaten up the good pasture, but you must tread down with your feet the residue of your pastures? and to have drunk of the deep waters, but you must foul the residue with your feet?

19 And as for my flock, they eat that which you have trodden with your feet; and they drink that which you have fouled with your feet.

20 Therefore thus says the Lord GOD to them; Behold, I, even I, will judge between the fat cattle and between the lean cattle.

21 Because you have thrust with side and with shoulder, and pushed all the diseased with your horns, till you have scattered them abroad;

22 Therefore will I save my flock, and they shall no more be a prey; and I will judge between cattle and cattle.

23 And I will set up one shepherd over them, and he shall feed them, even my servant David; he shall feed them, and he shall be their shepherd.

24 And I the LORD will be their God, and my servant David a prince among them; I the LORD have spoken it.

25 And I will make with them a covenant of peace, and will cause the evil beasts to cease out of the land: and they shall dwell safely in the wilderness, and sleep in the woods.

26 And I will make them and the places round about my hill a blessing; and I will cause the shower to come down in his season; there shall be showers of blessing.

27 And the tree of the field shall yield her fruit, and the earth shall yield her increase, and they shall be safe in their land, and shall know that I am the LORD, when I have broken the bands of their yoke, and delivered them out of the hand of those that served themselves of them.

28 And they shall no more be a prey to the heathen, neither shall the beast of the land devour them; but they shall dwell safely, and none shall make them afraid.

29 And I will raise up for them a plant of renown, and they shall be no more consumed with hunger in the land, neither bear the shame of the heathen any more.

30 Thus shall they know that I the LORD their God am with them, and that they, even the house of Israel, are my people, says the Lord GOD.

31 And you my flock, the flock of my pasture, are men, and I am your God, says the Lord GOD.

CHAPTER 35

MOREOVER the word of the LORD came to me, saying,

2 Son of man, set your face against mount Seir, and prophesy against it,

3 And say to it, Thus says the Lord GOD; Behold, O mount Seir, I am against you, and I will stretch out my hand against you, and I will make you most desolate.

4 I will lay your cities waste, and you shall be desolate, and you shall know that I am the LORD.

5 Because you have had a perpetual hatred, and have shed the blood of the children of Israel by the force of the sword in the time of their calamity, in the time that their iniquity had an end:

6 Therefore, as I live, says the Lord GOD, I will prepare you to blood, and blood shall pursue you: since you have not hated blood, even blood shall pursue you.

34:31 See John 10:1-18.

7 Thus will I make mount Seir most desolate, and cut off from it him that passes out and him that returns.

8 And I will fill his mountains with his slain men: in your hills, and in your valleys, and in all your rivers, shall they fall that are slain with the sword.

9 I will make you perpetual desolations, and your cities shall not return: and you shall know that I am the LORD.

10 Because you have said, These two nations and these two countries shall be mine, and we will possess it; whereas the LORD was there:

11 Therefore, as I live, says the Lord GOD, I will even do according to your anger, and according to your envy which you have used out of your hatred against them; and I will make myself known among them, when I have judged you.

12 And you shall know that I am the LORD, and that I have heard all your blasphemies which you have spoken against the mountains of Israel, saying, They are laid desolate, they are given us to consume.

13 Thus with your mouth you have boasted against me, and have multiplied your words against me: I have heard them.

14 Thus says the Lord GOD; When the whole earth rejoices, I will make you desolate.

15 As you did rejoice at the inheritance of the house of Israel, because it was desolate, so will I do to you: you shall be desolate, O mount Seir, and all Idumea, even all of it: and they shall know that I am the LORD.

CHAPTER 36

ALSO, you son of man, prophesy to the mountains of Israel, and say, You mountains of Israel, hear the word of the LORD:

2 Thus says the Lord GOD; Because the enemy has said against you, Aha, even the ancient high places are ours in possession:

3 Therefore prophesy and say, Thus says the Lord GOD; Because they have made you desolate, and swallowed you up on every side, that you might be a possession to the residue of the heathen, and you are taken up in the lips of talkers, and are an infamy of the people:

4 Therefore, you mountains of Israel, hear the word of the Lord GOD; Thus says the Lord GOD to the mountains, and to the hills, to the rivers, and to the valleys, to the desolate wastes, and to the cities that are forsaken, which became a prey and derision to the residue of the heathen that are round about;

5 Therefore thus says the Lord GOD; Surely in the fire of my jealousy have I spoken against the residue of the heathen, and against all Idumea, which have appointed my land into their possession with the joy of all their heart, with despiteful minds, to cast it out for a prey.

6 Prophesy therefore concerning the land of Israel, and say to the mountains, and to the hills, to the rivers, and to the valleys, Thus says the Lord GOD; Behold, I have spoken in my jealousy and in my fury, because you have borne the shame of the heathen:

7 Therefore thus says the Lord GOD; I have lifted up my hand, Surely the heathen that are about you, they shall bear their shame.

8 But you, O mountains of Israel, you shall shoot forth your branches, and yield your fruit to my people of Israel; for they are at hand to come.

9 For, behold, I am for you, and I will turn to you, and you shall be tilled and sown:

10 And I will multiply men upon you, all the house of Israel, even all of it: and the cities shall be inhabited, and the wastes shall be built:

11 And I will multiply upon you man and beast; and they shall increase and bring fruit: and I will settle you after your old estates, and will do better to you than at your beginnings: and you shall know that I am the LORD.

12 Yea, I will cause men to walk upon you, even my people Israel; and they shall possess you, and you shall be their inheritance, and you shall no more henceforth bereave them of men.

13 Thus says the Lord GOD; Because they say to you, You devour up men, and have bereaved your nations:

14 Therefore you shall devour men no more, neither bereave your nations any more, says the Lord GOD.

15 Neither will I cause men to hear in you the shame of the heathen any more, neither shall you bear the reproach of the people any more, neither shall you cause your nations to fall any more, says the Lord GOD.

16 Moreover the word of the LORD came to me, saying,

17 Son of man, when the house of Israel dwelt in their own land, they defiled it by their own way and by their doings: their way was before me as the uncleanness of a removed woman.

18 Therefore I poured my fury upon them for the blood that they had shed upon the land, and for their idols wherewith they had polluted it:

19 And I scattered them among the heathen, and they were dispersed through the countries: according to their way and according to their doings I judged them.

20 And when they entered to the heathen, where they went, they profaned my holy name, when they said to them, These are the people of the LORD, and are gone forth out of his land.

21 But I had pity for my holy name, which the house of Israel had profaned among the heathen, where they went.

22 Therefore say to the house of Israel, thus says the Lord GOD; I do not this for your sakes, O house of Israel, but for my holy name's sake, which you have profaned among the heathen, where you went.

23 And I will sanctify my great name, which was profaned among the heathen, which you have profaned in the midst of them; and the heathen shall know that I am the LORD, says the Lord GOD, when I shall be sanctified in you before their eyes.

24 For I will take you from among the heathen, and gather you out of all countries, and will bring you into your own land.

25 Then will I sprinkle clean water upon you, and you shall be clean: from all your filthiness, and from all your idols, will I cleanse you.

26 A new heart also will I give you, and a new spirit will I put within you: and I will take away the stony heart out of your flesh, and I will give you a heart of flesh.

27 And I will put my spirit within you, and cause you to walk in my statutes, and you shall keep my judgments, and do them.

28 And you shall dwell in the land that I gave to your fathers; and you shall be my people, and I will be your God.

29 I will also save you from all your uncleanness: and I will call for the corn, and will increase it, and lay no famine upon you.

30 And I will multiply the fruit of the tree, and the increase of the field, that you shall receive no more reproach of famine among the heathen.

31 Then shall you remember your own evil ways, and your doings that were not good, and shall lothe yourselves in your own sight for your iniquities and for your abominations.

36:24-27 This is the wonderful promise of God that finds fulfillment on conversion. God takes our heart of stone and gives us a heart of flesh. He causes us to love the things we once hated and hate the things we once loved. We are born again (see John 3:3), new creatures in Christ (see 2 Corinthians 5:17). He gives us His mind, written on the tables of our heart so that we desire to walk in His will (see 1 Peter 1:23).

Revivals begin with God's own people;
the Holy Spirit touches their heart anew,
and gives them new fervor
and compassion, and zeal,
new light and life,
and when He has thus come to you,
He next goes forth
to the valley of dry bones...
Oh, what responsibility this lays
on the Church of God!

Andrew A. Bonar

1810-1892
SCOTTISH MINISTER
ACTIVE IN THE KILSYTH REVIVAL
OF 1839-1840

32 Not for your sakes do I this, says the Lord GOD, let it be known to you: be ashamed and confounded for your own ways, O house of Israel.

33 Thus says the Lord GOD; In the day that I shall have cleansed you from all your iniquities I will also cause you to dwell in the cities, and the wastes shall be built.

34 And the desolate land shall be tilled, whereas it lay desolate in the sight of all that passed by.

35 And they shall say, This land that was desolate is become like the garden of Eden; and the waste and desolate and ruined cities are become fenced, and are inhabited.

36 Then the heathen that are left round about you shall know that I the LORD build the ruined places, and plant that that was desolate: I the LORD have spoken it, and I will do it.

37 Thus says the Lord GOD; I will yet for this be enquired of by the house of Israel, to do it for them; I will increase them with men like a flock.

38 As the holy flock, as the flock of Jerusalem in her solemn feasts; so shall the waste cities be filled with flocks of men: and they shall know that I am the LORD.

CHAPTER 37

THE hand of the LORD was upon me, and carried me out in the spirit of the LORD, and set me down in the midst of the valley which was full of bones,

2 And caused me to pass by them round about: and, behold, there were very many in the open valley; and, lo, they were very dry.

3 And he said to me, Son of man, can these bones live? And I answered, O Lord GOD, you know.

4 Again he said to me, Prophesy upon these bones, and say to them, O you dry bones, hear the word of the LORD.

5 Thus says the Lord GOD to these bones; Behold, I will cause breath to enter into you, and you shall live:

6 And I will lay sinews upon you, and will bring up flesh upon you, and cover you with skin, and put breath in you, and you shall live; and you shall know that I am the LORD.

7 So I prophesied as I was commanded: and as I prophesied, there was a noise, and behold a shaking, and the bones came together, bone to his bone.

8 And when I beheld, lo, the sinews and the flesh came up upon them, and the skin covered them above: but there was no breath in them.

9 Then said he to me, Prophesy to the wind, prophesy, son of man, and say to the wind, Thus says the Lord GOD;

Come from the four winds, O breath, and breathe upon these slain, that they may live.

10 So I prophesied as he commanded me, and the breath came into them, and they lived, and stood up upon their feet, an exceeding great army.

11 Then he said to me, Son of man, these bones are the whole house of Israel: behold, they say, Our bones are dried, and our hope is lost: we are cut off for our parts.

12 Therefore prophesy and say to them, Thus says the Lord GOD; Behold, O my people, I will open your graves, and cause you to come up out of your graves, and bring you into the land of Israel.

13 And you shall know that I am the LORD, when I have opened your graves, O my people, and brought you up out of your graves,

14 And shall put my spirit in you, and you shall live, and I shall place you in your own land: then shall you know that I the LORD have spoken it, and performed it, says the LORD.

15 The word of the LORD came again to me, saying,

16 Moreover, you son of man, take one stick for yourself, and write upon it, For Judah, and for the children of Israel his companions: then take another stick, and write upon it, For Joseph, the stick of Ephraim and for all the house of Israel his companions:

17 And join them one to another into one stick; and they shall become one in your hand.

18 And when the children of your people shall speak to you, saying, Will you not show us what you mean by these?

19 Say to them, Thus says the Lord GOD; Behold, I will take the stick of Joseph, which is in the hand of Ephraim, and the tribes of Israel his fellows, and will put them with him, even with the stick of Judah, and make them one stick, and they shall be one in my hand.

20 And the sticks whereon you write shall be in your hand before their eyes.

21 And say to them, Thus says the Lord GOD; Behold, I will take the children of Israel from among the heathen, wherever they have gone, and will gather them on every side, and bring them into their own land:

22 And I will make them one nation in the land upon the mountains of Israel; and one king shall be king to them all: and they shall be no more two nations, neither shall they be divided into two kingdoms any more at all.

23 Neither shall they defile themselves any more with their idols, nor with their detestable things, nor with any of their transgressions: but I will save them out of all their dwellingplaces, wherein they have sinned, and will cleanse them: so shall they be my people, and I will be their God.

24 And David my servant shall be king over them; and they all shall have one shepherd: they shall also walk in my judgments, and observe my statutes, and do them.

25 And they shall dwell in the land that I have given to Jacob my servant, wherein your fathers have dwelt; and they shall dwell therein, even they, and their children, and their children's children for ever: and my servant David shall be their prince for ever.

26 Moreover I will make a covenant of peace with them; it shall be an everlasting covenant with them: and I will place them, and multiply them, and will set my sanctuary in the midst of them for evermore.

27 My tabernacle also shall be with them: yea, I will be their God, and they shall be my people.

28 And the heathen shall know that I the LORD do sanctify Israel, when my sanctuary shall be in the midst of them for evermore.

THE VISION OF THE VALLEY OF DRY BONES

Ezekiel 37:1-10

While these verses are directed at the "whole house of Israel," it is easy to see their evangelistic application. The world sits in the valley of the shadow of death. Those who do not know the Lord are dry bones, dead in their sins (see Ephesians 2:1). There is no life, no hope…until the breath of the Spirit of God breathes life into them through the power of the gospel.

CHAPTER 38

AND the word of the LORD came to me, saying,

2 Son of man, set your face against Gog, the land of Magog, the chief prince of Meshech and Tubal, and prophesy against him,

3 And say, Thus says the Lord GOD; Behold, I am against you, O Gog, the chief prince of Meshech and Tubal:

4 And I will turn you back, and put hooks into your jaws, and I will bring you forth, and all your army, horses and horsemen, all of them clothed with all sorts of armour, even a great company with bucklers and shields, all of them handling swords:

5 Persia, Ethiopia, and Libya with them; all of them with shield and helmet:

6 Gomer, and all his bands; the house of Togarmah of the north quarters, and all his bands: and many people with you.

7 Be prepared, and prepare for yourself, you, and all your company that are assembled about you, and be a guard to them.

8 After many days you shall be visited: in the latter years you shall come into the land that is brought back from the sword, and is gathered out of many people, against the mountains of Israel, which have been always waste: but it is brought forth out of the nations, and they shall dwell safely all of them.

9 You shall ascend and come like a storm, you shall be like a cloud to cover the land, you, and all your bands, and many people with you.

10 Thus says the Lord GOD; It shall also come to pass, that at the same time shall things come into your mind, and you shall think an evil thought:

11 And you shall say, I will go up to the land of unwalled villages; I will go to them that are at rest, that dwell safely, all of them dwelling without walls, and having neither bars nor gates,

12 To take a spoil, and to take a prey; to turn your hand upon the desolate places that are now inhabited, and upon the people that are gathered out of the nations, which have acquired cattle and goods, that dwell in the midst of the land.

13 Sheba, and Dedan, and the merchants of Tarshish, with all the young lions thereof, shall say to you, Are you come to take a spoil? have you gathered your company to take a prey? to carry away silver and gold, to take away cattle and goods, to take a great spoil?

14 Therefore, son of man, prophesy and say to Gog, Thus says the Lord GOD; In that day when my people of Israel dwell safely, shall you not know it?

15 And you shall come from your place out of the north parts, you, and many people with you, all of them riding upon horses, a great company, and a mighty army:

16 And you shall come up against my people of Israel, as a cloud to cover the land; it shall be in the latter days, and I will bring you against my land, that the heathen may know me, when I shall be sanctified in you, O Gog, before their eyes.

17 Thus says the Lord GOD; Are you he of whom I have spoken in old time by my servants the prophets of Israel, which prophesied in those days many years that I would bring you against them?

18 And it shall come to pass at the same time when Gog shall come against the land of Israel, says the Lord GOD, that my fury shall come up in my face.

19 For in my jealousy and in the fire of my wrath have I spoken, Surely in that day there shall be a great shaking in the land of Israel;

20 So that the fishes of the sea, and the fowls of the heaven, and the beasts of the field, and all creeping things that creep upon the earth, and all the men that are

---

38:1-23 See Luke 21:26 comment.

upon the face of the earth, shall shake at my presence, and the mountains shall be thrown down, and the steep places shall fall, and every wall shall fall to the ground.

21 And I will call for a sword against him throughout all my mountains, says the Lord GOD: every man's sword shall be against his brother.

22 And I will plead against him with pestilence and with blood; and I will rain upon him, and upon his bands, and upon the many people that are with him, an overflowing rain, and great hailstones, fire, and brimstone.

23 Thus will I magnify myself, and sanctify myself; and I will be known in the eyes of many nations, and they shall know that I am the LORD.

CHAPTER 39

THEREFORE, you son of man, prophesy against Gog, and say, Thus says the Lord GOD; Behold, I am against you, O Gog, the chief prince of Meshech and Tubal:

2 And I will turn you back, and leave but the sixth part of you, and will cause you to come up from the north parts, and will bring you upon the mountains of Israel:

3 And I will smite your bow out of your left hand, and will cause your arrows to fall out of your right hand.

4 You shall fall upon the mountains of Israel, you, and all your bands, and the people that is with you: I will give you to the ravenous birds of every sort, and to the beasts of the field to be devoured.

5 You shall fall upon the open field: for I have spoken it, says the Lord GOD.

6 And I will send a fire on Magog, and among them that dwell carelessly in the isles: and they shall know that I am the LORD.

7 So will I make my holy name known in the midst of my people Israel; and I will not let them pollute my holy name any more: and the heathen shall know that I am the LORD, the Holy One in Israel.

8 Behold, it is come, and it is done, says the Lord GOD; this is the day whereof I have spoken.

9 And they that dwell in the cities of Israel shall go forth, and shall set on fire and burn the weapons, both the shields and the bucklers, the bows and the arrows, and the handstaves, and the spears, and they shall burn them with fire seven years:

10 So that they shall take no wood out of the field, neither cut down any out of the forests; for they shall burn the weapons with fire: and they shall spoil those that spoiled them, and rob those that robbed them, says the Lord GOD.

11 And it shall come to pass in that day, that I will give to Gog a place there of graves in Israel, the valley of the passengers on the east of the sea: and it shall stop the noses of the passengers: and there shall they bury Gog and all his multitude: and they shall call it The valley of Hamongog.

12 And seven months shall the house of Israel be burying of them, that they may cleanse the land.

13 Yea, all the people of the land shall bury them; and it shall be to them a renown the day that I shall be glorified, says the Lord GOD.

14 And they shall sever out men of continual employment, passing through the land to bury with the passengers those that remain upon the face of the earth, to cleanse it: after the end of seven months shall they search.

15 And the passengers that pass through the land, when any sees a man's bone, then shall he set up a sign by it, till the buriers have buried it in the valley of Hamongog.

16 And also the name of the city shall be Hamonah. Thus shall they cleanse the land.

17 And, you son of man, thus says the Lord GOD; Speak to every feathered fowl, and to every beast of the field,

Assemble yourselves, and come; gather yourselves on every side to my sacrifice that I do sacrifice for you, even a great sacrifice upon the mountains of Israel, that you may eat flesh, and drink blood.

18 You shall eat the flesh of the mighty, and drink the blood of the princes of the earth, of rams, of lambs, and of goats, of bullocks, all of them fatlings of Bashan.

19 And you shall eat fat till you be full, and drink blood till you be drunken, of my sacrifice which I have sacrificed for you.

20 Thus you shall be filled at my table with horses and chariots, with mighty men, and with all men of war, says the Lord GOD.

21 And I will set my glory among the heathen, and all the heathen shall see my judgment that I have executed, and my hand that I have laid upon them.

22 So the house of Israel shall know that I am the LORD their God from that day and forward.

23 And the heathen shall know that the house of Israel went into captivity for their iniquity: because they trespassed against me, therefore hid I my face from them, and gave them into the hand of their enemies: so fell they all by the sword.

24 According to their uncleanness and according to their transgressions have I done to them, and hid my face from them.

25 Therefore thus says the Lord GOD; Now will I bring again the captivity of Jacob, and have mercy upon the whole house of Israel, and will be jealous for my holy name;

26 After that they have borne their shame, and all their trespasses whereby they have trespassed against me, when they dwelt safely in their land, and none made them afraid.

27 When I have brought them again from the people, and gathered them out of their enemies' lands, and am sanctified in them in the sight of many nations;

28 Then shall they know that I am the LORD their God, which caused them to be led into captivity among the heathen: but I have gathered them to their own land, and have left none of them any more there.

29 Neither will I hide my face any more from them: for I have poured out my spirit upon the house of Israel, says the Lord GOD.

CHAPTER 40

IN the five and twentieth year of our captivity, in the beginning of the year, in the tenth day of the month, in the fourteenth year after that the city was smitten, in the selfsame day the hand of the LORD was upon me, and brought me there.

2 In the visions of God brought he me into the land of Israel, and set me upon a very high mountain, by which was as the frame of a city on the south.

3 And he brought me there, and, behold, there was a man, whose appearance was like the appearance of brass, with a line of flax in his hand, and a measuring reed; and he stood in the gate.

4 And the man said to me, Son of man, behold with your eyes, and hear with your ears, and set your heart upon all that I shall show you; for to the intent that I might show them to you are you brought here: declare all that you see to the house of Israel.

5 And behold a wall on the outside of the house round about, and in the man's hand a measuring reed of six cubits long by the cubit and an hand breadth: so he measured the breadth of the building, one reed; and the height, one reed.

6 Then he came to the gate which looks toward the east, and went up the stairs thereof, and measured the threshold of the gate, which was one reed broad; and the other threshold of the gate, which was one reed broad.

7 And every little chamber was one reed long, and one reed broad; and between

the little chambers were five cubits; and the threshold of the gate by the porch of the gate within was one reed.

8 He measured also the porch of the gate within, one reed.

9 Then measured he the porch of the gate, eight cubits; and the posts thereof, two cubits; and the porch of the gate was inward.

10 And the little chambers of the gate eastward were three on this side, and three on that side; they three were of one measure: and the posts had one measure on this side and on that side.

11 And he measured the breadth of the entry of the gate, ten cubits; and the length of the gate, thirteen cubits.

12 The space also before the little chambers was one cubit on this side, and the space was one cubit on that side: and the little chambers were six cubits on this side, and six cubits on that side.

13 He measured then the gate from the roof of one little chamber to the roof of another: the breadth was five and twenty cubits, door against door.

14 He made also posts of threescore cubits, even to the post of the court round about the gate.

15 And from the face of the gate of the entrance to the face of the porch of the inner gate were fifty cubits.

16 And there were narrow windows to the little chambers, and to their posts within the gate round about, and likewise to the arches: and windows were round about inward: and upon each post were palm trees.

17 Then brought he me into the outward court, and, lo, there were chambers, and a pavement made for the court round about: thirty chambers were upon the pavement.

18 And the pavement by the side of the gates over against the length of the gates was the lower pavement.

19 Then he measured the breadth from the forefront of the lower gate to the forefront of the inner court without, an hundred cubits eastward and northward.

20 And the gate of the outward court that looked toward the north, he measured the length thereof, and the breadth thereof.

21 And the little chambers thereof were three on this side and three on that side; and the posts thereof and the arches thereof were after the measure of the first gate: the length thereof was fifty cubits, and the breadth five and twenty cubits.

22 And their windows, and their arches, and their palm trees, were after the measure of the gate that looks toward the east; and they went up to it by seven steps; and the arches thereof were before them.

23 And the gate of the inner court was over against the gate toward the north, and toward the east; and he measured from gate to gate an hundred cubits.

24 After that he brought me toward the south, and behold a gate toward the south: and he measured the posts thereof and the arches thereof according to these measures.

25 And there were windows in it and in the arches thereof round about, like those windows: the length was fifty cubits, and the breadth five and twenty cubits.

26 And there were seven steps to go up to it, and the arches thereof were before them: and it had palm trees, one on this side, and another on that side, upon the posts thereof.

27 And there was a gate in the inner court toward the south: and he measured from gate to gate toward the south an hundred cubits.

28 And he brought me to the inner court by the south gate: and he measured the south gate according to these measures;

29 And the little chambers thereof, and the posts thereof, and the arches thereof, according to these measures: and there were windows in it and in the arches thereof round about: it was fifty cubits long, and five and twenty cubits broad.

30 And the arches round about were five and twenty cubits long, and five cubits broad.

31 And the arches thereof were toward the utter court; and palm trees were upon the posts thereof: and the going up to it had eight steps.

32 And he brought me into the inner court toward the east: and he measured the gate according to these measures.

33 And the little chambers thereof, and the posts thereof, and the arches thereof, were according to these measures: and there were windows therein and in the arches thereof round about: it was fifty cubits long, and five and twenty cubits broad.

34 And the arches thereof were toward the outward court; and palm trees were upon the posts thereof, on this side, and on that side: and the going up to it had eight steps.

35 And he brought me to the north gate, and measured it according to these measures;

36 The little chambers thereof, the posts thereof, and the arches thereof, and the windows to it round about: the length was fifty cubits, and the breadth five and twenty cubits.

37 And the posts thereof were toward the utter court; and palm trees were upon the posts thereof, on this side, and on that side: and the going up to it had eight steps.

38 And the chambers and the entries thereof were by the posts of the gates, where they washed the burnt offering.

39 And in the porch of the gate were two tables on this side, and two tables on that side, to slay thereon the burnt offering and the sin offering and the trespass offering.

40 And at the side without, as one goeth up to the entry of the north gate, were two tables; and on the other side, which was at the porch of the gate, were two tables.

41 Four tables were on this side, and four tables on that side, by the side of the gate; eight tables, whereupon they slew their sacrifices.

42 And the four tables were of hewn stone for the burnt offering, of a cubit and an half long, and a cubit and an half broad, and one cubit high: whereupon also they laid the instruments wherewith they slew the burnt offering and the sacrifice.

43 And within were hooks, a hand broad, fastened round about: and upon the tables was the flesh of the offering.

44 And without the inner gate were the chambers of the singers in the inner court, which was at the side of the north gate; and their prospect was toward the south: one at the side of the east gate having the prospect toward the north.

45 And he said to me, This chamber, whose prospect is toward the south, is for the priests, the keepers of the charge of the house.

46 And the chamber whose prospect is toward the north is for the priests, the keepers of the charge of the altar: these are the sons of Zadok among the sons of Levi, which come near to the LORD to minister to him.

47 So he measured the court, an hundred cubits long, and an hundred cubits broad, foursquare; and the altar that was before the house.

48 And he brought me to the porch of the house, and measured each post of the porch, five cubits on this side, and five cubits on that side: and the breadth of the gate was three cubits on this side, and three cubits on that side.

49 The length of the porch was twenty cubits, and the breadth eleven cubits, and he brought me by the steps whereby they went up to it: and there were pillars by the posts, one on this side, and another on that side.

CHAPTER 41

AFTERWARD he brought me to the temple, and measured the posts, six cubits broad on the one side, and six cubits broad on the other side, which was the breadth of the tabernacle.

2 And the breadth of the door was ten cubits; and the sides of the door were five cubits on the one side, and five cubits on the other side: and he measured the length thereof, forty cubits: and the breadth, twenty cubits.

3 Then went he inward, and measured the post of the door, two cubits; and the door, six cubits; and the breadth of the door, seven cubits.

4 So he measured the length thereof, twenty cubits; and the breadth, twenty cubits, before the temple: and he said to me, This is the most holy place.

5 After he measured the wall of the house, six cubits; and the breadth of every side chamber, four cubits, round about the house on every side.

6 And the side chambers were three, one over another, and thirty in order; and they entered into the wall which was of the house for the side chambers round about, that they might have hold, but they had not hold in the wall of the house.

7 And there was an enlarging, and a winding about still upward to the side chambers: for the winding about of the house went still upward round about the house: therefore the breadth of the house was still upward, and so increased from the lowest chamber to the highest by the midst.

8 I saw also the height of the house round about: the foundations of the side chambers were a full reed of six great cubits.

9 The thickness of the wall, which was for the side chamber without, was five cubits: and that which was left was the place of the side chambers that were within.

10 And between the chambers was the wideness of twenty cubits round about the house on every side.

11 And the doors of the side chambers were toward the place that was left, one door toward the north, and another door toward the south: and the breadth of the place that was left was five cubits round about.

12 Now the building that was before the separate place at the end toward the west was seventy cubits broad; and the wall of the building was five cubits thick round about, and the length thereof ninety cubits.

13 So he measured the house, an hundred cubits long; and the separate place, and the building, with the walls thereof, an hundred cubits long;

14 Also the breadth of the face of the house, and of the separate place toward the east, an hundred cubits.

15 And he measured the length of the building over against the separate place which was behind it, and the galleries thereof on the one side and on the other side, an hundred cubits, with the inner temple, and the porches of the court;

16 The door posts, and the narrow windows, and the galleries round about on their three stories, over against the door, cieled with wood round about, and from the ground up to the windows, and the windows were covered;

17 To that above the door, even to the inner house, and without, and by all the wall round about within and without, by measure.

18 And it was made with cherubims and palm trees, so that a palm tree was between a cherub and a cherub; and every cherub had two faces;

19 So that the face of a man was toward the palm tree on the one side, and the face of a young lion toward the palm tree on the other side: it was made through all the house round about.

20 From the ground to above the door were cherubims and palm trees made, and on the wall of the temple.

21 The posts of the temple were squared, and the face of the sanctuary; the appearance of the one as the appearance of the other.

22 The altar of wood was three cubits high, and the length thereof two cubits; and the corners thereof, and the length thereof, and the walls thereof, were of wood: and he said to me, This is the table that is before the LORD.

23 And the temple and the sanctuary had two doors.

24 And the doors had two leaves apiece, two turning leaves; two leaves for the one door, and two leaves for the other door.

25 And there were made on them, on the doors of the temple, cherubims and palm trees, like as were made upon the walls; and there were thick planks upon the face of the porch without.

26 And there were narrow windows and palm trees on the one side and on the other side, on the sides of the porch, and upon the side chambers of the house, and thick planks.

CHAPTER 42

THEN he brought me forth into the utter court, the way toward the north: and he brought me into the chamber that was over against the separate place, and which was before the building toward the north.

2 Before the length of an hundred cubits was the north door, and the breadth was fifty cubits.

3 Over against the twenty cubits which were for the inner court, and over against the pavement which was for the utter court, was gallery against gallery in three stories.

4 And before the chambers was a walk to ten cubits breadth inward, a way of one cubit; and their doors toward the north.

5 Now the upper chambers were shorter: for the galleries were higher than these, than the lower, and than the middlemost of the building.

6 For they were in three stories, but had not pillars as the pillars of the courts: therefore the building was straitened more than the lowest and the middlemost from the ground.

7 And the wall that was without over against the chambers, toward the utter court on the forepart of the chambers, the length thereof was fifty cubits.

8 For the length of the chambers that were in the utter court was fifty cubits: and, lo, before the temple were an hundred cubits.

9 And from under these chambers was the entry on the east side, as one goeth into them from the utter court.

10 The chambers were in the thickness of the wall of the court toward the east, over against the separate place, and over against the building.

11 And the way before them was like the appearance of the chambers which were toward the north, as long as they, and as broad as they: and all their goings out were both according to their fashions, and according to their doors.

12 And according to the doors of the chambers that were toward the south was a door in the head of the way, even the way directly before the wall toward the east, as one enters into them.

13 Then said he to me, The north chambers and the south chambers, which are before the separate place, they be holy chambers, where the priests that approach the LORD shall eat the most holy things: there shall they lay the most holy things, and the meat offering, and the sin offering, and the trespass offering; for the place is holy.

14 When the priests enter therein, then shall they not go out of the holy place into the utter court, but there they shall lay their garments wherein they minister; for they are holy; and shall put on other garments, and shall approach to those things which are for the people.

15 Now when he had made an end of measuring the inner house, he brought me forth toward the gate whose prospect

is toward the east, and measured it round about.

16 He measured the east side with the measuring reed, five hundred reeds, with the measuring reed round about.

17 He measured the north side, five hundred reeds, with the measuring reed round about.

18 He measured the south side, five hundred reeds, with the measuring reed.

19 He turned about to the west side, and measured five hundred reeds with the measuring reed.

20 He measured it by the four sides: it had a wall round about, five hundred reeds long, and five hundred broad, to make a separation between the sanctuary and the profane place.

CHAPTER 43

AFTERWARD he brought me to the gate, even the gate that looks toward the east:

2 And, behold, the glory of the God of Israel came from the way of the east: and his voice was like a noise of many waters: and the earth shined with his glory.

3 And it was according to the appearance of the vision which I saw, even according to the vision that I saw when I came to destroy the city: and the visions were like the vision that I saw by the river Chebar; and I fell upon my face.

4 And the glory of the LORD came into the house by the way of the gate whose prospect is toward the east.

5 So the spirit took me up, and brought me into the inner court; and, behold, the glory of the LORD filled the house.

6 And I heard him speaking to me out of the house; and the man stood by me.

7 And he said to me, Son of man, the place of my throne, and the place of the soles of my feet, where I will dwell in the midst of the children of Israel for ever, and my holy name, shall the house of Israel no more defile, neither they, nor their kings, by their whoredom, nor by the carcases of their kings in their high places.

8 In their setting of their threshold by my thresholds, and their post by my posts, and the wall between me and them, they have even defiled my holy name by their abominations that they have committed: therefore I have consumed them in my anger.

9 Now let them put away their whoredom, and the carcases of their kings, far from me, and I will dwell in the midst of them for ever.

10 You son of man, show the house to the house of Israel, that they may be ashamed of their iniquities: and let them measure the pattern.

11 And if they be ashamed of all that they have done, show them the form of the house, and the fashion thereof, and the goings out thereof, and the comings in thereof, and all the forms thereof, and all the ordinances thereof, and all the forms thereof, and all the laws thereof: and write it in their sight, that they may keep the whole form thereof, and all the ordinances thereof, and do them.

12 This is the law of the house; Upon the top of the mountain the whole limit thereof round about shall be most holy. Behold, this is the law of the house.

13 And these are the measures of the altar after the cubits: The cubit is a cubit and an hand breadth; even the bottom shall be a cubit, and the breadth a cubit, and the border thereof by the edge thereof round about shall be a span: and this shall be the higher place of the altar.

14 And from the bottom upon the ground even to the lower settle shall be two cubits, and the breadth one cubit; and from the lesser settle even to the greater settle shall be four cubits, and the breadth one cubit.

15 So the altar shall be four cubits; and from the altar and upward shall be four horns.

16 And the altar shall be twelve cubits long, twelve broad, square in the four squares thereof.

17 And the settle shall be fourteen cubits long and fourteen broad in the four

squares thereof; and the border about it shall be half a cubit; and the bottom thereof shall be a cubit about; and his stairs shall look toward the east.

18 And he said to me, Son of man, thus says the Lord GOD; These are the ordinances of the altar in the day when they shall make it, to offer burnt offerings thereon, and to sprinkle blood thereon.

19 And you shall give to the priests the Levites that are of the seed of Zadok, which approach me, to minister to me, says the Lord GOD, a young bullock for a sin offering.

20 And you shall take of the blood thereof, and put it on the four horns of it, and on the four corners of the settle, and upon the border round about: thus shall you cleanse and purge it.

21 You shall take the bullock also of the sin offering, and he shall burn it in the appointed place of the house, without the sanctuary.

22 And on the second day you shall offer a kid of the goats without blemish for a sin offering; and they shall cleanse the altar, as they did cleanse it with the bullock.

23 When you have made an end of cleansing it, you shall offer a young bullock without blemish, and a ram out of the flock without blemish.

24 And you shall offer them before the LORD, and the priests shall cast salt upon them, and they shall offer them up for a burnt offering to the LORD.

25 Seven days shall you prepare every day a goat for a sin offering: they shall also prepare a young bullock, and a ram out of the flock, without blemish.

26 Seven days shall they purge the altar and purify it; and they shall consecrate themselves.

27 And when these days are expired, it shall be, that upon the eighth day, and so forward, the priests shall make your burnt offerings upon the altar, and your peace offerings; and I will accept you, says the Lord GOD.

CHAPTER 44

THEN he brought me back the way of the gate of the outward sanctuary which looks toward the east; and it was shut.

2 Then said the LORD to me; This gate shall be shut, it shall not be opened, and no man shall enter in by it; because the LORD, the God of Israel, has entered in by it, therefore it shall be shut.

3 It is for the prince; the prince, he shall sit in it to eat bread before the LORD; he shall enter by the way of the porch of that gate, and shall go out by the way of the same.

4 Then brought he me the way of the north gate before the house: and I looked, and, behold, the glory of the LORD filled the house of the LORD: and I fell upon my face.

5 And the LORD said to me, Son of man, mark well, and behold with your eyes, and hear with your ears all that I say to you concerning all the ordinances of the house of the LORD, and all the laws thereof; and mark well the entering in of the house, with every going forth of the sanctuary.

6 And you shall say to the rebellious, even to the house of Israel, Thus says the Lord GOD; O you house of Israel, let it suffice you of all your abominations,

7 In that you have brought into my sanctuary strangers, uncircumcised in heart, and uncircumcised in flesh, to be in my sanctuary, to pollute it, even my house, when you offer my bread, the fat and the blood, and they have broken my covenant because of all your abominations.

8 And you have not kept the charge of my holy things: but you have set keepers of my charge in my sanctuary for yourselves.

9 Thus says the Lord GOD; No stranger, uncircumcised in heart, nor uncircumcised in flesh, shall enter into my sanctuary, of any stranger that is among the children of Israel.

10 And the Levites that are gone away far from me, when Israel went astray, which went astray away from me after their idols; they shall even bear their iniquity.

11 Yet they shall be ministers in my sanctuary, having charge at the gates of the house, and ministering to the house: they shall slay the burnt offering and the sacrifice for the people, and they shall stand before them to minister to them.

12 Because they ministered to them before their idols, and caused the house of Israel to fall into iniquity; therefore have I lifted up my hand against them, says the Lord GOD, and they shall bear their iniquity.

13 And they shall not come near me, to do the office of a priest to me, nor to come near to any of my holy things, in the most holy place: but they shall bear their shame, and their abominations which they have committed.

14 But I will make them keepers of the charge of the house, for all the service thereof, and for all that shall be done therein.

15 But the priests the Levites, the sons of Zadok, that kept the charge of my sanctuary when the children of Israel went astray from me, they shall come near to me to minister to me, and they shall stand before me to offer to me the fat and the blood, says the Lord GOD:

16 They shall enter into my sanctuary, and they shall come near to my table, to minister to me, and they shall keep my charge.

17 And it shall come to pass, that when they enter in at the gates of the inner court, they shall be clothed with linen garments; and no wool shall come upon them, whiles they minister in the gates of the inner court, and within.

18 They shall have linen bonnets upon their heads, and shall have linen breeches upon their loins; they shall not gird themselves with any thing that causes sweat.

19 And when they go forth into the utter court, even into the utter court to the people, they shall put off their garments wherein they ministered, and lay them in the holy chambers, and they shall put on other garments; and they shall not sanctify the people with their garments.

20 Neither shall they shave their heads, nor suffer their locks to grow long; they shall only poll their heads.

21 Neither shall any priest drink wine, when they enter into the inner court.

22 Neither shall they take for their wives a widow, nor her that is put away: but they shall take maidens of the seed of the house of Israel, or a widow that had a priest before.

23 And they shall teach my people the difference between the holy and profane, and cause them to discern between the unclean and the clean.

24 And in controversy they shall stand in judgment; and they shall judge it according to my judgments: and they shall keep my laws and my statutes in all my assemblies; and they shall hallow my sabbaths.

25 And they shall come at no dead person to defile themselves: but for father, or for mother, or for son, or for daughter, for brother, or for sister that has had no husband, they may defile themselves.

26 And after he is cleansed, they shall reckon to him seven days.

27 And in the day that he goeth into the sanctuary, in the inner court, to minister in the sanctuary, he shall offer his sin offering, says the Lord GOD.

28 And it shall be to them for an inheritance: I am their inheritance: and you shall give them no possession in Israel: I am their possession.

29 They shall eat the meat offering, and the sin offering, and the trespass offering: and every dedicated thing in Israel shall be theirs.

30 And the first of all the firstfruits of all things, and every oblation of all, of

every sort of your oblations, shall be the priest's: you shall also give to the priest the first of your dough, that he may cause the blessing to rest in your house.

31 The priests shall not eat of any thing that is dead of itself, or torn, whether it be fowl or beast.

CHAPTER 45

MOREOVER, when you shall divide by lot the land for inheritance, you shall offer an oblation to the LORD, an holy portion of the land: the length shall be the length of five and twenty thousand reeds, and the breadth shall be ten thousand. This shall be holy in all the borders thereof round about.

2 Of this there shall be for the sanctuary five hundred in length, with five hundred in breadth, square round about; and fifty cubits round about for the suburbs thereof.

3 And of this measure shall you measure the length of five and twenty thousand, and the breadth of ten thousand: and in it shall be the sanctuary and the most holy place.

4 The holy portion of the land shall be for the priests the ministers of the sanctuary, which shall come near to minister to the LORD: and it shall be a place for their houses, and an holy place for the sanctuary.

5 And the five and twenty thousand of length, and the ten thousand of breadth shall also the Levites, the ministers of the house, have for themselves, for a possession for twenty chambers.

6 And you shall appoint the possession of the city five thousand broad, and five and twenty thousand long, over against the oblation of the holy portion: it shall be for the whole house of Israel.

7 And a portion shall be for the prince on the one side and on the other side of the oblation of the holy portion, and of the possession of the city, before the oblation of the holy portion, and before the possession of the city, from the west side westward, and from the east side eastward: and the length shall be over against one of the portions, from the west border to the east border.

8 In the land shall be his possession in Israel: and my princes shall no more oppress my people; and the rest of the land shall they give to the house of Israel according to their tribes.

9 Thus says the Lord GOD; Let it suffice you, O princes of Israel: remove violence and spoil, and execute judgment and justice, take away your exactions from my people, says the Lord GOD.

10 You shall have just balances, and a just ephah, and a just bath.

11 The ephah and the bath shall be of one measure, that the bath may contain the tenth part of a homer, and the ephah the tenth part of a homer: the measure thereof shall be after the homer.

12 And the shekel shall be twenty gerahs: twenty shekels, five and twenty shekels, fifteen shekels, shall be your maneh.

13 This is the oblation that you shall offer; the sixth part of an ephah of an homer of wheat, and you shall give the sixth part of an ephah of an homer of barley:

14 Concerning the ordinance of oil, the bath of oil, you shall offer the tenth part of a bath out of the cor, which is an homer of ten baths; for ten baths are an homer:

15 And one lamb out of the flock, out of two hundred, out of the fat pastures of Israel; for a meat offering, and for a burnt offering, and for peace offerings, to make reconciliation for them, says the Lord GOD.

16 All the people of the land shall give this oblation for the prince in Israel.

17 And it shall be the prince's part to give burnt offerings, and meat offerings, and drink offerings, in the feasts, and in the new moons, and in the sabbaths, in all solemnities of the house of Israel: he shall prepare the sin offering, and the meat offering, and the burnt offering,

and the peace offerings, to make reconciliation for the house of Israel.

18 Thus says the Lord GOD; In the first month, in the first day of the month, you shall take a young bullock without blemish, and cleanse the sanctuary:

19 And the priest shall take of the blood of the sin offering, and put it upon the posts of the house, and upon the four corners of the settle of the altar, and upon the posts of the gate of the inner court.

20 And so you shall do the seventh day of the month for every one that errs, and for him that is simple: so shall you reconcile the house.

21 In the first month, in the fourteenth day of the month, you shall have the passover, a feast of seven days; unleavened bread shall be eaten.

22 And upon that day shall the prince prepare for himself and for all the people of the land a bullock for a sin offering.

23 And seven days of the feast he shall prepare a burnt offering to the LORD, seven bullocks and seven rams without blemish daily the seven days; and a kid of the goats daily for a sin offering.

24 And he shall prepare a meat offering of an ephah for a bullock, and an ephah for a ram, and a hin of oil for an ephah.

25 In the seventh month, in the fifteenth day of the month, shall he do the like in the feast of the seven days, according to the sin offering, according to the burnt offering, and according to the meat offering, and according to the oil.

CHAPTER 46

THUS says the Lord GOD; The gate of the inner court that looks toward the east shall be shut the six working days; but on the sabbath it shall be opened, and in the day of the new moon it shall be opened.

2 And the prince shall enter by the way of the porch of that gate without, and shall stand by the post of the gate, and the priests shall prepare his burnt offering and his peace offerings, and he shall worship at the threshold of the gate: then he shall go forth; but the gate shall not be shut until the evening.

3 Likewise the people of the land shall worship at the door of this gate before the LORD in the sabbaths and in the new moons.

4 And the burnt offering that the prince shall offer to the LORD in the sabbath day shall be six lambs without blemish, and a ram without blemish.

5 And the meat offering shall be an ephah for a ram, and the meat offering for the lambs as he shall be able to give, and a hin of oil to an ephah.

6 And in the day of the new moon it shall be a young bullock without blemish, and six lambs, and a ram: they shall be without blemish.

7 And he shall prepare a meat offering, an ephah for a bullock, and an ephah for a ram, and for the lambs according as his hand shall attain to, and an hin of oil to an ephah.

8 And when the prince shall enter, he shall go in by the way of the porch of that gate, and he shall go forth by the way thereof.

9 But when the people of the land shall come before the LORD in the solemn feasts, he that enters in by the way of the north gate to worship shall go out by the way of the south gate; and he that enters by the way of the south gate shall go forth by the way of the north gate: he shall not return by the way of the gate whereby he came in, but shall go forth over against it.

10 And the prince in the midst of them, when they go in, shall go in; and when they go forth, shall go forth.

45:20 We still violate the God's Law, even if we sin in ignorance. Even though someone is ignorant of the law of gravity, they suffer the consequences of violating its laws. God does, however, take ignorance into account (see Acts 17:30).

11 And in the feasts and in the solemnities the meat offering shall be an ephah to a bullock, and an ephah to a ram, and to the lambs as he is able to give, and an hin of oil to an ephah.

12 Now when the prince shall prepare a voluntary burnt offering or peace offerings voluntarily to the LORD, one shall then open him the gate that looks toward the east, and he shall prepare his burnt offering and his peace offerings, as he did on the sabbath day: then he shall go forth; and after his going forth one shall shut the gate.

13 You shall daily prepare a burnt offering to the LORD of a lamb of the first year without blemish: you shall prepare it every morning.

14 And you shall prepare a meat offering for it every morning, the sixth part of an ephah, and the third part of an hin of oil, to temper with the fine flour; a meat offering continually by a perpetual ordinance to the LORD.

15 Thus shall they prepare the lamb, and the meat offering, and the oil, every morning for a continual burnt offering.

16 Thus says the Lord GOD; If the prince give a gift to any of his sons, the inheritance thereof shall be his sons'; it shall be their possession by inheritance.

17 But if he give a gift of his inheritance to one of his servants, then it shall be his to the year of liberty; after it shall return to the prince: but his inheritance shall be his sons' for them.

18 Moreover the prince shall not take of the people's inheritance by oppression, to thrust them out of their possession; but he shall give his sons inheritance out of his own possession: that my people be not scattered every man from his possession.

19 After he brought me through the entry, which was at the side of the gate, into the holy chambers of the priests, which looked toward the north: and, behold, there was a place on the two sides westward.

20 Then he said to me, This is the place where the priests shall boil the trespass offering and the sin offering, where they shall bake the meat offering; that they bear them not out into the utter court, to sanctify the people.

21 Then he brought me forth into the utter court, and caused me to pass by the four corners of the court; and, behold, in every corner of the court there was a court.

22 In the four corners of the court there were courts joined of forty cubits long and thirty broad: these four corners were of one measure.

23 And there was a row of building round about in them, round about them four, and it was made with boiling places under the rows round about.

24 Then he said to me, These are the places of them that boil, where the ministers of the house shall boil the sacrifice of the people.

CHAPTER 47

AFTERWARD he brought me again to the door of the house; and, behold, waters issued out from under the threshold of the house eastward: for the forefront of the house stood toward the east, and the waters came down from under from the right side of the house, at the south side of the altar.

2 Then brought he me out of the way of the gate northward, and led me about the way without to the utter gate by the way that looks eastward; and, behold, there ran out waters on the right side.

3 And when the man that had the line in his hand went forth eastward, he measured a thousand cubits, and he brought me through the waters; the waters were to the ankles.

4 Again he measured a thousand, and brought me through the waters; the waters were to the knees. Again he measured a thousand, and brought me through; the waters were to the loins.

5 Afterward he measured a thousand; and it was a river that I could not pass

over: for the waters were risen, waters to swim in, a river that could not be passed over.

6 And he said to me, Son of man, have you seen this? Then he brought me, and caused me to return to the brink of the river.

7 Now when I had returned, behold, at the bank of the river were very many trees on the one side and on the other.

8 Then he said to me, These waters issue out toward the east country, and go down into the desert, and go into the sea: which being brought forth into the sea, the waters shall be healed.

9 And it shall come to pass, that every thing that lives, which moves, wherever the rivers shall come, shall live: and there shall be a very great multitude of fish, because these waters shall come there: for they shall be healed; and every thing shall live where the river comes.

10 And it shall come to pass, that the fishers shall stand upon it from Engedi even to Eneglaim; they shall be a place to spread forth nets; their fish shall be according to their kinds, as the fish of the great sea, exceeding many.

11 But the miry places thereof and the marishes thereof shall not be healed; they shall be given to salt.

12 And by the river upon the bank thereof, on this side and on that side, shall grow all trees for meat, whose leaf shall not fade, neither shall the fruit

47:1-2

How committed are we to reaching the lost? Too often we creep out into the waters of evangelism, but only up to our ankles. We would find a new liberty if we abandoned ourselves to the task of bringing others to the river of life.

thereof be consumed: it shall bring forth new fruit according to his months, because their waters they issued out of the sanctuary: and the fruit thereof shall be for meat, and the leaf thereof for medicine.

13 Thus says the Lord GOD; This shall be the border, whereby you shall inherit the land according to the twelve tribes of Israel: Joseph shall have two portions.

14 And you shall inherit it, one as well as another: concerning the which I lifted up my hand to give it to your fathers: and this land shall fall to you for inheritance.

15 And this shall be the border of the land toward the north side, from the great sea, the way of Hethlon, as men go to Zedad;

16 Hamath, Berothah, Sibraim, which is between the border of Damascus and the border of Hamath; Hazarhatticon, which is by the coast of Hauran.

17 And the border from the sea shall be Hazarenan, the border of Damascus, and the north northward, and the border of Hamath. And this is the north side.

18 And the east side you shall measure from Hauran, and from Damascus, and from Gilead, and from the land of Israel by Jordan, from the border to the east sea. And this is the east side.

19 And the south side southward, from Tamar even to the waters of strife in Kadesh, the river to the great sea. And this is the south side southward.

20 The west side also shall be the great sea from the border, till a man come over against Hamath. This is the west side.

21 So shall you divide this land to you according to the tribes of Israel.

22 And it shall come to pass, that you shall divide it by lot for an inheritance to you, and to the strangers that sojourn among you, which shall beget children among you: and they shall be to you as born in the country among the children of Israel; they shall have inheritance with you among the tribes of Israel.

23 And it shall come to pass, that in what tribe the stranger sojourns, there you shall give him his inheritance, says the Lord GOD.

CHAPTER 48

NOW these are the names of the tribes. From the north end to the coast of the way of Hethlon, as one goeth to Hamath, Hazarenan, the border of Damascus northward, to the coast of Hamath; for these are his sides east and west; a portion for Dan.

2 And by the border of Dan, from the east side to the west side, a portion for Asher.

3 And by the border of Asher, from the east side even to the west side, a portion for Naphtali.

4 And by the border of Naphtali, from the east side to the west side, a portion for Manasseh.

5 And by the border of Manasseh, from the east side to the west side, a portion for Ephraim.

6 And by the border of Ephraim, from the east side even to the west side, a portion for Reuben.

7 And by the border of Reuben, from the east side to the west side, a portion for Judah.

8 And by the border of Judah, from the east side to the west side, shall be the offering which you shall offer of five and twenty thousand reeds in breadth, and in length as one of the other parts, from the east side to the west side: and the sanctuary shall be in the midst of it.

9 The oblation that you shall offer to the LORD shall be of five and twenty thousand in length, and of ten thousand in breadth.

10 And for them, even for the priests, shall be this holy oblation; toward the north five and twenty thousand in length, and toward the west ten thousand in breadth, and toward the east ten thousand in breadth, and toward the south five and twenty thousand

in length: and the sanctuary of the LORD shall be in the midst thereof.

11 It shall be for the priests that are sanctified of the sons of Zadok; which have kept my charge, which went not astray when the children of Israel went astray, as the Levites went astray.

12 And this oblation of the land that is offered shall be to them a thing most holy by the border of the Levites.

13 And over against the border of the priests the Levites shall have five and twenty thousand in length, and ten thousand in breadth: all the length shall be five and twenty thousand, and the breadth ten thousand.

14 And they shall not sell of it, neither exchange, nor alienate the firstfruits of the land: for it is holy to the LORD.

15 And the five thousand, that are left in the breadth over against the five and twenty thousand, shall be a profane place for the city, for dwelling, and for suburbs: and the city shall be in the midst thereof.

16 And these shall be the measures thereof; the north side four thousand and five hundred, and the south side four thousand and five hundred, and on the east side four thousand and five hundred, and the west side four thousand and five hundred.

17 And the suburbs of the city shall be toward the north two hundred and fifty, and toward the south two hundred and fifty, and toward the east two hundred and fifty, and toward the west two hundred and fifty.

18 And the residue in length over against the oblation of the holy portion shall be ten thousand eastward, and ten thousand westward: and it shall be over against the oblation of the holy portion; and the increase thereof shall be for food to them that serve the city.

19 And they that serve the city shall serve it out of all the tribes of Israel.

20 All the oblation shall be five and twenty thousand by five and twenty thousand: you shall offer the holy obla-

tion foursquare, with the possession of the city.

21 And the residue shall be for the prince, on the one side and on the other of the holy oblation, and of the possession of the city, over against the five and twenty thousand of the oblation toward the east border, and westward over against the five and twenty thousand toward the west border, over against the portions for the prince: and it shall be the holy oblation; and the sanctuary of the house shall be in the midst thereof.

22 Moreover from the possession of the Levites, and from the possession of the city, being in the midst of that which is the prince's, between the border of Judah and the border of Benjamin, shall be for the prince.

23 As for the rest of the tribes, from the east side to the west side, Benjamin shall have a portion.

24 And by the border of Benjamin, from the east side to the west side, Simeon shall have a portion.

25 And by the border of Simeon, from the east side to the west side, Issachar a portion.

26 And by the border of Issachar, from the east side to the west side, Zebulun a portion.

27 And by the border of Zebulun, from the east side to the west side, Gad a portion.

28 And by the border of Gad, at the south side southward, the border shall be even from Tamar to the waters of strife in Kadesh, and to the river toward the great sea.

29 This is the land which you shall divide by lot to the tribes of Israel for inheritance, and these are their portions, says the Lord GOD.

30 And these are the goings out of the city on the north side, four thousand and five hundred measures.

31 And the gates of the city shall be after the names of the tribes of Israel: three gates northward; one gate of Reuben, one gate of Judah, one gate of Levi.

32 And at the east side four thousand and five hundred: and three gates; and one gate of Joseph, one gate of Benjamin, one gate of Dan.

33 And at the south side four thousand and five hundred measures: and three gates; one gate of Simeon, one gate of Issachar, one gate of Zebulun.

34 At the west side four thousand and five hundred, with their three gates; one gate of Gad, one gate of Asher, one gate of Naphtali.

35 It was round about eighteen thousand measures: and the name of the city from that day shall be, The LORD is there.

Daniel 2:25

Daniel

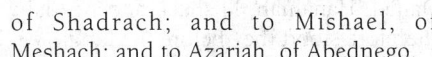

CHAPTER 1

IN the third year of the reign of Jehoiakim king of Judah came Nebuchadnezzar king of Babylon to Jerusalem, and besieged it.

2 And the Lord gave Jehoiakim king of Judah into his hand, with part of the vessels of the house of God: which he carried into the land of Shinar to the house of his god; and he brought the vessels into the treasure house of his god.

3 And the king spoke to Ashpenaz the master of his eunuchs, that he should bring certain of the children of Israel, and of the king's seed, and of the princes;

4 Children in whom was no blemish, but well favoured, and skilful in all wisdom, and cunning in knowledge, and understanding science, and such as had ability in them to stand in the king's palace, and whom they might teach the learning and the tongue of the Chaldeans.

5 And the king appointed them a daily provision of the king's meat, and of the wine which he drank: so nourishing them three years, that at the end thereof they might stand before the king.

6 Now among these were of the children of Judah, Daniel, Hananiah, Mishael, and Azariah:

7 To whom the prince of the eunuchs gave names: for he gave to Daniel the name of Belteshazzar; and to Hananiah,

of Shadrach; and to Mishael, of Meshach; and to Azariah, of Abednego.

8 But Daniel purposed in his heart that he would not defile himself with the portion of the king's meat, nor with the wine which he drank: therefore he requested of the prince of the eunuchs that he might not defile himself.

9 Now God had brought Daniel into favour and tender love with the prince of the eunuchs.

10 And the prince of the eunuchs said to Daniel, I fear my lord the king, who has appointed your meat and your drink: for why should he see your faces worse liking than the children which are of your sort? then shall you make me endanger my head to the king.

11 Then said Daniel to Melzar, whom the prince of the eunuchs had set over Daniel, Hananiah, Mishael, and Azariah,

12 Prove your servants, I beseech you, ten days; and let them give us pulse to eat, and water to drink.

13 Then let our countenances be looked upon before you, and the countenance of the children that eat of the portion of the king's meat: and as you see, deal with your servants.

14 So he consented to them in this matter, and proved them ten days.

15 And at the end of ten days their countenances appeared fairer and fatter in flesh than all the children which did eat the portion of the king's meat.

16 Thus Melzar took away the portion of their meat, and the wine that they should drink; and gave them pulse.

17 As for these four children, God gave them knowledge and skill in all learning and wisdom: and Daniel had understanding in all visions and dreams.

18 Now at the end of the days that the king had said he should bring them in, then the prince of the eunuchs brought them in before Nebuchadnezzar.

19 And the king communed with them; and among them all was found none like Daniel, Hananiah, Mishael, and Azariah: therefore stood they before the king.

20 And in all matters of wisdom and understanding, that the king enquired of them, he found them ten times better than all the magicians and astrologers that were in all his realm.

21 And Daniel continued even to the first year of king Cyrus.

CHAPTER 2

AND in the second year of the reign of Nebuchadnezzar Nebuchadnezzar dreamed dreams, wherewith his spirit was troubled, and his sleep brake from him.

2 Then the king commanded to call the magicians, and the astrologers, and the sorcerers, and the Chaldeans, for to show the king his dreams. So they came and stood before the king.

3 And the king said to them, I have dreamed a dream, and my spirit was troubled to know the dream.

4 Then the Chaldeans spoke to the king in Syriack, O king, live for ever: tell your servants the dream, and we will show the interpretation.

5 The king answered and said to the Chaldeans, The thing is gone from me: if you will not make known to me the dream, with the interpretation thereof, you shall be cut in pieces, and your houses shall be made a dunghill.

6 But if you show the dream, and the interpretation thereof, you shall receive of me gifts and rewards and great honour: therefore show me the dream, and the interpretation thereof.

7 They answered again and said, Let the king tell his servants the dream, and we will show the interpretation of it.

8 The king answered and said, I know of certainty that you would gain the time, because you see the thing is gone from me.

9 But if you will not make known to me the dream, there is but one decree for you: for you have prepared lying and corrupt words to speak before me, till the time be changed: therefore tell me the dream, and I shall know that you can show me the interpretation thereof.

10 The Chaldeans answered before the king, and said, There is not a man upon the earth that can show the king's matter: therefore there is no king, lord, nor ruler, that asked such things at any magician, or astrologer, or Chaldean.

11 And it is a rare thing that the king requires, and there is none other that can show it before the king, except the gods, whose dwelling is not with flesh.

12 For this cause the king was angry and very furious, and commanded to destroy all the wise men of Babylon.

13 And the decree went forth that the wise men should be slain; and they sought Daniel and his fellows to be slain.

14 Then Daniel answered with counsel and wisdom to Arioch the captain of the king's guard, which was gone forth to slay the wise men of Babylon:

Chapter 2 describes a succession of five empires or national entities. "Historians have confirmed that the succession of empires predicted in this chapter followed one another just as predicted here. Hundreds of years before these nations ever formed, Daniel foresaw the rise and fall of Assyria, Medo-Persia with Elam, Greece, Rome, western and eastern European nations."

Richard Gunther

15 He answered and said to Arioch the king's captain, Why is the decree so hasty from the king? Then Arioch made the thing known to Daniel.

16 Then Daniel went in, and desired of the king that he would give him time, and that he would show the king the interpretation.

17 Then Daniel went to his house, and made the thing known to Hananiah, Mishael, and Azariah, his companions:

18 That they would desire mercies of the God of heaven concerning this secret; that Daniel and his fellows should not perish with the rest of the wise men of Babylon.

19 Then was the secret revealed to Daniel in a night vision. Then Daniel blessed the God of heaven.

20 Daniel answered and said, Blessed be the name of God for ever and ever: for wisdom and might are his:

21 And he changes the times and the seasons: he removes kings, and sets up kings: he gives wisdom to the wise, and knowledge to them that know understanding:

22 He reveals the deep and secret things: he knows what is in the darkness, and the light dwells with him.

23 I thank you, and praise you, O God of my fathers, who have given me wisdom and might, and have made known to me now what we desired of you: for you have now made known to us the king's matter.

24 Therefore Daniel went in to Arioch, whom the king had ordained to destroy the wise men of Babylon: he went and said thus to him; Destroy not the wise men of Babylon: bring me in before the king, and I will show to the king the interpretation.

> To know how to use knowledge is to have wisdom.
>
> **CHARLES H. SPURGEON**
> 1834-1892
> BRITISH EVANGELIST

25 Then Arioch brought in Daniel before the king in haste, and said thus to him, I have found a man of the captives of Judah, that will make known to the king the interpretation.

26 The king answered and said to Daniel, whose name was Belteshazzar, Are you able to make known to me the dream which I have seen, and the interpretation thereof?

27 Daniel answered in the presence of the king, and said, The secret which the king has demanded, the wise men, the astrologers, the magicians, the soothsayers, cannot show to the king;

28 But there is a God in heaven that reveals secrets, and makes known to the king Nebuchadnezzar what shall be in the latter days. Your dream, and the visions of your head upon your bed, are these;

29 As for you, O king, your thoughts came into your mind upon your bed, what should come to pass hereafter: and he that reveals secrets makes known to you what shall come to pass.

30 But as for me, this secret is not revealed to me for any wisdom that I have more than any living, but for their sakes that shall make known the interpretation to the king, and that you might know the thoughts of your heart.

2:11-14 The wisdom of man is foolishness with God. The wisest of the wise of this world are but bumbling, brainless, babbling baboons when it comes to understanding the simplest of the simple things of God. The natural mind cannot receive them (see 1 Corinthians 2:14). The simplest Christian has the mind of Christ (1 Corinthians 2:16). He has access to the wisdom of God. The godless wisdom of this world can give no explanation as to why we exist, what causes death, and what is death's antidote. These mysteries are revealed by the Spirit of God to all who trust in the Savior.

31 You, O king, saw, and behold a great image. This great image, whose brightness was excellent, stood before you; and the form thereof was terrible.

32 This image's head was of fine gold, his breast and his arms of silver, his belly and his thighs of brass,

33 His legs of iron, his feet part of iron and part of clay.

34 You saw till that a stone was cut out without hands, which smote the image upon his feet that were of iron and clay, and brake them to pieces.

35 Then was the iron, the clay, the brass, the silver, and the gold, broken to pieces together, and became like the chaff of the summer threshingfloors; and the wind carried them away, that no place was found for them: and the stone that smote the image became a great mountain, and filled the whole earth.

36 This is the dream; and we will tell the interpretation thereof before the king.

37 You, O king, are a king of kings: for the God of heaven has given you a kingdom, power, and strength, and glory.

38 And wherever the children of men dwell, the beasts of the field and the fowls of the heaven has he given into your hand, and has made you ruler over them all. You are this head of gold.

39 And after you shall arise another kingdom inferior to you, and another third kingdom of brass, which shall bear rule over all the earth.

40 And the fourth kingdom shall be strong as iron: forasmuch as iron breaks in pieces and subdues all things: and as iron that breaks all these, shall it break in pieces and bruise.

41 And whereas you saw the feet and toes, part of potters' clay, and part of iron, the kingdom shall be divided; but there shall be in it of the strength of the iron, forasmuch as you saw the iron mixed with miry clay.

42 And as the toes of the feet were part of iron, and part of clay, so the kingdom shall be partly strong, and partly broken.

43 And whereas you saw iron mixed with miry clay, they shall mingle themselves with the seed of men: but they shall not cleave one to another, even as iron is not mixed with clay.

44 And in the days of these kings shall the God of heaven set up a kingdom, which shall never be destroyed: and the kingdom shall not be left to other people, but it shall break in pieces and consume all these kingdoms, and it shall stand for ever.

45 Forasmuch as you saw that the stone was cut out of the mountain without hands, and that it brake in pieces the iron, the brass, the clay, the silver, and the gold; the great God has made known to the king what shall come to pass hereafter: and the dream is certain, and the interpretation thereof sure.

46 Then the king Nebuchadnezzar fell upon his face, and worshipped Daniel, and commanded that they should offer an oblation and sweet odours to him.

47 The king answered Daniel, and said, Of a truth it is, that your God is a God of gods, and a Lord of kings, and a revealer of secrets, seeing you could reveal this secret.

48 Then the king made Daniel a great man, and gave him many great gifts, and made him ruler over the whole province of Babylon, and chief of the governors over all the wise men of Babylon.

49 Then Daniel requested of the king, and he set Shadrach, Meshach, and Abednego, over the affairs of the province of Babylon: but Daniel sat in the gate of the king.

2:44 What does the Bible mean when it speaks of taking the Kingdom of God by force? For an answer, see Matthew 11:12-13.

CHAPTER 3

NEBUCHADNEZZAR the king made an image of gold, whose height was threescore cubits, and the breadth thereof six cubits: he set it up in the plain of Dura, in the province of Babylon.

2 Then Nebuchadnezzar the king sent to gather together the princes, the governors, and the captains, the judges, the treasurers, the counsellors, the sheriffs, and all the rulers of the provinces, to come to the dedication of the image which Nebuchadnezzar the king had set up.

3 Then the princes, the governors, and captains, the judges, the treasurers, the counsellors, the sheriffs, and all the rulers of the provinces, were gathered together to the dedication of the image that Nebuchadnezzar the king had set up; and they stood before the image that Nebuchadnezzar had set up.

4 Then an herald cried aloud, To you it is commanded, O people, nations, and languages,

5 That at what time you hear the sound of the cornet, flute, harp, sackbut, psaltery, dulcimer, and all kinds of music, you fall down and worship the golden image that Nebuchadnezzar the king has set up:

6 And whoever does not fall down and worship shall the same hour be cast into the midst of a burning fiery furnace.

7 Therefore at that time, when all the people heard the sound of the cornet, flute, harp, sackbut, psaltery, and all kinds of music, all the people, the nations, and the languages, fell down and worshipped the golden image that Nebuchadnezzar the king had set up.

8 Therefore at that time certain Chaldeans came near, and accused the Jews.

9 They spoke and said to the king Nebuchadnezzar, O king, live for ever.

10 You, O king, have made a decree, that every man that shall hear the sound of the cornet, flute, harp, sackbut, psaltery, and dulcimer, and all kinds of music, shall fall down and worship the golden image:

11 And whoever does not fall down and worship, that he should be cast into the midst of a burning fiery furnace.

12 There are certain Jews whom you have set over the affairs of the province of Babylon, Shadrach, Meshach, and Abednego; these men, O king, have not regarded you: they do not serve your gods, nor worship the golden image which you have set up.

13 Then Nebuchadnezzar in his rage and fury commanded to bring Shadrach, Meshach, and Abednego. Then they brought these men before the king.

14 Nebuchadnezzar spoke and said to them, Is it true, O Shadrach, Meshach, and Abednego, do you not serve my gods, nor worship the golden image which I have set up?

15 Now if you are ready that at what time you hear the sound of the cornet, flute, harp, sackbut, psaltery, and dulcimer, and all kinds of music, you fall down and worship the image which I have made; well: but if you do not worship, you shall be cast the same hour into the midst of a burning fiery furnace;

3:12 These godly Jews refused to transgress the First and the Second Commandments by bowing before idols.

3:16 King Nebuchadnezzar exalted himself above God. This is normal human behavior. Sinful men stand in judgment over God. They question His decrees. They imagine themselves to be more subtle than God, imagining that they can outwit Him by sinning and then repenting at the last minute. They suppose that he is blind to their sin. They can see, but He is blind, they presume. They slur His character by thinking that He will tolerate their hypocrisy. Like the arrogant king of Babylon, they think that God lacks even the power to deliver from their mighty hands.

and who is that God that shall deliver you out of my hands?

16 Shadrach, Meshach, and Abednego, answered and said to the king, O Nebuchadnezzar, we are not careful to answer you in this matter.

17 If it be so, our God whom we serve is able to deliver us from the burning fiery furnace, and he will deliver us out of your hand, O king.

18 But if not, be it known to you, O king, that we will not serve your gods, nor worship the golden image which you have set up.

19 Then was Nebuchadnezzar full of fury, and the form of his visage was changed against Shadrach, Meshach, and Abednego: therefore he spoke, and commanded that they should heat the furnace one seven times more than it was wont to be heated.

20 And he commanded the most mighty men that were in his army to bind Shadrach, Meshach, and Abednego, and to cast them into the burning fiery furnace.

21 Then these men were bound in their coats, their hosen, and their hats, and their other garments, and were cast into the midst of the burning fiery furnace.

22 Therefore because the king's commandment was urgent, and the furnace exceeding hot, the flames of the fire slew those men that took up Shadrach, Meshach, and Abednego.

23 And these three men, Shadrach, Meshach, and Abednego, fell down bound into the midst of the burning fiery furnace.

24 Then Nebuchadnezzar the king was astonished, and rose up in haste, and spoke, and said to his counsellors, Did not we cast three men bound into the midst of the fire? They answered and said to the king, True, O king.

25 He answered and said, Lo, I see four men loose, walking in the midst of the fire, and they have no hurt; and the form of the fourth is like the Son of God.

26 Then Nebuchadnezzar came near to the mouth of the burning fiery furnace, and spoke, and said, Shadrach, Meshach, and Abednego, you servants of the most high God, come forth, and come here. Then Shadrach, Meshach, and Abednego, came forth of the midst of the fire.

27 And the princes, governors, and captains, and the king's counsellors, being gathered together, saw these men, upon whose bodies the fire had no power, nor was an hair of their head singed, neither were their coats changed, nor the smell of fire had passed on them.

28 Then Nebuchadnezzar spoke, and said, Blessed be the God of Shadrach, Meshach, and Abednego, who has sent his angel, and delivered his servants that trusted in him, and have changed the king's word, and yielded their bodies, that they might not serve nor worship any god, except their own God.

29 Therefore I make a decree, That every people, nation, and language, which speak any thing amiss against the God of Shadrach, Meshach, and Abednego, shall be cut in pieces, and their houses shall be made a dunghill: because there is no other God that can deliver after this sort.

3:18 The three faithful men refused to compromise—even at the loss of their lives. As we can see from their words, "But if not... ."their conviction didn't come from a promise that God would deliver them. They were full of faith. They lived by faith, and they were prepared to die in faith. We, too, are called to be faithful in the face of death. Neither do we have a promise of deliverance from the hands of ungodly men. God allowed Stephen to be martyred, as well as eleven of the original apostles and millions of other martyrs down through the ages (see note for Acts 7:55: "History reveals the fate of the apostles.")

3:19 The smiling face of the world changes when we refuse to compromise the issue of sin.

SHADRACH, MESHACH AND ABEDNEGO IN THE FIERY FURNACE

Daniel 3:24

I t is a great testimony to the world if they see that we are not bound by ties to fiery
trials. Our joy can remain even in the midst of a furnace because our names are
written in heaven.

30 Then the king promoted Shadrach, Meshach, and Abednego, in the province of Babylon.

CHAPTER 4

NEBUCHADNEZZAR the king, to all people, nations, and languages, that dwell in all the earth; Peace be multiplied to you.

2 I thought it good to show the signs and wonders that the high God has done for me.

3 How great are his signs! and how mighty are his wonders! his kingdom is an everlasting kingdom, and his dominion is from generation to generation.

4 I Nebuchadnezzar was at rest in my house, and flourishing in my palace:

5 I saw a dream which made me afraid, and the thoughts upon my bed and the visions of my head troubled me.

6 Therefore made I a decree to bring in all the wise men of Babylon before me, that they might make known to me the interpretation of the dream.

7 Then came in the magicians, the astrologers, the Chaldeans, and the soothsayers: and I told the dream before them; but they did not make known to me the interpretation thereof.

8 But at the last Daniel came in before me, whose name was Belteshazzar, according to the name of my God, and in whom is the spirit of the holy gods: and before him I told the dream, saying,

9 O Belteshazzar, master of the magicians, because I know that the spirit of the holy gods is in you, and no secret troubles you, tell me the visions of my dream that I have seen, and the interpretation thereof.

10 Thus were the visions of my head in my bed; I saw, and behold a tree in the midst of the earth, and the height thereof was great.

11 The tree grew, and was strong, and the height thereof reached to heaven, and the sight thereof to the end of all the earth:

12 The leaves thereof were fair, and the fruit thereof much, and in it was meat for all: the beasts of the field had shadow under it, and the fowls of the heaven dwelt in the boughs thereof, and all flesh was fed of it.

13 I saw in the visions of my head upon my bed, and, behold, a watcher and an holy one came down from heaven;

14 He cried aloud, and said thus, Hew down the tree, and cut off his branches, shake off his leaves, and scatter his fruit: let the beasts get away from under it, and the fowls from his branches:

15 Nevertheless leave the stump of his roots in the earth, even with a band of iron and brass, in the tender grass of the field; and let it be wet with the dew of heaven, and let his portion be with the beasts in the grass of the earth:

16 Let his heart be changed from man's, and let a beast's heart be given to him; and let seven times pass over him.

17 This matter is by the decree of the watchers, and the demand by the word of the holy ones: to the intent that the living may know that the most High rules in the kingdom of men, and gives it to whoever he will, and sets up over it the basest of men.

18 This dream I king Nebuchadnezzar have seen. Now you, O Belteshazzar, declare the interpretation thereof, forasmuch as all the wise men of my kingdom are not able to make known to me the interpretation: but you are able; for the spirit of the holy gods is in you.

19 Then Daniel, whose name was

4:15-16, 25, 30 God's Law strips a man of his pride (verse 30). It shows him that he has the heart of a beast and brings him to a point of understanding that the Most High rules the kingdom of men and gives it to whomsoever He will (verse 25). Like the prodigal son of Jesus' parable, when the sinner sees his sinfulness in the bright light of God's Law, he sees that his desire is for pig food and he comes to his senses (verses 34-37). Also see Luke 15:16-19.

Belteshazzar, was astonished for one hour, and his thoughts troubled him. The king spoke, and said, Belteshazzar, let not the dream, or the interpretation thereof, trouble you. Belteshazzar answered and said, My lord, the dream be to them that hate you, and the interpretation thereof to your enemies.

20 The tree that you saw, which grew, and was strong, whose height reached to the heaven, and the sight thereof to all the earth;

21 Whose leaves were fair, and the fruit thereof much, and in it was meat for all; under which the beasts of the field dwelt, and upon whose branches the fowls of the heaven had their habitation:

22 It is you, O king, that have grown and become strong: for your greatness is grown, and reaches to heaven, and your dominion to the end of the earth.

23 And whereas the king saw a watcher and an holy one coming down from heaven, and saying, Hew the tree down, and destroy it; yet leave the stump of the roots thereof in the earth, even with a band of iron and brass, in the tender grass of the field; and let it be wet with the dew of heaven, and let his portion be with the beasts of the field, till seven times pass over him;

24 This is the interpretation, O king, and this is the decree of the most High, which is come upon my lord the king:

25 That they shall drive you from men, and your dwelling shall be with the beasts of the field, and they shall make you to eat grass as oxen, and they shall wet you with the dew of heaven, and seven times shall pass over you, till you know that the most High rules in the kingdom of men, and gives it to whoever he will.

> Nearly all men can stand adversity, but if you want to test a man's character, give him power.
>
> **ABRAHAM LINCOLN**
>
> 1809-1865
>
> 16TH PRESIDENT
>
> OF THE UNITED STATES

26 And whereas they commanded to leave the stump of the tree roots; your kingdom shall be sure to you, after that you shall have known that the heavens do rule.

27 Therefore, O king, let my counsel be acceptable to you, and break off your sins by righteousness, and your iniquities by showing mercy to the poor; if it may be a lengthening of your tranquillity.

28 All this came upon the king Nebuchadnezzar.

29 At the end of twelve months he walked in the palace of the kingdom of Babylon.

30 The king spoke, and said, Is not this great Babylon, that I have built for the house of the kingdom by the might of my power, and for the honour of my majesty?

31 While the word was in the king's mouth, there fell a voice from heaven, saying, O king Nebuchadnezzar, to you it is spoken; The kingdom is departed from you.

32 And they shall drive you from men, and your dwelling shall be with the beasts of the field: they shall make you to eat grass as oxen, and seven times shall pass over you, until you know that the most High rules in the kingdom of men, and gives it to whomsoever he will.

33 The same hour was the thing fulfilled upon Nebuchadnezzar: and he was driven from men, and did eat grass as oxen, and his body was wet with the dew of heaven, till his hairs were grown like eagles' feathers, and his nails like birds' claws.

34 And at the end of the days I Nebuchadnezzar lifted up my eyes to heaven, and my understanding returned to me, and I blessed the most High, and I praised and honoured him that lives

for ever, whose dominion is an everlasting dominion, and his kingdom is from generation to generation:

35 And all the inhabitants of the earth are reputed as nothing: and he doeth according to his will in the army of heaven, and among the inhabitants of the earth: and none can stay his hand, or say to him, What have you done?

36 At the same time my reason returned to me; and for the glory of my kingdom, my honour and brightness returned to me; and my counsellors and my lords sought to me; and I was established in my kingdom, and excellent majesty was added to me.

37 Now I Nebuchadnezzar praise and extol and honour the King of heaven, all whose works are truth, and his ways judgment: and those that walk in pride he is able to abase.

CHAPTER 5

BELSHAZZAR the king made a great feast to a thousand of his lords, and drank wine before the thousand.

2 Belshazzar, whiles he tasted the wine, commanded to bring the golden and silver vessels which his father Nebuchadnezzar had taken out of the temple which was in Jerusalem; that the king, and his princes, his wives, and his concubines, might drink therein.

3 Then they brought the golden vessels that were taken out of the temple of the house of God which was at Jerusalem; and the king, and his princes, his wives, and his concubines, drank in them.

4 They drank wine, and praised the gods of gold, and of silver, of brass, of iron, of wood, and of stone.

5 In the same hour came forth fingers of a man's hand, and wrote over against the candlestick upon the plaster of the wall of the king's palace: and the king saw the part of the hand that wrote.

6 Then the king's countenance was changed, and his thoughts troubled him, so that the joints of his loins were loosed, and his knees smote one against another.

7 The king cried aloud to bring in the astrologers, the Chaldeans, and the soothsayers. And the king spoke, and said to the wise men of Babylon, Whoever shall read this writing, and show me the interpretation thereof, shall be clothed with scarlet, and have a chain of gold about his neck, and shall be the third ruler in the kingdom.

8 Then came in all the king's wise men: but they could not read the writing, nor make known to the king the interpretation thereof.

9 Then was king Belshazzar greatly troubled, and his countenance was changed in him, and his lords were astonished.

10 Now the queen by reason of the words of the king and his lords came into the banquet house: and the queen spoke and said, O king, live for ever: do not let your thoughts trouble you, nor let your countenance be changed:

11 There is a man in your kingdom, in whom is the spirit of the holy gods; and in the days of your father light and understanding and wisdom, like the wisdom of the gods, was found in him; whom the king Nebuchadnezzar your father, the king, I say, your father, made master of the magicians, astrologers, Chaldeans, and soothsayers;

12 Forasmuch as an excellent spirit, and knowledge, and understanding, interpreting of dreams, and showing of hard sentences, and dissolving of doubts, were found in the same Daniel, whom the king named Belteshazzar: now let Daniel be called, and he will show the interpretation.

13 Then was Daniel brought in before the king. And the king spoke and said to Daniel, Are you that Daniel, which are of the children of the captivity of Judah, whom the king my father brought out of Jewry?

14 I have even heard of you, that the spirit of the gods is in you, and that light

DANIEL INTERPRETING THE WRITING ON THE WALL

Daniel 5:5-6 and 25

God gave His Law. "...so terrible was the sight, that Moses said, 'I exceedingly fear and quake'" (Hebrews 12:21). We are called to do what Daniel did, to interpret the spiritual nature of God's Law for a sin-loving world. God has numbered our days and weighed them in the balance of His Law. Salvation is only through repentence and trust in the Savior.

and understanding and excellent wisdom is found in you.

15 And now the wise men, the astrologers, have been brought in before me, that they should read this writing, and make known to me the interpretation thereof: but they could not show the interpretation of the thing:

16 And I have heard of you, that you can make interpretations, and dissolve doubts: now if you can read the writing, and make known to me the interpretation thereof, you shall be clothed with scarlet, and have a chain of gold about your neck, and shall be the third ruler in the kingdom.

17 Then Daniel answered and said before the king, Let your gifts be to yourself, and give your rewards to another; yet I will read the writing to the king, and make known to him the interpretation.

18 O king, the most high God gave Nebuchadnezzar your father a kingdom, and majesty, and glory, and honour:

19 And for the majesty that he gave him, all people, nations, and languages, trembled and feared before him: whom he would he slew; and whom he would he kept alive; and whom he would he set up; and whom he would he put down.

20 But when his heart was lifted up, and his mind hardened in pride, he was deposed from his kingly throne, and they took his glory from him:

21 And he was driven from the sons of men; and his heart was made like the beasts, and his dwelling was with the wild asses: they fed him with grass like oxen, and his body was wet with the dew of heaven; till he knew that the most high God ruled in the kingdom of men, and that he appoints over it whomsoever he will.

22 And you his son, O Belshazzar, have not humbled your heart, though you knew all this;

23 But have lifted up yourself against the Lord of heaven; and they have brought the vessels of his house before you, and you, and your lords, your wives, and your concubines, have drunk wine in them; and you have praised the gods of silver, and gold, of brass, iron, wood, and stone, which see not, nor hear, nor know: and the God in whose hand your breath is, and whose are all your ways, have you not glorified:

24 Then was the part of the hand sent from him; and this writing was written.

25 And this is the writing that was written, MENE, MENE, TEKEL, UPHARSIN.

26 This is the interpretation of the thing: MENE; God has numbered your kingdom, and finished it.

27 TEKEL; You are weighed in the balances, and are found wanting.

28 PERES; Your kingdom is divided, and given to the Medes and Persians.

29 Then commanded Belshazzar, and they clothed Daniel with scarlet, and put a chain of gold about his neck, and made a proclamation concerning him, that he should be the third ruler in the kingdom.

30 In that night was Belshazzar the king of the Chaldeans slain.

31 And Darius the Median took the kingdom, being about threescore and two years old.

CHAPTER 6

IT pleased Darius to set over the kingdom an hundred and twenty princes, which should be over the whole kingdom;

2 And over these three presidents; of whom Daniel was first: that the princes might give accounts to them, and the king should have no damage.

3 Then this Daniel was preferred above the presidents and princes, because an excellent spirit was in him; and the king thought to set him over the whole realm.

4 Then the presidents and princes sought to find occasion against Daniel concerning the kingdom; but they could find none occasion nor fault; forasmuch as he was faithful, neither was there any error or fault found in him.

5 Then said these men, We shall not find any occasion against this Daniel, except we find it against him concerning the law of his God.

6 Then these presidents and princes assembled together to the king, and said thus to him, King Darius, live for ever.

7 All the presidents of the kingdom, the governors, and the princes, the counsellors, and the captains, have consulted together to establish a royal statute, and to make a firm decree, that whoever shall ask a petition of any God or man for thirty days, save of you, O king, he shall be cast into the den of lions.

8 Now, O king, establish the decree, and sign the writing, that it be not changed, according to the law of the Medes and Persians, which does not alter.

9 Therefore king Darius signed the writing and the decree.

10 Now when Daniel knew that the writing was signed, he went into his house; and his windows being open in his chamber toward Jerusalem, he kneeled upon his knees three times a day, and prayed, and gave thanks before his God, as he did aforetime.

11 Then these men assembled, and found Daniel praying and making supplication before his God.

12 Then they came near, and spoke before the king concerning the king's decree; Have you not signed a decree, that every man that shall ask a petition of any God or man within thirty days, save of you, O king, shall be cast into the den of lions? The king answered and said, The thing is true, according to the law of the Medes and Persians, which does not alter.

13 Then answered they and said before the king, That Daniel, which is of the children of the captivity of Judah, does not regard you, O king, nor the decree that you have signed, but makes his peti-

tion three times a day.

14 Then the king, when he heard these words, was sore displeased with himself, and set his heart on Daniel to deliver him: and he laboured till the going down of the sun to deliver him.

15 Then these men assembled to the king, and said to the king, Know, O king, that the law of the Medes and Persians is, That no decree nor statute which the king establishes may be changed.

16 Then the king commanded, and they brought Daniel, and cast him into the den of lions. Now the king spoke and said to Daniel, Your God whom you serve continually, he will deliver you.

17 And a stone was brought, and laid upon the mouth of the den; and the king sealed it with his own signet, and with the signet of his lords; that the purpose might not be changed concerning Daniel.

18 Then the king went to his palace, and passed the night fasting: neither were instruments of music brought before him: and his sleep went from him.

19 Then the king arose very early in the morning, and went in haste to the den of lions.

20 And when he came to the den, he cried with a lamentable voice to Daniel: and the king spoke and said to Daniel, O Daniel, servant of the living God, is your God, whom you serve continually, able to deliver you from the lions?

21 Then said Daniel to the king, O king, live for ever.

22 My God has sent his angel, and has shut the lions' mouths, that they have not hurt me: forasmuch as before him innocency was found in me; and also before you, O king, have I done no hurt.

23 Then was the king exceedingly glad for him, and commanded that they should take Daniel up out of the den. So

---

6:10 Daniel would not compromise his faith in God, not even in the face of death.

DANIEL IN THE DEN OF LIONS

Daniel 6:16-22

For us, God also stopped the mouths of the ten hungry lions of the Ten Commandments; He sent the Messiah to assume our curse and save us from destruction by their sharp teeth. Lion's dens are no fun. But they surely drive us to prayer, and that can only be good. (See Hebrews 12:5-6.)

Daniel was taken up out of the den, and no manner of hurt was found upon him, because he believed in his God.

24 And the king commanded, and they brought those men which had accused Daniel, and they cast them into the den of lions, them, their children, and their wives; and the lions had the mastery of them, and brake all their bones in pieces or ever they came at the bottom of the den.

25 Then king Darius wrote to all people, nations, and languages, that dwell in all the earth; Peace be multiplied to you.

26 I make a decree, That in every dominion of my kingdom men tremble and fear before the God of Daniel: for he is the living God, and stedfast for ever, and his kingdom that which shall not be destroyed, and his dominion shall be even to the end.

27 He delivers and rescues, and he works signs and wonders in heaven and in earth, who has delivered Daniel from the power of the lions.

28 So this Daniel prospered in the reign of Darius, and in the reign of Cyrus the Persian.

CHAPTER 7

IN the first year of Belshazzar king of Babylon Daniel had a dream and visions of his head upon his bed: then he wrote the dream, and told the sum of the matters.

2 Daniel spoke and said, I saw in my vision by night, and, behold, the four winds of the heaven strove upon the great sea.

3 And four great beasts came up from the sea, diverse one from another.

4 The first was like a lion, and had eagle's wings: I beheld till the wings thereof were plucked, and it was lifted up from the earth, and made stand upon the feet as a man, and a man's heart was given to it.

5 And behold another beast, a second, like to a bear, and it raised up itself on one side, and it had three ribs in the mouth of it between the teeth of it: and they said thus to it, Arise, devour much flesh.

6 After this I beheld, and lo another, like a leopard, which had upon the back of it four wings of a fowl; the beast had also four heads; and dominion was given to it.

7 After this I saw in the night visions, and behold a fourth beast, dreadful and terrible, and strong exceedingly; and it had great iron teeth: it devoured and brake in pieces, and stamped the residue with the feet of it: and it was diverse from all the beasts that were before it; and it had ten horns.

8 I considered the horns, and, behold, there came up among them another little horn, before whom there were three of the first horns plucked up by the roots: and, behold, in this horn were eyes like the eyes of man, and a mouth speaking great things.

9 I beheld till the thrones were cast down, and the Ancient of days did sit, whose garment was white as snow, and the hair of his head like the pure wool: his throne was like the fiery flame, and his wheels as burning fire.

10 A fiery stream issued and came forth from before him: thousand thousands ministered to him, and ten thousand times ten thousand stood before him: the judgment was set, and the books were opened.

11 I beheld then because of the voice of the great words which the horn spoke: I beheld even till the beast was slain, and his body destroyed, and given to the burning flame.

12 As concerning the rest of the beasts,

6:24 When a man fights against the ways of God, he often passes his godless sentiments onto his loved ones and leads his family into a fearful fate.

they had their dominion taken away: yet their lives were prolonged for a season and time.

13 I saw in the night visions, and, behold, one like the Son of man came with the clouds of heaven, and came to the Ancient of days, and they brought him near before him.

14 And there was given him dominion, and glory, and a kingdom, that all people, nations, and languages, should serve him: his dominion is an everlasting dominion, which shall not pass away, and his kingdom that which shall not be destroyed.

15 I Daniel was grieved in my spirit in the midst of my body, and the visions of my head troubled me.

16 I came near to one of them that stood by, and asked him the truth of all this. So he told me, and made me know the interpretation of the things.

17 These great beasts, which are four, are four kings, which shall arise out of the earth.

18 But the saints of the most High shall take the kingdom, and possess the kingdom for ever, even for ever and ever.

19 Then I would know the truth of the fourth beast, which was diverse from all the others, exceeding dreadful, whose teeth were of iron, and his nails of brass; which devoured, brake in pieces, and stamped the residue with his feet;

20 And of the ten horns that were in his head, and of the other which came up, and before whom three fell; even of that horn that had eyes, and a mouth that spoke very great things, whose look was more stout than his fellows.

21 I beheld, and the same horn made war with the saints, and prevailed against them;

22 Until the Ancient of days came, and judgment was given to the saints of the most High; and the time came that the saints possessed the kingdom.

23 Thus he said, The fourth beast shall be the fourth kingdom upon earth, which shall be diverse from all kingdoms, and shall devour the whole earth, and shall tread it down, and break it in pieces.

24 And the ten horns out of this kingdom are ten kings that shall arise: and another shall rise after them; and he shall be diverse from the first, and he shall subdue three kings.

25 And he shall speak great words against the most High, and shall wear out the saints of the most High, and think to change times and laws: and they shall be given into his hand until a time and times and the dividing of time.

26 But the judgment shall sit, and they shall take away his dominion, to consume and to destroy it to the end.

27 And the kingdom and dominion, and the greatness of the kingdom under the whole heaven, shall be given to the people of the saints of the most High, whose kingdom is an everlasting kingdom, and all dominions shall serve and obey him.

28 Hitherto is the end of the matter. As for me Daniel, my cogitations much troubled me, and my countenance changed in me: but I kept the matter in my heart.

CHAPTER 8

IN the third year of the reign of king Belshazzar a vision appeared to me, even to me Daniel, after that which appeared to me at the first.

2 And I saw in a vision; and it came to pass, when I saw, that I was at Shushan in the palace, which is in the province of Elam; and I saw in a vision, and I was by the river of Ulai.

3 Then I lifted up my eyes, and saw, and, behold, there stood before the river a ram which had two horns: and the two horns were high; but one was higher than the other, and the higher came up last.

4 I saw the ram pushing westward, and northward, and southward; so that no beasts might stand before him, neither was there any that could deliver out of

his hand; but he did according to his will, and became great.

5 And as I was considering, behold, an he goat came from the west on the face of the whole earth, and touched not the ground: and the goat had a notable horn between his eyes.

6 And he came to the ram that had two horns, which I had seen standing before the river, and ran to him in the fury of his power.

7 And I saw him come close to the ram, and he was moved with anger against him, and smote the ram, and brake his two horns: and there was no power in the ram to stand before him, but he cast him down to the ground, and stamped upon him: and there was none that could deliver the ram out of his hand.

8 Therefore the he goat grew very great: and when he was strong, the great horn was broken; and for it came up four notable ones toward the four winds of heaven.

9 And out of one of them came forth a little horn, which grew exceeding great, toward the south, and toward the east, and toward the pleasant land.

10 And it grew great, even to the host of heaven; and it cast down some of the host and of the stars to the ground, and stamped upon them.

11 Yea, he magnified himself even to the prince of the host, and by him the daily sacrifice was taken away, and the place of the sanctuary was cast down.

12 And an host was given him against the daily sacrifice by reason of transgression, and it cast down the truth to the ground; and it practised, and prospered.

13 Then I heard one saint speaking, and another saint said to that certain saint which spoke, How long shall be the vision concerning the daily sacrifice, and the transgression of desolation, to give both the sanctuary and the host to be trodden under foot?

14 And he said to me, For two thousand and three hundred days; then shall the sanctuary be cleansed.

15 And it came to pass, when I, even I Daniel, had seen the vision, and sought for the meaning, then, behold, there stood before me as the appearance of a man.

16 And I heard a man's voice between the banks of Ulai, which called, and said, Gabriel, make this man to understand the vision.

17 So he came near where I stood: and when he came, I was afraid, and fell upon my face: but he said to me, Understand, O son of man: for at the time of the end shall be the vision.

18 Now as he was speaking with me, I was in a deep sleep on my face toward the ground: but he touched me, and set me upright.

19 And he said, Behold, I will make you know what shall be in the last end of the indignation: for at the time appointed the end shall be.

20 The ram which you saw having two horns are the kings of Media and Persia.

21 And the rough goat is the king of Grecia: and the great horn that is between his eyes is the first king.

22 Now that being broken, whereas four stood up for it, four kingdoms shall stand up out of the nation, but not in his power.

23 And in the latter time of their kingdom, when the transgressors are come to the full, a king of fierce countenance, and understanding dark sentences, shall stand up.

24 And his power shall be mighty, but not by his own power: and he shall destroy wonderfully, and shall prosper, and practise, and shall destroy the mighty and the holy people.

25 And through his policy also he shall cause craft to prosper in his hand; and he shall magnify himself in his heart, and by peace shall destroy many: he shall also stand up against the Prince of princes; but he shall be broken without hand.

26 And the vision of the evening and the morning which was told is true:

> Have you noticed how much praying for revival has been going on of late
> and how little revival has resulted?
> I believe the problem is that we have been trying to substitute praying for obeying,
> and it simply will not work.
> To pray for revival while ignoring the plain precept laid down in scripture
> is to waste a lot of words and get nothing for our trouble.
> Prayer will become effective when we stop using it as a substitute for obedience.

AIDEN WILSON TOZER

1897 - 1963

therefore shut up the vision; for it shall be for many days.

27 And I Daniel fainted, and was sick certain days; afterward I rose up, and did the king's business; and I was astonished at the vision, but none understood it.

CHAPTER 9

IN the first year of Darius the son of Ahasuerus, of the seed of the Medes, which was made king over the realm of the Chaldeans;

2 In the first year of his reign I Daniel understood by books the number of the years, whereof the word of the LORD came to Jeremiah the prophet, that he would accomplish seventy years in the desolations of Jerusalem.

3 And I set my face to the Lord God, to seek by prayer and supplications, with fasting, and sackcloth, and ashes:

4 And I prayed to the LORD my God, and made my confession, and said, O Lord, the great and dreadful God, keeping the covenant and mercy to them that love him, and to them that keep his commandments;

5 We have sinned, and have committed iniquity, and have done wickedly, and have rebelled, even by departing from your precepts and from your judgments:

6 Neither have we hearkened to your servants the prophets, which spoke in your name to our kings, our princes, and our fathers, and to all the people of the land.

7 O LORD, righteousness belongs to you, but to us confusion of faces, as at this day; to the men of Judah, and to the inhabitants of Jerusalem, and to all Israel, that are near, and that are far off, through all the countries where you have driven them, because of their trespass that they have trespassed against you.

8 O Lord, to us belongs confusion of face, to our kings, to our princes, and to our fathers, because we have sinned against you.

9 To the Lord our God belong mercies and forgivenesses, though we have rebelled against him;

10 Neither have we obeyed the voice of the LORD our God, to walk in his laws, which he set before us by his servants the prophets.

11 Yea, all Israel have transgressed your law, even by departing, that they might not obey your voice; therefore the curse is poured upon us, and the oath that is written in the law of Moses the servant of God, because we have sinned against him.

12 And he has confirmed his words, which he spoke against us, and against our judges that judged us, by bringing upon us a great evil: for under the whole heaven has not been done as has been done upon Jerusalem.

13 As it is written in the law of Moses, all this evil is come upon us: yet made we not our prayer before the LORD our God, that we might turn from our iniquities, and understand your truth.

14 Therefore has the LORD watched upon the evil, and brought it upon us: for the LORD our God is righteous in all

his works which he doeth: for we obeyed not his voice.

15 And now, O Lord our God, that have brought your people forth out of the land of Egypt with a mighty hand, and have made yourself a name, as at this day; we have sinned, we have done wickedly.

16 O LORD, according to all your righteousness, I beseech you, let your anger and your fury be turned away from your city Jerusalem, your holy mountain: because for our sins, and for the iniquities of our fathers, Jerusalem and your people are become a reproach to all that are about us.

17 Now therefore, O our God, hear the prayer of your servant, and his supplications, and cause your face to shine upon your sanctuary that is desolate, for the Lord's sake.

18 O my God, incline your ear, and hear; open your eyes, and behold our desolations, and the city which is called by your name: for we do not present our supplications before you for our righteousnesses, but for your great mercies.

19 O Lord, hear; O Lord, forgive; O Lord, hearken and do; defer not, for your own sake, O my God: for your city and your people are called by your name.

20 And whiles I was speaking, and praying, and confessing my sin and the sin of my people Israel, and presenting my supplication before the LORD my God for the holy mountain of my God;

21 Yea, whiles I was speaking in prayer, even the man Gabriel, whom I had seen in the vision at the beginning, being caused to fly swiftly, touched me about the time of the evening oblation.

22 And he informed me, and talked with me, and said, O Daniel, I am now come forth to give you skill and understanding.

23 At the beginning of your supplications the commandment came forth, and I am come to show you; for you are greatly beloved: therefore understand the matter, and consider the vision.

24 Seventy weeks are determined upon your people and upon your holy city, to finish the transgression, and to make an end of sins, and to make reconciliation for iniquity, and to bring in everlasting righteousness, and to seal up the vision and prophecy, and to anoint the most Holy.

25 Know therefore and understand, that from the going forth of the commandment to restore and to build Jerusalem to the Messiah the Prince shall be seven weeks, and threescore and two weeks: the street shall be built again, and the wall, even in troublous times.

26 And after threescore and two weeks shall Messiah be cut off, but not for himself: and the people of the prince that shall come shall destroy the city and the sanctuary; and the end thereof shall be with a flood, and to the end of the war desolations are determined.

27 And he shall confirm the covenant with many for one week: and in the midst of the week he shall cause the sacrifice and the oblation to cease, and for the overspreading of abominations he shall make it desolate, even until the consummation, and that determined shall be poured upon the desolate.

> " Before I can preach love, mercy, and grace, I must preach sin, Law, and judgment "
>
> **JOHN WESLEY**
> 1703 - 1791
> **BRITISH EVANGELIST AND FOUNDER OF METHODISM**

CHAPTER 10

IN the third year of Cyrus king of Persia a thing was revealed to Daniel, whose name was called Belteshazzar; and the thing was true, but the time appointed was long: and he understood the thing, and had understanding of the vision.

2 In those days I Daniel was mourning three full weeks.

3 I ate no pleasant bread, neither came flesh nor wine in my mouth, neither did I anoint myself at all, till three whole weeks were fulfilled.

4 And in the four and twentieth day of the first month, as I was by the side of the great river, which is Hiddekel;

5 Then I lifted up my eyes, and looked, and behold a certain man clothed in linen, whose loins were girded with fine gold of Uphaz:

6 His body also was like the beryl, and his face as the appearance of lightning, and his eyes as lamps of fire, and his arms and his feet like in colour to polished brass, and the voice of his words like the voice of a multitude.

7 And I Daniel alone saw the vision: for the men that were with me saw not the vision; but a great quaking fell upon them, so that they fled to hide themselves.

8 Therefore I was left alone, and saw this great vision, and there remained no strength in me: for my comeliness was turned in me into corruption, and I retained no strength.

9 Yet heard I the voice of his words: and when I heard the voice of his words, then was I in a deep sleep on my face, and my face toward the ground.

10 And, behold, an hand touched me, which set me upon my knees and upon the palms of my hands.

11 And he said to me, O Daniel, a man greatly beloved, understand the words that I speak to you, and stand upright: for to you am I now sent. And when he had spoken this word to me, I stood trembling.

> "The Law cuts into the core of the evil;
> it reveals the seat of the malady, and informs us
> that the leprosy lies deep within."
>
> **CHARLES H. SPURGEON**
> **1834-1892**
> **FOREMOST PREACHER**
> **OF THE 19TH CENTURY**

12 Then said he to me, Fear not, Daniel: for from the first day that you set your heart to understand, and to chasten yourself before your God, your words were heard, and I am come for your words.

13 But the prince of the kingdom of Persia withstood me one and twenty days: but, lo, Michael, one of the chief princes, came to help me; and I remained there with the kings of Persia.

14 Now I am come to make you understand what shall befall your people in the latter days: for yet the vision is for many days.

15 And when he had spoken such words to me, I set my face toward the ground, and I became dumb.

16 And, behold, one like the similitude of the sons of men touched my lips: then I opened my mouth, and spoke, and said to him that stood before me, O my lord, by the vision my sorrows are turned upon me, and I have retained no strength.

17 For how can the servant of this my lord talk with this my lord? for as for me, straightway there remained no strength in me, neither is there breath left in me.

18 Then there came again and touched me one like the appearance of a man, and he strengthened me,

19 And said, O man greatly beloved, fear not: peace be to you, be strong, yea, be strong. And when he had spoken to me, I was strengthened, and said, Let my lord speak; for you have strengthened me.

20 Then said he, Do you know why I have come to you? and now will I return to fight with the prince of Persia: and when I am gone forth, lo, the prince of Grecia shall come.

21 But I will show you that which is noted in the scripture of truth: and there is none that holds with me in these things, but Michael your prince.

CHAPTER 11

ALSO I in the first year of Darius the Mede, even I, stood to confirm and to strengthen him.

2 And now will I show you the truth. Behold, there shall stand up yet three kings in Persia; and the fourth shall be far richer than they all: and by his strength through his riches he shall stir up all against the realm of Grecia.

3 And a mighty king shall stand up, that shall rule with great dominion, and do according to his will.

4 And when he shall stand up, his kingdom shall be broken, and shall be divided toward the four winds of heaven; and not to his posterity, nor according to his dominion which he ruled: for his kingdom shall be plucked up, even for others beside those.

5 And the king of the south shall be strong, and one of his princes; and he shall be strong above him, and have dominion; his dominion shall be a great dominion.

6 And in the end of years they shall join themselves together; for the king's daughter of the south shall come to the king of the north to make an agreement: but she shall not retain the power of the arm; neither shall he stand, nor his arm: but she shall be given up, and they that brought her, and he that begat her, and he that strengthened her in these times.

7 But out of a branch of her roots shall one stand up in his estate, which shall come with an army, and shall enter into the fortress of the king of the north, and shall deal against them, and shall prevail:

8 And shall also carry captives into Egypt their gods, with their princes, and with their precious vessels of silver and of gold; and he shall continue more years than the king of the north.

9 So the king of the south shall come into his kingdom, and shall return into his own land.

10 But his sons shall be stirred up, and shall assemble a multitude of great forces: and one shall certainly come, and overflow, and pass through: then shall he return, and be stirred up, even to his fortress.

11 And the king of the south shall be moved with anger, and shall come forth and fight with him, even with the king of the north: and he shall set forth a great multitude; but the multitude shall be given into his hand.

12 And when he has taken away the multitude, his heart shall be lifted up; and he shall cast down many ten thousands: but he shall not be strengthened by it.

13 For the king of the north shall return, and shall set forth a multitude greater than the former, and shall certainly come after certain years with a great army and with much riches.

14 And in those times there shall many stand up against the king of the south: also the robbers of your people shall exalt themselves to establish the vision; but they shall fall.

15 So the king of the north shall come, and cast up a mount, and take the most fenced cities: and the arms of the south shall not withstand, neither his chosen people, neither shall there be any strength to withstand.

16 But he that comes against him shall do according to his own will, and none shall stand before him: and he shall stand in the glorious land, which by his hand shall be consumed.

17 He shall also set his face to enter with the strength of his whole kingdom, and upright ones with him; thus shall he do: and he shall give him the daughter of women, corrupting her: but she shall not stand on his side, neither be for him.

18 After this shall he turn his face to the isles, and shall take many: but a prince for his own behalf shall cause the

reproach offered by him to cease; without his own reproach he shall cause it to turn upon him.

19 Then he shall turn his face toward the fort of his own land: but he shall stumble and fall, and not be found.

20 Then shall stand up in his estate a raiser of taxes in the glory of the kingdom: but within few days he shall be destroyed, neither in anger, nor in battle.

21 And in his estate shall stand up a vile person, to whom they shall not give the honour of the kingdom: but he shall come in peaceably, and obtain the kingdom by flatteries.

22 And with the arms of a flood shall they be overflown from before him, and shall be broken; yea, also the prince of the covenant.

23 And after the league made with him he shall work deceitfully: for he shall come up, and shall become strong with a small people.

24 He shall enter peaceably even upon the fattest places of the province; and he shall do that which his fathers have not done, nor his fathers' fathers; he shall scatter among them the prey, and spoil, and riches: yea, and he shall forecast his devices against the strong holds, even for a time.

25 And he shall stir up his power and his courage against the king of the south with a great army; and the king of the south shall be stirred up to battle with a very great and mighty army; but he shall not stand: for they shall forecast devices against him.

26 Yea, they that feed of the portion of his meat shall destroy him, and his army shall overflow: and many shall fall down slain.

27 And both of these kings' hearts shall be to do mischief, and they shall speak lies at one table; but it shall not prosper: for yet the end shall be at the time appointed.

28 Then shall he return into his land with great riches; and his heart shall be against the holy covenant; and he shall do exploits, and return to his own land.

29 At the time appointed he shall return, and come toward the south; but it shall not be as the former, or as the latter.

30 For the ships of Chittim shall come against him: therefore he shall be grieved, and return, and have indignation against the holy covenant: so shall he do; he shall even return, and have intelligence with them that forsake the holy covenant.

31 And arms shall stand on his part, and they shall pollute the sanctuary of strength, and shall take away the daily sacrifice, and they shall place the abomination that makes desolate.

32 And such as do wickedly against the covenant shall he corrupt by flatteries: but the people that do know their God shall be strong, and do exploits.

33 And they that understand among the people shall instruct many: yet they shall fall by the sword, and by flame, by captivity, and by spoil, many days.

34 Now when they shall fall, they shall be aided with a little help: but many shall cleave to them with flatteries.

35 And some of them of understanding shall fall, to try them, and to purge, and to make them white, even to the time of the end: because it is yet for a time appointed.

36 And the king shall do according to his will; and he shall exalt himself, and magnify himself above every god, and shall speak marvellous things against the God of gods, and shall prosper till the indignation be accomplished: for that that is determined shall be done.

37 Neither shall he regard the God of his fathers, nor the desire of women, nor regard any god: for he shall magnify himself above all.

38 But in his estate shall he honour the God of forces: and a god whom his fathers knew not shall he honour with gold, and silver, and with precious stones, and pleasant things.

39 Thus shall he do in the most strong holds with a strange god, whom he shall acknowledge and increase with glory: and he shall cause them to rule over many, and shall divide the land for gain.

40 And at the time of the end shall the king of the south push at him: and the king of the north shall come against him like a whirlwind, with chariots, and with horsemen, and with many ships; and he shall enter into the countries, and shall overflow and pass over.

41 He shall enter also into the glorious land, and many countries shall be overthrown: but these shall escape out of his hand, even Edom, and Moab, and the chief of the children of Ammon.

42 He shall stretch forth his hand also upon the countries: and the land of Egypt shall not escape.

43 But he shall have power over the treasures of gold and of silver, and over all the precious things of Egypt: and the Libyans and the Ethiopians shall be at his steps.

44 But tidings out of the east and out of the north shall trouble him: therefore he shall go forth with great fury to destroy, and utterly to make away many.

45 And he shall plant the tabernacles of his palace between the seas in the glorious holy mountain; yet he shall come to his end, and none shall help him.

CHAPTER 12

AND at that time shall Michael stand up, the great prince which stands for the children of your people: and there shall be a time of trouble, such as never was since there was a nation even to that same time: and at that time your people shall be delivered, every one that shall be found written in the book.

2 *And many of them that sleep in the dust of the earth shall awake, some to everlasting life, and some to shame and everlasting contempt.*

3 *And they that be wise shall shine as the brightness of the firmament; and*

they that turn many to righteousness as the stars for ever and ever.

4 But you, O Daniel, shut up the words, and seal the book, even to the time of the end: many shall run to and fro, and knowledge shall be increased.

5 Then I Daniel looked, and, behold, there stood other two, the one on this side of the bank of the river, and the other on that side of the bank of the river.

6 And one said to the man clothed in linen, which was upon the waters of the river, How long shall it be to the end of these wonders?

7 And I heard the man clothed in linen, which was upon the waters of the river, when he held up his right hand and his left hand to heaven, and swore by him that lives for ever that it shall be for a time, times, and an half; and when he shall have accomplished to scatter the power of the holy people, all these things shall be finished.

8 And I heard, but I understood not: then said I, O my Lord, what shall be the end of these things?

9 And he said, Go your way, Daniel: for the words are closed up and sealed till the time of the end.

10 Many shall be purified, and made white, and tried; but the wicked shall do wickedly: and none of the wicked shall understand; but the wise shall understand.

11 And from the time that the daily sacrifice shall be taken away, and the abomination that makes desolate set up, there shall be a thousand two hundred and ninety days.

12 Blessed is he that waits, and comes to the thousand three hundred and five and thirty days.

13 But you go your way till the end be: for you shall rest, and stand in your lot at the end of the days.

Hosea

CHAPTER 1

THE word of the LORD that came to Hosea, the son of Beeri, in the days of Uzziah, Jotham, Ahaz, and Hezekiah, kings of Judah, and in the days of Jeroboam the son of Joash, king of Israel.
2 The beginning of the word of the LORD by Hosea. And the LORD said to Hosea, Go, take to you a wife of whoredoms and children of whoredoms: for the land has committed great whoredom, departing from the LORD.
3 So he went and took Gomer the daughter of Diblaim; which conceived, and bare him a son.
4 And the LORD said to him, Call his name Jezreel; for yet a little while, and I will avenge the blood of Jezreel upon the house of Jehu, and will cause to cease the kingdom of the house of Israel.
5 And it shall come to pass at that day, that I will break the bow of Israel, in the valley of Jezreel.
6 And she conceived again, and bare a daughter. And God said to him, Call her name Loruhamah: for I will no more have mercy upon the house of Israel; but I will utterly take them away.
7 But I will have mercy upon the house of Judah, and will save them by the LORD their God, and will not save them by bow, nor by sword, nor by battle, by horses, nor by horsemen.
8 Now when she had weaned Loruhamah, she conceived, and bare a son.

9 Then said God, Call his name Loammi: for you are not my people, and I will not be your God.
10 Yet the number of the children of Israel shall be as the sand of the sea, which cannot be measured nor numbered; and it shall come to pass, that in the place where it was said to them, You are not my people, there it shall be said to them, You are the sons of the living God.
11 Then shall the children of Judah and the children of Israel be gathered together, and appoint themselves one head, and they shall come up out of the land: for great shall be the day of Jezreel.

CHAPTER 2

SAY to your brethren, Ammi; and to your sisters, Ruhamah.
2 Plead with your mother, plead: for she is not my wife, neither am I her husband: let her therefore put away her whoredoms out of her sight, and her adulteries from between her breasts;
3 Lest I strip her naked, and set her as in the day that she was born, and make her as a wilderness, and set her like a dry land, and slay her with thirst.
4 And I will not have mercy upon her children; for they be the children of whoredoms.
5 For their mother has played the harlot: she that conceived them has done shamefully: for she said, I will go after my lovers, that give me my bread and

my water, my wool and my flax, my oil and my drink.

6 Therefore, behold, I will hedge up your way with thorns, and make a wall, that she shall not find her paths.

7 And she shall follow after her lovers, but she shall not overtake them; and she shall seek them, but shall not find them: then shall she say, I will go and return to my first husband; for then was it better with me than now.

8 For she did not know that I gave her corn, and wine, and oil, and multiplied her silver and gold, which they prepared for Baal.

9 Therefore will I return, and take away my corn in the time thereof, and my wine in the season thereof, and will recover my wool and my flax given to cover her nakedness.

10 And now will I discover her lewdness in the sight of her lovers, and none shall deliver her out of my hand.

11 I will also cause all her mirth to cease, her feast days, her new moons, and her sabbaths, and all her solemn feasts.

12 And I will destroy her vines and her fig trees, whereof she has said, These are my rewards that my lovers have given me: and I will make them a forest, and the beasts of the field shall eat them.

13 And I will visit upon her the days of Baalim, wherein she burned incense to them, and she decked herself with her earrings and her jewels, and she went after her lovers, and forgot me, says the LORD.

14 Therefore, behold, I will allure her, and bring her into the wilderness, and speak comfortably to her.

15 And I will give her her vineyards from thence, and the valley of Achor for a door of hope: and she shall sing there, as in the days of her youth, and as in the day when she came up out of the land of Egypt.

16 And it shall be at that day, says the LORD, that you shall call me Ishi; and shall call me no more Baali.

17 For I will take away the names of Baalim out of her mouth, and they shall no more be remembered by their name.

18 And in that day will I make a covenant for them with the beasts of the field and with the fowls of heaven, and with the creeping things of the ground: and I will break the bow and the sword and the battle out of the earth, and will make them to lie down safely.

19 And I will betroth you to me for ever; yea, I will betroth you to me in righteousness, and in judgment, and in lovingkindness, and in mercies.

20 I will even betroth you to me in faithfulness: and you shall know the LORD.

21 And it shall come to pass in that day, I will hear, says the LORD, I will hear the heavens, and they shall hear the earth;

22 And the earth shall hear the corn, and the wine, and the oil; and they shall hear Jezreel.

23 And I will sow her to me in the earth; and I will have mercy upon her that had not obtained mercy; and I will say to them which were not my people, You are my people; and they shall say, You are my God.

CHAPTER 3

THEN said the LORD to me, Go yet, love a woman beloved of her friend, yet an adulteress, according to the love of the LORD toward the children of Israel, who look to other gods, and love flagons of wine.

2 So I bought her to me for fifteen pieces of silver, and for an homer of barley, and an half homer of barley:

3 And I said to her, You shall abide for me many days; you shall not play the harlot, and you shall not be for another man: so will I also be for you.

4 For the children of Israel shall abide many days without a king, and without a prince, and without a sacrifice, and without an image, and without an ephod, and without teraphim:

THE FUNCTION OF THE LAW

4:1-3 **There is a controversy between God and the world.** When truth is not preached, mercy isn't understood, and the world therefore lacks the knowledge of God. The result is an idolatrous perception of God. The world isn't offended when the Church preaches that God loves them, but when the truths of Judgment Day, God's Law, sin, hell and righteousness are preached, those who do not know the Lord become offended. The direct result of failing to preach His truth is lawlessness, transgression of the moral Law, such as swearing, lying, killing, stealing and committing adultery. Following lawlessness is judgment upon the land-- draughts, etc.

5 Afterward shall the children of Israel return, and seek the LORD their God, and David their king; and shall fear the LORD and his goodness in the latter days.

CHAPTER 4

HEAR the word of the LORD, you children of Israel: for the LORD has a controversy with the inhabitants of the land, because there is no truth, nor mercy, nor knowledge of God in the land.

2 By swearing, and lying, and killing, and stealing, and committing adultery, they break out, and blood touches blood.

3 Therefore shall the land mourn, and every one that dwells therein shall languish, with the beasts of the field, and with the fowls of heaven; yea, the fishes of the sea also shall be taken away.

4 Yet let no man strive, nor reprove another: for your people are as they that strive with the priest.

5 Therefore shall you fall in the day, and the prophet also shall fall with you in the night, and I will destroy your mother.

6 My people are destroyed for lack of knowledge: because you have rejected knowledge, I will also reject you, that you shall be no priest to me: seeing you have forgotten the law of your God, I will also forget your children.

7 As they were increased, so they sinned against me: therefore will I change their glory into shame.

8 They eat up the sin of my people, and they set their heart on their iniquity.

9 And there shall be, like people, like priest: and I will punish them for their ways, and reward them their doings.

10 For they shall eat, and not have enough: they shall commit whoredom, and shall not increase: because they have left off to take heed to the LORD.

11 Whoredom and wine and new wine take away the heart.

12 My people ask counsel at their stocks, and their staff declares to them: for the spirit of whoredoms has caused them to err, and they have gone a whoring from under their God.

13 They sacrifice upon the tops of the mountains, and burn incense upon the hills, under oaks and poplars and elms, because the shadow thereof is good: therefore your daughters shall commit whoredom, and your spouses shall commit adultery.

14 I will not punish your daughters when they commit whoredom, nor your spouses when they commit adultery: for themselves are separated with whores, and they sacrifice with harlots: therefore

4:6 This is perhaps the most commonly quoted verse in the Old Testament, but rarely do you hear it quoted in full. People who lack knowledge of God's Law have no knowledge of sin (see Romans 7:7), and those who have no knowledge of sin cannot repent; and if they don't repent, the Bible warns that they will perish (Luke 13:3).

THE FUNCTION OF THE LAW

"I was alive without the Law once: but when the commandment came, sin revived" (Romans 7:9). So it is with the work-righteous and the proud unbelievers. Because they do not know the Law of God, which is directed against them, it is impossible for them to know their sin. Therefore also they are not amenable to instruction. If they would know the Law, they would also know their sin; and sin to which they are now dead would become alive in them.

Martin Luther

the people that does not understand shall fall.

15 Though you, Israel, play the harlot, yet let not Judah offend; and do not come to Gilgal, neither go up to Bethaven, nor swear, The LORD lives.

16 For Israel slides back as a backsliding heifer: now the LORD will feed them as a lamb in a large place.

17 Ephraim is joined to idols: let him alone.

18 Their drink is sour: they have committed whoredom continually: her rulers with shame do love, You give.

19 The wind has bound her up in her wings, and they shall be ashamed because of their sacrifices.

CHAPTER 5

HEAR this, O priests; and hearken, you house of Israel; and you give ear, O house of the king; for judgment is toward you, because you have been a snare on Mizpah, and a net spread upon Tabor.

2 And the revolters are profound to make slaughter, though I have been a rebuker of them all.

3 I know Ephraim, and Israel is not hid from me: for now, O Ephraim, you commit whoredom, and Israel is defiled.

4 They will not frame their doings to turn to their God: for the spirit of whoredoms is in the midst of them, and they have not known the LORD.

5 And the pride of Israel does testify to his face: therefore shall Israel and Ephraim fall in their iniquity: Judah also shall fall with them.

6 They shall go with their flocks and with their herds to seek the LORD; but they shall not find him; he has withdrawn himself from them.

7 They have dealt treacherously against the LORD: for they have begotten strange children: now shall a month devour them with their portions.

8 Blow the cornet in Gibeah, and the trumpet in Ramah: cry aloud at Bethaven, after you, O Benjamin.

9 Ephraim shall be desolate in the day of rebuke: among the tribes of Israel have I made known that which shall surely be.

10 The princes of Judah were like them that remove the bound: therefore I will pour out my wrath upon them like water.

11 Ephraim is oppressed and broken in judgment, because he willingly walked after the commandment.

12 Therefore will I be to Ephraim as a moth, and to the house of Judah as rottenness.

13 When Ephraim saw his sickness, and Judah saw his wound, then went Ephraim to the Assyrian, and sent to king Jareb: yet could he not heal you, nor cure you of your wound.

14 For I will be to Ephraim as a lion, and as a young lion to the house of Judah: I, even I, will tear and go away; I will take away, and none shall rescue him.

15 I will go and return to my place, till they acknowledge their offence, and seek my face: in their affliction they will seek me early.

CHAPTER 6

COME, and let us return to the LORD: for he has torn, and he will heal us; he has smitten, and he will bind us up.

2 After two days will he revive us: in the third day he will raise us up, and we shall live in his sight.

3 Then shall we know, if we follow on to know the LORD: his going forth is prepared as the morning; and he shall come to us as the rain, as the latter and former rain to the earth.

4 O Ephraim, what shall I do to you? O Judah, what shall I do to you? for your goodness is as a morning cloud, and as the early dew it goeth away.

5 Therefore have I hewed them by the prophets; I have slain them by the words of my mouth: and your judgments are as the light that goeth forth.

6 For I desired mercy, and not sacrifice; and the knowledge of God more than burnt offerings.

7 But they like men have transgressed the covenant: there have they dealt treacherously against me.

8 Gilead is a city of them that work iniquity, and is polluted with blood.

9 And as troops of robbers wait for a man, so the company of priests murder in the way by consent: for they commit lewdness.

10 I have seen an horrible thing in the house of Israel: there is the whoredom of Ephraim, Israel is defiled.

11 Also, O Judah, he has set an harvest for you, when I returned the captivity of my people.

CHAPTER 7

WHEN I would have healed Israel, then the iniquity of Ephraim was discovered, and the wickedness of Samaria: for they commit falsehood; and the thief comes in, and the troop of robbers spoils without.

2 And they consider not in their hearts that I remember all their wickedness: now their own doings have beset them about; they are before my face.

3 They make the king glad with their wickedness, and the princes with their lies.

4 They are all adulterers, as an oven heated by the baker, who ceases from raising after he has kneaded the dough, until it be leavened.

5 In the day of our king the princes have made him sick with bottles of wine; he stretched out his hand with scorners.

6 For they have made ready their heart like an oven, whiles they lie in wait: their baker sleeps all the night; in the morning it burns as a flaming fire.

7 They are all hot as an oven, and have devoured their judges; all their kings are fallen: there is none among them that calls to me.

8 Ephraim, he has mixed himself among the people; Ephraim is a cake not turned.

9 Strangers have devoured his strength, and he does not know it: yea, gray hairs are here and there upon him, yet he does not know it.

10 And the pride of Israel testifies to his face: and they do not return to the LORD their God, nor seek him for all this.

11 Ephraim also is like a silly dove without heart: they call to Egypt, they go to Assyria.

12 When they shall go, I will spread my net upon them; I will bring them down as the fowls of the heaven; I will chastise them, as their congregation has heard.

13 Woe to them! for they have fled from me: destruction to them! because they have transgressed against me: though I have redeemed them, yet they have spoken lies against me.

14 And they have not cried to me with their heart, when they howled upon their beds: they assemble themselves for corn and wine, and they rebel against me.

15 Though I have bound and strengthened their arms, yet do they imagine mischief against me.

16 They return, but not to the most High: they are like a deceitful bow: their princes shall fall by the sword for the rage of their tongue: this shall be their derision in the land of Egypt.

CHAPTER 8

SET the trumpet to your mouth. He shall come as an eagle against the house of the LORD, because they have transgressed my covenant, and trespassed against my law.

2 Israel shall cry to me, My God, we know you.

3 Israel has cast off the thing that is good: the enemy shall pursue him.

4 They have set up kings, but not by me: they have made princes, and I knew it not: of their silver and their gold have they made them idols, that they may be cut off.

5 Your calf, O Samaria, has cast you off; my anger is kindled against them: how long will it be ere they attain to innocency?

6 For from Israel was it also: the workman made it; therefore it is not God: but the calf of Samaria shall be broken in pieces.

7 For they have sown the wind, and they shall reap the whirlwind: it has no stalk; the bud shall yield no meal: if so be it yield, the strangers shall swallow it up.

8 Israel is swallowed up: now shall they be among the Gentiles as a vessel wherein is no pleasure.

9 For they are gone up to Assyria, a wild ass alone by himself: Ephraim has hired lovers.

10 Yea, though they have hired among the nations, now will I gather them, and they shall sorrow a little for the burden of the king of princes.

11 Because Ephraim has made many altars to sin, altars shall be to him to sin.

12 I have written to him the great things of my law, but they were counted as a strange thing.

13 They sacrifice flesh for the sacrifices of my offerings, and eat it; but the LORD does not accept them; now will he remember their iniquity, and visit their sins: they shall return to Egypt.

14 For Israel has forgotten his Maker, and builds temples; and Judah has multiplied fenced cities: but I will send a fire upon his cities, and it shall devour the palaces thereof.

CHAPTER 9

REJOICE not, O Israel, for joy, as other people: for you have gone a whoring from your God, you have loved a reward upon every cornfloor.

2 The floor and the winepress shall not feed them, and the new wine shall fail in her.

3 They shall not dwell in the LORD's land; but Ephraim shall return to Egypt, and they shall eat unclean things in Assyria.

4 They shall not offer wine offerings to the LORD, neither shall they be pleasing to him: their sacrifices shall be to them as the bread of mourners; all that eat thereof shall be polluted: for their bread for their soul shall not come into the house of the LORD.

> " I fear the preachers have been
> more studious to please
> than to awaken,
> or there would have been
> a deeper work. "
>
> **JOHN WESLEY**
> 1703 - 1791
> BRITISH EVANGELIST
> AND FOUNDER OF METHODISM

5 What will you do in the solemn day, and in the day of the feast of the LORD?

6 For, lo, they are gone because of destruction: Egypt shall gather them up, Memphis shall bury them: the pleasant

places for their silver, nettles shall possess them: thorns shall be in their tabernacles.

7 The days of visitation are come, the days of recompence are come; Israel shall know it: the prophet is a fool, the spiritual man is mad, for the multitude of your iniquity, and the great hatred.

8 The watchman of Ephraim was with my God: but the prophet is a snare of a fowler in all his ways, and hatred in the house of his God.

9 They have deeply corrupted themselves, as in the days of Gibeah: therefore he will remember their iniquity, he will visit their sins.

10 I found Israel like grapes in the wilderness; I saw your fathers as the firstripe in the fig tree at her first time: but they went to Baalpeor, and separated themselves to that shame; and their abominations were according as they loved.

11 As for Ephraim, their glory shall fly away like a bird, from the birth, and from the womb, and from the conception.

12 Though they bring up their children, yet will I bereave them, that there shall not be a man left: yea, woe also to them when I depart from them!

13 Ephraim, as I saw Tyrus, is planted in a pleasant place: but Ephraim shall bring forth his children to the murderer.

14 Give them, O LORD: what will you give? give them a miscarrying womb and dry breasts.

15 All their wickedness is in Gilgal: for there I hated them: for the wickedness of their doings I will drive them out of my house, I will love them no more: all their princes are revolters.

16 Ephraim is smitten, their root is dried up, they shall bear no fruit: yea, though they bring forth, yet will I slay even the beloved fruit of their womb.

17 My God will cast them away, because they did not hearken to him: and they shall be wanderers among the nations.

CHAPTER 10

ISRAEL is an empty vine, he brings forth fruit to himself: according to the multitude of his fruit he has increased the altars; according to the goodness of his land they have made goodly images.

2 Their heart is divided; now shall they be found faulty: he shall break down their altars, he shall spoil their images.

3 For now they shall say, We have no king, because we feared not the LORD; what then should a king do to us?

4 They have spoken words, swearing falsely in making a covenant: thus judgment springs up as hemlock in the furrows of the field.

5 The inhabitants of Samaria shall fear because of the calves of Bethaven: for the people thereof shall mourn over it, and the priests thereof that rejoiced on it, for the glory thereof, because it is departed from it.

6 It shall be also carried to Assyria for a present to king Jareb: Ephraim shall receive shame, and Israel shall be ashamed of his own counsel.

7 As for Samaria, her king is cut off as the foam upon the water.

8 The high places also of Aven, the sin of Israel, shall be destroyed: the thorn and the thistle shall come up on their altars; and they shall say to the mountains, Cover us; and to the hills, Fall on us.

9 O Israel, you have sinned from the days of Gibeah: there they stood: the battle in Gibeah against the children of iniquity did not overtake them.

10 It is in my desire that I should chastise them; and the people shall be gathered against them, when they shall bind themselves in their two furrows.

9:7 Unrepentant sin comes back with a terrible vengeance, both on individuals and on nations.

11 And Ephraim is as an heifer that is taught, and loves to tread out the corn; but I passed over upon her fair neck: I will make Ephraim to ride; Judah shall plow, and Jacob shall break his clods.

12 Sow to yourselves in righteousness, reap in mercy; break up your fallow ground: for it is time to seek the LORD, till he come and rain righteousness upon you.

13 You have plowed wickedness, you have reaped iniquity; you have eaten the fruit of lies: because you trusted in your way, in the multitude of your mighty men.

14 Therefore shall a tumult arise among your people, and all your fortresses shall be spoiled, as Shalman spoiled Betharbel in the day of battle: the mother was dashed in pieces upon her children.

15 So shall Bethel do to you because of your great wickedness: in a morning shall the king of Israel utterly be cut off.

CHAPTER 11

WHEN Israel was a child, then I loved him, and called my son out of Egypt.

2 As they called them, so they went from them: they sacrificed to Baalim, and burned incense to graven images.

3 I taught Ephraim also to go, taking them by their arms; but they knew not that I healed them.

4 I drew them with cords of a man, with bands of love: and I was to them as they that take off the yoke on their jaws, and I laid meat for them.

5 He shall not return into the land of Egypt, and the Assyrian shall be his king, because they refused to return.

6 And the sword shall abide on his cities, and shall consume his branches, and devour them, because of their own counsels.

7 And my people are bent to backsliding from me: though they called them to the most High, none at all would exalt him.

8 How shall I give you up, Ephraim? how shall I deliver you, Israel? how shall I make you as Admah? how shall I set you as Zeboim? my heart is turned within me, my repentings are kindled together.

9 I will not execute the fierceness of my anger, I will not return to destroy Ephraim: for I am God, and not man; the Holy One in the midst of you: and I will not enter into the city.

10 They shall walk after the LORD: he shall roar like a lion: when he shall roar, then the children shall tremble from the west.

11 They shall tremble as a bird out of Egypt, and as a dove out of the land of Assyria: and I will place them in their houses, says the LORD.

12 Ephraim compasses me about with lies, and the house of Israel with deceit: but Judah yet rules with God, and is faithful with the saints.

CHAPTER 12

EPHRAIM feeds on wind, and follows after the east wind: he daily increases lies and desolation; and they do make a covenant with the Assyrians, and oil is carried into Egypt.

2 The LORD has also a controversy with Judah, and will punish Jacob according to his ways; according to his doings will he recompense him.

3 He took his brother by the heel in the womb, and by his strength he had power with God:

10:12 This is a summation of the Christian message to the world. The only way to reap the mercy of God is to obtain the righteousness of His Law, which comes from God through the "hearing of faith" (see Galatians 3:2 and Matthew 5:20).

11:1 This a Messianic prophecy. See Matthew 2:15.

4 Yea, he had power over the angel, and prevailed: he wept, and made supplication to him: he found him in Bethel, and there he spoke with us;

5 Even the LORD God of hosts; the LORD is his memorial.

6 Therefore turn to your God: keep mercy and judgment and wait on your God continually.

7 He is a merchant, the balances of deceit are in his hand: he loves to oppress.

8 And Ephraim said, Yet I am become rich, I have found me out substance: in all my labours they shall find none iniquity in me that were sin.

9 And I that am the LORD your God from the land of Egypt will yet make you to dwell in tabernacles, as in the days of the solemn feast.

10 I have also spoken by the prophets, and I have multiplied visions, and used similitudes, by the ministry of the prophets.

11 Is there iniquity in Gilead? surely they are vanity: they sacrifice bullocks in Gilgal; yea, their altars are as heaps in the furrows of the fields.

12 And Jacob fled into the country of Syria, and Israel served for a wife, and for a wife he kept sheep.

13 And by a prophet the LORD brought Israel out of Egypt, and by a prophet was he preserved.

14 Ephraim provoked him to anger most bitterly: therefore shall he leave his blood upon him, and his reproach shall his LORD return to him.

CHAPTER 13

WHEN Ephraim spoke trembling, he exalted himself in Israel; but when he offended in Baal, he died.

2 And now they sin more and more, and have made them molten images of their silver, and idols according to their own understanding, all of it the work of the craftsmen: they say of them, Let the men that sacrifice kiss the calves.

3 Therefore they shall be as the morning cloud and as the early dew that passes away, as the chaff that is driven with the whirlwind out of the floor, and as the smoke out of the chimney.

4 Yet I am the LORD your God from the land of Egypt, and you shall know no god but me: for there is no saviour beside me.

5 I did know you in the wilderness, in the land of great drought.

6 According to their pasture, so were they filled; they were filled, and their heart was exalted; therefore have they forgotten me.

7 Therefore I will be to them as a lion: as a leopard by the way will I observe them:

8 I will meet them as a bear that is bereaved of her whelps, and will rend the caul of their heart, and there will I devour them like a lion: the wild beast shall tear them.

9 O Israel, you have destroyed yourself; but in me is your help.

10 I will be your king: where is any other that may save you in all your cities? and your judges of whom you said, Give me a king and princes?

11 I gave you a king in my anger, and took him away in my wrath.

12 The iniquity of Ephraim is bound up; his sin is hid.

13 The sorrows of a travailing woman shall come upon him: he is an unwise son; for he should not stay long in the place of the breaking forth of children.

14 I will ransom them from the power of the grave; I will redeem them from death: O death, I will be your plagues; O grave, I will be your destruction: repentance shall be hid from my eyes.

13:14 Words cannot express the wonder of this promise from God. Through Jesus' sacrifice on the Cross, He destroyed the power of the grave. We have been redeemed from death by the precious blood of Christ. The enemy has been overcome and will eventually be vanquished forever. God promised this and will not change His mind.

15 Though he be fruitful among his brethren, an east wind shall come, the wind of the LORD shall come up from the wilderness, and his spring shall become dry, and his fountain shall be dried up: he shall spoil the treasure of all pleasant vessels.

16 Samaria shall become desolate; for she has rebelled against her God: they shall fall by the sword: their infants shall be dashed in pieces, and their women with child shall be ripped up.

CHAPTER 14

O Israel, return to the LORD your God; for you have fallen by your iniquity.

2 Take with you words, and turn to the LORD: say to him, Take away all iniquity, and receive us graciously: so will we render the calves of our lips.

3 Asshur shall not save us; we will not ride upon horses: neither will we say any more to the work of our hands, You are our gods: for in you the fatherless find mercy.

4 I will heal their backsliding, I will love them freely: for my anger is turned away from him.

5 I will be as the dew to Israel: he shall grow as the lily, and cast forth his roots as Lebanon.

6 His branches shall spread, and his beauty shall be as the olive tree, and his smell as Lebanon.

7 They that dwell under his shadow shall return; they shall revive as the corn, and grow as the vine: the scent thereof shall be as the wine of Lebanon.

8 Ephraim shall say, What have I to do any more with idols? I have heard him, and observed him: I am like a green fir tree. From me is your fruit found.

9 Who is wise, and he shall understand these things? prudent, and he shall know them? for the ways of the LORD are right, and the just shall walk in them: but the transgressors shall fall therein.

Joel

CHAPTER 1

THE word of the LORD that came to Joel the son of Pethuel.

2 Hear this, you old men, and give ear, all you inhabitants of the land. Has this been in your days, or even in the days of your fathers?

3 Tell your children of it, and let your children tell their children, and their children another generation.

4 That which the palmerworm has left has the locust eaten; and that which the locust has left has the cankerworm eaten; and that which the cankerworm has left has the caterpiller eaten.

5 Awake, you drunkards, and weep; and howl, all you drinkers of wine, because of the new wine; for it is cut off from your mouth.

6 For a nation is come up upon my land, strong, and without number, whose teeth are the teeth of a lion, and he has the cheek teeth of a great lion.

7 He has laid my vine waste, and barked my fig tree: he has made it clean bare, and cast it away; the branches thereof are made white.

8 Lament like a virgin girded with sackcloth for the husband of her youth.

9 The meat offering and the drink offering is cut off from the house of the LORD; the priests, the LORD's ministers, mourn.

10 The field is wasted, the land mourns; for the corn is wasted: the new wine is dried up, the oil languishes.

11 Be ashamed, O you husbandmen; howl, O you vinedressers, for the wheat and for the barley; because the harvest of the field is perished.

12 The vine is dried up, and the fig tree languishes; the pomegranate tree, the palm tree also, and the apple tree, even all the trees of the field, are withered: because joy is withered away from the sons of men.

13 Gird yourselves, and lament, you priests: howl, you ministers of the altar: come, lie all night in sackcloth, you ministers of my God: for the meat offering and the drink offering is withholden from the house of your God.

14 You sanctify a fast, call a solemn assembly, gather the elders and all the inhabitants of the land into the house of the LORD your God, and cry to the LORD,

15 Alas for the day! for the day of the LORD is at hand, and as a destruction from the Almighty shall it come.

1:3 Christian parents who don't have daily family devotions and don't make time to build a solid Christian foundation in their children's impressionable years should not be mystified when the children, in their teenage years, turn from the things of God (see Psalm 78:4). For more on this topic, see Kirk Cameron's commentary, beginning on page 1117.

16 Is not the meat cut off before our eyes, yea, joy and gladness from the house of our God?

17 The seed is rotten under their clods, the garners are laid desolate, the barns are broken down; for the corn is withered.

18 How do the beasts groan! the herds of cattle are perplexed, because they have no pasture; yea, the flocks of sheep are made desolate.

19 O LORD, to you will I cry: for the fire has devoured the pastures of the wilderness, and the flame has burned all the trees of the field.

20 The beasts of the field cry also to you: for the rivers of waters are dried up, and the fire has devoured the pastures of the wilderness.

CHAPTER 2

B LOW the trumpet in Zion, and sound an alarm in my holy mountain: let all the inhabitants of the land tremble: for the day of the LORD comes, for it is nigh at hand;

2 A day of darkness and of gloominess, a day of clouds and of thick darkness, as the morning spread upon the mountains: a great people and a strong; there has not been ever the like, neither shall be any more after it, even to the years of many generations.

3 A fire devours before them; and behind them a flame burns: the land is as the garden of Eden before them, and behind them a desolate wilderness; yea, and nothing shall escape them.

4 The appearance of them is as the appearance of horses; and as horsemen, so shall they run.

5 Like the noise of chariots on the tops of mountains shall they leap, like the noise of a flame of fire that devours the stubble, as a strong people set in battle array.

6 Before their face the people shall be much pained: all faces shall gather blackness.

7 They shall run like mighty men; they shall climb the wall like men of war; and they shall march every one on his ways, and they shall not break their ranks:

8 Neither shall one thrust another; they shall walk every one in his path: and when they fall upon the sword, they shall not be wounded.

9 They shall run to and fro in the city; they shall run upon the wall, they shall climb up upon the houses; they shall enter in at the windows like a thief.

10 The earth shall quake before them; the heavens shall tremble: the sun and the moon shall be dark, and the stars shall withdraw their shining:

11 And the LORD shall utter his voice before his army: for his camp is very great: for he is strong that executes his word: for the day of the LORD is great and very terrible; and who can abide it?

12 Therefore also now, says the LORD, turn even to me with all your heart, and with fasting, and with weeping, and with mourning:

13 And rend your heart, and not your garments, and turn to the LORD your God: for he is gracious and merciful, slow to anger, and of great kindness, and repents him of the evil.

14 Who knows if he will return and repent, and leave a blessing behind him; even a meat offering and a drink offering to the LORD your God?

15 Blow the trumpet in Zion, sanctify a fast, call a solemn assembly:

16 Gather the people, sanctify the congregation, assemble the elders, gather the children, and those that suck the breasts: let the bridegroom go forth of his chamber, and the bride out of her closet.

17 Let the priests, the ministers of the LORD, weep between the porch and the

---

2:1-10 See Luke 21:26 comment.

This Father of Five Teaches His Little Ones the Ten Commandments

Train up a child in the way he should go:
and when he is old, he will not depart from it.
PROVERBS 22:6

OK, this one is for parents... I love being a father. I'm taking the crash-course in parenting. I have five children under five years old. Yep—my kids are five, four, three, two, and one. Two boys and three girls...can you imagine what it'll be like when they're all teenagers at the same time, experimenting with life's options and dating at the same time? If it's true that small children have small problems and big kids have big problems, then in 10 years I'm going to fake my own death and move to Tahiti!

Growing up in this world of ungodly values and immoral lifestyles, our kids are already facing difficult challenges, and it's our responsibility as parents to give them a solid foundation upon which they can build their lives, dreams, and convictions. I find great comfort in this wonderful proverb: "Train up a child in the way he should go, and when he is old, he will not depart from it."

Now as much as I'd love for this verse of scripture to be a guaranteed promise of perfect Christian children as long as we raise them in a godly home, I know it doesn't always work that way. Many godly parents in the Bible and today, too, have had sons and daughters who did not walk with the Lord.

But I do know that the principle of preparing the soil for the seed of the gospel can and should start when a child is young. And I believe that the

*. . .awaken their conscience
and prepare the soil of their hearts
for the life-giving seed of the gospel.*

Kirk Cameron
AMERICAN ACTOR
BORN 1970
PANORAMA CITY, CALIFORNIA

promise of this scripture verse is that if a child learns to turn from sin and trust in Jesus when he is young, then, as he grows older, he will not depart from his Savior because God has already set him apart for His own glory.

Since we know that only the Holy Spirit can actually transform our children from the cute little "me-centered" people that they are into God-loving, God-fearing followers of Christ, the question is: "What should I be doing as a parent? How can I train my child "in the way he should go" so that he or she will continue on God's path and become a life-long follower of Jesus Christ?"

While there are many great books on the subject (*Shepherding a Child's Heart* by Ted Tripp is our favorite and we refer to it regularly), here is a simple suggestion that has been working very well with our children.

Deut. 6:1-7 "These are the commandments which the Lord your God commanded you...And you shall teach them diligently to your children, and shall talk of them when you sit in your house, and when you walk by the way, and when you lie down, and when you rise up."

This verse means, in simple terms, teach your children the Ten Commandments so that they know them backwards and forwards. This isn't to improve their memory or to help them win an Awana contest; it is to awaken their conscience and prepare the soil of their hearts for the life-giving seed of the gospel.

A personal understanding of the moral Law of God is foundational for anyone (including our children) to become a Christian. God commanded Abraham that he teach it to his children for a reason. Here's why; Galatians 3:24 reads, "The Law is our schoolmaster to lead us to Christ." So God's Moral Law (summed up in the 10 Commandments) is a schoolmaster to lead us (and our children) to Jesus Christ. Here's how it works:

1. We know that in order for a child (as well as an adult) to be saved, he or she must turn from their sin and trust in Jesus to save them. If our children are going to personally turn from their sin, they must know what his or her sin is.

2. The 10 Commandments show your child what sin is. Romans 3, verse 19 says, "By the Law is the knowledge of sin." 1 John 3:4 says, "Sin is transgression of the Law." Paul says in Romans 7:7, "I would not have known what sin was except through the Law." So Paul is saying that he would not have known what sin was unless the Law (10 Commandments) showed him. The 10 Commandments are what made Paul understand that he had sinned against God, helped him see that he was spiritually "dead," and in need of God's forgiveness and new life. (See Romans 7:7-12)

The 10 Commandments are like a mirror. They reveal that our hearts are dirty and in need of cleansing. What would you and I do if we didn't have a mirror to look into each morning? Without a mirror, we'd never know whether our face was clean or dirty. In the same way, it is only when we look into the mirror of the 10 Commandments that we can see that our heart is dirty and in desperate need of cleansing. Once children (and others) understand that they are guilty of sin, they are able (with the help of the Holy Spirit) to turn to Jesus to wash that sin away.

3. Simply go through the 10 Commandments with your children, explain what each one means and ask them if they've kept it or broken it (maybe not the 7th one if your child is too young). Just ask them, "Have you ever told a lie? Have you ever taken something that you knew didn't belong to you? Have you always honored and obeyed your Dad and Mom? Have you always loved God more than the things He's given you (like toys, family, and friends)?" Your children will see very quickly that they have broken these Commandments. You may notice that they even feel guilty. That's good, because they are guilty—and closer to the Kingdom of God than ever before!

Now that they understand exactly how they've sinned against God and angered Him in the process, they can see their dilemma and need for God's forgiveness. Now, the good news about Jesus taking their punishment for them on the cross will make sense.

"God demonstrated His own love for us in that while we were still sinners, Christ died for us." (Romans 5:8)

"For God so loved the world, that He gave His one and only Son, that whoever believes in him will not perish, but have everlasting life" (John 3:16).

Once our children have a keen understanding of their sin, they can now begin to appreciate the great, matchless, and incomprehensible love of God. We know God loves us not because of a warm fuzzy feeling he gives us; we know God loves us because of what He did for us on the cross. He laid down His own life for us so that we could be forgiven and born again! We broke the Law and Jesus paid our fine—it's as simple as that.

4. Since there can be no salvation without God-given repentance, if our children don't eventually see their need for God's forgiveness, they can't repent, and without repentance, they cannot be saved. Each child has a conscience and knows basic right from wrong. Repentance is simply a determination to turn away from what is wrong.

If you're worried about frightening your child by talking about the seriousness of his or her sin, I've found that my own children are remarkably capable of handling this…because their conscience tells them that it's true and they know that their Mom and Dad and God love them very much and are willing to forgive them. We must first convince them of the disease of sin before they will appreciate the cure of Jesus. Remind them that if they will surrender their hearts to Jesus, God will also give them a "new heart" and help them to begin to love and obey Him like never before.

Last night, my 4 year old daughter Isabella started crying very hard and explained that Jack (her five year old brother) had pushed her off the top of her baby brother's crib and hurt her head. Jack, with a look of complete shock and confusion, said, "I didn't do anything. She just fell all by herself. I think I might have scared her or something." As we comforted Isabella, I asked my son very directly, "Did you push your sister and make her fall?" Jack stood firm and denied any culpability. My wife also asked Jack if he was lying or telling the truth. Jack again said he did not push his sister. I asked both children to wait in their rooms for me to come talk with them. As I spoke with Jack, I told him that I was going to ask him one more question. I told him that if he was honest and told me the truth, he would not be in trouble. But if he did not tell me the truth, he would be in BIG trouble. He replied with, "What if I've already not told you the truth?" I told him that he must tell me the truth now, regardless of what he's already told me.

Jack looked down at the floor, wrinkled up his face, and began squirming in his chair like a worm on a hook. He knew I was serious, and he was now engaged in a wrestling match with his conscience. Jack finally confessed, "Yes. I pushed her." I told him to tell his mother what he had told me. I took three minutes to discuss the seriousness of lying. It was one of the Commandments that Jack knew so well. We talked about the fact that when he lies to his dad and mom, he is also lying to Jesus. We talked about the fact that in order to lie, Jack had to turn away from Jesus to do it.

I tried, as best as I could, to stir up his God-given conscience and help him see the seriousness of his deceit in the eyes of God. I told Jack that a deceitful heart is rotten in God's eyes and that's why he needs the new heart that Jesus can give him. I showed him how to kneel in prayer when you're really sorry and told him I was going to leave him to be alone with Jesus so that he could talk to him and ask for His forgiveness. I left Jack's room and closed the door (except for a crack through which I could hear him praying.)

Jack got on his knees, and I could hear him say, "Dear God, I'm sorry I lied to my mommy and daddy and You. I pushed my sister off the crib. Will you please forgive me? Will you please take the trash out of my heart and give me a new heart? And please keep it clean and pure all the time so I don't do sinful things. I ask this in Jesus' name. Amen."

I, a father in tears outside his door, was thanking God for making repentance and faith something that even a child can understand. I don't know if my son has been born again, but God does, and I take comfort in His promise that He will be faithful to anyone who calls upon His name.

altar, and let them say, Spare your people, O LORD, and do not give your heritage to reproach, that the heathen should rule over them: why should they say among the people, Where is their God?

18 Then will the LORD be jealous for his land, and pity his people.

19 Yea, the LORD will answer and say to his people, Behold, I will send you corn, and wine, and oil, and you shall be satisfied therewith: and I will no more make you a reproach among the heathen:

20 But I will remove far off from you the northern army, and will drive him into a land barren and desolate, with his face toward the east sea, and his hinder part toward the utmost sea, and his stink shall come up, and his ill savour shall come up, because he has done great things.

21 Fear not, O land; be glad and rejoice: for the LORD will do great things.

22 Do not be afraid, you beasts of the field: for the pastures of the wilderness do spring, for the tree bears her fruit, the fig tree and the vine do yield their strength.

23 Be glad then, you children of Zion, and rejoice in the LORD your God: for he has given you the former rain moderately, and he will cause to come down for you the rain, the former rain, and the latter rain in the first month.

24 And the floors shall be full of wheat, and the vats shall overflow with wine and oil.

25 And I will restore to you the years that the locust has eaten, the cankerworm, and the caterpiller, and the palmerworm, my great army which I sent among you.

26 And you shall eat in plenty, and be satisfied, and praise the name of the LORD your God, that has dealt wondrously with you: and my people shall never be ashamed.

27 And you shall know that I am in the midst of Israel, and that I am the LORD your God, and none else: and my people shall never be ashamed.

28 And it shall come to pass afterward, that I will pour out my spirit upon all flesh; and your sons and your daughters shall prophesy, your old men shall dream dreams, your young men shall see visions:

29 And also upon the servants and upon the handmaids in those days will I pour out my spirit.

30 And I will show wonders in the heavens and in the earth, blood, and fire, and pillars of smoke.

31 The sun shall be turned into darkness, and the moon into blood, before the great and terrible day of the LORD come.

32 And it shall come to pass, that whoever shall call on the name of the LORD shall be delivered: for in mount Zion and in Jerusalem shall be deliverance, as the LORD has said, and in the remnant whom the LORD shall call.

CHAPTER 3

FOR, behold, in those days, and in that time, when I shall bring again the captivity of Judah and Jerusalem,

2 I will also gather all nations, and will bring them down into the valley of Jehoshaphat, and will plead with them there for my people and for my heritage Israel, whom they have scattered among the nations, and parted my land.

3 And they have cast lots for my people; and have given a boy for an harlot, and sold a girl for wine, that they might drink.

4 Yea, and what have you to do with me, O Tyre, and Zidon, and all the coasts of Palestine? will you render me a

---

2:32 "Whosoever" means "anyone." No one can say that God's invitation doesn't include them. Jesus said, "He that comes to me, I will in no wise cast out" (John 6:37). The gospel applies universally.

*The missionary church
is a praying church.
The history of missions
is a history of prayer.
Everything vital to the success
of the world's evangelization
hinges on prayer.
Are thousands of missionaries
and tens of thousands
of native workers needed?
"Pray ye therefore the Lord
of the harvest,
that He send forth laborers
into His harvest."*

John R. Mott

1865-1955

NOBEL PEACE PRIZE CO-WINNER
OF 1946

will return your recompence upon your own head:

8 And I will sell your sons and your daughters into the hand of the children of Judah, and they shall sell them to the Sabeans, to a people far off: for the LORD has spoken it.

9 You proclaim this among the Gentiles; Prepare war, wake up the mighty men, let all the men of war draw near; let them come up:

10 Beat your plowshares into swords and your pruninghooks into spears: let the weak say, I am strong.

11 Assemble yourselves, and come, all you heathen, and gather yourselves together round about: there cause your mighty ones to come down, O LORD.

12 Let the heathen be wakened, and come up to the valley of Jehoshaphat: for there will I sit to judge all the heathen round about.

13 You put in the sickle, for the harvest is ripe: come, get you down; for the press is full, the fats overflow; for their wickedness is great.

14 Multitudes, multitudes in the valley of decision: for the day of the LORD is near in the valley of decision.

15 The sun and the moon shall be darkened, and the stars shall withdraw their shining.

16 The LORD also shall roar out of Zion, and utter his voice from Jerusalem; and the heavens and the earth shall shake: but the LORD will be the hope of his people, and the strength of the children of Israel.

17 So shall you know that I am the LORD your God dwelling in Zion, my holy mountain: then shall Jerusalem be holy, and there shall no strangers pass through her any more.

18 And it shall come to pass in that day, that the mountains shall drop down new wine, and the hills shall flow with milk, and all the rivers of Judah shall flow with waters, and a fountain shall come forth out of the house of the

recompence? and if you recompense me, swiftly and speedily will I return your recompence upon your own head;

5 Because you have taken my silver and my gold, and have carried into your temples my goodly pleasant things:

6 The children also of Judah and the children of Jerusalem have you sold to the Grecians, that you might remove them far from their border.

7 Behold, I will raise them out of the place where you have sold them, and

LORD, and shall water the valley of Shittim.

19 Egypt shall be a desolation, and Edom shall be a desolate wilderness, for the violence against the children of Judah, because they have shed innocent blood in their land.

20 But Judah shall dwell for ever, and Jerusalem from generation to generation.

21 For I will cleanse their blood that I have not cleansed: for the LORD dwells in Zion.

Amos

CHAPTER 1

THE words of Amos, who was among the herdmen of Tekoa, which he saw concerning Israel in the days of Uzziah king of Judah, and in the days of Jeroboam the son of Joash king of Israel, two years before the earthquake.

2 And he said, The LORD will roar from Zion, and utter his voice from Jerusalem; and the habitations of the shepherds shall mourn, and the top of Carmel shall wither.

3 Thus says the LORD; For three transgressions of Damascus, and for four, I will not turn away the punishment thereof; because they have threshed Gilead with threshing instruments of iron:

4 But I will send a fire into the house of Hazael, which shall devour the palaces of Benhadad.

5 I will break also the bar of Damascus, and cut off the inhabitant from the plain of Aven, and him that holds the sceptre from the house of Eden: and the people of Syria shall go into captivity to Kir, says the LORD.

6 Thus says the LORD; For three transgressions of Gaza, and for four, I will not turn away the punishment thereof; because they carried away captive the whole captivity, to deliver them up to Edom:

7 But I will send a fire on the wall of Gaza, which shall devour the palaces thereof:

8 And I will cut off the inhabitant from Ashdod, and him that holds the sceptre from Ashkelon, and I will turn my hand against Ekron: and the remnant of the Philistines shall perish, says the Lord GOD.

9 Thus says the LORD; For three transgressions of Tyrus, and for four, I will not turn away the punishment thereof; because they delivered up the whole captivity to Edom, and remembered not the brotherly covenant:

10 But I will send a fire on the wall of Tyrus, which shall devour the palaces thereof.

11 Thus says the LORD; For three transgressions of Edom, and for four, I will not turn away the punishment thereof; because he did pursue his brother with the sword, and did cast off all pity, and his anger did tear perpetually, and he kept his wrath for ever:

12 But I will send a fire upon Teman, which shall devour the palaces of Bozrah.

13 Thus says the LORD; For three transgressions of the children of Ammon, and for four, I will not turn away the punishment thereof; because they have ripped up the women with child of Gilead, that they might enlarge their border:

14 But I will kindle a fire in the wall of Rabbah, and it shall devour the palaces thereof, with shouting in the day of

AMOS

Amos 1:1-3

battle, with a tempest in the day of the whirlwind:

15 And their king shall go into captivity, he and his princes together, says the LORD.

CHAPTER 2

THUS says the LORD; For three transgressions of Moab, and for four, I will not turn away the punishment thereof; because he burned the bones of the king of Edom into lime:

2 But I will send a fire upon Moab, and it shall devour the palaces of Kirioth: and Moab shall die with tumult, with shouting, and with the sound of the trumpet:

3 And I will cut off the judge from the midst thereof, and will slay all the princes thereof with him, says the LORD.

4 Thus says the LORD; For three transgressions of Judah, and for four, I will not turn away the punishment thereof; because they have despised the law of the LORD, and have not kept his commandments, and their lies caused them to err, after the which their fathers have walked:

5 But I will send a fire upon Judah, and it shall devour the palaces of Jerusalem.

6 Thus says the LORD; For three transgressions of Israel, and for four, I will not turn away the punishment thereof; because they sold the righteous for silver, and the poor for a pair of shoes;

7 That pant after the dust of the earth on the head of the poor, and turn aside the way of the meek: and a man and his father will go in to the same maid, to profane my holy name:

8 And they lay themselves down upon clothes laid to pledge by every altar, and they drink the wine of the condemned in the house of their god.

9 Yet destroyed I the Amorite before them, whose height was like the height of the cedars, and he was strong as the oaks; yet I destroyed his fruit from above, and his roots from beneath.

10 Also I brought you up from the land of Egypt, and led you forty years through the wilderness, to possess the land of the Amorite.

11 And I raised up of your sons for prophets, and of your young men for Nazarites. Is it not even thus, O you children of Israel? says the LORD.

12 But you gave the Nazarites wine to drink; and commanded the prophets, saying, Prophesy not.

13 Behold, I am pressed under you, as a cart is pressed that is full of sheaves.

14 Therefore the flight shall perish from the swift, and the strong shall not strengthen his force, neither shall the mighty deliver himself:

15 Neither shall he stand that handles the bow; and he that is swift of foot shall not deliver himself: neither shall he that rides the horse deliver himself.

16 And he that is courageous among the mighty shall flee away naked in that day, says the LORD.

CHAPTER 3

HEAR this word that the LORD has spoken against you, O children of Israel, against the whole family which I brought up from the land of Egypt, saying,

2 You only have I known of all the families of the earth: therefore I will punish you for all your iniquities.

3 Can two walk together, except they be agreed?

4 Will a lion roar in the forest, when he has no prey? will a young lion cry out of his den, if he have taken nothing?

5 Can a bird fall in a snare upon the earth, where no gin is for him? shall one take up a snare from the earth, and have taken nothing at all?

6 Shall a trumpet be blown in the city, and the people not be afraid? shall there be evil in a city, and the LORD has not done it?

7 *Surely the Lord GOD will do nothing, but he reveals his secret to his servants the prophets.*

8 *The lion has roared, who will not fear? the Lord GOD has spoken, who can but prophesy?*

9 Publish in the palaces at Ashdod, and in the palaces in the land of Egypt, and

---

3:8 The Lion of the tribe of Judah has commanded us to preach the gospel to every creature (see Acts 4:20 and 1 Corinthians 9:16).

say, Assemble yourselves upon the mountains of Samaria, and behold the great tumults in the midst thereof, and the oppressed in the midst thereof.

10 For they know not to do right, says the LORD, who store up violence and robbery in their palaces.

11 Therefore thus says the Lord GOD; An adversary there shall be even round about the land; and he shall bring down your strength from you, and your palaces shall be spoiled.

12 Thus says the LORD; As the shepherd takes out of the mouth of the lion two legs, or a piece of an ear; so shall the children of Israel be taken out that dwell in Samaria in the corner of a bed, and in Damascus in a couch.

13 Hear, and testify in the house of Jacob, says the Lord GOD, the God of hosts,

14 That in the day that I shall visit the transgressions of Israel upon him I will also visit the altars of Bethel: and the horns of the altar shall be cut off, and fall to the ground.

15 And I will smite the winter house with the summer house; and the houses of ivory shall perish, and the great houses shall have an end, says the LORD.

CHAPTER 4

HEAR this word, you kine of Bashan, that are in the mountain of Samaria, which oppress the poor, which crush the needy, which say to their masters, Bring, and let us drink.

2 The Lord GOD has sworn by his holiness, that, lo, the days shall come upon you, that he will take you away with hooks, and your posterity with fishhooks.

3 And you shall go out at the breaches, every cow at that which is before her; and you shall cast them into the palace, says the LORD.

4 Come to Bethel, and transgress; at Gilgal multiply transgression; and bring your sacrifices every morning, and your tithes after three years:

5 And offer a sacrifice of thanksgiving with leaven, and proclaim and publish the free offerings: for this you like, O you children of Israel, says the Lord GOD.

6 And I also have given you cleanness of teeth in all your cities, and want of bread in all your places: yet have you not returned to me, says the LORD.

7 And also I have withholden the rain from you, when there were yet three months to the harvest: and I caused it to rain upon one city, and caused it not to rain upon another city: one piece was rained upon, and the piece whereupon it rained not withered.

8 So two or three cities wandered to one city, to drink water; but they were not satisfied: yet have you not returned to me, says the LORD.

9 I have smitten you with blasting and mildew: when your gardens and your vineyards and your fig trees and your olive trees increased, the palmerworm devoured them: yet have you not returned to me, says the LORD.

10 I have sent among you the pestilence after the manner of Egypt: your young men have I slain with the sword, and have taken away your horses; and I have made the stink of your camps to come up to your nostrils: yet have you not returned to me, says the LORD.

11 I have overthrown some of you, as God overthrew Sodom and Gomorrah, and you were as a firebrand plucked out of the burning: yet have you not returned to me, says the LORD.

12 Therefore thus will I do to you, O Israel: and because I will do this to you, prepare to meet your God, O Israel.

13 For, lo, he that forms the mountains, and creates the wind, and declares

---

4:6-10 At times, the power of hunger, thirst, pestilence and plague may not be enough to soften the hard hearts of wicked men.

to man what is his thought, that makes the morning darkness, and treads upon the high places of the earth, The LORD, The God of hosts, is his name.

CHAPTER 5

HEAR this word which I take up against you, even a lamentation, O house of Israel.

2 The virgin of Israel is fallen; she shall no more rise: she is forsaken upon her land; there is none to raise her up.

3 For thus says the Lord GOD; The city that went out by a thousand shall leave an hundred, and that which went forth by an hundred shall leave ten, to the house of Israel.

4 For thus says the LORD to the house of Israel, Seek me, and you shall live:

5 But seek not Bethel, nor enter into Gilgal, and pass not to Beersheba: for Gilgal shall surely go into captivity, and Bethel shall come to nought.

6 Seek the LORD, and you shall live; lest he break out like fire in the house of Joseph, and devour it, and there be none to quench it in Bethel.

7 You who turn judgment to wormwood, and leave off righteousness in the earth,

8 Seek him that makes the seven stars and Orion, and turns the shadow of death into the morning, and makes the day dark with night: that calls for the waters of the sea, and pours them out upon the face of the earth: The LORD is his name:

9 That strengthens the spoiled against the strong, so that the spoiled shall come against the fortress.

10 They hate him that rebukes in the gate, and they abhor him that speaks uprightly.

11 Forasmuch therefore as your treading is upon the poor, and you take from him burdens of wheat: you have built houses of hewn stone, but you shall not dwell in them; you have planted pleasant vineyards, but you shall not drink wine of them.

12 For I know your manifold transgressions and your mighty sins: they afflict the just, they take a bribe, and they turn aside the poor in the gate from their right.

13 Therefore the prudent shall keep silence in that time; for it is an evil time.

14 Seek good, and not evil, that you may live: and so the LORD, the God of hosts, shall be with you, as you have spoken.

15 Hate the evil, and love the good, and establish judgment in the gate: it may be that the LORD God of hosts will be gracious to the remnant of Joseph.

16 Therefore the LORD, the God of hosts, the LORD, says thus; Wailing shall be in all streets; and they shall say in all the highways, Alas! alas! and they shall call the husbandman to mourning, and such as are skilful of lamentation to wailing.

17 And in all vineyards shall be wailing: for I will pass through you, says the LORD.

18 Woe to you that desire the day of the LORD! to what end is it for you? the day of the LORD is darkness, and not light.

19 As if a man did flee from a lion, and a bear met him; or went into the house, and leaned his hand on the wall, and a serpent bit him.

20 Shall not the day of the LORD be darkness, and not light? even very dark, and no brightness in it?

21 I hate, I despise your feast days, and I will not smell in your solemn assemblies.

5:5-8 This is the message we have from God: "Seek me and live." He turns the shadow of death into morning through the rising of the Son.

5:12 God's Law shows the sinner that his "trivial" discrepancies are "manifold transgressions" and "mighty sins."

22 Though you offer me burnt offerings and your meat offerings, I will not accept them: neither will I regard the peace offerings of your fat beasts.

23 Take away from me the noise of your songs; for I will not hear the melody of your viols.

24 But let judgment run down as waters, and righteousness as a mighty stream.

25 Have you offered to me sacrifices and offerings in the wilderness forty years, O house of Israel?

26 But you have borne the tabernacle of your Moloch and Chiun your images, the star of your god, which you made to yourselves.

27 Therefore will I cause you to go into captivity beyond Damascus, says the LORD, whose name is The God of hosts.

CHAPTER 6

WOE to them that are at ease in Zion, and trust in the mountain of Samaria, which are named chief of the nations, to whom the house of Israel came!

2 Pass to Calneh, and see; and from thence you go to Hamath the great: then go down to Gath of the Philistines: be they better than these kingdoms? or their border greater than your border?

3 You that put far away the evil day, and cause the seat of violence to come near;

4 That lie upon beds of ivory, and stretch themselves upon their couches, and eat the lambs out of the flock, and the calves out of the midst of the stall;

5 That chant to the sound of the viol, and invent to themselves instruments of music, like David;

6 That drink wine in bowls, and anoint themselves with the chief ointments: but they are not grieved for the affliction of Joseph.

7 Therefore now shall they go captive with the first that go captive, and the banquet of them that stretched themselves shall be removed.

8 The Lord GOD has sworn by himself, says the LORD the God of hosts, I abhor the excellency of Jacob, and hate his palaces: therefore will I deliver up the city with all that is therein.

9 And it shall come to pass, if there remain ten men in one house, that they shall die.

10 And a man's uncle shall take him up, and he that burns him, to bring out the bones out of the house, and shall say to him that is by the sides of the house, Is there yet any with you? and he shall say, No. Then shall he say, Hold your tongue: for we may not make mention of the name of the LORD.

11 For, behold, the LORD commands, and he will smite the great house with breaches, and the little house with clefts.

12 Shall horses run upon the rock? will one plow there with oxen? for you have turned judgment into gall, and the fruit of righteousness into hemlock:

13 You which rejoice in a thing of nought, which say, Have we not taken to us horns by our own strength?

14 But, behold, I will raise up against you a nation, O house of Israel, says the LORD the God of hosts; and they shall afflict you from the entering in of Hemath to the river of the wilderness.

CHAPTER 7

THUS has the Lord GOD showed me; and, behold, he formed grasshoppers in the beginning of the shooting up of the latter growth; and, lo, it was the latter growth after the king's mowings.

2 And it came to pass, that when they had made an end of eating the grass of the land, then I said, O Lord GOD,

---

6:3 Those who live in the light of the great and terrible day of the Lord keep their heart from sin. They know that only in Christ can they have "boldness in the day of wrath."

forgive, I beseech you: by whom shall Jacob arise? for he is small.

3 The LORD repented for this: It shall not be, says the LORD.

4 Thus has the Lord GOD showed to me: and, behold, the Lord GOD called to contend by fire, and it devoured the great deep, and did eat up a part.

5 Then said I, O Lord GOD, cease, I beseech you: by whom shall Jacob arise? for he is small.

6 The LORD repented for this: This also shall not be, says the Lord GOD.

7 Thus he showed me: and, behold, the LORD stood upon a wall made by a plumbline, with a plumbline in his hand.

8 And the LORD said to me, Amos, what do you see? And I said, A plumbline. Then said the LORD, Behold, I will set a plumbline in the midst of my people Israel: I will not again pass by them any more:

9 And the high places of Isaac shall be desolate, and the sanctuaries of Israel shall be laid waste; and I will rise against the house of Jeroboam with the sword.

10 Then Amaziah the priest of Bethel sent to Jeroboam king of Israel, saying, Amos has conspired against you in the midst of the house of Israel: the land is not able to bear all his words.

11 For thus Amos has said, Jeroboam shall die by the sword, and Israel shall surely be led away captive out of their own land.

12 Also Amaziah said to Amos, go, you seer, flee away into the land of Judah, and there eat bread, and prophesy there:

13 But prophesy not again any more at Bethel: for it is the king's chapel, and it is the king's court.

14 Then answered Amos, and said to Amaziah, I was no prophet, neither was I a prophet's son; but I was an herdman, and a gatherer of sycamore fruit:

15 And the LORD took me as I followed the flock, and the LORD said to me, Go, prophesy to my people Israel.

16 Now therefore hear the word of the LORD: You say, Do not prophesy against Israel, and do not drop your word against the house of Isaac.

17 Therefore thus says the LORD; Your wife shall be an harlot in the city, and your sons and your daughters shall fall by the sword, and your land shall be divided by line; and you shall die in a polluted land: and Israel shall surely go into captivity forth of his land.

CHAPTER 8

THUS has the Lord GOD showed to me: and behold a basket of summer fruit.

2 And he said, Amos, what do you see? And I said, A basket of summer fruit. Then said the LORD to me, The end is come upon my people of Israel; I will not again pass by them any more.

3 And the songs of the temple shall be howlings in that day, says the Lord GOD: there shall be many dead bodies in every place; they shall cast them forth with silence.

4 Hear this, O you that swallow up the needy, even to make the poor of the land to fail,

5 Saying, When will the new moon be gone, that we may sell corn? and the sabbath, that we may set forth wheat, making the ephah small, and the shekel great, and falsifying the balances by deceit?

6 That we may buy the poor for silver, and the needy for a pair of shoes; yea, and sell the refuse of the wheat?

7 The LORD has sworn by the excellency of Jacob, Surely I will never forget any of their works.

8 Shall not the land tremble for this, and every one mourn that dwells in it? and it shall rise up wholly as a flood; and it shall be cast out and drowned, as by the flood of Egypt.

9 And it shall come to pass in that day, says the Lord GOD, that I will cause the sun to go down at noon, and I will darken the earth in the clear day:

10 And I will turn your feasts into mourning, and all your songs into lamentation; and I will bring up sackcloth upon all loins, and baldness upon every head; and I will make it as the mourning of an only son, and the end thereof as a bitter day.

11 Behold, the days come, says the Lord GOD, that I will send a famine in the land, not a famine of bread, nor a thirst for water, but of hearing the words of the LORD:

12 And they shall wander from sea to sea, and from the north even to the east, they shall run to and fro to seek the word of the LORD, and shall not find it.

13 In that day shall the fair virgins and young men faint for thirst.

14 They that swear by the sin of Samaria, and say, Your god, O Dan, lives; and, The manner of Beersheba lives; even they shall fall, and never rise up again.

CHAPTER 9

I saw the LORD standing upon the altar: and he said, Smite the lintel of the door, that the posts may shake: and cut them in the head, all of them; and I will slay the last of them with the sword: he that flees of them shall not flee away, and he that escapes of them shall not be delivered.

2 Though they dig into hell, thence shall my hand take them; though they climb up to heaven, thence will I bring them down:

3 And though they hide themselves in the top of Carmel, I will search and take them out thence; and though they be hid from my sight in the bottom of the sea, thence will I command the serpent, and he shall bite them:

4 And though they go into captivity before their enemies, thence will I command the sword, and it shall slay them: and I will set my eyes upon them for evil, and not for good.

5 And the Lord GOD of hosts is he that touches the land, and it shall melt, and all that dwell there shall mourn: and it shall rise up wholly like a flood; and shall be drowned, as by the flood of Egypt.

6 It is he that builds his stories in the heaven, and has founded his troop in the earth; he that calls for the waters of the sea, and pours them out upon the face of the earth: The LORD is his name.

7 Are you not as children of the Ethiopians to me, O children of Israel? says the LORD. Have not I brought up Israel out of the land of Egypt? and the Philistines from Caphtor, and the Syrians from Kir?

8 Behold, the eyes of the Lord GOD are upon the sinful kingdom, and I will destroy it from off the face of the earth; saving that I will not utterly destroy the house of Jacob, says the LORD.

9 For, lo, I will command, and I will sift the house of Israel among all nations, like as corn is sifted in a sieve, yet shall not the least grain fall upon the earth.

10 All the sinners of my people shall die by the sword, which say, The evil shall not overtake nor prevent us.

11 In that day will I raise up the tabernacle of David that is fallen, and close up the breaches thereof; and I will raise up his ruins, and I will build it as in the days of old:

12 That they may possess the remnant of Edom, and of all the heathen, which are called by my name, says the LORD that doeth this.

13 Behold, the days come, says the LORD, that the plowman shall overtake the reaper, and the treader of grapes him that sows seed; and the mountains shall drop sweet wine, and all the hills shall melt.

14 And I will bring again the captivity of my people of Israel, and they shall build the waste cities, and inhabit them; and they shall plant vineyards, and drink the wine thereof; they shall also make gardens, and eat the fruit of them.

15 And I will plant them upon their land, and they shall no more be pulled

up out of their land which I have given
them, says the LORD your God.

Obadiah

CHAPTER 1

THE vision of Obadiah. Thus says the Lord GOD concerning Edom; We have heard a rumour from the LORD, and an ambassador is sent among the heathen, Arise, and let us rise up against her in battle.

2 Behold, I have made you small among the heathen: you are greatly despised.

3 The pride of your heart has deceived you, you that dwells in the clefts of the rock, whose habitation is high; that says in his heart, Who shall bring me down to the ground?

4 Though you exalt yourself as the eagle, and though you set your nest among the stars, thence will I bring you down, says the LORD.

5 If thieves came to you, if robbers by night, (how are you cut off!) would they not have stolen till they had enough? if the grape gatherers came to you, would they not leave some grapes?

6 How are the things of Esau searched out! how are his hidden things sought up!

7 All the men of your confederacy have brought you even to the border: the men that were at peace with you have deceived you, and prevailed against you; that they eat your bread have laid a wound under you: there is none understanding in him.

8 Shall I not in that day, says the LORD, even destroy the wise men out of Edom, and understanding out of the mount of Esau?

9 And your mighty men, O Teman, shall be dismayed, to the end that every one of the mount of Esau may be cut off by slaughter.

10 For your violence against your brother Jacob shame shall cover you, and you shall be cut off for ever.

11 In the day that you stood on the other side, in the day that the strangers carried away captive his forces, and foreigners entered into his gates, and cast lots upon Jerusalem, even you were as one of them.

12 But you should not have looked on the day of your brother in the day that he became a stranger; neither should you have rejoiced over the children of Judah in the day of their destruction;

1:3 Pride deceives the human heart. Pride stops the search for God (see Psalm 10:4), and it blinds the eyes to reality. Pride makes a fool think that he is wise. It makes a grasshopper think that he's a giant. Pride tells a man that he is good when his heart is desperately wicked. It is the root of the tree of self-righteousness. Pride tells a man that he is right when the entire world can see that he is wrong. Thank God for His Law! It strips a man of the deceit of pride and humbles him by showing him the truth.

neither should you have spoken proudly in the day of distress.

13 You should not have entered into the gate of my people in the day of their calamity; yea, you should not have looked on their affliction in the day of their calamity, nor have laid hands on their substance in the day of their calamity;

14 Neither should you have stood in the crossway, to cut off those of his that did escape; neither should you have delivered up those of his that did remain in the day of distress.

15 For the day of the LORD is near upon all the heathen: as you have done, it shall be done to you: your reward shall return upon your own head.

16 For as you have drunk upon my holy mountain, so shall all the heathen drink continually, yea, they shall drink, and they shall swallow down, and they shall be as though they had not been.

17 But upon mount Zion shall be deliverance, and there shall be holiness; and the house of Jacob shall possess their possessions.

18 And the house of Jacob shall be a fire, and the house of Joseph a flame, and the house of Esau for stubble, and they shall kindle in them, and devour them; and there shall not be any remaining of the house of Esau; for the LORD has spoken it.

19 And they of the south shall possess the mount of Esau; and they of the plain the Philistines: and they shall possess the fields of Ephraim, and the fields of Samaria: and Benjamin shall possess Gilead.

20 And the captivity of this host of the children of Israel shall possess that of the Canaanites, even to Zarephath; and the captivity of Jerusalem, which is in Sepharad, shall possess the cities of the south.

21 And saviours shall come up on mount Zion to judge the mount of Esau; and the kingdom shall be the LORD's.

1:15 This is the law of sowing and reaping or, to use the modern idiom, "What goes around, comes around." Some wicked men may seem to have escaped this law by dying in peace and prosperity. But the grave will not hide men from God's justice.

1:21 "For Thine is the Kingdom and the power and the glory...forever" (Matthew 6:13).

Jonah

CHAPTER 1

N OW the word of the LORD came to Jonah the son of Amittai, saying,

2 Arise, go to Nineveh, that great city, and cry against it; for their wickedness is come up before me.

3 But Jonah rose up to flee to Tarshish from the presence of the LORD, and went down to Joppa; and he found a ship going to Tarshish: so he paid the fare thereof, and went down into it, to go with them to Tarshish from the presence of the LORD.

4 But the LORD sent out a great wind into the sea, and there was a mighty tempest in the sea, so that the ship was like to be broken.

5 Then the mariners were afraid, and every man cried to his god, and cast forth the wares that were in the ship into the sea, to lighten it of them. But Jonah was gone down into the sides of the ship; and he lay, and was fast asleep.

> If you want to run from God,
> the devil will always
> provide the transportation.
>
> **DR. JERRY VINES**
> Born 1937 in Carrolton, Georgia
> Pastor
> First Baptist Church of Jacksonville

1:2 For how to confront sinners, see Psalm 41:4 comment.

1:4-5 The storms of this life tell a thinking person that all is not well between humanity and God. The tempest of His anger sent the Genesis curse across the sea of humanity and this earthly abode. Earthquakes, hurricanes, floods, tornadoes, famine, drought, disease and death tell us that we don't have harmony with Heaven.

It is because of death that every sensible man cries out to his god. Every civilization has a measure of faith in some god. We have yet to discover an atheistic civilization. Primitive man is ignorant, but he's not that ignorant. In his darkened mind, he worships the sun or an idol made by his hands. He practices some form of sacrifice to try and appease his god because he can see that he lives on the brink of death.

He tries through his own religious effects to "lighten the ship." But religion cannot save him from death. His own labors are not able to deliver him. It's not by any works of righteousness that we are saved, but only according to His mercy (see also Ephesians 2:8-9).

1:6 Until God's Law comes in the hand of the captain of our salvation, we are asleep in our sins. It smites us and says, "Awake you who sleep, arise from the dead, and Christ shall give you light" (Ephesians 5:14). It is the sting of God's Law that causes the sinner to revive and also brings him to the point of death. The consciousness of sin once lay dormant within his sleeping breast until the Law did its wonderful work. It reveals to him that he will perish unless God intervenes with His great mercy.

*Less than two percent of believers
in this country
ever share their faith in Christ
with others.**

Dr. Bill Bright
1921-2003
FOUNDER OF CAMPUS CRUSADE
FOR CHRIST

6 So the shipmaster came to him, and said to him, What do you mean, O sleeper? arise, call upon your God, if so be that God will think upon us, that we perish not.

7 And they said every one to his fellow, come, and let us cast lots, that we may know for whose cause this evil is upon us. So they cast lots, and the lot fell upon Jonah.

8 Then said they to him, Tell us, we pray you, for whose cause this evil is upon us; What is your occupation? and where do you come from? what is your country? and of what people are you?

9 And he said to them, I am an Hebrew; and I fear the LORD, the God of heaven, which has made the sea and the dry land.

10 Then were the men exceedingly afraid, and said to him. Why have you done this? For the men knew that he fled from the presence of the LORD, because he had told them.

11 Then they said to him, What shall we do to you, that the sea may be calm to us? for the sea was growing more tempestuous.

12 And he said to them, Take me up, and cast me forth into the sea; so shall the sea be calm to you: for I know that for my sake this great tempest is upon you.

13 Nevertheless the men rowed hard to bring it to the land; but they could not: for the sea continued to grow more tempestuous against them.

14 Therefore they cried to the LORD, and said, We beseech you, O LORD, we beseech you, let us not perish for this man's life, and lay not upon us innocent blood: for you, O LORD, have done as it pleased you.

---

* *The Coming Revival*, p. 65.

1:7 God's incredible mercy came through the person of Jesus of Nazareth. His lot was to take the sin of the world upon Himself.

1:11-12 The more we sin, the more we provoke the tempestuous wrath of Almighty God. But wonder of wonders, this man from Nazareth said, "Pick me up and throw me into the sea of God's wrath." "Greater love hath no man than this, that a man lay down his life for his friends" John 15:13). The man Christ Jesus became sin for us, and in Him our sins are cast into the sea of God's forgetfulness. It is in Him that we have peace with God. The storm of God's anger is calm for all who trust in the Savior. Jesus likened His death on the cross to Jonah's experience in the belly of the whale (see Matthew 12:40).

1:13 Even when sinful men are presented with the Good News of the gospel--that they can be saved simply by God's grace through faith, they refuse to trust in the mercy of God. Their pride causes them to try and save themselves. Their guilt-ridden conscience drives them to works of righteousness that cannot save them. And the storm of God's wrath worsens.

15 So they took up Jonah, and cast him forth into the sea: and the sea ceased from her raging.

16 Then the men feared the LORD exceedingly, and offered a sacrifice to the LORD, and made vows.

17 Now the LORD had prepared a great fish to swallow up Jonah. And Jonah was in the belly of the fish three days and three nights.

CHAPTER 2

T HEN Jonah prayed to the LORD his God out of the fish's belly,

2 And said, I cried by reason of my affliction to the LORD, and he heard me; out of the belly of hell cried I, and you heard my voice.

3 For you had cast me into the deep, in the midst of the seas; and the floods compassed me about: all your billows and your waves passed over me.

4 Then I said, I am cast out of your sight; yet I will look again toward your holy temple.

5 The waters compassed me about, even to the soul: the depth closed me round about, the weeds were wrapped about my head.

6 I went down to the bottoms of the mountains; the earth with her bars was about me for ever: yet have you brought up my life from corruption, O LORD my God.

How each of us can identify with Jonah! We have been told to "go" also and speak to the world about its great wickedness that has come before God.

We may identify with the prophet, but God forbid that we should imitate him. He fled "from the presence of the Lord." A fish would do better to try and flee from the presence of the ocean. Although God may present Himself in certain places, it is to follow in the folly of Adam to imagine that we can run from His presence (see Genesis 3:8). God is omnipresent.

7 When my soul fainted within me I remembered the LORD: and my prayer came in to you, into your holy temple.

8 They that observe lying vanities forsake their own mercy.

9 But I will sacrifice to you with the voice of thanksgiving; I will pay that that I have vowed. Salvation is of the LORD.

10 And the LORD spoke to the fish, and it vomited out Jonah upon the dry land.

1:14 When all hope of saving themselves is stripped from them, men will turn to the mercy of God and trust in the innocent blood of the sinless Savior. They cry, "Not my will, but Yours be done" (Matthew 26:39).

1:15 When Jesus of Nazareth was taken by wicked hands and crucified, God was in Christ reconciling the world to Himself (see 2 Corinthians 5:19). God made Him who knew no sin to be sin for us.

2:2-6 Perhaps here we have insight into the sufferings of the Savior. The waters of the wrath of God encompassed Him as His soul was made an offering for sin. The crown of thorns was wrapped around His head as He took upon Himself the Genesis curse. Jesus Himself said that He went into the heart of the earth (Matthew 12:40), into the pit of death.

2:9 Salvation is of the Lord. This is the reason we should forsake any man-made methods for salvation and trust solely in God for our salvation. It is wrought by grace and grace alone; God saves men by grace and grace alone.

*A man's greatest misery
is to be without God
—that is to have no inward connection
to the One who is life and existence itself.*

Augustine
354-430
BISHOP OF HIPPO

CHAPTER 3

AND the word of the LORD came to Jonah the second time, saying,

2 Arise, go to Nineveh, that great city, and preach to it the preaching that I bid you.

3 So Jonah arose, and went to Nineveh, according to the word of the LORD. Now Nineveh was an exceeding great city of three days' journey.

4 And Jonah began to enter into the city a day's journey, and he cried, and said, Yet forty days, and Nineveh shall be overthrown.

5 So the people of Nineveh believed God, and proclaimed a fast, and put on sackcloth, from the greatest of them even to the least of them.

6 For word came to the king of Nineveh, and he arose from his throne, and he laid his robe from him, and covered him with sackcloth, and sat in ashes.

7 And he caused it to be proclaimed and published through Nineveh by the decree of the king and his nobles, saying, Let neither man nor beast, herd nor flock, taste any thing: let them not feed, nor drink water:

8 But let man and beast be covered with sackcloth, and cry mightily to God: yea, let them turn every one from his evil way, and from the violence that is in their hands.

9 Who can tell if God will turn and repent, and turn away from his fierce anger, that we perish not?

10 And God saw their works, that they turned from their evil way; and God repented of the evil, that he had said that he would do to them; and he did it not.

CHAPTER 4

BUT it displeased Jonah exceedingly, and he was very angry.

2 And he prayed to the LORD, and said, I pray you, O LORD, was not this my saying, when I was yet in my country? Therefore I fled before to Tarshish: for I knew that you are a gracious God, and merciful, slow to anger, and of great kindness, and you repent of the evil.

3 Therefore now, O LORD, take, I beseech you, my life from me; for it is better for me to die than to live.

4 Then said the LORD, Do you have good reason to be angry?

2:10 God spoke to death, and it could not hold Him.

3:5 When sinners accept the evangelistic message that their sin has placed them in great danger, they will repent and trust in the mercy of God in Christ.

3:7-8 May our King, too, cause the Good News of the gospel to be proclaimed and published throughout this world. This should be our constant prayer, that God will raise up and send forth messengers. Repentance from sin is more important than food or drink.

JONAH PREACHING TO THE NINEVITES

Jonah 3:3-4

You are not here in the world for yourself.
You have been sent here for others.
The world is waiting for you!

Catherine Booth

1829-1890
WITH HER HUSBAND, WILLIAM,
SHE FOUNDED
THE SALVATION ARMY
TO MINISTER
TO IMPOVERISHED LABORERS
OF VICTORIAN LONDON

5 So Jonah went out of the city, and sat on the east side of the city, and there made him a booth, and sat under it in the shadow, till he might see what would become of the city.

6 And the LORD God prepared a gourd, and made it to come up over Jonah, that it might be a shadow over his head, to deliver him from his grief. So Jonah was exceeding glad of the gourd.

7 But God prepared a worm when the morning rose the next day, and it smote the gourd that it withered.

8 And it came to pass, when the sun did arise, that God prepared a vehement east wind; and the sun beat upon the head of Jonah, that he fainted, and wished in himself to die, and said, It is better for me to die than to live.

9 And God said to Jonah, Do you have good reason to be angry for the gourd? And he said, I do have good reason to be angry, even to death.

10 Then said the LORD, You have had pity on the gourd, for the which you have not laboured, neither made it grow; which came up in a night, and perished in a night:

11 And should not I spare Nineveh, that great city, wherein are more then sixscore thousand persons that cannot discern between their right hand and their left hand; and also much cattle?

This generation of Christians
is responsible for this generation of souls
on the earth!

Keith Green

1953-1982
SINGER, SONGWRITER
AND PIONEER OF CONTEMPORARY
CHRISTIAN MUSIC

Micah

CHAPTER 1

THE word of the LORD that came to Micah the Morasthite in the days of Jotham, Ahaz, and Hezekiah, kings of Judah, which he saw concerning Samaria and Jerusalem.

2 Hear, all you people; hearken, O earth, and all that therein is: and let the Lord GOD be witness against you, the LORD from his holy temple.

3 For, behold, the LORD comes forth out of his place, and will come down, and tread upon the high places of the earth.

4 And the mountains shall be molten under him, and the valleys shall be cleft, as wax before the fire, and as the waters that are poured down a steep place.

5 For the transgression of Jacob is all this, and for the sins of the house of Israel. What is the transgression of Jacob? is it not Samaria? and what are the high places of Judah? are they not Jerusalem?

6 Therefore I will make Samaria as an heap of the field, and as plantings of a vineyard: and I will pour down the stones thereof into the valley, and I will discover the foundations thereof.

7 And all the graven images thereof shall be beaten to pieces, and all the hires thereof shall be burned with the fire, and all the idols thereof will I lay desolate: for she gathered it of the hire of an harlot, and they shall return to the hire of an harlot.

8 Therefore I will wail and howl, I will go stripped and naked: I will make a wailing like the dragons, and mourning as the owls.

9 For her wound is incurable; for it is come to Judah; he is come to the gate of my people, even to Jerusalem.

10 Do not declare it at Gath, do not weep at all: in the house of Aphrah roll yourself in the dust.

11 Pass away, you inhabitant of Saphir, having your shame naked: the inhabitant of Zaanan came not forth in the mourning of Bethezel; he shall receive of you his standing.

1:1-4 Notice the word "let" in verse 2. Those who allow God to speak to them will understand that He has witnessed every transgression of His Law. Those who refuse to hear will find to their horror that He has witnessed every secret sin, but then it will be too late to partake in His mercy. They will drink the wine of His wrath. They will see Him when He comes in flaming fire. How we must mediate on verses that warn us of that day, when mountains will melt under Him and great valleys will split like wax before the fire, like waters pouring down a steep place. In the light of these thoughts, do we plead with sinners? Are we horrified at their fate? Do our eyes run with water as we pray for them? If they don't, it may be because we have never truly mediated on the terror they must face at the coming of Almighty God.

12 For the inhabitant of Maroth waited carefully for good: but evil came down from the LORD to the gate of Jerusalem.

13 O you inhabitant of Lachish, bind the chariot to the swift beast: she is the beginning of the sin to the daughter of Zion: for the transgressions of Israel were found in you.

14 Therefore shall you give presents to Moreshethgath: the houses of Achzib shall be a lie to the kings of Israel.

15 Yet will I bring an heir to you, O inhabitant of Mareshah: he shall come to Adullam the glory of Israel.

16 Make you bald, and poll you for your delicate children; enlarge your baldness as the eagle; for they are gone into captivity from you.

CHAPTER 2

WOE to them that devise iniquity, and work evil upon their beds! when the morning is light, they practise it, because it is in the power of their hand.

2 And they covet fields, and take them by violence; and houses, and take them away: so they oppress a man and his house, even a man and his heritage.

3 Therefore thus says the LORD; Behold, against this family do I devise an evil, from which you shall not remove your necks; neither shall you go haughtily: for this time is evil.

4 In that day shall one take up a parable against you, and lament with a doleful lamentation, and say, We be utterly spoiled: he has changed the portion of my people: how has he removed it from me! turning away he has divided our fields.

5 Therefore you shall have none that shall cast a cord by lot in the congregation of the LORD.

6 Do not prophesy, say they to them that prophesy: they shall not prophesy to them, that they shall not take shame.

7 O you that are named the house of Jacob, is the spirit of the LORD straitened? are these his doings? do not my words do good to him that walks uprightly?

8 Even of late my people is risen up as an enemy: you pull off the robe with the garment from them that pass by securely as men averse from war.

9 The women of my people have you cast out from their pleasant houses; from their children have you taken away my glory for ever.

10 Arise, and depart; for this is not your rest: because it is polluted, it shall destroy you, even with a sore destruction.

11 If a man walking in the spirit and falsehood do lie, saying, I will prophesy to you of wine and of strong drink; he shall even be the prophet of this people.

12 I will surely assemble, O Jacob, all of you; I will surely gather the remnant of Israel; I will put them together as the sheep of Bozrah, as the flock in the midst of their fold: they shall make great noise by reason of the multitude of men.

13 The breaker is come up before them: they have broken up, and have passed through the gate, and are gone out by it: and their king shall pass before them, and the LORD on the head of them.

CHAPTER 3

AND I said, Hear, I pray you, O heads of Jacob, and you princes of the house of Israel; Is it not for you to know judgment?

2 Who hate the good, and love the evil; who pluck off their skin from off them, and their flesh from off their bones;

2:1-3 How this verse speaks of Hollywood, where evil men dig into the depths of their imaginations and make it a reality through their profession. They have the power in their hand to encourage violence in the land and to destroy the family unit by glamorization of adultery. They don't understand that God will bring upon them the fruit of their sin.

3 Who also eat the flesh of my people, and flay their skin from off them; and they break their bones, and chop them in pieces, as for the pot, and as flesh within the caldron.

4 Then shall they cry to the LORD, but he will not hear them: he will even hide his face from them at that time, as they have behaved themselves ill in their doings.

5 Thus says the LORD concerning the prophets that make my people err, that bite with their teeth, and cry, Peace; and he that puts not into their mouths, they even prepare war against him.

6 Therefore night shall be to you, that you shall not have a vision; and it shall be dark to you, that you shall not divine; and the sun shall go down over the prophets, and the day shall be dark over them.

7 Then shall the seers be ashamed, and the diviners confounded: yea, they shall all cover their lips; for there is no answer of God.

8 But truly I am full of power by the spirit of the LORD, and of judgment, and of might, to declare to Jacob his transgression, and to Israel his sin.

9 Hear this, I pray you, you heads of the house of Jacob, and princes of the house of Israel, that abhor judgment, and pervert all equity.

10 They build up Zion with blood, and Jerusalem with iniquity.

11 The heads thereof judge for reward, and the priests thereof teach for hire, and the prophets thereof divine for money: yet will they lean upon the LORD, and say, Is not the LORD among us? none evil can come upon us.

12 Therefore shall Zion for your sake be plowed as a field, and Jerusalem shall become heaps, and the mountain of the house as the high places of the forest.

CHAPTER 4

B UT in the last days it shall come to pass, that the mountain of the house of the LORD shall be established in the top of the mountains, and it shall be exalted above the hills; and people shall flow to it.

2 And many nations shall come, and say, Come, and let us go up to the mountain of the LORD, and to the house of the God of Jacob; and he will teach us of his ways, and we will walk in his paths: for the law shall go forth of Zion, and the word of the LORD from Jerusalem.

3 And he shall judge among many people, and rebuke strong nations afar off; and they shall beat their swords into plowshares, and their spears into pruninghooks: nation shall not lift up a sword against nation, neither shall they learn war any more.

4 But they shall sit every man under his vine and under his fig tree; and none shall make them afraid: for the mouth of the LORD of hosts has spoken it.

5 For all people will walk every one in the name of his god, and we will walk in the name of the LORD our God for ever and ever.

6 In that day, says the LORD, will I assemble her that halts, and I will gather her that is driven out, and her that I have afflicted;

7 And I will make her that halted a remnant, and her that was cast far off a

---

3:8 Jesus said that when we receive the Holy Spirit, we receive power (see Acts 1:8). Why have we been given this power? To be witnesses to Jesus' saving grace and against sin. We are to declare to the world the Law that God gave to Moses, which measures how all have sinned against God. Sin cannot be understood in truth until we realize that we are transgressors (see 1 John 3:4). Any knowledge of sin, without the light of God's Law, will be shallow. It is God's Law that shows sin to be exceedingly sinful (see Romans 7:13).

4:4 For millennia, peace among the nations has been but a dream. Such peace can only happen when God manifests Himself to the nations.

strong nation: and the LORD shall reign over them in mount Zion from henceforth, even for ever.

8 And you, O tower of the flock, the strong hold of the daughter of Zion, to you shall it come, even the first dominion; the kingdom shall come to the daughter of Jerusalem.

9 Now why do you cry out aloud? is there no king in you? is your counselor perished? for pangs have taken you as a woman in travail.

10 Be in pain, and labour to bring forth, O daughter of Zion, like a woman in travail: for now shall you go forth out of the city, and you shall dwell in the field, and you shall go even to Babylon; there shall you be delivered; there the LORD shall redeem you from the hand of your enemies.

11 Now also many nations are gathered against you, that say, Let her be defiled, and let our eye look upon Zion.

12 But they know not the thoughts of the LORD, neither understand they his counsel: for he shall gather them as the sheaves into the floor.

13 Arise and thresh, O daughter of Zion: for I will make your horn iron, and I will make your hoofs brass: and you shall beat in pieces many people: and I will consecrate their gain to the LORD, and their substance to the Lord of the whole earth.

CHAPTER 5

NOW gather yourself in troops, O daughter of troops: he has laid siege against us: they shall smite the judge of Israel with a rod upon the cheek.

2 But you, Bethlehem Ephratah, though you be little among the thousands of Judah, yet out of you shall he come forth to me that is to be ruler in Israel; whose goings forth have been from of old, from everlasting.

3 Therefore will he give them up, until the time that she which travails has brought forth: then the remnant of his brethren shall return to the children of Israel.

4 And he shall stand and feed in the strength of the LORD, in the majesty of the name of the LORD his God; and they shall abide: for now shall he be great to the ends of the earth.

5 And this man shall be the peace, when the Assyrian shall come into our land: and when he shall tread in our palaces, then shall we raise against him seven shepherds, and eight principal men.

6 And they shall waste the land of Assyria with the sword, and the land of Nimrod in the entrances thereof: thus shall he deliver us from the Assyrian, when he comes into our land, and when he treads within our borders.

7 And the remnant of Jacob shall be in the midst of many people as a dew from the LORD, as the showers upon the grass, that does not tarry for man, nor wait for the sons of men.

8 And the remnant of Jacob shall be among the Gentiles in the midst of many people as a lion among the beasts of the forest, as a young lion among the flocks of sheep: who, if he go through, both treads down, and tears in pieces, and none can deliver.

9 Your hand shall be lifted up upon your adversaries, and all your enemies shall be cut off.

10 And it shall come to pass in that day, says the LORD, that I will cut off your horses out of the midst of you, and I will destroy your chariots:

11 And I will cut off the cities of your land, and throw down all your strong holds:

12 And I will cut off witchcrafts out of your hand; and you shall have no more soothsayers:

5:2 This is a Messianic prophecy (see Matthew 2:6).

13 Your graven images also will I cut off, and your standing images out of the midst of you; and you shall no more worship the work of your hands.

14 And I will pluck up your groves out of the midst of you: so will I destroy your cities.

15 And I will execute vengeance in anger and fury upon the heathen, such as they have not heard.

CHAPTER 6

HEAR now what the LORD says; Arise, plead your case before the mountains, and let the hills hear your voice.

2 Hear, O mountains, the LORD's controversy, and you strong foundations of the earth: for the LORD has a controversy with his people, and he will plead with Israel.

3 O my people, what have I done to you? and wherein have I wearied you? testify against me.

4 For I brought you up out of the land of Egypt, and redeemed you out of the house of servants; and I sent before you Moses, Aaron, and Miriam.

5 O my people, remember now what Balak king of Moab consulted, and what Balaam the son of Beor answered him from Shittim to Gilgal; that you may know the righteousness of the LORD.

6 Wherewith shall I come before the LORD, and bow myself before the high God? shall I come before him with burnt offerings, with calves of a year old?

7 Will the LORD be pleased with thousands of rams, or with ten thousands of rivers of oil? shall I give my firstborn for my transgression, the fruit of my body for the sin of my soul?

8 He has showed you, O man, what is good; and what does the LORD require of you, but to do justly, and to love mercy, and to walk humbly with your God?

9 The LORD's voice cries to the city, and the man of wisdom shall see your name: hear the rod, and who has appointed it.

10 Are there yet the treasures of wickedness in the house of the wicked, and the scant measure that is abominable?

11 Shall I count them pure with the wicked balances, and with the bag of deceitful weights?

12 For the rich men thereof are full of violence, and the inhabitants thereof have spoken lies, and their tongue is deceitful in their mouth.

13 Therefore also will I make you sick in smiting you, in making you desolate because of your sins.

14 You shall eat, but not be satisfied; and your casting down shall be in the midst of you; and you shall take hold, but shall not deliver; and that which you deliver will I give up to the sword.

15 You shall sow, but you shall not reap; you shall tread the olives, but you shall not anoint you with oil; and sweet wine, but shall not drink wine.

16 For the statutes of Omri are kept, and all the works of the house of Ahab, and you walk in their counsels; that I should make you a desolation, and the inhabitants thereof an hissing: therefore you shall bear the reproach of my people.

CHAPTER 7

WOE is me! for I am as when they have gathered the summer fruits, as the grape gleanings of the vintage: there is no cluster to eat: my soul desired the firstripe fruit.

2 The good man is perished out of the earth: and there is none upright among

---

6:3 The Bible says that we hate God without cause (see John 15:25).

6:8 Rather than do that which is good and walk in humility with God, we walk away from Him in proud rebellion. The cross of Jesus is the great expression of God doing justly and loving mercy, so that we could walk humbly with Him. See Micah 7:18.

men: they all lie in wait for blood; they hunt every man his brother with a net.

3 That they may do evil with both hands earnestly, the prince asks, and the judge asks for a reward; and the great man, he utters his mischievous desire: so they wrap it up.

4 The best of them is as a brier: the most upright is sharper than a thorn hedge: the day of your watchmen and your visitation comes; now shall be their perplexity.

5 Do not trust in a friend, do not put confidence in a guide: keep the doors of your mouth from her that lies in your bosom.

6 For the son dishonours the father, the daughter rises up against her mother, the daughter in law against her mother in law; a man's enemies are the men of his own house.

7 Therefore I will look to the LORD; I will wait for the God of my salvation: my God will hear me.

8 Rejoice not against me, O my enemy: when I fall, I shall arise; when I sit in darkness, the LORD shall be a light to me.

9 I will bear the indignation of the LORD, because I have sinned against him, until he plead my cause, and execute judgment for me: he will bring me forth to the light, and I shall behold his righteousness.

10 Then she that is my enemy shall see it, and shame shall cover her which said to me, Where is the LORD your God? my eyes shall behold her: now shall she be trodden down as the mire of the streets.

11 In the day that your walls are to be built, in that day shall the decree be far removed.

12 In that day also he shall come even to you from Assyria, and from the forti- fied cities, and from the fortress even to the river, and from sea to sea, and from mountain to mountain.

13 Notwithstanding the land shall be desolate because of them that dwell therein, for the fruit of their doings.

14 Feed your people with your rod, the flock of your heritage, which dwell soli- tarily in the wood, in the midst of Carmel: let them feed in Bashan and Gilead, as in the days of old.

15 According to the days of your com- ing out of the land of Egypt will I show to him marvelous things.

16 The nations shall see and be con- founded at all their might: they shall lay their hand upon their mouth, their ears shall be deaf.

17 They shall lick the dust like a ser- pent, they shall move out of their holes like worms of the earth: they shall be afraid of the LORD our God, and shall fear because of you.

18 Who is a God like you, that pardons iniquity, and passes by the transgression of the remnant of his heritage? he does not retain his anger for ever, because he delights in mercy.

19 He will turn again, he will have compassion upon us; he will subdue our iniquities; and you will cast all their sins into the depths of the sea.

20 You will perform the truth to Jacob, and the mercy to Abraham, which you have sworn to our fathers from the days of old.

7:6 Jesus quoted this verse in regard to the persecution that comes to those who live godly in Christ Jesus (see Matthew 10:36, Mark 3:21, Luke 8:19 and John 7:5).

7:18 God's pardon and mercy is so evident in the cross of Calvary (also see Ezekiel 33:11 and John 1:17).

Nahum

CHAPTER 1

THE burden of Nineveh. The book of the vision of Nahum the Elkoshite.

2 God is jealous, and the LORD revenges; the LORD revenges, and is furious; the LORD will take vengeance on his adversaries, and he reserves wrath for his enemies.

3 The LORD is slow to anger, and great in power, and will not at all acquit the wicked: the LORD has his way in the whirlwind and in the storm, and the clouds are the dust of his feet.

4 He rebukes the sea, and makes it dry, and dries up all the rivers: Bashan languishes, and Carmel, and the flower of Lebanon languishes.

5 The mountains quake at him, and the hills melt, and the earth is burned at his presence, yea, the world, and all that dwell therein.

6 Who can stand before his indignation? and who can abide in the fierceness of his anger? his fury is poured out like fire, and the rocks are thrown down by him.

7 The LORD is good, a strong hold in the day of trouble; and he knows them that trust in him.

8 But with an overrunning flood he will make an utter end of the place thereof, and darkness shall pursue his enemies.

9 What do you imagine against the LORD? he will make an utter end: affliction shall not rise up the second time.

10 For while they be folden together as thorns, and while they are drunken as drunkards, they shall be devoured as stubble fully dry.

11 There is one come out of you, that imagines evil against the LORD, a wicked counselor.

12 Thus says the LORD; Though they be quiet, and likewise many, yet thus shall they be cut down, when he shall

---

1:1-7 Here is a revelation of God's divine attributes. He is jealous. He takes vengeance. He becomes furious and wrath-filled. Yet, this wrath-filled, jealous God is slow to anger. He holds back His terrible wrath because He is rich in mercy. He is not willing that any perish, but warns that He will by no means acquit the wicked. How do we know this? Primarily because He gives us His word that justice will be done. Reason also demands it. It is reasonable that murderers, rapists, thieves, etc., be punished. If His creation—massive tornadoes, huge clouds, the vast seas, rivers, flowers and mountains bow at His presence, how much more will sinful man be subject to His power? No one can stand before His indignation.

1:7 He gives us the good news of the gospel. It was His goodness that provided Jesus' sacrifice on the cross, and that is our stronghold in the Day of Trouble. It is there that wicked men are not merely acquitted, but also justified and made righteous before God.

1:9 See Psalm 2.

pass through. Though I have afflicted you, I will afflict you no more.

13 For now will I break his yoke from off you, and will burst your bonds in sunder.

14 And the LORD has given a commandment concerning you, that no more of your name be sown: out of the house of your gods will I cut off the graven image and the molten image: I will make your grave; for you are vile.

15 Behold upon the mountains the feet of him that brings good tidings, that publishes peace! O Judah, keep your solemn feasts, perform your vows: for the wicked shall no more pass through you; he is utterly cut off.

CHAPTER 2

HE that dashes in pieces is come up before your face: keep the munition, watch the way, make your loins strong, fortify your power mightily.

2 For the LORD has turned away the excellency of Jacob, as the excellency of Israel: for the emptiers have emptied them out, and marred their vine branches.

3 The shield of his mighty men is made red, the valiant men are in scarlet: the chariots shall be with flaming torches in the day of his preparation, and the fir trees shall be terribly shaken.

4 The chariots shall rage in the streets, they shall justle one against another in the broad ways: they shall seem like torches, they shall run like the lightnings.

5 He shall recount his worthies: they shall stumble in their walk; they shall make haste to the wall thereof, and the defence shall be prepared.

6 The gates of the rivers shall be opened, and the palace shall be dissolved.

7 And Huzzab shall be led away captive, she shall be brought up, and her maids shall lead her as with the voice of doves, tabering upon their breasts.

8 But Nineveh is of old like a pool of water: yet they shall flee away. Stand, stand, shall they cry; but none shall look back.

9 Take the spoil of silver, take the spoil of gold: for there is none end of the store and glory out of all the pleasant furniture.

1:15 God sees as beautiful, the lowly feet of those who preach His glorious gospel (see Romans 10:15).

2:4 Some see this as a prophecy of modern vehicles.

10 She is empty, and void, and waste: and the heart melts, and the knees smite together, and much pain is in all loins, and the faces of them all gather blackness.

11 Where is the dwelling of the lions, and the feeding place of the young lions, where the lion, even the old lion, walked, and the lion's whelp, and none made them afraid?

12 The lion did tear in pieces enough for his whelps, and strangled for his lionesses, and filled his holes with prey, and his dens with raven.

13 Behold, I am against you, says the LORD of hosts, and I will burn her chariots in the smoke, and the sword shall devour your young lions: and I will cut off your prey from the earth, and the voice of your messengers shall no more be heard.

CHAPTER 3

WOE to the bloody city! it is all full of lies and robbery; the prey does not depart;

2 The noise of a whip, and the noise of the rattling of the wheels, and of the pransing horses, and of the jumping chariots.

3 The horseman lifts up both the bright sword and the glittering spear: and there is a multitude of slain, and a great number of carcases; and there is none end of their corpses; they stumble upon their corpses:

4 Because of the multitude of the whoredoms of the well favoured harlot, the mistress of witchcrafts, that sells nations through her whoredoms, and families through her witchcrafts.

5 Behold, I am against you, says the LORD of hosts; and I will discover your skirts upon your face, and I will show the nations your nakedness, and the kingdoms your shame.

6 And I will cast abominable filth upon you, and make you vile, and will set you as a gazingstock.

7 And it shall come to pass, that all they that look upon you shall flee from you, and say, Nineveh is laid waste: who will bemoan her? where shall I seek comforters for you?

8 Are you better than populous No, that was situate among the rivers, that had the waters round about it, whose rampart was the sea, and her wall was from the sea?

9 Ethiopia and Egypt were her strength, and it was infinite; Put and Lubim were your helpers.

10 Yet was she carried away, she went into captivity: her young children also were dashed in pieces at the top of all the streets: and they cast lots for her honourable men, and all her great men were bound in chains.

11 You also shall be drunken: you shall be hid, you also shall seek strength because of the enemy.

12 All your strong holds shall be like fig trees with the firstripe figs: if they be shaken, they shall even fall into the mouth of the eater.

13 Behold, your people in the midst of you are women: the gates of your land shall be set wide open to your enemies: the fire shall devour your bars.

14 Draw your water for the siege, fortify your strong holds: go into clay, and tread the morter, make strong the brickkiln.

15 There shall the fire devour you; the sword shall cut you off, it shall eat you up like the cankerworm: make yourself many as the cankerworm, make yourself many as the locusts.

16 You have multiplied your merchants above the stars of heaven: the cankerworm spoils, and flees away.

17 Your crowned are as the locusts, and your captains as the great grasshoppers, which camp in the hedges in the cold day, but when the sun arises they flee away, and their place is not known where they are.

18 Your shepherds slumber, O king of Assyria: your nobles shall dwell in the

dust: your people are scattered upon the mountains, and no man gathers them.

19 There is no healing of your bruise; your wound is grievous: all that hear the news of you shall clap the hands over you: for upon whom has not your wickedness passed continually?

Habakkuk

CHAPTER 1

THE burden which Habakkuk the prophet did see.

2 O LORD, how long shall I cry, and you will not hear! even cry out to you of violence, and you will not save!

3 Why do you show me iniquity, and cause me to behold grievance? for spoiling and violence are before me: and there are that raise up strife and contention.

4 Therefore the law is slacked, and judgment never goes forth: for the wicked compass about the righteous; therefore wrong judgment proceeds.

5 Behold among the heathen, and regard, and wonder marvelously: for I will work a work in your days which you will not believe, though it be told you.

6 For, lo, I raise up the Chaldeans, that bitter and hasty nation, which shall march through the breadth of the land, to possess the dwelling places that are not their's.

7 They are terrible and dreadful: their judgment and their dignity shall proceed of themselves.

8 Their horses also are swifter than the leopards, and are more fierce than the evening wolves: and their horsemen shall spread themselves, and their horsemen shall come from far; they shall fly as the eagle that hastens to eat.

9 They shall come all for violence: their faces shall sup up as the east wind, and they shall gather the captivity as the sand.

10 And they shall scoff at the kings, and the princes shall be a scorn to them: they shall deride every strong hold; for they shall heap dust, and take it.

11 Then shall his mind change, and he shall pass over, and offend, imputing this his power to his god.

12 Are you not from everlasting, O LORD my God, my Holy One? we shall not die. O LORD, you have ordained them for judgment; and, O mighty God, you have established them for correction.

1:1-5 The Christian carries a "burden." We look around us at the unspeakable atrocities and carnage of humanity and cry out in despair to God. When we speak out about the fruits of sin, we find that the world contends with us. The unsaved suffer horribly with the disease of sin and yet refuse the cure.

One fruit of a sinful world is a system of law that eliminates any reference to God, who is the final authority, the one whose laws are perfect and just. When law excludes God, it produces erroneous judgments. But as desperate as things seem, God can do abundantly above all we ask or think. He allows us to see iniquity and see it for what it is so that we might be driven to prayer and see Him fulfill His wondrous purposes.

What is the testimony of your closet?
Can it bear witness
to your sighs and groans and tears
over the wickedness and desolations
of the world?

Charles Finney

1792 - 1875

AMERICAN EVANGELIST
AND EDUCATOR

13 You are of purer eyes than to behold evil, and can not look on iniquity: why do you look upon them that deal treacherously, and hold your tongue when the wicked devours the man that is more righteous than he?

14 And make men as the fishes of the sea, as the creeping things, that have no ruler over them?

15 They take up all of them with the angle, they catch them in their net, and gather them in their drag: therefore they rejoice and are glad.

16 Therefore they sacrifice to their net, and burn incense to their drag; because by them their portion is fat, and their meat plenteous.

17 Shall they therefore empty their net, and not spare continually to slay the nations?

CHAPTER 2

I will stand upon my watch, and set me upon the tower, and will watch to see what he will say to me, and what I shall answer when I am reproved.

2 And the LORD answered me, and said, Write the vision, and make it plain upon tables, that he may run that reads it.

3 For the vision is yet for an appointed time, but at the end it shall speak, and not lie: though it tarry, wait for it; because it will surely come, it will not tarry.

4 Behold, his soul which is lifted up is not upright in him: but the just shall live by his faith.

5 Yea also, because he transgresses by wine, he is a proud man, neither does he stay at home, who enlarges his desire as hell, and is as death, and cannot be satisfied, but gathers to himself all nations, and heaps up for himself all people:

6 Shall not all these take up a parable against him, and a taunting proverb against him, and say, Woe to him that increases that which is not his! how long? and to him that loads himself with thick clay!

7 Shall they not rise up suddenly that shall bite you, and awake that shall vex you, and you shall be for booties to them?

8 Because you have spoiled many nations, all the remnant of the people shall spoil you; because of men's blood, and for the violence of the land, of the city, and of all that dwell therein.

9 Woe to him that covets an evil covetousness to his house, that he may set his nest on high, that he may be delivered from the power of evil!

10 You have consulted shame to your house by cutting off many people, and have sinned against your soul.

2:4 Faith, and faith alone, makes us right with God (see Ephesians 2:8-9).

THE FUNCTION OF THE LAW IN EVANGELISM

1:4 **"I do not believe that any man can preach the gospel who does not preach the Law.**
Lower the Law, and you dim the light by which man perceives his guilt; this is a very serious loss to the sinner rather than a gain; for it lessens the likelihood of his conviction and conversion.

"I say you have deprived the gospel of its ablest auxiliary [its most powerful weapon] when you have set aside the Law. You have taken away from it the schoolmaster that is to bring men to Christ. They will never accept grace till they tremble before a just and holy Law. Therefore, the Law serves a most necessary purpose, and it must not be removed from its place."

Charles H. Spurgeon

11 For the stone shall cry out of the wall, and the beam out of the timber shall answer it.

12 Woe to him that builds a town with blood, and establishes a city by iniquity!

13 Behold, is it not of the LORD of hosts that the people shall labour in the very fire, and the people shall weary themselves for very vanity?

14 For the earth shall be filled with the knowledge of the glory of the LORD, as the waters cover the sea.

15 *Woe to him that gives his neighbour drink, that puts your bottle to him, and makes him drunken also, that you may look on their nakedness!*

16 You are filled with shame for glory: drink also, and let your foreskin be uncovered: the cup of the LORD's right hand shall be turned to you, and shameful spewing shall be on your glory.

17 For the violence of Lebanon shall cover you, and the spoil of beasts, which made them afraid, because of men's blood, and for the violence of the land, of the city, and of all that dwell therein.

18 What profits the graven image that the maker thereof has graven it; the molten image, and a teacher of lies, that the maker of his work trusts therein, to make dumb idols?

19 Woe to him that says to the wood, Awake; to the dumb stone, Arise, it shall teach! Behold, it is laid over with gold and silver, and there is no breath at all in the midst of it.

20 But the LORD is in his holy temple: let all the earth keep silence before him.

CHAPTER 3

A prayer of Habakkuk the prophet upon Shigionoth.

2 O LORD, I have heard your speech, and was afraid: O LORD, revive your work in the midst of the years, in the midst of the years make known; in wrath remember mercy.

3 God came from Teman, and the Holy One from mount Paran. Selah. His glory covered the heavens, and the earth was full of his praise.

4 And his brightness was as the light; he had horns coming out of his hand: and there was the hiding of his power.

5 Before him went the pestilence, and burning coals went forth at his feet.

6 He stood, and measured the earth: he beheld, and drove asunder the nations; and the everlasting mountains were scattered, the perpetual hills did bow: his ways are everlasting.

7 I saw the tents of Cushan in affliction: and the curtains of the land of Midian did tremble.

8 Was the LORD displeased against the rivers? was your anger against the rivers? was your wrath against the sea, that you did ride upon your horses and your chariots of salvation?

9 Your bow was made quite naked, according to the oaths of the tribes, even your word. Selah. You did cleave the earth with rivers.

10 The mountains saw you, and they trembled: the overflowing of the water passed by: the deep uttered his voice, and lifted up his hands on high.

11 The sun and moon stood still in their habitation: at the light of your arrows they went, and at the shining of your glittering spear. 12 You marched through the land in indignation, thou threshed the heathen in anger. 13 You went forth for the salvation of your people, even for salvation with your anointed; you wounded the head out of the house of the wicked, by discovering the foundation to the neck. Selah. 14 You did strike through with his staves the head of his villages: they came out as a whirlwind to scatter me: their rejoicing was as to devour the poor secretly. 15 You walked through the sea with your horses, through the heap of great waters.

> " God may appear
> to be overlooking sin,
> especially when evil seems to triumph
> in our day.
> Rest assured
> that within the very core nature
> of God is His justice.
> He cannot by nature overlook sin.
> And He has appointed a day
> in which He will judge the world
> in righteousness.
> You can be sure of that. "
>
> **JAY FOWLER**
> BORN 1977
> AMERICAN SCHOLAR
> OF THE BIBLE

16 When I heard, my belly trembled; my lips quivered at the voice: rottenness entered into my bones, and I trembled in myself, that I might rest in the day of trouble: when he comes up to the people, he will invade them with his troops. 17 Although the fig tree shall not blossom, neither shall fruit be in the vines; the labour of the olive shall fail, and the fields shall yield no meat; the flock shall be cut off from the fold, and there shall be no herd in the stalls: 18 Yet I will rejoice in the LORD, I will joy in the God of my salvation. 19 The LORD God is my strength, and he will make my feet like hinds' feet, and he will make me to walk upon my high places. To the chief singer on my stringed instruments.

Zephaniah

CHAPTER 1

THE word of the LORD which came to Zephaniah the son of Cushi, the son of Gedaliah, the son of Amariah, the son of Hizkiah, in the days of Josiah the son of Amon, king of Judah.

2 I will utterly consume all things from off the land, says the LORD.

3 I will consume man and beast; I will consume the fowls of the heaven, and the fishes of the sea, and the stumbling blocks with the wicked: and I will cut off man from off the land, says the LORD.

4 I will also stretch out my hand upon Judah, and upon all the inhabitants of Jerusalem; and I will cut off the remnant of Baal from this place, and the name of the Chemarims with the priests;

5 And them that worship the host of heaven upon the housetops; and them that worship and that swear by the LORD, and that swear by Malcham;

6 And them that are turned back from the LORD; and those that have not sought the LORD, nor inquired for him.

7 Hold your peace at the presence of the Lord GOD: for the day of the LORD is at hand: for the LORD has prepared a sacrifice, he has bid his guests.

8 And it shall come to pass in the day of the LORD's sacrifice, that I will punish the princes, and the king's children, and all such as are clothed with strange apparel.

9 In the same day also will I punish all those that leap on the threshold, which fill their masters' houses with violence and deceit.

10 And it shall come to pass in that day, says the LORD, that there shall be the noise of a cry from the fish gate, and an howling from the second, and a great crashing from the hills.

11 Howl, you inhabitants of Maktesh, for all the merchant people are cut down; all they that bear silver are cut off.

12 And it shall come to pass at that time, that I will search Jerusalem with candles, and punish the men that are settled on their lees: that say in their heart, The LORD will not do good, neither will he do evil.

13 Therefore their goods shall become a booty, and their houses a desolation: they shall also build houses, but not inhabit them; and they shall plant vineyards, but not drink the wine thereof.

14 The great day of the LORD is near, it is near, and hastens greatly, even the

---

1:12 The day will come when God reveals the secret sins of every sinner's heart. No darkened corner of the mind will be forgotten by God. Meanwhile, those sinners who have set up an idol in their heart remain in sin; the god they serve has no moral backbone. That god sees injustice and couldn't care less.

voice of the day of the LORD: the mighty man shall cry there bitterly.

15 That day is a day of wrath, a day of trouble and distress, a day of wasteness and desolation, a day of darkness and gloominess, a day of clouds and thick darkness,

16 A day of the trumpet and alarm against the fenced cities, and against the high towers.

17 And I will bring distress upon men, that they shall walk like blind men, because they have sinned against the LORD: and their blood shall be poured out as dust, and their flesh as the dung.

18 Neither their silver nor their gold shall be able to deliver them in the day of the LORD's wrath; but the whole land shall be devoured by the fire of his jealousy: for he shall make even a speedy riddance of all them that dwell in the land.

CHAPTER 2

G ATHER yourselves together, yea, gather together, O nation not desired;

2 Before the decree bring forth, before the day pass as the chaff, before the fierce anger of the LORD come upon you, before the day of the LORD's anger come upon you.

3 Seek the LORD, all you meek of the earth, which have carried out his judgment; seek righteousness, seek meekness: it may be you shall be hid in the day of the LORD's anger.

4 For Gaza shall be forsaken, and Ashkelon a desolation: they shall drive out Ashdod at the noon day, and Ekron shall be rooted up.

5 Woe to the inhabitants of the sea coast, the nation of the Cherethites! the word of the LORD is against you; O Canaan, the land of the Philistines, I will even destroy you, that there shall be no inhabitant.

6 And the sea coast shall be dwellings and cottages for shepherds, and folds for flocks.

7 And the coast shall be for the remnant of the house of Judah; they shall feed thereupon: in the houses of Ashkelon shall they lie down in the evening: for the LORD their God shall visit them, and turn away their captivity.

8 I have heard the reproach of Moab, and the revilings of the children of Ammon, whereby they have reproached my people, and magnified themselves against their border.

9 Therefore as I live, says the LORD of hosts, the God of Israel, Surely Moab shall be as Sodom, and the children of Ammon as Gomorrah, even the breeding of nettles, and saltpits, and a perpetual desolation: the residue of my people shall spoil them, and the remnant of my people shall possess them.

10 This shall they have for their pride, because they have reproached and magnified themselves against the people of the LORD of hosts.

11 The LORD will be terrible to them: for he will famish all the gods of the earth; and men shall worship him, every one from his place, even all the isles of the heathen.

12 You Ethiopians also, you shall be slain by my sword.

13 And he will stretch out his hand against the north, and destroy Assyria; and will make Nineveh a desolation, and dry like a wilderness.

14 And flocks shall lie down in the midst of her, all the beasts of the nations: both the cormorant and the bittern shall lodge in the upper lintels of it; their voice shall sing in the windows; desolation shall be in the thresholds; for he shall uncover the cedar work.

15 This is the rejoicing city that dwelt carelessly, that said in her heart, I am, and there is none beside me: how is she

---

2:3 It is the righteousness of Christ that will shelter the sinner in the day of the Lord's anger (See Romans 5:17).

THE FUNCTION OF THE LAW IN EVANGELISM

3:4   **False prophets,** whether during the time of Zephaniah, or the Pharisees in Jesus' day, or the false prophets of our day, all do "violence to the Law." They show contempt for the Law, refusing to preach it despite the example of Jesus (see Luke 10:25-26, 18:18-20) and despite the many other verses that speak of the Law's function, to bring sinners to the Savior (see Romans 3:19-20, 7:7, Galatians 3:24, 1 Timothy 1:10. Also see Amos 2:4 and Mark 7:9).

become a desolation, a place for beasts to lie down in! every one that passes by her shall hiss, and wag his hand.

CHAPTER 3

WOE to her that is filthy and polluted, to the oppressing city!

2 She obeyed not the voice; she received not correction; she trusted not in the LORD; she drew not near to her God.

3 Her princes within her are roaring lions; her judges are evening wolves; they gnaw not the bones till the morrow.

4 Her prophets are light and treacherous persons: her priests have polluted the sanctuary, they have done violence to the law.

5 The just LORD is in the midst thereof; he will not do iniquity: every morning he brings his judgment to light, he does not fail; but the unjust knows no shame.

6 I have cut off the nations: their towers are desolate; I made their streets waste, that none passes by: their cities are destroyed, so that there is no man, that there is none inhabitant.

7 I said, Surely you will fear me, you will receive instruction; so their dwelling should not be cut off, howsoever I punished them: but they rose early, and corrupted all their doings.

8 Therefore wait upon me, says the LORD, until the day that I rise up to the prey: for my determination is to gather the nations, that I may assemble the kingdoms, to pour upon them my indignation, even all my fierce anger: for all the earth shall be devoured with the fire of my jealousy.

9 For then will I turn to the people a pure language, that they may all call upon the name of the LORD, to serve him with one consent.

10 From beyond the rivers of Ethiopia my suppliants, even the daughter of my dispersed, shall bring my offering.

11 In that day shall you not be ashamed for all your doings, in which you have transgressed against me: for then I will take away out of the midst of you them that rejoice in your pride, and you shall no more be haughty because of my holy mountain.

12 I will also leave in the midst of you an afflicted and poor people, and they shall trust in the name of the LORD.

13 The remnant of Israel shall not do iniquity, nor speak lies; neither shall a deceitful tongue be found in their mouth: for they shall feed and lie down, and none shall make them afraid.

14 Sing, O daughter of Zion; shout, O Israel; be glad and rejoice with all the heart, O daughter of Jerusalem.

15 The LORD has taken away your judgments, he has cast out your enemy: the king of Israel, even the LORD, is in the midst of you: you shall not see evil any more.

16 In that day it shall be said to Jerusalem, Fear not: and to Zion, Do not let your hands be slack.

17 The LORD your God in the midst of you is mighty; he will save, he will rejoice over you with joy; he will rest in

3:17 In Christ, we find God's favor.; we can call God Almighty, Father, even Daddy, "Abba."

his love, he will joy over you with
singing.

18 I will gather them that are sorrowful
for the solemn assembly, who are of you,
to whom the reproach of it was a burden.

19 Behold, at that time I will undo all
that afflict you: and I will save her that
halts, and gather her that was driven out;
and I will get them praise and fame in
every land where they have been put to
shame.

20 At that time will I bring you again,
even in the time that I gather you: for I
will make you a name and a praise
among all people of the earth, when I
turn back your captivity before your
eyes, says the LORD.

Haggai

CHAPTER 1

IN the second year of Darius the king, in the sixth month, in the first day of the month, came the word of the LORD by Haggai the prophet to Zerubbabel the son of Shealtiel, governor of Judah, and to Joshua the son of Josedech, the high priest, saying,

2 Thus says the LORD of hosts, saying, This people say, The time is not come, the time that the LORD's house should be built.

3 Then came the word of the LORD by Haggai the prophet, saying,

4 Is it time for you yourselves to dwell in your cieled houses, and this house lie waste?

5 Now therefore thus says the LORD of hosts; Consider your ways.

6 You have sown much, and bring in little; you eat, but you have not enough; you drink, but you are not filled with drink; you clothe you, but there is none warm; and he that earns wages earns wages to put it into a bag with holes.

7 Thus says the LORD of hosts; Consider your ways.

8 Go up to the mountain, and bring wood, and build the house; and I will take pleasure in it, and I will be glorified, says the LORD.

9 You looked for much, and, lo it came to little; and when you brought it home, I did blow upon it. Why? says the LORD of hosts. Because of my house that is waste, and you run every man to his own house.

10 Therefore the heaven over you is stayed from dew, and the earth is stayed from her fruit.

11 And I called for a drought upon the land, and upon the mountains, and upon the corn, and upon the new wine, and upon the oil, and upon that which the ground brings forth, and upon men, and upon cattle, and upon all the labour of the hands.

12 Then Zerubbabel the son of Shealtiel, and Joshua the son of Josedech, the high priest, with all the remnant of the people, obeyed the voice of the LORD their God, and the words of Haggai the prophet, as the LORD their God had sent him, and the people did fear before the LORD.

13 Then Haggai, the LORD's messenger, spoke the LORD's message to the people, saying, I am with you, says the LORD.

14 And the LORD stirred up the spirit of Zerubbabel the son of Shealtiel, governor of Judah, and the spirit of Joshua the son of Josedech, the high priest, and the spirit of all the remnant of the people; and they came and did work in the house of the LORD of hosts, their God,

15 In the four and twentieth day of the sixth month, in the second year of Darius the king.

CHAPTER 2

IN the seventh month, in the one and twentieth day of the month, came the word of the LORD by the prophet Haggai, saying,

2 Speak now to Zerubbabel the son of Shealtiel, governor of Judah, and to Joshua the son of Josedech, the high priest, and to the residue of the people, saying,

3 Who is left among you that saw this house in her first glory? and how do you see it now? is it not in your eyes in comparison of it as nothing?

4 Yet now be strong, O Zerubbabel, says the LORD; and be strong, O Joshua, son of Josedech, the high priest; and be strong, all you people of the land, says the LORD, and work: for I am with you, says the LORD of hosts:

5 According to the word that I covenanted with you when you came out of Egypt, so my spirit remains among you: fear not.

6 For thus says the LORD of hosts; Yet once, it is a little while, and I will shake the heavens, and the earth, and the sea, and the dry land;

7 And I will shake all nations, and the desire of all nations shall come: and I will fill this house with glory, says the LORD of hosts.

8 The silver is mine, and the gold is mine, says the LORD of hosts.

9 The glory of this latter house shall be greater than of the former, says the LORD of hosts: and in this place will I give peace, says the LORD of hosts.

10 In the four and twentieth day of the ninth month, in the second year of Darius, came the word of the LORD by Haggai the prophet, saying,

11 Thus says the LORD of hosts; Ask now the priests concerning the law, saying,

12 If one bear holy flesh in the skirt of his garment, and with his skirt do touch bread, or pottage, or wine, or oil, or any meat, shall it be holy? And the priests answered and said, No.

13 Then said Haggai, If one that is unclean by a dead body touch any of these, shall it be unclean? And the priests answered and said, It shall be unclean.

14 Then answered Haggai, and said, So is this people, and so is this nation before me, says the LORD; and so is every work of their hands; and that which they offer there is unclean.

15 And now, I pray you, consider from this day and upward, from before a stone was laid upon a stone in the temple of the LORD:

16 Since those days were, when one came to an heap of twenty measures, there were but ten: when one came to the pressfat for to draw out fifty vessels out of the press, there were but twenty.

17 I smote you with blasting and with mildew and with hail in all the labours of your hands; yet you did not turn to me, says the LORD.

18 Consider now from this day and upward, from the four and twentieth day of the ninth month, even from the day that the foundation of the LORD's temple was laid, consider it.

19 Is the seed yet in the barn? yea, as yet the vine, and the fig tree, and the pomegranate, and the olive tree, has not brought forth: from this day will I bless you.

20 And again the word of the LORD came to Haggai in the four and twentieth day of the month, saying,

21 Speak to Zerubbabel, governor of Judah, saying, I will shake the heavens and the earth;

22 And I will overthrow the throne of kingdoms, and I will destroy the strength of the kingdoms of the heathen; and I will overthrow the chariots, and those that ride in them; and the horses and their riders shall come down, every one by the sword of his brother.

23 In that day, says the LORD of hosts, will I take you, O Zerubbabel, my servant, the son of Shealtiel, says the LORD, and will make you as a signet: for I have chosen you, says the LORD of hosts.

Zechariah

CHAPTER 1

IN the eighth month, in the second year of Darius, the word of the LORD came to Zechariah, the son of Berechiah, the son of Iddo the prophet, saying,

2 The LORD has been sore displeased with your fathers.

3 Therefore say to them, Thus says the LORD of hosts; Turn to me, says the LORD of hosts, and I will turn to you, says the LORD of hosts.

4 Do not be as your fathers, to whom the former prophets have cried, saying, Thus says the LORD of hosts; Turn now from your evil ways, and from your evil doings: but they did not hear, nor hearken to me, says the LORD.

5 Your fathers, where are they? and the prophets, do they live for ever?

6 But my words and my statutes, which I commanded my servants the prophets, did they not take hold of your fathers? and they returned and said, Like as the LORD of hosts thought to do to us, according to our ways, and according to our doings, so has he dealt with us.

7 Upon the four and twentieth day of the eleventh month, which is the month Sebat, in the second year of Darius, came the word of the LORD to Zechariah, the son of Berechiah, the son of Iddo the prophet, saying,

8 I saw by night, and behold a man riding upon a red horse, and he stood among the myrtle trees that were in the bottom; and behind him were there red horses, speckled, and white.

9 Then said I, O my lord, what are these? And the angel that talked with me said to me, I will show you what these be.

10 And the man that stood among the myrtle trees answered and said, These are they whom the LORD has sent to walk to and fro through the earth.

11 And they answered the angel of the LORD that stood among the myrtle trees, and said, We have walked to and fro through the earth, and, behold, all the earth sits still, and is at rest.

12 Then the angel of the LORD answered and said, O LORD of hosts, how long will you not have mercy on Jerusalem and on the cities of Judah, against which you have had indignation these threescore and ten years?

13 And the LORD answered the angel that talked with me with good words and comfortable words.

14 So the angel that communed with me said to me, Cry, saying, Thus says the LORD of hosts; I am jealous for Jerusalem and for Zion with a great jealousy.

15 And I am very sore displeased with the heathen that are at ease: for I was but a little displeased, and they helped forward the affliction.

16 Therefore thus says the LORD; I am returned to Jerusalem with mercies: my house shall be built in it, says the LORD

We give ourselves to prayer.
We preach a gospel that saves to the uttermost, and witness to its power.
We do not argue about worldliness; we witness.
We do not discuss philosophy; we preach the gospel.
We do not speculate about the destiny of sinners;
we pluck them as brands from the burning.
We ask no man's patronage. We beg no man's money.
We fear no man's frown...
Let no man join us who is afraid,
and we want none but those who are saved, sanctified
and aflame with the fire of the Holy Ghost.

SAMUEL CHADWICK
1860-1932
BRITISH PREACHER AND MISSIONARY

of hosts, and a line shall be stretched forth upon Jerusalem.

17 Cry yet, saying, Thus says the LORD of hosts; My cities through prosperity shall yet be spread abroad; and the LORD shall yet comfort Zion, and shall yet choose Jerusalem.

18 Then lifted I up my eyes, and saw, and behold four horns.

19 And I said to the angel that talked with me, What be these? And he answered me, These are the horns which have scattered Judah, Israel, and Jerusalem.

20 And the LORD showed me four carpenters.

21 Then said I, What come these to do? And he spoke, saying, These are the horns which have scattered Judah, so that no man did lift up his head: but these are come to fray them, to cast out the horns of the Gentiles, which lifted up their horn over the land of Judah to scatter it.

CHAPTER 2

I lifted up my eyes again, and looked, and behold a man with a measuring line in his hand.

2 Then I said, Where are you going? And he said to me, To measure Jerusalem, to see what is the breadth thereof, and what is the length thereof.

3 And, behold, the angel that talked with me went forth, and another angel went out to meet him,

4 And said to him, Run, speak to this young man, saying, Jerusalem shall be inhabited as towns without walls for the multitude of men and cattle therein:

5 For I, says the LORD, will be to her a wall of fire round about, and will be the glory in the midst of her.

6 Ho, ho, come forth, and flee from the land of the north, says the LORD: for I have spread you abroad as the four winds of the heaven, says the LORD.

7 Deliver yourself, O Zion, that dwells with the daughter of Babylon.

8 For thus says the LORD of hosts; After the glory has he sent me to the nations which spoiled you: for he that touches you touches the apple of his eye.

9 For, behold, I will shake my hand upon them, and they shall be a spoil to their servants: and you shall know that the LORD of hosts has sent me.

10 Sing and rejoice, O daughter of Zion: for, lo, I come, and I will dwell in the midst of you, says the LORD.

11 And many nations shall be joined to the LORD in that day, and shall be my people: and I will dwell in the midst of you, and you shall know that the LORD of hosts has sent me to you.

12 And the LORD shall inherit Judah his portion in the holy land, and shall choose Jerusalem again.

13 Be silent, O all flesh, before the LORD: for he is raised up out of his holy habitation.

CHAPTER 3

AND he showed me Joshua the high priest standing before the angel of the LORD, and Satan standing at his right hand to resist him.

2 And the LORD said to Satan, The LORD rebuke you, O Satan; even the LORD that has chosen Jerusalem rebuke you: is not this a brand plucked out of the fire?

3 Now Joshua was clothed with filthy garments, and stood before the angel.

4 And he answered and spoke to those that stood before him, saying, Take away the filthy garments from him. And to him he said, Behold, I have caused your iniquity to pass from you, and I will clothe you with change of raiment.

5 And I said, Let them set a fair mitre upon his head. So they set a fair mitre upon his head, and clothed him with garments. And the angel of the LORD stood by.

6 And the angel of the LORD protested to Joshua, saying,

7 Thus says the LORD of hosts; If you will walk in my ways, and if you will keep my charge, then you shall also judge my house, and shall also keep my courts, and I will give you places to walk among these that stand by.

8 Hear now, O Joshua the high priest, you, and your fellows that sit before you: for they are men wondered at: for, behold, I will bring forth my servant the BRANCH.

9 For behold the stone that I have laid before Joshua; upon one stone shall be seven eyes: behold, I will engrave the graving thereof, says the LORD of hosts, and I will remove the iniquity of that land in one day.

10 In that day, says the LORD of hosts, shall you call every man his neighbour under the vine and under the fig tree.

CHAPTER 4

AND the angel that talked with me came again, and waked me, as a man that is wakened out of his sleep.

2 And said to me, What do you see? And I said, I have looked, and behold a candlestick all of gold, with a bowl upon the top of it, and his seven lamps thereon, and seven pipes to the seven lamps, which are upon the top thereof:

3 And two olive trees by it, one upon the right side of the bowl, and the other upon the left side thereof.

4 So I answered and spoke to the angel that talked with me, saying, What are these, my lord?

5 Then the angel that talked with me answered and said to me, Do you not know what these things are? And I said, No, my lord.

6 Then he answered and spoke to me, saying, This is the word of the LORD to Zerubbabel, saying, Not by might, nor by power, but by my spirit, says the LORD of hosts.

7 Who are you, O great mountain? before Zerubbabel you shall become a plain: and he shall bring forth the headstone thereof with shoutings, crying, Grace, grace to it.

8 Moreover the word of the LORD came to me, saying,

3:2 Every Christian is a brand "plucked out of the fire." We have been saved from the fire that shall never be quenched, and our commission is to pull sinners "out of the fire, hating even the garment spotted by the flesh" (Jude 23).

4:6 We tend, in our carnality, to lean towards might and power, but God does all things by His Spirit. He created all things by His Spirit; we were born of His Spirit; we are baptized in His Spirit, and He leads us by the Spirit.

9 The hands of Zerubbabel have laid the foundation of this house; his hands shall also finish it; and you shall know that the LORD of hosts has sent me to you.

10 For who has despised the day of small things? for they shall rejoice, and shall see the plummet in the hand of Zerubbabel with those seven; they are the eyes of the LORD, which run to and fro through the whole earth.

11 Then answered I, and said to him, What are these two olive trees upon the right side of the candlestick and upon the left side thereof?

12 And I answered again, and said to him, What be these two olive branches which through the two golden pipes empty the golden oil out of themselves?

13 And he answered me and said, Do you not know what these are? And I said, No, my lord.

14 Then said he, These are the two anointed ones, that stand by the LORD of the whole earth.

CHAPTER 5

THEN I turned, and lifted up my eyes, and looked, and behold a flying roll.

2 And he said to me, What do you see? And I answered, I see a flying roll; the length thereof is twenty cubits, and the breadth thereof ten cubits.

3 Then said he to me, This is the curse that goes forth over the face of the whole earth: for every one that steals shall be cut off as on this side according to it; and every one that swears shall be cut off as on that side according to it.

4 I will bring it forth, says the LORD of hosts, and it shall enter into the house of the thief, and into the house of him that swears falsely by my name: and it shall remain in the midst of his house, and shall consume it with the timber thereof and the stones thereof.

5 Then the angel that talked with me went forth, and said to me, Lift up now your eyes, and see what is this that goes forth.

6 And I said, What is it? And he said, This is an ephah that goes forth. He said moreover, This is their resemblance through all the earth.

7 And, behold, there was lifted up a talent of lead: and this is a woman that sits in the midst of the ephah.

8 And he said, This is wickedness. And he cast it into the midst of the ephah; and he cast the weight of lead upon the mouth thereof.

9 Then lifted I up my eyes, and looked, and, behold, there came out two women, and the wind was in their wings; for they had wings like the wings of a stork: and they lifted up the ephah between the earth and the heaven.

10 Then said I to the angel that talked with me, Where do these bear the ephah?

11 And he said to me, To build it an house in the land of Shinar: and it shall be established, and set there upon her own base.

CHAPTER 6

AND I turned, and lifted up my eyes, and looked, and, behold, there came four chariots out from between two mountains; and the mountains were mountains of brass.

2 In the first chariot were red horses; and in the second chariot black horses;

3 And in the third chariot white horses; and in the fourth chariot grisled and bay horses.

4 Then I answered and said to the angel that talked with me, What are these, my lord?

5 And the angel answered and said to me, These are the four spirits of the heavens, which go forth from standing before the LORD of all the earth.

6 The black horses which are therein go forth into the north country; and the white go forth after them; and the grisled go forth toward the south country.

7 And the bay went forth, and sought to go that they might walk to and fro through the earth: and he said, Get you hence, walk to and fro through the earth. So they walked to and fro through the earth.

8 Then he cried out to me, and spoke to me, saying, Behold, these that go toward the north country have quieted my spirit in the north country.

9 And the word of the LORD came to me, saying,

10 Take of them of the captivity, even of Heldai, of Tobijah, and of Jedaiah, which are come from Babylon, and come the same day, and go into the house of Josiah the son of Zephaniah;

11 Then take silver and gold, and make crowns, and set them upon the head of Joshua the son of Josedech, the high priest;

12 And speak to him, saying, Thus says the LORD of hosts, saying, Behold the man whose name is The BRANCH; and he shall grow up out of his place, and he shall build the temple of the LORD:

13 Even he shall build the temple of the LORD; and he shall bear the glory, and shall sit and rule upon his throne; and he shall be a priest upon his throne: and the counsel of peace shall be between them both.

14 And the crowns shall be to Helem, and to Tobijah, and to Jedaiah, and to Hen the son of Zephaniah, for a memorial in the temple of the LORD.

15 And they that are far off shall come and build in the temple of the LORD, and you shall know that the LORD of hosts has sent me to you. And this shall come to pass, if you will diligently obey the voice of the LORD your God.

CHAPTER 7

A ND it came to pass in the fourth year of king Darius, that the word of the LORD came to Zechariah in the fourth day of the ninth month, even in Chisleu;

2 When they had sent to the house of God Sherezer and Regemmelech, and their men, to pray before the LORD,

3 And to speak to the priests which were in the house of the LORD of hosts, and to the prophets, saying, Should I weep in the fifth month, separating myself, as I have done these so many years?

4 Then came the word of the LORD of hosts to me, saying,

5 Speak to all the people of the land, and to the priests, saying, When you fasted and mourned in the fifth and seventh month, even those seventy years, did you at all fast for me, even to me?

6 And when you did eat, and when you did drink, did not you eat for yourselves, and drink for yourselves?

7 Should you not hear the words which the LORD has cried by the former prophets, when Jerusalem was inhabited and in prosperity, and the cities thereof round about her, when men inhabited the south and the plain?

8 And the word of the LORD came to Zechariah, saying,

9 Thus says the LORD of hosts, saying, Execute true judgment, and show mercy and compassions every man to his brother:

10 And oppress not the widow, nor the fatherless, the stranger, nor the poor; and let none of you imagine evil against his brother in your heart.

11 But they refused to hearken, and pulled away the shoulder, and stopped their ears, that they should not hear.

12 Yea, they made their hearts as an adamant stone, lest they should hear the law, and the words which the LORD of hosts has sent in his spirit by the former prophets: therefore came a great wrath from the LORD of hosts.

13 Therefore it is come to pass, that as he cried, and they would not hear; so

---

7:8-12 The unsaved refuse to hear; they pull away, stop their ears and harden their hearts "lest they should hear the Law." God's Ten Commandments offend them (see Romans 8:7).

they cried, and I would not hear, says the LORD of hosts:

14 But I scattered them with a whirlwind among all the nations whom they knew not. Thus the land was desolate after them, that no man passed through nor returned: for they laid the pleasant land desolate.

CHAPTER 8

AGAIN the word of the LORD of hosts came to me, saying,

2 Thus says the LORD of hosts; I was jealous for Zion with great jealousy, and I was jealous for her with great fury.

3 Thus says the LORD; I am returned to Zion, and will dwell in the midst of Jerusalem: and Jerusalem shall be called a city of truth; and the mountain of the LORD of hosts the holy mountain.

4 Thus says the LORD of hosts; There shall yet old men and old women dwell in the streets of Jerusalem, and every man with his staff in his hand for very age.

5 And the streets of the city shall be full of boys and girls playing in the streets thereof.

6 Thus says the LORD of hosts; If it be marvellous in the eyes of the remnant of this people in these days, should it also be marvellous in my eyes? says the LORD of hosts.

7 Thus says the LORD of hosts; Behold, I will save my people from the east country, and from the west country;

8 And I will bring them, and they shall dwell in the midst of Jerusalem: and they shall be my people, and I will be their God, in truth and in righteousness.

9 Thus says the LORD of hosts; Let your hands be strong, you that hear in these days these words by the mouth of the prophets, which were in the day that the foundation of the house of the LORD of hosts was laid, that the temple might be built.

10 For before these days there was no hire for man, nor any hire for beast; neither was there any peace to him that went out or came in because of the affliction: for I set all men every one against his neighbour.

11 But now I will not be to the residue of this people as in the former days, says the LORD of hosts.

12 For the seed shall be prosperous; the vine shall give her fruit, and the ground shall give her increase, and the heavens shall give their dew; and I will cause the remnant of this people to possess all these things.

13 And it shall come to pass, that as you were a curse among the heathen, O house of Judah, and house of Israel; so will I save you, and you shall be a blessing: fear not, but let your hands be strong.

14 For thus says the LORD of hosts; As I thought to punish you, when your fathers provoked me to wrath, says the LORD of hosts, and I repented not:

15 So again have I thought in these days to do well to Jerusalem and to the house of Judah: fear not.

16 These are the things that you shall do; Every man speak the truth to his neighbour; execute the judgment of truth and peace in your gates:

17 And let none of you imagine evil in your hearts against his neighbour; and love no false oath: for all these are things that I hate, says the LORD.

18 And the word of the LORD of hosts came to me, saying,

8:14 Skeptics often say that the fact that God "repents" proves that He has sin, from which He repents. But "repent," when used in reference to God, simply means "to change the mind." However, even in that sense, when God changes His mind, it doesn't mean that He decided that He was wrong and changed His attitude. Language cannot express the mind of God and therefore reverts to anthropomorphic statements to give light to our dark and ignorant minds about our supernatural Creator.

19 Thus says the LORD of hosts; The fast of the fourth month, and the fast of the fifth, and the fast of the seventh, and the fast of the tenth, shall be to the house of Judah joy and gladness, and cheerful feasts; therefore love the truth and peace.

20 Thus says the LORD of hosts; It shall yet come to pass, that there shall come people, and the inhabitants of many cities:

21 And the inhabitants of one city shall go to another, saying, Let us go speedily to pray before the LORD, and to seek the LORD of hosts: I will go also.

22 Yea, many people and strong nations shall come to seek the LORD of hosts in Jerusalem, and to pray before the LORD.

23 Thus says the LORD of hosts; In those days it shall come to pass, that ten men shall take hold out of all languages of the nations, even shall take hold of the skirt of him that is a Jew, saying, We will go with you: for we have heard that God is with you.

CHAPTER 9

THE burden of the word of the LORD in the land of Hadrach, and Damascus shall be the rest thereof: when the eyes of man, as of all the tribes of Israel, shall be toward the LORD.

2 And Hamath also shall border thereby; Tyrus, and Zidon, though it be very wise.

3 And Tyrus did build herself a strong hold, and heaped up silver as the dust, and fine gold as the mire of the streets.

4 Behold, the LORD will cast her out, and he will smite her power in the sea; and she shall be devoured with fire.

5 Ashkelon shall see it, and fear; Gaza also shall see it, and be very sorrowful, and Ekron; for her expectation shall be ashamed; and the king shall perish from Gaza, and Ashkelon shall not be inhabited.

6 And a bastard shall dwell in Ashdod, and I will cut off the pride of the Philistines.

7 And I will take away his blood out of his mouth, and his abominations from between his teeth: but he that remains, even he, shall be for our God, and he shall be as a governor in Judah, and Ekron as a Jebusite.

8 And I will encamp about my house because of the army, because of him that passes by, and because of him that returns: and no oppressor shall pass through them any more: for now have I seen with my eyes.

9 Rejoice greatly, O daughter of Zion; shout, O daughter of Jerusalem: behold, your King comes to you: he is just, and having salvation; lowly, and riding upon an ass, and upon a colt the foal of an ass.

10 And I will cut off the chariot from Ephraim, and the horse from Jerusalem, and the battle bow shall be cut off: and he shall speak peace to the heathen: and his dominion shall be from sea even to sea, and from the river even to the ends of the earth.

11 As for you also, by the blood of your covenant I have sent forth your prisoners out of the waterless pit.

12 Turn to the strong hold, you prisoners of hope: even to day do I declare that I will render double to you;

13 When I have bent Judah for me, filled the bow with Ephraim, and raised up your sons, O Zion, against your sons, O Greece, and made you as the sword of a mighty man.

14 And the LORD shall be seen over them, and his arrow shall go forth as the lightning: and the LORD God shall blow the trumpet, and shall go with whirlwinds of the south.

15 The LORD of hosts shall defend them; and they shall devour, and subdue with sling stones; and they shall drink, and make a noise as through wine; and

---

9:9 This is a direct reference to the Messiah (see Matthew 21:4-11).

they shall be filled like bowls, and as the corners of the altar.

16 And the LORD their God shall save them in that day as the flock of his people: for they shall be as the stones of a crown, lifted up as an ensign upon his land.

17 For how great is his goodness, and how great is his beauty! corn shall make the young men cheerful, and new wine the maids.

CHAPTER 10

ASK of the LORD rain in the time of the latter rain; so the LORD shall make bright clouds, and give them showers of rain, to every one grass in the field.

2 For the idols have spoken vanity, and the diviners have seen a lie, and have told false dreams; they comfort in vain: therefore they went their way as a flock, they were troubled, because there was no shepherd.

3 My anger was kindled against the shepherds, and I punished the goats: for the LORD of hosts has visited his flock the house of Judah, and has made them as his goodly horse in the battle.

4 Out of him came forth the corner, out of him the nail, out of him the battle bow, out of him every oppressor together.

5 And they shall be as mighty men, which tread down their enemies in the mire of the streets in the battle: and they shall fight, because the LORD is with them, and the riders on horses shall be confounded.

6 And I will strengthen the house of Judah, and I will save the house of Joseph, and I will bring them again to place them; for I have mercy upon them: and they shall be as though I had not cast them off: for I am the LORD their God, and will hear them.

7 And they of Ephraim shall be like a mighty man, and their heart shall rejoice as through wine: yea, their children shall

10:2-3

When those who profess to be shepherds of the flock of God fail to be faithful in their gospel proclamation, they fill the Church with false converts (goats among the sheep). See also Isaiah 56:11.

see it, and be glad; their heart shall rejoice in the LORD.

8 I will hiss for them, and gather them; for I have redeemed them: and they shall increase as they have increased.

9 And I will sow them among the people: and they shall remember me in far countries; and they shall live with their children, and turn again.

10 I will bring them again also out of the land of Egypt, and gather them out of Assyria; and I will bring them into the land of Gilead and Lebanon; and place shall not be found for them.

11 And he shall pass through the sea with affliction, and shall smite the waves in the sea, and all the deeps of the river shall dry up: and the pride of Assyria shall be brought down, and the sceptre of Egypt shall depart away.

12 And I will strengthen them in the LORD; and they shall walk up and down in his name, says the LORD.

CHAPTER 11

OPEN your doors, O Lebanon, that the fire may devour your cedars.

2 Howl, fir tree; for the cedar is fallen; because the mighty are spoiled: howl, O you oaks of Bashan; for the forest of the vintage is come down.

3 There is a voice of the howling of the shepherds; for their glory is spoiled: a

voice of the roaring of young lions; for the pride of Jordan is spoiled.

4 Thus says the LORD my God; Feed the flock of the slaughter;

5 Whose possessors slay them, and hold themselves not guilty: and they that sell them say, Blessed be the LORD; for I am rich: and their own shepherds pity them not.

6 For I will no more pity the inhabitants of the land, says the LORD: but, lo, I will deliver the men every one into his neighbour's hand, and into the hand of his king: and they shall smite the land, and out of their hand I will not deliver them.

7 And I will feed the flock of slaughter, even you, O poor of the flock. And I took for myself two staves; the one I called Beauty, and the other I called Bands; and I fed the flock.

8 Three shepherds also I cut off in one month; and my soul lothed them, and their soul also abhorred me.

9 Then said I, I will not feed you: that that dies, let it die; and that that is to be cut off, let it be cut off; and let the rest eat every one the flesh of another.

10 And I took my staff, even Beauty, and cut it asunder, that I might break my covenant which I had made with all the people.

11 And it was broken in that day: and so the poor of the flock that waited upon me knew that it was the word of the LORD.

12 And I said to them, If you think good, give me my price; and if not, forbear. So they weighed for my price thirty pieces of silver.

13 And the LORD said to me, Cast it to the potter: a goodly price that I was valued at of them. And I took the thirty pieces of silver, and cast them to the potter in the house of the LORD.

14 Then I cut asunder my other staff, even Bands, that I might break the brotherhood between Judah and Israel.

15 And the LORD said to me, Take for yourself yet the instruments of a foolish shepherd.

16 For, lo, I will raise up a shepherd in the land, which shall not visit those that be cut off, neither shall seek the young one, nor heal that that is broken, nor feed that that stands still: but he shall eat the flesh of the fat, and tear their claws in pieces.

17 Woe to the idol shepherd that leaves the flock! the sword shall be upon his arm, and upon his right eye: his arm shall be clean dried up, and his right eye shall be utterly darkened.

CHAPTER 12

THE burden of the word of the LORD for Israel, says the LORD, which stretches forth the heavens, and lays the foundation of the earth, and forms the spirit of man within him.

2 Behold, I will make Jerusalem a cup of trembling to all the people round about, when they shall be in the siege both against Judah and against Jerusalem.

3 And in that day will I make Jerusalem a burdensome stone for all people: all that burden themselves with it shall be cut in pieces, though all the people of the earth be gathered together against it.

4 In that day, says the LORD, I will smite every horse with astonishment, and his rider with madness: and I will open my eyes upon the house of Judah, and will smite every horse of the people with blindness.

5 And the governors of Judah shall say in their heart, The inhabitants of Jerusalem shall be my strength in the LORD of hosts their God.

6 In that day will I make the governors of Judah like an hearth of fire among the wood, and like a torch of fire in a sheaf; and they shall devour all the people round about, on the right hand and on the left: and Jerusalem shall be inhabited again in her own place, even in Jerusalem.

7 The LORD also shall save the tents of Judah first, that the glory of the house of David and the glory of the inhabitants of Jerusalem do not magnify themselves against Judah.

8 In that day shall the LORD defend the inhabitants of Jerusalem; and he that is feeble among them at that day shall be as David; and the house of David shall be as God, as the angel of the LORD before them.

9 And it shall come to pass in that day, that I will seek to destroy all the nations that come against Jerusalem.

10 And I will pour upon the house of David, and upon the inhabitants of Jerusalem, the spirit of grace and of supplications: and they shall look upon me whom they have pierced, and they shall mourn for him, as one mourns for his only son, and shall be in bitterness for him, as one that is in bitterness for his firstborn.

11 In that day shall there be a great mourning in Jerusalem, as the mourning of Hadadrimmon in the valley of Megiddon.

12 And the land shall mourn, every family apart; the family of the house of David apart, and their wives apart; the family of the house of Nathan apart, and their wives apart;

13 The family of the house of Levi apart, and their wives apart; the family of Shimei apart, and their wives apart;

14 All the families that remain, every family apart, and their wives apart.

CHAPTER 13

IN that day there shall be a fountain opened to the house of David and to the inhabitants of Jerusalem for sin and for uncleanness.

2 And it shall come to pass in that day, says the LORD of hosts, that I will cut off the names of the idols out of the land, and they shall no more be remembered: and also I will cause the prophets and the unclean spirit to pass out of the land.

3 And it shall come to pass, that when any shall yet prophesy, then his father and his mother that begat him shall say to him, You shall not live; for you speak lies in the name of the LORD: and his father and his mother that begat him shall thrust him through when he prophesies.

4 And it shall come to pass in that day, that the prophets shall be ashamed every one of his vision, when he has prophesied; neither shall they wear a rough garment to deceive:

5 But he shall say, I am no prophet, I am an husbandman; for man taught me to keep cattle from my youth.

6 And one shall say to him, What are these wounds in your hands? Then he shall answer, Those with which I was wounded in the house of my friends.

7 Awake, O sword, against my shepherd, and against the man that is my fellow, says the LORD of hosts: smite the shepherd, and the sheep shall be scattered: and I will turn my hand upon the little ones.

8 And it shall come to pass, that in all the land, says the LORD, two parts therein shall be cut off and die; but the third shall be left therein.

9 And I will bring the third part through the fire, and will refine them as silver is refined, and will try them as gold is tried: they shall call on my name, and I will hear them: I will say, It is my people: and they shall say, The LORD is my God.

CHAPTER 14

BEHOLD, the day of the LORD comes, and your spoil shall be divided in the midst of you.

2 For I will gather all nations against Jerusalem to battle; and the city shall be taken, and the houses rifled, and the women ravished; and half of the city

---

12:10 This is a direct reference to Jesus' crucifixion (see Psalm 22:16).

shall go forth into captivity, and the residue of the people shall not be cut off from the city.

3 Then shall the LORD go forth, and fight against those nations, as when he fought in the day of battle.

4 And his feet shall stand in that day upon the mount of Olives, which is before Jerusalem on the east, and the mount of Olives shall cleave in the midst thereof toward the east and toward the west, and there shall be a very great valley; and half of the mountain shall remove toward the north, and half of it toward the south.

5 And you shall flee to the valley of the mountains; for the valley of the mountains shall reach to Azal: yea, you shall flee, like as you fled from before the earthquake in the days of Uzziah king of Judah: and the LORD my God shall come, and all the saints with you.

6 And it shall come to pass in that day, that the light shall not be clear, nor dark:

7 But it shall be one day which shall be known to the LORD, not day, nor night: but it shall come to pass, that at evening time it shall be light.

8 And it shall be in that day, that living waters shall go out from Jerusalem; half of them toward the former sea, and half of them toward the hinder sea: in summer and in winter shall it be.

9 And the LORD shall be king over all the earth: in that day shall there be one LORD, and his name one.

10 All the land shall be turned as a plain from Geba to Rimmon south of Jerusalem: and it shall be lifted up, and inhabited in her place, from Benjamin's gate to the place of the first gate, to the corner gate, and from the tower of Hananeel to the king's winepresses.

11 And men shall dwell in it, and there shall be no more utter destruction; but Jerusalem shall be safely inhabited.

12 And this shall be the plague wherewith the LORD will smite all the people that have fought against Jerusalem; Their flesh shall consume away while they stand upon their feet, and their eyes shall consume away in their holes, and their tongue shall consume away in their mouth.

13 And it shall come to pass in that day, that a great tumult from the LORD shall be among them; and they shall lay hold every one on the hand of his neighbour, and his hand shall rise up against the hand of his neighbour.

14 And Judah also shall fight at Jerusalem; and the wealth of all the heathen round about shall be gathered together, gold, and silver, and apparel, in great abundance.

15 And so shall be the plague of the horse, of the mule, of the camel, and of the ass, and of all the beasts that shall be in these tents, as this plague.

16 And it shall come to pass, that every one that is left of all the nations which came against Jerusalem shall even go up from year to year to worship the King, the LORD of hosts, and to keep the feast of tabernacles.

17 And it shall be, that whichever will not come up of all the families of the earth to Jerusalem to worship the King, the LORD of hosts, even upon them shall be no rain.

18 And if the family of Egypt go not up, and come not, that have no rain; there shall be the plague, wherewith the LORD will smite the heathen that come not up to keep the feast of tabernacles.

19 This shall be the punishment of Egypt, and the punishment of all nations that come not up to keep the feast of tabernacles.

20 In that day shall there be upon the bells of the horses, HOLINESS TO THE LORD; and the pots in the LORD's house shall be like the bowls before the altar.

21 Yea, every pot in Jerusalem and in Judah shall be holiness to the LORD of hosts: and all they that sacrifice shall come and take of them, and seethe therein: and in that day there shall be no more the Canaanite in the house of the LORD of hosts.

Malachi

CHAPTER 1

THE burden of the word of the LORD to Israel by Malachi.

2 I have loved you, says the LORD. Yet you say, In what way have you loved us? Was not Esau Jacob's brother? says the LORD: yet I loved Jacob,

3 And I hated Esau, and laid his mountains and his heritage waste for the dragons of the wilderness.

4 Though Edom says, We are impoverished, but we will return and build the desolate places; thus says the LORD of hosts, They shall build, but I will throw down; and they shall call them, The border of wickedness, and, The people against whom the LORD has indignation for ever.

5 And your eyes shall see, and you shall say, The LORD will be magnified from the border of Israel.

6 A son honours his father, and a servant his master: if then I be a father, where is my honour? and if I be a master, where is my fear? says the LORD of hosts to you, O priests, that despise my name. And you say, How have we despised your name?

7 You offer polluted bread upon my altar; and you say, How have we polluted you? In that you say, The table of the LORD is contemptible.

8 And if you offer the blind for sacrifice, is it not evil? and if you offer the lame and sick, is it not evil? offer it now to your governor; will he be pleased with you, or accept your person? says the LORD of hosts.

9 And now, I pray you, beseech God that he will be gracious to us: this has been by your means: will he regard your persons? says the LORD of hosts.

10 Who is there even among you that would shut the doors for nought? neither do you kindle fire on my altar for nought. I have no pleasure in you, says the LORD of hosts, neither will I accept an offering at your hand.

11 For from the rising of the sun even to the going down of the same my name shall be great among the Gentiles; and in every place incense shall be offered to my name, and a pure offering: for my name shall be great among the heathen, says the LORD of hosts.

12 But you have profaned it, in that you say, The table of the LORD is polluted; and the fruit thereof, even his meat, is contemptible.

13 You said also, Behold, what a weariness is it! and you have snuffed at it, says

---

1:2-3 To say that God is "all loving," as the ungodly so often maintain, is to create an idol to worship. God is love, but He is also just, holy and righteous. He can choose to love or not to love. He is not a slave to sentiment.

the LORD of hosts; and you brought that which was torn, and the lame, and the sick; thus you brought an offering: should I accept this of your hand? says the LORD.

14 But cursed be the deceiver, which has in his flock a male, and vows, and sacrifices to the LORD a corrupt thing: for I am a great King, says the LORD of hosts, and my name is dreadful among the heathen.

CHAPTER 2

AND now, O you priests, this commandment is for you.

2 If you will not hear, and if you will not lay it to heart, to give glory to my name, says the LORD of hosts, I will even send a curse upon you, and I will curse your blessings: yea, I have cursed

> **If their houses were on fire,**
> thou wouldst run and help them;
> and wilt thou not help them
> when their souls
> are almost at the fire of hell?
>
> **RICHARD BAXTER**
> **1615-1691**
> **PURITAN LECTURER AND VICAR**
> **OF THE ENGLISH MIDLANDS**

them already, because you do not lay it to heart.

3 Behold, I will corrupt your seed, and spread dung upon your faces, even the dung of your solemn feasts; and one shall take you away with it.

4 And you shall know that I have sent this commandment to you, that my covenant might be with Levi, says the LORD of hosts.

5 My covenant was with him of life and peace; and I gave them to him for the fear wherewith he feared me, and was afraid before my name.

6 The law of truth was in his mouth, and iniquity was not found in his lips: he walked with me in peace and equity, and did turn many away from iniquity.

7 For the priest's lips should keep knowledge, and they should seek the law at his mouth: for he is the messenger of the LORD of hosts.

8 But you are departed out of the way; you have caused many to stumble at the law; you have corrupted the covenant of Levi, says the LORD of hosts.

9 Therefore have I also made you contemptible and base before all the people, according as you have not kept my ways, but have been partial in the law.

THE FUNCTION OF THE LAW

3:5 **The reason for sorcery, adultery, false witness and other transgressions of God's Law is a lack of the fear of God.** Never fear preaching the fear of God. It causes sinners to depart from sin (see Proverbs 16:6). Preach the thunderings and lightnings of Mount Sinai and preach future punishment!

The preaching of the Law without retribution will not be effective in winning souls for Christ. It has been well said that God's Law without consequence is nothing but good advice. The world will agree with "Thou shalt not kill." That makes sense. They will smile at "Thou shalt not commit adultery." They know it destroys families. They will give assent to "Thou shalt not bear false witness." They know that it breaks friendships. The Ten Commandments certainly are good advice. However, when you preach the Law with the message that God "will judge the world in righteousness" (as Paul preached in Athens, see Acts 17:22-31), your listeners will be provoked to say, "We will hear you again about this matter" (Acts 17:32). And sinners will be soundly saved.

10 Have we not all one father? has not one God created us? why do we deal treacherously every man against his brother, by profaning the covenant of our fathers?

11 Judah has dealt treacherously, and an abomination is committed in Israel and in Jerusalem; for Judah has profaned the holiness of the LORD which he loved, and has married the daughter of a strange god.

12 The LORD will cut off the man that does this, the master and the scholar, out of the tabernacles of Jacob, and him that offers an offering to the LORD of hosts.

13 And this have you done again, covering the altar of the LORD with tears, with weeping, and with crying out, insomuch that he does not regard the offering any more, or receives it with good will at your hand.

14 Yet you say, For what reason? Because the LORD has been witness between you and the wife of your youth, against whom you have dealt treacherously: yet is she your companion, and the wife of your covenant.

15 And did not he make one? Yet had he the residue of the spirit. And why one? That he might seek a godly seed.

Therefore take heed to your spirit, and let none deal treacherously against the wife of his youth.

16 For the LORD, the God of Israel, says that he hates divorce: for one covers violence with his garment, says the LORD of hosts: therefore take heed to your spirit, that you do not deal treacherously.

17 You have wearied the LORD with your words. Yet you say, How have we wearied him? When you say, Every one that does evil is good in the sight of the LORD, and he delights in them; or, Where is the God of judgment?

CHAPTER 3

BEHOLD, I will send my messenger, and he shall prepare the way before me: and the LORD, whom you seek, shall suddenly come to his temple, even the messenger of the covenant, whom you delight in: behold, he shall come, says the LORD of hosts.

2 But who may abide the day of his coming? and who shall stand when he appears? for he is like a refiner's fire, and like fullers' soap:

3 And he shall sit as a refiner and purifier of silver: and he shall purify the sons of Levi, and purge them as gold and

2:17 This is the theology of the ungodly. They weary God when they say that He delights in everyone or when they question His character (see Romans 3:12).

silver, that they may offer to the LORD an offering in righteousness.

4 Then shall the offering of Judah and Jerusalem be pleasant to the LORD, as in the days of old, and as in former years.

5 And I will come near to you to judgment; and I will be a swift witness against the sorcerers, and against the adulterers, and against false swearers, and against those that oppress the hireling in his wages, the widow, and the fatherless, and that turn aside the stranger from his right, and fear not me, says the LORD of hosts.

6 For I am the LORD, I change not; therefore you sons of Jacob are not consumed.

7 Even from the days of your fathers you are gone away from my ordinances, and have not kept them. Return to me, and I will return to you, says the LORD of hosts. But you said, How shall we return?

8 Will a man rob God? Yet you have robbed me. But you say, How have we robbed you? In tithes and offerings.

9 You are cursed with a curse: for you have robbed me, even this whole nation.

10 Bring all the tithes into the storehouse, that there may be meat in my house, and prove me now herewith, says the LORD of hosts, if I will not open you the windows of heaven, and pour you out a blessing, that there shall not be room enough to receive it.

11 And I will rebuke the devourer for your sakes, and he shall not destroy the fruits of your ground; neither shall your vine cast her fruit before the time in the field, says the LORD of hosts.

THE FUNCTION OF THE LAW

 **We are not to forget the Law once we have accepted the Savior.**

Does the student, after he graduates, forget the knowledge given by his schoolmaster?

That knowledge may now be used to instruct lost sinners on why they, too, need the Savior. (See Galations 3:24)

Thank God for all of the "Elijahs," who help to save us from God's curse because they are not afraid to speak of the "coming of the great and dreadful day of the Lord."

12 And all nations shall call you blessed: for you shall be a delightsome land, says the LORD of hosts.

13 Your words have been stout against me, says the LORD. Yet you say, What have we spoken so much against you?

14 You have said, It is vain to serve God: and what profit is it that we have kept his ordinance, and that we have walked mournfully before the LORD of hosts?

15 And now we call the proud happy; yea, they that work wickedness are set up; yea, they that tempt God are even delivered.

16 Then they that feared the LORD spoke often one to another: and the LORD hearkened, and heard it, and a book of remembrance was written before

---

3:6 There is not a God of the Old Testament and a different God of the New Testament, as some maintain (see Psalm 89:14 comment).

3:16 and 4:2 Notice in these verses the importance of the fear of the Lord—a doctrine that is despised by the world and also by many who profess to be part of the Church.

3:18 Are we "serving" God by seeking the lost? Or do we lift our hands in worship to God, but refuse to reach out our hands in evangelism for God? Worship without service is empty hypocrisy. It is to draw near to Him with our lips, but have our hearts far from Him. It is to worship Him in vain (see Mark 7:7). If the average church made as much noise about God on Mondays as it makes to God on Sundays, we would see revival.

him for them that feared the LORD, and that thought upon his name.

17 *And they shall be mine, says the LORD of hosts, in that day when I make up my jewels; and I will spare them, as a man spares his own son that serves him.*

18 *Then shall you return, and discern between the righteous and the wicked, between him that serves God and him that does not serve him.*

CHAPTER 4

FOR, behold, the day comes, that shall burn as an oven; and all the proud, yea, and all that do wickedly, shall be stubble: and the day that comes shall burn them up, says the LORD of hosts, that it shall leave them neither root nor branch.

2 *But to you that fear my name shall the Sun of righteousness arise with healing in his wings; and you shall go forth, and grow up as calves of the stall.*

3 *And you shall tread down the wicked; for they shall be ashes under the soles of your feet in the day that I shall do this, says the LORD of hosts.*

4 Remember the law of Moses my servant, which I commanded him in Horeb for all Israel, with the statutes and judgments.

5 Behold, I will send you Elijah the prophet before the coming of the great and dreadful day of the LORD:

More souls have been won for Christ by preachers who did what little they could, than by renowned evangelists.

Richard Wurmbrand
1909 - 2001
MESSIANIC JEW AND PASTOR
IMPRISONED AND TORTURED
FOR 14 YEARS
IN COMMUNIST ROMANIA
BECAUSE OF HIS FAITH

6 And he shall turn the heart of the fathers to the children, and the heart of the children to their fathers, lest I come and smite the earth with a curse.

The New Testament

Matthew

CHAPTER 1

THE book of the generation of Jesus Christ, the son of David, the son of Abraham.

2 Abraham begat Isaac; and Isaac begat Jacob; and Jacob begat Judas and his brethren;

3 And Judas begat Phares and Zara of Thamar; and Phares begat Esrom; and Esrom begat Aram;

4 And Aram begat Aminadab; and Aminadab begat Naasson; and Naasson begat Salmon;

5 And Salmon begat Booz of Rachab; and Booz begat Obed of Ruth; and Obed begat Jesse;

6 And Jesse begat David the king; and David the king begat Solomon of her that had been the wife of Urias;

7 And Solomon begat Roboam; and Roboam begat Abia; and Abia begat Asa;

8 And Asa begat Josaphat; and Josaphat begat Joram; and Joram begat Ozias;

9 And Ozias begat Joatham; and Joatham begat Achaz; and Achaz begat Ezekias;

10 And Ezekias begat Manasses; and Manasses begat Amon; and Amon begat Josias;

11 And Josias begat Jechonias and his brethren, about the time they were carried away to Babylon:

12 And after they were brought to Babylon, Jechonias begat Salathiel; and Salathiel begat Zorobabel;

13 And Zorobabel begat Abiud; and Abiud begat Eliakim; and Eliakim begat Azor;

14 And Azor begat Sadoc; and Sadoc begat Achim; and Achim begat Eliud;

15 And Eliud begat Eleazar; and Eleazar begat Matthan; and Matthan begat Jacob;

16 And Jacob begat Joseph the husband of Mary, of whom was born Jesus, who is called Christ.

17 So all the generations from Abraham to David are fourteen generations; and from David until the carrying away into Babylon are fourteen generations; and from the carrying away into Babylon to Christ are fourteen generations.

18 Now the birth of Jesus Christ was on this wise: When as his mother Mary was espoused to Joseph, before they came together, she was found with child of the Holy Spirit.

19 Then Joseph her husband, being a just man, and not willing to make her a public example, was minded to put her away privately.

20 But while he thought on these things, behold, the angel of the Lord appeared to him in a dream, saying, Joseph, you son of David, fear not to take to you Mary your

---

1:1 Some point to the different genealogies of Jesus as "errors" in the Bible. However, Matthew gives the paternal genealogy of the Messiah (through His legal father), and Luke (3:23) gives His maternal genealogy (through His mother).

wife: for that which is conceived in her is of the Holy Spirit.

21 And she shall bring forth a son, and you shall call his name JESUS: for he shall save his people from their sins.

22 Now all this was done, that it might be fulfilled which was spoken of the Lord by the prophet, saying,

23 Behold, a virgin shall be with child, and shall bring forth a son, and they shall call his name Emmanuel, which being interpreted is, God with us.

24 Then Joseph being raised from sleep did as the angel of the Lord had bidden him, and took to him his wife:

25 And knew her not till she had brought forth her firstborn son: and he called his name JESUS.

CHAPTER 2

NOW when Jesus was born in Bethlehem of Judea in the days of Herod the king, behold, there came wise men from the east to Jerusalem,

2 Saying, Where is he that is born King of the Jews? for we have seen his star in the east, and are come to worship him.

3 When Herod the king had heard these things, he was troubled, and all Jerusalem with him.

4 And when he had gathered all the chief priests and scribes of the people together, he demanded of them where Christ should be born.

5 And they said to him, In Bethlehem of Judea: for thus it is written by the prophet,

6 And you Bethlehem, in the land of Judah, are not the least among the princes of Judah: for out of you shall come a Governor, that shall rule my people Israel.

7 Then Herod, when he had privately called the wise men, inquired of them diligently what time the star appeared.

8 And he sent them to Bethlehem, and said, Go and search diligently for the young child; and when you have found him, bring me word again, that I may come and worship him also.

9 When they had heard the king, they departed; and, lo, the star, which they saw in the east, went before them, till it came and stood over where the young child was.

10 When they saw the star, they rejoiced with exceeding great joy.

11 And when they were come into the house, they saw the young child with Mary his mother, and fell down, and worshipped him: and when they had opened their treasures, they presented to him gifts; gold, and frankincense, and myrrh.

12 And being warned of God in a dream that they should not return to Herod, they departed into their own country another way.

13 And when they were departed, behold, the angel of the Lord appeared to Joseph in a dream, saying, Arise, and take the young child and his mother, and flee into Egypt, and be there until I bring you word: for Herod will seek the young child to destroy him.

14 When he arose, he took the young child and his mother by night, and departed into Egypt:

1:20–23 Some say this was not a "virgin" but merely a "young maiden." Isaiah 7:14 says that God Himself will give a "sign." A young maiden becoming pregnant is not a sign from God, but an everyday occurrence. A *virgin* conceiving is a supernatural sign. See also Luke 1:31–35.

2:1 Wise men still seek Him. How is it that these wise men, who were not Jews, were aware of the birth of the "King of the Jews"? That they not only understood who He was, but desired to worship Him (v. 2) shows that God is able to reveal Himself to people in all lands and call them to Himself. These wise men "rejoiced with exceeding great joy" as God used a star to guide them to the Christ Child, then they "fell down and worshiped Him" (vv. 9–11). They made great personal and financial sacrifices to see this Child: they traveled a great distance, spent months away from their homes, and gave extravagant gifts to this newborn King.

Those who are wise today will listen for His voice, follow His guidance, and be willing to sacrifice everything for so great a privilege as meeting the King. See Philippians 3:8.

15 And was there until the death of Herod: that it might be fulfilled which was spoken of the Lord by the prophet, saying, Out of Egypt have I called my son.

16 Then Herod, when he saw that he was mocked of the wise men, was exceeding wroth, and sent forth, and slew all the children that were in Bethlehem, and in all the coasts thereof, from two years old and under, according to the time which he had diligently inquired of the wise men.

17 Then was fulfilled that which was spoken by Jeremiah the prophet, saying,

18 In Rama was there a voice heard, lamentation, and weeping, and great mourning, Rachel weeping for her children, and would not be comforted, because they are not.

19 But when Herod was dead, behold, an angel of the Lord appeared in a dream to Joseph in Egypt,

20 Saying, Arise, and take the young child and his mother, and go into the land of Israel: for they are dead which sought the young child's life.

21 And he arose, and took the young child and his mother, and came into the land of Israel.

22 But when he heard that Archelaus did reign in Judea in the room of his father Herod, he was afraid to go there: notwithstanding, being warned of God in a dream, he turned aside into the parts of Galilee:

23 And he came and dwelt in a city called Nazareth: that it might be fulfilled which was spoken by the prophets, He shall be called a Nazarene.

CHAPTER 3

IN those days came John the Baptist, preaching in the wilderness of Judea,

2 And saying, **Repent: for the kingdom of heaven is at hand.**

3 For this is he that was spoken of by the prophet Isaiah, saying, The voice of one crying in the wilderness, **Prepare the way of the Lord, make his paths straight.**

3:1 Open-air preaching. John the Baptist was an open-air preacher. Jesus was an open-air preacher. He preached the greatest sermon of all time, the "Sermon on the Mount" in the open-air. Peter preached in the open-air at Pentecost and Paul chose to stand on Mars Hill and preach open-air to the Athenians.

If we are serious about reaching this world, let us follow in the footsteps of Jesus and the apostles and preach where sinners gather. In thirty minutes, a good open-air preacher can reach more sinners than the average church does in twelve months.

Thank God that the disciples didn't stay in the upper room. They didn't carpet the building, pad the pews, and then put a notice outside the front door saying, "Tonight: Gospel outreach service, 7 P.M.—all welcome." They went into the open air.

The gospel is for the world, not the Church. One-third of the word "gospel" is "go." Two-thirds of "God" is "go"; but like King Og, we seem to have it backwards. We take sinners to meetings rather than meetings to sinners. The Church prefers to fish on dry land rather than get its feet wet. *Charles Finney* put his finger on the reason why: "It is the great business of every Christian to save souls. People complain that they do not know how to take hold of this matter. Why, the reason is plain enough; they have never studied it. They have never taken the proper pains to qualify themselves for the work. If you do not make it a matter of study, how you may successfully act in building up the kingdom of Christ, you are acting a very wicked and absurd part as a Christian."

He who loves his neighbor as himself will be concerned for his eternal welfare. He who couldn't care less that every day multitudes of living people are being swallowed by the jaws of hell has a heart of stone indeed.

3:2 Repentance—its necessity for salvation. The first word John the Baptist preached to Israel was "repent." However, it must be remembered that Israel had the Law and therefore had the "knowledge of sin" (Romans 7:7). Unregenerate humanity needs the Moral Law to show them what sin is (1 John 3:4). Without the knowledge that the "schoolmaster" brings, they remain in ignorance about sin's true nature and therefore their need for biblical repentance. See Luke 13:3.

4 And the same John had his raiment of camel's hair, and a leathern girdle about his loins; and his meat was locusts and wild honey.

5 Then went out to him Jerusalem, and all Judea, and all the region round about Jordan,

6 And were baptized of him in Jordan, confessing their sins.

7 But when he saw many of the Pharisees and Sadducees come to his baptism, he said to them, **O generation of vipers, who has warned you to flee from the wrath to come?**

8 **Bring forth therefore fruits meet for repentance:**

9 **And think not to say within yourselves, We have Abraham to our father: for I say to you, that God is able of these stones to raise up children to Abraham.**

10 And now also the axe is laid to the root of the trees: therefore every tree which brings not forth good fruit is hewn down, and cast into the fire.

11 I indeed baptize you with water to repentance: but he that comes after me is mightier than I, whose shoes I am not worthy to bear: he shall baptize you with the Holy Spirit, and with fire:

12 Whose fan is in his hand, and he will thoroughly purge his floor, and gather his wheat into the garner; but he will burn up the chaff with unquenchable fire.

13 Then came Jesus from Galilee to Jordan to John, to be baptized of him.

14 But John forbad him, saying, I have need to be baptized of you, and you come to me?

15 And Jesus answering said to him, Suffer it to be so now: for thus it becomes us to fulfil all righteousness. Then he suffered him.

16 And Jesus, when he was baptized, went up straightway out of the water: and, lo, the heavens were opened to him, and he saw the Spirit of God descending like a dove, and lighting upon him:

17 And lo a voice from heaven, saying, This is my beloved Son, in whom I am well pleased.

CHAPTER 4

THEN was Jesus led up of the Spirit into the wilderness to be tempted of the devil.

2 And when he had fasted forty days and forty nights, he was afterward an hungered.

3 And when the tempter came to him, he said, If you are the Son of God, command that these stones be made bread.

4 But he answered and said, It is written, Man shall not live by bread alone, but by every word that proceeds out of the mouth of God.

5 Then the devil took him up into the holy city, and set him on a pinnacle of the temple,

6 And said to him, If you are the Son of God, cast yourself down: for it is written, He shall give his angels charge concerning you: and in their hands they shall bear you up, lest at any time you dash your foot against a stone.

7 Jesus said to him, It is written again, You shall not tempt the Lord your God.

8 Again, the devil took him up into an exceeding high mountain, and showed him all the kingdoms of the world, and the glory of them;

9 And said to him, All these things will I give you, if you will fall down and worship me.

10 Then said Jesus to him, Get you hence, Satan: for it is written, You shall worship the Lord your God, and him only shall you serve.

11 Then the devil left him, and, behold, angels came and ministered to him.

12 Now when Jesus had heard that John was cast into prison, he departed into Galilee;

4:6 "The devil can cite Scripture for his purpose." *William Shakespeare*

4:9 The devil tempted Jesus to become a Satan worshiper.

4:4 Archaeology and History Attest to the Reliability of the Bible

By Richard M. Fales, Ph.D.

No other ancient book is questioned or maligned like the Bible. Critics looking for the flyspeck in the masterpiece allege that there was a long span between the time the events in the New Testament occurred and when they were recorded. They claim another gap exists archaeologically between the earliest copies made and the autographs of the New Testament. In reality, the alleged spaces and so-called gaps exist only in the minds of the critics.

Manuscript Evidence. Aristotle's *Ode to Poetics* was written between 384 and 322 B.C. The earliest copy of this work is dated A.D. 1100, and there are only forty-nine extant manuscripts. The gap between the original writing and the earliest copy is 1,400 years. There are only seven extant manuscripts of Plato's *Tetralogies*, written 427–347 B.C. The earliest copy is A.D. 900—a gap of over 1,200 years. What about the New Testament? Jesus was crucified in A.D. 30. The New Testament was written between A.D. 48 and 95. The oldest manuscripts date to the last quarter of the first century, and the second oldest A.D. 125. This gives us a narrow gap of thirty-five to forty years from the originals written by the apostles.

From the early centuries, we have some 5,300 Greek manuscripts of the New Testament. Altogether, including Syriac, Latin, Coptic, and Aramaic, we have a whopping 24,633 texts of the ancient New Testament to confirm the wording of the Scriptures. So the bottom line is, there was no great period between the events of the New Testament and the New Testament writings. Nor is there a great time lapse between the original writings and the oldest copies. With the great body of manuscript evidence, it can be proved, beyond a doubt, that the New Testament says exactly the same things today as it originally did nearly 2,000 years ago.

Corroborating Writings. Critics also charge that there are no ancient writings about Jesus outside the New Testament. This is another ridiculous claim. Writings confirming His birth, ministry, death, and resurrection include Flavius Josephus (A.D. 93), the Babylonian Talmud (A.D. 70–200), Pliny the Younger's letter to the Emperor Trajan (approx. A.D. 100), the Annals of Tacitus (A.D. 115–117), Mara Bar Serapion (sometime after A.D. 73), and Suetonius' *Life of Claudius* and *Life of Nero* (A.D. 120). Another point of contention arises when Bible critics have knowingly or unknowingly misled people by implying that Old and New Testament books were either excluded from or added into the canon of Scripture at the great ecumenical councils of A.D. 336, 382, 397, and 419. In fact, one result of these gatherings was to confirm the Church's belief that the books already in the Bible were divinely inspired. Therefore, the Church, at these meetings, neither added to nor took away from the books of the Bible. At that time, the thirty-nine Old Testament books had already been accepted, and the New Testament, as it was written, simply grew up with the ancient Church. Each document, being accepted as it was penned in the first century, was then passed on to Christians of the next century. So, this foolishness about the Roman Emperor Constantine dropping books from the Bible is simply uneducated rumor.

Fulfilled Prophecies. Prophecies from the Old and New Testaments that have been fulfilled also add credibility to the Bible. The Scriptures predicted the rise and fall of great empires like Greece and Rome (Daniel 2:39, 40), and foretold the destruction of cities like Tyre and Sidon (Isaiah 23). Tyre's demise is recorded by ancient historians, who tell how Alexander the Great lay siege to the city for seven months. King Nebuchadnezzar of Babylon had failed in a 13-year attempt to capture the seacoast city and completely destroy its inhabitants. During the siege of 573 B.C., much of the population of Tyre moved to its new island home approximately half a mile from the land city. Here it remained surrounded by walls as high as 150 feet until judgment fell in 332 B.C. with the arrival of Alexander the Great. In the seven-month siege, he fulfilled the remainder of the prophecies (Zechariah 9:4; Ezekiel 26:12) concerning the city at sea by completely destroying Tyre, killing 8,000 of its inhabitants and selling 30,000 of its population into slavery. To reach the island, he

(continued on next page)

(4:4 continued)
scraped up the dust and rubble of the old land city of Tyre, just like the Bible predicted, and cast them into the sea, building a 200-foot-wide causeway out to the island.

Alexander's death and the murder of his two sons was also foretold in the Scripture. Another startling prophecy was Jesus' detailed prediction of Jerusalem's destruction, and the further spreading of the Jewish diaspora throughout the world, which is recorded in Luke 21. In A.D. 70, not only was Jerusalem destroyed by Titus, the future emperor of Rome, but another prediction of Jesus Christ in Matthew 24:1-2 came to pass—the complete destruction of the temple of God.

Messianic Prophecies. In the Book of Daniel, the Bible prophesied the coming of the one and only Jewish Messiah prior to the temple's demise. The Old Testament prophets declared He would be born in Bethlehem (Micah 5:2) to a virgin (Isaiah 7:14), be betrayed for thirty pieces of silver (Zechariah 11:12-13), die by crucifixion (Psalm 22), and be buried in a rich man's tomb (Isaiah 53:9). There was only one person who fits all of the messianic prophecies of the Old Testament who lived before A.D. 70: Jesus of Nazareth, the Son of Mary.

Yes, the Bible is an amazing book. (See also 1 Peter 1:25 footnote.)

13 And leaving Nazareth, he came and dwelt in Capernaum, which is upon the sea coast, in the borders of Zabulon and Nephthalim:
14 That it might be fulfilled which was spoken by Isaiah the prophet, saying,
15 The land of Zabulon, and the land of Nephthalim, by the way of the sea, beyond Jordan, Galilee of the Gentiles;
16 The people which sat in darkness saw great light; and to them which sat in the region and shadow of death light is sprung up.
17 From that time Jesus began to preach, and to say, **Repent: for the kingdom of heaven is at hand.**
18 And Jesus, walking by the sea of Galilee, saw two brethren, Simon called Peter, and Andrew his brother, casting a net into the sea: for they were fishers.
19 *And he said to them, Follow me, and I will make you fishers of men.*
20 And they straightway left their nets, and followed him.
21 And going on from there, he saw other two brethren, James the son of Zebedee, and John his brother, in a ship with Zebedee their father, mending their nets; and he called them.
22 And they immediately left the ship and their father, and followed him.
23 And Jesus went about all Galilee, teaching in their synagogues, and preaching the gospel of the kingdom, and healing all manner of sickness and all manner of disease among the people.
24 And his fame went throughout all Syria: and they brought to him all sick people that were taken with divers diseases and torments, and those which were possessed with devils, and those which were lunatic, and those that had the palsy; and he healed them.
25 And there followed him great multitudes of people from Galilee, and from Decapolis, and from Jerusalem, and from Judea, and from beyond Jordan.

CHAPTER 5

AND seeing the multitudes, he went up into a mountain: and when he was set, his disciples came to him:
2 And he opened his mouth, and taught them, saying,

4:16 This life is the valley of the shadow of death. Sinners sit in darkness—waiting to die. The light of the Savior banishes the shadow of death.

4:17 Like John the Baptist, Jesus' first word in preaching to Israel was "repent." Israel already had the "knowledge of sin" (which only the Law can bring), but now they needed to repent—to turn from their sins as revealed by the Law.

5:1 *The Sermon on the Mount*

This sermon not only reveals God's divine nature, it puts into our hands the most powerful of evangelistic weapons. It is the greatest evangelistic sermon ever preached by the greatest evangelist who ever lived. The straightedge of God's Law reveals how crooked we are:

v. 3: The unregenerate heart isn't poor in spirit. It is proud, self-righteous, and boastful (every man is pure in his own eyes—Proverbs 16:2).

v. 4: The unsaved don't mourn over their sin; they love the darkness and hate the light (John 3:19).

v. 5: The ungodly are not meek and lowly of heart. Their sinful condition is described in Romans 3:13–18.

v. 6: Sinners don't hunger and thirst after righteousness. Instead, they drink iniquity like water (Job 15:16).

v. 7: The world is shallow in its ability to show true mercy. It is by nature cruel and vindictive (Genesis 6:5).

v. 8: The heart of the unregenerate is not pure; it is desperately wicked (Jeremiah 17:9).

Those who are born again manifest the fruit of the Spirit, live godly in Christ Jesus (vv. 3–9), and therefore suffer persecution (vv. 10–12). However, their purpose on earth is to be salt and light: to be a moral influence, and to bring the light to those who sit in the shadow of death (vv. 13–16).

Look now at how the Messiah expounds the Law and makes it "honorable" (Isaiah 42:21). He establishes that He didn't come to destroy the Law (v. 17); not even the smallest part of it will pass away (v. 18). It will be the divine standard of judgment (James 2:12; Romans 2:12; Acts 17:31). Those who teach it "shall be called great in the kingdom of heaven" (v. 19). The Law should be taught to sinners because it was made for them (1 Timothy 1:8–10), and is a "schoolmaster" that brings the "knowledge of sin" (Romans 3:19,20; 7:7). Its function is to destroy self-righteousness and bring sinners to the cross (Galatians 3:24).

The righteousness of the scribes and Pharisees was merely outward, but God requires truth in the inward parts (Psalm 51:6). Jesus shows this by unveiling the Law's *spiritual* nature (Romans 7:14). The Sixth Commandment forbids murder. However, Jesus shows that it also condemns anger "without cause," and even evil-speaking (vv. 21–26): "Every idle word that men shall speak, they shall give an account thereof in the day of judgment" (Matthew 12:36). The Seventh Commandment forbids adultery, but Jesus revealed that this also includes lust, and it even condemns divorce, except in the case of sexual sin of the spouse (vv. 27–32).

Jesus opens up the Ninth Commandment (vv. 33–37), and then shows that love is the spirit of the Law—"The end of the commandment is charity out of a pure heart..." (1 Timothy 1:5). This is summarized in what is commonly called the Golden Rule: "All things whatsoever you would that men should do to you, do you even so to them: *for this is the Law and the prophets*" (Matthew 7:12, emphasis added). "Owe no man any thing, but to love one another: for he that loves another has fulfilled the law. For this, You shall not commit adultery, You shall not kill, You shall not steal, You shall not bear false witness, You shall not covet; and if there be any other commandment, it is briefly comprehended in this saying, namely, You shall love your neighbor as yourself. Love works no ill to his neighbor: therefore love is the fulfilling of the law" (Romans 13:8–10).

When a sinner is born again he is able to do this (vv. 38–47). He now possesses "the divine nature" (2 Peter 1:4). In Christ he is made perfect and thus satisfies the demands of a "perfect" Law (Psalm 19:7; James 1:25). Without the righteousness of Christ he cannot be perfect as his Father in heaven is perfect (v. 48). The Law annihilated his self-righteousness leaving him undone and condemned. His only hope was in the cross of Jesus Christ. After his conversion, knowledge of the Law that brought him there keeps him at the foot of the cross.

John Wesley said, "Therefore I cannot spare the Law one moment, no more than I can spare Christ, seeing I now want it as much to keep me to Christ, as I ever wanted it to bring me to Him. Otherwise this 'evil heart of unbelief' would immediately 'depart from the living God.' Indeed each is continually sending me to the other—the Law to Christ, and Christ to the Law."

3 Blessed are the poor in spirit: for theirs is the kingdom of heaven.

4 Blessed are they that mourn: for they shall be comforted.

5 Blessed are the meek: for they shall inherit the earth.

> We have grasped the mystery of the atom and rejected the Sermon on the Mount...The world has achieved brilliance without conscience. Ours is a world of nuclear giants and ethical infants.
>
> **GENERAL OMAR BRADLEY**

6 Blessed are they which do hunger and thirst after righteousness: for they shall be filled.

7 Blessed are the merciful: for they shall obtain mercy.

8 Blessed are the pure in heart: for they shall see God.

9 Blessed are the peacemakers: for they shall be called the children of God.

10 Blessed are they which are persecuted for righteousness' sake: for theirs is the kingdom of heaven.

11 Blessed are you, when men shall revile you, and persecute you, and shall say all manner of evil against you falsely, for my sake.

12 Rejoice, and be exceeding glad: for great is your reward in heaven: for so persecuted they the prophets which were before you.

13 You are the salt of the earth: but if the salt has lost his savour, wherewith shall it be salted? it is thenceforth good for nothing, but to be cast out, and to be trodden under foot of men.

14 *You are the light of the world. A city that is set on an hill cannot be hid.*

15 *Neither do men light a candle, and put it under a bushel, but on a candlestick; and*

5:2 Sin, righteousness, and judgment. "The Sermon on the Mount is the greatest example we have of how to 'reprove the world of sin, of righteousness, and of judgment.' In Matthew chapter 5, Christ reproves the multitudes of sin by showing the essence of the Law. In chapter 6, He teaches on true righteousness, the essence of which is to cause men to glorify our Father which is in heaven, not to draw attention to ourselves. Then, in chapter 7, He teaches concerning judgment. He warns the multitudes that if they judge others as guilty for doing the same things they themselves are practicing, instead of pulling the log out of their own eye first, they are obviously hypocrites. If we will follow this method of preaching the gospel, then we can expect the Holy Spirit to help us. For Jesus Himself promised that this divine Helper would reprove the world of sin, of righteousness, and of judgment. He does this by causing our words to make saving impressions on the minds of men." *Joel Crumpton*

5:6 We should come to the Savior thirsting for *righteousness*, not *happiness* as modern evangelism maintains—"Riches profit not in the day of wrath: but *righteousness* delivers from death" (Proverbs 11:4, emphasis added).

5:7 Jesus didn't come to destroy the Law and the prophets, but to fulfill them (Matthew 5:17). It was our transgressions that necessitated the Savior. If we hadn't sinned, there would have been no need for a sacrifice. We broke the Law, and Jesus paid the fine. God loved the world with such passion that He sent His only Son to the cross of Calvary, so that we might trust in Him alone. In so doing, we would not perish under the wrath of His Law, but have everlasting life (John 3:16).

5:13 "The pulpit, not the media, is to be the most powerful voice in our land." *Bill Gothard*

5:14 Set on a hill. Some people say that religion is a personal thing and it should be kept to oneself. However, Jesus tells us that the gospel of salvation is the good news of everlasting life and is for this dying world. We should be set on a hill. We should be preaching on the housetops, lifting up our voice like a trumpet to show this people their transgression. The Bible tells us that God's Law is light (Proverbs 6:23). When the light of the Law and the glorious gospel of Christ shine together, they expose and banish the shadows of sin and death.

POINTS FOR OPEN-AIR PREACHING

Never Fear Hecklers

5:10–12

The best thing that can happen to an open-air meeting is to have a good heckler. Jesus gave us some of the greatest gems of Scripture because someone either made a statement or asked a question in an open-air setting. A good heckler can increase a crowd of 20 people to 200 in a matter of minutes. The air becomes electric. Suddenly, you have 200 people listening intently to how you will answer a heckler. All you have to do is remember the attributes of 2 Timothy 2:23–26: be patient, gentle, humble, etc. Don't worry if you can't answer a question. Just say, "I can't answer that, but I'll try to get the answer for you if you really want to know." With Bible "difficulties," I regularly fall back on the powerful statement of *Mark Twain*: "Most people are bothered by those passages of Scripture they don't understand, but for me I have always noticed that the passages that bother me are those I do understand."

A "good" heckler is one who will provoke your thoughts. He will stand up, speak up, then shut up so that you can preach. Occasionally, you will get hecklers who have the first two qualifications, but they just won't be quiet. If they will not let you get a word in, move your location. Most of the crowd will follow. Better to have 10 listeners who can hear than 200 who can't. If the heckler follows, move again . . . then the crowd will usually turn on him.

One ploy that often works with a heckler who is out solely to hinder the gospel is to wait until he is quiet and say to the crowd (making sure the heckler is listening also), "I want to show you how people are like sheep. When I move, watch this man follow me because he can't get a crowd by himself." His pride usually keeps him from following.

If you have a "mumbling heckler" who won't speak up, ignore him and talk over the top of him. This will usually get him angry enough to speak up and draw hearers. There is a fine line between him getting angry enough to draw a crowd, and hitting you; you will find it in time.

If you are fortunate enough to get a heckler, don't panic. Show him genuine respect, not only because he can double your crowd, but because the Bible says to honor all men, so you don't want to offend him unnecessarily. Ask the heckler his name, so that if you want to ask him a question and he is talking to someone, you don't have to say, "Hey you!"

Often, people will walk through the crowd so they can get close to you and will whisper something like, "I think you are a #@*!$!" Answer loud enough for the crowd to hear, "God bless you." Do it with a smile so that it looks as though the person has just whispered a word of encouragement to you. This will stop him from doing it again. The Bible says to bless those who curse you, and to do good to those who hate you.

Remember that you are not fighting against flesh and blood. Hecklers will stoop very low and be cutting and cruel in their remarks. If you have some physical disability, they will play on it. Try to smile back at them. Look past the words. If you are reviled for the name of Jesus, "rejoice, and be exceeding glad." Read Matthew 5:10–12 until it is written on the corridors of your mind.

The most angry hecklers are usually what we call "backsliders." These are actually false converts who never slid forward in the first place. They "asked Jesus into their heart" but never truly repented. Ask him, "Did you know the Lord?" (see Hebrews 8:11). If he answers "Yes," then he is admitting that he is willfully denying Him, and if he answers "No," then he was never a Christian in the first place—"This is eternal life, that they might know you, the only true God, and Jesus Christ, whom you have sent" (John 17:3). See 1 Corinthians 2:4 footnote.

---

it gives light to all that are in the house.

16 *Let your light so shine before men, that they may see your good works, and glorify your Father who is in heaven.*

17 Think not that I am come to destroy the law, or the prophets: I am not come to destroy, but to fulfil.

18 For verily I say to you, Till heaven and earth pass, one jot or one tittle shall in no wise pass from the law, till all be fulfilled.

19 Whosoever therefore shall break one

SPIRITUAL NATURE OF THE LAW

5:22 "Herein is the Law of God above all other laws, that it is a spiritual law. Other laws may forbid compassing and imagining, which are treason in the heart, but cannot take cognizance thereof, unless there be some overt act; but the Law of God takes notice of the iniquity regarded in the heart, though it go no further." *Matthew Henry*

"The precepts of philosophy, and of the Hebrew code, laid hold of actions only. [Jesus] pushed His scrutinies into the heart of man, erected His tribunal in the region of his thoughts, and purified the waters at the fountain head." *Thomas Jefferson*

of these least commandments, and shall teach men so, he shall be called the least in the kingdom of heaven: but whosoever shall do and teach them, the same shall be called great in the kingdom of heaven. **20** For I say to you, That except your righteousness shall exceed the righteousness of the scribes and Pharisees, you shall in no case enter into the kingdom of heaven.

21 You have heard that it was said by them of old time, You shall not kill; and whosoever shall kill shall be in danger of the judgment:

22 But I say to you, That whosoever is angry with his brother without a cause shall be in danger of the judgment: and whosoever shall say to his brother, Raca, shall be in danger of the council: but whosoever shall say, You fool, shall be in danger of hell fire.

23 Therefore if you bring your gift to the altar, and there remember that your brother has anything against you;

24 Leave there your gift before the altar, and go your way; first be reconciled to your brother, and then come and offer your gift.

25 Agree with your adversary quickly, while you are in the way with him; lest at any time the adversary deliver you to the judge, and the judge deliver you to the officer, and you be cast into prison.

26 Verily I say to you, You shall by no means come out thence, till you have paid the uttermost farthing.

27 You have heard that it was said by them of old time, You shall not commit adultery:

28 But I say to you, That whosoever looks on a woman to lust after her has committed adultery with her already in his heart.

5:16 "If doing a good act in public will excite others to do more good, then 'Let your light shine to all.' Miss no opportunity to do good." *John Wesley*

5:20 **Self-righteousness.** These words would have astounded Jesus' hearers. If anyone was righteous, it was the scribes and Pharisees. Their hope of life from the Law was therefore shattered. That is what we must do: shatter the self-righteous beliefs of those poor souls who try to earn salvation. Jesus shows us how in the following verses by explaining that God requires truth even in the inward parts. He considers hatred to be murder (1 John 3:15). If we as much as have anger without cause, we are in danger of judgment (v. 22). If we have lust in our hearts, God considers us to be adulterers (v. 28). Sin is so serious, Jesus said that it would be better to be blind than to go to hell because of a lustful eye.

5:21,22 **God sees the thought-life:** He weighs our motives and judges the intent of the hearts: "Whoever hates his brother is a murderer" (1 John 3:15). See Matthew 5:27,28 footnote.

5:22 **Hell:** For verses warning of its reality, see Matthew 5:29,30.

5:27,28 **God knows what's in the heart:** "For God will bring every work into judgment, including every secret thing, whether good or evil" (Ecclesiastes 12:14). "But after your hardness and impenitent heart you treasure up to yourself wrath against the day of wrath and revelation of the righteous judgment of God; who will render to every man according to his deeds" (Romans 2:5,6). See Mark 7:20–23 footnote.

5:28

"What should I say if someone asks, 'Have you ever lusted?'"

An individual may challenge you on this issue while you're going through the Ten Commandments with him. Take care when answering. There is such a thing as being too candid. A U.S. president became synonymous with the word "lust" because he lacked discretion in answering this question. Soften your answer with, "I have broken *all* of the Ten Commandments in spirit, if not in letter." That will not only defuse the issue, but will give you opportunity to explain that we all have a sin nature and need God's forgiveness.

29 And if your right eye offend you, pluck it out, and cast it from you: for it is profitable for you that one of your members should perish, and not that your whole body should be cast into hell.

30 And if your right hand offend you, cut if off, and cast it from you: for it is profitable for you that one of your members should perish, and not that your whole body should be cast into hell.

31 It has been said, Whosoever shall put away his wife, let him give her a writing of divorcement:

32 But I say to you, That whosoever shall put away his wife, saving for the cause of fornication, causes her to commit adultery: and whosoever shall marry her that is divorced commits adultery.

33 Again, you have heard that it has been said by them of old time, You shall not forswear yourself, but shall perform to the Lord your oaths:

34 But I say to you, Swear not at all; neither by heaven; for it is God's throne:

35 Nor by the earth; for it is his footstool: neither by Jerusalem; for it is the city of the great King.

36 Neither shall you swear by your head, because you can not make one hair white or black.

37 But let your communication be, Yea, yea; Nay, nay: for whatsoever is more than these comes of evil.

38 You have heard that it has been said, An eye for an eye, and a tooth for a tooth:

39 But I say to you, That you resist not evil: but whosoever shall smite you on your right cheek, turn to him the other also.

40 And if any man will sue you at the law, and take away your coat, let him have your cloak also.

41 And whosoever shall compel you to go a mile, go with him two.

42 Give to him that asks you, and from him that would borrow of you turn not away.

43 You have heard that it has been said, You shall love your neighbour, and hate your enemy.

44 But I say to you, Love your enemies, bless them that curse you, do good to them that hate you, and pray for them which despitefully use you, and persecute you;

45 That you may be the children of your Father which is in heaven: for he makes his sun to rise on the evil and on the good, and sends rain on the just and on the unjust.

46 For if you love them which love you,

5:28 Men will often try to justify lust by saying that there's nothing wrong with looking at a pretty girl. True, the Bible doesn't condemn looking at a pretty girl; it condemns "lust." The conscience knows the difference.

5:29,30 Hell: For verses warning of its reality, see Matthew 10:28.

QUESTIONS & OBJECTIONS

5:38 *"When the Bible says 'an eye for an eye,' it encourages us to take the law in our own hands by avenging wrongdoing."*

This verse is so often misquoted by the world. Many believe it is giving a license to take matters into our own hands and render evil for evil. In reality, it is referring to civil law concerning restitution. If someone steals your ox, he is to restore the ox. If someone steals and wrecks your car, he is to buy you another one…a car for a car, an eye for an eye, a tooth for a tooth.

The spirit of what Jesus is saying here is radically different from the "sue the shirt off the back of your neighbor" society in which we live.

---

what reward have you? do not even the publicans the same?

47 And if you salute your brethren only, what do you more than others? do not even the publicans so?

48 Be therefore perfect, even as your Father which is in heaven is perfect.

CHAPTER 6

TAKE heed that you do not your alms before men, to be seen of them: otherwise you have no reward of your Father which is in heaven.

2 Therefore when you do your alms, do not sound a trumpet before you, as the

---

5:44 There are several reasons why as Christians we should pray for those who persecute us: 1) we are commanded to; 2) prayer is an antidote against bitterness; and 3) it can lead to the salvation of the persecutor.

5:44 Capital punishment. Some maintain that this verse shows Jesus did not believe in capital punishment. However, just because we have love for an enemy doesn't give us the right to allow him to escape punishment for murder. The Bible says, "Let every soul be subject to the higher powers. For there is no power but of God: the powers that be are ordained of God. Whosoever therefore resists the power, resists the ordinance of God: and they that resist shall receive to themselves damnation…*But if you do that which is evil, be afraid; for he bears not the sword in vain: for he is the minister of God, a revenger to execute wrath upon him that does evil*" (Romans 13:1–4, emphasis added).

The Bible says that if I deliberately take a life, I should lose my own: "Whoso kills any person, the murderer shall be put to death by the mouth of witnesses: but one witness shall not testify against any person to cause him to die. Moreover you shall take no satisfaction for the life of a murderer, which is guilty of death: but he shall be surely put to death" (Numbers 35:30,31). Genesis 9:6 says, "Whoso sheds man's blood, by man shall his blood be shed: for in the image of God made he man." This shows the value that God places on human life. The seriousness of a crime is revealed in the punishment dealt to the criminal. It is interesting to note that when Oklahoma City bomber Timothy McVeigh requested the death penalty, 250 relatives of the victims he killed asked to watch his execution. Their desire to actually see justice done shows the value they place on the loved one they lost. Despite claims to the contrary, capital punishment does deter crime. The person executed will not do it again.

Still, there are respected Christian leaders whose conscience will not allow them to advocate capital punishment. This is understandable in light of the fact that innocent people fall through the cracks of a godless justice system. However, despite civil law's imperfections, we are told to be subject to the governing authorities.

It was God who instigated the death penalty in the beginning. The Judge of the Universe pronounced the death sentence upon all humanity when He said, "The soul that sins, it shall die" (Ezekiel 18:20).

hypocrites do in the synagogues and in the streets, that they may have glory of men. Verily I say to you, They have their reward.

3 But when you do alms, let not your left hand know what your right hand does:

4 That your alms may be in secret: and your Father which sees in secret himself shall reward you openly.

5 And when you pray, you shall not be as the hypocrites are: for they love to pray standing in the synagogues and in the corners of the streets, that they may be seen of men. Verily I say to you, They have their reward.

6 But you, when you pray, enter into your closet, and when you have shut your door, pray to your Father which is in secret; and your Father which sees in secret shall reward you openly.

7 But when you pray, use not vain repetitions, as the heathen do: for they think that they shall be heard for their much speaking.

8 Be not therefore like to them: for your Father knows what things you have need of, before you ask him.

9 After this manner therefore pray: Our Father who is in heaven, Hallowed be your name.

10 Your kingdom come. Your will be done in earth, as it is in heaven.

> Before we can pray "Thy Kingdom come," we must be willing to pray "my kingdom go."
>
> **ALAN REDPATH**

11 Give us this day our daily bread.

12 And forgive us our debts, as we forgive our debtors.

13 And lead us not into temptation, but deliver us from evil: For yours is the kingdom, and the power, and the glory, for ever. Amen.

14 For if you forgive men their trespas-

5:48 Be perfect. Some believe Jesus didn't really mean "perfect" here, because that would require that we be "without defect, flawless." Instead, they think He was telling us to be "mature." If that were true, then He would be saying, "Be therefore mature, even as your Father which is in heaven is mature." However, calling God "mature" implies that He was once immature. Such a thought is contrary to Scripture. God never changes (Malachi 3:6); He has always been perfect and doesn't need to mature.

Throughout the Sermon on the Mount Jesus expounded the perfect Law of a perfect Creator. God's work is perfect (Deuteronomy 32:4), His way is perfect (Psalm 18:30), and His Law is perfect (Psalm 19:7; James 1:25). Jesus then climaxes His exposition with the demand of the Law—perfection in thought, word, and deed.

In magnifying the Law and making it honorable, He put righteousness beyond the reach of sinful humanity. He destroyed the vain hope that we can get right with a perfect Creator by our own imperfect efforts, i.e., by the works of the Law. (See Mark 7:5–13 footnote.)

Instead, we must seek righteousness by another means—through faith alone in the Savior (Romans 3:21,22). In doing so, Jesus was showing us the right use of the Law—as a "schoolmaster to bring us to Christ" (Galatians 3:24). This is what Jesus did with the rich young ruler. The young man asked, "Good Master, what good thing shall I do, that I may have eternal life?" (Matthew 19:16). Jesus corrected his misuse of the word "good," gave him five of the Ten Commandments, and then said, "If you will be perfect..." The young man's hope of "doing" something to be saved was dashed and he went away sorrowful. However, this is not a negative incident; it is positive when a sinner's vain hope is dashed. If he cannot find salvation "by the works of the Law," he may just seek it "by the hearing of faith" (Galatians 3:2). This is why we should use the Law when reasoning with the lost and press home its requirement of absolute perfection. (See James 2:10,11.) On hearing the demands of a perfect Law, it is not uncommon to hear a guilty sinner say, "Wow! Nobody's perfect." That's the point of the Law.

Our mission is to preach Christ and to warn sinners, "that we may present every man perfect in Christ Jesus" (Colossians 1:28).

6:9   *Prayer—"Wait for a Minute"*

God always answers prayer. Sometimes He says yes; sometimes He says no; and sometimes He says, "Wait for a minute." And since to the Lord a day is as a thousand years (2 Peter 3:8), that could mean a ten-year wait for us. So ask in faith, but rest in peace-filled patience.

Surveys show that more than 90% of Americans pray daily. No doubt they pray for health, wealth, happiness, etc. They also pray when grandma gets sick, and when grandma doesn't get better (or dies), many end up disillusioned or bitter. This is because they don't understand what the Bible says about prayer. It teaches, among other things, that our sin will keep God from even hearing our prayer (Psalm 66:18), and that if we pray with doubt, we will not get an answer (James 1:6,7).

Here's how to be heard:

- Pray with faith (Hebrews 11:6).
- Pray with clean hands and a pure heart (Psalm 24:3,4).
- Pray genuine heartfelt prayers, rather than vain repetitions (Matthew 6:7).
- Make sure you are praying to the God revealed in the Scriptures (Exodus 20:3–6).

1. How do you "pray with faith"? Someone once told me, "Ray, you're a man of great faith in God," thinking they were paying me a compliment. They weren't. What if I said to you, "I'm a man of great faith in my doctor"? It's a compliment to the doctor. If I have great faith in him, it means that I see him as being a man of integrity, a man of great ability—that he is trustworthy. I give "glory" to the man through my faith in him. The Bible says that Abraham "staggered not at the promise of God through unbelief; but was strong in faith, giving glory to God; and being fully persuaded that, what he had promised, he was able also to perform" (Romans 4:20,21). Abraham was a man of great faith in God. Remember, that is not a compliment to Abraham. He merely caught a glimpse of God's incredible ability, His impeccable integrity, and His wonderful faithfulness to keep every promise He makes. His faith gave "glory" to a faithful God.

As far as God is concerned, if you belong to Jesus, you are a VIP. You can boldly come before the throne of grace (Hebrews 4:16). You have access to the King *because you are the son or daughter of the King*. When you were a child, did you have to grovel to get your needs met by your mom or dad? I hope not.

So, when you pray, don't say, "Oh God, I *hope* you will supply my needs." Instead say something like, "Father, thank You that You keep *every* promise You make. Your Word says that You will supply *all* my needs according to Your riches in glory by Christ Jesus (Philippians 4:19). Therefore, I thank You that You will do this thing for my family. I ask this in the wonderful name of Jesus. Amen."

2. How do you get "clean hands and a pure heart"? Simply by confessing your sins to God through Jesus Christ, whose blood cleanses from all sin (1 John 1:7–9). God will not only forgive your every sin, He promises to *forget* them (Hebrews 8:12). He will even justify you based on the sacrifice of the Savior. This means He will count it as though you have never sinned in the first place. He will make you pure in His sight—sinless. He will even "purge" your conscience, so that you will no longer have a sense of guilt that you sinned. That's what it means to be "justified by faith." That's why you need to soak yourself in Holy Scripture; read the letters to the churches and see the wonderful things God has done for us through the cross of Calvary. If you don't bother to read the "will," you won't have any idea what has been given to you.

3. How do you pray "genuine heartfelt prayers"? Simply by keeping yourself in the love of God. If the love of God is in you, you will never pray hypocritical or selfish prayers. Just talk to your heavenly Father as candidly and intimately as a young child, nestled on Daddy's lap, would talk to his earthly father. How would you feel if every day your child pulled out a pre-written statement to dryly recite to you, rather than pouring out the events and emotions of that day? God wants to hear from your heart. When your prayer-life is pleasing to God, He will reward you openly (Matthew 6:6).   *(continued)*

(6:9 continued)

4. How do you know you're praying to "the God revealed in Scripture"? Study the Word. Don't accept the image of God portrayed by the world, even though it appeals to the natural mind. A kind, gentle Santa Claus figure, dispensing good things with no sense of justice or truth, appeals to guilty sinners.

Look to the thunderings and lightnings of Mount Sinai. Gaze at Jesus on the cross of Calvary—hanging in unspeakable agony because of the justice of a holy God. Such thoughts tend to banish idolatry.

For the next principle of growth, see 2 Corinthians 4:4 footnote.

ses, your heavenly Father will also forgive you:

15 But if you forgive not men their trespasses, neither will your Father forgive your trespasses.

16 Moreover when you fast, be not, as the hypocrites, of a sad countenance: for they disfigure their faces, that they may appear to men to fast. Verily I say to you, They have their reward.

17 But you, when you fast, anoint your head, and wash your face;

18 That you appear not to men to fast, but to your Father which is in secret: and your Father, which sees in secret, shall reward you openly.

19 Lay not up for yourselves treasures upon earth, where moth and rust corrupts, and where thieves break through and steal:

20 But lay up for yourselves treasures in heaven, where neither moth nor rust corrupts, and where thieves do not break through nor steal:

21 For where your treasure is, there will your heart be also.

22 The light of the body is the eye: if therefore your eye be single, your whole body shall be full of light.

23 But if your eye be evil, your whole body shall be full of darkness. If therefore the light that is in you be darkness, how great is that darkness!

24 **No man can serve two masters: for either he will hate the one, and love the other; or else he will hold to the one, and despise the other. You cannot serve God and mammon.**

25 Therefore I say to you, Take no thought for your life, what you shall eat, or what you shall drink; nor yet for your body, what you shall put on. Is not the life more than meat, and the body than raiment?

26 Behold the fowls of the air: for they sow not, neither do they reap, nor gather into barns; yet your heavenly Father feeds them. Are you not much better than they?

27 Which of you by taking thought can add one cubit to his stature?

28 And why take thought for raiment? Consider the lilies of the field, how they grow; they toil not, neither do they spin:

29 And yet I say to you, That even Solomon in all his glory was not arrayed like one of these.

30 Wherefore, if God so clothe the grass of the field, which to day is, and tomorrow is cast into the oven, shall he not much more clothe you, O you of little faith?

31 Therefore take no thought, saying, What shall we eat? or, What shall we drink? or, Wherewithal shall we be clothed?

32 (For after all these things do the Gentiles seek:) for your heavenly Father knows that you have need of all these things.

6:12 See Proverbs 26:12 footnote.

6:26 Man is the pinnacle of God's earthly creation. He is not a mere part of the evolutionary process having to yield to the rights of animals. Jesus said that mankind is "much better" than birds and sheep (Matthew 12:12). He is to subdue the earth and have dominion over it (Genesis 1:28) by bringing its vast resources into submission. All were created for him by the infinite genius and loving hand of Almighty God. See also Psalm 8:6–8 footnote.

THE FUNCTION OF THE LAW

7:6 "Just as the world was not ready for the New Testament before it received the Old, just as the Jews were not prepared for the ministry of Christ until John the Baptist had gone before Him with his claimant call to repentance, so the unsaved are in no condition today for the gospel till the Law be applied to their hearts, for 'by the Law is the knowledge of sin.' It is a waste of time to sow seed on ground which has never been ploughed or spaded! To present the vicarious sacrifice of Christ to those whose dominant passion is to take fill of sin, is to give that which is holy to the dogs." *A. W. Pink*

33 But seek first the kingdom of God, and his righteousness; and all these things shall be added to you.

34 Take therefore no thought for the morrow: for the morrow shall take thought for the things of itself. Sufficient to the day is the evil thereof.

CHAPTER 7

J UDGE not, that you be not judged.
2 For with what judgment you judge, you shall be judged: and with what measure you mete, it shall be measured to you again.
3 And why behold the mote that is in your brother's eye, but consider not the beam that is in your own eye?

4 Or how will you say to your brother, Let me pull out the mote out of your eye; and, behold, a beam is in your own eye?
5 You hypocrite, first cast out the beam out of your own eye; and then shall you see clearly to cast out the mote out of your brother's eye.
6 Give not that which is holy to the dogs, neither cast your pearls before swine, lest they trample them under their feet, and turn again and rend you.
7 Ask, and it shall be given you; seek, and you shall find; knock, and it shall be opened to you:
8 For every one that asks receives; and he that seeks finds; and to him that knocks it shall be opened.
9 Or what man is there of you, whom if his son ask bread, will he give him a stone?
10 Or if he ask a fish, will he give him a serpent?
11 If you then, being evil, know how to give good gifts to your children, how much more shall your Father which is in heaven give good things to them that ask him?
12 Therefore all things whatsoever you would that men should do to you, do you even so to them: for this is the law and the prophets.
13 Enter in at the strait gate: for wide is the gate, and broad is the way, that leads

6:31–33 Seek first His kingdom. Think about how the Lord must feel when He sees us spending so much more energy satisfying and gratifying self while neglecting our commitments to Him. We spend so little time obeying His commandment to warn sinners to flee from the wrath to come. When we consider what He's done for us, our excuses fall short. It is as we seek *first* His kingdom that "all these things shall be added to you" (v. 33).

"The unmortified Christian and the heathen are of the same religion, and the deity they truly worship is the god of this world. What shall we eat? What shall we drink? What shall we wear? And how shall we pass away our time? Which way may we gather and perpetuate our names and families in the earth? It is a mournful reflection, but a truth which will not be denied, that these worldly lusts fill up a great part of the study, care and conversation of Christendom.

"The false notion that they may be children of God while in a state of disobedience to his holy commandments, and disciples of Jesus though they revolt from his cross, and members of his true church, which is without spot or wrinkle, notwithstanding their lives are full of spots and wrinkles, is of all other deceptions upon themselves the most pernicious to their eternal condition for they are at peace in sin and under a security in their transgression." *William Penn*

to destruction, and many there be which go in thereat:

14 Because strait is the gate, and narrow is the way, which leads to life, and few there be that find it.

15 Beware of false prophets, which come to you in sheep's clothing, but inwardly they are ravening wolves.

16 You shall know them by their fruits. Do men gather grapes of thorns, or figs of thistles?

17 Even so every good tree brings forth good fruit; but a corrupt tree brings forth evil fruit.

18 A good tree cannot bring forth evil fruit, neither can a corrupt tree bring forth good fruit.

19 Every tree that brings not forth good fruit is hewn down, and cast into the fire.

20 Wherefore by their fruits you shall know them.

21 Not every one that says to me, Lord, Lord, shall enter into the kingdom of heaven; but he that does the will of my Father which is in heaven.

22 Many will say to me in that day, Lord, Lord, have we not prophesied in your name? and in your name have cast out devils? and in your name done many wonderful works?

23 And then will I profess to them, I nev-er knew you: depart from me, you that work iniquity.

24 Therefore whosoever hears these sayings of mine, and does them, I will liken him to a wise man, which built his house upon a rock:

25 And the rain descended, and the floods came, and the winds blew, and beat upon that house; and it fell not: for it was founded upon a rock.

> The number one reason people don't share their faith is that their walk doesn't match their talk.
>
> **MARK CAHILL**

26 And every one that hears these sayings of mine, and does them not, shall be likened to a foolish man, which built his house upon the sand:

27 And the rain descended, and the floods came, and the winds blew, and beat upon that house; and it fell: and great was the fall of it.

28 And it came to pass, when Jesus had ended these sayings, the people were astonished at his doctrine:

29 For he taught them as one having authority, and not as the scribes.

7:15 In Deuteronomy 18:20–22, the Bible proclaims capital punishment for a prophet who wasn't one hundred percent correct. Many think that the 16th-century astrologer Nostradamus was a prophet from God. However, only those who are ignorant of Bible prophecy will be impressed with the prophecies of Nostradamus. He was a false prophet who read the Bible in secret, stole its prophecies, and claimed them as his own.

7:22,23 These are perhaps the most frightening verses in the Bible. Vast multitudes of professing Christians fit into the category spoken of here. They call Jesus "Lord," but they practice lawlessness. They profess faith in Jesus, but have no regard for the divine Law. They tell "fibs" or "white" lies, take things that belong to others, have a roaming eye for the opposite sex, etc. They are liars, thieves, and adulterers at heart, who will be cast from the gates of heaven into the jaws of hell.

7:26 False converts. The foolish man was the one who heard the sayings of Jesus, but did not obey them. It's not the world that hears the sayings of Jesus and doesn't obey them. Most know only the "Golden Rule" and "Judge not," and even then their understanding is darkened. However, the Church is filled with false converts who sit among God's people and hear His words, but don't obey them. They build their house on sand rather than on the firm foundation of Jesus Christ and His words. *A. W. Tozer* said, "It is my opinion that tens of thousands of people, if not millions, have been brought into some kind of religious experience by accepting Christ, and they have not been saved." See Matthew 13:24–30 footnote.

CHAPTER 8

WHEN he was come down from the mountain, great multitudes followed him.

2 And, behold, there came a leper and worshipped him, saying, Lord, if you will, you can make me clean.

3 And Jesus put forth his hand, and touched him, saying, I will; be clean. And immediately his leprosy was cleansed.

4 And Jesus said to him, See you tell no man; but go your way, show yourself to the priest, and offer the gift that Moses commanded, for a testimony to them.

5 And when Jesus was entered into Capernaum, there came to him a centurion, beseeching him,

6 And saying, Lord, my servant lies at home sick of the palsy, grievously tormented.

7 And Jesus said to him, I will come and heal him.

8 The centurion answered and said, Lord, I am not worthy that you should come under my roof: but speak the word only, and my servant shall be healed.

9 For I am a man under authority, having soldiers under me: and I say to this man, Go, and he goes; and to another, Come, and he comes; and to my servant, Do this, and he does it.

10 When Jesus heard it, he marveled, and said to them that followed, Verily I say to you, I have not found so great faith, no, not in Israel.

11 And I say to you, That many shall come from the east and west, and shall sit down with Abraham, and Isaac, and Jacob, in the kingdom of heaven.

12 But the children of the kingdom shall be cast out into outer darkness: there shall be weeping and gnashing of teeth.

13 And Jesus said to the centurion, Go your way; and as you have believed, so be it done to you. And his servant was healed in the selfsame hour.

14 And when Jesus was come into Peter's house, he saw his wife's mother laid, and sick of a fever.

15 And he touched her hand, and the fever left her: and she arose, and ministered to them.

16 When the even was come, they brought to him many that were possessed with devils: and he cast out the spirits with his word, and healed all that were sick:

17 That it might be fulfilled which was spoken by Isaiah the prophet, saying, Him-

---

8:2 Was Jesus God in human form? See John 8:58.

Jehovah's Witnesses: Was Jesus God, manifest in human form? The Bible tells us: "As Peter was coming in, Cornelius met him, and fell down at his feet, and worshipped him. But Peter took him up, saying, Stand up; I myself also am a man" (Acts 10:25,26). Peter refused worship in light of the Law that said, "You shall worship the Lord your God, and Him only you shall serve." In Revelation 19:10, when the apostle John saw an angel, he said, "I fell at his feet to worship him. And he said to me, See you do it not: I am your fellow-servant, and of your brethren that have the testimony of Jesus: worship God." Even the angel of the Lord refused to be worshipped.

However, here are many more verses showing that Jesus allowed Himself to be worshipped, simply because He was God "manifest in the flesh": "While he spoke these things to them, behold, there came a certain ruler, and worshipped him, saying, My daughter is even now dead: but come and lay your hand upon her, and she shall live" (Matthew 9:18); "Then they that were in the ship came and worshipped him, saying, Of a truth you are the Son of God" (Matthew 14:33): "Then she came and worshipped him, saying, Lord, help me" (Matthew 15:25); "And as they went to tell his disciples, behold, Jesus met them, saying, All hail. And they came and held him by the feet, and worshipped him" (Matthew 28:9); "When they saw him, they worshipped him: but some doubted" (Matthew 28:17). He received their worship because He was "the image of the invisible God" (Colossians 1:15)—"*God was manifest in the flesh*, justified in the Spirit, seen of angels, preached to the Gentiles, believed on in the world, received up into glory" (1 Timothy 3:16, emphasis added). See also chart "The Deity of Jesus" at John 10:36.

QUESTIONS & OBJECTIONS

8:14   *"How should I witness to someone who belongs to a denomination, who I suspect isn't trusting the Savior?"*

The most effective way to speak about the issues of eternity to a religious person is not to get sidetracked from the essentials of salvation. Upon hearing a person's background, we may feel an obligation to speak to issues such as infant baptism, transubstantiation, etc. However, it is wise rather to build on the points of agreement between the Bible and the person's denomination, such as the virgin birth, the cross, and so on.

One point of agreement will almost certainly be the Ten Commandments. They are the key to bringing any religious person to a saving knowledge of the gospel. After someone is converted to Jesus Christ, the Bible will come alive and he will be led into all truth by the indwelling Holy Spirit. God's Word will then give him light, and he will forsake religious tradition as he is led by God.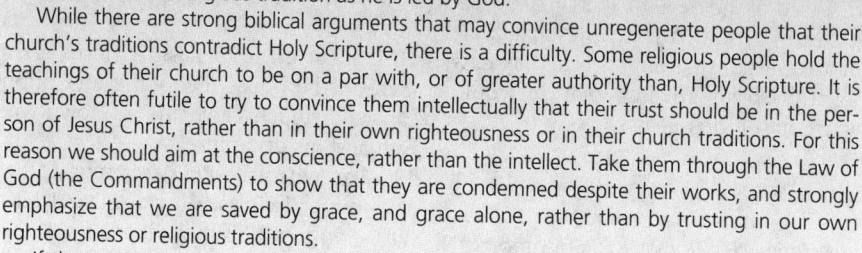

While there are strong biblical arguments that may convince unregenerate people that their church's traditions contradict Holy Scripture, there is a difficulty. Some religious people hold the teachings of their church to be on a par with, or of greater authority than, Holy Scripture. It is therefore often futile to try to convince them intellectually that their trust should be in the person of Jesus Christ, rather than in their own righteousness or in their church traditions. For this reason we should aim at the conscience, rather than the intellect. Take them through the Law of God (the Commandments) to show that they are condemned despite their works, and strongly emphasize that we are saved by grace, and grace alone, rather than by trusting in our own righteousness or religious traditions.

If they are open to the gospel, and are interested in what God's Word says in reference to their church's teachings, they will listen to Scripture. For example, in Matthew 8:14 we see that Peter (whom the Roman Catholic church maintains was the first pope) was married, as were many of the other apostles (see 1 Corinthians 9:5).

---

self took our infirmities, and bare our sicknesses.

18 Now when Jesus saw great multitudes about him, he gave commandment to depart to the other side.

19 And a certain scribe came, and said to him, Master, I will follow you wherever you go.

20 And Jesus said to him, The foxes have holes, and the birds of the air have nests; but the Son of man has no where to lay his head.

21 **And another of his disciples said to him, Lord, suffer me first to go and bury my father.**

22 **But Jesus said to him, Follow me; and let the dead bury their dead.**

23 And when he was entered into a ship, his disciples followed him.

24 And, behold, there arose a great tempest in the sea, insomuch that the ship was covered with the waves: but he was asleep.

25 And his disciples came to him, and awoke him, saying, Lord, save us: we perish.

26 And he said to them, Why are you fearful, O you of little faith? Then he arose, and rebuked the winds and the sea; and there was a great calm.

27 But the men marveled, saying, What manner of man is this, that even the winds and the sea obey him!

28 And when he was come to the other side into the country of the Gergesenes, there met him two possessed with devils, coming out of the tombs, exceeding fierce, so that no man might pass by that way.

29 And, behold, they cried out, saying, What have we to do with you, Jesus, you Son of God? are you come here to torment us before the time?

30 And there was a good way off from them an herd of many swine feeding.

31 So the devils besought him, saying, If you cast us out, suffer us to go away into the herd of swine.

32 And he said to them, Go. And when they were come out, they went into the herd of swine: and, behold, the whole herd of swine ran violently down a steep place into the sea, and perished in the waters.

33 And they that kept them fled, and went their ways into the city, and told every thing, and what was befallen to the possessed of the devils.

34 And, behold, the whole city came out to meet Jesus: and when they saw him, they besought him that he would depart out of their coasts.

. . . . .

Learn how to prove God's existence. See Romans 1:20 footnote.

. . . . . .

CHAPTER 9

AND he entered into a ship, and passed over, and came into his own city.

2 And, behold, they brought to him a man sick of the palsy, lying on a bed: and Jesus seeing their faith said to the sick of the palsy; Son, be of good cheer; your sins be forgiven you.

3 And, behold, certain of the scribes said within themselves, This man blasphemes.

4 And Jesus knowing their thoughts said, Why do you think evil in your hearts?

5 For whether is easier, to say, Your sins be forgiven you; or to say, Arise, and walk?

6 But that you may know that **the Son of man has power on earth to forgive sins,** (then said he to the sick of the palsy,) Arise, take up your bed, and go to your house.

7 And he arose, and departed to his house.

8 But when the multitudes saw it, they marveled, and glorified God, which had given such power to men.

9 And as Jesus passed forth from thence,

THE FUNCTION OF THE LAW

9:12 "Sinners that think they need no physician will not endure the healer's hand. The Law is therefore necessary to give knowledge of sin, so that proud man, who thought he was whole, may be humbled by the discovery of his own great wickedness, and sigh and pant after the grace that is set forth in Christ." *Martin Luther*

he saw a man, named Matthew, sitting at the receipt of custom: and he said to him, Follow me. And he arose, and followed him.

10 And it came to pass, as Jesus sat at meat in the house, behold, many publicans and sinners came and sat down with him and his disciples.

11 And when the Pharisees saw it, they said to his disciples, Why does your Master eat with publicans and sinners?

12 But when Jesus heard that, he said to them, They that be whole need not a physician, but they that are sick.

13 But go and learn what that means, I will have mercy, and not sacrifice: for **I am not come to call the righteous, but sinners to repentance.**

14 Then came to him the disciples of John, saying, Why do we and the Pharisees fast oft, but your disciples fast not?

15 And Jesus said to them, Can the children of the bridechamber mourn, as long as the bridegroom is with them? but the days will come, when the bridegroom shall be taken from them, and then shall they fast.

16 No man puts a piece of new cloth to an old garment, for that which is put in to fill it up takes from the garment, and the rent is made worse.

17 Neither do men put new wine into old bottles: else the bottles break, and the wine runs out, and the bottles perish: but they put new wine into new bottles, and both are preserved.

18 While he spoke these things to them, behold, there came a certain ruler, and

worshipped him, saying, My daughter is even now dead: but come and lay your hand upon her, and she shall live.

19 And Jesus arose, and followed him, and so did his disciples.

20 And, behold, a woman, which was diseased with an issue of blood twelve years, came behind him, and touched the hem of his garment:

21 For she said within herself, If I may but touch his garment, I shall be whole.

22 But Jesus turned him about, and when he saw her, he said, Daughter, be of good comfort; your faith has made you whole. And the woman was made whole from that hour.

23 And when Jesus came into the ruler's house, and saw the minstrels and the people making a noise,

24 He said to them, Give place: for the maid is not dead, but sleeps. And they laughed him to scorn.

25 But when the people were put forth, he went in, and took her by the hand, and the maid arose.

26 And the fame hereof went abroad into all that land.

27 And when Jesus departed thence, two blind men followed him, crying, and saying, You Son of David, have mercy on us.

28 And when he was come into the house, the blind men came to him: and Jesus said to them, Do you believe that I am able to do this? They said to him, Yes, Lord.

29 Then touched he their eyes, saying, According to your faith be it to you.

30 And their eyes were opened; and Jesus straitly charged them, saying, See that no man know it.

31 But they, when they were departed, spread abroad his fame in all that country.

32 As they went out, behold, they brought to him a dumb man possessed with a devil.

33 And when the devil was cast out, the dumb spoke: and the multitudes marveled, saying, It was never so seen in Israel.

34 But the Pharisees said, He casts out devils through the prince of the devils.

35 And Jesus went about all the cities and villages, teaching in their synagogues, and preaching the gospel of the kingdom, and healing every sickness and every disease among the people.

36 But when he saw the multitudes, he was moved with compassion on them, because they fainted, and were scattered abroad, as sheep having no shepherd.

37 *Then said he to his disciples, The harvest truly is plenteous, but the laborers are few;*

38 *Pray therefore the Lord of the harvest, that he will send forth laborers into his harvest.*

9:20 Evolution and blood. "Platelets" play an important role in preventing the loss of blood by beginning a chain reaction that results in blood clotting. As blood begins to flow from a cut or scratch, platelets respond to help the blood clot and to stop the bleeding after a short time.

Platelets promote the clotting process by clumping together and forming a plug at the site of a wound and then releasing proteins called "clotting factors." These proteins start a series of chemical reactions that are extremely complicated. Every step of the clotting must go smoothly if a clot is to form. If one of the clotting factors is missing or defective, the clotting process does not work. A serious genetic disorder known as "hemophilia" results from a defect in one of the clotting factor genes. Because they lack one of the clotting factors, hemophilia sufferers may bleed uncontrollably from even small cuts or scrapes.

To form a blood clot there must be twelve specific individual chemical reactions in our blood. If evolution is true, and if this 12-step process didn't happen in the first generation (i.e., if any one of these specific reactions failed to operate in their exact reaction and order), no creatures would have survived. They all would have bled to death!

9:38 If we are not laborers, we won't obey this command, because our conscience will condemn us. The devil therefore gets two victories: not only does the professing Christian not labor in the harvest fields, but neither does he pray for laborers.

"It is true that [many] are praying for world-wide revival. But it would be more timely, and more scriptural, for prayer to be made to the Lord of the harvest, that He would raise up and thrust forth laborers who would fearlessly and faithfully preach those truths which are calculated to bring about a revival."

A. W. Pink

CHAPTER 10

AND when he had called to him his twelve disciples, he gave them power against unclean spirits, to cast them out, and to heal all manner of sickness and all manner of disease.

2 Now the names of the twelve apostles are these; The first, Simon, who is called Peter, and Andrew his brother; James the son of Zebedee, and John his brother;

3 Philip, and Bartholomew; Thomas, and Matthew the publican; James the son of Alphaeus, and Lebbaeus, whose surname was Thaddaeus;

4 Simon the Canaanite, and Judas Iscariot, who also betrayed him.

5 These twelve Jesus sent forth, and commanded them, saying, Go not into the way of the Gentiles, and into any city of the Samaritans enter not:

6 But go rather to the lost sheep of the house of Israel.

7 *And as you go, preach, saying, The kingdom of heaven is at hand.*

8 *Heal the sick, cleanse the lepers, raise the dead, cast out devils: freely you have received, freely give.*

9 *Provide neither gold, nor silver, nor brass in your purses,*

10 *Nor scrip for your journey, neither two coats, neither shoes, nor yet staves: for the workman is worthy of his meat.*

11 *And into whatsoever city or town you shall enter, inquire who in it is worthy; and there abide till you go thence.*

12 *And when you come into an house, salute it.*

13 *And if the house be worthy, let your peace come upon it: but if it be not worthy, let your peace return to you.*

14 *And whosoever shall not receive you, nor hear your words, when you depart out of that house or city, shake off the dust of your feet.*

15 Verily I say to you, It shall be more tolerable for the land of Sodom and Gomorrha in the day of judgment, than for that city.

16 Behold, I send you forth as sheep in the midst of wolves: be therefore wise as serpents, and harmless as doves.

17 But beware of men: for they will deliver you up to the councils, and they will scourge you in their synagogues;

18 And you shall be brought before governors and kings for my sake, for a testimony against them and the Gentiles.

19 But when they deliver you up, take no thought how or what you shall speak: for it shall be given you in that same hour what you shall speak.

10:16 These verses contradict the "God loves you and has a wonderful plan for your life" promise of modern evangelism. It promises a life of roses without thorns. In reality, Jesus told His disciples that He was sending them among sharp thorns. Their own families would betray them and have them put to death for their faith (v. 21). This is the life Jesus promised believers: we would be hated for His name's sake and would be persecuted. See also John 15:18–21 footnote.

10:22 *God's Love: The Biblical Presentation*

The modern message of the gospel is "God loves you and has a wonderful plan for your life." However, our idea of "wonderful" and the world's may be a little different. Take a sinner through the pages of the Book of Acts and show him the terrifying scene of boulders breaking the bones of Stephen. Then smile and whisper, "*Wonderful...*" Listen together to the sound of a cat-o'-nine-tails as it rips the flesh off the back of the apostle Paul. Follow together the word "suffering" through the Epistles, and see if you can get the world to whisper, "Wonderful!" After such a ride down Honesty Road, they may think the pleasures of sin are a little more attractive than the call to "suffer affliction with the people of God." *John MacArthur* said, "We need to adjust our presentation of the gospel. We cannot dismiss the fact that God hates sin and punishes sinners with eternal torment. How can we begin a gospel presentation by telling people on their way to hell that God has a wonderful plan for their lives?"

Who in the world is going to listen if we are so blatantly honest about the Christian life? Perhaps not as many as are attracted by the talk of a wonderful plan. However, the answer to our dilemma is to make the issue one of righteousness, rather than happiness. This is what Jesus did. He used the Ten Commandments to show sinners the righteous standard of God (Luke 10:25-27; 18:18–20). Once the world sees the perfect standard by which they will be judged, they will begin to fear God, and through the fear of the Lord, men depart from sin (Proverbs 16:6). They will begin to

hunger and thirst after the righteousness that is in Jesus Christ alone.

If you study the New Testament you will see that God's love is almost always given in direct correlation to the cross: herein is love, for God so loved, God commended His love, etc. (See John 3:16; Romans 5:5,6,8; Galatians 2:20; Ephesians 2:4,5; 5:2,25; 1 John 3:16; 4:10; and Revelation 1:5, among others.) The cross is the focal point of God's love for the world. How can we point to the cross without making reference to sin? How can we refer to sin without the Law (Romans 7:7)? The biblical way to express God's love to a sinner is to show him how great his sin is (using the Law—see Romans 7:13; Galatians 3:24), and then give him the incredible grace of God in Christ. This was the key to reaching so many on the Day of Pentecost. They were "devout" Jews who knew the Law and its holy demands, and therefore readily accepted the mercy of God in Christ to escape its fearful wrath.

When you use the Law to show the world their true state, get ready for sinners to thank you. For the first time in their lives, they will see the Christian message as an expression of love and concern for their eternal welfare, rather than of merely proselytizing for a better lifestyle while on this earth.

---

20 For it is not you that speak, but the Spirit of your Father which speaks in you.
21 And the brother shall deliver up the brother to death, and the father the child: and the children shall rise up against their parents, and cause them to be put to death.
22 And you shall be hated of all men for my name's sake: but he that endures to the end shall be saved.
23 But when they persecute you in this city, flee into another: for verily I say to you, You shall not have gone over the cities of Israel, till the Son of man be come.
24 The disciple is not above his master, nor the servant above his lord.
25 It is enough for the disciple that he

10:23 Don't wait around to be martyred. Leave when trouble brews. Paul once left a potential explosive situation by being lowered down a wall in a basket. Sometimes backing off can be humbling, but wise.

be as his master, and the servant as his lord. If they have called the master of the house Beelzebub, how much more shall they call them of his household?

26 *Fear them not therefore: for there is nothing covered, that shall not be revealed; and hid, that shall not be known.*

27 *What I tell you in darkness, that speak in light: and what you hear in the ear, that preach upon the housetops.*

28 *And fear not them which kill the body, but are not able to kill the soul: but rather fear him which is able to destroy both soul and body in hell.*

29 Are not two sparrows sold for a farthing? and one of them shall not fall on the ground without your Father.

30 But the very hairs of your head are all numbered.

31 Fear not therefore, you are of more value than many sparrows.

32 **Whosoever therefore shall confess me before men, him will I confess also before my Father which is in heaven.**

33 **But whosoever shall deny me before men, him will I also deny before my Father which is in heaven.**

34 Think not that I am come to send peace on earth: I came not to send peace, but a sword.

35 For I am come to set a man at variance against his father, and the daughter against her mother, and the daughter in law against her mother in law.

36 And a man's foes shall be they of his own household.

37 **He that loves father or mother more than me is not worthy of me: and he that loves son or daughter more than me is not worthy of me.**

38 **And he that takes not his cross, and follows after me, is not worthy of me.**

39 He that finds his life shall lose it: and he that loses his life for my sake shall find it.

40 He that receives you receives me, and he that receives me receives him that sent me.

41 He that receives a prophet in the name of a prophet shall receive a prophet's reward; and he that receives a righteous man in the name of a righteous man shall receive a righteous man's reward.

42 And whosoever shall give to drink to one of these little ones a cup of cold water only in the name of a disciple, verily I say to you, he shall in no wise lose his reward.

10:23 Did Jesus say that He would return during the lifetime of His disciples? "Another alternative is to take the promise literally and immediately and to interpret the phrase 'before the Son of Man comes' as a reference to the fact that Jesus rejoined the disciples after their mission. This view may be supported by several facts. First, the phrase 'before the Son of Man comes' is never used by Matthew to describe the Second Coming. Second, it fits with a literal understanding of the first part of the verse. The disciples went literally and immediately into 'the cities of Israel' to preach, and Jesus literally and immediately rejoined them after their itinerant ministry." *Norman Geisler* and *Thomas Howe, When Critics Ask*

10:27,28 **Faithful, not fearful, witnesses.** We are to be faithful witnesses for Jesus. When it comes to preaching the gospel, we are to fear only God.

If you are fearful when it comes to witnessing, here's something you can do that doesn't take much courage. Go into a phone booth. Open the phone book to the Yellow Pages. Find "Abortion" and slip a tract in the page. Then look for the category "Escorts" and slip a tract in there. Many phone booths have a door, so you can go in, close the door and do this without fear of being seen. You are not breaking the law, and simply leaving a gospel tract in those two places may not only keep someone from making a terrible life-changing decision, but it may bring them to faith in the Savior.

10:28 **Hell:** For verses warning of its reality, see Matthew 18:9.

10:37 "People, who need people to walk with God, don't walk with God. They walk with people." *Emeal Zwayne*

"We must all mutually share in the knowledge that our existence only attains its true value when we have experienced in ourselves the truth of the declaration: 'He who loses his life shall find it.'"

Albert Schweitzer

CHAPTER 11

A ND it came to pass, when Jesus had made an end of commanding his twelve disciples, he departed thence to teach and to preach in their cities.

2 Now when John had heard in the prison the works of Christ, he sent two of his disciples,

3 And said to him, are you he that should come, or do we look for another?

4 Jesus answered and said to them, Go and show John again those things which you do hear and see:

5 The blind receive their sight, and the lame walk, the lepers are cleansed, and the deaf hear, the dead are raised up, and the poor have the gospel preached to them.

6 **And blessed is he, whosoever shall not be offended in me.**

7 And as they departed, Jesus began to say to the multitudes concerning John, What did you go out into the wilderness to see? A reed shaken with the wind?

8 But what did you go out for to see? A man clothed in soft raiment? behold, they that wear soft clothing are in kings' houses.

9 But what did you go out for to see? A prophet? yea, I say to you, and more than a prophet.

10 For this is he, of whom it is written, Behold, I send my messenger before your face, which shall prepare your way before you.

11 Verily I say to you, Among them that are born of women there has not risen a greater than John the Baptist: notwithstanding he that is least in the kingdom of heaven is greater than he.

12 And from the days of John the Baptist until now the kingdom of heaven suffers violence, and the violent take it by force.

13 For all the prophets and the law prophesied until John.

14 And if you will receive it, this is Elijah, which was for to come.

15 He that has ears to hear, let him hear.

16 But whereunto shall I liken this generation? It is like unto children sitting in the markets, and calling to their fellows,

---

11:11 "If God has called you to be a missionary, your Father would be grieved for you to shrivel down into a king." *Charles Spurgeon*

11:12,13 The Law and the prophets were doing their job in Israel. The prophets established the inspiration of Holy Scripture, while the Law brought the knowledge of sin. When John began to preach that Israel should repent, they flocked to him for the baptism of repentance because the Law convinced them of sin. Just as a drowning man may become "violent" to be saved (and at times have to be knocked out by a lifeguard), so the Law makes a man *desperate* to be saved. It makes him take hold of the kingdom of God "by force."

11:14 This verse is often used to try and justify belief in reincarnation. However, Elijah wasn't reincarnated as John the Baptist. John merely came in the "spirit and power of Elijah" (Luke 1:17). It is appointed unto man *once* to die (see Hebrews 9:27).

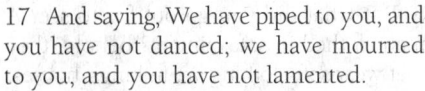
17 And saying, We have piped to you, and you have not danced; we have mourned to you, and you have not lamented.

18 For John came neither eating nor drinking, and they said, He has a devil.

19 The Son of man came eating and drinking, and they said, Behold a man gluttonous, and a winebibber, a friend of publicans and sinners. But wisdom is justified of her children.

20 Then began he to upbraid the cities wherein most of his mighty works were done, because they repented not:

21 Woe to you, Chorazin! woe to you, Bethsaida! for if the mighty works, which were done in you, had been done in Tyre and Sidon, they would have repented long ago in sackcloth and ashes.

22 But I say to you, It shall be more tolerable for Tyre and Sidon at the day of judgment, than for you.

23 And you, Capernaum, which are exalted to heaven, shall be brought down to hell: for if the mighty works, which have been done in you, had been done in Sodom, it would have remained until this day.

24 But I say to you, That it shall be more tolerable for the land of Sodom in the day of judgment, than for you.

25 At that time Jesus answered and said, I thank you, O Father, Lord of heaven and earth, because you have hid these things from the wise and prudent, and have revealed them to babes.

26 Even so, Father: for so it seemed good in your sight.

27 All things are delivered to me of my Father: and no man knows the Son, but the Father; neither knows any man the Father, save the Son, and he to whomsoever the Son will reveal him.

28 **Come to me, all you that labor and are heavy laden, and I will give you rest.**

29 **Take my yoke upon you, and learn of me; for I am meek and lowly in heart: and you shall find rest to your souls.**

30 **For my yoke is easy, and my burden is light.**

CHAPTER 12

AT that time Jesus went on the sabbath day through the corn; and his disciples were an hungered, and began to pluck the ears of corn, and to eat.

2 But when the Pharisees saw it, they said to him, Behold, your disciples do that which is not lawful to do upon the sabbath day.

3 But he said to them, Have you not read what David did, when he was an hungered, and they that were with him;

4 How he entered into the house of God, and did eat the shewbread, which was not lawful for him to eat, neither for them which were with him, but only for the priests?

5 Or have you not read in the law, how that on the sabbath days the priests in the temple profane the sabbath, and are blameless?

6 But I say to you, That in this place is one greater than the temple.

7 But if you had known what this means, I will have mercy, and not sacrifice, you would not have condemned the guiltless.

8 For the Son of man is Lord even of the sabbath day.

9 And when he was departed thence, he went into their synagogue:

10 And, behold, there was a man which had his hand withered. And they asked him, saying, Is it lawful to heal on the sabbath days? that they might accuse him.

11 And he said to them, What man shall there be among you, that shall have one sheep, and if it fall into a pit on the sabbath day, will he not lay hold on it, and lift it out?

12 How much then is a man better than a sheep? Wherefore it is lawful to do well on the sabbath days.

> Mass crusades, to which I have committed my life, will never finish the job; but one to one will.
> **BILLY GRAHAM**

13 Then said he to the man, Stretch forth your hand. And he stretched it forth; and it was restored whole, like as the other.

14 Then the Pharisees went out, and held a council against him, how they might destroy him.

15 But when Jesus knew it, he withdrew himself from thence: and great multitudes followed him, and he healed them all;

16 And charged them that they should not make him known:

17 That it might be fulfilled which was spoken by Isaiah the prophet, saying,

18 Behold my servant, whom I have chosen; my beloved, in whom my soul is well pleased: I will put my Spirit upon him, and he shall show judgment to the Gentiles.

19 He shall not strive, nor cry; neither shall any man hear his voice in the streets.

20 A bruised reed shall he not break, and smoking flax shall he not quench, till he send forth judgment to victory.

21 And in his name shall the Gentiles trust.

22 Then was brought to him one possessed with a devil, blind, and dumb: and he healed him, insomuch that the blind and dumb both spoke and saw.

23 And all the people were amazed, and said, Is not this the son of David?

24 But when the Pharisees heard it, they said, This fellow does not cast out devils, but by Beelzebub the prince of the devils.

25 And Jesus knew their thoughts, and said to them, Every kingdom divided against itself is brought to desolation; and every city or house divided against itself shall not stand:

26 And if Satan cast out Satan, he is divided against himself; how shall then his kingdom stand?

27 And if I by Beelzebub cast out devils, by whom do your children cast them out? therefore they shall be your judges.

28 But if I cast out devils by the Spirit of God, then the kingdom of God is come to you.

29 Or else how can one enter into a strong man's house, and spoil his goods, except he first bind the strong man? and then he will spoil his house.

30 He that is not with me is against me; and he that gathers not with me scatters abroad.

31 Wherefore I say to you, All manner of sin and blasphemy shall be forgiven to men: but the blasphemy against the Holy Spirit shall not be forgiven to men.

32 And whosoever speaks a word against the Son of man, it shall be forgiven him: but whosoever speaks against the Holy Spirit, it shall not be forgiven him, neither in this world, neither in the world to come.

33 Either make the tree good, and his fruit good; or else make the tree corrupt, and his fruit corrupt: for the tree is known by his fruit.

34 O generation of vipers, how can you, being evil, speak good things? for out of the abundance of the heart the mouth speaks.

35 A good man out of the good treasure of the heart brings forth good things: and an evil man out of the evil treasure brings forth evil things.

36 But I say to you, That every idle word that men shall speak, they shall

QUESTIONS & OBJECTIONS

12:39 *"If God gives me some 'sign,' then I will believe."*

The unsaved often want a "sign" from God. This is in spite of the testimony of creation, their conscience, the Bible, and the Christian. The cross is the only thing that can truly convince a sinner of the reality of who Jesus is. Once they understand that the holes in His hands and His feet are there because of their own sin, they will fall at His feet and cry, "My Lord and my God!"

give account thereof in the day of judgment.

37 For by your words you shall be justified, and by your words you shall be condemned.

38 Then certain of the scribes and of the Pharisees answered, saying, Master, we would see a sign from you.

39 But he answered and said to them, An evil and adulterous generation seeks after a sign; and there shall no sign be given to it, but the sign of the prophet Jonah:

40 For as Jonah was three days and three nights in the whale's belly; so shall the Son of man be three days and three nights in the heart of the earth.

41 The men of Nineveh shall rise in judgment with this generation, and shall condemn it: because they repented at the preaching of Jonah; and, behold, a greater

than Jonah is here.

42 The queen of the south shall rise up in the judgment with this generation, and shall condemn it: for she came from the uttermost parts of the earth to hear the wisdom of Solomon; and, behold, a greater than Solomon is here.

43 When the unclean spirit is gone out of a man, he walks through dry places, seeking rest, and finds none.

44 Then he says, I will return into my house from whence I came out; and when he is come, he finds it empty, swept, and garnished.

45 Then goes he, and takes with himself seven other spirits more wicked than himself, and they enter in and dwell there: and the last state of that man is worse than the first. Even so shall it be also to this wicked generation.

12:36 Idle words divide the body. In 1 Kings 3:16–27, the Bible tells of two harlots claiming to be the mother of one child. Solomon revealed his God-given wisdom by suggesting that the child be cut in two, thus exposing the true mother. The false mother preferred to divide the body rather than back down from her claim.

It is interesting to note that both women dwelt in the same house, just as both the wheat and the tares sit alongside each other in the House of God (Matthew 13:24–30,38). Each of the women called Solomon "lord," and both the wheat and tares call Jesus "Lord" (Matthew 7:21). It is not always easy to discern the wheat from the tares because it takes the wisdom of Solomon to do so. Here is wisdom—*the false convert will show his spirit by, without hesitation, dividing the Body of Christ in two, rather than gracefully making a withdrawal.* He will cut a body of believers in half with vicious gossip. He sows discord among the brethren. He is a slave to his tongue, which is a "world of iniquity...set on fire of hell" (James 3:6).

However, the true convert sets a watch at the door of his mouth, and will immediately back away from words that would divide a local church. He knows that "the beginning of strife is as when one lets out water" (Proverbs 17:14). He doesn't become involved in idle talk. He is a peacemaker, a child of God. The fear of God is his guide. He knows that there is not a word on his tongue that God doesn't know, and that on Judgment Day he will give an account for every idle word he speaks.

12:40 How long was Jesus in the tomb? To first-century Jews, any part of a day could be counted as if it were a full day, just as a child born December 31 at 11:59 p.m. is deductible for income-tax purposes for the full year. "Three days and three nights" may simply refer to three twenty-four-hour days (sunset-to-sunset periods), and Jesus was in fact in the tomb during part of three different days.

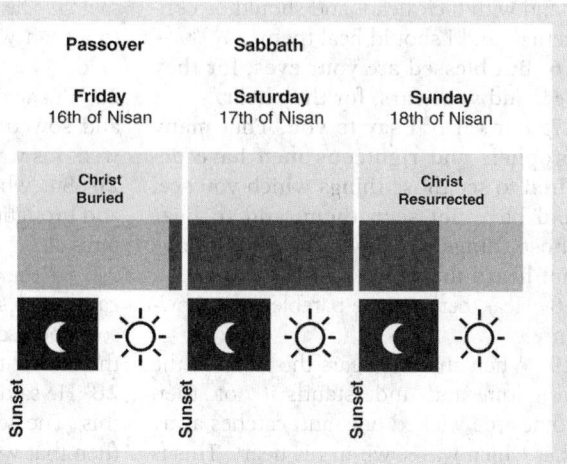

46 While he yet talked to the people, behold, his mother and his brethren stood without, desiring to speak with him.

47 Then one said to him, Behold, your mother and your brethren stand without, desiring to speak with you.

48 But he answered and said to him that told him, Who is my mother? and who are my brethren?

49 And he stretched forth his hand toward his disciples, and said, Behold my mother and my brethren!

50 For whosoever shall do the will of my Father which is in heaven, the same is my brother, and sister, and mother.

CHAPTER 13

THE same day went Jesus out of the house, and sat by the sea side.

2 And great multitudes were gathered together to him, so that he went into a ship, and sat; and the whole multitude stood on the shore.

3 And he spoke many things to them in parables, saying, Behold, a sower went forth to sow;

4 And when he sowed, some seeds fell by the way side, and the fowls came and devoured them up:

5 Some fell upon stony places, where they had not much earth: and forthwith they sprung up, because they had no deepness of earth:

6 And when the sun was up, they were scorched; and because they had no root, they withered away.

7 And some fell among thorns; and the thorns sprung up, and choked them:

8 But other fell into good ground, and brought forth fruit, some an hundredfold, some sixtyfold, some thirtyfold.

9 Who has ears to hear, let him hear.

10 And the disciples came, and said to him, Why do you speak to them in parables?

11 He answered and said to them, Because it is given to you to know the mysteries of the kingdom of heaven, but to them it is not given.

12 For whosoever has, to him shall be given, and he shall have more abundance: but whosoever has not, from him shall be taken away even that he has.

13 Therefore speak I to them in parables: because they seeing see not; and hearing they hear not, neither do they understand.

14 And in them is fulfilled the prophecy of Isaiah, which says, By hearing you shall hear, and shall not understand; and seeing you shall see, and shall not perceive:

15 For this people's heart is waxed gross, and their ears are dull of hearing, and their eyes they have closed; lest at any time they should see with their eyes, and hear with their ears, and should under-

stand with their heart, and should be converted, and I should heal them.

16 But blessed are your eyes, for they see: and your ears, for they hear.

17 **For verily I say to you, That many prophets and righteous men have desired to see those things which you see, and have not seen them; and to hear those things which you hear, and have not heard them.**

18 Hear therefore the parable of the sower.

19 When any one hears the word of the kingdom, and understands it not, then comes the wicked one, and catches away that which was sown in his heart. This is he which received seed by the way side.

20 But he that received the seed into stony places, the same is he that hears the word, and anon with joy receives it;

21 Yet has he no root in himself, but endures for a while: for when tribulation or persecution arises because of the word, by and by he is offended.

22 He also that received seed among the thorns is he that hears the word; and the care of this world, and the deceitfulness of riches, choke the word, and he becomes unfruitful.

23 But he that received seed into the good ground is he that hears the word, and understands it; which also bears fruit, and brings forth, some an hundredfold, some sixty, some thirty.

24 Another parable put he forth to them, saying, The kingdom of heaven is likened to a man which sowed good seed in his field:

25 But while men slept, his enemy came and sowed tares among the wheat, and went his way.

26 But when the blade was sprung up, and brought forth fruit, then appeared the tares also.

27 So the servants of the householder came and said to him, Sir, did not you sow good seed in your field? from whence then has it tares?

28 He said to them, An enemy has done this. The servants said to him, Will you then that we go and gather them up?

29 But he said, Nay; lest while you gather up the tares, you root up also the wheat with them.

30 Let both grow together until the harvest: and in the time of harvest I will say to the reapers, Gather together first the tares, and bind them in bundles to burn them: but gather the wheat into my barn.

31 Another parable put he forth to them, saying, The kingdom of heaven is like to a grain of mustard seed, which a man took, and sowed in his field:

32 Which indeed is the least of all seeds: but when it is grown, it is the greatest among herbs, and becomes a tree, so that the birds of the air come and lodge in the branches thereof.

33 Another parable spoke he to them; The kingdom of heaven is like to leaven,

---

13:16 These are not the words of merely a "great teacher." These are the words of God in human form. He was speaking of Himself—blessed are those who see Him and hear His words. He was either the greatest egotist who ever lived, or He was the source of life in the flesh.

13:19 The key difference between the "wayside" hearer in this verse and the "good soil" hearer in verse 19 is understanding. This is why we must use the Law as a "schoolmaster" to bring the knowledge of sin (Galatians 3:24; Romans 3:20). Unless there is understanding as to his true plight, the sinner will not flee to the Savior.

"I had rather be fully understood by ten than admired by ten thousand." *Jonathan Edwards*

13:24–30 The wheat and the tares are the true and the false converts sitting alongside each other until the time of harvest. (See vv. 37–43.) For more on true and false converts, see Matthew 25:12 footnote.

"There are probably more unsaved church people than we can begin to imagine." *Gary Labro*

which a woman took, and hid in three measures of meal, till the whole was leavened.

34 All these things spoke Jesus to the multitude in parables; and without a parable spoke he not to them:

35 That it might be fulfilled which was spoken by the prophet, saying, I will open my mouth in parables; I will utter things which have been kept secret from the foundation of the world.

36 Then Jesus sent the multitude away, and went into the house: and his disciples came to him, saying, Declare to us the parable of the tares of the field.

37 He answered and said to them, He that sows the good seed is the Son of man;

38 The field is the world; the good seed are the children of the kingdom; but the tares are the children of the wicked one;

39 The enemy that sowed them is the devil; the harvest is the end of the world; and the reapers are the angels.

40 As therefore the tares are gathered and burned in the fire; so shall it be in the end of this world.

41 The Son of man shall send forth his angels, and they shall gather out of his kingdom all things that offend, and them which do iniquity;

42 And shall cast them into a furnace of fire: there shall be wailing and gnashing of teeth.

43 Then shall the righteous shine forth as the sun in the kingdom of their Father. Who has ears to hear, let him hear.

44 Again, the kingdom of heaven is like to treasure hid in a field; the which when a man has found, he hides, and for joy thereof goes and sells all that he has, and buys that field.

45 Again, the kingdom of heaven is like to a merchant man, seeking goodly pearls:

46 Who, when he had found one pearl of great price, went and sold all that he had, and bought it.

47 Again, the kingdom of heaven is like to a net, that was cast into the sea, and gathered of every kind:

48 Which, when it was full, they drew to shore, and sat down, and gathered the good into vessels, but cast the bad away.

49 So shall it be at the end of the world: the angels shall come forth, and sever the wicked from among the just,

50 And shall cast them into the furnace of fire: there shall be wailing and gnashing of teeth.

51 Jesus said to them, Have you understood all these things? They said to him, Yea, Lord.

52 Then said he to them, Therefore every scribe which is instructed unto the kingdom of heaven is like to a man that is an householder, which brings forth out of his treasure things new and old.

53 And it came to pass, that when Jesus had finished these parables, he departed thence.

54 And when he was come into his own country, he taught them in their synagogue, insomuch that they were astonished, and said, Whence has this man this wisdom, and these mighty works?

55 Is not this the carpenter's son? is not his mother called Mary? and his brethren, James, and Joses, and Simon, and Judas?

56 And his sisters, are they not all with us? Whence then has this man all these things?

57 And they were offended in him. But Jesus said to them, A prophet is not without honor, save in his own country, and in his own house.

58 And he did not many mighty works there because of their unbelief.

CHAPTER 14

AT that time Herod the tetrarch heard of the fame of Jesus,

2 And said to his servants, This is John the Baptist; he is risen from the dead;

13:34,35 Messianic prophecy fulfilled: "I will open my mouth in a parable: I will utter dark sayings of old" (Psalm 78:2). See Matthew 26:15 footnote.

and therefore mighty works do show forth themselves in him.

3 For Herod had laid hold on John, and bound him, and put him in prison for Herodias' sake, his brother Philip's wife.

4 For John said to him, It is not lawful for you to have her.

5 And when he would have put him to death, he feared the multitude, because they counted him as a prophet.

6 But when Herod's birthday was kept, the daughter of Herodias danced before them, and pleased Herod.

7 Whereupon he promised with an oath to give her whatsoever she would ask.

8 And she, being before instructed of her mother, said, Give me here John Baptist's head in a charger.

9 And the king was sorry: nevertheless for the oath's sake, and them which sat with him at meat, he commanded it to be given her.

10 And he sent, and beheaded John in the prison.

11 And his head was brought in a charger, and given to the damsel: and she brought it to her mother.

12 And his disciples came, and took up the body, and buried it, and went and told Jesus.

13 When Jesus heard of it, he departed thence by ship into a desert place apart: and when the people had heard thereof, they followed him on foot out of the cities.

14 And Jesus went forth, and saw a great multitude, and was moved with compassion toward them, and he healed their sick.

15 And when it was evening, his disciples came to him, saying, This is a desert place, and the time is now past; send the multitude away, that they may go into the villages, and buy themselves victuals.

16 But Jesus said to them, They need not depart; you give them to eat.

17 And they said to him, We have here but five loaves, and two fishes.

18 He said, Bring them here to me.

19 And he commanded the multitude to sit down on the grass, and took the five loaves, and the two fishes, and looking up to heaven, he blessed, and broke, and gave the loaves to his disciples, and the disciples to the multitude.

20 And they did all eat, and were filled: and they took up of the fragments that remained twelve baskets full.

21 And they that had eaten were about five thousand men, beside women and children.

22 And straightway Jesus constrained his disciples to get into a ship, and to go before him to the other side, while he sent the multitudes away.

23 And when he had sent the multitudes away, he went up into a mountain apart to pray: and when the evening was come, he was there alone.

24 But the ship was now in the midst of the sea, tossed with waves: for the wind was contrary.

25 And in the fourth watch of the night Jesus went to them, walking on the sea.

26 And when the disciples saw him walk-

14:15–21 Sharing the Bread of Life. Compare this incident with 2 Kings 4:42–44, in which one hundred men were fed twenty loaves of barley bread. The Lord instructed Elisha, "Give unto the people, that they may eat...They shall eat, and shall leave thereof." In both incidents, the people were given bread to eat and had some left over. We have eaten from the Bread of Life, and now we must take that Bread to a starving world.

"The disciples watched miraculous healings for hours and then approached the Master and told Him three things: 1) the hour was late; 2) they were in a 'deserted place'; and 3) the multitude needed to eat. Jesus told His disciples that they should be the source of the multitude being fed. The boy's lunch (John 6:9) was the best they could bring, and Jesus did a miracle when they brought the best they had. Then He had them pick up what remained. There were twelve baskets, for twelve disciples. I believe Jesus was saying: 'Now that I showed you how, go feed your own multitude.'" *Mike Smalley*

ing on the sea, they were troubled, saying, It is a spirit; and they cried out for fear.

27 But straightway Jesus spoke to them, saying, Be of good cheer; it is I; be not afraid.

28 And Peter answered him and said, Lord, if it be you, bid me come to you on the water.

29 And he said, Come. And when Peter was come down out of the ship, he walked on the water, to go to Jesus.

30 But when he saw the wind boisterous, he was afraid; and beginning to sink, he cried, saying, Lord, save me.

31 And immediately Jesus stretched forth his hand, and caught him, and said to him, O you of little faith, wherefore did you doubt?

32 And when they were come into the ship, the wind ceased.

33 Then they that were in the ship came and worshipped him, saying, Of a truth you are the Son of God.

34 And when they were gone over, they came into the land of Gennesaret.

35 And when the men of that place had knowledge of him, they sent out into all that country round about, and brought to him all that were diseased;

36 And besought him that they might only touch the hem of his garment: and as many as touched were made perfectly whole.

CHAPTER 15

THEN came to Jesus scribes and Pharisees, which were of Jerusalem, saying,

2 Why do your disciples transgress the tradition of the elders? for they wash not their hands when they eat bread.

3 But he answered and said to them, Why do you also transgress the commandment of God by your tradition?

4 For God commanded, saying, Honor your father and mother: and, He that curses father or mother, let him die the death.

5 But you say, Whosoever shall say to his father or his mother, It is a gift, by whatsoever you might be profited by me;

6 And honor not his father or his mother, he shall be free. Thus have you made the commandment of God of none effect by your tradition.

> Save some, O Christians! By all means, save some. From yonder flames and outer darkness, and the weeping, wailing, and gnashing of teeth, seek to save some! Let this, as in the case of the apostle, be your great, ruling object in life, that by all means you might save some.
>
> **CHARLES SPURGEON**

7 You hypocrites, well did Isaiah prophesy of you, saying,

8 This people draws near to me with their mouth, and honors me with their lips; but their heart is far from me.

9 But in vain they do worship me, teaching for doctrines the commandments of men.

10 And he called the multitude, and said to them, Hear, and understand:

11 Not that which goes into the mouth defiles a man; but that which comes out of the mouth, this defiles a man.

12 Then came his disciples, and said to him, Do you know that the Pharisees were offended, after they heard this saying?

13 But he answered and said, Every plant,

14:28 Peter said, "Lord, if it be you, bid me come to you on the water." Peter had the concept, and Jesus put His blessing on Peter's idea. Peter knew Jesus intimately—he knew the mind of the Master. He knew that his desire wasn't an impertinent presumption, but just a longing to follow the Lord into the realm of the supernatural. Jesus said, "If any man serve me, let him follow me; and where I am, there shall also my servant be: if any man serve me, him will my Father honor" (John 12:26).

which my heavenly Father has not planted, shall be rooted up.

14 Let them alone: they be blind leaders of the blind. And if the blind lead the blind, both shall fall into the ditch.

15 Then answered Peter and said to him, Declare to us this parable.

16 And Jesus said, Are you also yet without understanding?

17 Do not you yet understand, that whatsoever enters in at the mouth goes into the belly, and is cast out into the draught?

18 But those things which proceed out of the mouth come forth from the heart; and they defile the man.

19 For out of the heart proceed evil thoughts, murders, adulteries, fornications, thefts, false witness, blasphemies:

20 These are the things which defile a man: but to eat with unwashed hands defiles not a man.

21 Then Jesus went thence, and departed into the coasts of Tyre and Sidon.

22 And, behold, a woman of Canaan came out of the same coasts, and cried to him, saying, Have mercy on me, O Lord, you Son of David; my daughter is grievously vexed with a devil.

23 But he answered her not a word. And his disciples came and besought him, saying, Send her away; for she cries after us.

24 But he answered and said, I am not sent but to the lost sheep of the house of Israel.

25 Then came she and worshipped him,

saying, Lord, help me.

26 But he answered and said, It is not meet to take the children's bread, and to cast it to dogs.

27 And she said, Truth, Lord: yet the dogs eat of the crumbs which fall from their masters' table.

28 Then Jesus answered and said to her, O woman, great is your faith: be it to you even as you will. And her daughter was made whole from that very hour.

29 And Jesus departed from thence, and came near to the sea of Galilee; and went up into a mountain, and sat down there.

30 And great multitudes came to him, having with them those that were lame, blind, dumb, maimed, and many others, and cast them down at Jesus' feet; and he healed them:

31 Insomuch that the multitude wondered, when they saw the dumb to speak, the maimed to be whole, the lame to walk, and the blind to see: and they glorified the God of Israel.

32 Then Jesus called his disciples to him, and said, I have compassion on the multitude, because they continue with me now three days, and have nothing to eat: and I will not send them away fasting, lest they faint in the way.

33 And his disciples said to him, Whence should we have so much bread in the wilderness, as to fill so great a multitude?

34 And Jesus said to them, How many loaves have you? And they said, Seven, and a few little fishes.

15:19 The spiritual nature of the Law. Notice how the sins named are transgressions of the Moral Law—the Ten Commandments. If civil law can prove that you are planning to assassinate the president, you can be prosecuted and severely punished. That law, however, is limited in its search for evidence—it can't see what a man thinks. Not so with the all-seeing eye of our Creator. His Law searches the heart. He sees "evil thoughts," and requires truth in the inward parts (Psalm 51:6). To *think* hatred is to commit murder (1 John 3:15) and transgress the Sixth Commandment. To *think* lustfully is to commit adultery (Matthew 5:27-28) and transgress the Seventh. Fornication breaks the same Commandment (Galatians 5:19). Then Jesus names theft (Eighth Commandment), false witness (Ninth), and blasphemies (Third). A person cannot lust without breaking the Tenth, and by their nature, these sins transgress the remaining four Commandments. All sin traces in some way back to the Moral Law, for sin is transgression of the Law (1 John 3:4). This is why the Law must be used to bring the knowledge of sin to religious people who are trusting in their own righteous deeds for their salvation.

35 And he commanded the multitude to sit down on the ground.

36 And he took the seven loaves and the fishes, and gave thanks, and broke them, and gave to his disciples, and the disciples to the multitude.

37 And they did all eat, and were filled: and they took up of the broken meat that was left seven baskets full.

38 And they that did eat were four thousand men, beside women and children.

39 And he sent away the multitude, and took ship, and came into the coasts of Magdala.

CHAPTER 16

THE Pharisees also with the Sadducees came, and tempting desired him that he would show them a sign from heaven.

2 He answered and said to them, When it is evening, you say, It will be fair weather: for the sky is red.

3 And in the morning, It will be foul weather to day: for the sky is red and lowring. O you hypocrites, you can discern the face of the sky; but can you not discern the signs of the times?

4 A wicked and adulterous generation seeks after a sign; and there shall no sign be given to it, but the sign of the prophet Jonah. And he left them, and departed.

5 And when his disciples were come to the other side, they had forgotten to take bread.

6 Then Jesus said to them, Take heed and beware of the leaven of the Pharisees and of the Sadducees.

7 And they reasoned among themselves, saying, It is because we have taken no bread.

8 Which when Jesus perceived, he said to them, O you of little faith, why reason among yourselves, because you have brought no bread?

9 Do you not yet understand, neither remember the five loaves of the five thousand, and how many baskets you took up?

10 Neither the seven loaves of the four thousand, and how many baskets you took up?

11 How is it that you do not understand that I spoke it not to you concerning bread, that you should beware of the leaven of the Pharisees and of the Sadducees?

12 Then understood they how that he bade them not beware of the leaven of bread, but of the doctrine of the Pharisees and of the Sadducees.

13 When Jesus came into the coasts of Caesarea Philippi, he asked his disciples, saying, Whom do men say that I the Son of man am?

14 And they said, Some say that you are John the Baptist: some, Elijah; and others, Jeremias, or one of the prophets.

15 **He said to them, But who do you say that I am?**

16 **And Simon Peter answered and said, You are the Christ, the Son of the living God.**

17 **And Jesus answered and said to him, Blessed are you, Simon Barjona: for flesh and blood has not revealed it to you, but my Father which is in heaven.**

18 **And I say also to you, That you are Peter, and upon this rock I will build my church; and the gates of hell shall not prevail against it.**

16:17 Don't see it as your job to convince a Muslim, Mormon, or other unbeliever that Jesus is God. That's the Father's job. Our part is to share the simple message of the gospel.

16:18 Jesus is not saying that Peter is the "rock" upon which He will build His Church. That would contradict Scripture. First Corinthians 3:11 makes it clear that Jesus is the only foundation, and the "rock" is the revelation that He is the Christ, the Son of the Living God. See Romans 9:33.

16:18 "Give me one hundred preachers who fear nothing but sin and desire nothing but God, and I care not a straw whether they be clergymen or laymen, such alone will shake the gates of hell and set up the kingdom of God upon earth." *John Wesley*

SPRINGBOARDS FOR PREACHING AND WITNESSING

Money or Water?

16:26

If you were offered a handful of $1,000 bills or a glass of cool water, which would you choose? The $1,000 bills, of course—*anyone in his right mind would.* However, if you were crawling through a desert, dying of thirst, and you were offered a glass of water or a handful of $1,000 bills, which would you take? The water, of course—*anyone in his right mind would.* That's called "circumstantial priorities." Your priorities change according to your circumstances.

If there were a way to find *everlasting* life, would you want to know about it? The answer is "yes," of course—*anyone in his right mind would.* What the Bible contains may surprise you. The Scriptures speak of riches beyond our wildest dreams—the "riches" of everlasting life—and they are offered in the form of cool, clear water: "Let him that is athirst come. And whosoever will, let him take the water of life freely" (Revelation 22:17). At the moment, you may not be interested in the offer, but on Judgment Day your circumstances will radically change. Then it will be too late.

19 And I will give to you the keys of the kingdom of heaven: and whatsoever you shall bind on earth shall be bound in heaven: and whatsoever you shall loose on earth shall be loosed in heaven.

20 Then charged he his disciples that they should tell no man that he was Jesus the Christ.

21 From that time forth began Jesus to show to his disciples, how that he must go to Jerusalem, and suffer many things of the elders and chief priests and scribes, and be killed, and be raised again the third day.

22 Then Peter took him, and began to rebuke him, saying, Be it far from you, Lord: this shall not be to you.

23 But he turned, and said to Peter, Get you behind me, Satan: you are an offence to me: for you savour not the things that be of God, but those that be of men.

24 **Then said Jesus to his disciples, If any man will come after me, let him deny himself, and take up his cross, and follow me.**

25 **For whosoever will save his life shall lose it: and whosoever will lose his life for my sake shall find it.**

26 **For what is a man profited, if he shall gain the whole world, and lose his own soul? or what shall a man give in exchange for his soul?**

27 For the Son of man shall come in the glory of his Father with his angels; and then he shall reward every man according to his works.

28 Verily I say to you, There be some standing here, which shall not taste of death, till they see the Son of man coming in his kingdom.

CHAPTER 17

AND after six days Jesus took Peter, James, and John his brother, and brought them up into an high mountain apart,

16:23 If you are going to do something in the area of evangelism, be sure you set your face like a "flint" to do so (Isaiah 50:7). A flint is a very hard stone that produces sparks when struck. That's what Peter found when he tried to deter Jesus from doing God's will. The enemy will try to discourage you, and where you least expect it.

16:27 Second coming of Jesus: See Matthew 24:27.

17:1–8 The new birth is a Mount of Transfiguration experience. It is divine revelation as to who Jesus is: He is the One to whom the Law (Moses) and the prophets (Elijah) testify. Those who hear the voice of the Father hear the voice of the Son. They fall on their faces before Jesus and see no one but Him.

2 And was transfigured before them: and his face did shine as the sun, and his raiment was white as the light.

3 And, behold, there appeared to them Moses and Elijah talking with him.

4 Then answered Peter, and said to Jesus, Lord, it is good for us to be here: if you will, let us make here three tabernacles; one for you, and one for Moses, and one for Elijah.

5 While he yet spoke, behold, a bright cloud overshadowed them: and behold a voice out of the cloud, which said, This is my beloved Son, in whom I am well pleased; hear him.

6 And when the disciples heard it, they fell on their face, and were sore afraid.

7 And Jesus came and touched them, and said, Arise, and be not afraid.

8 And when they had lifted up their eyes, they saw no man, save Jesus only.

9 And as they came down from the mountain, Jesus charged them, saying, Tell the vision to no man, until the Son of man be risen again from the dead.

10 And his disciples asked him, saying, Why then say the scribes that Elijah must first come?

11 And Jesus answered and said to them, Elijah truly shall first come, and restore all things.

12 But I say to you, That Elijah is come already, and they knew him not, but have done to him whatsoever they listed. Likewise shall also the Son of man suffer of them.

13 Then the disciples understood that he spoke to them of John the Baptist.

14 And when they were come to the multitude, there came to him a certain man, kneeling down to him, and saying,

15 Lord, have mercy on my son: for he is lunatic, and sore vexed: for often he

"God loves with a great love the man whose heart is bursting with a passion for the impossible."

William Booth

falls into the fire, and oft into the water.

16 And I brought him to your disciples, and they could not cure him.

17 Then Jesus answered and said, O faithless and perverse generation, how long shall I be with you? how long shall I suffer you? bring him here to me.

18 And Jesus rebuked the devil; and he departed out of him: and the child was cured from that very hour.

19 Then came the disciples to Jesus apart, and said, Why could not we cast him out?

20 And Jesus said to them, Because of your unbelief: for verily I say to you, If you have faith as a grain of mustard seed, you shall say to this mountain, Remove hence to yonder place; and it shall remove; and nothing shall be impossible to you.

21 Howbeit this kind goes not out but by prayer and fasting.

17:10 See Matthew 11:13 footnote.

17:20 "The prayer power has never been tried to its full capacity. If we want to see mighty works of Divine power and grace wrought in the place of weakness, failure and disappointment, let us answer God's standing challenge, 'Call to me, and I will answer you, and show you great and mighty things, which you do not know' [Jeremiah 33:3]." *Hudson Taylor*

22 And while they abode in Galilee, Jesus said to them, The Son of man shall be betrayed into the hands of men:

23 And they shall kill him, and the third day he shall be raised again. And they were exceeding sorry.

24 And when they were come to Capernaum, they that received tribute money came to Peter, and said, Does not your master pay tribute?

25 He said, Yes. And when he was come into the house, Jesus prevented him, saying, What do you think, Simon? of whom do the kings of the earth take custom or tribute? of their own children, or of strangers?

26 Peter said to him, Of strangers. Jesus said to him, Then are the children free.

27 Notwithstanding, lest we should offend them, go to the sea, and cast an hook, and take up the fish that first comes up; and when you have opened his mouth, you shall find a piece of money: that take, and give to them for me and you.

CHAPTER 18

AT the same time came the disciples to Jesus, saying, Who is the greatest in the kingdom of heaven?

2 **And Jesus called a little child to him, and set him in the midst of them,**

3 And said, Verily I say to you, Except you be converted, and become as little children, you shall not enter into the kingdom of heaven.

4 Whosoever therefore shall humble himself as this little child, the same is greatest in the kingdom of heaven.

5 And whoso shall receive one such little child in my name receives me.

6 But whoso shall offend one of these little ones which believe in me, it were better for him that a millstone were hanged about his neck, and that he were drowned in the depth of the sea.

7 Woe to the world because of offences! for it must needs be that offences come; but woe to that man by whom the offence comes!

8 **Wherefore if your hand or your foot offend you, cut them off, and cast them from you: it is better for you to enter into life halt or maimed, rather than having two hands or two feet to be cast into everlasting fire.**

9 **And if your eye offend you, pluck it out, and cast it from you: it is better for you to enter into life with one eye, rather than having two eyes to be cast into hell fire.**

10 Take heed that you despise not one of these little ones; for I say to you, That in heaven their angels do always behold the face of my Father which is in heaven.

11 For the Son of man is come to save that which was lost.

12 *How do you think? if a man has an hundred sheep, and one of them be gone astray, does he not leave the ninety and nine, and go into the mountains, and seek*

18:9 Hell: For verses warning of its reality, see Matthew 23:33.

that which is gone astray?

13 *And if so be that he find it, verily I say to you, he rejoices more of that sheep, than of the ninety and nine which went not astray.*

14 *Even so it is not the will of your Father which is in heaven, that one of these little ones should perish.*

15 Moreover if your brother shall trespass against you, go and tell him his fault between you and him alone: if he shall hear you, you have gained your brother.

16 But if he will not hear you, then take with you one or two more, that in the mouth of two or three witnesses every word may be established.

17 And if he shall neglect to hear them, tell it to the church: but if he neglect to hear the church, let him be to you as an heathen man and a publican.

18 Verily I say to you, Whatsoever you shall bind on earth shall be bound in heaven: and whatsoever you shall loose on earth shall be loosed in heaven.

19 Again I say to you, That if two of you shall agree on earth as touching any thing that they shall ask, it shall be done for them of my Father which is in heaven.

20 For where two or three are gathered together in my name, there am I in the midst of them.

21 Then came Peter to him, and said, Lord, how oft shall my brother sin against me, and I forgive him? till seven times?

22 Jesus said to him, I say not to you, Until seven times: but, Until seventy times seven.

23 Therefore is the kingdom of heaven likened to a certain king, which would take account of his servants.

24 And when he had begun to reckon, one was brought to him, which owed him ten thousand talents.

25 But forasmuch as he had not to pay, his lord commanded him to be sold, and his wife, and children, and all that he had, and payment to be made.

26 The servant therefore fell down, and worshipped him, saying, Lord, have patience with me, and I will pay you all.

27 Then the lord of that servant was moved with compassion, and loosed him, and forgave him the debt.

28 But the same servant went out, and found one of his fellow-servants, which owed him an hundred pence: and he laid hands on him, and took him by the throat, saying, Pay me that you owe.

29 And his fellow-servant fell down at his feet, and besought him, saying, Have patience with me, and I will pay you all.

30 And he would not: but went and cast him into prison, till he should pay the debt.

31 So when his fellow-servants saw what was done, they were very sorry, and came and told to their lord all that was done.

32 Then his lord, after that he had called him, said to him, O you wicked servant, I forgave you all that debt, because you desired me:

33 Should not you also have had compassion on your fellow-servant, even as I had pity on you?

34 And his lord was wroth, and delivered him to the tormentors, till he should pay all that was due to him.

35 So likewise shall my heavenly Father do also to you, if you from your hearts forgive not every one his brother their trespasses.

CHAPTER 19

A ND it came to pass, that when Jesus had finished these sayings, he departed from Galilee, and came into the coasts of Judea beyond Jordan;

2 And great multitudes followed him; and he healed them there.

18:11 "We would not see nor realize it (what a distressing and horrible fall in which we lie), if it were not for the Law, and we would have to remain forever lost, if we were not again helped out of it through Christ. Therefore the Law and the gospel are given to the end that we may learn to know both how guilty we are and to what we should again return." *Martin Luther*

QUESTIONS & OBJECTIONS

19:16 *"I need to get my life cleaned up first."*

Those who think that they can clean up their lives don't see their true plight. They are standing guilty before a wrath-filled God. They have been condemned by His Law (John 3:18; Romans 3:19). If a man commits rape and murder and admits to the judge that he is guilty, will the judge let him go just because the man says he will clean up his life? He is in debt to the law and must be punished. We may be able to clean up our lives in the sight of man, but not in the sight of God. The only way we can be cleansed is to repent and trust in the Savior.

3 The Pharisees also came to him, tempting him, and saying to him, Is it lawful for a man to put away his wife for every cause?

4 And he answered and said to them, Have you not read, that he who made them at the beginning made them male and female,

5 And said, For this cause shall a man leave father and mother, and shall cleave to his wife: and they twain shall be one flesh?

6 Wherefore they are no more twain, but one flesh. What therefore God has joined together, let not man put asunder.

7 They said to him, Why did Moses then command to give a writing of divorcement, and to put her away?

8 He said to them, Moses because of the hardness of your hearts suffered you to put away your wives: but from the beginning it was not so.

9 And I say to you, Whosoever shall put away his wife, except it be for fornication, and shall marry another, commits adultery: and whoso marries her which is put away does commit adultery.

10 His disciples said to him, If the case of the man be so with his wife, it is not good to marry.

11 But he said to them, All men cannot receive this saying, save they to whom it is given.

12 For there are some eunuchs, which were so born from their mother's womb: and there are some eunuchs, which were made eunuchs of men: and there be eunuchs, which have made themselves eunuchs for the kingdom of heaven's sake. He that is able to receive it, let him re-

19:3–6 Jesus confirmed that the creation of Adam and Eve was a real historical event when He quoted Genesis 1:27 and 2:24 in His teaching. Genesis is quoted more than sixty times in seventeen books of the New Testament. See also Mark 10:6–9 and 2 Corinthians 11:3 footnotes.

19:4 Evolution—the origin of sexes. Almost all forms of complex life have both male and female—horses, dogs, humans, moths, monkeys, fish, elephants, birds, etc. The male needs the female to reproduce, and the female needs the male to reproduce. *One cannot carry on life without the other.* Which then came first according to the evolutionary theory? If a male came into being before a female, how did the male of each species reproduce *without* females? How is it possible that a male and a female each spontaneously came into being, yet they have complex, complementary reproductive systems? If each sex was able to reproduce without the other, why (and how) would they have developed a reproductive system that requires both sexes in order for the species to survive? See Psalm 139:14 and Mark 10:6 footnotes.

"I myself am convinced that the theory of evolution, especially the extent to which it has been applied, will be one of the great jokes in the history books of the future. Posterity will marvel that so flimsy and dubious an hypothesis could be accepted with the incredible credulity that it has." *Malcolm Muggeridge*, British journalist and philosopher

ceive it.

13 Then were there brought to him little children, that he should put his hands on them, and pray: and the disciples rebuked them.

14 But Jesus said, Suffer little children, and forbid them not, to come to me: for of such is the kingdom of heaven.

15 And he laid his hands on them, and departed thence.

16 And, behold, one came and said to him, Good Master, what good thing shall I do, that I may have eternal life?

17 And he said to him, Why do you call me good? there is none good but one, that is, God: but if you will enter into life, keep the commandments.

18 He said to him, Which? Jesus said, You shall do no murder, You shall not commit adultery, You shall not steal, You shall not bear false witness,

19 Honor your father and your mother: and, You shall love your neighbour as yourself.

20 The young man said to him, All these things have I kept from my youth up: what lack I yet?

21 Jesus said to him, If you will be perfect, go and sell what you have, and give to the poor, and you shall have treasure in heaven: and come and follow me.

22 But when the young man heard that saying, he went away sorrowful: for he had great possessions.

23 Then said Jesus to his disciples, Verily I say to you, That a rich man shall hardly enter into the kingdom of heaven.

24 And again I say to you, It is easier for a camel to go through the eye of a needle, than for a rich man to enter into the kingdom of God.

25 When his disciples heard it, they were exceedingly amazed, saying, Who then can be saved?

26 But Jesus beheld them, and said to them, With men this is impossible; but with God all things are possible.

27 Then answered Peter and said to him, Behold, we have forsaken all, and fol-

USING THE LAW IN EVANGELISM

19:17–22 Here is the Master Evangelist showing us how to deal with a proud, self-righteous person—a typical sinner. This is noticeably different from the approach of modern evangelism. When the man asked how he could obtain eternal life, Jesus did not ask, "Would you like to have the assurance that if you died tonight you would go straight to heaven? You can have that confidence right now simply by acknowledging that you have sinned against God, and by trusting in the finished work of Calvary's cross. Would you like me to lead you in prayer right now so that you can have that assurance?" Instead, Jesus pointed him to the Law so that he could recognize his sin. Biblical evangelism is always "Law to the proud, grace to the humble." *John Newton* said, "My grand point in preaching is to break the hard heart and to heal the broken one."

This young man is a prime example of an unregenerate person. He had no understanding of the word "good." Jesus reproved him, then gently gave him five horizontal Commandments—those dealing with his fellow man. When the man revealed his self-righteousness, Jesus showed him that in his vertical relationship with God he had transgressed the First of the Ten Commandments. God wasn't foremost in his life. The rich young man loved his money, and the Scriptures make it clear that we cannot serve God and mammon (money). The Law brought him "the knowledge of sin."

In light of the way most Christians share the gospel, Jesus failed because He didn't get a "decision." However, heaven doesn't rejoice over "decisions." It reserves its rejoicing for repentance, and there can be no repentance without a God-given knowledge of sin—and that, according to Scripture, can come only by the Law (Romans 7:7). See Mark 10:17 and John 4:7 comments.

lowed you; what shall we have therefore?

28 And Jesus said to them, Verily I say to you, That you which have followed me, in the regeneration when the Son of man shall sit in the throne of his glory, you also shall sit upon twelve thrones, judging the twelve tribes of Israel.

29 And every one that has forsaken houses, or brethren, or sisters, or father, or mother, or wife, or children, or lands, for my name's sake, shall receive an hundredfold, and shall inherit everlasting life.
30 But many that are first shall be last; and the last shall be first.

CHAPTER 20

FOR the kingdom of heaven is like to a man that is an householder, which went out early in the morning to hire laborers into his vineyard.
2 And when he had agreed with the laborers for a penny a day, he sent them into his vineyard.
3 And he went out about the third hour, and saw others standing idle in the marketplace,
4 And said to them; Go also into the vineyard, and whatsoever is right I will give you. And they went their way.
5 Again he went out about the sixth and ninth hour, and did likewise.
6 And about the eleventh hour he went out, and found others standing idle, and said to them, Why do you stand here all the day idle?
7 They said to him, Because no man has hired us. He said to them, Go also into the vineyard; and whatsoever is right, that shall you receive.
8 So when even was come, the lord of the vineyard said to his steward, Call the laborers, and give them their hire, beginning from the last to the first.

9 And when they came that were hired about the eleventh hour, they received every man a penny.
10 But when the first came, they supposed that they should have received more; and they likewise received every man a penny.
11 And when they had received it, they murmured against the goodman of the house,
12 Saying, These last have wrought but one hour, and you have made them equal to us, which have borne the burden and heat of the day.
13 But he answered one of them, and said, Friend, I do you no wrong: did not you agree with me for a penny?
14 Take what is yours, and go your way: I will give to this last, even as to you.
15 Is it not lawful for me to do what I will with mine own? Is your eye evil, because I am good?
16 So the last shall be first, and the first last: for many be called, but few chosen.
17 And Jesus going up to Jerusalem took the twelve disciples apart in the way, and said to them,
18 Behold, we go up to Jerusalem; and the Son of man shall be betrayed to the chief priests and to the scribes, and they shall condemn him to death,
19 And shall deliver him to the Gentiles to mock, and to scourge, and to crucify him: and the third day he shall rise again.
20 Then came to him the mother of Zebedee's children with her sons, worship-

---

19:24 The eye of a needle. A common interpretation is that Jerusalem had a main gate, beside which was a smaller gate called "the eye of a needle." When the main gate was closed, a camel had to forsake its load, then get on its knees and crawl through the smaller gate to enter the city. This is what a rich man must do to enter the celestial city. He must forsake his riches and humble himself to enter. Interesting though it may sound, it is unlikely that this is correct, because of the response of both the disciples and Jesus. If that's what Jesus was saying, the disciples would have more than likely responded with something like, "That makes sense." Instead, they were "exceedingly amazed." What Jesus had said *astonished* them. He didn't then respond to their astonishment by saying that it was "difficult" for a camel to get through the eye of the needle. Rather, He used the word "impossible." It would seem therefore that the analogy was to a literal camel and a literal needle.

"The gate of heaven, though it is so wide that the greatest sinner may enter, is nevertheless so low that pride can never pass through it." *Charles Spurgeon*

ping him, and desiring a certain thing of him.

21 And he said to her, What do you want? She said to him, Grant that these my two sons may sit, the one on your right hand, and the other on the left, in your kingdom.

22 But Jesus answered and said, You know not what you ask. Are you able to drink of the cup that I shall drink of, and to be baptized with the baptism that I am baptized with? They said to him, We are able.

23 And he said to them, You shall drink indeed of my cup, and be baptized with the baptism that I am baptized with: but to sit on my right hand, and on my left, is not mine to give, but it shall be given to them for whom it is prepared of my Father.

24 And when the ten heard it, they were moved with indignation against the two brethren.

25 But Jesus called them to him, and said, You know that the princes of the Gentiles exercise dominion over them, and they that are great exercise authority upon them.

26 But it shall not be so among you: but whosoever will be great among you, let him be your minister;

27 And whosoever will be chief among you, let him be your servant:

28 Even as the Son of man came not to be ministered unto, but to minister, and to give his life a ransom for many.

29 And as they departed from Jericho, a great multitude followed him.

30 And, behold, two blind men sitting by the way side, when they heard that Jesus passed by, cried out, saying, Have mercy on us, O Lord, you Son of David.

31 And the multitude rebuked them, because they should hold their peace: but they cried the more, saying, Have mercy on us, O Lord, you Son of David.

32 And Jesus stood still, and called them, and said, What will you that I shall do to you?

33 They said to him, Lord, that our eyes may be opened.

34 So Jesus had compassion on them, and touched their eyes: and immediately their eyes received sight, and they followed him.

· · · · ·

*For the Bible's uniqueness,
see Psalm 119:105 footnote.*

· · · · ·

CHAPTER 21

AND when they drew near to Jerusalem, and were come to Bethphage, to the mount of Olives, then sent Jesus two disciples,

2 Saying to them, Go into the village over against you, and straightway you shall find an ass tied, and a colt with her: loose them, and bring them to me.

3 And if any man says anything to you, you shall say, The Lord has need of them; and straightway he will send them.

4 All this was done, that it might be fulfilled which was spoken by the prophet, saying,

5 Tell the daughter of Zion, Behold, your King comes to you, meek, and sitting upon an ass, and a colt the foal of an ass.

6 And the disciples went, and did as Jesus commanded them,

7 And brought the ass, and the colt, and put on them their clothes, and they set

---

20:28 "If the sinless Christ, who is literally God in human flesh and Lord of all, would so humble Himself for us, we dare not denigrate humility or aspire to self-esteem instead of lowliness...Do you want to be blessed? Develop a servant's heart. If Jesus can step down from His glorious equality with God to become a man, and then further humble Himself to be a servant and wash the feet of twelve undeserving sinners—then humble Himself to die so horribly on our behalf, surely we ought to be willing to suffer any indignity to serve Him." *John MacArthur*, "Humility," *Moody Magazine*

him thereon.

8 And a very great multitude spread their garments in the way; others cut down branches from the trees, and strawed them in the way.

9 And the multitudes that went before, and that followed, cried, saying, Hosanna to the Son of David: Blessed is he that comes in the name of the Lord; Hosanna in the highest.

10 And when he was come into Jerusalem, all the city was moved, saying, Who is this?

11 And the multitude said, This is Jesus the prophet of Nazareth of Galilee.

12 And Jesus went into the temple of God, and cast out all them that sold and bought in the temple, and overthrew the tables of the moneychangers, and the seats of them that sold doves,

13 And said to them, It is written, My house shall be called the house of prayer; but you have made it a den of thieves.

14 And the blind and the lame came to him in the temple; and he healed them.

15 And when the chief priests and scribes saw the wonderful things that he did, and the children crying in the temple, and saying, Hosanna to the Son of David; they were sore displeased,

16 And said to him, Hear what these say? And Jesus said to them, Yea; have you never read, Out of the mouth of babes and sucklings you have perfected praise?

17 And he left them, and went out of the city into Bethany; and he lodged there.

18 Now in the morning as he returned into the city, he hungered.

19 And when he saw a fig tree in the way, he came to it, and found nothing thereon, but leaves only, and said to it, Let no fruit grow on you henceforward

for ever. And presently the fig tree withered away.

20 And when the disciples saw it, they marveled, saying, How soon is the fig tree withered away!

21 Jesus answered and said to them, Verily I say to you, If you have faith, and doubt not, you shall not only do this which is done to the fig tree, but also if you shall say to this mountain, Be removed, and be cast into the sea; it shall be done.

22 And all things, whatsoever you shall ask in prayer, believing, you shall receive.

23 And when he was come into the temple, the chief priests and the elders of the people came to him as he was teaching, and said, By what authority do you do these things? and who gave you this authority?

24 And Jesus answered and said to them, I also will ask you one thing, which if you tell me, I in like wise will tell you by what authority I do these things.

25 The baptism of John, whence was it? from heaven, or of men? And they reasoned with themselves, saying, If we shall say, From heaven; he will say to us, Why did you not then believe him?

26 But if we shall say, Of men; we fear the people; for all hold John as a prophet.

27 And they answered Jesus, and said, We cannot tell. And he said to them, Neither tell I you by what authority I do these things.

28 But what do you think? A certain man had two sons; and he came to the first, and said, Son, go work to day in my vineyard.

29 He answered and said, I will not: but afterward he repented, and went.

30 And he came to the second, and said likewise. And he answered and said, I

21:12,13 See Mark 11:15 footnote. "Genuine outrage is not just a permissible reaction to the hard-pressed Christian; God himself feels it, and so should the Christian in the presence of pain, cruelty, violence, and injustice. God, who is the Father of Jesus Christ, is neither impersonal nor beyond good and evil. By the absolute immutability of His character, He is implacably opposed to evil and outraged by it." *Os Guinness*

"Tolerance is a virtue for those who have no convictions." *G. K. Chesterton*

go, sir: and went not.

31 Which of the two did the will of his father? They said to him, The first. Jesus said to them, Verily I say to you, That the publicans and the harlots go into the kingdom of God before you.

32 For John came to you in the way of righteousness, and you believed him not: but the publicans and the harlots believed him: and you, when you had seen it, repented not afterward, that you might believe him.

> Preaching the gospel is to us a matter of life and death; we throw our whole soul into it. We live and are happy if you believe in Jesus and are saved. But we are almost ready to die if you refuse the gospel of Christ.
>
> **CHARLES SPURGEON**

33 Hear another parable: There was a certain householder, which planted a vineyard, and hedged it round about, and dug a winepress in it, and built a tower, and let it out to husbandmen, and went into a far country:

34 And when the time of the fruit drew near, he sent his servants to the husbandmen, that they might receive the fruits of it.

35 And the husbandmen took his servants, and beat one, and killed another, and stoned another.

36 Again, he sent other servants more than the first: and they did to them likewise.

37 But last of all he sent to them his son, saying, They will reverence my son.

38 But when the husbandmen saw the son, they said among themselves, This is the heir; come, let us kill him, and let us seize on his inheritance.

39 And they caught him, and cast him out of the vineyard, and slew him.

40 When the lord therefore of the vineyard comes, what will he do to those husbandmen?

41 They said to him, He will miserably destroy those wicked men, and will let out his vineyard to other husbandmen, which shall render him the fruits in their seasons.

42 Jesus said to them, Did you never read in the scriptures, The stone which the builders rejected, the same is become the head of the corner: this is the Lord's doing, and it is marvelous in our eyes?

43 Therefore say I to you, The kingdom of God shall be taken from you, and given to a nation bringing forth the fruits thereof.

44 And whosoever shall fall on this stone shall be broken: but on whomsoever it shall fall, it will grind him to powder.

45 And when the chief priests and Pharisees had heard his parables, they perceived that he spoke of them.

46 But when they sought to lay hands on him, they feared the multitude, because they took him for a prophet.

CHAPTER 22

A ND Jesus answered and spoke to them again by parables, and said,

2 The kingdom of heaven is like to a certain king, which made a marriage for his son,

3 And sent forth his servants to call them that were bidden to the wedding: and they would not come.

4 Again, he sent forth other servants, saying, Tell them which are bidden, Behold, I have prepared my dinner: my oxen and

---

21:44 Those who fall upon the stone of Jesus Christ are broken. He will not despise a broken and contrite heart. However, when Jesus comes in flaming fire, taking vengeance on those who do not know God (2 Thessalonians 1:8), His judgment will "grind them to powder." When you grind something to powder, you do a thorough job. He will judge right down to the thoughts and intents of the heart.

my fatlings are killed, and all things are ready: come to the marriage.

5 But they made light of it, and went their ways, one to his farm, another to his merchandise:

6 And the remnant took his servants, and entreated them spitefully, and slew them.

7 But when the king heard thereof, he was wroth: and he sent forth his armies, and destroyed those murderers, and burned up their city.

8 Then said he to his servants, The wedding is ready, but they which were bidden were not worthy.

9 Go therefore into the highways, and as many as you shall find, bid to the marriage.

10 So those servants went out into the highways, and gathered together all as many as they found, both bad and good: and the wedding was furnished with guests.

11 And when the king came in to see the guests, he saw there a man which had not on a wedding garment:

12 And he said to him, Friend, how did you come in here not having a wedding garment? And he was speechless.

13 Then said the king to the servants, Bind him hand and foot, and take him away, and cast him into outer darkness; there shall be weeping and gnashing of teeth.

14 For many are called, but few are chosen.

15 Then went the Pharisees, and took counsel how they might entangle him in his talk.

16 And they sent out to him their disciples with the Herodians, saying, Master, we know that you are true, and teach the way of God in truth, neither care you for any man: for you regard not the person of men.

17 Tell us therefore, What do you think? Is it lawful to give tribute to Caesar, or not?

18 But Jesus perceived their wickedness, and said, Why tempt me, you hypocrites?

19 Show me the tribute money. And they brought to him a penny.

20 And he said to them, Whose is this image and superscription?

21 They said to him, Caesar's. Then said he to them, Render therefore to Caesar the things which are Caesar's; and to God the things that are God's.

22 When they had heard these words, they marveled, and left him, and went their way.

23 The same day came to him the Sadducees, which say that there is no resurrection, and asked him,

> Believe what you do believe, or else you will never persuade anybody else to believe it.
>
> **CHARLES SPURGEON**

24 Saying, Master, Moses said, If a man die, having no children, his brother shall marry his wife, and raise up seed to his brother.

25 Now there were with us seven brethren: and the first, when he had married a wife, deceased, and, having no issue, left his wife to his brother:

26 Likewise the second also, and the third, to the seventh.

27 And last of all the woman died also.

28 Therefore in the resurrection whose wife shall she be of the seven? for they all had her.

29 Jesus answered and said to them, You do err, not knowing the scriptures, nor the power of God.

30 For in the resurrection they neither marry, nor are given in marriage, but are as the angels of God in heaven.

31 But as touching the resurrection of the dead, have you not read that which

---

22:29 This is the error of the ungodly. They are ignorant of Holy Scripture and they have a darkened understanding of the power of God.

was spoken to you by God, saying,

32 I am the God of Abraham, and the God of Isaac, and the God of Jacob? God is not the God of the dead, but of the living.

33 And when the multitude heard this, they were astonished at his doctrine.

34 But when the Pharisees had heard that he had put the Sadducees to silence, they were gathered together.

35 Then one of them, which was a lawyer, asked him a question, tempting him, and saying,

36 Master, which is the great commandment in the law?

37 Jesus said to him, You shall love the Lord your God with all your heart, and with all your soul, and with all your mind.

38 This is the first and great commandment.

39 And the second is like it, You shall love your neighbour as yourself.

40 On these two commandments hang all the law and the prophets.

41 While the Pharisees were gathered together, Jesus asked them,

42 Saying, What do you think of Christ? whose son is he? They said to him, The Son of David.

43 He said to them, How then does David in spirit call him Lord, saying,

44 The LORD said to my Lord, Sit on my right hand, till I make your enemies your footstool?

45 If David then called him Lord, how is he his son?

46 And no man was able to answer him a word, neither dared any man from that day forth ask him any more questions.

CHAPTER 23

T HEN spoke Jesus to the multitude, and to his disciples,

2 Saying, The scribes and the Pharisees sit in Moses' seat:

3 All therefore whatsoever they bid you observe, that observe and do; but do not after their works: for they say, and do not do.

4 For they bind heavy burdens and grievous to be borne, and lay them on men's shoulders; but they themselves will not move them with one of their fingers.

5 But all their works they do for to be seen of men: they make broad their phylacteries, and enlarge the borders of their garments,

6 And love the uppermost rooms at feasts, and the chief seats in the synagogues,

7 And greetings in the markets, and to be called of men, Rabbi, Rabbi.

8 But be not called Rabbi: for one is your Master, even Christ; and all you are brethren.

9 And call no man your father upon the earth: for one is your Father, which is in heaven.

10 Neither be called masters: for one is

22:36–40   At war with the Law. "There is a war between you and God's Law. The Ten Commandments are against you. The first comes forward and says, 'Let him be cursed. For he denies Me. He has another god beside Me. His god is his belly and he yields his homage to his lust.' All the Ten Commandments, like ten great cannons, are pointed at you today. For you have broken all of God's statutes and lived in daily neglect of all His commands.

"Soul, thou wilt find it a hard thing to go at war with the Law. When the Law came in peace, Sinai was altogether on a smoke and even Moses said, 'I exceeding fear and quake!' What will you do when the Law of God comes in terror; when the trumpet of the archangel shall tear you from your grave; when the eyes of God shall burn their way into your guilty soul; when the great books shall be opened and all your sin and shame shall be punished…Can you stand against an angry Law in that Day?" *Charles Spurgeon*

23:9   Jesus commanded His followers not to call any man "father." The Pharisees loved to be seen and praised by men. They cherished their titles—Rabbi (Matthew 23:8) and Father (Acts 7:2; 22:1). Jesus condemned these titles because of their hypocrisy. Paul used them rightly in reference to those whom he had begotten through the gospel (1 Corinthians 4:15).

your Master, even Christ.

11 But he that is greatest among you shall be your servant.

12 And whosoever shall exalt himself shall be abased; and he that shall humble himself shall be exalted.

13 But woe to you, scribes and Pharisees, hypocrites! for you shut up the kingdom of heaven against men: for you neither go in yourselves, neither suffer them that are entering to go in.

14 Woe to you, scribes and Pharisees, hypocrites! for you devour widows' houses, and for a pretence make long prayer: therefore you shall receive the greater damnation.

15 Woe to you, scribes and Pharisees, hypocrites! for you compass sea and land to make one proselyte, and when he is made, you make him twofold more the child of hell than yourselves.

16 Woe to you, you blind guides, which say, Whosoever shall swear by the temple, it is nothing; but whosoever shall swear by the gold of the temple, he is a debtor!

17 You fools and blind: for whether is greater, the gold, or the temple that sanctifies the gold?

18 And, Whosoever shall swear by the altar, it is nothing; but whosoever swears by the gift that is upon it, he is guilty.

19 You fools and blind: for whether is greater, the gift, or the altar that sanctifies the gift?

20 Whoso therefore shall swear by the altar, swears by it, and by all things thereon.

21 And whoso shall swear by the temple, swears by it, and by him that dwells therein.

22 And he that shall swear by heaven, swears by the throne of God, and by him that sits thereon.

23 Woe to you, scribes and Pharisees, hypocrites! for you pay tithe of mint and anise and cummin, and have omitted the weightier matters of the law, judgment, mercy, and faith: these ought you to have done, and not to leave the other undone.

24 You blind guides, which strain at a gnat, and swallow a camel.

25 Woe to you, scribes and Pharisees, hypocrites! for you make clean the outside of the cup and of the platter, but within they are full of extortion and excess.

26 You blind Pharisee, cleanse first that which is within the cup and platter, that the outside of them may be clean also.

27 Woe to you, scribes and Pharisees, hypocrites! for you are like whited sepulchres, which indeed appear beautiful outward, but are within full of dead men's bones, and of all uncleanness.

28 Even so you also outwardly appear righteous to men, but within you are full of hypocrisy and iniquity.

29 Woe to you, scribes and Pharisees, hypocrites! because you build the tombs of the prophets, and garnish the sepulchres of the righteous,

30 And say, If we had been in the days of our fathers, we would not have been partakers with them in the blood of the prophets.

31 Wherefore be witnesses to yourselves, that you are the children of them which killed the prophets.

32 Fill up then the measure of your fathers.

33 You serpents, you generation of vipers, how can you escape the damnation of hell?

34 Wherefore, behold, I send to you prophets, and wise men, and scribes: and some of them you shall kill and crucify; and some of them shall you scourge in your synagogues, and persecute them from city to city:

35 That upon you may come all the righteous blood shed upon the earth, from the blood of righteous Abel to the blood of Zacharias son of Barachias, whom you slew between the temple and the altar.

36 Verily I say to you, All these things shall come upon this generation.

37 O Jerusalem, Jerusalem, you that kill the prophets, and stone them which are sent to you, how often would I have gathered your children together, even as a hen gathers her chickens under her wings, and you would not!

38 Behold, your house is left to you desolate.

39 For I say to you, You shall not see me henceforth, till you shall say, Blessed is he that comes in the name of the Lord.

CHAPTER 24

AND Jesus went out, and departed from the temple: and his disciples came to him for to show him the buildings of the temple.

2 And Jesus said to them, Do you not see all these things? verily I say to you, There shall not be left here one stone upon another, that shall not be thrown down.

3 And as he sat upon the mount of Olives, the disciples came to him privately, saying, Tell us, when shall these things be? and what shall be the sign of your coming, and of the end of the world?

4 And Jesus answered and said to them, Take heed that no man deceive you.

5 For many shall come in my name, saying, I am Christ; and shall deceive many.

6 And you shall hear of wars and rumors of wars: see that you be not troubled: for all these things must come to pass, but the end is not yet.

7 For nation shall rise against nation, and kingdom against kingdom: and there shall be famines, and pestilences, and earthquakes, in divers places.

8 All these are the beginning of sorrows.

9 Then shall they deliver you up to be afflicted, and shall kill you: and you shall be hated of all nations for my name's sake.

10 And then shall many be offended, and shall betray one another, and shall hate one another.

11 And many false prophets shall rise, and shall deceive many.

12 And because iniquity shall abound, the love of many shall wax cold.

13 But he that shall endure to the end, the same shall be saved.

14 And this gospel of the kingdom shall be preached in all the world for a witness to all nations; and then shall the end

---

23:33 Hell: For verses warning of its reality, see Matthew 25:41.

24:2 Historian Josephus wrote of the temple's destruction by Romans in A.D. 70: "They carried away every stone of the sacred temple, partially in a frenzied search for every last piece of the gold ornamentation melted in the awful heat of the fire. They then plowed the ground level, and since it had already been sown with its defenders' blood, they sowed it with salt" (*Wars of the Jews*). See also Mark 13:2.

24:3 For more signs of the end times, see Mark 13:4.

24:7 The Bible informs us that in the last days there will be earthquakes in different places. This was stated 2,000 years ago, and there is little historical data regarding the size, frequency, and location of earthquakes. One thing is certain: earthquakes in different places are a sign of these times.

come.

15 When you therefore shall see the abomination of desolation, spoken of by Daniel the prophet, stand in the holy place, (whoso reads, let him understand:)
16 Then let them which be in Judea flee into the mountains:
17 Let him which is on the housetop not come down to take any thing out of his house:
18 Neither let him which is in the field return back to take his clothes.
19 And woe to them that are with child, and to them that give suck in those days!
20 But pray that your flight be not in the winter, neither on the sabbath day:
21 For then shall be great tribulation, such as was not since the beginning of the world to this time, no, nor ever shall be.
22 And except those days should be shortened, there should no flesh be saved: but for the elect's sake those days shall be shortened.
23 Then if any man shall say to you, Lo, here is Christ, or there; believe it not.
24 For there shall arise false Christs, and false prophets, and shall show great signs and wonders; insomuch that, if it were possible, they shall deceive the very elect.
25 Behold, I have told you before.
26 Wherefore if they shall say to you, Behold, he is in the desert; go not forth: behold, he is in the secret chambers; believe it not.
27 For as the lightning comes out of the east, and shines even to the west; so shall also the coming of the Son of man be.
28 For wherever the carcass is, there will

the eagles be gathered together.
29 Immediately after the tribulation of those days shall the sun be darkened, and the moon shall not give her light, and the stars shall fall from heaven, and the powers of the heavens shall be shaken:
30 And then shall appear the sign of the Son of man in heaven: and then shall all the tribes of the earth mourn, and they shall see the Son of man coming in the clouds of heaven with power and great glory.
31 And he shall send his angels with a great sound of a trumpet, and they shall gather together his elect from the four winds, from one end of heaven to the other.
32 Now learn a parable of the fig tree; When his branch is yet tender, and puts forth leaves, you know that summer is near:
33 So likewise you, when you shall see all these things, know that it is near, even at the doors.
34 Verily I say to you, This generation shall not pass, till all these things be fulfilled.
35 Heaven and earth shall pass away, but my words shall not pass away.
36 But of that day and hour knows no man, no, not the angels of heaven, but my Father only.
37 But as the days of Noah were, so shall also the coming of the Son of man be.
38 For as in the days that were before the flood they were eating and drinking, marrying and giving in marriage, until the day that Noah entered into the ark,
39 And knew not until the flood came, and took them all away; so shall also the

24:14 "No one is beyond the reach of God to present the gospel to them." *Garry T. Ansdell, D.D.*
24:27 **Second coming of Jesus:** See Matthew 24:39.
24:35 God is able to ensure that His written Word, the Bible, will endure. See Psalm 119:105 footnote.
24:37–39 Jesus referred to Noah as an actual historical person, and the Flood as a bona fide historical event.
24:39 **Second coming of Jesus:** See Matthew 25:31.

24:38,39 Points to Ponder About the Flood and Noah's Ark

By Dr. Kent Hovind

Second Peter 3:3–8 tells us that people who scoff at the Bible are "willingly ignorant" of the Creation and the Flood. In order to understand science and the Bible, we must not be ignorant of those two great events in Earth's history.

1. Over 500 Flood legends from all parts of the world have been found. Most have similarities to the Genesis account.

2. Noah's ark was built only to float, not to sail anywhere. Many ark scholars believe that the ark was a "barge" shape, not a pointed "boat" shape. This would greatly increase the cargo capacity. Scoffers have pointed out that the largest sailing ships were less than 300 feet because of the problem of twisting and flexing the boat. These ships had giant masts and sails to catch the wind. Noah's ark needed neither of those and therefore had far less torsional stress.

3. Even using the small 18-inch cubit (my height is 6'1" and I have a 21-inch cubit), the ark was large enough to hold all the required animals, people, and food with room to spare.

4. The length-to-width ratio of 6 to 1 is what shipbuilders today often use. This is the best ratio for stability in stormy weather.

5. The ark may have had a "moon-pool" in the center. The larger ships would have a hole in the center of the bottom of the boat with walls extending up into the ship. There are several reasons for this feature:

a) It allowed water to go up into the hole as the ship crested waves. This would be needed to relieve strain on longer ships.

b) The rising and lowering water acted as a piston to pump fresh air in and out of the ship. This would prevent the buildup of dangerous gasses from all the animals on board.

c) The hole was a great place to dump waste into the ocean without going outside.

6. The ark may have had large drogue (anchor) stones suspended over the sides to keep it more stable in rough weather. Many of these stones have been found in the region where the ark landed.

7. Noah lived for 950 years. Many Bible schol-

ars believe the pre-Flood people were much larger than modern man. Skeletons over 11 feet tall have been found. If Noah were taller, his cubit (elbow to fingertip) would have been much larger also. This would make the ark larger by the same ratio.

8. God told Noah to bring two of each kind (seven of some), not of each species or variety. Noah had only two of the dog kind, which would include the wolves, coyotes, foxes, mutts, etc. The "kind" grouping is probably closer to our modern family division in taxonomy, and would greatly reduce the number of animals on the ark. Animals have diversified into many varieties in the last 4,400 years since the Flood. This diversification is not anything similar to great claims that the evolutionists teach.

9. Noah did not have to get the animals. God brought them to him (Genesis 6:20, "shall come to thee").

10. Only land-dwelling, air-breathing animals had to be included on the ark ("in which is the breath of life," Genesis 7:15,22).

11. Many animals sleep, hibernate, or become very inactive during bad weather.

12. All animals (and people) were vegetarian before and during the Flood according to Genesis 1:20–30 with Genesis 9:3.

13. The pre-Flood people were probably much smarter and more advanced than people today. The longer life spans, Adam's direct contact with God, and the fact that they could glean the wisdom of many generations that were still alive would greatly expand their knowledge base.

14. The Bible says that the highest mountains were covered by 15 cubits [20 feet] of water (Genesis 7:20). This is half the height of the ark. The ark was safe from scraping bottom at all times.

15. The large mountains, as we have them

(continued on next page)

(24:38,39 continued)
today, did not exist until after the Flood when "the mountains arose and the valleys sank down" (Psalm 104:5–9; Genesis 8:3–8).

16. There is enough water in the oceans right now to cover the earth 8,000 feet deep if the surface of the earth were smooth.

17. Many claim to have seen the ark in recent times in the area in which the Bible says it landed. There are two primary schools of thought about the actual site of the ark. Much energy and time have been expended to prove both views. Some believe the ark is on Mt. Ararat, covered by snow (CBS showed a one-hour special in 1993 about this site). Others believe the ark is seventeen miles south of Mt. Ararat in a valley called "the valley of eight" (eight souls on the ark). The Bible says the ark landed in the "mountains" of Ararat, not necessarily on the mountain itself.

18. The continents were not separated until 100–300 years after the Flood (Genesis 10:25). The people and animals had time to migrate anywhere on earth by then.

19. The top 3,000 feet of Mount Everest (26,000–29,000 feet) is made up of sedimentary rock packed with seashells and other ocean-dwelling animals.

20. Sedimentary rock is found all over the world. Sedimentary rock is formed in water.

21. Petrified clams in the closed position (found all over the world) testify to their rapid burial while they were still alive, even on top of Mount Everest.

22. Bent rock layers, fossil graveyards, and polystrata fossils are best explained by a Flood.

23. People choose to not believe in the Flood because it speaks of the judgment of God on sin (2 Peter 3:3–8).

coming of the Son of man be.

40 Then shall two be in the field; the one shall be taken, and the other left.

41 Two women shall be grinding at the mill; the one shall be taken, and the other left.

42 Watch therefore: for you know not what hour your Lord does come.

43 But know this, that if the goodman of the house had known in what watch the thief would come, he would have watched, and would not have suffered his house to be broken up.

44 Therefore be also ready: for in such an hour as you think not the Son of man comes.

45 Who then is a faithful and wise servant, whom his lord has made ruler over his household, to give them meat in due season?

46 Blessed is that servant, whom his lord when he comes shall find so doing.

47 Verily I say to you, That he shall make him ruler over all his goods.

48 But and if that evil servant shall say in his heart, My lord delays his coming;

49 And shall begin to smite his fellow-servants, and to eat and drink with the drunken;

50 The lord of that servant shall come in a day when he looks not for him, and in an hour that he is not aware of,

51 And shall cut him asunder, and appoint him his portion with the hypocrites: there shall be weeping and gnashing of teeth.

CHAPTER 25

THEN shall the kingdom of heaven be likened to ten virgins, which took their lamps, and went forth to meet the bridegroom.

2 And five of them were wise, and five were foolish.

3 They that were foolish took their lamps, and took no oil with them:

4 But the wise took oil in their vessels with their lamps.

5 While the bridegroom tarried, they all slumbered and slept.

6 And at midnight there was a cry made, Behold, the bridegroom comes; go out to meet him.

7 Then all those virgins arose, and trimmed their lamps.

8 And the foolish said to the wise, Give us of your oil; for our lamps are gone out.

9 But the wise answered, saying, Not so;

lest there be not enough for us and you: but go rather to them that sell, and buy for yourselves.

10 And while they went to buy, the bridegroom came; and they that were ready went in with him to the marriage: and the door was shut.

11 Afterward came also the other virgins, saying, Lord, Lord, open to us.

12 But he answered and said, Verily I say to you, I know you not.

13 Watch therefore, for you know neither the day nor the hour wherein the Son of man comes.

14 For the kingdom of heaven is as a man traveling into a far country, who called his own servants, and delivered to them his goods.

15 And to one he gave five talents, to another two, and to another one; to every man according to his several ability; and straightway took his journey.

16 Then he that had received the five talents went and traded with the same, and made them another five talents.

17 And likewise he that had received two, he also gained another two.

18 But he that had received one went and dug in the earth, and hid his lord's money.

19 After a long time the lord of those servants came, and reckoned with them.

20 And so he that had received five talents came and brought other five talents, saying, Lord, you delivered to me five talents: behold, I have gained beside them five talents more.

21 His lord said to him, Well done, you good and faithful servant: you have been faithful over a few things, I will make you ruler over many things: enter into the joy of your lord.

22 He also that had received two talents came and said, Lord, you delivered to me two talents: behold, I have gained two other talents beside them.

23 His lord said to him, Well done, good and faithful servant; you have been faithful over a few things, I will make you ruler over many things: enter into the joy of your lord.

24 Then he which had received the one talent came and said, Lord, I knew you that you are an hard man, reaping where you have not sown, and gathering where you have not strawed:

25 And I was afraid, and went and hid your talent in the earth: lo, there you have what is yours.

26 His lord answered and said to him, You wicked and slothful servant, you knew that I reap where I sowed not, and gather where I have not strawed:

27 You ought therefore to have put my money to the exchangers, and then at my coming I should have received mine own with usury.

28 Take therefore the talent from him, and give it to him which has ten talents.

29 For to every one that has shall be given, and he shall have abundance: but from him that has not shall be taken away even that which he has.

30 And cast the unprofitable servant into outer darkness: there shall be weeping

---

25:12 False converts. The foolish virgins called Him "Lord," but He said, "I know you not." They were false converts. Jesus warned, "Not every one that says to me, Lord, Lord, shall enter the kingdom of heaven, but he that does the will of my Father which is in heaven. Many will say to me in that day, Lord, Lord, have we not prophesied in your name? and in your name have cast out devils? and in your name done many wonderful works? And then will I profess to them, I never knew you: depart from me, you that work iniquity" (Matthew 7:21–23). This is why we must forsake traditional quick-fix evangelism and do all things according to the pattern given to us in Scripture. For the key to biblical evangelism, see Luke 11:52 footnote.

"The vast majority of people who are members of churches in America today are not Christians. I say that without the slightest fear of contradiction. I base it on empirical evidence of twenty-four years of examining thousands of people." *Dr. D. James Kennedy*

and gnashing of teeth.

31 When the Son of man shall come in his glory, and all the holy angels with him, then shall he sit upon the throne of his glory:

32 And before him shall be gathered all nations: and he shall separate them one from another, as a shepherd divides his sheep from the goats:

33 And he shall set the sheep on his right hand, but the goats on the left.

34 Then shall the King say to them on his right hand, Come, you blessed of my Father, inherit the kingdom prepared for you from the foundation of the world:

35 For I was an hungered, and you gave me meat: I was thirsty, and you gave me drink: I was a stranger, and you took me in:

36 Naked, and you clothed me: I was sick, and you visited me: I was in prison, and you came to me.

37 Then shall the righteous answer him, saying, Lord, when did we see you an hungered, and fed you? or thirsty, and gave you drink?

38 When did we see you a stranger, and took you in? or naked, and clothed you?

39 Or when did we see you sick, or in prison, and came to you?

40 And the King shall answer and say to them, Verily I say to you, Inasmuch as you have done it to one of the least of these my brethren, you have done it to me.

41 Then shall he say also to them on the left hand, Depart from me, you cursed, into everlasting fire, prepared for the devil and his angels:

42 For I was an hungered, and you gave me no meat: I was thirsty, and you gave me no drink:

43 I was a stranger, and you took me not in: naked, and you clothed me not: sick,

and in prison, and you visited me not.

44 Then shall they also answer him, saying, Lord, when saw we you an hungered, or athirst, or a stranger, or naked, or sick, or in prison, and did not minister to you?

45 Then shall he answer them, saying, Verily I say to you, Inasmuch as you did it not to one of the least of these, you did it not to me.

46 And these shall go away into everlasting punishment: but the righteous into life eternal.

> I desire to have both heaven and hell in my eye.
>
> **JOHN WESLEY**

CHAPTER 26

AND it came to pass, when Jesus had finished all these sayings, he said to his disciples,

2 You know that after two days is the feast of the passover, and the Son of man is betrayed to be crucified.

3 Then assembled together the chief priests, and the scribes, and the elders of the people, to the palace of the high priest, who was called Caiaphas,

4 And consulted that they might take Jesus by subtlety, and kill him.

5 But they said, Not on the feast day, lest there be an uproar among the people.

6 Now when Jesus was in Bethany, in the house of Simon the leper,

7 There came to him a woman having an alabaster box of very precious ointment, and poured it on his head, as he sat at meat.

8 But when his disciples saw it, they had indignation, saying, To what purpose is this waste?

25:31 Second coming of Jesus: See Matthew 26:64.

25:32 Judgment Day: For verses that warn of its reality, see John 5:28,29.

25:41 Hell: For verses warning of its reality, see Mark 9:43–48.

9 For this ointment might have been sold for much, and given to the poor.

10 When Jesus understood it, he said to them, Why trouble the woman? for she has wrought a good work upon me.

11 For you have the poor always with you; but me you have not always.

12 For in that she has poured this ointment on my body, she did it for my burial.

13 Verily I say to you, Wherever this gospel shall be preached in the whole world, there shall also this, that this woman has done, be told for a memorial of her.

14 Then one of the twelve, called Judas Iscariot, went to the chief priests,

15 And said to them, What will you give me, and I will deliver him to you? And they covenanted with him for thirty pieces of silver.

16 And from that time he sought opportunity to betray him.

17 Now the first day of the feast of unleavened bread the disciples came to Jesus, saying to him, Where will you that we prepare for you to eat the passover?

18 And he said, Go into the city to such a man, and say to him, The Master says, My time is at hand; I will keep the passover at your house with my disciples.

19 And the disciples did as Jesus had appointed them; and they made ready the passover.

20 Now when the even was come, he sat down with the twelve.

21 And as they did eat, he said, Verily I say to you, that one of you shall betray me.

22 And they were exceeding sorrowful, and began every one of them to say to him, Lord, is it I?

23 And he answered and said, He that dips his hand with me in the dish, the same shall betray me.

24 The Son of man goes as it is written of him: but woe to that man by whom the Son of man is betrayed! it had been good for that man if he had not been born.

25 Then Judas, which betrayed him, answered and said, Master, is it I? He said to him, You have said.

26 And as they were eating, Jesus took bread, and blessed it, and broke it, and gave it to the disciples, and said, Take, eat; this is my body.

27 And he took the cup, and gave thanks, and gave it to them, saying, Drink all of it;

28 For this is my blood of the new testament, which is shed for many for the remission of sins.

29 But I say to you, I will not drink henceforth of this fruit of the vine, until that day when I drink it new with you in my Father's kingdom.

30 And when they had sung a hymn, they went out into the mount of Olives.

31 Then said Jesus to them, All you shall be offended because of me this night: for it is written, I will smite the shepherd, and the sheep of the flock shall be scattered abroad.

32 But after I am risen again, I will go before you into Galilee.

33 Peter answered and said to him, Though all men shall be offended because of you, yet will I never be offended.

34 Jesus said to him, Verily I say to you,

26:15 Messianic prophecy fulfilled: "And I said unto them, If you think good, give me my price; and if not, forbear. So they weighed for my price thirty pieces of silver" (Zechariah 11:12). See Matthew 26:60 footnote.

26:26 This can only have been a *symbolic* statement. The bread was obviously not His *physical* body, as He was standing in front of them.

26:27,28 This could not have been Jesus' literal blood, because He was present with them. His words were *spiritual*. After Jesus told His disciples that they must eat of His flesh and drink of His blood, He said that the words that He spoke were spirit and life (John 6:63). When we are born of the Spirit (John 3:3–7), we "taste and see that the Lord is good" (Psalm 34:8).

That this night, before the cock crow, you shall deny me thrice.

35 Peter said to him, Though I should die with you, yet will I not deny you. Likewise also said all the disciples.

36 Then came Jesus with them to a place called Gethsemane, and said to the disciples, Sit here, while I go and pray yonder.

37 And he took with him Peter and the two sons of Zebedee, and began to be sorrowful and very heavy.

38 Then said he to them, My soul is exceeding sorrowful, even to death: tarry here, and watch with me.

39 And he went a little further, and fell on his face, and prayed, saying, O my Father, if it be possible, let this cup pass from me: nevertheless not as I will, but as you will.

40 And he came to the disciples, and found them asleep, and said to Peter, What, could you not watch with me one hour?

41 Watch and pray, that you enter not into temptation: the spirit indeed is willing, but the flesh is weak.

42 He went away again the second time, and prayed, saying, O my Father, if this cup may not pass away from me, except I drink it, your will be done.

43 And he came and found them asleep again: for their eyes were heavy.

44 And he left them, and went away again, and prayed the third time, saying the same words.

45 Then came he to his disciples, and said to them, Sleep on now, and take your rest: behold, the hour is at hand, and the Son of man is betrayed into the hands of sinners.

46 Rise, let us be going: behold, he is at hand that does betray me.

47 And while he yet spoke, lo, Judas, one of the twelve, came, and with him a great multitude with swords and staves, from the chief priests and elders of the people.

48 Now he that betrayed him gave them a sign, saying, Whomsoever I shall kiss, that same is he: hold him fast.

49 And forthwith he came to Jesus, and said, Hail, master; and kissed him.

50 And Jesus said to him, Friend, wherefore are you come? Then came they, and laid hands on Jesus, and took him.

51 And, behold, one of them which were with Jesus stretched out his hand, and drew his sword, and struck a servant of the high priest's, and smote off his ear.

52 Then said Jesus to him, Put up again your sword into his place: for all they that take the sword shall perish with the sword.

53 Think that I cannot now pray to my Father, and he shall presently give me more than twelve legions of angels?

54 But how then shall the scriptures be fulfilled, that thus it must be?

55 In that same hour said Jesus to the multitudes, Are you come out as against a thief with swords and staves for to take me? I sat daily with you teaching in the temple, and you laid no hold on me.

56 But all this was done, that the scriptures of the prophets might be fulfilled. Then all the disciples forsook him, and fled.

57 And they that had laid hold on Jesus led him away to Caiaphas the high priest, where the scribes and the elders were assembled.

58 But Peter followed him afar off to

26:41 Watch and pray. "Real praying is a costly exercise but it pays far more than it costs. It is not easy work but it is most profitable of all work. We can accomplish more by time and strength put into prayer than we can by putting the same amount of time and strength into anything else." *R. A. Torrey, The Power of Prayer*

"Do you ever get that wistful feeling that there are other things more effective, even more desirable, than prayer? This explains why far too many of us are busy in attempting great things for God, rather than expecting great things from God in a humble attitude of prayer." *Robert Foster*

the high priest's palace, and went in, and sat with the servants, to see the end.

59 Now the chief priests, and elders, and all the council, sought false witness against Jesus, to put him to death;

60 But found none: yea, though many false witnesses came, yet found they none. At the last came two false witnesses,

61 And said, This fellow said, I am able to destroy the temple of God, and to build it in three days.

62 And the high priest arose, and said to him, Do you answer nothing? what is it which these witness against you?

63 But Jesus held his peace. And the high priest answered and said to him, I adjure you by the living God, that you tell us whether you be the Christ, the Son of God.

64 Jesus said to him, You have said: nevertheless I say to you, Hereafter shall you see the Son of man sitting on the right hand of power, and coming in the clouds of heaven.

65 Then the high priest tore his clothes,

saying, He has spoken blasphemy; what further need have we of witnesses? behold, now you have heard his blasphemy.

66 What do you think? They answered and said, He is guilty of death.

67 Then did they spit in his face, and buffeted him; and others smote him with the palms of their hands,

68 Saying, Prophesy to us, you Christ, Who is he that smote you?

69 Now Peter sat without in the palace: and a damsel came to him, saying, You also were with Jesus of Galilee.

70 But he denied before them all, saying, I know not what you say.

71 And when he was gone out into the porch, another maid saw him, and said to them that were there, This fellow was also with Jesus of Nazareth.

72 And again he denied with an oath, I do not know the man.

73 And after a while came to him they that stood by, and said to Peter, Surely you also are one of them; for your speech betrays you.

26:54   Archaeology confirms the Bible. The Scriptures make more than 40 references to the great Hittite Empire. However, until one hundred years ago there was no archaeological evidence to substantiate the biblical claim that the Hittites existed. Skeptics claimed that the Bible was in error, until their mouths were suddenly stopped. In 1906, Hugo Winckler uncovered a huge library of 10,000 clay tablets, which completely documented the lost Hittite Empire. We now know that at its height, the Hittite civilization rivaled Egypt and Assyria in its glory and power. See Luke 1:27 footnote.

"It may be stated categorically that no archaeological discovery has ever controverted a Biblical reference. Scores of archaeological findings have been made which confirm in clear outline or exact detail historical statements in the Bible. And, by the same token, proper evaluation of Biblical descriptions has often led to amazing discoveries." *Dr. Nelson Glueck*

"Archaeology has confirmed countless passages which have been rejected by critics as unhistorical or contradictory to known facts...Yet archaeological discoveries have shown that these critical charges...are wrong and that the Bible is trustworthy in the very statements which have been set aside as untrustworthy...We do not know of any cases where the Bible has been proved wrong." *Dr. Joseph P. Free*

26:60   Messianic prophecy fulfilled: "Deliver me not over unto the will of mine enemies: for false witnesses are risen up against me, and such as breathe out cruelty" (Psalm 27:12). See Matthew 26:62,63 footnote.

26:62,63   Messianic prophecy fulfilled: "He was oppressed, and he was afflicted, yet he opened not his mouth: he is brought as a lamb to the slaughter, and as a sheep before her shearers is dumb, so he opened not his mouth" (Isaiah 53:7). See Matthew 27:39–44 footnote.

26:64   Second coming of Jesus: See Mark 8:38.

74 Then began he to curse and to swear, saying, I know not the man. And immediately the cock crew.

75 And Peter remembered the word of Jesus, which said to him, Before the cock crow, you shall deny me thrice. And he went out, and wept bitterly.

CHAPTER 27

WHEN the morning was come, all the chief priests and elders of the people took counsel against Jesus to put him to death:

2 And when they had bound him, they led him away, and delivered him to Pontius Pilate the governor.

3 Then Judas, which had betrayed him, when he saw that he was condemned, repented himself, and brought again the thirty pieces of silver to the chief priests and elders,

4 Saying, I have sinned in that I have betrayed the innocent blood. And they said, What is that to us? You see to that.

5 And he cast down the pieces of silver in the temple, and departed, and went and hanged himself.

6 And the chief priests took the silver pieces, and said, It is not lawful for to put them into the treasury, because it is the price of blood.

7 And they took counsel, and bought with them the potter's field, to bury strangers in.

8 Wherefore that field was called, The field of blood, to this day.

9 Then was fulfilled that which was spoken by Jeremiah the prophet, saying, And they took the thirty pieces of silver, the price of him that was valued, whom they of the children of Israel did value;

10 And gave them for the potter's field,

as the Lord appointed me.

11 And Jesus stood before the governor: and the governor asked him, saying, are you the King of the Jews? And Jesus said to him, It is as you say.

12 And when he was accused of the chief priests and elders, he answered nothing.

13 Then said Pilate to him, Hear not how many things they witness against you?

14 And he answered him to never a word; insomuch that the governor marveled greatly.

15 Now at that feast the governor was accustomed to release to the people a prisoner, whom they would.

16 And they had then a notable prisoner, called Barabbas.

17 Therefore when they were gathered together, Pilate said to them, Whom will you that I release to you? Barabbas, or Jesus which is called Christ?

18 For he knew that for envy they had delivered him.

19 When he was set down on the judgment seat, his wife sent to him, saying, Have nothing to do with that just man: for I have suffered many things this day in a dream because of him.

20 But the chief priests and elders persuaded the multitude that they should ask Barabbas, and destroy Jesus.

21 The governor answered and said to them, Which of the two will you that I release to you? They said, Barabbas.

22 Pilate said to them, What shall I do then with Jesus which is called Christ? They all say to him, Let him be crucified.

23 And the governor said, Why, what evil has he done? But they cried out the more, saying, Let him be crucified.

24 When Pilate saw that he could prevail nothing, but that rather a tumult was

---

27:5 "I have had few difficulties, many friends, great success; I have gone from wife to wife, and from house to house, visited great countries of the world, but I am fed up with inventing devices to fill up 24 hours of the day." Suicide note of cartoonist *Ralph Barton*

27:9,10 Notice that Scripture doesn't say "that which was *written in* Jeremiah." This was "spoken" by Jeremiah the prophet, but it was not recorded in the Book of Jeremiah. A similar prophecy was given in Zechariah 11:12,13.

made, he took water, and washed his hands before the multitude, saying, I am innocent of the blood of this just person: you see to it.

25 Then answered all the people, and said, His blood be on us, and on our children.

26 Then released he Barabbas to them: and when he had scourged Jesus, he delivered him to be crucified.

27 Then the soldiers of the governor took Jesus into the common hall, and gathered to him the whole band of soldiers.

28 And they stripped him, and put on him a scarlet robe.

29 And when they had platted a crown of thorns, they put it upon his head, and a reed in his right hand: and they bowed the knee before him, and mocked him, saying, Hail, King of the Jews!

30 And they spit upon him, and took the reed, and smote him on the head.

31 And after that they had mocked him, they took the robe off from him, and put his own raiment on him, and led him away to crucify him.

32 And as they came out, they found a man of Cyrene, Simon by name: him they compelled to bear his cross.

33 And when they were come to a place called Golgotha, that is to say, a place of a skull,

34 They gave him vinegar to drink mingled with gall: and when he had tasted thereof, he would not drink.

35 And they crucified him, and parted his garments, casting lots: that it might be fulfilled which was spoken by the prophet, They parted my garments among them, and upon my vesture did they cast lots.

36 And sitting down they watched him there;

37 And set up over his head his accusation written, THIS IS JESUS THE KING OF THE JEWS.

38 Then were there two thieves crucified with him, one on the right hand, and another on the left.

39 And they that passed by reviled him, wagging their heads,

40 And saying, You that destroy the temple, and build it in three days, save yourself. If you be the Son of God, come down from the cross.

41 Likewise also the chief priests mocking him, with the scribes and elders, said,

42 He saved others; himself he cannot save. If he be the King of Israel, let him now come down from the cross, and we will believe him.

43 He trusted in God; let him deliver him now, if he will have him: for he said, I am the Son of God.

44 The thieves also, which were crucified with him, cast the same in his teeth.

45 Now from the sixth hour there was darkness over all the land to the ninth hour.

46 And about the ninth hour Jesus cried with a loud voice, saying, Eli, Eli, lama sabachthani? that is to say, My God, my God, why have you forsaken me?

47 Some of them that stood there, when they heard that, said, This man calls for Elijah.

27:26–29 Paintings of a "suffering Savior" on the cross can never do justice to the agonies He suffered for us. Isaiah 52:14 tells us "His visage was so marred more than any man, and His form more than the sons of men."

27:39–44 **Messianic prophecy fulfilled:** "But I am a worm, and no man; a reproach of men, and despised of the people. All they that see me laugh me to scorn: they shoot out the lip, they shake the head, saying, He trusted on the LORD that he would deliver him: let him deliver him, seeing he delighted in him!" (Psalm 22:6–8). See Mark 14:10 footnote.

27:46 "The pain was absolutely unbearable. In fact, it was literally beyond words to describe; they had to invent a new word: *excruciating*. Literally, excruciating means 'out of the cross.'" *Alexander Metherell, M.D., Ph.D.* (quoted in *The Case for Christ* by *Lee Strobel*)

48 And straightway one of them ran, and took a sponge, and filled it with vinegar, and put it on a reed, and gave him to drink.

49 The rest said, Let be, let us see whether Elijah will come to save him.

50 Jesus, when he had cried again with a loud voice, yielded up the ghost.

51 And, behold, the veil of the temple was rent in twain from the top to the bottom; and the earth did quake, and the rocks rent;

52 And the graves were opened; and many bodies of the saints which slept arose,

> She is a traitor to the Master who sent her if she is so beguiled by the beauties of taste and art as to forget that to "preach Christ...and Him crucified" is the only object for which she exists among the sons of men. The business of the Church is salvation of souls.
>
> **CHARLES SPURGEON**

53 And came out of the graves after his resurrection, and went into the holy city, and appeared to many.

54 Now when the centurion, and they that were with him, watching Jesus, saw the earthquake, and those things that were done, they feared greatly, saying, Truly this was the Son of God.

55 And many women were there beholding afar off, which followed Jesus from Galilee, ministering to him:

56 Among which was Mary Magdalene, and Mary the mother of James and Joses, and the mother of Zebedee's children.

57 When the even was come, there came a rich man of Arimathaea, named Joseph, who also himself was Jesus' disciple:

58 He went to Pilate, and begged the body of Jesus. Then Pilate commanded the body to be delivered.

59 And when Joseph had taken the body, he wrapped it in a clean linen cloth,

60 And laid it in his own new tomb, which he had hewn out in the rock: and he rolled a great stone to the door of the sepulchre, and departed.

61 And there was Mary Magdalene, and the other Mary, sitting over against the sepulchre.

62 Now the next day, that followed the day of the preparation, the chief priests and Pharisees came together to Pilate,

63 Saying, Sir, we remember that that deceiver said, while he was yet alive, After three days I will rise again.

64 Command therefore that the sepulchre be made sure until the third day, lest his disciples come by night, and steal him away, and say to the people, He is risen from the dead: so the last error shall be worse than the first.

65 Pilate said to them, You have a watch: go your way, make it as sure as you can.

66 So they went, and made the sepulchre sure, sealing the stone, and setting a watch.

CHAPTER 28

IN the end of the sabbath, as it began to dawn toward the first day of the week, came Mary Magdalene and the other Mary to see the sepulchre.

2 And, behold, there was a great earthquake: for the angel of the Lord descended from heaven, and came and rolled back the stone from the door, and sat upon it.

3 His countenance was like lightning, and his raiment white as snow:

4 And for fear of him the keepers did shake, and became as dead men.

5 And the angel answered and said to the women, Fear not: for I know that you seek Jesus, which was crucified.

6 He is not here: for he is risen, as he said. Come, see the place where the Lord lay.

7 And go quickly, and tell his disciples that he is risen from the dead; and, behold, he goes before you into Galilee; there shall you see him: lo, I have told you.

8 And they departed quickly from the

QUESTIONS & OBJECTIONS

28:9 *"There are contradictions in the resurrection accounts. Did Christ appear first to the women or to His disciples?"*

Both Matthew and Mark list women as the first to see the resurrected Christ. Mark says, "He appeared first to Mary Magdalene" (16:9). But Paul lists Peter (Cephas) as the first one to see Christ after His resurrection (1 Corinthians 15:5).

Jesus appeared first to Mary Magdalene, then to the other women, and then to Peter. Paul was not giving a complete list, but only the important one for his purpose. Since only men's testimony was considered legal or official in the first century, it is understandable that the apostle would not list the women as witnesses in his defense of the resurrection here.

The order of the appearances of Christ is as follows:

CHRIST'S RESURRECTION APPEARANCES

APPEARED TO:	REFERENCES:
1. Mary	John 20:10–18
2. Mary and women	Matthew 28:1–10
3. Peter	1 Corinthians 15:5
4. Two disciples	Luke 24:13–35
5. Ten apostles	Luke 24:36–49; John 20:19–23
6. Eleven apostles	John 20:24–31
7. Seven apostles	John 21
8. All apostles	Matthew 28:16–20; Mark 16:14–18
9. 500 brethren	1 Corinthians 15:6
10. James	1 Corinthians 15:7
11. All apostles	Acts 1:4–8
12. Paul	Acts 9:1–9; 1 Corinthians 15:8

sepulchre with fear and great joy; and did run to bring his disciples word.

9 And as they went to tell his disciples, behold, Jesus met them, saying, All hail. And they came and held him by the feet, and worshipped him.

10 Then said Jesus to them, Be not afraid: go tell my brethren that they go into Galilee, and there shall they see me.

11 Now when they were going, behold, some of the watch came into the city, and showed to the chief priests all the things that were done.

12 And when they were assembled with the elders, and had taken counsel, they gave large money to the soldiers,

13 Saying, Say, His disciples came by night, and stole him away while we slept.

14 And if this come to the governor's ears, we will persuade him, and secure you.

15 So they took the money, and did as they were taught: and this saying is commonly reported among the Jews until this

---

28:9 If Jesus was not God, He would have been transgressing the Law of God by receiving their worship.

POINTS FOR OPEN-AIR PREACHING

28:19,20 *Make the Bullet Hit the Target*

It is obvious from Scripture that God requires us not only to preach to sinners, but also to teach them. The servant of the Lord must be "able to teach, patient, in meekness instructing" those who oppose them (2 Timothy 2:24,25). For a long while I thought I was to leap among sinners, scatter the seed, then leave. But our responsibility goes further. We are to bring the sinner to a point of understanding his need before God. Psalm 25:8 says, "Good and upright is the LORD: therefore will he teach sinners in the way." Psalm 51:13 adds, "Then will I teach transgressors your ways; and sinners shall be converted to you." The Great Commission is to teach sinners: "teach all nations...teaching them to observe all things" (Matthew 28:19,20). The disciples obeyed the command "daily in the temple, and in every house, they ceased not to *teach* and preach Jesus Christ" (Acts 5:42, emphasis added).

The "good-soil" hearer is he who "hears...and *understands*" (Matthew 13:23). Philip the evangelist saw fit to ask his potential convert, the Ethiopian, "Do you understand what you are reading?" Some preachers are like a loud gun that misses the target. It may sound effective, but if the bullet misses the target, the exercise is in vain. He may be the largest-lunged, chandelier-swinging, pulpit-pounding preacher this side of the Book of Acts. He may have great teaching on faith, and everyone he touches may fall over, but if the sinner leaves the meeting failing to understand his desperate need of God's forgiveness, then the preacher has failed. He has missed the target, which is the understanding of the sinner. This is why the Law of God must be used in preaching. It is a "schoolmaster" to bring "the knowledge of sin." It teaches and instructs. A sinner will come to "know His will, and approve the things that are more excellent," if he is "instructed out of the Law" (Romans 2:18). See Acts 20:21 footnote.

day.

16 Then the eleven disciples went away into Galilee, into a mountain where Jesus had appointed them.

17 And when they saw him, they worshipped him: but some doubted.

18 *And Jesus came and spoke to them, saying, All power is given to me in heaven and* *in earth.*

19 *Go therefore, and teach all nations, baptizing them in the name of the Father, and of the Son, and of the Holy Spirit:*

20 *Teaching them to observe all things whatsoever I have commanded you: and, lo, I am with you alway, even to the end of the world. Amen.*

28:19 "We cannot pick and choose which commands of our Lord we will follow. Jesus Christ's last command to the Christian community was, 'You are to go into all the world and preach the Good News to everyone, everywhere' (Mark 16:15, TLB). This command, which the Church calls the Great Commission, was not intended merely for the eleven remaining disciples, or just for the apostles or for those in present times who may have the gift of evangelism. This command is the duty of every man and woman who confesses Christ as Lord." *Dr. Bill Bright*

"Men are mirrors, or 'carriers' of Christ to other men. Usually it is those who know Him who bring Him to others. That's why the Church, the whole body of Christians showing Him to one another, is so important. It is so easy to think that the Church has a lot of different objects—education, building, missions, holding services...The Church exists for no other purpose but to draw men into Christ, to make them little Christs. If they are not doing that, all the cathedrals, clergy, missions, sermons, even the Bible itself, are simply a waste of time. God became man for no other purpose. It is even doubtful, you know, whether the whole universe was created for any other reason." *C. S. Lewis*

Mark

CHAPTER 1

THE beginning of the gospel of Jesus Christ, the Son of God;

2 As it is written in the prophets, Behold, I send my messenger before your face, which shall prepare your way before you.

3 The voice of one crying in the wilderness, Prepare the way of the Lord, make his paths straight.

4 John did baptize in the wilderness, and preach the baptism of repentance for the remission of sins.

5 And there went out to him all the land of Judea, and they of Jerusalem, and were all baptized of him in the river of Jordan, confessing their sins.

6 And John was clothed with camel's hair, and with a girdle of a skin about his loins; and he did eat locusts and wild honey;

7 And preached, saying, There comes one mightier than I after me, the latchet of whose shoes I am not worthy to stoop down and unloose.

8 I indeed have baptized you with water: but he shall baptize you with the Holy Spirit.

9 And it came to pass in those days, that Jesus came from Nazareth of Galilee, and was baptized of John in Jordan.

10 And straightway coming up out of the water, he saw the heavens opened, and the Spirit like a dove descending upon him:

11 And there came a voice from heaven, saying, You are my beloved Son, in whom I am well pleased.

12 And immediately the Spirit drove him into the wilderness.

13 And he was there in the wilderness forty days, tempted of Satan; and was with the wild beasts; and the angels ministered to him.

14 Now after that John was put in prison, Jesus came into Galilee, preaching the gospel of the kingdom of God,

15 And saying, The time is fulfilled, and the kingdom of God is at hand: repent, and believe the gospel.

THE FUNCTION OF THE LAW

1:3 Commenting on the Law's capacity to bring the knowledge of sin, Bible commentator *Matthew Henry* said, "Of this excellent use is the Law: it converts the soul, opens the eyes, prepares the way of the Lord in the desert, rends the rocks, levels the mountains, makes a people prepared for the Lord."

1:15 Jesus preached repentance because His hearers knew the Law. Since He was sent to "the lost sheep of the house of Israel" (Matthew 15:24), His ministry was originally confined to Jews. The Scriptures often use the phrase "to the Jew first." Romans 3:1,2 tells us that Jews had the advantage of having the Law of God. They knew what sin was, and therefore understood their need for repentance. Those without a knowledge of sin (which only the Law can bring—see Romans 7:7) need to hear the message of the Law before they are able (with God's help) to repent.

QUESTIONS & OBJECTIONS

1:4,5 "*Is water baptism essential to salvation?*"

While we should preach that all men are commanded to repent and be baptized (Acts 2:38), adding any other requirement to salvation by grace becomes "works" in disguise. Even though numerous Scriptures speak of the importance of water baptism, adding *anything* to the work of the cross demeans the sacrifice of the Savior. It implies that His finished work wasn't enough. But the Bible makes clear that we are saved by grace, and grace alone (Ephesians 2:8,9). Baptism is simply a step of obedience to the Lord following our repentance and confession of sin. Our obedience—water baptism, prayer, good works, fellowship, witnessing, etc.—issues from our faith in Christ. Salvation is not what we do, but Who we have: "He that has the Son has life" (1 John 5:12). See Acts 2:38 footnotes.

16 Now as he walked by the sea of Galilee, he saw Simon and Andrew his brother casting a net into the sea: for they were fishers.

17 *And Jesus said to them, Come after me, and I will make you to become fishers of men.*

18 And straightway they forsook their nets, and followed him.

19 And when he had gone a little further thence, he saw James the son of Zebedee, and John his brother, who also were in the ship mending their nets.

20 And straightway he called them: and they left their father Zebedee in the ship with the hired servants, and went after him.

21 And they went into Capernaum; and straightway on the sabbath day he entered into the synagogue, and taught.

22 And they were astonished at his doctrine: for he taught them as one that had authority, and not as the scribes.

23 And there was in their synagogue a man with an unclean spirit; and he cried out,

24 Saying, Let us alone; what have we to do with you, you Jesus of Nazareth? are you come to destroy us? I know you who you are, the Holy One of God.

25 And Jesus rebuked him, saying, Hold your peace, and come out of him.

26 And when the unclean spirit had torn him, and cried with a loud voice, he came out of him.

27 And they were all amazed, insomuch that they questioned among themselves, saying, What thing is this? what new doctrine is this? for with authority commands he even the unclean spirits, and they do obey him.

28 And immediately his fame spread abroad throughout all the region round about Galilee.

29 And forthwith, when they were come out of the synagogue, they entered into the house of Simon and Andrew, with James and John.

30 But Simon's wife's mother lay sick of a fever, and anon they tell him of her.

31 And he came and took her by the hand, and lifted her up; and immediately the fever left her, and she ministered to them.

32 And at even, when the sun did set, they brought to him all that were diseased, and them that were possessed with devils.

33 And all the city was gathered together at the door.

34 And he healed many that were sick of divers diseases, and cast out many devils; and suffered not the devils to speak, because they knew him.

35 And in the morning, rising up a great while before day, he went out, and departed into a solitary place, and there prayed.

36 And Simon and they that were with him followed after him.

🔍 1:17 *The Parable of the Fishless Fishermen*

Fellowship. They were surrounded by streams and lakes full of hungry fish. They met regularly to discuss the call to fish, the abundance of fish, and the thrill of catching fish. They got excited about fishing!

Someone suggested that they needed a philosophy of fishing, so they carefully defined and redefined fishing, and the purpose of fishing. They developed fishing strategies and tactics. Then they realized that they had been going at it backwards. They had approached fishing from the point of view of the fisherman, and not from the point of view of the fish. How do fish view the world? How does the fisherman appear to the fish? What do fish eat, and when? These are all good things to know. So they began research studies, and attended conferences on fishing. Some traveled to faraway places to study different kinds of fish with different habits. Some got doctorates in fishology. But no one had yet gone fishing.

So a committee was formed to send out fishermen. As prospective fishing places outnumbered fishermen, the committee needed to determine priorities. A priority list of fishing places was posted on bulletin boards in all of the fellowship halls. But still, no one was fishing. A survey was launched to find out why. Most did not answer the survey, but from those who did, it was discovered that some felt called to study fish, a few to furnish fishing equipment, and several to go around encouraging the fishermen. What with meetings, conferences, and seminars, they just simply didn't have time to fish.

Now, Jake was a newcomer to the Fisherman's Fellowship. After one stirring meeting of the Fellowship, he went fishing and caught a large fish. At the next meeting, he told his story and was honored for his catch. He was told that he had a special "gift of fishing." He was then scheduled to speak at all the Fellowship chapters and tell how he did it.

With all the speaking invitations and his election to the board of directors of the Fisherman's Fellowship, Jake no longer had time to go fishing. But soon he began to feel restless and empty. He longed to feel the tug on the line once again. So he cut the speaking, he resigned from the board, and he said to a friend, "Let's go fishing." They did, just the two of them, and they caught fish. The members of the Fisherman's Fellowship were many, the fish were plentiful, but the fishers were few!   *Anonymous*

37 And when they had found him, they said to him, All men seek for you.
38 And he said to them, Let us go into the next towns, that I may preach there also: for therefore came I forth.
39 And he preached in their synagogues throughout all Galilee, and cast out devils.
40 And there came a leper to him, beseeching him, and kneeling down to him, and saying to him, If you will, you can make me clean.
41 And Jesus, moved with compassion, put forth his hand, and touched him, and said to him, I will; be clean.
42 And as soon as he had spoken, immediately the leprosy departed from him, and he was cleansed.
43 And he straitly charged him, and forthwith sent him away;
44 And said to him, See you say nothing

1:35 Prayer—the secret weapon: See Mark 6:46. There are some days in which we think we are too busy to take time for prayer. But the busier our schedules become, the more we need to ask God to order our day and invite Him to work through us to accomplish His will. "I have so much to do [today] that I should spend the first three hours in prayer." *Martin Luther*

"I have been driven many times upon my knees by the overwhelming conviction that I had nowhere else to go. My own wisdom, and that of all about me, seemed insufficient for that day." *Abraham Lincoln*

to any man: but go your way, show yourself to the priest, and offer for your cleansing those things which Moses commanded, for a testimony to them.

45 But he went out, and began to publish it much, and to blaze abroad the matter, insomuch that Jesus could no more openly enter into the city, but was without in desert places: and they came to him from every quarter.

CHAPTER 2

AND again he entered into Capernaum, after some days; and it was noised that he was in the house.

2 And straightway many were gathered together, insomuch that there was no room to receive them, no, not so much as about the door: and he preached the word to them.

3 And they come to him, bringing one sick of the palsy, which was borne of four.

4 And when they could not come near to him for the press, they uncovered the roof where he was: and when they had broken it up, they let down the bed wherein the sick of the palsy lay.

5 When Jesus saw their faith, he said to the sick of the palsy, Son, your sins be forgiven you.

6 But there were certain of the scribes sitting there, and reasoning in their hearts,

7 Why does this man thus speak blasphemies? who can forgive sins but God only?

8 And immediately when Jesus perceived in his spirit that they so reasoned within themselves, he said to them, Why reason these things in your hearts?

9 Whether is it easier to say to the sick of the palsy, Your sins be forgiven you; or to say, Arise, and take up your bed, and walk?

10 **But that you may know that the Son of man has power on earth to forgive sins,** (he said to the sick of the palsy,)

11 I say to you, Arise, and take up your bed, and go your way into your house.

12 And immediately he arose, took up the bed, and went forth before them all; insomuch that they were all amazed, and glorified God, saying, We never saw it on this fashion.

13 And he went forth again by the sea side; and all the multitude resorted to him, and he taught them.

14 And as he passed by, he saw Levi the son of Alphaeus sitting at the receipt of custom, and said to him, Follow me. And he arose and followed him.

15 And it came to pass, that, as Jesus sat at meat in his house, many publicans and sinners sat also together with Jesus and his disciples: for there were many, and they followed him.

16 And when the scribes and Pharisees saw him eat with publicans and sinners, they said to his disciples, How is it that he eats and drinks with publicans and sinners?

17 When Jesus heard it, he said to them, **They that are whole have no need of the physician, but they that are sick: I came not to call the righteous, but sinners to repentance.**

18 And the disciples of John and of the Pharisees used to fast: and they come and said to him, Why do the disciples of John and of the Pharisees fast, but your disciples fast not?

19 And Jesus said to them, Can the children of the bridechamber fast, while the bridegroom is with them? as long as they have the bridegroom with them, they cannot fast.

20 But the days will come, when the bridegroom shall be taken away from them, and then shall they fast in those

---

2:2 "In my preaching of the Word, I took special notice of this one thing, namely, that the Lord did lead me to begin where His Word begins with sinners; that is, to condemn all flesh, and to open and allege that the curse of God, by the Law, doth belong to and lay hold on all men as they come into the world, because of sin." *John Bunyan*

days.

21 No man also sews a piece of new cloth on an old garment: else the new piece that filled it up takes away from the old, and the rent is made worse.

22 And no man puts new wine into old bottles: else the new wine does burst the bottles, and the wine is spilled, and the bottles will be marred: but new wine must be put into new bottles.

23 And it came to pass, that he went through the corn fields on the sabbath day; and his disciples began, as they went, to pluck the ears of corn.

24 And the Pharisees said to him, Behold, why do they do on the sabbath day that which is not lawful?

25 And he said to them, Have you never read what David did, when he had need, and was an hungered, he, and they that were with him?

26 How he went into the house of God in the days of Abiathar the high priest, and did eat the shewbread, which is not lawful to eat but for the priests, and gave also to them which were with him?

27 And he said to them, The sabbath was made for man, and not man for the sabbath:

28 Therefore the Son of man is Lord also of the sabbath.

CHAPTER 3

A ND he entered again into the synagogue; and there was a man there which had a withered hand.

2 And they watched him, whether he would heal him on the sabbath day; that they might accuse him.

3 And he said to the man which had the withered hand, Stand forth.

4 And he said to them, Is it lawful to do good on the sabbath days, or to do evil? to save life, or to kill? But they held their peace.

5 And when he had looked round about on them with anger, being grieved for the hardness of their hearts, he said to the man, Stretch forth your hand. And he stretched it out: and his hand was restored whole

"In every true searcher of Nature there is a kind of religious reverence, for he finds it impossible to imagine that he is the first to have thought out the exceedingly delicate threads that connect his perceptions."

Albert Einstein

as the other.

6 And the Pharisees went forth, and straightway took counsel with the Herodians against him, how they might destroy him.

7 But Jesus withdrew himself with his disciples to the sea: and a great multitude from Galilee followed him, and from Judea,

8 And from Jerusalem, and from Idumaea, and from beyond Jordan; and they about Tyre and Sidon, a great multitude, when they had heard what great things he did, came to him.

9 And he spoke to his disciples, that a small ship should wait on him because of the multitude, lest they should throng him.

10 For he had healed many; insomuch that they pressed upon him for to touch him, as many as had plagues.

11 And unclean spirits, when they saw him, fell down before him, and cried, saying, You are the Son of God.

12 And he straitly charged them that they should not make him known.

13 And he went up into a mountain, and

called to him whom he would: and they came to him.

14 And he ordained twelve, that they should be with him, and that he might send them forth to preach,

15 And to have power to heal sicknesses, and to cast out devils:

16 And Simon he surnamed Peter;

17 And James the son of Zebedee, and John the brother of James; and he surnamed them Boanerges, which is, The sons of thunder:

18 And Andrew, and Philip, and Bartholomew, and Matthew, and Thomas, and James the son of Alphaeus, and Thaddaeus, and Simon the Canaanite,

19 And Judas Iscariot, which also betrayed him: and they went into an house.

20 And the multitude came together again, so that they could not so much as eat bread.

21 And when his friends heard of it, they went out to lay hold on him: for they said, He is beside himself.

22 And the scribes which came down from Jerusalem said, He has Beelzebub, and by the prince of the devils casts he out devils.

23 And he called them to him, and said to them in parables, How can Satan cast out Satan?

24 And if a kingdom be divided against itself, that kingdom cannot stand.

25 And if a house be divided against itself, that house cannot stand.

26 And if Satan rise up against himself, and be divided, he cannot stand, but has an end.

27 No man can enter into a strong man's house, and spoil his goods, except he will first bind the strong man; and then he will spoil his house.

28 Verily I say to you, All sins shall be forgiven to the sons of men, and blasphemies wherewith soever they shall blaspheme:

29 But he that shall blaspheme against the Holy Spirit has never forgiveness, but is in danger of eternal damnation:

30 Because they said, He has an unclean spirit.

31 There came then his brethren and his mother, and, standing without, sent to him, calling him.

32 And the multitude sat about him, and they said to him, Behold, your mother and your brethren without seek for you.

33 And he answered them, saying, Who is my mother, or my brethren?

34 And he looked round about on them which sat about him, and said, Behold my mother and my brethren!

35 For whosoever shall do the will of God, the same is my brother, and my sister, and mother.

CHAPTER 4

A ND he began again to teach by the sea side: and there was gathered to him a great multitude, so that he entered into a ship, and sat in the sea; and the whole multitude was by the sea on the land.

2 And he taught them many things by

3:29 The unpardonable sin. It is often maintained that the "unpardonable sin" is when someone "rejects Jesus Christ as Lord and Savior." However, verse 30 defines exactly what the sin is. The scribes said that Jesus did His miracles by an "unclean spirit," attributing the work of the Holy Spirit to Satan's power. If sinners do not acknowledge the Holy Spirit's work in their lives as being from God, they cannot be saved.

It is only by the Holy Spirit that men are convicted of their sin (John 16:8) and can understand the salvation God offers (1 Corinthians 2:12–14). Those who are "stiffnecked and uncircumcised in heart and…always resist the Holy Ghost" (Acts 7:51) will therefore die in their sins. Anyone who rejects the Holy Spirit's convicting influence and does not repent will not be forgiven, "neither in this world, neither in the world to come" (Matthew 12:32).

3:31–35 Jesus here affords Mary with no more honor than any believer. See also Luke 8:20,21; 11:27,28.

parables, and said to them in his doctrine,

3 Hearken; Behold, there went out a sower to sow:

4 And it came to pass, as he sowed, some fell by the way side, and the fowls of the air came and devoured it up.

5 And some fell on stony ground, where it had not much earth; and immediately it sprang up, because it had no depth of earth:

6 But when the sun was up, it was scorched; and because it had no root, it withered away.

> That is the reason we have so many "mushroom" converts, because their stony ground is not plowed up; they have not got a conviction of the Law; they are stony-ground hearers.
>
> **GEORGE WHITEFIELD**

7 And some fell among thorns, and the thorns grew up, and choked it, and it yielded no fruit.

8 And other fell on good ground, and did yield fruit that sprang up and increased; and brought forth, some thirty, and some sixty, and some an hundred.

9 And he said to them, He that has ears to hear, let him hear.

10 And when he was alone, they that were about him with the twelve asked of him the parable.

11 And he said to them, to you it is given to know the mystery of the kingdom of God: but to them that are without, all these things are done in parables:

12 That seeing they may see, and not perceive; and hearing they may hear, and not understand; lest at any time they should be converted, and their sins should be forgiven them.

13 And he said to them, Do you not know this parable? and how then will you know all parables?

14 The sower sows the word.

15 And these are they by the way side, where the word is sown; but when they have heard, Satan comes immediately, and takes away the word that was sown in their hearts.

16 And these are they likewise which are sown on stony ground; who, when they have heard the word, immediately receive it with gladness;

17 And have no root in themselves, and so endure but for a time: afterward, when affliction or persecution arises for the word's sake, immediately they are offended.

18 And these are they which are sown among thorns; such as hear the word,

19 And the cares of this world, and the

4:13 The key to the parables. The parable of the sower is the key to unlock the mysteries of all the other parables. If we understand this parable (that when the gospel is preached there are true and false conversions), then all the parables Jesus told will make sense: the foolish virgins (false) and the wise virgins (genuine), the good and bad fish, the wheat and tares, etc. See also John 1:13 and 3:16 footnotes.

4:14 Sowing the seed of the gospel. A student at Jacksonville University in Florida was given a tract. The student crumpled the pamphlet up and tossed it into a trash bin in his dorm. Later, his dorm mate picked it out of the trash, read it, and was soundly saved. He is now a pastor of a church in Florida.

"A Christian I met in a home group said his job was raking litter off the Avon River. It was dull, boring work and he often wondered what life was all about. One day he raked a soggy piece of paper off the water and decided it was interesting enough to keep, so he carefully placed it in his bag and took it home. That evening he dried the paper in front of a heater and carefully unfolded it, then he read it...it was a gospel tract. He became a Christian that evening." *Richard Gunther*

"Nothing surpasses a tract for sowing the seed of the Good News." *Billy Graham*

See next page for ideas on where to distribute tracts. See also 1 Corinthians 9:22 and Revelation 22:2 footnotes.

Where to Leave Tracts

- At pay phones
- In shopping carts
- In clothes pockets in stores
- In letters to loved ones
- With a generous tip
- On seats in restaurant lobbies
- With fast-food employees, cashiers, flight attendants, cab drivers, and gas station workers
- In restrooms
- At rest areas
- On ATM machines and bank counters
- In envelopes with bill payments
- In elevators
- On hotel dressers for the maid
- On ice machines
- On newspaper racks
- In waiting rooms of doctors' offices and hospitals
- On seats at airports, subways, and bus stations
- In plane seat pockets
- Inside magazines
- In cabs
- In laundromats

deceitfulness of riches, and the lusts of other things entering in, choke the word, and it becomes unfruitful.

20 And these are they which are sown on good ground; such as hear the word, and receive it, and bring forth fruit, some thirtyfold, some sixty, and some an hundred.

21 And he said to them, Is a candle brought to be put under a bushel, or under a bed? and not to be set on a candlestick?

22 For there is nothing hid, which shall not be manifested; neither was any thing kept secret, but that it should come abroad.

23 If any man have ears to hear, let him hear.

24 And he said to them, Take heed what you hear: with what measure you mete, it shall be measured to you: and to you that hear shall more be given.

25 For he that has, to him shall be given: and he that has not, from him shall be taken even that which he has.

26 And he said, So is the kingdom of God, as if a man should cast seed into the ground;

27 And should sleep, and rise night and day, and the seed should spring and grow up, he knows not how.

28 For the earth brings forth fruit of herself; first the blade, then the ear, after that the full corn in the ear.

29 But when the fruit is brought forth, immediately he puts in the sickle, because the harvest is come.

30 And he said, Whereunto shall we liken the kingdom of God? or with what comparison shall we compare it?

31 It is like a grain of mustard seed, which, when it is sown in the earth, is less than all the seeds that be in the earth:

32 But when it is sown, it grows up, and becomes greater than all herbs, and shoots out great branches; so that the fowls of the air may lodge under the shadow of it.

33 And with many such parables spoke he the word to them, as they were able to hear it.

34 But without a parable spoke he not to them: and when they were alone, he expounded all things to his disciples.

35 And the same day, when the even was come, he said to them, Let us pass over to the other side.

36 And when they had sent away the multitude, they took him even as he was in the ship. And there were also with him

---

4:31 Skeptics claim that this verse is an error: "The mustard seed average size is approximately 1.0 millimeter in diameter. The basil seed average is .5 millimeter, the daisy seed is .4 millimeter, the lavender seed is .35 millimeter. Obviously these three seeds are smaller than the mustard seed." However, the mustard seed in Israel was less than .35 millimeters. We can know this as absolute fact, because here we have the Maker of the mustard seed telling us so. See John 1:3.

other little ships.

37 And there arose a great storm of wind, and the waves beat into the ship, so that it was now full.

38 And he was in the hinder part of the ship, asleep on a pillow: and they awake him, and say to him, Master, care not that we perish?

39 And he arose, and rebuked the wind, and said to the sea, Peace, be still. And the wind ceased, and there was a great calm.

40 And he said to them, Why are you so fearful? how is it that you have no faith?

41 And they feared exceedingly, and said one to another, What manner of man is this, that even the wind and the sea obey him?

· · · · · ·

*For the Holy Spirit's role in salvation,
see John 16:8–11 footnote.*

· · · · · ·

CHAPTER 5

A ND they came over to the other side of the sea, into the country of the Gadarenes.

2 And when he was come out of the ship, immediately there met him out of the tombs a man with an unclean spirit,

3 Who had his dwelling among the tombs; and no man could bind him, no, not with chains:

4 Because that he had been often bound with fetters and chains, and the chains had been plucked asunder by him, and the fetters broken in pieces: neither could any man tame him.

5 And always, night and day, he was in the mountains, and in the tombs, crying, and cutting himself with stones.

6 But when he saw Jesus afar off, he ran and worshipped him,

7 And cried with a loud voice, and said, What have I to do with you, Jesus, you Son of the most high God? I adjure you by God, that you torment me not.

8 For he said to him, Come out of the man, you unclean spirit.

9 And he asked him, What is your name? And he answered, saying, My name is Legion: for we are many.

10 And he besought him much that he would not send them away out of the country.

11 Now there was there near to the mountains a great herd of swine feeding.

12 And all the devils besought him, saying, Send us into the swine, that we may enter into them.

13 And forthwith Jesus gave them leave. And the unclean spirits went out, and entered into the swine: and the herd ran violently down a steep place into the sea, (they were about two thousand;) and were choked in the sea.

14 And they that fed the swine fled, and told it in the city, and in the country. And they went out to see what it was that was done.

15 And they come to Jesus, and see him that was possessed with the devil, and had the legion, sitting, and clothed, and in his right mind: and they were afraid.

16 And they that saw it told them how it befell to him that was possessed with the devil, and also concerning the swine.

17 And they began to pray him to depart out of their coasts.

18 And when he was come into the ship, he that had been possessed with the devil prayed him that he might be with him.

19 Howbeit Jesus suffered him not, but said to him, Go home to your friends, and tell them how great things the Lord has done for you, and has had compassion on you.

20 And he departed, and began to publish in Decapolis how great things Jesus had done for him: and all men did marvel.

21 And when Jesus was passed over again by ship to the other side, much people gathered to him: and he was near to the sea.

22 And, behold, there came one of the rulers of the synagogue, Jairus by name; and when he saw him, he fell at his feet,

23 And besought him greatly, saying, My little daughter lies at the point of death:

I pray you, come and lay your hands on her, that she may be healed; and she shall live.

24 And Jesus went with him; and much people followed him, and thronged him.

25 And a certain woman, which had an issue of blood twelve years,

26 And had suffered many things of many physicians, and had spent all that she had, and was nothing bettered, but rather grew worse,

27 When she had heard of Jesus, came in the press behind, and touched his garment.

28 For she said, If I may touch but his clothes, I shall be whole.

29 And straightway the fountain of her blood was dried up; and she felt in her body that she was healed of that plague.

30 And Jesus, immediately knowing in himself that virtue had gone out of him, turned him about in the press, and said, Who touched my clothes?

31 And his disciples said to him, You see the multitude thronging you, and you say, Who touched me?

32 And he looked round about to see her that had done this thing.

33 But the woman fearing and trembling, knowing what was done in her, came and fell down before him, and told him all the truth.

34 And he said to her, Daughter, your faith has made you whole; go in peace, and be whole of your plague.

35 While he yet spoke, there came from the ruler of the synagogue's house certain which said, Your daughter is dead: why trouble the Master any further?

36 As soon as Jesus heard the word that was spoken, he said to the ruler of the synagogue, Be not afraid, only believe.

37 And he suffered no man to follow him, save Peter, and James, and John the brother of James.

38 And he came to the house of the ruler of the synagogue, and saw the tumult, and them that wept and wailed greatly.

39 And when he was come in, he said to them, Why make this ado, and weep? the damsel is not dead, but sleeps.

40 And they laughed him to scorn. But when he had put them all out, he took the father and the mother of the damsel, and them that were with him, and entered in where the damsel was lying.

41 And he took the damsel by the hand, and said to her, Talitha cumi; which is, being interpreted, Damsel, I say to you, arise.

42 And straightway the damsel arose, and walked; for she was of the age of twelve years. And they were astonished with a great astonishment.

43 And he charged them straitly that no man should know it; and commanded that something should be given her to eat.

CHAPTER 6

AND he went out from thence, and came into his own country; and his disciples follow him.

2 And when the sabbath day was come, he began to teach in the synagogue: and many hearing him were astonished, saying, From whence has this man these things? and what wisdom is this which is given to him, that even such mighty works are wrought by his hands?

3 Is not this the carpenter, the son of Mary, the brother of James, and Joses, and of Juda, and Simon? and are not his sisters

---

6:3 Jesus' siblings. Jesus had four brothers and at least two sisters. Therefore Mary was no longer a virgin *after* she gave birth to Jesus. The Greek word used here is *adelphos*—brother (not half-brother). It is also unlikely that these were the cousins of Jesus or Jewish brethren. These children were spoken of as being with Mary, without a shadow of a hint that they were not her children. The word "mother" is mentioned at the same time (Mark 3:31; Luke 8:19; John 2:12; Acts 1:14). Likewise, Matthew 1:25 does not say that Mary remained a virgin for life, but that she had no physical union with her husband *until* Jesus was born.

"By a Carpenter mankind was made, and only by that Carpenter can mankind be remade."
Deriderius Erasmas

here with us? And they were offended at him.

4 But Jesus said to them, A prophet is not without honor, but in his own country, and among his own kin, and in his own house.

5 And he could there do no mighty work, save that he laid his hands upon a few sick folk, and healed them.

6 And he marveled because of their unbelief. And he went round about the villages, teaching.

7 And he called to him the twelve, and began to send them forth by two and two; and gave them power over unclean spirits;

8 And commanded them that they should take nothing for their journey, save a staff only; no scrip, no bread, no money in their purse:

9 But be shod with sandals; and not put on two coats.

10 And he said to them, In what place soever you enter into an house, there abide till you depart from that place.

11 And whosoever shall not receive you, nor hear you, when you depart thence, shake off the dust under your feet for a testimony against them. Verily I say to you, It shall be more tolerable for Sodom and Gomorrha in the day of judgment, than for that city.

12 And they went out, and preached that men should repent.

13 And they cast out many devils, and anointed with oil many that were sick, and healed them.

14 And king Herod heard of him; (for his name was spread abroad:) and he said, That John the Baptist was risen from the dead, and therefore mighty works do show

forth themselves in him.

15 Others said, That it is Elijah. And others said, That it is a prophet, or as one of the prophets.

16 But when Herod heard thereof, he said, It is John, whom I beheaded: he is risen from the dead.

17 For Herod himself had sent forth and laid hold upon John, and bound him in prison for Herodias' sake, his brother Philip's wife: for he had married her.

18 For John had said to Herod, It is not lawful for you to have your brother's wife.

> You and I must continue to drive at men's hearts till they are broken. Then we must keep on preaching Christ crucified until their hearts are bound up.
>
> **CHARLES SPURGEON**

19 Therefore Herodias had a quarrel against him, and would have killed him; but she could not:

20 For Herod feared John, knowing that he was a just man and an holy, and observed him; and when he heard him, he did many things, and heard him gladly.

21 And when a convenient day was come, that Herod on his birthday made a supper to his lords, high captains, and chief estates of Galilee;

22 And when the daughter of the said Herodias came in, and danced, and pleased Herod and them that sat with him, the king said to the damsel, Ask of me whatsoever you will, and I will give it you.

23 And he sware to her, Whatsoever you shall ask of me, I will give it you, to the half of my kingdom.

6:23 The power of lust. Lust blinds a man to reason (v. 22), leading him to yield up to "half his kingdom." He will abandon his wife, his children, his home, and his reputation, and run off with another woman. Herod feared John the Baptist because he knew that John was a just and holy man. He even protected him and heard him gladly, yet because of Herod's sinful eye he further violated the Law of God and had John murdered. Herod feared man more than he feared God (v. 26).

Those who don't fear God will lie to you, steal from you, and even kill you if they think they can get away with it. In truth, lust doesn't want half of your kingdom, it wants your head on a plate. See James 1:15.

24 And she went forth, and said to her mother, What shall I ask? And she said, The head of John the Baptist.

25 And she came in straightway with haste to the king, and asked, saying, I will that you give me by and by in a charger the head of John the Baptist.

26 And the king was exceeding sorry; yet for his oath's sake, and for their sakes which sat with him, he would not reject her.

27 And immediately the king sent an executioner, and commanded his head to be brought: and he went and beheaded him in the prison,

28 And brought his head in a charger, and gave it to the damsel: and the damsel gave it to her mother.

29 And when his disciples heard of it, they came and took up his corpse, and laid it in a tomb.

30 And the apostles gathered themselves together to Jesus, and told him all things, both what they had done, and what they had taught.

31 And he said to them, Come yourselves apart into a desert place, and rest a while: for there were many coming and going, and they had no leisure so much as to eat.

32 And they departed into a desert place by ship privately.

33 And the people saw them departing, and many knew him, and ran afoot there out of all cities, and outwent them, and came together to him.

34 And Jesus, when he came out, saw much people, and was moved with compassion toward them, because they were as sheep not having a shepherd: and he began to teach them many things.

35 And when the day was now far spent, his disciples came to him, and said, This is a desert place, and now the time is far passed:

36 Send them away, that they may go into the country round about, and into the villages, and buy themselves bread: for they have nothing to eat.

37 He answered and said to them, You give them to eat. And they said to him, Shall we go and buy two hundred pennyworth of bread, and give them to eat?

38 He said to them, How many loaves have you? Go and see. And when they knew, they said, Five, and two fishes.

39 And he commanded them to make all sit down by companies upon the green grass.

40 And they sat down in ranks, by hundreds, and by fifties.

41 And when he had taken the five loaves and the two fishes, he looked up to heaven, and blessed, and broke the loaves, and gave them to his disciples to set before them; and the two fishes divided he among them all.

42 And they did all eat, and were filled.

43 And they took up twelve baskets full of the fragments, and of the fishes.

44 And they that did eat of the loaves were about five thousand men.

45 And straightway he constrained his disciples to get into the ship, and to go to the other side before to Bethsaida, while he sent away the people.

46 And when he had sent them away, he departed into a mountain to pray.

47 And when even was come, the ship was in the midst of the sea, and he alone on the land.

48 And he saw them toiling in rowing; for the wind was contrary to them: and about the fourth watch of the night he came to them, walking upon the sea, and would have passed by them.

49 But when they saw him walking upon the sea, they supposed it had been a spirit, and cried out:

50 For they all saw him, and were troubled. And immediately he talked with them, and said to them, Be of good cheer: it is I; be not afraid.

51 And he went up to them into the ship; and the wind ceased: and they were

---

6:46 Prayer—the secret weapon: See Luke 5:16.

sore amazed in themselves beyond measure, and wondered.

52 For they considered not the miracle of the loaves: for their heart was hardened.

53 And when they had passed over, they came into the land of Gennesaret, and drew to the shore.

54 And when they were come out of the ship, straightway they knew him,

55 And ran through that whole region round about, and began to carry about in beds those that were sick, where they heard he was.

56 And wherever he entered, into villages, or cities, or country, they laid the sick in the streets, and besought him that they might touch if it were but the border of his garment: and as many as touched him were made whole.

CHAPTER 7

THEN came together to him the Pharisees, and certain of the scribes, which came from Jerusalem.

2 And when they saw some of his disciples eat bread with defiled, that is to say, with unwashed, hands, they found fault.

3 For the Pharisees, and all the Jews, except they wash their hands oft, eat not, holding the tradition of the elders.

4 And when they come from the market, except they wash, they eat not. And many other things there be, which they have received to hold, as the washing of cups, and pots, brazen vessels, and of tables.

5 Then the Pharisees and scribes asked him, Why walk not your disciples according to the tradition of the elders, but eat bread with unwashed hands?

6 He answered and said to them, Well has Isaiah prophesied of you hypocrites, as it is written, This people honors me with their lips, but their heart is far from me.

7 Howbeit in vain do they worship me, teaching for doctrines the commandments of men.

8 For laying aside the commandment of God, you hold the tradition of men, as the washing of pots and cups: and many other such like things you do.

9 And he said to them, Full well you reject the commandment of God, that you may keep your own tradition.

10 For Moses said, Honor your father and your mother; and, Whoso curses father or mother, let him die the death:

11 But you say, If a man shall say to his father or mother, It is Corban, that is to say, a gift, by whatsoever you might be profited by me; he shall be free.

12 And you suffer him no more to do anything for his father or his mother;

13 Making the word of God of none effect through your tradition, which you have delivered: and many such like things do you.

14 And when he had called all the people to him, he said to them, Hearken to me every one of you, and understand:

15 There is nothing from without a man, that entering into him can defile him: but the things which come out of him, those are they that defile the man.

16 If any man have ears to hear, let him hear.

17 And when he was entered into the house from the people, his disciples asked him concerning the parable.

18 And he said to them, Are you so without understanding also? Do you not perceive, that whatsoever thing from without enters into the man, it cannot defile him;

19 Because it enters not into his heart, but into the belly, and goes out into the

---

7:5–13 The Bible says that the Messiah would magnify the Law and make it honorable (Isaiah 42:21). Jesus did this many times, particularly in the Sermon on the Mount. The Pharisees had dishonored the Law by merely giving God lip service. They made the Commandment void through their tradition, teaching for doctrines the commandments of men. The Savior brought honor back to the Law by teaching that the Law was spiritual by nature, and that outward observance was not enough. God required truth in the inward parts (the thought-life, intent, and motives).

THE FUNCTION OF THE LAW

7:21 "Now, if you have your hearts broken up by the Law, you will find the heart is more deceitful than the devil. I can say this myself, I am very much afraid of mine, it is so bad. The heart is like a dark cellar, full of lizards, cockroaches, beetles, and all kinds of reptiles and insects, which in the dark we see not, but the Law takes down the shutters and lets in the light, and so we see the evil. Thus sin becoming apparent by the Law, it is written the Law makes the offense to abound." *Charles Spurgeon*

draught, purging all meats?

20 And he said, That which comes out of the man, that defiles the man.

21 For from within, out of the heart of men, proceed evil thoughts, adulteries, fornications, murders,

22 Thefts, covetousness, wickedness, deceit, lasciviousness, an evil eye, blasphemy, pride, foolishness:

23 All these evil things come from within, and defile the man.

24 And from thence he arose, and went into the borders of Tyre and Sidon, and entered into an house, and would have no man know it: but he could not be hid.

25 For a certain woman, whose young daughter had an unclean spirit, heard of him, and came and fell at his feet:

26 The woman was a Greek, a Syrophenician by nation; and she besought him that he would cast forth the devil out of her daughter.

27 But Jesus said to her, Let the children first be filled: for it is not meet to take the children's bread, and to cast it to the dogs.

28 And she answered and said to him, Yes, Lord: yet the dogs under the table eat of the children's crumbs.

29 And he said to her, For this saying go your way; the devil is gone out of your daughter.

30 And when she was come to her house, she found the devil gone out, and her daughter laid upon the bed.

31 And again, departing from the coasts of Tyre and Sidon, he came to the sea of Galilee, through the midst of the coasts of Decapolis.

32 And they bring to him one that was deaf, and had an impediment in his speech; and they beseech him to put his hand upon him.

33 And he took him aside from the multitude, and put his fingers into his ears, and he spit, and touched his tongue;

34 And looking up to heaven, he sighed, and said to him, Ephphatha, that is, Be opened.

35 And straightway his ears were opened, and the string of his tongue was loosed, and he spoke plain.

36 And he charged them that they should tell no man: but the more he charged them, so much the more a great deal they published it;

37 And were beyond measure astonished, saying, He has done all things well: he makes both the deaf to hear, and the dumb to speak.

CHAPTER 8

IN those days the multitude being very great, and having nothing to eat, Jesus called his disciples to him, and said to

---

7:20–23 Man's heart is sinful. Jeremiah 17:9 affirms the condition of man's heart: "The heart is deceitful above all things, and desperately wicked: who can know it?" Verse 10 then warns us that God not only knows the secret things of the heart but will reward us accordingly: "I the Lord search the heart, I try the reins, even to give every man according to his ways, and according to the fruit of his doings." See Mark 12:29–31 footnote.

7:21,22 Notice that what defiles a man is directly referenced to the Moral Law (the Ten Commandments): adulteries (Seventh), fornications (Seventh), murders (Sixth), thefts (Eighth), covetousness (Tenth), blasphemy (Third). Sin is transgression of the Law (1 John 3:4).

them,

2 I have compassion on the multitude, because they have now been with me three days, and have nothing to eat:

3 And if I send them away fasting to their own houses, they will faint by the way: for divers of them came from far.

4 And his disciples answered him, From whence can a man satisfy these men with bread here in the wilderness?

5 And he asked them, How many loaves have you? And they said, Seven.

6 And he commanded the people to sit down on the ground: and he took the seven loaves, and gave thanks, and broke, and gave to his disciples to set before them; and they did set them before the people.

7 And they had a few small fishes: and he blessed, and commanded to set them also before them.

8 So they did eat, and were filled: and they took up of the broken meat that was left seven baskets.

9 And they that had eaten were about four thousand: and he sent them away.

10 And straightway he entered into a ship with his disciples, and came into the parts of Dalmanutha.

11 And the Pharisees came forth, and began to question with him, seeking of him a sign from heaven, tempting him.

12 And he sighed deeply in his spirit, and said, Why does this generation seek after a sign? verily I say to you, There shall no sign be given to this generation.

13 And he left them, and entering into the ship again departed to the other side.

14 Now the disciples had forgotten to take bread, neither had they in the ship with them more than one loaf.

15 And he charged them, saying, Take heed, beware of the leaven of the Pharisees, and of the leaven of Herod.

16 And they reasoned among themselves, saying, It is because we have no bread.

17 And when Jesus knew it, he said to them, Why do you reason, because you have no bread? Do you not yet perceive, neither understand? have you your heart

yet hardened?

18 Having eyes, do you not see? and having ears, do you not hear? and do you not remember?

19 When I broke the five loaves among five thousand, how many baskets full of fragments did you take up? They said to him, Twelve.

20 And when the seven among four thousand, how many baskets full of fragments did you take up? And they said, Seven.

21 And he said to them, How is it that you do not understand?

> As the fisherman longs to take the fish in his net, as the hunter pants to bear home his spoil, as the mother pines to clasp her lost child to her bosom, so do we faint for the salvation of souls.
>
> **CHARLES SPURGEON**

22 And he came to Bethsaida; and they brought a blind man to him, and besought him to touch him.

23 And he took the blind man by the hand, and led him out of the town; and when he had spit on his eyes, and put his hands upon him, he asked him if he saw anything.

24 And he looked up, and said, I see men as trees, walking.

25 After that he put his hands again upon his eyes, and made him look up: and he was restored, and saw every man clearly.

26 And he sent him away to his house, saying, Neither go into the town, nor tell it to any in the town.

27 And Jesus went out, and his disciples, into the towns of Caesarea Philippi: and by the way he asked his disciples, saying to them, Whom do men say that I am?

28 And they answered, John the Baptist: but some say, Elijah; and others, One of the prophets.

29 And he said to them, But whom do you say that I am? And Peter answered

and said to him, You are the Christ.

30 And he charged them that they should tell no man of him.

31 And he began to teach them, that the Son of man must suffer many things, and be rejected of the elders, and of the chief priests, and scribes, and be killed, and after three days rise again.

32 And he spoke that saying openly. And Peter took him, and began to rebuke him.

33 But when he had turned about and looked on his disciples, he rebuked Peter, saying, Get behind me, Satan: for you savour not the things that be of God, but the things that be of men.

34 And when he had called the people to him with his disciples also, he said to them, **Whosoever will come after me, let him deny himself, and take up his cross, and follow me.**

. . . . . .

For the biblical way to confront sinners, see Psalm 41:4 footnote.

. . . . . .

35 **For whosoever will save his life shall lose it; but whosoever shall lose his life for my sake and the gospel's, the same shall save it.**

36 **For what shall it profit a man, if he shall gain the whole world, and lose his own soul?**

37 **Or what shall a man give in exchange for his soul?**

38 **Whosoever therefore shall be ashamed of me and of my words in this** adulterous and sinful generation; of him also shall the Son of man be ashamed, when he comes in the glory of his Father with the holy angels.

CHAPTER 9

AND he said to them, Verily I say to you, That there be some of them that stand here, which shall not taste of death, till they have seen the kingdom of God come with power.

2 And after six days Jesus took with him Peter, and James, and John, and led them up into an high mountain apart by themselves: and he was transfigured before them.

3 And his raiment became shining, exceeding white as snow; so as no fuller on earth can white them.

4 And there appeared to them Elijah with Moses: and they were talking with Jesus.

5 And Peter answered and said to Jesus, Master, it is good for us to be here: and let us make three tabernacles; one for you, and one for Moses, and one for Elijah.

6 For he knew not what to say; for they were sore afraid.

7 And there was a cloud that overshadowed them: and a voice came out of the cloud, saying, This is my beloved Son: hear him.

8 And suddenly, when they had looked round about, they saw no man any more, save Jesus only with themselves.

9 And as they came down from the mountain, he charged them that they should tell no man what things they had seen, till the Son of man were risen from the dead.

8:33 If you are going to do anything for the kingdom of God, be ready for unexpected discouragement. This may come through a Christian brother or sister—the place least expected. Satan spoke directly through Peter in an attempt to stop Jesus from doing the will of the Father. It was David's elder brother who tried to discourage him from slaying Goliath. See 1 Samuel 17:28.

8:38 Here's an effective way to unashamedly share your faith and show that you care about strangers: When you're eating in a restaurant, tell the waiter, "We're going to be asking the blessing for our food in a minute, and wanted to know if there's anything you'd like us to pray for?"

8:38 Second coming of Jesus: See Luke 12:40.

9:4 See Luke 9:30 footnote.

10 And they kept that saying with themselves, questioning one with another what the rising from the dead should mean.

11 And they asked him, saying, Why say the scribes that Elijah must first come?

12 And he answered and told them, Elijah verily comes first, and restores all things; and how it is written of the Son of man, that he must suffer many things, and be set at nought.

13 But I say to you, That Elijah is indeed come, and they have done to him whatsoever they listed, as it is written of him.

14 And when he came to his disciples, he saw a great multitude about them, and the scribes questioning with them.

15 And straightway all the people, when they beheld him, were greatly amazed, and running to him saluted him.

16 And he asked the scribes, What do you question with them?

17 And one of the multitude answered and said, Master, I have brought to you my son, which has a dumb spirit;

18 And wherever he takes him, he tears him: and he foams, and gnashes with his teeth, and pines away: and I spoke to your disciples that they should cast him out; and they could not.

19 He answered him, and said, O faithless generation, how long shall I be with you? how long shall I suffer you? bring him to me.

20 And they brought him to him: and when he saw him, straightway the spirit tare him; and he fell on the ground, and wallowed foaming.

21 And he asked his father, How long is it ago since this came to him? And he said, Of a child.

22 And often it has cast him into the fire, and into the waters, to destroy him: but if you can do any thing, have compassion on us, and help us.

23 Jesus said to him, If you can believe, all things are possible to him that believes.

24 And straightway the father of the child cried out, and said with tears, Lord, I believe; help mine unbelief.

"Most people are bothered by those passages of Scriptures they don't understand, but for me I have always noticed that the passages that bother me are those I do understand."

Mark Twain

25 When Jesus saw that the people came running together, he rebuked the foul spirit, saying to him, You dumb and deaf spirit, I charge you, come out of him, and enter no more into him.

26 And the spirit cried, and rent him sore, and came out of him: and he was as one dead; insomuch that many said, He is dead.

27 But Jesus took him by the hand, and lifted him up; and he arose.

28 And when he was come into the house, his disciples asked him privately, Why could not we cast him out?

29 And he said to them, This kind can come forth by nothing, but by prayer and fasting.

30 And they departed thence, and passed through Galilee; and he would not that any man should know it.

31 For he taught his disciples, and said to them, The Son of man is delivered into the hands of men, and they shall kill him; and after that he is killed, he shall rise the third day.

32 But they understood not that saying,

QUESTIONS & OBJECTIONS

9:47   *"Hell isn't a place. This life is hell."*

Skeptics who say this are trying to dismiss the reality of hell. They might like to think that life as we know it couldn't get any worse, but the sufferings in this life will be heaven compared to the suffering in the next life—for those who die in their sins. This life is the closest thing to hell that Christians will ever know, and the closest thing to heaven that sinners will ever know.

For a biblical description of hell, see Revelation 1:18 footnote.

and were afraid to ask him.

33 And he came to Capernaum: and being in the house he asked them, What was it that you disputed among yourselves by the way?

34 But they held their peace: for by the way they had disputed among themselves, who should be the greatest.

35 And he sat down, and called the twelve, and said to them, If any man desire to be first, the same shall be last of all, and servant of all.

36 And he took a child, and set him in the midst of them: and when he had taken him in his arms, he said to them,

37 Whosoever shall receive one of such children in my name, receives me: and whosoever shall receive me, receives not me, but him that sent me.

38 And John answered him, saying, Master, we saw one casting out devils in your name, and he followed not us: and we forbad him, because he followed not us.

39 But Jesus said, Forbid him not: for there is no man which shall do a miracle in my name, that can lightly speak evil of me.

40 For he that is not against us is on our part.

41 For whosoever shall give you a cup of water to drink in my name, because you

belong to Christ, verily I say to you, he shall not lose his reward.

42 And whosoever shall offend one of these little ones that believe in me, it is better for him that a millstone were hanged about his neck, and he were cast into the sea.

43 And if your hand offends you, cut it off: it is better for you to enter into life maimed, than having two hands to go into hell, into the fire that never shall be quenched:

44 Where their worm dies not, and the fire is not quenched.

45 And if your foot offends you, cut it off: it is better for you to enter halt into life, than having two feet to be cast into hell, into the fire that never shall be quenched:

46 Where their worm dies not, and the fire is not quenched.

47 And if your eye offends you, pluck it out: it is better for you to enter into the kingdom of God with one eye, than having two eyes to be cast into hell fire:

48 Where their worm dies not, and the fire is not quenched.

49 For every one shall be salted with fire, and every sacrifice shall be salted with salt.

50 Salt is good: but if the salt has lost

9:34,35 "Not everybody could be famous, but everybody can be great because greatness is determined by service." *Martin Luther King, Jr.*

9:43–48 **Hell:** For verses warning of its reality, see Luke 16:23.

"There is a dreadful hell, and everlasting pains; where sinners must with devils dwell, in darkness, fire, and chains." *Isaac Watts*

his saltiness, wherewith will you season it? Have salt in yourselves, and have peace one with another.

CHAPTER 10

AND he arose from thence, and came into the coasts of Judea by the farther side of Jordan: and the people resort to him again; and, as he was wont, he taught them again.

2 And the Pharisees came to him, and asked him, Is it lawful for a man to put away his wife? tempting him.

3 And he answered and said to them, What did Moses command you?

4 And they said, Moses suffered to write a bill of divorcement, and to put her away.

5 And Jesus answered and said to them, For the hardness of your heart he wrote you this precept.

6 But from the beginning of the creation God made them male and female.

7 For this cause shall a man leave his father and mother, and cleave to his wife;

8 And they twain shall be one flesh: so then they are no more twain, but one flesh.

9 What therefore God has joined together, let not man put asunder.

10 And in the house his disciples asked him again of the same matter.

11 And he said to them, Whosoever shall put away his wife, and marry another, commits adultery against her.

12 And if a woman shall put away her husband, and be married to another, she commits adultery.

13 And they brought young children to him, that he should touch them: and his disciples rebuked those that brought them.

14 But when Jesus saw it, he was much displeased, and said to them, Suffer the little children to come to me, and forbid

---

9:50 Salty Christians. "Salvation is a radical thing. It is a call to all that Christ has demanded us to do. Real Christianity will make a salty difference, in our family, in our waking up, in our work, in our relationships, in the way we spend our money, and in the way we spend our leisure time. Real Christianity is not casual. It is dynamic. It goes beyond mere intellectual assent to correct doctrine.

"Real Christians who want to know real Christianity, who are not content with games and masks and only images of the truth, must rise from our comfortable pews and leave our 'one-stop Christian service centers' and go out into the world and make a salty difference!" *Guy Rice Doud, Joy in the Journey*

10:6 God made them male and female. If every creature "evolved" with no Creator, there are numerous problems. Take for instance the first bird. Was it male or female? Let's say it was a male. How did it produce offspring without a mate? If a female evolved, why did it evolve with differing reproductive organs? Did it evolve by chance, or did it evolve because it knew that it was needed by the male of the species? How did it know what needed to be evolved if its brain hadn't yet evolved? Did the bird breathe? Did it breathe before it evolved lungs? How did it do this? Why did it evolve lungs if it was happily surviving without them? Did the bird have a mouth? How did it eat before it had evolved a mouth? Where did the mouth send the food before a stomach evolved? How did the bird have energy if it didn't eat (because it didn't yet have a mouth)? How did the bird see what there was to eat before its eyes evolved? Evolution is intellectual suicide. It is an embarrassment. (See Romans 1:21,22.)

"Evolution is a fairy tale for grown-ups. This theory has helped nothing in the progress of science. It is useless." *Professor Louis Bounoure,* Director of Research, National Center of Scientific Research

"Scientists who go about teaching that evolution is a fact of life are great con-men, and the story they are telling may be the greatest hoax ever. In explaining evolution, we do not have one iota of fact." *Dr. T. N. Tahmisian,* Atomic Energy Commission

10:6–9 By quoting from both chapters 1 and 2 of Genesis, Jesus shows that these chapters are not contradictory, as some claim. Chapter 2 merely gives the details of chapter 1. A sports commentator is not in error when (after a game) he gives in-depth analysis and fails to repeat every detail in chronological order. He is merely reviewing the completed game by mentioning the highlights.

10:18 *"I'm as good as any Christian!"*

A Christian, by himself, isn't good. Jesus said that only God is good. The only "goodness," or righteousness, that the believer has comes from Christ (2 Corinthians 5:21; Philippians 3:9). The Bible tells us that, without Christ, man is corrupt and filthy; "there is none that does good, no, not one" (Psalm 14:3). See also Romans 3:9 footnote.

them not: for of such is the kingdom of God.

15 Verily I say to you, Whosoever shall not receive the kingdom of God as a little child, he shall not enter therein.

16 And he took them up in his arms, put his hands upon them, and blessed them.

17 And when he was gone forth into the way, there came one running, and kneeled to him, and asked him, Good Master, what shall I do that I may inherit eternal life?

USING THE LAW IN EVANGELISM

10:17 This man came running and fell to his knees before Jesus. His earnest and humble heart would seem to make him a prime candidate as a potential convert. Yet, instead of giving him the message of God's grace, Jesus used the Law to expose the man's hidden sin. This man was a transgressor of the First of the Ten Commandments. His money was his god, and one cannot serve God and mammon. Verse 21 reveals that it was love that motivated the Savior to speak in this way to this rich young man. Love will be concerned with the desire for a genuine conversion, rather than a sense of accomplishment in leading someone in a sinner's prayer whose heart isn't right with God. (See also Matthew 19:17–22.)

18 And Jesus said to him, Why do you call me good? there is none good but one, that is, God.

19 You know the commandments, Do not commit adultery, Do not kill, Do not steal, Do not bear false witness, Defraud not, Honor your father and mother.

20 And he answered and said to him, Master, all these have I observed from my youth.

21 Then Jesus beholding him loved him, and said to him, One thing you lack: go your way, sell whatsoever you have, and give to the poor, and you shall have treasure in heaven: and come, take up the cross, and follow me.

22 And he was sad at that saying, and went away grieved: for he had great possessions.

23 And Jesus looked round about, and said to his disciples, How hardly shall they that have riches enter into the kingdom of God!

24 And the disciples were astonished at his words. But Jesus answered again, and said to them, Children, how hard is it for them that trust in riches to enter into the kingdom of God!

25 **It is easier for a camel to go through the eye of a needle, than for a rich man to enter into the kingdom of God.**

26 And they were astonished out of measure, saying among themselves, Who

10:21 "Christianity has always insisted that the cross we bear precedes the crown we wear." *Martin Luther King, Jr.*

"No pain, no palm; no thorns, no throne; no gall, no glory; no cross, no crown..." *William Penn*

then can be saved?

27 And Jesus looking upon them said, With men it is impossible, but not with God: for with God all things are possible.

28 Then Peter began to say to him, Lo, we have left all, and have followed you.

29 And Jesus answered and said, Verily I say to you, There is no man that has left house, or brethren, or sisters, or father, or mother, or wife, or children, or lands, for my sake, and the gospel's,

30 But he shall receive an hundredfold now in this time, houses, and brethren, and sisters, and mothers, and children, and lands, with persecutions; and in the world to come eternal life.

> The diver plunges deep to find pearls, and we must accept any labor or hazard to win a soul.
>
> **CHARLES SPURGEON**

31 But many that are first shall be last; and the last first.

32 And they were in the way going up to Jerusalem; and Jesus went before them: and they were amazed; and as they followed, they were afraid. And he took again the twelve, and began to tell them what things should happen to him,

33 Saying, Behold, we go up to Jerusalem; and the Son of man shall be delivered to the chief priests, and to the scribes; and they shall condemn him to death, and shall deliver him to the Gentiles:

34 And they shall mock him, and shall scourge him, and shall spit upon him, and shall kill him: and the third day he shall rise again.

35 And James and John, the sons of Zebedee, come to him, saying, Master, we would that you should do for us whatsoever we shall desire.

36 And he said to them, What would you that I should do for you?

37 They said to him, Grant to us that we may sit, one on your right hand, and the other on your left hand, in your glory.

38 But Jesus said to them, You know not what you ask: can you drink of the cup that I drink of? and be baptized with the baptism that I am baptized with?

39 And they said to him, We can. And Jesus said to them, You shall indeed drink of the cup that I drink of; and with the baptism that I am baptized withal shall you be baptized:

40 But to sit on my right hand and on my left hand is not mine to give; but it shall be given to them for whom it is prepared.

41 And when the ten heard it, they began to be much displeased with James and John.

42 But Jesus called them to him, and said to them, You know that they which are accounted to rule over the Gentiles exercise lordship over them; and their great ones exercise authority upon them.

43 But so shall it not be among you: but whosoever will be great among you, shall be your minister:

44 And whosoever of you will be the chiefest, shall be servant of all.

45 For even the Son of man came not to be ministered unto, but to minister, and to give his life a ransom for many.

46 And they came to Jericho: and as he went out of Jericho with his disciples and a great number of people, blind Bartimaeus, the son of Timaeus, sat by the highway side begging.

47 And when he heard that it was Jesus of Nazareth, he began to cry out, and say, Jesus, you Son of David, have mercy on me.

48 And many charged him that he should hold his peace: but he cried the more a great deal, You Son of David, have mercy on me.

49 And Jesus stood still, and commanded him to be called. And they called the

---

10:44 "A Christian man is the most free lord of all, subject to no one. A Christian man is the dutiful servant of all, subject to everyone." *Martin Luther*

11:15 *"Jesus wasn't sinless—He became angry when He cleared the temple."*

The temple of God was filled with the day's equivalent of money-grabbing televangelists. Jesus called it a "den of thieves" (v. 17), because the moneychangers were not interested in God but in taking financial advantage of those who came to worship. Anger at hypocrisy isn't a sin—it's a virtue.

blind man, saying to him, Be of good comfort, rise; he calls you.

50 And he, casting away his garment, rose, and came to Jesus.

51 And Jesus answered and said to him, What will you that I should do to you? The blind man said to him, Lord, that I might receive my sight.

52 And Jesus said to him, Go your way; your faith has made you whole. And immediately he received his sight, and followed Jesus in the way.

CHAPTER 11

AND when they came near to Jerusalem, to Bethphage and Bethany, at the mount of Olives, he sent forth two of his disciples,

2 And said to them, Go your way into the village over against you: and as soon as you enter into it, you shall find a colt tied, whereon never a man sat; loose him, and bring him.

3 And if any man say to you, Why are you doing this? say that the Lord has need of him; and straightway he will send him here.

4 And they went their way, and found the colt tied by the door without in a place where two ways met; and they loosened him.

5 And certain of them that stood there said to them, What are you doing, loosing the colt?

6 And they said to them even as Jesus had commanded: and they let them go.

7 And they brought the colt to Jesus, and cast their garments on him; and he sat upon him.

8 And many spread their garments in the way: and others cut down branches off the trees, and strawed them in the way.

9 And they that went before, and they that followed, cried, saying, Hosanna; Blessed is he that comes in the name of the Lord:

10 Blessed be the kingdom of our father David, that comes in the name of the Lord: Hosanna in the highest.

11 And Jesus entered into Jerusalem, and into the temple: and when he had looked round about upon all things, and now the eventide was come, he went out to Bethany with the twelve.

12 And on the morrow, when they were come from Bethany, he was hungry:

13 And seeing a fig tree afar off having leaves, he came, if haply he might find any thing thereon: and when he came to it, he found nothing but leaves; for the time of figs was not yet.

14 And Jesus answered and said to it, No man eat fruit of you hereafter for ever. And his disciples heard it.

15 And they come to Jerusalem: and Jesus went into the temple, and began to cast out them that sold and bought in the temple, and overthrew the tables of the moneychangers, and the seats of them that sold doves;

16 And would not suffer that any man should carry any vessel through the temple.

17 And he taught, saying to them, Is it not written, My house shall be called of all nations the house of prayer? but you have made it a den of thieves.

18 And the scribes and chief priests heard

it, and sought how they might destroy him: for they feared him, because all the people were astonished at his doctrine.

19 And when even was come, he went out of the city.

20 And in the morning, as they passed by, they saw the fig tree dried up from the roots.

21 And Peter calling to remembrance said to him, Master, behold, the fig tree which you cursed is withered away.

22 And Jesus answering said to them, Have faith in God.

23 For verily I say to you, That whosoever shall say to this mountain, Be removed, and be cast into the sea; and shall not doubt in his heart, but shall believe that those things which he said shall come to pass; he shall have whatsoever he says.

24 Therefore I say to you, What things soever you desire, when you pray, believe that you receive them, and you shall have them.

25 And when you stand praying, forgive, if you have anything against any: that your Father also which is in heaven may forgive you your trespasses.

26 But if you do not forgive, neither will your Father which is in heaven forgive your trespasses.

27 And they came again to Jerusalem: and as he was walking in the temple, there came to him the chief priests, and the scribes, and the elders,

28 And said to him, By what authority do you these things? and who gave you this authority to do these things?

29 And Jesus answered and said to them, I will also ask of you one question, and answer me, and I will tell you by what authority I do these things.

30 The baptism of John, was it from heaven, or of men? answer me.

31 And they reasoned with themselves, saying, If we shall say, From heaven; he will say, Why then did you not believe him?

32 But if we shall say, Of men; they feared the people: for all men counted John, that he was a prophet indeed.

33 And they answered and said to Jesus, We cannot tell. And Jesus answering said to them, Neither do I tell you by what authority I do these things.

CHAPTER 12

AND he began to speak to them by parables. A certain man planted a vineyard, and set an hedge about it, and dug a place for the winefat, and built a tower, and let it out to husbandmen, and went into a far country.

2 And at the season he sent to the husbandmen a servant, that he might receive from the husbandmen of the fruit of the vineyard.

3 And they caught him, and beat him, and sent him away empty.

4 And again he sent to them another servant; and at him they cast stones, and wounded him in the head, and sent him away shamefully handled.

5 And again he sent another; and him they killed, and many others; beating some, and killing some.

6 Having yet therefore one son, his well-beloved, he sent him also last to them, saying, They will reverence my son.

7 But those husbandmen said among themselves, This is the heir; come, let us kill him, and the inheritance shall be ours.

8 And they took him, and killed him, and cast him out of the vineyard.

9 What shall therefore the lord of the

11:22 Faith in God. "It's amazing how many people find it difficult to have faith in a perfect God, but they trust their lives without question to fallible men—the eighth leading cause of death in the U.S. is 'medical mistakes'" (*ABC News*, November 30, 1999).

11:23 Prayer—the secret weapon: This is an open invitation for Christians to beseech God for genuine revival. We should never be satisfied until every living human being is safe in Christ: "Show me a thoroughly satisfied man and I will show you a failure." *Thomas Edison*

11:25 *How to Witness to Mormons*

There are at least two approaches to use in witnessing to Mormons. We can either debate the doctrines of Mormonism (baptism for the dead, "burning" in the bosom, Joseph Smith as a prophet of God, the validity of the *Book of Mormon*, the Trinity, "God was once a man," "protective" underwear, etc.), or we can present the gospel biblically. One creates an atmosphere of contention and often leaves the Christian feeling frustrated, while the other creates an atmosphere of concern for the eternal welfare of the Mormon. Our goal should be to win a soul to Christ rather than merely win a doctrinal argument.

One point of frustration for the Christian is that Mormons often agree when they hear words such as "salvation," or Jesus as "Savior." The problem is that *their* understanding of the words differs from the biblical revelation of the words. "Salvation" for a Mormon can mean the salvation of all humanity—when the "Savior" will eventually raise everyone from the dead.

Rather than speak of "going to heaven," the Christian should ask what the Mormon has to do to be at peace with the "heavenly Father." This is language they can understand, and will reveal the basis for their salvation. Are they trusting in self-righteousness, or solely in the righteousness of Christ?

Mark J. Cares writes: "Although Mormons commonly appear self-assured and self-righteous, many are undergoing great stress. This is because Mormonism holds up perfection as an attainable goal. The one Bible passage the Mormon church constantly holds up before its membership is Matthew 5:48: 'Be ye therefore perfect, even as your Father which is in heaven is perfect.' They then expound on it with numerous exhortations to strive for perfection. Spencer W. Kimball, for example, wrote: 'Being perfect means to triumph over sin. This is a mandate from the Lord. He is just and wise and kind. He would never require anything from his children which was not for their benefit and which was not attainable. Perfection therefore is an achievable goal' (*Life and Teachings of Jesus and His Apostles*, Church of Jesus Christ of Latter-day Saints).

"This emphasis on perfection permeates every aspect of a Mormon's life. Its most common form is the unending demand on them to be 'worthy.' Every privilege in Mormonism is conditioned on a person's worthiness. Kimball wrote: 'All blessings are conditional. I know of none that are not' (*Remember Me*, Church of Jesus Christ of Latter-day Saints).

"Christians need to recognize that this constant striving for perfection—and the resultant stress it produces—offers an excellent opening to talk to Mormons about Jesus and the imputed perfection we receive through Him.

"**Reinforce their predicament.** Average hard-working Mormons view this striving for perfection as a heavy but manageable burden. They can cultivate illusions of perfection because the Mormon church has greatly watered down the concept of sin. Consequently, the Christian witness needs to show Mormons both the severity of their predicament and the impossibility of their becoming perfect. In other words, they need to have a face-to-face confrontation with the stern message of God's Law, because 'through the Law we become conscious of sin' (Romans 3:21).

"The Law must first convince Mormons of the severity of their predicament. The best way to accomplish this is to tell them, lovingly but firmly, that they are going to 'outer darkness.' (Outer darkness is the closest concept in Mormonism to an eternal hell.) Most Mormons have never been told this, nor have they ever considered that possibility for themselves, since Mormonism teaches that nearly everyone will enter one of Mormonism's three kingdoms of heaven. Therefore, until you introduce the thought of eternal suffering, they will not feel any real urgency to take your witness to heart. On the contrary, most, if they are willing to talk at all, will view any religious conversation as nothing more than an interesting intellectual discussion.

"Christians often hesitate to be this blunt. They feel that if anything will turn Mormons off, telling them that they are going to outer darkness surely will. I shared that fear when I began using this approach. To my amazement, however, rejection wasn't the reaction I

(continued)

(11:25 continued)
received. Most have been shocked, but they were also eager to know why I would say such a thing. The key is to speak this truth *with love*, in such a way that our concern for their souls is readily apparent.

"Alerting Mormons to the very real danger of their going to outer darkness opens the door to telling them the *basis* for that judg-ment—which is, they are not meeting God's requirement for living with Him (they are not *presently* perfect). The key to explaining this is the present imperative, *be perfect*, in Matthew 5:48."

See Luke 18:20 footnote for how to go through the Law, and 1 Corinthians 15:58 footnote on how not to be discouraged in witnessing.

---

vineyard do? he will come and destroy the husbandmen, and will give the vineyard to others.

10 And have you not read this scripture; The stone which the builders rejected is become the head of the corner:

11 This was the Lord's doing, and it is marvelous in our eyes?

12 And they sought to lay hold on him, but feared the people: for they knew that he had spoken the parable against them: and they left him, and went their way.

13 And they sent to him certain of the Pharisees and of the Herodians, to catch him in his words.

14 And when they were come, they said to him, Master, we know that you are true, and care for no man: for you regard not the person of men, but teach the way of God in truth: Is it lawful to give tribute to Caesar, or not?

15 Shall we give, or shall we not give? But he, knowing their hypocrisy, said to them, Why tempt me? bring me a penny, that I may see it.

16 And they brought it. And he said to them, Whose is this image and superscription? And they said to him, Caesar's.

17 And Jesus answering said to them, Render to Caesar the things that are Caesar's, and to God the things that are God's. And they marveled at him.

18 Then came to him the Sadducees, which say there is no resurrection; and they asked him, saying,

19 Master, Moses wrote to us, If a man's brother die, and leave his wife behind him, and leave no children, that his brother should take his wife, and raise up seed to his brother.

20 Now there were seven brethren: and the first took a wife, and dying left no seed.

21 And the second took her, and died, neither left he any seed: and the third likewise.

22 And the seven had her, and left no seed: last of all the woman died also.

23 In the resurrection therefore, when they shall rise, whose wife shall she be of them? for the seven had her to wife.

24 And Jesus answering said to them, Do you not therefore err, because you know not the scriptures, neither the power of God?

25 For when they shall rise from the dead, they neither marry, nor are given in marriage; but are as the angels which are in heaven.

26 And as touching the dead, that they rise: have you not read in the book of Moses, how in the bush God spoke to him, saying, I am the God of Abraham, and the God of Isaac, and the God of Jacob?

27 He is not the God of the dead, but the God of the living: you therefore do greatly err.

28 And one of the scribes came, and having heard them reasoning together, and perceiving that he had answered them well, asked him, Which is the first commandment of all?

29 And Jesus answered him, The first of all the commandments is, Hear, O Israel; The Lord our God is one Lord:

30 And you shall love the Lord your God with all your heart, and with all your soul, and with all your mind, and

PRINCIPLES OF GROWTH FOR THE NEW AND GROWING CHRISTIAN

12:41–44 *Tithing—The Final Frontier*

It has been said that the wallet is the "final frontier." It is the final area to be conquered—the last thing that comes to God in surrender. Jesus spoke much about money. He said that we cannot serve God and mammon (Matthew 6:24). "Mammon" was the common Aramaic word for riches, which is related to a Hebrew word signifying "that which is to be trusted." In other words, we cannot trust God and money. Either money is our source of joy, our great love, our sense of security, the supplier of our needs—or God is.

When you open your purse or wallet, give generously and regularly to your local church. A guide of how much you should give can be found in the "tithe" of the Old Testament: 10 percent of your income. Whatever amount you give, make sure you give *something* to the work of God (see Malachi 3:8–11). Give because you *want* to, not because you *have* to. God loves a cheerful giver (2 Corinthians 9:6,7), so learn to hold your money with a loose hand.

with all your strength: this is the first commandment.

31 And the second is like, namely this, You shall love your neighbour as yourself. There is none other commandment greater than these.

32 And the scribe said to him, Well, Master, you have said the truth: for there is one God; and there is none other but he:

33 And to love him with all the heart, and with all the understanding, and with all the soul, and with all the strength, and to love his neighbour as himself, is more than all whole burnt offerings and sacrifices.

34 And when Jesus saw that he answered discreetly, he said to him, You are not far from the kingdom of God. And no man after that dared ask him any question.

35 And Jesus answered and said, while he taught in the temple, How say the scribes that Christ is the Son of David?

36 For David himself said by the Holy Spirit, The Lord said to my Lord, Sit on my right hand, till I make your enemies your footstool.

37 David therefore himself calls him Lord; and whence is he then his son? And the common people heard him gladly.

38 And he said to them in his doctrine, Beware of the scribes, which love to go in long clothing, and love salutations in the marketplaces,

39 And the chief seats in the synagogues, and the uppermost rooms at feasts:

40 Which devour widows' houses, and for a pretence make long prayers: these shall receive greater damnation.

41 And Jesus sat over against the treasury, and beheld how the people cast money into the treasury: and many that were rich cast in much.

42 And there came a certain poor widow, and she threw in two mites, which make a farthing.

43 And he called to him his disciples, and said to them, Verily I say to you, That this poor widow has cast more in, than all they which have cast into the treasury:

44 For all they did cast in of their abundance; but she of her want did cast in all that she had, even all her living.

12:29–31 No one has ever kept the Commandments: "The Lord looked down from heaven upon the children of men, to see if there were any that did understand, and seek God. They are all gone aside, they are all together become filthy: there is no one that does good, no, not one" (Psalm 14:2,3). See Romans 2:15,16 footnote.

12:34 It is understanding of the Law that brings a sinner closer to the kingdom of God.

CHAPTER 13

AND as he went out of the temple, one of his disciples said to him, Master, see what manner of stones and what buildings are here!

2 And Jesus answering said to him, See these great buildings? There shall not be left one stone upon another, that shall not be thrown down.

3 And as he sat upon the mount of Olives over against the temple, Peter and James and John and Andrew asked him privately,

4 Tell us, when shall these things be? and what shall be the sign when all these things shall be fulfilled?

5 And Jesus answering them began to say, Take heed lest any man deceive you:

6 For many shall come in my name, saying, I am Christ; and shall deceive many.

7 And when you shall hear of wars and rumours of wars, be not troubled: for such things must needs be; but the end shall not be yet.

8 For nation shall rise against nation, and kingdom against kingdom: and there shall be earthquakes in divers places, and there shall be famines and troubles: these are the beginnings of sorrows.

9 But take heed to yourselves: for they shall deliver you up to councils; and in the synagogues you shall be beaten: and you shall be brought before rulers and kings for my sake, for a testimony against them.

10 And the gospel must first be published among all nations.

11 But when they shall lead you, and deliver you up, take no thought beforehand what you shall speak, neither premeditate: but whatsoever shall be given you in that hour, that speak: for it is not you that speak, but the Holy Spirit.

12 Now the brother shall betray the brother to death, and the father the son; and children shall rise up against their parents, and shall cause them to be put to death.

13 And you shall be hated of all men for my name's sake: but he that shall endure to the end, the same shall be saved.

14 But when you shall see the abomination of desolation, spoken of by Daniel the prophet, standing where it ought not, (let him that reads understand,) then let them that be in Judea flee to the mountains:

15 And let him that is on the housetop not go down into the house, neither enter therein, to take any thing out of his house:

16 And let him that is in the field not turn back again for to take up his garment.

17 But woe to them that are with child, and to them that give suck in those days!

13:2 Fulfilled prophecy. This prophecy was fulfilled in A.D. 70 when Titus destroyed Jerusalem. "Now the outward face of the temple in its front wanted nothing that was likely to surprise either men's minds or their eyes; for it was covered all over with plates of gold of great weight, and, at the first rising of the sun, reflected back a very fiery splendor, and made those who forced themselves to look upon it to turn their eyes away, just as they would have done at the sun's own rays. But this temple appeared to strangers, when they were coming to it at a distance, like a mountain covered with snow; for as to those parts of it that were not gilt, they were exceeding white. On its top it had spikes with sharp points, to prevent any pollution of it by birds sitting upon it. Of its stones, some of them were forty-five cubits in length, five in height, and six in breadth." (*The History of the Destruction of Jerusalem, The Works of Flavius Josephus*)

"[The wall] was so thoroughly laid even with the ground by those that dug it up to the foundation, that there was left nothing to make those that came thither believe it had ever been inhabited." *Josephus, The Wars of the Jews* (See also Matthew 24:2.)

13:4 For more signs of the end times, see Luke 21:7.

13:10 "The world can be witnessed to in a single generation. We can welcome Him back with our present of the finished task set by Him so long ago when He said, 'This gospel of the kingdom must be preached for a witness to all nations; then shall the end come.'" *Winkie Pratney*

18 And pray that your flight be not in the winter.

19 For in those days shall be affliction, such as was not from the beginning of the creation which God created to this time, neither shall be.

20 And except that the Lord had shortened those days, no flesh should be saved: but for the elect's sake, whom he has chosen, he has shortened the days.

21 And then if any man shall say to you, Lo, here is Christ; or, lo, he is there; believe him not:

22 For false Christs and false prophets shall rise, and shall show signs and wonders, to seduce, if it were possible, even the elect.

23 But take heed: behold, I have foretold you all things.

24 But in those days, after that tribulation, the sun shall be darkened, and the moon shall not give her light,

25 And the stars of heaven shall fall, and the powers that are in heaven shall be shaken.

26 And then shall they see the Son of man coming in the clouds with great power and glory.

27 And then shall he send his angels, and shall gather together his elect from the four winds, from the uttermost part of the earth to the uttermost part of heaven.

28 Now learn a parable of the fig tree; When her branch is yet tender, and puts forth leaves, you know that summer is near:

29 So you in like manner, when you shall see these things come to pass, know that it is near, even at the doors.

30 Verily I say to you, that this generation shall not pass, till all these things be done.

31 Heaven and earth shall pass away: but my words shall not pass away.

32 But of that day and that hour knows no man, no, not the angels which are in heaven, neither the Son, but the Father.

33 Take heed, watch and pray: for you know not when the time is.

34 For the Son of man is as a man taking a far journey, who left his house, and gave authority to his servants, and to every man his work, and commanded the porter to watch.

35 Watch therefore: for you know not when the master of the house comes, at even, or at midnight, or at the cockcrowing, or in the morning:

36 Lest coming suddenly he find you sleeping.

37 And what I say to you I say to all, Watch.

. . . . . .

For how to use the Ten Commandments in witnessing, see Psalm 51:6 footnote.

. . . . . .

CHAPTER 14

AFTER two days was the feast of the passover, and of unleavened bread: and the chief priests and the scribes sought how they might take him by craft, and put him to death.

2 But they said, Not on the feast day, lest there be an uproar of the people.

3 And being in Bethany in the house of Simon the leper, as he sat at meat, there came a woman having an alabaster box of ointment of spikenard very precious; and she broke the box, and poured it on his head.

4 And there were some that had indignation within themselves, and said, Why was this waste of the ointment made?

5 For it might have been sold for more than three hundred pence, and have been given to the poor. And they murmured against her.

6 And Jesus said, Let her alone; why trouble her? she has wrought a good work on me.

7 For you have the poor with you always, and whenever you will you may do them good: but me you have not always.

8 She has done what she could: she is come beforehand to anoint my body to the burying.

9 Verily I say to you, Wherever this gospel shall be preached throughout the whole world, this also that she has done shall be spoken of for a memorial of her.

10 And Judas Iscariot, one of the twelve, went to the chief priests, to betray him to them.

11 And when they heard it, they were glad, and promised to give him money. And he sought how he might conveniently betray him.

12 And the first day of unleavened bread, when they killed the passover, his disciples said to him, Where will you that we go and prepare that you may eat the passover?

13 And he sent forth two of his disciples, and said to them, Go into the city, and there shall meet you a man bearing a pitcher of water: follow him.

14 And wherever he shall go in, say to the goodman of the house, The Master says, Where is the guestchamber, where I shall eat the passover with my disciples?

15 And he will show you a large upper room furnished and prepared: there make ready for us.

16 And his disciples went forth, and came into the city, and found as he had said to them: and they made ready the passover.

17 And in the evening he came with the twelve.

18 And as they sat and did eat, Jesus said, Verily I say to you, One of you which eats with me shall betray me.

19 And they began to be sorrowful, and to say to him one by one, Is it I? and another said, Is it I?

20 And he answered and said to them, It is one of the twelve, that dips with me in the dish.

21 The Son of man indeed goes, as it is written of him: but woe to that man by whom the Son of man is betrayed! good were it for that man if he had never been born.

22 And as they did eat, Jesus took bread, and blessed, and broke it, and gave to them, and said, Take, eat: this is my body.

23 And he took the cup, and when he had given thanks, he gave it to them: and they all drank of it.

24 And he said to them, This is my blood of the new testament, which is shed for many.

25 Verily I say to you, I will drink no more of the fruit of the vine, until that day that I drink it new in the kingdom of God.

26 And when they had sung a hymn, they went out into the mount of Olives.

27 And Jesus said to them, All you shall be offended because of me this night: for it is written, I will smite the shepherd, and the sheep shall be scattered.

28 But after that I am risen, I will go before you into Galilee.

29 But Peter said to him, Although all shall be offended, yet will not I.

30 And Jesus said to him, Verily I say to you, That this day, even in this night, before the cock crow twice, you shall deny me thrice.

31 But he spoke the more vehemently, If I should die with you, I will not deny you in any wise. Likewise also said they all.

32 And they came to a place which was named Gethsemane: and he said to his disciples, Sit here, while I shall pray.

33 And he took with him Peter and James and John, and began to be sore amazed, and to be very heavy;

34 And said to them, My soul is exceeding sorrowful to death: tarry here, and watch.

35 And he went forward a little, and fell

14:10 Messianic prophecy fulfilled: "Yea, mine own familiar friend, in whom I trusted, which did eat of my bread, has lifted up his heel against me" (Psalm 41:9). See Mark 14:65 footnote.

14:24 The wine wasn't His literal blood, which was still in His body. He was referring to it as being *symbolic* of His blood.

on the ground, and prayed that, if it were possible, the hour might pass from him.

36 And he said, Abba, Father, all things are possible to you; take away this cup from me: nevertheless not what I will, but what you will.

37 And he came, and found them sleeping, and said to Peter, Simon, do you sleep? Couldn't you watch one hour?

38 Watch and pray, lest you enter into temptation. The spirit truly is ready, but the flesh is weak.

39 And again he went away, and prayed, and spoke the same words.

40 And when he returned, he found them asleep again, (for their eyes were heavy,) neither did they know what to answer him.

41 And he came the third time, and said to them, Sleep on now, and take your rest: it is enough, the hour is come; behold, the Son of man is betrayed into the hands of sinners.

42 Rise up, let us go; lo, he that betrays me is at hand.

43 And immediately, while he yet spoke, came Judas, one of the twelve, and with him a great multitude with swords and staves, from the chief priests and the scribes and the elders.

44 And he that betrayed him had given them a token, saying, Whomsoever I shall kiss, that same is he; take him, and lead him away safely.

45 And as soon as he was come, he went straightway to him, and said, Master, master; and kissed him.

46 And they laid their hands on him, and took him.

47 And one of them that stood by drew a sword, and smote a servant of the high priest, and cut off his ear.

48 And Jesus answered and said to them, Are you come out, as against a thief, with swords and with staves to take me?

49 I was daily with you in the temple teaching, and you took me not: but the scriptures must be fulfilled.

50 And they all forsook him, and fled.

51 And there followed him a certain young man, having a linen cloth cast about his naked body; and the young men laid hold on him:

52 And he left the linen cloth, and fled from them naked.

53 And they led Jesus away to the high priest: and with him were assembled all the chief priests and the elders and the scribes.

54 And Peter followed him afar off, even into the palace of the high priest: and he sat with the servants, and warmed himself at the fire.

> If you are saved, the work is only half done until you are employed to bring others to Christ.
>
> **CHARLES SPURGEON**

55 And the chief priests and all the council sought for witness against Jesus to put him to death; and found none.

56 For many bare false witness against him, but their witness agreed not together.

57 And there arose certain, and bare false witness against him, saying,

58 We heard him say, I will destroy this temple that is made with hands, and within three days I will build another made without hands.

59 But neither so did their witness agree together.

60 And the high priest stood up in the midst, and asked Jesus, saying, Do you answer nothing? what is it which these witness against you?

61 But he held his peace, and answered nothing. Again the high priest asked him,

---

14:38 "The reason why many fail in battle is because they wait until the hour of battle. The reason why others succeed is because they have gained their victory on their knees long before the battle came...Anticipate your battles; fight them on your knees before temptation comes, and you will always have victory." *R. A. Torrey*

and said to him, are you the Christ, the Son of the Blessed?

62 And Jesus said, I am: and you shall see the Son of man sitting on the right hand of power, and coming in the clouds of heaven.

63 Then the high priest rent his clothes, and said, What need we any further witnesses?

64 You have heard the blasphemy: what do you think? And they all condemned him to be guilty of death.

65 And some began to spit on him, and to cover his face, and to buffet him, and to say to him, Prophesy: and the servants did strike him with the palms of their hands.

66 And as Peter was beneath in the palace, there came one of the maids of the high priest:

67 And when she saw Peter warming himself, she looked upon him, and said, And you also were with Jesus of Nazareth.

68 But he denied, saying, I know not, neither understand I what you say. And he went out into the porch; and the cock crew.

69 And a maid saw him again, and began to say to them that stood by, This is one of them.

70 And he denied it again. And a little after, they that stood by said again to Peter, Surely you are one of them: for you are a Galilaean, and your speech agrees thereto.

71 But he began to curse and to swear, saying, I know not this man of whom you speak.

72 And the second time the cock crew. And Peter called to mind the word that Jesus said to him, Before the cock crow twice, you shall deny me thrice. And when he thought thereon, he wept.

CHAPTER 15

AND straightway in the morning the chief priests held a consultation with the elders and scribes and the whole council, and bound Jesus, and carried him away, and delivered him to Pilate.

2 And Pilate asked him, Are you the King of the Jews? And he answering said to him, It is as you say.

3 And the chief priests accused him of many things: but he answered nothing.

4 And Pilate asked him again, saying, Do you answer nothing? behold how many things they witness against you.

5 But Jesus yet answered nothing; so that Pilate marveled.

6 Now at that feast he released to them one prisoner, whomsoever they desired.

7 And there was one named Barabbas, which lay bound with them that had made insurrection with him, who had committed murder in the insurrection.

8 And the multitude crying aloud began to desire him to do as he had ever done to them.

9 But Pilate answered them, saying, Will you that I release to you the King of the Jews?

10 For he knew that the chief priests had delivered him for envy.

11 But the chief priests moved the people, that he should rather release Barabbas to them.

12 And Pilate answered and said again to them, What will you then that I shall do to him whom you call the King of the Jews?

13 And they cried out again, Crucify him.

14 Then Pilate said to them, Why, what evil has he done? And they cried out the more exceedingly, Crucify him.

15 And so Pilate, willing to content the people, released Barabbas to them, and

---

14:65 **Messianic prophecy fulfilled:** "I gave my back to those who struck me, and my cheeks to those who plucked out the beard; I did not hide my face from shame and spitting" (Isaiah 50:6). See Mark 15:24 footnote.

15:12 "Public opinion is held in reverence. It settles everything. Some think it is the voice of God." *Mark Twain*

delivered Jesus, when he had scourged him, to be crucified.

16 And the soldiers led him away into the hall, called Praetorium; and they called together the whole band.

17 And they clothed him with purple, and platted a crown of thorns, and put it about his head,

18 And began to salute him, Hail, King of the Jews!

19 And they smote him on the head with a reed, and did spit upon him, and bowing their knees worshipped him.

20 And when they had mocked him, they took off the purple from him, and put his own clothes on him, and led him out to crucify him.

21 And they compelled one Simon a Cyrenian, who passed by, coming out of the country, the father of Alexander and Rufus, to bear his cross.

22 And they brought him to the place Golgotha, which is, being interpreted, The place of a skull.

23 And they gave him to drink wine mingled with myrrh: but he received it not.

24 And when they had crucified him, they parted his garments, casting lots upon them, what every man should take.

25 And it was the third hour, and they crucified him.

26 And the superscription of his accusation was written over, THE KING OF THE JEWS.

27 And with him they crucified two thieves; the one on his right hand, and the other on his left.

28 And the scripture was fulfilled, which says, And he was numbered with the transgressors.

29 And they that passed by railed on him, wagging their heads, and saying, Ah, you that destroy the temple, and build it in three days,

30 Save yourself, and come down from the cross.

31 Likewise also the chief priests mocking said among themselves with the scribes, He saved others; himself he cannot save.

32 Let Christ the King of Israel descend now from the cross, that we may see and believe. And they that were crucified with him reviled him.

33 And when the sixth hour was come, there was darkness over the whole land until the ninth hour.

34 And at the ninth hour Jesus cried with a loud voice, saying, Eloi, Eloi, lama sabachthani? which is, being interpreted, My God, my God, why have you forsaken me?

35 And some of them that stood by, when they heard it, said, Behold, he calls Elijah.

36 And one ran and filled a sponge full of vinegar, and put it on a reed, and gave him to drink, saying, Let alone; let us see whether Elijah will come to take him down.

37 And Jesus cried with a loud voice, and gave up the ghost.

38 And the veil of the temple was rent in twain from the top to the bottom.

39 And when the centurion, which stood over against him, saw that he so cried out, and gave up the ghost, he said, Truly this man was the Son of God.

40 There were also women looking on afar off: among whom was Mary Magdalene, and Mary the mother of James the less and of Joses, and Salome;

41 (Who also, when he was in Galilee, followed him, and ministered to him;) and many other women which came up with him to Jerusalem.

42 And now when the even was come, because it was the preparation, that is, the day before the sabbath,

43 Joseph of Arimathaea, an honorable counsellor, which also waited for the kingdom of God, came, and went in boldly

---

15:24 Messianic prophecy fulfilled: "They part my garments among them, and cast lots upon my vesture" (Psalm 22:18). See Luke 1:32,33 footnote.

15:26 *Contradictions in the Bible—Why Are They There?*

The Bible has many *seeming* contradictions within its pages. For example, the four Gospels give four differing accounts as to what was written on the sign that hung on the cross. Matthew said, "This is Jesus the King of the Jews" (27:37). However, Mark contradicts that with "The King of the Jews" (15:26). Luke says something different: "This is the King of the Jews" (23:38), and John maintains that the sign said "Jesus of Nazareth the King of the Jews" (19:19). Those who are *looking* for contradictions may therefore say, "See—the Bible is *full* of mistakes!" and choose to reject it entirely as being untrustworthy.

However, those who trust God have no problem harmonizing the Gospels. There is no contradiction if the sign simply said, "This is Jesus of Nazareth the King of the Jews." The godly base their confidence on two truths: 1) "all Scripture is given by inspiration of God" (2 Timothy 3:16); and 2) an elementary rule of Scripture is that God has deliberately included *seeming* contradictions in His Word to "snare" the proud. He has "hidden" things from the "wise and prudent" and "revealed them to babes" (Luke 10:21), purposely choosing foolish things to confound the wise (1 Corinthians 1:27).

If an ungodly man refuses to humble himself and obey the gospel, and instead desires to build a case against the Bible, God gives him enough material to build his own gallows.

This incredible principle is clearly illustrated in the account of the capture of Zedekiah, king of Judah. Jeremiah the prophet told Zedekiah that God would judge him. He was informed that he would be "delivered into the hand of the king of Babylon" (Jeremiah 32:4). This is confirmed in Jeremiah 39:5–7 where we are told that he was captured and brought to King Nebuchadnezzar, then they "bound him with chains, to carry him to Babylon." However, in Ezekiel 12:13, God Himself warned, "I will bring him to Babylon...yet he shall not see it, though he shall die there" (emphasis added). Here is material to build a case against the Bible! It is an *obvious* mistake. Three Bible verses say that the king would go to Babylon, and yet the Bible in another place says that he would not see Babylon. How can someone be taken somewhere and not see it? It makes no sense at all—unless Zedekiah was *blinded*. And that is precisely what happened. Zedekiah saw Nebuchadnezzar face to face, saw his sons killed before his eyes, then "the king of Babylon...put out Zedekiah's eyes" before taking him to Babylon (Jeremiah 39:6,7). This is the underlying principle behind the many "contradictions" of Holy Scripture (such as how many horses David had, who was the first to arrive at the tomb after the resurrection of Jesus, etc.).

God has turned the tables on proud, arrogant, self-righteous man. When he proudly stands outside of the kingdom of God, and seeks to justify his sinfulness through evidence he thinks discredits the Bible, he doesn't realize that God has simply lowered the door of life, so that only those who are prepared to exercise faith, and bow in humility may enter.

It is interesting to note that the *seeming* contradictions in the four Gospels attest to the fact that there was no corroboration between the writers.

---

to Pilate, and craved the body of Jesus.

44 And Pilate marveled if he were already dead: and calling to him the centurion, he asked him whether he had been any while dead.

45 And when he knew it of the centurion, he gave the body to Joseph.

46 And he bought fine linen, and took him down, and wrapped him in the linen, and laid him in a sepulchre which was hewn out of a rock, and rolled a stone to the door of the sepulchre.

47 And Mary Magdalene and Mary the mother of Joses beheld where he was laid.

CHAPTER 16

AND when the sabbath was past, Mary Magdalene, and Mary the mother of James, and Salome, had bought sweet spices, that they might come and anoint him.

2 And very early in the morning the first

15:39 The Witness
(An interesting insight into what may have been…)

By Danny Hotea

As was my custom, I rose early that day to pay homage to the gods by prayers and burnt offerings. To which I vowed my obedience on that fateful morning, I cannot now remember. There were so many.

Leaving the place of worship, I endeavored to sit quietly and read the creeds of Rome as written by the emperor himself. It was my duty not only as a centurion, but as a Roman citizen, to understand the purpose of almighty Caesar and Rome. However, just as I began pouring over the open scroll, a nameless messenger came panting with word from Pontius Pilate, governor of Judea, ordering my garrison to his palace immediately.

I arrived with three hundred men as if by flight. The sun had hardly risen, and the air held an unseen weight, as if to distinguish this day from all others. The men, all clad in leather and metal with swords swaying from their belts and spears stabbing at the sky in protest of their unusually early arousal, wobbled restlessly in rigid formation, awaiting my command. The sound of spiked sandals scraping the stone palace floor echoed down the long, stone hallway adding tension to mystery. They undoubtedly supposed that I knew the reason for it all. But I didn't—until another messenger came with another scroll describing our purpose exactly.

Jerusalem was a place known for its concentrated reserve of mindless zealots. And I had experience in stamping out the feeble efforts of disorderly vagrants and disorganized militias meant to unshackle the Jews from Rome's iron grip. One in particular came to mind as I read the final sentence of that day's orders. It was the most recent and pathetic uprising. A small army of poorly armed religious rebels managed to assassinate an insignificant gatekeeper in the governor's palace. The idea that a handful of superstitious peasants could overthrow Rome was ridiculous and, if it weren't so sad, it would be laughable. Their leader had been a thin, sweaty man with hardly any beard, balding head and shifting eyes. A Jew. A brainless dreamer suffering from resentment. His name was Barabbas. He was hardly a match for Rome. I caught him in the streets attempting to hide beneath a vendor's blankets after his pitiful militia had been butchered and left for the dogs. I was his judge and jury. And since only Romans have the right to a trial, I stuffed him in a smaller-than-usual cell after the garrison had their day's exercise of beating him with rods and slapping him with gloved fists.

That day had another experience for me altogether.

As we pushed our way into the Praetorium hauling the scourged offender to the platform, where another Man stood, the mob sang out in a chorus of hatred, "Crucify Him!" The governor addressed the riotous masses with careful words, offering them a choice between the bloodied and uncondemned Man now occupying the platform with him, or the pathetic zealot, Barabbas, who had failed an attempt to destroy Rome. Immediately they sent out blood-curdling screams consenting to the murder of the One and the release of the other. It was apparent, by their screams, that this Man had not offended Rome. He had offended the Jews.

A messenger interrupted the procedure, which was doubtlessly an urgent matter, after which I was signaled to bring Him into the governor's inner court.

The conversation that took place proved this Man's character. He spoke only when questioned and claimed that the governor's authority was given to him by the Offender's Father, which made little sense to me at the time. When He said He was a King, I wondered whether Barabbas, the sweaty zealot, had similar thoughts. But, all in all, this Man had authority incomparable to any I had seen before. This fact was startling considering I had seen the Caesar and all his delegates more often than Pontius himself.

What seemed like moments later, my garrison had elbowed their way through the riotous crowds to the place of execution, hauling two offenders of Rome and One offender of the Jews.

His head had been crowned with thorns, no doubt a torturous invention of the guiltless soldiers in my garrison. His beard replaced with bleeding flesh. His back opened wide by a

Roman scourge to an infectious environment full of illness bred in the hearts of vehement enemies. Yet, it seemed that these were the slightest of His pains judging by the weight of grief He bore on His countenance. His visage carried an eternal load of unfamiliar burdens.

As was my custom, I drove the first nail into the left wrist of each offender inaugurating their torturous departure from this world and instructing my garrison how to proceed with the crucifixion. The two vagrants wrestled pathetically against the soldier's grip that held their filthy arms against the knotted wood, spitting out blasphemies against the gods of Rome and sprinkling our faces with bloody specs of mucus. But they could do little more than wiggle their palms and claw at my wrists with their broken nails until the iron spike impaled the wrist and its owner's arm was pinned against the wood, twitching like a wounded animal. I often delighted in the sound of their ear-splitting screams and hellish moans that filled the air and the sight of their epileptic convulsions of agony as their crosses were set upright. It became somewhat of a drama to which I looked forward with secret pleasure, even more than the gladiators and the chariot races where countless men had lost their lives to entertain Rome. I could hardly keep from smiling, at times.

But this Man, although He was innocent, displayed no reluctance in placing His arm against the wood. His eyes fastened on the soldier holding His arm and on me, His sadistic executioner. I expected the typical reaction as the iron penetrated His skin. But this Man was not typical in any sense of the word. Instead of spraying my face with spittle, He groaned and looked away, scrapping His thorny crown against the lumber behind His head. Unlike the other two, this Man did not moan in melodies of agony as the cross sat upright, disjointing its resident. Tears ran down His scabbed face as He viewed the masses streaming past the foot of His cross. Their venomous words struck the air like frothy waves pounding some seaside cliff. And, unlike the other two, whose hoarse-voiced cursing baptized each passerby with vulgar threats and swollen words of every sort, He spoke kindly to a few standing at the foot of His cross. Had He not been a Jew, I would have been compelled to defend His dying reputation for sheer sympathy's sake.

At the instant before He died, the sky blackened as if it had been split open like a carcass and all its guilt bled out onto the clouds. The earth convulsed, shaking and tossing my men and me like mere toys. At that instant I knew this Man was no mere Man.

He wielded an exclusive power. The image of Rome, as if it were a colossal statue carved of iron, lay in heaps beneath His cross as a mound of chaff vulnerable to the slightest breath of wind. The sight of His emaciated corpse stabbed at my conscience. Had I done wrong? If not, then why such agony of heart? I was bleeding now and my zeal for Rome poured from the bowels of my heart like the streamlets coursing from His side and brow. He had slain me; not I Him. His naked body, reduced to shards of stinking flesh hanging lifelessly on the cross, seemed more alive than I did standing with my hand-polished helmet and Roman embroidery hanging like empirical curtains from my shoulders. I was ashamed of myself.

I turned away to prevent my tears from being noticed. Regret welled up in my soul and poured out onto my cheeks with burning tears. I tried desperately to compose myself to no avail. Once more, I turned to look at Him, and my knees betrayed me to the ground beneath. My forehead kissed the ground in an unguarded slump. I gritted my teeth and formed the words, "Truly, this was the Son of God!"

I have never been the same since.

---

day of the week, they came to the sepulchre at the rising of the sun.

3 And they said among themselves, Who shall roll away the stone from the door of the sepulchre?

4 And when they looked, they saw that the stone was rolled away: for it was very great.

5 And entering into the sepulchre, they saw a young man sitting on the right side, clothed in a long white garment; and they were fearful.

6 And he said to them, Be not fearful: You seek Jesus of Nazareth, which was crucified: he is risen; he is not here: behold the place where they laid him.

7 But go your way, tell his disciples and Peter that he goes before you into Galilee:

16:6 "How many angels were at the tomb—one or two?"

The question has arisen simply because Matthew and Mark mention one angel, whereas Luke and John refer to two. There is no conflict if there were two angels but Matthew and Mark quote the one who was a spokesperson.

there shall you see him, as he said to you.

8 And they went out quickly, and fled from the sepulchre; for they trembled and were amazed: neither said they any thing to any man; for they were afraid.

9 Now when Jesus was risen early the first day of the week, he appeared first to Mary Magdalene, out of whom he had cast seven devils.

10 And she went and told them that had been with him, as they mourned and wept.

11 And they, when they had heard that he was alive, and had been seen of her, believed not.

12 After that he appeared in another form to two of them, as they walked, and went into the country.

13 And they went and told it to the residue: neither believed they them.

14 Afterward he appeared to the eleven as they sat at meat, and upbraided them with their unbelief and hardness of heart, because they believed not them which had seen him after he was risen.

15 And he said to them, Go into all the world, and preach the gospel to every creature.

16 He that believes and is baptized shall be saved; but he that believes not shall be damned.

17 And these signs shall follow them that believe; In my name shall they cast out devils; they shall speak with new tongues;

18 They shall take up serpents; and if they drink any deadly thing, it shall not hurt them; they shall lay hands on the sick, and they shall recover.

19 So then after the Lord had spoken to them, he was received up into heaven, and sat on the right hand of God.

20 And they went forth, and preached everywhere, the Lord working with them, and confirming the word with signs following. Amen.

16:15 Here is a fascinating thing. The original Greek meaning of "Go into all the world, and preach the gospel to every creature" opens up some interesting thoughts. The word for "go" is very captivating. It is *poreuomai*, meaning "go." The word "all" also carries with it gripping connotations. It is *hapas*, and actually means "all." And if that doesn't rivet you, look closely at the word "every." It is *pas*, and literally means "every." So when Jesus commanded us, "Go into all the world, and preach the gospel to every creature," to be true and faithful to the original text, what He was actually saying was, "Go into all the world, and preach the gospel to every creature." We are so fortunate to have access to knowledge like this.

"Here is our commissioning and sending. There are no exceptions—every Christian is commanded to go!" *Trevor Yaxley*

If the command to "preach the gospel to every creature" were given only to the eleven disciples, preaching of the gospel would have stopped when they died. *Every* Christian is a "disciple." The word in Greek is *mathetes* and simply means "a learner." It is used in reference to the eleven, as well as to believers such as Joseph of Arimathea (Matthew 27:57), Ananias (Acts 9:10), and others (Acts 9:36; 16:1; 21:16). In Luke 14:26,27 Jesus used the term in reference to *any* who would believe in Him.

16:17,18 In reference to true converts, Jesus said, "By their *fruits* you shall know them" (Matthew 7:20), not by their gifts. Many false converts have had "power" gifts. See Matthew 7:21–23.

Luke

FORASMUCH as many have taken in hand to set forth in order a declaration of those things which are most surely believed among us,

2 Even as they delivered them to us, which from the beginning were eyewitnesses, and ministers of the word;

3 It seemed good to me also, having had perfect understanding of all things from the very first, to write to you in order, most excellent Theophilus,

4 That you might know the certainty of those things, wherein you have been instructed.

5 There was in the days of Herod, the king of Judea, a certain priest named Zacharias, of the course of Abia: and his wife was of the daughters of Aaron, and her name was Elizabeth.

6 And they were both righteous before God, walking in all the commandments and ordinances of the Lord blameless.

7 And they had no child, because that Elizabeth was barren, and they both were now well stricken in years.

8 And it came to pass, that while he executed the priest's office before God in the order of his course,

9 According to the custom of the priest's office, his lot was to burn incense when he went into the temple of the Lord.

10 And the whole multitude of the people were praying without at the time of incense.

11 And there appeared to him an angel of the Lord standing on the right side of the altar of incense.

12 And when Zacharias saw him, he was troubled, and fear fell upon him.

13 But the angel said to him, Fear not, Zacharias: for your prayer is heard; and your wife Elizabeth shall bear you a son, and you shall call his name John.

14 And you shall have joy and gladness; and many shall rejoice at his birth.

15 For he shall be great in the sight of the Lord, and shall drink neither wine nor strong drink; and he shall be filled with the Holy Spirit, even from his mother's womb.

16 And many of the children of Israel shall he turn to the Lord their God.

17 And he shall go before him in the spirit and power of Elijah, to turn the hearts of the fathers to the children, and the disobedient to the wisdom of the just; to make ready a people prepared for the Lord.

18 And Zacharias said to the angel, Whereby shall I know this? for I am an old man, and my wife well stricken in years.

1:3 **Historical accuracy.** "Given the large portion of the New Testament written by him, it's extremely significant that Luke has been established to be a scrupulously accurate historian, even in the smallest details. One prominent archaeologist carefully examined Luke's references to thirty-two countries, fifty-four cities, and nine islands, finding not a single mistake." *John McRay*

19 And the angel answering said to him, I am Gabriel, that stands in the presence of God; and am sent to speak to you, and to show you these glad tidings.

20 And, behold, you shall be dumb, and not able to speak, until the day that these things shall be performed, because you believe not my words, which shall be fulfilled in their season.

21 And the people waited for Zacharias, and marveled that he tarried so long in the temple.

22 And when he came out, he could not speak to them: and they perceived that he had seen a vision in the temple: for he beckoned to them, and remained speechless.

23 And it came to pass, that, as soon as the days of his ministration were accomplished, he departed to his own house.

24 And after those days his wife Elizabeth conceived, and hid herself five months, saying,

25 Thus has the Lord dealt with me in the days wherein he looked on me, to take away my reproach among men.

26 And in the sixth month the angel Gabriel was sent from God to a city of Galilee, named Nazareth,

27 To a virgin espoused to a man whose name was Joseph, of the house of David; and the virgin's name was Mary.

28 And the angel came in to her, and said, Hail, you that are highly favored, the Lord is with you: blessed are you among women.

29 And when she saw him, she was troubled at his saying, and cast in her mind what manner of salutation this should be.

30 And the angel said to her, Fear not, Mary: for you have found favor with God.

31 And, behold, you shall conceive in your womb, and bring forth a son, and shall call his name JESUS.

32 He shall be great, and shall be called the Son of the Highest: and the Lord God shall give to him the throne of his father David:

33 And he shall reign over the house of Jacob for ever; and of his kingdom there shall be no end.

34 Then said Mary to the angel, How shall this be, seeing I know not a man?

35 And the angel answered and said to her, The Holy Spirit shall come upon you, and the power of the Highest shall overshadow you: therefore also that holy thing which shall be born of you shall be called the Son of God.

36 And, behold, your cousin Elizabeth, she has also conceived a son in her old age: and this is the sixth month with her, who was called barren.

37 For with God nothing shall be impossible.

38 And Mary said, Behold the handmaid of the Lord; be it to me according to your word. And the angel departed from her.

39 And Mary arose in those days, and went into the hill country with haste, into

---

1:27 Archaeology confirms the Bible. Following the 1993 discovery in Israel of a stone containing the inscriptions "House of David" and "King of Israel," *Time* magazine stated, "This writing—dated to the 9th century B.C., only a century after David's reign—described a victory by a neighboring king over the Israelites...The skeptics' claim that David never existed is now hard to defend." *Time*, December 18, 1995

"In extraordinary ways, modern archeology is affirming the historical core of the Old and New Testaments, supporting key portions of crucial biblical stories." *Jeffery L. Sheler*, "Is the Bible True?" *Reader's Digest*, June 2000 (See also Matthew 26:54 footnote.)

1:31–35 See Matthew 1:20–23 footnote.

1:32,33 Messianic prophecy fulfilled: "Of the increase of his government and peace there shall be no end, upon the throne of David, and upon his kingdom, to order it, and to establish it with judgment and with justice from henceforth, even for ever. The zeal of the LORD of hosts will perform this" (Isaiah 9:7). See Luke 3:33 footnote.

a city of Juda;

40 And entered into the house of Zacharias, and saluted Elizabeth.

41 And it came to pass, that, when Elizabeth heard the salutation of Mary, the babe leaped in her womb; and Elizabeth was filled with the Holy Spirit:

42 And she spoke out with a loud voice, and said, Blessed are you among women, and blessed is the fruit of your womb.

43 And whence is this to me, that the mother of my Lord should come to me?

44 For, lo, as soon as the voice of your salutation sounded in mine ears, the babe leaped in my womb for joy.

45 And blessed is she that believed: for there shall be a performance of those things which were told her from the Lord.

46 And Mary said, My soul does magnify the Lord,

47 And my spirit has rejoiced in God my Savior.

48 For he has regarded the low estate of his handmaiden: for, behold, from henceforth all generations shall call me blessed.

49 For he that is mighty has done to me great things; and holy is his name.

50 And his mercy is on them that fear him from generation to generation.

51 He has showed strength with his arm; he has scattered the proud in the imagination of their hearts.

52 He has put down the mighty from their seats, and exalted them of low degree.

53 He has filled the hungry with good things; and the rich he has sent empty away.

54 He has helped his servant Israel, in remembrance of his mercy;

55 As he spoke to our fathers, to Abraham, and to his seed for ever.

56 And Mary abode with her about three months, and returned to her own house.

57 Now Elizabeth's full time came that she should be delivered; and she brought forth a son.

58 And her neighbours and her cousins heard how the Lord had showed great mercy upon her; and they rejoiced with her.

59 And it came to pass, that on the eighth day they came to circumcise the child; and they called him Zacharias, after the name of his father.

60 And his mother answered and said, Not so; but he shall be called John.

61 And they said to her, There is none of your kindred that is called by this name.

62 And they made signs to his father, how he would have him called.

63 And he asked for a writing table, and wrote, saying, His name is John. And they marveled all.

64 And his mouth was opened immediately, and his tongue loosed, and he spoke, and praised God.

> I trust that you will find no rest for your feet till you have been the means of leading many to that blessed Savior who is your confidence and hope.
>
> **CHARLES SPURGEON**

65 And fear came on all that dwelt round about them: and all these sayings were noised abroad throughout all the hill country of Judea.

66 And all they that heard them laid them up in their hearts, saying, What manner of child shall this be! And the hand of the Lord was with him.

67 And his father Zacharias was filled with the Holy Spirit, and prophesied, saying,

68 Blessed be the Lord God of Israel; for he has visited and redeemed his people,

69 And has raised up an horn of salvation for us in the house of his servant David;

70 As he spoke by the mouth of his holy prophets, which have been since the world began:

71 That we should be saved from our enemies, and from the hand of all that hate us;

72 To perform the mercy promised to our fathers, and to remember his holy cov-

enant;

73 The oath which he sware to our father Abraham,

74 That he would grant to us, that we being delivered out of the hand of our enemies might serve him without fear,

75 In holiness and righteousness before him, all the days of our life.

76 And you, child, shall be called the prophet of the Highest: for you shall go before the face of the Lord to prepare his ways;

77 To give knowledge of salvation to his people by the remission of their sins,

78 Through the tender mercy of our God; whereby the dayspring from on high has visited us,

79 To give light to them that sit in darkness and in the shadow of death, to guide our feet into the way of peace.

80 And the child grew, and waxed strong in spirit, and was in the deserts till the day of his showing to Israel.

CHAPTER 2

A ND it came to pass in those days, that there went out a decree from Caesar Augustus, that all the world should be taxed.

2 (And this taxing was first made when Cyrenius was governor of Syria.)

3 And all went to be taxed, every one into his own city.

4 And Joseph also went up from Galilee, out of the city of Nazareth, into Judea, to the city of David, which is called Bethlehem; (because he was of the house and lineage of David:)

5 To be taxed with Mary his espoused wife, being great with child.

6 And so it was, that, while they were there, the days were accomplished that she should be delivered.

7 And she brought forth her firstborn son, and wrapped him in swaddling clothes, and laid him in a manger; because there was no room for them in the inn.

8 And there were in the same country shepherds abiding in the field, keeping watch over their flock by night.

9 And, lo, the angel of the Lord came upon them, and the glory of the Lord shone round about them: and they were sore afraid.

10 And the angel said to them, Fear not: for, behold, I bring you good tidings of great joy, which shall be to all people.

11 For to you is born this day in the city of David a Savior, which is Christ the Lord.

12 And this shall be a sign to you; You shall find the babe wrapped in swaddling clothes, lying in a manger.

13 And suddenly there was with the angel a multitude of the heavenly host praising God, and saying,

14 Glory to God in the highest, and on earth peace, good will toward men.

15 And it came to pass, as the angels were gone away from them into heaven, the shepherds said one to another, Let us now go even to Bethlehem, and see this thing which is come to pass, which the Lord has made known to us.

16 And they came with haste, and found Mary, and Joseph, and the babe lying in a manger.

17 And when they had seen it, they made known abroad the saying which was told them concerning this child.

18 And all they that heard it wondered at those things which were told them by the shepherds.

1:74 **Fear of man.** When God commissioned Moses to go speak to Pharaoh, Moses revealed that he had a problem. His seeming humility ("Who am I...?") was actually the fear of man (Exodus 3:11; 4:1). Although he argued with God that he wasn't eloquent, God promised to be with him and teach him what to say (Exodus 4:10–14). Likewise, we have no excuse for entertaining the fear of man when it comes to seeking the lost, because we are not called to use eloquent speech. We have the indwelling Christ, and through Him and His strength we can "do all things" (Philippians 4:13).

1:79 See Psalm 23:4 footnote.

19 But Mary kept all these things, and pondered them in her heart.

20 And the shepherds returned, glorifying and praising God for all the things that they had heard and seen, as it was told to them.

21 And when eight days were accomplished for the circumcising of the child, his name was called JESUS, which was so named of the angel before he was conceived in the womb.

22 And when the days of her purification according to the law of Moses were accomplished, they brought him to Jerusalem, to present him to the Lord;

23 (As it is written in the law of the Lord, Every male that opens the womb shall be called holy to the Lord;)

24 And to offer a sacrifice according to that which is said in the law of the Lord, A pair of turtledoves, or two young pigeons.

25 And, behold, there was a man in Jerusalem, whose name was Simeon; and the same man was just and devout, waiting for the consolation of Israel: and the Holy Spirit was upon him.

26 And it was revealed to him by the Holy Spirit, that he should not see death, before he had seen the Lord's Christ.

27 And he came by the Spirit into the temple: and when the parents brought in the child Jesus, to do for him after the custom of the law,

28 Then took he him up in his arms, and blessed God, and said,

29 Lord, now let you your servant depart in peace, according to your word:

30 For mine eyes have seen your salvation,

31 Which you have prepared before the face of all people;

32 A light to lighten the Gentiles, and the glory of your people Israel.

33 And Joseph and his mother marveled at those things which were spoken of him.

34 And Simeon blessed them, and said to Mary his mother, Behold, this child is set for the fall and rising again of many in Israel; and for a sign which shall be spoken against;

35 (Yea, a sword shall pierce through your own soul also,) that the thoughts of many hearts may be revealed.

36 And there was one Anna, a prophetess, the daughter of Phanuel, of the tribe of Aser: she was of a great age, and had lived with an husband seven years from her virginity;

37 And she was a widow of about fourscore and four years, which departed not from the temple, but served God with fastings and prayers night and day.

38 And she coming in that instant gave thanks likewise to the Lord, and spoke of him to all them that looked for redemption in Jerusalem.

39 And when they had performed all things according to the law of the Lord, they returned into Galilee, to their own city Nazareth.

40 And the child grew, and waxed strong in spirit, filled with wisdom: and the grace of God was upon him.

41 Now his parents went to Jerusalem every year at the feast of the passover.

42 And when he was twelve years old, they went up to Jerusalem after the custom of the feast.

43 And when they had fulfilled the days, as they returned, the child Jesus tarried behind in Jerusalem; and Joseph and his mother knew not of it.

44 But they, supposing him to have been in the company, went a day's journey; and they sought him among their kinsfolk and acquaintance.

45 And when they found him not, they turned back again to Jerusalem, seeking him.

46 And it came to pass, that after three

2:46 Jesus was not disobedient to Joseph and Mary as some assert. If anything, they were irresponsible in assuming (for a whole day) that their twelve-year-old son was with the company when He was not (v. 44).

days they found him in the temple, sitting in the midst of the doctors, both hearing them, and asking them questions.

47 And all that heard him were astonished at his understanding and answers.

48 And when they saw him, they were amazed: and his mother said to him, Son, why have you thus dealt with us? behold, your father and I have sought you sorrowing.

49 And he said to them, How is it that you sought me? Did you not know that I must be about my Father's business?

50 And they understood not the saying which he spoke to them.

51 And he went down with them, and came to Nazareth, and was subject to them: but his mother kept all these sayings in her heart.

52 And Jesus increased in wisdom and stature, and in favor with God and man.

CHAPTER 3

NOW in the fifteenth year of the reign of Tiberius Caesar, Pontius Pilate being governor of Judea, and Herod being tetrarch of Galilee, and his brother Philip tetrarch of Ituraea and of the region of Trachonitis, and Lysanias the tetrarch of Abilene,

2 Annas and Caiaphas being the high priests, the word of God came to John the son of Zacharias in the wilderness.

3 And he came into all the country about Jordan, preaching the baptism of repentance for the remission of sins;

4 As it is written in the book of the words of Isaiah the prophet, saying, The voice of

---

THE FUNCTION OF THE LAW

3:4 "Ever more the Law *must* prepare the way for the gospel. To overlook this in instructing souls is almost certain to result in false hope, the introduction of a false standard of Christian experience, and to fill the Church with false converts…Time will make this plain." *Charles Finney*

---

one crying in the wilderness, Prepare the way of the Lord, make his paths straight.

5 Every valley shall be filled, and every mountain and hill shall be brought low; and the crooked shall be made straight, and the rough ways shall be made smooth;

6 And all flesh shall see the salvation of God.

7 Then said he to the multitude that came forth to be baptized of him, O generation of vipers, who has warned you to flee from the wrath to come?

8 Bring forth therefore fruits worthy of repentance, and begin not to say within yourselves, We have Abraham to our father: for I say to you, That God is able of these stones to raise up children to Abraham.

9 And now also the axe is laid to the root of the trees: every tree therefore which brings not forth good fruit is hewn down, and cast into the fire.

10 And the people asked him, saying, What shall we do then?

11 He answered and said to them, He that has two coats, let him impart to him that has none; and he that has meat, let him do likewise.

3:1,2 Archaeology confirms the Bible. A hidden burial chamber, dating to the first century, was discovered in 1990 two miles from the Temple Mount. One bore the bones of a man in his 60s, with the inscription "Yehosef bar Qayafa" —meaning "Joseph, son of Caiaphas." Experts believe this was Caiaphas, the high priest of Jerusalem, who was involved in the arrest of Jesus, interrogated him, and handed Him over to Pontius Pilate for execution.

A few decades earlier, excavations at Caesarea Maritama, the ancient seat of Roman government in Judea, uncovered a stone slab whose complete inscription may have read: "Pontius Pilate, the prefect of Judea, has dedicated to the people of Caesarea a temple in honor of Tiberius."

The discovery is truly significant, establishing that the man depicted in the Gospels as Judea's Roman governor had the authority ascribed to him by the Gospel writers. *Jeffery L. Sheler*, "Is the Bible True?" *Reader's Digest*, June 2000

"Jews don't need to be 'saved'; they're already God's chosen people. Even the New Testament says 'so all Israel shall be saved.'"

3:7–9

The gospel was first preached to the Jews. They were commanded to repent and trust the Savior (Acts 2:38), and warned that if they didn't repent, they would perish (Luke 13:3). John the Baptist preached fearful words to those who, simply because they were Jews, thought that they need not repent. The Bible says, "Then said he to the multitude that came forth to be baptized of him, O generation of vipers, who has warned you to flee from the wrath to come? Bring forth therefore fruits worthy of repentance, and begin not to say within yourselves, We have Abraham to our father: for I say to you, That God is able of these stones to raise up children to Abraham. And now also the axe is laid to the root of the trees: every tree therefore which brings not forth good fruit is hewn down, and cast into the fire" (Luke 3:7–9).

12 Then came also publicans to be baptized, and said to him, Master, what shall we do?

13 And he said to them, Exact no more than that which is appointed you.

14 And the soldiers likewise demanded of him, saying, And what shall we do? And he said to them, Do violence to no man, neither accuse any falsely; and be content with your wages.

15 And as the people were in expectation, and all men mused in their hearts of John, whether he were the Christ, or not;

16 John answered, saying to them all, I indeed baptize you with water; but one mightier than I comes, the latchet of whose shoes I am not worthy to unloose: he shall baptize you with the Holy Spirit and with fire:

17 Whose fan is in his hand, and he will thoroughly purge his floor, and will gather the wheat into his garner; but the chaff he will burn with fire unquenchable.

18 And many other things in his exhortation preached he to the people.

19 But Herod the tetrarch, being reproved by him for Herodias his brother Philip's wife, and for all the evils which Herod had done,

20 Added yet this above all, that he shut up John in prison.

21 Now when all the people were baptized, it came to pass, that Jesus also being baptized, and praying, the heaven was opened,

22 And the Holy Spirit descended in a bodily shape like a dove upon him, and a voice came from heaven, which said, You are my beloved Son; in you I am well pleased.

23 And Jesus himself began to be about thirty years of age, being (as was supposed) the son of Joseph, which was the son of Heli,

24 Which was the son of Matthat, which was the son of Levi, which was the son of Melchi, which was the son of Janna, which was the son of Joseph,

25 Which was the son of Mattathias, which was the son of Amos, which was

3:21 "More than twenty times the Gospels call attention to Jesus' practice of prayer. It is given special mention during events of momentous decision in His life—His baptism (Luke 3:21); the selection of the twelve apostles (Luke 6:12); on the Mount of Transfiguration (Luke 9:29); the Last Supper (Matthew 26:27); in Gethsemane (Luke 22:39–46); and on the cross (Luke 23:46)." *Robert E. Coleman*

3:23 Some point to the different genealogies of Jesus as "errors" in the Bible. However, Luke gives the maternal genealogy of the Messiah (through His mother) and Matthew (1:1) gives His paternal genealogy (through His legal father).

the son of Naum, which was the son of Esli, which was the son of Nagge,

26 Which was the son of Maath, which was the son of Mattathias, which was the son of Semei, which was the son of Joseph, which was the son of Juda,

27 Which was the son of Joanna, which was the son of Rhesa, which was the son of Zorobabel, which was the son of Salathiel, which was the son of Neri,

28 Which was the son of Melchi, which was the son of Addi, which was the son of Cosam, which was the son of Elmodam, which was the son of Er,

29 Which was the son of Jose, which was the son of Eliezer, which was the son of Jorim, which was the son of Matthat, which was the son of Levi,

30 Which was the son of Simeon, which was the son of Juda, which was the son of Joseph, which was the son of Jonan, which was the son of Eliakim,

31 Which was the son of Melea, which was the son of Menan, which was the son of Mattatha, which was the son of Nathan, which was the son of David,

32 Which was the son of Jesse, which was the son of Obed, which was the son of Booz, which was the son of Salmon, which was the son of Naasson,

33 Which was the son of Aminadab, which was the son of Aram, which was the son of Esrom, which was the son of Phares, which was the son of Juda,

34 Which was the son of Jacob, which was the son of Isaac, which was the son of Abraham, which was the son of Thara, which was the son of Nachor,

35 Which was the son of Saruch, which was the son of Ragau, which was the son of Phalec, which was the son of Heber, which was the son of Sala,

36 Which was the son of Cainan, which was the son of Arphaxad, which was the son of Sem, which was the son of Noah, which was the son of Lamech,

37 Which was the son of Mathusala, which was the son of Enoch, which was the son of Jared, which was the son of Maleleel, which was the son of Cainan,

38 Which was the son of Enos, which was the son of Seth, which was the son of Adam, which was the son of God.

CHAPTER 4

AND Jesus being full of the Holy Spirit returned from Jordan, and was led by the Spirit into the wilderness,

2 Being forty days tempted of the devil. And in those days he did eat nothing: and when they were ended, he afterward hungered.

3 And the devil said to him, If you be the Son of God, command this stone that it be made bread.

4 And Jesus answered him, saying, It is written, That man shall not live by bread alone, but by every word of God.

5 And the devil, taking him up into an high mountain, showed to him all the kingdoms of the world in a moment of time.

6 And the devil said to him, All this power will I give you, and the glory of them: for that is delivered to me; and to whomsoever I will I give it.

7 If you therefore will worship me, all shall be yours.

8 And Jesus answered and said to him, Get behind me, Satan: for it is written, You shall worship the Lord your God, and him only shall you serve.

9 And he brought him to Jerusalem, and set him on a pinnacle of the temple, and

---

3:33 Messianic prophecy fulfilled: "The scepter shall not depart from Judah, nor a lawgiver from between his feet, until Shiloh come; and to him shall the gathering of the people be" (Genesis 49:10). See Luke 23:32–34 footnote.

4:4 "If you wish to know God, you must know His Word. If you wish to perceive His power, you must see how He works by His Word. If you wish to know His purpose before it comes to pass, you can only discover it by His Word." *Charles Spurgeon*

said to him, If you be the Son of God, cast yourself down from hence:

10 For it is written, He shall give his angels charge over you, to keep you:

11 And in their hands they shall bear you up, lest at any time you dash your foot against a stone.

12 And Jesus answering said to him, It is said, You shall not tempt the Lord your God.

13 And when the devil had ended all the temptation, he departed from him for a season.

14 And Jesus returned in the power of the Spirit into Galilee: and there went out a fame of him through all the region round about.

15 And he taught in their synagogues, being glorified of all.

16 And he came to Nazareth, where he had been brought up: and, as his custom was, he went into the synagogue on the sabbath day, and stood up for to read.

17 And there was delivered to him the book of the prophet Isaiah. And when he had opened the book, he found the place where it was written,

18 The Spirit of the Lord is upon me, because he has anointed me to preach the gospel to the poor; he has sent me to heal the brokenhearted, to preach deliverance to the captives, and recovering of sight to the blind, to set at liberty them that are bruised,

19 **To preach the acceptable year of the Lord.**

20 And he closed the book, and he gave it again to the minister, and sat down. And the eyes of all them that were in the synagogue were fastened on him.

21 And he began to say to them, This day is this scripture fulfilled in your ears.

22 And all bare him witness, and wondered at the gracious words which pro-

---

4:8   To worship is to change. "Just as worship begins in holy expectancy, it ends in holy obedience. If worship does not propel us into greater obedience, it has not been worship. To stand before the Holy One of eternity is to change…In worship an increased power steals into the heart sanctuary, an increased compassion grows in the soul." *Richard J. Foster, Celebration of Discipline*

4:10,11   When Jesus was being tempted, the devil quoted Scripture but twisted its meaning. Jesus responded by countering with the true application of God's Word (vv. 4–13). We must know the truth in order to counter error, or we will be misled by those who take Scripture out of context and misinterpret it. That's why we should not "live by bread alone, but by every word of God" (v. 4).

4:18   Who is the gospel for? Jesus gives us a summation of who the gospel is for: the poor, the brokenhearted, the captives, the blind, the bruised (oppressed). Jesus is not referring to those who lack financial resources when He speaks of the *poor*. The word means "meek, humble, lowly" and refers to the "poor in spirit" (Matthew 5:3)—the blessed ones to whom the kingdom of God belongs. The poor are those who know that they are destitute of righteousness.

The *brokenhearted* refers not to unhappy people who have been jilted by a sweetheart, but to those who, like Peter and Isaiah, are contrite and sorrowing for their sin. *Matthew Henry* wrote of Jesus, "For He was sent to heal the brokenhearted, to give peace to those that were troubled and humbled for sins, and to bring them to rest who were weary and heavy-laden, under the burden of guilt and corruption."

The *captives* are those "taken captive by [the devil] at his will" (2 Timothy 2:26).

The *blind* are those whom "the god of this world has blinded…[to] the light of the glorious gospel of Christ" (2 Corinthians 4:4).

The *oppressed* are those who are "oppressed of the devil" (Acts 10:38).

The gospel of grace is for the humble, not the proud. God resists the proud, but gives grace to the humble (James 4:6). The Scriptures tell us, "Every one that is proud in heart is an abomination to the Lord" (Proverbs 16:5). He sets on high those who are lowly, and those who mourn are lifted to safety (Job 5:11). God looks on the man who is poor and of a contrite spirit, and who trembles at His Word (Isaiah 66:2). Only the sick need a physician, and only those who are convinced of the disease of sin will appreciate and appropriate the cure of the gospel.

ceeded out of his mouth. And they said, Is not this Joseph's son?

23 And he said to them, You will surely say to me this proverb, Physician, heal yourself: whatsoever we have heard done in Capernaum, do also here in your country.

24 And he said, Verily I say to you, No prophet is accepted in his own country.

25 But I tell you of a truth, many widows were in Israel in the days of Elijah, when the heaven was shut up three years and six months, when great famine was throughout all the land;

26 But to none of them was Elisha sent, save to Sarepta, a city of Sidon, to a woman that was a widow.

27 And many lepers were in Israel in the time of Elijah the prophet; and none of them was cleansed, saving Naaman the Syrian.

28 And all they in the synagogue, when they heard these things, were filled with wrath,

29 And rose up, and thrust him out of the city, and led him to the brow of the hill whereon their city was built, that they might cast him down headlong.

30 But he passing through the midst of them went his way,

31 And came down to Capernaum, a city of Galilee, and taught them on the sabbath days.

32 And they were astonished at his doctrine: for his word was with power.

33 And in the synagogue there was a man, which had a spirit of an unclean devil, and cried out with a loud voice,

34 Saying, Let us alone; what have we to do with you, Jesus of Nazareth? are you come to destroy us? I know you who you are; the Holy One of God.

35 And Jesus rebuked him, saying, Hold your peace, and come out of him. And when the devil had thrown him in the midst, he came out of him, and hurt him not.

36 And they were all amazed, and spoke among themselves, saying, What a word is this! for with authority and power he commands the unclean spirits, and they come out.

37 And the fame of him went out into every place of the country round about.

. . . . . .

For evidence of the Bible's reliability, see Matthew 4:4 footnote.

. . . . . .

38 And he arose out of the synagogue, and entered into Simon's house. And Simon's wife's mother was taken with a great fever; and they besought him for her.

39 And he stood over her, and rebuked the fever; and it left her: and immediately she arose and ministered to them.

40 Now when the sun was setting, all they that had any sick with divers diseases brought them to him; and he laid his hands on every one of them, and healed them.

41 And devils also came out of many, crying out, and saying, You are Christ the Son of God. And he rebuking them suffered them not to speak: for they knew

---

4:40 Scientific facts in the Bible. For ages, scientists believed in a geocentric view of the universe. The differences between night and day were believed to be caused by the sun revolving around the earth. Today, we know that the earth's rotation on its axis is responsible for the sun's rising and setting. But 4,000 or more years ago, it was written, "Have you commanded the morning since your days; and caused the day spring [dawn] to know his place?...It [the earth] is turned as clay to the seal" (Job 38:12,14). The picture here is of a clay vessel being turned or rotated upon the potter's wheel—an accurate analogy of the earth's rotation. See also Hebrews 11:3 footnote.

"The study of the Book of Job and its comparison with the latest scientific discoveries has brought me to the matured conviction that the Bible is an inspired book and was written by the One who made the stars." *Charles Burckhalter,* Chabot Observatory

that he was Christ.

42 And when it was day, he departed and went into a desert place: and the people sought him, and came to him, and stayed him, that he should not depart from them.

43 And he said to them, I must preach the kingdom of God to other cities also: for therefore am I sent.

44 And he preached in the synagogues of Galilee.

CHAPTER 5

A ND it came to pass, that, as the people pressed upon him to hear the word of God, he stood by the lake of Gennesaret,

2 And saw two ships standing by the lake: but the fishermen were gone out of them, and were washing their nets.

3 And he entered into one of the ships, which was Simon's, and prayed him that he would thrust out a little from the land. And he sat down, and taught the people out of the ship.

4 Now when he had left speaking, he said to Simon, Launch out into the deep, and let down your nets for a draught.

5 And Simon answering said to him, Master, we have toiled all the night, and have taken nothing: nevertheless at your word I will let down the net.

6 And when they had this done, they enclosed a great multitude of fishes: and their net broke.

7 And they beckoned to their partners, which were in the other ship, that they should come and help them. And they came, and filled both the ships, so that they began to sink.

8 When Simon Peter saw it, he fell down at Jesus' knees, saying, Depart from me; for I am a sinful man, O Lord.

9 For he was astonished, and all that were with him, at the draught of the fishes which they had taken:

10 *And so was also James, and John, the sons of Zebedee, which were partners with Simon. And Jesus said to Simon, Fear not; from henceforth you shall catch men.*

11 And when they had brought their ships to land, they forsook all, and followed him.

12 And it came to pass, when he was in a certain city, behold a man full of leprosy: who seeing Jesus fell on his face, and besought him, saying, Lord, if you will, you can make me clean.

13 And he put forth his hand, and touched him, saying, I will: be clean. And immediately the leprosy departed from him.

14 And he charged him to tell no man: but go, and show yourself to the priest, and offer for your cleansing, according as Moses commanded, for a testimony to them.

15 But so much the more went there a fame abroad of him: and great multitudes came together to hear, and to be healed by him of their infirmities.

16 And he withdrew himself into the wilderness, and prayed.

17 And it came to pass on a certain day, as he was teaching, that there were Pharisees and doctors of the law sitting by, which were come out of every town of Galilee, and Judea, and Jerusalem: and the power of the Lord was present to heal

---

5:16 Prayer—the secret weapon: Prayer was the ignition to every revival fire in history. Prayer was the key to the doorway of ministry for every preacher used by God in the past. For the soldier of Christ, true prayer should be a way of life, not just a call for help in the heat of battle.

A man was once cutting a tree stump with an obviously blunt axe. He was only bruising the bark as sweat poured from his beaded brow. Someone suggested that he stop for a moment and sharpen the axe, to which he replied, "I'm too busy chopping the tree to stop for anything." If he would only stop for a moment and sharpen the axe, he would slice through the tree with far greater ease.

Stop at the beginning of each day, and "sharpen the axe" through prayer. Seek first the kingdom of God and you will slice through that day with far greater ease. See Luke 6:12.

them.

18 And, behold, men brought in a bed a man which was taken with a palsy: and they sought means to bring him in, and to lay him before him.

19 And when they could not find by what way they might bring him in because of the multitude, they went upon the housetop, and let him down through the tiling with his couch into the midst before Jesus.

20 And when he saw their faith, he said to him, Man, your sins are forgiven you.

21 And the scribes and the Pharisees began to reason, saying, Who is this which speaks blasphemies? Who can forgive sins, but God alone?

22 But when Jesus perceived their thoughts, he answering said to them, What do you reason in your hearts?

23 Whether is easier, to say, Your sins be forgiven you; or to say, Rise up and walk?

24 **But that you may know that the Son of man has power upon earth to forgive sins, (he said to the sick of the palsy,) I say to you, Arise, and take up your couch, and go into your house.**

25 And immediately he rose up before them, and took up that whereon he lay, and departed to his own house, glorifying God.

26 And they were all amazed, and they glorified God, and were filled with fear, saying, We have seen strange things to day.

27 And after these things he went forth, and saw a publican, named Levi, sitting at the receipt of custom: and he said to him, Follow me.

28 And he left all, rose up, and followed him.

29 And Levi made him a great feast in his own house: and there was a great company of publicans and of others that sat down with them.

30 But their scribes and Pharisees murmured against his disciples, saying, Why do you eat and drink with publicans and sinners?

31 And Jesus answering said to them, They that are whole need not a physician; but they that are sick.

32 I came not to call the righteous, but sinners to repentance.

33 And they said to him, Why do the disciples of John fast often, and make prayers, and likewise the disciples of the Pharisees; but yours eat and drink?

34 And he said to them, Can you make the children of the bridechamber fast, while the bridegroom is with them?

35 But the days will come, when the bridegroom shall be taken away from them, and then shall they fast in those days.

36 And he spoke also a parable to them; No man puts a piece of a new garment upon an old; if otherwise, then both the new makes a rent, and the piece that was taken out of the new agrees not with the old.

37 And no man puts new wine into old bottles; else the new wine will burst the bottles, and be spilled, and the bottles shall perish.

38 But new wine must be put into new bottles; and both are preserved.

39 No man also having drunk old wine straightway desires new: for he says, The old is better.

CHAPTER 6

AND it came to pass on the second sabbath after the first, that he went through the corn fields; and his disciples plucked the ears of corn, and did eat, rubbing them in their hands.

2 And certain of the Pharisees said to them, Why do you that which is not lawful to do on the sabbath days?

3 And Jesus answering them said, Have you not read so much as this, what David did, when himself was an hungered, and they which were with him;

5:32 Repentance—its necessity for salvation. See Luke 13:2-3.

4 How he went into the house of God, and did take and eat the shewbread, and gave also to them that were with him; which it is not lawful to eat but for the priests alone?

5 And he said to them, That the Son of man is Lord also of the sabbath.

6 And it came to pass also on another sabbath, that he entered into the synagogue and taught: and there was a man whose right hand was withered.

7 And the scribes and Pharisees watched him, whether he would heal on the sabbath day; that they might find an accusation against him.

8 But he knew their thoughts, and said to the man which had the withered hand, Rise up, and stand forth in the midst. And he arose and stood forth.

9 Then said Jesus to them, I will ask you one thing; Is it lawful on the sabbath days to do good, or to do evil? to save life, or to destroy it?

10 And looking round about upon them all, he said to the man, Stretch forth your hand. And he did so: and his hand was restored whole as the other.

11 And they were filled with madness; and communed one with another what they might do to Jesus.

12 And it came to pass in those days, that he went out into a mountain to pray, and continued all night in prayer to God.

13 And when it was day, he called to him his disciples: and of them he chose twelve, whom also he named apostles;

14 Simon, (whom he also named Peter,) and Andrew his brother, James and John, Philip and Bartholomew,

15 Matthew and Thomas, James the son of Alphaeus, and Simon called Zelotes,

16 And Judas the brother of James, and Judas Iscariot, which also was the traitor.

17 And he came down with them, and

"[The Bible] is a Book worth more than all the other books which were ever printed."

Patrick Henry

stood in the plain, and the company of his disciples, and a great multitude of people out of all Judea and Jerusalem, and from the sea coast of Tyre and Sidon, which came to hear him, and to be healed of their diseases;

18 And they that were vexed with unclean spirits: and they were healed.

19 And the whole multitude sought to touch him: for there went virtue out of him, and healed them all.

20 And he lifted up his eyes on his disciples, and said, Blessed be you poor: for yours is the kingdom of God.

21 Blessed are you that hunger now: for you shall be filled. Blessed are you that weep now: for you shall laugh.

22 Blessed are you, when men shall hate you, and when they shall separate you from their company, and shall reproach you, and cast out your name as evil, for the Son of man's sake.

6:12 Prayer—the secret weapon: See Luke 22:41. "The one concern of the devil is to keep Christians from praying. He fears nothing from prayerless studies, prayerless works, and prayerless religion. He laughs at our toil, mocks at our wisdom, but trembles when we pray." *Samuel Chadwick*

QUESTIONS & OBJECTIONS

6:27 *"Religion has caused more wars than anything else in history."*

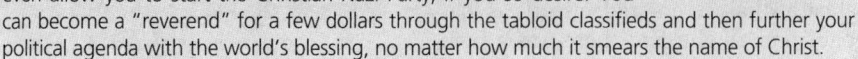

It is true that man has used religion for political gain. Nazi Germany had "God with us" engraved in German on the belts of Nazi soldiers. America said, "Praise the Lord and pass the ammunition." The law may even allow you to start the Christian Nazi Party, if you so desire. You can become a "reverend" for a few dollars through the tabloid classifieds and then further your political agenda with the world's blessing, no matter how much it smears the name of Christ.

Jesus tells us in John 16:2,3 that there will be some who, in their error, commit atrocities and murder in the name of God: "The time is coming that whosoever kills you will think that he does God service." However, He informs us that these are not true believers: "And these things will they do to you, because they have not known the Father, nor me." (See also 1 John 3:15.)

Jesus told His followers to love their enemies. So if a man puts a knife into someone's back in the name of Christianity, something obviously isn't right. If we human beings can detect it, how much more will God? He will deal with it on Judgment Day.

"I know that the Lord is always on the side of right. But it is my constant anxiety and prayer that I—and this nation—should be on the Lord's side." *Abraham Lincoln*

23 Rejoice in that day, and leap for joy: for, behold, your reward is great in heaven: for in the like manner did their fathers to the prophets.

24 But woe to you that are rich! for you have received your consolation.

25 Woe to you that are full! for you shall hunger. Woe to you that laugh now! for you shall mourn and weep.

26 Woe to you, when all men shall speak well of you! for so did their fathers to the false prophets.

27 But I say to you which hear, Love your enemies, do good to them which hate you,

28 Bless them that curse you, and pray for them which despitefully use you.

29 And to him that smites you on the one cheek offer also the other; and him that takes away your cloak forbid not to take your coat also.

30 Give to every man that asks of you; and of him that takes away your goods ask them not again.

31 And as you would that men should do to you, do you also to them likewise.

32 For if you love them which love you, what thanks do you have? for sinners also love those that love them.

6:26 A soft gospel. Those who speak about "the love of Jesus," but refuse to preach the gospel of love revealed in the bloodied cross, *will* have the smile of the world. Their listeners have itching ears and they are more than pleased to have them scratched with a soft gospel. They are of the world; they speak of the world and the world gladly hears them. Jesus gave warning to those who fall into this subtle trap: "Woe to you, when all men shall speak well of you!"

The cross is the only God-given means of salvation from death, and we will bear reproach as long as we cling to its frame. It is only for a season—some day we will exchange it for a crown. In the meantime, let our faith in Jesus be spoken of throughout the whole world whether it be with a smile or a frown. The praise of men is a volatile minefield of pleasant flowers. In a moment it can swing from a fragrant "Hosanna!" to an explosive "Crucify Him!" Ask any baseball hero who has had a bad season. God's approval, however, is eternal.

6:27 The Church is commanded to love her enemies, just as Israel was instructed to do in Exodus 23:4,5.

6:28 This is the spirit in which we should share our faith. See Colossians 4:5,6.

QUESTIONS & OBJECTIONS

6:37 *"Judge not lest you be judged. You therefore have no right to judge me when it comes to my sins!"*

The world often takes this verse out of context and uses it to accuse Christians of being "judgmental" when they speak of sin. In the context of the verse Jesus is telling His disciples not to judge one another, something the Bible condemns (Romans 14:10; James 4:11). In Luke 6:41,42 He speaks of seeing a speck in a *brother's* eye. In John 7:24 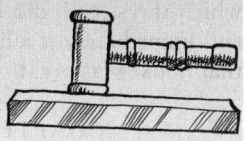 He said, "Judge not according to the appearance, but judge righteous judgment." If someone steals, lies, commits adultery or murder, etc., the Christian can make a (righteous) moral judgment and say that the actions were morally wrong, and that these sins will have eternal consequences. *Chuck Colson* said, "True tolerance is not a total lack of judgment. It's knowing what should be tolerated—and refusing to tolerate that which shouldn't."

33 And if you do good to them which do good to you, what thank have you? for sinners also do even the same.

34 And if you lend to them of whom you hope to receive, what thank have you? for sinners also lend to sinners, to receive as much again.

35 But love your enemies, and do good, and lend, hoping for nothing again; and your reward shall be great, and you shall be the children of the Highest: for he is kind to the unthankful and to the evil.

36 Be therefore merciful, as your Father also is merciful.

37 Judge not, and you shall not be judged: condemn not, and you shall not be condemned: forgive, and you shall be forgiven:

38 Give, and it shall be given to you; good measure, pressed down, and shaken together, and running over, shall men give into your bosom. For with the same measure that you mete withal it shall be measured to you again.

39 And he spoke a parable to them, Can the blind lead the blind? shall they not both fall into the ditch?

40 The disciple is not above his master: but every one that is perfect shall be as his master.

41 And why behold the mote that is in your brother's eye, but perceive not the beam that is in your own eye?

42 Either how can you say to your brother, Brother, let me pull out the mote that is in your eye, when you yourself behold not the beam that is in your own eye? You hypocrite, cast out first the beam out of your own eye, and then shall you see clearly to pull out the mote that is in your brother's eye.

43 For a good tree brings not forth corrupt fruit; neither does a corrupt tree bring forth good fruit.

44 For every tree is known by his own fruit. For of thorns men do not gather figs, nor of a bramble bush gather they grapes.

45 A good man out of the good treasure of his heart brings forth that which is good; and an evil man out of the evil treasure of his heart brings forth that which is evil: for of the abundance of the heart his mouth speaks.

46 And why do you call me, Lord, Lord, and do not the things which I say?

47 Whosoever comes to me, and hears my sayings, and does them, I will show you to whom he is like:

48 He is like a man which built an house, and dug deep, and laid the foundation on a rock: and when the flood arose, the stream beat vehemently up-

6:38 "You gain by giving that which you can't buy with money." *Dr. Edwin Cole*

on that house, and could not shake it: for it was founded upon a rock.

49 But he that hears, and does not, is like a man that without a foundation built an house upon the earth; against which the stream did beat vehemently, and immediately it fell; and the ruin of that house was great.

CHAPTER 7

N OW when he had ended all his sayings in the audience of the people, he entered into Capernaum.

2 And a certain centurion's servant, who was dear to him, was sick, and ready to die.

3 And when he heard of Jesus, he sent to him the elders of the Jews, beseeching him that he would come and heal his servant.

4 And when they came to Jesus, they besought him instantly, saying, That he was worthy for whom he should do this:

5 For he loves our nation, and he has built us a synagogue.

6 Then Jesus went with them. And when he was now not far from the house, the centurion sent friends to him, saying to him, Lord, trouble not yourself: for I am not worthy that you should enter under my roof:

7 Wherefore neither thought I myself worthy to come to you: but say in a word, and my servant shall be healed.

8 For I also am a man set under authority, having under me soldiers, and I say to one, Go, and he goes; and to another, Come, and he comes; and to my servant, Do this, and he does it.

9 When Jesus heard these things, he marveled at him, and turned him about, and said to the people that followed him, I say to you, I have not found so great faith, no, not in Israel.

10 And they that were sent, returning to the house, found the servant whole that had been sick.

11 And it came to pass the day after, that he went into a city called Nain; and many of his disciples went with him, and much people.

12 Now when he came near to the gate of the city, behold, there was a dead man carried out, the only son of his mother, and she was a widow: and much people of the city was with her.

13 And when the Lord saw her, he had compassion on her, and said to her, Weep not.

14 And he came and touched the coffin: and they that bare him stood still. And he said, Young man, I say to you, Arise.

15 And he that was dead sat up, and began to speak. And he delivered him to his mother.

16 And there came a fear on all: and they glorified God, saying, That a great prophet is risen up among us; and, That God has visited his people.

17 And this rumour of him went forth throughout all Judea, and throughout all the region round about.

18 And the disciples of John showed him of all these things.

19 And John calling to him two of his disciples sent them to Jesus, saying, are you he that should come? or look we for another?

20 When the men were come to him, they said, John Baptist has sent us to you, saying, are you he that should come? or look we for another?

21 And in that same hour he cured many of their infirmities and plagues, and of evil spirits; and to many that were blind he gave sight.

22 Then Jesus answering said to them, Go your way, and tell John what things you have seen and heard; how that the blind see, the lame walk, the lepers are cleansed, the deaf hear, the dead are raised, to the poor the gospel is preached.

6:46 "You cannot say, 'No, Lord,' and mean both words; one annuls the other. If you say no to Him, then He is not your Lord." *D. James Kennedy*

without, desiring to see you.

21 And he answered and said to them, My mother and my brethren are these which hear the word of God, and do it.

22 Now it came to pass on a certain day, that he went into a ship with his disciples: and he said to them, Let us go over to the other side of the lake. And they launched forth.

23 But as they sailed he fell asleep: and there came down a storm of wind on the lake; and they were filled with water, and were in jeopardy.

24 And they came to him, and awoke him, saying, Master, master, we perish. Then he arose, and rebuked the wind and the raging of the water: and they ceased, and there was a calm.

25 And he said to them, Where is your faith? **And they being afraid wondered, saying one to another, What manner of man is this! for he commands even the winds and water, and they obey him.**

> One of the earliest things a minister should do when he leaves college and settles in a country town or village is to begin open-air speaking.
>
> **CHARLES SPURGEON**

26 And they arrived at the country of the Gadarenes, which is over against Galilee.

27 And when he went forth to land, there met him out of the city a certain man, which had devils long time, and ware no clothes, neither abode in any house, but in the tombs.

28 When he saw Jesus, he cried out, and fell down before him, and with a loud voice said, What have I to do with you, Jesus, you Son of God most high? I beseech you, torment me not.

29 (For he had commanded the unclean spirit to come out of the man. For oftentimes it had caught him: and he was kept bound with chains and in fetters; and he broke the bands, and was driven of the devil into the wilderness.)

30 And Jesus asked him, saying, What is your name? And he said, Legion: because many devils were entered into him.

31 And they besought him that he would not command them to go out into the deep.

32 And there was there an herd of many swine feeding on the mountain: and they besought him that he would suffer them to enter into them. And he suffered them.

33 Then went the devils out of the man, and entered into the swine: and the herd ran violently down a steep place into the lake, and were choked.

34 When they that fed them saw what was done, they fled, and went and told it in the city and in the country.

35 Then they went out to see what was done; and came to Jesus, and found the man, out of whom the devils were departed, sitting at the feet of Jesus, clothed, and in his right mind: and they were afraid.

36 They also which saw it told them by what means he that was possessed of the devils was healed.

37 Then the whole multitude of the country of the Gadarenes round about besought him to depart from them; for they were taken with great fear: and he went up into the ship, and returned back again.

38 Now the man out of whom the devils were departed besought him that he might be with him: but Jesus sent him away, saying,

39 Return to your own house, and show how great things God has done to you. And he went his way, and published throughout the whole city how great things Jesus had done to him.

40 And it came to pass, that, when Jesus was returned, the people gladly received him: for they were all waiting for him.

41 And, behold, there came a man named Jairus, and he was a ruler of the synagogue: and he fell down at Jesus' feet, and besought him that he would come into his house:

42 For he had one only daughter, about twelve years of age, and she lay a dying. But as he went the people thronged him.

43 And a woman having an issue of blood twelve years, which had spent all her living upon physicians, neither could be healed of any,

44 Came behind him, and touched the border of his garment: and immediately her issue of blood stopped.

45 And Jesus said, Who touched me? When all denied, Peter and they that were with him said, Master, the multitude throng you and press you, and you say, Who touched me?

46 And Jesus said, Somebody has touched me: for I perceive that virtue is gone out of me.

47 And when the woman saw that she was not hid, she came trembling, and falling down before him, she declared to him before all the people for what cause she had touched him and how she was healed immediately.

48 And he said to her, Daughter, be of good comfort: your faith has made you whole; go in peace.

49 While he yet spoke, there came one from the ruler of the synagogue's house, saying to him, Your daughter is dead; trouble not the Master.

50 But when Jesus heard it, he answered him, saying, Fear not: believe only, and she shall be made whole.

51 And when he came into the house, he suffered no man to go in, save Peter, and James, and John, and the father and the mother of the maiden.

52 And all wept, and bewailed her: but he said, Weep not; she is not dead, but sleeps.

53 And they laughed him to scorn, knowing that she was dead.

54 And he put them all out, and took her by the hand, and called, saying, Maid, arise.

55 And her spirit came again, and she arose straightway: and he commanded to give her meat.

56 And her parents were astonished: but he charged them that they should tell no man what was done.

CHAPTER 9

THEN he called his twelve disciples together, and gave them power and authority over all devils, and to cure dis-

---

8:39 How to witness to family members. Here's some advice that may save you a great deal of grief. As a new Christian, I did almost irreparable damage by acting like a wild bull in a crystal showroom. I bullied my mom, my dad, and many of my friends into making a "decision for Christ." I was sincere, zealous, loving, kind, and stupid. I didn't understand that salvation doesn't come through making a "decision," but through *repentance*, and repentance is God-given (2 Timothy 2:25). The Bible teaches that no one can come to the Son unless the Father "draws" him (John 6:44). If you are able to get a "decision" but the person has no conviction of sin, you will almost certainly end up with a stillborn on your hands.

In my "zeal without knowledge" I actually alienated the very ones I was so desperately trying to reach. There is nothing more important to you than the salvation of your loved ones, and you don't want to blow it. If you do, you may find that you don't have a second chance. Fervently pray for them, thanking God for their salvation. Let them *see* your faith. Let them *feel* your kindness, your genuine love, and your gentleness. Buy gifts for no reason. Do chores when you are not asked to. Go the extra mile. Put yourself in their position. You know that you have found everlasting life—*death has lost its sting!* Your joy is unspeakable. But as far as they are concerned, you've been brainwashed and have become part of a weird sect. So your loving actions will speak more loudly than ten thousand eloquent sermons.

For this reason you should avoid *verbal* confrontation until you have knowledge that will guide your zeal. Pray for wisdom and sensitivity to God's timing. You may have only one shot, so make it count. Keep your cool. If you don't, you may end up with a lifetime of regret. *Believe* me. It is better to hear a loved one or a close friend say, "Tell me about your faith in Jesus Christ," rather than you saying, "Sit down. I want to talk to you." Continue to persevere in prayer for them, that God would open their eyes to the truth.

eases.

2 And he sent them to preach the kingdom of God, and to heal the sick.

3 And he said to them, Take nothing for your journey, neither staves, nor scrip, neither bread, neither money; neither have two coats apiece.

4 And whatsoever house you enter into, there abide, and thence depart.

5 And whosoever will not receive you, when you go out of that city, shake off the very dust from your feet for a testimony against them.

6 And they departed, and went through the towns, preaching the gospel, and healing every where.

7 Now Herod the tetrarch heard of all that was done by him: and he was perplexed, because that it was said of some, that John was risen from the dead;

8 And of some, that Elijah had appeared; and of others, that one of the old prophets was risen again.

9 And Herod said, John have I beheaded: but who is this, of whom I hear such things? And he desired to see him.

10 And the apostles, when they were returned, told him all that they had done. And he took them, and went aside privately into a desert place belonging to the city called Bethsaida.

11 And the people, when they knew it, followed him: and he received them, and spoke to them of the kingdom of God, and healed them that had need of healing.

12 And when the day began to wear away, then came the twelve, and said to him, Send the multitude away, that they may go into the towns and country round about, and lodge, and get victuals: for we are here in a desert place.

13 But he said to them, You give them to eat. And they said, We have no more but five loaves and two fishes; except we should go and buy meat for all this people.

14 For they were about five thousand men. And he said to his disciples, Make them sit down by fifties in a company.

15 And they did so, and made them all sit down.

16 Then he took the five loaves and the two fishes, and looking up to heaven, he blessed them, and broke, and gave to the disciples to set before the multitude.

17 And they did eat, and were all filled: and there was taken up of fragments that remained to them twelve baskets.

18 And it came to pass, as he was alone praying, his disciples were with him: and he asked them, saying, Whom say the people that I am?

19 They answering said, John the Baptist; but some say, Elijah; and others say, that one of the old prophets is risen again.

20 He said to them, But whom say you that I am? Peter answering said, The Christ of God.

21 And he straitly charged them, and commanded them to tell no man that thing;

> No sort of defense is needed for preaching out of doors; but it would need very potent arguments to prove that a man had done his duty who has never preached beyond the walls of his meeting place.
>
> **CHARLES SPURGEON**

22 Saying, The Son of man must suffer many things, and be rejected of the elders and chief priests and scribes, and be slain, and be raised the third day.

23 **And he said to them all, If any man will come after me, let him deny himself, and take up his cross daily, and follow me.**

24 **For whosoever will save his life shall lose it: but whosoever will lose his life for my sake, the same shall save it.**

25 **For what is a man advantaged, if he gain the whole world, and lose himself, or be cast away?**

26 **For whosoever shall be ashamed of me and of my words, of him shall the Son of man be ashamed, when he shall come in his own glory, and in his Father's, and of the holy angels.**

27 But I tell you of a truth, there be some standing here, which shall not taste of death, till they see the kingdom of God.

28 And it came to pass about an eight days after these sayings, he took Peter and John and James, and went up into a mountain to pray.

29 And as he prayed, the fashion of his countenance was altered, and his raiment was white and glistering.

30 And, behold, there talked with him two men, which were Moses and Elijah:

31 Who appeared in glory, and spoke of his decease which he should accomplish at Jerusalem.

32 But Peter and they that were with him were heavy with sleep: and when they were awake, they saw his glory, and the two men that stood with him.

33 And it came to pass, as they departed from him, Peter said to Jesus, Master, it is good for us to be here: and let us make three tabernacles; one for you, and one for Moses, and one for Elijah: not knowing what he said.

34 While he thus spoke, there came a cloud, and overshadowed them: and they feared as they entered into the cloud.

35 And there came a voice out of the cloud, saying, This is my beloved Son: hear him.

36 And when the voice was past, Jesus was found alone. And they kept it close, and told no man in those days any of those things which they had seen.

37 And it came to pass, that on the next day, when they were come down from the hill, much people met him.

38 And, behold, a man of the company cried out, saying, Master, I beseech you, look upon my son: for he is mine only child.

39 And, lo, a spirit takes him, and he suddenly cries out; and it tears him that he foams again, and bruising him hardly departs from him.

40 And I besought your disciples to cast him out; and they could not.

9:25 "[A] watchful eye must be kept on ourselves lest, while we are building great monuments of renown and bliss here, we neglect to have our names enrolled in the Annals of Heaven." *James Madison*

9:30   The Mount of Transfiguration. When Jesus was transfigured on the Holy Mountain, Moses and Elijah appeared in a vision and communed with Him. Moses represented the Law and Elijah represented the prophets.

Scripture gives us insight into what they spoke about: they communed about the cross (vv. 30,31). When Peter suggested paying homage to Moses, Elijah, and Jesus, it seems God wasn't impressed with the proposal. He spoke from heaven, telling the disciples to listen to Jesus. Then Moses and Elijah disappeared, and Jesus was left alone with the disciples.

When a person hears from the Father and understands who Jesus is, Moses and Elijah disappear. We see only Jesus. He is the Alpha and Omega, the Beginning and the End, the Author and Finisher of our faith. He is the only One to whom we bow the knee. Too many who profess to have heard the Father's voice spend too much time at the feet of Moses, bowing their knee to the Law. They are legalists who have no zeal for the lost. Their only concern is "touch not, taste not, handle not" (Colossians 2:21).

Many also spend too much time bowing down to Elijah. Prophecy is their joy. Prophecy shouldn't have us gazing into the future—it should have us gazing at the Savior and His will for the lost.

Charles Spurgeon said, "Here is another who spent all his time in interpreting the prophecies, so that everything he reads of in the newspapers he could see in Daniel or Revelation. Some say he is wise, but I would rather spend my time in winning souls. I would sooner bring one sinner to Jesus than unravel all the mysteries of the divine Word, for salvation is the one thing we are to live for."

The death and resurrection of the Savior didn't occur so that we could dabble in the future, but to open the door of salvation to hell-bound sinners. Those who hear the Father's voice hear the Son. They walk in His steps. They come down from the mountain to continue His work on earth: to seek and save that which is lost.

41 And Jesus answering said, O faithless and perverse generation, how long shall I be with you, and suffer you? Bring your son here.

42 And as he was yet a coming, the devil threw him down, and tare him. And Jesus rebuked the unclean spirit, and healed the child, and delivered him again to his father.

43 And they were all amazed at the mighty power of God. But while they wondered every one at all things which Jesus did, he said to his disciples,

44 Let these sayings sink down into your ears: for the Son of man shall be delivered into the hands of men.

45 But they understood not this saying, and it was hid from them, that they perceived it not: and they feared to ask him of that saying.

46 Then there arose a reasoning among them, which of them should be greatest.

47 And Jesus, perceiving the thought of their heart, took a child, and set him by him,

48 And said to them, Whosoever shall receive this child in my name receives me: and whosoever shall receive me receives him that sent me: for he that is least among you all, the same shall be great.

49 And John answered and said, Master, we saw one casting out devils in your name; and we forbad him, because he followed not with us.

50 And Jesus said to him, Forbid him not: for he that is not against us is for us.

51 And it came to pass, when the time was come that he should be received up, he steadfastly set his face to go to Jerusalem,

52 And sent messengers before his face: and they went, and entered into a village of the Samaritans, to make ready for him.

53 And they did not receive him, because his face was as though he would go to Jerusalem.

54 And when his disciples James and John saw this, they said, Lord, will you that we command fire to come down from heaven, and consume them, even as Elijah did?

55 But he turned, and rebuked them, and said, You know not what manner of spirit you are of.

56 For the Son of man is not come to destroy men's lives, but to save them. And they went to another village.

57 And it came to pass, that, as they went in the way, a certain man said to him, Lord, I will follow you wherever you go.

58 And Jesus said to him, Foxes have holes, and birds of the air have nests; but the Son of man has not where to lay his head.

59 *And he said to another, Follow me. But he said, Lord, suffer me first to go and bury my father.*

60 *Jesus said to him, Let the dead bury their dead: but you go and preach the kingdom of God.*

61 And another also said, Lord, I will follow you; but let me first go bid them farewell, which are at home at my house.

62 And Jesus said to him, **No man, hav-**

9:62 "Backsliders"—who are they? It is fairly common to hear someone give a testimony by saying something like: "I gave my heart to Jesus when I was a child. Then I fell away from the Lord and became involved in drugs, robbery, rape, murder, pornography, gambling, adultery, extortion, and other things I would rather not mention. All this time I still knew the Lord. Then I came back to Him when I was thirty years old."

These words usually come from those who don't understand that the Bible speaks many times of true and false conversion. Almost all of those we place in the category of "backsliders" are not backsliders. They never slid forward in the first place. They are false converts—"stony-ground" or "thorny-ground" hearers (Mark 4:16–19), who fall away in a time of temptation, tribulation, or persecution. The true convert puts his hand to the plow and doesn't look back, because he is fit for the kingdom. "Backsliders" don't just *look* back, they actually *go* back, showing that something was radically wrong.

ing put his hand to the plough, and looking back, is fit for the kingdom of God.

CHAPTER 10

AFTER these things the Lord appointed other seventy also, and sent them
two and two before his face into every
city and place, where he himself would
come.

2 *Therefore said he to them, The harvest
truly is great, but the laborers are few: pray
therefore the Lord of the harvest, that he
would send forth laborers into his harvest.*

3 Go your ways: behold, I send you forth
as lambs among wolves.

4 Carry neither purse, nor scrip, nor
shoes: and salute no man by the way.

5 And into whatsoever house you enter,
first say, Peace be to this house.

6 And if the son of peace be there, your
peace shall rest upon it: if not, it shall turn
to you again.

7 And in the same house remain, eating
and drinking such things as they give: for
the laborer is worthy of his hire. Go not
from house to house.

8 And into whatsoever city you enter,
and they receive you, eat such things as
are set before you:

9 And heal the sick that are therein, and
say to them, The kingdom of God is come
near to you.

10 But into whatsoever city you enter,
and they receive you not, go your ways
out into the streets of the same, and say,

11 Even the very dust of your city, which
cleaves on us, we do wipe off against
you: notwithstanding be sure of this, that
the kingdom of God is come near to you.

12 But I say to you, that it shall be more
tolerable in that day for Sodom, than for
that city.

13 Woe to you, Chorazin! woe to you,
Bethsaida! for if the mighty works had
been done in Tyre and Sidon, which have
been done in you, they had a great while
ago repented, sitting in sackcloth and
ashes.

14 But it shall be more tolerable for Tyre
and Sidon at the judgment, than for you.

15 And you, Capernaum, which are exalted to heaven, shall be thrust down to
hell.

16 He that hears you hears me; and he
that despises you despises me; and he
that despises me despises him that sent
me.

17 And the seventy returned again with
joy, saying, Lord, even the devils are subject to us through your name.

18 And he said to them, I beheld Satan
as lightning fall from heaven.

19 Behold, I give to you power to tread
on serpents and scorpions, and over all the
power of the enemy: and nothing shall by
any means hurt you.

20 Notwithstanding in this rejoice not,
that the spirits are subject to you; but rather rejoice, because your names are written
in heaven.

21 **In that hour Jesus rejoiced in spirit, and said, I thank you, O Father, Lord
of heaven and earth, that you have hid
these things from the wise and prudent,
and have revealed them to babes: even
so, Father; for so it seemed good in your
sight.**

22 All things are delivered to me of my
Father: and no man knows who the Son
is, but the Father; and who the Father is,
but the Son, and he to whom the Son will
reveal him.

10:14 The world often mocks the thought of hell, by saying that God is unjust in sending all sinners there regardless of whether their sins are menial or heinous. God's punishment, however, will
be according to righteousness. Here we see that the more sinful cities of Chorazin and Bethsaida
will receive a more harsh judgment than Tyre and Sidon. For a description of hell, see Revelation
1:18 footnote.

10:20 "The joy of heaven will arm us against the assaults of our spiritual enemies and put our
mouths out of taste for those pleasures with which the tempter baits his hooks." *Matthew Henry*

PRINCIPLES OF GROWTH FOR THE NEW AND GROWING CHRISTIAN

10:2 *Evangelism—Our Most Sobering Task*

Late in December 1996, a large family gathered for a joyous Christmas. There were so many gathered that night, five of the children slept in the converted garage, kept warm during the night by an electric heater placed near the door.

During the early hours of the morning, the heater suddenly burst into flames, blocking the doorway. In seconds the room became a blazing inferno. The frantic 911 call revealed the unspeakable terror as one of the children could be heard screaming, *"I'm on fire!"* The distraught father rushed into the flames to try to save his beloved children, receiving burns to 50% of his body. Tragically, all five children burned to death. They died because steel bars on the windows thwarted their escape. There was only one door, and it was blocked by the flames.

Imagine you're back in time, just minutes before the heater burst into flames. You peer through the darkness at the peaceful sight of five sleeping youngsters, knowing that at any moment the room will erupt into an inferno and burn the flesh of horrified children. *Can you in good conscience walk away?* No! You *must* awaken them and warn them to run from that death trap!

The world sleeps peacefully in the darkness of ignorance. There is only one Door by which they may escape death. The steel bars of sin prevent their salvation, and at the same time call for the flames of Eternal Justice. What a fearful thing Judgment Day will be! The fires of the wrath of Almighty God will burn for eternity. The Church has been entrusted with the task of awakening them before it's too late. We cannot turn our backs and walk away in complacency. *Think of how the father ran into the flames.* His love knew no bounds. Our devotion to the sober task God has given us will be in direct proportion to our love for the lost. There are only a few who run headlong into the flames to warn them to flee (Luke 10:2). *Please* be one of them. We really have no choice. The apostle Paul said, "Woe is to me, if I preach not the gospel!" (1 Corinthians 9:16).

The "Prince of Preachers," *Charles Spurgeon*, said, "We need to be ashamed at the bare suspicion of unconcern." A Christian *cannot* be apathetic about the salvation of the world. The love of God in him will motivate him to seek and save that which is lost.

You probably have a limited amount of time after your conversion to impact your unsaved friends and family with the gospel. After their initial shock, they will put you in a neat little ribbon-tied box, and keep you at arm's length. So it's important that you take advantage of the short time you have while you still have their ears. For advice on how to do this, see Luke 8:39 footnote.

It is important to realize that we should share our faith with others *whenever* we can. The Bible says that there are only two times we should do this: "in season, and out of season" (2 Timothy 4:2). The apostle Paul *pleaded* for prayer for his own personal witness. He said, "[Pray] for me, that utterance may be given to me, that I may open my mouth boldly, to make known the mystery of the gospel, for which I am an ambassador in bonds: that therein I may speak boldly, as I ought to speak" (Ephesians 6:19,20).

Remember that you have the sobering responsibility of speaking to other peoples' loved ones. Perhaps another Christian has prayed earnestly that God would use a faithful witness to speak to his beloved mom or dad, and *you* are the answer to that prayer. You are the true and faithful witness God wants to use.

Keep the fate of the ungodly before your eyes. Too many of us settle down on a padded pew and become introverted. Our world becomes a monastery without walls. Our friends are confined solely to those *within* the Church, when Jesus was the "friend of sinners." So take the time to deliberately befriend the lost for the sake of their salvation. Remember that each and every person who dies in his sins has an appointment with the Judge of the Universe. Hell opens wide its terrible jaws. There is no more sobering task than to be entrusted with the gospel of salvation—working with God for the eternal well-being of dying humanity.

For the next principle of growth, see Hebrews 6:18 footnote.

23 And he turned him to his disciples, and said privately, Blessed are the eyes which see the things that you see:

24 For I tell you, that many prophets and kings have desired to see those things which you see, and have not seen them; and to hear those things which you hear, and have not heard them.

25 And, behold, a certain lawyer stood up, and tempted him, saying, Master, what shall I do to inherit eternal life?

26 He said to him, What is written in the law? how do you read it?

27 And he answering said, You shall love the Lord your God with all your heart, and with all your soul, and with all your strength, and with all your mind; and your neighbour as yourself.

28 And he said to him, You have answered right: this do, and you shall live.

29 But he, willing to justify himself, said to Jesus, And who is my neighbour?

30 And Jesus answering said, A certain man went down from Jerusalem to Jericho, and fell among thieves, which stripped him of his raiment, and wounded him, and departed, leaving him half dead.

31 And by chance there came down a certain priest that way: and when he saw him, he passed by on the other side.

32 And likewise a Levite, when he was at the place, came and looked on him, and passed by on the other side.

33 But a certain Samaritan, as he journeyed, came where he was: and when he saw him, he had compassion on him,

34 And went to him, and bound up his wounds, pouring in oil and wine, and set him on his own beast, and brought him to an inn, and took care of him.

35 And on the morrow when he departed, he took out two pence, and gave them to the host, and said to him, Take care of him; and whatsoever you spend more, when I come again, I will repay you.

36 Which now of these three, do you think, was neighbour to him that fell among the thieves?

37 And he said, He that showed mercy on him. Then said Jesus to him, Go, and do likewise.

38 Now it came to pass, as they went, that he entered into a certain village: and a certain woman named Martha received him into her house.

39 And she had a sister called Mary, which also sat at Jesus' feet, and heard his word.

40 But Martha was cumbered about much serving, and came to him, and said, Lord, do you not care that my sister has left me to serve alone? bid her therefore that she help me.

41 And Jesus answered and said to her,

10:26 This man was proud and self-righteous. He "stood up" and tested Jesus. He needed the Law to humble him and bring him the knowledge of sin. When the Law accused him, he tried to justify his guilt—"But he, willing to justify himself, said to Jesus, And who is my neighbor?" Jesus then explained the spiritual nature of the Commandments to show the man how far he had fallen short of the glory of God that is revealed in the Law (vv. 30–37).

10:27 Love God with the whole heart. Three children were watching a new television set their father had just purchased for them. When their dad arrived home, they didn't even get up and greet him at the door. Instead, they were watching TV. The father walked over to it, turned it off and said, "Kids, I purchased that television set because I love you and want you to be happy. But if it comes between you and your love for me, I am going to sell it, because you are loving the gift more than the giver."

If we love anything more than God (our mother, father, brother, sister, spouse, children, job, sports, or even our own life), we are loving the gift more than the Giver. This is called "inordinate affection." To love anything more than we love God is to transgress the First Commandment. See Luke 14:26 footnote.

10:34 "When you see that men have been wounded by the Law, then it is time to pour in the gospel oil." *Samuel Bolton*

Martha, Martha, you are careful and troubled about many things:

42 But one thing is needful: and Mary has chosen that good part, which shall not be taken away from her.

CHAPTER 11

AND it came to pass, that, as he was praying in a certain place, when he ceased, one of his disciples said to him, Lord, teach us to pray, as John also taught his disciples.

2 And he said to them, When you pray, say, Our Father which art in heaven, Hallowed be your name. Your kingdom come. Your will be done, as in heaven, so in earth.

3 Give us day by day our daily bread.

4 And forgive us our sins; for we also forgive every one that is indebted to us. And lead us not into temptation; but deliver us from evil.

5 And he said to them, Which of you shall have a friend, and shall go to him at midnight, and say to him, Friend, lend me three loaves;

6 For a friend of mine in his journey is come to me, and I have nothing to set before him?

7 And he from within shall answer and say, Trouble me not: the door is now shut, and my children are with me in bed; I cannot rise and give you.

8 I say to you, Though he will not rise and give him, because he is his friend, yet because of his importunity he will rise and give him as many as he needs.

9 And I say to you, Ask, and it shall be given you; seek, and you shall find; knock, and it shall be opened to you.

10 For every one that asks receives; and he that seeks finds; and to him that knocks it shall be opened.

11 If a son shall ask bread of any of you

that is a father, will he give him a stone? or if he ask a fish, will he for a fish give him a serpent?

12 Or if he shall ask an egg, will he offer him a scorpion?

13 If you then, being evil, know how to give good gifts to your children: how much more shall your heavenly Father give the Holy Spirit to them that ask him?

14 And he was casting out a devil, and it was dumb. And it came to pass, when the devil was gone out, the dumb spoke; and the people wondered.

15 But some of them said, He casts out devils through Beelzebub the chief of the devils.

16 And others, tempting him, sought of him a sign from heaven.

17 But he, knowing their thoughts, said to them, Every kingdom divided against itself is brought to desolation; and a house divided against a house falls.

18 If Satan also be divided against himself, how shall his kingdom stand? because you say that I cast out devils through Beelzebub.

19 And if I by Beelzebub cast out devils, by whom do your sons cast them out? therefore shall they be your judges.

20 But if I with the finger of God cast out devils, no doubt the kingdom of God is come upon you.

21 When a strong man armed keeps his palace, his goods are in peace:

22 But when a stronger than he shall come upon him, and overcome him, he takes from him all his armor wherein he trusted, and divides his spoils.

23 He that is not with me is against me: and he that gathers not with me scatters.

24 When the unclean spirit is gone out of a man, he walks through dry places, seeking rest; and finding none, he says, I will return to my house whence I came

---

11:2 Prayer. "Prayer is the open admission that without Christ we can do nothing. And prayer is the turning away from ourselves to God in the confidence that He will provide the help we need. Prayer humbles *us* as needy and exalts *God* as all-sufficient." *John Piper*

"Prayer doesn't get man's will done in heaven; it gets God's will done on earth." *Ronald Dunn*

Sting Operation

11:39

Some years ago, Southern California police carried out an interesting "sting" operation. They had a list of thousands of wanted criminals who had somehow evaded jail. Instead of risking their lives by going and attempting to arrest each one, they sent all the criminals a letter telling them they had won a large amount of money in a drawing.

The police put signs and banners on a building, and placed balloons and even a clown on the outside to create a festive atmosphere to welcome the "winners." As each criminal entered the building, he heard music and celebration. He was then ushered into a room where he smiled as his hand was shaken. The facial expression changed from one of joy to unbelief as each was told, "Congratulations—you have just won time in prison!" Dozens of criminals made their way through the main doors, were arrested and ushered out the back door. It was interesting that many of these lawbreakers declared, "I *thought* it was a sting operation!" but their greed wouldn't let them stay away.

out.

25 And when he comes, he finds it swept and garnished.

26 Then he goes, and takes to him seven other spirits more wicked than himself; and they enter in, and dwell there: and the last state of that man is worse than the first.

27 And it came to pass, as he spoke these things, a certain woman of the company lifted up her voice, and said to him, Blessed is the womb that bare you, and the paps which you have sucked.

28 But he said, Yes rather, blessed are they that hear the word of God, and keep it.

29 And when the people were gathered thick together, he began to say, This is an evil generation: they seek a sign; and there shall no sign be given it, but the sign of Jonah the prophet.

30 For as Jonah was a sign to the Ninevites, so shall also the Son of man be to this generation.

31 The queen of the south shall rise up in the judgment with the men of this generation, and condemn them: for she came from the utmost parts of the earth to hear the wisdom of Solomon; and, behold, a greater than Solomon is here.

32 The men of Ninevah shall rise up in the judgment with this generation, and shall condemn it: for they repented at the preaching of Jonah; and, behold, a greater than Jonah is here.

33 No man, when he has lighted a candle, puts it in a secret place, neither under a bushel, but on a candlestick, that they which come in may see the light.

34 The light of the body is the eye: therefore when your eye is single, your whole body also is full of light; but when your eye is evil, your body also is full of darkness.

35 Take heed therefore that the light which is in you be not darkness.

36 If your whole body therefore be full of light, having no part dark, the whole shall be full of light, as when the bright shining of a candle does give you light.

37 And as he spoke, a certain Pharisee besought him to dine with him: and he went in, and sat down to meat.

38 And when the Pharisee saw it, he marveled that he had not first washed before dinner.

39 And the Lord said to him, Now do you Pharisees make clean the outside of the cup and the platter; but your inward part is full of ravening and wickedness.

11:27,28 Rather than exalting Mary above the rest of the common people, Jesus said that the greater blessing belongs to those who hear the Word of God and obey it.

40 You fools, did not he that made that which is without make that which is within also?

41 But rather give alms of such things as you have; and, behold, all things are clean to you.

42 But woe to you, Pharisees! for you tithe mint and rue and all manner of herbs, and pass over judgment and the love of God: these ought you to have done, and not to leave the other undone.

43 Woe to you, Pharisees! for you love the uppermost seats in the synagogues, and greetings in the markets.

44 Woe to you, scribes and Pharisees, hypocrites! for you are as graves which appear not, and the men that walk over them are not aware of them.

45 Then answered one of the lawyers, and said to him, Master, thus saying you reproach us also.

46 And he said, Woe to you also, you lawyers! for you load men with burdens grievous to be borne, and you yourselves touch not the burdens with one of your fingers.

47 Woe to you! for you build the sepulchres of the prophets, and your fathers killed them.

48 Truly you bear witness that you allow the deeds of your fathers: for they indeed killed them, and you build their sepulchres.

49 Therefore also said the wisdom of God, I will send them prophets and apostles, and some of them they shall slay and persecute:

50 That the blood of all the prophets, which was shed from the foundation of the world, may be required of this generation;

51 From the blood of Abel to the blood of Zacharias, which perished between the altar and the temple: verily I say to you, It shall be required of this generation.

52 Woe to you, lawyers! for you have taken away the key of knowledge: you entered not in yourselves, and them that were entering in you hindered.

53 And as he said these things to them, the scribes and the Pharisees began to urge him vehemently, and to provoke him to speak of many things:

54 Laying wait for him, and seeking to catch something out of his mouth, that they might accuse him.

CHAPTER 12

IN the mean time, when there were gathered together an innumerable multitude of people, insomuch that they trode one upon another, he began to say to his disciples first of all, Beware of the leaven of the Pharisees, which is hypocrisy.

2 **For there is nothing covered, that shall not be revealed; neither hid, that shall not be known.**

3 Therefore whatsoever you have spoken in darkness shall be heard in the light; and that which you have spoken in the ear in closets shall be proclaimed upon the housetops.

4 **And I say to you my friends, Be not afraid of them that kill the body, and after that have no more that they can do.**

5 **But I will forewarn you whom you shall fear: Fear him, which after he has killed has power to cast into hell; yea, I say to you, Fear him.**

6 Are not five sparrows sold for two far-

12:5 "People will never set their faces decidedly towards heaven, and live like pilgrims, until they really feel that they are in danger of hell...Let us expound and beat out the Ten Commandments, and show the length, and breadth, and depth, and height of their requirements. This is the way of our Lord in the Sermon on the Mount [Matthew 5:30]. We cannot do better than follow His plan. We may depend on it: men will never come to Jesus, and stay with Jesus, and live for Jesus, unless they really know why they are to come, and what is their need. Those whom the Spirit draws to Jesus are those whom the Spirit has convinced of sin. Without thorough conviction of sin, men may seem to come to Jesus and follow Him for a season, but they will soon fall away and return to the world." *J. C. Ryle, Holiness*

11:52 *The Key to Reaching the Lost*

Have you ever thought, "There must be a key to reaching the lost"? There is—and it's rusty through lack of use. The Bible does actually call it "the key," and its purpose is to bring us to Christ, to unlock the Door of the Savior (John 10:9).

Much of the Church still doesn't even know it exists. Not only is it biblical, but it can be shown through history that the Church used it to unlock the doors of revival. The problem is that it was lost around the turn of the twentieth century. Keys have a way of getting lost.

Jesus used it. So did Paul (Romans 3:19,20), Timothy (1 Timothy 1:8–11), and James (James 2:10). Stephen used it when he preached (Acts 7:53). Peter found that it had been used to open the door to release 3,000 imprisoned souls on the Day of Pentecost. Jesus said that the lawyers had "taken away" the key, and even refused to use it to let people enter into the kingdom of God.

The Pharisees didn't take it away. Instead, they bent it out of shape so that it wouldn't do its work (Mark 7:8). Jesus returned it to its true shape, just as the Scriptures prophesied that He would do (Isaiah 42:21).

Satan has tried to prejudice the modern Church against the key. He has maligned it, misused it, twisted it, and, of course, hidden it—he hates it because of what it does. Perhaps you are wondering what this key is. I will tell you. All I ask is that you set aside your traditions and prejudices and look at what God's Word says on the subject.

In Acts 28:23 the Bible tells us that Paul sought to persuade his hearers "concerning Jesus, both out of the law of Moses, and out of the prophets." Here we have two effective means of persuading the unsaved "concerning Jesus."

Let's first look at how the prophets can help persuade sinners concerning Jesus. Fulfilled prophecy *proves* the inspiration of Scripture. The predictions of the prophets present a powerful case for the inspiration of the Bible. Any skeptic who reads the prophetic words of Isaiah, Ezekiel, Joel, etc., or the words of Jesus in Matthew 24 cannot but be challenged that this is no ordinary book.

The other means by which Paul persuaded sinners concerning Jesus was "out of the law of Moses." The Bible tells us that the Law of Moses is good if it is used lawfully (1 Timothy 1:8). It was given by God as a "schoolmaster" to bring us to Christ (Galatians 3:24). Paul wrote that he "had not known sin, but by the law" (Romans 7:7). The Law of God (the Ten Commandments) is evidently the "key of knowledge" Jesus spoke of in Luke 11:52. He was speaking to "lawyers"—those who should have been teaching God's Law so that sinners would receive the "knowledge of sin," and thus recognize their need of the Savior.

Prophecy speaks to the *intellect* of the sinner, while the Law speaks to his *conscience*. One produces *faith* in the Word of God; the other brings *knowledge* of sin in the heart of the sinner. The Law is the God-given "key" to unlock the Door of salvation. See Matthew 19:17–22 footnote and Romans 3:19,20.

"I do not believe that any man can preach the gospel who does not preach the Law. The Law is the needle, and you cannot draw the silken thread of the gospel through a man's heart unless you first send the needle of the Law to make way for it." *Charles Spurgeon*

things, and not one of them is forgotten before God?

7 But even the very hairs of your head are all numbered. Fear not therefore: you are of more value than many sparrows.

8 Also I say to you, Whosoever shall confess me before men, him shall the Son of man also confess before the angels of God:

9 But he that denies me before men shall be denied before the angels of God.

10 And whosoever shall speak a word

12:8 "Our Lord needs no secret agents! Those who are not willing to confess Christ publicly are not willing to confess Christ. Perhaps acceptance of Christ begins as a very personal and private experience, but it can never stay that way." *Guy Rice Doud, Joy in the Journey*

12:20   *"I'll wait until I am old, then I'll get right with God."*

You may not get the chance. God may just lose patience with you and end your life. Perhaps you don't think He would do such a thing. Then read Genesis 38:7 to see how God killed a man who was wicked. Jesus told of a man who boasted that he had so many goods that he would have to build bigger barns. God called the man a fool and took his life that night.

Those who say they will repent in their own time lack the fear of God. Their understanding of His nature is erroneous. If they caught a glimpse of His holiness, His righteousness, and His consuming justice, they wouldn't trifle with His mercy. Such arrogance needs to be confronted with the thunders of Mount Sinai. He is not wise who thinks he can outwit his Creator, enjoy a lifetime of sin, and repent at the last minute. Deathbed repentance is very rare. God killed a husband and wife because they told a lie (Acts 5:1–10). He lost patience with them. Most people think that God's patience is eternal. It evidently is not. The Bible says that it is through the fear of the Lord that men depart from sin (Proverbs 16:6). If they don't fear God, they will be complacent about their eternal salvation (Matthew 10:28).

against the Son of man, it shall be forgiven him: but to him that blasphemes against the Holy Spirit it shall not be forgiven.

11 *And when they bring you to the synagogues, and to magistrates, and powers, take no thought how or what thing you shall answer, or what you shall say:*

12 *For the Holy Spirit shall teach you in the same hour what you ought to say.*

13 And one of the company said to him, Master, speak to my brother, that he divide the inheritance with me.

14 And he said to him, Man, who made me a judge or a divider over you?

15 **And he said to them, Take heed, and beware of covetousness: for a man's life consists not in the abundance of the things which he possesses.**

16 **And he spoke a parable to them, saying, The ground of a certain rich man brought forth plentifully:**

17 **And he thought within himself, saying, What shall I do, because I have no room where to bestow my fruits?**

18 **And he said, This will I do: I will pull down my barns, and build greater; and there will I bestow all my fruits and my goods.**

19 **And I will say to my soul, Soul, you have much goods laid up for many years; take your ease, eat, drink, and be merry.**

20 **But God said to him, You fool, this night your soul shall be required of you: then whose shall those things be, which you have provided?**

21 **So is he that lays up treasure for himself, and is not rich toward God.**

22 And he said to his disciples, Therefore I say to you, Take no thought for your life, what you shall eat; neither for the body, what you shall put on.

23 The life is more than meat, and the body is more than raiment.

24 Consider the ravens: for they neither sow nor reap; which neither have storehouse nor barn; and God feeds them: how much more are you better than the fowls?

25 And which of you with taking thought can add to his stature one cubit?

26 If you then be not able to do that thing which is least, why take thought for the rest?

27 Consider the lilies how they grow: they toil not, they spin not; and yet I say to you, that Solomon in all his glory was not arrayed like one of these.

28 If then God so clothe the grass, which is to day in the field, and tomorrow is cast into the oven; how much more will he

clothe you, O you of little faith?

29 And seek not what you shall eat, or what you shall drink, neither be of doubtful mind.

30 For all these things do the nations of the world seek after: and your Father knows that you have need of these things.

31 But rather seek the kingdom of God; and all these things shall be added to you.

32 Fear not, little flock; for it is your Father's good pleasure to give you the kingdom.

33 Sell what you have, and give alms; provide yourselves bags which wax not old, a treasure in the heavens that fails not, where no thief approaches, neither moth corrupts.

34 For where your treasure is, there will your heart be also.

35 *Let your loins be girded about, and your lights burning;*

36 *And you yourselves like to men that wait for their lord, when he will return from the wedding; that when he comes and knocks, they may open to him immediately.*

37 Blessed are those servants, whom the lord when he comes shall find watching: verily I say to you, that he shall gird himself, and make them to sit down to meat, and will come forth and serve them.

38 And if he shall come in the second watch, or come in the third watch, and find them so, blessed are those servants.

39 And this know, that if the goodman of the house had known what hour the thief would come, he would have watched, and not have suffered his house to be broken through.

40 Be therefore ready also: for the Son of man comes at an hour when you think not.

41 Then Peter said to him, Lord, speak you this parable to us, or even to all?

42 And the Lord said, Who then is that faithful and wise steward, whom his lord shall make ruler over his household, to give them their portion of meat in due season?

43 Blessed is that servant, whom his lord when he comes shall find so doing.

44 Of a truth I say to you, that he will make him ruler over all that he has.

45 But and if that servant say in his heart, My lord delays his coming; and shall begin to beat the menservants and maidens, and to eat and drink, and to be drunken;

46 The lord of that servant will come in a day when he looks not for him, and at an hour when he is not aware, and will cut him in sunder, and will appoint him his portion with the unbelievers.

47 And that servant, which knew his lord's will, and prepared not himself, neither did according to his will, shall be beaten with many stripes.

48 But he that knew not, and did commit things worthy of stripes, shall be beaten with few stripes. For to whomsoever much is given, of him shall be much required: and to whom men have committed much, of him they will ask the more.

49 I am come to send fire on the earth; and what will I if it be already kindled?

50 But I have a baptism to be baptized with; and how am I straitened till it be accomplished!

51 Suppose that I am come to give peace on earth? I tell you, Nay; but rather division:

52 For from henceforth there shall be five in one house divided, three against two, and two against three.

53 The father shall be divided against the son, and the son against the father; the mother against the daughter, and the daughter against the mother; the mother in law against her daughter in law, and the daughter in law against her mother in law.

54 And he said also to the people, When you see a cloud rise out of the west, straightway you say, There comes a shower; and so it is.

12:40 Second coming of Jesus: See Luke 21:27.

55 And when you see the south wind blow, you say, There will be heat; and it comes to pass.

56 You hypocrites, you can discern the face of the sky and of the earth; but how is it that you do not discern this time?

57 Yea, and why even of yourselves judge you not what is right?

58 When you go with your adversary to the magistrate, as you are in the way, give diligence that you may be delivered from him; lest he hale you to the judge, and the judge deliver you to the officer, and the officer cast you into prison.

59 I tell you, you shall not depart thence, till you have paid the very last mite.

· · · · · ·

Does God really expect us to be perfect?
See Matthew 5:48 footnote.

· · · · · ·

CHAPTER 13

THERE were present at that season some that told him of the Galileans, whose blood Pilate had mingled with their sacrifices.

2 And Jesus answering said to them, Suppose that these Galilaeans were sinners above all the Galileans, because they suffered such things?

3 I tell you, Nay: but, except you repent, you shall all likewise perish.

4 Or those eighteen, upon whom the tower in Siloam fell, and slew them, do you think that they were sinners above all men that dwelt in Jerusalem?

5 **I tell you, Nay: but, except you repent, you shall all likewise perish.**

6 He spoke also this parable; A certain man had a fig tree planted in his vineyard; and he came and sought fruit thereon, and found none.

7 Then said he to the dresser of his vineyard, Behold, these three years I come seeking fruit on this fig tree, and find none: cut it down; why does it cumber the ground?

8 And he answering said to him, Lord, let it alone this year also, till I shall dig about it, and dung it:

9 And if it bear fruit, well: and if not, then after that you shall cut it down.

10 And he was teaching in one of the synagogues on the sabbath.

11 And, behold, there was a woman which had a spirit of infirmity eighteen years, and was bowed together, and could in no wise lift up herself.

12 And when Jesus saw her, he called her to him, and said to her, Woman, you are loosed from your infirmity.

13 And he laid his hands on her: and immediately she was made straight, and glorified God.

14 And the ruler of the synagogue answered with indignation, because that Jesus had healed on the sabbath day, and said to the people, There are six days in which men ought to work: in them therefore come and be healed, and not on the sabbath day.

15 The Lord then answered him, and said, You hypocrite, does not each one of you on the sabbath loose his ox or his ass from the stall, and lead him away to watering?

13:2 Repentance—its necessity for salvation. See Luke 24:47.

13:3 Hosea 4:6 tells us why sinners will perish. "My people are destroyed for lack of knowledge: because you have rejected knowledge, I will also reject you...: seeing you have forgotten the law of your God, I will also forget your children." The reason God's people were destroyed was a lack of knowledge *of God's Law*. A sinner who is ignorant of the Moral Law has no understanding of the nature of sin (Romans 7:7–9). If he doesn't understand what sin is, he will not repent; and if he fails to repent, he will perish. He perishes through lack of knowledge of the Law.

"The gospel has not been clearly preached if the hearer doesn't know that not to make a decision is a decision." *Dan Arnold*

16 And ought not this woman, being a daughter of Abraham, whom Satan has bound, lo, these eighteen years, be loosed from this bond on the sabbath day?

17 And when he had said these things, all his adversaries were ashamed: and all the people rejoiced for all the glorious things that were done by him.

18 Then said he, to what is the kingdom of God like? and whereunto shall I resemble it?

19 It is like a grain of mustard seed, which a man took, and cast into his garden; and it grew, and waxed a great tree; and the fowls of the air lodged in the branches of it.

20 And again he said, Whereunto shall I liken the kingdom of God?

21 It is like leaven, which a woman took and hid in three measures of meal, till the whole was leavened.

22 And he went through the cities and villages, teaching, and journeying toward Jerusalem.

23 **Then said one to him, Lord, are there few that be saved? And he said to them,**

24 **Strive to enter in at the strait gate: for many, I say to you, will seek to enter in, and shall not be able.**

25 When once the master of the house is risen up, and has shut to the door, and you begin to stand without, and to knock at the door, saying, Lord, Lord, open to us; and he shall answer and say to you, I know not from where you are:

26 Then shall you begin to say, We have eaten and drunk in your presence, and you have taught in our streets.

27 But he shall say, I tell you, I know not from where you are; depart from me, all you workers of iniquity.

28 There shall be weeping and gnashing of teeth, when you shall see Abraham, and Isaac, and Jacob, and all the prophets, in the kingdom of God, and you yourselves thrust out.

29 And they shall come from the east, and from the west, and from the north, and from the south, and shall sit down in the kingdom of God.

30 And, behold, there are last which shall be first, and there are first which shall be last.

31 The same day there came certain of the Pharisees, saying to him, Get out, and depart hence: for Herod will kill you.

32 And he said to them, Go, and tell that fox, Behold, I cast out devils, and I do cures to day and tomorrow, and the third day I shall be perfected.

33 Nevertheless I must walk to day, and tomorrow, and the day following: for it cannot be that a prophet perish out of Jerusalem.

34 O Jerusalem, Jerusalem, which kills the prophets, and stones them that are sent to you; how often would I have gathered your children together, as a hen does gather her brood under her wings, and you would not!

35 Behold, your house is left to you desolate: and verily I say to you, You shall not see me, until the time come when you shall say, Blessed is he that comes in the name of the Lord.

CHAPTER 14

AND it came to pass, as he went into the house of one of the chief Pharisees to eat bread on the sabbath day, that they watched him.

2 And, behold, there was a certain man before him which had the dropsy.

3 And Jesus answering spoke to the lawyers and Pharisees, saying, Is it lawful to heal on the sabbath day?

4 And they held their peace. And he took him, and healed him, and let him go;

5 And answered them, saying, Which of

13:20,21 This is a picture of the false convert in the midst of God's people: "This shall have its accomplishment in the destruction of the corrupt and hypocritical part of the Church." *Matthew Henry*

14:26 *"Jesus taught hatred by saying that a Christian should 'hate' his father and mother."*

This is called "hyperbole"—a statement of extremes, contrasting love with hate for emphasis' sake. The Bible often does this (Proverbs 13:24; 29:24). Jesus tells us that the first and greatest Commandment is to love God with all of our heart, soul, and mind (Matthew 22:37,38). As much as we treasure our spouse and family, and even our own life, there should be no one whom we love and value more than God, no one who takes precedence in our life. To place love for another (including ourself) above God is idolatry.

you shall have an ass or an ox fallen into a pit, and will not straightway pull him out on the sabbath day?

6 And they could not answer him again to these things.

7 And he put forth a parable to those which were bidden, when he marked how they chose out the chief rooms; saying to them,

8 When you are bidden of any man to a wedding, sit not down in the highest room; lest a more honorable man than you be bidden of him;

9 And he that bade you and him come and say to you, Give this man place; and you begin with shame to take the lowest room.

10 But when you are bidden, go and sit down in the lowest room; that when he that bade you comes, he may say to you, Friend, go up higher: then shall you have worship in the presence of them that sit at meat with you.

11 **For whosoever exalts himself shall be abased; and he that humbles himself shall be exalted.**

12 Then said he also to him that bade him, When you make a dinner or a supper, call not your friends, nor your brethren, neither your kinsmen, nor your rich neighbours; lest they also bid you again, and a recompense be made you.

13 But when you make a feast, call the poor, the maimed, the lame, the blind:

14 And you shall be blessed; for they cannot recompense you: for you shall be recompensed at the resurrection of the just.

15 And when one of them that sat at meat with him heard these things, he said to him, Blessed is he that shall eat bread in the kingdom of God.

16 Then said he to him, A certain man made a great supper, and bade many:

17 And sent his servant at supper time to say to them that were bidden, Come; for all things are now ready.

18 And they all with one consent began to make excuse. The first said to him, I have bought a piece of ground, and I must needs go and see it: I pray you have me excused.

19 And another said, I have bought five yoke of oxen, and I go to prove them: I pray you have me excused.

20 And another said, I have married a wife, and therefore I cannot come.

21 So that servant came, and showed his lord these things. Then the master of the house being angry said to his servant, Go out quickly into the streets and lanes of the city, and bring in here the poor, and the maimed, and the halt, and the blind.

22 And the servant said, Lord, it is done as you have commanded, and yet there is room.

23 *And the lord said to the servant, Go out into the highways and hedges, and compel them to come in, that my house may be filled.*

24 *For I say to you, That none of those men which were bidden shall taste of my supper.*

25 And there went great multitudes with him: and he turned, and said to them,

26 **If any man come to me, and hate not his father, and mother, and wife, and**

children, and brethren, and sisters, yea, and his own life also, he cannot be my disciple.

27 And whosoever does not bear his cross, and come after me, cannot be my disciple.

28 For which of you, intending to build a tower, sits not down first, and counts the cost, whether he has sufficient to finish it?

29 Lest haply, after he has laid the foundation, and is not able to finish it, all that behold it begin to mock him,

30 Saying, This man began to build, and was not able to finish.

31 Or what king, going to make war against another king, sits not down first, and consults whether he be able with ten thousand to meet him that comes against him with twenty thousand?

32 Or else, while the other is yet a great way off, he sends an ambassage, and desires conditions of peace.

33 So likewise, whosoever he be of you that forsakes not all that he has, he cannot be my disciple.

34 Salt is good: but if the salt have lost his savour, wherewith shall it be seasoned?

35 It is neither fit for the land, nor yet for the dunghill; but men cast it out. He that has ears to hear, let him hear.

CHAPTER 15

THEN drew near to him all the publicans and sinners for to hear him.

2 And the Pharisees and scribes murmured, saying, This man receives sinners, and eats with them.

3 And he spoke this parable to them, saying,

4 What man of you, having an hundred sheep, if he lose one of them, does not leave the ninety and nine in the wilderness, and go after that which is lost, until he find it?

5 And when he has found it, he lays it

"The salvation of a single soul is more important than the production or preservation of all the epics and tragedies in the world."

C. S. Lewis

on his shoulders, rejoicing.

6 And when he comes home, he calls together his friends and neighbours, saying to them, Rejoice with me; for I have found my sheep which was lost.

7 I say to you, that likewise joy shall be in heaven over one sinner that repents, more than over ninety and nine just persons, which need no repentance.

8 Either what woman having ten pieces of silver, if she lose one piece, does not light a candle, and sweep the house, and seek diligently till she find it?

9 And when she has found it, she calls her friends and her neighbours together, saying, Rejoice with me; for I have found the piece which I had lost.

10 Likewise, I say to you, there is joy in the presence of the angels of God over one sinner that repents.

11 And he said, A certain man had two sons:

12 And the younger of them said to his father, Father, give me the portion

---

15:10 Heaven doesn't rejoice over those who make "decisions." It reserves its rejoicing for sinners who repent.

of goods that falls to me. And he divided to them his living.

13 And not many days after the younger son gathered all together, and took his journey into a far country, and there wasted his substance with riotous living.

14 And when he had spent all, there arose a mighty famine in that land; and he began to be in want.

15 And he went and joined himself to a citizen of that country; and he sent him into his fields to feed swine.

16 And he would fain have filled his belly with the husks that the swine did eat: and no man gave to him.

17 And when he came to himself, he said, How many hired servants of my father's have bread enough and to spare, and I perish with hunger!

18 I will arise and go to my father, and will say to him, Father, I have sinned against heaven, and before you,

19 And am no more worthy to be called your son: make me as one of your hired servants.

20 And he arose, and came to his father. But when he was yet a great way off, his father saw him, and had compassion, and ran, and fell on his neck, and kissed him.

21 And the son said to him, Father, I have sinned against heaven, and in your sight, and am no more worthy to be called your son.

22 But the father said to his servants, Bring forth the best robe, and put it on him; and put a ring on his hand, and shoes on his feet:

23 And bring here the fatted calf, and kill it; and let us eat, and be merry:

24 For this my son was dead, and is alive again; he was lost, and is found. And they began to be merry.

25 Now his elder son was in the field: and as he came and drew near to the house, he heard music and dancing.

26 And he called one of the servants, and asked what these things meant.

27 And he said to him, Your brother is come; and your father has killed the fatted calf, because he has received him safe and sound.

28 And he was angry, and would not go in: therefore came his father out, and entreated him.

29 And he answering said to his father, Lo, these many years do I serve you, neither transgressed I at any time your commandment: and yet you never gave me a kid, that I might make merry with my friends:

30 But as soon as this your son was come, which has devoured your living with harlots, you have killed for him the fatted calf.

31 And he said to him, Son, you are ever with me, and all that I have is yours.

32 It was meet that we should make merry, and be glad: for this your brother was dead, and is alive again; and was lost, and is found.

CHAPTER 16

AND he said also to his disciples, There was a certain rich man, which had a steward; and the same was accused to him that he had wasted his goods.

15:21 All sin is against God. Often sinners will try to justify their vices because there is no "victim" involved (such as in adult pornography). However, *all* sin is an offense against God. When Joseph was sexually propositioned by Potiphar's wife, he spoke of it as being a sin against God (Genesis 39:9). When David sinned with Bathsheba, he acknowledged that he had sinned against the LORD (2 Samuel 12:13). The prodigal son recognized that he had sinned against heaven (Luke 15:21). God is always the offended Party when someone commits sin. However, the real victim of sin will be the sinner. His sin will damn him, because he is a victim of his own foolishness.

15:32 "The evangelist who preaches for eternity is never great on numbers. He is not apt to count hundreds of converts where there is no restitution, no confession, and no glad cry which proclaims, "The lost is found, the dead is made alive again!" *E. M. Bounds*

2 And he called him, and said to him, How is it that I hear this of you? give an account of your stewardship; for you may be no longer steward.

3 Then the steward said within himself, What shall I do? for my lord takes away from me the stewardship: I cannot dig; to beg I am ashamed.

4 I am resolved what to do, that, when I am put out of the stewardship, they may receive me into their houses.

5 So he called every one of his lord's debtors to him, and said to the first, How much do you owe to my lord?

6 And he said, An hundred measures of oil. And he said to him, Take your bill, and sit down quickly, and write fifty.

7 Then said he to another, And how much do you owe? And he said, An hundred measures of wheat. And he said to him, Take your bill, and write fourscore.

8 And the lord commended the unjust steward, because he had done wisely: for the children of this world are in their generation wiser than the children of light.

9 And I say to you, Make to yourselves friends of the mammon of unrighteousness; that, when you fail, they may receive you into everlasting habitations.

10 He that is faithful in that which is least is faithful also in much: and he that is unjust in the least is unjust also in much.

11 If therefore you have not been faithful in the unrighteous mammon, who will commit to your trust the true riches?

12 And if you have not been faithful in that which is another man's, who shall give you that which is your own?

13 No servant can serve two masters: for either he will hate the one, and love the other; or else he will hold to the one, and despise the other. You cannot serve God and mammon.

14 And the Pharisees also, who were covetous, heard all these things: and they derided him.

15 And he said to them, You are they which justify yourselves before men; but God knows your hearts: for that which is highly esteemed among men is abomination in the sight of God.

16 The law and the prophets were until John: since that time the kingdom of God is preached, and every man presses into it.

17 And it is easier for heaven and earth to pass, than one tittle of the law to fail.

18 Whosoever puts away his wife, and marries another, commits adultery: and whosoever marries her that is put away from her husband commits adultery.

19 There was a certain rich man, which was clothed in purple and fine linen, and fared sumptuously every day:

20 And there was a certain beggar named Lazarus, which was laid at his gate, full of sores,

21 And desiring to be fed with the crumbs which fell from the rich man's table: moreover the dogs came and licked his sores.

22 And it came to pass, that the beggar died, and was carried by the angels into Abraham's bosom: the rich man also died, and was buried;

23 And in hell he lift up his eyes, being in torments, and saw Abraham afar off, and Lazarus in his bosom.

24 And he cried and said, Father Abraham, have mercy on me, and send Laza-

---

16:10 If I am not a straight-shooter with a pistol, He won't let me near the cannon.

16:13 If you were given $1,000 every time you witnessed to someone, would you be more zealous in your evangelism? If so, you are serving money rather than God.

16:15 A little girl was once looking at a sheep as it ate green grass. She thought to herself how nice and white the sheep looked against the green grass. Then it began to snow. The little girl then thought how dirty the sheep looked against the white snow. It was the same sheep, but with a different background. When we compare ourselves to the background of man's standards, we come up reasonably clean. However, when we compare ourselves to the snow-white righteousness of the Law of God, we see that we are all as an unclean thing, and our righteous deeds are as filthy rags (Isaiah 64:6).

SPRINGBOARDS FOR PREACHING AND WITNESSING

The Rush

16:17

You've always wanted to skydive, but the thought scared you too much to try it. That is, until you met someone who had made over 100 jumps. He talked you into it by explaining how safe it was. His enthusiasm was contagious. He spoke of the freedom of falling through the air...the adrenaline rush...the unspeakable exhilaration.

Now you are standing on the edge of a plane, looking down on the earth far, far below. Everything has been checked. *Double-checked.* This is safer than driving on the freeway—a thought that helps you deal with the fear. Modern parachutes are state-of-the-art. Besides, there is a backup chute. Still, your heart is beating with apprehension.

Suddenly, you *jump!* You have trained so much for this moment, you instinctively spread your hands and legs. The speed is unbelievable. The power of the air forcing itself against your body is incredible. It's like a dream. You are defying the law of gravity, racing through the air at more than 120 mph!

The earth is coming closer. All normal sense of time lost. Speed, thrust of air, unspeakable joy. You glance at the altimeter on your wrist. Only another ten seconds and you will pull the rip cord and feel the jolt of the parachute opening. All that you had been told was true. The adrenaline rush is like nothing you have experienced. If only it could last a little longer. Reluctantly, you pull the cord. It opens, *but there is no jolt!*

You tilt your head back to see a horrifying sight: the parachute has twisted and is trailing like a flapping streamer. Your heart races with fear, pounding in your chest. Your eyes bulge in terror. Your chest heaves as you gasp for air. You try to keep a clear mind and remember your training...pull the second cord. *Nothing happens!* You pull again. Again! Harder. *Harder!* Nothing. Your throat lets out a scream, a groan of panic. Your heart is pounding so hard you think your chest will burst. Sweat breaks through your skin. A thousand thoughts speed through your mind. Your family! Your fate!...Safer than driving on the freeway! You whisper, "What a fool I was...to think that I could defy the law of gravity." Now a merciless law waits for the moment of impact. The ground accelerates toward you. No words

can describe the terror gripping your mind. A voice is speaking to you. It is the voice of good sense. It is the voice you ignored so often: "You have played the fool. You have given up your life, your most precious possession, for a cheap thrill. You have exchanged your loved ones for a rush of adrenaline. What a fool...*what a fool!*"

One word stands alone to describe how you feel about what you've done. One word screams within the corridors of your terrified mind as the earth races toward you, as death readies to embrace you. One word, a word that you have never understood fully until this moment. That terrible word is *remorse!*

The world, the flesh, and the devil whisper to you about how pleasurable sin is. That God isn't angry at sin. God is love. It is safe to jump into the arms of iniquity and abandon yourself to a free fall through its vast domain.

You go where angels fear to tread. But it is worth it. The rush is everything sin promised. You drink in iniquity like water. You love the darkness. Conscience speaks again and again, but you ignore its warning. You are defying the Moral Law and loving every minute.

Now you stand before the Judge on Judgment Day. You pull your first line by telling God what a good person you are. Nothing happens. The Moral Law rushes at you. In panic, you pull the second line and tell God that you believed in Him. *Again, nothing happens.* It is no use. Your mouth is stopped. The Moral Law accelerates toward you even faster, promising to so impact you that it will "grind you to powder" (Luke 20:18). Death and hell wait to embrace you. Unspeakable terror fills your heart. Conscience speaks so clearly now: "What a fool you have been. You rejected the mercy of God in Jesus Christ. You have given up your loved ones in exchange for the joys of a sinful lifestyle. You relinquished your most precious possession, *your very life*, for the cheap thrill of sin. What a fool! What a fool!" One word will stay with you for eternity. One

(continued on next page)

rus, that he may dip the tip of his finger in water, and cool my tongue; for I am tormented in this flame.

25 But Abraham said, Son, remember that you in your lifetime received your good things, and likewise Lazarus evil things: but now he is comforted, and you are tormented.

26 And beside all this, between us and you there is a great gulf fixed: so that they which would pass from here to you cannot; neither can they pass to us, that would come from thence.

27 Then he said, I pray you therefore, father, that you would send him to my father's house:

28 For I have five brethren; that he may testify to them, lest they also come into this place of torment.

29 Abraham said to him, They have Moses and the prophets; let them hear them.

30 And he said, Nay, father Abraham: but if one went to them from the dead, they will repent.

31 And he said to him, If they hear not Moses and the prophets, neither will they be persuaded, though one rose from the dead.

CHAPTER 17

THEN said he to the disciples, It is impossible but that offences will come: but woe to him, through whom they come!

2 It were better for him that a millstone were hanged about his neck, and he cast into the sea, than that he should offend one of these little ones.

3 Take heed to yourselves: If your brother trespass against you, rebuke him; and if he repent, forgive him.

4 And if he trespass against you seven times in a day, and seven times in a day turn again to you, saying, I repent; you shall forgive him.

5 And the apostles said to the Lord, Increase our faith.

6 And the Lord said, If you had faith as a grain of mustard seed, you might say to this sycamine tree, Be plucked up by the root, and be planted in the sea; and it should obey you.

7 But which of you, having a servant plowing or feeding cattle, will say to him by and by, when he is come from the field, Go and sit down to meat?

8 And will not rather say to him, Make ready wherewith I may sup, and gird yourself, and serve me, till I have eaten and drunken; and afterward you shall eat and drink?

9 Does he thank that servant because he did the things that were commanded him? I think not.

10 So likewise, when you shall have done all those things which are commanded you, say, We are unprofitable servants: we have done that which was our duty to do.

11 And it came to pass, as he went to Jerusalem, that he passed through the midst of Samaria and Galilee.

16:23 Hell: For verses warning of its reality, see Revelation 20:15.

16:24 "Love your fellowmen, and cry about them if you cannot bring them to Christ. If you cannot save them, you can weep over them. If you cannot give them a drop of water in hell, you can give them your heart's tears while they are still in this body." *Charles Spurgeon*

17:4 "Forgiveness is not just an occasional act: it is a permanent attitude." *Martin Luther King, Jr.*

12 And as he entered into a certain village, there met him ten men that were lepers, which stood afar off:

13 And they lifted up their voices, and said, Jesus, Master, have mercy on us.

14 And when he saw them, he said to them, Go show yourselves to the priests. And it came to pass, that, as they went, they were cleansed.

15 And one of them, when he saw that he was healed, turned back, and with a loud voice glorified God,

16 And fell down on his face at his feet, giving him thanks: and he was a Samaritan.

17 And Jesus answering said, Were there not ten cleansed? but where are the nine?

18 There are not found that returned to give glory to God, save this stranger.

19 And he said to him, Arise, go your way: your faith has made you whole.

20 And when he was demanded of the Pharisees, when the kingdom of God should come, he answered them and said, The kingdom of God comes not with observation:

21 Neither shall they say, Lo here! or, lo there! for, behold, the kingdom of God is within you.

22 And he said to the disciples, The days will come, when you shall desire to see one of the days of the Son of man, and you shall not see it.

23 And they shall say to you, See here; or, see there: go not after them, nor follow them.

24 For as the lightning, that lightens out of the one part under heaven, shines to the other part under heaven; so shall also the Son of man be in his day.

25 But first must he suffer many things, and be rejected of this generation.

26 And as it was in the days of Noah, so shall it be also in the days of the Son

of man.

27 They did eat, they drank, they married wives, they were given in marriage, until the day that Noah entered into the ark, and the flood came, and destroyed them all.

28 Likewise also as it was in the days of Lot; they did eat, they drank, they bought, they sold, they planted, they built;

29 But the same day that Lot went out of Sodom it rained fire and brimstone from heaven, and destroyed them all.

> The conscience of a man, when he is really quickened and awakened by the Holy Spirit, speaks the truth. It rings the great alarm bell. And if he turns over in his bed, that great alarm bell rings out again and again, "The wrath to come! The wrath to come! The wrath to come."
>
> **CHARLES SPURGEON**

30 Even thus shall it be in the day when the Son of man is revealed.

31 In that day, he which shall be upon the housetop, and his stuff in the house, let him not come down to take it away: and he that is in the field, let him likewise not return back.

32 Remember Lot's wife.

33 **Whosoever shall seek to save his life shall lose it; and whosoever shall lose his life shall preserve it.**

34 I tell you, in that night there shall be two men in one bed; the one shall be taken, and the other shall be left.

35 Two women shall be grinding together; the one shall be taken, and the other left.

36 Two men shall be in the field; the one shall be taken, and the other left.

37 And they answered and said to him,

17:26,27 Jesus referred to Noah as an actual historical person, and the Flood as a bona fide historical event. See Matthew 24:38,39 for details on the Flood.

17:32 Some dismiss the Book of Genesis as just an allegory, but Jesus believed the Genesis account of Lot's wife.

Where, Lord? And he said to them, Wherever the body is, there will the eagles be gathered together.

CHAPTER 18

AND he spoke a parable to them to this end, that men ought always to pray, and not to faint;

2 Saying, There was in a city a judge, which feared not God, neither regarded man:

3 And there was a widow in that city; and she came to him, saying, Avenge me of mine adversary.

4 And he would not for a while: but afterward he said within himself, Though I fear not God, nor regard man;

5 Yet because this widow troubles me, I will avenge her, lest by her continual coming she weary me.

6 And the Lord said, Hear what the unjust judge says.

7 And shall not God avenge his own elect, which cry day and night to him, though he bear long with them?

8 I tell you that he will avenge them speedily. Nevertheless when the Son of man comes, shall he find faith on the earth?

9 **And he spoke this parable to certain which trusted in themselves that they were righteous, and despised others:**

10 **Two men went up into the temple to pray; the one a Pharisee, and the other a publican.**

11 **The Pharisee stood and prayed thus with himself, God, I thank you, that I am not as other men are, extortioners, unjust, adulterers, or even as this publican.**

12 **I fast twice in the week, I give tithes of all that I possess.**

"To be a Christian without prayer is no more possible than to be alive without breathing."

Martin Luther

13 **And the publican, standing afar off, would not lift up so much as his eyes to heaven, but smote upon his breast, saying, God be merciful to me a sinner.**

14 **I tell you, this man went down to his house justified rather than the other: for every one that exalts himself shall be abased; and he that humbles himself shall be exalted.**

15 **And they brought to him also infants, that he would touch them: but when his disciples saw it, they rebuked them.**

16 **But Jesus called them to him, and said, Suffer little children to come to me, and forbid them not: for of such is the kingdom of God.**

17 **Verily I say to you, Whosoever shall not receive the kingdom of God as a lit-**

18:1 Prayerlessness. "Prayerlessness is an insult to God. Every prayerless day is a statement by a helpless individual, 'I do not need God today.' Failing to pray reflects idolatry—a trust in substitutes for God. We rely on our money instead of God's provision. We rest on our own flawed thinking rather than on God's perfect wisdom. We take charge of our lives rather than trusting God. Prayerlessness short-circuits the working of God. Neglecting prayer, therefore, is not a weakness; it is a sinful choice." *Ben Jennings, The Arena of Prayer*

18:21 *"What if someone says they've never lied, stolen, lusted, blasphemed—if they deny having any sin at all?"*

Ask the person if he has kept the First of the Ten Commandments. Has he always loved God above all else—with all of his heart, soul, mind, and strength (Mark 12:30)? If he says that he has, gently say, "The Bible says that 'there is none that seeks after God' (Romans 3:11). *Nobody* (except Jesus Christ) has kept the First of the Ten Commandments. One of you is lying—either you or God—and the Bible says that it is *impossible* for God to lie" (Hebrews 6:18; Titus 1:2).

tle child shall in no wise enter therein.

18 And a certain ruler asked him, saying, Good Master, what shall I do to inherit eternal life?

19 And Jesus said to him, Why call me good? none is good, save one, that is, God.

20 You know the commandments, Do not commit adultery, Do not kill, Do not steal, Do not bear false witness, Honor your father and your mother.

21 And he said, All these have I kept from my youth up.

22 Now when Jesus heard these things, he said to him, Yet you lack one thing: sell all that you have, and distribute to the poor, and you shall have treasure in heaven: and come, follow me.

23 And when he heard this, he was very sorrowful: for he was very rich.

24 And when Jesus saw that he was very sorrowful, he said, How hardly shall they that have riches enter into the kingdom of God!

25 For it is easier for a camel to go through a needle's eye, than for a rich man to enter into the kingdom of God.

26 And they that heard it said, Who then can be saved?

27 And he said, The things which are impossible with men are possible with God.

28 Then Peter said, Lo, we have left all, and followed you.

29 And he said to them, Verily I say to you, There is no man that has left house, or parents, or brethren, or wife, or children, for the kingdom of God's sake,

30 Who shall not receive manifold more in this present time, and in the world to come life everlasting.

31 Then he took to him the twelve, and said to them, Behold, we go up to Jerusalem, and all things that are written by the prophets concerning the Son of man shall be accomplished.

32 For he shall be delivered to the Gentiles, and shall be mocked, and spitefully entreated, and spitted on:

33 And they shall scourge him, and put him to death: and the third day he shall rise again.

34 And they understood none of these things: and this saying was hid from them, neither knew they the things which were spoken.

35 And it came to pass, that as he was come near to Jericho, a certain blind man sat by the way side begging:

36 And hearing the multitude pass by, he asked what it meant.

37 And they told him, that Jesus of Nazareth passes by.

18:20 Jesus gave him five "horizontal" Commandments having to do with his fellow man. When he said that he had kept them, Jesus then used the First of the Ten Commandments to show this man that his god was his money, and you cannot serve God and money.

18:24,25 There is hope for the rich: see Luke 19:2.

38 And he cried, saying, Jesus, you Son of David, have mercy on me.

39 And they which went before rebuked him, that he should hold his peace: but he cried so much the more, You Son of David, have mercy on me.

40 And Jesus stood, and commanded him to be brought to him: and when he was come near, he asked him,

41 Saying, What will you that I shall do to you? And he said, Lord, that I may receive my sight.

42 And Jesus said to him, Receive your sight: your faith has saved you.

43 And immediately he received his sight, and followed him, glorifying God: and all the people, when they saw it, gave praise to God.

CHAPTER 19

AND Jesus entered and passed through Jericho.

2 And, behold, there was a man named Zacchaeus, which was the chief among the publicans, and he was rich.

3 And he sought to see Jesus who he was; and could not for the press, because he was little of stature.

4 And he ran before, and climbed up into a sycamore tree to see him: for he was to pass that way.

5 And when Jesus came to the place, he looked up, and saw him, and said to him, Zacchaeus, make haste, and come down; for to day I must abide at your house.

6 And he made haste, and came down, and received him joyfully.

7 And when they saw it, they all murmured, saying, That he was gone to be guest with a man that is a sinner.

8 And Zacchaeus stood, and said to the Lord; Behold, Lord, the half of my goods I give to the poor; and if I have taken any thing from any man by false accusation, I restore him fourfold.

9 And Jesus said to him, This day is salvation come to this house, forasmuch as he also is a son of Abraham.

10 For the Son of man is come to seek and to save that which was lost.

11 And as they heard these things, he added and spoke a parable, because he was near to Jerusalem, and because they thought that the kingdom of God should immediately appear.

12 He said therefore, A certain nobleman went into a far country to receive for himself a kingdom, and to return.

13 And he called his ten servants, and delivered them ten pounds, and said to them, Occupy till I come.

14 But his citizens hated him, and sent a message after him, saying, We will not have this man to reign over us.

15 And it came to pass, that when he was returned, having received the kingdom, then he commanded these servants to be called to him, to whom he had given the money, that he might know how much every man had gained by trading.

16 Then came the first, saying, Lord, your pound has gained ten pounds.

17 And he said to him, Well, you good servant: because you have been faithful in a very little, have authority over ten cities.

18 And the second came, saying, Lord, your pound has gained five pounds.

19 And he said likewise to him, Be also over five cities.

19:10 "Christ said, 'I came into this world for one reason—to reach and save lost souls!' Yet, this was not only Jesus' mission. He made it our mission as well: 'And he said unto them, Go ye into all the world, and preach the gospel to every creature'" (Mark 16:15). *David Wilkerson*

19:17 "Dietrich Bonhoeffer wrote that 'only he who believes is obedient, and only he who is obedient believes.' Neither proposition can stand alone. Christians often think we are doing the Lord's work when we are not. Jesus himself warned us about this. We cannot serve two masters. The one we choose will determine whether at our death we hear, 'Well done, good and faithful servant,' or 'I never knew you.'" *Daniel L. Weiss*

20 And another came, saying, Lord, behold, here is your pound, which I have kept laid up in a napkin:

21 For I feared you, because you are an austere man: you take up that you laid not down, and reap that you did not sow.

22 And he said to him, Out of your own mouth will I judge you, you wicked servant. You knew that I was an austere man, taking up that I laid not down, and reaping that I did not sow:

23 Why didn't you then give my money into the bank, that at my coming I might have required mine own with usury?

24 And he said to them that stood by, Take from him the pound, and give it to him that has ten pounds.

25 (And they said to him, Lord, he has ten pounds.)

26 For I say to you, That to every one which has shall be given; and from him that has not, even that he has shall be taken away from him.

> He that pleads for Christ should himself be moved with the prospect of Judgment Day.
>
> **CHARLES SPURGEON**

27 But those mine enemies, which would not that I should reign over them, bring here, and slay them before me.

28 And when he had thus spoken, he went before, ascending up to Jerusalem.

29 And it came to pass, when he was come near to Bethphage and Bethany, at the mount called the mount of Olives, he sent two of his disciples,

30 Saying, Go into the village over against you; in the which at your entering you shall find a colt tied, whereon yet never man sat: loose him, and bring him here.

31 And if any man ask you, Why do you loose him? thus shall you say to him, Because the Lord has need of him.

32 And they that were sent went their way, and found even as he had said to them.

33 And as they were loosing the colt, the owners thereof said to them, Why do you loose the colt?

34 And they said, The Lord has need of him.

35 And they brought him to Jesus: and they cast their garments upon the colt, and they set Jesus thereon.

36 And as he went, they spread their clothes in the way.

37 And when he was come near, even now at the descent of the mount of Olives, the whole multitude of the disciples began to rejoice and praise God with a loud voice for all the mighty works that they had seen;

38 Saying, Blessed be the King that comes in the name of the Lord: peace in heaven, and glory in the highest.

39 And some of the Pharisees from among the multitude said to him, Master, rebuke your disciples.

40 And he answered and said to them, I tell you that, if these should hold their peace, the stones would immediately cry out.

41 And when he was come near, he beheld the city, and wept over it,

42 Saying, If you had known, even you, at least in this your day, the things which belong to your peace! but now they are hid from your eyes.

43 For the days shall come upon you, that your enemies shall cast a trench about you, and compass you round, and keep you in on every side,

44 And shall lay you even with the ground, and your children within you; and they shall not leave in you one stone upon another; because you knew not the time of your visitation.

45 And he went into the temple, and began to cast out them that sold therein, and them that bought;

46 Saying to them, It is written, My house is the house of prayer: but you have made it a den of thieves.

47 And he taught daily in the temple. But the chief priests and the scribes and the chief of the people sought to destroy

him,

48 And could not find what they might do: for all the people were very attentive to hear him.

CHAPTER 20

AND it came to pass, that on one of those days, as he taught the people in the temple, and preached the gospel, the chief priests and the scribes came upon him with the elders,

2 And spoke to him, saying, Tell us, by what authority do you these things? or who is he that gave you this authority?

3 And he answered and said to them, I will also ask you one thing; and answer me:

4 The baptism of John, was it from heaven, or of men?

5 And they reasoned with themselves, saying, If we shall say, From heaven; he will say, Why then did you not believe him?

6 But and if we say, Of men; all the people will stone us: for they are persuaded that John was a prophet.

7 And they answered, that they could not tell whence it was.

8 And Jesus said to them, Neither tell I you by what authority I do these things.

9 Then began he to speak to the people this parable; A certain man planted a vineyard, and let it forth to husbandmen, and went into a far country for a long time.

10 And at the season he sent a servant to the husbandmen, that they should give him of the fruit of the vineyard: but the husbandmen beat him, and sent him away empty.

11 And again he sent another servant: and they beat him also, and entreated him shamefully, and sent him away empty.

12 And again he sent a third: and they wounded him also, and cast him out.

13 Then said the lord of the vineyard, What shall I do? I will send my beloved son: it may be they will reverence him when they see him.

14 But when the husbandmen saw him, they reasoned among themselves, saying,

This is the heir: come, let us kill him, that the inheritance may be ours.

15 So they cast him out of the vineyard, and killed him. What therefore shall the lord of the vineyard do to them?

16 He shall come and destroy these husbandmen, and shall give the vineyard to others. And when they heard it, they said, God forbid.

17 And he beheld them, and said, What is this then that is written, The stone which the builders rejected, the same is become the head of the corner?

18 **Whosoever shall fall upon that stone shall be broken; but on whomsoever it shall fall, it will grind him to powder.**

19 And the chief priests and the scribes the same hour sought to lay hands on him; and they feared the people: for they perceived that he had spoken this parable against them.

I would freely give my eyes if you might but see Christ, and I would willingly give my hands if you might but lay hold on Him.

CHARLES SPURGEON

20 And they watched him, and sent forth spies, which should feign themselves just men, that they might take hold of his words, that so they might deliver him to the power and authority of the governor.

21 And they asked him, saying, Master, we know that you say and teach rightly, neither accept you the person of any, but teach the way of God truly:

22 Is it lawful for us to give tribute to Caesar, or no?

23 But he perceived their craftiness, and said to them, Why tempt me?

24 Show me a penny. Whose image and superscription has it? They answered and said, Caesar's.

25 And he said to them, Render therefore to Caesar the things which be Caesar's, and to God the things which be God's.

26 And they could not take hold of his words before the people: and they mar-

veled at his answer, and held their peace.

27 Then came to him certain of the Sadducees, which deny that there is any resurrection; and they asked him,

28 Saying, Master, Moses wrote to us, If any man's brother die, having a wife, and he die without children, that his brother should take his wife, and raise up seed to his brother.

29 There were therefore seven brethren: and the first took a wife, and died without children.

30 And the second took her to wife, and he died childless.

31 And the third took her; and in like manner the seven also: and they left no children, and died.

32 Last of all the woman died also.

33 Therefore in the resurrection whose wife of them is she? for seven had her to wife.

34 And Jesus answering said to them, The children of this world marry, and are given in marriage:

35 But they which shall be accounted worthy to obtain that world, and the resurrection from the dead, neither marry, nor are given in marriage:

36 Neither can they die any more: for they are equal to the angels; and are the children of God, being the children of the resurrection.

37 Now that the dead are raised, even Moses showed at the bush, when he calls the Lord the God of Abraham, and the God of Isaac, and the God of Jacob.

38 For he is not a God of the dead, but of the living: for all live to him.

39 Then certain of the scribes answering said, Master, you have well said.

40 And after that they dared not ask him any question at all.

41 And he said to them, How say they that Christ is David's son?

42 And David himself said in the book of Psalms, The LORD said to my Lord, Sit you on my right hand,

43 Till I make your enemies your footstool.

44 David therefore calls him Lord, how is he then his son?

45 Then in the audience of all the people he said to his disciples,

46 Beware of the scribes, which desire to walk in long robes, and love greetings in the markets, and the highest seats in the synagogues, and the chief rooms at feasts;

47 Which devour widows' houses, and for a show make long prayers: the same shall receive greater damnation.

CHAPTER 21

AND he looked up, and saw the rich men casting their gifts into the treasury.

2 And he saw also a certain poor widow casting in there two mites.

3 And he said, Of a truth I say to you, that this poor widow has cast in more than they all:

4 For all these have of their abundance cast in to the offerings of God: but she of her penury has cast in all the living that she had.

5 And as some spoke of the temple, how it was adorned with goodly stones and gifts, he said,

6 As for these things which you behold, the days will come, in the which there shall not be left one stone upon another, that shall not be thrown down.

7 And they asked him, saying, Master, but when shall these things be? and what sign will there be when these things shall come to pass?

8 And he said, Take heed that you be not deceived: for many shall come in my name, saying, I am Christ; and the time draws near: go not therefore after them.

9 But when you shall hear of wars and commotions, be not terrified: for these

---

20:47 See Matthew 11:24 footnote.

21:7 For more signs of the end times, see 1 Timothy 4:1.

21:24 "*If the Jews are God's 'chosen people,' why have they been so oppressed?*"

Israel's blessings were dependent upon her obedience. If the nation sinned, it would be chastened. This is God's warning to the Jews, followed by His promised restoration: "The Lord shall scatter you among all people, from the one end of the earth to the other, and there you shall serve other gods, which neither you nor your fathers have known, even wood and stone. And among these nations shall you find no ease, neither shall the sole of your foot have rest: but the Lord shall give you there a trembling heart, and failing eyes, and sorrow of mind" (Deuteronomy 28:64,65).

"In the latter years you shall come into the land that is brought back from the sword, and is gathered out of many people, against the mountains of Israel, which have been always waste: but it is brought forth out of the nations, and they shall dwell safely all of them" (Ezekiel 38:8).

things must first come to pass; but the end is not by and by.

10 Then said he to them, Nation shall rise against nation, and kingdom against kingdom:

11 And great earthquakes shall be in divers places, and famines, and pestilences; and fearful sights and great signs shall there be from heaven.

12 But before all these, they shall lay their hands on you, and persecute you, delivering you up to the synagogues, and into prisons, being brought before kings and rulers for my name's sake.

13 And it shall turn to you for a testimony.

14 Settle it therefore in your hearts, not to meditate before what you shall answer:

15 For I will give you a mouth and wisdom, which all your adversaries shall not be able to gainsay nor resist.

16 And you shall be betrayed both by parents, and brethren, and kinsfolks, and friends; and some of you shall they cause to be put to death.

17 And you shall be hated of all men for my name's sake.

18 But there shall not an hair of your head perish.

19 In your patience possess your souls.

20 And when you shall see Jerusalem compassed with armies, then know that the desolation thereof is near.

21 Then let them which are in Judea flee to the mountains; and let them which are in the midst of it depart out; and let not them that are in the countries enter therein.

22 For these be the days of vengeance, that all things which are written may be fulfilled.

23 But woe to them that are with child, and to them that give suck, in those days! for there shall be great distress in the land, and wrath upon this people.

24 And they shall fall by the edge of the sword, and shall be led away captive into all nations: and Jerusalem shall be trodden down of the Gentiles, until the times of the Gentiles be fulfilled.

25 And there shall be signs in the sun, and in the moon, and in the stars; and upon the earth distress of nations, with perplexity; the sea and the waves roaring;

26 Men's hearts failing them for fear, and for looking after those things which

21:26 It has been said that there are three types of people in this world: those who are fearful, those who don't know enough to be fearful, and those who know their Bibles.

are coming on the earth: for the powers of heaven shall be shaken.

27 And then shall they see the Son of man coming in a cloud with power and great glory.

28 And when these things begin to come to pass, then look up, and lift up your heads; for your redemption draws near.

29 And he spoke to them a parable; Behold the fig tree, and all the trees;

30 When they now shoot forth, you see and know of your own selves that summer is now near at hand.

31 So you likewise, when you see these things come to pass, know that the kingdom of God is near at hand.

32 Verily I say to you, This generation shall not pass away, till all be fulfilled.

33 Heaven and earth shall pass away: but my words shall not pass away.

34 And take heed to yourselves, lest at any time your hearts be overcharged with surfeiting, and drunkenness, and cares of this life, and so that day come upon you unawares.

35 For as a snare shall it come on all them that dwell on the face of the whole earth.

36 Watch therefore, and pray always, that you may be accounted worthy to escape all these things that shall come to pass, and to stand before the Son of man.

37 And in the day time he was teaching in the temple; and at night he went out, and abode in the mount that is called the mount of Olives.

38 And all the people came early in the morning to him in the temple, for to hear him.

CHAPTER 22

NOW the feast of unleavened bread drew near, which is called the Passover.

21:26 Russia and Israel. A number of books of the Bible speak of future events. Ezekiel 38 (written approximately 600 B.C.) prophesies that in these times ("the latter days," v. 16), Russia (referred to as the "Prince of Rosh," see *Smith's Bible Dictionary*, p. 584) will combine with Iran, Libya (in Hebrew called "Put"), and communistic Ethiopia (in Hebrew called "Cush") and attack Israel (vv. 5–8). This will take place after an Israeli peace initiative has been successful (v. 11). The Bible even gives the Russian reasoning for and the direction of the attack (vv. 10–15), as well as the location of the battle (Armageddon—Revelation 16:16). This is generally interpreted as meaning "the mountain of Megiddo," which is located on the north side of the plains of Jezreel. Russia has had a foothold in the Middle East for many years: "The Soviets are entrenched around the rim of the Middle East heartland, in Afghanistan, South Yemen, Ethiopia, and Libya" ("Countdown in the Middle East," *Reader's Digest*, May 1982).

Israel will never have lasting peace until she obeys God. If she will obey His statutes and keep His commandments, He will give her rain in due season, an abundance of food, freedom from fear, victory over the enemy, and peace within the land (Leviticus 26:1–13). Sadly, from what we see of the Scriptures, Israel will only seek God as a last resort, when she sees that she cannot prevail against the might and power of the Russian invasion (Joel 2:12–20). Deuteronomy 4:30 gives warning that it would take tribulation to turn Israel to God in the latter days. When Israel finally turns to God in true repentance, He will take pity on His people and remove far from them the "northern army" (Joel 2:20).

Another sign of the latter days will be a clear understanding of the judgments and the will of God. No other generation has seen Russia mustering forces against Israel, the Arab-Israeli conflict in the Middle East and the Jews in Jerusalem. No other generation has had the scientific knowledge to help it understand "strange" Scriptures, nor have they had access to the Bible as we have. We can understand perfectly the times in which we live: "The anger of the Lord shall not return, until he has executed, and till he has performed the thoughts of his heart: in the latter days you shall consider it perfectly" (Jeremiah 23:20). Keep one eye on the Middle East—and the other toward the heavens. See also Revelation 9:9 and 16:16 footnotes.

21:27 Second coming of Jesus: See Acts 1:11.

2 And the chief priests and scribes sought how they might kill him; for they feared the people.

3 Then entered Satan into Judas surnamed Iscariot, being of the number of the twelve.

4 And he went his way, and communed with the chief priests and captains, how he might betray him to them.

5 And they were glad, and covenanted to give him money.

6 And he promised, and sought opportunity to betray him to them in the absence of the multitude.

7 Then came the day of unleavened bread, when the passover must be killed.

8 And he sent Peter and John, saying, Go and prepare us the passover, that we may eat.

9 And they said to him, Where will you that we prepare?

10 And he said to them, Behold, when you are entered into the city, there shall a man meet you, bearing a pitcher of water; follow him into the house where he enters in.

11 And you shall say to the goodman of the house, The Master said to you, Where is the guestchamber, where I shall eat the passover with my disciples?

12 And he shall show you a large upper room furnished: there make ready.

13 And they went, and found as he had said to them: and they made ready the passover.

14 And when the hour was come, he sat down, and the twelve apostles with him.

15 And he said to them, With desire I have desired to eat this passover with you before I suffer:

16 For I say to you, I will not any more eat thereof, until it be fulfilled in the kingdom of God.

17 And he took the cup, and gave thanks, and said, Take this, and divide it among yourselves:

18 For I say to you, I will not drink of the fruit of the vine, until the kingdom of God shall come.

19 And he took bread, and gave thanks, and broke it, and gave to them, saying, This is my body which is given for you: this do in remembrance of me.

20 Likewise also the cup after supper, saying, This cup is the new testament in my blood, which is shed for you.

21 But, behold, the hand of him that betrays me is with me on the table.

22 And truly the Son of man goes, as it was determined: but woe to that man by whom he is betrayed!

23 And they began to inquire among themselves, which of them it was that should do this thing.

24 And there was also a strife among them, which of them should be accounted the greatest.

25 And he said to them, The kings of the Gentiles exercise lordship over them; and they that exercise authority upon them are called benefactors.

26 But you shall not be so: but he that is greatest among you, let him be as the younger; and he that is chief, as he that does serve.

27 For whether is greater, he that sits at meat, or he that serves? is not he that sits at meat? but I am among you as he that serves.

28 You are they which have continued with me in my temptations.

29 And I appoint to you a kingdom, as my Father has appointed to me;

30 That you may eat and drink at my table in my kingdom, and sit on thrones judging the twelve tribes of Israel.

31 And the Lord said, Simon, Simon, behold, Satan has desired to have you, that he may sift you as wheat:

32 But I have prayed for you, that your faith fail not: and when you are converted, strengthen your brethren.

33 And he said to him, Lord, I am ready to go with you, both into prison, and to death.

34 And he said, I tell you, Peter, the cock shall not crow this day, before that you shall thrice deny that you know me.

35 And he said to them, When I sent you without purse, and scrip, and shoes, did you lack any thing? And they said,

Nothing.

36 Then said he to them, But now, he that has a purse, let him take it, and likewise his scrip: and he that has no sword, let him sell his garment, and buy one.

37 For I say to you, that this that is written must yet be accomplished in me, And he was reckoned among the transgressors: for the things concerning me have an end.

38 And they said, Lord, behold, here are two swords. And he said to them, It is enough.

39 And he came out, and went, as he was wont, to the mount of Olives; and his disciples also followed him.

40 And when he was at the place, he said to them, Pray that you enter not into temptation.

41 And he was withdrawn from them about a stone's cast, and kneeled down, and prayed,

42 Saying, Father, if you be willing, remove this cup from me: nevertheless not my will, but yours, be done.

43 And there appeared an angel to him from heaven, strengthening him.

44 And being in an agony he prayed more earnestly: and his sweat was as it were great drops of blood falling down to the ground.

"He who kneels the most, stands best."

D. L. Moody

45 And when he rose up from prayer, and was come to his disciples, he found them sleeping for sorrow,

46 And said to them, Why do you sleep? rise and pray, lest you enter into temptation.

47 And while he yet spoke, behold a multitude, and he that was called Judas, one of the twelve, went before them, and drew near to Jesus to kiss him.

22:31,32 The purpose of sifting. "In Luke 22:31, the word *sift* is translated from the Greek *siniazo*, meaning 'to sift, shake in a sieve; by inward agitation to try one's faith to the verge of overthrow.'

"Jesus did not pray that Simon Peter would escape this intense shaking. He prayed that his faith would not fail in the process...Satan had requested permission to shake Simon Peter so severely that he would lose his faith, but God had a different purpose for the shaking. He allowed the enemy to shake everything in Simon Peter that *needed* to be shaken.

"There are five purposes for shaking an object: 1) to bring it closer to its foundation; 2) to remove what is dead; 3) to harvest what is ripe; 4) to awaken it; and 5) to unify or mix together so it can no longer be separated. As a result of this tremendous shaking, all of Simon Peter's self-confidence would be gone, and all that would remain was God's sure foundation. He would be awakened to his true condition, the dead would be removed and the ripe fruit harvested, bringing him closer to his true foundation. He would no longer function independently but would be interdependent on the Lord." *John Bevere, The Bait of Satan*

22:41 Prayer—the secret weapon: See Acts 1:14.

22:44 This is not just hyperbole like "sweating bullets," but is an actual medical condition known as *hematidrosis*.

48 But Jesus said to him, Judas, do you betray the Son of man with a kiss?

49 When they which were about him saw what would follow, they said to him, Lord, shall we smite with the sword?

50 And one of them smote the servant of the high priest, and cut off his right ear.

51 And Jesus answered and said, Suffer you thus far. And he touched his ear, and healed him.

52 Then Jesus said to the chief priests, and captains of the temple, and the elders, which were come to him, Have you come out, as against a thief, with swords and staves?

53 When I was daily with you in the temple, you stretched forth no hands against me: but this is your hour, and the power of darkness.

54 Then took they him, and led him, and brought him into the high priest's house. And Peter followed afar off.

55 And when they had kindled a fire in the midst of the hall, and were set down together, Peter sat down among them.

56 But a certain maid beheld him as he sat by the fire, and earnestly looked upon him, and said, This man was also with him.

57 And he denied him, saying, Woman, I know him not.

58 And after a little while another saw him, and said, You are also of them. And Peter said, Man, I am not.

59 And about the space of one hour after another confidently affirmed, saying, Of a truth this fellow also was with him: for he is a Galilaean.

60 And Peter said, Man, I know not what you say. And immediately, while he yet spoke, the cock crew.

61 And the Lord turned, and looked upon Peter. And Peter remembered the word of the Lord, how he had said to him, Before the cock crow, you shall deny me thrice.

62 And Peter went out, and wept bitterly.

63 And the men that held Jesus mocked him, and smote him.

64 And when they had blindfolded him, they struck him on the face, and asked him, saying, Prophesy, who is it that smote you?

65 And many other things blasphemously spoke they against him.

66 And as soon as it was day, the elders of the people and the chief priests and the scribes came together, and led him into their council, saying,

67 Are you the Christ? tell us. And he said to them, If I tell you, you will not believe:

68 And if I also ask you, you will not answer me, nor let me go.

69 Hereafter shall the Son of man sit on the right hand of the power of God.

70 Then said they all, are you then the Son of God? And he said to them, You say that I am.

71 And they said, What need we any further witness? for we ourselves have heard of his own mouth.

22:47 Modern evangelism. The Bible tells us that Judas led a "multitude" to Jesus. His motive, however, wasn't to bring them to the Savior for salvation. Modern evangelism is also bringing "multitudes" to Jesus. Their motive may be different from Judas's, but the end result is the same. Just as the multitudes that Judas directed to Christ fell back from the Son of God, statistics show that up to 90% of those coming to Christ under the methods of modern evangelism fall away from the faith. Their latter end becomes worse than the first. They openly crucify the Son of God afresh.

In their zeal without knowledge, those who prefer the ease of modern evangelism to biblical evangelism betray the cause of the gospel with a kiss. What may look like love for the sinner's welfare is in truth eternally detrimental to him.

Like Peter (v. 51), our zeal without knowledge is actually cutting off the ears of sinners. Those we erroneously call "backsliders" won't listen to our reasonings. As far as they are concerned, they have tried it once, and it didn't work. What a victory for the prince of darkness, and what an unspeakable tragedy for the Church!

CHAPTER 23

AND the whole multitude of them arose, and led him to Pilate.

2 And they began to accuse him, saying, We found this fellow perverting the nation, and forbidding to give tribute to Caesar, saying that he himself is Christ a King.

3 And Pilate asked him, saying, are you the King of the Jews? And he answered him and said, You say it.

4 Then said Pilate to the chief priests and to the people, I find no fault in this man.

5 And they were the more fierce, saying, He stirs up the people, teaching throughout all Jewry, beginning from Galilee to this place.

6 When Pilate heard of Galilee, he asked whether the man were a Galilaean.

7 And as soon as he knew that he belonged to Herod's jurisdiction, he sent him to Herod, who himself also was at Jerusalem at that time.

8 And when Herod saw Jesus, he was exceeding glad: for he was desirous to see him of a long season, because he had heard many things of him; and he hoped to have seen some miracle done by him.

9 Then he questioned with him in many words; but he answered him nothing.

10 And the chief priests and scribes stood and vehemently accused him.

11 And Herod with his men of war set him at nought, and mocked him, and arrayed him in a gorgeous robe, and sent him again to Pilate.

12 And the same day Pilate and Herod were made friends together: for before they were at enmity between themselves.

13 And Pilate, when he had called together the chief priests and the rulers and the people,

14 Said to them, You have brought this man to me, as one that perverts the people: and, behold, I, having examined him before you, have found no fault in this man touching those things whereof you accuse him:

15 No, nor yet Herod: for I sent you to him; and, lo, nothing worthy of death is done to him.

16 I will therefore chastise him, and release him.

17 (For of necessity he must release one to them at the feast.)

18 And they cried out all at once, saying, Away with this man, and release to us Barabbas:

19 (Who for a certain sedition made in the city, and for murder, was cast into prison.)

20 Pilate therefore, willing to release Jesus, spoke again to them.

21 But they cried, saying, Crucify him, crucify him.

22 And he said to them the third time, Why, what evil has he done? I have found no cause of death in him: I will therefore chastise him, and let him go.

23 And they were instant with loud voices, requiring that he might be crucified. And the voices of them and of the chief priests prevailed.

24 And Pilate gave sentence that it should be as they required.

25 And he released to them him that for sedition and murder was cast into prison, whom they had desired; but he delivered Jesus to their will.

26 And as they led him away, they laid hold upon one Simon, a Cyrenian, coming out of the country, and on him they laid the cross, that he might bear it after Jesus.

27 And there followed him a great company of people, and of women, which also bewailed and lamented him.

28 But Jesus turning to them said, Daughters of Jerusalem, weep not for me, but weep for yourselves, and for your children.

29 For, behold, the days are coming, in the which they shall say, Blessed are the barren, and the wombs that never bare, and the paps which never gave suck.

30 Then shall they begin to say to the mountains, Fall on us; and to the hills, Cover us.

31 For if they do these things in a green tree, what shall be done in the dry?

32 And there were also two other, malefactors, led with him to be put to death.

33 And when they were come to the place, which is called Calvary, there they crucified him, and the malefactors, one on the right hand, and the other on the left.
34 Then said Jesus, Father, forgive them; for they know not what they do. And they parted his raiment, and cast lots.
35 And the people stood beholding. And the rulers also with them derided him, saying, He saved others; let him save himself, if he be Christ, the chosen of God.
36 And the soldiers also mocked him, coming to him, and offering him vinegar,
37 And saying, If you be the king of the Jews, save yourself.
38 And a superscription also was written over him in letters of Greek, and Latin, and Hebrew, THIS IS THE KING OF THE JEWS.
39 And one of the malefactors which were hanged railed on him, saying, If you be Christ, save yourself and us.
40 But the other answering rebuked him, saying, Do you not fear God, seeing you are in the same condemnation?
41 And we indeed justly; for we receive the due reward of our deeds: but this man has done nothing amiss.
42 And he said to Jesus, Lord, remember me when you come into your kingdom.
43 And Jesus said to him, Verily I say to you, To day shall you be with me in paradise.
44 And it was about the sixth hour, and there was a darkness over all the earth until the ninth hour.
45 And the sun was darkened, and the veil of the temple was rent in the midst.
46 And when Jesus had cried with a loud voice, he said, Father, into your hands I commend my spirit: and having said thus, he gave up the ghost.
47 Now when the centurion saw what was done, he glorified God, saying, Certainly this was a righteous man.

48 And all the people that came together to that sight, beholding the things which were done, smote their breasts, and returned.
49 And all his acquaintance, and the women that followed him from Galilee, stood afar off, beholding these things.
50 And, behold, there was a man named Joseph, a counsellor; and he was a good man, and a just:
51 (The same had not consented to the counsel and deed of them;) he was of Arimathaea, a city of the Jews: who also himself waited for the kingdom of God.
52 This man went to Pilate, and begged the body of Jesus.
53 And he took it down, and wrapped it in linen, and laid it in a sepulchre that was hewn in stone, wherein never man before was laid.
54 And that day was the preparation, and the sabbath drew on.
55 And the women also, which came with him from Galilee, followed after, and beheld the sepulchre, and how his body was laid.
56 And they returned, and prepared spices and ointments; and rested the sabbath day according to the commandment.

CHAPTER 24

NOW upon the first day of the week, very early in the morning, they came to the sepulchre, bringing the spices which they had prepared, and certain others with them.
2 And they found the stone rolled away from the sepulchre.
3 And they entered in, and found not the body of the Lord Jesus.
4 And it came to pass, as they were much perplexed thereabout, behold, two men stood by them in shining garments:
5 **And as they were afraid, and bowed down their faces to the earth, they said**

23:32–34 Messianic prophecy fulfilled: "He has poured out his soul unto death: and he was numbered with the transgressors; and he bare the sin of many, and made intercession for the transgressors" (Isaiah 53:12). See Luke 24:39 footnote.

23:53   *The Hands of the Carpenter*

It was Joseph of Arimathaea who had the honor of taking the body of Jesus down from the cross. Think what it would be like to have to pull the cold and lifeless hands of the Son of God from the thick, barbed Roman nails. These were carpenter's hands, which once held nails and wood, now being held by nails and wood. These were the hands that broke bread and fed multitudes, now being broken to feed multitudes. They once applied clay to a blind man's eyes, touched lepers, healed the sick, washed the disciple's feet, and took children in His arms. These were the hands that, more than once, loosed the cold hand of death, now held firmly by its icy grip.

These were the fingers that wrote in the sand when the adulterous woman was cast at His feet, and for the love of God, fashioned a whip that purged His Father's house. These were the same fingers that took bread and dipped it in a dish, and gave it to Judas as a gesture of deep love and friendship. Here was the Bread of Life itself, being dipped in the cup of suffering, as the ultimate gesture of God's love for the evil world that Judas represented.

Joseph's shame, that he had been afraid to own the Savior, sickened him as he tore the blood-sodden feet from the six-inch cold steel spikes that fastened them to the cross. These were the "beautiful feet" of Him that preached the gospel of peace, that Mary washed with her hair, that walked upon the Sea of Galilee, now crimson with a sea of blood.

As Joseph reached out his arms to get Him down from the cross, perhaps he stared for an instant at the inanimate face of the Son of God. His heart wrenched as he looked upon Him whom they had pierced. This face, which once radiated with the glory of God on the Mount of Transfiguration, which so many had looked upon with such veneration, was now blood-stained from the needle-sharp crown of thorns, deathly pale and twisted from unspeakable suffering as the sin of the world was laid upon Him.

His eyes, which once sparkled with the life of God, now stared at nothingness, as He was brought into the dust of death. His lips, which spoke such gracious words and calmed the fears of so many, were swollen and bruised from the beating given to Him by the hardened fists of cruel soldiers.

As it is written, "His visage was so marred more than any man" (Isaiah 52:14).

Nicodemus may have reached up to help Joseph with the body. As the cold blood of the Lamb of God covered his hand he was reminded of the blood of the Passover lamb he had seen shed so many times. The death of each spotless animal had been so quick and merciful, but this death had been unspeakably cruel, vicious, inhumane, and brutal. It seemed that all the hatred that sin-loving humanity had for the Light formed itself into a dark and evil spear, and was thrust with cruel delight into the perfect Lamb of God.

Perhaps as he carefully pried the crown from His head, looked at the gaping hole in His side, the deep mass of abrasions upon His back, and the mutilated wounds in His hands and feet, a sense of outrage engrossed him, that this could happen to such a Man as this. But the words of the prophet Isaiah rang within his heart:

> "He was wounded for our transgressions, he was bruised for our iniquities
> ...the Lord has laid on him the iniquity of us all...as a lamb to the slaughter
> ...for the transgression of my people he was stricken...yet it pleased the Lord to bruise him...by his knowledge shall my righteous servant justify many" (Isaiah 53:5–11).

Jesus of Nazareth was stripped of His robe, that we might be robed in pure righteousness. He suffered a deathly thirst, that our thirst for life might be quenched. He agonized under the curse of the Law, that we might relish the blessing of the gospel. He took upon Himself the hatred of the world, so that we could experience the love of God. Hell was let loose upon Him so that heaven could be let loose upon us. Jesus of Nazareth tasted the bitterness of death, so that we might taste the sweetness of life everlasting. The Son of God willingly passed over His life, that death might freely pass over the sons and daughters of Adam.

(continued on next page)

(23:53 continued)

May Calvary's cross be as real to us as it was to those who stood on its bloody soil on that terrible day. May we also gaze upon the face of the crucified Son of God, and may shame grip our hearts if ever the fear of man comes near our souls. May we identify with the apostle Paul, who could have gloried in his

dramatic and miraculous experience on the road to Damascus. Instead, he whispered in awe of God's great love:

"God forbid that I should glory, save in the cross of our Lord Jesus Christ, by whom the world is crucified unto me, and I unto the world" (Galatians 6:14).

to them, Why do you seek the living among the dead?

6 He is not here, but is risen: remember how he spoke to you when he was yet in Galilee,

7 Saying, The Son of man must be delivered into the hands of sinful men, and be crucified, and the third day rise again.

8 And they remembered his words,

9 And returned from the sepulchre, and told all these things to the eleven, and to all the rest.

10 It was Mary Magdalene, and Joanna, and Mary the mother of James, and other women that were with them, which told these things to the apostles.

11 And their words seemed to them as idle tales, and they believed them not.

12 Then arose Peter, and ran to the sepulchre; and stooping down, he beheld the linen clothes laid by themselves, and departed, wondering in himself at that which was come to pass.

13 And, behold, two of them went that same day to a village called Emmaus, which was from Jerusalem about threescore furlongs.

14 And they talked together of all these things which had happened.

15 And it came to pass, that, while they communed together and reasoned, Jesus himself drew near, and went with them.

16 But their eyes were withheld that they should not know him.

17 And he said to them, What manner of communications are these that you have one to another, as you walk, and are sad?

18 And the one of them, whose name was Cleopas, answering said to him, are you only a stranger in Jerusalem, and have not known the things which are come to pass therein these days?

19 And he said to them, What things? And they said to him, Concerning Jesus of Nazareth, which was a prophet mighty in deed and word before God and all the people:

20 And how the chief priests and our rulers delivered him to be condemned to death, and have crucified him.

21 But we trusted that it had been he which should have redeemed Israel: and beside all this, to day is the third day since these things were done.

22 Yea, and certain women also of our company made us astonished, which were early at the sepulchre;

23 And when they found not his body, they came, saying, that they had also seen a vision of angels, which said that he was alive.

24 And certain of them which were with us went to the sepulchre, and found it even so as the women had said: but him

24:1 Who arrived at the tomb first? There seems to be a contradiction as to who arrived first at the tomb. However, there is no contradiction when the Gospels are read in harmony. When the women arrived at the edge of the garden, they looked and saw that the stone had been rolled back from the tomb. Mary concluded that the body had been stolen, and ran back to Peter and John in Jerusalem. The other women continued to the tomb, and went on inside where they encountered the angels.

they saw not.

25 Then he said to them, O fools, and slow of heart to believe all that the prophets have spoken:

26 **Ought not Christ to have suffered these things, and to enter into his glory?**

27 And beginning at Moses and all the prophets, he expounded to them in all the scriptures the things concerning himself.

28 And they drew near to the village, where they went: and he made as though he would have gone further.

29 But they constrained him, saying, Abide with us: for it is toward evening, and the day is far spent. And he went in to tarry with them.

30 And it came to pass, as he sat at meat with them, he took bread, and blessed it, and broke, and gave to them.

31 And their eyes were opened, and they knew him; and he vanished out of their sight.

32 And they said one to another, Did not our heart burn within us, while he talked with us by the way, and while he opened to us the scriptures?

33 And they rose up the same hour, and returned to Jerusalem, and found the eleven gathered together, and them that were with them,

34 Saying, The Lord is risen indeed, and has appeared to Simon.

35 And they told what things were done in the way, and how he was known of them in breaking of bread.

36 And as they thus spoke, Jesus himself stood in the midst of them, and said to them, Peace be to you.

37 But they were terrified and fearful, and supposed that they had seen a spirit.

38 And he said to them, Why are you troubled? and why do thoughts arise in your hearts?

39 Behold my hands and my feet, that it is I myself: handle me, and see; for a spirit has not flesh and bones, as you see me have.

> Let eloquence be flung to the dogs rather than souls be lost. What we want is to win souls. They are not won by flowery speeches.
>
> **CHARLES SPURGEON**

40 And when he had thus spoken, he showed them his hands and his feet.

41 And while they yet believed not for joy, and wondered, he said to them, Have you here any meat?

42 And they gave him a piece of a broiled fish, and of an honeycomb.

43 And he took it, and did eat before them.

44 And he said to them, These are the words which I spoke to you, while I was yet with you, that all things must be ful-

---

24:25 "About this time there lived Jesus, a wise man, if indeed one ought to call him a man. For he was one who wrought surprising feats and was a teacher of such people as accepted the truth gladly. He won over many Jews and many Greeks. He was the Christ. When Pilate, upon hearing him accused by men of the highest standing among us, had condemned him to be crucified, those who had in the first place come to love him did not give up their affection for him. On the third day he appeared to them restored to life, for the prophets of God had prophesied these and countless other marvelous things about him. And the tribe of Christians, so called after him, has still to this day not disappeared." *Josephus, Testimonium Flavianum*

24:39 Messianic prophecy fulfilled: "For dogs have compassed me: the assembly of the wicked have enclosed me: they pierced my hands and my feet" (Psalm 22:16). See John 1:11 footnote.

24:43 Jesus' resurrected body was physical. He was visible, could be touched, and could eat food. He was not a spirit, but had flesh and bones. Our resurrected bodies will also be physical; see Romans 8:23.

QUESTIONS & OBJECTIONS

24:44,45 *"What if someone claims to have read the Bible and says it's just a book of fairy tales?"*

Call his bluff. Gently ask, "What is the thread of continuity that runs through the Bible—the consistent theme from the Old Testament through the New Testament?" More than likely he won't know. So say, "The Old Testament was God's promise that He would destroy death. The New Testament tells how He did it." Then appeal directly to the conscience by asking if he has kept the Ten Commandments. See John 4:7–26 and 2 Timothy 3:16 footnotes.

filled, which were written in the law of Moses, and in the prophets, and in the psalms, concerning me.

45 Then opened he their understanding, that they might understand the scriptures,

46 And said to them, Thus it is written, and thus it behoved Christ to suffer, and to rise from the dead the third day:

47 And that repentance and remission of sins should be preached in his name among all nations, beginning at Jerusalem.

48 And you are witnesses of these things.

49 And, behold, I send the promise of my Father upon you: but tarry in the city of Jerusalem, until you be endued with power from on high.

50 And he led them out as far as to Bethany, and he lifted up his hands, and blessed them.

51 And it came to pass, while he blessed them, he was parted from them, and carried up into heaven.

52 And they worshipped him, and returned to Jerusalem with great joy:

53 And were continually in the temple, praising and blessing God. Amen.

24:47 Repentance—its necessity for salvation. See Acts 2:38.

"There are many who speak only of the forgiveness of sin, but who say little or nothing about repentance. If there is nevertheless no forgiveness of sins without repentance, so also forgiveness of sins cannot be understood without repentance. Therefore, if forgiveness of sins is preached without repentance, it follows that the people imagine they have already received the forgiveness of sins, and thereby they become cocksure and fearless, which is then greater error and sin than all the error that preceded our time." *Melanchthon*

John

CHAPTER 1

IN the beginning was the Word, and the Word was with God, and the Word was God.

2 The same was in the beginning with God.

3 All things were made by him; and without him was not any thing made that was made.

4 In him was life; and the life was the light of men.

5 And the light shines in darkness; and the darkness comprehended it not.

6 There was a man sent from God, whose name was John.

7 The same came for a witness, to bear witness of the Light, that all men through him might believe.

8 He was not that Light, but was sent to bear witness of that Light.

9 That was the true Light, which lights every man that comes into the world.

10 He was in the world, and the world was made by him, and the world knew him not.

11 He came to his own, and his own received him not.

12 **But as many as received him, to them gave he power to become the sons of God, even to them that believe on his name:**

13 **Which were born, not of blood, nor of the will of the flesh, nor of the will of man, but of God.**

14 And the Word was made flesh, and dwelt among us, (and we beheld his glory, the glory as of the only begotten of the Father,) full of grace and truth.

1:3,4 Rejection of the Bible's account of creation as given in the Book of Genesis could rightly be called "Genocide," because it eradicated man's purpose of existence and left a whole generation with no certainty as to its beginning. Consequently, theories and tales of our origin have crept like primeval slime from the minds of those who don't know God. This intellectual genocide has given the godless a temporary license to labor to the extremes of their imagination, giving birth to painful conjecture of human beginnings. They speak in *speculation*, the uncertain language of those who drift aimlessly across the endless sea of secular philosophy.

The Scriptures, on the other hand, deal only with truth and certainty. They talk of fact, reality, and purpose for man's existence. The darkness of the raging sea of futility retreats where the lighthouse of Genesis begins.

1:9 On the Day of Judgment no one can plead ignorance. God has given light to every man. (See also 2 Corinthians 4:6.)

1:11 Messianic prophecy fulfilled: "He is despised and rejected of men; a man of sorrows, and acquainted with grief: and we hid as it were our faces from him; he was despised, and we esteemed him not" (Isaiah 53:3). See John 1:32 comment.

1:13 New birth—its necessity for salvation: See John 3:7.

1:13 The "Sinner's Prayer"—To Pray or Not To Pray?

The question often arises about what a Christian should do if someone is repentant. Should we lead him in what's commonly called a "sinner's prayer" or simply instruct him to seek after God? Perhaps the answer comes by looking to the natural realm. As long as there are no complications when a child is born, all the doctor needs to do is *guide the head*. The same applies spiritually. When someone is "born of God," all we need to do is guide the head—make sure that they *understand* what they are doing.

Philip the evangelist did this with the Ethiopian eunuch. He asked him, "Do you understand what you read?" (Acts 8:30). In the parable of the sower, the true convert (the "good soil" hearer) is he who hears "and understands." This understanding comes by the Law in the hand of the Spirit (Romans 7:7). If a sinner is ready for the Savior, it is because he has been drawn by the Holy Spirit (John 6:44). This is why we must be careful to allow the Holy Spirit to do His work and not rush in where angels fear to tread. Praying a sinner's prayer with someone who isn't genuinely repentant may leave you with a stillborn in your hands. Therefore, rather than *lead* him in a prayer of repentance, it is wise to encourage him to pray himself.

When Nathan confronted David about his sin, he didn't lead the king in a prayer of repentance. If a man committed adultery, and his wife is willing to take him back, should you have to write out an apology for him to read to her? No. Sorrow for his betrayal of her trust should spill from his lips. She doesn't want eloquent words, but simply sorrow of heart. The same applies to a prayer of repentance. The words aren't as important as the presence of "godly sorrow." The sinner should be told to repent—to confess and forsake his sins. He could do this as a whispered prayer, then you could pray for him. If he's not sure what to say, perhaps David's prayer of repentance (Psalm 51) could be used as a model, but his own words are more desirable.

---

15 John bare witness of him, and cried, saying, This was he of whom I spoke, He that comes after me is preferred before me: for he was before me.

16 And of his fulness have all we received, and grace for grace.

17 For the law was given by Moses, but grace and truth came by Jesus Christ.

18 No man has seen God at any time; the only begotten Son, which is in the bosom of the Father, he has declared him.

19 And this is the record of John, when the Jews sent priests and Levites from Jerusalem to ask him, Who are you?

20 And he confessed, and denied not; but confessed, I am not the Christ.

21 And they asked him, What then? are you Elijah? And he said, I am not. Are you that prophet? And he answered, No.

22 Then said they to him, Who are you?

1:13 How to get false converts. Our aim should be to ensure that sinners are born of the Spirit—of the will of God and not of the will of man. Too many of our "decisions" are not a work of the Spirit, but a work of our sincere but manipulative practices. It is simple to secure a decision for Jesus by using this popular method: "Do you know whether you are going to heaven when you die? God wants you to have that assurance. All you need to do is: 1) realize that you are a sinner ('All have sinned, and come short of the glory of God'), and 2) believe that Jesus died on the cross for you. Would you like me to pray with you right now so that you can give your heart to Jesus? Then you will have the assurance that you are going to heaven when you die." For the *biblical* way to present the gospel, see John 4:7–26 comment. For more on false converts, see Matthew 25:12 comment.

1:17 "A wrong understanding of the harmony between Law and grace would produce 'error on the left and the right hand.'" *John Newton*

QUESTIONS & OBJECTIONS

1:18 *"I will believe if God will appear to me."*

A proud and ignorant sinner who says this has no understanding of the nature of His Creator. No man has ever seen the essence of God. (When God "appeared" to certain men in the Old Testament, He manifested Himself in other forms, such as a burning bush or "the Angel of the Lord.") When Moses asked to see God's glory, God told him, "I will make all my goodness pass before you,...[but] you cannot see my face: for there shall no man see me, and live" (Exodus 33:18–23). If all of God's "goodness" were shown to a sinner, he would instantly die. God's "goodness" would just spill wrath upon evil man.

However, the Lord told Moses, "It shall come to pass, while my glory passes by, that I will put you in a cleft of the rock, and will cover you with My hand while I pass by." The only way a sinner can live in the presence of a holy God is to be hidden in the Rock of Jesus Christ (1 Corinthians 10:4).

that we may give an answer to them that sent us. What do you say of yourself?

23 He said, I am the voice of one crying in the wilderness, Make straight the way of the Lord, as said the prophet Isaiah.

24 And they which were sent were of the Pharisees.

25 And they asked him, and said to him, Why do you baptize then, if you be not that Christ, nor Elijah, neither that prophet?

26 John answered them, saying, I baptize with water: but there stands one among you, whom you know not;

27 He it is, who coming after me is preferred before me, whose shoe's latchet I am not worthy to unloose.

28 These things were done in Bethabara beyond Jordan, where John was baptizing.

29 **The next day John saw Jesus coming to him, and said, Behold the Lamb of God, which takes away the sin of the world.**

30 This is he of whom I said, After me comes a man which is preferred before me: for he was before me.

31 And I knew him not: but that he should be made manifest to Israel, there-

fore am I come baptizing with water.

32 And John bare record, saying, I saw the Spirit descending from heaven like a dove, and it abode upon him.

33 And I knew him not: but he that sent me to baptize with water, the same said to me, Upon whom you shall see the Spirit descending, and remaining on him, the same is he which baptizes with the Holy Spirit.

34 And I saw, and bare record that this is the Son of God.

35 Again the next day after John stood, and two of his disciples;

36 And looking upon Jesus as he walked, he said, Behold the Lamb of God!

37 And the two disciples heard him speak, and they followed Jesus.

38 Then Jesus turned, and saw them following, and said to them, What do you seek? They said to him, Rabbi, (which is to say, being interpreted, Master,) where do you dwell?

39 He said to them, Come and see. They came and saw where he dwelt, and abode with him that day: for it was about the tenth hour.

40 One of the two which heard John

1:32 Messianic prophecy fulfilled: "And the spirit of the LORD shall rest upon him, the spirit of wisdom and understanding, the spirit of counsel and might, the spirit of knowledge and of the fear of the LORD" (Isaiah 11:2). See John 6:14 comment.

"I believe that lack of efficient personal work is one of the failures of the Church today. The people of the Church are like squirrels in a cage. Lots of activity, but accomplishing nothing. It doesn't require a Christian life to sell oyster soup or run a bazaar or a rummage sale..."

Billy Sunday

speak, and followed him, was Andrew, Simon Peter's brother.

41 He first found his own brother Simon, and said to him, We have found the Messiah, which is, being interpreted, the Christ.

42 And he brought him to Jesus. And when Jesus beheld him, he said, You are Simon the son of Jonah: you shall be called Cephas, which is by interpretation, A stone.

43 The day following Jesus went forth into Galilee, and found Philip, and said to him, Follow me.

44 Now Philip was of Bethsaida, the city of Andrew and Peter.

45 Philip found Nathanael, and said to him, We have found him, of whom Moses in the law, and the prophets, did write, Jesus of Nazareth, the son of Joseph.

46 And Nathanael said to him, Can there any good thing come out of Nazareth? Philip said to him, Come and see.

47 Jesus saw Nathanael coming to him, and said of him, Behold an Israelite indeed, in whom is no guile!

48 Nathanael said to him, Where do you know me from? Jesus answered and said to him, Before that Philip called you, when you were under the fig tree, I saw you.

49 Nathanael answered and said to him, Rabbi, you are the Son of God; you are the King of Israel.

50 Jesus answered and said to him, Be-

1:41 After we have found the Messiah, we are to tell others about Him. The only "failure" when it comes to reaching out to the lost is not to be doing it.

"Many churches report no new members on confession of faith. Why these meager results with this tremendous expenditure of energy and money? Why are so few people coming into the Kingdom? I will tell you—there is not a definite effort put forth to persuade a definite person to receive a definite Savior at a definite time, and that definite time is now." *Billy Sunday*

"Our forefathers must be asking, 'How is it that we did so much with so little, and you do so little with so much?'" *R. Albert Mohler Jr.*

1:46   Come and see. Jesus called Philip to follow Him, then Philip immediately found Nathanael and told him about the Savior. Nathanael's question is a typical reaction of the contemporary world to those who follow the Savior. To the cynical, Christians are intellectual wimps, prudes, rejects—unlearned cripples who need some sort of crutch to get them through life. So it is understandable for them to ask, "Can any good thing come out of Christianity?" Down through the ages, its good name has been tainted with the stained brush of hypocrisy, dead religion, and more recently, fanatical sects and televangelism.

Philip merely answered Nathanael's cynicism with the same thing Jesus said to Andrew—"Come and see." Skeptic, come and see. Atheist, come and see. Intellectual, come and see. Just come with a humble and teachable heart, and you who are sightless *will* see and know that this Man from Nazareth is the Son of God.

cause I said to you, I saw you under the fig tree, do you believe? you shall see greater things than these.

51 And he said to him, Verily, verily, I say to you, Hereafter you shall see heaven open, and the angels of God ascending and descending upon the Son of man.

CHAPTER 2

AND the third day there was a marriage in Cana of Galilee; and the mother of Jesus was there:

2 And both Jesus was called, and his disciples, to the marriage.

3 And when they wanted wine, the mother of Jesus said to him, They have no wine.

4 Jesus said to her, Woman, what have I to do with you? mine hour is not yet come.

5 **His mother said to the servants, Whatsoever he says to you, do it.**

6 And there were set there six waterpots of stone, after the manner of the purifying of the Jews, containing two or three firkins apiece.

7 Jesus said to them, Fill the waterpots with water. And they filled them up to the brim.

8 And he said to them, Draw out now, and bear to the governor of the feast. And they bare it.

9 When the ruler of the feast had tasted the water that was made wine, and knew not whence it was: (but the servants which drew the water knew;) the governor of the feast called the bridegroom,

10 And said to him, Every man at the beginning does set forth good wine; and when men have well drunk, then that which is worse: but you have kept the good wine until now.

11 This beginning of miracles did Jesus in Cana of Galilee, and manifested forth his glory; and his disciples believed on him.

12 After this he went down to Capernaum, he, and his mother, and his brethren, and his disciples: and they continued there not many days.

13 And the Jews' passover was at hand, and Jesus went up to Jerusalem,

14 And found in the temple those that sold oxen and sheep and doves, and the changers of money sitting:

15 And when he had made a scourge of small cords, he drove them all out of the temple, and the sheep, and the oxen; and poured out the changers' money, and over-

---

1:47 Nathanael was "an Israelite indeed, in whom is no guile." He was a Jew in *deed*, not just in *word*. As an honest Jew he didn't twist the Law, as did the Pharisees. He read it in truth. The Law and the prophets had pointed him to Jesus and he was therefore ready to come to the Savior.

2:13–17 Cleansing the temple. When Jesus went to the temple, He found it to be filled with those buying and selling merchandise. According to the Jewish historian Josephus, at each Passover, over 250,000 animals were sacrificed. The priests sold licenses to the dealers and therefore would have had a great source of income from the Passover. When the Bible called them "changers of money," it was an appropriate term.

There is, however, another theft going on in another temple. Mankind was made as a dwelling place for his Creator. God made him a little lower than the angels, crowned him with glory and honor, and set him over the works of His hands (Hebrews 2:7), yet sin has given the dwelling place to the devil. The thief, who came to steal, kill, and destroy, is making merchandise out of mankind. Instead of the heart of man being a temple of the Living God (2 Corinthians 6:16)—a house of prayer—iniquity has made it a den of thieves.

When someone repents and calls upon the name of Jesus Christ, He turns the tables on the devil. The ten stinging cords of the Ten Commandments in the hand of the Savior cleanse the temple of sin. *Charles Spurgeon* had a resolute grasp of the Law. In preaching to sinners, he said, "I would that this whip would fall upon your backs, that you might be flogged out of your self-righteousness and made to fly to Jesus Christ and find shelter there."

2:15 This is the Lord's righteous indignation at Israel's equivalent of money-hungry televangelists.

2:6–11 *The Significance of the First Miracle*

1. The turning of water into blood was the first of the public miracles that Moses did in Egypt (Exodus 7:20), and the water into wine was the first of the public miracles that Jesus did in the world (John 2:11).

2. The signs that God gave to Egypt in the Old Testament were plagues, destruction, and death, and the signs that Jesus did in the world in the New Testament were healings, blessings, and life.

3. The turning of water to blood initiated Moses (a type of the Savior—Deuteronomy 18:15) leading his people out of the bondage of Egypt into an earthly liberty; the turning of water into wine initiated Jesus taking His people out of the bondage of the corruption of the world into the glorious liberty of the children of God (Romans 8:21).

4. The turning of water to blood culminated in the firstborn in Egypt being delivered to death, while turning the water into wine culminated in the life of the Firstborn being delivered from death (Colossians 1:18).

5. The Law was a ministration of death, the gospel a ministration of life. One was written on cold tablets of stone, the other on the warm fleshly tablets of the heart. One was a ministration of sin unto condemnation and bondage, the other a ministration of righteousness unto life and liberty (2 Corinthians 3:7–9).

6. When Moses changed the water into blood, we are told that all the fish in the river died. When Jesus initiated the new covenant, the catch of the fish are made alive in the net of the kingdom of God (Matthew 4:19).

7. The river of blood was symbolic of death for Egypt, but the water into wine is symbolic of life for the world. The letter of the Law kills, but the Spirit makes alive (2 Corinthians 3:6).

8. When Moses turned the waters of Egypt into blood, the river reeked and made the Egyptians search for another source of water supply (Exodus 7:21,24). When the Law of Moses does its work in the sinner, it makes life odious for him. The weight of sin on his back becomes unbearable as he begins to labor and be heavy laden under its weight. Like the Egyptians, he begins to search for another spring of water; he begins to "thirst for righteousness," because he knows that without a right standing with God, he will perish.

9. Moses turned water into blood, and Jesus' blood turned into water (1 John 5:6). They both poured from His side (John 19:34), perhaps signifying that both Law and grace found harmony in the Savior's death—"Mercy and truth are met together; righteousness and peace have kissed each other" (Psalm 85:10).

10. The water of the old covenant ran out. It could do nothing but leave the sinner with a thirst for righteousness. But as with the wine at Cana, God saved the best until last. The new wine given on the Day of Pentecost (Acts 2:13; Ephesians 5:18) was the Bridegroom giving us the new and "better" covenant (Hebrews 8:5,6).

---

threw the tables;

16 And said to them that sold doves, Take these things hence; make not my Father's house an house of merchandise.

17 And his disciples remembered that it was written, The zeal of your house has eaten me up.

18 Then answered the Jews and said to him, What sign do you show to us, seeing that you do these things?

19 **Jesus answered and said to them, Destroy this temple, and in three days I will raise it up.**

20 Then said the Jews, Forty and six years was this temple in building, and will you rear it up in three days?

21 But he spoke of the temple of his body.

22 When therefore he was risen from the dead, his disciples remembered that he had said this to them; and they believed the scripture, and the word which Jesus had said.

23 Now when he was in Jerusalem at the passover, in the feast day, many believed in his name, when they saw the

QUESTIONS & OBJECTIONS

3:3

"I have been born again many times."

Like Nicodemus, many people have no concept of what it means to be born again. He thought Jesus was speaking of a physical rebirth. Others see the experience as being a spiritual "tingle" when they think of God or a warm fuzzy feeling when they enter a building they erroneously call a "Church." Or maybe they are of the impression that one is born again when one is "christened" or "confirmed." However, the new birth spoken of by Jesus is absolutely essential for sinners to enter heaven. If they are not born again, they will not enter the kingdom of God. Therefore it is necessary to establish the fact that one becomes a Christian by being born again, pointing out that Jesus Himself said that the experience was crucial. The difference between *believing* in Jesus and being born again is like believing in a parachute, and putting one on. The difference will be seen when you jump. (See Romans 13:14.)

How is one born again? Simply through repentance toward God and faith in the Lord Jesus Christ. Confess and forsake your sins, and trust in Jesus alone for your eternal salvation. When you do, you receive spiritual life through the Holy Spirit who comes to live within you. See Ephesians 4:18 and 1 Peter 1:23 comments.

---

miracles which he did.

24 But Jesus did not commit himself to them, because he knew all men,

25 And needed not that any should testify of man: for he knew what was in man.

CHAPTER 3

THERE was a man of the Pharisees, named Nicodemus, a ruler of the Jews:

2 The same came to Jesus by night, and said to him, Rabbi, we know that you are a teacher come from God: for no man can do these miracles that you do, except God be with him.

3 Jesus answered and said to him, Verily, verily, I say to you, Except a man be born again, he cannot see the kingdom of God.

4 Nicodemus said to him, How can a man be born when he is old? can he enter the second time into his mother's womb, and be born?

5 Jesus answered, Verily, verily, I say to you, Except a man be born of water and of the Spirit, he cannot enter into the kingdom of God.

6 That which is born of the flesh is flesh; and that which is born of the Spirit is spirit.

7 Marvel not that I said to you, You must be born again.

8 The wind blows where it lists, and you hear the sound thereof, but can not

---

2:24,25 "We may deceive all the people sometimes; we may deceive some of the people all the time, but not all the people all the time, and not God at any time." *Abraham Lincoln*

"Character is what you are in the dark." *D. L. Moody*

3:2 Grace to the humble. Nicodemus was a humble Jew (he acknowledged the deity of the Son of God), and he knew the Law (he was a "master of Israel," v. 10); therefore, Jesus gave him the good news of the gospel. He was convinced of the disease of sin and consequently ready to hear of the cure.

3:3 "These verses aren't necessarily about what Nicodemus asked Jesus; they are about what Jesus knew. The last verse of the previous chapter said that He knew what was in man. Jesus knew what was in the heart of Nicodemus: he was a Law-breaker, and he needed to be born again." *Garry T. Ansdell, D.D.*

USING THE LAW IN EVANGELISM

3:16   "If I had my way, I would declare a moratorium on public preaching of 'the plan of salvation' in America for one to two years. Then I would call on everyone who has use of the airwaves and the pulpits to preach the holiness of God, the righteousness of God, and the Law of God, until sinners would cry out, 'What must we do to be saved?' Then I would take them off in a corner and whisper the gospel to them. Don't use John 3:16. Such drastic action is needed because we have gospel-hardened a generation of sinners by telling them how to be saved before they have any understanding why they need to be saved." *Paris Reidhead*

9 Nicodemus answered and said to him, How can these things be?

10 Jesus answered and said to him, Are you a master of Israel, and know not these things?

11 Verily, verily, I say to you, We speak that we do know, and testify that we have seen; and you receive not our witness.

12 If I have told you earthly things, and you believe not, how shall you believe, if I tell you of heavenly things?

13 And no man has ascended up to heaven, but he that came down from heaven, even the Son of man which is in heaven.

14 And as Moses lifted up the serpent in the wilderness, even so must the Son of man be lifted up:

15 That whosoever believes in him should not perish, but have eternal life.

16 For God so loved the world, that he

tell whence it comes, and where it goes: so is every one that is born of the Spirit.

3:7 New birth—its necessity for salvation. This is a fulfillment of Ezekiel 36:26: "A new heart also will I give you, and a new spirit will I put within you: and I will take away the stony heart out of your flesh, and I will give you an heart of flesh." Man cannot enter heaven in his spiritually dead state; he must be born again to have spiritual life. Jesus said that He is life (John 14:6; John 11:25,26), and that we must come to Him to have life (John 5:39,40; 1 John 5:11,12). Those who trust in Christ are "born again, not of corruptible seed, but of incorruptible, by the word of God, which lives and abides for ever" (1 Peter 1:23). See 2 Corinthians 5:17.

"Ever since Adam sinned, the earth has been the land of the walking dead—spiritually dead. What is the disease that killed man? 'The wages of sin is death.' So from God's point of view, salvation involves the raising of spiritually dead men to life. But before God could give life to the dead, He had to totally eradicate the fatal disease that killed men—sin. So the cross was God's method of dealing with the disease called sin, and the resurrection of Christ was and is God's method of giving life to the dead!" *Bob George, Classic Christianity*

3:14,15 When fiery serpents were sent among Israel, they caused the Israelites to admit that they had sinned. The means of their salvation was to look up to a bronze serpent that Moses had placed on a pole. Those who had been bitten and were doomed to die could look at the bronze serpent and live (Numbers 21:6–9). In John 3:14,15, Jesus specifically cited this Old Testament passage in reference to salvation from sin.

The Ten Commandments are like ten biting serpents that carry with them the venomous curse of the Law. They drive sinners to look to the One lifted up on a cross, and those who look to Him will live. It was the Law of Moses that put Jesus on the cross. The Messiah became a curse for us, and redeemed us from the curse of the Law.

3:16,17 Salvation is possible for every person. See John 4:14.

3:16,17   God Himself provided our way of escape: "But God commends his love toward us, in that, while we were yet sinners, Christ died for us" (Romans 5:8). "For he has made him to be sin for us, who knew no sin; that we might be made the righteousness of God in him" (2 Corinthians 5:21). "But he was wounded for our transgressions, he was bruised for our iniquities: the chastisement of our peace was upon him; and with his stripes we are healed. All we like sheep have gone astray; we have turned every one to his own way; and the Lord has laid on him the iniquity of us all" (Isaiah 53:5,6). See Romans 10:9 comment.

🔍 3:16 *Is Repentance Necessary for Salvation?*

It is true that numerous Bible verses speak of the promise of salvation with no mention of repentance. These verses merely say to "believe" on Jesus Christ and you shall be saved (Acts 16:31; Romans 10:9). However, the Bible makes it clear that God is holy and man is sinful, and that sin makes a separation between the two (Isaiah 59:1-2). Without repentance from sin, wicked men cannot have fellowship with a holy God. We are *dead* in our trespasses and sins (Ephesians 2:1) and until we forsake them through repentance, we cannot be made alive in Christ. The Scriptures speak of "repentance unto life" (Acts 11:18). We turn *from* sin *to* the Savior. This is why Paul preached "repentance toward God, and faith toward our Lord Jesus Christ" (Acts 20:21).

The first public word Jesus preached was "repent" (Matthew 4:17). John the Baptist began his ministry the same way (Matthew 3:2). Jesus told His hearers that without repentance, they would perish (Luke 13:3). If belief is all that is necessary for salvation, then the logical conclusion is that one need never repent. However, the Bible tells us that a false convert "believes" and yet is not saved (Luke 8:13); he remains a "worker of iniquity." Look at the warning of Scripture: "If we say that we have fellowship with him, and walk in darkness, we lie, and do not the truth" (1 John 1:6). The Scriptures also say, "He that covers

his sins shall not prosper, but whoso confesses and forsakes them [repentance] shall have mercy" (Proverbs 28:13). Jesus said that there was joy in heaven over one sinner who "repents" (Luke 15:10). If there is no repentance, there is no joy because there is no salvation.

As Peter preached on the Day of Pentecost, he commanded his hearers to repent "for the remission of sins" (Acts 2:38). Without repentance, there is no remission of sins; we are still under God's wrath. Peter further said, "Repent...and be converted, that your sins may be blotted out" (Acts 3:19). We cannot be "converted" unless we repent. God Himself "commands *all* men *everywhere* [leaving no exceptions] to repent" (Acts 17:30). Peter said a similar thing at Pentecost: "Repent, and be baptized *every one* of you" (Acts 2:38).

If repentance wasn't necessary for salvation, why then did Jesus command that *repentance* be preached to all nations (Luke 24:47)? With so many Scriptures speaking of the necessity of repentance for salvation, one can only suspect that those who preach salvation without repentance are strangers to repentance themselves, and thus strangers to true conversion.

gave his only begotten Son, that whosoever believes in him should not perish, but have everlasting life.

17 For God sent not his Son into the world to condemn the world; but that the world through him might be saved. **18** He that believes on him is not condemned: but he that believes not is condemned already, because he has not believed in the name of the only begotten Son of God.

19 And this is the condemnation, that light is come into the world, and men loved darkness rather than light, because their deeds were evil.

20 For every one that does evil hates the light, neither comes to the light, lest his deeds should be reproved.

21 But he that does truth comes to the light, that his deeds may be made man-

---

3:19 Jesus said that we loved the darkness of sin rather than the light of righteousness, because the human heart finds pleasure in sin. If you don't believe it, visit the "adult" section of your local video store. Look at the covers to see the type of entertainment the hearts of men and women crave—unspeakable violence, inconceivable horror, and unending sexual perversion.

ifest, that they are wrought in God.

22 After these things came Jesus and his disciples into the land of Judea; and there he tarried with them, and baptized.

23 And John also was baptizing in Aenon near to Salim, because there was much water there: and they came, and were baptized.

24 For John was not yet cast into prison.

25 Then there arose a question between some of John's disciples and the Jews about purifying.

> Sin and hell are married unless repentance proclaims the divorce.
>
> **CHARLES SPURGEON**

26 And they came to John, and said to him, Rabbi, he that was with you beyond Jordan, to whom you bare witness, behold, the same baptizes, and all men come to him.

27 John answered and said, A man can receive nothing, except it be given him from heaven.

28 You yourselves bear me witness, that I said, I am not the Christ, but that I am sent before him.

29 He that has the bride is the bridegroom: but the friend of the bridegroom, which stands and hears him, rejoices great-

ly because of the bridegroom's voice: this my joy therefore is fulfilled.

30 He must increase, but I must decrease.

31 He that comes from above is above all: he that is of the earth is earthly, and speaks of the earth: he that comes from heaven is above all.

32 And what he has seen and heard, that he testifies; and no man receives his testimony.

33 He that has received his testimony has set to his seal that God is true.

34 For he whom God has sent speaks the words of God: for God gives not the Spirit by measure to him.

35 The Father loves the Son, and has given all things into his hand.

36 He that believes on the Son has everlasting life: and he that believes not the Son shall not see life; but the wrath of God abides on him.

CHAPTER 4

WHEN therefore the Lord knew how the Pharisees had heard that Jesus made and baptized more disciples than John,

2 (Though Jesus himself baptized not, but his disciples,)

3 He left Judea, and departed again into Galilee.

3:19,20 The same sunlight that melts wax also hardens clay. As God's light shines on man, the sinner's heart determines his response. One whose heart is tender will respond to God; one whose heart is bent on evil will harden his heart further against God and will remain in darkness. Sinners should note: After Pharaoh repeatedly hardened his heart against God (Exodus 8:15,32), God then hardened Pharaoh's heart (Exodus 10:27). Those who continually reject God will be given up to "uncleanness, vile affections, and a reprobate mind" (Romans 1:24,26,28).

3:36 The Greek word used here for the first occurrence of "believes" is *pisteuo*—which means "to trust." However, in the second occurrence in this verse ("he that believes not the Son shall not see life; but the wrath of God abides on him"), the word used for "believes" is *apeitheo*—which means "disobedient." The disobedient will not see the salvation of God, no matter what prayer they have prayed, because they refuse to surrender their will to the Lordship of Jesus Christ. He is coming "in flaming fire taking vengeance on them that know not God, and that *obey not the gospel of our Lord Jesus Christ*" (2 Thessalonians 1:8, emphasis added).

3:36 Those without Christ are dead in their sins, separated from the life of God, and will not have spiritual life unless they trust in Jesus Christ. Their sin makes them objects of God's wrath.

Somehow we think that time forgives sin. This is not so. The more we sin, the more we store up God's wrath. See Romans 2:5.

4 And he must needs go through Samaria.

5 Then came he to a city of Samaria, which is called Sychar, near to the parcel of ground that Jacob gave to his son Joseph.

6 Now Jacob's well was there. Jesus therefore, being wearied with his journey, sat thus on the well: and it was about the sixth hour.

7 There came a woman of Samaria to draw water: Jesus said to her, Give me to drink.

8 (For his disciples were gone away to the city to buy meat.)

9 Then said the woman of Samaria to him, How is it that you, being a Jew, ask drink of me, which am a woman of Samaria? for the Jews have no dealings with the Samaritans.

10 Jesus answered and said to her, If you knew the gift of God, and who it is that said to you, Give me to drink; you would have asked of him, and he would have given you living water.

11 The woman said to him, Sir, you have nothing to draw with, and the well is deep: from whence then have you that living

---

4:7 *Personal Witnessing—How Jesus Did It*

How to address the sinner's conscience and speak with someone who doesn't believe in hell

Verses 7–26 give us the Master's example of how to share our faith. Notice that Jesus spoke to the woman at the well when she was alone. We will often find that people are more open and honest when they are alone. So, if possible, pick a person who is sitting by himself. From these verses, we can see four clear principles to follow.

First: Jesus began in the natural realm (v. 7). This woman was unregenerate, and the Bible tells us "the natural man receives not the things of the Spirit of God" (1 Corinthians 2:14). He therefore spoke of something she could relate to—water. Most of us can strike up a conversation with a stranger in the natural realm. It may be a friendly "How are you doing?" or a warm "Good morning!" If the person responds with a sense of warmth, we may then ask, "Do you live around here?" and from there develop a conversation.

Second: Jesus swung the conversation to the spiritual realm (v. 10). He simply mentioned the things of God. This will take courage. We may say something like, "Did you go to church on Sunday?" or "Did you see that Christian TV program last week?" If the person responds positively, the question "Do you have a Christian background?" will probe his background. He may answer, "I went to church when I was a child, but I drifted away from it."

Another simple way to swing to the spiritual is to offer the person a gospel tract and ask, "Did you get one of these?" When he takes it, simply say, "It's a gospel tract. Do you come from a Christian background?"

Third: Jesus brought conviction using the Law of God (vv. 16–18). Jesus gently spoke to her conscience by alluding to the fact that she had transgressed the Seventh of the Ten Commandments. He used the Law to bring "the knowledge of sin" (see Romans 3:19,20). We can do the same by asking, "Do you think that you have kept the Ten Commandments?" Most people think they have, so quickly follow with, "Have you ever told a lie?" This *is* confrontational, but if it's asked in a spirit of love and gentleness, there won't be any offense. Remember that the "work of the Law [is] written in their hearts" and that the conscience will bear "witness" (Romans 2:15). Jesus confronted the rich young ruler in Luke 18:18–21 with five of the Ten Commandments and there was no offense. Have confidence that the conscience will do its work and affirm the truth of each Commandment. Don't be afraid to gently ask, "Have you ever stolen something, even if it's small?" Learn how to open up the spirituality of the Law and show how God considers lust to be the same as adultery (Matthew 5:27,28) and hatred the same as murder (1 John 3:15). Make sure you get an admission of guilt.

(continued on next page)

(4:7 continued)

Ask the person, "If God judges you by the Ten Commandments on Judgment Day, do you think you will be innocent or guilty?" If he says he will be innocent, ask, "Why is that?" If he admits his guilt, ask, "Do you think you will go to heaven or hell?"

From there the conversation may go one of three ways:

1. *He may confidently say, "I don't believe in hell."* Gently respond, "That doesn't matter. You still have to face God on Judgment Day *whether you believe in it or not.* If I step onto the freeway when a massive truck is heading for me and I say, 'I don't believe in trucks,' my lack of belief isn't going to change reality."

Then tenderly tell him he has *already* admitted to you that he has lied, stolen, and committed adultery in his heart, and that God gave him a conscience so that he would know right from wrong. His conscience and the conviction of the Holy Spirit will do the rest.

That's why it is essential to draw out an admission of guilt *before* you mention Judgment Day or the existence of hell.

2. *He may say that he's guilty, but that he will go to heaven.* This is usually because he thinks that God is "good," and that He will, therefore, overlook sin in his case. Point out that if a judge in a criminal case has a guilty murderer standing before him, the judge, if he is a good man, can't just let him go. He must ensure that the guilty man is punished. If God is good, He must (by nature) punish murderers, rapists, thieves, liars, adulterers, fornicators, and those who have lived in rebellion to the inner light that God has given to every man.

3. *He may admit that he is guilty and therefore going to hell.* Ask him if that concerns him. Speak to him about how much he values his eyes and how much more therefore he should value the salvation of his soul. (For the biblical description of hell, see Revelation 1:18 comment.) If possible, take the person through the linked verses in this Bible, beginning at the Matthew 5:21,22 comment.

Fourth: Jesus revealed Himself to her (v. 26). Once the Law has humbled the person, he is ready for grace. Remember, the Bible says that God resists the proud and gives grace to the humble (James 4:6). The gospel is for the humble (see Luke 4:18 comment). Only the sick need a physician, and only those who will admit that they have the disease of sin will truly embrace the cure of the gospel.

Learn how to present the work of the cross —that God sent His Son to suffer and die in our place. Tell the sinner of the love of God in Christ; that Jesus rose from the dead and defeated death. Take him back to civil law and say, "It's as simple as this: We broke God's Law, and Jesus paid our fine. If you will repent and trust in the Savior, God will forgive your sins and dismiss your case." Ask him if he understands what you have told him. If he is willing to confess and forsake his sins, and trust the Savior with his eternal salvation, have him pray and ask God to forgive him. Then pray for him. Get him a Bible. Instruct him to read it daily and obey what he reads, and encourage him to get into a Bible-believing, Christ-preaching church.

---

water?

12 Are you greater than our father Jacob, which gave us the well, and drank thereof himself, and his children, and his cattle?

13 **Jesus answered and said to her, Whosoever drinks of this water shall thirst again:**

14 **But whosoever drinks of the water that I shall give him shall never thirst; but the water that I shall give him shall be in him a well of water springing up into everlasting life.**

15 The woman said to him, Sir, give me this water, that I thirst not, neither come here to draw.

16 Jesus said to her, Go, call your husband, and come here.

17 The woman answered and said, I have no husband. Jesus said to her, You have well said, I have no husband:

18 For you have had five husbands; and he whom you now have is not your husband: in that you said truly.

19 The woman said to him, Sir, I per-

4:14 Salvation is possible for every person. See John 6:51.

ceive that you are a prophet.

20 Our fathers worshipped in this mountain; and you say, that in Jerusalem is the place where men ought to worship.

21 Jesus said to her, Woman, believe me, the hour comes, when you shall neither in this mountain, nor yet at Jerusalem, worship the Father.

22 You worship you know not what: we know what we worship: for salvation is of the Jews.

23 But the hour comes, and now is, when the true worshippers shall worship the Father in spirit and in truth: for the Father seeks such to worship him.

24 God is a Spirit: and they that worship him must worship him in spirit and in truth.

25 The woman said to him, I know that Messiah comes, which is called Christ: when he is come, he will tell us all things.

26 Jesus said to her, I that speak to you am he.

27 And upon this came his disciples, and marveled that he talked with the woman: yet no man said, What do you seek? or, Why do you talk with her?

28 The woman then left her waterpot, and went her way into the city, and said to the men,

29 Come, see a man, which told me all things that ever I did: is not this the Christ?

30 Then they went out of the city, and came to him.

31 In the mean while his disciples prayed him, saying, Master, eat.

32 But he said to them, I have meat to eat that you know not of.

33 Therefore said the disciples one to another, has any man brought him anything to eat?

34 *Jesus said to them, My meat is to do the will of him that sent me, and to finish his work.*

35 *Do you not say, There are yet four months, and then comes harvest? behold, I say to you, Lift up your eyes, and look on the fields; for they are white already to harvest.*

36 *And he that reaps receives wages, and gathers fruit to life eternal: that both he that sows and he that reaps may rejoice together.*

37 *And herein is that saying true, One sows, and another reaps.*

38 *I sent you to reap that whereon you bestowed no labour: other men laboured, and you are entered into their labours.*

39 And many of the Samaritans of that city believed on him for the saying of the woman, which testified, He told me all that ever I did.

40 So when the Samaritans were come to him, they besought him that he would tarry with them: and he abode there two days.

41 And many more believed because of his own word;

42 And said to the woman, Now we believe, not because of your saying: for we have heard him ourselves, and know that this is indeed the Christ, the Savior of the world.

4:34 The "meat" that nourished the Savior was to carry out the work of evangelism—to seek and to save that which was lost.

4:36 "I would think it a greater happiness to gain one soul to Christ than mountains of silver and gold to myself." *Matthew Henry*

4:37,38 **The measure of success.** Don't be tempted to measure evangelistic "success" by the number of "decisions" obtained. We tend to rejoice over decisions, when heaven reserves its rejoicing for repentance—"There is joy in the presence of the angels of God over one sinner that repents" (Luke 15:10). It is easy to get "decisions for Jesus" using the modern method of well-chosen words and psychological manipulation. Rather, see success as having the opportunity to sow the seed of God's Word into the hearts of your hearers. If you faithfully sow, someone else will reap. If you have the privilege of reaping, then someone has faithfully sown before you. One sows, another reaps, but it is God who gives the increase. See 1 Corinthians 3:6,7.

43 Now after two days he departed thence, and went into Galilee.
44 For Jesus himself testified, that a prophet has no honor in his own country.
45 Then when he was come into Galilee, the Galilaeans received him, having seen all the things that he did at Jerusalem at the feast: for they also went to the feast.
46 So Jesus came again into Cana of Galilee, where he made the water wine. And there was a certain nobleman, whose son was sick at Capernaum.
47 When he heard that Jesus was come out of Judea into Galilee, he went to him, and besought him that he would come down, and heal his son: for he was at the point of death.
48 Then said Jesus to him, Except you see signs and wonders, you will not believe.
49 The nobleman said to him, Sir, come down ere my child die.
50 Jesus said to him, Go your way; your son lives. And the man believed the word that Jesus had spoken to him, and he went his way.
51 And as he was now going down, his servants met him, and told him, saying, Your son lives.
52 Then inquired he of them the hour when he began to amend. And they said to him, Yesterday at the seventh hour the fever left him.
53 So the father knew that it was at the same hour, in the which Jesus said to him, Your son lives: and himself believed, and his whole house.
54 This is again the second miracle that Jesus did, when he was come out of Judea into Galilee.

CHAPTER 5

AFTER this there was a feast of the Jews; and Jesus went up to Jerusalem.
2 Now there is at Jerusalem by the sheep market a pool, which is called in the Hebrew tongue Bethesda, having five porches.
3 In these lay a great multitude of impotent folk, of blind, halt, withered, waiting for the moving of the water.
4 For an angel went down at a certain season into the pool, and troubled the water: whosoever then first after the troubling of the water stepped in was made whole of whatsoever disease he had.
5 And a certain man was there, which had an infirmity thirty and eight years.
6 When Jesus saw him lie, and knew that he had been now a long time in that case, he said to him, Will you be made whole?
7 The impotent man answered him, Sir, I have no man, when the water is troubled, to put me into the pool: but while I am coming, another steps down before me.

> When your will is God's will, you will have your will.
>
> **CHARLES SPURGEON**

8 Jesus said to him, Rise, take up your bed, and walk.
9 And immediately the man was made whole, and took up his bed, and walked: and on the same day was the sabbath.
10 The Jews therefore said to him that was cured, It is the sabbath day: it is not lawful for you to carry your bed.
11 He answered them, He that made me whole, the same said to me, Take up your bed, and walk.
12 Then asked they him, What man is that which said to you, Take up your bed, and walk?
13 And he that was healed did not know who it was: for Jesus had conveyed himself away, a multitude being in that place.
14 Afterward Jesus found him in the temple, and said to him, Behold, you are made whole: sin no more, lest a worse thing come to you.
15 The man departed, and told the Jews that it was Jesus, which had made him whole.
16 And therefore did the Jews persecute Jesus, and sought to slay him, because he had done these things on the sabbath day.

17 But Jesus answered them, My Father works hitherto, and I work.

18 Therefore the Jews sought the more to kill him, because he not only had broken the sabbath, but said also that God was his Father, making himself equal with God.

19 Then answered Jesus and said to them, Verily, verily, I say to you, The Son can do nothing of himself, but what he sees the Father do: for what things soever he does, these also does the Son likewise.

20 For the Father loves the Son, and shows him all things that himself does: and he will show him greater works than these, that you may marvel.

21 For as the Father raises up the dead, and quickens them; even so the Son quickens whom he will.

22 For the Father judges no man, but has committed all judgment to the Son:

23 That all men should honor the Son, even as they honor the Father. He that honors not the Son honors not the Father which has sent him.

24 **Verily, verily, I say to you, He that hears my word, and believes on him that sent me, has everlasting life, and shall not come into condemnation; but is passed from death to life.**

25 Verily, verily, I say to you, The hour is coming, and now is, when the dead shall hear the voice of the Son of God: and they that hear shall live.

26 For as the Father has life in himself; so has he given to the Son to have life in himself;

27 And has given him authority to execute judgment also, because he is the Son of man.

28 **Marvel not at this: for the hour is coming, in the which all that are in the graves shall hear his voice,**

29 **And shall come forth; they that have**

5:14 We once lay as feeble, fragile, and frail folk, helpless and hopeless, pathetically paralyzed by the devil—"taken captive to do his will" until Jesus spoke a word to us. We were on a deathbed of sin with no one able to help us, but we heard the voice of the Word of God saying: "Arise from the dead, and Christ shall give you light" (Ephesians 5:14).

Now a thankful heart for the unspeakable gift makes us want to be always in the presence of God. Unlike the healed man, however, we need not go to the temple to thank the Father, for He now abides in the heart of the believer. The work of Calvary has made the believer the temple of the Living God. See 2 Corinthians 6:16.

5:17 **Jesus' claims.** Jesus was either God in human form, or a crackpot. There is no middle ground. In verses 17–29 He said:

- Whatever He saw the Father do, He did.
- God showed Jesus everything He did and He had even greater things to show Him, which would cause the people to be astonished.
- Just as God raised the dead and gave life to them, so Jesus gives life to whoever He would.
- God Himself had appointed Jesus of Nazareth as the Judge of all mankind.
- Humanity should honor Jesus as much as they honor the Father.
- Those who didn't honor Jesus didn't honor God.
- All who heard His words and trusted in the Father escape the wrath of the Law.
- All who trusted Him passed from death to life.
- The hour would come when *everyone* in their graves would hear the voice of Jesus, and be raised from the dead.
- As God is the source of all life, so He has given Jesus life in Himself.

5:28 **Jesus' unique words:** Jesus is saying that His voice will raise *billions* who have died. Psalm 29:3–9 describes the powerful voice of God. See John 6:38 comment.

5:28,29 **Judgment Day:** For verses that warn of its reality, see Acts 17:31.

done good, to the resurrection of life; and they that have done evil, to the resurrection of damnation.

30 I can of mine own self do nothing: as I hear, I judge: and my judgment is just; because I seek not mine own will, but the will of the Father which has sent me.

31 If I bear witness of myself, my witness is not true.

32 There is another that bears witness of me; and I know that the witness which he witnesses of me is true.

33 You sent to John, and he bare witness to the truth.

34 But I receive not testimony from man: but these things I say, that you might be saved.

35 He was a burning and a shining light: and you were willing for a season to rejoice in his light.

36 But I have greater witness than that of John: for the works which the Father has given me to finish, the same works that I do, bear witness of me, that the Father has sent me.

37 And the Father himself, which has sent me, has borne witness of me. You have neither heard his voice at any time, nor seen his shape.

38 And you have not his word abiding in you: for whom he has sent, him you believe not.

39 Search the scriptures; for in them you think you have eternal life: and they are they which testify of me.

40 And you will not come to me, that you might have life.

41 I receive not honor from men.

42 But I know you, that you have not the love of God in you.

43 I am come in my Father's name, and you receive me not: if another shall come in his own name, him you will receive.

44 How can you believe, which receive honor one of another, and seek not the honor that comes from God only?

45 Do not think that I will accuse you to the Father: there is one that accuses you, even Moses, in whom you trust.

46 For had you believed Moses, you would have believed me: for he wrote of me.

47 But if you believe not his writings, how shall you believe my words?

· · · · · ·

For the Bible's inspiration,
see 2 Timothy 3:16 comment.

· · · · · ·

CHAPTER 6

AFTER these things Jesus went over the sea of Galilee, which is the sea of Tiberias.

2 And a great multitude followed him, because they saw his miracles which he did on them that were diseased.

3 And Jesus went up into a mountain, and there he sat with his disciples.

4 And the passover, a feast of the Jews, was nigh.

5 When Jesus then lifted up his eyes, and saw a great company come to him, he said to Philip, Whence shall we buy bread, that these may eat?

6 And this he said to prove him: for he himself knew what he would do.

7 Philip answered him, Two hundred pennyworth of bread is not sufficient for them, that every one of them may take a little.

8 One of his disciples, Andrew, Simon Peter's brother, said to him,

9 There is a lad here, which has five barley loaves, and two small fishes: but what are they among so many?

10 And Jesus said, Make the men sit down. Now there was much grass in the place. So the men sat down, in number about five thousand.

11 And Jesus took the loaves; and when

5:39,40 To see why sinners need to come to Jesus to have life, see John 3:7 comment and Ephesians 4:18 "Questions & Objections."

he had given thanks, he distributed to the disciples, and the disciples to them that were set down; and likewise of the fishes as much as they would.

12 When they were filled, he said to his disciples, Gather up the fragments that remain, that nothing be lost.

13 Therefore they gathered them together, and filled twelve baskets with the fragments of the five barley loaves, which remained over and above to them that had eaten.

14 Then those men, when they had seen the miracle that Jesus did, said, This is of a truth that prophet that should come into the world.

15 When Jesus therefore perceived that they would come and take him by force, to make him a king, he departed again into a mountain himself alone.

16 And when even was now come, his disciples went down to the sea,

17 And entered into a ship, and went over the sea toward Capernaum. And it was now dark, and Jesus was not come to them.

18 And the sea arose by reason of a great wind that blew.

19 So when they had rowed about five and twenty or thirty furlongs, they see Jesus walking on the sea, and drawing near to the ship: and they were afraid.

20 But he said to them, It is I; be not afraid.

21 Then they willingly received him into the ship: and immediately the ship was at the land where they went.

22 The day following, when the people which stood on the other side of the sea saw that there was none other boat there, save that one whereinto his disciples were entered, and that Jesus went not with his disciples into the boat, but that his disci-ples were gone away alone;

23 (Howbeit there came other boats from Tiberias near to the place where they did eat bread, after that the Lord had given thanks:)

24 When the people therefore saw that Jesus was not there, neither his disciples, they also took shipping, and came to Capernaum, seeking for Jesus.

25 And when they had found him on the other side of the sea, they said to him, Rabbi, when did you come here?

26 Jesus answered them and said, Verily, verily, I say to you, You seek me, not because you saw the miracles, but because you did eat of the loaves, and were filled.

27 **Labour not for the meat which perishes, but for that meat which endures to everlasting life, which the Son of man shall give to you: for him has God the Father sealed.**

28 Then said they to him, What shall we do, that we might work the works of God?

29 Jesus answered and said to them, This is the work of God, that you believe on him whom he has sent.

30 They said therefore to him, What sign do you show then, that we may see, and believe you? what do you work?

31 Our fathers did eat manna in the desert; as it is written, He gave them bread from heaven to eat.

32 Then Jesus said to them, Verily, verily, I say to you, Moses gave you not that bread from heaven; but my Father gives you the true bread from heaven.

33 For the bread of God is he which came down from heaven, and gives life to the world.

34 Then said they to him, Lord, evermore give us this bread.

35 **And Jesus said to them, I am the**

6:14 Messianic prophecy fulfilled: "The LORD your God will raise up to you a Prophet from your midst, of your brethren, like unto me; to him you shall hearken" (Deuteronomy 18:15). See John 19:29 comment.

6:28,29 Most religions teach that certain works are required in order to be saved. Here God tells us the only "work" he considers: "believe on him whom he has sent."

bread of life: he that comes to me shall never hunger; and he that believes on me shall never thirst.

36 But I said to you, That you also have seen me, and believe not.

37 **All that the Father gives me shall come to me; and him that comes to me I will in no wise cast out.**

38 For I came down from heaven, not to do mine own will, but the will of him that sent me.

39 And this is the Father's will which has sent me, that of all which he has given me I should lose nothing, but should raise it up again at the last day.

40 And this is the will of him that sent me, that every one which sees the Son, and believes on him, may have everlasting life: and I will raise him up at the last day.

41 The Jews then murmured at him, because he said, I am the bread which came down from heaven.

42 And they said, Is not this Jesus, the son of Joseph, whose father and mother we know? how is it then that he says, I came down from heaven?

43 Jesus therefore answered and said to them, Murmur not among yourselves.

44 **No man can come to me, except the Father which has sent me draw him:** and I will raise him up at the last day.

45 It is written in the prophets, And they shall be all taught of God. Every man therefore that has heard, and has learned of the Father, comes to me.

46 Not that any man has seen the Father, save he which is of God, he has seen the Father.

47 **Verily, verily, I say to you, He that believes on me has everlasting life.**

48 I am that bread of life.

49 Your fathers did eat manna in the wilderness, and are dead.

50 This is the bread which came down from heaven, that a man may eat thereof, and not die.

51 I am the living bread which came down from heaven: if any man eat of this bread, he shall live for ever: and the bread that I will give is my flesh, which I will give for the life of the world.

52 The Jews therefore strove among themselves, saying, How can this man give us his flesh to eat?

53 Then Jesus said to them, Verily, verily, I say to you, Except you eat the flesh of the Son of man, and drink his blood, you have no life in you.

54 Whoso eats my flesh, and drinks my blood, has eternal life; and I will raise him up at the last day.

6:38 Jesus' unique words: Jesus said that He "came down" from heaven, that He was pre-existent. He says elsewhere: "I am from above...I am not of this world" (8:23), and "I proceeded forth and came from God" (8:42). For more on His pre-existence, see John 17:5. See also John 6:47 comment.

6:45 Taught by God. "Read and read again, and do not despair of help to understand the will and mind of God though you think they are fast locked up from you. Neither trouble your heads though you have not commentaries and exposition. Pray and read, read and pray; for a little from God is better than a great deal from men. Also, what is from men is uncertain, and is often lost and tumbled over by men; but what is from God is fixed as a nail in a sure place. There is nothing that so abides with us as what we receive from God; and the reason why the Christians in this day are at such a loss as to some things is that they are contented with what comes from men's mouths, without searching and kneeling before God to know of Him the truth of things. Things we receive at God's hands come to us as truths from the minting house, though old in themselves, yet new to us. Old truths are always new to us if they come with the smell of heaven upon them." *John Bunyan*

6:47 Jesus' unique words: He was saying that He had the authority to grant *everlasting life* to all who trust in Him. See John 6:53,54 comment.

6:51 Salvation is possible for every person. See John 7:37.

Halloween—an incredible opportunity for sharing the gospel. See 1 Timothy 4:1 comment.

55 For my flesh is meat indeed, and my blood is drink indeed.

56 He that eats my flesh, and drinks my blood, dwells in me, and I in him.

57 As the living Father has sent me, and I live by the Father: so he that eats me, even he shall live by me.

58 This is that bread which came down from heaven: not as your fathers did eat manna, and are dead: he that eats of this bread shall live for ever.

59 These things said he in the synagogue, as he taught in Capernaum.

60 Many therefore of his disciples, when they had heard this, said, This is an hard saying; who can hear it?

61 When Jesus knew in himself that his disciples murmured at it, he said to them, Does this offend you?

62 What and if you shall see the Son of man ascend up where he was before?

63 It is the spirit that quickens; the flesh profits nothing: the words that I speak to you, they are spirit, and they are life.

64 But there are some of you that believe not. For Jesus knew from the beginning who they were that believed not, and who should betray him.

65 And he said, Therefore said I to you, that no man can come to me, except it were given to him of my Father.

66 From that time many of his disciples went back, and walked no more with him.

67 Then said Jesus to the twelve, Will you also go away?

68 Then Simon Peter answered him, Lord, to whom shall we go? you have the words of eternal life.

69 And we believe and are sure that you are that Christ, the Son of the living God.

70 Jesus answered them, Have not I chosen you twelve, and one of you is a devil?

71 He spoke of Judas Iscariot the son of Simon: for he it was that should betray him, being one of the twelve.

CHAPTER 7

AFTER these things Jesus walked in Galilee: for he would not walk in Jewry, because the Jews sought to kill him.

6:53,54 Jesus' unique words: These are the words of a madman . . . or God in human form. He was not advocating cannibalism, but was speaking in a spiritual sense. Just as we need to eat and drink in order to live, so we must "eat" the Bread of Life (John 6:48,51) and "drink" His "blood, which is shed for you" (Luke 22:20) in order to have spiritual life. Unless we trust in Christ, relying on Him daily for our life-sustaining nourishment, we have no life in us and remain dead in our sins. (See Ephesians 2:1 comment.) See also John 8:51 comment.

6:65 "The impulse to pursue God originates with God." *A. W. Tozer*

6:68 The uniqueness of Jesus. "This Jesus of Nazareth, without money and arms, conquered more millions than Alexander, Caesar, Mohammed, and Napoleon; without science and learning, He shed more light on things human and divine than all philosophers and scholars combined; without the eloquence of schools, He spoke such words of life as were never spoken before or since, and produced effects which lie beyond the reach of orator or poet; without writing a single line, He set more pens in motion, and furnished themes for more sermons, orations, discussions, learned volumes, works of art, and songs of praise than the whole army of great men of ancient and modern times." *Philip Schaff, The Person of Christ*

2 Now the Jews' feast of tabernacles was at hand.

3 His brethren therefore said to him, Depart hence, and go into Judea, that your disciples also may see the works that you do.

4 For there is no man that does any thing in secret, and he himself seeks to be known openly. If you do these things, show yourself to the world.

5 For neither did his brethren believe in him.

6 Then Jesus said to them, My time is not yet come: but your time is always ready.

7 The world cannot hate you; but me it hates, because I testify of it, that the works thereof are evil.

8 Go up to this feast: I go not up yet to this feast; for my time is not yet full come.

9 When he had said these words to them, he abode still in Galilee.

10 But when his brethren were gone up, then went he also up to the feast, not openly, but as it were in secret.

11 Then the Jews sought him at the feast, and said, Where is he?

12 And there was much murmuring among the people concerning him: for some said, He is a good man: others said, Nay; but he deceives the people.

13 Howbeit no man spoke openly of him for fear of the Jews.

14 Now about the midst of the feast Jesus went up into the temple, and taught.

15 And the Jews marveled, saying, How knows this man letters, having never learned?

16 Jesus answered them, and said, My doctrine is not mine, but his that sent me.

17 If any man will do his will, he shall know of the doctrine, whether it be of God, or whether I speak of myself.

18 He that speaks of himself seeks his own glory: but he that seeks his glory that sent him, the same is true, and no unrighteousness is in him.

19 Did not Moses give you the law, and yet none of you keeps the law? Why do you go about to kill me?

20 The people answered and said, You have a devil: who goes about to kill you?

21 Jesus answered and said to them, I have done one work, and you all marvel.

22 Moses therefore gave to you circumcision; (not because it is of Moses, but of the fathers;) and you on the sabbath day circumcise a man.

23 If a man on the sabbath day receive circumcision, that the law of Moses should not be broken; are you angry at me, because I have made a man every whit whole on the sabbath day?

24 Judge not according to the appearance, but judge righteous judgment.

25 Then said some of them of Jerusalem, Is not this he, whom they seek to kill?

26 But, lo, he speaks boldly, and they say nothing to him. Do the rulers know indeed that this is the very Christ?

27 Howbeit we know this man whence he is: but when Christ comes, no man knows whence he is.

28 Then cried Jesus in the temple as he taught, saying, You both know me, and you know whence I am: and I am not come of myself, but he that sent me is true, whom you know not.

29 But I know him: for I am from him,

7:17 In reference to creation, respected Bible teacher *Derek Prince* said, "I am simple-minded enough to believe that it happened the way the Bible described it. I have been a professor at Britain's largest university [Cambridge] for nine years. I hold various degrees and academic distinctions, and I feel in many ways I am quite sophisticated intellectually, but I don't feel in any way intellectually inferior when I say that I believe the Bible record of creation. Prior to believing the Bible I have studied many other attempts to explain man's origin and found them all unsatisfying and in many cases self-contradictory. I turned to study the Bible as a professional philosopher—not as a believer—and I commented to myself, 'At least it can't be any sillier than some of the other things I've heard,' and to my astonishment, I discovered it had the answer."

and he has sent me.

30 Then they sought to take him: but no man laid hands on him, because his hour was not yet come.

31 And many of the people believed on him, and said, When Christ comes, will he do more miracles than these which this man has done?

32 The Pharisees heard that the people murmured such things concerning him; and the Pharisees and the chief priests sent officers to take him.

33 Then said Jesus to them, Yet a little while am I with you, and then I go to him that sent me.

34 You shall seek me, and shall not find me: and where I am, there you cannot come.

35 Then said the Jews among themselves, Where will he go, that we shall not find him? will he go to the dispersed among the Gentiles, and teach the Gentiles?

36 What manner of saying is this that he said, You shall seek me, and shall not find me: and where I am, there you cannot come?

37 In the last day, that great day of the feast, Jesus stood and cried, saying, If any man thirst, let him come to me, and drink.

38 He that believes on me, as the scripture has said, out of his belly shall flow rivers of living water.

39 (But this spoke he of the Spirit, which they that believe on him should receive: for the Holy Spirit was not yet given; because that Jesus was not yet glorified.)

40 Many of the people therefore, when they heard this saying, said, Of a truth this is the Prophet.

41 Others said, This is the Christ. But

"I know men and I tell you that Jesus Christ is no mere man..." (See what Napolean had to say about Jesus in John 7:46.)

Napolean Bonaparte

some said, Shall Christ come out of Galilee?

42 Has not the scripture said, That Christ comes of the seed of David, and out of the town of Bethlehem, where David was?

43 So there was a division among the people because of him.

44 And some of them would have taken him; but no man laid hands on him.

45 Then came the officers to the chief priests and Pharisees; and they said to them, Why have you not brought him?

46 The officers answered, Never man spoke like this man.

47 Then answered them the Pharisees, Are you also deceived?

48 Have any of the rulers or of the Pharisees believed on him?

7:37 Salvation is possible for every person. See Acts 2:21.

7:46 The uniqueness of Jesus. "I know men and I tell you that Jesus Christ is no mere man. Between Him and every other person in the world there is no possible term of comparison. Alexander, Caesar, Charlemagne, and I have founded empires. But on what did we rest the creations of our genius? Upon force. Jesus Christ founded His empire upon love; and at this hour millions of men would die for Him." *Napoleon Bonaparte* (quoted in *Evidence That Demands a Verdict* by *Josh McDowell*)

How to Witness to a Moslem, a Roman Catholic, a Homosexual and an Intellectual

You are sitting on a plane next to a Moslem. You smile as you say, "Hi. How are you doing? Did you get one of these? It's a gospel tract." The man replies, "I'm a Moslem." You simply ask, "Would you consider yourself to be a good person?" When he says, "Yes I am." You then take him through the Ten Commandments to show him God's standard of goodness, beginning with, "Have you ever told a lie?"

You are sitting on a plane next to a Roman Catholic (there are millions of Catholics and Protestants who have never been born again and need to hear the gospel). You smile and say, "Hi. How are you doing? Did you get one of these? It's a gospel tract." He answers "I'm a Roman Catholic." At this point, you need not panic and think that you are going to have to deal with issues such as papal infallibility, the confessional, praying to the saints, purgatory, transubstantiation, Mariology, etc. You simply answer him with "Would you consider yourself to be a good person?" He says, "Yes I am." You then take him through the Ten Commandments to show him God's standard of goodness, beginning with "Have you ever told a lie?"

You are sitting on a plane next to a homosexual. You smile and say, "Hi. How are you doing? Did you get one of these? It's a gospel tract." He answers, "I'm gay." Don't talk to him about his sexual orientation. Simply answer with, "Would you consider yourself to be a good person?" He says, "Yes I am." You then take him through the Ten Commandments to show him God's standard of goodness, beginning with, "Have you ever told a lie?"

You are sitting on a plane next to an intellectual. You smile and say, "Hi. How are you doing? Did you get one of these? It's a gospel tract." He answers, "I'm an evolutionist, and I lean strongly towards the controversial spontaneous regeneration and the quantum embryonic theory of cosmological physics." Don't be intimidated. Simply answer with, "Would you consider yourself to be a good person?" He says, "Yes I do." You then take him through the Ten Commandments to show him God's standard of goodness, beginning with, "Have you ever told a lie?"

You may have noticed repetition. This is to make an incredibly important point. That point is the profound principle of circumnavigating the human intellect and speaking directly to the conscience. This is what Jesus did (see Mark 10:17--21). The reason for this is that the human mind is at war with God, it is not subject to the Law of God (Romans 8:7). For you to be effective, you have to find ground upon which there is agreement with the Law which brings the knowledge of sin (Romans 3:19-20), so that you can reason with him about sin, righteousness and judgment to come. The place of common ground is the conscience: "Which show the work of the law written in their hearts, their conscience also bearing witness..." (Romans 2:15). The sinful human mind is bent on argument with the Law, but the conscience will agree with it. So use the Law of God (as Jesus did) to speak directly to the conscience.

We tend to complicate the issue of witnessing by bringing up subjects that are irrelevant to the subject of salvation, and therefore confine ourselves to the intellect (the place of argument), rather than the conscience (the place of the knowledge of sin).

QUESTIONS & OBJECTIONS

8:9

"You are trying to make me feel guilty by quoting the Ten Commandments."

Ask the person which one of the Ten Commandments makes him feel guilty. Simply state, "The Bible says, 'You shall not steal.' If you feel guilty when you hear that, why do you think that is? Could it be because you *are* guilty?" God gave us our conscience so we would know when we break His Law; the guilt we feel when we do something wrong tells us that we need to repent. (See also Romans 2:15 comment.)

49 But this people who knows not the law are cursed.

50 Nicodemus said to them, (he that came to Jesus by night, being one of them,)

51 Does our law judge any man, before it hear him, and know what he does?

52 They answered and said to him, are you also of Galilee? Search, and look: for out of Galilee arises no prophet.

53 And every man went to his own house.

CHAPTER 8

JESUS went to the mount of Olives.

2 And early in the morning he came again into the temple, and all the people came to him; and he sat down, and taught them.

3 And the scribes and Pharisees brought to him a woman taken in adultery; and when they had set her in the midst,

4 They said to him, Master, this woman was taken in adultery, in the very act.

5 Now Moses in the law commanded us, that such should be stoned: but what do you say?

6 This they said, tempting him, that they might have to accuse him. But Jesus stooped down, and with his finger wrote on the ground, as though he heard them not.

7 So when they continued asking him, he lifted up himself, and said to them, He that is without sin among you, let him first cast a stone at her.

8 And again he stooped down, and wrote on the ground.

9 And they which heard it, being convicted by their own conscience, went out one by one, beginning at the eldest, even to the last: and Jesus was left alone, and the woman standing in the midst.

10 When Jesus had lifted up himself, and saw none but the woman, he said to her, Woman, where are those your accus-

USING THE LAW IN EVANGELISM

8:4,5 The wrath of the Law brought this woman to the feet of the Savior. That's the function of the Law: to condemn. Some may say that we shouldn't *condemn* anyone, when all the Law does is reveal to the sinner that he is "condemned already" (John 3:18). The Law shows him his danger and therefore his desperate need for the Savior. See Galatians 3:19 comment.

7:52 This showed their ignorance of Scripture (see Isaiah 9:1,2), and of the fact that Jesus was born in Bethlehem.

8:6 It is likely that Jesus wrote the Ten Commandments on the ground. They had been talking about the Law, and each of the men were convicted by their conscience (v. 9), which is the effect of the Law (Romans 2:15). The Law was written in stone (uncompromising), this was written in sand (removable)—*besides, what else does God write with His finger?* See Exodus 31:18.

QUESTIONS & OBJECTIONS

8:11 *"Jesus didn't condemn the woman caught in the act of adultery, but condemned those who judged her. Therefore you shouldn't judge others."*

The Christian is not "judging others" but simply telling the world of *God's* judgment —that God (not the Christian) has judged all the world as being guilty before Him (Romans 3:19,23). Jesus was able to offer that woman forgiveness for her sin, because He was on His way to die on the cross for her. She acknowledged Him as "Lord," but He still told her, "Go, and sin no more." If she didn't repent, she would perish.

ers? has no man condemned you?

11 She said, No man, Lord. And Jesus said to her, Neither do I condemn you: go, and sin no more.

12 Then spoke Jesus again to them, saying, I am the light of the world: he that follows me shall not walk in darkness, but shall have the light of life.

13 The Pharisees therefore said to him, You bear record of yourself; your record is not true.

14 Jesus answered and said to them, Though I bear record of myself, yet my record is true: for I know whence I came, and where I go; but you cannot tell whence I come, and where I go.

15 You judge after the flesh; I judge no man.

16 And yet if I judge, my judgment is true: for I am not alone, but I and the Father that sent me.

17 It is also written in your law, that the testimony of two men is true.

18 I am one that bears witness of myself, and the Father that sent me bears witness of me.

19 Then said they to him, Where is your Father? Jesus answered, You neither know me, nor my Father: if you had known me, you should have known my Father also.

20 These words spoke Jesus in the treasury, as he taught in the temple: and no man laid hands on him; for his hour was not yet come.

21 Then said Jesus again to them, I go my way, and you shall seek me, and shall die in your sins: where I go, you cannot come.

22 Then said the Jews, Will he kill himself? because he says, Where I go, you cannot come.

23 And he said to them, You are from beneath; I am from above: you are of this world; I am not of this world.

24 I said therefore to you, that you shall die in your sins: for if you believe not that I am he, you shall die in your sins.

25 Then said they to him, Who are thou? And Jesus said to them, Even the same that I said to you from the beginning.

26 I have many things to say and to judge of you: but he that sent me is true;

8:10–12 What a fearful thing it is when we face God's Law. The very stones call for our blood. The Law cries out for justice; it has no mercy. It demands, "The soul that sins shall die!" But the Judge who rules can, at His own discretion, administer the *spirit* of the Law, and its spirit says that mercy rejoices over judgment—God is rich in mercy to all who call upon Him.

The letter kills, but the Spirit brings life. God is not willing that the wrath of the Law fall upon guilty sinners, because He would rather acquit the criminal from the courtroom…and He can do so because of Calvary.

A. N. Martin said, "The moment God's Law ceases to be the most powerful factor in influencing the moral sensitivity of any individual or nation, there will be indifference to Divine wrath, and when indifference comes in it always brings in its train indifference to salvation."

and I speak to the world those things which I have heard of him.

27 They understood not that he spoke to them of the Father.

28 Then said Jesus to them, When you have lifted up the Son of man, then shall you know that I am he, and that I do nothing of myself; but as my Father has taught me, I speak these things.

29 And he that sent me is with me: the Father has not left me alone; for I do always those things that please him.

30 As he spoke these words, many believed on him.

31 Then said Jesus to those Jews which believed on him, If you continue in my word, then are you my disciples indeed;

32 And you shall know the truth, and the truth shall make you free.

33 They answered him, We are Abraham's seed, and were never in bondage to any man: how do you say, You shall be made free?

34 Jesus answered them, Verily, verily, I say to you, Whosoever commits sin is the servant of sin.

35 And the servant abides not in the house for ever: but the Son abides ever.

36 If the Son therefore shall make you free, you shall be free indeed.

37 I know that you are Abraham's seed; but you seek to kill me, because my word has no place in you.

38 I speak that which I have seen with my Father: and you do that which you have seen with your father.

39 They answered and said to him, Abraham is our father. Jesus said to them, If you were Abraham's children, you would

do the works of Abraham.

40 But now you seek to kill me, a man that has told you the truth, which I have heard of God: this did not Abraham.

41 You do the deeds of your father. Then said they to him, We are not born of fornication; we have one Father, even God.

42 Jesus said to them, If God were your Father, you would love me: for I proceeded forth and came from God; neither came I of myself, but he sent me.

43 Why do you not understand my speech? even because you cannot hear my word.

44 You are of your father the devil, and the lusts of your father you will do. He was a murderer from the beginning, and abode not in the truth, because there is no truth in him. When he speaks a lie, he speaks of his own: for he is a liar, and the father of it.

45 And because I tell you the truth, you believe me not.

46 Which of you convinces me of sin? And if I say the truth, why do you not believe me?

47 He that is of God hears God's words: you therefore hear them not, because you are not of God.

48 Then answered the Jews, and said to him, Say we not well that you are a Samaritan, and have a devil?

49 Jesus answered, I have not a devil; but I honor my Father, and you do dishonor me.

50 And I seek not mine own glory: there is one that seeks and judges.

51 Verily, verily, I say to you, If a man keeps my saying, he shall never see death.

8:44 Names of the enemy. The devil is called the god and prince of this world, and the ruler of darkness (2 Corinthians 4:4; John 12:31; Acts 26:18; Ephesians 6:12). He seeks to hinder the work of God and suppress God's Word (Matthew 13:38,39; 1 Thessalonians 2:18). He is a liar, the father of lies, and a murderer (John 8:44). The devil is your adversary and a devourer (1 Peter 5:8). He is the promoter of pride (Genesis 3:5; 1 Timothy 3:6), the stimulator of lust (Ephesians 2:2,3), and the tempter (Luke 4:1–13).

8:51 Jesus' unique words: *Anyone* who obeys Him would not die. This is not advocating works as a means of salvation, but obedience as a *sign* of our salvation. We keep His word because we love Him (John 14:23). See 1 John 2:17 and John 8:58 comment.

52 Then said the Jews to him, Now we know that you have a devil. Abraham is dead, and the prophets; and you say, If a man keeps my saying, he shall never taste of death.

53 Are you greater than our father Abraham, which is dead? and the prophets are dead: whom do you make yourself?

54 Jesus answered, If I honor myself, my honor is nothing: it is my Father that honors me; of whom you say, that he is your God:

55 Yet you have not known him; but I know him: and if I should say, I know him not, I shall be a liar like you: but I know him, and keep his saying.

56 Your father Abraham rejoiced to see my day: and he saw it, and was glad.

57 Then said the Jews to him, You are not yet fifty years old, and have you seen Abraham?

58 Jesus said to them, Verily, verily, I say to you, Before Abraham was, I am.

59 Then took they up stones to cast at him: but Jesus hid himself, and went out of the temple, going through the midst of them, and so passed by.

CHAPTER 9

AND as Jesus passed by, he saw a man which was blind from his birth.

2 And his disciples asked him, saying, Master, who did sin, this man, or his parents, that he was born blind?

3 Jesus answered, Neither has this man sinned, nor his parents: but that the works of God should be made manifest in him.

4 I must work the works of him that sent me, while it is day: the night comes, when no man can work.

5 As long as I am in the world, I am the light of the world.

6 When he had thus spoken, he spat on the ground, and made clay of the spittle, and he anointed the eyes of the blind man with the clay,

7 And said to him, Go, wash in the pool of Siloam, (which is by interpretation, Sent.) He went his way therefore, and washed, and came seeing.

8 The neighbours therefore, and they which before had seen him that he was blind, said, Is not this he that sat and begged?

9 Some said, This is he: others said, He

8:58 Jesus' unique words: Jesus was affirming that He was God manifest in the flesh. He is the Great "I AM"—the Eternal One who revealed Himself to Moses in the burning bush (Exodus 3:14). See John 11:25 comment.

8:58 Was Jesus God in human form? If I give you a small slice of cheese from a large block (the taste being constant throughout the whole block), and you spit out the cheese saying you hate the taste, then you reject the whole block. Jesus was God manifest in human form. If the Jews rejected Him, they rejected the Father also—he who is of God hears God's words. John later stated in his epistle, "Whosoever denies the Son, the same has not the Father: (but) he that acknowledges the Son has the Father also" (1 John 2:23). See John 10:30.

9:4 *John Wesley* was asked what he would do with his life if he knew that he would die at midnight the next day. His answer was something like this: "I would just carry on with what I am doing. I will arise at 5:00 a.m. for prayer, then take a house meeting at 6.00 a.m. At 12 noon, I will be preaching at an open-air meeting. At 3:00 p.m. I have another meeting in another town. At 6:00 p.m. I have a house meeting; at 10:00 p.m. I have a prayer meeting and at 12:00 midnight, I would go to be with my Lord."

If we knew we were to die at 12 o'clock tomorrow night, would we have to step up our evangelistic efforts, or could we in all good conscience carry on just as we are?

"The evangelistic harvest is always urgent. The destiny of men and of nations is always being decided. Every generation is strategic. We are not responsible for the past generation, and we cannot bear the full responsibility for the next one; but we do have our generation. God will hold us responsible as to how well we fulfill our responsibilities to this age and take advantage of our opportunities." *Billy Graham*

THE FUNCTION OF THE LAW

9:7 When we apply the tablets of the Law to the eyes of sinners, it causes them to have reason to go to the cleansing pool of the gospel. This man would not have had a *reason* to go to the pool, until he perceived that he was unclean. That's the function of the Law—to convince a man he is unclean (Romans 7:13). *Charles Spurgeon* said, "No man will ever put on the robe of Christ's righteousness till he is stripped of his fig leaves, nor will he wash in the fount of mercy till he perceives his filthiness. Therefore, my brethren, we must not cease to declare the Law, its demands, its threatenings, and the sinner's multiplied breaches of it."

is like him: but he said, I am he.

10 Therefore said they to him, How were your eyes opened?

11 He answered and said, A man that is called Jesus made clay, and anointed mine eyes, and said to me, Go to the pool of Siloam, and wash: and I went and washed, and I received sight.

12 Then said they to him, Where is he? He said, I know not.

13 They brought to the Pharisees him that beforetime was blind.

14 And it was the sabbath day when Jesus made the clay, and opened his eyes.

15 Then again the Pharisees also asked him how he had received his sight. He said to them, He put clay upon mine eyes, and I washed, and do see.

16 Therefore said some of the Pharisees, This man is not of God, because he keeps not the sabbath day. Others said, How can a man that is a sinner do such miracles? And there was a division among them.

17 They said to the blind man again, What do you say of him, that he has opened your eyes? He said, He is a prophet.

18 But the Jews did not believe concerning him, that he had been blind, and received his sight, until they called the parents of him that had received his sight.

19 And they asked them, saying, Is this your son, who you say was born blind? how then does he now see?

20 His parents answered them and said, We know that this is our son, and that he was born blind:

21 But by what means he now sees, we know not; or who has opened his eyes, we know not: he is of age; ask him: he shall speak for himself.

22 These words spoke his parents, because they feared the Jews: for the Jews had agreed already, that if any man did confess that he was Christ, he should be put out of the synagogue.

23 Therefore said his parents, He is of age; ask him.

24 Then again called they the man that was blind, and said to him, Give God the praise: we know that this man is a sinner.

25 He answered and said, Whether he be a sinner or no, I know not: one thing I know, that, whereas I was blind, now I see.

26 Then said they to him again, What did he to you? how opened he your eyes?

27 He answered them, I have told you already, and you did not hear: wherefore would you hear it again? will you also be his disciples?

28 Then they reviled him, and said, You are his disciple; but we are Moses' disciples.

29 We know that God spoke to Moses: as for this fellow, we know not from whence he is.

30 The man answered and said to them, Why herein is a marvelous thing, that you know not from whence he is, and yet

9:25 This is the testimony of the newly saved. There are many questions for which they have no answers. But one thing they do know: "Whereas I was blind, now I see." It has been well said that the man with an experience is not at the mercy of a man with an argument.

he has opened mine eyes.

31 Now we know that God hears not sinners: but if any man be a worshipper of God, and does his will, him he hears.

32 Since the world began was it not heard that any man opened the eyes of one that was born blind.

33 If this man were not of God, he could do nothing.

34 They answered and said to him, You were altogether born in sins, and do you teach us? And they cast him out.

35 Jesus heard that they had cast him out; and when he had found him, he said to him, Do you believe on the Son of God?

36 He answered and said, Who is he, Lord, that I might believe on him?

37 And Jesus said to him, You have both seen him, and it is he that talks with you.

38 And he said, Lord, I believe. And he worshipped him.

39 And Jesus said, For judgment I am come into this world, that they which see not might see; and that they which see might be made blind.

40 And some of the Pharisees which were with him heard these words, and said to him, Are we blind also?

41 Jesus said to them, If you were blind, you should have no sin: but now you say, We see; therefore your sin remains.

CHAPTER 10

VERILY, verily, I say to you, He that enters not by the door into the sheepfold, but climbs up some other way, the same is a thief and a robber.

2 But he that enters in by the door is the shepherd of the sheep.

3 To him the porter opens; and the sheep hear his voice: and he calls his own sheep by name, and leads them out.

4 And when he puts forth his own sheep, he goes before them, and the sheep follow him: for they know his voice.

5 And a stranger will they not follow, but will flee from him: for they know not the voice of strangers.

6 This parable spoke Jesus to them: but they understood not what things they were which he spoke to them.

7 **Then said Jesus to them again, Verily, verily, I say to you, I am the door of the sheep.**

8 **All that ever came before me are thieves and robbers: but the sheep did not hear them.**

9 **I am the door: by me if any man enter in, he shall be saved, and shall go in and out, and find pasture.**

10 **The thief comes not, but for to steal, and to kill, and to destroy: I am come that they might have life, and that they**

10:2 True believers are likened to sheep, which: know the voice of their shepherd; are easily led (they submit without resistance); flock together (in unity); need a shepherd (or they stray); were a type of Israel (Matthew 10:6); imitate one another; are productive (wool, leather, meat, and milk); were a sign of God's blessing (see Deuteronomy 7:13); will be divided from the "goats" at the Judgment; were offered in sacrifice.

10:9 A Hebrew servant who was given his freedom had the option to stay with a master he loved. If he chose to give up his freedom, his master took him to the doorpost and pierced his ear with an awl, "and he shall serve him forever" (Exodus 21:5,6). In the same way, the sinner, upon conversion, is given freedom from sin and becomes a servant of Jesus Christ (1 Corinthians 7:22), to serve Him forever. He presents his body as a living sacrifice. His ear is forever open to the Door of the Savior (John 10:9).

10:10 "Evangelism is about experiencing God. If you choose to be obedient, He will take you on a journey so exciting that your life will never be the same." *Bill Fay, Share Jesus Without Fear*

"Evangelism is the cure to the disease of church boredom." *Todd P. McCollum*

"I can tell you that there is no greater joy than leading someone to faith in Jesus Christ. Even if they reject your message, it still feels great to obey Christ. Yet regardless of how we feel, we need to remember this is what He has commanded." *D. James Kennedy*

might have it more abundantly.

11 I am the good shepherd: the good shepherd gives his life for the sheep.

12 But he that is an hireling, and not the shepherd, whose own the sheep are not, sees the wolf coming, and leaves the sheep, and flees: and the wolf catches them, and scatters the sheep.

13 The hireling flees, because he is an hireling, and cares not for the sheep.

14 I am the good shepherd, and know my sheep, and am known of mine.

15 As the Father knows me, even so know I the Father: and I lay down my life for the sheep.

16 And other sheep I have, which are not of this fold: them also I must bring, and they shall hear my voice; and there shall be one fold, and one shepherd.

17 Therefore does my Father love me, because I lay down my life, that I might take it again.

18 **No man takes it from me, but I lay it down of myself. I have power to lay it down, and I have power to take it again. This commandment have I received of my Father.**

19 There was a division therefore again among the Jews for these sayings.

20 And many of them said, He has a devil, and is mad; why do you hear him?

21 Others said, These are not the words of him that has a devil. Can a devil open the eyes of the blind?

22 And it was at Jerusalem the feast of the dedication, and it was winter.

23 And Jesus walked in the temple in Solomon's porch.

24 Then came the Jews round about him, and said to him, How long do you make us to doubt? If you be the Christ, tell us plainly.

25 Jesus answered them, I told you, and you believed not: the works that I do in my Father's name, they bear witness of me.

The Bible is unique and proves itself to be supernatural in origin.
See Psalm 119:105 comment.

26 But you believe not, because you are not of my sheep, as I said to you.

27 My sheep hear my voice, and I know them, and they follow me:

28 And I give to them eternal life; and they shall never perish, neither shall any man pluck them out of my hand.

29 My Father, which gave them me, is greater than all; and no man is able to pluck them out of my Father's hand.

30 I and my Father are one.

10:11 Hundreds of years earlier, David had written that the Lord was his shepherd, and now that Shepherd had become flesh. Here is a continuance of the most famous of psalms, Psalm 23. This was the "Great Shepherd" Himself (Hebrews 13:20), the One who takes away the "want" of the covetous human heart. He was the path of righteousness, who brought light to the valley of the shadow of death. Here was the Bread of Life, placed by God on a table in the presence of our enemies. Heaven's cup "ran over," and brought the Father's goodness and mercy to us, so that we might dwell in the House of the Lord forever.

10:16 The Mormons misrepresent this verse. It is an obvious reference to the Gentiles. See John 11:52; Romans 15:9–12; Ephesians 2:11–18.

10:27 See 2 Timothy 2:19 comment.

10:30 Was Jesus God in human form? See John 10:38.

31 Then the Jews took up stones again to stone him.

32 Jesus answered them, Many good works have I showed you from my Father; for which of those works do you stone me?

33 The Jews answered him, saying, For a good work we stone you not; but for blasphemy; and because that you, being a man, make yourself God.

34 Jesus answered them, Is it not written in your law, I said, You are gods?

35 If he called them gods, to whom the word of God came, and the scripture cannot be broken;

36 Do you say of him, whom the Father has sanctified, and sent into the world, You blaspheme; because I said, I am the Son of God?

> Preach Christ or nothing: don't dispute or discuss except with your eye on the cross.
>
> **CHARLES SPURGEON**

37 If I do not the works of my Father, believe me not.

38 But if I do, though you believe not me, believe the works: that you may know, and believe, that the Father is in me, and I in him.

39 Therefore they sought again to take him: but he escaped out of their hand,

40 And went away again beyond Jordan into the place where John at first baptized; and there he abode.

41 And many resorted to him, and said, John did no miracle: but all things that John spoke of this man were true.

42 And many believed on him there.

CHAPTER 11

NOW a certain man was sick, named Lazarus, of Bethany, the town of Mary and her sister Martha.

2 (It was that Mary which anointed the Lord with ointment, and wiped his feet with her hair, whose brother Lazarus was sick.)

3 Therefore his sisters sent to him, saying, Lord, behold, he whom you love is sick.

4 When Jesus heard that, he said, This sickness is not to death, but for the glory of God, that the Son of God might be glorified thereby.

5 Now Jesus loved Martha, and her sister, and Lazarus.

6 When he had heard therefore that he was sick, he abode two days still in the same place where he was.

7 Then after that said he to his disciples, Let us go into Judea again.

8 His disciples said to him, Master, the Jews of late sought to stone you; and you go there again?

9 Jesus answered, Are there not twelve hours in the day? If any man walk in the day, he stumbles not, because he sees the light of this world.

10 But if a man walk in the night, he stumbles, because there is no light in him.

11 These things said he: and after that he said to them, Our friend Lazarus sleeps; but I go, that I may awake him out of sleep.

12 Then said his disciples, Lord, if he sleep, he shall do well.

10:38 Was Jesus God in human form? See John 14:10.

11:6 God's ways are distinctively and consistently different from ours. God did not rescue Daniel out of the lion's den as we would have. He didn't turn off the fiery furnace into which Shadrach, Meshach, and Abed-Nego were cast, as we would. He didn't kill Pharaoh and save the Israelites from the Red Sea; instead He worked His wondrous purposes *in* the lion's den, *in* the furnace, and *in* the Red Sea. Lion's teeth, fire, and water are no big deal to the God who created them. Death, at the presence of the Light of the world, is but a shadow that quickly dissipates like a frightened and sickly child.

10:36 *The Deity of Jesus*

From *Christ Before the Manger* by *Ron Rhodes*

A strong argument for the deity of Christ is the fact that many of the names, titles, and attributes ascribed to Yahweh are also ascribed to Jesus Christ.

DESCRIPTION	FATHER	JESUS
Yahweh ("I AM")	Exodus 3:14 Deuteronomy 32:39 Isaiah 43:10	John 8:24 John 8:58 John 18:4–6
God	Genesis 1:1 Deuteronomy 6:4 Psalm 45:6,7	Isaiah 7:14 Isaiah 9:6 John 1:1,14 John 20:28 Titus 2:13 Hebrews 1:8 2 Peter 1:1 Matthew 1:23 1 John 5:20
Alpha and Omega (First and Last)	Isaiah 41:4 Isaiah 48:12 Revelation 1:8	Revelation 1:17,18 Revelation 2:8 Revelation 22:12–16
Lord	Isaiah 45:23	Matthew 12:8 Acts 7:59,60 Acts 10:36 Romans 10:12 1 Corinthians 2:8 1 Corinthians 12:3 Philippians 2:10,11
Savior	Isaiah 43:3 Isaiah 43:11 Isaiah 49:26 Isaiah 63:8 Luke 1:47 1 Timothy 4:10	Matthew 1:21 Luke 2:11 John 1:29 John 4:42 2 Timothy 1:10 Titus 2:13 Hebrews 5:9
King	Psalm 95:3 Isaiah 43:15 1 Timothy 6:14–16	Revelation 17:14 Revelation 19:16
Judge	Genesis 18:25 Deuteronomy 32:36 Psalm 50:4,6 Psalm 58:11 Psalm 75:7 Psalm 96:13	John 5:22 2 Corinthians 5:10 2 Timothy 4:1
Light	2 Samuel 22:29 Psalm 27:1	John 1:4,9 John 3:19 John 8:12 John 9:5

(continued)

(10:36 *continued*)

DESCRIPTION	FATHER	JESUS
Rock	Deuteronomy 32:3,4 2 Samuel 22:32 Psalm 89:26	Romans 9:33 1 Corinthians 10:3,4 1 Peter 2:4–8
Redeemer	Psalm 130:7,8 Isaiah 43:1 Isaiah 48:17 Isaiah 49:26 Isaiah 54:5	Acts 20:28 Ephesians 1:7 Hebrews 9:12
Our Righteousness	Isaiah 45:24	Jeremiah 23:6 Romans 3:21,22
Husband	Isaiah 54:5 Hosea 2:16	Matthew 25:1 Mark 2:18,19 2 Corinthians 11:2 Ephesians 5:25–32 Revelation 21:2,9
Shepherd	Genesis 49:24 Psalm 23:1 Psalm 80:1	John 10:11,16 Hebrews 13:20 1 Peter 2:25 1 Peter 5:4
Creator	Genesis 1:1 Job 33:4 Psalm 95:5,6 Psalm 102:24,25 Isaiah 40:28 Isaiah 43:1 Acts 4:24	John 1:2,3,10 Colossians 1:15–18 Hebrews 1:1–3,10
Giver of Life	Genesis 2:7 Deuteronomy 32:39 1 Samuel 2:6 Psalm 36:9	John 5:21 John 10:28 John 11:25
Forgiver of Sin	Exodus 34:6,7 Nehemiah 9:17 Daniel 9:9 Jonah 4:2	Matthew 9:2 Mark 2:1–12 Acts 26:18 Colossians 2:13 Colossians 3:13
Lord our Healer	Exodus 15:26	Acts 9:34
Omnipresent	Psalm 139:7–12 Proverbs 15:3	Matthew 18:20 Matthew 28:20 Ephesians 3:17 Ephesians 4:10
Omniscient	1 Kings 8:39 Jeremiah 17:10,16	Matthew 9:4 Matthew 11:27 Luke 5:4–6 John 2:25 John 16:30 John 21:17 Acts 1:24

(*continued*)

(10:36 continued)

DESCRIPTION	FATHER	JESUS
Omnipotent	Isaiah 40:10–31 Isaiah 45:5–13 Revelation 19:6	Matthew 28:18 Mark 1:29–34 John 10:18 Jude 24
Preexistent	Genesis 1:1	John 1:15,30 John 3:13,31,32 John 6:62 John 16:28 John 17:5
Eternal	Psalm 102:26,27 Habakkuk 3:6	Isaiah 9:6 Micah 5:2 John 8:58
Immutable	Malachi 3:6 James 1:17	Hebrews 13:8
Receiver of worship	Matthew 4:10 John 4:24 Revelation 5:14 Revelation 7:11 Revelation 11:16 Revelation 19:4,10	Matthew 2:8,11 Matthew 14:33 Matthew 28:9 John 9:38 Philippians 2:10,11 Hebrews 1:6
Hope	Jeremiah 17:7	1 Timothy 1:1
Speaker with divine authority	"Thus saith the Lord…" —used hundreds of times	Matthew 23:34–37 John 3:5 John 7:46 "Truly, truly, I say…"
Who raised Jesus from the dead?	Acts 2:24,32 Romans 8:11 1 Corinthians 6:14	John 2:19–22 John 10:17,18 Matthew 27:40
Who gets the glory?	Isaiah 42:8 Isaiah 48:11	Hebrews 13:21 John 17:5

13 Howbeit Jesus spoke of his death: but they thought that he had spoken of taking of rest in sleep.

14 Then said Jesus to them plainly, Lazarus is dead.

15 And I am glad for your sakes that I was not there, to the intent you may believe; nevertheless let us go to him.

16 Then said Thomas, which is called Didymus, to his fellow-disciples, Let us also go, that we may die with him.

17 Then when Jesus came, he found that he had lain in the grave four days already.

18 Now Bethany was near to Jerusalem, about fifteen furlongs off:

19 And many of the Jews came to Martha and Mary, to comfort them concerning their brother.

20 Then Martha, as soon as she heard that Jesus was coming, went and met him: but Mary sat still in the house.

21 Then said Martha to Jesus, Lord, if you had been here, my brother had not died.

22 But I know, that even now, whatsoever you will ask of God, God will give it you.

23 Jesus said to her, Your brother shall

11:14 How to Preach at a Funeral for Someone You Suspect Died Unsaved

By Mike Smalley

1. Start in the natural realm and swing to the spiritual.

2. Say something positive about the person who has died—either personally, or their marriage, kids, work ethic, their generation, etc. This should build rapport with the audience. Use a humorous story that relates to the above.

3. Don't feel pressured to mention where the deceased may have gone after death (God is the only One who truly knows).

4. Never insinuate that he went to heaven.

5. Use this as a springboard: "Good friends often remind us of things that we don't want to deal with, but that are very important. Bob, today, reminds us that we *all* must die."

6. Use anecdotes that convey eternal truths.

7. Go quickly but thoroughly through each of the Ten Commandments.

8. Warn briefly about sin, death, judgment, and eternity.

9. Give a clear gospel presentation.

10. Appeal to the audience to repent today.

"When anyone dies, I ask myself, 'Was I faithful?' Did I speak all the truth? And did I speak it from my very soul every time I preached?" *Charles Spurgeon*

---

rise again.

24 Martha said to him, I know that he shall rise again in the resurrection at the last day.

25 Jesus said to her, I am the resurrection, and the life: he that believes in me, though he were dead, yet shall he live:
26 **And whosoever lives and believes in me shall never die. Do you believe this?**
27 She said to him, Yea, Lord: I believe that you are the Christ, the Son of God, which should come into the world.

28 And when she had so said, she went her way, and called Mary her sister secretly, saying, The Master is come, and calls for you.

29 As soon as she heard that, she arose quickly, and came to him.

30 Now Jesus was not yet come into the town, but was in that place where Martha met him.

31 The Jews then which were with her in the house, and comforted her, when they saw Mary, that she rose up hastily and went out, followed her, saying, She goes to the grave to weep there.

32 Then when Mary was come where Jesus was, and saw him, she fell down at his feet, saying to him, Lord, if you had been here, my brother had not died.

33 When Jesus therefore saw her weeping, and the Jews also weeping which came with her, he groaned in the spirit, and was troubled,

34 And said, Where have you laid him? They said to him, Lord, come and see.

35 Jesus wept.

36 Then said the Jews, Behold how he loved him!

37 And some of them said, Could not this man, which opened the eyes of the blind, have caused that even this man should

---

11:25   The uniqueness of Jesus. "A man who was merely a man and said the sort of things Jesus said wouldn't be a great moral teacher. He'd either be a lunatic—on a level with the man who says he's a poached egg—or else he'd be the Devil of Hell. You must make your choice. Either this man was, and is, the Son of God: or else a madman or something worse. You can shut Him up for a fool, you can spit at Him and kill Him as a demon; or you can fall at His feet and call Him Lord and God. But don't let us come with any patronizing nonsense about His being a great human teacher. He hasn't left that open to us. He didn't intend to." *C. S. Lewis, The Case for Christianity*

11:25   Jesus' unique words: See John 14:6 comment.

not have died?

38 Jesus therefore again groaning in himself came to the grave. It was a cave, and a stone lay upon it.

39 Jesus said, Take away the stone. Martha, the sister of him that was dead, said to him, Lord, by this time he stinks: for he has been dead four days.

40 Jesus said to her, Said I not to you, that, if you would believe, you should see the glory of God?

41 Then they took away the stone from the place where the dead was laid. And Jesus lifted up his eyes, and said, Father, I thank you that you have heard me.

42 And I knew that you hear me always: but because of the people which stand by I said it, that they may believe that you have sent me.

43 And when he thus had spoken, he cried with a loud voice, Lazarus, come forth.

44 And he that was dead came forth, bound hand and foot with graveclothes: and his face was bound about with a napkin. Jesus said to them, Loose him, and let him go.

45 Then many of the Jews which came to Mary, and had seen the things which Jesus did, believed on him.

46 But some of them went their ways to the Pharisees, and told them what things Jesus had done.

47 Then gathered the chief priests and the Pharisees a council, and said, What do we? for this man does many miracles.

48 If we let him thus alone, all men will believe on him: and the Romans shall come and take away both our place and nation.

49 And one of them, named Caiaphas, being the high priest that same year, said to them, You know nothing at all,

50 Nor consider that it is expedient for us, that one man should die for the people, and that the whole nation perish not.

51 And this spoke he not of himself: but being high priest that year, he prophe-

---

11:35 In one sense, this verse is a mystery because Jesus knew what He was about to do. He was about to give Mary and Martha the greatest gift, outside of salvation, that they could ever hope for. Yet, He wept.

The prophets tell us that the Messiah would be a "man of sorrows, and acquainted with grief" (Isaiah 53:3). He was moved with compassion for the multitudes, wept over Jerusalem, and knew what it was to "weep with those who weep." Even though we have heaven before us, it pains the Head of the Body when the foot hurts. Jesus is a High Priest who is "touched with the feeling of our infirmities" (Hebrews 4:15).

11:43,44 The words of Jesus cut through the icy grip of death like a white-hot blade through soft powdered snow. The same Word that brought life in the beginning breathed life into the decomposing corpse of Lazarus. Suddenly, from the blackened shadow of the tomb appeared a figure, wrapped in grave clothes. As he stood at the entrance of the tomb (for tombs didn't need an exit until that day), his face and body were covered with grave clothes. God took him by the hand and led him to the light.

What a picture of what is before us! The hour is coming when all who are in their graves will hear His voice. The victory Lazarus had over death was bad news for the devil and the undertaker, but it was only a temporary triumph, for the undertaker would eventually get his deathly fee. Lazarus would ultimately depart from this earth, but the time is coming when death shall be no more. On that day, we will exchange these vile, perishing bodies for incorruptible bodies that will never feel pain, disease, or death:

> "So when this corruptible shall have put on incorruption, and this mortal shall have put on immortality, then shall be brought to pass the saying that is written, Death is swallowed up in victory" (1 Corinthians 15:54).

For those who trust in Jesus, this body is but a chrysalis, which may become wrinkled and crusty with age, but it is just a shell that will be dropped off as the new butterfly emerges.

sied that Jesus should die for that nation;

52 And not for that nation only, but that also he should gather together in one the children of God that were scattered abroad.

53 Then from that day forth they took counsel together for to put him to death.

54 Jesus therefore walked no more openly among the Jews; but went thence to a country near to the wilderness, into a city called Ephraim, and there continued with his disciples.

55 And the Jews' passover was near at hand: and many went out of the country up to Jerusalem before the passover, to purify themselves.

56 Then sought they for Jesus, and spoke among themselves, as they stood in the temple, What do you think, that he will not come to the feast?

57 Now both the chief priests and the Pharisees had given a commandment, that, if any man knew where he were, he should show it, that they might take him.

CHAPTER 12

THEN Jesus six days before the passover came to Bethany, where Lazarus was which had been dead, whom he raised from the dead.

2 There they made him a supper; and Martha served: but Lazarus was one of them that sat at the table with him.

3 Then took Mary a pound of ointment of spikenard, very costly, and anointed the feet of Jesus, and wiped his feet with her hair: and the house was filled with the odor of the ointment.

4 Then said one of his disciples, Judas Iscariot, Simon's son, which should betray him,

5 Why was not this ointment sold for three hundred pence, and given to the poor?

6 This he said, not that he cared for the poor; but because he was a thief, and had the bag, and bare what was put therein.

7 Then said Jesus, Let her alone: against the day of my burying has she kept this.

8 For the poor always you have with you; but me you have not always.

> Men have been helped to live by remembering that they must die.
>
> **CHARLES SPURGEON**

9 Much people of the Jews therefore knew that he was there: and they came not for Jesus' sake only, but that they might see Lazarus also, whom he had raised from the dead.

10 But the chief priests consulted that they might put Lazarus also to death;

11 Because that by reason of him many of the Jews went away, and believed on Jesus.

12 On the next day much people that were come to the feast, when they heard that Jesus was coming to Jerusalem,

13 Took branches of palm trees, and went forth to meet him, and cried, Hosanna: Blessed is the King of Israel that comes

---

12:9 The undertaker's nightmare. The Son of God created havoc for undertakers by speaking to their frigid merchandise. His voice was supernatural. A mere "Lazarus, come forth," spoken to a corpse meant a nightmarish dilemma for the Bethany funeral director, because he was left with no body to deal with. Up until that moment, his business was mortally secure. Four days after the death, he had everything wrapped up, when suddenly, three words unraveled his inanimate toil. Reimbursement of all funeral expenses was just the beginning of the bad dream. Death was his living, and if this stranger from Nazareth continued to speak around graves, his business itself would soon be terminal. Jesus Christ was the undertaker's nightmare because death bowed its vile knee to His voice, and the day is promised when all undertakers will hit the unemployment line!

The raising of Lazarus snatched the profit from the undertaker; but the incident happened *for* the inestimable profit of humanity. It was the long-awaited fulfillment of what was spoken of by the prophets of old. It was a beam of wondrous and glistening light in the most hopeless and darkest of all caves.

in the name of the Lord.

14 And Jesus, when he had found a young ass, sat thereon; as it is written,

15 Fear not, daughter of Zion: behold, your King comes, sitting on an ass's colt.

16 These things understood not his disciples at the first: but when Jesus was glorified, then remembered they that these things were written of him, and that they had done these things to him.

17 The people therefore that was with him when he called Lazarus out of his grave, and raised him from the dead, bare record.

18 For this cause the people also met him, for that they heard that he had done this miracle.

19 The Pharisees therefore said among themselves, Perceive how you prevail nothing? behold, the world is gone after him.

20 And there were certain Greeks among them that came up to worship at the feast:

21 The same came therefore to Philip, which was of Bethsaida of Galilee, and desired him, saying, Sir, we would see Jesus.

22 Philip came and told Andrew: and again Andrew and Philip tell Jesus.

23 And Jesus answered them, saying, The hour is come, that the Son of man should be glorified.

24 Verily, verily, I say to you, Except a corn of wheat fall into the ground and die, it abides alone: but if it die, it brings forth much fruit.

25 He that loves his life shall lose it; and he that hates his life in this world shall keep it to life eternal.

26 *If any man serve me, let him follow me; and where I am, there shall also my servant be: if any man serve me, him will my Father honor.*

27 Now is my soul troubled; and what shall I say? Father, save me from this hour: but for this cause came I to this hour.

28 Father, glorify your name. Then came there a voice from heaven, saying, I have both glorified it, and will glorify it again.

29 The people therefore, that stood by, and heard it, said that it thundered: others said, An angel spoke to him.

30 Jesus answered and said, This voice came not because of me, but for your sakes.

31 Now is the judgment of this world: now shall the prince of this world be cast out.

32 And I, if I be lifted up from the earth, will draw all men to me.

33 This he said, signifying what death he should die.

34 The people answered him, We have heard out of the law that Christ abides for ever: and how do you say, The Son of man must be lifted up? who is this Son of man?

35 Then Jesus said to them, Yet a little while is the light with you. Walk while you have the light, lest darkness come upon you: for he that walks in darkness knows not where he goes.

36 While you have light, believe in the light, that you may be the children of light. These things spoke Jesus, and departed, and did hide himself from them.

37 But though he had done so many miracles before them, yet they believed not on him:

38 That the saying of Isaiah the prophet might be fulfilled, which he spoke, Lord,

---

12:14 Instead of riding triumphantly through the streets of Jerusalem on a kingly white stallion, He chose to ride on a young donkey, a lowly beast of burden. Imagine how humbling it would be for the president of the United States to ride through New York on the back of a donkey. But this is what the King of kings did. This time He came in lowliness, humbling Himself and becoming obedient to the death of the cross. The next time He will come in flaming fire, on a white horse with ten thousands of His saints.

12:25 "The greatest proof of Christianity for others is not how far a man can logically analyze his reasons for believing, but how far in practice he will stake his life on his belief." *T. S. Eliot*

who has believed our report? and to whom has the arm of the Lord been revealed?

39 Therefore they could not believe, because that Isaiah said again,

40 He has blinded their eyes, and hardened their heart; that they should not see with their eyes, nor understand with their heart, and be converted, and I should heal them.

41 These things said Isaiah, when he saw his glory, and spoke of him.

42 Nevertheless among the chief rulers also many believed on him; but because of the Pharisees they did not confess him, lest they should be put out of the synagogue:

43 For they loved the praise of men more than the praise of God.

44 **Jesus cried and said, He that believes on me, believes not on me, but on him that sent me.**

45 **And he that sees me sees him that sent me.**

46 **I am come a light into the world, that whosoever believes on me should not abide in darkness.**

47 And if any man hear my words, and believe not, I judge him not: for I came not to judge the world, but to save the world.

48 He that rejects me, and receives not my words, has one that judges him: the word that I have spoken, the same shall judge him in the last day.

49 **For I have not spoken of myself; but the Father which sent me, he gave me a commandment, what I should say, and what I should speak.**

50 **And I know that his commandment is life everlasting: whatsoever I speak**

therefore, **even as the Father said to me, so I speak.**

CHAPTER 13

NOW before the feast of the passover, when Jesus knew that his hour was come that he should depart out of this world to the Father, having loved his own which were in the world, he loved them to the end.

2 And supper being ended, the devil having now put into the heart of Judas Iscariot, Simon's son, to betray him;

3 Jesus knowing that the Father had given all things into his hands, and that he was come from God, and went to God;

4 He rose from supper, and laid aside his garments; and took a towel, and girded himself.

5 After that he poured water into a basin, and began to wash the disciples' feet, and to wipe them with the towel wherewith he was girded.

6 Then came he to Simon Peter: and Peter said to him, Lord, do you wash my feet?

7 Jesus answered and said to him, What I do you know not now; but you shall know hereafter.

8 Peter said to him, You shall never wash my feet. Jesus answered him, If I wash you not, you have no part with me.

9 Simon Peter said to him, Lord, not my feet only, but also my hands and my head.

10 Jesus said to him, He that is washed needs not save to wash his feet, but is clean every whit: and you are clean, but not all.

11 For he knew who should betray him; therefore said he, You are not all clean.

12:38 One would think that a terminally ill world would gladly embrace the cure of the gospel, but few, so few believe our report.

13:2 While "the devil made me do it" will not be a valid defense on Judgment Day, if more people would believe that the devil is at work in their lives, our prisons would be less full and human suffering would be much less.

So often we hear of people feeling "compelled" to kill, and thinking the impulses were their own. If potential homosexuals understood the influence of unclean spirits, they would be less likely to follow every grimy impulse that comes into their minds. Those who believe that our battle is not against flesh and blood, but demonic personalities, will then be less prone to be tools of darkness.

12 So after he had washed their feet, and had taken his garments, and was set down again, he said to them, Do you know what I have done to you?

13 You call me Master and Lord: and you say well; for so I am.

14 If I then, your Lord and Master, have washed your feet; you also ought to wash one another's feet.

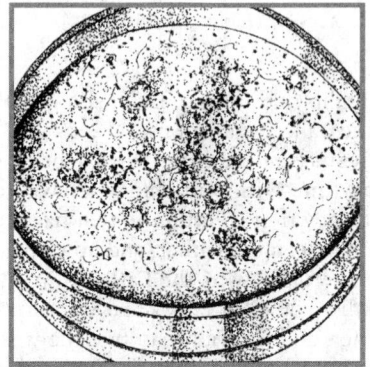

The Bible gives instructions on how to avoid diseases, thousands of years before man discovered their cause. See Hebrews 11:3 comment.

15 For I have given you an example, that you should do as I have done to you.

16 Verily, verily, I say to you, The servant is not greater than his lord; neither he that is sent greater than he that sent him.

17 If you know these things, happy are you if you do them.

18 I speak not of you all: I know whom I have chosen: but that the scripture may be fulfilled, He that eats bread with me has lifted up his heel against me.

19 Now I tell you before it come, that, when it is come to pass, you may believe that I am he.

20 Verily, verily, I say to you, He that receives whomsoever I send receives me; and he that receives me receives him that sent me.

21 When Jesus had thus said, he was troubled in spirit, and testified, and said, Verily, verily, I say to you, that one of you shall betray me.

22 Then the disciples looked one on another, doubting of whom he spoke.

23 Now there was leaning on Jesus' bosom one of his disciples, whom Jesus loved.

24 Simon Peter therefore beckoned to him, that he should ask who it should be of whom he spoke.

25 He then lying on Jesus' breast said to him, Lord, who is it?

26 Jesus answered, He it is, to whom I shall give a sop, when I have dipped it. And when he had dipped the sop, he gave it to Judas Iscariot, the son of Simon.

27 And after the sop Satan entered into him. Then said Jesus to him, That you do, do quickly.

28 Now no man at the table knew for what intent he spoke this to him.

29 For some of them thought, because Judas had the bag, that Jesus had said to him, Buy those things that we have need of against the feast; or, that he should give something to the poor.

30 He then having received the sop went immediately out: and it was night.

31 Therefore, when he was gone out, Jesus said, Now is the Son of man glorified, and God is glorified in him.

32 If God be glorified in him, God shall also glorify him in himself, and shall straightway glorify him.

33 Little children, yet a little while I am with you. You shall seek me: and as I said to the Jews, Where I go, you cannot come; so now I say to you.

34 A new commandment I give to you, That you love one another; as I have loved you, that you also love one another.

35 By this shall all men know that you are my disciples, if you have love one to another.

36 Simon Peter said to him, Lord, where are you going? Jesus answered him, Where I go, you can not follow me now; but you shall follow me afterwards.

37 Peter said to him, Lord, why cannot I follow you now? I will lay down my life for your sake.

38 Jesus answered him, Will you lay down your life for my sake? Verily, verily,

QUESTIONS & OBJECTIONS

14:6 *"It's intolerant to say that Jesus is the only way to God!"*

Jesus is the One who said that He is the only way to the Father. For Christians to say that there are other ways to find peace with God is to bear false testimony. In one sweeping statement, Jesus discards all other religions as a means of finding forgiveness of sins. This agrees with other Scriptures: "Neither is there salvation in any other: for there is no other name under heaven given among men, whereby we must be saved" (Acts 4:12), and "For there is one God, and one mediator between God and men, the man Christ Jesus" (1 Timothy 2:5).

I say to you, The cock shall not crow, till you have denied me thrice.

CHAPTER 14

LET not your heart be troubled: you believe in God, believe also in me.

2 In my Father's house are many mansions: if it were not so, I would have told you. I go to prepare a place for you.

3 And if I go and prepare a place for you, I will come again, and receive you to myself; that where I am, there you may be also.

4 And where I go you know, and the way you know.

5 Thomas said to him, Lord, we know not where you go; and how can we know the way?

6 Jesus said to him, I am the way, the truth, and the life: no man comes to the Father, but by me.

7 If you had known me, you should have known my Father also: and from henceforth you know him, and have seen him.

8 Philip said to him, Lord, show us the Father, and it suffices us.

9 Jesus said to him, Have I been so long time with you, and yet have you not known me, Philip? he that has seen me has seen the Father; and how do you say then, Show us the Father?

10 Do you not believe that I am in the Father, and the Father in me? the words that I speak to you I speak not of myself: but the Father that dwells in me, he does the works.

11 Believe me that I am in the Father, and the Father in me: or else believe me for the very works' sake.

12 *Verily, verily, I say to you, He that believes on me, the works that I do shall he do also; and greater works than these shall he do; because I go to my Father.*

13 And whatsoever you shall ask in my name, that will I do, that the Father may be glorified in the Son.

14 If you shall ask any thing in my name, I will do it.

14:2 Faith in God clears the muddy waters of fear. The Christian who has confidence in Jesus Christ knows that his eternal footsteps have been ordered by the Lord, and that there is a mansion prepared for him that his wildest imaginations could not conceive. If these things weren't so, Jesus would have told us. *He is not a liar.* His word is sure and steadfast, a mooring for the soul, and those who come into the harbor of a calm faith in God have perfect peace in the troubled storms of this world.

14:6 **Jesus' unique words:** *Paige Patterson* stated, "It comes down to a question of truth. Every false religious expression is a religion of darkness. That doesn't mean there are no good things in that faith. But if Jesus is to be taken seriously when He says, 'No one comes to the Father but through Me,' every other proposal is one of darkness." See John 14:21 comment.

14:10 **Was Jesus God in human form?** See John 17:22.

QUESTIONS & OBJECTIONS

14:21 *"I made a commitment, but nothing happened."*

Some people don't get past "square one" because they trust in their feelings rather than God. His promises are true, despite our feelings. If I make a promise to my wife, that promise is true whether she is feeling happy or sad. If she doubts my word, then she brings a slur to my integrity.

Anyone who genuinely repents and trusts in Christ will be saved. The Bible makes this promise: "He that has my commandments, and keeps them, he it is that loves me: and he that loves me shall be loved of my Father, and I will love him, and will manifest myself to him" [John 14:21]. There's the promise, and there's the condition. Any person who loves and obeys Jesus will begin a supernatural relationship with Him and the Father. He said, "And this is life eternal, that they might know you the only true God, and Jesus Christ, whom you have sent" (John 17:3). That doesn't mean you will hear voices or see visions. God will instead make you a new person from within. He will send His Spirit to live within you. You will have a new heart with new desires. You will suddenly become conscious of God and His creation. The Bible will open up to you and become a living Word, and you will have an inner witness that you are saved, that your name is written in heaven, and that death has lost its sting (1 John 5:10–12).

15 If you love me, keep my commandments.

16 And I will pray the Father, and he shall give you another Comforter, that he may abide with you for ever;

17 Even the Spirit of truth; whom the world cannot receive, because it sees him not, neither knows him: but you know him; for he dwells with you, and shall be in you.

18 I will not leave you comfortless: I will come to you.

19 Yet a little while, and the world sees me no more; but you see me: because I live, you shall live also.

20 At that day you shall know that I am in my Father, and you in me, and I in you.

21 He that has my commandments, and keeps them, he it is that loves me: and he that loves me shall be loved of my Father, and I will love him, and will manifest myself to him.

22 Judas said to him, not Iscariot, Lord, how is it that you will manifest yourself to us, and not to the world?

23 Jesus answered and said to him, If a man love me, he will keep my words: and my Father will love him, and we will come to him, and make our abode with him.

24 He that loves me not keeps not my sayings: and the word which you hear is not mine, but the Father's which sent me.

25 These things have I spoken to you,

14:14 In 1 Kings 3:5, the LORD appeared to Solomon in a dream by night, and said, "Ask! What shall I give you?" God asks us the same question. Be like Solomon and ask for wisdom. God promises to give it liberally (James 1:5). He who gets wisdom loves his own soul (Proverbs 19:8). If you have wisdom, you will think right, do right, and speak right. Remember: He who wins souls is wise (Proverbs 11:30).

14:15 We show our love for God by our obedience. If we do not obey, we do not truly love Him (see vv. 23,24). There are many who call Him "Lord, Lord," but do not do what He says. Matthew 7:21–23 tells us their fearful fate.

14:21 Jesus' unique words: Jesus promises that He and the Father will reveal themselves to all who love and obey Him. This is the ultimate challenge to any skeptic. See John 17:5 comment.

SPRINGBOARDS FOR PREACHING AND WITNESSING

15:13

Revolting Natives

An African chief got wind of a mutiny being planned in his tribe. In an effort to quash the revolt, he called the tribe together and said that *anyone* caught in rebellion would be given one hundred lashes, *without mercy.*

A short time later, to the chief's dismay he found that his own brother was behind the revolt. He was trying to overthrow him so he could be head of the tribe. Everyone thought the chief would break his word. But being a just man, he had his brother tied to a tree. Then he had himself tied next to him, *and he took those one hundred lashes across his own bare flesh, in his brother's place.* In doing so, he not only kept his word (justice was done), but he also demonstrated his great love and forgiveness toward his brother.

being yet present with you.

26 But the Comforter, which is the Holy Spirit, whom the Father will send in my name, he shall teach you all things, and bring all things to your remembrance, whatsoever I have said to you.

27 Peace I leave with you, my peace I give to you: not as the world gives, give I to you. Let not your heart be troubled, neither let it be afraid.

28 You have heard how I said to you, I go away, and come again to you. If you loved me, you would rejoice, because I said, I go to the Father: for my Father is greater than I.

29 And now I have told you before it come to pass, that, when it is come to pass, you might believe.

30 Hereafter I will not talk much with you: for the prince of this world comes, and has nothing in me.

31 But that the world may know that I love the Father; and as the Father gave me commandment, even so I do. Arise, let us go hence.

CHAPTER 15

I AM the true vine, and my Father is the husbandman.

2 Every branch in me that bears not fruit he takes away: and every branch that bears fruit, he purges it, that it may bring forth more fruit.

3 Now you are clean through the word which I have spoken to you.

4 Abide in me, and I in you. As the branch cannot bear fruit of itself, except it abide in the vine; no more can you, except you abide in me.

5 I am the vine, you are the branches: He that abides in me, and I in him, the same brings forth much fruit: for without me you can do nothing.

6 If a man abide not in me, he is cast forth as a branch, and is withered; and men gather them, and cast them into the fire, and they are burned.

7 If you abide in me, and my words abide in you, you shall ask what you will, and it shall be done to you.

8 Herein is my Father glorified, that you bear much fruit; so shall you be my disciples.

9 As the Father has loved me, so have I loved you: continue in my love.

10 If you keep my commandments, you shall abide in my love; even as I have kept my Father's commandments, and abide in his love.

11 These things have I spoken to you, that my joy might remain in you, and that your joy might be full.

12 This is my commandment, That you love one another, as I have loved you.

13 Greater love has no man than this, that a man lay down his life for his friends.

14 You are my friends, if you do whatsoever I command you.

15 Henceforth I call you not servants; for the servant knows not what his lord does: but I have called you friends; for

all things that I have heard of my Father I have made known to you.

16 You have not chosen me, but I have chosen you, and ordained you, that you should go and bring forth fruit, and that your fruit should remain: that whatsoever you shall ask of the Father in my name, he may give it you.

17 These things I command you, that you love one another.

18 If the world hate you, you know that it hated me before it hated you.

19 If you were of the world, the world would love his own: but because you are not of the world, but I have chosen you out of the world, therefore the world hates you.

> There must be true and deep conviction of sin. This the preacher must labor to produce, for where this is not felt, the new birth has not taken place.
>
> **CHARLES SPURGEON**

20 Remember the word that I said to you, The servant is not greater than his lord. If they have persecuted me, they will also persecute you; if they have kept my saying, they will keep yours also.

21 But all these things will they do to you for my name's sake, because they know not him that sent me.

22 If I had not come and spoken to them, they had not had sin: but now they have no cloak for their sin.

23 He that hates me hates my Father also.

24 If I had not done among them the works which none other man did, they had not had sin: but now have they both seen and hated both me and my Father.

25 But this comes to pass, that the word might be fulfilled that is written in their law, They hated me without a cause.

26 But when the Comforter is come, whom I will send to you from the Father, even the Spirit of truth, which proceeds from the Father, he shall testify of me:

27 And you also shall bear witness, because you have been with me from the beginning.

CHAPTER 16

THESE things have I spoken to you, that you should not be offended.

2 They shall put you out of the synagogues: yea, the time comes, that whosoever kills you will think that he does God service.

3 And these things will they do to you, because they have not known the Father, nor me.

4 But these things have I told you, that when the time shall come, you may remember that I told you of them. And these things I said not to you at the beginning, because I was with you.

5 But now I go my way to him that sent me; and none of you asks me, Where are you going?

6 But because I have said these things to you, sorrow has filled your heart.

7 Nevertheless I tell you the truth; It is expedient for you that I go away: for if I go not away, the Comforter will not come to you; but if I depart, I will send him to you.

8 And when he is come, he will reprove the world of sin, and of righteousness, and of judgment:

9 Of sin, because they believe not on me;

10 Of righteousness, because I go to my Father, and you see me no more;

11 Of judgment, because the prince of this world is judged.

12 I have yet many things to say to you,

15:18–21 Some preachers promise a life of peace and happiness, but the Bible promises something else: *"All that will live godly in Christ Jesus shall suffer persecution"* (2 Timothy 3:12). See Matthew 10:16 and Philippians 1:29 comments.

but you cannot bear them now.

13 Howbeit when he, the Spirit of truth, is come, he will guide you into all truth: for he shall not speak of himself; but whatsoever he shall hear, that shall he speak: and he will show you things to come.

14 He shall glorify me: for he shall receive of mine, and shall show it to you.

15 All things that the Father has are mine: therefore said I, that he shall take of mine, and shall show it to you.

16 A little while, and you shall not see me: and again, a little while, and you shall see me, because I go to the Father.

17 Then said some of his disciples among themselves, What is this that he said to us, A little while, and you shall not see me: and again, a little while, and you shall see me: and, Because I go to the Father?

18 They said therefore, What is this that he says, A little while? we cannot tell what he says.

19 Now Jesus knew that they were desirous to ask him, and said to them, Do you inquire among yourselves of that I said, A little while, and you shall not see me: and again, a little while, and you shall see me?

20 Verily, verily, I say to you, That you shall weep and lament, but the world shall rejoice: and you shall be sorrowful, but your sorrow shall be turned into joy.

21 A woman when she is in travail has sorrow, because her hour is come: but as soon as she is delivered of the child, she remembers no more the anguish, for joy that a man is born into the world.

22 And you now therefore have sorrow: but I will see you again, and your heart

---

16:8–11 The Holy Spirit's role in salvation. The question may arise about the Holy Spirit's role in the salvation of sinners. The answer is clear from Scripture. We are drawn by, convicted by, born of, and kept by the Holy Spirit. Why then do we need to use the Law when witnessing? Why don't we just leave the salvation of sinners up to the Holy Spirit? Simply because, just as God has condescended to choose the foolishness of preaching to save those who believe, so He has chosen the Moral Law to bring the knowledge of sin.

Jesus Himself tells us how the Holy Spirit works in the salvation of the lost. He said that when the Holy Spirit comes "he will reprove the world of sin [which is *transgression* of the Law—1 John 3:4], and of righteousness [which is *of* the Law—Romans 8:4], and of judgment [which is *by* the Law—Romans 2:12]. So when we use the Law to bring the knowledge of sin to the lost, we simply become instruments the Holy Spirit uses to lead sinners to the Savior.

"When 100 years ago earnest scholars decreed that the Law had no relationship to the preaching of the gospel, they deprived the Holy Spirit in the area where their influence prevailed of the only instrument with which He had ever armed Himself to prepare sinners for grace." *Paris Reidhead*

"The Holy Spirit convicts us...He shows us the Ten Commandments; the Law is the schoolmaster that leads us to Christ. We look in the mirror of the Ten Commandments, and we see ourselves in that mirror." *Billy Graham*

16:9 Why will sinners go to hell? Much damage has been done to the cause of the gospel by telling the world that they will go to hell "because they don't believe in Jesus." This makes no sense to the ungodly. It seems unreasonable that God would eternally damn them for not believing something. However, the verse can be explained this way: If a man jumps out of a plane without a parachute, he will perish because he transgressed the law of gravity. Had he put on a parachute, he would have been saved. In one sense, he perished because he didn't put on the parachute. But the primary reason he died was because he broke the law of gravity.

If a sinner refuses to trust in Jesus Christ when he passes through the door of death, he will perish. This isn't because he refused to trust the Savior, but because he transgressed the Law of God. Had he "put on the Lord Jesus Christ" (Romans 13:14), he would have been saved; but because he refused to repent, he will suffer the full consequences of his sin. Sin is not "failing to believe in Jesus." Sin is "transgression of the Law" (1 John 3:4).

QUESTIONS & OBJECTIONS

17:3 *"I don't believe that God is knowable."*

It is amazing how it's human nature to assume that because we believe or don't believe something, that makes it true. Some may not believe in the law of gravity, and may feel thay have "evidence" to back up their belief. However, gravity exists whether they believe in it or not. The truth is, God is knowable. Jesus testified, "And this is life eternal, that they might know you the only true God, and Jesus Christ, whom you have sent" (John 17:3). We not only have the testimony of the Scriptures to tell us this, but we have the testimony of multitudes of Christians who know the Lord personally. It is more truthful to say, "I don't *want* to know God." Sinful man runs from Him as did Adam in the garden of Eden.

shall rejoice, and your joy no man takes from you.

23 And in that day you shall ask me nothing. Verily, verily, I say to you, Whatsoever you shall ask the Father in my name, he will give it you.

24 Hitherto have you asked nothing in my name: ask, and you shall receive, that your joy may be full.

25 These things have I spoken to you in proverbs: but the time comes, when I shall no more speak to you in proverbs, but I shall show you plainly of the Father.

26 At that day you shall ask in my name: and I say not to you, that I will pray the Father for you:

27 For the Father himself loves you, because you have loved me, and have believed that I came out from God.

28 I came forth from the Father, and am come into the world: again, I leave the world, and go to the Father.

29 His disciples said to him, Lo, now you speak plainly, and speak no proverb.

30 Now are we sure that you know all things, and need not that any man should ask you; by this we believe that you came forth from God.

31 Jesus answered them, Do you now believe?

32 Behold, the hour comes, yea, is now come, that you shall be scattered, every man to his own, and shall leave me alone: and yet I am not alone, because the Father is with me.

33 These things I have spoken to you, that in me you might have peace. In the world you shall have tribulation: but be of good cheer; I have overcome the world.

· · · · ·

For what great leaders have said about the Bible, see page 1590.

· · · · ·

CHAPTER 17

THESE words spoke Jesus, and lifted up his eyes to heaven, and said, Father, the hour is come; glorify your Son, that your Son also may glorify you:

2 As you have given him power over all flesh, that he should give eternal life to as many as you have given him.

3 And this is life eternal, that they might know you the only true God, and Jesus Christ, whom you have sent.

4 I have glorified you on the earth: I have finished the work which you gave me to do.

5 And now, O Father, glorify me with your own self with the glory which I had with you before the world was.

6 I have manifested your name to the men which you gave me out of the world: yours they were, and you gave them me; and they have kept your word.

7 Now they have known that all things whatsoever you have given me are of you.

8 For I have given to them the words

SPRINGBOARDS FOR PREACHING AND WITNESSING

Experiential Faith

17:3 Our faith isn't intellectual; it is experiential. We don't know *about* God, we know *Him*. At the University of Chicago Divinity School, each year they have what is called "Baptist Day." It is a day when the school invites all the Baptists in the area to the school because they want the Baptist dollars to keep coming in.

On this day each one is to bring a lunch to be eaten outdoors in a grassy picnic area. Every "Baptist Day" the school would invite one of the greatest minds to lecture in the theological education center. One year they invited Dr. Paul Tillich. Dr. Tillich spoke for two-and-a-half hours proving that the resurrection of Jesus was false. He quoted scholar after scholar and book after book. He concluded that since there was no such thing as the historical resurrection, the religious tradition of the Church was groundless, emotional mumbo-jumbo, because it was based on a relationship with a risen Jesus, who, in fact, never rose from the dead in any literal sense. He then asked if there were any questions.

After about 30 seconds, an old preacher with a head of short-cropped, woolly white hair stood up in the back of the audience. "Docta Tillich, I got one question," he said as all eyes turned toward him. He reached into his lunch sack and pulled out an apple and began eating it. "Docta Tillich *(crunch, munch)*, my question is a simple one *(crunch, munch)*. Now, I ain't never read them books you read *(crunch, munch)*, and I can't recite the Scriptures in the original Greek *(crunch, munch)*. I don't know nothin' about Niebuhr and Heidegger *(crunch, munch)*." He finished the apple. "All I wanna know is: This apple I just ate—was it bitter or sweet?"

Dr. Tillich paused for a moment and answered in exemplary scholarly fashion: "I cannot possibly answer that question, for I haven't tasted your apple." The white-haired preacher dropped the apple core into his crumpled paper bag, looked up at Dr. Tillich and said calmly, "Neither have you tasted my Jesus."

The 1,000-plus in attendance could not contain themselves. The auditorium erupted with applause and cheers. Dr. Tillich thanked his audience and promptly left the platform.

"Taste and see that the Lord is good: blessed is the man that trusts in him" (Psalm 34:8). It has been well said, "The man with an experience is not at the mercy of a man with an argument."

which you gave me; and they have received them, and have known surely that I came out from you, and they have believed that you did send me.

9 I pray for them: I pray not for the world, but for them which you have given me; for they are yours.

10 And all mine are yours, and yours are mine; and I am glorified in them.

11 And now I am no more in the world, but these are in the world, and I come to you. Holy Father, keep through your own name those whom you have given me, that they may be one, as we are.

12 While I was with them in the world, I kept them in your name: those that you gave me I have kept, and none of them is lost, but the son of perdition; that the scripture might be fulfilled.

13 And now come I to you; and these things I speak in the world, that they might have my joy fulfilled in themselves.

14 I have given them your word; and the world has hated them, because they are not of the world, even as I am not of the world.

15 I pray not that you should take them out of the world, but that you should keep

17:5 Jesus' unique words: Jesus declared that He was with the Father before the world came into existence, and that the Father loved Him before the foundation of the world (v. 24). Hebrews 7:3 tells us that He had no beginning. He not only existed before Abraham (John 8:58), He existed before the creation of the world (John 1:1–3).

them from the evil.

16 They are not of the world, even as I am not of the world.

17 Sanctify them through your truth: your word is truth.

18 As you have sent me into the world, even so have I also sent them into the world.

19 And for their sakes I sanctify myself, that they also might be sanctified through the truth.

20 Neither pray I for these alone, but for them also which shall believe on me through their word;

21 That they all may be one; as you, Father, are in me, and I in you, that they also may be one in us: that the world may believe that you have sent me.

22 And the glory which you gave me I have given them; that they may be one, even as we are one:

23 I in them, and you in me, that they may be made perfect in one; and that the world may know that you have sent me, and have loved them, as you have loved me.

"Let men of science and learning expound their knowledge and prize and probe with their researches every detail of the records which have been preserved to us from those dim ages. All they will do is fortify the grand simplicity and essential accuracy of the recorded truths which have lighted so far the pilgrimage of men."

Winston Churchill

17:14 Do you feel discouraged by negative reactions to the gospel? You shouldn't. According to the Gospels, the religious leaders tried to kill Jesus ten times. Let's look to Scripture and see what happened when Paul preached the biblical gospel:

Acts 13:45: The crowd began "contradicting and blaspheming."

Acts 13:50: Paul and Barnabas were persecuted and thrown out of the region.

Acts 14:5: The crowd plotted to stone them, forcing them to flee.

Acts 14:19: Paul was stoned and left for dead.

Acts 16:23: Both Paul and Silas were beaten with "many stripes" and thrown in prison.

Acts 18:6: Paul's hearers "opposed themselves, and blasphemed."

Acts 19:26–28: His hearers were "full of wrath" and seized Paul's companions.

Acts 20:23: The Holy Spirit warned Paul that bonds and afflictions awaited him wherever he preached the gospel.

Acts 22:21,22: His listeners called for his death.

Acts 23:1,2: As soon as he began to speak, he was smacked in the mouth.

Acts 23:10. After Paul spoke there was "great dissension" in the crowd and he was nearly "pulled in pieces."

Acts 23:12,13: More than forty Jews conspired to murder him.

Acts 24:5: He is called a "pestilent fellow," a "mover of sedition," and a "ringleader" of a "sect."

17:22 Was Jesus God in human form? See Colossians 1:15,16.

24 Father, I will that they also, whom you have given me, be with me where I am; that they may behold my glory, which you have given me: for you loved me before the foundation of the world.

25 O righteous Father, the world has not known you: but I have known you, and these have known that you have sent me.

26 And I have declared to them your name, and will declare it: that the love wherewith you have loved me may be in them, and I in them.

CHAPTER 18

WHEN Jesus had spoken these words, he went forth with his disciples over the brook Cedron, where was a garden, into the which he entered, and his disciples.

2 And Judas also, which betrayed him, knew the place: for Jesus often resorted there with his disciples.

3 Judas then, having received a band of men and officers from the chief priests and Pharisees, came there with lanterns and torches and weapons.

4 Jesus therefore, knowing all things that should come upon him, went forth, and said to them, Whom do you seek?

5 They answered him, Jesus of Nazareth. Jesus said to them, I am he. And Judas also, which betrayed him, stood with them.

6 As soon then as he had said to them, I am he, they went backward, and fell to the ground.

7 Then asked he them again, Whom do you seek? And they said, Jesus of Nazareth.

8 Jesus answered, I have told you that I am he: if therefore you seek me, let these go their way:

9 That the saying might be fulfilled, which he spoke, Of them which you gave me have I lost none.

10 Then Simon Peter having a sword drew it, and smote the high priest's servant, and cut off his right ear. The servant's name was Malchus.

11 Then said Jesus to Peter, Put up your sword into the sheath: the cup which my Father has given me, shall I not drink it?

12 Then the band and the captain and officers of the Jews took Jesus, and bound him,

13 And led him away to Annas first; for he was father in law to Caiaphas, which was the high priest that same year.

14 Now Caiaphas was he, which gave counsel to the Jews, that it was expedient that one man should die for the people.

15 And Simon Peter followed Jesus, and so did another disciple: that disciple was known to the high priest, and went in with Jesus into the palace of the high priest.

16 But Peter stood at the door without. Then went out that other disciple, which was known to the high priest, and spoke to her that kept the door, and brought in Peter.

17 Then said the damsel that kept the door to Peter, are you not also one of this man's disciples? He said, I am not.

18 And the servants and officers stood there, who had made a fire of coals; for it was cold: and they warmed themselves: and Peter stood with them, and warmed himself

19 The high priest then asked Jesus of his disciples, and of his doctrine.

20 Jesus answered him, I spoke openly to the world; I ever taught in the synagogue, and in the temple, where the Jews always resort; and in secret have I said nothing.

21 Why do you ask me? ask them which heard me, what I have said to them: behold, they know what I said.

22 And when he had thus spoken, one of the officers which stood by struck Jesus

---

18:17 Who of us who know the Lord cannot identify with Peter? We have felt the paralyzing power of the fear of man grip our hearts and fasten our lips. Peter stood by the fire and warmed his cold body, but what he really needed was a fiery coal from the altar of God to touch his frozen lips.

with the palm of his hand, saying, Do you answer the high priest so?

23 Jesus answered him, If I have spoken evil, bear witness of the evil: but if well, why do you smite me?

24 Now Annas had sent him bound to Caiaphas the high priest.

25 And Simon Peter stood and warmed himself. They said therefore to him, are not you also one of his disciples? He denied it, and said, I am not.

26 One of the servants of the high priest, being his kinsman whose ear Peter cut off, said, Did not I see you in the garden with him?

27 Peter then denied again: and immediately the cock crew.

28 Then led they Jesus from Caiaphas to the hall of judgment: and it was early; and they themselves went not into the judgment hall, lest they should be defiled; but that they might eat the passover.

29 Pilate then went out to them, and said, What accusation do you bring against this man?

30 They answered and said to him, If he were not a malefactor, we would not have delivered him up to you.

31 Then said Pilate to them, You take him, and judge him according to your law. The Jews therefore said to him, It is not lawful for us to put any man to death:

32 That the saying of Jesus might be fulfilled, which he spoke, signifying what death he should die.

33 Then Pilate entered into the judgment hall again, and called Jesus, and said to him, Are you the King of the Jews?

34 Jesus answered him, Do you say this thing of yourself, or did others tell it of me?

35 Pilate answered, Am I a Jew? Your own nation and the chief priests have delivered you to me: what have you done?

36 Jesus answered, My kingdom is not of this world: if my kingdom were of this world, then would my servants fight, that I should not be delivered to the Jews: but now is my kingdom not from hence.

37 Pilate therefore said to him, Are you a king then? Jesus answered, You say that I am a king. To this end was I born, and for this cause came I into the world, that I should bear witness to the truth. Every one that is of the truth hears my voice.

38 Pilate said to him, What is truth? And when he had said this, he went out again to the Jews, and said to them, I find in him no fault at all.

39 But you have a custom, that I should release to you one at the passover: will you therefore that I release to you the King of the Jews?

40 Then cried they all again, saying, Not this man, but Barabbas. Now Barabbas was a robber.

· · · · ·

For witnessing to those who don't speak English, see page 1691 for the entire gospel in picture form.

· · · · ·

CHAPTER 19

THEN Pilate therefore took Jesus, and scourged him.

2 And the soldiers platted a crown of thorns, and put it on his head, and they put on him a purple robe,

3 And said, Hail, King of the Jews! and they smote him with their hands.

4 Pilate therefore went forth again, and said to them, Behold, I bring him forth

---

19:1,2 It was plain that the direction that Pilate was taking was not a good one, and he knew it. He could see that it was going to land him on ground he preferred not to touch. He tried vainly to alter his course by having Jesus scourged, in the hope that it would appease the Jews. After the whipping, the twisted soldiers twisted a crown of thorns and put it on His head. This was perhaps symbolic of the Messiah taking upon Himself the curse placed upon creation when Adam sinned (Genesis 3:18).

to you, that you may know that I find no fault in him.

5 Then came Jesus forth, wearing the crown of thorns, and the purple robe. And Pilate said to them, Behold the man!

6 When the chief priests therefore and officers saw him, they cried out, saying, Crucify him, crucify him. Pilate said to them, You take him, and crucify him: for I find no fault in him.

7 The Jews answered him, We have a law, and by our law he ought to die, because he made himself the Son of God.

8 When Pilate therefore heard that saying, he was the more afraid;

> We must school and train ourselves to deal personally with the unconverted. We must not excuse ourselves, but force ourselves to the irksome task until it becomes easy.
>
> **CHARLES SPURGEON**

9 And went again into the judgment hall, and said to Jesus, Where are you from? But Jesus gave him no answer.

10 Then said Pilate to him, Do you not speak to me? Do you not know that I have power to crucify you, and have power to release you?

11 Jesus answered, You could have no power at all against me, except it were given you from above: therefore he that delivered me to you has the greater sin.

12 And from thenceforth Pilate sought to release him: but the Jews cried out, saying, If you let this man go, you are not Caesar's friend: whosoever makes himself a king speaks against Caesar.

13 When Pilate therefore heard that saying, he brought Jesus forth, and sat down in the judgment seat in a place that is called the Pavement, but in the Hebrew, Gabbatha.

14 And it was the preparation of the passover, and about the sixth hour: and he said to the Jews, Behold your King!

15 But they cried out, Away with him, away with him, crucify him. Pilate said to

them, Shall I crucify your King? The chief priest answered, We have no king but Caesar.

16 Then delivered he him therefore to them to be crucified. And they took Jesus, and led him away.

17 And he bearing his cross went forth into a place called the place of a skull, which is called in the Hebrew Golgotha:

18 Where they crucified him, and two others with him, on either side one, and Jesus in the midst.

19 And Pilate wrote a title, and put it on the cross. And the writing was, JESUS OF NAZARETH THE KING OF THE JEWS.

20 This title then read many of the Jews: for the place where Jesus was crucified was near to the city: and it was written in Hebrew, and Greek, and Latin.

21 Then said the chief priests of the Jews to Pilate, Write not, The King of the Jews; but that he said, I am King of the Jews.

22 Pilate answered, What I have written I have written.

23 Then the soldiers, when they had crucified Jesus, took his garments, and made four parts, to every soldier a part; and also his coat: now the coat was without seam, woven from the top throughout.

24 They said therefore among themselves, Let us not rend it, but cast lots for it, whose it shall be: that the scripture might be fulfilled, which says, They parted my raiment among them, and for my vesture they did cast lots. These things therefore the soldiers did.

25 Now there stood by the cross of Jesus his mother, and his mother's sister, Mary the wife of Cleophas, and Mary Magdalene.

26 When Jesus therefore saw his mother, and the disciple standing by, whom he loved, he said to his mother, Woman, behold your son!

27 Then said he to the disciple, Behold your mother! And from that hour that disciple took her to his own home.

28 After this, Jesus knowing that all

19:33,34 *"Is it possible that Jesus simply fainted on the cross, and revived while He was in the tomb?"*

Jesus had been whipped and beaten, and was bleeding from His head, back, hands, and feet for at least six hours. While he was on the cross, a soldier pierced His side with a spear and blood and water gushed out. Professional soldiers would certainly have completed their assigned task and ensured his death.

"It is impossible that a being who had stolen half-dead out of the sepulcher, who crept about weak and ill, wanting medical treatment, who required bandaging, strengthening, and indulgence, and who still at last yielded to his sufferings, could have given to the disciples the impression that he was a conqueror over death and the grave, the Prince of Life: an impression which lay at the bottom of their future ministry. Such a resuscitation could only have weakened the impression which he had made upon them in life and in death, at the most could only have given it an elegiac voice, but could by no possibility have changed their sorrow into enthusiasm, have elevated their reverence into worship." *Strauss, New Life of Jesus* (quoted in *Who Moved the Stone?* by *Frank Morison*)

things were now accomplished, that the scripture might be fulfilled, said, I thirst.

29 Now there was set a vessel full of vinegar: and they filled a sponge with vinegar, and put it upon hyssop, and put it to his mouth.

30 When Jesus therefore had received the vinegar, he said, It is finished: and he bowed his head, and gave up the ghost.

31 The Jews therefore, because it was the preparation, that the bodies should not remain upon the cross on the sabbath day, (for that sabbath day was an high day,) besought Pilate that their legs might be broken, and that they might be taken away.

32 Then came the soldiers, and broke the legs of the first, and of the other which was crucified with him.

33 But when they came to Jesus, and saw that he was dead already, they broke not his legs:

34 But one of the soldiers with a spear pierced his side, and forthwith came there out blood and water.

35 And he that saw it bare record, and his record is true: and he knows what he said is true, that you might believe.

19:29 Messianic prophecy fulfilled: "They gave me also gall for my meat; and in my thirst they gave me vinegar to drink" (Psalm 69:21). See John 19:33,36 comment.

19:31,32 Archaeology confirms the Bible. "During the past four decades, spectacular discoveries have produced data corroborating the historical backdrop of the Gospels. In 1968, for example, the skeletal remains of a crucified man were found in a burial cave in northern Jerusalem ...There was evidence that his wrists may have been pierced with nails. The knees had been doubled up and turned sideways and an iron nail (still lodged in the heel bone of one foot) driven through both heels. The shinbones appeared to have been broken, perhaps corroborating the Gospel of John." *Jeffery L. Sheler*, "Is the Bible True?" *Reader's Digest*, June 2000

19:33,34 "Clearly the weight of historical and medical evidence indicates that Jesus was dead before the wound to His side was inflicted and supports the traditional view that the spear, thrust between his right rib, probably perforated not only the right lung but also the pericardium and heart and thereby ensured His death. Accordingly, interpretations based on the assumption that Jesus did not die on the cross appear to be at odds with modern medical knowledge." *Journal of the American Medical Society*, March 21, 1986

36 For these things were done, that the scripture should be fulfilled, A bone of him shall not be broken.

37 And again another scripture says, They shall look on him whom they pierced.

38 And after this Joseph of Arimathaea, being a disciple of Jesus, but secretly for fear of the Jews, besought Pilate that he might take away the body of Jesus: and Pilate gave him leave. He came therefore, and took the body of Jesus.

39 And there came also Nicodemus, which at the first came to Jesus by night, and brought a mixture of myrrh and aloes, about an hundred pound weight.

40 Then took they the body of Jesus, and wound it in linen clothes with the spices, as the manner of the Jews is to bury.

41 Now in the place where he was crucified there was a garden; and in the garden a new sepulchre, wherein was never man yet laid.

42 There laid they Jesus therefore because of the Jews' preparation day; for the sepulchre was near at hand.

CHAPTER 20

THE first day of the week came Mary Magdalene early, when it was yet dark, to the sepulchre, and saw the stone taken away from the sepulchre.

2 Then she ran, and came to Simon Peter, and to the other disciple, whom Jesus loved, and said to them, They have taken away the Lord out of the sepulchre, and we know not where they have laid him.

3 Peter therefore went forth, and that other disciple, and came to the sepulchre.

4 So they ran both together: and the other disciple did outrun Peter, and came first to the sepulchre.

5 And he stooping down, and looking in, saw the linen clothes lying; yet went he not in.

6 Then came Simon Peter following him, and went into the sepulchre, and saw the linen clothes lie,

7 And the napkin, that was about his head, not lying with the linen clothes, but wrapped together in a place by itself.

8 Then went in also that other disciple, which came first to the sepulchre, and he saw, and believed.

9 For as yet they knew not the scripture, that he must rise again from the dead.

10 Then the disciples went away again to their own home.

11 But Mary stood without at the sepulchre weeping: and as she wept, she stooped down, and looked into the sepulchre,

12 And saw two angels in white sitting, the one at the head, and the other at the feet, where the body of Jesus had lain.

13 And they said to her, Woman, why are you weeping? She said to them, Because they have taken away my Lord, and I know not where they have laid him.

14 And when she had thus said, she turned herself back, and saw Jesus standing, and knew not that it was Jesus.

15 Jesus said to her, Woman, why are you weeping? whom do you seek? She, supposing him to be the gardener, said to him, Sir, if you have borne him hence, tell me where you have laid him, and I will take him away.

16 Jesus said to her, Mary. She turned herself, and said to him, Rabboni; which is to say, Master.

17 Jesus said to her, Touch me not; for I am not yet ascended to my Father: but go to my brethren, and say to them, I ascend to my Father, and your Father; and to my God, and your God.

18 Mary Magdalene came and told the

19:33,36 Messianic prophecy fulfilled: As Exodus 12:46 instructs, none of the Passover lamb's bones were to be broken. When Jesus, our Passover Lamb, was sacrificed for our sins, none of His bones were broken. See Acts 2:31 comment.

20:18 The first evangelist was a woman. She took the good news of the resurrection to the men, who were hiding behind locked doors.

disciples that she had seen the Lord, and that he had spoken these things to her.

19 Then the same day at evening, being the first day of the week, when the doors were shut where the disciples were assembled for fear of the Jews, came Jesus and stood in the midst, and said to them, Peace be to you.

20 And when he had so said, he showed to them his hands and his side. Then were the disciples glad, when they saw the Lord.

21 Then said Jesus to them again, Peace be to you: as my Father has sent me, even so send I you.

22 And when he had said this, he breathed on them, and said to them, Receive the Holy Spirit:

23 Whose soever sins you remit, they are remitted to them; and whose soever sins you retain, they are retained.

24 But Thomas, one of the twelve, called Didymus, was not with them when Jesus came.

25 The other disciples therefore said to him, We have seen the Lord. But he said to them, Except I shall see in his hands the print of the nails, and put my finger into the print of the nails, and thrust my hand into his side, I will not believe.

26 And after eight days again his disciples were within, and Thomas with them: then came Jesus, the doors being shut, and stood in the midst, and said, Peace be to you.

27 Then said he to Thomas, reach here your finger, and behold my hands; and reach here your hand, and thrust it into

20:22 Why did Jesus breathe on His disciples and say, "Receive the Holy Spirit," when He had already told them that the Holy Spirit could come only after His ascension (John 16:7)? Perhaps it was at that moment that the Body of Christ on earth was conceived within the womb. Perhaps it was then that He *planted* the seed of the life of the Church, but after the gestation period, on the Day of Pentecost, the Body of Christ was then *birthed* on earth.

The first seed of Adam's race began with the breath of God (Genesis 2:7), but the "last Adam" began with the breath of God in Christ. The first man had been formed from the dust of the ground, and when the Lord God breathed into his nostrils the breath of life, he became a "living soul," but Christ was made a "quickening spirit" (1 Corinthians 15:45).

Jesus picked up fallen dust from the ground of Israel, shaped them for three years, and now He breathed life into them, as He did in Genesis with the dust He had formed into Adam's body. It was but a gentle breath at conception, which became a rushing mighty wind on the Day of Pentecost (Acts 2:2), and caused the living Body of Christ to stand on its feet on earth.

20:23 If someone has turned from sin and is trusting in Jesus Christ alone for his eternal salvation, every believer has power to inform him that his sin is forgiven, based on his professed faith in the Savior.

my side: and be not faithless, but believing.

28 **And Thomas answered and said to him, My Lord and my God.**

29 **Jesus said to him, Thomas, because you have seen me, you have believed: blessed are they that have not seen, and yet have believed.**

30 And many other signs truly did Jesus in the presence of his disciples, which are not written in this book:

31 But these are written, that you might believe that Jesus is the Christ, the Son of God; and that believing you might have life through his name.

CHAPTER 21

AFTER these things Jesus showed himself again to the disciples at the sea of Tiberias; and on this wise showed he himself.

2 There were together Simon Peter, and Thomas called Didymus, and Nathanael of Cana in Galilee, and the sons of Zebedee, and two other of his disciples.

3 Simon Peter said to them, I go a fishing. They said to him, We also go with you. They went forth, and entered into a ship immediately; and that night they caught nothing.

4 But when the morning was now come, Jesus stood on the shore: but the disciples knew not that it was Jesus.

5 Then Jesus said to them, Children, have you any meat? They answered him, No.

6 And he said to them, Cast the net on the right side of the ship, and you shall find. They cast therefore, and now they were not able to draw it for the multitude of fishes.

7 Therefore that disciple whom Jesus loved said to Peter, It is the Lord. Now when Simon Peter heard that it was the Lord, he girt his fisher's coat to him, (for he was naked,) and did cast himself into the sea.

> A dead calm is our enemy, a storm may prove our helper. Controversy may arouse thought, and through thought may come the Divine change.
>
> **CHARLES SPURGEON**

8 And the other disciples came in a little ship; (for they were not far from land, but as it were two hundred cubits,) dragging the net with fishes.

9 As soon then as they were come to land, they saw a fire of coals there, and fish laid thereon, and bread.

10 Jesus said to them, Bring of the fish which you have now caught.

11 Simon Peter went up, and drew the net to land full of great fishes, an hundred and fifty and three: and for all there were so many, yet was not the net broken.

20:26 Scientific facts in the Bible. Babies are circumcised on the eighth day because this is the day that the coagulating factor in the blood, called prothrombin, is the highest. Medical science has discovered that this is when the human body's immune system is at its peak.

Just as the eighth day was the God-given timing for circumcision (Genesis 17:12), there is a God-given timing for every person who is "circumcised with the circumcision made without hands" (Colossians 2:11). Jesus appeared to Thomas on the eighth day. What Thomas saw cut away the flesh of his unbelieving heart. He became a Jew inwardly as his circumcision became "that of the heart, in the spirit, and not in the letter" (Romans 2:29). Thomas bowed his heart to Jesus of Nazareth as his Lord and his God. He needed a miracle, and God graciously gave it to him.

Each of us is dealt with individually by God; some get incredible spiritual manifestations at conversion. Others quietly trust the promises of God, and God reveals Himself to them through faith rather than feelings of great joy. What matters is not *how* each of us came to Christ, but that we became new creatures in Christ, because that is the *real* miracle that proves the reality of salvation. This is what Paul meant when he wrote, "For in Christ Jesus neither circumcision avails anything, nor uncircumcision, but a new creature" (Galatians 6:15).

"God, if you are there, strike me dead!"
(See Proverb 3:34 comment.)

Benito Mussolini

12 Jesus said to them, Come and dine. And none of the disciples dared ask him, Who are you? knowing that it was the Lord.

13 Jesus then came, and took bread, and gave, and fish likewise.

14 This is now the third time that Jesus showed himself to his disciples, after that he was risen from the dead.

15 So when they had dined, Jesus said to Simon Peter, Simon, son of Jonah, do you love me more than these? He said to him, Yea, Lord; you know that I love you. He said to him, Feed my lambs.

16 He said to him again the second time, Simon, son of Jonah, do you love me? He said to him, Yea, Lord; you know that I love you. He said to him, Feed my sheep.

17 He said to him the third time, Simon, son of Jonah, do you love me? Peter was grieved because he said to him the third time, Do you love me? And he said to him, Lord, you know all things; you know that I love you. Jesus said to him, Feed my sheep.

18 Verily, verily, I say to you, When you were young, you girded yourself, and walked where you would: but when you shall be old, you shall stretch forth your hands, and another shall gird you, and carry you where you would not.

19 This spoke he, signifying by what death he should glorify God. And when he had spoken this, he said to him, Follow me.

20 Then Peter, turning about, saw the disciple whom Jesus loved following; which also leaned on his breast at supper, and said, Lord, which is he that betrays you?

21 Peter seeing him said to Jesus, Lord, and what shall this man do?

22 Jesus said to him, If I will that he tarry till I come, what is that to you? You follow me.

23 Then went this saying abroad among the brethren, that that disciple should not die: yet Jesus said not to him, He shall not die; but, If I will that he tarry till I come, what is that to you?

24 This is the disciple which testifies of these things, and wrote these things: and we know that his testimony is true.

25 And there are also many other things which Jesus did, the which, if they should be written every one, I suppose that even the world itself could not contain the books that should be written. Amen.

Acts 3:6

Then Peter said, "Silver and gold have I none; but such as I have, give I to thee: In the name of Jesus Christ of Nazareth, rise up and walk . . ."

Acts

CHAPTER 1

THE former treatise have I made, O Theophilus, of all that Jesus began both to do and teach,

2 Until the day in which he was taken up, after that he through the Holy Spirit had given commandments to the apostles whom he had chosen:

3 To whom also he showed himself alive after his passion by many infallible proofs, being seen of them forty days, and speaking of the things pertaining to the kingdom of God:

4 And, being assembled together with them, commanded them that they should not depart from Jerusalem, but wait for the promise of the Father, which, said he, you have heard of me.

5 For John truly baptized with water; but you shall be baptized with the Holy Spirit not many days hence.

6 When they therefore were come together, they asked of him, saying, Lord, will you at this time restore again the kingdom to Israel?

7 And he said to them, It is not for you to know the times or the seasons, which the Father has put in his own power.

8 *But you shall receive power, after that the Holy Spirit is come upon you: and you shall be witnesses to me both in Jerusalem, and in all Judea, and in Samaria, and to the uttermost part of the earth.*

9 And when he had spoken these things, while they beheld, he was taken up; and a cloud received him out of their sight.

10 And while they looked steadfastly toward heaven as he went up, behold, two men stood by them in white apparel;

11 *Which also said, You men of Galilee, why do you stand gazing up into heaven? this same Jesus, which is taken up from you into heaven, shall so come in like manner as you have seen him go into heaven.*

1:5 Water baptism doesn't save us. In Acts 2:38, Peter's hearers repented and believed the gospel *before* they were baptized. In Acts 10:47, those who believed the gospel received the Holy Spirit (they passed from death to life) *before* they were baptized.

1:8 "Oh my friends, we are loaded down with countless church activities, while the *real* work of the church, that of evangelizing the world and winning the lost, is almost entirely neglected!" *Oswald J. Smith*

1:10,11 The inference is, "Don't stand here gazing up into the heavens. God has granted everlasting life to sinful humanity. Go and wait for the power to take the gospel to the world." We haven't been saved to gaze up to heaven, but to take the light to those who sit in the dark shadow of death. How can any person, who professes to have the love of God in him, sit passively while sinners die daily and go to hell? Paul said, "Woe is to me, if I preach not the gospel!" (1 Corinthians 9:16).

1:11 Second coming of Jesus: See 1 Corinthians 4:5.

12 Then returned they to Jerusalem from the mount called Olivet, which is from Jerusalem a sabbath day's journey.

13 And when they were come in, they went up into an upper room, where abode both Peter, and James, and John, and Andrew, Philip, and Thomas, Bartholomew, and Matthew, James the son of Alphaeus, and Simon Zelotes, and Judas the brother of James.

14 These all continued with one accord in prayer and supplication, with the women, and Mary the mother of Jesus, and with his brethren.

15 And in those days Peter stood up in the midst of the disciples, and said, (the number of names together were about an hundred and twenty,)

16 Men and brethren, this scripture must needs have been fulfilled, which the Holy Spirit by the mouth of David spoke before concerning Judas, which was guide to them that took Jesus.

17 For he was numbered with us, and had obtained part of this ministry.

18 Now this man purchased a field with the reward of iniquity; and falling headlong, he burst asunder in the midst, and all his bowels gushed out.

19 And it was known to all the dwellers at Jerusalem; insomuch as that field is called in their proper tongue, Akeldama, that is to say, The field of blood.

20 For it is written in the book of Psalms, Let his habitation be desolate, and let no man dwell therein: and his bishopric let another take.

21 Wherefore of these men which have companied with us all the time that the Lord Jesus went in and out among us,

22 Beginning from the baptism of John, to that same day that he was taken up from us, must one be ordained to be a witness with us of his resurrection.

23 And they appointed two, Joseph called Barsabas, who was surnamed Justus, and Matthias.

24 And they prayed, and said, You, Lord, which know the hearts of all men, show whether of these two you have chosen,

25 That he may take part of this ministry and apostleship, from which Judas by transgression fell, that he might go to his own place.

26 And they gave forth their lots; and the lot fell upon Matthias; and he was numbered with the eleven apostles.

CHAPTER 2

AND when the day of Pentecost was fully come, they were all with one accord in one place.

2 And suddenly there came a sound from heaven as of a rushing mighty wind, and it filled all the house where they were sitting.

3 And there appeared to them cloven tongues like as of fire, and it sat upon each of them.

4 And they were all filled with the Holy Spirit, and began to speak with other tongues, as the Spirit gave them utterance.

5 And there were dwelling at Jerusalem Jews, devout men, out of every nation under heaven.

6 Now when this was noised abroad, the multitude came together, and were confounded, because that every man heard them speak in his own language.

7 And they were all amazed and marveled, saying one to another, Behold, are not all these which speak Galilaeans?

8 And how hear we every man in our own tongue, wherein we were born?

9 Parthians, and Medes, and Elamites, and

1:14 Prayer—the secret weapon: See Acts 4:24.

1:18 When a hanging body decomposes, this will be the grisly result.

1:21–26 As Israel crossed over the Jordan on dry ground, God instructed them to place twelve stones as immovable witnesses—a memorial to tell the Israelite children what God had done for them (Joshua 4:1–7). Likewise, the Church was established with twelve witnesses so that we would know and tell what God has done for us through Christ.

POINTS FOR OPEN-AIR PREACHING

How to Draw a Crowd

2:14

One of the most difficult things to do is draw a crowd to hear the gospel. Today's society has been programmed to want immediate action, and open-air preaching isn't too attractive to guilty sinners. Therefore we have to be as wise as serpents and as gentle as doves. A serpent gets its heart's desire subtly. Our desire is for sinners to gather under the sound of the gospel.

Ask people passing by what they think is the greatest killer of drivers in the U.S. This stirs their curiosity. Some begin calling out "Alcohol!" or "Falling asleep at the wheel!" Tell them it's not and repeat the question a few more times, saying that you will give a dollar to the person who gets the answer. Tell them that they will never guess what it is that kills more drivers than anything else in America. A few more shouts emit from the crowd. People are now waiting around for the answer. What is it that kills more drivers than anything else in the United States? What is it that could be the death of you and me? You won't believe this, but it is "trees." Millions of them line our highways, waiting for a driver to kill. When one is struck, the tree stays still, sending the driver into eternity.

Then tell the crowd that you have another question for them. Ask what they think is the most common food on which people choke to death in U.S. restaurants. Over the next few minutes, go through the same scenario. People call out "Steak!" "Chicken bones!" Believe it or not, the answer is "hard-boiled egg yoke."

By now you have a crowd that is enjoying what is going on. Ask them what they think is the most dangerous job in America. Someone calls out "cop." It's not. Someone else may name another dangerous profession like "fire fighter." Say, "Good one...but wrong." Give a suggestion by saying, "Why doesn't someone say 'electrician'?" Someone takes the suggestion and says, "Electrician!" Say, "Sorry, it's not electrician." The most dangerous job in the United States...is to be the president. Out of forty or so, four have been murdered while on the job.

Then tell the crowd you have another question. "Does anyone in the crowd consider himself to be a "good person"? By now you will have noted who in the crowd has the self-confidence to speak out. Point to one or two and ask, "Sir, do you consider yourself to be a good person?" The Bible tells us that "every man will proclaim his own goodness" (Proverbs 20:6), and he does. He smiles and says, "Yes, I do consider myself to be a good person." Ask him if he has ever told a lie. Has he stolen, lusted, blasphemed, etc.? That's when all heaven breaks loose. There is conviction of sin. Sinners hear the gospel, and angels rejoice.

> **MORE QUESTIONS FOR CROWD DRAWING**
> - Who wrote, "Ask not what your country can do for you. Ask what you can do for your country"? *(President Kennedy's speechwriter)*
> - What is the only fish that can blink with both eyes? *(A shark)*
> - Who was John Lennon's first girlfriend? *(Thelma Pickles)*
> - How long does it take the average person to fall asleep: 2 minutes, 7 minutes, or 4 hours? *(7 minutes)*
> - How long is a goldfish's memory span: 3 seconds, 3 minutes, or 3 hours? *(3 seconds)*
> - How many muscles does a cat have in each ear: 2, 32, or 426? *(32)*

the dwellers in Mesopotamia, and in Judea, and Cappadocia, in Pontus, and Asia,

10 Phrygia, and Pamphylia, in Egypt, and in the parts of Libya about Cyrene, and strangers of Rome, Jews and proselytes,

11 Cretes and Arabians, we do hear them speak in our tongues the wonderful works of God.

12 And they were all amazed, and were in doubt, saying one to another, What means this?

13 Others mocking said, These men are full of new wine.

14 But Peter, standing up with the eleven, lifted up his voice, and said to them, You men of Judea, and all you that dwell at Jerusalem, be this known to you, and hearken to my words:

15 For these are not drunken, as you suppose, seeing it is but the third hour of the day.

16 But this is that which was spoken by the prophet Joel;

17 And it shall come to pass in the last days, said God, I will pour out of my Spirit upon all flesh: and your sons and your daughters shall prophesy, and your young men shall see visions, and your old men shall dream dreams:

18 And on my servants and on my handmaidens I will pour out in those days of my Spirit; and they shall prophesy:

19 And I will show wonders in heaven above, and signs in the earth beneath; blood, and fire, and vapor of smoke:

20 The sun shall be turned into darkness, and the moon into blood, before that great and notable day of the Lord come:

21 And it shall come to pass, that whosoever shall call on the name of the Lord shall be saved.

22 You men of Israel, hear these words; Jesus of Nazareth, a man approved of God among you by miracles and wonders and signs, which God did by him in the midst of you, as you yourselves also know:

23 Him, being delivered by the determinate counsel and foreknowledge of God, you have taken, and by wicked hands have crucified and slain:

24 Whom God has raised up, having loosed the pains of death: because it was not possible that he should be held by it.

25 For David speaks concerning him, I foresaw the Lord always before my face, for he is on my right hand, that I should not be moved:

26 Therefore did my heart rejoice, and my tongue was glad; moreover also my flesh shall rest in hope:

27 Because you will not leave my soul in hell, neither will you suffer your Holy One to see corruption.

28 You have made known to me the ways of life; you shall make me full of joy with your countenance.

29 Men and brethren, let me freely speak to you of the patriarch David, that he is both dead and buried, and his sepulchre is with us to this day.

30 Therefore being a prophet, and knowing that God had sworn with an oath to him, that of the fruit of his loins, according to the flesh, he would raise up Christ to sit on his throne;

31 He, seeing this before spoke of the resurrection of Christ, that his soul was not left in hell, neither his flesh did see corruption.

32 This Jesus has God raised up, whereof we all are witnesses.

33 Therefore being by the right hand of God exalted, and having received of the Father the promise of the Holy Spirit, he has shed forth this, which you now see and hear.

34 For David is not ascended into the heavens: but he said himself, The Lord said to my Lord, Sit on my right hand,

35 Until I make your foes your footstool.

36 Therefore let all the house of Israel know assuredly, that God has made that same Jesus, whom you have crucified, both Lord and Christ.

37 Now when they heard this, they were pricked in their heart, and said to Peter and to the rest of the apostles, Men and brethren, what shall we do?

38 Then Peter said to them, Repent, and be baptized every one of you in the name of Jesus Christ for the remission

---

2:21 Salvation is possible for every person. See Romans 10:13.

2:31 Messianic prophecy fulfilled: "For thou wilt not leave my soul in hell; neither wilt thou suffer thine Holy One to see corruption" (Psalm 16:10). See 1 Peter 2:24 comment.

2:38 Repentance—its necessity for salvation. See Acts 3:19.

PRINCIPLES OF GROWTH FOR THE NEW AND GROWING CHRISTIAN

2:38 *Water Baptism—Sprinkle or Immerse?*

The Bible says, "Repent, and be baptized every one of you in the name of Jesus Christ for the remission of sins…" (Acts 2:38). There is no question about whether you *should* be baptized. The questions are how, when, and by whom?

It would seem clear from Scripture that those who were baptized were fully immersed in water. Here's one reason why: "John also was baptizing in Aenon near to Salim, because there was much water there" (John 3:23). If John were merely sprinkling believers, he would have needed only a cupful of water. Baptism by immersion also pictures our death to sin, burial, and resurrection to new life in Christ. (See Romans 6:4; Colossians 2:12.)

The Philippian jailer and his family were baptized at midnight, the same hour they believed (Acts 16:30–33). The Ethiopian eunuch was baptized as soon as he believed (Acts 8:35–37), as was Paul (Acts 9:17,18). Baptism is a step of obedience, and God blesses our obedience. So what are you waiting for?

Who should baptize you? It is clear from Scripture that other believers had the privilege, but check with your pastor; he may want the honor himself.

For the next principle of growth, see Mark 12:41–44 comment.

of sins, and you shall receive the gift of the Holy Spirit.

39 For the promise is to you, and to your children, and to all that are afar off, even as many as the Lord our God shall call.

40 And with many other words did he testify and exhort, saying, Save yourselves from this untoward generation.

41 Then they that gladly received his word were baptized: and the same day there were added to them about three thousand souls.

42 And they continued steadfastly in the apostles' doctrine and fellowship, and in breaking of bread, and in prayers.

43 And fear came upon every soul: and many wonders and signs were done by the apostles.

44 And all that believed were together, and had all things common;

45 And sold their possessions and goods, and parted them to all men, as every man had need.

46 And they, continuing daily with one accord in the temple, and breaking bread from house to house, did eat their meat with gladness and singleness of heart,

47 Praising God, and having favor with all the people. And the Lord added to the church daily such as should be saved.

USING THE LAW IN EVANGELISM

2:37 Peter's audience was composed of "devout men" (2:5) who were gathered at Pentecost to celebrate the giving of God's Law on Mount Sinai. Even though these were godly Jews, Peter told them that they were "lawless"—that they had violated God's Law by murdering Jesus (v. 23). He drove home that fact by saying, "Therefore let all the house of Israel know assuredly, that God has made that same Jesus, *whom you have crucified*, both Lord and Christ" (v. 36, emphasis added). It was then that they saw that their sin was personal. They were "pricked in their heart" and cried out for help. Only after the Law convicted them of their guilt did Peter tell his hearers the good news of the fine being paid for them in Christ (v. 38).

CHAPTER 3

NOW Peter and John went up together into the temple at the hour of prayer, being the ninth hour.

2 And a certain man lame from his mother's womb was carried, whom they laid daily at the gate of the temple which is called Beautiful, to ask alms of them that

POINTS FOR OPEN-AIR PREACHING

Crowd Etiquette

3:4

If you have other Christians with you, have them form an audience and look as though they are listening to your preaching. This will encourage others to stop and listen. Tell the Christians to never stand with their back to the preacher. I have seen open-air meetings when a fellow laborer is preaching for the first time, and what are the Christians doing? They are talking among themselves. Why then should anyone stop and listen if those in front of the speaker aren't even attentive? It is so easy to chat with friends when you've heard the gospel a million times before. I have found myself doing it, but it is so disheartening for the preacher to speak to the backs of a crowd.

Also, instruct Christians not to argue with hecklers. That will ruin an open-air meeting. I have seen an old lady hit a heckler with her umbrella and turn the crowd from listening to the gospel to watching the fight she has just started. Who can blame them? Remember, the enemy will do everything he can to distract your listeners. Don't let him. See 2 Timothy 2:24–26 comment.

entered into the temple;

3 Who seeing Peter and John about to go into the temple asked an alms.

4 And Peter, fastening his eyes upon him with John, said, Look on us.

5 And he gave heed to them, expecting to receive something of them.

6 Then Peter said, Silver and gold have I none; but such as I have give I you: In the name of Jesus Christ of Nazareth rise up and walk.

7 And he took him by the right hand, and lifted him up: and immediately his feet and ankle bones received strength.

8 And he leaping up stood, and walked, and entered with them into the temple, walking, and leaping, and praising God.

9 And all the people saw him walking and praising God:

10 And they knew that it was he which sat for alms at the Beautiful gate of the temple: and they were filled with wonder and amazement at that which had happened to him.

11 And as the lame man which was healed held Peter and John, all the people ran together to them in the porch that is called Solomon's, greatly wondering.

12 And when Peter saw it, he answered to the people, You men of Israel, why do you marvel at this? or why do you look so earnestly on us, as though by our own power or holiness we had made this man to walk?

13 The God of Abraham, and of Isaac, and of Jacob, the God of our fathers, has glorified his Son Jesus; whom you delivered up, and denied him in the presence of Pilate, when he was determined to let

2:44–46 The need for church. "None of us is self-sufficient in our spiritual lives. We need God, and we need each other. A lot of people go to church because they think God takes roll. For them, the important thing is to make sure their name gets checked off every Sunday on the heavenly roster. But that's not the way it works. Church is not some kind of moral obligation, some habit or tradition that is 'the right thing to do.' Church is a place where we worship God, share our faith with the community of believers, build each other up, and get empowered to go out into the world and *live out our faith!*

"Similarly, some people think of their spiritual life as if they were one person in a telephone booth, talking to God on a private line. They don't want to be bothered by the demands of 'organized religion' and don't think they need anyone else. 'Oh yeah, I'm spiritual,' they say, 'I just don't like church.' To those folks I say: You cannot grow spiritually in isolation." *Rich DeVos, Hope From My Heart: Ten Lessons for Life*

him go.

14 But you denied the Holy One and the Just, and desired a murderer to be granted to you;

15 And killed the Prince of life, whom God has raised from the dead; whereof we are witnesses.

16 And his name through faith in his name has made this man strong, whom you see and know: yes, the faith which is by him has given him this perfect soundness in the presence of you all.

17 And now, brethren, I realize that through ignorance you did it, as did also your rulers.

18 But those things, which God before had showed by the mouth of all his prophets, that Christ should suffer, he has so fulfilled.

> The open-air speaker's calling is as honorable as it is arduous, as useful as it is laborious. God alone can sustain you in it, but with Him at your side you will have nothing to fear.
>
> **CHARLES SPURGEON**

19 Repent therefore, and be converted, that your sins may be blotted out, when the times of refreshing shall come from the presence of the Lord;

20 And he shall send Jesus Christ, which before was preached to you:

21 Whom the heaven must receive until the times of restitution of all things, which God has spoken by the mouth of all his holy prophets since the world began.

22 For Moses truly said to the fathers, A prophet shall the Lord your God raise up to you of your brethren, like to me; him shall you hear in all things whatsoever he shall say to you.

23 And it shall come to pass, that every soul, which will not hear that prophet,

shall be destroyed from among the people.

24 Yes, and all the prophets from Samuel and those that follow after, as many as have spoken, have likewise foretold of these days.

25 You are the children of the prophets, and of the covenant which God made with our fathers, saying to Abraham, And in your seed shall all the kindreds of the earth be blessed.

26 To you first God, having raised up his Son Jesus, sent him to bless you, in turning away every one of you from his iniquities.

CHAPTER 4

AND as they spoke to the people, the priests, and the captain of the temple, and the Sadducees, came upon them,

2 Being grieved that they taught the people, and preached through Jesus the resurrection from the dead.

3 And they laid hands on them, and put them in hold to the next day: for it was now eventide.

4 Howbeit many of them which heard the word believed; and the number of the men was about five thousand.

5 And it came to pass on the morrow, that their rulers, and elders, and scribes,

6 And Annas the high priest, and Caiaphas, and John, and Alexander, and as many as were of the kindred of the high priest, were gathered together at Jerusalem.

7 And when they had set them in the midst, they asked, By what power, or by what name, have you done this?

8 Then Peter, filled with the Holy Spirit, said to them, You rulers of the people, and elders of Israel,

9 If we this day be examined of the good deed done to the impotent man, by what means he is made whole;

10 Be it known to you all, and to all the people of Israel, that by the name of Jesus Christ of Nazareth, whom you crucified, whom God raised from the dead, even by

---

3:19 Repentance—its necessity for salvation. See Acts 17:30.

4:12 Is Suffering the Entrance to Heaven?

In January 2000, a well-known ex-televangelist said on a worldwide TV talk show, "I believe that every person who died in the Holocaust went to heaven." He was very sincere, and if he was seeking the commendation of the world, he surely got it with that statement. Who wouldn't consider what he said to be utterly compassionate? However, let's look at the implications of his heartfelt beliefs. His statement seemed to limit salvation to the *Jews* who died in the Holocaust, because he added that "their blood laid a foundation for the nation of Israel." If the slaughtered Jews made it to heaven, did the many *Gypsies* who died in the Holocaust also obtain eternal salvation? If his statement includes Gentiles, is the salvation he spoke of limited to those who died at the hands of Nazis? Did the many *Frenchmen* who met their death at the hands of cruel Nazis go to heaven also?

Perhaps he was saying that the death of Jesus on the cross covered *all* of humanity, and that all will eventually be saved—something called "universalism." This means that salvation will also come to Hitler and the Nazis who killed the Jews. However, I doubt if he was saying that. Such a statement would have brought the scorn of his Jewish host, and of the world whose compassion has definite limits.

If pressed, he probably didn't mean that only the Jews in the camps went to heaven, because that smacks of *racism*. He was likely saying that those who died were saved because they died in such *tragic circumstances*. Then Jesus was lying when He said, "I am the

way, the truth, and the life: no man comes to the Father, but by me" (John 14:6). There is another way to heaven—death in a Nazi concentration camp. Does that mean that the many Jews who died under *communism* went to heaven? Or is salvation limited to *German* concentration camps?

If their salvation came because of the grim circumstances surrounding their death, does a Jew therefore enter heaven after suffering for hours before dying in a car wreck...if he was killed by a drunk driver who happened to be German? Bear in mind that his suffering may have been much greater than someone who died within minutes in a Nazi gas chamber.

Many unsaved think we *can* merit entrance into heaven by our suffering. Their error was confirmed by this sincere, compassionate man of God. They may now disregard the truth, "Neither is there salvation in any other: for there is no other name under heaven given among men, whereby we must be saved" (Acts 4:12). They can now save themselves by the means of their own death...if they suffer enough.

The ex-televangelist was concerned that his indiscretions of the 1980s brought discredit to the kingdom of God. However, those actions fade into history compared to the damage done by saying that there is another means of salvation outside of Jesus Christ, on a program watched by untold millions around the world. Who on earth needs to repent and trust in Jesus, if millions entered the kingdom without being born again? No one.

him does this man stand here before you whole.

11 This is the stone which was set at nought of you builders, which is become the head of the corner.

12 Neither is there salvation in any other: for there is no other name under heaven given among men, whereby we must be saved.

13 Now when they saw the boldness of Peter and John, and perceived that they were unlearned and ignorant men, they marveled; and they took knowledge of

them, that they had been with Jesus.

14 And beholding the man which was healed standing with them, they could say nothing against it.

15 But when they had commanded them to go aside out of the council, they conferred among themselves,

16 Saying, What shall we do to these men? for that indeed a notable miracle has been done by them is manifest to all them that dwell in Jerusalem; and we cannot deny it.

17 But that it spread no further among

the people, let us straitly threaten them, that they speak henceforth to no man in this name.

18 And they called them, and commanded them not to speak at all nor teach in the name of Jesus.

19 But Peter and John answered and said to them, Whether it be right in the sight of God to hearken to you more than to God, you judge.

20 *For we cannot but speak the things which we have seen and heard.*

21 So when they had further threatened them, they let them go, finding nothing how they might punish them, because of the people: for all men glorified God for that which was done.

22 For the man was above forty years old, on whom this miracle of healing was showed.

23 And being let go, they went to their own company, and reported all that the chief priests and elders had said to them.

24 And when they heard that, they lifted up their voice to God with one accord, and said, Lord, you are God, which have made heaven, and earth, and the sea, and all that in them is:

25 Who by the mouth of your servant David have said, Why did the heathen rage, and the people imagine vain things?

26 The kings of the earth stood up, and the rulers were gathered together against the Lord, and against his Christ.

27 For of a truth against your holy child Jesus, whom you have anointed, both Herod, and Pontius Pilate, with the Gentiles, and the people of Israel, were gathered together,

28 For to do whatsoever your hand and your counsel determined before to be done.

29 And now, Lord, behold their threatenings: and grant to your servants, that with all boldness they may speak your word,

30 By stretching forth your hand to heal; and that signs and wonders may be done by the name of your holy child Jesus.

31 *And when they had prayed, the place was shaken where they were assembled together; and they were all filled with the Holy Spirit, and they spoke the word of God with boldness.*

32 And the multitude of them that believed were of one heart and of one soul: neither said any of them that anything of the things which he possessed was his own; but they had all things common.

33 And with great power gave the apostles witness of the resurrection of the Lord Jesus: and great grace was upon them all.

34 Neither was there any among them that lacked: for as many as were possessors of lands or houses sold them, and brought the prices of the things that were sold,

35 And laid them down at the apostles' feet: and distribution was made to every man according as he had need.

36 And Joses, who by the apostles was surnamed Barnabas, (which is, being interpreted, The son of consolation,) a Levite, and of the country of Cyprus,

37 Having land, sold it, and brought the money, and laid it at the apostles' feet.

4:24 Prayer—the secret weapon: See Acts 12:12.

4:24 Fossil evidence points to creation. "The creation account in Genesis and the theory of evolution could not be reconciled. One must be right and the other wrong. The story of the fossils agrees with the account of Genesis. In the oldest rocks we did not find a series of fossils covering the gradual changes from the most primitive creatures to developed forms but rather, in the oldest rocks, developed species suddenly appeared. Between every species there was a complete absence of intermediate fossils." *D. B. Gower* (biochemist), "Scientist Rejects Evolution," *Kentish Times*

4:29 When we are afraid to witness to sinners, we can stand firmly upon the wonderful promise of God given in Isaiah 41:10. We need not fear or be dismayed because He is with us. He will strengthen, help, and uphold us with His righteous right hand.

CHAPTER 5

BUT a certain man named Ananias, with Sapphira his wife, sold a possession,

2 And kept back part of the price, his wife also being privy to it, and brought a certain part, and laid it at the apostles' feet.

3 But Peter said, Ananias, why has Satan filled your heart to lie to the Holy Spirit, and to keep back part of the price of the land?

4 Whiles it remained, was it not your own? and after it was sold, was it not in your own power? why have you conceived this thing in your heart? you have not lied to men, but to God.

5 And Ananias hearing these words fell down, and gave up the ghost: and great fear came on all them that heard these things.

6 And the young men arose, wound him up, and carried him out, and buried him.

7 And it was about the space of three hours after, when his wife, not knowing what was done, came in.

8 And Peter answered to her, Tell me whether you sold the land for so much? And she said, Yes, for so much.

9 Then Peter said to her, How is it that you have agreed together to tempt the Spirit of the Lord? behold, the feet of them which have buried your husband are at the door, and shall carry you out.

10 Then fell she down straightway at his feet, and yielded up the ghost: and the young men came in, and found her dead, and, carrying her forth, buried her by her husband.

11 And great fear came upon all the church, and upon as many as heard these things.

12 And by the hands of the apostles were many signs and wonders wrought among the people; (and they were all with one accord in Solomon's porch.

13 And of the rest no man dared join himself to them: but the people magnified them.

14 And believers were the more added to the Lord, multitudes both of men and wo-

"We have been assured, Sir, in the Sacred Writings, that 'except the Lord build the house, they labor in vain that build it.' I firmly believe this; and I also believe that without his concurring aid we shall succeed in this political building no better than the builders of Babel."

Benjamin Franklin

men.)

15 Insomuch that they brought forth the sick into the streets, and laid them on beds and couches, that at the least the shadow of Peter passing by might overshadow some of them.

16 There came also a multitude out of the cities round about to Jerusalem, bringing sick folks, and them which were vexed with unclean spirits: and they were healed every one.

17 Then the high priest rose up, and all they that were with him, (which is the sect of the Sadducees,) and were filled with indignation,

18 And laid their hands on the apostles, and put them in the common prison.

19 But the angel of the Lord by night opened the prison doors, and brought them forth, and said,

20 Go, stand and speak in the temple to the people all the words of this life.

21 And when they heard that, they entered into the temple early in the morn-

ing, and taught. But the high priest came, and they that were with him, and called the council together, and all the senate of the children of Israel and sent to the prison to have them brought.

22 But when the officers came, and found them not in the prison, they returned, and told,

23 Saying, The prison truly found we shut with all safety, and the keepers standing without before the doors: but when we had opened, we found no man within.

24 Now when the high priest and the captain of the temple and the chief priests heard these things, they doubted of them whereunto this would grow.

25 Then came one and told them, saying, Behold, the men whom you put in prison are standing in the temple, and teaching the people.

26 Then went the captain with the officers, and brought them without violence: for they feared the people, lest they should have been stoned.

27 And when they had brought them, they set them before the council: and the high priest asked them,

28 Saying, Did not we straitly command you that you should not teach in this name? and, behold, you have filled Jerusalem with your doctrine, and intend to bring this man's blood upon us.

29 Then Peter and the other apostles answered and said, We ought to obey God rather than men.

30 The God of our fathers raised up Jesus, whom you slew and hanged on a tree.

31 Him has God exalted with his right hand to be a Prince and a Savior, for to give repentance to Israel, and forgiveness of sins.

32 And we are his witnesses of these things; and so is also the Holy Spirit, whom God has given to them that obey him.

33 When they heard that, they were cut to the heart, and took counsel to slay them.

34 Then stood there up one in the council, a Pharisee, named Gamaliel, a doctor of the law, had in reputation among all the people, and commanded to put the apostles forth a little space;

35 And said to them, You men of Israel, take heed to yourselves what you intend to do as touching these men.

36 For before these days rose up Theudas, boasting himself to be somebody; to whom a number of men, about four hundred, joined themselves: who was slain; and all, as many as obeyed him, were scattered, and brought to nought.

37 After this man rose up Judas of Galilee in the days of the taxing, and drew away much people after him: he also perished; and all, even as many as obeyed him, were dispersed.

38 And now I say to you, Refrain from these men, and let them alone: for if this counsel or this work be of men, it will come to nought:

39 But if it be of God, you cannot overthrow it; lest haply you be found even to fight against God.

40 And to him they agreed: and when they had called the apostles, and beaten them, they commanded that they should not speak in the name of Jesus, and let them go.

41 And they departed from the presence of the council, rejoicing that they were counted worthy to suffer shame for his name.

42 And daily in the temple, and in every house, they ceased not to teach and preach Jesus Christ.

· · · · · ·

For how to witness to Jews,
see Romans 3:1 comment.

· · · · · ·

CHAPTER 6

AND in those days, when the number of the disciples was multiplied, there arose a murmuring of the Grecians against the Hebrews, because their widows were neglected in the daily ministration.

2 Then the twelve called the multitude

of the disciples to them, and said, It is not reason that we should leave the word of God, and serve tables.

3 Wherefore, brethren, look out among you seven men of honest report, full of the Holy Spirit and wisdom, whom we may appoint over this business.

4 But we will give ourselves continually to prayer, and to the ministry of the word.

5 And the saying pleased the whole multitude: and they chose Stephen, a man full of faith and of the Holy Spirit, and Philip, and Prochorus, and Nicanor, and Timon, and Parmenas, and Nicolas a proselyte of Antioch:

6 Whom they set before the apostles: and when they had prayed, they laid their hands on them.

7 And the word of God increased; and the number of the disciples multiplied in Jerusalem greatly; and a great company of the priests were obedient to the faith.

8 *And Stephen, full of faith and power, did great wonders and miracles among the people.*

9 Then there arose certain of the synagogue, which is called the synagogue of the Libertines, and Cyrenians, and Alexandrians, and of them of Cilicia and of Asia, disputing with Stephen.

10 And they were not able to resist the wisdom and the spirit by which he spoke.

11 Then they suborned men, which said, We have heard him speak blasphemous words against Moses, and against God.

12 And they stirred up the people, and the elders, and the scribes, and came upon him, and caught him, and brought him to the council,

13 And set up false witnesses, which said, This man ceases not to speak blasphemous words against this holy place, and the law:

14 For we have heard him say, that this Jesus of Nazareth shall destroy this place, and shall change the customs which Moses delivered us.

15 And all that sat in the council, looking steadfastly on him, saw his face as it had been the face of an angel.

CHAPTER 7

THEN said the high priest, Are these things so?

2 And he said, Men, brethren, and fathers, hearken; The God of glory appeared to our father Abraham, when he was in Mesopotamia, before he dwelt in Haran,

3 And said to him, Get you out of your country, and from your kindred, and come into the land which I shall show you.

4 Then came he out of the land of the Chaldaeans, and dwelt in Charran: and from thence, when his father was dead, he removed him into this land, wherein you now dwell.

5 And he gave him none inheritance in it, no, not so much as to set his foot on: yet he promised that he would give it to him for a possession, and to his seed after him, when as yet he had no child.

6 And God spoke on this wise, That his seed should sojourn in a strange land; and that they should bring them into bondage, and entreat them evil four hundred years.

7 And the nation to whom they shall be in bondage will I judge, said God: and after that shall they come forth, and serve me in this place.

8 And he gave him the covenant of circumcision: and so Abraham begat Isaac, and circumcised him the eighth day; and

---

7:5 The Bible's fascinating facts. In the Book of Beginnings, in Genesis 16:12, God said that Ishmael (the progenitor of the Arab race, see *Time*, April 4, 1988) would be a "wild man...and every man's hand [will be] against him; and he shall dwell in the presence of all his brethren." Almost four thousand years later, who could deny that this prophecy is being fulfilled in the Arab race? The Arabs and the Jews are "brethren" having Abraham as their ancestor. The whole Middle East conflict is caused by their dwelling together.

Isaac begat Jacob; and Jacob begat the twelve patriarchs.

9 And the patriarchs, moved with envy, sold Joseph into Egypt: but God was with him,

10 And delivered him out of all his afflictions, and gave him favor and wisdom in the sight of Pharaoh king of Egypt; and he made him governor over Egypt and all his house.

11 Now there came a dearth over all the land of Egypt and Canaan, and great affliction: and our fathers found no sustenance.

12 But when Jacob heard that there was corn in Egypt, he sent out our fathers first.

13 And at the second time Joseph was made known to his brethren; and Joseph's kindred was made known to Pharaoh.

14 Then sent Joseph, and called his father Jacob to him, and all his kindred, threescore and fifteen souls.

15 So Jacob went down into Egypt, and died, he, and our fathers,

16 And were carried over into Sychem, and laid in the sepulchre that Abraham bought for a sum of money of the sons of Emmor the father of Sychem.

17 But when the time of the promise drew nigh, which God had sworn to Abraham, the people grew and multiplied in Egypt,

18 Till another king arose, which knew not Joseph.

19 The same dealt subtly with our kindred, and evil entreated our fathers, so that they cast out their young children, to the end they might not live.

20 In which time Moses was born, and was exceeding fair, and nourished up in his father's house three months:

21 And when he was cast out, Pharaoh's daughter took him up, and nourished him for her own son.

22 And Moses was learned in all the wisdom of the Egyptians, and was mighty in words and in deeds.

23 And when he was full forty years old, it came into his heart to visit his brethren the children of Israel.

24 And seeing one of them suffer wrong, he defended him, and avenged him that was oppressed, and smote the Egyptian:

25 For he supposed his brethren would have understood how that God by his hand would deliver them: but they understood not.

26 And the next day he showed himself to them as they strove, and would have set them at one again, saying, Sirs, you are brethren; why do you wrong one to another?

27 But he that did his neighbour wrong thrust him away, saying, Who made you a ruler and a judge over us?

28 Will you kill me, as you did the Egyptian yesterday?

29 Then fled Moses at this saying, and was a stranger in the land of Madian,

---

7:22 Don't be concerned that you aren't "gifted" as a speaker when it comes to reaching the lost. Moses "was learned in all the wisdom of the Egyptians, and was mighty in words and in deeds," yet God didn't use him to deliver Israel until 40 years later. It took all that time of tending sheep to produce in him a meekness of character. We are told, "The meek will he guide in judgment: and the meek will he teach his way" (Psalm 25:9). The "wisdom" that Moses gained in Egypt was not wisdom from above. When he saw injustice, he took the law into his own hands and committed murder. God doesn't need the wisdom of this world. He merely desires a pure, humble, peace-loving, compassionate soul to use as a mouthpiece for the gospel. He wants us to be a lighthouse of His love. The moment we receive the Spirit of Christ, we receive the gift of those virtues. We don't need to tend sheep for 40 years when we have the character of the Good Shepherd manifesting through us.

7:26 "We do wrong, we think wrong, and our efforts to deal with wrong are themselves corrupted by wrong." *Chuck Colson*

where he begat two sons.

30 And when forty years were expired, there appeared to him in the wilderness of mount Sinai an angel of the Lord in a flame of fire in a bush.

31 When Moses saw it, he wondered at the sight: and as he drew near to behold it, the voice of the Lord came to him,

32 Saying, I am the God of your fathers, the God of Abraham, and the God of Isaac, and the God of Jacob. Then Moses trembled, and dared not behold.

33 Then said the Lord to him, Put off your shoes from your feet: for the place where you stand is holy ground.

34 I have seen, I have seen the affliction of my people which is in Egypt, and I have heard their groaning, and am come down to deliver them. And now come, I will send you into Egypt.

35 This Moses whom they refused, saying, Who made you a ruler and a judge? the same did God send to be a ruler and a deliverer by the hand of the angel which appeared to him in the bush.

36 He brought them out, after that he had showed wonders and signs in the land of Egypt, and in the Red sea, and in the wilderness forty years.

37 This is that Moses, which said to the children of Israel, A prophet shall the Lord your God raise up to you of your brethren, like to me; him shall you hear.

38 This is he, that was in the church in the wilderness with the angel which spoke to him in the mount Sinai, and with our fathers: who received the lively oracles to give to us:

39 To whom our fathers would not obey, but thrust him from them, and in their hearts turned back again into Egypt,

40 Saying to Aaron, Make us gods to go before us: for as for this Moses, which

brought us out of the land of Egypt, we know not what is become of him.

41 And they made a calf in those days, and offered sacrifice to the idol, and rejoiced in the works of their own hands.

42 Then God turned, and gave them up to worship the host of heaven; as it is written in the book of the prophets, O you house of Israel, have you offered to me slain beasts and sacrifices by the space of forty years in the wilderness?

43 Yes, you took up the tabernacle of Moloch, and the star of your god Remphan, figures which you made to worship them: and I will carry you away beyond Babylon.

44 Our fathers had the tabernacle of witness in the wilderness, as he had appointed, speaking to Moses, that he should make it according to the fashion that he had seen.

45 Which also our fathers that came after brought in with Jesus into the possession of the Gentiles, whom God drove out before the face of our fathers, to the days of David;

46 Who found favor before God, and desired to find a tabernacle for the God of Jacob.

47 But Solomon built him an house.

48 Howbeit the most High dwells not in temples made with hands; as said the prophet,

49 Heaven is my throne, and earth is my footstool: what house will you build me? said the Lord: or what is the place of my rest?

50 Has not my hand made all these things?

51 You stiff-necked and uncircumcised in heart and ears, you do always resist the Holy Spirit: as your fathers did, so do you.

52 Which of the prophets have not your

7:33 Moses was told to remove his sandals because by God's presence even the ground on which he stood was made holy. Through faith in Christ, the believer himself is made holy. Now his feet are shod with the gospel of peace (Ephesians 6:15), to take the word of salvation to those who stand on unholy ground.

7:39 When you turn your back on God, any way you go is a wrong direction.

History reveals the fate of the apostles:

PHILIP: Stoned to death, Phrygia, A.D. 54

PETER: Crucified, Rome, A.D. 69

PAUL: Beheaded, Rome, A.D. 69

ANDREW: Crucified, Achaia, A.D. 70

MATTHEW: Beheaded, Ethiopia, A.D. 70

THOMAS: Speared to death, Calamino, A.D. 70

JAMES (THE LESS): Clubbed to death, Jerusalem, A.D. 63

JOHN: Abandoned, Isle of Patmos, A.D. 63

fathers persecuted? and they have slain them which showed before of the coming of the Just One; of whom you have been now the betrayers and murderers:

53 Who have received the law by the disposition of angels, and have not kept it.

54 When they heard these things, they were cut to the heart, and they gnashed on him with their teeth.

55 But he, being full of the Holy Spirit, looked up steadfastly into heaven, and saw the glory of God, and Jesus standing

---

7:55 Honesty Road. As I was open-air preaching one day, a man looked to the heavens not to see the glory of God, but to shout obscenities at Jesus Christ that would make your hair curl in tight knots. He concluded his conversation by telling the Lord to strike him dead. He then turned to me and screamed, "Nothing happened!" I said, "Yes, it did. You have just stored up wrath for yourself, which will be revealed on the Day of Wrath."

Why would a man lack *any* fear of God? I believe it's because we insist on telling a sinful world that God loves them and has a wonderful plan for their lives. This is the gospel according to the contemporary Church. We give the world a choice: Do they choose God's wonderful plan, or is their own life's plan more wonderful? For the answer to this dilemma and the biblical way to witness, see Matthew 10:22 comment.

on the right hand of God,

56 And said, Behold, I see the heavens opened, and the Son of man standing on the right hand of God.

57 Then they cried out with a loud voice, and stopped their ears, and ran upon him with one accord,

58 And cast him out of the city, and stoned him: and the witnesses laid down their clothes at a young man's feet, whose name was Saul.

59 And they stoned Stephen, calling upon God, and saying, Lord Jesus, receive my spirit.

60 And he kneeled down, and cried with a loud voice, Lord, lay not this sin to their charge. And when he had said this, he fell asleep.

CHAPTER 8

AND Saul was consenting to his death. And at that time there was a great persecution against the church which was at Jerusalem; and they were all scattered abroad throughout the regions of Judea and Samaria, except the apostles.

2 And devout men carried Stephen to his burial, and made great lamentation over him.

3 As for Saul, he made havoc of the church, entering into every house, and haling men and women committed them to prison.

4 *Therefore they that were scattered abroad went every where preaching the word.*

5 Then Philip went down to the city of Samaria, and preached Christ to them.

6 And the people with one accord gave heed to those things which Philip spoke, hearing and seeing the miracles which he did.

7 For unclean spirits, crying with loud voice, came out of many that were pos-

sessed with them: and many taken with palsies, and that were lame, were healed.

8 And there was great joy in that city.

9 But there was a certain man, called Simon, which beforetime in the same city used sorcery, and bewitched the people of Samaria, giving out that himself was some great one:

10 To whom they all gave heed, from the least to the greatest, saying, This man is the great power of God.

11 And to him they had regard, because for a long time he had bewitched them with sorceries.

12 But when they believed Philip preaching the things concerning the kingdom of God, and the name of Jesus Christ, they were baptized, both men and women.

13 Then Simon himself believed also: and when he was baptized, he continued with Philip, and wondered, beholding the miracles and signs which were done.

14 Now when the apostles which were at Jerusalem heard that Samaria had received the word of God, they sent to them Peter and John:

15 Who, when they were come down, prayed for them, that they might receive the Holy Spirit:

16 (For as yet he was fallen upon none of them: only they were baptized in the name of the Lord Jesus.)

17 Then laid they their hands on them, and they received the Holy Spirit.

18 And when Simon saw that through laying on of the apostles' hands the Holy Spirit was given, he offered them money,

19 Saying, Give me also this power, that on whomsoever I lay hands, he may receive the Holy Spirit.

20 But Peter said to him, Your money perish with you, because you have thought that the gift of God may be purchased with

---

7:59 "You can kill us, but you cannot do us any real harm." *Justin Martyr* (martyred A.D. 165)

8:19 Using God's power. "Waste of power is a tragedy. God does not waste the great power of His Spirit on those who want it simply for their own sake, to be more holy, or good, or gifted. His great task is to carry on the work for which Jesus sacrificed His throne and His life—the redemption of fallen humanity." *Alan Redpath, The Life of Victory*

money.

21 You have neither part nor lot in this matter: for your heart is not right in the sight of God.

22 Repent therefore of this your wickedness, and pray God, if perhaps the thought of your heart may be forgiven you.

23 For I perceive that you are in the gall of bitterness, and in the bond of iniquity.

24 Then answered Simon, and said, Pray to the Lord for me, that none of these things which you have spoken come upon me.

25 And they, when they had testified and preached the word of the Lord, returned to Jerusalem, and preached the gospel in many villages of the Samaritans.

26 And the angel of the Lord spoke to Philip, saying, Arise, and go toward the south to the way that goes down from Jerusalem to Gaza, which is desert.

27 And he arose and went: and, behold, a man of Ethiopia, an eunuch of great authority under Candace queen of the Ethiopians, who had the charge of all her treasure, and had come to Jerusalem for to worship,

28 Was returning, and sitting in his chariot read Isaiah the prophet.

29 Then the Spirit said to Philip, Go near, and join yourself to this chariot.

30 And Philip ran there to him, and heard him read the prophet Isaiah, and said, Do you understand what you read?

31 And he said, How can I, except some man should guide me? And he desired Philip that he would come up and sit with him.

32 The place of the scripture which he read was this, He was led as a sheep to the slaughter; and like a lamb dumb before his shearer, so opened he not his mouth:

33 In his humiliation his judgment was taken away: and who shall declare his generation? for his life is taken from the earth.

34 And the eunuch answered Philip, and said, I pray you, of whom does the prophet speak? of himself, or of some other man?

> No man who preaches the gospel without zeal is sent from God to preach at all.
>
> **CHARLES SPURGEON**

35 Then Philip opened his mouth, and began at the same scripture, and preached to him Jesus.

36 **And as they went on their way, they came to a certain water: and the eunuch said, See, here is water; what does hinder me to be baptized?**

37 **And Philip said, If you believe with all your heart, you may. And he answered and said, I believe that Jesus Christ is the Son of God.**

38 And he commanded the chariot to stand still: and they went down both into

---

8:26,27 "God has placed you where He has placed no one else. No one else in the world has the same relationships you have. No one will stand in the same grocery store line at exactly the same moment you do. No one else will come across a hungering diplomat in the desert at exactly the same time you do. God hasn't put you in those places merely to model the truth. Listen for the voice of the Spirit to whisper in your ear. Watch for the stranger on the road. And be aware of your opportunities to go where He would send you." *Chuck Swindoll*

8:35   Wisdom in witnessing. The Scriptures tell us, "He who wins souls is wise" (Proverbs 11:30). If we are wise, we will discern the condition of a person's heart. If he is a sincere Nicodemus, tell him the good news; if he is like the arrogant lawyer (Luke 10:25–29) who has no understanding of sin, righteousness, and judgment, use the Law to stir his conscience and will. If he is not conscious of his sin, use the Law to convict him. If he has a knowledge of sin, give him the gospel. (See Matthew 19:17–22 comment.)

When the fruit is ripe, it should practically fall off the tree, as with the Ethiopian eunuch. God led Philip to a soul that was ripe for salvation! If you have to twist and pull an apple off a branch, you will probably find it to be sour.

the water, both Philip and the eunuch; and he baptized him.

39 And when they were come up out of the water, the Spirit of the Lord caught away Philip, that the eunuch saw him no more: and he went on his way rejoicing.

40 But Philip was found at Azotus: and passing through he preached in all the cities, till he came to Caesarea.

CHAPTER 9

AND Saul, yet breathing out threatenings and slaughter against the disciples of the Lord, went to the high priest,

2 And desired of him letters to Damascus to the synagogues, that if he found any of this way, whether they were men or women, he might bring them bound to Jerusalem.

3 And as he journeyed, he came near Damascus: and suddenly there shined round about him a light from heaven:

4 And he fell to the earth, and heard a voice saying to him, Saul, Saul, why do you persecute me?

5 And he said, Who are you, Lord? And the Lord said, I am Jesus whom you persecute: it is hard for you to kick against the pricks.

6 And he trembling and astonished said, Lord, what will you have me to do? And the Lord said to him, Arise, and go into the city, and it shall be told you what you must do.

7 And the men which journeyed with him stood speechless, hearing a voice, but seeing no man.

8 And Saul arose from the earth; and when his eyes were opened, he saw no man: but they led him by the hand, and brought him into Damascus.

9 And he was three days without sight, and neither did eat nor drink.

10 And there was a certain disciple at Damascus, named Ananias; and to him said the Lord in a vision, Ananias. And he said, Behold, I am here, Lord.

11 And the Lord said to him, Arise, and go into the street which is called Straight, and inquire in the house of Judas for one called Saul, of Tarsus: for, behold, he prays,

12 And has seen in a vision a man named Ananias coming in, and putting his hand on him, that he might receive his sight.

13 Then Ananias answered, Lord, I have heard by many of this man, how much evil he has done to your saints at Jerusalem:

14 And here he has authority from the chief priests to bind all that call on your name.

15 But the Lord said to him, Go your way: for he is a chosen vessel to me, to bear my name before the Gentiles, and kings, and the children of Israel:

16 For I will show him how great things he must suffer for my name's sake.

17 And Ananias went his way, and entered into the house; and putting his hands on him said, Brother Saul, the Lord, even

---

8:39 God does the "follow-up." The exciting thing about true conversion is that there will be little need for what is commonly called "follow-up." A true convert will not need to be followed. He will put his hand to the plow and not look back (Luke 9:62). Of course, he will have to be fed, discipled, and nurtured. These things are biblical and most necessary. This can be done simply by encouraging him to read the Bible daily, answering questions he may have, and teaching him principles of fellowship, prayer, evangelism, etc.

Sometimes there is confusion between "follow-up" (we need to follow the new convert because he will fall away if we don't) and discipleship (instructing him to continue in the word of Christ—John 8:31). Look what happened after the Ethiopian eunuch was saved—he was left without follow-up. The Spirit of God transported Philip away and left the new convert in the wilderness. This is because his salvation wasn't dependent on Philip, but upon his relationship with the indwelling Lord. Those whom God saves, He keeps. If He is the author of their faith, He will be the finisher. If He has begun a good work in them, He will complete it. He is able to keep them from falling and present them faultless before the presence of His glory with exceeding joy.

Jesus, that appeared to you in the way as you came, has sent me, that you might receive your sight, and be filled with the Holy Spirit.

18 And immediately there fell from his eyes as it had been scales: and he received sight forthwith, and arose, and was baptized.

*The Buddhist seeks salvation by works.
For how to witness to him,
the comment following 2 John.*

19 And when he had received meat, he was strengthened. Then was Saul certain days with the disciples which were at Damascus.

20 And straightway he preached Christ in the synagogues, that he is the Son of God.

21 But all that heard him were amazed, and said; Is not this he that destroyed them which called on this name in Jerusalem, and came here for that intent, that he might bring them bound to the chief priests?

22 But Saul increased the more in strength, and confounded the Jews which dwelt at Damascus, proving that this is very Christ.

23 And after that many days were fulfilled, the Jews took counsel to kill him:

24 But their laying await was known of Saul. And they watched the gates day and night to kill him.

25 Then the disciples took him by night, and let him down by the wall in a basket.

26 And when Saul was come to Jerusalem, he assayed to join himself to the disciples: but they were all afraid of him, and believed not that he was a disciple.

27 But Barnabas took him, and brought him to the apostles, and declared to them how he had seen the Lord in the way, and that he had spoken to him, and how he had preached boldly at Damascus in the name of Jesus.

28 And he was with them coming in and going out at Jerusalem.

29 And he spoke boldly in the name of the Lord Jesus, and disputed against the Grecians: but they went about to slay him.

30 Which when the brethren knew, they brought him down to Caesarea, and sent him forth to Tarsus.

31 Then had the churches rest throughout all Judea and Galilee and Samaria, and were edified; and walking in the fear of the Lord, and in the comfort of the Holy Spirit, were multiplied.

32 And it came to pass, as Peter passed throughout all quarters, he came down also to the saints which dwelt at Lydda.

33 And there he found a certain man named Aeneas, which had kept his bed

---

9:22 Don't be discouraged if, as a new Christian you feel inadequate to share your faith. The very fact that you were once enjoying the pleasures of sin and are now walking that path of righteousness is a testimony that Jesus is the Christ. Many no doubt heard of the conversion of Saul of Tarsus without hearing him preach. A changed life is a testimony in itself.

9:31 **Fear of the Lord.** "The fear of the Lord involves a sober awareness of what He loves, of what He despises, and of the consequences of disobedience and rebellion against Him. It leads to a sincere desire to please Him, heartfelt gratefulness for His mercy, and unending delight in His loving presence. So when we choose to 'fear the Lord' we will heed Romans 12:9, 'Abhor what is evil. Cling to what is good.'" *Berit Kjos*

9:37 "What should I say to someone who has lost a loved one through cancer?"

Be very careful not to give the impression that God was punishing the person for his sins. Instead, speak about the fact that all around us we can see the evidence of a "fallen creation." Explain how in the beginning there was no disease, pain, suffering, or death. But when sin entered the world, it brought suffering with it. Then gently turn the conversation away from the person who died to the person who is still living. Ask if he has been thinking about God, and if he has kept the Ten Commandments. Then take the opportunity to go through the spiritual nature of God's Law. Someone who has lost a loved one often begins to ask soul-searching questions about God, death, and eternity. Many people are so hard-hearted that it takes a tragedy to make them receptive to God.

eight years, and was sick of the palsy.

34 And Peter said to him, Aeneas, Jesus Christ makes you whole: arise, and make your bed. And he arose immediately.

35 And all that dwelt at Lydda and Saron saw him, and turned to the Lord.

36 Now there was at Joppa a certain disciple named Tabitha, which by interpretation is called Dorcas: this woman was full of good works and almsdeeds which she did.

37 And it came to pass in those days, that she was sick, and died: whom when they had washed, they laid her in an upper chamber.

38 And forasmuch as Lydda was near to Joppa, and the disciples had heard that Peter was there, they sent to him two men, desiring him that he would not delay to come to them.

39 Then Peter arose and went with them. When he was come, they brought him into the upper chamber: and all the widows stood by him weeping, and showing the coats and garments which Dorcas made, while she was with them.

40 But Peter put them all forth, and kneeled down, and prayed; and turning him to the body said, Tabitha, arise. And she opened her eyes: and when she saw Peter, she sat up.

41 And he gave her his hand, and lifted her up, and when he had called the saints and widows, presented her alive.

42 And it was known throughout all Joppa; and many believed in the Lord.

43 And it came to pass, that he tarried many days in Joppa with one Simon a tanner.

CHAPTER 10

THERE was a certain man in Caesarea called Cornelius, a centurion of the band called the Italian band,

2 A devout man, and one that feared God with all his house, which gave many alms to the people, and prayed to God always.

3 He saw in a vision evidently about the ninth hour of the day an angel of God coming in to him, and saying to him, Cornelius.

4 And when he looked on him, he was afraid, and said, What is it, Lord? And he said to him, Your prayers and your alms are come up for a memorial before God.

5 And now send men to Joppa, and call for one Simon, whose surname is Peter:

6 He lodges with one Simon a tanner, whose house is by the sea side: he shall tell you what you ought to do.

7 And when the angel which spoke to Cornelius was departed, he called two of his household servants, and a devout sol-

dier of them that waited on him continually;

8 And when he had declared all these things to them, he sent them to Joppa.

9 On the morrow, as they went on their journey, and drew near to the city, Peter went up upon the housetop to pray about the sixth hour:

10 And he became very hungry, and would have eaten: but while they made ready, he fell into a trance,

11 And saw heaven opened, and a certain vessel descending to him, as it had been a great sheet knit at the four corners, and let down to the earth:

12 Wherein were all manner of four-footed beasts of the earth, and wild beasts, and creeping things, and fowls of the air.

13 And there came a voice to him, Rise, Peter; kill, and eat.

14 But Peter said, Not so, Lord; for I have never eaten any thing that is common or unclean.

15 And the voice spoke to him again the second time, What God has cleansed, that call not common.

16 This was done thrice: and the vessel was received up again into heaven.

17 Now while Peter doubted in himself what this vision which he had seen should mean, behold, the men which were sent from Cornelius had made inquiry for Simon's house, and stood before the gate,

18 And called, and asked whether Simon, which was surnamed Peter, were lodged there.

19 While Peter thought on the vision, the Spirit said to him, Behold, three men seek you.

20 Arise therefore, and get down, and go with them, doubting nothing: for I have sent them.

21 Then Peter went down to the men which were sent to him from Cornelius; and said, Behold, I am he whom you seek: what is the cause wherefore you are come?

22 And they said, Cornelius the centurion, a just man, and one that fears God, and of good report among all the nation of the Jews, was warned from God by an holy angel to send for you into his house, and to hear words of you.

23 Then called he them in, and lodged them. And on the morrow Peter went away with them, and certain brethren from Joppa accompanied him.

24 And the morrow after they entered into Caesarea. And Cornelius waited for them, and had called together his kinsmen and near friends.

25 And as Peter was coming in, Cornelius met him, and fell down at his feet, and worshipped him.

26 But Peter took him up, saying, Stand up; I myself also am a man.

> If people are to be saved by a message, it must contain at least some measure of knowledge. There must be light as well as fire.
>
> **CHARLES SPURGEON**

27 And as he talked with him, he went in, and found many that were come together.

28 And he said to them, You know how that it is an unlawful thing for a man that is a Jew to keep company, or come to one of another nation; but God has showed me that I should not call any man common or unclean.

29 Therefore came I to you without gainsaying, as soon as I was sent for: I ask therefore for what intent you have sent for me?

30 And Cornelius said, Four days ago I was fasting until this hour; and at the ninth hour I prayed in my house, and, behold, a man stood before me in bright clothing,

31 And said, Cornelius, your prayer is heard, and your alms are had in remembrance in the sight of God.

32 Send therefore to Joppa, and call here Simon, whose surname is Peter; he is lodged in the house of one Simon a tanner by the sea side: who, when he comes, shall speak to you.

33 Immediately therefore I sent to you;

and you have well done that you are come. Now therefore are we all here present before God, to hear all things that are commanded you of God.

34 Then Peter opened his mouth, and said, Of a truth I perceive that God is no respecter of persons:

35 But in every nation he that fears him, and works righteousness, is accepted with him.

36 The word which God sent to the children of Israel, preaching peace by Jesus Christ: (he is Lord of all:)

37 That word, I say, you know, which was published throughout all Judea, and began from Galilee, after the baptism which John preached;

38 How God anointed Jesus of Nazareth with the Holy Spirit and with power: who went about doing good, and healing all that were oppressed of the devil; for God was with him.

39 And we are witnesses of all things which he did both in the land of the Jews, and in Jerusalem; whom they slew and hanged on a tree:

40 Him God raised up the third day, and showed him openly;

41 Not to all the people, but to witnesses chosen before of God, even to us, who did eat and drink with him after he rose from the dead.

42 And he commanded us to preach to the people, and to testify that it is he which was ordained of God to be the Judge of quick and dead.

43 To him give all the prophets witness, that through his name whosoever believes in him shall receive remission of sins.

44 While Peter yet spoke these words, the Holy Spirit fell on all them which heard the word.

45 And they of the circumcision which believed were astonished, as many as came with Peter, because that on the Gentiles also was poured out the gift of the Holy Spirit.

46 For they heard them speak with tongues, and magnify God. Then answered Peter,

47 Can any man forbid water, that these should not be baptized, which have received the Holy Spirit as well as we?

48 And he commanded them to be baptized in the name of the Lord. Then prayed they him to tarry certain days.

10:38   The Trinity at work in redemption. "In every major phase of the redemption, each Person of the Godhead is directly involved. Their involvement in each successive phase may be set out as follows:

1. *Incarnation.* The Father incarnated the Son in the womb of Mary by the Holy Spirit (see Luke 1:35).
2. *Baptism in the Jordan River.* The Spirit descended on the Son, and the Father spoke His approval from heaven (see Matthew 3:14–17).
3. *Public ministry.* The Father anointed the Son with the Spirit (see Acts 10:38).
4. *The crucifixion.* Jesus offered Himself to the Father through the Spirit (see Hebrews 9:14).
5. *The resurrection.* The Father resurrected the Son by the Spirit (see Acts 2:32; Romans 1:4).
6. *Pentecost.* From the Father the Son received the Spirit, whom He then poured out on His disciples (see Acts 2:33).

Each Person of the Godhead—and I mean this reverently—was jealous to be included in the process of redeeming humanity." *Derek Prince, Atonement*

10:47   Baptism. If we are saved by being water baptized (as certain Scriptures *seem* to imply), then we are saved by works and not grace. The Holy Spirit fell on the Gentles *before* they were baptized. This means they were saved (by God's grace) *before* they went near water. Paul said that Christ sent him not to baptize, but to preach (1 Corinthians 1:17). That's because it is the gospel that saves us, not our works in response to it. As this verse shows, baptism is an act of obedience *after* salvation.

CHAPTER 11

AND the apostles and brethren that were in Judea heard that the Gentiles had also received the word of God.

2 And when Peter was come up to Jerusalem, they that were of the circumcision contended with him,

3 Saying, You went in to men uncircumcised, and did eat with them.

4 But Peter rehearsed the matter from the beginning, and expounded it by order to them, saying,

5 I was in the city of Joppa praying: and in a trance I saw a vision, A certain vessel descend, as it had been a great sheet, let down from heaven by four corners; and it came even to me:

6 Upon the which when I had fastened mine eyes, I considered, and saw fourfooted beasts of the earth, and wild beasts, and creeping things, and fowls of the air.

7 And I heard a voice saying to me, Arise, Peter; slay and eat.

8 But I said, Not so, Lord: for nothing common or unclean has at any time entered into my mouth.

9 But the voice answered me again from heaven, What God has cleansed, that call not common.

10 And this was done three times: and all were drawn up again into heaven.

11 And, behold, immediately there were three men already come to the house where I was, sent from Caesarea to me.

12 And the spirit bade me go with them, nothing doubting. Moreover these six brethren accompanied me, and we entered into the man's house:

13 And he showed us how he had seen an angel in his house, which stood and said to him, Send men to Joppa, and call for Simon, whose surname is Peter;

14 Who shall tell you words, whereby you and all your house shall be saved.

15 And as I began to speak, the Holy Spirit fell on them, as on us at the beginning.

16 Then remembered I the word of the Lord, how that he said, John indeed baptized with water; but you shall be baptized with the Holy Spirit.

17 Forasmuch then as God gave them the like gift as he did to us, who believed on the Lord Jesus Christ; what was I, that I could withstand God?

18 When they heard these things, they held their peace, and glorified God, saying, Then has God also to the Gentiles granted repentance to life.

19 Now they which were scattered abroad upon the persecution that arose about Stephen traveled as far as Phenice, and Cyprus, and Antioch, preaching the word to none but to the Jews only.

20 And some of them were men of Cyprus and Cyrene, which, when they were come to Antioch, spoke to the Grecians, preaching the Lord Jesus.

21 And the hand of the Lord was with them: and a great number believed, and turned to the Lord.

Each individual is unique from the moment of conception. For how we are fearfully and wonderfully made, see Psalm 139:14 comment.

22 Then tidings of these things came to the ears of the church which was in Jerusalem: and they sent forth Barnabas, that he should go as far as Antioch.

23 Who, when he came, and had seen the grace of God, was glad, and exhorted them all, that with purpose of heart they would cleave to the Lord.

24 For he was a good man, and full of the Holy Spirit and of faith: and much people was added to the Lord.

25 Then departed Barnabas to Tarsus, for to seek Saul:

26 And when he had found him, he brought him to Antioch. And it came to pass, that a whole year they assembled themselves with the church, and taught much people. And the disciples were called Christians first in Antioch.

27 And in these days came prophets from Jerusalem to Antioch.

28 And there stood up one of them named Agabus, and signified by the spirit that there should be great dearth throughout all the world: which came to pass in the days of Claudius Caesar.

29 Then the disciples, every man according to his ability, determined to send relief to the brethren which dwelt in Judea:

30 Which also they did, and sent it to the elders by the hands of Barnabas and Saul.

CHAPTER 12

NOW about that time Herod the king stretched forth his hands to vex certain of the church.

2 And he killed James the brother of John with the sword.

3 And because he saw it pleased the Jews, he proceeded further to take Peter also. (Then were the days of unleavened bread.)

4 And when he had apprehended him, he put him in prison, and delivered him to

THE FUNCTION OF THE LAW

12:7 "The very first end of the Law [is], namely, convicting men of sin; awakening those who are still asleep on the brink of hell...The ordinary method of God is to convict sinners by the Law, and that only. The gospel is not the means which God hath ordained, or which our Lord Himself used, for this end." *John Wesley*

"Few, very few, are ever awakened or convinced by the encouragements and promises of the gospel, but almost all by the denunciations of the law." *Timothy Dwight*

four quaternions of soldiers to keep him; intending after Easter to bring him forth to the people.

5 Peter therefore was kept in prison: but prayer was made without ceasing of the church to God for him.

6 And when Herod would have brought him forth, the same night Peter was sleeping between two soldiers, bound with two chains: and the keepers before the door kept the prison.

7 And, behold, the angel of the Lord came upon him, and a light shined in the prison: and he smote Peter on the side, and raised him up, saying, Arise up quickly. And his chains fell off from his hands.

8 And the angel said to him, Gird your-

12:6 The chains of sin and death. Peter lay soundly asleep in Herod's prison. This is faith in action. Faith snoozes, even in a storm. Stephen had been stoned, James had just been killed with a sword,...and Peter sleeps like a parishioner in the back row of a dead church. He was bound with chains between two soldiers. More guards stood before the door of the prison. Suddenly an angel of the Lord appeared and stood by him, "and a light shined in the prison." There is a strong inference that the light didn't awaken Peter from his sleep, because the Scriptures then tell us that the angel struck him on the side. As he arose, his chains fell off, he girded himself, tied on his shoes, put on his garment, and followed the angel. After that, the iron gate leading to the city opened of its own accord, and Peter was free.

The sinner is in the prison of his sins. He is taken captive by the devil. He is bound by the chains of sin, under the sentence of death. He is asleep in his sins. He lives in a dream world. But it isn't the gospel light that will awaken him. How can "Good News" alarm a sinner? Rather, the Law must strike him. He needs to be struck with the lightning of Sinai and awakened by its thunderings. That will rouse him to his plight of being on the threshold of death. Then he will arise and the gospel will remove the chains of sin and death. It will be "the power of God unto salvation." Then he will gird himself with truth, tie on his gospel shoes, put on his garment of righteousness, follow the Lord, and the iron gate of the Celestial City will open of its own accord.

self, and bind on your sandals. And so he did. And he said to him, Cast your garment about you, and follow me.

9 And he went out, and followed him; and did not know that it was true which was done by the angel; but thought he saw a vision.

10 When they were past the first and the second ward, they came to the iron gate that leads to the city; which opened to them of his own accord: and they went out, and passed on through one street; and forthwith the angel departed from him.

11 And when Peter was come to himself, he said, Now I know of a surety, that the Lord has sent his angel, and has delivered me out of the hand of Herod, and from all the expectation of the people of the Jews.

12 And when he had considered the thing, he came to the house of Mary the mother of John, whose surname was Mark; where many were gathered together praying.

13 And as Peter knocked at the door of the gate, a damsel came to hearken, named Rhoda.

14 And when she knew Peter's voice, she opened not the gate for gladness, but ran in, and told how Peter stood before the gate.

15 And they said to her, You are mad. But she constantly affirmed that it was even so. Then said they, It is his angel.

16 But Peter continued knocking: and when they had opened the door, and saw him, they were astonished.

17 But he, beckoning to them with the hand to hold their peace, declared to them how the Lord had brought him out of the prison. And he said, Go show these things to James, and to the brethren. And he departed, and went into another place.

18 Now as soon as it was day, there was no small stir among the soldiers, what was become of Peter.

19 And when Herod had sought for him,

and found him not, he examined the keepers, and commanded that they should be put to death. And he went down from Judea to Caesarea, and there abode.

20 And Herod was highly displeased with them of Tyre and Sidon: but they came with one accord to him, and, having made Blastus the king's chamberlain their friend, desired peace; because their country was nourished by the king's country.

21 And upon a set day Herod, arrayed in royal apparel, sat upon his throne, and made an oration to them.

22 And the people gave a shout, saying, It is the voice of a god, and not of a man.

23 And immediately the angel of the Lord smote him, because he gave not God the glory: and he was eaten of worms, and gave up the ghost.

24 But the word of God grew and multiplied.

25 And Barnabas and Saul returned from Jerusalem, when they had fulfilled their ministry, and took with them John, whose surname was Mark.

. . . . . .

For questions to ask evolutionists,
see Proverbs 3:19 comment.

. . . . . .

CHAPTER 13

NOW there were in the church that was at Antioch certain prophets and teachers; as Barnabas, and Simeon that was called Niger, and Lucius of Cyrene, and Manaen, which had been brought up with Herod the tetrarch, and Saul.

2 As they ministered to the Lord, and fasted, the Holy Spirit said, Separate me Barnabas and Saul for the work whereunto I have called them.

3 And when they had fasted and prayed, and laid their hands on them, they sent them away.

4 So they, being sent forth by the Holy

12:12 Prayer—the secret weapon: See Acts 21:5.

Spirit, departed to Seleucia; and from thence they sailed to Cyprus.

5 And when they were at Salamis, they preached the word of God in the synagogues of the Jews: and they had also John as their minister.

6 And when they had gone through the isle to Paphos, they found a certain sorcerer, a false prophet, a Jew, whose name was Bar-jesus:

7 Which was with the deputy of the country, Sergius Paulus, a prudent man; who called for Barnabas and Saul, and desired to hear the word of God.

8 But Elymas the sorcerer (for so is his name by interpretation) withstood them, seeking to turn away the deputy from the faith.

9 Then Saul, (who also is called Paul,) filled with the Holy Spirit, set his eyes on him,

10 And said, O full of all subtlety and all mischief, you child of the devil, you enemy of all righteousness, will you not cease to pervert the right ways of the Lord?

11 And now, behold, the hand of the Lord is upon you, and you shall be blind, not seeing the sun for a season. And immediately there fell on him a mist and a darkness; and he went about seeking some to lead him by the hand.

12 Then the deputy, when he saw what was done, believed, being astonished at the doctrine of the Lord.

13 Now when Paul and his company loosed from Paphos, they came to Perga in Pamphylia: and John departing from them returned to Jerusalem.

14 But when they departed from Perga, they came to Antioch in Pisidia, and went into the synagogue on the sabbath day, and sat down.

15 And after the reading of the law and the prophets the rulers of the synagogue sent to them, saying, You men and brethren, if you have any word of exhortation for the people, say on.

16 Then Paul stood up, and beckoning with his hand said, Men of Israel, and you that fear God, give audience.

17 The God of this people of Israel chose our fathers, and exalted the people when they dwelt as strangers in the land of Egypt, and with an high arm brought he them out of it.

18 And about the time of forty years suffered he their manners in the wilderness.

19 And when he had destroyed seven nations in the land of Canaan, he divided their land to them by lot.

20 And after that he gave to them judges about the space of four hundred and fifty years, until Samuel the prophet.

21 And afterward they desired a king: and God gave to them Saul the son of Cis, a man of the tribe of Benjamin, by the space of forty years.

22 And when he had removed him, he raised up to them David to be their king; to whom also he gave testimony, and said, I have found David the son of Jesse, a man after mine own heart, which shall fulfil all my will.

23 Of this man's seed has God according to his promise raised to Israel a Savior, Jesus:

24 When John had first preached before his coming the baptism of repentance to all the people of Israel.

25 And as John fulfilled his course, he said, Whom do you think that I am? I am not he. But, behold, there comes one after me, whose shoes of his feet I am not worthy to loose.

26 Men and brethren, children of the stock of Abraham, and whosoever among you fears God, to you is the word of this salvation sent.

13:22 The psalms reveal that David was sometimes vindictive and even hateful in prayer. However, he proved to be "a man after [God's] own heart" in his dealings with King Saul. He was full of mercy and grace in the face of murderous hostility. This may be because he had the good sense to pour his heart out to God, dealing with his anger in the privacy of prayer.

27 For they that dwell at Jerusalem, and their rulers, because they knew him not, nor yet the voices of the prophets which are read every sabbath day, they have fulfilled them in condemning him.

28 And though they found no cause of death in him, yet desired they Pilate that he should be slain.

29 And when they had fulfilled all that was written of him, they took him down from the tree, and laid him in a sepulchre.

30 But God raised him from the dead:

31 And he was seen many days of them which came up with him from Galilee to Jerusalem, who are his witnesses to the people.

32 And we declare to you glad tidings, how that the promise which was made to the fathers,

33 God has fulfilled the same to us their children, in that he has raised up Jesus again; as it is also written in the second psalm, You are my Son, this day have I begotten you.

34 And as concerning that he raised him up from the dead, now no more to return to corruption, he said on this wise, I will give you the sure mercies of David.

35 Wherefore he said also in another psalm, You shall not suffer your Holy One to see corruption.

36 For David, after he had served his own generation by the will of God, fell on sleep, and was laid to his fathers, and saw corruption:

37 But he, whom God raised again, saw no corruption.

38 Be it known to you therefore, men and brethren, that through this man is preached to you the forgiveness of sins:

39 And by him all that believe are justified from all things, from which you could not be justified by the law of Moses.

40 Beware therefore, lest that come upon you, which is spoken of in the prophets;

41 Behold, you despisers, and wonder, and perish: for I work a work in your days, a work which you shall in no wise believe, though a man declare it to you.

> Some have used the terrors of the Lord to terrify, but Paul used them to persuade.
>
> **CHARLES SPURGEON**

42 And when the Jews were gone out of the synagogue, the Gentiles besought that these words might be preached to them the next sabbath.

43 Now when the congregation was broken up, many of the Jews and religious proselytes followed Paul and Barnabas: who, speaking to them, persuaded them to continue in the grace of God.

44 And the next sabbath day came almost the whole city together to hear the word of God.

45 But when the Jews saw the multitudes, they were filled with envy, and spoke against those things which were spoken by Paul, contradicting and blaspheming.

46 Then Paul and Barnabas waxed bold, and said, It was necessary that the word of God should first have been spoken to you: but seeing you put it from you, and

---

13:38,39 Notice to whom Paul was speaking. This was to Jews who knew the Law (v. 15). He therefore preached the gospel of grace—Christ crucified and risen from the dead.

13:39 Justification. "[Justification] is the judicial act of God, by which He pardons all the sins of those who believe in Christ, and accounts, accepts, and treats them as righteous in the eye of the Law, i.e., as conformed to all its demands. In addition to the pardon of sin, justification declares that all the claims of the Law are satisfied in respect of the justified. It is the act of a judge and not of a sovereign. The Law is not relaxed or set aside, but is declared to be fulfilled in the strictest sense; and so the person justified is declared to be entitled to all the advantages and rewards arising from perfect obedience to the Law." *Easton Bible Dictionary*

QUESTIONS & OBJECTIONS

13:47 *"If I submit to God, I'll just become a puppet!"*

"A brilliant young man questioned Dr. Henrietta Mears about surrendering his life to God. He was convinced that becoming a Christian would mean the destruction of his personality, that he'd be altered in some strange way, and that he'd lose control of his own mind. He feared becoming a mere puppet in God's hands.

"So Miss Mears asked him to watch as she turned on a lamp. One moment it was dark, then she turned on the switch. She explained, 'The lamp surrendered itself to the electric current and light has filled the room. The lamp didn't destroy its personality when it surrendered to the current. On the contrary—the very thing happened for which the lamp was created: it gave light.'"
Vonette Bright, Renew a Steadfast Spirit Within Me

judge yourselves unworthy of everlasting life, lo, we turn to the Gentiles.

47 For so has the Lord commanded us, saying, I have set you to be a light of the Gentiles, that you should be for salvation to the ends of the earth.

48 And when the Gentiles heard this, they were glad, and glorified the word of the Lord: and as many as were ordained to eternal life believed.

49 And the word of the Lord was published throughout all the region.

50 But the Jews stirred up the devout and honorable women, and the chief men of the city, and raised persecution against Paul and Barnabas, and expelled them out of their coasts.

51 But they shook off the dust of their feet against them, and came to Iconium.

52 And the disciples were filled with joy, and with the Holy Spirit.

CHAPTER 14

AND it came to pass in Iconium, that they went both together into the synagogue of the Jews, and so spoke, that a great multitude both of the Jews and also of the Greeks believed.

2 But the unbelieving Jews stirred up the Gentiles, and made their minds evil affected against the brethren.

3 Long time therefore abode they speaking boldly in the Lord, which gave testimony to the word of his grace, and grant-

ed signs and wonders to be done by their hands.

4 But the multitude of the city was divided: and part held with the Jews, and part with the apostles.

5 And when there was an assault made both of the Gentiles, and also of the Jews with their rulers, to use them despitefully, and to stone them,

6 They were ware of it, and fled to Lystra and Derbe, cities of Lycaonia, and to the region that lies round about:

7 And there they preached the gospel.

8 And there sat a certain man at Lystra, impotent in his feet, being a cripple from his mother's womb, who never had walked:

9 The same heard Paul speak: who steadfastly beholding him, and perceiving that he had faith to be healed,

10 Said with a loud voice, Stand upright on your feet. And he leaped and walked.

11 And when the people saw what Paul had done, they lifted up their voices, saying in the speech of Lycaonia, The gods are come down to us in the likeness of men.

12 And they called Barnabas, Jupiter; and Paul, Mercurius, because he was the chief speaker.

13 Then the priest of Jupiter, which was before their city, brought oxen and garlands to the gates, and would have done sacrifice with the people.

14 Which when the apostles, Barnabas

14:15 "Missing Link" Still Missing

"Did dinos soar? Imaginations certainly took flight over *Archaeoraptor Liaoningensis*, a birdlike fossil with a meat-eater's tail that was spirited out of northeastern China, 'discovered' at a Tucson, Arizona, gem and mineral show last year, and displayed at the National Geographic Society in Washington, D.C. Some 110,000 visitors saw the exhibit, which closed January 17; millions more read about the find in November's *National Geographic*. Now, paleontologists are eating crow. Instead of 'a true missing link' connecting dinosaurs to birds, the specimen appears to be a composite, its unusual appendage likely tacked on by a Chinese farmer, not evolution.

"*Archaeoraptor* is hardly the first 'missing link' to snap under scrutiny. In 1912, fossil remains of an ancient hominid were found in England's Piltdown quarries and quickly dubbed man's ape-like ancestor. It took decades to reveal the hoax." *U.S. News & World Report*, February 14, 2000

"Darwin admitted that millions of 'missing links,' transitional life forms, would have to be discovered in the fossil record to prove the accuracy of his theory that all species had gradually evolved by chance mutation into new species. [See next page.] Unfortunately for his theory, despite hundreds of millions spent on searching for fossils worldwide for more than a century, the scientists have failed to locate *a single missing link* out of the millions that must exist if their theory of evolution is to be vindicated." *Grant R. Jeffery, The Signature of God*

"There are gaps in the fossil graveyard, places where there should be intermediate forms, but where there is nothing whatsoever instead. No paleontologist...denies that this is so. It is simply a fact. Darwin's theory and the fossil record are in conflict." *David Berlinsky*

"Scientists concede that their most cherished theories are based on embarrassingly few fossil fragments and that huge gaps exist in the fossil record." *Time* magazine, Nov. 7, 1977

"The evolutionists seem to know everything about the missing link except the fact that it is missing." *G. K. Chesterton*

and Paul, heard of, they rent their clothes, and ran in among the people, crying out, **15** And saying, Sirs, why do you these things? We also are men of like passions with you, and preach to you that you should turn from these vanities to the living God, which made heaven, and earth, and the sea, and all things that are therein:

16 Who in times past suffered all nations to walk in their own ways.

17 Nevertheless he left not himself with-

14:15 Evolutionary fraud. "Charles Dawson, a British lawyer and amateur geologist, announced in 1912 his discovery of pieces of a human skull and an apelike jaw in a gravel pit near the town of Piltdown, England...Dawson's announcement stopped the scorn cold. Experts instantly declared Piltdown Man (estimated to be 300,000 to one million years old) the evolutionary find of the century. Darwin's missing link had been identified.

"Or so it seemed for the next 40 or so years. Then, in the early fifties...scientists began to suspect misattribution. In 1953, that suspicion gave way to a full-blown scandal: Piltdown Man was a hoax. Radiocarbon tests proved that its skull belonged to a 600-year old woman, and its jaw to a 500-year old orangutan from the East Indies." *Our Times: The Illustrated History of the 20th Century*

The Piltdown Man fraud wasn't an isolated incident. The famed Nebraska Man was derived from a single tooth, which was later found to be from an extinct pig. Java Man, found in the early 20th century, was nothing more than a piece of skull, a fragment of a thigh bone, and three molar teeth. The rest came from the deeply fertile imaginations of plaster of Paris workers. Java Man is now regarded as fully human. Heidelberg Man came from a jawbone, a large chin section, and a few teeth. Most scientists reject the jawbone because it's similar to that of modern man. Still, many evolutionists believe that he's 250,000 years old. No doubt they pinpointed (continued on next page)

out witness, in that he did good, and gave us rain from heaven, and fruitful seasons, filling our hearts with food and gladness.

18 And with these sayings scarce restrained they the people, that they had not done sacrifice to them.

19 And there came there certain Jews from Antioch and Iconium, who persuaded the people, and, having stoned Paul, drew him out of the city, supposing he had been dead.

20 Howbeit, as the disciples stood round about him, he rose up, and came into the city: and the next day he departed with Barnabas to Derbe.

21 And when they had preached the gospel to that city, and had taught many, they returned again to Lystra, and to Iconium, and Antioch,

22 Confirming the souls of the disciples, and exhorting them to continue in the faith, and that we must through much tribulation enter into the kingdom of God.

23 And when they had ordained them

"As by this theory innumerable transitional forms must have existed, why do we not find them embedded in countless numbers in the crust of the earth? The number of intermediate links between all living and extinct species must have been inconceivably great!"

Charles Darwin

(14:15 continued) his birthday with carbon dating. However, *Time* magazine (June 11, 1990) published a science article subtitled, "Geologists show that carbon dating can be way off." And don't look to Neanderthal Man for any evidence of evolution. He died of exposure. His skull was exposed as being fully human, not ape. Not only was his stooped posture found to be caused by disease, but he spoke and was artistic and religious.

"Shells from *living* snails were carbon dated as being 27,000 years old." *Science* magazine, vol. 224, 1984 (emphasis added)

14:17 Scientific facts in the Bible. Job stated, "[God] made a decree for the rain, and a way for the lightning of the thunder" (Job 28:26). Centuries later, scientists began to discern the "decrees [rules] for the rain." Rainfall is part of a process called the "water cycle." The sun evaporates water from the ocean. The water vapor then rises and becomes clouds. This water in the clouds falls back to earth as rain, and collects in streams and rivers, then makes its way back to the ocean. That process repeats itself again and again. About 300 years ago, Galileo discovered this cycle. But amazingly the Scriptures described it centuries before. The prophet Amos (9:6) wrote that God "calls for the water of the sea, and pours them out upon the face of the earth." Scientists are just beginning to fully understand God's "decrees for the rain."

14:19 Open-air preaching. "The [street] preachers needed to have faces set like flints, and so indeed they had. John Furz says, 'As soon as I began to preach, a man came forward and presented a gun at my face; swearing that he would blow my brains out if I spoke another word. However, I continued speaking and he continued swearing, sometimes putting the muzzle of the gun to my mouth, sometimes against my ear. While we were singing the last hymn, he got behind me, fired the gun, and burned off part of my hair.'

"After this, my brethren, we ought never to speak of petty interruptions or annoyances. The proximity of a blunderbuss in the hands of a son of Belial is not very conducive to collected thought and clear utterance." *Charles Spurgeon*

elders in every church, and had prayed with fasting, they commended them to the Lord, on whom they believed.

24 And after they had passed throughout Pisidia, they came to Pamphylia.

25 And when they had preached the word in Perga, they went down into Attalia:

26 And thence sailed to Antioch, from whence they had been recommended to the grace of God for the work which they fulfilled.

27 And when they were come, and had gathered the church together, they rehearsed all that God had done with them, and how he had opened the door of faith to the Gentiles.

28 And there they abode long time with the disciples.

CHAPTER 15

AND certain men which came down from Judea taught the brethren, and said, Except you be circumcised after the manner of Moses, you cannot be saved.

2 When therefore Paul and Barnabas had no small dissension and disputation with them, they determined that Paul and Barnabas, and certain other of them, should go up to Jerusalem to the apostles and elders about this question.

3 And being brought on their way by the church, they passed through Phenice and Samaria, declaring the conversion of the Gentiles: and they caused great joy to all the brethren.

4 And when they were come to Jerusalem, they were received of the church, and of the apostles and elders, and they declared all things that God had done with them.

5 But there rose up certain of the sect of the Pharisees which believed, saying, That it was needful to circumcise them, and to command them to keep the law of Moses.

6 And the apostles and elders came together for to consider of this matter.

7 And when there had been much disputing, Peter rose up, and said to them, Men and brethren, you know how that a good while ago God made choice among us, that the Gentiles by my mouth should hear the word of the gospel, and believe.

8 And God, which knows the hearts, bare them witness, giving them the Holy Spirit, even as he did to us;

9 And put no difference between us and them, purifying their hearts by faith.

10 Now therefore why do you tempt God, to put a yoke upon the neck of the disciples, which neither our fathers nor we were able to bear?

11 But we believe that through the grace of the Lord Jesus Christ we shall be saved, even as they.

12 Then all the multitude kept silence, and gave audience to Barnabas and Paul, declaring what miracles and wonders God had wrought among the Gentiles by them.

13 And after they had held their peace, James answered, saying, Men and brethren, hearken to me:

14 Simeon has declared how God at the first did visit the Gentiles, to take out of them a people for his name.

15 And to this agree the words of the prophets; as it is written,

16 After this I will return, and will build again the tabernacle of David, which is fallen down; and I will build again the ruins thereof, and I will set it up:

17 That the residue of men might seek after the Lord, and all the Gentiles, upon whom my name is called, said the Lord, who does all these things.

18 Known to God are all his works from the beginning of the world.

19 Wherefore my sentence is, that we

15:18   God doesn't think as we do. He is omniscient—He knows all things. That means He never has an idea. If a concept suddenly came to Him, then He would be ignorant of the thought before it formed in His mind. However, God doesn't have thoughts "come to His mind." Because He is omniscient, His mind has all thoughts resident.

trouble not them, which from among the Gentiles are turned to God:

20 But that we write to them, that they abstain from pollutions of idols, and from fornication, and from things strangled, and from blood.

21 For Moses of old time has in every city them that preach him, being read in the synagogues every sabbath day.

22 Then pleased it the apostles and elders, with the whole church, to send chosen men of their own company to Antioch with Paul and Barnabas; namely, Judas surnamed Barsabas, and Silas, chief men among the brethren:

> My main business is the saving of souls. This one thing I do.
>
> **CHARLES SPURGEON**

23 And they wrote letters by them after this manner; The apostles and elders and brethren send greeting to the brethren which are of the Gentiles in Antioch and Syria and Cilicia:

24 Forasmuch as we have heard, that certain which went out from us have troubled you with words, subverting your souls, saying, You must be circumcised, and keep the law: to whom we gave no such commandment:

25 It seemed good to us, being assembled with one accord, to send chosen men to you with our beloved Barnabas and Paul,

26 Men that have hazarded their lives for the name of our Lord Jesus Christ.

27 We have sent therefore Judas and Silas, who shall also tell you the same things by mouth.

28 For it seemed good to the Holy Spirit, and to us, to lay upon you no greater burden than these necessary things;

29 That you abstain from meats offered to idols, and from blood, and from things strangled, and from fornication: from which if you keep yourselves, you shall do well. Fare you well.

30 So when they were dismissed, they came to Antioch: and when they had gathered the multitude together, they delivered the epistle:

31 Which when they had read, they rejoiced for the consolation.

32 And Judas and Silas, being prophets also themselves, exhorted the brethren with many words, and confirmed them.

33 And after they had tarried there a space, they were let go in peace from the brethren to the apostles.

34 Notwithstanding it pleased Silas to abide there still.

35 Paul also and Barnabas continued in Antioch, teaching and preaching the word of the Lord, with many others also.

36 And some days after Paul said to Barnabas, Let us go again and visit our brethren in every city where we have preached the word of the Lord, and see how they do.

37 And Barnabas determined to take with them John, whose surname was Mark.

38 But Paul thought it not good to take him with them, who departed from them from Pamphylia, and went not with them to the work.

39 And the contention was so sharp between them, that they departed asunder one from the other: and so Barnabas took Mark, and sailed to Cyprus;

40 And Paul chose Silas, and departed, being recommended by the brethren to the grace of God.

41 And he went through Syria and Cilicia, confirming the churches.

CHAPTER 16

THEN came he to Derbe and Lystra: and, behold, a certain disciple was there, named Timotheus, the son of a certain woman, which was a Jewess, and believed; but his father was a Greek:

2 Which was well reported of by the brethren that were at Lystra and Iconium.

3 Him would Paul have to go forth with him; and took and circumcised him because of the Jews which were in those quarters: for they knew all that his father was a Greek.

4 And as they went through the cities, they delivered them the decrees for to keep, that were ordained of the apostles and elders which were at Jerusalem.

5 And so were the churches established in the faith, and increased in number daily.

6 Now when they had gone throughout Phrygia and the region of Galatia, and were forbidden of the Holy Spirit to preach the word in Asia,

7 After they were come to Mysia, they assayed to go into Bithynia: but the Spirit suffered them not.

8 And they passing by Mysia came down to Troas.

9 And a vision appeared to Paul in the night; There stood a man of Macedonia, and prayed him, saying, Come over into Macedonia, and help us.

10 And after he had seen the vision, immediately we endeavored to go into Macedonia, assuredly gathering that the Lord had called us for to preach the gospel to them.

11 Therefore loosing from Troas, we came with a straight course to Samothracia, and the next day to Neapolis;

12 And from thence to Philippi, which is the chief city of that part of Macedonia, and a colony: and we were in that city abiding certain days.

13 And on the sabbath we went out of the city by a river side, where prayer was wont to be made; and we sat down, and spoke to the women which resorted there.

14 And a certain woman named Lydia, a seller of purple, of the city of Thyatira, which worshipped God, heard us: whose heart the Lord opened, that she attended to the things which were spoken of Paul.

15 And when she was baptized, and her household, she besought us, saying, If you have judged me to be faithful to the Lord, come into my house, and abide there. And she constrained us.

16 And it came to pass, as we went to prayer, a certain damsel possessed with a spirit of divination met us, which brought her masters much gain by soothsaying:

16:6 "I think a good rule of thumb to follow would be to presume the Lord wants you to share the gospel with everyone unless He leads you not to." *Danny Lehmann*

16:16 Those who think they are contacting their dead loved ones through the occult are actually contacting "familiar spirits" (demons), a forbidden practice (Leviticus 19:31; 20:6; Deuteronomy 18:10–12).

16:16–18 The woman (or the demon) was speaking the truth. These men *were* servants of the Most High God, and they *were* showing the way of salvation. Why then was Paul grieved? Satan is very subtle. Rather than openly oppose the truth, he will often attempt to conceal it by maintaining that the occult and God are compatible. If you are open-air preaching, don't be surprised to have someone who is obviously demonically controlled loudly agree with you, so that it looks to the crowd that you are both preaching the same message. This *is* very frustrating.

For two years I was heckled almost daily by a woman named Petra. She dressed in black, carried a wooden staff, and said she was a prophet to the nation. As in the days of Noah, only eight would be saved. She maintained that she was one of them, and that she determined who the other seven would be. She also claimed that my spirit visited her spirit in the night (it did not!). My problem was that she would "Amen" much of what I preached, adding her thoughts at the points I made. She would do this at the top of her very loud voice. It must have appeared to newcomers to the crowd that we were a team, preaching the same thing. This was why I was delighted when (every now and then) she would get angry with something I said and let out a string of cuss words, revealing to the crowd that we were *not* on the same side.

The question arises as to whether Paul did the right thing by casting out the demon. I'm not sure he did. If the woman wasn't repentant, she may have received seven more demons (Matthew 12:43–45). After his action, great persecution came against the disciples, but God in His goodness worked it out for their good, and for the good of the Philippian jailer and his family (see vv. 24–34).

17 The same followed Paul and us, and cried, saying, These men are the servants of the most high God, which show to us the way of salvation.

18 And this did she many days. But Paul, being grieved, turned and said to the spirit, I command you in the name of Jesus Christ to come out of her. And he came out the same hour.

19 And when her masters saw that the hope of their gains was gone, they caught Paul and Silas, and drew them into the marketplace to the rulers,

20 And brought them to the magistrates, saying, These men, being Jews, do exceedingly trouble our city,

21 And teach customs, which are not lawful for us to receive, neither to observe, being Romans.

22 And the multitude rose up together against them: and the magistrates tore off their clothes, and commanded to beat them.

23 And when they had laid many stripes upon them, they cast them into prison, charging the jailor to keep them safely:

24 Who, having received such a charge, thrust them into the inner prison, and made their feet fast in the stocks.

25 And at midnight Paul and Silas prayed, and sang praises to God: and the prison-ers heard them.

26 And suddenly there was a great earthquake, so that the foundations of the prison were shaken: and immediately all the doors were opened, and every one's bands were loosed.

27 And the keeper of the prison awaking out of his sleep, and seeing the prison doors open, he drew out his sword, and would have killed himself, supposing that the prisoners had been fled.

28 But Paul cried with a loud voice, saying, Do yourself no harm: for we are all here.

29 Then he called for a light, and sprang in, and came trembling, and fell down before Paul and Silas,

30 And brought them out, and said, Sirs, what must I do to be saved?

31 And they said, Believe on the Lord Jesus Christ, and you shall be saved, and your house.

32 And they spoke to him the word of the Lord, and to all that were in his house.

33 And he took them the same hour of the night, and washed their stripes; and was baptized, he and all his, straightway.

34 And when he had brought them into his house, he set meat before them, and rejoiced, believing in God with all his house.

35 And when it was day, the magistrates

16:25 Ira Sankey, before he became D. L. Moody's famous song leader (and a powerful preacher himself), was assigned to night duty in the American Civil War. While he was on duty, he lifted his eyes toward heaven and began to sing, praising the Lord while he was alone. At least, he thought he was alone.

Years later, after the war had ended, Sankey was on a ship traveling across the Atlantic Ocean. Since he was now a famous singer, a crowd of people approached him and asked him to sing. He lifted his eyes toward heaven and sang a beautiful hymn.

After his song, a man from the crowd asked him if, on a certain night during the Civil War, he had performed night duty for a certain infantry unit. "Yes, I did," was his reply.

The man continued, "I was on the opposite side of the war, and I was hiding in a bush near your camp. With my rifle aimed at your head, I was about to shoot you when you looked toward heaven and began to sing. I thought, 'Well, I like music, and this guy has a nice voice. I'll sit here, let him sing the song,…and then shoot him. He's not going anywhere.' But then I realized what you were singing. It was the same hymn my mother used to sing at my bedside when I was a child. And it's the same hymn you sang tonight! I tried, but that night during the Civil War, I was powerless to shoot you."

Ira Sankey pointed that man to Christ. He and thousands of others were saved under Sankey's ministry. All this stemmed from the fact that Sankey praised the Lord at all times.

17:2

"Christians can't use 'circular reasoning' by trying to prove the Bible by quoting from the Bible!"

The "circular reasoning" argument is absurd. That's like saying you can't prove that the President lives in the White House by *looking into* the White House. It is looking into the White House that will provide the necessary proof. The fulfilled prophecies, the amazing consistency, and the many scientific statements of the Bible prove it to be the Word of God. They provide evidence that it is supernatural in origin.

See also Psalm 119:105 comment.

---

sent the serjeants, saying, Let those men go.

36 And the keeper of the prison told this saying to Paul, The magistrates have sent to let you go: now therefore depart, and go in peace.

37 But Paul said to them, They have beaten us openly uncondemned, being Romans, and have cast us into prison; and now do they thrust us out privately? nay verily; but let them come themselves and fetch us out.

38 And the serjeants told these words to the magistrates: and they feared, when they heard that they were Romans.

39 And they came and besought them, and brought them out, and desired them to depart out of the city.

40 And they went out of the prison, and entered into the house of Lydia and when they had seen the brethren, they comforted them, and departed.

CHAPTER 17

NOW when they had passed through Amphipolis and Apollonia, they came to Thessalonica, where was a synagogue of the Jews:

2 And Paul, as his manner was, went in to them, and three sabbath days reasoned with them out of the scriptures,

3 Opening and alleging, that Christ must needs have suffered, and risen again from the dead; and that this Jesus, whom I preach to you, is Christ.

4 And some of them believed, and consorted with Paul and Silas; and of the devout Greeks a great multitude, and of the chief women not a few.

5 But the Jews which believed not, moved with envy, took to them certain lewd fellows of the baser sort, and gathered a company, and set all the city on an uproar, and assaulted the house of Jason, and sought to bring them out to the people.

6 And when they found them not, they drew Jason and certain brethren to the rulers of the city, crying, These that have turned the world upside down are come here also;

7 Whom Jason has received: and these all do contrary to the decrees of Caesar, saying that there is another king, one Jesus.

8 And they troubled the people and the rulers of the city, when they heard these things.

9 And when they had taken security of Jason, and of the others, they let them go.

10 And the brethren immediately sent away Paul and Silas by night to Berea: who coming there went into the synagogue of the Jews.

11 **These were more noble than those in Thessalonica, in that they received the word with all readiness of mind, and searched the scriptures daily, whether those things were so.**

12 Therefore many of them believed; also of honorable women which were Greeks, and of men, not a few.

13 But when the Jews of Thessalonica had knowledge that the word of God was preached of Paul at Berea, they came there also, and stirred up the people.

POINTS FOR OPEN-AIR PREACHING

17:22   *Give Yourself a Lift*

If you are going to preach in the open-air, elevate yourself. For eighteen months, I preached without any elevation and hardly attracted any listeners. As soon as I did it "soapbox" style, people stopped to listen. Their attitude was "What has this guy got to say?" They had an excuse to stop.

Also, elevation will give you protection. I was once almost eaten by an angry 6'6" gentleman who kept fuming, "God is love!" We were eye to eye…while I was elevated. On another occasion, a very heavy gentleman who had a mean countenance placed it about 6" from mine and whispered, "Jesus said to love your enemies." I nodded in agreement. Then he asked in a deep voice, "Who is your enemy?" I shrugged. His voice deepened and spilled forth in a chilling tone, *"Lucifer!"* I was standing beside my stepladder at the time so he pushed me backwards with his stomach. He kept doing so until I was moved back about 20 feet. I prayed, "Wisdom, Lord," then said, "You are either going to hit me or hug me." He hugged me and walked off. That wouldn't have happened if I had been elevated.

Elevation will also give you added authority. Often hecklers will walk right up to you and ask questions quietly. This is an attempt to stifle the preaching, and it will work if you are not higher than your heckler. If they come too close to me, I talk over their heads and tell them to go back to the heckler's gallery. They actually obey me because they get the impression I am bigger than they are.

When Ezra preached the Law, he was elevated (Nehemiah 8:4,5). John Wesley used elevation to preach. Jesus preached the greatest sermon ever on a mount (Matthew 5–7), and Paul went up Mars' Hill to preach (Acts 17:22). So if you can't find a hilltop to preach from, use a soapbox or a stepladder. See Acts 3:4 comment.

14 And then immediately the brethren sent away Paul to go as it were to the sea: but Silas and Timotheus abode there still.

15 And they that conducted Paul brought him to Athens: and receiving a commandment to Silas and Timotheus for to come to him with all speed, they departed.

16 *Now while Paul waited for them at Athens, his spirit was stirred in him, when he saw the city wholly given to idolatry.*

17 *Therefore disputed he in the synagogue with the Jews, and with the devout persons, and in the market daily with them that met with him.*

18 Then certain philosophers of the Epicureans, and of the Stoicks, encountered him. And some said, What will this babbler say? other some, He seems to be a setter forth of strange gods: because he preached to them Jesus, and the resurrection.

19 And they took him, and brought him to Areopagus, saying, May we know what this new doctrine, whereof you speak, is?

20 For you bring certain strange things to our ears: we would know therefore what these things mean.

21 (For all the Athenians and strangers which were there spent their time in nothing else, but either to tell, or to hear some new thing.)

22 Then Paul stood in the midst of Mars' hill, and said, You men of Athens, I perceive that in all things you are too superstitious.

23 For as I passed by, and beheld your devotions, I found an altar with this inscription, TO THE UNKNOWN GOD. Whom therefore you ignorantly worship, him declare I to you.

24 God that made the world and all things therein, seeing that he is Lord of heaven and earth, dwells not in temples made with hands;

25 Neither is worshipped with men's hands, as though he needed any thing,

17:22 *How to Witness to Muslims*

In Acts 17:22–31 the apostle Paul built on areas of "common ground" as he prepared his listeners for the good news of the gospel. Even though he was addressing Gentiles whose beliefs were erroneous, he didn't rebuke them for having a doctrine of devils— "The things which the Gentiles sacrifice, they sacrifice to devils, and not to God" (1 Corinthians 10:20). Neither did he present the great truth that Jesus of Nazareth was Almighty God manifest in human form. This may have initially offended his hearers and closed the door to the particular knowledge he wanted to convey. Instead, he built on what they already knew. He first established that there is a Creator who made all things. He then exposed their sin of transgression of the First and Second of the Ten Commandments. Then he preached future punishment for sin.

There are three main areas of common ground upon which Christians may stand with Muslims. First, that there is one God—the Creator of all things. The second area is the fact that Jesus of Nazareth was a prophet of God. The Bible makes this clear: "And He shall send Jesus Christ, ... For Moses truly said to the fathers, A prophet shall the Lord your God raise up to you of your brethren, like to me; him shall you hear in all things whatsoever he shall say to you" (Acts 3:20–22).

The Qur'an (Koran) says: "Behold! The angel said 'O Mary! Allah giveth you Glad Tidings of a word from Him. His name will be (Christ Jesus) the son of Mary, held in honor in this world and the hereafter and of (the company of) those nearest to Allah'" (Surah 3:45). In Surah 19:19, the angel said to Mary, "I am only a messenger of thy Lord to announce to you a gift of a holy son." Surah 3:55 says, "Allah said: 'O Jesus! I will take you and raise you to Myself.'"

It is because of these and other references to Jesus in the Qur'an that a Muslim will not object when you establish that Jesus was a prophet from God.

This brings us to the third area of common ground. Muslims also respect Moses as a prophet of God. Therefore, there should be little contention when Christians speak of God (as Creator), Jesus the prophet, and the Law of the prophet Moses.

Most Muslims do have some knowledge of their sinfulness, but few see sin in its true light. It is therefore essential to take them through the spiritual nature of the Ten Commandments. While it is true that the Law of Moses begins with, "I am the Lord your God, you shall have no other gods before Me," it may be unwise to tell a Muslim, at that point, that Allah is a false god. Such talk may close the door before you are able to speak to his conscience. It is wise rather to present the Law in a similar order in which Jesus gave it in Luke 18:20. He addressed the man's sins of the flesh. He spoke directly to sins that have to do with his fellow man. Therefore, ask your hearer if he has ever told a lie. When (if) he admits that he has, ask him what that makes him. Don't call him a liar. Instead, gently press him to tell you what someone is called who has lied. Try to get him to say that he is a "liar."

Then ask him if he has ever stolen something, even if it's small. If he has, ask what that makes him (a thief). Then quote from the Prophet Jesus: "Whosoever looks on a woman to lust after her has committed adultery with her already in his heart" (Matthew 5:27). Ask if he has ever looked at a woman with lust. If he is reasonable, he will admit that he has sinned in that area. Then gently tell him that, *by his own admission*, he is a "lying, thieving adulterer-at-heart." Say, "If God judges you by the Law of Moses on Judgment Day, will you be innocent or guilty?"

At this point, he will more than likely say that he will be innocent, because he confesses his sins to God. However, the Qur'an says: "Every soul that has sinned, if it possessed all that is on earth, would fain give it in ransom" (Surah 10:54). In other words, if he possessed the *whole world* and offered it to God as a sacrifice for his sins, it wouldn't be enough to provide atonement for his sins.

Imagine that a criminal is facing a $50,000 fine. He is penniless, so he sincerely tells the judge that he is sorry for a crime and vows never to do it again. The judge won't let him go on the basis of his sorrow, or his vow never to commit the crime again. Of course, he

(continued on next page)

(17:22 continued)
should be sorry for what he has done, and of course, he shouldn't break the law again. The judge will, however, let him go if someone else pays the fine for him.

Now tell him that Moses gave instructions to Israel to shed the blood of a spotless lamb to provide a temporary atonement for their sin; and that Jesus was the Lamb that God provided to make atonement for the sins of the world. Through faith in Jesus, he can have atonement with God. All his sin can be washed away—once and for all. God can grant him the gift of everlasting life through faith in Jesus Christ on the basis of His death and resurrection.

The uniqueness of Jesus of Nazareth was that He claimed He had power on earth to forgive sins (Matthew 9:2–6). No other prophet of any of the great religions made this claim. Only Jesus can provide peace with God. This is why He said, "I am the way, the truth, and the life: no man comes to the Father, but by me" (John 14:6). God commands sinners to repent and trust in Jesus as Lord and Savior, or they will perish.

To try to justify himself, your listener may say something like, "The Bible has changed. It has been altered. There are many different versions, but the Koran has never changed." Explain to him that there are many different versions, printed in different languages and in modern English, to help people understand the Bible, but the content of the Scriptures remains the same. The Dead Sea Scrolls prove that God has preserved the Scriptures. Tell him that the 100% accurate prophecies of Matthew 24, Luke 21, and 2 Timothy 3 prove that this is the Book of the Creator.

Your task is to present the truth of the gospel. It is God who makes it come alive (1 Corinthians 3:6,7). It is God who brings conviction of sin (John 16:7,8). It is God who reveals who Jesus is (Matthew 16:16,17). All God requires is your faithful presentation of the truth (Matthew 25:21).

seeing he gives to all life, and breath, and all things;

26 And has made of one blood all nations of men for to dwell on all the face of the earth, and has determined the times before appointed, and the bounds of their habitation;

27 That they should seek the Lord, if haply they might feel after him, and find him, though he be not far from every one of us:

28 For in him we live, and move, and have our being; as certain also of your own poets have said, For we are also his offspring.

29 Forasmuch then as we are the offspring of God, we ought not to think that the Godhead is like to gold, or silver, or

17:24 **Evolution should not be taught.** *Dr. Colin Patterson*, senior paleontologist, British Museum of Natural History, gave a keynote address at the American Museum of Natural History, New York City, in 1981. In it, he explained his sudden "anti-evolutionary" view: "One morning I woke up and…it struck me that I had been working on this stuff for twenty years and there was not one thing I knew about it. That's quite a shock to learn that one can be misled so long…I've tried putting a simple question to various people: 'Can you tell me anything you know about evolution, any one thing, any one thing that is true?' I tried that question on the geology staff at the Field Museum of Natural History and the only answer I got was silence. I tried it on the members of the Evolutionary Morphology Seminar in the University of Chicago, a very prestigious body of evolutionists, and all I got there was silence for a long time and eventually one person said, 'I do know one thing—it ought not to be taught in high school.'"

17:26 Mormons believe that God cursed Cain with black skin and a flat nose. However, the "mark" was set upon Cain *before* the Flood. In that Flood all flesh perished except for Noah, his wife, his three sons, and their wives. If the curse upon Cain was dark skin, the only way the race could have survived was for Noah to be a direct descendent of Cain. However, Noah's genealogy didn't come from Cain, but from Seth (Genesis 5:3,6–32).

QUESTIONS & OBJECTIONS

17:26 *"Where do all the races come from?"*

Some have wondered, if we are all descendents of Adam and Eve, why are there so many races? The Bible informed us 2,000 years ago that God has made all nations from "one blood." We are all of the same race—the "human race," descendents of Adam and Eve, something science is slowly coming to realize.

Reuters news service reported the following article by Maggie Fox:

> Science may have caught up with the Bible, which says that Adam and Eve are the ancestors of all humans alive today.

> Peter Underhill of Stanford University in California remarked on findings published in the November 2000 issue of the journal *Nature Genetics*...Geneticists have long agreed there is no genetic basis to race—only to ethnic and geographic groups.

> "People look at a very conspicuous trait like skin color and they say, 'Well, this person's so different'...but that's only skin deep," Underhill said. "When you look at the level of the Y chromosome you find that, gee, there is very little difference between them. And skin color differences are strictly a consequence of climate."

stone, graven by art and man's device.

30 And the times of this ignorance God winked at; but now commands all men every where to repent:

31 Because he has appointed a day, in the which he will judge the world in righteousness by that man whom he has ordained; whereof he has given assurance to all men, in that he has raised him from the dead.

32 And when they heard of the resurrection of the dead, some mocked: and others said, We will hear you again of this matter.

33 So Paul departed from among them.

34 Howbeit certain men clave to him, and believed: among the which was Dionysius the Areopagite, and a woman named Damaris, and others with them.

USING THE LAW IN EVANGELISM

17:29 Paul was preaching the essence of the First and Second Commandments to show his hearers that they were idolaters. See Acts 28:23 comment.

17:30 Repentance—its necessity for salvation. See Acts 20:21.

"If my six-year-old daughter was out on the road playing in front of my house and I saw a huge truck barreling around the corner, what would I do in that moment? Out of my love for my daughter I would not gently invite her to step away from the street. I would *command* her to change her direction, and get off the road! Why? Because of my love for her. I know that the truck would not be able to stop in time and it would run her over and kill her. The same is true of the Father's love for us. Out of His love, he commands us to repent, because at any moment the truck of sin and death could run us over for playing on the road of rebellion!" *Rob Price*

17:31 Judgment Day: For verses that warn of its reality, see Romans 2:16. We preach Christ and Him crucified for the sins of the world, seeking to warn every man of the great and coming Day of the Lord, in which God will judge the world in righteousness. The standard of judgment will be a perfect Law (Psalm 19:7), and those who fail to meet its perfect requirements will come under its terrible wrath. See also Acts 18:9 comment.

CHAPTER 18

AFTER these things Paul departed from Athens, and came to Corinth;

2 And found a certain Jew named Aquila, born in Pontus, lately come from Italy, with his wife Priscilla; (because that Claudius had commanded all Jews to depart from Rome:) and came to them.

3 And because he was of the same craft, he abode with them, and wrought: for by their occupation they were tentmakers.

4 And he reasoned in the synagogue every sabbath, and persuaded the Jews and the Greeks.

5 And when Silas and Timotheus were come from Macedonia, Paul was pressed in the spirit, and testified to the Jews that Jesus was Christ.

6 And when they opposed themselves, and blasphemed, he shook his raiment, and said to them, Your blood be upon your own heads; I am clean: from henceforth I will go to the Gentiles.

7 And he departed thence, and entered into a certain man's house, named Justus, one that worshipped God, whose house joined hard to the synagogue.

8 And Crispus, the chief ruler of the synagogue, believed on the Lord with all his house; and many of the Corinthians hearing believed, and were baptized.

9 Then spoke the Lord to Paul in the night by a vision, Be not afraid, but speak, and hold not your peace:

10 For I am with you, and no man shall set on you to hurt you: for I have much people in this city.

11 And he continued there a year and six months, teaching the word of God among them.

12 And when Gallio was the deputy of Achaia, the Jews made insurrection with one accord against Paul, and brought him to the judgment seat,

---

18:4 Paul did not go to the synagogue to keep the Sabbath holy. He went there to *reason* with the Jews about Christ. His manner was to become like a Jew to the Jews. His heart's desire was to reach his own nation with the gospel. See 1 Corinthians 9:20–22.

18:9 "God [has] appointed a day in which He will judge the world, and we sigh and cry until it shall end the reign of wickedness, and give rest to the oppressed. Brethren, we must preach the coming of the Lord, and preach it somewhat more than we have done, *because it is the driving power of the gospel*. Too many have kept back these truths, and thus the bone has been taken out of the arm of the gospel. Its point has been broken; its edge has been blunted. The doctrine of judgment to come is the power by which men are to be aroused. There is another life; the Lord will come a second time; judgment will arrive; the wrath of God will be revealed. *Where this is not preached, I am bold to say the gospel is not preached.*

"It is absolutely necessary to the preaching of the gospel of Christ that men be warned as to what will happen if they continue in their sins. Ho, ho sir surgeon, you are too delicate to tell the man that he is ill! You hope to heal the sick without their knowing it. You therefore flatter them; and what happens? They laugh at you; they dance upon their own graves. At last they die! Your delicacy is cruelty; your flatteries are poisons; *you are a murderer*. Shall we keep men in a fool's paradise? Shall we lull them into soft slumbers from which they will awake in hell? Are we to become helpers of their damnation by our smooth speeches? In the name of God we will not." *Charles Spurgeon*

18:10 Never be discouraged by thinking that you are the only one God can use to reach the lost. Elijah, fearing that all the other prophets had been killed, said, "I, even I only, am left; and they seek my life, to take it away" (1 Kings 19:10). Yet God had reserved 7,000 faithful followers who hadn't bowed their knee to worship Baal (v. 18). Because God has His laborers, we need never panic when it comes to our loved ones being reached with the gospel. If we faithfully reach out and touch the lives of other peoples' loved ones, God (in His perfect timing) can use others to touch the lives of the ones we love so dearly. Claim your family in prayer, then thank God for His faithfulness in answering those prayers.

13 Saying, This fellow persuades men to worship God contrary to the law.

14 And when Paul was now about to open his mouth, Gallio said to the Jews, If it were a matter of wrong or wicked lewdness, O you Jews, reason would that I should bear with you:

15 But if it be a question of words and names, and of your law, you look to it; for I will be no judge of such matters.

16 And he drove them from the judgment seat.

17 Then all the Greeks took Sosthenes, the chief ruler of the synagogue, and beat him before the judgment seat. And Gallio cared for none of those things.

> The great benefit of open-air preaching is that we get so many new comers to hear the gospel who otherwise would never hear it.
>
> **CHARLES SPURGEON**

18 And Paul after this tarried there yet a good while, and then took his leave of the brethren, and sailed thence into Syria, and with him Priscilla and Aquila; having shorn his head in Cenchrea: for he had a vow.

19 And he came to Ephesus, and left them there: but he himself entered into the synagogue, and reasoned with the Jews.

20 When they desired him to tarry longer time with them, he consented not;

21 But bade them farewell, saying, I must by all means keep this feast that comes in Jerusalem: but I will return again to you, if God will. And he sailed from Ephesus.

22 And when he had landed at Caesarea, and gone up, and saluted the church, he went down to Antioch.

23 And after he had spent some time there, he departed, and went over all the country of Galatia and Phrygia in order, strengthening all the disciples.

24 And a certain Jew named Apollos, born at Alexandria, an eloquent man, and mighty in the scriptures, came to Ephesus.

25 This man was instructed in the way of the Lord; and being fervent in the spirit, he spoke and taught diligently the things of the Lord, knowing only the baptism of John.

26 And he began to speak boldly in the synagogue: whom when Aquila and Priscilla had heard, they took him to them, and expounded to him the way of God more perfectly.

27 And when he was disposed to pass into Achaia, the brethren wrote, exhorting the disciples to receive him: who, when he was come, helped them much which had believed through grace:

28 For he mightily convinced the Jews, and that publicly, showing by the scriptures that Jesus was Christ.

CHAPTER 19

AND it came to pass, that, while Apollos was at Corinth, Paul having passed through the upper coasts came to Ephesus: and finding certain disciples,

2 He said to them, Have you received the Holy Spirit since you believed? And they said to him, We have not so much as heard whether there be any Holy Spirit.

3 And he said to them, to what then were you baptized? And they said, to John's

---

18:19 "The proper goal in apologetics is not to force someone to admit that we have proved our position, but simply to remove objections so that a nonbeliever cannot hide behind intellectual objections." *John S. Hammett*

18:26 "It is better to be divided by truth than united in error; it is better to speak truth that hurts and then heals than to speak a lie; it is better to be hated for telling the truth than to be loved for telling a lie; it is better to stand alone with truth than to be wrong with the multitude...The religion of today is 'get-along-ism.' It is time for men and women of God to stand, [even] if they have to stand alone." *Adrian Rogers*

I Have a Problem

"FATHER, I HAVE a problem. It's weighing heavy on me. It's all I can think about, night and day. Before I bring it to you in prayer, I suppose I should pray for those who are less fortunate than me—those in this world who have hardly enough food for this day, and for those who don't have a roof over their heads at night. I also pray for families who have lost loved ones in sudden death, for parents whose children have leukemia, for the many people who are dying of brain tumors, for the hundreds of thousands who are laid waste with other terrible cancers, for people whose bodies have been suddenly shattered in car wrecks, for those who are lying in hospitals with agonizing burns over their bodies, whose faces have been burned beyond recognition. I pray for people with emphysema, whose eyes fill with terror as they struggle for every breath merely to live, for those who are tormented beyond words by irrational fears, for the elderly who are wracked with the pains of aging, whose only 'escape' is death.

"I pray for people who are watching their loved ones fade before their eyes through the grief of Alzheimer's disease, for the many thousands who are suffering the agony of AIDS, for those who are in such despair that they are contemplating suicide, for people who are tormented by the demons of alcoholism and drug addiction. I pray for children who have been abandoned by their parents, for those who are sexually abused, for wives held in quiet despair, beaten and abused by cruel drunken husbands, for people whose minds have been destroyed by mental disorders, for those who have lost everything in floods, tornadoes, hurricanes, and earthquakes. I pray for the blind, who never see the faces of the ones they love or the beauty of a sunrise, for those whose bodies are deformed by painful arthritis, for the many whose lives will be taken from them today by murderers, for those wasting away on their death-beds in hospitals.

"Most of all, I cry out for the millions who don't know the forgiveness that is in Jesus Christ... for those who in a moment of time will be swept into hell by the cold hand of death, and find to their utter horror the unspeakable vengeance of eternal fire. They will be eternally damned to everlasting punishment. O God, I pray for them.

"Strange. I can't seem to remember what my problem was. In Jesus' name I pray. Amen."

together.

9 And there sat in a window a certain young man named Eutychus, being fallen into a deep sleep: and as Paul was long preaching, he sunk down with sleep, and fell down from the third loft, and was taken up dead.

10 And Paul went down, and fell on him, and embracing him said, Trouble not yourselves; for his life is in him.

11 When he therefore was come up again, and had broken bread, and eaten, and talked a long while, even till break of day, so he departed.

12 And they brought the young man alive, and were not a little comforted.

> That sin must die, or you will perish by it. Depend on it, that sin which you would save from the slaughter will slaughter you.
>
> **CHARLES SPURGEON**

13 And we went before to ship, and sailed to Assos, there intending to take in Paul: for so had he appointed, minding himself to go afoot.

14 And when he met with us at Assos, we took him in, and came to Mitylene.

15 And we sailed thence, and came the next day over against Chios; and the next day we arrived at Samos, and tarried at Trogyllium; and the next day we came to Miletus.

16 For Paul had determined to sail by Ephesus, because he would not spend the time in Asia: for he hasted, if it were possible for him, to be at Jerusalem the day of Pentecost.

17 And from Miletus he sent to Ephesus, and called the elders of the church.

18 And when they were come to him, he said to them, You know, from the first day that I came into Asia, after what manner I have been with you at all seasons,

19 Serving the Lord with all humility of mind, and with many tears, and temptations, which befell me by the lying in wait of the Jews:

20 And how I kept back nothing that was profitable to you, but have showed you, and have taught you publicly, and from house to house,

21 Testifying both to the Jews, and also to the Greeks, repentance toward God, and faith toward our Lord Jesus Christ.

22 And now, behold, I go bound in the spirit to Jerusalem, not knowing the things that shall befall me there:

23 Save that the Holy Spirit witnesses in every city, saying that bonds and afflictions abide me.

24 *But none of these things move me, neither count I my life dear to myself, so that I might finish my course with joy, and the ministry, which I have received of the Lord Jesus, to testify the gospel of the grace of God.*

25 And now, behold, I know that you all, among whom I have gone preaching

---

20:9 Eutychus had some good excuses for dozing off:
- Paul's sermon was long.
- The many lights no doubt made the room hot.
- He was a young man staying up until midnight.
- He was "overcome" by sleep.

It is the midnight hour. We sit on the window of eternity. We can fall into eternity in a heartbeat. If the stale air of this world's influence makes us sink into a sleep of apathy, we must seek refreshing from the presence of the Lord. When our Christian life seems to be a dry and lifeless sermon without end, and the joy of feeding on God's Word is no longer in our hearts, we must get on our knees and return to our first love.

20:21 Repentance—its necessity for salvation. See 2 Peter 3:9.

POINTS FOR OPEN-AIR PREACHING

20:21

Aim for Repentance Rather Than a Decision

As you witness, divorce yourself from the thought that you are merely seeking "decisions for Christ." What we should be seeking is repentance within the heart. This is the purpose of the Law, to bring the knowledge of sin. How can a man repent if he doesn't know what sin is? If there is no repentance, there is no salvation. Jesus said, "Unless you repent, you shall all likewise perish" (Luke 13:3). God is not willing that any should perish, but that all should come to repentance (2 Peter 3:9).

Many don't understand that the salvation of a soul is not a resolution to change a way of life, but "repentance toward God, and faith toward our Lord Jesus Christ." The modern concept of success in evangelism is to relate how many people were "saved" (that is, how many prayed the "sinner's prayer"). This produces a "no decisions, no success" mentality. This shouldn't be, because Christians who seek decisions in evangelism become discouraged after a time of witnessing if "no one came to the Lord." The Bible tells us that as we sow the good seed of the gospel, one sows and another reaps. If you faithfully sow the seed, someone will reap. If you reap, it is because someone has sown in the past, but it is God who causes the seed to grow. If His hand is not on the person you are leading in a prayer of committal, if there is not *God-given* repentance, then you will end up with a stillbirth on your hands, and that is nothing to rejoice about. We should measure our success by how faithfully we sowed the seed. In that way, we will avoid becoming discouraged.

"If you have not repented, you will not see the inside of the kingdom of God." *Billy Graham*

the kingdom of God, shall see my face no more.

26 *Wherefore I take you to record this day, that I am pure from the blood of all men.*

27 *For I have not shunned to declare to you all the counsel of God.*

28 Take heed therefore to yourselves, and to all the flock, over the which the Holy Spirit has made you overseers, to feed the church of God, which he has purchased with his own blood.

29 For I know this, that after my departing shall grievous wolves enter in among you, not sparing the flock.

30 Also of your own selves shall men arise, speaking perverse things, to draw away disciples after them.

31 Therefore watch, and remember, that by the space of three years I ceased not to warn every one night and day with tears.

32 And now, brethren, I commend you to God, and to the word of his grace, which is able to build you up, and to give you an inheritance among all them which are sanctified.

33 I have coveted no man's silver, or gold, or apparel.

34 Yes, you yourselves know, that these hands have ministered to my necessities, and to them that were with me.

35 I have showed you all things, how that so laboring you ought to support the weak, and to remember the words of the Lord Jesus, how he said, It is more blessed to give than to receive.

36 And when he had thus spoken, he

20:24 A missionary society wrote to *David Livingstone* and suggested that if he could ensure them of safe roads, they would send him some help. He responded with the following note: "If you have men who will only come if they have a good road, I don't want them. I want men who will come if there is no road at all."

20:26 "My anxious desire is that every time I preach, I may clear myself of blood of all men; that if I step from this platform to my coffin, I may have told out all I knew of the way of salvation." *Charles Spurgeon*

kneeled down, and prayed with them all.

37 And they all wept sore, and fell on Paul's neck, and kissed him,

38 Sorrowing most of all for the words which he spoke, that they should see his face no more. And they accompanied him to the ship.

CHAPTER 21

AND it came to pass, that after we were gotten from them, and had launched, we came with a straight course to Coos, and the day following to Rhodes, and from thence to Patara:

2 And finding a ship sailing over to Phenicia, we went aboard, and set forth.

3 Now when we had discovered Cyprus, we left it on the left hand, and sailed into Syria, and landed at Tyre: for there the ship was to unload her burden.

4 And finding disciples, we tarried there seven days: who said to Paul through the Spirit, that he should not go up to Jerusalem.

5 And when we had accomplished those days, we departed and went our way; and they all brought us on our way, with wives and children, till we were out of the city: and we kneeled down on the shore, and prayed.

6 And when we had taken our leave one of another, we took ship; and they returned home again.

7 And when we had finished our course from Tyre, we came to Ptolemais, and saluted the brethren, and abode with them one day.

8 And the next day we that were of Paul's company departed, and came to Caesarea: and we entered into the house of Philip the evangelist, which was one of the seven; and abode with him.

9 And the same man had four daughters, virgins, which did prophesy.

10 And as we tarried there many days, there came down from Judea a certain prophet, named Agabus.

11 And when he was come to us, he took Paul's girdle, and bound his own hands and feet, and said, Thus says the Holy Spirit, So shall the Jews at Jerusalem bind the man that owns this girdle, and shall deliver him into the hands of the Gentiles.

12 And when we heard these things, both we, and they of that place, besought him not to go up to Jerusalem.

13 *Then Paul answered, Why do you weep and break my heart? for I am ready not to be bound only, but also to die at Jerusalem for the name of the Lord Jesus.*

14 And when he would not be persuaded, we ceased, saying, The will of the Lord be done.

15 And after those days we took up our carriages, and went up to Jerusalem.

16 There went with us also certain of the disciples of Caesarea, and brought with

---

20:27 How to witness. Here is a suggested structure of a gospel message:

Begin in the natural realm if you are not in a normal church setting. Perhaps you could springboard off some well-publicized tragedy, then ask if your hearers ever wonder how they are going to die. Say that we will all die because we have broken an eternal law—the Law of God, often referred to as the Ten Commandments. Then open up each Commandment, emphasizing its spiritual nature (lust is seen by God as adultery, hatred is murder—that God sees man's thoughts, and nothing is hidden from His eyes).

Stress the fact of Judgment Day—that God is holy and will bring every work into judgment, including every secret thing whether it is good or evil. Don't be afraid to use the word "hell." Tell them that it is God's place of punishment for sin. Emphasize that He doesn't want them to go there, that He has made provision for their forgiveness. Then preach Christ and Him crucified, risen from the dead. Thoroughly lace the message with God's Word—verbally quote relevant Scriptures. Then preach the necessity of repentance (that it's *commanded*), and the importance of faith in and obedience *to* God's Word. See Acts 20:21 comment.

21:5 Prayer—the secret weapon: See Mark 11:23.

POINTS FOR OPEN-AIR PREACHING

21:30   *Raw Nerves*

When you're preaching open-air, don't let angry reactions from the crowd concern you. A dentist knows where to work on a patient when he touches a raw nerve. When you touch a raw nerve in the heart of the sinner, it means that you are in business. Anger is a thousand times better than apathy. Anger is a sign of conviction. If I have an argument with my wife and suddenly realize that I am in the wrong, I can come to her in a repentant attitude and apologize, or I can save face by lashing out in anger.

Read Acts 19 and see how Paul was a dentist with an eye for decay. He probed raw nerves wherever he went. At one point, he had to be carried shoulder height by soldiers because of the "violence of the people" (Acts 21:36). Now there's a successful preacher! He didn't seek the praise of men. John Wesley told his evangelist trainees that when they preached, people should either get angry or get converted. No doubt, he wasn't speaking about the "Jesus loves you" gospel, but about sin, Law, righteousness, judgment, and hell. See Matthew 28:19,20 comment.

them one Mnason of Cyprus, an old disciple, with whom we should lodge.

17 And when we were come to Jerusalem, the brethren received us gladly.

18 And the day following Paul went in with us to James; and all the elders were present.

19 And when he had saluted them, he declared particularly what things God had wrought among the Gentiles by his ministry.

20 And when they heard it, they glorified the Lord, and said to him, You see, brother, how many thousands of Jews there are which believe; and they are all zealous of the law:

21 And they are informed of you, that you teach all the Jews which are among the Gentiles to forsake Moses, saying that they ought not to circumcise their children, neither to walk after the customs.

22 What is it therefore? the multitude must needs come together: for they will hear that you are come.

23 Do therefore this that we say to you: We have four men which have a vow on them;

24 Them take, and purify yourself with them, and be at charges with them, that they may shave their heads: and all may know that those things, whereof they were informed concerning you, are nothing; but that you yourself also walk orderly, and keep the law.

25 As touching the Gentiles which believe, we have written and concluded that they observe no such thing, save only that they keep themselves from things offered to idols, and from blood, and from strangled, and from fornication.

26 Then Paul took the men, and the next day purifying himself with them entered into the temple, to signify the accomplishment of the days of purification, until that an offering should be offered for every one of them.

27 And when the seven days were almost ended, the Jews which were of Asia, when they saw him in the temple, stirred up all the people, and laid hands on him,

28 Crying out, Men of Israel, help: This is the man, that teaches all men every where against the people, and the law, and this place: and further brought Greeks also into the temple, and has polluted this holy place.

29 (For they had seen before with him in the city Trophimus an Ephesian, whom they supposed that Paul had brought into the temple.)

30 And all the city was moved, and the people ran together: and they took Paul, and drew him out of the temple: and forthwith the doors were shut.

31 And as they went about to kill him, tidings came to the chief captain of the

band, that all Jerusalem was in an uproar.

32 Who immediately took soldiers and centurions, and ran down to them: and when they saw the chief captain and the soldiers, they left beating of Paul.

33 Then the chief captain came near, and took him, and commanded him to be bound with two chains; and demanded who he was, and what he had done.

34 And some cried one thing, some another, among the multitude: and when he could not know the certainty for the tumult, he commanded him to be carried into the castle.

35 And when he came upon the stairs, so it was, that he was borne of the soldiers for the violence of the people.

36 For the multitude of the people followed after, crying, Away with him.

37 And as Paul was to be led into the castle, he said to the chief captain, May I speak to you? Who said, Can you speak Greek?

38 Are you not that Egyptian, which before these days made an uproar, and lead out into the wilderness four thousand men that were murderers?

39 But Paul said, I am a man which am a Jew of Tarsus, a city in Cilicia, a citizen of no mean city: and, I beseech you, suffer me to speak to the people.

40 And when he had given him license, Paul stood on the stairs, and beckoned with the hand to the people. And when there was made a great silence, he spoke to them in the Hebrew tongue, saying,

CHAPTER 22

MEN, brethren, and fathers, hear my defence which I make now to you.

2 (And when they heard that he spoke in the Hebrew tongue to them, they kept the more silence: and he said,)

3 I am verily a man which am a Jew, born in Tarsus, a city in Cilicia, yet brought up in this city at the feet of Gamaliel, and taught according to the perfect manner of the law of the fathers, and was zealous toward God, as you all are this day.

4 And I persecuted this way to the death, binding and delivering into prisons both men and women.

5 As also the high priest does bear me witness, and all the estate of the elders: from whom also I received letters to the brethren, and went to Damascus, to bring them which were there bound to Jerusalem, for to be punished.

> The greatest enemy to human souls is the self-righteous spirit which makes men look to themselves for salvation.
>
> **CHARLES SPURGEON**

6 And it came to pass, that, as I made my journey, and was come near to Damascus about noon, suddenly there shone from heaven a great light round about me.

7 And I fell to the ground, and heard a voice saying to me, Saul, Saul, why do you persecute me?

8 And I answered, Who are you, Lord? And he said to me, I am Jesus of Nazareth, whom you persecute.

9 And they that were with me saw indeed the light, and were afraid; but they heard not the voice of him that spoke to me.

10 And I said, What shall I do, Lord? And the Lord said to me, Arise, and go into Damascus; and there it shall be told you of all things which are appointed for you to do.

11 And when I could not see for the glory

22:9 Contradiction in the Bible? Some may think that this is a mistake in the Scriptures, because in Acts 9:7 Paul said that those who were with him *heard* the voice. However, John 12:29 gives us insight into what God's voice sounds like. People *heard* His voice but thought that it thundered (see also 2 Samuel 22:14; Job 37:4,5; 40:9). They obviously heard it but the words were not coherent to them.

"Labor to keep alive in your breast that spark of celestial fire called conscience."

George Washington

of that light, being led by the hand of them that were with me, I came into Damascus.

12 And one Ananias, a devout man according to the law, having a good report of all the Jews which dwelt there,

13 Came to me, and stood, and said to me, Brother Saul, receive your sight. And the same hour I looked up upon him.

14 And he said, The God of our fathers has chosen you, that you should know his will, and see that Just One, and should hear the voice of his mouth.

15 For you shall be his witness to all men of what you have seen and heard.

16 And now why do you tarry? arise, and be baptized, and wash away your sins, calling on the name of the Lord.

17 And it came to pass, that, when I was come again to Jerusalem, even while I prayed in the temple, I was in a trance;

18 And saw him saying to me, Make haste, and get quickly out of Jerusalem: for they will not receive your testimony concerning me.

19 And I said, Lord, they know that I imprisoned and beat in every synagogue them that believed on you:

20 And when the blood of your martyr Stephen was shed, I also was standing by, and consenting to his death, and kept the raiment of them that slew him.

21 And he said to me, Depart: for I will send you far hence to the Gentiles.

22 And they gave him audience to this word, and then lifted up their voices, and said, Away with such a fellow from the earth: for it is not fit that he should live.

23 And as they cried out, and cast off their clothes, and threw dust into the air,

24 The chief captain commanded him to be brought into the castle, and bade that he should be examined by scourging; that he might know wherefore they cried so against him.

25 And as they bound him with thongs, Paul said to the centurion that stood by, Is it lawful for you to scourge a man that is a Roman, and uncondemned?

26 When the centurion heard that, he went and told the chief captain, saying, Take heed what you do: for this man is a Roman.

27 Then the chief captain came, and said to him, Tell me, are you a Roman? He said, Yes.

28 And the chief captain answered, With a great sum obtained I this freedom. And Paul said, But I was free born.

29 Then straightway they departed from him which should have examined him: and the chief captain also was afraid, after he knew that he was a Roman, and because he had bound him.

30 On the morrow, because he would have known the certainty wherefore he was accused of the Jews, he loosed him from his bands, and commanded the chief priests and all their council to appear, and brought Paul down, and set him before them.

CHAPTER 23

AND Paul, earnestly beholding the council, said, Men and brethren, I have lived in all good conscience before God until this day.

2 And the high priest Ananias commanded them that stood by him to smite him
on the mouth.

3 Then said Paul to him, God shall smite
you, you whited wall: for you sit to judge
me after the law, and command me to be
smitten contrary to the law?

4 And they that stood by said, Do you
revile God's high priest?

5 Then said Paul, I knew not, brethren,
that he was the high priest: for it is written, You shall not speak evil of the ruler
of your people.

6 But when Paul perceived that the one
part were Sadducees, and the other Pharisees, he cried out in the council, Men
and brethren, I am a Pharisee, the son of
a Pharisee: of the hope and resurrection
of the dead I am called in question.

7 And when he had so said, there arose
a dissension between the Pharisees and
the Sadducees: and the multitude was
divided.

8 For the Sadducees say that there is no
resurrection, neither angel, nor spirit: but
the Pharisees confess both.

9 And there arose a great cry: and the
scribes that were of the Pharisees' part
arose, and strove, saying, We find no evil
in this man: but if a spirit or an angel has
spoken to him, let us not fight against
God.

10 And when there arose a great dissension, the chief captain, fearing lest Paul
should have been pulled in pieces of them,
commanded the soldiers to go down,
and to take him by force from among
them, and to bring him into the castle.

11 And the night following the Lord
stood by him, and said, Be of good cheer,
Paul: for as you have testified of me in
Jerusalem, so must you bear witness also
at Rome.

12 And when it was day, certain of the
Jews banded together, and bound themselves under a curse, saying that they
would neither eat nor drink till they had
killed Paul.

13 And they were more than forty which
had made this conspiracy.

14 And they came to the chief priests
and elders, and said, We have bound ourselves under a great curse, that we will eat
nothing until we have slain Paul.

15 Now therefore you with the council
signify to the chief captain that he bring
him down to you tomorrow, as though
you would inquire something more perfectly concerning him: and we, or ever he
come near, are ready to kill him.

16 And when Paul's sister's son heard
of their lying in wait, he went and entered into the castle, and told Paul.

> I have known what it is to use up all
> my ammunition, and then I have, as it
> were, rammed myself into the great
> gospel gun and fired myself at the
> hearers—all my experience of God's
> goodness, all my consciousness of sin,
> and all my sense of the power of the
> gospel.
>
> **CHARLES SPURGEON**

17 Then Paul called one of the centurions
to him, and said, Bring this young man
to the chief captain: for he has a certain
thing to tell him.

18 So he took him, and brought him to
the chief captain, and said, Paul the prisoner called me to him, and prayed me to
bring this young man to you, who has
something to say to you.

19 Then the chief captain took him by
the hand, and went with him aside privately, and asked him, What is that you
have to tell me?

20 And he said, The Jews have agreed to
desire you that you would bring down
Paul tomorrow into the council, as though
they would inquire somewhat of him more
perfectly.

21 But do not yield to them: for there lie
in wait for him of them more than forty
men, which have bound themselves with
an oath, that they will neither eat nor
drink till they have killed him: and now
are they ready, looking for a promise from

you.

22 So the chief captain then let the young man depart, and charged him, See you tell no man that you have showed these things to me.

23 And he called to him two centurions, saying, Make ready two hundred soldiers to go to Caesarea, and horsemen three-score and ten, and spearmen two hundred, at the third hour of the night;

24 And provide them beasts, that they may set Paul on, and bring him safe to Felix the governor.

25 And he wrote a letter after this manner:

26 Claudius Lysias to the most excellent governor Felix sends greeting.

27 This man was taken of the Jews, and should have been killed of them: then came I with an army, and rescued him, having understood that he was a Roman.

28 And when I would have known the cause wherefore they accused him, I brought him forth into their council:

29 Whom I perceived to be accused of questions of their law, but to have nothing laid to his charge worthy of death or of bonds.

30 And when it was told me how that the Jews laid wait for the man, I sent straightway to you, and gave commandment to his accusers also to say before you what they had against him. Farewell.

31 Then the soldiers, as it was commanded them, took Paul, and brought him by night to Antipatris.

32 On the morrow they left the horsemen to go with him, and returned to the castle:

33 Who, when they came to Caesarea, and delivered the epistle to the governor, presented Paul also before him.

34 And when the governor had read the letter, he asked of what province he was. And when he understood that he was of Cilicia;

35 I will hear you, said he, when your accusers are also come. And he commanded him to be kept in Herod's judgment hall.

CHAPTER 24

AND after five days Ananias the high priest descended with the elders, and with a certain orator named Tertullus, who informed the governor against Paul.

2 And when he was called forth, Tertullus began to accuse him, saying, Seeing that by you we enjoy great quietness, and that very worthy deeds are done to this nation by your providence,

3 We accept it always, and in all places, most noble Felix, with all thankfulness.

4 Notwithstanding, that I be not further tedious to you, I pray you that you would hear us of your clemency a few words.

5 For we have found this man a pestilent fellow, and a mover of sedition among all the Jews throughout the world, and a ringleader of the sect of the Nazarenes:

6 Who also has gone about to profane the temple: whom we took, and would have judged according to our law.

7 But the chief captain Lysias came upon us, and with great violence took him away out of our hands,

8 Commanding his accusers to come to you: by examining of whom yourself may take knowledge of all these things, whereof we accuse him.

9 And the Jews also assented, saying that these things were so.

10 Then Paul, after that the governor had beckoned to him to speak, answered, Forasmuch as I know that you have been of many years a judge to this nation, I do the more cheerfully answer for myself:

11 Because that you may understand, that there are yet but twelve days since I went up to Jerusalem for to worship.

24:5 The apostle Paul was called a "pestilent fellow," a "mover of sedition," and a "ringleader" of a "sect." The prophet Elijah was called a "troubler of Israel" (1 Kings 18:17). Those who stand for righteousness will be considered troublemakers in the world's eyes.

QUESTIONS & OBJECTIONS

24:25 *"Is 'hell-fire' preaching effective?"*

Preaching the reality of hell, without using the Law to bring the knowledge of sin, can do a great deal of damage to the cause of the gospel. A sinner cannot conceive of the thought that God would send anyone to hell, as long as he is deceived into thinking that God's standard of righteousness is the same as his. Paul "reasoned" with Felix regarding righteousness, temperance, and judgment to come (Acts 24:25). This is the righteousness that is of the Law and judgment by the Law. Felix "trembled" because he suddenly understood that his intemperance made him a guilty sinner in the sight of a holy God. The reality of hell suddenly became *reasonable* to him when the Law was used to bring the knowledge of sin.

Imagine if the police burst into your home, arrested you, and shouted, "You are going away for a long time!" Such conduct would probably leave you bewildered and angry. What they have done seems unreasonable.

However, imagine if the law burst into your home and instead told you specifically why you were in trouble: "We have discovered 10,000 marijuana plants growing in your back yard. You are going away for a long time!" At least then you would understand *why* you are in trouble. Knowledge of the law you have transgressed furnished you with that understanding. It makes judgment *reasonable*. Hell-fire preaching without use of the Law to show the sinner why God is angry with him will more than likely leave him bewildered and angry—for what he considers *unreasonable* punishment.

12 And they neither found me in the temple disputing with any man, neither raising up the people, neither in the synagogues, nor in the city:

13 Neither can they prove the things whereof they now accuse me.

14 But this I confess to you, that after the way which they call heresy, so worship I the God of my fathers, believing all things which are written in the law and in the prophets:

15 And have hope toward God, which they themselves also allow, that there shall be a resurrection of the dead, both of the just and unjust.

16 And herein do I exercise myself, to have always a conscience void of offence toward God, and toward men.

17 Now after many years I came to bring alms to my nation, and offerings.

18 Whereupon certain Jews from Asia found me purified in the temple, neither with multitude, nor with tumult.

19 Who ought to have been here before you, and object, if they had anything against me.

20 Or else let these same here say, if they have found any evil doing in me, while I stood before the council,

21 Except it be for this one voice, that I cried standing among them, Touching the resurrection of the dead I am called in question by you this day.

22 And when Felix heard these things, having more perfect knowledge of that way, he deferred them, and said, When Lysias the chief captain shall come down, I will know the uttermost of your matter.

23 And he commanded a centurion to keep Paul, and to let him have liberty, and that he should forbid none of his acquaintance to minister or come to him.

24 And after certain days, when Felix came with his wife Drusilla, which was a Jewess, he sent for Paul, and heard him concerning the faith in Christ.

25 And as he reasoned of righteousness, temperance, and judgment to come Felix trembled, and answered, Go your way for this time; when I have a convenient season, I will call for you.

26 He hoped also that money should

have been given him of Paul, that he might loose him: wherefore he sent for him the oftener, and communed with him.

27 But after two years Porcius Festus came into Felix' room: and Felix, willing to show the Jews a pleasure, left Paul bound.

CHAPTER 25

NOW when Festus was come into the province, after three days he ascended from Caesarea to Jerusalem.

2 Then the high priest and the chief of the Jews informed him against Paul, and besought him,

3 And desired favor against him, that he would send for him to Jerusalem, laying wait in the way to kill him.

4 But Festus answered, that Paul should be kept at Caesarea, and that he himself would depart shortly there.

5 Let them therefore, said he, which among you are able, go down with me, and accuse this man, if there be any wickedness in him.

6 And when he had tarried among them more than ten days, he went down to Caesarea; and the next day sitting on the judgment seat commanded Paul to be brought.

7 And when he was come, the Jews which came down from Jerusalem stood round about, and laid many and grievous complaints against Paul, which they could not prove.

8 While he answered for himself, Neither against the law of the Jews, neither against the temple, nor yet against Caesar, have I offended any thing at all.

9 But Festus, willing to do the Jews a pleasure, answered Paul, and said, Will you go up to Jerusalem, and there be judged of these things before me?

10 Then said Paul, I stand at Caesar's judgment seat, where I ought to be judged: to the Jews have I done no wrong, as you very well know.

11 For if I be an offender, or have committed any thing worthy of death, I refuse not to die: but if there be none of these things whereof these accuse me, no man may deliver me to them. I appeal to Caesar.

12 Then Festus, when he had conferred with the council, answered, have you appealed to Caesar? to Caesar shall you go.

13 And after certain days king Agrippa and Bernice came to Caesarea to salute Festus.

14 And when they had been there many days, Festus declared Paul's cause to the king, saying, There is a certain man left in bonds by Felix:

15 About whom, when I was at Jerusalem, the chief priests and the elders of the Jews informed me, desiring to have judgment against him.

16 To whom I answered, It is not the manner of the Romans to deliver any man to die, before that he which is accused have the accusers face to face, and have license to answer for himself concerning the crime laid against him.

17 Therefore, when they were come here, without any delay on the morrow I sat on the judgment seat, and commanded the man to be brought forth.

18 Against whom when the accusers stood up, they brought none accusation of such things as I supposed:

19 But had certain questions against him of their own superstition, and of one Jesus, which was dead, whom Paul affirmed to be alive.

20 And because I doubted of such manner of questions, I asked him whether he would go to Jerusalem, and there be judged of these matters.

21 But when Paul had appealed to be reserved to the hearing of Augustus, I commanded him to be kept till I might send him to Caesar.

22 Then Agrippa said to Festus, I would

24:25 "What we think about God influences our friendship with him…The Bible is our only safe source of knowledge about God—and it requires thinking. God's persistent invitation in every age remains: "'Come now, let us *reason* together,' says the Lord' (Isaiah 1:18)." *Joni Eareckson Tada*

also hear the man myself. Tomorrow, said he, you shall hear him.

23 And on the morrow, when Agrippa was come, and Bernice, with great pomp, and was entered into the place of hearing, with the chief captains, and principal men of the city, at Festus' commandment Paul was brought forth.

24 And Festus said, King Agrippa, and all men which are here present with us, you see this man, about whom all the multitude of the Jews have dealt with me, both at Jerusalem, and also here, crying that he ought not to live any longer.

25 But when I found that he had committed nothing worthy of death, and that he himself has appealed to Augustus, I have determined to send him.

26 Of whom I have no certain thing to write to my lord. Wherefore I have brought him forth before you, and specially before you, O king Agrippa, that, after examination had, I might have somewhat to write.

27 For it seems to me unreasonable to send a prisoner, and not withal to signify the crimes laid against him.

CHAPTER 26

THEN Agrippa said to Paul, You are permitted to speak for yourself. Then Paul stretched forth the hand, and answered for himself:

2 I think myself happy, king Agrippa, because I shall answer for myself this day before you touching all the things whereof I am accused of the Jews:

3 Especially because I know you to be expert in all customs and questions which are among the Jews: wherefore I beseech you to hear me patiently.

4 My manner of life from my youth, which was at the first among mine own nation at Jerusalem, know all the Jews;

5 Which knew me from the beginning, if they would testify, that after the most strait sect of our religion I lived a Pharisee.

6 And now I stand and am judged for the hope of the promise made of God to our fathers:

7 To which promise our twelve tribes, instantly serving God day and night, hope to come. For which hope's sake, king Agrippa, I am accused of the Jews.

8 Why should it be thought a thing incredible with you, that God should raise the dead?

9 I verily thought with myself, that I ought to do many things contrary to the name of Jesus of Nazareth.

10 Which thing I also did in Jerusalem: and many of the saints did I shut up in prison, having received authority from the chief priests; and when they were put to death, I gave my voice against them.

11 And I punished them oft in every synagogue, and compelled them to blaspheme; and being exceedingly mad against them, I persecuted them even to strange cities.

> The early disciples were fishers of men —while modern disciples are often little more than aquarium keepers.
>
> **UNKNOWN**

12 Whereupon as I went to Damascus with authority and commission from the chief priests,

13 At midday, O king, I saw in the way a light from heaven, above the brightness of the sun, shining round about me and them which journeyed with me.

14 And when we were all fallen to the earth, I heard a voice speaking to me, and saying in the Hebrew tongue, Saul, Saul, why do you persecute me? it is hard for you to kick against the pricks.

15 And I said, Who are you, Lord? And he said, I am Jesus whom you persecute.

16 But rise, and stand upon your feet: for I have appeared to you for this purpose, to make you a minister and a witness both of these things which you have seen, and of those things in the which I will appear to you;

17 *Delivering you from the people, and from the Gentiles, to whom now I send you,*

18 *To open their eyes, and to turn them*

from darkness to light, and from the power of Satan to God, that they may receive forgiveness of sins, and inheritance among them which are sanctified by faith that is in me.

19 Whereupon, O king Agrippa, I was not disobedient to the heavenly vision:

20 But showed first to them of Damascus, and at Jerusalem, and throughout all the coasts of Judea, and then to the Gentiles, that they should repent and turn to God, and do works meet for repentance.

21 For these causes the Jews caught me in the temple, and went about to kill me.

22 Having therefore obtained help of God, I continue to this day, witnessing both to small and great, saying none other things than those which the prophets and Moses did say should come:

23 That Christ should suffer, and that he should be the first that should rise from the dead, and should show light to the people, and to the Gentiles.

24 And as he thus spoke for himself, Festus said with a loud voice, Paul, you are beside yourself; much learning does make you mad.

25 But he said, I am not mad, most noble Festus; but speak forth the words of truth and soberness.

26 For the king knows of these things, before whom also I speak freely: for I am persuaded that none of these things are hidden from him; for this thing was not done in a corner.

27 **King Agrippa, do you believe the**

prophets? I know that you believe.

28 **Then Agrippa said to Paul, You almost persuade me to be a Christian.**

29 **And Paul said, I would to God, that not only you, but also all that hear me this day, were both almost, and altogether such as I am, except these bonds.**

30 And when he had thus spoken, the king rose up, and the governor, and Bernice, and they that sat with them:

31 And when they were gone aside, they talked between themselves, saying, This man does nothing worthy of death or of bonds.

32 Then said Agrippa to Festus, This man might have been set at liberty, if he had not appealed to Caesar.

CHAPTER 27

AND when it was determined that we should sail into Italy, they delivered Paul and certain other prisoners to one named Julius, a centurion of Augustus' band.

2 And entering into a ship of Adramyttium, we launched, meaning to sail by the coasts of Asia; one Aristarchus, a Macedonian of Thessalonica, being with us.

3 And the next day we touched at Sidon. And Julius courteously entreated Paul, and gave him liberty to go to his friends to refresh himself.

4 And when we had launched from thence, we sailed under Cyprus, because the winds were contrary.

5 And when we had sailed over the sea of

26:20 The problem with modern evangelism. Many Christian obtain "decisions" by using the following method: "Do you know that you are going to heaven when you die?" Most will say, "I hope so." The Christian then says, "You can know so. The Bible says 'All have sinned.' Jesus died on the cross for our sins, and if you give your heart to Him today, you can know for sure that you are going to heaven. Would you like to have that assurance that you will go to heaven when you die?" He will almost always say, "Yes." The person is then led in what is commonly called a "sinner's prayer."

There are a few difficulties with the popular approach: 1) There is no mention of Judgment Day—the very reason men are commanded to repent; 2) There is no mention of hell; and 3) The Law isn't used to bring the knowledge of sin. The apostle Paul said that the Law was the only means by which he came to know what sin was (Romans 7:7). The modern approach may get a decision or gain a church member, but if there is no biblical repentance, there will be a false conversion. See John 4:7–26 comment.

QUESTIONS & OBJECTIONS

26:28

"What should I say to someone who acknowledges his sins, but says, 'I just hope God is forgiving'?"

These people could be referred to as "awakened, but not alarmed." Explain that God *is* forgiving—but only to those who repent of their sins. Ask him, "If you died right now, where would you go?" If he says, "Hell," ask if that concerns him. If it does concern him, ask, "What are you going to do?" Then tell him that God *commands* him to repent and trust the Savior. If it doesn't concern him, speak of the value of his life, the threat of *eternal* damnation, and the biblical description of hell. Caution him that he doesn't have the promise of tomorrow, and plead with him to come to his senses.

Cilicia and Pamphylia, we came to Myra, a city of Lycia.

6 And there the centurion found a ship of Alexandria sailing into Italy; and he put us therein.

7 And when we had sailed slowly many days, and scarce were come over against Cnidus, the wind not suffering us, we sailed under Crete, over against Salmone;

8 And, hardly passing it, came to a place which is called The fair havens; near whereunto was the city of Lasea.

9 Now when much time was spent, and when sailing was now dangerous, because the fast was now already past, Paul admonished them,

10 And said to them, Sirs, I perceive that this voyage will be with hurt and much damage, not only of the lading and ship, but also of our lives.

11 Nevertheless the centurion believed the master and the owner of the ship, more than those things which were spoken by Paul.

12 And because the haven was not commodious to winter in, the more part advised to depart thence also, if by any means they might attain to Phenice, and there to winter; which is an haven of Crete, and lies toward the south west and north west.

13 And when the south wind blew softly, supposing that they had obtained their purpose, loosing thence, they sailed close by Crete.

14 But not long after there arose against it a tempestuous wind, called Euroclydon.

15 And when the ship was caught, and could not bear up into the wind, we let her drive.

16 And running under a certain island which is called Clauda, we had much work to come by the boat:

17 Which when they had taken up, they used helps, undergirding the ship; and, fearing lest they should fall into the quicksands, strake sail, and so were driven.

18 And we being exceedingly tossed with a tempest, the next day they lightened the ship;

19 And the third day we cast out with our own hands the tackling of the ship.

20 And when neither sun nor stars in many days appeared, and no small tempest lay on us, all hope that we should be saved was then taken away.

21 But after long abstinence Paul stood forth in the midst of them, and said, Sirs, you should have hearkened to me, and not have loosed from Crete, and to have gained this harm and loss.

22 And now I exhort you to be of good cheer: for there shall be no loss of any man's life among you, but of the ship.

23 For there stood by me this night the angel of God, whose I am, and whom I serve,

24 Saying, Fear not, Paul; you must be brought before Caesar: and, lo, God has given you all them that sail with you.

25 Wherefore, sirs, be of good cheer: for I believe God, that it shall be even as it was told me.

26 Howbeit we must be cast upon a certain island.

27 But when the fourteenth night was come, as we were driven up and down in Adria, about midnight the shipmen deemed that they drew near to some country;

28 And sounded, and found it twenty fathoms: and when they had gone a little further, they sounded again, and found it fifteen fathoms.

What comes into our minds when we think about God is the most important thing about us.

A. W. TOZER

29 Then fearing lest we should have fallen upon rocks, they cast four anchors out of the stern, and wished for the day.

30 And as the shipmen were about to flee out of the ship, when they had let down the boat into the sea, under colour as though they would have cast anchors out of the foreship,

31 Paul said to the centurion and to the soldiers, Except these abide in the ship, you cannot be saved.

32 Then the soldiers cut off the ropes of the boat, and let her fall off.

33 And while the day was coming on, Paul besought them all to take meat, saying, This day is the fourteenth day that you have tarried and continued fasting, having taken nothing.

34 Wherefore I pray you to take some meat: for this is for your health: for there shall not an hair fall from the head of any of you.

35 And when he had thus spoken, he took bread, and gave thanks to God in presence of them all: and when he had broken it, he began to eat.

36 Then were they all of good cheer, and they also took some meat.

37 And we were in all in the ship two hundred threescore and sixteen souls.

38 And when they had eaten enough, they lightened the ship, and cast out the wheat into the sea.

39 And when it was day, they knew not the land: but they discovered a certain creek with a shore, into the which they were minded, if it were possible, to thrust in the ship.

40 And when they had taken up the anchors, they committed themselves to the sea, and loosed the rudder bands, and hoisted up the mainsail to the wind, and made toward shore.

41 And falling into a place where two seas met, they ran the ship aground; and the forepart stuck fast, and remained unmoveable, but the hinder part was broken with the violence of the waves.

42 And the soldiers' counsel was to kill the prisoners, lest any of them should swim out, and escape.

43 But the centurion, willing to save Paul, kept them from their purpose; and commanded that they which could swim should cast themselves first into the sea, and get to land:

44 And the rest, some on boards, and some on broken pieces of the ship. And so it came to pass, that they escaped all safe to land.

CHAPTER 28

AND when they were escaped, then they knew that the island was called Melita.

2 And the barbarous people showed us no little kindness: for they kindled a fire, and received us every one, because of the present rain, and because of the cold.

3 And when Paul had gathered a bundle of sticks, and laid them on the fire, there came a viper out of the heat, and fastened on his hand.

4 And when the barbarians saw the venomous beast hang on his hand, they said among themselves, No doubt this man is a murderer, whom, though he has escaped the sea, yet vengeance suffers not to

live.

5 And he shook off the beast into the fire, and felt no harm.

6 Howbeit they looked when he should have swollen, or fallen down dead suddenly: but after they had looked a great while, and saw no harm come to him, they changed their minds, and said that he was a god.

7 In the same quarters were possessions of the chief man of the island, whose name was Publius; who received us, and lodged us three days courteously.

8 And it came to pass, that the father of Publius lay sick of a fever and of a bloody flux: to whom Paul entered in, and prayed, and laid his hands on him, and healed him.

9 So when this was done, others also, which had diseases in the island, came, and were healed:

10 Who also honored us with many honors; and when we departed, they laded us with such things as were necessary.

11 And after three months we departed in a ship of Alexandria, which had wintered in the isle, whose sign was Castor and Pollux.

12 And landing at Syracuse, we tarried there three days.

13 And from thence we fetched a compass, and came to Rhegium: and after one day the south wind blew, and we came the next day to Puteoli:

14 Where we found brethren, and were desired to tarry with them seven days: and so we went toward Rome.

15 And from thence, when the brethren heard of us, they came to meet us as far as Appiiforum, and The three taverns: whom when Paul saw, he thanked God, and took courage.

16 And when we came to Rome, the centurion delivered the prisoners to the captain of the guard: but Paul was suffered to dwell by himself with a soldier that

USING THE LAW IN EVANGELISM

28:23 Notice that Paul used *both* prophecy and the Law of Moses in his evangelism. Prophecy appeals to a man's intellect and creates faith in the Word of God. As he realizes that the Bible is no ordinary book—that it contains numerous indisputable prophecies that prove its supernatural origin—he begins to give Scripture credibility. However, the Law of Moses appeals to a man's conscience and brings conviction of sin. A "decision" for Jesus purely in the realm of the intellect—with no biblical knowledge of sin, which comes only by the Law (Romans 7:7)—will almost certainly produce a false convert. See Romans 2:21 comment.

kept him.

17 And it came to pass, that after three days Paul called the chief of the Jews together: and when they were come together, he said to them, Men and brethren, though I have committed nothing against the people, or customs of our fathers, yet was I delivered prisoner from Jerusalem into the hands of the Romans.

18 Who, when they had examined me, would have let me go, because there was no cause of death in me.

19 But when the Jews spoke against it, I was constrained to appeal to Caesar; not that I had anything to accuse my nation of.

20 For this cause therefore have I called for you, to see you, and to speak with you: because that for the hope of Israel I am bound with this chain.

21 And they said to him, We neither received letters out of Judea concerning you, neither any of the brethren that came showed or spoke any harm of you.

22 But we desire to hear of you what you think: for as concerning this sect, we know that every where it is spoken against.

23 And when they had appointed him a day, there came many to him into his

---

28:23 The goal of evangelism is to persuade people concerning Jesus. He is the way, the truth, and the life. There is salvation in no other name.

THE FUNCTION OF THE LAW

28:23 "The Law's part in transformation is to make a person aware of his sin and of his need for divine forgiveness and redemption and to set the standard of acceptable morality.

"Until a person acknowledges his basic sinfulness and inability to perfectly fulfill the demands of God's Law, he will not come repentantly to seek salvation. Until he despairs of himself and his own sinfulness, he will not come in humble faith to be filled with Christ's righteousness. A person who says he wants salvation but refuses to recognize and repent of his sin deceives himself.

"Grace means nothing to a person who does not know he is sinful and that such sinfulness means he is separated from God and damned. It is therefore pointless to preach grace until the impossible demands of the Law and the reality of guilt before God are preached." *John MacArthur*

lodging; to whom he expounded and testified the kingdom of God, persuading them concerning Jesus, both out of the law of Moses, and out of the prophets, from morning till evening.

24 And some believed the things which were spoken, and some believed not.

25 And when they agreed not among themselves, they departed, after that Paul had spoken one word, Well spoke the Holy Spirit by Isaiah the prophet to our fathers,

26 Saying, Go to this people, and say, Hearing you shall hear, and shall not understand; and seeing you shall see, and not perceive:

27 For the heart of this people is waxed gross, and their ears are dull of hearing, and their eyes have they closed; lest they should see with their eyes, and hear with their ears, and understand with their heart, and should be converted, and I should heal them.

28 Be it known therefore to you, that the salvation of God is sent to the Gentiles, and that they will hear it.

29 And when he had said these words, the Jews departed, and had great reasoning among themselves.

30 And Paul dwelt two whole years in his own hired house, and received all that came in to him,

31 Preaching the kingdom of God, and teaching those things which concern the Lord Jesus Christ, with all confidence, no man forbidding him.

"*The great of the kingdom have been those who loved God more than others did.*"

A. W. TOZER

Romans

CHAPTER 1

PAUL, a servant of Jesus Christ, called to be an apostle, separated to the gospel of God,

2 (Which he had promised before by his prophets in the holy scriptures,)

3 Concerning his Son Jesus Christ our Lord, which was made of the seed of David according to the flesh;

4 And declared to be the Son of God with power, according to the spirit of holiness, by the resurrection from the dead:

5 By whom we have received grace and apostleship, for obedience to the faith among all nations, for his name:

6 Among whom are you also the called of Jesus Christ:

7 To all that be in Rome, beloved of God, called to be saints: Grace to you and peace from God our Father, and the Lord Jesus Christ.

8 *First, I thank my God through Jesus Christ for you all, that your faith is spoken of throughout the whole world.*

9 For God is my witness, whom I serve with my spirit in the gospel of his Son, that without ceasing I make mention of you always in my prayers;

10 Making request, if by any means now at length I might have a prosperous journey by the will of God to come to you.

11 For I long to see you, that I may impart to you some spiritual gift, to the end you may be established;

12 That is, that I may be comforted together with you by the mutual faith both of you and me.

13 Now I would not have you ignorant, brethren, that oftentimes I purposed to come to you, (but was let hitherto,) that I might have some fruit among you also, even as among other Gentiles.

14 *I am debtor both to the Greeks, and to the Barbarians; both to the wise, and to the unwise.*

15 *So, as much as in me is, I am ready to preach the gospel to you that are at Rome also.*

16 *For I am not ashamed of the gospel of Christ: for it is the power of God to salvation to every one that believes; to the Jew first, and also to the Greek.*

17 For therein is the righteousness of God revealed from faith to faith: as it is written, The just shall live by faith.

18 For the wrath of God is revealed from heaven against all ungodliness and unrighteousness of men, who hold the truth in unrighteousness;

19 Because that which may be known of God is manifest in them; for God has showed it to them.

20 For the invisible things of him from the creation of the world are clearly seen, being understood by the things that are made, even his eternal power and God-

---

1:14 So long as there is a human being who does not know Jesus Christ, I am his debtor to serve him until he does. *Oswald Chambers*

head; so that they are without excuse:

21 Because that, when they knew God, they glorified him not as God, neither were thankful; but became vain in their imaginations, and their foolish heart was darkened.

22 Professing themselves to be wise, they became fools,

23 And changed the glory of the uncorruptible God into an image made like to corruptible man, and to birds, and four-footed beasts, and creeping things.

24 Wherefore God also gave them up to uncleanness through the lusts of their own hearts, to dishonor their own bodies between themselves:

25 Who changed the truth of God into a lie, and worshipped and served the creature more than the Creator, who is blessed for ever. Amen.

26 For this cause God gave them up to vile affections: for even their women did change the natural use into that which is against nature:

27 And likewise also the men, leaving the natural use of the woman, burned in their lust one toward another; men with men working that which is unseemly, and receiving in themselves that recompense of their error which was meet.

28 And even as they did not like to retain God in their knowledge, God gave them over to a reprobate mind, to do those things which are not convenient;

29 Being filled with all unrighteousness, fornication, wickedness, covetousness, maliciousness; full of envy, murder, debate, deceit, malignity; whisperers,

30 Backbiters, haters of God, despiteful, proud, boasters, inventors of evil things, disobedient to parents,

31 Without understanding, covenant-

1:20 Faith in God is not blind faith; it is based on the fact of God's existence seen clearly through creation.

This most beautiful system of the sun, planets, and comets could only proceed from the counsel and dominion of an intelligent and powerful Being.   *Sir Isaac Newton*

The more I study nature, the more I stand amazed at the work of the Creator.   *Louis Pasteur*

1:20   How to prove God's existence. When I look at a building, how do I know that there was a builder? I can't see him, hear him, touch, taste, or smell him. Of course, the build*ing* is proof that there was a build*er*. In fact, I couldn't want better evidence that there was a builder than to have the building in front of me. I don't need faith to know that there was a builder. All I need is eyes that can see and a brain that works.

Likewise, when I look at a painting, how can I know that there was a painter? Again, the paint-*ing*is proof positive that there was a painter. I don't need faith to believe in a painter because I can see the clear evidence.

The same principle applies with the existence of God. When I look at creation, how can I *know* that there was a Creator? I can't see Him, hear Him, touch Him, taste Him, or smell Him. How can I know that He exists? Why, creation shows me that there is a Creator. *I couldn't want better proof that a Creator exists than to have the creation in front of me.* I don't need faith to believe in a Creator; all I need is eyes that can see and a brain that works: For the invisible things of Him from the creation of the world are clearly seen, being understood by the things that are made, even His eternal power and Godhead; so that they are without excuse (Romans 1:20).

If, however, I want the builder to *do* something for me, *then* I need to have faith in him. The same applies to God: Without faith it is impossible to please Him: for He that comes to God must believe that He is, and that He is a rewarder of them that diligently seek Him (Hebrews 11:6).

1:27   Homosexuality. Despite claims to the contrary, no scientific evidence has been found that homosexuals are born that way. In fact, God's Word is clear that sexual activity is to be only within the bounds of marriage, between one man and one woman. Homosexuality goes against God's created order and expressed will. If a homosexual claims to be born that way, gently explain that all people are born with a sin nature, but that our nature makes us children of wrath. (See Jude 7 comment.) See also 1 Timothy 1:8-10 comment.

2:12 *"Will people who have never heard the gospel all go to hell because they haven't heard about Jesus Christ?"*

No one will go to hell because they haven't heard of Jesus Christ. The heathen will go to hell for murder, rape, adultery, lust, theft, lying, etc. Sin is not *failing to hear the gospel*. Rather, sin is the transgression of the Law (1 John 3:4). If we really care about the lost, we will become missionaries and take the good news of God's forgiveness in Christ to them. See John 16:9 comment.

breakers, without natural affection, implacable, unmerciful:

32 Who knowing the judgment of God, that they which commit such things are worthy of death, not only do the same, but have pleasure in them that do them.

CHAPTER 2

THEREFORE you are inexcusable, O man, whosoever you are that judge: for wherein you judge another, you condemn yourself; for you that judge do the same things.

2 But we are sure that the judgment of God is according to truth against them which commit such things.

3 And do you think this, O man, that judge them which do such things, and do the same, that you shall escape the judgment of God?

4 Or do you despise the riches of his goodness and forbearance and longsuffering; not knowing that the goodness of God leads you to repentance?

5 But after your hardness and impenitent heart you treasure up to yourself wrath against the day of wrath and revelation of the righteous judgment of God;

6 Who will render to every man according to his deeds:

7 To them who by patient continuance in well doing seek for glory and honor and immortality, eternal life:

8 But to them that are contentious, and do not obey the truth, but obey unrighteousness, indignation and wrath,

9 Tribulation and anguish, upon every soul of man that does evil, of the Jew first, and also of the Gentile;

10 But glory, honor, and peace, to every man that works good, to the Jew first, and also to the Gentile:

11 For there is no respect of persons with God.

12 For as many as have sinned without law shall also perish without law: and as many as have sinned in the law shall be judged by the law;

13 (For not the hearers of the law are just before God, but the doers of the law shall be justified.

14 For when the Gentiles, which have not the law, do by nature the things contained in the law, these, having not the law, are a law to themselves:

15 Which show the work of the law written in their hearts, their conscience also bearing witness, and their thoughts

---

2:4 This verse is sandwiched between statements of God's judgment and wrath. If Paul was saying that we should speak only of God's goodness to sinners, he wasn't practicing what he preached.

I never knew but one person in the whole course of my ministry who acknowledged that the first motions of religion in his own heart arose from a sense of the goodness of God, What shall I render to the Lord, who has dealt so bountifully with me? But I think all besides who have come within my notice have rather been first awakened to fly from the wrath to come by the passion of fear. *Isaac Watts*

2:15 Conscience is the internal perception of God's moral Law. *Oswald Chambers*

USING THE LAW IN EVANGELISM

2:21   Here Paul uses the Law to bring the knowledge of sin.

Dr. J Gresham Machen said, "A new and more powerful proclamation of [the] Law is perhaps the most pressing need of the hour; men would have little difficulty with the gospel if they had only learned the lesson of the Law." See James 2:8 comment.

the mean while accusing or else excusing one another;)

16 In the day when God shall judge the secrets of men by Jesus Christ according to my gospel.

17 Behold, you are called a Jew, and rest in the law, and make your boast of God,

18 And know his will, and approve the things that are more excellent, being instructed out of the law;

19 And are confident that you yourself are a guide of the blind, a light of them which are in darkness,

20 An instructor of the foolish, a teacher of babes, which have the form of knowledge and of the truth in the law.

21 You therefore which teach another, do you not teach yourself? you that preach a man should not steal, do you steal?

22 You that say a man should not commit adultery, do you commit adultery? you that abhor idols, do you commit sacrilege?

23 You that make your boast of the law, through breaking the law do you dishonor God?

24 For the name of God is blasphemed among the Gentiles through you, as it is written.

25 For circumcision verily profits, if you keep the law: but if you be a breaker of the law, your circumcision is made uncircumcision.

26 Therefore if the uncircumcision keep the righteousness of the law, shall not his uncircumcision be counted for circumcision?

27 And shall not uncircumcision which is by nature, if it fulfil the law, judge you, who by the letter and circumcision do transgress the law?

28 For he is not a Jew, which is one outwardly; neither is that circumcision, which is outward in the flesh:

29 But he is a Jew, which is one inwardly; and circumcision is that of the heart, in the spirit, and not in the letter; whose praise is not of men, but of God.

. . . . . .

How did the apostles die?
See Acts 7:55.

. . . . . .

CHAPTER 3

WHAT advantage then has the Jew? or what profit is there of circumcision?

2 Much every way: chiefly, because that to them were committed the oracles of God.

3 For what if some did not believe? shall their unbelief make the faith of God without effect?

4 God forbid: yea, let God be true, but every man a liar; as it is written, That you

---

2:15 The sinner's conscience. God has given light to every man. The word con-science means with knowledge. The conscience is the headline warning of sin; the Scriptures give the fine print. No man can say he doesn't know that it's wrong to murder or commit adultery. That knowledge is written in bold print on his heart. However, in the Scriptures we see the true nature of sin: that God requires truth even in the inward parts (Psalm 51:6). The fine print reveals that lust is adultery of the heart, hatred is murder of the heart, etc.

2:15,16 There are two witnesses to our crimes: Our conscience and God Himself accuse us. See 1 Corinthians 6:9,10 comment.

2:16 Judgment Day: For verses that warn of its reality, see Romans 14:10.

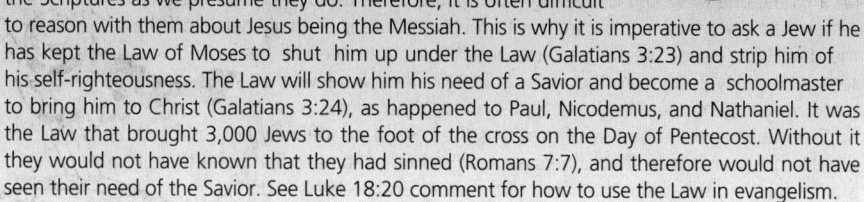

QUESTIONS & OBJECTIONS

 3:1   *"How should I witness to a Jew?"*

Sadly, many of today's Jews profess godliness but don't embrace the Scriptures as we presume they do. Therefore, it is often difficult to reason with them about Jesus being the Messiah. This is why it is imperative to ask a Jew if he has kept the Law of Moses to shut him up under the Law (Galatians 3:23) and strip him of his self-righteousness. The Law will show him his need of a Savior and become a schoolmaster to bring him to Christ (Galatians 3:24), as happened to Paul, Nicodemus, and Nathaniel. It was the Law that brought 3,000 Jews to the foot of the cross on the Day of Pentecost. Without it they would not have known that they had sinned (Romans 7:7), and therefore would not have seen their need of the Savior. See Luke 18:20 comment for how to use the Law in evangelism.

might be justified in your sayings, and might overcome when you are judged.

5 But if our unrighteousness commend the righteousness of God, what shall we say? Is God unrighteous who takes vengeance? (I speak as a man)

6 God forbid: for then how shall God judge the world?

7 For if the truth of God has more abounded through my lie to his glory; why yet am I also judged as a sinner?

8 And not rather, (as we be slanderously reported, and as some affirm that we say,) Let us do evil, that good may come? whose damnation is just.

9 What then? are we better than they? No, in no wise: for we have before proved both Jews and Gentiles, that they are all under sin;

10 As it is written, There is none righteous, no, not one:

11 There is none that understands, there is none that seeks after God.

12 They are all gone out of the way, they are together become unprofitable; there is none that does good, no, not one.

13 Their throat is an open sepulchre; with their tongues they have used deceit; the poison of asps is under their lips:

14 Whose mouth is full of cursing and bitterness:

15 Their feet are swift to shed blood:

16 Destruction and misery are in their ways:

17 And the way of peace have they not known:

18 There is no fear of God before their eyes.

19 Now we know that what things soever the law says, it says to them who are under the law: that every mouth may be stopped, and all the world may become guilty before God.

THE FUNCTION OF THE LAW

 3:19   "The purpose of the Law is to stop the sinner's mouth of justification. The Law tells him what sin is (see 1 John 3:4) and stops him proclaiming his own goodness. Its intent is to drive him to the cross. *John Wesley* said, The first use of [the Law], without question, is to convince the world of sin. By this is the sinner discovered to himself. All his fig-leaves are torn away, and he sees that he is wretched and poor and miserable, blind and naked. The Law flashes conviction on every side. He feels himself a mere sinner. He has nothing to pay. His mouth is stopped and he stands guilty before God.

"Ask Paul why [the Law] was given. Here is his answer: That every mouth may be stopped, and all the world may become guilty before God (Romans 3:19). The Law stops every man's mouth. I can always tell a man who is near the kingdom of God; his mouth is stopped. This, then, is why God gives us the Law to show us ourselves in our true colors" *D. L. Moody*

QUESTIONS & OBJECTIONS

3:9 *"Do you think that Christians are better than non-Christians?"*

The Christian is no better than a non-Christian, but he is infinitely *better off*. It is like two men on a plane, one of whom is wearing a parachute while the other is not. Neither is better than the other, but the man with the parachute is certainly better off than the man who is not wearing a parachute. The difference will be seen when they jump from the plane at 20,000 feet. Jesus warned that if we jump into death without Him, we would perish.

Even harsher than the law of gravity is the Law of an infinitely holy and just Creator. Scripture states that sinners are God's enemy (Romans 5:10) and that it is a fearful thing to fall into the hands of the living God (Hebrews 10:31).

20 Therefore by the deeds of the law there shall no flesh be justified in his sight: for by the law is the knowledge of sin.

21 But now the righteousness of God

THE FUNCTION OF THE LAW

3:20 "Sin is like smog it is not visible while you are in its midst. The Law takes the sinner above the smog of his own perspective and shows him heaven's viewpoint. It gives the sinner knowledge of his sin. *John Bunyan* stated, "The man who does not know the nature of the Law cannot know the nature of sin."

"The trouble with people who are not seeking for a Savior and for salvation is that they do not understand the nature of sin. It is the peculiar function of the Law to bring such an understanding to a man's mind and conscience. That is why great evangelical preachers 300 years ago in the time of the Puritans, and 200 years ago in the time of Whitefield and others, always engaged in what they called a preliminary Law work." *Martyn Lloyd-Jones*

"The first duty of the gospel preacher is to declare God's Law and show the nature of sin." *Martin Luther*

without the law is manifested, being witnessed by the law and the prophets;

22 Even the righteousness of God which is by faith of Jesus Christ to all and upon all them that believe: for there is no difference:

23 **For all have sinned, and come short of the glory of God;**

24 Being justified freely by his grace through the redemption that is in Christ Jesus:

25 Whom God has set forth to be a propitiation through faith in his blood, to declare his righteousness for the remission of sins that are past, through the forbearance of God;

26 To declare, I say, at this time his righteousness: that he might be just, and the justifier of him which believes in Jesus.

27 Where is boasting then? It is excluded. By what law? of works? Nay: but by the law of faith.

28 Therefore we conclude that a man is justified by faith without the deeds of the law.

29 Is he the God of the Jews only? is he not also of the Gentiles? Yes, of the Gentiles also:

3:19 Every unredeemed human being, Jew or Gentile, is under the Law of God and accountable to God. The final verdict, then, is that unredeemed mankind has no defense whatever and is guilty of all charges. The defense must rest, as it were, before it has opportunity to say anything, because the omniscient and all-wise God has infallibly demonstrated the impossibility of any grounds of acquittal. Absolute silence is the only possible response. *John MacArthur*

30 Seeing it is one God, which shall justify the circumcision by faith, and uncircumcision through faith.
31 Do we then make void the law through faith? God forbid: yea, we establish the law.

CHAPTER 4

WHAT shall we say then that Abraham our father, as pertaining to the flesh, has found?
2 For if Abraham were justified by works, he has whereof to glory; but not before God.
3 For what do the Scriptures say? Abraham believed God, and it was counted to him for righteousness.
4 Now to him that works is the reward not reckoned of grace, but of debt.
5 But to him that works not, but believes on him that justifies the ungodly, his faith is counted for righteousness.
6 Even as David also describes the blessedness of the man, to whom God imputes righteousness without works,
7 **Saying, Blessed are they whose iniquities are forgiven, and whose sins are covered.**
8 Blessed is the man to whom the Lord will not impute sin.
9 Came this blessedness then upon the circumcision only, or upon the uncircumcision also? for we say that faith was reckoned to Abraham for righteousness.
10 How was it then reckoned? when he was in circumcision, or in uncircumcision? Not in circumcision, but in uncircumcision.
11 And he received the sign of circumcision, a seal of the righteousness of the faith which he had yet being uncircumcised: that he might be the father of all them that believe, though they be not circumcised; that righteousness might be imputed to them also:
12 And the father of circumcision to them who are not of the circumcision only, but who also walk in the steps of that faith of our father Abraham, which he had being yet uncircumcised.
13 For the promise, that he should be the heir of the world, was not to Abraham, or to his seed, through the law, but through the righteousness of faith.
14 For if they which are of the law be heirs, faith is made void, and the promise made of no effect:

> I would sooner bring one sinner to Jesus than unravel all the mysteries of the Word, for salvation is the thing we are to live for.
>
> **CHARLES SPURGEON**

15 Because the law works wrath: for where no law is, there is no transgression.
16 Therefore it is of faith, that it might be by grace; to the end the promise might be sure to all the seed; not to that only which is of the law, but to that also which is of the faith of Abraham; who is the father of us all,
17 (As it is written, I have made you a father of many nations,) before him whom he believed, even God, who quickens the dead, and calls those things which be not as though they were.
18 Who against hope believed in hope, that he might become the father of many nations; according to that which was spoken, So shall your seed be.
19 And being not weak in faith, he considered not his own body now dead, when he was about an hundred years old, neither yet the deadness of Sara's womb:
20 He staggered not at the promise of God through unbelief; but was strong in

---

4:20 There is a wise saying: If it sounds too good to be true, it probably is. That is solid advice when you are dealing with sinful mankind. But the promises of God of forgiveness of sin, of peace with God through trusting in the Savior, of a new heaven and a new earth come from a faithful Creator, and there is no greater insult to God than not to believe His promises.

faith, giving glory to God;

21 And being fully persuaded that, what he had promised, he was able also to perform.

22 And therefore it was imputed to him for righteousness.

23 Now it was not written for his sake alone, that it was imputed to him;

24 But for us also, to whom it shall be imputed, if we believe on him that raised up Jesus our Lord from the dead;

25 Who was delivered for our offences, and was raised again for our justification.

CHAPTER 5

THEREFORE being justified by faith, we have peace with God through our Lord Jesus Christ:

2 By whom also we have access by faith into this grace wherein we stand, and rejoice in hope of the glory of God.

3 And not only so, but we glory in tribulations also: knowing that tribulation works patience;

4 And patience, experience; and experience, hope:

5 And hope makes not ashamed; because the love of God is shed abroad in our hearts by the Holy Spirit which is given to us.

6 **For when we were yet without strength, in due time Christ died for the ungodly.**

7 **For scarcely for a righteous man will one die: yet peradventure for a good** man some would even dare to die.

8 **But God commends his love toward us, in that, while we were yet sinners, Christ died for us.**

9 **Much more then, being now justified by his blood, we shall be saved from wrath through him.**

10 For if, when we were enemies, we were reconciled to God by the death of his Son, much more, being reconciled, we shall be saved by his life.

11 And not only so, but we also joy in God through our Lord Jesus Christ, by whom we have now received the atonement.

12 **Wherefore, as by one man sin entered into the world, and death by sin; and so death passed upon all men, for that all have sinned:**

13 (For until the law sin was in the world: but sin is not imputed when there is no law.

14 Nevertheless death reigned from Adam to Moses, even over them that had not sinned after the similitude of Adam's transgression, who is the figure of him that was to come.

15 But not as the offence, so also is the free gift. For if through the offence of one many be dead, much more the grace of God, and the gift by grace, which is by one man, Jesus Christ, has abounded to many.

16 And not as it was by one that sinned, so is the gift: for the judgment was by

---

5:8 "God proved His love on the cross. When Christ hung, and bled, and died, it was God saying to the world, I love you." *Billy Graham*

5:14 Many years ago, a man jumped off a high bridge in an effort to end his life. Fortunately, he lived through the ordeal but broke his back as a result of the fall, and ended up in a wheelchair. His attempt to take his life caused a great deal of distress, to those in control of the bridge, to paramedics, to traffic, and especially to his family. Authorities wanted to press charges against him but they couldn't; since this was the city's first suicide attempt, they had no law forbidding such an act. He escaped the consequences of the law of man, but suffered the painful consequences of breaking another law, the law of gravity.

In the same way, every person in Adam still sinned and therefore suffered the consequences of breaking the then unwritten moral Law, "the soul that sins, it shall die" (Ezekiel 18:4). Death reigned as king, with a dominion from Adam to Moses. They didn't partake from the Tree of Knowledge of Good and Evil as did Adam, but they still sinned against God.

5:12 "Why is there suffering? That proves there is no 'loving' God."

Study the soil for a moment. It naturally produces weeds. No one plants them; no one waters them. They even stubbornly push through cracks of a dry sidewalk. Millions of useless weeds sprout like there's no tomorrow, strangling our crops and ruining our lawns. Pull them out by the roots, and there will be more tomorrow. They are nothing but a curse!

Consider how much of the earth is uninhabitable. There are millions of square miles of barren deserts in Africa and other parts of the world. Most of Australia is nothing but miles and miles of useless desolate land.

Not only that, but the earth is constantly shaken with massive earthquakes. Its shores are lashed with hurricanes; tornadoes rip through creation with incredible fury; devastating floods soak the land; and terrible droughts parch the soil. Sharks, tigers, lions, snakes, spiders, and disease-carrying mosquitoes attack humanity and suck its life's blood. The earth's inhabitants are afflicted with disease, pain, suffering, and death.

Think of how many people are plagued with cancer, Alzheimer's, multiple sclerosis, heart disease, emphysema, Parkinson's, and a number of other debilitating illnesses. Consider all the children with leukemia, or people born with crippling diseases or without the mental capability to even feed themselves. All these things should convince thinking minds that something is radically wrong.

Did God blow it when He created humanity? What sort of tyrant must our Creator be if this was His master plan?

Sadly, many use the issue of suffering as an excuse to reject any thought of God, when its existence is the *very reason* we should accept Him. Suffering stands as terrible testimony to the truth of the explanation given by the Word of God.

But how can we know that the Bible is true? Simply by studying the prophecies of Matthew 24, Luke 21, and 2 Timothy 3. A few minutes of openhearted inspection will convince any honest skeptic that this is no ordinary book. It is the supernatural testament of our Creator about why there is suffering... and what we can do about it.

The Bible tells us that God cursed the earth because of Adam's transgression. Weeds *are* a curse. So is disease. Sin and suffering cannot be separated. The Scriptures inform us that we live in a *fallen* creation. In the beginning, God created man perfect, and he lived in a perfect world without suffering. *It was heaven on earth.* When sin came into the world, death and misery came with it.

Those who understand the message of Holy Scripture eagerly await a new heaven and a new earth wherein dwells righteousness. In that coming Kingdom there will be no more pain, suffering, disease, or death. We are told that no eye has ever seen, nor has any ear heard, neither has any man's mind ever imagined the wonderful things that God has in store for those who love Him (1 Corinthians 2:9). Think for a moment what it would be like if food grew with the fervor of weeds. Consider how wonderful it would be if the deserts became incredibly fertile, if creation stopped devouring humanity. Imagine if the weather worked *for* us instead of against us, if disease completely disappeared, if pain was a thing of the past, if death was no more.

The dilemma is that we are like a child whose insatiable appetite for chocolate has caused his face to break out with ugly sores. He looks in the mirror and sees a sight that makes him depressed. But instead of giving up his beloved chocolate, he consoles himself by stuffing more into his mouth. Yet, the source of his pleasure is actually the *cause* of his suffering.

The whole face of the earth is nothing but ugly sores of suffering. Everywhere we look we see unspeakable pain. But instead of believing God's explanation and asking Him to forgive us and change our appetite, we run deeper into sin's sweet embrace. There we find solace in its temporal pleasures, thus intensifying our pain, both in this life and in the life to come.

one to condemnation, but the free gift is of many offences to justification.

17 For if by one man's offence death reigned by one; much more they which receive abundance of grace and of the gift of righteousness shall reign in life by one, Jesus Christ.)

18 Therefore as by the offence of one judgment came upon all men to condemnation; even so by the righteousness of one the free gift came upon all men to justification of life.

19 For as by one man's disobedience many were made sinners, so by the obedience of one shall many be made righteous.

20 Moreover the law entered, that the offence might abound. But where sin abounded, grace did much more abound:

21 That as sin has reigned to death, even so might grace reign through righteousness to eternal life by Jesus Christ our Lord.

CHAPTER 6

WHAT shall we say then? Shall we continue in sin, that grace may abound?

2 God forbid. How shall we, that are dead to sin, live any longer therein?

3 Do you not know, that so many of us as were baptized into Jesus Christ were baptized into his death?

4 Therefore we are buried with him by baptism into death: that like as Christ was raised up from the dead by the glory of the Father, even so we also should walk in newness of life.

5 For if we have been planted together in the likeness of his death, we shall be also in the likeness of his resurrection:

6 Knowing this, that our old man is crucified with him, that the body of sin might be destroyed, that henceforth we should not serve sin.

7 For he that is dead is freed from sin.

8 Now if we be dead with Christ, we believe that we shall also live with him:

9 Knowing that Christ being raised from the dead dies no more; death has no more dominion over him.

10 For in that he died, he died to sin once: but in that he lives, he lives to God.

11 Likewise reckon you also yourselves to be dead indeed to sin, but alive to God through Jesus Christ our Lord.

12 Let not sin therefore reign in your mortal body, that you should obey it in the lusts thereof.

13 Neither yield your members as instruments of unrighteousness to sin: but yield yourselves to God, as those that are alive from the dead, and your members as instruments of righteousness to God.

14 For sin shall not have dominion over you: for you are not under the law, but under grace.

15 What then? shall we sin, because we are not under the law, but under grace? God forbid.

16 Do you not know, that to whom you yield yourselves servants to obey, his servants you are to whom you obey; whether of sin to death, or of obedience to righteousness?

5:2 "God's grace cannot be faithfully preached to unbelievers until His Law is preached and man's corrupt nature is exposed. It is impossible for a person to fully realize his need for God's grace until he sees how terribly he has failed the standards of God's Law. It is impossible for him to realize his need for mercy until he realizes the magnitude of his guilt." *John MacArthur*

6:6 See 1 John 2:19 comment.

6:14 In Christ we are sheltered under the umbrella of grace from the rain of the wrath of the Law. Paul is not saying that the Law has been done away with. Jesus Himself said that He hadn't come to do away with the Law. We establish the Law in Christ (Romans 3:31). We corroborate it. It still remains as the standard of God's righteousness, and it will be the means by which He will judge the world.

17 But God be thanked, that you were the servants of sin, but you have obeyed from the heart that form of doctrine which was delivered you.

18 Being then made free from sin, you became the servants of righteousness.

19 I speak after the manner of men because of the infirmity of your flesh: for as you have yielded your members servants to uncleanness and to iniquity to iniquity; even so now yield your members servants to righteousness to holiness.

20 For when you were the servants of sin, you were free from righteousness.

21 What fruit had you then in those things whereof you are now ashamed? for the end of those things is death.

22 But now being made free from sin, and become servants to God, you have your fruit to holiness, and the end everlasting life.

23 **For the wages of sin is death; but the gift of God is eternal life through Jesus Christ our Lord.**

CHAPTER 7

DO you not know, brethren, (for I speak to them that know the law,) how that the law has dominion over a man as long as he lives?

2 For the woman which has an husband is bound by the law to her husband so long as he lives; but if the husband be dead, she is loosed from the law of her husband.

3 So then if, while her husband lives, she be married to another man, she shall be called an adulteress: but if her husband be dead, she is free from that law; so that she is no adulteress, though she be married to another man.

4 Wherefore, my brethren, you also are become dead to the law by the body of Christ; that you should be married to another, even to him who is raised from the dead, that we should bring forth fruit to God.

5 For when we were in the flesh, the motions of sins, which were by the law, did work in our members to bring forth fruit to death.

6 But now we are delivered from the law, that being dead wherein we were held; that we should serve in newness of spirit, and not in the oldness of the letter.

7 What shall we say then? Is the law sin? God forbid. Nay, I had not known sin, but by the law: for I had not known lust, except the law had said, You shall not covet.

8 But sin, taking occasion by the commandment, wrought in me all manner of concupiscence. For without the law sin was dead.

9 For I was alive without the law once: but when the commandment came, sin revived, and I died.

10 And the commandment, which was

7:7 "Even with the light of nature, and the light of conscience, and the light of tradition, there are some things we should never have believed to be sins had we not been taught so by the Law." *Charles Spurgeon*

7:9 "It is right for a preacher of the gospel first, by a revelation of the Law and of sin, to rebuke everything and make sin of everything that is not the living fruit of the Spirit and faith in Christ, so that men may be led to know themselves and their own wretchedness, and become humble and ask for help.

"No one knows that lime has heat until he pours water upon it. Then the heat has occasion to show itself. The water did not create the heat in the lime, but it has made itself manifest. It is similar to the will of man and the Law.

"I was alive without the law once: but when the commandment came, sin revived (Romans 7:9). So it is with the work-righteous and the proud unbelievers. Because they do not know the Law of God, which is directed against them, it is impossible for them to know their sin. Therefore also they are not amenable to instruction. If they would know the Law, they would also know their sin; and sin to which they are now dead would become alive in them." *Martin Luther*

THE FUNCTION OF THE LAW

7:11 "To slay the sinner is then the first use of the Law, to destroy the life and strength wherein he trusts and convince him that he is dead while he lives; not only under the sentence of death, but actually dead to God, void of all spiritual life, dead in trespasses and sins." *John Wesley*

ordained to life, I found to be to death.

11 For sin, taking occasion by the commandment, deceived me, and by it slew me.

12 Wherefore the law is holy, and the commandment holy, and just, and good.

13 Was then that which is good made death to me? God forbid. But sin, that it might appear sin, working death in me by that which is good; that sin by the commandment might become exceeding sinful.

14 For we know that the law is spiritual: but I am carnal, sold under sin.

15 For that which I do I allow not: for what I would, that do I not; but what I hate, that do I.

16 If then I do that which I would not, I consent to the law that it is good.

17 Now then it is no more I that do it, but sin that dwells in me.

18 For I know that in me (that is, in my flesh,) dwells no good thing: for to will is present with me; but how to perform that which is good I find not.

19 For the good that I would I do not: but the evil which I would not, that I do.

20 Now if I do that I would not, it is no more I that do it, but sin that dwells in me.

. . . . . .

For last words of famous people, see 1 Corinthians 15:55 comment.

. . . . . .

21 I find then a law, that, when I would do good, evil is present with me.

22 For I delight in the law of God after the inward man:

23 But I see another law in my members, warring against the law of my mind, and bringing me into captivity to the law of sin which is in my members.

7:10 The Law is not in fault, but our evil and wicked nature; even as a heap of lime is still and quiet until water be poured thereon, but then it begins to smoke and burn, not from the fault of the water, but from the nature and kind of the lime which will not endure it. *Augustine*

7:18,19 There is disagreement about whether Paul is speaking of his pre-conversion experience or the battle the Christian has with sin. It would seem that both interpretations may be applied. God bless the Christian who is able to obtain "sinless perfection." He is a better man than most Christians. Rather, the majority of believers can identify with *George Whitefield*:

> After we are renewed, yet we are renewed but in part, indwelling sin continues in us, there is a mixture of corruption in every one of our duties; so that after we are converted, were Jesus Christ only to accept us according to our works, our works would damn us, for we cannot put up a prayer but it is far from that perfection which the moral Law requireth. I do not know what you may think, but I can say that I cannot pray but I sin; I cannot preach to you or others but I sin; I can do nothing without sin; and, as one expresseth it, my repentance wants to be repented of, and my tears to be washed in the precious blood of my dear Redeemer.

7:22 "Never, never let us despise [the Law]. It is the symptom of an ignorant ministry, and unhealthy state of religion, when the Law is reckoned unimportant. The true Christian delights in God's Law." *J. C. Ryle*

In speaking of the Christian's attitude to the Law, John Wesley said, "Yea, love and value it for the sake of Him from whom it came, and of Him to whom it leads. Let it be thy glory and joy, next to the cross of Christ. Declare its praise, and make it honorable before all men."

(Can Hinduism provide deliverance from sin? See Romans 7:24,25 comment.)

Mahatma Ghandi

24 O wretched man that I am! who shall deliver me from the body of this death?

25 I thank God through Jesus Christ our Lord. So then with the mind I myself serve the law of God; but with the flesh the law of sin.

CHAPTER 8

THERE is therefore now no condemnation to them which are in Christ Jesus, who walk not after the flesh, but after the Spirit.

2 For the law of the Spirit of life in Christ Jesus has made me free from the law of sin and death.

3 For what the law could not do, in that it was weak through the flesh, God sending his own Son in the likeness of sinful flesh, and for sin, condemned sin in the flesh:

4 That the righteousness of the law might be fulfilled in us, who walk not after the flesh, but after the Spirit.

5 For they that are after the flesh do mind the things of the flesh; but they that are after the Spirit the things of the Spirit.

6 For to be carnally minded is death; but to be spiritually minded is life and peace.

7 Because the carnal mind is enmity against God: for it is not subject to the law of God, neither indeed can be.

8 So then they that are in the flesh cannot please God.

9 But you are not in the flesh, but in the Spirit, if so be that the Spirit of God dwell in you. Now if any man have not the Spirit of Christ, he is none of his.

10 And if Christ be in you, the body is dead because of sin; but the Spirit is life because of righteousness.

11 But if the Spirit of him that raised up Jesus from the dead dwell in you, he that raised up Christ from the dead shall also quicken your mortal bodies by his Spirit

---

7:24,25 Mahatma Ghandi acknowledged the inability of his religion to atone for sin. Despite his moral lifestyle and good works, he admitted, "It is a constant torture to me that I am still so far from Him whom I know to be my very life and being. I know it is my own wretchedness and wickedness that keeps me from Him." All works-based religions lead to futility and death. It is only in Jesus Christ that sinners can find forgiveness for their sins and deliverance from death and hell.

8:2 A higher Law. One hundred fifty years ago it would have been thought insane that a jumbo jet, filled with people, could fly. The law of gravity made it impossible for even a feather to remain in the air. Yet, we know that when a certain object moves at a particular speed, it moves out of the law of gravity into a higher law, the law of aerodynamics, even though the law of gravity still remains. The world thinks the Christian is insane to live for Jesus Christ. But we know that, even though there is the law of sin and death, we live in a higher law the law of the Spirit of life in Christ Jesus.

8:6   "Let no man think of fighting hell's legions if he is still fighting an internal warfare. Carnage without will sicken him if he has carnality within. It is the man who has surrendered to the Lord who will never surrender to his enemies." *Leonard Ravenhill*

QUESTIONS & OBJECTIONS

8:22 *"Mother Nature sure blew it..."*

Hurricanes, tornadoes, floods, droughts, and earthquakes kill tens of thousands of people each year. Multitudes endure crippling diseases, endless suffering, and unspeakable pain (see Romans 5:12 comment). Many non-Christians credit a heartless Mother Nature for giving us all this grief. They fail to consider that Mother Nature has a Senior Partne—Father God.

However, if God is responsible for all this heartache, that presents an interesting dilemma. If God is an all-loving Father figure, as we are told, we seem to have three choices: 1) God blew it when He made everything (He's creative but incompetent); 2) God is a tyrant, who gets His kicks from seeing kids die of leukemia; 3) something between God and man is radically wrong. These are our choices...and those who take time to consider the evidence will lean toward number three. Something between man and God is radically wrong, and the Bible tells us what it is.

There is a war going on. We are told that mankind is an enemy of God in his mind through wicked works (Colossians 1:21). That's not too hard to see. Man is continually committing violent acts such as murder and rape, lying, stealing, etc., as the daily news confirms. He uses God's name as a curse word, while Mother Nature gets the glory for His creation—unless there's a horrible disaster; then man calls that an act of God.

An applicable acronym for WAR is We Are Right. Any country going to war does so because it has the conviction that it is in the right. However, a quick look at God's Law shows us who is right and who is wrong. We, not God, are the guilty party. If we want His blessing back on our nation and in our lives, we must make peace with Him, and that is possible only through faith in Jesus Christ.

that dwells in you.

12 Therefore, brethren, we are debtors, not to the flesh, to live after the flesh.

13 For if you live after the flesh, you shall die: but if you through the Spirit do mortify the deeds of the body, you shall live.

14 For as many as are led by the Spirit of God, they are the sons of God.

15 For you have not received the spirit of bondage again to fear; but you have received the Spirit of adoption, whereby we cry, Abba, Father.

16 The Spirit itself bears witness with our spirit, that we are the children of God:

17 And if children, then heirs; heirs of God, and joint-heirs with Christ; if so be that we suffer with him, that we may be also glorified together.

18 For I reckon that the sufferings of this present time are not worthy to be compared with the glory which shall be revealed in us.

19 For the earnest expectation of the creature waits for the manifestation of the sons of God.

20 For the creature was made subject to vanity, not willingly, but by reason of him who has subjected the same in hope,

21 Because the creature itself also shall be delivered from the bondage of corruption into the glorious liberty of the children of God.

22 For we know that the whole creation groans and travails in pain together until now.

23 And not only they, but ourselves also, which have the firstfruits of the Spirit, even we ourselves groan within ourselves, waiting for the adoption, to wit, the redemption of our body.

24 For we are saved by hope: but hope that is seen is not hope: for what a man sees, why does he yet hope for?

25 But if we hope for that we see not, then do we with patience wait for it.

26 Likewise the Spirit also helps our infirmities: for we know not what we should

pray for as we ought: but the Spirit itself makes intercession for us with groanings which cannot be uttered.

27 And he that searches the hearts knows what is the mind of the Spirit, because he makes intercession for the saints according to the will of God.

28 And we know that all things work together for good to them that love God, to them who are the called according to his purpose.

29 For whom he did foreknow, he also did predestinate to be conformed to the image of his Son, that he might be the firstborn among many brethren.

> The gospel isn't a treasure to be hoarded; it's a gift to be shared.
>
> **GREG LAURIE**

30 Moreover whom he did predestinate, them he also called: and whom he called, them he also justified: and whom he justified, them he also glorified.

31 What shall we then say to these things? If God be for us, who can be against us?

32 He that spared not his own Son, but delivered him up for us all, how shall he not with him also freely give us all things?

33 Who shall lay any thing to the charge of God's elect? It is God that justifies.

34 Who is he that condemns? It is Christ that died, yes rather, that is risen again, who is even at the right hand of God,

who also makes intercession for us.

35 Who shall separate us from the love of Christ? shall tribulation, or distress, or persecution, or famine, or nakedness, or peril, or sword?

36 As it is written, For your sake we are killed all the day long; we are accounted as sheep for the slaughter.

37 Nay, in all these things we are more than conquerors through him that loved us.

38 For I am persuaded, that neither death, nor life, nor angels, nor principalities, nor powers, nor things present, nor things to come,

39 Nor height, nor depth, nor any other creature, shall be able to separate us from the love of God, which is in Christ Jesus our Lord.

CHAPTER 9

I SAY the truth in Christ, I lie not, my conscience also bearing me witness in the Holy Spirit,

2 That I have great heaviness and continual sorrow in my heart.

3 For I could wish that myself were accursed from Christ for my brethren, my kinsmen according to the flesh:

4 Who are Israelites; to whom pertain the adoption, and the glory, and the covenants, and the giving of the law, and the service of God, and the promises;

5 Whose are the fathers, and of whom as concerning the flesh Christ came, who is

---

8:39 The cost of our redemption was the blood of God's Son. The Father's love for us was and is so great, He didn't hesitate for a moment, but delivered Him up freely for us like a lamb for the slaughter. If that is the case, then what good thing will He hold back from those who walk uprightly in Christ! What demon can make one peep, or mutter an accusation against us, when we have such evidence of God's love set before our eyes? What trial could ever separate us from the devotion of God in Christ?

Shall the Shepherd, who put His life in great jeopardy by climbing down a precipice to rescue a lost sheep, carry it back carelessly? Will He now let it starve after He risked His very life to rescue it? Will He now stand by idly and let wolves devour the sheep? The Chief Shepherd descended into death itself to deliver us. He has already proven His great love by willingly giving His life for the sheep, so no tribulation, distress, persecution, famine, or even sharp sword will cut us off from such love.

9:1 "When a man calls himself an atheist, he is not attacking God; he is attacking his own conscience." *Michael Pearl*

over all, God blessed for ever. Amen.

6 Not as though the word of God has taken none effect. For they are not all Israel, which are of Israel:

7 Neither, because they are the seed of Abraham, are they all children: but, In Isaac shall your seed be called.

8 That is, they which are the children of the flesh, these are not the children of God: but the children of the promise are counted for the seed.

9 For this is the word of promise, At this time will I come, and Sara shall have a son.

10 And not only this; but when Rebecca also had conceived by one, even by our father Isaac;

11 (For the children being not yet born, neither having done any good or evil, that the purpose of God according to election might stand, not of works, but of him that calls;)

12 It was said to her, The elder shall serve the younger.

13 As it is written, Jacob have I loved, but Esau have I hated.

14 What shall we say then? Is there unrighteousness with God? God forbid.

15 For he said to Moses, I will have mercy on whom I will have mercy, and I will have compassion on whom I will have compassion.

16 So then it is not of him that wills, nor of him that runs, but of God that shows mercy.

17 For the scripture said to Pharaoh, Even for this same purpose have I raised you up, that I might show my power in you, and that my name might be declared throughout all the earth.

18 Therefore has he mercy on whom he will have mercy, and whom he will he hardens.

19 You will say then to me, Why does he yet find fault? For who has resisted his will?

20 Nay but, O man, who are you that reply against God? Shall the thing formed say to him that formed it, Why have you made me thus?

21 Has not the potter power over the clay, of the same lump to make one vessel to honor, and another to dishonor?

22 What if God, willing to show his wrath, and to make his power known, endured with much longsuffering the vessels of wrath fitted to destruction:

23 And that he might make known the riches of his glory on the vessels of mercy, which he had before prepared to glory,

24 Even us, whom he has called, not of the Jews only, but also of the Gentiles?

9:2,3 A letter from an atheist:

"You are really convinced that you've got all the answers. You've really got yourself tricked into believing that you're 100% right. Well, let me tell you just one thing. Do you consider yourself to be compassionate of other humans? If you're right about God, as you say you are, and you believe that, then how can you sleep at night? When you speak with me, you are speaking with someone who you believe is walking directly into eternal damnation, into an endless onslaught of horrendous pain which your loving god created, yet you stand by and do nothing.

"If you believed one bit that thousands every day were falling into an eternal and unchangeable fate, you should be running the streets mad with rage at their blindness. That's equivalent to standing on a street corner and watching every person that passes you walk blindly directly into the path of a bus and die, yet you stand idly by and do nothing. You're just twiddling your thumbs, happy in the knowledge that one day that Walk signal will shine your way across the road.

"Think about it. Imagine the horrors hell must have in store if the Bible is true. You're just going to allow that to happen and not care about saving anyone but yourself? If you're right, then you are an uncaring, unemotional and purely selfish (expletive) that has no right to talk about subjects such as love and caring." From *Intelligent Design Vs. Evolution* (Bridge-Logos)

If we have great heaviness and sorrow in *our* heart for the lost, we'll warn them of the reality of hell (see 2 Thessalonians 1:7-9 comment) and how to avoid it. See John 4:7 comment for witnessing tips.

QUESTIONS & OBJECTIONS

10:3   *"Why are there so many different religions?"*

It has been well said that religion is man's way of trying to deal with his guilt. Different religions have different ways of attempting to rid their adherants of sin and its consequences. They fast, pray, deny themselves legitimate pleasures, or chasten themselves, often to a point of inflicting pain. They do this because they have a concept of what they think God (or the gods) is like, so they seek to establish their own righteousness, being ignorant of God's righteousness.

The Good News of the Christian faith is that no one need suffer the pains of religious works. Christ's blood can cleanse our conscience from the dead works of religion (Hebrews 9:14). Jesus took our punishment upon Himself, and He is the only One who can save us from sin and death. See Acts 4:12 and John 14:6.

25 As he said also in Hosea, I will call them my people, which were not my people; and her beloved, which was not beloved.

26 And it shall come to pass, that in the place where it was said to them, You are not my people; there shall they be called the children of the living God.

27 Isaiah also cries concerning Israel, Though the number of the children of Israel be as the sand of the sea, a remnant shall be saved:

28 For he will finish the work, and cut it short in righteousness: because a short work will the Lord make upon the earth.

29 And as Isaiah said before, Except the Lord of Sabaoth had left us a seed, we had been as Sodom, and been made like to Gomorrah.

30 What shall we say then? That the Gentiles, which followed not after righteousness, have attained to righteousness, even the righteousness which is of faith.

31 But Israel, which followed after the law of righteousness, has not attained to the law of righteousness.

32 Wherefore? Because they sought it not by faith, but as it were by the works of the law. For they stumbled at that stumblingstone;

33 As it is written, Behold, I lay in Zion a stumblingstone and rock of offence: and whosoever believes on him shall not be ashamed.

CHAPTER 10

BRETHREN, my heart's desire and prayer to God for Israel is, that they might be saved.

2 For I bear them record that they have a zeal of God, but not according to knowledge.

3 For they being ignorant of God's righteousness, and going about to establish their own righteousness, have not submitted themselves to the righteousness of God.

4 For Christ is the end of the law for righteousness to every one that believes.

5 For Moses describes the righteousness which is of the law, That the man which does those things shall live by them.

6 But the righteousness which is of faith speaks on this wise, Say not in your heart,

9:32 For those who are trusting in good works, see Ephesians 2:8,9 and Titus 3:5.

10:1 The heart of a person who is close to God must be consumed with prayer for the salvation of the world. The theme will permeate his prayers.

Who shall ascend into heaven? (that is, to bring Christ down from above:)

7 Or, Who shall descend into the deep? (that is, to bring up Christ again from the dead.)

8 **But what does it say? The word is near you, even in your mouth, and in your heart: that is, the word of faith, which we preach;**

9 **That if you shall confess with your mouth the Lord Jesus, and shall believe in your heart that God has raised him from the dead, you shall be saved.**

10 **For with the heart man believes to righteousness; and with the mouth confession is made to salvation.**

11 **For the scripture says, Whosoever believes on him shall not be ashamed.**

12 **For there is no difference between the Jew and the Greek: for the same Lord over all is rich to all that call upon him.**

13 **For whosoever shall call upon the name of the Lord shall be saved.**

14 *How then shall they call on him in whom they have not believed? and how shall they believe in him of whom they have not heard? and how shall they hear without a preacher?*

15 *And how shall they preach, except they be sent? as it is written, How beautiful are the feet of them that preach the gospel of peace, and bring glad tidings of good things!*

16 But they have not all obeyed the gospel. For Isaiah says, Lord, who has believed our report?

17 So then faith comes by hearing, and hearing by the word of God.

18 But I say, Have they not heard? Yes verily, their sound went into all the earth, and their words to the ends of the world.

19 But I say, Did not Israel know? First Moses says, I will provoke you to jealousy by them that are no people, and by a foolish nation I will anger you.

20 But Isaiah is very bold, and says, I was found of them that sought me not; I was made manifest to them that asked not after me.

21 But to Israel he says, All day long I have stretched forth my hands to a disobedient and gainsaying people.

CHAPTER 11

I SAY then, has God cast away his people? God forbid. For I also am an Israelite, of the seed of Abraham, of the tribe of Benjamin.

10:9 We must confess and forsake our sins to receive God's mercy: Here is a model prayer of repentance, from Psalm 51: Have mercy upon me, O God, according to your lovingkindness: according to the multitude of Your tender mercies blot out my transgressions. Wash me thoroughly from my iniquity, and cleanse me from my sin. For I acknowledge my transgressions, and my sin is ever before me. Against You, You only, have I sinned, and done this evil in Your sight. I believe that Jesus suffered and died in my place. I believe that He rose from the dead. I put my trust in Him this day as my Lord and my Savior. I will read Your Word daily and obey what I read. In Jesus' name I pray. Amen.

10:12 Here are God's promises to those who call upon Him: If we confess our sins, He is faithful and just to forgive us our sins, and to cleanse us from all unrighteousness (1 John 1:9). He who believes in the Son of God has the witness in himself; he who does not believe God has made Him a liar, because he has not believed the testimony that God has given of His Son. And this is the testimony: that God has given us eternal life, and this life is in His Son. He who has the Son has life; he who does not have the Son of God does not have life. These things I have written to you who believe in the name of the Son of God, that you may know that you have eternal life, and that you may continue to believe in the name of the Son of God (1 John 5:10-13).

10:13 Salvation is possible for every person. See also 1 Timothy 2:4.

10:15 If we take the gospel to a world that desperately needs to hear it, God considers even the lowest part of us to be beautiful.

2 God has not cast away his people which he foreknew. Do you not know what the scripture said of Elijah? how he makes intercession to God against Israel, saying,

3 Lord, they have killed your prophets, and dug down your altars; and I am left alone, and they seek my life.

4 But what said the answer of God to him? I have reserved to myself seven thousand men, who have not bowed the knee to the image of Baal.

5 Even so then at this present time also there is a remnant according to the election of grace.

6 And if by grace, then is it no more of works: otherwise grace is no more grace. But if it be of works, then is it no more grace: otherwise work is no more work.

7 What then? Israel has not obtained that which he seeks for; but the election has obtained it, and the rest were blinded

8 (According as it is written, God has given them the spirit of slumber, eyes that they should not see, and ears that they should not hear;) to this day.

9 And David said, Let their table be made a snare, and a trap, and a stumbling block, and a recompense to them:

10 Let their eyes be darkened, that they may not see, and bow down their back always.

11 I say then, Have they stumbled that they should fall? God forbid: but rather through their fall salvation is come to the Gentiles, for to provoke them to jealousy.

12 Now if the fall of them be the riches of the world, and the diminishing of them the riches of the Gentiles; how much more their fulness?

13 For I speak to you Gentiles, inasmuch as I am the apostle of the Gentiles, I magnify mine office:

14 If by any means I may provoke to emulation them which are my flesh, and might save some of them.

15 For if the casting away of them be the reconciling of the world, what shall the receiving of them be, but life from the dead?

16 For if the firstfruit be holy, the lump is also holy: and if the root be holy, so are the branches.

17 And if some of the branches be broken off, and you, being a wild olive tree, were grafted in among them, and with them partake of the root and fatness of the olive tree;

18 Boast not against the branches. But if you boast, you bear not the root, but the root you.

19 You will say then, The branches were broken off, that I might be grafted in.

20 Well; because of unbelief they were broken off, and you stand by faith. Be not high-minded, but fear:

> God, send me anywhere, only go with me. Lay any burden on me, only sustain me. And sever any tie in my heart except the tie that binds my heart to Yours.
>
> **DAVID LIVINGSTONE**

21 For if God spared not the natural branches, take heed lest he also spare not you.

22 Behold therefore the goodness and severity of God: on them which fell, severity; but toward you, goodness, if you continue in his goodness: otherwise you also shall be cut off.

23 And they also, if they abide not still in unbelief, shall be grafted in: for God is able to graft them in again.

24 For if you were cut out of the olive tree which is wild by nature, and were grafted contrary to nature into a good olive tree: how much more shall these, which be the natural branches, be grafted into their own olive tree?

25 For I would not, brethren, that you should be ignorant of this mystery, lest you should be wise in your own conceits; that blindness in part is happened to Israel, until the fulness of the Gentiles be come in.

26 And so all Israel shall be saved: as it is written, There shall come out of Zion

the Deliverer, and shall turn away ungodliness from Jacob:

27 For this is my covenant to them, when I shall take away their sins.

28 As concerning the gospel, they are enemies for your sakes: but as touching the election, they are beloved for the fathers' sakes.

29 For the gifts and calling of God are without repentance.

30 For as you in times past have not believed God, yet have now obtained mercy through their unbelief:

31 Even so have these also now not believed, that through your mercy they also may obtain mercy.

32 For God has concluded them all in unbelief, that he might have mercy upon all.

33 O the depth of the riches both of the wisdom and knowledge of God! how unsearchable are his judgments, and his ways past finding out!

34 For who has known the mind of the Lord? or who has been his counsellor?

35 Or who has first given to him, and it shall be recompensed to him again?

36 For of him, and through him, and to him, are all things: to whom be glory for ever. Amen.

CHAPTER 12

I BESEECH you therefore, brethren, by the mercies of God, that you present your bodies a living sacrifice, holy, acceptable to God, which is your reasonable service.

2 And be not conformed to this world: but be transformed by the renewing of your mind, that you may prove what is that good, and acceptable, and perfect, will of God.

3 For I say, through the grace given to me, to every man that is among you, not to think of himself more highly than he ought to think; but to think soberly, according as God has dealt to every man

the measure of faith.

4 For as we have many members in one body, and all members have not the same office:

5 So we, being many, are one body in Christ, and every one members one of another.

6 Having then gifts differing according to the grace that is given to us, whether prophecy, let us prophesy according to the proportion of faith;

7 Or ministry, let us wait on our ministering: or he that teaches, on teaching;

8 Or he that exhorts, on exhortation: he that gives, let him do it with simplicity; he that rules, with diligence; he that shows mercy, with cheerfulness.

9 Let love be without dissimulation. Abhor that which is evil; cleave to that which is good.

10 Be kindly affectionate one to another with brotherly love; in honor preferring one another;

11 Not slothful in business; fervent in spirit; serving the Lord;

12 Rejoicing in hope; patient in tribulation; continuing instant in prayer;

13 Distributing to the necessity of saints; given to hospitality.

14 Bless them which persecute you: bless, and curse not.

15 Rejoice with them that do rejoice, and weep with them that weep.

16 Be of the same mind one toward another. Mind not high things, but condescend to men of low estate. Be not wise in your own conceits.

17 Recompense to no man evil for evil. Provide things honest in the sight of all men.

18 If it be possible, as much as lies in you, live peaceably with all men.

19 Dearly beloved, avenge not yourselves, but rather give place to wrath: for it is written, Vengeance is mine; I will repay, says the Lord.

12:1 "If Jesus Christ be God and died for me, no sacrifice I make can be too great for Him."
C.T. Studd

"I was honored today with having a few stones, dirt, rotten eggs, and pieces of dead cats thrown at me."

George Whitefield

20 Therefore if your enemy hunger, feed him; if he thirst, give him drink: for in so doing you shall heap coals of fire on his head.

21 Be not overcome of evil, but overcome evil with good.

· · · · · ·

Are there contradictions in the Bible? See Mark 15:26 comment.

· · · · · ·

CHAPTER 13

LET every soul be subject to the higher powers. For there is no power but of God: the powers that be are ordained of God.

2 Whosoever therefore resists the power, resists the ordinance of God: and they that resist shall receive to themselves damnation.

3 For rulers are not a terror to good works, but to the evil. Will you then not be afraid of the power? do that which is good, and you shall have praise of the same:

4 For he is the minister of God to you for good. But if you do that which is evil, be afraid; for he bears not the sword in vain: for he is the minister of God, a revenger to execute wrath upon him that does evil.

5 Wherefore you must needs be subject, not only for wrath, but also for conscience sake.

6 For for this cause you pay tribute also: for they are God's ministers, attending continually upon this very thing.

7 Render therefore to all their dues: tribute to whom tribute is due; custom to whom custom; fear to whom fear; honor to whom honor.

8 Owe no man any thing, but to love one another: for he that loves another has fulfilled the law.

9 For this, You shall not commit adultery, You shall not kill, You shall not steal, You shall not bear false witness, You shall not covet; and if there be any other commandment, it is briefly comprehended in this saying, namely, You shall love your neighbor as yourself.

10 Love works no ill to his neighbor: therefore love is the fulfilling of the law.

11 *And that, knowing the time, that now it is high time to awake out of sleep: for now is our salvation nearer than when we believed.*

12 *The night is far spent, the day is at hand: let us therefore cast off the works of darkness, and let us put on the armor of light.*

13 Let us walk honestly, as in the day; not in rioting and drunkenness, not in chambering and wantonness, not in strife

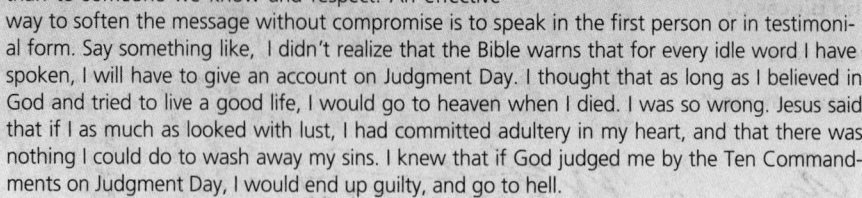

QUESTIONS & OBJECTIONS

14:12   *"How do I witness to someone I know?"*

For most of us, it is far easier to witness to a stranger than to someone we know and respect. An effective way to soften the message without compromise is to speak in the first person or in testimonial form. Say something like, I didn't realize that the Bible warns that for every idle word I have spoken, I will have to give an account on Judgment Day. I thought that as long as I believed in God and tried to live a good life, I would go to heaven when I died. I was so wrong. Jesus said that if I as much as looked with lust, I had committed adultery in my heart, and that there was nothing I could do to wash away my sins. I knew that if God judged me by the Ten Commandments on Judgment Day, I would end up guilty, and go to hell.

It was when I acknowledged my sins that I began to understand why Jesus died. It was to take the punishment for my sins, and the sins of the world. Then, depending on the person's openness, you may ask, How do you think you will do on Judgment Day, if God judges you by the Ten Commandments?

and envying.

14 But put on the Lord Jesus Christ, and make not provision for the flesh, to fulfil the lusts thereof.

CHAPTER 14

HIM that is weak in the faith receive, but not to doubtful disputations.
2 For one believes that he may eat all things: another, who is weak, eats herbs.
3 Let not him that eats despise him that eats not; and let not him which eats not judge him that eats: for God has received him.
4 Who are you that judge another man's servant? to his own master he stands or falls. Yes, he shall be held up: for God is able to make him stand.
5 One man esteems one day above another: another esteems every day alike. Let every man be fully persuaded in his own mind.
6 He that regards the day, regards it to the Lord; and he that regards not the day, to the Lord he does not regard it. He that

eats, eats to the Lord, for he gives God thanks; and he that eats not, to the Lord he eats not, and gives God thanks.
7 For none of us lives to himself, and no man dies to himself.
8 For whether we live, we live to the Lord; and whether we die, we die to the Lord: whether we live therefore, or die, we are the Lord's.
9 For to this end Christ both died, and rose, and revived, that he might be Lord both of the dead and living.
10 But why do you judge your brother? or why do you set at nought your brother? for we shall all stand before the judgment seat of Christ.
11 For it is written, As I live, says the Lord, every knee shall bow to me, and every tongue shall confess to God.
12 So then every one of us shall give account of himself to God.
13 Let us not therefore judge one another any more: but judge this rather, that no man put a stumblingblock or an occasion to fall in his brother's way.

13:14 Salvation comes through trusting Jesus Christ in the same way you trust a parachute. You don't just believe in it, you *put it on*. See Galatians 3:27.

14:2 Vegetarianism. See 1 Timothy 4:3 comment.

14:10 Judgment Day: For verses that warn of its reality, see 2 Corinthians 5:10.

14 I know, and am persuaded by the Lord Jesus, that there is nothing unclean of itself: but to him that esteems any thing to be unclean, to him it is unclean.

15 But if your brother be grieved with your meat, now you do not walk charitably. Destroy not him with your meat, for whom Christ died.

16 Let not then your good be evil spoken of:

17 For the kingdom of God is not meat and drink; but righteousness, and peace, and joy in the Holy Spirit.

18 For he that in these things serves Christ is acceptable to God, and approved of men.

19 Let us therefore follow after the things which make for peace, and things wherewith one may edify another.

20 For meat destroy not the work of God. All things indeed are pure; but it is evil for that man who eats with offence.

21 It is good neither to eat flesh, nor to drink wine, nor any thing whereby your brother stumbles, or is offended, or is made weak.

22 Do you have faith? have it to yourself before God. Happy is he that condemns not himself in that thing which he allows.

23 And he that doubts is damned if he eat, because he eats not of faith: for whatsoever is not of faith is sin.

CHAPTER 15

WE then that are strong ought to bear the infirmities of the weak, and not to please ourselves.

2 Let every one of us please his neighbor for his good to edification.

3 For even Christ pleased not himself; but, as it is written, The reproaches of them that reproached you fell on me.

4 For whatsoever things were written beforetime were written for our learning, that we through patience and comfort of the scriptures might have hope.

5 Now the God of patience and consolation grant you to be likeminded one toward another according to Christ Jesus:

6 That you may with one mind and one mouth glorify God, even the Father of our Lord Jesus Christ.

7 Wherefore receive one another, as Christ also received us to the glory of God.

8 Now I say that Jesus Christ was a minister of the circumcision for the truth of God, to confirm the promises made to the fathers:

9 And that the Gentiles might glorify God for his mercy; as it is written, For this cause I will confess to you among the Gentiles, and sing to your name.

> No pursuit of mortal men is to be compared with that of soul-winning.
> **CHARLES SPURGEON**

10 And again he says, Rejoice, you Gentiles, with his people.

11 And again, Praise the Lord, all you Gentiles; and laud him, all you people.

12 And again, Isaiah says, There shall be a root of Jesse, and he that shall rise to reign over the Gentiles; in him shall the Gentiles trust.

13 Now the God of hope fill you with all joy and peace in believing, that you may abound in hope, through the power of the Holy Spirit.

14 And I myself also am persuaded of you, my brethren, that you also are full of goodness, filled with all knowledge, able also to admonish one another.

15 Nevertheless, brethren, I have written the more boldly to you in some sort, as putting you in mind, because of the grace that is given to me of God,

16 That I should be the minister of Jesus Christ to the Gentiles, ministering the gospel of God, that the offering up of the Gentiles might be acceptable, being sanc-

15:16 "Consider as sin any minute of life spent on something other than saving souls for eternity from this world doomed to destruction." *Richard Wurmbrand*

Memorize the Ten Commandments

Memorize the Ten Commandments using these special picture figures. Then test your memory, and grade yourself. Put each picture in your mind, and it will remind you of each commandment.

1. "You shall have no other gods before Me"
(God should be Number One)

2. "You shall not make yourself any graven image"
(Don't bow down to anything but God)

3. "You shall not take the name of the Lord your God in vain"
(Don't use your lips to dishonor God)

4. "Remember the Sabbath Day to keep it holy"
(Don't neglect the things of God)

5. "Honor your Father and your Mother"

6. "You shall not kill"

7. "You shall not commit adultery"
(Adultery leaves a heart broken)

8. "You shall not steal"

9. "You shall not lie"
(a lying nine)

10. "You shall not covet"
(want what others have)

tified by the Holy Spirit.

17 I have therefore whereof I may glory through Jesus Christ in those things which pertain to God.

18 For I will not dare to speak of any of those things which Christ has not wrought by me, to make the Gentiles obedient, by word and deed,

19 **Through mighty signs and wonders, by the power of the Spirit of God; so that from Jerusalem, and round about to Illyricum, I have fully preached the gospel of Christ.**

20 Yea, so have I strived to preach the gospel, not where Christ was named, lest I should build upon another man's foundation:

21 But as it is written, To whom he was not spoken of, they shall see: and they that have not heard shall understand.

22 For which cause also I have been much hindered from coming to you.

23 But now having no more place in these parts, and having a great desire these many years to come to you;

24 Whenever I take my journey into Spain, I will come to you: for I trust to see you in my journey, and to be brought on my way thitherward by you, if first I be somewhat filled with your company.

25 But now I go to Jerusalem to minister to the saints.

26 For it has pleased them of Macedonia and Achaia to make a certain contribution for the poor saints which are at Jerusalem.

27 It has pleased them verily; and their debtors they are. For if the Gentiles have been made partakers of their spiritual things, their duty is also to minister to them in carnal things.

28 When therefore I have performed this, and have sealed to them this fruit, I will come by you into Spain.

29 And I am sure that, when I come to you, I shall come in the fulness of the blessing of the gospel of Christ.

30 Now I beseech you, brethren, for the Lord Jesus Christ's sake, and for the love of the Spirit, that you strive together with me in your prayers to God for me;

31 That I may be delivered from them that do not believe in Judea; and that my service which I have for Jerusalem may be accepted of the saints;

32 That I may come to you with joy by the will of God, and may with you be refreshed.

33 Now the God of peace be with you all. Amen.

CHAPTER 16

I COMMEND to you Phebe our sister, which is a servant of the church which is at Cenchrea:

2 That you receive her in the Lord, as becomes saints, and that you assist her in whatsoever business she has need of you: for she has been a succourer of many, and of myself also.

3 Greet Priscilla and Aquila my helpers in Christ Jesus:

4 Who have for my life laid down their own necks: to whom not only I give thanks, but also all the churches of the Gentiles.

5 Likewise greet the church that is in their house. Salute my wellbeloved Epaenetus, who is the firstfruits of Achaia to Christ.

6 Greet Mary, who bestowed much labor on us.

7 Salute Andronicus and Junia, my kinsmen, and my fellow-prisoners, who are of note among the apostles, who also were in Christ before me.

8 Greet Amplias my beloved in the Lord.

9 Salute Urbane, our helper in Christ,

16:5 Believers in many countries today must meet secretly in homes to worship. These house churches follow the New Testament model for fellowship, prayer , and study of the Scriptures better than do many modern churches that have the finest facilities. The true Church is actually the body of believers, and can worship the Lord with or without a building.

and Stachys my beloved.

10 Salute Apelles approved in Christ. Salute them which are of Aristobulus' household.

11 Salute Herodion my kinsman. Greet them that be of the household of Narcissus, which are in the Lord.

12 Salute Tryphena and Tryphosa, who labor in the Lord. Salute the beloved Persis, which labored much in the Lord.

13 Salute Rufus chosen in the Lord, and his mother and mine.

14 Salute Asyncritus, Phlegon, Hermas, Patrobas, Hermes, and the brethren which are with them.

15 Salute Philologus, and Julia, Nereus, and his sister, and Olympas, and all the saints which are with them.

16 Salute one another with an holy kiss. The churches of Christ salute you.

17 Now I beseech you, brethren, mark them which cause divisions and offences contrary to the doctrine which you have learned; and avoid them.

18 For they that are such serve not our Lord Jesus Christ, but their own belly; and by good words and fair speeches deceive the hearts of the simple.

19 For your obedience is come abroad to all men. I am glad therefore on your behalf: but yet I would have you wise to that which is good, and simple concerning evil.

20 And the God of peace shall bruise Satan under your feet shortly. The grace of our Lord Jesus Christ be with you. Amen.

21 Timotheus my workfellow, and Lucius, and Jason, and Sosipater, my kinsmen, salute you.

22 I Tertius, who wrote this epistle, salute you in the Lord.

23 Gaius mine host, and of the whole church, salutes you. Erastus the chamberlain of the city salutes you, and Quartus a brother.

24 The grace of our Lord Jesus Christ be with you all. Amen.

25 Now to him that is of power to stablish you according to my gospel, and the preaching of Jesus Christ, according to the revelation of the mystery, which was kept secret since the world began,

26 But now is made manifest, and by the scriptures of the prophets, according to the commandment of the everlasting God, made known to all nations for the obedience of faith:

27 To God only wise, be glory through Jesus Christ for ever. Amen.

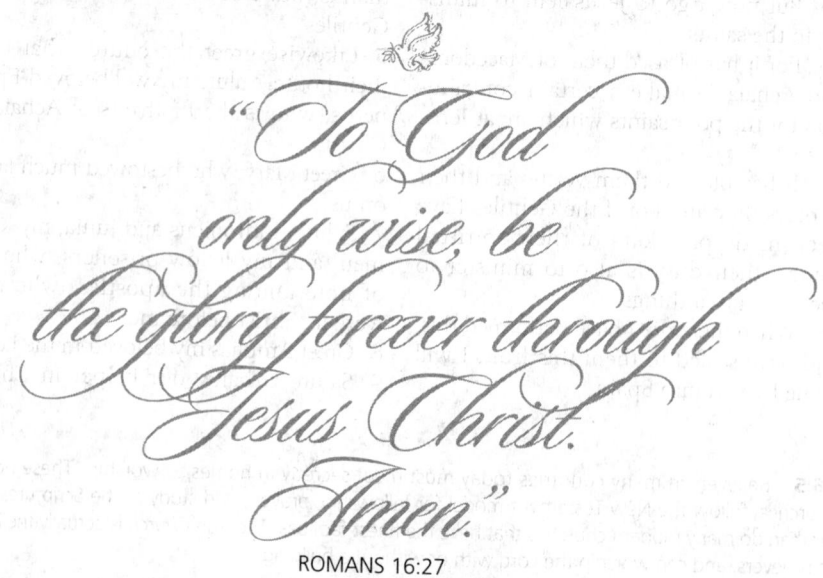

"To God only wise, be the glory forever through Jesus Christ. Amen."

ROMANS 16:27

1 Corinthians

CHAPTER 1

PAUL, called to be an apostle of Jesus Christ through the will of God, and Sosthenes our brother,

2 To the church of God which is at Corinth, to them that are sanctified in Christ Jesus, called to be saints, with all that in every place call upon the name of Jesus Christ our Lord, both theirs and ours:

3 Grace be to you, and peace, from God our Father, and from the Lord Jesus Christ.

4 I thank my God always on your behalf, for the grace of God which is given you by Jesus Christ;

5 That in every thing you are enriched by him, in all utterance, and in all knowledge;

6 Even as the testimony of Christ was confirmed in you:

7 So that you come behind in no gift; waiting for the coming of our Lord Jesus Christ:

8 Who shall also confirm you to the end, that you may be blameless in the day of our Lord Jesus Christ.

9 God is faithful, by whom you were called to the fellowship of his Son Jesus Christ our Lord.

10 Now I beseech you, brethren, by the name of our Lord Jesus Christ, that you all speak the same thing, and that there be no divisions among you; but that you be perfectly joined together in the same mind and in the same judgment.

11 For it has been declared to me of you, my brethren, by them which are of the house of Chloe, that there are contentions among you.

12 Now this I say, that every one of you says, I am of Paul; and I of Apollos; and I of Cephas; and I of Christ.

13 Is Christ divided? was Paul crucified for you? or were you baptized in the name of Paul?

14 I thank God that I baptized none of you, but Crispus and Gaius;

15 Lest any should say that I had baptized in mine own name.

16 And I baptized also the household of Stephanas: besides, I know not whether I baptized any other.

17 For Christ sent me not to baptize, but to preach the gospel: not with wisdom of words, lest the cross of Christ should be made of none effect.

18 For the preaching of the cross is to them that perish foolishness; but to us which are saved it is the power of God.

19 For it is written, I will destroy the wisdom of the wise, and will bring to nothing the understanding of the prudent.

1:18 "To convince the world of the truth of Christianity, it must first be convinced of sin. It is only sin that renders Christ intelligible." *Andrew Murray, The Spirit of Christ*

SPRINGBOARDS FOR PREACHING AND WITNESSING

The Sinking Ship

1:18 Imagine for a moment that you are standing on the seashore gazing at a large ocean liner. The sun is shining. There is no wind and the sea is calm. To your amazement, about thirty people suddenly dive off the end of the ship and cling to a lifeboat.

You shake your head in disbelief at their foolishness. Then without warning, the great ocean liner strikes an iceberg and suddenly sinks, taking all on board with it.

Those who *looked* like fools in abandoning the ship were actually wise, and those who seemed wise by staying on board were, in truth, fools.

The world scoffs at those who abandon the ship of this world and cling to the lifeboat of the Savior. But Christians know that this great pleasure-cruiser will eventually come into contact with the immovable iceberg of the Law of God, sink into hell...and take all those on board with it.

20 Where is the wise? where is the scribe? where is the disputer of this world? has not God made foolish the wisdom of this world?

21 For after that in the wisdom of God the world by wisdom knew not God, it pleased God by the foolishness of preaching to save them that believe.

22 For the Jews require a sign, and the Greeks seek after wisdom:

23 But we preach Christ crucified, to the Jews a stumblingblock, and to the Greeks foolishness;

24 But to them which are called, both Jews and Greeks, Christ the power of God, and the wisdom of God.

25 Because the foolishness of God is wiser than men; and the weakness of God is stronger than men.

26 For you see your calling, brethren, how that not many wise men after the flesh, not many mighty, not many noble, are called:

27 But God has chosen the foolish things of the world to confound the wise; and God has chosen the weak things of the world to confound the things which are mighty;

1:23 There were some in John Wesley's day who refused to preach the Law to bring the knowledge of sin. They justified their method by saying that they preached "Christ and Him crucified." So Wesley points to Paul's method of preaching Christ crucified:

"... when Felix sent for Paul, on purpose that he might hear him concerning the faith in Christ; instead of preaching Christ in *your* sense (which would probably have caused the Governor, either to mock or to contradict and blaspheme,) he reasoned of righteousness, temperance, and judgment to come, till Felix (hardened as he was) trembled, (Acts 24:24,25). Go thou and tread in his steps. Preach Christ to the careless sinner, by reasoning of righteousness, temperance, and judgment to come!" *John Wesley*

1:25 "Everything that can be invented has been invented." *Charles H. Duell*, Commissioner, U.S. Office of Patents, 1899

1:27,28 Many years ago, I ran a children's club. At the end of the club I told about one hundred kids to line up for some candy. There was an immediate rush, and the line sorted itself into what I saw as being a line of greed. The bigger, selfish kids were at the front, and the small and timid ones were at the back. I then did something that gave me great satisfaction. I told them to turn about face. Everyone did. Then I said to stay where they were, and I took great delight in going to the other end of the line and giving the candy to the smaller, timid kids first.

In a world where the rich get richer and the poor get stomped on, we are informed that God

POINTS FOR OPEN-AIR PREACHING

2:4

Watch for "Red Herrings" or "Rabbit Trails"

The Bible warns us to avoid foolish questions because they start arguments (2 Timothy 2:23). Most of us have fallen into the trap of jumping at every objection to the gospel. However, these questions can often be arguments in disguise to sidetrack you from the weightier matters of the Law. While apologetics (arguments for God's existence, creation vs. evolution, etc.) are legitimate in evangelism, they should merely be bait, with the Law of God being the hook that brings the conviction of sin. Those who witness solely in the realm of apologetical argument may just get an intellectual decision rather than a repentant conversion. The sinner may come to a point of acknowledging that the Bible is the Word of God, and Jesus is Lord but even the devil knows that.

Always pull the sinner back to his responsibility before God on Judgment Day, as Jesus did in Luke 13:1-5. Whenever you are in an open-air situation, be wary of so-called Christians who are intent on distracting workers from witnessing. They argue about prophecy, of how much water one should baptize with, or in whose name they should be baptized. It is grievous to see five or six Christians standing around arguing with some sectarian nitpicker, while sinners are sinking into hell. See Acts 21:30 comment.

28 And base things of the world, and things which are despised, has God chosen, yes, and things which are not, to bring to nothing things that are:
29 That no flesh should glory in his presence.
30 But of him are you in Christ Jesus, who of God is made to us wisdom, and righteousness, and sanctification, and redemption:
31 That, according as it is written, He that glories, let him glory in the Lord.

CHAPTER 2

*A*ND I, brethren, when I came to you, came not with excellency of speech or of wisdom, declaring to you the testimony of God.
2 For I determined not to know any thing among you, save Jesus Christ, and him crucified.
3 And I was with you in weakness, and in fear, and in much trembling.
4 And my speech and my preaching was not with enticing words of man's wisdom,

has gone to the other end of the line with the message of everlasting life. How has He done that? Simply by choosing that which is weak, base, and despised. You can see this by asking a skeptic, Do you believe that the following biblical accounts actually happened?

Adam and Eve, Noah's ark, Jonah and the whale, Joshua and the walls of Jericho, Samson and his long hair, Daniel and the lion's den, Moses and the Red Sea

Of course he doesn't. To say that he believed such fantastic stories would mean that he would have to surrender his intellectual dignity. Who in their right mind would ever do that? The answer is simply *those who understand that God has chosen foolish, base, weak, and despised things of the world to confound those who think they are wise.*

2:1–4 Qualifications for Evangelism:
1. A witness need not have excellency of speech or of wisdom. He should simply declare what he has seen and heard.
2. He must not get sidetracked with unnecessary details, but focus on the essentials of Christ's death on the cross.
3. He must have weakness (not trusting in his own strength or ability).
4. He must have fear (in Greek, *phobos*, that which is caused by being scared).
5. He must have much trembling (awareness of his insufficiency).
Do you meet these qualifications?

QUESTIONS & OBJECTIONS

2:14 *"I've tried to read the Bible, but I can't understand it."*

The Scriptures tell us that the "natural man" cannot understand the things of the Spirit of God. Most Americans would find it difficult to understand the Chinese language. However, a child who is *born* into a Chinese family can understand every word. That's why you must be born again with God's Spirit living within you (John 3:3). The moment you become part of God's family, the Bible will begin to make sense.

but in demonstration of the Spirit and of power:

5 *That your faith should not stand in the wisdom of men, but in the power of God.*

6 Howbeit we speak wisdom among them that are perfect: yet not the wisdom of this world, nor of the princes of this world, that come to nothing:

7 But we speak the wisdom of God in a mystery, even the hidden wisdom, which God ordained before the world to our glory:

8 Which none of the princes of this world knew: for had they known it, they would not have crucified the Lord of glory.

9 But as it is written, Eye has not seen, nor ear heard, neither have entered into the heart of man, the things which God has prepared for them that love him.

10 But God has revealed them to us by his Spirit: for the Spirit searches all things,

yes, the deep things of God.

11 For what man knows the things of a man, save the spirit of man which is in him? even so the things of God knows no man, but the Spirit of God.

12 Now we have received, not the spirit of the world, but the spirit which is of God; that we might know the things that are freely given to us of God.

13 Which things also we speak, not in the words which man's wisdom teaches, but which the Holy Spirit teaches; comparing spiritual things with spiritual.

14 But the natural man receives not the things of the Spirit of God: for they are foolishness to him: neither can he know them, because they are spiritually discerned.

15 But he that is spiritual judges all things, yet he himself is judged of no man.

16 For who has known the mind of the Lord, that he may instruct him? But we

2:5 If someone has been converted to the Christian faith by the wisdom of men, all it would take is the wisdom of *unconverted* men to talk him out of his faith. However, if he is transformed by the power of God, he is not solely motivated to Christianity by his intellect. The Holy Spirit has convicted him of sin, righteousness, and judgment. The motivation is the Law of God working upon his conscience. That has given him the knowledge that he has offended a holy God. His repentance is therefore directed at God, who responds in mercy. Those who are converted by God cannot be *talked out* of their faith because they were not *talked into* it.

2:11 "Groanings which cannot be uttered are often prayers which cannot be refused." *Spurgeon*

2:16 The Mind of God. We can get a glimpse of the incredible mind of God simply by looking at His creation. Take one (very) small part the mind of man: The brain is a soft lump of tissue weighing about 3 pounds. It is one of the most watery organs of the body, its outer tissue being 85% water. There is very little relationship between brain size and intelligence. Some very bright people have smaller brains than those who are less intelligent. The brain feels no pain because it has no pain receptors. It floats in fluid inside the skull, and the fluid (derived from blood) acts as a shock absorber. The brain stops growing in size at about age 15. *(continued on next page)*

have the mind of Christ.

CHAPTER 3

AND I, brethren, could not speak to you as to spiritual, but as to carnal, even as to babes in Christ.

2 I have fed you with milk, and not with meat: for hitherto you were not able to bear it, neither yet now are you able.

3 For you are yet carnal: for whereas there is among you envying, and strife, and divisions, are you not carnal, and walk as men?

4 For while one says, I am of Paul; and another, I am of Apollos; are you not carnal?

5 Who then is Paul, and who is Apollos, but ministers by whom you believed, even as the Lord gave to every man?

6 I have planted, Apollos watered; but God gave the increase.

7 *So then neither is he that plants any thing, neither he that waters; but God that gives the increase.*

8 *Now he that plants and he that waters are one: and every man shall receive his own reward according to his own labor.*

9 For we are laborers together with God: you are God's husbandry, you are God's building.

10 According to the grace of God which is given to me, as a wise masterbuilder, I have laid the foundation, and another built thereon. But let every man take heed how he build thereupon.

11 **For other foundation can no man lay than that is laid, which is Jesus Christ.**

12 Now if any man build upon this foundation gold, silver, precious stones, wood, hay, stubble;

13 Every man's work shall be made manifest: for the day shall declare it, because it shall be revealed by fire; and the fire shall try every man's work of what sort it is.

14 If any man's work abide which he has built thereupon, he shall receive a

---

Its surface is covered with folds. If it were laid out flat, the brain surface would cover two average student desks. The brain has four times as many nerve cells as there are people on Earth. With its 10 billion neurons, it can record 86 million bits of information each day of our lives. Supporting, protecting, and nourishing these 10 billion neurons are 100 billion glia cells, which make up half the mass of the brain.

The brain continues sending out electrical wave signals as long as 37 hours after death. Since nerve cells can't reproduce, you have fewer of them as you get older. Persons of 70 or 80 may have only 75% of the nerve cells they were born with. Nerve impulses travel more quickly than cars do, with some up to 250 miles per hour. If all the nerves were laid end to end, they would stretch almost 45 miles. If all the nerve cell connections axons and dendrites from a human brain could be placed end to end, they would encircle the earth many times. The dendrites alone could stretch an estimated 100,000 miles.

Let's now look to the heavens: They defined the exact shape of the closest major galaxy, a beautiful spiral named Andromeda, containing more than 300 billion stars. The nearest of these is (an incredible) thirteen quintillion (13,000,000,000,000,000,000) miles, or 2.2 million light-years, beyond the Milky Way, a distance calculated by comparing the star's apparent brightness with a star of similar brightness and known distance from Earth. And beyond Andromeda lay billions of other galaxies. *Solar System* (Time-Life Books)

The incredible complexity of the human brain and the vastness of the heavens speak of the awesome power of the Creator's mind, and together, declare the glory of God (Psalm 19:1).

2:16 Evolutionist *Stephen Hawking* wrote, "It would be very difficult to explain why the universe should have begun in just this way, except as the act of a God who intended to create beings like us." *(A Brief History of Time).* He also stated: "Then we shall ... be able to take part in the discussion of the question of why it is that we and the universe exist. If we find the answer to that, it would be the ultimate triumph of human reason for then we would know the mind of God."

3:6,7 See John 4:37,38 comment.

3:17 *"Does someone go to hell for committing suicide?"*

Those who are adamant that a person who takes his life is committing a mortal sin, and will go to hell, are basing their belief on church doctrine rather than on the Bible. Scripture is silent on the subject. There are no verses that say, He who takes his own life shall be damned. According to Scripture, only *one* sin does not have forgiveness, and that is blasphemy of the Holy Spirit (see Mark 3:29 comment). That means there *is* forgiveness for every other sin.

Some quote 1 Corinthians 3:17, which says that God will destroy someone who defiles the temple of the Holy Spirit. Yet, there is disagreement about what it means to *defile* the temple. Does this include suicide? Does it include illicit drug abuse (slow suicide), prescription drug abuse, cigarettes (deliberately breathing in poisons that will eventually kill), tattoos, over-eating (digging a grave with your spoon), or alcohol abuse?

God forbid that we add to the pain of someone who has lost a loved one through the tragedy of suicide, by making a judgment about their eternal destiny. God is the ultimate Judge, and we should therefore leave the issue in His hands. It would be wise to follow the biblical example and not come to any verdict in the case of suicide.

reward.

15 If any man's work shall be burned, he shall suffer loss: but he himself shall be saved; yet so as by fire.

16 Do you not know that you are the temple of God, and that the Spirit of God dwells in you?

17 If any man defile the temple of God, him shall God destroy; for the temple of God is holy, which temple you are.

18 Let no man deceive himself. If any man among you seems to be wise in this world, let him become a fool, that he may be wise.

19 For the wisdom of this world is foolishness with God. For it is written, He takes the wise in their own craftiness.

20 And again, The Lord knows the thoughts of the wise, that they are vain.

21 Therefore let no man glory in men. For all things are yours;

22 Whether Paul, or Apollos, or Cephas, or the world, or life, or death, or things present, or things to come; all are yours;

3:13,14 If we work on marble, it will perish; if on brass, time will efface it; if we rear up temples, they will crumble into dust; but if we work on immortal minds and imbue them with principles, with the just fear of God and the love of our fellow men, we engrave on those tablets something that will brighten to all eternity.   *Daniel Webster*

3:19 The World's Ignorant Maxims:

1. *"All good things must come to an end."* This isn't true for the Christian; see Ephesians 2:4-7. **2.** *"Which came first, the chicken or the egg?"* The chicken; see Genesis 1:20. **3.** *"There's no such thing as a free lunch."* See Matthew 14:19. **4.** *"You can't take it with you."* The Christian's works follow him; see Revelation 14:13. **5.** *"There are only two things in life that are sure—death and taxes."* Plenty of people avoid taxes; none avoid death. See Hebrews 9:27. **6.** *"Crime doesn't pay."* It *does*...up until Judgment Day; see Romans 2:6. **7.** *"As miserable as sin."* Sin gives pleasure; see Hebrews 11:25. **8.** *"That's impossible!"* With God, *nothing* is impossible; see Mark 10:27. **9.** *"No one knows!"* God does; see 1 John 3:20. **10.** *"It's the perfect crime."* Judgment Day will prove that there is no such thing as a crime that escapes justice; see Hebrews 4:13. **11.** *"Seeing is believing."* Any magician knows that isn't true. The eyes are easily fooled; see Proverbs 28:26. **12.** *"God helps those who help themselves."* God helps those who *cannot* help themselves; see Romans 5:6.

The Bible tells us that it is the Law of the Lord that make wise the simple. (See Psalm 19:7 comment.)

23 And you are Christ's; and Christ is God's.

CHAPTER 4

LET a man so account of us, as of the ministers of Christ, and stewards of the mysteries of God.
2 Moreover it is required in stewards, that a man be found faithful.
3 But with me it is a very small thing that I should be judged of you, or of man's judgment: yes, I judge not mine own self.
4 For I know nothing by myself; yet am I not hereby justified: but he that judges me is the Lord.
5 Therefore judge nothing before the time, until the Lord come, who both will bring to light the hidden things of darkness, and will make manifest the counsels of the hearts: and then shall every man have praise of God.
6 And these things, brethren, I have in a figure transferred to myself and to Apollos for your sakes; that you might learn in us not to think of men above that which is written, that no one of you be puffed up for one against another.
7 For who makes you to differ from another? and what have you that you did not receive? now if you did receive it, why do you glory, as if you had not received it?

8 Now you are full, now you are rich, you have reigned as kings without us: and I would to God you did reign, that we also might reign with you.
9 For I think that God has set forth us the apostles last, as it were appointed to death: for we are made a spectacle to the world, and to angels, and to men.
10 *We are fools for Christ's sake, but you are wise in Christ; we are weak, but you are strong; you are honorable, but we are despised.*
11 Even to this present hour we both hunger, and thirst, and are naked, and are buffeted, and have no certain dwellingplace;
12 *And labor, working with our own hands: being reviled, we bless; being persecuted, we suffer it:*
13 *Being defamed, we entreat: we are made as the filth of the world, and are the offscouring of all things to this day.*
14 I write not these things to shame you, but as my beloved sons I warn you.
15 For though you have ten thousand instructors in Christ, yet you do not have many fathers: for in Christ Jesus I have begotten you through the gospel.
16 Wherefore I beseech you, be followers of me.
17 For this cause have I sent to you Timotheus, who is my beloved son, and faithful in the Lord, who shall bring you

---

4:5 **Second coming of Jesus:** See Philippians 4:5.

4:15 See Matthew 23:9 comment.

4:16 Pastors often ask me how they can be more effective in reaching their city. This is what I tell them. Ask your congregation how many are concerned for their city. There will be a forest of hands. Ask how many are praying daily for the city. Many hands will appear. Then ask how many are sharing their faith on a regular basis. Give a gauge by asking how many have verbally spoken of the way of salvation to twelve people in the preceding twelve months. About 5 percent will raise their hands.

I once attended an interdenominational prayer meeting, where I could tell who attended a particular church simply by the way they prayed. I could recognize phrases of their pastors in their prayers. It confirmed that congregations imitate their pastor. This is why I would advise a pastor to join a secular health club, or a golf club, or somewhere where he will rub shoulders with the ungodly. I encourage him to regularly tell his congregation of his witnessing experiences and to share his fears to show not only that he agrees to witness to the unsaved, but that he has the same fears they have. In this way he can lead the flock of God, and it won't be long before they imitate him.

into remembrance of my ways which be in Christ, as I teach every where in every church.

18 Now some are puffed up, as though I would not come to you.

19 But I will come to you shortly, if the Lord will, and will know, not the speech of them which are puffed up, but the power.

20 For the kingdom of God is not in word, but in power.

21 What do you want? shall I come to you with a rod, or in love, and in the spirit of meekness?

In many ministries, there is not enough of probing the heart and arousing the conscience by the revelation of man's alienation from God, and by the declaration of the selfishness and the wickedness of such a state.

CHARLES SPURGEON

CHAPTER 5

IT is reported commonly that there is fornication among you, and such fornication as is not so much as named among the Gentiles, that one should have his father's wife.

2 And you are puffed up, and have not rather mourned, that he that has done this deed might be taken away from among you.

3 For I verily, as absent in body, but present in spirit, have judged already, as though I were present, concerning him that has so done this deed,

4 In the name of our Lord Jesus Christ, when you are gathered together, and my spirit, with the power of our Lord Jesus Christ,

5 To deliver such an one to Satan for the destruction of the flesh, that the spirit may be saved in the day of the Lord Jesus.

6 Your glorying is not good. Do you not know that a little leaven leavens the whole lump?

7 Purge out therefore the old leaven, that you may be a new lump, as you are unleavened. For even Christ our passover is sacrificed for us:

8 Therefore let us keep the feast, not with old leaven, neither with the leaven of malice and wickedness; but with the unleavened bread of sincerity and truth.

9 *I wrote to you in an epistle not to company with fornicators:*

10 *Yet not altogether with the fornicators of this world, or with the covetous, or extortioners, or with idolaters; for then you would need to go out of the world.*

11 But now I have written to you not to keep company, if any man that is called a brother be a fornicator, or covetous, or an idolater, or a railer, or a drunkard, or an extortioner; with such an one no not to eat.

12 For what have I to do to judge them also that are without? do you not judge them that are within?

13 But them that are without God judges. Therefore put away from among yourselves that wicked person.

CHAPTER 6

DARE any of you, having a matter against another, go to law before the unjust, and not before the saints?

2 Do you not know that the saints shall judge the world? and if the world shall be judged by you, are you unworthy to judge the smallest matters?

3 Do you not know that we shall judge angels? how much more things that pertain to this life?

4 If then you have judgments of things pertaining to this life, set them to judge who are least esteemed in the church.

5 I speak to your shame. Is it so, that there is not a wise man among you? no, not one that shall be able to judge between his brethren?

6 But brother goes to law with brother, and that before the unbelievers.

7 Now therefore there is utterly a fault among you, because you go to law one with another. Why do you not rather take wrong? why do you not rather suf-

fer yourselves to be defrauded?

8 Nay, you do wrong, and defraud, and that your brethren.

9 Do you not know that the unrighteous shall not inherit the kingdom of God? Be not deceived: neither fornicators, nor idolaters, nor adulterers, nor effeminate, nor abusers of themselves with mankind,

10 Nor thieves, nor covetous, nor drunkards, nor revilers, nor extortioners, shall inherit the kingdom of God.

11 And such were some of you: but you are washed, but you are sanctified, but you are justified in the name of the Lord Jesus, and by the Spirit of our God.

12 All things are lawful to me, but all things are not expedient: all things are lawful for me, but I will not be brought under the power of any.

13 Meats for the belly, and the belly for meats: but God shall destroy both it and them. Now the body is not for fornication, but for the Lord; and the Lord for the body.

14 And God has both raised up the Lord, and will also raise up us by his own power.

15 Do you not know that your bodies are the members of Christ? shall I then take the members of Christ, and make them the members of an harlot? God forbid.

16 What? Do you not know that he which is joined to an harlot is one body? for two, said he, shall be one flesh.

17 But he that is joined to the Lord is one spirit.

18 Flee fornication. Every sin that a man does is without the body; but he that commits fornication sins against his own body.

19 What? Do you not know that your body is the temple of the Holy Spirit which is in you, which you have of God, and you are not your own?

20 For you are bought with a price: therefore glorify God in your body, and in your spirit, which are God's.

CHAPTER 7

NOW concerning the things whereof you wrote to me: It is good for a man not to touch a woman.

2 Nevertheless, to avoid fornication, let every man have his own wife, and let every woman have her own husband.

3 Let the husband render to the wife due benevolence: and likewise also the wife to the husband.

4 The wife has not power of her own body, but the husband: and likewise also the husband has not power of his own body, but the wife.

5 Defraud not one the other, except it be with consent for a time, that you may give yourselves to fasting and prayer; and come together again, that Satan tempt you not for your incontinency.

6 But I speak this by permission, and not of commandment.

7 For I would that all men were even as

6:9,10 Sinners will not enter the kingdom of God: Who can say, I have made my heart clean, I am pure from my sin? (Proverbs 20:9). For there is not a just man on earth who does good and does not sin (Ecclesiastes 7:20). If we say that we have no sin, we deceive ourselves, and the truth is not in us (1 John 1:8). For all have sinned, and come short of the glory of God (Romans 3:23). See Revelation 21:8 comment.

6:9–11 Homosexuals are deceived if they think they find in Scripture that their lifestyle is okay with God, and that they cannot change. This list of sins (which encompass most, if not all, of the Ten Commandments) makes it clear who will not be included in the kingdom of God. However, Paul says to those who are now believers, And such were some of you (v. 11). No matter what their sins, God can wash sinners clean and make them righteous in His sight. See Jude 7 comment.

6:19 Coming under the loving Lordship of Jesus Christ means an end to our rights as well as to our wrongs. It means the end of life on our own terms. *Larry Tomczak*

I myself. But every man has his proper gift of God, one after this manner, and another after that.

8 I say therefore to the unmarried and widows, It is good for them if they abide even as I.

9 But if they cannot contain, let them marry: for it is better to marry than to burn.

10 And to the married I command, yet not I, but the Lord, Let not the wife depart from her husband:

11 But and if she depart, let her remain unmarried, or be reconciled to her husband: and let not the husband put away his wife.

12 But to the rest speak I, not the Lord: If any brother has a wife that believes not, and she be pleased to dwell with him, let him not put her away.

13 And the woman which has an husband that believes not, and if he be pleased to dwell with her, let her not leave him.

14 For the unbelieving husband is sanctified by the wife, and the unbelieving wife is sanctified by the husband: else were your children unclean; but now are they holy.

15 But if the unbelieving depart, let him depart. A brother or a sister is not under bondage in such cases: but God has called us to peace.

16 For how do you know, O wife, whether you shall save your husband? or how do you know, O man, whether you shall save your wife?

17 But as God has distributed to every man, as the Lord has called every one, so let him walk. And so ordain I in all churches.

18 Is any man called being circumcised? let him not become uncircumcised. Is any called in uncircumcision? let him not be circumcised.

19 Circumcision is nothing, and uncircumcision is nothing, but the keeping of the commandments of God.

20 Let every man abide in the same calling wherein he was called.

21 Are you called being a servant? care not for it: but if you may be made free, use it rather.

22 For he that is called in the Lord, being a servant, is the Lord's freeman: likewise also he that is called, being free, is Christ's servant.

23 You are bought with a price; be not the servants of men.

24 Brethren, let every man, wherein he is called, therein abide with God.

25 Now concerning virgins I have no commandment of the Lord: yet I give my judgment, as one that has obtained mercy

---

7:2–5 Biblical sexuality. The gift of sex came from God; it didn't come about through an evolutionary process. It was given by God for procreation and pleasure. Scripture says that the only time a husband and wife should refrain from the joys of sex is when they are praying and fasting. The Bible also says that a man should be ravished (enraptured) always with her love (Proverbs 5:18 20). The only stipulation is that it is his wife he is to be enraptured with not the woman down the street.

Those who forsake marriage thinking that they can enjoy sex outside the bonds of the institution risk getting AIDS and numerous other sexually transmitted diseases several of which are incurable. It is interesting to note that a man and a woman can engage in sex ten thousand times within marriage and never even once risk contracting any sexually transmitted disease.

One who commits fornication (from the Greek *Porneia*, illicit sexual intercourse) takes what could lawfully be his as a gift from God, and corrupts it. He is like a child who one night steals a crisp, new twenty-dollar bill from his father's wallet, not realizing that his father intended to give it to him as a gift in the morning.

The fornicator not only sins against God and incurs the wrath of eternal justice, but he sins against his conscience, and his own body (1 Corinthians 6:18). Fornicators will not inherit the kingdom of God (1 Corinthians 6:9).

of the Lord to be faithful.

26 I suppose therefore that this is good for the present distress, I say, that it is good for a man so to be.

27 Are you bound to a wife? seek not to be loosed. Are you loosed from a wife? seek not a wife.

28 But and if you marry, you have not sinned; and if a virgin marry, she has not sinned. Nevertheless such shall have trouble in the flesh: but I spare you.

29 *But this I say, brethren, the time is short: it remains, that both they that have wives be as though they had none;*

30 *And they that weep, as though they wept not; and they that rejoice, as though they rejoiced not; and they that buy, as though they possessed not;*

31 *And they that use this world, as not abusing it: for the fashion of this world passes away.*

32 But I would have you without carefulness. He that is unmarried cares for the things that belong to the Lord, how he may please the Lord:

33 But he that is married cares for the things that are of the world, how he may please his wife.

34 There is difference also between a wife and a virgin. The unmarried woman cares for the things of the Lord, that she may be holy both in body and in spirit: but she that is married cares for the things of the world, how she may please her husband.

35 And this I speak for your own profit; not that I may cast a snare upon you, but for that which is comely, and that you may attend upon the Lord without distraction.

36 But if any man think that he behaves himself uncomely toward his virgin, if she pass the flower of her age, and need so require, let him do what he will, he sins not: let them marry.

37 Nevertheless he that stands steadfast in his heart, having no necessity, but has

power over his own will, and has so decreed in his heart that he will keep his virgin, does well.

38 So then he that gives her in marriage does well; but he that gives her not in marriage does better.

39 The wife is bound by the law as long as her husband lives; but if her husband be dead, she is at liberty to be married to whom she will; only in the Lord.

40 But she is happier if she so abide, after my judgment: and I think also that I have the Spirit of God.

· · · · ·

For how to speak with someone who doesn't believe in the afterlife, see Psalm 49:15 comment.

· · · · ·

CHAPTER 8

N OW as touching things offered to idols, we know that we all have knowledge. Knowledge puffs up, but charity edifies.

2 And if any man think that he knows anything, he knows nothing yet as he ought to know.

3 But if any man love God, the same is known of him.

4 As concerning therefore the eating of those things that are offered in sacrifice to idols, we know that an idol is nothing in the world, and that there is none other God but one.

5 For though there be that are called gods, whether in heaven or in earth, (as there be gods many, and lords many,)

6 But to us there is but one God, the Father, of whom are all things, and we in him; and one Lord Jesus Christ, by whom are all things, and we by him.

7 Howbeit there is not in every man that knowledge: for some with conscience of the idol to this hour eat it as a thing offered to an idol; and their conscience be-

---

8:4 See Psalm 115:4-9 comment.

ing weak is defiled.

8 But meat commends us not to God: for neither, if we eat, are we the better; neither, if we eat not, are we the worse.

9 But take heed lest by any means this liberty of yours become a stumbling-block to them that are weak.

10 For if any man see you which have knowledge sit at meat in the idol's temple, shall not the conscience of him which is weak be emboldened to eat those things which are offered to idols;

11 And through your knowledge shall the weak brother perish, for whom Christ died?

12 But when you sin so against the brethren, and wound their weak conscience, you sin against Christ.

13 Wherefore, if meat make my brother to offend, I will eat no flesh while the world stands, lest I make my brother to offend.

CHAPTER 9

AM I not an apostle? am I not free? have I not seen Jesus Christ our Lord? are not you my work in the Lord?

2 If I be not an apostle to others, yet doubtless I am to you: for the seal of mine apostleship are you in the Lord.

3 Mine answer to them that do examine me is this,

4 Have we not power to eat and to drink?

5 Have we not power to lead about a sister, a wife, as well as other apostles, and as the brethren of the Lord, and Cephas?

6 Or I only and Barnabas, have not we power to forbear working?

7 Who goes a warfare any time at his own charges? who plants a vineyard, and eats not of the fruit thereof? or who feeds a flock, and eats not of the milk of the flock?

8 Say I these things as a man? or said not the law the same also?

9 For it is written in the law of Moses, You shall not muzzle the mouth of the ox that treads out the corn. Does God take care for oxen?

10 Or said he it altogether for our sakes? For our sakes, no doubt, this is written: that he that plows should plow in hope; and that he that threshes in hope should be partaker of his hope.

11 If we have sown to you spiritual things, is it a great thing if we shall reap your carnal things?

12 If others be partakers of this power over you, are not we rather? Nevertheless we have not used this power; but suffer all things, lest we should hinder the gospel of Christ.

13 Do you not know that they which minister about holy things live of the things of the temple? and they which wait at the alter are partakers with the alter?

14 *Even so has the Lord ordained that they which preach the gospel should live of the gospel.*

15 But I have used none of these things: neither have I written these things, that it should be so done to me: for it were better for me to die, than that any man should make my glorying void.

8:9 Although we have incredible liberty as Christians, we are servants of all. If something we are at liberty to do offends an unsaved person, we must stop doing it, for the sake of the gospel. It has been well said that if Paul saw a Jew, he would hide his ham sandwich behind his back. We need to walk in that same spirit.

9:16 Second Kings 7:9 tells of lepers who had seen a great victory and initially kept the good news to themselves. But their consciences spoke to them of their moral obligation to not remain silent: Then they said one to another, We do not well: this day is a day of good tidings, and we hold our peace. How much more should we feel an obligation to take the Good News of everlasting life to a dying world? We must speak about what we have seen and heard. Like Paul, we are debtors to those who haven't heard the gospel (Romans 1:14). Woe to us if we do not preach the gospel.

16 *For though I preach the gospel, I have nothing to glory of: for necessity is laid upon me; yes, woe is to me, if I preach not the gospel!*

17 For if I do this thing willingly, I have a reward: but if against my will, a dispensation of the gospel is committed to me.

18 What is my reward then? Verily that, when I preach the gospel, I may make the gospel of Christ without charge, that I abuse not my power in the gospel.

19 *For though I be free from all men, yet have I made myself servant to all, that I might gain the more.*

20 *And to the Jews I became as a Jew, that I might gain the Jews; to them that are under the law, as under the law, that I might gain them that are under the law;*

21 *To them that are without law, as without law, (being not without law to God, but under the law to Christ,) that I might gain them that are without law.*

22 *To the weak became I as weak, that I might gain the weak: I am made all things to all men, that I might by all means save some.*

23 *And this I do for the gospel's sake, that I might be partaker thereof with you.*

24 Do you not know that they which run in a race run all, but one receives the prize? So run, that you may obtain.

25 And every man that strives for the mastery is temperate in all things. Now they do it to obtain a corruptible crown; but we an incorruptible.

26 I therefore so run, not as uncertainly; so fight I, not as one that beats the air:

27 But I keep under my body, and bring it into subjection: lest that by any means, when I have preached to others, I myself should be a castaway.

9:22 Gospel tracts—how to use them. If Paul meant by all means, he no doubt would have used gospel tracts as a means to reach the lost. A Christian book relates the true story of a diver who saw a piece of paper clutched in the shell of an oyster. The man grabbed it, found that it was a gospel tract and said, "I can't hold out any longer. His mercy is so great that He has caused His Word to follow me even to the bottom of the ocean." God used a tract to save the man.

Why should a Christian use tracts? Simply because *God* uses them. He used a tract to save the great missionary Hudson Taylor, as well as innumerable others. That fact alone should be enough incentive for a Christian to always use tracts to reach the lost, but there are even more reasons why we should use them. Here are a few:

- Tracts can provide an opening for us to share our faith. We can watch people's reactions as we give them tracts, and see if they are open to listening to spiritual things.
- They can do the witnessing for us. If we are too timid to speak to someone about the things of God, we can at least give them a tract, or leave it lying around so that someone will pick it up.
- They speak to the individuals when they are ready. They don't read it until they want to.
- They can find their way into people's homes when we can't.
- They don't get into arguments; they just state their case.

Dr. Oswald J. Smith said, "The only way to carry out the Great Commission will be by the means of the printed page." *Charles Spurgeon* stated, "When preaching and private talk are not available, you need to have a tract ready...Get good striking tracts, or none at all. But a touching gospel tract may be the seed of eternal life. Therefore, do not go out without your tracts."

If you want people to accept your literature, try to greet them before offering them a tract. If you can get them to respond to a warm Good morning, or How are you doing? That will almost always break the ice and they will take it. After the greeting, don't ask, Would you like this? They will probably respond, What is it? Instead, say, Did you get one of these? That question has a twofold effect. You stir their curiosity and make them ask, One of what? That's when you hand it to them. It also makes them feel as though they are missing out on something. So they are.   *(continued on next page)*

CHAPTER 10

MOREOVER, brethren, I would not that you should be ignorant, how that all our fathers were under the cloud, and all passed through the sea;

2 And were all baptized unto Moses in the cloud and in the sea;

3 And did all eat the same spiritual meat;

4 And did all drink the same spiritual drink: for they drank of that spiritual Rock that followed them: and that Rock was Christ.

5 But with many of them God was not well pleased: for they were overthrown in the wilderness.

6 Now these things were our examples, to the intent we should not lust after evil things, as they also lusted.

7 Neither be idolaters, as were some of them; as it is written, The people sat down to eat and drink, and rose up to play.

8 Neither let us commit fornication, as some of them committed, and fell in one day three and twenty thousand.

9 Neither let us tempt Christ, as some of them also tempted, and were destroyed of serpents.

10 Neither murmur, as some of them also murmured, and were destroyed of the destroyer.

11 Now all these things happened to them for ensamples: and they are written for our admonition, upon whom the ends of the world are come.

12 Wherefore let him that thinks he

(9:22 continued) Perhaps you almost pass out at the thought of passing out a tract. Don't worry; you are not alone. We *all* battle fear. The answer to fear is found in the prayer closet. Ask God to give you a compassion that will swallow your fears. Meditate on the fate of the ungodly. Give hell some deep thought. Confront what it is that makes you fearful.

Do you like roller coasters? Some Christians want to try bungee-jumping or sky diving. Isn't it strange? We are prepared to risk our lives for the love of fear and yet we are willing to let a sinner go to hell for fear of giving out a tract. Ask yourself how many piles of bloodied stones you can find where Christians have been stoned to death for preaching the gospel. How much singed soil can you find where they have been burned at the stake? Part of our fear is a fear of rejection. We are fearful of looking foolish. That's a subtle form of pride. The other part of our battle with fear comes directly from the enemy. He knows that fear paralyzes. We must resist the devil and his lies. If God is with us, nothing can be against us.

Never underestimate the power of a gospel tract. After *George Whitefield* read one called The Life of God in the Soul of a Man, he said, "God showed me I must be born again or be damned. He went on to pray, Lord, if I am not a Christian, or if I am not a real one, for Jesus Christ's sake show me what Christianity is, that I may not be damned at last!" Then his journal tells us that from that moment...did I know that I must become a new creature."

If you have never given out tracts, why not begin today? Leave them in a shopping cart, or put them in the mail when you pay bills. Then each night as you shut your eyes to go to sleep, you will have something very special to pray about that God will use the tract you put somewhere. You will also have a deep sense of satisfaction that you played a small part in carrying out the Great Commission to reach this dying world with the gospel of everlasting life. Don't waste your life. Do something for the kingdom of God while you are able to. Always remember: treat every day as though it were your last; one day you will be right. See also Mark 4:14 and Revelation 22:2 comments.

10:1 This chapter shows how subtle idolatry can be. If we create an idol of God in our minds, that idol will not speak to us when we fall into the sin of lust. However, if we keep before us the true revelation of God's omniscient holiness, when Potiphar's wife calls we will flee from sexual sin. Despite our protests that lust easily overcomes our weak wills, verse 13 leaves each of us without excuse. See how that verse is linked to verse 14.

10:4 Just as Moses struck the rock to bring forth life-sustaining water for the Israelites in the desert (Exodus 17:6), it was Moses' Law that came down upon the Rock (Christ) at the cross.

stands take heed lest he fall.

13 There has no temptation taken you but such as is common to man: but God is faithful, who will not suffer you to be tempted above that you are able; but will with the temptation also make a way to escape, that you may be able to bear it.

14 Wherefore, my dearly beloved, flee from idolatry.

15 I speak as to wise men; judge what I say.

16 The cup of blessing which we bless, is it not the communion of the blood of Christ? The bread which we break, is it not the communion of the body of Christ?

17 For we being many are one bread, and one body: for we are all partakers of that one bread.

18 Behold Israel after the flesh: are not they which eat of the sacrifices partakers of the alter?

19 What say I then? that the idol is any thing, or that which is offered in sacrifice to idols is any thing?

20 But I say, that the things which the Gentiles sacrifice, they sacrifice to devils, and not to God: and I would not that you should have fellowship with devils.

21 You cannot drink the cup of the Lord, and the cup of devils: you cannot be par-

10:14 Idolatry. Those who deny the fact that God is angry at sin insinuate that sinful man (with his measure of desire to see justice) is more just than God. This is an incredible affront to the integrity of God. The following *Time* magazine letter to the editor epitomizes idolatry (the oldest sin in the Book):

> Excellent topic! I truly enjoyed reading Does Heaven Exist? I am a devout Christian, and I don't give much thought to heaven. My spirituality isn't based on an anthropomorphic, kick-butt God who will throw four generations of children into eternal damnation because some distant forefather ticked him off [see Proverbs 28:5]. Heaven is the flip side of the absolutely barbaric notion of hell that evolved under that kick-butt mindset. To me, God is a symbol for something unfathomable, an utter mystery that fills my heart with joy and my spirit with song.

10:20 To many, Eastern religions have a sense of romantic mysticism. It must therefore be a surprise to find that India has 220 million cows that are worshiped as the supreme givers of life (God). The cow's hooves are bathed in religious ceremonies. Their urine is considered holy and is used to anoint believers. The animal's dung is also applied to the skin of the faithful in religious rituals. They believe that all the gods inhabit some part of the cow's body. A Christian revival in India would not only provide eternal salvation for the country, but would also release enough meat to feed their hungry population.

takers of the Lord's table, and of the table of devils.

22 Do we provoke the Lord to jealousy? are we stronger than he?

23 All things are lawful for me, but all things are not expedient: all things are lawful for me, but all things edify not.

24 Let no man seek his own, but every man another's wealth.

25 Whatsoever is sold in the shambles, that eat, asking no question for conscience sake:

26 For the earth is the Lord's, and the fulness thereof.

27 If any of them that believe not bid you to a feast, and you be disposed to go; whatsoever is set before you, eat, asking no question for conscience sake.

28 But if any man say to you, This is offered in sacrifice to idols, eat not for his sake that showed it, and for conscience sake: for the earth is the Lord's, and the fulness thereof:

29 Conscience, I say, not your own, but of the other: for why is my liberty judged of another man's conscience?

30 For if I by grace be a partaker, why am I evil spoken of for that for which I give thanks?

31 Whether therefore you eat, or drink, or whatsoever you do, do all to the glory of God.

32 Give none offence, neither to the Jews, nor to the Gentiles, nor to the church of God:

33 Even as I please all men in all things, not seeking mine own profit, but the profit of many, that they may be saved.

CHAPTER 11

B E *followers of me, even as I also am of Christ.*

2 Now I praise you, brethren, that you remember me in all things, and keep the ordinances, as I delivered them to you.

3 But I would have you know, that the head of every man is Christ; and the head of the woman is the man; and the head of Christ is God.

4 Every man praying or prophesying, having his head covered, dishonors his head.

5 But every woman that prays or prophesies with her head uncovered dishonors her head: for that is even all one as if she were shaven.

> If any man's life at home is unworthy, he should go several miles away before he stands up to preach. When he stands up, he should say nothing.
>
> **CHARLES SPURGEON**

6 For if the woman be not covered, let her also be shorn: but if it be a shame for a woman to be shorn or shaven, let her be covered.

7 For a man indeed ought not to cover his head, forasmuch as he is the image and glory of God: but the woman is the glory of the man.

8 For the man is not of the woman; but the woman of the man.

9 Neither was the man created for the woman; but the woman for the man.

10 For this cause ought the woman to have power on her head because of the angels.

11 Nevertheless neither is the man without the woman, neither the woman without the man, in the Lord.

12 For as the woman is of the man, even so is the man also by the woman; but all things of God.

13 Judge in yourselves: is it comely that a woman pray to God uncovered?

14 Does not even nature itself teach you, that, if a man have long hair, it is a shame to him?

15 But if a woman have long hair, it is a glory to her: for her hair is given her for

---

11:8 It has been well said that woman was made from Adam's rib close to his heart, under his protective arm (Genesis 2:21,22).

a covering.

16 But if any man seem to be contentious, we have no such custom, neither the churches of God.

17 Now in this that I declare to you I praise you not, that you come together not for the better, but for the worse.

18 For first of all, when you come together in the church, I hear that there be divisions among you; and I partly believe it.

19 For there must be also heresies among you, that they which are approved may be made manifest among you.

20 When you come together therefore into one place, this is not to eat the Lord's supper.

21 For in eating every one takes before other his own supper: and one is hungry, and another is drunken.

22 What? have you not houses to eat and to drink in? or do you despise the church of God, and shame them that have not? What shall I say to you? shall I praise you in this? I praise you not.

23 For I have received of the Lord that which also I delivered to you, That the Lord Jesus the same night in which he was betrayed took bread:

24 And when he had given thanks, he broke it, and said, Take, eat: this is my body, which is broken for you: this do in remembrance of me.

25 After the same manner also he took the cup, when he had supped, saying, This cup is the new testament in my blood: this do, as oft as you drink it, in remembrance of me.

26 For as often as you eat this bread, and drink this cup, you do show the Lord's death till he come.

27 Wherefore whosoever shall eat this bread, and drink this cup of the Lord, unworthily, shall be guilty of the body and blood of the Lord.

28 But let a man examine himself, and so let him eat of that bread, and drink of that cup.

29 For he that eats and drinks unworthily, eats and drinks damnation to himself, not discerning the Lord's body.

30 For this cause many are weak and sickly among you, and many sleep.

31 For if we would judge ourselves, we should not be judged.

32 But when we are judged, we are chastened of the Lord, that we should not be condemned with the world.

33 Wherefore, my brethren, when you come together to eat, tarry one for an-

---

11:9 Earth's population refutes evolution. "The evolutionary scientists who believe that man existed for over a million years have an almost insurmountable problem. Using the assumption of forty-three years for an average human generation, the population growth over a million years would produce 23,256 consecutive generations. We calculate the expected population by starting with one couple one million years ago and use the same assumptions of a forty-three-year generation and 2.5 children per family...The evolutionary theory of a million years of growth would produce trillions × trillions × trillions × trillions of people that should be alive today on our planet. To put this in perspective, this number is vastly greater than the total number of atoms in our vast universe. If mankind had lived on earth for a million years, we would all be standing on enormously high mountains of bones from the trillions of skeletons of those who had died in past generations. However, despite the tremendous archeological and scientific investigation in the last two centuries, the scientists have not found a fraction of the trillions of skeletons predicted by the theory of evolutionary scientists." Grant R. Jeffery, The Signature of God

One common ancestor. Researchers suggest that virtually all modern men 99% of them, says one scientist are closely related genetically and share genes with one male ancestor, dubbed Y-chromosome Adam.

"We are finding that humans have very, very shallow genetic roots which go back very recently to one ancestor. That indicates that there was an origin in a specific location on the globe, and then it spread out from there." U.S. News & World Report, December 4, 1995

other.

34 And if any man hunger, let him eat at home; that you come not together to condemnation. And the rest will I set in order when I come.

CHAPTER 12

N OW concerning spiritual gifts, brethren, I would not have you ignorant.
2 You know that you were Gentiles, carried away to these dumb idols, even as you were led.
3 Wherefore I give you to understand, that no man speaking by the Spirit of God calls Jesus accursed: and that no man can say that Jesus is the Lord, but by the Holy Spirit.
4 Now there are diversities of gifts, but the same Spirit.
5 And there are differences of administrations, but the same Lord.
6 And there are diversities of operations, but it is the same God which works all in all.
7 But the manifestation of the Spirit is given to every man to profit withal.
8 For to one is given by the Spirit the word of wisdom; to another the word of knowledge by the same Spirit;
9 To another faith by the same Spirit; to another the gifts of healing by the same Spirit;
10 To another the working of miracles; to another prophecy; to another discerning of spirits; to another divers kinds of tongues; to another the interpretation of tongues:
11 But all these work that one and the selfsame Spirit, dividing to every man severally as he will.
12 For as the body is one, and has many members, and all the members of that one body, being many, are one body: so also is Christ.
13 For by one Spirit are we all baptized into one body, whether we be Jews or Gentiles, whether we be bond or free; and have been all made to drink into one Spirit.
14 For the body is not one member, but many.
15 If the foot shall say, Because I am not the hand, I am not of the body; is it therefore not of the body?
16 And if the ear shall say, Because I am not the eye, I am not of the body; is it therefore not of the body?
17 If the whole body were an eye, where were the hearing? If the whole were hearing, where were the smelling?
18 But now has God set the members every one of them in the body, as it has pleased him.
19 And if they were all one member, where were the body?
20 But now are they many members, yet but one body.
21 And the eye cannot say to the hand, I have no need of you: nor again the head to the feet, I have no need of you.
22 Nay, much more those members of the body, which seem to be more feeble, are necessary:
23 And those members of the body, which we think to be less honorable, upon these we bestow more abundant honor; and our uncomely parts have more abundant comeliness.
24 For our comely parts have no need: but God has tempered the body together, having given more abundant honor to that part which lacked:
25 That there should be no schism in the body; but that the members should have the same care one for another.
26 And whether one member suffer, all the members suffer with it; or one member be honored, all the members rejoice with it.
27 Now you are the body of Christ, and members in particular.
28 And God has set some in the church,

12:25   "Satan always hates Christian fellowship; it is his policy to keep Christians apart. Anything which can divide saints from one another he delights in." *Charles Spurgeon*

13:2 *Speaking the Truth in Love to Jehovah's Witnesses*

By Clint DeBoer

I was raised as a Jehovah's Witness and remained one until age 11. Coming out of this cult, I entered my teenage years as a bitter atheist where I remained until I graduated from college. Through God's amazing grace I was saved in 1994 after reading the Bible and realizing that it was indeed the true Word of God.

Repeatedly God has blessed me with the passion and privilege to witness to the Jehovah's Witnesses. You've almost certainly had them come knocking on your door on a Saturday afternoon and you may have even engaged a Jehovah s Witness in a theological discussion. In talking to other Christians I find that when presented with a face-to-face encounter with a Jehovah's Witness there are usually two responses:

1) A frontal assault via debate or heated discussion; or

2) A polite no thanks, I'm already a Christian, followed by an all too abrupt closing of the door.

For the mature Christian, what's usually missing is the realization that this is a true witnessing opportunity one that has arrived right at your doorstep.

In my earliest attempts at grabbing the proverbial bull by the horns, I tried engaging them in direct debates, often quoting from several texts I had studied regarding the cultic practices of the Jehovah's Witnesses. After several failed attempts at conversion, often ending with thoroughly frustrated Jehovah's Witnesses unwilling to ever return to my residence, I arrived at a startling realization: Jehovah's Witnesses are real people with real needs and real feelings. They can feel frustration, anger, fear, and confusion. I then realized that the reason my frontal assaults on the Jehovah's Witnesses never seemed to work was because I had not put myself in their place and taken their feelings into account.

A wise man once said, When you want to get someone's attention, you don't shine a flashlight in their eyes. In presenting my arguments and facts without giving them time to prepare, I had forgotten that they were human beings searching for the truth. I had not been speaking this truth in love.

Months later, when I was again presented with an opportunity to speak with Jehovah's Witnesses at my door, I engaged them in conversation, and agreed to do a weekly Bible study with them in order to further discuss what exactly they believed. They agreed, with the understanding that along the way I would ask questions whenever we arrived at a topic or subject with which I disagreed or failed to understand. The amazing difference was that instead of blindsiding them with questions and points of contention, I was giving them an opportunity to prepare themselves for a topic of discussion.

More importantly, though, I began to care about them personally and yearn for their salvation.

In this way, I am able to meet with Witnesses on a weekly basis and take them off the streets, focusing on critical topics such as the requirement that one be born again to enter the kingdom of God, the unbiblical theology of a two-class system of believers, and the true identity of Jesus Christ.

---

first apostles, secondarily prophets, thirdly teachers, after that miracles, then gifts of healings, helps, governments, diversities of tongues.

29 Are all apostles? are all prophets? are all teachers? are all workers of miracles?

30 Have all the gifts of healing? do all speak with tongues? do all interpret?

31 But covet earnestly the best gifts: and yet show I to you a more excellent way.

CHAPTER 13

THOUGH I speak with the tongues of men and of angels, and have not charity, I am become as sounding brass, or a tinkling cymbal.

2 And though I have the gift of prophecy, and understand all mysteries, and all knowledge; and though I have all faith, so that I could remove mountains, and have not charity, I am nothing.

3 And though I bestow all my goods to feed the poor, and though I give my body to be burned, and have not charity, it profits me nothing.

4 Charity suffers long, and is kind; charity envies not; charity vaunts not itself, is not puffed up,

5 Does not behave itself unseemly, seeks not her own, is not easily provoked, thinks no evil;

6 Rejoices not in iniquity, but rejoices in the truth;

7 Bears all things, believes all things, hopes all things, endures all things.

8 Charity never fails: but whether there be prophecies, they shall fail; whether there be tongues, they shall cease; whether there be knowledge, it shall vanish away.

9 For we know in part, and we prophesy in part.

10 But when that which is perfect is come, then that which is in part shall be done away.

11 When I was a child, I spoke as a child, I understood as a child, I thought as a child: but when I became a man, I put away childish things.

12 For now we see through a glass, darkly; but then face to face: now I know in part; but then shall I know even as also I am known.

13 And now abides faith, hope, charity, these three; but the greatest of these is charity.

CHAPTER 14

FOLLOW after charity, and desire spiritual gifts, but rather that you may prophesy.

2 For he that speaks in an unknown tongue speaks not to men, but to God: for no man understands him; howbeit in the spirit he speaks mysteries.

3 But he that prophesies speaks to men to edification, and exhortation, and comfort.

4 He that speaks in an unknown tongue edifies himself; but he that prophesies edifies the church.

5 I would that you all spoke with tongues, but rather that you prophesied: for greater is he that prophesies than he that speaks with tongues, except he interpret, that the church may receive edifying.

6 Now, brethren, if I come to you speaking with tongues, what shall I profit you, except I shall speak to you either by revelation, or by knowledge, or by prophesying, or by doctrine?

> Love will find a way. Indifference will find an excuse.
> **ANONYMOUS**

7 And even things without life giving sound, whether pipe or harp, except they give a distinction in the sounds, how shall it be known what is piped or harped?

8 For if the trumpet give an uncertain sound, who shall prepare himself to the battle?

9 So likewise you, except you utter by the tongue words easy to be understood, how shall it be known what is spoken? for you shall speak into the air.

10 There are, it may be, so many kinds of voices in the world, and none of them is without signification.

11 Therefore if I know not the meaning of the voice, I shall be to him that speaks a barbarian, and he that speaks shall be a barbarian to me.

12 Even so you, forasmuch as you are zealous of spiritual gifts, seek that you may excel to the edifying of the church.

13 Wherefore let him that speaks in an unknown tongue pray that he may interpret.

14 For if I pray in an unknown tongue, my spirit prays, but my understanding is unfruitful.

15 What is it then? I will pray with the spirit, and I will pray with the understanding also: I will sing with the spirit, and I will sing with the understanding also.

16 Else when you shall bless with the

spirit, how shall he that occupies the room of the unlearned say Amen at your giving of thanks, seeing he understands not what you say?

17 For you verily give thanks well, but the other is not edified.

18 I thank my God, I speak with tongues more than you all:

19 Yet in the church I had rather speak five words with my understanding, that by my voice I might teach others also, than ten thousand words in an unknown tongue.

20 Brethren, be not children in understanding: howbeit in malice be children, but in understanding be men.

21 In the law it is written, With men of other tongues and other lips will I speak to this people; and yet for all that will they not hear me, says the Lord.

22 Wherefore tongues are for a sign, not to them that believe, but to them that believe not: but prophesying serves not for them that believe not, but for them which believe.

23 If therefore the whole church be come together into one place, and all speak with tongues, and there come in those that are unlearned, or unbelievers, will they not say that you are mad?

24 But if all prophesy, and there come in one that believes not, or one unlearned, he is convinced of all, he is judged of all:

25 And thus are the secrets of his heart made manifest; and so falling down on his face he will worship God, and report that God is in you of a truth.

26 How is it then, brethren? when you come together, everyone of you has a psalm, has a doctrine, has a tongue, has a revelation, has an interpretation. Let all things be done to edifying.

27 If any man speak in an unknown tongue, let it be by two, or at the most by three, and that by course; and let one interpret.

28 But if there be no interpreter, let him keep silence in the church; and let him speak to himself, and to God.

29 Let the prophets speak two or three,

"We do not know one-millionth of one percent about anything." (See 1 Corinthians 8:2.)

Thomas Edison

and let the other judge.

30 If any thing be revealed to another that sits by, let the first hold his peace.

31 For you may all prophesy one by one, that all may learn, and all may be comforted.

32 And the spirits of the prophets are subject to the prophets.

33 For God is not the author of confusion, but of peace, as in all churches of the saints.

34 Let your women keep silence in the churches: for it is not permitted to them to speak; but they are commanded to be under obedience, as also says the law.

35 And if they will learn any thing, let them ask their husbands at home: for it is a shame for women to speak in the church.

36 What? came the word of God out from you? or came it to you only?

37 If any man think himself to be a prophet, or spiritual, let him acknowledge that the things that I write to you are the commandments of the Lord.

38 But if any man be ignorant, let him be ignorant.

39 Wherefore, brethren, covet to prophesy, and forbid not to speak with tongues.
40 Let all things be done decently and in order.

CHAPTER 15

MOREOVER, brethren, I declare to you the gospel which I preached to you, which also you have received, and wherein you stand;
2 By which also you are saved, if you keep in memory what I preached to you, unless you have believed in vain.
3 For I delivered to you first of all that which I also received, how that Christ died for our sins according to the scriptures;
4 And that he was buried, and that he rose again the third day according to the scriptures:
5 And that he was seen of Cephas, then of the twelve:
6 After that, he was seen of above five hundred brethren at once; of whom the greater part remain to this present, but some are fallen asleep.
7 After that, he was seen of James; then of all the apostles.
8 And last of all he was seen of me also, as of one born out of due time.

9 For I am the least of the apostles, that am not meet to be called an apostle, because I persecuted the church of God.
10 But by the grace of God I am what I am: and his grace which was bestowed upon me was not in vain; but I labored more abundantly than they all: yet not I, but the grace of God which was with me.

> It was not the volume of sin that sent Christ to the cross; it was the fact of sin.
>
> **RAVI ZACHARIAS**

11 Therefore whether it were I or they, so we preach, and so you believed.
12 Now if Christ be preached that he rose from the dead, how say some among you that there is no resurrection of the dead?
13 But if there be no resurrection of the dead, then is Christ not risen:
14 And if Christ be not risen, then is our preaching vain, and your faith is also vain.
15 Yes, and we are found false witnesses of God; because we have testified of God that he raised up Christ: whom he

---

15:6 "The fact that Abraham Lincoln was born, became president, or was assassinated cannot be proven using scientific methods. To be scientific it must be *repeatable* (as in the testing of gravity). The proofs that Lincoln did exist and was a historical figure are: 1) the written evidence; 2) eyewitness testimony; and 3) physical evidence that remains to this day the Ford Theatre, birth records, and newspaper articles regarding his election. All these facts are acceptable in a court of law as proof to a judge and jury.

"The resurrection of Jesus Christ from the dead is evidential: 1) the empty tomb still exists; 2) His birth record is documented all the way back to Adam and Eve; 3) the four Gospels record His death; 4) the location, and even the names of the political leaders who sentenced Him are historically recorded; 5) there were more than five hundred eyewitnesses who saw Jesus after the resurrection, recorded by the New Testament writers; 6) the very existence of the Christian faith, based on His death and resurrection; 7) the cultural and political evidence of the time, including the Roman calendar separating all of time into Before Christ (B.C.) and in the year of our Lord (A.D.)." *Garry T. Ansdell, D.D.*

15:10 "There is nothing but God's grace. We walk upon it; we breathe it; we live and die by it; it makes the nails and axles of the universe." *Robert Louis Stevenson*

15:14 If Jesus Christ didn't rise from the tomb, then the Bible is a fraud and any hope of resurrection is therefore in vain. However, God has given us irrefutable evidence in His Word to strengthen our faith in His promises historical, scientific, medical, archeological, and prophetic evidence.

QUESTIONS & OBJECTIONS

15:22 *"If God is perfect, why did He make an imperfect creation?"*

The Bible tells us that the Genesis creation was good. There was no sin and therefore no suffering or death. Why then did God give Adam and Eve the ability to sin, knowing full well that they would sin and bring death and pain to the human race? Some believe that if Adam had been created without the ability to choose, then he would have been a robot. A father *cannot* make his children love him. They choose to love him because they have a free will. Others point out that humanity would never have seen the depth of the love of God, as displayed in the cross, unless Adam had sinned, and that fact could be one reason why God allowed sin to enter the world.

raised not up, if so be that the dead rise not.

16 For if the dead rise not, then is not Christ raised:

17 And if Christ be not raised, your faith is vain; you are yet in your sins.

18 Then they also which are fallen asleep in Christ are perished.

19 If in this life only we have hope in Christ, we are of all men most miserable.

20 But now is Christ risen from the dead, and become the firstfruits of them that slept.

21 For since by man came death, by man came also the resurrection of the dead.

22 For as in Adam all die, even so in Christ shall all be made alive.

23 But every man in his own order: Christ the firstfruits; afterward they that are Christ's at his coming.

24 Then comes the end, when he shall have delivered up the kingdom to God, even the Father; when he shall have put down all rule and all authority and power.

25 For he must reign, till he has put all enemies under his feet.

26 The last enemy that shall be destroyed is death.

27 For he has put all things under his feet. But when he says, all things are put under him, it is manifest that he is excepted, which did put all things under him.

28 And when all things shall be subdued to him, then shall the Son also himself be subject to him that put all things under him, that God may be all in all.

29 Else what shall they do which are baptized for the dead, if the dead rise not at all? why are they then baptized for the dead?

30 And why stand we in jeopardy every hour?

31 I protest by your rejoicing which I have in Christ Jesus our Lord, I die daily.

32 If after the manner of men I have

15:17 "How can anyone lose who chooses to become a Christian? If, when he dies, there turns out to be no God and his faith was in vain, he has lost nothing. In fact, he has been happier in life than his nonbelieving friends. If, however, there is a God and a heaven and hell, then he has gained heaven and his skeptical friends will have lost everything in hell!" *Blaise Pascal*

15:29 Some believe in baptizing for the dead, which Paul mentions in these verses. Note that Paul does not say "we," but "they," thus distancing himself from the practice. See Acts 2:38 comment for the biblical basis for baptism.

15:31 "We are not merely imperfect creatures who must be improved: we are, as Newman said, rebels who must lay down our arms...To surrender a self-will inflamed and swollen with years of usurpation is a kind of death...Hence the necessity to die daily: however often we think we have broken the rebellious self, we shall still find it alive." *C. S. Lewis, The Problem of Pain*

QUESTIONS & OBJECTIONS

15:39 "*Evolution disproves the Bible!*"

The Book of Genesis tells us that *everything* was created by God nothing evolved.

Every creature was given the ability to reproduce *after its own kind* as is stated ten times in Genesis 1. Dogs do not produce cats. Neither do cats and dogs have a common ancestry. Dogs began as dogs and are still dogs. They vary in species from Chihuahuas to Saint Bernards, but you will not find a "dat" or a "cog" (part cat/dog) throughout God's creation. Frogs don't reproduce oysters, cows don't have lambs, and pregnant pigs don't give birth to rabbits. God made monkeys as monkeys, and man as man. Each creature brings forth after its own kind. That's no theory; that's a fact.

Why then should we believe that man comes from another species? If evolution is true, then it is proof that the Bible is false. However, the whole of creation stands in contradiction to the theory of evolution. Dr. Kent Hovind of Florida has a standing offer of $250,000 to anyone who can give any

empirical evidence (scientific proof) for evolution. Evolutionis true science fiction. His website is www.drdino.com.

fought with beasts at Ephesus, what advantage is it to me, if the dead rise not? let us eat and drink; for tomorrow we die.

33 Be not deceived: evil communications corrupt good manners.

34 Awake to righteousness, and sin not; for some have not the knowledge of God: I speak this to your shame.

35 But some man will say, How are the dead raised up? and with what body do they come?

36 You fool, that which you sow is not quickened, except it die:

37 And that which you sow, you sow not that body that shall be, but bare grain, it may chance of wheat, or of some other grain:

38 But God gives it a body as it has pleased him, and to every seed his own body.

39 All flesh is not the same flesh: but there is one kind of flesh of men, another flesh of beasts, another of fishes, and another of birds.

40 There are also celestial bodies, and bodies terrestrial: but the glory of the celestial is one, and the glory of the terrestrial is another.

41 There is one glory of the sun, and another glory of the moon, and another glory of the stars: for one star differs from another star in glory.

42 So also is the resurrection of the dead. It is sown in corruption; it is raised in incorruption:

43 It is sown in dishonor; it is raised in glory: it is sown in weakness; it is raised in power:

44 It is sown a natural body; it is raised a spiritual body. There is a natural body,

---

15:34 **False converts.** Paul acknowledges that there were false converts in their midst; to their shame, some among them did not know God, were dead to righteousness, and were continuing to sin. We also should feel a sense of shame at the state of the lukewarm contemporary Church, where only 2 percent have any real concern for the salvation of the world.

15:39 "This notion of species as "natural kinds" fits splendidly with creationist tenets of a pre-Darwinian age. *Louis Agassiz* even argued that species are God's individual thoughts, made incarnate so that we might perceive both His majesty and His message. Species, Agassiz wrote, are instituted by the Divine Intelligence as the categories of His mode of thinking. But how could a division of the organic world into discrete entities be justified by an evolutionary theory that proclaimed ceaseless change as the fundamental fact of nature?" *Stephen J. Gould*, professor of geology and paleontology, Harvard University

15:45   *"Adam was a mythical figure who never really lived."*

Adam is a key figure in Scripture. He is described as the first Adam, the one who brought sin into the world. He made it necessary for Jesus, the last Adam, to atone for all humans, and then rise from the grave with the promise of complete redemption for fallen man and fallen creation. If Adam was just a myth, we would not be able to fully understand the work of Jesus.

If Adam and Eve were not real, then we ought to doubt whether their children were real too, and their children…and then we ought to doubt the first 11 chapters of Genesis, and so on. All the genealogies accept Adam as being a literal person, so their children Cain and Abel (Genesis 4:9,10; Luke 11:50,51) must be real too. Jesus was descended from Adam, and it is impossible to be descended from a myth.

and there is a spiritual body.

45 And so it is written, The first man Adam was made a living soul; the last Adam was made a quickening spirit.

46 Howbeit that was not first which is spiritual, but that which is natural; and afterward that which is spiritual.

47 The first man is of the earth, earthy: the second man is the Lord from heaven.

48 As is the earthy, such are they also that are earthy: and as is the heavenly, such are they also that are heavenly.

49 And as we have borne the image of the earthy, we shall also bear the image of the heavenly.

50 Now this I say, brethren, that flesh and blood cannot inherit the kingdom of God; neither does corruption inherit incorruption.

51 Behold, I show you a mystery; We shall not all sleep, but we shall all be changed,

52 In a moment, in the twinkling of an eye, at the last trump: for the trumpet shall sound, and the dead shall be raised incorruptible, and we shall be changed.

53 For this corruptible must put on incorruption, and this mortal must put on immortality.

54 So when this corruptible shall have put on incorruption, and this mortal shall have put on immortality, then shall be brought to pass the saying that

is written, Death is swallowed up in victory.

55 O death, where is your sting? O grave, where is your victory?

56 The sting of death is sin; and the strength of sin is the law.

57 But thanks be to God, who gives us the victory through our Lord Jesus Christ.

58 Therefore, my beloved brethren, be steadfast, unmoveable, always abounding in the work of the Lord, forasmuch as you know that your labor is not in vain in the Lord.

CHAPTER 16

NOW concerning the collection for the saints, as I have given order to the churches of Galatia, even so do.

2 Upon the first day of the week let every one of you lay by him in store, as God has prospered him, that there be no gatherings when I come.

3 And when I come, whomsoever you shall approve by your letters, them will I send to bring your liberality to Jerusalem.

4 And if it be meet that I go also, they shall go with me.

5 Now I will come to you, when I shall pass through Macedonia: for I do pass through Macedonia.

6 And it may be that I will abide, yes, and winter with you, that you may bring

15:55   *Last Words of Famous People*

Fearful Last Words:

Cardinal Borgia: I have provided in the course of my life for everything except death, and now, alas, I am to die unprepared.

Elizabeth the First: All my possessions for one moment of time.

Kurt Cobain (suicide note): Frances and Courtney, I'll be at your altar. Please keep going Courtney, for Frances. For her life will be so much happier without me. I love you. *I love you.*

Ludwig van Beethoven: Too bad, too bad! It's too late!

Thomas Hobbs: I am about to take my last voyage, a great leap in the dark.

Anne Boleyn: O God, have pity on my soul. O God, have pity on my soul.

Prince Henry of Wales: Tie a rope round my body, pull me out of bed, and lay me in ashes, that I may die with repentant prayers to an offended God. O! I in vain wish for that time I lost with you and others in vain recreations.

Socrates: All of the wisdom of this world is but a tiny raft upon which we must set sail when we leave this earth. If only there was a firmer foundation upon which to sail, perhaps some divine word.

Sigmund Freud: The meager satisfaction that man can extract from reality leaves him starving.

Tony Hancock (British comedian): Nobody will ever know I existed. Nothing to leave behind me. Nothing to pass on. Nobody to mourn me. That's the bitterest blow of all.

Phillip III, King of France: What an account I shall have to give to God! How I should like to live otherwise than I have lived.

Luther Burbank: I don't feel good.

Voltaire (skeptic): I am abandoned by God and man! I will give you half of what I am worth if you will give me six months life. Then I shall go to hell; and you will go with me. O Christ! O Jesus Christ! (The talented French writer once said of Jesus, Curse the wretch! He stated, Every sensible man, every honorable man, must hold the Christian sect in horror... Christianity is the most ridiculous, the most absurd and bloody religion that has ever infected the world.)

He also boasted, In twenty years Christianity will be no more. My single hand shall destroy the edifice it took twelve apostles to rear. Some years later, Voltaire's house was used by the Geneva Bible Society to print Bibles.

Philosophical Last Words:

Aldus Huxley (humanist): It is a bit embarrassing to have been concerned with the human problem all one's life and find at the end that one has no more to offer by way of advice than Try and be a little kinder.

Karl Marx: Go on, get out! Last words are for fools who haven't said enough!

Napoleon: I marvel that where the ambitious dreams of myself and of Alexander and of Caesar should have vanished into thin air, a Judean peasant Jesus should be able to stretch his hands across the centuries, and control the destinies of men and nations.

Leonardo da Vinci: I have offended God and mankind because my work did not reach the quality it should have.

Tolstoy: Even in the valley of the shadow of death, two and two do not make six.

Benjamin Franklin: A dying man can do nothing easy.

Grotius: I have lived my life in a laborious doing of nothing.

Unexpected Demise:

H. G. Wells: Go away: I'm alright.

General John Sedgwick (during the heat of battle in 1864): They couldn't hit an elephant at this distance!

Bing Crosby: That was a great game of golf.

Mahatma Ghandi: I am late by ten minutes. I hate being late. I like to be at the prayer punctually at the stroke of five.

Diana (Spencer), Princess of Wales: My God. What's happened? (per police files)

Douglas Fairbanks, Sr.: Never felt better.

Franklin D. Roosevelt: I have a terrific headache.

Sal Mineo: (stabbed through the heart): Oh God! No! Help! Someone help!

Jesse James: It's awfully hot today.

Lee Harvey Oswald: I will be glad to discuss this proposition with my attorney, and that after I talk with one, we could either discuss it with him or discuss it with my attorney, if the attorney thinks it is a wise thing to do, but at the present time I have nothing more to say to you.

Unusual Last Words:

Vincent Van Gogh: I shall never get rid of this depression.

James Dean: My fun days are over.

Oscar Wilde: My wallpaper and I are fighting a duel to the death. One or the other of us has to go...

W. C. Fields: I'm looking for a loophole.

Louis XVII: I have something to tell you ...

Assurance of Salvation:

Jonathan Edwards: Trust in God and you shall have nothing to fear.

Patrick Henry: Doctor, I wish you to observe how real and beneficial the religion of Christ is to a man about to die... In his will he wrote: This is all the inheritance I give to my dear family. The religion of Christ which will give them one which will make them rich indeed.

John Owen: I am going to Him whom my soul loveth, or rather who has loved me with an everlasting love, which is the sole ground of all my consolation.

D. L. Moody: I see earth receding; heaven is opening. God is calling me.

Lew Wallace (author of *Ben Hur*): Thy will be done.

Alexander Hamilton: I have a tender reliance on the mercy of the Almighty, through the merits of the Lord Jesus Christ. I am a sinner. I look to Him for mercy.

William Shakespeare: I commend my soul into the hands of God my Creator, hoping and assuredly believing, through the only merits of Jesus Christ my Savior, to be made partaker of life everlasting; and my body to the earth, whereof it was made.

Martin Luther: Into Thy hands I commend my spirit! Thou hast redeemed me, O God of truth.

John Milton (British poet): Death is the great key that opens the palace of Eternity.

Sir Walter Raleigh (at his execution): So the heart be right, it is no matter which way the head lieth.

Daniel Webster (just before his death): The great mystery is Jesus Christ the gospel. What would the condition of any of us be if we had not the hope of immortality?...Thank God, the gospel of Jesus Christ brought life and immortality to light. His last words were: I still live.

General William Booth (to his son): And the homeless children, Bramwell, look after the homeless. Promise me...

David Livingstone: Build me a hut to die in. I am going home.

Charles Dickens: I commit my soul to the mercy of God, through our Lord and Savior Jesus Christ, and I exhort my dear children humbly to try and guide themselves by the teaching of the New Testament.

Andrew Jackson: My dear children, do not grieve for me...I am my God's. I belong to Him. I go but a short time before you, and...I hope and trust to meet you all in heaven.

Isaac Watts (hymn-writer): It is a great mercy that I have no manner of fear or dread of death. I could, if God please, lay my head back and die without terror this afternoon.

me on my journey wherever I go.

7 For I will not see you now by the way; but I trust to tarry a while with you, if the Lord permit.

8 But I will tarry at Ephesus until Pentecost.

9 For a great door and effectual is opened to me, and there are many adversaries.

10 Now if Timotheus come, see that he may be with you without fear: for he works the work of the Lord, as I also do.

11 Let no man therefore despise him: but conduct him forth in peace, that he may come to me: for I look for him with the brethren.

12 As touching our brother Apollos, I greatly desired him to come to you with the brethren: but his will was not at all to come at this time; but he will come when he shall have convenient time.

13 Watch, stand fast in the faith, quit you like men, be strong.

14 Let all your things be done with charity.

15 I beseech you, brethren, (you know the house of Stephanas, that it is the first-fruits of Achaia, and that they have addicted themselves to the ministry of the saints,)

16 That you submit yourselves to such, and to every one that helps with us, and labors.

17 I am glad of the coming of Stephanas and Fortunatus and Achaicus: for that which was lacking on your part they have supplied.

18 For they have refreshed my spirit and yours: therefore acknowledge them that are such.

19 The churches of Asia salute you. Aquila and Priscilla salute you much in the Lord, with the church that is in their house.

20 All the brethren greet you. Greet one another with an holy kiss.

21 The salutation of me Paul with mine own hand.

22 If any man love not the Lord Jesus Christ, let him be Anathema Maranatha.

23 The grace of our Lord Jesus Christ be with you.

24 My love be with you all in Christ Jesus. Amen.

"Grace is love that cares and stoops and rescues."

JOHN R. W. STOTT

15:58 Discouragement in witnessing. It is easy to become discouraged after trying to reason with sinners. But to do so is to demean the influence of the Holy Spirit in our witness. If the salvation of a single soul depended solely upon us, we *should* be depressed if we see little visible and immediate fruit for our labors. However, the Bible tells us that salvation is of the Lord. We *do* play a part as a co-laborer with Christ. He may instruct us to roll the stone away, but it is the Lord alone who calls the sinner from the tomb of his deathly state. He gives us opportunity, but He opens the heart of the sinner, and it is Him alone that makes the sinner come to life.

Our confidence should then be in *Him*. Jesus said, With God, nothing shall be impossible. We therefore can *always* abound in the Lord, knowing that our labors (even with cults) are not in vain. His Word cannot return void. Our part is simply to be true and faithful in our witness, then to stand back and watch the miracle work of our God. Who knows, perhaps the words we placed in the heart of the person may bear fruit years after they were spoken, and we will have the joy of unwrapping the grave clothes when God, in His time, calls them.

2 Corinthians

CHAPTER 1

PAUL, an apostle of Jesus Christ by the will of God, and Timothy our brother, to the church of God which is at Corinth, with all the saints which are in all Achaia:

2 Grace be to you and peace from God our Father, and from the Lord Jesus Christ.

3 Blessed be God, even the Father of our Lord Jesus Christ, the Father of mercies, and the God of all comfort;

4 Who comforts us in all our tribulation, that we may be able to comfort them which are in any trouble, by the comfort wherewith we ourselves are comforted of God.

5 For as the sufferings of Christ abound in us, so our consolation also abounds by Christ.

6 And whether we be afflicted, it is for your consolation and salvation, which is effectual in the enduring of the same sufferings which we also suffer: or whether we be comforted, it is for your consolation and salvation.

7 And our hope of you is steadfast, knowing, that as you are partakers of the sufferings, so shall you be also of the consolation.

8 For we would not, brethren, have you ignorant of our trouble which came to us in Asia, that we were pressed out of measure, above strength, insomuch that we despaired even of life:

9 But we had the sentence of death in ourselves, that we should not trust in ourselves, but in God which raises the dead:

10 Who delivered us from so great a death, and does deliver: in whom we trust that he will yet deliver us;

11 You also helping together by prayer for us, that for the gift bestowed upon us by the means of many persons thanks may be given by many on our behalf.

12 For our rejoicing is this, the testimony of our conscience, that in simplicity and godly sincerity, not with fleshly wisdom, but by the grace of God, we have had our conversation in the world, and more abundantly toward you.

13 For we write none other things to you, than what you read or acknowledge; and I trust you shall acknowledge even to the end;

14 As also you have acknowledged us in part, that we are your rejoicing, even as you also are ours in the day of the Lord Jesus.

15 And in this confidence I was minded to come to you before, that you might

---

1:4,5 This chapter is in direct conflict with the message of modern evangelism, which promises a life of happiness, joy, peace, and fulfillment. The truth is that the Christian life is flavored with trials that keep us on our knees.

have a second benefit;

16 And to pass by you into Macedonia, and to come again out of Macedonia to you, and of you to be brought on my way toward Judea.

17 When I therefore was thus minded, did I use lightness? or the things that I purpose, do I purpose according to the flesh, that with me there should be yes yes, and no no?

18 But as God is true, our word toward you was not yes and no.

19 For the Son of God, Jesus Christ, who was preached among you by us, even by me and Silvanus and Timotheus, was not yes and no, but in him was yes.

20 For all the promises of God in him are yes, and in him Amen, to the glory of God by us.

21 Now he which stablishes us with you in Christ, and has anointed us, is God;

22 Who has also sealed us, and given the earnest of the Spirit in our hearts.

23 Moreover I call God for a record upon my soul, that to spare you I came not as yet to Corinth.

24 Not for that we have dominion over your faith, but are helpers of your joy: for by faith you stand.

CHAPTER 2

BUT I determined this with myself, that I would not come again to you in heaviness.

2 For if I make you sorry, who is he then that makes me glad, but the same which is made sorry by me?

3 And I wrote this same to you, lest, when I came, I should have sorrow from them of whom I ought to rejoice; having confidence in you all, that my joy is the joy of you all.

4 For out of much affliction and anguish of heart I wrote to you with many tears; not that you should be grieved, but that you might know the love which I have more abundantly to you.

5 But if any have caused grief, he has not grieved me, but in part: that I may not overcharge you all.

6 Sufficient to such a man is this punishment, which was inflicted of many.

7 So that contrariwise you ought rather to forgive him, and comfort him, lest perhaps such a one should be swallowed up with overmuch sorrow.

8 Wherefore I beseech you that you would confirm your love toward him.

9 For to this end also did I write, that I might know the proof of you, whether you be obedient in all things.

10 To whom you forgive any thing, I forgive also: for if I forgave any thing, to whom I forgave it, for your sakes forgave I it in the person of Christ;

11 Lest Satan should get an advantage of us: for we are not ignorant of his devices.

12 Furthermore, when I came to Troas to preach Christ's gospel, and a door was opened to me of the Lord,

13 I had no rest in my spirit, because I found not Titus my brother: but taking my leave of them, I went from thence into Macedonia.

14 Now thanks be to God, which always causes us to triumph in Christ, and makes manifest the savour of his knowledge by us in every place.

15 *For we are to God a sweet savour of Christ, in them that are saved, and in them that perish:*

16 *To the one we are the savour of death to death; and to the other the savour of life to life. And who is sufficient for these things?*

17 *For we are not as many, which corrupt the word of God: but as of sincerity, but as of God, in the sight of God speak we in Christ.*

2:17 Opticians now offer glasses with titanium frames. Titanium twists and bends but retains its integrity. It always goes back to its original shape. That's what a Christian should be like. We bend; we are flexible on certain issues. However, we always retain our integrity. We refuse to compromise the truth of God's Word. See also 2 Corinthians 4:2.

2:17 The Gospel: Why not preach that Jesus gives happiness, peace, and joy?

Two men are seated on a plane. The first is given a parachute and told to put it on as it would improve his flight. He's a little skeptical at first, since he can't see how wearing a parachute on a plane could possibly improve his flight.

He decides to experiment and see if the claims are true. As he puts it on, he notices the weight of it upon his shoulders and he finds he has difficulty in sitting upright. However, he consoles himself with the fact he was told that the parachute would improve his flight. So he decides to give it a little time.

As he waits he notices that some of the other passengers are laughing at him for wearing a parachute on a plane. He begins to feel somewhat humiliated. As they continue to point and laugh at him, he can stand it no longer. He slinks in his seat, unstraps the parachute and throws it to the floor. Disillusionment and bitterness fill his heart, because as far as he was concerned he was told an outright lie.

The second man is given a parachute, *but listen to what he is told.* He's told to put it on because at any moment he'll be jumping 25,000 feet out of the plane. He gratefully puts the parachute on. He doesn't notice the weight of it upon his shoulders, nor that he can't sit upright. His mind is consumed with the thought of what would happen to him if he jumped without the parachute.

Let's now analyze the motive and the result of each passenger's experience. The first man's motive for putting the parachute on was solely to improve his flight. The result of his experience was that he was humiliated by the passengers, disillusioned, and somewhat embittered against those who gave him the parachute. As far as he's concerned, it will be a long time before anyone gets one of those things on his back again.

The second man put the parachute on solely to escape the jump to come. And because of his knowledge of what would happen to him if he jumped without it, he has a deep-rooted joy and peace in his heart knowing that he's saved from sure death. This knowledge gives him the ability to withstand the mockery of the other passengers. His atti-

tude toward those who gave him the parachute is one of heartfelt gratitude.

Now listen to what the modern gospel says: Put on the Lord Jesus Christ. He'll give you love, joy, peace, fulfillment, and lasting happiness. In other words, Jesus will improve your flight. The sinner responds, and in an experimental fashion puts on the Savior to see if the claims are true. And what does he get? The promised temptation, tribulation, and persecution the other passengers mock him. So what does he do? He takes off the Lord Jesus Christ; he's offended for the Word's sake; he's disillusioned and somewhat embittered...and quite rightly so.

He was promised peace, joy, love, and fulfillment, and all he got were trials and humiliation. His bitterness is directed at those who gave him the so-called "good news." His latter end becomes worse than the first, and he's another inoculated and bitter backslider.

Instead of preaching that Jesus improves the flight, we should be warning sinners that they have to jump out of a plane. That it's appointed for man to die once and then face judgment (Hebrews 9:27). When a sinner understands the horrific consequences of breaking the Law of God, he will flee to the Savior, solely to escape the wrath that's to come. If we are true and faithful witnesses, that's what we'll be preaching: that there is wrath to come that God commands all men everywhere to repent: *because* he has appointed a day in which he will judge the world in righteousness (Acts 17:30,31).

The issue isn't one of happiness, but one of righteousness. It doesn't matter how happy a sinner is, or how much he is enjoying the pleasures of sin for a season, without the righteousness of Christ, he will perish on the day of wrath. Proverbs 11:4 says, Riches profit not in the day of wrath: but righteousness delivers from death. Peace and joy are legitimate *fruits* of salvation, but it's not legitimate to use these fruits as a drawing card for

(continued on next page)

(2:17 continued)

salvation. If we continue to do so, the sinner will respond with an impure motive, lacking repentance.

Can you remember why the *second* passenger had joy and peace in his heart? It was because he knew that the parachute was going to save him from sure death. In the same way, as believers we have joy and peace in believing because we know that the righteousness of Christ is going to deliver us from the wrath that is to come.

With that thought in mind, let's take a close look at an incident aboard the plane. We have a brand-new flight attendant. It's her first day. She's carrying a tray of boiling hot coffee. She wants to leave an impression upon the passengers and she certainly does! As she's walking down the aisle she trips over someone's foot and slops the hot coffee all over the lap of our second passenger. What's his reaction as that boiling liquid hits his tender flesh? Does he go, Man that hurt! ? Yes,

he does. But then does he rip the parachute from his shoulders, throw it to the floor, and say, The stupid parachute! ? No, why should he? He didn't put the parachute on for a better flight. He put it on to save him from the jump to come. If anything, the hot coffee incident causes him to cling tighter to the parachute and even look forward to the jump.

If we have put on the Lord Jesus Christ for the right motive to flee from the wrath that's to come when tribulation strikes, when the flight gets bumpy, we won't get angry at God, and we won't lose our joy and peace. Why should we? We didn't come to Christ for a better lifestyle, but to flee from the wrath to come.

If anything, tribulation drives the true believer *closer* to the Savior. Sadly, we have multitudes of professing Christians who lose their joy and peace when the flight gets bumpy. Why? They are the product of a man-centered gospel. They came lacking repentance, without which they cannot be saved.

CHAPTER 3

D O we begin again to commend ourselves? or need we, as some others, epistles of commendation to you, or letters of commendation from you?

2 You are our epistle written in our hearts, known and read of all men:

3 Forasmuch as you are manifestly declared to be the epistle of Christ ministered by us, written not with ink, but with the Spirit of the living God; not in tables of stone, but in fleshy tables of the heart.

4 And such trust have we through Christ to God-ward:

THE FUNCTION OF THE LAW

3:5,6   God be thanked when the Law so works as to take off the sinner from all confidence in himself! To make the leper confess that he is incurable is going a great way toward compelling him to go to that divine Savior, who alone is able to heal him. This is the whole end of the Law toward men whom God will save. *Charles Spurgeon*

5 Not that we are sufficient of ourselves to think any thing as of ourselves; but our sufficiency is of God;

6 Who also has made us able ministers of the new testament; not of the letter, but of the spirit: for the letter kills, but the spirit gives life.

7 But if the ministration of death, written and engraven in stones, was glorious, so that the children of Israel could not steadfastly behold the face of Moses for the glory of his countenance; which glory was to be done away:

8 How shall not the ministration of the spirit be rather glorious?

9 For if the ministration of condemnation be glory, much more does the ministration of righteousness exceed in glory.

10 For even that which was made glorious had no glory in this respect, by reason of the glory that excels.

11 For if that which is done away was glorious, much more that which remains is glorious.

12 Seeing then that we have such hope, we use great plainness of speech:

13 And not as Moses, which put a veil

over his face, that the children of Israel could not steadfastly look to the end of that which is abolished:

14 But their minds were blinded: for until this day remains the same veil untaken away in the reading of the old testament; which veil is done away in Christ.

15 But even to this day, when Moses is read, the veil is upon their heart.

16 Nevertheless when it shall turn to the Lord, the veil shall be taken away.

17 Now the Lord is that Spirit: and where the Spirit of the Lord is, there is liberty.

18 But we all, with open face beholding as in a glass the glory of the Lord, are changed into the same image from glory to glory, even as by the Spirit of the Lord.

CHAPTER 4

*T*HEREFORE *seeing we have this ministry, as we have received mercy, we faint not;*

2 *But have renounced the hidden things of dishonesty, not walking in craftiness, nor handling the word of God deceitfully; but by manifestation of the truth commending ourselves to every man's conscience in the sight of God.*

3 **But if our gospel be hid, it is hid to them that are lost:**

4 In whom the god of this world has blinded the minds of them which believe not, lest the light of the glorious gospel of Christ, who is the image of God, should shine to them.

5 **For we preach not ourselves, but Christ Jesus the Lord; and ourselves your servants for Jesus' sake.**

6 For God, who commanded the light to shine out of darkness, has shined in our hearts, to give the light of the knowledge of the glory of God in the face of Jesus Christ.

7 But we have this treasure in earthen vessels, that the excellency of the power may be of God, and not of us.

8 We are troubled on every side, yet not distressed; we are perplexed, but not in despair;

9 Persecuted, but not forsaken; cast down, but not destroyed;

10 Always bearing about in the body the dying of the Lord Jesus, that the life also of Jesus might be made manifest in our body.

11 For we which live are always deliv-

3:12 "The big problem is that many Christians speak with forked tongues. They speak a strange lingo called the language of Zion and can only be understood by using a special unscrambler, which most [people] do not possess. So we have to learn to speak plainly and not in code." *Dan Wooding*

3:14–16 "Be cold, sober, wise, circumspect. Keep yourself low by the ground avoiding high questions. Expound the Law truly and open the veil of Moses to condemn all flesh and prove all men sinners, and set at broach the mercy of our Lord Jesus, and let wounded consciences drink of Him." *William Tyndale*

3:18 We often delight in sifting gnats, making issues out of things that aren't important. If someone becomes a Christian, some in the Church seem intent on shaping him to be conformed to their own image, rather than the image of Christ. They feel that he should dress, look, believe, speak, eat, and breathe just as they do.

When someone comes to the Lord, he may not look as we think he should. His hair may be long, his clothes may be radical, he may have an earring in his ear, but if these things are wrong God will speak in his ear. In the meantime, He may be ministering to him about the need to return stolen goods, or about seeking forgiveness from those he has wronged in the past. Those are the things that matter to God.

4:2 "I believe in preaching without compromise against sin." *Franklin Graham*

"Some evangelists are prepared to be anything to anybody as long as they get somebody at the altar for something." *Leonard Ravenhill*

PRINCIPLES OF GROWTH FOR THE NEW AND GROWING CHRISTIAN

 **4:4** *Warfare—Praise the Lord and Pass the Ammunition*

Before you became a Christian, you floated downstream with the other dead fish. But now, God has put His life within you, and you will find yourself swimming against a threefold current: the world, the devil, and the flesh. Let's look at these three resistant enemies.

Our first enemy is the world, which refers to the sinful, rebellious, world system. The world loves the darkness and hates the light (John 3:20), and is governed by the prince of the power of the air (Ephesians 2:2). The Bible says the Christian has escaped the corruption that is in the world through lust. Lust is unlawful desire, and is the life's blood of the world whether it be the lust for sexual sin, for power, for money, for material things. Lust is a monster that will never be gratified, so don't feed it. It will grow bigger and bigger until it weighs heavy upon your back, and will be the death of you (James 1:15).

There is nothing wrong with sex, power, money, or material things, but when desire for these becomes predominant, it becomes idolatry. We are told, Love not the world, neither the things that are in the world. If any man love the world, the love of the Father is not in him ; whoever is a friend of the world is the enemy of God (1 John 2:15; James 4:4).

The second enemy is the devil, who is the god of this world (2 Corinthians 4:4). He was your spiritual father before you joined the family of God (John 8:44; Ephesians 2:2). Jesus called the devil a thief who came to steal, kill, and destroy (John 10:10).

The way to overcome him and his demons is to make sure you are outfitted with the spiritual armor of God (Ephesians 6:10-20). Become intimately familiar with it. Sleep in it. Never take it off. Bind the sword to your hand so you never lose its grip. The reason for this brings us to the third enemy.

The third enemy is what the Bible calls the "flesh." This is your sinful nature. The domain for the battle is your mind.

If you have a mind to, you *will* be attracted to the world and all its sin. The mind is the control panel for the eyes and the ears, the center of your appetites. All sin begins in the heart (Proverbs 4:23; Matthew 15:19). We think of sin before we commit it. James 1:15 warns that lust brings forth sin, and sin when it s conceived brings forth death. Every day of life, we have a choice. To sin or not to sin that is the question. The answer is the fear of God. If you don't fear God, you will sin to your sinful heart's delight.

Did you know that God kills people? He killed a man for what he did sexually (Genesis 38:9,10), killed another man for being greedy (Luke 12:15-21), and killed a husband and wife for lying (Acts 5:1-10). Knowledge of God's goodness His righteous judgments against evil should put the fear of God in us and help us to not indulge in sin.

If we know that the eye of the Lord is in every place beholding the evil and the good, and that He will bring every work to judgment, we will live accordingly. Such weighty thoughts are valuable, for by the fear of the Lord men depart from evil (Proverbs 16:6).

For the next principle of growth, see Hebrews 10:25 comment.

---

ered to death for Jesus' sake, that the life also of Jesus might be made manifest in our mortal flesh.

12 So then death works in us, but life in you.

13 *We having the same spirit of faith, according as it is written, I believed, and therefore have I spoken; we also believe, and therefore speak;*

14 Knowing that he which raised up

4:6 Just as in the beginning the earth was without form and void, and in darkness (Genesis 1:2), the understanding of unregenerate man is darkened (Ephesians 4:18). It is without form and void until God says, "Let there be light."

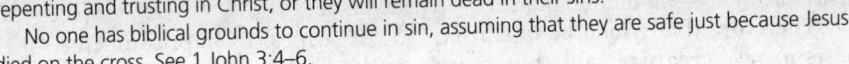

5:14,15 *"Because Jesus died on the cross, we are all forgiven of every sin."*

The forgiveness that is in Jesus Christ is conditional upon "repentance toward God, and faith toward our Lord Jesus Christ" (Acts 20:21). It is a gift that God offers to everyone, but individuals must receive it by repenting and trusting in Christ, or they will remain dead in their sins.

No one has biblical grounds to continue in sin, assuming that they are safe just because Jesus died on the cross. See 1 John 3:4–6.

the Lord Jesus shall raise up us also by Jesus, and shall present us with you.

15 For all things are for your sakes, that the abundant grace might through the thanksgiving of many redound to the glory of God.

16 For which cause we faint not; but though our outward man perish, yet the inward man is renewed day by day.

17 For our light affliction, which is but for a moment, works for us a far more exceeding and eternal weight of glory;

18 While we look not at the things which are seen, but at the things which are not seen: for the things which are seen are temporal; but the things which are not seen are eternal.

CHAPTER 5

FOR we know that if our earthly house of this tabernacle were dissolved, we have a building of God, an house not made with hands, eternal in the heavens.

2 For in this we groan, earnestly desiring to be clothed upon with our house which is from heaven:

3 If so be that being clothed we shall not be found naked.

4 For we that are in this tabernacle do groan, being burdened: not for that we would be unclothed, but clothed upon, that mortality might be swallowed up of life.

5 Now he that has wrought us for the selfsame thing is God, who also has given to us the earnest of the Spirit.

6 Therefore we are always confident, knowing that, whilst we are at home in the body, we are absent from the Lord:

7 (For we walk by faith, not by sight:)

8 We are confident, I say, and willing rather to be absent from the body, and to be present with the Lord.

9 Wherefore we labor, that, whether present or absent, we may be accepted of him.

10 For we must all appear before the judgment seat of Christ; that every one may receive the things done in his body, according to that he has done, whether it be good or bad.

11 *Knowing therefore the terror of the Lord, we persuade men; but we are made manifest to God; and I trust also are made manifest in your consciences.*

12 For we commend not ourselves again to you, but give you occasion to glory on our behalf, that you may have somewhat to answer them which glory in appearance, and not in heart.

13 For whether we be beside ourselves, it is to God: or whether we be sober, it is for your cause.

14 For the love of Christ constrains us; because we thus judge, that if one died

---

5:10 Judgment Day: For verses that warn of its reality, see 2 Thessalonians 1:7–9.

5:11 "We fear men so much because we fear God so little. One fear causes another. When man's terror scares you, turn your thoughts to the wrath of God." *William Gurnall*

for all, then were all dead:

15 And that he died for all, that they which live should not henceforth live to themselves, but to him which died for them, and rose again.

16 Wherefore henceforth know we no man after the flesh: yes, though we have known Christ after the flesh, yet now henceforth know we him no more.

17 Therefore if any man be in Christ, he is a new creature: old things are passed away; behold, all things are become new.

18 And all things are of God, who has reconciled us to himself by Jesus Christ, and has given to us the ministry of reconciliation;

19 *To wit, that God was in Christ, reconciling the world to himself, not imputing their trespasses to them; and has committed to us the word of reconciliation.*

20 Now then we are ambassadors for Christ, as though God did beseech you by us: we pray you in Christ's stead, be reconciled to God.

21 For he has made him to be sin for us, who knew no sin; that we might be made the righteousness of God in him.

CHAPTER 6

WE then, as workers together with him, beseech you also that you receive not the grace of God in vain.

2 (For he says, I have heard you in a time accepted, and in the day of salva-tion have I succoured you: behold, now is the accepted time; **behold, now is the day of salvation**.)

3 Giving no offence in any thing, that the ministry be not blamed:

4 But in all things approving ourselves as the ministers of God, in much patience, in afflictions, in necessities, in distresses,

5 In stripes, in imprisonments, in tumults, in labors, in watchings, in fastings;

6 By pureness, by knowledge, by longsuffering, by kindness, by the Holy Spirit, by love unfeigned,

7 By the word of truth, by the power of God, by the armor of righteousness on the right hand and on the left,

8 By honor and dishonor, by evil report and good report: as deceivers, and yet true;

9 As unknown, and yet well known; as dying, and, behold, we live; as chastened, and not killed;

10 As sorrowful, yet always rejoicing; as poor, yet making many rich; as having nothing, and yet possessing all things.

11 O you Corinthians, our mouth is open to you, our heart is enlarged.

12 You are not straitened in us, but you are straitened in your own bowels.

13 Now for a recompense in the same, (I speak as to my children,) be you also enlarged.

14 Be not unequally yoked together with

5:17 New birth—its necessity for salvation. See Titus 3:5. "It is easier to denature plutonium than to denature the evil spirit of man." *Albert Einstein*

5:21 "Christians are continually trying to *change* their lives; but God calls us to experience the ex-changed life. Christianity is not a self-improvement program. It isn't a reformation project. It is resurrection! It is new life! And it is expressed in terms of a total exchange of identity. Jesus Christ identified Himself with us in our death in order that we might be identified with Him in His resurrection. We give Christ all that we were—spiritually dead, guilty sinners—and Christ gives us all that He is—resurrected life, forgiveness, righteousness, acceptance." *Bob George, Classic Christianity* (See Galatians 2:20.)

6:1 "It's very sobering to find how many people whom I would presume to be saved feel little or no urgency regarding their spiritual condition, the condition of the church, or that of our nation …Whereas I once thought the battlefield was 'out there' among those rejecting Christ, I see things differently now…The front-line of the battle is in the hearts of God's people." *Rob Cummins* (quoted in *The Transforming Power of Fasting and Prayer* by Bill Bright)

SPRINGBOARDS FOR PREACHING AND WITNESSING

The Olympic High Diver

6:2

An Olympic gold-medalist high-diving champion was once plagued with insomnia. As he tossed and turned upon his bed, he began thinking deeply about the success he had attained in his field. He meditated on the gold medals he had won. To his dismay he realized that his success had not achieved what he had hoped. The excitement of winning, the photographers, the medals, and the fame had given him some sense of pleasure, but the fact of death awaiting him left him with a complete sense of futility.

He rose from the bed and made his way to his diving pool. Because of a full moon, he didn't even bother to turn the lights on. As he climbed the high diving board, he watched his shadow cast by the moonlight on the far wall. The routine had become so commonplace to him that he could confidently walk that board in the semi-darkness.

At the end of the diving board, he prepared for the dive. He placed his feet together, then pulled his arms up to a horizontal position. As he did so, his eyes caught a glimpse of his shadow on the far wall. All he could see was a perfect cross. His mind immediately raced back to his Sunday school days: "God commends his love toward us, in that, while we were yet sinners, Christ died for us" (Romans 5:8). All of a sudden he felt unclean as he considered the Commandments he had broken. The sinless Son of God had come to pay the penalty for his sins. With tears in his eyes, the great athlete turned around, slowly made his way down to the bottom of the diving board, fell to his knees, and yielded his life to Jesus Christ. He was able to go back to bed and sleep peacefully.

In the morning he arose with a new sense of forgiveness of his sins. He made his way back to the pool, but to his utter astonishment, *it was completely empty*. The previous evening, the caretaker had emptied it and was just beginning the process of refilling.

unbelievers: for what fellowship has righteousness with unrighteousness? and what communion has light with darkness?

15 And what concord has Christ with Belial? or what part has he that believes with an infidel?

16 And what agreement has the temple of God with idols? for you are the temple of the living God; as God has said, I will dwell in them, and walk in them; and I will be their God, and they shall be my people.

17 **Wherefore come out from among them, and be separate, says the Lord, and touch not the unclean thing; and I will receive you,**

18 **And will be a Father to you, and you shall be my sons and daughters,**

said the Lord Almighty.

CHAPTER 7

HAVING therefore these promises, dearly beloved, let us cleanse ourselves from all filthiness of the flesh and spirit, perfecting holiness in the fear of God.

2 Receive us; we have wronged no man, we have corrupted no man, we have defrauded no man.

3 I speak not this to condemn you: for I have said before, that you are in our hearts to die and live with you.

4 Great is my boldness of speech toward you, great is my glorying of you: I am filled with comfort, I am exceeding joyful in all our tribulation.

5 For, when we were come into Mace-

7:4 "Receive every inward and outward trouble, every disappointment, pain, uneasiness, temptation, darkness and desolation with both hands, as to a true opportunity and blessed occasion of dying to self and entering into a fuller fellowship with thy self-denying, suffering Savior." *John Wesley*

donia, our flesh had no rest, but we were troubled on every side; without were fightings, within were fears.

6 Nevertheless God, that comforts those that are cast down, comforted us by the coming of Titus;

7 And not by his coming only, but by the consolation wherewith he was comforted in you, when he told us your earnest desire, your mourning, your fervent mind toward me; so that I rejoiced the more.

> You must have, more or less, a distinct sense of the dreadful wrath of God and of the terrors of the judgment to come, or you will lack energy in your work and so lack one of the essentials of success.
>
> **CHARLES SPURGEON**

8 For though I made you sorry with a letter, I do not repent, though I did repent: for I perceive that the same epistle has made you sorry, though it were but for a season.

9 Now I rejoice, not that you were made sorry, but that you sorrowed to repentance: for you were made sorry after a godly manner, that you might receive damage by us in nothing.

10 For godly sorrow works repentance to salvation not to be repented of: but the sorrow of the world works death.

11 For behold this selfsame thing, that you sorrowed after a godly sort, what carefulness it wrought in you, yes, what clearing of yourselves, yes, what indignation, yes, what fear, yes, what vehement desire, yes, what zeal, yes, what revenge! In all things you have approved yourselves to be clear in this matter.

12 Wherefore, though I wrote to you, I did it not for his cause that had done the wrong, nor for his cause that suffered wrong, but that our care for you in the sight of God might appear to you.

13 Therefore we were comforted in your comfort: yes, and exceedingly the more joyed we for the joy of Titus, because his spirit was refreshed by you all.

14 For if I have boasted any thing to him of you, I am not ashamed; but as we spoke all things to you in truth, even so our boasting, which I made before Titus, is found a truth.

15 And his inward affection is more abundant toward you, whilst he remembered the obedience of you all, how with fear and trembling you received him.

16 I rejoice therefore that I have confidence in you in all things.

CHAPTER 8

MOREOVER, brethren, we make known to you the grace of God bestowed on the churches of Macedonia;

7:10 Godly sorrow. A pastor was once approached by his six-year-old son who said he wanted to "ask Jesus into his heart." The father, suspecting that the child lacked the knowledge of sin, told him that he could do so when he was older, then sent him off to bed.

A short time later, the boy got out of bed and asked his father if he could give his life to the Savior. The father still wasn't persuaded of the son's understanding, so, not wanting the child's salvation to be spurious, he sent him back to his room.

A third time the son returned. This time the father questioned him about whether he had broken any of the Ten Commandments. The young boy didn't think he had. When asked if he was a liar, the child said he wasn't. The father thought for a moment, then asked him how many lies he had to tell to be a liar. When it was established that one lie made a person a liar, the child thought for a moment, realized he had lied, and broke down in uncontrollable tears. When the father then asked if he wanted to "ask Jesus into his heart," the child *cringed* and shook his head. He was fearful because now he knew that he had sinned against God. At this point, he could do more than experimentally "ask Jesus into his heart." He could find a place of godly sorrow, repentance toward God, and faith toward our Lord Jesus Christ (Acts 20:21).

"If your sorrow is because of certain consequences which have come on your family because of your sin, this is remorse, not true repentance. If, on the other hand, you are grieved because you also sinned against God and His holy laws, then you are on the right road." (See 2 Corinthians 7:10.)

Billy Graham

2 How that in a great trial of affliction the abundance of their joy and their deep poverty abounded to the riches of their liberality.

3 For to their power, I bear record, yes, and beyond their power they were willing of themselves;

4 Praying us with much entreaty that we would receive the gift, and take upon us the fellowship of the ministering to the saints.

5 And this they did, not as we hoped, but first gave their own selves to the Lord, and to us by the will of God.

6 Insomuch that we desired Titus, that as he had begun, so he would also finish in you the same grace also.

7 Therefore, as you abound in every thing, in faith, and utterance, and knowledge, and in all diligence, and in your love to us, see that you abound in this grace also.

8 I speak not by commandment, but by occasion of the forwardness of others, and to prove the sincerity of your love.

9 For you know the grace of our Lord Jesus Christ, that, though he was rich, yet for your sakes he became poor, that you through his poverty might be rich.

10 And herein I give my advice: for this is expedient for you, who have begun before, not only to do, but also to be forward a year ago.

11 Now therefore perform the doing of it; that as there was a readiness to will, so there may be a performance also out of that which you have.

12 For if there be first a willing mind, it is accepted according to that a man has, and not according to that he has not.

13 For I mean not that other men be eased, and you burdened:

14 But by an equality, that now at this time your abundance may be a supply for their want, that their abundance also may be a supply for your want: that there may be equality:

15 As it is written, He that had gathered much had nothing over; and he that had gathered little had no lack.

16 But thanks be to God, which put the same earnest care into the heart of Titus for you.

17 For indeed he accepted the exhortation; but being more forward, of his own accord he went to you.

18 And we have sent with him the brother, whose praise is in the gospel throughout all the churches;

19 And not that only, but who was also chosen of the churches to travel with us with this grace, which is administered by us to the glory of the same Lord, and declaration of your ready mind:

20 Avoiding this, that no man should blame us in this abundance which is administered by us:

21 Providing for honest things, not only in the sight of the Lord, but also in the sight of men.

22 And we have sent with them our brother, whom we have oftentimes proved

diligent in many things, but now much more diligent, upon the great confidence which I have in you.

23 Whether any do inquire of Titus, he is my partner and fellow-helper concerning you: or our brethren be inquired of, they are the messengers of the churches, and the glory of Christ.

24 Wherefore show to them, and before the churches, the proof of your love, and of our boasting on your behalf.

CHAPTER 9

FOR as touching the ministering to the saints, it is superfluous for me to write to you:

2 For I know the forwardness of your mind, for which I boast of you to them of Macedonia, that Achaia was ready a year ago; and your zeal has provoked very many.

3 Yet have I sent the brethren, lest our boasting of you should be in vain in this behalf; that, as I said, you may be ready:

4 Lest haply if they of Macedonia come with me, and find you unprepared, we (that we say not, you) should be ashamed in this same confident boasting.

5 Therefore I thought it necessary to exhort the brethren, that they would go before to you, and make up beforehand your bounty, whereof you had notice before, that the same might be ready, as a matter of bounty, and not as of covetousness.

6 But this I say, He which sows sparingly shall reap also sparingly; and he which sows bountifully shall reap also bountifully.

7 Every man according as he purposes in his heart, so let him give; not grudgingly, or of necessity: for God loves a cheerful giver.

8 And God is able to make all grace abound toward you; that you always having all sufficiency in all things, may abound to every good work:

9 (As it is written, He has dispersed abroad; he has given to the poor: his righteousness remains for ever.

10 Now he that ministers seed to the sower both minister bread for your food, and multiply your seed sown, and increase the fruits of your righteousness;)

11 Being enriched in every thing to all bountifulness, which causes through us thanksgiving to God.

12 For the administration of this service not only supplies the want of the saints, but is abundant also by many thanksgivings to God;

13 Whiles by the experiment of this ministration they glorify God for your professed subjection to the gospel of Christ, and for your liberal distribution to them, and to all men;

14 And by their prayer for you, which long after you for the exceeding grace of God in you.

15 Thanks be to God for his unspeakable gift.

CHAPTER 10

NOW I Paul myself beseech you by the meekness and gentleness of Christ, who in presence am base among you, but being absent am bold toward you:

2 But I beseech you, that I may not be bold when I am present with that confidence, wherewith I think to be bold against some, which think of us as if we walked according to the flesh.

3 For though we walk in the flesh, we

9:2 "If you never have sleepless hours, if you never have weeping eyes, if your hearts never swell as if they would burst, you need not anticipate that you will be called zealous. You do not know the beginning of true zeal, for the foundation of Christian zeal lies in the heart. The heart must be heavy with grief and yet must beat high with holy ardor. The heart must be vehement in desire, panting continually for God's glory, or else we shall never attain to anything like the zeal which God would have us know." *Charles Spurgeon*

do not war after the flesh:

4 (For the weapons of our warfare are not carnal, but mighty through God to the pulling down of strong holds;)

5 Casting down imaginations, and every high thing that exalts itself against the knowledge of God, and bringing into captivity every thought to the obedience of Christ;

6 And having in a readiness to revenge all disobedience, when your obedience is fulfilled.

7 Do you look on things after the outward appearance? If any man trust to himself that he is Christ's, let him of himself think this again, that, as he is Christ's, even so are we Christ's.

8 For though I should boast somewhat more of our authority, which the Lord has given us for edification, and not for your destruction, I should not be ashamed:

9 That I may not seem as if I would terrify you by letters.

10 For his letters, say they, are weighty and powerful; but his bodily presence is weak, and his speech contemptible.

11 Let such an one think this, that, such as we are in word by letters when we are absent, such will we be also in deed when we are present.

12 For we dare not make ourselves of the number, or compare ourselves with some that commend themselves: but they measuring themselves by themselves, and comparing themselves among themselves, are not wise.

13 But we will not boast of things without our measure, but according to the measure of the rule which God has dis-tributed to us, a measure to reach even to you.

14 For we stretch not ourselves beyond our measure, as though we reached not to you: for we are come as far as to you also in preaching the gospel of Christ:

15 Not boasting of things without our measure, that is, of other men's labors; but having hope, when your faith is increased, that we shall be enlarged by you according to our rule abundantly,

16 To preach the gospel in the regions beyond you, and not to boast in another man's line of things made ready to our hand.

17 But he that glories, let him glory in the Lord.

18 For not he that commends himself is approved, but whom the Lord commends.

CHAPTER 11

WOULD to God you could bear with me a little in my folly: and indeed bear with me.

2 For I am jealous over you with godly jealousy: for I have espoused you to one husband, that I may present you as a chaste virgin to Christ.

3 But I fear, lest by any means, as the serpent beguiled Eve through his subtlety, so your minds should be corrupted from the simplicity that is in Christ.

4 For if he that comes preaches another Jesus, whom we have not preached, or if you receive another spirit, which you have not received, or another gospel, which you have not accepted, you might well bear with him.

5 For I suppose I was not a whit behind

11:3 Notice that Paul believed the Genesis account of the Fall. See 2 Peter 3:6 comment.

11:3 When the serpent deceived Eve, he cast doubt on God's Word, causing her to mistrust God Himself (Genesis 3:1–5). God said, "You shall surely die," but Eve chose to believe that God was deceitful. To partake of the fruit was an act of rebellion against the God who had not only given Adam and Eve life but had lavished His goodness upon them.

We must remember that Satan is the father of lies (John 8:44), and he usually uses enough of the truth to make the lie believable. Here Paul cautions believers to reject any message that differs from the true gospel as revealed in the Word of God. See Ephesians 4:18 and Luke 4:1–13 comments.

the very chiefest apostles.

6 But though I be rude in speech, yet not in knowledge; but we have been thoroughly made manifest among you in all things.

7 Have I committed an offence in abasing myself that you might be exalted, because I have preached to you the gospel of God freely?

8 I robbed other churches, taking wages of them, to do you service.

9 And when I was present with you, and wanted, I was chargeable to no man: for that which was lacking to me the brethren which came from Macedonia supplied: and in all things I have kept myself from being burdensome to you, and so will I keep myself.

10 As the truth of Christ is in me, no man shall stop me of this boasting in the regions of Achaia.

11 Wherefore? because I love you not? God knows.

12 But what I do, that I will do, that I may cut off occasion from them which desire occasion; that wherein they glory, they may be found even as we.

13 For such are false apostles, deceitful workers, transforming themselves into the apostles of Christ.

14 And no marvel; for Satan himself is transformed into an angel of light.

15 Therefore it is no great thing if his ministers also be transformed as the ministers of righteousness; whose end shall be according to their works.

16 I say again, Let no man think me a fool; if otherwise, yet as a fool receive me, that I may boast myself a little.

17 That which I speak, I speak it not after the Lord, but as it were foolishly, in this confidence of boasting.

18 Seeing that many glory after the flesh, I will glory also.

19 For you suffer fools gladly, seeing you yourselves are wise.

20 For you suffer, if a man bring you into bondage, if a man devour you, if a man take of you, if a man exalt himself, if a man smite you on the face.

"Thrice was I beaten with rods, once was I stoned, thrice I suffered shipwreck, a night and a day I have been in the deep..." (v. 25).

For other trials and tribulations Paul suffered for preaching the gospel, see John 17:14.

21 I speak as concerning reproach, as though we had been weak. Howbeit whereinsoever any is bold, (I speak foolishly,) I am bold also.

22 Are they Hebrews? so am I. Are they Israelites? so am I. Are they the seed of Abraham? so am I.

23 Are they ministers of Christ? (I speak as a fool) I am more; in labors more abundant, in stripes above measure, in prisons more frequent, in deaths oft.

24 Of the Jews five times received I forty stripes save one.

25 Thrice was I beaten with rods, once was I stoned, thrice I suffered shipwreck, a night and a day I have been in the deep;

26 In journeyings often, in perils of waters, in perils of robbers, in perils by mine own countrymen, in perils by the heathen, in perils in the city, in perils in the wilderness, in perils in the sea, in perils among false brethren;

27 In weariness and painfulness, in watchings often, in hunger and thirst, in fastings often, in cold and nakedness.

28 Beside those things that are without, that which comes upon me daily, the care of all the churches.

29 Who is weak, and I am not weak? who is offended, and I burn not?

30 If I must needs glory, I will glory of the things which concern mine infirmities.

31 The God and Father of our Lord Jesus Christ, which is blessed for evermore, knows that I lie not.

32 In Damascus the governor under Aretas the king kept the city of the Damascenes with a garrison, desirous to apprehend me:

33 And through a window in a basket was I let down by the wall, and escaped his hands.

CHAPTER 12

I T is not expedient for me doubtless to glory. I will come to visions and revelations of the Lord.

2 I knew a man in Christ above fourteen years ago, (whether in the body, I cannot tell; or whether out of the body, I cannot tell: God knows;) such an one caught up to the third heaven.

3 And I knew such a man, (whether in the body, or out of the body, I cannot tell: God knows;)

4 How that he was caught up into paradise, and heard unspeakable words, which it is not lawful for a man to utter.

5 Of such an one will I glory: yet of myself I will not glory, but in mine infirmities.

6 For though I would desire to glory, I shall not be a fool; for I will say the truth: but now I forbear, lest any man should think of me above that which he sees me to be, or that he hears of me.

7 And lest I should be exalted above measure through the abundance of the revelations, there was given to me a thorn in the flesh, the messenger of Satan to buffet me, lest I should be exalted above measure.

8 For this thing I besought the Lord thrice, that it might depart from me.

9 And he said to me, My grace is sufficient for you: for my strength is made perfect in weakness. Most gladly therefore will I rather glory in my infirmities, that the power of Christ may rest upon me.

10 Therefore I take pleasure in infirmities, in reproaches, in necessities, in persecutions, in distresses for Christ's sake: for when I am weak, then am I strong.

11 I am become a fool in glorying; you have compelled me: for I ought to have been commended of you: for in nothing am I behind the very chiefest apostles, though I be nothing.

12 Truly the signs of an apostle were wrought among you in all patience, in signs, and wonders, and mighty deeds.

> We spend our entire lives acting out our concept of God.
> **JACK TAYLOR**

13 For what is it wherein you were inferior to other churches, except it be that I myself was not burdensome to you? forgive me this wrong.

14 Behold, the third time I am ready to come to you; and I will not be burdensome to you: for I seek not yours, but you: for the children ought not to lay up for the parents, but the parents for the children.

15 And I will very gladly spend and be spent for you; though the more abundantly I love you, the less I be loved.

16 But be it so, I did not burden you: nevertheless, being crafty, I caught you with guile.

17 Did I make a gain of you by any of them whom I sent to you?

12:9 "God whispers to us in our pleasures, speaks to us in our conscience, but shouts in our pains: It is His megaphone to rouse a deaf world." *C. S. Lewis, The Problem of Pain*

12:11 "God creates out of nothing. Therefore until man is nothing, God can make nothing out of him." *Martin Luther*

12:15 "You have nothing to do but to save souls. Therefore spend and be spent in this work." *John Wesley*

18 I desired Titus, and with him I sent a brother. Did Titus make a gain of you? walked we not in the same spirit? walked we not in the same steps?

19 Again, do you think that we excuse ourselves to you? we speak before God in Christ: but we do all things, dearly beloved, for your edifying.

20 For I fear, lest, when I come, I shall not find you such as I would, and that I shall be found to you such as you would not: lest there be debates, envyings, wraths, strifes, backbitings, whisperings, swellings, tumults:

21 And lest, when I come again, my God will humble me among you, and that I shall bewail many which have sinned already, and have not repented of the uncleanness and fornication and lasciviousness which they have committed.

· · · · · ·

To find out where the races came from, see Acts 17:26 comment.

· · · · · ·

CHAPTER 13

THIS is the third time I am coming to you. In the mouth of two or three witnesses shall every word be established.

2 I told you before, and foretell you, as if I were present, the second time; and being absent now I write to them which heretofore have sinned, and to all other, that, if I come again, I will not spare:

3 Since you seek a proof of Christ speaking in me, which toward you is not weak, but is mighty in you.

4 For though he was crucified through weakness, yet he lives by the power of God. For we also are weak in him, but we shall live with him by the power of God toward you.

5 Examine yourselves, whether you be in the faith; prove your own selves. Do you not know your own selves, how that Jesus Christ is in you, except you be reprobates?

6 But I trust that you shall know that we are not reprobates.

7 Now I pray to God that you do no evil; not that we should appear approved, but that you should do that which is honest, though we be as reprobates.

8 For we can do nothing against the truth, but for the truth.

9 For we are glad, when we are weak, and you are strong: and this also we wish, even your perfection.

10 Therefore I write these things being absent, lest being present I should use sharpness, according to the power which the Lord has given me to edification, and not to destruction.

11 Finally, brethren, farewell. Be perfect, be of good comfort, be of one mind, live in peace; and the God of love and peace shall be with you.

12 Greet one another with an holy kiss.

13 All the saints salute you.

14 The grace of the Lord Jesus Christ, and the love of God, and the communion of the Holy Spirit, be with you all. Amen.

13:3 The Christian life. "The Christian life is more than difficult; it is humanly impossible to live. Only Jesus Christ can live it through you as He dwells within you. The Christian life is not a person trying to imitate Christ; rather, it is Christ imparting His life to and living His life through the person. The Christian life is not what you do for Him; it is what He does for and through you. He wants to think with your mind, express Himself through your emotions, and speak through your voice, though you may be unconscious of it." *Dr. Bill Bright*

13:5 See 1 John 4:8 comment.

Galatians

CHAPTER 1

PAUL, an apostle, (not of men, neither by man, but by Jesus Christ, and God the Father, who raised him from the dead;)

2 And all the brethren which are with me, to the churches of Galatia:

3 Grace be to you and peace from God the Father, and from our Lord Jesus Christ,

4 Who gave himself for our sins, that he might deliver us from this present evil world, according to the will of God and our Father:

5 To whom be glory for ever and ever. Amen.

6 I marvel that you are so soon removed from him that called you into the grace of Christ to another gospel:

7 Which is not another; but there be some that trouble you, and would pervert the gospel of Christ.

8 But though we, or an angel from heaven, preach any other gospel to you than that which we have preached to you, let him be accursed.

9 As we said before, so say I now again, If any man preach any other gospel to you than that you have received, let him be accursed.

10 For do I now persuade men, or God? or do I seek to please men? for if I yet pleased men, I should not be the servant of Christ.

11 But I certify you, brethren, that the gospel which was preached of me is not

---

1:3 Many who don't know the Savior claim to have made their "peace with God." But there is no peace with God without accepting the grace of God, which is given only to those who repent.

1:4 Jesus willingly "gave" Himself for the sins of the world. No one took His life from Him.

1:6 These are strong words from the same apostle who wrote the "love chapter" of 1 Corinthians 13. His words reveal his passion for the truth and his knowledge of the consequences of preaching "a different gospel." This should make the gospel preacher strive to make sure his hearers understand that salvation is by grace alone. Any message saying that we must add anything to the work of the cross to be saved is another gospel.

"Satan, the God of all dissension, stirreth up daily new sects, and last of all, which of all other I should never have foreseen or once suspected, he has raised up a sect such as teach...that men should not be terrified by the Law, but gently exhorted by the preaching of the grace of Christ." *Martin Luther*

1:8 "Avoid a sugared gospel as you would shun sugar of lead. Seek that gospel which rips up and tears and cuts and wounds and hacks and even kills, for that is the gospel that makes alive again. And when you have found it, give good heed to it. Let it enter into your inmost being. As the rains soaks into the ground, so pray the Lord to let His gospel soak into your soul." *Charles Spurgeon*

after man.

12 For I neither received it of man, neither was I taught it, but by the revelation of Jesus Christ.

13 For you have heard of my conversation in time past in the Jews' religion, how that beyond measure I persecuted the church of God, and wasted it:

14 And profited in the Jews' religion above many my equals in mine own nation, being more exceedingly zealous of the traditions of my fathers.

15 But when it pleased God, who separated me from my mother's womb, and called me by his grace,

· · · · · ·

Does God "hate the sin but love the sinner"? See 1 Timothy 1:8–10 "Questions & Objections."

· · · · · ·

16 To reveal his Son in me, that I might preach him among the heathen; immediately I conferred not with flesh and blood:

17 Neither went I up to Jerusalem to them which were apostles before me; but I went into Arabia, and returned again to Damascus.

18 Then after three years I went up to Jerusalem to see Peter, and abode with him fifteen days.

19 But other of the apostles saw I none, save James the Lord's brother.

20 Now the things which I write to you, behold, before God, I lie not.

21 Afterwards I came into the regions of Syria and Cilicia;

22 And was unknown by face to the churches of Judea which were in Christ:

23 But they had heard only, That he which persecuted us in times past now preaches the faith which once he destroyed.

24 And they glorified God in me.

CHAPTER 2

THEN fourteen years after I went up again to Jerusalem with Barnabas, and took Titus with me also.

2 And I went up by revelation, and communicated to them that gospel which I preach among the Gentiles, but privately to them which were of reputation, lest by any means I should run, or had run, in vain.

3 But neither Titus, who was with me, being a Greek, was compelled to be circumcised:

4 And that because of false brethren unawares brought in, who came in privately to spy out our liberty which we have in Christ Jesus, that they might bring us into bondage:

5 To whom we gave place by subjection, no, not for an hour; that the truth of the gospel might continue with you.

6 But of these who seemed to be somewhat, (whatsoever they were, it makes no matter to me: God accepts no man's person:) for they who seemed to be somewhat in conference added nothing to me:

7 But contrariwise, when they saw that the gospel of the uncircumcision was committed to me, as the gospel of the circumcision was to Peter;

8 (For he that wrought effectually in Peter to the apostleship of the circumcision, the same was mighty in me toward the Gentiles:)

9 And when James, Cephas, and John, who seemed to be pillars, perceived the grace that was given to me, they gave to me and Barnabas the right hands of fellowship; that we should go to the heathen, and they to the circumcision.

10 Only they would that we should re-

1:16 God also wants to reveal His Son in us. We can do this by following in Paul's steps and preaching Jesus Christ and Him crucified.

2:4 The Bible speaks of false brethren, false apostles, false prophets, false teachers, and false conversion (Mark 4:3–20).

member the poor; the same which I also was forward to do.

11 But when Peter was come to Antioch, I withstood him to the face, because he was to be blamed.

12 For before that certain came from James, he did eat with the Gentiles: but when they were come, he withdrew and separated himself, fearing them which were of the circumcision.

13 And the other Jews dissembled likewise with him; insomuch that Barnabas also was carried away with their dissimulation.

14 But when I saw that they walked not uprightly according to the truth of the gospel, I said to Peter before them all, If you, being a Jew, live after the manner of Gentiles, and not as do the Jews, why compel the Gentiles to live as do the Jews?

15 We who are Jews by nature, and not sinners of the Gentiles,

16 Knowing that a man is not justified by the works of the law, but by the faith of Jesus Christ, even we have believed in Jesus Christ, that we might be justified by the faith of Christ, and not by the works of the law: for by the works of the law shall no flesh be justified.

17 But if, while we seek to be justified by Christ, we ourselves also are found sinners, is therefore Christ the minister of sin? God forbid.

18 For if I build again the things which I destroyed, I make myself a transgressor.

THE FUNCTION OF THE LAW

2:19 The Law's function is to bring death to the sinner in the same way civil law brings capital punishment to a guilty murderer. However, our offense was paid for by the Savior, leaving us free to receive the pardon of the gospel. The Law has no demand on the Christian.

19 For I through the law am dead to the law, that I might live to God.

20 I am crucified with Christ: nevertheless I live; yet not I, but Christ lives in me: and the life which I now live in the flesh I live by the faith of the Son of God, who loved me, and gave himself for me.

21 I do not frustrate the grace of God: for if righteousness come by the law, then Christ is dead in vain.

CHAPTER 3

O FOOLISH Galatians, who has bewitched you, that you should not obey the truth, before whose eyes Jesus Christ has been evidently set forth, crucified among you?

2 This only would I learn of you, Did you receive the Spirit by the works of the law, or by the hearing of faith?

3 Are you so foolish? having begun in the Spirit, are you now made perfect by the flesh?

4 Have you suffered so many things in vain? if it be yet in vain.

2:10 Good works are a legitimate form of evangelism. When the Salvation Army first began, their message was "soap, soup, and salvation." See Titus 3:8.

2:16 For those trusting in good works, see Galatians 3:11. "Neither the Jewish Law of ten commands nor its law of ceremonies was ever intended to save anybody. By a set of pictures it set forth the way of salvation, but it was not itself the way. It was a map, not a country; a model of the road, not the road itself." *Charles Spurgeon*

2:20 Dying to self. "The path toward humility is death to self. When self is dead, humility has been perfected. Jesus humbled Himself unto death, and by His example the way is opened for us to follow. A dead man or woman does not react to an offense. The truth is, if we become offended by the words of others, then death to self has not been finished. When we humble ourselves despite injustice and there is perfect peace of heart, then death to self is complete. Death is the seed, while humility is the ripened fruit." *Alice Smith, Beyond the Veil: God's Call to Intimate Intercession* (See also Galatians 5:24.)

5 He therefore that ministers to you the Spirit, and works miracles among you, does he do it by the works of the law, or by the hearing of faith?

6 Even as Abraham believed God, and it was accounted to him for righteousness.

7 Know therefore that they which are of faith, the same are the children of Abraham.

8 And the scripture, foreseeing that God would justify the heathen through faith, preached before the gospel to Abraham, saying, In you shall all nations be blessed.

9 So then they which be of faith are blessed with faithful Abraham.

10 For as many as are of the works of the law are under the curse: for it is written, Cursed is every one that continues not in all things which are written in the book of the law to do them.

11 But that no man is justified by the law in the sight of God, it is evident: for, The just shall live by faith.

12 And the law is not of faith: but, The man that does them shall live in them.

13 **Christ has redeemed us from the curse of the law, being made a curse for us: for it is written, Cursed is every one that hangs on a tree:**

14 That the blessing of Abraham might come on the Gentiles through Jesus Christ; that we might receive the promise of the Spirit through faith.

15 Brethren, I speak after the manner of men; Though it be but a man's covenant, yet if it be confirmed, no man disannuls, or adds thereto.

16 Now to Abraham and his seed were the promises made. He said not, And to seeds, as of many; but as of one, And to your seed, which is Christ.

17 And this I say, that the covenant, that was confirmed before of God in Christ, the law, which was four hundred and thirty years after, cannot disannul, that it should make the promise of none effect.

18 For if the inheritance be of the law, it is no more of promise: but God gave it to Abraham by promise.

19 Wherefore then serve the law? It was added because of transgressions, till the seed should come to whom the promise was made; and it was ordained by angels in the hand of a mediator.

20 Now a mediator is not a mediator of one, but God is one.

21 Is the law then against the promises of God? God forbid: for if there had been a law given which could have given life, verily righteousness should have been by the law.

22 But the scripture has concluded all under sin, that the promise by faith of Jesus Christ might be given to them that believe.

23 But before faith came, we were kept under the law, shut up to the faith which should afterwards be revealed.

24 Wherefore the law was our schoolmaster to bring us to Christ, that we might be justified by faith.

25 But after that faith is come, we are no longer under a schoolmaster.

26 For you are all the children of God by faith in Christ Jesus.

27 For as many of you as have been baptized into Christ have put on Christ.

28 There is neither Jew nor Greek, there is neither bond nor free, there is neither male nor female: for you are all one in Christ Jesus.

29 And if you be Christ's, then are you Abraham's seed, and heirs according to the promise.

3:10 Those who try to keep the Law are usually ignorant of its holy demands. It requires perfection in thought, word, and deed. The proclamation of the spiritual nature of the Law (that God requires truth in the inward parts) strips a sinner of self-righteousness. See James 2:10 comment.

3:11 No one will earn their way into heaven by keeping the Ten Commandments. They were not given for that purpose. The Law is like a mirror. All it can do is reflect what we are in truth—unclean and desperately in need of cleansing. For those trusting in good works, see Ephesians 2:8,9.

3:19   *What is the Purpose of the Law?*

By Charles Spurgeon

"Beloved, the Law is a great deluge which would have drowned the world with worse than the water of Noah's flood; it is a great fire which would have burned the earth with a destruction worse than that which fell on Sodom; it is a stern angel with a sword, athirst for blood, and winged to slay; it is a great destroyer sweeping down the nations; it is the great messenger of God's vengeance sent into the world. Apart from the gospel of Jesus Christ, the Law is nothing but the condemning voice of God thundering against mankind. 'Wherefore then serveth the Law?' seems a very natural question. Can the Law be of any benefit to man? Can the Judge who puts on a black cap and condemns us all, this Lord Chief Justice Law, can he help in salvation? Yes, he can; and you shall see how he does it, if God shall help us while we preach.

"Now, if you are unrepentant, you have never obeyed your Maker. Every step you have taken has added to your crimes. When God has fanned your heaving lungs, you have breathed out your poisonous breath in rebellion against Him. How should God feel toward you? You have walked over the principles of righteousness with your unsanctified feet. You have lifted up your hands, filled with poisoned weapons, against the throne of the Almighty. You have spurned every principle of right, of love and of happiness. You are the enemy of God, the foe of man and a child of the devil in league with hell. Ought not God hate you with all His heart?

"Yet, in the midst of your rebellion He has borne with you. All this you have done, and He has kept silent. Dare you think that He will never reprove?

"Lo, I see, the Law given upon Mount Sinai. The very hill doth quake with fear. Lightnings and thunders are the attendants of those dreadful syllables which make the hearts of Israel to melt. Sinai seemeth altogether on the smoke. The Lord came from Paran, and the Holy One from Mount Sinai; 'He came with ten thousands of his saints.' Out of His mouth went a fiery Law for them. It was a dread Law even when it was given, and since then from that Mount of Sinai an awful lava of ven-geance has run down, to deluge, to destroy, to burn, and to consume the whole human race, if it had not been that Jesus Christ had stemmed its awful torrent and bidden its waves of fire be still. If you could see the world without Christ in it, simply under the Law, you would see a world in ruins, a world with God's black seal put upon it, stamped and sealed for condemnation; you would see men, who, if they knew their condition, would have their hands on their loins and be groaning all their days—you would see men and women condemned, lost, and ruined; and in the uttermost regions you would see the pit that is digged for the wicked, into which the whole earth must have been cast if the Law had its way, apart from the gospel of Jesus Christ our Redeemer.

"My hearer, does not the Law of God convince you of sin? Under the hand of God's Spirit does it not make you feel that you have been guilty, that you deserve to be lost, that you have incurred the fierce anger of God? Look here: have you not broken these Ten Commandments; even in the letter, have you not broken them? Who is there among you who has always honored his mother and father? Who is there among you who has always spoken the truth? Have we not sometimes borne false witness against our neighbors? Is there one person here who has not made to himself another god, and loved himself, or his business, or his friends, more than he has Jehovah, the God of the whole earth? Which of you has not coveted his neighbor's house, or his manservant, or his ox, or his donkey? We are all guilty with regard to every letter of the Law; we have all of us transgressed the Commandments.

"And if we really understood these Commandments, and felt that they condemned us, they would have this useful influence on us of showing us our danger, and so leading us to fly to Christ. But, my hearers, does not this Law condemn you, because even if you should say you have not broken the letter of it, yet you have violated the spirit of it. What, though you have never killed, yet we are told, he that is angry with his brother is a murderer.

(continued on next page)

(3:19 continued)

"This Law does not only mean what it says in words, but it has deep things hidden in its bowels. It says, 'Thou shall not commit adultery,' but it means as Jesus has it, 'He that looketh on a woman to lust after her has committed adultery with her already in his heart.' It says, 'Thou shall not take the name of the Lord thy God in vain.' It meaneth that we should reverence God in every place, and have His fear before our eyes, and should always pay respect to His ordinances and evermore walk in His fear and love. My brethren, surely there is not one here so foolhardy in self-righteousness as to say, 'I am innocent.' The spirit of the Law condemns us. And this is its useful property; it humbles us, makes us know we are guilty, and so we are led to receive the Savior."

THE FUNCTION OF THE LAW

3:24 "Lower the Law and you dim the light by which man perceives his guilt; this is a very serious loss to the sinner rather than a gain; for it lessens the likelihood of his conviction and conversion. I say you have deprived the gospel of its ablest auxiliary [its most powerful weapon] when you have set aside the Law. You have taken away from it the schoolmaster that is to bring men to Christ...*They will never accept grace till they tremble before a just and holy Law.* Therefore the Law serves a most necessary purpose, and it must not be removed from its place." *Charles Spurgeon*

CHAPTER 4

NOW I say, That the heir, as long as he is a child, differs nothing from a servant, though he be lord of all;

2 But is under tutors and governors until the time appointed of the father.

3 Even so we, when we were children, were in bondage under the elements of the world:

4 But when the fulness of the time was come, God sent forth his Son, made of a woman, made under the law,

5 To redeem them that were under the law, that we might receive the adoption of sons.

6 And because you are sons, God has sent forth the Spirit of his Son into your hearts, crying, Abba, Father.

7 Wherefore you are no more a servant, but a son; and if a son, then an heir of God through Christ.

8 Howbeit then, when you knew not God, you did service to them which by nature are no gods.

9 But now, after that you have known God, or rather are known of God, how can you turn again to the weak and beggarly elements, whereunto you desire again to be in bondage?

10 You observe days, and months, and times, and years.

11 I am afraid of you, lest I have bestowed upon you labor in vain.

12 Brethren, I beseech you, be as I am; for I am as you are: you have not injured me at all.

13 You know how through infirmity of the flesh I preached the gospel to you at

---

3:21 "Although the Law disclosed and increases sin, it is still not against the promises of God but is, in fact, for them. For in its true and proper work and purpose it humbles a man and prepares him—if he uses the Law correctly—to yearn and seek for grace." *Martin Luther*

4:5 There is no difference between Jew and Gentile. Both must be put "under the Law" first, before the gospel can redeem them. Why would any sinner see any need to be redeemed, if he didn't first see himself as a lawbreaker? Until each Commandment is applied to the conscience, sinners will not see sin as being "exceedingly sinful." The Law must also be preached in conjunction with future punishment. It has been well observed that "Law without consequence is nothing but good advice." The world must be made to understand that God is going to judge the world "in righteousness."

QUESTIONS & OBJECTIONS

"How can you know that you are saved?"

A two-year-old boy was once staring at a heater, fascinated by its bright orange glow. His father saw him and warned, "Don't touch that heater, son. It may look pretty, but it's hot." The little boy believed him, and moved away from the heater.

Some time later, after his father had left the room, the boy thought, "I wonder if it really is hot." He then reached out to touch it and see for himself. The second his flesh burned, he stopped *believing* it was hot; he now *knew* it was hot! He had moved out of the realm of *belief* into the realm of *experience*.

Christians believed in God's existence before their conversion. However, when they obeyed the Word of God, turned from their sins, and embraced Jesus Christ, they stopped merely believing. The moment they reached out and touched the heater bar of God's mercy, they moved out of *belief* into the realm of *experience*. This experience is so radical, Jesus referred to it as being "born again."

The Bible says that those who don't know God are spiritually dead (Ephesians 2:1; 4:18). We are born with physical life, but not spiritual life. Picture unbelievers as corpses walking around who, by repenting and placing their faith in Christ, receive His very life. There is a radical difference between a corpse and a living, breathing human, just as there is when sinners pass from spiritual death to life. The apostle Paul said if you are "in Christ," you are a brand new creature (2 Corinthians 5:17).

Those who now have God's Spirit living in them will love what He loves and desire to do His will; they will have a hunger for His Word, a love for other believers, and a burden for the lost. The Holy Spirit also confirms in their spirit that they are now children of God (Romans 8:16). Those who believe on the name of the Son of God can *know* that they have eternal life (1 John 5:12,13).

Paul wrote to the church at Corinth, "My speech and my preaching were not with enticing words of man's wisdom, but in demonstration of the Spirit and of power: that your faith should not stand in the wisdom of men, but in the power of God" (1 Corinthians 2:4,5). What Paul was saying was, "I deliberately didn't talk you into your faith, but I let God's power transform you." He didn't reach them through an intellectual assent, but through the realm of personal experience.

Suppose two people—a heater manufacturer and a skin specialist—walked into the room just after that child had burned his hand on the heater. Both assured the boy that he couldn't possibly have been burned. But all the experts, theories, and arguments in the world will not dissuade that boy, because of his experience.

Those who have been transformed by God's power need never fear scientific or other arguments, because the man with an experience is not at the mercy of a man with an argument. "For our gospel came not to you in word only, but also in power, and in the Holy Spirit, and in much assurance..." (1 Thessalonians 1:5).

the first.

14 And my temptation which was in my flesh you despised not, nor rejected; but received me as an angel of God, even as Christ Jesus.

15 Where is then the blessedness you spoke of? for I bear you record, that, if it had been possible, you would have plucked out your own eyes, and have given them to me.

16 Am I therefore become your enemy, because I tell you the truth?

17 They zealously affect you, but not well; yes, they would exclude you, that you might affect them.

18 But it is good to be zealously affect-

ed always in a good thing, and not only when I am present with you.

19 My little children, of whom I travail in birth again until Christ be formed in you,

20 I desire to be present with you now, and to change my voice; for I stand in doubt of you.

21 Tell me, you that desire to be under the law, do you not hear the law?

22 For it is written, that Abraham had two sons, the one by a bondmaid, the other by a freewoman.

> The preacher's work is to throw sinners down in utter helplessness, so that they may be compelled to look up to Him who alone can help them.
>
> **CHARLES SPURGEON**

23 But he who was of the bondwoman was born after the flesh; but he of the freewoman was by promise.

24 Which things are an allegory: for these are the two covenants; the one from the mount Sinai, which genders to bondage, which is Agar.

25 For this Agar is mount Sinai in Arabia, and answers to Jerusalem which now is, and is in bondage with her children.

26 But Jerusalem which is above is free, which is the mother of us all.

27 For it is written, Rejoice, you barren that bear not; break forth and cry, you that travail not: for the desolate has many more children than she which has an husband.

28 Now we, brethren, as Isaac was, are the children of promise.

29 But as then he that was born after the flesh persecuted him that was born after the Spirit, even so it is now.

30 Nevertheless what do the Scriptures say? Cast out the bondwoman and her son: for the son of the bondwoman shall not be heir with the son of the free-

woman.

31 So then, brethren, we are not children of the bondwoman, but of the free.

CHAPTER 5

STAND fast therefore in the liberty wherewith Christ has made us free, and be not entangled again with the yoke of bondage.

2 Behold, I Paul say to you, that if you be circumcised, Christ shall profit you nothing.

3 For I testify again to every man that is circumcised, that he is a debtor to do the whole law.

4 Christ is become of no effect to you, whosoever of you are justified by the law; you are fallen from grace.

5 For we through the Spirit wait for the hope of righteousness by faith.

6 For in Jesus Christ neither circumcision avails anything, nor uncircumcision; but faith which works by love.

7 You did run well; who did hinder you that you should not obey the truth?

8 This persuasion comes not of him that calls you.

9 A little leaven leavens the whole lump.

10 I have confidence in you through the Lord, that you will be none otherwise minded: but he that troubles you shall bear his judgment, whosoever he be.

11 And I, brethren, if I yet preach circumcision, why do I yet suffer persecution? then is the offence of the cross ceased.

12 I would they were even cut off which trouble you.

13 For, brethren, you have been called to liberty; only use not liberty for an occasion to the flesh, but by love serve one another.

14 For all the law is fulfilled in one word, even in this; You shall love your neighbour as yourself.

15 But if you bite and devour one an-

5:11 The cross will cause offense to the proud and self-righteous—those whose understanding is darkened. To those who understand their need of grace (the humble), it is a tree of life.

QUESTIONS & OBJECTIONS

5:14 "I believe I will go to heaven because I live by the Golden Rule."

Much of the world knows the Golden Rule simply as "do unto others as you would have them do unto you" (see Luke 6:31). According to this verse, if we can live by this rule and love our neighbor as much as we love ourselves, we fulfill the Law. Ask those who claim to do this if they have ever lied, stolen, hated, or looked with lust. If they have broken any of these Commandments, then they haven't loved those they have lied to, stolen from, etc. This will show them that they have *violated* the Golden Rule. They are under God's wrath (John 3:36), desperately needing the Savior's cleansing blood.

other, take heed that you be not consumed one of another.

16 This I say then, Walk in the Spirit, and you shall not fulfill the lust of the flesh.

17 For the flesh lusts against the Spirit, and the Spirit against the flesh: and these are contrary the one to the other: so that you cannot do the things that you would.

18 But if you be led of the Spirit, you are not under the law.

19 Now the works of the flesh are manifest, which are these; Adultery, fornication, uncleanness, lasciviousness,

20 Idolatry, witchcraft, hatred, variance, emulations, wrath, strife, seditions, heresies,

21 Envyings, murders, drunkenness, revellings, and such like: of the which I tell you before, as I have also told you in time past, that they which do such things shall not inherit the kingdom of God.

5:16 Ten Ways to Break the Stronghold of Pornography

1 Would you ever take pornography to church and look at it during worship? You may as well, because God is just as present in your bedroom as He is in the church building.

2 Face the fact that you may not be saved. Examine yourself to ensure that Christ is living in you (2 Corinthians 13:5). See Romans 6:11–22; 8:1–14; Ephesians 5:3–8.

3 Realize that when you give yourself to pornography, you are committing adultery (Matthew 5:27,28).

4 Grasp the serious nature of your sin. Jesus said that it would be better for you to be blind and go to heaven, than for your eye to cause you to sin and end up in hell (Matthew 5:29).

5 Those who profess to be Christians yet give themselves to pornographic material evidently lack the fear of God (Proverbs 16:6). Cultivate the fear of God by reading Proverbs 2:1–5.

6 Read Psalm 51 and make it your own prayer.

7 Memorize James 1:14,15 and 1 Corinthians 10:13. Follow Jesus' example (Matthew 4:3–11) and quote the Word of God when you are tempted (see Ephesians 6:12–20).

8 Make no provision for your flesh (Romans 13:14; 1 Peter 2:11). Get rid of every access to pornographic material—the Internet, printed literature, TV, videos, and movies. Stop feeding the fire.

9 Guard your heart with all diligence (Proverbs 4:23). Don't let the demonic realm have access to your thought-life. If you give yourself to it, you will become its slave (Romans 6:16). Read the Bible daily, without fail. As you submit to God, the devil will flee (James 4:7,8).

10 The next time temptation comes, do fifty push-ups, then fifty sit-ups. If you are still burning, repeat the process (see 1 Corinthians 9:27).

22 But the fruit of the Spirit is love, joy, peace, longsuffering, gentleness, goodness, faith,

23 Meekness, temperance: against such there is no law.

24 And they that are Christ's have crucified the flesh with the affections and lusts.

25 If we live in the Spirit, let us also walk in the Spirit.

26 Let us not be desirous of vain glory, provoking one another, envying one another.

CHAPTER 6

BRETHREN, if a man be overtaken in a fault, you which are spiritual, restore such an one in the spirit of meekness; considering yourself, lest you also be tempted.

2 Bear one another's burdens, and so fulfil the law of Christ.

3 For if a man think himself to be something, when he is nothing, he deceives himself.

4 But let every man prove his own work, and then shall he have rejoicing in himself alone, and not in another.

5 For every man shall bear his own burden.

6 Let him that is taught in the word communicate to him that teaches in all good things.

7 Be not deceived; God is not mocked: for whatsoever a man sows, that shall he also reap.

8 For he that sows to his flesh shall of the flesh reap corruption; but he that sows to the Spirit shall of the Spirit reap life everlasting.

9 And let us not be weary in well doing: for in due season we shall reap, if we faint not.

10 As we have therefore opportunity, let us do good to all men, especially to them who are of the household of faith.

11 You see how large a letter I have written to you with mine own hand.

12 As many as desire to make a fair show in the flesh, they constrain you to be circumcised; only lest they should suffer persecution for the cross of Christ.

13 For neither they themselves who are circumcised keep the law; but desire to have you circumcised, that they may glory in your flesh.

14 But God forbid that I should glory, save in the cross of our Lord Jesus Christ, by whom the world is crucified to me, and I to the world.

15 For in Christ Jesus neither circumcision avails anything, nor uncircumcision, but a new creature.

16 And as many as walk according to this rule, peace be on them, and mercy, and upon the Israel of God.

17 From henceforth let no man trouble me: for I bear in my body the marks of the Lord Jesus.

18 Brethren, the grace of our Lord Jesus Christ be with your spirit. Amen.

5:19 Men will often deceive themselves by believing that the Ten Commandments condemn only adultery, leaving them free to have sex outside the bonds of marriage. However, the Law condemns all unlawful sex. First Timothy 1:8–10 tells us that the Law was also made for fornicators (whoremongers).

6:7 "Many people think they can break the Ten Commandments right and left and get by with it. That reminds me of the whimsical story of the man who jumped off the Empire State Building in New York City. As he went sailing by the fiftieth floor, a man looked out the window and said to him, 'Well, how is it?' The falling man replied, 'So far, so good.' That is not where the law of gravity enforces itself. Fifty more floors down and the man will find out, 'So far, not so good.' The interesting thing is that a law must be enforced to be a law and therefore God says in Ezekiel 18:4, 'The soul that sins, it shall die.' The Law must be enforced and the breaker of the Law must pay the penalty." *J. Vernon McGee*

6:14 "All heaven is interested in the cross of Christ, all hell terribly afraid of it, while men are the only beings who more or less ignore its meaning." *Oswald Chambers*

EPHESIANS

Ephesians

CHAPTER 1

P AUL, an apostle of Jesus Christ by the will of God, to the saints which are at Ephesus, and to the faithful in Christ Jesus:

2 Grace be to you, and peace, from God our Father, and from the Lord Jesus Christ.

3 Blessed be the God and Father of our Lord Jesus Christ, who has blessed us with all spiritual blessings in heavenly places in Christ:

4 According as he has chosen us in him before the foundation of the world, that we should be holy and without blame before him in love:

5 Having predestinated us to the adoption of children by Jesus Christ to himself, according to the good pleasure of his will,

6 To the praise of the glory of his grace, wherein he has made us accepted in the beloved.

7 In whom we have redemption through his blood, the forgiveness of sins, according to the riches of his grace;

8 Wherein he has abounded toward us in all wisdom and prudence;

9 Having made known to us the mystery of his will, according to his good pleasure which he has purposed in himself:

10 That in the dispensation of the fulness of times he might gather together in one all things in Christ, both which are in heaven, and which are on earth; even in him:

11 In whom also we have obtained an in-

1:1 Sainthood. There are those who believe that someone must be dead for many years, and have performed miracles, before he can be "exalted" to sainthood. Not so. Paul is writing to *living* people and, as he often begins his letters, he refers to them as "saints." The word "saint" comes from the same Hebrew root as "sanctified" and "holy," which mean "set apart." The moment we are born again, God sets us apart from the world (sanctifies us) for His use. In addressing the Corinthian church, Paul writes: "to them that are *sanctified* in Christ Jesus, called to be *saints*, with *all* that in every place call upon the name of Jesus Christ our Lord" (1 Corinthians 1:2). A saint is not someone who has lived a "holy" life, but a forgiven sinner who has called upon the name of Jesus and been made righteous by the grace of God.

1:9 The will of God is no longer a mystery ("having *made* known..."). The next verse makes His will clear: He wants to gather the redeemed together. We can work within His will by seeking to save that which is lost. He is not willing that *any* perish, but that *all* come to repentance. He has commanded us to "Go." We don't need to wait for another moment. To wait upon God for His will, when it is so plainly given, is to sit in disobedience. If you are paralyzed by fear, leave a gospel tract in a shopping cart. Crawl before you walk. Do *something* to bring the message of eternal salvation to a dying world.

1533

QUESTIONS & OBJECTIONS

1:7 *"I know I'm a sinner, but I confess my sins to God daily. I tell Him that I'm sorry and I won't sin again."*

If you find yourself in court with a $50,000 fine, will a judge let you go simply because you say you're sorry and you won't commit the crime again? Of course not. You *should* be sorry for breaking the law and, of course, you shouldn't commit the crime again. But only when someone pays your $50,000 fine will you be free from the demands of the law.

God will not forgive a sinner on the basis that he is sorry. Of course we should be sorry for sin—we have a conscience to tell us that adultery, rape, lust, murder, hatred, lying, stealing, etc., are wrong. And of course we shouldn't sin again. However, God will only release us from the demands for eternal justice on the basis that someone else paid our fine. Two thousand years ago, Jesus Christ died on the cross to pay for the sins of the world. His words on the cross were, "It is finished!" In other words, the debt has been paid in full. All who repent and trust in Him receive forgiveness of sins. Their case is dismissed on the basis of His suffering death.

heritance, being predestinated according to the purpose of him who works all things after the counsel of his own will:

12 That we should be to the praise of his glory, who first trusted in Christ.

13 In whom you also trusted, after that you heard the word of truth, the gospel of your salvation: in whom also after that you believed, you were sealed with that holy Spirit of promise,

14 Which is the earnest of our inheritance until the redemption of the purchased possession, to the praise of his glory.

15 Wherefore I also, after I heard of your faith in the Lord Jesus, and love to all the saints,

16 Cease not to give thanks for you,

making mention of you in my prayers;

17 That the God of our Lord Jesus Christ, the Father of glory, may give to you the spirit of wisdom and revelation in the knowledge of him:

18 The eyes of your understanding being enlightened; that you may know what is the hope of his calling, and what the riches of the glory of his inheritance in the saints,

19 And what is the exceeding greatness of his power toward us who believe, according to the working of his mighty power,

20 Which he wrought in Christ, when he raised him from the dead, and set him at his own right hand in the heavenly places,

---

1:13 Many think that to "believe" in Jesus is merely an intellectual assent. However, when the Bible speaks of believing in Jesus Christ, it means to *trust* in Him in the same way you trust yourself to an elevator. It is more than a mere acknowledgment of its ability to transport.

1:19 Our God's power is so great that He could easily turn 800 billion enemy tanks into fine powder with the flutter of an eyelash. Never, never lose sight of the victory! Don't let the lies of enemy propaganda penetrate your mind. Remember the command, "Fear not; for I am with you: be not dismayed; for I am your God: I will strengthen you;...yes, I will uphold you with the right hand of my righteousness" (Isaiah 41:10).

To be discouraged is to dishonor God. If He is with us we must never lose courage. A blind, anemic, weak-kneed flea on crutches would have a greater chance of defeating a herd of a thousand wild stampeding elephants than the enemy has of defeating God!

SPRINGBOARDS FOR PREACHING AND WITNESSING

The Love of God

2:4,5 Imagine a place on the earth that never saw the sun. Day in, day out, it is covered with thick clouds. From the time a person was born until the time he died he never saw even a glimpse of the sun. Suppose you visited this place and tried to convince the inhabitants of the reality, the beauty, and the power of the sun. "Where I come from," you say, "a huge yellow ball rises up over the sea each day and floats across the sky, no strings attached, giving warmth and light to those upon the earth. The reason you don't experience it is because you are cut off from it by the clouds." Although the thought may seem fantastic to those people, the fact that they don't believe in it does not change the reality that it exists.

21 Far above all principality, and power, and might, and dominion, and every name that is named, not only in this world, but also in that which is to come:
22 And has put all things under his feet, and gave him to be the head over all things to the church,
23 Which is his body, the fulness of him that fills all in all.

CHAPTER 2

AND you has he quickened, who were dead in trespasses and sins;
2 Wherein in time past you walked according to the course of this world, according to the prince of the power of the air, the spirit that now works in the children of disobedience:
3 Among whom also we all had our conversation in times past in the lusts of our flesh, fulfilling the desires of the flesh and of the mind; and were by nature the children of wrath, even as others.
4 But God, who is rich in mercy, for his great love wherewith he loved us,
5 Even when we were dead in sins, has quickened us together with Christ, (by grace you are saved;)
6 And has raised us up together, and made us sit together in heavenly places in Christ Jesus:
7 That in the ages to come he might show the exceeding riches of his grace in his kindness toward us through Christ Jesus.
8 For by grace are you saved through faith; and that not of yourselves: it is the gift of God:
9 Not of works, lest any man should boast.
10 For we are his workmanship, created in Christ Jesus to good works, which God has before ordained that we should walk in them.
11 Wherefore remember, that you being in time past Gentiles in the flesh, who are called Uncircumcision by that which is called the Circumcision in the flesh made by hands;
12 That at that time you were without Christ, being aliens from the commonwealth of Israel, and strangers from the covenants of promise, having no hope, and without God in the world:

2:3 Unsaved people often try to justify themselves when confronted with their sinfulness, by saying, "It's only *natural* that we sin." They're right—sin does come naturally to us. We naturally lie, steal, lust, etc. The lifestyles of the ungodly can be clearly seen in soap operas, movies, talk shows, and tabloids. However, because it's natural doesn't make it right. By nature we are children of wrath. See Titus 3:3 comment.

2:8,9 These verses make it clear that no one will be saved through their own goodness. Nothing we can do could ever merit everlasting life. It can come only as a gift, by the grace of God. Note that we are not saved *by* our faith—it is not faith itself that saves us. Faith is the medium God uses to extend His grace to us. For those trusting in good works, see Titus 3:5.

13 But now in Christ Jesus you who sometimes were far off are made near by the blood of Christ.

14 For he is our peace, who has made both one, and has broken down the middle wall of partition between us;

15 Having abolished in his flesh the enmity, even the law of commandments contained in ordinances; for to make in himself of twain one new man, so making peace;

16 And that he might reconcile both to God in one body by the cross, having slain the enmity thereby:

17 And came and preached peace to you which were afar off, and to them that were nigh.

18 For through him we both have access by one Spirit to the Father.

19 Now therefore you are no more strangers and foreigners, but fellowcitizens with the saints, and of the household of God;

20 And are built upon the foundation of the apostles and prophets, Jesus Christ himself being the chief corner stone;

21 In whom all the building fitly framed together grows to an holy temple in the Lord:

22 In whom you also are built together for an habitation of God through the Spirit.

. . . . .

To read about the power of lust, see Mark 6:23 comment.

. . . . .

CHAPTER 3

FOR this cause I Paul, the prisoner of Jesus Christ for you Gentiles,

2 If you have heard of the dispensation of the grace of God which is given me toward you:

3 How that by revelation he made known to me the mystery; (as I wrote before in few words,

4 Whereby, when you read, you may understand my knowledge in the mystery of Christ)

5 Which in other ages was not made known to the sons of men, as it is now revealed to his holy apostles and prophets by the Spirit;

> Your one business in life is to lead men to believe in Jesus Christ by the power of the Holy Spirit. Every other thing should be made subservient to this one objective.
>
> **CHARLES SPURGEON**

6 That the Gentiles should be fellowheirs, and of the same body, and partakers of his promise in Christ by the gospel:

7 Whereof I was made a minister, according to the gift of the grace of God given to me by the effectual working of his power.

8 To me, who am less than the least of all saints, is this grace given, that I should preach among the Gentiles the unsearchable riches of Christ;

9 And to make all men see what is the fellowship of the mystery, which from the beginning of the world has been hid in God, who created all things by Jesus Christ:

10 To the intent that now to the principalities and powers in heavenly places might be known by the church the manifold wisdom of God,

11 According to the eternal purpose which he purposed in Christ Jesus our Lord:

2:13 There is nothing more valuable in the universe than the precious blood of our Savior. We were separated from God and without hope, but the blood of Jesus brought us to God.

3:7 It is God's power, working in us through His Holy Spirit, that equips us to share the gospel. (See Acts 1:8.) God provides the ability; all He wants from us is our *availability*.

12 In whom we have boldness and access with confidence by the faith of him.

13 Wherefore I desire that you faint not at my tribulations for you, which is your glory.

14 For this cause I bow my knees to the Father of our Lord Jesus Christ,

15 Of whom the whole family in heaven and earth is named,

16 That he would grant you, according to the riches of his glory, to be strengthened with might by his Spirit in the inner man;

17 That Christ may dwell in your hearts by faith; that you, being rooted and grounded in love,

18 May be able to comprehend with all saints what is the breadth, and length, and depth, and height;

19 And to know the love of Christ, which passes knowledge, that you might be filled with all the fulness of God.

20 Now to him that is able to do ex-ceeding abundantly above all that we ask or think, according to the power that works in us,

21 To him be glory in the church by Christ Jesus throughout all ages, world without end. Amen.

CHAPTER 4

I THEREFORE, the prisoner of the Lord, beseech you that you walk worthy of the vocation wherewith you are called,

2 With all lowliness and meekness, with longsuffering, forbearing one another in love;

3 Endeavouring to keep the unity of the Spirit in the bond of peace.

4 There is one body, and one Spirit, even as you are called in one hope of your calling;

5 One Lord, one faith, one baptism,

6 One God and Father of all, who is above all, and through all, and in you all.

7 But to every one of us is given grace

3:9 Life's origins—the ever-changing mind of science. According to an NBC News report in August 1999, there was a "remarkable" discovery in Australia. They said the *Journal of Science* reported that they had found what they considered to be proof that life appeared on earth 2.7 billion years ago—a billion years earlier than previously thought. They now admit that they were wrong in their first estimate (a mere 1,000,000,000 years off), but with this discovery they are now sure that they have the truth…until their next discovery.

CBS News reported in October 1999 that discoveries were made of the bones of an unknown animal in Asia that may be as much as 40 million years old. This changed scientific minds as to *where* man first originated. Scientists once believed that primates evolved in Africa, but now they think they may be wrong, and that man's ancestors may have originated in Asia. So they believe …until the next discovery.

USA Today (March 21, 2001) reported, "Paleontologists have discovered a new skeleton in the closet of human ancestry that is likely to force science to revise, if not scrap, current theories of human origins." *Reuters* reported that the discovery left "scientists of human evolution…*confused*," saying, "Lucy may not even be a direct human ancestor after all."

What is science? "We are invited, brethren, most earnestly to go away from the old-fashioned belief of our forefathers because of the supposed discoveries of science. What is science? The method by which man tries to hide his ignorance. It should not be so, but so it is. You are not to be dogmatical in theology, my brethren, it is wicked; but for scientific men it is the correct thing. You are never to assert anything very strongly; but scientists may boldly assert what they cannot prove, and may demand a faith far more credulous than any we possess. Forsooth, you and I are to take our Bibles and shape and mould our belief according to the ever-shifting teachings of so-called scientific men. What folly is this! Why, the march of science, falsely so called, through the world may be traced by exploded fallacies and abandoned theories. Former explorers once adored are now ridiculed; the continual wreckings of false hypotheses is a matter of universal notoriety. You may tell where the supposed learned have encamped by the debris left behind of suppositions and theories as plentiful as broken bottles." *Charles Spurgeon*

according to the measure of the gift of Christ.

8 Wherefore he says, When he ascended up on high, he led captivity captive, and gave gifts to men.

9 (Now that he ascended, what is it but that he also descended first into the lower parts of the earth?

10 He that descended is the same also that ascended up far above all heavens, that he might fill all things.)

11 And he gave some, apostles; and some, prophets; and some, evangelists; and some, pastors and teachers;

12 For the perfecting of the saints, for the work of the ministry, for the edifying of the body of Christ:

13 Till we all come in the unity of the faith, and of the knowledge of the Son of God, to a perfect man, to the measure of the stature of the fulness of Christ:

14 That we henceforth be no more children, tossed to and fro, and carried about with every wind of doctrine, by the sleight of men, and cunning craftiness, whereby they lie in wait to deceive;

15 But speaking the truth in love, may grow up into him in all things, which is the head, even Christ:

16 From whom the whole body fitly joined together and compacted by that which every joint supplies, according to the effectual working in the measure of every part, makes increase of the body to the edifying of itself in love.

17 This I say therefore, and testify in the Lord, that you henceforth walk not as other Gentiles walk, in the vanity of their mind,

18 Having the understanding darkened, being alienated from the life of God through the ignorance that is in them, because of the blindness of their heart:

19 Who being past feeling have given themselves over to lasciviousness, to work all uncleanness with greediness.

20 But you have not so learned Christ;

21 If so be that you have heard him, and have been taught by him, as the truth is in Jesus:

22 That you put off concerning the former conversation the old man, which is corrupt according to the deceitful lusts;

23 And be renewed in the spirit of your mind;

24 And that you put on the new man, which after God is created in righteousness and true holiness.

4:11 Often Christians pass off their responsibility to reach out to the lost by saying that it's not their "gifting." However, there is no such thing as the "gift of evangelism." That's like saying, "He has the gift of feeding starving children." It is not a gift. Rather, he has love enough to take food to the hungry. Another word for *evangelism* is "love." The Scriptures here are speaking of the God-given ability of the evangelist to equip the saints for the work of ministry.

"It occurred to me that in our work with secular organizations, the leader shapes the heart and passion of the corporate entity. In our work with non-profit organizations, we have found the same principle to be operative. When it comes to the focus of the organization, the people who serve there tend to take on many of the core personality traits of the leader toward fulfilling the mandate of the organization. If this is true, and most churches seem to lack the fervor and focus for evangelism, is it reasonable to conclude that it may be because of the lack of zeal most pastors have for identifying, befriending, loving and evangelizing non-Christian people?" *George Barna, Evangelism That Works*

4:18 When New Age followers say, "I am God," rather than revealing their delusions of grandeur, they are revealing their darkened understanding of their concept of God. The god of this world has blinded their minds. If, in their ignorance, sinners continually harden their hearts against the truth of God, they will eventually be unable to feel the Holy Spirit's conviction, and will be given over to a life of sin (Romans 1:21–24).

To reach them we must use God's Law to provide understanding (Romans 3:20). It breaks the hard heart, and reveals to the sinner that he is cut off from the life of God (Romans 7:9).

QUESTIONS & OBJECTIONS

4:18 *"Adam didn't die the day God said he would!"*

He certainly did. He died spiritually. The moment he sinned, he became "dead in trespasses and sins" (Ephesians 2:1). Ezekiel 18:4 says, "The soul that sins, it shall die." It is because we are born spiritually dead that Jesus came to give us spiritual life (John 5:40; 10:10; 14:6; etc.). This is why Jesus told us that we must be born again (John 3:3). When we repent of our sins and believe in Jesus Christ, the Bible tells us that we "pass from death to life" (John 5:24; Romans 6:13; 1 John 3:14).

"We are born dead in trespasses and sins, alienated, cut off, detached from the life of God. The day that man believed the devil's lie (which is sin), he forfeited the life that distinguished him from the animal kingdom—the life of God. When sin came in, the life went out." *Ian Thomas*

25 Wherefore putting away lying, speak every man truth with his neighbour: for we are members one of another.

26 Be angry, and sin not: let not the sun go down upon your wrath:

27 Neither give place to the devil.

28 Let him that stole steal no more: but rather let him labor, working with his hands the thing which is good, that he may have to give to him that needs.

29 Let no corrupt communication proceed out of your mouth, but that which is good to the use of edifying, that it may minister grace to the hearers.

30 And grieve not the holy Spirit of God, whereby you are sealed to the day of redemption.

31 Let all bitterness, and wrath, and anger, and clamour, and evil speaking, be put away from you, with all malice:

32 And be kind one to another, tenderhearted, forgiving one another, even as God for Christ's sake has forgiven you.

CHAPTER 5

BE therefore followers of God, as dear children;

2 And walk in love, as Christ also has loved us, and has given himself for us an offering and a sacrifice to God for a sweet-smelling savour.

3 But fornication, and all uncleanness, or covetousness, let it not be once named among you, as becomes saints;

4 Neither filthiness, nor foolish talking, nor jesting, which are not convenient: but rather giving of thanks.

5 For this you know, that no whoremonger, nor unclean person, nor covetous man, who is an idolater, has any inheritance in the kingdom of Christ and of God.

6 Let no man deceive you with vain words: for because of these things comes the wrath of God upon the children of disobedience.

7 Be not therefore partakers with them.

8 For you were sometimes darkness, but now are you light in the Lord: walk as children of light:

9 (For the fruit of the Spirit is in all goodness and righteousness and truth;)

10 Proving what is acceptable to the Lord.

4:29 If you wouldn't say it in prayer, don't say it at all.

5:5 A covetous person transgresses the Tenth, First, and Second Commandments. When he loves material things more than he loves God, he is setting his affections on the gift, rather than on the Giver. What father wouldn't be grieved if his beloved child loved his toys more than the father who gave him the toys? A child should love his father first and foremost. He should love the *giver* more than the *gift*.

PRINCIPLES OF GROWTH FOR THE NEW AND GROWING CHRISTIAN

5:20 *Thanksgiving—Do the Right Thing*

For the Christian, every day should be Thanksgiving Day. We should be thankful even in the midst of problems. The apostle Paul said, "I am exceedingly joyful in all our tribulation" (2 Corinthians 7:4). He knew that God was working all things together for his good, even his trials (Romans 8:28).

Problems *will* come your way. God will see to it personally that you grow as a Christian. He will allow storms, to send your roots deep into the soil of His Word. We also pray more in the midst of problems. It's been well said that you will see more from your knees than on your tip-toes.

A man once watched a butterfly struggling to get out of its cocoon. In an effort to help it, he took a razor blade and carefully slit the edge of the cocoon. The butterfly escaped from its problem...but immediately died. It is God's way to have the butterfly struggle. It is the struggle that causes its tiny heart to beat fast, and send the life's blood into its wings.

Trials have their purpose. They make us struggle in the cocoon in which we often find ourselves. It is there that the life's blood of faith in God helps us spread our wings.

Faith and thanksgiving are close friends. If you have faith in God, you will be thankful because you know His loving hand is upon you, even though you are in a lion's den. That will give you a deep sense of joy, which is the barometer of the depth of faith you have in God. Let me give you an example. Imagine if I said I'd give one million dollars to everyone who ripped out the last page of this book and mailed it to me. Of course, you don't believe I would do that. But imagine if you did, and that you knew 1,000 people who had sent in the page, and every one received their million dollars—no strings attached. More than that, you actually called me, and I assured you personally that I would keep my word. If you believed me, *wouldn't* you have joy? If you didn't believe me—no joy. The amount of joy you have would be a barometer of how much you believed my promise.

We have so much for which to be thankful. God has given us "exceeding great and precious promises" that are more to be desired than gold. Do yourself a big favor: believe those promises, thank God continually for them, and "let your joy be full."

For the next principle of growth, see Acts 2:38 comment.

---

11 And have no fellowship with the unfruitful works of darkness, but rather reprove them.

12 For it is a shame even to speak of those things which are done of them in secret.

13 But all things that are reproved are made manifest by the light: for whatsoever does make manifest is light.

14 Wherefore he says, Awake you that sleep, and arise from the dead, and Christ shall give you light.

15 See then that you walk circumspectly, not as fools, but as wise,

16 Redeeming the time, because the days are evil.

17 Wherefore be not unwise, but understanding what the will of the Lord is.

18 And be not drunk with wine, wherein is excess; but be filled with the Spirit;

19 Speaking to yourselves in psalms and hymns and spiritual songs, singing and making melody in your heart to the Lord;

20 Giving thanks always for all things to God and the Father in the name of our Lord Jesus Christ;

21 Submitting yourselves one to another in the fear of God.

22 Wives, submit yourselves to your own husbands, as to the Lord.

5:17 Those who don't understand the will of the Lord are unwise. See Ephesians 1:9 comment.

23 For the husband is the head of the wife, even as Christ is the head of the church: and he is the savior of the body. **24** Therefore as the church is subject to Christ, so let the wives be to their own husbands in every thing. **25** Husbands, love your wives, even as Christ also loved the church, and gave himself for it; **26** That he might sanctify and cleanse it with the washing of water by the word, **27** That he might present it to himself a glorious church, not having spot, or wrinkle, or any such thing; but that it should be holy and without blemish.

> The only real argument against the Bible is an unholy life. When a man argues against the Word of God, follow him home, and see if you cannot discover the reason of his enmity to the Word of the Lord. It lies in some sort of sin.
>
> **CHARLES SPURGEON**

28 So ought men to love their wives as their own bodies. He that loves his wife loves himself. **29** For no man ever yet hated his own flesh; but nourishes and cherishes it, even as the Lord the church: **30** For we are members of his body, of his flesh, and of his bones. **31** For this cause shall a man leave his father and mother, and shall be joined to his wife, and they two shall be one flesh. **32** This is a great mystery: but I speak concerning Christ and the church. **33** Nevertheless let every one of you in particular so love his wife even as himself; and the wife see that she reverence her husband.

CHAPTER 6

CHILDREN, obey your parents in the Lord: for this is right. **2** Honor your father and mother; (which is the first commandment with promise;) **3** That it may be well with you, and you may live long on the earth. **4** And, you fathers, provoke not your children to wrath: but bring them up in the nurture and admonition of the Lord. **5** Servants, be obedient to them that are your masters according to the flesh, with fear and trembling, in singleness of your heart, as to Christ; **6** Not with eye-service, as men-pleasers; but as the servants of Christ, doing the will of God from the heart; **7** With good will doing service, as to the Lord, and not to men: **8** Knowing that whatsoever good thing any man does, the same shall he receive

---

5:22–25 See Proverbs 31:10 comment.

6:1,2 Teaching children God's Law. Paul uses the Commandment to bring the knowledge of sin. The biblical way to bring a child to the Savior is to teach him God's Law. Immediately after Moses had read the Ten Commandments to Israel, he said that they should teach them to their children as they sit and as they walk, when they lie down and rise up. The Commandments should be placed where they can be constant reminders (see Deuteronomy 6:4–9). Why should our children be taught the Ten Commandments? Simply because they will show the child what sin is. As the child matures and discovers sin in his heart, and he begins to understand that God requires truth in the inward parts, the threat of the Law will drive him to the foot of a blood-stained cross. What child can look at Ephesians 6:1,2 and say that he is guiltless and therefore free of its warning? To help children memorize the Ten Commandments, see page 1476.

6:4 "I am much afraid that schools will prove to be the great gates of hell unless they diligently labor in explaining the Holy Scriptures, engraving them in the hearts of youth. I advise no one to place his child where the Scriptures do not reign paramount. Every institution in which men are not increasingly occupied with the Word of God must become corrupt." *Martin Luther* (See also Proverbs 4:1–5 comment.)

of the Lord, whether he be bond or free.

9 And, you masters, do the same things to them, forbearing threatening: knowing that your Master also is in heaven; neither is there respect of persons with him.

10 Finally, my brethren, be strong in the Lord, and in the power of his might.

11 Put on the whole armor of God, that you may be able to stand against the wiles of the devil.

12 For we wrestle not against flesh and blood, but against principalities, against powers, against the rulers of the darkness of this world, against spiritual wickedness in high places.

13 Wherefore take to you the whole armor of God, that you may be able to withstand in the evil day, and having done all, to stand.

14 Stand therefore, having your loins girt about with truth, and having on the breastplate of righteousness;

15 And your feet shod with the preparation of the gospel of peace;

16 Above all, taking the shield of faith, wherewith you shall be able to quench all the fiery darts of the wicked.

17 And take the helmet of salvation, and the sword of the Spirit, which is the word of God:

18 Praying always with all prayer and supplication in the Spirit, and watching thereunto with all perseverance and supplication for all saints;

19 *And for me, that utterance may be given to me, that I may open my mouth boldly, to make known the mystery of the gospel,*

20 *For which I am an ambassador in bonds: that therein I may speak boldly, as I ought to speak.*

21 But that you also may know my affairs, and how I do, Tychicus, a beloved brother and faithful minister in the Lord, shall make known to you all things:

22 Whom I have sent to you for the same purpose, that you might know our affairs, and that he might comfort your hearts.

23 Peace be to the brethren, and love with faith, from God the Father and the Lord Jesus Christ.

24 Grace be with all them that love our Lord Jesus Christ in sincerity. Amen.

6:10 "Do not pray for easy lives. Pray to be stronger men. Do not pray for tasks commensurate with your strength. Pray for strength commensurate with your tasks." *Phillips Brooks*

6:15 **Don't go barefoot.** In verse 11 we are told to put on the *whole* armor of God. Many Christians are truthful. They have their heart free of sin, they are sure of their salvation, they rightly use the Word of God. But they are shoeless—they are not prepared to share the gospel. Those who do not advance the cause of the gospel are stationary soldiers; any evangelistic movement is too painful for them. If they are not seeking to save the lost, they are not taking ground for the kingdom of God. Paul climaxed his admonition to the Ephesians by highlighting what the battle is for. He pleads with them to pray for him to have boldness to reach out to the unsaved, citing his moral responsibility (v. 20).

6:17 "We must thrust the sword of the Spirit into the hearts of men." *Charles Spurgeon*

6:18 "Let's move from theology to kneeology! Power for victory in spiritual warfare is found in prayer." *Robert R. Lawrence*

6:19 Beware of the subtlety of passive prayer. We have been commanded to *preach* the gospel. Make sure you don't pacify a guilty conscience by simply *praying* for the salvation of the lost, but not preaching to them. It is the gospel that is the power of God unto salvation. How shall they hear without a preacher? See Romans 10:14.

Philippians

CHAPTER 1

PAUL and Timotheus, the servants of Jesus Christ, to all the saints in Christ Jesus which are at Philippi, with the bishops and deacons:

2 Grace be to you, and peace, from God our Father, and from the Lord Jesus Christ.

3 I thank my God upon every remembrance of you,

4 Always in every prayer of mine for you all making request with joy,

5 For your fellowship in the gospel from the first day until now;

6 Being confident of this very thing, that he which has begun a good work in you will perform it until the day of Jesus Christ:

7 Even as it is meet for me to think this of you all, because I have you in my heart; inasmuch as both in my bonds, and in the defence and confirmation of the gospel, you all are partakers of my grace.

8 For God is my record, how greatly I long after you all in the bowels of Jesus Christ.

9 And this I pray, that your love may abound yet more and more in knowledge and in all judgment;

10 That you may approve things that are excellent; that you may be sincere and without offence till the day of Christ;

11 Being filled with the fruits of righteousness, which are by Jesus Christ, to the glory and praise of God.

12 But I would you should understand, brethren, that the things which happened to me have fallen out rather to the furtherance of the gospel;

13 So that my bonds in Christ are manifest in all the palace, and in all other places;

14 And many of the brethren in the Lord, waxing confident by my bonds, are much more bold to speak the word

---

1:6 Do you ever think about how many faces there are upon the earth? As you line up in a store, do you sometimes feel like a tiny grain of sand in the massive desert? Then lift your head and look to the heavens—God Almighty is your Maker. Like a giant heavenly zoom lens, He focused in on you from eternity. He foreknew every sinew of your fearfully and wonderfully made body. He is the lover of your soul. He breathed life into your human frame, and is at work in you to will and do of His good pleasure.

His good pleasure is to conform you to the image of His Son. Never let discouragement fall upon your mind, for God will complete the good work He has begun in you. He picked you out of the ranks of the masses, called you by His Grace, justified you through faith, and glorified you in Christ.

1:14 The Church should never dread persecution, as it can work *for* rather than *against* the furtherance of the gospel. The winds of persecution only spread the flames of the gospel.

without fear.

15 Some indeed preach Christ even of envy and strife; and some also of good will:

16 The one preach Christ of contention, not sincerely, supposing to add affliction to my bonds:

17 But the other of love, knowing that I am set for the defence of the gospel.

18 What then? notwithstanding, every way, whether in pretence, or in truth, Christ is preached; and I therein do rejoice, yes, and will rejoice.

19 For I know that this shall turn to my salvation through your prayer, and the supply of the Spirit of Jesus Christ,

20 According to my earnest expectation and my hope, that in nothing I shall be ashamed, but that with all boldness, as always, so now also Christ shall be magnified in my body, whether it be by life, or by death.

21 *For to me to live is Christ, and to die is gain.*

22 But if I live in the flesh, this is the fruit of my labor: yet what I shall choose I do not know.

23 For I am in a strait betwixt two, having a desire to depart, and to be with Christ; which is far better:

24 Nevertheless to abide in the flesh is more needful for you.

25 And having this confidence, I know that I shall abide and continue with you all for your furtherance and joy of faith;

26 That your rejoicing may be more abundant in Jesus Christ for me by my coming to you again.

27 *Only let your conversation be as it becomes the gospel of Christ: that whether I come and see you, or else be absent, I may hear of your affairs, that you stand fast in one spirit, with one mind striving together for the faith of the gospel;*

28 *And in nothing terrified by your adversaries: which is to them an evident token of perdition, but to you of salvation, and that of God.*

29 For to you it is given in the behalf of Christ, not only to believe on him, but also to suffer for his sake;

30 Having the same conflict which you saw in me, and now hear to be in me.

CHAPTER 2

IF there be therefore any consolation in Christ, if any comfort of love, if any fellowship of the Spirit, if any bowels and mercies,

2 Fulfil my joy, that you be likeminded, having the same love, being of one accord, of one mind.

3 Let nothing be done through strife or vainglory; but in lowliness of mind let each esteem other better than themselves.

4 *Look not every man on his own things, but every man also on the things of others.*

5 Let this mind be in you, which was also in Christ Jesus:

6 Who, being in the form of God, thought it not robbery to be equal with God:

7 But made himself of no reputation, and took upon him the form of a ser-

---

1:18 Paul rejoiced even though Christ was preached from the mouth of a hypocrite. This is because the quality is in the seed, not in the sower. This gives great consolation to those of us who lack what is commonly called "ability."

1:20 Paul lived for the furtherance of the gospel. God's will was his will.

1:29 "Suffering and sacrifice are essential to the Christian life just as they were essential to Christ's life. 'When Christ calls a man,' [Dietrich] Bonhoeffer wrote, 'He bids him come and die' *(The Cost of Discipleship).* This doesn't always—or even usually—necessitate our physical deaths, but Christ calls us first and foremost to die to sin and to ourselves. Leave your home, sell everything you own, turn the other cheek, do not store up earthly treasures, love your enemies, take up your cross and follow me. None of Christ's commands call believers to a life of comfort. All require patience, suffering, and sacrifice." *Daniel L. Weiss*

vant, and was made in the likeness of men:

8 And being found in fashion as a man, he humbled himself, and became obedient to death, even the death of the cross.

9 Wherefore God also has highly exalted him, and given him a name which is above every name:

10 That at the name of Jesus every knee should bow, of things in heaven, and things in earth, and things under the earth;

11 And that every tongue should confess that Jesus Christ is Lord, to the glory of God the Father.

12 Wherefore, my beloved, as you have always obeyed, not as in my presence only, but now much more in my absence, work out your own salvation with fear and trembling.

13 For it is God which works in you both to will and to do of his good pleasure.

14 *Do all things without murmurings and disputings:*

15 *That you may be blameless and harmless, the sons of God, without rebuke, in the midst of a crooked and perverse nation, among whom you shine as lights in the world;*

16 *Holding forth the word of life; that I may rejoice in the day of Christ, that I have not run in vain, neither labored in vain.*

17 Yes, and if I be offered upon the sacrifice and service of your faith, I joy, and rejoice with you all.

18 For the same cause also do you joy, and rejoice with me.

19 But I trust in the Lord Jesus to send Timotheus shortly to you, that I also may be of good comfort, when I know your state.

> Preach Christ or nothing: don't dispute or discuss except with your eye on the cross.
>
> **CHARLES SPURGEON**

20 For I have no man likeminded, who will naturally care for your state.

21 For all seek their own, not the things which are Jesus Christ's.

22 But you know the proof of him, that, as a son with the father, he has served with me in the gospel.

23 Him therefore I hope to send presently, so soon as I shall see how it will

---

2:8   The death of the cross. "Oh sinner, why provoke your Maker? Your judgment does not linger and your damnation does not slumber. When the Law was broken and mankind was exposed to its fearful penalty, God offered justice to the universe and mercy for sinners, which He displayed in the atonement. To make this universal offer of pardon without justice would violate His Law. A due regard for public interest forbade the Lawgiver to forgive and set aside the penalty without finding a way to secure obedience to the Law. Therefore, His compassion for mankind and His regard for the Law were so great that He was willing to suffer in the person of His Son, who became a substitute for the penalty of the Law. This was the most stupendous exhibition of self-denial that was ever made: the Father giving His only begotten and beloved Son; the Son veiling the glories of His uncreated Godhead and becoming obedient to death, even the death of the cross, that we may never die." *Charles Finney*

2:13 "I used to ask God to help me. Then I asked if I might help Him. I ended up by asking Him to do His work through me." *Hudson Taylor*

2:15 Too often the Church becomes exclusive. We fellowship only with Christians—a monastery without walls. We become salt among salt, light among light. In reality, the Church should be "in the midst...among whom...in the world." Verse 16 tells us what we should be doing "in the midst."

"I would not give much for your religion unless it can be seen. Lamps do not talk, but they do shine." *Charles Spurgeon*

go with me.

24 But I trust in the Lord that I also myself shall come shortly.

25 Yet I supposed it necessary to send to you Epaphroditus, my brother, and companion in labor, and fellowsoldier, but your messenger, and he that ministered to my wants.

26 For he longed after you all, and was full of heaviness, because that you had heard that he had been sick.

27 For indeed he was sick near to death: but God had mercy on him; and not on him only, but on me also, lest I should have sorrow upon sorrow.

28 I sent him therefore the more carefully, that, when you see him again, you may rejoice, and that I may be the less sorrowful.

29 Receive him therefore in the Lord with all gladness; and hold such in reputation:

30 Because for the work of Christ he was near to death, not regarding his life, to supply your lack of service toward me.

. . . . . .

For the new birth—its necessity for salvation, see John 1:13 comment.

. . . . . .

CHAPTER 3

FINALLY, my brethren, rejoice in the Lord. To write the same things to you, to me indeed is not grievous, but for you it is safe.

2 Beware of dogs, beware of evil workers, beware of the concision.

3 For we are the circumcision, which worship God in the spirit, and rejoice in Christ Jesus, and have no confidence in the flesh.

4 Though I might also have confidence in the flesh. If any other man thinks that he has whereof he might trust in the flesh, I more:

5 Circumcised the eighth day, of the stock of Israel, of the tribe of Benjamin, an Hebrew of the Hebrews; as touching the law, a Pharisee;

6 Concerning zeal, persecuting the church; touching the righteousness which is in the law, blameless.

7 But what things were gain to me, those I counted loss for Christ.

8 Yes doubtless, and I count all things but loss for the excellency of the knowledge of Christ Jesus my Lord: for whom I have suffered the loss of all things, and do count them but dung, that I may win Christ,

9 And be found in him, not having mine own righteousness, which is of the law, but that which is through the faith of Christ, the righteousness which is of God by faith:

10 That I may know him, and the power of his resurrection, and the fellowship of his sufferings, being made conformable to his death;

11 If by any means I might attain to the resurrection of the dead.

12 Not as though I had already attained,

3:8 The greatest discovery. Dr. James Simpson, born in 1811, was responsible for the discovery of chloroform's anesthetic qualities, leading to its medical use worldwide. He also laid a solid foundation for gynecology and predicted the discovery of the X-ray. Dr. Simpson was president of the Royal Medical Society and Royal Physician to the Queen, the highest medical position of his day. He once stated, "Christianity works because it is supremely true and therefore supremely livable. There is nothing incompatible between religion and science."

When asked what his greatest discovery was, Dr. Simpson replied: "It was not chloroform. It was to know I am a sinner and that I could be saved by the grace of God. A man has missed the whole meaning of life if he has not entered into an active, living relationship with God through Christ." The greatest discovery in history has not been the law of gravity, calculus, telescopes, or the telegraph. The greatest discovery an individual could ever make is finding Jesus Christ and making Him both Lord and Savior.

"Man is never so tall as when he kneels before God—never so great as when he humbles himself before God. And the man who kneels to God can stand up to anything."

Louis H. Evans

16 Nevertheless, whereto we have already attained, let us walk by the same rule, let us mind the same thing.

17 Brethren, be followers together of me, and mark them which walk so as you have us for an ensample.

18 (For many walk, of whom I have told you often, and now tell you even weeping, that they are the enemies of the cross of Christ:

19 Whose end is destruction, whose God is their belly, and whose glory is in their shame, who mind earthly things.)

20 For our conversation is in heaven; from whence also we look for the Savior, the Lord Jesus Christ:

21 Who shall change our vile body, that it may be fashioned like to his glorious body, according to the working whereby he is able even to subdue all things to himself.

CHAPTER 4

THEREFORE, my brethren dearly beloved and longed for, my joy and crown, so stand fast in the Lord, my dearly beloved.

2 I beseech Euodias, and beseech Syntyche, that they be of the same mind in the Lord.

3 And I entreat you also, true yokefellow, help those women which labored with me in the gospel, with Clement also, and with other my fellowlaborers, whose names are in the book of life.

4 Rejoice in the Lord always: and again I say, Rejoice.

either were already perfect: but I follow after, if that I may apprehend that for which also I am apprehended of Christ Jesus.

13 Brethren, I count not myself to have apprehended: but this one thing I do, forgetting those things which are behind, and reaching forth to those things which are before,

14 I press toward the mark for the prize of the high calling of God in Christ Jesus.

15 Let us therefore, as many as be perfect, be thus minded: and if in any thing you be otherwise minded, God shall reveal even this to you.

3:13 "Oh God, let this horrible war quickly come to an end that we may all return home and engage in the only work that is worthwhile—and that is the salvation of men." *General "Stonewall" Jackson*

3:21 New bodies for Christians. The unsaved have no idea of our hope. They presume that when we die we will spend eternity in heaven as a spirit or an angel. In truth, God's kingdom is coming to earth, and God's will *will* be done on earth as it is in heaven. We will become neither spirits nor angels, but we will have new bodies similar to the resurrected body of the Savior, never again to be plagued by disease, decay, death, or even dandruff. See Luke 24:36–43.

4:3 True companions are those who "labor" in the gospel. These are the ones of whom Jesus said there was a great lack (Luke 10:2). The fruit of genuine converts (those whose names are in the Book of Life) is a concern for the lost. Love cannot sit in passivity while sinners sink into hell.

5 Let your moderation be known to all men. The Lord is at hand.

6 Be careful for nothing; but in every thing by prayer and supplication with thanksgiving let your requests be made known to God.

7 And the peace of God, which passes all understanding, shall keep your hearts and minds through Christ Jesus.

8 Finally, brethren, whatsoever things are true, whatsoever things are honest, whatsoever things are just, whatsoever things are pure, whatsoever things are lovely, whatsoever things are of good report; if there be any virtue, and if there be any praise, think on these things.

9 Those things, which you have both learned, and received, and heard, and seen in me, do: and the God of peace shall be with you.

10 But I rejoiced in the Lord greatly, that now at the last your care of me has flourished again; wherein you were also careful, but you lacked opportunity.

11 Not that I speak in respect of want: for I have learned, in whatsoever state I am, therewith to be content.

12 I know both how to be abased, and I know how to abound: every where and in all things I am instructed both to be full and to be hungry, both to abound and to suffer need.

13 *I can do all things through Christ who strengthens me.*

14 Notwithstanding you have well done, that you did communicate with my affliction.

15 Now you Philippians know also, that in the beginning of the gospel, when I departed from Macedonia, no church communicated with me as concerning giving and receiving, but you only.

16 For even in Thessalonica you sent once and again to my necessity.

17 Not because I desire a gift: but I desire fruit that may abound to your account.

18 But I have all, and abound: I am full, having received of Epaphroditus the things which were sent from you, an odor of a sweet smell, a sacrifice acceptable, well-pleasing to God.

19 But my God shall supply all your need according to his riches in glory by Christ Jesus.

20 Now to God and our Father be glory for ever and ever. Amen.

21 Salute every saint in Christ Jesus. The brethren which are with me greet you.

22 All the saints salute you, chiefly they that are of Caesar's household.

23 The grace of our Lord Jesus Christ be with you all. Amen.

4:5 Second coming of Jesus: See 1 Thessalonians 5:2.

4:6 "Realistically, the way you regard prayer is the way you regard God, for prayer is communicating with Him. No other way exists in which to relate with Him! Put simply, low levels of prayer signal a demotion of God in our attitude. High levels of prayer indicate an expectation for a fullness of His presence and power." *Ben Jennings, The Arena of Prayer*

4:13 Although God assured the prophet Jeremiah that He formed him, knew him, sanctified and ordained him, he still was paralyzed by the fear of man (Jeremiah 1:5,6). When the fear of man seeks to paralyze us, we must stop saying "I cannot speak," and instead say, "I can do all things through Christ who strengthens me." This verse obliterates every excuse we try to offer for not preaching the gospel to every creature. It counters the fear of man, the fear of rejection, the fear of public speaking, and the fear of offering a stranger a gospel tract.

Hudson Taylor said, "All God's giants have been weak men, who did great things for God because they believed that God would be with them."

Colossians

CHAPTER 1

PAUL, an apostle of Jesus Christ by the will of God, and Timotheus our brother,

2 To the saints and faithful brethren in Christ which are at Colosse: Grace be to you, and peace, from God our Father and the Lord Jesus Christ.

3 We give thanks to God and the Father of our Lord Jesus Christ, praying always for you,

4 Since we heard of your faith in Christ Jesus, and of the love which you have to all the saints,

5 For the hope which is laid up for you in heaven, whereof you heard before in the word of the truth of the gospel;

6 Which is come to you, as it is in all the world; and brings forth fruit, as it does also in you, since the day you heard of it, and knew the grace of God in truth:

7 As you also learned of Epaphras our dear fellow-servant, who is for you a faithful minister of Christ;

8 Who also declared to us your love in the Spirit.

9 For this cause we also, since the day we heard it, do not cease to pray for you, and to desire that you might be filled with the knowledge of his will in all wisdom and spiritual understanding;

10 That you might walk worthy of the Lord to all pleasing, being fruitful in every good work, and increasing in the knowledge of God;

11 Strengthened with all might, according to his glorious power, to all patience and longsuffering with joyfulness;

12 Giving thanks to the Father, which has made us meet to be partakers of the inheritance of the saints in light:

13 Who has delivered us from the power of darkness, and has translated us into the kingdom of his dear Son:

14 In whom we have redemption through his blood, even the forgiveness of sins:

15 Who is the image of the invisible God, the firstborn of every creature:

16 For by him were all things created, that are in heaven, and that are in earth, visible and invisible, whether they be thrones, or dominions, or principalities, or powers: all things were created by him, and for him:

17 And he is before all things, and by

1:3,4 Some people applaud when sinners step forward to make a decision for Christ. It is more biblical to hold the applause until the genuineness of their repentance is evidenced by "fruit." See verse 6.

1:15,16 Was Jesus God in human form? The One who created all things and brought life into being is the Word of God, who became flesh in the person of Jesus of Nazareth (John 1:3,4,14). See Colossians 2:9.

QUESTIONS & OBJECTIONS

1:20 *"I've made my peace with the 'Man upstairs.'"*

When people refer to God as "the Man upstairs," they reveal that they have no concept of (nor living relationship with) Him. They will use such words because they feel uncomfortable saying His name. Often they will have a measure of reverence for God, but not enough to obey Him. Ask if the person thinks he will go to heaven when he dies. He'll almost certainly say he will, and a little probing will reveal that he's trusting in his own goodness to save him. However, the only way sinners can have peace with the God they have offended is through the shed blood of the Savior.

Therefore, it's important to take the person through the Ten Commandments and strip him of his self-righteousness and his false sense of assurance of salvation. As you do so, you may feel bad that you are making him uncomfortable, but if you care about his eternal salvation, you must ask yourself, "Which is worse: a few moments of conviction under the sound of God's Law, or eternity in the Lake of Fire?" Unless there is a knowledge of sin (which comes by the Law—Romans 7:7), there will be no repentance.

him all things consist.

18 And he is the head of the body, the church: who is the beginning, the first-born from the dead; that in all things he might have the preeminence.

19 For it pleased the Father that in him should all fulness dwell;

20 And, having made peace through the blood of his cross, by him to reconcile all things to himself; by him, I say, whether they be things in earth, or things in heaven.

21 And you, that were sometime alienated and enemies in your mind by wicked works, yet now has he reconciled

22 In the body of his flesh through death, to present you holy and unblameable and unreproveable in his sight:

23 If you continue in the faith grounded and settled, and be not moved away from the hope of the gospel, which you have heard, and which was preached to every creature which is under heaven;

whereof I Paul am made a minister;

24 Who now rejoice in my sufferings for you, and fill up that which is behind of the afflictions of Christ in my flesh for his body's sake, which is the church:

25 Whereof I am made a minister, according to the dispensation of God which is given to me for you, to fulfil the word of God;

26 Even the mystery which has been hid from ages and from generations, but now is made manifest to his saints:

27 To whom God would make known what is the riches of the glory of this mystery among the Gentiles; which is Christ in you, the hope of glory:

28 *Whom we preach, warning every man, and teaching every man in all wisdom; that we may present every man perfect in Christ Jesus:*

29 Whereunto I also labor, striving according to his working, which works in me mightily.

1:21 This runs contrary to the secular concept of man's relationship to his Creator. We are alienated from God, separated from Him by our iniquities (Isaiah 59:2). We are His enemies, and our works are wicked.

1:27 Salvation doesn't come from *what* we know, but from *Who* we know. Jesus said, "This is life eternal, that they might know you the only true God, and Jesus Christ, whom you have sent" (John 17:3).

CHAPTER 2

FOR I would that you knew what great conflict I have for you, and for them at Laodicea, and for as many as have not seen my face in the flesh;

2 That their hearts might be comforted, being knit together in love, and to all riches of the full assurance of understanding, to the acknowledgement of the mystery of God, and of the Father, and of Christ;

3 In whom are hid all the treasures of wisdom and knowledge.

4 And this I say, lest any man should beguile you with enticing words.

5 For though I be absent in the flesh, yet am I with you in the spirit, joying and beholding your order, and the steadfastness of your faith in Christ.

6 As you have therefore received Christ Jesus the Lord, so walk in him:

7 Rooted and built up in him, and stablished in the faith, as you have been taught, abounding therein with thanksgiving.

8 Beware lest any man spoil you through philosophy and vain deceit, after the tradition of men, after the rudiments of the world, and not after Christ.

9 For in him dwells all the fulness of

1:28 Our primary task. A lighthouse keeper gained a reputation as being a very kind man. He would give free fuel to ships that miscalculated the amount of fuel needed to reach their destination port. One night during a storm, lightning struck his lighthouse and put out his light. He immediately turned on his generator, but it soon ran out of fuel, and he had given his reserves to passing ships. During the dark night, a ship struck the rocks and many lives were lost.

At his trial, the judge knew of the lighthouse keeper's reputation as a kind man and wept as he gave sentence. He accused the lighthouse keeper of neglecting his primary responsibility—to keep the light shining.

The Church can so often get caught up in legitimate acts of kindness—standing for political righteousness, feeding the hungry, etc.—but our primary task is to warn sinners of danger. We are to keep the light of the gospel shining so that sinners can avoid the jagged-edged rocks of wrath and escape being eternally damned.

> My friend, I stand in judgment now,
> and feel that you're to blame somehow.
> On earth I walked with you by day,
> and never did you show the way.
>
> You knew the Savior in truth and glory,
> But never did you tell the story.
> My knowledge then was very dim.
> You could have led me safe to Him.
> Though we lived together, here on earth,
>
> you never told me of the second birth.
> And now I stand before eternal hell,
> because of heaven's glory you did not tell!
> *(Anonymous)*

"Each person we meet on a daily basis who does not know Christ is hell-bound. That may make some folks bristle—but it's a fact. When we refuse to warn people that their actions and lifestyles have eternal consequences, we're not doing them any favors. If everybody feels good about his or her sin, why would anyone repent?" *Franklin Graham*

"If they are breathing...they need Jesus." *Mark Cahill*

2:9 Was Jesus God in human form? Some may ask how Jesus could be both God and man. It has been well said that when God, the Creator and Sustainer of the universe, became a man, He didn't cease to be God. He created a body, and then filled that body as a hand fills a glove (Hebrews 10:5). See 1 Timothy 3:16.

2:16 Freedom from Sabbath-keeping

Some today insist that Christians must keep the Sabbath day, that those who worship on the first day of the week (Sunday) are in great error. They reason that "Sun-day" comes from the pagan worship of the Sun god, that Jesus and Paul kept the Sabbath day as an example for us to follow, and that the Roman Catholic church is responsible for the change in the day of worship. Those who continue to worship on Sunday will receive the mark of the beast.

Let's briefly look at these arguments. First, nowhere does the Fourth Commandment say that Christians are to *worship* on the Sabbath. It commands that we *rest* on that day: "Remember the Sabbath day, to keep it holy. Six days shall you labor, and do all your work: But the seventh day is the Sabbath of the LORD your God: in it you shall not do any work …For in six days the LORD made heaven and earth, the sea, and all that in them is, and rested the seventh day: wherefore the LORD blessed the Sabbath day, and hallowed it" (Exodus 20:8–11).

Sabbath-keepers worship on Saturday. However, the word "Satur-day" comes from the Latin for "Saturn's day," a pagan day of worship of the planet Saturn (astrology).

If a Christian's salvation depends upon his keeping a certain day, surely God would have told us. At one point, the apostles gathered specifically to discuss the relationship of believers to the Law of Moses. Acts 15:5–11, 24–29 was God's opportunity to make His will clear to His children. All He had to do to save millions from damnation was say, "Remember to keep the Sabbath holy," and millions of Christ-centered, God-loving, Bible-believing Christians would have gladly kept it. Instead, the only commands the apostles gave were to "abstain from meats offered to idols, and from blood, and from things strangled, and from fornication."

There isn't even one command in the New Testament for Christians to keep the Sabbath holy. In fact, we are told not to let others judge us regarding Sabbaths (Colossian 2:16), and that man was not made for the Sabbath, but the Sabbath for man (Mark 2:27). The Sabbath was given as a sign to Israel (Exodus 31:13–17); nowhere is it given as a sign to the Church. Thousands of years after the Commandment was given we can still see the sign that separates Israel from the world—they continue to keep the Sabbath holy.

The apostles came together on the first day of the week to break bread (Acts 20:7). The collection was taken on the first day of the week (1 Corinthians 16:2). When do Sabbath-keepers gather together to break bread or take up the collection? It's not on the same day as the early Church. They tell us that the Roman Catholic church changed their day of worship from Saturday to Sunday, but what has that got to do with the disciples keeping the first day of the week? That was the Roman Catholic church in the early centuries, not the Church of the Book of Acts.

Romans 14:5–10 tells us that one man esteems one day of the week above another; another esteems every day alike. Then Scripture tells us that everyone should be fully persuaded in his own mind. We are not to judge each other regarding the day on which we worship.

Jesus did keep the Sabbath. He had to keep the whole Law to be the perfect sacrifice. The Bible makes it clear that the Law has been satisfied in Christ. The reason Paul went to the synagogue each Sabbath wasn't to keep the Law; that would have been contrary to everything he taught about being saved by grace alone (Ephesians 2:8,9). It was so he could preach the gospel to the Jews, as evident in the Book of Acts. Paul had an incredible evangelistic zeal for Israel to be saved (Romans 10:1). To the Jew he became as a Jew, that he might win the Jews (1 Corinthians 9:19,20). That meant he went to where they gathered on the day they gathered.

D. L. Moody said, "The Law can only chase a man to Calvary, no further." Christ redeemed us from the curse of the Law so we are no longer in bondage to it. If we try to keep one part of the Law (even out of love for God), we are obligated to keep the whole Law (Galatians 3:10)—all 613 precepts.

If those who insist on keeping the Sabbath were as zealous about the salvation of the lost as they are about other Christians keeping the Sabbath, we would see revival.

the Godhead bodily.

10 And you are complete in him, which is the head of all principality and power:

11 In whom also you are circumcised with the circumcision made without hands, in putting off the body of the sins of the flesh by the circumcision of Christ:

12 Buried with him in baptism, wherein also you are risen with him through the faith of the operation of God, who has raised him from the dead.

13 And you, being dead in your sins and the uncircumcision of your flesh, has he quickened together with him, having forgiven you all trespasses;

14 Blotting out the handwriting of ordinances that was against us, which was contrary to us, and took it out of the way, nailing it to his cross;

15 And having spoiled principalities and powers, he made a show of them openly, triumphing over them in it.

16 Let no man therefore judge you in meat, or in drink, or in respect of an holyday, or of the new moon, or of the sabbath days:

17 Which are a shadow of things to come; but the body is of Christ.

18 Let no man beguile you of your reward in a voluntary humility and worshipping of angels, intruding into those things which he has not seen, vainly puffed up by his fleshly mind,

19 And not holding the Head, from which all the body by joints and bands having nourishment ministered, and knit together, increases with the increase of God.

20 Wherefore if you be dead with Christ from the rudiments of the world, why, as though living in the world, are you subject to ordinances,

21 (Touch not; taste not; handle not;

THE FUNCTION OF THE LAW

2:21 Some may wonder whether using the Law in evangelism produces legalism. When the Law is used to show a sinner that sin is "exceedingly sinful"—that nothing can commend him to God—he clings to the cross knowing that he is saved by grace and grace alone. This knowledge gives the Christian the understanding that even after a lifetime of good works, fasting, praying, seeking the lost, etc., his "works" don't commend him to God—he is still saved by grace and grace alone.

However, when the Law *isn't* used before the cross, and a sinner simply makes a "decision for Christ," he comes with a lack of understanding about the true nature of sin. After his commitment, he thinks that his good works, his fasting, praying, evangelism, etc., commend him to God. He is the one who thinks that what he eats, what he wears, and what he does become relevant to his salvation. He is the one who is liable to say "touch not, taste not, handle not"—the one who becomes "legalistic." Using the Law in evangelism before the cross liberates a new convert from legalism.

22 Which all are to perish with the using;) after the commandments and doctrines of men?

23 Which things have indeed a show of wisdom in will worship, and humility, and neglecting of the body; not in any honor to the satisfying of the flesh.

CHAPTER 3

IF you then be risen with Christ, seek those things which are above, where Christ sits on the right hand of God.

2 Set your affection on things above, not on things on the earth.

3 For you are dead, and your life is hid with Christ in God.

2:16 "I am no preacher of the old legal Sabbath. I am a preacher of the gospel. The Sabbath of the Jew is to him a task; the Lord's Day of the Christian, the first day of the week, is to him a joy, a day of rest, of peace, and of thanksgiving. And if you Christian men can earnestly drive away all distractions, so that you can really rest today, it will be good for your bodies, good for your souls, good mentally, good spiritually, good temporally, and good eternally." *Charles Spurgeon*

4 When Christ, who is our life, shall appear, then shall you also appear with him in glory.

5 Mortify therefore your members which are upon the earth; fornication, uncleanness, inordinate affection, evil concupiscence, and covetousness, which is idolatry:

6 For which things' sake the wrath of God comes on the children of disobedience:

7 In the which you also walked some time, when you lived in them.

8 But now you also put off all these; anger, wrath, malice, blasphemy, filthy communication out of your mouth.

9 Lie not one to another, seeing that you have put off the old man with his deeds;

10 And have put on the new man, which is renewed in knowledge after the image of him that created him:

11 Where there is neither Greek nor Jew, circumcision nor uncircumcision, Barbarian, Scythian, bond nor free: but Christ is all, and in all.

12 Put on therefore, as the elect of God, holy and beloved, bowels of mercies, kindness, humbleness of mind, meekness, longsuffering;

13 Forbearing one another, and forgiving one another, if any man have a quarrel against any: even as Christ forgave you, so also do.

14 And above all these things put on charity, which is the bond of perfectness.

15 And let the peace of God rule in your hearts, to the which also you are called in one body; and be thankful.

16 Let the word of Christ dwell in you richly in all wisdom; teaching and admonishing one another in psalms and hymns and spiritual songs, singing with grace in your hearts to the Lord.

> I am told that Christians do not love each other. I am very sorry if that be true, but I rather doubt it, for I suspect that those who do not love each other are not Christians.
>
> **CHARLES SPURGEON**

17 And whatsoever you do in word or deed, do all in the name of the Lord Jesus, giving thanks to God and the Father by him.

18 Wives, submit yourselves to your own husbands, as it is fit in the Lord.

19 Husbands, love your wives, and be not bitter against them.

20 Children, obey your parents in all things: for this is well pleasing to the Lord.

21 Fathers, provoke not your children to anger, lest they be discouraged.

22 Servants, obey in all things your masters according to the flesh; not with eyeservice, as men-pleasers; but in singleness of heart, fearing God:

3:3 "There was a day when I died, utterly died, died to George Mueller, his opinions, preferences, tastes, and will—died to the world, its approval or censure—died to the approval or blame even of my brethren and friends—and since then I have only to show myself approved to God." *George Mueller*

3:6 The Bible calls us children of disobedience. Children know naturally how to be selfish and lie. Rebellion is rooted deep in the human heart until we are born again and become children of God (John 1:12).

3:10 Feminists bristle at the Bible's statement that God made man in *His* image. This verse doesn't mean that God is a man, or that He looks like man (John 4:24). It means that when God made man and woman, He endowed them with a mind, emotions, and will. Humans are rational, moral beings with an inherent God-consciousness. However, in revealing Himself to mankind, God describes Himself in the male gender using terms such as Father, Son, Bridegroom, etc. Those who consider God to be female and call Him "Mother" are engaging in idolatry. To change who God has revealed Himself to be is to create a god in their own image.

23 And whatsoever you do, do it heartily, as to the Lord, and not to men;

24 Knowing that of the Lord you shall receive the reward of the inheritance: for you serve the Lord Christ.

25 But he that does wrong shall receive for the wrong which he has done: and there is no respect of persons.

. . . . . .

For scientific facts in the Bible,
see Hebrews 11:3 comment.

. . . . . .

CHAPTER 4

M ASTERS, give to your servants that which is just and equal; knowing that you also have a Master in heaven.

2 Continue in prayer, and watch in the same with thanksgiving;

3 Withal praying also for us, that God would open to us a door of utterance, to speak the mystery of Christ, for which I am also in bonds:

4 That I may make it manifest, as I ought

to speak.

5 Walk in wisdom toward them that are without, redeeming the time.

6 Let your speech be always with grace, seasoned with salt, that you may know how you ought to answer every man.

7 All my state shall Tychicus declare to you, who is a beloved brother, and a faithful minister and fellow-servant in the Lord:

8 Whom I have sent to you for the same purpose, that he might know your estate, and comfort your hearts;

9 With Onesimus, a faithful and beloved brother, who is one of you. They shall make known to you all things which are done here.

10 Aristarchus my fellow-prisoner salutes you, and Marcus, sister's son to Barnabas, (touching whom you received commandments: if he come to you, receive him;)

11 And Jesus, which is called Justus, who are of the circumcision. These only are my fellow-workers to the kingdom of God, which have been a comfort to me.

4:3,4 Paul asks the Colossian church to pray that God would open doors of opportunity for him to evangelize. Reaching out to the unsaved was the apostle's number one priority (see Romans 9:1–3). He often uses the phrase "as I ought to speak." He didn't see evangelism as a ministry only for people with a "gift" to reach the unsaved; he saw it as a moral responsibility, as each of us should. The only "gift" we need for evangelizing is the Holy Spirit, and every born-again believer has received Him.

4:4 Witnessing to telemarketers. If you are ever bugged by telemarketers, take the opportunity to share your faith. Simply say, "May I ask *you* a question?" Telemarketers will usually say yes. Ask, "Have you kept the Ten Commandments?" Then ask, "Have you ever told a lie?" Most admit to at least telling "fibs" or "white lies." When they admit it, ask what that makes them. If they refuse to call themselves a liar, say, "If *I* told a lie, what would I be called?" When they say, "Liar," ask, "Have you ever stolen something, even if it's small?" Be gentle and loving in your tone. Then say, "Jesus said that if you look with lust, you commit adultery in your heart. Have you ever looked with lust?"

Don't be afraid to inquire how they will do on Judgment Day—will they be innocent or guilty...heaven or hell? The worst thing that can happen is that they hang up in your ear. If that happens, you can rejoice that they were convicted enough to do so. You not only had the privilege of planting the seed of God's Word in the heart of a stranger, but you proved yourself to be faithful to the Lord, you conquered the fear of man, and now you can rejoice that you were rejected for the sake of righteousness. If they hang up, spend a moment in prayer for them. If they are open to hearing more, take them through the cross, repentance, and faith. Ask if they have a Bible at home, encourage them to read it daily, and then thank them for listening to you.

4:5,6 This is the spirit in which we should share our faith. See 1 Thessalonians 5:14.

"When thou prayest, rather let thy heart be without words than thy words be without heart."

John Bunyan

12 Epaphras, who is one of you, a servant of Christ, salutes you, always laboring fervently for you in prayers, that you may stand perfect and complete in all the will of God.

13 For I bear him record, that he has a great zeal for you, and them that are in Laodicea, and them in Hierapolis.

14 Luke, the beloved physician, and Demas, greet you.

15 Salute the brethren which are in Laodicea, and Nymphas, and the church which is in his house.

16 And when this epistle is read among you, cause that it be read also in the church of the Laodiceans; and that you likewise read the epistle from Laodicea.

17 And say to Archippus, Take heed to the ministry which you have received in the Lord, that you fulfil it.

18 The salutation by the hand of me Paul. Remember my bonds. Grace be with you. Amen.

4:12 Transforming prayer. "Prayer can move mountains. It can change human hearts, families, neighborhoods, cities, and nations. It's the ultimate source of power because it is, in reality, the power of Almighty God.

"Prayer can do what political action cannot, what education cannot, what military might cannot, and what planning committees cannot. All these are impotent by comparison.

"By prayer the kingdom of God is built, and by prayer the kingdom of Satan is destroyed. Where there is no prayer, there are no great works, and there is no building of the kingdom. Where there is much prayer and fervent prayer, there are great gains for the kingdom: God's rule is established, His power is directed, His will is done, society is transformed, lost persons are saved, and saints are enabled to 'stand against the devil's schemes' (Eph. 6:11). If that isn't enough to compel us to 'devote [ourselves] to prayer' and 'always [wrestle] in prayer' (Col. 4:2,12), I don't know what is!" *Alvin J. Vander Griend, "Your Prayers Matter," Discipleship Journal*

1 Thessalonians

CHAPTER 1

PAUL, and Silvanus, and Timotheus, to the church of the Thessalonians which is in God the Father and in the Lord Jesus Christ: Grace be to you, and peace, from God our Father, and the Lord Jesus Christ.

2 We give thanks to God always for you all, making mention of you in our prayers;

3 Remembering without ceasing your work of faith, and labor of love, and patience of hope in our Lord Jesus Christ, in the sight of God and our Father;

4 Knowing, brethren beloved, your election of God.

5 *For our gospel came not to you in word only, but also in power, and in the Holy Spirit, and in much assurance; as you know what manner of men we were among you for your sake.*

6 And you became followers of us, and of the Lord, having received the word in much affliction, with joy of the Holy Spirit:

7 So that you were ensamples to all that believe in Macedonia and Achaia.

8 For from you sounded out the word of the Lord not only in Macedonia and Achaia, but also in every place your faith to God-ward is spread abroad; so that we need not to speak any thing.

9 **For they themselves show of us what manner of entering in we had to you, and how you turned to God from idols to serve the living and true God;**

10 **And to wait for his Son from heaven, whom he raised from the dead, even Jesus, which delivered us from the wrath to come.**

CHAPTER 2

For yourselves, brethren, know our entrance in to you, that it was not in vain:

2 But even after that we had suffered before, and were shamefully entreated, as you know, at Philippi, we were bold in our God to speak to you the gospel of God with much contention.

3 For our exhortation was not of deceit, nor of uncleanness, nor in guile:

4 *But as we were allowed of God to be put*

1:5 God backs up His Word with power. When the unsaved ask for proof, we have it. If any person obeys the command to repent and trust Jesus Christ, he will experience the power of the gospel. God will transform him on the inside by giving him a new heart with new desires. Instead of drinking in iniquity like water, he will begin to thirst after righteousness. He will be born again. God will make him a new creature, all of which will give him "much assurance."

1:9 This reveals the essence of Paul's message to the Thessalonians. He preached against their sin of idolatry (transgression of the First and Second Commandments). This is also the essence of his message to the Athenians (see Acts 17:29).

QUESTIONS & OBJECTIONS

2:13   *"There is no absolute truth. You can't be sure of anything!"*

Those who say that there are no absolutes are often very adamant about their belief. If they say that they are *absolutely* sure, then they are wrong because their own statement is an absolute. If they are not 100 percent sure, then there is a chance that they are wrong and they are risking their eternal salvation by trusting in a wrong belief. God tells us that there is an objective, absolute truth that is not subject to man's interpretations or whims, on which we can base our eternity. That truth is the Word of God (John 17:7).

in trust with the gospel, even so we speak; not as pleasing men, but God, which tries our hearts.

5 For neither at any time used we flattering words, as you know, nor a cloak of covetousness; God is witness:

6 Nor of men sought we glory, neither of you, nor yet of others, when we might have been burdensome, as the apostles of Christ.

7 But we were gentle among you, even as a nurse cherishes her children:

8 So being affectionately desirous of you, we were willing to have imparted to you, not the gospel of God only, but also our own souls, because you were dear to us.

9 For you remember, brethren, our labor and travail: for laboring night and day, because we would not be chargeable to any of you, we preached to you the gospel of God.

10 You are witnesses, and God also, how holy and justly and unblameably we behaved ourselves among you that believe:

11 As you know how we exhorted and comforted and charged every one of you, as a father does his children,

12 That you would walk worthy of God, who has called you to his kingdom and glory.

13 For this cause also thank we God without ceasing, because, when you received the word of God which you heard of us, you received it not as the word of men, but as it is in truth, the word of God, which effectually works also in you that believe.

14 For you, brethren, became followers of the churches of God which in Judea are in Christ Jesus: for you also have suffered like things of your own countrymen, even as they have of the Jews:

15 Who both killed the Lord Jesus, and their own prophets, and have persecuted us; and they please not God, and are contrary to all men:

16 Forbidding us to speak to the Gentiles that they might be saved, to fill up their sins always: for the wrath is come upon them to the uttermost.

17 But we, brethren, being taken from you for a short time in presence, not in heart, endeavored the more abundantly to see your face with great desire.

18 Wherefore we would have come to you, even I Paul, once and again; but Satan hindered us.

19 For what is our hope, or joy, or crown

2:4 It is a great betrayal of trust to fashion our message to please men. We must never fail to call hell "hell" and sin "sin," rather than use timid clichés such as a "Christless eternity" and "indiscretions."

"Never mind *who* frowns, if God smiles." *Catherine Booth*

2:9,10 We must strive to be devout, just, and blameless in the sight of a sinful world. God forbid that any soul should stumble because they see what they perceive to be hypocrisy in our lives.

of rejoicing? Are not even you in the presence of our Lord Jesus Christ at his coming?

20 For you are our glory and joy.

. . . . . .

*For how to witness to homosexuals,
see 1 Timothy 1:8–10 comment.*

. . . . . .

CHAPTER 3

WHEREFORE when we could no longer forbear, we thought it good to be left at Athens alone;

2 And sent Timotheus, our brother, and minister of God, and our fellowlaborer in the gospel of Christ, to establish you, and to comfort you concerning your faith:

3 That no man should be moved by these afflictions: for yourselves know that we are appointed thereunto.

4 For verily, when we were with you, we told you before that we should suffer tribulation; even as it came to pass, and you know.

5 For this cause, when I could no longer forbear, I sent to know your faith, lest by some means the tempter have tempted you, and our labor be in vain.

6 But now when Timotheus came from you to us, and brought us good tidings of your faith and charity, and that you have good remembrance of us always, desiring greatly to see us, as we also to see you:

7 Therefore, brethren, we were comforted over you in all our affliction and distress by your faith:

8 For now we live, if you stand fast in the Lord.

9 For what thanks can we render to God again for you, for all the joy wherewith we joy for your sakes before our God;

10 Night and day praying exceedingly that we might see your face, and might perfect that which is lacking in your faith?

11 Now God himself and our Father, and our Lord Jesus Christ, direct our way to you.

12 And the Lord make you to increase and abound in love one toward another, and toward all men, even as we do toward you:

13 To the end he may stablish your hearts unblameable in holiness before God, even our Father, at the coming of our Lord Jesus Christ with all his saints.

> In proportion as a church is holy, in that proportion will its testimony for Christ be powerful.
>
> **CHARLES SPURGEON**

CHAPTER 4

FURTHERMORE then we beseech you, brethren, and exhort you by the Lord Jesus, that as you have received of us how you ought to walk and to please God, so you would abound more and more.

2 For you know what commandments we gave you by the Lord Jesus.

3 For this is the will of God, even your

2:16 Some lack the fear of God and believe that it is their right to suppress the truth of God's Word. However, those who hinder the progress of the gospel will come under the severe wrath of the Almighty. It would be better that a millstone be placed around their neck and they be cast into the depths of the sea, rather than hinder a single person from coming to peace with their Creator.

We can take strong consolation in the fact that God will have His way. Whoever calls upon the name of the Lord *shall* be saved and the wicked *will* be punished. He has delusions of grandeur indeed who thinks he can stop the will of God from coming to pass. Though hand join in hand, the wicked will not go unpunished (Proverbs 11:21). God will judge the world in righteousness. It would be infinitely easier to build a bacon-burger restaurant on the Temple Mount in Jerusalem than to stop God from saving those who call upon Him and from having His Day of Justice.

Two Prayers

. . . .

"**D**EAR GOD, I have sinned against You by breaking Your Commandments. Despite the conscience You gave me, I have looked with lust and therefore committed adultery in my heart. I have lied, stolen, failed to love You, failed to love my neighbor as myself, and failed to keep the Sabbath holy. I have been covetous, harbored hatred in my heart and therefore been guilty of murder in Your sight. I have used Your holy name in vain, have made a god to suit myself, and because of the nature of my sin, I have dishonored my parents. If I stood before You in Your burning holiness on Judgment Day, if every secret sin I have committed and every idle word I have spoken came out as evidence of my crimes against You, I would be utterly guilty, and justly deserve hell. I am unspeakably thankful that Jesus took my place by suffering and dying on the cross. He was bruised for my iniquities. He paid my fine so that I could leave the courtroom. He revealed how much You love me. I believe that He then rose from the dead (according to the Scriptures). I now confess and forsake my sin and yield myself to Him to be my Lord and Savior. I will no longer live for myself. I present my body, soul, and spirit to You as a living sacrifice, to serve You in the furtherance of Your Kingdom. I will read Your Word daily and obey what I read. It is solely because of Calvary's cross that I will live forever. I am eternally Yours. In Jesus' name I pray. Amen."

"Choose you this day whom you will serve..."

"**S**ATAN, the Bible tells me that you are the god of this world. You are the father of lies. You deceive the nations and blind the minds of those who do not believe. God warns that I cannot enter His Kingdom because I have lied, stolen, looked with lust and therefore committed adultery in my heart. I have harbored hatred, which the Bible says is the same as murder. I have blasphemed, refused to put God first, violated the Sabbath, coveted other people's goods, dishonored my parents, and have been guilty of the sin of idolatry—I even made a god to suit myself. I did all this despite the presence of my conscience. I know that it was God who gave me life. I have seen the splendor of a sunrise. I have heard the sounds of nature. I have enjoyed pleasures of an incredible array of food, all of which came from His generous hand. I realize that if I die in my sins I will never know pleasure again. I know that Jesus Christ shed His life's blood for my sins and rose again to destroy the power of death, but today I refuse to confess and forsake my sins. On the Day of Judgment, if I am cast into the Lake of Fire I will have no one to blame but myself. It is not God's will that I perish. He commended His love toward me through the death of His Son, who came to give me life. It was you who came to kill, steal, and destroy. You are my spiritual father. I choose to continue to serve you and do your will. This is because I love the darkness and hate the light. If I do not come to my senses, I will be eternally yours. Amen."

sanctification, that you should abstain from fornication:

4 That every one of you should know how to possess his vessel in sanctification and honor;

5 Not in the lust of concupiscence, even as the Gentiles which know not God:

6 That no man go beyond and defraud his brother in any matter: because that the Lord is the avenger of all such, as we also have forewarned you and testified.

7 For God has not called us to uncleanness, but to holiness.

8 He therefore that despises, despises not man, but God, who has also given to us his holy Spirit.

9 But as touching brotherly love you need not that I write to you: for you yourselves are taught of God to love one another.

10 And indeed you do it toward all the brethren which are in all Macedonia: but we beseech you, brethren, that you increase more and more;

11 And that you study to be quiet, and to do your own business, and to work with your own hands, as we commanded you;

12 That you may walk honestly toward them that are without, and that you may have lack of nothing.

13 But I would not have you to be ignorant, brethren, concerning them which are asleep, that you sorrow not, even as others which have no hope.

14 For if we believe that Jesus died and rose again, even so them also which sleep in Jesus will God bring with him.

15 For this we say to you by the word of the Lord, that we which are alive and remain to the coming of the Lord shall not prevent them which are asleep.

16 For the Lord himself shall descend from heaven with a shout, with the voice of the archangel, and with the trump of God: and the dead in Christ shall rise first:

17 Then we which are alive and remain

shall be caught up together with them in the clouds, to meet the Lord in the air: and so shall we ever be with the Lord.

18 Wherefore comfort one another with these words.

The Dead Sea Scrolls confirm that the Bible hasn't changed through the years. See 1 Peter 1:25 comment.

CHAPTER 5

BUT of the times and the seasons, brethren, you have no need that I write to you.

2 For yourselves know perfectly that the day of the Lord so comes as a thief in the night.

3 For when they shall say, Peace and safety; then sudden destruction comes upon them, as travail upon a woman with child; and they shall not escape.

4 But you, brethren, are not in darkness, that that day should overtake you as a thief.

5 You are all the children of light, and the children of the day: we are not of the night, nor of darkness.

6 Therefore let us not sleep, as do others; but let us watch and be sober.

7 For they that sleep sleep in the night; and they that be drunken are drunken in the night.

8 But let us, who are of the day, be sober, putting on the breastplate of faith

---

5:2 Second coming of Jesus: See Hebrews 9:28.

and love; and for an helmet, the hope of salvation.

9 For God has not appointed us to wrath, but to obtain salvation by our Lord Jesus Christ,

10 Who died for us, that, whether we wake or sleep, we should live together with him.

11 Wherefore comfort yourselves together, and edify one another, even as also you do.

12 And we beseech you, brethren, to know them which labor among you, and are over you in the Lord, and admonish you;

13 And to esteem them very highly in love for their work's sake. And be at peace among yourselves.

14 Now we exhort you, brethren, warn them that are unruly, comfort the feeble-minded, support the weak, be patient toward all men.

15 See that none render evil for evil to any man; but ever follow that which is good, both among yourselves, and to all men.

16 Rejoice evermore.

17 Pray without ceasing.

18 In every thing give thanks: for this is the will of God in Christ Jesus concerning you.

19 Quench not the Spirit.

20 Despise not prophesyings.

21 Prove all things; hold fast that which is good.

22 Abstain from all appearance of evil.

23 And the very God of peace sanctify you wholly; and I pray God your whole spirit and soul and body be preserved blameless to the coming of our Lord Jesus Christ.

24 Faithful is he that calls you, who also will do it.

25 Brethren, pray for us.

26 Greet all the brethren with an holy kiss.

27 I charge you by the Lord that this epistle be read to all the holy brethren.

28 The grace of our Lord Jesus Christ be with you. Amen.

5:14 This is the spirit in which we should share our faith. See 2 Timothy 2:24.

5:17 *General "Stonewall" Jackson*, one of the country's greatest generals, gives a good example of how to "pray without ceasing":

> "When we take our meals, there is the grace. When I take a draught of water, I always pause...to lift up my heart to God in thanks and prayer for the water of life. Whenever I [send] a letter...I send a petition along with it, for God's blessing upon its mission and upon the person to whom it is sent.

> "When I [open] a letter...I stop to pray to God that He may prepare me for its contents...When I go to my class-room and await the arrangement of the cadets in their places, that is my time to intercede with God for them."

5:17 "Prayers are not limited to place and time. If you are not in the right place to pray, you're not in the right place." *Chuck Missler*

"Prayer is the shield to the soul, a delight to God, and a scourge to Satan." *John Bunyan*

5:20 The Bible's fascinating facts. In Isaiah 66:7,8 (700 B.C.), the prophet Isaiah gives a strange prophecy: "Before she travailed, she brought forth; before her pain came, she was delivered of a man child. Who has heard such a thing? Who has seen such things? Shall the earth be made to bring forth in one day? Or shall a nation be born at once? For as soon as Zion travailed, she brought forth her children." In 1922 the League of Nations gave Great Britain the mandate (political authority) over Palestine. On May 14, 1948, Britain withdrew her mandate, and the nation of Israel was "born in a day." There are more than 25 Bible prophecies concerning Palestine that have been literally fulfilled. Probability estimations conclude that the chances of these being accidentally fulfilled are less than one chance in 33 million.

2 Thessalonians

CHAPTER 1

PAUL, and Silvanus, and Timotheus, to the church of the Thessalonians in God our Father and the Lord Jesus Christ:

2 Grace to you, and peace, from God our Father and the Lord Jesus Christ.

3 We are bound to thank God always for you, brethren, as it is meet, because that your faith grows exceedingly, and the charity of every one of you all toward each other abounds;

4 So that we ourselves glory in you in the churches of God for your patience and faith in all your persecutions and tribulations that you endure:

5 Which is a manifest token of the righteous judgment of God, that you may be counted worthy of the kingdom of God, for which you also suffer:

6 Seeing it is a righteous thing with God to recompense tribulation to them that trouble you;

7 And to you who are troubled rest with us, when the Lord Jesus shall be revealed from heaven with his mighty angels,

8 In flaming fire taking vengeance on them that know not God, and that obey not the gospel of our Lord Jesus Christ:

9 Who shall be punished with everlasting destruction from the presence of the Lord, and from the glory of his power;

10 When he shall come to be glorified in his saints, and to be admired in all them that believe (because our testimony among you was believed) in that day.

11 Wherefore also we pray always for you, that our God would count you worthy of this calling, and fulfil all the good pleasure of his goodness, and the work of faith with power:

12 That the name of our Lord Jesus Christ may be glorified in you, and you in him, according to the grace of our God and the Lord Jesus Christ.

CHAPTER 2

NOW we beseech you, brethren, by the coming of our Lord Jesus Christ, and by our gathering together to him,

2 That you be not soon shaken in mind, or be troubled, neither by spirit, nor by

---

1:6 The world doesn't understand why the Christian turns the other cheek. This isn't because he is weak. Rather than take the law into his own hands, he simply commits himself to "Him who judges righteously." If God sees fit to repay, He will. The Scriptures tell us, "Vengeance is mine; I will repay, says the Lord" (Romans 12:19).

1:7–9 Judgment Day: Such a thought should stir in us a passion for evangelism. It is a fearful thing to fall into the hands of the living God. For verses that warn of its reality, see 2 Timothy 4:1.

1:10 Our beliefs govern our actions. Those who don't believe that they are in danger of God's wrath will not flee from it.

"I never thought much of the courage of a lion-tamer. Inside the cage he is at least safe from people."

George Bernard Shaw

word, nor by letter as from us, as that the day of Christ is at hand.

3 Let no man deceive you by any means: for that day shall not come, except there come a falling away first, and that man of sin be revealed, the son of perdition;

4 Who opposes and exalts himself above all that is called God, or that is worshipped; so that he as God sits in the temple of God, showing himself that he is God.

5 Do you not remember, that, when I was yet with you, I told you these things?

6 And now you know what withholds that he might be revealed in his time.

7 For the mystery of iniquity does already work: only he who now lets will let, until he be taken out of the way.

8 And then shall that Wicked be revealed, whom the Lord shall consume with the spirit of his mouth, and shall destroy with the brightness of his coming:

9 Even him, whose coming is after the working of Satan with all power and signs and lying wonders,

10 And with all deceivableness of unrighteousness in them that perish; because they received not the love of the truth, that they might be saved.

11 And for this cause God shall send them strong delusion, that they should believe a lie:

12 That they all might be damned who believed not the truth, but had pleasure in unrighteousness.

13 But we are bound to give thanks always to God for you, brethren beloved of the Lord, because God has from the beginning chosen you to salvation through sanctification of the Spirit and belief of the truth:

14 Whereunto he called you by our gospel, to the obtaining of the glory of our Lord Jesus Christ.

> I further believe, although certain persons deny it, that the influence of fear is to be exercised over the minds of men, and that it ought to operate upon the mind of the preacher himself: "Noah...moved with fear, prepared an ark to the saving of his house" (Hebrews 11:7).
>
> **CHARLES SPURGEON**

15 Therefore, brethren, stand fast, and hold the traditions which you have been taught, whether by word, or our epistle.

16 Now our Lord Jesus Christ himself, and God, even our Father, who has loved us, and has given us everlasting consolation and good hope through grace,

17 Comfort your hearts, and stablish you in every good word and work.

2:11,12   If sinners refuse to truly embrace the gospel, God in His righteousness will give them over to "powerful delusion" and a "depraved mind" (Romans 1:28). Those who refuse to come to the light will be given over to darkness. See John 3:19,20 comment.

CHAPTER 3

FINALLY, brethren, pray for us, that the word of the Lord may have free course, and be glorified, even as it is with you:

2 And that we may be delivered from unreasonable and wicked men: for all men have not faith.

3 But the Lord is faithful, who shall stablish you, and keep you from evil.

4 And we have confidence in the Lord touching you, that you both do and will do the things which we command you.

5 And the Lord direct your hearts into the love of God, and into the patient waiting for Christ.

6 Now we command you, brethren, in the name of our Lord Jesus Christ, that you withdraw yourselves from every brother that walks disorderly, and not after the tradition which he received of us.

7 For yourselves know how you ought to follow us: for we behaved not ourselves disorderly among you;

8 Neither did we eat any man's bread for nothing; but wrought with labor and travail night and day, that we might not be chargeable to any of you:

9 Not because we have not power, but to make ourselves an ensample to you to follow us.

10 For even when we were with you, this we commanded you, that if any would not work, neither should he eat.

11 For we hear that there are some which walk among you disorderly, working not at all, but are busybodies.

12 Now them that are such we command and exhort by our Lord Jesus Christ, that with quietness they work, and eat their own bread.

13 But you, brethren, be not weary in well doing.

14 And if any man obey not our word by this epistle, note that man, and have no company with him, that he may be ashamed.

Archaeological discoveries confirm the Bible's account of historical events. See Matthew 26:54 comment.

15 Yet count him not as an enemy, but admonish him as a brother.

16 Now the Lord of peace himself give you peace always by all means. The Lord be with you all.

17 The salutation of Paul with mine own hand, which is the token in every epistle: so I write.

18 The grace of our Lord Jesus Christ be with you all. Amen.

3:1 Paul again requests prayer for the evangelistic enterprise. "The word of the Lord" refers to the salvation message. "Unreasonable and wicked men" (v. 2) continually seek to stop the gospel from having "free course."

Hinduism

ORIGIN: India, about 1500 B.C. to 2500 B.C.

FOUNDER: No single person

ADHERENTS: 1998 worldwide: 825–850 million; India 780 million; Bangladesh 20 million; Nepal 20 million; Indonesia 7 million; Sri Lanka 3 million; Pakistan 2 million. In Fiji, Guyana, Mauritius, Surinam, and Trinidad and Tobago, over 20 percent of their people practice Hinduism. A considerable number of Hindus live in Africa, Myanmar, and the United Kingdom. U.S.: Estimated 1.5 to 2 million.

SCRIPTURES: *Vedas*, *Upanishads*, epics, *Puranas*, and the *Bhagavad Gita* explain the essence of Hinduism. Hinduism is the world's oldest surviving organized religion. It is a complex family of sects whose copious scriptures, written over a period of almost 2,000 years (1500 B.C.–A.D. 250), allow a diverse belief system. Hinduism has no single creed and recognizes no final truth. At its core, Hinduism has a pagan background in which the forces of nature and human heroes are personified as gods and goddesses. They are worshiped with prayers and offerings. Hinduism can be divided into Popular Hinduism, characterized by the worship of gods through offerings, rituals, and prayers; and Philosophical Hinduism, the complex belief system understood by those who can study ancient texts, meditate, and practice yoga.

GOD: God (*Brahman*) is the one impersonal, ultimate, but unknowable, spiritual Reality. Sectarian Hinduism personalizes Brahman as *Brahma* (Creator, with four heads symbolizing creative energy), *Vishnu* (Preserver, the god of stability and control), and *Shiva* (Destroyer, god of endings). Most Hindus worship two of Vishnu's 10 mythical incarnations: Krishna and Rama. On special occasions, Hindus may worship other gods, as well as family and individual deities. Hindus claim that there are 330 million gods. In Hinduism, belief in astrology, evil spirits, and curses also prevails.

Christian Response: If God (Ultimate Reality) is impersonal, then the impersonal must be greater than the personal. Our life experiences reveal that the personal is of more value than the impersonal. Even Hindus treat their children as having more value than a rock in a field.

The Bible teaches that God is personal and describes Him as having personal attributes. The Bible regularly describes God in ways used to describe human personality. God talks, rebukes, feels, becomes angry, is jealous, laughs, loves, and even has a personal name (Gen. 1:3; 6:6, 12; Ex. 3:15; 16:12; 20:5; Lev. 20:23; Deut. 5:9; 1 Sam. 26:19; Ps. 2:4; 59:9; Hos. 1:8–9; Amos 9:4; Zeph. 3:17). The Bible also warns Christians to avoid all forms of idolatry (Gen. 35:2; Ex. 23:13; Josh. 23:7; Ezek. 20:7; 1 Cor. 10:20). No idol or pagan deity is a representation of the true God. They are all false deities and must be rejected.

CREATION: Hindus accept various forms of pantheism and reject the Christian doctrine of creation. According to Hinduism, Brahman alone exists; everything is ultimately an illusion (*maya*). God emanated itself to cause the illusion of creation. There is no beginning or conclusion to creation, only endless repetitions or cycles of creation and destruction. History has little value since it is based on an illusion.

Christian Response: Christianity affirms the reality of the material world and the genuineness of God's creation. The Bible declares that all is not God. God is present in His creation but He is not to be confused with it. The Bible teaches that in the beginning God created that which was not God (Gen. 1:1ff; Heb 11:3). The Bible contradicts pantheism by teaching creation rather than pantheistic emanation. The Bible issues strong warnings to those who confuse God with His creation (Rom. 1:22–23). God created the world at a definite time and will consummate His creation (2 Pet. 2:12–13). Christianity is founded upon the historical event of God's incarnation in Jesus Christ (John 1:1–14).

MAN: The eternal soul (*atman*) of man is a manifestation or "spark" of Brahman mysteriously trapped in the physical body. *Samsara*, repeated lives or reincarnations, are required before the soul can be liberated (*moksha*) from the body. An individual's present life is determined by the law of *karma* (actions, words, and thoughts in previous lifetimes). The physical body is ultimately an illusion (*maya*) with little inherent or permanent worth. Bodies generally are cremated, and the eternal soul goes to an intermediate state of punishment or reward before rebirth in another body. Rebirths are experienced until karma has been removed to allow the soul's re-absorption into Brahman.

Christian Response: People are created in God's image (Gen. 12:7). The body's physical resurrection and eternal worth are emphasized in John 2:18–22 and 1 Corinthians 15. The Bible declares, "And as it is appointed unto men once to die, but after this the judgment: so Christ was once offered to bear the sins of many" (Heb. 9:27–28, KJV). Since we die only once, reincarnation cannot be true. Instead of reincarnation, the Bible teaches resurrection (John 5:25). At death, Christians enjoy a state of conscious fellowship with Christ (Matt. 22:32; 2 Cor. 5:8; Phil. 1:23) to await the resurrection and heavenly reward. A person's eternal destiny is determined by his or her acceptance or rejection of Jesus Christ as Savior and Lord (John 3:36; Rom. 10:9–10).

SIN: Hindus have no concept of rebellion against a holy God. Ignorance of unity with Brahman, desire, and violation of *dharma* (one's social duty) are humanity's problems.

Christian Response: Sin is not ignorance of unity with Brahman, but is rather a willful act of rebellion against God and His commandments (Eccl. 7:20; Rom. 1:28–32; 2:1–16; 3:9,19; 11:32; Gal. 3:22; 1 John 1:8–10). The Bible declares, "All have sinned and fall short of the glory of God" (Rom. 3:23, NIV).

SALVATION: There is no clear concept of salvation in Hinduism. *Moksha* (freedom from infinite being and self-hood and final self-realization of the truth) is the goal of existence. *Yoga* and meditation (especially *raja-yoga*) taught by a *guru* (religious teacher) is one way to attain *moksha*. The other valid paths for *moksha* are: the way of works (*karma marga*), the way of knowledge (*jnana marga*), and the way of love and devotion (*bhakti marga*). Hindus hope to eventually get off the cycle of reincarnation. They believe the illusion of personal existence will end and they will become one with the impersonal God.

Christian Response: Salvation is a gift from God through faith in Jesus Christ (Eph. 2:8–10). Belief in reincarnation opposes the teaching of the Bible (Heb. 9:27). The Christian hope of eternal life means that all true believers in Christ

will not only have personal existence but personal fellowship with God. It is impossible to earn one's salvation by good works (Titus 3:1–7). Religious deeds and exercises cannot save (Matt. 7:22–23; Rom 9:32; Gal. 2:16; Eph. 2:8–9).

WORSHIP: Hindu worship has an almost endless variety with color symbolism, offerings, fasting, and dance as integral parts. Most Hindus daily worship an image of their chosen deity, with chants (*mantras*), flowers, and incense. Worship, whether in a home or temple, is primarily individualistic rather than congregational.

HINDUS IN THE UNITED STATES

- Traditional movements include the Ramakrishna Mission and Vedanta Societies, Sri Aurobindo Society, Satya Sai Baba Movement, Self-Realization Fellowship, and International Sivananda Yoga Society.

- Hindu-based sects include the International Society for Krishna Consciousness (Hare Krishna), Transcendental Meditation, Vedanta Society, Self-Realization Fellowship, Theosophy, and Eckankar.

- Sects that have "Americanized" Hindu concepts include Church of Christ, Scientists (Christian Science); Unity School of Christianity; and several groups within the New Age Movement.

WITNESSING TO HINDUS

- Pray and trust the Holy Spirit to use the gospel message to reach the heart and mind of your Hindu friend.

- Share your personal faith in Jesus Christ as your Lord and Savior. Keep your testimony short.

- Stress the uniqueness of Jesus Christ as God's revelation of Himself.

- Stress the necessity of following Jesus to the exclusion of all other deities.

- Keep the gospel presentation Christ-centered.

- Share the assurance of salvation that God's grace gives you and about your hope in the resurrection. Make sure you communicate that your assurance is derived from God's grace and not from your good works or your ability to be spiritual (1 John 5:13).

- Give a copy of the New Testament. If a Hindu desires to study the Bible, begin with the Gospel of John. Point out passages that explain salvation.

N.S.R.K. Ravi, Interfaith Evangelism Team. Copyright 1999 North American Mission Board of the Southern Baptist Convention, Alpharetta, Georgia. All rights reserved. Reprinted with permission.

The Great Commission

"Go into all the world, and preach the gospel to every creature" *(Mark 16:15)*.

"Have you no wish for others to be saved? Then you are not saved yourself. Be sure of that." *Charles Spurgeon*

"If you do not make it a matter of study, how you may successfully act in building up the kingdom of Christ, you are acting a very wicked and absurd part as a Christian." *Charles Finney*

"The harvest truly is plenteous, but the laborers are few; pray therefore the Lord of the harvest, that he will send forth laborers into his harvest" *(Matthew 9:37,38)*.

"Oh my friends, we are loaded down with countless church activities, while the real work of the church, that of evangelizing the world and winning the lost, is almost entirely neglected!"
Oswald J. Smith

"Why call you me, Lord, Lord, and do not the things which I say?" *(Luke 6:46)*.

(See John 4:7 comment on how to effectively share your faith.)

1 Timothy

CHAPTER 1

PAUL, an apostle of Jesus Christ by the commandment of God our Savior, and Lord Jesus Christ, which is our hope;

2 To Timothy, my own son in the faith: Grace, mercy, and peace, from God our Father and Jesus Christ our Lord.

3 As I besought you to abide still at Ephesus, when I went into Macedonia, that you might charge some that they teach no other doctrine,

4 Neither give heed to fables and endless genealogies, which minister questions, rather than godly edifying which is in faith: so do.

5 Now the end of the commandment is charity out of a pure heart, and of a good conscience, and of faith unfeigned:

6 From which some having swerved have turned aside to vain jangling;

7 Desiring to be teachers of the law; understanding neither what they say, nor whereof they affirm.

8 But we know that the law is good, if a man use it lawfully;

9 Knowing this, that the law is not made for a righteous man, but for the lawless and disobedient, for the ungodly and for sinners, for unholy and profane, for murderers of fathers and murderers of mothers, for manslayers,

10 For whoremongers, for them that defile themselves with mankind, for menstealers, for liars, for perjured persons, and if there be any other thing that is contrary to sound doctrine;

11 According to the glorious gospel of the blessed God, which was committed to my trust.

12 And I thank Christ Jesus our Lord, who has enabled me, for that he counted me faithful, putting me into the ministry;

13 Who was before a blasphemer, and a persecutor, and injurious: but I obtained mercy, because I did it ignorantly in unbelief.

14 And the grace of our Lord was ex-

1:5 In the context of this passage (vv. 5–11), Paul is speaking of the Law of God when he refers to the "commandment." Its purpose is to bring a sinner to genuine conversion, with the evidence of the fruit of love from a pure heart, a good conscience, and true faith. The purpose of a mirror is to send us to the water that we might be made clean. The purpose of the Law is to reveal sin and send us to be washed clean by the blood of Jesus Christ.

1:8 The way to use the Law "lawfully" is to use it in evangelism as a "schoolmaster" to bring sinners to Christ (Galatians 3:24). See verses 9, 10.

"I have found by long experience that the severest threatenings of the Law of God have a prominent place in leading men to Christ. They must see themselves lost before they will cry for mercy. They will not escape from danger until they see it." *A. B. Earle*

THE FUNCTION OF THE LAW

1:8 "As that which is straight discovers that which is crooked, so there is no way of coming to that knowledge of sin which is necessary to repentance, but by comparing our hearts and lives with the Law.

"Paul had a very quick and piercing judgment and yet never attained the right knowledge of indwelling sin till the Spirit by the Law made it known to him. Though brought up at the feet of Gamaliel, a doctor of the Law, though himself a strict observer of it, yet without the Law. He had the letter of the Law, but he had not the spiritual meaning of it—the shell, but not the kernel. He had the Law in his hand and in his head, but he had it not in his heart. But when the commandment came (not to his eyes only, but to his heart), sin revived, as the dust in a room rises when the sunshine is let into it. Paul then saw that in sin which he had never seen before—sin in its consequences, sin with death at the heels of it, sin and the curse entailed upon it. 'The Spirit, by the commandment, convinced me that I was in a state of sin, and in a state of death because of sin.' Of this excellent use is the Law; it is a lamp and a light; it opens the eyes, prepares the way of the Lord." *Matthew Henry*

ceeding abundant with faith and love which is in Christ Jesus.
15 **This is a faithful saying, and worthy of all acceptation, that Christ Jesus came into the world to save sinners; of whom I am chief.**
16 Howbeit for this cause I obtained mercy, that in me first Jesus Christ might show forth all longsuffering, for a pattern to them which should hereafter believe on him to life everlasting.
17 Now to the King eternal, immortal, invisible, the only wise God, be honor and glory for ever and ever. Amen.
18 This charge I commit to you, son Timothy, according to the prophecies which went before on you, that you by them might war a good warfare;
19 Holding faith, and a good conscience; which some having put away concerning faith have made shipwreck:
20 Of whom is Hymenaeus and Alexander; whom I have delivered to Satan, that they may learn not to blaspheme.

CHAPTER 2

I EXHORT therefore, that, first of all, supplications, prayers, intercessions, and giving of thanks, be made for all men;
2 For kings, and for all that are in authority; that we may lead a quiet and peaceable life in all godliness and honesty.
3 **For this is good and acceptable in the sight of God our Savior;**
4 **Who will have all men to be saved, and to come to the knowledge of the**

1:12 Here are three wonderful truths for evangelism:
1. God has enabled you to be His witness (Acts 1:8).
2. God considers you faithful, entrusting you with the stewardship of the gospel (1 Corinthians 9:16,17).
3. God has placed you into the ministry (Mark 16:15).

2:1 Intercessory prayer. "God gave us intercessory prayer so we could partner with Him in transforming society, saving the lost, and establishing His kingdom. To be sure, God is perfectly capable of doing these things without us. He is all-wise, full of love, and almighty. In His wisdom He always knows what is best. In His love He always chooses what is best. And in His power He is able to do what is best. He doesn't need us. Nevertheless, in His sovereign good pleasure, He has chosen to involve us, through our prayers, in accomplishing His will. Our intercessory prayers are important to God; they should also be important to us." *Alvin J. Vander Griend, "Your Prayers Matter," Discipleship Journal*

2:4 Salvation is possible for every person. See 2 Peter 3:9.

QUESTIONS & OBJECTIONS

 1:8–10 *"How should I witness to a homosexual?"*

Rather than offend homosexuals by directly confronting the issue of their sinful lifestyle, modern evangelism often tries to soften the approach by saying that "God hates the sin, but loves the sinner." This isn't a new concept. *Charles Finney* stated, "God is not angry merely against the sin abstracted from the sinner, but against the sinner himself. Some persons have labored hard to set up this ridiculous and absurd abstraction, and would fain make it appear that God is angry at sin, yet not at the sinner. He hates the theft, but loves the thief. He abhors adultery, but is pleased with the adulterer. Now this is supreme nonsense. The sin has no moral character apart from the sinner. The act is nothing apart from the actor. The very thing that God hates and disapproves is not the mere event—the thing done in distinction from the doer; but it is the *doer himself*. It grieves and displeases Him that a rational moral agent, under His government, should array himself against his own God and Father, against all that is right and just in the universe. This is the thing that offends God. The sinner himself is the direct and the only object of his anger.

"So the Bible shows. God is angry with the wicked [Psalm 7:11], not with the abstract sin. If the wicked turn not, God will whet His sword—He has bent His bow and made it ready—not to shoot at the *sin*, but the *sinner*—the wicked man who has done the abominable thing. This is the only doctrine of either the Bible or of common sense on this subject" *(The Guilt of Sin)*.

The biblical way to witness to a homosexual is not to argue with him about his lifestyle but to use the Law to bring the knowledge of sin. This will show him that he is guilty of breaking God's holy Law, and he is damned *despite* his sexual preference. The Law was made for homosexuals, as well as other lawbreakers. See Psalm 5:5 and 2 Peter 2:6–8 comments.

truth.

5 For there is one God, and one mediator between God and men, the man Christ Jesus;

6 Who gave himself a ransom for all, to be testified in due time.

7 Whereunto I am ordained a preacher, and an apostle, (I speak the truth in Christ, and lie not;) a teacher of the Gentiles in faith and verity.

8 I will therefore that men pray every where, lifting up holy hands, without wrath and doubting.

9 In like manner also, that women adorn themselves in modest apparel, with shamefacedness and sobriety; not with broided hair, or gold, or pearls, or costly array;

10 But (which becomes women professing godliness) with good works.

11 Let the woman learn in silence with all subjection.

12 But I suffer not a woman to teach, nor to usurp authority over the man, but to be in silence.

2:5 "We know God only through Jesus Christ. Without this Mediator, is taken away all communication with God; through Jesus Christ we know God. All those who have pretended to know God, and prove Him without Jesus Christ, have only impotent proofs.

"But, to prove Jesus Christ we have the prophecies which are good and valid proofs. And those prophecies, being fulfilled, and truly proved by the event, indicate the certainty of these truths, and therefore the truth of the divinity of Jesus Christ. In Him, and by Him, then, we know God. Otherwise, and without Scripture, without original sin, without a necessary Mediator, we can not absolutely prove God, nor teach a good doctrine and sound morals." *Blaise Pascal*

2:8 "The neglect of prayer is a grand hindrance to holiness." *John Wesley*

2:14 *"God made me like this. Sin is His fault!"*

If this won't work in a civil court, it certainly won't work on Judgment Day. Even with an expert defense lawyer, it would take a pretty inept judge to fall for the old "God made me do it" defense. We are responsible moral agents. The "buck" stopped at Adam. He tried to blame both God and Eve for his sin; Eve blamed the serpent. It is human nature to try, but it doesn't work with God.

13 For Adam was first formed, then Eve.
14 And Adam was not deceived, but the woman being deceived was in the transgression.
15 Notwithstanding she shall be saved in childbearing, if they continue in faith and charity and holiness with sobriety.

CHAPTER 3

THIS is a true saying, If a man desire the office of a bishop, he desires a good work.
2 A bishop then must be blameless, the husband of one wife, vigilant, sober, of good behavior, given to hospitality, able to teach;
3 Not given to wine, no striker, not greedy of filthy lucre; but patient, not a brawler, not covetous;
4 One that rules well his own house, having his children in subjection with all gravity;
5 (For if a man know not how to rule his own house, how shall he take care of the church of God?)
6 Not a novice, lest being lifted up with pride he fall into the condemnation of the devil.

7 Moreover he must have a good report of them which are without; lest he fall into reproach and the snare of the devil.
8 Likewise must the deacons be grave, not double-tongued, not given to much wine, not greedy of filthy lucre;
9 Holding the mystery of the faith in a pure conscience.
10 And let these also first be proved; then let them use the office of a deacon, being found blameless.
11 Even so must their wives be grave, not slanderers, sober, faithful in all things.
12 Let the deacons be the husbands of one wife, ruling their children and their own houses well.
13 For they that have used the office of a deacon well purchase to themselves a good degree, and great boldness in the faith which is in Christ Jesus.
14 These things write I to you, hoping to come to you shortly:
15 But if I tarry long, that you may know how you ought to behave yourself in the house of God, which is the church of the living God, the pillar and ground of the truth.
16 And without controversy great is the

2:14 Why God created the serpent and allowed him to tempt Eve is a great mystery. However, those who would be quick to accuse God of wrongdoing would be wise to lay a hand on their mouth. We don't have to question His integrity because we know that all of His judgments are true and altogether righteous (Psalm 19:9). See also 2 Corinthians 11:3 comment.

3:9 "Without God there is no virtue because there is no prompting of the conscience...without God there is a coarsening of the society; without God democracy will not and cannot long endure...If we ever forget that we are One Nation Under God, then we will be a nation gone under." *Ronald Reagan*

3:16 Was Jesus God in human form? See Hebrews 1:1–3.

3:16   *Jehovah's Witnesses: Witnessing Tips*

By David A. Reed, Ex-Jehovah's Witness elder

Encounters between Christians and Jehovah's Witnesses typically revolve around a discussion of deity. The reason for this is twofold. First, this is the area where Watchtower theology deviates most dramatically from orthodox Christianity. In contrast to the Trinitarian concept of one God in three Persons—Father, Son, and Holy Spirit—the JWs have been taught to believe that God the Father alone is "Jehovah," the only true God; that Jesus Christ is Michael the archangel, the first angelic being created by God; and that the Holy Spirit is neither God nor a person, but rather God's impersonal "active force." Second, the subject of deity is a frequent confrontational focus because *both* Jehovah's Witnesses and Christians (at least those who like to witness to JWs) feel confident and well-prepared to defend their stand and attack the opposing viewpoint.

Due to the profound theological differences, such discussions often take the form of spiritual trench warfare—a long series of arguments and counterarguments, getting nowhere and ending in mutual frustration. But this need not be the case, especially if the Christian will "become all things to all men" by taking a moment to put himself in the Witness's shoes, so to speak (see 1 Corinthians 9:22). In the JW's mind he himself is a worshiper of the true God of the Bible, while you are a lost soul who has been misled by the devil into worshiping a pagan three-headed deity. He is, no doubt, quite sincere in these beliefs and feels both threatened and offended by the doctrine of the Trinity. To give any serious consideration to your arguments in support of the Trinity is simply unthinkable to the JW; he would be sinning against Jehovah God to entertain such a thought.

So, in order to make any headway with the Witness, it is necessary to bridge the gap—to find common ground that will enable him to rethink his theology. Rather than plunging into a defense of "the doctrine of the Trinity," which can be mind-boggling even to a Christian, take things one step at a time.

A good first step would be to consider the question, "Is Jesus Christ really an angel?" It will be frightening to the Jehovah's Witness to open this cherished belief of his to critical re-examination, but not nearly as frightening as to start off discussing evidence that God is tri-une.

Since the Watchtower Society speaks of "Jesus Christ, whom we understand from the Scriptures to be Michael the archangel" (*The Watchtower,* February 15, 1979, p. 31), put the JW on the spot and ask him to show you "the Scriptures" that say Jesus is Michael. There are none. The Watchtower Society *New World Translation* (NWT) mentions Michael five times as: 1) "one of the foremost princes" (Dan. 10:13); 2) "the prince of [Daniel's] people" (Dan. 10:21); 3) "the great prince who is standing in behalf of the sons of [Daniel's] people" (Dan. 12:1); 4) "the archangel" who "had a difference with the devil and was disputing about Moses' body" but "did not dare to bring a judgment against him in abusive terms" (Jude 9); and 5) a participant in heavenly conflict when "Michael and his angels battled with the dragon" (Rev. 12:7).

Ask the Jehovah's Witness which one of these verses says that Michael is Jesus Christ. Help him to see that it is necessary to read Scripture *plus* a complicated Watchtower argument to reach that conclusion. Rather than being merely *"one of* the foremost princes," Jesus Christ is "Lord of lords and King of kings" (Rev. 17:14, NWT) and is "far above every government and authority and power and lordship and every name named, not only in this system of things, but also in that to come" (Ephesians 1:21, NWT). And, unlike "Michael who did not dare condemn the Devil with insulting words, but said, 'The Lord rebuke you!'" (Jude 9, *Today's English Version*), Jesus Christ displayed His authority over the devil when He freely commanded him, "Go away, Satan!" (Matthew 4:10, NWT).

In arguing that Jesus is Michael the archangel, the Watchtower Society also points to another verse that does not use the name Michael but says that "the Lord himself will descend from heaven with a commanding call, with an archangel's voice and with God's trumpet..." (1 Thessalonians 4:16, NWT).

(continued on next page)

(3:16 continued)
However, the expression "with an archangel's voice" simply means that the archangel, like God's trumpet, will herald the coming of the Lord, not that the Lord is an archangel.

Point out to the JW that none of the verses he has attempted to use as proof-texts even comes close to stating that Jesus Christ is Michael the archangel. In fact, Scripture clearly teaches the opposite: namely, that the Son of God is *superior* to the angels. The entire first chapter of Hebrews is devoted to this theme. Have the Witness read Hebrews chapter one aloud with you, and, as you do so, interrupt to point out the sharp contrast between angels and the Son of God. "For to what angel did God ever say, 'Thou are my Son...?' And again, when he brings the first-born into the world, he says, 'Let all God's angels worship him'" (vv. 5,6, *Revised Standard Version*).

Remind the JW that angels consistently refuse worship ("Be careful! Do not do that! ...Worship God," Revelation 22:8,9, NWT), but the Father's command concerning the Son is, "Let all God's angels worship him" (Hebrews 1:6). That is how the Watchtower's own *New World Translation* read for some 20 years until, in 1970, the Society changed it to read "do obeisance to him" instead of "worship him"—part of their consistent campaign to eliminate from their Bible all references to the deity of Christ. (See John 10:36 comment.)

True, you have not yet proved the "doctrine of the Trinity" in this discussion. But you have laid a good foundation by giving the Jehovah's Witness convincing evidence that Jesus Christ is not an angel (he is now faced with the question of who Jesus really is), and you have shown that the Watchtower Society has misled him, even resorting to altering Scripture to do so. Now you are in a much better position to go on to present the gospel.

mystery of godliness: God was manifest in the flesh, justified in the Spirit, seen of angels, preached to the Gentiles, believed on in the world, received up into glory.

CHAPTER 4

NOW the Spirit speaks expressly, that in the latter times some shall depart from the faith, giving heed to seducing spirits, and doctrines of devils;

2 Speaking lies in hypocrisy; having their conscience seared with a hot iron;

3 Forbidding to marry, and commanding to abstain from meats, which God has created to be received with thanksgiving of them which believe and know

---

4:1 For more signs of the end times, see 2 Timothy 3:1.

4:1 Halloween. The celebration can be traced back to the Druid festival of the dead. The Roman Pantheon, built by Emperor Hadrian in A.D. 100 as a temple to the goddess Cybele and other Roman gods, became the principle place of worship. In 609, Emperor Phocas seized Rome and gave the Pantheon to Pope Boniface IV. Boniface consecrated it to the Virgin Mary and kept using the temple to pray for the dead, only now it was "Christianized," as men added the unscriptural teaching of purgatory. In 834, Gregory IV extended the feast for all the church and it became known as All Saint's Day, still remembering the dead.

Samhain, a Druid god of the dead, was honored at Hallowe'en ("All Hallows Eve") in Britain, Germany, France, and the Celtic countries. Samhain called together all wicked souls who died within the past year and who were destined to inhabit animals. The Druids believed that souls of the dead came back to their homes to be entertained by those still living. Suitable food and shelter were provided for these spirits or else they would cast spells, steal infants, destroy crops, kill farm animals, and create terror as they haunted the living. This is the action that "Trick-or-Treat" copies today. The Samhain celebration used nuts, apples, skeletons, witches, and black cats. Divination and auguries were practiced as well as magic to seek answers for the future. Even today witchcraft practitioners declare October 31 as the most favorable time to practice their arts.

Many Christians use Halloween as an opportunity to reach out to the lost by giving candy and gospel tracts to those who knock on their door during Halloween. *What other day do scores of people come to your door for gospel tracts?*

QUESTIONS & OBJECTIONS

 4:2   *"I don't feel guilty."*

People often don't feel guilty when they sin because they have "seared" their conscience. They have removed the batteries from the smoke detector of their conscience, so that they can sin without interruption. The way to resurrect a deadened conscience is to go through each of the Ten Commandments, reminding the person that they know that it's wrong to lie, steal, commit adultery, etc. Always preach the Law along with future punishment, then pray that the Holy Spirit will come upon them and cause them to be convicted of sin, righteousness, and judgment to come.

the truth.

4 For every creature of God is good, and nothing to be refused, if it be received with thanksgiving:

5 For it is sanctified by the word of God and prayer.

6 If you put the brethren in remembrance of these things, you shall be a good minister of Jesus Christ, nourished up in the words of faith and of good doctrine, whereunto you have attained.

7 But refuse profane and old wives' fables, and exercise yourself rather to godliness.

8 For bodily exercise profits little: but godliness is profitable to all things, having promise of the life that now is, and of that which is to come.

9 This is a faithful saying and worthy of all acceptation.

10 For therefore we both labor and suffer reproach, because we trust in the living God, who is the Savior of all men, specially of those that believe.

11 These things command and teach.

12 Let no man despise your youth; but be an example of the believers, in word, in conversation, in charity, in spirit, in faith, in purity.

13 Till I come, give attendance to reading, to exhortation, to doctrine.

THE FUNCTION OF THE LAW

 4:2 "When once God the Holy Spirit applies the Law to the conscience, secret sins are dragged to light, little sins are magnified to their true size, and things apparently harmless become exceedingly sinful. Before that dread searcher of the hearts and trier of the reins makes His entrance into the soul, it appears righteous, just, lovely, and holy; but when He reveals the hidden evils, the scene is changed. Offenses which were once styled peccadilloes, trifles, freaks of youth, follies, indulgences, little slips, etc., then appear in their true color, as breaches of the Law of God, deserving condign punishment." *Charles Spurgeon*

"The proper effect of the Law is to lead us out of our tents and tabernacles, that is to say, from the quietness and security wherein we dwell, and from trusting in ourselves, and to bring us before the presence of God, to reveal his wrath to us, and to set us before our sins." *Martin Luther*

4:3,4 Vegetarianism. One of the signs of the end of this age is that people would try to impose a vegetarian lifestyle on others, but the Scriptures tell us that *every* creature of God is good for food, and *nothing* is to be refused.

Vegetarianism is not always the blessing it is made out to be. In India in 1942, three million people died of starvation. Alongside the bodies of men, women, and children lay the carcasses of hundreds of thousands of "sacred" cows—potential beef-steaks. They were God-given protein that would have saved the lives of multitudes. See Psalm 66:15 and Revelation 22:3 comments.

14 Neglect not the gift that is in you, which was given you by prophecy, with the laying on of the hands of the presbytery.

15 Meditate upon these things; give yourself wholly to them; that your profiting may appear to all.

16 Take heed to yourself, and to the doctrine; continue in them: for in doing this you shall both save yourself, and them that hear you.

CHAPTER 5

REBUKE not an elder, but entreat him as a father; and the younger men as brethren;

2 The elder women as mothers; the younger as sisters, with all purity.

3 Honor widows that are widows indeed.

4 But if any widow have children or nephews, let them learn first to show piety at home, and to requite their parents: for that is good and acceptable before God.

5 Now she that is a widow indeed, and desolate, trusts in God, and continues in supplications and prayers night and day.

6 But she that lives in pleasure is dead while she lives.

7 And these things give in charge, that they may be blameless.

8 But if any provide not for his own, and specially for those of his own house, he has denied the faith, and is worse than an infidel.

9 Let not a widow be taken into the number under threescore years old, having been the wife of one man,

10 Well reported of for good works; if she have brought up children, if she have lodged strangers, if she have washed the saints' feet, if she have relieved the afflicted, if she have diligently followed every good work.

11 But the younger widows refuse: for when they have begun to wax wanton against Christ, they will marry;

12 Having damnation, because they have cast off their first faith.

13 And withal they learn to be idle, wandering about from house to house; and not only idle, but tattlers also and busybodies, speaking things which they ought not.

> Try after sermons to talk to strangers. The preacher may have missed the mark, but you need not miss it. Or the preacher may have struck the mark, and you can help to make the impression deeper by a kind word.
>
> **CHARLES SPURGEON**

14 I will therefore that the younger women marry, bear children, guide the house, give none occasion to the adversary to speak reproachfully.

15 For some are already turned aside after Satan.

16 If any man or woman that believes have widows, let them relieve them, and let not the church be charged; that it may relieve them that are widows indeed.

17 Let the elders that rule well be counted worthy of double honor, especially they who labor in the word and doctrine.

18 For the scripture says, You shall not muzzle the ox that treads out the corn.

4:7 The way to prevent injuries and pain is to keep yourself fit. Exercise. After warning Timothy to refuse false doctrine, Paul told him to exercise himself to godliness. Paul kept fit through exercise. He said, "Herein do I exercise myself, to have always a conscience void of offense toward God, and toward men" (Acts 24:16). Do the same. Listen to the voice of conscience. It's your friend, not your enemy.

5:5 "I have no confidence at all in polished speech or brilliant literary effort to bring about a revival, but I have all the confidence in the world in the poor saint who would weep her eyes out because people are living in sin." *Charles Spurgeon*

6:1 *"Isn't it blasphemous to call the Bible 'God's Word' when it makes Him look so bad?"*

I am going to tell you some things about my father that will make him look bad. He regularly left my mother to fend for herself. I was once horrified to hear that he deliberately killed a helpless animal. Not only that, but he hit me (often).

Here's the information that's missing: The reason he left my mom during the day was to work to earn money to take care of her and their children. He killed the animal because it had been run over by a car and was suffering. He regularly chastened me because he loved me enough to teach me right from wrong (I was a brat).

Portions of the Bible that "make God look bad" merely reveal that we lack understanding. I never once questioned my dad's integrity, because I trusted him (see Mark 10:15).

And, The laborer is worthy of his reward.

19 Against an elder receive not an accusation, but before two or three witnesses.

20 Them that sin rebuke before all, that others also may fear.

21 I charge you before God, and the Lord Jesus Christ, and the elect angels, that you observe these things without preferring one before another, doing nothing by partiality.

22 Lay hands suddenly on no man, neither be partaker of other men's sins: keep yourself pure.

23 Drink no longer water, but use a little wine for your stomach's sake and your often infirmities.

24 Some men's sins are open beforehand, going before to judgment; and some men they follow after.

25 Likewise also the good works of some are manifest beforehand; and they that are otherwise cannot be hid.

· · · · · ·

For how to address the sinner's conscience, see John 4:7 comment.

· · · · · ·

CHAPTER 6

LET as many servants as are under the yoke count their own masters worthy of all honor, that the name of God and his doctrine be not blasphemed.

2 And they that have believing masters, let them not despise them, because they are brethren; but rather do them service, because they are faithful and beloved, partakers of the benefit. These things teach and exhort.

3 If any man teach otherwise, and consent not to wholesome words, even the words of our Lord Jesus Christ, and to the doctrine which is according to godliness;

4 He is proud, knowing nothing, but doting about questions and strifes of words, whereof comes envy, strife, railings, evil surmisings,

5 Perverse disputings of men of corrupt minds, and destitute of the truth, supposing that gain is godliness: from such withdraw yourself.

6 But godliness with contentment is great gain.

7 For we brought nothing into this world, and it is certain we can carry nothing out.

8 And having food and raiment let us be therewith content.

9 But they that will be rich fall into temptation and a snare, and into many foolish and hurtful lusts, which drown men in destruction and perdition.

10 For the love of money is the root of all evil: which while some coveted after, they have erred from the faith, and pierced themselves through with many sorrows.

11 But you, O man of God, flee these things; and follow after righteousness, godliness, faith, love, patience, meekness.

6:20 "Didn't the Church persecute Galileo?"

Skeptics often try to demean Scripture by saying that the Christian Church persecuted Galileo when he maintained that the earth circled the sun. As a professor of astronomy at the University of Pisa, Galileo was required to teach the accepted theory of his time that the sun and all the planets revolved around the Earth. Later at the University of Padua he was exposed to a new theory, proposed by Nicolaus Copernicus, that the Earth and all the other planets revolved around the sun. Galileo's observations with his new telescope convinced him of the truth of Copernicus's sun-centered or heliocentric theory. Galileo's support for the heliocentric theory got him into trouble with the *Roman Catholic church*. In 1633 during the Inquisition he was convicted of heresy and ordered to recant (publicly withdraw) his support of Copernicus. The Roman Catholic church sentenced him to life imprisonment, but because of his advanced age allowed him to serve his term under house arrest at his villa outside of Florence, Italy. The Christian Church therefore should not be blamed for his imprisonment. It was the Roman Catholic church that persecuted Galileo.

"Under the sentence of imprisonment Galileo remained till his death in 1642. It is, however, untrue to speak of him as in any proper sense a 'prisoner.' As his Protestant biographer, von Gebler, tells us, 'One glance at the truest historical source for the famous trial would convince anyone that Galileo spent altogether twenty-two days in the buildings of the Holy Office [during the Inquisition], and even then not in a prison cell with barred windows, but in the handsome and commodious apartment of an official of the Inquisition.'" *(Catholic Encyclopedia)*

12 *Fight the good fight of faith, lay hold on eternal life, whereunto you are also called, and have professed a good profession before many witnesses.*

13 I give you charge in the sight of God, who quickens all things, and before Christ Jesus, who before Pontius Pilate witnessed a good confession;

14 That you keep this commandment without spot, unrebukeable, until the appearing of our Lord Jesus Christ:

15 Which in his times he shall show, who is the blessed and only Potentate, the King of kings, and Lord of lords;

16 Who only has immortality, dwelling in the light which no man can approach unto; whom no man has seen, nor can see: to whom be honor and power everlasting. Amen.

17 Charge them that are rich in this world, that they be not high-minded, nor trust in uncertain riches, but in the living God, who gives us richly all things to enjoy;

18 That they do good, that they be rich in good works, ready to distribute, willing to communicate;

19 Laying up in store for themselves a good foundation against the time to come, that they may lay hold on eternal life.

20 O Timothy, keep that which is committed to your trust, avoiding profane and vain babblings, and oppositions of science falsely so called:

21 Which some professing have erred concerning the faith. Grace be with you. Amen.

6:18 "Do all the good you can, by all the means you can, in all the places you can, at all the times you can, to all the people you can, as long as you ever can." *John Wesley*

2 Timothy

CHAPTER 1

PAUL, an apostle of Jesus Christ by the will of God, according to the promise of life which is in Christ Jesus,

2 To Timothy, my dearly beloved son: Grace, mercy, and peace, from God the Father and Christ Jesus our Lord.

3 I thank God, whom I serve from my forefathers with pure conscience, that without ceasing I have remembrance of you in my prayers night and day;

4 Greatly desiring to see you, being mindful of your tears, that I may be filled with joy;

5 When I call to remembrance the unfeigned faith that is in you, which dwelt first in your grandmother Lois, and your mother Eunice; and I am persuaded that in you also.

6 Wherefore I put you in remembrance that you stir up the gift of God, which is in you by the putting on of my hands.

7 *For God has not given us the spirit of fear; but of power, and of love, and of a sound mind.*

8 *Be not therefore ashamed of the testimony of our Lord, nor of me his prisoner: but you be a partaker of the afflictions of the gospel according to the power of God;*

9 *Who has saved us, and called us with an holy calling, not according to our works, but according to his own purpose and grace, which was given us in Christ Jesus before the world began,*

10 *But is now made manifest by the appearing of our Savior Jesus Christ, who has abolished death, and has brought life and immortality to light through the gospel:*

11 *Whereunto I am appointed a preacher, and an apostle, and a teacher of the Gentiles.*

12 For the which cause I also suffer these things: nevertheless I am not ashamed: for I know whom I have believed, and am persuaded that he is able to keep that which I have committed to him against that day.

13 Hold fast the form of sound words, which you have heard of me, in faith and love which is in Christ Jesus.

14 That good thing which was committed to you keep by the Holy Spirit which dwells in us.

15 This you know, that all they which are in Asia be turned away from me; of whom are Phygellus and Hermogenes.

16 The Lord give mercy to the house of Onesiphorus; for he oft refreshed me, and

---

1:8,9 "We want the power of God to be manifested, but sometimes we fail to seek purity on our part." Anonymous testimony (quoted in *The Transforming Power of Fasting and Prayer* by *Bill Bright*)

1:10 "Surely God would not have created such a being as man, with an ability to grasp the infinite, to exist only for a day. No, no, man was made for immortality." *Abraham Lincoln*

was not ashamed of my chain:

17 But, when he was in Rome, he sought me out very diligently, and found me.

18 The Lord grant to him that he may find mercy of the Lord in that day: and in how many things he ministered to me at Ephesus, you know very well.

CHAPTER 2

YOU therefore, my son, be strong in the grace that is in Christ Jesus.

2 And the things that you have heard of me among many witnesses, the same commit to faithful men, who shall be able to teach others also.

3 You therefore endure hardness, as a good soldier of Jesus Christ.

4 No man that wars entangles himself with the affairs of this life; that he may please him who has chosen him to be a soldier.

5 And if a man also strive for masteries, yet is he not crowned, except he strive lawfully.

6 The husbandman that labors must be first partaker of the fruits.

7 Consider what I say; and the Lord give you understanding in all things.

8 Remember that Jesus Christ of the seed of David was raised from the dead according to my gospel:

9 Wherein I suffer trouble, as an evil doer, even to bonds; but the word of God is not bound.

10 Therefore I endure all things for the elect's sakes, that they may also obtain the salvation which is in Christ Jesus with eternal glory.

11 It is a faithful saying: For if we be dead with him, we shall also live with him:

12 **If we suffer, we shall also reign with him: if we deny him, he also will deny us:**

13 **If we believe not, yet he abides faithful: he cannot deny himself.**

14 Of these things put them in remembrance, charging them before the Lord that they strive not about words to no profit, but to the subverting of the hearers.

15 Study to show yourself approved to God, a workman that needs not to be ashamed, rightly dividing the word of truth.

16 But shun profane and vain babblings: for they will increase to more ungodliness.

17 And their word will eat as does a canker: of whom is Hymenaeus and Philetus;

18 Who concerning the truth have erred, saying that the resurrection is past already; and overthrow the faith of some.

19 Nevertheless the foundation of God stands sure, having this seal, The Lord knows them that are his. And, Let every one that names the name of Christ depart from iniquity.

20 But in a great house there are not

2:3 "A barracks is meant to be a place where real soldiers were to be fed and equipped for war, not a place to settle down in or as a comfortable snuggery in which to enjoy ourselves. I hope that if ever they, our soldiers, do settle down God will burn their barracks over their heads!" *Catherine Booth*

2:19 **True and false converts.** False converts lack genuine contrition for sin. They make a profession of faith but are deficient in biblical repentance—"They profess that they know God; but in works they deny him, being abominable, and disobedient, and to every good work reprobate" (Titus 1:16). A true convert, however, has a knowledge of sin and has godly sorrow, truly repents, and produces the "things that accompany salvation" (Hebrews 6:9). This is evident by the fruit of the Spirit, the fruit of righteousness, etc. However, only God truly knows the genuine from the false.

"Our churches are full of the nicest, kindest people who have never known the despair of guilt or the breathless wonder of forgiveness." *P. T. Forsyth*

2:19 *"The church is full of hypocrites."*

Hypocrites may show up at a church building every Sunday, but there are no hypocrites in the Church (Christ's body). *Hypocrite* comes from the Greek word for "actor," or pretender. Hypocrisy is "the practice of professing beliefs, feelings, or virtues that one does not hold." The Church is made up of true believers; hypocrites are "pretenders" who sit among God's people. God knows those who love Him, and the Bible warns that He will sort out the true converts from the false on the Day of Judgment. All hypocrites will end up in hell (Matthew 24:51).

only vessels of gold and of silver, but also of wood and of earth; and some to honor, and some to dishonor.

21 If a man therefore purge himself from these, he shall be a vessel to honor, sanctified, and meet for the master's use, and prepared to every good work.

22 Flee also youthful lusts: but follow righteousness, faith, charity, peace, with them that call on the Lord out of a pure heart.

23 But foolish and unlearned questions avoid, knowing that they do gender strifes.

24 And the servant of the Lord must not strive; but be gentle to all men, able to teach, patient,

25 In meekness instructing those that oppose themselves; if God peradventure will give them repentance to the acknowledging of the truth;

26 And that they may recover themselves out of the snare of the devil, who are taken captive by him at his will.

CHAPTER 3

This know also, that in the last days perilous times shall come.

2 **For men shall be lovers of their own selves, covetous, boasters, proud, blasphemers, disobedient to parents, unthankful, unholy,**

3 **Without natural affection, trucebreakers, false accusers, incontinent, fierce, despisers of those that are good,**

4 **Traitors, heady, high-minded, lovers of pleasures more than lovers of God;**

5 **Having a form of godliness, but denying the power thereof: from such turn away.**

6 For of this sort are they which creep into houses, and lead captive silly women laden with sins, led away with divers lusts,

7 Ever learning, and never able to come to the knowledge of the truth.

8 Now as Jannes and Jambres withstood Moses, so do these also resist the truth:

2:21 "When you are willing, God will call you. When you are prepared, God will empower you. When you are empowered, God will test you. When you are tested, God will strengthen you. When you are strengthened, God will use you, and when you are used, God will reward you." *Ross Rhodes*

"Clay is molded into a vessel, but the ultimate use of the vessel depends on the part where nothing exists. Doors and windows are cut out of the wall of a house, but the ultimate use of the house depends on the parts where nothing exists. I wish to become such a useful nothing." *Richard Wurmbrand*

2:24 This is the spirit in which we should share our faith. It has been well said, "Never argue with a fool. Someone watching might not be able to tell the difference." As we witness, we must be kind and gentle to those who oppose us. It is not our job to convince them with brilliant arguments, but simply to share the truth, so that God may bring them to repentance. See 2 Timothy 4:2.

POINTS FOR OPEN-AIR PREACHING

"Watch It, Blind Man!"

2:24–26

There is one passage in Scripture to which I point for all those who want to witness or preach in the open-air. It is 2 Timothy 2:24–26. Memorize it. Scripture tells us that sinners are blind. They *cannot* see. What would you think if I were to stomp up to a blind man who had just stumbled, and say, "Watch where you're going, blind man!"? Such an attitude is completely unreasonable. The man *cannot* see.

The same applies to the lost—spiritual sight is beyond their ability. Look at the words used in Scripture: "Except a man be born again, he *cannot see* the kingdom of God...The god of this world has *blinded* the minds of them which believe not...But the natural man receives not the things of the Spirit of God: for they are foolishness to him: neither *can* he know them...Having the understanding *darkened*...because of the *blindness* of their heart...Ever learning, and *never able* to come to the knowledge of the truth."

With these thoughts in mind, read 2 Timothy 2:24–26 again and look at the adjectives used by Paul to describe the attitude we are to have with sinners: "must not strive...be gentle...patient...in meekness." Just as it is unreasonable to be impatient with a blind man, so it is with the sinner. See Matthew 5:10–12 comment.

men of corrupt minds, reprobate concerning the faith.

9 But they shall proceed no further: for their folly shall be manifest to all men, as theirs also was.

10 But you have fully known my doctrine, manner of life, purpose, faith, long-suffering, charity, patience,

11 Persecutions, afflictions, which came to me at Antioch, at Iconium, at Lystra;

2:26 Warning sinners of judgment. Jeremiah warned King Zedekiah repeatedly that God would judge His people. The prophet pleaded with the king, but still he would not do what Jeremiah said. One cannot but wonder what the king thought about after he was blinded and bound with chains (Jeremiah 39:6–8). Perhaps his thoughts were of the last thing he saw—the unspeakable agony of seeing his own beloved sons butchered before his eyes. Perhaps the words of Jeremiah flashed before his tormented mind, warning him that all of Israel (including his sons) could have been saved if he had obeyed the voice of the Lord. We can't begin to imagine the remorse he felt.

How this must typify the ungodly who have been bound by the bronze fetters of sin, "taken captive by [the devil] at his will." We warn that there is judgment coming (both temporal and eternal) to those who live for the devil, but most remain in unbelief. Their master is he who came "to steal, and to kill, and to destroy" (John 10:10). He blinds the minds of those who don't believe. Like Zedekiah, so many see their own sons and daughters die before their very eyes. AIDS and other sin-related diseases, as well as alcohol, drugs, and suicide, kill many before their time. Multitudes give themselves to the burning fires of sexual lust, and so the devil breaks down the walls of entire nations.

Yet, there is still time to warn them. There is still time to pray that God will open their understanding. God told Jeremiah to tell an Ethiopian named Ebedmelech that He would deliver him from judgment. He said, "For I will surely deliver you, and you shall not fall by the sword, but your life shall be for a prey to you: because you have put your trust in me, says the Lord" (Jeremiah 39:18). This is the message we are to deliver. He who keeps his life will lose it, but those who trust in the Lord will be safe on the Day of Judgment. On that Day, the sword of the Word of God will not fall upon him, because it fell on the Savior two thousand years ago.

3:1 For more signs of the end times, see 2 Peter 3:3.

3:5 "The chief danger of the 20th century will be religion without the Holy Spirit, Christianity without Christ, forgiveness without repentance, salvation without regeneration, politics without God, and heaven without hell." *General William Booth*

what persecutions I endured: but out of them all the Lord delivered me.

12 Yes, and all that will live godly in Christ Jesus shall suffer persecution.

13 But evil men and seducers shall wax worse and worse, deceiving, and being deceived.

14 But continue in the things which you have learned and have been assured of, knowing of whom you have learned them;

15 And that from a child you have known the holy scriptures, which are able to make you wise to salvation through faith which is in Christ Jesus.

16 All scripture is given by inspiration of God, and is profitable for doctrine, for reproof, for correction, for instruction in righteousness:

17 That the man of God may be perfect, thoroughly furnished to all good works.

CHAPTER 4

I CHARGE you therefore before God, and the Lord Jesus Christ, who shall judge the quick and the dead at his appearing and his kingdom;

2 *Preach the word; be instant in season, out of season; reprove, rebuke, exhort with*

"The New Testament is the very best book that ever was or ever will be known in the world."

Charles Dickens

all longsuffering and doctrine.

3 For the time will come when they will not endure sound doctrine; but after their own lusts shall they heap to themselves teachers, having itching ears;

4 And they shall turn away their ears from the truth, and shall be turned to fa-

---

3:16 The Bible's Inspiration. "The authors, speaking under the inspiration of the Holy Spirit, ...wrote on hundreds of controversial subjects with absolute harmony from the beginning to the end. There is one unfolding story from Genesis to Revelation: the redemption of mankind through the Messiahthe Old Testament through the coming Messiah, the New Testament from the Messiah that has come. In Genesis, you have paradise lost, in Revelation you have paradise gained. You can't understand Revelation without understanding Genesis. It's all interwoven on hundreds of controversial subjects.

"Now here's the picture: 1,600 years, 60 generations, 40-plus authors, different walks of life, different places, different times, different moods, different continents, three languages, writing on hundreds of controversial subjects and yet when they are brought together, there is absolute harmony from beginning to end...There is no other book in history to even compare to the uniqueness of this continuity. "*Josh McDowell*

"We account the Scriptures of God to be the most sublime philosophy. I find more sure marks of authenticity in the Bible than in any profane history whatsoever." *Sir Isaac Newton*

"The Bible is endorsed by the ages. Our civilization is built upon its words. In no other Book is there such a collection of inspired wisdom, reality, and hope." *Dwight D. Eisenhower*

3:16,17 What better good work can there be than to use the Law of God to bring sinners to repentance? For the biblical way to witness, see John 4:7-26 comment.

4:1 Judgment Day: For verses that warn of its reality, see Hebrews 9:27.

4:2 This is the spirit in which we should share our faith. See Titus 3:2,3.

bles.

5 *But watch in all things, endure afflic-tions, do the work of an evangelist, make full proof of your ministry.*

6 For I am now ready to be offered, and the time of my departure is at hand.

7 I have fought a good fight, I have fin-ished my course, I have kept the faith:

8 Henceforth there is laid up for me a crown of righteousness, which the Lord, the righteous judge, shall give me at that day: and not to me only, but to all them also that love his appearing.

9 Do your diligence to come shortly to me:

10 For Demas has forsaken me, having loved this present world, and is departed to Thessalonica; Crescens to Galatia, Titus to Dalmatia.

11 Only Luke is with me. Take Mark, and bring him with you: for he is prof-itable to me for the ministry.

12 And Tychicus have I sent to Ephesus.

13 The cloak that I left at Troas with Carpus, when you come, bring with you, and the books, but especially the parch-ments.

14 Alexander the coppersmith did me much evil: the Lord reward him accord-ing to his works:

15 Of whom be you ware also; for he has greatly withstood our words.

16 At my first answer no man stood with me, but all men forsook me: I pray God that it may not be laid to their charge.

17 Notwithstanding the Lord stood with me, and strengthened me; that by me the preaching might be fully known, and that all the Gentiles might hear: and I was delivered out of the mouth of the lion.

. . . . . .

For how to use gospel tracts, see 1 Corinthians 9:22 comment.

. . . . . .

18 And the Lord shall deliver me from every evil work, and will preserve me to his heavenly kingdom: to whom be glory for ever and ever. Amen.

19 Salute Prisca and Aquila, and the household of Onesiphorus.

20 Erastus abode at Corinth: but Tro-phimus have I left at Miletum sick.

21 Do your diligence to come before winter. Eubulus greets you, and Pudens, and Linus, and Claudia, and all the breth-ren.

22 The Lord Jesus Christ be with your spirit. Grace be with you. Amen.

4:2 "When it comes to seeking and saving the lost, it's always hunting season. We should be ready to preach the gospel to everyone we meet.

"What we want in the Church of Christ is a band of well-trained sharpshooters, who will pick the peo-ple out individually and be always on the watch for all who come into the place, not annoying them, but making sure that they do not go away without having had a personal warning, invita-tion, and exhortation to come to Christ." *Charles Spurgeon*

4:3,4 "Scratching people where they itch and addressing their felt needs is a stratagem of the poor steward of the oracles of God. This was the recipe for success for the false prophets of the Old Testament." *R. C. Sproul*

Titus

CHAPTER 1

PAUL, a servant of God, and an apostle of Jesus Christ, according to the faith of God's elect, and the acknowledging of the truth which is after godliness;

2 *In hope of eternal life, which God, that cannot lie, promised before the world began;*

3 *But has in due times manifested his word through preaching, which is committed to me according to the commandment of God our Savior;*

4 To Titus, mine own son after the common faith: Grace, mercy, and peace, from God the Father and the Lord Jesus Christ our Savior.

5 For this cause left I you in Crete, that you should set in order the things that are wanting, and ordain elders in every city, as I had appointed you:

6 If any be blameless, the husband of one wife, having faithful children not accused of riot or unruly.

7 For a bishop must be blameless, as the steward of God; not self-willed, not soon angry, not given to wine, no striker, not given to filthy lucre;

8 But a lover of hospitality, a lover of good men, sober, just, holy, temperate;

9 *Holding fast the faithful word as he has been taught, that he may be able by sound doctrine both to exhort and to convince the gainsayers.*

10 For there are many unruly and vain talkers and deceivers, specially they of the circumcision:

11 Whose mouths must be stopped, who subvert whole houses, teaching things which they ought not, for filthy lucre's sake.

12 One of themselves, even a prophet of their own, said, The Cretians are always liars, evil beasts, slow bellies.

13 This witness is true. Wherefore rebuke them sharply, that they may be sound in the faith;

14 Not giving heed to Jewish fables, and commandments of men, that turn from the truth.

15 To the pure all things are pure: but to them that are defiled and unbelieving is nothing pure; but even their mind and conscience is defiled.

16 They profess that they know God; but in works they deny him, being abom-

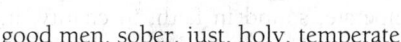

1:1 The world cries out for truth. They have no idea of their origin, why they exist, or what death holds in store for them. Sin has left them lost and in darkness. The truth will set them free (John 8:31,32), but there can be no understanding of the truth without repentance and faith. It comes *after* godliness.

1:9 The steward of God is not to see himself as being above the lowly task of evangelism.

1:11 The way to stop the mouth is to use the Law of God. See Romans 3:19 comment.

1:15 Those who defile the conscience remove the battery from their own smoke detector.

inable, and disobedient, and to every good work reprobate.

· · · · · ·

For alleged mistakes in the Bible, see Mark 15:26 comment.

· · · · · ·

CHAPTER 2

B UT speak the things which become sound doctrine:

2 That the aged men be sober, grave, temperate, sound in faith, in charity, in patience.

3 The aged women likewise, that they be in behavior as becomes holiness, not false accusers, not given to much wine, teachers of good things;

4 That they may teach the young women to be sober, to love their husbands, to love their children,

5 To be discreet, chaste, keepers at home, good, obedient to their own husbands, that the word of God be not blasphemed.

6 Young men likewise exhort to be sober minded.

7 In all things showing yourself a pattern of good works: in doctrine showing uncorruptness, gravity, sincerity,

8 Sound speech, that cannot be condemned; that he that is of the contrary part may be ashamed, having no evil thing to say of you.

9 Exhort servants to be obedient to their own masters, and to please them well in all things; not answering again;

10 Not purloining, but showing all good fidelity; that they may adorn the doctrine of God our Savior in all things.

11 For the grace of God that brings salvation has appeared to all men,

12 Teaching us that, denying ungodliness and worldly lusts, we should live soberly, righteously, and godly, in this present world;

13 Looking for that blessed hope, and the glorious appearing of the great God and our Savior Jesus Christ;

14 Who gave himself for us, that he might redeem us from all iniquity, and purify to himself a peculiar people, zealous of good works.

15 These things speak, and exhort, and rebuke with all authority. Let no man despise you.

CHAPTER 3

P UT them in mind to be subject to principalities and powers, to obey magistrates, to be ready to every good work,

2 To speak evil of no man, to be no brawlers, but gentle, showing all meekness to all men.

3 For we ourselves also were sometimes foolish, disobedient, deceived, serving divers lusts and pleasures, living in mal-

---

1:16 There are many who profess to know God, but they lack the things that accompany salvation the fruit of righteousness, holiness, repentance, good works, and the fruit of the Spirit. We must repent, turn to God, and do works befitting repentance (Acts 26:20).

2:6–8 We must be sober-minded, rich in good works, sound in doctrine, living in the fear of God and without corruption, all for the sake of our testimony.

3:2 This is the spirit in which we should share our faith. See James 3:17.

3:3 This is why we should never have a holier-than-thou attitude toward the unsaved (see also 1 Corinthians 6:9-11).

3:3 The deceitfulness of sin. Two women from Southern California were about to cross the Mexican border to return to the U.S. when they saw what looked like a very small, sick animal in the ditch beside their car. As they examined it in the darkness of the night, they saw that it was a tiny Chihuahua. There they decided to take it home with them and nurse it back to health. However, because they were afraid that they were breaking the law, they put it in the trunk of their car, and drove across the border. Once they were in the U.S., they retrieved the animal and nursed

ice and envy, hateful, and hating one another.

4 But after that the kindness and love of
God our Savior toward man appeared,

**5 Not by works of righteousness which
we have done, but according to his
mercy he saved us, by the washing of
regeneration, and renewing of the Holy
Spirit;**

6 Which he shed on us abundantly
through Jesus Christ our Savior;

7 That being justified by his grace, we
should be made heirs according to the
hope of eternal life.

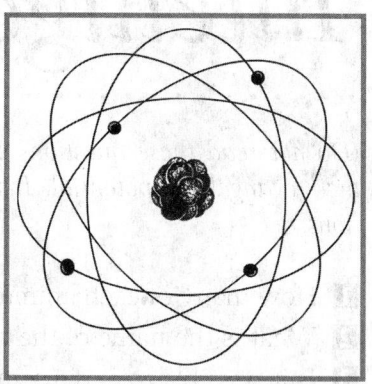

*The Bible tells us that God created every-
thing with things that are not seen.
See Hebrews 11:3 comment.*

> He is no Christian who does not seek
> to serve his God. The very motto of
> the Christian should be "I serve."
>
> **CHARLES SPURGEON**

8 This is a faithful saying, and these
things I will that you affirm constantly,
that they which have believed in God
might be careful to maintain good works.
These things are good and profitable to
men.

9 But avoid foolish questions, and genealogies, and contentions, and strivings
about the law; for they are unprofitable
and vain.

10 A man that is an heretic after the
first and second admonition reject;

11 Knowing that he that is such is sub-
verted, and sins, being condemned of
himself.

12 When I shall send Artemas to you,
or Tychicus, be diligent to come to me
to Nicopolis: for I have determined there
to winter.

13 Bring Zenas the lawyer and Apollos
on their journey diligently, that nothing
be wanting to them.

14 And let ours also learn to maintain
good works for necessary uses, that they
be not unfruitful.

15 All that are with me salute you. Greet
them that love us in the faith. Grace be
with you all. Amen.

---

it until they arrived home.

One of the women was so concerned for the ailing dog that she actually took it to bed with
her, and reached out several times during the night to touch the tiny animal and reassure it that
she was still present.

The dog was so sick the next morning, she decided to take it to the veterinarian. That's when
she found out that the animal wasn't a tiny sick dog. It was a Mexican water rat, dying of rabies.

The world, in the blackness of its ignorance, thinks that sin is a puppy to be played with. It is the
light of God's Law that enlightens the sinner to the fact that he is in bed with a deadly rat.

We were once deceived, serving divers lusts and pleasures, but now, if we are truly converted, our eyes have been opened. We see sin for the sugar-coated venom that it is.

3:5 New birth—its necessity for salvation. See 1 Peter 1:3.

3:5 For those trusting in good works, see Galatians 2:16 comment.

3:10 It is wise to avoid those brethren who only want to argue about doctrine. Rather, put your
energy into reaching the lost.

Intelligence Tests

(Do not read these questions yourself. If you do, you will fail to see their evangelistic potential. Instead, have someone ask you the questions.)

1 How many of each animal did Moses take into the ark?
2 What is the name of the raised print that deaf people use?
3 Is it possible to end a sentence with the word "the"?
4 Spell the word "shop." What do you do when you come to a green light?
5 It is noon. You look at the clock. The big hand is on three. The little hand is on five. What time is it?
6 Spell the word "silk." What do cows drink?
7 Listen carefully: You are the driver of a train. There are thirty people on board. At the first stop ten people get off. At the next stop five people get on. Now for the question: What is the name of the train driver?

Answers:

1 None. It was Noah.
2 Deaf people don't use raised print.
3 The question is an example of one.
4 Go.
5 Noon.
6 Water.
7 You are the driver of the train.

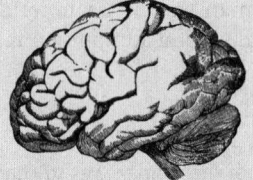

The Bible warns, "He who trusts his own heart is a fool" (Proverbs 28:26). The tests are an excellent way to humble an unsaved person and show him that he can't trust his own judgments. This may be followed with, "If you make a mistake with something as simple as this, could you be wrong in your beliefs about God, Judgment Day, the existence of hell, etc.?"

Philemon

PAUL, a prisoner of Jesus Christ, and Timothy our brother, to Philemon our dearly beloved, and fellow-laborer,

2 And to our beloved Apphia, and Archippus our fellow-soldier, and to the church in your house:

3 Grace to you, and peace, from God our Father and the Lord Jesus Christ.

4 I thank my God, making mention of you always in my prayers,

5 Hearing of your love and faith, which you have toward the Lord Jesus, and toward all saints;

6 That the communication of your faith may become effectual by the acknowledging of every good thing which is in you in Christ Jesus.

7 For we have great joy and consolation in your love, because the bowels of the saints are refreshed by you, brother.

8 Wherefore, though I might be much bold in Christ to enjoin you that which is convenient,

9 Yet for love's sake I rather beseech you, being such an one as Paul the aged, and now also a prisoner of Jesus Christ.

10 I beseech you for my son Onesimus,

whom I have begotten in my bonds:

11 Which in time past was to you unprofitable, but now profitable to you and to me:

12 Whom I have sent again: therefore receive him, that is, mine own bowels:

13 Whom I would have retained with me, that in your stead he might have ministered to me in the bonds of the gospel:

14 But without your mind would I do nothing; that your benefit should not be as it were of necessity, but willingly.

15 For perhaps he therefore departed for a season, that you should receive him for ever;

16 Not now as a servant, but above a servant, a brother beloved, specially to me, but how much more to you, both in the flesh, and in the Lord?

17 If you count me therefore a partner, receive him as myself.

18 If he has wronged you, or owes you anything, put that on my account;

19 I Paul have written it with mine own hand, I will repay it: albeit I do not say to you how you owe to me even your own

---

4–6 For the communication of our faith to be effectual (active, operative, and powerful), we must not confine our love to the Lord Jesus and the saints. Philemon's love went beyond the walls of the church building. He communicated his faith. This is what made Paul prayerfully thankful.

11 Now that the runaway slave was a Christian, upon return to Philemon he would be profitable. The world gains unspeakable profit from the presence of Christians. People who once were filled with corruption, upon conversion live as law-abiding, useful members of society. Onesimus (useful) would be a faithful servant for God's kingdom. He would work not only for his earthly master, but also for his heavenly Master, to whom he had submitted himself as a willing slave.

self besides.

20 Yes, brother, let me have joy of you in the Lord: refresh my bowels in the Lord.

21 Having confidence in your obedience I wrote to you, knowing that you will also do more than I say.

22 But withal prepare me also a lodging: for I trust that through your prayers I shall be given to you.

23 There salute you Epaphras, my fellow-prisoner in Christ Jesus;

24 Marcus, Aristarchus, Demas, Lucas, my fellow-laborers.

25 The grace of our Lord Jesus Christ be with your spirit. Amen.

. . . . . .

For untrue things the world says, see 1 Corinthians 3:19 comment.

. . . . . .

The Bible is the best book in the world. It contains more than all the libraries I have seen.

John Adams

Great Leaders Speak About the Bible

Here is a Book worth more than all the other books which were ever printed. *Patrick Henry*

That book, Sir, is the Rock upon which our republic rests. *Andrew Jackson*

The more profoundly we study this wonderful Book, and the more closely we observe its divine precepts, the better citizens we will become and the higher will be our destiny as a nation. *William McKinley*

The best religion the world has ever known is the religion of the Bible. It builds up all that is good. *Rutherford B. Hayes*

There are a good many problems before the American people today, and before me as President, but I expect to find the solution of those problems just in the proportion that I am faithful in the study of the Word of God. *Woodrow Wilson*

The whole inspiration of our civilization springs from the teachings of Christ and the lessons of the prophets. To read the Bible for these fundamentals is a necessity of American life. *Herbert Hoover*

I say to you, Search the Scriptures! The Bible is the book of all others, to be read at all ages, and in all conditions of human life; not to be read once or twice or thrice through, and then laid aside, but to be read in small portions of one or two chapters every day, and never to be intermitted, unless by some overruling necessity. *John Quincy Adams*

We cannot read the history of our rise and development as a nation, without reckoning the place the Bible has occupied in shaping the advances of the Republic. *Franklin D. Roosevelt*

Within the covers of the Bible are all the answers for all the problems men face. The Bible can touch hearts, order minds and refresh souls. *Ronald Reagan*

In all my perplexities and distresses, the Bible has never failed to give me light and strength. *Robert E. Lee*

I have read the Bible through many times, and now make it a practice to read it through once every year. It is a book of all others for lawyers, as well as divines; and I pity the man who cannot find in it a rich supply of thought and of rules for conduct. It fits a man for life it prepares him for death. *Daniel Webster*

Hebrews

CHAPTER 1

GOD, who at sundry times and in divers manners spoke in time past to the fathers by the prophets,

2 Has in these last days spoken to us by his Son, whom he has appointed heir of all things, by whom also he made the worlds;

3 Who being the brightness of his glory, and the express image of his person, and upholding all things by the word of his power, when he had by himself purged our sins, sat down on the right hand of the Majesty on high;

4 Being made so much better than the angels, as he has by inheritance obtained a more excellent name than they.

5 For to which of the angels said he at any time, You are my Son, this day have I begotten you? And again, I will be to him a Father, and he shall be to me a Son?

6 And again, when he brought in the first begotten into the world, he says, And let all the angels of God worship him.

7 And of the angels he says, Who makes his angels spirits, and his ministers a flame of fire.

8 But to the Son he says, Your throne, O God, is for ever and ever: a sceptre of righteousness is the sceptre of your kingdom.

9 You have loved righteousness, and hated iniquity; therefore God, even your God, has anointed you with the oil of gladness above your fellows.

10 And, You, Lord, in the beginning have laid the foundation of the earth; and the heavens are the works of your hands:

11 They shall perish; but you remain; and

1:1 The Bible's inspiration. The Bible doesn't attempt to defend its inspiration. But here is an interesting thing: Genesis opens with the words, "God said," nine times in the first chapter. The statement, "Thus says the Lord," appears 23 times in the last Old Testament book, Malachi. So you have, "God says," from Genesis to Malachi. "The Lord spoke," appears 560 times in the first five books of the Bible and at least 3,800 times in the whole of the Old Testament! Isaiah claims at least 40 times that his message came directly from the Lord; Ezekiel, 60 times; and Jeremiah, 100 times.

There are about 3,856 verses directly or indirectly concerned with prophecy in Scripture. God's challenge to the world is, "Prove Me now...I the LORD have spoken it; it shall come to pass." (see Malachi 3:10; Ezekiel 24:14). Mormons, Buddhists, and Muslims have their own sacred writings, but the element of proven prophecy is absent in them. The destruction of Tyre, the invasion of Jerusalem, the fall of Babylon and Rome each event was accurately predicted in the Bible and later fulfilled to the smallest detail. See Matthew 4:4 comment.

"Defend the Bible? I would as soon defend a lion!" *Charles Spurgeon*

1:2,3 "There is a Being who made all things, who holds all things in His power, and is therefore to be feared." *Sir Isaac Newton*

1:11 See Psalm 102:25,26 comment.

they all shall wax old as does a garment;

12 And as a vesture shall you fold them up, and they shall be changed: but you are the same, and your years shall not fail.

13 But to which of the angels said he at any time, Sit on my right hand, until I make your enemies your footstool?

14 Are they not all ministering spirits, sent forth to minister for them who shall be heirs of salvation?

CHAPTER 2

Therefore we ought to give the more earnest heed to the things which we have heard, lest at any time we should let them slip.

2 For if the word spoken by angels was steadfast, and every transgression and disobedience received a just recompense of reward;

3 How shall we escape, if we neglect so great salvation; which at the first began to be spoken by the Lord, and was confirmed to us by them that heard him;

4 God also bearing them witness, both with signs and wonders, and with divers miracles, and gifts of the Holy Spirit, according to his own will?

5 For to the angels has he not put in subjection the world to come, whereof we speak.

6 But one in a certain place testified, saying, What is man, that you are mindful of him? or the son of man, that you visit him?

7 You made him a little lower than the angels; you crowned him with glory and honor, and did set him over the works of your hands:

8 You have put all things in subjection under his feet. For in that he put all in subjection under him, he left nothing that is not put under him. But now we see not yet all things put under him.

9 **But we see Jesus, who was made a little lower than the angels for the suf-**

fering of death, crowned with glory and honor; that he by the grace of God should taste death for every man.

10 For it became him, for whom are all things, and by whom are all things, in bringing many sons to glory, to make the captain of their salvation perfect through sufferings.

11 For both he that sanctifies and they who are sanctified are all of one: for which cause he is not ashamed to call them brethren,

12 Saying, I will declare your name to my brethren, in the midst of the church will I sing praise to you.

13 And again, I will put my trust in him. And again, Behold I and the children which God has given me.

> No sinner looks to the Savior with a dry eye or a hard heart. Aim, therefore, at heart-breaking, at bringing home condemnation to the conscience and weaning the mind from sin. Be not content till the whole mind is deeply and vitally changed in reference to sin.
>
> **CHARLES SPURGEON**

14 Forasmuch then as the children are partakers of flesh and blood, he also himself likewise took part of the same; that through death he might destroy him that had the power of death, that is, the devil;

15 And deliver them who through fear of death were all their lifetime subject to bondage.

16 For verily he took not on him the nature of angels; but he took on him the seed of Abraham.

17 Wherefore in all things it behoved him to be made like to his brethren, that he might be a merciful and faithful high priest in things pertaining to God, to

---

2:6 "Young man, the secret of my success is that at an early age I discovered I was not God." *Oliver Wendell Holmes, Jr.*

SPRINGBOARDS FOR PREACHING AND WITNESSING

The Titanic

2:10

The story of the Titanic has incredibly close parallels to the biblical plan of salvation. Just as the great pleasure ship struck an iceberg and sank, this great world with all its inhabitants is slowly sinking into the cold grip of death. As with the Titanic, where only those passengers who believed that they were in impending danger looked to the lifeboats, so only those who believe that they are in mortal danger will look to the Lifeboat of the Savior, Jesus Christ. The great iceberg that will take the world to an icy grave is the Moral Law—the Ten Commandments.

Here is the evidence that we are sinking: Jesus said that if we look with lust, we commit adultery in our heart. No one who has had sex outside of marriage, or any liar, or any thief will enter heaven. The Bible says that if we hate someone, we are guilty of murder. We fail to put God first. We make a god in our image. We break all the Commandments. If we stay with the ship, we will perish on the Day of Judgment, when all of our sins come out as evidence of our guilt. God, however, is rich in mercy and doesn't want anyone to go to hell. He made a way for us to be saved. Jesus Christ, the One whom the Bible calls the Captain of our salvation, gave His life so that we could have a place in the lifeboat. He took our punishment upon Himself, suffering on the cross for us. We broke God's Law, but He paid our fine. Then He rose from the dead, defeating death. The moment we repent and trust in Him alone for our eternal salvation, God will forgive us and grant us the gift of eternal life.

Don't hesitate. You may wait until it's too late! It was reported that some of the lifeboats that left the Titanic early were only half full. Many more on board could have been saved, but they refused to believe that the great unsinkable ship was sinking. They perished because their faith was misguided. Don't be like them. Believe the gospel. Repent and trust Jesus Christ today...and God will never let you down.

make reconciliation for the sins of the people.

18 For in that he himself has suffered being tempted, he is able to succour them that are tempted.

CHAPTER 3

WHEREFORE, holy brethren, partakers of the heavenly calling, consider the Apostle and High Priest of our profession, Christ Jesus;

2 Who was faithful to him that appointed him, as also Moses was faithful in all his house.

3 For this man was counted worthy of more glory than Moses, inasmuch as he who has built the house has more honor than the house.

4 For every house is built by some man; but he that built all things is God.

5 And Moses verily was faithful in all his house, as a servant, for a testimony of those things which were to be spoken after;

6 But Christ as a son over his own house; whose house are we, if we hold fast the confidence and the rejoicing of the hope firm to the end.

7 Wherefore (as the Holy Spirit says, Today if you will hear his voice,

8 Harden not your hearts, as in the provocation, in the day of temptation in the wilderness:

9 When your fathers tempted me, proved me, and saw my works forty years.

10 Wherefore I was grieved with that generation, and said, They do always err in their heart; and they have not known my ways.

11 So I sware in my wrath, They shall not enter into my rest.)

12 Take heed, brethren, lest there be in any of you an evil heart of unbelief, in departing from the living God.

THE FUNCTION OF THE LAW

 3:12 While [every true believer] cries out, O what love have I unto thy Law! All the day long is my study in it; he sees daily, in that divine mirror, more and more of his own sinfulness. He sees more and more clearly that he is fullness a sinner in all things that neither his heart nor his ways are right before God, and that every moment sends him to Christ.

Therefore I cannot spare the Law one moment, no more than I can spare Christ, seeing I now want it as much to keep me to Christ, as I ever wanted it to bring me to Him. Otherwise this evil heart of unbelief would immediately depart from the living God. Indeed each is continually sending me to the other-the Law to Christ, and Christ to the Law. *John Wesley*

13 But exhort one another daily, while it is called Today; lest any of you be hardened through the deceitfulness of sin.
14 For we are made partakers of Christ, if we hold the beginning of our confidence steadfast to the end;
15 While it is said, Today if you will hear his voice, harden not your hearts, as in the provocation.

16 For some, when they had heard, did provoke: howbeit not all that came out of Egypt by Moses.
17 But with whom was he grieved forty years? was it not with them that had sinned, whose carcasses fell in the wilderness?
18 And to whom sware he that they should not enter into his rest, but to them that believed not?
19 So we see that they could not enter in because of unbelief.

CHAPTER 4

LET us therefore fear, lest, a promise being left us of entering into his rest, any of you should seem to come short of it.
2 For to us was the gospel preached, as well as to them: but the word preached did not profit them, not being mixed with faith in them that heard it.
3 For we which have believed do enter into rest, as he said, As I have sworn in my wrath, if they shall enter into my rest: although the works were finished from the foundation of the world.
4 For he spoke in a certain place of the seventh day on this wise, And God did

4:4 Creation in six days. Most theologians throughout church history agree that in using the phrase "the evening and the morning were the first day," the Scriptures are speaking of a literal 24-hour day, rather than a period of years.

"To understand the meaning of "day" in Genesis 1, we need to determine how the Hebrew word for 'day,' *yom*, is used in the context of Scripture ... A number, and the phrase 'evening and morning,' are used for each of the six days of creation (Genesis 1:5,8,13,19,23,31). Outside Genesis 1, *yom* is used with a number 410 times, and each time it means an ordinary day: why would Genesis 1 be the exception? Outside Genesis 1, *yom* is used with the word 'evening' or 'morning' 23 times. 'Evening' and 'morning' appear in association, but without *yom*, 38 times. All 61 times the text refers to an ordinary day; why would Genesis 1 be the exception? In Genesis 1:5, *yom* occurs in context with the word 'night.' Outside of Genesis 1, 'night' is used with *yom* 53 times and each time it means an ordinary day. Why would Genesis 1 be the exception? Even the usage of the word 'light' with *yom* in this passage determines the meaning as ordinary day." *Ken Ham*, et al., *The Answers Book* (revised and expanded)

"So far as I know, there is no professor of Hebrew or Old Testament at any world-class university who does not believe that the writer(s) of Genesis 1:11 intended to convey to their readers the idea that (a) creation took place in a series of six days which were the same as the days of 24 hours we now experience; (b) the figures contained in the Genesis genealogies provided by simple addition a chronology from the beginning of the world up to later stages in the biblical story; (c) Noah's Flood was understood to be worldwide and extinguish all human and animal life except for those in the ark." *Dr. James Barr*, professor of Hebrew, Oxford University

rest the seventh day from all his works.

5 And in this place again, If they shall enter into my rest.

6 Seeing therefore it remains that some must enter therein, and they to whom it was first preached entered not in because of unbelief:

7 Again, he limits a certain day, saying in David, Today, after so long a time; as it is said, **Today if you will hear his voice, harden not your hearts.**

8 For if Jesus had given them rest, then would he not afterward have spoken of another day.

9 There remains therefore a rest to the people of God.

10 For he that is entered into his rest, he also has ceased from his own works, as God did from his.

11 Let us labor therefore to enter into that rest, lest any man fall after the same example of unbelief.

12 For the word of God is quick, and powerful, and sharper than any two-edged sword, piercing even to the dividing asunder of soul and spirit, and of the joints and marrow, and is a discerner of the thoughts and intents of the heart.

13 **Neither is there any creature that is not manifest in his sight: but all things are naked and opened to the eyes of him**

THE FUNCTION OF THE LAW

4:12 "It is the ordinary method of the Spirit of God to convict sinners by the Law. It is this which, being set home on the conscience, generally breaketh the rocks in pieces. It is more especially this part of the Word of God which is quick and powerful, full of life and energy and sharper than any two-edged sword." *John Wesley*

"The Law cuts into the core of the evil, it reveals the seat of the malady, and informs us that the leprosy lies deep within." *Charles Spurgeon*

---

with whom we have to do.

14 Seeing then that we have a great high priest, that is passed into the heavens, Jesus the Son of God, let us hold fast our profession.

15 For we have not an high priest which cannot be touched with the feeling of our infirmities; but was in all points tempted like as we are, yet without sin.

16 Let us therefore come boldly to the throne of grace, that we may obtain mercy, and find grace to help in time of need.

CHAPTER 5

FOR every high priest taken from among men is ordained for men in

---

4:4 The creation days. Some of the early church fathers believed that God created everything in only one day, or in an instant. To counter this teaching, *Martin Luther* wrote: When Moses writes that God created Heaven and Earth and whatever is in them in six days, then let this period continue to have been six days, and do not venture to devise any comment according to which six days were one day. But, if you cannot understand how this could have been done in six days, then grant the Holy Spirit the honor of being more learned than you are. For you are to deal with Scripture in such a way that you bear in mind that God Himself says what is written. But since God is speaking, it is not fitting for you to wantonly turn His Word in the direction you wish it to go.

4:7 Isaiah 55:6 exhorts the lost to "seek the Lord while He may be found, call upon Him while He is near." God's offer of grace will end, so sinners are commanded to seek the Lord while He may be found. They must then "call" upon Him. An intellectual belief in His existence is not saving faith. Romans 10:13 says, "whoever *calls* upon the name of the Lord shall be saved."

4:12 Soldier of Christ, throw away your sheath, it is not part of your armor. Strap the two-edged sword firmly in your hand. The way to keep the sword on hand is to have it in your mouth. In Jeremiah 1:7 9, God told the prophet not to be afraid to speak. God then put His words in the mouth of Jeremiah, and in chapter 5 we are given a report of his transformation: "Thus says the Lord God of hosts, Because you speak this word, behold, I will make my words in your mouth fire, and this people wood, and it shall devour them" (v. 14).

things pertaining to God, that he may offer both gifts and sacrifices for sins:

2 Who can have compassion on the ignorant, and on them that are out of the way; for that he himself also is compassed with infirmity.

3 And by reason hereof he ought, as for the people, so also for himself, to offer for sins.

4 And no man takes this honor to himself, but he that is called of God, as was Aaron.

5 So also Christ glorified not himself to be made an high priest; but he that said to him, You are my Son, today have I begotten you.

6 As he said also in another place, You are a priest for ever after the order of Melchisedec.

7 Who in the days of his flesh, when he had offered up prayers and supplications with strong crying and tears to him that was able to save him from death, and was heard in that he feared;

8 Though he were a Son, yet learned he obedience by the things which he suffered;

9 And being made perfect, he became the author of eternal salvation to all them that obey him;

10 Called of God an high priest after the order of Melchisedec.

11 Of whom we have many things to say, and hard to be uttered, seeing you are dull of hearing.

12 For when for the time you ought to be teachers, you have need that one teach you again which be the first principles of the oracles of God; and are become such as have need of milk, and not of strong meat.

13 For every one that uses milk is unskilful in the word of righteousness: for he is a babe.

14 But strong meat belongs to them that are of full age, even those who by reason of use have their senses exercised to discern both good and evil.

CHAPTER 6

THEREFORE leaving the principles of the doctrine of Christ, let us go on to perfection; not laying again the foundation of repentance from dead works, and of faith toward God,

2 Of the doctrine of baptisms, and of laying on of hands, and of resurrection of the dead, and of eternal judgment.

3 And this will we do, if God permit.

4 For it is impossible for those who were once enlightened, and have tasted of the heavenly gift, and were made partakers of the Holy Spirit,

5 And have tasted the good word of God,

4:15   Some believe that because Scripture says Jesus was in all points tempted like as we are that He must have struggled with temptations to lie, steal, sin sexually, etc. But Scripture explains that all the attractions of this world fit into three categories: the lust of the flesh, the lust of the eyes, and the pride of life (1 John 2:16). Jesus was tempted by the devil in these three areas and, as the second Adam, He successfully passed the tests. These are the same tests that the first Adam underwent and failed (Genesis 3:6). Adam and Eve saw that the tree was good for food (lust of the flesh; compare Luke 4:3,4), was pleasant to the eyes (lust of the eyes; compare Luke 4:5 8), and was desirable to make one wise (pride of life; compare Luke 4:9-12). We will pass the test and not succumb to these temptations by following Jesus' example. He quoted the truths of the Word of God, using the sword of the Spirit to vanquish the lies of the enemy.

4:16   If you have a zeal for the lost, you will be a target for the enemy of your soul. He wants you to be beset by sin. His devious obsession is for iniquity to defile your conscience, and therefore take away your confidence before God. God forbid that we should allow that to happen. May each of us be so saturated in prayer and in the grace of God that we can boldly come before His throne with our head held high in faith and effectively stand in the gap for a dark and sinful world.

5:9   "I don't believe in any religion apart from doing the will of God." *Catherine Booth*

PRINCIPLES OF GROWTH FOR THE NEW AND GROWING CHRISTIAN

6:18   *Faith—Elevators Can Let You Down*

I have heard people say, I just find it hard to have faith in God, not realizing the implications of their words. These are the same people who often accept the daily weather forecast, believe the newspapers, and trust their lives to a pilot they have never seen whenever they board a plane. We exercise faith every day. We rely on our car's brakes. We trust history books, medical journals, and elevators. Yet elevators can let us down. History books can be wrong. Planes can crash. How much more then should we trust the sure and true promises of Almighty God. He will never let us down...if we trust Him.

Cynics often argue, "You cant trust the Bible; it's full of mistakes." It is. The first mistake was when man rejected God, and the Scriptures show men and women making the same tragic mistake again and again. It's also full of what *seem to be* contradictions. For example, the Scriptures tell us that with God nothing shall be impossible (Luke 1:37); there is nothing Almighty God can't do. Yet we are also told that it is impossible for God to lie (Hebrews 6:18). So there is something God cannot do! Isn't that an obvious mistake in the Bible? No, it isn't.

Lying, deception, bearing false witness, etc., is so repulsive to God, so disgusting to Him, so against His holy character, that the Scriptures draw on the strength of the word impossible to substantiate the claim. He cannot, could not, and would not lie.

That means that in a world where we are continually let down, we can totally rely on, trust in, and count on His promises. They are sure, certain, indisputable, true, trustworthy, reliable, faithful, unfailing, dependable, steadfast, and an anchor for the soul. In other words, you can truly believe them, and because of that, you can throw yourself blindfolded and without reserve, into His mighty hands. He will *never, ever* let you down. Do you believe that?

For the next principle of growth, see 1 Peter 2:2 comment.

and the powers of the world to come,

6 If they shall fall away, to renew them again to repentance; seeing they crucify to themselves the Son of God afresh, and put him to an open shame.

7 For the earth which drinks in the rain that comes oft upon it, and brings forth herbs meet for them by whom it is dressed, receives blessing from God:

8 But that which bears thorns and briers is rejected, and is near to cursing; whose end is to be burned.

9 But, beloved, we are persuaded better things of you, and things that accompany salvation, though we thus speak.

10 For God is not unrighteous to forget your work and labor of love, which you have showed toward his name, in that you have ministered to the saints, and do minister.

11 And we desire that every one of you do show the same diligence to the full assurance of hope to the end:

12 That you be not slothful, but followers of them who through faith and patience inherit the promises.

13 For when God made promise to Abraham, because he could swear by no greater, he sware by himself,

14 Saying, Surely blessing I will bless you, and multiplying I will multiply you.

15 And so, after he had patiently endured, he obtained the promise.

16 For men verily swear by the greater: and an oath for confirmation is to them an end of all strife.

17 Wherein God, willing more abundantly to show to the heirs of promise the immutability of his counsel, confirmed it by an oath:

18 That by two immutable things, in which it was impossible for God to lie, we might have a strong consolation, who have fled for refuge to lay hold upon the hope set before us:

19 Which hope we have as an anchor

of the soul, both sure and steadfast, and which enters into that within the veil;

20 Whither the forerunner is for us entered, even Jesus, made an high priest for ever after the order of Melchisedec.

. . . . . .

Check out "The Rush."
See Luke 16:17 comment.

. . . . . .

CHAPTER 7

FOR this Melchisedec, king of Salem, priest of the most high God, who met Abraham returning from the slaughter of the kings, and blessed him;

2 To whom also Abraham gave a tenth part of all; first being by interpretation King of righteousness, and after that also King of Salem, which is, King of peace;

3 Without father, without mother, without descent, having neither beginning of days, nor end of life; but made like to the Son of God; abides as a priest continually.

4 Now consider how great this man was, to whom even the patriarch Abraham gave the tenth of the spoils.

5 And verily they that are of the sons of Levi, who receive the office of the priesthood, have a commandment to take tithes of the people according to the law, that is, of their brethren, though they come out of the loins of Abraham:

6 But he whose descent is not counted from them received tithes of Abraham, and blessed him that had the promises.

7 And without all contradiction the less is blessed of the better.

8 And here men that die receive tithes; but there he receives them, of whom it is witnessed that he lives.

9 And as I may so say, Levi also, who receives tithes, paid tithes in Abraham.

10 For he was yet in the loins of his father, when Melchisedec met him.

11 If therefore perfection were by the Levitical priesthood, (for under it the people received the law,) what further need was there that another priest should rise after the order of Melchisedec, and not be called after the order of Aaron?

12 For the priesthood being changed, there is made of necessity a change also of the law.

13 For he of whom these things are spoken pertains to another tribe, of which no man gave attendance at the altar.

14 For it is evident that our Lord sprang out of Judah; of which tribe Moses spoke nothing concerning priesthood.

15 And it is yet far more evident: for that after the similitude of Melchisedec there arose another priest,

16 Who is made, not after the law of a carnal commandment, but after the power of an endless life.

17 For he testifies, You are a priest for ever after the order of Melchisedec.

18 For there is verily a disannulling of the commandment going before for the weakness and unprofitableness thereof.

19 For the law made nothing perfect, but the bringing in of a better hope did; by the which we draw near to God.

> To be a soul winner is the happiest thing in this world. And with every soul you bring to Jesus Christ, you seem to get a new heaven here upon earth.
>
> **CHARLES SPURGEON**

20 And inasmuch as not without an oath he was made priest:

21 (For those priests were made without an oath; but this with an oath by him that said to him, The Lord sware and will not repent, You are a priest for ever after the order of Melchisedec:)

22 By so much was Jesus made a surety of a better testament.

23 And they truly were many priests, because they were not suffered to continue by reason of death:

24 But this man, because he continues ever, has an unchangeable priesthood.

25 Wherefore he is able also to save them to the uttermost that come to God by him, seeing he ever lives to make in-

Solid Ice

8:6

There once was a man who was traveling on foot through a snowstorm in a strange country. He had to get to a certain town by nightfall and was somewhat perturbed when he came to an ice-covered river. *How thick was the ice?* Could he trust it to hold him? He began crawling on the ice on his stomach, inch-by-inch, tapping with his fingers. Sweat poured from his forehead. He was filled with the fear that at any moment he could plunge to an icy death.

An hour later, he had progressed only about 40 feet. He suddenly stopped crawling. He could hear singing! He turned his head to see a horse and cart, laden with people. The driver was singing at the top of his voice as he drove his cart across the ice. The driver knew that lake was solid ice and his faith was such that he had total confidence, with not an ounce of fear. Such are the solid promises of God.

tercession for them.

26 For such an high priest became us, who is holy, harmless, undefiled, separate from sinners, and made higher than the heavens;

27 Who needs not daily, as those high priests, to offer up sacrifice, first for his own sins, and then for the people's: for this he did once, when he offered up himself.

28 For the law makes men high priests which have infirmity; but the word of the oath, which was since the law, makes the Son, who is consecrated for evermore.

CHAPTER 8

NOW of the things which we have spoken this is the sum: We have such an high priest, who is set on the right hand of the throne of the Majesty in the heavens;

2 A minister of the sanctuary, and of the true tabernacle, which the Lord pitched, and not man.

3 For every high priest is ordained to offer gifts and sacrifices: wherefore it is of necessity that this man have somewhat also to offer.

4 For if he were on earth, he should not be a priest, seeing that there are priests that offer gifts according to the law:

5 Who serve to the example and shadow of heavenly things, as Moses was admonished of God when he was about to make the tabernacle: for, See, said he, that you make all things according to the pattern showed to you in the mount.

6 But now has he obtained a more excellent ministry, by how much also he is the mediator of a better covenant, which

8:5 Following the God-given pattern. When God spoke to Moses about the tabernacle, He told him to do all things according to the pattern. He didn't say, "Do the best you can." It had to be 100% accurate, according to the instructions God had given him. How much more then should we follow the pattern God has given us for bringing men and women into the knowledge of eternal salvation? Our failure to use the Law lawfully, as a schoolmaster to bring sinners to Christ (Galatians 3:24), has resulted in the ruin of millions of souls, something which will not be fully realized until Judgment Day.

The pattern of evangelistic endeavor is made plain in the Book of Romans. To obtain God s blessing, we must never deviate from the biblical paradigm set so clearly before us in the inspired words of the apostle Paul. *Winston Churchill* noted that the nose of the bulldog is slanted backward so he can continue to breathe without letting go. Get your teeth into the importance of using the Law of God to bring the knowledge of sin, and don t let it go for any reason. Let it be said of you, The Law of his God is in his heart; none of his steps shall slide (Psalm 37:31). See 2 Corinthians 2:17 comment.

was established upon better promises.

7 For if that first covenant had been faultless, then should no place have been sought for the second.

8 For finding fault with them, he says, Behold, the days come, says the Lord, when I will make a new covenant with the house of Israel and with the house of Judah:

9 Not according to the covenant that I made with their fathers in the day when I took them by the hand to lead them out of the land of Egypt; because they continued not in my covenant, and I regarded them not, says the Lord.

10 For this is the covenant that I will make with the house of Israel after those days, says the Lord; I will put my laws into their mind, and write them in their hearts: and I will be to them a God, and they shall be to me a people:

11 And they shall not teach every man his neighbour, and every man his brother, saying, Know the Lord: for all shall know me, from the least to the greatest.

12 For I will be merciful to their unrighteousness, and their sins and their iniquities will I remember no more.

13 In that he says, A new covenant, he has made the first old. Now that which decays and waxes old is ready to vanish away.

CHAPTER 9

THEN verily the first covenant had also ordinances of divine service, and a worldly sanctuary.

2 For there was a tabernacle made; the first, wherein was the candlestick, and the table, and the showbread; which is called the sanctuary.

3 And after the second veil, the tabernacle which is called the Holiest of all;

"O Lord, Almighty and everlasting God, by Thy holy Word Thou hast created the heaven, and the earth, and the sea; blessed and glorified be Thy name, and praised be Thy majesty, which hath deigned to use us, Thy humble servants, that Thy holy name may be proclaimed in this second part of the earth."

Christopher Columbus

4 Which had the golden censer, and the ark of the covenant overlaid round about with gold, wherein was the golden pot that had manna, and Aaron's rod that budded, and the tables of the covenant;

5 And over it the cherubims of glory shadowing the mercyseat; of which we cannot now speak particularly.

6 Now when these things were thus ordained, the priests went always into the first tabernacle, accomplishing the service of God.

7 But into the second went the high priest alone once every year, not without blood, which he offered for himself, and for the errors of the people:

8 The Holy Spirit thus signifying, that

8:10   God puts His Law into our minds, giving us a new mind, "the mind of Christ" (1 Corinthians 2:16), and renewing us in the spirit of our minds. He gives us a "new and living way" (Hebrews 10:20). Now God's ways are our ways and God's thoughts become our thoughts. We are led by the Spirit, walking in His ways (Psalm 119:3). This is the miracle of the new birth. We are completely new creatures in Christ (2 Corinthians 5:17).

the way into the holiest of all was not yet made manifest, while as the first tabernacle was yet standing:

9 Which was a figure for the time then present, in which were offered both gifts and sacrifices, that could not make him that did the service perfect, as pertaining to the conscience;

10 Which stood only in meats and drinks, and divers washings, and carnal ordinances, imposed on them until the time of reformation.

11 But Christ being come an high priest of good things to come, by a greater and more perfect tabernacle, not made with hands, that is to say, not of this building;

12 Neither by the blood of goats and calves, but by his own blood he entered in once into the holy place, having obtained eternal redemption for us.

13 For if the blood of bulls and of goats, and the ashes of an heifer sprinkling the unclean, sanctifies to the purifying of the flesh:

14 How much more shall the blood of Christ, who through the eternal Spirit offered himself without spot to God, purge your conscience from dead works to serve the living God?

15 And for this cause he is the mediator of the new testament, that by means of death, for the redemption of the transgressions that were under the first testament, they which are called might receive the promise of eternal inheritance.

16 For where a testament is, there must also of necessity be the death of the testator.

17 For a testament is of force after men are dead: otherwise it is of no strength at all while the testator lives.

18 Whereupon neither the first testament was dedicated without blood.

THE FUNCTION OF THE LAW

9:14 "You understand that the work of the Law is the revealing of sin. Furthermore, when I speak of sin, I include all kinds of sn: external, internal, hypocrisy, unbelief, love of self, and contempt for or ignorance of God, which are certainly the very roots of all human works. In the justification of sinners the first work of God is to reveal our sin; to confound our conscience, make us tremble, terrify us, briefly, to condemn us.

"The beginning of repentance consists of that work of the Law by which the Spirit of God terrifies and confounds consciences... Just as the Christian life must certainly begin with the knowledge of sin, so Christian doctrine must begin with the function of the Law." *Melanchthon*

---

19 For when Moses had spoken every precept to all the people according to the law, he took the blood of calves and of goats, with water, and scarlet wool, and hyssop, and sprinkled both the book, and all the people,

20 Saying, This is the blood of the testament which God has enjoined to you.

21 Moreover he sprinkled with blood both the tabernacle, and all the vessels of the ministry.

22 And almost all things are by the law purged with blood; and without shedding of blood is no remission.

23 It was therefore necessary that the patterns of things in the heavens should be purified with these; but the heavenly things themselves with better sacrifices than these.

24 For Christ is not entered into the holy places made with hands, which are the figures of the true; but into heaven itself, now to appear in the presence of

---

9:22 Forgiveness of sin requires the shedding of blood: God was the first person to kill an animal, as recorded in Genesis 3:21. As Adam and Eve sinned and lost their righteousness, God shed the blood of an innocent animal to provide a covering for them. The fig leaves of self-righteousness will not cover a sinner on the Day of Judgment. God alone can provide the covering through the shed blood of the Savior (1 John 1:7-10). See John 3:16,17 and Psalm 51:6 comments.

God for us:

25 Nor yet that he should offer himself often, as the high priest enters into the holy place every year with blood of others;

26 For then must he often have suffered since the foundation of the world: but now once in the end of the world has he appeared to put away sin by the sacrifice of himself.

27 And as it is appointed to men once to die, but after this the judgment:

28 So Christ was once offered to bear the sins of many; and to them that look for him shall he appear the second time without sin to salvation.

CHAPTER 10

F OR the law having a shadow of good things to come, and not the very image of the things, can never with those sacrifices which they offered year by year continually make the comers thereunto perfect.

2 For then would they not have ceased to be offered? because that the worshippers once purged should have had no more conscience of sins.

3 But in those sacrifices there is a remembrance again made of sins every year.

4 For it is not possible that the blood of bulls and of goats should take away sins.

5 Wherefore when he came into the world, he says, Sacrifice and offering you would not, but a body have you prepared me:

6 In burnt offerings and sacrifices for sin you have had no pleasure.

7 Then said I, Lo, I come (in the volume of the book it is written of me,) to do your will, O God.

8 Above when he said, Sacrifice and offering and burnt offerings and offering for sin you would not, neither had pleasure therein; which are offered by the law;

9 Then said he, Lo, I come to do your will, O God. He takes away the first, that he may establish the second.

10 By the which will we are sanctified through the offering of the body of Jesus Christ once for all.

11 And every priest stands daily ministering and offering oftentimes the same sacrifices, which can never take away sins:

12 But this man, after he had offered one sacrifice for sins for ever, sat down on the right hand of God;

13 From henceforth expecting till his enemies be made his footstool.

14 For by one offering he has perfected for ever them that are sanctified.

15 Whereof the Holy Spirit also is a witness to us: for after that he had said before,

16 This is the covenant that I will make with them after those days, said the Lord, I will put my laws into their hearts, and in their minds will I write them;

17 And their sins and iniquities will I remember no more.

9:27 Judgment Day: For verses that warn of its reality, see 2 Peter 2:4,5,9.

9:27 Reincarnation. This verse shows that there is no such thing as reincarnation. It is merely wishful thinking for guilty sinners. Many of the world's largest religions teach their adherents that if they don't get it right in this lifetime, they'll have multiple opportunities in future lives. That people don't need to trust in Jesus before they die is one of Satan's greatest lies. See Psalm 49:15 comment.

9:28 Second coming of Jesus: See Hebrews 10:37.

10:16 This is the promise of the gospel of salvation. The experience of "conversion" is when God puts His Law in the heart of those who repent and trust in the Savior. He causes them to walk in His statutes (Ezekiel 36:26,27), and gives believers the desire to obey the Moral Law. The Christian no longer desires to lie, steal, covet, commit adultery, etc.; he has a new heart with new desires. He is a new creature in Christ (2 Corinthians 5:17). See Psalm 40:7-9 comment.

PRINCIPLES OF GROWTH FOR THE NEW AND GROWING CHRISTIAN

10:25   *Fellowship—Flutter by Butterfly*

Pray about where you should fellowship. Make sure your church home calls sin what it is: sin. Do they believe the promises of God? Are they loving? Does the pastor treat his wife with respect? Is he a man of the Word? Does he have a humble heart and a gentle spirit? Listen closely to his teaching. It should glorify God, magnify Jesus, and edify the believer.

One evidence that you have been truly saved is that you will have a love for other Christians (1 John 3:14). You will want to fellowship with them. The old saying that birds of a feather flock together is true of Christians. You gather together for the breaking of bread (communion), for teaching from the Word, and for fellowship. You share the same inspirations, illuminations, inclinations, temptations, aspirations, motivations, and perspirations. You are working together for the same thing: the furtherance of the kingdom of God on earth. This is why you attend church—not because you have to, but because you want to.

Don't become a spiritual butterfly. If you are flitting from church to church, how will your pastor know what type of food you are digesting? The Bible says that your shepherd is accountable to God for you (Hebrews 13:17), so make yourself known to your pastor. Pray for him regularly. Pray also for his wife, his family, and the elders. Being a pastor is no easy task. Most people don't realize how long it takes to prepare a fresh sermon each week. They don't appreciate the time spent in prayer and in study of the Word. If the pastor repeats a joke or a story, remember, he's human. So give him a great deal of grace, and double honor. Never murmur about him. If you don't like something he has said, pray about it, then leave the issue with God. If that doesn't satisfy you, leave the church, rather than divide it through murmuring and complaining. God hates those who cause division among the brethren (Proverbs 6:16-19). See Psalm 92:13 comment.

For the next principle of growth, see Ephesians 5:20 comment.

18 Now where remission of these is, there is no more offering for sin.

19 Having therefore, brethren, boldness to enter into the holiest by the blood of Jesus,

20 By a new and living way, which he has consecrated for us, through the veil, that is to say, his flesh;

21 And having an high priest over the house of God;

22 Let us draw near with a true heart in full assurance of faith, having our hearts sprinkled from an evil conscience, and our bodies washed with pure water.

23 Let us hold fast the profession of our faith without wavering; (for he is faithful that promised;)

24 And let us consider one another to provoke to love and to good works:

25 Not forsaking the assembling of ourselves together, as the manner of some is; but exhorting one another: and so much the more, as you see the day approaching.

26 For if we sin wilfully after that we have received the knowledge of the truth, there remains no more sacrifice for sins,

27 But a certain fearful looking for of judgment and fiery indignation, which shall devour the adversaries.

10:22 The sinner's conscience. "O soul! Thou are at war with thy conscience. Thou hast tried to quiet it, but it will prick you. Oh, there be some of you to whom conscience is a ghost haunting you by day and night. You know the good, though you choose the evil; you prick your fingers with the thorn of conscience when you try to pluck the rose of sin." *Charles Spurgeon*

10:23 "Never be afraid to trust an unknown future to a known God." *Corrie ten Boom*

QUESTIONS & OBJECTIONS

10:31

"You are using scare tactics by talking about hell and Judgment Day."

In the late 1980s, TV commercials in the U.S. asked, What goes through the mind of a driver who is not wearing a seat belt in a head-on collision? Then they showed a crash dummy having its head crushed by a steering wheel in a collision, and said, *"The steering wheel!"* Those were scare tactics, but no one complained because they were *legitimate* scare tactics. That s what happens in a head-on collision if you are foolish enough to not put on a seat belt.

To warn of hell is fearful, but it is *absolutely* legitimate, because the Bible says that it is a *fearful* thing for a sinner to fall into the hands of the living God.

28 He that despised Moses' law died without mercy under two or three witnesses:

29 Of how much sorer punishment, do you suppose, shall he be thought worthy, who has trodden under foot the Son of God, and has counted the blood of the covenant, wherewith he was sanctified, an unholy thing, and has done despite to the Spirit of grace?

30 For we know him that has said, Vengeance belongs to me, I will recompense, says the Lord. And again, The Lord shall judge his people.

31 It is a fearful thing to fall into the hands of the living God.

32 But call to remembrance the former days, in which, after you were illuminated, you endured a great fight of afflictions;

33 Partly, whilst you were made a gazingstock both by reproaches and afflictions; and partly, whilst you became companions of them that were so used.

34 For you had compassion of me in my bonds, and took joyfully the spoiling of your goods, knowing in yourselves that you have in heaven a better and an enduring substance.

35 Cast not away therefore your confidence, which has great recompense of reward.

36 For you have need of patience, that, after you have done the will of God, you might receive the promise.

37 For yet a little while, and he that shall come will come, and will not tarry.

38 Now the just shall live by faith: but if any man draw back, my soul shall have no pleasure in him.

39 But we are not of them who draw back to perdition; but of them that believe to the saving of the soul.

CHAPTER 11

NOW faith is the substance of things hoped for, the evidence of things not seen.

2 For by it the elders obtained a good report.

3 Through faith we understand that the worlds were framed by the word of God, so that things which are seen were not made of things which do appear.

4 By faith Abel offered to God a more excellent sacrifice than Cain, by which he obtained witness that he was righteous, God testifying of his gifts: and by it he being dead yet speaks.

5 By faith Enoch was translated that he should not see death; and was not found, because God had translated him: for before his translation he had this testimony, that he pleased God.

6 But without faith it is impossible to please him: for he that comes to God must believe that he is, and that he is a

10:37 Second coming of Jesus: See James 5:8.

11:3 Scientific Facts in the Bible

1. Only in recent years has science discovered that everything we see is composed of invisible atoms. Here, Scripture tells us that the things which are seen were not made of things which do appear.

2. Medical science has only recently discovered that blood-clotting in a newborn reaches its peak on the eighth day, then drops. The Bible consistently says that a baby must be circumcised on the eighth day.

3. At a time when it was believed that the earth sat on a large animal or a giant (1500 B.C.), the Bible spoke of the earth's free float in space: "He ... hangs the earth upon nothing" (Job 26:7).

4. The prophet Isaiah also tells us that the earth is round: It is he that sits upon the circle of the earth (Isaiah 40:22). This is not a reference to a flat disk, as some skeptic maintain, but to a sphere. Secular man discovered this 2,400 years later. At a time when science believed that the earth was flat, it was the Scriptures that inspired Christopher Columbus to sail around the world (see Proverbs 3:6 comment).

5. God told Job in 1500 B.C.: Can you send lightnings, that they may go, and say to you, Here we are? (Job 38:35). The Bible here is making what appears to be a scientifically ludicrous statement that light can be *sent*, and then manifest itself in speech. But did you know that radio waves travel at the speed of light? This is why you can have *instantaneous* wireless communication with someone on the other side of the earth. Science didn't discover this until 1864 when British scientist James Clerk Maxwell suggested that electricity and light waves were two forms of the same thing (*Modern Century Illustrated Encyclopedia*).

6. Job 38:19 asks, Where is the way where light dwells? Modern man has only recently discovered that light (electromagnetic radiation) has a way, traveling at 186,000 miles per second.

7. Science has discovered that stars emit radio waves, which are received on earth as a high pitch. God mentioned this in Job 38:7: When the morning stars sang together ...

8. Most cosmologists (scientists who study the structures and evolution of the universe) agree that the Genesis account of creation, in imagining an initial void, may be uncannily close to the truth (*Time*, Dec. 1976).

9. Solomon described a cycle of air currents two thousand years before scientists discovered them. The wind goes toward the south, and turns about unto the north; it whirls about continually, and the wind returns again according to his circuits (Ecclesiastes 1:6).

10. Science expresses the universe in five terms: time, space, matter, power, and motion. Genesis 1:1,2 revealed such truths to the Hebrews in 1450 B.C.: In the beginning [*time*] God created [*power*] the heaven [*space*] and the earth [*matter*]...And the Spirit of God moved [*motion*] upon the face of the waters. The first thing God tells man is that He controls all aspects of the universe.

11. The great biological truth concerning the importance of blood in our body's mechanism has been fully comprehended only in recent years. Up until 120 years ago, sick people were bled, and many died because of the practice. If you lose your blood, you lose your life. Yet Leviticus 17:11, written 3,000 years ago, declared that blood is the source of life: For the life of the flesh is in the blood.

12. All things were made by Him (see John 1:3), including dinosaurs. Why then did the dinosaur disappear? The answer may be in Job 40:15-24. In this passage, God speaks about a great creature called behemoth. Some commentators think this was a hippopotamus. However, the hippo's tail isn't like a large tree, but a small twig. Following are the characteristics of this huge animal: It was the largest of all the creatures God made; was plant-eating (herbivorous); had its strength in its hips and a tail like a large tree. It had very strong bones, lived among the trees, drank massive amounts of water, and was not disturbed by a raging river. He appears impervious to attack because his nose could pierce through snares, but Scripture says, He that made him can make his sword to approach unto him. In other words, God caused this, the largest of all the

(continued on next page)

(11:3 continued)
creatures He had made, to become extinct.

13. *Encyclopedia Britannica* documents that in 1845, a young doctor in Vienna named Dr. Ignaz Semmelweis was horrified at the terrible death rate of women who gave birth in hospitals. As many as 30 percent died after giving birth. Semmelweis noted that doctors would examine the bodies of patients who died, then, without washing their hands, go straight to the next ward and examine expectant mothers. This was their normal practice, because the presence of microscopic diseases was unknown. Semmelweis insisted that doctors wash their hands before examinations, and the death rate immediately dropped to 2 percent.

Look at the specific instructions God gave His people for when they encounter disease: "And when he that has an issue is cleansed of his issue; then he shall number to himself seven days for his cleansing, and wash his clothes, and bathe his flesh in running water, and shall be clean" (Leviticus 15:13). Until recent years, doctors washed their hands in a bowl of water, leaving invisible germs on their hands. However, the Bible says specifically to wash hands under running water.

14. Luke 17:34-36 says the Second Coming of Jesus Christ will occur while some are asleep at night and others are working at daytime activities in the field. This is a clear indication of a revolving earth, with day and night at the same time.

15. During the devastating Black Death of the fourteenth century, patients who were sick or dead were kept in the same rooms as the rest of the family. People often wondered why the disease was affecting so many people at one time. They attributed these epidemics to bad air or evil spirits. However, careful attention to the medical commands of God as revealed in Leviticus would have saved untold millions of lives. Arturo Castiglione wrote about the overwhelming importance of this biblical medical law: *The laws against leprosy in Leviticus 13 may be regarded as the first model of sanitary legislation* (*A History of Medicine*). *Grant R. Jeffery, The Signature of God*

With all these truths revealed in Scripture, how could a thinking person deny that the Bible is supernatural in origin? There is no other book in any of the world's religions (Vedas, Bhagavad-Gita, Koran, Book of Mormon, etc.) that contains scientific truth. In fact, they contain statements that are clearly unscientific. *Hank Hanegraaff* said, "Faith in Christ is not some blind leap into a dark chasm, but a faith based on established evidence."

rewarder of them that diligently seek him.
7 By faith Noah, being warned of God of things not seen as yet, moved with fear, prepared an ark to the saving of his house; by the which he condemned the world, and became heir of the righteousness which is by faith.

11:6 The need for faith. The key that unlocks the door of salvation is faith. Without faith, we cannot please God. Try establishing any sort of friendship without faith. Walk up to a woman and introduce yourself. When she tells you her name, say, "I don't believe you," Watch her reaction. When she tells you where she works, say that you don't believe that either. Carry on like that for a while, and before long you may be nursing a black eye. Your lack of faith in her is a strong insinuation that she is a liar.

If she, a mere mortal, feels insulted by your lack of faith in her word, how much more do unbelievers insult Almighty God by refusing to believe His Word. In doing so, they are saying that God isn't worth trusting and that He is a liar and a deceiver. The Bible says, "He that believes not God has made him a liar" (1 John 5:10). It also says, "Take heed, brethren, lest there be in any of you *an evil heart of unbelief...*" (Hebrews 3:12, emphasis added). The command of the Scriptures is, "Have faith in God" (Mark 11:22). If a meaningful human relationship can't be established without faith, what sort of relationship could we expect to have with God, if by our unbelief we continue to call Him a liar?

8 By faith Abraham, when he was called to go out into a place which he should after receive for an inheritance, obeyed; and he went out, not knowing where he went.

9 By faith he sojourned in the land of promise, as in a strange country, dwelling in tabernacles with Isaac and Jacob, the heirs with him of the same promise:

10 For he looked for a city which has foundations, whose builder and maker is God.

11 Through faith also Sara herself received strength to conceive seed, and was delivered of a child when she was past age, because she judged him faithful who had promised.

12 Therefore sprang there even of one, and him as good as dead, so many as the stars of the sky in multitude, and as the sand which is by the sea shore innumerable.

13 These all died in faith, not having received the promises, but having seen them afar off, and were persuaded of them, and embraced them, and confessed that they were strangers and pilgrims on the earth.

14 For they that say such things declare plainly that they seek a country.

15 And truly, if they had been mindful of that country from whence they came out, they might have had opportunity to have returned.

16 But now they desire a better country, that is, an heavenly: wherefore God is not ashamed to be called their God:

for he has prepared for them a city.

17 By faith Abraham, when he was tried, offered up Isaac: and he that had received the promises offered up his only begotten son,

18 Of whom it was said, That in Isaac shall your seed be called:

19 Accounting that God was able to raise him up, even from the dead; from whence also he received him in a figure.

20 By faith Isaac blessed Jacob and Esau concerning things to come.

21 By faith Jacob, when he was dying, blessed both the sons of Joseph; and worshipped, leaning upon the top of his staff.

22 By faith Joseph, when he died, made mention of the departing of the children of Israel; and gave commandment concerning his bones.

23 By faith Moses, when he was born, was hid three months of his parents, because they saw he was a proper child; and they were not afraid of the king's commandment.

24 **By faith Moses, when he was come to years, refused to be called the son of Pharaoh's daughter;**

25 **Choosing rather to suffer affliction with the people of God, than to enjoy the pleasures of sin for a season;**

26 **Esteeming the reproach of Christ greater riches than the treasures in Egypt: for he had respect to the recompense of the reward.**

27 By faith he forsook Egypt, not fearing the wrath of the king: for he endured, as

---

11:7 The writer of the Book of Hebrews believed the Genesis account of Noah's Flood.

11:11 Scientific facts in the Bible. Genesis 3:15 reveals that a female possesses a seed for childbearing. This was not the common knowledge until a few centuries ago. It was widely believed that only the male possessed the seed of life and that the woman was nothing more than a glorified incubator.

11:25 As we witness, we should remember that there *is* pleasure in sin for a season. Contrary to the claims of modern evangelism, the world *can* find happiness without Jesus. The prophet Jeremiah complained to the Lord, "Why does the way of the wicked prosper? Why are those happy who deal so treacherously?" (Jeremiah 12:1). However, this sinful world cannot find *righteousness* without Jesus, and it is righteousness that they will need on the Day of Wrath (Proverbs 11:4). See Revelation 6:15 comment.

QUESTIONS & OBJECTIONS

11:25 *"I'm doing fine. I don't need God."*

Many people feel this way because of the modern gospel message. It says that Jesus will help their marriage, remove their drug problem, fill the emptiness in their heart, give them peace and joy, etc. In doing so, it restricts the gospel's field of influence. If the message of the cross is for people who have bad marriages, are lonely, and have problems, then those who are happy'won t see their need for the Savior.

In truth, the forgiveness of God in Jesus Christ is for people with bad marriages and people with good marriages. It is for the happy and the sad. It is for people with problems and for those without problems. It is for those who are miserable in their sins, and for those who are enjoying the pleasures of sin for a season. Those who think they are doing fine need to be confronted with a holy Law that they have violated a multitude of times. Then they will see themselves through the eyes of the Judge of the Universe and will flee to the Savior. See also Luke 4:18 comment.

seeing him who is invisible.

28 Through faith he kept the passover, and the sprinkling of blood, lest he that destroyed the firstborn should touch them.

29 By faith they passed through the Red sea as by dry land: which the Egyptians trying to do were drowned.

30 By faith the walls of Jericho fell down, after they were compassed about seven days.

31 By faith the harlot Rahab perished not with them that believed not, when she had received the spies with peace.

32 And what shall I more say? for the time would fail me to tell of Gideon, and of Barak, and of Samson, and of Jephthae;

of David also, and Samuel, and of the prophets:

33 Who through faith subdued kingdoms, wrought righteousness, obtained promises, stopped the mouths of lions,

34 Quenched the violence of fire, escaped the edge of the sword, out of weakness were made strong, waxed valiant in fight, turned to flight the armies of the aliens.

35 Women received their dead raised to life again: and others were tortured, not accepting deliverance; that they might obtain a better resurrection:

36 And others had trial of cruel mockings and scourgings, yes, moreover of bonds and imprisonment:

SPRINGBOARDS FOR PREACHING AND WITNESSING

The New Convert

11:29

A new convert was reading his Bible when he called out, "Wow! Praise the Lord!"

A liberal minister heard him, and asked him what the noise was about. The young Christian replied with great enthusiasm, "This is incredible. It says here that God performed a miracle of deliverance by opening up the Red Sea for the Jews to march through!"

The minister replied, "Owing to tidal patterns around that time of year, the Red Sea was a swamp that was only three inches deep."

Somewhat subdued, the young man continued reading, but soon exclaimed, "Wow! Praise the Lord!" "What s the matter now?" asked the minister. To which the Christian replied, *"God has just drowned the whole Egyptian army in three inches of water!"*

Over 3,000 times, the Bible speaks of its inspiration by God. His Word is true, and you can believe every word of it.

37 They were stoned, they were sawn asunder, were tempted, were slain with the sword: they wandered about in sheepskins and goatskins; being destitute, afflicted, tormented;

38 (Of whom the world was not worthy:) they wandered in deserts, and in mountains, and in dens and caves of the earth.

39 And these all, having obtained a good report through faith, received not the promise:

40 God having provided some better thing for us, that they without us should not be made perfect.

CHAPTER 12

WHEREFORE seeing we also are compassed about with so great a cloud of witnesses, let us lay aside every weight, and the sin which does so easily beset us, and let us run with patience the race that is set before us,

2 Looking to Jesus the author and finisher of our faith; who for the joy that was set before him endured the cross, despising the shame, and is set down at the right hand of the throne of God.

3 For consider him that endured such contradiction of sinners against himself, lest you be wearied and faint in your minds.

4 You have not yet resisted to blood, striving against sin.

5 And you have forgotten the exhortation which speaks to you as to children, My son, despise not the chastening of the Lord, nor faint when you are rebuked of him:

6 For whom the Lord loves he chastens, and scourges every son whom he receives.

7 If you endure chastening, God deals with you as with sons; for what son is he whom the father chastens not?

8 But if you be without chastisement, whereof all are partakers, then are you bastards, and not sons.

9 Furthermore we have had fathers of our flesh which corrected us, and we gave them reverence: shall we not much rather be in subjection to the Father of spirits, and live?

10 For they verily for a few days chastened us after their own pleasure; but he for our profit, that we might be partakers of his holiness.

11 Now no chastening for the present seems to be joyous, but grievous: nevertheless afterward it yields the peaceable fruit of righteousness to them which are exercised thereby.

12 Wherefore lift up the hands which hang down, and the feeble knees;

13 And make straight paths for your feet, lest that which is lame be turned out of

---

12:3 Evangelistic discouragement. "One night when [Dwight L.] Moody was going home, it suddenly occurred to him that he had not spoken to a single person that day about accepting Christ. A day lost, he thought to himself. But as he walked up the street he saw a man by a lamppost. He promptly walked up to the man and asked, 'Are you a Christian?'

"Moody did not find soul-winning easy. In fact, even Christians often criticized him for having zeal without knowledge. Others called him "Crazy Moody." Once when he spoke to a perfect stranger about Christ, the man said, "That is none of your business ... If you were not a sort of preacher I would knock you into the gutter for your impertinence.'

"The next day, a businessman friend sent for Moody. The businessman told Moody that the stranger he had spoken to was a friend of his. 'Moody, you've got zeal without knowledge. You insulted a friend of mine on the street last night. You went up to him, a perfect stranger, and asked him if he were a Christian.'

"Moody went out of his friend's office almost brokenhearted. For some time he worried about this. Then late one night a man pounded on the door of his home. It was the stranger he had supposedly insulted. The stranger said, 'Mr. Moody, I have not had a good night's sleep since that night you spoke to me under the lamppost, and I have come around at this unearthly hour of the night for you to tell me what I have to do to be saved.'" *Harry Albus*

Optical Illusions

. . . .

Seeing is believing?

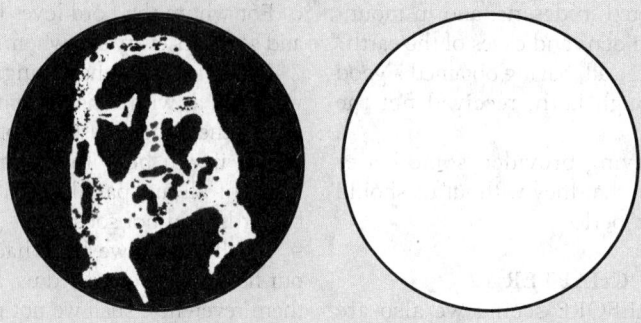

1. Stare intently at the four dots in the center of the left image for 40 seconds. Then stare at the empty circle for 30 seconds.

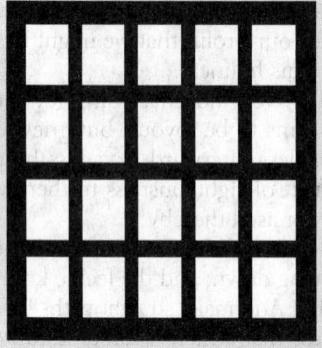

2. Are there dots between the white boxes?

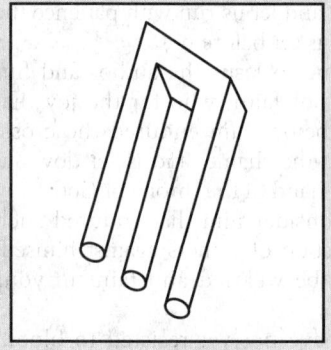

3. How many "prongs" —three or four?

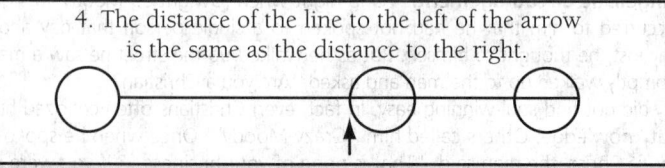

4. The distance of the line to the left of the arrow is the same as the distance to the right.

The Atheist Test: Imagine a circle represents all the knowledge in the universe (someone who had all knowledge would know every hair on every head, every thought of every heart, every grain of sand, every event in human history, etc.). Let's surmise that you know an incredible 1 percent of all knowledge. Is it possible that, in the 99 percent of the knowledge you haven't yet come across, there is ample evidence to prove that God does exist?

(See John 20:25 comment.)

the way; but let it rather be healed.

14 Follow peace with all men, and holiness, without which no man shall see the Lord:

15 Looking diligently lest any man fail of the grace of God; lest any root of bitterness springing up trouble you, and thereby many be defiled;

16 Lest there be any fornicator, or profane person, as Esau, who for one morsel of meat sold his birthright.

17 For you know how that afterward, when he would have inherited the blessing, he was rejected: for he found no place of repentance, though he sought it carefully with tears.

18 For you are not come to the mount that might be touched, and that burned with fire, nor to blackness, and darkness, and tempest,

19 And the sound of a trumpet, and the voice of words; which voice they that heard entreated that the word should not be spoken to them any more:

20 (For they could not endure that which was commanded, And if so much as a beast touch the mountain, it shall be stoned, or thrust through with a dart:

21 And so terrible was the sight, that Moses said, I exceedingly fear and quake:)

22 But you are come to mount Zion, and to the city of the living God, the heavenly Jerusalem, and to an innumerable company of angels,

23 To the general assembly and church of the firstborn, which are written in heaven, and to God the Judge of all, and to the spirits of just men made perfect,

24 And to Jesus the mediator of the new covenant, and to the blood of sprinkling, that speaks better things than that of Abel.

25 **See that you refuse not him that speaks. For if they escaped not who refused him that spoke on earth, much more shall not we escape, if we turn away from him that speaks from heaven:**

26 **Whose voice then shook the earth: but now he has promised, saying, Yet once more I shake not the earth only, but also heaven.**

27 And this word, Yet once more, signifies the removing of those things that are shaken, as of things that are made, that those things which cannot be shaken may remain.

28 **Wherefore we receiving a kingdom which cannot be moved, let us have grace, whereby we may serve God acceptably with reverence and godly fear:**

29 **For our God is a consuming fire.**

For how to convince a sinner of the reasonableness of judgment, see Psalm 55:15 comment.

CHAPTER 13

LET brotherly love continue.

2 Be not forgetful to entertain strangers: for thereby some have entertained angels unawares.

3 Remember them that are in bonds, as bound with them; and them which suffer adversity, as being yourselves also in the body.

12:29 Our God is a consuming fire, and we try to reduce Him to something we can handle or are comfortable with...We are religious consumers. We want our religion to be convenient. It's the perpetual job of writers, preachers, the church and the gospel to help people respond to God as He reveals Himself. *Eugene Peterson*

4 **Marriage is honorable in all, and the bed undefiled: but whoremongers and adulterers God will judge.**

5 Let your conversation be without covetousness; and be content with such things as you have: for he has said, I will never leave you, nor forsake you.

6 *So that we may boldly say, The Lord is my helper, and I will not fear what man shall do to me.*

7 Remember them which have the rule over you, who have spoken to you the word of God: whose faith follow, considering the end of their conversation.

8 Jesus Christ the same yesterday, and today, and for ever.

9 Be not carried about with divers and strange doctrines. For it is a good thing that the heart be established with grace; not with meats, which have not profited them that have been occupied therein.

10 We have an altar, whereof they have no right to eat which serve the tabernacle.

11 For the bodies of those beasts, whose blood is brought into the sanctuary by the high priest for sin, are burned without the camp.

12 Wherefore Jesus also, that he might sanctify the people with his own blood, suffered without the gate.

13 Let us go forth therefore to him without the camp, bearing his reproach.

14 For here have we no continuing city, but we seek one to come.

15 By him therefore let us offer the sacrifice of praise to God continually, that is, the fruit of our lips giving thanks to his name.

16 But to do good and to communicate forget not: for with such sacrifices God is well pleased.

17 Obey them that have the rule over you, and submit yourselves: for they watch for your souls, as they that must give account, that they may do it with joy, and not with grief: for that is unprofitable for you.

18 Pray for us: for we trust we have a good conscience, in all things willing to live honestly.

19 But I beseech you the rather to do this, that I may be restored to you the sooner.

> Only by imitating the spirit and manner of the Lord Jesus shall we become wise to win souls.
> **CHARLES SPURGEON**

20 Now the God of peace, that brought again from the dead our Lord Jesus, that great shepherd of the sheep, through the blood of the everlasting covenant,

21 Make you perfect in every good work to do his will, working in you that which is well-pleasing in his sight, through Jesus Christ; to whom be glory for ever and ever. Amen.

22 And I beseech you, brethren, suffer the word of exhortation: for I have written a letter to you in few words.

23 Know that our brother Timothy is set at liberty; with whom, if he come shortly, I will see you.

24 Salute all them that have the rule over you, and all the saints. They of Italy salute you.

25 Grace be with you all. Amen.

13:8 Jesus has never changed. He has no variableness or shadow of turning (James 1:17). Hebrews 1:12 says of Him, You are the same, and your years shall not fail.

James

CHAPTER 1

JAMES, a servant of God and of the Lord Jesus Christ, to the twelve tribes which are scattered abroad, greeting.

2 My brethren, count it all joy when you fall into divers temptations;

3 Knowing this, that the trying of your faith works patience.

4 But let patience have her perfect work, that you may be perfect and entire, wanting nothing.

5 If any of you lack wisdom, let him ask of God, that gives to all men liberally, and upbraides not; and it shall be given him.

6 But let him ask in faith, nothing wavering. For he that wavers is like a wave of the sea driven with the wind and tossed.

7 For let not that man think that he shall receive any thing of the Lord.

8 A double minded man is unstable in all his ways.

9 Let the brother of low degree rejoice in that he is exalted:

10 But the rich, in that he is made low: because as the flower of the grass he shall pass away.

11 For the sun is no sooner risen with a burning heat, but it withers the grass, and the flower thereof falls, and the grace of the fashion of it perishes: so also shall the rich man fade away in his ways.

12 Blessed is the man that endures temptation: for when he is tried, he shall receive the crown of life, which the Lord has promised to them that love him.

13 Let no man say when he is tempted, I am tempted of God: for God cannot be tempted with evil, neither tempts he any man:

14 But every man is tempted, when he is drawn away of his own lust, and enticed.

15 Then when lust has conceived, it brings forth sin: and sin, when it is finished, brings forth death.

16 Do not err, my beloved brethren.

17 Every good gift and every perfect gift

1:3 Satan tempts us in order to bring out the worst in us; God tests us to bring out the best. (See verse 12.)

1:5 One mark of wisdom is the saving of souls (Proverbs 11:30). With an open-ended promise such as this, we should plead with God for wisdom (see Proverbs 2:1-7). Proverbs 19:8 tells us that he who gets wisdom loves his own soul.

1:15 The ungodly hold firmly onto the lighted stick of dynamite called sin. They relish its flickering flame. Lust may delight the human heart, but its terrible consequences are sin, death, and hell.

"Human nature rises against restraint: I had not known lust except the Law had said, Thou shall not covet. The depravity of man is excited to rebellion by the promulgation of laws. So evil are we, that we conceive at once the desire to commit an act, simply because it is forbidden." *Charles Spurgeon*

THE FUNCTION OF THE LAW

1:25 "God, being a perfect God, had to give a perfect Law, and the Law was given not to save men, but to measure them. I want you to understand this clearly, because I believe hundreds and thousands stumble at this point. They try to save themselves by trying to keep the Law; but it was never meant for men to save themselves by." *D. L. Moody*

is from above, and comes down from the Father of lights, with whom is no variableness, neither shadow of turning.

18 Of his own will begat he us with the word of truth, that we should be a kind of firstfruits of his creatures.

19 **Wherefore, my beloved brethren, let every man be swift to hear, slow to speak, slow to wrath:**

20 **For the wrath of man works not the righteousness of God.**

21 Wherefore lay apart all filthiness and superfluity of naughtiness, and receive with meekness the engrafted word, which is able to save your souls.

22 But be doers of the word, and not hearers only, deceiving your own selves.

23 For if any be a hearer of the word, and not a doer, he is like unto a man beholding his natural face in a glass:

24 For he beholds himself, and goes his way, and straightway forgets what manner of man he was.

25 But whoso looks into the perfect law of liberty, and continues therein, he being not a forgetful hearer, but a doer of the work, this man shall be blessed in his deed.

26 If any man among you seem to be religious, and bridles not his tongue, but deceives his own heart, this man's religion is vain.

27 Pure religion and undefiled before God and the Father is this, To visit the fatherless and widows in their affliction, and to keep himself unspotted from the world.

CHAPTER 2

MY brethren, have not the faith of our Lord Jesus Christ, the Lord of glory, with respect of persons.

2 For if there come to your assembly a man with a gold ring, in goodly apparel, and there come in also a poor man in vile raiment;

3 And you have respect to him that wears the gay clothing, and say to him, Sit here in a good place; and say to the poor, Stand there, or sit here under my footstool:

4 Are you not then partial in yourselves, and are become judges of evil thoughts?

5 Hearken, my beloved brethren, has not God chosen the poor of this world rich in faith, and heirs of the kingdom which he has promised to them that love him?

6 But you have despised the poor. Do not rich men oppress you, and draw you before the judgment seats?

7 Do not they blaspheme that worthy name by the which you are called?

8 If you fulfil the royal law according to the scripture, You shall love your neighbour as yourself, you do well:

9 But if you have respect to persons, you commit sin, and are convinced of the law as transgressors.

10 For whosoever shall keep the whole law, and yet offend in one point, he is guilty of all.

1:22 This is particularly applicable to the many commands to evangelize this world.

1:23–25 The only way you and I can see ourselves in truth is to look into a mirror. Yet a mirror can only do its job and reflect truth if there is bright light. In Scripture, the Law of God is called both a mirror (James 1:23-25; 2:11,12) and light (Proverbs 6:23). Many of today's converts aren't shown the mirror of the Law. We think that a long look at what they are in truth will be too painful for them, so "All have sinned" is all we tell them. Without the conviction of their own sin, they are stillborn with no life in them.

THE FUNCTION OF THE LAW

2:10 "It is of great importance that the sinner should be made to feel his guilt, and not to the impression that he is unfortunate. Do not be afraid, but show him the breadth of the divine Law, and the exceeding strictness of its precepts. Make him see how it condemns his thoughts and life. By a convicted sinner, I mean one who feels himself condemned by the Law of God, as a guilty sinner.

"I remark that this [the Law] is the rule, and the only just rule by which the guilt of sin can be measured...Every man need only consult his own conscience faithfully and he will see that it is equally affirmed by the mind's own intuition to be right." *Charles Finney*

11 For he that said, Do not commit adultery, said also, Do not kill. Now if you commit no adultery, yet if you kill, you are become a transgressor of the law.

12 So speak, and so do, as they that shall be judged by the law of liberty.

13 For he shall have judgment without mercy, that has showed no mercy; and mercy rejoices against judgment.

14 What does it profit, my brethren, though a man say he has faith, and have not works? can faith save him?

15 If a brother or sister be naked, and destitute of daily food,

16 And one of you say to them, Depart in peace, be you warmed and filled; notwithstanding you give them not those things which are needful to the body; what does it profit?

17 Even so faith, if it has not works, is dead, being alone.

18 Yes, a man may say, You have faith, and I have works: show me your faith without your works, and I will show you my faith by my works.

19 **You believe that there is one God; you do well: the devils also believe, and tremble.**

20 **But will you know, O vain man, that faith without works is dead?**

21 Was not Abraham our father justified by works, when he had offered Isaac his son upon the altar?

22 See how faith wrought with his works, and by works was faith made perfect?

23 And the scripture was fulfilled which says, Abraham believed God, and it was imputed to him for righteousness: and he was called the Friend of God.

24 You see then how that by works a man is justified, and not by faith only.

25 Likewise also was not Rahab the harlot justified by works, when she had received the messengers, and had sent them out another way?

2:7 Witnessing to blasphemers. If you hear God's name taken in vain, don't tell the person it's offensive; use it as an opening for the gospel. Greet him, talk about something in the natural realm, then give him a gospel tract. Gently say, "I noticed that you used God's name in vain. Do you know what you're actually doing when you do that?" Most people will say no. Then say, "Instead of using a filthy word to express disgust, you're putting God's name in place of that word. That's called 'blasphemy,' and the Bible says, 'The Lord will not hold him guiltless who takes His name in vain.'"

2:8 Using the Law in evangelism. In verses 8-12 James uses the Law (in conjunction with future punishment) to bring the knowledge of sin. See John 8:4,5 comment.

2:10 Galatians 3:10 warns that the sinner must continue to do *all* things that are written in the Law. The strict demands of the Law cannot be kept by sinful man and should send the sinner to the Savior. See Matthew 5:48 comment.

"God's Law is unified; it all hangs together and is inseparable. It is like hitting a window with a hammer. You may hit it only once, and that rather lightly, but the whole window is shattered." *John MacArthur*

2:16 "Science may have found a cure for most evils; but it has found no remedy for the worst of them all: the apathy of human beings." *Helen Keller*

26 For as the body without the spirit is dead, so faith without works is dead also.

CHAPTER 3

MY brethren, be not many masters, knowing that we shall receive the greater condemnation.

2 For in many things we offend all. If any man offend not in word, the same is a perfect man, and able also to bridle the whole body.

3 Behold, we put bits in the horses' mouths, that they may obey us; and we turn about their whole body.

4 Behold also the ships, which though they be so great, and are driven of fierce winds, yet are they turned about with a very small helm, wherever the governor lists.

5 Even so the tongue is a little member, and boasts great things. Behold, how great a matter a little fire kindles!

6 And the tongue is a fire, a world of iniquity: so is the tongue among our members, that it defiles the whole body, and sets on fire the course of nature; and it is set on fire of hell.

7 For every kind of beasts, and of birds, and of serpents, and of things in the sea, is tamed, and has been tamed of mankind:

8 But the tongue can no man tame; it is an unruly evil, full of deadly poison.

9 Therewith bless we God, even the Father; and therewith curse we men, which are made after the similitude of God.

10 Out of the same mouth proceeds blessing and cursing. My brethren, these things ought not so to be.

> What can be wiser than in the highest sense to bless our fellow men to snatch a soul from the gulf that yawns, to lift it up to the heaven that glorifies, to deliver an immortal from the thralldom of Satan, and to bring him into the liberty of Christ?
>
> **CHARLES SPURGEON**

11 Does a fountain send forth at the same place sweet water and bitter?

12 Can the fig tree, my brethren, bear olive berries? either a vine, figs? so can no fountain both yield salt water and fresh.

13 Who is a wise man and endued with

2:17 Faith without works. A Christian farmer in western Kansas felt sure that God spoke to him to give his $40,000 hail insurance to missions. So, in faith he gave the money, trusting that God would protect his crop. Sure enough, the hail came and severely damaged all his neighbr's crops, but not his.

In contrast, there is a well-known story about a brilliant tightrope artist named Blondin, who pushed a wheelbarrow across Niagara Falls. After he had walked to the other side, the crowd roared with applause at his amazing feat.

He asked a small boy in the crowd if he believed that Blondin could walk back. The boy said, Yes, sir! He then asked if the boy thought he could do it with him in the wheelbarrow. The boy said he believed he could do it, to which the famous tightrope walker said, *"Good! Jump in then and I will take you!"* The boy would not get in.

Here are two different types of faith. The farmer had faith that he had heard from God; he was so sure that he was prepared to step out. But the boy's faith was (understandably) lacking; he wasn't prepared to step out, and get in. Many sincere folks have a measure of faith in Jesus, but they have never *trusted* in Him. In that sense, their faith, because it doesn't have works with it, is dead.

2:20 "What is it [evolution] based upon? Upon nothing whatever but faith, upon belief in the reality of the unseen, belief in the fossils that cannot be produced, belief in the embryological experiments that refuse to come off. It is faith unjustified by work." *Arthur N. Field*

3:6 The tongue weighs practically nothing, but so few people are able to hold it.

Here we are told that the tongue is set on fire by hell. At Pentecost, God gave man a new tongue set on fire by heaven. The mouths of men reveal their wicked hearts. See Romans 3:13,14.

knowledge among you? let him show out of a good conversation his works with meekness of wisdom.

14 But if you have bitter envying and strife in your hearts, glory not, and lie not against the truth.

15 This wisdom descends not from above, but is earthly, sensual, devilish.

16 For where envying and strife is, there is confusion and every evil work.

17 But the wisdom that is from above is first pure, then peaceable, gentle, and easy to be entreated, full of mercy and good fruits, without partiality, and without hypocrisy.

18 And the fruit of righteousness is sown in peace of them that make peace.

CHAPTER 4

FROM whence come wars and fightings among you? come they not hence, even of your lusts that war in your members?

2 You lust, and have not: you kill, and desire to have, and cannot obtain: you fight and war, yet you have not, because you ask not.

3 You ask, and receive not, because you ask amiss, that you may consume it upon your lusts.

4 **You adulterers and adulteresses, do you not know that the friendship of the world is enmity with God? whosoever therefore will be a friend of the world is the enemy of God.**

5 Do you think that the scripture said in vain, The spirit that dwells in us lusts to envy?

6 **But he gives more grace. Wherefore he says, God resists the proud, but gives grace to the humble.**

7 **Submit yourselves therefore to God. Resist the devil, and he will flee from you.**

8 **Draw near to God, and he will draw near to you. Cleanse your hands, you sinners; and purify your hearts, you double minded.**

9 **Be afflicted, and mourn, and weep: let your laughter be turned to mourning, and your joy to heaviness.**

10 **Humble yourselves in the sight of the Lord, and he shall lift you up.**

11 Speak not evil one of another, brethren. He that speaks evil of his brother, and judges his brother, speaks evil of the law, and judges the law: but if you judge the law, you are not a doer of the law, but a judge.

12 There is one lawgiver, who is able to

3:17 This is the spirit in which we should share our faith. See Proverbs 15:1.

Beware of religious types. They tend to gravitate toward the evangelistic enterprise. They will contend with you about doctrine and steal your time from the work of evangelism. You will recognize them by their lack of gentleness, mercy, and willingness to yield to reason.

4:2–4 Using the Law in evangelism. James here uses the Law once again to bring the knowledge of sin, speaking of lust, adultery, murder, and covetousness.

4:6 Biblical evangelism is always *Law to the proud and grace to the humble*. With the Law we break the hard heart; with the gospel we heal the broken one. See Matthew 19:17-22 comment.

4:9,10 These are the inner workings of a genuinely repentant heart affliction, mourning, weeping (contrition), heaviness, and humility. These are the ones the Lord lifts up. See Psalm 147:6.

4:12 The idea for the American government's divided powers came directly from Scripture. Isaiah 33:22 says, "For the Lord is our Judge [the judicial branch], the Lord is our Lawgiver [the legislative branch], the Lord is our King [the executive branch]." Our Founding Fathers knew that separated powers were needed because of man's inherent sinfulness and desire for control, and what better model could there be for a government than the Lord who governs the universe!

"The teachings of the Bible are so interwoven and entwined with our whole civic and social life that it would be literally—I do not mean figuratively, I mean literally—impossible for us to figure out ourselves what life would be if these teachings were removed." *Theodore Roosevelt*

SPRINGBOARDS FOR PREACHING AND WITNESSING

The Will to Live

4:14

Millions of people spend dozens of hours each week watching dead people on TV. From Elvis to Lucy to Jimmy Stewart, the faces of folks who no longer exist entertain us. Time not only snatched their looks, it snatched their lives. Today, good-looking Hollywood stars are making movies so that tomorrow's generation can also pass the time by watching dead people on TV.

Time makes today tomorrow's memory. Each weekend seems to pass us by like blurred telephone poles flashing past the window of the speeding train of life.

If I purchased a new car and saw in the owner's manual that it had a certain type of engine, I shouldn't be surprised to lift the hood and find the engine to be exactly as the manual stated. The maker's handbook gives me insight into the unseen workings of the vehicle. This is also true with human beings. The Maker's manual tells us how each of us thinks and why we react the way we do. It lifts the hood and reveals the inner workings of homo sapiens.

In doing so, the Bible discloses an often-overlooked tool that we can use to reach the lost. That tool is the fear of death. For the Christian who may find such an approach to be negative, it may be looked at in a *positive* light. The tool may also be called "the will to live." Every human being in his right mind has a fear of death (Hebrews 2:15). *He doesn't want to die.* He sits wide-eyed, staring out the window of the speeding train watching life pass him by.

Here is how to use that tool when speaking to an unsaved person: Let's assume that the average person dies at 70 years old. Then if you are 20 years old, you have just 2,500 weekends left to live. If you have turned 30, you have 2,000 weekends left until the day you die. If you are 40 years old, you have only 1,500 weekends left. If you are 50, then you have just 1,000 weekends, and if you are 60, you have a mere 500 weekends left until the day death comes to you.

Even as a Christian that thought concerns me. I somehow can relate to "weekends," while "years" puts death into the distance. It shakes me enough to ask myself, "*What I am doing with my life?*" It sickens me that I am doing so little to reach the lost. It also deeply concerns me that I have dry eyes when I pray. My train will take me into the presence of God. For those trusting in Jesus Christ, death has been defeated. But the train of the unregenerate will take them to horrific disaster. Their end will be eternal hell. In light of such terrible thoughts, all my activities outside of warning the world of their destination seem trivial.

It has been wisely stated that every one of us is unique...*just like everyone else.* In truth, each unique individual is uniquely predictable. Every sinner has a fear of death. No one can deny that he naturally has a will to live. Therefore, it makes sense to confront him with reality by reminding him that he has an appointment to keep. Bluntly tell him how many weekends he has left. Then appeal to his reason by saying, "If there was one chance in a million that Jesus Christ has abolished death, and has brought life and immortality to light through the gospel, you owe it to your good sense just to look into it."

---

save and to destroy: who are you that judge another?

13 Go to now, you that say, Today or tomorrow we will go into such a city, and continue there a year, and buy and sell, and get gain:

14 Whereas you know not what shall be on the morrow. For what is your life? It is even a vapor, that appears for a little time, and then vanishes away.

15 For that you ought to say, If the Lord will, we shall live, and do this, or that.

16 But now you rejoice in your boastings: all such rejoicing is evil.

17 Therefore to him that knows to do good, and does it not, to him it is sin.

4:17 "To sin by silence when they should protest makes cowards out of men." *Abraham Lincoln*

CHAPTER 5

GO to now, you rich men, weep and howl for your miseries that shall come upon you.

2 Your riches are corrupted, and your garments are motheaten.

3 Your gold and silver is cankered; and the rust of them shall be a witness against you, and shall eat your flesh as it were fire. You have heaped treasure together for the last days.

4 Behold, the hire of the laborers who have reaped down your fields, which is of you kept back by fraud, cries: and the cries of them which have reaped are entered into the ears of the Lord of sabaoth.

5 You have lived in pleasure on the earth, and been wanton; you have nourished your hearts, as in a day of slaughter.

6 You have condemned and killed the just; and he does not resist you.

7 Be patient therefore, brethren, to the coming of the Lord. Behold, the husbandman waits for the precious fruit of the earth, and has long patience for it, until he receive the early and latter rain.

8 Be also patient; stablish your hearts: for the coming of the Lord draws nigh.

9 Grudge not one against another, brethren, lest you be condemned: behold, the judge stands before the door.

10 Take, my brethren, the prophets, who have spoken in the name of the Lord, for an example of suffering affliction, and of patience.

11 Behold, we count them happy which endure. You have heard of the patience of Job, and have seen the end of the Lord; that the Lord is very pitiful, and of tender mercy.

12 But above all things, my brethren, swear not, neither by heaven, neither by the earth, neither by any other oath: but let your yes be yes; and your no, no; lest you fall into condemnation.

13 Is any among you afflicted? let him pray. Is any merry? let him sing psalms.

14 Is any sick among you? let him call for the elders of the church; and let them pray over him, anointing him with oil in the name of the Lord:

15 And the prayer of faith shall save the sick, and the Lord shall raise him up; and if he has committed sins, they shall be forgiven him.

16 Confess your faults one to another, and pray one for another, that you may be healed. The effectual fervent prayer of a righteous man avails much.

17 Elijah was a man subject to like passions as we are, and he prayed earnestly that it might not rain: and it rained not on the earth by the space of three years and six months.

18 And he prayed again, and the heaven gave rain, and the earth brought forth her fruit.

19 *Brethren, if any of you do err from the truth, and one convert him;*

20 *Let him know, that he which converts the sinner from the error of his way shall save a soul from death, and shall hide a multitude of sins.*

5:8   Second coming of Jesus: See Jude 14.

5:16   "Prayer is the honest thoughts of the heart and mind converted into a form of communication, either verbal or mental, directed toward God." *Emeal Zwayne*

5:20   There is no higher calling than to turn a sinner from the error of his ways. A surgeon may extend someone's life, but death eventually takes the person. Our work has *eternal* consequences.

Mormonism

OFFICIAL NAME: Church of Jesus Christ of Latter-day Saints (LDS, Mormons)

FOUNDER: Joseph Smith Jr., on April 6, 1830

CURRENT LEADER: Gordon B. Hinckley (b. 1910)

HEADQUARTERS: Salt Lake City, Utah

MEMBERSHIP (1998): Worldwide: 10.3 million in 28,670 wards and branches in 162 countries; United States: 5.1 million in all 50 states and D.C.; Canada: 152,000.

MISSIONARIES (1998): 58,700

The Church of Jesus Christ of Latter-day Saints was founded by Joseph F. Smith Jr. (1805-1844). Smith claimed to have had a visitation from God in 1820 in which God directed him to establish the true church. Consequently he organized the Mormon Church on April 6, 1830, with six original members. Beginning with a few hundred followers, the church moved to Ohio, Missouri, and Illinois before Smith's death at the hands of a mob at the Carthage, Ill., jail. Smith had been arrested for encouraging the destruction of the *Expositor*, a Nauvoo, Ill., newspaper. After Smith's death, Brigham Young was affirmed as president of the church by a majority of the church's leaders and led several thousand followers to Utah where they established Salt Lake City in 1847. Joseph Smith's widow, Emma, resided in Independence, Mo. Those who affirmed her son, Joseph Smith, as the true successor of his father and as prophet of the church helped found the Reorganized Church of Jesus Christ of Latter Day Saints, now headquartered in Independence, Mo., in 1852.

MAJOR BELIEFS OF MORMONS

ONE TRUE CHURCH: The Mormon church claims to be the only true church. In God's supposed revelation to Joseph Smith, Jesus Christ told him to join no other church for they were all wrong...their creeds were an abomination ...those professors [members] were all corrupt (*The Pearl of Great Price*, Joseph Smith History 1:19). Mormons teach that after the New Testament all churches became heretical and no true saints existed until the Church of the Latter-day Saints was organized, hence their name. Non-Mormons are thus called Gen-

tiles. The new revelations given to Smith, the institution of the prophet and apostles in the church, the restoration of the divine priesthoods, and the temple ceremonies make the church authentic. True and full salvation or exaltation is found only in the LDS Church.

Biblical Response: The true church of Jesus Christ has had an ongoing presence and witness in the world since Pentecost. Jesus Christ promised that His church, *true* baptized and regenerate believers, would not fail (Matt. 16:17-18). The marks of a true church include faithfulness to the teaching of the first apostles (Acts 2:42), not the creation of new doctrines.

AUTHORITY OF THE PROPHET: The *president* or *prophet* of the Church is thought to be the sole spokesman and revelator of God. Joseph Smith was the initial prophet, but each successive president holds that position. Through him God's will can be made known to the church. All revelations are made scripture and no Mormon can attain godhood without accepting Joseph Smith as a true prophet. The Mormon scriptures state that Latter-day Saints shalt give heed unto all his [the prophet's] words and commandments...For his word ye shall receive as if from mine [God's] own mouth (*Doctrine and Covenants* 21:4-5).

Biblical Response: Old and New Testament prophets were God's spokesmen. Their words were always consistent with the Bible and pointed to God's Son, Jesus Christ. A test of genuineness for prophets was that any prediction they proclaimed would come true (Deut. 18:20-22). For example, Joseph Smith predicted that the temple of the church would be built in Independence, Mo., within his lifetime (*Doctrine and Covenants* 84:2-5). No temple has yet been built there. New Testament prophets spoke, along with teachers, pastors, and evangelists, in evangelizing with and edifying the church (Eph. 4:11-13).

MORMON SCRIPTURE: Mormons accept four books as scripture and the word of God. The King James Version of the Bible is one of them, but only as far as it is translated correctly, seemingly allowing for possible questions about its authority. Joseph Smith made over 600 corrections to its text. Other standard works are the *Book of Mormon*, *Doctrine and Covenants*, and *The Pearl of Great Price*. The Bible is missing plain and precious parts according to the *Book of Mormon* (1 Nephi 13:26) which the other three volumes complete. The *Book of Mormon* has the fullness of the gospel and tells the story of a supposed migration of Israelites in 600 B.C. to the American continent. These Israelites subsequently lapsed into apostasy, although their story was preserved on golden plates written in Reformed Egyptian. Joseph Smith, it is said, translated the plates by the "gift and power of God" (*Doctrine and Covenants* 135:3). Reformed Egyptian does not exist as a language. The golden plates were returned to the angel Moroni after they were transcribed and Moroni returned them to heaven. The *Book of Mormon* does not contain explicit Mormon doctrine. *Doctrine and Covenants* contains the revelations of the Mormon prophets 138 in number along with two declarations. Here most of Mormon doctrine can be found including the priesthood, baptism for the dead, godhood, and polygamy. *The Pearl of Great Price* contains Smith's religious history, the Articles of Faith, the Book of Abraham, and the Book of Moses.

Biblical Response: The Bible explicitly warns against adding to or detracting from its teaching (Rev. 22:18; Deut. 4:2). The New Testament contains the inspired and totally accurate witness of contemporary disciples and followers of Jesus. It alone claims to be fully inspired of God and usable for the establishment of doctrine (2 Tim. 3:15 17; 2 Pet. 1:19 21).

ESTABLISHMENT OF TEMPLES: The first Mormon temple was constructed in Kirtland, Ohio, in 1836. Subsequently, a temple was constructed in Nauvoo, Ill., in 1846. Presently there are at least 53 operating temples throughout the world including the one finished in Salt Lake City in 1893. The purpose and function of temples are for the practice of eternal ordinances, including primarily baptism for the dead, endowments, and celestial marriages. Baptism in the Mormon church, for both the living and the dead, is essential for the fullness of salvation. The dead often are baptized by proxy, which affords them after death the opportunity to become Mormons. Celestial marriage for "time and eternity" is also a temple ordinance. It is necessary for godhood and seals the marriage forever. Temples form an essential part of Mormon salvation. Only Mormons in possession of a temple recommended by their bishop may enter a temple.

Biblical Response: The Temple of the Old Testament was a place of symbolic sacrifice forefiguring the sacrifice of Christ. Worship in the Jewish temple in Jerusalem was a practice of early Jewish believers (Acts 2:46). Otherwise, there is no mention of any such practice in the New Testament. Never was the Jewish temple used for baptism for the dead, marriage, or other secret ceremonies. It was the place in the Old Testament where the glory of God occasionally dwelt. Today the individual believer is God's dwelling place and not a physical building (1 Cor. 3:16).

GOD IS AN EXALTED MAN: Elohim, the god of this universe, was previously a man in a prior existence. As a result of having kept the requirements of Mormonism, he was exalted to godhood and inherited his own universe. God is confined to a body of flesh and bones (*Doctrine and Covenants* 130:22) and yet is thought to be omniscient and omnipotent. He obviously cannot be omnipresent. There are infinite numbers of gods with their own worlds. These, too, were previously men. The Holy Ghost, Jesus Christ, and Heavenly Father comprise three separate and distinct gods. Heavenly Father sires spiritual children in heaven destined for human life on earth. All humans, as well as Jesus Christ and Lucifer, are god's heavenly children. (See *Doctrine and Covenants* 130:22; God, Jesus, and the Spirit thus had beginnings.)

Biblical Response: God is Spirit and is not confined to a physical body (John 4:24). Jesus Christ was incarnated through a miraculous and non-physical conception through the Virgin Mary. He was fully God from the beginning (John 1:1). Together with the person of the Holy Spirit, they form the triune (three-in-one) eternal God.

JESUS IS GOD'S "SON": Jesus was Heavenly Father's firstborn spirit child in heaven. He was begotten by God through Mary as in a literal, full and complete sense: in the same sense in which he is the son of Mary (Bruce McConkie, *A New Witness for the Articles of Faith* [Salt Lake City: Deseret Book Co., 1993], 67). These two elements of Jesus being literally God's son form his uniqueness in Mormon theology. In the Garden of Gethsemane, as well as on the cross, Jesus atoned for Adam's sin and guaranteed all humankind resurrection and immortality. Jesus visited the Israelites or Indians of North

America after his resurrection and established the true church among them. We are the spiritual, but literal, younger brothers and sisters of Christ. Some Mormon documents claim that Jesus was married at Cana in Galilee (Mark 2) and had children himself.

Biblical Response: Jesus is viewed as God, the Word or Son, eternally existent with the Father and worthy of identity as God (John 1:1-14). He was born of the Virgin Mary who had conceived him supernaturally by the Holy Spirit. He lived a perfect life, died on the cross for the sins of the world, and was raised from the dead. He will come again and reign as Lord of lords.

HUMANS ARE GODS IN EMBRYO: Every human being has the potential of becoming a god by keeping the requirements of Mormonism. A well-known statement within Mormonism is, "As man is, god once was; as god is, man may become." From a prior spirit existence in heaven, humans may be born on earth in order to exercise freedom to choose good or evil and to have a body for the resurrection. Basically humans are good, but they will be punished for their sin. But by keeping Mormon teaching and obeying the church and the Prophet, after the resurrection, worthy Mormon males may pass the celestial guards, bring their wives with them, and achieve a status similar to Elohim, the god of this world. The consequences of their sin are erased by their allegiance to the tenets of Mormonism. In resurrection faithful Mormons receive exaltation to godhood and will exercise dominion over their world.

Biblical Response: Human beings are God's special creation. There is no evidence from Scripture of preexistence; rather God acknowledges that it was in the womb of our mothers that He formed us (Isaiah 44:2). A sinful nature is part of humanity's experience. Liberation from the power and presence of sin is experienced as a result of faith in Christ. At that point God's image is begun to be remade in every Christian. Although the believer is being transformed to Christlikeness, the Bible does not teach literal godhood as the inheritance of the saints (Rom. 8:29; Rev. 1:5-6).

MORMON PLAN OF SALVATION: The Mormon plan of salvation is built on the idea that all people have eternal life, but only the most faithful Mormons have godhood or enter the celestial Kingdom. In order to obtain this ultimate step, Mormons must exercise faith in the God of Mormonism, its Christ, and the Church of Jesus Christ of Latter-day Saints; exercise repentance; and be baptized in the LDS Church. Additionally Mormons must keep the Word of Wisdom by abstaining from alcohol, tobacco, and caffeine; tithe to the church; attend weekly sacrament meetings; support the Mormon prophet; do temple works; and be active in their support of the church.

Biblical Response: Salvation, according to the Bible, is due to God's grace and love. He provided Jesus as the sacrifice for the sins of the world. It is through faith in the crucified and risen Jesus that we may be saved. Works are excluded (John 1:12; 3:16; Rom. 10:9-13; Eph. 2:8-9).

EVANGELIZING MORMONS

- Know clearly the Christian faith and the gospel.
- Be aware of the unique Mormon doctrines as presented here.
- Remember, Mormons use Christian vocabulary (gospel, atonement, god) but radically redefine their meanings. Define clearly what you mean when you use biblical words.
- Present a clear testimony of your faith in Christ alone for your salvation.
- Show your Mormon friend that the Bible teaches salvation alone through the cross of Christ (John 3:16; Rom. 10:4,10-13; Eph. 2:8-9). Emphasize that salvation is a gift to be received, not a merit to be earned.
- Warn the Mormon about trusting in feelings (i.e., the burning in the bosom) for a validation of Mormonism's truth claim. Without historical, objective verification, feelings are useless.
- When Mormons use a Bible verse, read carefully the verses before and afterward to make clear the exact meaning and purpose of the passage. Don't let them take Bible verses out of context. Read carefully the full reference in the Bible before deciding what any one verse means.
- Keep the central doctrines of the faith as the focus of your discussion.
- Do the basics: pray, trust the Holy Spirit, and be loving, patient, and steadfast.

1 Peter

CHAPTER 1

Peter, an apostle of Jesus Christ, to the strangers scattered throughout Pontus, Galatia, Cappadocia, Asia, and Bithynia,

2 Elect according to the foreknowledge of God the Father, through sanctification of the Spirit, to obedience and sprinkling of the blood of Jesus Christ: Grace to you, and peace, be multiplied.

3 Blessed be the God and Father of our Lord Jesus Christ, which according to his abundant mercy has begotten us again to a lively hope by the resurrection of Jesus Christ from the dead,

4 To an inheritance incorruptible, and undefiled, and that fades not away, reserved in heaven for you,

5 Who are kept by the power of God through faith to salvation ready to be revealed in the last time.

6 Wherein you greatly rejoice, though now for a season, if need be, you are in heaviness through manifold temptations:

7 That the trial of your faith, being much more precious than of gold that perishes though it be tried with fire, might be found unto praise and honor and glory at the appearing of Jesus Christ:

8 Whom having not seen, you love; in whom, though now you see him not, yet believing, you rejoice with joy unspeakable and full of glory:

9 Receiving the end of your faith, even the salvation of your souls.

10 Of which salvation the prophets have inquired and searched diligently, who prophesied of the grace that should come

---

1:3 **New birth—its necessity for salvation.** See 1 Peter 1:23.

1:4 **The beloved son.** A true story is told of a millionaire who had a portrait of his beloved son painted before the son went to war. He was tragically killed in battle, and shortly afterward, the heartbroken millionaire died.

His will stated that all his riches were to be auctioned, specifying that the painting must sell first.

Many showed up at the auction, where a mass of the rich man's wealth was displayed. When the painting was held up for sale, there were no bids made. It was an unknown painting by an unknown painter of the rich man's uncelebrated son, so sadly, there was little interest.

After a few moments, a butler who worked for the man remembered how much the millionaire loved his son, decided to bid for it, and purchased the portrait for a very low price.

Suddenly, to everyone's surprise the auctioneer brought down his gavel and declared the auction closed. The rich man's will had secretly specified that the person who cared enough to purchase the painting of his beloved son was also to be given all the riches of his will.

This is precisely what God has done through the gospel. He who accepts the beloved Son of God also receives all the riches of His will the gift of eternal life and pleasures for evermore. They become joint heirs with the Son (Romans 8:16,17).

to you:

11 Searching what, or what manner of time the Spirit of Christ which was in them did signify, when it testified beforehand the sufferings of Christ, and the glory that should follow.

12 To whom it was revealed, that not to themselves, but to us they did minister the things, which are now reported to you by them that have preached the gospel to you with the Holy Spirit sent down from heaven; which things the angels desire to look into.

13 Wherefore gird up the loins of your mind, be sober, and hope to the end for the grace that is to be brought to you at the revelation of Jesus Christ;

14 As obedient children, not fashioning yourselves according to the former lusts in your ignorance:

15 But as he which has called you is holy, so be holy in all manner of conversation;

16 Because it is written, Be holy; for I am holy.

17 And if you call on the Father, who without respect of persons judges according to every man's work, pass the time of your sojourning here in fear:

18 Forasmuch as you know that you were not redeemed with corruptible things, as silver and gold, from your vain conversation received by tradition from your fathers;

19 But with the precious blood of Christ, as of a lamb without blemish and without spot:

20 Who verily was foreordained before the foundation of the world, but was manifest in these last times for you,

21 Who by him do believe in God, that raised him up from the dead, and gave him glory; that your faith and hope might be in God.

22 Seeing you have purified your souls in obeying the truth through the Spirit to unfeigned love of the brethren, see that you love one another with a pure heart fervently:

23 Being born again, not of corruptible seed, but of incorruptible, by the word of God, which lives and abides for ever.

24 **For all flesh is as grass, and all the glory of man as the flower of grass. The grass withers, and the flower thereof falls away:**

25 But the word of the Lord endures for ever. And this is the word which by the

---

1:8 The source of joy. Joy is not the same as pleasure or happiness. A wicked and evil man may have pleasure, while any ordinary mortal is capable of being happy. Pleasure generally comes from things, and always through the senses; happiness comes from humans through fellowship. Joy comes from loving God and neighbor. Pleasure is quick and violent, like a flash of lightning. Joy is steady and abiding, like a fixed star. Pleasure depends on external circumstances, such as money, food, travel, etc. Joy is independent of them, for it comes from a good conscience and love of God. *Fulton J. Sheen*

1:15 To ask that God's love should be content with us as we are is to ask that God should cease to be God: because He is what He is, His love must, in the nature of things, be impeded and repelled by certain stains in our present character, and because He already loves us He must labor to make us lovable. *C. S. Lewis*

1:23 New birth—its necessity for salvation. If you speak to someone who professes to know God and you are not certain of their salvation, simply ask if they have been born again (see John 3:1-7). If you find that they are not sure (this is one sign that they haven't: 1 John 5:10) or they say that they haven't, here is how you can bring focus to its importance. Tell them that the difference between *believing* in God and being *born again* is like the difference between *believing* in a parachute and *putting it on*. There's a big difference when you jump from the plane. Then say, "Do you know what convinced me that I had to be born again? It was the Ten Commandments." Then take them through the spiritual nature of the Law, which brings the knowledge of sin (Romans 7:7). See 1 John 5:1.

1:25 *The Dead Sea Scrolls—*
"The greatest manuscript discovery of all times."

By William F. Albright

The discovery of the Dead Sea Scrolls (DSS) at Qumran in 1949 had significant effects in corroborating evidence for the Scriptures. The ancient texts, found hidden in pots in cliff-top caves by a monastic religious community, confirm the reliability of the Old Testament text. These texts, which were copied and studied by the Essenes, include one complete Old Testament book (Isaiah) and thousands of fragments, representing every Old Testament book except Esther.

The manuscripts date from the third century B.C. to the first century A.D. and give the earliest window found so far into the texts of the Old Testament books and their predictive prophecies. The Qumran texts have become an important witness for the divine origin of the Bible, providing further evidence against the criticism of such crucial books as Daniel and Isaiah.

Dating the Manuscripts. Carbon-14 dating is a reliable form of scientific dating when applied to uncontaminated material several thousand years old. Results indicated an age of 1917 years with a 200-year (10 percent) variant.

Paleography (ancient writing forms) and orthography (spelling) indicated that some manuscripts were inscribed before 100 B.C. Albright set the date of the complete Isaiah scroll to around 100 B.C. There can happily not be the slightest doubt in the world about the genuineness of the manuscript.

Archaeological Dating. Collaborative evidence for an early date came from archaeology. Pottery accompanying the manuscripts was late Hellenistic (c. 150-63 B.C.) and Early Roman (c. 63 B.C. to A.D. 100). Coins found in the monastery ruins proved by their inscriptions to have been minted between 135 B.C. and A.D. 135. The weave and pattern of the cloth supported an early date. There is no reasonable doubt that the Qumran manuscripts came from the century before Christ and the first century A.D.

Significance of the Dating. Previous to the DSS, the earliest known manuscript of the Old Testament was the Masoretic Text (A.D. 900) and two others (dating about A.D. 1000) from which, for example, the King James version of the Old Testament derived its translation. Perhaps most would have considered the Masoretic text as a very late text and therefore questioned the reliability of the Old Testament wholesale. The Dead Sea Scrolls eclipse these texts by 1,000 years and provide little reason to question their reliability, and further, present only confidence for the text. The beauty of the Dead Sea Scrolls lies in the close match they have with the Masoretic text demonstrable evidence of reliability and preservation of the authentic text through the centuries. So the discovery of the DSS provides evidence for the following:

1) Confirmation of the Hebrew Text
2) Support for the Masoretic Text
3) Support for the Greek translation of the Hebrew Text (the Septuagint). Since the New Testament often quotes from the Greek Old Testament, the DSS furnish the reader with further confidence for the Masoretic texts in this area where it can be tested.

(Generated from *Norman Geisler*, Dead Sea Scrolls, *Baker Encyclopedia of Christian Apologetics*)

---

gospel is preached to you.

CHAPTER 2

WHEREFORE laying aside all malice, and all guile, and hypocrisies, and envies, and all evil speakings,

2 As newborn babes, desire the sincere milk of the word, that you may grow thereby:

3 If so be you have tasted that the Lord is gracious.

4 To whom coming, as to a living stone,

2:2   Had the doctrines of Jesus been preached always as pure as they came from His lips, the whole civilized world would now have been Christians. *Thomas Jefferson*

PRINCIPLES OF GROWTH FOR THE NEW AND GROWING CHRISTIAN

2:2   *Feeding on the Word—Daily Nutrition*

A healthy baby has a healthy appetite. If you have truly been born of the Spirit of God, you *will* have a healthy appetite. The Bible says, "As newborn babes, desire the sincere milk of the word, that you may grow thereby" (1 Peter 2:2). Feed yourself daily without fail. Job said, "I have esteemed the words of His mouth more than my necessary food" (Job 23:12). The more you eat, the quicker you will grow, and the less bruising you will have. Speed up the process and save yourself some pain. Vow to read God's Word every day, *without fail*. Say to yourself, "No Bible, no breakfast. No read, no feed." Be like Job, and put your Bible *before* your belly. If you do that, God promises that you will be like a fruitful, strong, and healthy tree (Psalm 1). Each day, find somewhere quiet and thoroughly soak your soul in the Word of God.

There may be times when you read through its pages with great enthusiasm, and other times when it seems dry and even boring. But food profits your body whether you enjoy it or not. As a child, you no doubt ate desserts with great enthusiasm. Perhaps vegetables weren't so exciting. If you were a normal child, you probably had to be *encouraged* to eat them at first. Then, as you matured in life you were taught to discipline yourself to eat vegetables, because they benefit you physically even though they may not bring pleasure to your taste buds.

For the next principle of growth, see Matthew 6:9 comment.

disallowed indeed of men, but chosen of God, and precious,

5 You also, as lively stones, are built up a spiritual house, an holy priesthood, to offer up spiritual sacrifices, acceptable to God by Jesus Christ.

6 Wherefore also it is contained in the scripture, Behold, I lay in Zion a chief corner stone, elect, precious: and he that believes on him shall not be confounded.

7 To you therefore which believe he is precious: but to them which be disobedient, the stone which the builders disallowed, the same is made the head of the corner,

8 And a stone of stumbling, and a rock of offence, even to them which stumble at the word, being disobedient: whereunto also they were appointed.

9 But you are a chosen generation, a royal priesthood, an holy nation, a peculiar people; that you should show forth the praises of him who has called you out of darkness into his marvelous light:

10 Which in time past were not a people, but are now the people of God: which had not obtained mercy, but now have obtained mercy.

11 Dearly beloved, I beseech you as strangers and pilgrims, abstain from fleshly lusts, which war against the soul;

12 Having your conversation honest among the Gentiles: that, whereas they speak against you as evildoers, they may by your good works, which they shall behold, glorify God in the day of visitation.

13 Submit yourselves to every ordinance of man for the Lord's sake: whether it be to the king, as supreme;

14 Or to governors, as to them that are sent by him for the punishment of evildoers, and for the praise of them that do well.

15 For so is the will of God, that with well doing you may put to silence the ig-

2:7 Perhaps the number one fruit of salvation will be that Jesus will become precious to the believer. See 1 Corinthians 16:22.

2:15 Good works are a legitimate form of evangelism. Since the way to a man's heart is often through his taste buds, buying him a hamburger may reach him more effectively than an argument.

Kindness has converted more sinners than zeal, eloquence, or learning. *Frederick W. Faber*

QUESTIONS & OBJECTIONS

2:15 *"How should I witness to my coworkers?"*

When we interact with people on a daily basis, we have many opportunities for sharing our faith.

First, be sure you are respectful to your employer and set a good example in your work ethic by working as to the Lord (Colossians 3:23). When others around you grumble and complain, if you have a calm, forgiving, steadfast spirit, it will make an impression. As you respond in a Christlike way to angry coworkers and stressful circumstances, people will see a difference in your life.

Always be friendly and courteous, and show genuine interest in your coworkers' lives. Invite them out to lunch to get better acquainted. Share their joys and sorrows by congratulating them in their good times and offering to pray for them in their bad times. Be sure you *do* pray for them, then follow up by asking them about the situation you prayed for. They will be moved by your concern.

If coworkers are discussing what they did during the previous weekend, you can share your excitement about attending church services or a special church event. Ask others if they have any plans for celebrating Christmas or Easter; be nonjudgmental of their answer, but be ready (if asked) to explain why you celebrate as you do. Displaying a favorite Scripture or a devotional calendar, or reading your Bible during lunchtime may prompt others to inquire about your faith.

Bringing home-baked goods or leaving a small gift with a note on a coworker's desk can sometimes have a greater impact than a thousand eloquent sermons. We can show our faith *by* our works. Others may not like a tree of righteousness, but they cannot help but like its fruit. Pray for opportunities to share the gospel, being careful not to infringe on your boss's time.

norance of foolish men:

16 As free, and not using your liberty for a cloak of maliciousness, but as the servants of God.

17 Honor all men. Love the brotherhood. Fear God. Honor the king.

18 Servants, be subject to your masters with all fear; not only to the good and gentle, but also to the froward.

19 For this is thankworthy, if a man for conscience toward God endure grief, suffering wrongfully.

20 For what glory is it, if, when you are buffeted for your faults, you shall take it patiently? but if, when you do well, and suffer for it, you take it patiently, this is acceptable with God.

21 For even hereunto were you called: because Christ also suffered for us, leaving us an example, that you should follow his steps:

22 Who did no sin, neither was guile found in his mouth:

23 Who, when he was reviled, reviled not again; when he suffered, he threatened not; but committed himself to him that judges righteously:

24 Who his own self bare our sins in his own body on the tree, that we, being dead to sins, should live to righteousness: by whose stripes you were healed.

25 For you were as sheep going astray; but are now returned to the Shepherd and Bishop of your souls.

CHAPTER 3

LIKEWISE, you wives, be in subjection to your own husbands; that, if

2:24 Messianic prophecy fulfilled: But he was wounded for our transgressions, he was bruised for our iniquities: the chastisement of our peace was upon him; and with his stripes we are healed (Isaiah 53:5). See Matthew 13:34,35 comment.

any obey not the word, they also may without the word be won by the conversation of the wives;

2 While they behold your chaste conversation coupled with fear.

3 Whose adorning let it not be that outward adorning of plaiting the hair, and of wearing of gold, or of putting on of apparel;

4 But let it be the hidden man of the heart, in that which is not corruptible, even the ornament of a meek and quiet spirit, which is in the sight of God of great price.

5 For after this manner in the old time the holy women also, who trusted in God, adorned themselves, being in subjection to their own husbands:

6 Even as Sara obeyed Abraham, calling him lord: whose daughters you are, as long as you do well, and are not afraid with any amazement.

7 Likewise, you husbands, dwell with them according to knowledge, giving honor to the wife, as to the weaker vessel, and as being heirs together of the grace of life; that your prayers be not hindered.

8 Finally, be all of one mind, having compassion one of another, love as brethren, be pitiful, be courteous:

9 Not rendering evil for evil, or railing for railing: but contrariwise blessing; knowing that you are thereunto called, that you should inherit a blessing.

10 For he that will love life, and see good days, let him refrain his tongue from evil, and his lips that they speak no guile:

11 Let him eschew evil, and do good; let him seek peace, and ensue it.

12 For the eyes of the Lord are over the righteous, and his ears are open to their prayers: but the face of the Lord is against them that do evil.

13 And who is he that will harm you, if you be followers of that which is good?

14 But and if you suffer for righteousness' sake, happy are you: and be not afraid of their terror, neither be troubled;

15 But sanctify the Lord God in your hearts: and be ready always to give an answer to every man that asks you a reason of the hope that is in you with meekness and fear:

16 Having a good conscience; that, whereas they speak evil of you, as of evil-doers, they may be ashamed that falsely accuse your good conversation in Christ.

17 For it is better, if the will of God be so, that you suffer for well doing, than for evil doing.

18 **For Christ also has once suffered for sins, the just for the unjust, that he might bring us to God, being put to death in the flesh, but quickened by the Spirit:**

19 By which also he went and preached to the spirits in prison;

3:1,2 Do not preach to loved ones, or express frustration or anger because they don't believe. Win them with your works rather than your words. Buy them gifts, do them favors, show them love and kindness. Make sure that you are free from the slightest hint of hypocrisy.

3:8,9 Witnessing tips. When you approach a careless individual, be sure to treat him kindly. Let him see that you are talking with him, not because you seek a quarrel with him, but because you love his soul and desire his best good in time and eternity. If you are harsh and overbearing, you will probably drive him farther away from the way of life.

Be serious! Avoid all lightness of manner or language. Levity will produce anything but a right impression. You ought to feel that you are engaged in a very serious work, which is going to affect the character of your friend or neighbor and probably determine his destiny for eternity. Who could trifle and use levity in such circumstances if his heart were sincere?

Be respectful. Some think it is necessary to be abrupt, rude, and coarse in their discussions with the careless and impenitent. No mistake can be greater. The apostle Peter has given us a better rule on the subject, where he says: Be pitiful, be courteous: not rendering evil for evil, or railing for railing: but contrariwise blessing. *Charles Finney*

QUESTIONS & OBJECTIONS

3:12 **"If God is a God of love, why hasn't He dealt with evil?"**

In Dr. Robert Morey s book *The New Atheism and the Erosion of Freedom*, he talks with an atheist about this issue. The atheist assumes that everything is relative, and there are no absolutes. (He is absolutely sure of that). Morey replies that the first thing an atheist must do is prove the existence of evil. By what process can an atheist identify evil? He must have a universal absolute to do so. Without an absolute reference point for good (which only God can provide), no one can identify what is good or evil. Thus without the existence of God, there is no "evil" or "good" in an absolute sense. Everything is relative. The problem of evil does not negate the existence of God. It actually requires it.

Many assume that because evil still exists today, God has not dealt with it. How can atheists assume that God has not already solved the problem of evil in such a way that neither His goodness nor omnipotence is limited? On what grounds do they limit what God can and cannot do to solve the problem? God has already solved the problem of evil. And He did it in a way in which He did not contradict His nature or the nature of man.

We assume God will solve the problem of evil in one single act. But why can't He deal with evil in a progressive way? Can't He deal with it throughout time as we know it, and then bring it to the climax on the Day of Judgment?

God sent His Son to die on the cross in order to solve the problem of evil. Christ atoned for evil and secured the eventual removal of all evil from the earth. One day evil will be quarantined in one spot called hell. Then there will be a perfect world devoid of all evil. If God declared that all evil would, at this moment, cease to exist, you and I and all of humanity would go up in a puff of smoke. Divine judgment demands that sin be punished. *Ron Meade*

20 Which sometime were disobedient, when once the longsuffering of God waited in the days of Noah, while the ark was being prepared, wherein few, that is, eight souls were saved by water.

21 The like figure whereunto even baptism does also now save us (not the putting away of the filth of the flesh, but the

3:15 Fear of questions. In a terrible accident at a railroad crossing, a train smashed into a car and pushed it nearly four hundred yards down the track. Though no one was killed, the driver took the train company to court.

At the trial, the engineer insisted that he had given the driver ample warning by waving his lantern back and forth for nearly a minute. He even stood and convincingly demonstrated how he'd done it. The court believed his story, and the suit was dismissed.

"Congratulations," the lawyer said to the engineer when it was over. "You did superbly under cross-examination."

"Thanks," he said, "but he sure had me worried. I was afraid he was going to ask if the lantern was lit!"

In a similar way, we often go through our lives afraid that someone will ask us a particular question. If someone asks me why I believe in God and not evolution, what will I say?...What if someone asks me how I can possibly believe in the resurrection?...What should I say if someone asks me why I believe the Bible truly is the Word of God, or why I believe that it teaches this or that?

Instead of being detrimental as in the case of the engineer above, though, such questions provide us with an opportunity to share our faith. Don't be afraid for anyone to ask! *Alan Smith*

3:20 Peter believed the Genesis account of Noah's Flood that it was a worldwide deluge in which only eight people were saved.

QUESTIONS & OBJECTIONS

Q 4:1   *"Do you sin, as a Christian?"*

If a Christian sins, it is *against* his will. One who is regenerate *falls* rather than *dives* into sin; he resists rather than embraces it. Any dead fish can float downstream. It takes a live one to swim against the flow. Christians still experience temptations and can sometimes fall into sin, but they are no longer slaves to sin (Romans 6:6). They have God's Holy Spirit within them to help them say no to temptation, and to convict their conscience of wrongdoing when they do sin.

answer of a good conscience toward God,) by the resurrection of Jesus Christ:

22 Who is gone into heaven, and is on the right hand of God; angels and authorities and powers being made subject to him.

CHAPTER 4

FORASMUCH then as Christ has suffered for us in the flesh, arm yourselves likewise with the same mind: for he that has suffered in the flesh has ceased from sin;

2 That he no longer should live the rest of his time in the flesh to the lusts of men, but to the will of God.

3 For the time past of our life may suffice us to have wrought the will of the Gentiles, when we walked in lasciviousness, lusts, excess of wine, revellings, banquetings, and abominable idolatries:

4 Wherein they think it strange that you run not with them to the same excess of riot, speaking evil of you:

5 Who shall give account to him that is ready to judge the quick and the dead.

6 For for this cause was the gospel preached also to them that are dead, that they might be judged according to men in the flesh, but live according to God in the spirit.

7 But the end of all things is at hand: be therefore sober, and watch to prayer.

8 And above all things have fervent charity among yourselves: for charity shall cover the multitude of sins.

9 Use hospitality one to another without grudging.

10 As every man has received the gift, even so minister the same one to another, as good stewards of the manifold grace of God.

11 *If any man speak, let him speak as the oracles of God; if any man minister, let him do it as of the ability which God gives: that God in all things may be glorified through Jesus Christ, to whom be praise and dominion for ever and ever. Amen.*

12 Beloved, think it not strange concerning the fiery trial which is to try you, as though some strange thing happened to you:

13 But rejoice, inasmuch as you are partakers of Christ's sufferings; that, when his glory shall be revealed, you may be glad also with exceeding joy.

14 If you are reproached for the name of Christ, happy are you; for the spirit of glory and of God rests upon you: on their part he is evil spoken of, but on your part he is glorified.

15 But let none of you suffer as a murderer, or as a thief, or as an evildoer, or as a busybody in other men's matters.

16 Yet if any man suffer as a Christian, let him not be ashamed; but let him glo-

---

4:5 *Daniel Webster* (1782-1852), politician and diplomat, is considered one of the greatest orators in American history. When asked, "What is the greatest thought that ever passed through your mind?" Webster responded, "My accountability to God."

Science Confirms the Bible

THE BIBLE (2,000–3,000 years ago)	SCIENCE THEN	SCIENCE NOW
The earth is a sphere (Isaiah 40:22).	The earth was a flat disk.	The earth is a sphere.
Innumerable stars (Jeremiah 33:22).	Only 1,100 stars.	Innumerable stars.
Free float of earth in space (Job 26:7).	Earth sat on a large animal.	Free float of earth in space.
Creation made of invisible elements (Hebrews 11:3).	Science was ignorant on the subject.	Creation made of invisible elements (atoms).
Each star is different (1 Corinthians 15:41).	All stars were the same.	Each star is different.
Light moves (Job 38:19,20).	Light was fixed in place.	Light moves.
Air has weight (Job 28:25).	Air was weightless.	Air has weight.
Winds blow in cyclones (Ecclesiastes 1:6).	Winds blew straight.	Winds blow in cyclones.
Blood is the source of life and health (Leviticus 17:11).	Sick people must be bled.	Blood is the source of life and health.
Ocean floor contains deep valleys and mountains (2 Samuel 22:16; Jonah 2:6).	The ocean floor was flat.	Ocean floor contains deep valleys and mountains.
Ocean contains springs (Job 38:16).	Ocean fed only by rivers and rain.	Ocean contains springs.
When dealing with disease, hands should be washed under running water (Leviticus 15:13).	Hands washed in still water.	When dealing with disease, hands should be washed under running water.

(See Hebrews 11:3 comment.)

rify God on this behalf.

17 For the time is come that judgment must begin at the house of God: and if it first begin at us, what shall the end be of them that obey not the gospel of God?

18 And if the righteous scarcely be saved, where shall the ungodly and the sinner appear?

19 Wherefore let them that suffer according to the will of God commit the keeping of their souls to him in well doing, as to a faithful Creator.

CHAPTER 5

THE elders which are among you I exhort, who am also an elder, and a witness of the sufferings of Christ, and also a partaker of the glory that shall be revealed:

2 Feed the flock of God which is among you, taking the oversight thereof, not by constraint, but willingly; not for filthy lucre, but of a ready mind;

3 Neither as being lords over God's heritage, but being ensamples to the flock.

4 And when the chief Shepherd shall appear, you shall receive a crown of glory that fades not away.

5 Likewise, you younger, submit yourselves to the elder. Yes, all of you be subject one to another, and be clothed with humility: for God resists the proud, and gives grace to the humble.

6 Humble yourselves therefore under the mighty hand of God, that he may exalt you in due time:

7 Casting all your care upon him; for he cares for you.

8 Be sober, be vigilant; because your adversary the devil, as a roaring lion, walks about, seeking whom he may devour:

9 Whom resist steadfast in the faith, knowing that the same afflictions are accomplished in your brethren that are in the world.

10 But the God of all grace, who has called us to his eternal glory by Christ Jesus, after that you have suffered a while, make you perfect, stablish, strengthen, settle you.

11 To him be glory and dominion for ever and ever. Amen.

12 By Silvanus, a faithful brother to you, as I suppose, I have written briefly, exhorting, and testifying that this is the true grace of God wherein you stand.

13 The church that is at Babylon, elected together with you, salutes you; and so does Marcus my son.

14 Greet one another with a kiss of charity. Peace be with you all that are in Christ Jesus. Amen.

RIDDLE:
Name nine people who were saved from drowning by an ark.

ANSWER:
Eight members of Noah's family were saved by an ark in the Flood (Genesis 7:13), and the infant Moses was also saved by an ark (Exodus 2:3).
(See 1 Peter 3:20.)

4:14 When we share our faith, we are in a win/win situation. If people accept what we say, we win. If we plant the seed of God's Word, we win; and even if we are rejected, we win. This is because the Bible says that when that happens, the Spirit of glory and of God rests upon us. When we contend for the faith and are rejected, we are to rejoice and leap for joy, for great is our reward in heaven (Luke 6:22,23). It is a winning situation every single time that you share your faith!
Mark Cahill

5:3 A message prepared in the mind reaches a mind; a message prepared in a life reaches a life.
Bill Gothard

2 Peter

CHAPTER 1

SIMON Peter, a servant and an apostle of Jesus Christ, to them that have obtained like precious faith with us through the righteousness of God and our Savior Jesus Christ:

2 Grace and peace be multiplied to you through the knowledge of God, and of Jesus our Lord,

3 According as his divine power has given to us all things that pertain to life and godliness, through the knowledge of him that has called us to glory and virtue:

4 Whereby are given to us exceeding great and precious promises: that by these you might be partakers of the divine nature, having escaped the corruption that is in the world through lust.

5 And beside this, giving all diligence, add to your faith virtue; and to virtue knowledge;

6 And to knowledge temperance; and to temperance patience; and to patience godliness;

7 And to godliness brotherly kindness; and to brotherly kindness charity.

8 For if these things be in you, and abound, they make you that you shall neither be barren nor unfruitful in the knowledge of our Lord Jesus Christ.

9 But he that lacks these things is blind, and cannot see afar off, and has forgotten that he was purged from his old sins.

10 Wherefore the rather, brethren, give diligence to make your calling and election sure: for if you do these things, you shall never fall:

11 For so an entrance shall be ministered to you abundantly into the everlasting kingdom of our Lord and Savior Jesus Christ.

12 Wherefore I will not be negligent to put you always in remembrance of these things, though you know them, and be established in the present truth.

13 Yes, I think it meet, as long as I am in this tabernacle, to stir you up by putting you in remembrance;

14 Knowing that shortly I must put off this my tabernacle, even as our Lord Jesus Christ has showed me.

15 Moreover I will endeavour that you may be able after my decease to have these things always in remembrance.

16 For we have not followed cunningly devised fables, when we made known to you the power and coming of our Lord Jesus Christ, but were eyewitnesses of his majesty.

17 For he received from God the Father honor and glory, when there came such a voice to him from the excellent glory, This is my beloved Son, in whom I am well pleased.

18 And this voice which came from heaven we heard, when we were with him in the holy mount.

19 We have also a more sure word of prophecy; whereunto you do well that you take heed, as to a light that shines in a dark place, until the day dawn, and the day star arise in your hearts:

QUESTIONS & OBJECTIONS

1:21 *"Didn't men write the Bible?"*

Absolutely. When you write a letter, do *you* write the letter, or does the pen? Obviously you do; the pen is merely the instrument you use. God used men as instruments to write His letter to humanity. They ranged from kings to common fishermen, but the 66 books of the Bible were all given by inspiration of God. Proof that this Book is supernatural can be seen with a quick study of its prophecies. See Psalm 119:105 comment.

20 Knowing this first, that no prophecy of the scripture is of any private interpretation.

21 For the prophecy came not in old time by the will of man: but holy men of God spoke as they were moved by the Holy Spirit.

CHAPTER 2

BUT there were false prophets also among the people, even as there shall be false teachers among you, who privately shall bring in damnable heresies, even denying the Lord that bought them, and bring upon themselves swift destruction.

2 And many shall follow their pernicious ways; by reason of whom the way of truth shall be evil spoken of.

3 And through covetousness shall they with feigned words make merchandise of you: whose judgment now of a long time lingers not, and their damnation slumbers not.

4 For if God spared not the angels that sinned, but cast them down to hell, and delivered them into chains of darkness, to be reserved to judgment;

5 And spared not the old world, but saved Noah the eighth person, a preacher of righteousness, bringing in the flood upon the world of the ungodly;

6 And turning the cities of Sodom and Gomorrha into ashes condemned them with an overthrow, making them an ensample to those that after should live ungodly;

7 And delivered just Lot, vexed with the

1:19 It is important to point out that it isn't the Bible that converts people. The first Christians didn't have the Bible as we know it. The New Testament hadn't been compiled, and there was no such thing as the printing press. Besides, many couldn't read. Rather, they were converted by the spoken message of the gospel. It is the gospel that is "the power of God to salvation" (Romans 1:16). Until God gives light to His Word, it will remain a dry history book to its reader.

1:21 The idea conveyed is that just as the wind controls the sails of a boat, so also the breath of God controlled the writers of the Bible. The end result was exactly what God intended. *Josh McDowell*

2:4,5,9 Judgment Day: For verses that warn of its reality, see 2 Peter 3:7.

2:5 The Bible's fascinating facts. In Genesis 6, God gave Noah the dimensions of the 1.5 million cubic foot ark he was to build. In 1609 at Hoorn in Holland, a ship was built after that same pattern, revolutionizing shipbuilding. By 1900 every large ship on the high seas was inclined toward the proportions of the ark (as verified by "Lloyd's Register of Shipping" in the *World Almanac*).

2:6–8 Witnessing to homosexuals. I had an angry lesbian heckle me one Friday night while speaking in Santa Monica in front of a large crowd. I was so pleased to have the Law of God as a weapon. When she insisted that she was born with homosexual desires, I told her that I was too. I was born with a capacity to be a homosexual, to fornicate, commit adultery, lie, and steal. I said

filthy conversation of the wicked:

8 (For that righteous man dwelling among them, in seeing and hearing, vexed his righteous soul from day to day with their unlawful deeds;)

9 The Lord knows how to deliver the godly out of temptations, and to reserve the unjust to the day of judgment to be punished:

10 But chiefly them that walk after the flesh in the lust of uncleanness, and despise government. Presumptuous are they, self-willed, they are not afraid to speak evil of dignities.

11 Whereas angels, which are greater in power and might, bring not railing accusation against them before the Lord.

12 But these, as natural brute beasts, made to be taken and destroyed, speak evil of the things that they understand not; and shall utterly perish in their own corruption;

13 And shall receive the reward of unrighteousness, as they that count it pleasure to riot in the day time. Spots they are and blemishes, sporting themselves with their own deceivings while they feast with you;

14 Having eyes full of adultery, and that cannot cease from sin; beguiling unstable souls: an heart they have exercised with covetous practices; cursed children:

15 Which have forsaken the right way, and are gone astray, following the way of Balaam the son of Bosor, who loved the wages of unrighteousness;

16 But was rebuked for his iniquity: the dumb ass speaking with man's voice forbad the madness of the prophet.

> I believe that the most damnable thing a man can do is to preach the gospel merely as an actor and turn the worship of God into a kind of theatrical performance.
>
> **CHARLES SPURGEON**

17 These are wells without water, clouds that are carried with a tempest; to whom the mist of darkness is reserved for ever.

18 For when they speak great swelling words of vanity, they allure through the lusts of the flesh, through much wantonness, those that were clean escaped from them who live in error.

19 While they promise them liberty, they themselves are the servants of corruption: for of whom a man is overcome, of the same is he brought in bondage.

20 For if after they have escaped the pollutions of the world through the knowl-

---

that it was called "sin," and that we all had it in our nature. It diffused her intent on making me seem like a gay-basher. I could see the frustration on her face when she wasn't able to take the discourse in the direction she wanted. Instead of seeming the poor victim, she found herself in the public hot-seat of having sinned against God.

The way to witness to a homosexual is simply to follow the biblical guidelines and use the Law. See Matthew 19:17 22 comment.

2:9 Using a Survey to Share Your Faith. Begin by asking: Do you have a moment to answer a couple of quick questions for a survey?

1) Do you believe in the existence of any type of God or Higher Power? *(Yes___ No___)*

2) If there truly was a coming Day of Judgment when God would give every person either everlasting life or everlasting punishment, do you think it would be important for people to know what they would need to do to receive everlasting life? *(Yes___ No___)*

3) If there truly was a coming Day of Judgment, do you think you would know how a person could receive everlasting life? *(Yes___ No___)* If so, how?

2:14 These workers of iniquity violate God's Law by transgressing the Seventh and Tenth Commandments.

edge of the Lord and Savior Jesus Christ, they are again entangled therein, and overcome, the latter end is worse with them than the beginning.

21 For it had been better for them not to have known the way of righteousness, than, after they have known it, to turn from the holy commandment delivered to them.

22 But it is happened to them according to the true proverb, The dog is turned to his own vomit again; and the sow that was washed to her wallowing in the mire.

CHAPTER 3

THIS second epistle, beloved, I now write to you; in both which I stir up your pure minds by way of remembrance:

2 That you may be mindful of the words which were spoken before by the holy prophets, and of the commandment of us the apostles of the Lord and Savior:

3 Knowing this first, that there shall come in the last days scoffers, walking after their own lusts,

4 And saying, Where is the promise of his coming? for since the fathers fell asleep, all things continue as they were from the beginning of the creation.

5 For this they willingly are ignorant of, that by the word of God the heavens were of old, and the earth standing out of the water and in the water:

6 Whereby the world that then was, be-

2:21 When sinners make professions of faith and refuse to have any regard for God's Moral Law, their latter end becomes worse than the first. They fall away and become hardened (inoculated) against the truth. It would have been better for them not to have known the way of righteousness (the gospel) than, after they have known it, to turn from the holy commandment (the Moral Law).

The Law cannot condemn the Christian (Romans 8:1), but those who are truly converted will not transgress its precepts. Those who do, prove to be "workers of iniquity" (lawlessness). See Matthew 7:21-23. This is why we must thunder out the precepts of God's Law before we offer sinners the pardon of the gospel. If they don't see the serious nature of sin, they will still toy with its pleasures after they make a profession of faith.

2:22 Some argue that sins such as pornography are wrong because they are harmful to society. However, you have more chance of convincing a pig that the mud in which he wallows is harmful to him. The reason he wallows is to cool his flesh. The only practical way to stop a pig wallowing in the mire is to kill him. That's the function of the Law: it nails the sin-loving sinner to the cross. It deals directly with the sinful nature. Sin is wrong not because it's harmful to society; it is wrong because God says that it's wrong.

3:3 Signs of the end times (combined from Matthew 24; Mark 13; Luke 21; 1 Timothy 4; and 2 Timothy 3): There will be false Christs; wars and rumors of wars; nation rising against nation; famines; disease (pestilence); false prophets who will deceive many; and lawlessness (forsaking of the Ten Commandments). The gospel will be preached in all the world. There will be earthquakes in various places; signs from heaven (in the sun, moon, and stars); and persecution against Christians in all nations. Men's hearts will fail them for fear of the future; they will be selfish, materialistic, arrogant, proud. Homosexuality will increase; there will be blasphemy; cold-heartedness; intemperance; brutality; rebellious youth; hatred of those who stand up for righteousness; ungodliness; pleasure-seeking; much hypocrisy. False Bible teachers will have many followers, be money-hungry, and slander the Christian faith (2 Peter 2:1-3).

Men will scoff and say that there was no such thing as the flood of Noah and that these signs have always been around. Their motivation for hating the truth will be their love of lust (2 Peter 3:1-7). The Scriptures tell us that they make one big mistake. Their understanding of God is erroneous. They don't understand that God's time frame is not the same as ours. They think (in their ignorance) that God's continued silence means that He doesn't see their sins. In truth, He is merely holding back His wrath, waiting for them to repent and escape the damnation of hell.

Jesus warned that the sign to look for was the repossession of Jerusalem by the Jews. That happened in 1967, after 2,000 years, bringing into culmination all the signs of the times.

QUESTIONS & OBJECTIONS

3:3–6

"The number of fossils in some areas is enormous. How could earth have supported all those creatures at the same time?"

This question shows a common false assumption that many people make. They assume the earth today is the same as it has always been. Today's earth is seventy percent under water. There are scriptural and scientific indications that the pre-Flood world had greater air pressure, higher percentages of oxygen and carbon dioxide, much more land (above sea level), less water (on the earth's surface), and a canopy of water to filter out the harmful effects of the sun. This would cause there to be many times more plants and animals on the earth than there are today. The added air pressure would diffuse more gasses into the water and support a much greater fish population. Aquatic plant life per cubic mile would multiply also.

Second Peter 3 tells us that the scoffers in the last days will be willingly ignorant of how God created the heavens and the earth. They would also be ignorant of the Flood. These two great events must be considered before making any statements about the conditions on earth today. Only about three percent of the earth today is habitable for man. The rest is under water, ice, deserts, mountains, etc. If the earth before the Flood were, say, seventy percent habitable, it could have supported a huge population. The vast amount and worldwide distribution of fossils shows that the Flood was global and that God hates sin enough to judge the entire world. *Dr. Kent Hovind*

About 85% of the rock surface around the world is made up of sedimentary rock, indicating that at some time in the past, the world was covered by water. *Peter and Paul Lalonde, 301 Startling Proofs & Prophecies*

---

ing overflowed with water, perished:

7 But the heavens and the earth, which are now, by the same word are kept in store, reserved to fire against the day of judgment and perdition of ungodly men.

8 But, beloved, be not ignorant of this one thing, that one day is with the Lord as a thousand years, and a thousand years as one day.

9 The Lord is not slack concerning his promise, as some men count slackness; but is longsuffering to us-ward, not willing that any should perish, but that all should come to repentance.

10 But the day of the Lord will come as a thief in the night; in the which the heavens shall pass away with a great noise, and the elements shall melt with fervent heat, the earth also and the works that are therein shall be burned up.

11 Seeing then that all these things shall be dissolved, what manner of persons ought you to be in all holy conversation and godliness,

12 Looking for and hastening to the coming of the day of God, wherein the heavens being on fire shall be dissolved, and the elements shall melt with fervent heat?

13 Nevertheless we, according to his

3:6 Peter believed the Genesis account of Noah's Flood.

3:7 Judgment Day: For verses that warn of its reality, see Jude 14,15.

3:8 Because God is eternal and outside of the dimension of time, to Him one day is the same as a thousand years. In the same way, a person who is in space, outside of the influence of gravity, will find that one ounce is the same as a thousand pounds.

3:9 Salvation is possible for every person. See John 3:16,17.

QUESTIONS & OBJECTIONS

Q **3:9**   *"Why does God allow evil?"*

Why does God allow evil men and women to live? Should He instead kill them before they do evil deeds? Should He judge murderers and rapists now? What about thieves and liars, adulterers, fornicators, those who lust, and those who hate? If God judged evil today, all unconverted men and women would perish under His wrath. Thank God that He is patiently waiting for them to turn to the Savior and be saved from His terrible wrath.

promise, look for new heavens and a new earth, wherein dwells righteousness.

14 Wherefore, beloved, seeing that you look for such things, be diligent that you may be found of him in peace, without spot, and blameless.

15 And account that the longsuffering of our Lord is salvation; even as our beloved brother Paul also according to the wisdom given to him has written to you;

16 As also in all his epistles, speaking in them of these things; in which are some things hard to be understood, which they that are unlearned and unstable wrest, as they do also the other scriptures, to their own destruction.

17 You therefore, beloved, seeing you know these things before, beware lest you also, being led away with the error of the wicked, fall from your own steadfastness.

18 But grow in grace, and in the knowledge of our Lord and Savior Jesus Christ. To him be glory both now and for ever. Amen.

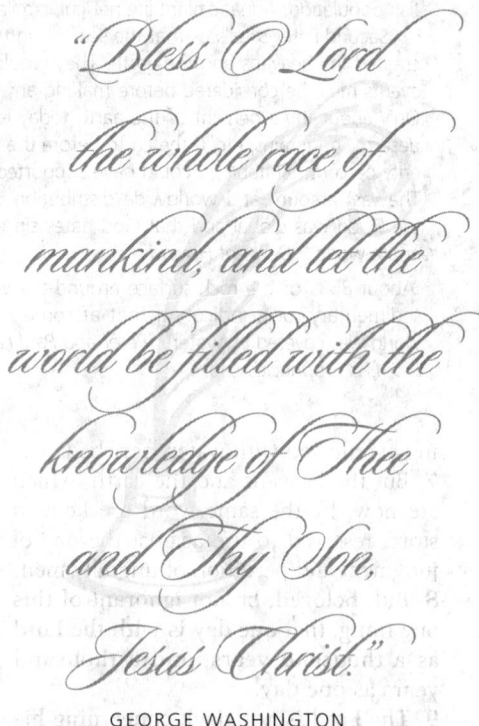

"Bless O Lord the whole race of mankind, and let the world be filled with the knowledge of Thee and Thy Son, Jesus Christ."

GEORGE WASHINGTON

3:16 Never feel as though you have to be able to explain every Bible verse. Even Peter admits that some things Paul wrote are hard to understand. In doing so, he also puts his seal of approval on the fact that Paul's letters were not the mere writings of a man, but Scriptures.

1 John

CHAPTER 1

THAT which was from the beginning, which we have heard, which we have seen with our eyes, which we have looked upon, and our hands have handled, of the Word of life;

2 (For the life was manifested, and we have seen it, and bear witness, and show to you that eternal life, which was with the Father, and was manifested to us;)

3 That which we have seen and heard declare we to you, that you also may have fellowship with us: and truly our fellowship is with the Father, and with his Son Jesus Christ.

4 And these things write we to you, that your joy may be full.

5 This then is the message which we have heard of him, and declare to you, that God is light, and in him is no darkness at all.

6 If we say that we have fellowship with him, and walk in darkness, we lie, and do not the truth:

7 But if we walk in the light, as he is in the light, we have fellowship one with another, and the blood of Jesus Christ his Son cleanses us from all sin.

8 **If we say that we have no sin, we deceive ourselves, and the truth is not in us.**

9 **If we confess our sins, he is faithful and just to forgive us our sins, and to cleanse us from all unrighteousness.**

10 **If we say that we have not sinned, we make him a liar, and his word is not in us.**

CHAPTER 2

MY little children, these things write I to you, that you sin not. And if any man sin, we have an advocate with the Father, Jesus Christ the righteous:

2 And he is the propitiation for our sins: and not for ours only, but also for the sins of the whole world.

3 **And hereby we do know that we know him, if we keep his commandments.**

4 **He that says, I know him, and keeps**

1:9 The Christian who sins. The great foundational truth respecting the believer in relationship to his sins is the fact that his salvation comprehends the forgiveness of all his trespasses past, present and future so far as condemnation is concerned (see Romans 8:1, Colossians 2:13; John 3:18; John 5:24). Since Christ has vicariously borne all sin and since the believer's standing in Christ is complete, he is perfected forever in Christ. When a believer sins, he is subjected to chastisement from the Father, but never to condemnation with the world (see 1 Corinthians 11:31,32). By confession the Christian is forgiven and restored to fellowship (see 1 John 1:9). It needs to be remembered that were it not for Christ's finished work on the cross and His present intercession in heaven, the least sin would result in his banishment from God's presence and eternal ruin. *Unger's Bible Dictionary*

THE FUNCTION OF THE LAW

1:7 The Law also shows us our great need—our need of cleansing, cleansing with the water and the blood. It discovers to us our filthiness, and this naturally leads us to feel that we must be washed from it if we are ever to draw near to God. So the Law drives us to accept Christ as the only Person who can cleanse us, and make us fit to stand within the veil in the presence of the Most High.

The Law is the surgeon's knife that cuts out the proud flesh that the wound may heal. The Law by itself only sweeps and raises the dust, but the gospel sprinkles clean water upon the dust, and all is well in the chamber of the soul. The Law kills, the gospel makes alive; the Law strips, and then Jesus Christ comes in and robes the soul in beauty and glory. All the commandments, and all the types direct us to Christ, if we will but heed their evident intent. *Charles Spurgeon*

not his commandments, is a liar, and the truth is not in him.

5 But whoso keeps his word, in him verily is the love of God perfected: hereby know we that we are in him.

6 He that said he abides in him ought himself also so to walk, even as he walked.

7 Brethren, I write no new commandment to you, but an old commandment which you had from the beginning. The old commandment is the word which you have heard from the beginning.

8 Again, a new commandment I write to you, which thing is true in him and in you: because the darkness is past, and the true light now shines.

9 He that says he is in the light, and hates his brother, is in darkness even until now.

10 He that loves his brother abides in the light, and there is none occasion of stumbling in him.

11 But he that hates his brother is in darkness, and walks in darkness, and knows not where he goes, because that darkness has blinded his eyes.

12 I write to you, little children, because your sins are forgiven you for his name's sake.

13 I write to you, fathers, because you have known him that is from the beginning. I write to you, young men, because you have overcome the wicked one. I write to you, little children, because you have known the Father.

14 I have written to you, fathers, because you have known him that is from the beginning. I have written to you, young men, because you are strong, and the word of God abides in you, and you have overcome the wicked one.

15 **Love not the world, neither the things that are in the world. If any man love the world, the love of the Father is not in him.**

16 For all that is in the world, the lust of the flesh, and the lust of the eyes, and the pride of life, is not of the Father, but is of the world.

17 And the world passes away, and the lust thereof: but he that does the will of God abides for ever.

18 Little children, it is the last time: and as you have heard that antichrist shall come, even now are there many antichrists; whereby we know that it is the last time.

19 They went out from us, but they were not of us; for if they had been of us, they would no doubt have continued with us: but they went out, that they might be made manifest that they were not all of us.

2:11 The Incarnation is the ultimate reason why the service of God cannot be divorced from the service of man. He who says he loves God and hates his brother is a liar. *Dietrich Bonhoeffer*

2:16 See Hebrews 4:15 comment.

2:19 I have left my religious conversion behind and settled into a comfortable state of atheism. I have come to think that religion has caused more harm than any other idea since the beginning of time. *Larry Flynt* (publisher of "Hustler" magazine, in his autobiography *An Unseemly Man*)

QUESTIONS & OBJECTIONS

2:19 *"I was once a born-again Christian. Now I believe it's all rubbish!"*

When a person maintains that he was once a Christian, but came to his senses, he is saying that he once knew the Lord (see John 17:3). Ask him, "Did you know the Lord?" He will then be forced to say, "I *thought* I did!" This gives you license to gently say, "If you don't *know* so, then you probably didn't." If he didn't know the Lord, he was therefore never a Christian (1 John 5:11-13,20). Explain to him that the Bible speaks of false conversion, in which a stony ground hearer receives the Word with joy and gladness. Then, in a time of tribulation, temptation, and persecution, falls away. If he is open to reason, take him through the Ten Commandments, into the message of the cross, and the necessity of repentance and faith in the Savior.

20 But you have an unction from the Holy One, and you know all things.

21 I have not written to you because you know not the truth, but because you know it, and that no lie is of the truth.

22 Who is a liar but he that denies that Jesus is the Christ? He is antichrist, that denies the Father and the Son.

23 Whosoever denies the Son, the same has not the Father: (but) he that acknowledges the Son has the Father also.

> The most terrible warning to impenitent men in all the world is the death of Christ. For if God spared not His only Son, on whom was only laid imputed sin, will He spare sinners whose sins are their own?
>
> **CHARLES SPURGEON**

24 Let that therefore abide in you, which you have heard from the beginning. If that which you have heard from the beginning shall remain in you, you also shall continue in the Son, and in the Father.

25 And this is the promise that he has promised us, even eternal life.

26 These things have I written to you concerning them that seduce you.

27 But the anointing which you have received of him abides in you, and you need not that any man teach you: but as the same anointing teaches you of all

things, and is truth, and is no lie, and even as it has taught you, you shall abide in him.

28 And now, little children, abide in him; that, when he shall appear, we may have confidence, and not be ashamed before him at his coming.

29 If you know that he is righteous, you know that every one that does righteousness is born of him.

CHAPTER 3

BEHOLD, what manner of love the Father has bestowed upon us, that we should be called the sons of God: therefore the world knows us not, because it knew him not.

2 Beloved, now are we the sons of God, and it does not yet appear what we shall be: but we know that, when he shall appear, we shall be like him; for we shall see him as he is.

3 And every man that has this hope in him purifies himself, even as he is pure.

4 **Whosoever commits sin transgresses also the law: for sin is the transgression of the law.**

5 And you know that he was manifested to take away our sins; and in him is no sin.

6 Whosoever abides in him sins not: whosoever sins has not seen him, neither known him.

7 Little children, let no man deceive you:

QUESTIONS & OBJECTIONS

3:12 **"Where did Cain get his wife?"**

Many ask this question thinking they've found a "mistake" in the Bible that there must have been other people besides Adam and Eve. Scripture tells us that Adam is "the first man" (1 Corinthians 15:45); that there were no other humans when he was created, because God said, "It is not good that the man should be alone" (Genesis 2:18); and that Eve is "the mother of all living" (Genesis 3:20). Cain and Abel, then, must have married distant sisters. All of the first-generation siblings married each other in order to populate the earth. At that time there was no law against incest. But as the population grew large enough, and as the risk of genetic problems increased because of sin's curse, God outlawed marriage between siblings.

he that does righteousness is righteous, even as he is righteous.

8 He that commits sin is of the devil; for the devil sinned from the beginning. For this purpose the Son of God was manifested, that he might destroy the works of the devil.

9 Whosoever is born of God does not commit sin; for his seed remains in him: and he cannot sin, because he is born of God.

10 In this the children of God are manifest, and the children of the devil: whosoever does not righteousness is not of God, neither he that loves not his brother.

11 For this is the message that you heard from the beginning, that we should love one another.

12 Not as Cain, who was of that wicked one, and slew his brother. And wherefore slew he him? Because his own works were evil, and his brother's righteous.

13 Marvel not, my brethren, if the world hate you.

14 We know that we have passed from death to life, because we love the brethren. He that loves not his brother abides in death.

15 Whosoever hates his brother is a murderer: and you know that no murderer has eternal life abiding in him.

16 Hereby perceive we the love of God,

3:12 The cool impudence of Cain is an indication of the state of heart which led up to his murdering his brother; and it was also a part of the result of his having committed that terrible crime. He would not have proceeded to the cruel deed of bloodshed if he had not first cast off the fear of God and been ready to defy his Maker. *Charles Spurgeon*

3:13 **Hypocrisy in the Church.** It's interesting to note that the world hates hypocrisy in the Church. They detest the pretender. Does that mean that they *want* the Christian to be genuine? Do they *want* us to be true and faithful in our witness and therefore speak of sin, righteousness, and judgment? Do they want us to live in holiness rather than in compromise? Does the world really want us to speak up against pornography, greed, adultery, abortion, homosexuality, fornication, and other sins they so love? In their eyes we are damned if we do, and damned if we don't.

3:15 Always be ready to earnestly contend for the faith (Jude 3). Learn how to prove God's existence. Study the theory of evolution and the evidence for creation. Become proficient in presenting the spiritual nature of God's Law. Say, *I can do all things through Christ who strengthens me,* and thereby walk above the snare of the fear of man.

Note that this verse is not a prescription for what is commonly called "lifestyle evangelism." We are not being told to wait until we are asked about our faith; we may be waiting for a long time. As soldiers of Christ, we are not only to *defend* the faith, but we are to *advance* the cause of the gospel. The word "go" in the Great Commission, means just that—go.

because he laid down his life for us: and we ought to lay down our lives for the brethren.

17 But whoso has this world's good, and sees his brother have need, and shuts up his bowels of compassion from him, how dwells the love of God in him?

18 My little children, let us not love in word, neither in tongue; but in deed and in truth.

19 And hereby we know that we are of the truth, and shall assure our hearts before him.

20 For if our heart condemn us, God is greater than our heart, and knows all things.

21 Beloved, if our heart condemn us not, then have we confidence toward God.

22 And whatsoever we ask, we receive of him, because we keep his commandments, and do those things that are pleasing in his sight.

23 And this is his commandment, That we should believe on the name of his Son Jesus Christ, and love one another, as he gave us commandment.

24 And he that keeps his commandments dwells in him, and he in him. And hereby we know that he abides in us, by the Spirit which he has given us.

CHAPTER 4

BELOVED, believe not every spirit, but try the spirits whether they are of God: because many false prophets are gone out into the world.

2 Hereby know you the Spirit of God: Every spirit that confesses that Jesus Christ is come in the flesh is of God:

3 And every spirit that confesses not that Jesus Christ is come in the flesh is not of God: and this is that spirit of antichrist, whereof you have heard that it should come; and even now already is it in the world.

4 You are of God, little children, and have overcome them: because greater is he that is in you, than he that is in the world.

5 They are of the world: therefore speak they of the world, and the world hears them.

6 *We are of God: he that knows God hears us; he that is not of God hears not us. Hereby know we the spirit of truth, and the spirit of error.*

7 Beloved, let us love one another: for love is of God; and every one that loves is born of God, and knows God.

8 He that loves not knows not God; for God is love.

9 **In this was manifested the love of God toward us, because that God sent his only begotten Son into the world, that we might live through him.**

10 **Herein is love, not that we loved God, but that he loved us, and sent his Son to be the propitiation for our sins.**

11 Beloved, if God so loved us, we ought also to love one another.

12 No man has seen God at any time. If we love one another, God dwells in us, and his love is perfected in us.

3:16 You are more sinful than you ever dared to believe, but you are more loved than you ever dared to hope. *Mark Liederbach*

4:4 Confidence in witnessing. When you represent the Lord Jesus Christ as His disciple, you can be assured that you are representing the One who possesses all power, wisdom, and authority. You have everything when you have Him. Jesus said: I tell you the truth, anyone who has faith in me will do what I have been doing. He will do even greater things than these, because I am going to the Father (John 14:12). No power can resist you as you go in obedience and faith as His ambassador (2 Corinthians 5:19,20). You have the promise, The one who is in you is greater than the one who is in the world (1 John 4:4). Also, you are assured that even the gates of hell will not prevail against you (Matthew 16:18). The more you understand who Christ is and all that He has done and will do for you and through you, the more completely you will want to trust, obey, and serve Him. *Dr. Bill Bright*

4:8 The Firefighters

Imagine seeing a group of firefighters polishing their engine outside a burning building with people trapped at a top floor window. Obviously, there is nothing wrong with cleaning a fire-engine, *but not while people are trapped in a burning building!* Instead of ignoring their cries, the firefighters should have an overwhelming sense of urgency to rescue them. That's the spirit that should be behind the task of evangelism. But according to Dr. Bill Bright of Campus Crusade for Christ, Only 2 percent of believers in America regularly share their faith with others. That means that 98 percent of the professing Body of Christ are lukewarm when it comes to obeying the Great Commission (Mark 16:15).

Oswald J. Smith said, "Oh my friends, we are loaded down with countless church activities, while the *real* work of the Church, that of evangelizing and winning the lost, is almost entirely neglected." We have polished the engines of worship, prayer, and praise and neglected the sober task given to us by God. A firefighter who ignores his responsibilities and allows people to perish in flames is not a firefighter; he is an impostor. How could we ignore our responsibility and allow the world to walk blindly into the fires of hell? If God's love dwells in us, we must warn them. The Bible tells us to have compassion... save with fear, pulling them out of the fire; hating even the garment spotted by the flesh (Jude 22,23). If we don't have love and compassion, then we don't know God; we are impostors (1 John 4:8).

Charles Spurgeon said, "Have you no wish for others to be saved? Then you are not saved yourself. Be sure of that." Please, examine yourself to see if you are in the faith (2 Corinthians 13:5). Don't be part of the great multitude who called Jesus Lord, but refused to obey Him. It will be professing *believers* who will hear those fearful words, I never knew you: depart from me (Matthew 7:21 23).

Backward Christian Soldiers

Backward Christian soldiers, fleeing from the fight
With the cross of Jesus nearly out of sight.
Christ, our rightful master, stands against the foe
But forward into battle, we are loathe to go.

Like a mighty tortoise moves the Church of God
Brothers, we are treading where we've always trod.
We are much divided, many bodies we
Having many doctrines, not much charity.

Crowns and thorns may perish, kingdoms rise and wane,
But the Church of Jesus hidden does remain.
Gates of hell should never 'gainst the Church prevail.
We have Christ's own promise, but think that it will fail.

Sit here then, ye people, join our useless throng,
Blend with ours your voices in a feeble song.
Blessings, ease and comfort, ask from Christ the King
With our modern thinking, we don't do a thing.
(Anonymous)

If God is speaking to you about your lack of evangelistic concern, pray something like this now:

Father, please forgive me for my lack of love for this dying world. From this day forward I will strive to be a "true and faithful witness." Please give me the wisdom to know what to say to reach the lost. In Jesus' name I pray. Amen.

13 Hereby know we that we dwell in him, and he in us, because he has given us of his Spirit.

14 And we have seen and do testify that the Father sent the Son to be the Savior of the world.

5:10   *"I find it difficult to have faith in God."*

If you don't believe someone, it means you think that he is a liar. The Bible says that those who don't believe God accuse Him of lying. Martin Luther said, "What greater insult...can there be to God, than to not believe His promises." See Hebrews 11:6 comment.

15 Whosoever shall confess that Jesus is the Son of God, God dwells in him, and he in God.

16 And we have known and believed the love that God has to us. God is love; and he that dwells in love dwells in God, and God in him.

17 Herein is our love made perfect, that we may have boldness in the day of judgment: because as he is, so are we in this world.

18 *There is no fear in love; but perfect love casts out fear: because fear has torment. He that fears is not made perfect in love.*

19 We love him, because he first loved us.

20 If a man say, I love God, and hates his brother, he is a liar: for he that loves not his brother whom he has seen, how can he love God whom he has not seen?

21 And this commandment have we from him, That he who loves God love his brother also.

· · · · · ·

For two forms of the "Sinner's Prayer," see page 1560.

· · · · · ·

CHAPTER 5

WHOSOEVER believes that Jesus is the Christ is born of God: and every one that loves him that begat loves

him also that is begotten of him.

2 By this we know that we love the children of God, when we love God, and keep his commandments.

3 For this is the love of God, that we keep his commandments: and his commandments are not grievous.

4 For whatsoever is born of God overcomes the world: and this is the victory that overcomes the world, even our faith.

5 Who is he that overcomes the world, but he that believes that Jesus is the Son of God?

> The Church has developed a theology that doesn't require much repentance. We have a theology that is uncomfortable with the very term, "Jesus is Lord."
>
> **DR. PAUL A. CEDAR**

6 This is he that came by water and blood, even Jesus Christ; not by water only, but by water and blood. And it is the Spirit that bears witness, because the Spirit is truth.

7 For there are three that bear record in heaven, the Father, the Word, and the Holy Spirit: and these three are one.

8 And there are three that bear witness in earth, the spirit, and the water, and the blood: and these three agree in one.

9 If we receive the witness of men, the witness of God is greater: for this is the witness of God which he has testified of

---

4:20   I really only love God as much as I love the person I love the least.   *Dorothy Day*

I shall allow no man to belittle my soul by making me hate him.   *Booker T. Washington*

5:1 New birth—its necessity for salvation. See John 1:13.

5:12,13 "*I hope I'm going to heaven when I die.*"

Of all the things that you should be sure of, it is your eternal destiny. To say, "I hope I'm going to heaven," is like standing at the open door of a plane 25,000 feet in the air and, when asked, "Have you got your parachute on?" answering with, "I hope so." You want to *know* so and you can, simply by obeying the gospel. If you repent and place your faith in Jesus Christ, He will give you eternal life and you can *know* that your eternity is secure. These verses also make clear that those who refuse to trust in the Son of God can likewise *know* that they do not have eternal life, they will remain dead in their sins.

his Son.

10 He that believes on the Son of God has the witness in himself: he that believes not God has made him a liar; because he believes not the record that God gave of his Son.

11 And this is the record, that God has given to us eternal life, and this life is in his Son.

12 He that has the Son has life; and he that has not the Son of God has not life.

13 These things have I written to you that believe on the name of the Son of God; that you may know that you have eternal life, and that you may believe on the name of the Son of God.

14 And this is the confidence that we have in him, that, if we ask any thing according to his will, he hears us:

15 And if we know that he hear us, whatsoever we ask, we know that we have the petitions that we desired of him.

16 If any man see his brother sin a sin which is not to death, he shall ask, and he shall give him life for them that sin not to death. There is a sin to death: I do not say that he shall pray for it.

17 All unrighteousness is sin: and there is a sin not to death.

18 We know that whosoever is born of God sins not; but he that is begotten of God keeps himself, and that wicked one touches him not.

19 And we know that we are of God, and the whole world lies in wickedness.

20 And we know that the Son of God is come, and has given us an understanding, that we may know him that is true, and we are in him that is true, even in his Son Jesus Christ. This is the true God, and eternal life.

21 Little children, keep yourselves from idols. Amen.

5:14 Prayer begins with God. God prompts His people to pray and then acts in response to their prayers. Things happen or don't happen because of prayer. This does not mean God can be manipulated through prayer to do what we want if what we want is contrary to His will. Instead, God reveals His will to us by His Word and works in us by His Spirit so that we know His will and pray in accord with it. Then, in responding to our prayers, He accomplishes both His will and ours, and, in the process, involves us. *Alvin J. Vander Griend,* Your Prayers Matter, *Discipleship Journal*

2 John

THE elder to the elect lady and her children, whom I love in the truth; and not I only, but also all they that have known the truth;

2 For the truth's sake, which dwells in us, and shall be with us for ever.

3 Grace be with you, mercy, and peace, from God the Father, and from the Lord Jesus Christ, the Son of the Father, in truth and love.

4 I rejoiced greatly that I found of your children walking in truth, as we have received a commandment from the Father.

5 And now I beseech you, lady, not as though I wrote a new commandment to you, but that which we had from the beginning, that we love one another.

6 And this is love, that we walk after his commandments. This is the commandment, That, as you have heard from the beginning, you should walk in it.

7 For many deceivers are entered into the world, who confess not that Jesus Christ is come in the flesh. This is a deceiver and an antichrist.

8 Look to yourselves, that we lose not those things which we have wrought, but that we receive a full reward.

9 Whosoever transgresses, and abides not in the doctrine of Christ, has not God. He that abides in the doctrine of Christ, he has both the Father and the Son.

10 If there come any to you, and bring not this doctrine, receive him not into your house, neither bid him God speed:

11 For he that bids him God speed is partaker of his evil deeds.

12 Having many things to write to you, I would not write with paper and ink: but I trust to come to you, and speak face to face, that our joy may be full.

13 The children of your elect sister greet you. Amen.

---

7 Religions and Christian sects that deny the great truth that God was manifest in the flesh are deceivers and are antichrist in spirit. See 1 John 4:2; 1 Timothy 3:16.

9 Those who object to Christianity's claim that there is only one way to God usually argue that we should be tolerant of all religions. In that case, they should practice what they preach and be tolerant of the Christian claim. Jesus is *the* way, *the* truth, and *the* life. No one comes to the Father except through Him (John 14:6). See 1 John 2:23.

Buddhism

FOUNDER: Siddhartha Gautama, a prince from northern India near modern Nepal who lived about 563 483 B.C.

SCRIPTURES: Various, but the oldest and most authoritative are compiled in the Pali Canon.

ADHERENTS: 613 million worldwide; 1 million in the United States.

GENERAL DESCRIPTION: Buddhism is the belief system of those who follow the Buddha, the Enlightened One, a title given to its founder. The religion has evolved into three main schools:

1. *Theravada* or the Doctrine of the Elders (38%) is followed in Sri Lanka (Ceylon), Myanmar (Burma), Thailand, Cambodia (Kampuchea), and Vietnam.

2. *Mahayana* or the Greater Vehicle (56%) is strong in China, Korea, and Japan.

3. *Vajrayana*, also called Tantrism or Lamaism, (6%) is rooted in Tibet, Nepal, and Mongolia. Theravada is closest to the original doctrines. It does not treat the Buddha as deity and regards the faith as a worldview, not a type of worship. Mahayana has accommodated many different beliefs, and worships the Buddha as a god. Vajrayana has added elements of shamanism and the occult and includes taboo-breaking (intentional immorality) as a means of spiritual enlightenment.

GROWTH IN THE UNITED STATES: Buddhists regard the United States as a prime mission field, and the number of Buddhists in this country is growing rapidly due to surges in Asian immigration, endorsement by celebrities such as Tina Turner and Richard Gere, and positive exposure in major movies such as *Siddhartha*, *The Little Buddha*, and *What's Love Got to Do with It?* Buddhism is closely related to the New Age Movement and may to some extent be driving it. Certainly Buddhist growth is benefiting from the influence of New Age thought on American life.

HISTORIC BACKGROUND: Buddhism was founded as a form of atheism that rejected more ancient beliefs in a permanent, personal, creator God (Ishvara) who controlled the eternal destiny of human souls. Siddhartha Gautama rejected more ancient theistic beliefs because of

difficulty he had over reconciling the reality of suffering, judgment, and evil with the existence of a good and holy God.

CORE BELIEFS: Buddhism is an impersonal religion of self-perfection, the end of which is death (extinction) not life. The essential elements of the Buddhist belief system are summarized in the Four Noble Truths, the Noble Eightfold Path, and several additional key doctrines. The Four Noble Truths affirm that (1) life is full of suffering (*dukkha*); (2) suffering is caused by craving (*samudaya*); (3) suffering will cease only when craving ceases (*nirodha*); and (4) this can be achieved by following the Noble Eightfold Path consisting of right views, right aspiration, right speech, right conduct, right livelihood, right effort, right mindfulness, and right contemplation. Other key doctrines include belief that nothing in life is permanent (*anicca*), that individual selves do not truly exist (*anatta*), that all is determined by an impersonal law of moral causation (*karma*), that reincarnation is an endless cycle of continuous suffering, and that the goal of life is to break out of this cycle by finally extinguishing the flame of life and entering a permanent state of pure nonexistence (*nirvana*).

BRIDGES FOR EVANGELIZING BUDDHISTS

The gospel can be appealing to Buddhists if witnessing focuses on areas of personal need where the Buddhist belief system is weak. Some major areas include:

Suffering: Buddhists are deeply concerned with overcoming suffering, but must deny that suffering is real. Christ faced the reality of suffering and overcame it by solving the problem of sin, which is the real source of suffering. Now, those who trust in Christ can rise above suffering in this life because they have hope of a future life free of suffering. We fix our eyes not on what is seen [suffering], but on what is unseen [eternal life free of suffering]. For what is seen [suffering] is temporary, but what is unseen [future good life with Christ] is eternal (2 Cor. 4:18, NIV).

Meaningful Self: Buddhists must work to convince themselves they have no personal significance, even though they live daily as though they do. Jesus taught that each person has real significance. Each person is made in God's image with an immortal soul and an eternal destiny. Jesus demonstrated the value of people by loving us so much that He sacrificed His life in order to offer eternal future good life to anyone who trusts Him. God demonstrates His own love for us in this: While we were still sinners, Christ died for us (Rom. 5:8, NIV).

Future Hope: The hope of nirvana is no hope at all—only death and extinction. The hope of those who put their trust in Christ is eternal good life in a new heaven and new earth in which God will wipe every tear from their eyes. There will be no more death or mourning or crying or pain, for the old order of things [suffering] has passed [will pass] away (Rev. 21:4, NIV).

Moral Law: Because karma, the Buddhist law of moral cause and effect, is completely rigid and impersonal, life for a Buddhist is very oppressive. Under karma, there can be no appeal, no mercy, and no escape except through unceasing effort at self-perfection. Christians understand that the moral force governing the universe is a personal God who listens to those who pray, who has mercy on those who repent, and who with love personally controls for good the lives of those who follow Christ. In all things God works for the good of those who love him (Rom. 8:28, NIV).

Merit: Buddhists constantly struggle to earn merit by doing good deeds, hoping to collect enough to break free from the life of suffering. They also believe saints can transfer surplus merit to the undeserving. Jesus taught no one can ever collect enough merit on his own to earn everlasting freedom from suffering. Instead, Jesus Christ, who has unlimited merit (righteousness) by virtue of His sinless life, meritorious death, and resurrection, now offers His unlimited merit as a free gift to anyone who will become His disciple. For it is by grace you have been saved, through faith and this not from yourselves, it is the gift of God not by works, so that no one can boast (Eph. 2:8 9, NIV).

Desire: Buddhists live a contradiction; they seek to overcome suffering by rooting out desire, but at the same time they cultivate desire for self-control, meritorious life, and nirvana. Christians are consistent; we seek to reject evil desires and cultivate good desires according to the standard of Christ. "Flee the evil desires of youth and pursue righteousness, faith, love and peace, along with those who call on the Lord out of a pure heart" (2 Tim. 2:22, NIV).

JESUS AND THE EIGHTFOLD PATH

Because Buddhists think a good life consists of following the Eightfold Path, the stages of the path can be used to introduce them to Christ as follows:

Right views: Jesus is the way, the truth, and the life (John 14:6), and there is salvation in no one else (Acts 4:12).

Right aspiration: Fights and quarrels come from selfish desires and wrong motives (Jas. 4:1-3); right desires and motives honor God (1 Cor. 10:31).

Right speech: A day of judgment is coming when God will hold men accountable for every careless word they have spoken (Matt. 12:36).

Right conduct: The one who loves Jesus must obey Him (John 14:21), and those who live by God's wisdom will produce good acts/fruit (Jas. 3:17).

Right livelihood: God will care for those who put Him first (Matt. 6:31,33), and all work must be done for God's approval (2 Tim. 2:15).

Right effort: Like runners in a race, followers of Christ must throw off every hindrance in order to give Him their best efforts (Heb. 12:1-2).

Right mindfulness: The sinful mind cannot submit to God's law (Rom. 8:7), and disciples of Christ must orient their minds as He did (Phil. 2:5).

Right contemplation: The secret of true success, inner peace, self-control, and lasting salvation is submission to Jesus Christ as Savior and Lord and setting your heart and mind on things above where He now sits in glory waiting to bring the present order of sin and suffering to an end (Col. 3:1-4).

WHEN WITNESSING TO BUDDHISTS

1. Avoid terms such as new birth, rebirth, regeneration, or born again. Use alternatives such as endless freedom from suffering, guilt, and sin, new power for living a holy life, promise of eternal good life without suffering, or gift of unlimited merit.

2. Emphasize the uniqueness of Christ.

3. Focus on the gospel message and do not get distracted by details of Buddhist doctrine.

4. Understand Buddhist beliefs enough to discern weaknesses that can be used to make the gospel appealing (see Bridges for Evangelizing Buddhists and Jesus and the Eightfold Path).

5. While using bridge concepts (see Bridges for Evangelizing Buddhists), be careful not to reduce Christian truth to a form of Buddhism. Buddhism has been good at accommodating other religions. Do not say Buddhism is good, but Christianity is easier.

6. Share your own testimony, especially your freedom from guilt, assurance of heaven (no more pain), and personal relationship with Christ.

7. Prepare with prayer. Do not witness in your own strength.

Evangelistic Survey

- Where do people go to when they die?
- What do you think God is like?
- If you could ask God one thing, what would it be?
- Should God punish murderers? If so, how should He punish them?
- What do you think a person has to do to go to heaven?
- Do you consider yourself to be a "good" person?
- How many of the Ten Commandments can you name?
- Do you think you have kept the Ten Commandments?
- Where would you go if you died tonight?
- Do you believe there is such a place as hell?
- If there was a way to avoid death, would you be interested?
- Do you think the Bible's claim, that someone can know that they have everlasting life, is true?
- Who do you think Jesus was?
- What is stopping you from asking God for forgiveness and being converted right now?

3 John

THE elder to the wellbeloved Gaius, whom I love in the truth.

2 Beloved, I wish above all things that you may prosper and be in health, even as your soul prospers.

3 For I rejoiced greatly, when the brethren came and testified of the truth that is in you, even as you walk in the truth.

4 I have no greater joy than to hear that my children walk in truth.

5 Beloved, you do faithfully whatsoever you do to the brethren, and to strangers;

6 Which have borne witness of your charity before the church: whom if you bring forward on their journey after a godly sort, you shall do well:

7 Because that for his name's sake they went forth, taking nothing of the Gentiles.

8 We therefore ought to receive such, that we might be fellow-helpers to the truth.

9 I wrote to the church: but Diotrephes, who loves to have the preeminence among them, receives us not.

10 Wherefore, if I come, I will remember his deeds which he does, prating against us with malicious words: and not content therewith, neither does he himself receive the brethren, and forbids them that would, and casts them out of the church.

11 Beloved, follow not that which is evil, but that which is good. He that does good is of God: but he that does evil has not seen God.

12 Demetrius has good report of all men, and of the truth itself: yes, and we also bear record; and you know that our record is true.

> Satan always hates Christian fellowship; it is his policy to keep Christians apart. Anything which can divide saints from one another he delights in.
>
> **CHARLES SPURGEON**

13 I had many things to write, but I will not with ink and pen write to you:

14 But I trust I shall shortly see you, and we shall speak face to face. Peace be to you. Our friends salute you. Greet the friends by name.

---

9 Loving to have preeminence is not a fruit of godliness. Those who want it will manifest their unregenerate hearts with malicious words. They will divide the Body of Christ for their own ends, as did Diotrephes.

Test Your I.Q.

Read OUT LOUD the wording in the three triangles:

READ this sentence:

FINISHED FILES ARE THE RE-SULTS OF YEARS OF SCIENTIFIC STUDY COMBINED WITH THE EXPERIENCE OF YEARS

Now count aloud the F's in the box. Count them only ONCE; do not look back and count them again.

Answers: The words "the" and "a" are repeated. There are six F's.

Here is another I.Q. test:

This one is more important. Answer Yes or No OUT LOUD:

1. Is there a God?
2. Does God care about right and wrong?
3. Are God's standards the same as ours?
4. Will God punish sin?
5. Is there a hell?
6. Can you avoid hell by living a good life?

Answers:

1. Yes. 2. Yes. 3. No. 4. Yes. 5. Yes. 6. No.

Jude

JUDE, the servant of Jesus Christ, and brother of James, to them that are sanctified by God the Father, and preserved in Jesus Christ, and called:

2 Mercy to you, and peace, and love, be multiplied.

3 *Beloved, when I gave all diligence to write to you of the common salvation, it was needful for me to write to you, and exhort you that you should earnestly contend for the faith which was once delivered to the saints.*

4 For there are certain men crept in unawares, who were before of old ordained to this condemnation, ungodly men, turning the grace of our God into lasciviousness, and denying the only Lord God, and our Lord Jesus Christ.

5 I will therefore put you in remembrance, though you once knew this, how that the Lord, having saved the people out of the land of Egypt, afterward destroyed them that believed not.

6 And the angels which kept not their first estate, but left their own habitation, he has reserved in everlasting chains under darkness to the judgment of the great day.

7 Even as Sodom and Gomorrha, and the cities about them in like manner, giving themselves over to fornication, and going after strange flesh, are set forth for an example, suffering the vengeance of eternal fire.

8 Likewise also these filthy dreamers defile the flesh, despise dominion, and speak evil of dignities.

9 Yet Michael the archangel, when contending with the devil he disputed about

USING THE LAW IN EVANGELISM

3 Regarding the Law's use in evangelism, *Martin Luther* stated: "This now is the Christian teaching and preaching, which God be praised, we know and possess, and it is not necessary at present to develop it further, but only to offer the admonition that it be maintained in Christendom with all diligence. For Satan has attacked it hard and strong from the beginning until present, and gladly would he completely extinguish it and tread it under foot."

3 Never lose sight of the mandate of the Church: to contend earnestly for the faith. The battle in which we find ourselves is for the salvation of lost sinners.

When people inquire as to the relevance of our gospel, we must not be tricked into going on the defensive. We must immediately take the offensive, for our Lord Himself has promised that the gates of hell shall not withstand the assault of His Church. *Dr. Leighton Ford*

4 False converts have crept in unawares and sit amid God's people. They think that salvation and sin are compatible. They are actually workers of iniquity. See Matthew 7:21-23.

7

"God made me to be a homosexual, so He doesn't want me to change."

Homosexuals argue that they did not make a conscious decision to be that way, so it must be natural. They *are* born that way just as all of us are born with a sin nature and sinful desires (Ephesians 2:1-3). Tell them that it *is* natural for them, and for all of us, to be tempted to do things that God says are wrong. In the same way, pedophiles and adulterers (alcoholics, drug addicts, etc.) don't make a conscious decision to choose that self-destructive lifestyle; they simply give in to their sinful desires. However, although sin is natural for unbelievers, that doesn't mean God wants them to remain that way. God can set them free from their sinful nature (Romans 7:23-8:2), give them new desires (Ephesians 4:22-24), and help them withstand temptations (1 Corinthians 10:13). See 1 Corinthians 6:9-11 comment.

the body of Moses, dared not bring against him a railing accusation, but said, The Lord rebuke you.

10 But these speak evil of those things which they know not: but what they know naturally, as brute beasts, in those things they corrupt themselves.

11 Woe to them! for they have gone in the way of Cain, and ran greedily after the error of Balaam for reward, and perished in the gainsaying of Core.

> Preach with this object, that men may quit their sins and fly to Christ for pardon, that by His blessed Spirit they may be renovated and become as much in love with everything that is holy as they are now in love with everything that is sinful.
>
> **CHARLES SPURGEON**

12 These are spots in your feasts of charity, when they feast with you, feeding themselves without fear: clouds they are without water, carried about of winds;

trees whose fruit withers, without fruit, twice dead, plucked up by the roots;

13 Raging waves of the sea, foaming out their own shame; wandering stars, to whom is reserved the blackness of darkness for ever.

14 And Enoch also, the seventh from Adam, prophesied of these, saying, Behold, the Lord comes with ten thousands of his saints,

15 To execute judgment upon all, and to convince all that are ungodly among them of all their ungodly deeds which they have ungodly committed, and of all their hard speeches which ungodly sinners have spoken against him.

16 These are murmurers, complainers, walking after their own lusts; and their mouth speaks great swelling words, having men's persons in admiration because of advantage.

17 But, beloved, remember the words which were spoken before of the apostles of our Lord Jesus Christ;

18 How that they told you there should be mockers in the last time, who should walk after their own ungodly lusts.

---

14 Second coming of Jesus: See Revelation 1:7.

15 With the help of God, we are to convince the ungodly that their deeds and their speech are offensive to their Creator, and will bring swift judgment upon them.

19 These be they who separate themselves, sensual, having not the Spirit.

20 But you, beloved, building up yourselves on your most holy faith, praying in the Holy Spirit,

21 Keep yourselves in the love of God, looking for the mercy of our Lord Jesus Christ to eternal life.

22 And of some have compassion, making a difference:

23 And others save with fear, pulling them out of the fire; hating even the garment spotted by the flesh.

24 Now to him that is able to keep you from falling, and to present you faultless before the presence of his glory with exceeding joy,

25 To the only wise God our Savior, be glory and majesty, dominion and power, both now and ever. Amen.

"Before I can preach love, mercy, and grace, I must preach sin, Law, and judgment."

John Wesley

18,19 A failure to preach the Commandments of God has left an entire generation without the fear of God. They are mockers in these last days. Scripture sheds light on their secret sins, lust and sensuality.

20 What is the reason that some believers are so much brighter and holier than others? I believe the difference, in nineteen cases out of twenty, arises from different habits about private prayer. I believe that those who are not eminently holy pray little, and those who are eminently holy pray much. *J. C. Ryle*

23 The world says you can't confront people with Jesus; you'll run them off. Where are you going to run them to? Hell number 2? *Darrell Robinson*

Revelation 21:2

I John saw the holy city, new Jerusalem, coming down from God out of heaven, prepared as a bride adorned for her husband . . .

Revelation

CHAPTER 1

THE Revelation of Jesus Christ, which God gave to him, to show to his servants things which must shortly come to pass; and he sent and signified it by his angel to his servant John:

2 Who bare record of the word of God, and of the testimony of Jesus Christ, and of all things that he saw.

3 Blessed is he that reads, and they that hear the words of this prophecy, and keep those things which are written therein: for the time is at hand.

4 John to the seven churches which are in Asia: Grace be to you, and peace, from him which is, and which was, and which is to come; and from the seven Spirits which are before his throne;

5 And from Jesus Christ, who is the faithful witness, and the first begotten of the dead, and the prince of the kings of the earth. To him that loved us, and washed us from our sins in his own blood,

6 And has made us kings and priests to God and his Father; to him be glory and dominion for ever and ever. Amen.

7 Behold, he comes with clouds; and every eye shall see him, and they also which pierced him: and all kindreds of the earth shall wail because of him. Even so, Amen.

8 I am Alpha and Omega, the beginning and the ending, says the Lord, which is, and which was, and which is to come, the Almighty.

9 I John, who also am your brother, and companion in tribulation, and in the kingdom and patience of Jesus Christ, was in the isle that is called Patmos, for the word of God, and for the testimony of Jesus Christ.

10 I was in the Spirit on the Lord's day, and heard behind me a great voice, as of a trumpet,

11 Saying, I am Alpha and Omega, the first and the last: and, What you see, write in a book, and send it to the seven churches which are in Asia; to Ephesus, and to Smyrna, and to Pergamos, and to Thyatira, and to Sardis, and to Philadelphia, and to Laodicea.

12 And I turned to see the voice that spoke with me. And being turned, I saw seven golden candlesticks;

13 And in the midst of the seven candlesticks one like to the Son of man, clothed with a garment down to the foot, and girt about the paps with a golden girdle.

14 His head and his hairs were white like wool, as white as snow; and his eyes were as a flame of fire;

15 And his feet like to fine brass, as if they burned in a furnace; and his voice as the sound of many waters.

16 And he had in his right hand seven stars: and out of his mouth went a sharp

---

1:7 Second coming of Jesus: See Revelation 3:11.

1:7 *"The Bible teaches that the earth is flat."*

This is often claimed because the Bible says said that every eye will see Jesus at His Second Coming. However, it would seem that His coming will envelop the entire earth. (See Hebrews 11:3 comment.)

two-edged sword: and his countenance was as the sun shines in his strength.

17 And when I saw him, I fell at his feet as dead. And he laid his right hand upon me, saying to me, Fear not; I am the first and the last:

18 I am he that lives, and was dead; and, behold, I am alive for evermore, Amen; and have the keys of hell and of death.

19 Write the things which you have seen, and the things which are, and the things which shall be hereafter;

20 The mystery of the seven stars which you saw in my right hand, and the seven golden candlesticks. The seven stars are the angels of the seven churches: and the seven candlesticks which you saw are the seven churches.

CHAPTER 2

TO the angel of the church of Ephesus write; These things says he that holds the seven stars in his right hand, who walks in the midst of the seven golden candlesticks;

2 I know your works, and your labor, and your patience, and how you can not bear them which are evil: and you have tried them which say they are apostles, and are not, and have found them liars:

3 And have borne, and have patience, and for my name's sake have labored, and have not fainted.

4 Nevertheless I have somewhat against you, because you have left your first love.

5 Remember therefore from whence you are fallen, and repent, and do the first works; or else I will come to you quickly, and will remove your candlestick out of his place, except you repent.

6 But this you have, that you hate the deeds of the Nicolaitans, which I also hate.

7 He that has an ear, let him hear what the Spirit says to the churches; To him that overcomes will I give to eat of the tree of life, which is in the midst of the paradise of God.

8 And to the angel of the church in Smyrna write; These things says the first and the last, which was dead, and is alive;

9 I know your works, and tribulation, and poverty, (but you are rich) and I know the blasphemy of them which say they are Jews, and are not, but are the synagogue of Satan.

1:17 Perfection of mercy and love. "If you have studied the matchless purity of [Jesus'] character with adoring admiration, you must have been amazed at the absolute perfection of his manhood, and the glory of His moral and spiritual character. At such times, if you have had a true sense of your own position, you have been ready to sink into the dust, and you have exclaimed, 'Shall He wash my feet? Shall he give himself for me? Can it be that He could have loved one so stained and polluted, so mean and so beggarly, so altogether unworthy even to live, much less to be loved by such an altogether lovely one?'

"But I pray you always to remember, when you think of His perfection, that He has perfection of mercy as well as of holiness, and perfection of love to sinners as well as perfection of hatred of sin; and that, guilty as you are, you must never doubt His affection, for He has pledged you in His heart's blood, and proved His love by His death." *Charles Spurgeon*

QUESTIONS & OBJECTIONS

1:18

"Hell is just a metaphor for the grave."

There are three words translated "hell" in Scripture:

Gehenna (Greek): The place of punishment (Matthew 5:22,29; 10:28; and James 3:6)

Hades (Greek): The abode of the dead (Matthew 11:23; 16:18, Luke 16:23; Acts 2:27)

Sheol (Hebrew): The grave (Psalm 9:17; 16:10)

There are those who accept that hell is a place of punishment, but believe that the punishment is to be annihilated—to cease conscious existence. They can't conceive that the punishment of the wicked will be conscious and *eternal*. If they are correct, then a man like Adolph Hitler, who was responsible for the deaths of millions, is being "punished" merely with eternal sleep. His fate is simply to return to the non-existent state he was in before he was born, where he doesn't even know that he is being punished.

However, Scripture paints a different story. The rich man who found himself in hell (Luke 16:19–31) was conscious. He was able to feel pain, to thirst, and to experience remorse. He wasn't asleep in the grave; he was in a place of "torment."

If hell is a place of knowing nothing or a reference to the grave into which we go at death, Jesus's statements about hell make no sense. He said that if your hand, foot, or eye causes you to sin, it would be better to remove it than to "go into hell, into the fire that never shall be quenched: where their worm dies not, and the fire is not quenched" (Mark 9:43–48).

The Bible refers to the fate of the unsaved with such fearful words as the following:

"Shame and everlasting contempt" (Daniel 12:2)

"Everlasting punishment" (Mathew 25:46)

"Weeping and gnashing of teeth" (Matthew 24:51)

"Fire unquenchable" (Luke 3:17)

"Indignation and wrath, tribulation and anguish" (Romans 2:8,9)

"Everlasting destruction from the presence of the Lord" (2 Thessalonians 1:9)

"Eternal fire...the blackness of darkness for ever" (Jude 7,13)

Revelation 14:10,11 tells us the final, eternal destiny of the sinner: "He shall be tormented with fire and brimstone...the smoke of their torment ascended up for ever and ever: and they have no rest day or night."

---

10 Fear none of those things which you shall suffer: behold, the devil shall cast some of you into prison, that you may be tried; and you shall have tribulation ten days: be faithful to death, and I will give you a crown of life.

11 He that has an ear, let him hear what the Spirit says to the churches; He that overcomes shall not be hurt of the second death.

12 And to the angel of the church in Pergamos write; These things says he which has the sharp sword with two edges;

13 I know your works, and where you dwell, even where Satan's seat is: and you hold fast my name, and have not denied my faith, even in those days wherein Antipas was my faithful martyr, who was slain among you, where Satan dwells.

14 But I have a few things against you, because you have there them that hold the doctrine of Balaam, who taught Balak to cast a stumblingblock before the children of Israel, to eat things sacrificed to idols, and to commit fornication.

15 So have you also them that hold the doctrine of the Nicolaitans, which thing I hate.

Hitler's Nazi Germany had "God with us" engraved on the belts of Nazi soldiers. See Luke 6:27 comment. Lest we forget.

16 Repent; or else I will come to you quickly, and will fight against them with the sword of my mouth.

17 He that has an ear, let him hear what the Spirit says to the churches; To him that overcomes will I give to eat of the hidden manna, and will give him a white stone, and in the stone a new name written, which no man knows saving he that receives it.

18 And to the angel of the church in Thyatira write; These things says the Son of God, who has his eyes like to a flame of fire, and his feet are like fine brass;

19 I know your works, and charity, and service, and faith, and your patience, and your works; and the last to be more than the first.

20 Notwithstanding I have a few things against you, because you suffer that woman Jezebel, which calls herself a prophetess, to teach and to seduce my servants to commit fornication, and to eat things sacrificed to idols.

21 And I gave her space to repent of her fornication; and she repented not.

22 Behold, I will cast her into a bed, and them that commit adultery with her into great tribulation, except they repent of their deeds.

23 And I will kill her children with death; and all the churches shall know that I am he which searches the reins and hearts: and I will give to every one of you according to your works.

24 But to you I say, and to the rest in Thyatira, as many as have not this doctrine, and which have not known the depths of Satan, as they speak; I will put upon you none other burden.

25 But that which you have already hold fast till I come.

26 And he that overcomes, and keeps my works to the end, to him will I give power over the nations:

27 And he shall rule them with a rod of iron; as the vessels of a potter shall they be broken to shivers: even as I received of my Father.

28 And I will give him the morning star.

29 He that has an ear, let him hear what the Spirit says to the churches.

CHAPTER 3

AND to the angel of the church in Sardis write; These things says he that has the seven Spirits of God, and the seven stars; I know your works, that you have a name that you live, and are dead.

2 Be watchful, and strengthen the things which remain, that are ready to die: for I have not found your works perfect before God.

3 Remember therefore how you have received and heard, and hold fast, and repent. If therefore you shall not watch, I will come on you as a thief, and you shall not know what hour I will come upon you.

4 You have a few names even in Sardis which have not defiled their garments; and they shall walk with me in white: for they are worthy.

5 He that overcomes, the same shall be clothed in white raiment; and I will not blot out his name out of the book of life, but I will confess his name before my

Father, and before his angels.

6 He that has an ear, let him hear what the Spirit says to the churches.

7 And to the angel of the church in Philadelphia write; These things says he that is holy, he that is true, he that has the key of David, he that opens, and no man shuts; and shuts, and no man opens;

8 I know your works: behold, I have set before you an open door, and no man can shut it: for you have a little strength, and have kept my word, and have not denied my name.

9 Behold, I will make them of the synagogue of Satan, which say they are Jews, and are not, but do lie; behold, I will make them to come and worship before your feet, and to know that I have loved you.

10 Because you have kept the word of my patience, I also will keep you from the hour of temptation, which shall come upon all the world, to try them that dwell upon the earth.

11 Behold, I come quickly: hold that fast which you have, that no man take your crown.

12 Him that overcomes will I make a pillar in the temple of my God, and he shall go no more out: and I will write upon him the name of my God, and the name of the city of my God, which is new Jerusalem, which comes down out of heaven from my God: and I will write upon him my new name.

13 He that has an ear, let him hear what the Spirit says to the churches.

14 And to the angel of the church of the Laodiceans write; These things says the Amen, the faithful and true witness, the beginning of the creation of God;

15 *I know your works, that you are neither cold nor hot: I would you were cold or hot.*

16 *So then because you are lukewarm, and neither cold nor hot, I will spue you out of my mouth.*

17 Because you say, I am rich, and increased with goods, and have need of nothing; and know not that you are wretched, and miserable, and poor, and blind, and naked:

18 I counsel you to buy of me gold tried in the fire, that you may be rich; and white raiment, that you may be clothed, and that the shame of your nakedness do not appear; and anoint your eyes with eyesalve, that you may see.

19 As many as I love, I rebuke and chasten: be zealous therefore, and repent.

20 **Behold, I stand at the door, and knock: if any man hear my voice, and open the door, I will come in to him, and will sup with him, and he with me.**

21 To him that overcomes will I grant to sit with me in my throne, even as I also overcame, and am set down with my Father in his throne.

22 He that has an ear, let him hear what the Spirit says to the churches.

CHAPTER 4

AFTER this I looked, and, behold, a door was opened in heaven: and the first voice which I heard was as it were of a trumpet talking with me; which said, Come up here, and I will show you things

---

3:11 Second coming of Jesus: See Revelation 16:15.

3:14–19 Here is a perfect description of the contemporary Church, especially in America, with its beautiful facilities, the finest music, and state-of-the-art technology. It has busied itself in everything but the will of God—to seek and save the lost. The word "evangelism" has as much attraction for the modern Church as the word "righteousness" has for the world.

3:16 "The Christian world is in a deep sleep; nothing but a loud shout can awaken them out of it!" *George Whitefield*

"We are not a generation marked by passion. Passion can be lost in programs and progress reports and institutions and calendars. In doing what is good, we may fail to do what is best." *R. Albert Mohle Jr.*

which must be hereafter.

2 And immediately I was in the spirit: and, behold, a throne was set in heaven, and one sat on the throne.

3 And he that sat was to look upon like a jasper and a sardine stone: and there was a rainbow round about the throne, in sight like to an emerald.

4 And round about the throne were four and twenty seats: and upon the seats I saw four and twenty elders sitting, clothed in white raiment; and they had on their heads crowns of gold.

5 And out of the throne proceeded lightnings and thunderings and voices: and there were seven lamps of fire burning before the throne, which are the seven Spirits of God.

6 And before the throne there was a sea of glass like to crystal: and in the midst of the throne, and round about the throne, were four beasts full of eyes before and behind.

7 And the first beast was like a lion, and the second beast like a calf, and the third beast had a face as a man, and the fourth beast was like a flying eagle.

8 And the four beasts had each of them six wings about him; and they were full of eyes within: and they rest not day and night, saying, Holy, holy, holy, Lord God Almighty, which was, and is, and is to come.

9 And when those beasts give glory and honor and thanks to him that sat on the throne, who lives for ever and ever,

10 The four and twenty elders fall down before him that sat on the throne, and worship him that lives for ever and ever, and cast their crowns before the throne, saying,

11 You are worthy, O Lord, to receive glory and honor and power: for you have created all things, and for your pleasure

they are and were created.

CHAPTER 5

A ND I saw in the right hand of him that sat on the throne a book written within and on the backside, sealed with seven seals.

2 And I saw a strong angel proclaiming with a loud voice, Who is worthy to open the book, and to loose the seals thereof?

3 And no man in heaven, nor in earth, neither under the earth, was able to open the book, neither to look thereon.

4 And I wept much, because no man was found worthy to open and to read the book, neither to look thereon.

5 And one of the elders said to me, Weep not: behold, the Lion of the tribe of Judah, the Root of David, has prevailed to open the book, and to loose the seven seals thereof.

6 And I beheld, and, lo, in the midst of the throne and of the four beasts, and in the midst of the elders, stood a Lamb as it had been slain, having seven horns and seven eyes, which are the seven Spirits of God sent forth into all the earth.

7 And he came and took the book out of the right hand of him that sat upon the throne.

8 And when he had taken the book, the four beasts and four and twenty elders fell down before the Lamb, having every one of them harps, and golden vials full of odors, which are the prayers of saints.

9 And they sung a new song, saying, You are worthy to take the book, and to open the seals thereof: for you were slain, and have redeemed us to God by your blood out of every kindred, and tongue, and people, and nation;

10 And have made us to our God kings and priests: and we shall reign on the earth.

4:11 This is the reason for our existence on earth. The entire creation was made for the pleasure of God. That doesn't mean that we are "God's toys" as some would suggest. Just as a father is pleased when he sees that his children have pleasure, so our pleasure is God's pleasure. Those who love God will have "pleasures for evermore" (Psalm 16:11).

11 And I beheld, and I heard the voice of many angels round about the throne and the beasts and the elders: and the number of them was ten thousand times ten thousand, and thousands of thousands;

12 Saying with a loud voice, Worthy is the Lamb that was slain to receive power, and riches, and wisdom, and strength, and honor, and glory, and blessing.

13 And every creature which is in heaven, and on the earth, and under the earth, and such as are in the sea, and all that are in them, heard I saying, Blessing, and honor, and glory, and power, be to him that sits upon the throne, and to the Lamb for ever and ever.

14 And the four beasts said, Amen. And the four and twenty elders fell down and worshipped him that lives for ever and ever.

CHAPTER 6

AND I saw when the Lamb opened one of the seals, and I heard, as it were the noise of thunder, one of the four beasts saying, Come and see.

2 And I saw, and behold a white horse: and he that sat on him had a bow; and a crown was given to him: and he went forth conquering, and to conquer.

3 And when he had opened the second seal, I heard the second beast say, Come and see.

4 And there went out another horse that was red: and power was given to him that sat thereon to take peace from the earth, and that they should kill one another: and there was given to him a great sword.

5 And when he had opened the third seal, I heard the third beast say, Come and see. And I beheld, and lo a black horse; and he that sat on him had a pair of balances in his hand.

6 And I heard a voice in the midst of the four beasts say, A measure of wheat for a penny, and three measures of barley for a penny; and see you hurt not the oil and the wine.

7 And when he had opened the fourth seal, I heard the voice of the fourth beast say, Come and see.

8 And I looked, and behold a pale horse: and his name that sat on him was Death, and Hell followed with him. And power was given to them over the fourth part of the earth, to kill with sword, and with hunger, and with death, and with the beasts of the earth.

9 And when he had opened the fifth seal, I saw under the altar the souls of them that were slain for the word of God, and for the testimony which they held:

10 And they cried with a loud voice, saying, How long, O Lord, holy and true, do you not judge and avenge our blood on them that dwell on the earth?

11 And white robes were given to every one of them; and it was said to them, that they should rest yet for a little season, until their fellow-servants also and their brethren, that should be killed as they were, should be fulfilled.

12 And I beheld when he had opened the sixth seal, and, lo, there was a great earthquake; and the sun became black as sackcloth of hair, and the moon became as blood;

13 And the stars of heaven fell to the earth, even as a fig tree casts her untimely figs, when she is shaken of a mighty wind.

14 **And the heaven departed as a scroll when it is rolled together; and every mountain and island were moved out**

6:10,11 Never fear the thought that you are causing sinners to fear by referring to the Judgment. Judgment Day is the climax of the ages. It is an event for which the very creation cries out (Romans 8:21,22). It has done so from the blood of Abel to the last injustice of this age.

With God, justice delayed is not justice denied. Every transgression against the Moral Law will receive just recompense—in His time. God loves justice...and He will have it.

of their places.

15 And the kings of the earth, and the great men, and the rich men, and the chief captains, and the mighty men, and every bondman, and every free man, hid themselves in the dens and in the rocks of the mountains;

16 And said to the mountains and rocks, Fall on us, and hide us from the face of him that sits on the throne, and from the wrath of the Lamb:

17 For the great day of his wrath is come; and who shall be able to stand?

CHAPTER 7

AND after these things I saw four angels standing on the four corners of the earth, holding the four winds of the earth, that the wind should not blow on the earth, nor on the sea, nor on any tree.

2 And I saw another angel ascending from the east, having the seal of the living God: and he cried with a loud voice to the four angels, to whom it was given to hurt the earth and the sea,

3 Saying, Hurt not the earth, neither the sea, nor the trees, till we have sealed the servants of our God in their foreheads.

4 And I heard the number of them which were sealed: and there were sealed an hundred and forty and four thousand of all the tribes of the children of Israel.

5 Of the tribe of Judah were sealed twelve thousand. Of the tribe of Reuben were sealed twelve thousand. Of the tribe of Gad were sealed twelve thousand.

6 Of the tribe of Aser were sealed twelve thousand. Of the tribe of Nepthalim were sealed twelve thousand. Of the tribe of Manasses were sealed twelve thousand.

7 Of the tribe of Simeon were sealed twelve thousand. Of the tribe of Levi were sealed twelve thousand. Of the tribe of Issachar were sealed twelve thousand.

8 Of the tribe of Zabulon were sealed twelve thousand. Of the tribe of Joseph were sealed twelve thousand. Of the tribe of Benjamin were sealed twelve thousand.

9 After this I beheld, and, lo, a great multitude, which no man could number, of all nations, and kindreds, and people, and tongues, stood before the throne, and before the Lamb, clothed with white robes, and palms in their hands;

10 And cried with a loud voice, saying, Salvation to our God which sits upon the throne, and to the Lamb.

11 And all the angels stood round about the throne, and about the elders and the four beasts, and fell before the throne on their faces, and worshipped God,

12 Saying, Amen: Blessing, and glory, and wisdom, and thanksgiving, and honor, and power, and might, be to our God for ever and ever. Amen.

13 And one of the elders answered, saying to me, What are these which are arrayed in white robes? and whence came they?

14 And I said to him, Sir, you know. And he said to me, These are they which came out of great tribulation, and have washed

---

6:15 Note the truth of Proverbs 11:4: "Riches profit not in the day of wrath: but righteousness delivers from death." Those who are unrighteous—no matter how wealthy or prominent, great or mighty—all will be cowering in fear of a holy God's wrath.

6:16,17 Concern for the lost. The very thought of this terrible day should motivate the hardest heart into urgent evangelism.

"You blame me for weeping; but how can I help it when you will not weep for yourselves, although your own immortal souls are on the verge of destruction, and ought I know, you are hearing your last sermon, and may never have opportunity to have Christ offered to you." *George Whitefield*

"If you haven't got tears in your eyes, let them hear tears in your voice!" *Catherine Booth*

7:4–8 These are not Jehovah's Witnesses who have been born again, as the Jehovah's Witnesses claim. The 144,000 are from the twelve tribes of Israel.

their robes, and made them white in the blood of the Lamb.

15 Therefore are they before the throne of God, and serve him day and night in his temple: and he that sits on the throne shall dwell among them.

16 They shall hunger no more, neither thirst any more; neither shall the sun light on them, nor any heat.

17 For the Lamb which is in the midst of the throne shall feed them, and shall lead them to living fountains of waters: and God shall wipe away all tears from their eyes.

CHAPTER 8

AND when he had opened the seventh seal, there was silence in heaven about the space of half an hour.

2 And I saw the seven angels which stood before God; and to them were given seven trumpets.

3 And another angel came and stood at the altar, having a golden censer; and there was given to him much incense, that he should offer it with the prayers of all saints upon the golden altar which was before the throne.

4 And the smoke of the incense, which came with the prayers of the saints, ascended up before God out of the angel's hand.

5 And the angel took the censer, and filled it with fire of the altar, and cast it into the earth: and there were voices, and thunderings, and lightnings, and an earthquake.

6 And the seven angels which had the seven trumpets prepared themselves to sound.

7 The first angel sounded, and there followed hail and fire mingled with blood, and they were cast upon the earth: and the third part of trees was burnt up, and all green grass was burnt up.

8 And the second angel sounded, and as it were a great mountain burning with fire was cast into the sea: and the third part of the sea became blood;

9 And the third part of the creatures which were in the sea, and had life, died; and the third part of the ships were destroyed.

10 And the third angel sounded, and there fell a great star from heaven, burning as it were a lamp, and it fell upon the third part of the rivers, and upon the fountains of waters;

11 And the name of the star is called Wormwood: and the third part of the waters became wormwood; and many men died of the waters, because they were made bitter.

12 And the fourth angel sounded, and

7:17 How we long for this day, and how the world will eternally regret beyond words its rejection of the gospel.

the third part of the sun was smitten, and the third part of the moon, and the third part of the stars; so as the third part of them was darkened, and the day shone not for a third part of it, and the night likewise.

13 And I beheld, and heard an angel flying through the midst of heaven, saying with a loud voice, Woe, woe, woe, to the inhabiters of the earth by reason of the other voices of the trumpet of the three angels, which are yet to sound!

CHAPTER 9

AND the fifth angel sounded, and I saw a star fall from heaven to the earth: and to him was given the key of the bottomless pit.

2 And he opened the bottomless pit; and there arose a smoke out of the pit, as the smoke of a great furnace; and the sun and the air were darkened by reason of the smoke of the pit.

3 And there came out of the smoke locusts upon the earth: and to them was given power, as the scorpions of the earth have power.

4 And it was commanded them that they should not hurt the grass of the earth, neither any green thing, neither any tree; but only those men which have not the seal of God in their foreheads.

5 And to them it was given that they should not kill them, but that they should be tormented five months: and their torment was as the torment of a scorpion, when he strikes a man.

6 And in those days shall men seek death, and shall not find it; and shall desire to die, and death shall flee from them.

7 And the shapes of the locusts were like to horses prepared to battle; and on their heads were as it were crowns like gold, and their faces were as the faces of men.

8 And they had hair as the hair of women, and their teeth were as the teeth of lions.

9 And they had breastplates, as it were breastplates of iron; and the sound of their wings was as the sound of chariots of many horses running to battle.

10 And they had tails like to scorpions, and there were stings in their tails: and their power was to hurt men five months.

11 And they had a king over them, which is the angel of the bottomless pit, whose name in the Hebrew tongue is Abaddon, but in the Greek tongue has his name Apollyon.

12 One woe is past; and, behold, there come two woes more hereafter.

13 And the sixth angel sounded, and I heard a voice from the four horns of the golden altar which is before God,

14 Saying to the sixth angel which had the trumpet, Loose the four angels which are bound in the great river Euphrates.

15 And the four angels were loosed, which were prepared for an hour, and a day, and a month, and a year, for to slay the third part of men.

16 And the number of the army of the horsemen were two hundred thousand thousand: and I heard the number of them.

17 And thus I saw the horses in the vision, and them that sat on them, having breastplates of fire, and of jacinth, and brimstone: and the heads of the horses were as the heads of lions; and out of their

---

9:9 Joel 2:1–10 relates a striking account of the coming Battle of Armageddon, the greatest of all battles. As this vision (which seems to entail flame-throwing tank warfare) was given to him approximately 2,800 years ago, the prophet relates it to the only thing he has seen in battle—horse-drawn chariots. Think of modern warfare and compare: fire goes before them (v. 3); they burn what is behind them (v. 3); they destroy everything in their path (v. 3); they move at the speed of a horse (30–40 mph, v. 4); their rumbling sounds like the noise of many chariots and the roar of a fire (v. 5); they climb over walls (v. 7); they don't break ranks (v. 7); the sword can't stop them (v. 8); they climb into houses (v. 9); they make the earth quake (v. 10).

mouths issued fire and smoke and brimstone.

18 By these three was the third part of men killed, by the fire, and by the smoke, and by the brimstone, which issued out of their mouths.

19 For their power is in their mouth, and in their tails: for their tails were like to serpents, and had heads, and with them they do hurt.

20 And the rest of the men which were not killed by these plagues yet repented not of the works of their hands, that they should not worship devils, and idols of gold, and silver, and brass, and stone, and of wood: which neither can see, nor hear, nor walk:

21 Neither repented they of their murders, nor of their sorceries, nor of their fornication, nor of their thefts.

· · · · · ·

Why not preach that Jesus
gives happiness?
See 2 Corinthians 2:17 comment.

· · · · · ·

CHAPTER 10

AND I saw another mighty angel come down from heaven, clothed with a cloud: and a rainbow was upon his head, and his face was as it were the sun, and his feet as pillars of fire:

2 And he had in his hand a little book open: and he set his right foot upon the sea, and his left foot on the earth,

3 And cried with a loud voice, as when a lion roars: and when he had cried, seven thunders uttered their voices.

4 And when the seven thunders had uttered their voices, I was about to write: and I heard a voice from heaven saying to me, Seal up those things which the seven thunders uttered, and write them not.

5 And the angel which I saw stand upon the sea and upon the earth lifted up his hand to heaven,

6 And sware by him that lives for ever and ever, who created heaven, and the

things that therein are, and the earth, and the things that therein are, and the sea, and the things which are therein, that there should be time no longer:

7 But in the days of the voice of the seventh angel, when he shall begin to sound, the mystery of God should be finished, as he has declared to his servants the prophets.

8 And the voice which I heard from heaven spoke to me again, and said, Go and take the little book which is open in the hand of the angel which stands upon the sea and upon the earth.

9 And I went to the angel, and said to him, Give me the little book. And he said to me, Take it, and eat it up; and it shall make your belly bitter, but it shall be in your mouth sweet as honey.

10 And I took the little book out of the angel's hand, and ate it up; and it was in my mouth sweet as honey: and as soon as I had eaten it, my belly was bitter.

11 And he said to me, You must prophesy again before many peoples, and nations, and tongues, and kings.

CHAPTER 11

AND there was given me a reed like to a rod: and the angel stood, saying, Rise, and measure the temple of God, and the altar, and them that worship therein.

2 But the court which is without the temple leave out, and measure it not; for it is given to the Gentiles: and the holy city shall they tread under foot forty and two months.

3 And I will give power to my two witnesses, and they shall prophesy a thousand two hundred and threescore days, clothed in sackcloth.

4 These are the two olive trees, and the two candlesticks standing before the God of the earth.

5 And if any man will hurt them, fire proceeds out of their mouth, and devours their enemies: and if any man will hurt them, he must in this manner be killed.

6 These have power to shut heaven, that it rain not in the days of their prophecy:

and have power over waters to turn them to blood, and to smite the earth with all plagues, as often as they will.

7 And when they shall have finished their testimony, the beast that ascended out of the bottomless pit shall make war against them, and shall overcome them, and kill them.

8 And their dead bodies shall lie in the street of the great city, which spiritually is called Sodom and Egypt, where also our Lord was crucified.

9 And they of the people and kindreds and tongues and nations shall see their dead bodies three days and an half, and shall not suffer their dead bodies to be put in graves.

10 And they that dwell upon the earth shall rejoice over them, and make merry, and shall send gifts one to another; because these two prophets tormented them that dwelt on the earth.

11 And after three days and an half the Spirit of life from God entered into them, and they stood upon their feet; and great fear fell upon them which saw them.

12 And they heard a great voice from heaven saying to them, Come up here. And they ascended up to heaven in a cloud; and their enemies beheld them.

13 And the same hour was there a great earthquake, and the tenth part of the city fell, and in the earthquake were slain of men seven thousand: and the remnant were fearful, and gave glory to the God of heaven.

14 The second woe is past; and, behold, the third woe comes quickly.

15 And the seventh angel sounded; and there were great voices in heaven, saying, The kingdoms of this world are become the kingdoms of our Lord, and of his Christ; and he shall reign for ever

and ever.

16 And the four and twenty elders, which sat before God on their seats, fell upon their faces, and worshipped God,

17 Saying, We give you thanks, O Lord God Almighty, which are, and was, and are to come; because you have taken to you your great power, and have reigned.

18 And the nations were angry, and your wrath is come, and the time of the dead, that they should be judged, and that you should give reward to your servants the prophets, and to the saints, and them that fear your name, small and great; and should destroy them which destroy the earth.

19 And the temple of God was opened in heaven, and there was seen in his temple the ark of his testament: and there were lightnings, and voices, and thunderings, and an earthquake, and great hail.

CHAPTER 12

AND there appeared a great wonder in heaven; a woman clothed with the sun, and the moon under her feet, and upon her head a crown of twelve stars:

2 And she being with child cried, travailing in birth, and pained to be delivered.

3 And there appeared another wonder in heaven; and behold a great red dragon, having seven heads and ten horns, and seven crowns upon his heads.

4 And his tail drew the third part of the stars of heaven, and did cast them to the earth: and the dragon stood before the woman which was ready to be delivered, for to devour her child as soon as it was born.

5 And she brought forth a man child, who was to rule all nations with a rod of iron: and her child was caught up to God, and to his throne.

6 And the woman fled into the wilder-

11:18 These days, some would have us believe that those who "destroy the earth" are people who are not environmentally conscious. There are many who worship "Mother Earth" and think that those who harvest forests, utilize fossil fuels, and don't recycle should be punished. God has made us stewards of His creation, but we are to worship only Him, the Creator. Sinners who refuse to acknowledge Almighty God are the objects of wrath spoken of here.

They loved not their lives unto death:

"Now I have given up on everything else. I have found it to be the only way to really know Christ and to experience the mighty power that brought Him back to life again, and to find out what it means to suffer and to die with Him. So, whatever it takes, I will be one who lives in the fresh newness of life of those who are alive from the dead."

Cassie Bernall, *17, Columbine martyr*

"I have no more personal friends at school. But you know what? I am not going to apologize for speaking the name of Jesus. I am not going to justify my faith to them, and I am not going to hide the light that God has put into me. If I have to sacrifice everything, I will. I will take it. If my friends have to become my enemies for me to be with my best friend, Jesus, then that's fine with me."

Rachel Scott, *Columbine martyr*

"Father take my life, yes, my blood if Thou wilt, and consume it with Thine enveloping fire. I would not save it, for it is not mine to save. Have it Lord, have it all. Pour out my life as in oblation for the world. Blood is the only value as it flows before Thine altar."

Jim Elliot, *martyr (written at age 21)*

ness, where she has a place prepared of God, that they should feed her there a thousand two hundred and threescore days.

7 And there was war in heaven: Michael and his angels fought against the dragon; and the dragon fought and his angels,

8 And prevailed not; neither was their place found any more in heaven.

9 And the great dragon was cast out, that old serpent, called the Devil, and Satan, which deceives the whole world: he was cast out into the earth, and his angels were cast out with him.

10 And I heard a loud voice saying in heaven, Now is come salvation, and strength, and the kingdom of our God, and the power of his Christ: for the accuser of our brethren is cast down, which accused them before our God day and night.

11 And they overcame him by the blood of the Lamb, and by the word of their testimony; and they loved not their lives

12:9 The god of this world blinds the minds of those who do not believe (2 Corinthians 4:4). If they would *believe*, they would see their danger, and therefore obey the command to repent and be saved.

12:11 Here are the keys to victory in the Christian life:

1) Trust in the blood of Jesus. If sin enters our heart, we must confess it and the blood of Jesus Christ will cleanse us from all sin (1 John 1:7–9). If we do that, then the accuser will have nothing for which to accuse us before the throne of God (v. 10).

2) Our testimony is that Jesus Christ died for our sins and rose again, defeating the grave. Satan has been stripped of the power of death (Hebrews 2:14).

3) We don't live to ourselves, but for the will of God. We love Jesus more than our life (Luke 14:26).

unto the death.

12 Therefore rejoice, you heavens, and you that dwell in them. Woe to the inhabiters of the earth and of the sea! for the devil is come down to you, having great wrath, because he knows that he has but a short time.

13 And when the dragon saw that he was cast to the earth, he persecuted the woman which brought forth the man child.

14 And to the woman were given two wings of a great eagle, that she might fly into the wilderness, into her place, where she is nourished for a time, and times, and half a time, from the face of the serpent.

15 And the serpent cast out of his mouth water as a flood after the woman, that he might cause her to be carried away of the flood.

16 And the earth helped the woman, and the earth opened her mouth, and swallowed up the flood which the dragon cast out of his mouth.

17 And the dragon was wroth with the woman, and went to make war with the remnant of her seed, which keep the commandments of God, and have the testimony of Jesus Christ.

· · · · ·

For evolution and its clash with the Bible, see 1 Corinthians 15:39 comment.

· · · · ·

CHAPTER 13

AND I stood upon the sand of the sea, and saw a beast rise up out of the sea, having seven heads and ten horns, and upon his horns ten crowns, and upon his heads the name of blasphemy.

2 And the beast which I saw was like to a leopard, and his feet were as the feet of a bear, and his mouth as the mouth of a lion: and the dragon gave him his power, and his seat, and great authority.

3 And I saw one of his heads as it were wounded to death; and his deadly wound was healed: and all the world wondered after the beast.

4 And they worshipped the dragon which gave power to the beast: and they worshipped the beast, saying, Who is like to the beast? who is able to make war with him?

5 And there was given to him a mouth speaking great things and blasphemies; and power was given to him to continue forty and two months.

6 And he opened his mouth in blasphemy against God, to blaspheme his name, and his tabernacle, and them that dwell in heaven.

7 And it was given to him to make war with the saints, and to overcome them: and power was given him over all kindreds, and tongues, and nations.

8 And all that dwell upon the earth shall worship him, whose names are not written in the book of life of the Lamb slain from the foundation of the world.

9 If any man have an ear, let him hear.

10 He that leads into captivity shall go into captivity: he that kills with the sword must be killed with the sword. Here is the patience and the faith of the saints.

11 And I beheld another beast coming up out of the earth; and he had two horns like a lamb, and he spoke as a dragon.

12 And he exercises all the power of the first beast before him, and causes the earth and them which dwell therein to worship the first beast, whose deadly wound was healed.

13 And he does great wonders, so that he makes fire come down from heaven on the earth in the sight of men,

14 And deceives them that dwell on the earth by the means of those miracles which he had power to do in the sight of the beast; saying to them that dwell on the earth, that they should make an image to the beast, which had the wound by a sword, and did live.

15 And he had power to give life to the image of the beast, that the image of the beast should both speak, and cause that as many as would not worship the image of the beast should be killed.

16 And he causes all, both small and

great, rich and poor, free and bond, to receive a mark in their right hand, or in their foreheads:

17 And that no man might buy or sell, save he that had the mark, or the name of the beast, or the number of his name.

18 Here is wisdom. Let him that has understanding count the number of the beast: for it is the number of a man; and his number is Six hundred threescore and six.

CHAPTER 14

AND I looked, and, lo, a Lamb stood on the mount Zion, and with him an hundred forty and four thousand, having his Father's name written in their foreheads.

2 And I heard a voice from heaven, as the voice of many waters, and as the voice of a great thunder: and I heard the voice of harpers harping with their harps:

3 And they sung as it were a new song before the throne, and before the four beasts, and the elders: and no man could learn that song but the hundred and forty and four thousand, which were redeemed from the earth.

4 These are they which were not defiled with women; for they are virgins. These are they which follow the Lamb wherever he goes. These were redeemed from among men, being the firstfruits to God and to the Lamb.

5 And in their mouth was found no guile: for they are without fault before the throne of God.

6 And I saw another angel fly in the midst of heaven, having the everlasting gospel to preach to them that dwell on the earth, and to every nation, and kindred, and tongue, and people,

7 Saying with a loud voice, Fear God, and give glory to him; for the hour of his judgment is come: and worship him that made heaven, and earth, and the sea, and the fountains of waters.

8 And there followed another angel, saying, Babylon is fallen, is fallen, that great city, because she made all nations drink of the wine of the wrath of her fornication.

9 And the third angel followed them, saying with a loud voice, If any man worship the beast and his image, and receive his mark in his forehead, or in his hand,

10 The same shall drink of the wine of the wrath of God, which is poured out without mixture into the cup of his indig-

---

14:6 We have the great honor of preaching "the everlasting gospel," which is for *all* who dwell on the earth.

14:7 Law of probabilities refutes evolution. "The chance that higher life forms might have emerged in this way is comparable to the chance that a tornado sweeping through a junkyard might assemble a Boeing 747 from the materials therein." *Sir Fred Hoyle*, professor of astronomy, Cambridge University

"The likelihood of the formation of life from inanimate matter is one out of $10^{40,000}$ ...It is big enough to bury Darwin and the whole theory of evolution. There was no primeval soup, neither on this planet nor on any other, and if the beginnings of life were not random, they must therefore have been the product of purposeful intelligence." *Sir Fred Hoyle, Evolution from Space*

"I believe that Darwin's mechanism for evolution doesn't explain much of what is seen under a microscope. Cells are simply too complex to have evolved randomly. Intelligence was required to produce them." *Michael J. Behe*

"Evolution is unproved and unprovable. We believe it only because the only alternative is special creation, and that is unthinkable" *Sir Arthur Keith* (author of Foreword to *The Origin of Species*, 100th edition)

"In fact, evolution became in a sense a scientific religion; almost all scientists have accepted it and many are prepared to 'bend' their observations to fit in with it." *H. S. Lipson*, professor of physics, University of Manchester, UK

nation; and he shall be tormented with fire and brimstone in the presence of the holy angels, and in the presence of the Lamb:

11 And the smoke of their torment ascended up for ever and ever: and they have no rest day nor night, who worship the beast and his image, and whosoever receives the mark of his name.

12 Here is the patience of the saints: here are they that keep the commandments of God, and the faith of Jesus.

13 And I heard a voice from heaven saying to me, Write, Blessed are the dead which die in the Lord from henceforth: Yes, says the Spirit, that they may rest from their labors; and their works do follow them.

14 And I looked, and behold a white cloud, and upon the cloud one sat like to the Son of man, having on his head a golden crown, and in his hand a sharp sickle.

> If persecution should arise, you should be willing to part with all that you possess—with your liberty, with your life itself, for Christ—or you cannot be His disciple.
>
> **CHARLES SPURGEON**

15 And another angel came out of the temple, crying with a loud voice to him that sat on the cloud, Thrust in your sickle, and reap: for the time is come for you to reap; for the harvest of the earth is ripe.

16 And he that sat on the cloud thrust in his sickle on the earth; and the earth was reaped.

17 And another angel came out of the temple which is in heaven, he also having a sharp sickle.

18 And another angel came out from the altar, which had power over fire; and cried with a loud cry to him that had the sharp sickle, saying, Thrust in your sharp sickle, and gather the clusters of the vine

of the earth; for her grapes are fully ripe.

19 And the angel thrust in his sickle into the earth, and gathered the vine of the earth, and cast it into the great winepress of the wrath of God.

20 And the winepress was trodden without the city, and blood came out of the winepress, even to the horse bridles, by the space of a thousand and six hundred furlongs.

CHAPTER 15

AND I saw another sign in heaven, great and marvelous, seven angels having the seven last plagues; for in them is filled up the wrath of God.

2 And I saw as it were a sea of glass mingled with fire: and them that had gotten the victory over the beast, and over his image, and over his mark, and over the number of his name, stand on the sea of glass, having the harps of God.

3 And they sing the song of Moses the servant of God, and the song of the Lamb, saying, Great and marvelous are your works, Lord God Almighty; just and true are your ways, you King of saints.

4 Who shall not fear you, O Lord, and glorify your name? for you only are holy: for all nations shall come and worship before you; for your judgments are made manifest.

5 And after that I looked, and, behold, the temple of the tabernacle of the testimony in heaven was opened:

6 And the seven angels came out of the temple, having the seven plagues, clothed in pure and white linen, and having their breasts girded with golden girdles.

7 And one of the four beasts gave to the seven angels seven golden vials full of the wrath of God, who lives for ever and ever.

8 And the temple was filled with smoke from the glory of God, and from his power; and no man was able to enter into the temple, till the seven plagues of the seven angels were fulfilled.

14:13 If we die in the Lord, our works follow us. No good deed will be forgotten by God.

CHAPTER 16

AND I heard a great voice out of the temple saying to the seven angels, Go your ways, and pour out the vials of the wrath of God upon the earth.

2 And the first went, and poured out his vial upon the earth; and there fell a noisome and grievous sore upon the men which had the mark of the beast, and upon them which worshipped his image.

3 And the second angel poured out his vial upon the sea; and it became as the blood of a dead man: and every living soul died in the sea.

4 And the third angel poured out his vial upon the rivers and fountains of waters; and they became blood.

5 And I heard the angel of the waters say, You are righteous, O Lord, which are, and was, and shall be, because you have judged thus.

6 For they have shed the blood of saints and prophets, and you have given them blood to drink; for they are worthy.

7 And I heard another out of the altar say, Even so, Lord God Almighty, true and righteous are your judgments.

8 And the fourth angel poured out his vial upon the sun; and power was given to him to scorch men with fire.

9 And men were scorched with great heat, and blasphemed the name of God, which has power over these plagues: and they repented not to give him glory.

10 And the fifth angel poured out his vial upon the seat of the beast; and his kingdom was full of darkness; and they gnawed their tongues for pain,

11 And blasphemed the God of heaven because of their pains and their sores, and repented not of their deeds.

12 And the sixth angel poured out his vial upon the great river Euphrates; and the water thereof was dried up, that the way of the kings of the east might be prepared.

13 And I saw three unclean spirits like frogs come out of the mouth of the dragon, and out of the mouth of the beast, and out of the mouth of the false prophet.

14 For they are the spirits of devils, working miracles, which go forth to the kings of the earth and of the whole world, to gather them to the battle of that great day of God Almighty.

15 Behold, I come as a thief. Blessed is he that watches, and keeps his garments, lest he walk naked, and they see his shame.

16 And he gathered them together into a place called in the Hebrew tongue Armageddon.

17 And the seventh angel poured out his vial into the air; and there came a great voice out of the temple of heaven, from

---

16:15 Second coming of Jesus: See Revelation 22:20.

16:16 Ezekiel 39, written over 2,500 years ago, speaks of God's judgment upon the enemies of Israel. Verses 12–15 describe what will happen after what many see as the Battle of Armageddon:

> And seven months shall the house of Israel be burying of them, that they may cleanse the land...And they shall sever out men of continual employment, passing through the land to bury with the passengers those that remain upon the face of the earth, to cleanse it: after the end of seven months shall they search. And the passengers that pass through the land, when any sees a man's bone, then shall he set up a sign by it, till the buriers have buried it in the valley of Hamongog.

Before the days of nuclear warfare, this portion of the Bible would have made no sense to the reader. We are told that even the weapons left by the enemy will have to be burned (Ezekiel 39:9). So many will die that it will take those specially employed for the purpose seven months to bury the dead (v. 14). The Scriptures are very specific about the method of burial. When even a bone is found by searchers, a special marker is to be placed near the bone until the buriers have buried it. This would seem to be a clear reference to radioactive contamination after nuclear war. This thought is confirmed in Joel 2:30, which speaks of "pillars of smoke."

Did the Church persecute Galileo?
See 1 Timothy 6:20 comment.

Galileo

the throne, saying, It is done.

18 And there were voices, and thunders, and lightnings; and there was a great earthquake, such as was not since men were upon the earth, so mighty an earthquake, and so great.

19 And the great city was divided into three parts, and the cities of the nations fell: and great Babylon came in remembrance before God, to give to her the cup of the wine of the fierceness of his wrath.

20 And every island fled away, and the mountains were not found.

21 And there fell upon men a great hail out of heaven, every stone about the weight of a talent: and men blasphemed God because of the plague of the hail; for the plague thereof was exceeding great.

CHAPTER 17

AND there came one of the seven angels which had the seven vials, and talked with me, saying to me, Come here; I will show to you the judgment of the great whore that sits upon many waters:

2 With whom the kings of the earth have committed fornication, and the inhabitants of the earth have been made drunk with the wine of her fornication.

3 So he carried me away in the spirit into the wilderness: and I saw a woman sit upon a scarlet colored beast, full of names of blasphemy, having seven heads and ten horns.

4 And the woman was arrayed in purple and scarlet color, and decked with gold and precious stones and pearls, having a golden cup in her hand full of abominations and filthiness of her fornication:

5 And upon her forehead was a name written, MYSTERY, BABYLON THE GREAT, THE MOTHER OF HARLOTS AND ABOMINATIONS OF THE EARTH.

6 And I saw the woman drunken with the blood of the saints, and with the blood of the martyrs of Jesus: and when I saw her, I wondered with great admiration.

7 And the angel said to me, Wherefore did you marvel? I will tell you the mystery of the woman, and of the beast that carries her, which has the seven heads and ten horns.

8 The beast that you saw was, and is not; and shall ascend out of the bottomless pit, and go into perdition: and they that dwell on the earth shall wonder, whose names were not written in the book of life from the foundation of the world, when they behold the beast that was, and is not, and yet is.

9 And here is the mind which has wisdom. The seven heads are seven mountains, on which the woman sits.

10 And there are seven kings: five are fallen, and one is, and the other is not yet come; and when he comes, he must continue a short space.

11 And the beast that was, and is not, even he is the eighth, and is of the seven, and goes into perdition.

12 And the ten horns which you saw are ten kings, which have received no kingdom as yet; but receive power as kings one hour with the beast.

13 These have one mind, and shall give their power and strength to the beast.

14 These shall make war with the Lamb, and the Lamb shall overcome them: for

he is Lord of lords, and King of kings: and they that are with him are called, and chosen, and faithful.

15 And he said to me, The waters which you saw, where the whore sits, are peoples, and multitudes, and nations, and tongues.

16 And the ten horns which you saw upon the beast, these shall hate the whore, and shall make her desolate and naked, and shall eat her flesh, and burn her with fire.

17 For God has put in their hearts to fulfil his will, and to agree, and give their kingdom to the beast, until the words of God shall be fulfilled.

18 And the woman which you saw is that great city, which reigns over the kings of the earth.

CHAPTER 18

AND after these things I saw another angel come down from heaven, having great power; and the earth was lightened with his glory.

2 And he cried mightily with a strong voice, saying, Babylon the great is fallen, is fallen, and is become the habitation of devils, and the hold of every foul spirit, and a cage of every unclean and hateful bird.

3 For all nations have drunk of the wine of the wrath of her fornication, and the kings of the earth have committed fornication with her, and the merchants of the earth are waxed rich through the abundance of her delicacies.

4 And I heard another voice from heaven, saying, Come out of her, my people, that you be not partakers of her sins, and that you receive not of her plagues.

5 For her sins have reached to heaven, and God has remembered her iniquities.

6 Reward her even as she rewarded you, and double to her double according to her works: in the cup which she has filled fill to her double.

7 How much she has glorified herself, and lived deliciously, so much torment and sorrow give her: for she said in her heart, I sit a queen, and am no widow, and shall see no sorrow.

8 Therefore shall her plagues come in one day, death, and mourning, and famine; and she shall be utterly burned with fire: for strong is the Lord God who judges her.

9 And the kings of the earth, who have committed fornication and lived deliciously with her, shall bewail her, and lament for her, when they shall see the smoke of her burning,

10 Standing afar off for the fear of her torment, saying, Alas, alas, that great city Babylon, that mighty city! for in one hour is your judgment come.

11 And the merchants of the earth shall weep and mourn over her; for no man buys their merchandise any more:

12 The merchandise of gold, and silver, and precious stones, and of pearls, and fine linen, and purple, and silk, and scarlet, and all thyine wood, and all manner vessels of ivory, and all manner vessels of most precious wood, and of brass, and iron, and marble,

13 And cinnamon, and odors, and ointments, and frankincense, and wine, and oil, and fine flour, and wheat, and beasts, and sheep, and horses, and chariots, and slaves, and souls of men.

14 And the fruits that your soul lusted after are departed from you, and all things which were dainty and goodly are departed from you, and you shall find them no more at all.

15 The merchants of these things, which were made rich by her, shall stand afar off for the fear of her torment, weeping and wailing,

16 And saying, Alas, alas, that great city, that was clothed in fine linen, and purple, and scarlet, and decked with gold, and precious stones, and pearls!

17 For in one hour so great riches is come to nothing. And every shipmaster, and all the company in ships, and sailors, and as many as trade by sea, stood afar off,

18 And cried when they saw the smoke of her burning, saying, What city is like to this great city!

19 And they cast dust on their heads,

The Resurrection:
Does Circumstantial Evidence Confirm It?

Timothy McVeigh, the man behind the Oklahoma City bombing, had a date with death. On June 11, 2001, he received a lethal injection for killing 168 innocent people, even though no one saw him commit this heinous crime. All the evidence against McVeigh was circumstantial.

Indirect testimony: That's what circumstantial evidence is. It's an accumulation of facts from which one can draw intelligent conclusions.

As a newspaper reporter covering the courts, former journalist Lee Strobel saw how circumstantial evidence is used to expose what really happened during a crime. So, in the midst of a spiritual quest, Strobel began to wonder: Could circumstantial evidence verify that the resurrection of Christ really happened?

Well, he took his question to philosopher J. P. Moreland. In a challenging voice, Strobel asked Moreland: "Can you give me five pieces of solid circumstantial evidence that convince you Jesus rose from the dead?"

Certainly, Moreland responded. **First**, there's the evidence of the skeptics. Some of those who were most hostile to Jesus prior to His death became His most ardent supporters afterwards.

Second, the ancient Jews had a number of immensely important religious rituals. These included the offering of animal sacrifices, obeying the Mosaic law, and keeping the Sabbath. But within five weeks of Jesus' death, more than 10,000 Jews had suddenly altered or abandoned these rituals. Moreland asked: Why would they relinquish rites that had long given them their national identity? The implication is that something enormously significant had occurred.

Third, we see the emergence of new rituals: the sacraments of Communion and Baptism. The early Jews baptized in the name of the Father, the Son, and the Holy Spirit, "which," Moreland said, "meant they had elevated Jesus to the full status of God."

Fourth, we see the rapid rise of a new Church, beginning shortly after the death of Jesus. Within twenty years this new Church (begun by the companions of a dead carpenter) had reached Caesar's palace in Rome, and eventually spread throughout the Roman empire.

And **fifth**, Moreland said, there's the most convincing circumstantial evidence of all: the fact that every one of Jesus' disciples was willing to suffer and die for his beliefs. These men spent the rest of their lives witnessing about Christ. They frequently went without food; they were mocked, beaten, and thrown into prison. In the end, all but one died a painful martyr's death.

Would they have done this for a lie? Of course not. They did it because they were convinced beyond a doubt that they had seen the risen Christ.

Even if we doubted 2,000-year-old evidence, we have all the circumstantial evidence we could possibly want—right in front of us. It is, Moreland said, "the ongoing encounter with the resurrected Christ that happens all over the world, in every culture, to people from all kinds of backgrounds and personalities. They all will testify that more than any single thing in their lives, Jesus Christ has changed them."

Circumstantial evidence earned Timothy McVeigh a death sentence. But sacred circumstantial evidence about the resurrection of Jesus Christ can lead all of us, including McVeigh, to a much better verdict: everlasting life in the presence of God.

From "BreakPoint with Charles Colson," April 19, 2001, reprinted with permission of Prison Fellowship, PO Box 17500, Washington, DC 20041-7500, www.pfm.org. (Edited to indicate McVeigh's June 2001 execution. CNN)

and cried, weeping and wailing, saying, Alas, alas, that great city, wherein were made rich all that had ships in the sea by reason of her costliness! for in one hour is she made desolate.

20 Rejoice over her, you heaven, and you holy apostles and prophets; for God has avenged you on her.

21 And a mighty angel took up a stone like a great millstone, and cast it into the sea, saying, Thus with violence shall that great city Babylon be thrown down, and shall be found no more at all.

22 And the voice of harpers, and musicians, and of pipers, and trumpeters, shall be heard no more at all in you; and no craftsman, of whatsoever craft he be, shall be found any more in you; and the sound of a millstone shall be heard no more at all in you;

23 And the light of a candle shall shine no more at all in you; and the voice of the bridegroom and of the bride shall be heard no more at all in you: for your merchants were the great men of the earth; for by your sorceries were all nations deceived.

24 And in her was found the blood of prophets, and of saints, and of all that were slain upon the earth.

CHAPTER 19

AND after these things I heard a great voice of much people in heaven, saying, Alleluia; Salvation, and glory, and honor, and power, to the Lord our God:

2 For true and righteous are his judgments: for he has judged the great whore, which did corrupt the earth with her fornication, and has avenged the blood of his servants at her hand.

3 And again they said, Alleluia. And her smoke rose up for ever and ever.

4 And the four and twenty elders and the four beasts fell down and worshipped God that sat on the throne, saying, Amen; Alleluia.

5 And a voice came out of the throne, saying, Praise our God, all you his servants, and you that fear him, both small and great.

6 And I heard as it were the voice of a great multitude, and as the voice of many waters, and as the voice of mighty thunderings, saying, Alleluia: for the Lord God omnipotent reigns.

7 Let us be glad and rejoice, and give honor to him: for the marriage of the Lamb is come, and his wife has made herself ready.

8 And to her was granted that she should be arrayed in fine linen, clean and white: for the fine linen is the righteousness of saints.

9 And he said to me, Write, Blessed are they which are called to the marriage supper of the Lamb. And he said to me, These are the true sayings of God.

10 And I fell at his feet to worship him. And he said to me, See you do it not: I am your fellow-servant, and of your brethren that have the testimony of Jesus: worship God: for the testimony of Jesus is the spirit of prophecy.

11 And I saw heaven opened, and behold a white horse; and he that sat upon him was called Faithful and True, and in righteousness he does judge and make war.

12 His eyes were as a flame of fire, and on his head were many crowns; and he had a name written, that no man knew, but he himself.

13 And he was clothed with a vesture dipped in blood: and his name is called The Word of God.

14 And the armies which were in heaven followed him upon white horses, clothed in fine linen, white and clean.

15 And out of his mouth goes a sharp sword, that with it he should smite the nations: and he shall rule them with a rod of iron: and he treads the winepress of the fierceness and wrath of Almighty God.

16 And he has on his vesture and on his thigh a name written, KING OF KINGS, AND LORD OF LORDS.

17 And I saw an angel standing in the sun; and he cried with a loud voice, saying to all the fowls that fly in the midst

of heaven, Come and gather yourselves together to the supper of the great God;

18 That you may eat the flesh of kings, and the flesh of captains, and the flesh of mighty men, and the flesh of horses, and of them that sit on them, and the flesh of all men, both free and bond, both small and great.

19 And I saw the beast, and the kings of the earth, and their armies, gathered together to make war against him that sat on the horse, and against his army.

20 And the beast was taken, and with him the false prophet that wrought miracles before him, with which he deceived them that had received the mark of the beast, and them that worshipped his image. These both were cast alive into a lake of fire burning with brimstone.

21 And the remnant were slain with the sword of him that sat upon the horse, which sword proceeded out of his mouth: and all the fowls were filled with their flesh.

CHAPTER 20

AND I saw an angel come down from heaven, having the key of the bottomless pit and a great chain in his hand.

2 And he laid hold on the dragon, that old serpent, which is the Devil, and Satan, and bound him a thousand years,

3 And cast him into the bottomless pit, and shut him up, and set a seal upon him, that he should deceive the nations no more, till the thousand years should be fulfilled: and after that he must be loosed a little season.

4 And I saw thrones, and they sat upon them, and judgment was given to them: and I saw the souls of them that were beheaded for the witness of Jesus, and for the word of God, and which had not worshipped the beast, neither his image, neither had received his mark upon their foreheads, or in their hands; and they lived and reigned with Christ a thousand years.

5 But the rest of the dead lived not again until the thousand years were finished. This is the first resurrection.

6 Blessed and holy is he that has part in the first resurrection: on such the second death has no power, but they shall be priests of God and of Christ, and shall reign with him a thousand years.

7 And when the thousand years are expired, Satan shall be loosed out of his prison,

8 And shall go out to deceive the nations which are in the four quarters of the earth, Gog and Magog, to gather them together to battle: the number of whom is as the sand of the sea.

9 And they went up on the breadth of the earth, and compassed the camp of the saints about, and the beloved city: and fire came down from God out of heaven, and devoured them.

10 And the devil that deceived them was cast into the lake of fire and brimstone, where the beast and the false prophet are, and shall be tormented day and night for ever and ever.

11 And I saw a great white throne, and him that sat on it, from whose face the

---

20:11 No hiding from God. "Whither can the enemies of God flee? If up to heaven their high-flown impudence could carry them, His right hand of holiness would hurl them thence, or, if under hell's profoundest wave they dive, to seek a sheltering grave, His left hand would pluck them out of the fire, to expose them to the fiercer light of His countenance. Nowhere is there a refuge from the Most High. The morning beams cannot convey the fugitive so swiftly as the almighty Pursuer would follow him; neither can the mysterious lightning flash, which annihilates time and space, journey so rapidly as to escape His far-reaching hand. 'If I mount up to heaven, thou art there; if I make my bed in hell, thou art there.'

"It was said of the Roman Empire under the Caesars that the whole world was only one great prison for Caesar, for if any man offended the emperor it was impossible for him to escape. If he crossed the Alps, could not Caesar find him out in Gaul? If he sought to hide himself in the Indies,

QUESTIONS & OBJECTIONS

21:4 *"How can people be happy in heaven, knowing that their unsaved loved ones are suffering in hell?"*

Those who ask such questions fall into the category of those who asked Jesus a similar question. The Sadducees said that a certain woman had seven consecutive husbands, so whose wife will she be in heaven (Mark 12:23)? Jesus answered by saying that they neither knew the Scriptures nor the power of God. The unregenerate mind has no concept of God's mind or His infinite power. If God can speak the sun into existence; if He can see every thought of every human heart at the same time; if He can create the human eye with its 137,000,000 light-sensitive cells, then He can handle the minor details of our eternal salvation.

John writes that in heaven "we shall be like him; for we shall see him as he is" (1 John 3:2), so perhaps we will be fully satisfied that God is perfectly just and merciful, and that He gave every individual the opportunity to accept or reject Him. However He works it out, God promises that there will not be sorrow or crying in heaven. Our focus in heaven won't be on our loss, but on our gain.

earth and the heaven fled away; and there was found no place for them.

12 And I saw the dead, small and great, stand before God; and the books were opened: and another book was opened, which is the book of life: and the dead were judged out of those things which were written in the books, according to their works.

13 And the sea gave up the dead which were in it; and death and hell delivered up the dead which were in them: and they were judged every man according to their works.

14 And death and hell were cast into the lake of fire. This is the second death.

15 And whosoever was not found written in the book of life was cast into the lake of fire.

CHAPTER 21

AND I saw a new heaven and a new earth: for the first heaven and the first earth were passed away; and there was no more sea.

2 And I John saw the holy city, new Jerusalem, coming down from God out of heaven, prepared as a bride adorned for her husband.

3 And I heard a great voice out of heaven saying, Behold, the tabernacle of God is with men, and he will dwell with them, and they shall be his people, and God himself shall be with them, and be their God.

4 And God shall wipe away all tears

even the swarthy monarchs there knew the power of the Roman arms, so that they would give no shelter to a man who had incurred imperial vengeance. And yet, perhaps, a fugitive from Rome might have prolonged his miserable life by hiding in the dens and caves of the earth.

"But oh! sinner, there is no hiding from God. The mountains cannot cover you from Him, even if they would, neither can the rocks conceal you. See, then, at the very outset how this throne should awe our minds with terror. Founded in right, sustained by might, and universal in its dominion, look ye and see the throne which John of old beheld." *Charles Spurgeon*

20:15 Hell: It should be grievous for any Christian to make light of or joke about hell. This verse should break our hearts, drive us to weep for the unsaved, and then motivate us to put legs to our prayers and plead with sinners to turn to the Savior. For verses warning of its reality, see Revelation 21:8.

from their eyes; and there shall be no more death, neither sorrow, nor crying, neither shall there be any more pain: for the former things are passed away.

5 And he that sat upon the throne said, Behold, I make all things new. And he said to me, Write: for these words are true and faithful.

6 And he said to me, It is done. I am Alpha and Omega, the beginning and the end. I will give to him that is athirst of the fountain of the water of life freely.

7 He that overcomes shall inherit all things; and I will be his God, and he shall be my son.

8 But the fearful, and unbelieving, and the abominable, and murderers, and whoremongers, and sorcerers, and idolaters, and all liars, shall have their part in the lake which burns with fire and brimstone: which is the second death.

> Young men and old men, and sisters of all ages, if you love the Lord, get a passion for souls. Do you not see them? They are going down to hell by the thousands.
>
> **CHARLES SPURGEON**

9 And there came to me one of the seven angels which had the seven vials full of the seven last plagues, and talked with me, saying, Come here, I will show you the bride, the Lamb's wife.

10 And he carried me away in the spirit to a great and high mountain, and showed me that great city, the holy Jerusalem, descending out of heaven from God,

11 Having the glory of God: and her light was like to a stone most precious, even like a jasper stone, clear as crystal;

12 And had a wall great and high, and had twelve gates, and at the gates twelve angels, and names written thereon, which are the names of the twelve tribes of the children of Israel:

13 On the east three gates; on the north three gates; on the south three gates; and on the west three gates.

14 And the wall of the city had twelve foundations, and in them the names of the twelve apostles of the Lamb.

15 And he that talked with me had a golden reed to measure the city, and the gates thereof, and the wall thereof.

16 And the city lies foursquare, and the length is as large as the breadth: and he measured the city with the reed, twelve thousand furlongs. The length and the breadth and the height of it are equal.

17 And he measured the wall thereof, an hundred and forty and four cubits, according to the measure of a man, that is, of the angel.

18 And the building of the wall of it was of jasper: and the city was pure gold, like to clear glass.

19 And the foundations of the wall of the city were garnished with all manner of precious stones. The first foundation was jasper; the second, sapphire; the third, a chalcedony; the fourth, an emerald;

20 The fifth, sardonyx; the sixth, sardius; the seventh, chrysolite; the eighth, beryl; the ninth, a topaz; the tenth, a chrysoprasus; the eleventh, a jacinth; the twelfth, an amethyst.

21 And the twelve gates were twelve pearls; every several gate was of one pearl: and the street of the city was pure gold, as it were transparent glass.

22 And I saw no temple therein: for the Lord God Almighty and the Lamb are the temple of it.

21:8 Hell: For verses warning of its reality, see Matthew 5:22.

God isn't willing that any perish. "Behold, the LORD's hand is not shortened, that it cannot save; neither his ear heavy, that it cannot hear: but your iniquities have separated between you and your God, and your sins have hid his face from you, that he will not hear" (Isaiah 59:1,2). See Hebrews 9:22 comment.

23 And the city had no need of the sun, neither of the moon, to shine in it: for the glory of God did lighten it, and the Lamb is the light thereof.

24 And the nations of them which are saved shall walk in the light of it: and the kings of the earth do bring their glory and honor into it.

25 And the gates of it shall not be shut at all by day: for there shall be no night there.

26 And they shall bring the glory and honor of the nations into it.

27 **And there shall in no wise enter into it any thing that defiles, neither whatsoever works abomination, or makes a lie: but they which are written in the Lamb's book of life.**

CHAPTER 22

AND he showed me a pure river of water of life, clear as crystal, proceeding out of the throne of God and of the Lamb.

2 In the midst of the street of it, and on either side of the river, was there the tree of life, which bare twelve manner of fruits, and yielded her fruit every month: and the leaves of the tree were for the healing of the nations.

3 And there shall be no more curse: but the throne of God and of the Lamb shall be in it; and his servants shall serve him:

4 And they shall see his face; and his name shall be in their foreheads.

5 And there shall be no night there; and they need no candle, neither light of the sun; for the Lord God gives them light: and they shall reign for ever and ever.

6 And he said to me, These sayings are faithful and true: and the Lord God of the holy prophets sent his angel to show to his servants the things which must shortly be done.

7 Behold, I come quickly: blessed is he that keeps the sayings of the prophecy of this book.

8 And I John saw these things, and heard them. And when I had heard and seen, I fell down to worship before the feet of the angel which showed me these things.

9 Then said he to me, See you do it not:

22:2   Charles Spurgeon on Tracts:

"I well remember distributing them in a town in England where tracts had never been distributed before, and going from house to house, and telling in humble language the things of the kingdom of God. I might have done nothing, if I had not been encouraged by finding myself able to do something…[Tracts are] adapted to those persons who have but little power and little ability, but nevertheless, wish to do something for Christ. They have not the tongue of the eloquent, but they may have the hand of the diligent. They cannot stand and preach, but they can stand and distribute here and there these silent preachers…They may buy their thousand tracts, and these they can distribute broadcast.

"I look upon the giving away of a religious tract as only the first step for action not to be compared with many another deed done for Christ; but were it not for the first step we might never reach to the second, but that first attained, we are encouraged to take another, and so at the last…There is a real service of Christ in the distribution of the gospel in its printed form, a service the result of which heaven alone shall disclose, and the judgment day alone discover. How many thousands have been carried to heaven instrumentally upon the wings of these tracts, none can tell.

"I might say, if it were right to quote such a Scripture, 'The leaves were for the healing of the nations'—verily they are so. Scattered where the whole tree could scarcely be carried, the very leaves have had a medicinal and a healing virtue in them and the real word of truth, the simple statement of a Savior crucified and of a sinner who shall be saved by simply trusting in the Savior, has been greatly blessed, and many thousand souls have been led into the kingdom of heaven by this simple means. *Let each one of us, if we have done nothing for Christ, begin to do something now. The distribution of tracts is the first thing.*"

See also Mark 4:14 and 1 Corinthians 9:22 comments.

for I am your fellow-servant, and of your brethren the prophets, and of them which keep the sayings of this book: worship God.

10 And he said to me, Seal not the sayings of the prophecy of this book: for the time is at hand.

11 He that is unjust, let him be unjust still: and he which is filthy, let him be filthy still: and he that is righteous, let him be righteous still: and he that is holy, let him be holy still.

12 And, behold, I come quickly; and my reward is with me, to give every man according as his work shall be.

13 I am Alpha and Omega, the beginning and the end, the first and the last.

14 Blessed are they that do his commandments, that they may have right to the tree of life, and may enter in through the gates into the city.

15 **For without are dogs, and sorcerers, and whoremongers, and murderers, and idolaters, and whosoever loves and makes a lie.**

16 I Jesus have sent mine angel to testify to you these things in the churches. I am the root and the offspring of David, and the bright and morning star.

17 **And the Spirit and the bride say, Come. And let him that hears say, Come. And let him that is athirst come. And whosoever will, let him take the water of life freely.**

18 For I testify to every man that hears the words of the prophecy of this book, If any man shall add to these things, God shall add to him the plagues that are written in this book:

19 And if any man shall take away from the words of the book of this prophecy, God shall take away his part out of the book of life, and out of the holy city, and from the things which are written in this book.

20 He which testifies these things says, Surely I come quickly. Amen. Even so, come, Lord Jesus.

21 The grace of our Lord Jesus Christ be with you all. Amen.

22:3 A magnificent doe stands with its foal and drinks in the cool water from a mountain stream. The sun sparkles off the dew on deep green leaves of native tree branches. The mother gently caresses her offspring as it begins to also drink from the brook. The scene is one of incredible serenity...the picture of innocence. What more could optimize the beauty of God's creation?

Suddenly a mountain lion leaps from a tree and digs its sharp claws deeply into the mother's neck, dragging the helpless creature to the ground. As it holds its terrified prey in a death grip, its powerful jaws bite into the jugular vein, turning the mountain stream crimson with the creature's blood.

It is a strong consolation to know that this isn't the way God planned it in the beginning. Animals were not created to devour each other; they were created to be vegetarian (Genesis 1:29,30). The original creation was "good" and was not filled with violence and bloodshed. We live in a *fallen* creation (Romans 8:20–23). As a result of Adam's sin, the perfect creation was cursed and death was introduced into the world (Romans 5:12). The day will come when the entire creation will be delivered from the "bondage of corruption" and there will be no more curse. In the new heaven and new earth, "the wolf and the lamb shall feed together, and the lion shall eat straw like the bullock...They shall not hurt nor destroy in all my holy mountain" (Isaiah 65:25). See also Isaiah 11:6–9.

Closing Words of Comfort

RARELY DO I become involved in counseling; I leave that to the expertise of the local pastor. However, I was awakened one morning by my wife, Sue. She said, "There is someone in the living room and he desperately wants to talk to you." I protested, "But it's not even 7 A.M.... and I don't do counseling!"

Nevertheless, I made my way into the living room and found a man whose eyes flashed with despair. I had met him a few months earlier when he purchased a series of our tapes, but this day he looked like a different man. It turned out that his whole life seemed to be falling to pieces. There were terrible problems at work, at home, and even in his church. Everything had suddenly gone wrong. I looked him in the eye and asked, "You didn't pray that God would 'break' you, did you?" He looked back at me and said, "I asked God to break me and grind me to powder..."

Make sure you realize what you are saying at church when you sing words like "Refiner's fire, my heart's one desire, is to be holy." I hum the song. Let me tell you why.

We may think that we are asking God for the "warm fuzzies," but the refining fire is what Job went through, and God may just give you your heart's one desire if you keep asking Him. After the service, you find that someone has just crashed into your new car. That week you discover that God has let the devil get at you and your house has burned to the ground, your spouse and children have been killed, and someone forgot to pay the insurance premium.

The loss of your family, car, and home and financial collapse give you a complete nervous breakdown. Well, rejoice —because you are getting your heart's one desire. Read the Book of Job. I've been through the Refiner's fire and I never want to go through it again. My prayer is, "If it is possible, let this cup pass from me." Jesus had to suffer; there was no alternative for Him. But there is an alternative for us. If we chasten ourselves, perhaps we will not be chastened by God. Instead of praying that God will break me, I say, "Please, Lord, be gentle on your servant. 'Neither chasten me in your hot displeasure' [Psalm 38:1]. Help me to see the areas that I need to change."

If we discipline ourselves to pray and read the Word, we may avoid the Refiner's fire. If we draw close to Him, we won't need a lion's den to bring us to our knees. If we scatter abroad, preaching the Word everywhere, we may not need a Saul of Tarsus to breathe out slaughter against us. If we cut off unfruitful branches, we won't feel the pain of the Husbandman's sharp pruning sheers. Read the last chapters of Job and learn the lesson, so that you won't have to go through the earlier chapters. Scripture was written for our instruction. Lay your hand on your mouth and quickly bow to the sovereignty of God.

THE FIERY TRIAL

Let me share something very personal. In June 1985, I had just finished preaching in a small country church when a lean-looking young man approached me and said, "I wish I was like you." I managed a smile, but held onto the words that came to mind. *You don't know what you are saying.* Little did he know that at that moment I was going through sheer terror. I had been praying earlier that day when suddenly it seemed that all hell was let loose in my mind. It was as though God had removed every hedge of protection from me and a thousand spirits of terror invaded my thoughts. I fell upon the floor. I wept. I cried out to God. I exorcised myself, to no avail. There is no way I can describe the experience of the following months other than to say that it was like being held over a black pit of insanity by a spider's web.

When I arrived home from that series of meetings, Sue asked how they went. I said, "The meetings were fine," then broke down. I felt so crushed within my mind that I was unable to have family devotions, or even eat a meal at the table with my family for over twelve months.

I diagnosed myself as having a "wounded spirit." Before God could use me, I needed to have a broken spirit:

> But this is the man to whom I will look and have regard: he who is humble and of a broken or wounded spirit, and who trembles at My word and reveres My commands (Isaiah 66:2, *Amplified Bible*).

It was A. W. Tozer who said, "Before God uses a man, God will break the man."

It took years to overcome that experience. At one point, I couldn't even gather enough courage to go to my home church. I wanted to, but irrational fear was paralyzing me. The first Sunday after the initial experience, I was in my bedroom trying to gather strength to go with my family to church. The fear was so strong, I would actually lose my breath even while I lay in bed. My son, who was seven at the time, came into the bedroom and handed me a note. He had written out a few Scriptures he thought I should read, although he had no idea what I was going through. These were the verses:

> The Lord is my helper, and I will not fear what man shall do to me (Hebrews 13:6).

> But the path of the just is as the shining light, that shines more and more unto the perfect day (Proverbs 4:18).

> Greater is he that is in you, than he that is in the world (1 John 4:4).

Then he had written the words, "I love you, Dad!"

HOW TO SPEED UP THE PROCESS

If there is a cry in your heart to be used by God, then you may go through a similar experience. I don't want to unnecessarily alarm you, but if you understand why it is happening and what you can do to speed up the process, it will help. If God in His great wisdom sees fit to use the Refiner's fire (if He takes you through a fiery trial), then it is only "if need be" (1 Peter 1:6). Pray that you may avoid it, but this is often normal procedure in being prepared for ministry. A wild horse is no good to a rider. It can't be trusted. It needs its spirit broken so that it will willingly yield to the desire of the rider. So, let me share with you a few words of comfort, so that if you find yourself hanging over a dark chasm of insanity by the spider web of faith, you will know why, and realize that the web is unbreakable.

You are asleep in bed, when suddenly a creak of the floor causes you to open your eyes in the semi-dark room. Towering over you stands the ugly sight of a huge man, wearing a stocking over his face, with a gun pointed at your head.

Suddenly, your heart races with fear. Your mouth becomes dry. Terror paralyzes you. You can see his evil lips smile in delight at having another human being under his power. Time stands still. Your racing heart is taking too much blood into your brain, feeding it an oversupply of oxygen, making your mind go blank. This inability to respond, even mentally, brings a panic that causes your breathing to become erratic. The over-action of the heart has also speedily lifted your body temperature to a point where cold sweat is forming on your brow, back, and legs.

With malicious intent, the intruder slowly moves the gun to the temple of your moistened brow. You can feel its cold barrel against your warm skin. The reality of what is happening tells you that this is no mere nightmare.

Adrenaline is being pumped throughout your body. Your mind is instinctively screaming *Run!* and yet you know that if you move, you are dead. With both hands on the gun, the cruel intruder slowly cocks the weapon. You see his white teeth grit in perverted delight. *You are going to die!* Unspeakable terror grips your mind. Perspiration pours out of your flesh. Your mouth is totally dry. It's as though your heart is pounding through your chest. Your breath seems to have drained from your lungs and you can feel your eyes bulge with overwhelming dread...

That's what an attack of irrational fear feels like. There is no intruder, no gun, and no threat of death. Yet there are those same, very real, worse-than-nightmarish symptoms.

According to estimates, three million people in the U.S. have panic attacks. These are characterized by rapid heartbeat, dizziness, shortness of breath, and fear of losing control, going crazy, or dying.

The unsaved who experience panic attacks are often driven to drugs, alcohol, despair, or insanity. The Christian who suffers doesn't do so in vain, but there is a sense of guilt on top of the fear. The experience doesn't seem to match the Bible's description of a faith-filled Christian. He says, "I *will not* fear"...*and yet he still fears*. His will is incapacitated.

For those who have prayed, and prayed, and prayed for deliverance, and still find themselves in such a predicament, there are strong consolations.

The apostle Paul was no stranger to fear. He said, "For, when we were come into Macedonia, our flesh had no rest, but we were troubled on every side; without were fightings, *within were fears*" (2 Corinthians 7:5, emphasis added).

Look at these verses from 2 Corinthians 12:7–9:

> And lest I should be exalted above measure through the abundance of the revelations, there was given to me a thorn in the flesh, the messenger of Satan to buffet me, lest I should be exalted above measure. For this thing I besought the Lord thrice, that it might depart from me. And he said to me, My grace is sufficient for you: for my strength is made perfect in weakness. Most gladly therefore will I rather glory in my infirmities, that the power of Christ may rest upon me.

Paul asked for deliverance from this demonic attack three times. Yet God chose to leave him with it. Some say it was a sickness, but that doesn't seem to be what the Bible teaches. It says it was a "messenger of Satan" (a demon) that buffeted him.

Why then did God allow demonic oppression to come against His apostle? He wanted to use Paul, but He didn't want him to fall through pride and fail in his calling. The demonic oppression was to keep him humble as God gave him an abundance of revelations. He had to remain small in his own eyes. The Greek word for "buffet" is *kolaphizo*, which means to "rap with the fist." Its root word is *kolos*, which means "dwarf."

Satan fires arrows only at those who have potential for the kingdom of God. You have great potential to be used by God in these last days. Instead of saying, "But God can't use me when I am paralyzed by fear," say, "Because His strength is made perfect in my weakness, God can use me for His glory *because the fear I am plagued by actually keeps me in weakness.*"

EXAMINE YOURSELF

Today, there are many who name the name of Christ, but who never "depart from iniquity." They are false converts who "ask Jesus into their heart," but are actually unconverted because they have never truly repented. So it is important that you examine yourself to see if you are in the faith (2 Corinthians 13:5). Those who allow sin in their lives are actually opening themselves up to demonic influence. The Bible instructs us to "neither give place to the devil" (Ephesians 4:27).

Afflictions only work together for our good, if we are "called according to [God's] purpose" (Romans 8:28). Therefore, the following are questions each of us need to ask ourselves:

Do I honor my parents? Do I value them implicitly? God commands that we honor our parents, then Scripture warns, "that it may be well with you, and you may live long on the earth" (Ephesians 6:3). In other words, if you don't value your parents, all will not be well with you. I have found that many people have demonic problems because they *hate* their parents.

Is there any unconfessed sin in my life? Is there any bitterness, resentment, or jealousy? Have I been hurt by someone in the past whom I can't find it within my heart to forgive? Then I am giving place to the devil. If I won't forgive and forget, I'm like a man who is stung to death by one bee. You could understand someone being stung to death by a *swarm* of bees, but we can do something about one bee. The sad thing about someone who becomes bitter is that all they need to do to deal with their problem is to swat the thing through repentance. God says He will not forgive us if we will not forgive from our heart (Matthew 6:15).

Has there been any occult activity in my life in the past? Do I have idols (even as souvenirs) in my home? Is there any pornography? I need to prayerfully walk around in the house and ask God if there is anything that is unpleasing to Him. Then I must consider the same thing within the temple of my own body. Am I a glutton? Do I feed filth into my mind through my eyes or through my ears? Do my hands touch only what is pleasing in His sight? Are my words kind and loving? Are the meditations of my mind pleasing to God?

The only way to know if you are a Christian is by your fruit. There are a number of fruits in Scripture: the fruit of praise, the fruit of thanksgiving, the fruit of holiness, the fruit of repentance, the fruit of righteousness, and the fruit of the Spirit— love, joy, peace, patience, goodness, gentleness, faith, meekness, and temperance.

A key to overcoming trials is to understand that they are *relative*. The next time Satan tries to make you feel sorry for yourself in the midst of a trial, ask yourself, "Would I like to trade places with someone who has a horrible terminal disease? Would I like to trade places with a burn victim who has been burned over 90% of his body?" We can't imagine the agonies those in such a predicament go through. Have you ever burned yourself on a toaster? Think what it must be like for those poor people. Such sober thoughts bring our problem into perspective, and should make us want to thank God for His many blessings. Not only for what we have, but also for those things we don't have—like unspeakable pain.

The fruit of thanksgiving should be evident in the Christian, not only for temporal blessings, but for the cross. Paul was persecuted beyond measure, merely for his faith in God, yet he said, "Thanks be to God for his unspeakable gift" (2 Corinthians 9:15).

As Christians, we should have the fruit of holiness. We should be separated from this world, with all of its corruption, to God. We should have evidence of our repentance. If we have stolen, we will return what isn't ours. We will set right (where possible) that which we have wronged. Lastly, we will possess the fruit of the Spirit. If we are rooted and grounded in Him, we will have the fruits of His character hanging from the branches of our lives. Do we have love that cares for others? Do we care enough about the salvation of sinners to put feet to our prayers and take the gospel to them? Love is not passive. It will not be self-indulgent while others suffer. It is empathetic.

GOOD REASON

If we haven't given place to the devil, what is he doing in our lives? There must be good reason for him to be there. The only reasonable conclusion is that God has given permission. This happened in the Book of Job. God allowed Satan to buffet Job so that he would grow in his faith in God. As I have said before, God has given us the Book of Job for our admonition and instruction.

Study the following verse from the *Amplified Bible*:

It is God who is all the while effectually at work in you [energizing and creating in you the power and desire], both to will and to work for His good pleasure and satisfaction and delight (Philippians 2:13).

We have established that God is at work in you. You have this demonic "buffeting" from which God will not presently deliver you because He is doing a good work in you. Therefore, what should be your attitude to this good work He is doing? It should be one of joy—*because your joy is evidence of how much you trust God.* If you trust Him, then you will rejoice for His goodness, and that joy will be strength to you.

Take for instance a world champion boxer. His coach loves him to a point where he wants him above all things to be a winner. So what does the coach do—buy him a sofa, a TV, and potato chips? No. Instead, he places weights on his shoulders and resistance against his arms. He will even look around for the toughest sparring partner he can find. If the boxer doesn't understand what his trainer is doing, if he doesn't have faith in his methods, he will get depressed and lose heart. But if he knows what's going on, he will rejoice now in the trials because he sees, through the eyes of faith, the finished product.

That's why God is letting the devil loose on you: to make you strong. Paul says,

For our light affliction, which is but for a moment [in the light of eternity], works for us a far more exceeding and eternal weight of glory (2 Corinthians 4:17).

Afflictions work *for* us, not against us, if we are in God's will. How is your joy when the Trainer brings the resistance your way? How much faith do you have in Him? The joy you have will be your measuring rod.

For you, O God, have proved us: you have tried us, as silver is tried. You have caused men to ride over our heads; we went through fire and through water: but you brought us out into a wealthy place (Psalm 66:10,12).

God takes us through the fires of persecution, tribulation, and temptation to purify us, not to burn us. He takes us through water to cleanse us, not to drown us. Look at the reason God chastens His children, given in Hebrews 12:9–15:

> Furthermore we have had fathers of our flesh which corrected us, and we gave them reverence: shall we not much rather be in subjection to the Father of spirits, and live? For they verily for a few days chastened us after their own pleasure; but he for our profit, that we might be partakers of his holiness. Now no chastening for the present seems to be joyous, but grievous: nevertheless afterward it yields the peaceable fruit of righteousness to them which are exercised thereby.
>
> Wherefore lift up the hands which hang down, and the feeble knees; and make straight paths for your feet, lest that which is lame be turned out of the way; but let it rather be healed. Follow peace with all men, and holiness, without which no man shall see the Lord: looking diligently lest any man fail of the grace of God; lest any root of bitterness springing up trouble you, and thereby many be defiled.

In other words, get it together. Don't fall into discouragement, which is essentially a lack of faith in God. If you let your arms hang down in depression instead of rejoicing that God is working all things out for your good, you are saying that God isn't faithful, that His promises aren't worth believing, that He is actually a liar. There is no greater insult to God than to not believe His promises. The result of unbelief will be depression, discouragement, self-pity, resentment, then bitterness, which you will end up spreading to others.

If you have never thanked God for His promises, for His faithfulness, for the fact that He is working with you, in you, and for you—if you have been joyless, or even despised what has been happening to you and moved into bitterness—then repent of the sin of mistrust. How insulted you would be if you were a faithful and loving trainer, and your boxer, for whose good you are laboring, began to despise you for what you were doing.

On the other hand, if you are "exercised thereby," the result will be the "peaceable fruit of righteousness." In other words, you will end up living a life that is in complete righteousness, and bring a smile to the heart of your heavenly Father.

Look at Hebrews 12:11. Notice the word "afterward." That one word was my light in the dark tunnel. It meant there was an end to my terror, a light at the end of the tunnel that wasn't a train heading for me. Write down the word "afterward," and put it somewhere where you will be reminded that you have hope—and "hope never disappoints or deludes or shames us" (Romans 5:5, *Amplified*).

Guard against condemnation. You are no "less spiritual" than those who seem to have complete victory. If you don't believe it, think of the experience of Oswald Chambers, author of the mega-bestselling devotional *My Utmost For His Highest*. Now there's a man whose life and words have been an inspiration to millions. He was "spiritual" in the truest sense of the word. However, the great author had four years in his life of which he said, "God used me during those years for the conversion of souls, but I had no conscious communion with Him. The Bible was the dullest, most uninteresting book in existence" (*Oswald Chambers: Abandoned to God*). He described those four years as "hell on earth." However, he found that there was an "afterward," saying,

> But those of you who know the experience know very well how God brings one to the point of utter despair, and I got to the place where I did not care whether everyone knew how bad I was, I cared not for another on earth, saving to get out of my present condition (ibid).

If you have panic attacks or agoraphobia (fear of open spaces), don't fall into the deep pit of self-pity, because it has ugly bedfellows—discouragement, joylessness, condemnation, despair, and hopelessness. The sides of the pit of self-pity are very slippery, but there is one firm foothold. It is the uplifting stairs of thanksgiving. Let me explain how you can get your foot into it.

AN ATTITUDE OF THANKSGIVING

Sue and I were visiting an elderly lady named Helen, a 93-year-old who had broken her hip. She was unhappy because the food in the convalescent home wasn't very good. One day Mary walked into Helen's room. Mary was in her late seventies and had to be permanently fed through a tube that ran from a bottle directly into her stomach. Mary never tasted food or drink, and barring a miracle from God, she would never taste food or liquid again. Mary's condition made Helen thankful that at least she could have the pleasure of food and drink, even if it wasn't up to standard.

Then there was Robert. Robert had a good clear brain, but he had chronic emphysema. He couldn't breathe. Whenever she looked into his room, he was sitting on his bed, leaning over with his hand on his forehead. He gasped for every breath, twenty-four hours a day. Robert's problem made Mary thankful that at least she could breathe.

The point is that, despite your tormenting fears, you won't have to look too far for people who are suffering so badly that their problems dwarf yours. If you don't believe me, try being Robert for two minutes. Pinch your nose with one hand, then with the other one hold your lips together so that a meager amount of air gets into your mouth. Don't cheat. Do that for 120 long seconds. Feel the sweat break out on your forehead. Feel the panic. After two minutes of gasping for your breath, when you let go you will begin to thank God that you can breathe, and that will bring your problems into perspective. I'm not demeaning your fears. I'm offering you a way to lift yourself out of the pit of pity.

So next time you are attacked in some way, pull yourself together with a prayer of heartfelt thanksgiving, and say,

> Father, I thank You that all things work together for my good; that it is You who are at work in me to will and do of Your good pleasure. Your strength is made perfect in my weakness. I will not let this attack discourage me because Your grace is sufficient for me. You will help me through it. When I think of the sufferings of many, many others, I feel ashamed for having any self-pity. I will therefore rejoice in the God of my salvation and give You thanks in and for everything. In Jesus' name I pray. Amen.

Your constant battle with trials will make you no stranger to them. Like a tree that is constantly beaten about by the wind, your roots will be deep. You will find, if you have an acquaintance with fear, etc., that you can live with it where others can't. You will be able to do things that others can't. The roots of your faith in God will be deeper than the roots of those who have never been ravaged by the winds of terror. Affliction works *for* us. God doesn't let the wind blow to destroy, but to strengthen. You will be able to go places and do things that others would fear to do, because those things that should (rationally) produce fear pale in significance compared to the average attack of irrational fear.

Again, do you believe God is at work in you to will and do of His good pleasure? Then rejoice, and let the joy of the Lord be your strength. There is a world weighed in the balance and found wanting. Don't fiddle while Rome burns. Your problems and fears are nothing compared to the terrible plight of the sinner. Eternal hell is his destiny. Lift up hands that hang down, lift up your heart through faith, then lift up your voice like a trumpet and show this people their transgression.

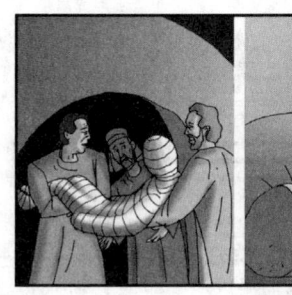

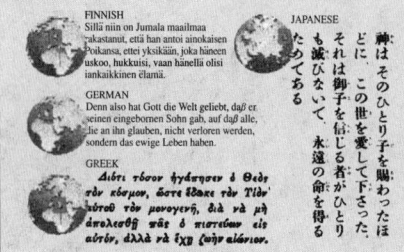

FINNISH
Sillä niin on Jumala maailmaa rakastanut, että hän antoi ainokaisen Poikansa, ettei yksikään, joka häneen uskoo, hukkuisi, vaan hänellä olisi iankaikkinen elämä.

GERMAN
Denn also hat Gott die Welt geliebt, daß er seinen eingebornen Sohn gab, auf daß alle, die an ihn glauben, nicht verloren werden, sondern das ewige Leben haben.

GREEK
Διότι τόσον ἠγάπησεν ὁ Θεὸς τὸν κόσμον, ὥστε ἔδωκε τὸν Υἱὸν αὐτοῦ τὸν μονογενῆ, διὰ νὰ μὴ ἀπολεσθῇ πᾶς ὁ πιστεύων εἰς αὐτόν, ἀλλὰ νὰ ἔχῃ ζωὴν αἰώνιον.

JAPANESE
神は、そのひとり子を賜わったほどに、この世を愛して下さった。それは御子を信じる者がひとりも滅びないで、永遠の命を得るためである

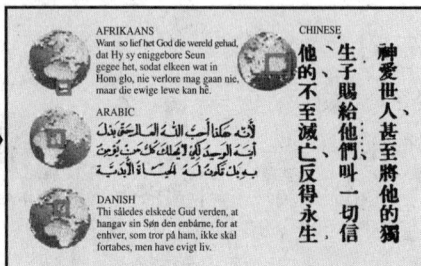

AFRIKAANS
Want so lief het God die wêreld gehad, dat Hy sy eniggebore Seun gegee het, sodat elkeen wat in Hom glo, nie verlore mag gaan nie, maar die ewige lewe kan hê.

ARABIC
لأنه هكذا أحب الله العالم حتى بذل ابنه الوحيد لكي لا يهلك كل من يؤمن به بل تكون له الحياة الأبدية

DANISH
Thi således elskede Gud verden, at hangav sin Søn den enbårne, for at enhver, som tror på ham, ikke skal fortabes, men have evigt liv.

CHINESE
神愛世人、甚至將他的獨生子賜給他們叫一切信他的不至滅亡反得永生

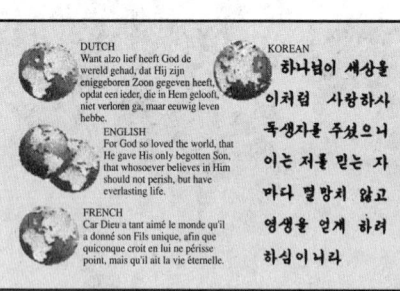

DUTCH
Want alzo lief heeft God de wereld gehad, dat Hij zijn eniggeboren Zoon gegeven heeft, opdat een ieder, die in Hem gelooft, niet verloren ga, maar eeuwig leven hebbe.

ENGLISH
For God so loved the world, that He gave His only begotten Son, that whosoever believes in Him should not perish, but have everlasting life.

FRENCH
Car Dieu a tant aimé le monde qu'il a donné son Fils unique, afin que quiconque croit en lui ne périsse point, mais qu'il ait la vie éternelle.

KOREAN
하나님이 세상을 이처럼 사랑하사 독생자를 주셨으니 이는 저를 믿는 자마다 멸망치 않고 영생을 얻게 하려 하심이니라

HEBREW
כִּי־כָכָה אָהַב הָאֱלֹהִים אֶת־הָעוֹלָם עַד אֲשֶׁר נָתַן אֶת־בְּנוֹ אֶת־יְחִידוֹ לְמַעַן לֹא־יֹאבַד כָּל־הַמַּאֲמִין בּוֹ כִּי אִם־יִחְיֶה חַיֵּי עוֹלָם׃

HINDI
क्योंकि परमेश्वर ने संसार से ऐसा प्रेम रखा कि उस ने अपना एकलौता पुत्र दे दिया, कि जो कोई उस पर विश्वास करे, नाश न हो परन्तु अनन्त जीवन पाए।

TURKISH
Çünkü Tanrı dünyayı o kadar çok sevdi ki, biricik Oğlunu verdi. Öyle ki, O'na iman edenlerin hiçbiri mahvolmasın, ama hepsi sonsuz yaşama kavuşsun.

ICELANDIC
Því að svo elskaði Guð heiminn, að hann gaf son sinn eingetinn, til þess að hver, sem á hann trúir, glatist ekki, heldur hafi eilíft líf.

ITALIAN
Poiché Iddio ha tanto amato il mondo, che ha dato il suo unigenito Figliuolo, affinché chiunque crede in lui non perisca, ma abbia vita eterna.

NORWEGIAN
For så har Gud elsket verden at han gav sin Sønn, den enbårne, forat hver den som tror på ham, ikke skal fortapes, men ha evig liv.

POLISH
Ponieważ Bóg tak świat kochał, że dał swego syna jedynego, aby kto wierzy w Niego nie zginął, lecz żył wiecznie.

RUSSIAN
Ибо так возлюбил Бог мир, что отдал Сына Своего единородного, дабы всякий, верующий в Него, не погиб, но имел жизнь вечную,

PORTUGESE
Porque Deus amou o mundo de tal maneira, que deu o seu Filho unigênito, para que todo aquêle que nêle crê não pereça, mas tenha a vida eterna.

SPANISH
Porque de tal manera amó Dios al mundo, que ha dado a su Hijo unigénito, para que todo aquel que en él cree, no se pierda, mas tenga vida eterna.

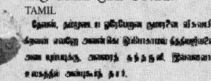

SINHALESE
මක්නිසාද දෙවියන්වහන්සේ තමන් වහන්සේගේ ඒකජාතක පුත්‍රයානන් දුන්සේක; ඒ කුමකටද යත්, උන් වහන්සේ කෙරෙහි විශ්වාස කරන සෑම කෙනෙකුන් විනාශ නොවී සදාකාල ජීවනය ලැබෙන පිණිස ය.

TAMIL
தேவன், தம்முடைய ஒரேபேறான குமாரனை விசுவாசிக்கிறவன் எவனோ அவன் கெட்டுப்போகாமல் நித்தியஜீவனை அடையும்படிக்கு, அவரைத் தந்தருளி, இவ்வளவாய் உலகத்தில் அன்புகூர்ந்தார்.

VIETNAMESE
Vì Đức Chúa Trời thương yêu thế-gian đến nỗi đã ban Con độc sanh của Ngài, hầu cho hễ ai tin Con ấy không hư-mất, nhưng được sự sống đời đời.

SWAHILI
Kwa maana jinsi hii Mungu aliupenda ulimwengu, hata akamtoa Mwanawe pekee, ili kila mtu amwaminiye asipotee; bali awe na uzima wa milele.

SWEDISH
Ty så älskade Gud världen, att han utgav sin enfödde Son, på det att var och en som tror på honom skall icke förgås, utan hava evigt liv.

Bibliography

Behe, Michael. *Darwin's Black Box*. New York: Free Press, 1996.

Darwin, Charles. *The Origin of Species*. London: Dent, and New York: E. P. Dutton, 1972.

Bevere, John. *The Bait of Satan*. Orlando: Creation House, 1994.

Bright, Bill. *The Transforming Power of Fasting & Prayer*. Orlando: New Life Publications, 1997.

Bright, Bill. *The Coming Revival*. Orlando: NewLife Publications, 1995.

Comfort, Ray. *Scientific Facts in The Bible*. Orlando, FL: Bridge-Logos Publishers, 2001.

DeVos, Richard M. *Hope from My Heart*. Nashville: J. Countryman, 2000.

Geisler, Norman L. *When Critics Ask*. Victor Books, 1992.

George, Bob. *Classic Christianity*. Eugene, Or: Harvest House, 1989.

Glennon, Lorraine. *Our Times: The Illustrated History of the 20th Century*. Atlanta: Turner Pub. 1995.

Hoyle, Sir Fred. *Evolution from Space*. London: Dent, 1981.

Ham, Ken. *The Answers Book*. El Cajon, Ca: Master Books, 1992.

Henry, Matthew. *Commentary on the Whole Bible, Genesis to Revelation*. Grand Rapids: Zondervan 1961.

Jeffrey, Grant R. *The Signature of God*. Nashville: Word Pub., 1998.

Jennings, Ben A. *The Arena of Prayer*. Orlando: New Life Publications, 1999.

Josephus, Flavius. *The Wars of the Jews*. London: J.M. Dent & Sons, Ltd. and New York: E.P. Dutton & Co. Inc., 1928.

Kennedy, D. James . *What If Jesus Had Never Been Born?* Nashville: T. Nelson Publishers, 1994.

Lewis, C. S. *The Problem of Pain*. New York: The Macmillan Company, 1944.

Lewis, C. S. *The Case for Christianity*. New York: Collier Books, 1989.

McDowell, Josh. *More Evidence that Demands a Verdict*. San Bernardino, CA: Here's Life Publishers 1981.

Morris, Henry Madison. *What Is Creation Science?* El Cajon, CA: Master Books, 1987.

Murray, Andrew. *The Spirit of Christ.* Minneapolis: Bethany House Publishers, 1979.

Packer, J. I. *Faithfulness and Holiness: The Witness of J.C. Ryle.* Wheaton, Ill: Crossway Books, 2002.

Prince, Derek. *Atonement.* Grand Rapids: Chosen Books, 2000.

Rose, Millicent. *The Dore Bible Illustrations.* Mineola: New York, Dover Publications, Inc., 1974.

Schaff, Philip. *The Person of Christ.* New York, American Tract Society 1913.

Smith, Alice. *Beyond the Veil.* Ventura, CA: Renew, 1997.

Spurgeon, Charles Haddon. *Lectures to My Students.* New York: Sheldon, 1860.

Spurgeon, Charles Haddon. *The Soul Winner.* Grand Rapids: Zondervan, 1948.

Torrey, R. A.. *The Power of Prayer.* New Kensington, PA: Whitaker House, 2000.

Tozer, A. W. *Knowledge of the Holy.* New York: Walker, 1996.

Yancey, Philip. *What's So Amazing About Grace?* Grand Rapids: Zondervan, 1997

Index

SCRIPTURE REFERENCES indicate that a comment about the subject can be found at that verse. For example, at Ps. 106:35-39, you will find a comment about abortion. At Ps. 33:12, you will find a comment about John Adams. (Additional Scripture verses relating to the subject are in parenthesis.)

Abortion, Ps. 106:35–39; 127:3; 139:16
  (Exod. 21:22-25; Ps. 82:3-4; Ps. 127:3;
  Ps. 139:13-16; Jer. 1:5; Jer. 7:30-34);
  Ps. 127:3; Isa. 57:5
Absolutes, 1 Thess. 2:13; 1 Pet. 3:12
Adam, Ps. 136:7–9; Prov. 4:1–5;
  Matt. 19:3–6; 24:38,39; Luke 23:53;
  John 3:7; 17:3; 19:1,2; 20:22; Gen. 22;
  Acts 17:26; Rom. 5:12; 5:14;
  1 Cor. 1:27,28; 11:8; 11:9; 15:6; 15:22;
  15:45; 2 Cor. 11:3; 1 Tim. 2:14;
  Heb. 4:15; 9:22; James 5, 1 John 3:12;
  Rev. 22:3.
  didn't die the day God said he would!
    Eph. 4:18
  long life of, Gen. 5:3
  mythical figure who never really lived.
    1 Cor. 15:45
Adams, John, Ps. 33:12
Adultery, Ps. 41:4; 50:16; 51:6; 55:15;
  103:17; 107:17; Prov. 21:2; Matt. 5:1;
  15:19; John 4:7; 8:11; John 21;
  Acts 17:22; Rom. 14:12; Gal. 3:19; 5:16;
  5:19; 1 Thess. 4; Heb. 2:10
  (Gen. 20:3; 2 Sam. 12:14; Job 24:15-18;
  Job 31:1; Job 31:9-12; Prov. 2:16-19;
  Prov. 5:3-22; Prov. 6:24-29;
  Prov. 6:32-33; Prov. 7:5-23;
  Prov. 9:13-18; Prov. 22:14;
  Prov. 23:27-28; Prov. 29:3;
  Prov. 30:18-20; Prov. 31:3; Isa. 57:3-4;
  Jer. 3:1; Jer. 5:7-8; Jer. 7:9-10; Jer. 23:10;
  Ezek. 18:5-6; Ezek. 18:9; Hos. 4:1-2;
  Hos. 4:11; Matt. 5:28; Matt. 5:32;
  Matt. 15:19; Matt. 19:9; Mark 7:21;

Mark 10:11-12; Mark 10:19; Luke 16:18;
  John 10:10; Acts 15:20; Acts 15:29; Rom.
  1:28-29; Rom. 1:32; Rom. 7:3;
  1 Cor. 5:9-10; 1 Cor. 6:15-16;
  1 Cor. 6:18; 1 Cor. 10:8; 2 Cor. 12:21;
  Gal. 5:19; Gal. 5:21; 1 Tim. 1:9-10; 2
  Tim. 3:6; James 2:11; 1 Pet. 4:3-4;
  2 Pet. 2:9-10; 2 Pet. 2:14; Jude 1:7;
  Rev. 2:20-22; Rev. 9:21)
  Repercussions of, Exod. 20:14
Advocate, Job 16:21 (1 John 2:1)
Afterlife, Ps. 49:15 [See Life, everlasting]
Agassiz, Louis, 1 Cor. 15:39
Air,
  currents, Heb. 11:3
  weight of, Job 28:25
Albus, Harry, Heb. 12:3
Alcohol, Ps. 107:17; Prov. 20:1; Acts 19;
  1 Cor. 3:17; 2 Tim. 2:26; James 5; Jude 7
  (Lev. 10:9; Num. 6:3; Num. 28:7;
  Deut. 14:26; Deut. 29:6; Judg. 13:4;
  Judg. 13:7; Judg. 13:14; Prov. 20:1;
  Prov. 31:4; Prov. 31:6; Isa. 5:11;
  Isa. 5:22; Isa. 24:9; Isa. 28:1-29)
Alleine, Joseph, Ps. 126:6
Amalek, Ps. 109:15 (Gen. 36:12;
  1 Chron. 1:36)
Animals and men, the difference, Gen. 1:25
Angels
  at Jesus' tomb, Mark 16:6
  appearing to Balaam, Num. 23:23
Ansdell, Garry, Matt. 24:14; John 3:3;
  1 Cor. 15:6
Apostles, fate of, Acts 7

Arabs, Acts 7:5
  Descended from, Gen. 21:18
Archaeology confirms the Bible, Matt. 4:4;
  26:54; Luke 1:27; 3:1,2; John 19:31,32;
  1 Pet. 1:25
Ark, Matt. 24:38,39; 1 Cor. 1:27,28;
  Heb. 4:4; 2 Pet. 2:5 (Gen. 6:14-16
  Gen. 6:18; Gen. 7:8; Matt. 24:38;
  Heb. 11:7; 1 Pet. 3:20 Gen. 6:19-20;
  Gen. 7:1-16); I Sam. 6:13
Armageddon, Luke 21:26; Rev. 9:9; 16:16
Armor of God, 2 Cor. 4:4; Eph. 6:15;
  Heb. 4:12
Arnold, Dan, Luke 13:3
Atheism, Ps.53:1; 1 John 2:19 (Ps. 10:4;
  Ps. 14:1; Ps. 53:1; Prov. 30:9; Jer. 5:12;
  1 John 2:22)
Atheist, Ps. 14:1; Rom. 9:1
  letter from, Rom. 9:2,3
Atoms, Heb. 10:31
Augustine, Prov. 15:8; Rom. 7:20; Jon. 2
Authenticity of Gen., Gen. 1:1
Backslider, Matt. 5:10–12; Luke 9:62; 22:47;
  2 Cor. 2:17 (Lev. 26:14-42; Deut. 4:9;
  Deut. 8:11-14; Deut. 28:15-68;
  Deut. 29:18-28; Deut. 32:15-30;
  Josh. 24:20-27; 1 Kings 9:6-9;
  2 Chron. 15:2-4; Ezra 8:22; Job 34:26-27;
  Ps. 44:20-21; Ps. 73:27; Ps. 85:8;
  Ps. 125:5; Prov. 2:17; Prov. 14:14;
  Prov. 24:16; Prov. 26:11; Jer. 17:13;
  Ezek. 3:20; Ezek. 18:24; Ezek. 18:26;
  Ezek. 23:35; Ezek. 33:12-13;
  Ezek. 33:18; Hos. 11:7-8; Jon. 2:4;
  Matt. 5:13; Matt. 12:45; Matt. 24:12;
  Matt. 26:31; Mark 4:7; Mark 4:15-19;
  Mark 8:38; Mark 9:50; Luke 9:62;
  Luke 11:21-26; Luke 17:32; John 6:67;
  John 15:6; 1 Cor. 10:1-13;
  2 Cor. 12:20-21; Gal. 1:6-7; Gal. 3:1;
  Gal. 4:9-11; Gal. 5:7; 1 Tim. 1:19;
  1 Tim. 5:15; 1 Tim. 6:10; 1 Tim. 6:20-21;
  2 Tim. 1:8; 2 Tim. 2:12; 2 Tim. 4:10;
  Heb. 3:12-13; Heb. 4:1; Heb. 4:11;
  Heb. 5:11-12; Heb. 6:4-8; Heb. 10:26-29;
  Heb. 10:38-39; Heb. 11:14-15;
  Heb. 12:15; 2 Pet. 1:9; 2 Pet. 2:20-21;
  2 John 1:9; Rev. 2:4-5; Rev. 2:21-23;
  Rev. 3:2-3; Rev. 21:8)
  Identity of, Jer. 3:8
Bacteria, Exod. 22:31
Baptism, Matt. 8:14; Mark 1:4,5; Acts 1:5;
  2:38; 10:47; 1 Cor. 15:29; James 5;
  Rev. 18 (Matt. 28:19; Mark 16:16;
  John 3:5; John 3:22; John 4:1-2;

Acts 1:22; Acts 2:41; Acts 8:12-13;
  Acts 8:16; Acts 8:36-38; Acts 9:18;
  Acts 10:46-48; Acts 16:14-15; Acts 16:33;
  Acts 18:8; Acts 18:25; Acts 19:4-5;
  Acts 22:16; Rom. 6:3-4; 1 Cor. 1:13-17; 1
  Cor. 10:1-2; 1 Cor. 12:13; 1 Cor. 15:29;
  Gal. 3:27; Eph. 4:5; Eph. 5:26; Col. 2:12;
  Heb. 6:2; 1 Pet. 3:18; 1 Pet. 3:21)
  for the dead, 1 Cor. 15:29
Barna, George, Eph. 4:11
Barr, James, Heb. 4:4
Barton, Ralph, Matt. 27:5
Baxter, Richard, Mal. 2
Beethoven, Ludwig van, Ps. 139:16;
  1 Cor. 15:55
Behe, Michael J., Ps. 139:14; Rev. 14:7
Beliefs, mistaken, Isa. 28:16; Ps. 139:16
Bernall, Cassie, Rev 12
Bevere, John, Ps. 92:13; Luke 22:31,32
Bible, Ps. 22:28; 33:12; 67:4; 119:14;
  Prov. 23:12; John 7:17; 1 Pet. 2:2;
  Rev. 16:16; Ps. 119:105
  confirmed by archaeology,
    Matt. 4:4; 26:54; Luke 1:27; 3:1,2;
    John 19:31,32; 1 Pet. 1:25
  study of, Gen. 1:1
  fascinating facts in, Ps. 38:11; Acts 7:5;
    1 Thess. 5:20; 2 Pet. 2:5
  hasn't changed, Ps. 119:160
  in schools, Prov. 22:6; Eph. 6:4
  inspiration of, Heb. 1:1; 1 Pet. 1:21
  necessity of , Ps. 1:1–3
  not understandable, 1 Cor. 2:14
  Questions and Objections rgarding,
    Ps. 119:162; Ps. 109:15; Ps. 89:14;
    Ps. 147:9, Ps. 109:15
    has changed down through the ages.
      Ps. 119:160
    wrong when it call the hare a cud-
      chewing animal. Ps. 147:9
    many versions of proves that it has
      mistakes. Prov. 30:5
    scripture that says "an eye for an eye,"
      encourages us to avenge wrongdo
      ing. Matt. 5:38
    response to someone who says the
      Bible is just a book of fairy tales?
      Luke 24:44,45
    Christians quoting from, Acts 17:2
    tried to read the Bible, but I can't un
      derstand it. 1 Cor. 2:14
    wrong to call the Bible "God's Word"
      when it makes Him look so bad?
      1 Tim. 6:1
    written by men? 2 Pet. 1:21

teaches that the earth is flat. Rev. 1:7
quotes of, Ps. 73; Ps. 119:14; 119:72;
  Ps. 119; 119:97; 119:104;
  Prov. 14:34; 2 Tim. 3:16; 2 Tim. 4;
  Philem.
read every day, Job 23:12
reliability of, Matt. 4:4; Luke 1:3;
scientific facts in, Ps. 8:8; 19:5,6; 33:6;
  95:4,5; 102:25,26; 104:2; 104:19;
  135:7; Luke 4:40; John 20:26;
  Acts 14:17; Heb. 11:3; 11:11
uniqueness of, Ps. 119:105
versions of, Prov. 30:5
(See also Dead Sea Scrolls)
Big Bang, Gen. 1:9; Ps. 19:1–4
confirmed by science, 1 Pet. 4
Blanchard, P., Prov. 4:1–5
Blasphemy, Isa. 53:3 (Matt. 12:31-32;
  Matt. 15:19; Mark 3:29-30;
  Mark 7:21-23; Luke 12:10; John 19:7;
  Rom. 2:24; 1 Cor. 12:3; Col. 3:8; 2
  Thess. 2:4; 2 Tim. 3:2; Heb. 10:29;
  James 2:7; James 3:10; James 5:12;
  2 Pet. 3:3; Rev. 13:1; Rev. 13:6;
  Rev. 16:9; Rev. 16:11; Rev. 16:21;
  Rev. 17:3)
Blessings on nation, Ps. 33:12 and Lev. 26:1
Blind, the sinner who is, Job 24:15
  (John 9:25; Rom. 2:19; 2 Pet. 1:9;
  Rev. 3:17)
Blood, Matt. 9:20; Heb. 11:3
  (is the life, Gen. 9:4; Lev. 17:11;
  Lev. 17:14; Lev. 19:16; Deut. 12:23;
  Matt. 27:4; Matt. 27:24)
Boldness, in Day of wrath, Amos 6:3
  (of the righteous, Prov. 14:26; Prov. 28:1;
  Eph. 3:12; Heb. 4:16; Heb. 10:19; Heb.
  13:6; 1 John 2:28; 1 John 4:17)
  (in prayer, Abraham: Gen. 18:23-32,
  Moses: Exod. 33:12-18)
Boleyn, Anne, 1 Cor. 15:55
Bolton, Sam., Luke 10:34
Bonaparte, Napoleon, John 7
Bonar, Andrew A., Ezek. 36
Bonhoeffer, Dietrich, Luke 19:17; Phil. 1:29;
  1 John 2:11
Boom, Corrie Ten: Num. 23
Booth, Catherine: Jon. 4; 1 Thess. 2:4;
  2 Tim. 2:3; Heb. 5:9; Rev. 6:16,17
Booth, William, Ps. 90:12; 1 Cor. 15:55;
  2 Tim. 3:5; Jer. 1; Josh. 11; Duet. 18

Born again, Matt. 5:1; John 3:3; Acts 4:12;
  1 Cor. 2:14; 9:22; 13:2; Gal. 4:6; Eph.
  1:1; 4:18; Col. 3:6; 4:3,4; 1 Thess. 1:5;
  2 Tim. 2:24–26; 1 John 2:19; Rev. 7:4–8
  (See also New Birth)
Bounds, E. M., Luke 15:32
Bounoure, Louis, Mark 10:6
Borgia, Cardinal, 1 Cor. 15:55
Bradley, General Omar, Matt. 5
Brain, human, 1 Cor. 2:16
Bright, Bill, Matt. 28:19; 2 Cor. 6:1; 13:3;
  2 Tim. 1:8,9; 1 John 4:4; 4:8; Jon. 1
Bright, Vonette, Acts 13:47
Brooks, Phillips, Eph. 6:10
Browning, E.B.: Ex. 3
Buddhism, Heb. 1:1
  beliefs of, 2 John
Bunyan, John, Mark 2:2; John 6:45;
  Rom. 3:20; Col. 4; 1 Thess. 5:17
Burbank, Luther, 1 Cor. 15:55
Burden, for the lost, Lam. 3:48; Mic. 1:1
Burden, of the Christian, Hab. 1:1
  (of oppressions, Isa. 58:6; Matt. 23:4;
  Luke 11:46; Gal. 6:2)
Cahill, Mark, Matt. 7; Col. 1:28; 1 Pet. 4:14
Cameron, Kirk, family, Joel 2 This Father of
  Five Teaches His Little Ones the Ten
  Commandments
Campus Crusade for Christ, Preface; 1 John
  4:8; Jon. 1
Capital punishment, Matt. 5:44; 7:15
  (Gen. 9:6; Exod. 21:14; Lev. 20:10; Deut.
  13:9)
Carbon dating, Ps. 146:6; Acts 14:15
Carlyle, Thomas, Ps. 36:2
Cedar, Paul A., 1 John 5
Chadwick, Sam., Luke 6:12; Zech. 1;
  Ezek. 7
Cain's wife, Gen. 4:17
Chambers, Oswald, Lev. 18
Chambers, Oswald, Rom. 1:14; 2:15;
  Gal. 6:14
Chantry, Walter, Prov. 6:23
Chapel of the Air, Ps. 49:17
Chesterton, G. K., Ps. 45; Matt. 21:12,13;
  Acts 14:15; Isa. 27
Children, sinful nature of, Prov. 20:11;
  29:15; Col. 3:6
training of, Prov. 4:1–5; 22:6; Eph. 6:4
teaching Ten Commandments to,
  Eph. 6:1,2; Rom. 15
Christ,
  forsaken on cross, Ps. 22:1
  suffering on cross, Ps. 22:6–8; 22:14;
  Matt. 27:26–29; 27:46

(His suffering, Isa. 53: 4-12; Luke 24:26;
Luke 24:46-47; John 6:51; John 10:11;
John 10:15; John 11:50-52; Rom. 4:25;
Rom. 5:6-8; Rom. 14:15; 1 Cor. 1:17-18;
1 Cor. 1:23-24; 1 Cor. 8:11; 1 Cor. 15:3;
2 Cor. 5:14-15; Gal. 1:4; Gal. 2:20-21;
Eph. 5:2; Eph. 5:25; 1 Thess. 5:9-10;
Heb. 2:9-10; Heb. 2:14; Heb. 2:18;
Heb. 5:8-9; Heb. 9:15-16; Heb. 9:28;
Heb. 10:10; Heb. 10:18-20; 1 Pet. 2:21;
1 Pet. 2:24; 1 Pet. 3:18; 1 Pet. 4:1;
1 John 3:16)
Christians,
    as salt, Matt. 5:1; Mark 9:50; Phil. 2:15
    sin of, 1 Pet. 4:1; 1 John 1:9
Church, world threatened by, Neh. 4:1
Churches, Rev. 3:14–19; Josh. 4:1-7
    house, Rom. 16:5
    need for, Acts 2:44–46
    selecting, Ps. 92:13; Heb. 10:25
Churchill, Winston, Prov. 19:17; John 17;
    Heb. 8:5
Circumcision, John 20:26 (Gen. 17:12-13;
    Lev. 12:3; Phil. 3:5)
Cobain, Kurt, 1 Cor. 15:55
Cole, Edwin, Luke 6:38
Columbus, Christopher, Prov. 3:6; Heb. 9;
    Heb. 11:3
Co-laborers, Neh. 2:8
Colson, Chuck, Luke 6:37; Acts 7:26;
    Rev. 18
Communion, Matt. 26:26; 26:27,28;
    Mark 14:24
Compton, Arthur H., Ps. 25:14
Confession,
    (of Christ, Matt. 3:11; Matt. 7:21-23;
        Matt. 10:32-33; Luke 12:8;
        John 1:15-18; John 9:22-38;
        John 12:42-43; Acts 8:35-37;
        Acts 18:5; Acts 19:4-5; Rom. 10:9-11;
        1 Cor. 12:3; 1 John 1:6; 1 John 2:4;
        1 John 4:2-3;
        1 John 4:15)
    of sin, Ps. 32:5 (Lev. 16:21; Num. 14:40;
        2 Sam. 24:10; 2 Sam. 24:17;
        1 Chron. 21:17; 2 Chron. 29:6;
        Ezra 9:4-7; Ezra 9:10-15; Neh. 1:6-9;
        Neh. 9:2-3; Neh. 9:5-38; Job 7:20;
        Job 9:20; Job 13:23; Job 40:4;
        Job 42:5-6; Ps. 32:5; Ps. 38:3-4;
        Ps. 38:18; Ps. 40:11-12; Ps. 41:4;
        Ps. 51:2-5; Ps. 69:5; Ps. 73:21-22;
        Ps. 106:6; Ps. 119:59-60; Ps. 119:176;
        Ps. 130:3; Isa. 6:5; Isa. 26:13;
        Isa. 59:12-15; Isa. 64:5-7;
        Jer. 3:21-22; Jer. 3:25; Jer. 8:14-15;
        Jer. 14:7; Jer. 14:20; Jer. 31:18-19;
        Lam. 1:18; Lam. 1:20; Lam. 3:40-42;
        Dan. 9:5-6; Dan. 9:8-11; Dan. 9:15;
        Luke 15:17-21; 1 Cor. 15:9;
        James 5:16; 1 John 1:8-10)
Conscience, Prov. 30:20; Matt. 5; Luke 17;
    John 4:7; Rom. 2:15; 9:1; 1 Tim. 4:2;
    Heb. 10:22 (Job 15:21; Job 15:24;
    Job 27:6; Prov. 20:12; Matt. 5:15-16;
    Matt. 6:22-23; Luke 11:33-36; Acts 23:1;
    Acts 24:16; Rom. 7:15-23; Rom. 9:1;
    Rom. 14:1-23; 1 Cor. 8:7; 1 Cor. 8:9-13;
    1 Cor. 10:27-32; 2 Cor. 1:12; 2 Cor. 4:2;
    2 Cor. 5:11; 1 Tim. 1:5; 1 Tim. 1:19;
    1 Tim. 3:9; Heb. 9:14; Heb. 10:22;
    Heb. 13:18; 1 Pet. 2:19; 1 Pet. 3:16;
    1 Pet. 3:21; 1 John 3:20-21)
Constellations, distant, Job 38:31
Contradictions in Bible, Gen. 1:2; Gen. 1:26;
    Ps. 12:6,7; 147:9; Matt. 1:1; 27:9,10;
    28:9; Mark 4:31; 15:26; 16:6; Luke 3:23;
    Acts 22:9
    (Also see Bible)
Coolidge, Calvin, Ps. 67:4
Conversion, Ezek. 36:24; Jer. 32:40
Copeland, Lynn, Acknowledgments,
    Ps. 127:3
Courage, Neh. 7:2 (Prov. 28:1; Ezek. 2:6;
    Ezek. 3:9; 1 Cor. 16:13; Phil. 1:27-28; 2
    Tim. 1:7)
Creation, John 7:17; Rev. 4:11; 22:3
    dictionary definition of, Gen. 1:31
    Age of, Gen. 1:1
    Questions about, Gen. 1:27
    completion of, Ps. 33:6
    days of, Col. 2:16; Heb. 4:4
    design in, Ps. 19:1–4; 25:14; Ps. 33:8
    evidence for, Prov. 3:19
    proof of God as Creator, Rom. 1:20
    imperfection of, 1 Cor. 15:22
    marvels of, Job 37:1
Criswell, Wallie Amos, Isa. 29
Crosby, Bing, 1 Cor. 15:55
Cross, Matt. 10:22
Cross, hard-hearted sinners, Lam. 1:12
Cross, the message, Hos. 13:14
Cross, suffering of Jesus, Jon. 2:2
Crucifixion, Mark 15:39; Luke 23:53;
    John 19:31,32; 19:33,34 (Ps. 22:1-18)
Crumpton, Joel, Matt. 5:2
Cummins, Rob, 2 Cor. 6:1
Death, Psalm 90
Darwin, Charles, Ps. 104:24; 139:14;
    Acts 14; Gen. 2

On evolution's absurdity, Gen. 2:6
Darwinian, Ps. 25:14; 104:24; 139:14;
    146:6; Acts 14:15; Rev. 14:7
David,
    prayer of, Ps. 58:6; Acts 13:22
    sin of, Ps. 41:4; John 1:13
da Vinci, Leonardo, 1 Cor. 15:55
Day, Dorothy, 1 John 4:20
Dead Sea Scrolls, Ps. 119:160; Acts 17:22;
    1 Pet. 1:25
Dean, James, 1 Cor. 15:55
Death, Ps. 49:15
    average age of, Ps. 90
    fear of, James 4:14 and Job 4:20
        (Heb. 2:15)
    nearness of, Ps. 90
    shadow of, Ps. 23:4; Matt. 4:16; 5:14;
        John 10:11; Acts 1:10,11
    destruction of, Hos. 13:14
    of the wicked, Ezek. 33:11
Declaration of Independence, U.S., Ps. 113:3
Denominations, reason for, Ps. 1:6
Destruction, why sinners perish, Hos. 4:6
DeVos, Rich, Acts 2:44-46
Devotions, family, Joel 1:3 and Deut. 4:10
Diana, Princess of Wales, 1 Cor. 15:55
Dickens, Charles, 1 Cor. 15:55
Dinosaur, Ps. 146:6; Acts 14:15; Heb. 11:3
Discouragement, Isa. 42:1
Disease, protections against, Ps. 38:11;
    Heb. 11:3
Divorce, Ps. 107:17 (Mal. 2:14-16;
    Matt. 5:31-32; Matt. 19:3-12; Mark 10:2;
    Luke 16:18; 1 Cor. 7:10-17)
Doud, Guy Rice, Mark 9:50; Luke 12:8
Drake, Jordan, Ps. 119:105
Drake, Justin, Ps. 119:105
Dunn, Ronald, Luke 11:2
Dwight, Timothy, Acts 12:7
Earle, A. B., 1 Tim. 1:8
Earth,
    round, Heb. 11:3
    free-floating, Heb. 11:3
Edison, Thomas, Mark 11:23; 1 Cor. 14
Education, Prov. 4:1-5; 22:6; Eph. 6:4
Edwards, Jonathan, Ps. 55; Ps. 140:2,3;
    Matt. 13:19; 1 Cor. 15:55; Ex. 20; Ezra 7
Einstein, Albert, Ps. 33:8; 119:105; Mark 3;
    2 Cor. 5:17, Heb. 11:29; Gen. 2:1;
    Gen. 2; Gen. 2:7
    On appreciation of Creator, Gen. 1:31
Eisenhower, Dwight, Ps. 53:1; 2 Tim. 3:16
Electricity, Heb. 11:3
Eliot, T. S., John 12:25
Elizabeth the First, 1 Cor. 15:55

Elliot, Jim, Rev. 12
End times, Luke 21:26; Rev. 9:9; 16:16
    signs of, Matt. 24:3; Mark 13:4;
        Luke 21:7; 1 Tim. 4:1; 2 Tim. 3:1;
        2 Pet. 3:3
Entropy
    (See Thermodynamics, Second Law of)
Environmentalists, Rev. 11:18
Error of the wicked, Ezek. 8:12
Evangelism, Judges 7:3-7; Luke 10:2;
    Col. 1:28; Heb. 8:5; Ezek. 37:1-10 and
    47:1-2; Isa. 41:10; Isa. 52:7; Jer. 20:9;
    Jon. 2; Jon. 3:3-4
    Christian's responsibility for, Ezek. 33:3
    enemy's attacks upon, Neh. 6:9
    enemy's frustrations, Neh. 6:3
    in relation to walls of Jericho falling
        down, Josh. 6:1-20
    reading the law in the hearing of the
        people, Neh. 8:2-9
    obligation, 2 Kings 7:9
    reason the Church exists, Neh. 3:1
    task for all believers, Neh. 5:16
    (See also Tracts; Witnessing, Personal
    Witnessing)
Evans, Louis, Phil. 3
Eve, Prov. 4:1-5; Matt. 19:3-6; Acts 17:26;
    1 Cor. 1:27,28; 11:8; 15:6; 15:22; 15:45;
    2 Cor. 11:3; 1 Tim. 2:14; Heb. 4:15; 9:22;
    1 John 3:12 (Gen. 1:26-28; Gen. 2:21-24;
    Gen. 3:1-24; Gen. 4:1-2; Gen. 4:25;
    Gen. 5:3-4; 2 Cor. 11:3; 1 Tim. 2:13-14)
Evolution, Gen. 1:24; Gen. 2:8 and 2:25;
    Neh. 9:6; Ps. 19:1-4; 90:2; Acts 17:24;
    1 Cor. 15:39; Eph. 3:9; James 2:20;
    2 Pet. 3:3-6; Ps. 19:1-4; Ps. 136:7-9
    and blood platelets, Matt. 9:20
    and carbon dating, Ps. 146:6; Acts 14:15
    circular reasoning of, Ps. 146:6
    contradictions in, Matt. 19:4
    fraudulent claims of, Acts 14:15
    law of probabilities refutes, Rev. 14:7
    population refutes, 1 Cor. 11:9
    questions on, Prov. 3:19; Mark 10:6
    Questions and Objections regarding,
        Doesn't the Big Bang theory disprove
        the Genesis account of creation?
            Ps. 19:1
        The young-earth theory is wrong be
        cause we see stars millions of light-
        years away. Ps. 136:7
        Where do all the races come from?
            Acts 17:26
        Evolution disproves the Bible!
            1 Cor. 15:39

Adam was a mythical figure who never really lived. 1 Cor. 15:45

How could earth have supported so many huge creatures at the same time? 2 Pet. 3:3

Evolutionists,
  questions for, Gen. 1:27
  discouragement in, Ps. 105:17–19; Matt. 16:23; Mark 8:33; John 17:14; Acts 18:10; 1 Cor. 15:58; Heb. 12:3
  key to reaching the lost, Luke 11:52
  lifestyle, Prov. 11:30; Acts 9:22
  modern, Luke 22:47; Acts 26:20; 2 Cor. 1:4,5; 2:17; Heb. 11:25
  motivation for, Ps. 1:1–3; Luke 16:13; John 10:10; Acts 1:10,11; 1 Cor. 9:16
  qualifications for, 1 Cor. 2:1–4; 1 Tim. 1:12

Excuses for disbelief
  When you're dead, you're dead. Ps. 49:15
  I'll wait until I am old, then I'll get right with God. Luke 12:20
  If I submit to God, I'll just become a puppet! Acts 13:47
  I don't believe God can be known. John 17:3
  There is no absolute truth. You can't be sure of anything! 1 Thess. 2:13
  God made me like this. Sin is His fault! 1 Tim. 2:14
  I was once a born-again Christian. Now I believe it's all rubbish! 1 John 2:19

Exultation of self, Dan. 3:16

Eye,
  complexity of, Ps. 139:14
  marvels of, Job 39:26

Faber, Frederick W., 1 Pet. 2:15

Fairbanks, Douglas Sr., 1 Cor. 15:55

Faith,
  great, Job 13:15
  in coming Messiah, Job 19:25
  true, Dan. 3:18
  (definition of, Heb. 11:1)
  (pleasing to God, 11:5,6)
  (heroes of, Heb. 11:7-40)
  questions and objections, Deut. 30:19
    If God gives me a sign, then I will believe. Matt. 12:39
    I will believe if God will appear to me. John 1:18
    I made a commitment, but nothing happened. John 14:21
    Seeing is believing. If I can't see it, I don't believe it exists. John 20:25

I find it difficult to have faith in God. 1 John 5:10

Faithfulness in preaching, Jer. 23:28 and 26:2

Fales, Richard M., Matt. 4:4

Fallen creation, Jon. 1:4

False converts, Prov. 14:14; Matt. 6:31–33; 7:22,23; 7:26; 12:36; 13:24–30; 25:12; Mark 16:17,18; Luke 3:4; 9:62; 13:20,21; John 1:13; Acts 28:23; 1 Cor. 15:34; 2 Cor. 2:17; Col. 3; 2 Tim. 2:19; Titus 1:16; 2 Pet. 2:21; 1 John 2:11; 2:19; Jude 4; Jude 8

False converts, in leadership, Ezra 2:62

Family, sentiments, Dan. 6:24

Fasting, Ps. 35:13 (Ezra 8:21-23; Ps. 35:13; Ps. 69:10; Isa. 58:3-7; Jer. 14:12; Dan. 10:2-3; Joel 1:14; Joel 2:12-13; Zech. 7:5; Zech. 8:19; Matt. 6:16-18; Matt. 9:14-15; Matt. 17:21; Acts 27:9; Acts 27:33-34; 1 Cor. 7:5)

Fay, Bill, John 10:10

Fear,
  of death, Job 7:6 (Heb. 2:15)
  of man, Ps. 56:11; 91:1; 118:6; Matt. 10:27,28; Acts 4:29
  and inability of man, Exod. 4:10
  of the Lord, Prov. 2:1-5; Acts 7:55; 9:31; Jude 18,19
  of the Lord, Neh. 1:11

Feet, beauty of, Nah. 1:15

Fellowship, Prov. 18:1; 1 Cor. 12:25; Phil. 2:15; Heb. 10:25; 3 John

Field, Arthur N., James 2:20

Fields, W. C., 1 Cor. 15:55

Finished nature of creation, Gen. 2:1

Finney, Charles, Ps. 5:5; Matt. 3:1; Luke 3:4; Phil. 2:8; 1 Tim. 1:8–10; James 2:10; 1 Pet. 3:8,9; Hab. 1

Flavel, John, Ps. 122

Flood, Matt. 24:37–39; 24:38,39; Luke 17:26,27; Acts 17:26; Gal. 3:19; Heb. 4:4; 11:7; 1 Pet. 3:20; 1 Pet. 5; 2 Pet. 3:3; 3:3–6; 3:6

Flynt, Larry, 1 John 2:19

Follow-up, Acts 8:39

Ford, Leighton, Jude 3

Forgiveness, Luke 17:4; 2 Cor. 5:14,15 (Exod. 23:4-5; Prov. 19:11; Prov. 24:17; Prov. 24:29; Prov. 25:21-22; Eccles. 7:21; Matt. 5:7; Matt. 5:39-41; Matt. 5:43-48; Matt. 6:12; Matt. 6:14-15; Matt. 18:21-35; Mark 11:25-26; Luke 6:27-37; Luke 11:4; Luke 17:3-4; Rom. 12:14; Rom. 12:17; Rom. 12:19-21; 1 Cor. 4:12-13;

Eph. 4:32; Col. 3:13; Philem. 1:10;
Philem. 1:18; 1 Pet. 3:9)
Forsyth, P. T., 2 Tim. 2:19
Fossils, Ps. 146:6; Matt. 24:38,39; Acts 4:24;
14:15; Eph. 3:9; James 2:20; 2 Pet. 3:3–6;
Jude
Foster, Richard, Luke 4:8
Foster, Robert, Matt. 26:41
Fowler, Jay, Gen. 18:1; 2 Chron. 30; Hab. 3
Franklin, Benjamin, Acts 5; 1 Cor. 15:55
Free, Joseph P., Matt. 26:54
Freud, Sigmund, 1 Cor. 15:55
Fruitfulness, Ps. 1:1–3
Futility of life, Job 7:6
Gallop, George, Gen. 2
Galileo, Galilei, Ps. 25:14; Acts 14:17;
1 Tim. 6:20; Rev. 16
Geisler, Norman, Ps. 5:5; 37:9; Matt. 10:23;
1 Pet. 1:25
George, Bob, John 3:7; 2 Cor. 5:21
Ghandi, Mahatma, Rom 7; Rom. 7:24,25;
1 Cor. 10:20; 15:55
Glueck, Nelson, Matt. 26:54
Gunther, Richard,
On creation finished, Gen. 2:1;
On soil substance, Gen. 2:7
God,
all-loving? Jer. 4:2
Anger toward sinners Ps. 5:5; 7:11–13;
Gal. 3:19; 1 Tim. 1:8–10
attributes of, Nah. 1:1
character of, Ps. 89:14; 97:2; 135:14;
Matt. 21:12,13; 1 Tim. 6:1; Heb. 6:18
His love, Deut. 23:5
love of, Ps. 5:5; 145:8; Matt. 10:22;
Rom. 8:39; Eph. 2:4,5; Rev. 1:17;
love for, Luke 10:27; John 14:15
mind of, 1 Cor. 2:16
nature of, Nah. 1
omnipresence of, Psa 139:2
omniscience of, Ps. 44:21; 94:7–10;
Ezek. 8:15; Matt. 5:21,22; 5:27,28;
Acts 15:18; Rev. 20:11
origin of, Ps. 90:2
peace with, Prov. 28:9; Mark 11:25;
John 14:6; Acts 17:22; Rom. 4:20;
8:22; Gal. 1:3; Col. 1:20
promises of, Ps. 31:19; 55:22; 91:1;
103:17; Acts 4:29; Rom. 4:20; 10:12;
Eph. 1:19; Heb. 8:6; James 1:5
proving existence of, Rom. 1:20; Gal. 4:6;
1 Thess. 1:5
will of, Ps. 37:4; Prov. 6:6–8; 10:32;
Eph. 1:9; 1 Thess. 2:16; Heb. 5:9;
Rev. 3:14–19; 12:11

greatness of, Jer. 32:17
ignored, Job 26:14
path of, Job 28:7
sovereignty of and man's responsibility to-
ward, Exod. 10:27
unchanging nature of, Neh. 9:17
Questions and Objetions regarding;
Ps. 90:2
Belief in, Ex. 33:18-23
God of wrath or mercy? Ps. 89:14
Who made God? Ps. 90:2
The First Commandment proves He
isn't the only God! Ps. 115:4
Does the Bible saying "God repented"
show He is capable of sin?
Ps. 135:14
If Hitler and a dear old lady who never
accepted Jesus both go to hell, God is
unfair., Matt. 11:24
My God would never create hell.
Matt. 18:9
I don't believe that God can be known.
John 17:3
What to say to someone who admits
sinning, but says, "I just hope God
is forgiving"? Acts 26:28
Suffering proves there is no "loving"
God." Rom. 5:12
If God is perfect, why did He make an
imperfect creation? 1 Cor. 15:22
God made me like this. Sin is His
fault! 1 Tim. 2:14
Why Does the Old Testament Show a
God of Wrath and the New Testament
a God of Mercy? Ps. 89:14
The Bibles says 'God repented.'
Doesn't that show He is capable of
sin? Ps. 135:14;
If God is a God of love, why hasn't He
dealt with evil? 1 Pet. 3:12
Why does God allow evil? 2 Pet. 3:9
I want nothing to do with a God killed
people all through the Bible. Rev. 8:11
If God forsook Jesus on the Cross, it
proves Jesus was a fake. Ps. 22:1
Jesus wasn't sinless—He became angry
when He cleared the temple.
Mark 11:15
Jesus taught hatred – he said you
should hate your father and mother.
Luke 14:26
You shouldn't judge others because
Jesus condemned those who judged.
John 8:11

It's intolerant to say that Jesus is the only way to God! John 14:6
Jesus fainted on the cross, and revived while He was in the tomb. John 19:33
Will people who have never heard about Jesus go to hell? Rom. 2:12
Goliath, Prov. 10:32; Mark 8:33
  (1 Sam. 17:1-58; 1 Sam. 21:9;
  1 Sam. 22:10)
  (his sons, 2 Sam. 21:15-22;
  1 Chron. 20:4-8)
Golden Rule, Matt. 5:1; 7:26; Gal. 5:14
Goodness,
  of Creation, (1:4,10,12,18,21,25,31)
  of God, Ps. 34:8,9; John 1:18; 1 Pet. 3:12
  of man, Ps. 14:1–3; 53:1–3; Prov. 16:2;
  20:6; Mark 10:18
  of the Law, Ps. 14:1–3
Good works, John 6:28,29
  of sinners, Prov. 2:27, 16:10; 20:9;
  21:27; Rom. 9:32; Gal. 2:10
  of Christians, Prov. 27:10; Gal. 2:16;
  3:11; Col. 1:28; 1 Tim. 6:18; 2 Tim.
  3:16,17; 1 Pet. 2:15; 3:1,2
  (See also Works)
Gothard, Bill, Matt. 5:13; 1 Pet. 5:3
Gould, Stephen J., Ps. 104:24; 1 Cor. 15:39
Gospel,
  Intended for whom, Luke 4:18;
  Heb. 11:25
  to be preached universally, Amos 3:8
  universal, Joel 2:32
Gossip, damage of, Prov. 11:13; Matt. 12:36
Gower, D. B., Acts 4:24
Graham, Billy, Matt. 12; Mark 4:14; John
  9:4; 16:8–11; Acts 20:21; Rom. 5:8; 2
  Cor. 8; Ex. 14
Graham, Franklin, 2 Cor. 4:2; Col. 1:28
Grant, Ulysses S., Ps. 119
Great Commission, Matt. 28:19; Mark
  16:15; Luke 19:10; 1 Cor. 9:22; 2 Thess.;
  1 John 3:15; 4:8
Greed, Luke 11:39
Green, Keith, Jon. 4
Grace, salvation by, Jon. 1:13 (Eph. 2:8,9)
Grotius, 1 Cor. 15:55
Guilt, John 8:9; Rom. 10:3; 1 Tim. 4:2;
  Exod. 20:14
  Questions and Objections regarding,
    You're trying to make me feel guilty by
      quoting the Ten Commandments.
      John 8:9
    I don't feel guilty. 1 Tim. 4:2
Guinness, Os, Matt. 21:12,13
Gunther, Richard, Job 26:8; Job 28:25; Job

38:24; Job 38:31; Mark 4:14; Gen. 5:3; 2
  Kings 20:7; Gen. 2:1, 2:7, 2:17, 5:3, 10:5;
  Eccl. 1:6; Ex. 22:31; 2 Kings 20; Dan. 1
  On Gen. authenticity, Gen. 1:1
  on long life, Gen. 5:3
Gurnall, William, Job 32; 2 Cor. 5:11
Halloween, 1 Tim. 4:1
Ham, Ken, Ps. 90:2; Heb. 4:4
Hamilton, Alexander, 1 Cor. 15:55
Hammett, John S., Acts 18:26
Hancock, Tony, 1 Cor. 15:55
Hanegraaff, Hank, Heb. 11:3
Hearts, hardness of, Amos 4:6; Zech. 7:8
  (Ezek. 3:7; Ezek. 11:19; Ezek. 36:26;
  Mark 6:52; Mark 10:5; Mark 16:14;
  John 12:40; Rom. 1:21; Rom. 2:5)
Hatred, Luke 14:26 (Lev. 19:17; Ps. 25:19;
  Ps. 35:19; Prov. 10:12; Prov. 10:18;
  Prov. 15:17; Prov. 26:24-26; Matt. 5:43-
  44; Matt. 6:15; Matt. 10:22; John 15:18-
  19; John 15:23-25; John 17:14; Gal. 5:19-
  20; Eph. 4:31; Col. 3:8; 1 John 2:9; 1
  John 2:11; 1 John 3:10; 1 John 3:13-15;
  1 John 4:20)
Hawking, Stephen, Prov. 3:19; 1 Cor. 2:16;
  Gen. 2:25
Hayes, Rutherford B., Philem.
Heaven, Acts 4:12; 1 John 5:12,13
  (2 Cor. 5:1; 2 Cor. 12:2-4; Eph. 1:18;
  Col. 1:5-6; Col. 1:12; Col. 3:4; 1 Thess.
  2:12; 1 Thess. 4:17; 2 Thess. 1:7; 2 Thess.
  2:14; Heb. 10:34; Heb. 11:10;
  Heb. 11:16; Heb. 12:22-24; Heb. 12:28;
  Heb. 13:14; 1 Pet. 1:4; 2 Pet. 1:11;
  2 Pet. 3:13; Rev. 2:7; Rev. 3:21; Rev. 4:4;
  Rev. 5:9; Rev. 7:9; Rev. 7:13-17;
  Rev. 14:1-3; Rev. 15:2; Rev. 21:1-5;
  Rev. 21:9-11; Rev. 21:18-19; Rev. 21:21-
  25; Rev. 21:27-22:5)
Heaven and Hell,
  Questions and Objections regarding,
    I don't mind going to hell. All my
      friends will be there. Ps. 55:15
    Could you be wrong about Judgment
      Day and the existence of hell? Ps. 76:8
    My God would never create hell.
      Matt. 18:9
    Hell isn't a place. This life is hell.
      Mark 9:47
    Is "hell-fire" preaching effective?
      Acts 24:25
    Will people who have never heard
      about Jesus go to hell? Rom. 2:12
    Does someone go to hell for commit
      ting suicide? 1 Cor. 3:17

You are using scare tactics by talking about hell and Judgment Day. Heb. 10:31
I hope I'm going to heaven when I die. 1 John 5:12,13
Hell is just a metaphor for the grave. Rev. 1:18
How can people be happy in heaven when their unsaved loved ones are in hell? Rev. 21:4
Heavens, 1 Cor. 2:16
  lights in, Ps. 104:19; 136:7–9; 147:4
  stretching out, Ps. 104:2
Hecklers, Matt. 5:10–12; Acts 3:4;
  16:16–18; 17:22; 21:30; 1 Cor. 2:4;
  2 Pet. 2:6–8
Hell, Mark 9:47; Heb. 10:31; Jude 23
  degrees of punishment in, Matt. 11:24;
  Luke 10:14
  description of, Rev. 1:18
  friends will be there, Ps. 55:15; Rev. 21:4
  reality of, Ps. 76; Ps. 76:8; Prov. 11:21;
  Matt. 5:22; 5:29,30; 10:28; 18:9; 23:33;
  25:41; Mark 9:43–48; Luke 16:23;
  Rev. 20:15; 21;8
  reason for, John 16:9; Rom. 2:12
  reasonableness of, Ps. 55:15; Acts 24:25
Henry, Matt., Ps. 8:5; 19:7–11; 22:6–8;
  22:18; Matt. 5:22; Luke 4:18; 10:20;
  13:20,21; John 4:36; 1 Tim. 1:8; Ex. 33;
  2 Sam. 14; Neh. 8; Nah. 1
Henry, Patrick, Luke 6; 1 Cor. 15:55;
  Philem.
Henry, Prince of Wales, 1 Cor. 15:55
Herschel, John Frederick, Ps. 33:8
Herschel, William, Ps. 33:8
Hinduism, Ps. 115:4–9; Rom. 7:24,25
  beliefs of, 2 Thess. 3
Hitler, Adolf, Matt. 11:24; Acts 4:12;
  Rev. 1:18; Rev. 2
Hittite Empire, Matt. 26:54
Hoagland, Paul, Prov. 4:1–5
Hobbs, Thomas, 1 Cor. 15:55
Hollywood, evil imaginations of, Mic. 2:1
Holmes, Oliver Wendell Jr., Heb. 2:6
Holy Spirit, John 20:22
  role in salvation, John 16:8–11;
  Acts 10:38
  power to witness, Mic. 3:8
Homosexuality, John 13:2; Rom. 1:27;
  1 Cor. 6:9–11; 1 Tim. 1:8–10;
  2 Pet. 2:6–8; 3:3; Jude 7; Ezek. 16:49;
  Isa. 3:9
  God made me to be a homosexual, so He doesn't want me to change. Jude 7

How to Confront Sinners, Ps. 41:4
How to Use the Ten Commandments in Witnessing, Ps. 51:6
How to Witness to Mormons, Mark 11:25
How to Witness to Muslims, Acts 17:22
Hoover, Herbert, Philem.
Horse, marvels of, Job 39:19
Hovind, Kent, Ps. 146:6; Prov. 3:19;
  Matt. 24:38,39; 1 Cor. 15:39;
  2 Pet. 3:3–6;
  Jude; Gen. 2
Howe, Thomas, Ps. 5:5; 37:9; Matt. 10:23
Hoyle, Fred, Ps. 33:6; Rev. 14:7
Humanism, Prov. 4:1–5
Human sacrifice, God condoning? Gen. 22:2
  (Lev. 18:21; Lev. 20:2-5; Deut. 12:31)
Humbling of the Law, Dan. 4:15
Humilty, walking with God in, Mic. 6:8
Huxley, Aldus, 1 Cor. 15:55
Hypocrisy, Job 20:5; Matt. 23:9; 23:13–16;
  Mark 11:15; John 1:46; 1 Thess. 2:9,10;
  2 Tim. 2:19; Heb. 9:14; 1 Pet. 3:1,2;
  1 John 3:13
  The church is full of hypocrites. 2 Tim. 2:19
Idolatry, Dan. 3:12; Ps. 106:35–39; 115:4–9;
  Matt. 18:9; 1 Cor. 10:1; 10:14; Col. 3:10;
  Ex. 32:1-6
Ignatius, Peter Kreeft, Deut. 30
Imaginations, evil, Mic. 2:1 (Gen. 6:5;
  Gen. 8:21; Deut. 29:19-20;
  1 Chron. 28:9; Prov. 6:16-18; Matt. 5:28;
  Rom. 1:21)
Immune system, Ps. 90:2; John 20:26
In-depth Comments
  About Abortion, Ps. 127:3
  An Interesting Quiz, Ps. 139:16
  Bible Stands Alone , Ps. 119:105
  Contradictions in the Bible—Why Are They There? Mark 15:26
  Dead Sea Scrolls 1 Pet,.1:25
  Archaeology and History Attest to the Deity of Jesus, John 10:36
  Firefighters, 1 John 4:8
  Freedom from Sabbath-keeping, Col. 2:16
  God's Love: The Biblical Presentation, Matt. 10:22
  Gospel: Why not preach that Jesus gives happiness, peace, and joy? 2 Cor. 2:17
  Hands of the Carpenter Luke 23:53
  How to Preach at a Funeral for Someone
  How to Witness to Muslims, Acts 17:22
  How to Preach at a Funeral for Someone You Suspect Died Unsaved, John 11:14

Is Repentance Necessary for Salvation?
John 3:16
Is Suffering the Entrance to Heaven?,
Acts 4:12
Jehovah's Witnesses: Witnessing Tips,
1 Tim. 3:16
Key to Reaching the Lost, Luke 11:52
Last Words of Famous People,
1 Cor. 15:55
"Missing Link" Still Missing, Acts 14:15
Points to Ponder About the Flood and
Noah's Ark, Matt. 24:38,39
Parable of the Fishless Fishermen,
Mark 1:17
Personal Witnessing— How Jesus Did It,
John 4:7
Questions for Evolutionists, Prov. 3:19
Reliability of the Bible, Matt. 4:4
Significance of the First Miracle
Performed by Moses, John 2:6–11
Sermon on the Mount, Matt. 5:1
Speaking the Truth in Love to Jehovah's
Witnesses, 1 Cor. 13:2
"Sinner's Prayer"— To Pray or Not To
Pray? John 1:13
Ten Ways to Break the Stronghold of
Pornography, Gal. 5:16
What is the Purpose of the Law? Gal. 3:19
Witness, Mark 15:39
Iniquity, Ps. 32:1,2
Instinct, Ps. 32:9
Irreducible complexity, Ps. 139:14
Islam, Gen. 21:18 (See also Muslim)
Israel, Luke 21:26; 1 Thess. 5:20
crossing Jordan, Josh. 3:14–17
Jackson, Andrew, 1 Cor. 15:55
Jackson, Stonewall, Phil. 3:13; 1 Thess. 5:17
James, Jesse, 1 Cor. 15:55
Jefferson, Thomas, Ps. 1:6; Matt. 5:22;
1 Pet. 2:2
Jeffery, Grant R., Acts 14:15; 1 Cor. 11:9;
Heb. 11:3
Jehovah's Witnesses, Matt. 8:2; Rev. 7:4–8
witnessing to, 1 Cor. 13:2; 1 Tim. 3:16
Jennings, Ben, Luke 18:1; Phil. 4:6
Jesus (See also Christ), Ps. 22:1
cleansing of temple, John 2:13–17
deity of, Matt. 8:2; John 10:36
genealogy of, Matt. 1:1; Luke 3:23
"not sinless," Mark 11:15
only way to God, John 14:6
Second Coming of, Matt. 10:23; 16:27;
24:27; 24:39; 25:31; 26:64; Mark 8:38;
Luke 12:40; 21:27; Acts 1:11; 1 Cor. 4:5;
Phil. 4:5; 1 Thess. 5:2; Heb. 9:28; 10:37;

11:3; James 5:8; Jude 14; Rev. 1:7; 3:11;
16:15; 22:20
siblings of, Mark 6:3
temptation of, Luke 4:10,11; Heb. 4:15
time in tomb, Matt. 12:40
unique words of, John 5:28; 6:38; 6:47;
6:53,54; 8:51; 8:58; 11:25; 14:6; 14:21;
17:5
uniqueness of, John 6:68; 7:46; 11:25;
Acts 17:22; 1 Cor. 10:20; 2 Thess. 3;
2 John
love for, Song of Sol. 2:16
physical description, Gen. 49:10
Jews, Luke 3:7–9; Acts 13:39
oppression of, Luke 21:24
history of, Ezek. 11:17
regaining Jerusalem, Ezek. 33:13
Joy, Ps. 62 (Isa. 25:9; Isa. 29:19; Isa. 30:29;
Isa. 35:1-2; Isa. 35:10; Isa. 41:16;
Isa. 44:23; Isa. 49:13; Isa. 51:11;
Isa. 52:9; Isa. 55:12; Isa. 56:7; Isa. 61:3;
Isa. 61:7; Isa. 61:10; Isa. 65:14;
Isa. 65:18-19; Isa. 66:10-12; Isa. 66:14;
Jer. 15:16; Jer. 31:12-14; Jer. 31:25-26;
Jer. 33:6; Jer. 33:11; Joel 2:23; Nah. 1:15;
Hab. 3:18; Matt. 25:21; Luke 1:47;
Luke 2:10; Luke 6:22-23; Luke 10:20;
Luke 15:6-8; Luke 15:10-32; Luke 24:52-
53; John 16:20; John 16:22; John 16:24;
John 16:33; John 17:13; Acts 2:28;
Acts 8:8; Acts 8:39; Acts 13:52;
Acts 16:25; Acts 16:34; Rom. 5:2;
Rom. 5:11; Rom. 12:12; Rom. 14:17;
Rom. 15:13; 2 Cor. 1:12; 2 Cor. 1:24;
2 Cor. 6:10; 2 Cor. 7:4; 2 Cor. 8:2;
2 Cor. 12:10; Gal. 5:22; Eph. 5:18-19;
Phil. 3:3; Phil. 4:4; Col. 1:11;
1 Thess. 1:6; 1 Thess. 5:16; Heb. 10:34;
James 1:2; James 5:13; 1 Pet. 1:8;
1 Pet. 4:13; 1 John 1:4; Jude 1:24)
Judas, Ps. 109:8; Prov. 10:7; Luke 22:47;
23:53; John 21 (Prophecies concerning,
Ps. 41:9; Ps. 109:8; Zech. 11:12-13;
Matt. 26:21-25; Mark 14:18-21;
Luke 22:21-23; John 13:18-26;
John 17:12; Acts 1:16; Acts 1:20 – Betrays
the Lord, Matt. 26:47-50; Mark 14:43-45;
Luke 22:47-49; John 18:2-5;
Acts 1:16-25)
Judgment,
of others, Luke 6:37; John 8:11
of God, Job 14:14; Ezek. 18:25

Judgment Day, Ps. 2:12; 7:11–13; 76:8; Acts 18:9
  reality of, Prov. 11:21; Matt. 25:32; John 5:28,29; Acts 17:31; Rom. 2:16; 14:10; 2 Cor. 5:10; 2 Thess. 1:8–10; 2 Tim. 4:1; Heb. 9:27; 2 Pet. 2:4,5,9; 3:7; Jude 14,15; Rev. 6:10,11; Eccl. 12:13
Justice, of God, Job 34:21
Justification, Acts 13:39 (Gen. 15:6; Ps. 32:2; Isa. 53:11; Isa. 54:17; Isa. 61:10; Jer. 23:6; Hab. 2:4; Zech. 3:4; John 5:24; Acts 13:39; Rom. 1:16-17; Rom. 2:13; Rom. 3:21-22; Rom. 3:24-26; Rom. 3:28; Rom. 3:30; Rom. 4:3; Rom. 4:5-5:1; Rom. 5:9; Rom. 5:11-21; Rom. 6:22; Rom. 7:1-8:1; Rom. 8:30-31; Rom. 8:33-34; Rom. 9:30-32; Rom. 10:1-21; 1 Cor. 1:30; 1 Cor. 6:11; 2 Cor. 5:19; 2 Cor. 5:21; Gal. 2:14-21; Gal. 3:6; Gal. 3:8-9; Gal. 3:11; Gal. 3:21-24; Gal. 4:21-31; Gal. 5:4-6; Eph. 6:14; Phil. 3:8-9; Col. 2:13-14; Titus 3:7; Heb. 11:4; Heb. 11:7; James 2:20-23; James 2:26)
Keith, Arthur, Rev. 14:7
Keith, Edwin, 1 Cor. 2:11
Keller, Helen, James 2:16
Kelvin, Lord, Ps. 25:14
Kennedy, D. James, Ps. 33:8; Matt. 25:12; Luke 6:46; John 10:10
Kepler, Johann, Ps. 25:14
King, Martin Luther, Jr., Mark 10:21; Luke 17:4
Kingdom, everlasting, Dan. 4:3
Kjos, Berit, Acts 9:31
Labro, Gary, Matt. 13:24–30
Lalonde, Paul, 2 Pet. 3:3–6
Lalonde, Peter, 2 Pet. 3:3–6
Lamb of God, Gen. 22:8; Exodus 12:29; (John 1:29; Rev. 6:16; Rev. 7:9-10; Rev. 7:14; Rev. 7:17; Rev. 12:11; Rev. 13:8; Rev. 14:1; Rev. 14:4; Rev. 15:3; Rev. 17:14; Rev. 19:7; Rev. 21:9; Rev. 21:14; Rev. 21:22-23; Rev. 21:27-22:1; Rev. 22:3)
Language,
  barriers, Gen. 11:9
  origin, Gen. 10:5
Laurie, Greg, Ps. 119:16
Law of God, Ex. 14:16; Ps. 19:7–11; 51:6; 119:18; Ex. 14:16; Judg. 16:25-30; Ex. 33; Ex. 35:1; Num. 2; Num. 7; Deut. 6:5-9; Deut. 17:11; Job 8:3; Job 13:23; Job 40:4; Ps. 1; Ps. 5:5;

Ps. 19:1-11; Ps. 143:2; Esther 9:13; Hab. 1:4; Hos. 4:1-3; Hos. 4; Isa. 4:4; Isa. 42; Isa. 53; Jer. 6:13-14; Jer. 17:9; Jer. 31:33; Josh. 1:7; Mal. 2:5-8; Mal. 3:5; Mal. 4:4; Neh. 8:9; Zeph. 3:4
  and Christians, Lev. 3; Lev. 19:11
  at war with, Matt. 22:36–40
  converts the soul, Ps. 19:7
  Father of Five Teaches His Little Ones the Ten Commandments Joel 2
  function of, Exod. 14:16; Job 5:18; Jon. 1:6; Ps. 5:5; 19:7–11; 143:2; Prov. 6:23; Matt. 7:6; 9:12; Mark 1:3; 7:21; Luke 3:4; John 8:4,5; 9:7; Acts 12:7; 28:23; Rom. 3:19; 3:20; 7:11; 2 Cor. 3:5,6; Gal. 2:19; 3:19; 3:24; Col. 2:21; 1 Tim. 1:5; 1:8; 4:2; Heb. 3:12; 4:12; 9:14; James 1:25; 2:10; 2 Pet. 2:22; 1 John 1:7
  hated, Neh. 9:26
  perfection of, 19:7–11; James 1:25; Hab. 1:4
  relevance to Christian, Prov. 6:23–30, Lev. 3
  reveals sin, Amos 5:12
  spiritual nature of, Ps. 19:7–11; Matt. 5:22; 15:19; Luke 10:26; Acts 17:22; 20:27; Gal. 3:10; 1 Pet. 1:23; 1 John 3:15
  using in evangelism, Matt. 19:17–22; Mark 10:17; John 3:16; 8:4,5; Acts 2:37; 17:29; 28:23; Rom. 2:21; James 2:8; 4:2–4; Jude 3
  violation of, Ezek. 45:20
  without mercy, Num. 15:32
  written in heart, Ps. 40:7–9
  preaching, Ex. 23
Lee, Robert E., Philem.; Ex. 14
Legalism, Prov. 15:15; Luke 9:30; Col. 2:21
Lehmann, Danny, Acts 16:6
Lenin, Vladimir, Prov. 4:1–5
Lewis, C. S., Ps. 76; Ps. 90:7,8; Matt. 28:19; Luke 15; John 11:25; 1 Cor. 15:31; 2 Cor. 12:9; 1 Pet. 1:15; Num. 24; Gen. 5
  on pain, Gen. 5:3
Liederbach, Mark, 1 John 3:16
Life,
  offered by God, Amos 5:5
  sanctity of, Ps. 127:3; 139:16; Matt. 5:44
  longevity (Gen. 6:3; Exod. 20:12; 1 Kings 3:11-14; Job 5:26; Ps. 21:4; Ps. 34:11-13; Ps. 90:10; Ps. 91:16; Prov. 3:1-2; Prov. 3:16; Prov. 9:11; Prov. 10:27; Isa. 65:20; 1 Pet. 3:10-11)

everlasting (Ps. 21:4; Ps. 121:8; Ps. 133:3;
Isa. 25:8; Dan. 12:2; Matt. 19:16-21;
Matt. 19:29; Matt. 25:46; Mark 10:30;
Luke 18:18; Luke 18:30; Luke 20:36;
John 3:14-16; John 4:14; John 5:24-
25; John 5:29; John 5:39; John 6:27;
John 6:40; John 6:47; John 6:50-58;
John 6:68; John 10:10; John 10:27-28;
John 12:25; John 12:50; John 17:2-3;
Acts 13:46; Acts 13:48; Rom. 2:7;
Rom. 5:21; Rom. 6:22-23;
1 Cor. 15:53-54; 2 Cor. 5:1; Gal. 6:8;
1 Tim. 1:16; 1 Tim. 4:8; 1 Tim. 6:12;
1 Tim. 6:19; 2 Tim. 1:10; Titus 1:2;
Titus 3:7; 1 John 2:25; 1 John 3:15; 1
John 5:11-13; 1 John 5:20; Jude 1:21;
Rev. 1:18) [see Afterlife]
Light, Heb. 11:3 (Gen. 1:3-5; Ps. 74:16;
Isa. 45:7; 2 Cor. 4:6)
Lincoln, Abraham, Ps. 119:14; 119:104;
Prov. 17; Prov. 28:13; Mark 1:35;
Luke 6:27; John 2:24,25; 1 Cor. 15:6;
2 Tim. 1:10; James 4:17; Dan. 4
Lipson, H. S., Rev. 14:7
Livingstone, David, Acts 20:24; Rom. 11
Lloyd-Jones, Dr. Martyn, Rom. 3:20;
Lev. 19; Ex. 21; Duet. 17
Louis XVII, 1 Cor. 15:55
Love for God, Ps. 5:5; Rev. 1:17
Lust, Prov. 27:20; Matt. 5:28; Mark 6:23
(Gen. 3:6; Exod. 20:17; Job 31:9-12;
Ps. 81:12; Prov. 6:24-25; Matt. 5:28;
Mark 4:19; John 8:44; 1 Cor. 9:27;
1 Cor. 10:6-7; Eph. 4:22; 1 Tim. 6:9;
2 Tim. 2:22; 2 Tim. 4:3-4; Titus 2:12;
James 1:14-15; James 4:1-3; 1 Pet. 2:11;
1 Pet. 4:3; 2 Pet. 2:18; 2 Pet. 3:3;
1 John 2:16-17; Jude 1:16; Jude 1:18)
Luther, Martin, Ps. 1:6; 82:7; Matt. 9:12;
18:11; Mark 1:35; 9:34,35; 10:44;
Luke 18; Rom. 3:20; 7:9; 1 Cor. 15:55;
2 Cor. 12:11; Gal. 1:6; 3:21; Eph. 6:4;
1 Tim. 4:2; Heb. 4:4; 1 John 5:10; Jude 3;
Judg. 6; Num. 7; 1 Sam. 12, 13;
2 Kings 13; Lev. 25; Ex. 20; 2 Cor. 14,
Hos. 4
Lying, Gen. 12:13 (John 8:44-45; Eph. 4:25;
Eph. 4:29; Col. 3:9; 1 Tim. 1:9-10;
1 Tim. 4:2; 1 Pet. 3:10; 1 Pet. 3:16;
Rev. 21:8; Rev. 21:27; Rev. 22:15)
MacArthur, John, Matt. 10:22; 20:28;
Acts 28:23; Rom. 3:19; 5:20; James 2:10
Machen, J. Gresham, Rom. 2:21
Macroevolution, Ps. 90:2

Madison, James, Ps. 22:28; Luke 9:25
Man,
dominion of, Ps. 8:6; Matt. 6:26
fear of, Ps. 56:11; Luke 1:74; John 18:17;
Phil. 4:13
made in God's image, Ps. 32:9
master of his own destiny, Ps. 89:48
(See also sinners)
Marijuana, Prov. 27:25
Marx, Karl, 1 Cor. 15:55
Marriage, biblical pattern for, Prov. 31:10
Martin, A. N., John 8:10–12
Martyr, Justin, Acts 7:59
Martyrdom, Jer. 26:8
Martyrs, Ps. 76:8; Acts 7; Acts 7:59; Rev. 12,
14, 18
Mary, Mark 3:31–35; 6:3; Luke 8:20, 21;
11:27, 28
Maury, Matt., Ps. 8:8
McCollum, Todd P., John 10:10
McDowell, Josh, John 7:46; 2 Tim. 3:16;
2 Pet. 1:21
McGee, J. Vernon, Gal. 6:7
McKinley, William, Philem.
McRay, John, Luke 1:3
Meade, Ron, 1 Pet. 3:12
Melanchthon, Luke 24:47; Heb. 9:14
Mercy of God, Lam. 3:22-36
Message of the Christian, Hos. 10:12
Metherell, Alexander, Matt. 27:46
Microevolution, Ps. 90:2
Middle East, Luke 21:26; Acts 7:5
Milton, John, 1 Cor. 15:55
Mineo, Sal, 1 Cor. 15:55
Miracle, significance of first by Moses,
John 2:6–11
"Missing link," Acts 14:15
Mohler, R. Albert Jr., John 1:41; Rev. 3:16
Money, the love of, Ezek. 7:19; Isa. 52:3
Moody, D. L., Luke 22; John 2:24,25;
Rom. 3:19; 1 Cor. 15:55; Col. 2:16;
Heb. 12:3; James 1:25; Josh. 2
Moreland, J. P., Rev. 18
Morey, Robert, 1 Pet. 3:12; Gen. 22
Mormonism, Matt. 16:17; John 10:16;
Acts 17:26; Heb. 1:1
beliefs of, James 5
Mormons, how to witness to, Mark 11:25
Morris, Henry M., Ps. 25:14
Morse, Sam., Ps. 25:14
Moses, Ps. 78:5,6; 103:17; 104:19; 109:15;
Matt. 22:36–40; Luke 1:74; 9:30;
John 1:18; 2:6–11; 3:14,15; 8:58;
Acts 7:22; 7:33; 17:22; Rom. 5:14;
1 Cor. 10:4; Eph. 6:1,2; 1 Tim. 3:16;

Titus; Heb. 4:4; 8:5; 1 Pet. 5 (Exod. 3:10;
     Exod. 4:5; Exod. 4:11-12; Exod. 6:13;
     Exod. 7:2; Exod. 17:16; Exod. 19:3-9;
     Exod. 33:11; Num. 11:17; Num. 12:7-8;
     Num. 36:13; Deut. 1:3; Deut. 5:31;
     Deut. 18:15; Deut. 18:18; Deut. 34:10;
     Deut. 34:12)
Mote, Richard, Ps. 1:6
Moth, peppered, Ps. 104:24
Mother Nature, Rom. 8:22
Mott, John R., Joel 3
Mueller, George, Ps. 78; Col. 3:3
Muggeridge, Malcolm, Matt. 19:4
Murder,
     the first, Gen. 4:9
     in Ten Commandments
     (Prov. 6:16-17; Prov. 12:6; Prov. 28:17;
     Isa. 26:21; Isa. 59:3; Isa. 59:7; Jer. 2:34;
     Jer. 7:9-10; Jer. 19:4; Jer. 22:3;
     Ezek. 22:9; Ezek. 35:6; Hos. 1:4;
     Hos. 4:1-3; Hab. 2:10; Hab. 2:12;
     Matt. 5:21-22; Matt. 15:19; Matt. 19:18;
     Mark 7:21; Mark 10:19; Luke 18:20;
     Rom. 13:9; Gal. 5:19-21; 1 Tim. 1:9;
     James 2:11; 1 Pet. 4:15; 1 John 3:12;
     1 John 3:15; Rev. 9:21; Rev. 21:8;
     Rev. 22:15)
Murray, Andrew, 1 Cor. 1:18
Muslim, Matt. 16:17; Heb. 1:1
     how to witness to, Acts 17:22
     (See also Islam)
Mussolini, Benito, Prov. 3:34; John 21
Mysteries, Dan. 2:11
Napoleon, John 7
Nation,
     blessings on, Ps. 33:12; Prov. 29:2
     iniquity in, Prov. 28:4
     reliance on God, Ps. 67:4; Prov. 28:13
Natural selection, Ps. 90:2; 104:24
Nature, God's purpose in, Ps. 25:14
Nazis, Luke 6:27; Acts 4:12; Rev. 2
Neighbor,
     identity of, Luke 10:26
     interest of, Prov. 29:2
     love for, Ps. 49:7; Prov. 3:27,28;
     Matt. 3:1; Gal. 5:14; 1 Pet. 1:8
     witness to, Prov. 27:10; 1 Pet. 3:8,9
New Age, Prov. 26:12; Eph. 4:18
New Birth, Matt. 17:1-8; John 1:13; 3:3;
     3:7; John 15; 2 Cor. 5:17; Titus 3:5;
     Heb. 8:10; 1 Pet. 1:3; 1:23; 1 John 5:1;
     2 John
New creature, in Christ, Job 14:4
     (2 Cor. 5:17; Gal. 6:15)

Newcombe, Jerry, Ps. 33:8
Newton, Sir Isaac, Job 38:24; Ps. 25:14;
     Ps. 63; Rom. 1:20; 2 Tim. 3:16;
     Heb. 1:2,3
Newton, John, Ps. 35; Ps. 119:18;
     Matt. 19:17-22; John 1:17
Noah, Matt. 24:37-39; 24:38,39;
     Luke 17:26,27; Acts 16:16-18; 17:26;
     1 Cor. 1:27,28; Titus 3; Heb. 4:4; 11:7;
     1 Pet. 3:20; 1 Pet. 5; 2 Pet. 2:5; 3:3; 3:6
     (Gen. 6:14-22; Gen. 7:8; Gen. 8:20;
     Gen. 8:22; Gen. 9:9-17; Gen. 9:28-29;
     Matt. 24:38; Luke 17:27)
Obedience, Isa. 6:1
     as key to success, Josh. 1:6
Ocean,
     Currents of, Ps. 8:8
     Floor of, Ps. 95:4,5
Occult, Acts 16:16 (Lev. 19:26-28;
     Lev. 19:31; Lev. 20:6; Deut. 18:9-14)
Omniscience of God, Ezek. 8:15
Open-air preaching, Prov. 15:1; 21:24;
     Matt. 3:1, Luke 8; Acts 3, 18
     Aim for Repentance Rather Than a
     Decision, Acts 20:21
     Crowd Etiquette, Acts 3:4
     Give Yourself a Lift, Acts 17:22
     How to Draw a Crowd, Acts 2:14
     Make the Bullet Hit the Target,
         Matt. 28:19
     Never Fear Hecklers, Matt. 5:10
         points for, Matt. 5:10-12; 28:19,20;
         Acts 2:14; 3:4; 7:55; 14:19; 16:16-18;
         17:22; 20:21; 21:30; 1 Cor. 2:4;
         2 Tim. 2:24-26
     questions for crowd-drawing, Acts 2:14
     Raw Nerves, Acts 21:30
     Watch for "Red Herrings" or "Rabbit
     Trails," 1 Cor. 2:4
     "Watch It, Blind Man!" 2 Tim. 2:24-26
Oscar Wilde, 1 Cor. 15:55
Oswald, Lee Harvey, 1 Cor. 15:55
Owen, John, 1 Cor. 15:55
Packer, J. I., Prov. 6:23
Pain, commentary by C. S. Lewis, Gen. 5:3
Palau, Luis, Ps. 94:1; Ps. 147
Parables, key to, Mark 4:13
Parker, Gary E., Ps. 25:14
Pascal, Blaise, Ps. 25:14; 1 Cor. 15:17;
     1 Tim. 2:5; Deut. 30
Passion,
     for the lost, Jer. 4:19
Passover, and salvation, Exod. 12:1; Ex.
     12:1-16 ; Exod. 12:29

Pasteur, Louis, Ps. 25:14; Ps. 106;
Rom. 1:20
Pastors, 1 Cor. 4:16; Eph. 4:11; Heb. 10:25
Patterson, Colin, Acts 17:24
Patterson, Paige, John 14:6
Pearl, Michael, Rom. 9:1
Penn, William, Ps. 22; Matt. 6:31–33;
Mark 10:21
Perfection, Matt. 5:48; Rom. 7:18,19
Personal Witnessing
How do I reach my neighbors with the
gospel? Prov. 27:10
How do I witness to a person in a denom-
ination, but who isn't trusting Christ?
Matt. 8:14
What should I say to someone who has
lost a loved one through cancer?
Acts 9:37
How should I witness to a Jew? Rom. 3:1
How do I witness to someone I know?
Rom. 14:12
How should I witness to a homosexual? 1
Tim. 1:8–10
How should I witness to my coworkers? 1
Pet. 2:15
Peterson, Eugene, Heb. 12:29
Philip III, King of France, 1 Cor. 15:55
Pink, A. W., Matt. 7:6 and Matt. 9
Piper, John, Luke 11:2
Plucked from the fire, every Christian,
Zech. 3:2
Pornography, Luke 9:62; 15:21; 2 Pet. 2:22;
1 John 3:13
breaking stronghold of, Gal. 5:16
Poverty, spiritual, Ps. 40:17
Pratney, Winkie, Mark 13:10
Prayer, Ps. 58:6; Matt. 6:9; 17:20; 26:41;
Mark 14:38; Luke 3:21; 11:2; Col. 4:12;
1 Thess. 5:17; 1 Tim. 2:1; 1 John 5:14;
Ezek. 22:30; Neh. 1:4 and 4:8; Ezra 9:1-6
choice of two, 1 Thess. 4
in restaurant, Mark 8:38
lack of, Luke 18:1
model, of repentance, Ps. 89
secret weapon of, Mark 6:46; 11:23;
Luke 5:16; 6:12; 22:41; Acts 1:14; 4:24;
12:12; 21:5
sinner's, of repentance, John 1:13
when not heard by God, Isa. 59:1
Preaching, Zechariah 10:2-3
at funeral, John 11:14
"hell-fire," Acts 24:25; Heb. 10:31
(Also see open-air preaching)
Price, Rob, Acts 17:30

Pride, Ps. 34:2; Job 35:10; Obad. 1:3
(Matt. 23:6-8; Matt. 23:10-12; Mark 7:21-
22; Mark 10:43; Mark 12:38-39;
Luke 1:51-52; Luke 9:46; Luke 11:43;
Luke 14:8-9; Luke 18:14; Luke 20:45-47;
Rom. 1:22; Rom. 1:29-30; Rom. 11:17-
21; Rom. 11:25; Rom. 12:3; Rom. 12:16;
1 Cor. 1:29; 1 Cor. 3:18; 1 Cor. 4:6-8;
1 Cor. 4:10; 1 Cor. 5:2; 1 Cor. 5:6;
1 Cor. 8:1-2; 1 Cor. 10:12; 1 Cor. 13:4;
1 Cor. 14:38; 2 Cor. 10:5; 2 Cor. 10:12;
2 Cor. 10:18; 2 Cor. 12:7; Gal. 6:3;
Eph. 4:17; Phil. 2:3; 1 Tim. 2:9;
1 Tim. 3:6; 1 Tim. 6:3-4; 1 Tim. 6:17;
2 Tim. 3:2; 2 Tim. 3:4; James 3:1;
James 4:6; 1 Pet. 5:3; 1 Pet. 5:5;
1 John 2:16; Rev. 3:17-18; Rev. 18:7-80
Man is the master of his own destiny!
Ps. 89:48
Prince, Derek, John 7:17; Acts 10:38
Principles of Growth for the New and
Growing Christian
Daily Nutrition, 1 Pet. 2:2
Evangelism—Our Most Sobering Task,
Luke 10:2
Faith—Elevators Can Let You Down,
Heb. 6:18
Fellowship—Flutter by Butterfly,
Heb. 10:25
Prayer—"Wait for a Minute", Matt. 6:9
Thanksgiving—Do the Right Thing,
Eph. 5:20
Warfare—Praise the Lord and Pass the
Ammunition , 2 Cor. 4:4
Water Baptism— Sprinkle or Immerse?
Acts 2:38
Tithing—The Final Frontier,
Mark 12:41–44
Promised land, Num. 13
Prophecy, 1 Tim. 2:5
messianic, Ps. 16:10; 22:12–18; 22:16;
22:18; 27:12; 34:20; 40:7–9; 41:9; 69:9;
69:21; 78:2; 110; 118:22; Matt. 4:4
fulfilled, Matt. 4:4; 13:34,35; 26:15;
26:60; 26:62,63; 27:39–44; Mark 13:2;
14:10; 14:65; 15:24; Luke 1:32,33; 3:33;
23:32–34; 24:39; John 1:11; 1:32; 6:14;
19:29; 19:33,36; Acts 2:31; 1 Pet. 2:24
Prophets, false, Ezek. 13:10
Protestant Church, Ps. 1:6
Qua'ran, concerning Arab descent from
Abraham, Gen. 21:18
Quarantine, Ps. 38:11
Rabbits, Ps. 147:9

Races, origin of, Acts 17:26

Radiometric dating, Ps. 146:6

Raleigh, Walter, 1 Cor. 15:55

Ravenhill, Leonard, Rom. 8:6; 2 Cor. 4:2

Reader, John, Ps. 104:24

Reagan, Ronald, 1 Tim. 3:9; Philem.

Rebellion of sinners, Ezek. 20:8
  (Prov. 17:11); Isa. 57:4

Record of Christian Work, Oct. 1908,
  Eccl. 3; May 1909, Ezra 8

Redpath, Alan, Acts 8:19

Reidhead, Paris, John 3:16; 16:8–11;
  1 Chron. 16

Reincarnation, 2 Thess. 3; Heb. 9:27; 2 John

Religion,
  Questions and Objections regarding,
    Ps. 1:6
  caused more wars than anything else in
  history. Luke 6:27
  many denominations Ps. 1:6
  many different religions? Rom. 10:3
  Why is Christianity better than other religions? 1 Cor. 10:20

Religions,
  harm of, Luke 6:27; 1 John 2:19
  other compared to Christianity,
    1 Cor. 10:20
  reason for, Rom. 10:3

Repentance,
  model prayer of, Ps. 89; Rom. 10:9
  necessary for salvation, Ps. 103:17;
    Matt. 3:2; 4:17; Luke 13:2; 24:47;
    Acts 2:38; 3:19; 17:30; 20:21;
    John 3:16; 2 Pet. 3:9
  of God, Ps. 135:14; Zech. 8:14
  preaching, Mark 1:15

Resurrection, Matt. 28:9; Luke 24:43;
  I Kings 17:23
  evidence for,1 Cor. 15:6; 15:14; Rev. 16
  of Christ, Isa. 14:19
  of the just, Isa. 25:8
  of Christians, John 11:43,44; Phil. 3:21

Rhodes, Ron, John 10:36

Rhodes, Ross, 2 Tim. 2:21

Rifkin, Jeremy, Prov. 26:12

Righteousness, no attraction for the world,
  Isa. 51:7

Robinson, Darrell, Jude 23

Rogers, Adrian, Acts 18:26

Roosevelt, Franklin D., 1 Cor. 15:55;
  Philem.

Roosevelt, Theodore, Ps.73; Ps. 119:72;
  James 4:12

Ruse, Michael, Ps. 25:14

Rush, Benjamin, Prov. 22:6

Russia, Luke 21:26

Ryle, J. C., Luke 12:51; Rom. 7:22; Jude 20;
  Num. 33; Ex. 35, 40; Isa. 4:4

Sabbath, Acts 18:4; Col. 2:16; Rev. 18

Sainthood, Eph. 1:1

Salvation, Exodus 12:29; Daniel 16-22;
  Isa. 55:1-3; Num. 21
  by grace, Job 9:2
  from God, Ps. 3:8
  nature of, Jer. 3:23
  Questions and Objections regarding,
    How can you know that you're saved?
    Gal. 4:6
    I have been born again many times.
    John 3:3
    Is water baptism essential to salvation?
    Mark 1:4,5
    Jews don't need to be saved because
    the NT says "all Israel shall be saved."
    Luke 3:7–9

Sangster, W.E., Judg. 6

Satan, Matt. 4:6; 4:9; Luke 4:10,11
  comments on by C.H. Spurgeon, Gen. 3:1
  influence of, John 13:2; 1 Cor. 12:25;
  2 Cor. 4:4; 11:3; Gal. 1:6
  names of, John 8:44

Savior, need for, Deut. 4:24

Schaff, Philip, John 6:68

Schweitzer, Albert, Matt. 10

Schools, Prov. 4:1–5; 22:6; John 17:3;
  Acts 17:24; Eph. 6:4

Science,
  and the Bible, Eccl. 1:16
  defined, Eph. 3:9

Scientists,
  creationist, Ps. 25:14
  faith of, Ps. 33:6
  bias of, Ps. 104:24
  thoughts of, Gen. 2:1

Scott, Rachel, Rev. 12

Second coming (see Jesus)

Sedgwick, John, 1 Cor. 15:55

Self-righteousness, Gen. 3:7; Prov. 10:2;
  Matt. 5:20; 19:17–22; Luke 10:26; 16:15;
  Acts 22; Gal. 3:10; Col. 1:20
  (Prov. 12:15; Prov. 14:12; Prov. 16:2;
  Prov. 20:6; Prov. 21:2; Isa. 5:21;
  Isa. 28:17; Isa. 28:20; Isa. 47:7;
  Isa. 50:11; Isa. 64:6; Hab. 2:4; Matt. 7:22-
  23; Matt. 9:10-13; Matt. 16:6;
  Matt. 19:16-22; Matt. 22:12-13;
  Matt. 23:29-31; Mark 2:16; Mark 8:15;
  Mark 10:17-22; Luke 5:30; Luke 7:36-50;
  Luke 10:25-37; Luke 15:2; Luke 15:25-
  32; Luke 16:14-15; Luke 18:9-14;

Luke 18:18-23; John 9:34; John 9:39-41; Rom. 2:17-20; Rom. 3:27; Rom. 10:3; Rom. 11:19-21; 2 Cor. 1:9; 2 Cor. 10:17-18; Gal. 6:3; Rev. 3:17-18)

Questions and Objections regarding,
> A long time ago I was a liar and a thief, but now I try to be a good person. Prov. 20:9
> Do you think Christians are better than non-Christians? Rom. 3:9
> I believe I will go to heaven because I live by the Golden Rule. Gal. 5:14
> I'm as good as any Christian! Mark 10:18
> I'm doing fine. I don't need God. Heb. 11:25
> I need to get my life cleaned up first. Matt. 19:16
> I've broken the Ten Commandments, but I do good things for people. Prov. 16:10
> I've made my peace with the "Man up stairs." Col. 1:20
> Man is the master of his own destiny! Ps. 89:48
> What if someone denies having any sin at all? Luke 18:21

Sermon on the Mount, Matt. 3:1; 5:1; 5:2; 5:48; Mark 7:5–13; Luke 12:5
Service, professed, Mal. 3:18
Sex, biblical, Prov. 5:19
Sexes, origin of, Matt. 19:4; Mark 10:6
Sexual sin, resisting, Prov. 2:12
Sexuality, biblical, Prov. 6:6–8; 1 Cor. 7:2–5; Gal. 5:19; Lev. 18
Shakespeare, William, Matt. 4:6; 1 Cor. 15:55
Shame, no longer in Christ, Job 22:26
Shaw, George Bernard, 2 Thess. 2
Sheen, Fulton J., 1 Pet. 1:8
Sheler, Jeffery, Luke 1:27; 3:1,2; John 19:31,32
Sign, demanded by unsaved, Matt. 12:39; John 1:18
Simpson, James, Phil. 3:8
Sin, Ps. 32:1,2; Prov. 9:17; Deut. 21:18; Ps. 103:17; Ps. 41:4
> against God, Luke 15:21
> consequences of, Hos. 9:7; Hab. 1:1
> pleasure of, Isa. 40:6
> power of, Jer. 2:29
> confession of, Prov. 28:13
> denied by sinners, Luke 18:21
> deceitfulness of, Titus 3:3
> forgivable, Ps. 103:17

Heaven's silence, Job 12:6
> results of, Ps. 107:17
> sorrow for, Isa. 61:3
> mourning over ruins of Jerusalem, Lam. 1:1; Neh. 2:17
> unpardonable, Mark 3:29
Questions and Objections regarding,
> Because Jesus died on the cross, we are all forgiven of every sin. 2 Cor. 5:14,15
> Do you sin, as a Christian? 1 Pet. 4:1
> Every day I confess my sins to God and say I'm sorry and won't sin again. Eph. 1:7
> God made me like this. Sin is His fault! 1 Tim. 2:14
> God couldn't forgive my sin. Ps. 103:17
> "Judge not lest you be judged." – so you have no right to judge me. Luke 6:37
> What if someone admits sinning, but says, "I just hope God is forgiving"? Acts 26:28
> What if someone denies having any sin at all? Luke 18:21
> What should I say if someone asks, "Have you ever lusted?" Matt. 5:28
> You shouldn't talk about sin because Jesus didn't condemn anybody. Matt. 23:13
Sinners, Mark 10:18; Rom. 3:9
> concern for, Ps. 119:136; 126:6; Luke 16:24; 2 Cor. 9:2; Rev. 6:16,17; Rev. 21
> condemning, Matt. 23:13–16
> confronting biblically, Ps. 41:4
> depraved heart of, Ps. 5:9; Mark 7:20–23; John 3:19
> how to confront, Ps. 41:4
> natural state of, Ps. 92:5,6; Eph. 2:3
> thoughts of, Ps. 10:3
> wickedness of, Ps. 8:5
"Sinner's prayer," John 1:13
Slavery, Footnote, Exod. 21:5-6
Smalley, Mike, Matt. 14:15–21; John 11:14
Smith, Alan, 1 Pet. 3:15
Smith, Alice, Gal. 2:20
Smith, Oswald J., 1 Cor. 9:22; Acts 1:8; 2 Thess. 2; 1 John 4:8
Socrates, 1 Cor. 15:55
Solomon Receiving the Queen of Sheba, 2 Chron. 9

Sorrow
  for lost, Ps. 49:7
  godly, Ps. 41:4; 51:14; 130:1–4;
    John 1:13; 2 Cor. 7:10
Soil, man made of same substance as,
  Gen. 2:7
Scott, John, Ex. 33
Spence, Mark A., Prov. 6:23
Springboards for Preaching and Witnessing
  Bible and All It Contains , Ps. 119:162
  Experiential Faith, John 17:3
  Hang in There, Job 6:11
  Key, Prov. 14:12
  Love of God, Eph. 2:4,5
  New Convert, Heb. 11:29
  Olympic High Diver, 2 Cor. 6:2
  Revolting Natives, John 15:13
  Rush, Luke 16:17
  Sinking Ship, 1 Cor. 1:18
  Solid Ice, Heb. 8:6
  Sting Operation, Luke 11:39
  Titanic, Heb. 2:10
  Water or Money? Matt. 16:26
  Will to Live, James 4:14
Spirit, God does all things by, Zech. 4:6
Sproul, R. C., Ps. 21:9; 2 Tim. 4:3,4
Spurgeon, Charles, Ps. 10, 22:14, 68,
    119:136; 126:6, 132, 137, 145, 150;
    Prov. 4, 7, 11:30, 24; Matt. 11:11, 15,
    19:24, 22:36–40; Prov. 21; Prov. 22;
    Matt. 27; Mark 6; Mark 8; Mark 10;
    Mark 14; Luke 1; Luke 4:4; Luke 7;
    Luke 8; Luke 9; Luke 9:30; 11:52; 16:24;
    Luke 17; Luke 19; Luke 20; Luke 24;
    John 2:13–17; John 3; John 5; John 9:7;
    John 10; John 11:14; John 12; John 15;
    John 19; John 21; Acts 3; Acts 8; Acts 10;
    Acts 13; Acts 14:19; Acts 15; Acts 18:9;
    Acts 18; Acts 20; Acts 20:26; Acts 22;
    Acts 23; Rom 4; Rom. 7:7; Rom. 15;
    1 Cor. 4; 1 Cor. 9:22; 1 Cor. 11;
    1 Cor. 12:25; 2 Cor. 3:5,6; 2 Cor. 7;
    2 Cor. 9:2; Gal. 1:8; 2:16; 3:19; Gal. 4;
    Eph. 3; Eph. 3:9; Eph. 5; Eph. 6:17;
    Phil. 2; Phil. 2:15; Col. 2:16; Col. 3; 1
    Thess. 3; 2 Thess. 2; 2 Thess. 5; 1 Tim. 5;
    1 Tim. 5:5; 2 Tim. 4:2; Titus 3; Heb. 1:1;
    Heb. 2; Heb. 4:12; Heb. 7; Heb. 10:22;
    Heb. 13; James 1:15; James 2; 2 Pet. 2;
    1 John 2; 1 John 3:12; 4:8; 3 John; Jude;
    Rev. 1:17; Rev. 14; Rev. 20:11; Rev. 21;
    Rev. 22:2; Gen. 3:1; Gen 4:9; Gen. 20:18;
    Gen. 21:5-6; Num. 10; Ex. 15; Ex. 16;
    Ex. 25; Gen. 3; Hab. 3; Dan. 2; Dan. 10
  On murder, Gen. 4:9

  On sin, Gen. 3:1
Stars, Ps. 136:7–9; 147:4
Steindl-Rast, David, Ps. 62
Stevenson, Robert Louis, 1 Cor. 15:10
Stewardship, Ps. 24:1; 1 Tim. 1:12;
    2 Tim. 4:3,4; Titus 1:9; Rev. 11:18
Stott, John. R. W, 2 Cor. 16
Strobel, Lee, Rev. 18
Stubbornness for the Kingdom, Ezek. 3:8
Studd, C. T., Rom. 12:1; Ex. 25
Success, biblical formula for, Ps. 1:1–3
Success, key to, Josh. 1:6
Suffering,
  way to enter heaven?, Acts 4:12
  reason for, Rom. 5:12
  (for Christ, Acts 9:16; Rom. 8:17-23;
    Rom. 8:26; 1 Cor. 4:12-13; 2 Cor. 1:7;
    2 Cor. 4:11-18; Phil. 1:29; Phil. 2:27-30;
    Phil. 3:10; Col. 1:24; 2 Thess. 1:4-5;
    2 Tim. 2:12; James 5:10; 1 Pet. 4:13-14;
    1 Pet. 5:10)
Suicide, Acts 19; Rom. 5:14; 1 Cor. 3:17;
    2 Tim. 2:26
Sun, circuit of, Ps. 19:5,6
Sunday, Billy, John 1; John 1:41
Swindoll, Chuck, Acts 8:26,27
Tada, Joni Eareckson, Acts 24:25; 2 Sam. 22
Tahmisian, T. N., Mark 10:6
Taylor, Hudson, Matt. 17:20; 1 Cor. 9:22;
    Phil. 2:13; 4:13
Taylor, Jack, 2 Chron. 12
Taylor, James H., 2 Chron. 36; Ruth 4
Temple,
  built by King Solomon, I Kings 5:5-6
Ten Boom, Corrie, Num. 22; Heb. 10:23
Ten Commandments, Numbers 21;
  Ps. 22:28; Joshua 6:1-20; Daniel 6:16-22;
  Joel 2; Nehemiah 8:2-9; John 3:14-15;
  John 7; John 8:6; Gal. 6:7; Ps. 32:5;
  Ps. 51:6; Ps. 1:18
  breaking all, Ps. 32:5
  how to memorize, Ex. 21
  teaching to children, Joel 2,
    Ps. 78:5,6; Rom.15
  use in witnessing, Ps. 51:6; Luke 12:5;
    John 8:9
  to memorize, Exod. 21
  Questions and Objections regarding,
    What if someone says, "I've broken
    every one of the Ten
    Commandments"? Ps. 32:5
    You're trying to make me feel guilty by
    quoting the Ten Commandments.
      John 8:9
  (See also Law)

Thanksgiving, Ezra 3:11

Thermodynamics, Second Law of, Ps. 33:6; 102:25,26

Time, created by God, Ps. 90:4

Titanic, Prov. 15; Heb. 2:10

Tithing, Mark 12:41–44 (2 Chron. 31:11-12; Neh. 10:38-39; Neh. 12:44; Neh. 13:5; Neh. 13:12; Mal. 3:10)

Tolerance, Matt. 21:12,13; Luke 6:37; 2 John 9

Tolstoy, Leo 1 Cor. 15:55

Tomczak, Larry, 1 Cor. 6:19

Torrey, R. A., Matt. 26:41; 2 Kings 24

Tozer, A. W., Job 34; Ps. 95:6; Prov. 28:5; Matt. 7:26; John 6:65; Acts 27; Acts 28; Dan. 8

Tracts, Matt. 10:27,28; Mark 4:14; Mark 4; John 4:7; 1 Cor. 9:22; Eph. 1:9; Phil. 4:13; 1 Tim. 4:1; James 2:7; Rev. 22:2

Trials of life, Jon. 1:4 (Ps. 55:16-23; Ps. 119:65-72; 1 Pet. 1:7; 1 Pet. 4:12; 1 Pet. 5:7); Dan. 3:24; Dan. 6:16-22

Transfiguration of Jesus, Matt. 17:1–8, Luke 3:21; 9:30; 23:53

Transgression, Ps. 32:1,2; 51:13–17

Trials, benefit of, Ps. 66:10–12; Luke 22:31,32; 1 Cor. 7:4; 2 Cor. 12:9; Eph. 5:20

Trinity, in redemption, Acts 10:38

Truth, opposition to, Ezek. 12:2

Twain, Mark, Ps. 119; Matt. 5:10–12; Mark 15:12

Tyndale, William, 2 Cor. 3:14–16

United States, sins of, Deut.28:15

Unpardonable sin, Mark 3:29 (2 Kings 24:4; Matt. 12:31-32; Luke 12:10; Heb. 6:4-6; 1 John 5:16)

Van Gogh, Vincent, 1 Cor. 15:55

Vander Griend, Alvin J., Col. 4:12; 1 Tim. 2:1; 1 John 5:14

Varney, Mark, Ps. 104:24

Vegetarianism, Ps. 66:15; Rom. 14:2; 1 Tim. 4:3

Virgin birth, Isa. 7:14; Matt. 1:20–23

Vision, Valley of Dry Bones, Ezek. 37:1–10

Voice of the Lord, Ps. 29:3–9

Voltaire, Ps. 119:105; 1 Cor. 15:55

Wallace, Lew, 1 Cor. 15:55

Washington, Booker T., 1 John 4:20

Washington, George, Ps. 51:7; 67:4; Acts 22; 2 Pet. 3

Water cycle, Ps. 135:7

Water, sitting in the sky, Job 26:8

Waters, Ethel, Ps. 139:16

Watts, Isaac, Mark 9:43–48; Rom. 2:4; 1 Cor. 15:55

Weapons always ready, Neh. 4:17

Webster, Dan., Ps. 33:12; 119:97; Prov. 28:4; 1 Cor. 3:13,14; 15:55; Philem.; 1 Pet. 4:5

Webster, Noah, Prov. 14:34; 29:2

Weiss, Dan. L., Luke 19:17; Phil. 1:29

Wells, H. G., 1 Cor. 15:55

Wesley, John, Ps. 139:16; Matt. 5:1; 5:16; 16:18; Matt. 25; John 9:4; Acts 12:7; 21:30; Rom. 3:19; 7:11; 7:22; 1 Cor. 1:23; 2 Cor. 7:4; 12:15; 1 Tim. 2:8; 6:18; Heb. 3:12; 4:12; Jude; Judg. 7; Lev. 4; Num. 2; Hos. 9; Dan. 9

West, Ronald, R., Ps. 146:6

Wheeler, John, Prov. 3:19; Gen 2:25

Whitefield, George, Mark 4; Rom. 3:20; 7:18,19; Rom. 12; 1 Cor. 9:22; Rev. 3:16; 6:16,17; Ex. 19 and 23; Isa. 44

Wickedness, of human heart, Job 10:7 and 15:15 (Gen. 6:5; Gen. 8:21; 1 Sam. 17:28; Prov. 6:14; Prov. 6:18; Prov. 11:20; Eccles. 8:11; Eccles. 9:3; Jer. 4:14; Jer. 4:18; Jer. 17:9; Rom. 1:21)

Wilkerson, David, Luke 19:10

Wilson, Woodrow, Philem. and Gen 3:7

Winthrop, Robert, Ps. 22:28

Wisdom, of man and of God, Dan. 2:11 (Ps. 111:10; Prov. 1:5; Prov. 1:7; Prov. 1:20-2:20; Prov. 3:13-26; Prov. 8:1-9:6; Prov. 10:8; Prov. 10:13-14; Prov. 10:21; Prov. 10:23; Prov. 11:12; Prov. 12:8; Prov. 12:15; Prov. 14:6-8; Prov. 14:16; Prov. 14:33; Prov. 15:2; Prov. 15:7; Prov. 15:14; Prov. 15:33; Prov. 16:16; Prov. 16:20-24; Prov. 17:10; Prov. 17:24; Prov. 18:15; Prov. 19:8; Prov. 19:20; Prov. 21:11; Prov. 22:17-21; Prov. 23:12; Prov. 23:19; Prov. 23:23; Prov. 24:13-14; Prov. 28:5; Prov. 28:7; Prov. 29:3; Col. 3:16; James 3:13); 1 Kings 3:27; Dan. 5:5-6 and 25

Witnessing, Mark 8:38; Acts 20:26; Eph. 1:9; 1 Pet. 3:8,9; Ps. 41:4; Ps. 41:4 effectiveness in, Prov. 30:25–28; John 4:37,38; 1 Cor. 4:16; 2 Cor. 7 fear in, Ps. 56:11; 91:1; 118:6; Matt. 10:27,28; Acts 4:29; Eph. 1:19; Phil. 4:13; 1 Pet. 3:15 Jesus' example of, John 4:7 to acquaintances, Rom. 14:12 to blasphemers, James 2:7 to Buddhists, 2 John to coworkers, 1 Pet. 2:15

to family members, Luke 8:39;
    Acts 18:10; 1 Pet. 3:1,2
to Hindus, 2 Thess. 3
to homosexuals, 1 Tim. 1:8–10; 2
    Pet. 2:6–8
to Jehovah's Witnesses, 1 Cor. 13:2;
    1 Tim. 3:16
to Jews, Rom. 3:1
to Mormons, Mark 11:25
to Muslims, Acts 17:22
to neighbors, Prov. 27:10
to non-English speakers,
    Closing Words of Comfort, Wordless
    Gospel
to someone in denomination, Matt. 8:14
to telemarketers, Col. 4:4
to the bereaved, Acts 9:37
using survey, 2 Pet. 2:9; 2 John
using Ten Commandments, Ps. 51:6
using tracts (see Tracts)
wisdom in, Acts 8:35
(See also Evangelism & Personal
    Witnessing)
Women, oppressed by Christianity,
    Prov. 31:10
Wooding, Dan, 2 Cor. 3:12
Word, becoming flesh, Gen. 1:3; Jer. 8:1-12
    (title of Jesus, John 1:1; John 1:14;
    1 John 5:7; Rev. 19:13)
Works (see Good works)
World threatened by the Church, Neh. 4:1
Wrath of God, Ps. 21:9; 89:14; 90:7,8;
    Rom. 2:4; 2 Cor. 2:17; 2 Cor. 7; Rev. 8:11
    warning of, Ps. 2:12; 7:11–13; 50:16;
        Acts 18:9; Gal. 4:5; 2 Tim. 2:26; Heb.
        10:31; 1 John 2
    of the Law, Mic. 1:1
Wurmbrand, Richard, Ps. 33:8; 143:2;
    Prov. 16:32; Rom. 15:16; 2 Tim. 2:21;
    Mal. 4
Wycliffe, John, Deut. 13
Yancey, Philip, Ps. 75:1
Yaxley, Trevor, Mark 16:15
Young-earth theory, Ps. 136:7–9
Zacharias, Ravi, 1 Cor. 15
Zeal,
    for the lost, Ps. 49:7; Luke 8:39; 9:30;
        16:30; Acts 8; 2 Cor. 9:2; Eph. 4:11;
        Col. 2:16; Heb. 4:16
    for the truth, Job 32:2
Zwayne, Emeal, Ps. 56:11; Matt. 10:37;
    James 5:16; Lev. 3

Ray Comfort has spoken in approximately 850 churches in almost every denomination. Dr. D. James Kennedy, Bill Gothard, David Wilkerson and many other Christian leaders have commended his ministry. He has written extensively on evangelism, including writing for Billy Graham's *Decision* magazine. The Moody Bible Institute, Leighton Ford Ministries, Institute in basic Life Principles, and the Institute for Scientific & Biblical Research use his literature. He has written more than 60 books and is a regular platform speaker at the Southern Baptist State Conferences. His videos have been seen by more than 30,000 pastors. He also co-hosts The Way of the Master Radio (www.wayofthemasterradio.com) and the award-winning television program The Way of the Master with actor Kirk Cameron.

CREATION

Adam and Eve driven from Garden

Cain slays Abel

Noah Builds Ark

The Flood

Tower of Babel built

Jericho founded, world's first walled town

Society in Japan based on hunting, fishing and gathering

Japanese pottery with geometric motifs. Greek farmers clear forests for farming

3,500 First great Sumerian civilizations emerge along Nile-Egypt and Mesopotamia

4,236- first date in Egyptian calendar

First use of plow by farmers in Britain

Llamas and alpacas domesticated in Peru; widespread cultivation of maize, potatoes and corn in North, Central and South America.

Farming begins in China

3,500 Invention of the wheel in Mesopotamia

3,372 first date in Maya calendar

3,200 Earliest surviving evidence of writing in Temple at Urk in Mesopotamia

c. 2,600 Building of Stonehenge, Britain

2,572-2,464 Great Pyramids of Cheops, Giza, completed, one of the Seven Wonders of the World

Abraham chosen by God

God destroys Sodom and Gomorrah

---

c. 2,000 Rise of Old Babylon

1,760 Hammurabi's Code-greatest warrior-ruler of Babylon created code written in cuneiform, first exercise in history to develop a civilized way of life. The Codes addressed criminal civil matters, from murder to family disputes. Isaac born to Abraham and Sarai

c. 1,600 Minonans erect palace at Knossos, in Crete.

Rise of Dong-Son culture in Vietnam, spreads across Southeast Asia

Egyptians develop mathematics

1,678 Joseph, favorite son of Jacob, sold by his brothers to be a slave

1,666 Joseph 2nd in command in Egypt

1,657 Children of Jacob (who is now called Israel) follow Joseph to live in Egypt

1,595 Hittites from Anatolia penetrate northern borders of the Babylonian empire

1,523-1,027 Bronze and jade objects are created during the Shang dynasty in China

c. 900 Olmec civilization in Mexico. Villages along Mexican Gulf Coast have irrigation system

Earliest known Native American town in North America - Mississippi

Development of the Hindu culture of Ganges valley

1,600-717 The Hittites smelt and forge iron, technique increased carbon content of iron

1,391-1,353 Reign of Pharoah Amemhotep II Egypt's Golden Age

1,304-1,237 Pharaoh Ramses II's kingdom-Nubia to the Nile Delta.

---

daughter

1,250-1,210 Moses leads Jewish people in flight from Egypt to Palestine

Moses gives the Ten Commandments to the Jews

The Ark of the Covenant is constructed

Moses dies and the Israelites cross into the Promised Land

c. 1,400 Battle of Jericho; walls of the city collapse

Caste system-rigid hierarchical structure in Indian society

Siege of Troy

Rule of Judges among the Israelites

Gideon leads small army into victory over the Midianites.

Samson betrayed by Deliah

1,100 Phoenicians develop script, which will become the basis of all European scripts.

Time of the Jewish prophets

Samuel anoints Saul to be King of Israel

Samuel anoints David to be King

1,003 David, King of Israel, establishes capital at Jerusalem

971 David dies; his son Solomon succeeds him as king

960 Solomon builds Temple on Mount Morriah

Great period of Tyre in Phoenicia

Culture of Villanova flourishes in Italy

Rheoboam in kingdom of Judea

Damascus is center of power and trade

c. 900 Foundation of Sparta, Greece-city of military training and strength

Elijah taken up in a whirlwind in a chariot of fire

C.850 Homer composes The Illiad and The Odyssey

814 Phoenicians found City of Carthage

Sardinia known for distinctive architecture and bronze sculptures

Isaiah, the prophet

Micah

Beginning of Etruscan period in Italy

Chariots introduced into Italy by Etruscans

776 first Olympic games held in Greece

753 Legendary foundation of Rome on banks of Tiber, by Romulus, first of seven kings

715 King Numa Pompilius, of Rome, establishes 12-month calendar.

700 first coins used in Lydia, Turkey

650 Greek historian Herodotus noted Phoenicians circumnavigate Africa

Lifetime of Jeremiah, Ezekiel, Daniel, Zechariah

City of Jerusalem falls to Babylonians; Solomon's Temple destroyed

551 Confucious born

550 Siddhartha Gautama Buddah, founder of Buddism, born

...of law issued in China.

Roman Republic founded; Etruscans driven ...m city

Roman Monarchy replaced by two consuls elected by popular assemblies

278 First Roman treaty with Carthage

437 Completion of the Parthenon, Greece

Life of Nehemiah

399 Trial and execution of Socrates

387 Plato founded academy in Athens

336-323 Alexander the Great succeeded King Philip II of Macedonia. Alexander conquered Asia Minor, Armenia, Palestine, Egypt and Persia; his empire reached from Indus Valley to eastern sections of Mediterranean and northern portions of Africa

312 Construction of Appian Way-route from Rome to Brindisi, approx 350 miles

297-280 **425** foot-tall lighthouse at port in Alexandria is built; One of the Seven Wonders of the World

275 The mathematician Euclid sets principles of geometry in Elements

284 Ptolemy founded Museum in Alexandria dedicated to Muses

Start of translation of Hebrew holy scriptures into Greek

224 The Colossus of Rhodes, 100 foot statue of sun-god Helios, one of the Seven Wonders of the World, destroyed by earthquake

---

221 The Great Wall of China built, 2,600-mile-long wall

215 Roman army defeats Hannibal at battle of Zama

Rome now a major Mediterranean power

551 Confucianism becomes state religion in China

206 Zhang Qian established "Silk Roads," links central Asia to the Mediterranean

Roman roads link Italy with Spain, also coast roads from Alps to the Rhone

Roman trading posts extend from southwest coast of India to southern edge of Sahara Desert

119 3/4's of goods carried on "Silk Road" from China to Europe

70-63 Rule of Pompey over Roman Empire

64 Pompey annexes Judea as a Roman province

55 Caesar invades Britain

52 Caesar begins his Roman conquest of Gaul

50 Cleopatra becomes Queen of Egypt

Rome's civil war ends in defeat of Mark Anthony & Cleopatra at Actium, Greece

Pompey, sole consul, commands Caesar to disband army

Caesar crosses Rubicon river, marches into Italy

Pompey is murdered in Egypt

Julius Caesar is the supreme ruler of Rome

---

44 March 15th, Julius Caesar assassinated in Rome, an event that marks the beginning of the decline of the Roman Empire

Roman Senate appoints Herod the Great as King of Judea

6-4 Birth of Jesus Christ in Bethlehem

Death of Herod the Great

Roman Empire divided by three sons associated with the Murder of the Innocents

Pontius Pilate serves as Procurator of Judea

John the Baptist denounces Herod Antipas for incestuous marriage to Herodias

27 April 30, Crucifixion of Jesus Christ in Palestine at Golgatha

29 Descent of the Holy Spirit on Pentecost

35 Stephen, first Christian martyr

36-68 Buddhism flourishes in Asia

37 On Road to Damascus, Syria, Saul of Tarsus converted to Christianity by vision of Jesus Christ; now named Paul, he begins missionary work

64 Rome; Emperor Nero, Great Fire; persecution of Christians

66 First Jewish revolt against Rome. Jesus brother, James, and Paul martyred

First apostle martyred-James

The apostle Peter crucified

54 The apostle Philip dies

---

63 James (the Less) dies

64 Barnabas, a missionary who traveled with Paul, dies

64 The apostle Mark dies

Jews rise up against Romans in Judea

68-70 Dead Sea Scrolls hidden in caves

69 The apostle Paul dies

69 The apostle Peter dies

70 The apostle Matthew dies

70 The apostle Thomas dies

70 The apostle Andrew dies

70 AD September 7, under siege by Vespasian's son, Titus, Jerusalem falls to Romans, and the Temple is destroyed

70 The apostle Luke dies

90s Early church structure established, bishops, presbyters, and deacons

95 John the Apostle, while on the Isle of Patmos, receives his Revelation of Jesus Christ

c.100 AD Buddhism reaches China from Asia and India

105 Paper invented

100-c.165 Justin Martyr describes the liturgical worship of the Church, centered in the Eucharist

c.130-c.200 Irenaeus

c.150-c.212 Tertullian

220 Iron-smelting develops in East Africa

250 Persecution of Christians under Decius

303 Persecution of Christians under Diocletian

313 Constantine I grants tolerance to the Christians in the Roman Empire

325 Council of Nicaea settles heretical challenge to the Christian faith

331-420 Jerome

354-430 Augustine of Hippo

361 Birth of Attila the Hun

387 Augustine converted to Christianity

397 North African Council, Carthage, determines canon; Jerome translates Vulgate

440 Pope Leo I proclaims supremacy of papacy in governing Christianity

450 Chief Hawaii-Loa discovers Hawaiian Islands

450 Bodhidharma founds Zen Buddhism, India; takes to China

451 Council of Chalcedon affirms apostolic doctrine of two natures in Christ, divine and human

476 Fall of Rome to Goths

525 Dionysius Exiguus sets birth of Jesus and Christian calendar at Dec. 23, AD1

537 King Arthur killed at Camelot

542-594 Plague cuts population of Europe in half

622 Birth of Islamic religion

640 Library of Alexandria with 30,000 manuscripts completely destroyed

700 Beowulf composed between 700-750

732 Battle of Poitiers- victory from Franks kept Islam out of Christian Europe

800 Charlemagne crowned Holy Roman emperor

831 Dublin founded

982 Greenland discovered by, Eric the Red

988 Vladimir converts, brings Christianity to Kiev and Russia

1000 Viking Leif Erickson discovers North America

1000 Gunpowder discovered in China

1054 East-West church schism

1085 King Alfonso VI conquers Toledo, the old Visigothic capital, and discovers the works of Aristotle, Plato, and Muhammed abu-Muhammed al-Ghazali

1096 First Christian crusade to the Holy Land

1100s Norman, then Gothic, cathedrals are built

1118 The fall of Zaragoza to Christian forces

1170 Murder of Thomas Becket, Archbishop of Canterbury

1182 Magnetic compass discovered

1204 Sack of Constantinople by Rome adds to the estrangement between East and West

1207 Genghis Khan overruns Asia

1225-1274 Thomas Aquinas

1270 eighth and last Christian crusade

1298 Marco Polo writes The Travels of Marco Polo

1325 Aztecs build their capital, Tenochtitlan,

1337-1453 Hundred Years War between France and England

1342-1400 Chaucer, English author, The Canterbury Tales

1347 Black Plague kills 75 million - halts economic growth in Europe for 200 years

1350-1527 Approximate dates of the Renaissance

1362-1415 Jan Huss, must important Czech religious reformer

1368 China, Ming Dynasty

1330-c. 1384 John Wycliffe translates the Bible into English

1378-1417 Great Schism brings an end to papal domination

1380-1471 Thomas A Kempis, author of The Imitation of Christ, first pub.1427

1386-1466 Donatello, great Florentine sculptor

1431 Joan of Arc burned at the stake in France

1452-1519 Leonardo da Vinci sculptor, architect, engineer, and scientist

1453 Fall of Constantinople to the Turks

1450 Johann Gutenberg invents the printing press

1455 Gutenberg prints the first Bible

1469-1527 Niccolo Machiavelli, Italian Philosopher, author of The Prince

1473-1543 Nicolaus Copernicus, Polish Astronomer, founder of modern astronomy

1475-1564 Michelangelo, sculptor and painter in Florence; The Pieta, Moses, David and the Sistine Chapel

1488 The Portuguese rounded the cape of Africa

1492 Columbus discovers America - 1495 proves the world is round

1497 The Florentine John Cabot discovered the North American continent

1483-1546 Martin Luther

1490-1536 William Tyndale

1509-1564 John Calvin

1489-1556 Thomas Cranmer

1491-1556 Ignatius Loyola

1514-1572 John Knox

1500s Spanish conquer Aztec, Inca civilizations in the New World

1502 Shidism becomes state religion in Persia

1516-1587 John Foxe, author of The Foxe's Book of Martyrs, pub. 1563

1517 Martin Luther posts his 95 theses, Protestant Reformation begins

1525 William Tyndale translates the New Testament from Greek into English

1533-1584 Ivan the Terrible rules Russia

1534 Society of Jesus (Jesuits) founded

1536 Tyndale strangled and burned

1536 King Henry VIII breaks with the Church of Rome and founds The Church of England

1542 Inquisition begins

1545 Council of Trent convenes

1549 Book of Common Prayer

1560 Geneva Bible

1564 Birth of Shakespeare

1572 Saint Bartholomew Day Massacre of 50,000 Protestants in France

1600s English, French, Dutch colonize North America, East and West Indies, South Africa; kill or enslave and evangelize native peoples

1607 Authorized King James Version of the Bible

1607 Jamestown, first English settlement in North America

1623-1662 Blaise Pascal

1616-1683 John Owen

John Bunyan

...91 Brother Lawrence, author of The ...ce of the Presence of God, pub. in parts ...1, 1741

1620 Pilgrims, aboard the Mayflower, land at Plymouth Rock

1628-1688 John Bunyan, author of The Pilgrim's Progress, first pub. 1668

1633 Galileo convicted of heresy for writing Dialogue on Great World Systems

1640-1660 English Civil War and Protectorate

1648 Westminster Confession

1648-1717 Madame Jeanne Guyon, author of Experiencing Union with God Through Inner Prayer and the Way and Results of Union with God, pub. 1685

1662-1714 Mathew Henry

1667 John Milton publishes Paradise Lost

1703-1758 Jonathan Edwards

1714-1770 George Whitfield

1720-1750 Great Awakening in America

1703-1790 John Wesley

1763 Seven Year War in Europe

1760 The Industrial Revolution begins in England

1781 American Revolution

1799 French Revolution

1792-1875 Charles Finney

1795-1835 Second Great Awakening in America

1703-1758 Johnathan Edwards

1703-1791 John Wesley

1707-1788 Charles Wesley

1714-1770 George Whitefield

1800s Missionary organizations translate Bible into many languages

1815 Defeat of Napoleon

1820s Independence of most Latin American countries

1828 Noah Webster publishes An American Dictionary of the English Language

1828-1917 Andrew Murray, author of With Christ in the School of Prayer, first pub. 1885

1759-1833 William Wilberforce

1761-1834 William Carey

1780-1845 Elizabeth Fry

1792-1875 Charles Finney

1805-1898 George Muller

1813-1873 David Livingstone

1834-1892 C.H. Spurgeon

1837-1899 D.L. Moody

1829-1912 General Wm. Booth, founder of the Salvation Army

1856-1928 R.A. Torrey

1832-1911 Hannah Whitall Smith, author of The Christian's Secret to a Happy Life, first pub. 1875

1892 Charles H. Spurgeon, author of Morning By Morning

1837-1897 Dwight Lyman Moody

1844 Samuel Frank Morse invents the telegraph

1845 Irish Potato famine - nearly 1 million people die

1848 Karl Marx publishes Das Capital

1857-1858 Third Great Awakening in America Prayer Meeting Revival

1859 Darwin publishes The Origin of Species

1851-1897 Henry Drummond, author of The Greatest Thing in the World, first pub. 1884

1857-1946 Charles Sheldon, author of In His Steps, first pub. 1896

1861-1864 American Civil War

1867-1934 Madame Marie Curie, discovers radium, wins Nobel Prize in 1903 for physics and in 1911 for chemistry

1867 Alexander Graham Bell invents the telephone

1881-1955 Sir Alexander Fleming discovers penicillin in 1929

1886-1952 A.W. Pink

1898-1900 Boxer Rebellion in China

1898-1963 C.S. Lewis

1901 American Standard Version of the Bible first pub.

1906-1909 Azusa Street Revival, California

1912-1984 Francis A. Schaeffer

1914-1918 World War I

1914 Jonas Salk born, US bacteriologist, develops the Salk Vaccine to innoculate against polio

1917 Bolshevik Revolution in Russia

1923 J. Gresham Machen, fundamentalist leader, writes Christianity and Liberalism

1926 Scope Trial pits literal reading vs. modern understanding of the Bible

1929 American Stock Market crashes, starts 12-year long Great Depression

1939-1945 World War II

1947 Dead Sea Scrolls found

1948 State of Israel established

1949 Communist revolution in China; Christianity suppressed

1952 Revised Standard Version of the Bible published

1959 Chinese invade Tibet

1960s Civil Rights movement US

1960s Post colonial independence of most African and Asian countries

1969 Neil Armstrong walks on the moon

1989 Berlin Wall comes down - opens Eastern Germany to Christianity

1989 New Revised Standard Version of the Bible first pub. Dead Sea Scrolls made widely available

1990s Internet technology globalizes communication; economy globalizes

1906-1945 Dietrich Bonhoeffer

1991 Communist Government in Russia crumbles; Christianity regains its liberty

1998 Another space travel for John Glenn, age 77, worlds oldest astronaut

2001 September 11th Terrorist Attack on U.S.